SCHOLARSHIPS, FELLOWSHIPS AND LOANS

ISSN 1058-5699

SCHOLARSHIPS, FELLOWSHIPS AND LOANS

A GUIDE TO EDUCATION-RELATED FINANCIAL AID PROGRAMS FOR STUDENTS AND PROFESSIONALS

Volume One

Sponsors and Their Scholarships: A–H

Thirty-Fourth Edition

GALE
CENGAGE Learning

Farmington Hills, Mich • San Francisco • New York • Waterville, Maine
Meriden, Conn • Mason, Ohio • Chicago

GALE
CENGAGE Learning

Scholarships, Fellowships and Loans, 34th Edition

Project Editor: Bohdan Romaniuk

Editorial Support Services: Wayne Fong

Composition and Electronic Prepress: Gary Leach

Manufacturing: Rita Wimberley

© 2017 Gale, Cengage Learning

ALL RIGHTS RESERVED. No part of this work covered by the copyright herein may be reproduced or distributed in any form or by any means, except as permitted by U.S. copyright law, without the prior written permission of the copyright owner.

This publication is a creative work fully protected by all applicable copyright laws, as well as by misappropriation, trade secret, unfair competition, and other applicable laws. The authors and editors of this work have added value to the underlying factual material herein through one or more of the following: unique and original selection, coordination, expression, arrangement, and classification of the information.

For product information and technology assistance, contact us at
Gale Customer Support, 1-800-877-4253.
For permission to use material from this text or product, submit all requests online at www.cengage.com/permissions.
Further permissions questions can be emailed to
permissionrequest@cengage.com

While every effort has been made to ensure the reliability of the information presented in this publication, Gale, a part of Cengage Learning, does not guarantee the accuracy of the data contained herein. Gale accepts no payment for listing; and inclusion in the publication of any organization, agency, institution, publication, service, or individual does not imply endorsement of the editors or publisher. Errors brought to the attention of the publisher, and verified to the satisfaction of the publisher, will be corrected in future editions.

EDITORIAL DATA PRIVACY POLICY: Does this product contain information about you as an individual? If so, for more information about our editorial data privacy policies, please see our Privacy Statement at www.gale.cengage.com.

Gale
27500 Drake Rd.
Farmington Hills, MI, 48331-3535

ISBN-13: 978-1-4103-1886-2 (3 vol. set)
ISBN-13: 978-1-4103-1887-9 (vol. 1)
ISBN-13: 978-1-4103-1888-6 (vol. 2)
ISBN-13: 978-1-4103-1889-3 (vol. 3)

ISSN 1058-5699

This title is also available as an e-book.
ISBN-13: 978-1-4103-1902-9
Contact your Gale sales representative for ordering information.

Printed in the United States of America
1 2 3 4 5   20 19 18 17 16

Contents

Volume 1

Highlights vii
Introduction ix
User's Guide. xiii
Federal Programs xvii
AmeriCorps xix
State Higher Education Agencies xxi
Abbreviations xxv
Sponsors and Their Scholarships: A-H 1

Volume 2

Highlights vii
Introduction ix
User's Guide. xiii
Federal Programs xvii
AmeriCorps xix
State Higher Education Agencies xxi
Abbreviations xxv
Sponsors and Their Scholarships: I-T 693

Volume 3

Highlights vii
Introduction ix
User's Guide. xiii
Federal Programs xvii
AmeriCorps xix
State Higher Education Agencies xxi
Abbreviations xxv
Sponsors and Their Scholarships: U-Z 1337
Field of Study Index 1469
Legal Residence Index. 1571
Place of Study Index 1647
Special Recipient Index 1721
Sponsor and Scholarship Index 1745

Highlights

This edition of *Scholarships, Fellowships and Loans* (SFL) provides access to nearly 8,000 sources of education-related financial aid for students and professionals at all levels. *SFL*'s scope ranges from undergraduate and vocational/technical education through post-doctoral and professional studies. Students and others interested in education funding will find comprehensive information on a variety of programs in all educational areas, including:

- Architecture
- Area and Ethnic Studies
- Art
- Business
- Communications
- Computer Science
- Education
- Engineering
- Health Science
- Humanities
- Industrial Arts
- Language
- Law
- Literature
- Liberal Arts
- Library Science
- Life Science
- Medicine
- Mathematics
- Performing Arts
- Philosophy
- Physical Sciences
- Social Sciences
- Theology and Religion

SFL Provides Detailed Information on Awards

SFL provides all the information students need to complete their financial aid search. Entries include: administering organization name and address; purpose of award; qualifications and restrictions; selection criteria; award amount and number of awards granted; application details and deadlines; detailed contact information.

Additionally, look for the section on federal financial aid following the User's Guide for a quick summary of programs sponsored by the U.S. government, as well as information on the AmeriCorps program. There is also a section that lists higher education agencies by state.

Five Indexes Allow Quick and Easy Access to Awards

Whether you are a high school student looking for basic undergraduate financial aid, a scientist investigating research grants, or a professional attempting to finance additional career training, SFL aids your search by providing access to awards through the following indexes:

Field of Study Index categorizes awards by very specific subject fields.

Legal Resident Index targets awards restricted to applicants from specific geographic locations.

Place of Study Index provides a handy guide to awards granted for study within specific states, provinces, or countries.

Special Recipient Index lists awards that are reserved for candidates who qualify by virtue of their gender, organizational affiliation, minority or ethnic background.

Sponsor and Scholarship Index provides a complete alphabetical listing of all awards and their administering organizations.

Catchwords

SFL includes catchwords of the organization on each corresponding page, to aid the user in finding a particular entry.

Introduction

As we make our way through difficult economic times, there is a growing need for a more highly-trained and educated work force. From political discussions and debates to reports from future-oriented think tanks and other groups, there is agreement that postsecondary education is a key to success. Yet how are students and their families to afford the already high (and constantly rising) cost of higher education? Searching for financial aid can be very tedious and difficult, even though hundreds of millions of dollars in aid reportedly go unclaimed every year.

Scholarships, Fellowships and Loans (SFL), the most comprehensive single directory of education-related financial aid available, can save you time, effort, and money by helping you to focus your search within the largest pool of awards and avoid pursuing aid for which you do not qualify. In most cases, the detailed descriptions contain enough information to allow you to decide if a particular scholarship is right for you to begin the application process. *SFL* lists nearly 8,000 major awards available to U.S. and Canadian students for study throughout the world. Included are:

- scholarships, fellowships, and grants, which do not require repayment;
- loans, which require repayment either monetarily or through service;
- scholarship loans, which are scholarships that become loans if the recipient does not comply with the award's terms;
- internships and work study programs, which provide training, work experience, and (usually) monetary compensation; and
- awards and prizes that recognize excellence in a particular field.

Also included are other forms of assistance offered by associations, corporations, religious groups, fraternal organizations, foundations, and other private organizations and companies. *SFL* includes a broad representation of government-funded awards at the national and state levels, as well as a representative sampling of lesser-known and more narrowly focused awards, such as those of a strictly local nature or programs sponsored by small organizations. Financial aid programs administered and funded by individual colleges or universities are not included in *SFL*. Both need- and merit-based awards are included. Competition-based awards and prizes are included when they offer funds that support study or research and are intended to encourage further educational or professional growth.

Students of All Types Can Benefit

Traditional students as well as those returning to school, non-degree learners, those in need of retraining, and established professionals can use the funding sources listed in *SFL* for formal and non-formal programs of study at all levels:

- high school
- vocational
- undergraduate
- graduate
- postgraduate
- doctorate
- postdoctorate
- professional development

Content and Arrangement

Scholarships, Fellowships and Loans is organized into a main section containing descriptive listings of award programs and their administering organizations, and five indexes.

The main section, Sponsors and Their Scholarships, is arranged alphabetically by name of administering organization. Entries for each organization's awards appear immediately following the entry on the organization. Each entry contains detailed contact and descriptive information, often providing users with all the information they need to make a decision about applying.

INTRODUCTION

The indexes provide a variety of specific access points to the information contained within the organization and award listings, allowing users to easily identify awards of interest.

Practical Tips on How to Find Financial Aid

While there are many education-related financial aid programs for students of all types and study levels, the competition for available funds is steadily increasing. You will improve the likelihood of meeting your financial aid goals if you:

- carefully assess your particular needs and preferences;
- consider any special circumstances or conditions that might qualify you for aid; and
- carefully research available aid programs.

The following pages list some general guidelines for making your way through the search and application process.

Start Your Search Early

Any search for financial aid is likely to be more successful if you begin early. If you allow enough time to complete all of the necessary steps, you will be more likely to identify a wide variety of awards for which you qualify with plenty of time to meet their application deadlines. This can increase your chances of obtaining aid.

Some experts recommend that you start this process up to two years before you think you will need financial assistance. While you will probably be able to obtain some support if you allow less time, you might overlook some important opportunities.

Some awards are given on a first-come, first-served basis, and if you do not file your application early enough, the aid will already be distributed. In many cases, if your application is late you will not be considered, even if you have met all of the other criteria.

An early start will also allow you to identify organizations that offer scholarships to members or participants, such as student or professional associations, in time to establish membership or otherwise meet their qualifying criteria.

Assess Your Needs and Goals

The intended recipients for financial aid programs and the purposes for which awards are established can vary greatly. Some programs are open to almost anyone, while others are restricted to very specific categories of recipients. The majority of awards fall somewhere in between. Your first step in seeking financial aid is to establish your basic qualifications as a potential recipient. The following are some general questions to ask yourself to help define your educational and financial needs and goals:

- What kinds of colleges or universities interest me?
- What careers or fields of study interest me?
- Do I plan to earn a degree?
- Am I only interested in financial aid that is a gift, or will I consider a loan or work study?
- In what parts of the country am I willing to live and study?

Leave No Stone Unturned

After you have defined your goals, the next step is to identify any special factors that might make you eligible for aid programs offered only to a restricted group. Examine this area carefully, and remember that even minor or unlikely connections may be worth checking. The most common qualifications and restrictions involve:

- citizenship
- community involvement or volunteer work
- creative or professional accomplishment
- employer
- financial need
- gender
- merit or academic achievement
- military or veteran status
- organization membership (such as a union, association, or fraternal group)
- place of residence
- race or ethnic group
- religious affiliation

With many awards, you may be eligible if your spouse, parents, or guardians meet certain criteria by status or affiliations. You should be aware of your parents' affiliations even if you don't live with one (or both) of them, or if they are deceased. And given enough lead time, it may be possible for you (or your parents) to join a particular organization, or establish necessary residence, in time for you to be eligible for certain funds.

Contact Financial Aid Offices

Most colleges, universities, and other educational institutions offer their own financial aid programs. Their financial aid offices may also have information on privately sponsored awards that are specifically designated for students at those institutions. Contact their respective financial aid offices to request applications and details for all of the aid programs they sponsor and/or administer.

Use *SFL* to Identify Awards Sponsored by Private Organizations and Corporations

Scholarships, Fellowships and Loans (SFL) is the most comprehensive single source of information on major education-related financial aid programs sponsored and administered by private organizations and companies for use by students and professionals. Using *SFL* as a starting point, you can quickly compile a substantial list of financial aid programs for which you may qualify by following these simple steps:

- Compile an initial list of awards offered in your field of study.

- If you have already chosen your field of study, look in the Field of Study Index to find listings of awards grouped by more precise disciplines (such as Accounting or Journalism). If you choose this approach, your initial list is likely to be shorter but more focused. Eliminate awards that cannot be used at your chosen level of study or that do not meet your financial needs. Are you an undergraduate only interested in scholarships? Are you a graduate student willing to participate in an internship or take out a loan? Consult the User's Guide to determine which of the study level categories and award types apply to your particular situation. Both indexes clearly note the study levels at which awards may be used. The Field of Study Index also lists the type of financial aid provided.

- Eliminate awards by citizenship, residence, and other restrictions (minority status, ethnic background, gender, organizational affiliation) that make you ineligible.

- If your list is based on the Field of Study Index, you will need to look under the section for qualifications in each descriptive listing to see what requirements apply.

- Read the descriptive listings for each of the award programs left on your list. The descriptive listings should contain all the information you need to decide if you qualify and should apply for each of the awards on your list.

Expand Your List of Possibilities

If you are willing to take the initiative and do a little extra digging, you should be able to add to your list of institution-related and privately sponsored programs. In most cases, the best possibilities fall into these two areas:

Government Agencies and Programs. The Sponsors and Their Scholarships main section includes a broad representation of award programs sponsored by federal and state governments. Since these listings are not meant to be exhaustive, you should be able to identify additional programs by contacting the government agencies responsible for education-related financial aid programs listed here. On the federal level, contact the U.S. Department of Education at 400 Maryland Ave., SW, Washington, DC 20202, or on their website at http://www.ed.gov, for up-to-date information on U.S. Government award programs. For a broad overview of federal financial aid, consult the Federal Programs section. Similarly, you may contact your state department of education for details on what is offered in your particular state. Please see the State Higher Education Agencies section for state-by-state listings.

Local Sources of Awards. A surprisingly large number of financial aid programs are sponsored by small and/or local organizations. *SFL* contains a representative sampling of such programs to encourage you to seek similar programs in your own geographic area. High school guidance counselors are often aware of local programs as well, and they can usually tell you how to get in touch with the sponsoring or administering organizations. Local newspapers are also rich sources of information on financial aid programs.

Allow Enough Time for the Application Process

The amount of time needed to complete the application process for individual awards will vary, so you should pay close attention to application deadlines. Some awards carry application deadlines that require you to apply a year or more before your studies will begin. In general, allow plenty of time to:

- Write for official applications. You may not be considered for some awards unless you apply with the correct forms.

- Read all instructions carefully.

- Take note of application deadlines.

- Accurately and completely file all required supporting material, such as essays, school transcripts, and financial records. If you fail to answer certain questions, you may be disqualified even if you are a worthy candidate.

- Give references enough time to submit their recommendations. Teachers in particular get many requests for letters of recommendation and should be given as much advance notice as possible.

Make Sure You Qualify

Finally, don't needlessly submerge yourself in paperwork. If you find you don't qualify for a particular award, don't apply for it. Instead, use your time and energy to find and apply for more likely sources of aid.

Available in Electronic Format

Scholarships, Fellowships and Loans is also available online as part of the Gale Directory Library and the Gale Virual Reference Library. For more information, call 1-800-877-GALE.

Comments and Suggestions Welcome

We welcome reader suggestions regarding new and previ-

INTRODUCTION

ously unlisted organizations and awards. Please send your suggestions to:

Scholarships, Fellowships and Loans
Gale, Cengage Learning
27500 Drake Rd.
Farmington Hills, MI 48331-3535
Phone: (248) 699-4253
Toll-free: 800-347-4253
Fax: (248) 699-8070
Email: Bob.Romaniuk@cengage.com

User's Guide

Scholarships, Fellowships and Loans is comprised of a main section containing descriptive listings on award programs and their administering organizations, and five indexes that aid users in identifying relevant information. Each of these sections is described in detail below.

Sponsors and Their Scholarships

SFL contains two types of descriptive listings:

- brief entries on the organizations that sponsor or administer specific award programs
- descriptive entries on the award programs themselves

Entries are arranged alphabetically by administering organization; awards administered by each organization follow that organization's listings. Entries contain detailed contact and descriptive information. Users are strongly encouraged to read the descriptions carefully and pay particular attention to the various eligibility requirements before applying for awards.

The following sample organization and award entries illustrate the kind of information that is or might be included in these entries. Each item of information is preceded by a number, and is explained in the paragraph with the same number on the following pages.

Sample Entry

▮1▮ 3445
▮2▮ Microscopy Society of America
▮3▮ 4 Barlows Landing Rd., Ste. 8 Woods Hole, MA 02543
▮4▮ *Ph:* (508) 563-1155
▮5▮ *Fax:* (508) 563-1211
▮6▮ *Free:* 800-538-3672
▮7▮ *E-mail:* businessofficemsa.microscopy.com
▮8▮ *URL:* http://www.msa.microscopy.com
▮9▮ 3446
▮10▮ MSA Presidential Student Awards
▮11▮ *(Graduate, Undergraduate/*
▮12▮ *Award*

▮13▮ Purpose: To recognize outstanding original research by students. ▮14▮ Focus: Biological Clinical Sciences—Microscopy, Physical Sciences—Microscopy. ▮15▮ Qualif.: Candidate may be of any nationality, but must be enrolled at a recognized college or university in the United States at the time of the MSA annual meeting. ▮16▮ Criteria: Selection is done based on the applicant's career objectives, academic record, and financial need. ▮17▮ Funds Avail.: Registration and round-trip travel to the MSA annual meeting, plus a stipend to defray lodging and other expenses. ▮18▮ Duration: Annual. ▮19▮ Number awarded: 5. ▮20▮ To Apply: Write to MSA for application form and guidelines. ▮21▮ Deadline: March 15. ▮22▮ Remarks: Established in 1979. ▮23▮ Contact: Alternate phone number: 800-538-EMSA.

Descriptions of Numbered Elements

▮1▮ **Organization Entry Number.** Administering organizations are listed alphabetically. Each entry is followed by an alphabetical listing of its awards. All entries (organization and award) are numbered in a single sequence. These numbers are used as references in the indexes.

▮2▮ **Organization Name.** The name of the organization administering the awards that follow.

▮3▮ **Mailing Address.** The organization's permanent mailing address is listed when known; in some cases an award address is given.

▮4▮ **Telephone Number.** The general telephone number for the administering organization. Phone numbers pertaining to specific awards are listed under "Contact" in the award description.

▮5▮ **Fax Number.** The facsimile number for the administering organization. Fax numbers pertaining to specific awards are included under "Contact" in the award description.

▮6▮ **Toll-free Number.** The toll-free number for the administering organization. Toll-free numbers pertaining to specific awards are included under "Contact" in the award description.

▮7▮ **E-mail Address.** The electronic mail address for the administering organization. Electronic mail addresses pertaining to specific awards are included under "Contact" in the award description.

▮8▮ **URL.** The web address for the administering organization.

▮9▮ **Award Entry Number.** Awards are listed alphabetically following the entry for their administering organizations. All entries (organization and award) are numbered in a single sequence. These numbers are used as references in the indexes.

▮10▮ **Award Name.** Names of awards are always listed. Organization titles or acronyms have been added to generic award names (for example, MSA Undergraduate Scholarships, Canadian Council Fiction Writing Grant, etc.) to avoid confusion.

❚11❚ Study Level. The level of study for which the award may be used. One or more of the following terms will be listed:

- All: not restricted to a particular level.
- High School: study at the secondary level.
- Vocational: study leading to postsecondary awards, certificates, or diplomas requiring less than two years of study.
- 2 Year: study leading to a bachelor's degree within two years
- 4 Year: study leading to a bachelor's degree within four years
- Undergraduate: study immediately beyond the secondary level, including associate, colleges and universities, junior colleges, technical institutes leading to a bachelor's degree, and vocational technical schools.
- Graduate: study leading to an M.A., M.S., LL.B., LL.M., and other intermediate degrees.
- Master's: study leading specifically to a master's degree, such as a M.A., M.S., or M.B.A.
- Postgraduate: study beyond the graduate level not specifically leading to a degree.
- Doctorate: study leading to a Ph.D., Ed.D., Sc.D., M.D., D.D.S., D.O., J.D., and other terminal degrees.
- Postdoctorate: study beyond the doctorate level; includes awards intended for professional development when candidates must hold a doctoral degree to qualify.
- Professional Development: career development not necessarily restricted by study.

❚12❚ Award Type. The type or category of award. One or more of the following terms will be listed:

- Award: generally includes aid given in recognition and support of excellence, including awards given through music and arts competitions. Non-monetary awards and awards given strictly for recognition are not included.
- Fellowship: awards granted for graduate- or postgraduate-level research or education that do not require repayment.
- Grant: includes support for research, travel, and creative, experimental, or innovative projects.
- Internship: training and work experience programs. Internships that do not include compensation of some type are not included.
- Loan: aid that must be repaid either monetarily or through service. Some loans are interest-free, others are not.
- Prize: funds awarded as the result of a competition or contest. Prizes that are not intended to be used for study or to support professional development are not included.
- Scholarships: support for formal educational programs that does not require repayment.
- Scholarship Loan: a scholarship that becomes a loan if the recipient does not comply with the terms.
- Work Study: combined study and work program for which payment is received.
- Other: anything that does not fit the other categories, such as a travel award.

❚13❚ Purpose. The purpose for which the award is granted is listed here when known.

❚14❚ Focus. The field(s) of study that the recipient must be pursuing.

❚15❚ Qualif. Information regarding applicant eligibility. Some examples of qualification requirements include the following: academic record, citizenship, financial need, organizational affiliation, minority or ethnic background, residency, and gender.

❚16❚ Criteria Information concerning selection criteria.

❚17❚ Funds Avail. The award dollar amounts are included here along with other relevant funding information, such as the time period covered by the award, a breakdown of expenses covered (e.g., stipends, tuition and fees, travel and living allowances, equipment funds, etc.), the amount awarded to the institution, loan repayment schedules, service-in-return-for-funding agreements, and other obligations.

❚18❚ Duration. Frequency of the award.

❚19❚ Number awarded. Typical number of awards distributed.

❚20❚ To Apply. Application guidelines, requirements, and other information.

❚21❚ Deadline. Application due dates, notification dates (the date when the applicant will be notified of receipt or denial of award), disbursement dates, and other relevant dates.

❚22❚ Remarks. Any additional information concerning the award.

❚23❚ Contact. When contact information differs from that given for the administering organization, relevant addresses, telephone and fax numbers, and names of specific contact persons are listed here. When the address is that of the administering organization, the entry number for the organization is provided.

Indexes

Field of Study Index classifies awards by one or more of 450 specific subject categories, allowing users to easily target their search by specific area of study. Citations are arranged alphabetically under all appropriate subject terms. Each citation is followed by the study level and award type, which appear in parentheses and can be used to narrow the search even further.

USER'S GUIDE

Legal Residence Index lists awards that are restricted by the applicant's residence of legal record. Award citations are arranged alphabetically by country and subarranged by region, state or province (for U.S. and Canada). Each citation is followed by the study level and award type, which appear in parentheses and can be used to eliminate inappropriate awards.

Place of Study Index lists awards that carry restrictions on where study can take place. Award citations are arranged alphabetically under the following geographic headings:

- United States
- United States—by Region
- United States—by State
- Canada
- Canada—by Province
- International
- International—by Region
- International—by Country

Each citation is followed by the study level and award type, which appear in parentheses.

Special Recipient Index lists awards that carry restrictions or special qualifying factors relating to applicant affiliation. This index allows users to quickly identify awards relating to the following categories:

- African American
- Asian American
- Association Membership
- Disabled
- Employer Affiliation
- Ethnic Group Membership
- Fraternal Organization Membership
- Hispanic American
- Military
- Minority
- Native American
- Religious Affiliation
- Union Affiliation
- Veteran

Awards are listed under all appropriate headings. Each citation includes information on study level and award type, which appear in parentheses and can be used to further narrow the search. Users interested in awards restricted to particular minorities should also look under the general Minorities heading, which lists awards targeted for minorities but not restricted to any particular minority group.

Sponsor and Scholarship Index lists, in a single alphabetic sequence, all of the administering organizations, awards, and acronyms included in *SFL*.

Federal Programs

Federal aid for college students is available through a variety of programs administered by the U.S. Department of Education. Most colleges and universities participate in federal programs, but there are exceptions. Contact a school's financial aid office to find out if it is a participating institution. If it participates, the student works with financial aid counselors to determine how much aid can be obtained.

Aid for students comes in three forms: grants (gifts to the student), loans (which must be repaid), and work-study jobs (a job for the student while enrolled in which his/her pay is applied to his school account). These types of aid are further explained below. More information can be found at http://www.ed.gov.

Grants

Pell Grants are intended to provide funds for any undergraduate student (who does not already have a degree) who wishes to attend college regardless of family financial background. They are available through the financial aid office at the school. The maximum Pell Grant award for the 2016-2017 award year (July 1, 2016 to June 30, 2017) is $5,815.

Federal Supplemental Educational Opportunity Grants (FSEOG) are intended for students with exceptional financial need, these grants are typically for smaller amounts (between $100 and $4,000) than Pell Grants. They are available on a limited basis.

Loans

Student loans are available a variety of ways. Loans may not be taken out for more than the cost of attendance at the school, which is determined by the financial aid administrator. Grants and other forms of aid are taken into consideration when determining the amount a student will be allowed to borrow. Loan amounts may be reduced if a student receives other forms of aid. Loans are divided into two types, subsidized and unsubsidized:

Subsidized loans: the federal government pays the interest on the loan until after schooling is complete.

Unsubsidized loans: the student incurs the interest charges while in school, but payment of the charges may be deferred until schooling is complete. The advantage of unsubsidized loans is that there are usually fewer restrictions against obtaining them. Amounts available through these programs vary depending on academic level. The total debt a student or a student's parents may accumulate for that student is $31,000 for a dependent undergraduate student, $57,500 for an independent undergraduate student (with a limit of $23,000 in subsidized loans), and $138,500 for a graduate or professional student (with a limit of $65,500 in subsidized loans) or $224,000 for health professionals.

Available Funding Programs Direct Loan Program

These low-interest loans bypass lending institutions such as banks. They are a direct arrangement between the government and the student (administered by the school). There are four repayment options for the Direct Loan program: the Income Contingent Repayment Plan, the Extended Repayment Plan, the Graduated Repayment Plan, and the Standard Repayment Plan.

Direct subsidized loans may be taken out for a maximum of $3,500 by incoming freshmen, $4,500 for sophomores, and $5,500 for juniors and seniors. The amounts for independent undergraduate students range from $9,500 to $12,500 per year for direct loans. Independent students face some restrictions on the amount of subsidized funds they can receive from the program. At least half of the funds borrowed through the Direct Loan program by independent students must come from unsubsidized loans. Graduate students may borrow up to $20,500 directly in unsubsidized loans.

Direct PLUS Loans Direct PLUS loans are federal loans that graduate or professional degree students and parents of dependent undergraduate students can use to help pay education expenses. The U.S. Department of Education makes Direct PLUS loans to eligible borrowers through schools participating in the program. The Maximum amount to be borrowed is the cost of attending the shool minus other forms of aid already obtained. For 2016-2017 the fixed rate for a Direct PLUS loan is 6.31%.

With the Direct PLUS loan, students or parents fill out a Direct PLUS Loan Application, available at the school's financial aid office. The funds are disbursed to the school. Students and parents may choose from three repayment plans: Standard, Extended, or Graduated.

Perkins Loan Program The Perkins Loan program allows students who have unusual financial need to borrow funds not otherwise available from other loan or grant programs. Up to $5,500 is available to undergraduates each year (up to $8,000 for graduate students). These loans have a fixed interest rate of 5%. Perkins Loans must be repaid within ten years.

Federal Work-Study Program Work-study is an arrangement that allows students to work on campus while they are enrolled to help pay their expenses. The federal government pays the majority of the student's wages, although the department where the student works also contributes. The employment must be relevant to the student's field of study and only so much time per semester may be devoted to the job. If the student earns the amount of aid prior to the end of the semester, work is terminated for the duration of the award period.

Other Considerations

Application: Applying for federal student aid is free. All federal aid is obtained by first completing a Free Application for Federal Student Aid (FAFSA). After the application is submitted, it will be processed by the Department of Education. The student then receives a Student Aid Report (SAR), which contains a figure for Expected Family Contribution. This is the amount that the student should plan on providing from non-federal sources in order to attend school.

Dependency: If a student is eligible for independent status, more money may be available in the form of loans. The interest rates and the programs for repayment, however, are the same. Independent status provides more financial aid for students who do not have the benefit of parental financial contributions.

Deadline: FAFSA deadlines are set by federal and state agencies, as well as individual schools, and vary widely. Applicants are encouraged to apply as soon as possible after January 1 of the year they plan to enroll, but no earlier.

Special Circumstances: The financial aid counselor at the school will often listen to extenuating circumstances such as unexpected medical expenses, private education expenses for other family members, or recent unemployment when evaluating requests for assistance.

Contact Information for Federal Financial Aid Programs

Call (800)433-3243 to have questions answered; (319) 337-5665 to find out if your application has been processed; (800) 730-8913 (TTY) if you are hearing impaired; (800) 647-8733 to report fraud, waste, or abuse of federal student aid funds; or visit http://www.ed.gov for application forms, guidelines, and general information.

AmeriCorps

President Clinton launched this volunteer community service program in September 1993 through the *National and Community Service Trust Act*, aimed at helping college-bound young people pay for their education while serving their communities. AmeriCorps volunteers receive minimum wage, health benefits, and a grant toward college for up to two years.

Funds for the program are distributed by the federal government in the form of grants to qualifying organizations and community groups with the goal of achieving direct results in addressing the nation's critical education, human services, public safety, and environmental needs at the community level. The program provides meaningful opportunities for Americans to serve their country in organized efforts, fostering citizen responsibility, building community, and providing educational opportunities for those who make a substantial commitment to service.

The AmeriCorps programs are run by not-for-profit organizations or partnerships, institutions of higher learning, local governments, school or police districts, states, Native American tribes, and federal agencies. Examples of participating programs include Habitat for Humanity, the American Red Cross, Boys and Girls Clubs, and local community centers and places of worship. Volunteers have nearly 1,000 different groups from which to choose. The AmeriCorps Pledge: "I will get things done for America to make our people safer, smarter, and healthier. I will bring Americans together to strengthen our communities. Faced with apathy, I will take action. Faced with conflict, I will seek a common ground. Faced with adversity, I will persevere. I will carry this commitment with me this year and beyond. I am an AmeriCorps Member and I am going to get things done."

Eligibility and Selection for Service in AmeriCorps

Citizens and legal resident aliens who are 17 years of age or older are eligible to serve in AmeriCorps before, during, or after post-secondary education. In general, participants must be high school graduates or agree to achieve their GED prior to receiving education awards. Individual programs select service participants on a nondiscriminatory and nonpolitical basis. There are national and state-wide recruiting information systems and a national pool of potential service volunteers.

Term of Service

One full-time term of service is a minimum of 1,700 hours over the course of one year or less; or a part-time term, which can range from 300 hours to 900 hours. Short-term service (such as a summer program) provides eligibility for reduced part-time status.

Compensation

You will receive a modest living allowance, health insurance, student loan deferment, and training. After you complete your term of service, you will receive an education award to help pay for your education. Serve part-time and you will receive a portion of the full amount. The amount is tied to the maximum amount of the U.S. Department of Education's Pell Grant. Prior to fiscal year 2010, the amount of an education award had remained the same since the AmeriCorps program began. Effective fiscal year 2017, which began October 1, 2016, the award is $5,815 for a year of full-time service, and is pro-rated for part-time service.

How Can I Use an Award?

These awards may be used to repay qualified existing or future student loans, to pay all or part of the cost of attending a qualified institute of higher education (including some vocational programs), or to pay expenses while participating in an approved school-to-work program. Awards must be used within seven years of completion of service.

Contact

Individuals interested in participating in AmeriCorps national service programs should apply directly. For basic program information, individuals can call the AmeriCorps Information Hotline at 1-800-942-2677 or visit their Web site at http://www.nationalservice.gov/programs/americorps.

State Higher Education Agencies

The following is an alphabetic state-by-state listing of agencies located in the United States. Many of these agencies administer special federal award programs, as well as state-specific awards, such as the Tuition Incentive Program (TIP) offered by the state of Michigan for low-income students to receive free tuition at community colleges. Financial aid seekers should contact the agency in their home state for more information.

ALABAMA

Alabama Comm. on Higher Education
100 N. Union St.
P.O. Box 302000
Montgomery, AL 36104
(334)242-1998
http://www.ache.state.al.us

ALASKA

Alaska Comm. on Postsecondary Education
P.O. Box 110505
Juneau, AK 99811-0505
(907)465-2962
http://acpe.alaska.gov

ARIZONA

Arizona Comm. for Postsecondary Education
2020 N. Central Ave.,
Ste. 650
Phoenix, AZ 85004-4503
(602)258-2435
http://highered.az.gov

ARKANSAS

Arkansas Dept. of Higher Education
423 Main St., Ste. 400
Little Rock, AR 72201
(501)371-2000
http://www.adhe.edu

CALIFORNIA

California Student Aid Comm.
PO Box 419026
Rancho Cordova, CA 95741-9026
(888)224-7268
http://www.csac.ca.gov

COLORADO

Colorado Dept. of Higher Education
1560 Broadway, Ste. 1600
Denver, CO 80202
(303)862-3001
http://highered.colorado.gov

CONNECTICUT

Connecticut Dept. of Higher Education
61 Woodland St.
Hartford, CT 06105-2326
(860)947-1800
http://www.ctdhe.org

DELAWARE

Delaware Dept. of Higher Education Scholarship/incentive Loan Program
The Townsend Building
401 Federal St.
Dover, DE 19901
(302)735-4000
http://www.doe.k12.de.us/Page/316

DISTRICT OF COLUMBIA

District of Columbia Office of the State Superintendent of Education
810 1st St., NE, 9th Fl.
Washington, DC 20002
(202)727-6436
http://osse.dc.gov

FLORIDA

Office of Student Financial Assistance
Dept. of Education
325 W. Gaines St.
Turlington Bldg., Ste. 1514
Tallahassee, FL 32399-0400
(800)366-3475
http://www.floridastudentfinancialaid.org

GEORGIA

Georgia Student Finance Comm.
2082 E. Exchange Pl.
Tucker, GA 30084
(800)436-7442
http://gsfc.georgia.gov

HAWAII

Hawaii Board of Regents
2444 Dole St.,
Bachman Hall, Rm. 209
Honolulu, HI 96822
(808)956-8213
http://www.hawaii.edu/offices/bor/

IDAHO

Idaho State Board of Education
PO Box 83720
Boise, ID 83720-0037
(208)334-2270
http://www.boardofed.idaho.gov

ILLINOIS

Illinois Student Assistance Comm.
1755 Lake Cook Rd.
Deerfield, IL 60015-5209
(800)899-4722
http://www.isac.org

INDIANA

Indiana Comm. for Higher Education
101 W. Ohio St., Ste. 300
Indianapolis, IN 46204-4206

STATE HIGHER EDUCATION AGENCIES

(888)528-4719
http://www.in.gov/che

IOWA

Iowa College Student Aid Comm.
430 E. Grand Ave., Fl. 3
Des Moines, IA 50309-1920
(877)272-4456
http://www.iowacollegeaid.gov

KANSAS

Kansas Board of Regents
1000 SW Jackson St., Ste. 520
Topeka, KS 66612-1368
(785)296-3421
http://www.kansasregents.org

KENTUCKY

Kentucky Higher Education Assistance Authority
100 Airport Rd.
Frankfort, KY 40602-0798
(800)928-8926
http://www.kheaa.com

LOUISIANA

Louisiana Office of Student Financial Assistance
602 N. Fifth St.
Baton Rouge, LA 70802
(225)219-1012
http://www.osfa.state.la.us

MAINE

Finance Authority of Maine (FAME)
5 Community Dr.
P.O. Box 949
Augusta, ME 04332-0949
(207)623-3263
http://www.famemaine.com

MARYLAND

Maryland Higher Education Comm.
6 N. Liberty St.
Baltimore, MD 21201
(410)767-3301
http://www.mhec.state.md.us

MASSACHUSETTS

Massachusetts Dept. of Higher Education
One Ashburton Pl., Rm. 1401
Boston, MA 02108-1696

(617)994-6950
http://www.mass.edu

MICHIGAN

Michigan Higher Education Student Loan Authority
Student Scholarships and Grants
P.O. Box 30462
Lansing, MI 48909-7962
(888)447-2687
http://www.michigan.gov/mistudentaid

MINNESOTA

Minnesota Office of Higher Education
1450 Energy Park Dr., Ste. 350
St. Paul, MN 55108-5227
(651)642-0567
http://www.ohe.state.mn.us/index.cfm

MISSISSIPPI

Mississippi Institutions of Higher Learning
3825 Ridgewood Rd.
Jackson, MS 39211
(601)432-6198
http://www.ihl.state.ms.us

MISSOURI

Missouri Dept. of Higher Education
205 Jefferson St.
P.O.Box 1469
Jefferson City, MO 65102-1469
(573)751-2361
http://www.dhe.mo.gov/

MONTANA

Montana Board of Regents
Office of Commissioner of Higher Education
Montana University System
2500 Broadway St.
PO Box 203201
Helena, MT 59620-3201
(406)444-6570
http://www.mus.edu

NEBRASKA

Nebraska Coordinating Comm. for Postsecondary Education
P.O. Box 95005
Lincoln, NE 68509-5005
(402)471-2847
http://ccpe.nebraska.gov

NEVADA

Nevada Department of Education
700 E. Fifth St.
Carson City, NV 89701
(775)687-9200
http://www.doe.nv.gov

(Southern Office)
9890 S. Maryland Pkwy., 2nd Fl.
Las Vegas, NV 89183
(702)486-6458

NEW HAMPSHIRE

New Hampshire Higher Education Comm.
101 Pleasant St.
Concord, NH 03301-3494
(603)271-3494
http://www.state.nh.us/postsecondary

NEW JERSEY

Higher Education Student Assistance Authority
P.O. Box 545
Trenton, NJ 08625-0545
(800)792-8670
http://www.hesaa.org

NEW MEXICO

New Mexico Higher Education Dept.
2048 Galisteo St.
Santa Fe, NM 87505-2100
(505)476-8400
http://www.hed.state.nm.us

NEW YORK

New York State Higher Education Svcs. Corp.
99 Washington Ave.
Albany, NY 12255
(888)697-4372
http://www.hesc.ny.gov

NORTH CAROLINA

North Carolina State Education Assistance Authority
PO Box 14103
Research Triangle Park, NC 27709

STATE HIGHER EDUCATION AGENCIES

(919)549-8614
http://www.ncseaa.edu

NORTH DAKOTA

North Dakota University System
North Dakota Student Financial Assistance Program
10th Fl., State Capitol
600 E. Boulevard Ave., Dept. 215
Bismarck, ND 58505-0230
(701)328-2960
http://www.ndus.edu

OHIO

Ohio Department of Higher Education
25 S. Front St.
Columbus, OH 43215
(614)466-6000
http://www.ohiohighered.org

OKLAHOMA

Oklahoma State Regents for Higher Education
Oklahoma Guaranteed Loan Program
655 Research Pkwy.
Suite 200
Oklahoma City, OK 73104
(405)225-9100
http://www.okhighered.org

OREGON

Oregon Student Access Comm.
1500 Valley River Dr., Ste. 100
Eugene, OR 97401
(541)687-7400
http://www.osac.state.or.us

PENNSYLVANIA

Pennsylvania Higher Education Assistance Agency
1200 N. 7th St.
Harrisburg, PA 17102-1444
(800)692-7392
http://www.pheaa.org

RHODE ISLAND

Rhode Island Higher Education Assistance Authority
560 Jefferson Blvd., Ste. 100
Warwick, RI 02886-1304
(401)736-1100
http://www.riheaa.org

SOUTH CAROLINA

South Carolina Comm. on Higher Education
1122 Lady St., Ste. 300
Columbia, SC 29201
(803)737-2260
http://www.che.sc.gov/

SOUTH DAKOTA

South Dakota Board of Regents
306 E. Capitol Ave., Ste. 200
Pierre, SD 57501
(605)773-3455
http://www.sdbor.edu/

TENNESSEE

Tennessee Higher Education Comm.
Parkway Towers
404 James Robertson Pkwy., Ste. 1900
Nashville, TN 37243-0830
(615)741-3605
https://www.tn.gov/thec

TEXAS

Texas Higher Education Coordinating Board
1200 E. Anderson Ln.
Austin, TX 78752
(512)427-6101
http://www.thecb.state.tx.us

UTAH

Utah State Board of Regents
Board of Regents Building, The Gateway
60 South 400 West
Salt Lake City, UT 84101-1284
(800)418-8757
http://higheredutah.org

VERMONT

Vermont Student Assistance Corp.
10 E. Allen St.
P.O. Box 2000
Winooski, VT 05404
(800)642-3177
http://www.services.vsac.org/wps/wcm/connect/vsac/VSAC

VIRGINIA

State Council of Higher Education for Virginia
James Monroe Bldg.
101 N. 14th St., 10th Fl.
Richmond, VA 23219
(804)225-2600
http://www.schev.edu

WASHINGTON

Washington Student Achievement Council
917 Lakeridge Way
Olympia, WA 98502
(360)753-7800
http://www.wsac.wa.gov

WEST VIRGINIA

West Virginia Higher Education Policy Comm.
1018 Kanawha Blvd., E., Ste. 700
Charleston, WV 25301
(304)558-2101
http://www.hepc.wvnet.edu

WISCONSIN

Wisconsin Higher Education Aids Board
131 W. Wilson St., Ste. 902
P.O. Box 7885
Madison, WI 53707-7885
(608)267-2206
http://heab.state.wi.us

WYOMING

Wyoming Community College Comm.
2300 Capitol Ave., 5th Fl., Ste. B
Cheyenne, WY 82002
(307)777-7763
http://www.communitycolleges.wy.edu

Abbreviations

U.S. State Abbreviations

AK	Alaska
AL	Alabama
AR	Arkansas
AZ	Arizona
CA	California
CO	Colorado
CT	Connecticut
DC	District of Columbia
DE	Delaware
FL	Florida
GA	Georgia
GU	Guam
HI	Hawaii
IA	Iowa
ID	Idaho
IL	Illinois
IN	Indiana
KS	Kansas
KY	Kentucky
LA	Louisiana
MA	Massachusetts
MD	Maryland
ME	Maine
MI	Michigan
MN	Minnesota
MO	Missouri
MS	Mississippi
MT	Montana
NC	North Carolina
ND	North Dakota
NE	Nebraska
NH	New Hampshire
NJ	New Jersey
NM	New Mexico
NV	Nevada
NY	New York
OH	Ohio
OK	Oklahoma
OR	Oregon
PA	Pennsylvania
PR	Puerto Rico
RI	Rhode Island
SC	South Carolina
SD	South Dakota
TN	Tennessee
TX	Texas
UT	Utah
VA	Virginia
VI	Virgin Islands
VT	Vermont
WA	Washington
WI	Wisconsin
WV	West Virginia
WY	Wyoming

Canadian Province Abbreviations

AB	Alberta
BC	British Columbia
MB	Manitoba
NB	New Brunswick
NL	Newfoundland and Labrador
NS	Nova Scotia
NT	Northwest Territories
ON	Ontario
PE	Prince Edward Island
QC	Quebec
SK	Saskatchewan
YT	Yukon Territory

Other Abbreviations

ACT	American College Testing Program
B.A.	Bachelor of Arts
B.Arch.	Bachelor of Architecture
B.F.A.	Bachelor of Fine Arts
B.S.	Bachelor of Science
B.Sc.	Bachelor of Science
CSS	College Scholarship Service
D.D.S.	Doctor of Dental Science/Surgery
D.O.	Doctor of Osteopathy
D.Sc.	Doctor of Science
D.S.W.	Doctor of Social Work
D.V.M.	Doctor of Veterinary Medicine
D.V.M.S.	Doctor of Veterinary Medicine and Surgery
D.V.S.	Doctor of Veterinary Science
FAFSA	Free Application for Federal Student Aid
FWS	Federal Work Study
GED	General Education Development Certificate
GPA	Grade Point Average
GRE	Graduate Record Examination
J.D.	Doctor of Jurisprudence
LL.B.	Bachelor of Law
LL.M.	Master of Law
LSAT	Law School Admission Test
M.A.	Master of Arts
M.Arch.	Master of Architecture
M.B.A.	Master of Business Administration
M.D.	Doctor of Medicine
M.Div.	Master of Divinity
M.F.A.	Master of Fine Arts
MIA	Missing in Action
M.L.S.	Master of Library Science
M.N.	Master of Nursing
M.S.	Master of Science
M.S.W.	Master of Social Work
O.D.	Doctor of Optometry
Pharm.D.	Doctor of Pharmacy
Ph.D.	Doctor of Philosophy
POW	Prisoner of War
PSAT	Preliminary Scholastic Aptitude Test
ROTC	Reserve Officers Training Corps
SAR	Student Aid Report
SAT	Scholastic Aptitude Test
Sc.D.	Doctor of Science
TDD	Telephone Device for the Deaf
Th.d.	Doctor of Theology
U.N.	United Nations
U.S.	United States

Sponsors and Their Scholarships

1 ■ 101st Airborne Division Association
PO Box 929
Fort Campbell, KY 42223-0929
Ph: (931)431-0199
Fax: (931)431-0195
E-mail: 101exec@comcast.net
URL: www.screamingeagle.org

2 ■ Chappie Hall Scholarship Program
(Undergraduate/Scholarship)

Purpose: To provide financial assistance to students who have the potential to become assets to the nation. **Focus:** General studies/Field of study not specified. **Qualif.:** Applicants must maintain an overall "C" or better grade average during the past school year. Their parents, grandparent, husband or wife is (or if deceased was) a regular or life (not Associate) member of the 101st Airborne Division Association. **Criteria:** Major factors to be considered in the evaluation and rating of applicants are eligibility, career objectives, academic record, and insight gained from the letter requesting consideration and letters of recommendation.

Funds Avail.: No specific amount. **Duration:** Annual. **To Apply:** Applicants must complete and submit the following required documents: a typed personal letter; proof of membership of parent, grandparent, husband, or wife in the 101st Airborne Division Association; a transcript of school records; two letters of recommendation; small photo (head and shoulders) to be used for publication in "The screaming Eagle" if scholarship grant is awarded; letter of acceptance from a university or college and the address of the department of office at the university or college where a scholarship check could be mailed; and not less than 250-word essay, but not exceeding 300 words on patriotism. **Deadline:** May 6.

3 ■ 180 Medical, Inc.
8516 NW Expy.
Oklahoma City, OK 73162
Ph: (877)688-2729
Free: 888-718-0633
URL: www.180medical.com

4 ■ 180 Medical College Scholarship Program
(Undergraduate, Graduate/Scholarship)

Purpose: To help young adults with spinal cord injuries, transverse myelitis, spina bifida, neurogenic bladder or ostomy (ileostomy, colostomy or urostomy) to pursue their goals. **Focus:** Spinal cord injuries and research. **Qualif.:** Applicants must be students attending a two-year, four-year or graduate school program and legal residents of United States; must be under a physicians' care for a spinal cord injury, transverse myelitis, spina bifida, neurogenic bladder or ostomy (ileostomy, colostomy or urostomy). **Criteria:** Selection will be based on the committee's criteria.

Funds Avail.: $1,000. **To Apply:** Applicants must submit the following materials: application form; typed questions and essay that can be found at the online application form; physician's statement of diagnosis; most recent official transcript; document verifying acceptance by college or current enrollment. **Deadline:** June 1. **Contact:** scholarships@180medical.com.

5 ■ 1Dental.com
2501 Parkview Dr., Ste. 210
Fort Worth, TX 76155
Ph: (817)377-2200
URL: www.1dental.com

6 ■ 1Dental Dentistry Scholarships *(Undergraduate/Scholarship)*

Purpose: To provide financial assistance for the aspiring dentist. **Focus:** Dentistry. **Qualif.:** Applicants must be U.S. residents, enrolled in high school as a high school student or higher and not related to any 1Dental.com employees. **Criteria:** Selection will be based on the committee's criteria.

Funds Avail.: $1,000. **Duration:** Non-renewable. **Number Awarded:** 1. **To Apply:** Applicants must submit a 500 words essay answering to the question "What recent or upcoming technology you think will reshape - or is already reshaping - the field of dentistry?" including full name, address, phone number, name of high school or college they're attending, school address, current GPA, grade level and any important information about the applicant. **Deadline:** December 21. **Contact:** scholarship@1dental.com.

7 ■ 4-H Alberta
c/o Marguerite Stark, Director
97 E Lake Ramp NE
Airdrie, AB, Canada T4A 0C3
Ph: (403)948-8510
Fax: (403)948-2069
E-mail: info@4h.ab.ca
URL: www.4h.ab.ca
Facebook: www.facebook.com/4halberta

Awards are arranged alphabetically below their administering organizations

8 ■ Grande Prairie 4-H District Scholarships
(Undergraduate/Scholarship)

Purpose: To financially support deserving student members of the Organization who seek for continuing education. **Focus:** General studies/Field of study not specified. **Qualif.:** Applicants must be Grande Prairie 4-H District member students for 3 years and residents of Alberta based on Student Finance Regulations who have minimum year residency in Alberta immediately prior to the application date and enrolled full-time in a post secondary program recognized by Alberta Advanced Education. **Criteria:** Applicants will be evaluated based on their financial need, commitment to living and working in northern Alberta for a specified amount of time upon graduation, and reasonable good prospects for employment in northern Alberta after graduation. **Funds Avail.:** $1,000. **Duration:** Annual. **Number Awarded:** 2. **To Apply:** Applicants must submit complete Provincial 4-H Scholarship application and NADC scholarship application; a letter (at least 200 words) detailing their involvement with 4-H after leaving the Grande Prairie district and two (2) letters of reference. **Contact:** Grande Prairie 4-H District, Scholarship Committee, Unit 90, 10001 - 101 Ave., Grande Prairie, AB T8V 0X9; Email: vandergn@xplornet.com.

9 ■ Provincial and Regional 4-H Scholarships
(Undergraduate/Scholarship)

Purpose: To financially support deserving student members of the Organization who seek to continue their education. **Focus:** General studies/Field of study not specified. **Qualif.:** Applicants must be past or present members of Alberta 4-H Club for a minimum of 3 years and/or a full-time post-secondary students at an officially recognized institution. **Criteria:** Recipients are selected based on a set of criteria designed by the Selection Committee made up of representatives from Alberta 4-H Council, 4-H Foundation of Alberta, 4-H Branch. **Funds Avail.:** Up to $2,500. **Number Awarded:** Varies. **To Apply:** Applicants must register and log-in to the online application form at 4-H Alberta website; and must include an original photo along with the official transcript request for the last year's education. **Deadline:** May 5.

10 ■ Servus Credit Union 4-H Scholarships
(Undergraduate/Scholarship)

Purpose: To provide financial assistance for Alberta 4-H members for their further education. **Focus:** General studies/Field of study not specified. **Qualif.:** Applicants must be Alberta 4-H members who have been involved for a minimum of three years; entering their first year of study at a postsecondary institution in Alberta within one year of graduation from high school; and reside in the following Servus Credit Union trade areas: Andrew, Devon, Drayton Valley, Elk Point, Entwistle, Fort Saskatchewan, Gibbons, Lamont, Leduc, Legal, Morinville, Mundare, Myrnam, Plamondon, Sangudo, St. Paul, Stony Plain and Wabamun. **Criteria:** Recipients are selected based on their demonstrated outstanding 4-H achievement, leadership skills, community involvement and academic standing. **Funds Avail.:** No specific amount. **To Apply:** Applicants must submit application form and the complete materials needed to avail the scholarship. **Deadline:** May 5.

11 ■ AACC International
3340 Pilot Knob Rd.
Saint Paul, MN 55121-2055
Ph: (651)454-7250
Fax: (651)454-0766
E-mail: aacc@scisoc.org
URL: www.aaccnet.org
Facebook: www.facebook.com/AACCInternational
LinkedIn: www.linkedin.com/in/aacci
Twitter: twitter.com/aaccintl

12 ■ American Association of Cereal Chemists Graduate Fellowships *(Graduate/Fellowship)*

Purpose: To encourage graduate research in grain-based food science and technology. **Focus:** Food science and technology. **Qualif.:** Applicants must be current AACC International Student Division members; must be enrolled in a graduate study by the time the fellowship becomes effective or be current graduate students pursuing a course of study leading to an MS or a PhD degree; educational institutions where recipients have been enrolled must be conducting fundamental investigations for the advancement of cereal science and technology, including oilseeds; must be enrolled in an academic schedule that meets the minimum requirements of the university involved, for full-time graduate studies. **Criteria:** Applications will be sent to each member of the AACCI selection jury for review. Material in excess of that requested will not be included. **Funds Avail.:** Up to $3,000. **Duration:** Annual. **To Apply:** Applicants may visit the website to download an application form; must submit copies of transcripts, letter of application describing the career plans, and three letters of recommendation. **Deadline:** March 4. **Contact:** AACCI Foundation Headquarters; Email: cscheller@scisoc.org.

13 ■ AACE International
1265 Suncrest Towne Centre Dr.
Morgantown, WV 26505-1876
Ph: (304)296-8444
Fax: (304)291-5728
E-mail: info@aacei.org
URL: www.aacei.org
LinkedIn: www.linkedin.com/groups/8285063/profile
Twitter: twitter.com/AACE_Tweets

14 ■ AACE International Competitive Scholarships
(Undergraduate/Scholarship)

Purpose: To advance the study of cost engineering and cost management through the integrative process of total cost management. **Focus:** Business administration; Construction; Engineering, Agricultural; Engineering, Architectural; Engineering, Chemical; Engineering, Civil; Engineering, Electrical; Engineering, Industrial; Engineering, Mechanical; Management; Manufacturing. **Qualif.:** Applicants must be full-time students pursuing a related degree in engineering and other related courses, as well as cost management; meet a minimum 3.0 or equivalent GPA. **Criteria:** Selection will be on a competitive basis. Recipients will be chosen based on academic performance, extracurricular activities and an essay on the value of study of cost engineering or total cost management. **Funds Avail.:** $2,000 to $8,000. **Duration:** Annual. **To Apply:** Applicants must fill out the online application completely within given time period. **Deadline:** February 7.

15 ■ AASP - The Palynological Society (AASP)
University of N Carolina at Pembroke
Geology, Old Main 213
Pembroke, NC 28372

Awards are arranged alphabetically below their administering organizations

Ph: (910)521-6478
E-mail: aaspwebmaster@gmail.com
URL: www.palynology.org

16 ■ American Association of Stratigraphic Palynologists Student Scholarships *(Graduate/Scholarship)*

Purpose: To support studies in palynology. **Focus:** Earth sciences; Geology. **Qualif.:** Applicants must be beginning graduate students or advanced graduate students. **Criteria:** Selection is based on applicant's qualifications and the quality of proposed project.

Funds Avail.: No specific amount. **Duration:** Annual. **To Apply:** Applicants must submit four copies of completed application form (available at the AASP Awards Committee Chair, or can be downloaded from the website).

17 ■ Paleontological Society Student Research Grants *(Graduate, Undergraduate/Grant)*

Purpose: To support research in the field or any aspect related to paleontology. **Focus:** Earth sciences; Geology. **Qualif.:** Applicants must be undergraduate or graduate student members of the Paleontological Society conducting a research on any aspect of paleontology. **Criteria:** Awards are based upon scholastic ability, potential, professional interest, character and financial need.

Funds Avail.: $3,000 each. **Duration:** Annual. **Number Awarded:** 2. **To Apply:** Applicants must submit a completed application form (available at the website) and a letter of support from research advisor. **Deadline:** March 31.

18 ■ AAUW Legal Advocacy Fund (AAUW/LAF)
1111 16th St. NW
Washington, DC 20036
Ph: (202)785-7700
Fax: (202)872-1425
Free: 800-326-2289
E-mail: connect@aauw.org
URL: www.aauw.org
Facebook: www.facebook.com/AAUW.National
Twitter: twitter.com/aauw

19 ■ AAUW American Fellowships *(Doctorate, Postdoctorate/Fellowship)*

Purpose: To support female doctoral candidates completing dissertations or scholars seeking funds for postdoctoral research leave from accredited institutions. **Focus:** General studies/Field of study not specified. **Qualif.:** Applicants for postdoctoral fellowships must be U.S. citizens and must hold a Ph.D., Ed.D., D.B.A., M.F.A., D.M.; Applicants for the summer/short-term must be U.S. citizens and hold a doctorate or M.F.A. degree; Applicants for dissertation must be U.S. citizens or permanent residents, must be in a program other than an engineering program, must be in or entering the final year of dissertation, must have a dissertation proposal approved by the committee, must have all course work completed and have passed all preliminary exams. **Criteria:** Candidates will be evaluated on the basis of scholarly excellence, teaching experience, and active commitment to helping women and girls through service in their communities, professions, or fields of research.

Funds Avail.: No specific amount. **Duration:** Annual. **Number Awarded:** Varies. **To Apply:** Applicants must comply to the rules regarding the application process. Complete application must consist of: application with budget information, narrative autobiography, statement of project (description of project, design, research methodology and excepted contribution to knowledge); clear statement of financial need; name(s) of the university, institution, or other location where study will be carried out; and three recommendations. All documents must be postmarked by the deadline in hard copy format: Transcript(s)/Proof of Doctorate; Institution Certification Form; Institution Letter; and Filing Fee ($40). **Deadline:** November 15.

20 ■ AAUW Career Development Grants *(Graduate, Advanced Professional, Professional development/Grant)*

Purpose: To support women who hold a bachelor's degree and are preparing to advance their careers, change careers, or re-enter the work force. **Focus:** General studies/Field of study not specified. **Qualif.:** Applicants must be US citizens or permanent residents who hold a bachelor's degree or specialized training in technical or professional fields. **Criteria:** Special consideration is given to AAUW members, women of color, and women pursuing their first advanced degree or credentials in nontraditional fields.

Funds Avail.: $2,000-$12,000. **Duration:** Annual. **To Apply:** Questions on the application form must be answered. Applicants must submit all the required components: proposed budget and narrative; recommendation to be completed online; and filing fee of $35. **Deadline:** December 15. **Remarks:** Established in 1972.

21 ■ AAUW International Fellowships *(Master's, Doctorate, Postdoctorate/Fellowship)*

Purpose: To award a full-time study or research in the United States to women who are not United States citizens or permanent residents. **Focus:** General studies/Field of study not specified. **Qualif.:** Applicants must be citizens in a country other than the United States, or must hold a non-immigrant visa if applicants reside in the United States; must complete an academic degree (either in the US or abroad) equivalent to a US bachelor's degree; must intend to devote herself full-time to her proposed academic plan during the fellowship year; must intend to return to her home country to pursue a professional career; and must be proficient in English, unless applicants can verify that their native language is English or that she received her undergraduate degree from or will have completed one semester of full-time study in her discipline at a university in the United States. **Criteria:** Award is given based on academic and professional qualifications; the need of the applicant's country for the specialized knowledge and skills that she plans to acquire; applicant's commitment to the advancement of women and girls in her home country as demonstrated by her previous work and her proposed study or research; documented evidence of prior community or civic service in the home country, particularly activities that contributed to the improvement of the lives of women and girls; quality and feasibility of the proposed plan of study or research and proposed time schedule; planned confirmed place of work after returning to home country; English proficiency; financial need; and country of residence at the time of application (Preference will be given to women who reside in their home country at the time of application).

Funds Avail.: No specific amount. **Duration:** Annual. **Number Awarded:** 5. **To Apply:** Applications must be submitted online. Applications and supporting documents will not be accepted via fax or e-mail. The following requirements must be submitted before the deadline: application form which includes research program/thesis/course work proposal, three recommendations and filing fee of $30. **Deadline:** December 1. **Remarks:** Established in 1917.

22 ■ AAUW Selected Professions Fellowships
(Graduate, Master's, Doctorate/Fellowship)

Purpose: To award women who intend to pursue a full-time course of study at accredited institutions during the fellowship year. **Focus:** Architecture; Business administration; Computer and information sciences; Engineering; Law; Mathematics and mathematical sciences; Medicine; Statistics. **Qualif.:** Applicants must be U.S. citizens or permanent residents who are full-time students. **Criteria:** Panel of academic and practicing professionals who work in the respective selected professions fields will review and evaluate all fellowship applications for recommendation to the Program Committee of the AAUW Educational Foundation Board. Final fellowship selections are approved by the Foundation Board of Directors. **Funds Avail.:** $25,000. **Duration:** Annual. **To Apply:** Applicants must accomplish complete application package which consist of: application; budget information for Administrative and Internal Revenue Service Purposes; narrative autobiography; detailed statement of thesis or special project (applicable to engineering and medical students only); statement of applicants' career plans and professional goals; three letters of recommendation; and dean's letter (applicable to medical students). Applicants must also submit supporting documents such as: official transcripts and a bound set of reproductions of a range of the applicants' design projects. 10 to 12 samples may be submitted in the portfolio, no larger than 8" x 10" in size (applicable to architecture students only). **Deadline:** January 10. **Remarks:** Established in 1970.

23 ■ Aboriginal Nurses Association of Canada (ANAC)
50 Driveway
Ottawa, ON, Canada K2P 1E2
Ph: (613)724-4677
E-mail: info@anac.on.ca
URL: www.anac.on.ca
Twitter: twitter.com/aboriginalnurse

24 ■ Baxter Corporation - Jean Goodwill Scholarships *(Graduate/Scholarship)*

Purpose: To encourage and help nurses of Aboriginal ancestry to obtain the specialized knowledge they require. **Focus:** Nursing. **Qualif.:** Applicants must be students who are graduating from a registered nurse course and are accepted into one of the following specialized training programs: community health nursing, outpost nursing, midwifery; must be or will be enrolled in a bachelor level nursing program; can be graduate nurses already serving in isolated communities and who are accepted into community health nursing, outpost nursing or midwifery program. **Criteria:** Applicants are selected based on the selection board's review of the application materials. Preference will be given to applicants of aboriginal ancestry who intend to serve in the North. **Funds Avail.:** 2,500 Canadian dollars. **Duration:** Annual. **To Apply:** Applicants must submit complete application and must received by the President of the Aboriginal Nurses Association of Canada. **Deadline:** July 1.

25 ■ Abraham Lincoln Brigade Archives
799 Broadway, Ste. 341
New York, NY 10003
Ph: (212)674-5398
Fax: (212)674-2101
E-mail: info@alba-valb.org
URL: www.alba-valb.org

26 ■ George Watt Prize *(Undergraduate, Graduate/Prize)*

Purpose: To recognize the best essay made by students. **Focus:** Human rights. **Qualif.:** Candidates must be undergraduate or graduate students from the United States and elsewhere. **Criteria:** Selection will be based on the committee's criteria. **Funds Avail.:** $250. **Duration:** Annual. **Number Awarded:** 2. **To Apply:** Interested applicants must submit an essay or thesis chapter about any aspect of the Spanish Civil War, the global political or cultural struggles against fascism in the 1920s and 1930s, or the lifetime histories and contributions of the Americans who fought in support of the Spanish Republic from 1936 to 1938. Submissions must be between 3,500 and 7,500 words; must be in Spanish or English; must have been produced to fulfill an undergraduate or graduate course requirement; must be in MS Word or PDF format. Submit applications by email with the name of the award on the subject line. Entries must include a cover page with name, address, email, and telephone number. **Deadline:** August 1.

27 ■ Frederick B. Abramson Memorial Foundation
PO Box 7810
Washington, DC 20044-7810
Ph: (202)470-5425
Fax: (202)318-2482
E-mail: info@abramsonfoundation.org
URL: abramsonfoundation.org

28 ■ Frederick B. Abramson Memorial Foundation Scholarships *(Undergraduate/Scholarship)*

Purpose: To help defer college expenses at a four-year accredited institution. **Focus:** General studies/Field of study not specified. **Qualif.:** Applicants must: be graduating from any public senior high school located in the District of Columbia; be residents of District of Columbia; have admitted to and committed to attend any accredited four-year college in the US as candidates for any degree; have demonstrated commitment to community service and social change; have demonstrated financial need; have at least 2.75 GPA or better, at least 1500 between math and verbal SATs and at least a score of 3 and above in the essay section; and, have family income of less than $70,000. **Criteria:** Recipients will be selected based on financial need, academic standing, and upon the decision of the Foundation Board of Directors. **Funds Avail.:** $2,000 to $5,000. **Duration:** Annual. **Number Awarded:** Varies. **To Apply:** Applicants must submit an application form, along with the following requirements: essay; two letters of recommendation in which one is from the councilor and one is from the teacher; a copy of College Financial Aid Application or Student Aid Report; official transcript through midterm period of second semester of senior year including the SAT scores; budget for preferred college; letter of acceptance from college of choice; and a financial aid award letter from college of choice. **Deadline:** April 29. **Contact:** Scholarship Committee; Phone: 202-470-5425; Fax: 202-318-2482; Email: info@abramsonfoundation.org.

Awards are arranged alphabetically below their administering organizations

29 ■ Academy of Criminal Justice Sciences (ACJS)
7339 Hanover Pky., Ste. A
Greenbelt, MD 20770
Ph: (301)446-6300
Fax: (301)446-2819
Free: 800-757-2257
URL: www.acjs.org

30 ■ Affirmative Action Student Scholarship Mini-Grant Travel Awards *(Undergraduate, Master's, Doctorate/Grant)*

Purpose: To promote the involvement of all minority groups in the academy. **Focus:** Criminal justice; Law. **Qualif.:** Applicants must be members of a group who have experienced historical discrimination (i.e., African American, Asian American, Native American, persons of Hispanic descent); enrolled in criminal justice, criminology or related programs; available for undergraduates, masters, and doctoral students. **Criteria:** Recipients are selected based on the AACJS Affirmative Action Committee panel's review of application materials.

Funds Avail.: Maximum of $600. **Duration:** Annual. **Number Awarded:** 2. **To Apply:** Applicants must submit a completed manuscript (not more than 30 pages in length) examining criminal justice/ criminological issue; a 10-page, double-spaced, typed proposal discussing: (a) the nature of the research topic, (b) why the research is important, and where relevant, (c) the methods used, (d) the findings of the research, and (e) the theoretical, methodological, and/or policy implications of the results. **Deadline:** October 15. **Contact:** Melchor De Guzman, melchordgizman@yahoo.com.

31 ■ Academy for Eating Disorders (AED)
12100 Sunset Hills Rd., Ste. 130
Reston, VA 20190
Ph: (703)234-4079
Fax: (703)435-4390
E-mail: info@aedweb.org
URL: www.aedweb.org
Facebook: www.facebook.com/AcademyforEatingDisorders
LinkedIn: www.linkedin.com/groups/1208317/profile
Twitter: twitter.com/aedweb

32 ■ AED Student Early Career Investigator Travel Fellowships *(Undergraduate, Graduate, Postdoctorate, Postgraduate/Fellowship)*

Purpose: To support the students and early career investigators in attending the International Conference on Eating Disorders (ICED). **Focus:** Mental health; Psychology. **Qualif.:** Applicants must be student members, and early career investigators, of AED as of the deadline of the application. **Criteria:** Selection will be based on the committee's criteria.

Funds Avail.: Up to $1,500. **To Apply:** Applicants should submit the following materials: AED common application form; the Student/Early Career Travel Fellowship Application; a brief statement describing their career goals and how the fellowship will further these goals; two letters of endorsement; and, if there is, an abstract for the International Conference on Eating Disorders. All applications should be submitted electronically to the AED Headquarters. **Deadline:** January 12. **Contact:** Submit applications at earlycareer@aedweb.org.

33 ■ AED Student Research Grants *(Undergraduate, Graduate, Postgraduate/Grant)*

Purpose: To support innovative and cutting-edge research on eating disorders. **Focus:** Mental health; Psychology. **Qualif.:** Applicants must be student members of AED by the deadline of the grants application and must be nominated by non-student members of AED. **Criteria:** Selection will be based on the committee's criteria.

Funds Avail.: $1,000 each. **Number Awarded:** 2. **To Apply:** Applicants should submit the following materials: AED common application form; a current curriculum vita; a two-page, single-spaced Research Plan outlining the specific aims of the project, the background literature, the study procedure and methods and the timeline for completion (within the research plan, applicants should provide a brief statement that indicates: 1) whether the research fulfills a degree requirement (i.e., a thesis, a dissertation; please take note that the information on whether the research is for a degree is not a requirement, but is helpful information for the review committee); and 2) how the funds will be spent in the conduct of the research); and, a detailed Budget that lists materials and other items and their costs. For the nominators of the applicants, they should submit: a nomination letter (no longer than 500 words); and an additional letter of support from a faculty member from the nominees' institution or in the eating disorders field (no longer than 500 words). All application materials should be sent electronically to the AED Headquarters. **Deadline:** January 12. **Contact:** Email applications at grants@aedweb.org.

34 ■ Academy of Laser Dentistry (ALD)
9900 W Sample Rd., Ste. 400
Coral Springs, FL 33065-4079
Ph: (954)346-3776
Fax: (954)757-2598
Free: 877-527-3776
URL: www.laserdentistry.org
Facebook: www.facebook.com/AcademyofLaserDentistry
LinkedIn: www.linkedin.com/company/academy-of-laser-dentistry
Twitter: twitter.com/aldteam

35 ■ Dr. Eugene M. Seidner Student Scholarship Program *(Undergraduate, Graduate/Scholarship)*

Purpose: To promote the advancement of dental laser education and clinical research. **Focus:** Dentistry. **Qualif.:** Applicants must be either undergraduate or graduate dental students in a general or specialty program, and they are eligible through their first year after graduation of an accredited dental program. **Criteria:** Selection will be based on the committee's criteria.

Funds Avail.: $500 (Top 1); $250 (Top 2); $100 (Top 3). **Duration:** Annual. **Number Awarded:** 3. **To Apply:** Students must be nominated by their dental university faculty or ALD members. Nominated applicants must provide the following and must be sent electronically: student scholarship application; abstract for presentation; and, letter of reference. Selected students are required to submit their abstract for publication in the Journal of Laser Dentistry. Scholarship Application and Letter of Reference Form can be retrieved at the website. **Deadline:** June 30 (for the application and abstract); September 1 (for the letter of reference). **Remarks:** Established in 2004. **Contact:** Submit applications via email at memberservices@laserdentistry.org.

36 ■ Academy of Medical-Surgical Nurses (AMSN)
PO Box 56
Pitman, NJ 08071-0056
Ph: (856)256-2422
Fax: (856)589-7463
Free: 866-877-2676
E-mail: amsn@ajj.com
URL: www.amsn.org
Facebook: www.facebook.com/MedSurgNurses
LinkedIn: www.linkedin.com/company/academy-of-medical-surgical-nurses
Twitter: twitter.com/medsurgnurses

37 ■ AMSN Career Mobility Scholarship Awards
(Undergraduate, Doctorate/Scholarship)

Purpose: To provide financial assistance to AMSN members who wish to further their education. **Focus:** Medicine; Nursing; Surgery. **Qualif.:** Applicants must be members of AMSN for at least one year. **Criteria:** Applicants will be selected based on the jury's review of application materials and other supporting documents.

Funds Avail.: $2,000. **Duration:** Annual. **Number Awarded:** Up to 9. **To Apply:** Applicants must submit a completed application form; a brief description (one page, double-spaced with size 12 font) discussing how additional education will enhance the care of Adult Medical-Surgical patient; and a self-addressed stamped postcard. Electronic submission is preferred; otherwise applicant must submit additional nine blinded photocopies of application and of required documentation. **Deadline:** March 31.

38 ■ Academy of Model Aeronautics (AMA)
5161 E Memorial Dr.
Muncie, IN 47302
Fax: (765)289-4248
Free: 800-435-9262
URL: www.modelaircraft.org
Facebook: www.facebook.com/modelaviation
Twitter: twitter.com/modelaircraft

39 ■ AMA/Charles H. Grant Scholarships
(Undergraduate/Scholarship)

Purpose: To assist students in their educational pursuits. **Focus:** Aeronautics. **Qualif.:** Applicants must be full members of AMA for 36 months prior to applying; must be high school graduates; accepted by a college/university offering a certificate or degree program. **Criteria:** Applicants will be rated based on grade average, test results, modeling activities and citizenship achievement.

Funds Avail.: Approximately $40,000. **Duration:** Annual. **To Apply:** Applicants must submit a completed application form. **Contact:** Jessy Symmes at 765-287-1256 Ext. 516.

40 ■ Telford Scholarships *(Undergraduate/Scholarship)*

Purpose: To assist students in their educational pursuits. **Focus:** Aeronautics. **Qualif.:** Applicants must be full members of AMA 36 months prior to applying; high school graduates; accepted by a college/university offering a degree program; and have participated in any of AMA and FAI activities/events. **Criteria:** Applications will be evaluated by the AMA Scholarship Committee. Selection is based on the participation in competition activity by AMA and FAI.

Funds Avail.: No Specific amount. **Duration:** Annual. **To Apply:** Applicant must submit a Contest Classification form to list competitions that applicant participated in.

41 ■ Academy of Motion Picture Arts and Sciences (AMPAS)
8949 Wilshire Blvd.
Beverly Hills, CA 90211
Ph: (310)247-3000
Fax: (310)859-9619
E-mail: membership@oscars.org
URL: www.oscars.org

42 ■ Academy of Motion Picture Arts and Sciences Student Academy Awards *(Undergraduate/Award)*

Purpose: To encourage and reward excellence in filmmaking at the collegiate level. **Focus:** Media arts. **Qualif.:** Filmmaker must be a full-time student in a degree-granting program at an accredited US college or university. The film must have been made in a teacher-student relationship within the curricular structure of that institution. If the filmmaker has graduated or left such a program, the film may be submitted no later than one year from the filmmaker's date of departure. For foreign filmmakers, applicants must be enrolled in CILECT-affiliated colleges and universities outside the borders of the United States and must have previous professional experience. **Criteria:** Submitted entries will be judged on four categories: Animation, Documentary, Narrative and Alternative.

Funds Avail.: No specific amount. **Duration:** Annual. **Number Awarded:** Varies. **To Apply:** All entries must be submitted electronically. The maximum running time allowed for entries in all categories is 40 minutes. Domestic applicants must print a hard copy of their entry form and submit it together with their DVD to the appropriate Regional Coordinator. To be officially completed, the hard copy must contain the applicant's signature(s) and the signature of their supervising faculty advisor. For foreign applicants, all entries submitted must be in English, subtitled in English or dubbed in English. Entries will be accepted in the 16mm, 35mm and 70mm format or in the Digital Betacam format. Film prints submitted must be composite, with optical or magnetic soundtracks. **Remarks:** Established in 1972.

43 ■ The Academy of Neonatal Nursing
1425 N McDowell Blvd., Ste. 105
Petaluma, CA 94954
Ph: (707)568-2168
Fax: (707)569-0786
URL: www.academyonline.org

44 ■ Academy of Neonatal Nursing Conference Scholarships *(Professional development/Scholarship)*

Purpose: To support members in attending the annual National Neonatal Nurses Meeting. **Focus:** Nursing, Neonatal. **Qualif.:** Applicants must be members of the Academy in good standing for at least one year; must have a minimum of two years of neonatal practice experience;

Awards are arranged alphabetically below their administering organizations

must be professionally active neonatal nurses; and have not been recipients of an ANN Conference Scholarship within the past 5 years. **Criteria:** Selection will be based on the committee's criteria. Preference will be given to nurses who demonstrate active involvement in professional or community service activities.

Funds Avail.: No specific amount. **Number Awarded:** Up to 3. **To Apply:** Applicants must submit the following: completed application; a brief written explanation, no more than one paragraph, of how they intend to share information from the conference with their unit colleagues or work group; a list of contact hours obtained in the last year, including title of offering and provider; and a current curriculum vitae. **Deadline:** June 1.

45 ■ ANN Ingrid Josefin Ridky Academic Scholarships (Undergraduate, Graduate/Scholarship)

Purpose: To support those members who are pursuing academic advancement in neonatal nursing. **Focus:** Nursing, Neonatal. **Qualif.:** Applicants must be members of the Academy in good standing for at least one year; must have a minimum of two years of neonatal practice experience, with at least one of these years completed in the past 18 months; must be enrolled in a nursing academic degree program or a neonatal postgraduate program for one of the following: Bachelor of Nursing, Master of Nursing, Doctoral Degree in Nursing, or Post Master Certificate in a Nursing Specialty; must have successfully completed two required courses in that program; must have a GPA of 3.0 or higher; must be professionally active neonatal nurses; and have not been recipients of an ANN scholarship within the past 5 years. **Criteria:** Selection will be based on the committee's criteria.

Funds Avail.: $1,000. **To Apply:** Applicants must submit the following: completed application; a letter from their advisors or the deans of the university or other institutions of learning stating that they are enrolled in a degree program and have successfully completed two courses toward that degree; transcript of grades achieved (proof of GPA); and an essay of 200 words or less, stating why they are pursuing their education and how attainment of the degree will benefit them in their professional role as neonatal nurses. Use plain bond paper for this essay, not letterhead. **Deadline:** June 1.

46 ■ Academy of Television Arts and Sciences Foundation
5220 Lankershim Blvd.
North Hollywood, CA 91601
Ph: (818)754-2800
URL: www.emmys.com/foundation
Facebook: www.facebook.com/televisionacad

47 ■ Mister Rogers Memorial Scholarship (Graduate, Master's, Doctorate/Scholarship)

Purpose: To provide financial assistance to students pursuing a degree in a children's media related course. **Focus:** Child development; Education, Early childhood; Filmmaking; Media arts; Music; Radio and television. **Qualif.:** Applicants must be graduate students of accredited colleges and universities; must demonstrate a commitment, through coursework or experience, to any combination of at least two of the following fields: early childhood education; child development/child psychology; film/television production; music; animation; and production of cross-platform entertainment. **Criteria:** Applications are evaluated by a committee formed yearly by the two governors representing the Television Academy's Children's Programming Peer Group.

Funds Avail.: $10,000 each. **Duration:** Annual. **Number Awarded:** 2. **To Apply:** Applicants must complete the application form available online; must attach background information about the plan for the use of the scholarship money and a proposed detailed budget on how the scholarship funds will be used; must submit a recommendation letter from two persons, either faculty members or professionals from the children's media industry who have worked with the applicant.

48 ■ Accounting and Financial Women's Alliance (AFWA)
2365 Harrodsburg Rd., Ste. A325
Lexington, KY 40504
Ph: (859)219-3532
Fax: (859)219-3577
Free: 800-326-2163
E-mail: afwa@afwa.org
URL: www.afwa.org
LinkedIn: www.linkedin.com/company/accounting-&-financial-women%27s-alliance?trk=company_name

49 ■ AFWA Masters Degree Scholarships (Undergraduate, Master's/Scholarship)

Purpose: To support the costs of attending a masters program towards an accounting or finance degree. **Focus:** Accounting; Finance. **Qualif.:** Applicants must be students who have applied to a masters degree program by the time of the application and are majoring in accounting or finance; must have a minimum cumulative college GPA of 3.0 on a 4.0 scale or the equivalent. **Criteria:** Scholarship recipients will be selected on the basis of leadership, character and communication skills, scholastic average and financial need.

Funds Avail.: No specific amount. **Duration:** Annual. **To Apply:** Applicants must submit a completed application form; 150-250 words essay about their goals and objectives, what impact they want to have on the accounting and financial world, community involvement and leadership examples; endorsement form to be submitted online by a chapter or AFWA member; and a copy and the original academic transcript from school. **Deadline:** April 1.

50 ■ AFWA Undergraduate Scholarships (Undergraduate/Scholarship)

Purpose: To defray the cost of attending 3rd, 4th or 5th year towards an accounting or finance degree. **Focus:** Accounting; Finance. **Qualif.:** Applicants must be students who have completed their sophomore year of college and are majoring in accounting or finance. Applicants must have a minimum cumulative GPA of 3.0 on a 4.0 scale. **Criteria:** Recipients are selected on the basis of leadership, character and communication skills, scholastic average and financial need.

Funds Avail.: No specific amount. **Duration:** Annual. **To Apply:** Applicants must submit a completed application form; 150 to 250-word essay about their goals and objectives, what impact they wants to have on the accounting world and most likes about accounting; three references (two references must be from accounting faculty); and a copy and the original academic transcript from school.

Awards are arranged alphabetically below their administering organizations

51 ■ Acoustical Society of America (ASA)

c/o Elaine Moran, Office Manager
1305 Walt Whitman Rd., Ste. 300
Melville, NY 11747-4300
Ph: (516)576-2360
Fax: (516)576-2377
E-mail: asa@aip.org
URL: acousticalsociety.org

52 ■ Acoustical Society of America Minority Fellowships (Graduate/Fellowship)

Purpose: To support minority students in their pursuit of graduate-level degrees in acoustics. **Focus:** Speech and language pathology/Audiology. **Qualif.:** Applicants must be permanent residents or citizens of the United States at the time of application; members of an ethnic minority group (Hispanic, African-American or Native American) that are underrepresented in the sciences; and accepted into, or good academic standing in, a graduate degree program. **Criteria:** Selection is based on academic record, personal statement and letters of recommendation from three instructors or employers.

Funds Avail.: No specific amount. **To Apply:** Applicants must submit a completed application form along with official transcripts of all college and university study; Graduate Record Exam scores; a personal statement; and three letters of recommendation. **Remarks:** Established in 1992.

53 ■ Frederick V. Hunt Postdoctoral Research Fellowships in Acoustics (Postdoctorate/Fellowship)

Purpose: To further the science of, and education in acoustics. **Focus:** Speech and language pathology/Audiology. **Qualif.:** Applicants must be conducting a research on a topic in acoustics at a chosen institution. **Criteria:** Selection is based on the submitted application and materials.

Funds Avail.: No specific amount. **Duration:** Annual. **Number Awarded:** 1. **To Apply:** Applicants may contact the Society for the application information.

54 ■ Raymond H. Stetson Scholarships in Phonetics and Speech Science (Graduate/Scholarship)

Purpose: To facilitate the research efforts of promising graduate students. **Focus:** Speech and language pathology/Audiology. **Qualif.:** Applicants must be members of the Acoustical Society of America prior to, or at the time of, the application deadline. Evidence of good academic standing in a graduate degree program is also required. **Criteria:** Selection is based on the applicants' academic record, personal statement, letters of recommendation, the research paper and relevance of the research area.

Funds Avail.: No specific amount. **Duration:** Annual. **To Apply:** Applicants must submit a completed application form together with official transcripts of university graduate study; a personal statement; a current curriculum vitae; a research paper; and two letters of recommendation. **Remarks:** Established in 1998. **Contact:** Acoustical Society of America, at the above address.

55 ■ Action Institute for the Study of Religion and Liberty

98 E Fulton St.
Grand Rapids, MI 49503
Ph: (616)454-3080
Fax: (616)454-9454
Free: 800-345-2286
E-mail: info@acton.org
URL: www.acton.org
Facebook: www.facebook.com/ActonInstitute
LinkedIn: www.linkedin.com/company/acton-institute
Twitter: twitter.com/actoninstitute

56 ■ Calihan Academic Fellowships (Graduate, Professional development/Fellowship, Grant)

Purpose: To provide scholarships and research grants to future scholars and religious leaders whose academic work shows outstanding potential. **Focus:** Economics; Philosophy; Religion; Theology. **Qualif.:** Applicants must be seminarians or graduate students in theology, philosophy, religion, economics, or in related fields. Strong academic performance is essential; must have a demonstrated interest in the themes of the Acton Institute; must display the potential to advance the themes of the Acton Institute. Awards are open to all qualified persons irrespective of race, sex, national or ethnic origin, age, citizenship, religious affiliation, or disability. **Criteria:** Selection shall be based on the following criteria: strong academic performance; having a demonstrated interest in the themes of the Institute; and able to display the potential to advance the themes of the Institute.

Funds Avail.: Maximum of $3,000, but typically range from $500 to $1,000. **Duration:** Semiannual. **Number Awarded:** Varies. **To Apply:** Applicants must complete the following requirements: a signed application form; a one-page proposal that outlines what they intend to accomplish with the scholarship; a two-page essay that describes their intellectual development, future plans and career goals; a recent paper they have already written relevant to the themes promoted by the Acton Institute (if such is not in English, please provide an English abstract or summary); and, official transcripts from their current university and each university where they have received a degree in which notarized copies are also acceptable. **Deadline:** July 15 (Fall term); October 15 (Spring term).

57 ■ Calihan Travel Grants (Graduate/Grant)

Purpose: To provide financial assistance to students who have been selected to present, at an academic conference, research relevant to themes promoted by the Acton Institute. **Focus:** Economics; Philosophy; Religion; Theology. **Qualif.:** Applicants must be seminarians or graduate students in theology, philosophy, religion, economics, or related fields; must have a strong academic performance; must have a demonstrated interest in the themes of the Acton Institute; must display the potential to contribute to the advancement of a free and virtuous society. Awards are open to all qualified persons irrespective of age, race, sex, national or ethnic origin, citizenship, religious affiliation, or disability. **Criteria:** Selection will be based on the criteria of the research staff of the Acton Institute.

Funds Avail.: Up to $3,000. **To Apply:** Applicants must complete and submit the following requirements: stated purpose of travel; if applicable, abstract of paper/research; description of how one's conference paper, research travel or conference attendance is connected to themes promoted by the Acton Institute; disclosure of educational history; two academic references; estimated conference expenses: travel, room and board, registration fees, other expenses directly related to the conference/research; disclosure of additional sources of funding.

58 ■ Novak Awards (Doctorate/Monetary)

Purpose: To support emerging scholars for outstanding new research into the interrelation of religion and economic

Awards are arranged alphabetically below their administering organizations

liberty. **Focus:** Business; Economics; Philosophy; Religion; Theology. **Qualif.:** Candidates must be scholars who have received a doctorate from an accredited domestic or international program in the previous five calendar years or current doctoral candidates in the process of completing their dissertations; must be studying theology, religion, economics, philosophy, business or a related field; must have a strong academic performance; must have a demonstrated interest in the relationship between religion, economic liberty and the free and virtuous society. Important principles in this relationship include the recognition of human dignity, the importance of the rule of law, limited government, religious liberty and freedom in economic life; must display the potential to contribute to the advancement of a free and virtuous society. The award is open to all qualified persons irrespective of race, sex, age, national or ethnic origin, citizenship, religious affiliation, or disability. **Criteria:** Selection will be based on the committee's criteria.

Funds Avail.: $10,000. **Duration:** Annual. **To Apply:** Professors, university faculty members and other scholars may nominate qualified individuals for the Novak Award by completing the online nomination form. Those scholars nominated for the Novak Award will be contacted via email and asked to submit an application. A completed application consists of the following: a signed application form, available at the website; a curriculum vitae; a 500-word essay that describes applicants' intellectual development, future plans and career goals; a research paper, refereed published article or other scholarly work, such as a book, monograph or a conference paper on a theme relevant to religion and economic liberty or a related theme; two letters of recommendation from professors or other established scholars in applicants' field. **Deadline:** February 15 for the nomination; March 15 for the application.

59 ■ The Actuarial Foundation
475 N Martingale Road Ste 600
Schaumburg, IL 60173-2226
Ph: (847)706-3535
E-mail: info@Actfnd.org
URL: www.actuarialfoundation.org

60 ■ Actuarial Diversity Scholarship *(Undergraduate/Scholarship)*

Purpose: To promote diversity within the profession through an annual scholarship program for Black/African American, Hispanic, Native North American and Pacific Islander students. **Focus:** Actuarial science; Mathematics and mathematical sciences; Minorities. **Qualif.:** Each applicant must have the intent on pursuing a career in the actuarial profession; must have at least one birth parent who is a member of one of the following minority groups: Black/African American, Hispanic, Native North American, Pacific Islander; will be a full-time undergraduate student at a U.S. accredited educational institution; minimum GPA of 3.0 (on a 4.0 scale), emphasis on math or actuarial courses; and, entering college freshmen must have a minimum ACT math score of 28 or SAT math score of 600. **Criteria:** Actuarial exams will be an important factor in evaluating scholarship qualifications for applicants entering their junior year and beyond. Additionally, exams passed will also be a consideration for previous award recipients applying to renew the scholarship.

Funds Avail.: $1,000 for high school senior; $2,000 for college freshman; $3,000 for college sophomore; $4,000 for college junior. **Duration:** Annual. **To Apply:** Applicants must visit the Foundation's website for the online application process. Applicants must complete and submit all the requirements on or before the deadline. **Deadline:** May 2. **Remarks:** Established in 1977. **Contact:** Additional information can be asked through The Actuarial Foundation at scholarships@actfnd.org.

61 ■ Caribbean Actuarial Scholarship *(Undergraduate/Scholarship)*

Purpose: To support undergraduate actuarial students who demonstrate strong record of accomplishment, leadership qualities and commitment to become actuary. **Focus:** Actuarial science; Mathematics and mathematical sciences. **Qualif.:** Each applicant must be undergraduate student attending the University of the West Indies (UWI); must be entering second or third year; must be enrolled in the UWI actuarial science program; must have a minimum GPA of 3.0 or equivalent. **Criteria:** Selection will be based on the committee's criteria.

Funds Avail.: $1,500 for student entering second year of studies; $2,500 for student entering third year of studies. **Duration:** Annual. **To Apply:** Applicants must visit the website for the online application process. Applicants must complete and submit the application on or before the deadline. **Deadline:** July 14. **Remarks:** Established in 2008. **Contact:** scholarships@actfnd.org.

62 ■ Curtis E. Huntington Memorial Scholarship *(Undergraduate/Scholarship)*

Purpose: To recognize the remarkably positive impact Huntington had on the students and on the actuarial profession. **Focus:** Actuarial science; Mathematics and mathematical sciences. **Qualif.:** Each applicant must be full-time college senior (seniors are undergraduate students who will receive their degree no later than August of the current year); must obtain a minimum cumulative GPA of 3.0 (on 4.0 scale); must be nominated by a professor at the affiliated school (only one nomination per school is accepted); and, successfully completed at least one actuarial exam. **Criteria:** Selection will be based on the committee's criteria.

Funds Avail.: $2,000. **Duration:** Annual. **To Apply:** Applicants must visit the website for the online application process. Applicants must complete and submit the application on or before the deadline. **Deadline:** June 17. **Contact:** scholarships@actfnd.org.

63 ■ Elizabeth M. Mauro Reimbursement Awards *(Advanced Professional/Award)*

Purpose: To recognize the limited resources available and to support career changers aspiring to transition into the actuarial profession. **Focus:** Actuarial science. **Qualif.:** Applicants must be 25 years or older by application deadline date; must not receive reimbursement for these exam registration fees and/or study materials from any other reimbursement program (including employee programs); must be U.S. citizens; and have passed at least one actuarial exam within the twenty-four months prior to the application due date. **Criteria:** Selection will be based on the committee's criteria.

Funds Avail.: $1,000. **Duration:** Annual. **Number Awarded:** 2. **To Apply:** Applicants must meet all the eligibility requirements; must include a resume, documentation of actuarial exams passed, and one-page personal statement detailing the desire and plan to enter the actuarial profession with the completed application. Applicants must electronically complete and submit the application. **Dead-**

line: August 8. **Contact:** programs@actfnd.org.

64 ■ Actuary of Tomorrow - Stuart A. Robertson Memorial Scholarship *(Undergraduate/Scholarship)*

Purpose: To recognize and encourage the academic achievements of undergraduate students pursuing a career in actuarial science. **Focus:** Actuarial science; Mathematics and mathematical sciences. **Qualif.:** Applicant must be full-time students entering as a sophomore, junior or senior at a U.S accredited educational institution; must obtain a minimum cumulative GPA of 3.0 (on 4.0 scale); and, successfully completed two actuarial exams. **Criteria:** Selection will be based on the committee's criteria.

Funds Avail.: $9,000. **Duration:** Annual. **To Apply:** Applicants must visit the website for the online application process. Applicants must complete and submit all the required materials on or before the deadline. **Deadline:** June 1. **Contact:** scholarships@actfnd.org.

65 ■ Adelante Fund
Highpoint Twr.
8415 Datapoint Dr., Ste. 400
San Antonio, TX 78229
Ph: (210)692-1971
Fax: (210)855-6213
E-mail: info@adelantefund.org
URL: www.adelantefund.org
Facebook: www.facebook.com/adelante.fund

66 ■ Adelante Fund Hope Scholarships, CPS Energy Dependents *(Undergraduate/Scholarship)*

Purpose: To support Hispanic students in their educational pursuit. **Focus:** General studies/Field of study not specified. **Qualif.:** Applicant must be an incoming freshman or undergraduate college student; attend an accredited college/university in San Antonio recognized by the U.S. Department of Education; have and maintain a 2.5 GPA or above based on a 4.0 scale; and be involved in community service. **Criteria:** Selection is based on the application materials.

Funds Avail.: $1,500-3,000. **To Apply:** Applicants must submit a completed application together with the required documents. **Deadline:** June 24. **Remarks:** Active or retired CPS Energy guardians or parents must obtain a signature from a HOPE officer on the Scholarship Eligibility Form found on the CPS Energy Intranet.

67 ■ Adelante Fund Hope Scholarships, San Antonio, TX Students *(Undergraduate/Scholarship)*

Purpose: To support Hispanic students in their educational pursuit. **Focus:** General studies/Field of study not specified. **Qualif.:** Applicant must be an incoming freshman or undergraduate college student; attend an accredited college/university in San Antonio recognized by the U.S. Department of Education; have and maintain a 2.5 GPA or above based on a 4.0 scale; and be involved in community service. **Criteria:** Selection is based on the application materials.

Funds Avail.: $3,000. **To Apply:** Applicants must submit a completed application together with the required documents. **Deadline:** May 31.

68 ■ MillerCoors Engineering and Sciences Scholarships *(Undergraduate/Scholarship)*

Purpose: To support Hispanic students in their educational pursuit. **Focus:** Biochemistry; Computer and information sciences; Engineering, Electrical; Engineering, Mechanical. **Qualif.:** Applicant must be eligible for college junior or senior status and pursue a degree in Electrical Engineering, Mechanical Engineering, Computer Science or Bio-Chemistry. Must be a US citizen or Legal Permanent Resident; be of Hispanic descent; maintain a GPA of 3.0 or above (on a 4.0 scale); and must attend a partnering university. **Criteria:** Selection is based on the application materials.

Funds Avail.: $3,000. **Duration:** Annual. **To Apply:** Applicants must submit a completed application together with the required documents. **Deadline:** May 29.

69 ■ MillerCoors National Scholarships *(Undergraduate/Scholarship)*

Purpose: To support Hispanic students in their educational pursuit. **Focus:** Accounting; Business; Communications; Economics; Marketing and distribution; Public relations. **Qualif.:** Applicant must be eligible for college junior or senior status and pursue a degree in International Business, General Business, Economics, Finance, Accounting, Marketing, Public Relations, General Communications or Sales. Must be a US citizen or Legal Permanent Resident; be of Hispanic descent; maintain a GPA of 3.0 or above (on a 4.0 scale); and must attend a partnering university. **Criteria:** Selection is based on the application materials submitted.

Funds Avail.: $3,000. **Duration:** Annual. **To Apply:** Applicants must submit a completed application together with the required documents. **Deadline:** May 29.

70 ■ Adler Pollock & Sheehan, P.C.
One Citizens Plaza, 8th Fl.
Providence, RI 02903-1345
Ph: (401)274-7200
Fax: (401)751-0604
URL: www.apslaw.com

71 ■ Adler Pollock & Sheehan Diversity Scholarships *(Undergraduate/Scholarship)*

Purpose: To support and encourage more diverse candidates to enter the practice of law and to diversify and enrich both the firm and profession. **Focus:** Law. **Qualif.:** Applicants must: be members of a diverse group; be entering first year students at an ABA accredited law school anywhere in the US; have permanent residence in Massachusetts or Rhode Island; have a strong academic achievement; have demonstrated financial need. **Criteria:** Scholarship will be given to students who have demonstrated commitment to academic excellence and commitment to the community.

Funds Avail.: $10,000. **Duration:** Annual. **To Apply:** Applicants must submit the following: a completed application form; one-page typed essay; a certified copy of college transcript; an acceptance letter from an ABA accredited law school and written notice of intention to attend; a copy of their FAFSA and any other financial aid application, as well as any financial aid they have been offered by the law school they will be attending and by any other source; copies of applicants' and their parents' federal and state tax returns filed in the most recent year; photo ID; proof of Legal Residency in US; two letters of recommendation from persons who are not related to the applicants and who are familiar with the students' academic achievements, character and commitment to the community. **Deadline:** June 1. **Contact:** Call 617-482-0600; or email at diversitycomm@apslaw.com.

Awards are arranged alphabetically below their administering organizations

72 ■ Administrative Sciences Association of Canada (ASAC)
c/o University of Windsor
Odette School of Business
Odette Bldg., Rm. 446
401 Sunset Ave.
Windsor, ON, Canada N9B 3P4
Ph: (519)253-3000
Fax: (519)973-7073
E-mail: templer@uwindsor.ca
URL: www.asac.ca

73 ■ ASAC-CJAS PhD Research Grant Awards
(Doctorate/Grant)

Purpose: To support Canadian PhD students during their doctoral research. **Focus:** Business administration. **Qualif.:** Applicants must be full-time Canadian PhD students at Canadian universities in the areas of administrative sciences and business administration; must have successfully completed their examination and have not yet defended their dissertation. **Criteria:** Applications will be assessed based on the quality and originality of the proposal, research/scholarly achievements of the applicant, and special circumstances or other factors deemed appropriate in a particular instance.

Funds Avail.: $2,500. **Duration:** Biennial. **Number Awarded:** 1. **To Apply:** Applicants must submit curriculum vitae, two letters of reference, transcript from current program of study, certificate(s) of approval for research involving the use of human subjects from the host university and budget justification. **Deadline:** December 31. **Contact:** Andrew Templer, Odette School of Business, University of Windsor, Odette Building Room 316B, 401 Sunset Avenue Windsor, Ontario N9B 3P4; Email at templer@uwindsor.ca.

74 ■ ADSC: The International Association of Foundation Drilling
8445 Freeport Pky., Ste. 325
Irving, TX 75063
Ph: (469)359-6000
Fax: (469)359-6007
E-mail: adsc@adsc-iafd.com
URL: www.adsc-iafd.com
Facebook: www.facebook.com/adsc.iafd
LinkedIn: www.linkedin.com/in/adsc-iafd-45505b2a
Twitter: twitter.com/ADSC_IAFD

75 ■ International Association of Foundation Drilling Scholarships for Civil Engineering Students
(Graduate/Scholarship)

Purpose: To support full-time civil engineering students in their continuing education. **Focus:** Engineering, Civil. **Qualif.:** Applicants must be full-time civil engineering students currently enrolled in an ABET or CEAB accredited engineering program or graduates from such a program, and must plan to enter or continue graduate school during the current academic year. **Criteria:** Recipients are selected based on academic performance and financial need.

Funds Avail.: $3,000. **Duration:** Annual. **To Apply:** Applicants must submit a completed application form; current, official transcript of academic records and two letters of reference from persons familiar with their academic or professional experience.

76 ■ International Association of Foundation Drilling Scholarships for Part-time Civil Engineering Graduate School Students
(Graduate/Scholarship)

Purpose: To assist part-time civil engineering students in their continuing education. **Focus:** Engineering, Civil. **Qualif.:** Applicants must be part-time civil engineering students currently enrolled in an ABET or CEAB accredited engineering program or graduates from such a program, and must plan to enter or continue graduate school during the current academic year. **Criteria:** Recipients are selected based on academic performance and financial need.

Funds Avail.: $1,500. **Duration:** Annual. **To Apply:** Applicants must submit a completed application form; current, official transcript of academic record; and two letters of reference from persons familiar with the academic or professional experience.

77 ■ Advertising Production Club of New York (APC)
Showtime Networks
1633 Broadway
New York, NY 10019
Ph: (212)716-7767
E-mail: info@apc-ny.org
URL: www.apc-nyc.org

78 ■ APC High School Scholarship Awards
(Undergraduate/Scholarship)

Purpose: To provide financial assistance to those studying graphic arts and communications. **Focus:** Communications; Graphic art and design. **Qualif.:** Applicants must be graduating high school students with graphic arts/communications curriculum; must have "B" average upon graduation; and must have plan to attend an accredited college program in a full-time basis. **Criteria:** Preference will be given to those individuals who have not previously been awarded a scholarship through the APC.

Funds Avail.: No specific amount. **Duration:** Annual. **To Apply:** Guidelines and application forms are available from the Advertising Production Club office or can be downloaded from the APC website; must submit a completed hard copy of the application form together with the registration receipt for the new semester, college transcript and acceptance letter; and must present an identification and confirmation by the high school principal.

79 ■ Advocates' Society (AS)
2700-250 Yonge St.
Toronto, ON, Canada M5B 2L7
Ph: (416)597-0243
Fax: (416)597-1588
E-mail: mail@advocates.ca
URL: www.advocates.ca
LinkedIn: www.linkedin.com/company/the-advocates'
 -society
Twitter: twitter.com/advocates_soc

80 ■ Catzman Awards for Professionalism and Civility
(Advanced Professional, Professional development/Award)

Purpose: To recognize individuals who have demonstrated a high degree of professionalism and civility in the practice of law. **Focus:** Law. **Qualif.:** Candidates must show profes-

Awards are arranged alphabetically below their administering organizations

sionalism and civility, and have made contributions to legal education. **Criteria:** Recipients will be selected by the selection committee. Criteria shall be determined by as well by the selection body.

Funds Avail.: No specific amount. **Duration:** Annual. **To Apply:** Applicants must provide a brief statement outlining the reasons for the nomination, current curriculum vitae and two letters of support. **Remarks:** Established in 2008. **Contact:** The Advocates' Society, at the above address.

81 ■ David Stockwood Memorial Prize (Advanced Professional, Professional development/Prize)

Purpose: To honor individuals who made contributions to advocacy-related fields. **Focus:** Law. **Qualif.:** Applicants must be the authors of a previously unpublished, advocacy-related article. **Criteria:** Papers will be evaluated based on their merit by a panel.

Funds Avail.: $1,000. **Duration:** Biennial; in even-numbered years. **To Apply:** Articles must be a maximum of 3,500 words in length and should be submitted in Word format. **Contact:** Robin Black, Director, Marketing and Membership, robin@advocates.ca.

82 ■ Aerospace States Association (ASA)
107 S West St., Ste. 510
Alexandria, VA 22314
Ph: (202)257-4872
Fax: (703)548-8784
URL: aerostates.org

83 ■ Edward A. O'Connor Founder's Scholarships (Undergraduate/Scholarship)

Purpose: To help students pursue their education in an aerospace-related field. **Focus:** Aerospace sciences. **Qualif.:** Applicants must be sophomore or junior undergraduate students pursuing an aerospace-related field. **Criteria:** Selection will be based on submitted materials.

Funds Avail.: $2,000. **Duration:** Annual. **Number Awarded:** Varies. **To Apply:** Applicants must complete the application form; must submit a copy of official transcript; must submit a two-page, typed statement describing the educational career goals and interests, and how this can be related to aerospace fields; must also submit one letter of recommendation. **Contact:** ASA Education Committee Vice Chair, Dr. Stephanie Wright at swright@udel.edu.

84 ■ AFCEA International
4400 Fair Lakes Ct.
Fairfax, VA 22033-3899
Ph: (703)631-6100
Fax: (703)631-6169
Free: 800-336-4583
URL: www.afcea.org

85 ■ AFCEA Cyber Studies and Intelligence Scholarships (Undergraduate, Graduate/Scholarship)

Purpose: To provide scholarship to the general public. **Focus:** Computer and information sciences; Engineering; Information science and technology; National security. **Qualif.:** Applicants must: be sophomore, junior or senior undergraduate students and graduate students enrolled full time in an eligible degree-granting program; be U.S. citizens currently enrolled at the time of application in a two-year or four-year accredited college or university in the United States; obtain minimum overall GPA of 3.0 on a 4.0 scale; be majoring in a field directly related to the support of U.S. cyber security enterprises with relevance to the mission of AFCEA such as cyber security, cyber attack, computer science, digital forensics, information technology, or electronic engineering. Distance-learning programs are eligible. **Criteria:** Recipients are selected based on demonstrated academic excellence, leadership, and financial need.

Funds Avail.: Amount varies. **Duration:** Annual. **Number Awarded:** Varies. **To Apply:** Applicants must fill up completely the provided application form. Applicants must also submit two letters of recommendation printed in school stationery and with signature from field-of-study professors; and official transcript of all college level study. Submission of all the mentioned requirements must be by either electronic or walk-in.

86 ■ AFCEA Scholarship for Working Professionals (Undergraduate, Graduate/Scholarship)

Purpose: To provide scholarship to those students pursuing an undergraduate or graduate degree while employed. **Focus:** Communications; Engineering; Mathematics and mathematical sciences; Physics. **Qualif.:** Applicants must be: U.S. citizens attending an accredited college or university in the United States as either traditional or distance learning students; and, majoring in any of the following: electrical, chemical, systems or aerospace engineering; mathematics; physics; technical management; computer information systems; computer science or related fields. They must have an overall GPA of 3.0. For graduates, they must have completed at least two postgraduate-level courses and are enrolled in an eligible degree-granting master's degree program. Undergraduate candidates must be at least second year students attending an accredited college or university in the United States. **Criteria:** Recipients will be selected based on committee's review of applications.

Funds Avail.: $250 each. **Duration:** Annual. **Number Awarded:** 4. **To Apply:** Applicants may apply online at the AFCEA web site. **Contact:** Call Roy Nielsen via phone at 405-739-4060.

87 ■ AFCEA Science, Technology, Engineering and Math Teachers Scholarships (Graduate/Scholarship, Grant)

Purpose: To promote science, mathematics or information technology education at the US Secondary School, and support graduate students to become STEM teachers. **Focus:** Education; Engineering; Mathematics and mathematical sciences; Science; Technology. **Qualif.:** Applicants must be U.S. citizens who are graduate students attending an accredited U.S. college or university on-campus and majoring in secondary education for the purpose of teaching STEM (science, technology, engineering or math) subjects in a U.S. middle/intermediate and high schools. **Criteria:** Selection will be on competitive basis.

Funds Avail.: $2,500 to $5,000. **Duration:** Annual. **To Apply:** Applicants may visit the website for further information. **Deadline:** April 22. **Contact:** Contact via e-mail: edfoundation@afcea.org.

88 ■ Afghanistan and Iraq War Veterans Scholarship (Undergraduate/Scholarship)

Purpose: To provide scholarships to students connected to the US military. **Focus:** Communications; Engineering; Information science and technology; Intelligence service; Mathematics and mathematical sciences; Physics. **Qualif.:**

Awards are arranged alphabetically below their administering organizations

Applicants must be active-duty and honorably discharged U.S. military veterans and reservists and National Guard personnel of the Enduring Freedom-Afghanistan or Iraqi Freedom Operations. Also, they must be currently enrolled and attending either two year or four year level at any accredited colleges or universities in the United States. Distance-learning or online programs affiliated with a major U.S. institution are also eligible. **Criteria:** Recipients will be selected based on the committee's review of application.

Funds Avail.: $2,500. **Duration:** Annual. **To Apply:** Applicants may apply online at AFCEA web site. Additional requirements are the following: copy of either a Certificate of Service or Discharge Form DD214; current transcript issued by the school Registrar's Office and at least two letters of recommendation from relevant faculty. **Deadline:** April 15.

89 ■ Lt. General Douglas D. Buchholz Memorial Scholarship *(Undergraduate/Scholarship)*

Purpose: To provide scholarships to enlisted soldiers designated at Fort Gordon, Georgia. **Focus:** Communications; Engineering; Mathematics and mathematical sciences; Physics. **Qualif.:** Applicants must: be currently active enlisted soldiers assigned to Fort Gordon, Georgia; have completed a minimum of 15 semester hours/25 quarter hours; be currently enrolled either full or part time in an accredited US college; and, have a minimum GPA of 2.5 on a 4.0 scale. **Criteria:** Recipients will be selected based on recommendation of Scholarship Board under the guidance of the Fort Gordon Command Sergeant Major.

Funds Avail.: $2,000. **Duration:** Annual. **To Apply:** Students may apply online at the AFCEA web site. **Contact:** Mr. Joseph S. Yavorsky, at president@afcea-augusta.org.

90 ■ Disabled War Veterans Scholarships *(Undergraduate/Scholarship)*

Purpose: To provide scholarships to disabled students connected to the US military. **Focus:** Communications; Engineering; Information science and technology; Intelligence service; Mathematics and mathematical sciences; Physics. **Qualif.:** Applicants must be: active-duty service personnel, honorably discharged U.S. military veterans, reservists, and National Guard personnel who are disabled because of wounds received during combat service in Enduring Freedom-Afghanistan or Iraqi Freedom Operations; currently enrolled and attending either a two-year or four-year in an accredited college or university in the United States; and, enrolled in an accredited distance learning or online degree granting program affiliated with major, accredited two year or four year college or university in the United States. **Criteria:** Recipients will be selected based on academic excellence, leadership and financial need.

Funds Avail.: $2,500. **Duration:** Annual. **To Apply:** Applicants may apply online at AFCEA web site. Additional requirements are the following: copy of either a Certificate of Service or Discharge Form DD214; current transcript issued by the school Registrar's Office and at least two letters of recommendation from relevant faculty. **Deadline:** November 13.

91 ■ Ralph W. Shrader Diversity Scholarship *(Graduate/Scholarship)*

Purpose: To provide educational opportunities for talented individuals pursuing advanced degrees at the master's level. **Focus:** Computer and information sciences; Engineering, Chemical; Engineering, Electrical; Mathematics and mathematical sciences; Physics. **Qualif.:** Applicants must be U.S. citizens currently enrolled full time in a master's degree program in an accredited university in the United States. They must currently be enrolled in their second semester and at least two (2) semester-equivalent courses per semester at a four-year accredited college or university (HBCU or non-HBCU) in the United States at the time of application. A current overall GPA of 3.5 or higher on a 4.0 scale at the time of application. **Criteria:** Recipients will be selected based on academic excellence.

Funds Avail.: $3,000. **Duration:** Annual. **To Apply:** Applicants may apply online at the AFCEA web site.

92 ■ African American Success Foundation (AASF)
7027 W Broward Blvd., No. 313
Fort Lauderdale, FL 33317
Ph: (954)792-1117
E-mail: info@blacksuccessfoundation.org
URL: www.blacksuccessfoundation.org

93 ■ Lydia Donaldson Tutt-Jones Memorial Research Grant *(Graduate, Other, Master's/Grant)*

Purpose: To provide financial support to students and professionals who conduct research study of African American success, particularly in the area of education. **Focus:** African-American studies. **Qualif.:** Applicants must be graduate students and professionals. Students must be recommended by a faculty mentor who agrees to oversee the project and the submission of a publishable caliber paper upon its completion. **Criteria:** Selection will be based on the committee's criteria.

Funds Avail.: No specific amount. **Duration:** Annual. **To Apply:** Applicants must submit the following: a letter of interest in applying for the award; curriculum vitae; a description of the proposed research project (please give project a title) including a timeline; a letter of recommendation from their faculty mentor, if students, or from their department chairperson, agency head or officer of their professional association, if professionals. An original and five copies of the application materials should be submitted along with a stamped, self-addressed post card that will be used to acknowledge receipt of their application. **Deadline:** June 5.

94 ■ AfterCollege
98 Battery St., Ste. 502
San Francisco, CA 94111
Ph: (415)263-1300
Fax: (415)263-1307
Free: 877-725-7721
E-mail: info@aftercollege.com
URL: www.aftercollege.com

95 ■ Aerospace Corporation Science and Engineering Student Scholarships *(Undergraduate, Graduate/ Scholarship)*

Purpose: To support students in their continuing education. **Focus:** Computer and information sciences; Engineering, Aerospace/Aeronautical/Astronautical; Engineering, Electrical; Engineering, Mechanical; Information science and technology; Mathematics and mathematical sciences. **Qualif.:** Applicants must be U.S. citizens and currently enrolled students working toward a degree (BA, BS, MS, PhD) in the fields of electrical engineering, computer sci-

Awards are arranged alphabetically below their administering organizations

ence, mechanical engineering, aerospace engineering, information systems, and mathematics; must have a minimum 3.0 GPA. **Criteria:** Selection of applicants will be based on AfterCollege profiles. GPA, honors, awards, scholarships, skills and all other information provided on the profile will also be considered.

Funds Avail.: $500. **Duration:** Quarterly. **Number Awarded:** 1 per quarter. **To Apply:** Applicants must submit their succinct but impactful, resume-style personal statements (250 words or less) that describe their respective goals and values that they bring in an academic and/or professional context. They may visit the AfterCollege website to create a free AfterCollege account and profile and submit the online application. Chosen finalists will be contacted via email and will be asked to submit a copy of their unofficial transcript verifying GPA. **Deadline:** March 31; June 30; September 30; December 31.

96 ■ AfterCollege-AACN Scholarships (Undergraduate, Master's, Doctorate/Scholarship)

Purpose: To support students who are seeking a baccalaureate, master's or doctoral degree in nursing. **Focus:** Nursing. **Qualif.:** Applicants must already be enrolled at an AACN member institution. Special consideration will be given to students in a graduate program with the goal of becoming a nurse educator; students completing an RN-to-BSN or RN-to-MSN program; and those enrolled in an accelerated program. **Criteria:** Selection will be based on the committee's criteria.

Funds Avail.: $10,000 ($2,500 will be awarded each quarter). **To Apply:** Applicants must visit the website to create a free AfterCollege account and profile and submit the online application. Finalists are contacted and may be asked to submit letters of recommendation, published articles, awards/honors, etc. to the selection committee. **Deadline:** March 31; June 30; September 30; December 31.

97 ■ AfterCollege Business Student Scholarships (Undergraduate, Graduate, Doctorate/Scholarship)

Purpose: To help deserving students cover expenses during school and propel them forward into rewarding careers after college. **Focus:** Business. **Qualif.:** Applicants must be current students working toward a degree (AA, AS, BA, BS, MS, PhD) in a field of business, which can include (but is not limited to): Accounting, Advertising, Business Administration, Economics, Finance, Human Resources, International Relations, Management, Political Science, Public Relations, etc.; must have a minimum of 3.0 GPA; must be members of AfterCollege. **Criteria:** Selection will be based on the committee's criteria.

Funds Avail.: $500. **Duration:** Annual. **To Apply:** Interested applicants may visit the website to create a free AfterCollege account and profile and submit the online application. Finalists will be contacted by email and may be asked to submit the following: copy of unofficial transcript verifying GPA. **Deadline:** March 31.

98 ■ AfterCollege Engineering Student Scholarships (Undergraduate, Graduate, Doctorate, Master's/Scholarship)

Purpose: To support current students working toward a degree in a field of engineering. **Focus:** Engineering. **Qualif.:** Applicants must be current students working toward a degree (AA, AS, AAS, BA, BS, MS and PhD) in a field of engineering; must have a minimum of 3.0 GPA; must be members of AfterCollege. **Criteria:** AfterCollege profiles are used as criteria to select the scholarship recipient. Primarily looking for a succinct but impactful, resume-style personal statement that describes your goals and the value that you bring in an academic and/or professional context (we recommend 250 words or less). May also consider GPA, honors, awards, scholarships, skills and all other information provided on your profile.

Funds Avail.: $500. **Duration:** Annual. **Number Awarded:** 1 per quarter. **To Apply:** Interested applicants may visit the website to create a free AfterCollege account and profile and submit the online application. Chosen finalists will be contacted by email and will be asked to submit a copy of their unofficial transcript verifying GPA. **Deadline:** March 31; June 30: September 30; December 31.

99 ■ AfterCollege Occupational Therapy Scholarships (Master's, Doctorate/Scholarship)

Purpose: To help deserving students cover expenses during school and propel them forward into rewarding careers after college. **Focus:** Occupational therapy. **Qualif.:** Student in good standing in an accredited program in the field of occupational therapy; have and carry a minimum 3.0 cumulative GPA; must be a full-time student while under the scholarship; must be a member of a department/student organization that is working with AfterCollege. **Criteria:** Selection will be based on the committee's criteria.

Funds Avail.: $500. **Duration:** Annual. **Number Awarded:** 2. **To Apply:** Interested applicants may visit the website to create a free AfterCollege account and profile and submit an online application. Finalists will be contacted by email and may be asked to submit the following: copy of unofficial transcripts verifying GPA; recommendation letter from Program Director.

100 ■ AfterCollege Physical Therapist Student Scholarships (Undergraduate, Master's, Doctorate/Scholarship)

Purpose: To help deserving students cover expenses during school and propel them forward into rewarding careers after college. **Focus:** Physical therapy. **Qualif.:** Applicants must be students working towards a master's or doctorate degree in Physical Therapy or in a 2-year Physical Therapist Assistant program; must have a minimum of 3.0 GPA; must be members of AfterCollege. **Criteria:** Selection will be based on the committee's criteria.

Funds Avail.: $500. **Duration:** Annual. **To Apply:** Interested applicants may visit the website to create a free AfterCollege account and profile and submit the online application. Finalists will be contacted by email and may be asked to submit the following: copy of unofficial transcript verifying GPA; letter of recommendation from Program Director. **Deadline:** March 31; June 30; September 30; and December 31.

101 ■ AfterCollege Science Student Scholarships (Undergraduate, Graduate, Doctorate/Scholarship)

Purpose: To help deserving students cover expenses during school and propel them forward into rewarding careers after college. **Focus:** Science. **Qualif.:** Applicants must be current students working toward a degree (AA, AS, BA, BS, MS and PhD) in one of the many fields of science, including but not limited to: Astronomy, Biology, Chemistry, Geology, Meteorology, Oceanography, Physics, Zoology, etc.; must have a minimum of 3.0 GPA; must be members of AfterCollege. **Criteria:** Selection will be based on the committee's criteria.

Funds Avail.: No specific amount. **To Apply:** Interested

Awards are arranged alphabetically below their administering organizations

applicants must visit the website to create a free AfterCollege account and profile and submit the online application. Finalists will be contacted by email and may be asked to submit the following: copy of unofficial transcript verifying GPA; letter of recommendation from Program Director.

102 ■ AfterCollege STEM Inclusion Scholarships (Undergraduate, Graduate/Scholarship)

Purpose: To support students who are about to learn more on STEM education. **Focus:** Engineering; Mathematics and mathematical sciences; Science; Technology. **Qualif.:** Applicants must be currently enrolled students working toward a degree in the fields of science, technology, engineering or mathematics from a group underrepresented in their field of study; must have a minimum 3.0 GPA. **Criteria:** Selection of applicants will be based on AfterCollege profiles. GPA, honors, awards, scholarships, skills and all other information provided on the profile will also be considered.

Funds Avail.: $500. **Duration:** Quarterly. **Number Awarded:** 1 per quarter. **To Apply:** Applicants must submit their succinct but impactful, resume-style personal statements (250 words or less) that describe their respective goals and values that they bring in an academic and/or professional context. They may visit the AfterCollege website to create a free AfterCollege account and profile and submit the online application. Chosen finalists will be contacted via email and will be asked to submit a copy of their unofficial transcript verifying GPA. **Deadline:** March 31; June 30; September 30; December 31.

103 ■ AfterCollege Succurro Scholarships (Undergraduate, Graduate, Doctorate/Scholarship)

Purpose: To help deserving students cover expenses during school and propel them forward into rewarding careers after college. **Focus:** General studies/Field of study not specified. **Qualif.:** Applicants must be current students enrolled in an accredited program, working toward a degree (AA, AS, BA, BS, MA, MS, PhD) in any discipline; must have a minimum of 2.5 GPA; must be members of AfterCollege. **Criteria:** Selection will be based on the committee's criteria.

Funds Avail.: $1,000. **To Apply:** Interested applicants are required to visit the website to create a free AfterCollege account and profile and submit the online application. Finalists will be contacted by email and may be asked to submit the following: a copy of unofficial transcript verifying GPA. **Deadline:** June 30.

104 ■ Med Technology and Clinical Lab Science Scholarships (Undergraduate/Scholarship)

Purpose: To help deserving students cover expenses during school and propel them forward into rewarding careers after college. **Focus:** Medical technology. **Qualif.:** Applicants must be current students working toward a degree (AA, AS, BA, BS, MS, PhD) in Medical Technology or Clinical Laboratory Science; must have a minimum 3.0 GPA; must be members of AfterCollege. **Criteria:** Selection will be based on the committee's criteria.

Funds Avail.: $500. **To Apply:** Interested applicants may visit the website to create a free AfterCollege account and profile and submit the online application. Finalists will be contacted by email and may be asked to submit the following: a copy of unofficial transcript verifying GPA; a letter of recommendation from Program Director. **Deadline:** March 31; June 30; September 30; December 31.

105 ■ Mutual of Omaha Finance Careers Scholarships (Undergraduate, Graduate/Scholarship)

Purpose: To support current students preparing for a future in finance or related industries. **Focus:** Accounting; Actuarial science; Banking; Finance; Insurance and insurance-related fields; Management; Risk management. **Qualif.:** Applicants must be currently enrolled students working toward a bachelor's, master's or doctorate degree in accounting, actuarial sciences, banking, economics, finance, financial management, insurance, risk management or related majors; must have a minimum 3.0 GPA. **Criteria:** Applicants are selected based on AfterCollege profiles. GPA, honors, awards, scholarships, skills and all other information provided on the profile will also be considered.

Funds Avail.: $500. **Duration:** Quarterly. **Number Awarded:** 1 per quarter. **To Apply:** Applicants must submit their resume-style personal statements (250 words or less) that describe their respective goals and values that they bring in an academic and/or professional context. They may visit the AfterCollege website to create a free AfterCollege account and profile and submit the online application. Chosen finalists will be contacted via email and will be asked to submit a copy of their unofficial transcript verifying GPA. **Deadline:** March 31; June 30; September 30; December 31.

106 ■ Mutual of Omaha Sales and Marketing Student Scholarships (Undergraduate, Graduate/Scholarship)

Purpose: To support students interested in a career in sales or marketing. **Focus:** Marketing and distribution. **Qualif.:** Applicants must be currently enrolled students working toward a bachelor's or master's degree and interested in a future career in sales or marketing; must have a minimum 3.0 GPA. **Criteria:** Selection of applicants will be based on AfterCollege profiles. GPA, honors, awards, scholarships, skills and all other information provided on the profile will also be considered.

Funds Avail.: $500. **Duration:** Quarterly. **Number Awarded:** 1 per quarter. **To Apply:** Applicants must submit their succinct but impactful, resume-style personal statements (250 words or less) that describe their respective goals and values that they bring in an academic and/or professional context. They may visit the AfterCollege website to create a free AfterCollege account and profile and submit the online application. Chosen finalists will be contacted via email and will be asked to submit a copy of their unofficial transcript verifying GPA. **Deadline:** March 31; June 30; September 30; December 31.

107 ■ NSA Electrical Engineering Student Scholarships (Undergraduate, Graduate, Doctorate/Scholarship)

Purpose: To help deserving students cover expenses during school and propel them forward into rewarding careers after college. **Focus:** Engineering, Electrical. **Qualif.:** Applicants must be currently enrolled students pursuing a degree in the field of electrical engineering; must have a minimum of 3.0 GPA; must be members of AfterCollege; must be U.S. citizens. **Criteria:** Selection will be based on the committee's criteria.

Funds Avail.: $500. **To Apply:** Interested applicants may visit the website to create a free AfterCollege account and profile and complete the online application. Finalists will be contacted by email and may be asked to submit the follow-

Awards are arranged alphabetically below their administering organizations

ing: copy of unofficial transcript verifying GPA. **Deadline:** March 31.

108 ■ **NSA Mathematics and Computer Science Student Scholarships** (Undergraduate, Graduate, Doctorate/Scholarship)

Purpose: To help deserving students cover expenses during school and propel them forward into rewarding careers after college. **Focus:** Computer and information sciences; Engineering, Computer; Mathematics and mathematical sciences. **Qualif.:** Applicants must be current students working toward a degree (AA, AS, BA, BA, MS and PhD) in the fields of computer science, computer engineering, or mathematics; must have a minimum of 3.0 GPA; must be members of AfterCollege; must be U.S. citizens. **Criteria:** Selection will be based on the committee's criteria.

Funds Avail.: $500. **Duration:** Annual. **To Apply:** Interested applicants may visit the website to create a free AfterCollege account and profile and submit the online application. Finalists will be contacted by email and may be asked to submit the following: copy of unofficial transcript verifying GPA. **Deadline:** March 31; June 30; September 30; December 31.

109 ■ **NYU Langone Medical Center Science Student Scholarships** (Undergraduate, Graduate/Scholarship)

Purpose: To support students who are about to learn more on life sciences. **Focus:** Biology; Biology, Molecular; Genetics; Life sciences; Neuroscience. **Qualif.:** Applicants must be full-time students pursuing a bachelor's, master's or doctoral degree in a Life Science major; must be enrolled in a life sciences program in an accredited college or university in Maine, New Hampshire, Massachusetts, Rhode Island, Connecticut, New York, New Jersey, Delaware, Maryland, Pennsylvania, Virginia, West Virginia, DC, or Vermont; must have a minimum 3.5 GPA. **Criteria:** Selection of applicants will be based on AfterCollege profiles. GPA, honors, awards, scholarships, skills and all other information provided on the profile will also be considered.

Funds Avail.: $500. **Duration:** Quarterly. **Number Awarded:** 1 per quarter. **To Apply:** Applicants must submit their succinct but impactful, resume-style personal statements (250 words or less) that describe their respective goals and values that they bring in an academic and/or professional context. They may visit the AfterCollege website to create a free AfterCollege account and profile and submit the online application. Chosen finalists will be contacted via email and will be asked to submit a copy of their unofficial transcript verifying GPA. **Deadline:** March 31; June 30; September 30; December 31.

110 ■ **Aging Gracefully across Environments using Technology to Support Wellness, Engagement and Long Life (AGE-WELL)**
12th Fl. Research
550 University Ave.
Toronto, ON, Canada
Ph: (416)597-3422
Fax: (416)597-3031
E-mail: info@agewell-nce.ca
URL: agewell-nce.ca

111 ■ **AGE-WELL Graduate Student and Postdoctoral Awards in Technology and Aging** (Master's, Doctorate, Postdoctorate/Award)

Purpose: To provide a unique training environment that exposes trainees to multi-disciplinary research environments and to its industry and community partners. **Focus:** Technology. **Qualif.:** Applicants must: have received at least some financial support from additional sources; participate full-time in their respective program at a Canadian post-secondary institution; be engaged in academic study/research aligned with the mission and vision of AGE-WELL. Applicants for doctoral awards are restricted to those entering the first or second year of their program. **Criteria:** All applications will be reviewed by a team of field experts using the following criteria: Scholarly Merit and Quality of Proposed Research (40%); Fit with AGE-WELL Goals and Priorities (40%); Quality of Training environment (20%).

Funds Avail.: $10,000 to $20,000. **Duration:** Annual. **To Apply:** Applicants must complete and submit the following: online application form; two confidential letters of support (one must be from the proposed supervisor); formal evidence of enrollment in a Master's or Doctoral program or Post-Doctoral position; formal evidence of awarded funding for the current academic year; curriculum vitae. **Deadline:** July 15. **Contact:** support@forum.agewell-nce.ca.

112 ■ **Agricultural Institute of Canada (AIC)**
176 Gloucester St., Ste. 320
Ottawa, ON, Canada K2P 0A6
Ph: (613)232-9459
Fax: (613)594-5190
Free: 888-277-7980
E-mail: office@aic.ca
URL: www.aic.ca
Twitter: twitter.com/AgInstitute

113 ■ **Dr. Karl C. Ivarson Scholarships** (Master's, Doctorate/Scholarship)

Purpose: To support students pursuing studies in soil science. **Focus:** Soil science. **Qualif.:** Applicants must hold Canadian citizenship or landed immigrant status; must be registered full-time in a master or doctorate program in the area of soil science. Applicants may pursue course electronically or by attending classes on campus. **Criteria:** Recipients are selected on the basis of scholastic ability, areas of study, leadership and career interests.

Funds Avail.: No specific amount. **Number Awarded:** 2. **To Apply:** Applicants must submit an official transcript; and letter from the university confirming that their enrollment in current program are required. **Deadline:** October 31. **Remarks:** Established in 2005.

114 ■ **Douglas McRorie Memorial Scholarships** (Doctorate, Master's/Scholarship)

Purpose: To provide financial support to post-graduate masters or PhD students specializing in agricultural business, economics, finance or trade. **Focus:** Agribusiness; Economics; Finance. **Qualif.:** Applicants must hold Canadian citizenship or landed immigrant status; must be post-graduates in the area of agricultural business, economics, finance or trade. **Criteria:** Selection will be based on the following criteria: agricultural post-graduate; emphasis in agricultural business/commerce/trade; strong academic record; good leadership potential; excellence in previous performance.

Awards are arranged alphabetically below their administering organizations

Funds Avail.: 3,000 Canadian dollars for Masters level (2); 5,000 Canadian dollars for PhD level (1). **Number Awarded:** 3. **To Apply:** Applicants must submit a completed application form; official transcript of records; letter of enrollment verification; and letters of recommendation from faculty advisors. **Deadline:** February 22. **Remarks:** Established in 1990.

115 ■ Agriculture Future of America (AFA)
PO Box 414838
Kansas City, MO 64141-4838
Ph: (816)472-4232
Fax: (816)472-4239
Free: 888-472-4232
E-mail: afa@agfuture.org
URL: www.agfuture.org
Facebook: www.facebook.com/agriculturefutureofamerica
Twitter: twitter.com/AgFutureAmerica

116 ■ Agriculture Future of America Community Scholarships (Undergraduate/Scholarship)

Purpose: To support local students preparing for a career in the agriculture and food industry. **Focus:** Agriculture, Economic aspects. **Qualif.:** Applicants must be graduating high school seniors planning to pursue a bachelor's degree in an agriculture-related program. **Criteria:** Recipients are selected based on an interview; an essay of 300-500 words describing the student's perception on the future of agriculture; community service; study group activities; general factors; GPA of 3.0/4.0.

Funds Avail.: $3,200. **To Apply:** Applicants must contact AFA to request an application form.

117 ■ Agriculture Future of America Scholarships (Undergraduate/Scholarship)

Purpose: To support academic development through partnerships with rural communities, agriculture organizations, colleges and universities. **Focus:** Agriculture, Economic aspects. **Qualif.:** Applicants must be students who plan to pursue a four year degree in an agriculture-related field; must have a cumulative GPA of 3.0 or higher at the time of selection **Criteria:** Recipients are selected based on academic performance.

Funds Avail.: No specific amount. **To Apply:** Applicants must contact AFA to request an application form.

118 ■ Ahepa Buckeye Scholarship Foundation
c/o Marian Capranica, Secretary
601 Tall Pines Dr.
Toledo, OH 43615
Ph: (330)372-1869
URL: www.bsf.buckeyedistrict11.org

119 ■ Ahepa Buckeye Scholarship Awards (Undergraduate/Scholarship)

Purpose: To provide financial support to students in pursuing their higher educational career. **Focus:** General studies/Field of study not specified. **Qualif.:** Applicant must be an active member of the AHEPA, Daughters of Penelope, Sons of Pericles, Maids of Athena, or whose parent(s) have been active members of the Senior Orders for three consecutive years. **Criteria:** Recipient is selected based on scholastic achievement and financial need.

Funds Avail.: No specific amount. **Number Awarded:** 2. **To Apply:** Applicant must submit most recent high school transcript; letter of acceptance from accredited college university; IRS from 1040. For college student submit an official transcript of grades including cumulative grade point average up to the date of application and grades for the semester or term.

120 ■ Air Force Association (AFA)
1501 Lee Hwy.
Arlington, VA 22209-1198
Ph: (703)247-5800
Fax: (703)247-5853
Free: 800-727-3337
E-mail: membership@afa.org
URL: www.afa.org/home

121 ■ Air Force Association/Grantham Scholarships (Undergraduate/Scholarship)

Purpose: To promote aerospace education, specifically the study of science, mathematics and technology. **Focus:** Aerospace sciences. **Qualif.:** Candidates must have a high school diploma or GED and must be members of AFA or their dependents. **Criteria:** Selection will be based on the committee's criteria.

Funds Avail.: No specific amount. **To Apply:** Applicants must submit a completed application form; a two-page, double-spaced essay describing the applicant's academic and career goals and explaining why he/she is interested in pursuing his/her degree via an online degree program, an explanation why this is the right time in the applicant's life and why he/she would be committed to continuing his/her education to get a degree; two letters of recommendation (These should be character references with descriptions of the applicant's performance and his/her potential as a student); and proof of GED completion or high school transcripts (or college transcripts if applicable). College transcript(s) and proof of undergraduate degree are required for the graduate programs. Applicants will be required to provide the information requested on a feedback form six months after the scholarship is awarded.

122 ■ Captain Jodi Callahan Memorial Scholarships (Graduate, Master's/Scholarship)

Purpose: To provide scholarships for active duty of Air Force, full-time Air National Guard or full-time Air Force Reserve. **Focus:** General studies/Field of study not specified. **Qualif.:** Applicants must be active duty Air Force, full time Air National Guard or full time Air Force Reserve (officer or enlisted) pursuing a Master's Degree in a non-technical field of study. A minimum Grade Point Average of 3.0 on a scale of 4.0 is required. **Criteria:** Selection will be based on the committee's criteria.

Funds Avail.: $1,000. **Duration:** Annual. **To Apply:** Applicants must complete both online portion and mail required documents by the deadline to be considered: one letter of recommendation from the Air Force supervisor or commander; proof of acceptance into an accredited college/university; and proof of Grade Point Average. Applicant's essay should describe academic goals and how he/she expects his/her degree to enhance his/her service to the Air Force. The letter of recommendation should include a character reference, a description of applicant's performance and an assessment of his/her potential as an Air Force leader and volunteer. **Deadline:** June 30. **Remarks:**

The scholarship is in memory of Captain Jodi Callahan who was an AFA Under-Forty National Director and a Trustee of the former Aerospace Education Foundation. The scholarship is made possible through contributions to the Jodi Callahan Memorial Fund by her family and friends. **Contact:** Lynette Cross, Manager, National Aerospace Awards, Air Force Association, at LCross@afa.org.

123 ■ Mike and Gail Donley Spouse Scholarships *(Undergraduate, Graduate, Postgraduate/Scholarship)*

Purpose: To encourage Air Force spouses worldwide to pursue associate, bachelor or graduate/postgraduate degrees. **Focus:** General studies/Field of study not specified. **Qualif.:** Applicants must be spouses of Air Force Active Duty, Air National Guard, Air Force Reserve or Department of the Air Force Civilian employees. Spouses who are themselves Air Force personnel, or in ROTC, are not eligible. **Criteria:** Selection will be based on the committee's criteria and applicants' eligibility.

Funds Avail.: $30,000 ($2,500 each). **Duration:** Annual. **Number Awarded:** 12. **To Apply:** Applicants must include the following in their application: an original or copy of the most recent college/university transcript or a report card from the applicants' last semester verifying their minimum 3.5 GPA or higher; proof of acceptance into a regionally accredited community college/college/university (this may consist of a short letter on college/university stationery from either the admissions office or the registrar); a two-page double-spaced essay, describing the applicants' academic and career goals and the motivation which led them to this decision and describing how Air Force and other local community activities in which they are involved will enhance their goals; two letters of recommendation (should be character references and descriptions of performance and potential as a student, employee or volunteer); a letter of endorsement from the local AFA Chapter would be welcomed and encouraged (the two letters must be from the different sources). Letters from previous or present professors, employers and volunteer organizations referencing the work of the applicants are encouraged. **Deadline:** April 30. **Remarks:** The Air Force Association (AFA) has named its spouse scholarship program "The Mike & Gail Donley Spouse Scholarship" to provide a lasting tribute to the former Secretary of the Air Force and his wife for their exemplary support of the Air Force Family.

124 ■ Lt. Colonel Romeo and Josephine Bass Ferretti Scholarships *(Undergraduate/Scholarship)*

Purpose: To provide educational assistance for graduating high school students. **Focus:** Engineering; Mathematics and mathematical sciences; Science; Technology. **Qualif.:** Applicants must be minor dependents of active duty or retired Air Force, Air Force Reserve or Air National Guard enlisted airmen. They must be students pursuing an undergraduate degree in the area of science, technology, engineering or math (STEM). **Criteria:** Recipients will be selected by committee based upon high academic achievement, good character and financial need.

Funds Avail.: $2,500. **Duration:** Annual. **To Apply:** Applicants must submit a completed application form, a two-page essay describing the academic achievements and goals, one letter of recommendation, an official and original high school transcript, proof of acceptance and a photo. **Deadline:** June 30. **Remarks:** The scholarship is made possible by a bequest from the estate of Lt Col Romeo and Josephine Bass Ferretti. **Contact:** Lynette Cross, Manager, National Aerospace Awards, Air Force Association, at LCross@afa.org.

125 ■ Pitsenbarger Awards *(Undergraduate/Grant, Award)*

Purpose: To provide a one-time grant to selected top USAF enlisted personnel. **Focus:** Aerospace sciences. **Qualif.:** Applicants must be top USAF enlisted personnel graduating from the Community College of the Air Force (CCAF) who plan to pursue a baccalaureate degree. **Criteria:** Selection is determined at the ESO by a committee of individuals appointed by the base education officer. The committee considers job performance, scholastic achievement, education goals and leadership qualities. Need is not a principle criterion.

Funds Avail.: $400. **Duration:** Annual. **To Apply:** Applicants must submit the following requirements: completed application form; a proof of current enrollment or intent to enroll in an accredited program leading to baccalaureate degree; citations and awards representing activities; narrative statement describing extracurricular activities and explaining their significance; and Commander's endorsement

126 ■ Michael Wilson Scholarships *(Undergraduate/Scholarship)*

Purpose: To support Air Force ROTC cadtes in their education. **Focus:** Aerospace sciences. **Qualif.:** Applicants must be current Air Force ROTC cadets in good standing, enrolled full-time as incoming juniors or seniors for the academic year at the Professional Air Force ROTC Officer Course program and attend both the Aerospace Studies class and Leadership Lab each semester. They must have a cumulative 2.8 GPA or better on a 4.0 scale. **Criteria:** Selection will be based on the committee's criteria.

Funds Avail.: $15,000. **Duration:** Annual. **Number Awarded:** 2. **To Apply:** Applicants must submit complete three essays with a uniform format prescribed by the organization. Such must be submitted along with other requirements asked. **Remarks:** The scholarship program was created by the Air Force Association (AFA) in partnership with Brian Wilson. **Contact:** Staff Sergeant Darryl Andrews at 334-953-2607 or via e-mail to Darryl.Andrews@maxwell.af.mil.

127 ■ Air Force Sergeants Association (AFSA)

5211 Auth Rd.
Suitland, MD 20746
Ph: (301)899-3500
Fax: (301)899-8136
Free: 800-638-0594
E-mail: staff@hqafsa.org
URL: www.hqafsa.org

128 ■ Air Force Sergeants Association Scholarship Program *(Undergraduate/Scholarship)*

Purpose: To provide financial assistance to the studies of dependent children of the enlisted Total Air Force members. **Focus:** General studies/Field of study not specified. **Qualif.:** Applicants must be dependent youth of AFSA or AFSA Auxiliary members and must be students attending an accredited academic institution. **Criteria:** Recipients are selected based on applicant's academic record, character, leadership skills, writing ability, versatility and potential for success.

Funds Avail.: Amount varies. **Duration:** Annual. **To Apply:** Applicants must submit a completed application form; a copy of proof of sponsor's military status (copy of DD 214,

Awards are arranged alphabetically below their administering organizations

copy of the sponsor's ID and discharge letter); official transcript of grades (high school graduates must include all grades from 9th to 12th grades, college applicants must include cumulative record of grades); a letter of recommendation written on the official school stationary with original signature (for high school graduate, letter must be written by the school principal or counselor; for college student, letter must be written by a college professor); a typed paragraph of the applicant's objectives (double-spaced) answering the question, "What do you plan to do with the education you receive?"; essay (double-spaced) answering the question, "What is the most urgent problem facing society today?" and a typed, double-spaced two-page essay about a current, controversial issue; two self-addressed, stamped, blank postcards. High school graduates must include a valid record of combined SAT I or ACT scores (must be recorded on an official school transcript). **Deadline:** March 31. **Remarks:** Established in 1968.

129 ■ Air Force Sergeants Association Chapter 155
1 Polk Ave.
Portsmouth, NH 03801-5729
E-mail: webmaster@afsa155.org
URL: www.afsa155.org
Facebook: www.facebook.com/afsa155

130 ■ AFSA Chapter 155 Division 1 Scholarships - Category 1 *(Undergraduate/Scholarship)*

Purpose: To support students pursuing their educational goals. **Focus:** General studies/Field of study not specified. **Qualif.:** Applicants must be graduating high school seniors entering 1st year college, whose parents, grandparents and/or guardians are current members of AFSA/Auxiliary; must have a GPA of 3.0. **Criteria:** Recipients are selected based on their submitted applications.

Funds Avail.: $500. **Duration:** Annual. **Number Awarded:** 1. **To Apply:** Applicants must submit a completed application form (available at the website), two (2) letters of recommendation, one (1) letter from student guidance/counselor, results from SAT/ACT or equivalent, class rank or mid-term for the current year and a 5"x7" photograph. **Deadline:** April 3. **Contact:** Clifford Wittman at wittmancm@yahoo.com.

131 ■ AFSA Chapter 155 Division 1 Scholarships - Category 2 *(Undergraduate/Scholarship)*

Purpose: To support students pursuing their educational goals. **Focus:** General studies/Field of study not specified. **Qualif.:** Applicants must be 2nd, 3rd and 4th year college students up to 26 years age, whose parents, grandparents and/or guardians are current members of AFSA/Auxiliary; have a GPA of 3.0. **Criteria:** Recipients are selected based on their submitted applications.

Funds Avail.: $500. **Duration:** Annual. **Number Awarded:** 1. **To Apply:** Applicants must submit a completed application form (available at the website), one (1) letter from student guidance/counselor, one (1) letter from senior faculty member and a 5"x7" photograph. **Deadline:** April 3. **Contact:** Clifford Wittman at wittmancm@yahoo.com.

132 ■ AFSA Chapter 155 Division 1 Scholarships - Category 3 *(Undergraduate/Scholarship)*

Purpose: To support students pursuing their educational goals. **Focus:** General studies/Field of study not specified. **Qualif.:** Applicants must be AFSA/Auxiliary members seeking to complete advanced schooling at a credited college or trade school; must have a GPA of 3.0. **Criteria:** Recipients are selected based on their submitted applications.

Funds Avail.: $500. **Duration:** Annual. **Number Awarded:** 1. **To Apply:** Applicants must submit a completed application form (available at the website) and a 5"x7" photograph. **Deadline:** April 3. **Contact:** Clifford Wittman at wittmancm@yahoo.com.

133 ■ Master Sergeant William Sowers Memorial Scholarships *(Undergraduate/Scholarship)*

Purpose: To support students for their continuing education. **Focus:** General studies/Field of study not specified. **Qualif.:** Applicants must be members, or dependent of a parent, grandparent and/or legal guardian, who are current members of AFSA Chapter 155. **Criteria:** Recipients are selected based on their submitted applications.

Funds Avail.: $1,000. **To Apply:** Applicants must submit a completed application form (available at the website). **Deadline:** August 15. **Contact:** Raymond L. Drapeau at rddrapeau@comcast.net.

134 ■ Air Traffic Control Association (ATCA)
1101 King St., Ste. 300
Alexandria, VA 22314
Ph: (703)299-2430
Fax: (703)299-2437
E-mail: info@atca.org
URL: www.atca.org
Facebook: www.facebook.com/AirTrafficControlAssociation

135 ■ Air Traffic Control Association Full-time Employee Student Scholarships *(Other/Scholarship)*

Purpose: To provide financial assistance to full-time employees enrolled in advanced study programs that enhance employee's skills in aviation-related position. **Focus:** Aviation; Transportation. **Qualif.:** Applicants must have an attendance equal to at least half-time (6 semester hours or the equivalent) and a minimum of 30 semester or 45 hours still to be completed before graduation; must be enrolled or accepted in a two-year or greater air traffic control program at an institution approved and/or listed by the Federal Aviation Administration as directly supporting the FAA's college training initiative; must be enrolled or accepted in an accredited college or university and planning to continue the following academic year; must be enrolled in course work related to their aviation-related career and leading to a bachelor's degree or greater; must be engaged in full-time employment in an aviation-related field; must be enrolled in course work designed to enhance the applicants' skill in an air traffic control or other aviation-related discipline. **Criteria:** Selection will be based on the committee's criteria.

Funds Avail.: No specific amount. **Duration:** Annual. **To Apply:** Applicants must provide two letters of recommendation (from present or previous teachers, professors, instructors, supervisors, or managers) from within the last 12 months; submit certified transcript of all college coursework. If less than 30 semester or 45 quarter hours of college coursework have been completed, all high school transcripts are also required, work or experience that supports the applicant's educational and/or aviation career goals must be addressed in the application and/or essay; financial need must be addressed in the application and/or essay;

submit a paper on the subject, "How My Education Efforts Will Enhance My Potential Contribution To Aviation." which should be typed, doubled spaced, 400 words maximum. **Deadline:** May 1.

136 ■ Air Traffic Control Association Non-employee Student Scholarships *(Undergraduate/Scholarship)*

Purpose: To provide financial assistance to students enrolled in aviation related program of study leading to a bachelor's degree or greater. **Focus:** Aviation. **Qualif.:** Applicants must have attendance equal to at least half-time (6 semester hours or the equivalent) and a minimum of 30 semester or 45 hours still to be completed before graduation; must be enrolled or accepted in a two-year or greater air traffic control program at an institution approved and/or listed by the Federal Aviation Administration as directly supporting the FAA's college training initiative; must be enrolled or accepted in an accredited college or university and planning to continue the following academic year; must be enrolled in course work related to his/her aviation-related career and leading to a bachelor's degree or greater; must be engaged in full-time employment in an aviation-related field; must be enrolled in course work designed to enhance the applicant's skill in an air traffic control or other aviation-related discipline. **Criteria:** Recipient will be selected by the Scholarship Selection Committee based on set of criteria.

Funds Avail.: No amount mentioned. **Duration:** Annual. **To Apply:** Applicants must provide two letters of recommendation (from present or previous teachers, professors, instructors, supervisors, or managers) from within the last 12 months; submit certified transcript of all college coursework. If less than 30 semester or 45 quarter hours of college coursework have been completed, all high school transcripts are also required, work or experience that supports the applicant's educational and/or aviation career goals must be addressed in the application and/or essay; financial need must be addressed in the application and/or essay; submit a paper on the subject, "How My Education Efforts Will Enhance My Potential Contribution To Aviation." which should be typed, doubled spaced, 400 words maximum. **Deadline:** May 1.

137 ■ Gabe A. Hartl Scholarships *(Undergraduate/Scholarship)*

Purpose: To provide financial assistance to students enrolled in air traffic control curriculum at FAA approved institution. **Focus:** Transportation. **Qualif.:** Applicants must have an attendance equal to at least half-time (6 semester hours or the equivalent) and a minimum of 30 semester or 45 hours still to be completed before graduation; must be enrolled or accepted in a two-year or greater air traffic control program at an institution approved and/or listed by the Federal Aviation Administration as directly supporting the FAA's college training initiative; must be enrolled or accepted in an accredited college or university and planning to continue the following academic year; must be enrolled in course work related to their aviation-related career and leading to a bachelor's degree or greater; must be engaged in full-time employment in an aviation-related field; must be enrolled in course work designed to enhance the applicants' skill in an air traffic control or other aviation-related disciplines. **Criteria:** Selection will be based on the committee's criteria.

Funds Avail.: No specific amount. **Duration:** Annual. **To Apply:** Applicants must provide two letters of recommendation (from present or previous teachers, professors, instructors, supervisors, or managers) from within the last 12 months; submit certified transcript of all college coursework. If less than 30 semester or 45 quarter hours of college coursework have been completed, all high school transcripts are also required, work or experience that supports the applicant's educational and/or aviation career goals must be addressed in the application and/or essay; financial need must be addressed in the application and/or essay; submit a paper on the subject, "How My Education Efforts Will Enhance My Potential Contribution To Aviation." which should be typed, doubled spaced, 400 words maximum. **Deadline:** May 1.

138 ■ Air & Waste Management Association (A&WMA)

1 Gateway Ctr., 3rd Fl.
420 Fort Duquesne Blvd.
Pittsburgh, PA 15222-1435
Ph: (412)232-3444
Fax: (412)232-3450
Free: 800-270-3444
E-mail: info@awma.org
URL: www.awma.org
Facebook: www.facebook.com/
 AirandWasteManagementAssociation
LinkedIn: www.linkedin.com/company/445959
Twitter: twitter.com/AirandWaste

139 ■ A&WMA Scholarships *(Graduate/Scholarship)*

Purpose: To promote education in air quality and waste management. **Focus:** Air pollution; Environmental law; Waste management. **Qualif.:** Applicant must be a full-time graduate student pursuing courses of study and research leading to careers in air quality, waste management, environmental management/policy/law and/or sustainability. **Criteria:** Selection is based on the application materials submitted.

Funds Avail.: No specific amount. **Duration:** Annual. **To Apply:** Applicants are required to create a scholarship account online, and upload supporting documents.

140 ■ Dave Benferado Scholarships *(Graduate/Scholarship)*

Purpose: To support the future of fields of air and waste management and to help students improve their knowledge and skills in air pollution control and waste minimization research. **Focus:** Air pollution; Waste management. **Qualif.:** Applicants must be full-time graduate students pursuing courses of study and research leading to careers in air quality, waste management, environmental management/policy/law, and/or sustainability during the academic year. **Criteria:** Selection will be based on the committee's criteria.

Funds Avail.: No specific amount. **To Apply:** Applicants may contact the Foundation for the application process and other information. **Deadline:** January 12. **Contact:** Robin Lebovitz, A&WMA Educational Programs Associate at rlebovitz@awma.org.

141 ■ Milton Feldstein Memorial Scholarships *(Graduate/Scholarship)*

Purpose: To support the future of fields of air and waste management and to help students improve their knowledge and skills in air quality research. **Focus:** Air pollution; Waste management. **Qualif.:** Applicants must be full-time graduate students pursuing courses of study and research lead-

Awards are arranged alphabetically below their administering organizations

ing to careers in air quality, waste management, environmental management/policy/law, and/or sustainability during the academic year. **Criteria:** Selection will be based on the committee's criteria.

Funds Avail.: $7,500. **To Apply:** Applicants may contact the Foundation for the application process and other information. **Deadline:** January 12. **Contact:** Robin Lebovitz, A&WMA Educational Programs Associate at rlebovitz@awma.org.

142 ■ Jacqueline Shields Memorial Scholarships
(Graduate/Scholarship)

Purpose: To support the future of fields of air and waste management and to help students improve their knowledge and skills in waste management research and study. **Focus:** Air pollution; Waste management. **Qualif.:** Applicants must be full-time graduate students pursuing courses of study and research leading to careers in air quality, waste management, environmental management/policy/law, and/or sustainability during the academic year. **Criteria:** Selection will be based on the committee's criteria.

Funds Avail.: No specific amount. **To Apply:** Applicants may contact the Foundation for the application process and other information. **Deadline:** January 12. **Contact:** Robin Lebovitz, A&WMA Educational Programs Associate at rlebovitz@awma.org.

143 ■ Richard Stessel Memorial Scholarships
(Graduate/Scholarship)

Purpose: To support the future of fields of air and waste management and to help students improve their knowledge and skills in solid and hazardous waste research. **Focus:** Air pollution; Waste management. **Qualif.:** Applicants must be full-time graduate students pursuing courses of study and research leading to careers in air quality, waste management, environmental management/policy/law, and/or sustainability during the academic year. **Criteria:** Selection will be based on the committee's criteria.

Funds Avail.: No specific amount. **To Apply:** Applicants may contact the Foundation for the application process and other information **Deadline:** January 12. **Contact:** Robin Lebovitz, A&WMA Educational Programs Associate at rlebovitz@awma.org.

144 ■ Air and Waste Management Association - Golden West Section (A&WMA-GWS)
1277 Treat Blvd., Ste. 500
Walnut Creek, CA 94597
Ph: (925)335-3468
E-mail: info@awma-gws.org
URL: www.awma-gws.org

145 ■ GWS Scholarships *(Undergraduate, Graduate/Scholarship)*

Purpose: To assist students pursuing careers in the areas of atmospheric, energy and environmental science and engineering, environmental management and sustainability, air pollution control, and waste management. **Focus:** Air pollution; Atmospheric science; Environmental science; Public health; Toxicology; Waste management; Water resources. **Qualif.:** Applicants must be: graduate or undergraduate students accepted into a full-time program pursuing courses of study and/or research leading to careers ranging from atmospheric science, environmental science and engineering, air pollution, waste management and water resources to toxicology and public health; and, attending a college/university in the Section's geographic area. **Criteria:** Awards will be given based on academic record and career goals. Consideration may also be given to financial need.

Funds Avail.: Up to $3,500 each. **Duration:** Annual. **Number Awarded:** Varies. **To Apply:** Applicants must submit a completed scholarship application together with the statement of professional goals; transcripts/grade point average; a resume/work experience and letters of recommendation. Application package must be submitted in duplicate (do not staple duplicate copy). **Deadline:** March 14.

146 ■ Air and Waste Management Association - Louisiana Section
c/o Sharon Duke
PO Box 640608
Kenner, LA 70064-0608
Ph: (504)472-9993
Fax: (504)472-9963
URL: la-awma.org

147 ■ AWMA Louisiana Section Scholarships
(Undergraduate, Graduate/Scholarship)

Purpose: To promote education in air quality and waste management. **Focus:** Engineering; Natural sciences; Physical sciences; Public health. **Qualif.:** Applicants must: be full-time students attending a college/university located within the geographical area of the Section (Louisiana and the Sabine River Region of Eastern Texas); be at least juniors (undergraduates) and no higher than master's level graduate students; have at least two semesters (or three quarters) of schooling remaining at the time of the award; be pursuing a bachelors or master's degree with a major in engineering, physical or natural science, or public health; show through course work, projects, personal interest, etc. a desire to promote air pollution control and/or solid or hazardous waste management; and, have at least an overall "B" average (3.00 or higher on a scale of 4.00) including all course work through the last completed semester. **Criteria:** Selection shall be based on academic record, plan of study, career goals, recommendations, and financial status.

Funds Avail.: $2,500 (2 recipients); $5,000 (1 recipient). **Duration:** Annual. **Number Awarded:** Varies. **To Apply:** Applicants must submit a completed General Application Information Sheet together with a 1-2 page resume; 1-2 page interest and award statement; current transcripts; letter or recommendation from a major professor or department head (envelope should be signed across) and a list of current financial awards. **Deadline:** April 24. **Contact:** Louisiana Section Scholarship Award, c/o Karen J. Blakemore, Phelps Dunbar, LLP, P.O. Box 4412 Baton Rouge, Louisiana 70821-4412; E-mail: Karen.blakemore@phelps.com.

148 ■ Air and Waste Management Association - Niagara Frontier Section (AWMA-NFS)
PO Box 384
Williamsville, NY 14231
E-mail: awmanfsinfo@gmail.com
URL: awmanfs.wildapricot.org

149 ■ AWMA Niagara Frontier Section College Scholarships *(Graduate, Undergraduate/Scholarship)*

Purpose: To support students in their educational pursuits. **Focus:** General studies/Field of study not specified. **Qua-**

Awards are arranged alphabetically below their administering organizations

lif.: Applicants must be full-time undergraduate or graduate students attending a recognized college/university located within the NY State counties (Allegany, Cattaraugus, Chautauqua, Erie, Niagara and Wyoming).; must be children or spouses of a current member. **Criteria:** Selection is based on applicant's environmental interests, academic record, leadership in school and the community, future academic and career potential, without consideration of sex, race, national origin, financial need, age or physical disability.

Funds Avail.: $500-$1,000. **Duration:** One academic year. **Number Awarded:** Varies. **To Apply:** Applicants must submit a completed application form (Section I, Section II, and Section III) along with grade transcripts. **Deadline:** April 13.

150 ■ Dave Sauer Memorial College Scholarships
(Undergraduate/Scholarship)

Purpose: To support students in their educational pursuits. **Focus:** General studies/Field of study not specified. **Qualif.:** Applicants must be high school seniors in good academic standing, attending a recognized high school located within the New York State counties (Allegany, Cattaraugus, Chautauqua, Erie, Niagara or Wyoming) and will attend a recognized college/university. **Criteria:** Selection is based on academic record, leadership in school and community activities and future academic and career potential, without consideration of sex, race, religion, national origin, financial need, age or physical disability.

Funds Avail.: $500-$1,000. **Duration:** One academic year. **Number Awarded:** Varies. **To Apply:** Applicants must submit a completed application form (Sections I through IV) together with a high school transcript(s) covering the sophomore and junior years. **Deadline:** April 13.

151 ■ Air and Waste Management Association - Northern and Central New Jersey Chapter (A&WMA NCNJ)
c/o Mr. Jerry Marcus, Scholarship Chair
Stonehenge Associates, LLC
304 Highland Ave.
Upper Montclair, NJ 07043
Ph: (973)746-2372
URL: www.mass-awma.net/nj-chapter.html

152 ■ NCNJ-AWMA Undergraduate Scholarship
(Undergraduate/Scholarship)

Purpose: To encourage qualified students to enter careers in environmental science. **Focus:** Environmental science; Environmental technology. **Qualif.:** Applicant must be a full-time (9 credits or more) undergraduate college student; pursuing courses of study leading to a career (or postgraduate study) in the environmental sciences/engineering or environmental management or related fields; a resident of New Jersey within the chapter area (Northern and Central New Jersey); or attending a college/university within the chapter area. **Criteria:** Selection is based on the application materials submitted for review.

Funds Avail.: $1,000 each. **Duration:** Annual. **Number Awarded:** 2. **To Apply:** Applicant must submit a completed application form or a copy of the applicant's resume, college transcript, letter of recommendation, and one-page essay on the applicant's experience and interest in environmental issues. **Deadline:** April 25. **Contact:** Mr. Jerry Z. Marcus, QEP, Stonehenge Associates, LLC, 304 Highland Avenue, Upper Montclair, NJ 07043; Phone: (973) 746-2372; E-mail: Jaziem@aol.com.

153 ■ Aircraft Electronics Association (AEA)
3570 NE Ralph Powell Rd.
Lees Summit, MO 64064
Ph: (816)347-8400
Fax: (816)347-8405
E-mail: info@aea.net
URL: www.aea.net
Facebook: www.facebook.com/AircraftElectronicsAssociation

154 ■ Aircraft Owners and Pilots Association Scholarships *(Undergraduate/Scholarship)*

Purpose: To provide financial support to students pursuing a career in avionics and/or aircraft maintenance through technical training and education at a learning institution. **Focus:** Aviation. **Qualif.:** Applicants must be high school seniors and/or college students planning to or attending an accredited school in an avionics or aircraft repair program. **Criteria:** Selection of candidates will be based on their application materials.

Funds Avail.: $2,000. **Duration:** Annual. **To Apply:** Applicants must submit complete and signed application form; recent high school or college transcript; 300-word typed-written essay. **Deadline:** February 15.

155 ■ David Arver Memorial Scholarships
(Undergraduate/Scholarship)

Purpose: To promote and secure the future of aviation by furthering the education of students and technicians from AEA member companies. **Focus:** Aviation. **Qualif.:** Applicants must be high school seniors and/or college students planning to or attend an accredited school in an avionics or aircraft repair program. **Criteria:** Selection of candidates will be based on their application materials.

Funds Avail.: $1,000. **To Apply:** Applicants must submit the completed application form; official transcript of grades; one 300-word essay. **Deadline:** April 1.

156 ■ Dutch and Ginger Arver Scholarships
(Undergraduate/Scholarship)

Purpose: To promote and secure the future of aviation by furthering the education of students and technicians from AEA member companies. **Focus:** Aviation. **Qualif.:** Applicants must be seniors and/or college students planning to attend an accredited school in an avionics or aircraft repair program. **Criteria:** Selection of candidates will be based on the criteria of the scholarship committee.

Funds Avail.: $1,000. **To Apply:** Applicants must submit the completed application form; official transcript of grades; one 300-word essay. **Deadline:** April 1.

157 ■ Johnny Davis Memorial Scholarships
(Undergraduate/Scholarship)

Purpose: To provide financial support to students pursuing a career in avionics and/or aircraft maintenance through technical training and education at a learning institution. **Focus:** Aviation. **Qualif.:** Applicants must be high school seniors and/or college students planning to or attending an accredited school in an avionics or aircraft repair program. **Criteria:** Selection of candidates will be based on their application materials.

Awards are arranged alphabetically below their administering organizations

Funds Avail.: $1,000. **Duration:** Annual. **To Apply:** Applicants must submit complete and signed application form; recent high school or college transcript; 300-word typed-written essay. **Deadline:** February 15.

158 ■ Duncan Aviation Scholarships *(Undergraduate/Scholarship)*

Purpose: To promote and secure the future of aviation by furthering the education of students and technicians from AEA member companies. **Focus:** Aviation. **Qualif.:** Applicants must be high school seniors and/or college students planning to or currently attending an accredited school in an avionics or aircraft repair program. **Criteria:** Selection of candidates will be based on the criteria of the scholarship committee.

Funds Avail.: $1,000. **To Apply:** Applicants are advised to contact the foundation for application forms and other required materials. **Deadline:** April 1.

159 ■ Field Aviation Co., Inc. Scholarships *(Undergraduate/Scholarship)*

Purpose: To support individuals intending to pursue their career in aircraft electronics and aviation maintenance industry. **Focus:** Aviation. **Qualif.:** Applicants must be high school seniors and/or college students planning to or attending an accredited college/university in an aircraft repair program. The educational institutions must be located in Canada. **Criteria:** Selection of candidates will be based on the decision of the Scholarship Committee.

Funds Avail.: $1,000. **To Apply:** Applicants are advised to contact the foundation for application forms and other required materials. **Deadline:** April 1.

160 ■ Garmin Scholarships *(Undergraduate/Scholarship)*

Purpose: To provide support to individuals intending to pursue their career in aircraft electronics and aviation maintenance industry. **Focus:** Aviation. **Qualif.:** Applicants must be seniors and/or college students planning to or attending an accredited school in an avionics or aircraft repair program. **Criteria:** Selection of candidates will be based on their application materials.

Funds Avail.: $2,000. **Duration:** Annual. **To Apply:** Applicants are advised to contact the foundation for application forms and other required materials. **Deadline:** April 1.

161 ■ Lowell Gaylor Memorial Scholarships *(Undergraduate/Scholarship)*

Purpose: To promote and secure the future of aviation by furthering the education of students and technicians from AEA member companies. **Focus:** Aviation. **Qualif.:** Applicants must be high school seniors and/or college students who plan to or attending an accredited school in an avionics or aircraft repair program. **Criteria:** Selection of candidates will be based on their application materials.

Funds Avail.: $1,000. **To Apply:** Applicants are advised to contact the foundation for application forms and other required materials. **Deadline:** April 1.

162 ■ Bud Glover Memorial Scholarships *(Undergraduate/Scholarship)*

Purpose: To promote and secure the future of aviation by furthering the education of students and technicians from AEA member companies. **Focus:** Aviation. **Qualif.:** Applicants must be high school seniors and/or college students who are planning to attend an accredited school in an avionics or aircraft repair program. **Criteria:** Selection of candidates will be based on their application materials.

Funds Avail.: $1,500. **To Apply:** Applicants must submit the completed application form; official transcript of grades; one 300-word essay. **Deadline:** February 15.

163 ■ Leon Harris/Les Nichols Memorial Scholarships to Spartan College of Aeronautics & Technology *(Undergraduate/Scholarship)*

Purpose: To promote and secure the future of aviation by furthering the education of students and technicians from AEA member companies. **Focus:** Aviation. **Qualif.:** Applicants must be student planning to pursue an Associate's Degree in Applied Science in Aviation Electronics (avionics) at Spartan College of Aeronautics and Technology campus in Tulsa, Oklahoma. **Criteria:** Selection of candidates will be based on their application materials.

Funds Avail.: $35,000. **To Apply:** Applicants must submit a completed application form together with official transcript of grades and a 300-word essay. **Deadline:** April 1.

164 ■ Don C. Hawkins Memorial Scholarships *(Undergraduate/Scholarship)*

Purpose: To provide financial support to students pursuing a career in aircraft electronics and aircraft maintenance through technical training and education at a learning institution. **Focus:** Aviation. **Qualif.:** Applicants must be high school seniors and/or college students planning to or attending an accredited school in an avionics or aircraft repair program. **Criteria:** Selection of candidates will be based on their application materials.

Funds Avail.: $1,000. **To Apply:** Applicants must submit complete and signed application form; recent high school or college transcript; 300-word typed-written essay. **Deadline:** February 15.

165 ■ Honeywell Avionics Scholarships *(Undergraduate/Scholarship)*

Purpose: To provide support to students pursuing a career in avionics and/or aircraft maintenance through technical training and education at a learning institution. **Focus:** Aviation. **Qualif.:** Applicants must be high school, college, or vocational/technical school students planning to or attending an accredited school in an avionics or aircraft repair program. **Criteria:** Selection of candidates will be based on the decision of the Scholarship Committee.

Funds Avail.: $1,000. **Duration:** Annual. **To Apply:** Applicants must submit complete and signed application form; recent high school or college transcript; 300-word typed-written essay. **Deadline:** February 15.

166 ■ L-3 Communications Avionics Systems Scholarships *(Undergraduate/Scholarship)*

Purpose: To provide financial support to students pursuing a career in avionics and/or aircraft maintenance through technical training and education at a learning institution. **Focus:** Aviation. **Qualif.:** Applicants must be high school, college, or vocational/technical school students planning to or attending an accredited school in an avionics or aircraft repair program. **Criteria:** Selection of candidates will be based on the decision of the Scholarship Committee.

Funds Avail.: $2,500. **Duration:** Annual. **To Apply:** Applicants must submit complete and signed application form; recent high school or college transcript; 300-word typed-written essay. **Deadline:** February 15.

Awards are arranged alphabetically below their administering organizations

AIRCRAFT ELECTRONICS ASSOCIATION — Sponsors and Their Scholarships

167 ■ Mid-Continent Instrument Scholarships
(Undergraduate/Scholarship)

Purpose: To support individuals intending to pursue their career in aircraft electronics and aviation maintenance industry. **Focus:** Aviation. **Qualif.:** Applicants must be high school seniors and/or college students planning to or attending an accredited school in an avionics or aircraft repair program. **Criteria:** Selection of candidates will be based on the criteria of the Scholarship Committee.

Funds Avail.: $1,000. **To Apply:** Applicants are advised to contact the foundation for application forms and other required materials. **Deadline:** April 1.

168 ■ Monte R. Mitchell Global Scholarships
(Undergraduate/Scholarship)

Purpose: To promote and secure the future of aviation by furthering the education of students and technicians from AEA member companies. **Focus:** Aviation. **Qualif.:** Applicants must be European students pursuing a degree in aviation maintenance technology, avionics or aircraft repair at an accredited school located in Europe or the United States. **Criteria:** Selection of candidates will be based on the criteria of the scholarship committee.

Funds Avail.: $1,500. **Duration:** Annual. **To Apply:** Application form can be downloaded at the website. Applicants must complete and submit the application form and other required materials. **Deadline:** April 1.

169 ■ Chuck Peacock Memorial Scholarships
(Undergraduate/Scholarship)

Purpose: To promote and secure the future of aviation by furthering the education of students and technicians from AEA member companies. **Focus:** Aviation. **Qualif.:** Applicants must be high school seniors and/or college students who are planning to attend an accredited school in an aviation management program. **Criteria:** Selection of candidates will be based on their application materials.

Funds Avail.: $1,000. **To Apply:** Applicants must submit the completed application form; official transcript of grades; one 300-word essay. **Deadline:** April 1.

170 ■ Rockwell Collins Scholarships
(Undergraduate/Scholarship)

Purpose: To promote and secure the future of aviation by furthering the education of students and technicians from AEA member companies. **Focus:** Aviation. **Qualif.:** Applicants must be high school seniors and/or college students planning to or attending an accredited school in an avionics or aircraft repair program. **Criteria:** Selection of candidates will be based on the criteria of the Scholarship Committee.

Funds Avail.: $1,000. **To Apply:** Applicants are advised to contact the foundation for application forms and other required materials.

171 ■ Thomas J. Slocum Memorial Scholarships to Redstone College *(Undergraduate/Scholarship)*

Purpose: To promote and secure the future of aviation by furthering the education of students and technicians from AEA member companies. **Focus:** Aviation. **Qualif.:** Applicants must be students who plans to attend Westwood College of Aviation Technology in Broomfield, Colorado in the avionics program. **Criteria:** Selection of candidates will be based on their application materials.

Funds Avail.: $1,000. **To Apply:** Applicants must submit the completed application form together with official transcript of grades and 300-word essay. **Deadline:** April 1.

172 ■ Sporty's/Cincinnati Avionics Scholarships
(Undergraduate, Vocational/Occupational/Scholarship)

Purpose: To provide support to individuals intending to pursue their career in aircraft electronics and aviation maintenance industry. **Focus:** Aviation. **Qualif.:** Applicants must be high school, college, or vocational/technical school students planning to or attending an accredited school in an avionics or aircraft repair program. **Criteria:** Selection of candidates will be based on the decision of the Scholarship Committee.

Funds Avail.: No specific amount. **Duration:** Annual. **Number Awarded:** Varies. **To Apply:** Applicants are advised to contact the foundation for application forms and other required materials. **Deadline:** February 15. **Contact:** Mike Adamson, Executive Director, at 816-347-8400 or send email to mikea@aea.net.

173 ■ Kei Takemoto Memorial Scholarships
(Undergraduate/Scholarship)

Purpose: To provide financial support to students pursuing a career in aircraft electronics and aircraft maintenance through technical training and education at a learning institution. **Focus:** Aviation. **Qualif.:** Applicants must be high school seniors and/or college students planning to or are attending an accredited school in an avionics or aircraft repair program. **Criteria:** Candidates will be selected based on the scholarship criteria.

Funds Avail.: No specific amount. **Duration:** Annual. **To Apply:** Applicants must submit complete and signed application form; recent high school or college transcript; 300-word typed-written essay. **Deadline:** February 15.

174 ■ Lee Tarbox Memorial Scholarships
(Undergraduate/Scholarship)

Purpose: To promote and secure the future of aviation by furthering the education of students and technicians from AEA member companies. **Focus:** Aviation. **Qualif.:** Applicants must be high school seniors and/or college students who are planning to attend an accredited school in an avionics or aircraft repair program. **Criteria:** Selection of candidates will be based on their application materials.

Funds Avail.: $2,500. **To Apply:** Applicants must submit the completed application form; official transcript of grades; one 300-word essay. **Deadline:** April 1.

175 ■ Tom Taylor Memorial Scholarships to Spartan College of Aeronautics and Technology
(Undergraduate/Scholarship)

Purpose: To promote and secure the future of aviation by furthering the education of students and technicians from AEA member companies. **Focus:** Aviation. **Qualif.:** Applicants must have a desire to pursue their associates degree in Applied Science or a diploma in Aviation Maintenance Technology at Spartan College of Aeronautics & Technology's campus in Tulsa, Oklahoma; must not be currently enrolled in the AMT program at Spartan. **Criteria:** Selection will be based on the submitted application materials.

Funds Avail.: $35,000. **To Apply:** Applicants must submit the completed application form, official transcript of grades and a 300-word essay. **Deadline:** April 1.

176 ■ Texas State Technical College Scholarships
(Undergraduate/Scholarship)

Purpose: To promote and secure the future of aviation by furthering the education of students and technicians from

Awards are arranged alphabetically below their administering organizations

AEA member companies. **Focus:** Aviation. **Qualif.:** Applicants must be students intending to pursue an associate's degree in avionics. **Criteria:** Selection of candidates will be based on the criteria of the scholarship committee.

Funds Avail.: $1,000. **To Apply:** Application form can be obtain at the website. Submit completed application form together with transcript, questions and essay to the AEA Educational Foundation. **Deadline:** February 15.

177 ■ Airport Minority Advisory Council Educational and Scholarship Program (AMAC-ESP)
2001 Jefferson Davis Hwy., Ste. 500
Arlington, VA 22202
Ph: (703)414-2622
Fax: (703)414-2686
E-mail: amac.info@amac-org.com
URL: amac-org.com/?p=247

178 ■ AMACESP Student Scholarships *(Undergraduate/Scholarship)*

Purpose: To provide financial assistance for education and outreach to full-time college students interested in pursuing aviation careers. **Focus:** Aviation. **Qualif.:** Applicant must be a U.S. citizen; must be admitted by an accredited school or university for the current school term in which he/she is applying for; must have a minimum GPA of 2.5; must demonstrates involvement in community activities, extracurricular activities, interest and desire to pursue a career in the aviation/airport industry; and must be seeking a degree in aviation, business administration, accounting, architecture, engineering or finance. **Criteria:** Recipient will be selected by the AMACESP Scholarship Selection Committees based on a set of criteria.

Funds Avail.: $2,000. **Number Awarded:** 4. **To Apply:** Applicant must complete a current Scholarship Application; enclose transcripts to show proof of 2.5 GPA; a one-page essay (750 words or less) on overcoming barriers towards career goals; dedication to succeed in aviation and how AMAC can help; overcoming issues in the aviation industry; and two letters of recommendation from persons who are not relatives that can comment on his/her academic and career goals. Applicant must also submit one 5" x 7" (400x600 pixels) digital color photograph, and a two-paragraph biography summarizing employment, volunteer work, awards, and academic accomplishments. **Contact:** Call 703-414-2622 or email: delianny.almonte@amac-org.com.

179 ■ Airports Council International - North America (ACI-NA)
1615 L St. NW, Ste. 300
Washington, DC 20036
Ph: (202)293-8500
Fax: (202)331-1362
Free: 888-424-7767
E-mail: memberservices@aci-na.org
URL: www.aci-na.org

180 ■ ACI-NA Scholarships *(Graduate, Undergraduate/Scholarship)*

Purpose: To provide educational assistance to students at an accredited educational institution working towards a degree and a career in airport management or airport administration. **Focus:** Aviation. **Qualif.:** Applicants must be officially enrolled in an accredited college or university in either an undergraduate program focused on airport management and/or airport operations, or a graduate program focused on research on airport management or airport operations; must reside and attend school in U.S. or Canada; and must maintain a minimum GPA of 3.0 at the time of application. **Criteria:** Applicants are evaluated based on demonstrated academic excellence and leadership; economic needs; and impact of the airport industry.

Funds Avail.: $5,000. **Duration:** Annual. **Number Awarded:** Up to 3. **To Apply:** Applicants must submit scholarship application (Form 101-06); official school transcript; two recent letters of recommendation, with one from a former or current professor/instructor and the other letter from someone other than a professor/instructor that has knowledge of the student's leadership qualities; a (300-500 word) personal statement which emphasizes the applicant's interest in airport management or airport operations; and a current resume (maximum of two pages). **Deadline:** April 15. **Remarks:** Established in 1993. **Contact:** University Aviation Association at 334-844-2434.

181 ■ Akron Bar Association Foundation
57 S Broadway
Akron, OH 44308
Ph: (330)253-5007
Fax: (330)253-2140
URL: www.akronbar.org

182 ■ Akron Bar Association Foundation Scholarships *(Undergraduate/Scholarship)*

Purpose: To provide scholarships to students enrolled in a law school. **Focus:** Law. **Qualif.:** Applicants must be U.S. citizens attending a law school in Ohio. **Criteria:** Selection will be based on grade point average, affiliation with Summit County, history of community involvement, and financial need.

Funds Avail.: No specific amount. **Duration:** Annual. **To Apply:** Applicants must send an updated resume, a completed application, a certified transcript from their school(s), two letters of recommendation, and a FERPA release form. Send all application checklist to Akron Bar Foundation by email or fax. **Deadline:** March or April. **Contact:** Email: development@akronbar.org; Fax: 330-253-2140.

183 ■ Alabama Commission on Higher Education
100 N Union St.
Montgomery, AL 36104-3758
Ph: (334)242-1998
Fax: (334)242-0268
URL: www.ache.alabama.gov

184 ■ ACHE/American Legion Auxiliary Scholarships *(Undergraduate/Scholarship)*

Purpose: To support the education of Alabama students. **Focus:** General studies/Field of study not specified. **Qualif.:** Applicants must be the son, daughter, grandson, granddaughter of veterans of World War I, World War II, Korea, or Vietnam and who are residents of Alabama; and must be attending an institutions having on-campus housing. **Criteria:** Selection will be based on the committee's criteria.

Awards are arranged alphabetically below their administering organizations

Funds Avail.: No specific amount. To Apply: Applications are available from the American Legion Department Headquarters. Deadline: April 1. Contact: American Legion Department Headquarters, American Legion Auxiliary, 120 North Jackson Street, Montgomery, AL 36104; Phone: 334-262-1176.

185 ■ ACHE Junior and Community College Athletic Scholarships (Undergraduate/Scholarship)

Purpose: To support the education of Alabama students though defraying their expenses. Focus: General studies/Field of study not specified. Qualif.: Applicants must be full-time students enrolled in public junior and community colleges in Alabama. Criteria: Selection is based on demonstrated athletic ability determined through try-outs.

Funds Avail.: No specific amount. Duration: One academic year. To Apply: Applicants must contact the coach, athletic director, or financial aid officer at any public junior or community college in Alabama in order to be considered.

186 ■ ACHE Junior and Community College Performing Arts Scholarships (Undergraduate/Scholarship)

Purpose: To support the education of Alabama students though defraying their expenses. Focus: Performing arts. Qualif.: Applicant must be a full-time student enrolled in public junior and community colleges in Alabama. Criteria: Selection is based on demonstrated talent determined through competitive auditions.

Funds Avail.: No specific amount. Duration: One academic year. To Apply: Applicant must contact the financial aid office at any public junior or community college in Alabama. Competitive auditions will also be scheduled as part of the application process.

187 ■ ACHE Police Officers and Firefighters Survivors' Educational Assistance Programs (Undergraduate/Scholarship)

Purpose: To assist the education of the dependents or spouses of police officers or firefighters killed in the line of duty in Alabama. Focus: General studies/Field of study not specified. Qualif.: Applicant must be the dependent or the spouse of a police officer or firefighter killed in the line of duty; must be enrolled in an undergraduate program at a public post-secondary educational institution in Alabama. Criteria: Selection will be based on the submitted application.

Funds Avail.: No specific amount. To Apply: Applicant must submit completed application form and must include necessary documentations such as copy of natural child's birth certificate, adoption papers, marriage certificate and a death certificate or medical certification for the police officer or firefighter killed or permanently disabled as result of service in the line of duty. Contact: Wanda Rowe, AL Comm. on Higher Education; PO Box 302000, Montgomery, AL 36130-2000; Email: cnewton@ache.state.al.us.

188 ■ ACHE Senior Adult Scholarships (Undergraduate/Scholarship)

Purpose: To provide support to senior citizens by giving them a free tuition program. Focus: General studies/Field of study not specified. Qualif.: Applicant must be a senior citizen (aged 60 and over) who meets the admission requirements to attend a public two-year post-secondary institution in Alabama. Criteria: Preference will be given to an applicant who meet the admission requirements.

Funds Avail.: No specific amount. To Apply: Applicant must contact the financial aid office at any public two-year post-secondary educational institutions in Alabama in order to be considered.

189 ■ ACHE Two-Year College Academic Scholarships (Undergraduate/Scholarship)

Purpose: To provide educational assistance to students who are in need. Focus: General studies/Field of study not specified. Qualif.: Applicant must be a student accepted for enrollment at public two-year post-secondary educational institutions in Alabama. Criteria: Selection is based on demonstrated academic merit as determined by the institutional scholarship committee. Priorities will be given to in-state residents.

Funds Avail.: No specific amount. Duration: One academic year. To Apply: Application forms are available at the financial aid office at any public two-year post-secondary educational institution in Alabama.

190 ■ Alabama Gi Dependents' Educational Benefit Program (Undergraduate/Scholarship)

Purpose: To support the education of Alabama students. Focus: General studies/Field of study not specified. Qualif.: Applicant must be a dependent or spouses of eligible Alabama veterans attending a public postsecondary educational institutions in Alabama; enrolled as an undergraduate student. Criteria: Selection will be based on the submitted application.

Funds Avail.: No specific amount. To Apply: Application forms may be obtained from the Alabama State Department of Veterans Affairs or from any county veterans service officer. Contact: Alabama State Department of Veterans Affairs, PO Box 1509, Montgomery, AL 36102-1509 334-242-5077.

191 ■ Alabama National Guard Educational Assistance Program (Undergraduate/Scholarship)

Purpose: To provide educational fees and book/supplies for Alabama National Guard members. Focus: General studies/Field of study not specified. Qualif.: Applicants must be students who are active members in good standing with a federally recognized unit of the Alabama National Guard; must be residents of Alabama and at least 17 years old; must be enrolled in an accredited college, university, community college, or technical college and have completed basic training and advanced individual training. Criteria: Selection will be based on the submitted application.

Funds Avail.: Limited to $1,000 per semester, and no more than $2,000 per year. To Apply: Applications are available from Alabama National Guard units. Forms must be signed by a representative of the Alabama Military Department and the financial aid officer at the college/university.

192 ■ Alabama Scholarships for Dependents of Blind Parents (Undergraduate/Scholarship)

Purpose: To support the education of students from families in which the head of the family is blind and whose family income is insufficient to provide educational benefits. Focus: General studies/Field of study not specified. Qualif.: Applicants must be Alabama residents; having a family in which the head of the family is blind or with family income is insufficient to provide educational benefits for attendance at an Alabama postsecondary institution. Criteria: Selection will be based on need.

Funds Avail.: No specific amount. To Apply: Interested

Awards are arranged alphabetically below their administering organizations

applicants may contact Debra Culver for the application process and other information. **Contact:** Debra Culver, Rehab. Specialist, Alabama Department of Rehabilitation Services, 2129 East South Blvd., Montgomery, AL 36116-2455; Phone: 800-441-7607; 334-613-2248; 256-362-0638.

193 ■ Alabama Student Assistance Programs
(Undergraduate/Scholarship)

Purpose: To provide support to students in pursuing their educational goal. **Focus:** General studies/Field of study not specified. **Qualif.:** Applicants must be undergraduate students; and must be Alabama residents attending an eligible Alabama institution; in need of financial assistance and not enrolled in a course of study leading to a religious profession. **Criteria:** Selection will be based on need.

Funds Avail.: $300 to $5,000. **Duration:** One academic year. **To Apply:** Applicants must submit the Free Application for Federal Student Aid available from high school guidance office or the financial aid office at the institution planning to attend.

194 ■ Alabama Student Grant Programs
(Undergraduate, Vocational/Occupational/Grant)

Purpose: To provide educational assistance to students who are in need. **Focus:** General studies/Field of study not specified. **Qualif.:** Applicants must be part-time or full-time undergraduate students; must be Alabama resident; must not be enrolled in a course of study leading to a religious vocation; must enrolled in the following schools: Amridge University, Birmingham Southern College, Concordia College, Faulkner University, Huntingdon College, Judson College, Miles College, Oakwood University, Samford University, South University, Spring Hill College, Stillman College, U.S. Sports Academy and University of Mobile. **Criteria:** Selection will be based on the committee's criteria.

Funds Avail.: Up to $1200 per academic year. **To Apply:** Applications are available to the financial aid office of the institution where applicants are planning to attend.

195 ■ Alabama Dietetic Association (ALDA)
PO Box 240757
Montgomery, AL 36124
Ph: (334)260-7970
Fax: (334)272-7128
E-mail: alda@gmsal.com
URL: www.eatrightalabama.org
Facebook: www.facebook.com/groups/37031827726/?fref=ts
Twitter: twitter.com/alda_rd

196 ■ Birmingham District Alabama Dietetic Association Scholarships *(Graduate, Undergraduate/Scholarship)*

Purpose: To encourage and reward students majoring in the field of human nutrition, dietetics, foods, nutrition, or food systems management or admitted or enrolled in a dietetic internship who have demonstrated ability and potential in the field of dietetics and nutrition by aiding them financially. **Focus:** Nutrition. **Qualif.:** Applicants must be junior or senior undergraduate students, graduate students, or dietetic interns majoring in the field of human nutrition, dietetics, foods, nutrition, or food systems management or admitted or enrolled in a dietetic internship; must be legal residents of the following counties: Jefferson, Cullman, Walker, Bibb, Chilton, Shelby, Talladega, St. Clair and/ or an active member in the Birmingham District Dietetic Association and student members of the American Dietetic Association; must have cumulative grade point average of 3.0 or above in major courses of study. **Criteria:** Selection is based on the scholarship; potential in the field of dietetics and nutrition ascertained by, for example: leadership in activities within and outside school, professional interest, honors, activities, and work or volunteer experience; financial need; letters of recommendation; and letter of application.

Funds Avail.: $500. **To Apply:** Applicants must submit a completed application form together with the official computed cumulative GPA (all post secondary work related to dietetics) authenticated by a faculty member; a letter of application including statements relating to financial need, immediate and future goals, leadership activities, and personal attributes such as initiation and motivation for meeting physical, emotional, and family demands as well as graduate school requirements; and resume including personal contact data, education, honors, and awards, involvement in clubs and organizations including offices held, professional and leadership activities, and work on volunteer experience.

197 ■ North Alabama Dietetic Association Scholarships *(Graduate, Undergraduate/Scholarship)*

Purpose: To encourage and reward students majoring in the field of human nutrition, dietetics, foods, nutrition, or food systems management or admitted or enrolled in a dietetic internship who have demonstrated ability and potential in the field of dietetics and nutrition by aiding them financially. **Focus:** Nutrition. **Qualif.:** Applicants must be junior or senior students majoring in the field of human nutrition dietetics, food, nutrition, or food systems management or admitted or enrolled in a dietetic internship; must be student members of the American Dietetic Association; must have cumulative grade point average of 2.5, and 3.0 or above in major sources of study; must be legal residents of North Alabama. **Criteria:** Selection is based on the scholarship; potential in the field of dietetics and nutrition ascertained by, for example: leadership in activities within and outside school, professional interest, honors, activities, and work or volunteer experience; financial need; letters of recommendation; and letter of application.

Funds Avail.: $500. **Duration:** Annual. **To Apply:** Applicants must submit a completed application form together with the official computed cumulative GPA (all post secondary work related to dietetics) authenticated by a faculty member; letter of application including statements relating to financial need, immediate and future goals, leadership activities, and personal attributes such as initiation and motivation for meeting physical, emotional, and family demands as well as graduate school requirements; and resume including personal contact data, education, honors, and awards, involvement in clubs and organizations including offices held, professional and leadership activities, and work on volunteer experience.

198 ■ Northeast Alabama District Dietetic Association Scholarships *(Graduate, Undergraduate/Scholarship)*

Purpose: To encourage and reward students majoring in the field of human nutrition, dietetics, foods, nutrition, or food systems management or admitted or enrolled in a dietetic internship who have demonstrated ability and potential in the field of dietetics and nutrition by aiding them financially. **Focus:** Nutrition. **Qualif.:** Applicants must be junior or senior students majoring in the field of human

Awards are arranged alphabetically below their administering organizations

nutrition dietetics, food, nutrition, or food systems management or admitted or enrolled in a dietetic internship; must have active, associate, or student membership in the Academy of Nutrition and Dietetics; must have cumulative grade point average of 2.5, and 3.0 or above in major sources of study; must be legal resident of one of the following counties: Calhoun, DeKalb, Cherokee, Cleburne, Etowah, Marshall, St. Clair or Talladega, or volunteered in a healthcare facility in one of the stated counties. **Criteria:** Selection is based on the scholarship; potential in the field of dietetics and nutrition ascertained by, for example: leadership in activities within and outside school, professional interest, honors, activities, and work or volunteer experience; financial need; letters of recommendation; and letter of application.

Funds Avail.: $500. **Duration:** Annual. **To Apply:** Applicants must submit a completed application form together with the official computed cumulative GPA (all post secondary work related to dietetics) authenticated by a faculty member; letter of application including statements relating to financial need, immediate and future goals, leadership activities, and personal attributes such as initiation and motivation for meeting physical, emotional, and family demands as well as graduate school requirements; and resume including personal contact data, education, honors, and awards, involvement in clubs and organizations including offices held, professional and leadership activities, and work on volunteer experience.

199 ■ William E. Smith Scholarships (Graduate/Scholarship)

Purpose: To reward full time graduate students who have demonstrated ability and potential in the field of dietetics and nutrition by aiding them financially during graduate study. **Focus:** Nutrition. **Qualif.:** Applicants must be full-time graduate students in the field of dietetics and nutrition. **Criteria:** Selection is based on the scholarship; potential in the field of dietetics and nutrition ascertained by, for example: leadership in activities within and outside school, professional interest, honors, activities, and work or volunteer experience; financial need; letters of recommendation; and letter of application.

Funds Avail.: $1,000. **Duration:** Annual. **To Apply:** Applicants must submit completed application form together with the official computed cumulative GPA (all post secondary work related to dietetics) authenticated by a faculty member; letter of application including statements relating to financial need, immediate and future goals, leadership activities, and personal attributes such as initiation and motivation for meeting physical, emotional, and family demands as well as graduate school requirements; and resume including personal contact data, education, honors, and awards, involvement in clubs and organizations including offices held, professional and leadership activities, and work on volunteer experience.

200 ■ Southeast Alabama Dietetic Association Scholarships (Graduate, Undergraduate/Scholarship)

Purpose: To encourage and reward students majoring in the field of human nutrition, dietetics, foods, nutrition, or food systems management or admitted or enrolled in a dietetic internship who have demonstrated ability and potential in the field of dietetics and nutrition by aiding them financially. **Focus:** Nutrition. **Qualif.:** Applicant must be a junior or senior majoring in the field of human nutrition, dietetics, foods, nutrition, or food systems management or admitted or enrolled in a dietetic internship; must be a legal resident of one of the following counties: Houston, Geneva, Covington, Coffee, Dale, Henry, Pike, or Barbour; or must have been employed or volunteered in a healthcare facility in one of the stated counties; or must be the child or grandchild of an active or former member of the SE Alabama Dietetic Association; and must have a cumulative GPA of 2.5 or above on a 4.0 scale, and a 3.0 or above on a 4.0 scale in major courses of study. **Criteria:** Selection is based on the scholarship; potential in the field of dietetics and nutrition ascertained by, for example: leadership in activities within and outside school, professional interest, honors, activities, and work or volunteer experience; financial need; letters of recommendation; and letter of application.

Funds Avail.: $750. **Duration:** Annual. **To Apply:** Applicant must submit a completed application form together with the official computed cumulative GPA (all post secondary work related to dietetics) authenticated by a faculty member; a letter of application including statements relating to financial need, immediate and future goals, leadership activities, and personal attributes such as initiation and motivation for meeting physical, emotional, and family demands as well as graduate school requirements; and resume including personal contact data, education, honors, and awards, involvement in clubs and organizations including offices held, professional and leadership activities, and work on volunteer experience.

201 ■ Wood Fruitticher Grocery Company, Inc. Scholarships (Graduate, Undergraduate/Scholarship)

Purpose: To encourage and reward junior level undergraduate students or full or part time graduate students in American Dietetic Association (ADA). **Focus:** Nutrition. **Qualif.:** Applicant must have been enrolled in an ADA accredited Alabama college/university for at least one quarter or one semester. **Criteria:** Selection is based on the scholarship; potential in the field of dietetics and nutrition ascertained by, for example: leadership in activities within and outside school, professional interest, honors, activities, and work or volunteer experience; financial need; letters of recommendation; and letter of application.

Funds Avail.: $1,000. **Duration:** Annual. **To Apply:** Applicant must submit a completed application form together with the official computed cumulative GPA (all post secondary work related to dietetics) authenticated by a faculty member; a letter of application including statements relating to financial need, immediate and future goals, leadership activities, and personal attributes such as initiation and motivation for meeting physical, emotional, and family demands as well as graduate school requirements; and resume including personal contact data, education, honors, and awards, involvement in clubs and organizations including offices held, professional and leadership activities, and work on volunteer experience.

202 ■ Alabama Horse Council (AHC)

PO Box 553
Columbiana, AL 35051
Ph: (205)678-2882
URL: www.alabamahorsecouncil.org

203 ■ Alabama Horse Council Scholarships (Undergraduate/Scholarship)

Purpose: To provide educational support to outstanding youth in Alabama pursuing higher education in a college or any university. **Focus:** Equine studies. **Qualif.:** Applicants or their parents/grandparents must be current members of

Awards are arranged alphabetically below their administering organizations

AHC; must be majoring in a field of study for a career in the equine industry; must have demonstrated record of activity in the equine industry prior to college application. **Criteria:** Recipients are selected based on their submitted applications thru mailing.

Funds Avail.: $1,000. **Duration:** Annual. **To Apply:** Applicants must submit 4 copies of: one page-cover form; two letters of references attesting to the applicant's commitment to the equine industry, activity in the industry and character; short (500 word maximum) essay about how horses have shaped the lives and the goals that applicant want to pursue in the horse industry; and a list of activities and honors received. **Deadline:** December 18.

204 ■ Alabama Law Foundation
PO Box 4129
Montgomery, AL 36103
Ph: (334)387-1600
URL: www.alfinc.org

205 ■ William Verbon Black Scholarships *(Undergraduate/Scholarship)*

Purpose: To assist and support full-time students at the University of Alabama School of Law. **Focus:** Law. **Qualif.:** Applicants must be students at the University of Alabama School of Law. **Criteria:** Selection will be based on academic achievement, but consideration is also given to consciousness, dependability, civic involvement, financial need and dedication to the highest ethical standards.

Funds Avail.: No specific amount. **To Apply:** Interested students must contact the foundation for the application process and other information.

206 ■ Johnston Cabaniss Scholarships *(Graduate/Scholarship)*

Purpose: To support students in furthering their law education. **Focus:** Law. **Qualif.:** Applicants must be residents of Alabama and must be law students entering second year at any accredited law school in the United States. **Criteria:** Selection will be based on the committee's criteria.

Funds Avail.: $5,000-first place; $1,000-second place. **Duration:** Annual. **Number Awarded:** Varies. **To Apply:** Applicants may download an application form via ALFINC website. Applicants must submit a completed application form with school transcript attached. **Remarks:** Established in 1987.

207 ■ Justice Janie L. Shores Scholarships *(Undergraduate/Scholarship)*

Purpose: To award scholarship to female Alabama residents. **Focus:** Law. **Qualif.:** Applicants must be female Alabama residents attending an Alabama law school. **Criteria:** Selection will be based on the committee's criteria.

Funds Avail.: No specific amount. **To Apply:** Applicants must visit the website for the online application process. **Deadline:** May 1. **Remarks:** Established in 1995.

208 ■ Alamo Area Paralegal Association (AAPA)
PO Box 90037
San Antonio, TX 78209
Ph: (210)734-7077
Fax: (210)734-9965
E-mail: membership@alamoparalegals.org
URL: www.alamoparalegals.org

209 ■ Alamo Area Paralegal Association Educational Scholarships *(Undergraduate, Professional development/Scholarship)*

Purpose: To promote excellence, education, ethical conduct and the enhancement of the paralegal profession. **Focus:** Paralegal studies. **Qualif.:** Applicants must be current voting, associate, or student members of AAPA. **Criteria:** Selection will be based on the committee's criteria.

Funds Avail.: Varies. **Duration:** Annual. **To Apply:** Applicants must provide a written essay on a topic listed in the application. The winner of the first scholarship category must submit proof of payment of tuition/CLE registration fees in order to receive award disbursement. **Deadline:** June 2.

210 ■ Alamogordo Music Theatre (AMT)
PO Box 266
Alamogordo, NM 88311
E-mail: amt88310@gmail.com
URL: alamogordomusictheatre.org
Facebook: www.facebook.com/alamogordomusictheatre

211 ■ Don Fox Memorial Scholarship *(Undergraduate/Scholarship)*

Purpose: To help students pay for their education. **Focus:** Arts. **Qualif.:** Applicants must be graduating high school seniors; must be planning to major in some aspect of fine arts; must have a minimum of 3.0 GPA (on a 4.0 scale). **Criteria:** Selection will be based on the committee's criteria.

Funds Avail.: No specific amount. **Duration:** Annual. **Number Awarded:** April 1. **To Apply:** Applicants must complete the application form provided by Alamogordo. Submit the application to AMT office and must attach a copy of high school transcript.

212 ■ Martha Julian Memorial Scholarship *(Undergraduate/Scholarship)*

Purpose: To help students pay for their education. **Focus:** Art. **Qualif.:** Applicants must be students pursuing a degree in the fine arts; must be graduating seniors or continuing college students; must have a minimum of 3.0 GPA (on a 4.0 scale). **Criteria:** Preference will be given to those majoring in some aspect of fine arts; financial need will be considered.

Funds Avail.: No specific amount. **Duration:** Annual. **To Apply:** Applicants must complete the application form provided by Alamogordo. Submit the application to AMT office and must attach a copy of high school transcript. **Deadline:** April 1.

213 ■ Ted Lewis Memorial Scholarship *(Undergraduate/Scholarship)*

Purpose: To provide support a graduating senior or continuing college student. **Focus:** Arts. **Qualif.:** Applicants must be graduating seniors or continuing college students; must have a minimum of 3.0 GPA on a 4.0 scale **Criteria:** Selection will be based on the committee's criteria.

Funds Avail.: No specific amount. **Duration:** Annual. **To Apply:** Applicants must complete the application form provided by Alamogordo. Submit the application to AMT office. **Deadline:** April 1.

214 ■ Alaska Airmen Association
4451 Aircraft Dr.
Anchorage, AK 99502

Awards are arranged alphabetically below their administering organizations

Ph: (907)245-1251
Fax: (907)245-1259
Free: 800-464-7030
E-mail: info@alaskaairmen.org
URL: alaskaairmen.org

215 ■ John P. Culhane Professional Pilot Scholarships *(Undergraduate/Scholarship)*

Purpose: To promote development in aviation careers. **Focus:** Aviation. **Qualif.:** Applicants must be enrolled in an aviation-related program at an accredited college, university, trade school or approved training center or be in current training with a certified Flight Instructor or A&P Mechanic; must have completed one year of a commercial aviation training program or at least 25% of the work toward it; must maintain a minimum GPA of 3.0 if enrolled in an accredited college, university or trade school program; must be legal U.S. residents and have no felony convictions. **Criteria:** Recipients are selected based on commitment to aviation goals; interest in both general and commercial aviation in Alaska; evidence of financial need; personal and career goals.

Funds Avail.: $2,500. **Duration:** Annual. **To Apply:** Applicants must provide a letter of recommendation from one of their current instructors attesting to the commitment of the applicant to the program; must submit a completed application form; school transcripts; proof of U.S. citizenship. **Deadline:** March 31. **Contact:** Alaska Airmen Association, Scholarship Committee, 4200 Floatplane Dr., Anchorage, AK 99502; Fax: 907-245-1259; Email: dee.hanson@alaskaairmen.org.

216 ■ F. Atlee Dodge Maintenance Scholarships *(Undergraduate/Scholarship)*

Purpose: To promote development in aviation careers. **Focus:** Aviation. **Qualif.:** Applicants must be enrolled in an aviation-related program at an accredited college, university, trade school, approved training center or be in current training with a certified Flight Instructor or A&P Mechanic; must have completed one year of a commercial aviation training program or at least 25% of the work; must maintain a minimum GPA of 3.0 if enrolled in an accredited college, university or trade school program; must be legal U.S. residents and have no felony convictions. **Criteria:** Recipients are selected based on commitment to aviation goals; interest in both general and commercial aviation in Alaska; evidence of financial need; personal and career goals.

Funds Avail.: $2,500. **To Apply:** Applicants must provide a letter of recommendation from one of their current instructors attesting to the commitment of the applicant to the program; must submit a completed application form; school transcripts; proof of U.S. citizenship. **Deadline:** March 31. **Contact:** Alaska Airmen Association, Scholarship Committee, 4200 Floatplane Dr., Anchorage, AK 99502; Fax: 907-245-1259; Email: dee.hanson@alaskaairmen.org.

217 ■ Bob Reeve Aviation Management Scholarships *(Undergraduate/Scholarship)*

Purpose: To promote development in aviation careers. **Focus:** Aviation. **Qualif.:** Applicants must be enrolled in an aviation-related program with an accredited college, university, trade school, approved training center or be in current training with a certified Flight Instructor or A&P Mechanic; must have completed one year of a commercial aviation training program or at least 25% of the work; must maintain a minimum GPA of 3.0 if enrolled in an accredited college, university or trade school program; must be legal U.S. residents and have no felony convictions. **Criteria:** Recipients are selected based on commitment to aviation goals; interest in both general and commercial aviation in Alaska; evidence of financial need; personal and career goals.

Funds Avail.: $2,500. **Duration:** Annual. **To Apply:** Applicants must provide a letter of recommendation from one of their current instructors attesting to the commitment of the applicant to the program; must submit a completed application form; school transcripts; proof of U.S. citizenship. **Deadline:** March 31. **Contact:** Alaska Airmen Association, Scholarship Committee, 4200 Floatplane Dr., Anchorage, AK 99502; Fax: 907-245-1259; Email: dee.hanson@alaskaairmen.org.

218 ■ Alaska Broadcasters Association (ABA)

c/o Cathy Hiebert, Executive Director
700 W 41st St., Ste. 102
Anchorage, AK 99503
Ph: (907)258-2424
Fax: (907)258-2414
E-mail: akbagold@gci.net
URL: www.alaskabroadcasters.org
Facebook: www.facebook.com/pages/AlaskaBroadcastersAssociation/376061105799719

219 ■ Linda Simmons Memorial Scholarships *(Undergraduate/Scholarship)*

Purpose: To provide encouragement and financial assistance to students who have demonstrated their interest in the communications arts. **Focus:** Broadcasting. **Qualif.:** Candidate must be pursuing a degree or certified course of study in an accredited junior/community college, college, university or professional trade school; must be pursuing radio and/or television broadcasting or broadcast engineering as a major course of study. Application from candidates pursuing major studies in journalism, public relations or advertising will be considered if there are no qualified candidates with broadcast communications or broadcast engineering majors; must be residents of the State of Alaska. Student must demonstrate excellence in the following areas: academic performance; discipline/attitude; attendance. **Criteria:** Selection will be based on the submitted application materials.

Funds Avail.: $2,000. **Duration:** Annual. **To Apply:** Applicants must submit a formal application sheet; short written essay expressing applicant's personal goals; and three letters of reference that address the following criteria: academic performance, discipline/attitude and attendance. **Deadline:** April 1. **Remarks:** Established in 2001.

220 ■ Alaska Community Foundation

3201 C St., Ste. 110
Anchorage, AK 99503
Ph: (907)334-6700
Fax: (907)334-5780
Free: 855-336-6701
E-mail: info@alaskacf.org
URL: www.alaskacf.org

221 ■ Nordic Ski Association of Anchorage Scholarships *(Undergraduate/Scholarship)*

Purpose: To encourage scholastic performance, cross-country skiing and participation in community ski activities.

Awards are arranged alphabetically below their administering organizations

Focus: General studies/Field of study not specified. **Qualif.:** Applicants must: be Alaska residents who are high school seniors or currently enrolled college students; be members of the high school cross-country ski team during their junior and senior years; have individual or family memberships in the NSAA; and, have a cumulative GPA of at least 2.7 on a 4.0 scale. **Criteria:** Preference will be given to students attending college in Alaska. Applicants will be selected based on their academic performance and application materials.
Funds Avail.: $1,500. **Duration:** Annual. **To Apply:** Application forms are available at the Nordic Skiing Association of Anchorage website. Applicants must have: a letter of recommendation, list of personal achievements and honors, a brief statement describing any community service, a maximum 500-word essay on the "benefits you have received from skiing", and a copy of official transcripts from all high school or university works. **Deadline:** March 31. **Contact:** The Alaska Community Foundation at szerkel@alaskacf.org.

222 ■ Alaska Space Grant Program (ASGP)
306 Tanana Loop, Duckering Hall 207
Fairbanks, AK 99775
Ph: (907)474-6833
E-mail: ua-spacegrant-dept@alaska.edu
URL: spacegrant.alaska.edu
Facebook: www.facebook.com/Alaska-Space-Grant-Program-164327900265148/

223 ■ ASGP Graduate Research Fellowships
(Graduate/Fellowship)
Purpose: To support students in conducting research projects fostering the vision of NASA. **Focus:** Engineering; Mathematics and mathematical sciences; Science; Space and planetary sciences; Technology. **Qualif.:** Applicants must be graduate students enrolled at an Alaskan institution of higher education during the period of the award; must be U.S. citizens and in good academic standing; must be women or individuals from underrepresented groups, specifically, Alaska Natives, Native Americans, African Americans, Hispanics, Pacific Islanders, and person with disabilities. **Criteria:** Applications are ranked based on the following criteria: scholastic achievement; strength of recommendations and; proposed project merit. Preference may be given to women and individuals from underrepresented groups.
Funds Avail.: Up to $15,000. **To Apply:** Applicants are required to identify faculty mentors with whom they intend to work and who are available to write a letter of collaboration. Applicants must submit the following requirements: completed application form; match authorization; budget form; project description maximum of 3 pages; letter of collaboration from mentors and; academic transcript. All requirements must submit in one compiled PDF file. **Deadline:** April 1. **Contact:** Rebecca Lees, rblees@alaska.edu, 907-474-6833.

224 ■ Alberta Association on Gerontology (AAG)
Edmonton Ctr.
Edmonton, AB, Canada T5J 4N1
E-mail: info@albertaaging.ca
URL: www.albertaaging.ca

225 ■ Alberta Association of Gerontology Student Awards *(Graduate/Award)*
Purpose: To assist with the costs associated with a student's coursework, research or attendance at a workshop or conference. **Focus:** Gerontology. **Qualif.:** Applicants must be Albertans registered in a graduate degree program in an accredited post secondary institution; must not be in the last term of their program; must demonstrate interest in any aspect of aging; must agree to contribute an article for an edition of the AAGmag (e.g., a written summary of research). **Criteria:** Selection will be based on academic merit as illustrated by grades and educational attainment, relevant work/volunteer, current studies/research plans, future commitment to the field of gerontology and an indication of how this award will be used to support the applicant's interest in gerontology.
Funds Avail.: $1,000. **Duration:** Annual. **Number Awarded:** 2. **To Apply:** A complete application package consists of: a two-page cover letter that includes a description of the applicant's current studies or research, relevant volunteer/work experience and future plans in gerontology (academic, research, practice); a completed award application form; a copy of the applicant's curriculum vitae; a copy of post-secondary education transcripts (they do not need to be original); a letter from the student's supervisor. **Deadline:** March 31.

226 ■ Alberta Association of Gerontology Student Awards - Edmonton Chapter *(Graduate, Undergraduate/Award)*
Purpose: To assist with the costs associated with a student's coursework, research or attendance at a workshop or conference. **Focus:** Gerontology. **Qualif.:** Applicants must be registered in a degree, diploma or certificate program in an accredited post-secondary institution (undergraduate, graduate, and diploma students); reside in Edmonton or surrounding communities; not be in the last term of their program; demonstrate an interest in any aspect of aging; agree to contribute an article for an edition of the AAGmag (e.g., a written summary of their research or studies). **Criteria:** Selection will be based on academic merit as illustrated by grades and educational attainment, relevant work/volunteer, current studies/research plans, future commitment to the field of gerontology and an indication of how this award will be used to support the applicant's interest in gerontology. Preference will be given to full-time students, graduate students and current AAG members.
Funds Avail.: $1,000. **Duration:** Annual. **To Apply:** A complete application package consists of: a one-page cover letter that includes a description of the applicant's current studies or research as well as future plans in gerontology (academic, research, practice); a completed award application form; a copy of the applicant's curriculum vitae; a copy of post-secondary education transcripts (they do not need to be original) or verification of the student's studies or research (e.g., current timetable, a letter from the student's supervisor). **Deadline:** March 31.

227 ■ Alberta Barley Commission
6815 8th St. NE, No. 200
Calgary, AB, Canada T2E 7H7
Ph: (403)291-9111
Fax: (403)291-0190
Free: 800-265-9111
E-mail: barleyinfo@albertabarley.com
URL: www.albertabarley.com

228 ■ Eugene Boyko Memorial Scholarships
(Undergraduate/Scholarship)
Purpose: To recognize and encourage students studying in the field of crop production and/or crop processing

Awards are arranged alphabetically below their administering organizations

technology studies. **Focus:** Agricultural sciences. **Qualif.:** Applicants must be: Canadian citizens or permanent Canadian residents living in Alberta; attending a post-secondary institution in Alberta; enrolled full-time in the second or subsequent year of post-secondary study. **Criteria:** Selection will be based on academic achievement in their previous year of post-secondary studies.

Funds Avail.: 500 Canadian Dollars. **Duration:** Annual. **To Apply:** Application forms are available from Alberta Scholarship Programs and from Alberta post-secondary institutions. Mail completed application and an official transcript to Alberta Scholarship Programs.

229 ■ Alberta Blue Cross
10009 108th St. NW
Edmonton, AB, Canada T5J 3C5
Ph: (780)498-8000
Fax: (780)425-4627
Free: 800-661-6995
E-mail: webcommunications@ab.bluecross.ca
URL: www.ab.bluecross.ca
Facebook: www.facebook.com/AlbertaBlueCross?sk=wall
Twitter: www.twitter.com/ABBluecross

230 ■ Alberta Blue Cross Scholarships for Aboriginal Students (Undergraduate/Scholarship)

Purpose: To provide support for young Albertans in their quest for higher skills and meaningful employment. **Focus:** General studies/Field of study not specified. **Qualif.:** Applicants must: be registered Indians, Inuit or Metis; have been a resident of Alberta the during previous year of study; have completed the final year of high school and be entering into the first year of post-secondary studies at an accredited Alberta post-secondary institute. **Criteria:** Selection is based on scholastic achievement in Alberta Grade 12 diploma examinations, financial need and community involvement.

Funds Avail.: Amount varies. **Duration:** Annual. **Number Awarded:** 3. **To Apply:** Applicants must submit a completed application form along with a copy of Alberta Education High School transcript; a list or description of involvement in the community and school-sponsored events over the past two years; two letters of reference on letterhead paper; proof of Aboriginal status; a letter confirming attendance from one of the accredited post-secondary educational institution; and a short essay about the application and the reasons for applying for the scholarship. **Deadline:** September 30.

231 ■ Alberta Child Care Association (ACCA)
10025 - 106 St., Ste. 110
Edmonton, AB, Canada T5J 1G4
Ph: (780)421-7544
Fax: (780)428-0080
E-mail: nataliew.accna@telus.net
URL: www.albertachildcare.org

232 ■ Alberta Child Care Association Professional Development Grants (Professional development/Grant)

Purpose: To assist a Child Development Supervisor (CDS) to attend approved workshops, conferences, post-secondary credit courses and participate in professional learning communities. **Focus:** Child care. **Qualif.:** Applicants are individuals with a valid Child Development Supervisor certificate issued by the Alberta Child Care Certification office that are: working as paid staff members or family child care consultants/coordinators in a licensed child care program or contracted family day home agency in Alberta, and working a minimum of 80 hours a month in a licensed child care program or family day home agency; or 40 hours each month in a licensed out-of-school care program. **Criteria:** Selection will be based on the aforesaid qualifications.

Funds Avail.: No specific amount. **Duration:** Annual. **To Apply:** Applicants may verify the application process through the program website. **Remarks:** Professional Development Grants are funding for three distinct approaches: workshops and conferences; postsecondary programs and courses; and professional learning communities.

233 ■ Alberta Equestrian Federation (AEF)
251 Midpark Blvd. SE, Ste. 100
Calgary, AB, Canada T2X 1S3
Ph: (403)253-4411
Fax: (403)252-5260
Free: 877-463-6233
E-mail: info@albertaequestrian.com
URL: www.albertaequestrian.com
Facebook: www.facebook.com/AlbertaEquestrian
Twitter: twitter.com/ab_equestrian

234 ■ AEF Educational Scholarship (Undergraduate/Scholarship)

Purpose: To support active members who exemplify the objectives, vision and mission of the AEF, and interested in pursuing an equine-related post secondary education. **Focus:** General studies/Field of study not specified. **Qualif.:** Applicants must: be AEF members for two consecutive years; be Canadian citizens or hold landed immigrant status; over 18 years of age; and, have not been awarded an AEF scholarship. **Criteria:** Selection will be based on the committee's criteria.

Funds Avail.: 750 Canadian Dollars. **Duration:** Annual. **To Apply:** Applicant must submit the following requirements through mail: application form; essay; two letters of reference; curriculum vitae; proof of citizenship; survey; scholarship committee application. **Deadline:** May 31.

235 ■ Alberta Foundation for the Arts
10708 - 105 Ave.
Edmonton, AB, Canada T5H 0A1
Ph: (780)427-9968
URL: www.affta.ab.ca

236 ■ AFA Aboriginal Traditional Arts Individual Project Grants (Professional development/Grant)

Purpose: To support the development of Aboriginal artists, or artists working on Aboriginal cultural themes, who seek to express and share Aboriginal culture and perspectives in a contemporary or traditional context. **Focus:** Culture; Media arts. **Qualif.:** Applicants must be Canadian citizens or landed immigrants and have their primary residence in Alberta for one full year before applying for a grant. Ensembles must be made up of members who meet the individual criteria. Applicants, including ensembles, must

Awards are arranged alphabetically below their administering organizations

not be incorporated with provincial or federal corporate registries. **Criteria:** Selection will be based on the submitted application and supporting materials.
Funds Avail.: Maximum of 15,000 Canadian Dollars. **Duration:** Annual. **To Apply:** Applicants must provide the following in the application package: a completed application form and signed Applicant Agreement with original signature. Ensembles must designate one member who is the contact person for all requirements of the grant; must submit the required materials if the applicants are under the age of 18 years at the time of application; an application checklist must be completed and submitted with the application; a detailed description of the project, which demonstrates the project's connection to historical practice in a specific Aboriginal community. Protocols and permission from the community to use traditional tribal knowledge must be addressed. Include a letter of agreement with mentor, elder or cultural resource person, and an outline of the objectives, planned activities, expected results and benefits; a balanced project budget detailing revenues and expenditures in Canadian dollars. Total revenues must equal total expenditures; a professional resume. Applicants must also include the following: for art production, a list of all principals involved in the project and their resumes; for marketing or research, official invitations, confirmation or itineraries, as applicable; for marketing, a detailed marketing plan; for mentorship, training or career development. Applicants who have been accepted into a mentorship must provide a letter of agreement as proof of acceptance and support from the mentor, elder or cultural resource person and a detailed description, schedule and budget for the course of study. Applicants are encourage to submit additional support materials that may assist in the assessment process. These may include press clippings, invitations, reference letters, reviews, catalogues, scripts, published books or storyboards. Applicants must submit applications in the following format to allow for ease of use by juries: submit four complete, assembled application packages (one original and three copies of the application forms and all printed attachments) along with one copy of audio and/or visual support materials; assemble the parts of the packages in the same order as the checklist for this grant; clip applications into four packages. Do not bind or use folders, page covers or binders; remember to make one additional copy of the complete application package and keep it for your records. Audio and/or visual support materials such as CD, videocassette or DVD must be clearly labeled with the applicant's name on the media. All media must be compatible with Microsoft Windows operating system and NTSC VHS video standards. The applicant is responsible for providing support materials that comply with the viewing capabilities of the AFA. Only one copy of these support materials is required. **Deadline:** February 1 or September 1.

237 ■ AFA Art Acquisition by Application Grants (Professional development/Grant)

Purpose: To support individual artists through the purchase of art produced by Albertan artists and offers an opportunity for Albertans to experience the legacy of Alberta's visual arts community. **Focus:** Arts. **Qualif.:** Artists must be Canadian citizens or landed immigrants; have their primary residence in Alberta for one full year before applying to the program; have met the reporting requirements of any previously applied for AFA grant programs; have had at least one public exhibition featuring their work. Interested artists may submit artworks in one or more of the following categories: painting; sculpture; fibre art; ceramics; drawing; printmaking (excluding reproductions); photography; glass; mixed media (including new media). **Criteria:** Selection will be based on the expert jury's criteria.
Funds Avail.: No specific amount. **Duration:** Annual. **To Apply:** Applicants must submit one copy of the complete, assembled application package (application form and all attachments). Staple or clip applications and do not use folders, page covers or binders. Applicants to this program must provide the following in the application package: A completed and signed Application Form and Artist Agreement. If a galley/agent is submitting on the artists' behalf, they must designate one person as the contact for all requirements of the submission and must complete the Application Form, or the artist must complete and sign with an original signature the Authorization for Submission by a Commercial Gallery/Agent and the Artist Agreement; the artists' current resume and an artist statement including background information on the works submitted. A visual representation of the proposed artworks to be purchased by the AFA. This must be submitted as follows: digital image files on CD-ROM. Submission of artwork images on CD-ROM, available for purchase, must be compatible with Microsoft Windows operating system; images must be provided on one CD-ROM clearly labeled with the name of the artist who produced the artworks and the name of the gallery or agent if applicable; each image on the disc must be labelled with the artists name, title of the work and be ordered and numbered corresponding to the Artwork Submission List ("1_Lastname_title.jpg"); image must be in JPEG format, 2280 x 1750 pixel range and between 1-2MB in size; for galleries submitting multiple submissions on one disk, each artist's images must be in a separate folder and labeled; images may represent from 1 to 5 artworks as listed on the Artwork Submission List; an artwork comprised of more than one part/component where the individual parts/components can also be sold separately is considered to be more than one artwork. Applicants must also submit a completed Artwork Submission List. Applicants requesting the return of their CD-ROM must provide a stamped, self-addressed envelope. **Deadline:** April 1.

238 ■ AFA Cultural Relations Project Grants (Professional development/Grant)

Purpose: To support professional artists and arts organizations in any arts discipline that will represent Alberta at a national or international level, and encourage professional artists in community residencies in partnership with an Albertan or Western Canadian community organization. **Focus:** Arts; Culture. **Qualif.:** Applicants must be Canadian citizens or landed immigrants; have their primary residence in Alberta for one full year before applying for a grant. In order to be eligible for a project grant from this fund, an organization must: be incorporated as a not-for-profit and be in good standing with Corporate Registry in Alberta, Saskatchewan, Manitoba or British Columbia; demonstrate responsible fiscal management. Eligible projects include: projects taking place outside of Canada that, in the opinion of the AFA support the development and promotion of Alberta art internationally; projects taking place in Canada but outside of Alberta that, in the opinion of the AFA, support the development and promotion of Alberta art Nationally; artists in the community residencies: (i) applications jointly submitted by an Alberta artist or arts organization and an incorporated not-for-profit Western Canadian organization for a community residency of up to 12 months; (ii) up to three months of collaborative research and development for a 10-12 months residency program; (iii) applications serving more than one community; (iv) applications between an artist and an incorporated for-profit company or organization. **Criteria:** Preference will be given

Awards are arranged alphabetically below their administering organizations

to projects that meet any of the following criteria: projects destined for those countries designated as a priority by the Government of Alberta; projects with confirmed support from the Government of Canada and/or the Canada Council for the Arts; project with clearly demonstrated support from the host community; projects that introduce Alberta artists to new audiences; increase artistic activity in a community, encourage development of future artists and arts audiences, or encourage linkages between artists and the broader community.

Funds Avail.: No specific amount. **Duration:** Annual. **To Apply:** Applicants to this program must provide the following in the application package: A complete Application Form, Applicants Agreement, and Application checklist (Attachment VII of the Individual Artists Project Grant Program Application Form or Attachment XII of the Organization Project Grant Program Application Form). Organizations must designate one member who is the contact person for all requirements of the grant. Projects involving more than one artist must be submitted by an organization or by an individual submitting as an ensemble/group. Separate individual artist applications will not be accepted for the same project; the organization's most recent annual financial statement, approved and signed by two board members other than the Treasurer, demonstrating responsible fiscal management; a copy of the organization's most recent return to a Western Canadian Corporate Registry; a detailed description of the project, including an outline of the objectives, planned activities, and expected results and benefits (for Development applications for Artists in the Community projects, a description of the proposed community needs assessment must be included); a balanced project budget detailing revenues (including the amount requested from the AFA) and expenditures. Total revenues must equal total expenditures; artists in the Community Residencies must provide a signed contract or Memorandum of Understanding between the artist and the organization or municipality that clearly outlines the terms and conditions of the residency and the rights and obligations of each party; a resume of the artist(s) or arts company profile of those representing Alberta in the project; applicants must also include any applicable itinerary, travel confirmations and funding confirmations. Applicants must also include letter(s) or invitation from the host organization. Applicants are encouraged to submit additional support materials that may assist in the assessment process. These may include press clippings, invitations, reference letters, reviews, catalogues, scripts, CD's, DVD's and storyboards. Only one copy of these materials is required. First time applicants must include three letters of reference from recognized peers who attest that the applicant maintains a standard of professionalism that will represent Alberta artists in a positive light. Applicants must submit one original copy of the complete, assembled application package (Application Form, Applicant Agreement and all printed attachments). Staple or clip applications and do not use folders, page covers or binders. Audio and/or visual support materials such as CD, videocassette or DVD must be clearly labelled with the applicant's name. Use separate discs for different file types. All media must be compatible with Microsoft Windows operating system and NTSC VHS video standards. The applicant is responsible for providing support materials that comply with the viewing capabilities of the AFA. An Application Checklist must be completed and submitted with the application.

239 ■ AFA Dance Project Grants *(Professional development/Grant)*

Purpose: To support the development of individual Alberta artists, arts administrators or an ensemble of artists by providing a grant from a specific dance project in a limited time period. **Focus:** Arts; Dance. **Qualif.:** Applicants must be Canadian citizens or landed immigrants; have their primary residence in Alberta for one full year before applying for a grant. In order to be eligible from a project grants, ensembles must be made up of members who meet the individual criteria. Applicants, including ensembles, must not be incorporated with provincial or federal corporate registries. Eligible projects must meet the criteria in one of the following categories: Art production includes the development, creation and production of any dance work. Alberta individual artists that have been contracted by commissioners to create a specific work may apply under this category; Training and career development includes a workshop, master class summer program, professional development or professional course of study in dance. Dancers, dance instructors, designers, arts administrators and technicians may apply; Marketing includes projects that promote, market or distribute the work of Alberta dance artists; Research includes activities that support or result in the development of a dance project. **Criteria:** Selection will be based on the jury's criteria.

Funds Avail.: 15,000 Canadian Dollars; and may include up to 3,000 Canadian Dollars per month subsistence allowance. **Duration:** Annual. **To Apply:** Applicants must provide the following in the application package: a completed Application Form and signed Applicant Agreement with original signature. Ensembles must designate one member who is the contact person for all requirements of the grant. This applicant must sign the Applicant Agreement and complete the Application Form; must submit the required materials if the applicants are under the age of 18 years at the time of application; an application checklist must be completed and submitted with the application; a detailed description of the project, including an outline of the objectives, planned activities, timelines and expected results and benefits; a balanced project budget detailing revenues (including the amount requested from the AFA) and expenditures in Canadian dollars. Total revenues must equal total expenditures; an artistic resume of no more than four pages. Students may submit a description of their dance background, including level of training, performing arts activities and other relevant dance history. Applicants must also include: for art production, a list of all principals involved in the project and their resumes. To assist in the assessment process, applicants are encouraged to submit a video of previous productions of their work, or of the work-in-progress. Commission applicants are encouraged to submit a completed and signed contract with the commissioner and a plan for the exhibition, presentation, display, publication, screening or performance of the commissioned work; for marketing or research, official invitations, confirmations or itineraries, as applicable; for marketing, a detailed marketing plan; for training or career development: (i) applicants who have been accepted into a specific course must provide proof of acceptance and a detailed description, schedule and budget for the study program; (ii) applicants who have not already been accepted into a course must submit a detailed description, schedule and budget for the preferred choice. In addition, two alternate program choices should be submitted, with detailed description, schedules and budgets for each choice; (iii) for dance training programs, artists must submit two audition pieces on one VHS NTSC video cassette or DVD that is playable in a

Awards are arranged alphabetically below their administering organizations

commercial DVD player. The two audition pieces together must not exceed 4 minutes in length, and must duplicate the experience of a live audition, including full body shot composition, without props or costume. One audition piece must relate to the program of study, such as classical, contemporary, jazz, modern, folk or heritage dance. The second piece must be in a contrasting style; (iv) non-performing artists must provide a resume, portfolio or videocassette/DVD of their work. Applicants are encouraged to submit additional support materials that may assist in the assessment process. These may include press clippings, invitations, reference letters, reviews, catalogues, scripts published books or storyboards. Applicants must submit applications in the following format to allow ease of use by juries: submit four complete, assembled application packages (one original and three copies of the application forms and all printed attachments) along with one copy of audio and/or visual support materials; assemble the parts of the packages in the same order as the checklist for this grant; clip application into four packages. Do not bind or use folders, page covers or binders; remember to make one additional copy of the complete application package and keep it for your records. Audio and/or visual support materials such as CD, videocassette or DVD must be clearly labelled with the applicant's name on the media. Use separate discs for different file types. All media must be compatible with Microsoft Windows operating system and NTSC VHS video standards. **Deadline:** February 1; September 1.

240 ■ AFA Film and Video Arts Project Grants *(Professional development/Grant)*

Purpose: To support the development of individual Alberta artists, arts administrators or an ensemble of artists by providing a grant for a specific film and video arts project. **Focus:** Arts; Filmmaking; Video. **Qualif.:** Applicants must be Canadian citizens or landed immigrants; have their primary residence in Alberta for one full year before applying for a grant. In order to be eligible for a project grant, an ensemble must be made up of members who meet the individual criteria. Applicants, including ensembles, must not be incorporated with provincial or federal corporate registries. Eligible projects must meet the criteria in one of the following categories: (a) Art production: the creation of a new work in film and video arts. Eligible projects may be a distinct phase of a new work, such as script or screenplay writing, pre-production, production and post-production. Eligible genres include, but are not limited to, narrative shorts and features, experimental shorts, documentary and animation; (b) Marketing: a program of activity for a specific period of time to disseminate a completed film and video arts work and/or to develop audiences and markets for an artist's work. Eligible projects include, but are not limited to, film festival submissions, on-line distribution and promotion initiatives, attendance at screenings, exhibitions, presentations or conferences featuring the artist's work and award presentations by invitations; (c) Research: a program of activity for a specific period of time that supports or results in the development of new work in film and video arts. Eligible projects include, but are not limited to, experimentation, exploration and research (including research for documentaries) related to production; (d) Training and career development: a course or program of study to develop an artist's training in film and video arts. Eligible projects include, but are not limited to, workshops, master classes, retreats, mentorship programs and professional courses. **Criteria:** Selection will be based on the jury's criteria. **Funds Avail.:** 15,000 Canadian Dollars; and may include up to 3,000 Canadian Dollars per month subsistence allowance. **Duration:** Annual. **To Apply:** Applicants must provide the following in the application package: a completed Application Form and signed Applicant Agreement with original signature. Ensembles must designate one member who is the contact person for all requirements of the grant. Applicants must sign the Applicant Agreement and complete the Application Form; must submit the required materials if the applicants are under the age of 18 years at the time of application; an application checklist must be completed and submitted with the application; a detailed description of the project, including an outline of the objectives, planned activities, timelines and expected results and benefits; a balanced project budget detailing revenues (including the amount requested from the AFA) and expenditures in Canadian dollars. Total revenues must equal total expenditures; an artistic resume of no more than four pages. Students may submit a description of their dance background, including level of training, performing arts activities and other relevant dance history. Applicants must also include: for all categories, film and video work, scripts or storyboards of previous productions or of the work in progress to aid the assessment process. Video submissions must be a JPEG or GIF video file on VHS NTSC videocassette or one CD or DVD compatible with Microsoft Windows operating system; for art production, a list of all principals involved in the project and their resumes. Commission applicants are encouraged to submit a completed and signed contract with the commissioner and a plan for the screening, exhibition or presentation of the commissioned work; for marketing ore research, official invitations, confirmation or itineraries, as applicable; for training or career development: (i) applicants who have been accepted into a specific course must provide proof of acceptance and a detailed description, schedule and budget for the study program; applicants who have not already been accepted into a course must submit a detailed description, schedule and budget for the preferred choice. In addition, two alternate program choices should be submitted, with detailed description, schedules and budgets for each choice. Applicants are encouraged to submit additional support materials that may assist in the assessment process. These may include press clippings, invitations, reference letters, reviews, catalogues, scripts published books or storyboards. Applicants must submit applications in the following format to allow ease of use by juries: submit four complete, assembled application packages (one original and three copies of the application forms and all printed attachments) along with one copy of audio and/or visual support materials; assemble the parts of the packages in the same order as the checklist for this grant; clip application into four packages. Do not bind or use folders, page covers or binders; remember to make one additional copy of the complete application package and keep it for your records. Audio and/or visual support materials such as CD, videocassette or DVD must be clearly labelled with the applicant's name on the media. Use separate discs for different file types. All media must be compatible with Microsoft Windows operating system and NTSC VHS video standards. **Deadline:** February 1 and September 1.

241 ■ AFA Literary Arts Project Grants *(Professional development/Grant)*

Purpose: To support the development of individual Alberta artists, arts administrators or an ensemble of artists by providing a grant for a specific literary arts project in a limited time period. **Focus:** Arts; Literature. **Qualif.:** Applicants must be Canadian citizens or landed immigrants; have their primary residence in Alberta for one full year

before applying for a grant. In order to be eligible from a project grants, ensembles must be made up of members who meet the individual criteria. Applicants, including ensembles, must not be incorporated with provincial or federal corporate registries. Eligible projects must meet the criteria in one of the following categories: (a) Art production: the creation of a new literary work. Eligible projects may be a distinct phase of a new work, such as a first draft or a final draft, in one of the eligible literary genres; (b) Marketing: a program of activity for a specific period of time to disseminate a completed literary work and/or to develop audiences and markets for an artists' work. Eligible projects include, but are not limited to, promotional reading tours and book launches; on-line marketing initiatives such as book trailers; attendance at literary festivals, non-academic conference or award presentation by invitation; (c) Research: a program of activity for a specific period of time that supports or results in the development of new work in the literary arts. Eligible projects include, but are not limited to, experimentation, exploration and research of primary materials; (d) training and career development: a course or program of study to develop a writer's training in one or more of the eligible literary genres, including literary translation. Eligible projects include, but are not limited to, workshops, master classes, retreats, mentorship programs and professional courses. Except for projects in the training and career development category, eligible applicants must be professional writers who have had literary works professional published or produced. Professional literary publications or productions are literary works: (a) that have gone through an editorial process made by an independent editor/editorial board or that have gone through a dramaturgical process; (b) that have been published or produced by organizations with a majority of paid contributors who are not principals of the publishing or producing organization; (c) for which the writer has received compensation either as royalties, fees or honoraria, or as in-kind remuneration in the form of complimentary copies or a complimentary subscription; (d) of which the writer owns copyright; (e) that are available and accessible to the general public. Eligible literary arts genres are defined as the following: novels, short fiction, poetry, literary non-fiction, graphic novels, plays, young adult fiction and picture books. Professional writers of literary work are those who meet at least one of the following publication or production requirements: (a) a literary book published in print or as an e-book by a professional publishing house; (b) a minimum of two texts of short fiction, such as short stories or excerpts from a novel, published on two separate occasions in print or online literary magazines or periodicals, or in print or e-book anthologies published by professional publishing houses; (c) a minimum of five poems published on at least two separate occasions in print or online literary magazines or periodicals, or in print or e-book anthologies published by professional publishing houses; (d) a minimum of two texts of literary non-fiction published on two separate occasions in print or online literary magazines or periodicals, or in print or e-book anthologies published by professional publishing houses; (e) a play professionally produced. Applicants with a publishing or producing history established outside of Canada must provide in their artistic resumes evidence that their publications or productions are professional literary work. A statement of editorial and copyright policy of the publishes or producers may be required. **Criteria:** Selection will be based on the jury's criteria.
Funds Avail.: 15,000 Canadian Dollars; and may include up to 3,000 Canadian Dollars per month subsistence allowance. **Duration:** Annual. **To Apply:** Applicants must provide the following in the application package: a completed Application Form and signed Applicant Agreement with original signature. Ensembles must designate one member who is the contact person for all requirements of the grant. Applicants must sign the Applicant Agreement and complete the Application Form; must submit the required materials if the applicants are under the age of 18 years at the time of application; an application checklist must be completed and submitted with the application; a detailed description of the project, including an outline of the objectives, planned activities, timelines and expected results and benefits; a balanced project budget detailing revenues (including the amount requested from the AFA) and expenditures in Canadian dollars. Total revenues must equal total expenditures; an artistic resume of no more than four pages that includes a current list of literary works professionally published and produce. Applicants must identify the title, publisher, genre, year published/produced, and length/duration for each work. The artistic resume should also include other literary arts activities such as level of training, readings, performances and self-published works, if applicable. Applicants must also include the following: for all categories, a writing sample of no more than 15 pages, preferably from a work in progress. The writing sample must be a clean copy on white, 8.5 x 11 paper, single-sided, 1.5 or double-spaced and in 12-pt. font; for art production or research involving literary translation projects, a sample manuscript of original text along with a translated version in English; for art production or research involving anthology projects, an agreement with, or expression of interest from, a publisher including a clear statement that identifies the publisher's proposed financial contribution for such costs as editing, legal fees and postage, as well as the publisher's role in the selection of anthology materials; for marketing or research, official invitations, confirmations or itineraries, as applicable; for marketing, a detailed marketing plan; for training or career development: (a) applicants who have been accepted into a specific course must provide proof of acceptance and a detailed description, schedule and budget for the program; (b) applicants who have not already been accepted into a specific course must submit a detailed description, schedule and budget for the preferred choice. In addition, at least two alternate program choices should be submitted, with detailed descriptions, schedules and budgets for each choice. Applicants are encouraged to submit additional support materials that may assist in the assessment process. These may include press clippings, invitations, reference letters, reviews, catalogues, scripts, published books or storyboards. Applicants must submit applications in the following format to allow for ease of use by juries: submit four complete, assembled application packages (one original and three copies of the application forms and all printed attachments) along with one copy of audio and/or visual support materials; assemble the parts of the packages in the same order as the checklist for this grant; clip applications into four packages. Do not bind or use folders, page covers or binders; remember to make one additional copy of the complete application package and keep it for your records. Audio and/or visual support materials such as CD, videocassette or DVD must be clearly labelled with the applicant's name on the media. Use separate discs for different file types. All media must be compatible with Microsoft Windows operating system and NTSC VHS video standards. **Deadline:** February 1; September 1.

Awards are arranged alphabetically below their administering organizations

242 ■ AFA Music Project Grants *(Professional development/Grant)*

Purpose: To support the development of individual Alberta artists, arts administrators or an ensemble of artists by providing a grant for a specific music project in a limited time period. **Focus:** Music. **Qualif.:** Applicants must be Canadian citizens or landed immigrants; have their primary residence in Alberta for one full year before applying for a grant. In order to be eligible for a project grants, ensembles must be made up of members who meet the individual criteria. Applicants, including ensembles, must not be incorporated with provincial or federal corporate registries. Eligible projects must meet the criteria in one of the following categories: (a) Art production demo recording project, not intended for sale, including full production support and basic press kit expenses, or commercial recording projects, intended for sale, including support for pre-production and song development (basic recording); (b) Marketing includes, but is not limited to, marketing and promotion of a commercial release, costs associated with performances at special events by invitation, and promotional tours. Recording artists marketing a commercial recording or producing a music video must have released a commercial recording prior to applying; (c) Research includes activities that support or result in the development of a music project; (d) Training and career development includes a course or program of study to develop an artist's training in music. Eligible projects include, but are not limited to, workshop, master classes, summer program mentorship program, or professional course of study in performance, recording arts or composition. **Criteria:** Selection will be based on the jury's criteria.

Funds Avail.: 15,000 Canadian Dollars; and may include up to 3,000 Canadian Dollars per month subsistence allowance. **Duration:** Annual. **To Apply:** Applicants must provide the following in the application package: A completed application form and signed Applicant Agreement with original signature. Ensembles must designate one member who is the contact person for all requirements of the grant. Applicants must sign the Applicant Agreement and complete the Application Form; must submit the required materials if the applicants are under the age of 18 years at the time of application; an application checklist must be completed and submitted with the application; a detailed description of the project, including an outline of the objectives, planned activities, timelines and expected results and benefits; a balanced project budget detailing revenues (including the amount requested from the AFA) and expenditures in Canadian dollars. Total revenues must equal total expenditures; an artistic resume of no more than four pages that includes past training, most recent performance highlights, compositions, discography, and ensemble experience. Applicants must also include the following: (a) for art production, include a demo recording, commercial recording, signed contract with the commissioner and a plan for the exhibition, presentation, display, publication, screening or performance of the commissioned work (commission applicants); for all other art production projects include one copy of audio material, including two musical selections; (b) for marketing, include: any official invitations, confirmations or itineraries; a detailed marketing plan; one copy of audio material, including two musical selection, A final copy of a commercially released recording is required for the marketing of commercial recordings or music videos; (c) for research, include: any official invitations, confirmations or itineraries; one copy of audio material, including two musical selections, if applicable; (d) for training or career development: (i) applicants who have been accepted into a specific course must submit: proof of acceptance; a detailed description; a program schedule; budget for the study program; one copy of audio material, including two musical selections. For performance programs, the two selections must be of contrasting style; (ii) applicants who have not already been accepted into a course must submit the following information for the preferred study programs including: a detailed description; a program schedule; budget for each study program; one copy of audio material, including two musical selections. For performance programs, the two selections must be of contrasting style. Applicants are encouraged to submit additional support materials that may assist in the assessment process. These may include press clippings, invitations, reference letters, reviews, catalogues, scripts, published books or storyboards. Applicants must submit applications in the following format to allow for ease of use by juries: submit four complete, assembled application packages (one original and three copies of the application form and all printed attachments) along with one copy of audio and/or visual support materials; assemble the parts of the packages in the same order as the checklist for this grant; clip applications into four packages. Do not bind or use folders, page covers or binders; remember to make one additional copy of the complete application package and keep it for your records. Audio and/or visual support materials such as CD, videocassette or DVD must be clearly labelled with the applicant's name on the media. Use separate discs for different file types. All media must be compatible with Microsoft Windows operating system and NTSC VHS video standards. The applicant is responsible for providing support materials that comply with the viewing capabilities of the AFA. **Deadline:** February 1; September 1.

243 ■ AFA Theatre & Performance Art Project Grants *(Professional development/Grant)*

Purpose: To support the development of individual Alberta artists, arts administrators or an ensemble of artist by providing a grant for a specific theatre and/or performance art project in a limited time period. **Focus:** Performing arts; Theater arts. **Qualif.:** Applicants must be Canadian citizens or landed immigrants; have their primary residence in Alberta for one full year before applying for a grant. In order to be eligible for project grants, ensembles must be made up of members who meet the individual criteria. Applicants, including ensembles, must not be incorporated with provincial or federal corporate registries. Eligible projects must meet the criteria in one of the following categories: Art production includes the development, creation and production of any theatre/performance art work. Alberta individual artists/ensembles that have been contracted by commissioners to create a specific work; Marketing includes projects that promote, market or distribute the work of Alberta theatre/performance arts artists; Research includes activities that support or result in the development of a theatre/performance arts project; Training and career development includes a workshop, master class, summer program, professional development or professional course of study in theatre/performance art Theatre/Performance artists, drama instructors, designers and technicians. **Criteria:** Selection will be based on the jury's criteria.

Funds Avail.: 15,000 Canadian Dollars; and may include up to 3,000 Canadian Dollars per month subsistence allowance. **Duration:** Annual. **To Apply:** Applicants must provide the following in the application package: a completed Application Form and signed Applicant Agreement with original signature. Ensembles must designate one member who is the contact person for all requirements of the grant. Applicants must sign the Applicant Agreement and complete the Application Form; must submit the required materials if the applicants are under the age of 18 years at the time of application; an application checklist must be completed and submitted with the application; a detailed description of the project, including an outline of the objectives, planned activities, timelines and expected results and benefits; a balanced project budget detailing revenues (including the amount requested from the AFA) and expenditures in Canadian dollars. Total revenues must equal total expenditures; an artistic resume of no more than four pages that includes a description of their theatre/performance art background, including level of training, performing arts activities and other relevant artistic history. Applicants must also include the following: for art production, a list of all principals involved in the project and their resumes. To assist in the assessment process, applicants are encouraged to submit a video of previous productions of their work, or of the work-in-progress. Commission applicants are encourage to submit a completed and signed contract with the commissioner and a plan for the workshop, exhibition, presentation, display, publication, screening or performance of the commissioned work; for marketing or research, official invitations, confirmations or itineraries, as applicable; for marketing, a detailed marketing plan; for training or career development: (i) applicants who have been accepted into a specific course must provide proof of acceptance and a detailed description, schedule and budget for the study program; (ii) applicants who have not already been accepted into a course must submit a detailed description, schedule and budget for the preferred choice. In addition, at least two alternate program choices should be submitted, with detailed descriptions, schedules and budgets for each choice. Applicants are encouraged to submit additional support materials that may assist in the assessment process. These may include press clippings, invitations, reference letters, reviews, catalogues, scripts, published books or storyboards. Applicants must submit applications in the following format to allow for ease of use by juries: submit four complete, assembled application packages (one original and three copies of the application form and all printed attachments) along with one copy of audio and/or visual support materials; assemble the parts of the packages in the same order as the checklist for this grant; clip applications into four packages. Do not bind or use folders, page covers or binders; remember to make one additional copy of the complete application package and keep it for your records. Audio and/or visual support materials such as CD, videocassette or DVD must be clearly labelled with the applicant's name on the media. Use separate discs for different file types. All media must be compatible with Microsoft Windows operating system and NTSC VHS video standards. The applicant is responsible for providing support materials that comply with the viewing capabilities of the AFA. **Deadline:** February 1; September 1.

244 ■ AFA Visual Arts and New Media Project Grants (Professional development/Grant)
Purpose: To support the development of individual Alberta artists, arts administrators or an ensemble of artists by providing a grant for a specific literary arts project in a limited time period. **Focus:** Media arts; Visual arts. **Qualif.:** Applicants must be Canadian citizens or landed immigrants; have their primary residence in Alberta for one full year before applying for a grant. In order to be eligible from a project grants, ensembles must be made up of members who meet the individual criteria. Applicants, including ensembles, must not be incorporated with provincial or federal corporate registries. Eligible projects must meet the criteria in one of the following categories: Art production includes creation of new work in any visual arts medium. Visual arts media may include but are not limited to drawing, painting, sculpture, printmaking, clay, glass, wood, metal fibre or any combination of media. New media may include CD-ROM, Internet and other computer-assisted art; Marketing includes, but is not limited to, attending an exhibition opening, visual arts festival, workshop or award presentation by invitation and projects that promote and market the work of new media artists; Research includes activities that support or result in the development of a visual arts/new media project; training and career development includes a workshop, master class, mentorship program or professional course of study in visual arts or new media. **Criteria:** Selection will be based on the jury's criteria.
Funds Avail.: 15,000 Canadian Dollars; and may include up to 3,000 Canadian Dollars per month subsistence allowance. **Duration:** Annual. **To Apply:** Applicants must provide the following in the application package: A completed application form and signed Applicant Agreement with original signature. Ensembles must designate one member who is the contact person for all requirements of the grant. Applicants must sign the Applicant Agreement and complete the Application Form; must submit the required materials if the applicants are under the age of 18 years at the time of application; an application checklist must be completed and submitted with the application; a detailed description of the project, including an outline of the objectives, planned activities, timelines and expected results and benefits; a balanced project budget detailing revenues (including the amount requested from the AFA) and expenditures in Canadian dollars. Total revenues must equal total expenditures; an artistic resume of no more than four pages. Applicants must also include the following: (a) for art production, one set of no more than ten images of completed work in JPEG or GIF format. Images should be of recent work completed within last five years. The selection must be clearly marked with the applicant's name, Provide a numbered inventory of the images, including title, medium, size and year of execution. Present the images chronologically. Acceptable formats are: (i) one CD or DVD compatible with Microsoft operating system. Images must be JPEG format with a resolution of 72 dpi. A maximum size of 1024 x 798 pixels and 500K (o.5MG). Use RGB or SRGB color mode only (no CMYK). DVDs must be plug and play; (ii) one JPEG or GIF video file of no more than 5 minutes in length on VHS NTSC videocassette, CD or DVD compatible with Microsoft Windows operating system; (iii) an audio CD sample. Commission applicants are encouraged to submit a completed and signed contract with the commissioner and a plan for the exhibition, presentation, display, publication, screening or performance of the commissioned work; (b) for marketing or research, official invitations, confirmations or itineraries, as applicable; (c) for marketing, a detailed marketing plan; (d) for training or career development: (i) applicants who have been accepted into a specific course must provide proof of acceptance and a detailed description, schedule and budget for the study program; (ii) applicants who have not already been accepted into a course must submit a detailed description, schedule and budget for the preferred choice. In addition, at least two alternate program choices should be submitted, with detailed descriptions, schedules and budgets for each choice. Applicants are encouraged to submit additional support materials that may assist in the assessment process. These may include press clippings, invitations, reference letters, reviews, catalogues, scripts, published

Awards are arranged alphabetically below their administering organizations

books or storyboards. Applicants must submit applications in the following format to allow for ease of use by juries: submit four complete, assembled application packages (one original and three copies of the application form and all printed attachments) along with one copy of audio and/or visual support materials; assemble the parts of the packages in the same order as the checklist for this grant; clip applications into four packages. Do not bind or use folders, page covers or binders; remember to make one additional copy of the complete application package and keep it for your records. Audio and/or visual support materials such as CD, videocassette or DVD must be clearly labelled with the applicant's name on the media. Use separate discs for different file types. All media must be compatible with Microsoft Windows operating system and NTSC VHS video standards. The applicant is responsible for providing support materials that comply with the viewing capabilities of the AFA. **Deadline:** February 1; September 1.

245 ■ Alberta Holstein Association
RR 1
Didsbury, AB, Canada T0M 0W0
Ph: (403)335-5916
Fax: (403)335-4751
E-mail: info@albertaholstein.ca
URL: www.albertaholstein.ca
Facebook: www.facebook.com/Alberta-Holstein-Association-270585993034177/?ref=tn_tnmn

246 ■ Alberta Holstein Association Scholarships (Undergraduate/Scholarship)

Purpose: To encourage students to pursue their education by providing educational funds for deserving undergraduate students. **Focus:** Agriculture, Economic aspects. **Qualif.:** Applicants must have completed at least the first year of university/college; and must be returning to school within the calendar year; must be regular junior member of the Alberta Branch Holstein Canada, or a son/daughter of a member. **Criteria:** Recipient will be selected based on farm involvement, community participation, extracurricular activities and academic standings.

Funds Avail.: $500 each. **Duration:** Annual. **Number Awarded:** 4. **To Apply:** Applicants must submit a completed application form available from the website, a 500 to 1000-word essay explaining their farm involvement, and volunteer experience along with future employment ambitions. **Deadline:** October 31. **Contact:** Heidi Voegeli-Bleiker at info@albertaholstein.ca; Phone: 403-335-5916.

247 ■ Alberta Indian Investment Corporation (AIIC)
PO Box 180
Enoch, AB, Canada T7X 3Y3
Ph: (780)470-3600
Fax: (780)470-3605
Free: 888-308-6789
E-mail: info@aiicbusiness.org
URL: www.aiicbusiness.org

248 ■ Sam Bull Memorial Scholarships (Undergraduate/Scholarship)

Purpose: To encourage and assist Treaty First Nations people in the pursuit of post-secondary education studies. **Focus:** Law; Political science. **Qualif.:** Applicants must be First Nation persons who are: residents of Alberta; and are post-secondary students enrolled full-time in a university program of law and political science. **Criteria:** Recipients will be evaluated by the selection committee based on academic performance, chosen area of study in relation to First Nation community development and future career aspirations.

Funds Avail.: 1,000 Canadian Dollars. **Duration:** Annual. **To Apply:** Applicants may contact the AIIC office for further information on application details. **Deadline:** February 15.

249 ■ Senator James Gladstone Memorial Scholarships (Graduate, Undergraduate/Scholarship)

Purpose: To encourage and assist Treaty First Nations people in the pursuit of post-secondary education studies. **Focus:** Business; Economics; Finance. **Qualif.:** Applicants must be First Nation persons who are: residents of Alberta; and are post-secondary students enrolled full-time in a university program of business, finance or economics. **Criteria:** Recipients will be evaluated by the selection committee based on strong academic performance, chosen area of study in relation to First Nation business/economic development and future career aspirations.

Funds Avail.: 750 Canadian Dollars per year (for colleges); 1,000 Canadian Dollars per year (for universities). **Duration:** Annual. **Number Awarded:** 2. **To Apply:** Applicants may contact the AIIC office for further information on application details. **Deadline:** February 15.

250 ■ Alberta Innovates - Health Solutions
1500, 10104 - 103 Ave.
Edmonton, AB, Canada T5J 4A7
Ph: (780)423-5727
Fax: (780)429-3509
Free: 877-423-5727
E-mail: health@aihealthsolutions.ca
URL: www.aihealthsolutions.ca

251 ■ AIHS Graduate Studentships (Master's, Doctorate, Professional development/Fellowship)

Purpose: To provide opportunities for individuals undertaking health-related research areas in pursuit of a Master's or PhD at an Alberta university. **Focus:** Health sciences; Medical research. **Qualif.:** Applicants must be currently enrolled in a graduate program at an Alberta university undertaking health-related training leading to a thesis-based graduate degree; must have completed their first year of graduate training at the time of award implementation. The Graduate Studentship is tenable only at an Alberta university. **Criteria:** Applicants will be assessed with a focus on the graduate trainee, their career plan and the anticipated benefits they would gain from the opportunities provided by the proposed training environment(s) as measured by the following criteria: academic track record; relevant work and/or research experience; career development plans; supervisory team, the research and the mentorship environment; and research proposal. All applications will undergo a rigorous review process by a committee whose membership is both interdisciplinary and cross-sectoral.

Funds Avail.: 30,000 Canadian Dollars stipend, plus an allowance of 2,000 for research and career development. **Duration:** Up to 4 years. **To Apply:** Interested applicants must review the AIHS Training and Early Career Development Programs Graduate Studentship Program Guide before applying. **Contact:** Carolina Koutras, PhD, Program

Manager, Training and Early Career Development; Phone: 780-306-1329; E-mail: carolina.koutras@aihealthsolutions.ca or Kathy Morrison, Senior Coordinator, Grants Processing; Phone: 780-423-5727 ext. 229; E-mail: kathy.morrison@aihealthsolutions.ca.

252 ■ AIHS Media Fellowships - CBC Radio (Undergraduate, Graduate/Fellowship)

Purpose: To strengthen the relationship between scientists and the media, as well as to provide young scientists, at a critical stage in their careers, the opportunity to observe and participate in how events and ideas become news. **Focus:** Media arts; Medicine. **Qualif.:** Applicants must be undergraduate- or graduate-level university students at a degree granting institution in Alberta with a strong background in biomedical science; must be continuing their university studies in the fall in any discipline; must demonstrate excellent writing skills; and must work well independently or as part of a team. **Criteria:** Selection will be based on the aforesaid qualifications and compliance with the application process. Applications are evaluated by members of the Media Fellowship Review Committees. Two separate committees are utilized in the review process: one panel to review applications submitted from the Calgary region, and one panel for the Edmonton region. Committees include representatives from CBC, AIHS, and past media fellows. **Funds Avail.:** No specific amount. **To Apply:** Applicants must review the Media Fellowship Program Guide and the Media Fellowship Application Instructions when submitting your application package. **Deadline:** March 4. **Contact:** Dwayne Brunner, Manager, Media Relations; E-mail: dwayne.brunner@aihealthsolutions.ca; Phone: 877-423-5727 ext. 224 or Kari Larson, Coordinator, Grants Processing; E-mail: kari.larson@aihealthsolutions.ca; Phone: 780-423-5727 ext. 289.

253 ■ AIHS Postgraduate Fellowships (Postgraduate, Advanced Professional/Fellowship)

Purpose: To support individuals who are pursuing postgraduate health-related research at an Alberta university. **Focus:** Health sciences; Medical research. **Qualif.:** Applicants must hold a PhD and/or professional health degree (e.g., MD, DDS, DVM or DPharm) without clinical accreditation in Canada, and be accepted or currently hold a postgraduate appointment at a university in Alberta. **Criteria:** Applicants will be assessed on the following criteria: academic track record; relevant work and/or research experience; career development plans; supervisory team, the research and the mentorship environment; and, research proposal. All applications will undergo a rigorous review process by a committee whose membership is both interdisciplinary and intersectoral. **Funds Avail.:** 50,000 Canadian Dollars per annum, plus 5,000 for research and career development. **Duration:** Up to 3 years. **To Apply:** Interested applicants must review the AIHS Training and Early Career Development Opportunity Postgraduate Fellowship Program Guide before applying. **Deadline:** October 1. **Contact:** Carolina Koutras, PhD, Program Manager, Training and Early Career Development; Phone: 780-306-1329; E-mail: carolina.koutras@aihealthsolutions.ca or Kathy Morrison, Senior Coordinator, Grants Processing; Phone: 780-423-5727 ext. 229; E-mail: kathy.morrison@aihealthsolutions.ca.

254 ■ AIHS Cy Frank Fellowships: Impact Assessment (Doctorate, Professional development/Fellowship)

Purpose: To provide an opportunity for the successful recipients to gain practice-based experience in impact assessment in the health research and innovation environment. **Focus:** Health sciences; Medical research; Social sciences. **Qualif.:** Applicants are required to hold a PhD in health sciences or related social science discipline; demonstrate the relevance of the Fellowship to their career goals in the application; and identify the support of an academic advisor with an academic appointment at an Alberta university. For out of province applicants, please contact the AIHS for questions about the latter requirement. **Criteria:** Applicants will be assessed on the following criteria: academic track record; relevant work and/or research experience; career development plans; supervisory team, the research and the mentorship environment; and, research proposal. All applications will undergo a review process by a committee comprised of professional evaluators, academics in the area of evaluation research, and AIHS Performance Management and Evaluation staff. Applications will be assessed on the following criteria: academic excellence of applicants; academic excellence of academic advisors; relevance and quality of work, research, and/or evaluation experience; motivation to develop knowledge and practice in health research and innovation, evaluation, and evaluation research; and alignment of the applicants' skills and career aspirations to the objectives of the AIHS Cy Frank Fellowship. **Funds Avail.:** 70,000 Canadian Dollars per year. **Duration:** Up to 3 years. **To Apply:** Interested applicants must review the AIHS Cy Frank Fellowship Information Document before applying. **Remarks:** The Fellowship is named in honor of Dr. Cy Frank whose vision for a transformed health system included positioning Alberta as a leader in the assessment of health research and innovation. The AIHS Cy Frank Fellowship in Impact Assessment is one way in which we aim to carry forward his legacy and commit to his vision. **Contact:** Performance Management and Evaluation (PME) team at pme@aihealthsolutions.ca.

255 ■ Alberta Innovates - Technology Futures (AITF)
250 Karl Clark Rd.
Edmonton, AB, Canada T6N 1E4
Ph: (780)450-5111
Fax: (780)450-5333
E-mail: referral@albertainnovates.ca
URL: www.albertatechfutures.ca
Facebook: www.facebook.com/AlbertaInnovates
LinkedIn: www.linkedin.com/company/alberta-innovates
---technology-futures
Twitter: www.twitter.com/TechFuturesAB

256 ■ Alberta Innovates Graduate Student Scholarships (Graduate/Scholarship)

Purpose: To enable promising students to succeed in areas of scientific research which are strategically important to Alberta. **Focus:** Energy-related areas; Environmental technology; Health sciences; Information science and technology. **Qualif.:** Candidates must be Canadian citizens who hold a new NSERC (Natural Sciences and Engineering Research Council of Canada) or international and Canadian candidates who do not hold an NSERC award, studying at an Alberta university to do graduate work in one of the following research areas: Information and Communication Technology, Nanotechnology and Omics; in and of themselves or additionally which support the areas of Health, Bio-industries, Energy and Environment. If candidates are not yet registered at an Alberta university, their

Awards are arranged alphabetically below their administering organizations

eligibility to apply for the GSS is contingent upon meeting all eligibility requirements for admission to an Alberta university. Candidates should contact the university of their choice for information on those requirements. **Criteria:** Each Alberta university will review all applications and evaluate them based on excellence and strategic alignment in areas of scientific research important to Alberta.

Funds Avail.: Amount varies. **Duration:** Annual. **Number Awarded:** Varies. **To Apply:** Application processes are specific to the applicant's university of choice.

257 ■ Alberta Innovates - Technology Futures Graduate Student Scholarships in ICT *(Doctorate, Graduate, Master's/Scholarship)*

Purpose: To help Alberta attract and retain world-class graduate students studying in an ICT related area. **Focus:** Information science and technology. **Qualif.:** Applicants must be entering or currently in a full-time graduate program at an Alberta university, in any discipline, working towards a research-based master's or doctoral degree. **Criteria:** Selection is based on the excellence of the student and the proposed research.

Funds Avail.: $26,500/year for Marter's students; $31,500/year for Doctoral students. **To Apply:** Applicants must submit an original, signed application form along with official transcripts or certified copies of transcripts in sealed envelopes (if not sent directly to Alberta Ingenuity office); and three letters of reference in sealed envelopes (if not sent directly to Alberta Ingenuity office).

258 ■ Alberta Innovates - Technology Futures Graduate Student Scholarships in Nanotechnology *(Doctorate, Graduate/Scholarship)*

Purpose: To help Alberta attract and retain world class Master's and Doctoral students in the nanotechnology field. **Focus:** Engineering; Science. **Qualif.:** Applicants must be entering or currently in a full-time graduate program at an Alberta university in a science or engineering-related discipline working towards a research-based master's or doctoral degree. **Criteria:** Selection is based on excellence of the student and the proposed research.

Funds Avail.: $26,500/year for Master's students; $31,500/year for Doctoral students. **To Apply:** Applicants must submit an original, signed application form along with official transcripts or certified copies of transcripts in sealed envelopes (if not sent directly to Alberta Ingenuity office); and three letters of reference in sealed envelopes (if not sent directly to Alberta Ingenuity office).

259 ■ Alberta Innovates - Technology Futures Graduate Student Scholarships in Omics *(Doctorate, Graduate/Scholarship)*

Purpose: To enable academically superior graduate students, in a natural science or engineering discipline, to undertake full-time research training at an Alberta university, leading to a research-based Master's or Doctoral degree. **Focus:** Engineering; Science. **Qualif.:** Applicants must be entering or currently in a full-time graduate program at an Alberta university in a science or engineering-related discipline working towards a research-based master's or doctoral degree. **Criteria:** Selection is based on excellence of the student and the proposed research.

Funds Avail.: Up to $26,500 for a Master's student or up to $31,5000 for a Doctoral student per year. **Duration:** Four years. **To Apply:** Applicants must submit an original, signed application form along with official transcripts or certified copies of transcripts in sealed envelopes (if not sent directly to Alberta Ingenuity office); and three letters of reference in sealed envelopes (if not sent directly to Alberta Ingenuity office).

260 ■ Alberta Learning Information Service - Alberta Scholarship Program

Box 28000 Sta. Main
Edmonton, AB, Canada T5J 4R4
Ph: (780)427-8640
Fax: (780)427-1288
E-mail: scholarships@gov.ab.ca
URL: alis.alberta.ca/index.html

261 ■ Alberta Award for the Study of Canadian Human Rights and Multiculturalism *(Doctorate, Graduate/Award)*

Purpose: To encourage the pursuit of studies in Canadian human rights, cultural diversity and multiculturalism. **Focus:** Human rights. **Qualif.:** Applicant must be: a Canadian citizen or permanent resident; enrolled or planning to enroll as a full-time graduate student (Master's or Doctoral level) at an Alberta public post-secondary institution; taking a program of study that supports the purpose of this scholarship; planning to do research that is within a Canadian context and will ultimately benefit Albertans. **Criteria:** Recipients will be selected based on information provided on application form; submitted essay; and curriculum vitae.

Funds Avail.: 10,000 Canadian Dollars - Master's level; 15,000 Canadian Dollars - Doctoral level. **Number Awarded:** 2. **To Apply:** Applicants may obtain an application form from Graduate and Awards Offices at post-secondary institutions and through Alberta Scholarship Programs at Alberta Learning Information Service's website. Applicant must submit an application form; essay; curriculum vitae and any attachment. **Deadline:** February 1.

262 ■ Alberta Centennial Scholarships - Alberta *(Undergraduate/Scholarship)*

Purpose: To support Alberta students in their pursuit of higher education. **Focus:** General studies/Field of study not specified. **Qualif.:** Applicants must be Canadian citizens or permanent residents of Canada and Alberta entering any level of post-secondary study at any university, college, technical institute or apprenticeship program in Canada. **Criteria:** Selection will be based on students' involvement in volunteer activities in and outside school, citizenship and community service.

Funds Avail.: 2,005 Canadian Dollars each. **Duration:** Annual. **Number Awarded:** 25. **To Apply:** Application is via selection. Each high school in Alberta will select recipients for the Premier's Citizenship Award, and from those recipients a selection committee will select twenty-five recipients for the scholarship. Applicants may contact high school counselor for more information. **Deadline:** June 1. **Remarks:** The scholarship is sponsored by the Government of Alberta to commemorate the Province of Alberta's Centennial.

263 ■ ALIS Fellowships for Full-time Studies in French *(Undergraduate/Fellowship)*

Purpose: To assist Albertans in pursuing post-secondary studies taught in French. **Focus:** Canadian studies; French studies. **Qualif.:** Applicants must be Alberta residents,

Awards are arranged alphabetically below their administering organizations

Canadian citizens or permanent residents plan to register full-time in a post-secondary program of at least one semester in length. In addition, applicants must be enrolled in a minimum of three courses per semester in which the course content and the language of instruction are in French. **Criteria:** Selection will be based on academic achievement.

Funds Avail.: 500 Canadian Dollars-1,000 Canadian Dollars. **Duration:** Annual. **To Apply:** Applicants may obtain application form from the website or from the Students Awards Office at Alberta post-secondary institutions that offer programs taught in French and from Alberta Scholarship Programs. Applicants must include proof of Canadian citizenship: either a photocopy of Canadian birth certificate, passport or immigration papers. College applicants must include a transcript. **Deadline:** November 15.

264 ■ ALIS Graduate Student Scholarships
(Graduate/Scholarship)

Purpose: To reward the outstanding academic achievement of students studying at the Masters level. **Focus:** General studies/Field of study not specified. **Qualif.:** Applicants must be enrolled in the second year of a Masters program. Students must be Canadian citizens or landed immigrants and attending a post-secondary institution in Alberta. **Criteria:** Selection will be based on the committee's criteria.

Funds Avail.: 3,000 Canadian Dollars each. **Duration:** Annual. **To Apply:** No application required. Students are nominated by the faculty of graduate studies.

265 ■ ALIS International Education Awards - Ukraine *(Undergraduate/Scholarship)*

Purpose: To enable Alberta post-secondary students, post-graduates, professionals and scholars to undertake career-related training, research or study in Ukraine, and Ukrainian post-secondary students, post-graduates, professionals and scholars to undertake career-related training, research or study in Alberta. **Focus:** General studies/Field of study not specified. **Qualif.:** Eligible applicants are Canadian citizens/permanent residents and Ukrainian residents. Canadian citizens/permanent residents must be Alberta residents, preferably attending or associated with an Alberta post-secondary institution or apprenticeship/co-op program. They must be either enrolled in a post-secondary institution at senior level, graduate students, recent post-graduates, or professionals or scholars. Students applying to take a course or applying to study for one or two semesters at a post-secondary institution in Ukraine are also eligible. On the other hand, Ukrainian residents must be citizens or residents of Ukraine, preferably attending or associated with a post-secondary teaching or research institution, or apprenticeship/co-op program. They must be either enrolled in a post-secondary institution at senior level, graduate students, recent post-graduates, or professionals or scholars. Students applying to take a course or applying to study for one or two semesters at a post-secondary institution in Alberta are also eligible. **Criteria:** Recipients will be selected based on demonstrated past accomplishments and potential for improving relations between Ukraine and Alberta.

Funds Avail.: 5,000 Canadian Dollars each. **Duration:** Annual. **Number Awarded:** 5. **To Apply:** Applicants may retrieve application forms available from the Alberta Scholarship Programs' office, Alberta Colleges and Universities, the Canadian Embassy in Kyiv and the Ministry of Education of Ukraine. In total, five copies of the completed application form must be submitted (an original plus four photocopies). Such requirement does not apply to academic transcripts and reference letters. **Deadline:** February 1. **Remarks:** Established in 2003.

266 ■ Janet and Horace Allen Scholarships
(Undergraduate/Scholarship)

Purpose: To recognize the academic excellence of a student from Crowsnest Pass high School in the area of the sciences. **Focus:** Science. **Qualif.:** Applicant must be an Alberta resident and plan to enroll full-time in a post-secondary program of at least one semester in length. **Criteria:** Recipient will be selected on the basis of achieving the highest average on two of the following Grade 12 courses at the 30 level: Biology, Chemistry, Physics or Science.

Funds Avail.: 1,500 Canadian Dollars. **Duration:** Annual. **Number Awarded:** 1. **To Apply:** Applicant may obtain an application form from Alberta Scholarship Programs and Crowsnest Pass High School. **Deadline:** June 1.

267 ■ Arts Graduate Scholarships *(Graduate/Scholarship)*

Purpose: To provide assistance to students who demonstrated outstanding ability in the arts pursue graduate study. **Focus:** Arts. **Qualif.:** Applicants must be residents of Alberta enrolled or planning to enroll full-time either in music, dance, literary arts or visual arts at a Master's level or equivalent level; must demonstrate an outstanding ability in arts; and must be Canadian Citizens or permanent residents. There is a lifetime maximum of two awards per student. Scholarships are for study at graduate faculties and equivalent institutions anywhere in the world. **Criteria:** Recipients are chosen by a Selection Committee appointed by the presidents of the universities in Alberta. Applicants are judged on previous academic accomplishments; program of study; appraiser's evaluations; answers to the essay question; and general impressions from the application form.

Funds Avail.: 15,000 Canadian Dollars. **To Apply:** Applicants must submit a completed application form; and two letters of reference. Original and four signed unstapled copies of application form and attachments must be submitted. **Deadline:** February 15.

268 ■ Theodore R. Campbell Scholarships
(Undergraduate/Scholarship)

Purpose: To reward the accomplishments of an aboriginal student from Blue Quills First Nations College. **Focus:** General studies/Field of study not specified. **Qualif.:** Applicants must be Alberta residents and have completed the first year towards an Education degree at Blue Quills First Nations College. **Criteria:** Selection will be based on the academic achievement during first year of study.

Funds Avail.: 1,500 Canadian Dollars. **To Apply:** Application forms are available from Alberta Scholarship Programs and from the Research and Planning Office at Blue Quills First Nations College. **Deadline:** June 1.

269 ■ Carmangay Home and School Association Scholarships *(Undergraduate/Scholarship)*

Purpose: To recognize the accomplishments of students who attended Carmangay School and to commemorate the closing of the school. **Focus:** General studies/Field of study not specified. **Qualif.:** Applicants must: be Canadian citizens or landed immigrants and residents of Alberta ac-

Awards are arranged alphabetically below their administering organizations

cording to Alberta Heritage Scholarship Fund regulations; have attended Carmangay School for at least one complete school year; have achieved a high academic standing in their Grade 12 year at an Alberta high school; and plan on entering full-time studies at a recognized post-secondary institution. **Criteria:** Selection will be based on the academic achievement in Grade 12, demonstrated leadership and community involvement. Applicants must provide proof of attendance at Carmangay School either by reference letter or other documentation.

Funds Avail.: 2,500 Canadian Dollars. **To Apply:** Application forms are available from regional school counselors and from the office of Alberta Scholarship Programs. Applicants must mail their application form to Alberta Scholarship Programs. **Deadline:** August 1. **Remarks:** Established in 2001.

270 ■ Robert C. Carson Memorial Bursary
(Undergraduate/Scholarship)

Purpose: To provide financial assistance to aboriginal students who have successfully completed the first year of a program relating to criminal justice, criminology or law. **Focus:** Criminal justice; Criminology; Law. **Qualif.:** Applicants must be Alberta residents and full-time students enrolled in the second year of either Law Enforcement or Criminal Justice. The qualifying Alberta institutions are: Lethbridge Community College, Mount Royal College, Grant MacEwan College, the University of Calgary or the University of Alberta. **Criteria:** Recipients are nominated by the educational institution they are attending. Preference will be given to non-sponsored aboriginal students.

Funds Avail.: 500 Canadian Dollars. **Number Awarded:** 5. **To Apply:** Application forms are available from the Institution's Student Award Office. **Deadline:** October 1.

271 ■ Laurence Decore Awards for Student Leadership *(Undergraduate/Scholarship)*

Purpose: To recognize those post-secondary students who have demonstrated outstanding dedication and leadership to fellow students and to their community. **Focus:** General studies/Field of study not specified. **Qualif.:** Applicants must be Alberta residents who are currently enrolled in a minimum of three courses at a designated Alberta post-secondary institution. **Criteria:** Recipients will be selected based on applicant's involvement in either government or student societies, clubs or organization.

Funds Avail.: 1,000 Canadian Dollars. **To Apply:** Applicants do not need to apply. Schools may submit a nomination for this scholarship. **Deadline:** March 1.

272 ■ Earl and Countess of Wessex - World Championships in Athletics Scholarships
(Undergraduate/Scholarship)

Purpose: To recognize the top male and female Alberta students who have excelled in track and field. **Focus:** Athletics. **Qualif.:** Applicants must be Canadian citizens or landed immigrants and residents of Alberta, according to Alberta Scholarship Programs regulations; must have completed Grade 12 in Alberta in the same year they apply for the scholarship; must be planning on continuing their studies at a post-secondary institution in Alberta; and participating on that institution's track and field team. **Criteria:** Selection will be based on students' placing in provincial and national championships, AADP standards, best performances, Mercier scores and recommendations from the applicants' coaches. Academic achievement will also be a consideration.

Funds Avail.: 3,000 Canadian Dollars each. **Duration:** Annual. **Number Awarded:** 2. **To Apply:** Applicants may obtain an application form from all Alberta high schools and from Alberta Scholarship Programs. **Deadline:** October 1.

273 ■ Lois Hole Humanities and Social Sciences Scholarships *(Undergraduate/Scholarship)*

Purpose: To recognize student leadership and community service. **Focus:** Humanities; Social sciences. **Qualif.:** Applicants must be students enrolled full-time in the second or subsequent year of post-secondary study in the Faculty of Humanities, the Faculty of Social Sciences or the Faculty of Arts, at the University of Alberta, the University of Calgary, the University of Lethbridge, Athabasca University, MacEwan University or Mount Royan University. **Criteria:** Selection will be based on academic merit, demonstrated leadership and community service.

Funds Avail.: 5,000 Canadian Dollars. **Number Awarded:** 6. **To Apply:** Applicants may contact the Student Awards Office at participating educational institutions for other application requirements. **Deadline:** October 15 for University of Alberta and Athabasca University; November 15 for University Lethbridge and the University of Calgary.

274 ■ Helen and George Kilik Scholarships
(Undergraduate/Scholarship)

Purpose: To assist students from Olds High School who are pursuing post-secondary education. **Focus:** General studies/Field of study not specified. **Qualif.:** Candidate must be a Canadian citizen or permanent resident and an Alberta resident; have completed all high school studies at Olds High school and intend to pursue post-secondary studies; must demonstrate financial need; and involvement in extracurricular activities. **Criteria:** Selection will be based on academic achievement particularly in math and science.

Funds Avail.: 1,000 Canadian Dollars. **Duration:** Annual. **Number Awarded:** 1. **To Apply:** Applicant may obtain an application from Olds High School or Alberta Scholarship Programs. **Deadline:** June 1.

275 ■ Anna and John Kolesay Memorial Scholarships *(Undergraduate/Scholarship)*

Purpose: To support those students who are academically excellent and have plan to enter in Faculty Education. **Focus:** General studies/Field of study not specified. **Qualif.:** Applicant must be: a Canadian citizen or permanent resident and an Alberta resident; from a family where neither parent obtained a university degree; enrolling full-time in the first year of a program in a Faculty of Education. **Criteria:** Selection is based on the highest average obtained on three Grade 12 subjects: one of English 30, or English 30-1, 30-2, or Francais 30 30-2 and two other subjects at the 30 level; Social studies, Mathematics, Science, Biology, Chemistry, Physics and a language.

Funds Avail.: 1,500 Canadian Dollars. **To Apply:** Application form can be obtained from Alberta Scholarship Programs and at Alberta high schools. **Deadline:** July 1.

276 ■ Jason Lang Scholarships *(Undergraduate/Scholarship)*

Purpose: To reward the outstanding academic achievement of Alberta post-secondary students who are continuing full-time in an undergraduate program in Alberta. **Focus:** Dentistry; Law; Medicine; Pharmacy. **Qualif.:** Nominees must be enrolled full-time in an undergraduate or professional program, such as Law, Medicine, Pharmacy or

Awards are arranged alphabetically below their administering organizations

Dentistry at an eligible Alberta post-secondary institution. These include publicly-funded colleges, technical institutes, universities, private colleges accredited to grant degrees and the Banff Centre. Also, they must be progressing in their post-secondary program and continuing their full-time post-secondary studies at an eligible Alberta educational institution. Nominees must be Canadian citizens or permanent residents and Alberta residents. **Criteria:** Selection will be based on Committee's criteria. Recipients are nominated on the basis of achieving a minimum GPA of 3.2 on a 4.0 scale in the previous academic year while maintaining enrollment in at least 80% of a full course load.
Funds Avail.: 1,000 Canadian Dollars. **Duration:** Annual. **To Apply:** Recipients are nominated by the Awards Office at participating Alberta institutions where they have obtained qualifying grades. For information on the nomination process and eligibility, contact the Awards Office.

277 ■ Language Teacher Bursary Program Awards
(Other/Award)

Purpose: To assist certified Alberta teachers to take a summer post-secondary program in a language other than English or language pedagogy course at an institution outside of Canada. **Focus:** Foreign languages. **Qualif.:** Applicants must: be Canadian citizens or individuals lawfully admitted to Canada for permanent residence and residents of Alberta; hold a valid Alberta professional teaching certificate; have been teaching in Alberta for a minimum of three years by the end of the current school year; demonstrate a background in language learning or have recently initiated the study of this language; plan to take a summer program of at least four weeks duration in a language/language teaching methodology other than English, or related field at an institution outside of Canada; must have not previously been awarded a Language Teacher Bursary. **Criteria:** Recipients will be selected based on statement of the program; course rigour; school authority endorsement; and potential benefit for both teacher and the school authority.
Funds Avail.: Approximately 5,000 Canadian Dollars. **To Apply:** Application form can be obtained from the website. Completed application form must be submitted to your local school authority for endorsement. Once endorsement has been given, the school authority will mail your application to Alberta Scholarship Programs. **Deadline:** February 10.

278 ■ Languages In Teacher Education Scholarships
(Undergraduate/Scholarship)

Purpose: To reward Alberta students enrolled in a recognized Alberta teacher preparation program taking courses that will allow them to teach languages other than English in Alberta schools. **Focus:** Foreign languages. **Qualif.:** Applicants must be: Canadian citizens or individuals lawfully admitted to Canada for permanent residence in Alberta. Visa students are not eligible for this award. Applicants must be registered full-time in their final two years of a recognized Alberta teacher preparation program at an Alberta faculty of education and intend to teach in Alberta schools upon completion of their program. **Criteria:** Selection will be based on the committee's criteria.
Funds Avail.: 2,500 Canadian Dollars. **Duration:** Annual. **Number Awarded:** 16. **To Apply:** No applications required. Students will be nominated by their post-secondary institution.

279 ■ Sir James Lougheed Awards of Distinction
(Doctorate, Graduate/Award)

Purpose: To provide Alberta students in graduate programs with the opportunity for study outside of Alberta at institutions anywhere in the world. **Focus:** General studies/Field of study not specified. **Qualif.:** Applicants must be: Canadian citizens or landed immigrants; Alberta residents; enrolled or planning to enroll full-time in a graduate program at an institution outside of Alberta. Doctoral students must have completed at least one full year of graduate study or a master's degree. **Criteria:** Recipients will be selected based on previous academic achievements; program of study; appraiser's evaluations; answers to the essay question; and general impression of application form. Recipients will also assessed in the following quantifiable areas: GPA; number of research contributions; number of other contributions such as academic, community, professional activities; and number of previous awards.
Funds Avail.: 15,000 Canadian Dollars for Masters level; 20,000 Canadian Dollars for Doctoral level. **Number Awarded:** Up to 15. **To Apply:** An application form can be obtained from Alberta Scholarship Program, however, applicants cannot send their application electronically. Submit the original and four signed unstapled copies of the completed application form and attachments. This requirement does not apply to academic transcripts and appraisals, these documents must be sent directly to Alberta Scholarship Programs. **Deadline:** February 15.

280 ■ Louise McKinney Post-secondary Scholarships
(Undergraduate/Scholarship)

Purpose: To recognize exceptional academic achievement and encourage outstanding students to continue their studies at the post-secondary level. **Focus:** General studies/Field of study not specified. **Qualif.:** Applicants must be residents of Alberta and in their second or subsequent year of full-time study; must have plan to enroll in a university, college, or technical institute; and class standing must be in the top two percent of their program. Alberta students studying outside the province because their program of study is not offered in Alberta will be considered for a scholarship if their class standing is in the top two percent of their program. **Criteria:** Selection will be based on the committee's criteria.
Funds Avail.: 2,500 Canadian Dollars. **To Apply:** Students studying in-province are nominated by the Student Awards Office at participating Alberta post-secondary institutions. Other students may contact the Awards Office to determine their eligibility.

281 ■ Dr. Ernest and Minnie Mehl Scholarships
(Undergraduate/Scholarship)

Purpose: To encourage students to pursue a post-secondary education and to recognize and reward exceptional academic at the senior high school level. **Focus:** General studies/Field of study not specified. **Qualif.:** Applicants must be Canadian citizens or landed immigrants who have completed their Grade 12 in Alberta at a school that follows the Alberta Education Curriculum. Applicants must be continuing their studies at a degree granting post-secondary institution in Canada. University transfer programs are acceptable. **Criteria:** Selection will be based on the average obtained on Diploma Examinations in one of English 30-1, 30-2 or Francais 30, 30-2 and Social Studies 30, 30-1 or 30-2 plus any three other subjects: Pure Mathematics 30, Applied Mathematics 30, Biology 30, Chemistry 30, Physics 30 or Science 30. Financial need will also be considered.
Funds Avail.: 3,500 Canadian Dollars. **Number Awarded:** 1. **To Apply:** No application is required. The recipient will be selected from applications received for an Alexander

Awards are arranged alphabetically below their administering organizations

Rutherford Scholarship. **Deadline:** May 1.

282 ■ Charles S. Noble Scholarships for Study at Harvard *(Undergraduate/Scholarship)*

Purpose: To provide students the opportunity to pursue undergraduate studies at Harvard. **Focus:** General studies/ Field of study not specified. **Qualif.:** Applicants must be Alberta residents who plan to apply or enrolled full-time in any year of study in an undergraduate program at Harvard. **Criteria:** Selection will be based on the committee's criteria.

Funds Avail.: 10,000 Canadian Dollars. **Number Awarded:** 3. **To Apply:** Applicants may obtain an application form from the Office of Admissions at Harvard and from the Alberta Heritage Scholarship Fund. **Deadline:** May 15.

283 ■ Northern Alberta Development Council Bursary Awards *(Undergraduate/Award)*

Purpose: To increase the number of trained professionals in Northern Alberta and to encourage students from Northern Alberta to obtain a post-secondary education. **Focus:** General studies/Field of study not specified. **Qualif.:** Applicants must be residents of Alberta, and planning to enroll in a full-time post-secondary program. Applicants must also be within two years of completion of their post-secondary program. **Criteria:** Selection will be based on the committee's criteria.

Funds Avail.: 6,000 Canadian Dollars - 12,000 Canadian Dollars. **To Apply:** Applicants may obtain an application form from www.benorth.ca. Application forms for these bursaries are also available from Alberta Scholarship Programs, Student Awards Offices and from the Northern Alberta Development Council. **Deadline:** April 30.

284 ■ Northern Alberta Development Council Bursary Partnership Program *(Undergraduate/Award)*

Purpose: To assist students in pursuing a post-secondary education. **Focus:** General studies/Field of study not specified. **Qualif.:** Applicants must be residents of Alberta and plan to enroll full-time in a post-secondary program. In addition, applicants must demonstrate financial need and be willing to live and work in northern Alberta after completion of the program. **Criteria:** Selection will be based on the committee's criteria.

Funds Avail.: 1,750 Canadian Dollars. **To Apply:** Applicants may obtain an application form from www.benorth.ca. Application form for these bursaries are also available from Alberta Scholarship Programs, Student Awards Offices and from the Northern Alberta Development Council.

285 ■ Persons Case Scholarships *(Undergraduate, Graduate/Scholarship)*

Purpose: To assist students whose studies will ultimately contribute to the advancement of women, or who are studying in fields where members of their gender are traditionally few in number. **Focus:** General studies/Field of study not specified. **Qualif.:** Applicants must be residents of Alberta and enrolled full-time at a post-secondary institution in Alberta. In addition, applicants must be enrolled in a program that is either non-traditional for their sex, or a program that will contribute to the advancement of women. Students studying out-of-province may be considered for this award if their program of study is not available in Alberta. **Criteria:** Recipients will be selected based on program of studies; academic achievement; and personal essay.

Funds Avail.: Up to 5,000 Canadian Dollars. **To Apply:** Application form can be obtained from the website. Applicants must submit the following requirements with their complete application form: official transcript of all-post secondary studies; short essay of two or three pages outlining why the issues they are studying are important to them and how their studies, activities and community contribute to the advancement of women; curriculum vitae/resume outlining academic achievement, volunteer experience, awards won, etc. In total, submit six copies of the completed application form, and six copies of all attachments (the original and five photocopies). **Deadline:** September 30.

286 ■ Prairie Baseball Academy Scholarships *(Undergraduate/Scholarship)*

Purpose: To reward the athletic and academic excellence of baseball players and to provide an incentive and means for these players to continue with their post-secondary education. **Focus:** General studies/Field of study not specified. **Qualif.:** Applicants must be Alberta residents and enrolled full-time at a post-secondary institution in Alberta; must be participants in the Prairie Baseball Academy; and must have achieved a minimum GPA of 2.0 on a 4.0 scale in the previous semester. **Criteria:** Selection will be based on academic achievement, community involvement and baseball achievements.

Funds Avail.: 500 Canadian Dollars - 2,500 Canadian Dollars. **To Apply:** Applicants may obtain an application form from Alberta Scholarship Programs and from the Prairie Baseball Academy. **Deadline:** October 15.

287 ■ Queen Elizabeth II Graduate Scholarship Program *(Doctorate, Graduate/Scholarship)*

Purpose: To reward the high level of achievement of students pursuing graduate studies in Alberta. **Focus:** General studies/Field of study not specified. **Qualif.:** Applicants must be Canadian citizens or landed immigrants and enrolled full-time in a faculty of graduate studies in Alberta. **Criteria:** Selection will be based on the committee's criteria.

Funds Avail.: 10,800 Canadian Dollars-Masters level; 15,000 Canadian Dollars-Doctoral level. **To Apply:** Applicants may contact the faculty of graduate studies at their institution for more information about the nomination process.

288 ■ Registered Apprenticeship Program/CTS Scholarships (RAP) *(Undergraduate/Scholarship)*

Purpose: To provide assistance to those high school students who are taking Registered Apprenticeship Program. **Focus:** General studies/Field of study not specified. **Qualif.:** Applicant must: be a Canadian citizen or landed immigrant and a resident of Alberta; have completed the requirements for a high school diploma of the current year or earlier; be registered as an Alberta apprentice in a trade while still attending high school; have completed a minimum of 250 hours of on-the-job training and work experience in their chosen trade; plan to continue in an approved regular apprenticeship program after completing high school; have at least one period of technical training left to complete the apprenticeship. **Criteria:** Selection will be based on the committee's criteria.

Funds Avail.: 1,000 Canadian Dollars. **Duration:** Annual. **To Apply:** Application form can be obtained from Alberta Scholarship Program. Applications must be supported by: one or two paragraph (written or typed) autobiography confirming plans to continue their apprenticeship program and detailing why a career in that trade is a good fit for

Awards are arranged alphabetically below their administering organizations

them; completed employer recommendation form; recommendation letter from a high school teacher or counselor. **Deadline:** June 30.

289 ■ Rutherford Scholars *(Undergraduate/Scholarship)*

Purpose: To provide assistance to those students who are in need. **Focus:** General studies/Field of study not specified. **Qualif.:** Applicants must be in the top ten students as determined on the first writing of Diploma Examination. **Criteria:** Recipients are selected on the basis of results obtained on Diploma Examinations in one of: English 30-1, 30-2 or Francais 30, 30-2, Social Studies 30 plus three other subjects. Averages normally are in the 96.0 to 98.8 percent range. Only the first writing of the diploma exam will be considered.

Funds Avail.: 2,500 Canadian Dollars. **To Apply:** No application is required. Recipients are selected from all Alexander Rutherford Scholarship applications received before the deadline. **Deadline:** August 1.

290 ■ Alexander Rutherford Scholarships for High School Achievement *(Undergraduate/Scholarship)*

Purpose: To provide assistance to those students who are pursuing post-secondary studies. **Focus:** General studies/Field of study not specified. **Qualif.:** Applicants must be Canadian citizens or permanent residents and Alberta residents and plan to enroll full-time in a post-secondary program or apprenticeship program. Students must have a minimum combined average based on five designated courses in at least one grade: Grade 10, 11 or 12. The minimum average, value of the award and courses that can be used depend on the student's graduation year. **Criteria:** Selection will be based on the committee's criteria.

Funds Avail.: Up to 2,500 Canadian Dollars. **To Apply:** Applicants must provide the following: (1) Alberta Student Number; (2) High School Code; (3) Social Insurance Number; (4) photocopy of permanent resident card or landed immigration long form; (5) Alberta residency; (6) post-secondary studies; and (7) signed and dated application form. There is no limit to apply for the scholarship except that the applicant must be planning to pursue post-secondary studies. Students who apply after the application deadline may not be recognized at their high school awards ceremony. High school grades obtained through upgrading at a post-secondary institution are not accepted. Eligible students who complete high school outside of Alberta must submit an official transcript of their high school marks from that province. **Deadline:** May 1 and December 1.

291 ■ Dr. Robert and Anna Shaw Scholarships *(Undergraduate/Scholarship)*

Purpose: To recognize and reward the academic and leadership accomplishments of three students graduating from Sexsmith Secondary School who are entering post-secondary studies. **Focus:** Agriculture, Economic aspects; Art; Art industries and trade; Engineering. **Qualif.:** Applicants must be Alberta residents and plan to enroll full-time in a post-secondary program related to agriculture, engineering/trades or fine arts; and must have completed their grade 12 at Sexsmith secondary school. **Criteria:** Selection will be based on academic accomplishments, leadership qualities, community spirit; involvement in extracurricular activities and a student's commitment to place the welfare of others above their own needs.

Funds Avail.: 500 Canadian Dollars. **Number Awarded:** 3.

To Apply: Applicants may obtain application form from Alberta Scholarship Programs and from the Counseling Office at Sexsmith Secondary School. **Deadline:** June 1.

292 ■ Dr. Robert Norman Shaw Scholarships *(Undergraduate/Scholarship)*

Purpose: To recognize and reward the exceptional achievement of a student graduating from Sexsmith Secondary School who is entering post-secondary studies in a health-related field. **Focus:** Health sciences. **Qualif.:** Applicant must have completed Grade 12 at Sexsmith Secondary School; be an Alberta resident and plan to enroll full-time in a health-related post-secondary program of at least one semester in length. **Criteria:** Selection will be based on the highest average on five 30 level Grade 12 subjects: English or Francais, Mathematics, Social Studies, Biology, Chemistry, Physics or Science.

Funds Avail.: $1,500. **Duration:** Annual. **Number Awarded:** 1. **To Apply:** Each applicant may retrieve a copy of the application form in the website and from the Counseling Office at Sexsmith Secondary School. **Deadline:** June 1. **Remarks:** Applicants will be notified of the results of the competition in September. The award will be disbursed in November after Alberta Scholarship Programs confirms full-time enrollment in post-secondary studies.

293 ■ Alberta Teachers' Association (ATA)
11010 142 St. NW
Edmonton, AB, Canada T5N 2R1
Ph: (780)447-9400
Fax: (780)455-6481
Free: 800-232-7208
E-mail: postmaster@ata.ab.ca
URL: www.teachers.ab.ca/Pages/Home.aspx
Facebook: www.facebook.com/ABteachers

294 ■ Alberta Teachers Association Doctoral Fellowships in Education *(Doctorate/Fellowship)*

Purpose: To recognize academic excellence and to help defray the financial costs of university study. **Focus:** Education. **Qualif.:** Applicants must hold a permanent Alberta teaching certificate and have at least five years of successful teaching; must be at the highest level of membership (associate, if applicants are not qualified for active membership); must be entering or enrolled first year of full-time study in a doctoral program in education at an accredited or recognized Alberta public university; must have plan to continue a career in Alberta; not have received a previous award; and be members in good standing. **Criteria:** Recipients will be selected based on academic standing, contribution to the association and commitment to public and excellence in teaching.

Funds Avail.: $15,000 each. **Duration:** Annual. **Number Awarded:** 2. **To Apply:** Applicants must obtain and complete the application form; official transcripts of all post-secondary academic and professional courses; three letters of reference attesting the applicant's excellence as a teacher and contributions to the association; and any proof that will provide information of entering the full-time study in a doctoral program. **Deadline:** February 29. **Contact:** Mardi Veinot, Administrative Officer, Scholarship Subcommittee; Phone: 780-447-9470 or 1-800-232-7208; E-mail: mardi.veinot@ata.ab.ca.

295 ■ Alberta Teachers Association Educational Research Award *(Other/Scholarship)*

Purpose: To support academic research in Alberta's universities to improve teaching and learning. **Focus:** Edu-

Awards are arranged alphabetically below their administering organizations

cation. **Qualif.:** Applicants must be faculty of education members or seasonal lecturers at an Alberta university who have undertaken quality research on classroom teaching and learning. **Criteria:** To qualify for an award, the research must meet the following categories: 1) be directly related to school and classroom practice; 2) be focused on school teaching and/or learning; 3) research must be current, ongoing or completed within the last two years; 4) be related to critical issues; 5) have involved classroom teachers and/or students; 6) be applicable to the Alberta context; 7) have practical benefits to teachers; and 8) have high quality in terms of purpose, methodology and originality.

Funds Avail.: $5,000. **Duration:** Annual. **To Apply:** Applicants must fill-out the application form and attach a detailed description of the research. **Deadline:** May 13. **Contact:** J-C Couture at jc.couture@ata.ab; Phone: 780-447-9462.

296 ■ John Mazurek Memorial-Morgex Insurance Scholarship *(Other/Scholarship)*

Purpose: To help students pursue their professional development in the field of business education and/or the use of computer technology in education from a Canadian public institution. **Focus:** Computer and information sciences; Nursing. **Qualif.:** Applicants must hold a permanent Alberta teaching certificate; have completed at least five years of successful teaching; be at the highest level of membership (associate, if applicants are not qualified for active membership); and be members in good standing. The area of study must focus on business education and computer technology in education from a recognized Canadian public institution. **Criteria:** Scholarship will be awarded to applicants who possess the following: 1) area of study focusing on business education or the use of computer technology in education; 2) contributions to association and commitment to public education; and 3) excellence in teaching.

Funds Avail.: $2,500. **To Apply:** Applicants must complete the application form and include two letters of reference attesting the excellence of teaching and contributions to the association. **Deadline:** February 29. **Contact:** Mardi Veinot, Administrative Officer, Scholarship Subcommittee; Phone: 780-447-9470 or 1-800-232-7208; E-mail: mardi.veinot@ata.ab.ca.

297 ■ Nadene M. Thomas Graduate Research Scholarships *(Graduate/Scholarship)*

Purpose: To financially assist graduate students conducting research on health issues. **Focus:** Education. **Qualif.:** Applicants must hold a permanent Alberta teaching certificate; have completed at least five years of successful teaching in Alberta; must be the highest level of membership (associate, if applicants are not qualified for active membership); must intend to continue a career in education; must be registered graduate students in an education degree program at a recognized Canadian university; must conduct research focusing on health issues affecting teacher's working conditions; must not be previous awardees; and must be members in good standing. **Criteria:** Recipients will be selected based on the following categories: 1) applicant's academic standing; 2) contributions to the association and commitment to the public; 3) excellence in teaching; and 4) applicability of the research on health issues affecting teacher's working condition.

Funds Avail.: $5,000. **Duration:** Annual. **To Apply:** Applicants must complete the application form; include official transcripts of all post-secondary academic and professional courses; include three letters of reference attesting the excellence of teaching, contributions to the association and post-secondary work; and must provide a written proof that they have been accepted into a graduate program in education at a recognized Canadian university. **Deadline:** February 29. **Contact:** Mardi Veinot, Administrative Officer, Scholarship Subcommittee; Phone: 780-447-9470 or 1-800-232-7208; E-mail: mardi.veinot@ata.ab.ca.

298 ■ Albuquerque Community Foundation (ACF)

624 Tijeras Ave. NW
Albuquerque, NM 87102
Ph: (505)883-6240
Fax: (505)883-3629
E-mail: foundation@albuquerquefoundation.org
URL: www.albuquerquefoundation.org
Facebook: www.facebook.com/AlbuquerqueCommunityFoundation/?ref=ts
LinkedIn: www.linkedin.com/company/albuquerque-community-foundation
Twitter: twitter.com/abqfoundation

299 ■ Robby Baker Memorial Scholarships *(Undergraduate/Scholarship)*

Purpose: To provide financial support to those deserving students who are coping with dyslexia. **Focus:** General studies/Field of study not specified. **Qualif.:** Applicants must: be La Cueva High School graduating senior students who are coping with dyslexia or other reading disability; have earned a minimum of 2.0 GPA; and, must be enrolled as full time students in an accredited college or university. **Criteria:** Selection shall be based on the aforementioned qualifications and compliance with the application details.

Funds Avail.: $750. **Duration:** Annual. **Number Awarded:** 1. **To Apply:** Applicants must submit a completed application form and two references from teachers or counselors. **Deadline:** March 18. **Remarks:** Established in 2003. **Contact:** Albuquerque Community Foundation, at the above address.

300 ■ Notah Begay III Scholarship Program *(Undergraduate/Scholarship)*

Purpose: To provide financial assistance to Native American athletes attending college. **Focus:** General studies/Field of study not specified. **Qualif.:** Applicants must be Native American scholar athletes having a minimum GPA 3.0, and attending a community college, four-year college or university on a full time basis. **Criteria:** Preference will be given to those students who meet the criteria.

Funds Avail.: $1,400 each. **Duration:** Annual. **Number Awarded:** 1 or 2. **To Apply:** Applicants must submit the following: copy of FAFSA, Student Aid Report or statement of financial aid; proof of tribal enrollment or Certificate of Indian Blood (minimum 25%); one reference from a current academic teacher or counselor; one reference from an athletic coach; include in your personal statement how you plan to give back to your community after college; high school transcript; copy of SAT and/or ACT scores; resume; and personal essay stating the following: 1) reason(s) of pursuing a post-secondary education; 2) plans of study; 3) career goals; and 4) challenges have been experienced in continuing education. **Deadline:** March 18. **Remarks:** Established in 1999. **Contact:** Albuquerque Community Foundation, at the above address.

Awards are arranged alphabetically below their administering organizations

301 ■ Bryan Cline Memorial Soccer Scholarship Program *(Undergraduate/Scholarship)*

Purpose: To support the education of graduating senior varsity soccer players. **Focus:** General studies/Field of study not specified. **Qualif.:** Applicants must be graduating senior students from Eldorado High School (EHS) who will attend a college or university full-time. **Criteria:** Preference will be given to those students who meet the criteria. **Funds Avail.:** $800 each. **Duration:** Annual. **Number Awarded:** 2 (1 male; 1 female). **To Apply:** Applicants must submit a completed application form including the name of your varsity soccer team coach and two letters of reference (one from a teacher or counselor and one from a soccer coach). **Deadline:** March 18. **Remarks:** Established in 1986. **Contact:** Albuquerque Community Foundation, at the above address.

302 ■ Excel Staffing Companies Scholarships for Excellence in Continuing Education *(Undergraduate/Scholarship)*

Purpose: To assist individuals who demonstrate a commitment towards reaching a career goal. **Focus:** General studies/Field of study not specified. **Qualif.:** Applicants must: be individuals who are employed full time while attending school part time; be residents of Albuquerque; have a minimum of 3.0 GPA; and, be working with a minimum of 30 hours per week. **Criteria:** Selection shall be based on the aforementioned qualifications and compliance with the application details. **Funds Avail.:** $1,000 each. **Duration:** Annual. **Number Awarded:** 4. **To Apply:** Applicants must submit a completed application form along with a resume including employment, community service, and awards or honors (maximum 4 pages); statement outlining career goals in relation to academic pursuits and financial need (grammar, spelling and punctuation do count); current/most recent transcript verifying minimum 3.0 cumulative GPA; letter from employer verifying employment of at least 30 hours per week; and letter of reference verifying community service and/or volunteer commitment (optional). Attached (sealed) or sent under separate cover: up to two letters of reference from a current or recent instructor or counselor (1-page, 1-side). **Deadline:** June 4. **Remarks:** Established in 1989. **Contact:** Albuquerque Community Foundation, at the above address.

303 ■ New Mexico Manufactured Housing Association Scholarship Program *(Undergraduate/Scholarship)*

Purpose: To provide scholarship awards to New Mexico graduating high school seniors residing in a manufactured home. **Focus:** General studies/Field of study not specified. **Qualif.:** Applicants must: live in a mobile/manufactured home; have earned a minimum GPA 3.0; and, attend a college or university full time. **Criteria:** Preference will be given to those students who meet the criteria. **Funds Avail.:** $1,000 each. **Duration:** Annual. **Number Awarded:** 1 or 2. **To Apply:** Applicants must submit the following: written statement of financial need; proof of residency in a mobile/manufactured home: a copy of title or rental agreement or retail installment contract or county tax assessment; one reference from a teacher or counselor (1 page, 1 side only). **Deadline:** March 18. **Remarks:** Established in 1996. **Contact:** Albuquerque Community Foundation, at the above address.

304 ■ Barnes W. Rose, Jr. and Eva Rose Nichol Scholarship Fund *(Undergraduate/Scholarship)*

Purpose: To provide financial assistance to those AHS graduating students who are in need. **Focus:** Engineering. **Qualif.:** Applicants must: be graduates of Albuquerque High School who demonstrate math and/or science interest and skill through SAT/ACF scores and/or strong grades in appropriate high school classes; have a minimum of 3.6 GPA; demonstrate financial need; and attend a college or university in pursuit of an engineering degree. **Criteria:** Selection shall be based on the aforementioned qualifications and compliance with the application details. **Funds Avail.:** $700. **Duration:** Annual. **Number Awarded:** Varies. **To Apply:** Applicants must submit a completed application form and a minimum of one reference from an Albuquerque High School Math or Science teacher. **Deadline:** March 18. **Remarks:** Established in 2003. **Contact:** Albuquerque Community Foundation, at the above address.

305 ■ Sussman-Miller Educational Assistance Award Program *(Undergraduate/Scholarship)*

Purpose: To provide financial assistance to address the 'gap' in financial aid packages for both students graduating from high school and those continuing their education. **Focus:** General studies/Field of study not specified. **Qualif.:** Applicants must be: graduating high school seniors who will attend any out-of-state college or an in-state private school; graduating high school seniors who will attend a New Mexico public college/university and any students already attending college in or out of the state; and, federal financial aid recipients. **Criteria:** Preference will be given to those students who meet the criteria. **Funds Avail.:** Between $500 and $2,000. **Duration:** Annual. **Number Awarded:** Varies. **To Apply:** Applicants must check the available website for the required materials. **Deadline:** April 23 (for those who will attend out-of-state schools/in-state private schools); June 26 (for those who will attend New Mexico state public schools). **Remarks:** Established in 1994. **Contact:** Albuquerque Community Foundation, at the above address.

306 ■ Woodcock Family Education Scholarship Program *(Undergraduate/Scholarship)*

Purpose: To support students of exceptional promise in the fields of science and math. **Focus:** Mathematics and mathematical sciences; Science. **Qualif.:** Applicants must: be Albuquerque graduating high school seniors; with strong math and/or science credentials; attend a college or university full time; and, have a minimum GPA of 3.8 or minimum ACT composite score of 30 or minimum Math SAT of 680. **Criteria:** Preference will be given to those students who meet the criteria. **Funds Avail.:** $10,000 each. **Duration:** Annual; up to 4 years. **Number Awarded:** 3. **To Apply:** Applicants must attach these to their application packet: career goals in personal statement must include those in the field of math or science; one reference from a math or science teacher; one or more references from other teachers, internship or work programs, or community services. **Deadline:** March 18. **Remarks:** Established in 1993. **Contact:** Albuquerque Community Foundation, at the above address.

307 ■ Alden Kindred of America (AKA)
105 Alden St.
Duxbury, MA 02332
Ph: (781)934-9092

Awards are arranged alphabetically below their administering organizations

E-mail: info@alden.org
URL: www.alden.org

308 ■ Donnell B. Young Scholarships
(Undergraduate/Scholarship)

Purpose: To provide educational assistance to incoming college students. **Focus:** General studies/Field of study not specified. **Qualif.:** Applicants must be members of the Alden Kindred of America, Inc.; must be graduating high school students who are lineage members of the Alden Kindred of America, Inc. **Criteria:** Recipient will be selected based on the submitted research paper.

Funds Avail.: No specific amount. **Number Awarded:** 1. **To Apply:** Applicants must submit their high school transcripts (mailed directly by their school). A typewritten research paper of 750-1000 words is a strict requirement. The topic must be extracted from the Early American Period (1620-1750). The preface of the research paper should contain a short paragraph about the reason of the application for the scholarship. Footnotes and bibliography of references should be included. Volunteer work and personal information including hobbies and interests must also be provided. All application forms must have two references (one personal and one from the school). **Deadline:** March 1.

309 ■ Aleut Foundation
703 W Tudor Rd., Ste. 102
Anchorage, AK 99503-6650
Ph: (907)646-1929
Fax: (907)646-1949
Free: 800-232-4882
E-mail: taf@thealeutfoundation.org
URL: www.thealeutfoundation.org

310 ■ Andrew Gronholdt Arts Scholarship Awards
(Undergraduate, Vocational/Occupational, Graduate, Master's/Scholarship)

Purpose: To help students pursue their education in the Arts field. **Focus:** Arts. **Qualif.:** Applicants must be two-year/vocational, undergraduate, graduate or master's degree students; must have at least 3.0 GPA and must be full-time majoring in the Arts field. **Criteria:** Recipients will be selected based on submitted materials.

Funds Avail.: No specific amount. **To Apply:** Applicants must complete the application form; must submit a letter of acceptance, two letters of recommendation, personal statement, birth certificate, class schedule and an official transcript. **Contact:** taf@thealeutfoundation.org.

311 ■ Lillie Hope-McGarvey Health Scholarship Awards
(Undergraduate, Vocational/Occupational, Graduate, Master's/Scholarship)

Purpose: To provide financial assistance to students majoring in healthcare. **Focus:** Health care services; Medicine. **Qualif.:** Applicants must be enrolled in a two-year/vocational, undergraduate, graduate or master's degree healthcare program; must maintain at least 3.0 GPA. **Criteria:** Recipients will be selected based on submitted materials.

Funds Avail.: Amount not specified. **To Apply:** Applicants must complete the application form; must submit an official transcript, letter of acceptance, two letters of recommendation, personal statement, birth certificate, class schedule and an official transcript.

312 ■ Gabe Stepetin Business Scholarship Awards
(Undergraduate, Vocational/Occupational, Graduate, Master's/Scholarship)

Purpose: To provide financial assistance to students interested in pursuing a business field. **Focus:** Business. **Qualif.:** Applicants must be two-year/vocational, undergraduate, graduate and master's degree students; must have at least 3.0 GPA; must be enrolled full-time majoring in the business field. **Criteria:** Recipients will be chosen based on submitted materials.

Funds Avail.: Amount not specified. **To Apply:** Applicants must complete an application form; must submit a letter of acceptance, two letters of recommendation, personal statement, birth certificate, class schedule and an official transcript. **Contact:** taf@thealeutfoundation.org.

313 ■ Alexander Graham Bell Association for the Deaf and Hard of Hearing (AG Bell)
3417 Volta Pl. NW
Washington, DC 20007
Ph: (202)337-5220
E-mail: info@agbell.org
URL: www.agbell.org
Twitter: twitter.com/AGBellAssoc

314 ■ AG Bell College Scholarship Awards
(Undergraduate, Graduate/Scholarship)

Purpose: To support students diagnosed with a moderate to profound hearing loss prior to learning, listening and talking and who are seeking to continue their undergraduate or graduate level education in any field of study. **Focus:** Hearing and deafness. **Qualif.:** Applicants must be enrolled in or applied to a mainstream and accredited college/university as full-time students. **Criteria:** Award will be given to applicant who has been diagnosed with a moderate to profound hearing loss prior to acquiring a spoken language (pre-lingual hearing loss); Applicants hearing loss must be bilateral and in the moderate to profound range; Spoken communication must be the student's primary mode of communication.

Funds Avail.: $2,500-$10,000. **Duration:** Annual. **Number Awarded:** Varies. **To Apply:** Applicants must submit an application, with pages in numbered order; For children who use hearing aids, an unaided Audiogram performed within the last twelve (12) months or for those with cochlear implants, the most recent mapping report (first page only); Verification of the student's application, acceptance or enrollment to a mainstream and accredited university/college; Official transcripts for the most recent two years completed of high school or college; Student essay; Recommendation from a hearing health professional (maximum of two single-sided pages); Recommendation from a current AG Bell member (Maximum of two single-sided pages). If you do not know an AG Bell member, please provide a recommendation from an educational or therapeutic professional; Recommendation from a non-relative who is familiar with the family's financial need (maximum of two single-sided pages). **Contact:** Questions may be directed to financialaid@agbell.org.

315 ■ A.G. Bell School Age Financial Aid Program
(Undergraduate/Scholarship)

Purpose: To help students with their educational costs such as tuition, room and board, books, equipment, auditory and speech language support services, academic tutoring, transportation, and other school-related expenses. **Focus:** General studies/Field of study not specified; Hearing and deafness. **Qualif.:** Applicants' eligibility are as follows: bilateral hearing loss or Auditory Neuropathy (AN) must have been diagnosed before the children's fourth birthday; children's hearing loss must be in the moderate to profound range; primary mode of communication is Listening and Spoken Language; enrolled or registered as full-time students for the school year beginning in the fall of the given year between grades one and twelve in a mainstream parochial, independent or private elementary or secondary school; and, residents of United States (including territories) or Canada. **Criteria:** Selection shall be based on the premises that the students are with hearing loss who use listening and spoken language and who are in first through twelfth grades and attending a parochial, private or independent (not public) mainstream school.

Funds Avail.: $500-$1,500. **Duration:** Annual. **Number Awarded:** 1. **To Apply:** Applicants must submit the following: an application, with pages in numbered order; for children who use hearing aids, an unaided Audiogram performed within the last twelve months or for those with cochlear implants, the most recent mapping report (first page only); verification of the child's enrollment, and a narrative from a teacher or principal on the child's progress on school letterhead; recommendation from a hearing health professional (maximum of two single-sided pages); recommendation from a current AG Bell member (Maximum of two single-sided pages). If you do not know an AG Bell member, please provide a recommendation from an educational or therapeutic professional; recommendation from a non-relative who is familiar with the family's financial need (maximum of two single-sided pages). **Deadline:** May 13. **Contact:** financialaid@agbell.org.

316 ■ George H. Nofer Scholarships for Law and Public Policy (Graduate/Scholarship)

Purpose: To support students with hearing impairments thrive in an educational setting. **Focus:** Hearing and deafness; Public administration. **Qualif.:** Applicants must be full-time graduate students with a pre-lingual bilateral hearing loss in the moderately-severe to profound range, use listening and spoken language as their primary method of communication, and who are attending an accredited mainstream law school or a masters or doctoral program in public policy or public administration. **Criteria:** Selection shall be based on the premises that the students are with hearing loss who use listening and spoken language and who are in first through twelfth grades and attending a parochial, private or independent (not public) mainstream school.

Funds Avail.: $5,000 each. **Duration:** Annual. **Number Awarded:** Up to 3. **To Apply:** Applicants must submit an application, with pages in numbered order; For students who use hearing aids, an unaided Audiogram performed within the last twelve months or for those with cochlear implants, the most recent mapping report (first page only); Official transcripts for the most recent two completed years of college. For third year applicants, a transcript of your previous year of study will suffice. Verification of the student's application, acceptance or enrollment to a mainstream and accredited university/college (a readable photocopy of a letter, tuition notice, or other correspondence is acceptable); Student essay (as indicated in the application); Recommendation from a hearing health professional (maximum of two single-sided pages); Recommendation from a current AG Bell member (Maximum of two single-sided pages). If you do not know an AG Bell member, please provide a recommendation from an educational or therapeutic professional; Recommendation from a non-relative who is familiar with the family's financial need (maximum of two single-sided pages). **Deadline:** April 22. **Contact:** financialaid@agbell.org.

317 ■ Alex's Lemonade Stand Foundation (ALSF)
333 E Lancaster Ave., No. 414
Wynnewood, PA 19096
Ph: (610)649-3034
Fax: (610)649-3038
Free: 866-333-1213
URL: www.alexslemonade.org
Facebook: www.facebook.com/alexslemonade
LinkedIn: www.linkedin.com/company/alex%27s-lemonade-stand-foundation

318 ■ Alex's Lemonade Stand Foundation Epidemiology Grants (Doctorate, Master's, Professional development/Grant)

Purpose: To support research of investigators who have a specific focus on the epidemiology, early detection or the prevention of childhood cancer. **Focus:** Epidemiology; Oncology. **Qualif.:** Applicants should be at least at the Assistant, Associate or Full Professor level; must be MD or PhD; must have a history of formal training in disciplines that are relevant to the proposed research or a track record of conducting similar research; critical to these application are innovative proposals that have the potential to generate new insight into the causes of childhood cancer; must demonstrate feasibility. **Criteria:** Selection will be based on the committee's criteria.

Funds Avail.: $100,000 per year. **Duration:** Annual; two years. **To Apply:** Applicants must first complete the online form then upload the application in one PDF. Applicants can request a password or sign in by going to the Guidelines and Submission page of www.alsfgrants.org. All applications must be submitted using the ALSF's online submission process. **Deadline:** December 15. **Contact:** Kay Schaul at 610-649-3034 or e-mail grants@alexslemonade.org.

319 ■ Alex's Lemonade Stand Foundation Innovation Grants (Other/Grant)

Purpose: To provide critical and significant seed funding for experienced investigators with a novel and promising approach to finding causes and cures for childhood cancers. **Focus:** Oncology. **Qualif.:** Applicants must be experienced investigators with a novel and promising approach in finding causes and cures for childhood cancers. **Criteria:** Selection will be based on the committee's criteria.

Funds Avail.: Up to $125,000. **Duration:** Annual; two years. **To Apply:** Applicants must submit an approved letter of intent before application will be submitted. All requests must be submitted using ALSF's online application process. Applicants can request a password or sign in by going to the Guidelines and Submission page. **Deadline:** March 2. **Contact:** Kay Schaul, 610-649-3034, grants@alexslemonade.org.

320 ■ Alex's Lemonade Stand Foundation Young Investigator Grants (Doctorate, Master's, Professional development/Grant)

Purpose: To eradicate childhood cancer through basic research, career development and helping to streamline

Awards are arranged alphabetically below their administering organizations

translational clinical research. **Focus:** Oncology. **Qualif.:** Applicants must be researchers and physicians who have promising research ideas; must be at the early stages of their research careers; must hold an MD or PhD either in an accredited fellowship program or within six years from the completion of a three-year fellowship program at the time the funding will start. PhD applicants must be within six years granting the PhD at the time the funding will start. Post-doctoral are encouraged to apply, but must also be within the six-year time frame; must not currently hold an independent NIH grant. Applicants may currently have a NIH K Award; research mentors must be identified and the application must document their involvement in experimental design and execution. **Criteria:** Selection will be based on the committee's criteria.

Funds Avail.: $50,000. **Duration:** Annual. **To Apply:** Applicants can request a password or sign in by going to the Guidelines and Submission page of www.alsfgrants.org. All requests must be submitted using ALSF's online application process. **Deadline:** December 15. **Contact:** Kay Schaul; Email: grants@AlexsLemonade.org.

321 ■ All Star Association
1050 Monarch St., Ste. 101
Lexington, KY 40513
Fax: (859)255-3647
Free: 800-930-3644
E-mail: lexoffice@allstarassociation.com
URL: allstarassociation.com

322 ■ John D. Utterback Scholarship Program
(Undergraduate/Scholarship)

Purpose: To financially support those students who are continuing their studies. **Focus:** Food science and technology. **Qualif.:** Applicants must be high school or college students enrolled in food science, marketing, business, nutrition, packaging, or AG education programs; must be employees and/or their dependents. **Criteria:** Applicants will be selected based on their academic performance, courses related to food science, apparent commitment to a career in dairy/beverage/food industry; involvement in extra-curricular activities, and by the evidence of leadership ability, initiative, character and integrity.

Funds Avail.: Maximum of $15,000. **Duration:** Annual. **Number Awarded:** Up to 5. **To Apply:** Applicants must complete and print the online questionnaire; must have the official transcript from all high schools, colleges and universities attended; must submit a request letter of recommendation from a faculty member familiar with the applicant's scholastic performance; must have a recent photograph. Applicants must complete and submit the application form and other supporting documents on or before the deadline. **Deadline:** June 15.

323 ■ Allegheny County Bar Foundation (ACBF)
400 Koppers Bldg.
436 7th Ave.
Pittsburgh, PA 15219-1826
Ph: (412)402-6641
URL: www.acbf.org
Facebook: www.facebook.com/alleghenycountybarfoundation

324 ■ Daniel B. Dixon Scholarships *(Undergraduate/Scholarship)*

Purpose: To support a law student attending the University of Pittsburgh School of Law. **Focus:** Law. **Qualif.:** Applicants must be law students attending the University of Pittsburgh School of Law who have completed their first or second year and who have demonstrated an interest in real estate law. **Criteria:** Selection is based on academic excellence and financial need.

Funds Avail.: $1,000. **Duration:** Annual. **Number Awarded:** 1. **To Apply:** Applicants must submit a completed application form together with the essay, recommendation, transcripts and proof of class rank (most recent grade reports). **Deadline:** June 15. **Remarks:** Established in 2007. **Contact:** Erin Rhodes, Programs & Projects Coordinator, Allegheny County Bar Foundation; 400 Koppers Bldg., 436 7th Ave., Pittsburgh, PA 15219; Phone: 412-402-6641; Email: erhodes@acba.org.

325 ■ Kennedy T. Friend Scholarships *(Graduate, Undergraduate/Scholarship)*

Purpose: To provide support to the children of the Bar of Allegheny County in pursuing their educational goals. **Focus:** General studies/Field of study not specified. **Qualif.:** Applicants must be sons/daughters of a "member of the Bar of Allegheny County", and enrolled at Yale University in New Haven, Connecticut or at the University of Paris in France. **Criteria:** Applicants must meet the qualification to receive the award.

Funds Avail.: Varies. **Duration:** Annual. **To Apply:** Applicants must submit an application form together with a copy of Attorney's Annual Fee application, written confirmation of registration from the school, and a list of courses to be taken. **Contact:** Joshua Pie, Trust Administrator; 2 PNC Plaza-7th Fl., 620 Liberty Ave., Pittsburgh, PA 1522; Phone: 412-768-7587.

326 ■ F.C. Grote Fund Scholarships *(Graduate, Undergraduate/Scholarship)*

Purpose: To support the education of a student at the University of Pittsburgh School of Law and the University of Pennsylvania Law School. **Focus:** Law. **Qualif.:** Applicants must be students at the University of Pittsburgh School of Law or the University of Pennsylvania Law School. **Criteria:** Selection is based on the application materials submitted.

Funds Avail.: $5,000. **Duration:** Annual. **To Apply:** Applicants must submit a completed application form. **Deadline:** April 15. **Contact:** Lorrie K. Albert; Email: lalbert@acba.org.

327 ■ Honorable Carol Los Mansmann Memorial Scholarships *(Graduate, Undergraduate/Scholarship)*

Purpose: To support an outstanding female law student attending Duquesne University School of Law. **Focus:** Law. **Qualif.:** Applicants must be female law students attending Duquesne University School of Law who demonstrates a potential for leadership and a commitment to the advancement of women; must be enrolled in the School of Law and must have completed first year of the day division or second year of the evening or part-time day division; must be ranked in the top half of the class. **Criteria:** Selection is based on a combination of academic achievement, involvement in extracurricular and other activities, financial need and an essay.

Funds Avail.: $3,000. **Duration:** Annual. **To Apply:** Applicants must submit a completed application including transcripts and proof of class rank (most recent grade reports). **Deadline:** April 15. **Contact:** Erin Rhodes, Programs & Projects Coordinator; 400 Koppers Bldg., 436 7th Ave., Pittsburgh, PA 15219; Phone: 412-402-6641; Fax: 412-261-3622; Email: erhodes@acba.org.

328 ■ Honorable Joseph H. Ridge Memorial Scholarships *(Undergraduate/Scholarship)*

Purpose: To support the education of a student at Duquesne Law School. **Focus:** Law. **Qualif.:** Applicants must be students of Duquesne Law School and must also be graduates of Central Catholic High School. **Criteria:** Scholarship will be awarded to the highest ranking member of the graduating class at Duquesne Law School.

Funds Avail.: No specific amount. **To Apply:** Applicants must submit a letter stating interest in the scholarship; proof of graduation from Central Catholic High School; and Duquesne Law School transcript and class rank. **Deadline:** June 15.

329 ■ James I. Smith, III Notre Dame Law School Scholarship Fund *(Graduate, Undergraduate/Scholarship)*

Purpose: To provide scholarships to law students from Allegheny County enrolled at Notre Dame Law School. **Focus:** Law. **Qualif.:** Applicants must be Allegheny County students enrolled at Notre Dame Law School. **Criteria:** Selection is based on the application materials submitted.

Funds Avail.: No specific amount. **To Apply:** Applicants must submit completed applications and include an estimated budget. Application must be signed by an authorized representative of the law school. **Deadline:** April 15.

330 ■ Alliance Defending Freedom (ADF)
15100 N 90th St.
Scottsdale, AZ 85260-2769
Ph: (480)444-0020
Fax: (480)444-0025
Free: 800-835-5233
E-mail: grants@alliancedefendingfreedom.org
URL: www.alliancedefendingfreedom.org
Facebook: www.facebook.com/AllianceDefendingFreedom
LinkedIn: www.linkedin.com/company/alliance-defending-freedom
Twitter: twitter.com/alliancedefends

331 ■ Alliance Defending Freedom - Blackstone Legal Fellowships *(Undergraduate/Fellowship)*

Purpose: To train law students who will rise to positions of influence and leadership as legal scholars, litigators, policy makers and judges. **Focus:** Law. **Qualif.:** Applicants must be exceptionally capable and highly motivated first year law students (second year law students are also welcome to apply). **Criteria:** Selection is based on demonstrated Christian commitment, motivation to engage in popular legal culture, leadership potential in a legal context, evidence of oral and written communication skills, and academic achievement.

Funds Avail.: No specific amount. **Duration:** nine weeks. **To Apply:** Applicants must complete the application online.

332 ■ Alliance for Equality of Blind Canadians (AEBC)
PO Box 20262
Kelowna, BC, Canada V1Y 9H2
Free: 800-561-4774
E-mail: info@blindcanadians.ca
URL: www.blindcanadians.ca
Facebook: www.facebook.com/blindcanadians

333 ■ AEBC Toronto Chapter Scholarships *(Undergraduate/Scholarship)*

Purpose: To support outstanding blind, deaf-blind and partially blind Canadian students in their educational pursuits. **Focus:** General studies/Field of study not specified. **Qualif.:** Applicants must: be blind, deaf-blind or partially sighted; be Canadian citizens or landed immigrants; be attending a post-secondary program (college, university or vocational) with a full-time course load or at a 40% course load if accompanied by an explanation; and Ontario residents studying in Ontario. **Criteria:** Selection is based on academic performance, community involvement and overcoming adversity.

Funds Avail.: $1,500. **Duration:** Annual. **Number Awarded:** Varies. **To Apply:** Applicants must complete the application form online. In addition, applicants must submit a current or most recent average academic grade, calculated in percent; a personal letter; and a reference letter.

334 ■ Business, Education and Technology Scholarships *(Graduate, Undergraduate/Scholarship)*

Purpose: To support outstanding blind, deaf-blind and partially blind Canadian students in their educational pursuits. **Focus:** General studies/Field of study not specified. **Qualif.:** Applicant must be blind, deaf-blind or partially sighted; a Canadian citizen or landed immigrant; and attending a post-secondary program (college, university or vocational) with a full-time course load or at a 40% course load if accompanied by an explanation. **Criteria:** Selection is based on academic performance, community involvement and overcoming adversity.

Funds Avail.: No specific amount. **Duration:** Annual. **To Apply:** Applicant must complete the application form online. In addition, applicant must submit a current or most recent average academic grade, calculated in percent; a personal letter; and a reference letter. **Contact:** scholarship@blindcanadians.ca.

335 ■ Alan H. Neville Memorial Scholarships *(Undergraduate/Scholarship)*

Purpose: To support outstanding blind, deaf-blind and partially blind Canadian students in their educational pursuits. **Focus:** General studies/Field of study not specified. **Qualif.:** Applicants must: be blind, deaf-blind or partially sighted; be Canadian citizens or landed immigrants; and attending a post-secondary program (college, university or vocational) with a full-time course load or at a 40% course load if accompanied by an explanation. **Criteria:** Selection is based on academic performance, community involvement and overcoming adversity.

Funds Avail.: $1,000. **Duration:** Annual. **To Apply:** Applicants must complete the application form online. In addition, applicants must submit a current or most recent average academic grade, calculated in percent; a personal letter; and a reference letter. **Contact:** scholarship@blindcanadians.ca.

336 ■ AEBC Rick Oakes Scholarships for the Arts *(Undergraduate/Scholarship)*

Purpose: To support outstanding blind, deaf-blind and partially blind Canadian students in their educational pursuits. **Focus:** General studies/Field of study not speci-

Awards are arranged alphabetically below their administering organizations

fied. **Qualif.:** Applicants must: be blind, deaf-blind or partially sighted; be Canadian citizens or landed immigrants; be attending a post-secondary program (college, university or vocational) with a full-time course load or at a 40% course load if accompanied by an explanation. **Criteria:** Selection is based on academic performance, community involvement and overcoming adversity.

Funds Avail.: $1,000. **Duration:** Annual. **Number Awarded:** 1. **To Apply:** Applicants must complete the application form online. In addition, applicants must submit a current or most recent average academic grade, calculated in percent; a personal letter; and a reference letter.

337 ■ Alliance of Technology and Women (ATW)
c/o Marilyn Kibler-Colon, President
Services for Airline Solutions at Sabre
3150 Sabre Dr.
Southlake, TX 76092
E-mail: info@dfwatw.org
URL: www.dfwatw.org
Twitter: www.twitter.com/DFW_ATW

338 ■ GREAT MINDS Collegiate Scholarship Program *(Undergraduate/Scholarship)*

Purpose: To help young girls become more interested in technology. **Focus:** Engineering; Mathematics and mathematical sciences; Science; Technology. **Qualif.:** Applicants must be first-time students or adult learners returning to school to pursue a new career; must be enrolled in an Associate's or Bachelor's Degree program; may have diverse levels of life experience, academic merit, age, race and religion. **Criteria:** Recipients are chosen on the basis of volunteer service, passion for technology, leadership activities, scholastic grades, letters of recommendation and previous awards. Demonstrated passion and spirit is weighted most heavily in the selection process.

Funds Avail.: No specific amount. **To Apply:** Applicants must submit a completed application form.

339 ■ Alpha Chi (AX)
Alpha Chi National College Honor Scholarship Society
915 E Market Ave.
Searcy, AR 72149
Ph: (501)279-4443
Fax: (501)279-4589
Free: 800-477-4225
E-mail: office@alphachihonor.org
URL: www.alphachihonor.org

340 ■ H. Y. Benedict Fellowships *(Graduate/Fellowship)*

Purpose: To provide financial support to individuals for their first year of graduate study toward the master's, doctorate, or professional degree at any recognized institution. **Focus:** General studies/Field of study not specified. **Qualif.:** Nominees must be enrolled as graduate students with the baccalaureate degree during the school year in which application is made and must identify the graduate or professional school(s) to which they have applied for study the following fall. **Criteria:** Selection will be based on the committee's criteria.

Funds Avail.: $2,500. **Duration:** Annual. **Number Awarded:** 10. **To Apply:** Nominees must submit the official nomination form completed, signed by the sponsor and included with the entry; a letter of application from the student outlining their plans for study and detailing their extracurricular activities, maximum length of two pages, double-spaced; an academic paper or other appropriate work in the students' major field; one letter of recommendation/evaluation from a faculty member in the field represented by the paper or project addressed to the significance of the work; a self-addressed, stamped envelope. **Deadline:** February 15. **Contact:** scholarships@alphachihonor.org.

341 ■ Edwin W. Gaston Scholarships *(Undergraduate/Scholarship)*

Purpose: To provide financial support for the education of senior undergraduate students. **Focus:** General studies/Field of study not specified. **Qualif.:** Nominee must be a senior year undergraduate student. **Criteria:** Nominee must be enrolled for the fall semester as a full-time student in undergraduate study toward the baccalaureate degree.

Funds Avail.: $2,500. **Duration:** Annual. **Number Awarded:** 2. **To Apply:** Nominee must submit the official nomination form completed, signed by the sponsor and included with the entry; a letter of application from the student outlining his/her plans for study and detailing his/her extracurricular activities, maximum length of two pages, double-spaced; an academic paper or other appropriate work in the student's major field; one letter of recommendation/evaluation from a faculty member in the field represented by the paper or project addressed to the significance of the work; a self-addressed, stamped envelope. **Deadline:** February 15. **Contact:** scholarships@alphachihonor.org.

342 ■ Alfred H. Nolle Scholarships *(Undergraduate/Scholarship)*

Purpose: To provide financial support for the education of senior undergraduate students. **Focus:** General studies/Field of study not specified. **Qualif.:** Nominees must be full-time undergraduate senior students; must be enrolled for the fall semester as full-time students in undergraduate study toward the baccalaureate degree. **Criteria:** Selection will be based on the committee's criteria.

Funds Avail.: $1,500. **Duration:** Annual. **Number Awarded:** 10. **To Apply:** Nominees must submit a completed official nomination form, signed by the sponsor and included with the entry; a letter of application from students outlining their plans for study and detailing their extracurricular activities, maximum length of two pages, double-spaced; an academic paper or other appropriate work in the students' major field; one letter of recommendation/evaluation from a faculty member in the field represented by the paper or project addressed to the significance of the work; a self-addressed, stamped envelope. **Deadline:** February 15. **Contact:** scholarships@alphachihonor.org.

343 ■ Joseph E. Pryor Graduate Fellowships *(Graduate/Fellowship, Scholarship)*

Purpose: To provide financial assistance to individuals for full-time graduate or professional study (beyond the baccalaureate level). **Focus:** General studies/Field of study not specified. **Qualif.:** Applicants must be active alumni members and graduate student members at Alpha Chi institutions at the time of application. **Criteria:** Candidates will be evaluated based on criteria by the Pryor Fellowship Committee. Only complete applications will be given consideration.

Awards are arranged alphabetically below their administering organizations

Funds Avail.: $5,000 to a student who has completed at least two years of graduate or professional study and $3,000 to a first or second year student of graduate or professional study. **Duration:** Annual. **Number Awarded:** 2. **To Apply:** Applicants must submit evidence of outstanding scholarship; 300-500 word essay introducing their academic/professional goals, but not indicating financial need; two letters of recommendation from employers or professors or other persons qualified to give an evaluation; two complete official transcripts sealed by registrar; copy of official results of GRE, LSAT, MCAT or equivalent to applicant's discipline; and completed application form. **Deadline:** February 15. **Contact:** scholarships@alphachihonor.org.

344 ■ Robert W. Sledge Fellowships *(Graduate/Fellowship)*

Purpose: To provide financial support to individuals for their first year of graduate study toward the master's, doctorate or professional degree at any recognized institution. **Focus:** General studies/Field of study not specified. **Qualif.:** Nominees must be enrolled graduate students with the baccalaureate degree during the school year in which application is made and must identify the graduate or professional school(s) to which they have applied for study the following fall. **Criteria:** Selection will be based on the committee's criteria.

Funds Avail.: $3,500. **Duration:** Annual. **Number Awarded:** 2. **To Apply:** Nominees must submit the official nomination form completed, signed by the sponsor and included with the entry; a letter of application from the student outlining their plans for study and detailing their extracurricular activities, maximum length of two pages, double-spaced; an academic paper or other appropriate work in the students' major field; one letter of recommendation/evaluation from a faculty member in the field represented by the paper or project addressed to the significance of the work; a self-addressed, stamped envelope. **Deadline:** February 15. **Contact:** scholarships@alphachihonor.org.

345 ■ Alpha Chi Omega
5939 Castle Creek Pky.
North Dr.
Indianapolis, IN 46250
Ph: (317)579-5050
Fax: (317)579-5051
E-mail: axoinfo@alphachiomega.org
URL: www.alphachiomega.org

346 ■ Alpha Chi Omega Love and Loyalty Grants *(Professional development/Grant)*

Purpose: To support the educational, literary and charitable pursuits of Alpha Chi Omega, and encourage efforts that create well-rounded real, strong women. **Focus:** General studies/Field of study not specified. **Qualif.:** Awarded to the Alpha Chi Omega Fraternity, collegiate and alumnae chapters, and individual alumnae and collegiate members. **Funds Avail.:** Varies. **Duration:** Annual. **To Apply:** An application form is available on the web site. **Contact:** Amber Latta, assistant director-grants and stewardship via email at alatta@alphachiomega.org.

347 ■ Alpha Chi Sigma Fraternity, Inc.
6296 Rucker Rd., Ste. B
Indianapolis, IN 46220
Ph: (317)357-5944
Fax: (317)351-9702
Free: 800-252-4369
E-mail: national@alphachisigma.org
URL: www.alphachisigma.org
LinkedIn: www.linkedin.com/company/alpha-chi-sigma-fraternity

348 ■ Alpha Chi Sigma Scholarship Awards *(Graduate, Undergraduate/Scholarship)*

Purpose: To encourage and recognize outstanding scholarship among Collegiate members of Alpha Chi Sigma Fraternity. **Focus:** General studies/Field of study not specified. **Qualif.:** Nominees must have been members of Alpha Chi Sigma Fraternity for at least one year, and enrolled in an institution of higher learning at the time of nomination. Undergraduate nominees must have completed the Junior year at the time of nomination. Graduate nominees may be nominated based upon their undergraduate and graduate records upon the completion of their first year of graduate study. Graduate students may also be nominated, based upon their graduate records alone, after admission to candidacy for the terminal degree in the field of graduate study. **Criteria:** Nominees will be evaluated by the appointed award committee with established criteria.

Funds Avail.: $1,000. **To Apply:** Application process is done through nomination. Nominee must submit the following checklist: 1) biographical sketch; 2) two letters of recommendation by faculty of the institution from where the student is enrolled; 3) transcripts of all academic works; 4) photograph; 5) address and telephone number of a candidate including summer address if different; and 6) other information that may support the application of a nominee such as abstracts of presentations of meetings, or reprints of scientific publications. **Deadline:** February 1. **Remarks:** Established in 1913.

349 ■ Alpha Delta Gamma (ADG)
1100 Rockhurst Rd.
Kansas City, MO 64110
E-mail: president@alphadeltagamma.org
URL: www.alphadeltagamma.org

350 ■ Alpha Delta Gamma Educational Foundation Scholarships *(Undergraduate, Graduate/Scholarship)*

Purpose: To support and promote educational opportunities for the members of Alpha Delta Gamma National Fraternity. **Focus:** General studies/Field of study not specified. **Qualif.:** Applicants must be members of Alpha Delta Gamma National Fraternity. **Criteria:** Selection shall be based on the aforementioned applicants' qualifications and compliance with the application details.

Funds Avail.: Amount varies. **Duration:** Annual. **Number Awarded:** 2. **To Apply:** Applicants must submit a statement from the financial office of the college or university attended; one letter of recommendation from Chapter moderator; one letter of recommendation from a current instructor; no larger than 5X7 photo; a letter from the ADG National Treasurer stating the applicant's membership standing; one-page biographical sketch; and one copy of transcript of records. **Deadline:** June 15. **Contact:** Alpha Delta Gamma Educational Foundation, c/o Michael Blackstock, 2063 Dellwood Drive, Atlanta, GA 30309; Email: adgef@adgef.com.

Awards are arranged alphabetically below their administering organizations

351 ■ Alpha Kappa Alpha Educational Advancement Foundation (AKA-EAF)
5656 S Stony Island Ave.
Chicago, IL 60637
Ph: (773)947-0026
Fax: (773)947-0277
Free: 800-653-6528
E-mail: akaeaf@akaeaf.net
URL: www.akaeaf.org

352 ■ Alpha Kappa Alpha - Educational Advancement Foundation Financial Need-Based Scholarships *(Graduate, Undergraduate/Scholarship)*
Purpose: To provide financial support to undergraduate and graduate students for the advancement of education. **Focus:** General studies/Field of study not specified. **Qualif.:** Applicants must be full-time undergraduate and/or graduate students currently enrolled in an accredited degree-granting institution; have a minimum GPA of 2.5 ("C" average); and demonstrate community service and involvement. **Criteria:** Recipients are selected based on financial need.
Funds Avail.: No specific amount. **Duration:** Annual. **To Apply:** Applicants must submit all the required application information. For undergraduate: completed application form including personal statement; three recommendation letters; and official transcripts (please open, scan, and add as an attachment). For graduate: completed application form; current resume; documentation of project/research, scholarly pursuit, etc. (two double-spaced typewritten pages; three recommendation letters not be dated earlier than January of the current year; official transcripts (please open, scan, and add as an attachment); and, if first time graduate students, please include a copy of the acceptance letter. **Deadline:** April 15 (undergraduate); August 15 (graduate).

353 ■ Alpha Kappa Alpha - Educational Advancement Foundation Merit Scholarships *(Graduate, Undergraduate/Scholarship)*
Purpose: To provide financial support to undergraduate and graduate students for the advancement of education. **Focus:** General studies/Field of study not specified. **Qualif.:** Applicants must be full-time undergraduate and/or graduate students currently enrolled in an accredited degree-granting institution; have a minimum GPA of 3.0 ("B" average); and demonstrate community service and involvement. **Criteria:** Selection shall be based on the aforesaid qualifications.
Funds Avail.: No specific amount. **Duration:** Annual. **To Apply:** Applicants must submit all the required application information. For undergraduate: completed application form including personal statement; three recommendation letters; and official transcripts (please open, scan, and add as an attachment). For graduate: completed application form; current resume; documentation of project/research, scholarly pursuit, etc. (two double-spaced typewritten pages; three recommendation letters not be dated earlier than January of the current year; official transcripts (please open, scan, and add as an attachment); and, if first time graduate students, please include a copy of the acceptance letter. **Deadline:** April 15 (undergraduate); August 15 (graduate).

354 ■ Youth Partners Accessing Capital (PAC) *(Undergraduate/Scholarship)*
Purpose: To develop leadership among undergraduates in the areas of criteria development, evaluation, and fund management. **Focus:** General studies/Field of study not specified. **Qualif.:** Applicants must be members of the Alpha Kappa Alpha Sorority, Inc.; at least college sophomores who have a minimum 3.0 of GPA. **Criteria:** Applicants are evaluated based on demonstrated exceptional academic achievement; financial need; and leadership or volunteerism in civic or campus activities.
Funds Avail.: No specific amount. **Duration:** Annual. **To Apply:** Applicants may check the website for further information. **Deadline:** April 15. **Remarks:** Established in 1997.

355 ■ Alpha Phi Sigma
3301 College Ave.
Fort Lauderdale, FL 33314
Ph: (954)262-7004
Fax: (954)262-3646
E-mail: headquarters@alphaphisigma.org
URL: www.alphaphisigma.org

356 ■ V.A. Leonard Scholarships *(Graduate, Undergraduate/Scholarship)*
Purpose: To assist students in their educational pursuits. **Focus:** General studies/Field of study not specified. **Qualif.:** Applicants must be Alpha Phi Sigma members. **Criteria:** Recipients are selected based on academic achievement, professional recommendations and extracurricular activities.
Funds Avail.: No specific amount. **Duration:** Annual. **To Apply:** Applicants must submit required materials and documents following the stipulated guidelines. **Remarks:** Established in 1982.

357 ■ Regina B. Shearn Scholarships *(Graduate, Undergraduate/Scholarship)*
Purpose: To assist students in their educational pursuits. **Focus:** General studies/Field of study not specified. **Qualif.:** Applicants must be Alpha Phi Sigma members. Applicants are not eligible to receive the same scholarship two years in succession. **Criteria:** Selection is based on academic performance, leadership and service, personal statement and evaluation reports.
Funds Avail.: No specific amount. **Duration:** Annual. **To Apply:** Applicants must submit required materials and documents following the stipulated guidelines. **Remarks:** Established in 2001.

358 ■ Alpha Tau Omega (ATO)
1 N Pennsylvania St., 12th Fl.
Indianapolis, IN 46204
Ph: (317)684-1865
Fax: (317)684-1862
E-mail: board@ato.org
URL: www.ato.org/default.aspx

359 ■ Alpha Tau Omega Graduate Scholarships *(Graduate/Scholarship)*
Purpose: To provide students the highest standard of educational programs and scholarships who demonstrated leadership. **Focus:** General studies/Field of study not specified. **Qualif.:** Applicants must be students either enrolled or accepted into an accredited graduate program; must be full-time students during the academic year; must

be initiated members of ATO in good standing; must have a minimum cumulative GPA of 3.5 on a 4.0 scale. **Criteria:** Selection will be based on academic achievements; demonstrated leadership in ATO; and demonstrated leadership on campus and in the community.

Funds Avail.: No specific amount. **Number Awarded:** 4. **To Apply:** Applicants must apply online at www.ato.org and answer all questions in essay format. Applicants must also attach their transcript and three letters of recommendation. **Deadline:** March 31.

360 ■ Alpha Tau Omega Undergraduate Scholarships *(Undergraduate/Scholarship)*

Purpose: To provide students the highest standard of educational programs and scholarships who demonstrated leadership. **Focus:** General studies/Field of study not specified. **Qualif.:** Applicants must be students who have at least one undergraduate year remaining before graduation. **Criteria:** Selection will be based on the committee's criteria.

Funds Avail.: No specific amount. **To Apply:** Applicants must apply online at www.ato.org and answer all questions in essay format. Applicants must also attach their transcript and three letters of recommendation. **Deadline:** March 31.

361 ■ William D. Krahling Excellence in Journalism Scholarships *(Undergraduate/Scholarship)*

Purpose: To provide students the highest standard of educational programs and scholarships who demonstrated leadership. **Focus:** Journalism. **Qualif.:** Applicants must be students majoring in journalism or a related field; must have completed one academic year of undergraduate education and have at least one undergraduate year remaining. **Criteria:** Selection will be based on the committee's criteria.

Funds Avail.: No specific amount. **To Apply:** Applicants must apply online at www.ato.org and answer all questions in essay format. Applicants must also attach their transcript and three letters of recommendation. **Deadline:** March 31.

362 ■ Lawrence A. Long Memorial Law Scholarships *(Undergraduate/Scholarship)*

Purpose: To provide educational programs and scholarships of the highest standards. **Focus:** General studies/Field of study not specified. **Qualif.:** Applicants must be students who are enrolled or accepted into an accredited law school and must be full-time students during the academic year. **Criteria:** Selection will be based on academic achievements; demonstrated leadership in ATO; and demonstrated leadership on campus and in the community.

Funds Avail.: No specific amount. **To Apply:** Applicants must apply online at www.ato.org and answer all questions in essay format. Applicants must also attach their transcript and three letters of recommendation. **Deadline:** March 31.

363 ■ J. Milton Richardson Theological Fellowships *(Graduate/Fellowship)*

Purpose: To provide students the highest standard of educational programs and scholarships who plans to attend graduate school in theology or seminary. **Focus:** Theology. **Qualif.:** Applicant must be an ATO member who plans to attend or is enrolled in an accredited graduate school in theology or the seminary, and who intends to become a member of the clergy. **Criteria:** Selection will be based on the committee's criteria.

Funds Avail.: No specific amount. **To Apply:** Applicants must apply online at www.ato.org and answer all questions in essay format. Applicants must also attach their transcript and three letters of recommendation. **Deadline:** March 31. **Remarks:** Established in 1981.

364 ■ ALS Canada
3000 Steeles Ave. E, Ste. 200
Markham, ON, Canada L3R 4T9
Ph: (905)248-2052
Fax: (905)248-2019
Free: 800-267-4257
URL: www.als.ca

365 ■ ALS Canada Bridge Grants *(Professional development/Grant)*

Purpose: To support key ALS grants falling below the CIHR Operating Grant funding threshold. **Focus:** Amyotrophic lateral sclerosis. **Qualif.:** Applicants must be those applying for the CIHR Transitional Operating Grant competition. **Criteria:** Selection will be based on the committee's criteria.

Funds Avail.: 100,000 Canadian Dollars each (200,000 Canadian Dollars for exceptional applications). **Number Awarded:** 4. **To Apply:** Applicants may contact the ALS Canada for the application process and other required materials.

366 ■ ALS Canada Doctoral Research Awards *(Doctorate, Professional development/Fellowship)*

Purpose: To encourage young scientists to pursue ALS research. **Focus:** Amyotrophic lateral sclerosis. **Qualif.:** Applicants must be Ph.D. students within two years of starting degree and proposing ALS research at a Canadian institution or Canadian citizens working abroad. **Criteria:** Selection will be based on the committee's criteria.

Funds Avail.: 25,000 Canadian Dollars per year. **Duration:** Three years. **To Apply:** Applicants may contact the ALS Canada for the application process and other required materials. **Deadline:** April 15.

367 ■ ALS Canada and Tim E. Noel Postdoctoral Fellowships *(Postdoctorate, Professional development/Fellowship)*

Purpose: To encourage young scientists to pursue ALS research. **Focus:** Amyotrophic lateral sclerosis. **Qualif.:** Applicants must be postdoctorals within two years of achieving Ph.D. and proposing ALS research at a Canadian institution or Canadian citizens working abroad. **Criteria:** Selection will be based on the committee's criteria.

Funds Avail.: 55,000 Canadian Dollars per year. **Duration:** Three years. **Number Awarded:** Up to 2. **To Apply:** Applicants may contact the ALS Canada for the application process and other required materials. **Deadline:** April 15.

368 ■ Alter-Cine Foundation
5369 ave. De l'Esplanade
Montreal, QC, Canada H2T 2Z8
Ph: (514)273-7136
Fax: (514)273-8280
URL: altercine.org

369 ■ Documentary Film Grants *(Professional development/Grant)*

Purpose: To help filmmakers in having the opportunity to assist in the production of a documentary project. **Focus:**

Filmmaking. **Qualif.:** Applicants must be filmmakers born and living in Africa, Asia, or Latin America. **Criteria:** Selection will be based on the committee's criteria. **Funds Avail.:** A total of 10,000 Canadian dollars. **Duration:** Annual. **To Apply:** Interested applicants must complete the application form, available online, including a synopsis that describes the content, characters, situations, theme, and the treatment and style of the project; a VHS cassette or a DVD of a completed documentary work; must have financial plan; and two support letters from partners. **Deadline:** August 15.

370 ■ Alzheimer Society of Canada (ASC)
20 Eglinton Ave. W, Ste. 1600
Toronto, ON, Canada M4R 1K8
Ph: (416)488-8772
Fax: (416)322-6656
Free: 800-616-8816
E-mail: info@alzheimer.ca
URL: www.alzheimer.ca
Facebook: www.facebook.com/AlzheimerSociety
Twitter: twitter.com/AlzSociety

371 ■ Firefly Foundation/ASRP Spark Award *(Postdoctorate, Advanced Professional/Grant)*
Purpose: To support unique, creative research ideas that will impact brain health and prevent, defer or effectively treat neurodegenerative disease. **Focus:** Alzheimer's disease. **Qualif.:** Applicants must be within the 18 months of completing their Ph.D. and pursue their postdoctoral fellowship in Canada. **Criteria:** Selection will be based on the research proposals of the applicants. **Funds Avail.:** 100,000 Canadian Dollars per year (50,000 per annum). **Duration:** Up to 2 years. **To Apply:** Applicants are required to submit proposals for studies using the Alzheimer Society of Canada (ASC) online application system for work that explicitly address the Firefly Foundation's mission to find treatment for prevention or cures to eradicate neurodegenerative disease. **Remarks:** The Spark Award is a partnership program between the Firefly Foundation and the Alzheimer Society of Canada, through its Alzheimer Society Research Program. **Contact:** Research Department, Alzheimer Society of Canada, at research@alzheimer.ca.

372 ■ NBHRF/ASRP Doctoral Training Awards *(Doctorate/Grant)*
Purpose: To encourage doctoral degree students to pursue research related to Alzheimer's Disease. **Focus:** Alzheimer's disease; Medical research. **Qualif.:** Applicants must be Canadian citizens or permanent residents of Canada; must be working towards a Ph.D. degree pertaining to research in Alzheimer's Disease (AD) at a New Brunswick institution; and must be responsible to an appropriate supervisor at a New Brunswick institution, who is in a field relevant to AD. **Criteria:** Selection will be based on the aforementioned qualifications. **Funds Avail.:** 22,000 Canadian Dollars per annum, including a research allowance worth 500/year. **Duration:** Up to 3 years. **To Apply:** Candidates must apply to the ASRP regular research grants competition. They must also notify NBHRF of their ASRP application by email and attach to it all documents and materials submitted to the regular ASRP competition. The ASRP/NBHRF will make awards to the top-ranked applicants and will work with institutions in New Brunswick to administer awards. **Remarks:** The awards are co-sponsored by the New Brunswick Health Research Foundation and Alzheimer Society of Canada.

373 ■ Alzheimer's Association
225 N Michigan Ave., 17th Fl.
Chicago, IL 60601-7633
Ph: (312)335-8700
Free: 866-699-1246
E-mail: info@alz.org
URL: www.alz.org

374 ■ New Investigator Research Grant *(Postdoctorate/Grant)*
Purpose: To provide newly independent investigators with funding that will allow them to develop preliminary data, to test procedures and to develop hypotheses. **Focus:** Alzheimer's disease. **Qualif.:** Applicants must be assistant professors or above at their respective institution; must be investigators who have less than ten years of research experience after receipt of their terminal degree. **Criteria:** Selection will be based on the committee's criteria. **Funds Avail.:** $100,000. **Duration:** Annual; up to 2 years. **To Apply:** Interested applicants must submit their letter of intent, and a budget summary for the proposed research project. **Deadline:** May 1. **Contact:** Alzheimer's Association at grantsapp@alz.org.

375 ■ Part the Cloud Translational Research Funds *(Postgraduate/Grant)*
Purpose: To provide support for early phase studies of potential Alzheimer's therapeutics or validation of biological markers in of disease progression. **Focus:** Alzheimer's disease. **Qualif.:** Applicants must be non-profit and small for-profit agencies, or researchers with full-time staff or faculty appointments. **Criteria:** Selection will be based on the committee's criteria. **Funds Avail.:** $600,000. **Duration:** Annual; 2-3 years. **Number Awarded:** Up to 6. **To Apply:** Interested applicants must submit letter of intent, annual progress and financial reports, and budget summary for the proposed research. **Deadline:** August 8. **Contact:** Alzheimer's Association at grantsapp@alz.org.

376 ■ U.S.-U.K. Young Investigator Exchange Fellowship *(Postdoctorate/Fellowship)*
Purpose: To provide new investigators with funding that will allow them to develop preliminary or pilot data. **Focus:** Alzheimer's disease. **Qualif.:** Applicants must be investigators based in the United States or United Kingdom who have less than ten years of research experience after receipt of their terminal degree. **Criteria:** Selection will be based on the committee's criteria. **Funds Avail.:** $300,000 for U.S. and 160,000 British Pounds for U.K. **Duration:** Annual; 3 years. **To Apply:** Interested applicants must complete and submit the application form and letter of intent which includes the name of principal investigator, contact information, academic rank/position title, title of the fellowship project, area of focus of the submission, brief rationale for the proposal limited to 3,000 characters, employer and identification number, a current non-profit verification for the institution, and employment verification letter. **Deadline:** April 18.

377 ■ The Zenith Fellows Award Program (Zenith) *(Postdoctorate/Fellowship)*
Purpose: To provide major support for investigators who have: contributed significantly to the field of Alzheimer's

disease research; made significant contributions to other areas of science and now focusing on problems related to Alzheimer's disease; and are likely to make substantial contributions in the future. **Focus:** Alzheimer's disease. **Qualif.:** Applicants must be independent investigators as evidenced by their academic appointment, external multi-year grant support on which the they are the principal investigators, independent laboratory operation, and quality of publication record. **Criteria:** Selection will be based on the committee's criteria.

Funds Avail.: $450,000. **Duration:** Annual; up to 3 years. **To Apply:** Interested applicants must complete and submit the application form available online, and must provide a budget summary for the proposed research project. **Deadline:** May 1. **Remarks:** Established in 1991.

378 ■ Amato Sanita Attorney at Law
1518 Walnut St., Ste. 808A
Philadelphia, PA 19102
Ph: (215)699-3355
Fax: (215)893-1410
E-mail: info@criminallawpennsylvania.com
URL: criminallawpennsylvania.com

379 ■ The Amato Sanita Brighter Future Scholarships (Undergraduate, Graduate, Advanced Professional/Scholarship)

Purpose: To assist a student who exemplifies the pursuit of a better world through education. **Focus:** General studies/Field of study not specified. **Qualif.:** Applicants must be those seeking to enroll in undergraduate, graduate, or law school programs in the United States; and must be in good academic standing, with a minimum cumulative GPA of 3.0 or greater based on the most recent transcript available from the current institution or one attended immediately prior. **Criteria:** Selection will be based on the aforesaid qualifications and compliance with the application process.

Funds Avail.: $500. **To Apply:** Interested applicants must send the following via U.S. mail or fax: a completed application; a 500-word letter of intent that identifies a problem and explains how the applicants intend to use their education as a way to begin solving that problem and creating a brighter future; and academic transcript. **Deadline:** January 1.

380 ■ Ambucs Resource Center
4285 Regency Dr.
Greensboro, NC 27410
Fax: (336)852-6830
Free: 800-838-1845
E-mail: ambucs@ambucs.org
URL: www.ambucs.org/who-are-we/resource-center

381 ■ AMBUCS Scholarships for Therapists Program (Graduate, Undergraduate/Scholarship)

Purpose: To ensure that a new generation of therapists will continue to enhance the lives of people with disabilities. **Focus:** Occupational therapy; Physical therapy; Speech and language pathology/Audiology. **Qualif.:** Applicant must be a citizen of the United States; with documented financial need; with good scholastic standing; be accepted at the junior or senior undergraduate, or graduate level in a program which qualifies the applicant for clinical practice in occupational therapy, physical therapy, speech and language pathology and hearing audiology; and must express an intent to enter clinical practice in chosen field of therapy in the United States upon completion of course of study for which aid is requested. **Criteria:** Awards are based on financial need, US citizenship, and commitment to local community, demonstrated academic accomplishment, character for compassion integrity and career objectives.

Funds Avail.: No specific amount. **Duration:** Annual. **To Apply:** Applicants must may visit the website for the online application. **Deadline:** April 15.

382 ■ Americal Division Veterans Association (ADVA)
4493 Highway 64 W
Henderson, TX 75652
Ph: (830)377-8115
URL: americal.org/cmsaml

383 ■ American Division Veterans Association Scholarships (Undergraduate/Scholarship)

Purpose: To support high school graduate students planning to attend a college. **Focus:** General studies/Field of study not specified. **Qualif.:** Applicants must be children and grandchildren, including those by adoption, of current and deceased ADVA members, provided the deceased member held good membership standing at the time of death, and to any child or adopted child of an American Division soldier who was killed or died while on active duty with the division. **Criteria:** Recipient shall be selected based on financial need.

Funds Avail.: $500. **Duration:** Annual. **Number Awarded:** 1. **To Apply:** Applicant must submit a letter from the sponsor attesting to the applicant's eligibility according to ADVA Scholarship Fund Purpose and By-Laws; a letter of admission from the applicant's college or vocational school of choice; a letter from the applicant's high school principal attesting to the applicant's character if applicant is attending or has graduated from high school (If currently attending a college education, applicant may disregard this reference letter); two letters of recommendation from current teachers concerning the applicant's progress in current classes or subjects; a photocopy of the applicant's high school or college transcript; a detailed statement of the applicant's academic accomplishments, extracurricular activities, and community service involvement; an applicant must submit a 200-300 word essay on subjects pertaining to American Division history, national pride, loyalty to the nation, and patriotism. **Deadline:** April 1. **Remarks:** Established in 1994. **Contact:** William Bruinsma, 5425 Parmalee Road, Middleville, Michigan 49333; E-mail: wb3379@gmail.com.

384 ■ American Academy of Ambulatory Care Nursing (AAACN)
E Holly Ave.
Pitman, NJ 08071-0056
Free: 800-262-6877
E-mail: aaacn@ajj.com
URL: www.aaacn.org

385 ■ AAACN Conference Scholarships for Nursing Students (Undergraduate/Scholarship)

Purpose: To support students who are seeking initial nursing licensure. **Focus:** Nursing. **Qualif.:** Applicants must be

Awards are arranged alphabetically below their administering organizations

nursing students with financial need and willing to contribute their knowledge to the Association and publish their articles for ViewPoint publication. **Criteria:** Selection will be based on the committees' criteria.

Funds Avail.: $1,000. **Duration:** Annual. **To Apply:** Applicants must be recommended by a current member of the AAACN and must submit a complete application form together with CV/resume. **Deadline:** November 15.

386 ■ AAACN Education Scholarships
(Undergraduate/Scholarship)

Purpose: To assist students with their tuition, books, and academic supplies to purse nursing education. **Focus:** Nursing. **Qualif.:** Applicants must be members of AAACN for a minimum of two continuous years with financial need and have the willingness to give back to the Association and publish their articles for the ViewPoint publication. **Criteria:** Selection will be based on the committees' criteria.

Funds Avail.: $1,000. **Duration:** Annual. **To Apply:** Applicants must submit the complete application form together with the applicants' CV/resume. **Deadline:** November 15.

387 ■ AAACN Research Grants *(Undergraduate/Grant)*

Purpose: To assist individuals who are conducting either nursing research or EBP project. **Focus:** Nursing. **Qualif.:** Applicants must be members of AAACN for a minimum of two continuous years with financial need and willing to contribute their knowledge to the Association and publish their articles for the ViewPoint publication, also applicants must have the eager to submit abstract for a podium or poster presentation of the research study/EBP project and its outcome. **Criteria:** Selection will be based on the committees' criteria.

Funds Avail.: $1,000. **Duration:** Annual. **To Apply:** Applicants must submit the complete application form together with the applicants' CV/resume. **Deadline:** November 15.

388 ■ AAACN Scholarships *(Undergraduate/Scholarship)*

Purpose: To provide financial support for researches. **Focus:** Nursing. **Qualif.:** Applicants must be members of American Academy of Ambulatory Care Nursing (AAACN) for a minimum of two years; currently enrolled in an accredited school of nursing or a program deemed by the committee to advance the profession of nursing; request for payment of tuition, books, academic supplies; proof of acceptance in course; must submit a research abstract and proof of acceptance of research study by academic institution or Investigational Review Board employing or sponsoring institutions; willing to present research findings at AAACN Annual Conference following receipt of award; willing to publish article in Viewpoint describing a research study and outcome. **Criteria:** Recipient will be selected by the AAACN Committee.

Funds Avail.: $500-$1,000. **Duration:** Annual. **Number Awarded:** Varies. **To Apply:** Applicants must complete an application form and must provide a current enrollment or proof of acceptance in an accredited school of nursing or other academic program. Applicants are required to submit two copies of the application form. **Deadline:** November 15. **Contact:** Applications can be addressed to A.J. Jannetti at the above address or email reichartp@ajj.com.

389 ■ Candia Baker Laughlin Certification Scholarships *(Undergraduate/Scholarship)*

Purpose: To cover the exam fee, study materials, and other expenses related to achieving certification. **Focus:** Nursing. **Qualif.:** Applicants must be members of AAACN for a minimum of two continuous years with financial need and eligible to sit for the exam. Applicants must have the willingness to give back to the Association, contribute their knowledge, become certified in Ambulatory Care and write an article for the ViewPoint publication. **Criteria:** Selection will be based on the committees' criteria.

Funds Avail.: $1,000. **Duration:** Annual. **To Apply:** Applicants must submit the complete application form together with the applicants' CV/resume. **Deadline:** November 15.

390 ■ American Academy of Attorney-CPAs (AAA-CPA)
PO Box 706
Warrendale, PA 15095
Ph: (703)352-8064
Fax: (703)352-8073
Free: 888-272-2889
E-mail: info@attorney-cpa.com
URL: www.attorney-cpa.com

391 ■ Attorney-CPA Foundation Scholarships *(Postgraduate/Scholarship)*

Purpose: To promote the study and understanding of the fields of Law and Accounting and other related professions. **Focus:** Accounting; Law. **Qualif.:** Applicants must be graduating law students who have obtained CPA Certificate. **Criteria:** Selection will be based on the committee's criteria.

Funds Avail.: No specific amount. **Duration:** Annual. **To Apply:** Applicants may contact the AAA-CPA or the Attorney-CPA Foundation for more information.

392 ■ American Academy of Audiology (AAA)
11480 Commerce Park Dr., Ste. 220
Reston, VA 20191
Ph: (703)790-8466
Fax: (703)790-8631
Free: 800-222-2336
E-mail: infoaud@audiology.org
URL: www.audiology.org
Facebook: www.facebook.com/audiology
LinkedIn: www.linkedin.com/company/american-academy-of-audiology
Twitter: twitter.com/AcademyofAuD

393 ■ New Investigator Research Grant *(Doctorate/Grant)*

Purpose: To support new investigators who have completed a doctoral degree and do not have significant sources of research funding. **Focus:** Speech and language pathology/Audiology. **Qualif.:** Applicants must have been granted the doctoral degree in audiology or hearing science within the past five years; must have a mentor with expertise in the research area to be investigated and who will be prepared to foster the advancement in the development and prosecution of the research. **Criteria:** The Academy Research Committee will evaluate applications on the following attributes: rationale/purpose; methods; overall clarity; importance of work; innovation; and budget

Funds Avail.: Up to $10,000. **Duration:** Annual. **To Apply:** Applications will be submitted using the Academy's online grant submission system. Applicants shall be required to upload several PDF documents. The body of the proposal

Awards are arranged alphabetically below their administering organizations

should adhere to the following requirements: font should be a minimum of size 12 or no smaller than 6 characters per inch; should be single-spaced with no more than 6 lines per vertical inch; should be a minimum of 1 inch for all borders. **Deadline:** October 1.

394 ■ Student Investigator Research Grant - General Audiology/Hearing Science *(Graduate, Doctorate/Grant)*

Purpose: To support doctoral students working towards doctoral degree in audiology or hearing science who are completing a research project as part of their course of study. **Focus:** Speech and language pathology/Audiology. **Qualif.:** Applicants must be doctoral students working towards a doctoral degree in audiology or hearing science who are completing a research project as a part of their course of study; must be currently enrolled in a non-profit tax-exempt institution in the United States or Canada, public or private, as this is where grant funds will be issued; must conduct their research project under the advice and guidance of a mentor. **Criteria:** The Academy Research Committee will evaluate applications on the following attributes: rationale/purpose, methods, overall clarity, importance of work, innovation, and budget. **Funds Avail.:** $5,000. **Duration:** Annual. **To Apply:** Applications must be submitted using the Academy's online grant submission system. No paper copies will be accepted. Applicants will be required to upload several PDF documents. The body of the proposal should adhere to the following requirements: font should be a minimum of size 12 or smaller than 6 characters per inch; single-spaced with no more than 6 lines per vertical inch; margins should be a minimum of 1 inch for all borders. **Deadline:** October 1. **Contact:** American Academy of Audiology, at the above address.

395 ■ Student Investigator Research Grant - Hearing Aids, Clinical Protocols and Patient Outcomes *(Graduate, Doctorate/Grant)*

Purpose: To support doctoral students working towards doctoral degree in audiology or hearing science who are completing a research project as part of their course of study. **Focus:** Speech and language pathology/Audiology. **Qualif.:** Applicants must be doctoral students working towards a doctoral degree in audiology or hearing science who are completing a research project as a part of their course of study; must be currently enrolled in a non-profit tax-exempt institution in the United States or Canada, public or private, as this is where grant funds will be issued; must conduct their research project under the advice and guidance of a mentor. **Criteria:** The Academy Research Committee will evaluate applications on the following attributes: rationale/purpose, methods, overall clarity, importance of work, innovation, and budget. **Funds Avail.:** Up to $5,000. **Duration:** Annual. **To Apply:** Applications must be submitted using the Academy's online grant submission system. No paper copies will be accepted. Applicants will be required to upload several PDF documents. The body of the proposal should adhere to the following requirements: font should be a minimum of size 12 or smaller than 6 characters per inch; single-spaced with no more than 6 lines per vertical inch; margins should be a minimum of 1 inch for all borders. **Deadline:** October 1.

396 ■ Student Investigator Research Grant - Vestibular *(Graduate, Doctorate/Grant)*

Purpose: To support doctoral students working towards doctoral degree in audiology or hearing science who are completing a research project as part of their course of study. **Focus:** Speech and language pathology/Audiology. **Qualif.:** Applicants must be doctoral students working towards a doctoral degree in audiology or hearing science who are completing a research project as a part of their course of study; must be currently enrolled in a non-profit tax-exempt institution in the United States or Canada, public or private, as this is where grant funds will be issued; must conduct their research project under the advice and guidance of a mentor. **Criteria:** The Academy Research Committee will evaluate applications on the following attributes: rationale/purpose, methods, overall clarity, importance of work, innovation, and budget. **Funds Avail.:** Up to $5,000. **Duration:** Annual. **To Apply:** Applications must be submitted using the Academy's online grant submission system. No paper copies will be accepted. Applicants will be required to upload several PDF documents. The body of the proposal should adhere to the following requirements: font should be a minimum of size 12 or smaller than 6 characters per inch; single-spaced with no more than 6 lines per vertical inch; margins should be a minimum of 1 inch for all borders. **Deadline:** October 1. **Contact:** American Academy of Audiology, at the above address or Email: molek@audiology.org.

397 ■ Student Summer Research Fellowship *(Undergraduate, Graduate/Fellowship)*

Purpose: To expose students who are interested in research or wishing to pursue a career in research to a stimulating research environment under the guidance of a mentor. **Focus:** Speech and language pathology/Audiology. **Qualif.:** Applicants must be either of the following: undergraduate students interested in pursuing a research doctorate in audiology or hearing science; or, graduate students who are currently enrolled in a research doctoral program in audiology or hearing science; or, graduate students who are enrolled in an AuD program with plans to pursue a research doctorate degree in audiology or hearing science. **Criteria:** Selection will be based on the committee's criteria. **Funds Avail.:** $2,500. **Duration:** Annual. **To Apply:** Application process is divided for student applicants, both student applicants and mentors, and mentors. Such process can be determined through the Academy's website. In general, applicants who are students must complete the online application and must secure three recommendation letters from mentors, department chairpersons, and academic advisors. **Deadline:** October 1. **Contact:** American Academy of Audiology, at the above address.

398 ■ American Academy for Cerebral Palsy and Developmental Medicine (AACPDM)

555 E Wells St., Ste. 1100
Milwaukee, WI 53202-3800
Ph: (414)918-3014
Fax: (414)276-2146
E-mail: info@aacpdm.org
URL: www.aacpdm.org

399 ■ AACPDM Student Scholarships *(Professional development/Scholarship)*

Purpose: To support individuals who are conducting lessons and research regarding the health and general status of children and adults with cerebral palsy, developmental disorders and other childhood onset disabilities. **Focus:** Child development; Disabilities; Mental health. **Qualif.:** Ap-

Awards are arranged alphabetically below their administering organizations

plicants must be student members of AACPDM who are enrolled in a full-time degree program or be medical trainees (medical students, residents or fellows), and authors of abstracts submitted to the Annual Meeting. **Criteria:** Selection will be based on the committee's criteria.

Funds Avail.: $1,000. **To Apply:** Applications are accepted online only. Those who are not yet members must apply for membership before gaining access to the online application. As part of the online application process, applicants will be required to upload the following documents: a brief statement (1-2 paragraphs) outlining why they wish to have an AACPDM Scholarship; a letter of support from their Program Chief, Clinical Head or authorized official indicating that they are in a good standing with the program; curriculum vitae of no more than two pages; and a copy of their submitted abstracts.

400 ■ AACPDM Transformative Practice Grants
(Professional development/Grant)

Purpose: To facilitate the translation of evidence-based clinical management strategies into practice. **Focus:** Clinical laboratory sciences. **Qualif.:** Applicants must be current AACPDM members and have not received an AACPDM Transformative Practice Grant within the past five years. **Criteria:** Selection will be based on the applications which are going to be evaluated on the following criteria: effectiveness of the proposed management strategy proposed for implementation is supported by research evidence; evidence that the experts have had previous success with implementation of the strategy and that the applications were completed in collaboration with the experts; the proposed activities represent active approaches to implementation; the evaluation plans are reasonable and will provide indications as to the extent the management strategy was implemented; budgets are reasonable and aligned with the proposed activities; and the degree of readiness of the host institution for change.

Funds Avail.: $4,000. **To Apply:** Applicants may check the website for further information on the application process. **Deadline:** March 13.

401 ■ American Academy of Clinical Toxicology (AACT)
6728 Old McLean Village Dr.
McLean, VA 22101
Ph: (703)556-9222
Fax: (703)556-8729
E-mail: admin@clintox.org
URL: www.clintox.org

402 ■ AACT Junior Investigator Research Grants
(Professional development/Grant)

Purpose: To support clinical toxicology research and the development of new investigators' research skills. **Focus:** Toxicology. **Qualif.:** Applicants must be principal investigators who are new researchers within 5 years of completion of their terminal degree or postgraduate training or have professional experience greater than 5 years and no more than two externally funded research projects as principal investigators; must have senior investigators participate on the research team as mentors/advisors; and must be members of AACT in good standing. **Criteria:** Selection will be based on the applicants' eligibility and applications.

Funds Avail.: $30,000. **Duration:** Two years. **To Apply:** Applications for the research grant should emphasize study objectives that focus on clinical toxicology research, sound research methods that support the study objectives, interdisciplinary collaborations, the potential for the project to be replicated, and prudent use of grant funds. The application and any appended pages should be sent as an email attachment to the AACT office, either as a Word document (.doc) or as a PDF file. In addition, the signature page (Page 5) should be sent by "fax" to the AACT office. **Deadline:** November 1.

403 ■ AACT Toxicology Trainee Research Grants
(Professional development/Grant)

Purpose: To support clinical toxicology research and the development of toxicology trainees' research skills. **Focus:** Toxicology. **Qualif.:** Applicants must be principal investigators who are clinical/medical toxicology fellows-in-training within 5 years of completion of their terminal degree; must have senior investigators participate on the research team as mentors/advisors; and must be members of AACT in good standing. **Criteria:** Selection will be based on the applicants' eligibility and applications.

Funds Avail.: $4,000 ($3,000 for research study; $1,000 for travel to NACCT to present the results of the project). **To Apply:** Applications for the research grant should emphasize study objectives that focus on clinical toxicology research, sound research methods that support the study objectives, interdisciplinary collaborations, the potential for the project to be replicated, and prudent use of grant funds. The application and any appended pages should be sent as an email attachment to the AACT office, either as a Word document (.doc) or as a PDF file. In addition, the signature page (Page 5) should be sent by "fax" to the AACT office. **Deadline:** April 1.

404 ■ American Academy of Cosmetic Dentistry (AACD)
402 W Wilson St.
Madison, WI 53703
Ph: (608)222-8583
Fax: (608)222-9540
Free: 800-543-9220
E-mail: info@aacd.com
URL: www.aacd.com

405 ■ AACD Dentist Fellowships *(Professional development/Fellowship)*

Purpose: To provide the highest level of achievement for members in accordance with the AACD's mission of education and excellence. **Focus:** Dentistry. **Qualif.:** Applicants must be members of the American Academy of Cosmetic Dentistry; must have attended three of the most recent five annual AACD scientific sessions. **Criteria:** Selection criteria will be based on the committee's criteria.

Funds Avail.: Amount not specified. **Duration:** Annual. **To Apply:** Interested applicants may visit the website to obtain the application form. Applicants must submit 50 cases of different patients to the executive office and must pay the $550 (USD) application fee.

406 ■ AACD Laboratory Fellowships *(Professional development/Fellowship)*

Purpose: To provide means for accredited members in attaining highest level of achievement and excellence in cosmetic dentistry. **Focus:** Dentistry. **Qualif.:** Applicants must be members of the American Academy of Cosmetic

Awards are arranged alphabetically below their administering organizations

Dentistry. **Criteria:** Selection criteria will be based on the committee's criteria.

Funds Avail.: Amount not specified. **Duration:** Annual. **To Apply:** Interested applicants may visit the website to obtain the application form. Applicants must submit 50 cases of different patients to the executive office and must pay the $550 (USD) application fee.

407 ■ American Academy of Dermatology (AAD)
930 E Woodfield Rd.
Schaumburg, IL 60173
Ph: (847)240-1280
Fax: (847)240-1859
Free: 866-503-7546
E-mail: MRC@aad.org
URL: www.aad.org
Facebook: www.facebook.com/AADskin
Twitter: twitter.com/AADskin

408 ■ International Society Annual Meeting Travel Grant (Professional development/Grant)

Purpose: To promote and give participants the opportunity to meet foreign colleagues, and establish long-lasting professional relationship. **Focus:** Dermatology. **Qualif.:** Applicants must be dermatology residents, fellows, or young dermatologists (within five years of completing residency) from the United States and Canada willing to travel in Asia, Europe, and Latin America for dermatology meetings. **Criteria:** Preference will be given to those who have one year of complete training, and with letter of recommendation.

Funds Avail.: No specific amount. **Duration:** Annual. **To Apply:** Interested applicants may contact the American Academy of Dermatology for application process and other details. **Deadline:** August 28. **Contact:** Jaime Campbell-Kraus at jcampbell-kraus@aad.org.

409 ■ American Academy of Neurology (AAN)
201 Chicago Ave.
Minneapolis, MN 55415-1126
Ph: (612)928-6000
Fax: (612)454-2746
Free: 800-879-1960
E-mail: memberservices@aan.com
URL: www.aan.com
Facebook: www.facebook.com/
 AmericanAcademyofNeurology
Twitter: twitter.com/AANMember

410 ■ AAN Clinical Research Training Fellowships (Other/Fellowship)

Purpose: To support clinical research training in the neurosciences. **Focus:** Neurology. **Qualif.:** Applicants must be neurologists and clinical investigators interested in academic careers in clinical research; and must be AAN members who have completed less than five years of residency. **Criteria:** Applicants' applications are evaluated by the Clinical Research Subcommittee of the Science Committee of the AAN based on the applicant's ability and promises as clinician-scientists based on prior record of achievement and career plan, letters of reference and curriculum vitae; quality and nature of the training to be provided and the institutional, departmental and mentor-specific training environment; quality and originality of the research plan. Priorities will be given to those applicants who have taken their research career at an early stage.

Funds Avail.: $55,000 per year for two years plus $10,000 per year for tuition fee. **Duration:** Annual. **To Apply:** Applicants must submit one complete copy of the letter of nomination from the Chair of the department of neurology, including assurance that clinical service responsibilities will be restricted to no more than 20 percent of the fellow's time; three-page research plan; copy of a current curriculum vitae; two letters of reference supporting applicants' potential for a clinical, academic research career and qualifications for the fellowship; listing of the applicants' and mentor's current and pending for support, other than the fellowship, using NIH format; letters from proposed mentor detailing the support of and commitment to the applicant and the proposed research and training plan; copy of the proposed mentor's NIH Biosketch; and document describing arrangements for formal course work including quantitative clinical epidemiology, biostatistics, study design, data analysis and ethics. **Contact:** Kristin Roehl, Email: kroehl@aan.com; Phone: 612-928-6082.

411 ■ AAN International Scholarship Award (Professional development/Scholarship)

Purpose: To provide eligible international candidates the opportunity to attend and participate in the Annual Meeting. **Focus:** Neurology. **Qualif.:** Applicant must be a resident living outside of the United States and Canada at the time of application. **Criteria:** Selection will be based on committee's criteria.

Funds Avail.: Up to $2,500. **Duration:** Annual. **Number Awarded:** Varies. **To Apply:** All nominees must provide a curriculum vitae, including a list of publications, and must submit an abstract for the Annual Meeting. **Deadline:** October 26.

412 ■ AAN Medical Student Summer Research Scholarships (Graduate/Scholarship)

Purpose: To provide financial support for projects in either institutional, clinical or laboratory settings where there are ongoing programs of research, service, or training, or for a private practice. **Focus:** Neurology. **Qualif.:** Applicants must be first or second-year medical student members who have a supporting preceptor and a project with clearly defined goals; or either third-year medical student members who are on the official summer break will also be considered with accompanying documentation, whose project is conducted through U.S. or Canadian institution of the students' choice and jointly designed by the students and sponsoring institutions. **Criteria:** Preference will be given to those applicants from schools with established SIGN chapters. More than one student from an institution may apply, but only one student will be selected from an institution.

Funds Avail.: $3,000. **Duration:** Annual. **Number Awarded:** Up to 20. **To Apply:** Applicants must submit completed application form; (1-2 page) project proposal and curriculum vitae; two letters of recommendation: one from the project preceptor and one from the SIGN faculty advisor; and completed tax form with institution information. **Deadline:** February 5. **Contact:** Cheryl Alementi, Phone: 612-928-6073; E-mail: calementi@aan.com.

413 ■ American Academy of Optometry (AAO)
2909 Fairgreen St.
Orlando, FL 32803
Ph: (321)710-3937

Awards are arranged alphabetically below their administering organizations

Fax: (407)893-9890
Free: 800-969-4226
E-mail: aaoptom@aaoptom.org
URL: www.aaopt.org
Facebook: www.facebook.com/AAOPT
LinkedIn: www.linkedin.com/groups/90580/profile
Twitter: twitter.com/aaopt

414 ■ AOF/Johnson & Johnson Vision Care - Innovation in Education Grants *(Advanced Professional, Professional development/Grant)*

Purpose: To aid recently appointed faculty in advancing their teaching skills in the areas of improving delivery of information to students, new methodologies, increasing the use of new technology in all teaching settings, and the promotion of online learning tools. **Focus:** Optometry. **Qualif.:** Applicants must be faculty members at a North American optometric institution with less than 10 years experience as faculty members. **Criteria:** Selection shall be based on the aforementioned applicants' qualifications and compliance with the application details. Priority will be given to innovative and creative projects of the applicants..

Funds Avail.: Amount varies. **Duration:** Annual. **To Apply:** Applicants must submit a proposal electronically and must contain the following components: introduction; background and significance; specific aims; preliminary studies; and study design and methods. These sections should total no more than Three pages. References (maximum of one page) Budget and budget justification (maximum of one page) Biographical sketch(es) of Principal and one co-investigator only (maximum of two pages for each investigator) Education/training; research and professional experience; honors and awards publications (refereed) for the last three years and representative earlier publications. **Contact:** Tracy Kitts, Foundation Coordinator: Phone: 321-710-3936; Email: AOF@aaoptom.org.

415 ■ William C. Ezell Fellowships *(Postdoctorate/Fellowship)*

Purpose: To encourage talented persons to pursue full-time careers in optometric research and education. **Focus:** Optometry. **Qualif.:** Applicants must be post-graduate students, continuing a full-time study and training in research that leads to a Masters or PhD degree. **Criteria:** Applicants fellowship applications will be reviewed by the Research Committee of the American Academy of Optometry and recommendations will then be sent to the AOF Board which approves and funds the Ezell Fellowships.

Funds Avail.: $8,000. **Duration:** Annual. **Number Awarded:** Varies. **To Apply:** Applicants must submit application form together with three letters of recommendation from the persons qualified to comment on his/her educational qualifications, research abilities and potential and current and future teaching capabilities; one-page statement describing the applicant's educational objectives, future research and/or teaching interest and career objectives; and a copy of scientific publications, copies of papers in press must be included. Applications and documents must be submitted electronically indicating the Ezell Fellowship (plus applicants' last name) in the subject line. Attachments in .pdf are highly preferred, although MS Word is acceptable. **Deadline:** March 1. **Remarks:** Established in 1949. **Contact:** aof@aaoptom.org.

416 ■ Terrance N. Ingraham Pediatric Optometry Residency Support *(Graduate/Fellowship)*

Purpose: To promote the practice and development of the field of Pediatric Optometry by providing incentive and support to sustain talented optometric residents who demonstrate a passion and commitment to practice, research, and education in the field of children's vision. **Focus:** Optometry. **Qualif.:** Applicants must be optometrists in an advanced practice pediatric/vision therapy residency program through a North-American school or college of optometry. **Criteria:** Applicants will be evaluated primarily on the basis of their educational background and their ability and potential as teachers, researchers, and practitioners in the field of pediatric optometry. Preference will be given to applicants with an interest in the utilization of soft contact lenses in pediatric populations. Proposals will be reviewed by a peer review committee established by the American Optometric Foundation with the assistance of the American Academy of Optometry Binocular Vision, Perception, and Pediatric Optometry Section chairs.

Funds Avail.: $2,750 each. **Duration:** Annual. **Number Awarded:** 2. **To Apply:** Applications and letters of recommendation must be submitted electronically (preferably as a PDF file) to the contact provided. Please include "Residency Award" and the applicant's last name in the subject line. Applications require the following: cover page that lists applicant name, any degrees, facility of residency, accredited optometric institution under which serving residency, current and permanent address information, email and daytime and evening phone contact information; applicant's education, clinical, research, and teaching experience typically in the form of a CV; a brief description of the residency program and the names and email addresses of the three people the applicant have contacted to submit letters of recommendation; one-page statement of career goals and list the date/status of when AAO membership was obtained; and, letters of recommendation from persons qualified to comment on educational qualifications, research abilities, and potential. One of which must be the Residency Director or Program Coordinator of the Institution. These should be emailed separately by the recommender. **Deadline:** June 8. **Contact:** Tracy Kitts, Foundation Coordinator: Phone 321-710-3936; Email: AOF@aaoptom.org.

417 ■ Antoinette M. Molinari Memorial Scholarships *(Doctorate/Scholarship)*

Purpose: To assist an exceptional student who has extraordinary financial needs and, as such, would have difficulty meeting the financial requirements of attending optometry school. **Focus:** Optometry. **Qualif.:** Eligible applicants must be pursuing a Doctorate of Optometry degree through a full-time course of study and maintain a grade point average of 3.5 (4 point scale) or higher for all course work taken thus far in optometry school. Students must currently hold a first to third year student status during the open application period and be a student member of the American Academy of Optometry (AAO). **Criteria:** Major criteria for selection is financial need, but academic and leadership potential are also important considerations.

Funds Avail.: $7,000. **Duration:** Annual. **Number Awarded:** 1. **To Apply:** Applicants must submit a completed application form; three letters of reference from persons who can attest the applicant's educational qualifications, leadership potential, and financial needs; one-page statement describing the educational and career objectives; and an official transcript of optometry course work. Application materials (aside from the transcript that is mailed) must be sent in an electronic format (preferably a PDF) to the contact provided. Please include the words "Molinari" and the "institution name" in the subject title. **Deadline:** June 15. **Contact:** Tracy Kitts, Foundation Coordinator: Phone: 321-710-3936; Email: AOF@aaoptom.org.

Awards are arranged alphabetically below their administering organizations

418 ■ Sheldon Wechsler and George Mertz Contact Lens Residency Awards *(Professional development, Advanced Professional/Award)*

Purpose: To promote the practice and development of the field of optometry by providing incentive and support to talented optometric residents who demonstrate a passion and commitment to practice, research, and education. **Focus:** Optometry. **Qualif.:** Applicant must be an optometrist continuing a contact lens residency program at a North-American school or college of optometry. **Criteria:** Applicants will be evaluated primarily on the basis of their educational background and their ability and potential as teachers, researchers and practitioners in the field of contact lenses. **Funds Avail.:** $2,750. **Duration:** Annual. **Number Awarded:** 2. **To Apply:** Applicants must submit a summary of the their education, research and teaching experience; description of the residency program and plans for the next academic year; one-page statement of the applicant's career goals; and three letters of reference. **Deadline:** June 8. **Contact:** Tracy Kitts, Foundation Coordinator; Phone: 321-710-3936; Email: aof@aaoptom.org.

419 ■ American Academy of Periodontology (AAP)

737 N Michigan Ave., Ste. 800
Chicago, IL 60611-6660
Ph: (312)787-5518
URL: www.perio.org
Facebook: www.facebook.com/PerioNews
Twitter: twitter.com/PerioNews

420 ■ American Academy of Periodontology Educator Scholarships *(Postdoctorate/Scholarship)*

Purpose: To provide financial relief to students intending to pursue a career as a full-time teacher at a U.S. periodontal program upon graduation from a U.S. periodontal postdoctoral training program. **Focus:** Dentistry. **Qualif.:** Applicants must be student members of the AAP who have been accepted into or are currently enrolled in a U.S. periodontal postdoctoral training program and who intend to enter full-time teaching in a U.S. program. **Criteria:** Applicants are evaluated based on merit and financial need. **Funds Avail.:** $25,000. **Duration:** Annual. **To Apply:** Applicants must submit completed application form; dental school transcripts; periodontal program transcripts; curriculum vitae; letter of nomination from the periodontal program director or the designated mentor; two letters of recommendation; and essay of approximately 1,000 words which addresses their commitment to education. **Deadline:** June 1. **Contact:** Robert Vitas, Executive Director, at bob@perio.org.

421 ■ American Academy of Periodontology Dr. D. Walter Cohen Teaching Fellowships *(Postdoctorate/Fellowship)*

Purpose: To assist third-year periodontal residents in launching their careers as educators. **Focus:** Dentistry. **Qualif.:** Applicants must be in the first three years of their full-time teaching employment as defined by the institution at a U.S. periodontal program or have accepted a full-time faculty position at a U.S. periodontal program; must be students or active members of American Academy of Periodontology (AAP). Individuals who have not yet begun working as educators but who present a letter stating they have accepted a full-time teaching position may also apply. **Criteria:** Applications will be reviewed by a Selection Committee appointed by the Foundation President. Finalists will be invited to attend a mandatory personal interview during the Annual Meeting. If applicants will reach the final level, Selection Committee will call writers of recommendation letters and individuals mentioned by name in the applicant's personal statements and/or application letters. **Funds Avail.:** $10,000. **Duration:** Annual. **To Apply:** Applicants must submit completed application form; dental school transcripts; periodontal program transcripts; curriculum vitae; letter of nomination from the periodontal chair or other appropriate individual from their employing institution; two letters of recommendation; and essay of approximately 1,000 words which addresses their commitment to education. **Deadline:** June 1. **Contact:** Robert Vitas, Executive Director, at bob@perio.org.

422 ■ Bud and Linda Tarrson Fellowships *(Professional development/Fellowship)*

Purpose: To support professionals in their teaching and research in periodontology. **Focus:** Dentistry. **Qualif.:** Applicants must be either full-time faculty members at the instructor or assistant level or part-time faculty members. They must be affiliated for 10 years or less with a degree-granting institution, and their career goal must be teaching and research in periodontology. **Criteria:** Applicants are evaluated based on their work on academic field. **Funds Avail.:** Maximum of $36,000 ($12,000 per year). **Duration:** Annual; up to three years. **To Apply:** Applicants must submit completed application form; letter of nomination; recommendations; curriculum vitae; and personal statement. **Deadline:** May 1. **Contact:** Robert Vitas, Executive Director, at bob@perio.org.

423 ■ American Academy in Rome

7 E 60 St.
New York, NY 10022-1001
Ph: (212)751-7200
Fax: (212)751-7220
E-mail: info@aarome.org
URL: www.aarome.org

424 ■ Rome Prize *(Doctorate, Graduate/Prize, Award)*

Purpose: To foster the pursuit of advanced research and independent study in the fine arts and humanities. **Focus:** Arts; Humanities. **Qualif.:** Applicants must be U.S. citizens at the time of application. U.S. citizens and foreign nationals who have lived in the United States for three years may apply for the National Endowment for the Humanities post-doctoral fellowships. Graduate students in the humanities may apply for pre-doctoral fellowships. **Criteria:** Selection will be based on the applicant's achievements and the potential for future development. Jurors will consider the quality of submitted application materials and what interviews reveal about an applicant's past achievements and future goals. **Funds Avail.:** Up to $5,000 each. **Duration:** Annual. **Number Awarded:** 30. **To Apply:** Applicants may visit the website to get the online application. **Deadline:** November 1.

425 ■ American Acne and Rosacea Society (AARS)

201 Claremont Ave.
Montclair, NJ 07042

Awards are arranged alphabetically below their administering organizations

Ph: (973)783-4575
Fax: (973)783-4576
Free: 888-744-3376
E-mail: info@aarsmember.org
URL: www.acneandrosacea.org/site.php

426 ■ American Acne and Rosacea Society Mentorship Grant *(Professional development/Grant)*

Purpose: To assist young dermatologists to become leaders and experts in the field by acquiring academic skills which may not be available at their training institutions. **Focus:** Dermatology. **Qualif.:** Applicants must be dermatology residents, fellows, and recent graduates (within 5 years) of U.S. dermatology residency; and the sponsor of the applicants must be a member of the AARS. **Criteria:** Selection will be based on the committee's criteria.

Funds Avail.: $3,000. **Duration:** Annual. **To Apply:** Interested applicants must provide a short discussion of the aims and relevance of the project. The discussion should state what specific goals they hopes to achieve with the mentorship experience and the expected duration of mentorship. Academic/leadership potential of the applicants must be demonstrated either from the applicants' application or department chair's support letters. **Deadline:** December 31.

427 ■ American Antiquarian Society (AAS)
185 Salisbury St.
Worcester, MA 01609-1634
Ph: (508)755-5221
Fax: (508)753-3311
E-mail: library@americanantiquarian.org
URL: www.americanantiquarian.org
Facebook: www.facebook.com/American.Antiquarian
Twitter: www.twitter.com/AmAntiquarian

428 ■ AAS-American Historical Print Collectors Society Fellowships *(Doctorate/Fellowship)*

Purpose: To support research using prints. **Focus:** United States studies. **Qualif.:** Applicants must be enrolled in doctoral degree of accredited institutions or universities. **Criteria:** Recipients are selected based on: significance or importance of the project; appropriateness of the proposed study to AAS collections.

Funds Avail.: No specific amount. **Duration:** Annual. **To Apply:** Applicants must fill out the online application form. **Deadline:** January 15.

429 ■ AAS-American Society for Eighteenth Century Studies Fellowships *(Postdoctorate/Fellowship)*

Purpose: To enable scholars to spend an uninterrupted block of time doing research in the AAS library. **Focus:** General studies/Field of study not specified. **Qualif.:** Applicants must be ABD graduate or postdoctoral students, holding the PhD or equivalent degree at the time of the application. **Criteria:** Recipients are selected based on: significance or importance of the project; appropriateness of the proposed study to the AAS collections.

Funds Avail.: $1,850 per month or $1,350 per month including housing in the society's fellows' residence. **Duration:** One to two months. **To Apply:** Applicants must fill out the online application form. **Deadline:** January 15. **Contact:** Email: academicfellowships@mwa.org.

430 ■ AAS Fellowships for Creative and Performing Artists and Writers *(Professional development/Fellowship, Award)*

Purpose: To improve the ways in which an understanding of history is communicated to the American people. **Focus:** Culture; Filmmaking; History, American; Journalism; Performing arts; Writing. **Qualif.:** Applicants must have work for the general public which produces imaginative, non-formulaic works dealing with pre-twentieth century American history. **Criteria:** Recipients are selected based on the quality of performed task.

Funds Avail.: $1,850 stipend; (Room fees range from $700 to $500 per month.). **Number Awarded:** 3. **To Apply:** Applicants must provide a cover sheet; two letters of reference; a current resume including a listing of any awards, scholarship, or grant received; a statement of not more than five-typed, double spaced pages briefly summarizing the applicants educational and professional background and goals, describing the research for the project including readings in primary and secondary sources, and indicating the nature of the research program proposed for the AAS fellowship; ten copies of representative samples of previous works must included for the distribution of the committee. **Deadline:** October 5.

431 ■ AAS National Endowment for the Humanities Long-Term Fellowships *(Postdoctorate/Fellowship)*

Purpose: To enable scholars to spend an uninterrupted block of time doing research in the AAS library. **Focus:** Humanities. **Qualif.:** Applicants must have completed their formal professional training; maybe foreign nationals who have been residents in the United States for at least three years immediately preceding the application deadline. Applicants must have received a PhD within the last 3 years. **Criteria:** Recipients are selected based on: significance or importance of the project; appropriateness of the proposed study to the AAS collections.

Funds Avail.: No specific amount. **Duration:** 4 to 12 months. **To Apply:** Applicants must fill out the online application form. **Deadline:** January 15.

432 ■ AAS-Northeast Modern Language Association Fellowships *(Undergraduate/Fellowship)*

Purpose: To enable scholars to spend an uninterrupted block of time doing research in the AAS library. **Focus:** History, American. **Qualif.:** Applicants are not necessarily members of NEMLA. **Criteria:** Recipients are selected based on: significance or importance of the project; appropriateness of the proposed study to the AAS collections.

Funds Avail.: $1,850 per month or $1,350 per month including housing in the society's fellows' residence. **To Apply:** Applicants must fill out the online application form. **Deadline:** January 15. **Contact:** Email: academicfellowships@mwa.org.

433 ■ Stephen Botein Fellowships *(Doctorate/Fellowship)*

Purpose: To enable scholars to spend an uninterrupted block of time doing research in the AAS library. **Focus:** Culture; History, American. **Qualif.:** Applicants must be enrolled in doctoral degree of accredited institution or universities; must be engaged in scholarly research and writing including doctoral dissertation in any field of American history and culture. **Criteria:** Recipients are selected based on: significance or importance of the project; appropriateness of the proposed study to the AAS collections.

Awards are arranged alphabetically below their administering organizations

Funds Avail.: $1,850 per month or $1,350 per month including housing in the society's fellows' residence. **Duration:** Annual. **To Apply:** Applicants must fill out the online application form. **Deadline:** January 15. **Contact:** Email: academicfellowships@mwa.org.

434 ■ ACLS Frederick Burkhardt Residential Fellowships *(Other/Fellowship)*

Purpose: To support individuals for their research projects in humanities and related social sciences. **Focus:** Humanities; Social sciences. **Qualif.:** Applicants must be recently tenured humanists; must be employed in a tenured position at a degree granting academic institution in the United States. **Criteria:** Recipients are selected based on the quality of the proposal and required qualifications.

Funds Avail.: $75,000 cash plus funds for research costs and related scholarly activities of up to $5,000 and for relocation up to $2,000. **Duration:** Annual; One academic year. **To Apply:** Applicants must visit the website for the online fellowship application system. Applicants must submit no more than ten pages, double-spaced proposal; no more than three pages bibliography; no more than two pages publications list; three reference letters. Applicants must provide an institutional statement. **Deadline:** September 23.

435 ■ Jenny d'Héricourt Fellowships *(Doctorate/Fellowship)*

Purpose: To assist individuals to do a research on any topic supported by the collections of the Society. **Focus:** Culture; History; Literature. **Qualif.:** Applicants must hold a PhD and residents of France. **Criteria:** Selection will be based on the committee's criteria.

Funds Avail.: 1,800 Euros. **Duration:** Annual; one to two months. **Number Awarded:** 1. **To Apply:** Applicants must complete the application form online and must submit the following materials: current CV; description of the proposed research project (no longer than two double-spaced pages); one-page bibliography of relevant secondary literature; list of other sources of funding for the project; two letters of recommendation.

436 ■ The "Drawn to Art" Fellowships *(Doctorate/Fellowship)*

Purpose: To enable scholars, advanced graduate students and others to spend an uninterrupted block of time doing research in the AAS library. **Focus:** Art; Culture. **Qualif.:** Applicants must be enrolled in doctoral degree of accredited institution or universities. **Criteria:** Recipients are selected based on: significance or importance of the project; appropriateness of the proposed study to the AAS collections.

Funds Avail.: $1,850 per month or $1,350 per month including housing in the society's fellows' residence. **To Apply:** Applicants must fill out the online application form. **Deadline:** January 15. **Contact:** Mr. Paul Erickson, academicfellowships@mwa.org.

437 ■ The Christoph Daniel Ebeling Fellowships *(Postdoctorate, Postgraduate/Fellowship)*

Purpose: To enable scholars and advanced graduate students to spend an uninterrupted block of time doing research in the AAS library. **Focus:** United States studies. **Qualif.:** Applicants must be scholars in American Studies doing dissertation or rehabilitation research at universities in Germany. **Criteria:** Recipients are selected based on: significance or importance of the project; appropriateness of the proposed study to the AAS collections.

Funds Avail.: No specific amount. **Duration:** One or two months. **To Apply:** Applicants must fill out the online application form. **Deadline:** January 15.

438 ■ Hench Post-Dissertation Fellowship *(Postdoctorate/Fellowship)*

Purpose: To provide scholars with time and resources to extend research and/or to revise the dissertation for publication. **Focus:** Art history; History; Literature; Music; Political science; United States studies. **Qualif.:** A minimum of twelve-month fellowship for scholars no more than three years beyond receipt of their doctorate. Intended to provide the recipient with time and resources to extend research and revise the dissertation written for publication. Anything relevant to the society's library collections and programmatic scope of American history and culture through 1876 is eligible. Applicants must come from such fields as history, literature, American studies, political science, art history, music history, and others relating to America. **Criteria:** Recipients are selected based on: appropriateness of the project to the AAS collections and interests; likelihood that the revised dissertation will make a highly significant books.

Funds Avail.: $35,000. **Duration:** Annual. **To Apply:** Applicant must fill out the on-line application form. **Deadline:** October 15. **Remarks:** Established in 1998.

439 ■ Lapides Fellowships in Pre-1865 Juvenile Literature and Ephemera *(Graduate, Postdoctorate/Fellowship)*

Purpose: To support projects examining the creative, artistic, cultural, technological, or commercial aspects of American juvenile literature and ephemera produces between the Puritan Era and the Civil War. **Focus:** Culture; History; Literature. **Qualif.:** Applicants must be postdoctoral scholars or graduate students at work on doctoral dissertations. **Criteria:** Selection will be based on the committee's criteria.

Funds Avail.: $1,850. **Duration:** Annual; 1 to 2 months. **To Apply:** Applicants must complete the application form online and must submit the following materials: current CV; description of the proposed research project (no longer than two double-spaced pages); one-page bibliography of relevant secondary literature; list of other sources of funding for the project; two letters of recommendation. **Deadline:** January 15. **Contact:** Cheryl McRell, Program Administrator at cmcrell@mwa.org.

440 ■ Jay and Deborah Last Fellowships *(Doctorate/Fellowship)*

Purpose: To support research on American art, visual culture, or other projects that will make substantial use of graphic materials as primary sources. **Focus:** Art; Culture. **Qualif.:** Applicants must be enrolled in doctoral degree of accredited institution or universities. **Criteria:** Recipients are selected based on: significance or importance of the project; appropriateness of the proposed study to the AAS collections.

Funds Avail.: No specific amount. **Duration:** One, two or three months. **To Apply:** Applicants must fill out the online application form. **Deadline:** January 15.

441 ■ The Legacy Fellowships *(Doctorate/Fellowship)*

Purpose: To enable scholars, advanced graduate students and others to spend an uninterrupted block of time doing research in the AAS library. **Focus:** Culture; History,

Awards are arranged alphabetically below their administering organizations

American. **Qualif.:** Applicants must be enrolled in doctoral degree of accredited institution or universities; must be engaged in scholarly research and writing including doctoral dissertation in any field of American history and culture. **Criteria:** Recipients are selected based on: significance or importance of the project; appropriateness of the proposed study to the AAS collections.

Funds Avail.: $1,850 per month or $1,350 per month including housing in the society's fellows' residence. **Duration:** Annual. **To Apply:** Applicants must fill out the online application form. **Deadline:** January 15. **Contact:** Mr. Paul Erickson, academicfellowships@mwa.org.

442 ■ Barbara L. Packer Fellowships *(Doctorate, Postdoctorate/Fellowship)*

Purpose: To support individuals engaged in scholarly research and writing related to the Transcendentalists in general. **Focus:** Culture; History; Literature. **Qualif.:** Applicants must be doctoral or postdoctoral scholars. **Criteria:** Applicants will be selected based on the scholarly qualifications, the scholarly significance or importance of the project, and the appropriateness of the proposed study to the Society's collections.

Funds Avail.: $1,350 - $1,850. **Duration:** Monthly. **To Apply:** Interested applicants may contact the Society for the application process and other information. **Deadline:** January 15. **Contact:** academicfellowships@mwa.org.

443 ■ Kate B. and Hall J. Peterson Fellowships *(Doctorate/Fellowship)*

Purpose: To enable scholars to spend an uninterrupted block of time doing research in the AAS library. **Focus:** Culture; History, American. **Qualif.:** Applicants must be enrolled in doctoral degree of accredited institution or universities; must be engaged in scholarly research and writing including doctoral dissertation in any field of American history and culture. **Criteria:** Recipients are selected based on: significance or importance of the project; appropriateness of the proposed study to the AAS collections.

Funds Avail.: $1,850 per month or $1,350 per month including housing in the society's fellows' residence. **Duration:** One, two or three months. **To Apply:** Applicants must fill out the online application form. **Deadline:** January 15. **Contact:** Email: academicfellowships@mwa.org.

444 ■ The Reese Fellowships *(Doctorate/Fellowship)*

Purpose: To enable scholars, advanced graduate students and others to spend an uninterrupted block of time doing research in the AAS library. **Focus:** United States studies. **Qualif.:** Applicants must be enrolled in doctoral degree of accredited institution or universities. **Criteria:** Recipients are selected based on: significance or importance of the project; appropriateness of the proposed study to the AAS collections.

Funds Avail.: $1,850 per month or $1,350 per month including housing in the society's fellows' residence. **To Apply:** Applicants must fill out the online application form. **Deadline:** January 15. **Contact:** Mr. Paul Erickson, academicfellowships@mwa.org.

445 ■ Justin G. Schiller Fellowships *(Doctorate, Postdoctorate/Fellowship)*

Purpose: To support research from any disciplinary perspective on the production, distribution, literary content, or historical context of American children's books to 1876. **Focus:** Culture; History. **Qualif.:** Applicants must be doctoral or postdoctoral scholars. **Criteria:** Selection will be based on the committee's criteria.

Funds Avail.: $1,850 per month. **Duration:** Annual; One to two months. **To Apply:** Applicants must complete the application form online and must submit the following materials: current CV; description of the proposed research project (no longer than two double-spaced pages); one-page bibliography of relevant secondary literature; list of other sources of funding for the project; two letters of recommendation. **Deadline:** January 15. **Contact:** Cheryl McRell, Program Administrator at cmcrell@mwa.org.

446 ■ The Joyce Tracy Fellowships *(Doctorate/Fellowship)*

Purpose: To enable scholars, advanced graduate students and others to spend an uninterrupted block of time doing research in the AAS library. **Focus:** Culture; History, American. **Qualif.:** Applicants must be enrolled in doctoral degree of accredited institution or universities; must be engaged in scholarly research and writing including doctoral dissertation in any field of American history and culture. **Criteria:** Recipients are selected based on: significance or importance of the project; appropriateness of the proposed study to the AAS collections.

Funds Avail.: $1,850 per month or $1,350 per month including housing in the society's fellows' residence. **To Apply:** Applicants must fill out the online application form. **Deadline:** January 15. **Contact:** Mr. Paul Erickson, academicfellowships@mwa.org.

447 ■ American Art Therapy Association (AATA)
4875 Eisenhower Ave., Ste. 240
Alexandria, VA 22304
Ph: (703)548-5860
Fax: (703)783-8468
Free: 888-290-0878
E-mail: info@arttherapy.org
URL: www.arttherapy.org
Facebook: www.facebook.com/
  TheAmericanArtTherapyAssociation
Twitter: twitter.com/ArtTherapyOrg

448 ■ American Art Therapy Association Anniversary Scholarships *(Graduate/Scholarship)*

Purpose: To encourage the growth of the profession by rewarding excellence and enabling access to information and resources for the members who are selected by the Scholarship Committee. **Focus:** Art therapy. **Qualif.:** Applicants must be student members with a current GPA of at least 3.25 who can demonstrate financial need and acceptance or enrollment in an American Art Therapy Association approved graduate art therapy program. **Criteria:** Selection shall be based on the aforementioned qualifications and compliance with the application details.

Funds Avail.: No specific amount. **Duration:** Annual. **To Apply:** Applicants must submit a completed application form. Other documents to be submitted are: financial form; letters of recommendation; financial information forms; and, documentation indicating acceptance or enrollment in an AATA-approved art therapy program. Please do not bind or staple documents or include extraneous information with the application.

449 ■ Myra Levick Scholarships *(Graduate/Scholarship)*

Purpose: To promote education in art therapy. **Focus:** Art therapy. **Qualif.:** Applicant must be an active student

Awards are arranged alphabetically below their administering organizations

member of AATA; accepted or attending an AATA approved graduate art therapy program; have a GPA of 3.0; and demonstrated financial need. **Criteria:** Selection is based on the application.

Funds Avail.: $900. **Number Awarded:** 1. **To Apply:** Applicant must submit a completed application form; one official academic transcript; two academic or work-related, signed letters of recommendation; student financial information form; one essay (maximum of two pages, double spaced, typewritten) including the biography and stating the future role as an art therapist; and documentation of acceptance or enrollment in an American Art Therapy Association approved art therapy program. **Deadline:** April 1.

450 ■ Rawley Silver Awards for Excellence (Graduate/Scholarship)

Purpose: To promote education in art therapy. **Focus:** Art therapy. **Qualif.:** Applicant must be an active student member of AATA; accepted or attending an AATA approved graduate art therapy program; and have an excellent academic record. **Criteria:** Selection is based on the application.

Funds Avail.: $900. **Number Awarded:** 1. **To Apply:** Applicants must submit a completed application form together with official academic transcripts; two academic/work related letters of recommendations; student financial information form; a two-page essay (biography); and proof of acceptance in an AATA approved graduate art therapy program. Submit the original and four more copies of the complete required application packets. **Deadline:** April 1.

451 ■ Rawley Silver Research Award (Postgraduate, Postdoctorate/Award)

Purpose: To support an art therapy research project by a voting member of the American Art Therapy Association. **Focus:** Art therapy. **Qualif.:** Applicants must be voting members of AATA and may only submit one proposal. **Criteria:** Reviewers will evaluate proposals considering the following: qualifications of the researcher, quality of the proposed research, and plan for dissemination.

Funds Avail.: $750 - $1,000. **Duration:** Annual. **To Apply:** Applicants must have a completed research, not yet initiated research but approved by a review board, or a research in progress; must have a proposal including the rationale, methodology, ethical and multicultural considerations, plan for dissemination, and reference list; and a completed application form. The proposal document may be a maximum of four pages, and must include one copy with author identification and one copy without author identification or any other identifying information such as location of study. Proposal must be submitted via email in A.P.A. style. **Deadline:** April 1. **Contact:** American Art Therapy Association, at the above address or Email: info@arttherapy.org.

452 ■ American Association for the Advancement of Science (AAAS)

1200 New York Ave. NW
Washington, DC 20005
Ph: (202)326-6400
URL: www.aaas.org
Facebook: www.facebook.com/AAAS.Science
LinkedIn: www.linkedin.com/company/aaas
Twitter: twitter.com/AAAS

Awards are arranged alphabetically below their administering organizations

453 ■ AAAS Mass Media Science and Engineering Fellowship (Undergraduate, Graduate, Postdoctorate/Fellowship, Award)

Purpose: To increase public understanding of science and technology. **Focus:** Engineering; Media arts; Science technologies. **Qualif.:** Applicants must be enrolled as college or university students (graduate, doctoral, or upper level undergraduates) or within one year of a completed degree in the physical, biological, geological, health, engineering, computer, or social sciences or mathematics in order to apply. The Fellowship is open to international students who are already studying in the United States and who hold visas that allow them to receive payment for work during the summer. Such is also open to US citizens studying abroad, as long as they can pay their way back into the US for the Fellowship. **Criteria:** Recipients will be selected based on telephone interview made by the AAAS staff.

Funds Avail.: $500/week. **Duration:** Annual; Up to 10 weeks. **Number Awarded:** 15-20. **To Apply:** Applicants must fill out the online application form. They must also submit the following: a copy of resume including honors, awards and relevant activities; one brief sample of their writing (two-to-three pages on any subject written in terms appropriate for the general public); journal articles; three letters of recommendation; transcript of the undergraduate and graduate work. **Deadline:** January 15. **Contact:** Dione L. Rossiter, Project Director, at drossite@aaas.org; phone:202-306-6645.

454 ■ AAAS Science and Technology Policy Fellowships (Professional development/Fellowship)

Purpose: To provide professional development opportunity to individuals interested in learning about the science-policy interface while applying their scientific and technical knowledge and analytical skills to the federal policy realm. **Focus:** Engineering; Science; Science technologies. **Qualif.:** Applicants must: hold a doctoral level science degree or a master's in engineering; have solid scientific and technical credentials and three references; exhibit integrity, problem-solving ability, flexibility and leadership qualities; be U.S. citizens who are committed to serving society; have good verbal and written communication skills; and, not federal employees. AAAS seeks candidates from a broad array of backgrounds and a diversity of geographic, disciplinary, gender, and ethnic perspectives as well as disability status. Fellows represent the spectrum of career stages - from recent doctoral graduates to faculty on sabbatical and retired scientists, and sectors - from academia and industry to nonprofit organizations. **Criteria:** Selection will be based on the aforesaid qualifications and compliance with the application process.

Funds Avail.: $75,000 to $100,000 per year. **Duration:** Annual. **To Apply:** Applicants must provide a profile indicating name and contact information; candidates' data; candidates' statement providing the qualifications for the fellowship and career goals; reasons for applying for the fellowship. They must also submit curriculum vitae; extracurricular activities; and references including three recommendation letters. **Remarks:** Established in 1973. **Contact:** AAAS Science & Technology Policy Fellowships at fellowships@aaas.org.

455 ■ American Association of Advertising Agencies (AAAA)

1065 Avenue of Americas, 16th Fl.
New York, NY 10018
Ph: (212)682-2500

E-mail: research@aaaa.org
URL: www.aaaa.org/Pages/default.aspx
Facebook: www.facebook.com/aaaaorg
LinkedIn: www.linkedin.com/company/american-association-of-advertising-agencies

456 ■ ANA Multicultural Excellence Scholarship Fund (MAIP) (Graduate, Undergraduate/Internship)

Purpose: To provide scholarships to MAIP interns upon completion of the internship program. **Focus:** Advertising. **Qualif.:** Applicants must be undergraduate and graduate students; must be African Americans, Asian Americans, Hispanic Americans and Native Americans. **Criteria:** Recipients will be selected based on submitted materials.

Funds Avail.: No specific amount. **To Apply:** Applicants must contact the AAAA office to clarify guidelines and required procedures. **Remarks:** Established in 2003. **Contact:** American Association of Advertising Agencies, at the above address.

457 ■ Bill Bernbach Diversity Scholarships (Undergraduate/Scholarship)

Purpose: To provide financial assistance to creatively talented, culturally diverse students seeking an education in copywriting, art direction and design at designated colleges and portfolio schools. **Focus:** Advertising. **Qualif.:** Applicants must be African Americans, Native Americans, or Hispanic Americans; must be full-time students in their final year at one of the following 4A's participating portfolio schools: Miami Ad School, Ad Center at Virginia Commonwealth University, Portfolio Center, Creative Circus, University of Texas at Austin, Art Center of Design at Pasadena; must be U.S. citizens or permanent residents; must hold a bachelor's degree from an accredited college or university. **Criteria:** Awards will be given to those applicants who best meet the criteria.

Funds Avail.: $5,000. **Duration:** Annual. **Number Awarded:** 5. **To Apply:** Applicants must contact the tuition office of the participating schools. **Deadline:** May 30. **Remarks:** Established in 1998. **Contact:** American Association of Advertising Agencies, at the above address, or Email: bbscholarship@ny.ddb.com.

458 ■ Operation JumpStart Scholarships (Graduate/Scholarship)

Purpose: To provide financial assistance to aspiring multicultural art directors and copywriters. **Focus:** Advertising. **Qualif.:** Applicants must be registered as incoming graduates or portfolio school students at one of six designated OJS III portfolio schools: Miami Ad School, Ad Center at Virginia Commonwealth University, Portfolio Center, Creative Circus, University of Texas at Austin, or Pratt Institute; either be full-time juniors at one of two designated OJS III colleges (Minneapolis College of Art and Design or the Art Center College of Design at Pasadena); must be African Americans, Asian Americans, Hispanic Americans, Native Americans, multiracial or multiethnic; must show a creative talent and promise; must be U.S. citizens or permanent residents. **Criteria:** Awards will be given to those applicants who best meet the criteria and demonstrated financial need.

Funds Avail.: $10,000. **Duration:** Annual. **To Apply:** Applicants must request an application form from the aforementioned schools. **Remarks:** Established in 1998. **Contact:** American Association of Advertising Agencies, at the above address.

459 ■ American Association of Anatomists (AAA)
9650 Rockville Pke.
Bethesda, MD 20814-3999
Ph: (301)634-7910
Fax: (301)634-7965
E-mail: info@anatomy.org
URL: www.anatomy.org
Facebook: www.facebook.com/Anatomists
Twitter: www.twitter.com/anatomymeeting

460 ■ AAA Postdoctoral Fellowship Program (Postdoctorate/Fellowship)

Purpose: To provide salary support to AAA members working in any aspect of biology relevant to the anatomical sciences. **Focus:** Biology. **Qualif.:** Applicants must be current AAA members and are expected to remain members for the duration of the fellowship. Candidates should be working on a research project encompassing any aspect of biology that is relevant to the anatomical sciences. Approaches can include (but are not limited to) cellular, molecular, genetic or histological techniques, and/or emphasize development, evolution, morphology or human health. Candidate should have all requirements of doctoral degree completed at the time of submission of fellowship application. **Criteria:** Selection will be based on the committee's criteria.

Funds Avail.: $20,000. **Duration:** Annual. **Number Awarded:** 1. **To Apply:** Applications should be submitted electronically. Each application must include the following: curriculum vitae, NIH four-page format; four-page research proposal with the formats given by AAA; letter from the department chair stating that the candidates have completed all requirements of doctoral degrees at the time of application; evidence of an application to their institution's IACUC or IRB, as appropriate; letter describing other salary and research support available to the postdoc in the sponsor laboratory; and, three letters of recommendation, including one from the sponsor and one written by an AAA member (who may also be the sponsor). **Deadline:** June 1.

461 ■ American Association for Applied Linguistics (AAAL)
Bldg. 14, Ste. 100
1827 Powers Ferry Rd.
Atlanta, GA 30339
Ph: (678)229-2892
Fax: (678)229-2777
Free: 866-821-7700
E-mail: info@aaal.org
URL: www.aaal.org

462 ■ Graduate Student Travel Grants (Doctorate, Master's/Grant)

Purpose: To support graduate student members by helping them to attend the Association's Annual Meeting. **Focus:** Linguistics; Travel and tourism. **Qualif.:** Applicants must be student members of AAAL at the time of application and enrolled in a university Master's or Ph.D. program in applied linguistics or a related field. **Criteria:** The primary consideration in granting the award is the academic merit of the student's proposal submitted to the conference.

Funds Avail.: No specific amount. **Duration:** Annual. **To Apply:** Graduate students who are eligible to apply will be notified by the conference chair and may submit their ap-

Awards are arranged alphabetically below their administering organizations

plication once they have confirmed their intention to attend the conference and arrange for their academic advisor to send a letter of recommendation. Specific information about the application submission process will be distributed to the students eligible to apply. **Deadline:** December 1. **Remarks:** Established in 1996.

463 ■ American Association of Blacks in Energy (AABE)
1625 K St. NW, Ste. 405
Washington, DC 20006
Ph: (202)371-9530
Fax: (202)371-9218
E-mail: info@aabe.org
URL: www.aabe.org
Facebook: www.facebook.com/AABENational
Twitter: twitter.com/_AABE

464 ■ American Association of Blacks in Energy Scholarships (Undergraduate/Scholarship)

Purpose: To help increase the number of African Americans and other misrepresented minorities in energy-related fields. **Focus:** Energy-related areas. **Qualif.:** Applicants must have at least an overall "B" academic average and a "B" average in mathematics and science courses; must be graduating high school seniors who have applied to one or more accredited colleges/universities; must be planning to major in engineering, mathematics, or the physical sciences; must demonstrate financial need; and must be members of one of the underrepresented minority groups in the sciences and related areas of technology. **Criteria:** Applicants are evaluated based on criteria designed by the organization's National Scholarship Committee.

Funds Avail.: $3,000. **Duration:** Annual. **To Apply:** Applicants must submit completed AABE application form; high school transcript; two letters of reference (one academic, one non-academic); and parent(s) or guardian(s) official verification of income (copy of signed tax return for previous year or W2 or a verified FAFSA form). **Deadline:** March 4. **Remarks:** The scholarships are awarded among students from the AABE chapters.

465 ■ American Association of Bovine Practitioners (AABP)
3320 Skyway Dr., Ste. 802
Opelika, AL 36801
Ph: (334)821-0442
Fax: (334)821-9532
E-mail: aabphq@aabp.org
URL: www.aabp.org
Facebook: www.facebook.com/AABPmembers

466 ■ AABP Amstutz Scholarships (Undergraduate/Scholarship)

Purpose: To support American and Canadian veterinary students. **Focus:** Veterinary science and medicine. **Qualif.:** Applicant must be enrolled in a college of veterinary medicine located in Canada and United States or the two Caribbean colleges of veterinary medicine accredited by the AVMA Council on Education and whose students undergo their fourth year clinical training primarily at US and Canadian schools, Ross University and St. George's University; and must be in second year of the veterinarian curriculum at the time of the application. **Criteria:** Applicants will be evaluated for the overall interest of the applicant in bovine practice, involvement in bovine medicine and bovine-related extracurricular activities, ability to express oneself in writing, and insightful answers to the essay questions.

Funds Avail.: $7,500. **Duration:** Annual. **Number Awarded:** Varies. **To Apply:** Applicants must submit a current cumulative school GPA and class rank; he/she must submit a biographical account that outlines the background of the cattle industry; an applicant must prepare a one-page or less list factors that stimulate the interest and involvement in bovine medicine and extracurricular activities; 500 characters or less description of plans following graduation from veterinary school; 2500 characters or less answer about the experiences that stimulate in pursuing a career in food/animal/bovine medicine; 2500 characters or less answering the question "What is our role today and in the future as a veterinarian in shaping public perception of food animal welfare in United States or Canada?"; an essay about the plans in using the money acquired from the award if considered; applicant must submit two letters of recommendation from either veterinarian or faculty members regarding the applicant's worthiness for the award. **Deadline:** May 31.

467 ■ AABP Bovine Veterinary Student Recognition Awards (Undergraduate/Scholarship)

Purpose: To provide awards to 3rd and/or 4th year veterinary students who are interested in dairy and/or beef veterinary medicine. **Focus:** Veterinary science and medicine. **Qualif.:** Applicant must be a student member of AABP enrolled at Veterinary Colleges and Schools during the 2nd year and/or 3rd year. **Criteria:** Award committee will evaluate the student's application based on interest in bovine medicine, work experience, academic and professional experience, career goals, and recommendation letter.

Funds Avail.: $1,500. **Number Awarded:** 14. **To Apply:** Applicant must fill out the on-line application form which outlines the background, work, and academic experience, primary interests in veterinary medicine, career goals and providing the name of a faculty sponsor. **Deadline:** March 15.

468 ■ AABP Education Grants (Undergraduate/Grant)

Purpose: To help expand the skills and knowledge base of the cattle production medicine practitioner. **Focus:** Veterinary science and medicine. **Qualif.:** Applicants must be AABP members who are incoming senior students or new graduates attending an accredited veterinary college advanced education program or another AABP approved continuing education endeavor. **Criteria:** Selection shall be based on the aforesaid qualifications and compliance with the application details.

Funds Avail.: $1,000. **Duration:** Annual. **To Apply:** Applicants must submit the following: a completed AABP Education Grant application form, including a letter of intent outlining the applicants' career goals (students) or current job description (recent graduates), prior experience with food animal production medicine, and goals for the advanced education program; brief course outline; letter of recommendation from a faculty member (who is also an AABP member) of the veterinary school the applicants graduated from or are currently enrolled in; and, a signed hold harmless agreement release form which must be emailed to the AABP office. Education Grant applications must be made online via the AABP website. Applications

Awards are arranged alphabetically below their administering organizations

can be edited once submitted up to the deadline date. **Deadline:** April 15.

469 ■ AABP Student Externship Program
(Undergraduate/Scholarship)

Purpose: To support veterinary students. **Focus:** Veterinary science and medicine. **Qualif.:** Applicant must be admitted to a veterinary school and completed his/her externship of at least two weeks in bovine practice; must be a student and AABP member; must be a full-time veterinary student at an American, Canadian, or Caribbean veterinary college or be a newly admitted freshman at such college. **Criteria:** Scholarship will be given to students who have an interest in food animal practice but who may not have extensive exposure to bovine practice or cattle industry; awards will be given to underclassmen and to externships where the practice provides some tangible support for the student, such as room or board.

Funds Avail.: $1000. **To Apply:** Applicant must complete the online application form including the dates of expected externship, practice where it is to take place, projected cost support to be provided by the practice and amount of aid requested, and student's career interests, prior experience with food producing animals, and goals for the externship; must provide a letter from the practice describing what the students will be doing; a letter from a faculty member at the student's veterinary college; and must submit a completed release agreement. **Deadline:** April and October 1.

470 ■ American Association for Cancer Research (AACR)
615 Chestnut St., 17th Fl.
Philadelphia, PA 19106-4406
Ph: (215)440-9300
Fax: (215)440-9313
Free: 866-423-3965
E-mail: aacr@aacr.org
URL: www.aacr.org
Facebook: www.facebook.com/aacr.org
Twitter: twitter.com/aacr

471 ■ AACR Scholar-in-Training Awards: Other Conferences and Meetings *(Graduate, Postdoctorate, Professional development/Grant)*

Purpose: To enhance the education and training of early career scientists by providing financial support for their attendance at AACR conferences and meetings. **Focus:** Medical research. **Qualif.:** Applicants must be graduate medical students, postdoctoral fellows or physicians-in-training. Associate members will receive priority for these awards. **Criteria:** Selection will be based on the qualitative rating of the abstract and the letter of recommendation.

Funds Avail.: No specific amount. **Duration:** Annual. **To Apply:** Applicants must submit an abstract for the conference and be listed as the presenter of the abstract; must submit a letter of recommendation from their program supervisor or department head that describes the quality of their clinical and/or experimental work.

472 ■ American Association for Cancer Research Minority Scholar Awards *(Graduate/Award)*

Purpose: To provide opportunities and support for research training and career development of minorities and for involving minority institutions in cancer research, research training, education and outreach. **Focus:** Oncology. **Qualif.:** Candidates must be full-time graduate students, medical students, residents, clinical or postdoctoral fellows, or junior faculty members; must be in the minority groups that have been defined by the National Cancer Institute as being traditionally underrepresented in cancer and biomedical research; must be citizens or permanent residents of the United States or Canada. **Criteria:** Selection will be based on the committee's criteria.

Funds Avail.: No specific amount. **To Apply:** Applicants may visit the website for the online application or to download a copy of the application. **Deadline:** December. **Contact:** AACR Minority Scholar in Cancer Research Awards, American Association for Cancer Research; Email: micr@aacr.org.

473 ■ Thomas J. Bardos Science Education Awards for Undergraduate Students *(Undergraduate/Award)*

Purpose: To inspire young science students to enter the field of cancer research and provide a unique educational opportunity for these students in the development of their careers in science. **Focus:** Science. **Qualif.:** Candidates must be full-time, third-year undergraduate students majoring in science; must be AACR members at the time of application. Student membership is free of charge. **Criteria:** Selection will be based on the committee's criteria.

Funds Avail.: No specific amount. **Duration:** 2 years. **To Apply:** Applicants may visit the website for the online application or to download a copy of the application. **Contact:** Membership Department at the above address or email at scienceeducation@aacr.org.

474 ■ Minority-Serving Institution Faculty Scholar Awards *(Doctorate/Award)*

Purpose: To increase the scientific knowledge base of faculty members at Minority-Serving Institutions, and to encourage them and their students to pursue careers in cancer research. **Focus:** Oncology. **Qualif.:** Candidates must have completed doctoral studies or clinical fellowships and hold full-time faculty status at an institution designated as a Minority-Serving Institution; must have acquired doctoral degrees in fields relevant to cancer research; must be citizens or permanent residents of the United States or Canada. **Criteria:** Selection will be based on the committee's criteria.

Funds Avail.: No specific amount. **To Apply:** Applicants may visit the website for the online application or to download a copy of the application. **Contact:** AACR Minority-Serving Institution Faculty Scholar in Cancer Research Awards, American Association for Cancer Research; Email: micr@aacr.org.

475 ■ Women in Cancer Research Scholar Awards *(Graduate, Postdoctorate/Award)*

Purpose: To support Women in Cancer Research scientists-in-training and presenters of meritorious scientific papers. **Focus:** Oncology. **Qualif.:** Applicants must be members of Women in Cancer Research; must be full time scientists-in-training who are graduate students, medical students, residents, clinical fellows or equivalent, or postdoctoral fellows; may be travelling from within the United States or abroad. There are no citizenship or residency requirements; must be first authors on abstracts submitted for consideration for presentation at the AACR Annual Meeting. **Criteria:** Selection will be based on the committee's criteria.

Funds Avail.: $1,000. **Duration:** Annual. **To Apply:** Eligible individuals should check the appropriate box in the Online Abstract Submission System and must submit their abstracts by the deadline. **Contact:** AACR-WICR Scholar Award Program, American Association for Cancer Research; Email: wicr@aacr.org.

476 ■ American Association of Candy Technologists (AACT)

711 W Water St.
Princeton, WI 54968
Ph: (920)295-6969
Fax: (920)295-6843
E-mail: aactinfo@gomc.com
URL: www.aactcandy.org

477 ■ AACT John Kitt Memorial Scholarship
(Undergraduate/Scholarship)

Purpose: To support the education of students involved in confectionery technology. **Focus:** Biology; Chemistry; Food science and technology. **Qualif.:** Applicants must be sophomores, juniors or seniors majoring in food science, chemical science, biological science, or related field at an accredited four-year college or university in North America. They must also have a GPA of 3.0, and be interested in confectionery technology. **Criteria:** Selection shall be based on the aforementioned qualifications and compliance with the application details.

Funds Avail.: $5,000 (two $2,500 installments). **Duration:** Annual. **To Apply:** Applicants must submit a completed application form together with a letter of recommendation; copy of college transcript; and a list of academic activities, experience, other activities, honors and awards, and a short statement of personal and professional goals. **Deadline:** April 1. **Contact:** The Warrell Corp., Att'n: Kevin Silva, 1250 Slate Hill Rd. Camp Hill, Pennsylvania; Email: kevins@warrellcorp.com.

478 ■ American Association of Colleges of Nursing (AACN)

1 Dupont Cir. NW, Ste. 530
Washington, DC 20036
Ph: (202)463-6930
Fax: (202)785-8320
E-mail: info@aacn.nche.edu
URL: www.aacn.nche.edu
Facebook: www.facebook.com/AACNursing
LinkedIn: www.linkedin.com/company/american-association-of-colleges-of-nursing
Twitter: twitter.com/AACNursing

479 ■ AfterCollege/AACN Nursing Scholarships
(Graduate, Undergraduate/Scholarship)

Purpose: To support students who are seeking a baccalaureate, master's or doctoral degree in nursing. **Focus:** Nursing. **Qualif.:** Applicants must be enrolled at an AACN member institution seeking baccalaureate, master's or doctoral degree in nursing; and have a GPA of 3.25 or higher. **Criteria:** Special consideration will be given to students in a graduate program with the goal of becoming a nurse educator; completing an RN to BSN or MSN program; and those enrolled in an accelerated nursing program.

Funds Avail.: $2,500. **Duration:** Quarterly. **Number Awarded:** 1. **To Apply:** Applicants are advised to visit the website for the application forms. **Deadline:** March 31; June 30; September 30; December 31. **Remarks:** The scholarship is being bestowed by AACN, in partnership with AfterCollege, Inc.

480 ■ Johnson and Johnson/AACN Minority Nurse Faculty Scholars *(Graduate/Scholarship)*

Purpose: To provide financial support to graduate nursing students from minority backgrounds who agree to teach in a school of nursing after graduation. **Focus:** Nursing. **Qualif.:** Applicants must be: enrolled full-time in an accredited graduate nursing program; U.S. citizens, permanent residents, refugees or qualified immigrants; be from underrepresented minority that are committed to teach nursing in the United States after successful completion of graduate studies. **Criteria:** Applications will be judged based on following criteria: 1) ability to contribute in nursing education field; 2) commitment to nursing education career in United States which includes mentoring, recruiting, and retaining underrepresented minority nurses; 3) ability to work with a mentor/advisor throughout the award period; 4) leadership potential; 5) development of goals which reflect education, research, and professional involvement; 6) quality, feasibility and innovativeness of the proposed research; and 7) school has made commitment to the academic career and professional development.

Funds Avail.: $18,000 each. **Duration:** Annual. **Number Awarded:** 5. **To Apply:** Applicants must submit the following: an application data sheet; three letters of reference with signatures; one-page letter (no more than 500 words) describing the personal and professional interest in nursing education; budget outline; Dean's Commitment statement; letter of acceptance to a Nursing school; original transcript of records; outlined program of study; curriculum vitae; goal identification form; and applicant's signature form. **Deadline:** May 1. **Contact:** Marta Okoniewski, Email: mokoniewski@aacn.nche.edu.

481 ■ American Association of Colleges of Osteopathic Medicine (AACOM)

5550 Friendship Blvd., Ste. 310
Chevy Chase, MD 20815-7231
Ph: (301)968-4100
Fax: (301)968-4101
E-mail: aacomas@aacom.org
URL: www.aacom.org/home
Facebook: www.facebook.com/AACOM-The-American-Association-of-Colleges-of-Osteopathic-Medicine-49933236324
Twitter: twitter.com/aacommunities

482 ■ AACOM Scholar in Residence Program
(Professional development/Scholarship)

Purpose: To provide opportunities for college of osteopathic medicine faculty to engage in focused study and develop their competencies in medical education as a scholar-in-residence at the AACOM headquarters in Chevy Chase, Maryland. **Focus:** Medicine, Osteopathic. **Qualif.:** Applicants must be nominated by their dean and, together with the dean and department chair, develop a proposal for study that will enhance both their own college's medical education and provide leadership to the greater osteopathic medical education community. **Criteria:** Selection shall be based on the aforementioned qualifications and compliance with the application details.

Awards are arranged alphabetically below their administering organizations

Funds Avail.: No specific amount. **Duration:** Quarterly. **To Apply:** Applicants must complete and electronically submit the application provided at the program website. **Deadline:** March 31; June 30; September 30; December 31. **Contact:** Luke Mortensen, PhD, AACOM Vice President for Medical Education; Phone: 301-948-4143; Email: meded@aacom.org.

483 ■ American Association of Colleges for Teacher Education (AACTE)

1307 New York Ave. NW, Ste. 300
Washington, DC 20005-4721
Ph: (202)293-2450
Fax: (202)457-8095
E-mail: aacte@aacte.org
URL: aacte.org
Facebook: www.facebook.com/AACTE
LinkedIn: www.linkedin.com/company/american-association-of-colleges-for-teacher-education
Twitter: twitter.com/aacte

484 ■ AACTE Outstanding Book Awards (Other/Recognition)

Purpose: To recognize as exemplary books that make a significant contribution to the knowledge base of educator preparation or of teaching and learning with implications for educator preparation. **Focus:** Teaching. **Criteria:** Recipients will be selected based on submitted published book. Priority will be given to works that address the four areas and eight action items identified in AACTE's research agenda and whose focus and style of presentation are consistent with the principles set forth in Research Standards and Guidelines.

Funds Avail.: Amount not specified. **Duration:** Annual. **To Apply:** Candidates must submit a letter of nomination addressing the criteria, seven copies of the book, brief professional biography at least 150 words and must include the contact information of the author(s) or the publisher's representative(s).

485 ■ AACTE Outstanding Dissertation Awards (Doctorate/Award)

Purpose: To recognize excellence in doctoral dissertation research that contributes to the knowledge base of teacher education or teaching and learning with implications for teacher education. **Focus:** Teaching. **Qualif.:** Candidates must be individuals receiving a doctorate in education from January 1 through June 30. **Criteria:** Evaluation will be based on quality of submitted research. Priority will be given to works that address the four areas and eight action items identified in AACTE's research agenda and whose focus and style of presentation are consistent with the principles set forth in Research Standards and Guidelines.

Funds Avail.: $1,000. **Duration:** Annual. **To Apply:** Candidates must submit an information sheet providing the dissertation adviser's contact information; letter of support from the dissertation's adviser and explaining the importance of dissertation's question, appropriateness and completeness of the study design and significance of the analysis and interpretations; a copy of dissertation's abstract and narrative (not to exceed 10 pages, double-spaced) that answers questions stated on the online application procedures.

486 ■ David G. Imig Awards for Distinguished Achievement in Teacher Education (Other/Recognition)

Purpose: To recognize distinguished achievements in the field of policy or research in teacher education. **Focus:** Teaching. **Qualif.:** Nominees need not be from an AACTE member institution or otherwise affiliated with AACTE, although there should be an obvious connection between the achievement recognized and AACTE's mission and work. **Criteria:** Recipients will be selected based on qualifications and submitted materials.

Funds Avail.: No specific amount. **Duration:** Annual. **To Apply:** Nominees must complete the online entry form. Nomination must contain a letter of recommendation describing how nominees fulfill the selection criteria and must include their curriculum vitae. **Contact:** American Association of Colleges for Teacher Education, at the above address.

487 ■ Margaret B. Lindsey Award for Distinguished Research in Teacher Education (Other/Award, Recognition)

Purpose: To support and recognize individuals whose research over the last decade has made a major impact on the field of teacher education. **Focus:** Teaching. **Qualif.:** Candidates must be individuals or groups conducting research together, who have made exceptional contributions to research in the field of educator preparation. **Criteria:** The selection criteria include evidence of distinguished achievement in the following: research in the field of educator preparation for at least a decade; publications in peer-reviewed professional journals; presentations at AACTE professional meetings; widely cited contributions with practical applications for the field.

Duration: Annual. **To Apply:** All entries must be made through AACTE's online submissions site. Application materials must include: a 300-word biographical sketch of the nominee; one or more letters of support describing how the nominee fulfills the selection criteria; curriculum vitae. **Deadline:** October 12.

488 ■ Edward C. Pomeroy Awards for Outstanding Contributions to Teacher Education (Other/Recognition)

Purpose: To recognize outstanding contributions to teacher education, either through distinguished service to the teacher education community through the development and promotion of outstanding practices in teacher education at the collegiate, state or national level. **Focus:** Teaching. **Qualif.:** Nominees must be individuals who have made exceptional contributions to AACTE, to a national or state organization involved in teacher education, or to persons responsible for the development of exemplary teacher education initiatives. **Criteria:** Award will be given to individuals who best meet the qualifications.

Funds Avail.: No specific amount. **Duration:** Annual. **To Apply:** Nominators must visit the website for the online nomination process. **Deadline:** October 12.

489 ■ American Association of Critical-Care Nurses (AACN)

101 Columbia
Aliso Viejo, CA 92656-4109
Ph: (949)362-2000
Fax: (949)362-2020

Awards are arranged alphabetically below their administering organizations

E-mail: info@aacn.org
URL: www.aacn.org
Facebook: www.facebook.com/aacnface
Twitter: twitter.com/aacnme

490 ■ AACN Continuing Professional Development Scholarships *(Advanced Professional, Other/Scholarship)*

Purpose: To provide financial assistance to students who want to acquire knowledge and skills beyond traditional academic nursing education. **Focus:** Nursing. **Qualif.:** Applicants must be current active members of AACN at the time of application and throughout the term of the funded activity. **Criteria:** Selection will be based on how applicants would assess and articulate gaps in their own knowledge and skills; how they set professional learning goals on the basis of identified gaps; how they identify and evaluate learning opportunities that will move them toward achieving their goals; and how they present a budget of expenses for funding the proposed learning activity.

Funds Avail.: $3,000. **Duration:** Annual. **To Apply:** Applicants must submit a completed application form and curriculum vitae in a separate Word document or PDF file. **Contact:** AACN, at the above address or E-mail at scholarships@aacn.org.

491 ■ American Association of Endodontists (AAE)

211 E Chicago Ave., Ste. 1100
Chicago, IL 60611-2691
Ph: (312)266-7255
Fax: (312)266-9867
Free: 800-872-3636
E-mail: info@aae.org
URL: www.aae.org
Facebook: www.facebook.com/endodontists
Twitter: www.twitter.com/savingyourteeth

492 ■ Endodontic Educator Fellowship Award *(Graduate/Fellowship)*

Purpose: To recognize the critical role that endodontic educators play in strengthening their specialty and to address the need for more endodontic specialists to teach in dental schools. **Focus:** Dentistry. **Qualif.:** Applicant must be a citizen or hold a permanent residency card for the United States or Canada. Applicant must have been accepted for the next academic year or enrolled in the first or second year of an Advanced Specialty Education Program in Endodontics that is accredited by, or has a reciprocal agreement with, the Commission on Dental Accreditation of the American Dental Association; and has been accepted into a Master's, Doctorate or postdoctoral training program (the degree-granting institution must be an accredited U.S. university). **Criteria:** Fellows are selected based on: Meeting the eligibility requirements; accuracy of information on the application form; official transcripts from previous degree or certification programs; strength of recommendations; strength of the personal essay; degree of support from program director/dean of current institution; and strength of interview with committee members.

Funds Avail.: $50,000 per year. **Duration:** Annual; five years. **To Apply:** Applicants must submit a completed application form along with three letters of recommendation; a typed essay; official transcripts from all undergraduate and graduate programs; and a copy of the applicants' employment contract. **Deadline:** April 15. **Contact:** Alyson Hall, development coordinator, at ahall@aae.org.

493 ■ Endodontic Research Grants *(Graduate/Grant)*

Purpose: To inspire and support research and the genesis of new knowledge in endodontics. **Focus:** Dentistry. **Qualif.:** Applicants must: be students of an advanced specialty education program in endodontics at a dental school that is accredited by or has a reciprocal agreement with the Commission on Dental Accreditation of the American Dental Association; be faculty members or researchers in endodontology or related fields (microbiology, pathology and physiology) of a dental school that is accredited by or has a reciprocal agreement with the Commission on Dental Accreditation of the ADA; be active members of the AAE. Dental school faculty or research staffs who are not endodontists are strongly encouraged to include an endodontist as a consultant or co-investigator. Postgraduate students must be AAE members. **Criteria:** Applications are evaluated based on: significance of research and its relation to the AAE Research Priorities; scientific merit and potential for discovering new information; excellence of research design and statistical methods and probability of successful completion; extent to which the project has been previously funded; extent to which alternative funding sources were sought; and extent to which the research can lead to future innovations in clinical endodontics, or future research that is funded by national or federal funding agencies.

Funds Avail.: $500. **Duration:** Semiannual. **To Apply:** Applicants must submit a CD containing the application form and all proposal materials. **Deadline:** February 7 spring and August 15 fall.

494 ■ American Association of Equine Practitioners (AAEP)

4033 Iron Works Pky.
Lexington, KY 40511
Ph: (859)233-0147
Fax: (859)233-1968
Free: 800-443-0177
E-mail: aaepoffice@aaep.org
URL: www.aaep.org
Facebook: www.facebook.com/American-Association-of-Equine-Practitioners-128570532690
Twitter: twitter.com/AAEPHorseDocs

495 ■ AAEP/ALSIC Scholarships *(Undergraduate/Scholarship)*

Purpose: To advance the health and welfare of horses by promoting the discovery and sharing of new knowledge; to enhance awareness of the need to the targeted research; to educate the public; to expand fundraising opportunities; to facilitate cooperation among funding agencies. **Focus:** Veterinary science and medicine. **Qualif.:** Applicants must be senior veterinary students who have indicated a strong desire to pursue a career in equine medicine at schools nationwide. **Criteria:** Consideration will be given to students who have demonstrated leadership qualities in any of a variety of equine-related areas including, but not limited to, involvement with the AAEP, community organizations or equined industry programs.

Funds Avail.: $2,500. **Number Awarded:** 8. **To Apply:** An applicant must fill out the online application form. Applicants must attach completed AAEP/ALSIC Scholarship Program Cover Sheet; one essay, not to exceed 1,500 words that

Awards are arranged alphabetically below their administering organizations

answers the three questions, "Why do you plan to enter equined practice and what events and/or individuals influenced your decision?", "What characteristics do you possess that uniquely qualify?"; a curriculum vitae, not to exceed two pages; a 2-page curriculum vitae. Evaluation form must be completed by a clinical instructor familiar with the applicant's performance and the other evaluation form must be completed by an equine practitioner in private practice; a self-addressed, stamped postcard by the AAEP as confirmation of receipt. **Deadline:** October 1.

496 ■ AAEP Foundation Past Presidents' Research Fellowships *(Graduate, Professional development/ Scholarship)*

Purpose: To emphasize the importance of equine research, and reward a researcher for his or her contributions. **Focus:** Veterinary science and medicine. **Qualif.:** An applicant must: be a graduate of an AVMA-accredited school/college of veterinary medicine; be a current AAEP member; a graduate student or resident; and, have completed a doctorate or residency program within the past 2 years. **Criteria:** Scholarship Committee will evaluate application based on the potential for proposed research to contribute to equine veterinary medicine; sincere intent for long-term career in equine veterinary research; experience within horse industry; experience and activity in equine veterinary medicine; experience with equine research; academic performance; and based on the professional accomplishments before and after graduation.

Funds Avail.: $5,000. **Duration:** Annual. **Number Awarded:** 1. **To Apply:** An applicant must attach the complete filled out AAEP Research Fellow Cover Sheet; he/she must prepare a maximum one-page cover letter outlining long-term research intent, as well as how it will impact equine veterinary medicine and positively affect horse health; an applicant must include how the scholarship will help in doing the research; a maximum two-page scientific abstract and budget of the intent research project; an applicant must obtain a curriculum vitae, a completed evaluation form, a signed and sealed letter of recommendations; and an applicant must provide a self-addressed, stamped postcard to be returned as confirmation of receipt; an applicant must attend the AAEP Convention; he/she must provide information to AAEP for AAEP Foundation Publications such as biographical sketch, benefits of fellowship, impact of research result, **Remarks:** Established in 2006.

497 ■ American Association of Family and Consumer Sciences (AAFCS)
400 N Columbus St., Ste. 202
Alexandria, VA 22314
Ph: (703)706-4600
Fax: (703)706-4663
Free: 800-424-8080
E-mail: staff@aafcs.org
URL: www.aafcs.org
Facebook: www.facebook.com/AAFCSheadquarters/ ?ref=ts
Twitter: www.twitter.com/aafcs

498 ■ American Association of Family and Consumer Sciences Undergraduate Scholarships *(Undergraduate/Scholarship)*

Purpose: To encourage undergraduate study in family and consumer sciences and its subspecialties. **Focus:** Science.

Qualif.: Applicants must be citizens or permanent residents of the United States; must be planning to pursue or currently pursuing a degree in family and consumer sciences or its specialties at the undergraduate level on a full-time basis; must be currently enrolled in an undergraduate program that will continue into the coming academic year or have been admitted to an undergraduate program for the coming academic year; must be willing to commit themselves to meet the specific requirements of the scholarship for which they are applying. **Criteria:** Recipients are selected based on ability to pursue undergraduate study; experience in relation to preparation for study in proposed field; special recognition and awards; participation in professional/community organizations and activities; evidence of professional commitment and leadership; significance of proposed area of study to families and individuals; professional goals; written communication and evaluation of applicant's recommendations.

Funds Avail.: $5,000 scholarship and $1,000 membership support. **To Apply:** Applicants must complete the application form; must have maximum of three evaluators; must obtain official or unofficial copies of transcript; must mail five hard copies of labeled CDs of the completed application form. **Contact:** Awards and Governance Manager at RAYona@aafcs.org; or call Roxana at 703-706-4608.

499 ■ American Association for Hand Surgery (AAHS)
500 Cummings Ctr., Ste. 4550
Beverly, MA 01915
Ph: (978)927-8330
Fax: (978)524-8890
URL: www.handsurgery.org

500 ■ American Association for Hand Surgery Annual Research Awards *(Other/Award)*

Purpose: To foster creativity and innovation in basic and/or clinical research in all areas pertinent to hand surgery. **Focus:** Surgery. **Qualif.:** Applicants must be residents, fellows, therapists and AAHS members. **Criteria:** Applicants are selected according to the potential of their research project.

Funds Avail.: No specific amount. **Duration:** Annual. **To Apply:** Applicants must submit an application form plus seven copies of investigators' demographic information, description of research and curriculum vitae for each researcher.

501 ■ American Association on Health and Disability (AAHD)
110 N Washington St., Ste. 328-J
Rockville, MD 20850
Ph: (301)545-6140
Fax: (301)545-6144
URL: www.aahd.us
Facebook: www.facebook.com/aahdus
LinkedIn: www.linkedin.com/company/ aahd?trk=hb_tab_compy_id_2841080
Twitter: twitter.com/AAHD1

502 ■ AAHD Scholarships *(Graduate, Undergraduate/ Scholarship)*

Purpose: To support students aiming a higher education in the disability and health field. **Focus:** Disabilities; Health education; Public health. **Qualif.:** Applicant must be enrolled in undergraduate or graduate school; have a documented disability and must provide documentation; be a US citizen or legal resident living in the US; and enrolled in, or accepted by, an accredited US four year university or graduate school on a full-time basis. **Criteria:** Preference will be given to students majoring in public health, disability studies, health promotion or a field related to disability and health.

Funds Avail.: $1,000. **Duration:** Annual. **To Apply:** Applicant must submit a completed application form together with a personal statement (maximum 3 pages-double spaced), including brief personal history, educational/career goals, extra-curricular activities, and reasons why he/she should be selected by the AAHD Scholarship Committee; three letters of recommendation (one must be from a teacher or academic advisor); and an official copy of high school transcript as well as college transcript (if applicable). Applicant must agree to allow AAHD to use his/her name, picture and/or story in future scholarship materials. **Deadline:** November 15.

503 ■ American Association of Healthcare Administrative Management (AAHAM)
11240 Waples Mill Rd., Ste. 200
Fairfax, VA 22030
Ph: (703)281-4043
Fax: (703)359-7562
E-mail: info@aaham.org
URL: www.aaham.org
Facebook: www.facebook.com/AAHAMNational

504 ■ National AAHAM Scholarships
(Undergraduate/Scholarship)

Purpose: To provide educational scholarship to individual AAHAM members and their dependents. **Focus:** General studies/Field of study not specified. **Qualif.:** Applicants must be individuals who have been National AAHAM members for at least one year and have paid their current dues by March 31 of the year in which applications are submitted. **Criteria:** Applicants are judged based on the established criteria by the review and selection committee comprised of the Chairmen of the Board and the current chairs of the Education and Finance Committees.

Funds Avail.: $2,500 National AAHAM member ADVANCEMENT IN HEALTHCARE; $1,000 Member or Dependent of member of National AAHAM. **Duration:** Annual. **Number Awarded:** 2 for National AAHAM member ADVANCEMENT IN HEALTHCARE; 4 for Member or Dependent of member of National AAHAM. **To Apply:** Applicants must submit all the required application information. **Deadline:** May 31. **Contact:** Awards and Governance Manager at RAYona@aafcs.org; or call Roxana at 703-706-4608.

505 ■ American Association of Immunologists (AAI)
1451 Rockville Pke., Ste. 650
Bethesda, MD 20814
Ph: (301)634-7178
Fax: (301)634-7887
E-mail: infoaai@aai.org
URL: www.aai.org

506 ■ AAI Careers in Immunology Fellowship Program *(Graduate, Doctorate, Postdoctorate/Fellowship)*

Purpose: To support the career development of immunologists by providing AAI regular members with one year of salary support for an AAI trainee member in their labs. **Focus:** Immunology. **Qualif.:** Applicants must be AAI Regular members, in good standing, who have predoctoral or postdoctoral degrees. **Criteria:** Selection will be based on the Fellowship Review Committee's criteria.

Funds Avail.: Varies. **Duration:** Annual. **To Apply:** Applicants are required to provide the following in the application package: completed Careers in Immunology Fellowship Application (Please note that the Funding Confirmation Form page must be signed by the Department Chair/Dean); the PI's CV/NIH Biosketch; the trainees' Curriculum Vitae; documentation from your department that is signed by the student's Program or Department Chair and confirms that the trainee has passed the candidacy/qualifying exam (for predoctoral trainees only). **Deadline:** March 16. **Contact:** AAI Careers in Immunology Fellowship to fellowships@aai.org.

507 ■ AAI Public Policy Fellows Program (PPFP)
(Doctorate, Postdoctorate/Fellowship)

Purpose: To help AAI members, early in their careers, better understand the role of the President and Administration, Congress, and the National Institutes of Health in determining the policies that affect biomedical research; and to teach participants how best to advocate for, and help shape, these policies that guide their careers. **Focus:** Immunology; Public health. **Qualif.:** Applicants must have received their Ph.D., M.D., or equivalent within the previous 10 years in immunology or a related field; must be members in good standing of AAI; must be committed to a career in biomedical research; must have excellent interpersonal and communication skills; and must have interest in public policy as it relates to biomedical research. **Criteria:** Selection will be based on the committee's criteria.

Duration: Annual. **Number Awarded:** Up to 10. **To Apply:** Applicants must submit the following on or before the designated deadline of application: AAI PPFP application form; curriculum vitae; and two references from AAI members (regular members in good standing who do not serve on the AAI Council or AAI Committee on Public Affairs) using the PPFP recommendation form.

508 ■ American Association for the Improvement of Boxing (AAIB)
86 Fletcher Ave.
Mount Vernon, NY 10552-3319
Ph: (914)664-4571
Fax: (914)664-3164
E-mail: aaib@verizon.net
URL: www.aaib.org

509 ■ AAIB Scholarships *(Undergraduate/Scholarship)*

Purpose: To provide educational opportunities and financial assistance to young boxers who wish to obtain tertiary level education. **Focus:** General studies/Field of study not specified. **Qualif.:** Applicant must be: a high school senior who has accepted by an accredited college or university; and, a current or former amateur boxer. **Criteria:** Applicant will be evaluated in the following areas: athletics (awards, honors,

Awards are arranged alphabetically below their administering organizations

or achievements); academics (same as in the athletics); and, community involvement.

Funds Avail.: No specific amount. **Duration:** Annual. **To Apply:** Application form is available in the website. The applicant must also sign a waiver authorizing the school to release records to be reviewed by the Scholarship Committee. **Deadline:** May 1.

510 ■ American Association on Intellectual and Developmental Disabilities (AAIDD)
501 3rd St. NW, Ste. 200
Washington, DC 20001
Ph: (202)387-1968
Fax: (202)387-2193
URL: aaidd.org

511 ■ AAIDD Fellowship (Advanced Professional, Professional development/Fellowship)

Purpose: To give recognition to those active members of the Association who exhibited significant contributions to the organization. **Focus:** Disabilities; Mental retardation. **Qualif.:** Applicants must be AAIDD members who have had at least seven years of continuous, active membership in the Association. **Criteria:** Selection will be based on the committee's criteria.

Funds Avail.: No specific amount. **Duration:** Annual. **To Apply:** Applicants must fill-up completely the application form provided by the Association. Submit the finished application form and other supplemental materials to the designated contact person. **Deadline:** October 31. **Contact:** Maria Alfaro at maria@aaidd.org.

512 ■ American Association of Japanese University Women (AAJUW)
2164 Calmette Ave.
Rowland Heights, CA 91748
E-mail: president@aajuw.org
URL: www.aajuw.org

513 ■ AAJUW Scholarships (Graduate, Undergraduate/Scholarship)

Purpose: To assist the advancement of women in education. **Focus:** General studies/Field of study not specified. **Qualif.:** Applicants must: be female students enrolled in an accredited California college/university; have junior, senior or graduate standing by Fall; attend (at own expense) the award ceremony; be contributors to U.S.-Japan relations, cultural exchanges and the development of leadership in the area of their designated field. **Criteria:** Selection is based on the application materials submitted.

Funds Avail.: $2,000. **Duration:** Annual. **Number Awarded:** Varies. **To Apply:** Applicants must submit a completed application form together with the following: a current resume; official transcript for the past two years of study (sealed and sent directly by the college/university to AAJUW); two letters of recommendation (addressed to AAJUW); and the essay (maximum to 2 typewritten pages, double-spaced, 8 1/2 x 11). **Deadline:** September 30.

514 ■ American Association for Justice (AAJ)
777 6th St. NW, Ste. 200
Washington, DC 20001
Ph: (202)965-3500
Free: 800-424-2725
E-mail: help@justice.org
URL: www.justice.org
Facebook: www.facebook.com/JusticeDotOrg
LinkedIn: www.linkedin.com/company/american-association-for-justice
Twitter: twitter.com/JusticeDotOrg

515 ■ AAJ Trial Advocacy Scholarships (Undergraduate/Scholarship)

Purpose: To assist law students in furthering their studies. **Focus:** Law. **Qualif.:** Applicants must be second and third year AAJ law student members; must be enrolled in an ABA-accredited law school. **Criteria:** Scholarships are given to applicants who: exhibit an interest and proficiency of skills in trial advocacy; express a desire to represent victims; demonstrate a commitment and dedication to AAJ mission through involvement in an AAJ student chapter and minority caucus activities; and show financial need.

Funds Avail.: $3,000. **To Apply:** Applicants must submit resume; 500-word essay on how the applicants will meet the criteria; up to three recommendations from a faculty adviser, trial advocacy professor, Dean, AAJ member, or trial lawyer; and a completed form verifying applicant's student status. **Contact:** Email: education@justice.org.

516 ■ Mike Eidson Scholarships (Graduate, Undergraduate/Scholarship)

Purpose: To provide a support system of women lawyers to network, socialize, form professional relationships and develop female leadership for AAJ. **Focus:** Law. **Qualif.:** Applicants must be 3L (or rising 4L in a night program) female students who have demonstrated a commitment to a career as a plaintiffs lawyer or criminal defense lawyer, along with dedication to upholding and defending the principles of the Constitution, and to the concept of a fair trial, the adversary system, and a just result for the injured, the accused and those whose rights are jeopardized. **Criteria:** Selection will be based on the committee's criteria.

Funds Avail.: $5,000. **Duration:** Annual. **To Apply:** Applicants must contact the Association for the application process. **Deadline:** May 1. **Remarks:** Established in 2008.

517 ■ The Leesfield/AAJ Law Student Scholarships (Undergraduate/Scholarship)

Purpose: To assist law students in furthering their studies. **Focus:** Law. **Qualif.:** Applicants must be first and second year AAJ law student members. **Criteria:** Recipients are selected based on submitted application materials.

Funds Avail.: $2,500. **Duration:** Annual. **To Apply:** Applicants must submit resume; statement of financial need; 500-word written request substantiating the applicant's commitment to preserving the civil justice system; three recommendations from a faculty adviser, trial advocacy professor, dean AAJ member, or trial lawyer; and a completed form verifying applicant's student status. **Deadline:** May 1.

518 ■ American Association of Law Libraries (AALL)
105 W Adams St., Ste. 3300
Chicago, IL 60603
Ph: (312)939-4764
Fax: (312)431-1097
URL: www.aallnet.org

Awards are arranged alphabetically below their administering organizations

AMERICAN ASSOCIATION OF LAW LIBRARIES

519 ■ AALL Leadership Academy Grants *(Professional development/Grant)*

Purpose: To provide a forum for the exchange of ideas and information on academic law libraries and to represent its members interests and concerns within the Association. **Focus:** Law; Library and archival sciences. **Qualif.:** Applicants must be ALL-SIS members who are accepted into the AALL Leadership Academy and who have not received and used any ALL-SIS grants in the past. **Criteria:** Preference is given to newer members of ALL-SIS who are active participants in the ALL-SIS, AALL and/or AALL Chapters.

Funds Avail.: $1,000. **To Apply:** Applicants must submit a completed application packet, available at the website, to the Chair of the ALL-SIS Awards Committee. The application packet must include the following: completed application; two letters of recommendation commenting on your potential to contribute to ALL-SIS, AALL and the field of law librarianship, and addressing the applicant's financial need for the grant; personal statement; current resume.

520 ■ AALL Minority Leadership Development Award *(Graduate/Award)*

Purpose: To nurture leaders for the future, and introduce minority law librarians to leadership opportunities within the Association. **Focus:** Law; Library and archival sciences. **Qualif.:** Applicants must be: members of a minority groups as defined by current US government guidelines; have a strong academic record and have earned a Master's degree in Library/Information Science; have no more than 5 years of professional (post-MLS or post-JD) library or information service work experience; be current members of AALL at the time application is submitted; have been members of AALL for at least 2 years or have 2 years of full time, professional law library work experience; demonstrate leadership potential. **Criteria:** Selection will be based on the committee's criteria.

Funds Avail.: No specific amount. **Duration:** Annual. **To Apply:** Applicants must submit the application package containing the following: completed application form; current resume or curriculum vitae; three letters of recommendation from individuals who can evaluate their law library employment experience or relevant graduate education commenting on their present and potential contributions to AALL and the field of law librarianship; a brief essay on how belonging to a minority group has influenced their career to date and on how the profession benefits from encouraging the leadership development of law librarians from minority groups; a brief essay on what leadership means to them and how this grant will help them realize their personal leadership goals. **Deadline:** February 1. **Remarks:** Established in 2001.

521 ■ AALL Research Funds *(Professional development/Grant)*

Purpose: To fund one or more projects of value to those professions that create, disseminate or use legal and law-related information. **Focus:** Law; Paralegal studies. **Qualif.:** Applicants should have experience with research projects, and an understanding of the creation, dissemination and/or use of legal and law related information. Applicants may be individuals or partnerships. **Criteria:** Preference will be given to members of AALL, working individually or in partnership with others. Selection will be based on the following: the pertinence of the research question, the appropriateness of the research and the feasibility of the work plan; the intellectual significance of the project, including its potential contribution to scholarship in librarianship, law librarianship or legal fields, and the likelihood that it will encourage research in a new direction; the qualification, expertise and level of commitment of the project director, and appropriateness of chosen staff; the promise of quality, usefulness and impact on scholarship of any resulting research product; the potential for success of the project.

Funds Avail.: $5,000 each. **Duration:** Annual. **Number Awarded:** 1 or more. **To Apply:** Applicants must provide a resume and statement of their qualifications for carrying out the project. The AALL grant proposal cover sheet must accompany all applications. Applicants must submit two copies of the proposal to the Research Committee Chair. Grant recipients will submit their final report and project results by the scheduled date. The project proposal must: demonstrate significance and originality in the context of existing literature and research; propose appropriate strategies for conducting the research based on the topic or issue selected, including a plan for systematic analysis that will produce objective and reliable results; show feasibility to be completed within the established time frame and budget; include a preferred means of disseminating project results. **Deadline:** April 1; December 1. **Remarks:** An endowment established by LexisNexis.

522 ■ AALL Scholarships for Continuing Education Classes *(Postgraduate/Scholarship)*

Purpose: To provide financial assistance to individuals who wish to pursue courses related to law librarianship. **Focus:** Library and archival sciences. **Qualif.:** Applicants must be law librarians with a degree from an ALA-accredited library school or an ABA-accredited law school, who are registered in continuing education courses related to law librarianship. Applicants must also be AALL members. **Criteria:** Applicants who are permanent residents of United States and Canada will be given preference.

Funds Avail.: No specific amount. **Duration:** Annual. **To Apply:** Applicants must submit a completed application form; course description and registration; personal statement; and letters of recommendation.

523 ■ AALL Technical Services SIS Active Member Grant *(Professional development/Grant)*

Purpose: To cover the cost of registration and travel expenses to support attendance at AALL sponsored educational events related to technical services. **Focus:** Law. **Qualif.:** Applicants must be active members of TS-SIS who have participated in TS-SIS and AALL activities, financial need and have not received a TS-SIS sponsored grant in past five (5) years. **Criteria:** Selection will be based on the committees' criteria.

Funds Avail.: Up to $1,000. **To Apply:** Each applicant must submit a resume that includes current position and relevant previous positions and application form (32 KB Word version) which includes: evidence of professional involvement; estimate of expenses for attending the event; statement of how much financial support will be provided by the applicant's employer; brief statement (200 words maximum) explaining how attendance will help applicant achieve professional goals; two (2) reference letters supporting the application by individuals who are familiar with the applicant's work or the applicant's interest in professional development as a technical services law librarian. **Deadline:** March 22.

Awards are arranged alphabetically below their administering organizations

524 ■ AALL Technical Services SIS Experienced Member General Grant *(Professional development/ Grant)*

Purpose: To cover the cost of registration to support attendance at AALL-sponsored educational events related to technical services. **Focus:** Law. **Qualif.:** Applicants must be members of TS-SIS for six or more years, financial need and have the desire for professional engagement. **Criteria:** Preference will be given to individuals who have not previously attended an AALL-sponsored educational event.

Funds Avail.: No specific amount. **To Apply:** Each applicant must submit a resume that includes current position and relevant previous positions; application form (32 KB Word version) which includes: estimate of expenses for attending the event; statement of how much financial support will be provided by the applicant's employer; brief statement (200 words maximum) explaining how attendance will help applicant achieve professional goals and; two (2) reference letters supporting the application by individuals who are familiar with the applicant's work or the applicant's interest in professional development as a technical services law librarian. **Deadline:** March 22.

525 ■ AALL Technical Services SIS Leadership Academy Grant *(Professional development/Grant)*

Purpose: To provide financial assistance to librarians who might not otherwise be able to attend an AALL-sponsored workshop due to limited financial resources. **Focus:** Law. **Qualif.:** Applicants must be members of TS-SIS. **Criteria:** Selection will be based on the committees' criteria.

Funds Avail.: Up to $1,000. **Duration:** Biennial. **To Apply:** Each applicant must submit a resume that includes current position and relevant positions and application form (32 KB Word version) which includes: evidence of professional involvement; itemized estimate of transportation, lodging, meals, and/or registration expenses for attending the Academy; statement of how much financial support will be provided by the applicant's employer; brief statement (200 words maximum) connecting attendance at Academy with service to TS-SIS; indicate whether applicant will be unable to attend the Academy without funding from this grant. Also submit a copy of Leadership Academy application (no letters required) and copy of notification of acceptance into the Academy and one letter of recommendation.

526 ■ AALL Technical Services SIS Management Institute Grant *(Professional development/Grant)*

Purpose: To provide financial assistance to librarians who might not otherwise be able to attend an AALL-sponsored workshop due to limited financial resources. **Focus:** Law. **Qualif.:** Applicants must be members of TS-SIS. **Criteria:** Selection will be based on the committees' criteria.

Funds Avail.: Up to $1,000. **Duration:** Biennial. **To Apply:** Each applicant must submit a resume that includes current position and relevant positions and application form (32 KB Word version) which includes: evidence of professional involvement; itemized estimate of transportation, lodging, meals, and/or registration expenses for attending the Institute; statement of how much financial support will be provided by the applicant's employer; statement describing their interest in the Institute and financial need; indicate whether the applicant will be unable to attend the Institute without funding from this grant. Also submit a copy of registration confirmation for the institute and one letter of recommendation.

527 ■ AALL Technical Services SIS New Member General Grant *(Professional development/Grant)*

Purpose: To cover the cost of registration to support attendance at AALL-sponsored educational events related to technical services. **Focus:** Law. **Qualif.:** Applicants must be members of TS-SIS for five or fewer years, financial need and have the desire for professional engagement. Applicants must have not received a TS-SIS sponsored educational grant previously. **Criteria:** Preference will be given to individuals who have not previously attended an AALL-sponsored educational event.

Funds Avail.: No specific amount. **To Apply:** Each applicant must submit a resume that includes current position and relevant previous positions; application form (32 KB Word version) which includes: estimate of expenses for attending the event; statement of how much financial support will be provided by the applicant's employer; brief statement (200 words maximum) explaining how attendance will help applicant achieve professional goals and; two (2) reference letters supporting the application by individuals who are familiar with the applicant's work or the applicant's interest in professional development as a technical services law librarian. **Deadline:** March 22.

528 ■ ALL-SIS Conference of Newer Law Librarians Grants *(Professional development/Grant)*

Purpose: To promote participation by newer academic law librarians in AALL and the ALL-SIS. **Focus:** Law; Library and archival sciences. **Qualif.:** Recipients must be ALL-SIS members with demonstrated financial need and agree to become a member of the New Academic Law Librarians Meeting (NALLM)/Mentoring Committee for the year following the grant. **Criteria:** Grant recipients will be chosen, in large part, based on demonstrated financial need.

Funds Avail.: $500. **Number Awarded:** Two. **To Apply:** Interested applicants must submit the following: a current resume; two letters of recommendation from current or former teachers or employers that discuss your potential to contribute to the field of academic law librarianship and your need for the grant.

529 ■ FCIL Schaffer Grants for Foreign Law Librarians *(Professional development/Grant)*

Purpose: To provide financial assistance to ensure the presence and participation of a foreign librarian at the AALL Annual Meeting. **Focus:** Law; Library and archival sciences. **Qualif.:** Applicants must be law librarians or other professional working in the legal information field, who is currently employed in a country other than the United States. Applicants must be in a position of significant responsibility for the dissemination, preservation and/or organization of legal information. Applicants may be from any type of law library. An applicant who would not otherwise have the opportunity to attend the AALL Annual Meeting is invited and encouraged to apply. Applicants must have sufficient English proficiency to fully participate in the conference without an interpreter. **Criteria:** Applications will be evaluated on the basis of the law librarian's ability to add to the Association's knowledge of law, legal information and law librarianship from a foreign perspective. Preference will be given to an applicant from an under-represented country or region, to someone who demonstrates financial need or to an applicant who has never attended an AALL Annual Meeting.

Funds Avail.: $2,000. **Duration:** Annual. **Number Awarded:** 1. **To Apply:** Applicants must submit an Application Form and a resume of their professional qualifications.

Awards are arranged alphabetically below their administering organizations

The Application Form should be filled out as completely as possible. Simultaneous electronic submission of a completed Application and resume is preferred but not required. All documents should be in English and should be sent together either electronically or traditional mail. **Remarks:** Established in 2001. **Contact:** Sherry Leysen at leysen@chapman.edu.

530 ■ Government Documents Special Interest Section - Veronica Maclay Student Grants *(Master's/Grant)*

Purpose: To promote and enhance the value of law libraries to the legal and public communities, to foster the profession of law librarianship, and to provide leadership in the field of legal information. **Focus:** Law; Library and archival sciences. **Qualif.:** Applicants must be students currently enrolled in an ALA accredited library and information studies master's program. **Criteria:** Preference will be given to LIS students who demonstrate interest in government information and a career in law librarianship.

Funds Avail.: $1,250. **To Apply:** Applicants must submit a completed application and recommendation letter in electronic format.

531 ■ Alan Holoch Memorial Grants *(Professional development/Grant)*

Purpose: To assist individuals with travel or registration expenses for the American Association of Law Libraries Annual Meeting. **Focus:** Law; Library and archival sciences. **Qualif.:** Applicants must be members of the Social Responsibilities Special Interest Section at the time of the application. **Criteria:** Preference will be given to members of the LGBTIQ community and those who have not received this grant in the past.

Funds Avail.: No specific amount. **Duration:** Annual. **To Apply:** Applicants must submit a completed application together with one letter of recommendation from either an employer or a colleague or peer. Recommendations should be sought from those who are familiar with the applicants. **Deadline:** April 1. **Contact:** Email Jane Larrington at jlarrington@sandiego.edu.

532 ■ AALL/Wolters Kluwer Law & Business Grants *(Professional development/Grant)*

Purpose: To fund one or more projects of value to those professions that create, disseminate or use legal and law-related information. **Focus:** Law; Paralegal studies. **Qualif.:** Applicants should have experience with research projects, and an understanding of the creation, dissemination and/or use of legal and law related information. Applicants may be individuals or partnerships. **Criteria:** Preference will be given to members of AALL, working individually or in partnership with others. Selection will be based on the following: the pertinence of the research question, the appropriateness of the research and the feasibility of the work plan; the intellectual significance of the project, including its potential contribution to scholarship in librarianship, law librarianship or legal fields, and the likelihood that it will encourage research in a new direction; the qualification, expertise and level of commitment of the project director, and appropriateness of chosen staff; the promise of quality, usefulness and impact on scholarship of any resulting research product; the potential for success of the project.

Funds Avail.: No specific amount. **To Apply:** Applicants must provide a resume and statement of their qualifications for carrying out the project. The proposal must: demonstrate significance and originality in the context of existing literature and research; propose appropriate strategies for conducting the research based on the topic or issue selected, including a plan for systematic analysis that will produce objective and reliable results; show feasibility to be completed within the established time frame and budget; include a preferred means of disseminating project results. Applicants must submit two copies of the project proposal to the Research Committee Chair. **Deadline:** December 12. **Contact:** Paula Davidson, Director of Finance and Administration, American Association of Law Libraries; Email: pdavidson@aall.org.

533 ■ Marcia J. Koslov Scholarship *(Professional development/Scholarship)*

Purpose: To provide funding for members to attend live seminars and conferences presented by the Institute for Court Management, the Center for Legal and Court Technology, the Equal Justice Conference or other programs that provide continuing education for state, court or county law librarians. **Focus:** Law; Library and archival sciences. **Qualif.:** Candidates must be current members of AALL who serve as librarians in state, court or county libraries. **Criteria:** Selection will be based on the committee's criteria. Preference will be given to permanent residents of the United States and Canada.

Funds Avail.: No specific amount. **Duration:** Annual. **To Apply:** Candidates must provide the following information: submit a copy of the seminar or conference information, which provides detail as to the content, faculty and educational goals of the program. Be sure that it also provides the registration and/or other fees necessary for attendance; submit a statement explaining why the applicant wants to pursue continuing professional education and why the live seminar or conference they are interested in attending will meet their objectives. The statement should also summarize the applicant's primary duties, responsibilities and career goals. This statement will help gauge the fit between what the course offers and the benefits the applicant hopes to receive from attendance; submit a resume providing evidence of work experience, academic achievement and professional participation. **Deadline:** April 1. **Contact:** Email at membership@aall.org.

534 ■ Marla Schwartz Education Grant *(Graduate, Professional development/Grant)*

Purpose: To support newer law librarians and graduate students in library/information studies programs in their attendance at AALL-sponsored educational events related to technical services. **Focus:** Law; Library and archival sciences. **Qualif.:** Applicants must be newer law librarians and graduate students in library/information studies programs. **Criteria:** Selection will be based on the following: financial need; individuals who have not previously attended an AALL sponsored educational event; individuals who have not previously received a TS-SIS sponsored educational grant; new or student members of TS-SIS who have demonstrated potential for professional development or scholarly activity.

Funds Avail.: No specific amount. **Duration:** Annual. **To Apply:** Applicants must submit an application which includes: a resume that includes current position and relevant previous positions and application form (32 KB Word version) which includes: estimate of expenses for attending the event; statement of how much financial support will be provided by the applicants' employers; expected graduation date (for student applicants); brief statement (200 words maximum) explaining how attendance will help

Awards are arranged alphabetically below their administering organizations

applicants achieve professional goals; two (2) reference letters supporting the application by individuals who are familiar with the applicants' work or the applicants' interest in professional development as technical services law librarians. **Deadline:** March 22.

535 ■ Marla Schwartz Grants *(Professional development, Graduate/Grant)*

Purpose: To enable other law librarians to attend conferences. **Focus:** Law; Library and archival sciences. **Qualif.:** Applicants do not need to be members of either AALL or TS-SIS. Applicants must be new law librarians and graduate students in library/information studies programs. **Criteria:** Selection will be based on the following: financial need; individuals who have not previously attended an AALL sponsored educational event; individuals who have not previously received a TS-SIS sponsored educational grant; new or student members of TS-SIS who have demonstrated potential for professional development or scholarly activity; students in library science/information studies program who may not be a member of either AALL or TS-SIS, but who plan careers in technical services law librarianship.

Funds Avail.: No specific amount. **To Apply:** Applicants must submit an application which includes: current position and relevant previous positions; estimate of expenses for attending the event; statement of how much financial support will be provided by the applicant's employer; expected graduation date; maximum of 200 words brief statement explaining why the applicant is applying for the grant; two references supporting the application by individuals who are familiar with the applicant's work or the applicant's interest in professional development as a technical services law librarian. **Remarks:** Established to honor Marla's memory and achievements.

536 ■ George A. Strait Minority Scholarship *(Graduate/Scholarship)*

Purpose: To support the education of minority students who wish to pursue their career goals in law librarianship. **Focus:** Library and archival sciences. **Qualif.:** Applicants must be college graduates with meaningful law library experience; members of a minority group as defined by current U.S. Government guidelines; degree candidates in an ALA-accredited library school or an ABA-accredited law school; intend to have a career in law librarianship; must have at least one quarter/semester remaining after the scholarship is awarded. **Criteria:** Recipients are selected based on application materials submitted and financial need.

Funds Avail.: No specific amount. **Duration:** Annual. **To Apply:** Applicants must submit a completed application form; course description and registration; personal statement; and three letters of recommendation.

537 ■ American Association for Marriage and Family Therapy (AAMFT)
112 S Alfred St.
Alexandria, VA 22314-3061
Ph: (703)838-9808
Fax: (703)838-9805
E-mail: central@aamft.org
URL: www.aamft.org/iMIS15/AAMFT
Facebook: www.facebook.com/TheAAMFT
LinkedIn: www.linkedin.com/company/aamft
Twitter: twitter.com/theaamft

538 ■ AAMFT Minority Fellowships *(Doctorate, Graduate/Fellowship)*

Purpose: To provide financial assistance to graduate students who wish to pursue their doctoral degrees in Marriage and Family therapy. **Focus:** Family/Marital therapy. **Qualif.:** Applicants must be American citizens or permanent residents with permanent resident registration card; must demonstrate a strong commitment to a career in ethnic minority mental health and substance abuse services; must be enrolled full-time in a Marriage and Family Therapy doctoral program. **Criteria:** Selection is based on the submitted application materials and financial need.

Funds Avail.: No specific amount. **Duration:** Annual. **To Apply:** Applicants must complete the application form available in the website; must submit two essays containing the following: (1) specific training interest and career goals and (2) the choice of university, training program, and advisor/mentor, and how their choices relate to minority mental health or specific training interest and career goals; must provide a curriculum vita/resume, three recommendation letters, and transcript for any college/university attended for at least a full academic year within the last 10 years.

539 ■ American Association of Medical Assistants (AAMA)
20 N Wacker Dr., Ste. 1575
Chicago, IL 60606
Ph: (312)899-1500
Fax: (312)899-1259
Free: 800-228-2262
URL: www.aama-ntl.org

540 ■ Maxine Williams Scholarships *(Undergraduate/Scholarship)*

Purpose: To provide educational assistance to deserving medical assisting students. **Focus:** Medical assisting. **Qualif.:** Applicants must be currently enrolled in and have completed a minimum of one quarter or a semester at a postsecondary medical assisting program accredited by Commission on Accreditation of Allied Health Education Programs (CAAHEP); and have a GPA of 3.0 or higher. **Criteria:** Selection is based on academic ability and financial need.

Funds Avail.: $1,000. **Duration:** Annual. **To Apply:** Applicants must request an application form electronically, including applicants' name, accreditation code and program's institution name, city and state. **Deadline:** February 15. **Remarks:** Established in 1959.

541 ■ American Association of Neurological Surgeons (AANS)
5550 Meadowbrook Dr.
Rolling Meadows, IL 60008-3852
Ph: (847)378-0500
Fax: (847)378-0600
Free: 888-566-2267
E-mail: info@aans.org
URL: www.aans.org

542 ■ AANS Medical Student Summer Research Fellowships (MSSRF) *(Undergraduate/Fellowship)*

Purpose: To provide medical students the opportunity to participate in neurosurgical research through a summer fel-

Awards are arranged alphabetically below their administering organizations

lowship within an academic department of neurosurgery in the United States or Canada. **Focus:** Neurology. **Qualif.:** Applicants must be American or Canadian medical students who wish to spend summer working in a neurosurgical laboratory, mentored by a neurosurgical investigator sponsor who is a member of the American Association of Neurological Surgeons (AANS). **Criteria:** Applicants will be judged based upon the scientific merits of the proposed project, the credentials of the applicant, letters of reference, the preceptor statement and the support provided by the sponsoring program/laboratory. **Funds Avail.:** $2,500 each. **Duration:** Annual. **Number Awarded:** Up to 20. **To Apply:** Applicants must submit applications which include the curriculum vitae and bio-sketch, a description of future plans, and a statement of why this fellowship is of interest to the applicants and why it would be beneficial to them. **Deadline:** February 1. **Remarks:** The fellowship is made possible by AANS, in association with Neurosurgery Research and Education Foundation (NREF). **Contact:** NREF Development office at grants@nref.org.

543 ■ William P. Van Wagenen Fellowships
(Undergraduate/Fellowship)

Purpose: To provide financial support to a post neurosurgical resident for foreign travel for scientific enrichment, prior to beginning an academic career in neurological surgery. **Focus:** Neurology. **Qualif.:** Applicants must be senior neurosurgical residents whose country of study is different from the country of residence in approved neurosurgery residency programs and whose intent is to pursue an academic career in neurological surgery. **Criteria:** Candidates will be evaluated by the Van Wagenen Selection Committee based on the originality and quality of proposal, thoroughness with which the plan for a period abroad has been designed, personal attributes, and the quality of the research environment. **Funds Avail.:** $120,000. **Duration:** One year. **To Apply:** Applicants must submit a completed application together with the letter of reference. **Deadline:** October 1. **Contact:** Neurosurgery Research and Education Foundation (NREF) of the American Association of Neurological Surgeons 847378-0500 or email at nref@aans.org.

544 ■ American Association of Neuroscience Nurses (AANN)
8735 W Higgins Rd., Ste. 300
Chicago, IL 60631
Ph: (847)375-4733
Fax: (847)375-6430
Free: 888-557-2266
E-mail: info@aann.org
URL: www.aann.org

545 ■ Certified Neuroscience Registered Nurse Recertification Grant Program *(Other/Grant)*

Purpose: To provide financial assistance to those who are due to recertify their CNRN credential. **Focus:** Neuroscience; Nursing. **Qualif.:** Applicants must be certified neuroscience registered nurses (CNRN's) who are AANN members in good standing working in the neuroscience nursing field. **Criteria:** Selection will be based on the committee's criteria. **Funds Avail.:** No specific amount. **To Apply:** Applicants must provide one complete, typed copy of the grant application (handwritten are not accepted); 2 recommendation letters; and two personal essays. Applications must be received by the AMWF office. **Deadline:** August 13. **Contact:** grants@AMWF.org.

546 ■ Integra Foundation NNF Research Grant Awards *(Other/Grant)*

Purpose: To help neuroscience nurses implement evidence-based changes in their practice setting. **Focus:** Neuroscience; Nursing. **Qualif.:** Applicants must be North American neuroscience nurses. **Criteria:** Selection will be based on the applicants' ability to effect change. **Funds Avail.:** Up to and around $2,500. **Duration:** Annual. **Number Awarded:** 4. **To Apply:** Applicants may check the website for further information. **Deadline:** August 15.

547 ■ American Association of Nurse Practitioners (AANP)
Bldg. II, Ste. 450
911 S MoPac Expy.
Austin, TX 78711-2846
Ph: (512)442-4262
Fax: (512)442-6469
E-mail: admin@aanp.org
URL: www.aanp.org
Facebook: www.facebook.com/AmericanAssociationofNPs
Twitter: twitter.com/aanp_news

548 ■ Education Advancement Scholarships *(Graduate, Master's, Doctorate/Scholarship)*

Purpose: To provide education assistance to the members of the organization and to enhance their skills in the field of nursing. **Focus:** Nursing. **Qualif.:** Applicants must: be US citizens or permanent residents; not be members of or relatives of current AANP Board; not be employees or relatives of employee of any current Funders; not be staffs or related to AANP staffs; be scheduled to complete an eligible graduate NP program. Moreover, applicants must be AANP members currently enrolled in an accredited NP graduate program in pursuit of an advanced degree or certification. **Criteria:** Applicants will receive an email upon successful submission. As well, applicants may log in at any time to review the status of application. All applicants will be notified once awards have been determined. **Funds Avail.:** No specific amount. **To Apply:** Applicants must complete and submit the application form together with the following documents: copy of NP Program of Study; copy of most recent official transcript; current GPA; two professional references; current CV/resume.

549 ■ American Association of Occupational Health Nurses (AAOHN)
330 N Wabash Ave., Ste. 2000
Chicago, IL 60611
Ph: (312)321-5173
Fax: (312)673-6719
E-mail: info@aaohn.org
URL: www.aaohn.org
Facebook: www.facebook.com/AAOHN
Twitter: twitter.com/AAOHN

550 ■ AAOHN Professional Development Scholarships - Academic Study *(Graduate, Undergraduate/Scholarship)*

Purpose: To provide opportunities to further professional education for occupational and environmental health professionals. **Focus:** Occupational safety and health. **Qualif.:** Undergraduate applicants must be registered nurses enrolled full or part time in a nationally accredited school of nursing baccalaureate program and demonstrate an interest in, and commitment to, occupational and environmental health. Graduate candidates must be registered nurses enrolled full or part time in a graduate program that has application to occupational and environmental health. **Criteria:** Selection will be based on professional goals; two recommendation letters; impact of education on career.

Funds Avail.: $2,500 each. **Duration:** Annual. **Number Awarded:** 2. **To Apply:** Applicants must submit documentation of enrollment status. They must also submit a narrative of 500 words or less (double-spaced with 1-inch margins in 12-point font) addressing the aforementioned selection criteria. **Deadline:** November 15. **Contact:** aaohngov@aaohn.org.

551 ■ AAOHN Professional Development Scholarships - Continuing Education *(Other/Scholarship)*

Purpose: To support occupational and environmental health professionals in attending and successfully completing continuing education activities that will further their professional development and continued competence. **Focus:** Occupational safety and health. **Qualif.:** Candidates must be employed in the field of occupational and environmental health nursing and demonstrate an interest in, and commitment to, occupational and environmental health. They must also be members of AAOHN. **Criteria:** Selection will be based on career goals; developing skills; financial support; commitment; and letter of support.

Funds Avail.: $1,500 each. **Duration:** Annual. **Number Awarded:** Varies. **To Apply:** Applicants must submit a 500 word or less narrative (double-spaced with one-inch margins in 12-point font) addressing: career goals as they pertain to applicant's professional development and continued competence; how continuing education will further applicant's goals; need for financial support; commitment to ongoing continuing education activities. Applicants must also submit a letter of support from their employer/supervisor and copy of continuing education activity brochure or other printed information describing the activity. **Deadline:** November 15. **Contact:** aaohngov@aaohn.org.

552 ■ American Association for Paralegal Education (AAFPE)
222 S Westmonte Dr., Ste. 101
Altamonte Springs, FL 32714
Ph: (407)774-7880
Fax: (407)774-6440
E-mail: info@aafpe.org
URL: www.aafpe.org

553 ■ AAFPE LEX Scholarships *(Undergraduate/Scholarship)*

Purpose: To support students pursue their education in legal studies. **Focus:** Paralegal studies. **Qualif.:** Applicants must be full or part-time students who have a LEX chapter. **Criteria:** Applicants will be evaluated based on submitted materials.

Funds Avail.: $500 each. **Duration:** Annual. **Number Awarded:** Up to 5. **To Apply:** Candidates must submit a completed LEX application form with a 500-word essay; transcript of records showing at least "B" average; and a letter of recommendation from a faculty member in the paralegal or legal assistant studies department of the qualifying institution. **Deadline:** January 15. **Contact:** AAfPE LEX Scholarship, at the above address.

554 ■ American Association of People with Disabilities (AAPD)
2013 H St. NW, 5th Fl.
Washington, DC 20006
Ph: (202)521-4316
Free: 800-840-8844
E-mail: communications@aapd.com
URL: www.aapd.com
Facebook: www.facebook.com/DisabilityPowered
Twitter: twitter.com/AAPD

555 ■ NBCUniversal Tony Coelho Media Scholarships *(Undergraduate, Graduate/Scholarship)*

Purpose: To assist students with disabilities in pursuing a communications or media related degree. **Focus:** Disabilities. **Qualif.:** Applicants must be any 2nd year associate's degree students, undergraduate sophomores, juniors or seniors, or graduate students who self-identifies as individuals with any type of disability and are pursuing a communications or media related degree. **Criteria:** Selection will be based on the committee's criteria.

Funds Avail.: $5,625. **Number Awarded:** 4. **To Apply:** Applicants must submit the following requirements: application form in word or in PDF format; resume; unofficial transcript; one letter of recommendation from a professor, academic advisor or mentor; and two essays. Applicants must write a 300 to 350 word essay on the following topics: "what inspired you to pursue a communications or media-related degree?" and "how will you use your degree to positively impact the disability community?". **Contact:** scholarship@aapd.com.

556 ■ American Association of Physicists in Medicine (AAPM)
1631 Prince St.
Alexandria, VA 22314
Ph: (571)298-1300
Fax: (571)298-1301
E-mail: 2016.aapm@aapm.org
URL: www.aapm.org
Facebook: www.facebook.com/AAPM.org

557 ■ AAPM Diversity Recruitment through Education and Mentoring Program (MUSE) *(Undergraduate/Fellowship)*

Purpose: To expose minority undergraduate university students to the field of medical physics by performing research or assisting with clinical service at a U.S. institutions. **Focus:** Physics. **Qualif.:** Applicants must have completed at least 2 years of undergraduate studies, but shall not have graduated; must be U.S. citizens, permanent residents, or eligible to live and work in the U.S.. Non-citizens and non-permanent residents must provide evidence at the time of application (e.g. visas and permits issued by INS) that they are authorized to work in the USA during the period of the fellowship. **Criteria:** Preference will be made to applicants who have declared a major or are eligible to declare a major in physics, engineering, or other science, which requires mathematics at least through differential equations and junior level courses in modern physics/quantum mechanics and electricity and magnetism or equivalent courses in engineering sciences. **Funds Avail.:** $4,000. **Duration:** Annual; 10 weeks. **To Apply:** Applicants must complete the AAPM-provided student application and all required supplementary information. **Contact:** Jacqueline Ogburn, Education Manager; Phone: 301-209-3394; E-mail: jackie@aapm.org.

558 ■ AAPM Fellowships for Graduate Study in Medical Physics *(Graduate/Fellowship)*

Purpose: To support students pursuing graduate studies leading to a doctoral degree in Medical Physics. **Focus:** Physics. **Qualif.:** Applicants must be graduates of an undergraduate program in physics or equivalent majors (engineering-physics, math-physics, or nuclear engineering or applied physics) from an accredited university or college in North America; have an undergraduate GPA of greater than 3.5; and must have submitted an application for graduate study to one of the accredited programs with subsequent acceptance. **Criteria:** Selection is based on the submitted application and materials. **Funds Avail.:** $13,000/year plus tuition support not exceeding $5,000/year. **Duration:** two years. **To Apply:** Applicants must submit a completed application form. **Deadline:** April 15. **Contact:** Jackie Ogburn at 301-209-3394 or jackie@aapm.org.

559 ■ AAPM Summer Undergraduate Fellowships *(Undergraduate/Fellowship)*

Purpose: To provide opportunities for undergraduate university students to gain experience in medical physics by performing research in a medical physics laboratory or assisting with clinical service at a clinical facility. **Focus:** Mathematics and mathematical sciences; Physics. **Qualif.:** Applicants must: have completed at least 2 years of undergraduate studies, but shall not have graduated; have declared a major or be eligible to declare a major in physics, engineering, or other science, which requires mathematics at least through differential equations and junior level courses in modern physics/quantum mechanics and electricity and magnetism or equivalent courses in engineering sciences; be U.S. citizens, permanent residents, or eligible to live and work in the U.S.. Non-citizens and non-permanent residents must provide evidence at the time of application (e.g. visas and permits issued by INS) that they are authorized to work in the USA during the period of the fellowship. **Criteria:** Selection is based on the submitted application and materials. **Funds Avail.:** $4,000. **Duration:** Annual; 10 weeks during the summer academic period. **To Apply:** Applicants must submit a completed application form and materials. **Deadline:** February 1.

560 ■ RSNA/AAPM Fellowships for Graduate Study in Medical Physics *(Graduate/Fellowship)*

Purpose: To support students pursuing graduate studies leading to a doctoral degree in Medical Physics. **Focus:** Physics. **Qualif.:** Applicant must be a graduate of an undergraduate program in physics or equivalent major from an accredited university or college in North America; have an undergraduate GPA of greater than 3.5; and must have submitted an application for graduate study at one of the accredited programs with subsequent acceptance. **Criteria:** Selection is based on the submitted application and materials. **Funds Avail.:** $13,000/year plus tuition support not exceeding $5,000/year. **Duration:** two years. **To Apply:** Applicants must submit a completed application form together with all post-secondary study transcripts; Graduate Record Exam results; two or three reference letters; and acceptance letter from the intended AAPM Accredited Program. **Deadline:** March 18. **Contact:** Jackie Ogburn at 301-209-3394 or jackie@aapm.org.

561 ■ American Association of Physics Teachers (AAPT)
1 Physics Ellipse
College Park, MD 20740-3841
Ph: (301)209-3311
Fax: (301)209-0845
E-mail: webmaster@aapt.org
URL: www.aapt.org
Facebook: www.facebook.com/AAPTHQ
Twitter: twitter.com/AAPTHQ

562 ■ Barbara Lotze Scholarships for Future Teachers *(Undergraduate/Scholarship)*

Purpose: To provide scholarships for future high school physics teachers. **Focus:** Physics. **Qualif.:** Applicants must be U.S. citizens attending U.S. schools. Undergraduate students who are enrolled or planning to enroll in physics teacher preparation curricula or high school seniors entering such programs are eligible to apply. **Criteria:** Recipients are selected based on merit. **Funds Avail.:** $2,000. **To Apply:** Applicants must submit a completed application form; transcripts of all relevant academic works; a letter to the Scholarship Committee; and proof of U.S. citizenship. **Deadline:** December 1.

563 ■ American Association of Plastic Surgeons (AAPS)
500 Cummings Ctr., Ste. 4550
Beverly, MA 01915
Ph: (978)927-8330
Fax: (978)524-0498
URL: www.aaps1921.org

564 ■ American Association of Plastic Surgeons Academic Scholars Program *(Professional development/Scholarship)*

Purpose: To assist surgeons in establishing a new and independent research program. **Focus:** Plastic surgery. **Qualif.:** Applicants must be plastic and reconstructive surgeons who have: completed the chief residency year within the preceding five years; and received a full-time faculty appointment in a department of surgery/plastic surgery at a medical school accredited by the Liaison Committee on Graduate Medical Education in the United States or by the Committee for Accreditation of Canadian Medical Schools in Canada. **Criteria:** Applicants who are not current recipients of major research grants are given preference. **Funds Avail.:** $30,000. **Duration:** Biennial. **To Apply:** Applicants must complete application online; must submit the research plan and budget; and supporting letters from the Chair of the Department/Division of Plastic Surgery. **Deadline:** November 2.

565 ■ American Association of Police Polygraphists (AAPP)
3223 Lake Ave., Unit 15c-168
Wilmette, IL 60091-1069

Awards are arranged alphabetically below their administering organizations

Ph: (847)635-3980
URL: www.policepolygraph.org
Facebook: www.facebook.com/www.americanassociation-ofpolicepolygraphists.org

566 ■ William "Buddy" Sentner Scholarship Awards *(Undergraduate/Scholarship)*

Purpose: To provide financial support to deserving graduating high school senior or student currently attending college. **Focus:** General studies/Field of study not specified. **Qualif.:** Applicants must be the children, grandchildren, nieces, nephews, adopted or dependents of an AAPP member; or have at least one parent, grandparent and other legal guardian who is a full, life, or honorably retired member. Applicants who have a deceased member will be accepted as long as he/she was in good standing with the AAPP at the time of death. **Criteria:** Recipients are selected based on Selection Committee's review of the application materials.

Funds Avail.: No specific amount. **Duration:** Annual. **To Apply:** Applicants must submit a completed application form; a recent official transcript of all courses and grades; and two character reference letters (from current institution's faculty and from a non-relative). Completed application package must be sent to the AAPP's Office. **Deadline:** February 15.

567 ■ American Association of Professional Apiculturists (AAPA)
c/o Dr. Juliana Rangel-Posada, President
Texas A&M University
401 Joe Routt Blvd.
College Station, TX 77843-2475
Ph: (979)845-3211
Fax: (517)353-4354
E-mail: bees@msu.edu
URL: aapa.cyberbee.net

568 ■ American Association of Professional Apiculturists Research Scholarships *(Graduate, Undergraduate/Scholarship)*

Purpose: To recognize and promote outstanding research by students in the field of apiculture. **Focus:** Entomology. **Qualif.:** Applicants must be undergraduate or graduate students working in North America with completed research on Apis; must be active AAPA members. **Criteria:** Award Committee will review proposals and rank them to the top three. Ranks will be based on scientific merit, presentation, originality and the overall value of the work within the field of apiculture.

Funds Avail.: $1,000. **Duration:** Annual. **To Apply:** Research proposal package must include a curriculum vitae of the nominee, one letter of recommendation, and a summary of the research problem not exceeding three pages including: objectives, significance, and methods. Nominees may also include: up to three publication reprints, submitted manuscripts or abstracts of theses or dissertations. Four copies of the proposal package should be sent to the Chair of the AAPA Student Award Committee at least one month prior to the annual meeting.

569 ■ American Association of Railroad Superintendents (AARS)
PO Box 200
Lafox, IL 60147-0200
E-mail: aars@railroadsuperintendents.org
URL: www.railroadsuperintendents.org

570 ■ Frank J. Richter Scholarships *(Graduate, Undergraduate/Scholarship)*

Purpose: To support the education of students enrolled at an accredited college or university in the U.S. or Canada. **Focus:** Transportation. **Qualif.:** Applicant must be enrolled full-time undergraduate or graduate student at an accredited college or university; demonstrated successful completion of the previous year's study by maintaining at least a 2.75 accumulated GPA on a scale of 1 to 4 with an "A" equal to 4; have accumulate enough credits from accredited schools in time for the Fall Semester to have obtained at least a sophomore level standing at the college or university of enrollment. **Criteria:** Preference will be given to applicants enrolled in the transportation field and all applicants will be considered.

Funds Avail.: $1,000. **Duration:** One year. **To Apply:** Applicants must submit a completed application form together with an official transcript from the schools attended; and two letters of recommendation. The application and narrative statement are to be submitted in one envelope. The transcripts and letters of recommendation must be sent directly to AARS from the appropriate person. **Deadline:** July 1.

571 ■ American Association of School Administrators (AASA)
1615 Duke St.
Alexandria, VA 22314
Ph: (703)528-0700
Fax: (703)841-1543
E-mail: info@aasa.org
URL: www.aasa.org
Facebook: www.facebook.com/AASApage
LinkedIn: www.linkedin.com/company/american-association-of-school-administrators
Twitter: twitter.com/aasahq

572 ■ AASA Educational Administration Scholarship Awards *(Postgraduate/Scholarship)*

Purpose: To provide incentive, honor and financial assistance for outstanding graduate students in school administration intending to make school superintendency a career. **Focus:** Educational administration. **Qualif.:** Applicants must be recommended by the chair of the school of education in which the applicants are currently enrolled. Only one application may be submitted from each college or university campus. **Criteria:** Recipients will be selected based on academic performance.

Funds Avail.: $2,500. **Duration:** Annual. **To Apply:** Applicants must submit completed application form available on the website; a declaration of mission consisting of no more than three separate statements (single-spaced, typewritten) addressing the following: an account of how you came to be interested in school administration, what you conceive the job of a school superintendent to be, what aspects of it chiefly appeal to you, what type of contribution you would like to make in this field, the particular kind of further training and experience which you believe most essential to your best performance, and how you would apply a scholarship toward achieving your professional goals; a succinct statement of an administrative problem you have already encountered, a description

Awards are arranged alphabetically below their administering organizations

of how you met it, and what, on reflection, you wish you had done about it. If you have had no administrative experience, select a problem in the field of classroom teaching or of student activities or discipline; no more than two paragraphs in which you describe specific instances in your training and experience which highlight your individual strengths and focus on your successes. These paragraphs should help the reader know you as an administrator; also submit a letter of recommendation (one original and five photocopies) from the dean of the school of education where applicant is currently enrolled; and letters of endorsement. **Deadline:** September 30. **Remarks:** Established in 1949.

573 ■ Stop Hunger Scholarships *(Undergraduate/Scholarship)*

Purpose: To support the education of students who have made a significant impact in the fight against hunger. **Focus:** General studies/Field of study not specified. **Qualif.:** Applicants must be enrolled in an accredited education institution (kindergarten through college) in the United States; and must have demonstrated ongoing commitment to their community by performing volunteer services impacting hunger in the United States at least within the last 12 months. **Criteria:** Recipients will be selected based on academic performance.

Funds Avail.: $5,000 each. **Duration:** Annual. **Number Awarded:** 5. **To Apply:** Applicants and nominators must supply a valid e-mail address. They must submit a completed application form. **Deadline:** December 5. **Remarks:** Established in 2007. **Contact:** Contact ISTS by e-mail at StopHunger@applyists.com or by phone at 615-320-3149.

574 ■ American Association of School Personnel Administrators (AASPA)

11863 W 112th St., Ste. 100
Overland Park, KS 66210-1375
Ph: (913)327-1222
Fax: (913)327-1223
E-mail: aaspa@aaspa.org
URL: www.aaspa.org
Facebook: www.facebook.com/AASchoolPersonnelA
Twitter: twitter.com/_AASPA_

575 ■ Leon Bradley Scholarship Program *(Undergraduate/Scholarship)*

Purpose: To assist minorities seeking their initial teaching certification and/or endorsement. **Focus:** Teaching. **Qualif.:** Applicants must have an overall GPA of 3.0 or better; must be high school graduate or equivalent status; must be licensed teachers; must be residing or currently matriculating at a college or university within the following states/provinces: Alabama, Florida, Georgia, Kentucky, North Carolina, South Carolina, Tennessee, or Virginia. **Criteria:** Selection will be based on work experience; other scholarship or financial aid support; and maintained overall GPA.

Funds Avail.: $2,500 for student's final year; $1,500 for minority paraprofessional career-charge; $1,500 for minority graduate student. **Duration:** Annual. **Number Awarded:** 4. **To Apply:** Applicants must complete an application form available in website. **Deadline:** May 31. **Contact:** Email: aaspa@aaspa.org.

576 ■ American Association of State Troopers (AAST)

1949 Raymond Diehl Rd.
Tallahassee, FL 32308
Fax: (850)385-8697
Free: 800-765-5456
URL: www.statetroopers.org
Facebook: www.facebook.com/StateTroopers

577 ■ American Association of State Troopers Scholarship Foundation First Scholarships *(Undergraduate/Scholarship)*

Purpose: To provide financial assistance for the education of students who are dependents of the members of American Association of State Troopers, Inc. **Focus:** Law enforcement. **Qualif.:** Applicants must be high school or college students who are dependents of trooper members by natural birth, legal adoption, step child, or legal guardian. **Criteria:** Applicants will be evaluated based on academic performance and financial need.

Funds Avail.: $500. **Duration:** Annual. **To Apply:** Applicants must submit an official transcript indicating a minimum 3.0 GPA (4.0 scale) at an accredited school; for high school students: final four-year high school transcripts; for college students: a current official college transcripts indicating all grades earned through the current year which he or she is applying for; letter of acceptance from an accredited college, state university or community college for the academic year; a 500-word, typed essay entitled, "How my Education Will Advance My Career Plans"; and a small photo attached to the bottom of the application as indicated. **Deadline:** July 31. **Contact:** Joan Breeding at joan@statetroopers.org.

578 ■ American Association of State Troopers Scholarship Foundation Second Scholarships *(Undergraduate/Scholarship)*

Purpose: To provide financial assistance for the education of students who are dependents of the members of American Association of State Troopers, Inc. **Focus:** Law enforcement. **Qualif.:** Applicants must be high school or college students who are dependents of trooper members by natural birth, legal adoption, step child, or legal guardian. **Criteria:** Applicants will be evaluated based on academic performance and financial need.

Funds Avail.: $1,000. **Duration:** Annual. **To Apply:** Applicants must submit an original and official transcript indicating the minimum 3.5 GPA (4.0 scale) maintained during the fall through spring semesters for which the scholarship award was granted; a letter or registration notice as proof of enrollment for the academic year; and a small photo attached to the bottom of the application as indicated. **Deadline:** July 31. **Contact:** Joan Breeding at joan@statetroopers.org.

579 ■ V.J. Johnson Memorial Scholarships *(Undergraduate/Scholarship)*

Purpose: To provide financial assistance to a student who intend to use their education to pursue a career in law enforcement. **Focus:** Law enforcement. **Qualif.:** Applicants must be high school or college students who are dependents of trooper members by natural birth, legal adoption, step child, or legal guardian (in Florida only). **Criteria:** Recipients will be selected based on academic performance and financial need.

Funds Avail.: $1,500. **Duration:** Annual. **To Apply:** Applicants must submit an original and official transcript indicating the minimum of 3.8 GPA (4.0 scale) maintained during the fall through spring semesters for which the second scholarship award was granted; a letter or registra-

Awards are arranged alphabetically below their administering organizations

tion notice as proof of enrollment for the academic year; a 500-word, typed essay entitled, "How my Education Will Advance My Plans for a Career in Law Enforcement"; and a small photo attached to the bottom of the application as indicated. **Deadline:** July 31. **Contact:** Joan Breeding at joan@statetroopers.org.

580 ■ American Association for the Study of Liver Diseases (AASLD)
1001 N Fairfax St., Ste. 400
Alexandria, VA 22314-1587
Ph: (703)299-9766
E-mail: aasld@aasld.org
URL: www.aasld.org

581 ■ AASLD Advanced/Transplant Hepatology Fellowships (Professional development/Fellowship)

Purpose: To prepare individuals to be eligible for certification in transplant hepatology by the American Board of Internal Medicine. **Focus:** Health sciences; Medicine. **Qualif.:** Applicants must be citizens or permanent residents of the United States or must have a student trainee visa to the United States; must be members of AASLD at the time of award application and maintain active membership for the duration of the award period; must have a faculty mentor who is active in hepatology at the applicants' sponsoring institution and be members of AASLD in good standing; must have been accepted to a U.S. transplant hepatology training program with. The sponsoring institution must have a United Network for Organ Sharing approved liver transplant program, which must be in good standing and must perform at least 10 liver transplantations per year. The program must have a full-time faculty member or members capable of teaching a curriculum with a broad-base of knowledge in transplant medicine and hepatology. **Criteria:** Applicants will be evaluated based upon their background and their commitment to a career in adult or pediatric clinical hepatology, Specifically, candidates will be reviewed based on: professional potential of the applicants; experience, productivity, and commitment of the faculty mentor(s); clinical and/or academic environment; quality of proposed clinical program.

Funds Avail.: $60,000. **Duration:** Annual. **To Apply:** To prepare an application: download the application [PDF]; use the forms provided in the application package as a cover pages (print or type responses); include only the required documents and provide signatures as requested; put the applicant's name (last name, first name) and the name of the award in the upper right-hand corner of each page; use half-inch margins (do not use lettering smaller than 10 point); assemble the application package in the order listed in the required documents section of this application; and, adhere to page limits and complete all sections. The completed application, letters of support or commitment, and other documents as applicable must be combined into and submitted as one PDF document. Name the PDF file as follows: 2017 AdvHep - Last Name, First Name (example: 2017 AdvHep - Smith, Jane). Submit the application via online. **Deadline:** December 1. **Contact:** E-mail at awards@aasld.org.

582 ■ AASLD Autoimmune Liver Diseases Pilot Research Awards (Graduate, Doctorate, Postdoctorate, Professional development/Award, Grant)

Purpose: To provide supplementary funding during the pilot phase of basic, translational or clinical research projects in autoimmune liver disease in preparation for future grant applications by the recipient. **Focus:** Health sciences; Medicine. **Qualif.:** Applicants must be at the pre-doctoral/graduate level, post-doctoral level, or junior faculty within five years of their faculty appointment date in an accredited North American academic institution a the award start date; must be members of the AASLD at the time of award application and maintain active membership for the duration of the award period; and must have their respective mentors who are AASLD members in good standing for the duration of the award period. **Criteria:** Candidates will be evaluated based upon their background, their commitment to a research career, the strength of their research project and the environment in which they will conduct the project. Applications will be reviewed based on the written materials submitted. Incomplete applications and applications that fail to adhere strictly to the instructions (including the submission deadline and page limitations) will not be reviewed. All decisions are final.

Funds Avail.: $20,000. **Duration:** Annual. **To Apply:** To prepare an application: download the application [PDF]; use the forms provided in the application package as a cover pages (print or type responses); include only the required documents and provide signatures as requested; put the applicant's name (last name, first name) and the name of the award in the upper right-hand corner of each page; use half-inch margins (do not use lettering smaller than 10 point); assemble the application package in the order listed in the required documents section of this application; and, adhere to page limits and complete all sections. The completed application, letters of support or commitment, and other documents as applicable must be combined into and submitted as one PDF document. Name the PDF file as follows: 2017 Autoimmune Pilot - last name, first name (example: 2017 Autoimmune Pilot - Smith, Jane). Submit the application via online. **Deadline:** December 1. **Contact:** E-mail at awards@aasld.org.

583 ■ AASLD Career Development Awards in Liver Transplantation (Professional development/Grant)

Purpose: To foster career development for an individual performing clinical and/or translational research in the field of liver transplantation. **Focus:** Health sciences; Medicine. **Qualif.:** Applicants must be members of AASLD at the time of the award application and maintain active membership for the duration of the award period (the applicants' respective sponsors should be research mentors and AASLD members in good standing as well); commence the award within the first five years of appointment as junior faculty members (with the rank of instructor or assistant professor) at a UNOS approved transplant center who spend 50 percent or more of their time in clinical transplantation or transplantation-related sciences; and show commitment to making substantial contributions to the field of liver transplantation. **Criteria:** Candidates will be evaluated based upon their background, their commitment to a research career, the strength of their research project and the environment in which they will conduct the project. Applications will be reviewed based on the written materials submitted. Incomplete applications and applications that fail to adhere strictly to the instructions (including the submission deadline and page limitations) will not be reviewed. All decisions are final.

Funds Avail.: $90,000 ($45,000 per year). **Duration:** Annual; up to 2 years. **To Apply:** To prepare an application: download the application [PDF]; use the forms provided in the application package as a cover pages (print or type responses); include only the required documents and

Awards are arranged alphabetically below their administering organizations

provide signatures as requested; put the applicant's name (last name, first name) and the name of the award in the upper right-hand corner of each page; use half-inch margins (do not use lettering smaller than 10 point); assemble the application package in the order listed in the required documents section of this application; and, adhere to page limits and complete all sections. The completed application, letters of support or commitment, and other documents as applicable must be combined into and submitted as one PDF document. Name the PDF file as follows: 2017 CarDev in LT - last name, first name (example: 2017 CarDev in LT - Smith, Jane). Submit the application via online. **Deadline:** December 1. **Contact:** E-mail at awards@aasld.org.

584 ■ AASLD Clinical and Translational Research Awards *(Professional development/Grant)*

Purpose: To foster career development for individuals performing clinical and/or translational research in a liver-related area and who have shown commitment to excellence at an early stage of their research study. **Focus:** Health sciences; Medicine. **Qualif.:** Applicants must be either advance fellows (i.e. will have completed at least two years of fellowship training/research at the start of the award) or junior faculty members (at or below the rank of Assistant Professor) for no more than five years at the start of the award in an accredited North American (U.S., Canada, or Mexico) academic institution (at least 50% effort should be devoted to research activities); and must be members of AASLD at the time of award application and maintain active membership for the duration of the award period (they must have their respective sponsors or co-sponsors who are AASLD members in good standing). **Criteria:** Candidates will be evaluated based upon their background, their commitment to a research career, the strength of their research project and the environment in which they will conduct the project. Applications will be reviewed based on the written materials submitted. Incomplete applications and applications that fail to adhere strictly to the instructions (including the submission deadline and page limitations) will not be reviewed. All decisions are final.

Funds Avail.: $150,000 ($75,000 per year). **Duration:** Annual; up to 2 years. **To Apply:** To prepare an application: download the application [PDF]; use the forms provided in the application package as a cover pages (print or type responses); include only the required documents and provide signatures as requested; put the applicant's name (last name, first name) and the name of the award in the upper right-hand corner of each page; use half-inch margins (do not use lettering smaller than 10 point); assemble the application package in the order listed in the required documents section of this application; and, adhere to page limits and complete all sections. The completed application, letters of support or commitment, and other documents as applicable must be combined into and submitted as one PDF document. Name the PDF file as follows: 2017 CTRA - last name, first name (example: 2017 CTRA - Smith, Jane). Submit the application via online. **Deadline:** December 1. **Contact:** E-mail at awards@aasld.org.

585 ■ AASLD NP/PA Clinical Hepatology Fellowships *(Professional development/Fellowship)*

Purpose: To provide salary and benefit support for certified and licensed Nurse Practitioners or Physician Assistants pursuing a full-year of training focused on clinical care in hepatology. **Focus:** Health sciences; Medical assisting; Nursing. **Qualif.:** Applicants must be fully certified and licensed nurse practitioners, physician assistants, clinical nurse specialist or advanced practice nurses; must have no more than 18 months of experience as midlevel provider in hepatology and/or transplant hepatology (adult and/or pediatric); must be members of AASLD at the time of award application and maintain active membership for the duration of the award period (Associate or Regular Members); must be mentored during the Fellowship period by an AASLD member Clinical Hepatologists who dedicates at least 50% of his/her time to the care of patients with liver diseases. **Criteria:** Applicants will be evaluated based upon their background and their commitment to a career in adult or pediatric clinical hepatology.

Funds Avail.: $78,000. **Duration:** Annual. **To Apply:** Applicants must download the application form in PDF; use the forms provided in the application package as a cover pages (print or type responses); include only the required documents and provide signatures as requested; put the applicant's name (last name, first name) and the name of the award in the upper right-hand corner of each page; use half-inch margins (do not use lettering smaller than 10 point); assemble the application package in the order listed in the required documents section of this application; and adhere to page limits and complete all sections. The completed application, letters of support or commitment, and other documents as applicable must be combined into and submitted as one PDF document. Name the PDF file as follows: 2017 NPPA - Last Name, First Name (example: 2017 NPPA - Smith, Jane). Submit the application via online. **Deadline:** February 2. **Contact:** E-mail at awards@aasld.org.

586 ■ AASLD Pinnacle Research Awards in Liver Disease *(Professional development/Grant)*

Purpose: To develop the potential of outstanding, young scientists and encourage research in liver physiology and disease. **Focus:** Health sciences; Medicine. **Qualif.:** Applicant must commence the award within the first five (5) years of his/her first faculty appointment (including prior appointments in universities outside of North America) (if the applicant does not have a faculty appointment at the time of application, a letter signed by the department chair confirming that the applicant will have a faculty appointment (a) no later than the Pinnacle Research Award start date and (b) for the full award cycle must be submitted); must be a member of AASLD at the time of award application and maintain active membership for the duration of the award period; must be sponsored by a research mentor (the mentor must be an AASLD member in good standing at the time of application and maintain active membership for the duration of the award period); and must be sponsored by a public or private non-profit institution accredited in the United States, Canada or Mexico engaged in health care and health-related research. **Criteria:** Each applicant will be evaluated based upon their background, their commitment to a research career, the scientific merit of their research project and the environment in which they will conduct the project. Applications will be reviewed based on the written materials submitted. Incomplete applications and applications that fail to adhere strictly to the instructions (including the submission deadline and page limitations) will not be reviewed. All decisions are final.

Funds Avail.: $300,000 ($100,000 per year). **Duration:** Annual; up to 3 years. **To Apply:** To prepare an application: download the application [PDF]; use the forms provided in the application package as a cover pages (print or type responses); include only the required documents and provide signatures as requested; put the applicant's name (last name, first name) and the name of the award in the

Awards are arranged alphabetically below their administering organizations

upper right-hand corner of each page; use half-inch margins (do not use lettering smaller than 10 point); assemble the application package in the order listed in the required documents section of this application; and, adhere to page limits and complete all sections. The completed application, letters of support or commitment, and other documents as applicable must be combined into and submitted as one PDF document. Name the PDF file as follows: 2017 Pinnacle in LT - last name, first name (example: 2017 Pinnacle in LT - Smith, Jane). Submit the application via online. **Deadline:** December 1. **Contact:** E-mail at awards@aasld.org.

587 ■ Afdhal/McHutchison LIFER Awards *(Postdoctorate, Professional development/Grant)*

Purpose: To develop independent and productive research careers in liver disease. **Focus:** Health sciences; Medicine. **Qualif.:** Applicants must be postdoctoral or clinical research fellows who have completed their most recent doctoral degree or medical residency within the past five years at the start of the grant term; must be either from North America, working at an academic, medical or research institution at the time of application and for the duration of the award, or outside of North America who have already been accepted into a fellowship position at a North American education institution at the time of application and for the duration of the award; and must be members of the AASLD at the time of award application and maintain active membership for the duration of the award period (they must have their respective mentors at the North American Institution who are AASLD members in good standing for the duration of the award). **Criteria:** Candidates will be evaluated based upon their background, their commitment to a research career, the strength of their research project and the environment in which they will conduct the project. Applications will be reviewed based on the written materials submitted. Incomplete applications and applications that fail to adhere strictly to the instructions (including the submission deadline and page limitations) will not be reviewed. All decisions are final.

Funds Avail.: $100,000. **Duration:** Annual; up to 2 years. **To Apply:** To prepare an application: download the application [PDF]; use the forms provided in the application package as a cover pages (print or type responses); include only the required documents and provide signatures as requested; put the applicant's name (last name, first name) and the name of the award in the upper right-hand corner of each page; use half-inch margins (do not use lettering smaller than 10 point); assemble the application package in the order listed in the required documents section of this application; and, adhere to page limits and complete all sections. The completed application, letters of support or commitment, and other documents as applicable must be combined into and submitted as one PDF document. Name the PDF file as follows: 2017 LIFER - Last Name, First Name (example: 2017 Autoimmune Pilot - Smith, Jane). Submit the application via online. **Deadline:** December 1. **Contact:** E-mail at awards@aasld.org.

588 ■ American Association for the Surgery of Trauma (AAST)
633 N St. Clair St., Ste. 2600
Chicago, IL 60611
Fax: (312)202-5064
Free: 800-789-4006
E-mail: aast@aast.org
URL: www.aast.org

Facebook: www.facebook.com/AASTtraumasurgeons
Twitter: twitter.com/traumadoctors

589 ■ AAST/ETHICON Research Grants in Local Wound Haemostatics and Hemorrhage Control Scholarships *(Graduate, Postgraduate/Grant)*

Purpose: To support post residency research of surgeons with a major commitment in trauma surgery. **Focus:** Surgery. **Qualif.:** Program is open for individuals intending to conduct clinical research in the areas of homeostasis and resuscitation only; must have commitment to trauma surgery academic research. **Criteria:** Recipients are selected based on the Scholarship Committee's review of application materials.

Funds Avail.: No specific amount. **To Apply:** Applicants must submit a completed application form including curriculum vitae, bibliography and research proposals. Applicants are also required to submit one typed original copy of the application form and 4 3-hole punched photocopies. Submit completed application to Robert C. Mackersie, M.D., AAST Sec.-Treas., Trauma/Critical Care, UCSF-San Francisco Gen. Hospital, at the above address.

590 ■ AAST/KCI Research Grant *(Doctorate/Grant)*

Purpose: To sponsor clinical research in the area of wound care. **Focus:** Surgery. **Qualif.:** Program is open to individuals intending to conduct clinical research in the area of wound care only. **Criteria:** Recipients are selected based on the Scholarship Committee's review of application materials.

Funds Avail.: No specific amount. **Duration:** Annual. **To Apply:** Applicants must submit a completed application form including curriculum vitae, bibliography and research proposals. Applicants are also required to submit one typed original copy of the application form and four 3-hole punched photocopies.

591 ■ AAST Medical Student, Resident and In-Training Fellow Scholarships *(Advanced Professional/Scholarship)*

Purpose: To support those who want to attend the AAST Annual Meetings. **Focus:** Surgery. **Qualif.:** Applicants must be medical students, residents, and in-training fellows who want attend the AAST annual meeting. **Criteria:** Recipients will be selected based on the Scholarship Committee's review of application materials.

Funds Avail.: $200 stipend for food/miscellaneous items. **Duration:** Annual. **To Apply:** Applicants must submit letters of recommendation, cover letter and curriculum vitae to Martin A. Croce, M.D., AAST Secretary-Treasurer. **Deadline:** June 1. **Contact:** For more information: Jermica Smith, AAST Project Specialist, at jsmith@aast.org.

592 ■ American Association for Thoracic Surgery (AATS)
500 Cummings Ctr., Ste. 4550
Beverly, MA 01915-6183
Ph: (978)927-8330
Fax: (978)524-0498
URL: www.aats.org
Facebook: www.facebook.com/AATS1917
Twitter: twitter.com/AATSHQ

593 ■ AATS Cardiothoracic Surgery Resident Poster Competition *(Professional development/Award)*

Purpose: To help offset the cost of travel and hotel accommodations at the AATS Annual Meeting. **Focus:** Health sci-

ences; Surgery. **Qualif.:** Participants must be cardiothoracic surgery residents and/or congenital heart surgery fellows from around the world. North American residents must be in their last year of either an ACGME-accredited or RCPSC-accredited cardiothoracic surgery residency program or congenital heart surgery fellowship in the United States or Canada. International residents must be in their last year of a cardiothoracic training program at an AATS Member's institution. **Criteria:** Selection will be based on the committee's criteria.
Funds Avail.: $500. **Duration:** Annual. **To Apply:** Participants must provide the Cardiothoracic Residents Committee with a brief abstract regarding the research on their posters. Posters may include research that has been previously presented and/or published. Details regarding poster format, presentation viewing hours, and grading formats will be provided once the AATS receives the completed application.

594 ■ AATS Medical Students Summer Intern Scholarships *(Undergraduate/Scholarship, Internship)*
Purpose: To broaden the educational experience of medical students in cardiothoracic surgery. **Focus:** Medicine. **Qualif.:** Applicants must be first or second year medical students in a North American medical school. **Criteria:** Recipients are selected based on the committee's review of application materials.
Funds Avail.: $2,500. **Duration:** Annual; Up to 8 weeks. **To Apply:** Applicants must complete an online application and include a one-page outline of what they hope to accomplish during their eight weeks internship. Applicants must also submit a letter of support from the host sponsor. **Remarks:** Established in 2007.

595 ■ AATS Perioperative/Team-Based Care Poster Competition *(Professional development/Award)*
Purpose: To provide an opportunity for professionals to participate in a scientific poster competition. **Focus:** Health sciences; Surgery. **Qualif.:** Participants must be non-MD cardiothoracic surgical team professionals (NPs, PAs, Perfusionists, and RNs). **Criteria:** Selection will be based on the submitted abstract.
Funds Avail.: $1,000. **Duration:** Annual. **To Apply:** Participants must submit an abstract electronically on the AATS Perioperative/Team-Based Care abstract submission website. Abstracts and posters may contain material that has been previously presented. The Posters should reflect the participants' research findings and/or new and innovative ideas for successful approaches in the management of the cardiothoracic patient. **Contact:** admin@aats.org.

596 ■ AATS Resident Critical Care Scholarships *(Professional development/Scholarship)*
Purpose: To assist individuals to attend the Cardiovascular-Thoracic (CVT) Critical Care Conference. **Focus:** Health sciences. **Qualif.:** Applicants must be residents enrolled in an ACGME-accredited cardiothoracic surgical training program in the United States or RCPSC-accredited residency program located in Canada. **Criteria:** Selection will be based on the submitted application materials.
Funds Avail.: $500. **Duration:** Annual. **Number Awarded:** Up to 35. **To Apply:** Interested applicants may visit the website to fill up the online scholarship application form. **Deadline:** July 15.

597 ■ AATS/STS Cardiothoracic Ethics Forum Scholarships *(Professional development/Scholarship)*
Purpose: To support CT surgeons who are interested in biomedical ethics and show promise of providing leadership for the continuing development and flourishing of ethics education for CT surgery. **Focus:** Health sciences; Surgery. **Qualif.:** Applicants must be members of The Society of Thoracic Surgeons or the American Association for Thoracic Surgery. **Criteria:** Selection will be based on the committee's criteria.
Funds Avail.: No specific amount. **To Apply:** Applicants must: identify a specific educational program that will advance their ethics knowledge and skills in preparation for participation and leadership in CT ethics programs; provide a curriculum vitae or resume that displays evidence of scholarly activity and leadership roles; submit a proposed plan of study (no longer than 500 words) that clearly states the educational insights and benefits that the scholarship will provide for their professional careers and for CT surgery as a specialty. **Deadline:** August 1. **Remarks:** Established in 2000. **Contact:** Robert M. Sade, MD at sader@musc.edu.

598 ■ American Association of University Women (AAUW)
1111 16th St. NW
Washington, DC 20036-4809
Ph: (202)785-7700
Fax: (202)872-1425
Free: 800-326-2289
E-mail: connect@aauw.org
URL: www.aauw.org
Facebook: www.facebook.com/AAUW.National
LinkedIn: www.linkedin.com/company/aauw
Twitter: twitter.com/aauw

599 ■ American Association of University Women American Fellowships *(Doctorate, Postdoctorate/Fellowship)*
Purpose: To support female doctoral candidates and scholars completing dissertations and seeking funds for postdoctoral research leave from accredited institutions. **Focus:** General studies/Field of study not specified. **Qualif.:** Applicants must be U.S. citizens or permanent residents. **Criteria:** Candidates are evaluated on the basis of scholarly excellence, teaching experience and active commitment to help women through service in their communities, professions, or fields of research.
Funds Avail.: No specific amount. **Duration:** Annual. **To Apply:** Applicants must check online for further information about the award. **Deadline:** November 15.

600 ■ American Association of University Women Career Development Grants *(Postgraduate/Grant)*
Purpose: To support women who hold bachelor's degree preparing to advance their careers, change careers, or re-enter the work force. **Focus:** General studies/Field of study not specified. **Qualif.:** Applicants must be U.S. citizens or permanent residents; must be AAUW members. **Criteria:** Primary consideration will be given to women of color who are pursuing their first advanced degree or credentials in non-traditional fields.
Funds Avail.: $2,000-$12,000. **Duration:** Annual. **To Apply:** Applicants must check online for further information about the award. **Deadline:** December 15.

601 ■ American Association of University Women International Fellowships *(Graduate, Postgraduate/Fellowship)*
Purpose: To provide fund for full-time study or research in the United States to women who are not United States

Awards are arranged alphabetically below their administering organizations

citizens or permanent residents. **Focus:** General studies/Field of study not specified. **Qualif.:** Applicant must be a citizen in a country other than the United States, or must hold a non-immigrant visa if residing in the United States. **Criteria:** Candidates are selected based on academic and professional qualifications, need for the specialized knowledge and skills of the country where she came from, commitment to the advancement of women and girls in her home country as demonstrated by her previous work and proposed study or research, documented evidence prior to her community service in the home country particularly activities concerning women and girls lives' improvement. **Funds Avail.:** $18,000 - $30,000. **Duration:** Annual. **Number Awarded:** Varies. **To Apply:** Applicant must check online for further information about the award. Applicants must submit the following supporting documents in a single packet: official transcript; proof of bachelor's degree; proof of doctorate degree (for Postdoctoral applicants); official report of TOEFL test scores or request for waiver; letter of admission; and acknowledgement postcard. **Deadline:** December 1. **Remarks:** Established in 1917.

602 ■ American Association of University Women Master's and First Professional Awards *(Other/Award)*

Purpose: To financially support women intending to pursue a full-time course of study at accredited institutions. **Focus:** Women's studies. **Qualif.:** Applicants must be U.S. citizens or permanent residents; must be full-time women who are enrolled at an accredited U.S. institution. **Criteria:** Selected Professions Fellowships are awarded for the following programs: Architecture (M.Arch, M.S.Arch), Computer/Information Sciences (M.S.), Engineering (M.E., M.S., Ph.D.), Engineering Dissertation Award also awarded Mathematics/Statistics (M.S.), and fellowships in the following degree programs are restricted to women of color, who have been underrepresented in these fields: Business Administration (M.B.A., E.M.B.A.), Law (J.D.), Medicine (M.D., D.O.). **Funds Avail.:** $18,000. **To Apply:** Applicants must check online for further information about the award. **Deadline:** December 1.

603 ■ American Association of University Women Selected Professions Fellowships *(Other/Fellowship)*

Purpose: To support women in professional degree programs in fields where female participation traditionally has been low. **Focus:** Architecture; Business administration; Computer and information sciences; Engineering; Law; Medicine. **Qualif.:** Applicants must be U.S. citizens or permanent residents. **Criteria:** Selection of candidates based upon the following programs: Architecture (M.Arch, M.S.Arch), Computer/Information Sciences (M.S.), Engineering (M.E., M.S., Ph.D.), Engineering Dissertation Award also awarded Mathematics/Statistics (M.S.), and fellowships in the following degree programs are restricted to women of color, who have been underrepresented in these fields: Business Administration (M.B.A., E.M.B.A.), Law (J.D.), Medicine (M.D., D.O.). **Funds Avail.:** $5,000-$18,000. **Duration:** Annual. **To Apply:** Applicants must check online for further information about the award. **Deadline:** January 10. **Remarks:** Established in 1970.

604 ■ American Association for Women in Community Colleges (AAWCC)
PO Box 3098
Gaithersburg, MD 20885
Ph: (301)442-3374
E-mail: info@aawccnatl.org
URL: www.aawccnatl.org
Facebook: www.facebook.com/AAWCCNatl
Twitter: www.twitter.com/AAWCCNatl

605 ■ American AZA Association for Women in Community Colleges Regional Scholarships *(Undergraduate/Scholarship)*

Purpose: To provide support to students pursuing doctoral studies. **Focus:** General studies/Field of study not specified. **Qualif.:** Applicants must be currently enrolled; and must have cumulative GPA of 3.2 or higher. **Criteria:** Selection will be based on submitted essay; GPA; Financial need; employment; extracurricular activities. **Funds Avail.:** No specific amount. **Duration:** Annual. **To Apply:** Applicants must submit scholarship application form; AAWCC fact sheet; and unofficial transcript. **Deadline:** March 1.

606 ■ American Association for Women in Community Colleges Scholarship LEADERS Institute *(Other/Scholarship)*

Purpose: To provide leadership development opportunities for women in Community Colleges across the country. **Focus:** General studies/Field of study not specified. **Qualif.:** Applicants must be faculty members who work in a community college. **Criteria:** Selection of recipients will be based on commitment to AAWCC, leadership plans, and the endorsement of a mentor from their home institution. **Funds Avail.:** $3,000. **To Apply:** Applicants must complete the application form available at the website. **Deadline:** February 15. **Contact:** Dr. Maureen Murphy at aawccleaders@brookdalecc.edu.

607 ■ American Association of Zoo Keepers (AAZK)
8476 E Speedway Blvd., Ste. 204
Tucson, AZ 85710-1728
Ph: (520)298-9688
E-mail: visitor@aazk.org
URL: www.aazk.org
Facebook: www.facebook.com/AAZKinc
LinkedIn: www.linkedin.com/company/american-association-of-zoo-keepers
Twitter: twitter.com/AAZKinc

608 ■ AAZK/AZA Advances in Animal Keeping Course Grants *(Professional development/Grant)*

Purpose: To assist members with costs associated with attending the Advances in Animal Keeping Course offered through AZA. **Focus:** Zoology. **Qualif.:** Applicants must be full-time keepers/aquarists in zoological parks and aquariums. Researchers other than zoo keepers may participate in the funded studies. The principal investigators, however, must be keepers/aquarists. **Criteria:** Selection will be based on the committee's criteria. **Funds Avail.:** No specific amount. **To Apply:** Application can be obtained at the members section of the AAZK website. Members are required to make an account or login at the website to access the Grant application. **Deadline:** March 1. **Contact:** Shelly Roach, Grants Committee Chair, at the above address.

Awards are arranged alphabetically below their administering organizations

AMERICAN ASTRONOMICAL SOCIETY

609 ■ AAZK Conservation, Preservation and Restoration Grants *(Professional development/Grant)*

Purpose: To encourage and support efforts in conservation conducted by AAZK members in zoological parks and aquariums around the world. **Focus:** Zoology. **Qualif.:** Applicants must be full-time keepers/aquarists in zoological parks and aquariums. Researchers other than zoo keepers may participate in the funded studies. The principal investigators, however, must be keepers/aquarists. **Criteria:** Selection will be based on the committee's criteria.

Funds Avail.: No specific amount. **To Apply:** Applications can be obtained at the members section of the AAZK website. Members are required to make an account or login at the website to access the Grant application. **Deadline:** March 1. **Contact:** Shelly Roach, Grants Committee Chair, at the above address.

610 ■ AAZK Professional Development Grants *(Professional development/Grant)*

Purpose: To assist AAZK members with costs associated with attending professional meetings or workshops or participating in field research. **Focus:** Zoology. **Qualif.:** Applicants must be professional members of AAZK in good standing, must be full-time keepers/aquarists in zoological parks and aquariums. Researchers other than zoo keepers may participate in the funded studies. The principal investigators, however, must be keepers/aquarists. **Criteria:** Selection will be based on the committee's criteria.

Funds Avail.: No specific amount. **To Apply:** Application can be obtained at the Members section of the AAZK website. Members are required to make an account or login at the website to access the Grant application. **Deadline:** March 1. **Contact:** Shelly Roach, Grants Committee Chair, at the above address.

611 ■ AAZK Research Grants *(Professional development/Grant)*

Purpose: To encourage and support efforts in noninvasive research conducted by AAZK members in zoological parks and aquariums around the world. **Focus:** Zoology. **Qualif.:** Applicants must be full-time keepers/aquarists in zoological parks and aquariums. Researchers other than zoo keepers may participate in the funded studies. The principal investigators, however, must be keepers/aquarists. **Criteria:** Selection will be based on the committee's criteria.

Funds Avail.: No specific amount. **To Apply:** Application can be obtained at the members section of the AAZK website. Members are required to make an account or login at the website to access the Grant application. **Deadline:** March 1. **Contact:** Shelly Roach, Grants Committee Chair, at the above address.

612 ■ American Astronomical Society (AAS)
2000 Florida Ave. NW, Ste. 400
Washington, DC 20009-1231
Ph: (202)328-2010
Fax: (202)234-2560
E-mail: aas@aas.org
URL: www.aas.org
Facebook: www.facebook.com/AmericanAstronomicalSociety

613 ■ Annie J. Cannon Award in Astronomy *(Doctorate/Award, Recognition)*

Purpose: To honor and recognize outstanding research and promise for future research by a postdoctoral woman researcher. **Focus:** Astronomy and astronomical sciences. **Qualif.:** Applicants must be North American female astronomers within five years of receiving their PhD in the year designated for the award. **Criteria:** Selection will be based on the committee's criteria.

Funds Avail.: $1,500. **Duration:** Annual. **Number Awarded:** 1. **To Apply:** Nominators should request that the nominee submit a research plan of no more than three pages describing their anticipated course of work for the next five years. The plan should be broadly accessible to astronomers with a range of scientific interests. **Deadline:** June 30. **Remarks:** Established in 1934.

614 ■ Chambliss Astronomy Achievement Student Awards *(Undergraduate, Graduate/Award)*

Purpose: To recognized exemplary research by undergraduate and graduate students who present at one of the poster sessions at the meetings of the AAS. **Focus:** Astronomy and astronomical sciences. **Qualif.:** Participants must be undergraduate and graduate students and must be members of the AAS. **Criteria:** Judging criteria are based on presentation and content, weighted so that content is 60% of the score.

Funds Avail.: No specific amount. **To Apply:** Work must have been done while the presenters were undergraduate or graduate students. Participants must submit the correct abstract form indicating that the poster is being submitted for consideration for the award. Participants must be present at their posters at the scheduled judging time to be eligible. **Deadline:** October 1 (winter); March 1 (summer).

615 ■ Chrétien International Research Grants *(Doctorate/Grant)*

Purpose: To promote research or projects related to astronomy. **Focus:** Astronomy and astronomical sciences. **Qualif.:** Applicants must be astronomers with PhD or equivalent. **Criteria:** Recipients are selected based on submitted proposals. Decisions will be made on the basis of quality research; importance of the proposed research to the international astronomy; ability of the applicant to carry out the research; and prudence of the budget estimates. Letters of reference will greatly affect the committee's decision. Preference will be given to individuals of high promise who are otherwise unfunded.

Funds Avail.: Up to $20,000. **Duration:** Annual. **To Apply:** Applicants must submit a description of research (maximum of three pages); a statement on the applicant's ability to finish the project; a proposed budget; description of other financial resources (if applicable); curriculum vitae and bibliography of recent papers; two reference letters from astronomers who know the applicant's work; other circumstances that might help in the selection process. **Deadline:** April 1. **Contact:** Applications and all supporting materials should be submitted electronically to: Kelly Clark, grants@aas.org.

616 ■ Rodger Doxsey Travel Prizes *(Graduate, Postdoctorate/Prize)*

Purpose: To assist graduate or postdoctoral students to enable the oral presentation of their dissertation research at the AAS meeting. **Focus:** Astronomy and astronomical sciences. **Qualif.:** Applicants must be graduate students or postdocs; must be planning to present their dissertation research at a meeting of the AAS in the form of an oral dissertation talk; must be attending a North American university or have recently graduated from a North American university. **Criteria:** Selection will be based on the scientific merit

Awards are arranged alphabetically below their administering organizations

of the dissertation research of the PhD.

Funds Avail.: No specific amount. **Duration:** only every winter meetings. **To Apply:** Applicants must submit their abstract by the "on-time" abstract submission deadline. Advisors of the applicants must submit a letter indicating that the applicant is within one year of receiving or receipt of the PhD. **Deadline:** October 1.

617 ■ American Australian Association (AAA)

50 Broadway, Ste. 2003
New York, NY 10004
Ph: (212)338-6860
Fax: (212)338-6864
E-mail: information@aaanyc.org
URL: www.americanaustralian.org
Facebook: www.facebook.com/americanaustralian
Twitter: twitter.com/_aaausa

618 ■ Morgan Stanley Pediatrics Fellowships
(Doctorate, Postdoctorate, Postgraduate, Graduate/Fellowship)

Purpose: To support Australian or American researchers who wish to conduct research in pediatrics at a top U.S. or Australian educational or research institution. **Focus:** Education, Early childhood; Medicine, Osteopathic; Medicine, Pediatric; Oncology. **Qualif.:** Applicant must be an Australian citizen or permanent resident; must be conducting postgraduate or post-doctoral research in the area of medicine particularly with a focus on early childhood. **Criteria:** Selection will be based on the committee's criteria.

Funds Avail.: Up to $40,000 a year. **Duration:** Annual. **To Apply:** Application form may be obtained online at www.americanaustralian.org. Applicant must submit a completed application form, budget for the research/study period, essays and letters of reference. **Deadline:** April 15. **Contact:** jhelum.bagchi@aaanyc.org.

619 ■ American Bar Association Commission on Homelessness and Poverty

1050 Connecticut Ave. NW, Ste. 400
Washington, DC 20036
Ph: (202)662-1693
Fax: (202)638-3844
URL: www.americanbar.org/groups/public_services/homelessness_poverty.html

620 ■ John J. Curtin, Jr. Fellowships
(Undergraduate/Fellowship)

Purpose: To provide stipends to law students working to help homeless and indigent people. **Focus:** Law. **Qualif.:** Candidates must be law school students working for a bar association or legal services program designed to prevent homeless for indigent clients or their advocates. Programs must have been operational for at least one year and must have an attorney on staff or easily available to supervise the intern. **Criteria:** Selection will be based on the committee's criteria.

Funds Avail.: $2,500. **Duration:** Annual. **Number Awarded:** 3. **To Apply:** Applicants must submit a cover letter, resume, application form and a prospective program's supporting statement. Applicants must be specific about the issues on which they plan to focus and what they hope to accomplish. Both the intern and the program will be expected to submit to the ABA Commission on Homelessness and Poverty and the Standing Committee on Legal Aid and Indigent Defendants reports on the summer internship experience. The intern should assess the quality of the supervision received, describe whether the written work assigned was challenging, discuss the opportunities to work with clients, and include a summary of what the student learned from the experience. The program supervisor should describe the student's contributions to the program and provide feedback as to what skills and abilities the Curtin Justice Fund Legal Internship Program should look for in future interns. **Deadline:** March 28. **Contact:** 202-662-1691 or homeless@americanbar.org.

621 ■ American Bar Foundation (ABF)

750 N Lake Shore Dr.
Chicago, IL 60611-4403
Ph: (312)988-6500
Fax: (312)988-6579
URL: www.americanbarfoundation.org/index.html

622 ■ ABF Doctoral/Post-Doctoral Fellowships
(Doctorate, Graduate/Fellowship)

Purpose: To encourage original and significant research on law, the legal profession, and legal institutions. **Focus:** Law. **Qualif.:** Applicants must: be Doctoral or Post-Doctoral candidates in social sciences; have completed all doctoral requirements except the dissertation; or students who will complete their dissertation prior to the beginning of the award. Research must be in the general area of socio-legal studies or in social scientific approaches to law. Dissertations must address issues in the field and show major contribution to social scientific understanding of law and legal process. **Criteria:** Selection is based on the submitted dissertation abstract or proposal.

Funds Avail.: $30,000. **Duration:** Annual; 12-month fellowship. **To Apply:** Applicants must submit a dissertation abstract or proposal; two letters of reference; a curriculum vitae; a transcript of graduate records; and a short sample of written work (optional). **Deadline:** December 15. **Contact:** Amanda Ehrhardt, Administrative Associate for Academic Affairs and Research Administration, American Bar Foundation; Phone: 312-988-6517; Email: aehrhardt@abfn.org.

623 ■ ABF Law and Social Science Dissertation Fellowship and Mentoring Program *(Graduate/Fellowship)*

Purpose: To promote education in Law and Social Sciences. **Focus:** Law; Social sciences. **Qualif.:** Applicants should be U.S. citizens and permanent residents who are students in a Ph.D. program in a social science department or an interdisciplinary program (third-, fourth-, and fifth-year graduate students who specialize in the field of law and social science and whose research interests include law and inequality). Humanities students pursuing empirically-based social science dissertations are welcome to apply. **Criteria:** Selection is based on the application.

Funds Avail.: $30,000 stipend; $1,500 for research and travel expenses; $2,500 for relocation expenses. **Duration:** Annual. **To Apply:** Applicants should submit: a 1-2 page letter of application; a 2-3 page description of a research project or interest that relates to law and inequality (broadly defined) with a statement of how the applicants became interested in the research topic; (3) a resume or curriculum vitae; (4) a writing sample (a paper written for a graduate-

Awards are arranged alphabetically below their administering organizations

level course or dissertation prospectus); and (5) three letters of recommendation from faculty members (including one from the faculty member who will serve as the departmental liaison – typically the applicants' respective advisors). **Deadline:** December 1. **Contact:** Amanda Ehrhardt; Phone: 312-988-6517; Email: aehrhardt@abfn.org.

624 ■ ABF Montgomery Summer Research Diversity Fellowships in Law and Social Science
(Undergraduate/Fellowship)

Purpose: To introduce students from diverse backgrounds to the rewards and demands of a research-oriented career in the field of law and social science. **Focus:** Law; Social sciences. **Qualif.:** Applicants must be American citizens and lawful permanent residents including, but not limited to, persons who are African American, Hispanic/Latino, Asian, Native American, or Puerto Rican, as well as other individuals who will add diversity to the field of law and social science, such as persons with disabilities and LGBTQ persons. They must have a Grade Point Average of at least 3.0 (on a 4.0 scale) and be moving toward an academic major in the social sciences or humanities. **Criteria:** Selection shall be based on the aforementioned qualifications and compliance with the application details.

Funds Avail.: $3,600 each. **Duration:** Annual. **Number Awarded:** Varies. **To Apply:** Applicants must provide the following along with the provided application form: two (2) brief essays on the topics indicated in the application form; official transcripts of all academic courses completed at the time of application; and, one letter of recommendation from a faculty member familiar with the student's work. **Deadline:** February 15. **Contact:** For further information: Phone: 312-988-6520; Email: fellowships@abfn.org.

625 ■ American Birding Association (ABA)
PO Box 744
Delaware City, DE 19706
Ph: (302)838-3660
Fax: (302)838-3651
Free: 800-850-2473
E-mail: info@aba.org
URL: www.aba.org
Facebook: www.facebook.com/birders
Twitter: twitter.com/aba

626 ■ ABA Scholarships *(Undergraduate/Scholarship)*

Purpose: To promote the pursuit of educational and other bird-related activities. **Focus:** Animal rights; Animal science and behavior. **Qualif.:** Scholarship is open to American Birding Association active members only. **Criteria:** Scholarship recipients will be selected based on scholastic ability, professional interest, character and financial need.

Funds Avail.: No specific amount. **Duration:** Annual. **To Apply:** Applicants must submit a completed application form available from the ABA office and can be downloaded from the website; an essay about the importance of a bird; a letter of recommendation from a teacher, bird club member or mentor. **Deadline:** March 1.

627 ■ Richard E. Andrews Memorial Scholarships
(Undergraduate/Scholarship)

Purpose: To provide financial assistance for young birders. **Focus:** Animal rights; Animal science and behavior. **Qualif.:** Scholarship is open to American Birding Association active members. **Criteria:** Scholarship recipients will be selected based on scholastic ability, professional interest, character and financial need.

Funds Avail.: No specific amount. **Duration:** Annual. **To Apply:** Applicants must submit a complete application form (available at the ABA office and can be downloaded from the website); an essay explaining why he/she deserves the Andrews Scholarships; and a letter of recommendation from a teacher, bird club member or mentor.

628 ■ American Board of Funeral Service Education (ABFSE)
3414 Ashland Ave., Ste. G
Saint Joseph, MO 64506-1333
Ph: (816)233-3747
Fax: (816)233-3793
E-mail: exdir@abfse.org
URL: www.abfse.org

629 ■ ABFSE National Scholarship Program
(Undergraduate/Scholarship)

Purpose: To provide financial awards to students enrolled in funeral service or mortuary science programs to assist them in obtaining their professional education. **Focus:** Funeral services; Mortuary science. **Qualif.:** Applicant must have at least completed one semester (or quarter) of study in a funeral service or mortuary science education accredited by the American Board of Funeral Service Education; must have one term or semester remaining in his/her program which will commence after the award date in order to be considered for a full award; must be a citizen of the United States. **Criteria:** Selection of scholarship recipients is competitive. Awards are made by the Scholarship Committee of ABFSE.

Funds Avail.: $500 - $2,500. **Duration:** One year. **To Apply:** Applicants must apply online. Applicant must submit the email confirmation, tax forms, letter of recommendation, enrollment verification, Federal Tax Form 1040, an essay (1-2 pages; double-spaced) addressing your decision and choice to pursue a funeral service education; and transcript of records to: ABFSE Scholarship Committee. **Deadline:** March 1 or September 1. **Contact:** scholarships@abfse.org.

630 ■ American Brain Tumor Association (ABTA)
8550 W Bryn Mawr Ave., Ste. 550
Chicago, IL 60631
Ph: (773)577-8750
Fax: (773)577-8738
Free: 800-886-2282
E-mail: info@abta.org
URL: www.abta.org

631 ■ ABTA Discovery Grant Program *(Professional development/Grant)*

Purpose: To recognize investigators who have given the outstanding high risk/high impact research related to adult or pediatric brain tumors. **Focus:** Medical research. **Qualif.:** Applicants must be investigators from sciences outside traditional biology fields that conducting high risk/high impact research deemed to have the potential to change current diagnostic or treatment paradigms. **Criteria:** Selection will be based on the committees' criteria.

Funds Avail.: $50,000. **Duration:** Up to one year. **To Ap-

Awards are arranged alphabetically below their administering organizations

ply: Applicants must submit a letter of intent and may contact the Association for the application process and other information.

632 ■ ABTA Medical Student Summer Fellowship Program *(Undergraduate/Grant, Fellowship)*

Purpose: To recognize medical students who have given the outstanding brain tumor research. **Focus:** Medical research. **Qualif.:** Applicants must be currently enrolled in the first, second or third year of medical school; must conduct the proposed research and training at the Mentors' Institution; must not have previously been a fellow on an ABTA Medical Student Summer Fellowship. The host institution must be a non-profit institution or organization in the United States or Canada; must not be a governmental institution and; must agree to adhere to the Policies and Procedures for ABTA Research Grants and Fellowship. Mentors must have a doctoral degree, including MD, PhD, DrPH, DO or equivalent; must hold a full-time faculty appointment with the applicants' institution; must currently conduct brain tumor research; must make a specific time commitment to supervise the training and advancement of the fellow. **Criteria:** Applications will be reviewed using the following criteria: research question and significance; applicant; training environment and mentor. **Funds Avail.:** $3,000. **Duration:** 10-12 weeks. **To Apply:** Applicants must complete the online application through the ABTA grant portal, www.abtagrants.org, together with the following components: lay summary; a not to exceed three pages, including figures and tables of project narrative - research project plan, career development plan and list of publications cited in the application narrative; biosketches - research biosketches are required for the applicants and mentors; letter of support from mentors and from institutions; budget period detail and; budget justification. **Deadline:** January 27.

633 ■ ABTA Translational Grant Program *(Postdoctorate/Grant)*

Purpose: To support the collection of the preclinical data researchers need to apply for major funding from other sources. **Focus:** Oncology. **Qualif.:** MDs must be within eight years of completion of their post-residency training and hold a faculty or junior faculty appointment; PhDs must be within three to ten years of having received their doctorate and hold a faculty or junior faculty appointment. If a candidate holds multiple postdoctoral degrees, the last conferred postdoctoral degree will be used to determine eligibility. **Criteria:** Selection will be based on the potential of the research, the caliber of the laboratory environment and the experience of the investigator. **Funds Avail.:** $75,000. **To Apply:** Applicants must visit the website for the online application. Gathering the following information/documents in advance will expedite the completion of the online application: the year of the doctorate was conferred; knowledge of previous ABTA funding history and the names of any other organizations to whom the applicants are submitting grant applications; applicants' NIH biosketch in PDF format; letter from department chair in PDF format; description of the institutional support, equipment, resources for data set analysis and other critical resources available for the proposed project. A text box is provided online; a 250 words, publishable summary of study for a non-expert reader. A text box is provided online; research proposal in PDF format, not to exceed five pages including images; the name and email address of the grant officer, within the institution, who will certify the applicants' application. All applications must be certified by a grant officer prior to submission; a note about grant officer edit and submission authority. The applicants can choose to give the grant officer the authority to edit/change the application and can choose to allow the grant officer to submit the application, once complete. These authorities can be manage once a grant officer has been entered by editing permissions in the named grant officer section; ABTA's new grant portal provides personalized user views. Applicants and grant officers see all questions and responses. The applicants can allow the grant officer to edit or submit the application.

634 ■ Basic Research Fellowship Program *(Postdoctorate/Fellowship)*

Purpose: To encourage talented scientists early in their careers to enter, or remain in, the field of brain tumor research. **Focus:** Oncology. **Qualif.:** Applicant must be post-doctorate student intending to pursue a career in neuro-oncology; The institution where the fellowship training will be performed is located in the US or Canada; must be within two years of residency completion **Criteria:** Candidates will be evaluated based on some criteria by members of the Association's distinguished Scientific Advisory Council which include the caliber of the applicants, training program, and proposed research. **Funds Avail.:** $100,000. **Duration:** Up to two years. **To Apply:** Applicants must be completed online. Applicants must also provide essays regarding: year doctorate was conferred, knowledge of your previous ABTA funding history (if awarded), career goals (500 words), previous research (500 words), biosketch (NIH-formatted PDF format), a letter of support from sponsor, training plan, and sponsor's biosketch (NIH-format), names and e-mail addresses for three references, description of the institutional resources for data set analysis, summary of study (250 word, publishable), research proposal (PDF format, five pages only), name and e-mail address of the grant officer, note about grant officer edit and submission authority. **Contact:** Deneen Hesser at the above address.

635 ■ American Bus Association (ABA)
111 K St. NE, 9th Fl.
Washington, DC 20002
Ph: (202)842-1645
Fax: (202)842-0850
Free: 800-283-2877
E-mail: abainfo@buses.org
URL: www.buses.org
Facebook: www.facebook.com/AmericanBusAssociation
Twitter: twitter.com/AmericanBusAssn

636 ■ ABA Diversity Scholarships *(Undergraduate/Scholarship)*

Purpose: To mobilize greater involvement in the transportation industry. **Focus:** Transportation; Travel and tourism. **Qualif.:** Applicants must have completed first year of studies; must be majoring or have a course of study relevant to the transportation, travel, and tourism industry at an accredited university; and must have a minimum of 3.0 GPA. **Criteria:** Recipients are selected on the basis of academic merit, character, leadership and financial need and dedication to advancing the transportation, travel and tourism industry.

Funds Avail.: $2,500. **Duration:** Annual. **To Apply:** Interested applicants may visit the website for the online application process and other details. **Deadline:** April 11.

637 ■ ABA Members Scholarships for ABA Bus and Tour Operators Only *(Undergraduate/Scholarship)*

Purpose: To financially assist deserving students who have potentials to be future leaders in the transportation, travel and tourism industry. **Focus:** Transportation; Travel and tourism. **Qualif.:** Applicant must be an employee or a dependent of ABA bus and tour member companies employed for at least one year; must be entering first year of college, university or professional training school by fall; must have a minimum of 3.0 GPA or an average of "B". **Criteria:** Applicants will be selected based on their academic merit, community service, extracurricular activities, leadership and anticipated financial need.

Funds Avail.: $2,500 each. **Duration:** Annual. **Number Awarded:** 7. **To Apply:** Interested applicants may visit the website for the online application process and other details. **Deadline:** April 11.

638 ■ ABA Members Scholarships for All ABA Member Companies *(Undergraduate, Graduate/Scholarship)*

Purpose: To financially assist deserving students who have potentials to be future leaders in the transportation, travel and tourism industry. **Focus:** Transportation; Travel and tourism. **Qualif.:** Applicants must be employees or dependent of ABA members companies employed for at least one year; must have completed their first year of studies and pursuing with reference to the field of transportation, travel and tourism industry; must have a minimum of 3.0 GPA or an average of "B". **Criteria:** Applicants will be selected based on their academic merit, community service, extracurricular activities, leadership and anticipated financial need.

Funds Avail.: $2,500 each. **Duration:** Annual. **Number Awarded:** 7. **To Apply:** Interested applicants may visit the website for the online application process and other details. **Deadline:** April 11.

639 ■ American Bus Association Academic Merit Scholarships *(Undergraduate, Graduate/Scholarship)*

Purpose: To financially assist deserving students who have a potential to be future leaders in the transportation, travel, and tourism industry. **Focus:** Transportation; Travel and tourism. **Qualif.:** Applicants must have completed first year of studies and majoring or have a course of study relevant to the transportation, travel and tourism industry at an accredited university; must have a minimum of 3.4 GPA or higher. **Criteria:** Applicants will be selected based on their academic record, personal promise, character and financial need. Applicants affiliated with ABA-member companies will be given priority.

Funds Avail.: $2,500 each. **Duration:** Annual. **Number Awarded:** 2. **To Apply:** Interested applicants may visit the website for the online application process and must also submit an essay (500 words) discussing the role they will play in advancing the future of the transportation, motor coach, travel, and tourism/hospitality industry.

640 ■ Peter L. Picknelly Honorary Scholarships *(Undergraduate/Scholarship)*

Purpose: To mobilize greater involvement in the transportation industry. **Focus:** Transportation; Travel and tourism. **Qualif.:** Applicant must be a bus driver or maintenance personnel, or dependent of ABA operator member; must be in a technical school with two-years or more transportation-related education programs; must maintain a 3.0 GPA; must have demonstrated desire and ability to participate in a learning program. **Criteria:** Recipients are selected on the basis of academic merit; extracurricular activities; commitment to complete the transportation program; and financial need.

Funds Avail.: $2,500. **Duration:** Annual. **To Apply:** Interested applicants may visit the website for the online application process and other details. **Deadline:** April 11.

641 ■ American Cancer Society (ACS)
250 Williams St. NW
Atlanta, GA 30303-1002
Free: 800-227-2345
URL: www.cancer.org
Facebook: www.facebook.com/AmericanCancerSociety
Twitter: twitter.com/americancancer

642 ■ ACS Doctoral Degree Scholarships in Cancer Nursing *(Doctorate, Graduate/Scholarship)*

Purpose: To strengthen nursing practice by providing assistance for advance preparation in the field of cancer nursing research. **Focus:** Nursing. **Qualif.:** Applicants must be currently enrolled in or applying to a doctoral degree program in nursing or a related field of research; must meet the requirements for doctoral study and must have been accepted by the institution to which they have applied at the time of funding; must have a current license to practice as registered nurses; must project a program of study that integrates cancer nursing and provides evidence of faculty support for the program of study. Scholarship recipients must take a minimum of 18 credit hours or 6 courses per year; must demonstrate a commitment to cancer nursing as evidenced by recent experience, education and/or research in the specialty area. **Criteria:** Selection will be based on the following criteria: relevant professional experience in oncology; involvement in professional organizations, including leadership roles; involvement in activities of the American Cancer Society or other relevant volunteer organizations; clear, explicit and realistic professional goals; consideration of program components, particularly oncology content, in selecting a doctoral program; conduct or plan to conduct research that is important, methodologically sound, and relevant to the health of persons affected with cancer or at risk for cancer; commitment from a faculty advisor who is experienced in the student's area of study and will provide guidance in academic and research activities; selection of a doctoral program which will support the student's professional goals and research; and dedication to cancer nursing research.

Funds Avail.: $15,000 per year. **Duration:** Annual; up to two years. **To Apply:** Interested applicants must visit the website for the electronic application process. **Deadline:** October 15.

643 ■ ACS Graduate Scholarships in Cancer Nursing Practice *(Graduate, Master's, Doctorate/Scholarship)*

Purpose: To provide support graduate students pursuing a master's degree in cancer nursing or doctorate of nursing practice. **Focus:** Nursing. **Qualif.:** Applicants must be currently enrolled in or applying to a master's or DNP degree graduate program with demonstrated integration of cancer content; must have a current license to practice as a registered nurse. Students in bridge programs must have passed the N-CLEX examination and updated their status with the ACS Program Office by the time the award begins; must be pursuing an advance degree and not solely a postmaster's certificate. **Criteria:** Award will be given to the successful applicants who: have work experience in oncology; are involved in cancer-related professional and academic organizations; are involved in cancer-related volunteer organizations; have published or contributed to scholarly publications, presentations and creative works; are the recipients of professional and academic awards and honors; have considered program content, faculty and clinical resources related to cancer in selecting a graduate program; have a focus for scholarly activity in a specific area of cancer nursing; have strong letters of recommendation from two qualified professionals; have made a career commitment to cancer nursing; have formed explicit and realistic professional goals.

Funds Avail.: $10,000. **Duration:** Up to two years. **To Apply:** Interested applicants must visit the website for the electronic application process **Deadline:** February 1.

644 ■ American Cancer Society - Postdoctoral Fellowships *(Doctorate/Fellowship)*

Purpose: To support the training of researchers who have received a doctoral degree to provide initial funding leading to an independent career in cancer research. **Focus:** Health care services. **Qualif.:** Applicants must have obtained their doctoral degree prior to activation of the fellowship; must be US citizens, non-citizen nationals or permanent residents of the United States. **Criteria:** Selection will be based on the committee's criteria.

Funds Avail.: $48,000, $50,000 and $52,000 plus $4,000 per year fellowship allowance. **Duration:** Annual. **To Apply:** Interested applicants must visit the website for the electronic grant application process. **Deadline:** April 1 and October 15.

645 ■ American Cancer Society - Research Scholar Grants *(Doctorate, Professional development/Grant)*

Purpose: To provide resources for investigator-initiated research in a variety of cancer-relevant areas. **Focus:** Medical research. **Qualif.:** Applicants must have an independent research or faculty position and meet one of the following criteria: must be independent investigators within first 6 years of independent career with no more than one current R01-like support; must be independent investigators at any stage of their career with any level of prior funding; or independent investigators at any stage of their career with any level of prior funding. **Criteria:** Selection will be based on the following: demonstrated intellectual independence and committed research facilities; time limit on applicants' eligibility; and current grant support.

Funds Avail.: $165,000 per year. **Duration:** Up to four years. **To Apply:** Applicants must visit the website for the electronic grant application process. **Deadline:** April 1 and October 15.

646 ■ Mentored Research Scholar Grant in Applied and Clinical Research *(Doctorate, Professional development/Grant)*

Purpose: To support junior faculty members to become independent investigators as either clinician scientists or cancer control researchers. **Focus:** Medical research. **Qualif.:** Applicants must: be within the first four years of a full-time faculty appointment or the equivalent; not be independent investigators; have four years or less postdoctoral research training/experience at the time of application; have a clinical doctoral degree; have a research doctoral degree in a clinical discipline or equivalent in nursing, nutrition, psychology, social work, etc.; or have a research doctoral degree in a cancer control discipline or equivalent in behavioral, epidemiologic, health policy, health services or psychosocial research. **Criteria:** Selection will be based on the following: applicants' academic and scientific qualifications, potential to succeed as an independent investigator and commitment to research as a career; the appropriateness of the mentors' research qualifications in the proposed project area, the role of the mentors on the project, research productivity and prior success in fostering the development of cancer researchers; submitted research and training plan; documentation of the institutional commitment to the research development of the applicants.

Funds Avail.: Up to $135,000 for the awardee and $10,000 for the mentors ($10,000 is included in the $135,000) per year. **Duration:** Up to five years. **To Apply:** Interested applicants must visit the website for the electronic grant application process. **Deadline:** April 1 and October 15.

647 ■ American Center for Mongolian Studies (ACMS)
c/o Ctr. for East Asian Studies
642 Williams Hall
255 S 36th St.
Philadelphia, PA 19104-6305
Ph: (360)356-1020
E-mail: admin@mongoliacenter.org
URL: mongoliacenter.org

648 ■ ACMS Intensive Mongolian Language Fellowship Program *(Undergraduate/Fellowship)*

Purpose: To provide opportunities to Intermediate-level students to enhance their communicative competence through systematic improvement of reading, writing, listening and speaking skills in an authentic environment. **Focus:** General studies/Field of study not specified. **Qualif.:** Applicants must be in their intermediate-level of the study and be current members of the ACMS. **Criteria:** Fellowships are awarded to applicants based on merit and need. Criteria for fellowship selection includes: 1) ability to complete coursework at the Intermediate level; 2) importance of learning a Mongolian language for the applicant's academic studies or career plans; and 3) commitment to attend classes and maintain an average minimum grade of B+.

Funds Avail.: Up to $2,000. **To Apply:** Applicants must submit a completed application form, resume or CV, short description of applicant's Mongolian Language Proficiency, description on how to further their career or studies through program participation, a letter of recommendation and relevant information on financial need. **Deadline:** March 1.

649 ■ ACMS Library Fellowships *(Graduate, Other/Fellowship)*

Purpose: To support students or faculty members in library science to conduct a short-term project and/or research in Mongolia. **Focus:** Library and archival sciences. **Qualif.:** Applicants must be U.S. citizens or permanent residents currently enrolled in or teaching in a college or university in United States; must be advanced graduate students or faculty members in library science and must be current members of ACMS. **Criteria:** Applicants will be selected based on their submitted research project.

Funds Avail.: Up to $4,000. **Number Awarded:** 1-2. **To**

Apply: Applicants must submit a cover sheet, curriculum vitae, (500-word each) personal statement and a research statement, and a letter of support from a Research Sponsor in Mongolia. All application materials should be submitted in English. **Deadline:** February 15. **Contact:** ACMS at apply@mongoliacenter.org.

650 ■ ACMS U.S.-Mongolia Field Research Fellowship Program *(Graduate, Undergraduate/Fellowship)*

Purpose: To support students who wish to conduct field research in Mongolia. **Focus:** General studies/Field of study not specified. **Qualif.:** Applicants must be U.S. citizens or permanent residents currently enrolled full-time in a university or college and must be current members of ACMS. Undergraduate applicants must have at least third year standing in their program while graduate applicants can be at a masters or pre-dissertation doctoral level. **Criteria:** Applicants will be evaluated based on submitted research projects.

Funds Avail.: $4,000. **Duration:** Annual. **To Apply:** Applicants must submit the required materials and must include a letter of support from their Research Sponsor responsible for overseeing their research program. **Deadline:** February 15. **Remarks:** Established in 2006.

651 ■ Enkhbaatar Demchig Field Research Fellowship Program *(Undergraduate/Fellowship)*

Purpose: To support Mongolian students working collaboratively with international scholars from North America on academic research projects conducted in Mongolia. **Focus:** General studies/Field of study not specified. **Qualif.:** Applicants must be citizens of Mongolia and must be enrolled full-time in a university in Mongolia or in North America. Undergraduate applicants must have at least third year standing in their program, while graduate applicants can be at a master's, pre-dissertation, doctoral or post-doctoral level. Research projects from any academic field, including the physical and natural sciences, social sciences, and humanities are eligible. **Criteria:** Selection will be based on the committee's criteria.

Funds Avail.: No specific amount. **To Apply:** Applicants must submit the following items: a cover sheet, which is available from the ACMS website; a curriculum vitae that include the applicants' current address and academic standing, institution, current level of study, information on past academic research and studies and relevant work experience; copies of all undergraduate and graduate university transcripts; a personal statement of up to 500 words that explains the applicants' interest in participating in the program, background and experience with field research, if any, and how the research experience supported by the program fits into the applicants' long term career goals; a research plan of up to 500 words that details the type of research to be conducted and its importance to the field of study; an indication of any source of support applied for or anticipated for the research work in Mongolia; a letter of support and CV from the Research Sponsor who has agreed to supervise the applicants' research project. The letter should describe the Research Sponsor's relationship to the applicants and clearly indicate plans to be present in Mongolia to supervise the project during the proposed field research period.

652 ■ American Center for Oriental Research
656 Beacon St., 5th Fl.
Boston, MA 02215
Ph: (617)353-6571
Fax: (617)353-6575
E-mail: acor@bu.edu
URL: www.bu.edu/acor

653 ■ ACOR-CAORC Post-Graduate Fellowships *(Doctorate, Postdoctorate/Award)*

Purpose: To support a research in any sub-discipline within the natural and social sciences or humanities. **Focus:** Humanities; Natural sciences; Social sciences. **Qualif.:** Applicants must hold the PhD degree or the equivalent terminal degree in their field at the time of application and be U.S. citizens. **Criteria:** Applications will be evaluated by the ACOR Fellowship Committee.

Funds Avail.: $32,400. **Duration:** Annual; two to six months. **To Apply:** Applicants may download an application form online and must be sent as email attachments. Fill in all pertinent sections using Times New Roman, 12 point font (or similar). Applicants should set their paper size to U.S. Letter and maintain one-inch margins on all four sides. The required Health Insurance and Waiver Forms will be mailed later to successful applicants. Letters of recommendation must come directly from their referees. **Deadline:** February 1.

654 ■ ACOR-CAORC Pre-Doctorate Fellowships *(Graduate, Doctorate/Fellowship)*

Purpose: To support students conducting research in Jordan. **Focus:** Aquaculture. **Qualif.:** Applicants must be U.S. citizens and enrolled graduate students at the time of application. **Criteria:** Selection will be based on the committee's criteria.

Funds Avail.: $23,800. **Duration:** Annual. **To Apply:** Applicants may download an application form online and must be sent as email attachments. Fill in all pertinent sections using Times New Roman, 12 point font (or similar). Applicants should set their paper size to U.S. Letter and maintain one-inch margins on all four sides. The required Health Insurance and Waiver Forms will be mailed later to successful applicants. Letters of recommendation must come directly from their referees. **Deadline:** February 1.

655 ■ Pierre and Patricia Bikai Fellowships *(Graduate/Fellowship)*

Purpose: To assist graduate students conducting archaeological research in Jordan. **Focus:** Archeology. **Qualif.:** Applicants must be graduate students of any nationality except Jordanian citizens. **Criteria:** Selection will be based on the committee's criteria.

Funds Avail.: $600 per month. **Duration:** Annual; up to 2 months. **Number Awarded:** 1-2. **To Apply:** Applicants may download an application form online and must be sent as email attachments. Fill in all pertinent sections using Times New Roman, 12 point font (or similar). Applicants should set their paper size to U.S. Letter and maintain one-inch margins on all four sides. The required Health Insurance and Waiver Forms will be mailed later to successful applicants. Letters of recommendation must come directly from their referees. **Deadline:** February 1.

656 ■ Bert and Sally de Vries Fellowships *(Undergraduate, Graduate/Fellowship)*

Purpose: To support students participating in archaeological excavations in Jordan. **Focus:** Archeology. **Qualif.:** Applicants must be undergraduate or graduate students of any nationality except Jordanian citizens for participation on an archaeological project or research in Jordan **Criteria:**

Awards are arranged alphabetically below their administering organizations

Selection will be based on the committee's criteria.

Funds Avail.: $1,200. **Duration:** Annual. **To Apply:** Applicants may download an application form online and must be sent as email attachments. Fill in all pertinent sections using Times New Roman, 12 point font (or similar). Applicants should set their paper size to U.S. Letter and maintain one-inch margins on all four sides. The required Health Insurance and Waiver Forms will be mailed later to successful applicants. Letters of recommendation must come directly from their referees. **Deadline:** February 1. **Remarks:** Established in 2004.

657 ■ Jennifer C. Groot Memorial Fellowships
(Undergraduate, Graduate/Fellowship)

Purpose: To assist students to enable their participation in an archaeological excavation or survey in Jordan. **Focus:** Archeology. **Qualif.:** Applicants must be U.S. or Canadian citizens; must be undergraduate or graduate students. **Criteria:** Selection will be based on the committee's criteria.

Funds Avail.: $1,500. **To Apply:** Applicants may download an application form online and must be sent as email attachments. Fill in all pertinent sections using Times New Roman, 12 point font (or similar). Applicants should set their paper size to U.S. Letter and maintain one-inch margins on all four sides. The required Health Insurance and Waiver Forms will be mailed later to successful applicants. Letters of recommendation must come directly from their referees. **Deadline:** February 1.

658 ■ Harrell Family Fellowships *(Graduate/Fellowship)*

Purpose: To assist in partial payment of essential expenses for graduate students. **Focus:** Archeology. **Qualif.:** Applicants must be graduate students of any nationality except Jordanian citizens for participation on an archaeological project in Jordan. **Criteria:** Selection will be based on the committee's criteria.

Funds Avail.: $1,800. **To Apply:** Applicants may download an application form online and must be sent as email attachments. Fill in all pertinent sections using Times New Roman, 12 point font (or similar). Applicants should set their paper size to U.S. Letter and maintain one-inch margins on all four sides. The required Health Insurance and Waiver Forms will be mailed later to successful applicants. Letters of recommendation must come directly from their referees. **Deadline:** February 1.

659 ■ Burton MacDonald and Rosemarie Sampson Fellowships *(Undergraduate, Graduate/Fellowship)*

Purpose: To encourage students to take part in archaeological excavations in Jordan. **Focus:** Archeology. **Qualif.:** Applicants must be Canadian citizens or Canadian landed immigrants; must be undergraduate or graduate students. **Criteria:** Selection will be based on the committee's criteria.

Funds Avail.: $600 per month. **To Apply:** Applicants may download an application form online and must be sent as email attachments. Fill in all pertinent sections using Times New Roman, 12 point font (or similar). Applicants should set their paper size to U.S. Letter and maintain one-inch margins on all four sides. The required Health Insurance and Waiver Forms will be mailed later to successful applicants. Letters of recommendation must come directly from their referees. **Deadline:** February 1.

660 ■ National Endowment for the Humanities Research Fellowships *(Doctorate/Fellowship)*

Purpose: To support research in the humanities and disciplines of the social sciences that have humanistic content and employ humanistic methods. **Focus:** Humanities; Social sciences. **Qualif.:** Applicants must have a PhD degree or equivalent professional training at the time of application. They must be U.S. citizens or have lived in the United States for the three years immediately preceding the application deadline. **Criteria:** Selection will be based on the ACOR NEH panel's criteria.

Funds Avail.: $25,200. **Duration:** Up to six months. **Number Awarded:** 1-2. **To Apply:** Applicants may download an application form online and must be sent as email attachments. Fill in all pertinent sections using Times New Roman, 12 point font (or similar). Applicants should set their paper size to U.S. Letter and maintain one-inch margins on all four sides. The required Health Insurance and Waiver Forms will be mailed later to successful applicants. Letters of recommendation must come directly from their referees. **Deadline:** February 1.

661 ■ Kenneth W. Russell Memorial Fellowships
(Undergraduate, Graduate/Fellowship)

Purpose: To assist students in the fields archaeology, anthropology, conservation, or related areas. **Focus:** Anthropology; Archeology; Conservation of natural resources. **Qualif.:** Applicants must be Jordanian citizens (research or study may take place in any country). Undergraduate students attending a higher educational institution in Jordan may also be eligible. **Criteria:** Selection will be based on the committee's criteria.

Funds Avail.: $1,800. **To Apply:** Applicants may download an application form online and must be sent as email attachments. Fill in all pertinent sections using Times New Roman, 12 point font (or similar). Applicants should set their paper size to U.S. Letter and maintain one-inch margins on all four sides. The required Health Insurance and Waiver Forms will be mailed later to successful applicants. Letters of recommendation must come directly from their referees. **Deadline:** February 1.

662 ■ James A. Sauer Memorial Fellowships
(Graduate/Fellowship)

Purpose: To support students participating in archaeological research in Jordan. **Focus:** Archeology. **Qualif.:** Applicants must be enrolled graduate students of U.S. or Canadian citizenship. **Criteria:** Selection will be based on the committee's criteria.

Funds Avail.: A stipend of $400. **Duration:** Annual. **To Apply:** Applicants may download an application form online and must be sent as email attachments. Fill in all pertinent sections using Times New Roman, 12 point font (or similar). Applicants should set their paper size to U.S. Letter and maintain one-inch margins on all four sides. The required Health Insurance and Waiver Forms will be mailed later to successful applicants. Letters of recommendation must come directly from their referees. **Deadline:** February 1.

663 ■ American Ceramic Society (ACerS)
600 N Cleveland Ave., Ste. 210
Westerville, OH 43082
Ph: (240)646-7054
Fax: (204)396-5637
Free: 866-721-3322
E-mail: customerservice@ceramics.org
URL: www.ceramics.org
Facebook: www.facebook.com/acersnews
Twitter: twitter.com/ACerSNews

Awards are arranged alphabetically below their administering organizations

664 ■ Electronics Division Lewis C. Hoffman Scholarships *(Undergraduate/Scholarship)*

Purpose: To encourage academic interest and excellence among undergraduate students. **Focus:** Engineering, Materials; Materials research/science. **Qualif.:** Applicant must be a junior-year student, or a student who has recently completed his or her junior year; must have acquired a total of 70 or more semester credits or equivalent quarter credits; must have extracurricular activities. **Criteria:** Applicants will be selected based on the application requirements.

Funds Avail.: $2,000. **To Apply:** Applicant must submit a recommendation letter from a faculty member in the department; must have a 500 word essay on the year's topic. **Deadline:** May 15. **Contact:** Rick Ubic; Phone: 208-426-2309; E-mail: RickUbic@BoiseState.edu.

665 ■ American Chemical Society - Rubber Division
411 Wolf Ledges, Ste. 201
Akron, OH 44311
Ph: (330)595-5531
Fax: (330)972-5269
URL: www.rubber.org

666 ■ ACS Rubber Division Undergraduate Scholarships *(Undergraduate/Scholarship)*

Purpose: To support the need of chemistry-related students for financial assistance in obtaining a college degree. **Focus:** Chemistry; Engineering, Chemical; Engineering, Mechanical; Physics. **Qualif.:** Applicants must be students entering their junior or senior year for the fall-spring academic year and may have a major area study in chemistry, physics, chemical or mechanical engineering, polymer science or any other technical discipline relevant to the rubber industry. **Criteria:** Awards are given based on academic merit.

Funds Avail.: Up to $5,000. **Duration:** Annual. **Number Awarded:** 3. **To Apply:** Applicants may visit the website to verify the application process and other pieces of information. **Deadline:** March 1.

667 ■ American Choral Directors Association - Texas Chapter
c/o Sharon Lutz, Executive Director
7900 Centre Park Dr., Ste. A
Austin, TX 78754
Ph: (512)474-2801
Fax: (512)474-7873
URL: www.tcda.net

668 ■ TCDA Carroll Barnes Student Scholarships *(Undergraduate/Scholarship)*

Purpose: To support active TCDA student members in their continuing education. **Focus:** Education, Music; Religion. **Qualif.:** Applicants must be Texas college/university undergraduate students in music education or church music majors with 60+ credit hours and must have maintained at least 3.0 GPA on a 4.0 system. **Criteria:** Selection shall be based on the aforementioned qualifications and compliance with the application details.

Funds Avail.: No specific amount. **Duration:** Annual. **To Apply:** Applicants must submit a current transcript; two sealed letters of recommendation (one from a current TCDA member); letter of application (typed or printed) detailing musical contributions and accomplishments, potential for success in the choral music profession, and professional qualifications.

669 ■ TCDA Jim and Glenda Casey Professional Scholarships *(Other/Scholarship)*

Purpose: To support active TCDA members in their professional development. **Focus:** Education, Music. **Qualif.:** Applicants must be enrolled in a Texas college/university and have three years of continuous active membership. **Criteria:** Selection shall be based on the aforementioned qualifications and compliance with the application details.

Funds Avail.: $500. **Duration:** Annual. **Number Awarded:** 1. **To Apply:** Applicants must submit a letter of application describing their qualifications, professional goals, and a description of the higher education or workshop certification sought. They must also submit their respective resume or curriculum vitae. **Contact:** Sharon Lutz at sharon@tcda.net or call 512-474-2801.

670 ■ TCDA Bill Gorham Student Scholarships *(Undergraduate/Scholarship)*

Purpose: To support active TCDA student members in their continuing education. **Focus:** Education, Music; Religion. **Qualif.:** Applicants must be Texas college/university undergraduate students in music education or church music majors with 60+ credit hours and must have maintained at least 3.0 GPA on a 4.0 system. **Criteria:** Selection shall be based on the aforementioned qualifications and compliance with the application details.

Funds Avail.: $1,000. **Duration:** Annual. **Number Awarded:** 1. **To Apply:** Applicants must submit a current transcript; two sealed letters of recommendation (one from a current TCDA member); letter of application (typed or printed) detailing musical contributions and accomplishments, potential for success in the choral music profession, and professional qualifications. **Contact:** Sharon Lutz at sharon@tcda.net or call 512-474-2801.

671 ■ TCDA Abbott IPCO Professional Scholarships *(Other/Scholarship)*

Purpose: To support active TCDA members in their professional development. **Focus:** Education, Music. **Qualif.:** Applicants must be enrolled in a Texas college/university and have three years of continuous active membership. **Criteria:** Selection shall be based on the aforementioned qualifications and compliance with the application details.

Funds Avail.: $1,000. **Duration:** Annual. **Number Awarded:** 1. **To Apply:** Applicants must submit a letter of application describing their qualifications, professional goals, and a description of the higher education or workshop certification sought. They must also submit their respective resume or curriculum vitae. **Contact:** Sharon Lutz at sharon@tcda.net or call 512-474-2801.

672 ■ TCDA Gandy Ink Professional Scholarships *(Professional development/Scholarship)*

Purpose: To support active TCDA members in their professional development. **Focus:** Education, Music; Religion. **Qualif.:** Applicants must be enrolled in a Texas college/university and have three years of continuous active membership. **Criteria:** Selection shall be based on the aforementioned qualifications and compliance with the application details.

Awards are arranged alphabetically below their administering organizations

Funds Avail.: $1,000. **Duration:** Annual. **To Apply:** Applicants must submit a letter of application describing their qualifications, professional goals, and a description of the higher education or workshop certification sought. They must also submit their respective resume or curriculum vitae. **Contact:** Sharon Lutz at sharon@tcda.net or call 512-474-2801.

673 ■ TCDA General Fund Scholarships (Undergraduate/Scholarship)

Purpose: To support active TCDA student members in their continuing education. **Focus:** Education, Music; Religion. **Qualif.:** Applicants must be Texas college/university undergraduate students in music education or church music majors with 60+ credit hours and must have maintained at least 3.0 GPA on a 4.0 system. **Criteria:** Selection shall be based on the aforementioned qualifications and compliance with the application details.
Funds Avail.: $1,000. **Duration:** Annual. **Number Awarded:** 1. **To Apply:** Applicants must submit a current transcript; two sealed letters of recommendation (one from a current TCDA member); letter of application (typed or printed) detailing musical contributions and accomplishments, potential for success in the choral music profession, and professional qualifications. **Contact:** Sharon Lutz at sharon@tcda.net or call 512-474-2801.

674 ■ TCDA Past Presidents Student Scholarships (Undergraduate/Scholarship)

Purpose: To support active TCDA student members in their continuing education. **Focus:** Education, Music; Religion. **Qualif.:** Applicants must be Texas college/university undergraduate students in music education or church music majors with 60+ credit hours and must have maintained at least 3.0 GPA on a 4.0 system. **Criteria:** Selection shall be based on the aforementioned qualifications and compliance with the application details.
Funds Avail.: $1,000. **Duration:** Annual. **Number Awarded:** 1. **To Apply:** Applicants must submit a current transcript; two sealed letters of recommendation (one from a current TCDA member); letter of application (typed or printed) detailing musical contributions and accomplishments, potential for success in the choral music profession, and professional qualifications. **Contact:** Sharon Lutz at sharon@tcda.net or call 512-474-2801.

675 ■ TCDA Cloys Webb Student Scholarships (Undergraduate/Scholarship)

Purpose: To support active TCDA student members in their continuing education. **Focus:** Education, Music; Religion. **Qualif.:** Applicants must be Texas college/university undergraduate students in music education or church music majors with 60+ credit hours and must have maintained at least 3.0 GPA on a 4.0 system. **Criteria:** Selection shall be based on the aforementioned qualifications and compliance with the application details.
Funds Avail.: $1,000. **Duration:** Annual. **Number Awarded:** 1. **To Apply:** Applicants must submit a current transcript; two sealed letters of recommendation (one from a current TCDA member); letter of application (typed or printed) detailing musical contributions and accomplishments, potential for success in the choral music profession, and professional qualifications. **Contact:** Sharon Lutz at sharon@tcda.net or call 512-474-2801.

676 ■ American Clan Gregor Society (ACGS)

c/o Jeanne Lehr, Registrar
11 Ballas Ct.
Saint Louis, MO 63131-3038
Ph: (801)899-6157
E-mail: info@acgsus.org
URL: www.acgsus.org
Facebook: www.facebook.com/americanclangregorsocietyus

677 ■ Dr. Edward May Magruder Medical Scholarships (Undergraduate/Scholarship)

Purpose: To provide educational assistance to the students of the University of Virginia School of Medicine. **Focus:** Medicine. **Qualif.:** Applicants who are ACGHS members, children of members, or others who have lineage to the Clan Gregor are welcome to apply. Applicants must also be enrolled at least half-time or full-time for Federal Title VII programs. Those applicants who are in default on a federal loan or owe a refund on a federal grant are disqualified. Registration in Selective Service is also required for the application. **Criteria:** Recipients will be selected based on their satisfactory academic progress and financial information.
Funds Avail.: Varies. **Duration:** Annual. **Number Awarded:** Varies. **To Apply:** Applicants must complete both the FAFSA and the UVA School of Medicine Application (refer and download from www.healthsystem.virginia.edu). Previous year U.S Tax Returns is also required for the completion of the requirements. **Deadline:** April 1 for entering students; April 15 for returning students. **Remarks:** Established in 1927. **Contact:** Ms. Nancy L. Zimmer, nlb3w@virginia.edu.

678 ■ American Classical League (ACL)

860 NW Washington Blvd., Ste. A
Hamilton, OH 45013
Ph: (513)529-7741
Fax: (513)529-7742
Free: 800-670-8346
E-mail: info@aclclassics.org
URL: www.aclclassics.org
Facebook: www.facebook.com/ACLClassics

679 ■ Glenn Knudsvig Memorial Scholarships (Graduate, Undergraduate/Scholarship)

Purpose: To encourage teaching profession of classics by providing educational fund for deserving teacher and undergraduate or graduate member of the American Classical League. **Focus:** Classical studies. **Qualif.:** Applicant must be a current JCL sponsor who has attended the most recent NJCL convention; teacher of Latin, Greek or Classics with less than five years of classroom experience and has never attended an ACL Institute; graduate student who plans to teach K-12 Latin, Greek or Classics; teacher whose student participated in the 2010 National Latin Exam and has never attended an ACL Institute. **Criteria:** Recipient is chosen based on merit.
Funds Avail.: $250-$1,500. **Duration:** Annual. **To Apply:** Application form and instructions are available at the website. **Deadline:** January 15.

680 ■ Arthur Patch McKinlay Scholarships (Graduate, Undergraduate/Scholarship)

Purpose: To provide educational fund for deserving teachers, undergraduate or graduate members of the American Classical League as they pursue careers in teaching classics. **Focus:** Classical studies. **Qualif.:** Applicant must be

Awards are arranged alphabetically below their administering organizations

an ACL member for the preceding three years and planning to teach classics at elementary through secondary level for the current school year. **Criteria:** Recipient is chosen based on a review of proposed bonafide study program. **Funds Avail.:** $250-$1,500. **Duration:** Annual. **To Apply:** Application form and instructions are available at the website. **Deadline:** January 15.

681 ■ Ed Phinney Commemorative Scholarships (Graduate, Undergraduate/Scholarship)

Purpose: To support teacher and student members of the American Classical League. **Focus:** Classical studies. **Qualif.:** Applicant must be a current member of the American Classical League; must have been an ACL member for year prior to applying (if applying to attend ACL Institute for the first time, only current ACL membership required.) **Criteria:** Award is given to an eligible and proficient undergraduate classic major or graduate student of classics intending to teach at the elementary through college level. **Funds Avail.:** $250-$1,500. **Duration:** Annual. **To Apply:** Application form and instructions are available at the website. **Deadline:** January 15.

682 ■ American College of Chiropractic Orthopedists (ACCO)

c/o Boyd M. Peterson, President
1155 N Mayfair Rd.
Wauwatosa, WI 53226
Ph: (414)955-7999
Fax: (414)955-0110
URL: www.accoweb.org

683 ■ F. Maynard Lipe Scholarship Award (Master's, Postgraduate/Scholarship)

Purpose: To provide financial assistance to the candidate enrolled in a post-graduate orthopedic program leading to diplomate status or the masters degree program leading to a health science degree in orthopedics. **Focus:** Medicine, Chiropractic; Medicine, Orthopedic. **Qualif.:** Applicant must be enrolled in a CCE approved College of Chiropractic Post-Graduate Orthopedics course leading to Diplomate or the Masters Degree Program leading to a Health Science Degree in Orthopedics. **Criteria:** Applicants will be evaluated by the ACCO assigned Scholarship Committee. Selection shall be based on the aforementioned qualifications and compliance with the application details. **Funds Avail.:** $500. **Duration:** Annual. **To Apply:** Applicants should submit an article (1,000-2,500 words) on a subject current to Chiropractic Orthopedics as decided by the Scholarship Awards Committee and approved by the ACCO executive board. Articles should be doubled-spaced on white 8 1/2 x 11 inch paper. Six copies should be submitted to the Secretary of the Executive Board, with five of them being "clean" (having no identification as to the author or college), and one with full identification. Articles should include: title page; abstract and index term page; text pages or body; footnoted pages; and reference pages. **Deadline:** December 31. **Contact:** Boyd Peterson, DC, FACO. Chairman, Lipe Scholarship Committee, Spine Care-Medical College of Wisconsin, 1155 N Mayfair Rd., Wauwatosa, Wisconsin 53226.

684 ■ American College of Gastroenterology (ACG)

6400 Goldsboro Rd., Ste. 200
Bethesda, MD 20817
Ph: (301)263-9000
Fax: (301)263-9025
E-mail: info@acg.gi.org
URL: gi.org
Facebook: www.facebook.com/AmCollegeGastro
Twitter: twitter.com/AmCollegeGastro

685 ■ International GI Training Grant Award (Professional development/Grant)

Purpose: To provide partial financial support to physicians outside of the United States and Canada to receive clinical or clinical research training or education in Gastroenterology and Hepatology in selected medical training centers in North America. **Focus:** Gastroenterology; Medical research. **Qualif.:** Applicants must be Physicians who are not citizens of nor are currently residing in the United States or Canada, and who are working in gastroenterology or related areas. **Funds Avail.:** $10,000. **Duration:** Annual. **To Apply:** Applicants must submit a completed application form, a personal statement that summarizes the reasons and objectives of additional training, a curriculum vitae, copies of all published articles and abstracts within the last five years and a completed application form from the host training center. Three letters of recommendation from the training preceptor/director, from an ACG Fellow and from a person of the applicants' choosing. **Deadline:** March 31.

686 ■ American College of Healthcare Executives (ACHE)

1 N Franklin St., Ste. 1700
Chicago, IL 60606-3529
Ph: (312)424-2800
Fax: (312)424-0023
E-mail: contact@ache.org
URL: www.ache.org
Facebook: www.facebook.com/ACHEConnect/
 timeline?ref=page_internal
Twitter: twitter.com/ACHEConnect

687 ■ Albert W. Dent Graduate Student Scholarships (Undergraduate/Scholarship)

Purpose: To help ACHE Student Associates finance their education. **Focus:** Health care services. **Qualif.:** Applicant must be a Student Associate in good standing in the American College of Healthcare Executives; must be enrolled in full-time study for the upcoming term; must demonstrate financial need; must be a U.S or Canadian citizen; must have not been a previous recipient of the scholarship. **Criteria:** Selection of applicants will be based on the Scholarship application criteria. **Funds Avail.:** $5,000. **Duration:** Annual. **Number Awarded:** Up to 20. **To Apply:** Applicants must submit and complete the application form available online; must submit a current curriculum vitae or resume; an official undergraduate and graduate transcript; must provide three current letters of recommendation and essay. **Deadline:** March 31.

688 ■ Foster G. McGaw Graduate Student Scholarships (Graduate/Scholarship)

Purpose: To provide financial aid to students in healthcare management graduate programs to help offset tuition costs, student loans and expenses. **Focus:** Health care services. **Qualif.:** Applicant must be a Student Associate in good standing in the American College of Healthcare Executives;

Awards are arranged alphabetically below their administering organizations

enrolled in full-time study for the upcoming fall term, which is the final year of classroom work in a healthcare management graduate program; must demonstrate financial need; must be a U.S or Canadian citizen; and not a previous recipient of the scholarship. **Criteria:** Selection of applicants will be based on the scholarship application criteria.

Funds Avail.: $5,000. **Duration:** Annual. **Number Awarded:** Up to 20. **To Apply:** Applicants must submit and complete the application form available online; must submit a current curriculum vitae or resume; an official undergraduate and graduate transcript; must provide three current letters of recommendation and essay. **Deadline:** March 31.

689 ■ American College of Medical Toxicology (ACMT)

10645 N Tatum Blvd., Ste. 200-111
Phoenix, AZ 85028
Ph: (623)533-6340
Fax: (623)533-6520
E-mail: info@acmt.net
URL: www.acmt.net
Facebook: www.facebook.com/medicaltoxicology
LinkedIn: www.linkedin.com/groups/3516408/profile
Twitter: twitter.com/acmt

690 ■ Michael P. Spadafora Medical Toxicology Travel Awards *(Professional development/Grant)*

Purpose: To encourage individuals to pursue Medical Toxicology fellowship training. **Focus:** Toxicology. **Qualif.:** Applicants must be any PGY-1 or PGY-2 (or a PGY-3 in a 4 year program) members of an ACGME or AOA accredited residency program. **Criteria:** Selection will be based on the committee's criteria.

Funds Avail.: $1,500. **Number Awarded:** 1. **To Apply:** Applicants should provide the following information: curriculum vitae; letter documenting verification of employment; letter of support from the applicant's program director; letter of nomination from a current ACMT member (if the program director is an ACMT member, then that letter will suffice); and 1-2 page essay describing the applicants' interest and background in Medical Toxicology. **Deadline:** August 1.

691 ■ American College of Nurse-Midwives Foundation (ACNM)

PO Box 380272
Cambridge, MA 02238-0272
Ph: (240)485-1850
Fax: (617)876-5822
E-mail: fdn@acnm.org
URL: www.midwife.org/ACNM-Foundation

692 ■ ACNM Foundation, Inc. Fellowships for Graduate Education *(Doctorate, Postdoctorate/Fellowship, Grant)*

Purpose: To provide financial assistance for midwives actively enrolled in doctoral or post-doctoral studies. **Focus:** Midwifery. **Qualif.:** Applicants must be certified nurse-midwives (CNM) or certified midwives (CM); must be current members of the American College of Nurse-Midwives (ACNM); must be actively enrolled in a doctoral or post-doctoral education program; and must be graduate students in good standing as verified by the Academic Program Director. **Criteria:** Applicants are evaluated based on financial need and academic achievement.

Funds Avail.: No specific amount. **Duration:** Annual. **To Apply:** Applicants must submit application form; academic/career goals and plans; academic director form; and two academic recommendations.

693 ■ ACNM Foundation Midwives of Color-Watson Midwifery Student Scholarship *(Undergraduate/Scholarship)*

Purpose: To increase the number of midwives of color. **Focus:** Midwifery; Nursing. **Qualif.:** Applicants must be student midwives of color. **Criteria:** Applicants will be judged based on demonstrated academic excellence and financial need.

Funds Avail.: No specific amount. **Duration:** Annual. **To Apply:** Applicants must submit application information form; statement of career goals and plans; financial assessment form; statement of financial need; program director form; and the faculty recommendation form.

694 ■ American College Personnel Association (ACPA)

1 Dupont Cir. NW, Ste. 300
Washington, DC 20036-1137
Ph: (202)835-2272
Fax: (202)296-3286
E-mail: info@acpa.nche.edu
URL: www.myacpa.org
Facebook: www.facebook.com/myACPA
LinkedIn: www.linkedin.com/company/american-college-personnel-association
Twitter: twitter.com/ACPA

695 ■ ACPA Foundation Annual Fund *(Professional development/Grant)*

Purpose: To support scholarship and research activities of ACPA members. **Focus:** General studies/Field of study not specified. **Qualif.:** Applicants must be currently enrolled in a college, university and institution. **Criteria:** Recipients will be selected based on the submitted project proposal.

Funds Avail.: Approximately $10,000. **Duration:** Annual. **To Apply:** Applicants must complete the online application form including the name and contact information.

696 ■ American College of Surgeons (ACS)

633 N St. Clair St.
Chicago, IL 60611-3211
Ph: (312)202-5000
Fax: (312)202-5001
Free: 800-621-4111
E-mail: postmaster@facs.org
URL: www.facs.org
Facebook: www.facebook.com/AmCollSurgeons
LinkedIn: www.linkedin.com/company/american-college-of-surgeons
Twitter: twitter.com/amcollsurgeons

697 ■ Health Policy Scholarship for General Surgeons *(Professional development/Scholarship)*

Purpose: To support general surgeons in terms of cost of tuition, travel, housing, and subsistence. **Focus:** Surgery.

Qualif.: Award is open to general surgeons who are members in good standing of the ACS. Applicants must be at least 30 years old up to 60 on the date that the completed application is filed. **Criteria:** Selection will be based on the committee's criteria.

Funds Avail.: $8,000. **Duration:** Annual. **Number Awarded:** 2. **To Apply:** Applications for these scholarships consist of the following items, submitted as a single PDF file: one copy of the applicants' current curriculum vitae; one copy of a one-page essay, discussing why the applicants wish to receive the scholarship. Application form can be downloaded at the website. **Deadline:** February 2. **Contact:** ACS Scholarships Administrator at 312-202-5281; or Email: kearly@facs.org.

698 ■ American College of Veterinary Ophthalmologists (ACVO)
PO Box 1311
Meridian, ID 83680
Ph: (208)466-7624
Fax: (208)466-7693
E-mail: office15@avco.org
URL: www.acvo.org

699 ■ ACVO Best Resident Manuscript Awards *(Undergraduate/Recognition)*

Purpose: To recognize the best manuscript made by a resident. **Focus:** Optometry; Veterinary science and medicine. **Qualif.:** Candidates must be residents in an ABVO-approved residency training program or individuals who have completed their ABVO-approved residency within 18 months of the application deadline; manuscript must be published, in press, or accepted without further revisions. **Criteria:** Selection will be based on the committees' criteria.

Funds Avail.: $500. **Duration:** Annual. **Number Awarded:** 3. **To Apply:** Candidates may contact the Association for the application process and other information. **Deadline:** August 1.

700 ■ American Concrete Institute (ACI)
38800 Country Club Dr.
Farmington Hills, MI 48331-3439
Ph: (248)848-3700
Fax: (248)848-3701
URL: www.concrete.org
Facebook: www.facebook.com/AmericanConcreteInstitute
LinkedIn: www.linkedin.com/in/concreteaci
Twitter: www.twitter.com/concreteaci

701 ■ ACI BASF Construction Chemicals Student Fellowships *(Graduate, Undergraduate/Fellowship)*

Purpose: To support high-potential undergraduate and graduate students whose studies relate to concrete. **Focus:** Construction; Engineering, Chemical. **Qualif.:** Applicants must be undergraduate or graduate students in the award year with an interest in the area of specialty chemicals for new construction and repair/rehabilitation. Students must be nominated by an ACI-Member Faculty. **Criteria:** Selection is based on the application materials and on the interview.

Funds Avail.: $7,000-$10,000. **Duration:** Annual. **To Apply:** Applicants must submit a completed application form together with a resume, an essay (maximum of 500 words), two completed online reference forms, all undergraduate and graduate transcripts and Internship Requirement Agreement. **Deadline:** October 15.

702 ■ ACI Cagley ACI Student Fellowships *(Graduate, Master's, Undergraduate/Fellowship)*

Purpose: To support high-potential undergraduate and graduate students whose studies relate to concrete. **Focus:** Design. **Qualif.:** Applicants must have an interest in a career in design; must be undergraduates or enrolled in Master's programs; and must be serving an internship with Cagley & Associates prior to the award year. Students must be nominated by an ACI-Member Faculty. **Criteria:** Selection is based on the application materials and on the interview.

Funds Avail.: $7,000-$10,000. **Duration:** Annual. **To Apply:** Applicants must submit a completed application form together with a resume; an essay (maximum of 500 words); two completed online reference forms; all undergraduate and graduate transcripts; and Internship Requirement Agreement. **Deadline:** October 15.

703 ■ ACI Foundation Scholarships *(Graduate/Scholarship)*

Purpose: To support high-potential graduate students whose studies relate to concrete. **Focus:** Architecture; Engineering; Materials research/science. **Qualif.:** Applicants must have been accepted for graduate study at an accredited college or university in an engineering, architecture, or materials science program (graduate study program shall be in the area of concrete with an emphasis on structural design, materials, construction, or any combination thereof), and must be full-time first or second-year graduate students during the entire scholarship year. **Criteria:** Selection is based on the submitted application and materials.

Funds Avail.: $3,000-$5,000. **Duration:** Annual. **To Apply:** Applicants must submit a completed application form along with a resume; an essay (maximum of 500 words); two completed Online Reference Forms; and all undergraduate and graduate transcripts. **Deadline:** October 18.

704 ■ ACI President's Fellowships *(Doctorate, Master's/Fellowship)*

Purpose: To support high-potential undergraduate and graduate students whose studies relate to concrete. **Focus:** Construction; Design. **Qualif.:** Applicants must be in Master's or Doctoral programs in either construction, design, or education programs and must be nominated by an ACI-Member Faculty. **Criteria:** Selection is based on the application materials and on the interview.

Funds Avail.: $7,000-$10,000. **Duration:** Up to two academic years. **To Apply:** Applicants must submit a completed application form together with a resume; an essay (maximum of 500 words); two completed online reference forms; all undergraduate and graduate transcripts; and Internship Requirement Agreement. **Deadline:** October 15.

705 ■ ACI W.R. Grace Scholarships *(Graduate/Scholarship)*

Purpose: To support high-potential graduate students whose studies relate to concrete. **Focus:** Architecture; Engineering; Materials research/science. **Qualif.:** Applicants must have been accepted for graduate study at an accredited college or university in an engineering, architec-

Awards are arranged alphabetically below their administering organizations

ture, or materials science program (graduate study program shall be in the area of concrete with an emphasis on structural design, materials, construction, or any combination thereof), and must be full-time first or second-year graduate students during the entire scholarship year. **Criteria:** Selection is based on the submitted application and materials.

Funds Avail.: No specific amount. **Duration:** Annual. **To Apply:** Applicants must submit a completed application form along with a resume; an essay (maximum of 500 words); two completed Online Reference Forms; and all undergraduate and graduate transcripts.

706 ■ ACI Baker Student Fellowships (Undergraduate, Graduate/Fellowship)

Purpose: To support high-potential undergraduate and graduate students whose studies relate to concrete. **Focus:** Construction; Engineering, Civil. **Qualif.:** Applicant must be an undergraduate student with an interest in a career in the construction industry; entering junior or senior year; studying in a civil engineering, structural engineering, or construction industry management program; serving an internship before the award period (this internship may be served with a firm other than Baker Concrete Construction); and must be nominated by an ACI-Member Faculty. **Criteria:** Selection is based on the application materials and on the interview.

Funds Avail.: $7,000-$10,000. **Duration:** Annual; Up to two academic years. **Number Awarded:** 2. **To Apply:** Applicants must submit a completed application form together with a resume; an essay (maximum of 500 words); two completed online reference forms; all undergraduate and graduate transcripts; and Internship Requirement Agreement. **Deadline:** October 15.

707 ■ ACI Elmer Baker Student Fellowships (Undergraduate, Graduate/Fellowship)

Purpose: To support high-potential undergraduate and graduate students whose studies relate to concrete. **Focus:** Construction. **Qualif.:** Applicant must be an undergraduate student entering junior or senior year with an interest in a career in the construction industry; serving an internship with Baker Concrete Construction before the award period; and must be nominated by an ACI-Member Faculty. **Criteria:** Selection is based on the application materials and on the interview.

Funds Avail.: $7,000-$10,000. **Duration:** Annual. **Number Awarded:** 1. **To Apply:** Applicants must submit a completed application form together with a resume; an essay (maximum of 500 words); two completed online reference forms; all undergraduate and graduate transcripts; and Internship Requirement Agreement. **Deadline:** October 15.

708 ■ Katharine & Bryant Mather Scholarship (Graduate/Scholarship)

Purpose: To support high-potential graduate students whose studies relate to concrete. **Focus:** Architecture; Engineering; Materials research/science. **Qualif.:** Applicants must have been accepted for graduate study at an accredited college or university in an engineering, architecture, or materials science program (graduate study program shall be in the area of concrete with an emphasis on structural design, materials, construction, or any combination thereof); must be full-time first or second-year graduate students during the entire scholarship year; and must be pursuing a research on sustainable development of concrete. **Criteria:** Selection is based on the submitted application and materials.

Funds Avail.: No specific amount. **To Apply:** Applicants must submit a completed application form along with a resume; an essay (maximum of 500 words); two completed Online Reference Forms; and all undergraduate and graduate transcripts. **Remarks:** Established in 1988. **Contact:** Julie Webb, Marketing Communications Specialist; Phone: 248-848-3148; Email: Julie.Webb@concrete.org.

709 ■ Kumar Mehta Scholarship (Graduate/Scholarship)

Purpose: To support high-potential graduate students whose studies relate to concrete. **Focus:** Architecture; Engineering; Materials research/science. **Qualif.:** Applicants must have been accepted for graduate study at an accredited college or university in an engineering, architecture, or materials science program (graduate study program shall be in the area of concrete with an emphasis on structural design, materials, construction, or any combination thereof); must be a full-time first or second-year graduate student during the entire scholarship year; and must be pursuing a research on sustainable development of concrete. **Criteria:** Selection is based on the submitted application and materials.

Funds Avail.: No specific amount. **To Apply:** Applicants must submit a completed application form along with a resume; an essay (maximum of 500 words); two completed Online Reference Forms; and all undergraduate and graduate transcripts. **Contact:** Julie Webb, Marketing Communications Specialist; Phone: 248-848-3148; Email: Julie.Webb@concrete.org.

710 ■ ACI Charles Pankow Foundation ACI Student Fellowships (Graduate, Undergraduate/Fellowship)

Purpose: To support high-potential undergraduate and graduate students whose studies relate to concrete. **Focus:** Construction. **Qualif.:** Applicant must be in an undergraduate or graduate class in the award year; serving an internship in a construction environment with the Charles Pankow Company prior to the award year; and must be nominated by an ACI-Member Faculty. **Criteria:** Selection is based on the application materials and on the interview.

Funds Avail.: $10,000. **Duration:** Annual. **To Apply:** Applicants must submit a completed application form together with a resume; an essay (maximum of 500 words); two completed online reference forms; all undergraduate and graduate transcripts; and Internship Requirement Agreement. **Deadline:** October 15.

711 ■ Bertold E. Weinberg Scholarship (Graduate/Scholarship)

Purpose: To support high-potential graduate students whose studies relate to concrete. **Focus:** Architecture; Engineering; Materials research/science. **Qualif.:** Applicants must have been accepted for graduate study at an accredited college or university in an engineering, architecture, or materials science program (graduate study program shall be in the area of concrete with an emphasis on structural design, materials, construction, or any combination thereof), and must be full-time first or second-year graduate students during the entire scholarship year. **Criteria:** Selection is based on the submitted application and materials.

Funds Avail.: No specific amount. **To Apply:** Applicants must submit a completed application form along with a resume; an essay (maximum of 500 words); two completed Online Reference Forms; and all undergraduate and graduate transcripts. **Contact:** Julie Webb, Marketing Com-

Awards are arranged alphabetically below their administering organizations

munications Specialist; Phone: 248-848-3148; Email: Julie.Webb@concrete.org.

712 ■ ACI Richard N. White Student Fellowships (Master's/Fellowship)

Purpose: To support high-potential undergraduate and graduate students whose studies relate to concrete. **Focus:** Engineering, Materials. **Qualif.:** Applicant must have an interest in materials enrolling in a Master's program during the award year and must be nominated by an ACI-Member Faculty. **Criteria:** Selection is based on the application materials and on the interview.

Funds Avail.: Amount varies. **To Apply:** Applicants must submit a completed application form together with a resume; an essay (maximum of 500 words); two completed online reference forms; all undergraduate and graduate transcripts; and Internship Requirement Agreement. **Contact:** Julie Webb, Marketing Communications Specialist; Phone: 248-848-3148; Email: Julie.Webb@concrete.org.

713 ■ American Conifer Society (ACS)
PO Box 1583
Maple Grove, MN 55311
Ph: (763)657-7251
E-mail: nationaloffice@conifersociety.org
URL: conifersociety.org

714 ■ American Conifer Society Scholarships (Undergraduate/Scholarship)

Purpose: To provide financial assistance to ACS members to pursue their education. **Focus:** Horticulture. **Qualif.:** Applicant must be a current ACS member. **Criteria:** Selection of applicant is based on merit in the field of agriculture.

Funds Avail.: $2,500. **Duration:** Annual. **To Apply:** Application form may be downloaded from The American Conifer Society Web Page: www.conifersociety.org. **Deadline:** June 1. **Contact:** Gerald P. Kral, ACS Scholarship Committee: 900 Winton Rd., N, Rochester, NY 14609; Email: gkral1@rochester.rr.com.

715 ■ American Constitution Society for Law and Policy (ACS)
1333 H St. NW, 11th Fl.
Washington, DC 20005
Ph: (202)393-6181
Fax: (202)393-6189
E-mail: info@acslaw.org
URL: www.acslaw.org
Facebook: www.facebook.com/acslaw
Twitter: twitter.com/ACSLaw

716 ■ ACS Law Fellowships (Graduate/Fellowship)

Purpose: To provide a recent law school graduate a year of legal experience and training. **Focus:** Law. **Qualif.:** Applicant must be a recent law school graduate from a U.S. law school; have a strong academic record; excellent research, writing and oral communication skills; strong interpersonal skills; and demonstrate initiative, organization and attention to detail. **Criteria:** Selection is based on the application materials.

Funds Avail.: No specific amount. **To Apply:** Applicants must send a cover letter; resume; 5-10 page, self-edited writing sample; and three references to ACS via U.S. mail.

717 ■ American Copy Editors Society Education Fund (ACES)
7 Avenida Vista Grande, Ste. B7, No. 467
Santa Fe, NM 87508
E-mail: info@copydesk.org
URL: www.copydesk.org/blog/category/education_fund

718 ■ Aubespin Scholarships (Undergraduate/Scholarship)

Purpose: To encourage young individuals to continue their career as potential professional copy editors. **Focus:** Editors and editing. **Qualif.:** Applicants must be college juniors, seniors or recently college graduate students who will take full-time copy editing jobs or internships. **Criteria:** Selection shall be based on the commitment to a career in copy editing, exemplary work and academic achievement, and recommendations from teachers and work supervisors.

Funds Avail.: $2,500. **Duration:** Annual. **Number Awarded:** 1. **To Apply:** Applicants should send, electronically, the following: an original essay on the aspects of copy editing most important in a multi-media world (must not exceed 500 words); resume; names and contact information for three references (supervisors and/or faculty members); and either (but not both) six headlines or tweets, or a mix thereof, that have been written, or the answers to the exercise given by the Society through the Educational Fund website. **Deadline:** November 16. **Contact:** Alex Cruden at alex@copydesk.org.

719 ■ American Council of Blind Students (ACBS)
American Council of the Blind
2200 Wilson Blvd., Ste. 650
Arlington, VA 22201-3354
Ph: (202)467-5081
Fax: (202)465-5085
Free: 800-424-8666
E-mail: info@acb.org
URL: acb.org

720 ■ American Council of the Blind Scholarships (Graduate, Undergraduate/Scholarship)

Purpose: To support blind students in their educational pursuits. **Focus:** General studies/Field of study not specified. **Qualif.:** Applicants must be undergraduate or graduate blind students. **Criteria:** Selection is based on the submitted application and materials.

Funds Avail.: No specific amount. **To Apply:** Application process must be completed online. In addition, applicants must submit a Certification of Legal Blindness from an ophthalmologist, optometrist, physician or other competent authority; certified transcripts; acceptance letter from a university for entering freshmen; high school transcripts (entering freshmen and sophomores) or undergraduate transcripts (graduate students); and a recommendation letter from a current or recent instructor. **Deadline:** March 1. **Contact:** Dee Theien; Email: deetheien@acbes.org; Phone: (612) 332-3242 or (800) 866-3242.

721 ■ American Council of Engineering Companies of Illinois (ACEC-IL)
5221 S 6th Street Rd., Ste. 120
Springfield, IL 62703
Ph: (217)529-7430

Awards are arranged alphabetically below their administering organizations

Fax: (217)529-2742
E-mail: info@acecil.org
URL: www.acecil.org

722 ■ American Council of Engineering Companies of Illinois Scholarships *(Undergraduate/Scholarship)*

Purpose: To assist engineering students of Illinois in reaching their goals of higher education. **Focus:** Engineering. **Qualif.:** Applicants must be U.S. citizens, specifically, Illinois engineering students currently enrolled and pursuing a bachelor's, master's or PhD degree in an Accreditation Board for Engineering and Technology (ABET)-accredited engineering program or in an accredited land surveying program located in the state of Illinois; may be students entering their junior, senior, fifth, master's or graduate year in the fall. **Criteria:** Applicants are evaluated based on academic merit.

Funds Avail.: No specific amount. **Duration:** Annual. **To Apply:** Applicants must submit the completed application form along with student's GPA; work experience; extracurricular college activities; recommendation from a professor, consulting engineering or land surveyor; and a 500-word essay.

723 ■ American Council on Germany (ACG)
14 E 60th St., Ste. 1000
New York, NY 10022
Ph: (212)826-3636
Fax: (212)758-3445
E-mail: info@acgusa.org
URL: www.acgusa.org
Facebook: www.facebook.com/acgusa
LinkedIn: www.linkedin.com/groups/3662105/profile
Twitter: twitter.com/acg_usa

724 ■ Dr. Guido Goldman Fellowships *(Doctorate, Postdoctorate/Fellowship)*

Purpose: To promote the study of German and European issues by American scholars. **Focus:** European studies; German studies. **Qualif.:** Applicants must be U.S. citizens; postgraduate students; or enrolled in PhD programs and finishing their dissertation. **Criteria:** Selection Committee will select applicants based on the contribution the project will make to an understanding of the economics and foreign relations of Germany, Europe and North America; the feasibility of the proposed project; the training of the applicant; and the scholarly potential of the applicant.

Funds Avail.: Covers the cost of pre-approved international and domestic travel and a per diem stipend of $200. **Duration:** Annual. **To Apply:** Applicants must submit a cover letter, outlining the applicant's professional and personal objectives for the fellowship; a 2-page project proposal; a current CV; and two letters of reference. **Deadline:** July 1. **Remarks:** Established in 2003. **Contact:** Robin Cammarota-Nicolson, Fellowship Coordinator at 212-826-3636 or rcammarota@acqusa.org.

725 ■ Dr. Richard M. Hunt Fellowships *(Doctorate, Postdoctorate/Fellowship)*

Purpose: To promote the study of German issues by American scholars. **Focus:** German studies. **Qualif.:** Applicants must be U.S. citizens; postgraduate students; or enrolled in PhD programs and finishing their dissertation. **Criteria:** The selection committee will evaluate applications based on the contribution the project will make to a better understanding of German history; the feasibility of the proposed project; the training of the applicant; and the scholarly potential of the applicant.

Funds Avail.: Covers the cost of pre-approved international and domestic travel and a per diem stipend of $200. **To Apply:** Applicants must submit a cover letter, outlining the applicant's professional and personal objectives for the fellowship; a 2-page project proposal; a current CV; and two letters of reference. **Deadline:** July 1. **Remarks:** Established in 2003. **Contact:** Robin Cammarota-Nicolson, Fellowship Coordinator at 212-826-3636 or rcammarota@acqusa.org.

726 ■ Anna-Maria and Stephen M. Kellen Fellowships *(Professional development/Fellowship)*

Purpose: To enable American and German professionals to conduct research and meet with their professional counterparts. **Focus:** Broadcasting; Journalism. **Qualif.:** Applicants must be mid-career journalists who hold German citizenship and live and work in Berlin. Working knowledge of the English language is a prerequisite for a fellowship. Journalists who are employed by a media organization are encouraged to apply. Freelance journalists are asked to demonstrate where resulting articles and/or related pieces could be published. **Criteria:** Selection will be based on the committee's criteria.

Funds Avail.: A daily stipend of $200 to cover housing, meals, and local transportation. **Duration:** Annual. **To Apply:** Applicants must complete and submit the following requirements: a cover letter outlining their personal and professional objectives for the fellowship; a project proposal of at least two pages detailing the background and scope of their project, the general sources and institutions with whom they would like to consult while in the United States and the relevance of the project; a current resume; two letters of recommendation; several recent writing clips. **Deadline:** August 28. **Contact:** Applications may be sent via e-mail to fellowships@acgusa.org.

727 ■ McCloy Fellowships in Agriculture *(Professional development/Fellowship)*

Purpose: To enable American and German professionals to conduct significant research in agriculture and meet with their professional counterparts. **Focus:** Agricultural sciences. **Qualif.:** Applicants must hold US or German citizenship. American applicants need not be fluent in German, although some background in the language could be helpful. German fellows visiting the United States should have a basic knowledge of English. Applicants who wish to build on their experience while at an earlier stage in their careers are preferred. **Criteria:** Applicants are chosen by the American Council on Germany in conjunction with the American Farm Bureau Federation and the Deutscher Bauernverband.

Funds Avail.: A daily allowance of $200 per individual. **Duration:** Annual. **Number Awarded:** Varies. **To Apply:** Applicants may contact Robin Cammarota-Nicolson for the application process and other information. **Contact:** Robin Cammarota-Nicolson, Fellowship Manager, at fellowships@acgusa.org.

728 ■ McCloy Fellowships in Environmental Policy *(Professional development/Fellowship)*

Purpose: To provide German and American midcareer professionals and academics with the opportunity to travel across the Atlantic for three weeks to undertake indepen-

Awards are arranged alphabetically below their administering organizations

dent research and meet with their counterparts to exchange best practices and foster professional and intellectual ties. **Focus:** Environmental law; Journalism. **Qualif.:** Applicants must be a German or US citizen; must be 45 years of age or younger at the time of the application deadline; must have a minimum of five years of relevant, full-time work experience; must earned a bachelor's degree (or equivalent); must have a track record of outstanding professional performance; and must have a sincere commitment to furthering the transatlantic relationship. **Criteria:** Selection will be based on the committee's criteria.

Funds Avail.: A daily stipend of $200 to cover housing, meals, and local transportation. **Duration:** Annual. **To Apply:** Applicants must submit the following requirements: a cover letter outlining their personal and professional objectives for the fellowship; a project proposal of at least two pages detailing the background and scope of their project, the general sources and institutions with whom they would like to consult while abroad and the relevance of the project for environmental policy and transatlantic relations; a current resume; two letters of recommendation. **Deadline:** May 1. **Contact:** American Council on Germany, at the above address. Or email: fellowships@acgusa.org.

729 ■ McCloy Fellowships in Journalism (Professional development/Fellowship)

Purpose: To provide print, broadcast, and new-media journalists in the relatively early stages of their career with the opportunity to travel to Europe or the United States for up to three weeks to conduct research and interviews and pursue stories of their own design. **Focus:** Journalism. **Qualif.:** Applicants must hold US or German citizenship; must 45 years of age or younger at the time of the application deadline; must have a minimum of five years of relevant, full-time work experience; must have earned a bachelor's degree (or equivalent); must have track record of outstanding professional performance; must have a sincere commitment to furthering the transatlantic relationship. **Criteria:** Selection will be based on the committee's criteria.

Funds Avail.: A daily stipend of $200 to cover housing, meals, and local transportation. **Duration:** Annual. **To Apply:** Applicants must submit the following requirements: a cover letter outlining what the applicants expect to gain in terms of personal and professional development from the fellowship; a current curriculum vitae; a project proposal of at least two pages detailing the background and scope of their proposed story or stories, the general sources with whom they plan to consult while abroad and the relevance of the project for transatlantic relations; two letters of recommendation. **Deadline:** June 1. **Contact:** American Council on Germany, at the above address. Or email: fellowships@acgusa.org.

730 ■ McCloy Fellowships in Urban Affairs (Professional development/Fellowship)

Purpose: To enable American and German professionals to conduct research and meet with their professional counterparts. **Focus:** Urban affairs/design/planning. **Qualif.:** Applicants must hold US or German citizenship. While in the United States, German fellows should tour US cities, take part in City Council meetings and attend a National League of Cities convention in Washington, DC. American fellows should meet with local officials, European Union agencies and members of the Deutscher Stadtetag while being hosted by fellowship alumni. **Criteria:** Applicants are selected by the American Council on Germany in conjunction with the National League of Cities and the Deutscher Stadtetag.

Funds Avail.: A daily allowance of $200. **Duration:** Annual. **To Apply:** Applicants may contact Robin Cammarota-Nicolson for the application process and other information.

731 ■ American Council of Independent Laboratories (ACIL)

1875 I St. NW, Ste. 500
Washington, DC 20006
Ph: (202)887-5872
Fax: (202)887-0021
E-mail: info@acil.org
URL: www.acil.org
Facebook: www.facebook.com/ACIL.info

732 ■ American Council of Independent Laboratories Scholarships (Undergraduate/Scholarship)

Purpose: To provide financial assistance for helping to ensure future generations of skilled employees for the laboratory testing community. **Focus:** Physical sciences. **Qualif.:** Applicants must be students attending their junior year or higher in a four-year, bachelor degree major in any of the physical sciences practiced by ACIL members: physics, chemistry, engineering, geology, biology, or environmental science in granting institution or graduate program within the United States. **Criteria:** Recipient will be selected based on academic achievement, career goals, leadership, and financial need.

Funds Avail.: $1,000 - $4,000. **Duration:** Annual. **To Apply:** Applicant must submit a completed application form, a brief resume or personal statement outlining the activities in college, including field of study and future plans; two letters of recommendation from faculty members of the university currently attending; transcript of grades; and information on any other scholarship or grant aid now receiving. **Deadline:** April 4.

733 ■ American Council of Learned Societies (ACLS)

633 3rd Ave., 8th Fl.
New York, NY 10017-6795
Ph: (212)697-1505
Fax: (212)949-8058
URL: www.acls.org
Facebook: www.facebook.com/ACLS1919/
Twitter: twitter.com/acls1919/

734 ■ ACLS African Humanities Fellowships (Postdoctorate/Fellowship)

Purpose: To support dissertations and projects in African studies in all disciplines of the humanities. **Focus:** African studies; Humanities. **Qualif.:** Applicants must be nationals and residents of a country in sub-Saharan Africa, with a current affiliation at an institution in Ghana, Nigeria, South Africa, Tanzania or Uganda. Applicants for Dissertation-Completion Fellowships should be in the final year of writing the dissertation at a university in Ghana, Nigeria, Tanzania or Uganda. Dissertation-Completion Fellowships are not available in South Africa. Applicants for Early Career Postdoctoral Fellowships must be working in Ghana, Nigeria, South Africa, Tanzania or Uganda and must have completed the PhD no more than five years ago. **Criteria:** Selection will be based on the committee's criteria.

Funds Avail.: No specific amount. **To Apply:** Projects must

Awards are arranged alphabetically below their administering organizations

be in the humanities and must be carried out in sub-Saharan Africa. Applicants must submit a completed application by email or may be mailed to the AHP/ACLS offices in New York. **Deadline:** November 2.

735 ■ ACLS Collaborative Research Fellowships *(Doctorate/Fellowship)*

Purpose: To offer small teams of two or more scholars the opportunity to collaborate intensively on a single, substantive project. **Focus:** Humanities; Social sciences. **Qualif.:** A collaborative project must constitute of at least two scholars who are each seeking salary-replacement stipends for six to twelve continuous months of supported research leave to pursue full-time collaborative research during the fellowship tenure. The project coordinator must have an appointment at a US-based institution of higher education. Other project members may be at institutions outside the United States or may be independent scholars; must hold a PhD degree or its equivalent in publications and professional experience at the time of application. **Criteria:** Proposals will be judged along the following criteria: (1) Intellectual significance of the project, including its ambition and scope, and its potential contribution to scholarship in the humanities; (2) Relevance of the research questions being posed, the appropriateness of research methods, the feasibility of the work plan, the appropriateness of the field work to be undertaken, the archival or source materials to be studied and the research site; (3) Qualifications, expertise and commitment of the project coordinator and collaborators; (4) Detail and soundness of the process and product of the collaboration, including dissemination plans; (5). Degree to which the proposed collaboration represents innovative practice in the applicants' disciplines and subfields; (6) Potential for success, including the likelihood that the work proposed will be completed and lead to distance results within the projected timeframe; where appropriate, the collaborators' previous record of success; and the size of the proposed budget in relation to anticipated results. **Funds Avail.:** Varies. **Duration:** A total tenure period of 24 months. **Number Awarded:** Varies. **To Apply:** Applications must include the following: completed application forms; participant information sheet, listing all collaborators and additional project members; 10-page Proposal (double space, in Times New Roman, 11-point font). The proposal should describe the intellectual significance of the research project and explain in detail the process and product of the collaboration; two-page bibliography that places the project in intellectual context and includes relevant work in all of the disciplines involved in the project; research plan, including a timeline of the proposed research activities that specifies the location, duration and names of individuals involved in each stage. This may be in the form of a graphic timeline or narrative description; budget statement, outlining salary replacement, costs of research assistance, travel and research materials; a no more than three pages publications list for each collaborator; two reference letters that provide explicit information on the proposed collaborative project and the collaborators. **Deadline:** September 23.

736 ■ ACLS Fellowships *(Advanced Professional, Professional development/Fellowship)*

Purpose: To help scholars devote to full-time research and writing. **Focus:** Humanities; Social sciences. **Qualif.:** Applicants must: be U.S. citizens or permanent residents as of the application deadline; have PhD degrees conferred at least two years before the application deadline; and, have a lapse of at least two years since the last supported research leave. **Criteria:** Recipients will be selected based on academic rank. **Funds Avail.:** $35,000 (Assistant Professors and career equivalent); $45,000 (Associate Professors and career equivalent); $70,000 (full Professors and career equivalent). **Duration:** Annual; From 6 to 12 consecutive months. **Number Awarded:** Varies. **To Apply:** Applications must be submitted online and must include: completed application form; proposal (no more than five pages, double spaced, in Times New Roman 11-point font); up to two additional pages of images, musical scores, or other similar supporting non-text materials [optional]; bibliography (no more than two pages); publications list (no more than two pages); and, two reference letters. **Deadline:** September 23.

737 ■ American Research in the Humanities in China Fellowships *(Doctorate/Fellowship)*

Purpose: To support research that reflects an understanding of the present Chinese academic and research environment. **Focus:** Humanities; Social sciences. **Qualif.:** Applicants must be citizens or permanent residents of the United States who have lived in the United States continuously for at least three years as of the application deadline date; must hold a PhD degree conferred prior to the application deadline. However, an established scholar who can demonstrate the equivalent of the PhD in publications and professional experience may also qualify. **Criteria:** Selection will be based on the committee's criteria. **Funds Avail.:** Up to $50,400. **Duration:** Annual; A tenure period of 4 to 12 months. **To Apply:** Applicants must submit a carefully formulated research proposal that reflects an understanding of the present Chinese academic and research environment. The proposal should include a persuasive statement of the need to conduct the research in China. Applications must include: completed application form; proposal (no more than five pages, double spaced, in Times New Roman 11-point font); up to three additional pages of images, musical scores or other similar supporting non-text materials; copies of correspondence with Chinese contacts; bibliography (no more than two pages); curriculum vitae (no more than five pages); three reference letters. **Deadline:** October 2.

738 ■ Frederick Burkhardt Residential Fellowships for Recently Tenured Scholars *(Advanced Professional, Professional development/Fellowship)*

Purpose: To support long-term, unusually ambitious projects in the humanities and related social sciences. **Focus:** Humanities; Social sciences. **Qualif.:** Application is open to recently tenured humanists (i.e. scholars who will have begun their first tenured contracts by the application deadline but began their first tenured contracts no earlier than the fall season semester or quarter). Applicants must be employed in any tenured position at any degree-granting academic institution in the United States, remaining so for the duration of the fellowship. **Criteria:** Peer reviewers in this program are asked to evaluate all eligible proposals according to the following criteria: potential of the project to advance the field of study; the ambition and scope of the proposed project; quality of the proposal with regard to its methodology, scope, theoretical framework, and grounding in the relevant scholarly literature; feasibility of the project and the likelihood that the applicant will execute the work within the proposed timeframe; scholarly record and career trajectory of the applicant; likelihood that residence at the specified center will increase significantly the applicants' ability to carry the project forward; commitment by the scholars' institution to assist in advancing the project. **Funds Avail.:** $75,000 each. **Duration:** Annual. **Number Awarded:** Up to 9. **To Apply:** Applications must be submit-

Awards are arranged alphabetically below their administering organizations

ted online and must include the following: completed application form; proposal of no more than 10 pages, double spaced, in Times New Roman 11-point font; bibliography of no more than three pages; publications list of no more than two pages; three reference letters; and institutional statement. Completed applications must be submitted through the ACLS Online Fellowship Application system (ofa.acls.org) no later than the fixed application deadline. **Deadline:** September 24.

739 ■ Comparative Perspectives on Chinese Culture and Society Grants *(Doctorate/Grant)*

Purpose: To promote interchange among scholars who may not otherwise have the opportunity to work together, and to support collaborative work in China studies. **Focus:** Chinese studies. **Qualif.:** The principal organizer must be affiliated with a university or research institution and must hold a PhD. There are no restrictions as to citizenship of participants or location of the project; however, it is expected the scholars from academic institutions in Taiwan will participate in conferences, workshops and planning meetings. **Criteria:** Selection will be based on the committee's criteria.

Funds Avail.: Up to $25,000 for conferences; $10,000 to $15,000 for workshops and seminars; up to $6,000 for planning meetings. **Duration:** Annual. **To Apply:** All proposals must include the following: application information sheet (available at the website); a description of the project and its purposes. Descriptions should be no more than five double-spaced pages; a budget for the proposed event, including a statement of any other funds available; a short bibliography of relevant sources; two-page CV of principal organizer; a list of those invited with their CVs (two pages maximum). This list should clearly differentiate between those who have agreed to participate in the event and those whose participation is not confirmed. This list should also specify paper writers and discussants. Participation of scholars from academic institutions in Taiwan is expected. Participation of scholars from outside the China field is strongly encouraged; for conferences only: an appendix containing abstracts (of approximately 150-200 words) for each paper to be presented at the conference. Submit the application materials as a single, searchable PDF file. **Deadline:** November 4.

740 ■ Dissertation Fellowships in East European Studies *(Doctorate/Fellowship)*

Purpose: To support dissertations in East European studies in all disciplines of the humanities and social sciences. **Focus:** European studies; Humanities; Social sciences. **Qualif.:** Applicants must be enrolled in a PhD program at a US university; must have completed all requirements for the PhD except the dissertation; may apply for one-year research and writing fellowships in sequence, but may not apply for a second year of funding in either category. **Criteria:** Fellowships will be granted based on the potential of the applicants, the quality and scholarly significance of the proposed work and its importance to the development of the field of East European studies.

Funds Avail.: $18,000. **Duration:** Annual. **To Apply:** Applicants project must pertain to at least one of the East European countries; must be in the humanities or social sciences; must aim to produce a PhD dissertation, written in English; must clearly state a plan of work that can be accomplished during the fellowship period. Applications must include the following: completed application form; proposal (no more than five pages, double spaced, in Times New Roman, 11-point font; up to two additional pages of images, musical scores or other similar supporting non-text materials; bibliography (no more than two pages); publications list (no more than two pages); three reference letters; institutional statement; language evaluation form(s). **Deadline:** November 15.

741 ■ Early Career Postdoctoral Fellowships in East European Studies *(Postdoctorate/Fellowship)*

Purpose: To support postdoctoral research and writing in East European studies in all disciplines of the humanities and social sciences. **Focus:** European studies; Humanities; Social sciences. **Qualif.:** Applicants must be US citizens; PhD must be conferred prior to the application deadline. However, established scholars who can demonstrate the equivalent of the PhD in publications and professional experience may also qualify; must be at an early career stage. **Criteria:** Selection will be based on the scholarly merit of the proposal, its importance to the development of the field and the scholarly potential and accomplishments of the applicants.

Funds Avail.: Up to $25,000. **Duration:** 6-12 months. **To Apply:** Applicants' projects must: pertain to at least one of the East European countries; be in the humanities or social sciences and must investigate aspects of East European societies, histories and cultures with a special regard for how they illuminate contemporary issues or the necessary backgrounds for understanding such issues; aim to produce a written scholarly product such as a book manuscript, to be written in English; must clearly state a plan of work that can be accomplished during the fellowship period. Applications must be submitted online and must include: completed application form; a no more than five pages, double spaced, in Times New Roman and 11-point font proposal; up to two additional pages of images, musical scores or other similar supporting non-text materials; no more than two pages bibliography; no more than two pages publications list; two reference letters. **Deadline:** November 9.

742 ■ Henry Luce Foundation/ACLS Dissertation Fellowships in American Art *(Graduate, Doctorate/Fellowship)*

Purpose: To provide support for young scholars who are in the phase of completing their dissertations, as well as to advance research after being awarded the PhD. **Focus:** Art history. **Qualif.:** Applicants must: be PhD candidates in a department of art history in the United States completing their dissertation which focuses on a topic in the history of the visual arts of the United States; be U.S. citizens or permanent residents; and, have completed all the requirements for the PhD except the dissertation before the beginning of the fellowship tenure. **Criteria:** Recipients will be selected based on academic standing and completed requirements.

Funds Avail.: $25,000 plus up to $2,000 as a travel allowance. **Duration:** Annual. **Number Awarded:** 10. **To Apply:** Applicants must complete the application form including statement of all university and external support received during graduate study; double-spaced proposal including a timeline for the expected completion of the dissertation writing and defense (not more than five pages); up to additional three pages of supporting materials; bibliography of not more than two pages; a completed chapter of the dissertation; three reference letters; a letter from the applicant's institution; and official transcript of graduate records. **Deadline:** October 21.

Awards are arranged alphabetically below their administering organizations

743 ■ Mellon/ACLS Dissertation Completion Fellowships *(Graduate, Doctorate/Fellowship)*

Purpose: To provide support for young scholars who are in the phase of completing their dissertations, as well as to advance research after being awarded the PhD. **Focus:** Humanities; Social sciences. **Qualif.:** Applicants must: be PhD candidates in a humanities or social science department in the United States; have all requirements for the PhD except the dissertation completed before beginning fellowship tenure; and, be no more than six years in the degree program. **Criteria:** Recipients will be selected based on academic standing and completed requirements.

Funds Avail.: $38,000 ($30,000 stipend, plus funds for research costs of up to $3,000 and for university fees of up to $5,000). **Duration:** Annual. **Number Awarded:** 65. **To Apply:** Applications must be submitted online and must include: completed application form; proposal (no more than ten pages, double spaced, in Times New Roman 11-point font); one-page timeline for the expected completion of dissertation writing and defense; up to three additional pages of images, musical scores, or other similar supporting non-text materials [optional]; bibliography (no more than two pages); completed chapter of the dissertation (that is neither the introduction, nor the conclusion, nor the literature review) of not more than 25 double-spaced pages, in Times New Roman 11-point font, or a representative 25-page excerpt from a longer chapter. The chapter must be in English, though citations may be in other languages (with translations provided); two reference letters; and, a statement from the applicant's institution (preferably from the applicant's department chair or dean). The provided form asks the institutional representative to (1) attest to the viability of the proposed timeline for completion; (2) stipulate that, in the event of an award, the university will not charge the student tuition or fees beyond a limit of $5,000 and will provide for any additional costs; and (3) pledge that if an ACLS award is made, the university will not provide the applicant with any subsequent aid. The person submitting the statement cannot be one of the reference letter writers. **Deadline:** October 21.

744 ■ Charles A. Ryskamp Research Fellowships *(Postgraduate, Postdoctorate, Professional development/Fellowship)*

Purpose: To support advanced assistant professors and untenured associate professors in the humanities and related science. **Focus:** Humanities; Social sciences. **Qualif.:** Applicants must be tenured-track assistant professors and untenured associate professors, hold the PhD or equivalent and be employed in tenure-track positions at degree granting academic institutions in the United States. **Criteria:** Recipients will be selected based on academic standing.

Funds Avail.: $64,000 plus $2,500 for research and travel. **Duration:** Annual; Up to 9 months. **Number Awarded:** 12. **To Apply:** Applications must be submitted online and must include: completed application form; proposal (no more than ten pages, double spaced, in Times New Roman 11-point font); bibliography (no more than two pages); publications list (no more than two pages); and, three reference letters including one from a tenured faculty member in the applicant's department. **Deadline:** September 24.

745 ■ American Councils for International Education
1828 L St. NW, Ste. 1200
Washington, DC 20036-5136
Ph: (202)833-7522
Fax: (202)833-7523
E-mail: info@americancouncils.org
URL: www.americancouncils.org
Facebook: www.facebook.com/AmericanCouncils
LinkedIn: www.linkedin.com/company/american-councils-for-international-education
Twitter: twitter.com/AC_Global

746 ■ American Councils for International Education Critical Language Scholarships *(Undergraduate, Graduate/Scholarship)*

Purpose: To provide opportunities to a diverse range of students from across the United States at every level of language learning. **Focus:** Linguistics. **Qualif.:** Applicants must be at least 18 years old, U.S. citizen and enrolled in an accredited U.S. degree-granting program at the undergraduate or graduate level. **Criteria:** Selection process is administered by American Councils for International Education with awards approved by the U.S. Department of State, Bureau of Educational and Cultural Affairs.

Funds Avail.: No specific amount. **To Apply:** Applicants must provide two letters of recommendation may be provided by an academic advisor, a current or past professor or someone who knows the applicant in a professional or volunteer capacity. For first year undergraduate students, please consider limiting the number of recommendations from high school teachers. For further application information kindly visits the society's website. **Contact:** cls@americancouncils.org.

747 ■ American Counsel Association (ACA)
3770 Ridge Pike
Collegeville, PA 19426
Ph: (610)489-3300
URL: www.amcounsel.org

748 ■ American Counsel Association Scholarships *(Undergraduate/Scholarship)*

Purpose: To provide scholarships to academically gifted and financially needy third-year law students. **Focus:** Law. **Qualif.:** Applicants must be enrolled in third year in a law school located within the Seventh Federal Judicial District. **Criteria:** Selection will be based upon academic excellence, financial need and commitment to public service.

Funds Avail.: No specific amount. **Duration:** Annual. **To Apply:** Interested applicants may contact the Foundation for the application process and other information.

749 ■ American Counseling Association (ACA)
6101 Stevenson Ave.
Alexandria, VA 22304
Ph: (703)823-9800
Fax: (703)823-0252
Free: 800-347-6647
E-mail: membership@counseling.org
URL: www.counseling.org
Facebook: www.facebook.com/American.Counseling.Association
LinkedIn: www.linkedin.com/groups/103440/profile
Twitter: twitter.com/CounselingViews

750 ■ Ross Trust Future School Counselors Essay Competition *(Master's, Doctorate/Award, Prize)*

Purpose: To help those who endeavor to become professional counselors. **Focus:** Counseling/Guidance. **Qualif.:**

Awards are arranged alphabetically below their administering organizations

Applicants must be master's and doctoral level students, and ACA members enrolled in counseling-related at an accredited college or university leading to a career as a professional school counselor at the elementary, middle or high school level. Only future school counselors who intend to function in pre-K-12 educational setting are eligible. **Criteria:** Selection of applicants will be based on the following: (a) Master's-level students must have an outstanding academic performance (based on a minimum of 15 graduate hours completed) and exemplary volunteer activities; (b) Doctoral-level students must have an outstanding academic performance (based on a minimum of 15 graduate hours completed), exemplary volunteer activities in schools and/or community, and scholarly research, writing and presentations.

Funds Avail.: No specific amount. **Duration:** Annual. **To Apply:** Applicants must have statement of career goals; must provide a description of volunteer experiences in schools and/or the community. For doctoral level scholarships, applicants must have statement reflecting research, writing and presentation activities. Essays must be 500 words or less in length, addressing the theme given by the Association.

751 ■ American Criminal Justice Association - Lambda Alpha Epsilon (ACJA-LAE)
PO Box 601047
Sacramento, CA 95860-1047
Ph: (916)484-6553
Fax: (916)488-2227
E-mail: acjalae@aol.com
URL: www.acjalae.org

752 ■ ACJA-LAE Student Paper Competitions
(Undergraduate, Graduate/Scholarship)

Purpose: To support financially and recognize the authors of best papers among graduate, upper, and lower divisions. **Focus:** Criminal justice; Paralegal studies. **Qualif.:** Candidates must be members of ACJA-LAE; must be enrolled in an accredited post-graduate program such as a Master's or Doctorate degree program; must be enrolled in an accredited undergraduate degree program who have completed a minimum of 70/105 semester hours of course work; must be enrolled in an accredited undergraduate degree program and have completed no more that 70/105 semester hours and no less than 12 semester hour/18 quarter hours. **Criteria:** Selection will be based on the submitted entries.

Funds Avail.: $150 for first place; $100 for second place; $50 for third place. **Duration:** Annual. **To Apply:** Application form can be downloaded at the website. Students' papers must be original which deal with issues and problems in the areas of criminology, law enforcement, juvenile justice, courts, corrections, prevention, planning and evaluation, career development or education in the field of criminal justice. Papers must be at least 1,500 words with a suggested maximum of 3,000 words (five to ten pages), typewritten, double-spaced on an 8-1/2" x 11" white quality paper. Any standard referencing format is acceptable for the organization of papers and citations. Three copies of the paper must be submitted along with the paper on CD or Flash Drive indicating what program and version was used for the word processing. Applicants must also submit three completed copies of the Student Paper Competition Application along with their papers. **Deadline:** December 31.

753 ■ American Criminal Justice Association - Lambda Alpha Epsilon Student Scholarships - Graduate Level *(Graduate, Master's, Doctorate/Scholarship)*

Purpose: To support students enrolled in a course of study in the criminal justice field. **Focus:** Criminal justice; Law. **Qualif.:** Applicants must be U.S. citizens or eligible non-citizens; must be members of ACJA/LAE chapter or Member-at-Large in good standing (both at the time of submission and at the time of the awards); must be enrolled in an accredited post-graduate program such as a Master's or Doctorate degree program in the criminal justice field; must achieved a minimum overall GPA of a 3.0 on a scale of 4.0. **Criteria:** Selection will be based on the committee's criteria.

Funds Avail.: $100-$400. **To Apply:** Applicants must submit five complete copies of application forms together with school transcripts, letters of recommendation from chapter officers and faculty advisors and a complete Career and Educational Goals Statement contained in packet. **Deadline:** December 31.

754 ■ American Criminal Justice Association - Lambda Alpha Epsilon Student Scholarships - Upper and Lower Division Levels *(Undergraduate/Scholarship)*

Purpose: To provide financial support to members who are upper or lower division students enrolled in a course of study in the criminal justice field. **Focus:** Criminal justice. **Qualif.:** Applicants must be upper or lower division students enrolled in a course of study in the criminal justice field. **Criteria:** Recipients will be selected based on: overall GPA of 3.0 or better on a scale of 4.0; GPA of basic courses completed in criminal justice or related field of study; and statement of career and educational goals.

Funds Avail.: $400 first place; $200 second place; $100 third place. **Duration:** Annual. **To Apply:** Applicants must fill out application form. Applicants must submit: five copies of school transcript; five copies of letters of recommendation from chapter officers and faculty advisors; career and educational goal statement. **Deadline:** December 31.

755 ■ Richard McGrath Memorial Fund Awards *(Undergraduate/Award)*

Purpose: To help the students pay the Conference Registration fee for the upcoming National Conference. **Focus:** Criminal justice; Paralegal studies. **Qualif.:** Candidates must be members of ACJA/LAE in good standing; must be currently enrolled in a degree-seeking program consistent with the criminal justice field; have been active in chapter and regional activities; must have attended at least one regional meeting. **Criteria:** Selection will be based on the committee's criteria.

Funds Avail.: No specific amount. **Duration:** Annual. **To Apply:** Nomination form can be obtained at the website. Complete and submit the nomination form to the regional president on or before the deadline. **Deadline:** December 1.

756 ■ American Culinary Federation (ACF)
180 Center Place Way
Saint Augustine, FL 32095
Fax: (904)824-4468
Free: 800-624-9458
E-mail: acf@acfchefs.net

Awards are arranged alphabetically below their administering organizations

URL: www.acfchefs.org
Facebook: www.facebook.com/ACFChefs
LinkedIn: www.linkedin.com/company/american-culinary-federation
Twitter: twitter.com/acfchefs

757 ■ Balestreri/Cutino Scholarships
(Undergraduate/Scholarship)

Purpose: To provide financial assistance to those studying culinary arts. **Focus:** Culinary arts. **Qualif.:** Applicant must be an exemplary student currently enrolled in an accredited, post-secondary college, with a major in either culinary or pastry arts, or be an ACFEF registered apprentice. Applicant must also have completed a grading or marking period (trimester, semester or quarter) and must have a career goal of becoming a chef or pastry chef. **Criteria:** Selection will be based by points on student's overall academic progress, financial need, extracurricular activities, participation in culinary activities, competitions and answers to essay questions.

Funds Avail.: No specific amount. **Duration:** Annual. **To Apply:** Applicant must submit a completed application form; two letters of recommendation from industry and/or culinary professionals (may not be related to the applicant in any manner); a Financial Aid Release Form completed by the financial aid office; sealed official transcript showing current GPA; and signed photo and/or photo in ACF publications. **Deadline:** May 1 or September 1. **Contact:** ACFEF Scholarships, Education Department, at the above address; e-mail: educate@acfchefs.net.

758 ■ Chaîne des Rôtisseurs Scholarships
(Undergraduate/Scholarship)

Purpose: To provide financial assistance to those studying culinary arts. **Focus:** Culinary arts. **Qualif.:** Applicant must be an exemplary student currently enrolled in an accredited, post-secondary college, with a major in either culinary or pastry arts, or be an ACFEF registered apprentice. Applicant must also have completed a grading or marking period (trimester, semester or quarter) and must have a career goal of becoming a chef or pastry chef. **Criteria:** Selection will be based by points on student's overall academic progress, financial need, extracurricular activities, participation in culinary activities, competitions and answers to essay questions.

Funds Avail.: No specific amount. **Duration:** Annual. **To Apply:** Applicant must submit a completed application form; two letters of recommendation from industry and/or culinary professionals (may not be related to the applicant in any manner); a Financial Aid Release Form completed by the financial aid office; sealed official transcript showing current GPA; and signed photo and/or photo in ACF publications. **Deadline:** May 1 or September 1. **Contact:** ACFEF Scholarships, Education Department, at the above address; e-mail: educate@acfchefs.net.

759 ■ Linda Cullen Memorial Scholarships
(Undergraduate/Scholarship)

Purpose: To provide financial assistance to those studying culinary arts. **Focus:** Culinary arts. **Qualif.:** Applicant must be an exemplary senior high school student eligible to graduate the same year as the scholarship is applied for. Applicant must also be currently accepted to an accredited, post-secondary college, with a major in either culinary or pastry arts, or must be an ACF registered apprentice; have a career goal of becoming a chef or pastry chef. **Criteria:** Selection will be based by points on student's overall academic progress, financial need, extracurricular activities, participation in culinary activities, competitions and answers to essay questions.

Funds Avail.: No specific amount. **Duration:** Annual. **To Apply:** Applicant must submit a completed application form; two letters of recommendation from industry and/or culinary professionals (may not be related to the applicant in any manner); a Financial Aid Release Form completed by the financial aid office; sealed official high school transcript showing current GPA; and signed photo and/or photo in ACF publications. **Deadline:** March 31. **Contact:** ACFEF Scholarships, Education Department, at the above address; e-mail: educate@acfchefs.net.

760 ■ Stanley "Doc" Jensen Scholarships
(Undergraduate/Scholarship)

Purpose: To provide financial assistance to those studying culinary arts. **Focus:** Culinary arts. **Qualif.:** Applicant must be an exemplary senior high school student eligible to graduate the same year as the scholarship is applied for. Applicant must also be currently accepted to an accredited, post-secondary college, with a major in either culinary or pastry arts, or must be an ACF registered apprentice; have a career goal of becoming a chef or pastry chef. **Criteria:** Selection will be based by points on student's overall academic progress, financial need, extracurricular activities, participation in culinary activities, competitions and answers to essay questions.

Funds Avail.: No specific amount. **Duration:** Annual. **To Apply:** Applicant must submit a completed application form; two letters of recommendation from industry and/or culinary professionals (may not be related to the applicant in any manner); a Financial Aid Release Form completed by the financial aid office; sealed official high school transcript showing current GPA; and signed photo and/or photo in ACF publications. **Contact:** ACFEF Scholarships, Education Department, at the above address; e-mail: educate@acfchefs.net.

761 ■ Andrew Macrina Scholarships *(Undergraduate/Scholarship)*

Purpose: To provide financial assistance to those studying culinary arts. **Focus:** Culinary arts. **Qualif.:** Applicant must be an exemplary senior high school student eligible to graduate the same year as the scholarship is applied for. Applicant must also be currently accepted to an accredited, post-secondary college, with a major in either culinary or pastry arts, or must be an ACF registered apprentice; have a career goal of becoming a chef or pastry chef. **Criteria:** Selection will be based by points on student's overall academic progress, financial need, extracurricular activities, participation in culinary activities, competitions and answers to essay questions.

Funds Avail.: No specific amount. **Duration:** Annual. **To Apply:** Applicant must submit a completed application form; two letters of recommendation from industry and/or culinary professionals (may not be related to the applicant in any manner); a Financial Aid Release Form completed by the financial aid office; sealed official high school transcript showing current GPA; and signed photo and/or photo in ACF publications. **Deadline:** March 31. **Contact:** ACFEF Scholarships, Education Department, at the above address; e-mail: educate@acfchefs.net.

762 ■ Ray and Gertrude Marshall Scholarships
(Undergraduate/Scholarship)

Purpose: To provide financial assistance to those studying culinary arts. **Focus:** Culinary arts. **Qualif.:** Applicant must

Awards are arranged alphabetically below their administering organizations

be an exemplary student currently enrolled in an accredited, post-secondary college, with a major in either culinary or pastry arts, or be an ACFEF registered apprentice. Applicant must also have completed a grading or marking period (trimester, semester or quarter) and must have a career goal of becoming a chef or pastry chef. **Criteria:** Selection will be based by points on student's overall academic progress, financial need, extracurricular activities, participation in culinary activities, competitions and answers to essay questions.

Funds Avail.: No specific amount. **Duration:** Annual. **To Apply:** Applicant must submit a completed application form; two letters of recommendation from industry and/or culinary professionals (may not be related to the applicant in any manner); a Financial Aid Release Form completed by the financial aid office; sealed official transcript showing current GPA; and signed photo and/or photo in ACF publications. **Deadline:** May 1 or September 1. **Contact:** ACFEF Scholarships, Education Department, at the above address; e-mail: educate@acfchefs.net.

763 ■ Hermann G. Rusch Scholarships (Other/Scholarship, Grant)

Purpose: To support professional chefs who wished to continue education or initial certification class. **Focus:** Culinary arts. **Qualif.:** For initial certification, applicants must pass an initial ACF certification class with a "C" grade or better. For continuing education, applicants must be certified by the American Culinary Federation as a Certified Chef d' Cuisine or higher; enrolled in a state accredited educational institution for the purpose of enhancing culinary skills or knowledge; an active member of the American Culinary Federation in good standing for three or more years. **Criteria:** Selection shall be based on the aforementioned applicants' qualifications and compliance with the application details.

Funds Avail.: Up to $500. **Duration:** Annual. **To Apply:** Application must be completed and signed by applicants. Verification of registration to the professional development course must be submitted, along with total cost of class. Applicants will be notified by mail of any grant award or denial. **Contact:** ACFEF Scholarships, Education Department, at the above address; e-mail: educate@acfchefs.net.

764 ■ Spice Box Grants (Advanced Professional/Grant)

Purpose: To support professional chefs who wish to continue their education or initial certification class. **Focus:** Culinary arts. **Qualif.:** For initial certification, applicants must pass an initial ACF certification class with a "C" grade or better. For continuing education, applicants must be certified by the American Culinary Federation as a Certified Chef d' Cuisine or higher; enrolled in a state accredited educational institution for the purpose of enhancing culinary skills or knowledge; an active member of the American Culinary Federation in good standing for three or more years. **Criteria:** Selection shall be based on the aforementioned applicants' qualifications and compliance with the application details.

Funds Avail.: Up to $500. **Duration:** Annual. **To Apply:** Application must be completed and signed by applicants. Verification of registration to the professional development course must be submitted, along with total cost of class. Applicants will be notified by mail of any grant award or denial. **Contact:** ACFEF Scholarships, Education Department, at the above address; e-mail: educate@acfchefs.net.

765 ■ Charlie Trotters's Culinary Education Foundation Scholarships (Other, Undergraduate/Scholarship)

Purpose: To support students in pursuing their career in culinary arts. **Focus:** Culinary arts. **Qualif.:** Applicants must be high school students, college students, professional chefs looking to further their education or become certified and student culinary teams currently competing at ACF regional and national conferences. **Criteria:** Recipients will be selected based on merit, work experience, culinary goals and skills and references.

Funds Avail.: No specific amount. **To Apply:** Applicants must submit a completed Culinary Trust Scholarship application form; a project proposal (two-page, double-spaced) illustrating their culinary goals; two letters of reference on business or personal letterhead; a current academic transcript; a non-refundable application fee of $35. **Deadline:** March 1.

766 ■ American Darts Organization (ADO)

230 N Crescent Way, Ste. K
Anaheim, CA 92801-6707
Ph: (714)254-0212
Fax: (714)254-0214
E-mail: president@adodarts.com
URL: www.adodarts.com

767 ■ American Darts Organization Memorial Scholarship (Undergraduate/Scholarship)

Purpose: To provide financial aid for college education of young Dart players throughout the United States. **Focus:** General studies/Field of study not specified. **Qualif.:** Applicants must be U.S. citizens or must have been domiciled in the United States for a period of two years and one day; must be members in good standing of the American Darts Organization; must be Regional/National winners in the ADO Youth Playoff Program; must be under twenty-one (21) years of age as of December 1st of the year in which they plans to attend college. **Criteria:** Selection will be based on the committee's criteria.

Funds Avail.: Amount varies. **Duration:** Annual. **Number Awarded:** Varies. **To Apply:** Interested applicants may contact the Organization for the application process and other information.

768 ■ American Dental Association (ADA)

211 E Chicago Ave.
Chicago, IL 60611-2678
Ph: (312)440-2500
Fax: (312)440-3542
Free: 800-947-4746
URL: www.ada.org
Facebook: www.facebook.com/AmericanDentalAssociation

769 ■ American Dental Association Allied Dental Student Scholarships (Undergraduate/Scholarship)

Purpose: To help dental assisting, dental hygiene, and dental laboratory technology student defray a part of their professional educational expenses. **Focus:** Dentistry. **Qualif.:** Applicants must be U.S. citizens; must be entering second year students at the time of application and currently attending or enrolled at a dental school accredited by the Commission on Dental Accreditation of the American Dental Association; must be enrolled as full-time students

Awards are arranged alphabetically below their administering organizations

with a minimum of 12 credit hours; must demonstrate a financial need of $1,000; must have a minimum accumulative grade point average of 3.5 based on a 4.0 scale; and two reference forms from two dental school representatives. **Criteria:** Applicants will be evaluated based on demonstrated financial need; academic achievement; biographical sketch questionnaire; and two completed reference forms.

Funds Avail.: Varies. **Duration:** One year. **Number Awarded:** Varies. **To Apply:** Applicants must submit an application form that is typed or printed in black ink, completed and signed by school officials; completed application form, including the Academic Achievement Record Form and Financial Needs Assessment Form signed by school official; a copy of the school's letter of acceptance, for entering first-year students; two completed reference forms, sealed and signed on the back flap of the envelope by the referrers (required forms must be used which are a part of the scholarship application form); typed, biographical sketch questionnaire (required form must be used which is a part of the scholarship application form); a self-addressed, stamped postcard, which can be mailed upon receipt of the application (if the applicants wishes to have verification that the application was received).

770 ■ American Dental Association Dental Assisting Scholarship Program (Undergraduate/Scholarship)

Purpose: To provide financial assistance for furthering education of students in pursuing the field of dentistry. **Focus:** Dentistry. **Qualif.:** Applicants must be U.S. citizens; must be entering students at the time of application and enrolled in a dental assisting program accredited by the Commission on Dental Accreditation of the American Dental Association; enrolled as full-time students with minimum of 12 credit hours; demonstrate a minimum financial need of $1,000; have minimum accumulative grade point average of 3.5 based on a 4.0 scale; and two reference forms: one from a dentist or dental assisting representative and/or one from a school representative which must be submitted as part of the application form. **Criteria:** Applicants will be evaluated based on demonstrated financial need; academic achievement; biographical sketch questionnaire; and two completed reference forms.

Funds Avail.: $1,000. **Duration:** Annual; One year. **Number Awarded:** 10. **To Apply:** Applicants must submit an application form that is typed or printed in black ink, completed and signed by school officials; completed application form including the Academic Achievement Record Form and Financial Needs Assessment Form signed by school official; a copy of the school's letter of acceptance for those incoming first-year students; two completed reference forms, sealed and signed on the back flap of the envelope by the referrers (required forms must be used which are a part of the scholarship application form); typed, biographical sketch questionnaire (required form must be used which is a part of the scholarship application form); a self-addressed, stamped postcard which can be mailed upon receipt of the application (if the applicants wishes to have verification that the application was received).

771 ■ American Dental Association Dental Hygiene Scholarship Program (Undergraduate/Scholarship)

Purpose: To help students in dental assisting, dental hygiene, and dental laboratory technology students defray a part of their professional education expenses. **Focus:** Dentistry. **Qualif.:** Applicants must be U.S. citizens; entering second year students at the time of application and currently attending or enrolled at a dental school accredited by the Commission on Dental Accreditation of the American Dental Association; enrolled as full-time students with a minimum of 12 credit hours; must demonstrate a financial need of $1,000; have a minimum accumulative grade point average of 3.5 based on a 4.0 scale; and two reference forms from two dental school representatives. **Criteria:** Applicants will be evaluated based on their demonstrated financial need; academic achievement; biographical sketch questionnaire; and two completed reference forms.

Funds Avail.: $1,000. **Duration:** Annual; One year. **To Apply:** Applicants must submit an application form that is typed or printed in black ink, completed and signed by school officials; completed application form including the Academic Achievement Record Form and Financial Needs Assessment Form signed by school official; a copy of the school's letter of acceptance for those incoming first-year students; two completed reference forms, sealed and signed on the back flap of the envelope by the referrers (required forms must be used which are a part of the scholarship application form); typed, biographical sketch questionnaire (required form must be used which is a part of the scholarship application form); a self-addressed, stamped postcard which can be mailed upon receipt of the application (if the applicants wishes to have verification that the application was received).

772 ■ American Dental Association Dental Laboratory Technology Scholarship Program (Undergraduate/Scholarship)

Purpose: To provide financial assistance for students to further their education in the field of dentistry. **Focus:** Dentistry. **Qualif.:** Applicants must be U.S. citizens (permanent resident status does not qualify); entering their final year as students at the time of application; must be currently attending a dental laboratory technology program accredited by the Commission on Dental Accreditation of the American Dental Association; must be enrolled as full-time students with minimum of 12 credit hours; must demonstrate financial need of $1,000; have a minimum accumulative grade point average of 3.5 based on a 4.0 scale; and must have two reference forms from two dental laboratory technology program representatives which must be submitted as part of the application form. **Criteria:** Applicants will be evaluated based on demonstrated financial need; academic achievement; biographical sketch questionnaire; and two completed reference forms.

Funds Avail.: $1,000. **Duration:** One year. **Number Awarded:** 5. **To Apply:** Applicants must submit an application form that is typed or printed in black ink, completed and signed by school officials; completed application form including the Academic Achievement Record Form and Financial Needs Assessment Form signed by school official; a copy of the school's letter of acceptance for those incoming first-year students; two completed reference forms, sealed and signed on the back flap of the envelope by the referrers (required forms must be used which are a part of the scholarship application form); typed, biographical sketch questionnaire (required form must be used which is a part of the scholarship application form); a self-addressed, stamped postcard which can be mailed upon receipt of the application (if applicants wish to have verification that their application was received).

773 ■ American Dental Association Minority Dental Student Scholarships (Undergraduate/Scholarship)

Purpose: To help pre-doctoral dental students defray a part of their professional education expenses. **Focus:** Dentistry. **Qualif.:** Applicants must be U.S. citizens; entering second year students at the time of application and currently attending or enrolled at a dental school accredited by the Commission on Dental Accreditation of the American Dental Association; enrolled as full-time students, a minimum of 12 credit hours; demonstrate a minimum financial need of $2,500; have a minimum accumulative grade point average of 3.0 based on a 4.0 scale; and two reference forms from two dental school representatives (i.e., professor or academic advisor) in support of the application must be submitted as part of the application form. **Criteria:** Applicants will be evaluated based on their demonstrated financial need, academic achievement, biographical sketch questionnaire and two completed reference forms.

Funds Avail.: $2,500. **Duration:** One year. **Number Awarded:** Varies. **To Apply:** Applicants must submit an application form that is typed or printed in black ink, completed and signed by school officials; completed application form, including the Academic Achievement Record Form and Financial Needs Assessment Form, which are a part of the application form, and signed by school official; a copy of the school's letter of acceptance, if entering first-year students; two completed reference forms, sealed and signed on the back flap of the envelopes by the referrers (required forms must be used which are a part of the scholarship application form); typed, biographical sketch questionnaire (required form must be used which is a part of the scholarship application form); a self-addressed, stamped postcard, which can be mailed upon receipt of the application (if the applicants wishes to have verification that the application was received).

774 ■ American Dental Hygienists' Association Institute for Oral Health (ADHA IOH)
444 N Michigan Ave., Ste. 3400
Chicago, IL 60611
Ph: (312)440-8900
E-mail: institute@adha.net
URL: www.adha.org/ioh

775 ■ ADHA IOH Sigma Phi Alpha Graduate Scholarships (Graduate/Scholarship)

Purpose: To provide financial assistance to dental hygiene students and dental hygienists who can demonstrate a commitment to further knowledge through academic achievement, professional excellence and desire to improve the public's overall health. **Focus:** Dental hygiene. **Qualif.:** Applicants must be Sigma Phi Alpha members pursuing a graduate degree in dental hygiene or any related fields; must demonstrate a cumulative GPA of at least 3.5 on a 4.0 scale; must be members of ADHA. **Criteria:** Applicants will be chosen based on submitted materials.

Funds Avail.: $1,000. **Duration:** Annual. **Number Awarded:** 1. **To Apply:** Applicants are required to have a specific goals statement and must submit a manuscript upon completion of the program.

776 ■ American Dental Hygienists' Association Institute for Oral Health Research Grants (Master's/Fellowship)

Purpose: To support professional advancement of dental hygiene educators. **Focus:** Dental hygiene. **Qualif.:** Applicants must be faculty members pursuing a Master's degree in dental hygiene education or doctoral work; must hold a valid license to practice dental hygiene; must be active members of ADHA. **Criteria:** Recipients will be selected based on demonstrated commitment to dental hygiene education, research, advancement of dental hygiene practice and academic record.

Funds Avail.: Amount varies. **Duration:** Annual. **Number Awarded:** Varies. **To Apply:** Applicants must contact ADHA Institute for Oral Health for application process. **Deadline:** February 28.

777 ■ Wilma Motley Memorial California Merit Scholarships (Undergraduate/Scholarship)

Purpose: To provide financial assistance to dental hygiene students and dental hygienists who can demonstrate a commitment to further knowledge through academic achievement, professional excellence and desire to improve the public's overall health. **Focus:** Dental hygiene. **Qualif.:** Applicants must be Registered Dental Hygienists in Alternative Practice (RDHAP) or individuals pursuing associate/certificate, baccalaureate, master's or doctorate degree in dental hygiene or related field; must be residents and attending a dental hygiene program in California; must demonstrate leadership experience and have GPA of at least 3.5 on a 4.0 scale; must be active members of ADHA. **Criteria:** Applicants will be awarded based on merit.

Funds Avail.: $2,000. **Duration:** Annual. **Number Awarded:** 3. **To Apply:** Applicants must contact ADHA Institute for Oral Health office to request an application form and to ask further information.

778 ■ Irene Woodall Graduate Scholarships (Master's/Scholarship)

Purpose: To provide financial assistance to dental hygiene students and dental hygienists who demonstrate a commitment to further knowledge through academic achievement, professional excellence and desire to improve the public's overall health. **Focus:** Dental hygiene. **Qualif.:** Applicants must be pursuing a Master's degree in dental hygiene or any related fields; must have a minimum GPA of 3.5 on a 4.0 scale; must be members of American Dental Hygienist's Association. **Criteria:** Scholarship will be awarded based on how well the applicant demonstrates the goal or achievement described.

Funds Avail.: $1,000. **Duration:** Annual. **To Apply:** Applicants must contact ADHA Institute for Oral Health office for further information. **Deadline:** February 1.

779 ■ American Diabetes Association (ADA)
1701 N Beauregard St.
Alexandria, VA 22311
Ph: (800)342-2383
Free: 800-342-2383
E-mail: diabetesforecast@pubservice.com
URL: www.diabetes.org
Facebook: www.facebook.com/AmericanDiabetesAssociation?loc=superfooter
Twitter: twitter.com/AmDiabetesAssn?loc=superfooter

780 ■ American Diabetes Association and Boehringer Ingelheim Research Award: Chronic Kidney Disease and Renal Insufficiency in the Setting of Diabetes (Doctorate, Professional development/Award)

Purpose: To funds research aimed at improving the care of people with diabetes and chronic kidney disease. **Focus:** Medical research. **Qualif.:** Applicants must hold a PhD, MD, PharmD, DO or DPM degree, or other science-related degree; must possess the necessary skills and training to

Awards are arranged alphabetically below their administering organizations

carry out proposed work; and must agree to devote sufficient time and effort to research. **Criteria:** Preference will be given on evaluated applications that has original study design with applicability to the scope of study, its potential impact, and its treatment and prevention to kidney disease and diabetes.

Funds Avail.: $1,005,000. **Duration:** Annual. **To Apply:** Applicants must complete the online application form and upload all supporting documents as an attachment in PDF format. **Deadline:** October 15.

781 ■ American Educational Research Association (AERA)

1430 K St. NW, Ste. 1200
Washington, DC 20005-2504
Ph: (202)238-3200
Fax: (202)238-3250
E-mail: webmaster@aera.net
URL: www.aera.net
Facebook: www.facebook.com/AERAEdResearch
LinkedIn: www.linkedin.com/company/american
-educational-research-association
Twitter: twitter.com/AERA_EdResearch

782 ■ AERA-AIR Fellows Program (Postdoctorate/Fellowship)

Purpose: To support early career scholars by providing intensive research and training opportunities to recent doctoral recipients in the fields and disciplines related to the scientific study of education and education processes; to increase the number of underrepresented minority professionals conducting advanced research or providing technical assistance. **Focus:** Education. **Qualif.:** Applicants must be U.S citizens and permanent residents; must have completed their PhD/EdD degrees within the three years prior to application. **Criteria:** Selection of applicants will be based on their research proposal.

Funds Avail.: $55,000-$65,000. **Duration:** Annual. **To Apply:** Applicants must complete the application form available online; must submit a letter of recommendation; transcript of records; personal statement; dissertation abstract; dissertation/doctoral thesis summary; writing sample; and curriculum vitae. **Contact:** George Wimberly at fellowships@aera.net.

783 ■ AERA-ETS Fellowship Program in Measurement and Education Research (Doctorate/Fellowship)

Purpose: To provide learning opportunities and practical experience to recent doctoral degree recipients and to early career research scientists in education research areas directed toward explaining student progress and achievement. **Focus:** Testing, educational/psychological. **Qualif.:** Applicants must be U.S citizens and permanent residents; must have completed their PhD/EdD degrees within the three years prior to application. **Criteria:** Selection of applicants will be based on the scholarship selection criteria.

Funds Avail.: $62,000. **Duration:** Annual. **Number Awarded:** Up to 2. **To Apply:** Applicants must complete the application form available online; must submit a letter of recommendation; transcript of records; personal statement; dissertation abstract; dissertation/doctoral thesis summary; writing sample; and curriculum vitae. **Contact:** George Wimberly at fellowships@aera.net.

784 ■ AERA Minority Fellowship Program in Education Research (Doctorate/Fellowship)

Purpose: To provide support for doctoral dissertation research and to advance education research by outstanding minority graduate students and to improve the quality and diversity of university faculties. **Focus:** Education. **Qualif.:** Applicant must be a U.S citizen and permanent resident; must work full-time on his or her dissertations and course requirements. **Criteria:** Selection will be based on the submitted application.

Funds Avail.: $19,000; and $1,000 in travel support to attend the AERA Annual Meeting. **Duration:** Annual. **To Apply:** Applicants must complete the application form available online; must submit a letter of recommendation and transcript of record. Application form and other supporting documents must be sent to AERA-AIR Fellows Program. **Contact:** fellowships@aera.net.

785 ■ American Enterprise Institute

1150 17th St. NW
Washington, DC 20036
Ph: (202)862-5800
Fax: (202)862-7177
E-mail: custserv@nbnbooks.com
URL: www.aei.org
Facebook: www.facebook.com/AEIonline
Twitter: twitter.com/AEI

786 ■ American Enterprise Institute National Research Initiative Fellowships (NRI) (Graduate/Fellowship)

Purpose: To help AEI collaborate with scholars who were doing important work on issues relevant to the Institute's interests and to provide the support needed for these scholars to have a greater influence on the policy debate. **Focus:** Economics; Law; Political science; Social sciences. **Qualif.:** Applicant must be a recent law school and business school graduate wishing to pursue public policy whose areas of study are economics, political and social science, law, or public policy. **Criteria:** Selection is based on academic performance, writing ability and references.

Funds Avail.: No specific amount. **To Apply:** Applicants must submit a statement of purpose; two letters of reference; curriculum vitae; graduate school transcripts; and one writing sample. **Remarks:** Established in 2002. **Contact:** The American Enterprise Institute, at the above address.

787 ■ American Federation for Aging Research (AFAR)

55 W 39th St., 16th Fl.
New York, NY 10018-0541
Ph: (212)703-9977
Fax: (212)997-0330
Free: 888-582-2327
E-mail: info@afar.org
URL: www.afar.org
Facebook: www.facebook.com/AFARorg/?ref=ts
Twitter: www.twitter.com/AFARorg

788 ■ Glenn/AFAR Scholarships for Research in the Biology of Aging (Graduate, Doctorate/Scholarship)

Purpose: To give students the chance to learn more about the field of aging research, as well as increase their understanding of the challenges involved in improving the quality of life for older people. **Focus:** Gerontology. **Qualif.:** Applicants must be MD, DO, PhD or combined degree students in good standing at a not-for-profit institution in the United States. **Criteria:** Applicants will be evaluated based on the following: qualifications and ability of the applicant, as demonstrated by academic performance, statement of purpose and letter of reference; merit and feasibility of the proposed research project and its relevance to aging; qualifications of the designated mentor, his or her endorsement of the research project, assurance of active supervision and demonstrated commitment to aging research and to the student; likelihood that the project will advance the applicant's interest and career in aging research; quality of the research environment.

Funds Avail.: $5,000. **Number Awarded:** 12. **To Apply:** Recipients will be required to submit a full report detailing their research methods and findings within 90 days of completing the research projects. Similarly, the mentor will be required to provide an evaluation of the student's performance and impressions of the impact of the program on the student's career. **Deadline:** January 15. **Contact:** afar@agingresearchfoundation.org.

789 ■ American Federation of Police and Concerned Citizens (AFP&CC)
6350 Horizon Dr.
Titusville, FL 32780
Ph: (321)264-0911
E-mail: policeinfo@aphf.org
URL: www.afp-cc.org

790 ■ American Federation of Police and Concerned Citizen Scholarships (Undergraduate/Scholarship)

Purpose: To assist family members and children of officers killed in the line of duty. **Focus:** Law enforcement. **Qualif.:** Applicants must: be the surviving sons or daughters of law enforcement officers killed in the line of duty; be enrolled in a minimum of 6 credit hours; and, maintain a 2.0 GPA. **Criteria:** Recipients will be selected based on financial need.

Funds Avail.: $1,000 to $4,000. **Duration:** Annual. **To Apply:** Applicants currently enrolled in college must submit a copy of their most recent school transcript. New college students must submit a high school transcript, ACT/SAT scores, and a copy of the acceptance letter from the institution he/she plans on attending.

791 ■ American Federation of Teachers - Oregon (AFT)
10228 SW Capitol Hwy.
Portland, OR 97219
Ph: (971)888-5665
Fax: (503)906-3533
E-mail: AFTOregon@aft-oregon.org
URL: or.aft.org
Facebook: www.facebook.com/aftoregon
Twitter: www.twitter.com/AFTOregon

792 ■ AFT-Oregon Union Plus Credit Card Scholarship (Undergraduate/Scholarship)

Purpose: To provide scholarships to the members and dependents or spouses who are attending or planning to attend a four-year college or university, a community college, technical college or trade school. **Focus:** General studies/Field of study not specified. **Qualif.:** Applicants must be participating union members from the U.S., Puerto Rico, Guam and the U.S. Virgin Islands and Canada; must be accepted into a U.S. accredited college or university, community college or technical or trade school at the time the award is issued. **Criteria:** Selection will be based on the committee's criteria.

Funds Avail.: $500 to $4,000. **Duration:** Annual. **To Apply:** Interested applicants may visit the union privilege website for other instructions for the application process. **Deadline:** January 31. **Remarks:** Established in 1992.

793 ■ Shirley J. Gold Scholarship (Undergraduate/Scholarship)

Purpose: To support AFT-Oregon members who are pursuing higher education at an accredited higher education institution. **Focus:** General studies/Field of study not specified. **Qualif.:** Applicants must be AFT-Oregon members planning to enroll in a college, university or trade program. **Criteria:** Selection shall be based on the aforementioned qualifications and compliance with the application details.

Funds Avail.: $1,000. **Duration:** Annual. **Number Awarded:** 1. **To Apply:** Applicants must complete the provided application form, as well as the writing assignment and provide a letter of reference. **Deadline:** January 31. **Contact:** Leahl@aft-oregon.org.

794 ■ Carl J. Mejel Scholarship (Undergraduate/Scholarship)

Purpose: To provide assistance to dependents of AFT-Oregon members who are graduating seniors and plan to pursue higher education. **Focus:** General studies/Field of study not specified. **Qualif.:** Applicants must be children or grandchildren of AFT members; must be graduating high school students planning to enroll in an accredited institution or trade program to continue their higher education of the current year. **Criteria:** Selection will be based on the committee's criteria.

Funds Avail.: $1,000. **Duration:** Annual. **To Apply:** Applicants must visit the website to obtain an application form. Applicants must also provide the following materials: a writing assignment and certification of original composition; at least two references in a stamped envelope addressed to AFT-Oregon, from a teacher or community leader who knows the applicants well and can attest to their outstanding qualities; a copy of applicants' current transcript from the college, university or trade program where they are enrolled. For college freshmen applicants, please provide a high school transcript. **Deadline:** January 31.

795 ■ AFT Robert Porter Scholarship Program (Undergraduate/Scholarship)

Purpose: To support graduating high school senior students who show outstanding service to their community and an understanding of the role unions can play to create a more just society. **Focus:** General studies/Field of study not specified. **Qualif.:** Applicants must be graduating high school seniors who are dependents of AFT members. **Criteria:** Selection will be based on the academic achievement, commitment to community services and school-related activities, demonstration of leadership, work experience, recommendations, special talents and skills, an essay and a commitment to advancing the interests of working people and building unions.

Funds Avail.: $8,000 each (for scholarship recipients); one-time $1,000 grants to 2 members from each division of the AFT. **Duration:** Annual; up to four years. **Number**

Awarded: Up to 4. **To Apply:** Applicants may verify the application process through the program website. **Deadline:** March 31.

796 ■ Albert F. Shanker Scholarship (Undergraduate/Scholarship)

Purpose: To provide assistance to members' dependents enrolled in higher education institutions. **Focus:** General studies/Field of study not specified. **Qualif.:** Applicants must be children or grandchildren of AFT-Oregon members; must be currently attending an accredited higher education, institution or trade program and planning to continue higher education in the current academic year. **Criteria:** Selection will be based on the committee's criteria.

Funds Avail.: $1,000. **Duration:** Annual. **To Apply:** Applicants must visit the website to obtain an application form. Applicants must also provide the following materials: a writing assignment and certification of original composition; at least two references in a stamped envelope addressed to AFT-Oregon, from a teacher or community leader who knows the applicants well and can attest to their outstanding qualities; a copy of applicants' current transcript from the college, university or trade program where they are enrolled. For college freshmen applicants, please provide a high school transcript. **Deadline:** January 31.

797 ■ American Floral Endowment (AFE)
1601 Duke St.
Alexandria, VA 22314-3406
Ph: (703)838-5211

798 ■ Ball Horticultural Company Scholarships (Undergraduate/Scholarship)

Purpose: To support junior or senior students pursuing a career in commercial floriculture. **Focus:** Horticulture. **Qualif.:** Applicants must be students currently enrolled in their third to fourth year of college; must be pursuing a career in commercial floriculture. **Criteria:** Recipients are selected based on academic performance.

Funds Avail.: $300-$4,000. **To Apply:** Applicants must complete the online application form; must submit two letters of recommendation and transcript of records. **Deadline:** May 1. **Contact:** Send your applications to AFE Scholarships at daker@afeendowment.org.

799 ■ Vic and Margaret Ball Student Intern Scholarships (Undergraduate/Internship)

Purpose: To give students the opportunity to gain practical floriculture/horticulture experience while training at a commercial production greenhouse or nursery. **Focus:** Horticulture. **Qualif.:** Applicants must be full-time undergraduate students who are currently enrolled in a floriculture/environmental horticulture program at a two or four year college/university within the United States; must be U.S. citizens; must maintain "C" or better GPA with satisfactory progress in a degree or certificate program. **Criteria:** Recipients are selected based on academic performance, financial need and interest in a horticulture career.

Funds Avail.: $1,500 (three months); $3,000 (four months); or $6,000 (six months). **Duration:** Semiannual. **To Apply:** Applicants must submit a completed and signed application form, official transcript from all institutions attended, a statement explaining past and current involvement in floriculture activities, your expectations from the program, and your future career goals; pictures of the student working at the intern location must be included. Applicants must have permission to interrupt studies for the length of the training period. **Deadline:** March 1; October 1.

800 ■ Harold Bettinger Scholarships (Undergraduate, Graduate/Scholarship)

Purpose: To further the advancement of education and science in the floriculture and environmental horticulture field by funding research and studies and financing scholarships and other educational activities for individuals interested in the field. **Focus:** Horticulture. **Qualif.:** Applicants must be sophomore or graduate students pursuing a career in business and/or marketing with the intent to apply it to a horticulture-related business. **Criteria:** Recipients are selected based on academic performance.

Funds Avail.: $300-$4,000. **To Apply:** Applicants must complete the online application form; must submit two letters of recommendation and transcript of records. **Deadline:** May 1. **Contact:** Send your applications to AFE Scholarships at daker@afeendowment.org.

801 ■ Leonard Bettinger Vocational Scholarships (Undergraduate, Vocational/Occupational/Scholarship)

Purpose: To further the advancement of education and science in the floriculture and environmental horticulture field by funding research and studies and financing scholarships and other educational activities for individuals interested in the field. **Focus:** Horticulture. **Qualif.:** Applicants must be vocational students in a one or two-year program who intend to become growers or greenhouse managers. **Criteria:** Recipients are selected based on academic performance.

Funds Avail.: $300-$4,000. **To Apply:** Applicants must complete the online application form; must submit two letters of recommendation and transcript of records. **Deadline:** May 1. **Contact:** Send your applications to AFE Scholarships at daker@afeendowment.org.

802 ■ James Bridenbaugh Memorial Scholarships (Undergraduate/Scholarship)

Purpose: To further the advancement of education and science in the floriculture and environmental horticulture field by funding research and studies and financing scholarships and other educational activities for individuals interested in the field. **Focus:** Horticulture. **Qualif.:** Applicants must be sophomore to senior students pursuing a career in floral design and marketing fresh flowers and plants. **Criteria:** Recipients are selected based on academic performance.

Funds Avail.: $300-$4,000. **To Apply:** Applicants must complete the online application form; must submit two letters of recommendation and transcript of records. **Deadline:** May 1. **Contact:** AFE Scholarships at daker@afeendowment.org.

803 ■ John Carew Memorial Scholarships (Graduate/Scholarship)

Purpose: To further the advancement of education and science in the floriculture and environmental horticulture field by funding research and studies and financing scholarships and other educational activities for individuals interested in the field. **Focus:** Horticulture. **Qualif.:** Applicants must be graduate students with an interest in greenhouse crops. **Criteria:** Recipients are selected based on academic performance.

Funds Avail.: $300-$4,000. **To Apply:** Applicants must complete the online application form; must submit two let-

Awards are arranged alphabetically below their administering organizations

AMERICAN FLORAL ENDOWMENT

ters of recommendation and transcript of records. **Deadline:** May 1. **Contact:** AFE Scholarships at daker@afeendowment.org.

804 ■ Earl Dedman Memorial Scholarships
(Undergraduate/Scholarship)

Purpose: To further the advancement of education and science in the floriculture and environmental horticulture field by funding research and studies and financing scholarships and other educational activities for individuals interested in the field. **Focus:** Horticulture. **Qualif.:** Applicants must be junior or senior students maintaining a minimum 3.0 GPA who are interested in becoming greenhouse growers. **Criteria:** Recipients are selected based on academic performance.

Funds Avail.: $300-$4,000. **To Apply:** Applicants must complete the online application form; must submit two letters of recommendation and transcript of records. **Deadline:** May 1. **Contact:** AFE Scholarships at daker@afeendowment.org.

805 ■ Markham-Colegrave International Scholarships *(Undergraduate/Scholarship)*

Purpose: To further the advancement of education and science in the floriculture and environmental horticulture field by funding research and studies and financing scholarships and other educational activities for individuals interested in the field. **Focus:** Horticulture. **Qualif.:** Applicants must be sophomore to graduate students pursuing a career in horticulture marketing through international travel, either from U.S. and Europe. **Criteria:** Recipients are selected based on academic performance.

Funds Avail.: $4,500. **Duration:** Biennial; awarded in even numbered years. **To Apply:** Applicants must send a completed online application form; must submit two letters of recommendation and transcript of records; relevant documentation of travel plans; **Deadline:** May 1. **Contact:** AFE Scholarships at daker@afeendowment.org.

806 ■ National Greenhouse Manufacturers Association Scholarships *(Undergraduate/Scholarship)*

Purpose: To further the advancement of education and science in the floriculture and environmental horticulture field by funding research and studies and financing scholarships and other educational activities for individuals interested in the field. **Focus:** Horticulture. **Qualif.:** Applicants must be junior, senior or graduate students pursuing a career in horticulture and bio-engineering or the equivalent at a four-year college. Applicants must maintain a 3.0 GPA. **Criteria:** Recipients are selected based on academic performance.

Funds Avail.: $300-$4,000. **Number Awarded:** Up to 6. **To Apply:** Applicants must send a completed online application form; must submit two letters of recommendation and transcript of records. **Deadline:** May 1. **Contact:** AFE Scholarships at daker@afeendowment.org.

807 ■ Mike and Flo Novovesky Scholarships
(Undergraduate/Scholarship)

Purpose: To support young married students who are working to put themselves through college. **Focus:** Horticulture. **Qualif.:** Applicants must be second year to graduating married students with a GPA of 2.5 or higher. The scholarship may also go to an undergraduate working his or her way through school with financial need and family obligations, depending on the availability of married applicants. **Criteria:** Recipients are selected based on academic performance.

Funds Avail.: $300-$4,000. **Duration:** Annual. **Number Awarded:** up to 6. **To Apply:** Applicants must complete the online application form; must submit two letters of recommendation and transcript of records. **Deadline:** May 1. **Contact:** AFE Scholarships at daker@afeendowment.org.

808 ■ Lawrence "Bud" Ohlman Memorial Scholarships *(Undergraduate/Scholarship)*

Purpose: To further the advancement of education and science in the floriculture and environmental horticulture field by funding research and studies and financing scholarships and other educational activities for individuals interested in the field. **Focus:** Horticulture. **Qualif.:** Applicants must be in their third to final year in college, with a career goal to become a bedding plant grower for an established business. **Criteria:** Recipients are selected based on academic performance.

Funds Avail.: $300-$4,000. **Duration:** Annual. **Number Awarded:** Up to 6. **To Apply:** Applicants must complete the online application form; must submit two letters of recommendation and transcript of records. **Deadline:** May 1. **Contact:** AFE Scholarships at daker@afeendowment.org.

809 ■ Jim Perry Vocational Scholarships
(Undergraduate, Vocational/Occupational/Scholarship)

Purpose: To further the advancement of education and science in the floriculture and environmental horticulture field by funding research and studies and financing scholarships and other educational activities for individuals interested in the field. **Focus:** Horticulture. **Qualif.:** Applicant must be a vocational student in a one or two-year program with the intent of becoming a grower or greenhouse manager. **Criteria:** Recipients are selected based on academic performance.

Funds Avail.: $300-$4,000. **Number Awarded:** Up to 6. **To Apply:** Applicants must complete the online application form; must submit two letters of recommendation and transcript of records. **Deadline:** May 1. **Contact:** AFE Scholarships at daker@afeendowment.org.

810 ■ James K. Rathmell Jr. Memorial Scholarships
(Undergraduate, Graduate/Scholarship)

Purpose: To further the advancement of education and science in the floriculture and environmental horticulture field by funding research and studies and financing scholarships and other educational activities for individuals interested in the field. **Focus:** Horticulture. **Qualif.:** Applicants must be in their third to final year of undergraduate studies or be graduate students; must plan to work or study outside of the United States. **Criteria:** Recipients are selected based on academic performance.

Funds Avail.: $300-$4,000. **Number Awarded:** Up to 6. **To Apply:** Applicants must complete the online application form; must submit two letters of recommendation and transcript of records, and specific plan for horticulture work/study outside of the USA. **Deadline:** May 1. **Contact:** Send your applications to AFE Scholarships at daker@afeendowment.org.

811 ■ Seed Companies Scholarships *(Undergraduate, Graduate/Scholarship)*

Purpose: To further the advancement of education and science in the floriculture and environmental horticulture field by funding research and studies and financing scholarships and other educational activities for individuals interested in

Awards are arranged alphabetically below their administering organizations

the field. **Focus:** Horticulture. **Qualif.:** Applicants must be third to final year or graduate students who are pursuing a career in the seed industry in sales, breeding, research or marketing. **Criteria:** Recipients are selected based on academic performance.

Funds Avail.: $300-$4,000. **Number Awarded:** Up to 6. **To Apply:** Applicants must complete the online application form; must submit two letters of recommendation and transcript of records. **Deadline:** May 1. **Contact:** Send your applications to AFE Scholarships at daker@afeendowment.org.

812 ■ John L. Tomasovic, Sr. Scholarships
(Undergraduate/Scholarship)

Purpose: To further the advancement of education and science in the floriculture and environmental horticulture field by funding research and studies and financing scholarships and other educational activities for individuals interested in the field. **Focus:** Horticulture. **Qualif.:** Applicants must be in their second to final year in college and pursuing a career in a horticulture-related field; must have 3.0-3.5 GPA. **Criteria:** Recipients are selected based on financial need and GPA.

Funds Avail.: $300-$4,000. **Duration:** Annual. **Number Awarded:** Up to 6. **To Apply:** Applicants must complete the online application form; must submit two letters of recommendation and transcript of records. **Deadline:** May 1. **Contact:** Send your applications to AFE Scholarships at daker@afeendowment.org.

813 ■ Edward Tuinier Memorial Scholarships
(Undergraduate/Scholarship)

Purpose: To further the advancement of education and science in the floriculture and environmental horticulture field by funding research and studies and financing scholarships and other educational activities for individuals interested in the field. **Focus:** Horticulture. **Qualif.:** Applicants must be in their second to final year in a floriculture program at Michigan State University. **Criteria:** Recipients are selected based on academic performance.

Funds Avail.: $300-$4,000. **Duration:** Annual. **To Apply:** Applicants must complete the online application form; must submit two letters of recommendation and transcript of records. **Deadline:** May 1. **Contact:** Send your applications to AFE Scholarships at daker@afeendowment.org.

814 ■ Jacob and Rita Van Namen Marketing Scholarships *(Undergraduate/Scholarship)*

Purpose: To further the advancement of education and science in the floriculture and environmental horticulture field by funding research and studies and financing scholarships and other educational activities for individuals interested in the field. **Focus:** Horticulture. **Qualif.:** Applicants must be in their second to final year in college; must be interested in agribusiness marketing and distribution of floral products. **Criteria:** Recipients are selected based on academic performance.

Funds Avail.: $300-$4,000. **To Apply:** Applicants must complete the online application form; must submit two letters of recommendation and transcript of records. **Deadline:** May 1. **Remarks:** Established in 1997. **Contact:** AFE Scholarships at daker@afeendowment.org.

815 ■ American Foreign Service Association (AFSA)
2101 E St. NW
Washington, DC 20037
Ph: (202)338-4045
Fax: (202)338-6820
E-mail: member@afsa.org
URL: www.afsa.org
Facebook: www.facebook.com/afsapage
Twitter: twitter.com/afsatweets

816 ■ American Foreign Service Association Scholarship Fund *(Undergraduate/Scholarship)*

Purpose: To provide financial assistance to students for their college education. **Focus:** General studies/Field of study not specified. **Qualif.:** Applicants must be students who attended or will be attending full-time (12 credit hours or more) as undergraduates at a 2 or 4 year accredited college, university, community college, art school or conservatory (stateside or overseas); have cumulative 2.0 GPA on a 4.0 scale; complete undergraduate in four years; and, demonstrate financial need. **Criteria:** Applicants will be evaluated on the basis of academic record and financial need.

Funds Avail.: Amount varies. **Duration:** Annual. **To Apply:** Applicants must submit the Scholarship Application accompanied with a copy of high school/college transcripts; students or parents must complete the CSS PROFILE. **Contact:** Lori Dec, Scholarship Director, dec@afsa.org.

817 ■ American Foundation for the Blind (AFB)
2 Penn Plz., Ste. 1102
New York, NY 10121-1100
Ph: (212)502-7600
URL: www.afb.org
Facebook: www.facebook.com/americanfoundationfortheblind
Twitter: www.twitter.com/afb1921

818 ■ Gladys C. Anderson Memorial Scholarships
(Graduate, Undergraduate/Scholarship)

Purpose: To provide scholarships in the field of classical or religious music to persons who are blind or visually impaired. **Focus:** Music, Classical. **Qualif.:** Applicant must be blind or visually impaired; be a female undergraduate or graduate student studying classical or religious music. **Criteria:** The scholarship committee will review only those applications that are complete with supporting documents and meet all scholarship requirements.

Funds Avail.: $1,000. **Number Awarded:** 1. **To Apply:** Applicants must complete the online application. In addition, applicants must submit official transcripts; proof of post-secondary acceptance; two letters of recommendation; proof of U.S. citizenship; proof of legal blindness. Supporting documents are to be collected and sent in one envelope to the AFB Scholarship Committee. **Deadline:** May 31.

819 ■ Karen D. Carsel Memorial Scholarships
(Graduate/Scholarship)

Purpose: To financially support the education of a blind or visually impaired graduate student. **Focus:** General studies/Field of study not specified. **Qualif.:** Applicant must be blind or visually impaired; and must be a full-time graduate student who presents evidence of economic need. **Criteria:** The scholarship committee will review only those applications that are complete with supporting documents and meet all scholarship requirements.

Awards are arranged alphabetically below their administering organizations

Funds Avail.: $500. Number Awarded: 1. To Apply: Applicants must complete the online application. In addition, applicants must submit official transcripts; proof of post-secondary acceptance; two letters of recommendation; proof of U.S. citizenship; and proof of legal blindness. Supporting documents are to be collected and sent in one envelope to the AFB Scholarship Committee. Deadline: May 31. Contact: AFB Information Center; Email: tannis@afb.net.

820 ■ Rudolph Dillman Memorial Scholarships (Graduate, Undergraduate/Scholarship)

Purpose: To provide scholarships in the field of rehabilitation and/or education to persons who are blind or visually impaired. **Focus:** Education; Rehabilitation, Physical/Psychological. **Qualif.:** Applicant must be blind or visually impaired; and an undergraduate or graduate student in the field of rehabilitation or education. **Criteria:** The scholarship committee will review only those applications that are complete with supporting documents and meet all scholarship requirements.

Funds Avail.: $2,500 each. **Duration:** Annual. **Number Awarded:** 4. **To Apply:** Applicants must complete the online application. In addition, applicants must submit official transcripts; proof of post-secondary acceptance; two letters of recommendation; proof of U.S. citizenship; and proof of legal blindness. Supporting documents are to be collected and sent in one envelope to the AFB Scholarship Committee. **Deadline:** May 31. **Contact:** AFB Information Center; Email: tannis@afb.net.

821 ■ R.L. Gillette Scholarships (Undergraduate/Scholarship)

Purpose: To provide scholarships in the field of literature or music to persons who are blind or visually impaired. **Focus:** Literature; Music. **Qualif.:** Applicant must be blind or visually impaired; must be a female student enrolled in a full-time four-year undergraduate degree program in literature or music. **Criteria:** The scholarship committee will review only those applications that are complete with supporting documents and meet all scholarship requirements.

Funds Avail.: $1,000 each. **Number Awarded:** 2. **To Apply:** Applicants must complete the online application. In addition, applicants must submit official transcripts; proof of post-secondary acceptance; two letters of recommendation; proof of U.S. citizenship; proof of legal blindness. Supporting documents are to be collected and sent in one envelope to the AFB Scholarship Committee. **Deadline:** May 31. **Contact:** AFB Information Center; Email: tannis@afb.net.

822 ■ Delta Gamma Foundation Florence Margaret Harvey Memorial Scholarships (Graduate, Undergraduate/Scholarship)

Purpose: To provide scholarships in the field of rehabilitation and/or education to persons who are blind or visually impaired. **Focus:** Education; Rehabilitation, Physical/Psychological. **Qualif.:** Applicant must be blind or visually impaired; and an undergraduate or graduate student in the field of rehabilitation or education. **Criteria:** The scholarship committee will review only those applications that are complete with supporting documents and meet all scholarship requirements.

Funds Avail.: $1,000. **Number Awarded:** 1. **To Apply:** Applicants must complete the online application. In addition, applicants must submit official transcripts; proof of post-secondary acceptance; two letters of recommendation; proof of U.S. citizenship; and proof of legal blindness. Supporting documents are to be collected and sent in one envelope to the AFB Scholarship Committee. **Deadline:** May 31. **Contact:** AFB Information Center; Email: tannis@afb.net.

823 ■ Paul and Ellen Ruckes Scholarships (Graduate, Undergraduate/Scholarship)

Purpose: To provide scholarships in the field of engineering or in computer, physical or life sciences to persons who are blind or visually impaired. **Focus:** Computer and information sciences; Engineering; Life sciences; Physical sciences. **Qualif.:** Applicant must be blind or visually impaired; and an undergraduate or graduate student in the field of engineering or in computer, physical or life sciences. **Criteria:** The scholarship committee will review only those applications that are complete with supporting documents and meet all scholarship requirements.

Funds Avail.: $2,000 each. **Number Awarded:** 2. **To Apply:** Applicants must complete the online application. In addition, applicants must submit official transcripts; proof of post-secondary acceptance; two letters of recommendation; proof of U.S. citizenship; and proof of legal blindness. Supporting documents are to be collected and sent in one envelope to the AFB Scholarship Committee. **Deadline:** May 31. **Contact:** AFB Information Center; Email: tannis@afb.net.

824 ■ Ferdinand Torres Scholarships (Graduate, Undergraduate/Scholarship)

Purpose: To financially support the education of a blind or visually impaired graduate student. **Focus:** General studies/Field of study not specified. **Qualif.:** Applicant must be a blind or visually impaired full-time undergraduate or graduate student. **Criteria:** Strong preference will be given to new immigrants to the United States, and to those residing in the New York City metropolitan area.

Funds Avail.: $3,500. **Duration:** Annual. **Number Awarded:** 1. **To Apply:** Applicants must complete the online application. In addition, applicants must submit official transcripts; proof of post-secondary acceptance; two letters of recommendation; proof of U.S. citizenship; proof of legal blindness; evidence of economic need; and proof of residence in the United States (e.g. telephone bill; utility bill). Immigrants must include a description of country of origin and reason for coming to the United States. Supporting documents are to be collected and sent in one envelope to the AFB Scholarship Committee. **Deadline:** May 31. **Contact:** AFB Information Center; Email: tannis@afb.net.

825 ■ American Foundation for Pharmaceutical Education (AFPE)
6076 Franconia Rd., Ste. C
Alexandria, VA 22310-1758
Ph: (703)875-3095
Fax: (703)875-3098
Free: 855-624-9526
E-mail: info@afpenet.org
URL: www.afpenet.org
Facebook: www.linkedin.com/company/american-foundation-for-pharmaceutical-education
Twitter: twitter.com/AFPEPharmEd

826 ■ AFPE Gateway Research Scholarships (Doctorate/Scholarship)

Purpose: To increase the number of students who undertake a faculty-mentored research program and decide to

Awards are arranged alphabetically below their administering organizations

enroll in graduate programs leading to a Ph.D. in the basic, clinical, or administrative pharmaceutical sciences. **Focus:** Pharmaceutical sciences. **Qualif.:** Scholars must be selected and nominated by a faculty member; must be enrolled in a Pharm.D. program; must have completed at least two years of college; must be enrolled in at least the first year of the professional pharmacy curriculum; be enrolled in a baccalaureate degree program; have completed at least one year of the degree program; must be enrolled for at least one full academic year after initiation of the award; and must be U.S. citizens. **Criteria:** Preference will be given to applications from students who need relevant research experience in order to have the basis to decide whether to pursue the Ph.D. degree in the pharmaceutical sciences. **Funds Avail.:** $5,000. **Duration:** Annual. **To Apply:** Applicants must complete the online application form, which can be downloaded from the website. The faculty member seeking support and who will be responsible for mentoring the research scholar must provide: a copy of the faculty member's curriculum vitae including education and training, experience in research and bibliography/publications; official copies of all of the students' college transcripts; a typewritten letter by the students (not more than one page) explaining their interest in a pharmaceutical science research experience and their potential career goal(s); two fully completed statements of recommendation and evaluation forms from the faculty and a professor who is familiar with both the faculty member and the students' work. **Deadline:** February 24. **Contact:** E-mail at office.manager@afpenet.org.

827 ■ AFPE Pre-Doctoral Fellowships in Pharmaceutical Sciences *(Doctorate/Fellowship)*

Purpose: To encourage outstanding pre-doctoral students who have completed at least three semesters of graduate study and have no more than three years remaining to continue their studies and earn a Ph.D. in the pharmaceutical sciences at a U.S. school or college of pharmacy. **Focus:** Pharmaceutical sciences. **Qualif.:** Applicants must have completed at least three semesters of graduate study toward a Ph.D. and have no more than three years remaining to obtain a Ph.D. degree in a graduate program in the pharmaceutical sciences administered by, or affiliated with a U.S. school or college of pharmacy. Students enrolled in joint Pharm.D./Ph.D programs are eligible to apply if they have completed the equivalent of three full semesters of graduate credit toward Ph.D., and if the Ph.D. degree will be awarded within three additional years; must be U.S. citizens or permanent residents. **Criteria:** Recipients will be selected by the Board of grant based on completed requirements. **Funds Avail.:** $10,000. **Duration:** Annual. **To Apply:** Applicants must complete the pre-doctoral fellowship form; statements of recommendation and evaluation forms from three college faculty members who are acquainted with the student's progress in graduate study; and official transcripts of all collegiate grades. Application must be signed by the Dean of the Pharmacy Department. **Deadline:** January 13.

828 ■ AFPE Pre-Doctoral Fellowships in Pharmaceutical Sciences for Underrepresented Minorities *(Doctorate, Graduate/Fellowship)*

Purpose: To identify and support those students who have the potential to become leaders in the pharmaceutical profession. **Focus:** Pharmaceutical sciences. **Qualif.:** Applicants must be Africa-American/Black students who have completed at least three semesters of graduate study toward the Ph.D. and who have no more than three years remaining to obtain the Ph.D. degree in a graduate program in the pharmaceutical sciences administered by, or affiliated with a U.S. school or college of pharmacy. Students enrolled in joint Pharm.D./Ph.D programs are eligible if they have completed the equivalent of three semesters of graduate credit toward Ph.D., and if the Ph.D. degree will be awarded within three additional years. Applicants must be U.S. citizens or permanent residents. **Criteria:** Recipients are selected based on academic achievement as decided by the Board of Grant based on the completed requirements. **Funds Avail.:** $10,000. **Duration:** Annual. **To Apply:** Applicants must complete the pre-doctoral fellowship form; statements of recommendation and evaluation forms from three college faculty members who are acquainted with applicants' progress in graduate study; and official transcripts of all collegiate grades. **Deadline:** January 13. **Contact:** E-mail Victoria Moses at office.manager@afpenet.org.

829 ■ American Foundation for Suicide Prevention (AFSP)
120 Wall St., 29th Fl.
New York, NY 10005
Ph: (212)363-3500
Fax: (212)363-6237
Free: 888-333-AFSP
E-mail: info@afsp.org
URL: afsp.org

830 ■ AFSP - Distinguished Investigator Grants *(Postgraduate/Grant)*

Purpose: To support the work of investigators from all disciplines that contribute to the understanding of suicide and suicide prevention. **Focus:** Suicide. **Qualif.:** Investigators from all academic disciplines are eligible to apply, and both basic science and applied research projects will be considered, providing the study has an essential focus on suicide prevention. Applicants must be at the level of associate professor or higher with an established record of research and publication on suicide. **Criteria:** Awards are given based on the research proposals; the qualifications, experience and productivity of the applicant, innovation, and the facilities available to the applicant for the purpose of the study. **Funds Avail.:** $100,000. **Duration:** Two Years. **To Apply:** Applicant may fill-up an application form online. The application must include the following sections: Cover sheet; Principal Investigator Assurance Form; Abstract; Certification for Protection of Human Subjects; Budget; Budget Justification; Biographical Information; Project Description; Project Timeline; References; and Appendices. Completed grant applications must be submitted electronically to grants@afsp.org. A compact disc (CD) containing the completed application must also be submitted to the American Foundation for Suicide Prevention, 120 Wall St., 22nd Floor, New York, NY 10005. **Deadline:** November 15. **Contact:** grantsmanager@afsp.org.

831 ■ AFSP Postdoctoral Research Fellowships *(Postgraduate/Fellowship)*

Purpose: To support the work of investigators from all disciplines that contribute to the understanding of suicide and suicide prevention. **Focus:** Suicide. **Qualif.:** Applicant must have received a Ph.D., M.D., or other doctoral degree within the preceding years and have not had more than three years of fellowship support. **Criteria:** Awards are given based on the research proposals; the qualifications, experience and productivity of the applicant, innovation, the facilities available to the applicant for the purpose of the study, and availability of a sufficient number of patients or subjects

Funds Avail.: $104,000. **Duration:** Two years. **To Apply:** Applicants may go online to fill out an application form. The application must include the following sections: Cover sheet; Principal Investigator Assurance Form; Abstract; Certification for Protection of Human Subjects; Budget; Budget Justification; Biographical Information; Project Description; Project Timeline; References; Research Training Plan; and Recommendation of Mentor. Completed grant applications must be submitted electronically to grants@afsp.org. A compact disc (CD) containing the completed application must also be submitted to the American Foundation for Suicide Prevention, 120 Wall St., 22nd Floor, New York, NY 10005. **Deadline:** November 15. **Contact:** grantsmanager@afsp.org.

832 ■ AFSP Standard Research Grants
(Postgraduate/Grant)

Purpose: To support the work of investigators from all disciplines that contribute to the understanding of suicide and suicide prevention. **Focus:** Suicide. **Qualif.:** Investigators from all academic disciplines are eligible to apply, and both basic science and applied research projects will be considered, providing the study has an essential focus on suicide prevention. **Criteria:** Awards are given based on the research proposals; the qualifications, experience and productivity of the applicant, innovation, the facilities available to the applicant for the purpose of the study, and availability of a sufficient number of patients or subjects

Funds Avail.: $90,000. **Duration:** Two years. **To Apply:** Applicant may fill-up an application form online. The application must include the following sections: Cover sheet; Principal Investigator Assurance Form; Abstract; Certification for Protection of Human Subjects; Budget; Budget Justification; Biographical Information; Project Description; Project Timeline; References; and Appendices. Completed grant applications must be submitted electronically to grants@afsp.org. A compact disc (CD) containing the completed application must also be submitted to the American Foundation for Suicide Prevention, 120 Wall St., 22nd Floor, New York, NY 10005. **Deadline:** November 15. **Contact:** grantsmanager@afsp.org.

833 ■ AFSP Young Investigator Grants
(Postgraduate/Grant)

Purpose: To support the work of investigators from all disciplines that contribute to the understanding of suicide and suicide prevention. **Focus:** Suicide. **Qualif.:** Applicant must be at the level of assistant professor or lower. **Criteria:** Awards are given based on the research proposals; the qualifications, experience and productivity of the applicant, innovation, the facilities available to the applicant for the purpose of the study, and availability of a sufficient number of patients or subjects

Funds Avail.: $85,000. Additional $5,000 per year for a mentor, who serves as an advisor to the applicant. **Duration:** Two years. **To Apply:** Applicants may apply and fill out the application form online. The application must include the following sections: Cover sheet; Principal Investigator Assurance Form; Abstract; Certification for Protection of Human Subjects; Budget; Budget Justification; Biographical Information; Project Description; Project Timeline; References; and Recommendation of Mentor. Completed grant applications must be submitted electronically to grants@afsp.org. A compact disc (CD) containing the completed application must also be submitted to the American Foundation for Suicide Prevention, 120 Wall St., 22nd Floor, New York, NY 10005. **Deadline:** November 15. **Contact:** Vinita Ling, Grants Manager; 212-363-3500 ext. 15.

834 ■ American Foundation for Suicide and Prevention Pilot Grants *(Postgraduate/Grant)*

Purpose: To support the work of investigators from all disciplines that contribute to the understanding of suicide and suicide prevention. **Focus:** Suicide. **Qualif.:** Any investigator at any level with research that will provide seed funding for new projects that have the potential to lead to larger investigations. **Criteria:** Awards are given based on the research proposals; the qualifications, experience and productivity of the applicant, innovation, the facilities available to the applicant for the purpose of the study, and availability of a sufficient number of patients or subjects

Funds Avail.: $30,000 over one or two years. **Duration:** Two years. **To Apply:** Applicants may go online to fill out an application form. The application must include the following sections: Cover sheet; Principal Investigator Assurance Form; Abstract; Certification for Protection of Human Subjects; Budget; Budget Justification; Biographical Information; Project Description; Project Timeline; References; Research Training Plan; and Recommendation of Mentor. Completed grant applications must be submitted electronically to grants@afsp.org. A compact disc (CD) containing the completed application must also be submitted to the American Foundation for Suicide Prevention, 120 Wall St., 22nd Floor, New York, NY 10005. **Deadline:** November 15. **Contact:** grantsmanager@afsp.org.

835 ■ American Foundry Society
1695 N Penny Ln.
Schaumburg, IL 60173
Ph: (847)824-0181
Fax: (847)824-7848
Free: 800-537-4237
URL: www.afsinc.org
Facebook: www.facebook.com/americanfoundrysociety
Twitter: twitter.com/AmerFoundrySoc

836 ■ H.H. Harris Foundation Scholarships *(Professional development, Undergraduate/Scholarship)*

Purpose: To provide educational aid to students and professionals in the metallurgical and casting of metals field. **Focus:** Metallurgy. **Qualif.:** Applicants must be students or professionals pursuing a career in the field of metallurgy or any related fields; and must be U.S. citizens. **Criteria:** Recipients will be selected based on submitted application.

Funds Avail.: $1,000. **Duration:** Annual. **To Apply:** Applicants must fill out the application form and are required to submit two letters of reference. **Deadline:** May 31.

837 ■ American Galvanizers Association (AGA)
6881 S Holy Cir., Ste. 108
Centennial, CO 80112
Ph: (720)554-0900
Fax: (720)554-0909

Awards are arranged alphabetically below their administering organizations

E-mail: aga@galvanizeit.org
URL: www.galvanizeit.org
Facebook: www.facebook.com/galvanizeit
LinkedIn: www.linkedin.com/company/american-galvanizers-association
Twitter: twitter.com/agagalvanizeit

838 ■ Galvanize the Future: Edgar K. Schutz Scholarships (Undergraduate, Graduate/Scholarship)

Purpose: To assist future specifiers with the rising cost of a college education, and teach these specifiers a little about hot-dip galvanizing. **Focus:** Architecture; Engineering, Civil; Engineering, Materials. **Qualif.:** Applicants must be full- or part-time, undergraduate or graduate students of any age enrolled at an accredited 4-year college/university only in North America during the school year. Qualifying majors include architecture, civil engineering, structural engineering, construction management, material science, or other related field. **Criteria:** Selection shall be based on relevance, accuracy, conciseness and ingenuity of the applicants' respective essays.

Funds Avail.: $2,500 (1st place); $1,500 (2nd place); $1,000 (3rd place). **Duration:** Annual. **Number Awarded:** 3. **To Apply:** Application is via online. Applicants must also submit their respective essays (1000-2000 words). **Deadline:** March 31.

839 ■ American Ground Water Trust (AGWT)
50 Pleasant St., Ste. 2
Concord, NH 03301
Ph: (603)228-5444
Fax: (603)228-6557
Free: 800-423-7748
E-mail: trustinfo@agwt.org
URL: www.agwt.org

840 ■ AGWT Baroid Scholarships (Undergraduate/Scholarship)

Purpose: To encourage high school students to consider careers specializing the provision and protection of ground water resources. **Focus:** Water resources. **Qualif.:** Applicants must be high school seniors planning to attend an undergraduate academic program of study at a four-year accredited university or college located in the United States; must have a minimum 3.0 GPA; must be US citizens or legal residents of the United States. **Criteria:** Selection will be based on the submitted materials.

Funds Avail.: $2,000. **Duration:** Annual. **To Apply:** Interested may obtain an application form online and must submit the following materials: biographical and achievement information, countersigned by a teacher at the applicants' high school; a 500-word essay and a 300-word description of the applicants' high school ground water project and/or practical environmental work experience; two letters of recommendation; documentary evidence of scholastic achievements and references. **Deadline:** June 1.

841 ■ AGWT Thomas M. Stetson Scholarships (Undergraduate/Scholarship)

Purpose: To encourage high school students to consider careers specializing the provision and protection of ground water resources. **Focus:** Water resources. **Qualif.:** Applicants must be high school seniors planning to attend a college or university located west of the Mississippi River; must have a minimum 3.0 GPA; must be US citizens or legal residents of the United States. **Criteria:** Selection will be based on the submitted application materials.

Funds Avail.: $2,000. **Duration:** Annual. **To Apply:** Interested may obtain an application form online and must submit the following materials: biographical and achievement information, countersigned by a teacher at the applicants' high school; a 500-word essay and a 300-word description of the applicants' high school ground water project and/or practical environmental work experience; two letters of recommendation; documentary evidence of scholastic achievements and references. **Deadline:** June 1.

842 ■ American Handel Society (AHS)
49 Christopher Hollow Rd.
Sandwich, MA 02563-2227
Ph: (860)768-4895
Fax: (860)768-4441
E-mail: info@americanhandelsociety.org
URL: www.americanhandelsociety.org

843 ■ J. Merrill Knapp Research Fellowship (Undergraduate/Fellowship)

Purpose: To support fellows for their scholarly projects related to Handel and his world. **Focus:** General studies/Field of study not specified. **Qualif.:** Applicants must be students at North American universities and residents of North America. **Criteria:** Preference will be given to advanced graduate student who has not previously held this fellowship.

Funds Avail.: $2,000. **Duration:** Periodic. **To Apply:** Applicants must submit curriculum vitae, a description of the project (not to exceed 750 words), a budget showing how and when the applicant plans to use the funds, and a description of other grants applied for or received for the same project; must have two recommendation letters. **Deadline:** March 1. **Remarks:** Established in 1989. **Contact:** Roger Freitas at rfreitas@esm.rochester.edu.

844 ■ American Head and Neck Society (AHNS)
11300 W Olympic Blvd., Ste. 600
Los Angeles, CA 90064
Ph: (310)437-0559
Fax: (310)437-0585
E-mail: admin@ahns.info
URL: www.ahns.info
Facebook: www.facebook.com/AHNSInfo

845 ■ AHNS/AAO-HNS Young Investigator Award (Other/Grant)

Purpose: To support research in neoplastic disease of the head and neck. **Focus:** Medical research. **Qualif.:** Applicants must be AHNS members (may be a candidate member). Also open to fellows and assistant professors. **Criteria:** Priority is given to investigators with outstanding research.

Funds Avail.: $20,000. **Duration:** Annual. **Number Awarded:** 1. **To Apply:** Applicants may contact the society for the application process and other requirements.

846 ■ AHNS Pilot Research Grants (Other/Grant)

Purpose: To support basic, translational or clinical researches in head and neck oncology. **Focus:** Medical

Awards are arranged alphabetically below their administering organizations

research. **Qualif.:** Applicants must be residents, fellows or junior faculty for pilot research in head and neck related topics; must be residents of U.S. or Canada, medical students, PhD or faculty members at the rank of associate professor or below. **Criteria:** Recipient is chosen based on reviewed quality of research project.

Funds Avail.: $10,000. **Duration:** Annual. **Number Awarded:** 2. **To Apply:** Applicants may contact the Society for the application process and other requirements.

847 ■ Ballantyne Resident Research Grants *(Other/Grant)*

Purpose: To support basic, translational or clinical researches in head and neck oncology. **Focus:** Medical research. **Qualif.:** Applicants must be residents, fellows or junior faculty for pilot research in head and neck related topics; must be residents of U.S. or Canada; must be medical students, Ph.D.s or faculty members at the rank of associate professor or below. **Criteria:** Recipient is chosen based on ability to meet mentioned criteria and potential of proposed research.

Funds Avail.: maximum total cost of $10,000. **Duration:** Annual. **Number Awarded:** 1. **To Apply:** Applicants may contact the Society for the application process and other requirements.

848 ■ American Hellenic Educational Progressive Association - District No. 1

2025 Ludovie Ln.
Decatur, GA 30033
Ph: (404)843-0180
URL: www.ahepadistrict1.org

849 ■ AHEPA Family District No. 1 Scholarships *(Graduate, Undergraduate/Scholarship)*

Purpose: To promote, encourage, induce and advance education at the college, university and graduate school level. **Focus:** General studies/Field of study not specified. **Qualif.:** Applicants must be one of the following: students in the graduating class of their high school and planning to attend full-time in an accredited college or university during the current calendar year; high school graduates planning to attend full-time in an accredited college or university during the calendar year; or attending an accredited college or university and will continue to attend full-time during the calendar year. **Criteria:** Recipients will be selected based on financial need, scholastic achievement, extra-curricular activities, athletic achievements, work and community service.

Funds Avail.: No specific amount. **Duration:** Annual. **To Apply:** Applicants must complete the application form; must submit transcript of records; must provide the name of the college or university to which they have been accepted or which they are planning to attend; must submit a typewritten and not to exceed 500 words essay; and must include two letters of recommendation which have been obtained within the past six months.

850 ■ American Historical Association (AHA)

400 A St. SE
Washington, DC 20003-3889
Ph: (202)544-2422
Fax: (202)544-8307
E-mail: info@historians.org

URL: www.historians.org
Facebook: www.facebook.com/AHAhistorians
LinkedIn: www.linkedin.com/groups/3810333/profile
Twitter: www.twitter.com/AHAhistorians

851 ■ American Historical Association Fellowships in Aerospace History *(Doctorate/Fellowship)*

Purpose: To provide funding support for a research project related to aerospace history; to encourage engagement in significant and sustained advanced research in all aspects of the history of aerospace from the earliest human interest in flight to the present including cultural and intellectual history, economic history, history of law and public policy, history of science, engineering and management. **Focus:** History. **Qualif.:** Applicants must possess a doctorate degree in history or in a closely related field; may either be enrolled as students having completed all coursework in a doctoral degree-granting program. **Criteria:** Recipients will be selected based on the significance of the research project.

Funds Avail.: $20,000. **Duration:** Annual; From 6 to 9 months. **To Apply:** Applicants must complete the application form and submit along with seven copies (each copy should contain one application form, proposal and CV, collated and paper clipped together); and letter of recommendations sealed in a separate envelope. **Deadline:** April 1. **Contact:** Prize Administrator at awards@historians.org.

852 ■ Albert J. Beveridge Grants for Research in the Western Hemisphere *(Doctorate/Grant)*

Purpose: To support research in the history of the Western hemisphere. **Focus:** History. **Qualif.:** Candidates must be PhD and junior scholars. **Criteria:** Preference will be given to those with specific research needs, such as the completion of a project or completion of a discrete segment thereof.

Funds Avail.: Not to exceed $1,000. **Duration:** Annual. **To Apply:** Interested applicants may contact the Research Grant Administrator for the application process and other information. **Deadline:** February 15.

853 ■ J. Franklin Jameson Fellowships in American History *(Professional development/Fellowship)*

Purpose: To support significant scholarly research in the collections of the Library Congress for one semester for scholars who are at an early stage in their careers in history. **Focus:** History. **Qualif.:** Applicants must hold a Ph.D. degree or equivalent; must have received this degree within the past seven years; and must have not published or had accepted for publication a book-length historical work. **Criteria:** Recipients are selected based on academic performance.

Funds Avail.: $5,000. **Duration:** Annual. **To Apply:** Applicants must submit an original and six copies of complete application including applicant's vita (not more than three to five pages in length); a statement concerning the proposed project and its relationship to the Library of Congress holdings; tentative schedule for residence of the fellowship; and three letters of recommendation. Letters should be written by individuals qualified to judge the project and address the applicant's fitness to undertake it. **Deadline:** April 1. **Remarks:** The fellowship is named in honor of J. Franklin Jameson, a founder of the Association, longtime managing editor of the American Historical Review, formerly Chief of the Manuscript Division of the Library of Congress, and the first incumbent of the library's chair of American history. **Contact:** Prize Administrator at awards@historians.org.

Awards are arranged alphabetically below their administering organizations

854 ■ Michael Kraus Research Grants *(Doctorate/Grant)*

Purpose: To support student's travel to a library or archive; microfilming, photography, or photocopying; borrowing or access fees; and similar research expenses. **Focus:** History. **Qualif.:** Applicants must be PhD candidates and junior scholars; must be members of AHA. **Criteria:** Selection will be based on the committee's criteria.

Funds Avail.: Up to $800. **Duration:** Annual. **To Apply:** Interested applicants may contact the Research Grant Administration for the application process and other information. **Deadline:** February 15.

855 ■ Littleton-Griswold Research Grants *(Doctorate/Grant)*

Purpose: To support research in U.S. legal history and in the general field of law and society. **Focus:** History. **Qualif.:** Applicants must be PhD candidates and junior scholars; must be members of AHA. **Criteria:** Preference will be given to those with specific research needs, such as the completion of a project or completion of a discrete segment thereof.

Funds Avail.: Up to $1,000. **Duration:** Annual. **To Apply:** Interested applicants may contact the Research Grant Administrator for the application process. **Deadline:** February 15.

856 ■ Bernadotte E. Schmitt Grants *(Doctorate/Grant)*

Purpose: To support research in the history of Europe, Africa, and Asia. **Focus:** History. **Qualif.:** Applicants must be PhD and junior scholars; must be members of AHA. **Criteria:** Preference will be given to those with specific research needs, such as the completion of a project or completion of a discrete segment thereof.

Funds Avail.: Not to exceed $1,000. **Duration:** Annual. **To Apply:** Interested applicants may contact the Research Grant Administrator for the application process and other information. **Deadline:** February 15.

857 ■ American Hotel & Lodging Educational Foundation (AH&LEF)

1250 I St. NW, Ste. 1100
Washington, DC 20005-3931
Ph: (202)289-3180
Fax: (202)289-3199
E-mail: foundation@ahlef.org
URL: www.ahlef.org
Facebook: www.facebook.com/AHLEF.org
LinkedIn: www.linkedin.com/company/american-hotel-&-lodging-educational-foundation
Twitter: twitter.com/AHLEFoundation

858 ■ AH&LEF American Express Scholarship *(Undergraduate/Scholarship)*

Purpose: To provide educational assistance to current lodging employees and their dependents. **Focus:** Hotel, institutional, and restaurant management. **Qualif.:** Applicants must be enrolled full-time or part-time; must be working a minimum of 20 hours per week at an AH & LA member hotel and with at least 12 months hotel experience. **Criteria:** Recipients are selected based on academic performance, hospitality work experience, financial need, extracurricular/professional attributes and honors, as well as personal attributes as defined in their career goal statement.

Funds Avail.: Baccalaureate Majors - $2,000 full-time enrollment; or $1,000 part-time; Associate Majors - $1,000 full-time enrollment; or $500 part-time. **Duration:** Annual. **To Apply:** Applicants must complete all the required sections of the application. **Remarks:** Established in 1994.

859 ■ American Express Professional Development Scholarships *(Other/Scholarship)*

Purpose: To support individuals in advancing their career by growing their industry knowledge or skill set. **Focus:** Hotel, institutional, and restaurant management. **Qualif.:** Applicants must be working a minimum of 35 hours per week at an AH&LA member hotel and with at least 12 months hotel experience. If applying for a certification, applicants must qualify the certification program. **Criteria:** Applicants are selected based on professional, community and extracurricular activities; industry-related work experience; and personal attributes including career goals and their response to questions.

Funds Avail.: No specific amount. **To Apply:** Applicants must submit an application form and attach the appropriate EI distance learning enrollment form or professional certification form. **Deadline:** January 1; April 1; July 1; and October 1.

860 ■ The Hyatt Hotels Fund For Minority Lodging Management Students *(Undergraduate/Scholarship)*

Purpose: To provide educational support to minority students in hotel management program. **Focus:** Hotel, institutional, and restaurant management. **Qualif.:** Applicant must be enrolled in at least 12 credit hours for the upcoming Fall and Spring semesters, or just the Fall semester if graduating this December; at least a sophomore in a four-year program at the time of application; a minority descent: African-American, Hispanic, American Indian, Alaskan Native, Asian or Pacific Islander; a U.S. citizen or permanent U.S. resident. **Criteria:** Recipients are selected based on academic performance, hospitality work experience, financial need, extracurricular/professional attributes and honors, as well as personal attributes as defined in their career goal statement.

Funds Avail.: $2,000 and a plaque. **Duration:** Annual. **To Apply:** Applicants must complete all the required sections of the application. **Deadline:** May 1. **Remarks:** Established in 1988.

861 ■ The Steve Hymans Extended Stay Scholarship Program *(Undergraduate/Scholarship)*

Purpose: To support students to achieve their educational goals. **Focus:** Hotel, institutional, and restaurant management. **Qualif.:** Applicant must be enrolled full-time or part-time; have a minimum of 3.0 GPA; be a U.S. citizen or permanent U.S. resident; and have at least some experience either working or interning (paid or unpaid) at a lodging property. **Criteria:** Applicants with experience at an extended stay property will be given preference.

Funds Avail.: $64,750. **Number Awarded:** 40. **To Apply:** Students will be nominated by their respective school. Student nominees must complete all the required sections of the application. Additionally, under separate cover, participating schools are required to send a nomination form confirming their nominees and providing suggested award amounts.

Awards are arranged alphabetically below their administering organizations

862 ■ The Arthur J. Packard Memorial Scholarship Competition *(Undergraduate/Scholarship)*

Purpose: To provide educational assistance to lodging management students. **Focus:** Hotel, institutional, and restaurant management. **Qualif.:** Applicants must be enrolled full-time for the upcoming Fall and Spring semesters majoring Hospitality Management; have a minimum GPA of 3.5 or higher; and must be U.S. residents. **Criteria:** Recipient are selected based on academic performance, hospitality work experience, financial need, extracurricular/professional attributes and honors, as well as personal attributes as defined in their career goal statement.
Funds Avail.: First-place winner $5,000; Second-place $3,000; Third-place $2,000. **Duration:** Annual. **To Apply:** Applicants must complete all the required sections of the application. **Deadline:** May 1.

863 ■ Pepsi Scholarships *(Undergraduate/Scholarship)*

Purpose: To provide financial support to those students who are pursuing hospitality-related degree programs. **Focus:** Hotel, institutional, and restaurant management. **Qualif.:** Applicants must be graduates of the Hospitality High School in Washington, D.C.; enrolled in at least 12 credit hours for the upcoming Fall and Spring semesters; worked at least 250 hours in the hotel/hospitality industry; and have a minimum 2.5 GPA. **Criteria:** Recipients are selected based on academic performance, hospitality work experience, financial need, extracurricular/professional attributes and honors, as well as personal attributes as defined in their career goal statement.
Funds Avail.: $500-$3,000 depending upon enrollment. **Duration:** Annual. **To Apply:** Applicants must complete all the required sections of the application; participating school must send a nomination form confirming its nominees and suggested award amount(s).

864 ■ Rama Scholarships for the American Dream *(Graduate, Undergraduate/Scholarship)*

Purpose: To provide educational assistance for lodging management students. **Focus:** Hotel, institutional, and restaurant management. **Qualif.:** Applicants must be enrolled in at least nine credit hours for the upcoming Fall and Spring semesters or just the Fall semester if graduating in December; must be undergraduate or graduate hospitality management majors; must have a minimum 2.5 GPA; and must be U.S. citizens or permanent U.S. residents. **Criteria:** Applicants who are students of Asian-Indian descent and other minority groups, as well as JHM employees and their dependents will be given preference.
Funds Avail.: $1,000-$3,000. **Duration:** Annual. **To Apply:** Applicants must complete all the required sections of the application. **Deadline:** May 1. **Remarks:** Established by JHM Hotels, Inc.

865 ■ American Indian College Fund
8333 Greenwood Blvd.
Denver, CO 80221-4488
Ph: (303)426-8900
Fax: (303)426-1200
Free: 800-776-3863
E-mail: info@collegefund.org
URL: www.collegefund.org

866 ■ Citi Foundation Scholarship Program *(Undergraduate/Scholarship)*

Purpose: To provide scholarship to Native students attending the following tribal colleges and universities in South Dakota. **Focus:** General studies/Field of study not specified. **Qualif.:** Applicants must have at least a 3.0 grade point average; must commit to organizing and participating in a career exploration day; must be American Indian or Alaskan Native with proof of enrollment; must be enrolled full-time at an eligible tribal college; and must have demonstrated exceptional academic achievement and financial need. **Criteria:** Preference will be given to those students who meet the criteria.
Funds Avail.: $50,000. **To Apply:** Applicants must complete the application process online.

867 ■ Coca-Cola First Generation Scholarships *(Undergraduate/Scholarship)*

Purpose: To provide financial assistance for students who are in need. **Focus:** General studies/Field of study not specified. **Qualif.:** Applicants must have at least a 3.0 grade point average; must be in first or second semester of college; must be the first member of their immediate family to attend college; must be American Indian or Alaskan Native with proof of enrollment; must be enrolled full-time at an eligible tribal college; and must have demonstrated exceptional academic achievement and financial need. **Criteria:** Preference will be given to those students who meet the criteria.
Funds Avail.: $5,000. **To Apply:** Applicants must complete the application process online.

868 ■ Vine Deloria Jr. Memorial Scholarships *(Graduate, Professional development/Scholarship)*

Purpose: To provide financial support for outstanding American Indian students who are pursuing a graduate degree. **Focus:** General studies/Field of study not specified. **Qualif.:** Applicants must be pursuing graduate or professional degree; must have a 3.0 GPA.. **Criteria:** Preference will be given to students who meet the criteria.
Funds Avail.: $1,000. **To Apply:** Applicants must complete the application process online.

869 ■ General Mills Foundation Scholarships *(Undergraduate/Scholarship)*

Purpose: To provide need-based scholarships for outstanding American Indian students. **Focus:** General studies/Field of study not specified. **Qualif.:** Applicants must have at least a 2.5 grade point average; must be American Indian or Alaskan Native with proof of enrollment; must be enrolled full-time at an eligible Minnesota or New Mexico tribal college; and must have demonstrated exceptional academic achievement and financial need. **Criteria:** Preference will be given to those who meet the criteria.
Funds Avail.: No specific amount. **To Apply:** Applicants must complete the application process online.

870 ■ Morgan Stanley Tribal Scholars Program *(Undergraduate/Scholarship)*

Purpose: To provide financial support to those students who are in need. **Focus:** Business. **Qualif.:** Applicants must have at least a 3.0 grade point average; must have declared a major in business or a related field; must be enrolled full-time at an eligible tribal college; must be American Indian or Alaskan Native with proof of enrollment; and must have demonstrated exceptional academic achievement. **Criteria:** Preference will be given to those students who meet the criteria.
Funds Avail.: $2,500-$5,000. **To Apply:** Applicants must complete the application process online.

Awards are arranged alphabetically below their administering organizations

AMERICAN INDIAN GRADUATE CENTER

871 ■ Nissan North America, Inc. Scholarships
(Undergraduate/Scholarship)

Purpose: To award scholarships to outstanding American Indian students who are currently enrolled in tribal colleges. **Focus:** General studies/Field of study not specified. **Qualif.:** Applicants must have at least a 2.5 grade point average; must be enrolled full-time at an eligible tribal college; must be American Indian or Alaskan Native with proof of enrollment or descendancy; and must have demonstrated exceptional academic achievement. **Criteria:** Preference will be given to students who meet the criteria.

Funds Avail.: $3,000. **To Apply:** Applicants must complete the application process online. **Contact:** Debra Reed at 800-776-3863 or dreed@collegefund.org.

872 ■ Sovereign Nations Scholarships
(Undergraduate/Scholarship)

Purpose: To provide financial support to those students who are in need. **Focus:** General studies/Field of study not specified. **Qualif.:** Applicants must have demonstrated exceptional academic achievement by maintaining a 3.0 or higher G.P.A.; must commit to working for their tribe or an Indian organization upon completion of their degree; must be enrolled full-time at an eligible tribal college; and must be American Indian or Alaskan Native with proof of enrollment or. **Criteria:** Preference will be given to those students who meet the criteria.

Funds Avail.: $2,000. **To Apply:** Applicants must complete the application process online.

873 ■ Woksape Oyate: "Wisdom of the People" Distinguished Scholars Awards *(Undergraduate/Scholarship)*

Purpose: To provide financial support to students who are in need. **Focus:** General studies/Field of study not specified. **Qualif.:** Applicants must be American Indian or Alaskan Native with proof of enrollment; must be enrolled full-time at an eligible tribal college; and must have demonstrated exceptional academic achievement. **Criteria:** Preference will be given to students who meet the criteria.

Funds Avail.: $8,000. **To Apply:** Applicants must complete the application process online. **Contact:** Debra Reed at 800-776-3863 or dreed@collegefund.org.

874 ■ American Indian Education Fund (AIEF)
PO Box 27491
Albuquerque, NM 87125
Free: 800-881-8694
E-mail: info@aiefprograms.org
URL: www.nrcprograms.org/site/
PageServer?pagename=aief_home

875 ■ Indian Health Service Professionals Program
(Undergraduate/Scholarship)

Purpose: To provide opportunity to those Indian students who want learn and succeed in their educational career. **Focus:** Health sciences. **Qualif.:** Applicants must be enrolled members of state or federally recognized tribes; must be undergraduate or graduate students who are majoring in any health-related pre-professional program. **Criteria:** Selection will be based on the committee's criteria.

Funds Avail.: No specific amount. **Duration:** Annual. **Number Awarded:** Approximately 500. **To Apply:** Applicants must: complete AIEF Scholarship Application; provide documentation of tribal enrollment for themselves or their parents; provide transcripts with ACT and GPA scores; attach an essay that outlines the following information: introduction, academics, career plans, service to the Native American community, leadership/community service, financial needs and unique circumstances. **Deadline:** June 15.

876 ■ International Order of the King's Daughters and Sons North American Indian Scholarship Program *(Undergraduate/Scholarship)*

Purpose: To provide opportunity to those Indian students who want learn and succeed in their educational career. **Focus:** General studies/Field of study not specified. **Qualif.:** Applicants must be: Native Americans who have (or whose parents have) a reservation number; undergraduates of any major. **Criteria:** Selection will be based on the committee's criteria.

Funds Avail.: $650. **Duration:** Annual. **Number Awarded:** Approximately 50. **To Apply:** Applicants must: complete AIEF Scholarship Application; provide documentation of tribal enrollment for themselves or their parents; provide transcripts with ACT and GPA scores; attach an essay that outlines the following information: introduction, academics, career plans, service to the Native American community, leadership/community service, financial needs and unique circumstances. **Deadline:** April 1.

877 ■ Native American Education Grants *(Graduate, Undergraduate/Grant)*

Purpose: To provide opportunity to those Indian students who want learn and succeed in their educational career. **Focus:** General studies/Field of study not specified. **Qualif.:** Applicants must be: enrolled members of federally recognized tribes; undergraduate or graduate students of any major. **Criteria:** Selection will be based on the committee's criteria.

Funds Avail.: No specific amount. **To Apply:** Applicants must: complete AIEF Scholarship Application; provide documentation of tribal enrollment for themselves or their parents; provide transcripts with ACT and GPA scores; attach an essay that outlines the following information: introduction, academics, career plans, service to the Native American community, leadership/community service, financial needs and unique circumstances.

878 ■ U.S. BIA Indian Higher Education Grants
(Undergraduate/Grant)

Purpose: To provide opportunity to those Indian students who want learn and succeed in their educational career. **Focus:** General studies/Field of study not specified. **Qualif.:** Applicants must be: Native American undergraduate students of any major; enrolled in a federally recognized tribe. **Criteria:** Awards will be given based on financial need.

Funds Avail.: $300-$900. **To Apply:** Applicants must: complete AIEF Scholarship Application; provide documentation of tribal enrollment for themselves or their parents; provide transcripts with ACT and GPA scores; attach an essay that outlines the following information: introduction, academics, career plans, service to the Native American community, leadership/community service, financial needs and unique circumstances. Applicants may contact their tribe's education office for more information.

879 ■ American Indian Graduate Center (AIGC)
3701 San Mateo Blvd. NE, No. 200
Albuquerque, NM 87110

Awards are arranged alphabetically below their administering organizations

Ph: (505)881-4584
Fax: (505)884-0427
Free: 800-628-1920
E-mail: web@aigcs.org
URL: www.aigcs.org
Facebook: www.facebook.com/American-Indian-Graduate-Center-100211176314

880 ■ Accenture American Indian Scholarship Program *(Graduate, Undergraduate/Scholarship)*

Purpose: To provide financial assistance to students who are seeking next level of education. **Focus:** Business; Engineering; Law; Medicine; Technology. **Qualif.:** Applicants must be American Indians who are incoming freshmen with a cumulative GPA of 3.25 or greater on a 4.0 scale at the end of the seventh semester of high school or graduates/professionals who have attained a cumulative GPA of 3.25 or greater on a 4.0 scale, as measured by undergraduate transcripts; must be enrolled members of a U.S. federally-recognized American Indian tribe or Alaska Native group; must be seeking a degree and career in fields of study including technology, engineering, medicine, law and business. **Criteria:** Applicants are evaluated on the basis of demonstrated character; personal merit evident through leadership in school, civic and extracurricular activities, academic achievement and motivation to serve and succeed; and commitment to the American Indian Community, locally and/or nationally.

Funds Avail.: No amount specified. **Duration:** Annual. **To Apply:** Applicants must submit completed application form; copy of certificate of Indian Blood (CIB); unofficial undergraduate and/or graduate academic transcripts; biographical data and/or resume; essay describing their character, personal merit and commitment to community and heritage; two personal letters of recommendation (one must come from an education professional who is familiar with their academic work and the other one must come from an individual having knowledge of their leadership and community service activities); and financial aid award letter from the institution they will attend. **Deadline:** May 1. **Remarks:** Established in 2005.

881 ■ AIGC Fellowships - Graduate *(Graduate/Fellowship)*

Purpose: To provide financial assistance to Native Americans and Alaska Native graduates or professional degree-seeking students in furthering their education. **Focus:** General studies/Field of study not specified. **Qualif.:** Applicants must be pursuing a post-baccalaureate graduate or professional degree as full-time students at an accredited institution in the U.S.; must be enrolled members of a federally-recognized American Indian or Alaska Native group or provide documentation of descendency; must possess one-fourth federally-recognized Indian blood. **Criteria:** Recipients are selected based on financial need.

Funds Avail.: $1,000 - $5,000. **Duration:** Annual. **To Apply:** Applicants must submit all the required application information including the Tribal Eligibility Certificate and Financial Need Form. **Deadline:** June 1.

882 ■ BIE-Loan for Service for Graduates *(Graduate/Loan)*

Purpose: To provide financial assistance to students who are seeking graduate and professional degree. **Focus:** General studies/Field of study not specified. **Qualif.:** Applicant must be an enrolled member of a United States federally-recognized American Indian tribe or Alaska Native group or possess one-fourth federally-recognized Indian blood; must have 3.0 GPA; and must be pursuing a graduate or a professional degree as a full-time student at an accredited institution in the United States. **Criteria:** Applicants are evaluated based on financial need.

Funds Avail.: No specific amount. **To Apply:** Applicants must submit all the required application information. **Deadline:** June 1.

883 ■ Wells Fargo American Indian Scholarships - Graduate *(Graduate/Scholarship)*

Purpose: To provide financial assistance to American Indian graduates in furthering their education. **Focus:** Accounting; Banking; Finance; Gaming industry; Information science and technology; Management. **Qualif.:** Applicants must be enrolled members of a United States federally-recognized American Indian tribe or Alaska Native group; must be pursuing career and degree fields relating to banking, resort management, gaming operations, management and administration, including accounting, finance, information technology and human resources; must be full-time graduate students at a U.S. accredited college or university; and must have a cumulative average GPA of 3.0 on a 4.0 scale at the time of application. **Criteria:** Applicants are evaluated based on financial need.

Funds Avail.: No specific amount. **To Apply:** Applicants must submit all the required application information. **Deadline:** May 1.

884 ■ American Indian Library Association (AILA)
c/o Heather Devine-Hardy, Membership Coordinator
PO Box 41296
San Jose, CA 95160
E-mail: ailawebsite@gmail.com
URL: www.ailanet.org
Facebook: www.facebook.com/ailanet

885 ■ AILA Virginia Mathews Memorial Scholarships *(Graduate/Scholarship)*

Purpose: To encourage the entry of qualified American Indians and Alaskan Natives into the library profession. **Focus:** Library and archival sciences. **Qualif.:** Applicants must be: enrolled members of a federally recognized tribe as evidenced by the CIBC card of the applicants, or be tribal members with official documentation; able to demonstrate sustained involvement in the American Indian community and sustained commitment to American Indian concerns and initiatives; admitted to a graduate program in library and/or information sciences accredited by the American Library Association; and, enrolled for a minimum of 6 hours each semester. **Criteria:** Preference will be given to applicants who are employed in a tribal library or who are currently employed in a library serving American Indian populations. Financial need will be considered.

Funds Avail.: $2,000. **Duration:** Annual. **To Apply:** Applicants must submit a completed scholarship application together with two letters of recommendation; evidence of enrollment in a federally recognized tribe or Alaskan village or a similar official document; a personal statement (maximum of 250 words) addressing past and future sustained involvement in American Indian communities and a resume. Submit complete application package to American Indian Library Association Treasurer, Dean Joan S.

Awards are arranged alphabetically below their administering organizations

Howland. **Deadline:** May 1. **Contact:** Holly Tomren-Chair, AILA Scholarship Review Board; Drexel Univ. Libraries, 3300 Market St., Philadelphia, PA 19104.

886 ■ American Indian Science and Engineering Society (AISES)
2305 Renard Pl. SE, Ste. 200
Albuquerque, NM 87106
Ph: (505)765-1052
Fax: (505)765-5608
E-mail: info@aises.org
URL: www.aises.org
Facebook: www.facebook.com/aises.org
Twitter: twitter.com/AISES

887 ■ AISES Intel Scholarships *(Graduate, Undergraduate/Scholarship)*

Purpose: To financially assist ethnic students in furthering their education. **Focus:** Computer and information sciences; Engineering, Chemical; Engineering, Computer; Engineering, Electrical; Engineering, Materials. **Qualif.:** Applicant must be a member of an American Indian tribe or otherwise considered to be an American Native by the tribe with which affiliation is claimed; or is at least 1/4 American Indian or Alaskan Native blood or considered to be an Alaskan Native by an Alaskan Native group to which affiliation is claimed; must be a full-time undergraduate or graduate student with at least 3.0 GPA at an accredited four-year college or university; must be majoring one of the following disciplines: a) Computer Science; b) Computer Engineering; or c) Electrical Engineering; and must be a current member of AISES. **Criteria:** Judges will evaluate the applications based on information that is provided, including but not limited to: 1) which school within the college/university the student is attending; 2) student's current or expected course curriculum; and 3) AISES current year funding levels.

Funds Avail.: $5,000 for undergraduates and $10,000 for graduate students. **Duration:** Annual. **Number Awarded:** Up to 5. **To Apply:** Applicant must complete an application form; must submit the most recent transcript and proof of tribal enrollment; two letters of recommendation; online resume. On a separate sheet, applicant must provide a personal statement of no more than 500 words. **Deadline:** May 31. **Contact:** American Indian Science and Engineering Society, at the above address.

888 ■ AISES Summer Internships *(Undergraduate, Graduate/Internship)*

Purpose: To promote an advanced study to the graduate level and assist students in developing professional networks. **Focus:** General studies/Field of study not specified. **Qualif.:** Applicants must be U.S. citizens or permanent residents; must be college/university sophomores, juniors, seniors, or graduate students at the time of application; must be enrolled on a full-time basis; must have 3.0 GPA on a 4.0 scale; and must be current AISES members. Specific eligibilities for the internship offices shall be provided by the AISES partners for internship program and such are specified at the program website. **Criteria:** Recipients will be selected based on submitted materials.

Funds Avail.: No specific amount. **Duration:** Annual; Program runs in 10 weeks every year. **Number Awarded:** 6 to 7. **To Apply:** Applicants must submit a completed and signed application form; must submit two letters of recommendation; most recent official transcript(s); professional resume; proof of citizenship; essay; and two letters of recommendation. **Deadline:** May 31. **Contact:** Katherine Cristiano at kcristiano@aises.org.

889 ■ A.T. Anderson Memorial Scholarships *(Graduate, Undergraduate/Scholarship)*

Purpose: To financially assist ethnic students in furthering their education. **Focus:** Engineering; Mathematics and mathematical sciences; Medicine; Natural resources; Science; Technology. **Qualif.:** Applicant must be a member of an American Indian tribe, an Alaska Native, or Native Hawaiian otherwise considered to be an American Indian by the tribe with which affiliation is claimed; or at least 1/4 American Indian blood or at least 1/4 Alaskan Native; must be a current AISES member; and have a 3.0 on a 4.0 scale cumulative GPA. **Criteria:** Judges will evaluate the applications based on information that is provided, including but not limited to: 1) which school within the college/university the student is attending; 2) student's current or expected course curriculum; and 3) AISES current year funding levels.

Funds Avail.: $1,000 for undergraduates; $2,000 for graduate students. **Duration:** Annual. **Number Awarded:** 20 to 40. **To Apply:** Applicants must complete an application form; must submit the most recent transcript and proof of tribal enrollment; two letters of recommendation; online resume. On a separate sheet, applicants must provide a personal statement with no more than 500 words. **Deadline:** May 31. **Contact:** American Indian Science and Engineering Society, at the above address.

890 ■ American Institute of Aeronautics and Astronautics (AIAA)
12700 Sunrise Valley Dr., Ste. 200
Reston, VA 20191-5807
Ph: (703)264-7500
Fax: (703)264-7551
Free: 800-639-2422
E-mail: custserv@aiaa.org
URL: www.aiaa.org
Facebook: www.facebook.com/AIAAfan
Twitter: twitter.com/aiaa

891 ■ AIAA Foundation Scholarship Program *(Graduate, Undergraduate/Scholarship)*

Purpose: To foster the professional development of those engaged in scientific and engineering activities; improves public understanding of the profession and its contributions; fosters education in engineering and science; promotes communication among engineers and scientists, as well as other professional groups; and stimulates outstanding professional accomplishments. **Focus:** Aeronautics; Astronautics. **Qualif.:** Applicant must: have completed at least one academic quarter or semester of full-time college work; have a college GPA of not less than the equivalent of a 3.3 on a 4.0 scale; be enrolled in an accredited college or university. Applicant does not have to be an AIAA student member in good standing to apply, but must become one before receiving a scholarship. Applicant's scholarship plan shall be such as to provide entry into some field of science or engineering encompassed by the technical activities of AIAA. Applicants shall not have, or subsequently receive, any other scholarship/award which, when combined with the AIAA Foundation award covers more than the cost of tuition. Applicant may be

Awards are arranged alphabetically below their administering organizations

students of any nationality, not restricted by the US State Department, in full-time study at any accredited college or university within the United States. **Criteria:** Selection will be based on the committee's criteria.

Funds Avail.: No specific amount. **Duration:** Annual. **To Apply:** The completed application must be received on or before the deadline. Students submitting their applications should include the essay (500-1000 words describing career goals); three references; official transcripts; and a research outline (for graduate students) of approved research topic (PDF format, 20 pages only, Times New Roman 10 pt font) and also make arrangements to have their official college transcripts sent directly to AIAA. Sophomore and junior students who have received one of these scholarship awards and wish to be considered for continuation of this award should arrange to have transcripts of their college academic record, and letters of recommendation from their faculty members and others supporting their continuance in the program sent to AIAA. **Deadline:** January 31.

892 ■ American Institute of Architects - Alaska
PO Box 244141
Anchorage, AK 99524
Ph: (907)276-2834
Fax: (907)276-2834
E-mail: contact@aiaalaska.org
URL: aiaalaska.org

893 ■ AIA Alaska Scholarships *(Graduate, Undergraduate/Scholarship)*

Purpose: To help Alaska resident students enroll in an accredited architectural program. **Focus:** Landscape architecture and design. **Qualif.:** Students must be permanent residents of the State of Alaska and have completed six or more semesters in a program leading to a Bachelor's Degree in Architecture or enrolled in a Master's Program in Architecture. **Criteria:** Selection will be based on overall ability, desire, determination and potential for successfully completing an architecture education and entering into architecture as a profession.

Funds Avail.: Up to $2,000. **Number Awarded:** 3. **To Apply:** Applicants must submit an application packet containing a personal letter stating need, qualifications and desire. In addition, a completed application form, resume and transcript, as well as a letter of recommendation from a faculty member, must be included in the package. **Deadline:** November 1.

894 ■ American Institute of Architects - Northeast Illinois (AIA NEI)
c/o Tracy J. Mitchell, Executive Director
1717 N Naper Blvd., Ste. 102
Naperville, IL 60563
Ph: (630)527-8550
Fax: (630)416-9798
URL: www.aianei.org
Facebook: www.facebook.com/#!/pages/AIA-Northeast-Illinois/157502574304228

895 ■ AIA Northeast Illinois Student Scholarships *(Undergraduate, Graduate/Scholarship)*

Purpose: To support students enrolled in an accredited architecture program. **Focus:** Architecture. **Qualif.:** Applicants must be U.S. citizens enrolled at one of the East Central or West Central accredited Architecture schools and have a home residence of record within the AIA/NEI Chapter boundaries (Cook, DuPage, Kane, and Kendall Counties, except that the territory shall not include the area within the city limits of Chicago, nor south of Interstate 55, nor east of the Edens Expressway). **Criteria:** Selection shall be based on the aforementioned applicants' qualifications and compliance with the application details.

Funds Avail.: $3,000 each. **Duration:** Annual. **Number Awarded:** 2. **To Apply:** Applicants must submit a completed application form including two letters of recommendation and a self-addressed, stamped postcard. **Deadline:** April 22.

896 ■ Arnold "Les" Larsen, FAIA, Memorial Scholarships *(Graduate/Scholarship)*

Purpose: To support students enrolled in an accredited architecture program. **Focus:** Architecture. **Qualif.:** Applicants must be U.S. citizens and enrolled in the Master's of Architecture program at either the University of Illinois at Chicago or at Urbana-Champaign. **Criteria:** Preference will be given to students who are participants in an AIAS chapter, demonstrated financial need and with a permanent residence within the AIA/NEI Chapter boundaries (DuPage, Kane, Kendall and suburban Cook Counties).

Funds Avail.: $1,000. **Duration:** Annual. **To Apply:** Applicants must submit a completed application form including two letters of recommendation and a self-addressed, stamped postcard. **Deadline:** April 22.

897 ■ American Institute of Bangladesh Studies (AIBS)
B488 Medical Science Ctr.
1300 University Ave.
Madison, WI 53706
Ph: (608)261-1471
E-mail: aibs@southasia.wisc.edu
URL: www.aibs.net

898 ■ AIBS Junior Fellowships *(Doctorate/Fellowship)*

Purpose: To support junior researchers with their travel expenses. **Focus:** General studies/Field of study not specified. **Qualif.:** Applicants must be U.S. citizens or permanent residents; must be in the ABD phase of their Ph.D. programs; and must be in the stage of data collection and writing. **Criteria:** Recipients are selected based on submitted applications and supporting materials.

Funds Avail.: $920 and allowances per month. **Duration:** Six to twelve months. **To Apply:** Applicants must send five copies each of application form (available on the website), curriculum vitae (maximum of three pages) and research proposal (maximum of ten pages).

899 ■ AIBS Senior Fellowships *(Doctorate/Fellowship)*

Purpose: To provide funding for a senior research fellowship in Bangladesh. **Focus:** General studies/Field of study not specified. **Qualif.:** Applicants must be U.S. citizens or permanent residents and must have a PhD degree. **Criteria:** Recipients are selected based on submitted applications and supporting materials.

Funds Avail.: $1,150 and allowances per month. **Duration: Six to twelve months. **To Apply:** Applicants must send five copies each of application form (available at the website), curriculum vitae (maximum of three pages), research proposal (maximum of ten pages) and transcript of records.

900 ■ American Institute of Certified Public Accountants (AICPA)
1211 Avenue of the Americas
New York, NY 10036-8775
Ph: (212)596-6200
Fax: (212)596-6213
E-mail: service@aicpa.org
URL: www.aicpa.org/Pages/default.aspx

901 ■ John L. Carey Scholarship Awards (Graduate/Scholarship)

Purpose: To encourage students to acquire professional accounting careers. **Focus:** Accounting. **Qualif.:** Applicants must be U.S. citizens or permanent residents; must be liberal arts and non-business degree holders who are pursuing both graduate studies in accounting and the CPA licensure; must obtained a liberal arts or other non-business undergraduate degree from a regionally accredited institution in the United States prior to enrolling in a graduate accounting program; must not earned more than 12 credits in accounting or business during their undergraduate program; must be planning to pursue the CPA licensure but not presently be CPAs; must be planning to pursue a graduate-level degree in an "accounting-related" major; must be AICPA student affiliate members; must demonstrate some financial need. **Criteria:** Recipients are selected based on academic achievement, leadership and future career interests in accounting.

Funds Avail.: $5,000. **Duration:** Annual. **Number Awarded:** 5. **To Apply:** Applicants must visit the website for the online application process. **Deadline:** April 1.

902 ■ American Institute of Chemical Engineers (AIChE)
120 Wall St., Fl. 23
New York, NY 10005-4020
Fax: (203)775-5177
Free: 800-242-4363
URL: www.aiche.org
Facebook: www.facebook.com/ChEnected
Twitter: www.twitter.com/ChEnected

903 ■ AIChE Minority Scholarship Awards for College Students (Undergraduate/Scholarship)

Purpose: To provide educational assistance for underrepresented chemical engineering undergraduate students. **Focus:** Engineering, Chemical. **Qualif.:** Applicants must be AIChE national student members at the time of application. **Criteria:** Selection of recipients will be based on academic record, participation in AIChE student and professional activities, career objectives and financial need.

Funds Avail.: $1,000 each. **Duration:** Annual. **Number Awarded:** Varies. **To Apply:** Nominations must be submitted containing the following items: from the students: a) a completed application form; b) a career essay not to exceed 300 words outlining the following: immediate plans after graduation and area(s) of chemical engineering of most interest; long-range career objectives; official transcript of college grades. Nominations from the college financial aid office must contain: a letter indicating that the student is eligible for financial aid based on their records; a letter of recommendation from the AIChE student chapter advisor, department chair, or chemical engineering faculty member containing, but not limited to, the following: verification of nominee's GPA and projected completion date; evaluation of the student's academic performance and participation in AIChE and other professional or civic activities. **Deadline:** July 1. **Contact:** AIChE Awards Administrator; Email: awards@aiche.org.

904 ■ AIChE Minority Scholarship Awards for Incoming College Freshmen (Undergraduate/Scholarship)

Purpose: To provide educational assistance for chemical engineering college freshmen. **Focus:** Engineering, Chemical. **Qualif.:** Applicants must be members of a minority group (i.e. African-American, Hispanic, Native American, or Alaskan Native) that is underrepresented in chemical engineering; must be high school graduates during the previous academic year and plan to enroll during the following academic year in a four-year university offering a science/engineering degree. **Criteria:** Recipients will be selected based on academic record, participation in school and work activities, reason for choosing science or engineering, and financial need.

Funds Avail.: $1,000 each. **Duration:** Annual. **Number Awarded:** 10. **To Apply:** Nominations must be submitted containing the following items from the student: a) completed application form; b) career essay not to exceed 300 words outlining the following: (1) college or university chosen to attend, (2) reasons for choosing science/engineering, (3) possible career choices that may be of interest; c) official transcript of high school grades. Nominations must also include documents from the parent/guardian which should contain a letter verifying financial need which includes a list of financial resources for educational support; and a letter of recommendation from the high school counselor, math teacher or science teacher containing, but not limited to, the following: a) verification of student's GPA and graduation date; b) verification of high school senior class average grade (if confidential, high school counselor statement is required); c) confirmation of minority group of student; d) information about the student's school, job and/or other activities. **Deadline:** July 1. **Contact:** AIChE Awards Administrator; Email: awards@aiche.org.

905 ■ John J. McKetta Undergraduate Scholarships (Undergraduate/Scholarship)

Purpose: To provide financial assistance for chemical engineering undergraduate students planning a career in the chemical engineering process industries. **Focus:** Engineering, Chemical. **Qualif.:** Nominees must be national student members of AIChE attending an ABET accredited schools in the US, Canada or Mexico who are in their junior or senior year of a 4-year program in Chemical Engineering or equivalent for a 5-year co-op program. Nominees must have maintained a minimum of 3.0/4.0 GPA. **Criteria:** Preference will be given to nominees from Mexican universities participating in ABET's Equivalent Education Program.

Funds Avail.: $5,000. **Duration:** Annual. **To Apply:** Nominees must submit a maximum two-page essay outlining career goals in the chemical engineering process industries (2 single-sided, single-spaced typed pages) and nominations must be accompanied by a minimum of two letters of

Awards are arranged alphabetically below their administering organizations

recommendation, one from AIChE student advisor and the other from either a departmental faculty member or technical work supervisor. **Deadline:** June 15. **Contact:** AIChE Awards Administrator; Email: awards@aiche.org.

906 ■ Donald F. and Mildred Topp Othmer National Scholarship Awards *(Undergraduate/Scholarship)*

Purpose: To provide financial assistance for AIChE national student members for their undergraduate education in chemical engineering. **Focus:** Engineering, Chemical. **Qualif.:** Nominees must be AIChE national student members at the time of the nomination. **Criteria:** Selection will be on the basis of academic achievement and involvement in student chapter activities.

Funds Avail.: $1,000 each. **Duration:** Annual. **Number Awarded:** 15. **To Apply:** Nominators must submit completed nomination form; letter of nomination from the AIChE Student Chapter Advisor containing, but not limited to, the following: a) verification of the nominees' GPAs and projected completion date; b) an evaluation of the nominees' academic performance and participation in AIChE Student Chapter and other professional activities; statement from the nominees (not to exceed 300 words) outlining their career plans and objectives in chemical engineering and including, but not limited to, the following: a) immediate plans after graduation and area(s) of chemical engineering of most interest; b) long-range career objectives. **Deadline:** June 15. **Contact:** AIChE Awards Administrator; Email: awards@aiche.org.

907 ■ American Institute for Conservation of Historic & Artistic Works
1156 15th St. NW, Ste. 320
Washington, DC 20005
Ph: (202)452-9545
Fax: (202)452-9328
E-mail: info@conservation-us.org
URL: www.conservation-us.org
Facebook: www.facebook.com/aiconservation
Twitter: twitter.com/conservators

908 ■ FAIC Latin American and Caribbean Scholars Program *(Other/Scholarship)*

Purpose: To provide financial support for conservation professionals from Latin America and the Caribbean to participate in the annual meeting. **Focus:** Latin American studies. **Qualif.:** Applicants must be Latin Americans. **Criteria:** Recipients will be selected based on quality of the essay, opportunities to attend international meetings, number of applicants, ability to communicate in English and availability of the financial support.

Funds Avail.: No specific amount. **To Apply:** Applicants must complete the application form and submit a curriculum vitae and an essay. For further information, applicants are advised to visit www.conservation-us.org/grants. **Deadline:** August 22. **Contact:** FAIC Scholarship Program; E-mail: faicgrants@conservation-us.org.

909 ■ Foundation of American Institute for Conservation Lecture Grants *(Other/Grant)*

Purpose: To provide funds and presentations of public lectures to help advance public awareness of conservation. **Focus:** Latin American studies. **Qualif.:** Applicants must be Latin American. **Criteria:** Recipients are selected based on the ability of the project to advance public awareness of conservation; number of people reached, other project outcomes; speaker's ability to communicate the proposed topic; and feasibility of project.

Funds Avail.: Up to $500. **Duration:** Annual. **To Apply:** Applicants must complete and submit the application form via email and must attach the following materials: letter of commitment from speaker; letter of commitment from site; letter of commitment from lecture coordinator; resume of speaker; brief information about sponsor (brochure or one-page description of organization and previous activities). If sending hard copies, two copies of the application and attachments must be delivered to the FAIC office. **Deadline:** February 15 and September 15. **Contact:** faicgrants@conservation-us.org.

910 ■ American Institute for Economic Research (AIER)
250 Division St.
Great Barrington, MA 01230-1000
Fax: (413)528-0103
Free: 888-528-1216
E-mail: info@aier.org
URL: www.aier.org
Facebook: www.facebook.com/AmericanInstituteForEconomicResearch
LinkedIn: www.linkedin.com/company/american-institute-for-economic-research
Twitter: twitter.com/aier

911 ■ American Institute for Economic Research Student Summer Fellowships *(Doctorate, Graduate, Undergraduate/Fellowship)*

Purpose: To train graduating college seniors who plan to enter doctoral programs in economics or an affiliated field, and those enrolled in such programs for no longer than two years. **Focus:** Economics; Political science. **Qualif.:** Applicants must be graduating college seniors planning to pursue a PhD in economics or in a related field; or, current graduate students enrolled in such program for no longer than two years. **Criteria:** Selection is based on academic achievement, interest in current economic problems, plans for future study, and potential for success.

Funds Avail.: No specific amount. **To Apply:** Applicants must submit a completed application form together with a vita/resume; personal statement (not to exceed three double-spaced typewritten pages); writing sample; outline of proposed course of study; official transcripts; and scholastic references. **Deadline:** April 1. **Contact:** Summer Fellowship Program Coordinator; E-Mail: fellowship@aier.org.

912 ■ American Institute of Iranian Studies (AIIrS)
c/o Dr. Erica Ehrenberg, Executive Director
118 Riverside Dr.
New York, NY 10024
E-mail: aiis@nyc.rr.com
URL: www.simorgh-aiis.org

913 ■ AIIrS Persian Language Study in Tehran Fellowships *(Graduate, Master's, Doctorate/Fellowship)*

Purpose: To promote advanced language study in Tehran at the Dehkhoda Institute. **Focus:** Linguistics. **Qualif.:** Applicants must be US citizens traveling on a US passport; enrolled in a Doctoral or Masters program in the humanities or social sciences; must have an approved research topic that requires the use of Persian; have completed at least one full academic year of Persian language study.

Funds Avail.: No specific amount. **Duration:** Annual. **To Apply:** Applications must include a curriculum vitae and be made in the form of a letter, giving the following information: citizenship; research plans, level of Persian attained and what degree of proficiency is required; academic affiliation and status; names, addresses and email addresses of two referees, including the primary academic advisor. **Deadline:** January 10 - application; January 15 - recommendation. **Contact:** American Institute of Iranian Studies, at the above address.

914 ■ Short-term Senior Fellowships in Iranian Studies *(Professional development/Fellowship)*

Purpose: To enable established scholars with research interests in the field of Iranian Studies to acquaint themselves with the range of academic activities and resources in Iran today. **Focus:** Area and ethnic studies; Humanities; Social sciences. **Qualif.:** Applicants must be US citizens traveling on a US passport. **Criteria:** Preference will be given to tenured faculty members and museum staff with some knowledge of Persian and a record of research in the humanities or the social sciences relating to Iran.

Funds Avail.: No specific amount. **Duration:** Annual. **To Apply:** Application should be made in the form of a letter explaining how the opportunity afforded by the fellowship would benefit the applicant's work.

915 ■ American Institute for Maghrib Studies (AIMS)

Marshall Bldg., Rm. 470
Center for Middle Eastern Studies
845 N Park Ave.
Tucson, AZ 85719-4871
Ph: (520)626-6498
Fax: (520)621-9257
E-mail: aims@aimsnorthafrica.org
URL: aimsnorthafrica.org
Facebook: www.facebook.com/
AmericanInstituteForMaghribStudies

916 ■ AIMS Long-term Research Grants *(Doctorate, Graduate/Grant)*

Purpose: To render fund for US scholars interested in conducting research on North Africa in any Maghrib country. **Focus:** General studies/Field of study not specified. **Qualif.:** Applicant must be a U.S. citizen graduate student, independent scholar and faculty in all disciplines currently enrolled in a M.A. or Ph.D. program; and must be a member of AIMS at the time of application. **Criteria:** Recipients will be selected based on submitted application and proposal.

Funds Avail.: Maximum of $15,000. **Duration:** Annual. **To Apply:** Applicant must submit completed grant application, proposal or research design (no more than 1500 words), proposed itinerary with approximate dates, budget, vitae indicating language proficiency and institutional affiliation, letters of recommendation from two referees, including the candidate's dissertation advisor, or in the case of applicants holding a Ph.D., the names of two persons who may be contacted for references, and one page summary of the proposed research in either French or Arabic. **Deadline:** January 31.

917 ■ AIMS Short-term Research Grants *(Doctorate/Grant)*

Purpose: To render fund for US scholars interested in conducting research on North Africa in any Maghrib country. **Focus:** General studies/Field of study not specified. **Qualif.:** Applicant must be a U.S. citizen graduate student, independent scholar and faculty in all disciplines currently enrolled in a M.A. or Ph.D. program; and must be a member of AIMS at the time of application. **Criteria:** Recipients will be selected based on submitted application and proposal.

Funds Avail.: Up to $6,000. **Duration:** 1-3 months. **Number Awarded:** 1. **To Apply:** Applicant must submit a completed grant application, proposal or research design, proposed itinerary with approximate dates, budget, vitae indicating language proficiency and institutional affiliation, letters of recommendation from two referees, including the candidate's dissertation advisor, or in the case of applicants holding a Ph.D., the names of two persons who may be contacted for references, and one page summary of the proposed research in either French or Arabic. **Deadline:** January 31.

918 ■ American Institute of Pakistan Studies (AIPS)

B488 Medical Science Ctr.
University of Wisconsin - Madison
1300 University Ave.
Madison, WI 53706
Ph: (608)265-1471
E-mail: aips@pakistanstudies-aips.org
URL: www.pakistanstudies-aips.org

919 ■ AIPS Long Term Fellowships *(Doctorate, Postdoctorate/Fellowship)*

Purpose: To promote academic study of Pakistan in the US and to encourage scholarly exchange between the US and Pakistan. **Focus:** Pakistani studies. **Qualif.:** Applicants must be US citizens and enrolled/employed full-time in an institution of higher education in the USA. Pre-doctoral applicants should have completed all requirements for the PhD except the dissertation. **Criteria:** Selection will be based on the Executive Committee's criteria

Funds Avail.: No specific amount. **To Apply:** Interested applicants may visit the website for the online application package. The proposal should include each the following elements: a precisely stated research question, a detailed statement indicating the research methodology to be employed, including tentative timelines and list of persons to contact and/or places to visit, and expected results. Describe the intellectual merit of the project and how it relates to the goals of AIPS to promote and disseminate knowledge on Pakistan in the United States and Pakistan. Also address the broader impact for your specific field and Pakistan studies as a whole. In the case of pre-doctoral fellowships, its relevance to the applicant's dissertation should be addressed, along with a timeline for the completion of the dissertation or that portion of the project for which funding is being requested from AIPS. Pre-doctoral application should also include a transcripts and a letter from the dissertation advisor.

920 ■ AIPS Post-Doctoral Fellowships *(Postdoctorate/Fellowship)*

Purpose: To promote academic study of Pakistan in the U.S., and encourage scholarly exchange between the U.S.

Awards are arranged alphabetically below their administering organizations

and Pakistan. **Focus:** Pakistani studies. **Qualif.:** Applicants must be U.S. citizens or enrolled/employed full-time in an institution of higher education in the U.S.A. **Criteria:** Selection shall be based on the aforementioned applicants' qualifications and compliance with the application details.

Funds Avail.: Amount varies. **Duration:** Annual. **Number Awarded:** Varies. **To Apply:** Applicants must submit a complete application package which includes: application checklist; application processing fee of $30; signed and dated application form; abstract; project statement (maximum of 5 pages); bibliography; budget proposal; curriculum vitae (maximum of 2 pages); one letter of recommendation (if submitted via email, the letters should come from the referees' own email account); and letter of affiliation.

921 ■ AIPS Pre-Doctoral Fellowships *(Doctorate, Graduate/Fellowship)*

Purpose: To promote academic study of Pakistan in the U.S., and encourage scholarly exchange between the U.S. and Pakistan. **Focus:** Pakistani studies. **Qualif.:** Applicants must be U.S. citizens or enrolled/employed full-time in an institution of higher education in the U.S.A. Pre-doctoral applicant should have completed all requirements for the PhD except the dissertation. **Criteria:** Selection shall be based on the aforementioned applicants' qualifications and compliance with the application details.

Funds Avail.: Amount varies. **Duration:** Annual. **Number Awarded:** Varies. **To Apply:** Applicants must submit a complete application package which includes: application checklist; application processing fee of $30; signed and dated application form; abstract; project statement (maximum of 5 pages); bibliography; budget proposal; curriculum vitae (maximum of 2 pages); two letters of recommendation (one must be from their respective dissertation advisors); letter of affiliation; and graduate transcripts.

922 ■ AIPS Short Term Fellowships *(Doctorate, Postdoctorate/Fellowship)*

Purpose: To promote academic study of Pakistan in the US and to encourage scholarly exchange between the US and Pakistan. **Focus:** Pakistani studies. **Qualif.:** Applicants must be US citizens and enrolled/employed full-time in an institution of higher education in the USA. **Criteria:** Selection will be based on the Executive Committee's criteria.

Funds Avail.: No specific amount. **To Apply:** Interested applicants may visit the website for the online application package. The proposal should include each the following elements: a precisely stated research question, a detailed statement indicating the research methodology to be employed, including tentative timelines and list of persons to contact and/or places to visit, and expected results. Describe the intellectual merit of the project and how it relates to the goals of AIPS to promote and disseminate knowledge on Pakistan in the United States and Pakistan. Also address the broader impact for your specific field and Pakistan studies as a whole. In the case of pre-doctoral fellowships, its relevance to the applicant's dissertation should be addressed, along with a timeline for the completion of the dissertation or that portion of the project for which funding is being requested from AIPS. Pre-doctoral application should also include a transcripts and a letter from the dissertation advisor. **Deadline:** March 20.

923 ■ American Institute of Physics (AIP)
1 Physics Ellipse
College Park, MD 20740
Ph: (301)209-3100
Free: 888-491-8833
URL: www.aip.org

924 ■ American Institute of Physics Congressional Science Fellowships *(Doctorate/Fellowship)*

Purpose: To help scientists broaden their experience through direct involvement with the legislative and policy processes. **Focus:** Physics. **Qualif.:** Applicants must be members in one or more of the 10 AIP Member Societies at the time of application; must be U.S. citizens; must have a PhD in physics or closely-related field prior to start of Fellowship term; must have an interest or experience in applying scientific knowledge to the solution of societal problems; must have excellent scientific credentials, outstanding interpersonal and communications skills and sound judgment and maturity in decision-making. **Criteria:** Selection will be based on the committee's criteria.

Funds Avail.: $75,000 per year. **Duration:** Annual. **To Apply:** Applicants must submit the following application materials: letter of intent, providing information regarding their reason for applying, scientific training and professional background, science policy interest and experience, attributes and experiences that would make applicants more effective in this position; a resume limited to two pages, with up to one additional page allowed for a list of key publications; three letters of recommendation to be submitted directly by applicant's references. Letters should be from those having direct knowledge of the applicants' character, professional competence and particular attributes or experience that would enhance the candidate's suitability for this position. Applicants must visit the website for the on-line application and instructions on submitting the application materials. **Deadline:** January 15. **Contact:** If you have any questions, please email scipolicyfellows@aip.org or Marissa Nielsen at mnielsen@aip.org.

925 ■ American Institute of Physics State Department Science Fellowships *(Doctorate/Fellowship)*

Purpose: To contribute scientific and technical expertise to the department and raise awareness of the value of scientific input. **Focus:** Physics. **Qualif.:** Applicants must be members in one or more of the 10 AIP Member Societies at the time of application; must be U.S. citizens; must have a PhD in physics or closely-related field prior to start of Fellowship term; must be eligible for security clearance; must have an interest or experience in S&T aspects of foreign policy; must have excellent scientific credentials, outstanding interpersonal and communications skills and sound judgment and maturity in decision-making. **Criteria:** Selection will be based on the committee's criteria.

Funds Avail.: $75,000. **Duration:** Annual. **To Apply:** Applicants must submit the following application materials: letter of intent, providing information regarding their reason for applying, scientific training and professional background, science policy interest and experience, attributes and experiences that would make applicants more effective in this position; a resume limited to two pages, with up to one additional page allowed for a list of key publications; three letters of recommendation to be submitted directly by applicant's references. Letters should be from those having direct knowledge of the applicants' character, professional competence and particular attributes or experience that would enhance the candidate's suitability for this position. Applicants must visit the website for the on-line application and instructions on submitting the application materials. **Deadline:** November 1.

Awards are arranged alphabetically below their administering organizations

926 ■ American Institute of Polish Culture (AIPC)
1440 79th St. Causeway, Ste. 117
Miami, FL 33141
Ph: (305)864-2349
Fax: (305)865-5150
E-mail: info@ampolinstitute.org
URL: www.ampolinstitute.org

927 ■ Harriet Irsay Scholarships (Graduate, Undergraduate/Scholarship)

Purpose: To provide financial support for American students of Polish descent who wish to continue their education after high school. **Focus:** Communications; Education; History; International affairs and relations; Journalism; Liberal arts; Media arts; Polish studies; Public relations. **Qualif.:** Applicant must be of Polish heritage; an American citizen or permanent resident; full-time graduate or undergraduate student in the field of communication, education, film, history, International Relation, journalism, liberal arts, polish studies, public relations; or graduate student in business programs with a thesis related to Poland, or graduate student with a thesis with Polish subject. **Criteria:** Recipients are selected on the basis of merits.

Funds Avail.: $1,000. **Number Awarded:** 10-15. **To Apply:** Applicants must submit a completed application form; school transcripts; resume; essay (200-400 words) about "Why should I receive the scholarship"; an article about Poland (maximum of 700 words); and three signed recommendation letters on a letterhead stationary from teachers or other person knowledgeable about the applicant's academic background. A non-refundable $10 processing fee (check or money order) must also be included. **Deadline:** July 19. **Contact:** For further information, applicants may e-mail admin@ampolinstitute.org.

928 ■ American Institute for Sri Lankan Studies (AISLS)
155 Pine St.
Belmont, MA 02478
URL: www.aisls.org

929 ■ AISLS Dissertation Planning Grants (Graduate/Grant)

Purpose: To enable graduate students intending to do dissertation research in Sri Lanka to make a pre-dissertation visit to Sri Lanka to investigate the feasibility of their topic, to sharpen their research design or to make other practical arrangements for future research. **Focus:** Humanities; Social sciences. **Qualif.:** Applicants must be graduate students enrolled at a US university; must have completed most of their graduate coursework by the time of application. **Criteria:** Proposals will be judged on the quality and on the potential of the dissertation research to strengthen scholarship on Sri Lanka.

Funds Avail.: $525 per week and $2,000 reimbursement for roundtrip. **Duration:** Annual. **To Apply:** The completed application should contain the following items: A one-page cover sheet, stating the applicants' name, mailing address, email address, home and office telephone, citizenship, major field of study, institutional affiliation, foreign languages including proficiency, proposed dates of project, project title and a brief project description; A curriculum vitae, not to exceed two pages and may include the name and email address of the applicants' dissertation supervisor; A copy of the applicants' official or unofficial graduate transcript; A project narrative, not to exceed two single-spaced pages; A one-page project bibliography, including a selected list of publications by other scholars or primary sources that have been or will be used in the project; A confidential letter of recommendation from the applicants' dissertation supervisor. This letter should cover the applicants' academic record and be specific about the applicants' progress to date within the graduate program concerned. This letter should be sent directly to John Rogers. The project narrative should cover the following topics: a summary of the proposed dissertation project, or, if the purpose of the planning grant is to define a dissertation project, a summary of the more general questions the applicants hopes to address in their dissertation; a description of what the applicants intends to do during the grant period; the applicants' competence to carry out their proposed project, including language training. Pages should have one-inch margins on all sides, 10 points or larger and should be printed on one side only. Every page should be numbered and include the name of the applicants in the upper right-hand corner. Five copies of the application, including the original, must be collated and fastened with staple in the following order: cover sheet, CV, project description, bibliography. A copy of the application should also be submitted in Word or PDF format by email. **Deadline:** December 1. **Contact:** John Rogers, AISLS, 155 Pine St., Belmont, MA 02478; E-mail: rogersjohnd@aol.com.

930 ■ AISLS Fellowships Program (Doctorate/Fellowship)

Purpose: To strengthen ties between US and Sri Lankan scholars. **Focus:** Humanities; Social sciences. **Qualif.:** Applicants must be US citizens; must hold a PhD or equivalent academic degree or show that they will hold such a degree before taking up the fellowship; must plan to spend at least two months in Sri Lanka. **Criteria:** Selection will be based on the submitted proposal.

Funds Avail.: $3,700/month and $2,000 for travel expenses. **To Apply:** The completed application should contain the following items: A one-page cover sheet, stating the applicants' name, mailing address, email address, home and office telephone, citizenship, major field of study, institutional affiliation, dates of previous research in Sri Lanka, proposed dates of project, project title and a brief description; A curriculum vitae, not to exceed three pages and may include information on such matters as gender and race/ethnicity; A description of the proposed study, not to exceed three single-spaced pages. It should cover the following topics: questions to be addressed by the project, the approach to be taken, work done to date, work to be accomplished during the fellowship period, the applicants' competence to carry out the project, how the project addresses the criteria of the competition, a statement of other support received or being sought for the project; A one-page project bibliography, including a selected list of publications by other scholars or primary sources that have been or will be used in the project. Pages should have one-inch margins on all sides, 10 points or larger and should be printed on one side only. Every page should be numbered and include the name of the applicants in the upper right-hand corner. Five copies of the application, including the original, must be collated and fastened with staple in the following order: cover sheet, CV, project description, bibliography. A copy of the application should also be submitted in Word or PDF format by email. **Deadline:** December 1.

Awards are arranged alphabetically below their administering organizations

AMERICAN INSTITUTE OF STEEL CONSTRUCTION

931 ■ AISLS Grants for Language Instruction (Doctorate/Grant)

Purpose: To provide funds that can be used to cover expenses for language instruction in Sinhala, Tamil, Pali or Arabic. **Focus:** Foreign languages. **Qualif.:** Applicants must be members of AISLS; must be US residents who hold a PhD or equivalent qualification; must be members of AISLS who are undertaking language instruction to support the needs of graduate study at a US university; must be faculty members at AISLS member institutions; must be graduate students at AISLS member institutions who are undertaking language instruction to support the needs of their program of study. **Criteria:** Selection will be based on the committee's criteria.

Funds Avail.: $400. **To Apply:** Interested applicants must submit a short curriculum vitae, a one-page statement that includes a description of the proposed instruction and how it supports their long-range research plans, a proposed timetable, and a budget. **Contact:** John Rogers, AISLS, 155 Pine St., Belmont, MA 02478; E-mail: rogersjohnd@aol.com.

932 ■ American Institute of Steel Construction (AISC)

1 E Wacker Dr., Ste. 700
Chicago, IL 60601-1802
Ph: (312)670-2400
Fax: (312)670-5403
E-mail: solutions@aisc.org
URL: www.aisc.org
Facebook: www.facebook.com/AISCdotORG
Twitter: twitter.com/aisc

933 ■ AISC/Great Lakes Fabricators and Erectors Association Fellowships (Graduate/Fellowship)

Purpose: To provide financial assistance to those studying civil engineering. **Focus:** Engineering, Architectural. **Qualif.:** Applicants must be full-time civil or architectural engineering students who are currently/or will be doing masters-level work at any graduate school in Michigan. **Criteria:** Applicants will be selected based on academic merit, faculty recommendation and jury's review of application materials.

Funds Avail.: $5,000. **Duration:** Annual. **Number Awarded:** 1. **To Apply:** Applicants must submit an official transcript; a reference and optional letter of reference; and a one-page detailed answers to the following: (a) Demonstrate concentration on steel related course work and/or thesis with a strong steel orientation, or (b) Demonstrate proposed course work and proposed thesis concentration in structural steel. **Deadline:** May 1. **Contact:** For more information: Maria Mnookin, Phone: 312-670-5418; Email: mnookin@aisc.org.

934 ■ AISC/Ohio Structural Steel Association Scholarships (Graduate/Scholarship)

Purpose: To provide financial assistance to those studying civil engineering. **Focus:** Engineering, Architectural; Engineering, Civil. **Qualif.:** Applicants must be residents of/ and full-time civil or architectural engineering students undertaking masters-level work in any graduate program from universities in Ohio. **Criteria:** Applicants will be selected based on academic merit and faculty recommendation. Preference will be given to applicants who are legal residents from Ohio.

Funds Avail.: $2,500. **Duration:** Annual. **Number Awarded:** 1. **To Apply:** Applicants must submit an official transcript; a reference and optional letter of reference; and a one-page detailed answers to the following: (a) Demonstrate concentration on steel related course work and/or thesis with a strong steel orientation, or (b) Demonstrate proposed course work and proposed thesis concentration in structural steel. **Deadline:** May 1. **Contact:** For more information: Maria Mnookin, Phone: 312-670-5418; Email: mnookin@aisc.org.

935 ■ AISC/Rocky Mountain Steel Construction Association Scholarships (Graduate/Scholarship)

Purpose: To provide financial assistance to those studying civil engineering. **Focus:** Engineering, Architectural; Engineering, Civil. **Qualif.:** Applicants must be undergraduate (senior) or full-time civil or architectural engineering students who are currently/or will be doing masters-level work in either Colorado or Wyoming. Applicants must be U.S. citizens. **Criteria:** Applicants will be selected based on academic merit, faculty recommendation and jury's review of the application materials.

Funds Avail.: $4,000. **Duration:** Annual. **Number Awarded:** 1. **To Apply:** Applicants must submit an official transcript; a reference and optional letter of reference; and a one-page detailed answers to the following: (a) Demonstrate concentration on steel related course work and/or thesis with a strong steel orientation, or (b) Demonstrate proposed course work and proposed thesis concentration in structural steel. **Deadline:** May 1. **Contact:** For more information: Maria Mnookin, 312-670-5418; e-mail: mnookin@aisc.org.

936 ■ AISC/Southern Association of Steel Fabricators Scholarships (Graduate/Scholarship)

Purpose: To provide financial assistance to those studying civil engineering. **Focus:** Engineering, Architectural; Engineering, Civil. **Qualif.:** Applicants must be full-time civil or architectural engineering students who are currently/or will be doing masters-level work at any graduate school in Alabama, Florida, Georgia, Kentucky, Louisiana, Mississippi and Tennessee. Applicants must be U.S. citizens. **Criteria:** Applicants will be selected based on academic merit, faculty recommendation and jury's review of the application materials.

Funds Avail.: $2,500. **Duration:** Annual. **Number Awarded:** 2. **To Apply:** Applicants must submit an official transcript; a reference and optional letter of reference; and one-page detailed answers to the following: (a) Demonstrate concentration on steel related course work and/or thesis with a strong steel orientation, or (b) Demonstrate proposed course work and proposed thesis concentration in structural steel. **Deadline:** May 1. **Contact:** For more information: Maria Mnookin, Phone: 312-670-5418; Email: mnookin@aisc.org.

937 ■ AISC Education Foundation - Fred R. Havens Fund (Undergraduate, Graduate/Scholarship)

Purpose: To provide financial assistance to those studying civil engineering. **Focus:** Engineering, Architectural; Engineering, Civil. **Qualif.:** Applicants must be U.S. citizens studying civil or architectural engineering full-time at universities in Missouri, Kansas or at MIT. Applicants must be graduates or undergraduate students who have completed one steel design course. **Criteria:** Undergraduate applicants are selected based on academic merit, faculty recommendation and evaluation of short essay and steel

Awards are arranged alphabetically below their administering organizations

design analysis/designs submitted while graduate students applying are evaluated. **Funds Avail.:** $5,000. **Duration:** Annual. **Number Awarded:** 1. **To Apply:** Undergraduate applicants must submit an official transcript; a reference and optional letter of reference; a two-page essay on their interest in steel structures and an original sample steel design analysis/design solution with calculations. In addition to the mentioned requirements, graduate applicants must submit an official transcript; a reference and optional letter of reference; and a one-page detailed which answers the following: (a) Demonstrate concentration on steel related course work and/or thesis with a strong steel orientation, or (b) Demonstrate proposed course work and proposed thesis concentration in structural steel. **Deadline:** May 1. **Contact:** For more information: Maria Mnookin, Phone: 312-670-5418; Email: mnookin@aisc.org.

938 ■ American Institute of Wine and Food (AIWF)
26384 Carmel Rancho Ln., Ste. 200E
Carmel, CA 93923
Ph: (401)683-2490
Fax: (502)456-1821
Free: 800-274-2493
E-mail: info@aiwf.org
URL: www.aiwf.org

939 ■ The AIWF/Patricia Tillinghast Memorial Scholarships *(Graduate, Undergraduate/Scholarship)*

Purpose: To provide educational financial support to a culinary arts student, a baking and pastry student and a continuing education student. **Focus:** Culinary arts. **Qualif.:** Applicant must be a Rhode Island resident for a minimum of 5 years; maintain a 3.5 - 4.0 GPA; a full-time student enrolled and attending a university/college; and be available to receive the scholarship at the annual Meet the Board event if chosen as a recipient. **Criteria:** Selection is based on academic standing and financial need.

Funds Avail.: No specific amount. **Duration:** Annual. **Number Awarded:** 3. **To Apply:** Applicants must write a letter to: The Board of Directors, AIWF Rhode Island Chapter, c/o John Philcox, 969 W Main Rd., Apt 6404, Middletown, RI 02842. The letter (1 page, 250 words) should contain experiences or future dreams in the culinary arts field and why you deserve to receive the scholarship. Applicants must include two letters of recommendation from faculty. **Deadline:** November 1. **Remarks:** Established in 1997. **Contact:** The Board of Directors, AIWF Rhode Island Chapter,c/o John Philcox, 969 West Main Road, Apt. 6404, Middletown, Rhode Island 02842.

940 ■ American Intellectual Property Law Education Foundation (AIPLEF)
4801 Woodway, Ste. 300 E
Houston, TX 77056-1884
E-mail: admin@aiplef.org
URL: www.aiplef.org

941 ■ Jan Jancin Competition Awards *(Undergraduate/Award)*

Purpose: To promote the study of intellectual property law. **Focus:** Law. **Qualif.:** Candidates must be law students nominated by their schools who have excelled in the study of intellectual property law. **Criteria:** Selection will be based on the committee's criteria.

Funds Avail.: $2,500 and $5,000. **Number Awarded:** 2. **To Apply:** Any law school may submit one nomination of a law student enrolled in their institution of the current year. The nomination should be no more than two pages and completed by a member of the faculty who has a direct knowledge of the student's work. Submit a nomination in the form of a letter of recommendation on Law School letterhead, enclosing a one-page written summation of the achievements from the nominee along with student's application summary and all of the following items: best grades in IP courses overall; outstanding achievement in specified IP courses; best IP paper written by a student; determination by a faculty consensus; or membership and activity in student IP organizations. **Deadline:** May 29.

942 ■ Sidney B. Williams, Jr. Scholarships *(Undergraduate/Scholarship)*

Purpose: To increase the number of underrepresented minority groups serving as intellectual property law practitioners in law firms and departments of corporations. **Focus:** Law. **Qualif.:** Applicants must be entering or attending law school. **Criteria:** Recipients are selected based on: demonstrated commitment to developing a career in intellectual property law; academic performance during the undergraduate, graduate and law school levels; financial need; leadership skills; and community activities or special accomplishments.

Funds Avail.: $10,000. **Duration:** Annual. **To Apply:** Applicants must submit completed scholarship application form; FAFSA form (or similar form) and other supporting documentation required. They must also submit: undergraduate transcript and graduate law transcript(if applicable); two letters of recommendation from, but not limited to former teachers, college administrators, community leaders, or other similar persons concerning the academic ability, character, reputation or professional aptitude of the applicant; evidence of being US citizens; personal or telephonic interview; and recent resume. **Deadline:** March 15. **Contact:** Deshuandra Walker, Manager, Student Support Programs, Thurgood Marshall College Fund; 1770 St. James Place, Suite 414, Houston, TX 77056; phone: 713.955.1073; fax: 202.448.1017; e-mail: deshuandra.walker@tmcfund.org.

943 ■ American Jersey Cattle Association (AJCA)
6486 E Main St.
Reynoldsburg, OH 43068-2362
Ph: (614)861-3636
Fax: (614)861-8040
URL: www.usjersey.com
Facebook: www.facebook.com/usjersey

944 ■ Cedarcrest Farms Scholarships *(Graduate, Undergraduate/Scholarship)*

Purpose: To financially support secondary students entering college freshmen through graduate school. **Focus:** General studies/Field of study not specified. **Qualif.:** Applicants must be junior member or lifetime member of the American Jersey Cattle Association. **Criteria:** Applicants are selected by an anonymous selection committee appointed by the AJCA President. Applicants must have minimum grade point average of 2.5 on a 4 point scale; and are selected by the following criteria: academic excellence, activities

Awards are arranged alphabetically below their administering organizations

and accomplishments, and personal goals and commitment in the Jersey dairy business.

Funds Avail.: Varies year to year. **Number Awarded:** Varies. **To Apply:** Applicants must submit complete scholarship application form and a copy of most recent transcript listing all completed coursework. Applicants must also provide (2) letters of recommendation. **Deadline:** July 1.

945 ■ Reuben R. Cowles Youth Awards
(Undergraduate/Award)

Purpose: To financially support secondary students entering as college freshmen through graduate school. **Focus:** General studies/Field of study not specified. **Qualif.:** Applicants must be junior members or lifetime members of the American Jersey Cattle Association, and residents of Florida, Georgia, North Carolina, South Carolina, Tennessee or Virginia; must be at least high school seniors but not older than 36 years old. **Criteria:** Applicants must have minimum grade point average of 2.5 on a 4 point scale.

Funds Avail.: No specific amount. **Number Awarded:** Varies. **To Apply:** Applicants must submit complete scholarship application form and a copy of most recent transcript listing all completed coursework. **Deadline:** July 1.

946 ■ American Jewish Archives (AJA)
3101 Clifton Ave.
Cincinnati, OH 45220-2404
Ph: (513)221-1875
Fax: (513)221-7812
URL: americanjewisharchives.org
Facebook: www.facebook.com/AmericanJewishArchives

947 ■ Loewenstein-Wiener Fellowship Award
(Professional development/Fellowship)

Purpose: To provide fellows with an opportunity to pursue their own research, interact and exchange ideas with research peers as well as with the faculty and students of HUC-JIR. **Focus:** Jewish studies. **Qualif.:** Applicants for the fellowship program must be conducting serious research in some area relating to the history of North American Jewry. **Criteria:** Selection will be based on the committee's criteria.

Funds Avail.: No specific amount. **Duration:** Annual. **To Apply:** Applicants must submit a fellowship application, available on the website, together with a five-page (maximum) research proposal that outlines the scope of their project and lists those collections at the American Jewish Archives that are crucial to their research. Applicants should also submit two letters of support, preferably from academic colleagues. For graduate and doctoral students, one of these two letters must be from their dissertation advisor. **Deadline:** February 19. **Remarks:** Established in 1976. **Contact:** Kevin Proffitt, Director of the Fellowship Program; Phone: 513-487-3004; Email: kproffitt@huc.edu.

948 ■ American Jewish Historical Society (AJHS)
15 W 16th St.
New York, NY 10011-6301
Ph: (212)294-6160
Fax: (212)294-6161
E-mail: publicservices@cjh.org
URL: www.ajhs.org
Facebook: www.facebook.com/AmericanJewishHistoricalSociety

Twitter: twitter.com/AJHSNYC

949 ■ Ruth B. Fein Prize *(Graduate/Prize)*

Purpose: To encourage interested students to undertake research in the field of American Jewish history. **Focus:** Area and ethnic studies. **Qualif.:** Candidates must be graduate students who will help undertake research at the American Jewish Historical Society. **Criteria:** Recipients will be selected based on qualifications.

Funds Avail.: Up to $1,000. **To Apply:** Candidates must submit a two-page description of the project, a letter of support from a graduate mentor and a detailed budget for travel expenses. **Deadline:** April 24. **Contact:** American Jewish Historical Society, at the above address or Email: to feinprize@ajhs.cjh.org.

950 ■ Pokross/Curhan Family Fund Prize *(Graduate, Undergraduate/Prize)*

Purpose: To assist undergraduate or graduate student pursuing an academic degree at an accredited academic institution. **Focus:** Area and ethnic studies. **Qualif.:** Candidates must be undergraduates and graduate students pursuing an academic degree at an accredited academic institution. **Criteria:** Recipients will be selected based on qualifications.

Funds Avail.: $1,000. **To Apply:** Candidates must send a two-page description of plans to produce an essay, thesis, dissertation, documentary, exhibition or other form of public program on an aspect of the American Jewish experience; and must submit a letter of support from an undergraduate or graduate mentor. **Contact:** American Jewish Historical Society, at the above address, or Email: pokrosscurhanprize@ajhs.cjh.org.

951 ■ American Judges Association (AJA)
300 Newport Ave.
Williamsburg, VA 23185-4147
Ph: (757)259-1841
Fax: (757)259-1520
E-mail: aja@ncsc.dni.us
URL: aja.ncsc.dni.us

952 ■ American Judges Association Law Student Essay Competition *(Undergraduate/Prize)*

Purpose: To support students who have original and unpublished work. **Focus:** Law. **Qualif.:** Applicants must be full-time law students enrolled in and attending an accredited law school in the United States or Canada. **Criteria:** Papers will be evaluated based on the following category: 1) writing quality and clarity; 2) interest of the topic and content to a broad segment of the judiciary; 3) analysis and reasoning; 4) timeliness, originality and creativity; 5) quality and use of the research; and 6) compliance with these rules.

Funds Avail.: $3,000 (1st Prize); $1,500 (2nd Prize); $1,000 (3rd Prize). **Duration:** Annual. **Number Awarded:** 3. **To Apply:** Applicants must submit a paper (double-spaced, 10-25 pages in length) discussing the topic given by the Committee. The cover page must be submitted in a separate document which includes the title, author's name and contact information.

953 ■ American Legion (AL)
700 N Pennsylvania St.
Indianapolis, IN 46206

Awards are arranged alphabetically below their administering organizations

Ph: (317)630-1200
Fax: (317)630-1223
E-mail: acy@legion.org
URL: www.legion.org
Facebook: www.facebook.com/americanlegionhq
LinkedIn: www.linkedin.com/company/the-american-legion
Twitter: twitter.com/AmericanLegion

954 ■ The American Legion Legacy Scholarships
(Undergraduate/Scholarship)

Purpose: To financially support the education of the dependents of active duty United States military and guard and reserve personnel. **Focus:** General studies/Field of study not specified. **Qualif.:** Applicants must be dependents of active duty United States military and guard and reserve personnel who were federalized and killed on active duty on or after September 11, 2001; must be high school seniors or high school graduates studying at an accredited institution of higher education within the United States. **Criteria:** Awards are given based on merit.

Funds Avail.: Amount varies. **To Apply:** Applicants must submit a completed scholarship application with a photocopy of the deceased veteran's Certificate of Death (DD 1300). **Deadline:** April 1. **Contact:** The American Legion Legacy Scholarship, e-mail: scholarships@legion.org.

955 ■ Eight and Forty Lung and Respiratory Disease Nursing Scholarships *(Other/Scholarship)*

Purpose: To assist registered nurses (RN) with advanced preparation for positions in supervision, administration or teaching. **Focus:** Nursing, Pediatric. **Qualif.:** Applicant must be a registered nurse with a current state license; must have graduated at a regionally accredited school of nursing or will be graduated by the application deadline; must be a registered nurse pursuing nursing education in the field of pediatric lung and respiratory diseases on a part-time or full-time basis; must be accepted by a regionally accredited school of nursing; must be a U.S. citizen; must have leadership qualities; and must have the ability to pursue full-time employment after school. **Criteria:** Awards are given based on personal and academic qualifications with consideration given to past experience and future employment plans as they relate to pediatric lung and respiratory disease nursing.

Funds Avail.: No specific amount. **To Apply:** Applicants must submit a completed scholarship application along with a current state Registered Nurse License or registration; three letters of recommendation; transcript of all college credit attempted; and letter of acceptance from an accredited school of nursing. **Contact:** The American Legion Americanism and Children & Youth Division, Attn: Eight and Forty Nursing Scholarship at the above address.

956 ■ National High School Oratorical Contest Scholarship *(Undergraduate/Scholarship)*

Purpose: To provide financial support for the education of deserving high school students. **Focus:** General studies/Field of study not specified. **Qualif.:** Candidates must be high school students. **Criteria:** Students must win the oratorical contest to acquire the scholarship.

Funds Avail.: Amount varies. **Number Awarded:** Varies. **To Apply:** Applicants may contact their Department (State) or the National Organization of the American Legion for more information about the scholarships. **Contact:** oratorical@legion.org.

957 ■ Samsung American Legion Scholarships
(Undergraduate/Scholarship)

Purpose: To assist the education of a child, grandchild, great grandchild, etc. or a legally adopted child of a U.S. wartime veteran. **Focus:** General studies/Field of study not specified. **Qualif.:** Applicants must be high school juniors who participates in either an American Legion Boys State or American Legion Auxiliary Girls State Program and be direct descendants (children, grandchildren, great grandchildren, etc. or legally adopted children) of a U.S. wartime veteran who served on active duty during one or more of the periods of war officially designated as eligibility dates for membership in The American Legion by the United States government. **Criteria:** Awards are given based on merit.

Funds Avail.: Up to $20,000. **Duration:** Annual. **Number Awarded:** Varies. **To Apply:** Applicants must submit a completed scholarship application along with a photocopy of the veteran's Certification of Release or Discharge from Active Duty (DD-214), to Boys/Girls State program. **Contact:** American Legion Boys State or American Legion Auxiliary Girls State Program at the above address or e-mail: scholarships@legion.org.

958 ■ American Legion Department of Vermont
126 State St.
Montpelier, VT 05601
Ph: (802)223-7131
Fax: (802)223-0318
Free: 800-501-7131
E-mail: alvthq@myfairpoint.net
URL: vtlegion.org

959 ■ American Legion Department of Vermont Scholarships *(Undergraduate, High School/Scholarship)*

Purpose: To support and give educational opportunity to qualified students. **Focus:** General studies/Field of study not specified. **Qualif.:** Applicants must be seniors attending a Vermont secondary school or a similar school in an adjoining state, whose parents are legal residents of the State of Vermont; must be seniors residing in an adjacent state whose normal high school attendance area is a Vermont secondary school. **Criteria:** Selection will be based on the committee's criteria.

Funds Avail.: Varies. **Duration:** Annual. **To Apply:** Applicants must complete and submit the application form available at the website. **Deadline:** April 1.

960 ■ American Library Association (ALA)
50 E Huron St.
Chicago, IL 60611-2795
Ph: (312)944-6780
Fax: (312)440-9374
Free: 800-545-2433
E-mail: ala@ala.org
URL: www.ala.org
Facebook: www.facebook.com/AmericanLibraryAssociation
LinkedIn: www.linkedin.com/company/american-library-association
Twitter: www.twitter.com/alalibrary

961 ■ David H. Clift Scholarships *(Graduate/Scholarship)*

Purpose: To aid those who are pursuing a master's degree in library sciences. **Focus:** Library and archival sciences.

Qualif.: Applicants must be American or Canadian citizens or permanent residents attending ALA accredited Master's Program and have no more than 12 semester hours towards MLS/MLIS/MIS prior to June 1 of year awarded. **Criteria:** Applicants will be evaluated based on academic excellence, leadership and evidence of commitment to a career in librarianship. **Funds Avail.:** $3,000. **Duration:** Annual. **Number Awarded:** 1. **To Apply:** Applicants must complete the online application. In addition, applicants must provide an official academic transcript from institutions. These can be submitted directly from the institution, or mailed in the unopened envelope as received from the degree-granting institutions along with any other materials. Only official (sealed) copies will be accepted. **Deadline:** March 1. **Contact:** ALA Library Reference Desk; Phone: 800-545-2433, ext. 2153; Fax: 312-280-3255; Email: library@ala.org.

962 ■ Christopher Hoy/ERT Scholarships *(Graduate/Scholarship)*

Purpose: To aid those who are pursuing a master's degree in library sciences. **Focus:** Library and archival sciences. **Qualif.:** Applicants must be American or Canadian citizens or permanent residents attending ALA accredited Master's Program and have no more than 12 semester hours towards MLS/MLIS/MIS prior to June 1 of year awarded. **Criteria:** Applicants will be evaluated based on academic excellence, leadership and evidence of commitment to a career in librarianship. **Funds Avail.:** $5,000. **Duration:** Annual. **Number Awarded:** 1. **To Apply:** Applicants are required to apply online. They may visit the program website for further application details. **Deadline:** March 1. **Contact:** Kimberly L. Sanders, Staff Liaison; Phone: 312-280-4279; Fax: 312-280-3256; Email: ksanders@ala.org.

963 ■ American Livebearer Association (ALA)
5 Zerbe St.
Cressona, PA 17929-1513
Ph: (570)385-0573
URL: www.livebearers.org
Facebook: www.facebook.com/AmericanLivebearerAssociation

964 ■ Vern Parish *(Graduate, Undergraduate/Scholarship)*

Purpose: To support education in the field of livebearing fish. **Focus:** Cooley's anemia; Fisheries sciences/management. **Qualif.:** Applicants must be agencies or college-student researchers working with livebearing fishes. **Criteria:** Selection will be based on the following criteria: significance; approach; student background; sponsor and environment. **Funds Avail.:** Varies. **Duration:** Annual. **To Apply:** Applicants must submit the following requirements: a project title; letter of nomination from the faculty sponsor; students' curriculum vitae; research statement. **Deadline:** March 30. **Remarks:** Established in 1997. **Contact:** Completed application should be submitted to: Earl Blewett, PhD, Biochemistry & Microbiology, Oklahoma State University - Center for Health Sciences; Email: earl.blewett@okstate.edu.

965 ■ American Liver Foundation (ALF)
39 Broadway, Ste. 2700
New York, NY 10006
Ph: (212)668-1000
Fax: (212)483-8179
Free: 800-465-4837
URL: www.liverfoundation.org

966 ■ ALF Postdoctoral Research Fellowship Award *(Postdoctorate, Professional development/Fellowship)*

Purpose: To support investigational work relating to liver physiology and disease. **Focus:** Medical research. **Funds Avail.:** $12,500. **Duration:** Annual. **Deadline:** December 4.

967 ■ American Liver Foundation Liver Scholar Awards *(Doctorate/Award)*

Purpose: To develop the potential of outstanding, young scientists and encouraging research in liver physiology and disease. **Focus:** Medical research. **Qualif.:** Applicants must be sponsored by a public or private non-profit institution accredited in the United States, Canada or Mexico engaged in health care and health-related research; an AASLD member in good standing; and sponsored by a research mentor. **Criteria:** Awards are made to eligible institutions and are for salary support only for the awardee. **Funds Avail.:** $225,000. **Duration:** Three years. **To Apply:** Applicants may download an application form online. Applicants must submit an application which contain the following section: Application Information; Summary and Abstract; Biographical Sketch; Research Plan; Research Facilities; Candidate's Statement; Letters of Commitment; Letters of Recommendation; Institution Review Board; Signatures. Original and eight (8) copies of the completed application must be received at ALF. **Deadline:** December 3. **Contact:** American Liver Foundation Research Department/Liver Scholars 1425 Pompton Avenue, Suite 3 Cedar Grove, NJ 07009.

968 ■ American Lung Association in the District of Columbia (ALA)
1301 Pennsylvania Ave. NW
Washington, DC 20004
Ph: (202)785-3355
Fax: (202)452-1805
Free: 800-548-8252
E-mail: lungdc@lunginfo.org
URL: www.lung.org/about-us/local-associations/washington-dc.html
Facebook: www.facebook.com/American-Lung-Association-in-the-District-of-Columbia-165138033580702
Twitter: twitter.com/AmericanLungDC

969 ■ ALA Allergic Respiratory Diseases Research Award *(Doctorate/Grant)*

Purpose: To support research that will advance the understanding of allergic respiratory disease. **Focus:** Health sciences; Public health. **Qualif.:** Applicant must hold a doctoral degree at the time of application; have a primary faculty appointment in an allergy/immunology division/section of an academic institution, be undertaking a project related to allergic respiratory disease, and have completed a training fellowship; must be United States citizens at the time of application or foreign nationals holding one of the following visa immigration statuses: permanent resident (Green Card), exchange visitor (J-1), temporary worker in a specialty occupation (H-1B), Canadian or Mexican citizen engaging in professional activities (TN), Australians in

Awards are arranged alphabetically below their administering organizations

Specialty Occupation (E-3 visa) or temporary worker with extraordinary abilities in the sciences (O-1); at the time of application and throughout the award, an applicant must be employed by a U.S. institution. **Criteria:** Selection will be based on scientific merit, innovation, and feasibility of the research plan, and its relevance to the mission of the American Lung Association; education and experience; sponsor's program, including the record of training academic scientists, the research productivity of the faculty and the quality of the research training program proposed for the applicant.
Funds Avail.: $75,000. **Duration:** Annual. **Number Awarded:** 2. **To Apply:** Applicants may visit the website for the application process. Submit one signed original plus two copies of all application materials. **Deadline:** December 15.

970 ■ American Lung Association Biomedical Research Grants *(Doctorate/Grant)*

Purpose: To provide seed monies to junior investigators who are researching the mechanism of lung disease and general lung biology. **Focus:** Health sciences; Public health. **Qualif.:** Applicant must hold a doctoral degree, be assured of a faculty appointment or equivalent institutional commitment (salary support, research space) by the start of the award. Applicants must have completed two years of post-doctoral research training by the start of the award. Applicants must be US citizens or foreign nationals holding one of the following visa immigration statuses: permanent resident (Green Card), student (F-1), exchange visitor (J-1), temporary worker in a specialty occupation (H-1, H-1B), Canadian or Mexican citizen engaging in professional activities (TC or TN), or temporary worker with extraordinary abilities in the sciences (O-1). Non-citizens must submit a notarized copy of proof of possession of a Green Card or F-1, J-1, H-1, H-1B, TC, TN or O-1 visas. **Criteria:** Selection will be based on scientific merit, innovation, and feasibility of the research plan, and its relevance to the mission of the American Lung Association; education and experience, publications and letters of recommendation; research environment; likelihood that the applicant will continue to have a career in lung and/or other relevant research; Department Chair letter clearly assuring faculty appointment with demonstrated institutional commitment before the start of an award.
Funds Avail.: $40,000. **Duration:** Annual. **To Apply:** Applicants may visit the website for the application process. Submit one signed original plus two copies of all application materials. **Deadline:** December 15.

971 ■ American Lung Association Clinical Patient Care Research Grants *(Doctorate/Grant)*

Purpose: To provide monies to investigators working on traditional clinical studies examining methods for improving patient care and treatment for lung disease. **Focus:** Health sciences; Public health. **Qualif.:** At the time of application, an applicant must hold a doctoral degree, be assured of faculty appointment or equivalent with demonstrated institutional commitment (salary support, research space) by the start of the award. Applicants must have completed two years of post-doctoral research training by the start of the award. Grantee organizations must be recognized academic or other non-profit research entities. **Criteria:** Selection will be based on scientific merit, innovation, and feasibility of the research plan, and its relevance to the mission of the American Lung Association; education and experience, publications and letters of recommendation; research environment; likelihood that the applicant will continue to have a career in lung and/or other relevant research; Department Chair letter clearly assuring faculty appointment with demonstrated institutional commitment before the start of an award.
Funds Avail.: $40,000. **Duration:** Annual. **To Apply:** Applicants may visit the website for the application process. Submit one signed original plus two copies of all application materials. **Deadline:** December 15.

972 ■ American Lung Association Dalsemer Research Grants *(Doctorate/Grant)*

Purpose: To provide seed monies to junior investigators who are researching the mechanism of lung disease and general lung biology. **Focus:** Health sciences; Public health. **Qualif.:** Applicant must hold a doctoral degree, be assured of faculty appointment or equivalent with demonstrated institutional commitment (salary support, research space) by the start of the award. Applicants must have completed two years of post-doctoral research training by the start of the award. Grantee organizations must be recognized academic or other non-profit research entities. Applicants must be US citizens or foreign nationals holding one of the following visa immigration statuses: permanent resident (Green Card), student (F-1), exchange visitor (J-1), temporary worker in a specialty occupation (H-1, H-1B), Canadian or Mexican citizen engaging in professional activities (TC or TN), or temporary worker with extraordinary abilities in the sciences (O-1). Non-citizens must submit a notarized copy of proof of possession of a Green Card or F-1, J-1, H-1, H-1B, TC, TN or O-1 visas. **Criteria:** Selection will be based on scientific merit, innovation, and feasibility of the research plan, and its relevance to the mission of the American Lung Association; education and experience, publications and letters of recommendation; research environment; likelihood that the applicant will continue to have a career in lung and/or other relevant research; Department Chair letter clearly assuring faculty appointment with demonstrated institutional commitment before the start of an award.
Funds Avail.: $40,000. **Duration:** Annual. **To Apply:** Applicants may visit the website for the application process. Submit one signed original plus two copies of all application materials. **Deadline:** December 15.

973 ■ American Lung Association DeSousa Awards *(Doctorate/Grant)*

Purpose: To support clinical, laboratory, epidemiological, or any other kind of research that focuses on bronchiectasis, infection with a typical Mycobacteria, and infection with Nocardia species. **Focus:** Health sciences; Public health. **Qualif.:** Applicants must hold a doctoral degree, be assured of faculty appointment or equivalent with demonstrated institutional commitment (salary support, research space) by the start of the award. Applicants must have completed two years of post-doctoral research training by the start of the award. Grantee organizations must be recognized academic or other non-profit research entities. Applicants must be US citizens or foreign nationals holding one of the following visa immigration statuses: permanent resident (Green Card), student (F-1), exchange visitor (J-1), temporary worker in a specialty occupation (H-1, H-1B), Canadian or Mexican citizen engaging in professional activities (TC or TN), or temporary worker with extraordinary abilities in the sciences (O-1). Non-citizens must submit a notarized copy of proof of possession of a Green Card or F-1, J-1, H-1, H-1B, TC, TN or O-1 visas. **Criteria:** Selection will be based on scientific merit, innovation, and feasibility of the research plan, and its relevance to the

Awards are arranged alphabetically below their administering organizations

mission of the American Lung Association; education and experience, publications and letters of recommendation; research environment; likelihood that the applicant will continue to have a career in lung and/or other relevant research; Department Chair letter clearly assuring faculty appointment with demonstrated institutional commitment before the start of an award.

Funds Avail.: No specific amount. **Duration:** Annual. **To Apply:** Applicants may visit the website for the application process. Submit one signed original plus two copies of all application materials.

974 ■ American Lung Association Lung Cancer Discovery Awards *(Doctorate/Grant)*

Purpose: To support the development of novel medical treatments, advancing current treatment options and/or finding a cure for lung cancer through clinical, laboratory, epidemiological, or any other king of research. **Focus:** Health sciences; Public health. **Qualif.:** Applicant must be a matriculating student in good standing in a full-time academic program leading to a doctoral degree in one of the above-mentioned fields. Applicants must be US citizens or foreign nationals holding one of the following visa immigration statuses: permanent resident (Green Card), student (F-1), exchange visitor (J-1), temporary worker in a specialty occupation (H-1, H-1B), Canadian or Mexican citizen engaging in professional activities (TC or TN), or temporary worker with extra-ordinary abilities in the sciences (O-1). Non-citizens must submit a notarized copy of proof of possession of a Green Card or F-1, J-1, H-1, H-1B, TC, TN or O-1 visas. **Criteria:** Selection will be based on scientific merit, innovation, and feasibility of the research plan, and its relevance to the mission of the American Lung Association; education and experience; sponsor's program, including the record of training academic scientists, the research productivity of the faculty and the quality of the research training program proposed for the applicant.

Funds Avail.: $100,000. **Duration:** Annual. **To Apply:** Applicants are required to submit a Letter of Intent to the American Lung Association. Letter of Intent must be an attached PDF file, no more than 3 pages, which must include: rationale for the project; planned specific aims; brief statement of the overall experimental approach; NIH Biosketch of the applicant (separate attached PDF file). Submit one signed original plus two copies of all application materials. **Deadline:** December 15.

975 ■ American Lung Association Senior Research Training Fellowships *(Doctorate/Fellowship)*

Purpose: To support the training of MDs and PhDs seeking further academic training as scientific investigators with the goal of pursuing a career in pulmonary medicine and long biology research. **Focus:** Health sciences; Public health. **Qualif.:** Applicants must hold a doctoral degree and must work in an academic or not-for-profit institution. MD or DO applicants must also have completed their clinical training, have some research experience, and be in their 3rd or 4th year of fellowship training. PhD applicants must be in their 1st or 2nd year of postdoctoral training. Persons with medical degrees, whose credentials show that they are on a career track which will not include the practice of medicine, must be in their 1st or 2nd year of full-time postdoctoral research. Applicants must be US citizens or foreign nationals holding one of the following visa immigration statuses: permanent resident (Green Card), student (F-1), exchange visitor (J-1), temporary worker in a specialty occupation (H-1, H-1B), Canadian or Mexican citizen engaging in professional activities (TC or TN), or temporary worker with extra-ordinary abilities in the sciences (O-1). Non-citizens must submit a notarized copy of proof of possession of a Green Card or F-1, J-1, H-1, H-1B, TC, TN or O-1 visas. **Criteria:** Selection will be based on the committee's criteria.

Funds Avail.: $32,500. **Duration:** Annual; 2 years. **To Apply:** Applicants may visit the website for the application process. Submit one signed original plus two copies of all application materials. **Deadline:** December 15.

976 ■ American Lung Association Social-Behavioral Research Grants *(Doctorate/Grant)*

Purpose: To provide seed monies to junior investigators working on various disciplines of social science examining risk factors affecting lung health. **Focus:** Health sciences; Public health. **Qualif.:** Applicant must hold a doctoral degree, be assured of faculty appointment or equivalent with demonstrated institutional commitment (salary support, research space) by the start of the award. Applicants must have completed two years of post-doctoral research training by the start of the award. Grantee organizations must be recognized academic or other non-profit research entities. Applicants must be US citizens or foreign nationals holding one of the following visa immigration statuses: permanent resident (Green Card), student (F-1), exchange visitor (J-1), temporary worker in a specialty occupation (H-1, H-1B), Canadian or Mexican citizen engaging in professional activities (TC or TN), or temporary worker with extra-ordinary abilities in the sciences (O-1). Non-citizens must submit a notarized copy of proof of possession of a Green Card or F-1, J-1, H-1, H-1B, TC, TN or O-1 visas. **Criteria:** Selection will be based on scientific merit, innovation, and feasibility of the research plan, and its relevance to the mission of the American Lung Association; education and experience, publications and letters of recommendation; research environment; likelihood that the applicant will continue to have a career in lung and/or other relevant research; Department Chair letter clearly assuring faculty appointment with demonstrated institutional commitment before the start of an award.

Funds Avail.: $40,000. **Duration:** Annual. **To Apply:** Applicants may visit the website for the application process. Submit one signed original plus two copies of all application materials. **Deadline:** December 15.

977 ■ Lung Health Dissertation Grants *(Graduate/Grant)*

Purpose: To support pre-doctoral dissertation research in the various disciplines of social science examining risk factors affecting lung health. **Focus:** Health sciences; Public health. **Qualif.:** Applicants must be a matriculating student in good standing in a full-time academic program leading to a doctoral degree in one of the above-mentioned fields. Applicants must be US citizens or foreign nationals holding one of the following visa immigration statuses: permanent resident (Green Card), student (F-1), exchange visitor (J-1), temporary worker in a specialty occupation (H-1, H-1B), Canadian or Mexican citizen engaging in professional activities (TC or TN), or temporary worker with extra-ordinary abilities in the sciences (O-1). Non-citizens must submit a notarized copy of proof of possession of a Green Card or F-1, J-1, H-1, H-1B, TC, TN or O-1 visas. The sponsor should be a recognized authority in the applicant's field of research and possess the necessary training resources. The sponsor must have an academic affiliated appointment and must be working in a not-for-profit institution. **Criteria:** Selection will be based on scientific merit, innovation, and feasibility of the research plan, and its relevance to the

Awards are arranged alphabetically below their administering organizations

mission of the American Lung Association; education and experience; sponsor's program, including the record of training academic scientists, the research productivity of the faculty and the quality of the research training program proposed for the applicant. **Funds Avail.:** $21,000. **Duration:** Annual. **Number Awarded:** 1. **To Apply:** Applicants may visit the website for the application process. Submit one signed original plus two copies of all application materials. **Deadline:** November 12.

978 ■ American Lung Association in New Jersey
PO Box 10188, No. 37214
Newark, NJ 07101-3188
Ph: (908)685-8040
E-mail: jgrinwald@lunginfo.org
URL: www.lung.org/about-us/local-associations/new-jersey.html

979 ■ American Lung Association Scholar Program
(Professional development/Grant)

Purpose: To foster laboratory, patient-centered and social-behavioral research designed to prevent and relieve the suffering associated with all lung diseases and corresponding risk factors. **Focus:** General studies/Field of study not specified. **Qualif.:** Applicants must be mid-career investigators and members of the American Lung Association. **Criteria:** Selection will be based on the committee's criteria.

Funds Avail.: No specific amount. **Duration:** Annual. **To Apply:** Interested applicants for these scholarships may reach the Association for further details and application process.

980 ■ American Marketing Association Foundation (AMAF)
311 S Wacker Dr., Ste. 5800
Chicago, IL 60606
Ph: (312)542-9000
Fax: (312)542-9001
URL: themarketingfoundation.org

981 ■ Richard A. Hammill Scholarship Fund
(Undergraduate/Scholarship)

Purpose: To support students who are enrolled in the Marketing Program. **Focus:** Marketing and distribution. **Qualif.:** Applicants must be students enrolled at Georgia State University. **Criteria:** Selection will be based on the committee's criteria.

Funds Avail.: No specific amount. **Duration:** Annual. **To Apply:** Interested applicants may apply online via the AMAF website. **Remarks:** Established in 2005.

982 ■ Robert J. Lavidge Nonprofit Marketing Research Scholarships *(Other/Scholarship)*

Purpose: To assist marketing professionals working in the nonprofit sector to further their marketing research related education. **Focus:** Marketing and distribution. **Qualif.:** Applicants must be nonprofit marketing professionals with an interest in furthering their marketing research education. **Criteria:** Individuals will be judged based on how they demonstrate participation in a marketing research educational program.

Funds Avail.: No specific amount. **Duration:** Annual. **To Apply:** Interested applicants may apply online via the AMAF website. **Remarks:** Established in 1999.

983 ■ Valuing Diversity PhD Scholarships
(Doctorate/Scholarship)

Purpose: To provide scholarship to underrepresented populations in the marketing profession. **Focus:** Marketing and distribution. **Qualif.:** Applicants must be U.S. citizens or permanent residents enrolled on campus, in a full-time AACSB-accredited marketing doctoral program and have successfully completed at least one year; must have not previously received a Valuing Diversity Scholarship. They must also be African American, Hispanic American, or Native American. **Criteria:** Selection will be based on the committee's criteria.

Funds Avail.: $1,000 each. **Duration:** Annual. **Number Awarded:** Varies. **To Apply:** Applicants must complete the online application found on the AMAF's website. Essays must be in Microsoft Word format. Essays should be two-pages, double-spaced, in 12 pt. type (approximately 500 words). Sources you mention in your essay should be credited on an additional page and do not count against the two-page maximum. Applicants must also submit two letters of recommendation. **Deadline:** April 30. **Remarks:** Established in 2003.

984 ■ American Mathematical Society (AMS)
201 Charles St.
Providence, RI 02904-2294
Ph: (401)455-4000
Fax: (401)331-3842
Free: 800-321-4267
E-mail: cust-serv@ams.org
URL: www.ams.org
Facebook: www.facebook.com/amermathsoc
LinkedIn: www.linkedin.com/company/american-mathematical-society?trk=fc_badge
Twitter: twitter.com/amermathsoc

985 ■ AMS Centennial Fellowships *(Postdoctorate/Fellowship)*

Purpose: To promote study and research in mathematics. **Focus:** Mathematics and mathematical sciences. **Qualif.:** Applicant must have held his/her doctoral degree for at least three years but not more than twelve years at the inception of the award. **Criteria:** Selection is based on the excellence of the applicant's research.

Funds Avail.: $82,000, plus allowance or $8,200. **Duration:** One year. **Number Awarded:** Varies. **To Apply:** Applicants must submit a completed application form along with the required materials. **Deadline:** December 1. **Contact:** prof-serv@ams.org.

986 ■ American Meat Science Association (AMSA)
1 E Main St., Ste. 200
Champaign, IL 61820
Ph: (217)356-5370
Fax: (217)356-5370
Free: 800-517-AMSA
E-mail: information@meatscience.org
URL: www.meatscience.org
Facebook: www.facebook.com/scienceofmeat

Awards are arranged alphabetically below their administering organizations

Twitter: twitter.com/meatscience

987 ■ AMSA Graduate Student Research Poster Competition Award *(Undergraduate, Doctorate, Master's/Award)*

Purpose: To recognize individuals who have made outstanding posters relevant to any aspect of meat science. **Focus:** Science. **Qualif.:** Applicants must be graduate (MS or PhD) or undergraduate students currently members of the American Meat Association at the time of entry. **Criteria:** Selection will be based on the committees' criteria.

Funds Avail.: No specific amount. **Number Awarded:** 4. **To Apply:** Applicants must submit electronic poster regarding meat science. **Contact:** Deidrrea Mabry, dmabry@meatscience.org.

988 ■ American Medical Association (AMA)
AMA Plaza
330 N Wabash Ave.
Chicago, IL 60611
Ph: (312)464-4430
Fax: (312)464-5226
Free: 800-621-8335
E-mail: amalibrary@ama-assn.org
URL: www.ama-assn.org

989 ■ AMA Foundation Minority Scholars Awards *(Graduate/Scholarship)*

Purpose: To encourage diversity in medicine and alleviates debt, and reward commitment to the elimination of healthcare disparities, outstanding academic achievements, leadership activities and community involvement. **Focus:** Medicine. **Qualif.:** Applicants must be current first or second year students and permanent residents or citizens of the U.S. They must also be African Americans, American Indians, Native Americans, Alaska Natives or Hispanics/Latinos. **Criteria:** Selection will be based on the applicant's academic standing.

Funds Avail.: No specific amount. **Duration:** Annual. **Number Awarded:** Varies. **To Apply:** Applicant must complete the application form. Detailed requirement will be sent by the AMA Foundation to each medical school's Office of the Dean, Office of the Student Affairs, and Office of Financial Aid. **Remarks:** The Minority Scholars Awards are supported in part by Pfizer Inc., with additional support from the American Society of Anesthesiologists, National Business Group on Health and generous individual contributions.

990 ■ AMA Foundation Physicians of Tomorrow Scholarships *(Graduate/Scholarship)*

Purpose: To support rising fourth year medical students (third year students who are approaching their final year of medical school). **Focus:** Medicine. **Qualif.:** Applicants must be current third year medical students who are entering their fourth year of study. **Criteria:** Recipients will be selected based on academic standing and financial need.

Funds Avail.: $10,000. **Duration:** Annual. **Number Awarded:** Varies. **To Apply:** Applicants must complete the application form. Detailed requirements will be sent by the AMA Foundation to each medical school's Office of the Dean, Office of the Student Affairs, and Office of Financial Aid.

991 ■ Arthur N. Wilson, MD, Scholarships *(Undergraduate/Scholarship)*

Purpose: To support a medical student who graduated from a high school in Southeast Alaska. **Focus:** Medicine. **Qualif.:** Applicants must be medical students who attended high school in Southeast Alaska. **Criteria:** Recipients will be selected based on academic standing and financial need.

Funds Avail.: $5,000. **Duration:** Annual. **Number Awarded:** 1. **To Apply:** Applicants must submit the following: completed application form; a one-page personal statement outlining the career goals in the field of medicine; a curriculum vitae; official transcript from the applicant's high school in Southeast Alaska; official medical school transcript; and letter of recommendation from a faculty member at the medical school or office of the dean. Applicants may apply directly to the American Medical Association (AMA) Foundation. **Deadline:** June 17.

992 ■ American Medical Society for Sports Medicine (AMSSM)
4000 W 114th St., Ste. 100
Leawood, KS 66211-2622
Ph: (913)327-1415
Fax: (913)327-1491
E-mail: office@amssm.org
URL: www.amssm.org
Twitter: twitter.com/theamssm

993 ■ AMSSM-ACSM Clinical Research Grants *(Professional development/Grant)*

Purpose: To foster original scientific investigations with a strong clinical focus among physician members of AMSSM and the ACSM. **Focus:** Medicine, Sports. **Qualif.:** Applicants must be physicians who are members of the AMSSM and the ACSM. **Criteria:** Selection will be based on the applicants' eligibility and their submitted applications.

Funds Avail.: Maximum of $20,000. **Duration:** Annual; up to two years. **To Apply:** Applicants may contact the AMSSM Foundation for the application process and other information.

994 ■ American Men's Studies Association (AMSA)
1080 S University Ave.
Ann Arbor, MI 48109-1106
Ph: (470)333-AMSA
E-mail: amsamail@gmail.com
URL: mensstudies.org

995 ■ Loren Frankel Memorial Scholarships *(Undergraduate, Graduate/Scholarship)*

Purpose: To support students engaged in the critical study of men and masculinities. **Focus:** Sexuality. **Qualif.:** Applicants must be undergraduate or graduate students. **Criteria:** Applicants will be evaluated based on content of the application, quality and the student's potential for making a contribution to the field of men's studies.

Funds Avail.: $500 per year. **To Apply:** Applicants must submit a maximum two-page document that includes brief biographical information, title and abstract of the paper and paragraph describing the importance of the project to professional and intellectual development. **Deadline:** January 15.

996 ■ American Meteorological Society (AMS)
45 Beacon St.
Boston, MA 02108-3693

Awards are arranged alphabetically below their administering organizations

Ph: (617)227-2425
Fax: (617)742-8718
E-mail: amsinfo@ametsoc.org
URL: www.ametsoc.org
Facebook: www.facebook.com/ametsoc
Twitter: twitter.com/ametsoc

997 ■ AMS Freshman Undergraduate Scholarships (Undergraduate/Scholarship)

Purpose: To encourage high school students to study in the atmospheric and related sciences. **Focus:** Meteorology. **Qualif.:** Applicant must be a U.S. citizen or hold a permanent resident status; entering the freshman year of college as a full-time student; and plan to pursue a degree in the atmospheric or related oceanic or hydrologic sciences. **Criteria:** Selection is based on the applicant's performance in high school including academic records, recommendation, scores from a national college exam and a written essay.

Funds Avail.: $2,500/year. **Duration:** two years. **To Apply:** Applicants must submit a completed application form together with an official high school transcript showing grades from the past three years; a letter of recommendation from a high school teacher or guidance counselor; and a copy of scores from a SAT or similar national college entrance exam. **Contact:** Donna Fernandez, Development and Student Program Manager; Phone: 617-227-2426 ext. 3907.

998 ■ AMS Graduate Fellowships in the History of Science (Graduate/Fellowship)

Purpose: To support students who wish to complete a dissertation on the history of science. **Focus:** Science--History. **Qualif.:** Applicants must be graduate students in good standing who proposes to complete a dissertation in the history of the atmospheric or related oceanic or hydrologic sciences. **Criteria:** Selection is based on the submitted application materials.

Funds Avail.: $15,000. **Duration:** one year. **To Apply:** Applicants must submit a cover letter with a curriculum vitae; official transcripts from undergraduate and graduate institutions; a typewritten, detailed description of the dissertation topic and proposed research plan (10 page maximum); and three letters of recommendation (including one from dissertation advisor). **Contact:** Donna Fernandez, Development and Student Program Manager; Phone: 617-227-2426 ext. 3907.

999 ■ AMS/Industry/Government Graduate Fellowships (Graduate/Fellowship)

Purpose: To attract promising young scientists to prepare for careers in the atmospheric and related oceanic and hydrologic fields. **Focus:** Meteorology. **Qualif.:** Applicants must be entering the first year of graduate school and provide evidence of acceptance as full-time students at an accredited U.S. institution at the time of the award; must pursue a related full-time course of study in the atmospheric or related oceanic or hydrologic sciences over a full academic year; must have a minimum GPA of 3.25 on a 4.0-point scale; must be U.S. citizens or hold permanent resident status. **Criteria:** Selection is based on the applicant's performance as an undergraduate student including academic records, recommendations and Graduate Record Examinations (GRE) scores.

Funds Avail.: No specific amount. **To Apply:** Applicants must submit a completed application form along with the written references, official transcripts and GRE score reports. **Contact:** Donna Fernandez, Development and Student Program Manager; Phone: 617-227-2426 ext. 3907.

1000 ■ AMS/Industry Minority Scholarships (Undergraduate/Scholarship)

Purpose: To help further the education of outstanding students pursuing a career in the atmospheric and related oceanic or hydrologic sciences. **Focus:** Meteorology. **Qualif.:** Applicants must be minority students entering the freshman year of college; planning to pursue a career in the atmospheric or related oceanic and hydrologic sciences; must be U.S. citizens or hold permanent resident status; and must be pursuing a degree at a U.S. institution. **Criteria:** Selection is based on the submitted application materials.

Funds Avail.: $3,000/year. **Duration:** Two years. **To Apply:** Applicants must submit a completed application form along with an official high school transcript showing grades from the past three years; a letter of recommendation from a high school teacher or guidance counselor; and a copy of scores from a SAT or similar national college entrance exam. All original materials should be mailed to the closest local chapter listed at the bottom of the application. Photocopies of the application, transcripts and essay should be mailed to the AMS Headquarters. **Contact:** Donna Fernandez; Phone 617-226-3907; Email: dfernandez@ametsoc.org.

1001 ■ AMS Undergraduate Named Scholarships (Undergraduate/Scholarship)

Purpose: To support students majoring in the atmospheric or related oceanic or hydrologic sciences. **Focus:** Meteorology. **Qualif.:** Applicant must be a full-time student entering the final year of undergraduate study; majoring in the atmospheric or related oceanic or hydrologic science, and/or must show clear intent to make the atmospheric or related sciences a career; enrolled full time in an accredited U.S. institution; and must have a cumulative GPA of at least a 3.25 on a scale of 4.0. **Criteria:** Selection is based on the applicant's performance as an undergraduate student including academic records and recommendation.

Funds Avail.: $7,500. **Duration:** Annual. **Number Awarded:** 25. **To Apply:** Applicants must submit a completed application form along with letters of reference and official transcripts. **Deadline:** March 31. **Contact:** Donna Fernandez, Development and Student Program Manager; Phone: 617-227-2426 ext. 3907.

1002 ■ American MidEast Leadership Network (AMLN)

PO Box 2156
Astoria, NY 11102
Ph: (347)924-9674
Fax: (917)591-2177
E-mail: info@amln.org
URL: amln.org

1003 ■ AMLN Scholarships for Arab American Students (Graduate, Undergraduate/Scholarship)

Purpose: To encourage Arab students to pursue higher education. **Focus:** General studies/Field of study not specified. **Qualif.:** Applicants must be of Arab heritage; U.S. citizens or legal permanent residents with permanent

Awards are arranged alphabetically below their administering organizations

resident card or passport stamped I-551; and high school seniors or undergraduate/graduate students enrolled full-time in a degree seeking program at an accredited U.S. college/university in the Tri state area (NJ, NY, CT). Undergraduate and graduate students must have earned at least 12 credits at a U.S. accredited college/university; have a minimum cumulative GPA of 3.00 on a 4.00 scale and must be active in the local Arab American community. **Criteria:** Selection shall be based on the aforementioned applicants' qualifications and compliance with the application details.

Funds Avail.: $1,000-$3,000. **Duration:** Annual. **To Apply:** Applicants may visit the website to verify the application process and other pieces of information. **Contact:** American MidEast Leadership Network, at the above address.

1004 ■ American Military Retirees Association (AMRA)
5436 Peru St., No. 1
Plattsburgh, NY 12901
Ph: (518)563-9479
Fax: (518)324-5204
Free: 800-424-2969
E-mail: info@amra1973.org
URL: amra1973.org
Facebook: www.facebook.com/AMRA1973

1005 ■ Sergeant Major Douglas R. Drum Memorial Scholarship Fund (Undergraduate/Scholarship)

Purpose: To protect and improve the benefits of the military retirees. **Focus:** General studies/Field of study not specified. **Qualif.:** Applicant must be a current member of AMRA, his/her dependent, child or grandchild; he/she must be pursuing a degree in an accredited college or university. **Criteria:** Scholarship Committee will evaluate the application based on the student's educational achievements, leadership abilities, character, citizenship, and community service.

Funds Avail.: $35,000. **Duration:** Annual; two semesters. **Number Awarded:** 24. **To Apply:** Applicants must present the award letter to the college/university and request that AMRA be billed for half the scholarship for the first semester and half the scholarship for the second semester; an applicant must submit a 750 word or less essay telling why an applicant deserve a scholarship from AMRA stating the Educational plans, achievements, leadership abilities, extracurricular and community activities, work experiences, character and citizenship traits, or any other circumstance that assist the committee during the selection process; an applicant must submit a letter of recommendation either from a teacher or professor, non-family member, past or current employer, from a project coordinator or a team leader. He/She must also submit a transcript of records, and signed student release form (available on the website) and record of accomplishment,. **Deadline:** March 9.

1006 ■ American Montessori Society (AMS)
116 E 16th St.
New York, NY 10003-2163
Ph: (212)358-1250
Fax: (212)358-1256
E-mail: ams@amshq.org
URL: amshq.org
Facebook: www.facebook.com/AmericanMontessoriSociety
Twitter: twitter.com/amshq

1007 ■ AMS Teacher Education Scholarships (Undergraduate/Scholarship)

Purpose: To support the growth of Montessori teachers. **Focus:** Education; Teaching. **Qualif.:** Applicant must be accepted or in the process of acceptance by an affiliated AMS teacher education program; Application is considered on the basis of financial need. **Criteria:** Selection of applicant will not be based on the gender, race, creed, color or national origin or sexual orientation. Applicants are considered on the basis of financial need, a compelling personal statement, three letters of recommendation and official verification of acceptance into an AMS Teacher Education Program.

Funds Avail.: $34,000. **Duration:** Annual. **Number Awarded:** 18. **To Apply:** Application forms are available on the website. Applicant must submit a personal statement, three recommendation letters, financial statement and appropriate tax form and verification of TEP acceptance. **Deadline:** May 1. **Contact:** Application form and supporting documents must be sent to Connie Murphy at the above address.

1008 ■ Teacher Education Scholarships (Advanced Professional/Scholarship)

Purpose: To support the growth of Montessori teachers of tomorrow. **Focus:** Teaching. **Qualif.:** Eligible to apply for scholarships are individuals who have been accepted, are in the process of being accepted, or are already enrolled in an AMS-affiliated teacher education program. **Criteria:** Selection shall be based on the committee's criteria. Applicants are considered on the basis of financial need, a compelling personal statement, 3 letters of recommendation, and official verification of acceptance into an AMS-affiliated program.

Funds Avail.: Varies. **Duration:** Annual. **Number Awarded:** Varies. **To Apply:** Application details can be found at the program website. **Deadline:** May 1.

1009 ■ American Music Therapy Association (AMTA)
8455 Colesville Rd., Ste. 1000
Silver Spring, MD 20910
Ph: (301)589-3300
Fax: (301)589-5175
E-mail: info@musictherapy.org
URL: www.musictherapy.org
Facebook: www.facebook.com/AMTAInc
Twitter: twitter.com/AMTAInc

1010 ■ AMTA Past Presidents' Conference Scholar Awards (Professional development/Award)

Purpose: To support AMTA members cover the cost of attending the AMTA annual conference. **Focus:** Music therapy. **Qualif.:** Applicants must be music therapists with a current credential of MT-BC or current professional designation of ACMT, CMT or RMT; must be professional members in good standing of AMTA. **Criteria:** Selection will be based on the committee's criteria.

Funds Avail.: $500. **Number Awarded:** 5. **To Apply:** Applicants must submit a maximum of one page narrative application. Statement of need and potential professional

Awards are arranged alphabetically below their administering organizations

development should be addressed within the narrative. **Deadline:** July 8.

1011 ■ AMTA Student Conference Scholar Awards *(Undergraduate, Graduate/Award)*

Purpose: To support students cover the expenses of attending the AMTA National Conference. **Focus:** Music therapy. **Qualif.:** Applicants must be undergraduate, undergraduate equivalency, or graduate students enrolled in a college or university program in music therapy approved by the American Music Therapy Association. All interns in clinical training are considered eligible through their parent academic institution. Applicants must be current student members of AMTA in the year in which they apply and the year in which the award is granted. **Criteria:** Selection will be based on the committee's criteria.

Funds Avail.: $250. **Number Awarded:** 2. **To Apply:** Applicants must submit a maximum of one page narrative application. Statement of need and potential development should be addressed within the narrative. **Deadline:** July 8.

1012 ■ Edwina Eustis Dick Scholarship for Music Therapy Interns *(Graduate/Scholarship)*

Purpose: To support the education of music therapy students. **Focus:** Music therapy. **Qualif.:** Applicants must be music therapy interns; must be current student members of AMTA in the year in which they apply and the year in which the award is granted. **Criteria:** Selection will be based on the committee's criteria.

Funds Avail.: $500. **Number Awarded:** 2. **To Apply:** Nomination for this award is required. Only AMTA-Approved Program Faculty may nominate students. Nominated candidates must provide the following materials: completed scholarship application form, signed and dated; personal, community, and college activities; college transcript; letter of recommendation which must be submitted by author from a music therapy professor, a professional familiar with the applicants' clinical skills or another person of the applicants' choice; participation in AMTA conferences, AMTA committees, presentations, and publications; a maximum of 800 words essay on long-term professional goals; a 400 words essay on how AMTA can impact the profession of music therapy. Any narrative must be double-spaced, 1-inch margins and in 12-point font. Narrative must be written for blind review, without specific reference to applicants' name or place of employment. **Deadline:** March 4.

1013 ■ Arthur Flagler Fultz Research Awards *(Professional development/Grant)*

Purpose: To encourage, promote and fund music therapy research and to explore new and innovative music therapy treatments. **Focus:** Music therapy. **Qualif.:** Applicants must be music therapists with a current credential of MT-BC or current professional designation of ACMT, CMT or RMT; must be a professional member in good standing of AMTA. **Criteria:** Selection will be based on the committee's criteria.

Funds Avail.: $15,000. **To Apply:** All applications must be typed and submitted electronically using Fultz application form available online. Download and save the application form as a new file using the Member number of the principal investigators and the word "Fultz". Feel free to contact the AMTA national office to know your member number. Applicants must also include all required forms and information in the order listed. **Deadline:** May 8. **Contact:** AMTA at fultz@musictherapy.org.

1014 ■ Anne Emery Kyllo Professional Scholarships *(Professional development/Scholarship)*

Purpose: To support professional music therapists in their efforts to expand their training and professional interactions through participation in continuing education opportunities. **Focus:** Music therapy. **Qualif.:** Applicants must be music therapists with a current credential of MT-BC or current professional designation of ACMT, CMT or RMT; must be professional members in good standing of AMTA. **Criteria:** Selection will be based on the committee's criteria.

Funds Avail.: $500. **Number Awarded:** 3. **To Apply:** Applicants must submit a maximum of two pages narrative application. Statement of need, potential professional development and client impact and strength/appropriateness of continuing education goals and opportunities should be included. **Deadline:** June 24.

1015 ■ Theodore Meyer Scholarships *(Undergraduate, Graduate/Scholarship)*

Purpose: To help individuals with mental health and/or addiction issues find a path to wellness and inspiration through the joy of music. **Focus:** Music therapy. **Qualif.:** Applicants must be undergraduate, undergraduate equivalency, or graduate students enrolled in a college or university program in music therapy approved by the American Music Therapy Association. All interns in clinical training are considered eligible through their parent academic institution. Applicants must be current student members of AMTA in the year in which they apply and the year in which the award is granted. **Criteria:** Selection will be based on the committee's criteria.

Funds Avail.: $1,000. **Duration:** Annual. **Number Awarded:** 1. **To Apply:** Students must provide two short essays. The first essay should detail an interest in mental health and addiction. The second essay should describe long-term professional goals. Each application narrative should be a maximum of two pages. **Deadline:** April 1.

1016 ■ Brian and Cathy Smith Memorial Fund *(Graduate/Scholarship)*

Purpose: To support the education of music therapy students. **Focus:** Music therapy. **Qualif.:** Candidates must be music therapy interns; must be current student members of AMTA in the year in which they apply and the year in which the award is granted. **Criteria:** Selection will be based on the committee's criteria.

Funds Avail.: $500. **Number Awarded:** 1. **To Apply:** Nomination for this award is required. Only AMTA-Approved Program Faculty may nominate students. Nominated candidate must provide the following materials: completed scholarship application form, signed and dated; personal, community, and college activities; college transcript; letter of recommendation which must be submitted by author from a music therapy professor, a professional familiar with the applicants' clinical skills or another person of the applicants' choice; participation in AMTA conferences, AMTA committees, presentations, and publications; a maximum of 800 words essay on long-term professional goals; a 400 words essay on how AMTA can impact the profession of music therapy. Any narrative must be double-spaced, 1-inch margins and in 12-point font. Narrative must be written for blind review, without specific reference to applicants' name or place of employment. **Deadline:** March 4.

1017 ■ Christine K. Stevens Development Scholarships *(Undergraduate, Graduate/Scholarship)*

Purpose: To support music therapy students in their efforts to expand their training in the use of percussion-based

Awards are arranged alphabetically below their administering organizations

strategies through continuing education opportunities with the research-based HealthRHYTHMS Group Empowerment Drumming program. **Focus:** Music therapy. **Qualif.:** Applicants must be undergraduate, undergraduate equivalency, or graduate students enrolled in a college or university program in music therapy approved by the American Music Therapy Association. All interns in clinical training are considered eligible through their parent academic institution. Applicants must be current student members of AMTA in the year in which they apply and the year in which the award is granted. **Criteria:** Selection will be based on the committee's criteria.

Funds Avail.: $599. **Number Awarded:** 2. **To Apply:** Nomination for this award is required. Only AMTA-Approved Program Faculty may nominate students. Nominated candidates must submit a maximum of one page narrative. Statement of need and potential professional development should be addressed within the narrative. **Deadline:** March 4.

1018 ■ Florence Tyson Grants to Study Music Psychotherapy (Professional development/Grant)

Purpose: To support professional music therapists in post-undergraduate training in music psychotherapy, music and psychotherapy, or psychotherapy. **Focus:** Music therapy. **Qualif.:** Applicants must be music therapists with a current credential of MT-BC or current professional designation of ACMT, CMT or RMT; must be professional members in good standing of AMTA. **Criteria:** Selection will be based on the committee's criteria.

Funds Avail.: No specific amount. **To Apply:** Applicants must submit a maximum of two pages application narrative describing how the study of music psychotherapy, music and psychotherapy, and/or psychotherapy is important to applicants' work as music therapists. Statement of need, potential professional development and client impact and strength/appropriateness of continuing education goals and opportunities should also be included. **Deadline:** June 24.

1019 ■ American Musicological Society (AMS)
6010 College Sta.
Brunswick, ME 04011-8451
Ph: (207)798-4243
Fax: (207)798-4254
Free: 877-679-7648
E-mail: ams@ams-net.org
URL: www.ams-net.org
Facebook: www.facebook.com/AMS.musicology
Twitter: twitter.com/AMS_musicology

1020 ■ Alvin H. Johnson AMS 50 Dissertation Fellowships (Doctorate/Fellowship)

Purpose: To provide financial assistance for full-time studies in musicology. **Focus:** Music. **Qualif.:** Applicants are those who are registered in good standing for a doctorate at a North American university and have completed all formal degree requirements except the dissertation at the time of full application. **Criteria:** Recipients will be selected on the basis of academic merit.

Funds Avail.: $21,000. **Duration:** Annual. **Number Awarded:** Up to 3. **To Apply:** Applicants should apply and submit applications online via the AMS website. Applicants are requested to upload the following information: a 150-word project description; a current dissertation prospectus of 12-15 pages (c. 3,000 to 4,000 words). The prospectus should include a detailed rationale of the project (supported by, but not limited to, an assessment of relevant secondary literature), an overview of each chapter, and a clear statement of progress to date, all written in prose; a sample chapter (preferably not an introductory chapter reviewing the literature); a curriculum vitae. Applicants should also arrange for a letter from the registrar or departmental Director of Graduate Studies attesting to ABD (all-but-dissertation) status. Send as an e-mail attachment to the contact provided. **Deadline:** December 15. **Contact:** a50-recomms@ams-net.org, or via AMS office fax (877-679-7648 or 207-798-4254).

1021 ■ Howard Mayer Brown Fellowship (Graduate/Fellowship)

Purpose: To increase the presence of minority scholars and teachers in musicology by providing financial aid. **Focus:** Music; Musicology. **Qualif.:** Applicants must be students who have completed at least one year of graduate work, intend to pursue a Ph.D. and are in good standing at their home institution. Applicant must show evidence of academic excellence and promise of continuing achievement in music scholarship. **Criteria:** Selection shall be based on the aforesaid qualifications and compliance with the application details.

Funds Avail.: $20,000. **Duration:** Annual. **Number Awarded:** Varies. **To Apply:** Applications may be made directly by the student, or the student may be nominated by a faculty member of the institution at which the student is enrolled or by a member of the Society at another institution. Supporting documents must include the following: a personal statement from the student (not to exceed five pages) summarizing applicants' musical and academic background and stating why they wished to pursue an advanced degree in musicology; a summary statement, not to exceed 250 words, outlining areas of research or specific topics presented in the personal statement; a curriculum vitae; samples of the applicants' work (typically not to exceed 30 pages total), such as term papers, thesis chapters, or any published material; letters of support from three faculty members, one of which may be the letter of nomination. Letters should address the applicants' general intellectual and musical ability and how these might contribute to a successful career in scholarship and teaching. One letter of support must include information about the students' expected funding (to the extent it can be predicted) for the given academic year. **Deadline:** December 15. **Contact:** Letters of recommendation should be sent as an e-mail attachment to: hmb-apps@ams-net.org, or AMS office fax (877-679-7648 or 207-798-4254). Inquiries should be sent to Prof. Charles Carson, chair of the committee, at ccarson@utexas.edu.

1022 ■ American National Red Cross
2025 East St. NW
Washington, DC 20006
Ph: (202)303-5214
Free: 800-733-2767
URL: www.redcross.org

1023 ■ Jane Delano Student Nurse Scholarships (Undergraduate, Graduate/Scholarship)

Purpose: To promote nursing as a career and the involvement of new nurses in the Red Cross. **Focus:** Nursing. **Qualif.:** Applicants must have served as Red Cross volunteers or employees within the past five (5) years; have

Awards are arranged alphabetically below their administering organizations

completed the equivalent of at least one year of college/university credits; be currently enrolled in an accredited United States nursing program; and, be currently enrolled as undergraduate or graduate students in good academic standing. **Criteria:** Selection will be based on Scholarship Selection Committee's criteria. Preference will be given to student nurse volunteers.

Funds Avail.: $3,000. **Duration:** Annual. **Number Awarded:** 2. **To Apply:** Applicants must submit the following: completed application form; application support documents including personal essay (attach to application), endorsement from the Red Cross Unit (attach form to application), and endorsement from Nursing School Dean (attach form to application). **Deadline:** May 11. **Contact:** Questions and application documents should be submitted via email to NationalAwards@redcross.org.

1024 ■ American Nephrology Nurses' Association (ANNA)
E Holly Ave.
Pitman, NJ 08071-0056
Ph: (856)256-2320
Fax: (856)589-7463
E-mail: anna@annanurse.org
URL: www.annanurse.org
Facebook: www.facebook.com/NephrologyNursing
Twitter: twitter.com/annanurses

1025 ■ American Nephrology Nurses' Association Evidence-Based Research Grants *(Other/Grant)*

Purpose: To encourage the discovery of new knowledge as well as the incorporation of the best scientific evidence currently available into the practice of nephrology nursing, with the ultimate goal of improving patient outcomes. **Focus:** Nephrology. **Qualif.:** Principal or co-principal investigators must be members of ANNA within the duration of the research project; must share equal responsibility with all other co-investigators for the conceptualization and implementation of the proposed research project; must provide an evidence of their experiences and credentials demonstrating the ability to complete the proposed EBP project and commitment to nephrology nursing; must have the option of contacting a member of the ANNA Research Committee to discuss ideas and use the assistance of the committee to connect them with appropriate mentors, if needed. **Criteria:** Funding will be based on established research, clinical practice priorities and availability of funds.

Funds Avail.: $5,000 each. **Duration:** Annual. **Number Awarded:** 3. **To Apply:** Proposal must demonstrate the following: significance and applicability of the EBP project to nephrology nursing or related therapies; for EBP research proposals, sound methodology in accordance with recognized nursing research guidelines; for other EBP, sound methodology and implementation strategies depending on the type of project; for EBP research projects, approval by the appropriate institutional review board; for other EBP projects, support from the institution where the project will be implemented; feasibility and likelihood of successful completion. Applicants must submit the following items in the order specified: cover letter; ANNA Evidence-based Practice Grant Application Checklist; cover sheet; Co-investigators/consultants/collaborators sheet; detailed budget and justification; abstract; research or project plan; timeline for the research/project completion; references; appendices; copy of IRB approval for research studies or letter of support for other projects; curriculum vitae; personal research articles if available; 8 x 10 professional headshot (black and white or color). Project proposals should be submitted by e-mail to the ANNA National Office. **Contact:** American Nephrology Nurses' Association, at the above address, or Email: to annascholarships@ajj.com.

1026 ■ American Nephrology Nurses' Association Research Grants *(Doctorate, Graduate/Grant)*

Purpose: To recognize an outstanding nephrology nurse researchers. **Focus:** Nephrology. **Qualif.:** The principal or co-principal investigators must be members of ANNA within the duration of the research project; must share equal responsibility with all other co-investigators for the conceptualization and implementation of the proposed research project; must provide an evidence of their commitment to nephrology nursing experiences and credentials; must be registered nurses who hold a master's or doctoral degree. The contributions of each of the team members must be identified and the application should describe how each investigator's role fits with their expertise and will facilitate completion of the research project. **Criteria:** Award funding will be based on established research priorities and availability of funds.

Funds Avail.: Up to $15,000. **Duration:** Annual. **Number Awarded:** 1. **To Apply:** Applicants must complete the entire grant application form according to the instructions. The proposal must demonstrate the following: applicability of investigation to nephrology, transplantation or related therapies; sound methodology in accordance with recognized nursing research guidelines; approval by the appropriate institutional review board; feasibility and likelihood of successful completion; a detailed budget for the proposed project should be outlined including costs that exceed the grant amount. While indirect costs may be included in the budget, ANNA does not fund indirect costs; a detailed timeline from the beginning to completion of the project must be included as well as list of specific dates and activities. Applicants must also include the following: a cover letter, indicating how the applicant(s) meet the criteria; a completed and signed cover sheet; a 250-word abstract; maximum of 12 pages, double-spaced research plan; references; appendices; budget sheet(s); and curriculum vitae of principal and all co-investigators, collaborators and consultants. **Deadline:** November 15. **Contact:** annascholarships@ajj.com.

1027 ■ ANNA Nephrology Nurse Researcher Awards *(Doctorate, Graduate/Award)*

Purpose: To recognize outstanding nephrology nurse researchers. **Focus:** Nephrology. **Qualif.:** Candidates must be full members of ANNA, have been members for a minimum of the last two years as of the award application deadline; actively involved in nephrology nursing related health care services; active participants in ANNA at the local, regional and national level; must preferably hold a master's or doctoral degree. **Criteria:** Selection will be based on the committee's criteria.

Funds Avail.: $1,000. **Duration:** Annual. **To Apply:** Nomination packet should include documentation of the following: a) nominee has conducted research which contributes towards advancement of nephrology nursing. The packet should include a list of research the nominee has completed with the following information: title of the research study; list of other researchers (if applicable); date of completion of the project or projected completion of the study; b) the nominee has shared his/her research findings, either through presentation at ANNA meeting or publication in appropriate journals. The nomination letter should provide the following: a list of presentations, including any co-presenters, with the title of the presentation, date, type of meeting and site of meeting; a list of publications in APA format, including other authors (if applicable), publication date, title of article, name of the journal, volume and issue and page numbers; c) additional comments that support the nominee as an outstanding nephrology nurse researcher. **Contact:** American Nephrology Nurses' Association, at the above address.

1028 ■ Barbara F. Prowant Nursing Research Grants *(Graduate/Grant)*

Purpose: To promote nursing research particularly in the area of nephrology. **Focus:** Nephrology. **Qualif.:** Principal investigators must be members of ANNA within the duration of the project; must be currently certified by the Nephrology Nursing Certification Commission; must be currently enrolled in a graduate program on the masters, doctorate or post-doctorate level; must provide evidences of their experiences and credentials demonstrating the ability to complete the proposed project and commitment to nephrology nursing; must have the option of contacting a member of the ANNA Research Committee to discuss ideas and use the assistance of the committee to connect them with appropriate mentors, if needed. **Criteria:** Funding will be based on scientific merit and availability of funds.

Funds Avail.: $5,000. **Duration:** Annual. **Number Awarded:** 1. **To Apply:** Proposal must demonstrate the following: significance and applicability of the project to nursing, education or related therapies; for research proposals, sound methodology in accordance with recognized nursing research guidelines; for other proposals, sound methodology and implementation strategies depending on the type of project; approval by the appropriate Institutional Review Board; support from institution where the project will be implemented; feasibility and likelihood of successful completion and support from faculty. Applicants must submit the following items in the order specified: cover letter; ANNA Evidence-based Practice Grant Application Checklist; cover sheet; Co-investigators/consultants/collaborators sheet; detailed budget and justification; abstract; research or project plan; timeline for research/project completion; references; appendices; copy of IRB approval for research studies or letter of support for other projects; curriculum vitae; personal research articles if available; 8 x 10 professional headshot (black and white or color). Project proposals should be submitted by e-mail to the ANNA National Office. **Deadline:** November 15. **Contact:** American Nephrology Nurses' Association, at the above address, or Email: to annascholarships@ajj.com.

1029 ■ American Neurotology Society (ANS)
c/o Kristen Bordignon, Administrator
4960 Dover St. NE
Saint Petersburg, FL 33703
Ph: (217)638-0801
Fax: (217)679-1677
E-mail: administrator@americanneurotologysociety.com
URL: www.americanneurotologysociety.com

1030 ■ ANS Research Grants *(Professional development/Grant)*

Purpose: To encourage and support academic research in sciences related to the investigation of otology and neurotology. **Focus:** Hearing and deafness; Otolaryngology; Otology. **Qualif.:** Applicants must be physician investigators in the United States and Canada. **Criteria:** Selection will be on a competitive basis.

Funds Avail.: $25,000 per year. **To Apply:** Applicants must submit, first, their letters of intent one month prior to deadline for the applications. Letters must state the grant mechanism for the proposal, the principal investigator and institution(s) for the work, provide a working title, and contain an abstract of no more than 500 words to summarize the proposal sufficiently in order to identify appropriate reviewers. To the extent possible, the abstract should note specific methods to be used so as to facilitate the selection of reviewers. Other information on the application process can be obtained at the website. Please take note that grant applications should be sent electronically only. **Deadline:** December 31 (letter of intent); January 31 (completed applications). **Contact:** John S. Oghalai, M.D., ANS Research Committee Chair, at joghalai@stanford.edu; and Kristen Bordignon, ANS Research Fund Administrator, at administrator@americanneurotologysociety.com.

1031 ■ American Nuclear Society (ANS)
555 N Kensington Ave.
La Grange Park, IL 60526
Ph: (708)352-6611
Fax: (708)352-0499
Free: 800-323-3044
E-mail: nuclear@ans.org
URL: www.ans.org
Facebook: www.facebook.com/www.ans.org
Twitter: twitter.com/ans_org

1032 ■ American Nuclear Society Incoming Freshman Scholarships *(Undergraduate/Scholarship)*

Purpose: To assist students who wish to complete their post-secondary education and prepare for careers in nuclear science and technology (NS&T). **Focus:** Engineering, Nuclear. **Qualif.:** Applicants must be graduating high school seniors who have the intention to pursue a degree in nuclear engineering. **Criteria:** Applicants are evaluated based on high school academic achievement; freshman college courses enrolled in; quality and content of 500-word essay; letters of recommendation by counselors and/or teachers; and other information.

Funds Avail.: $1,000. **Duration:** Annual. **Number Awarded:** 4. **To Apply:** Applicants must submit all the required application information. **Deadline:** April 1. **Contact:** Scholarship Coordinator; Phone: 800-323-3044; Fax: 708-579-8238.

1033 ■ American Nuclear Society Undergraduates Scholarships *(Undergraduate/Scholarship)*

Purpose: To help students complete their post-secondary education and prepare for careers in nuclear science and technology (NS&T). **Focus:** Engineering, Nuclear; Nuclear science. **Qualif.:** Applicants must be students who have completed at least one year in a course of study leading to a degree in nuclear science, nuclear engineering or a nuclear-related field. **Criteria:** Recipients are selected based on merit and financial need.

Funds Avail.: No specific amount. **Duration:** Annual. **To Apply:** Applicants must submit all the required application information.

1034 ■ Everitt P. Blizard Scholarships *(Graduate/Scholarship)*

Purpose: To support full-time graduate students in a program leading to an advanced degree in nuclear science, nuclear engineering, or a nuclear-related field. **Focus:** Nuclear science. **Qualif.:** Applicants must be students pursuing graduate studies in the field of radiation protection and shielding. **Criteria:** Selection will be based on the committee's criteria.

Funds Avail.: $3,000. **To Apply:** Interested applicants must visit the website to obtain an application form. Scholarship application, official transcripts, letter of sponsorship and three confidential reference forms must all be mailed together as a complete packet to ANS Headquarters, to the attention of the Scholarship Coordinator. **Deadline:** February 1.

1035 ■ Decommissioning, Decontamination and Reutilization Scholarships *(Graduate, Master's/Scholarship)*

Purpose: To support students who are pursuing higher education. **Focus:** Engineering; Science. **Qualif.:** Applicants must be students pursuing master's degrees in engineering or science with an emphasis on: decommissioning/decontamination; management/characterization of radioactive waste; restoration of the environment; nuclear engineering. **Criteria:** Selection will be based on the committee's criteria.

Funds Avail.: No specific amount. **Duration:** Annual. **To Apply:** Interested applicants must visit the website to obtain an application form. Scholarship application, official transcripts, letter of sponsorship and three confidential reference forms must all be mailed together as a complete packet to ANS Headquarters, to the attention of the Scholarship Coordinator. Applicants must also submit a description of long-term and short-term professional objectives. **Deadline:** February 1.

1036 ■ Allan F. Henry/Paul A. Greebler Scholarships *(Graduate/Scholarship)*

Purpose: To support full-time graduate students in a program leading to an advanced degree in nuclear science, nuclear engineering, or a nuclear-related field. **Focus:** Nuclear science. **Qualif.:** Applicants must be full-time graduate students of a North American university engaged in Masters or PhD research in the area of nuclear reactor physics or radiation transport. **Criteria:** Selection will be based on the committee's criteria.

Funds Avail.: $3,500. **Duration:** Annual. **To Apply:** Interested applicants must visit the website to obtain an application form. Scholarship application, official transcripts, letter of sponsorship and three confidential reference forms must all be mailed together as a complete packet to ANS Headquarters, to the attention of the Scholarship Coordinator. **Deadline:** February 1.

1037 ■ Saul Levine Memorial Scholarships *(Graduate/Scholarship)*

Purpose: To support full-time graduate students in a program leading to an advanced degree in nuclear science, nuclear engineering, or a nuclear-related field. **Focus:** Nuclear science. **Qualif.:** Applicants must be students of graduate education of meritorious nuclear engineering. **Criteria:** Selection will be based on the committee's criteria.

Funds Avail.: $3,000. **Duration:** Annual. **To Apply:** Interested applicants must visit the website to obtain an application form. Scholarship application, official transcripts, letter of sponsorship and three confidential reference forms must all be mailed together as a complete packet to ANS Headquarters, to the attention of the Scholarship Coordinator. **Deadline:** February 1.

1038 ■ Nuclear Criticality Safety Pioneers Scholarships *(Graduate/Scholarship)*

Purpose: To support full-time graduate students in a program leading to an advanced degree in nuclear science, nuclear engineering, or a nuclear-related field. **Focus:** Nuclear science. **Qualif.:** Applicants must be graduate students majoring in nuclear science/engineering, with the desired emphasis on areas supporting nuclear criticality safety. **Criteria:** Selection will be based on the following criteria: contributions to American Nuclear Society; financial need; professional accomplishments and career objectives; academic performance.

Funds Avail.: $3,000. **Duration:** Annual. **To Apply:** Interested applicants must visit the website to obtain an application form. Scholarship application, official transcripts, letter of sponsorship and three confidential reference forms must all be mailed together as a complete packet to ANS Headquarters, to the attention of the Scholarship Coordinator. **Deadline:** February 1.

1039 ■ James F. Schumar Scholarships *(Graduate/Fellowship)*

Purpose: To support full-time graduate students in a program leading to an advanced degree in nuclear science, nuclear engineering, or a nuclear-related field. **Focus:** Nuclear science. **Qualif.:** Applicants must be students pursuing graduate studies in material science and technology for nuclear applications. **Criteria:** Selection will be based on the committee's criteria.

Funds Avail.: $3,000. **Duration:** Annual. **To Apply:** Interested applicants must visit the website to obtain an application form. Scholarship application, official transcripts, letter of sponsorship and three confidential reference forms must all be mailed together as a complete packet to ANS Headquarters, to the attention of the Scholarship Coordinator. **Deadline:** February 1.

1040 ■ Glenn T. Seaborg Congressional Science and Engineering Fellowships *(Professional development/Fellowship)*

Purpose: To promote a better understanding of public policy procedures. **Focus:** Nuclear science. **Qualif.:** Applicants must be US citizens; must be ANS members for at least two years; must fulfill a PhD in a nuclear-related discipline and at least one year of experience in a nuclear field; must fulfill a PhD in another science or engineering discipline and at least two years experience in a nuclear field; must fulfill an MS in engineering with at least three years post-degree experience in a nuclear field. **Criteria:** Selection will be based on the following criteria: competence in nuclear science and technology; demonstrated ability to participate in public policy discussions; a demonstrated ability in written and oral communications; contributions to ANS.

Funds Avail.: $60,000. **Duration:** Annual. **To Apply:** Applicants must submit the following information in a word, PDF, or other compatible format: applicants' name; mailing address; maximum two pages academic and professional summary; maximum two-page statement explaining the reasons for applying, what they hope to accomplish and how the fellowship will benefit them and their employer; one or two letters of reference. **Deadline:** April 1.

1041 ■ American Nurses Foundation (ANF)
8515 Georgia Ave., Ste. 400
Silver Spring, MD 20910-3492

Awards are arranged alphabetically below their administering organizations

Ph: (301)628-5227
Fax: (301)628-5354
E-mail: anf@ana.org
URL: www.anfonline.org
Facebook: www.facebook.com/AmericanNursesAssociation
Twitter: twitter.com/ananursingworld

1042 ■ ANF/ANN-FNRE Nursing Research Grants
(Professional development/Grant)

Purpose: To support scientific research for advancing the practice of nursing, promoting health and preventing disease. **Focus:** Nursing, Neonatal. **Qualif.:** Applicants must be principal investigators who are licensed registered nurses and obtained at least one degree, either a baccalaureate degree or higher, in nursing. **Criteria:** Selection will be based on the applicants' proposals. Proposals are judged on scientific merit with critique based on the following criteria, which should be explicitly addressed in the proposal: significance; approach; innovation; environment; strength of investigators and research teams; attention to human subjects protection or other protections (animals); and justified budget. Preference will be given to applicants who are members of the Academy of Neonatal Nursing. If there are no member applications, or no high-quality proposals from members, non-member applicants will be considered, with the selected grantee required to become a member of ANN in order to receive funding.

Funds Avail.: $5,000. **To Apply:** Applicants may visit the website for the online application information. A nonrefundable application fee of $100.00 is required. **Deadline:** May 1. **Remarks:** The grants are made possible by the ANF, in partnership with the Academy of Neonatal Nursing and the Foundation for Neonatal Research and Education. **Contact:** For more information, contact Gisele Marshall at 301-628-5227 or email at gisele.marshall@ana.org.

1043 ■ ANF/ENRS Nursing Research Grants *(Professional development/Grant)*

Purpose: To support scientific research for advancing the practice of nursing, promoting health and preventing disease. **Focus:** Nursing. **Qualif.:** Applicants must be principal investigators who are licensed registered nurses and obtained at least one degree, either a baccalaureate degree or higher, in nursing. **Criteria:** Selection will be based on the Foundation's criteria. Preference will be given to applicants who are members of the ENRS. If there are no member applications, or no high-quality proposal from association members, non-member applicants will be considered, with the selected grantee required to become a member of ENRS in order to receive funding.

Funds Avail.: $5,000. **To Apply:** Applicants may visit the website for the online application information. A nonrefundable application fee of $100.00 is required. **Deadline:** May 1. **Remarks:** The grants are made possible by the ANF, in partnership with the Eastern Nursing Research Society. **Contact:** For more information, contact Gisele Marshall at 301-628-5227 or email at gisele.marshall@ana.org.

1044 ■ ANF/STTI Nursing Research Grants
(Master's, Doctorate/Grant)

Purpose: To support scientific research for advancing the practice of nursing, promoting health and preventing disease. **Focus:** Nursing. **Qualif.:** Applicants must be U.S. citizens and clinical nursing researchers who obtained either master's or doctorate degree, or enrolled in a doctoral program. **Criteria:** Selection will be based on the Foundation's criteria.

Funds Avail.: $7,500. **To Apply:** Applicants may visit the website for the online application information. A nonrefundable application fee of $100.00 is required. **Deadline:** May 1. **Remarks:** The grants are made possible by the ANF, in partnership with the Sigma Theta Tau International. **Contact:** For more information, contact Gisele Marshall at 301-628-5227 or email at gisele.marshall@ana.org.

1045 ■ American Occupational Therapy Foundation (AOTF)
4720 Montgomery Ln., Ste. 202
Bethesda, MD 20814-3449
Ph: (240)292-1079
Fax: (240)396-6188
E-mail: aotf@aotf.org
URL: www.aotf.org

1046 ■ Kappa Delta Phi Scholarship Program
(Postgraduate/Scholarship)

Purpose: To support students enrolled in a occupational therapy assistant programs. **Focus:** Occupational therapy. **Qualif.:** Applicant must be a member of the AOTF; must demonstrate a need for financial assistance; sustained a record of outstanding scholastic achievement. Postbaccalaureate applicant must be enrolled as a full-time student at the professional level in an accredited or developing occupational therapy educational program. **Criteria:** Recipients are selected based on the application and the materials submitted. Priority will be given to the residents of AZ, CA, FL, IA, IN, KY, MO, OH.

Funds Avail.: $2,000. **Duration:** Annual. **To Apply:** Applicants must complete the online application, (please visit AOTF website); must prepare two personal references; curriculum Director's statement; official transcripts; financial statement; and an essay.

1047 ■ Mary Minglen Scholarship Program
(Postgraduate/Scholarship)

Purpose: To support students enrolled in a occupational therapy assistant programs. **Focus:** Occupational therapy. **Qualif.:** Applicant must be a member of the AOTF; must demonstrate a need for financial assistance; sustained a record of outstanding scholastic achievement. Postbaccalaureate applicants must be enrolled as full-time students at the professional level in an accredited or developing occupational therapy educational program. **Criteria:** Recipients are selected based on the application and the materials submitted.

Funds Avail.: $1,200. **Duration:** Annual. **To Apply:** Applicants must complete the online application, (please visit AOTF website); must prepare two personal references; curriculum Director's statement; official transcripts; financial statement; and an essay. **Deadline:** October 30 for application; December 9 for references and program director statements.

1048 ■ NorthCoast Medical Scholarship Program
(Postgraduate/Scholarship)

Purpose: To support students enrolled in a occupational therapy assistant programs. **Focus:** Occupational therapy. **Qualif.:** Applicant must be a member of the AOTF; must demonstrate a need for financial assistance; sustain a record of outstanding scholastic achievement. Post-baccalaureate applicants must be enrolled as full-time students at the professional level in an accredited or developing occupational therapy educational program. **Criteria:** Recipients are selected based on the application and the materials submitted.

Funds Avail.: $5,000. **Duration:** Annual. **To Apply:** Applicants must complete the online application, (please visit AOTF website); must prepare two personal references; curriculum Director's statement; official transcripts; financial statement; and an essay.

1049 ■ Frank Oppenheimer Scholarship Program (Postgraduate/Scholarship)

Purpose: To support students enrolled in a occupational therapy assistant programs. **Focus:** Occupational therapy. **Qualif.:** Applicant must be a member of the AOTF; must demonstrate a need for financial assistance; sustained a record of outstanding scholastic achievement. Post-baccalaureate applicant must be enrolled as a full-time student at the professional level in an accredited or developing occupational therapy educational program. **Criteria:** Recipients are selected based on the application and the materials submitted.

Funds Avail.: $750. **Duration:** Annual. **To Apply:** Applicants must complete the online application, (please visit AOTF website); must prepare two personal references; curriculum Director's statement; official transcripts; financial statement; and an essay.

1050 ■ Edith Weingarten Scholarship Program (Postgraduate/Scholarship)

Purpose: To support students enrolled in a occupational therapy assistant programs. **Focus:** Occupational therapy. **Qualif.:** Applicant must be a member of the AOTF; must demonstrate a need for financial assistance; sustained a record of outstanding scholastic achievement. Post-baccalaureate applicant must be enrolled as a full-time student at the professional level in an accredited or developing occupational therapy educational program. **Criteria:** Recipients are selected based on the application and the materials submitted.

Funds Avail.: $1,000. **Duration:** Annual. **To Apply:** Applicants must complete the online application, (please visit AOTF website); must prepare two personal references; curriculum Director's statement; official transcripts; financial statement; and an essay.

1051 ■ Willard & Spackman Scholarship Program (Postgraduate/Scholarship)

Purpose: To support students enrolled in a occupational therapy assistant programs. **Focus:** Occupational therapy. **Qualif.:** Applicant must be a member of the AOTF; must demonstrate a need for financial assistance; sustained a record of outstanding scholastic achievement. Post-baccalaureate applicant must be enrolled as a full-time student at the professional level in an accredited or developing occupational therapy educational program. **Criteria:** Recipients are selected based on the application and the materials submitted.

Funds Avail.: $2,000 each. **Duration:** Annual. **Number Awarded:** 2. **To Apply:** Applicants must complete the online application, (please visit AOTF website); must prepare two personal references; curriculum Director's statement; official transcripts; financial statement; and an essay.

1052 ■ American Orff-Schulwerk Association (AOSA)
147 Bell St., Ste. 300
Chagrin Falls, OH 44022
Ph: (440)600-7329
Fax: (440)600-7332
URL: aosa.org
Facebook: www.facebook.com/groups/146906471237
Twitter: twitter.com/AOSA1968

1053 ■ AOSA Research Grants (Undergraduate/Grant)

Purpose: To promote philosophy and encourage research in varied applications of Orff Schulwerk. **Focus:** Education, Music; Music. **Qualif.:** Applicants must be active and expert AOSA members. **Criteria:** Applicants are evaluated based on merit.

Funds Avail.: No specific amount. **Duration:** Annual. **To Apply:** Applicants must submit a completed application form, a resume reflecting knowledge of or expertise in Orff Schulwerk, a letter of reference and a project proposal. Abstract should be maximum of 250 words. Requirements must be submitted to the AOSA Research Chair. **Deadline:** January 25.

1054 ■ AOSA Research Partnership Grants (Professional development/Grant)

Purpose: To support joint research related to Orff Schulwerk by music teachers and experienced researchers. **Focus:** Music. **Qualif.:** Applicants must be groups consisting of one practicing music teacher (must be a member of the AOSA) of grades PK-12 in a school setting and one faculty member with substantial research experience at a college or university. **Criteria:** Applicants are selected based on the panel's review of the application materials.

Funds Avail.: $500-$8,000. **Duration:** Annual. **To Apply:** Applicants must submit a completed application form; resume; letter of reference; and a proposal indicating the purpose, procedure, budget summary and timeline of the project. **Deadline:** January 25 and July 25.

1055 ■ Barbara Potter Scholarships (Professional development/Scholarship)

Purpose: To provide financial assistance for members of AOSA who wish to study at the Orff Institute in Salzburg, Austria. **Focus:** Music. **Qualif.:** Applicant must be a U.S. citizen or a resident of the United States for the past five years; must be an AOSA member; must be planning to study at the Orff Institute in Salzburg, Austria; must have completed Level III Orff Schulwerk Training; must demonstrate personal need of financial aid. **Criteria:** Applicants are selected based on the jury's review of application materials.

Funds Avail.: No specific amount. **Duration:** Biennial; in even-numbered years. **Number Awarded:** Varies. **To Apply:** Applicants must submit a completed application and agreement form; one-page resume; one-to-two pages project description and three reference letters. **Deadline:** January 15.

1056 ■ Shields-Gillespie Scholarships (Other/Scholarship)

Purpose: To support special creative projects that are associated with Orff Schulwerk and that will benefit the music education of children. **Focus:** Music. **Qualif.:** Applicant

Awards are arranged alphabetically below their administering organizations

must be a U.S. citizen or must have resided in the United States for the past five years; a current member of AOSA and must have been an AOSA member in good standing for one year; must be actively involved in teaching low-income preschool or kindergarten students; must have a strong motivation to study music; and demonstrated financial need. **Criteria:** Applicants are selected based on the jury's review of application materials.

Funds Avail.: No specific amount. **Duration:** Annual. **Number Awarded:** Varies. **To Apply:** Applicants must submit two copies of completed application and agreement form; one-page resume; one-to-two pages project description and three reference letters. If the application is for professional development, applicants must submit a financial statement and copies of two most recent income tax returns. **Deadline:** January 15.

1057 ■ American Oriental Society (AOS)
Hatcher Graduate Library
University of Michigan
Ann Arbor, MI 48109-1190
Ph: (734)764-7555
Fax: (734)647-4760
URL: www.umich.edu/~aos

1058 ■ Louise Wallace Hackney Fellowships for the Study of Chinese Art (Doctorate, Postdoctorate/Fellowship)

Purpose: To permit the study of Chinese art, with special relation to painting and its reflection of Chinese culture, **Focus:** Chinese studies. **Qualif.:** Applicants must have completed three years study of the Chinese language or its equivalent and must be able to demonstrate that they have already committed themselves to the serious study of this important area of oriental art; must be post-doctoral as well as doctoral students. **Criteria:** Applicants are selected by the two committees of specialists in the field.

Funds Avail.: $8,000. **Duration:** 12 months. **To Apply:** Applicants should submit the following materials in duplicate: (1) transcript of their undergraduate and graduate course work; (2) statement of personal finances; (3) three or four-page summary of the proposed project to be undertaken during the year of the fellowship award, appended with a financial statement explaining the expense involved in this study; (4) no less than three letters of recommendation. **Contact:** Jonathan Rodgers, jrodgers@umich.edu.

1059 ■ American Orthopedic Foot and Ankle Society (AOFAS)
9400 W Higgins Rd., Ste. 220
Rosemont, IL 60018-3315
Ph: (847)698-4654
Fax: (847)692-3315
Free: 800-235-4855
E-mail: aofasinfo@aofas.org
URL: www.aofas.org/Pages/Home.aspx
Facebook: www.facebook.com/aofas1
LinkedIn: www.linkedin.com/company/american-orthopaedic-foot-&-ankle-society
Twitter: twitter.com/aofas

1060 ■ AOFAS Research Grants Program (Graduate/Grant)

Purpose: To assist members and other orthopedists in providing the highest quality foot and ankle care to the public. **Focus:** Medicine, Orthopedic. **Qualif.:** Eligibility for grant funding is a benefit of membership in AOFAS, and the principle or co-principle project investigator must be an AOFAS active, candidate or international member. **Criteria:** Applications are reviewed and scored by the AOFAS Research Committee and its ad hoc reviewers on a blind basis using an NIH-style process. The committee makes recommendations to the AOFAS Board, which makes the final decision on funding.

Funds Avail.: $20,000. **Duration:** One year. **To Apply:** The grant application form and administrative policies and procedures are available online. **Deadline:** December 1. **Contact:** For additional questions, applicants must contact the AOFAS office at aofasinfo@aofas.org or call 847-698-4654.

1061 ■ Orthopaedic Foot and Ankle Fellowships (Graduate, Professional development/Fellowship)

Purpose: To assist members and other orthopedists in providing the highest quality foot and ankle care to the public. **Focus:** Medicine, Orthopedic. **Qualif.:** Applicants must be orthopedic surgeons and/or graduates from an allopathic or osteopathic medical school where in fellowship is dependent upon successful completion of an approved orthopaedic surgery residency program. **Criteria:** Recipients will be selected based on a consensus by foot and ankle fellowship directors.

Funds Avail.: No specific amount. **Duration:** Annual. **Number Awarded:** Varies. **To Apply:** Applicants may download an fellowship application form online. Upon completion of the requirements, the applicants must submit their application together with program application list, curriculum vitae, personal vitae, personal statement, four letters of reference directly from the referrer, and check list of programs. **Contact:** AOFAS Executive Office: Phone: 800-235-4855; or 847-698-4654; Email: aofasinfo@aofas.org.

1062 ■ American Osteopathic Foundation (AOF)
142 E Ontario St., Ste. 1450
Chicago, IL 60611
Ph: (312)202-8234
Fax: (312)202-8216
Free: 866-455-9383
E-mail: info@aof.org
URL: aof.org
Facebook: www.facebook.com/AmericanOsteopathicFoundation
Twitter: twitter.com/AOFDOgood

1063 ■ William G. Anderson, DO, Minority Scholarships (Undergraduate/Scholarship)

Purpose: To support and recognize an outstanding minority osteopathic medical student who is committed to osteopathic principals and practice, has excelled academically, and has proven to be a leader in addressing the educational, societal, and health needs of minorities. **Focus:** Medicine, Osteopathic. **Qualif.:** Applicants must be minority osteopathic medical students who have successfully completed their first-year of studies prior to the fall of the current year and will still be enrolled as osteopathic medical students during the same time. All applicants must be in good academic standing at an AOA accredited college of osteopathic medicine. **Criteria:** Applicants shall meet the following criteria: strong interest in osteopathic medicine, its philosophy and principles; excellent academic achievement; demonstrated leadership efforts in address-

Awards are arranged alphabetically below their administering organizations

ing the educational, societal, and health needs of minorities; demonstrated leadership efforts to eliminate inequities in medical education and health care; noteworthy accomplishments, awards and honors, clerkship or special projects, and extracurricular activities in which they have shown leadership abilities. Financial need can be considered but not the determinative factor in the selection. **Funds Avail.:** $7,500. **Duration:** Annual. **Number Awarded:** 1. **To Apply:** Applicants should submit the following requirements: completed application form; letters of recommendation/support from two references; letter from the Dean or dean's designee as an official document certifying that applicants are in good academic standing or confirming the students class ranking/academic standing; current Resume or Curriculum Vitae; and, official medical school academic transcript which may be mailed separately. **Remarks:** Established in 1998.

1064 ■ McCaughan Heritage Scholarships
(Undergraduate/Scholarship)

Purpose: To provide monetary scholarship to help defer the cost of students' osteopathic medical education. **Focus:** Medicine, Osteopathic. **Qualif.:** Applicants must be osteopathic medical students who are in their last year of studies; must be committed to the science, art and philosophy of osteopathic medicine; must be enrolled in an AOA approved college/school of osteopathic medicine. **Criteria:** Selection will be based on the following criteria: demonstrated commitment to the osteopathic profession, medicine and education; promotes osteopathic ideas and unity within the osteopathic community; participation in extracurricular activities that promote osteopathic medicine to the public; demonstrates, by word and deed, the desire to advance osteopathic medicine; presents a positive image and attitude about the osteopathic profession; exhibits a unique combination of character, moral, academic and ethical behavior. **Funds Avail.:** $5,000. **Number Awarded:** 1. **To Apply:** Applicants must submit the following in one packet: completed application form; letters of recommendation from 3 references; letter from Dean certifying that the applicants is in good academic standing and states the applicants' class ranking; personal statement from the applicant of not more than 2 pages; official medical school academic transcript; curriculum vitae or resume. **Contact:** Vicki Heck, Association Dir. of Communications; vheck@aof-foundation.org or at 312-202-8232.

1065 ■ Welch Scholars Grants *(Undergraduate/Grant)*

Purpose: To provide monetary aid to students in need at each college of osteopathic medicine. **Focus:** Medicine, Osteopathic. **Qualif.:** Applicants must be osteopathic medical students who have successfully completed their first-year of studies prior to the fall of the current year and will still be enrolled as osteopathic medical students during the same time. All applicants must be in good academic standing at an AOA accredited college of osteopathic medicine. **Criteria:** Recipients are chosen because of their outstanding academic achievement, participation in extracurricular activities, strong commitment toward osteopathic medicine and financial need. **Funds Avail.:** $2,000. **Duration:** Annual. **Number Awarded:** 1. **To Apply:** Applicants should submit the following requirements: completed application form; letters of recommendation/support from one reference; letter from the Dean or dean's designee as an official document certifying that applicants are in good academic standing or confirming the students class ranking/academic standing; letter from the Director of Financial Aid verifying discussing why the recipient was selected; personal statement; and official medical school academic transcript. **Remarks:** Established in 2001.

1066 ■ American Otological Society (AOS)
c/o Kristen Bordignon, Administrator
4960 Dover St. NE
Saint Petersburg, FL 33703
Ph: (217)638-0801
Fax: (727)800-9428
E-mail: administrator@americanotologicalsociety.org
URL: www.americanotologicalsociety.org

1067 ■ AOS Research Training Fellowships
(Graduate/Fellowship)

Purpose: To further the study on otosclerosis, Meniere's disease, and related ear disorders. **Focus:** Meniere's disease; Otology; Otosclerosis. **Qualif.:** Applicant must be a physician (resident or medical student). **Criteria:** Selection is based on the application materials and documents submitted. **Funds Avail.:** $35,000 for stipend, $5,000 for supplies. **Duration:** 1-2 years. **To Apply:** Applicants must submit a completed scholarship application together with the required materials. Applications must be accompanied by a documentation from the sponsor and institution that facilities and faculty are appropriate for the research training requested. **Deadline:** January 31. **Contact:** John P. Carey, M.D., Executive Secretary, Research Fund of the American Otological Society, Inc. Johns Hopkins University, School of Medicine, Department of Otolaryngology-Head & Neck Surgery 601 N. Caroline Street, JHOC 6255 Baltimore, MD 21287-0910, Tel: 352-751-0932, or E-mail: jcarey@jhmi.edu.

1068 ■ American Paint Horse Foundation (APHA)
2800 Meacham Blvd.
Fort Worth, TX 76161-0023
Ph: (817)834-2742
Fax: (817)834-3152
E-mail: aphaonline@apha.com
URL: apha.com/foundation

1069 ■ APHF Academic Scholarships
(Undergraduate/Scholarship)

Purpose: To support and encourage hard-working young horsemen and women who are striving every day to be the best both in the horse show arena and in their academic pursuits. **Focus:** General studies/Field of study not specified. **Qualif.:** Applicants must be members of the AjPHA or APHA for the past three years and pass a college entrance examination. Once they have been granted a scholarship, they must maintain a "B"/3.0 or better grade-point average to be eligible for renewal. **Criteria:** Recipients will be selected based on a review of submitted requirements. **Funds Avail.:** $1,000 each. **Duration:** Annual; Up to 4 years. **Number Awarded:** 54. **To Apply:** Interested applicants must review application requirements on application form. APHF scholarship checklist are the following: filled out personal and family information; completely listed all scholastic information; 500-word essay on educational plans and goals; a photograph; a transcript covering grades

Awards are arranged alphabetically below their administering organizations

10–12 indicating the required cumulative 3.0 or higher GPA adjusted to a 4-point scale; official copy of SAT or ACT results if scores are not listed in transcript; listed all APHA- and horse-related activities; noted all extracurricular and community involvement; three letters of reference (each provided with a recommendation form); and, a college transcript if applicable. If they meet requirements, completely fill out application. Mail completed scholarship application to APHA at the mailing address located on the front cover of application by the deadline. **Deadline:** March 1. **Contact:** APHF Director Laura Jesberg at 817-222-6412 or e-mail ljesberg@apha.com.

1070 ■ American Parkinson Disease Association (APDA)

135 Parkinson Ave.
Staten Island, NY 10305
Ph: (718)981-8001
Fax: (718)981-4399
Free: 800-223-2732
E-mail: apda@apdaparkinson.org
URL: www.apdaparkinson.org
Facebook: www.facebook.com/APDA.INC
LinkedIn: www.linkedin.com/company/american-parkinson-disease-association
Twitter: twitter.com/apdaparkinsons

1071 ■ APDA Medical Students Summer Fellowships *(Graduate, Professional development/Fellowship)*

Purpose: To provide stipend to enable medical students performing supervised laboratory or clinical research designed to clarify our understanding of Parkinson's disease, its nature, manifestations, etiology or treatment. **Focus:** Medicine. **Qualif.:** Applicants must be full-time medical students in good academic standing in an approved American medical school. The proposed research project must be performed in an academic medical center or recognized research institute in the United States; and be sponsored by a full-time faculty member or established institute scientist. The project must be part of the sponsor's ongoing research which performed under the sponsor's direct supervision. **Criteria:** Preference will be given to those who meet the qualifications. The applications will be reviewed by the APDA Scientific Advisory Board and approved by the APDA Executive Committee.

Funds Avail.: $4,000. **Duration:** Annual; 3 months per year. **Number Awarded:** 1. **To Apply:** Applicants must provide three pages of proposed work which contains: title, location, sponsors, goals and objectives, investigative methods, data analysis methods, significance of anticipated findings, resources and description of the proposed project. Also, it should be discussing the background rationale including preliminary results of work completed by the sponsors. One original and two hard copies of application should be submitted electronically. Submission of electronic applications to Heather Gray. **Deadline:** January 31. **Contact:** APDA, at the above address.

1072 ■ APDA Postdoctoral Research Fellowships *(Other/Fellowship)*

Purpose: To support postdoctoral scientists whose research training holds promise into new insights of geriatric psychology, pathophysiology, etiology and treatment of Parkinson's disease. **Focus:** Medicine, Geriatric; Parkinson's disease. **Qualif.:** Applicants must have completed their MD, DO, PhD, MD/PhD, DO/PhD or clinical residency program within two (2) years of the onset of the proposed study and must perform the research project at an academic institution within the United States. **Criteria:** Preference will be given to those who meet the criteria.

Funds Avail.: Up to $35,000. **Duration:** Annual. **To Apply:** Applicants must submit (three pages) research proposal which includes: background rationale, research plan/methods and goals; a description of where the research will be done and the resources available; a letter of reference and support from the mentor; a list of all current and pending support; the applicant's NIH-Biosketch; One (1) original of the application must be submitted to the attention of Heather Gray, National Office.. **Deadline:** March 11. **Contact:** E-mail Heather Gray at hgray@apdaparkinson.org.

1073 ■ APDA Research Grants *(Other/Grant)*

Purpose: To provide financial support to junior investigators intending to pursue research in Parkinson's disease. **Focus:** Parkinson's disease. **Qualif.:** Applicants must be affiliated with and perform the research project at an academic institution within the United States who are also junior investigators pursuing research in Parkinson's disease. **Criteria:** Selection of recipients will be based on merit.

Funds Avail.: $50,000. **Duration:** Annual; Every September 1 to August 1. **To Apply:** Applicants must complete online application and submit the three pages proposal; NIH Bio-sketch and references. One (1) original of the complete application must be submitted to the attention of Heather Gray, National office. **Deadline:** March 11. **Contact:** E-mail Heather Gray at hgray@apdaparkinson.org.

1074 ■ Dr. George C. Cotzias Memorial Fellowship *(Other/Fellowship)*

Purpose: To assist promising young neurologist in establishing careers in research, teaching and patient service relevant to the problems, causes, prevention, diagnosis and treatment of Parkinson's disease and related neurological movement disorders. **Focus:** Neurology. **Qualif.:** Applicant must be a physician and a U.S. citizen or a permanent resident of the U.S. who or has completed, training in a clinical discipline concerned with disorders of the nervous system (i.e. medical neurology, child neurology, neurosurgery, neuropathology); should be an instructor or assistant professor and demonstrate a clear commitment for the future at his or her sponsoring institution; must be no more than 8 years beyond receipt of their MD or OD degree and should be sponsored by a non-profit institution in the U.S. or its territories. Applicant should be no more than 6 years beyond completion of their clinical training at the time of submission and must be sponsored by a non-profit institution in the U.S. or its territories. **Criteria:** Selection will be based on the aforesaid qualifications and compliance with the application process.

Funds Avail.: $55,000 salary plus $25,000 for research expenses. **Duration:** Annual. **To Apply:** Applicant must submit the following requirements: an abstract of the proposed study; a budget for each year; resources provided or to be provided by the sponsoring institution; other sources of funding, to include sponsoring agency, amount and award period (indicate how the other sponsored research complements or supplements the present proposal); two letters of recommendation (one from the applicant's institutional sponsor and one from an academic colleague with knowledge of the applicant's professional

Awards are arranged alphabetically below their administering organizations

performance). One (1) original of the complete application must be submitted to the attention of Heather Gray, National office. **Deadline:** March 11. **Contact:** E-mail Heather Gray at hgray@apdaparkinson.org.

1075 ■ American Pediatric Surgical Nurses Association (APSNA)
1 Parkview Plz., Ste. 800
Oakbrook Terrace, IL 60181
Ph: (605)376-4742
Free: 855-984-1609
E-mail: webadmin@apsna.org
URL: www.apsna.org
Facebook: www.facebook.com/American-Pediatric-Surgical-Nurses-Association-225918394132411
Twitter: twitter.com/APSNAnurse

1076 ■ American Pediatric Surgical Nurses Association Educational Grants *(Other/Grant)*
Purpose: To assist APSNA members to further their professional education. **Focus:** Medicine, Pediatric; Nursing; Surgery. **Qualif.:** Applicant must be an APSNA member in good standing for at least one year; a registered nurse or advanced practice nurse with two years experience in pediatric surgical nursing involved in pediatric surgery patient care, education or research. **Criteria:** Recipients will be selected by the Education Committees based on potential leadership.

Funds Avail.: No specific amount. **Duration:** Annual. **To Apply:** Applicant must submit a completed application form; a documentation of program, conference or educational needs which the scholarship will be used; description of the program course; a current curriculum vitae; a letter of recommendation from co-worker; a cover letter to the Director at Large stating the applicant's credentials, experience and involvement in the pediatric surgical nursing practices and standards; and an essay about the importance of the award. **Deadline:** February 28.

1077 ■ American Philosophical Society (APS)
104 S 5th St.
Philadelphia, PA 19106-3387
Ph: (215)440-3400
Fax: (215)440-3423
E-mail: orders@dianepublishing.net
URL: amphilsoc.org

1078 ■ American Philosophical Society Library Resident Research Fellowships *(Doctorate/Fellowship)*
Purpose: To support research in the Society's collections. **Focus:** Humanities; Science. **Qualif.:** Applicants must be US citizens or foreign nationals; must hold a PhD or its equivalent and have passed their preliminary examinations; degreed independent scholars. **Criteria:** Preference will be given to the candidates who live 75 or more miles from Philadelphia.

Funds Avail.: $3,000 per month. **Duration:** Up to 3 months. **To Apply:** Interested applicants must visit the website for the online application process. **Deadline:** March 1.

1079 ■ Daland Fellowships in Clinical Investigation *(Doctorate, Postgraduate/Fellowship)*
Purpose: To provide financial support for research in the several branches of clinical medicine, including internal medicine, neurology, pediatrics, psychiatry and surgery. **Focus:** Biological and clinical sciences; Medicine, Pediatric; Neurology; Psychiatry; Surgery. **Qualif.:** Candidates must be both U.S. citizens and foreign nationals; have MD or MD/PhD degree for fewer than eight years; do not have more than two years of post-doctoral training and research; expecting to perform the research at an institution in the United States. **Criteria:** Fellowship recipients will be selected on the basis of merits.

Funds Avail.: $40,000 for first year and $40,000 for second year. **Duration:** Annual. **To Apply:** Applicants must submit a completed application form and letter of support form. Maintain the application format, do not include additional page. Three references are required. **Deadline:** September 15. **Contact:** Linda Musumeci, Dir. of Grants and Fellowships; Email: lmusumeci@amphilsoc.org; Phone: 215-440-3429.

1080 ■ John Hope Franklin Dissertation Fellowships *(Doctorate/Fellowship)*
Purpose: To support an outstanding doctoral student at an American university or an exceptional American doctoral student abroad who is completing the dissertation. **Focus:** General studies/Field of study not specified. **Qualif.:** Applicants must have completed all course work and examinations preliminary to the dissertation; devote full-time for twelve months with no teaching obligations-to research on the dissertation. **Criteria:** Fellowship recipients will be selected on the basis of merit.

Funds Avail.: No specific amount. **Duration:** Annual. **To Apply:** Applicants must submit completed on-line application form and letter of support form; must maintain the (three-page) format and must not be in 11pt. font smaller. References are required, referees must follow the format (must not exceed one-page) and must be sent electronically. **Contact:** Linda Musumeci, Dir. of Grants and Fellowships; Email: lmusumeci@amphilsoc.org; Phone: 215-440-3429.

1081 ■ Franklin Research Grants *(Doctorate/Grant)*
Purpose: To support research in all areas of knowledge leading to publication. **Focus:** General studies/Field of study not specified. **Qualif.:** Applicants must have a doctorate or have published work of doctoral character and quality. Pre-doctoral graduate students are not eligible. **Criteria:** Recipients will be selected based on the jury's review of the application materials.

Funds Avail.: Up to maximum of $6,000. **Duration:** Annual. **To Apply:** Applicants must submit a completed application form and letter of support form available at the website; must maintain the 4-page format and must not be in 11 point font smaller. Two references are required, referees must follow the format (must not exceed one page) and must be sent in a sealed envelope with the proposal or sent electronically. **Contact:** Linda Musumeci, Dir. of Grants and Fellowships; Email: lmusumeci@amphilsoc.org; Phone: 215-440-3429.

1082 ■ Lewis and Clark Fund for Exploration and Field Research *(Graduate, Postdoctorate/Grant)*
Purpose: To provide funds for projects related to the astrobiological field. **Focus:** Biological and clinical sciences. **Qualif.:** Applicant must be a post-doctoral student and a U.S. resident performing research anywhere in the world. Foreign applicant must be based at a U.S. institution or planning to carry out research in the United States. **Criteria:** Grant recipient will be selected on the basis of merits.

Awards are arranged alphabetically below their administering organizations

Funds Avail.: Up to $5,000. **Duration:** Annual. **To Apply:** Applicant must submit a completed application form and letter of support form available at the website; must maintain the 4-page format and must have a font size greater than 11pt. Applicant must also submit two references. Referees must also follow the format (must not exceed one page) and send their letters of support electronically. **Deadline:** February 1. **Contact:** Linda Musumeci, Dir. of Grants and Fellowships; Email: lmusumeci@amphilsoc.org; Phone: 215-440-3429.

1083 ■ Phillips Fund Grants for Native American Research *(Doctorate, Master's/Grant)*

Purpose: To provide assistance such as travel expenses, tapes, films and consultants' fee. **Focus:** Native American studies. **Qualif.:** Applicant must be a graduate student for research on masters theses or doctoral dissertations. **Criteria:** Grant recipient will be selected on the basis of merits.

Funds Avail.: $2,500-$3,500. **Duration:** Annual. **To Apply:** Applicant must submit a completed on-line application form and letter of support form; must maintain the (3-page) format and must not be in 11pt. font smaller. Two references are required, referees must follow the format (must not exceed one page); a brief formal report; copies of any tape recordings; transcriptions; microfilms; and must be sent in a sealed envelope with the proposal or sent electronically. **Deadline:** March 1. **Contact:** Linda Musumeci, Dir. of Grants and Fellowships; Email: lmusumeci@amphilsoc.org; Phone: 215-440-3429.

1084 ■ American Physical Society (APS)
1 Physics Ellipse
College Park, MD 20740-3844
Ph: (301)209-3200
Fax: (301)209-0865
URL: www.aps.org
Facebook: www.facebook.com/apsphysics
Twitter: twitter.com/APSphysics

1085 ■ Andreas Acrivos Dissertation Award in Fluid Dynamics *(Graduate, Doctorate/Award)*

Purpose: To support exceptional young scientists who have performed original doctoral thesis work of outstanding scientific quality and achievement in the area of fluid dynamics. **Focus:** Physics. **Qualif.:** Candidates must be doctoral students studying at any colleges or universities in the United States or in any education abroad program of any colleges or universities in the United States; must have completed their dissertations during the previous calendar year at a university within the United States. **Criteria:** Selection of applicants/nominees for the award depends on the bestowing organization.

Funds Avail.: $1,000; $1,500 travel allowance to attend the annual meeting. **Duration:** Annual. **To Apply:** Nominator may contact the Society for the nomination process and other details. **Deadline:** May. **Remarks:** Established in 1998. **Contact:** American Physical Society, at the above address.

1086 ■ Award for Outstanding Doctoral Dissertation in Laser Science *(Doctorate/Award)*

Purpose: To promote doctoral research in the Laser Science area and to encourage effective written and oral presentation of research results. **Focus:** Physics. **Qualif.:** Applicants must be doctoral students at any university in the United States or abroad who have passed their dissertation defense for the Ph.D. any time during the three calendar years preceding the Laser Science Conference and who are members of DLS. **Criteria:** Applicants will be chosen by the Dissertation Award Selection Committee based on the quality of the research and the written presentation.

Funds Avail.: $1,000. **Duration:** Annual. **To Apply:** Applicants must submit an abstract for a regular contributed talk to the Frontiers in Optics/Laser Science conference and check the box to opt in to the DLS Dissertation Award competition. The following materials must be submitted as a single PDF file to the email provided by the Society as an email attachment: letter from the research advisor, letter from the department chair certifying the date of the defense, two letters seconding the application, and summary of the dissertation, not to exceed 1,500 words excluding figures and references. **Deadline:** June 1. **Remarks:** Established in 2013. **Contact:** American Physical Society, at the above address.

1087 ■ Award for Outstanding Doctoral Thesis Research in Biological Physics *(Doctorate/Award)*

Purpose: To recognize doctoral thesis research of outstanding quality and achievement in any area of experimental, computational, engineering, or theoretical Biological Physics, broadly construed, and to encourage effective written and oral presentation of research results. **Focus:** Physics. **Qualif.:** Candidates must be doctoral students at any universities in the United States or abroad who have passed their thesis defense for the Ph.D. in any areas of experimental, computational, engineering, or theoretical Biological Physics, broadly construed, any time from October 1st two years before the year in which the award is to be presented until September 30th in the year before the award is to be presented except for those whose thesis advisors serve on the current Selection Committee. **Criteria:** Selection will be based on the committee's criteria.

Funds Avail.: $1,500; $500 to $1,000 travel allowance. **Duration:** Annual. **To Apply:** Application/nomination package must consists of the following: letter from the thesis advisor citing the specific contributions of the nominee and the significance of those contributions; letter from the department chair and/or relevant program director certifying the date of the thesis defense; two letters seconding the nomination; manuscript prepared by the nominee describing the thesis research not exceed 1,500 words excluding figures and references; abstract suitable for publication in the Bulletin of the APS not exceed 1,300 characters, and the name of the thesis supervisor and the institution should be indicated in a footnote; full curriculum vitae including publication list. **Deadline:** First Monday in October. **Remarks:** Established in 2009. **Contact:** American Physical Society, at the above address.

1088 ■ M. Hildred Blewett Fellowships *(Postdoctorate/Fellowship)*

Purpose: To enable women to return to physics research careers after having had to interrupt those careers. **Focus:** Physics. **Qualif.:** Applicants must currently be citizens, legal residents, or resident aliens of the United States or Canada who have completed work toward a PhD. **Criteria:** Selection shall be based on the aforesaid qualifications and compliance with the application details.

Funds Avail.: Up to $45,000. **Duration:** Annual. **To Apply:** Application forms are available on the website. Completed application form and other supporting documents being

Awards are arranged alphabetically below their administering organizations

asked by the Society must be sent electronically. Also, applicants must provide written proof from a U.S. or Canadian institution that they will have institutional affiliation during the tenure of the grant. **Deadline:** June 1. **Remarks:** Established in 2005. **Contact:** APS: Phone: 301-209-3231; Email: blewett@aps.org.

1089 ■ Dissertation Award in Hadronic Physics
(Doctorate/Award)

Purpose: To support outstanding young scientists who have performed original research in the area of hadronic physics. **Focus:** Physics. **Qualif.:** Eligible candidates must have received a Ph.D. in experimental or theoretical hadronic physics from a college or university in the United States, or, if a Ph.D. student at a non-US institution, must have conducted a significant part of their Ph.D. research within the USA (have resided in the USA for at least one-half of the official duration of their Ph.D. research program) or have been a member of the APS for a period of at least two-thirds of their Ph.D. research program. The Ph.D. degree must have been awarded within a two-year period ending the day before nominations are due. **Criteria:** Selection will be based on the committee's criteria.

Funds Avail.: $1,000 and a travel allowance of up to $1,500 to attend the biennial meeting. **Duration:** Biennial. **To Apply:** Applicants for the awards must submit the following: letter of not more than 5,000 characters evaluating the qualifications of the nominee(s); biographical sketch; list of the most important publications; at least two, but not more than four, seconding letters; up to five reprints or preprints. Nominations should include the following: the name and address of the candidates; a statement of the candidates' contribution to the research; a letter of support from the candidates' PhD dissertation advisor; two additional letters of support from physicists familiar with the candidate and the research; a copy of the candidates' dissertation. **Remarks:** Established in 2011.

1090 ■ Richard L. Greene Dissertation Award
(Doctorate/Award)

Purpose: To promote doctoral thesis research of exceptional quality and importance in experimental condensed matter or experimental materials physics. **Focus:** Physics. **Qualif.:** Nominees must be doctoral students who produced doctoral dissertations about experimental condensed matter or experimental materials physics, written in English and submitted to any college or university, worldwide. **Criteria:** Preference will be given to qualified women, members of underrepresented minority groups, and scientists from outside the United States.

Funds Avail.: $2,500; $1,500 travel allowance. **Duration:** Annual. **To Apply:** Nomination packet consists of the following materials: PDF of the Ph.D. thesis written in English; letter from the thesis advisor explaining the rationale for the nomination; two letters of support with at least one being from another institution; contact information for the nominee. Nominations must be submitted using the online electronic submission form. Letters can be signed electronically or physically. **Deadline:** September 1. **Remarks:** Established in 2013. **Contact:** American Physical Society, at the above address.

1091 ■ Nicholas Metropolis Award for Outstanding Doctoral Thesis Work in Computational Physics
(Doctorate/Award)

Purpose: To promote doctoral thesis research of outstanding quality and achievement in computational physics and to encourage effective written and oral presentation of research results. **Focus:** Physics. **Qualif.:** Nominations will be accepted for doctoral students (present or past) in any country for work performed as part of the requirements for a doctoral degree. Nominees must have pass their thesis defense not more than 18 months before the nomination deadline. **Criteria:** Preference will be given to qualified women, members of underrepresented minority groups, and scientists from outside United States.

Funds Avail.: $1,500 and $1,000 travel allowance. **Duration:** Annual. **To Apply:** Nomination package should include: letter of nomination accompanied by the thesis manuscript, publications and/or reports describing the work, curriculum vitae and graduate course records; letter from the nominees' thesis advisor; three independent letters of reference, at least one of which should be from outside the nominee's institution. Submit electronically one unified .pdf file, or a .tar file containing everything in a single directory to the current committee chair. **Deadline:** July 1. **Contact:** James Belak; Email: belak@llnl.gov.

1092 ■ Outstanding Doctoral Thesis in Astrophysics
(Doctorate/Award)

Purpose: To promote doctoral thesis in research in Astrophysics, and to encourage effective written and oral presentation of research results. **Focus:** Physics. **Qualif.:** Nominees for the award must be doctoral students at any university in the United States or abroad who have passed their thesis defense for the Ph.D. any time during the two calendar years prior to the year of the April APS meeting where the award is made, and whose thesis topic is appropriate for DAP (i.e. dealing with topics that are typically presented in DAP sponsored or co-sponsored sessions at the April APS meeting), and who are members of the DAP are eligible for the award. Student may be finalists in the competition only once. **Criteria:** The finalists will be chosen by the Thesis Award Selection Committee based on the quality of the thesis research and the written presentation.

Funds Avail.: $1,000; $750 for travel allowance. **Duration:** Annual. **Number Awarded:** 4. **To Apply:** Nomination packet consists of the following materials: letter from the thesis advisor citing the specific contributions of the nominee and the significance of those contributions; two letters from DAP members seconding the nomination; letter from the department chair certifying the date of the thesis defense; manuscript prepared by the nominee describing the thesis research not exceeding 1,500 words (excluding references) and maximum of 6 figures; and abstract prepared by the nominee suitable for publication in the April APS meeting Bulletin. **Deadline:** August 1. **Remarks:** Established in 2013.

1093 ■ Marshall N. Rosenbluth Outstanding Doctoral Thesis Award *(Doctorate/Award)*

Purpose: To provide recognition to exceptional young scientists who have performed original thesis work of outstanding scientific quality and achievement in the area of plasma physics. **Focus:** Physics. **Qualif.:** Candidates must be doctoral students at any colleges or universities in the United States or United States students abroad who have successfully passed the final thesis defense within the preceding 24 months of the current nomination deadline. **Criteria:** Preference will be given to qualified women and members of underrepresented minority groups.

Funds Avail.: $2,000 and $500 travel allowance. **Duration:** Annual. **To Apply:** Nominators may contact the Society for the nomination process and other details. **Remarks:** Established in 1985.

Awards are arranged alphabetically below their administering organizations

1094 ■ Mitsuyoshi Tanaka Dissertation Award in Experimental Particle Physics *(Doctorate/Award)*

Purpose: To support exceptional young scientists who have performed original doctoral thesis work of outstanding scientific quality and achievement in the area of experimental particle physics. **Focus:** Physics. **Qualif.:** Nominations will be accepted for doctoral students studying at a college or university in North America including their study-abroad programs, for dissertation research carried out in the field of experimental particle physics. **Criteria:** Preference will be given to qualified women and members of under-represented minority groups.

Funds Avail.: $1,500 and $1,000 travel allowance. **Duration:** Annual. **To Apply:** Nominators may contact the Society for the nominations process and other details. **Deadline:** July 1. **Remarks:** Established in 1999. **Contact:** Jonathan Link; Email: jmlink@vt.edu.

1095 ■ American Physical Therapy Association (APTA)
1111 N Fairfax St.
Alexandria, VA 22314-1488
Ph: (703)684-2782
Fax: (703)684-7343
Free: 800-999-2782
E-mail: memberservices@apta.org
URL: www.apta.org
Facebook: www.facebook.com/APTAfans
Twitter: twitter.com/aptatweets

1096 ■ APTA Minority Scholarships - Faculty Development Scholarships *(Postdoctorate/Scholarship)*

Purpose: To provide doctoral education support for minority faculty members, to acknowledge and reward those who demonstrate commitment to minority services and activities and show superior achievements in the profession of physical therapy. **Focus:** Physical therapy. **Qualif.:** Applicants must be U.S. citizens or legal permanent residents; must be members of one of the racial/ethnic minority groups (African-American or Black, Asian, Native Hawaiian or other Pacific Islander, American Indian/Alaska Native and Hispanic/Latino); must be physical therapists, full-time faculty members, teaching in an accredited or developing professional physical therapist education program; must possess a license to practice physical therapy in a U.S. jurisdiction or have met all the requirements for licensure in a U.S. jurisdiction; must be enrolled as students in a regionally accredited post-professional doctoral program whose content has a demonstrated relationship to physical therapy; must demonstrate continuous progress toward the completion of their post-professional doctoral program in a timely fashion; must demonstrate commitment to minority services and activities; must demonstrate a commitment to further the physical therapy profession through teaching and research; and must not have received the award in prior years. **Criteria:** Selection is based on demonstrated evidence of contributions in the area of minority affairs and services, contributions to the profession of physical therapy and scholastic achievement.

Funds Avail.: Amount varies. **Duration:** Annual. **To Apply:** Applicants must submit a completed typewritten application form along with the following: a copy of an official transcript from the Registrar's Office of all post-professional doctoral coursework; a personal essay which include a response to the four questions listed on the application; curriculum vitae; plan of study for attaining degree (signed by the applicants' faculty advisor); and the reference forms completed by the faculty advisor or chair of the dissertation committee. One original typewritten (or other computerized format) set and six collated, attached, duplicate sets of all materials must be submitted. **Deadline:** December 1.

1097 ■ APTA Minority Scholarships - Physical Therapist Assistant Students *(Undergraduate/Scholarship)*

Purpose: To acknowledge and reward demonstrated participation in minority affairs and service, the potential for superior achievements as a physical therapist assistant and academic excellence. **Focus:** Physical therapy. **Qualif.:** Applicants must be a U.S. citizens or legal permanent residents; must be members of a racial/ethnic minority group (African-American or Black, Asian, Native Hawaiian or other Pacific Islander, American Indian/Alaska Native or Hispanic/Latino); must be enrolled in the final academic year of an accredited or developing physical therapist assistant education program; must show evidence of contributions in the areas of minority affairs and services and high scholastic achievement; and must possess potential for excellence as physical therapist assistants. **Criteria:** Selection is based on demonstrated evidence of contributions in the area of minority affairs and services with an emphasis on contributions made while enrolled in the physical therapy education program; potential to contribute to the profession of physical therapy; and scholastic achievement.

Funds Avail.: No specific amount. **Duration:** Annual. **To Apply:** Applicants must submit a completed application form along with the following: one copy of an official transcript from the Registrar's Office of all physical therapist assistant coursework (when possible); a personal essay on professional goals and minority services including a response to the three questions listed on the application; a personal information fact sheet (curriculum vitae); and reference forms completed (typed or other computerized form) by the physical therapy academic program, a physical therapist clinician and from a resource to verify contributions to the minority community. Application package which consist of seven sets of materials (1 original and six duplicate sets collated) and one original transcript of physical therapy coursework must be received in the Department of Minority Affairs. **Deadline:** December 1.

1098 ■ APTA Minority Scholarships - Physical Therapist Students *(Undergraduate/Scholarship)*

Purpose: To acknowledge and reward demonstrated participation in minority affairs activities and services, the potential for superior achievements in the profession of physical therapy, appropriate display of professionalism as a future physical therapist and academic excellence. **Focus:** Physical therapy. **Qualif.:** Applicants must be U.S. citizens or a legal permanent residents; must be members of one of the racial/ethnic minority group (African-American or Black, Asian, Native Hawaiian or other Pacific Islander, American Indian/Alaska Native and Hispanic/Latino); must be enrolled in the final academic year of an accredited or developing professional physical therapist education program; must show evidence of contributions in the areas of minority affairs and services and high scholastic achievement; and must possess potential for superior achievements in the profession of physical therapy as well as professional excellence as a physical therapist. **Criteria:** Selection is based on demonstrated evidence of contributions in the area of minority affairs and services with an

Awards are arranged alphabetically below their administering organizations

emphasis on contributions made while enrolled in the physical therapy education program; potential to contribute to the profession of physical therapy; and scholastic achievement.

Funds Avail.: No specific amount. **Duration:** Annual. **To Apply:** Applicants must submit a completed application form along with the following: a copy of an official transcript from the Registrar's Office of all physical therapy coursework (when possible); a personal essay on professional goals and minority service including a response to the three questions listed on the first page of the application; a personal information fact sheet (curriculum vitae); and reference forms completed (typed or other computerized form) by the physical therapy academic program, a physical therapist clinician and from a resource to verify contributions to the minority community. Application package which consist of seven sets of materials (1 original and six duplicate sets collated) and one original transcript of physical therapy coursework must be received in the Department of Minority Affairs. **Deadline:** October 16. **Contact:** Eric Robertson, PT, DPT, OCS, FAAOMPT, Director; Phone: 510-675-4259; Email: Eric.K.Robertson@kp.org.

1099 ■ American Physiological Society (APS)
9650 Rockville Pke.
Bethesda, MD 20814-3991
Ph: (301)634-7164
Fax: (301)634-7241
URL: www.the-aps.org
Facebook: www.facebook.com/AmericanPhysiologicalSociety
Twitter: twitter.com/APSPhysiology

1100 ■ Porter Physiology Development Fellowship Awards *(Doctorate/Fellowship)*

Purpose: To encourage PhD students to pursue their education in physiological sciences. **Focus:** Physiology. **Qualif.:** Applicant must be a PhD student majoring physiological sciences; must be an ethnic minority who is a citizen or permanent resident of the United States; and must be a member of American Physiological Society (APS). **Criteria:** Applications will be judged based on potential for success including the following: 1) academic records; 2) statement of interest; 3) previous awards and experiences; and 4) recommendation letters; applicant's proposed training environment; clarity and quality of the research.

Funds Avail.: $23,500. **To Apply:** Applicant must submit an application form; documentation of educational background including transcript of records, a copy of acceptance letter to the graduate training program, current curriculum vitae, list of all undergraduate and graduate institutions have attended; must upload a biographical sketch; must provide the Advisor's or Program Director's contact information; must complete a proposed training or research plan; and must request the uploading of two letters of recommendation from an advisor or Program Director. **Deadline:** January 15.

1101 ■ Caroline tum Suden/Frances Hellebrandt Professional Opportunity Awards *(Postdoctorate, Other/Award)*

Purpose: To encourage professionals, pre-doctoral and post-doctoral students who want to enhance their knowledge in the field of physiological sciences. **Focus:** Physiol-

ogy. **Qualif.:** Applicants must be authors of an abstract submitted to American Physiological Society (APS); and must be members in good standing at the time of application. **Criteria:** Awards will be given to applicants who successfully submit their abstract. Abstracts must show a clearly stated hypothesis or aim, technical approach to the study, quantitative and statistical comparisons and clarity of the conclusion including the significance of the study.

Funds Avail.: $500 each. **Number Awarded:** 36. **To Apply:** Applicants must submit a copy of their abstract; a one-page own composition letter stating the following: 1) career goals; 2) research goals; 3) role in the research described in the abstract; and 4) reason(s) why they deserve to receive the award. Applicants must log on to www.the-aps.org/awardapps for the online application.

1102 ■ American Planning Association (APA)
205 N Michigan Ave., Ste. 1200
Chicago, IL 60601
Ph: (312)431-9100
Fax: (312)786-6700
E-mail: customerservice@planning.org
URL: www.planning.org

1103 ■ American Planning Association ENRE Student Fellowship Program *(Graduate/Fellowship)*

Purpose: To provide financial support for students interested and excelling in graduate level studies in planning related to natural resources, energy or the environment. **Focus:** Energy-related areas; Natural resources; Urban affairs/design/planning. **Qualif.:** Applicants must be second-year graduate students enrolled in a PAB-accredited graduate planning program focusing on issues related to the environment, natural resources or energy. Students must also have a GPA of B or above (3.0 on a 4.0 scale) and may be full or part-time, but must be classified as second year students. **Criteria:** Selection shall be based on the aforesaid qualifications, quality of application materials submitted, and connection of the students' course of study to Division's mission. Preference will be given to students with APA and Division memberships.

Funds Avail.: $1,250. **Duration:** Annual. **Number Awarded:** 2. **To Apply:** Applicants must submit their respective application forms; recommendation letters from their own thesis/project faculty advisors; an 800-word description of the student's master's thesis or project, including how it relates to the division's mission; a 600-word essay describing interest in environmental planning, experience and future goals; and, curriculum vitae or resume. Completed application with the five submission requirements listed should be submitted to the contact provided. **Deadline:** August 1. **Contact:** Danielle Bower at bowerdanielle@gmail.com.

1104 ■ Robert A. Catlin/David W. Long Memorial Fellowships *(Graduate/Fellowship)*

Purpose: To encourage the pursuit and achievement of the growing number of African American students entering the urban planning profession. **Focus:** Urban affairs/design/planning. **Qualif.:** Applicants must be African American undergraduate students who have been accepted in an urban planning program for graduate studies and graduate students, of the same affiliation, majoring in urban planning or a related field (environmental studies, geography, urban studies, urban policy etc.) Current graduate students may not be in the final semester of their programs. **Criteria:**

Awards are arranged alphabetically below their administering organizations

Selection shall be based on the aforementioned applicants' qualifications and compliance with the application details.

Funds Avail.: $1,500. **Duration:** Annual. **To Apply:** Applicants must download and complete the fellowship application. Other requirements include are personal statement, proof of enrollment in graduate planning program or letter of acceptance to graduate planning program, one recommendation letter, and academic transcript (unofficial). All materials must be received by the PBCD Vice Chairperson of Programs, via e-mail. **Deadline:** February 19. **Contact:** For more information, contact PBCD Vice Chairperson of Programs at planningandtheblackcommunity@gmail.com.

1105 ■ Holzheimer Memorial Student Scholarship for Economic Development Planning *(Graduate, Master's/Scholarship)*

Purpose: To support the travel or attendance of Master's students at the national APA meeting. **Focus:** Urban affairs/design/planning. **Qualif.:** Applicants must be Master's level students enrolled in PAB-accredited planning programs across the United States, as well as individuals who have graduated from those programs in the last year. **Criteria:** Scholarship is awarded on the basis of a letter of recommendation from a faculty member and an original student paper or work.

Funds Avail.: $2,000. **Duration:** Annual. **To Apply:** Applicants must submit their respective letters of recommendation from a full-time faculty member and original student papers or works (of 2,500 words or less) with substantive and relevant topics related to economic development and planning. **Deadline:** February 12. **Contact:** Margaret Cowell, Assistant Professor, Urban Affairs and Planning, Virginia Tech at: mmcowell@vt.edu.

1106 ■ Judith McManus Price Scholarships *(Undergraduate, Graduate/Scholarship)*

Purpose: To provide partial funding for women and minority students. **Focus:** Urban affairs/design/planning. **Qualif.:** Applicants must women and minority (African American, Hispanic American, or Native American) students enrolled in an approved Planning Accreditation Board (PAB) planning program who are citizens of the United States, intend to pursue careers as practicing planners in the public sector, and are able to demonstrate a genuine financial need. **Criteria:** Selection shall be based on the aforementioned applicants' qualifications and compliance with the application details.

Funds Avail.: $2,000-$4,000. **Duration:** Annual. **To Apply:** Applicants must submit a two- to five page background statement describing how their graduate education will be applied to career goals and why they chose planning as a career path; a completed and signed APA financial aid application; two letters of recommendation; written verification from the school's financial officer indicating the average cost of one academic year; resume; copy of acceptance letter from a PAB-accredited graduate planning school; a notarized statement of financial independence signed by the applicant's parents; and an official transcript. **Deadline:** April 30. **Contact:** To check on the status of application, send requests to students@planning.org.

1107 ■ American Political Science Association (APSP)
1527 New Hampshire Ave. NW
Washington, DC 20036-1206

Awards are arranged alphabetically below their administering organizations

Ph: (202)483-2512
Fax: (202)483-2657
E-mail: apsa@apsanet.org
URL: www.apsanet.org
Facebook: www.facebook.com/likeAPSA
Twitter: twitter.com/APSAtweets

1108 ■ APSA Congressional Fellowship for Communications Scholars and Journalists *(Advanced Professional, Professional development/Fellowship)*

Purpose: To give early-to-mid scholars and journalists an opportunity to learn more about Congress and the legislative process through direct participation. **Focus:** Communications; Journalism; Political science; Public administration. **Qualif.:** Applicants must be early and mid-career scholars and journalists with an interest in public policy and telecommunications. They may be scholars of telecommunications with a PhD or may be journalists who cover this topic with two to ten years of continuous, full-time professional experience in either print or broadcast journalism. U.S. citizenship or permanent residency is required. **Criteria:** Selection will be based on the aforesaid qualifications and compliance with the application process.

Funds Avail.: $50,000. **Duration:** Annual; Up to 9 and a half months. **To Apply:** Application must be submitted online and include: a detailed resume or curriculum vitae; 500-word personal statement explaining how participation in the fellowship relates to the applicants' professional goals; one writing sample (political scientists and communications scholars) or news article, broadcast script, or clip (journalists); and, the names and contact information for three professional references who have agreed to write letters of recommendation. **Contact:** APSA Congressional Fellowship Program office, at cfp@apsanet.org for more information.

1109 ■ APSA Congressional Fellowships for Journalists *(Advanced Professional, Professional development/Fellowship)*

Purpose: To give early-to mid career journalists an opportunity to learn more about Congress and the legislative process through direct participation. **Focus:** Broadcasting; Journalism; Political science. **Qualif.:** Applicants must be early and mid-career print and broadcast journalists who have a professional interest in Congress. Candidates must have a bachelor's degree and two to ten years of continuous, full-time professional experience in either print or broadcast journalism. U.S. citizenship or permanent residency is required. **Criteria:** Selection will be based on the aforesaid qualifications and compliance with the application process.

Funds Avail.: $50,000. **Duration:** Annual; Up to 9 and a half months. **To Apply:** Application must be submitted online and include: a detailed resume or curriculum vitae; 500-word personal statement explaining how participation in the fellowship relates to the applicants' professional goals; one writing sample (political scientists and communications scholars) or news article, broadcast script, or clip (journalists); and, the names and contact information for three professional references who have agreed to write letters of recommendation. **Contact:** APSA Congressional Fellowship Program office at cfp@apsanet.org for more information.

AMERICAN POLITICAL SCIENCE ASSOCIATION

1110 ■ APSA Congressional Fellowships for Political Scientists *(Advanced Professional, Professional development/Fellowship)*

Purpose: To give early-to-mid career political scientists an opportunity to learn more about Congress and the legislative process through direct participation. **Focus:** Political science. **Qualif.:** Applicants must have completed a PhD in the last 15 years or will have defended a dissertation in political science by November of the fellowship year. The program is open to scholars in all fields of study within political science who can show a scholarly interest in Congress and the legislative process. U.S. citizenship or permanent residency is required. **Criteria:** Selection will be based on the aforesaid qualifications and compliance with the application process.

Funds Avail.: $50,000. **Duration:** Annual; Up to 9 and a half months. **To Apply:** Application must be submitted online and include: a detailed resume or curriculum vitae; 500-word personal statement explaining how participation in the fellowship relates to the applicants' professional goals; one writing sample (political scientists and communications scholars) or news article, broadcast script, or clip (journalists); and, the names and contact information for three professional references who have agreed to write letters of recommendation. **Contact:** APSA Congressional Fellowship Program office at cfp@apsanet.org for more information.

1111 ■ APSA Fund for Latino Scholarship *(Undergraduate, Graduate/Scholarship)*

Purpose: To support Latino students and encourage them to enter the profession of political science. **Focus:** Political science. **Qualif.:** Applicants must be Latino or Latina graduate/undergraduate students. **Criteria:** Selection will be based on the committee's criteria.

Funds Avail.: $500-$1,000. **Duration:** Annual. **To Apply:** Applicants must submit: two-page application form available online that summarizes current research activities which are relevant to the grant. Form shall be submitted electronically time-stamped or hard-copy; must also include certification that the host institution, department or program will provide direct financial support at least equal to the maximum amount of grant from the Fund. **Deadline:** June 5. **Contact:** APSANET; Phone: 202-483-2512; Fax: +1 202-483-2657; E-mail: latinofund@apsanet.org.

1112 ■ APSA/Health and Aging Policy Fellowships *(Graduate, Advanced Professional, Professional development/Fellowship)*

Purpose: To make a positive contribution to the development and implementation of health policies that affect the older Americans. **Focus:** Adult education; Health care services; Health education; Social work. **Qualif.:** Applicants must be engaged in all career stages (i.e. early, mid, and late); must be U.S. citizens or permanent residents of the U.S. territories who have career plans that anticipate continued work in the U.S. after the fellowship period. **Criteria:** Recipients are selected based on the commitment to health and aging issues and improving the health and well-being of older Americans; potential for leadership in health policy; professional qualifications and achievements; impact of the fellowship experience on the applicant's career; and interpersonal and communication skills.

Funds Avail.: No specific amount. **Duration:** Annual. **Number Awarded:** 6. **To Apply:** Applicants must fill out and submit the application form which can be downloaded in the website of the program; an essay stating the reasons why the applicant needs the fellowship, description of his/her experiences or contributions in the health aging field, and plans for continued development of the health policy leadership skills after completing the fellowship; a curriculum vitae; a one-page biographical sketch; and the name and contact information of the institutional references and two professional references. **Deadline:** April 15. **Remarks:** The fellowship is supported by The Atlantic Philanthropies and administered by Columbia University. The goal of the program is to create a cadre of professional leaders who will serve as positive change agents in health and aging policy, helping to shape a healthy and productive future for older Americans. **Contact:** Harold Alan Pincus, M.D. at pincush@nyspi.columbia.edu or Kathleen Pike, Ph.D. at kmp2@columbia.edu.

1113 ■ APSA Minority Fellows Program *(Doctorate/Fellowship)*

Purpose: To support minority or underrepresented students applying to enter a doctoral program in political science. **Focus:** Political science. **Qualif.:** Applicants must be members of one of the following racial/ethnic minority groups (African Americans, Asian Pacific Americans, Latinos/as, and Native Americans); must be college/university seniors, college/university graduates, or students currently enrolled in a Master's Program applying for doctoral study at another political science program/institution; must demonstrate interests in teaching and potential for research in political science; must be United States citizen at time of award. **Criteria:** Selection will be based on the committee's criteria.

Funds Avail.: No specific amount. **Duration:** Annual. **To Apply:** Interested applicants may contact the Association for the application process and other details. **Deadline:** October 24.

1114 ■ APSA Small Research Grant Program *(Doctorate/Grant)*

Purpose: To support the research and further the careers of political scientists who are not employed at Ph.D. granting departments in the field. **Focus:** Political science. **Qualif.:** Applicants must be APSA members at the time of application. The principal investigators and co-authors must be one of the following: faculty members at a college or university that does not award a PhD in political science, public administration, public policy, international relations, government or politics and whose primary appointment is in one of these departments; or political scientists not affiliated with an academic institution and are either unemployed or working in a research organization such as a think tank. **Criteria:** Selection will be based on the committee's criteria.

Funds Avail.: $2,500. **Duration:** Annual. **To Apply:** Applicants must submit five single-spaced, single-sided pages proposal. Proposals should address a significant problem in political science, should specify research design, should state how the project relates to previous research and theoretical developments, should state how the project contributes to scholarship within the field. In addition to that are the following: title page, bibliography, itemized budget, and curriculum vitae. **Deadline:** March 1. **Contact:** APSA team at researchgrants@apsanet.org.

1115 ■ APSA U.S. Federal Executives Fellowships *(Advanced Professional, Professional development/Fellowship)*

Purpose: To give senior-level federal executives an opportunity to learn more about Congress and the legislative

Awards are arranged alphabetically below their administering organizations

process through direct participation. **Focus:** Political science. **Qualif.:** Nominees must be fellows who are employees of federal agencies and who are sponsored by their home institutions during the fellowship year. They must have a minimum grade of GS-13 or equivalent at the time of nomination, at least two years of federal service in the executive branch, and long-term career goals relevant to a Congressional experience. **Criteria:** Selection will be based on the nominees' aforesaid eligibility.

Funds Avail.: No specific amount. **Duration:** Annual. **To Apply:** Application is via nomination. Nominations are to be submitted to APSA by the headquarters-level training officer or coordinator for executive development. For the candidates, the department or agency must also submit: a detailed resume with contact information, current grade, work experience, education (degree dates and subject majors), summary of languages, special skills, and interests; a statement assessing the nominees' executive potential and need for training by the supervisor(s) or agency Executive Resources Board; and a 500-word statement by the nominees presenting a need for training, the relevance of training to career goals, and the utilization of training by the agency. **Deadline:** April 1. **Contact:** APSA Congressional Fellowship Program office at cfp@apsanet.org for more information.

1116 ■ Paul A. Volcker Endowment for Public Service Research and Education *(Doctorate/Grant)*

Purpose: To support individuals for their research activities such as travel to archives, travel to conduct interviews, administration and coding of survey instruments, research assistance and purchase of datasets. **Focus:** Government; Public administration. **Qualif.:** Applicants must be doctoral students who have successfully defended their dissertation prospectus and tenure-track assistant professors; must be APSA members at the time of application. **Criteria:** Selection will be based on the committee's criteria.

Funds Avail.: $3,000. **Duration:** Annual. **To Apply:** Applicants must submit five single-spaced pages written proposal which contains the following: project purpose; its contribution to scholarship within public administration and its applicability for practice and development; relation of the project to previous research and theoretical development; research design; itemized budget; and any other financial support that the applicant is already receiving or anticipates receiving. Additional contents to the proposal include cover letter, abstract, letter attesting to the quality of the research project, and curriculum vitae of no more than 3 pages. Applicants must submit their proposals, either electronically or three hard-copies to Paul A. Volcker Endowment for Public Administration Research and Education, Junior Scholar Research Grant Program, care of American Political Science Association. **Deadline:** June 21. **Contact:** APSA Centennial Center at volcker@apsanet.org.

1117 ■ American Political Science Association - Centennial Center for Political Science and Public Affairs
1527 New Hampshire Ave. NW
Washington, DC 20036
Ph: (202)483-2512
Fax: (202)483-2657
E-mail: center@apsanet.org
URL: www.apsanet.org

1118 ■ APSA Presidency Research Group Fellowships *(Graduate, Postdoctorate/Fellowship)*

Purpose: To provide supplemental support to people whose scholarly research brings them to the Washington area, to examine the relationships, institutions, and environment surrounding the President. **Focus:** History, American; Political science. **Qualif.:** Applicants must be APSA members; must be seniors or junior faculty members, post-doctoral fellows and advanced graduate students working at the Centennial Center or other research locations. **Criteria:** Selection will be based on the committee's criteria.

Funds Avail.: No specific amount. **Duration:** Annual. **To Apply:** A completed application must include the following: a completed two-page Visiting Scholar application form; a project proposal with budget and funding sources, not to exceed three double-spaced pages, 12 point font; and curriculum vitae. The following elements are requested as part of the project proposal: detailed description of the topic; the originality of the proposed study; summary of the basic ideas and hypotheses; the methodology to be used; the present status of the research, including how much has already been done in relevant collections and archives, and what the applicants would accomplish at the Center; the materials that will be used and where appropriate, the importance of Washington-area resources; an estimated budget for the course of research; outside funding sources contributing to time at Center. Applicants should have two letters of reference sent directly to the Center by the application deadline.

1119 ■ Marguerite Ross Barnett Research Grant *(Graduate, Postdoctorate/Grant)*

Purpose: To support political scientists who are in tenure-track and non-tenure track positions. To assist them in gaining tenure. **Focus:** Political science. **Qualif.:** Applicants must be APSA members; must be seniors or junior faculty members, post-doctoral fellows and advanced graduate students working at the Centennial Center or other research locations. **Criteria:** Applications are accepted on a rolling basis.

Funds Avail.: No specific amount. **Duration:** Biennial. **To Apply:** A completed application must include the following: a completed two-page Visiting Scholar application form; a project proposal with budget and funding sources, not to exceed three double-spaced pages, 12 point font; and curriculum vitae. The following elements are requested as part of the project proposal: detailed description of the topic; the originality of the proposed study; summary of the basic ideas and hypotheses; the methodology to be used; the present status of the research, including how much has already been done in relevant collections and archives, and what the applicants would accomplish at the Center; the materials that will be used and where appropriate, the importance of Washington-area resources; an estimated budget for the course of research; outside funding sources contributing to time at Center. Applicants should have two letters of reference sent directly to the Center by the application deadline.

1120 ■ Chun-tu Hsueh Fellowship for International Scholars *(Graduate, Postdoctorate/Grant)*

Purpose: To support international scholars, especially those from Asia, funding to cover short-term stays at the Centennial Center for Political Science & Public Affairs. **Focus:** Political science. **Qualif.:** Applicants must be APSA members; must be seniors or junior faculty members, post-doctoral fellows and advanced graduate students working

Awards are arranged alphabetically below their administering organizations

at the Centennial Center or other research locations. **Criteria:** Selection will be based on the committee's criteria.

Funds Avail.: No specific amount. **Duration:** Annual. **To Apply:** A completed application must include the following: a completed two-page Visiting Scholar application form; a project proposal with budget and funding sources, not to exceed three double-spaced pages, 12 point font; and curriculum vitae. The following elements are requested as part of the project proposal: detailed description of the topic; the originality of the proposed study; summary of the basic ideas and hypotheses; the methodology to be used; the present status of the research, including how much has already been done in relevant collections and archives, and what the applicants would accomplish at the Center; the materials that will be used and where appropriate, the importance of Washington-area resources; an estimated budget for the course of research; outside funding sources contributing to time at Center. Applicants should have two letters of reference sent directly to the Center by the application deadline.

1121 ■ Rita Mae Kelly Fund *(Graduate, Doctorate/Fellowship)*

Purpose: To support research on the intersection of gender, race, ethnicity, and political power. **Focus:** Political science. **Qualif.:** Applicants must be APSA members; must be seniors or junior faculty members, post-doctoral fellows and advanced graduate students working at the Centennial Center or other research locations. **Criteria:** Selection will be based on the committee's criteria.

Funds Avail.: No specific amount. **Duration:** Annual. **To Apply:** A completed application must include the following: a completed two-page Visiting Scholar application form; a project proposal with budget and funding sources, not to exceed three double-spaced pages, 12 point font; and curriculum vitae. The following elements are requested as part of the project proposal: detailed description of the topic; the originality of the proposed study; summary of the basic ideas and hypotheses; the methodology to be used; the present status of the research, including how much has already been done in relevant collections and archives, and what the applicants would accomplish at the Center; the materials that will be used and where appropriate, the importance of Washington-area resources; an estimated budget for the course of research; outside funding sources contributing to time at Center. Applicants should have two letters of reference sent directly to the Center by the application deadline.

1122 ■ Warren E. Miller Fellowship in Electoral Politics *(Advanced Professional, Graduate, Postdoctorate/Fellowship)*

Purpose: To support research residencies in national and comparative electoral politics. **Focus:** Political science. **Qualif.:** Applicants must be APSA members; must be seniors or junior faculty members, post-doctoral fellows and advanced graduate students working at the Centennial Center or other research locations. **Criteria:** Selection will be based on the committee's criteria.

Funds Avail.: No specific amount. **Duration:** Annual. **To Apply:** A completed application must include the following: a completed two-page Visiting Scholar application form; a project proposal with budget and funding sources, not to exceed three double-spaced pages, 12 point font; and curriculum vitae. The following elements are requested as part of the project proposal: detailed description of the topic; the originality of the proposed study; summary of the basic ideas and hypotheses; the methodology to be used; the present status of the research, including how much has already been done in relevant collections and archives, and what the applicants would accomplish at the Center; the materials that will be used and where appropriate, the importance of Washington-area resources; an estimated budget for the course of research; outside funding sources contributing to time at Center. Applicants should have two letters of reference sent directly to the Center by the application deadline.

1123 ■ Special Fund for the Study of Women and Politics *(Graduate, Postdoctorate/Grant)*

Purpose: To provide scholars conducting research on issues of women and politics with supplemental funding. **Focus:** Political science; Women's studies. **Qualif.:** Applicants must be APSA members; must be seniors or junior faculty members, post-doctoral fellows and advanced graduate students working at the Centennial Center or other research locations. **Criteria:** Selection will be based on the committee's criteria.

Funds Avail.: No specific amount. **Duration:** Annual. **To Apply:** A completed application must include the following: a completed two-page Visiting Scholar application form; a project proposal with budget and funding sources, not to exceed three double-spaced pages, 12 point font; and curriculum vitae. The following elements are requested as part of the project proposal: detailed description of the topic; the originality of the proposed study; summary of the basic ideas and hypotheses; the methodology to be used; the present status of the research, including how much has already been done in relevant collections and archives, and what the applicants would accomplish at the Center; the materials that will be used and where appropriate, the importance of Washington-area resources; an estimated budget for the course of research; outside funding sources contributing to time at Center. Applicants should have two letters of reference sent directly to the Center by the application deadline.

1124 ■ American Polygraph Association (APA)
PO Box 8037
Chattanooga, TN 37414-0037
Ph: (423)892-3992
Fax: (423)894-5435
Free: 800-272-8037
URL: www.polygraph.org

1125 ■ William J. Yankee Memorial Scholarships *(Undergraduate/Scholarship)*

Purpose: To provide financial assistance to deserving students. **Focus:** General studies/Field of study not specified. **Qualif.:** Applicants must have four-year degree from an accredited college or university; must attend an APA accredited basic polygraph examiner training course; must qualify for APA membership upon completion of training. **Criteria:** Selection of candidates will be based on academic success and a demonstrated interest in the field of polygraphing.

Funds Avail.: $5,000. **Duration:** Annual. **To Apply:** Applicants must submit an essay of up to 1000 words on detection of deception, interviewing, interrogation or related fields; must have at least two letters of recommendation. **Deadline:** June 1. **Contact:** Michael Gougler at directorgougler@polygraph.org.

Awards are arranged alphabetically below their administering organizations

1126 ■ American Psychiatric Association Alliance (APAA)
PO Box 285
North Boston, NY 14110
URL: www.apaalliance.org

1127 ■ Elsa Barton Educational Scholarship Fund
(Undergraduate, Vocational/Occupational/Scholarship)

Purpose: To provide financial assistance for post secondary educational needs of a spouse/partner or dependents of impaired, disabled, or deceased physicians unable to provide family income. **Focus:** General studies/Field of study not specified. **Qualif.:** Program is open for the spouse, partner, widow, or child of an impaired, disabled or deceased physician who could exhibit a need for additional financial resources in acquiring a post secondary education or vocational training. **Criteria:** Recipient is selected based on financial need.

Funds Avail.: No specific amount. **Duration:** Annual. **To Apply:** Applicants must submit a completed application form available on the website; a brief statement (300 words or less) on the applicant's professional or vocational goals, explanation of financial situation, amount of funding needed and purpose and list of financial aid or scholarships applicant receives or will be receiving; verification of financial need: CSS Financial Aid Profile, or FAFSA and applicant's Federal Income Tax returns (If applicant is a child of a physician, also include copies of both parents' Federal Income Tax Returns); proof of physician's inability to practice or a death certificate; and the applicant's relevant high school, university, or course of study transcripts. **Deadline:** April 15.

1128 ■ American Psychoanalytic Association (APSAA)
309 E 49th St.
New York, NY 10017-1601
Ph: (212)752-0450
E-mail: info@apsa.org
URL: www.apsa.org
Facebook: www.facebook.com/American.psychoanalysis
LinkedIn: www.linkedin.com/company/american-psychoanalytic-association
Twitter: twitter.com/psychoanalysis_

1129 ■ American Psychoanalytic Association Fellowships *(Doctorate, Postdoctorate, Other/Fellowship)*

Purpose: To encourage interest and involvement in psychoanalysis among future leaders, researchers and educators of mental health and academia. **Focus:** Psychology. **Qualif.:** Applicants must be nominated by their Department Chairs or Program Directors. Psychiatry applicants must be full-time general or child psychiatry residents, PGY-2 or higher, or fellows or psychiatrists who have become board eligible within the previous three years. Psychology applicants must hold a half-time position with an academic department or clinical training program; must have training, leadership, or research responsibilities. If predoctorate, must have completed the required coursework and be in or beyond the predoctoral internship. If postdoctorate, must have received the doctoral degree within the past five years. Social worker applicants must have an M.S.W., D.S.W., or PhD received within the past five years; must demonstrate a pursuit of applied psychoanalysis in one or more of the following areas: a part-time appointment with an academic department; a position in training, leadership, public policy, or research; an interdisciplinary position (at least part-time) offering an opportunity to teach through didactics or consultation. D.S.W. and PhD applicants must have begun their advanced degrees within five years of M.S.W. Academic and multidisciplinary applicants must be individuals from academia or non-mental health professions; must demonstrate a serious ongoing interest in psychoanalysis and its relationship to their primary field; must be curious about how psychoanalytic theory is used clinically; must be working in a position that influences others through education, writing, public speaking, research organizational leadership, performance, and/or artistic installations; must be no more than eight years postdoctorate (or its equivalent) or, if predoctorate, be nearing completion of degree. **Criteria:** Recipients will be selected based on demonstrated leadership ability in their discipline; have showed special aptitude in research, teaching, artistic, writing and/or clinical endeavors; have special interest in psychodynamics, psychoanalysis, applied psychoanalysis or community outreach/development.

Funds Avail.: No specific amount. **Duration:** Annual. **To Apply:** Applicants must submit a completed application form and other supporting materials. **Deadline:** February 9. **Remarks:** Established in 1991. **Contact:** American Psychoanalytic Association, at the above address.

1130 ■ American Psychological Association of Graduate Students (APAGS)
750 1st St. NE
Washington, DC 20002-4242
Ph: (202)336-5500
Fax: (202)336-5997
Free: 800-374-2721
URL: www.apa.org/apags
Facebook: www.facebook.com/APAGradStudents
Twitter: twitter.com/APAGradStudents

1131 ■ APAGS-CLGBTC Grant Program *(Graduate/Grant)*

Purpose: To fund a project that promotes training and educational experiences in Lesbian, Gay, Bisexual and Transgender Concerns practice. **Focus:** Psychology. **Qualif.:** Applicant must be a graduate student member of APAGS; enrolled as a student in good standing at an accredited university; must be in a masters or doctoral program. Undergraduates are not eligible for the scholarships. **Criteria:** Scholarship Selection Committee will review applications based on objective, qualitative and quantitative criteria.

Funds Avail.: $1,000. **To Apply:** Applicants must submit a title page; summary of the proposed project; evaluation; organization profile; appendix.

1132 ■ Ellin Bloch and Pierre Ritchie Diversity Dissertation Grant *(Graduate/Grant)*

Purpose: To encourage and support graduate students in their research in the field of psychology concerning diversity issues. **Focus:** Psychology. **Qualif.:** Applicant must be a graduate student member of APAGS; enrolled as a student in good standing at an accredited university; must be in a doctoral program. **Criteria:** Recipient is selected based on the relevance of the study to diversity.

Funds Avail.: $1,000. **Duration:** Annual. **To Apply:** Applicants must submit a cover letter that indicates the name of the nominee and the scholarship being applied for; graduate school affiliation; dissertation chair, current address, phone number and email address; a letter of recommendation supporting the application; an abbreviated dissertation proposal; and a curriculum vitae. **Deadline:** May 4.

1133 ■ Nancy B. Forest and L. Michael Honaker Master's Grant for Research in Psychology *(Graduate/Grant)*

Purpose: To support dissertation research related to the field of psychology. **Focus:** Psychology. **Qualif.:** Applicant must be a graduate student member of APAGS; enrolled as a student in good standing at an accredited university; must be in a masters or doctoral program. Undergraduates are not eligible for the scholarships. **Criteria:** Scholarship Selection Committee will review applications based on objective, qualitative and quantitative criteria.

Funds Avail.: $1,000. **Duration:** Annual. **To Apply:** Applicants must submit a cover letter that indicates the name of the scholarship; a curriculum vitae; a thesis proposal; and two letters of recommendation that supports the application. **Deadline:** May 4.

1134 ■ Scott Mesh Honorary Grant for Research in Psychology *(Graduate/Grant)*

Purpose: To support dissertation research related to the field of psychology. **Focus:** Psychology. **Qualif.:** Applicant must be a graduate student member of APAGS; enrolled as a student in good standing at an accredited university; must be in a masters or doctoral program. Undergraduates are not eligible for the scholarships. **Criteria:** Scholarship Selection Committee will review applications based on objective, qualitative and quantitative criteria.

Funds Avail.: $1,000. **Duration:** Annual. **To Apply:** Applicants must submit a cover letter that indicates the name of the scholarship; a curriculum vitae; a dissertation proposal; and two letters of recommendation (not to exceed two pages) that supports the application. **Deadline:** May 4.

1135 ■ David Pilon Scholarships for Training in Professional Psychology *(Graduate/Scholarship)*

Purpose: To promote supplement training and education experiences in professional practice. **Focus:** Psychology. **Qualif.:** Applicant must be a graduate student member of APAGS; must be enrolled as a student in good standing at an accredited university; must be in a masters or doctoral program. Undergraduates are not eligible for the scholarships. **Criteria:** Scholarship Selection Committee will review applications based on objective, qualitative and quantitative criteria.

Funds Avail.: $1,000. **Duration:** Annual. **To Apply:** Applicants must submit a cover letter that indicates the name of the scholarship; a curriculum vitae; a statement (maximum 1,000 words) addressing the applicant's short and long-term goals; a formal proposal; and two letters of recommendation that supports the application. **Deadline:** May 4.

1136 ■ American Psychological Foundation (APF)
750 1st St. NE
Washington, DC 20002-4241
Ph: (202)336-5843
Fax: (202)336-5812
E-mail: foundation@apa.org

URL: www.apa.org/apf

1137 ■ Annette Urso Rickel Foundation Dissertation Award for Public Policy *(Graduate/Scholarship)*

Purpose: To support dissertation research on public policy. **Focus:** Psychology. **Qualif.:** Applicants must be graduate students in psychology enrolled full-time in good standing in a regionally accredited institution in the U.S. or Canada; must completed doctoral candidacy, including dissertation approval by the committee; and must have demonstrated research competence and area commitment. **Criteria:** Selection will be based on the quality of proposed work, magnitude of incremental contribution, conformance with stated program goals, and the applicant's demonstration of scholarship and research competence.

Funds Avail.: $1,000. **Duration:** Annual. **To Apply:** Applicants must complete the online application form and must submit the following requirements: funding applications including scholarships, fellowships and grants; interim and final grant reports; nominations; letters of recommendation. **Deadline:** October 1. **Contact:** Samantha Edington, Program Officer, at sedington@apa.org.

1138 ■ APF/COGDOP Graduate Research Scholarships *(Doctorate, Graduate/Scholarship)*

Purpose: To help graduate students further their education in psychology. **Focus:** Psychology. **Qualif.:** Applicants must be graduate students enrolled in an interim master's program or doctoral program. **Criteria:** Selection is based on the research proposal and applicant's background.

Funds Avail.: Amount varies. **Number Awarded:** Varies. **To Apply:** Applicants must submit a completed application form along with a letter of recommendation (maximum of 3 pages) from the student's graduate research advisor with original signature; a brief outline (maximum of 3 pages) of the student's thesis or dissertation research project (even if in progress); a curriculum vitae and a transcript (unofficial/student copy is acceptable) of all graduate coursework completed. Each application must include five collated sets and submitted in one complete package. **Deadline:** June 30.

1139 ■ APF High School Psychology Teacher Network Grants *(Advanced Professional, Professional development/Grant)*

Purpose: To support the development of local and regional networks of psychology teachers. To support a local or regional teaching workshop or conference for high school psychology teachers. **Focus:** Psychology; Teaching. **Qualif.:** Program is open to local and regional networks of psychology teachers. **Criteria:** Applicants will be selected based on their written proposals.

Funds Avail.: $3,000. **Duration:** Annual. **To Apply:** Applicants must submit written proposals which include justification/rationale for how a specific project would build a new network of psychology teachers and enhance the teaching of high school psychology on a local basis, along with budget outlining the expected costs associated with the network, workshop or conference. **Deadline:** July 1. **Contact:** Martha Boenau at mboenau@apa.org.

1140 ■ APF Professional Development Awards for High School Psychology Teachers *(Advanced Professional, Professional development/Grant)*

Purpose: To help high school psychology teachers travel to and attend American Psychological Association Annual

Awards are arranged alphabetically below their administering organizations

Convention. **Focus:** Psychology. **Qualif.:** Applicants must: currently teach at least one high school psychology course and expect to teach psychology in the following academic year; high school teacher affiliates of the American Psychological Association. **Criteria:** Selection will be based on the committee's criteria.

Funds Avail.: Up to $500. **Duration:** Annual. **Number Awarded:** 5. **To Apply:** Applicants must use the official application form downloadable at the APF website. Application form must be typed or neatly printed and submitted with the applicants' resume or curriculum vitae. **Deadline:** April 1. **Contact:** Martha Boenau at mboenau@apa.org.

1141 ■ APF Visionary Grants *(Graduate/Grant)*

Purpose: To provide financial support for innovative research and programs that enhance the power of psychology and advance human potential in the present and in generations to come. **Focus:** Psychology. **Qualif.:** Applicants must be affiliated with nonprofit organizations; must have demonstrated competence and capacity to execute the proposed work. **Criteria:** Applicants will be evaluated based on the following criteria: innovative and potential impact qualities; quality, viability, promise for proposed work; criticality of proposed funding for proposed work; clear and comprehensive methodology.

Funds Avail.: $20,000. **Duration:** Annual. **To Apply:** Applicants must submit a no more than seven pages, one inch margin and 11 point font proposal and must include the following sections: goals and objectives; workplan and timeline; program evaluation/outcomes measures; personnel; budget. Applicants must also attach their organization's ITS determination letter. Completed application must be submitted online at http://forms.apa.org/apf/grants. **Deadline:** April 1. **Contact:** Samantha Edington, Program Officer, at sedington@apa.org.

1142 ■ Benton-Meier Neuropsychology Graduate Scholarships *(Graduate/Scholarship)*

Purpose: To financially support graduate students in Neuropsychology. **Focus:** Psychology. **Qualif.:** Applicants must be graduate students in psychology enrolled full time and in good standing at an accredited university. **Criteria:** Selection is based on the submitted proposal and application materials.

Funds Avail.: $2,500. **Number Awarded:** 2. **To Apply:** Applicants must submit a proposal together with a letter of recommendation from a faculty advisor and a curriculum vitae online. **Deadline:** June 1. **Contact:** American Psychological Foundation, at the above address.

1143 ■ William and Dorothy Bevan Scholarship *(Graduate, Master's, Doctorate/Scholarship)*

Purpose: To assist graduate students of psychology with research costs associated with the master's thesis or doctoral dissertation. **Focus:** Psychology. **Qualif.:** Applicants must be graduate students enrolled in interim master's program or doctoral program. **Criteria:** Selection will be based on the submitted proposals. Proposals will be rated on the description of the context for the research, the clarity and comprehensibility of the research question, the appropriateness of the research design, the general importance of the research and the use of requested funds. Secondary criteria are related to the students' background, including previous publications or presentations at conferences, awards won at the student's institution, the letter of recommendations from the major advisor, breadth of courses taken and grades in courses.

Funds Avail.: $5,000. **Duration:** Annual. **To Apply:** Applicants must submit five (5) collated sets of the following materials: completed application form available on the APF website; three-page maximum letter of recommendation from the nominees' graduate research advisor, with original signature; three-page maximum brief outline of the nominees' thesis or dissertation research project (even if in progress); and curriculum vitae and transcript (unofficial/student copy is acceptable) of all graduate coursework completed by the nominees. All application materials must be delivered in one complete package on or before the application deadline. **Deadline:** June 30. **Contact:** Samantha Edington, Program Officer, at sedington@apa.org.

1144 ■ Violet and Cyril Franks Scholarship *(Graduate/Scholarship)*

Purpose: To support graduate-level scholarly projects that use a psychological perspective to help understand and reduce stigma associated with mental illness. **Focus:** Psychology. **Qualif.:** Applicants must be graduate students in psychology enrolled full time and in good standing at an accredited university. **Criteria:** Selection is based on the submitted proposal and application materials.

Funds Avail.: $5,000. **Duration:** Annual. **To Apply:** Applicants must submit a proposal together with a letter of recommendation from a faculty advisor and a curriculum vitae online. **Deadline:** May 15.

1145 ■ William C. Howell Scholarship *(Graduate, Master's, Doctorate/Scholarship)*

Purpose: To assist graduate students of psychology with research costs associated with the master's thesis or doctoral dissertation. **Focus:** Psychology. **Qualif.:** Applicants must be graduate students enrolled in interim master's program or doctoral program. **Criteria:** Selection will be based on the submitted proposals. Proposals will be rated on the description of the context for the research, the clarity and comprehensibility of the research question, the appropriateness of the research design, the general importance of the research and the use of requested funds. Secondary criteria are related to the students' background, including previous publications or presentations at conferences, awards won at the student's institution, the letter of recommendations from the major advisor, breadth of courses taken and grades in courses.

Funds Avail.: $1,000. **Duration:** Annual. **To Apply:** Applicants must submit five (5) collated sets of the following materials: completed application form available on the APF website; three-page maximum letter of recommendation from the nominees' graduate research advisor, with original signature; three-page maximum brief outline of the nominees' thesis or dissertation research project (even if in progress); and curriculum vitae and transcript (unofficial/student copy is acceptable) of all graduate coursework completed by the nominees. All application materials must be delivered in one complete package on or before the application deadline. **Deadline:** June 30. **Contact:** Samantha Edington, Program Officer, at sedington@apa.org.

1146 ■ Peter and Malina James and Dr. Louis P. James Legacy Scholarships *(Graduate, Master's, Doctorate/Scholarship)*

Purpose: To assist graduate students of psychology with research costs associated with the master's thesis or doctoral dissertation. **Focus:** Psychology. **Qualif.:** Applicants must be graduate students enrolled in interim master's program or doctoral program. **Criteria:** Selection

Awards are arranged alphabetically below their administering organizations

will be based on the submitted proposals. Proposals will be rated on the description of the context for the research, the clarity and comprehensibility of the research question, the appropriateness of the research design, the general importance of the research and the use of requested funds. Secondary criteria are related to the students' background, including previous publications or presentations at conferences, awards won at the student's institution, the letter of recommendations from the major advisor, breadth of courses taken and grades in courses.

Funds Avail.: $1,000. **Duration:** Annual. **To Apply:** Applicants must submit five (5) collated sets of the following materials: completed application form available on the APF website; three-page maximum letter of recommendation from the nominees' graduate research advisor, with original signature; three-page maximum brief outline of the nominees' thesis or dissertation research project (even if in progress); and curriculum vitae and transcript (unofficial/student copy is acceptable) of all graduate coursework completed by the nominees. All application materials must be delivered in one complete package on or before the application deadline. **Deadline:** June 30. **Contact:** Samantha Edington, Program Officer, at sedington@apa.org.

1147 ■ Elizabeth Munsterberg Koppitz Child Psychology Graduate Fellowships *(Graduate, Doctorate/Fellowship)*

Purpose: To promote the advancement of knowledge and learning in the field of child psychology. **Focus:** Psychology. **Qualif.:** Applicants must have achieved doctoral candidacy. Students may apply before having passed the qualifying exams but proof of having advanced to doctoral candidacy will be required before funds are released. **Criteria:** Selection is based on the submitted proposal and application materials.

Funds Avail.: Up to $25,000. **Duration:** Annual. **Number Awarded:** Varies. **To Apply:** Applicants must submit a proposal (maximum of 7 pages, 1 inch margins, no smaller than 11 pt. font) together with a curriculum vitae, two recommendations (one from a graduate advisor and the other from the department chair or Director of Graduate Studies), and a copy of the IRB approval online. **Deadline:** November 15.

1148 ■ Harry and Miriam Levinson Scholarship *(Graduate, Master's, Doctorate/Scholarship)*

Purpose: To assist graduate students of psychology with research costs associated with the master's thesis or doctoral dissertation. **Focus:** Psychology. **Qualif.:** Applicants must be graduate students enrolled in interim master's program or doctoral program. **Criteria:** Selection will be based on the submitted proposals. Proposals will be rated on the description of the context for the research, the clarity and comprehensibility of the research question, the appropriateness of the research design, the general importance of the research and the use of requested funds. Secondary criteria are related to the students' background, including previous publications or presentations at conferences, awards won at the student's institution, the letter of recommendations from the major advisor, breadth of courses taken and grades in courses.

Funds Avail.: $5,000. **Duration:** Annual. **To Apply:** Applicants must submit five (5) collated sets of the following materials: completed application form available on the APF website; three-page maximum letter of recommendation from the nominees' graduate research advisor, with original signature; three-page maximum brief outline of the nominees' thesis or dissertation research project (even if in progress); and curriculum vitae and transcript (unofficial/student copy is acceptable) of all graduate coursework completed by the nominees. All application materials must be delivered in one complete package on or before the application deadline. **Deadline:** June 30. **Contact:** Samantha Edington, Program Officer, at sedington@apa.org.

1149 ■ Ruth G. and Joseph D. Matarazzo Scholarship *(Graduate, Master's, Doctorate/Scholarship)*

Purpose: To assist graduate students of psychology with research costs associated with the master's thesis or doctoral dissertation. **Focus:** Psychology. **Qualif.:** Applicants must be graduate students enrolled in interim master's program or doctoral program. **Criteria:** Selection will be based on the submitted proposals. Proposals will be rated on the description of the context for the research, the clarity and comprehensibility of the research question, the appropriateness of the research design, the general importance of the research and the use of requested funds. Secondary criteria are related to the students' background, including previous publications or presentations at conferences, awards won at the student's institution, the letter of recommendations from the major advisor, breadth of courses taken and grades in courses.

Funds Avail.: $3,000. **Duration:** Annual. **To Apply:** Applicants must submit five (5) collated sets of the following materials: completed application form available on the APF website; three-page maximum letter of recommendation from the nominees' graduate research advisor, with original signature; three-page maximum brief outline of the nominees' thesis or dissertation research project (even if in progress); and curriculum vitae and transcript (unofficial/student copy is acceptable) of all graduate coursework completed by the nominees. All application materials must be delivered in one complete package on or before the application deadline. **Deadline:** June 30. **Contact:** Samantha Edington, Program Officer, at sedington@apa.org.

1150 ■ Wayne F. Placek Grants *(Graduate, Doctorate/Grant)*

Purpose: To support researchers and encourage them to research on heterosexuals' attitudes and behaviors toward the LGBT people, their family, workplace and other special concerns of sectors of the LGBT people. **Focus:** Behavioral sciences; Psychology. **Qualif.:** Applicants must be either doctoral-level researchers or graduate students affiliated with an educational institution of a nonprofit research organization. **Criteria:** Selection process will be evaluated on relevance to Placek program goals, magnitude if incremental contribution, quality of proposed work, and the applicants' demonstration of scholarship and research competence.

Funds Avail.: $15,000. **Duration:** Annual. **To Apply:** Interested applicants must submit a completed application online with their proposal. **Deadline:** March 1. **Contact:** Samantha Edington, Program Officer, at sedington@apa.org.

1151 ■ Clarence J. Rosecrans Scholarship *(Graduate, Master's, Doctorate/Scholarship)*

Purpose: To assist graduate students of psychology with research costs associated with the master's thesis or doctoral dissertation. **Focus:** Psychology. **Qualif.:** Applicants must be graduate students enrolled in interim master's program or doctoral program. **Criteria:** Selection will be based on the submitted proposals. Proposals will be

Awards are arranged alphabetically below their administering organizations

rated on the description of the context for the research, the clarity and comprehensibility of the research question, the appropriateness of the research design, the general importance of the research and the use of requested funds. Secondary criteria are related to the students' background, including previous publications or presentations at conferences, awards won at the student's institution, the letter of recommendations from the major advisor, breadth of courses taken and grades in courses.

Funds Avail.: $2,000. **Duration:** Annual. **To Apply:** Applicants must submit five (5) collated sets of the following materials: completed application form available on the APF website; three-page maximum letter of recommendation from the nominees' graduate research advisor, with original signature; three-page maximum brief outline of the nominees' thesis or dissertation research project (even if in progress); and curriculum vitae and transcript (unofficial/student copy is acceptable) of all graduate coursework completed by the nominees. All application materials must be delivered in one complete package on or before the application deadline. **Deadline:** June 30. **Contact:** Samantha Edington, Program Officer, at sedington@apa.org.

1152 ■ Esther Katz Rosen Fund Grants (Graduate, Doctorate/Grant)

Purpose: To support activities related to the psychological understanding of gifted and talented children and adolescents. **Focus:** Psychology. **Qualif.:** Applicants must be affiliated with a school or education institution; must hold a doctoral degree from, or be graduate students at, an accredited university for research proposals. **Criteria:** Selection is based on the submitted proposal and application materials.

Funds Avail.: Up to $50,000. **Duration:** Annual. **Number Awarded:** Varies. **To Apply:** Applicants must submit a proposal (maximum of 10 pages, with 1 inch margins, no smaller than 11 pt. font) along with a curriculum vitae, two recommendations (one from a graduate advisor and the other from the department chair or Director of Graduate Studies) and a copy of the IRB approval (if applicable) online. **Deadline:** March 1. **Remarks:** Established in 1974.

1153 ■ Charles and Carol Spielberger Scholarships (Graduate, Master's, Doctorate/Scholarship)

Purpose: To assist graduate students of psychology with research costs associated with the master's thesis or doctoral dissertation. **Focus:** Psychology. **Qualif.:** Candidates must be graduate students enrolled in interim master's program or doctoral program. **Criteria:** Selection will be based on the following criteria: description of the context for the research; the clarity and comprehensibility of the research question; the appropriateness of the research design, the general importance of the research and the use of requested funds. Preference given for funds to actually conduct the research as opposed to tuition, travel, books and journals. Secondary criteria are related to the students' background, including previous publications or presentations at conferences, awards won at the students' institution, the letter of recommendations from the major advisor, breadth of courses taken and grades in courses.

Funds Avail.: $5,000. **Duration:** Annual. **To Apply:** Candidates must complete and submit the following materials: a completed application form; a curriculum vitae and a transcript of all graduate coursework completed by the nominees; a 3-page maximum letter of recommendation from the nominees' graduate research advisor, with original signature; a 3-page maximum brief outline of the nominees' thesis or dissertation research project. Outlines may be single or double-spaced and margin sized are at the discretion of each applicant. The 3-page outline may include up to two additional pages of references. **Deadline:** June 30. **Contact:** Samantha Edington, Program Officer, at sedington@apa.org.

1154 ■ American Psychology-Law Society (AP-LS)

750 1st St. NE
Washington, DC 20002-4242
Ph: (202)336-5500
E-mail: apls@ec.rr.com
URL: www.apadivisions.org/division-41/index.aspx

1155 ■ American Psychology-Law Society Dissertation Awards (Graduate/Award)

Purpose: To promote the interdisciplinary study of psychology and law. **Focus:** Law; Psychology. **Qualif.:** Applicants must be members of AP-LS and must defend their dissertation. **Criteria:** Selection will be based on the committee's criteria.

Funds Avail.: No specific amount. **Duration:** Annual. **To Apply:** Applicants must attach and submit the following items in Word or PDF format to aplsdissertations@gmail.com: the dissertation which was submitted to the student's university; the dissertation with all author, advisor and school identifying information removed; and a letter of support from the dissertation advisor. **Deadline:** January 1.

1156 ■ American Psychology-Law Society Early Career Professional Grants-In-Aid (Other/Grant)

Purpose: To support AP-LS members who are early career professionals in conducting research related to psychology and law. **Focus:** Law; Psychology. **Qualif.:** Applicants must be Early Career professionals, defined by APA as those within seven years of receiving their last degree. **Criteria:** Preference will be given to those applicants who have not ever received an AP-LS ECP Grant-In-Aid.

Funds Avail.: Up to $5,000. **Duration:** Annual. **To Apply:** Applicants must submit a cover sheet including all contact information for the primary investigator and the title of the proposal. The cover letter should include the status of the human subject review for the project; an abstract of 150-word or less describing the proposed research; a proposed budget with justifications; a curriculum vitae; a list of at least five suggested outside reviewers for the project with expertise in the area of the proposal. External reviewer suggestions must exclude those with a potential conflict of interest; a five-page maximum project description including the following: statement of the problem. A clear statement of the research problem and the significance of the problem to psychology and law; relation of the problem to the state of the field. A concise overview of the relevant empirical literature, theoretical background and/or law related to the project; project method. A detailed description of the methodology and analytical strategy to be employed, including an outline for expected completion of the project; anticipated contribution. A statement of the significance of the project within the field of psychology and law. **Deadline:** December 15. **Contact:** ECP Committee, Chair, Lora Levett, llevett@ufl.edu.

1157 ■ American Psychology-Law Society Student Grants-In-Aid (Graduate/Grant)

Purpose: To support empirical graduate research that addresses psycholegal issues. **Focus:** Law; Psychology. **Qua-**

lif.: Applicants must be graduate students who are student affiliate members of AP-LS. **Criteria:** Selection will be based on the committee's criteria.

Funds Avail.: $750. **To Apply:** Applicants must submit a maximum of 1500-word proposal, excluding references, in a Word or PDF format that includes the following: a cover sheet indicating the title of the project, name, address, phone number and email address of the investigator; an abstract of 100 words or less summarizing the project; purpose, theoretical rationale and significance of the project; procedure to be employed; specific amount requested, including a detailed budget; references. Applicants should include a discussion of the feasibility of the research. Applicants must submit a proof that IRB approval has been obtained for the project and the appropriate tax form W-9 for U.S. citizens and W-8BEN for international students. **Deadline:** September 30; January 31; January 1. **Contact:** American Psychology-Law Society, at the above address.

1158 ■ Saleem Shah Early Career Award *(Doctorate/Recognition)*

Purpose: To recognize early career excellence and contributions to the field of psychology and law. **Focus:** Law; Psychology. **Qualif.:** Candidates must have received the doctoral degree or the law degree, whichever comes later, if both have been earned within the last six years. **Criteria:** Selection will be based on the committee's criteria.

Funds Avail.: A total of $2,000. **Duration:** Annual. **To Apply:** Nominators must send a letter detailing the nominee's contributions to psychology and law, copy of the nominee's vita. Self-nominations will not be considered. **Deadline:** November 30.

1159 ■ American Public Power Association (APPA)

2451 Crystal Dr., Ste. 1000
Arlington, VA 22202-4804
Ph: (202)467-2900
URL: www.publicpower.org
Facebook: www.facebook.com/americanpublicpower
LinkedIn: www.linkedin.com/company/american-public-power-association
Twitter: twitter.com/publicpowerorg

1160 ■ DEED Student Research Grant/Internships *(Undergraduate, Graduate/Grant, Scholarship, Internship)*

Purpose: To introduce students to career opportunities in public power, support students entering technical programs and majors in short supply and high demand by the utility industry and to provide assistance to DEED members that sponsor scholarships. **Focus:** Energy-related areas. **Qualif.:** Applicants must be accepted or enrolled in a full-time vocational school or accredited college or university, this includes high school seniors through graduate students; must be studying an energy related discipline. **Criteria:** Selection of applicants will be based on the scholarship criteria: (a) Broad applicability of benefits to public power systems; (b) Close involvement of the host utility in project monitoring, sponsorship and guidance; (c) Major in an academic field related to the electric power or energy service industries; (d) Superior academic performance; (e) Special consideration to utilities who have not previously sponsored a student and to small utilities; (f) Educational and learning opportunities for student(s) in public power and utility field.

Funds Avail.: $4,000; up to $1,000 in travel funds to attend applicable conference. **Duration:** Annual. **To Apply:** Applicants must complete the information on the DEED Student Research Grant/Internship application cover sheet available online; must submit the original signature of the student, utility authority and school official as well as other information requested in required signature section; must have a single transcript of the student's academic record. **Deadline:** February 15 and October 1. **Contact:** DEED Administrator, 202-467-2960; Email: deed@publicpower.org.

1161 ■ American Public Transportation Foundation (APFT)

1666 K St. NW, Ste. 1100
Washington, DC 20006
Ph: (202)496-4803
Fax: (202)496-4323
URL: www.aptfd.org

1162 ■ Richard J. Bouchard AECOM Scholarships *(Undergraduate, Graduate/Scholarship)*

Purpose: To provide educational assistance to individuals in public transportation industry-related fields of study. **Focus:** Transportation. **Qualif.:** Applicants must: be enrolled in a fully accredited institution; have and maintain at least a 3.0 GPA (B) in course works that are relevant to the industry or required of a degree program; be either employed by or demonstrate a strong interest in entering the public transportation industry; and, be college sophomores (30 hours or more satisfactorily completed), juniors, seniors, or seeking advanced degree(s). **Criteria:** Selection shall be based on demonstrated interest in the public transportation industry as a career, academic achievement, essay content and quality, need for financial assistance and involvement in extracurricular citizenship and leadership activities.

Funds Avail.: No specific amount. **Duration:** Annual. **To Apply:** Applicants must submit a completed application form along with a description of internship program or supplemental educational program from nominating/sponsoring organization for nominee; a typed, double-spaced essay of 1,000 words or less on "In what segment of the public transportation industry will you make a career and why?"; three letters of recommendation; a copy of completed Free Application for Student Aid Form (FAFSA); official college transcript; verification of enrollment; and a copy of the fee schedule from the college/university for the academic year. **Deadline:** June 15. **Remarks:** The scholarship is awarded to the applicant dedicated to a career in public transportation planning and development. **Contact:** Lindsey Robertson, Senior Program Manager - Workforce Development, American Public Transportation Association; Address: 1300 I Street N.W., Suite 1200 East, Washington, DC 20005; Phone: 202-496-4818; Email lrobertson@apta.com.

1163 ■ Parsons Brinckerhoff-Jim Lammie Scholarships *(Undergraduate, Graduate/Scholarship)*

Purpose: To provide educational assistance to individuals in public transportation industry-related fields of study. **Focus:** Transportation. **Qualif.:** Applicants must: be enrolled in a fully accredited institution; have and maintain at least a 3.0 GPA (B) in course works that are relevant to the industry or required of a degree program; be either employed by or

Awards are arranged alphabetically below their administering organizations

AMERICAN PUBLIC TRANSPORTATION FOUNDATION

demonstrate a strong interest in entering the public transportation industry; and, be college sophomores (30 hours or more satisfactorily completed), juniors, seniors, or seeking advanced degree(s). **Criteria:** Selection shall be based on demonstrated interest in the public transportation industry as a career, academic achievement, essay content and quality, need for financial assistance and involvement in extracurricular citizenship and leadership activities. **Funds Avail.:** No specific amount. **Duration:** Annual. **To Apply:** Applicants must submit a completed application form along with a description of internship program or supplemental educational program from nominating/sponsoring organization for nominee; a typed, double-spaced essay of 1,000 words or less on "In what segment of the public transportation industry will you make a career and why?"; three letters of recommendation; a copy of completed Free Application for Student Aid Form (FAFSA); official college transcript; verification of enrollment; and a copy of the fee schedule from the college/university for the academic year. **Deadline:** June 15. **Remarks:** The scholarship is awarded to the applicant who is dedicated to a public transportation engineering career. **Contact:** Lindsey Robertson, Senior Program Manager - Workforce Development, American Public Transportation Association; Address: 1300 I Street N.W., Suite 1200 East, Washington, DC 20005; Phone: 202-496-4818; Email lrobertson@apta.com.

1164 ■ Florida Public Transportation Association Scholarships (FPTA) *(Undergraduate, Graduate/Scholarship)*

Purpose: To provide educational assistance to individuals in public transportation industry-related fields of study. **Focus:** Transportation. **Qualif.:** Applicants must: be enrolled in a fully accredited institution; have and maintain at least a 3.0 GPA (B) in course works that are relevant to the industry or required of a degree program; be either employed by or demonstrate a strong interest in entering the public transportation industry; and, be college sophomores (30 hours or more satisfactorily completed), juniors, seniors, or seeking advanced degree(s). **Criteria:** Selection shall be based on demonstrated interest in the public transportation industry as a career, academic achievement, essay content and quality, need for financial assistance and involvement in extracurricular citizenship and leadership activities. **Funds Avail.:** No specific amount. **Duration:** Annual. **To Apply:** Applicants must submit a completed application form along with a description of internship program or supplemental educational program from nominating/sponsoring organization for nominee; a typed, double-spaced essay of 1,000 words or less on "In what segment of the public transportation industry will you make a career and why?"; three letters of recommendation; a copy of completed Free Application for Student Aid Form (FAFSA); official college transcript; verification of enrollment; and a copy of the fee schedule from the college/university for the academic year. **Deadline:** June 15. **Remarks:** The scholarship is awarded to an applicant from the state of Florida, and sponsored by a Florida public transit system or the FPTA. **Contact:** Lindsey Robertson, Senior Program Manager - Workforce Development, American Public Transportation Association; Address: 1300 I Street N.W., Suite 1200 East, Washington, DC 20005; Phone: 202-496-4818; Email lrobertson@apta.com.

1165 ■ Jack R. Gilstrap Scholarships *(Undergraduate, Graduate/Scholarship)*

Purpose: To encourage and develop the next generation of transit professionals. **Focus:** Transportation. **Qualif.:** Applicants must: be enrolled in a fully accredited institution; have and maintain at least a 3.0 GPA (B) in course work that is relevant to the industry or required of a degree program; be either employed by or demonstrate a strong interest in entering the public transportation industry; and, be college sophomores (30 hours or more satisfactorily completed), juniors, seniors, or seeking advanced degree(s). **Criteria:** Selection shall be based on demonstrated interest in the public transportation industry as a career, academic achievement, essay content and quality, need for financial assistance and involvement in extracurricular citizenship and leadership activities. **Funds Avail.:** No specific amount. **Duration:** Annual. **To Apply:** Applicants must submit a completed application form along with a description of internship program or supplemental educational program from nominating/sponsoring organization for nominee; a typed, double-spaced essay of 1,000 words or less on "In what segment of the public transportation industry will you make a career and why?"; three letters of recommendation; a copy of completed Free Application for Student Aid Form (FAFSA); official college transcript; verification of enrollment; and a copy of the fee schedule from the college/university for the academic year. **Deadline:** June 15. **Remarks:** The scholarship is awarded to the applicant receiving the highest overall score. **Contact:** Lindsey Robertson, Senior Program Manager - Workforce Development, American Public Transportation Association; Address: 1300 I Street N.W., Suite 1200 East, Washington, DC 20005; Phone: 202-496-4818; Email lrobertson@apta.com.

1166 ■ Louis T. Klauder Scholarships *(Undergraduate, Graduate/Scholarship)*

Purpose: To provide educational assistance to individuals in public transportation industry-related fields of study. **Focus:** Engineering, Electrical; Engineering, Mechanical; Transportation. **Qualif.:** Applicants must: be enrolled in a fully accredited institution; have and maintain at least a 3.0 GPA (B) in course works that are relevant to the industry or required of a degree program; be either employed by or demonstrate a strong interest in entering the public transportation industry; and, be college sophomores (30 hours or more satisfactorily completed), juniors, seniors, or seeking advanced degree(s). **Criteria:** Selection shall be based on demonstrated interest in the public transportation industry as a career, academic achievement, essay content and quality, need for financial assistance and involvement in extracurricular citizenship and leadership activities. **Funds Avail.:** No specific amount. **Duration:** Annual. **To Apply:** Applicants must submit a completed application form along with a description of internship program or supplemental educational program from nominating/sponsoring organization for nominee; a typed, double-spaced essay of 1,000 words or less on "In what segment of the public transportation industry will you make a career and why?"; three letters of recommendation; a copy of completed Free Application for Student Aid Form (FAFSA); official college transcript; verification of enrollment; and a copy of the fee schedule from the college/university for the academic year. **Deadline:** June 15. **Remarks:** The scholarship is awarded to the applicant dedicated to a career in the rail transit industry as an electrical or mechanical engineer. **Contact:** Lindsey Robertson, Senior Program Manager - Workforce Development, American Public Transportation Association; Address: 1300 I Street N.W., Suite 1200 East, Washington, DC 20005; Phone: 202-496-4818; Email lrobertson@apta.com.

Awards are arranged alphabetically below their administering organizations

1167 ■ Reba Malone Scholarships *(Undergraduate, Graduate/Scholarship)*

Purpose: To provide educational assistance to individuals in public transportation industry-related fields of study. **Focus:** Marketing and distribution; Transportation. **Qualif.:** Applicants must: be enrolled in a fully accredited institution; have and maintain at least a 3.0 GPA (B) in course works that are relevant to the industry or required of a degree program; be either employed by or demonstrate a strong interest in entering the public transportation industry; and, be college sophomores (30 hours or more satisfactorily completed), juniors, seniors, or seeking advanced degree(s). **Criteria:** Selection shall be based on demonstrated interest in the public transportation industry as a career, academic achievement, essay content and quality, need for financial assistance and involvement in extracurricular citizenship and leadership activities.

Funds Avail.: No specific amount. **Duration:** Annual. **To Apply:** Applicants must submit a completed application form along with a description of internship program or supplemental educational program from nominating/sponsoring organization for nominee; a typed, double-spaced essay of 1,000 words or less on "In what segment of the public transportation industry will you make a career and why?"; three letters of recommendation; a copy of completed Free Application for Student Aid Form (FAFSA); official college transcript; verification of enrollment; and a copy of the fee schedule from the college/university for the academic year. **Deadline:** June 15. **Remarks:** The scholarship is awarded to the applicant dedicated to a career in marketing/communications. **Contact:** Lindsey Robertson, Senior Program Manager - Workforce Development, American Public Transportation Association; Address: 1300 I Street N.W., Suite 1200 East, Washington, DC 20005; Phone: 202-496-4818; Email lrobertson@apta.com.

1168 ■ Dan M. Reichard, Jr. Scholarships *(Undergraduate, Graduate/Scholarship)*

Purpose: To provide educational assistance to individuals in public transportation industry-related fields of study. **Focus:** Business administration; Transportation. **Qualif.:** Applicants must: be enrolled in a fully accredited institution; have and maintain at least a 3.0 GPA (B) in course works that are relevant to the industry or required of a degree program; be either employed by or demonstrate a strong interest in entering the public transportation industry; and, be college sophomores (30 hours or more satisfactorily completed), juniors, seniors, or seeking advanced degree(s). **Criteria:** Selection shall be based on demonstrated interest in the public transportation industry as a career, academic achievement, essay content and quality, need for financial assistance and involvement in extracurricular citizenship and leadership activities.

Funds Avail.: No specific amount. **Duration:** Annual. **To Apply:** Applicants must submit a completed application form along with a description of internship program or supplemental educational program from nominating/sponsoring organization for nominee; a typed, double-spaced essay of 1,000 words or less on "In what segment of the public transportation industry will you make a career and why?"; three letters of recommendation; a copy of completed Free Application for Student Aid Form (FAFSA); official college transcript; verification of enrollment; and a copy of the fee schedule from the college/university for the academic year. **Deadline:** June 15. **Remarks:** The scholarship is awarded to the applicant dedicated to a career in the business administration/management area of the transit industry. **Contact:** Lindsey Robertson, Senior Program Manager - Workforce Development, American Public Transportation Association; Address: 1300 I Street N.W., Suite 1200 East, Washington, DC 20005; Phone: 202-496-4818; Email lrobertson@apta.com.

1169 ■ Dr. George M. Smerk Scholarships *(Undergraduate, Graduate/Scholarship)*

Purpose: To provide educational assistance to individuals in public transportation industry-related fields of study. **Focus:** Transportation. **Qualif.:** Applicants must: be enrolled in a fully accredited institution; have and maintain at least a 3.0 GPA (B) in course works that are relevant to the industry or required of a degree program; be either employed by or demonstrate a strong interest in entering the public transportation industry; and, be college sophomores (30 hours or more satisfactorily completed), juniors, seniors, or seeking advanced degree(s). **Criteria:** Selection shall be based on demonstrated interest in the public transportation industry as a career, academic achievement, essay content and quality, need for financial assistance and involvement in extracurricular citizenship and leadership activities.

Funds Avail.: No specific amount. **Duration:** Annual. **To Apply:** Applicants must submit a completed application form along with a description of internship program or supplemental educational program from nominating/sponsoring organization for nominee; a typed, double-spaced essay of 1,000 words or less on "In what segment of the public transportation industry will you make a career and why?"; three letters of recommendation; a copy of completed Free Application for Student Aid Form (FAFSA); official college transcript; verification of enrollment; and a copy of the fee schedule from the college/university for the academic year. **Deadline:** June 15. **Remarks:** The scholarship is awarded to the applicant dedicated to a career in public transit management. **Contact:** Lindsey Robertson, Senior Program Manager - Workforce Development, American Public Transportation Association; Address: 1300 I Street N.W., Suite 1200 East, Washington, DC 20005; Phone: 202-496-4818; Email lrobertson@apta.com.

1170 ■ American Quarter Horse Youth Association (AQHYA)
1600 Quarter Horse Dr.
Amarillo, TX 79104
Ph: (806)376-4811
Fax: (806)349-6411
URL: www.aqha.com
Facebook: www.facebook.com/aqhayouth

1171 ■ American Quarter Horse Foundation Scholarships *(Undergraduate/Scholarship)*

Purpose: To develop and educate the future professionals. **Focus:** Education; Journalism; Nursing; Veterinary science and medicine. **Qualif.:** Applicant must be enrolled in college specializing degree programs such as education, nursing, journalism, veterinary and racing. **Criteria:** Applicant will be selected based on financial need, academic merit, equine involvement and civic activities.

Funds Avail.: No specific amount. **To Apply:** Applicant must fill out the application form and submit proof that he/she is currently enrolled in a college or university. **Deadline:** December 1. **Contact:** For more information, contact the Foundation at 806-378-5029 or e-mail at foundation@aqha.org.

1172 ■ American Quilt Study Group (AQSG)
1610 L St.
Lincoln, NE 68508-2509

Ph: (402)477-1181
Fax: (402)477-1181
E-mail: aqsg2@americanquiltstudygroup.org
URL: www.americanquiltstudygroup.org

1173 ■ Lucy Hilty Research Grants *(Graduate/Grant)*

Purpose: To provide support for research in the industry of quilting. **Focus:** Art. **Qualif.:** Applicants can be individuals or group affiliated with quilt-related studies. **Criteria:** Grantees will be selected according to the quality and impact of their projects; ability to complete the project; compatibility of the projects for the goal of AQSG; and how the projects will contribute to the quilting industry.

Funds Avail.: $2,000. **To Apply:** Application form is available at the website. Proposal should be limited to a cover letter and the application; include completed proposal description; must state the qualifications of the researcher; include letters of support from cooperating institutions or individuals; and a line-item budget for the amount of funding required. **Deadline:** February 1.

1174 ■ American Railway Engineering and Maintenance-of-Way Association (AREMA)

4501 Forbes Blvd., Ste. 130
Lanham, MD 20706
Ph: (301)459-3200
Fax: (301)459-8077
URL: www.arema.org
Facebook: www.facebook.com/American-Railway
 -Engineering-and-Maintenance-of-Way-Association
 -AREMA-113915328654319/?ref=bookmarks

1175 ■ American Railway Engineering and Maintenance-of-Way Association Scholarships *(Undergraduate/Scholarship)*

Purpose: To support the education of undergraduate engineering student who has potential interest in railway engineering careers. **Focus:** Engineering. **Qualif.:** Applicant must be enrolled as a full-time undergraduate student in a four or five year program leading to a Bachelor's degree in Engineering or Engineering Technology in a curriculum accredited by the Accreditation Board of Engineering and Technology; have completed at least one quarter or semester prior to the application; interest in railway engineering; and maintaining a minimum GPA of 2.0. **Criteria:** Selection is based on the materials submitted.

Funds Avail.: varies. **Duration:** varies. **Number Awarded:** varies. **To Apply:** Applicant must submit a completed AREMA data form together with a cover letter (maximum of 350 words); a resume; two letters of recommendation from a faculty member and another from a present employer, AREMA member or other responsible person; and a transcript from the schools attended and courses currently enrolled in. **Deadline:** March 11. **Remarks:** Staple application materials in the upper left hand corner and do not include any photos.

1176 ■ AREMA Committee 12 - Rail Transit Scholarships *(Undergraduate/Scholarship)*

Purpose: To support the education of a student who is also working full-time in the railway industry. **Focus:** Engineering. **Qualif.:** Applicants must be enrolled students who have completed at least one quarter or semester in an accredited engineering program or part time student working full time in the railway industry. They must also maintain a minimum GPA of 2.0 . **Criteria:** Selection shall be based on the aforementioned qualifications and compliance with the application details.

Funds Avail.: $4,000. **Duration:** Annual; One academic year. **Number Awarded:** 1. **To Apply:** Applicants must submit completed AREMA data form together with a cover letter (maximum of 350 words); a resume; two letters of recommendation, one from a faculty member, and another from a present employer, AREMA member, or other responsible person; and a transcript from the schools attended, and courses currently enrolled in. **Deadline:** December 11.

1177 ■ AREMA Committee 18 - Light Density and Short Line Railways Scholarships *(Undergraduate/Scholarship)*

Purpose: To support the education of an engineering student who has a potential interest in railway engineering careers. **Focus:** Engineering. **Qualif.:** Applicants must be enrolled students who have completed at least one quarter or semester in an accredited four or five year engineering or engineering technology undergraduate degree program. **Criteria:** Selection shall be based on the aforementioned qualifications and compliance with the application details.

Funds Avail.: $2,000. **Duration:** Annual; One academic year. **Number Awarded:** 1. **To Apply:** Applicants must submit completed AREMA data form together with a cover letter (maximum of 350 words); a resume; two letters of recommendation, one from a faculty member, and another from a present employer, AREMA member, or other responsible person; and a transcript from the schools attended, and courses currently enrolled in. **Deadline:** December 11.

1178 ■ AREMA Committee 24 - Education and Training Scholarships *(Undergraduate/Scholarship)*

Purpose: To support the education of an engineering student who has a potential interest in railway engineering careers. **Focus:** Engineering. **Qualif.:** Applicants must be current AREMA student members who have completed at least on quarter or semester in an accredited four or five year engineering or engineering technology undergraduate degree program; must have at least a 2.00 GPA (out of 4.00). **Criteria:** Selection shall be based on the aforementioned qualifications and compliance with the application details.

Funds Avail.: $2,000. **Duration:** Annual; One academic year. **Number Awarded:** 1. **To Apply:** Applicants must submit completed AREMA data form together with a cover letter (maximum of 350 words); a resume; two letters of recommendation, one from a faculty member, and another from a present employer, AREMA member, or other responsible person; and a transcript from the schools attended, and courses currently enrolled in. **Deadline:** December 11.

1179 ■ AREMA Committee 27 - Maintenance-of-Way Work Equipment Scholarships *(Undergraduate/Scholarship)*

Purpose: To support the education of those students whose family members work hard in the work equipment industry for railroads. **Focus:** Engineering. **Qualif.:** Applicants must be enrolled full-time students in a four or five year program leading to a Bachelor's degree in Engineering or Engineering Technology in a curriculum accredited by the Accreditation Board of Engineering and Technology; have completed at least one quarter or semester in college prior to the application; and have a GPA of 2.00. **Criteria:** Priority is given to Committee 27 family members or family members of those in the work equipment industry for railroads.

Funds Avail.: $6,000. **Duration:** Annual; One academic year. **Number Awarded:** Varies. **To Apply:** Applicants must submit completed AREMA data form together with a cover letter (maximum of 350 words); a resume; two letters of recommendation, one from a faculty member, and another from a present employer, AREMA member, or other responsible person; and a transcript from the schools attended, and courses currently enrolled in. **Deadline:** December 11.

1180 ■ AREMA Committee 33 - Electric Energy Utilization Scholarships (Undergraduate/Scholarship)

Purpose: To support the education of an engineering student who has a potential interest in railway engineering careers. **Focus:** Engineering. **Qualif.:** Applicants must have interests in railway engineering, maintaining a minimum GPA of 2.0, and be available for interview by the AREMA Scholarship Committee. **Criteria:** Selection shall be based on the aforementioned qualifications and compliance with the application details. Preference will be given to those applicants demonstrating an interest in the field of rail traction electrification systems engineering.

Funds Avail.: $1,000. **Duration:** Annual; One academic year. **Number Awarded:** 1. **To Apply:** Applicants must submit completed AREMA data form together with a cover letter (maximum of 350 words); a resume; two letters of recommendation, one from a faculty member, and another from a present employer, AREMA member, or other responsible person; and a transcript from the schools attended, and courses currently enrolled in. **Deadline:** December 11.

1181 ■ AREMA Michigan Tech Alumni Scholarships (Graduate, Undergraduate/Scholarship)

Purpose: To support the education of engineering students at Michigan Technological University. **Focus:** Engineering. **Qualif.:** Applicants must be undergraduate or graduate engineering student in good standing at Michigan Tech University. Scholarships are also available to Railroad Engineering and Activities Club (REAC) Members and Club Officers. **Criteria:** Selection shall be based on the aforementioned qualifications and compliance with the application details.

Funds Avail.: $1,000. **Duration:** Annual. **Number Awarded:** Varies. **To Apply:** Applicants may verify the application process through the program website. Also, applicants must also specify on the application if they are members of REAC. **Deadline:** December 11.

1182 ■ AREMA Presidential Spouse Scholarships (Undergraduate/Scholarship)

Purpose: To support the education of a female engineering student with a potential interest in railway engineering careers. **Focus:** Engineering. **Qualif.:** Applicants must be enrolled female students who have completed at least one quarter or semester in an accredited four or five year engineering or engineering technology undergraduate degree program. **Criteria:** Selection shall be based on the aforementioned qualifications and compliance with the application details.

Funds Avail.: $1,000. **Duration:** Annual. **Number Awarded:** 1. **To Apply:** Applicants must submit completed AREMA data form together with a cover letter (maximum of 350 words); a resume; two letters of recommendation, one from a faculty member, and another from a present employer, AREMA member, or other responsible person; and a transcript from the schools attended, and courses currently enrolled in. **Deadline:** December 11.

1183 ■ CSX Scholarships (Undergraduate/Scholarship)

Purpose: To support the education of an undergraduate engineering student who has potential interest in railway engineering careers. **Focus:** Engineering. **Qualif.:** Applicants must be enrolled full-time as undergraduate students in a four or five year program leading to a Bachelor's degree in Engineering or Engineering Technology in a curriculum accredited by the Accreditation Board of Engineering and Technology; have completed at least one quarter or semester prior to the application; interest in railway engineering; and maintaining a minimum GPA of 2.0. **Criteria:** Selection shall be based on the aforementioned qualifications and compliance with the application details.

Funds Avail.: $1,000. **Duration:** Annual. **Number Awarded:** 1. **To Apply:** Applicants must submit completed AREMA data form together with a cover letter (maximum of 350 words); a resume; two letters of recommendation, one from a faculty member, and another from a present employer, AREMA member, or other responsible person; and a transcript from the schools attended, and courses currently enrolled in. **Deadline:** December 11.

1184 ■ John J. Cunningham Memorial Scholarships (Undergraduate/Scholarship)

Purpose: To support the education of student in a professional field that has direct applications in the passenger rail sector. **Focus:** Engineering. **Qualif.:** Applicants must be junior or senior college students pursuing an undergraduate degree in a professional field that has direct applications in the passenger rail sector; must have at least a 2.00 GPA (out of 4.00). **Criteria:** Selection shall be based on the aforementioned qualifications and compliance with the application details.

Funds Avail.: $1,000. **Duration:** Annual; one academic year. **To Apply:** Applicants must submit completed AREMA data form together with a cover letter (maximum of 350 words); a resume; two letters of recommendation, one from a faculty member, and another from a present employer, AREMA member, or other responsible person; and a transcript from the schools attended, and courses currently enrolled in. **Deadline:** December 11.

1185 ■ Larry L. Etherton Scholarships (Graduate, Undergraduate/Scholarship)

Purpose: To support the continuing education of railway engineering students at the University of Illinois in the Engineering Department at Urbana-Champaign. **Focus:** Engineering. **Qualif.:** Applicants must be engineering students pursuing an undergraduate or graduate degree at the University of Illinois at Urbana-Champaign; must have at least a 2.00 GPA (out of 4.00). **Criteria:** Selection shall be based on the aforementioned qualifications and compliance with the application details.

Funds Avail.: $1,500. **Duration:** Annual. **Number Awarded:** 1. **To Apply:** Applicants must submit completed AREMA data form together with a cover letter (maximum of 350 words); a resume; two letters of recommendation, one

Awards are arranged alphabetically below their administering organizations

from a faculty member, and another from a present employer, AREMA member, or other responsible person; and a transcript from the schools attended, and courses currently enrolled in. **Deadline:** December 11.

1186 ■ Michael W. and Jean D. Franke Family Foundation Scholarships *(Graduate, Undergraduate/ Scholarship)*

Purpose: To support the continuing education of railway engineering students at the University of Illinois in the Engineering Department at Urbana-Champaign. **Focus:** Engineering. **Qualif.:** Applicants must be engineering students pursuing an undergraduate or graduate degree at the University of Illinois at Urbana-Champaign; must have at least a 2.00 GPA (out of 4.00). **Criteria:** Selection shall be based on the aforementioned qualifications and compliance with the application details.

Funds Avail.: $6,000. **Duration:** Annual. **Number Awarded:** 1. **To Apply:** Applicants must submit completed AREMA data form together with a cover letter (maximum of 350 words); a resume; two letters of recommendation, one from a faculty member, and another from a present employer, AREMA member, or other responsible person; and a transcript from the schools attended, and courses currently enrolled in. **Deadline:** December 11.

1187 ■ Michael and Gina Garcia Rail Engineering Scholarships *(Undergraduate, Graduate/Scholarship)*

Purpose: To support the education of an engineering student, especially to students already married or supporting a family. **Focus:** Engineering. **Qualif.:** Applicants must be enrolled in a four or five year program leading to a Bachelor's degree in Engineering or Engineering Technology at the University of Illinois of Urbana-Champaign. **Criteria:** Priority will be given to students who are already married or supporting a family.

Funds Avail.: $3,000. **Duration:** Annual. **Number Awarded:** 1. **To Apply:** Applicants must submit completed AREMA data form together with a cover letter (maximum of 350 words); a resume; two letters of recommendation, one from a faculty member, and another from a present employer, AREMA member, or other responsible person; and a transcript from the schools attended, and courses currently enrolled in. **Deadline:** Decemeber 11.

1188 ■ Norfolk Southern Foundation Scholarships *(Undergraduate/Scholarship)*

Purpose: To support the education of an engineering student. **Focus:** Engineering. **Qualif.:** Applicants must be enrolled full-time in a four or five year undergraduate program in Engineering or Engineering Technology in which the institution must be located in Norfolk Southern's service area (22 states, the District of Columbia and Ontario, Canada); have completed at least one quarter or semester in college prior to the application; and have a GPA of 2.00. **Criteria:** Selection shall be based on the aforementioned qualifications and compliance with the application details.

Funds Avail.: $1,000. **Duration:** Annual. **Number Awarded:** 1. **To Apply:** Applicants must submit completed AREMA data form together with a cover letter (maximum of 350 words); a resume; two letters of recommendation, one from a faculty member, and another from a present employer, AREMA member, or other responsible person; and a transcript from the schools attended, and courses currently enrolled in. **Deadline:** December 11.

1189 ■ REMSA Scholarships *(Undergraduate/ Scholarship)*

Purpose: To support the education of an undergraduate engineering student who has potential interest in railway engineering careers. **Focus:** Engineering. **Qualif.:** Applicants must be enrolled students who have completed at least one quarter or semester in an accredited four or five year engineering or engineering technology undergraduate degree program; must have at least a 2.00 GPA (out of 4.00). **Criteria:** Selection shall be based on the aforementioned qualifications and compliance with the application details.

Funds Avail.: $1,000. **Duration:** Annual. **Number Awarded:** 1. **To Apply:** Applicants must submit completed AREMA data form together with a cover letter (maximum of 350 words); a resume; two letters of recommendation, one from a faculty member, and another from a present employer, AREMA member, or other responsible person; and a transcript from the schools attended, and courses currently enrolled in. **Deadline:** December 11.

1190 ■ American Rental Association Foundation
1900 19th St.
Moline, IL 61265-4179
Ph: (309)764-2475
Fax: (309)764-1533
Free: 800-334-2177
E-mail: arafoundation@ararental.org
URL: foundation.ararental.org

1191 ■ American Rental Association Foundation Scholarships *(Graduate, Undergraduate, Vocational/ Occupational/Scholarship)*

Purpose: To provide scholarships to promising young students looking to enter the rental industry. **Focus:** Education, Industrial. **Qualif.:** Applicants must be students pursuing a field of study they will use while working in the rental industry or completing a rental-related vocational or certification program. **Criteria:** Selection of applicants will be based on the scholarship application criteria.

Funds Avail.: Amount varies. **Duration:** Annual. **Number Awarded:** Varies. **To Apply:** For further information, applicants are advised to contact the ARA Foundation. **Deadline:** February 2.

1192 ■ Ron Marshall Scholarships *(Undergraduate/ Scholarship)*

Purpose: To provide scholarships to promising young students looking to enter the rental industry. **Focus:** Education, Industrial. **Qualif.:** Applicants must be pursuing an education applicable to the rental industry. **Criteria:** Selection of applicants will be based on the scholarship application criteria.

Funds Avail.: $750. **Duration:** Annual. **Number Awarded:** 2. **To Apply:** Applicants are advised to contact the ARA Foundation. **Deadline:** February 2.

1193 ■ Dorothy Wellnitz Canadian Scholarships *(Undergraduate, Vocational/Occupational/Scholarship)*

Purpose: To provide scholarships to promising young students looking to enter the rental industry. **Focus:** Education, Industrial. **Qualif.:** Applicants must be pursuing an education program applicable to the rental industry; must be college and technical school students from Canada.

Awards are arranged alphabetically below their administering organizations

Criteria: Selection of applicants will be based on the scholarship application criteria.

Funds Avail.: $1,000. **Duration:** Annual. **Number Awarded:** 10. **To Apply:** For further information, applicants are advised to contact the ARA Foundation. **Deadline:** February 2.

1194 ■ American Research Center in Egypt (ARCE)

8700 Crownhill Blvd., Ste. 507
San Antonio, TX 78209-1130
Ph: (210)821-7000
Fax: (210)821-7007
E-mail: info@arce.org
URL: www.arce.org
Facebook: www.facebook.com/The-American-Research-Center-in-Egypt-113468798665292

1195 ■ ARCE Funded Fellowships (Doctorate, Postdoctorate/Fellowship)

Purpose: To provide sufficient funding to cover round-trip air transportation, living allowance, mentoring and a home base in Egypt for doctoral candidates in the all-but-dissertation stage and senior scholars conducting more advanced research. **Focus:** Anthropology; Archeology; Architecture; Art; Economics; History; Humanities; Literature; Political science; Religion. **Qualif.:** Applicants must be students enrolled in doctoral programs at North American universities or American postdoctoral scholars and professionals affiliated with universities and research institutions worldwide. **Criteria:** Selection will be based on the committee's criteria.

Funds Avail.: Amount varies. **Duration:** Annual. **Number Awarded:** Varies. **To Apply:** Applications can be obtained at the website. All materials must be submitted electronically. Forms requiring original signatures, including the MOHE forms and reference forms will need to be scanned and saved as PDF documents. Transcripts may be sent as PDF or JPG files. Applicants may also send their materials through fax to the ARCE San Antonio office to the attention of Ms. Djodi Deutsch, Academic Programs Coordinator. **Deadline:** January 15. **Contact:** Ms. Djodi Deutsch, Academic Programs Coordinator, or vai e-mail at fellows@arce.org.

1196 ■ ARCE Research Associates Fellowships (Doctorate, Postdoctorate, Professional development/ Fellowship)

Purpose: To provide sufficient funding to cover round-trip air transportation, living allowance, mentoring and a home base in Egypt for doctoral candidates in the all-but-dissertation stage and senior scholars conducting more advanced research. **Focus:** Anthropology; Archeology; Architecture; Art; Economics; History; Humanities; Literature; Political science; Religion. **Qualif.:** Applicants must be individuals enrolled in doctoral programs at North American universities, postdoctoral scholars, or professional scholars interested in conducting research in Egypt under an institutional auspice. **Criteria:** Selection will be based on the committee's criteria.

Funds Avail.: No specific amount. **Duration:** Annual. **To Apply:** Applications can be obtained at the website. All materials must be submitted electronically. Forms requiring original signatures, including the MOHE forms and reference forms will need to be scanned and saved as PDF documents. Transcripts may be sent as PDF or JPG files. Applicants may also send their materials through fax to the ARCE San Antonio office to the attention of Ms. Djodi Deutsch, Academic Programs Coordinator. **Deadline:** January 15. **Contact:** Ms. Djodi Deutsch, Academic Programs Coordinator, or e-mail at fellows@arce.org.

1197 ■ William P. McHugh Memorial Fund Award (Doctorate, Graduate/Fellowship)

Purpose: To financially support the students enrolled in a graduate program through education, training and research initiatives. **Focus:** Anthropology; Archeology; Architecture; Art; Economics; Education, Religious; History; Literature; Political science. **Qualif.:** Applicants must be U.S. citizens; must be students enrolled in doctoral programs at North America universities, or postdoctoral scholars and professionals affiliated with North American universities and research institutions; must be students of geo-archaeology and prehistory. **Criteria:** Selection of applicants will be based on the criteria given by the Scholarship Committee.

Funds Avail.: $600. **To Apply:** Applicants must complete the application form available on the website; must submit three letters of recommendation and Pre-doctoral students must submit a fourth recommendation attesting to their capacity in ancient or modern languages relating to their proposed research. **Deadline:** January 15.

1198 ■ The National Endowment for the Humanities Fellowships (Graduate/Fellowship)

Purpose: To financially support the students enrolled in a graduate program through education, training and research initiatives. **Focus:** Anthropology; Archeology; Architecture; Art; Economics; Education, Religious; History; Literature; Political science. **Qualif.:** Applicants must be U.S. citizens; must be students enrolled in doctoral programs at North America universities, or postdoctoral scholars and professionals affiliated with North American universities and research institutions. **Criteria:** Selection of applicants will be based on the criteria given by the Scholarship Committee.

Funds Avail.: No specific amount. **Duration:** 4-12 months. **Number Awarded:** 1-2. **To Apply:** Applicants must complete the application form available on the website; must submit three letters of recommendation and Pre-doctoral students must submit a fourth recommendation attesting to their capacity in ancient or modern languages relating to their proposed research.

1199 ■ The United States Department of State, Bureau of Educational & Cultural Affairs Fellowships (Graduate/Fellowship)

Purpose: To financially support the students enrolled in a graduate program through education, training and research initiatives. **Focus:** Anthropology; Archeology; Architecture; Art; Economics; Education, Religious; History; Literature; Political science. **Qualif.:** Applicants must be U.S. citizens; must be students enrolled in doctoral programs at North America universities, or postdoctoral scholars and professionals affiliated with North American universities and research institutions. **Criteria:** Selection of applicants will be based on the criteria given by the Scholarship Committee.

Funds Avail.: No specific amount. **Duration:** 3-12 months. **Number Awarded:** 6-7. **To Apply:** Applicants must complete the application form available on the website; must submit three letters of recommendation and Pre-doctoral students must submit a fourth recommendation attesting to

Awards are arranged alphabetically below their administering organizations

their capacity in ancient or modern languages relating to their proposed research. **Deadline:** January 15.

1200 ■ American Research Institute in Turkey (ARIT)
3260 S St.
Philadelphia, PA 19104-6324
Ph: (215)898-3474
URL: ccat.sas.upenn.edu/ARIT

1201 ■ ARIT Fellowships in the Humanities and Social Sciences in Turkey (Postdoctorate, Graduate/Fellowship)

Purpose: To promote American and Turkish research and exchange related to Turkey. **Focus:** History, Ancient; Humanities; Medieval studies; Modern languages; Social sciences. **Qualif.:** Applicants must be scholars and advanced graduate students engaged in research on ancient, medieval, or modern times in Turkey, in any field of the humanities and social sciences. Student applicants must have fulfilled all requirements for the doctorate except the dissertation by June of the current year, and before beginning any ARIT-sponsored research. **Criteria:** Recipients will be selected based on academic records and financial need. Preference will be given to applicants with projects of shorter duration.

Funds Avail.: No specific amount. **Duration:** Annual. **To Apply:** Applicants must provide complete application information; three letters of recommendation; a 100-word abstract of the project; letters of reference; and a copy of graduate transcript. **Deadline:** November 1.

1202 ■ ARIT National Endowment for the Humanities Advanced Fellowships for Research in Turkey (Postdoctorate/Fellowship)

Purpose: To promote American and Turkish research and exchange related to Turkey. **Focus:** Archeology; Art; History; Humanities; Linguistics; Literature; Social sciences. **Qualif.:** Applicants may be U.S. citizens or three-year residents of the U.S. (they may consult ARIT headquarters on questions of eligibility). Scholars who have completed all formal training by the application deadline and plan to carry out research in Turkey for four months or longer may apply. **Criteria:** Recipients will be selected based on academic records and financial need.

Funds Avail.: $4,200. **Duration:** Annual. **Number Awarded:** Varies. **To Apply:** Applicants must provide complete application information; three letters of recommendation; a 100-word abstract of the project; letters of reference; and a copy of graduate transcript. **Deadline:** November 1. **Contact:** Submit your application by e-mail to aritoffice@gmail.com.

1203 ■ ARIT Summer Fellowships for Intensive Advanced Turkish Language Study (Graduate, Undergraduate/Fellowship)

Purpose: To promote American and Turkish research and exchange related to Turkey. **Focus:** Foreign languages; General studies/Field of study not specified. **Qualif.:** Applicants must be: full-time students and scholars affiliated at academic institutions; citizens, nationals, or permanent residents of the United States; and, currently enrolled in an undergraduate or graduate level academic program, or faculty members. They must also have a minimum B average in current program of study and perform at the highest intermediate level on a proficiency-based admissions examination. **Criteria:** Recipients will be selected based on academic records and financial need.

Funds Avail.: No specific amount. **Duration:** Annual. **Number Awarded:** 15. **To Apply:** Applicants must submit complete application information; three letters of recommendation; letters of reference; and a copy of graduate transcript. Application fee in the amount of $25 via PayPal is required. **Deadline:** February 5. **Contact:** Director, Dr. Sylvia Onder; Division of Eastern Mediterranean Languages, Department of Arabic and Islamic Studies, Georgetown University; 210 North Poulton Hall, 1437 - 37th Street N.W., Washington D.C. 20007.

1204 ■ Critical Language Scholarships for Intensive Summer Institutes (Graduate, Undergraduate/Scholarship)

Purpose: To expand the number of Americans studying and mastering critical need foreign languages. **Focus:** Business; Engineering; Humanities; Science; Social sciences. **Qualif.:** Applicants must be U.S. citizens; must be currently enrolled in a degree-granting program at the undergraduate or graduate level; must have graduated from an undergraduate or graduate program no more than two years ago; undergraduate students must have completed at least one year of general college coursework by program start date (one year is defined as two semesters or three quarters); or students in all disciplines including business, engineering, science, the social sciences and humanities are encouraged to apply. **Criteria:** Recipients are selected based on academic record and potential to succeed in a rigorous academic setting; ability to adapt to a different cultural environment; diversity; plan for continuation of study of the language; and plan to use the language in future career.

Funds Avail.: No specific amount. **To Apply:** Applicants must submit a completed application form along with transcript of records and letters of recommendation. **Deadline:** November 1.

1205 ■ Getty Research Exchange Fellowship Program for Cultural Heritage Preservation (Doctorate/Fellowship)

Purpose: To support advanced regional research and exchanges between research centers in the Mediterranean and Middle East regions. **Focus:** General studies/Field of study not specified. **Qualif.:** Applicants must be Turkish citizens who have already obtained PhD; must have professional experience in the study or preservation of cultural heritage; must be willing to undertake specific research project in overseas research centers of another country. **Criteria:** Recipients are selected based on: the significance of the proposal; value of the collaboration proposed; feasibility of the research design; and applicant's research background.

Funds Avail.: Up to $4,000. **To Apply:** Applicants must fill out the application form; submit a project abstract and project description along with a letter of recommendation and 3-page curriculum vitae. **Deadline:** December 31.

1206 ■ Ilse Hanfmann, George Hanfmann and Machteld Mellink Fellowships (Doctorate/Fellowship)

Purpose: To enable nationals of the Republic of Turkey who are graduate students at or recent PhDs from Turkish universities in archaeology and related fields to study abroad (North America or elsewhere). **Focus:** General

Awards are arranged alphabetically below their administering organizations

studies/Field of study not specified. **Qualif.:** Applicants must be candidates for M.A. or Ph.D. degrees who have finished all course work and passed all qualifying examinations for the degree before entering the tenure of a Hanfmann Fellowship. Also eligible are scholars who have received their Ph.D. and have not yet reached 40 years of age. **Criteria:** Recipients will be selected based on achievement.

Funds Avail.: $15,000 to $45,000. **Duration:** Annual. **To Apply:** Applicants must submit a curriculum vitae; one-paragraph summary of the project; statement of purpose (no more than five double-spaced pages, and includes description of the project and its importance, a brief summary of the literature, the reasons for wanting to study or conduct research abroad, what institution this work would be conducted, and why such tenure abroad would be professionally advantageous to the present academic career); official transcript of undergraduate and graduate course work; demonstration of proficiency in the language or languages necessary for conducting research abroad; minimum of three letters of recommendation from scholars familiar with the applicant's work. **Deadline:** February 26.

1207 ■ American Respiratory Care Foundation
9425 N MacArthur Blvd., Ste. 100
Irving, TX 75063-4706
Ph: (972)243-2272
Fax: (972)484-2720
URL: www.arcfoundation.org

1208 ■ Advance Degree and Clinical Research Training Grants in Alpha-1 Antitrypsin Deficiency (Master's/Grant)

Purpose: To support an RT's getting advance training in research with the subject of the deliverable research project being a meritorious project regarding alpha-1 antitrypsin deficiency. **Focus:** Respiratory therapy. **Qualif.:** Applicants must be respiratory therapists who conduct research (clinical or translational), including detection, inhalation therapies, clinical care, diagnostics, and therapeutic tools in alpha-1 antitrypsin deficiency (AATD)-related lung disease. **Criteria:** The project must be deemed important and meritorious by the grant review committee and could involve any of a number of aspects regarding AATD, e.g., strategies in detection, therapy/ethical/legal/social issues, basic science, etc.

Funds Avail.: No specific amount. **To Apply:** Interested applicants may contact the Foundation for the application process and other information.

1209 ■ CareFusion Fellowships for Neonatal and Pediatric Therapists (Professional development/Fellowship)

Purpose: To foster projects in the field of neonatal and pediatric critical care. **Focus:** Health sciences; Medical research. **Qualif.:** Candidates must be researchers having high quality abstracts accepted for presentation at the AARC Congress of the current year. **Criteria:** Selection will be based on the Trustee's criteria.

Funds Avail.: No specific amount. **Duration:** Annual. **To Apply:** No formal application is required. All fellows will be selected by ARCF Trustees. Projects involving original research in mechanical ventilation issues using bench models, animal models or human subjects are encouraged. **Remarks:** Funded by VIASYS Healthcare.

1210 ■ Jeri Eiserman, RRT Professional Education Research Fellowships (Professional development/Fellowship)

Purpose: To support original university hospital research in respiratory care and airway management. **Focus:** Health sciences. **Qualif.:** Candidates must be researchers having high quality abstracts accepted for presentation at the AARC Congress of the current year. **Criteria:** Selection will be based on the Trustee's criteria.

Funds Avail.: No specific amount. **Duration:** Annual. **To Apply:** No formal application is required. All fellows will be selected by ARCF Trustees. Projects using bench models, animal model or human subjects are encouraged. **Remarks:** Funded by the Anesthesia and Respiratory Division of Teleflex in honor of Mrs. Jeri Eiserman's dedication to advancing the respiratory care profession, and her service as an extraordinary leader, role model and educator. Established in 2015.

1211 ■ Parker B. Francis Respiratory Research Grants (Advanced Professional, Professional development/Grant)

Purpose: To provide financial assistance for research programs dealing with respiratory care and related topics. **Focus:** Medical research; Respiratory therapy. **Qualif.:** Applicants must be physicians or respiratory care practitioners. **Criteria:** Selection will be based on the committee's criteria.

Funds Avail.: $10,000. **Duration:** Annual. **To Apply:** Applicants must submit a completed application and research materials to the foundation. Application form is available at the website. **Deadline:** December 31. **Remarks:** The grant is made possible through the provided endowment by the Parker B. Francis Foundation to the ARCF.

1212 ■ Monaghan/Trudell Fellowships for Aerosol Technique Development (Professional development/Fellowship)

Purpose: To support projects dealing with aerosol delivery issues. **Focus:** Health sciences; Medical research. **Qualif.:** Candidates must be researchers having high quality abstracts accepted for presentation at the AARC Congress of the current year. **Criteria:** Selection will be based on the Trustee's criteria.

Funds Avail.: No specific amount. **Duration:** Annual. **To Apply:** No formal application is required. All fellows will be selected by ARCF Trustees. Projects may include modeling, in-vitro, or clinical studies. The focus should be on developing cost-effective approaches to aerosol delivery. **Remarks:** Funded by Trudell Medical and Monaghan Medical in the United States. Established in 1993.

1213 ■ NBRC/AMP H. Frederic Helmholz, Jr., MD Educational Research Funds (Master's, Doctorate/Grant)

Purpose: To support a research with practical value to the respiratory care profession. **Focus:** Respiratory therapy. **Qualif.:** Candidates must be Master's or PhD students. **Criteria:** Selection will be based on the committee's criteria.

Funds Avail.: No specific amount. **To Apply:** Applicants must submit a proposal in a format prescribed by the American Respiratory Care Foundation Board of Trustees. Applicants may download a copy of the application form and the research plan online. **Contact:** ARCF Executive Office, at the above address.

Awards are arranged alphabetically below their administering organizations

1214 ■ Philips Respironics Fellowships in Mechanical Ventilation *(Professional development/Award)*
Purpose: To foster projects dealing with mechanical ventilation, especially outside of the intensive care unit. **Focus:** Health sciences. **Qualif.:** Candidates must be researchers having high quality abstracts accepted for presentation at the AARC Congress of the current year. **Criteria:** Selection will be based on the Trustee's criteria.
Funds Avail.: No specific amount. **Duration:** Annual. **To Apply:** No formal application is required. All fellows will be selected by ARCF Trustees. Projects can be device development, device evaluation, cost effectiveness analysis, or education programs. **Remarks:** Funded by Respironics, Inc. Established in 1993.

1215 ■ Philips Respironics Fellowships in Non-Invasive Respiratory Care *(Professional development/Fellowship)*
Purpose: To foster projects dealing with non-invasive techniques to provide ventilator support. **Focus:** Health sciences; Medical research. **Qualif.:** Candidates must be researchers having high quality abstracts accepted for presentation at the AARC Congress of the current year. **Criteria:** Selection will be based on the Trustee's criteria.
Funds Avail.: No specific amount. **Duration:** Annual. **To Apply:** No formal application is required. All fellows will be selected by ARCF Trustees. Projects can be device development, device evaluation, cost effectiveness analysis, or education programs. **Remarks:** Funded by Respironics, Inc. Established in 1993.

1216 ■ Charles W. Serby COPD Research Fellowships *(Professional development/Fellowship)*
Purpose: To promote research and education in the area of Chronic Obstructive Pulmonary Disease (COPD). **Focus:** Health sciences. **Qualif.:** Candidates must be researchers having high quality abstracts accepted for presentation at the AARC Congress of the current year. **Criteria:** Selection will be based on the Trustee's criteria.
Funds Avail.: No specific amount. **To Apply:** No formal application is required. All fellows will be selected by ARCF Trustees. **Remarks:** Funded by Boehringer Ingelheim Pharmaceuticals, Inc. in honor of Dr. Charles Serby's long-standing commitment to respiratory clinical research. Established in 2002.

1217 ■ Jerome M. Sullivan Research Funds *(Professional development/Grant)*
Purpose: To support investigators for their clinical or basic research in respiratory care and cardiopulmonary medicine. **Focus:** Health sciences. **Qualif.:** Applicants must be respiratory therapists or respiratory technicians. **Criteria:** Selection will be based on the committee's criteria.
Funds Avail.: $10,000. **Duration:** Annual. **To Apply:** Interested applicants may obtain an application form online. Application must: be typewritten, using single spacing and black ribbon; be stay within the margin limitations indicated on the form and continuation pages. Continuation pages must be 8 1/2" x 11" in a good quality white bond paper. Draw all graphs, diagrams, tables, and charts with black ink. Do not include oversized documents, graphs, diagrams, tables, and chairs in the body of the application; submit them in an appendix. **Deadline:** December 31.

1218 ■ American Road & Transportation Builders Association (ARTBA)
1219 28th St. NW
Washington, DC 20007
Ph: (202)289-4434
E-mail: info@artba.org
URL: www.artba.org
Facebook: www.facebook.com/ARTBAssociation
LinkedIn: www.linkedin.com/company/artba
Twitter: twitter.com/ARTBA

1219 ■ The Lanford Family Highway Worker Memorial Scholarship Program *(Undergraduate/Scholarship)*
Purpose: To provide financial assistance to the children or legally adopted children of highway workers killed or permanently disabled in the line of duty to pursue post-high school education. **Focus:** General studies/Field of study not specified. **Qualif.:** Applicants must be sons, daughters or legally adopted children of highway workers who died or became permanently disabled in roadway construction zone accidents and their parents have been employed by a transportation construction firm or a transportation public agency at the time of his or her death or disabling injury. **Criteria:** Candidates will be evaluated on the basis of their submitted application materials.
Funds Avail.: No specific amount. **Duration:** Annual. **To Apply:** Candidates must submit completed and signed award application form; proof of parent's death in line of duty (if parent is permanently disabled, candidates must submit documentation that shows disability as work-related); proof of guardianship if not living with surviving parent; an official copy of transcript and grade report from the school currently attended or most recently attended; a brief, typewritten statement explaining reasons for wanting to continue education accompanied by recent photo; completed and signed "Free Application for Federal Student Aid" (FAFSA) forms for the current year; federal tax return copy; copy of acceptance letter from the college, university, technical school where the applicants plan to attend; and two letters of recommendation from teachers in support of their application. **Deadline:** April 8. **Remarks:** Established in 1999.

1220 ■ American Roentgen Ray Society (ARRS)
44211 Slatestone Ct.
Leesburg, VA 20176-5109
Ph: (703)729-3353
Fax: (703)729-4839
Free: 866-940-2777
E-mail: info@arrs.org
URL: www.arrs.org
Facebook: www.facebook.com/AmericanRoentgenRaySociety
LinkedIn: www.linkedin.com/company/arrs
Twitter: twitter.com/ARRS_Radiology

1221 ■ American Roentgen Ray Society Scholarships *(Other/Scholarship)*
Purpose: To support study in a field selected by the scholars to attain their professional career goals. **Focus:** Radiology. **Qualif.:** Applicants must have earned MD or DO from an accredited institution; completed all the required residency or fellowship training or equivalent; must be full-time faculty appointment as lecturers, instructors, assistant professors or equivalent for no more than five years beyond completion of training; be certified by the American Board of Radiology or equivalent. **Criteria:** Recipients will be selected based on competence and promise

Awards are arranged alphabetically below their administering organizations

of the candidate in research, education or administration related to medical imaging, as indicated by the institution making the nomination and personal qualities of the candidate that indicate that he or she is a true scholar and leader with exceptional potential. **Funds Avail.:** No specific amount. **To Apply:** Applicants must submit a cover letter stating his or her address, phone and fax numbers and e-mail address, for use by the ARRS administrative office; a curriculum vitae; a three-page summary of the applicant's qualifications, goals and purpose of study; statements from the department and applicant regarding present interests in a specific area related to radiological sciences or education, and long-term scientific and professional objectives or aspirations as they may relate to his or her future career; statement from the Department Chair as to the department's commitment to provide time for the scholar to study, and a commitment ensuring his or her return to the faculty at the completion of the scholarship; and an estimated budget covering the scholar's program over the one or two-year period.

1222 ■ ARRS/Leonard Berlin Scholarships in Medical Professionalism (Other/Scholarship)

Purpose: To support study and research related to medical ethics, medico-legal principles, patient accountability, sensitivity to patient diversity and/or other topics encompassing medical professionalism. **Focus:** Ethics and bioethics. **Qualif.:** Applicants must: have an MD or DO from an accredited institution, or equivalent; have completed a radiology residency, and fellowship training where appropriate, or the equivalent; be certified by the American Board of Radiology or equivalent; and, be members of the ARRS at the time the application is submitted and for the duration of the award. **Criteria:** Recipients will be selected based on competence and promise of the candidate in research, education or administration related to medical imaging, as indicated by the institution making the nomination and personal qualities of the candidate that indicate that he or she is a true scholar and leader with exceptional potential. **Funds Avail.:** Total of $100,000. **Duration:** Annual; up to two years. **Number Awarded:** 1. **To Apply:** Applicants must submit a cover letter stating their address, phone and fax numbers and e-mail address, for use by the ARRS administrative office; a curriculum vitae including details of any other current or pending salary support; a three-page summary of the applicant's qualifications, goals and purpose of study; a description of course-work that will be undertaken; a listing of mentors, as appropriate to the proposal, and their contributions to the proposal; a letter of nomination from the Department Chair, or when applicable, the Radiology Group Director, and two additional letters of recommendation; and an estimated budget covering the scholar's program over the one or two-year period. **Deadline:** November 14. **Contact:** For additional information email nkhaliq@arrs.org.

1223 ■ American Romanian Orthodox Youth (AROY)

c/o Stephen Maxim, President
832 Indian Lake Rd.
Lake Orion, MI 48362
Ph: (586)260-3342
URL: www.roea.org/aroy.html

1224 ■ A.R.F.O.R.A. Undergraduate Scholarships for Women (Undergraduate/Scholarship)

Purpose: To support the continuing education of student members. **Focus:** General studies/Field of study not specified. **Qualif.:** Applicant must be a female voting member of a parish of the Romanian Orthodox Episcopate of America and accepted by a duly accredited university or college. **Criteria:** Selection is based on the application materials. **Funds Avail.:** $1,000. **Number Awarded:** 1. **To Apply:** Applicants must send a request for application to ARFORA/Martha Gavrila Scholarship c/o 222 Orchard Park Dr. New Castle, PA 16105. Three letters of recommendation must be mailed sealed with attached photo and must submit a formal letter projecting the plans of the applicant. **Deadline:** May 15.

1225 ■ Pamfil and Maria Bujea Family Orthodox Christian Seminarian Scholarships (Undergraduate/Scholarship)

Purpose: To support the education of students seeking ordination into priesthood or wish to serve the Church in a professional manner. **Focus:** Christian education; Religion; Theology. **Qualif.:** Applicants must be citizens or permanent residents of either Canada or the United States of American and show proof thereof. Students must furnish written proof of enrollment in the appropriate higher education program along with a transcripts of the students' grades at the designated institutions. **Criteria:** Award is limited to those who either seek ordination into the priesthood or who wish to serve the Church. **Funds Avail.:** $10,000. **Number Awarded:** 1. **To Apply:** Applicants must submit a completed application; a 300-word handwritten essay explaining their mission if they're assigned to Canada; and a posed photograph. Three letters of recommendation obtained sealed, from the authors, must be included with the application. One should be from the applicants' spiritual advisor/priest. **Deadline:** May 31. **Contact:** Application forms must be sent to PO Box 309, Grass Lake, MI 49240-0309.

1226 ■ A.R.F.O.R.A. Martha Gavrila Scholarships for Women (Postgraduate/Scholarship)

Purpose: To support the student members in post-graduate studies. **Focus:** General studies/Field of study not specified. **Qualif.:** Applicant must be a female voting member of a parish of the Romanian Orthodox Episcopate of America; a graduate of a duly accredited university/college; and accepted by a graduate school or a duly accredited university and specify her course of study. **Criteria:** Selection is based on the application materials. **Funds Avail.:** $1,000. **Duration:** One year. **Number Awarded:** 1. **To Apply:** Applicants must send a request for application to ARFORA/Martha Gavrila Scholarship c/o 222 Orchard Park Dr New Castle, PA 16105. Three letters of recommendation must be mailed sealed, directly to the attention of the Scholarship Committee. A photo must be included and a formal letter projecting the plans of the applicant. **Deadline:** May 15.

1227 ■ R.O.E.A. Dumitru Golea Goldy-Gemu Scholarships (Undergraduate/Scholarship)

Purpose: To support the continuing education of student members. **Focus:** General studies/Field of study not specified. **Qualif.:** Applicant must be of Romanian descent and a citizen or permanent resident of the United States or Canada; must be enrolled as a full-time undergraduate student in a recognized four-year educational institution. **Criteria:** Selection is based on the application. **Funds Avail.:** $1,500. **Number Awarded:** 2. **To Apply:** Applicant must submit a completed application form; three

Awards are arranged alphabetically below their administering organizations

letters of recommendation; 300 words handwritten essay explaining, "How Romanian heritage makes him/her become a better American/Canadian"; and recent photo for publication. In addition, applicant must submit written proof of enrollment: 1) For High School applicants: a copy of letter of acceptance from higher education program; 2) Current undergraduate applicants: a transcript of records at the institution; 3) Returning undergraduate applicants: a letter of acceptance from the institution. **Deadline:** May 31. **Contact:** Send application materials to Goldy Scholarship Committee PO Box 309 Grass Lake, MI 49240-0309.

1228 ■ A.R.O.Y. Stanitz Scholarships
(Undergraduate/Scholarship)

Purpose: To support the continuing education of student members. **Focus:** General studies/Field of study not specified. **Qualif.:** Applicants must be active AROY members; must be high school graduates; must be college students or those who intends to enroll in a school or college or university level. **Criteria:** Selection will be based on the submitted application.

Funds Avail.: $1,000. **Duration:** Annual. **Number Awarded:** 2. **To Apply:** Applicants must submit the following application materials: a biographical history including family; an educational background and grades; list of AROY and church activities; list of extra-curricular interests or achievements; reasons why applying for the scholarship; a photograph; and a letter of recommendation from parish priest or AROY advisors regarding parish and AROY activities. **Deadline:** July 1. **Remarks:** Established in 1971. **Contact:** Send all materials to William R. Stanitz/AROY Scholarship The Romanian Orthodox Episcopate of America PO Box 309 Grass Lake, MI 49240-0309.

1229 ■ The American-Scandinavian Foundation (ASF)
58 Park Ave. 38th St.
New York, NY 10016
Ph: (212)779-3587
E-mail: info@amscan.org
URL: www.amscan.org
Facebook: www.facebook.com/ASF-Scandinavia-House-75185450461
Twitter: twitter.com/ScanHouse

1230 ■ American-Scandinavian Foundation Fellowships and Grants to Study in America *(Graduate, Professional development/Fellowship, Grant)*

Purpose: To promote international understanding through educational and cultural exchange between the United States and Denmark, Finland, Iceland, Norway and Sweden. **Focus:** General studies/Field of study not specified. **Qualif.:** Applicants must be citizens of Denmark, Finland, Iceland, Norway or Sweden who wish to undertake study or research programs (usually at the graduate level) in the United States. **Criteria:** Selection will be based on the standards set by the respective countries of the awardees.

Funds Avail.: Over $500,000. **Duration:** Annual. **Number Awarded:** Varies. **To Apply:** In order to apply, applicants must contact the cooperating organizations of ASF.

1231 ■ American-Scandinavian Foundation Fellowships to Study in Scandinavia *(Graduate/Fellowship)*

Purpose: To support an individual to pursue research, study or creative arts projects. **Focus:** General studies/Field of study not specified. **Qualif.:** Applicants must have a well-defined research or study project that makes a stay in Scandinavia essential; must be US citizens or permanent residents; must have completed their undergraduate education by the start of their project in Scandinavia. **Criteria:** Priority is given to candidates at the graduate level for dissertation-related study or research.

Funds Avail.: Up to $23,000. **Duration:** Annual. **Number Awarded:** Varies. **To Apply:** Applicants must submit an official ASF form and supporting documents (letters of reference and academic transcripts) in sealed envelopes. They must also submit one original paper copy and one electronic copy of the following items: signed application form; project summary (not to exceed 200 words); budget form; project statement (not to exceed 1,200 words) and bibliography; curriculum vitae (not to exceed ten pages including publications listing); invitation and other relevant correspondence confirming the availability of overseas resources. **Deadline:** November 1.

1232 ■ American-Scandinavian Foundation Grants to Study in Scandinavia *(Graduate/Grant)*

Purpose: To support an individual to pursue research, study or creative arts projects. **Focus:** Arts. **Qualif.:** Applicants must have a well-defined research or study project that makes a stay in Scandinavia essential; must be US citizens or permanent residents; must have completed their undergraduate education by the start of their project in Scandinavia; must be post-graduate scholars, professionals and candidates in the arts to carry out research or study visits of one to three months duration. **Criteria:** Priority is given to candidates at the graduate level for dissertation-related study or research.

Funds Avail.: Up to $5,000. **Duration:** Annual. **Number Awarded:** Varies. **To Apply:** Applicants must submit an official ASF form and supporting documents (letters of reference and academic transcripts) in sealed envelopes. They must also submit one original paper copy and one electronic copy of the following items: signed application form; project summary (not to exceed 200 words); budget form; project statement (not to exceed 1,200 words) and bibliography; curriculum vitae (not to exceed ten pages including publications listing); invitation and other relevant correspondence confirming the availability of overseas resources. **Deadline:** November 1.

1233 ■ American-Scandinavian Foundation Translation Prize *(Other/Prize)*

Purpose: To support the most outstanding translations of poetry, fiction, drama or literary prose written by a Scandinavian author. **Focus:** General studies/Field of study not specified. **Qualif.:** Applicants must be outstanding English translators of poetry, fiction, drama or literary prose originally written in a Nordic language. **Criteria:** Selection will be based on the committee's criteria.

Funds Avail.: Varies. **Duration:** Annual. **Number Awarded:** 2. **To Apply:** An entry must consist of four legible copies of the translation, including a title page and a table of contents for the proposed book of which the manuscript submitted is a part and one copy of the work(s) in the original language. Applicants must also send photocopies of the following pages: a CV containing all contact information including email address for the translator; and a letter or other documents signed by the author, the author's agent or the author's estate granting permission for the translation to be entered in this competition and published in Scandinavian Review. Prose manuscripts must

Awards are arranged alphabetically below their administering organizations

not be longer than 50 pages and must not be longer than 25 pages for poetry. Manuscripts must be typed and double-spaced with numbered pages. **Deadline:** June 1.

1234 ■ ASF/Annika Teig/Skidmore, Owings and Merrill Fellowships *(Postgraduate/Fellowship)*

Purpose: To support Scandinavian citizens seeking experience in interior design at a leading architecture firm in New York City. **Focus:** Architecture. **Qualif.:** Applicants must be from Scandinavia who have studied or are currently studying architecture. **Criteria:** Selection shall be conducted by the review panel selected by SOM.

Funds Avail.: No specific amount. **Duration:** Annual. **To Apply:** Applicants must complete the online application through the SOM Career Center and submit a soft copy of the prescribed portfolio. **Deadline:** May 31. **Contact:** Online submission to teig.fellowship@som.com.

1235 ■ Leif and Inger Sjöberg Awards *(Advanced Professional, Professional development/Award, Grant, Prize)*

Purpose: To encourage the English translation of Scandinavian literature of the last two centuries. **Focus:** Literature; Translating. **Qualif.:** Applicants must be outstanding English translators of poetry, fiction, drama or literary prose originally written in a Nordic language. **Criteria:** Selection will be based on the committee's criteria.

Funds Avail.: $2,000. **Duration:** Annual. **To Apply:** An entry must consist of four legible copies of the translation, including a title page and a table of contents for the proposed book of which the manuscript submitted is a part as well as one copy of the work(s) in the original language. Applicants must also send photocopies of the following pages: a CV containing all contact information, including email address for the translator; and a letter or other document signed by the author, the author's agent or the author's estate granting permission for the translation to be entered in this competition and published in Scandinavian Review. Prose manuscripts must not be longer than 50 pages and must not be longer than 25 pages for poetry. Manuscripts must be typed and double-spaced with numbered pages. **Deadline:** June 1. **Contact:** American-Scandinavian Foundation, at the above address.

1236 ■ American Schools of Oriental Research (ASOR)
Boston University
656 Beacon St., 5th Fl.
Boston, MA 02215
Ph: (617)353-6570
Fax: (617)353-6575
E-mail: asor@bu.edu
URL: www.asor.org
Facebook: www.facebook.com/ASOR.org
LinkedIn: www.linkedin.com/company/american-schools-of-oriental-research?trk=company_name
Twitter: twitter.com/ASORResearch

1237 ■ Katherine Barton Platt Excavation Fellowships *(Other, Undergraduate/Fellowship)*

Purpose: To support the participation of ASOR members as volunteers or staff on excavation projects. **Focus:** General studies/Field of study not specified. **Qualif.:** Applicants must be current members of ASOR or students enrolled at an institutional member of ASOR. **Criteria:** Preference will be given to individuals who have not received a support through the heritage programs or other funding sources.

Funds Avail.: No specific amount. **To Apply:** Applicants must submit a completed application form and 250-350 words with photo (digital tiff, 300 dpi or higher). Reports and photos should be sent electronically with "Platt Report" in the subject heading. **Deadline:** February 17. **Contact:** American Schools of Oriental Research, at the above address.

1238 ■ American Senior Benefits Association (ASBA)
PO Box 300777
Chicago, IL 60630-0777
Free: 877-906-2722
E-mail: info@asbaonline.org
URL: www.asbaonline.org
Facebook: www.facebook.com/asbaonline/timeline/?ref=ts
Twitter: twitter.com/asbaonline

1239 ■ ASBA College Scholarship Grant Program *(Postgraduate/Scholarship)*

Purpose: To provide and support educational financial aid to members and their grandchildren. **Focus:** General studies/Field of study not specified. **Qualif.:** Applicant must be a dependent or grandchild of an ASBA member; enrolled at least one year in college or university. **Criteria:** Awards are given based on academic merit and evaluation of the submitted essay.

Funds Avail.: Up to $1,000. **Duration:** Annual. **To Apply:** Applicant must submit an application form (please visit the website); an essay; two letters of recommendation; official copies of high school/college transcript. **Deadline:** May 31.

1240 ■ American Sheep Industry Association (ASI)
9785 Maroon Cir., Ste. 360
Englewood, CO 80112
Ph: (303)771-3500
URL: www.sheepusa.org
Facebook: www.facebook.com/SheepUSA/
Twitter: twitter.com/SheepUSA

1241 ■ ASI Sheep Heritage Foundation Memorial Scholarship *(Graduate/Scholarship)*

Purpose: To provide financial support to a graduate-level student for research toward the advancement of the sheep, lamb, and wool industry. **Focus:** Animal science and behavior. **Qualif.:** Applicants must be graduate students involved in sheep and/or wool research in such areas as animal science, agriculture economics or veterinary medicine with proof of graduate school acceptance. **Criteria:** Selection will be based on the committee's criteria.

Funds Avail.: $3,000. **Duration:** Annual. **To Apply:** Applicants should complete an application, available on the website, and include two letters of reference. **Deadline:** June 1.

1242 ■ American Shotcrete Association (ASA)
38800 Country Club Dr.
Farmington Hills, MI 48331
Ph: (248)848-3780

Awards are arranged alphabetically below their administering organizations

Fax: (248)848-3740
E-mail: info@shotcrete.org
URL: www.shotcrete.org
Facebook: www.facebook.com/AmericanShotcreteAssociation

1243 ■ ASA Graduate Scholarships *(Graduate/Scholarship)*

Purpose: To attract, identify and assist outstanding graduate students pursuing careers within the field of concrete with a significant interest in the shotcrete process. **Focus:** Construction. **Qualif.:** Applicant must have been accepted for graduate study in the area of concrete at an accredited college/university within the U.S. or at Laval University in Canada, and be a full-time first or second-year (after bachelor's degree) graduate student during the entire scholarship year. **Criteria:** Selection is based on the essay, submitted data and reference.

Funds Avail.: $3,000. **Duration:** One academic year. **Number Awarded:** 2. **To Apply:** Applicants must submit a completed typed application form together with one-page resume; essay (1-page limit, 300 words or less, name must be on first page, include all scheduled classes for balance of academic year); two completed online reference forms; and all original undergraduate and graduate transcripts (mailed directly to ASA in sealed envelope with a university stamp). Application materials must be sent together via email in one package. All materials must be in English. **Deadline:** November 1.

1244 ■ American Society of Anesthesiologists (ASA)

1061 American Ln.
Schaumburg, IL 60173-4973
Ph: (847)825-5586
Fax: (847)825-1692
E-mail: communications@asahq.org
URL: www.asahq.org

1245 ■ Lansdale Public Policy Fellowship *(Advanced Professional, Professional development/Fellowship)*

Purpose: To provide opportunities for the fellows to gain understandings of the national health policy-making processes and contribute to the development of programs and legislation related to health care. **Focus:** Anesthesiology. **Qualif.:** Applicants must be ASA members; must be anesthesiologists interested in health policy issues at the federal government level. **Criteria:** Selection will be based on the committee's criteria.

Funds Avail.: $123,000. **Duration:** Annual. **To Apply:** Interested applicants should contact the Program Administrator for the application process and other details. **Contact:** Pat Daly; Phone: 202-289-2222; E-mail: p.daly@asawash.org.

1246 ■ American Society of Brewing Chemists (ASBC)

3340 Pilot Knob Rd.
Saint Paul, MN 55121-2097
Ph: (651)454-7250
Fax: (651)454-0766
E-mail: asbc@scisoc.org
URL: www.asbcnet.org/Pages/default.aspx
Facebook: www.facebook.com/BrewingChemists
LinkedIn: www.linkedin.com/groups/4662739/profile
Twitter: twitter.com/BrewingChemists

1247 ■ ASBC Foundation Graduate Scholarships *(Graduate/Scholarship)*

Purpose: To provide financial support to students who are pursuing MS or Ph.D. degrees in brewing science or related areas. **Focus:** Food science and technology; Nutrition. **Qualif.:** Applicants must be current ASBC student members enrolled in graduate studies by the time the graduate scholarship becomes effective, or be current graduate students pursuing a course of study leading to an MS or a Ph.D. degree. **Criteria:** Selection shall be based on the aforementioned candidates' qualifications and compliance with the application details.

Funds Avail.: Up to $5,000. **Duration:** Annual. **To Apply:** Applicants must submit a completed application form; copies of transcripts; a letter of application describing career plans; and three letters of recommendation. At least two of which are from deans, department heads and/or professors who have supervised the applicant's most recent academic work. Letters should present essential facts regarding scholastic record, capacity for work, extracurricular activities, career potential, ability to cooperate, character and personality and interest and capability in research. **Deadline:** April 1. **Contact:** ASBC Foundation Program Manager, Linda Schmitt at lschmitt@scisoc.org.

1248 ■ ASBC Foundation Undergraduate Scholarships *(Undergraduate/Scholarship)*

Purpose: To provide financial support to students who are children of active ASBC members. **Focus:** Food science and technology; Nutrition. **Qualif.:** Applicants must be: children of active ASBC members; enrolled as undergraduate students (juniors and seniors) at a college or university; and, actively pursuing a bachelor's degree. **Criteria:** Selection shall be based on the aforementioned candidates' qualifications and compliance with the application details.

Funds Avail.: Up to $1,000. **Duration:** Annual. **To Apply:** Applicants must submit a completed application form; copies of transcripts; a letter of application describing career plans; and three letters of recommendation with at least two from the academic adviser and/or faculty members familiar with the applicant's academic record. The confidential letter(s) should include a general appraisal of the scholarship, extracurricular activities and abilities in particular relation to the purposes and eligibility requirements of the scholarships. **Deadline:** April 1. **Contact:** ASBC Foundation Program Manager, Linda Schmitt at lschmitt@scisoc.org.

1249 ■ American Society of Business Publication Editors (ASBPE)

214 N Hale St.
Wheaton, IL 60187
Ph: (630)510-4588
Fax: (630)510-4501
E-mail: info@asbpe.org
URL: www.asbpe.org
Facebook: www.facebook.com/asbpe
Twitter: twitter.com/asbpe

1250 ■ ASBPE Young Leaders Scholarships *(Professional development/Scholarship)*

Purpose: To help young editors in their careers. **Focus:** Business; Editors and editing. **Qualif.:** Applicant must be

Awards are arranged alphabetically below their administering organizations

an editor; 30 years old or younger; worked as an editor in a business magazine for at least two years; must be sponsored by the applicant's chief editor; pursuing career in business press; and must not be a past winner of the ASBPE Young Leaders Scholarship. **Criteria:** Selection is based on merit.

Funds Avail.: No specific amount. **Duration:** Annual. **To Apply:** Application form is available at the website. **Deadline:** March 10. **Contact:** For further information, applicants may e-mail at asbpe.info@asbpe.org.

1251 ■ American Society of Certified Engineering Technicians (ASCET)
PO Box 95
Cape May Court House, NJ 08210
Ph: (609)600-2097
Fax: (609)600-2097
URL: www.ascet.org
Facebook: www.facebook.com/American-Society-of-Certified-Engineering-Technicians-546249435452001
LinkedIn: www.linkedin.com/company/american-society-of-certified-engineering-technicians
Twitter: twitter.com/ascet50

1252 ■ Joseph C. Johnson Memorial Grants
(Undergraduate/Grant, Scholarship)

Purpose: To diminish the cost of tuition, books, and lab fees for students. **Focus:** Engineering. **Qualif.:** Applicant must be an American citizen or a legal resident, a student, certified, regular, registered or associate member of ASCET; full or part-time student in an Engineering Technology program (students in a two year program should apply in the first year to receive the grant for their second year. Students in a four year program who apply in the third year may receive the grant for their fourth year); and be qualified for financial aid under the Federal College Work Study Program. Applicant must meet the following grade requirements: 2 points on a 3 point system, 3 points on a 4 point system, 4 points on a 5 point system, or 5 points on a 6 point system. **Criteria:** Priority will be given to applicants who have demonstrated financial need, as verified by the Dean or Registrar of Engineering Technology, or the Financial Aid Office at the institution the applicant attends.

Funds Avail.: $750. **Duration:** Annual. **To Apply:** Applicants must submit a fully accomplished printed or typewritten application form available online; a letter of recommendation from a faculty member of the Engineering Technology Department indicating the motivation, progress, achievements, and an evaluation of the applicant's potential in the field of Engineering Technology; letters of recommendation from two personal acquaintances, employers or former employers, outlining association, motivation and potential for success; a copy of transcript of records and be sure to pass all the requirements on time.

1253 ■ Joseph M. Parish Memorial Grants
(Undergraduate/Scholarship, Grant)

Purpose: To diminish the cost of tuition, books, and lab fees for students. **Focus:** Engineering. **Qualif.:** Applicants must meet the following: must have a minimum grade points average of 2 points on a 3 point system, 3 points on a 4 point system, 4 points on a 5 point system, or 5 points on a 6 point system; must be U.S. citizens or legal residents; must be student members of ASCET; must be full time students in an Engineering Technology program; must be qualified for financial aid under the Federal Work Study Program. **Criteria:** Priority will be given to applicants who have demonstrated financial need, as verified by the Dean or Registrar of Engineering Technology, or the Financial Aid Office at the institution the applicant is attending.

Funds Avail.: $500. **Duration:** Annual. **To Apply:** Applicants must submit a fully accomplished printed or typewritten application form available online; a letter of recommendation from a faculty member of the Engineering Technology Department indicating the motivation, progress, achievements, and an evaluation of the applicant's potential in the field of Engineering Technology; letters of recommendation from two personal acquaintances, employers or former employers, outlining association, motivation and potential for success; copy of transcript of records and be sure to pass all the requirements on time. **Deadline:** April 1.

1254 ■ Kurt H. and Donna M. Schuler Cash Grants
(Undergraduate/Scholarship, Grant)

Purpose: To offset the cost of educational expenses as desired. **Focus:** Engineering. **Qualif.:** Applicant must either be a student, certified, regular, registered, or associate member of ASCET; a high school senior in the last five months of the academic year who will be enrolled in an Engineering Technology curriculum no later than six months following selection for award; achieved passing grades in their present curriculum. **Criteria:** Priority will be given to applicants who show financial need, as verified by the Dean or Registrar of Engineering Technology, or the Financial Aid Office.

Funds Avail.: $400. **Duration:** Annual. **Number Awarded:** Varies. **To Apply:** Applicant must provide a copy of transcript; a letter of recommendation from a personal acquaintance, faculty member, or employer outlining motivation, progress, outstanding achievements, and an evaluation of the applicant's potential in the field of Engineering Technology. **Deadline:** April 1.

1255 ■ American Society of Cinematographers (ASC)
1782 N Orange Dr.
Los Angeles, CA 90078
Ph: (323)969-4333
Free: 800-448-0145
E-mail: office@theasc.com
URL: www.theasc.com
Facebook: www.facebook.com/AmericanCinematographer
Twitter: twitter.com/americancine

1256 ■ William A. Fraker Student Heritage Awards
(Graduate, Undergraduate/Award)

Purpose: To recognize cinematography students who made contributions to advance the art form. **Focus:** Cinema. **Qualif.:** Applicants must be undergraduate, graduate or recently graduated (within one year) cinematography students. **Criteria:** Applicants will be judged based on artful cinematography and effective creation of the images.

Funds Avail.: No specific amount. **Number Awarded:** 2. **To Apply:** Applicants must submit a film entry. **Deadline:** November 1. **Contact:** For more information, applicants must contact Lisa Muldowney at the above address; E-mail: lisam@cspr.com.

Awards are arranged alphabetically below their administering organizations

1257 ■ American Society for Clinical Laboratory Science (ASCLS)
1861 International Dr., Ste. 200
McLean, VA 22102
Ph: (571)748-3770
E-mail: ascls@ascls.org
URL: www.ascls.org
Facebook: www.facebook.com/ASCLS

1258 ■ Alpha Mu Tau Undergraduate Scholarships (Undergraduate/Scholarship)

Purpose: To provide financial assistance for professionals who are involved in advancement of clinical laboratory sciences. **Focus:** Clinical laboratory sciences. **Qualif.:** Applicants must be United States citizens or permanent residents of the United States; accepted into an NAACLS accredited program in Clinical Laboratory Science, to include Clinical Laboratory Science, Medical Technology, Clinical Laboratory Technician/Medical Laboratory Technician, Cytotechnology or Histotechnology. Graduate applicants must be enrolled in the year which the award is made. Undergraduate applicants must be entering in the year in which the award is made. **Criteria:** Candidates will be evaluated by the Scholarship Committee.

Funds Avail.: $1,500. **Duration:** Annual. **Number Awarded:** 3. **To Apply:** Applicants must submit a completed application form including all required documents (letter of admission, 2 letters of recommendation and 2 performance sheets are required) to the AMTF Scholarship Coordinator. **Deadline:** April 1. **Contact:** Joe Briden, AMTF Scholarship Coordinator, 7809 S 21st Dr., Phoenix, AZ 85041-7736.

1259 ■ AMTF Graduate Scholarships (Graduate/Scholarship)

Purpose: To support student members in their graduate studies. **Focus:** Medicine. **Qualif.:** Applicants must be U.S. citizens or permanent residents and ASCLS members who are accepted into or are in an approved Masters or Doctoral program in areas related to Clinical Laboratory Science including Clinical Laboratory Education or Management Programs. **Criteria:** Selection will be based on the committee's criteria.

Funds Avail.: $1,000 to $3,000. **Number Awarded:** Varies. **To Apply:** Applicants may visit the website for the instructions regarding application process. **Deadline:** April 1.

1260 ■ Dorothy Morrison Undergraduate Scholarships (Undergraduate/Scholarship)

Purpose: To provide financial assistance to professionals who are involved in advancement of clinical laboratory sciences. **Focus:** Clinical laboratory sciences. **Qualif.:** Applicants must be accepted into an NAACLS accredited program in Clinical Laboratory Science, to include Clinical Laboratory Science/Medical Technology, Clinical Laboratory Technician/Medical Laboratory Technician; must be entering or in their last year of study in the calendar year in which the award is made. **Criteria:** Applicants will be evaluated by the Scholarship Committee based on the aforesaid qualifications and compliance with the application process.

Funds Avail.: Amount varies. **Duration:** Annual. **Number Awarded:** Varies. **To Apply:** Applicants may verify the application process through the program website. **Deadline:** April 1.

1261 ■ American Society for Clinical Pathology (ASCP)
33 W Monroe St., Ste. 1600
Chicago, IL 60603
Ph: (312)541-4999
Fax: (312)541-4998
E-mail: info@ascp.org
URL: www.ascp.org
Facebook: www.facebook.com/ASCP.Chicago
Twitter: twitter.com/ASCP_Chicago

1262 ■ ASCP Phlebotomy Scholarships (Undergraduate/Scholarship)

Purpose: To support students for their outstanding academic performance. **Focus:** Medical technology. **Qualif.:** Applicants must be ASCP members; must be students enrolled in or recent graduates of an approved phlebotomy training program. **Criteria:** Selection will be based on the committee's criteria.

Funds Avail.: $500. **Duration:** Annual. **To Apply:** Interested applicants may contact the ASCP for the application and other information.

1263 ■ Siemens-ASCP Scholarship (Undergraduate/Scholarship)

Purpose: To defray education costs, promote the profession, and address the laboratory workforce shortage. **Focus:** Clinical laboratory sciences; Medical laboratory technology; Pathology. **Qualif.:** Applicants must be students in their final year of study in one of the following NAACLS-accredited programs: Cytogenetics Technologist; Cytotechnologist; Histotechnician; Histotechnologist; Molecular Biology Technologist; Medical Laboratory Technician/Clinical Laboratory Technician; Medical Laboratory Scientist/Medical Technologist/Clinical Laboratory Scientist; Pathologists' Assistants. Applicants must be ASCP members. **Criteria:** Selection will be based on the committee's criteria.

Funds Avail.: $1,000. **Duration:** Annual. **To Apply:** Interested applicants may contact the ASCP for the application process and other information. **Deadline:** November 14.

1264 ■ American Society of Colon and Rectal Surgeons (ASCRS)
85 W Algonquin Rd., Ste. 550
Arlington Heights, IL 60005
Ph: (847)290-9184
Fax: (847)290-9203
E-mail: ascrs@fascrs.org
URL: www.fascrs.org
Facebook: www.facebook.com/fascrs
LinkedIn: www.linkedin.com/company/the-american-society-of-colon-and-rectal-surgeons
Twitter: twitter.com/fascrs_updates

1265 ■ American Society of Colon and Rectal Surgeons International Fellowships (Other/Fellowship)

Purpose: To provide opportunities for surgeons to visit clinical, teaching and research activities in North America. **Focus:** Surgery. **Qualif.:** Applicants must have completed their training in colorectal surgery; have manifested interest in colon and rectal surgery as evidenced by practice, teaching, research or writings; have minimum of two years specialty colorectal practice experience; and must have a

Awards are arranged alphabetically below their administering organizations

commitment from a center to host the recipient. **Criteria:** To qualify for the fellowship, candidates should: 1) be proposed in writing by the chair of their department; 2) submit two letters of recommendation from individuals whom they have worked with; and 3) submit other supporting documents, including curriculum vitae.

Funds Avail.: Up to $50,000. **Duration:** one year. **To Apply:** Applicants must submit an application form; two letters of recommendation; completed activity profile; list of publications and presentations made at International meetings. **Deadline:** March 1.

1266 ■ American Society of Colon and Rectal Surgeons Travel Scholarships (Other/Scholarship)

Purpose: To help colorectal surgeons further their education. **Focus:** Surgery. **Qualif.:** Applicants must have completed general surgical training and must be currently involved in colorectal surgical training; must demonstrate a commitment to practice colorectal surgery; have a guarantee of one-third funding support within their colorectal society, organization, or group; and be willing to undertake the scholarship at the next meeting. **Criteria:** In order for candidates to qualify, they should: 1) be proposed in writing by the current President or an official nominee of the institution where they are trained; 2) submit references of recommendation from the Chairman of the Department where they are working; 3) submit curriculum vitae; and 4) submit a personal statement.

Funds Avail.: $4,000. **Duration:** Annual. **Number Awarded:** 4. **To Apply:** Applicants must submit a filled-out application form; two letters of recommendation (one from any official of the society where they undergo training and one from the Chairman of the Department where they are working); current activity profile; and list of publications, research work and presentations. **Deadline:** October 15.

1267 ■ American Society of Composers, Authors and Publishers Foundation (ASCAP)
1900 Broadway
New York, NY 10023-7142
Ph: (212)621-6219
Fax: (212)595-3342
E-mail: ascapfoundation@ascap.com
URL: www.ascapfoundation.org

1268 ■ Louis Armstrong Scholarships (Undergraduate/Scholarship)

Purpose: To provide educational support to students who wish to pursue education. **Focus:** Music. **Qualif.:** Applicant must be a junior-year student and enrolled full-time. **Criteria:** Selection will be based on abilities in music performance and composition.

Funds Avail.: No specific amount. **Duration:** Annual. **To Apply:** The ASCAP Foundation does not accept applications for this scholarship. Interested students should consult their financial aid office for application information.

1269 ■ Charlotte V. Bergen Scholarships (Undergraduate/Scholarship)

Purpose: To provide scholarship to young composers, aged 18 or under, to be used for music study at an accredited college or music conservatory. **Focus:** Music. **Qualif.:** Applicants must be citizens or permanent residents of the United States or enrolled students with Students Visas. **Criteria:** Selection will be based on the committee's criteria.

Funds Avail.: No specific amount. **Duration:** Annual. **To Apply:** Applicants must submit a completed application form, one reproduction of a manuscript or score, biographical information including music studies, background and experience and a list of compositions. Completed Application materials must be postmarked on or before the deadline.

1270 ■ Fran Morgenstern Davis Scholarships (Undergraduate/Scholarship)

Purpose: To provide educational support to students who are taking music composition. **Focus:** Music. **Qualif.:** Applicants must be full-time undergraduate music composition students at the Manhattan School of Music who demonstrate the potential to produce creative and original work and who also demonstrate financial need. **Criteria:** Selection will be based on the Manhattan School of Music faculty's criteria.

Funds Avail.: No specific amount. **Duration:** Annual. **Number Awarded:** 2. **To Apply:** Applicants must submit an application together with other required documents to the Manhattan School of Music.

1271 ■ John Denver Music Scholarships (Undergraduate/Scholarship)

Purpose: To provide young music students with an opportunity to attend summer music camp which they would otherwise not be able to afford. **Focus:** Music. **Qualif.:** Applicants must be students, aged 10-16, who demonstrate both musical promise and financial need. **Criteria:** Selection will be based on the committee's criteria.

Funds Avail.: No specific amount. **Duration:** Annual. **To Apply:** Applicants must submit an application to the Perry-Mansfield School in Steamboat Springs, Colorado. **Contact:** Perry-Mansfield School in Steamboat Springs, Colorado at p-m@cmn.ne.

1272 ■ Louis Dreyfus Warner-Chappell City College Scholarships (Undergraduate/Scholarship)

Purpose: To award scholarships to composition students for scores written for dance, film/video or theater. **Focus:** Music. **Qualif.:** Applicants must be students enrolled in either a B.A. or B.F.A. program at the City College/City University of New York. **Criteria:** Selection will be based on the committee's criteria.

Funds Avail.: No specific amount. **Duration:** Annual. **To Apply:** The ASCAP Foundation does not accept applications for this scholarship. Interested students should consult their school's financial aid office for application information.

1273 ■ Steve Kaplan TV and Film Studies Scholarships (Other/Scholarship)

Purpose: To provide financial assistance for an aspiring television and film composer to attend ASCAP's Film Scoring Workshop in Los Angeles. **Focus:** Filmmaking; Music. **Qualif.:** Applicants must be television and film composers. **Criteria:** Selection will be based on the committee's criteria.

Funds Avail.: No specific amount. **Duration:** Annual. **Number Awarded:** 1. **To Apply:** Interested applicants may contact the Foundation for the application information.

1274 ■ Leiber and Stoller Music Scholarships (Undergraduate/Scholarship)

Purpose: To provide assistance to young aspiring songwriters, musicians and vocalists. **Focus:** Music. **Qualif.:** Applicants must be incoming freshmen. **Criteria:** Selection

Awards are arranged alphabetically below their administering organizations

will be based on the committee's criteria.

Funds Avail.: No specific amount. **Duration:** Annual. **To Apply:** Interested students should consult their financial aid office for application information.

1275 ■ Rudy Perez Songwriting Scholarships
(Undergraduate/Scholarship)

Purpose: To provide educational opportunities to students to develop them as professionals. **Focus:** Music. **Qualif.:** Applicants must be aspiring Latino songwriters who demonstrates potential to produce creative and original work and also demonstrates financial need. **Criteria:** Selection will be based on the committee's criteria.

Funds Avail.: No specific amount. **Duration:** Annual. **To Apply:** The ASCAP Foundation does not accept applications for this scholarship. Interested students should consult their school's financial aid office for application information.

1276 ■ Betty Rose Scholarships *(Undergraduate/Scholarship)*

Purpose: To support students with their education. **Focus:** Filmmaking; Music. **Qualif.:** Applicant must be a college-level student working toward a career in scoring for film and/or television who is participating in ASCAP's Film and Television Scoring Workshop. **Criteria:** Selection will be based on the committee's criteria.

Funds Avail.: No specific amount. **Duration:** Annual. **Number Awarded:** Up to 20. **To Apply:** The ASCAP Foundation does not accept applications for this scholarship. Interested students should consult their school's financial aid office for application information.

1277 ■ American Society of Crime Laboratory Directors (ASCLD)
139A Technology Dr.
Garner, NC 27529
Ph: (919)773-2044
Fax: (919)861-9930
E-mail: office@ascld.org
URL: www.ascld.org
Facebook: www.facebook.com/ASCLD-758850184259771
LinkedIn: www.linkedin.com/company/american-society-of-crime-lab-directors-ascld-?trk=top_nav_home
Twitter: twitter.com/ascld_

1278 ■ American Society of Crime Laboratory Directors Scholarships *(Graduate, Undergraduate, Master's, Doctorate/Scholarship)*

Purpose: To provide opportunities to students intending to enter the forensic field. **Focus:** Science. **Qualif.:** Applicants must be juniors or senior students in a baccalaureate program; or graduate students (master's or doctorate) at an accredited university who are pursuing a degree in forensic science, forensic chemistry, physical or natural science; **Criteria:** Recipients will be selected based on their overall scholastic record especially in forensic science coursework, motivation or commitment to a forensic science career, personal statement and according to faculty or advisor's recommendation. At least three ASCLD members who are not affiliated with institutions from which students are applying will evaluate the pool of applicants. Applicants from FEPAC accredited programs will be given additional consideration.

Funds Avail.: $1,000. **Duration:** Annual. **To Apply:** Applicants must submit a completed application form; transcript of records; personal statement; and letter of recommendation of faculty members or a laboratory director. **Deadline:** April 15 and May 15.

1279 ■ American Society of Criminology (ASC)
1314 Kinnear Rd., Ste. 212
Columbus, OH 43212-1156
Ph: (614)292-9207
Fax: (614)292-6767
E-mail: asc@asc41.com
URL: www.asc41.com
Facebook: www.facebook.com/asc41
Twitter: twitter.com/ASCRM41

1280 ■ ASC Graduate Fellowships for Ethnic Minorities *(Doctorate/Fellowship)*

Purpose: To encourage students of color to enter the field of criminology and criminal justice. **Focus:** Criminal justice; Criminology. **Qualif.:** Applicants must be students of color, especially those from ethnic minority groups underrepresented in the field, including but not limited to, Asians, Africans, Indigenous peoples, and Hispanics, entering the field of criminology and criminal justice. **Criteria:** Selection shall be based on the aforementioned applicants' qualifications and compliance with the application details.

Funds Avail.: $6,000 each. **Duration:** Annual. **Number Awarded:** 3. **To Apply:** Applicants must complete and submit the following: proof of admission to a criminal justice, criminology, or related program of doctoral studies; up-to-date curriculum vitae; indication of race/ethnicity; copies of undergraduate or graduate transcripts; statement of need and prospects for financial assistance for graduate study; a letter describing career plans, salient experiences, and nature of interest in criminology and criminal justice; and, three letters of reference. **Deadline:** March 1. **Remarks:** Established in 1988. **Contact:** Alex Piquero; Email: apiquero@utdallas.edu.

1281 ■ Gene Carte Student Paper Competition Awards *(Undergraduate, Graduate/Prize)*

Purpose: To recognize students who have made outstanding scholarly works. **Focus:** Criminal justice; Criminology; Paralegal studies. **Qualif.:** Candidates must be students enrolled on a full-time basis in an academic program at either the undergraduate or graduate level. **Criteria:** Selection will be based on the committee's criteria.

Funds Avail.: $500 (First place); $300 (Second place); $200 (Third place). **To Apply:** Candidates may submit only one paper a year for consideration. Papers may be conceptual and/or empirical but must be directly related to criminology and must be a maximum of 7,500 words. The criminology format for the organization of text, citations and references should be used. Authors' names and departments should appear only on the title page. The next page of the manuscript should include the title and a 100-word abstract. The authors also need to submit an electronic copy of the manuscript, as well as a letter verifying their enrollment status as full-time students, cosigned by the dean, department chair or program director, all in electronic format. **Deadline:** April 15. **Remarks:** Established in 1971.

1282 ■ American Society for Eighteenth-Century Studies (ASECS)
PO Box 7867
Winston Salem, NC 27109-6253

Awards are arranged alphabetically below their administering organizations

Ph: (336)727-4694
Fax: (336)727-4697
E-mail: asecs@wfu.edu
URL: asecs.press.jhu.edu

1283 ■ ASECS Graduate Student Research Paper Awards *(Graduate/Award)*

Purpose: To recognize pioneering research contributions of the next generation of scholars of eighteenth-century studies. **Focus:** General studies/Field of study not specified. **Qualif.:** Applicants must be graduate scholars of the eighteenth-century studies. **Criteria:** Recipients will be selected based on submitted paper.

Funds Avail.: $200. **To Apply:** Applicants must submit four copies of a research essay (15-30 pages) that has not been previously published; and must submit a letter of endorsement from a mentoring professor which outlines the originality and contributions in the field of eighteenth-century studies. **Deadline:** January 1.

1284 ■ ASECS Innovative Course Design Competition *(Undergraduate/Award)*

Purpose: To encourage excellence in undergraduate teaching of the eighteenth century. **Focus:** General studies/Field of study not specified. **Qualif.:** Applicants must be undergraduate student members in any ASECS constituent disciplines. **Criteria:** Proposals will be evaluated based on relationship to design, readings, pedagogy and/or activities.

Funds Avail.: Amount not specified. **To Apply:** Applicants must submit five copies of a (three to five page) proposal. It should be for a new approach of teaching a unit within a course on the eighteenth century. **Deadline:** October 1. **Contact:** Applicants must submit their proposal to Byron R. Wells at the above address.

1285 ■ ASECS Women's Caucus Editing and Translation Fellowships *(Doctorate/Fellowship)*

Purpose: To support an editing or a translation work in progress of an eighteenth-century primary text on a feminist or a women's studies subject. **Focus:** Women's studies. **Qualif.:** Applicants must be ASECS members who have received a PhD degree. **Criteria:** Applicants will be evaluated based on submitted proposal.

Funds Avail.: $1,000. **Duration:** Annual. **To Apply:** Applicants must submit a project translated or edited by eighteenth-century women writers or works that significantly advance the women's experience in the eighteenth century; must include curriculum vitae, three to five page proposal outlining the project, a two-page bibliography of pertinent works, two letters of recommendation and a budget explaining the candidate's plans for using the funds. Winner will be asked to submit a brief written report on the progress of the project one year after receiving the award. Five copies of the proposal should be submitted to the ASECS office. **Deadline:** January 15. **Contact:** American Society for Eighteenth-Century Studies, at the above address.

1286 ■ Paula Backscheider Archival Fellowships *(Other/Fellowship)*

Purpose: To support researchers whose projects necessitate work in archives, repositories and special collections (public and private) in foreign countries and/or in the United States. **Focus:** General studies/Field of study not specified. **Qualif.:** Applicants must be members of ASECS. **Criteria:** Recipients will be selected based on submitted materials.

Funds Avail.: $1,000. **To Apply:** Applicants must submit an application form, curriculum vitae, one-page bibliography of major related books and articles, narrative description of the project and two letters of recommendation. **Deadline:** January 1. **Contact:** American Society for Eighteenth-Century Studies, at the above address.

1287 ■ Theodore E.D. Braun Research Travel Fellowships *(Other/Fellowship)*

Purpose: To support researchers, regardless of rank, who are working in French literary studies. **Focus:** Area and ethnic studies. **Qualif.:** Applicants must be ASECS members. **Criteria:** Recipients will be selected based on submitted materials.

Funds Avail.: $1,000. **To Apply:** Applicants must submit an application form, curriculum vitae, one-page bibliography of major related books and articles, narrative description of the project and two letters of recommendation. **Deadline:** January 1. **Contact:** American Society for Eighteenth-Century Studies, at the above address.

1288 ■ Emilie Du Chatelet Awards *(Doctorate/Award)*

Purpose: To support research in progress by independent or adjunct scholars on a feminist or women's studies subject. **Focus:** Women's studies. **Qualif.:** Applicants must be ASECS members who have received their PhD and who do not currently hold a tenured, tenure-track or job-secure position in a college or university. **Criteria:** Selection will be based on submitted project.

Funds Avail.: $500. **To Apply:** Applicants must include a curriculum vitae, one to three page research proposal outlining the project and candidate's plans for using the funds. Winner will be asked to submit a brief written report on the progress of the project after one year of receiving the award. **Deadline:** January 15.

1289 ■ James L. Clifford Prize *(Other/Prize, Monetary)*

Purpose: To recognize authors interested in eighteenth-century studies. **Focus:** General studies/Field of study not specified. **Qualif.:** Applicants must be author(s) of an article in outstanding study of some aspect of eighteenth-century culture; must be members of the ASECS at the time of submission. Articles must have appeared in print journal, festschrift or other serial publications. **Criteria:** Recipients will be selected based on submitted article.

Funds Avail.: $500. **Duration:** Annual. **To Apply:** Applicants must submit an article of no more than 15,000 words. Nominations must be submitted in PDF format with one hard copy. **Deadline:** January 1. **Remarks:** Established in 1976. **Contact:** Byron R. Wells, Executive Director, ASECS, at the above address or E-mail: asecs@wfu.edu.

1290 ■ A.C. Elias, Jr. Irish-American Research Travel Fellowships *(Other/Fellowship)*

Purpose: To support documentary scholarship in Ireland in the period between the Treaty of Limerick (1691) and the Act of Union (1800) to enable North American-based scholars to travel in Ireland and Irish-based scholars to travel in North America for furthering their research. **Focus:** General studies/Field of study not specified. **Qualif.:** Applicants must be ASECS members who are residents of North America, or members of ASEC's Irish sister organization, Eighteenth-Century Ireland Society who are residents of the Republic of Ireland or Northern Ireland. **Criteria:** Recipients will be selected based on submitted materials.

Funds Avail.: $2,500. **To Apply:** Applicants must submit an application form, curriculum vitae, one-page bibliography of major related books and articles, narrative description of the project and two letters of recommendation. **Deadline:** November 15. **Contact:** Prof. James E. May, Department of English, Pennsylvania State University, DuBois Campus, College Place, DuBois, PA 15801-3199; email: jem4@psu.edu; Dr. Máire Kennedy Divisional Librarian, Dublin and Irish Collections, Dublin City Libraries and Archive, 138-144 Pearse Street, Dublin 2, Ireland; email: maire.kennedy@dublincity.ie.

1291 ■ Louis Gottschalk Prize *(Other/Prize)*

Purpose: To recognize an outstanding historical or critical study on a subject of eighteenth-century interest. Books that are primarily translations are not eligible. **Focus:** History; Literature. **Qualif.:** Applicants must be authors of a scholarly book including commentaries, biographies, collections of essays by a single author and critical editions or written in any language; authors must be members of the society at the time of application. **Criteria:** Winner will be chosen based on submitted materials.

Funds Avail.: $1,000. **Duration:** Annual. **To Apply:** Publishers must submit five copies of a book. **Deadline:** November 15. **Remarks:** Established in 1976. **Contact:** Submission should be directed to this address: 2596 Reynolda Rd., Ste. C, Winston-Salem, NC 27106.

1292 ■ Hemlow Prize in Burney Studies *(Graduate/Prize)*

Purpose: To recognize the best essay written by students. **Focus:** General studies/Field of study not specified. **Qualif.:** Candidates must be graduate students. **Criteria:** Candidates will be judged based on essay's originality, coherence, use of source material, awareness of other work in the field and documentation.

Funds Avail.: $250. **Duration:** Annual. **To Apply:** Candidates must submit two copies of the essay (one appropriate for blind submission). **Deadline:** September 1. **Contact:** Dr. Laura Engel, engell784@duq.edu or by mail to Dr. Laura Engel, English Department, Duquesne University, 600 Forbes Avenue, Pittsburgh, PA 15282.

1293 ■ Oscar Kenshur Book Prize *(Other/Prize)*

Purpose: To recognize an outstanding monograph that has value to the field of eighteenth-century studies. **Focus:** Literature. **Qualif.:** Submissions in English from any discipline are welcome; authors can submit their work irrespective of citizenship. Multi-authored collections of essays and translations, as well as books by members of the Bloomington faculty, are not eligible. **Criteria:** Award will be given to applicants who best meet the requirements.

Funds Avail.: $1,000. **Duration:** Annual. **To Apply:** Authors or publishers must submit three copies of the book. For additional information, applicants must contact the Director of the Center for Eighteenth-Century Studies at Indiana University. **Deadline:** January 31. **Contact:** For further inquiries, applicants must contact Prof. Rebecca Spang, Director of the Center for Eighteenth-Century at Indiana University; rispang@indiana.edu.

1294 ■ Gwin J. and Ruth Kolb Research Travel Fellowships *(Doctorate, Other/Fellowship)*

Purpose: To supplement costs for younger eighteenth-century scholars to travel to distant collections in North America and abroad. **Focus:** General studies/Field of study not specified. **Qualif.:** Applicants must be members of ASECS who are faculty and independent scholars within the first five years of receipt of their PhD. Advanced doctoral candidates with a demonstrable need for specific collections necessary for their dissertation are also encouraged to apply. **Criteria:** Applicants will be evaluated based on submitted materials.

Funds Avail.: $500. **To Apply:** Applicants must submit an application form, curriculum vitae, one-page bibliography of major related books and articles, narrative description of the project and two letters of recommendation. **Deadline:** January 1. **Contact:** American Society for Eighteenth-Century Studies, at the above address.

1295 ■ Catharine Macaulay Prize *(Graduate/Prize)*

Purpose: To recognize student's paper in the field of feminist and gender studies. **Focus:** Women's studies. **Qualif.:** Applicants must be graduate students interested in the field of feminist and gender studies. **Criteria:** Recipients will be selected based on submitted paper.

Funds Avail.: $350. **To Apply:** Applicants must submit a paper. It should advance understanding of gender dynamics, women's experiences and/or women's contributions and offer a feminist analysis of any aspect to eighteenth-century culture and/or society. **Deadline:** September 1.

1296 ■ Robert R. Palmer Research Travel Fellowships *(Other/Fellowship)*

Purpose: To support documentary research related primarily to the history and culture of France. **Focus:** General studies/Field of study not specified. **Qualif.:** Applicants must be members of ASECS. **Criteria:** Recipients will be selected based on submitted materials.

Funds Avail.: $500. **To Apply:** Applicants must submit a completed application form, curriculum vitae, one-page bibliography of major related books and articles, narrative description of the project and two letters of recommendation. **Deadline:** January 1. **Contact:** American Society for Eighteenth-Century Studies, at the above address.

1297 ■ Hans Turley Prize in Queer Eighteenth-Century Studies *(Graduate, Other/Prize)*

Purpose: To recognize a student's paper on a topic in Lesbian, Gay, Bisexual, Transgender or Queer studies delivered at the ASECS Annual meeting. **Focus:** General studies/Field of study not specified. **Qualif.:** Applicants must be graduate students, untenured faculty members or independent scholars. **Criteria:** Recipients will be selected based on submitted paper.

Funds Avail.: No specific amount. **Duration:** Annual. **To Apply:** Applicants must submit a paper addressing issues on LGBT or Queer studies. **Deadline:** November 1. **Contact:** ASECS office, at the above address or by email to asecs@wfu.edu.

1298 ■ Aubrey L. Williams Research Travel Fellowships *(Doctorate/Fellowship)*

Purpose: To support documentary research in eighteenth-century English literature by American-based scholars. **Focus:** Literature. **Qualif.:** Applicants must be ASECS members and be residents of North America. **Criteria:** Recipients will be selected based on submitted materials.

Funds Avail.: $1,500. **To Apply:** Applicants must submit an application form, curriculum vitae, one-page bibliography of major related books and articles, narrative description of the project and two letters of recommendation. **Deadline:**

Awards are arranged alphabetically below their administering organizations

January 1. **Contact:** American Society for Eighteenth-Century Studies, at the above address.

1299 ■ American Society of Electroneurodiagnostic Technologists (ASET)
402 E Bannister Rd., Ste. A
Kansas City, MO 64131-3019
Ph: (816)931-1120
Fax: (816)931-1145
E-mail: info@aset.org
URL: www.aset.org/i4a/pages/index.cfm?pageid=1
Facebook: www.facebook.com/ASETLIVE59
Twitter: twitter.com/ASETLIVE

1300 ■ American Society of Electroneurodiagnostic Technologists Student Education Grants (ASET) *(Undergraduate/Grant)*

Purpose: To assist and encourage students to further their education in neurodiagnostic and for working professionals to continue their interests, enhance their knowledge and improve their skills in the field. **Focus:** Health sciences. **Qualif.:** Applicant must be a student enrolled full-time in a CAAHEP accredited END school; or an employee of ASET member companies or individuals. Relatives of the Foundation Selection Committee and the Foundation Board of Directors are not qualified for grants. **Criteria:** Selection Committees will review all submitted applications based on applicant's interest in pursuing a career; scholastic achievement including GPA; interest in pursuing a degree; upon references and recommendations by instructors, employers and other pertinent individuals. **Funds Avail.:** Up to $1,500. **Duration:** Annual. **To Apply:** Applicants must submit an application; copies of transcript; recommendations and reference letters; an outline of the proposed program of study. **Deadline:** July 1. **Contact:** Arlen Reimnitz, Executive Director; Email: arlene@aset.org.

1301 ■ ASET Scholarships *(Other/Scholarship)*

Purpose: To provide conference, seminars, and other educational opportunities to ASET members. **Focus:** Neuroscience. **Qualif.:** Applicant must be an ASET member who wishes to attend an ASET conference, seminar, and other educational opportunities. **Criteria:** Selection is based on financial need and educational needs. **Funds Avail.:** No specific amount. **Duration:** Annual. **Number Awarded:** Varies. **To Apply:** Application form is available at the website. Applicant must include a typed, signed statement and a recommendation letter from a supervisor.

1302 ■ American Society for Engineering Education (ASEE)
1818 N St. NW, Ste. 600
Washington, DC 20036-2479
Ph: (202)331-3500
E-mail: board@asee.org
URL: www.asee.org

1303 ■ ASEE/NSF Small Business Postdoctoral Research Diversity Fellowships *(Postdoctorate/Fellowship)*

Purpose: To encourage creative and highly-trained recipients of doctoral degrees in NSF-supported science, technology, engineering and mathematical disciplines to engage in hands-on research projects in their areas of expertise at the kind of small innovative businesses that historically have fueled the nation's economic regime. **Focus:** Business; Economics. **Qualif.:** Applicants must be U.S. citizens, U.S. nationals or U.S. permanent residents, and must have received a Ph.D. degree in a NSF-supported science, technology, engineering or mathematical (STEM) discipline in the seven years prior to the application date. **Criteria:** Selection will be based on the committee's criteria. **Funds Avail.:** Amount varies. **To Apply:** Applicants should submit the complete application, determined as the following: contact information, citizenship Status, academic background, awards and honors, and information for references entered; uploaded PDF resume reflecting past work history; PDF Transcripts uploaded for all institutions listed in Academic Background section; at least one (1) research proposal submitted for a specific research opportunity; and no less than three (3) submitted references. Submission of applications are through online process. **Contact:** For further information, please email aseensfip@asee.org or call 202-331-3548.

1304 ■ Naval Research Enterprise Internship Program (NREIP) *(Undergraduate, Graduate, Professional development/Internship)*

Purpose: To encourage participating students to pursue science and engineering careers; further education via mentoring by laboratory personnel and their participation in research; and make them aware of Department of Navy (DoN) research and technology efforts, which can lead to employment within the DoN. **Focus:** Naval art and science. **Qualif.:** Applicants must be U.S. citizens (sophomore, junior, senior, or graduate students) who are enrolled at a 4 year U.S. college or university deemed accredited by the U.S. Department of Education. Students attending two-year colleges, who meet the major and credit requirements, may be eligible at the laboratory's discretion. **Criteria:** NREIP interns will be selected based upon academic achievement, personal statements, recommendation, and career and research interests. **Funds Avail.:** $5,400 (sophomores); $8,100 (juniors and seniors); $10,800 (graduate-level students). **Number Awarded:** Varies. **To Apply:** Interested applicants may contact the NREIP Program Help Desk for the application process and other essential information. **Deadline:** December 19. **Contact:** NREIP Program Help Desk at nreip@asee.org.

1305 ■ Science, Mathematics And Research for Transformation Scholarship for Service Program (SMART) *(Undergraduate, Graduate/Scholarship)*

Purpose: To increase the number of civilian scientists and engineers working at Department of Defense laboratories. **Focus:** Engineering; Mathematics and mathematical sciences; Science; Technology. **Qualif.:** Applicants must be: U.S. citizens; 18 years old and above; able to participate in summer internships at Department of Defense (DoD) laboratories; willing to accept post-graduate employment with the DoD; students in good standing with a minimum cumulative GPA of 3.0 on a 4.0 scale; and, pursuing undergraduate or graduate degree in one of the science, technology, engineering and mathematics (STEM) disciplines. In addition, undergraduate applicants must be enrolled in a regionally accredited U.S. college/university and have their respective high school diplomas/GED's while graduate applicants can be either currently enrolled in a regionally accredited U.S. college or university or awaiting

Awards are arranged alphabetically below their administering organizations

notification of admission to such. **Criteria:** Selection shall be based on the aforementioned applicants' qualifications and compliance with the application details. **Funds Avail.:** $25,000-$38,000. **Duration:** Annual. **To Apply:** Applicants may visit the program website for further information regarding the application details/process. **Contact:** American Society for Engineering Education, at the above address.

1306 ■ American Society for Enology and Viticulture (ASEV)

PO Box 1855
Davis, CA 95617-1855
Ph: (530)753-3142
Fax: (530)753-3318
E-mail: society@asev.org
URL: www.asev.org

1307 ■ American Society for Enology and Viticulture Scholarships *(Graduate, Undergraduate/Scholarship)*

Purpose: To define questions in the wine industry and work towards answers based on the relevant and scientifically rigorous information on selected topics. **Focus:** Viticulture. **Qualif.:** Applicants must be undergraduate or graduate students accepted into a full-time accredited four year college or university program; be in their junior status for the upcoming academic year (45/60 quarter units); undergraduate students must have a minimum cumulative grade point average of 3.0; graduate students must have a minimum overall grade point average of 3.2. These averages must be based on a scale maximum of 4.0; have curriculum emphasizing enology, viticulture or science basic to the wine and grape industry. **Criteria:** Undergraduate and graduate students will be rated on a separate basis.

Funds Avail.: Vary from year to year. **Duration:** Annual. **To Apply:** Applicants must download the scholarship application form or contact ASEV office; fill out the application form after receiving the packet; must submit an original or copies of transcripts; two original letters of recommendation; (one-page) statement of intent; and list of planned courses for the upcoming academic year. **Deadline:** March 1. **Contact:** For inquiries send it to ASEV Scholarship Committee at PO Box 1855, Davis, California or contact their office.

1308 ■ American Society for Environmental History (ASEH)

Interdisciplinary Arts & Sciences Program
University of Washington
1900 Commerce St.
Tacoma, WA 98402
E-mail: director@aseh.net
URL: aseh.net

1309 ■ ASEH Minority Travel Grants *(Graduate, Other/Grant)*

Purpose: To support individuals present their research at ASEH's annual meetings. **Focus:** General studies/Field of study not specified. **Qualif.:** Applicants must be minority, low income scholars or graduate students. **Criteria:** Recipients will be selected based on qualifications and submitted materials. Special consideration will be given to first time applicants.

Funds Avail.: $500. **Duration:** Annual. **To Apply:** Applicants must submit a brief vita or resume (at least two pages); one-page statement outlining their interest/objectives in attending the ASEH conference. Applicants should specify the sources of funding already received and/or applied for. Documents should be e-mailed with the subject line "Madison Travel Grant." **Contact:** American Society for Environmental History, at the above address.

1310 ■ Rachel Carson Prize *(Other/Prize)*

Purpose: To recognize individuals who work in the field of environmental history. **Focus:** Environmental science; History. **Qualif.:** Candidates must be individuals who made the best dissertation in environmental history. **Criteria:** Applications will be evaluated based on submitted dissertation.

Funds Avail.: No specific amount. **Duration:** Annual. **To Apply:** Candidates must send three copies (hard or paper copies). If dissertation was approved between November 1 of the current year and October 31 of the following year, it should be submitted in PDF format as a single file, less than five megabytes. **Deadline:** November 16. **Contact:** Materials should be submitted electronically at director@aseh.net.

1311 ■ Alice Hamilton Prize *(Other/Prize)*

Purpose: To recognize individuals who work within the field of environmental history. **Focus:** General studies/Field of study not specified. **Qualif.:** Candidates must be authors of an article outside environmental history. **Criteria:** Candidates will be evaluated based on submitted articles.

Funds Avail.: No specific amount. **Duration:** Annual. **To Apply:** Candidates must send three copies (hard or paper copies) of an article. **Deadline:** November 16. **Contact:** Materials should be submitted electronically at director@aseh.net.

1312 ■ Samuel P. Hays Research Fellowships *(Other/Fellowship)*

Purpose: To advance the field of environmental history. **Focus:** Environmental science; History. **Qualif.:** Applicants must be practicing historians (either academic, public, or independent). **Criteria:** Recipients will be judged based on submitted materials.

Funds Avail.: $1,000. **To Apply:** Applicants must submit a two-page (500 words) statement explaining the project and how it is intended for the research funds; must submit a curriculum vitae no more than three pages in length. **Deadline:** November 16.

1313 ■ George Perkins Marsh Prize *(Other/Prize)*

Purpose: To recognize individuals who work in the field of environmental history. **Focus:** Environmental science; History. **Qualif.:** Candidates must be authors of a book in the field of environmental history. **Criteria:** Applications will be evaluated based on submitted books.

Funds Avail.: No specific amount. **Duration:** Annual. **To Apply:** Candidates must send three copies (hard or paper copies) of a book. **Deadline:** November 16. **Contact:** Mark Cioc, chair; Email: cioc@ucsc.edu.

1314 ■ E.V. and Nancy Melosi Travel Grants *(Graduate, Other/Grant)*

Purpose: To support individuals present their research at ASEH's annual meetings. **Focus:** General studies/Field of study not specified. **Qualif.:** Applicants must be graduate students, low income and international scholars. **Criteria:**

Awards are arranged alphabetically below their administering organizations

Recipients will be selected based on qualifications and submitted materials. Special consideration will be given to first time applicants.

Funds Avail.: $500. **Duration:** Annual. **To Apply:** Applicants must submit a brief vita or resume (at least two pages); one-page statement outlining their interest/objectives in attending the ASEH conference. Applicants should specify the sources of funding already received and/or applied for. Documents should be e-mailed with the subject line "Madison Travel Grant." **Contact:** American Society for Environmental History, at the above address.

1315 ■ Ellen Swallow Richards Travel Grants *(Graduate, Other/Grant)*

Purpose: To support individuals present their research at ASEH's annual meetings. **Focus:** General studies/Field of study not specified. **Qualif.:** Applicants must be graduate students, low income and international scholars. **Criteria:** Recipients will be selected based on qualifications and submitted materials. Special consideration will be given to first time applicants.

Funds Avail.: $500. **Duration:** Annual. **To Apply:** Applicants must submit a brief vita or resume (at least two pages); one-page statement outlining their interest/objectives in attending the ASEH conference. Applicants should specify the sources of funding already received and/or applied for. Documents should be e-mailed with the subject line "Madison Travel Grant."

1316 ■ Hal Rothman Dissertation Fellowships *(Doctorate, Graduate/Fellowship)*

Purpose: To recognize graduate students and to support archival research and travel. **Focus:** Environmental science; History. **Qualif.:** Candidates must be PhD students in the field of environmental history. **Criteria:** Recipients will be selected based on qualifications and submitted materials.

Funds Avail.: $1,000. **To Apply:** Candidates must submit a two-page (500 words) statement explaining the project and how it is intended for the research funds, curriculum vitae and a letter of recommendation from graduate advisors. **Deadline:** November 16. **Contact:** Materials should be submitted electronically at director@aseh.net.

1317 ■ Morgan and Jeanie Sherwood Travel Grants *(Graduate, Other/Grant)*

Purpose: To support individuals present their research at ASEH's annual meetings. **Focus:** General studies/Field of study not specified. **Qualif.:** Applicants must be graduate students, low income and international scholars. **Criteria:** Recipients will be selected based on qualifications and submitted materials. Special consideration will be given to first time applicants.

Funds Avail.: $500. **Duration:** Annual. **To Apply:** Applicants must submit a brief vita or resume (at least two pages); one-page statement outlining their interest/objectives in attending the ASEH conference. Applicants should specify the sources of funding already received and/or applied for. Documents should be e-mailed with the subject line "Madison Travel Grant."

1318 ■ John D. Wirth Travel Grants for International Scholars *(Graduate, Other/Grant)*

Purpose: To support individuals present their research at ASEH's annual meetings. **Focus:** General studies/Field of study not specified. **Qualif.:** Applicants must be graduate students, low-income and international scholars. **Criteria:** Recipients will be selected based on qualifications and submitted materials. Special consideration will be given to first time applicants.

Funds Avail.: $500. **Duration:** Annual. **To Apply:** Applicants must submit a brief vita or resume (at least two pages); one-page statement outlining their interest/objectives in attending the ASEH conference. Applicants should specify the sources of funding already received and/or applied for. Documents should be e-mailed with the subject line "Madison Travel Grant."

1319 ■ Donald Worster Travel Grants *(Graduate, Other/Grant)*

Purpose: To support individuals present their research at ASEH's annual meetings. **Focus:** General studies/Field of study not specified. **Qualif.:** Applicants must be graduate students, low income and international scholars. **Criteria:** Recipients will be selected based on qualifications and submitted materials. Special consideration will be given to first time applicants.

Funds Avail.: $500. **Duration:** Annual. **To Apply:** Applicants must submit a brief vita or resume (at least two pages); one-page statement outlining their interest/objectives in attending the ASEH conference. Applicants should specify the sources of funding already received and/or applied for. Documents should be e-mailed with the subject line "Madison Travel Grant." **Deadline:** January 21.

1320 ■ American Society of Genealogists (ASG)
c/o Joseph C. Anderson II, Secretary
5337 Del Roy Dr.
Dallas, TX 75229-3016
URL: www.fasg.org

1321 ■ ASG Scholar Awards *(Professional development/Scholarship)*

Purpose: To recognize talent and build genealogical expertise by providing promising genealogists the opportunity to receive advanced academic training in genealogy. **Focus:** Genealogy. **Qualif.:** Applicants should be genealogists, genealogical librarians, and researchers working in related fields. **Criteria:** Applicants will be selected by the ASG Scholarship Committee based on the aforesaid qualifications and compliance with application process.

Funds Avail.: $1,000. **Duration:** Annual. **To Apply:** Applicants must submit a published work or a manuscript of work in progress, to be judged by a panel of three Fellows. In addition, applicants should apply before the deadline fixed by the scholarship program by submitting three copies of items such as: a resume that emphasizes activities relating to genealogy and lists the applicants' publications in the field, if any (prior publications are not necessary); a manuscript or published work of at least 5,000 words, demonstrating an ability to conduct quality genealogical research, analyze results, and report findings in an appropriately documented fashion. If the submission is to be returned, it should be accompanied by an envelope or bagging with sufficient postage; and, a statement (100—150 words) which identifies the individuals' choice of program and explains why the individuals feel that attendance will enhance their growth as genealogical scholars. **Deadline:** September 31. **Remarks:** Established in 1996. **Contact:** Henry Z Jones, Jr., FASG Chair, ASG Scholarship Committee, at the above address.

Awards are arranged alphabetically below their administering organizations

1322 ■ American Society of Health-System Pharmacists (ASHP)
7272 Wisconsin Ave.
Bethesda, MD 20814
Ph: (301)664-8700
Fax: (301)657-1251
Free: 866-279-0681
E-mail: custserv@ashp.org
URL: www.ashp.org
Facebook: www.facebook.com/ASHPofficial
LinkedIn: www.linkedin.com/company/ashp
Twitter: twitter.com/ASHPOfficial

1323 ■ ASHP Student Research Awards (Doctorate/Award)

Purpose: To recognize pharmacy students for their published or unpublished paper that describes a completed research project related to medication use. **Focus:** Pharmacy. **Qualif.:** Applicants must be full-time students enrolled in a Doctor of Pharmacy program at an ACPE-accredited school/college of pharmacy; must be students who are authors of unpublished or published paper that describes a completed research project related to medication use. Article must be written between January 1 and December 31. **Criteria:** Recipients will be selected based on originality, impact, innovation and quality of the paper.

Funds Avail.: $1,500 honorarium plus $1,000 expense allowance. **To Apply:** Applicants must submit an application form and published/unpublished article.

1324 ■ John W. Webb Lecture Awards (Other/Recognition)

Purpose: To recognize hospital or health-system pharmacy practitioners and educators who have distinguished themselves with extraordinary dedication to foster excellence in pharmacy management. **Focus:** Pharmacy. **Qualif.:** Nominee must be hospital or health-system practitioners or educators. **Criteria:** Selection will be based on the committee's criteria.

Funds Avail.: No specific amount. **Duration:** Annual. **To Apply:** Nominations should be accompanied by a one-to-three page statement about why individuals are qualified for the award along with a copy of the nominee's curriculum vitae. **Deadline:** March 25. **Contact:** Section of Pharmacy Practice Managers, c/o Charles Daniels, B.S.Pharm., Ph.D., FASHP, Chair John W. Webb Lecture Award Selection Committee ASHP; Email: sections@ashp.org.

1325 ■ American Society of Heating, Refrigerating and Air-Conditioning Engineers (ASHRAE)
1791 Tullie Cir. NE
Atlanta, GA 30329
Ph: (404)636-8400
Fax: (404)321-5478
Free: 800-527-4723
E-mail: ashrae@ashrae.org
URL: www.ashrae.org
Facebook: www.facebook.com/ASHRAEupdates/?ref=ts

1326 ■ Henry Adams Scholarships (Undergraduate/Scholarship)

Purpose: To help reduce the financial burdens of obtaining an engineering education. **Focus:** Engineering. **Qualif.:** Applicants must be full-time undergraduate engineering students in ABET-accredited Engineering Technology program leading to bachelor degree, and have cumulative GPA of at least 3.0 on a scale where 4.0 is the highest. **Criteria:** Recipients will be selected based on financial need; leadership ability; and character.

Funds Avail.: $3,000. **Duration:** Annual. **To Apply:** Applicants must submit: an official transcript of college grades; letter of recommendation; and evaluation form from three references including professor or faculty advisor. **Deadline:** December 1. **Remarks:** The scholarship was established by Henry Adams, Inc, a consulting firm based in Baltimore, Maryland, in memory of its founder, a charter member and sixth president of ASHRAE's predecessor society, ASHVE, in 1899. **Contact:** Lois Benedict, ASHRAE Scholarship Administrator, at lbenedict@ashrae.org.

1327 ■ American Society of Heating, Refrigerating, and Air-Conditioning Memorial Scholarships (Undergraduate/Scholarship)

Purpose: To help reduce the financial burdens of obtaining an engineering education. **Focus:** Engineering. **Qualif.:** Applicants must be full-time undergraduates in an ABET-accredited Engineering Technology program leading to a Bachelor of Science or Engineering Degree and must have cumulative GPA of at least 3.0 on a 4.0 scale. **Criteria:** Recipients are selected based on the need for financial assistance; leadership ability; and character.

Funds Avail.: No specific amount. **Duration:** Annual. **To Apply:** Applicants must submit an official transcript of college grades; a letter of recommendation; and an evaluation form from three references including professor or faculty advisor. **Deadline:** December 1. **Contact:** Lois Benedict, at lbenedict@ashrae.org.

1328 ■ ASHARE Undergraduate Engineering Scholarships (Undergraduate/Scholarship)

Purpose: To help reduce the financial burdens of obtaining an engineering education. **Focus:** Engineering. **Qualif.:** Applicants must be full-time undergraduate engineering students in an ABET-accredited Engineering Technology program leading to a bachelor degree, and have cumulative GPA of at least 3.0 on a 4.0 scale. **Criteria:** Recipients will be selected based on the need for financial assistance, leadership ability, and character.

Funds Avail.: No specific amount. **Duration:** Annual. **To Apply:** Applicants must submit: an official transcript of college grades; a letter of recommendation; and an evaluation form from three references including professor or faculty advisor. **Deadline:** December 1. **Contact:** Lois Benedict, ASHRAE Scholarship Administrator, at lbenedict@ashrae.org.

1329 ■ Willis H. Carrier Scholarships (Undergraduate/Scholarship, Award)

Purpose: To help reduce the financial burdens of obtaining an engineering education. **Focus:** Engineering. **Qualif.:** Applicants must be full-time undergraduate engineering students in an ABET-accredited Engineering Technology program leading to a bachelor degree, and have cumulative GPA of at least 3.0 on a 4.0 scale. **Criteria:** Recipients will be selected based on need for financial assistance, leadership ability, and character.

Funds Avail.: $10,000. **Duration:** Annual. **Number Awarded:** 2. **To Apply:** Applicants must submit: an official transcript of college grades; a letter of recommendation; and an evaluation form from three references including

Awards are arranged alphabetically below their administering organizations

professor or faculty advisor. **Deadline:** December 1. **Remarks:** The scholarship was established by The Carrier Corporation in memory of its founder, who is known widely for his numerous and significant contributions to establishing air conditioning as an industry. Carrier installed the world's first scientifically designed air conditioning system in 1902. **Contact:** Lois Benedict, ASHRAE Scholarship Administrator, at lbenedict@ashrae.org.

1330 ■ Frank M. Coda Scholarships *(Undergraduate/Scholarship)*

Purpose: To help reduce the financial burdens of obtaining the engineering education. **Focus:** Engineering. **Qualif.:** Applicants must be full-time undergraduate engineering students in an ABET-accredited Engineering Technology program leading to a bachelor degree, and have cumulative GPA of at least 3.0 on a 4.0 scale. **Criteria:** Recipients will be selected based on the need for financial assistance, leadership ability, and character.

Funds Avail.: $5,000. **Duration:** Annual. **To Apply:** Applicants must submit: an official transcript of college grades; a letter of recommendation and an evaluation form from three references including professor or faculty advisor. **Deadline:** December 1. **Remarks:** The scholarship was established in memory of ASHRAE's former Executive Vice President, who served the Society from 1981-2004. **Contact:** Lois Benedict, ASHRAE Scholarship Administrator, at lbenedict@ashrae.org.

1331 ■ Duane Hanson Scholarships *(Undergraduate/Scholarship)*

Purpose: To help reduce the financial burdens of obtaining an engineering education. **Focus:** Engineering. **Qualif.:** Applicants must be full-time undergraduate engineering students in ABET-accredited Engineering Technology program leading to bachelor degree, and have cumulative GPA of at least 3.0 on a scale where 4.0 is the highest. **Criteria:** Recipients will be selected based on financial need; leadership ability; and character.

Funds Avail.: $5,000. **Duration:** Annual. **To Apply:** Applicants must submit: an official transcript of college grades; letter of recommendation; and evaluation form from three references including professor or faculty advisor. **Deadline:** December 1. **Remarks:** The scholarship is named after the president of Gayner Engineers, a consulting mechanical/electrical engineering firm in San Francisco, California. **Contact:** Lois Benedict, at lbenedict@ashrae.org.

1332 ■ Alwin B. Newton Scholarships *(Undergraduate/Scholarship)*

Purpose: To help reduce the financial burdens of obtaining an engineering education. **Focus:** Engineering. **Qualif.:** Applicants must be full-time undergraduate engineering students in an ABET-accredited Engineering Technology program leading to a bachelor degree, and have cumulative GPA of at least 3.0 on a scale of 4.0. **Criteria:** Recipients will be selected based on financial need; leadership ability; and character.

Funds Avail.: $5,000. **Duration:** Annual. **To Apply:** Applicants must submit: an official transcripts of college grades; a letter of recommendation; and an evaluation form from three references including a professor or faculty advisor. **Deadline:** December 1. **Remarks:** The scholarship was named for an industry pioneer, who was granted 219 patents during his lifetime. **Contact:** Lois Benedict, ASHRAE Scholarship Administrator, at lbenedict@ashrae.org.

1333 ■ Donald E. Nichols Scholarships *(Undergraduate/Scholarship)*

Purpose: To help reduce the financial burdens of obtaining an engineering education. **Focus:** Engineering. **Qualif.:** Applicants must be full-time undergraduate engineering students in an ABET-accredited Engineering Technology program leading to a bachelor degree at Tennessee Technological University. They must have cumulative GPA of at least 3.0 on a 4.0 scale. **Criteria:** Recipients will be selected based on the need for financial assistance, leadership ability, and character.

Funds Avail.: $3,000. **Duration:** Annual. **To Apply:** Applicants must submit: an official transcript of college grades; a letter of recommendation; and an evaluation form from three references including professor or faculty advisor. **Deadline:** December 1. **Remarks:** The scholarship is named for a former ASHRAE vice president and graduate of Tennessee Technological University. **Contact:** Lois Benedict, ASHRAE Scholarship Administrator, at lbenedict@ashrae.org.

1334 ■ Reuben Trane Scholarships *(Undergraduate/Scholarship)*

Purpose: To help reduce the financial burdens of obtaining the engineering education. **Focus:** Engineering. **Qualif.:** Applicants must be full-time undergraduate engineering students in an ABET-accredited Engineering Technology program leading to a bachelor Degree, and have cumulative GPA of at least 3.0 on a 4.0 scale. **Criteria:** Recipients will be selected based on the need for financial assistance, leadership ability, and character.

Funds Avail.: $5,000 per year. **Duration:** Annual; Up to 2 years. **To Apply:** Applicants must submit: an official transcript of college grades; a letter of recommendation; and an evaluation form from three references including professor or faculty advisor. **Deadline:** December 1. **Remarks:** The scholarship was established in memory of The Trane Company founder, an engineer, inventor and business executive, whose manufacturing enterprise ranks today as one of the world's largest in the HVAC&R industry. **Contact:** Lois Benedict, ASHRAE Scholarship Administrator, at lbenedict@ashrae.org.

1335 ■ American Society for Horticultural Science
1018 Duke St.
Alexandria, VA 22314
Ph: (703)836-4606
Fax: (703)836-2024
URL: www.ashs.org
Facebook: www.facebook.com/American-Society-for-Horticultural-Science-122634511137355
LinkedIn: www.linkedin.com/company/american-society-for-horticultural-science?trk=hb_tab_compy_id_1355991
Twitter: twitter.com/ASHS_Hort

1336 ■ American Society for Horticultural Science Student Travel Grants *(Graduate, Undergraduate/Grant)*

Purpose: To provide financial assistance to students in the area of horticulture. **Focus:** Horticulture. **Qualif.:** Applicants must be enrolled in horticultural science as a major course of study and must have submitted an abstract title or complete abstract for presentation at the ASHS Annual Conference. **Criteria:** Grants will be awarded on the basis

Awards are arranged alphabetically below their administering organizations

of merit and geographical distribution.

Funds Avail.: $500 (domestic graduate and undergraduate students); $750 (international students). **Duration:** Annual. **Number Awarded:** Varies. **To Apply:** Applicants must accomplish application and abstract. Application forms and instructions are available on the website. **Deadline:** April 4.

1337 ■ ASHS Industry Division Student Travel Grants *(Graduate, Undergraduate/Grant)*

Purpose: To provide financial assistance to students in the area of horticulture who are attending the ASHS Annual Conference. **Focus:** Horticulture. **Qualif.:** Applicants should be undergraduate and graduate Horticulture students. **Criteria:** Applicants will be selected based on academic achievement (30 points for 4.0 GPA), recommendation (20 points) and essay (50 points).

Funds Avail.: $1,000. **Duration:** Annual. **Number Awarded:** 2. **To Apply:** Applicants must submit transcripts, completed application, letter of recommendation from undergraduate advisor or faculty member and a 500-word essay outlining interest in horticulture and career goals. **Deadline:** May 15. **Remarks:** Established in 2004.

1338 ■ ASHS Scholars Awards *(Undergraduate/Scholarship)*

Purpose: To recognize and support scholastic achievement, and encourage career development in horticultural science at the undergraduate level. **Focus:** Horticulture. **Qualif.:** Applicants must be undergraduate students of any class standing at the time of the application and registered as full-time students (minimum 10 credit hours) actively pursuing a degree in horticulture. **Criteria:** Recipients are chosen based on excellence in academic and scholastic performance in the major (an area of horticulture) and supporting areas of science; participation in extracurricular, leadership and research activities relating to horticulture; participation in university and community service; demonstrated commitment to the horticulture science profession and related career fields; and related horticultural experiences.

Funds Avail.: $1,500. **Duration:** Annual. **Number Awarded:** 2. **To Apply:** Applicants must be nominated by the chair/head of the department in which they are majoring; must submit completed application supported by a 250-500 essay, complete resume, three letters of reference and official university/college transcripts. Forms and information are available on the website. **Deadline:** February 4.

1339 ■ Miklos Faust International Travel Awards *(Doctorate/Grant)*

Purpose: To promote international cooperation in fruit crops research and education. **Focus:** Horticulture. **Qualif.:** Applicants must be young scientists (less than 40 yrs. old) who are actively involved in fruit science research, and hold or pursuing a doctoral degree. **Criteria:** Applications are reviewed according to evidence of high originality and strong commitment to research in fruit science.

Funds Avail.: No specific amount. **Duration:** Quadrennial. **To Apply:** Applicants must submit the completed application form available at the website.

1340 ■ American Society of Interior Designers (ASID)
718 7th St. NW, 4th Fl.
Washington, DC 20001
Ph: (202)546-3480
Fax: (202)546-3240
E-mail: membership@asid.org
URL: www.asid.org

1341 ■ ASID Foundation Legacy Scholarships for Graduate Students *(Graduate/Scholarship)*

Purpose: To encourage talented practicing interior designers to advance their professional development through graduate study and research. **Focus:** Interior design. **Qualif.:** Applicants must be enrolled in or have applied for admission to a graduate-level interior design program at a degree-granting institution. Applicants must have been practicing designers for a period of at least five years prior to graduate school. **Criteria:** Selection will be based on academic/creative accomplishment.

Funds Avail.: $4,000. **Duration:** Annual. **Number Awarded:** 1. **To Apply:** Applicants must submit the following requirements: a maximum of 750 words personal statement; official school transcript(s); letter of recommendation; maximum of 100 words biographical statement; headshot picture. **Deadline:** March 12.

1342 ■ Irene Winifred Eno Grants *(Professional development/Grant)*

Purpose: To provide financial assistance to individuals or groups engaged in the creation of an educational program or an interior design research project dedicated to health, safety and welfare. **Focus:** Interior design. **Qualif.:** Applicants must be students, educators, interior design practitioners, institutions or other interior design-related groups. **Criteria:** Selection will be based on the project description, breakdown of potential use of funds and the marketing plan for the use/distribution of the end product of the project.

Funds Avail.: $5,000. **Duration:** Annual. **Number Awarded:** 1. **To Apply:** Applicants may apply online and submit a photo (300 dpi in jpeg or gif format) in the above address. **Deadline:** April 18.

1343 ■ American Society of International Law (ASIL)
2223 Massachusetts Ave. NW
Washington, DC 20008
Ph: (202)939-6000
Fax: (202)797-7133
URL: www.asil.org
Facebook: www.facebook.com/AmericanSocietyofInternationalLaw
Twitter: twitter.com/asilorg

1344 ■ ASIL Arthur C. Helton Fellowship Program *(Professional development/Fellowship)*

Purpose: To provide financial assistance for law students and young professionals to pursue field work and research on significant issues involving international law, human rights, humanitarian affairs, and related areas. **Focus:** Human rights; International affairs and relations; Law. **Qualif.:** Applicants must be: in the early stages of their academic and professional careers who demonstrate the potential to make significant contributions to the use and study of international law around the world; and, law students or practicing law profession, human rights professionals, scholars and other individuals seeking assistance in conducting international fieldwork and law-related research

Awards are arranged alphabetically below their administering organizations

Criteria: Recipients will be selected based on the performance in conducting research.

Funds Avail.: $2,000. **Duration:** Annual. **To Apply:** Applicants must complete the online application form including description of intended project and career statement; a writing sample; current CV or resume; evidence of law student status and/or date of graduation from a law school; and two letters of recommendation or support. **Deadline:** January 18. **Remarks:** Established in 2004. **Contact:** Helton Fellowship Program at fellowship@asil.

1345 ■ American Society of Landscape Architects (ASLA)
636 Eye St. NW
Washington, DC 20001-3736
Ph: (202)898-2444
Fax: (202)898-1185
Free: 888-999-2752
E-mail: info@asla.org
URL: www.asla.org

1346 ■ ASLA Council of Fellow Scholarships
(Undergraduate/Scholarship)

Purpose: To aid outstanding students who would not otherwise have an opportunity to continue a professional degree program in the area of landscape architecture due to unmet financial need, increase the interest and participation of economically disadvantaged and underrepresented populations in the study of landscape architecture through a more diverse population, and enrich the profession of landscape architecture through a more diverse population. **Focus:** Landscape architecture and design. **Qualif.:** Applicants must be permanent US citizens or permanent resident aliens who are Student ASLA members and third, fourth, or fifth-year undergraduates in Landscape Architecture Accreditation Board (LAAB) accredited programs of landscape architecture. **Criteria:** Recipients will be selected based on financial need.

Funds Avail.: $5,000 each. **Duration:** Annual. **Number Awarded:** 3. **To Apply:** Applicants must submit a 300-word essay about how the applicant envisions himself or herself contributing to the profession of landscape architecture; two letters of recommendation specifically addressing the quality of applicant's performance as a student of landscape architecture and promise as a professional (one letter of recommendation must come from a faculty member and the other one must be sent by a non-academic member); and a student aid report. **Deadline:** February 15. **Remarks:** Established in 2004. **Contact:** Landscape Architecture Foundation at scholarships@lafoundation.org; Phone: 202-331-7070 x13.

1347 ■ Peridian International, Inc./Rae L. Price, FASLA Scholarship *(Undergraduate/Scholarship)*

Purpose: To bring young creative individuals into the profession who may not otherwise have the financial ability to cover all the costs of their educational program. **Focus:** Landscape architecture and design. **Qualif.:** Applicants must be U.S. citizens who are undergraduate students in the final two years of study in Landscape Architecture at the UCLA Extension Program or Cal Poly Pomona. **Criteria:** Recipients will be selected based on the following: minimum "B" GPA and financial need.

Funds Avail.: $5,000. **Duration:** Annual. **Number Awarded:** 1. **To Apply:** Applicants must submit all of the following: online general scholarship form; photo; 150-word maximum bio for LAF website; two-page resume; financial aid form; two letters of recommendation; and, two-page maximum originally written essay in PDF format with specific formats provided. **Deadline:** February 15. **Contact:** Landscape Architecture Foundation at scholarships@lafoundation.org; Phone: 202-331-7070 x13.

1348 ■ American Society for Laser Medicine and Surgery (ASLMS)
2100 Stewart Ave., Ste. 240
Wausau, WI 54401-1709
Ph: (715)845-9283
Fax: (715)848-2493
Free: 877-258-6028
E-mail: information@aslms.org
URL: www.aslms.org
Facebook: www.facebook.com/aslms.connect
LinkedIn: www.linkedin.com/company/the-american-society-for-laser-medicine-and-surgery-inc-aslms-
Twitter: www.twitter.com/aslmsedu

1349 ■ ASLMS Research Grants *(Postdoctorate/Grant)*

Purpose: To support research projects designed to foster the development and use of lasers and other related technologies in medical and surgical applications. **Focus:** Medicine. **Qualif.:** Applicants must presently be enrolled in or have completed postdoctoral and/or residency training. All non-ASLMS members will be required to apply for and be accepted into ALSMS membership. **Criteria:** Selection will be based on the committee's criteria.

Funds Avail.: Up to $70,000. **To Apply:** Interested applicants must complete and submit a preapplication. Preapplications will be reviewed and scored with only the top scoring applications being selected to submit a full Grant Application. **Deadline:** January 11. **Contact:** ASLMS; Phone: 715-845-9283; E-mail: information@aslms.org.

1350 ■ ASLMS Student Research Grants
(Undergraduate, Graduate, Professional development/Grant)

Purpose: To support research projects designed to foster the development and use of lasers and other related technologies in medical and surgical applications. **Focus:** Medicine. **Qualif.:** Applicants must be undergraduate or graduate students, or employed by an organization in a capacity or classification due primarily to their student status. **Criteria:** Preference will be given to proposed research projects which have a direct implication for medical or surgical applications.

Funds Avail.: Up to $5,000. **To Apply:** Applicants must complete and submit the application available online. **Deadline:** January 11. **Contact:** ASLMS; Phone: 715-845-9283; E-mail: information@aslms.org.

1351 ■ A. Ward Ford Memorial Research Grants
(Postdoctorate, Professional development/Grant)

Purpose: To support direct clinical research investigating current use or potential new applications of laser or other light based therapy. **Focus:** Medicine. **Qualif.:** Applicants must be enrolled in or have completed an MD residency or PhD postdoctoral training at the time of application and must be members or applicants for membership in ASLMS at the time of the award. **Criteria:** Priority will be given to applicants who are interested in or entering an academic teaching or research position.

Funds Avail.: Up to $10,000. **Duration:** Annual. **To Apply:** Applications are accepted through the Community Foundation of North Central Wisconsin's online application system. Applicants must go to www.cfoncw.org to register online and to complete the application. Follow the prompts to the Grants and Scholarship page and click on the Apply Online button. Once registered, choose the A. Ward Ford Memorial Research Grant on the menu of Foundation grant opportunities. The complete application requirements must include the following: applicant's background, including training, previous positions, publications, previous research; clear presentation of the clinical problem or question to be researched; presentation of the research design; a detailed budget; evidence of the institutional or other support base for the research, including collaborators; IRB approval letter for human subjects research and proposal from the institution supporting the research; those in training positions will need to have a letter of support from the training program director and a designated mentor or research supervisor. **Deadline:** March 31. **Contact:** Dr. William Owen, Chair; Phone: 715-845-9555; E-mail: info@cfoncw.org.

1352 ■ Dr. Horace Furumoto Innovations Professional Development - Young Investigator Awards *(Professional development/Award)*

Purpose: To recognize and encourage the development of future technology innovators and leaders. **Focus:** Medicine. **Qualif.:** Candidates must be in an early stage in his or her career and/or professional development. Nonclinical professionals, particularly those who work in industry, are especially encouraged to apply and will receive special consideration. **Criteria:** Selection will be based on the individuals' potential development of innovations in the areas of lasers and/or related technologies in health care.

Funds Avail.: $9,000. **Duration:** Annual. **To Apply:** Candidates must be nominated by an ASLMS member. A nomination form can be obtained at the website and must be sent electronically. **Deadline:** August 31. **Remarks:** Established in 2001.

1353 ■ American Society for Legal History (ASLH)
c/o Patricia Minter, Membership Committee
Western Kentucky University
1906 College Heights Blvd., No. 21086
Bowling Green, KY 42101-1000
Fax: (270)793-0040
URL: aslh.net

1354 ■ Cromwell Fellowships *(Graduate/Fellowship)*

Purpose: To support research and writing in American legal history. **Focus:** History, American. **Qualif.:** Applicants must be graduate studies students currently enrolled in any institution, college or university. **Criteria:** Recipients will be selected based on the eligibility of applicants. Preference will be given to scholars at the early stage of their careers. The Committee for Research Fellowships and Awards of the American Society for Legal History (ASLH) reviews the applications and makes recommendations to the Foundation.

Funds Avail.: $5,000. **Duration:** Annual. **Number**

Awarded: 5 to 8. **To Apply:** Applicants should submit a description of their proposed project (double-spaced, maximum 6 pages, with working title), a budget, a timeline, and a short c.v. (no longer than 3 pages). Two letters of recommendation from academic referees. Applications must be submitted electronically (preferably in one .pdf file). **Deadline:** July 13. **Contact:** Cornelia H. Dayton, Committee Chair; e-mail: cornelia.dayton@uconn.edu.

1355 ■ American Society of Mammalogists (ASM)
c/o Christy Classi, CAE
PO Box 4973
Topeka, KS 66604
Ph: (785)550-6904
E-mail: asm@allenpress.com
URL: www.mammalsociety.org
Facebook: www.facebook.com/American.Society.of.Mammalogists
LinkedIn: www.linkedin.com/groups/4575484/profile
Twitter: twitter.com/mammalogists

1356 ■ American Society of Mammalogists - Fellowships in Mammalogy *(Graduate/Fellowship)*

Purpose: To recognize current accomplishments in mammalogy, service to ASM, and the potential for a productive, future role in professional mammalogy. **Focus:** Zoology. **Qualif.:** Applicants must be graduate student members of ASM enrolled at a college or university of the forthcoming academic year and be engaged in research in mammalogy. **Criteria:** Selection will be based on the committee's criteria.

Funds Avail.: $7,500. **Duration:** Annual. **To Apply:** Applicants must gather the following materials: curriculum vita, 3-5 pages in length and must include peer-reviewed publications, other publications, presentations to professional meetings, research grants, memberships in professional societies, honors and awards and professional service; Arrange for three letter of recommendation to be sent via email. One letter must be from applicants' advisor. Please make sure that applicants' and other providers of letters of recommendation include their name in the subject line of the email; names and contact information for three people who the applicants have asked to provide letters in support of their applications plus name and contact information for their department head or chairperson; summary of professional experience in mammalogy, research interests and career goals, limited to one page; abstract for thesis or dissertation research, limited to 150 words; brief statement describing how the applicants would use any support from ASM. Limited to one page; Description of thesis or dissertation research project organized under the following headings: Title, Introduction, Objective, Methods, Present Status of the Research, Significance and Literature Cited. Limited to five pages, double spaced, however, Literature Citations may be included on additional pages.

1357 ■ American Society of Mammalogists Grants-in-Aid of Research *(Graduate, Undergraduate/Grant)*

Purpose: To enhance and support graduate researchers by indentifying and funding research proposals pertaining to mammals. **Focus:** Zoology. **Qualif.:** Applicants must be graduate and undergraduate students who are members of the Society at the time of application. **Criteria:** Selection will be based on the committee's criteria.

Funds Avail.: Up to $1,500. **To Apply:** Applicants must complete the following materials: Research proposal,

Awards are arranged alphabetically below their administering organizations

limited to two pages, 12 pt. font, 0.5 inch margins. Literature cited may be on a separate page; itemized budget for the proposed work. Categorize each item as equipment, supplies or travel. Indicate expected source of funds and indicate with an X if a commitment has been made for that item. Give estimated total cost and amount requested from ASM; arrange for two letters of recommendation to be sent via email. One letter must be from applicants' advisor. Please make sure that the advisor includes the name of the applicants in the subject line of the email; if applicants have received a Grant-in-Aid of research previously, they will have to provide the year it was awarded, title of the proposal, amount awarded, status of any resulting publications and a brief summary of progress. For the attachments, please use this name convention: LAST NAME_DOCUMENT TYPE. **Deadline:** March 1. **Contact:** Karen Mabry at kmabry@nmsu.edu.

1358 ■ Graduate Student Honoraria - Elmer C. Birney Awards *(Master's, Doctorate/Award)*

Purpose: To recognize students who have been primarily responsible for the design and/or conduct of the submitted research project. **Focus:** Zoology. **Qualif.:** Applicants must be Master's or Doctoral student members of the Society. **Criteria:** Selection will be based on the originality, quality and presentation of research and the advisor's letter of support.

Funds Avail.: $2,000. **Duration:** Annual. **To Apply:** Applicants should submit a summary of their graduate research not exceeding 1,000 words with the following clearly labeled sections: Title, Project Significance/Theoretical Context, Methods, Results and Discussion/Interpretation. Include key figures/tables with concise captions to support the results. A reference letter should be addressed to the committee and be written by an individual familiar with the applicants' research, ideally, the research advisor/mentor or major professor. The letter must address the following: 1.) if the students will be prepared to present the research project in the plenary session of the upcoming annual meeting; 2.) the students' role in designing and conducting the research, especially in the case collaborative research. **Deadline:** February 15. **Contact:** Dr. Paul Stapp; phone: 657-278-2849; E-mail: pstapp@fullerton.edu.

1359 ■ Graduate Student Honoraria - A. Brazier Howell Awards *(Master's, Doctorate/Award)*

Purpose: To recognize students who have been primarily responsible for the design and/or conduct of the submitted research project. **Focus:** Zoology. **Qualif.:** Applicants must be Master's or Doctoral student members of the Society. **Criteria:** Selection will be based on the originality, quality and presentation of research and the advisor's letter of support.

Funds Avail.: $2,000. **Duration:** Annual. **To Apply:** Applicants should submit a summary of their graduate research not exceeding 1,000 words with the following clearly labeled sections: Title, Project Significance/Theoretical Context, Methods, Results and Discussion/Interpretation. Include key figures/tables with concise captions to support the results. A reference letter should be addressed to the committee and be written by an individual familiar with the applicants' research, ideally, the research advisor/mentor or major professor. The letter must address the following: 1.) if the students will be prepared to present the research project in the plenary session of the upcoming annual meeting; 2.) the students' role in designing and conducting the research, especially in the case collaborative research. **Deadline:** February 15.

1360 ■ Graduate Student Honoraria - Anna M. Jackson Awards *(Master's, Doctorate/Award)*

Purpose: To recognize excellence in pre-doctoral research. **Focus:** Zoology. **Qualif.:** Applicants must be Master's or Doctoral student members of the Society. **Criteria:** Selection will be based on originality, quality and presentation of the research and the advisor's letter of support.

Funds Avail.: No specific amount. **Duration:** Annual. **To Apply:** Applicants should submit a summary of their graduate research not exceeding 1,000 words with the following clearly labeled sections: Title, Project Significance/Theoretical Context, Methods, Results and Discussion/Interpretation. Include key figures/tables with concise captions to support the results. Reference letter should be addressed to the committee and be written by an individual familiar with the applicants' research, ideally, the research advisor/mentor or major professor. The letter must address the following: 1.) if the students will be prepared to present the research project in the Plenary Session of the upcoming Annual Meeting; 2.) the students' role in designing and conducting the research, especially in the case collaborative research. **Deadline:** February 15.

1361 ■ Albert R. and Alma Shadle Fellowships *(Graduate/Fellowship)*

Purpose: To recognize individuals who have made significant contributions to the American Society of Mammalogists. **Focus:** Zoology. **Qualif.:** Applicants must be enrolled as graduate students in a college or university in the United States for the forthcoming academic year and be engaged in research in any area of mammalogy. **Criteria:** Selection will be based on the committee's criteria.

Funds Avail.: No specific amount. **Duration:** Annual. **To Apply:** Applicants must gather the following materials: curriculum vita, 3-5 pages in length and must include peer-reviewed publications, other publications, presentations to professional meetings, research grants, memberships in professional societies, honors and awards and professional service; Arrange for three letter of recommendation to be sent via email. One letter must be from applicants' advisor. Please make sure that applicants' and other providers of letters of recommendation include their name in the subject line of the email; names and contact information for three people who the applicants have asked to provide letters in support of their applications plus name and contact information for their department head or chairperson; summary of professional experience in mammalogy, research interests and career goals, limited to one page; abstract for thesis or dissertation research, limited to 150 words; brief statement describing how the applicants would use any support from ASM. Limited to one page; Description of thesis or dissertation research project organized under the following headings: Title, Introduction, Objective, Methods, Present Status of the Research, Significance and Literature Cited. Limited to five pages, double spaced, however, Literature Citations may be included on additional pages.

1362 ■ American Society for Mass Spectrometry (ASMS)
Bldg. I-1
2019 Galisteo St.
Santa Fe, NM 87505
Ph: (505)989-4517
Fax: (505)989-1073
E-mail: office@asms.org
URL: www.asms.org

Awards are arranged alphabetically below their administering organizations

AMERICAN SOCIETY FOR MICROBIOLOGY

1363 ■ ASMS Research Awards *(Other/Grant)*

Purpose: To promote research done by young scientists in mass spectrometry. **Focus:** Science. **Qualif.:** Applicants must be academic scientists within four years of joining the term track faculty or equivalent in a North American university and who have not yet received awards under this program. **Criteria:** Recipients are selected based on applications and proposals.

Funds Avail.: $35,000. **Duration:** Annual. **Number Awarded:** 2. **To Apply:** Applicants must send seven sets of: one-page fiscal proposal and justification; list of current research support; curriculum vitae; and two letters of recommendation. **Deadline:** November 30. **Remarks:** Established in 1985. **Contact:** ASMS Awards, 2019 Galisteo St., Bldg. 1, Santa Fe, NM 87505.

1364 ■ American Society for Microbiology (ASM)

1752 N St. NW
Washington, DC 20036-2904
Ph: (202)942-9207
Fax: (202)942-9333
E-mail: service@asmusa.org
URL: www.asm.org
Facebook: www.facebook.com/asmfan
LinkedIn: www.linkedin.com/company/american-society-for-microbiology
Twitter: twitter.com/asmicrobiology

1365 ■ American Society for Microbiology International Fellowships for Africa *(Postdoctorate/Fellowship)*

Purpose: To promote American/African collaborations in microbiological research and training. **Focus:** Microbiology. **Qualif.:** Applicants must: be members of ASM or any other national microbiological society; actively involved in research in the microbiological sciences; have obtained or be in the process of obtaining masters, Ph.D. or other equivalent academic degree within the last five years; be nationals of non-developed Asian countries; and, be proficient in the use of the English language. **Criteria:** Recipients will be selected based on academic excellence of the applicant; depth of the applicant's research experience; quality and originality of work proposed during the fellowship; and relevance of the work proposed.

Funds Avail.: Up to $5,000. **Duration:** Annual; from 6 weeks to 6 months. **To Apply:** Applicants must fill out the application form.

1366 ■ American Society for Microbiology International Fellowships for Asia *(Postdoctorate/Fellowship)*

Purpose: To promote American/Asian collaborations in microbiological research and training. **Focus:** Microbiology. **Qualif.:** Applicants must: be members of ASM or any other national microbiological society; be actively involved in research in the microbiological sciences; have obtained or be in the process of obtaining masters, Ph.D. or other equivalent academic degree within the last five years; be nationals of non-developed Asian countries; and, be proficient in the use of the English language. **Criteria:** Recipients will be selected based on the academic excellence; depth of the applicant's research experience; quality and originality of work proposed during the fellowship; and relevance of the work proposed.

Funds Avail.: $5,000. **Duration:** Annual; From 6 weeks to 6 months. **To Apply:** Applicants must fill out the application form.

1367 ■ American Society for Microbiology International Fellowships for Latin America and the Caribbean *(Postdoctorate/Fellowship)*

Purpose: To promote American/Latin American collaborations in microbiological research and training. **Focus:** Microbiology. **Qualif.:** Applicants must: be members of ASM or any other national microbiological society; be actively involved in research in the microbiological sciences; have obtained, or be in a process of obtaining masters, Ph.D. or other equivalent academic degree within the last five years; be nationals of Latin American countries; and, be proficient in the use of the English language. **Criteria:** Preference will be given to applicants who can prove three years of membership in ASM or any other national microbiological society; and who have not previously had the opportunity to travel to a facility in another country

Funds Avail.: $4,000. **Duration:** Annual; From 6 weeks to 6 months. **To Apply:** Applicants must complete the application form; must submit an updated resume; copy honors and awards received; statement of career plans; potential collaborations and proposed research plans; budget; certificates; and letters of reference from academic advisors and/or supervisors.

1368 ■ American Society for Microbiology Undergraduate Research Fellowships *(Undergraduate/Fellowship)*

Purpose: To support highly competitive students who wish to pursue graduate careers in biology. **Focus:** Microbiology. **Qualif.:** Applicants must be U.S. citizens or permanent residents who are ASM members and enrolled as full-time matriculating undergraduate students during the academic year at an accredited U.S. Institution. They must be involved in a research project, have ASM members at their home institutions willing to serve as mentors, and not receive financial support for research during the Fellowship. **Criteria:** Recipients will be selected based on: academic achievement; relevant career objectives; potential contribution to overall project outcome; personal motivation to participate in the program; and achievement in previous research experiences.

Funds Avail.: Up to $4,000 plus $1,000 travel support. **Duration:** Annual. **To Apply:** Applicants must submit a complete application form. **Deadline:** February 1. **Contact:** ASM Undergraduate Research Fellowship Program at fellowships@asmusa.org.

1369 ■ ASM/CDC Program in Infectious Disease and Public Health Microbiology *(Postdoctorate/Fellowship)*

Purpose: To support the development of new approaches, methodologies, and knowledge in infectious disease prevention and control in areas within the public health mission of the CDC. **Focus:** Microbiology. **Qualif.:** Applicants must have earned their doctorate degree or completed primary residency within three years from proposed start date, and may not have a faculty position or enrolled in a graduate degree program during the fellowship. **Criteria:** Recipients will be selected based on: scientific merit and training potential of the research proposal; training resources; and have significance with the Centers for Diseases public health mission.

Funds Avail.: Up to $47,032 (annual stipend) which

Awards are arranged alphabetically below their administering organizations

includes $3,000 for health benefits; $500 relocation benefits, and $2,000 for professional development. **Duration:** Annual; Up to 2 years. **To Apply:** Applicants must fill out the application form. **Deadline:** January 15. **Contact:** ASM/CDC Postdoctoral Research Fellowship Program, fellowships@asmusa.org.

1370 ■ ASM Congressional Science Fellowships (Postdoctorate/Fellowship)

Purpose: To make practical contributions to more effective use of scientific knowledge in government, educate the scientific communities regarding public policy, and broaden the perspective of both the scientific and governmental communities regarding the value of such science-government interaction. **Focus:** Science. **Qualif.:** Applicants must: be citizens of the United States who are members of ASM for at least one year; have completed their Ph.D. by the time the fellowship begins; show competence in some aspect of microbiology; have broad background in science and technology; have interest and experience in applying scientific knowledge toward the solution of social problems; be articulate, literate, adaptable, interested in public policy problems; and, be able to work with a variety of people from diverse professional backgrounds. **Criteria:** Recipients will be selected based on the result of the interview.

Funds Avail.: $65,000. **Duration:** Annual. **To Apply:** Applicants must submit a letter indicating a desire to apply; three letters of references; and 1,000-word statement about the qualifications and career goals. **Deadline:** February 19. **Contact:** ASM Congressional Science Fellowship, at hgarvey@asmusa.org.

1371 ■ ASM Science Teaching Fellowships - Student (Undergraduate/Fellowship)

Purpose: To support students who are interested in a career as elementary or secondary school science teachers. **Focus:** Education. **Qualif.:** Applicants must be: enrolled as full-time matriculating undergraduates in an accredited U.S. institution; involved in educational outreach projects; and, science majors interested in education. They must have strong faculty ASM members in their home institutions willing to serve as co-mentors, and have not received any financial support for the project during the fellowship. **Criteria:** Recipients will be selected based on academic achievement; relevant career objectives; potential contribution to overall project outcome; personal motivation to participate in the program; achievement in previous teaching experience. Preference will be given to applicants whose projects will demonstrate the co-mentor's and institution's financial commitment and have significant impact on their ongoing educational efforts.

Funds Avail.: No specific amount. **Duration:** Annual. **To Apply:** Applicants must submit six copies of complete application form. **Deadline:** November 2.

1372 ■ ASM Undergraduate Research Capstone Program (Undergraduate/Fellowship)

Purpose: To increase the number of underrepresented undergraduate students who have demonstrated the ability to pursue graduate careers in microbiology. **Focus:** Microbiology. **Qualif.:** Applicants must: be enrolled as full-time matriculating undergraduates in an accredited U.S. institution; be either freshmen with college level research experience or sophomores, juniors, or seniors who will not graduate before the completion date of the summer program; be members of underrepresented group of microbiology; have taken introductory courses in biology, chemistry and preferably microbiology prior to submission of the application; have strong interests in obtaining a Ph.D. or M.D/Ph.D. in the microbiological sciences; and, have laboratory research experience. **Criteria:** Recipients will be selected based on academic achievement and to previous research experiences or independent projects; commitment to research; career goals as a research scientist; motivation to participate in the program; willingness to conduct research with an ASM member at a sponsoring U.S. institution; leadership skills; and involvement in activities that serve the needs of underrepresented groups.

Funds Avail.: $1,500 travel support. **Duration:** Annual. **To Apply:** Applicants must submit a complete application form. **Deadline:** January 20. **Contact:** ASM Undergraduate Research Capstone Program at fellowships@asmusa.org.

1373 ■ ASM Robert D. Watkins Graduate Research Fellowships (Postdoctorate/Fellowship)

Purpose: To increase the number of underrepresented groups completing doctoral degrees in the microbiological sciences. **Focus:** Microbiology. **Qualif.:** Applicants must: be formally admitted to a doctoral program in the microbiological sciences in an accredited U.S. institution; have successfully completed the first year of the graduate program; have successfully completed all graduate course work requirements for the doctoral degree by the date of activation of the fellowship; be student members of ASM; be mentored by ASM members; and, be U.S. citizens or permanent residents. **Criteria:** Recipients will be selected based on academic achievement; evidence of successful research plan developed in collaboration with research advisor/mentor; relevant career goals in the microbiological sciences; involvement in activities that serve the needs of underrepresented groups.

Funds Avail.: $63,000 ($21,000 a year). **Duration:** Annual; Up to 3 years. **To Apply:** Applicants must submit three letters of recommendation; and official transcript from all colleges and universities attended. **Deadline:** May 1. **Contact:** ASM Robert D. Watkins Graduate Research Fellowship, fellowships@asmusa.org.

1374 ■ American Society of Military Comptrollers (ASMC)
415 N Alfred St.
Alexandria, VA 22314
Ph: (703)549-0360
Fax: (703)549-3181
Free: 800-462-5637
URL: www.asmconline.org
Facebook: www.facebook.com/ASMCNationalHQ/?ref=ts
Twitter: twitter.com/asmctweets

1375 ■ American Society of Military Comptrollers National Scholarship Program (Undergraduate/Scholarship)

Purpose: To provide financial assistance to seniors to accomplish their future financial management baccalaureate educational goals. **Focus:** Accounting; Business administration; Economics; Finance; Resource management. **Qualif.:** Applicants must be students entering a field of study directly related to financial/resource management. **Criteria:** Recipients will be selected based on the selection panel's review of applications. The selection panel will make final recommendations to the ASMC National Executive Committee, who will approve the final award winners.

Funds Avail.: Amount varies. **Duration:** Annual. **Number Awarded:** Varies. **To Apply:** Applicants must have endorsement letters from ASMC chapters. Applicants must submit completed application form and three letters of recommendation from local ASMC chapter president, high school principal, academic dean, or guidance counselor, and a high school teacher.

1376 ■ American Society of Mining and Reclamation (ASMR)
1305 Weathervane
Champaign, IL 61821
Ph: (217)333-9489
URL: www.asmr.us

1377 ■ American Society of Mining and Reclamation Memorial Scholarships (Undergraduate/Scholarship, Recognition)

Purpose: To support deserving students from universities, colleges, or community colleges having curricula in a scientific discipline directly related to and leading toward a profession in reclamation related work. **Focus:** Conservation of natural resources; Engineering, Mining and Mineral; Environmental science; Mining. **Qualif.:** Applicants must be full-time students who have completed at least sophomore year of curriculum in a science discipline directly relating to and leading to a profession in reclamation, and have an adequate grade point of average, carry the curriculum-required hours and participated in other curricular activities. **Criteria:** Recipients will be selected based on the following: extracurricular activities; participation; and leadership. Preference will be given to students from schools having an ASMR student chapter.

Funds Avail.: Amount varies. **Duration:** Annual. **Number Awarded:** 3. **To Apply:** Applicants must complete the application form to be found at ASMR website. They must submit: a statement outlining education and career goals; three reference letters from two academic sources, including one from advisor; college transcripts; and resume with list of awards, honors and extracurricular activities listed. **Deadline:** March 31.

1378 ■ American Society of Naval Engineers (ASNE)
1452 Duke St.
Alexandria, VA 22314
Ph: (703)836-6727
Fax: (703)836-7491
E-mail: asnehq@navalengineers.org
URL: www.navalengineers.org

1379 ■ American Society of Naval Engineers Scholarships (ASNE) (Graduate, Undergraduate/Scholarship)

Purpose: To improve the profession of naval engineering by encouraging college students to enter the field of naval engineering and by providing support to naval engineers seeking advanced education in the field. **Focus:** Engineering, Naval. **Qualif.:** Applicants must be U.S. citizens who are either: undergraduate full-time students in their last years of undergraduate program at an accredited college or university, or graduate students on a full graduate program leading to an engineering or physical science degree at an accredited university. **Criteria:** Selection is focused on the applicants' academic record, work history, professional promise and interest in naval engineering, ASNE membership, extracurricular activities, as well as recommendations of college faculty, employers, and other character references. The scholarship program is merit-based, however, financial need may also be considered.

Funds Avail.: $3,000 for undergraduate students; $4,000 for graduate students. **Duration:** Annual. **Number Awarded:** Varies. **To Apply:** Applicants must complete and submit an application form available at the website. **Remarks:** Established in 1979. **Contact:** scholarships@navalengineers.org.

1380 ■ American Society of Nephrology (ASN)
1510 H St. NW, Ste. 800
Washington, DC 20005
Ph: (202)640-4660
Fax: (202)637-9793
E-mail: email@asn-online.org
URL: www.asn-online.org
Facebook: www.facebook.com/AmericanSocietyofNephrology
Twitter: www.twitter.com/ASNKidney

1381 ■ Carl W. Gottschalk Research Scholar Grants (Professional development/Grant)

Purpose: To provide financial assistance for the development of a general nephrology investigator. **Focus:** Medical research. **Qualif.:** Applicants must: be residents of North America; be active members of ASN; hold an M.D., Ph.D., or equivalent degree; be within seven years of initial faculty appointment at the time of the award activation; have a proposed project that is independent of previous mentors; and, devote 75% of their time to research. **Criteria:** Applicants will be assessed based on their potential and the proposed project for eventual funding by a NIH R01 grant or its equivalent; qualifications with respect to prior training, productivity and independence, as well as the scientific merit of the proposed project; and commitment to the development as an independent investigator.

Funds Avail.: $100,000 a year for up to two years. **Duration:** Annual. **To Apply:** Applicants must submit original and three paper copies of the application (including letter from department chair or Division Director), contact information and project title; applicants' biosketch (such as a NIH Biosketch), research project plan, letter of support from department head, and three letters of reference. **Contact:** grants@asn-online.org.

1382 ■ Norman Siegel Research Scholar Grants (Doctorate/Grant)

Purpose: To provide financial assistance for the development of a pediatric investigator. **Focus:** Medicine, Pediatric. **Qualif.:** Applicants must: be residents of North America; be active members of ASN; hold an M.D., Ph.D., or equivalent degree; be within seven years of initial faculty appointment at the time of the award activation; have a proposed project that is independent of previous mentors; and, devote 75% of their time to research. **Criteria:** Applicants will be assessed based on their potential and the proposed project for eventual funding by a NIH R01 grant or its equivalent; qualifications with respect to prior training, productivity and independence, as well as the scientific merit of the proposed project; and commitment to the development as independent investigators.

Awards are arranged alphabetically below their administering organizations

Funds Avail.: $100,000 a year for up to two years. **Duration:** Annual. **To Apply:** Applicants must submit original and three paper copies of the application (including letter from Department Chair or Division Director); contact information and project title; applicants' Biosketch (such as a NIH Biosketch); research project plan; and three letters of reference. **Contact:** ASN Foundation: Phone: 202-640-4665; Email: grants@asn-online.org.

1383 ■ American Society for Nondestructive Testing (ASNT)
1711 Arlingate Ln.
Columbus, OH 43228
Ph: (614)274-6003
Fax: (614)274-6899
Free: 800-222-2768
URL: www.asnt.org
Facebook: www.facebook.com/asntinfo
LinkedIn: www.linkedin.com/company/the-american-society-for-nondestructive-testing?trk=hb_tab_compy_id_1229427
Twitter: twitter.com/asntinfo

1384 ■ ASNT Fellowship Award (Graduate/Fellowship, Award)

Purpose: To fund a specific research in nondestructive testing. **Focus:** Engineering; Materials research/science; Testing, educational/psychological. **Qualif.:** Program is open to any institution with a graduate educational research program. **Criteria:** Applicant who has the most outstanding proposal about NDT research, investigation or development will be given preference and will be judged based on creativity, content, format, and readability.

Funds Avail.: $20,000. **Duration:** Annual. **Number Awarded:** Up to 5. **To Apply:** Applicant must submit an original and eight copies of the research proposal (maximum of 21 pages) consisting of a title page, table of contents, research proposal, program of study, research facilities, budget, research advisor, and background on potential graduate student. An original and eight (8) copies of the proposal shall be forwarded to ASNT. **Deadline:** October 15.

1385 ■ Robert B. Oliver ASNT Scholarships (Undergraduate/Scholarship)

Purpose: To assist students who have chosen a career in NDT. **Focus:** Materials research/science; Testing, educational/psychological. **Qualif.:** Applicants must be enrolled in a course work related to nondestructive testing (NDT) leading to an undergraduate degree, an associate degree or certificate program. **Criteria:** Applicant who has the most outstanding manuscript about NDT research, investigation or development will be given preference. The manuscript is judge based on creativity, content, format, and readability.

Funds Avail.: $2,500 each. **Duration:** Annual. **Number Awarded:** Up to 3. **To Apply:** Applicants must submit one original and four copies of student manuscript with original illustrations and photos (maximum of ten). Manuscripts must contain the title, author, complete references and must be limited to 5,000 words. International System of Units or SI is preferred for all measurements. Applicants must also submit a completed application form; student's curriculum; transcript; and verification of enrollment letter from an instructor. **Deadline:** February 15.

1386 ■ American Society of Podiatric Medical Assistants (ASPMA)
1000 W St. Joseph Hwy., Ste. 200
Lansing, MI 48915
Fax: (517)485-9408
Free: 888-882-7762
E-mail: aspmaex@aol.com
URL: www.aspma.org
Facebook: www.facebook.com/TheASPMA
Twitter: twitter.com/aspma

1387 ■ Zelda Walling Vicha Memorial Scholarships (Undergraduate/Scholarship)

Purpose: To assist the continuing education of podiatry students. **Focus:** Podiatry. **Qualif.:** Applicants must be fourth year podiatry students throughout the United States. **Criteria:** Selection shall be based on the financial need and high scholastic achievement throughout the podiatric schooling.

Funds Avail.: $2,000 each. **Duration:** Annual. **Number Awarded:** 2. **To Apply:** Applicants may verify the application process through the program website.

1388 ■ American Society for Quality (ASQ)
600 N Plankinton Ave.
Milwaukee, WI 53201
Ph: (414)272-8575
Fax: (414)272-1734
Free: 800-248-1946
URL: asq.org
Facebook: www.facebook.com/ASQ
LinkedIn: www.linkedin.com/company/asq

1389 ■ Richard A. Freund International Scholarships (Graduate/Scholarship)

Purpose: To support students for their graduate study of the theory and application of quality control, quality assurance, quality improvement, and total quality management. **Focus:** Quality assurance and control. **Qualif.:** Applicants must be undergraduate seniors or currently graduate students having a 3.25 GPA or higher. **Criteria:** Selection will be based on the committee's criteria.

Funds Avail.: $5,000. **Duration:** Annual. **To Apply:** Interested applicants are advise to visit the website to register and to give them access to download the application form. **Deadline:** April 1.

1390 ■ Ellis R. Ott Scholarships (Graduate, Master's/Scholarship)

Purpose: To provide financial assistance to students who are pursuing the degree of statistics and/or quality management field. **Focus:** Quality assurance and control; Statistics. **Qualif.:** Applicants must be students who are planning to enroll or currently enrolled in a masters degree or higher level in US or Canadian program that has concentration in applied statistics and/or quality management. **Criteria:** Recipients are selected based on the following criteria: demonstrated ability; academic achievement, including honors; career objectives; faculty recommendations; involvement in campus activities, including teaching and tutoring; and industrial exposure including part-time work and internships.

Funds Avail.: $7,500. **Duration:** Annual. **To Apply:** Ap-

Awards are arranged alphabetically below their administering organizations

plicants must submit completed application form; resume; undergraduate transcript; graduate transcript, for students who have graduate school experience; essay of no longer than one page, typewritten, no smaller than 10-point type, stating qualifications, career goals, reasons for seeking the scholarship; two letters of recommendation from professors in the current or intended field of study. **Deadline:** April 1. **Contact:** Dr. Lynne B. Hare at Email: lynnehare@verizon.net.

1391 ■ American Society for Radiation Oncology (ASTRO)
251 18th St. S, 8th Fl.
Arlington, VA 22202
Ph: (703)502-1550
Fax: (703)502-7852
Free: 800-962-7876
E-mail: info@astro.org
URL: www.astro.org
Facebook: www.facebook.com/American-Society-for-Radiation-Oncology-35768312349
LinkedIn: www.linkedin.com/company/american-society-for-radiation-oncology
Twitter: twitter.com/ASTRO_org

1392 ■ ASTRO Junior Faculty Career Research Training Awards *(Advanced Professional, Professional development/Grant)*

Purpose: To stimulate interest in radiation research early in junior faculty's careers by offering them the opportunity to have focused time for research projects in radiation oncology, biology, physics or outcomes/health services. **Focus:** Oncology. **Qualif.:** Applicants must be active members of ASTRO; must be board-eligible physicians or physicists in radiation oncology or radiobiologists within the first three years of junior faculty appointment; must have their respective institutions recognized as providing a rich environment for career development; and must possessed qualified faculty in clinical, translational or basic research to serve as mentors. **Criteria:** Selection will be based on ASTRO's criteria.

Funds Avail.: $100,000 per year. **Duration:** Two years. **Number Awarded:** 2. **To Apply:** Applicants must visit the website for the online application process. **Deadline:** March 27. **Contact:** ASTRO Research Department at research@astro.org.

1393 ■ ASTRO Minority Summer Fellowship Awards *(Postgraduate, Professional development/Fellowship)*

Purpose: To introduce medical students from backgrounds that are underrepresented in medicine to the discipline of radiation oncology early in their medical education. **Focus:** Oncology. **Qualif.:** Applicants must be trainees who are enrolled in a U.S. medical school; must be in good standing at the time the application is submitted; and must be able to identify a mentor/co-mentor (who should be an ASTRO member) with a successful record of research productivity. **Criteria:** Selection will be based on ASTRO's criteria.

Funds Avail.: Amount varies. **Number Awarded:** 3. **To Apply:** Applicants must visit the website for the online application process. **Deadline:** March 6.

1394 ■ ASTRO Residents/Fellows in Radiation Oncology Research Seed Grants *(Advanced Professional, Professional development/Grant)*

Purpose: To support residents or fellows who are planning a career focusing primarily on basic science or clinical research. **Focus:** Oncology. **Qualif.:** Applicants must be ASTRO members who are residents or fellows in the field of radiation oncology sciences. **Criteria:** Selection will be based on ASTRO's criteria.

Funds Avail.: $25,000 each. **Number Awarded:** 3. **To Apply:** Applicants must visit the website for the online application process. **Contact:** ASTRO Research Department at research@astro.org.

1395 ■ ASTRO/ROI Comparative Effectiveness Research Awards *(Professional development/Grant)*

Purpose: To develop comparative effectiveness research leaders within radiation oncology and to stimulate research focused on evaluating the effectiveness, complication profile, cost and cost-effectiveness of various radiation therapy treatments, as well as the comparative effectiveness when compared to other therapies. **Focus:** Oncology. **Qualif.:** Applicants must be ASTRO members who are board-certified or board-eligible physician in radiation oncology at the time the award commences and committed to a career that focuses primarily on academic radiation oncology. **Criteria:** Selection will be based on ASTRO's criteria.

Funds Avail.: $50,000 per year. **Duration:** Annual; up to two years. **Number Awarded:** 2. **To Apply:** Applicants must visit the website for the online application process. **Contact:** ASTRO Research Department at research@astro.org.

1396 ■ American Society of Radiologic Technologists Education and Research Foundation (ASRT)
15000 Central Ave. SE
Albuquerque, NM 87123-3909
Fax: (505)298-5063
Free: 800-444-2778
E-mail: foundation@asrt.org
URL: www.asrtfoundation.org

1397 ■ Jerman-Cahoon Student Scholarship *(Undergraduate/Scholarship)*

Purpose: To provide resources for radiologic technologists intending to improve patient care and to support education and research in the radiologic sciences. **Focus:** Radiology. **Qualif.:** Applicants must be entry-level students in radiography, sonography, magnetic resonance or nuclear medicine who are U.S. citizens, national or permanent residents enrolled in an accredited radiologic science program, and have a minimum program GPA of 3.0 on a 4.0 scale (B average). **Criteria:** Recipients will be selected based on the criteria set by the Scholarship Review Committee that reviews blinded application materials and prepare funding recommendations for the ASRT Foundation's Board of Trustees.

Funds Avail.: $2,500 each. **Duration:** Annual. **Number Awarded:** 6. **To Apply:** Application is via online. Visit the program website for the online application and gathering of other information about the scholarship. **Remarks:** The American Society of Radiologic Technologists established the Jerman-Cahoon Student Scholarship in honor of Edward C. Jerman, founder of the Society, and John B. Cahoon Jr., former ASRT president and one of the most highly respected educators the profession ever produced.

1398 ■ Royce Osborn Minority Scholarship *(Undergraduate/Scholarship)*

Purpose: To assist minority students in an entry-level radiography, sonography, magnetic resonance, radiation

Awards are arranged alphabetically below their administering organizations

therapy or nuclear medicine program. **Focus:** Radiology. **Qualif.:** Applicants must be students attending entry-level radiologic sciences program who are U.S. citizens, national or permanent residents enrolled in an accredited radiologic science program and have a minimum program GPA of 3.0 on a 4.0 scale (B average). **Criteria:** Recipients will be selected based on the criteria set by the Scholarship Review Committee that reviews blinded application materials and prepare funding recommendations for the ASRT Foundation's Board of Trustees.

Funds Avail.: $4,000 each. **Duration:** Annual. **Number Awarded:** 5. **To Apply:** Application is via online. Visit the program website for the online application and gathering of other information about the scholarship. **Remarks:** The scholarship was created in honor of Royce Osborn and is funded through an endowment from the ARRT, as well as through contributions from individual donors.

1399 ■ Professional Research Grants *(Professional development/Grant)*

Purpose: To support research and analysis of issues that affect the radiologic sciences. **Focus:** Radiology. **Qualif.:** Applicants must be radiologic technologists or radiation therapists; must be ASRT members who are also registered with the American Registry of Radiologic Technologists or ASRT members who hold an unrestricted state license. Proposed research projects must be for a period not to exceed two years. Acceptable areas of research include radiation therapy, dosimetry, medical imaging, and radiologic science education and administration. **Criteria:** Selection will be based on the following criteria: significant/relevance to the profession; qualification/resources of the principal investigator and associated personnel; adequate demonstration of study protocols, assurances and agreements; appropriateness of methodology/experimental design; soundness of budget; thoroughness of literature review.

Funds Avail.: $10,000. **To Apply:** Grant application can be obtained at the website. Applicants must complete and submit the full proposal via email or mail. Prior to submitting the full proposal, applicants may submit a letter of intent for preliminary review of their proposal concept. Letters of intent are reviewed by the ASRT Research Department and feedback will be provided regarding the proposed research relevancy, objective and methodology. **Deadline:** March 1 and August 1.

1400 ■ Siemens Clinical Advancement Scholarship *(Undergraduate, Master's/Scholarship)*

Purpose: To assist medical imaging professionals seeking to enhance their clinical practice skills and provide excellent patient care. **Focus:** Radiology. **Qualif.:** Applicants must: be students attending professional-level radiologic sciences program; be ASRT members; and, have applied to or currently be attending an accredited degree or certificate program. Furthermore, applicants eligible are those who attend bachelor's, or master's degree program in radiologic sciences or certificate in a specialty discipline such as CT, MR or sonography to enhance their clinical practice skills and provide excellent patient care. **Criteria:** Recipients will be selected based on the criteria set by the Scholarship Review Committee that reviews blinded application materials and prepare funding recommendations for the ASRT Foundation's Board of Trustees.

Funds Avail.: $5,000 each. **Duration:** Annual. **Number Awarded:** 4. **To Apply:** Application is via online. Visit the program website for the online application and gathering of other information about the scholarship. **Remarks:** The scholarships are funded by the Siemens Healthcare.

1401 ■ Varian Radiation Therapy Advancement Scholarship *(Undergraduate, Master's, Doctorate/Scholarship)*

Purpose: To ensure radiation therapists and medical dosimetrists can afford education that enhances their clinical practice skills and helps them provide excellent patient care. **Focus:** Radiology. **Qualif.:** Applicants must: be students attending professional-level radiologic sciences program; be ASRT members; and, have applied to or currently be attending an accredited degree or certificate program. Furthermore, applicants eligible are those who attend certificate, bachelor's, master's or doctoral degree program to enhance their clinical practice skills and provide excellent patient care. Current medical imaging technologists pursuing a certificate in radiation therapy also qualify for this scholarship. **Criteria:** Recipients will be selected based on the criteria set by the Scholarship Review Committee that reviews blinded application materials and prepare funding recommendations for the ASRT Foundation's Board of Trustees.

Funds Avail.: $5,000 each. **Duration:** Annual. **Number Awarded:** 19. **To Apply:** Application is via online. Visit the program website for the online application and gathering of other information about the scholarship. **Remarks:** The scholarships are funded by Varian Medical Systems because it believes in the power of education to make a difference for radiation therapists, as well as their patients.

1402 ■ American Society of Regional Anesthesia and Pain Medicine (ASRA)
4 Penn Center W, Ste. 401
Pittsburgh, PA 15222
Ph: (412)471-2718
Free: 855-795-ASRA
URL: www.asra.com
Facebook: www.facebook.com/pages/The-American-Society-of-Regional-Anesthesia-and-Pain-Medicine-ASRA/228281927234196
Twitter: www.twitter.com/asra_society

1403 ■ Chronic Pain Medicine Research Grants *(Professional development/Grant)*

Purpose: To promote and facilitate high quality research in pain medicine. **Focus:** Medicine. **Qualif.:** Applicants must be North American members of ASRA. **Criteria:** Selection will be based on the ASRA Research Committee's criteria.

Funds Avail.: Maximum of $100,000. **To Apply:** Applicants must provide the following: letter from the chair of the department confirming the availability of time and facilities for the project; budget; applicants' and co-investigators' curriculum vitae with a listing of any past or present research support; and research plan (the components can be verified at the website). Applications should be submitted in a PDF (electronic form) form to the chair of the Research Committee of the ASRA. **Deadline:** August 31. **Contact:** Email all applications to asraassistant@asra.com.

1404 ■ Carl Koller Memorial Research Grants *(Professional development/Grant)*

Purpose: To support clinical and laboratory studies related to any aspect of regional anesthesia and analgesia and their application to surgery. **Focus:** Anesthesiology. **Qua-**

Awards are arranged alphabetically below their administering organizations

lif.: Applicants must be North American members of ASRA. **Criteria:** Selection will be based on the ASRA Research Committee's criteria.

Funds Avail.: Maximum of $200,000. **Duration:** Biennial. **To Apply:** Applicants must provide the following: letter from the chair of the department confirming the availability of time and facilities for the project; budget; applicants' curriculum vitae with a listing of any past or present research support; and research plan (the components can be verified at the website). Applications should be submitted in a PDF (electronic form) form to the chair of the Research Committee of the ASRA. **Deadline:** November 30. **Contact:** Email all applications to asraassistant@asra.com.

1405 ■ American Society of Safety Engineers (ASSE)
520 N Northwest Hwy.
Park Ridge, IL 60068
Ph: (847)699-2929
Fax: (847)768-3434
E-mail: customerservice@asse.org
URL: www.asse.org
Facebook: www.facebook.com/ASSESafety
Twitter: twitter.com/ASSE_Safety

1406 ■ America Responds Memorial Scholarships (Undergraduate/Scholarship)

Purpose: To provide financial support to deserving students. **Focus:** Occupational safety and health. **Qualif.:** Applicant must be a U.S citizen; must be pursuing an undergraduate degree in occupational safety and health; must have experience working as an emergency responder. **Criteria:** Selection of applicants will be based on scholarship application criteria. Priority will be given to students who have an experience working as Emergency Responders.

Funds Avail.: $1,000. **Duration:** Annual. **Number Awarded:** 1. **To Apply:** Applicant must submit a transcript of records; verification by a safety faculty member; student's narrative; certification; and must attach a letter of recommendation. **Contact:** Matthew Sells at msells@asse.org.

1407 ■ American Society of Safety Engineers Construction Safety Scholarships (Undergraduate/Scholarship)

Purpose: To provide financial support to deserving students. **Focus:** Construction; Occupational safety and health. **Qualif.:** Applicant must be a student pursuing an undergraduate degree in occupational safety and health with an emphasis in construction safety. **Criteria:** Selection of applicants will be based on scholarship application criteria.

Funds Avail.: $2,000. **Duration:** Annual. **Number Awarded:** 1. **To Apply:** Applicant must submit a transcript of records; verification by a safety faculty member; student's narrative; certification; and must attach a letter of recommendation. **Contact:** Matthew Sells at msells@asse.org.

1408 ■ ASSE Diversity Committee Scholarships (Graduate, Undergraduate/Scholarship)

Purpose: To provide financial support to deserving students. **Focus:** Occupational safety and health. **Qualif.:** Applicant must be a student pursuing an undergraduate or graduate degree in occupational safety and health or a closely related field. **Criteria:** Scholarship is open to any individual regardless of race, ethnicity, gender, religion, personal beliefs, age, sexual orientation, physical challenges, geographic location, university or specific area of study.

Funds Avail.: $1,000. **Duration:** Annual. **Number Awarded:** 1. **To Apply:** Applicant must submit a transcript of records; verification by a safety faculty member; student's narrative; certification; and must attach a letter of recommendation. **Contact:** Matthew Sells at msells@asse.org.

1409 ■ Bechtel Group Foundation Scholarships for Safety & Health (Undergraduate/Scholarship)

Purpose: To provide financial support to deserving students. **Focus:** Construction; Occupational safety and health. **Qualif.:** Applicant must be a student pursuing an undergraduate degree in occupational safety and health with an emphasis in construction safety; and must be enrolled or planning to attend at Murray State in Murray, Montana Tech in Butte, of University of Central Missouri. **Criteria:** Selection of applicants will be based on scholarship application criteria. Priority will be given to students with an emphasis in construction safety attending Murray State in Murray, KY, Montana Tech in Butte, MT or Central Washington University in Ellensburg, WA.

Funds Avail.: $5,500 each. **Duration:** Annual. **Number Awarded:** 2. **To Apply:** Applicant must submit a transcript of records; verification by a safety faculty member; student's narrative; certification; and must attach a letter of recommendation. **Contact:** Matthew Sells at msells@asse.org.

1410 ■ Warren K. Brown Scholarships (Undergraduate/Scholarship)

Purpose: To provide financial support to deserving students. **Focus:** Occupational safety and health. **Qualif.:** Applicant must be a student pursuing an undergraduate degree in occupational safety & health or a closely related field at Murray State University in Murray, KY or Indiana State University in Terre Haute, IN. **Criteria:** Selection of applicants will be based on the scholarship application criteria.

Funds Avail.: $1,000. **Duration:** Annual. **Number Awarded:** 1. **To Apply:** Applicant must submit a transcript of records; verification by a safety faculty member; student's narrative; certification; and must attach a letter of recommendation. **Contact:** Matthew Sells at msells@asse.org.

1411 ■ CNA Foundation Scholarships (Graduate, Undergraduate/Scholarship)

Purpose: To provide financial support to deserving students. **Focus:** Occupational safety and health. **Qualif.:** Applicant must be a student pursuing an undergraduate or graduate degree in occupational safety & health or a closely related field. **Criteria:** Selection of applicants will be based on the scholarship application criteria.

Funds Avail.: $2,500. **Duration:** Annual. **Number Awarded:** 2. **To Apply:** Applicant must submit a transcript of records; verification by a safety faculty member; student's narrative; certification; and must attach a letter of recommendation. **Contact:** Matthew Sells at msells@asse.org.

1412 ■ Scott Dominguez - Craters of the Moon Chapter Scholarships (Graduate, Undergraduate/Scholarship)

Purpose: To provide financial support to deserving students. **Focus:** Occupational safety and health. **Qualif.:**

Awards are arranged alphabetically below their administering organizations

Applicant must be a student pursuing an undergraduate or graduate degree in occupational safety & health or a closely related field. Students who are employees or dependents of sponsoring organizations, serving the country through active duty in the armed forces or honorably discharged, members of Boy Scouts, Girl Scouts, FFA, 4H, etc. in previous years, recipients of awards from service organizations or have provided volunteer service to an ASSE chapter are also eligible. Part-time student must have a general or professional ASSE membership. **Criteria:** Priority will be given to students that reside within the Craters of the Moon Chapter, Idaho and the Region II area.

Funds Avail.: $1,000. **Duration:** Annual. **Number Awarded:** 1. **To Apply:** Applicant must submit a transcript of records; verification by a safety faculty member; student's narrative; certification; and must attach a letter of recommendation. **Contact:** Matthew Sells at msells@asse.org.

1413 ■ Gulf Coast Past President's Scholarships (Undergraduate/Scholarship)

Purpose: To provide financial support to deserving students. **Focus:** Occupational safety and health. **Qualif.:** Applicant must be a student pursuing an undergraduate degree in occupational safety and health or a closely related field; and must have a general or professional ASSE membership. **Criteria:** Selection of applicants will be based on scholarship application criteria.

Funds Avail.: $1,500 each. **Duration:** Annual. **Number Awarded:** 2. **To Apply:** Applicant must submit a transcript of records; verification by a safety faculty member; student's narrative; certification; and must attach a letter of recommendation. **Contact:** Matthew Sells at msells@asse.org.

1414 ■ George Gustafson HSE Memorial Scholarships (Graduate, Undergraduate/Scholarship)

Purpose: To provide financial support to deserving students. **Focus:** Occupational safety and health. **Qualif.:** Applicant must be a student pursuing an undergraduate or graduate degree in occupational safety & health or a closely related field; must be a resident of Texas and attending a Texas university. **Criteria:** Priority will be given to students from Texas attending a Texas University.

Funds Avail.: $2,000. **Duration:** Annual. **Number Awarded:** 1. **To Apply:** Applicant must submit a transcript of records; verification by a safety faculty member; student's narrative; certification; and must attach a letter of recommendation. **Contact:** Matthew Sells at msells@asse.org.

1415 ■ David Iden Memorial Safety Scholarships (Undergraduate/Scholarship)

Purpose: To provide financial support to students who seek higher education. **Focus:** Occupational safety and health. **Qualif.:** Applicant must be a student pursuing an undergraduate degree in occupational safety & health or a closely related field. **Criteria:** Selection of applicants will be based on the scholarship application criteria.

Funds Avail.: Varies. **Duration:** Annual. **To Apply:** Applicant must submit a transcript of records; verification by a safety faculty member; student's narrative; certification; and must attach a letter of recommendation.

1416 ■ Greater Baton Rouge Chapter - Don Jones Excellence in Safety Scholarships (Undergraduate/Scholarship)

Purpose: To provide financial support to deserving students. **Focus:** Occupational safety and health. **Qualif.:** Applicant must be a student pursuing a degree in occupational safety & health or a closely related field; must be attending any college or university within Louisiana or within the Southeast U.S. region; must be a student pursuing an associate or bachelor degree. A part-time student must have a general or professional ASSE membership. **Criteria:** Priority will be given to a student attending Southeastern Louisiana University in Hammond, Louisiana, attending any college or university within Louisiana, or any within the Southeast U.S. region.

Funds Avail.: $1,500. **Duration:** Annual. **Number Awarded:** 1. **To Apply:** Applicant must submit a transcript of records; verification by a safety faculty member; student's narrative; certification; and must attach a letter of recommendation. **Contact:** Matthew Sells at msells@asse.org.

1417 ■ Southwest Chapter Roy Kinslow Scholarships (Undergraduate/Scholarship)

Purpose: To provide financial support to deserving students. **Focus:** Occupational safety and health. **Qualif.:** Applicant must be a student pursuing an undergraduate degree in occupational safety & health or a closely related field at Southeastern Oklahoma State University in Durat, OK or for any student from the Southwest Chapter area attending a school within the Region III boundaries. **Criteria:** Selection of applicants will be based on scholarship application criteria.

Funds Avail.: $1,000. **Duration:** Annual. **Number Awarded:** 1. **To Apply:** Applicant must submit a transcript of records; verification by a safety faculty member; student's narrative; certification; and must attach a letter of recommendation. **Contact:** Matthew Sells at msells@asse.org.

1418 ■ James P. Kohn Memorial Scholarships (Graduate/Scholarship)

Purpose: To provide financial support to deserving students. **Focus:** Occupational safety and health. **Qualif.:** Applicants must be students pursuing a graduate degree in occupational safety and health or a closely related field. **Criteria:** Selection of applicants will be based on scholarship application criteria.

Funds Avail.: $1,000. **Duration:** Annual. **Number Awarded:** 1. **To Apply:** Applicanst must submit a transcript of records; verification by a safety faculty member; applicants' narrative; certification; and must attach a letter of recommendation. **Contact:** Matthew Sells at msells@asse.org.

1419 ■ Central Indiana ASSE Jim Kriner Memorial Scholarships (Graduate, Undergraduate/Scholarship)

Purpose: To provide financial support to deserving students. **Focus:** Occupational safety and health. **Qualif.:** Applicant must be a student pursuing an undergraduate or graduate degree in occupational safety & health or a closely related field. **Criteria:** Priority will be given to Indiana residents attending school in Indiana or anywhere in the U.S or to non-residents attending an Indiana university.

Funds Avail.: $1,000 (2); $3,000 (1.). **Duration:** Annual. **Number Awarded:** 3. **To Apply:** Applicant must submit a transcript of records; verification by a safety faculty member; student's narrative; certification; and must attach a letter of recommendation. **Contact:** Matthew Sells at msells@asse.org.

1420 ■ Liberty Mutual Scholarships (Undergraduate/Scholarship)

Purpose: To provide financial support to deserving students. **Focus:** Occupational safety and health. **Qualif.:**

Awards are arranged alphabetically below their administering organizations

Applicant must be a student pursuing an undergraduate degree in occupational safety & health or a closely related field. **Criteria:** Selection of applicants will be based on scholarship application criteria.

Funds Avail.: $4,000 each. **Duration:** Annual. **Number Awarded:** 2. **To Apply:** Applicant must submit a transcript of records; verification by a safety faculty member; student's narrative; certification; and must attach a letter of recommendation. **Contact:** Matthew Sells at msells@asse.org.

1421 ■ Marsh Risk Consulting Scholarships (Undergraduate/Scholarship)

Purpose: To provide financial support to student who seek higher education. **Focus:** Occupational safety and health. **Qualif.:** Applicant must be a student pursuing an undergraduate degree in occupational safety & health or a closely related field. **Criteria:** Selection of applicants will be based on the scholarship application criteria.

Funds Avail.: $1,500. **Number Awarded:** 1. **To Apply:** Applicant must submit a transcript of records; verification by a safety faculty member; student's narrative; certification; and must attach a letter of recommendation.

1422 ■ Rixio Medina and Associates Hispanics in Safety Scholarships (Graduate, Undergraduate/Scholarship)

Purpose: To provide financial support to deserving students. **Focus:** Occupational safety and health. **Qualif.:** Applicant must be a student pursuing an undergraduate or graduate degree in occupational safety & health or a closely related field; must be a bilingual student (Spanish-English). **Criteria:** Selection of applicants will be based on scholarship application criteria.

Funds Avail.: $4,000. **Duration:** . **Number Awarded:** 1. **To Apply:** Applicants must submit a transcript of records. For further information about the application form and requirements, applicants are advised to contact the ASSE Foundation. **Contact:** Matthew Sells at msells@asse.org.

1423 ■ North Florida Chapter Safety Education Scholarships (Graduate, Undergraduate/Scholarship)

Purpose: To provide financial support to deserving students. **Focus:** Occupational safety and health. **Qualif.:** Applicant must be a student pursuing an undergraduate or graduate degree in occupational safety & health or a closely related field; must be planning to attend in any Florida College or university. Part-time student must have a general or professional ASSE membership. **Criteria:** Priority will be given to part-time or full-time students who belong to the North Florida chapter, full-time students who attend any Florida college or university or to full-time students attending an ASAC/ABET accredited program nationwide.

Funds Avail.: $1,000. **Duration:** Annual. **Number Awarded:** 1. **To Apply:** Applicant must submit a transcript of records; verification by a safety faculty member; student's narrative; certification; and must attach a letter of recommendation. **Contact:** Matthew Sells at msells@asse.org.

1424 ■ Northeastern Illinois Chapter Scholarships (Graduate, Undergraduate/Scholarship)

Purpose: To provide financial support to deserving students. **Focus:** Occupational safety and health. **Qualif.:** Applicant must be a student pursuing an undergraduate or graduate degree in occupational safety & health or a closely related field; must attend Northeastern Illinois University or in any Northeastern Illinois region; must be members or offspring of Northeastern, IL chapter. **Criteria:** Selection of applicants will be based on scholarship application criteria. Preference will be given to students who attend Northern Illinois University in DeKalb, IL or in any Northeastern Illinois region.

Funds Avail.: $2,000. **Duration:** Annual. **Number Awarded:** 1. **To Apply:** Applicant must submit a transcript of records; verification by a safety faculty member; student's narrative; certification; and must attach a letter of recommendation. **Contact:** Matthew Sells at msells@asse.org.

1425 ■ PDC Scholarships (Undergraduate/Scholarship)

Purpose: To provide financial support to deserving students. **Focus:** Occupational safety and health. **Qualif.:** Applicant must be a student pursuing a degree in occupational safety & health or a closely related field. **Criteria:** Selection of applicants will be based on scholarship application criteria.

Funds Avail.: $700. **Duration:** Annual. **Number Awarded:** 1. **To Apply:** Applicants must submit a transcript of records; verification by a safety faculty member; student's narrative; certification; and must attach a letter of recommendation. **Contact:** Matthew Sells at msells@asse.org.

1426 ■ Harold F. Polston Scholarships (Graduate, Undergraduate/Scholarship)

Purpose: To provide financial support to deserving students. **Focus:** Occupational safety and health. **Qualif.:** Applicant must be a student pursuing an undergraduate or graduate degree in occupational safety & health or a closely related field. **Criteria:** Priority will be given to students that belong to the Middle Tennessee Chapter, those attending Middle Tennessee State University in Murfreesboro, TN or Murray State University in Murray, KY and those who live in the Region VII.

Funds Avail.: $1,500. **Duration:** Annual. **Number Awarded:** 1. **To Apply:** Applicants must submit a transcript of records; verification by a safety faculty member; student's narrative; certification; and must attach a letter of recommendation. **Contact:** Matthew Sells at msells@asse.org.

1427 ■ William C. Ray, CIH, CSP Arizona Scholarships (Graduate, Undergraduate/Scholarship)

Purpose: To provide financial support to those students who are enrolled in occupational safety and health programs or closely-related degree programs. **Focus:** Occupational safety and health. **Qualif.:** Applicant must be a student pursuing an undergraduate or graduate degree in occupational safety & health or a closely related field; must reside in Arizona. **Criteria:** Selection will be based on requirements. Priority will be given to students residing in Arizona or within the Region II area.

Funds Avail.: $2,500. **Duration:** Annual. **Number Awarded:** 2. **To Apply:** Applicant must submit a transcript of records; verification by a safety faculty member; student's narrative; certification; and must attach a letter of recommendation. **Contact:** Matthew Sells at msells@asse.org.

1428 ■ Region II Scholarships (Graduate, Undergraduate/Scholarship)

Purpose: To provide financial support to deserving students. **Focus:** Occupational safety and health. **Qualif.:** Applicant must be a student pursuing an undergraduate or graduate degree in occupational safety & health or a closely related field; must be a student that resides within the

Awards are arranged alphabetically below their administering organizations

Region II (MT, ID, WY, CO, UT, NV, AZ, NM) area. **Criteria:** Selection of applicants will be based on the scholarship application criteria. Preference will be given to students who reside within the Region II area.
Funds Avail.: $1,000. **Duration:** Annual. **Number Awarded:** 1. **To Apply:** Applicants must submit a transcript of records; verification by a safety faculty member; student's narrative; certification; and must attach a letter of recommendation. **Contact:** Matthew Sells at msells@asse.org.

1429 ■ Harry Taback 9/11 Memorial Scholarships (Undergraduate/Scholarship)

Purpose: To provide financial support to deserving students. **Focus:** Occupational safety and health. **Qualif.:** Applicant must be a student pursuing an undergraduate or graduate degree in occupational safety & health or a closely related field; must be a natural born U.S citizen. **Criteria:** Selection of applicants will be based on scholarship application criteria.
Funds Avail.: $1,000. **Duration:** Annual. **Number Awarded:** 1. **To Apply:** Applicant must submit a transcript of records; verification by a safety faculty member; student's narrative; certification; and must attach a letter of recommendation. **Contact:** Matthew Sells at msells@asse.org.

1430 ■ Thompson Scholarships for Women in Safety (Graduate/Scholarship)

Purpose: To provide financial support to deserving students. **Focus:** Engineering; Environmental technology; Fires and fire prevention; Industrial hygiene; Medicine; Occupational safety and health; Risk management. **Qualif.:** Applicant must be a woman pursuing a degree in safety engineering, safety management, occupational health nursing, occupational medicine, risk management, ergonomics, industrial hygiene, fire safety, environmental safety, environmental health or any other closely related field. **Criteria:** Selection will be based on the submitted application. Priority will be given to female students.
Funds Avail.: $1,000. **Duration:** Annual. **Number Awarded:** 1. **To Apply:** Applicants must submit a transcript of records. **Contact:** Matthew Sells at msells@asse.org.

1431 ■ UPS Diversity Scholarships (Undergraduate/Scholarship)

Purpose: To provide financial support to deserving students. **Focus:** Occupational safety and health. **Qualif.:** Applicant must be a student pursuing an undergraduate degree in occupational safety & health or a closely relative field; must be of minority ethnic descent or racial group and must be a U.S. citizen. **Criteria:** Selection of applicants will be based on scholarship application criteria.
Funds Avail.: $5,250 each. **Duration:** Annual. **Number Awarded:** 3. **To Apply:** Applicants must submit a transcript of records; for further information about the application form and requirements, applicants are advised to contact the ASSE Foundation. **Contact:** Matthew Sells at msells@asse.org.

1432 ■ American Society for Theatre Research (ASTR)
1000 Westgate Dr., Ste. 252
Saint Paul, MN 55114
Ph: (651)288-3429
Fax: (651)290-2266
E-mail: info@astr.org
URL: www.astr.org

1433 ■ ASTR Research Fellowships (Other/Fellowship)

Purpose: To underwrite some of the research expenses of scholars undertaking projects significant to the field of theatre and/or performance studies. **Focus:** Performing arts; Theater arts. **Qualif.:** Applicant must be holding a terminal degree and a member of ASTR for at least three years. **Criteria:** Selection is based on the merit of the project within the field of theatre or performance studies.
Funds Avail.: Up to $3,000. **Duration:** Annual. **Number Awarded:** Varies. **To Apply:** Applicants must submit a 150-word abstract of the project; a longer narrative description of the project indicating its procedures, goals and significance; a budget; a two-page curriculum vitae; and three letters of support from scholars in the proposed or related fields of study.

1434 ■ Helen Krich Chinoy Dissertation Research Fellowships (Doctorate/Fellowship)

Purpose: To financially support PhD candidates with their travel in conducting research projects connected to their dissertations. **Focus:** Theater arts. **Qualif.:** Applicants must be PhD candidates who have passed their qualifying exams within the last two years and have begun working on their dissertations. **Criteria:** Recipients will be selected based on clarity, originality and critical rigor.
Funds Avail.: A total of $3,000. **Number Awarded:** 3. **To Apply:** Applicants must submit a project abstract (100 words); description of the proposed project (500 words, including the nature of the project, research strategy, current status of the project and a rationale for the project); a statement on how the award will be used and how will it help the project; a curriculum vitae; and two letters of recommendation (one from the dissertation advisor, and another from a scholar familiar with the applicant's work). **Deadline:** April 28.

1435 ■ American Society of Travel Agents (ASTA)
675 N Washington St., Ste. 490
Alexandria, VA 22314
Ph: (703)739-2782
Free: 800-275-2782
E-mail: askasta@asta.org
URL: www.asta.org
Facebook: www.facebook.com/AmSocTrvlAgents/

1436 ■ America Express Travel Scholarships (Undergraduate/Scholarship)

Purpose: To encourage the pursuit of education and the growth and development of tomorrow's travel/tourism work force. **Focus:** Travel and tourism. **Qualif.:** Applicants must be travel/tourism students in either a two or four-year college/university or propriety travel school; have at least 3.0 GPA on a 4.0 scale; have relevant training in basic statistics or other social research method courses; have at least basic computer skills; and, be residents, citizens, or legal aliens of the United States or Canada. **Criteria:** Recipients will be selected based on academic standing.
Funds Avail.: $2,000. **Duration:** Annual. **Number Awarded:** 1. **To Apply:** Applicants must submit a proof of enrollment/acceptance at a travel school, community/junior college, college or university; an official school-printed

description or listing of the curriculum where they enrolled; proof of enrollments in travel and tourism courses, or letter from business colleague that can attest to each of the applicant's desire to pursue a career in the travel and tourism industry; four identical collated copies of applications and required materials (one original and three photocopies); and a 500-word statement detailing the student's plans in travel and tourism as well as the student's view of the travel industry's future. **Deadline:** April 1.

1437 ■ ASTA Alaska Airlines Scholarships
(Undergraduate/Scholarship)

Purpose: To encourage people to go into the travel and tourism business as their profession. **Focus:** Travel and tourism. **Qualif.:** Applicants must be travel/tourism students in either a four-year college/university or propriety travel school; have at least 3.0 GPA on a 4.0 scale; have relevant training in basic statistics or other social research method courses; have at least basic computer skills; and, be residents, citizens, or legal aliens of the United States or Canada. **Criteria:** Recipients will be selected based on academic standing.

Funds Avail.: $2,000. **Duration:** Annual. **Number Awarded:** 1. **To Apply:** Applicants must submit proof of enrollment/acceptance at a travel school, community/junior college, college or university; an official school-printed description or listing of the curriculum where they are enrolled; proof of enrollments in travel and tourism courses, or letter from business colleague that can attest to each of the applicant's desire to pursue a career in the travel and tourism industry; four identical collated copies of applications and required materials (one original and three photocopies); and a 500-word paper on why the applicant is pursuing a career in the travel and tourism industry, which must include at least two career goals. **Deadline:** April 1.

1438 ■ ASTA Holland America Line Graduate Research Scholarships *(Graduate/Scholarship)*

Purpose: To provide funding support to research projects in the travel and tourism field. **Focus:** Travel and tourism. **Qualif.:** Applicants must be graduate students who are residents, citizens, or legal aliens of the United States or Canada and have a cumulative or overall minimum 3.0 grade point average. **Criteria:** Selection will be based on the aforesaid qualifications and compliance with the application process.

Funds Avail.: $4,000. **Duration:** Annual. **Number Awarded:** 1. **To Apply:** Applicants must submit the following: a proof of enrollment/acceptance at a travel school, community/junior college, or university; an official school-printed description or listing of the curriculum where applicants are enrolled; a proof of enrollment in travel and tourism courses; and a letter of recommendation from a professor, employer, or business colleague that can attest to each of the applicant's desire to pursue a career in the travel and tourism industry. **Deadline:** April 1.

1439 ■ ASTA Rigby, Healy, Simmons Scholarships
(Graduate/Scholarship)

Purpose: To encourage serious academic study in the field of travel and tourism. **Focus:** Travel and tourism. **Qualif.:** Applicants must be travel/tourism students in either a four-year college/university or propriety travel school; have at least 3.0 GPA on a 4.0 scale; have relevant training in basic statistics or other social research method courses; must have at least basic computer skills; and, be residents, citizens, or legal aliens of the United States or Canada.

Criteria: Recipients will be selected based on academic standing.

Funds Avail.: $2,000. **Duration:** Annual. **Number Awarded:** 1. **To Apply:** Applicants must submit a proof of enrollment/acceptance at a travel school, community/junior college, college or university; an official school-printed description or listing of the curriculum where they are enrolled; proof of enrollments in travel and tourism courses, or letter from business colleague that can attest to each of the applicant's desire to pursue a career in the travel and tourism industry; four identical collated copies of applications and required materials (one original and three photocopies); and a 500-word statement suggesting improvements in the travel industry. **Deadline:** April 1.

1440 ■ Avis Budget Group Scholarships *(Graduate/Scholarship)*

Purpose: To help future travel professionals meet the need for broader business management skills, beyond those dealing solely with travel and tourism issues. **Focus:** Travel and tourism. **Qualif.:** Applicants must have a minimum of two years of full-time travel industry experience or an undergraduate degree in travel/tourism. They may be currently employed in the travel industry, or be currently enrolled in a minimum of two courses per semester in an accredited undergraduate or graduate level degree program in business or equivalent degree program. **Criteria:** Recipients will be selected based on merit.

Funds Avail.: $1,000. **Duration:** Annual. **Number Awarded:** 1. **To Apply:** Applicants must provide a proof of current employment in the travel industry; transcript from last academic term with proof of a GPA of 3.0 on a 4.0 scale, or if the applicants are returning to school after time spent in the workforce, applicant must submit transcript showing a GPA of 3.0 on 4.0 scale; and a brief essay (500-750 words) explaining how the degree program relates to applicant's future career in the travel industry. **Deadline:** April 1.

1441 ■ David J. Hallissey Memorial Internships
(Graduate, Undergraduate/Internship)

Purpose: To encourage academic research in the tourism field. **Focus:** Travel and tourism. **Qualif.:** Applicants must be travel/tourism students from Washington, DC metro area colleges/universities in undergraduate or graduate travel or tourism programs; have at least 3.0 GPA on a 4.0 scale; have relevant training in basic statistics or other social research method courses; have at least basic computer skills; and, be residents, citizens, or legal aliens of the United States or Canada. **Criteria:** Recipients will be selected based on academic standing.

Funds Avail.: $2,000. **Duration:** Annual. **Number Awarded:** 1. **To Apply:** Applicants must submit a proof of enrollment/acceptance at a travel school, community/junior college, college or university; an official school-printed description or listing of the curriculum where they are enrolled; proof of enrollment in travel and tourism courses, or letter from a business colleague that can attest to each of the applicant's desire to pursue a career in the travel and tourism industry. Complete application must consist of four identical collated copies of applications and required materials (one original and three photocopies). **Deadline:** April 1.

1442 ■ George Reinke Scholarships *(Other/Scholarship)*

Purpose: To support travel and tourism industry professionals who were completing their industry certification

Awards are arranged alphabetically below their administering organizations

programs. **Focus:** Travel and tourism. **Qualif.:** Applicants must be travel/tourism students in either a two or four-year college/university or propriety travel school; have at least 3.0 GPA on a 4.0 scale; have a relevant training in basic statistics or other social research method courses; have at least basic computer skills; and, be residents, citizens, or legal aliens of the United States or Canada. **Criteria:** Recipients will be selected based on academic standing.

Funds Avail.: No specific amount. **Duration:** Annual. **To Apply:** Applicants must submit proof of enrollment/acceptance at a travel school, community/junior college, college or university; an official school-printed description or listing of the curriculum where they are enrolled; proof of enrollments in travel and tourism courses, or letter from business colleague that can attest to each of the applicant's desire to pursue a career in the travel and tourism industry; four identical collated copies of applications and required materials (one original and three photocopies); and a 500-word paper explaining why applicant needs the scholarship. **Remarks:** The scholarship was established by George Reinke of Travel Unlimited (late Trans Mark Travel). He was a long-term ASTA member from Tulsa, Oklahoma, was an area director in 1980-84 and was on the ASTA Board and Southwest Chapter President in 1974-75.

1443 ■ Allegheny Branch of Mid-America Chapter - Nancy Stewart Professional Development Scholarships (Professional development/Scholarship)

Purpose: To fund research projects in the travel and tourism field. **Focus:** Travel and tourism. **Qualif.:** Applicants must have a minimum of three years of full-time travel industry experience; must be pursuing one of the Travel Institute's four certification program: CTC accreditation, Destination Specialist, Travel Career Development, Professional Management. **Criteria:** Recipients are selected based on the academic standing.

Funds Avail.: $3,000. **Duration:** Annual. **To Apply:** Applicants must provide a proof of current employment in the travel industry; transcript from last academic term with proof of a GPA of 3.0 on a 4.0 scale or if the applicant is returning to school after time spent in the workforce, submit a cover letter explaining why applicant is returning to school; a letter of intent to enroll in a Travel Institute course within one year and explaining what benefits they hope to obtain from the Travel Institute program or an application to the ASTA educational program; a letter of recommendation from the official ASTA employer to confirm the employment status; and an original headshot picture. **Deadline:** November 5.

1444 ■ American Sociological Association (ASA)
1430 K St. NW, Ste. 600
Washington, DC 20005
Ph: (202)383-9005
Fax: (202)638-0882
E-mail: customer@asanet.org
URL: www.asanet.org
Facebook: www.facebook.com/AmericanSociologicalAssociation
Twitter: twitter.com/ASANews

1445 ■ ASA Minority Fellowship Program (ASA MFP) (Graduate, Doctorate, Professional development/Fellowship)

Purpose: To support minority graduate students who have strong interests in and commitment to a research career in sociology. **Focus:** Discrimination, Sex; Education; Medicine; Minorities; Psychology; Sociology. **Qualif.:** Applicants must be: U.S. citizens, non-citizen nationals of the U.S., or have been lawfully admitted to the U.S. for permanent residence; members of any underrepresented racial/ethnic minority group in the U.S. (e.g. Blacks/African-Americans, Hispanics/Latinos, Asians or Pacific Islanders, or American Indians/Alaska Natives); and, enrolled in (and have completed one full academic year) in a program that grants the Ph.D. in sociology. **Criteria:** Fellows will be selected on the basis of their commitment to research, the focus of their research experience, academic achievement, scholarship, writing ability, research potential, financial need, and racial/ethnic minority background. The MFP Advisory Panel, a rotating, appointed group of senior scholars in sociology, shall select the recipients.

Funds Avail.: $18,000. **Duration:** Annual; Every August 1 to July 31. **To Apply:** Application package must include: fellowship application; essays; three recommendation letters of which one should be from the mentor; official transcripts from all the undergraduate and graduate institutions that you have been enrolled in; curriculum vita; and other supporting documents such as abstracts of published papers (the transcripts shall be separately transmitted while supports are optional). **Deadline:** January 31. **Contact:** ASA Minority Affairs Program: minority.affairs@asanet.org.

1446 ■ ASA Student Forum Travel Awards (Undergraduate, Graduate/Grant)

Purpose: To assist students by defraying the expenses associated with attending the ASA Annual Meeting. **Focus:** Sociology. **Qualif.:** Applicants must be students pursuing an undergraduate or graduate sociology degree in an academic institution and current student members of ASA at the time of application. **Criteria:** Selection will be based on the following: participation in the Annual Meeting program (e.g., paper sessions, roundtables); purpose for attending (e.g., workshop training, Honors Program participation); student financial need; availability of other forms of support, matching funds; and potential benefit to the students.

Funds Avail.: $225 each. **Number Awarded:** 25. **To Apply:** Applicants must complete the application form (in PDF file) and send via email or print out and mail one hard copy. **Deadline:** April 1. **Contact:** Email application at studentforum@asanet.org.

1447 ■ American Sokol Organization (ASO)
9126 Ogden Ave.
Brookfield, IL 60513-1943
Ph: (708)255-5397
E-mail: aso@american-sokol.org
URL: american-sokol.org
Facebook: www.facebook.com/americansokol
Twitter: twitter.com/AmericanSokol

1448 ■ American Sokol Merit Awards (Undergraduate/Scholarship, Recognition)

Purpose: To help incoming students pursue their studies in college. **Focus:** Education, Physical; Physical sciences. **Qualif.:** Applicants must be Sokol Youth or Sokol Adult members who are planning a full-time course or program in an accredited college. Applications must be made in advance of the year of study. **Criteria:** Applicants will be selected based on the following: regular attendance in American Sokol classes for at least three years (juniors may be included but must become American Sokol adult members at age 17); successful completion of Sokol Instructor School(s) - Unit, District, or National; teaching or assisting experience in Sokol gym classes; and service American Sokol Units, Districts, and/or National Organization.

Funds Avail.: $500. **Duration:** One year. **To Apply:** Successful candidates must submit a recommendation proof of the Unit or District Physical Director; a parent or guardian will be required to sign to the condition that if the candidate cannot submit the needed requirements completely, he or she should repay the whole amount of the award. **Deadline:** June 1. **Remarks:** The award was instituted by the XIIth American Sokol Convention to be paid from the American Sokol Future Leaders Fund.

1449 ■ American Speech Language Hearing Foundation (ASHF)
2200 Research Blvd.
Rockville, MD 20850-3289
Ph: (301)296-8700
Fax: (301)296-8567
E-mail: foundationprograms@asha.org
URL: www.ashfoundation.org/default.htm

1450 ■ American Speech Language Hearing Foundation Clinical Research Grants (Doctorate/Grant)

Purpose: To support investigations that will advance knowledge of the efficacy of treatment and assessment practices. **Focus:** Communications; Disabilities; Hearing and deafness; Speech and language pathology/Audiology. **Qualif.:** Applicants must have received a PhD or equivalent research doctorate within the discipline of communication sciences and disorders or related field and must demonstrate the potential and commitment to conducting independent research with a clear plan for applying for extramural research support. **Criteria:** Recipients will be selected based on the following: objectives and significance; experimental design and research method; innovation; facilities and resources; management plan and budget; investigator; mentor and mentoring plan; collaborators and collaboration plan. Priority will be given to proposals investigating promising approaches that have potential for improving the everyday functioning of individuals with, or at-risk for, communication and related impairments.

Funds Avail.: $50,000 to $75,000. **Duration:** Annual. **To Apply:** Applicants should prepare research proposals with the formats prescribed by the Foundation. Such must be submitted electronically. **Deadline:** April 25.

1451 ■ American Speech Language Hearing Foundation Endowed Scholarships (Graduate, Master's, Doctorate/Scholarship)

Purpose: To support the advancement of knowledge in the area of disabilities and to improve the lives of people with speech, language, or hearing disorders. **Focus:** Communications; Disabilities; Hearing and deafness; Minorities; Speech and language pathology/Audiology. **Qualif.:** Applicants must be enrolled or accepted in a master's or doctoral in communication sciences and disorders program in the United States (in full-time study for full academic year). **Criteria:** Recipients will be selected based on the criteria set by the Foundation.

Funds Avail.: $5,000 each. **Duration:** Annual. **Number Awarded:** 6. **To Apply:** Applicants must submit the following: online student information form; letter of application and modified vitae appendix; department information form; transcripts; and confidential recommendation letters. All of those must be submitted through online application system. **Deadline:** May 23.

1452 ■ American Speech Language Hearing Foundation General Scholarships (Graduate, Master's, Doctorate/Scholarship)

Purpose: To support the advancement of knowledge in the area of disabilities and to improve the lives of people with speech, language, or hearing disorders. **Focus:** Communications; Disabilities; Handicapped; Hearing and deafness; Speech and language pathology/Audiology. **Qualif.:** Applicants must be full-time master's or doctorate students who will be or who are currently enrolled in a graduate program in communication sciences and disorders. **Criteria:** Recipients will be selected based on the criteria set by the Foundation.

Funds Avail.: $5,000 each. **Duration:** Annual. **Number Awarded:** 15. **To Apply:** Applicants must submit the following: online student information form; letter of application and modified vitae appendix; department information form; transcripts; and confidential recommendation letters. All of those must be submitted through online application system. **Deadline:** May 23.

1453 ■ American Speech Language Hearing Foundation Scholarships for International Students (Graduate, Master's, Doctorate/Scholarship)

Purpose: To support the advancement of knowledge in the area of disabilities, and improve the lives of people with speech, language, or hearing disorders. **Focus:** Communications; Hearing and deafness; Speech and language pathology/Audiology. **Qualif.:** Applicants must be full-time international graduate students studying communication sciences and disorders in the United States and demonstrating outstanding achievement. **Criteria:** Recipients will be selected based on the aforesaid qualifications and compliance with the application process.

Funds Avail.: $5,000 each. **Duration:** Annual. **Number Awarded:** 2. **To Apply:** Applicants must submit the following: online student information form; letter of application and modified vitae appendix; department information form; transcripts; and confidential recommendation letters. All of those must be submitted through online application system. **Deadline:** May 23.

1454 ■ American Speech Language Hearing Foundation Scholarships for Minority Students (Graduate, Master's, Doctorate/Scholarship)

Purpose: To support the advancement of knowledge of minority students in the area of disabilities, as well as to improve the lives of people with speech, language, or hearing disorders. **Focus:** Communications; Hearing and deafness; Minorities; Speech and language pathology/Audiology. **Qualif.:** Applicants must be members of a racial or ethnic minority group and must be U.S. citizens. They must be graduate students enrolled full-time in a communication sciences and disorders program. **Criteria:** Recipients will be selected based on the aforesaid qualifications and compliance with the application process.

Funds Avail.: $5,000 each. **Duration:** Annual. **Number Awarded:** 2. **To Apply:** Applicants must submit the following: online student information form; letter of application

Awards are arranged alphabetically below their administering organizations

and modified vitae appendix; department information form; transcripts; and confidential recommendation letters. All of those must be submitted through online application system. **Deadline:** May 23.

1455 ■ ASHFoundation New Century Scholars Doctoral Scholarships *(Doctorate/Scholarship)*

Purpose: To support strong doctoral candidates who are committed to attaining the research doctoral degree and to working in the higher education academic community in the field of communication sciences and disorders in the United States. **Focus:** Communications; Disabilities; Speech and language pathology/Audiology. **Qualif.:** Applicants must be students who are accepted to, or currently enrolled in, a research doctoral program (PhD or equivalent) in communication sciences and disorders, and be NSSLHA or ASHA members. **Criteria:** Recipients will be selected based on the following: students with either full-time status (9 hours or more per semester requirement or the university equivalent for the quarter system) or part-time statuses; and commitment of having teacher-investigator career in communication sciences and disorders in the U.S.A.

Funds Avail.: $10,000 each. **Duration:** Annual. **Number Awarded:** 15. **To Apply:** Applicants must submit the following: online student information form; letter of application and modified vitae appendix; department information form; transcripts; and confidential recommendation letters. All of those must be submitted through online application system. **Deadline:** May 9.

1456 ■ ASHFoundation New Century Scholars Research Grants *(Doctorate/Grant)*

Purpose: To support investigations that will advance knowledge of the efficacy of treatment and assessment practices, and encourage innovative studies or unmet research. **Focus:** Communications; Disabilities; Hearing and deafness; Speech and language pathology/Audiology. **Qualif.:** Applicants must be scientists with research doctorate within the discipline of communication sciences and disorders or related field, and able to demonstrate the potential and commitment to conducting independent research with a clear plan for applying for extramural research support. **Criteria:** Recipients will be selected based on the following: objectives and significance; experimental design and research method; innovation; facilities and resources; management plan and budget; investigator; mentor and mentoring plan; collaborators and collaboration plan.

Funds Avail.: $25,000 each. **Duration:** Annual. **Number Awarded:** Up to 4. **To Apply:** Applicants should prepare research proposals with the formats prescribed by the Foundation. Such must be submitted electronically. **Deadline:** April 25.

1457 ■ ASHFoundation New Investigators Research Grants *(Doctorate/Grant)*

Purpose: To pursue doctoral research in audiology or speech-language pathology. **Focus:** Speech and language pathology/Audiology. **Qualif.:** Applicants must be new scientists earning their research doctorate (Ph.D.) in the discipline of communication sciences within the last 5 years. **Criteria:** Selection will be based on the committee's criteria for evaluation.

Funds Avail.: $10,000. **To Apply:** Applicants must provide their research proposals. Other documents include: investigator letter (limit 2 pages); abstract (limit 1 page); research plan (10 pages consist of specific aims, significance of research, design methods, procedures and evaluation, and facilities and resources); references (2 pages); management plan and budget (2 pages); human subjects); letter of institutional commitment; and letters of support. **Deadline:** April 24.

1458 ■ ASHFoundation Scholarships for NSSLHA Members *(Graduate/Scholarship)*

Purpose: To support NSSLHA student members in their graduate studies. **Focus:** Speech and language pathology/Audiology. **Qualif.:** Applicants must be undergraduate senior students with active national NSSLHA memberships and who will begin graduate study in the fall of the current year; and must be accepted for, or enrolled in, graduate study in a communication sciences and disorders program in the United States in which Master's programs in speech-language pathology or clinical doctoral programs in audiology must be accredited by the Council on Academic Accreditation in Audiology and Speech-Language Pathology (CAA). **Criteria:** Selection will be based on the committee's criteria.

Funds Avail.: $5,000 each. **Number Awarded:** Up to 3. **To Apply:** Applicants must complete the online Student Information Form and upload the following required materials through the online application system: letter of application (PDF file, limit 2 pages, 12-point font, single-spaced); letter of acceptance or statement of good standing (PDF file); transcript (PDF file); essay (PDF file, limit 5 pages, 12-point font, single-spaced) responding to the question provided at the website; and confidential recommendation letters. **Deadline:** May 22.

1459 ■ ASHFoundation Speech Science Research Grants *(Doctorate/Grant)*

Purpose: To support investigations that will advance knowledge of the efficacy of treatment and assessment practices; to help further research activities of new investigators that have particular relevance to audiology and/or speech language pathology. **Focus:** Communications; Speech and language pathology/Audiology. **Qualif.:** Applicants must have received a doctoral degree within the past five years and wish to further research activities in the areas of speech communication. **Criteria:** Recipients will be selected based on the clearly stated project aims; significance of the research and its potential impact on the clinical needs relevant to speech-language pathology or audiology; merit of the design for answering the question, including detailed account of the methodology to be used; adequate provision for evaluating the results of the project; explicit statement of how the objectives will be measured; indication of the facilities, resources, personnel and subjects to which the applicant would have access in order to carry out the activities described in the proposal; the perceived ability of the applicant to complete the proposed research within one year period; Management plan that clearly outlines the activities and timeliness.

Funds Avail.: $10,000. **Duration:** Biennial. **To Apply:** Applicants should prepare research proposals with the formats prescribed by the Foundation. Such must be submitted electronically. **Deadline:** April 25. **Remarks:** The Speech Science Research Grant is supported by the Dennis Klatt Memorial Fund. The grant is designed to further research activities of new investigators and to promulgate Dr. Klatt's work. It can be used to initiate new research or supplement an existing research study. Funds may be requested for a variety of purposes; for example, equipment, subjects, research assistants, or research-related travel.

Awards are arranged alphabetically below their administering organizations

AMERICAN STATISTICAL ASSOCIATION

1460 ■ ASHFoundation Student Research Grants in Audiology *(Doctorate/Grant)*

Purpose: To support investigations that will advance knowledge of the efficacy of treatment and assessment practices. To help further the research activities of new investigators whose research have particular relevance to audiology and/or speech language pathology. **Focus:** Communications; Disabilities; Handicapped; Hearing and deafness; Speech and language pathology/Audiology. **Qualif.:** Applicants must be doctoral (research or clinical) degree students enrolled in, or accepted for, study in audiology or hearing science at an academic program in the United States; enrolled for full-time study for the full academic year. **Criteria:** Recipients will be selected based on the following: clearly stated project aims; the significance of the research and its potential impact on the clinical needs relevant to speech-language pathology or audiology; the merit of the design for answering the question, including detailed account of the methodology to be used; adequate provision for evaluating the results of the project, explicit statement of how the objectives will be measured; indication of the facilities, resources, personnel and subjects to which the applicant would have access in order to carry out the activities described in the proposal; the perceived ability of the applicant to complete the proposed research within a one year period; and management plan that clearly outlines the activities and timeliness.

Funds Avail.: $2,000. **Duration:** Annual. **Number Awarded:** 2. **To Apply:** Applicants should prepare research proposals with the formats prescribed by the Foundation. Such must be submitted electronically. **Deadline:** May 23. **Remarks:** The grant is supported by the Ira M. Ventry and Brad Friedrich Memorial Funds and general contributions to the annual fund. The grant competition memorializes two individuals. Ira Ventry was an audiologist whose research interests and publications focused on supra-threshold hearing, conductive hearing loss, hearing screening in the elderly and hearing handicap assessment. Brad Friedrich lectured and published widely in the field of pediatric audiology and was known for his ability to diagnose difficult-to-test children.

1461 ■ ASHFoundation Student Research Grants in Early Childhood Language Development *(Doctorate, Master's/Grant)*

Purpose: To support investigations that will advance knowledge of the efficacy of treatment and assessment practices, and help further research activities of new investigators that have particular relevance to audiology and/or speech language pathology. **Focus:** Communications; Hearing and deafness; Speech and language pathology/Audiology. **Qualif.:** Applicants must have received a master's and doctoral degree in communication sciences and disorders and aim to conduct research in early childhood language development. They must be enrolled full-time within the academic year. **Criteria:** Recipients are selected based on the following: clearly stated project aims; the significance of the research and its potential impact on the clinical needs relevant to speech-language pathology or audiology; the merit of the design for answering the question, including detailed account of the methodology to be used; adequate provision for evaluating the results of the project, explicit statement of how the objectives will be measured; indication of the facilities, resources, personnel and subjects to which the applicant would have access in order to carry out the activities described in the proposal; the perceived ability of the applicant to complete the proposed research within one year period; and management plan that clearly outlines the activities and timeliness.

Funds Avail.: $2,000 each. **Duration:** Annual. **Number Awarded:** 2. **To Apply:** Applicants should prepare research proposals with the formats prescribed by the Foundation. Such must be submitted electronically. **Deadline:** May 23.

1462 ■ American Statistical Association (ASA)
732 N Washington St.
Alexandria, VA 22314-1943
Ph: (703)684-1221
Fax: (703)684-2037
Free: 888-231-3473
E-mail: asainfo@amstat.org
URL: www.amstat.org

1463 ■ ASA/NSF/BLS Fellowships *(Graduate/Fellowship)*

Purpose: To improve the collaboration between government and academic research. **Focus:** Government; Statistics. **Qualif.:** Applicants should have academically recognized research records and considerable expertise in their areas of proposed research. Moreover, applicants must be affiliated with a U.S. institution. **Criteria:** Recipients will be selected based on the proposed research project. Preference will be given to those who meet the criteria.

Funds Avail.: No specific amount. **Duration:** Annual. **To Apply:** Applicants must submit the following information via e-mail: a curriculum vitae; names and addresses of three references; a detailed research proposal that includes background information about research topic, significance of expected results; advantages of conducting research at the BLS; and detailed budget estimate (salary, relocation, travel expenses, research support). All of these must be compiled in one PDF file. **Deadline:** February 8. **Contact:** Joyce Narine at joyce@amstat.org; phone: 703-684-1221.

1464 ■ Edward C. Bryant Scholarship for an Outstanding Graduate Student in Survey Statistics *(Graduate/Scholarship)*

Purpose: To help support an outstanding graduate student in survey statistics. **Focus:** Statistics. **Qualif.:** Applicants must be full-time graduate school students. **Criteria:** Recipients will be chosen by the ASA Bryant Scholarship Award Committee. Criteria for the selection are the following: have the potential to contribute in survey statistics, experience in survey statistics; and performance in graduate studies.

Funds Avail.: $2,500. **Duration:** Annual. **Number Awarded:** 1. **To Apply:** Applicants must submit the provided application form and three letters of recommendation. **Deadline:** March 1. **Remarks:** Established in 1995. **Contact:** E-mail at awards@amstat.org.

1465 ■ Gertrude M. Cox Scholarships *(Graduate, Master's, Doctorate/Scholarship)*

Purpose: To encourage more women to enter statistically-oriented professions. **Focus:** Statistics. **Qualif.:** Applicants must be female citizens or permanent residents of United States or Canada who are admitted to full-time study in a graduate statistical program. **Criteria:** Awards will be given based on the qualifications prescribed by the Scholarship Committee and the bestowing organization in general.

Funds Avail.: $2,000. **Duration:** Annual. **To Apply:** Applicants must submit the completed application form,

Awards are arranged alphabetically below their administering organizations

academic reference letter and Cox status form. These forms are available at their website. **Deadline:** February 23. **Remarks:** Established in 1989.

1466 ■ Samuel S. Wilks Awards *(Advanced Professional/Award, Monetary)*

Purpose: To honor a distinguished individual who has made statistical contributions to the advancement of scientific or technical knowledge, ingenious application of existing knowledge, or successful activity in the fostering of cooperative scientific efforts that have been directly involved in matters of national defense or public interest. **Focus:** National security; Statistics; Technology. **Qualif.:** Nominee for the award must be a distinguished individual who has made statistical contributions to the advancement of scientific or technical knowledge, ingenious application of existing knowledge, or successful activity in the fostering of cooperative scientific efforts that have been directly involved in matters of national defense or public interest. **Criteria:** Selection of the awardee shall be based on the nominations wherein those nominated must possess the qualifications prescribed by the bestowing organization. The committee for the award will only choose from among the nominees submitted.

Funds Avail.: Total of $1,500. **Duration:** Annual. **Number Awarded:** 1. **To Apply:** Application for the award is by nomination. **Deadline:** April 1. **Remarks:** The Samuel S. Wilks Award is one of the ASA's most prestigious that honors the memory and distinguished career of Samuel S. Wilks. Established in 1964.

1467 ■ American Surgical Association (ASA)
500 Cummings Ctr., Ste. 4550
Beverly, MA 01915
Ph: (978)927-8330
Fax: (978)524-0498
URL: www.americansurgical.org

1468 ■ ACS/ASA Health Policy and Management Scholarships *(Professional development/Scholarship)*

Purpose: To subsidize the attendance and participation in the Executive Leadership Program in Health Policy and Management at Brandeis University. **Focus:** Health education. **Qualif.:** Applicants must be surgeons; must be members in good standing of both the ACS and ASA; must be between 30-60 years old; and planning to attend the Executive Leadership Program in Health Policy and Management at Brandeis University. **Criteria:** Scholarship recipients will be selected based on the Selection Committee's review of the application materials.

Funds Avail.: $8,000. **Duration:** One year. **To Apply:** Applicants must submit a completed application form, a copy of curriculum vitae and one-page essay that discusses why the applicant needs the scholarship to ASA Scholarships Section. **Deadline:** February 2.

1469 ■ American Swedish Institute (ASI)
2600 Park Ave.
Minneapolis, MN 55407-1090
Ph: (612)871-4907
E-mail: info@asimn.org
URL: www.asimn.org
Facebook: www.facebook.com/AmericanSwedishInstitute
Twitter: twitter.com/AmSwedInstitute

1470 ■ Lilly Lorenzen Scholarships *(Undergraduate/Scholarship)*

Purpose: To promote the study of Swedish heritage. **Focus:** Swedish studies. **Qualif.:** Applicants must be Minnesota residents who have knowledge of the Swedish language. **Criteria:** Recipients are selected based on the application materials.

Funds Avail.: $1,000. **To Apply:** Applicants must submit a completed application form and a transcript or a statement of professional and community achievement. **Deadline:** May 1. **Remarks:** Established in memory of Lilly Lorenzen, an instructor in Swedish University of Minnesota and the American Swedish Institute, and author of the book "Of Swedish Ways". **Contact:** Karin Krull, karink@asimn.org.

1471 ■ Malmberg Scholarships *(Undergraduate/Scholarship)*

Purpose: To provide financial assistance for individuals intending to study in Sweden. **Focus:** Swedish studies. **Qualif.:** Applicants must be U.S. citizens; enrolled in a degree-granting program in college/university or in a study or research that requires or can be enhanced by study in Sweden; and must have knowledge in the Swedish language. **Criteria:** Recipients are selected based on submitted application materials.

Funds Avail.: Up to $10,000. **Duration:** Nine months. **To Apply:** Applicants must submit a completed application form and a letter of invitation or affiliation from the Swedish institution/organization; a project summary (1000 words); transcript (optional if out of school for three years); resume; and two letters of recommendation. **Deadline:** November 15.

1472 ■ American Thoracic Society (ATS)
25 Broadway
New York, NY 10004
Ph: (212)315-8600
Fax: (212)315-6498
E-mail: atsinfo@thoracic.org
URL: www.thoracic.org
Facebook: www.facebook.com/americanthoracic
LinkedIn: www.linkedin.com/company/american-thoracic-society_2
Twitter: twitter.com/atscommunity

1473 ■ ATS Abstract Scholarships *(Undergraduate, Graduate, Doctorate/Scholarship)*

Purpose: To engage its members around the globe and to support their expenses. **Focus:** Health sciences. **Qualif.:** Applicants must be trainee members who are students, residents, fellows (holders of M.D. or Ph.D.) or equivalent; must be ATS members at the time of receiving the abstract scholarship. **Criteria:** Selection will be based on the committee's criteria.

Funds Avail.: No specific amount. **Number Awarded:** Varies. **To Apply:** Applicants must submit a meritorious abstract to be presented at the ATS International Conference; must attend the ATS International Conference and must fill the questionnaire of the abstract online submission program, indicating the applicants wish that will be consider for the scholarship.

1474 ■ International Trainee Scholarships (ITS) *(Doctorate/Scholarship)*

Purpose: To support expenses related to attending the ATS International Conference including registration, ac-

Awards are arranged alphabetically below their administering organizations

commodations and related daily costs such as meals and local transportation. **Focus:** Health sciences. **Qualif.:** Applicants must be trainees who are not at a U.S. or Canadian program at the time of application; must not be a U.S. or Canadian citizens; must be authors of an abstract accepted for presentation at the ATS International Conference; must not be a recipient of another travel award at the ATS International Conference; and the work in the abstract should not have been performed at a U.S. or Canadian institution. **Criteria:** Selection will be based on the committee's criteria.

Funds Avail.: No specific amount. **To Apply:** Applicants must submit the complete online ATS-ITS application and upload the necessary documents in PDF format within the online application. The necessary documents are abstract accepted for presentation at the ATS International Conference and Curriculum Vitae limited to one page based on career aspects of work in accepted IC abstract. **Deadline:** February 13.

1475 ■ American University School of Public Affairs
4400 Massachusetts Ave. NW
Washington, DC 20016-8001
Ph: (202)885-2940
Fax: (202)885-1000
E-mail: spagrad@american.edu
URL: www.american.edu/spa

1476 ■ Jane R. Glaser Scholarships (Undergraduate/Scholarship)

Purpose: To provide financial assistance to School of Public Administration students. **Focus:** Public administration. **Qualif.:** Applicants should be undergraduate students of School of Public Administration. **Criteria:** Recipients will be selected based on a review of applications, interviews and consultation with faculty and staff.

Funds Avail.: $2,500. **Duration:** Annual. **Number Awarded:** 1. **To Apply:** Applicants must submit one page formal recommendation from advisor; outline of grade point average; activities; reason for studying at Hebrew University; and statement stating interest in receiving the scholarship and studying abroad. **Remarks:** The scholarship was established by Patricia L. Glaser, BA/SPA'69 in honor of her mother, Jane R. Glaser.

1477 ■ American Veterinary Medical Association (AVMA)
1931 N Meacham Rd., Ste. 100
Schaumburg, IL 60173-4360
Fax: (847)925-1329
Free: 800-248-2862
URL: www.avma.org

1478 ■ AVMA Fellowship Program (Professional development/Fellowship)

Purpose: To support fellows in influencing key legislation affecting the veterinary profession. **Focus:** Veterinary science and medicine. **Qualif.:** Applicant fellows must be willing to serve for one year in Washington D.C. as scientific advisors to members of congress; and must have play vital roles in shaping and influencing key legislation affecting veterinary profession. **Criteria:** Selection will be based on the committee's criteria.

Funds Avail.: A stipend of $79,000; $6,000 to offset the cost of health insurance premiums. **Duration:** Annual. **To Apply:** Interested applicants may contact the Association for the application process and other details.

1479 ■ American Water Resources Association - Colorado Section
PO Box 9822
Denver, CO 80209
E-mail: webmaster@awracolorado.org
URL: www.awracolorado.org

1480 ■ Richard A. Herbert Memorial Scholarships (Undergraduate/Scholarship)

Purpose: To promote the education in water resources. **Focus:** Water resources. **Qualif.:** Applicants must be: enrolled as students in a degree program at any accredited Colorado public or private college or university; and, involved in research or independent study pertaining to hydrology, engineering, hydrogeology, aquatic biology, water law, water-resources policy or planning, environmental science or other topics concerning water resources in Colorado. **Criteria:** A standing committee of the AWRA-Colorado Section will review applications and make recommendations to the Board of Directors based on academic performance (GPA).

Funds Avail.: $500-$4,000. **Duration:** Annual. **To Apply:** Applicants must submit a completed application that includes their resume, abstract of current research and three letter of recommendation from a faculty advisor; a title page which include the applicants' full name, permanent mailing address, email address, phone number and type of scholarship; two page summary of academic interests and achievements, career goals and extracurricular interests; and transcript of records. **Contact:** Laurel Stadjuhar: Phone: 303-835-9914; Email: laurel@westsagewater.com; Beorn Courtney: Phone: 720-524-6115; Email: bcourtney@elementwaterinc.com.

1481 ■ American Water Works Association (AWWA)
6666 W Quincy Ave.
Denver, CO 80235
Ph: (303)794-7711
Fax: (303)347-0804
Free: 800-926-7337
E-mail: service@awwa.org
URL: www.awwa.org

1482 ■ ARCADIS Scholarships (Master's, Doctorate/Scholarship)

Purpose: To provide support to a master's or doctoral candidate student seeking a degree in the water industry. **Focus:** Water resources; Water supply industry. **Qualif.:** Applicants must be students pursuing graduate degree (master's or doctoral) in water industry. **Criteria:** Selection will be based on the potential to provide leadership in the water service industry and pursuit of graduate work advancing the science and engineering of drinking water.

Funds Avail.: $5,000. **To Apply:** Applicants may contact AWWA for the application process and other information.

1483 ■ AWWA American Water Scholarships (Master's, Doctorate/Scholarship)

Purpose: To assist the development of professionals interested in service to the water industry. **Focus:** Water resources; Water supply industry. **Qualif.:** Applicants must be students pursuing graduate degree (master's or doctoral). **Criteria:** Selection will be based on the committee's criteria.

Funds Avail.: $5,000. **Duration:** Annual. **To Apply:** Applicants may contact AWWA for the application process and other information.

1484 ■ HDR/Henry "Bud" Benjes Scholarships *(Master's/Scholarship)*

Purpose: To provide support to a student seeking a masters degree in the water industry. **Focus:** Water resources; Water supply industry. **Qualif.:** Applicants must be students pursuing master's degree in water industry. **Criteria:** Selection will be based on the committee's criteria.

Funds Avail.: $5,000. **To Apply:** Applicants may contact AWWA for the application process and other information.

1485 ■ Dave Caldwell Scholarships *(Graduate/Scholarship)*

Purpose: To benefit students pursuing engineering degree in the drinking water field. **Focus:** Engineering; Water resources; Water supply industry. **Qualif.:** Applicants must be female and/or minority students pursuing graduate degree in the drinking water field. **Criteria:** Selection will be based on the demonstrated ability to provide leadership in applied research and consulting in the drinking water field.

Funds Avail.: $10,000. **To Apply:** Applicants may contact AWWA for the application process and other information.

1486 ■ Thomas R. Camp Scholarships *(Graduate/Scholarship)*

Purpose: To support and encourage graduate students conducting applied research in the drinking water field. **Focus:** Water resources; Water supply industry. **Qualif.:** Applicants must be in pursuit of their respective graduate degrees (either masters or doctoral) at an institution of higher education located in Canada, Guam, Puerto Rico, Mexico or the United States. **Criteria:** Scholarship recipient will be selected based on academic record and potential to provide leadership in applied research and consulting in the drinking water field.

Funds Avail.: $5,000. **Duration:** Annual. **Number Awarded:** 1. **To Apply:** Applicants must submit a completed official application form; a two-page resume that includes educational history; official transcripts of all university education; official GRE Scores (quantitative, verbal and analytical) sent directly from the GRE Testing Center, or a photocopy of the official report; three letters of recommendation (one of which must be from the academic or research advisor); a one-page statement of educational plans and career objectives demonstrating or declaring an interest in the drinking water field; a two to three page proposed plan of research. **Remarks:** The scholarship is sponsored by CDM Smith. **Contact:** AWWA scholarship at scholarships@awwa.org.

1487 ■ Carollo Engineers Scholarships *(Master's/Scholarship)*

Purpose: To provide support to a master's student engaging in water-energy nexus issues for water, wastewater or water use. **Focus:** Water resources; Water supply industry. **Qualif.:** Applicants must be students pursuing master's degree. **Criteria:** Selection will be based on the committee's criteria.

Funds Avail.: $10,000. **Duration:** Annual. **To Apply:** Applicants may contact AWWA for the application process and other information.

1488 ■ Holly Cornell Scholarship *(Master's/Scholarship)*

Purpose: To support and encourage outstanding female and/or minority masters' students in pursuit of advanced training in the field of water supply and treatment. **Focus:** Water resources; Water supply industry. **Qualif.:** Applicants must be female and/or minority U.S. citizens, who are currently masters degree students anticipating completion of the requirements for a Masters degree in engineering. **Criteria:** Recipients are selected based on academic merit and potential to provide leadership in the field of water supply and treatment.

Funds Avail.: $7,500. **Duration:** Annual. **To Apply:** Applicants must submit a completed official application form; a two-page resume that includes educational history; official transcripts of all university education; official GRE Scores (quantitative, verbal, and analytical) sent directly from the GRE Testing Center, or a photocopy of the official report; three letters of recommendation (one of which must be from the academic or research advisor); a proposed curriculum of study; a brief (one to two pages) statement describing the student's career objectives. **Remarks:** The scholarship is sponsored by CH2M Hill, Inc. **Contact:** AWWA scholarship at scholarships@awwa.org.

1489 ■ Hazen and Sawyer Scholarships *(Master's/Scholarship)*

Purpose: To provide support to a student seeking a master's degree in the water science field. **Focus:** Water resources; Water supply industry. **Qualif.:** Applicants must be students pursuing master's degree in water science field. **Criteria:** Selection will be based on the applicants' potential to provide leadership in applied research and consulting in the drinking water field.

Funds Avail.: $5,000. **To Apply:** Applicants may contact AWWA for the application process and other information.

1490 ■ Larson Aquatic Research Support Scholarships (LARS) *(Graduate/Scholarship)*

Purpose: To provide support for students interested in careers in the fields of corrosion control, treatment and distribution of domestic and industrial water supplies, aquatic chemistry, and/or environmental chemistry. **Focus:** Biochemistry; Chemistry; Water resources; Water supply industry. **Qualif.:** Applicants must be students pursuing a masters or doctoral degree at an institution of higher education located in Canada, Guam, Puerto Rico, Mexico, or the United States. **Criteria:** Awards are given based on academic record and applicants' potential to provide leadership in the fields served by Dr. Larson.

Funds Avail.: $5,0000 (Master's student); $7,000 (Doctoral student). **Duration:** Annual. **Number Awarded:** 2. **To Apply:** Applicants must submit a completed application form; a two-page resume that includes educational history; official transcripts of all university education; official GRE Scores (quantitative, verbal and analytical) sent directly from the GRE Testing Center, or a photocopy of the official report; three letters of recommendation (one of which must be from the academic or research advisor); a proposed curriculum of study; a statement of educational plans and career objectives demonstrating or declaring an interest in an appropriate field of endeavor; a research plan, if applicable (required for Masters students conducting research

Awards are arranged alphabetically below their administering organizations

and all Ph.D. students). **Remarks:** Larson Aquatic Research Support Scholarships honor the memory of Dr. Thurston E. "Lars" Larson. **Contact:** AWWA scholarship at scholarships@awwa.org.

1491 ■ MWH Scholarships (Master's/Scholarship)

Purpose: To provide support to a master's student seeking a degree in the water industry. **Focus:** Water resources; Water supply industry. **Qualif.:** Applicants must be students seeking master's degree in water industry. **Criteria:** Selection will be based on the committee's criteria.

Funds Avail.: $5,000. **To Apply:** Applicants may contact AWWA for the application process and other information.

1492 ■ Abel Wolman Fellowships (Doctorate/Fellowship)

Purpose: To support promising doctoral students in the U.S., Canada and Mexico pursuing advanced training and research in the field of water supply and treatment. **Focus:** Water resources; Water supply industry. **Qualif.:** Applicants must complete the requirements for a Ph.D. within two years of the award and have citizenship or permanent residence in Canada, Mexico or the United States. **Criteria:** Fellowship recipients are selected based on academic record, significance of the proposed research to water supply and treatment and the applicants' potential to do high quality research.

Funds Avail.: No specific amount. **Duration:** Annual; up to two years. **To Apply:** Applicants must submit a completed official application form; a two-page resume that includes educational history; official transcripts of all university education; official GRE scores sent directly from the Testing Center or a photocopy of the official report; three letters of recommendation, one of which must be from the dissertation advisor; proposed curriculum of study; a brief description of the dissertation research, including a statement describing how the research will relate specifically to water supply and treatment (two pages of text plus two pages of figures and tables). **Deadline:** January 11. **Contact:** AWWA scholarship at scholarships@awwa.org.

1493 ■ American Water Works Association - Florida Section (FSAWWA)
1300 9th St., B-124
Saint Cloud, FL 34769
Ph: (407)957-8448
Fax: (407)957-8415
URL: www.fsawwa.org

1494 ■ Roy W. Likins Scholarships (Undergraduate, Graduate/Scholarship)

Purpose: To support students pursuing a degree related to drinking water industry. **Focus:** Water resources; Water supply industry. **Qualif.:** Applicants must be upper level undergraduate (over 65 credit hours) or graduate students enrolled in an accredited Florida Institution and currently majoring in an area related to the drinking water industry and have a minimum 3.0 grade point average based on a 4.0 system. **Criteria:** Evaluations will be made on the basis of academic performance, work experience, community and civic activities, honor, career goals, letters of recommendation, and evidence of leadership, motivation, character, and self-reliance.

Funds Avail.: $2,500. **Duration:** Annual. **To Apply:** Applicants must submit the following: completed application form (provided in Word or PDF format); official college transcripts for undergraduate and graduate courses; two recommendation letters; and a brief letter describing their interests in the scholarship.

1495 ■ American Water Works Association - Illinois Section
545 S Randall Rd.
Saint Charles, IL 60174
Ph: (866)521-3595
URL: www.isawwa.org

1496 ■ AWWA Illinois Section Safe Water Scholarship Awards (Undergraduate, Master's, Doctorate/Scholarship)

Purpose: To support the general public on the essential functions and importance of the water industry, the water cycle and water treatment, and career paths in the water industry. **Focus:** Water resources; Water supply industry. **Qualif.:** Applicants must be enrolled or accepted into a water-related secondary, continuing-education, or enrichment program for the academic year. Secondary education includes water system operator training programs, water-related technical school, community college, four-year college, Master's and Doctoral programs. **Criteria:** Selection will be based on the committee's criteria.

Funds Avail.: Around $5,000. **To Apply:** Interested applicants may contact the AWWA Illinois Section for the application process and other information. **Deadline:** January 31. **Contact:** Any questions regarding the scholarship application can be directed through email at laurie@isawwa.org or phone 866-521-3595 ext. 1.

1497 ■ American Water Works Association - Virginia Section (VA AWWA)
PO Box 11992
Lynchburg, VA 24506-1992
Ph: (757)363-1760
Fax: (757)363-1720
E-mail: vaawwa@vaawwa.org
URL: www.vaawwa.org

1498 ■ VA AWWA Graduate Student Scholarships (Graduate/Scholarship)

Purpose: To support graduate students from Virginia who have the intention to pursue a career in water industry. **Focus:** Water resources; Water supply industry. **Qualif.:** Applicants must be full- or part-time graduate students who are also members of AWWA attending school in Virginia, with the intention to of a career in the water industry. **Criteria:** Selection will be based on merit.

Funds Avail.: $2,000 to $2,500. **To Apply:** Applicants should submit the following requirements: resume indicating their academic and extracurricular performance and activities; unofficial or official up-to-date transcript or official semester schedule of school currently attending; completed VAAWWA Student Scholarship application; membership in the American Water Works Association; a reference letter from an instructor or professor; and one-page essay on a water topic of their choice. Applications should be submitted electronically to Beverly Noffsinger. **Deadline:** June 15. **Contact:** Beverly Noffsinger at bnoffy@gmail.com.

1499 ■ American Watercolor Society (AWS)
47 5th Ave.
New York, NY 10003-4679

Awards are arranged alphabetically below their administering organizations

Ph: (212)206-8986
Fax: (212)206-1960
E-mail: info@americanwatercolorsociety.org
URL: www.americanwatercolorsociety.com
Facebook: www.facebook.com/AmericanWatercolor

1500 ■ American Watercolor Society Scholarship Program for Art Teachers (Other/Scholarship)

Purpose: To enhance and improve the capabilities of teachers in watercolor media. **Focus:** Art; Painting. **Qualif.:** Applicants must be U.S. citizens and art teachers at a high school or college level institution in the United States. **Criteria:** Grantees are selected based on the application materials.

Funds Avail.: $500. **Duration:** Annual. **To Apply:** Applicants must complete and submit the application form, available at the website, at least three months in advance of the start date of the instruction.

1501 ■ American Welding Society (AWS)
8669 NW 36th St., Ste. 130
Miami, FL 33166-6672
Ph: (305)443-9353
Free: 800-443-9353
URL: www.aws.org

1502 ■ Howard E. and Wilma J. Adkins Memorial Scholarships (Undergraduate/Scholarship)

Purpose: To provide financial assistance to individuals interested in pursuing a career in welding engineering. **Focus:** Welding. **Qualif.:** Applicants must: be undergraduate students pursuing a four-year bachelors degree in welding engineering or welding engineering technology; be 18 years old and above; have a minimum of 2.8 overall grade point average; be citizens of the United States; and plan to attend an accredited engineering school within the United States. **Criteria:** Preference will be given to those individuals residing or attending school in the states of Wisconsin or Kentucky.

Funds Avail.: $2,500. **Duration:** Annual. **To Apply:** Applicants must complete the application form and submit it along with a high school diploma and a financial statement. Official transcripts must be sent directly to Registrar's Office. **Deadline:** February 15. **Remarks:** Established in 1994. **Contact:** The fund was established in memory of Mr. Howard E. Adkins, by family and friends.

1503 ■ American Welding Society District Scholarships (Undergraduate/Scholarship)

Purpose: To provide financial assistance to students preparing for a career in the welding and related joining technologies. **Focus:** Welding. **Qualif.:** Applicants must be high school graduates planning to enroll in a welding course program; must attend a school located in United States or its territories. **Criteria:** Recipients are selected based on academic standing.

Funds Avail.: No specific amount. **Duration:** Annual. **Number Awarded:** Varies. **To Apply:** Applicants must submit a financial statement; transcript of records; personal statement; biography and photo. **Deadline:** March 1. **Contact:** Nazdhia Prado-Pulido at nprado-pulido@aws.org.

1504 ■ American Welding Society Graduate Research Fellowships (Graduate/Fellowship)

Purpose: To advance opportunities for students preparing for a career in the welding and related joining technologies. **Focus:** Welding. **Qualif.:** Applicants must be graduate students who wish to pursue areas of research related to the welding and joining industry. **Criteria:** Recipients will be selected based on academic standing.

Funds Avail.: No specific amount. **Duration:** Annual. **To Apply:** Applicants must prepare the academic credentials; plans; research history; and proposal. Technical portion of proposal should be: 25-typewritten pages; with two megabytes; 12-point font; and Times New Roman.

1505 ■ American Welding Society International Scholarships (Undergraduate, Graduate/Scholarship)

Purpose: To provide financial assistance to international students who wish to pursue their education in welding and related joining technologies. **Focus:** Welding. **Qualif.:** Applicants must be full time international students pursuing undergraduate or graduate studies in joining sciences. They can be matriculating in accredited joining science programs at institutions anywhere in the world. Student must be in the top 20% of the institution's grading system. **Criteria:** Recipients are selected based on financial need and academic standing.

Funds Avail.: $2,500. **Duration:** Annual. **To Apply:** Applicants must submit a copy of the proposed curriculum; verification of enrollment to the institution; two letters of personal reference; two-page professional goal statement with a brief bibliography; transcript of grades or equivalent from each college; proof of country of citizenship; AWS membership number, if member; and financial information regarding tuition fees from the academic institution. **Deadline:** April 1.

1506 ■ American Welding Society National Scholarships (Undergraduate/Scholarship)

Purpose: To support students preparing for a career in the welding and related joining technologies. **Focus:** Welding. **Qualif.:** Applicants must be students pursuing a specific degree at an accredited four-year college or university. **Criteria:** Recipients are selected based on academic standing.

Funds Avail.: $2,500 each. **Duration:** Annual. **Number Awarded:** Varies. **To Apply:** Applicants must submit a financial statement; transcript of records; personal statement; biography; and photo. **Deadline:** February 15. **Remarks:** The AWS National Scholarships are awarded in various types. **Contact:** Vicki Pinsky at vpinsky@aws.org.

1507 ■ American Welding Society Past Presidents Scholarships (Undergraduate, Graduate/Scholarship)

Purpose: To provide financial assistance to individuals interested in pursuing a bachelor's degree in welding engineering, welding engineering technology, or an engineering program with an emphasis in welding. **Focus:** Welding. **Qualif.:** Applicants must be junior, senior, or graduate level (Masters or Ph.D.) students pursuing a degree in Welding Engineering or Welding Engineering Technology. **Criteria:** Recipients will be selected based on financial need.

Funds Avail.: $2,500. **Duration:** Annual. **Number Awarded:** 1. **To Apply:** Applicants must complete the application form and submit it along with one or more recommendation letters from community members, local AWS officers, and/or AWS district directors attesting to the applicant's leadership capability; and (300-500 word) essay on the applicant's objectives and aspirations in the field of welding. **Deadline:** February 15.

Awards are arranged alphabetically below their administering organizations

AMERICAN WELDING SOCIETY

1508 ■ Arsham Amirikian Engineering Scholarships
(Undergraduate/Scholarship)

Purpose: To provide financial assistance to an engineering student pursuing a career in the art of welding in civil and structural engineering. **Focus:** Engineering, Civil; Welding. **Qualif.:** Applicants must be U.S. citizens who are full-time undergraduate students pursuing a minimum four-year degree in a welding or welding related program at an accredited university. They must: be at least 18 years of age; be enrolled full-time; and, have a minimum 3.0 grade point average. **Criteria:** Recipients are selected based on financial need.

Funds Avail.: $2,500. **Duration:** Annual. **Number Awarded:** 1. **To Apply:** Applicants must submit an application; a high school diploma; and a financial statement. **Deadline:** February 15. **Contact:** Vicki Pinsky at vpinsky@aws.org.

1509 ■ Airgas - Jerry Baker Scholarships
(Undergraduate/Scholarship)

Purpose: To provide financial assistance to those individuals interested in pursuing a career in welding engineering. **Focus:** Welding. **Qualif.:** Applicants must be U.S. citizens who are full-time undergraduate students pursuing a minimum four-year degree in a welding or welding related program at an accredited university. They must: be at least 18 years of age; be enrolled full-time; and, have a minimum 2.5 overall GPA. **Criteria:** Recipients are selected based on need. Priority will be given to individuals who demonstrate an interest in pursuing a career with an industrial gas or welding equipment distributor with prior to work experience, clubs, organizations, or extracurricular activities. For individuals residing or attending schools in the states of Alabama, Georgia and Florida are also given preference.

Funds Avail.: $2,500. **Duration:** Annual. **Number Awarded:** 1. **To Apply:** Applicants must submit an application form and a high school diploma. **Deadline:** February 15. **Contact:** Vicki Pinsky at vpinsky@aws.org.

1510 ■ Jack R. Barckhoff Welding Management Scholarships *(Undergraduate/Scholarship)*

Purpose: To provide financial assistance to individuals interested in pursuing a career in welding engineering. **Focus:** Welding. **Qualif.:** Applicants must be college juniors pursuing a four-year bachelors degree in welding engineering at the Ohio State University; must be 18 years old and above; must have minimum of 2.5 overall grade point average; must be citizens of the United States and plan to attend an accredited engineering school within the United States; must be enrolled and must complete the two-hour credit course in Total Welding Management at the Ohio State University. **Criteria:** Recipients will be selected based on the financial need.

Funds Avail.: $2,500. **Duration:** Annual. **Number Awarded:** 2. **To Apply:** Applicants must complete the application form and submit it along with a high school diploma, financial statement and a transcript of records. They must also submit (300-500 word) essay on how they see their role once they have graduated in improving the world of welding and its industry in the United States and how they plan to use their education to improve the U.S. competitive position in welding and manufacturing. **Deadline:** February 15. **Remarks:** The scholarship namesake is a Life Member of AWS, a past chairman of his Local Section, an Associate Trustee of the AWS Foundation and received the AWS District Meritorious Award.

1511 ■ Edward J. Brady Memorial Scholarships
(Undergraduate/Scholarship)

Purpose: To provide financial assistance to individuals interested in pursuing a career in welding engineering. **Focus:** Welding. **Qualif.:** Applicant must be undergraduate students pursuing a four-year bachelors degree in welding engineering or welding engineering technology; must be 18 years old and above; must have a minimum of 2.5 overall grade point average; must be citizens of the United States; and must plan to attend an accredited engineering school within the United States. **Criteria:** Recipient are selected based on financial need. Priority will be given to welding engineering students.

Funds Avail.: $2,500. **Duration:** Annual. **Number Awarded:** 1. **To Apply:** Applicant must complete the application form and submit it along with a high school diploma and a financial statement. Official transcripts must be sent directly to the Registrar's Office. another requirement is a 300-500 words of essay answering the question "Why I Want to Pursue a Career in Welding?" **Deadline:** February 15. **Remarks:** The scholarship was named in honor of Edward J. Brady.

1512 ■ William A. and Ann M. Brothers Scholarships *(Undergraduate/Scholarship)*

Purpose: To provide financial assistance to those individuals interested in pursuing a career in welding. **Focus:** Welding. **Qualif.:** Applicants must be U.S. citizens who are full-time undergraduate students pursuing a minimum four-year degree in a welding or welding related program at an accredited university. They must: be at least 18 years of age; be enrolled full-time; and, have a minimum 2.5 overall GPA. **Criteria:** Recipients are selected based on financial need. Priority will be given to individuals residing or attending schools in the states of Ohio.

Funds Avail.: $2,500. **Duration:** Annual. **Number Awarded:** 1. **To Apply:** Applicants must submit an application form; high school diploma; and a financial statement. **Deadline:** February 15. **Contact:** Vicki Pinsky at vpinsky@aws.org.

1513 ■ Donald F. Hastings Scholarships
(Undergraduate/Scholarship)

Purpose: To provide financial assistance to those individuals interested in pursuing a career in welding engineering. **Focus:** Welding. **Qualif.:** Applicants must be U.S. citizens who are full-time undergraduate students pursuing a minimum four-year bachelor's degree in welding engineering (WE) or welding engineering technology (WET) at an accredited university. They must: be at least 18 years of age; be enrolled full-time; and, have a minimum 2.5 grade point average. **Criteria:** Recipients are selected based on financial need. Priority will be given to students residing or attending schools in the states of Ohio and California.

Funds Avail.: $2,500. **Duration:** Annual. **Number Awarded:** 1. **To Apply:** Applicants must submit an application; a high school diploma; and a financial statement. **Deadline:** February 15. **Contact:** Vicki Pinsky at vpinsky@aws.org.

1514 ■ Donald and Shirley Hastings Scholarships
(Undergraduate/Scholarship)

Purpose: To provide financial assistance to individuals interested in pursuing a career in welding engineering. **Focus:** Welding. **Qualif.:** Applicants must be U.S. citizens who are full-time undergraduate students pursuing a

Awards are arranged alphabetically below their administering organizations

minimum four-year bachelor's degree in welding engineering (WE) or welding engineering technology (WET) at an accredited university. They must: be at least 18 years of age; be enrolled full-time; and, have a minimum 2.5 grade point average. **Criteria:** Recipients are selected based on financial need. Priority will be given to students residing or attending schools in the states of Iowa, Ohio, or California.

Funds Avail.: $2,500. **Duration:** Annual. **Number Awarded:** 1. **To Apply:** Applicants must submit an application; a high school diploma; a copy of Free Application Financial Student Aid (FAFSA) and a financial statement. **Deadline:** February 15. **Contact:** Vicki Pinsky at vpinsky@aws.org.

1515 ■ William B. Howell Scholarships
(Undergraduate/Scholarship)

Purpose: To provide financial assistance to those individuals interested in pursuing a career in welding. **Focus:** Welding. **Qualif.:** Applicants must be U.S. citizens who are full-time undergraduate students pursuing a minimum four-year degree in a welding or welding related program at an accredited university. They must: be at least 18 years of age; be enrolled full-time; and, have a minimum 2.5 overall GPA. **Criteria:** Recipients are selected based on financial need. Priority will be given to individuals residing or attending school in the states of Florida, Michigan and Ohio.

Funds Avail.: $2,500. **Duration:** Annual. **Number Awarded:** 1. **To Apply:** Applicants must submit an application form; high school diploma; and financial statement. **Deadline:** February 15. **Contact:** Vicki Pinsky at vpinsky@aws.org.

1516 ■ Hypertherm International HyTech Leadership Scholarships *(Graduate/Scholarship)*

Purpose: To provide financial assistance to those individuals interested in pursuing a graduate degree in engineering management, with a focus on becoming a technical leader within the welding and cutting industry. **Focus:** Welding. **Qualif.:** Applicants must have completed a Bachelor of Science degree or be in their final year, and have been accepted for graduate work in engineering management at an accredited graduate school (with an average GPA of 2.8). They may be citizens of any country and plan to attend an academic institution located in any country. **Criteria:** Recipients will be selected based on financial need.

Funds Avail.: $2,500. **Duration:** Annual. **Number Awarded:** 1. **To Apply:** Applicants must complete the application form and personal statement addressing a proposed advanced academic and post-academic plan. **Deadline:** February 15.

1517 ■ ITW Welding Companies Scholarships
(Undergraduate/Scholarship)

Purpose: To provide financial assistance to individuals interested in pursuing a career in welding engineering. **Focus:** Welding. **Qualif.:** Applicants must be senior, full-time undergraduate students working towards a bachelors degree in welding engineering or welding engineering technology; must be 18 years old and above; must have a minimum of 3.0 overall grade point average; must be citizens of the United States; and must plan to attend an accredited engineering school within the United States. **Criteria:** Recipients are selected based on financial need. Priority will be given to students who exhibits a strong interest and with more experience in welding equipment.

Funds Avail.: $3,000. **Duration:** Annual. **Number Awarded:** 2. **To Apply:** Applicants must complete an application form and submit it along with a high school diploma and a financial statement. **Deadline:** February 15. **Contact:** Vicki Pinsky at 800-443-9353, ext 212.

1518 ■ Airgas - Terry Jarvis Memorial Scholarships
(Undergraduate/Scholarship)

Purpose: To provide financial assistance to those individuals interested in pursuing a career in welding engineering. **Focus:** Welding. **Qualif.:** Applicants must be U.S. citizens who are full-time undergraduate students pursuing a minimum four-year degree in a welding or welding related program at an accredited university. They must: be at least 18 years of age; be enrolled full-time; and, have at least a 2.8 overall grade point average with a 3.0 grade point average in engineering courses. They must also have the plan to attend an institution located within the United States or Canada. **Criteria:** Recipients are selected based on need. Priority will be given to those individuals who demonstrate an interest in pursuing a career with an industrial gas or welding equipment distributor prior to work experience, clubs, organizations, or extracurricular activities. For individuals residing or attending schools in the states of Alabama, Georgia, or Florida are also given preference.

Funds Avail.: $2,500. **Duration:** Annual. **Number Awarded:** 1. **To Apply:** Applicants must submit an application form and a high school diploma. **Deadline:** February 15. **Contact:** Vicki Pinsky at vpinsky@aws.org.

1519 ■ John C. Lincoln Memorial Scholarships
(Undergraduate/Scholarship)

Purpose: To provide financial assistance to individuals interested in pursuing a career in welding engineering. **Focus:** Welding. **Qualif.:** Applicants must be undergraduate students pursuing a four-year Bachelors Degree in a welding program at an accredited university; must have 2.5 overall grade point average; must be 18 years old and above; must be citizen of the United States and plan to attend an academic institution located within the United States. **Criteria:** Recipients are selected based on financial need. Priority will be given to those individuals residing or attending school in the States of Ohio and Arizona.

Funds Avail.: $3,500. **Duration:** Annual. **Number Awarded:** 1. **To Apply:** Applicants must complete the application form and submit it along with a high school diploma and a financial statement. **Deadline:** February 15. **Remarks:** The scholarship is named after the founder of The Lincoln Electric Company.

1520 ■ Miller Electric International WorldSkills Competition Scholarships *(Undergraduate/Scholarship)*

Purpose: To provide financial assistance to individuals interested in pursuing a bachelor's degree in welding engineering, welding engineering technology, or an engineering program with an emphasis in welding. **Focus:** Welding. **Qualif.:** Applicants must compete in the National Skills USA Competition for welding and advance to the AWS Weld Trials at the AWS International Welding and Fabricating Exposition and Convention. **Criteria:** Recipients will be selected based on financial need.

Funds Avail.: Maximum of $40,000. **Duration:** Biennial. **Number Awarded:** Varies. **To Apply:** Applicants must complete the National Skills USA Competition and complete the application form.

Awards are arranged alphabetically below their administering organizations

1521 ■ Robert L. Peaslee-Detroit Brazing and Soldiering Division Scholarships *(Undergraduate/Scholarship)*

Purpose: To provide financial assistance to individuals interested in pursuing a bachelor's degree in welding engineering, welding engineering technology, or an engineering program with an emphasis in welding. **Focus:** Welding. **Qualif.:** Applicants must be college junior or senior students pursuing a degree in Welding Engineering or Welding Engineering Technology; must have demonstrated leadership abilities; must be 18 years old and above; must be United States citizens and plan to attend an academic institution within the United States or Canada; must have 3.0 overall grade point average; must express an interest in the resistance welding process; must show emphasis on Brazing and Soldiering application in their coursework. **Criteria:** Recipients will be selected based on final decision of Selection Committee.

Funds Avail.: $2,500. **Duration:** Annual. **Number Awarded:** 1. **To Apply:** Applicants must submit an application form; two letters of reference; personal statement; an official transcript of records; statement of unmet financial needs; and verification of enrollment. Recipients are required to submit a photograph for publicity purposes. **Deadline:** February 15. **Remarks:** The fund was established by Robert L. Peaslee and the AWS Detroit Brazing and Soldering Division of the AWS Detroit Section. Established in 2004.

1522 ■ Ronald C. and Joyce Pierce - Mobile Section Named Scholarships *(Undergraduate/Scholarship)*

Purpose: To provide financial assistance to individuals interested in pursuing a bachelor's degree in welding engineering, welding engineering technology, or an engineering program with an emphasis in welding. **Focus:** Welding. **Qualif.:** Applicants must have a minimum 2.7 overall grade point average, and be full-time college sophomores, juniors, or seniors. **Criteria:** Selection will be based on financial need.

Funds Avail.: $5,000. **Duration:** Annual. **Number Awarded:** 3. **To Apply:** Applicants must submit an application form; a high school diploma; two letters of reference; personal statement; transcript of records; statement of the unmet financial need; and verification of enrollment. **Deadline:** February 15. **Contact:** Vicky Pinsky at vpinsky@aws.org.

1523 ■ Praxair International Scholarships *(Undergraduate/Scholarship)*

Purpose: To provide financial assistance to individuals interested in pursuing a bachelor's degree in welding engineering, welding engineering technology, or an engineering program with an emphasis in welding. **Focus:** Welding. **Qualif.:** Applicants must be undergraduate students pursuing a degree in Welding Engineering or Welding Engineering Technology. They must also: have demonstrated leadership abilities; be 18 years old and above and citizens of United States planning to attend an academic institution within the United States or Canada; and, maintain an overall GPA of 2.5. **Criteria:** Preference will be given to welding engineering students.

Funds Avail.: $2,500. **Duration:** Annual. **Number Awarded:** 1. **To Apply:** Applicants must an application form. Official transcript of records will be directed to the Office of Registrar. **Deadline:** February 15.

1524 ■ Resistance Welder Manufacturers' Association Scholarships *(Undergraduate/Scholarship)*

Purpose: To provide financial assistance to individuals interested in the resistance of welding process while pursuing a career in welding engineering. **Focus:** Welding. **Qualif.:** Applicants must be college junior students pursuing a degree in Welding Engineering or Welding Engineering Technology; must demonstrate leadership abilities; must be 18 years old and above; must be U.S. citizens and plan to attend an academic institution within the United States or Canada; must at least have a 3.0 overall grade point average; and must be working in a four-year degree in Welding Engineering or Technology. **Criteria:** Recipients are selected based on academic achievements and submitted materials.

Funds Avail.: $2,500. **Duration:** Annual. **To Apply:** Applicants must submit an application form along with a high school diploma and an essay of 500 words or less about why the applicant wishes to become involved in the resistance welding industry; two letters of recommendation (one must from advisor and the other one must from employer); personal statement; an official transcript of records; verification of enrollment; and statement of unmet financial needs. **Deadline:** February 15. **Remarks:** Established in 2005.

1525 ■ James A. Turner, Jr. Memorial Scholarships *(Undergraduate/Scholarship)*

Purpose: To provide financial assistance to those individuals interested in pursuing a management career in welding store operations or a welding distributorship. **Focus:** Welding. **Qualif.:** Applicants must be full-time students pursuing a four-year Bachelor of Business Degree leading to a management career in welding store operations or a welding distributorship; be employed for at least ten hours a week at a welding distributorship; must be 18 years old and above. **Criteria:** Recipients will be selected based on financial need.

Funds Avail.: $3,500. **Duration:** Annual. **Number Awarded:** 1. **To Apply:** Applicants must complete the application form and submit it along with a high school diploma and a financial statement. Official transcripts will be sent directly to the Registrar's Office. **Deadline:** February 15. **Remarks:** The scholarship is named in honor of James A. Turner, Jr.

1526 ■ Amos and Marilyn Winsand - Detroit Section Named Scholarships *(Undergraduate/Scholarship)*

Purpose: To provide financial assistance to those individuals interested in pursuing a career in welding engineering. **Focus:** Welding. **Qualif.:** Applicants must be enrolled in a two or four-year program and must be residents of Michigan or attending a Michigan College. **Criteria:** Recipients are selected based on financial need.

Funds Avail.: $2,500. **Duration:** Annual. **To Apply:** Applicants must submit an application form and a high school diploma.

1527 ■ American Wine Society Educational Foundation (AWSEF)
c/o Bonnie Huber, President
9 Summit Ave.
Butler, NJ 07405
Ph: (212)878-6277
E-mail: president@awsef.org
URL: www.awsef.org

Awards are arranged alphabetically below their administering organizations

1528 ■ American Wine Society Educational Foundation Scholarships *(Graduate/Scholarship)*

Purpose: To support full-time graduate students pursuing degrees in enology, viticulture, or health aspects of wine. **Focus:** Enology; Viticulture. **Qualif.:** Applicants must be full-time graduate students who have completed at least one semester in a graduate program leading to an MS, PhD, or equivalent in enology, viticulture, or health aspects of wine, and who express intent to work in one of these areas upon completion of the graduate degree (PhD candidates with an MS from another graduate program are eligible); must be North American (U.S., Canada, Mexico, Bahamas and West Indies Islands) citizens or permanent residents, enrolled in a degree located within North American institutions of higher learning. **Criteria:** Applications will be evaluated based on strength of application and accompanied letters of recommendation.

Funds Avail.: $3,500 each. **Duration:** Annual. **Number Awarded:** 7. **To Apply:** Applicants must submit a completed scholarship application form; current official transcripts of all college or university academic records; a written statement which indicates the applicant's intent to pursue a career in a wine or grape related area; a written recommendation from the applicant's academic advisor using the form supplied; three letters of recommendation including the academic advisor's written recommendation. **Deadline:** March 31. **Contact:** Patricia Graham, Vice President for Scholarships; Email: vpscholarships@awsef.org.

1529 ■ American Woman's Society of Certified Public Accountants (AWSCPA)
701 N Post Oak Rd., Ste. 635
Houston, TX 77024
Ph: (937)222-1872
Fax: (937)222-5794
Free: 800-297-2721
E-mail: info@awscpa.org
URL: awscpa.org
Facebook: www.facebook.com/American-Womans-Society-of-CPAs-192800737440746

1530 ■ AWSCPA National Scholarships *(Graduate/Scholarship)*

Purpose: To support students aspiring to become a Certified Public Accountant. **Focus:** Accounting. **Qualif.:** Applicant must meet the minimum education requirements to sit for the CPA exam within one year of scholarship awarding; must either be an entering Senior, 5th year student, graduate student or a graduate and eligible to take a review course within one year of scholarship awarding; must have a 3.0 GPA in accounting and a 3.0 GPA overall; and must either be a U.S. citizen or a permanent resident of the United States. **Criteria:** Selection is based on the application.

Funds Avail.: Becker CPA Review Course worth $3,065. **Duration:** One year. **To Apply:** Applicants must submit a completed scholarship application form together with a validated transcript and an essay of no longer than 1,000 words. Applicants can also apply online. **Deadline:** May 31. **Remarks:** Sponsored by Becker CPA Review. **Contact:** LInda Jone, CPA of Becker at 800-369-8545 or email at ljones@becker.com.

1531 ■ Americans for Informed Democracy (AID)
1220 L St. NW, Ste. 100-161
Washington, DC 20005
Ph: (202)709-6172
E-mail: info@aidemocracy.org
URL: www.aidemocracy.org

1532 ■ Americans for Informed Democracy Global Scholar Program *(Undergraduate/Scholarship)*

Purpose: To support and encourage students from all different fields, backgrounds and interests who have a strong academic records. **Focus:** International affairs and relations; Leadership, Institutional and community; Public affairs. **Qualif.:** Applicants must be high school or college students who have experienced honors or advanced placement-level courses. **Criteria:** Applicants will be evaluated based on academic records, extracurricular achievements and essay writing.

Funds Avail.: No specific amount. **To Apply:** Applicants must file online application. Applicants must also submit a short essay explaining "what issue in international affairs he/she has most interest, why and how will it fit into his or her future plans?".

1533 ■ AmeriGlide
3901A Commerce Park Dr.
Raleigh, NC 27610
Free: 800-790-1635
URL: www.ameriglide.com
Facebook: www.facebook.com/AmeriGlide
Twitter: www.twitter.com/AmeriGlide

1534 ■ AmeriGlide Achiever Scholarships *(Undergraduate/Scholarship)*

Purpose: To provide financial assistance for books or other school related supplies to deserving mobility challenged students. **Focus:** General studies/Field of study not specified. **Qualif.:** Applicants must: be enrolled at an accredited two or four year college; use a manual or electric wheelchair; have a minimum 3.0 GPA; be legal residents of the U.S. or hold a valid student visa. **Criteria:** Selection is based on the submitted application materials.

Funds Avail.: $2,500. **To Apply:** Applicants must submit an application form along with the essay and two character references from a teacher or any other non-related third party. **Deadline:** May 31.

1535 ■ amfAR, The Foundation for AIDS Research
120 Wall St., 13th Fl.
New York, NY 10005-3908
Ph: (212)806-1600
Fax: (212)806-1601
URL: www.amfar.org

1536 ■ Mathilde Krim Fellowships in Basic Biomedical Research *(Doctorate/Fellowship)*

Purpose: To encourage the investigators with limited experience and demonstrated interest in the field of HIV/AIDS to redirect or to embark on a career in biomedical, social or behavioral HIV/AIDS research. **Focus:** AIDS. **Qualif.:** Applicants must hold a research or clinical doctorate; must be positioned to secure an independent research position; must be mentored by an experienced investigator at the same US or international nonprofit research institution who is qualified to oversee the proposed research, has

Awards are arranged alphabetically below their administering organizations

successfully supervised postdoctoral fellows and is at the associate professor level or higher; be the main author on significant publications in leading international peer-reviewed journals; have made oral and poster presentations at major scientific conferences and meetings. **Criteria:** Selection will be based on the Scientific Advisory Committee's relevance, scientific merit and promise.

Funds Avail.: $150,000. **To Apply:** Applicants must visit the website to obtain a letter of intent form. The LOI format for this program has been simplified. Only the following will be required: face page; eligibility details; fellow's biographical sketch and list of publications, presentations and posters; mentor's biographical sketch and list of fellows supervised; career development questionnaire; resources and environment form. **Deadline:** July 31.

1537 ■ AMSUS - The Society of Federal Health Professionals

9320 Old Georgetown Rd.
Bethesda, MD 20814
Ph: (301)897-8800
Fax: (301)530-5446
Free: 800-761-9320
E-mail: amsus@amsus.org
URL: www.amsus.org

1538 ■ AMSUS Dentist Awards *(Professional development/Recognition)*

Purpose: To recognize the accomplishments of federal dentists who have made outstanding contributions as clinicians, researchers, educators or healthcare managers. **Focus:** Dentistry. **Qualif.:** Candidates must be federal dentists. **Criteria:** Recipients will be selected based on submitted narrative.

Funds Avail.: No specific amount. **Duration:** Annual. **To Apply:** The nomination process takes place electronically on the AMSUS website. In addition to the award recommendation, individual award nominations require a biography/resume/CV (no more than 3 pages in length) and letter of recommendation from the individual's supervisor, with commanding officer approval, be uploaded. Essay awards are submitted directly by the author through the AMSUS website. **Deadline:** June 30.

1539 ■ AMSUS Nursing Awards *(Advanced Professional/Recognition)*

Purpose: To recognize the accomplishments of federal nurses who have made outstanding contributions as clinicians, researchers, educators or healthcare managers. **Focus:** Nursing. **Qualif.:** Candidates must be federal nurses. **Criteria:** Recipients will be selected based on submitted narrative.

Funds Avail.: No specific amount. **Duration:** Annual. **To Apply:** The nomination process takes place electronically on the AMSUS website. In addition to the award recommendation, individual award nominations require a biography/resume/CV (no more than 3 pages in length) and letter of recommendation from the individual's supervisor, with commanding officer approval, be uploaded. Essay awards are submitted directly by the author through the AMSUS website. **Deadline:** June 30.

1540 ■ AMSUS Physician Awards *(Advanced Professional/Recognition)*

Purpose: To recognize the accomplishments of federal physicians who have made outstanding contributions as clinicians, researchers, educators or healthcare managers. **Focus:** Health care services. **Qualif.:** Candidates must be federal physicians. **Criteria:** Recipients will be selected based on submitted narrative.

Funds Avail.: No specific amount. **Duration:** Annual. **To Apply:** The nomination process takes place electronically on the AMSUS website. In addition to the award recommendation, individual award nominations require a biography/resume/CV (no more than 3 pages in length) and letter of recommendation from the individual's supervisor, with commanding officer approval, be uploaded. Essay awards are submitted directly by the author through the AMSUS website. **Deadline:** June 30.

1541 ■ Lewis L. Seaman Junior Enlisted Awards for Outstanding Operational Support *(Professional development/Recognition)*

Purpose: To recognize junior and senior enlisted medical healthcare professionals who have made a significant impact in the areas of patient care, clinical support or healthcare management and to their service's medical mission. **Focus:** Health care services. **Qualif.:** Candidates must be Active Duty, Reserve or Guard enlisted professionals of the Army, Navy, Air Force or Coast Guard who have exhibited outstanding accomplishments in advancing the healthcare mission of their service. **Criteria:** Recipients will be evaluated based on submitted performance from the previous calendar year.

Funds Avail.: No specific amount. **Duration:** Annual. **To Apply:** The nomination process takes place electronically on the AMSUS website. In addition to the award recommendation, individual award nominations require a biography/resume/CV (no more than 3 pages in length) and letter of recommendation from the individual's supervisor, with commanding officer approval, be uploaded. Essay awards are submitted directly by the author through the AMSUS website. **Deadline:** June 30. **Remarks:** Established in 1900.

1542 ■ Amusement & Music Operators Association (AMOA)

600 Spring Hill Ring Rd., Ste. 111
West Dundee, IL 60118
Ph: (847)428-7699
Fax: (847)428-7719
Free: 800-937-2662
URL: www.amoa.com

1543 ■ Wayne E. Hesch Memorial Scholarship *(Undergraduate, Graduate/Scholarship)*

Purpose: To provide financial support to students who are, or plan or hope to be engaged in the profession. **Focus:** General studies/Field of study not specified. **Qualif.:** Applicants must be undergraduate or graduate students endorsed by any AMOA member companies. **Criteria:** Selection will be based on the committee's criteria.

Funds Avail.: No specific amount. **Duration:** Annual. **To Apply:** Applicants must visit the Association's website to obtain an application form. Completed applications with applicants' most recent transcripts should be mailed to AMOA Education Foundation. **Deadline:** February 12. **Remarks:** Established in 1985.

1544 ■ AMVETS

4647 Forbes Blvd.
Lanham, MD 20706-4380

Awards are arranged alphabetically below their administering organizations

Ph: (301)459-9600
Fax: (301)459-7924
Free: 877-726-8387
E-mail: amvets@amvets.org
URL: www.amvets.org
Facebook: www.facebook.com/AMVETSHQ
LinkedIn: www.linkedin.com/company/79226
Twitter: twitter.com/AMVETSNational

1545 ■ AMVETS National Scholarships - Entering College Freshmen *(Undergraduate/Scholarship)*

Purpose: To assist deserving children and grandchildren of veterans in attaining post-secondary education. **Focus:** General studies/Field of study not specified. **Qualif.:** Applicant must be a graduating high school senior entering at the college freshmen level; must have a minimum high school GPA of 3.0; must be the child or grandchild of a United States veteran; must be a U.S. citizen; must have demonstrated academic promise and financial need; and must agree to authorize AMVETS to publicize the scholarship award, if selected. **Criteria:** Selection is based on academic promise, financial need and merit.

Funds Avail.: $1,000 per year. **Duration:** Annual; up to 4 years. **To Apply:** Applicant must submit a copy of the veteran's honorable discharge (Form DD 214). Dependents of current military personnel must submit a letter from the base commander certifying the active duty status of the parent; an official high school transcript (must be in the 4.0 grade scale or if in a different system, translated to the 4.0 scales); SAT and/or ACT scores; a complete and signed copy of the parent(s)'/guardian(s)' 1040 tax form (applicant's name must appear on the tax form); a copy of the applicant's Free Application for Federal Student Aid (FAFSA); essay (50-100 words); acceptance letter from the accredited school to be attended; proof of college expenses; and a resume detailing extracurricular activities, volunteer activities, community services and jobs held during the past four years. **Deadline:** April 30. **Contact:** AMVETS at the above address.

1546 ■ AMVETS National Scholarships - For Veterans *(Undergraduate/Scholarship)*

Purpose: To financially assist veterans who have exhausted government aid or who might not otherwise have the financial means to further their education. **Focus:** General studies/Field of study not specified. **Qualif.:** Applicant must be a U.S. veteran; a U.S. citizen; must demonstrate financial need; and must agree to authorize AMVETS to publicize the scholarship award, if selected. **Criteria:** Selection is based on academic promise, financial need and merit.

Funds Avail.: $1,000 per year. **Duration:** Up to 4 years. **To Apply:** Applicant must submit a copy of the veteran's honorable discharge or a letter certifying current service and eligibility for release from active duty prior to attending school; official college transcripts for all courses attempted and any degrees or certificates awarded (must be in the 4.0 grade scale, or if in a different system, translated to the 4.0 scales); a complete and signed copy of the applicant's 1040 tax form; a copy of the Free Application for Federal Student Aid (FAFSA); an essay (50-100 words); acceptance letter or a letter stating current student status from an accredited school; proof of college expenses; and a resume detailing military duty and awards, volunteer activities, community services and jobs held during the past four years. **Deadline:** April 30.

1547 ■ AMVETS National Scholarships - JROTC *(Undergraduate/Scholarship)*

Purpose: To support Junior ROTC cadets in pursuing study at an undergraduate college or university. **Focus:** General studies/Field of study not specified. **Qualif.:** Applicant must be an active JROTC cadet and currently a high school senior; have a minimum high school GPA of 3.0; be the child or grandchild of a U.S. veteran; a U.S. citizen; have demonstrated academic promise and financial need; and agree to authorize AMVETS to publicize the scholarship award, if selected. **Criteria:** Selection is based on academic promise, financial need and merit.

Funds Avail.: $1,000. **Duration:** Annual. **To Apply:** Applicant must submit a copy of the veteran's honorable discharge (Form DD 214). Dependents of current military personnel must submit a letter from the base commander certifying the active duty status of the parent; an official transcript including the first grading period of the current school year (must be in the 4.0 grade scale, or if in a different system, translated to the 4.0 scale); SAT and/or ACT scores; a complete and signed copy of the parent(s)'/guardian(s)'s 1040 tax form; a copy of the Free Application for Federal Student Aid (FAFSA); an essay (50-100 words); acceptance letter from the accredited school to attend; proof of college expenses; a letter from program commander verifying participation in ROTC/JROTC activities; and a resume detailing extracurricular activities, volunteer activities, community services and jobs held during the past four years. **Deadline:** April 30. **Contact:** AMVETS at the above address.

1548 ■ Anaheim Police Association (APA)

508 N Anaheim Blvd.
Anaheim, CA 92805
Ph: (714)635-0272
Fax: (714)635-3240
URL: anaheimpa.com
Facebook: www.facebook.com/AnaheimPA
Twitter: twitter.com/AnaheimPA

1549 ■ Anaheim Police Survivors and Scholarship Fund *(Undergraduate/Scholarship)*

Purpose: To provide financial assistance to the families of Anaheim Police Officers and other public safety personnel who are killed or severely injured in the line of duty. **Focus:** General studies/Field of study not specified. **Qualif.:** Applicants must: be entering students or recently high school graduates; continuing students (already enrolled in College Program) or returning students (entering college after a break in educational experience); and, children (natural or adopted) of Anaheim Police Officers or Anaheim Reserve Officers enrolled in at least twelve units. They must have cumulative GPA of 3.0 or higher. **Criteria:** Recipients are recommended by the American Police Officer's Honorary Association Scholarship Committee and approved by the Board of Trustees of Anaheim Police Survivors and Scholarship Fund.

Funds Avail.: No specific amount. **Duration:** Annual. **To Apply:** Applicants may contact the Trust, through Anaheim Police Association, for other information regarding the application process. **Remarks:** Established in 1979.

1550 ■ Anchor Environmental

720 Olive Way, Ste. 1900
Seattle, WA 98101

Ph: (206)287-9130
Fax: (206)287-9131
E-mail: info@anchorqea.com
URL: www.anchorqea.com

1551 ■ Anchor QEA Environmental Scholarships (Graduate/Scholarship)

Purpose: To assist students in fields related to water resources, surface and groundwater quality, coastal development, habitat restoration, and contaminated sediment management. **Focus:** Aquaculture; Environmental science; Fisheries sciences/management; Land management; Landscape architecture and design. **Qualif.:** Applicants must: be full-time graduate students or persons accepted to a graduate school in the United States; have undergraduate GPA equivalent of B average or higher; and, be majoring in fisheries, environmental sciences, planning/land use, landscape architecture, or coastal, geotechnical, or environmental engineering (any of which has an aquatic/waterfront emphasis). **Criteria:** Selection shall be based on the aforementioned applicants' qualifications and compliance with the application details.

Funds Avail.: $500 to $5,000. **Duration:** Annual. **Number Awarded:** Varies. **To Apply:** Applicants must submit a completed scholarship application form together with the letter(s) of recommendation (professional/academic) from professors, employers, etc.; a certified copy of undergraduate and graduate (if applicable) transcripts; a one-page essay on educational goals, reasons for selecting the major, future plans in the field and how the scholarship will help the student and a resume (optional). **Deadline:** November 17. **Contact:** scholarship@anchorqea.com.

1552 ■ The Anderson Group Summer Institute

PO Box 38334
Los Angeles, CA 90038-0334
Ph: (323)469-3050
E-mail: execsecretary@harpsociety.org
URL: www.harpsociety.org

1553 ■ The Anderson Group Summer Institute Scholarships (Other/Scholarship)

Purpose: To provide opportunity to members to go in AHS National Conference by covering their expenses. **Focus:** Music. **Qualif.:** Applicants must be active members of the American Harp Society with maximum age limit of 40 years old by April 15, 2011. **Criteria:** Recipients will be selected based on financial need and musical promise in the study of harp.

Funds Avail.: $1,000. **Duration:** Biennial; in odd-numbered years. **Number Awarded:** 2. **To Apply:** Applicants must submit biography including applicant's full name, legal residence, present address, telephone number, email address, proof of age, musical and academic education, personal profile, general analysis of financial need and long-range goals for harp-playing, hand-written statement, CD recording, and letter of reference.

1554 ■ Androscoggin County Chamber of Commerce

415 Lisbon St.
Lewiston, ME 04243-0059
Ph: (207)783-2249
Fax: (207)783-4481
URL: www.androscoggincounty.com

1555 ■ Androscoggin County Chamber of Commerce Adult Scholarships (Professional development/Scholarship)

Purpose: To support adults working for LA Metro Chamber member businesses. **Focus:** General studies/Field of study not specified. **Qualif.:** Applicants must be employed 20 or more hours by a member of the Androscoggin County Chamber of Commerce; must begin course within 6 months of receiving award; must be matriculated in college-level coursework applicable toward an Associates or Bachelor's degree; must be at least 25 years old. **Criteria:** Selection will be based on a scoring rubric.

Funds Avail.: $1,000. **Duration:** Annual; One year. **To Apply:** Applicants must submit a completed application, one-page typewritten essay, completed employer verification form, letter of reference/recommendation from employer.

1556 ■ Angus Foundation

3201 Frederick Ave.
Saint Joseph, MO 64506
Ph: (816)383-5100
Fax: (816)233-9703
E-mail: mjenkins@angusfoundation.org
URL: www.angusfoundation.org

1557 ■ Angus Foundation General Undergraduate Student Scholarships (Undergraduate/Scholarship)

Purpose: To support young men and women who are actively involved in the Angus breed pursuing an undergraduate degree in higher education. **Focus:** General studies/Field of study not specified. **Qualif.:** Applicants must have been members of National Junior Angus Association and are currently junior, regular or life members of the American Angus Association; must be graduating high school seniors or currently enrolled in a junior college, four-year college/university or other accredited institution of higher education. **Criteria:** Selection will be based on financial need, personal and/or family hardship, physical handicap, medical disability, other extenuating circumstances or combination thereof when determined such sufficiently exists to warrant special consideration by the Angus Foundation Scholarship Selection Committee for such purpose.

Funds Avail.: $1,000 to $5,000. **Duration:** Annual. **To Apply:** Applicants must complete the application form; must submit copy of the most recent high school or college transcript; must include three letters of recommendation and member code; and must be U.S. Postal service postmarked by the set deadline. **Deadline:** May 1.

1558 ■ Angus Foundation Graduate Student Degree Scholarship Program (Graduate/Scholarship)

Purpose: To support young men and women who are active in Angus breed pursuing an advanced degree in higher education. **Focus:** Animal science and behavior. **Qualif.:** Applicants must have been members of National Angus Association and currently be junior, regular or life members of the American Angus Association; must be currently enrolled in a graduate school pursuing a post-baccalaureate degree; must have a minimum of 3.0 GPA as continuing graduate students; must have not entered their first semester of graduate school. **Criteria:** Strong preference and priority will be given to applicants pursuing advanced degrees

Awards are arranged alphabetically below their administering organizations

related closely to the beef industry.

Funds Avail.: $5,000 each. **Duration:** Annual. **Number Awarded:** 5. **To Apply:** Applicants must submit signed and dated application form; must include a copy of the most recent college/university transcript, three letters of recommendation and member code. **Deadline:** May 1.

1559 ■ Angus/Talon Youth Educational Learning Program Endowment Fund (Graduate, Undergraduate/Scholarship)

Purpose: To support young men and women who are active in Angus breed pursuing an advanced degree in higher education. **Focus:** Animal science and behavior. **Qualif.:** Applicants must be either undergraduate or graduate students pursuing a degree related closely to the beef cattle industry. **Criteria:** Preference will be given to applicants who have successfully maintained academic progress.

Funds Avail.: Amount varies. **Duration:** Annual. **Number Awarded:** Varies. **To Apply:** Applicants must submit a signed and dated application form; must include a copy of the most recent college/university transcript, three letters of recommendation and member code.

1560 ■ Annapolis Rotary Club
PO Box 3175
Annapolis, MD 21403
E-mail: rachael.blair@atsverizon.net
URL: www.annapolisrotary.org

1561 ■ Rotary Club of Annapolis Scholarship (Undergraduate/Scholarship)

Purpose: To support graduating high school students defray their college expenses. **Focus:** General studies/Field of study not specified. **Qualif.:** Applicants must be graduating high school students who are residents of Anne Arundel County; must be attending high school in the Annapolis Area, including home schooled students; must be students planning to attend an accredited community college or university; must have a minimum GPA of 3.0. **Criteria:** Preference will be given to those who have demonstrated significant involvement in school and in the community.

Funds Avail.: $1,000. **Duration:** Annual. **Number Awarded:** 4. **To Apply:** Interested applicants must submit their complete Rotary Club of Annapolis Scholarship Application via mail. **Deadline:** March 1.

1562 ■ Anne Frank Center U.S.A. (AFC USA)
44 Park Pl.
New York, NY 10007-2500
Ph: (212)431-7993
Fax: (212)431-8375
E-mail: info@annefrank.com
URL: www.annefrank.com
Facebook: www.facebook.com/AnneFrankCenterUSA
LinkedIn: www.linkedin.com/company/the-anne-frank-center-usa
Twitter: twitter.com/AnneFrankCenter

1563 ■ Spirit of Anne Frank Outstanding Scholarship Award (Undergraduate/Scholarship)

Purpose: To support students who have proven themselves exceptional leaders in combating intolerance, prejudice and injustice in their communities. **Focus:** Human rights; Social sciences. **Qualif.:** Applicants must be high school seniors in the United States who will be attending a four-year college in the fall. Applicants must exhibit extraordinary leadership in combating intolerance and prejudice in their communities. **Criteria:** Winners are chosen based on their level of activism in their community in combating issues of prejudice, intolerance and inequality. This activism is detailed in the applicant's personal essay and in two supporting letters of recommendation.

Funds Avail.: $10,000. **Duration:** Annual. **To Apply:** Applicants must complete the online application form, which includes a 1,000-word personal essay and two supporting letters of recommendation that detail their commitment to social justice and their fight for equality in their community.

1564 ■ Annuity.org
189 S Orange Ave., Ste. 1600
Orlando, FL 32801
Free: 877-521-1463
URL: www.annuity.org

1565 ■ Annuity.org Scholarships (Undergraduate, Graduate/Scholarship)

Purpose: To encourage students to think about their financial future long before they graduate. **Focus:** General studies/Field of study not specified. **Qualif.:** Applicants must be high school seniors, undergraduate or graduate students enrolled in any U.S. college. **Criteria:** Selection will be based on the submitted essay. Essays will be verified on the following bases: grammar and style; original ideas; well-researched and plausible; investment advice; organized and persuasive writing; and foundational knowledge of finance.

Funds Avail.: $2,000 (for 1st place); $1,000 (for 2nd place). **Number Awarded:** 2. **To Apply:** Applicants must write an essay on the topic: "being responsible with your money today". Essay must be designed around a concept that is easy to understand but difficult to execute; must be of 700 to 1,400 words; must include cited works of at least three sources. Applicants must also provide contact information and proof of enrollment in U.S. college. **Deadline:** May 1. **Contact:** scholarship@annuity.org.

1566 ■ Antioch University New England - Center for Tropical Ecology and Conservation (CTEC)
40 Avon St.
Keene, NH 03431
Ph: (603)283-2328
Fax: (603)357-0718
Free: 800-553-8920
E-mail: bkaplin@antioch.edu
URL: www.antiochne.edu/centerfortropicalecology

1567 ■ CTEC Internships (Undergraduate/Internship)

Purpose: To support individuals who wish to conduct studies related to tropical ecology and conservation. **Focus:** Ecology; Environmental conservation. **Qualif.:** Applicants must be students who are interested to further their study relevant to tropical ecology and conservation. **Criteria:** Selection will be based on the committees' criteria.

Funds Avail.: No specific amount. **To Apply:** Applicant may contact the Center for application process and other information.

Awards are arranged alphabetically below their administering organizations

1568 ■ Anxiety and Depression Association of America (ADAA)
8701 Georgia Ave., Ste. 412
Silver Spring, MD 20910
Ph: (240)485-1001
Fax: (240)485-1035
E-mail: information@adaa.org
URL: www.adaa.org
Facebook: www.facebook.com/
  AnxietyAndDepressionAssociationOfAmerica
LinkedIn: www.linkedin.com/company/anxiety-and
  -depression-association-of-america?trk=tyah&trkInfo
  =clickedVertical%3Acompany%2CclickedEntityId%3
  A10281167%2Cidx%3A4-3-13%2CtarId%3A14498
  50364766%2Ctas%3Aanxiety+and
Twitter: twitter.com/Got_Anxiety

1569 ■ ADAA Career Development Travel Awards (Other/Award)

Purpose: To help young professionals with a career interest in fields related to anxiety disorders; to encourage mental health professionals to advance the field of study of disorders, including the causes, prevention, treatment options and other related issues. **Focus:** Mental health. **Qualif.:** Applicants must have completed their master's degree or are training for postgraduate degrees (MD, PhD, MPH, MSW, PsyD); must be Ph.D level scientists or clinicians who have received doctorates or completed postdoctoral fellowships within the past three years; must be physician-scientists or clinicians who have completed their residencies or research fellowships within the past three years. **Criteria:** Candidates will be judged based on the following criteria: (1) Evidence of commitment to the field of anxiety disorders; (2) Strength of current program and training; (3) Quality, extent and multidisciplinary nature of research; (4) Professional reference and personal statement (5) Interest in becoming involved with ADAA.

Funds Avail.: $500. **To Apply:** Applicant must submit the application form with attached curriculum vitae; an abstract following the guidelines; and a letter of recommendation from a mentor, supervisor, department chair or advisor. **Deadline:** November 7. **Contact:** Application materials must be sent to: Career Development Travel Awards, 8701 George Ave., Ste. 412, Silver Spring, MD 20910, e-mail: awards@adaa.org.

1570 ■ APA Division 54: Society of Pediatric Psychology (SPP)
PO Box 3968
Lawrence, KS 66046
Ph: (785)856-0713
Fax: (785)856-0759
E-mail: apadiv54@gmail.com
URL: www.apadivisions.org/division-54
Facebook: www.facebook.com/Society-of-Pediatric
  -Psychology-119656468096032

1571 ■ Lizette Peterson Homer Injury Prevention Grant Awards (Other, Undergraduate, Graduate/Grant)

Purpose: To support research related to the prevention of injuries in children and adolescents. **Focus:** Medicine, Pediatric. **Qualif.:** Applicants must be students and/or faculty members at an accredited university with demonstrated research competence and area commitment. **Criteria:** Selection will be based on the committee's criteria.

Funds Avail.: $5,000. **Duration:** Annual. **Number Awarded:** 1. **To Apply:** Applicants must submit the following: research proposal, which should be no more than four single spaced pages including (1) 100-word abstract, (2) description of the project with introduction, methods and procedures, (3) detailed budget, and (4) references (all in one MS Word document); a current curriculum vitae; supporting faculty supervisor letter (if the applicants are student); and proof of IRB approval or statement that IRB approval is pending. **Deadline:** October 1.

1572 ■ Marion and Donald Routh Student Research Grants (Undergraduate/Grant)

Purpose: To provide assistance to research related to the field of pediatric psychology. **Focus:** Medicine, Pediatric. **Qualif.:** Applicants must be student members of APA. **Criteria:** Recipients are selected based on committee's review of proposal.

Funds Avail.: $1,000. **Duration:** Annual. **To Apply:** Applicants must submit a summary of proposed research (maximum of 100 words); project objectives (maximum of 7 pages); a detailed budget; a statement about the qualifications, training, membership of the applicant; and a letter of recommendation by faculty supervisor, send materials by email in MS Word format. **Deadline:** October 1. **Contact:** Paul Robins, PhD, at robinsp@email.chop.edu.

1573 ■ APhA Foundation
2215 Constitution Ave NW
Washington, DC 20037
Ph: (202)429-7565
Fax: (202)638-3793
E-mail: info@aphafoundation.org
URL: www.pharmacist.com

1574 ■ Mary Louise Andersen Scholarship (Undergraduate/Scholarship)

Purpose: To support students who choose to invest their time in their school's APhA - ASP chapter to help shape the future of the profession while managing the demands of a full-time pharmacy curriculum. **Focus:** Pharmacy. **Qualif.:** Applicants must: complete at least one academic year in the professional sequence of courses; earn cumulative grade point average of at least 2.75 on a 4.0 scale (or equivalent grading system) in professional coursework during pharmacy school; be active members in the APhA Academy of Student Pharmacists (APhA-ASP). **Criteria:** Applicants will be evaluated on their potential to become leaders for the profession of pharmacy, as demonstrated by involvement in school and community activities and academic performance.

Funds Avail.: No specific amount. **Duration:** Annual. **Number Awarded:** 1. **To Apply:** Interested applicants may contact the Foundation for the application process and other information. **Contact:** Brian Wall at bwall@aphanet.org.

1575 ■ APhA Auxilliary Scholarship (Undergraduate/Scholarship)

Purpose: To support students who choose to invest their time in their school's APhA - ASP chapter to help shape the future of the profession while managing the demands of a full-time pharmacy curriculum. **Focus:** Pharmacy. **Qualif.:** Applicants must: complete at least one academic year in the professional sequence of courses; earn cumulative grade point average of at least 2.75 on a 4.0 scale (or

Awards are arranged alphabetically below their administering organizations

equivalent grading system) in professional coursework during pharmacy school; active members in the APhA Academy of Student Pharmacists (APhA-ASP). **Criteria:** Applicants will be evaluated on their potential to become leaders for the profession of pharmacy, as demonstrated by involvement in school and community activities and academic performance.

Funds Avail.: No specific amount. **Duration:** Annual. **Number Awarded:** 1. **To Apply:** Interested applicants may contact the Foundation for the application process and other information. **Contact:** Brian Wall, Executive Resident; Phone: 202-429-7503; E-mail: bwall@aphanet.org.

1576 ■ George F. Archambault Scholarship (Undergraduate/Scholarship)

Purpose: To support students who choose to invest their time in their school's APhA - ASP chapter to help shape the future of the profession while managing the demands of a full-time pharmacy curriculum. **Focus:** Pharmacy. **Qualif.:** Applicants must: complete at least one academic year in the professional sequence of courses; earn cumulative grade point average of at least 2.75 on a 4.0 scale (or equivalent grading system) in professional coursework during pharmacy school; be active members in the APhA Academy of Student Pharmacists (APhA-ASP). **Criteria:** Applicants will be evaluated on their potential to become leaders for the profession of pharmacy, as demonstrated by involvement in school and community activities and academic performance.

Funds Avail.: No specific amount. **Duration:** Annual. **Number Awarded:** 1. **To Apply:** Interested applicants may contact the Foundation for the application process and other related information. **Remarks:** Established in 2011. **Contact:** Brian Wall at bwall@aphanet.org.

1577 ■ Boyle Family Scholarship (Undergraduate/Scholarship)

Purpose: To support student pharmacists who will provide much needed pharmaceutical care. **Focus:** Pharmacy. **Qualif.:** Applicants must: complete at least one academic year in the professional sequence of courses; earn cumulative grade point average of at least 2.75 on a 4.0 scale (or equivalent grading system) in professional coursework during pharmacy school; be active members in the APhA Academy of Student Pharmacists (APhA-ASP). **Criteria:** Applicants will be evaluated on their potential to become leaders for the profession of pharmacy, as demonstrated by involvement in school and community activities and academic performance.

Funds Avail.: No specific amount. **Duration:** Annual. **Number Awarded:** 1. **To Apply:** Interested applicants may contact the Foundation for the application process and other related information. **Contact:** Brian Wall at bwall@aphanet.org.

1578 ■ Marvin and Joanell Dyrstad Scholarship (Undergraduate/Scholarship)

Purpose: To support students who choose to invest their time in their school's APhA - ASP chapter to help shape the future of the profession while managing the demands of a full-time pharmacy curriculum. **Focus:** Pharmacy. **Qualif.:** Applicants must: complete at least one academic year in the professional sequence of courses; earn cumulative grade point average of at least 2.75 on a 4.0 scale (or equivalent grading system) in professional coursework during pharmacy school; be active members in the APhA Academy of Student Pharmacists (APhA-ASP). **Criteria:** Applicants will be evaluated on their potential to become leaders for the profession of pharmacy, as demonstrated by involvement in school and community activities and academic performance.

Funds Avail.: No specific amount. **Duration:** Annual. **Number Awarded:** 1. **To Apply:** Interested applicants may contact the Foundation for the application process and other information. **Contact:** Brian Wall at bwall@aphanet.org.

1579 ■ Gloria Francke Scholarship (Undergraduate/Scholarship)

Purpose: To support students who choose to invest their time in their school's APhA - ASP chapter to help shape the future of the profession while managing the demands of a full-time pharmacy curriculum. **Focus:** Pharmacy. **Qualif.:** Applicants must complete at least one academic year in the professional sequence of courses; must earn cumulative grade point average of at least 2.75 on a 4.0 scale (or equivalent grading system) in professional coursework during pharmacy school; must be active members in the APhA Academy of Student Pharmacists (APhA-ASP). **Criteria:** Applicants will be evaluated on their potential to become leaders for the profession of pharmacy, as demonstrated by involvement in school and community activities and academic performance.

Funds Avail.: No specific amount. **Duration:** Annual. **Number Awarded:** 1. **To Apply:** Interested applicants may contact the Foundation for the application process and other information.

1580 ■ John A. Gans Scholarship (Undergraduate/Scholarship)

Purpose: To support students who choose to invest their time in their school's APhA - ASP chapter to help shape the future of the profession while managing the demands of a full-time pharmacy curriculum. **Focus:** Pharmacy. **Qualif.:** Applicants must: complete at least one academic year in the professional sequence of courses; earn cumulative grade point average of at least 2.75 on a 4.0 scale (or equivalent grading system) in professional coursework during pharmacy school; be active members in the APhA Academy of Student Pharmacists (APhA-ASP). **Criteria:** Applicants will be evaluated on their potential to become leaders for the profession of pharmacy, as demonstrated by involvement in school and community activities and academic performance.

Funds Avail.: No specific amount. **Duration:** Annual. **Number Awarded:** 1. **To Apply:** Interested applicants may contact the Foundation for the application process and other information. **Contact:** Brian Wall at bwall@aphanet.org.

1581 ■ Robert D. Gibson Scholarship (Undergraduate/Scholarship)

Purpose: To support students who choose to invest their time in their school's APhA - ASP chapter to help shape the future of the profession while managing the demands of a full-time pharmacy curriculum. **Focus:** Pharmacy. **Qualif.:** Applicants must: complete at least one academic year in the professional sequence of courses; earn cumulative grade point average of at least 2.75 on a 4.0 scale (or equivalent grading system) in professional coursework during pharmacy school; active members in the APhA Academy of Student Pharmacists (APhA-ASP). **Criteria:** Applicants will be evaluated on their potential to become leaders for the profession of pharmacy, as demonstrated by involve-

Awards are arranged alphabetically below their administering organizations

ment in school and community activities and academic performance.

Funds Avail.: No specific amount. **Duration:** Annual. **Number Awarded:** 1. **To Apply:** Interested applicants may contact the Foundation for the application process and other information. **Contact:** Brian Wall at bwall@aphanet.org.

1582 ■ Sam Kalman Scholarship (Undergraduate/Scholarship)

Purpose: To support students who choose to invest their time in their school's APhA - ASP chapter to help shape the future of the profession while managing the demands of a full-time pharmacy curriculum. **Focus:** Pharmacy. **Qualif.:** Applicants must: complete at least one academic year in the professional sequence of courses; earn cumulative grade point average of at least 2.75 on a 4.0 scale (or equivalent grading system) in professional coursework during pharmacy school; active members in the APhA Academy of Student Pharmacists (APhA-ASP). **Criteria:** Applicants will be evaluated on their potential to become leaders for the profession of pharmacy, as demonstrated by involvement in school and community activities and academic performance.

Funds Avail.: No specific amount. **Duration:** Annual. **Number Awarded:** 1. **To Apply:** Interested applicants may contact the Foundation for the application process and other information. **Contact:** Brian Wall, Executive Resident; Phone: 202-429-7503; E-mail: bwall@aphanet.org.

1583 ■ Juan and Esperanza Luna Scholarship (Undergraduate/Scholarship)

Purpose: To support students who choose to invest their time in their school's APhA - ASP chapter to help shape the future of the profession while managing the demands of a full-time pharmacy curriculum. **Focus:** Pharmacy. **Qualif.:** Applicants must: complete at least one academic year in the professional sequence of courses; earn cumulative grade point average of at least 2.75 on a 4.0 scale (or equivalent grading system) in professional coursework during pharmacy school; active members in the APhA Academy of Student Pharmacists (APhA-ASP). **Criteria:** Applicants will be evaluated on their potential to become leaders for the profession of pharmacy, as demonstrated by involvement in school and community activities and academic performance.

Funds Avail.: No specific amount. **Duration:** Annual. **Number Awarded:** 1. **To Apply:** Interested applicants may contact the Foundation for the application process and other information. **Remarks:** Established in 2013. **Contact:** Brian Wall, Executive Resident; Phone: 202-429-7503; E-mail: bwall@aphanet.org.

1584 ■ Paul Pumpian Scholarship (Undergraduate/Scholarship)

Purpose: To support students who choose to invest their time in their school's APhA - ASP chapter to help shape the future of the profession while managing the demands of a full-time pharmacy curriculum. **Focus:** Pharmacy. **Qualif.:** Applicants must complete at least one academic year in the professional sequence of courses; must earn a cumulative GPA of at least 2.75 on a 4.0 scale or equivalent grading system in professional coursework during pharmacy school; must be active members in the APhA Academy of Student Pharmacists. The applicants must show active participation in their chapter's activities but are not required to hold a leadership position. **Criteria:** Applicants will be evaluated on their potential to become leaders for the profession of pharmacy, as demonstrated by involvement in school and community activities and academic performance.

Funds Avail.: No specific amount. **Duration:** Annual. **To Apply:** Interested applicants may contact the Foundation for the application process and other information. **Contact:** Brian Wall, Executive Resident; Phone: 202-429-7503; E-mail: bwall@aphanet.org.

1585 ■ Colonel Jerry W. Ross Scholarship (Undergraduate/Scholarship)

Purpose: To support students who choose to invest their time in their school's APhA - ASP chapter to help shape the future of the profession while managing the demands of a full-time pharmacy curriculum. **Focus:** Pharmacy. **Qualif.:** Applicants must: complete at least one academic year in the professional sequence of courses; earn cumulative grade point average of at least 2.75 on a 4.0 scale (or equivalent grading system) in professional coursework during pharmacy school; active members in the APhA Academy of Student Pharmacists (APhA-ASP). **Criteria:** Applicants will be evaluated on their potential to become leaders for the profession of pharmacy, as demonstrated by involvement in school and community activities and academic performance.

Funds Avail.: No specific amount. **Duration:** Annual. **Number Awarded:** 1. **To Apply:** Interested applicants may contact the Foundation for the application process and other information. **Contact:** Brian Wall, Executive Resident; Phone: 202-429-7503; E-mail: bwall@aphanet.org.

1586 ■ Charles C. Thomas Scholarship (Undergraduate/Scholarship)

Purpose: To support students who choose to invest their time in their school's APhA - ASP chapter to help shape the future of the profession while managing the demands of a full-time pharmacy curriculum. **Focus:** Pharmacy. **Qualif.:** Applicants must: complete at least one academic year in the professional sequence of courses; earn cumulative grade point average of at least 2.75 on a 4.0 scale (or equivalent grading system) in professional coursework during pharmacy school; active members in the APhA Academy of Student Pharmacists (APhA-ASP). **Criteria:** Applicants will be evaluated on their potential to become leaders for the profession of pharmacy, as demonstrated by involvement in school and community activities and academic performance.

Funds Avail.: No specific amount. **Duration:** Annual. **Number Awarded:** 1. **To Apply:** Interested applicants may contact the Foundation for the application process and other information. **Contact:** Brian Wall, Executive Resident; Phone: 202-429-7503; E-mail: bwall@aphanet.org.

1587 ■ Aplastic Anemia and MDS International Foundation (AA&MDSIF)

100 Park Ave., Ste. 108
Rockville, MD 20850
Ph: (301)279-7202
Fax: (301)279-7205
Free: 800-747-2820
E-mail: help@aamds.org
URL: www.aamds.org
Facebook: www.facebook.com/aamds
Twitter: twitter.com/aamdsif

Awards are arranged alphabetically below their administering organizations

1588 ■ Matthew Debono Memorial Scholarship Funds (Undergraduate, Graduate/Scholarship)

Purpose: To assist students who are challenged with a bone marrow failure disease. **Focus:** Health sciences; Medicine. **Qualif.:** Applicants must have been diagnosed with aplastic anemia, MDS, PNH, or a combination of these diseases; must be a U.S. residents ages 35 and under; must be attending a school located in the United States; must be high school seniors or graduates who plan to enroll, or students who are already enrolled, in a full-time or part-time (minimum six credits) undergraduate or graduate course of study at an accredited two or four-year college, university, vocational-technical school or graduate school. **Criteria:** Selection will be based on the quality and completeness of the applicants' materials, their academic record, essays, financial need, and other criteria such as leadership, activities, awards and community service. **Funds Avail.:** $1,000-$2,000 each. **To Apply:** Applicants must submit the following requirements: official transcript; letter from a physician stating their diagnosis; essay and reference as part of the application process; Student Aid Report with the EFC (Estimated Family Contribution) amount; complete FAFSA (Free Application for Federal Student Aid) application form; school web page address that verifies the cost information provided on the application or copy of last tuition/room and board invoice. **Remarks:** Established in 1986.

1589 ■ Appalachian School of Law (ASL)
1169 Edgewater Dr.
Grundy, VA 24614
Ph: (276)935-4349
Fax: (276)935-8496
Free: 800-895-7411
E-mail: admissions@asl.edu
URL: www.asl.edu

1590 ■ Appalachian School of Law Merit Scholarship Program (Undergraduate/Scholarship)

Purpose: To support students financially in the form of credit against tuition charged. **Focus:** Law. **Qualif.:** Applicants must be at least incoming first year law students. **Criteria:** Recipients will be selected based on the Law School Admission Test (LSAT) and Undergraduate Grade Point Average (UGPA). Eligibility for retention of an award during the students' first three years in law school will be based on their academic performance. Scholarship will be awarded on a first come, first serve basis. **Funds Avail.:** Amount varies. **Duration:** Annual. **To Apply:** Applicants must complete and submit an online application available at the website; online certification page; two letters of recommendation; and 500 words or less describing professional goals and qualifications. **Contact:** Financial Aid Office, 800-895-7411 ext. 1211, or e-mail at financialaid@asl.edu.

1591 ■ Appel Law Firm, LLP
100 Pringle Ave., Ste. 730
Walnut Creek, CA 94596
Ph: (925)938-2000
URL: www.appellawyer.com

1592 ■ Auto Accident Law Firm Survivor Scholarships (Graduate/Scholarship)

Purpose: To assist students with their educational expenses. **Focus:** General studies/Field of study not specified. **Qualif.:** Applicants must be U.S. citizens or permanent residents; have sustained injuries from a car or truck accident or been affected by someone else's accident; enrolled in an accredited college or university within the United States; and have a cumulative GPA of 3.00 or higher. Graduate and Law school students are encouraged to apply. **Criteria:** Selection will be based on the committee's criteria.
Funds Avail.: $1,000. **To Apply:** Applicants must submit the following requirements: completed application; official copy of a current academic transcript; copy of a police report or other proof of the applicants' accident; and personal essay of not more than three pages describing the car accident, how it affected the applicants and what are the changes since the accident. **Deadline:** August 1.

1593 ■ Applied Motion Products, Inc.
404 Westridge Dr.
Watsonville, CA 95076
Ph: (831)761-6555
Fax: (831)761-6544
Free: 888-976-8640
E-mail: jgibbings@applied-motion.com
URL: www.applied-motion.com

1594 ■ The Make It Move Scholarships (Undergraduate/Scholarship)

Purpose: To assist those who want to turn their brilliant ideas into moving, working realities. **Focus:** General studies/Field of study not specified. **Qualif.:** Applicants must be U.S. citizens and international students enrolled in high school or an undergraduate/graduate program at an accredited U.S. institution. **Criteria:** Once entries are received, they will be reviewed by a selection committee compose of managing staff members of Applied Motion. The decision of the panel will be based on which students' creation best exemplified the originality, ingenuity, and mechanical skill to drive the advancement of today's technological society.
Funds Avail.: $1,000. **Duration:** Annual. **Number Awarded:** 1. **To Apply:** Applicants need to do the following: take your great idea, and turn it into an actual moving creation; film your final creation in action using instagram; include a short description about your creation; upload it to Instagram including the hashtag #ampmakeitmove. **Deadline:** October 16.

1595 ■ Appraisal Institute Education Trust
200 W Madison, Ste. 1500
Chicago, IL 60606
Ph: (312)335-4133
Fax: (312)335-4134
E-mail: educationtrust@appraisalinstitute.org
URL: www.aiedtrust.org

1596 ■ Appraisal Institute Education Trust Undergraduate Scholarships (Undergraduate/Scholarship)

Purpose: To help finance the education endeavors of individuals concentrating in real estate appraisal, land economics, real estate or allied fields. **Focus:** Land management; Real estate. **Qualif.:** Applicants must be students majoring in real estate appraisal, land economics, real estate or allied fields; must be sophomore, junior or

Awards are arranged alphabetically below their administering organizations

senior students seeking an associate or bachelor's degree; must be full- or part-time students in any U.S. degree granting college or university; must have a strong academic record. **Criteria:** Selection will be based on the applicants' academic excellence. Preference will be given to applicants with an appraisal internship.

Funds Avail.: $1,000. **Duration:** Annual. **To Apply:** Applicants must submit a completed application together with two-hundred (200) word personal statement discussing academic achievements, financial need, career aspirations, involvement in real estate field; and any qualifications considered relevant by the applicants; current resume; official copies of all college transcripts; two (2) letters of recommendation attesting to applicants' work ethic, character and pursuit of career in real estate appraisal, land economics, real estate or allied fields. Letters of recommendation should be sent directly to the Appraisal Institute Education Trust. **Deadline:** April 15. **Contact:** Appraisal Institute Education Trust at educationtrust@appraisalinstitute.org.

1597 ■ Arab American Institute (AAI)
1600 K St. NW, Ste. 601
Washington, DC 20006
Ph: (202)429-9210
Fax: (202)429-9214
E-mail: communications@aaiusa.org
URL: www.aaiusa.org
Facebook: www.facebook.com/ArabAmericanInstitute
Twitter: twitter.com/aaiusa

1598 ■ Barakat Trust and Barakat Foundation Scholarships *(Graduate, Postdoctorate/Scholarship)*

Purpose: To provide financial support for students and scholars of Islamic culture. **Focus:** General studies/Field of study not specified. **Qualif.:** Applicants must have completed at least a B.A. degree and have been accepted for graduate study or an apprenticeship at an accredited university or institution. **Criteria:** Selection will be based on the committee's criteria.

Funds Avail.: Amount varies. **Duration:** Annual. **To Apply:** Applicants may contact the Barakat Trust and Barakat Foundation for the application requirements. **Deadline:** February 15. **Contact:** Barakat Trust and Barakat Foundation, 2665 Kimball Pomona, CA 91767; rc101@earthlink.net.

1599 ■ Ameen Rihani Scholarship Program *(Undergraduate/Scholarship)*

Purpose: To promote academic excellence and provide an opportunity for outstanding student to reach their fullest potential. **Focus:** Literature; Philosophy; Political science. **Qualif.:** Applicants should be individuals who: are of Lebanese or other Arab descent; are citizens/legal permanent residents of the United States; have attained a cumulative GPA of at least 3.25 on a 4.0 scale; will enter a college or university as full-time, degree-seeking freshmen in the fall of the year; and, have demonstrated leadership abilities through participation in the community service, extracurricular or other activities. **Criteria:** Selection shall be based on the aforementioned qualifications and compliance with the application details.

Funds Avail.: $1,500. **To Apply:** Application is via nomination. Teachers, counselors, and principals are invited to nominate students with outstanding academic qualifications, particularly those who would promote success in the fields of literature, philosophy, or political science. **Deadline:** March 15. **Contact:** Ameen Rihani Scholarship Program, The Ameen Rihani Organization, 7979 Old Georgetown Rd., Ste. 700 Bethesda, MD 20814.

1600 ■ Arab American Medical Association Houston Chapter (AAMA)
John P. McGovern Bldg.
1515 Hermann Dr.
Houston, TX 77004-7126
Ph: (713)524-4267
Fax: (713)526-1434
E-mail: admin@aama-houston.org
URL: aama-houston.org

1601 ■ AAMA Houston Chapter Health Training Scholarships *(Other/Scholarship)*

Purpose: To support Arab students in their educational pursuit. **Focus:** Education, Medical; Medicine. **Qualif.:** Applicants must be of Arab heritage; enrolled full-time in an internationally recognized health care related school; accepted to spend greater than 3 months at one of Houston's medical institutions or any affiliated hospitals; willing to provide a written report describing his/her experience during the elective training; willing to attend AAMA meetings during the training months in Houston; and, become members of NAAMA/AAMA-Houston Chapter. **Criteria:** Selection shall be based on the aforementioned applicants' qualifications and compliance with the application details.

Funds Avail.: $750-$3,000. **Duration:** Annual. **To Apply:** Applicants must submit a completed scholarship application form along with an updated CV; a letter verifying enrollment in a medical/health institution/school; a letter of acceptance for elective training at any of the medical institutions in Houston and two letters or recommendation from current instructors.

1602 ■ Archaeological Institute of America (AIA)
656 Beacon St., 6th Fl.
Boston, MA 02215-2006
Ph: (617)353-9361
Fax: (617)353-6550
E-mail: aia@aia.bu.edu
URL: www.archaeological.org

1603 ■ AIA Graduate Student Travel Awards *(Graduate/Grant)*

Purpose: To assist graduate students who are presenting papers at the AIA Annual Meeting with their travel expenses. **Focus:** Archeology. **Qualif.:** Applicants must be graduate students and must be AIA members in good standing. **Criteria:** Selection will be based on the committee's criteria.

Funds Avail.: No specific amount. **To Apply:** Interested applicants may visit the website for the online application process. Applicants must attach their curriculum vitae and a scanned copy of their student ID or submit the attached documents through fax. **Deadline:** October 30. **Contact:** AIA Membership Department, Phone: 617-353-8705, Fax: 617-353-6550, Email: membership@aia.bu.edu; Megan Bernard, Phone: 617-353-8703, Email: mbernard@aia.bu.edu.

1604 ■ Archaeological Institute of America Fellowships for Study in the U.S. *(Postdoctorate/Fellowship)*

Purpose: To provide support to scholars who are pursuing highest quality on various aspects of archeology. **Focus:**

Awards are arranged alphabetically below their administering organizations

Archeology. **Qualif.:** Applicants who are archaeologists must have a PhD degree; architects must have their diploma. Both must demonstrate professional competence in archaeology in their applications. **Criteria:** Fellows will be selected on the basis of scholarly promise as indicated by the applicants' academic record, prior publications and the merits of the proposed research projects. Preference will be given to applicants who are at an early stage of their professional careers.

Funds Avail.: No specific amount. **To Apply:** Interested applicants must submit the following materials: a completed online application form; curriculum vitae, including a list of publications; two references. **Deadline:** November 1.

1605 ■ Archaeology of Portugal Fellowships
(Professional development/Fellowship)

Purpose: To support projects pertaining to the archaeology of Portugal. **Focus:** Archeology. **Qualif.:** Applicants must be Portuguese, American or other scholars; must be members of the AIA at the time of application and until the end of the fellowship term. **Criteria:** Selection will be based on the committee's criteria.

Funds Avail.: $4,000-$10,000. **To Apply:** Interested applicants may visit the website for the online application process. All materials including references and transcripts must be received on or before the deadline. **Deadline:** November 1. **Contact:** fellowships@aia.bu.edu; 617-358-4184.

1606 ■ Anna C. and Oliver C. Colburn Fellowships
(Doctorate/Fellowship)

Purpose: To support studies undertaken at the American School of Classical Studies at Athens, Greece for no more than a year. **Focus:** Archeology. **Qualif.:** Applicants must be citizens or permanent residents of the United States or Canada; must be members of the AIA at the time of application and until the end of the fellowship term; must be at the pre-doctoral stage or have received a PhD within five years of application. **Criteria:** Selection will be based on the committee's criteria.

Funds Avail.: $5,500 each. **Duration:** Biennial. **Number Awarded:** 5. **To Apply:** Applicants must visit the website for the online application process. Applicants must apply concurrently to the ASCSA for associate membership or associate student membership, but applicants may not be members of ASCSA during the year of application. All materials including references and transcripts must be submitted on or before the deadline. **Deadline:** January 15.

1607 ■ DAI Fellowships for Study in Berlin
(Doctorate/Fellowship)

Purpose: To encourage and support scholarship on various aspects of archaeology and promotes contact between North American and German archaeologists. **Focus:** Archeology. **Qualif.:** Applicants must be members of the Archaeological Institute of American and must be residents of a North American country. **Criteria:** Fellows will be selected on the basis of scholarly promise as indicated by the applicants' academic record, prior publications and the merits of the proposed research project. Preference will be given to applicants who are at an early stage of their professional careers.

Funds Avail.: No specific amount. **Duration:** Annual. **To Apply:** Applicants must send the following materials: a detailed research proposal, no more than three pages; a curriculum vitae; a publication list. **Deadline:** November 30.

1608 ■ Olivia James Traveling Fellowships
(Professional development/Fellowship)

Purpose: To support fellows to travel and study in Greece, Cyprus, the Aegean Islands, Sicily, Southern Italy, Asia Minor (Turkey) or Mesopotamia. **Focus:** Archeology. **Qualif.:** Applicants must be US citizens; must be members of the AIA at the time of application and until the end of the fellowship term. **Criteria:** Preference will be given to individuals engaged in dissertation research or to those who received their PhD within five years of the application deadline.

Funds Avail.: $25,000. **Duration:** Annual. **To Apply:** Interested applicants may visit the website for the online application process. All application materials including references and transcripts must be received on or before the deadline. **Deadline:** November 1. **Contact:** AIA Fellowship Coordinator, at the above address; or Email: fellowships@aia.bu.edu.

1609 ■ Samuel H. Kress Grants for Research and Publication in Classical Art and Architecture
(Professional development/Grant)

Purpose: To provide financial support to individuals who have publication activities critical to both current and future archaeological research. **Focus:** Archeology; Architecture; Art. **Qualif.:** Applicants must still be in the research stage and must have a publication contract in place with either a non-profit or commercial publisher. **Criteria:** Selection will be based on the committee's criteria.

Funds Avail.: $3,000. **To Apply:** Interested applicants may visit the website for the application process. Research may be undertaken at domestic or international universities, libraries or study centers or through excavation or preservation projects of Classical sites. Proposals must include a timetable for completion of the manuscript, specific plans for publication including budget information and a description of how the grant will be utilized. **Deadline:** November 1 and March 1.

1610 ■ Harriet and Leon Pomerance Fellowships
(Professional development/Fellowship)

Purpose: To support an individual project of a scholarly nature, related to Aegean Bronze Age Archaeology. **Focus:** Archeology. **Qualif.:** Applicants must be citizens or permanent residents of the United States or Canada, or be actively pursuing an advance degree at a North American College or University; must be members of the AIA at the time of application and until the end of the fellowship term. **Criteria:** Preference will be given to candidates whose project requires travel to the Mediterranean for the purpose of the fellowship.

Funds Avail.: $5,000. **Duration:** Annual. **To Apply:** Applicants must visit the website for the online application process. All materials including references and transcripts must be submitted on or before the deadline. **Deadline:** November 1. **Contact:** AIA Fellowship Coordinator, at the above address; or Email: fellowships@aia.bu.edu.

1611 ■ Jane C. Waldbaum Archaeological Field School Scholarships *(Undergraduate/Scholarship)*

Purpose: To help students pay their expenses associated with participation on an archaeological excavation or survey project. **Focus:** Archeology. **Qualif.:** Applicants must be juniors and senior undergraduate students who have not yet completed their first year of graduate school and currently enrolled at a college or university in United States or

Awards are arranged alphabetically below their administering organizations

Canada; must be at least 18 years old and have not previously participated in an archaeological excavation. **Criteria:** Applicants will be judged based on academic achievements and financial need.

Funds Avail.: $1,000. **To Apply:** Applicants must complete the online application form; must submit two copies of transcript; a brief cover letter (300 words or less) in the applicant's own words; an outline of anticipated expenses associated with participation on the project and a statement from the applicant indicating any other financial resources available to help cover expenses and two references for letters of recommendation from professors or academic advisors at the applicant's college or university. **Deadline:** March 1.

1612 ■ Helen M. Woodruff Fellowships *(Professional development/Fellowship)*

Purpose: To support pre- or post-doctoral fellowship for study of archaeology and classical studies. **Focus:** Archeology. **Qualif.:** Applicants must be citizens or permanent residents of the United States. **Criteria:** Selection will be based on the committee's criteria.

Funds Avail.: $10,000. **Duration:** Annual. **To Apply:** Interested applicants must contact the American Academy in Rome for the application process and other information. **Deadline:** November 1. **Contact:** Archaeological Institute of America, at the above address; or Email: fellowships@aia.bu.edu.

1613 ■ Architectural Precast Association (APA)
325 John Knox Rd., Ste. L103
Tallahassee, FL 32303
Ph: (850)205-5637
Fax: (850)222-3019
E-mail: info@archprecast.org
URL: www.archprecast.org
Facebook: www.facebook.com/APAMembers
Twitter: twitter.com/ArchPrecast?ref_src=twsrc%5Etfw

1614 ■ Tom Cory Memorial Scholarships *(Undergraduate/Scholarship)*

Purpose: To provide financial assistance for architecture students. **Focus:** Architecture. **Qualif.:** Applicants must have a cumulative GPA of 3.0 or higher; must have at least two semesters of school left to complete from date of award; must be involved in activities related to the architectural field. **Criteria:** Recipients are selected based on academic merit and committee's review of the application.

Funds Avail.: $2,000. **To Apply:** Applicants must send a completed application form; transcript of two years college through the last grading period to the date of application; letter of recommendation from a faculty member of the college; written description of the applicant's career plans after graduation; an essay explaining why the applicant have chosen the architectural field.

1615 ■ Arctic Institute of North America (AINA)
University of Calgary
2500 University Dr. NW
Calgary, AB, Canada T2N 1N4
Ph: (403)220-7515
Fax: (403)282-4609
E-mail: arctic@ucalgary.ca
URL: arctic.ucalgary.ca
Facebook: www.facebook.com/arcticinstituteofnorthamerica
Twitter: twitter.com/ArcticSynthesis

1616 ■ Lorraine Allison Scholarship *(Graduate/Scholarship)*

Purpose: To support academic excellence, a demonstrated commitment to northern research, and a desire for research results to be beneficial to northerners, especially Native northerners. **Focus:** Natural sciences; Social sciences. **Qualif.:** Applicants must be students enrolled at a Canadian university in a program of graduate study related to northern issues. **Criteria:** Candidates will be selected based on selection committee's review of the application materials.

Funds Avail.: 3,000 Canadian Dollars. **Duration:** Annual. **Number Awarded:** 1. **To Apply:** Applicant must provide a two-page description of the northern studies program and relevant project(s) being undertaken; must submit three letters of reference from the applicant's current or past professors; complete curriculum vitae with academic transcript and list of the current source and amounts of research funding, including scholarships, grants and bursaries. Materials should be submitted at above address. **Deadline:** January 15.

1617 ■ Jim Bourque Scholarship *(Undergraduate/Scholarship)*

Purpose: To provide support to Canadian Aboriginal student who intends to take, or is enrolled in, post-secondary training in education, environmental studies, traditional knowledge or telecommunications. **Focus:** Environmental technology; Telecommunications systems. **Qualif.:** Applicants must be Canadian students who are enrolled or intend to take, post-secondary education in environmental studies, traditional knowledge or telecommunications. **Criteria:** Scholarships are given based on financial need, relevance of study, achievements, return on investment and overall presentation of the application.

Funds Avail.: 1,000 Canadian Dollars. **Duration:** Annual. **Number Awarded:** 1. **To Apply:** Applicants must submit a description of their intended program of study and the reason for their choice of program (500 words); a copy of the recent high school or college/university transcript; letter of recommendation from a community leader; a statement of financial need; proof of enrollment to post-secondary institution; and must also provide a proof of Canadian Aboriginal descent. **Deadline:** July 15.

1618 ■ Arctic Physical Therapy Fairbanks
330 Old Steese Highway
Fairbanks, AK 99701
Ph: (907)374-3000
Fax: (907)374-3005
URL: www.physicaltherapyfairbanks.com

1619 ■ Arctic Physical Therapy Scholarship *(Undergraduate/Scholarship)*

Purpose: To support college and university students enrolled in college or university. **Focus:** General studies/Field of study not specified. **Qualif.:** Applicants must be attending college or university no later than January; attending college or university on a full-time or part-time basis by January; must have achieved a GPA of 3.0 or greater during their last academic year; must be attending a school in

Awards are arranged alphabetically below their administering organizations

the U.S. or Canada; must be U.S. or Canadian residents. **Criteria:** Selection will be based on the committee's criteria.

Funds Avail.: $500. **To Apply:** Applicants must apply online via website of the bestowing organization. They are also needed to answer the essay question provided by the bestowing organization. **Deadline:** August 31.

1620 ■ Arent Fox L.L.P.
1717 K St. NW
Washington, DC 20036
Ph: (202)857-6000
Fax: (202)857-6395
E-mail: matthew.clark@arentfox.com
URL: www.arentfox.com
LinkedIn: www.linkedin.com/company/arent-fox
Twitter: www.twitter.com/arentfox

1621 ■ Arent Fox Diversity Scholarships (Graduate, Juris Doctorate/Scholarship)

Purpose: To provide financial assistance to qualified individuals intending to pursue their law career. **Focus:** Law. **Qualif.:** Applicants must be in good standing at an ABA-accredited law school in the U.S. and have successfully completed their first year of a J.D. program. **Criteria:** Selection criteria are as follows: must be first-year law students; have excellent college and law school academic performance; have excellent oral and written communication skills; demonstrated leadership; authorized to work in U.S.; member of a diverse population that historically has been underrepresented in the legal profession; and, have a strong interest in joining the Firm as an associate after law school graduation

Funds Avail.: $15,000. **Duration:** Annual. **Number Awarded:** 3. **To Apply:** Applicants must submit the following: completed electronic application; personal statement; resume; undergraduate transcript; law school transcript; legal writing sample; contact information of three professional and academic references. **Deadline:** January 20.

1622 ■ Arizona Airports Association (AZAA)
107 S Southgate Dr.
Chandler, AZ 85226
Ph: (480)403-4618
Fax: (480)893-7775
E-mail: info@azairports.org
URL: www.azairports.org
Facebook: www.facebook.com/AzAirports
Twitter: twitter.com/AzAirports

1623 ■ Marty Rosness Student Scholarships (Undergraduate/Scholarship)

Purpose: To enhance careers in the aviation industry. **Focus:** Aviation. **Qualif.:** Applicants must be enrolled in a bachelor's or master's degree in an accredited aviation management programs in the state of Arizona. **Criteria:** Recipients are selected based on academic performance.

Funds Avail.: $1,250-$2,500. **Duration:** Annual. **Number Awarded:** 2. **To Apply:** Applicants must submit a completed application form; current copy of college academic transcript of records; resume; and must attach a sheet that includes a reference to the questions or sections from which the applicant is responding to. **Deadline:** March 16. **Contact:** Scholarship Committee Chair, Steve Johnston; Phone: 928-764-3330; E-mail: johnstons@lhcaz.gov.

1624 ■ Arizona Artist Blacksmith Association (AABA)
c/o Terry Porter, Secretary
2310 E Melrose St.
Gilbert, AZ 85297-1136
Ph: (602)509-1543
E-mail: president@azblacksmiths.org
URL: azblacksmiths.org

1625 ■ AABA Read Carlock Memorial Scholarship Fund (Other/Scholarship)

Purpose: To provide financial assistance to interested blacksmiths and/or immediate family members of AABA members for skills and abilities development. **Focus:** General studies/Field of study not specified. **Qualif.:** Applicants must be members of the Arizona Artist Blacksmith Association, as defined by Article 2 sections (a), (b, paragraphs I, II, III, and IV) of the AABA Bylaws, who have been members for at least one year prior to their application, or immediate family of those members. **Criteria:** Applicants are evaluated based on evidence of their strong desire for continued and serious investigation of the craft; quality of work as demonstrated by visual materials submitted with application; level of blacksmithing ability; record of professional activity and achievement; benefit to the Arizona Artist Blacksmith Association and demonstrated involvement with and commitment to AABA.

Funds Avail.: $1,000. **Duration:** Annual. **Number Awarded:** Varies. **To Apply:** Applicants must submit all the required application information.

1626 ■ Arizona Christian School Tuition Organization (ACSTO)
PO Box 6580
Chandler, AZ 85246
Ph: (480)820-0403
Fax: (480)820-2027
E-mail: social@acsto.org
URL: www.acsto.org

1627 ■ Original Tax Credit Scholarship (Undergraduate/Scholarship)

Purpose: To provide educational support to students who are in need. **Focus:** General studies/Field of study not specified. **Qualif.:** Applicants must be students planning to attend K-12 in a Christian private school. **Criteria:** Awards are given based on the submitted application.

Funds Avail.: No specific amount. **Duration:** Annual. **To Apply:** Applicants must complete the application form available online. **Remarks:** Established in 1998.

1628 ■ Overflow/PLUS Tax Credit Scholarships (Undergraduate/Scholarship)

Purpose: To give private schools additional help with their students' cost of tuition while still ensuring that the end result is budget positive for the state. **Focus:** Education. **Qualif.:** Applicants must meet one of these categories: Switchers - a student who switched from an Arizona public school to a private school in the previous school year after having attended the public school for at least 90 days (or one full semester) before switching (note: this does include charters); Kindergartners - automatically qualify once enrolled in Kindergarten (not pre-K); Pre-K w/a disability - a students with disabilities (and an IEP) enrolled in a preschool that offers services to students with disabilities; Military - students who are the dependents of a member of the U.S. Armed Forces who is stationed in Arizona pursuant to military orders; Corporate - a student who has already received a scholarship from the Corporate tax credit in a previous school year, and has continued in private school since and; Previous Overflow - students who have already received an Overflow/PLUS scholarship, and has continued in private school ever since, continue to qualify. In ordered to be considered, applicants must be enrolled in the school (or in the process), have completed scholarship application and submitted the required paperwork to verify qualification. **Criteria:** Selection will be based on the committees' criteria. **Funds Avail.:** No specific amount. **Duration:** Annual. **To Apply:** Switchers applicants need to complete a Public School Attendance Verification Form; Pre-K applicants with disabilities must submit a copy of the applicants' IEP; military families must submit a copy of their military orders indicating the Arizona station; Corporate applicants must complete an Corporate Scholarship Verification form or an award letter; and Overflow/PLUS applicants must submit a Overflow/PLUS Scholarship Verification form or a copy of their scholarship award letter from the STO that made the award. Kindergarten applicants do not need any additional documentation, they just have to be enrolled.

1629 ■ Arizona City/County Management Association (ACMA)
1820 W Washington St.
Phoenix, AZ 85007
Ph: (602)258-5786
Fax: (602)253-3874
E-mail: info@azmanagement.org
URL: www.azmanagement.org

1630 ■ Marvin A. Andrews Scholarships/Internships (Graduate/Internship, Scholarship)

Purpose: To financially assist Arizona graduate students in public administration who aspire to a career in local government management. **Focus:** Public administration. **Qualif.:** Applicants must be full-time students attending either Arizona State University, Northern Arizona University or the University of Arizona who have exhibited strong academic achievement. **Criteria:** Recipients are selected based on interest in local government administration, career plans, academic achievement, school and/or community honors and activities and financial need. **Funds Avail.:** $2,000. **To Apply:** Applicants must submit: completed application form; resume; two letters of recommendation; an official graduate-level transcript; a letter addressed to Robert Flatley, ACMA President addressing their interest in local government management, career goals and financial need or plans for using the scholarship. **Deadline:** December 1. **Contact:** Amy Price at aprice@azleague.org; Phone: 602-258-5786.

1631 ■ Charles A. Esser Memorial Scholarships (Graduate/Scholarship)

Purpose: To honor and financially assist Arizona graduate students in public administration who aspire to a career in local government management. **Focus:** Public administration. **Qualif.:** Applicants must be part-time MPA students attending either Arizona State University, Northern Arizona University or the University of Arizona who are currently working in local government; and with a 3.0 minimum GPA in previous college coursework (recommended – strong academic achievement). **Criteria:** Recipients are selected based on interest in local government administration, career plans, academic achievement, school and/or community honors and activities and financial need. **Funds Avail.:** $2,000. **Duration:** Annual. **To Apply:** Applicants must submit the following: completed application form; resume; two letters of recommendation; an official graduate-level transcript; a letter addressed to Robert Flatley, ACMA President addressing their interest in local government management, career goals and financial needs or plans for using the scholarship. **Deadline:** December 1. **Contact:** Amy Price at aprice@azleague.org; Phone: 602-258-5786.

1632 ■ Arizona Cowpuncher's Scholarship Organization (ACSO)
c/o Valerie Owen, President
12373 W Bajada Rd.
Peoria, AZ 85383-2590
E-mail: info@allaboutacso.com
URL: www.allaboutacso.com

1633 ■ ACSO Scholarships (Undergraduate/Scholarship)

Purpose: To provide funds for education programs beyond high school for young people of the Arizona ranching community. **Focus:** General studies/Field of study not specified. **Qualif.:** Applicants must be: U.S. citizens, and Arizona residents; high school graduates or continuing education students attending an accredited college or trade school; taking a minimum of 12 credit hours per semester equivalent and involved as owners or employees of ranches. **Criteria:** Selection shall be based on the aforementioned applicants' qualifications and compliance with the application details. **Funds Avail.:** No specific amount. **Duration:** Annual. **To Apply:** Applicants must submit the completed scholarship application form in an envelope together with an official birth certificate; two letters of recommendation from persons other than family members; and a letter of intent (which includes a summary of educational attainment, achievements and activities, personal goals, dollar amount for school related expenses, as well as other scholarships applied for and/or granted); and the name of the educational facility that the applicant is planning to attend including the mailing address of the financial aid or registrar office, the email address and contact numbers. **Deadline:** February 10. **Contact:** E-mail: info@allaboutacso.com; Snail Mail: The Arizona Cowpuncher's Scholarship Org., Inc., at the above address.

1634 ■ Arizona Hydrological Society (AHS)
PO Box 80652
Tucson, AZ 85728
Free: 866-931-3134
E-mail: info@azhydrosoc.org
URL: azhydrosoc.org
Facebook: www.facebook.com/azhydrosoc
LinkedIn: www.linkedin.com/company/arizona-hydrological-society

Awards are arranged alphabetically below their administering organizations

1635 ■ Arizona Hydrological Society Scholarships
(Graduate, Undergraduate/Scholarship)

Purpose: To encourage full-time students to excel in the field of hydrology, hydrogeology or any water-resource related fields. **Focus:** Hydrology. **Qualif.:** Applicants must be junior, senior or graduate students at any university or college in Arizona. **Criteria:** Recipients will be select based on GPA; strength of recommendation letter; application letter describing the interest and goals in hydrology and water resources; and degree of need.

Funds Avail.: $2,000. **Number Awarded:** 3. **To Apply:** Applicants must submit an application form; official transcripts; and at least one letter of recommendation. **Deadline:** April 30. **Contact:** For further information, applicants must contact Erin Young 1055 Hano Trail, Flagstaff, AZ 86001; Phone: 928-606-8422; E-mail: eyoung@flusol.com.

1636 ■ Arizona Nursery Association (ANA)
1430 W Broadway, Ste. 110
Tempe, AZ 85282
Ph: (480)966-1610
Fax: (480)966-0923
E-mail: info@azna.org
URL: azna.org
Facebook: www.facebook.com/Arizona-Nursery-Association-209851672369172/?fref=nf

1637 ■ Arizona Nursery Association Scholarships
(Undergraduate/Scholarship)

Purpose: To financially assist students in horticultural related curriculum. **Focus:** Horticulture. **Qualif.:** Applicants must be residents of Arizona currently or planning to be enrolled in a horticultural-related curriculum at a university, community college or continuing education program; must be currently employed in or have an interest in the nursery industry as a career; must have above-average scholastic achievement or at least two years work experience in the industry; must display involvement in extracurricular activities related to industry. **Criteria:** Recipients are selected based on academic performance.

Funds Avail.: $500-$3,000. **Duration:** Annual. **To Apply:** Applicants must complete the online application form. **Deadline:** April 15. **Contact:** Arizona Nursery Association at scholarship@azna.org.

1638 ■ Arizona Nurses Association (AzNA)
1850 E Southern Ave., Ste. 1
Tempe, AZ 85282
Ph: (480)831-0404
Fax: (480)839-4780
URL: aznurse.org
Facebook: www.facebook.com/arizonanursesassociation
Twitter: twitter.com/ArizonaNurses

1639 ■ Arizona Nurses Foundation Scholarships
(Doctorate, Graduate, Undergraduate/Scholarship)

Purpose: To enhance the development of Arizona nurses and further the nursing profession in Arizona. **Focus:** Nursing. **Qualif.:** Applicants must be undergraduate and graduate students enrolled in or accepted in an academic education program; must be enrolled part-time or full-time. **Criteria:** Recipients are selected based on potential for leadership in nursing; merit; commitment to professional nursing in Arizona; expressed need for financial assistance; and interest in teaching nursing in Arizona.

Funds Avail.: A.D.N. applicants: $500; BSN, RN-BSN, Masters: $1,000; doctoral applicants: $2,500. **Duration:** Annual. **To Apply:** Applicants must submit: completed application form; evidence of admission such as official or unofficial transcript of records; current courses schedule; copy of letter or certificate of admission or a written statement from an appropriate academic official; a brief statement describing the professional's activities; community service and other activities in the last three years that demonstrate the potential for leadership; a statement describing the need for financial assistance; one confidential reference form from an immediate supervisor, student's academic advisor or another faculty member. **Deadline:** March 1; October 1. **Contact:** Arizona Nurses Foundation, 1850 E Southern Ave., Ste. 1, Tempe, AZ, 85282, Phone: 480-831-0404, Email: wendy@aznurse.org.

1640 ■ Arizona Society of Certified Public Accountants (ASCPA)
4801 E Washington St., Ste. 225-B
Phoenix, AZ 85034
Ph: (602)252-4144
Fax: (602)252-1511
Free: 888-237-0700
URL: www.ascpa.com

1641 ■ ASCPA High School Scholarships
(Undergraduate/Scholarship, Monetary)

Purpose: To support students pursuing an accounting degree. **Focus:** Accounting. **Qualif.:** Applicants must be high school seniors enrolling in an Arizona university/community college as fulltime students majoring in accounting, and be legal U.S. residents and current residents of Arizona. **Criteria:** Selection is based on academic achievement (as documented through GPA, class ranking and standardized test scores) and community involvement and leadership potential (as demonstrated by the student's personal statement and letters of recommendation).

Funds Avail.: $500. **Number Awarded:** Up to 3. **To Apply:** Applicants must submit a completed application form along with a certified high school transcript (contains student's class rank, GPA and test scores); a personal statement on community involvement, career goals and desire to contribute to the community (maximum of 2 pages); and a one-page letter of recommendation from a teacher or a school official. **Deadline:** February 5. **Contact:** Sandra McKitrick; Phone: (602) 253-9631; Email: smckitrick@ascpa.com.

1642 ■ Future CPA Scholarships *(Undergraduate/Scholarship)*

Purpose: To support students pursuing an accounting degree. **Focus:** Accounting. **Qualif.:** Applicants must: be accounting major; be legal U.S. and Arizona residents; be full-time students (12 or more credits per semester or 24 credits per year); have earned at least 12 college/university credits at the time of application; have completed at least one accounting course at a college/university; and have a GPA of 3.0 or better. **Criteria:** Selection is based on academic achievement (as documented through GPA and success in accounting or accounting-related courses), likelihood of becoming a CPA and remaining in Arizona, and community involvement and leadership potential (as demonstrated by the student's personal statement and letter of recommendation).

Awards are arranged alphabetically below their administering organizations

Funds Avail.: No specific amount. **To Apply:** Applicants must submit a completed application form along with the college/university transcripts for all schools attended; resume (includes work experience and information such as extra-curricular activities, public service activities, awards and honors); a one-page essay on future career interests and professional goals (include 2-year and 5-year goals); and letter of recommendation from an instructor or employer. **Contact:** Arizona Society of Certified Public Accountants, at the above address.

1643 ■ Sam Gallant Memorial Scholarships *(Graduate, Undergraduate/Scholarship)*

Purpose: To support students pursuing an accounting degree. **Focus:** Accounting. **Qualif.:** Applicant must be an accounting major; have a 3.5 minimum GPA; be studying in an Arizona State University Main; an African American; and a legal U.S. resident. **Criteria:** Selection is based on the submitted application materials.

Funds Avail.: $1,000. **Number Awarded:** 1. **To Apply:** Applicants must complete a detailed scholarship application form together with a statement of career goals and a formal resume. Students may contact Arizona State University Main Campus for more information on the scholarship.

1644 ■ University Senior and Master's Program Scholarships *(Graduate/Scholarship)*

Purpose: To support students pursuing an accounting degree. **Focus:** Accounting. **Qualif.:** Applicants must: be accounting major who will begin their senior year or master's program; have a 3.5 minimum GPA; be studying in an Arizona public university (Arizona State University Main, University of Arizona and Northern Arizona University); and legal U.S. residents. **Criteria:** Selection is based on the submitted application materials.

Funds Avail.: $2,000. **Number Awarded:** 3. **To Apply:** Applicants must complete a detailed scholarship application form together with a statement of career goals and a formal resume. Students may contact the individual university for applications and to learn more about the process. **Contact:** Arizona Society of Certified Public Accountants, at the above address.

1645 ■ Arkansas Association of Family and Consumer Sciences (ARAFCS)
Little Rock, AR
E-mail: ArkAfcs@gmail.com
URL: arkafcs.weebly.com

1646 ■ ARAFCS Doctoral Scholarships *(Doctorate/Scholarship)*

Purpose: To encourage family and consumer sciences professionals by providing financial assistance for graduate education. **Focus:** General studies/Field of study not specified. **Qualif.:** Applicant must be a legal resident of Arkansas; must be a family and consumer sciences major at an Arkansas university; must have been admitted to a graduate program; must have at least 3.0 cumulative GPA and maintain a 3.0 GPA on a scale of 4.0 in graduate school; must have demonstrated qualities of leadership in AAFCS; must be a current member of AAFCS; must have been a member of the American and Arkansas Association of Family and Consumer Sciences for at least two of the last three years. **Criteria:** Applicants will be selected by the scholarship committee, chaired by the AAFCS Scholarship Chairperson, who will review applications and recommend the recipient to the AAFCS Board.

Funds Avail.: No specific amount.

1647 ■ ARAFCS Masters Scholarships *(Graduate/Scholarship)*

Purpose: To encourage family and consumer sciences professionals by providing financial assistance for graduate education. **Focus:** General studies/Field of study not specified. **Qualif.:** Applicant must be a legal resident of Arkansas; must be a family and consumer sciences major at an Arkansas university; must have been admitted to a graduate program; must have at least 3.0 cumulative GPA and maintain a 3.0 GPA on a scale of 4.0 in graduate school; must have demonstrated qualities of leadership in AAFCS; must be a current member of AAFCS; must have been a member of the American and Arkansas Association of Family and Consumer Sciences for at least two of the last three years. **Criteria:** Applicants will be selected by the scholarship committee, chaired by the AAFCS Scholarship Chairperson, who will review applications and recommend the recipient to the AAFCS Board.

Funds Avail.: No specific amount. **Duration:** Annual. **To Apply:** Applicants must complete the application form available on the website; must submit an official transcript of record. **Deadline:** January 31. **Contact:** Arkansas Association of Family and Consumer Sciences at the above address.

1648 ■ Arkansas Environmental Federation (AEF)
1400 W Markham St., Ste. 302
Little Rock, AR 72201
Ph: (501)374-0263
Fax: (501)374-8752
URL: netforum.avectra.com/eWeb/StartPage
  .aspx?Site=AEF

1649 ■ Randall Matthis for Environmental Studies Scholarships *(Graduate, Undergraduate/Scholarship)*

Purpose: To provide financial assistance for selected students from Arkansas universities. **Focus:** Environmental science; Health education; Natural resources. **Qualif.:** Applicants must be U.S. citizens residing in Arkansas and must be undergraduates or graduate students with at least 2.8 cumulative GPA based on 4.0 system. **Criteria:** Applicants are evaluated based on academic achievement and financial need.

Funds Avail.: $2,500. **Duration:** Annual. **Number Awarded:** 1. **To Apply:** Applicants must submit a completed application form; transcript of records; letter of nomination from a faculty member; and two additional letters of recommendation that address candidate's scholastic and personal attributes. **Deadline:** April 8.

1650 ■ Arkansas Green Industry Association (AGIA)
9 Shackleford Plz., Ste. 1
Little Rock, AR 72221-1715
Ph: (501)225-0029
Fax: (501)224-0988
E-mail: office@argia.org
URL: www.argia.org
Facebook: www.facebook.com/pages/Arkansas-Green
  -Industry-Association/105497262821260

Awards are arranged alphabetically below their administering organizations

Twitter: twitter.com/ArkansasAGIA

1651 ■ Arkansas Green Industry Association Professional Grants *(Professional development, Undergraduate/Grant)*

Purpose: To encourage young or new business owners and students to become involved in the AGIA by encouraging participation in AGIA events. **Focus:** Business; Horticulture. **Qualif.:** Applicants must be young or business owners for less than 3 years, or students or recent graduates in horticulture. **Criteria:** Selection will be based on the committees' criteria.

Funds Avail.: No specific amount. **Duration:** Periodic. **To Apply:** Applicants may contact the Association for application process and other information.

1652 ■ Arkansas Green Industry Association Student Scholarships *(Undergraduate/Scholarship)*

Purpose: To provide financial assistance to Arkansas students pursuing study in botany and related field. **Focus:** Botany. **Qualif.:** Applicants must be Arkansas residents; must have exhibited an interest in pursuing a career in nursery management, greenhouse management, garden center management, landscape contracting or other green industry related areas; should have a grade point average of 2.5 or GED equivalent. **Criteria:** Selection will be based on the committee's criteria.

Funds Avail.: No specific amount. **Duration:** Annual. **To Apply:** Applicants must submit the following requirements: an accomplished application form; a statement describing their educational interest; commitment/interest in the nursery and landscape industry; career plans. **Deadline:** April 1.

1653 ■ Arkansas Library Association (ArLA)
PO Box 958
Benton, AR 72018-0958
Ph: (501)860-7585
Fax: (501)778-4014
E-mail: arlib2@sbcglobal.net
URL: www.arlib.org

1654 ■ ArLA Scholarships *(Graduate/Scholarship)*

Purpose: To encourage a higher standard of professional training in Arkansas libraries. **Focus:** Library and archival sciences. **Qualif.:** Applicants must: be legal residents of the State of Arkansas who hold or are completing work toward a bachelor's degree from an accredited college or university; and, have been accepted at an American Library Association accredited program leading to a master's degree in library science or to an NCATE accredited program leading to a master's degree in library media (the course of study should be completed within three academic years after receipt of the award). **Criteria:** Selection shall be based on applicants' interest in librarianship as a profession, academic record and references.

Funds Avail.: $1,500 each. **Duration:** Annual. **Number Awarded:** 2. **To Apply:** Applicants must submit a completed application form together with an official graduate transcript or proof of enrollment; letter of application; resume; and three letters of reference from individuals qualified to address the academic and professional potential of the applicant. **Remarks:** The scholarships are classified into two: the Arkansas Library Association Annual Scholarship, and the Arkansas Library Association School Library Media Specialist (SLMS) Scholarship. Both are awarded at the annual conference. **Contact:** Lynda Hampel, Executive Administrator, Arkansas Library Association, at the above address.

1655 ■ Arkansas Nurses Association (ARNA)
1123 S University, Ste. 1015
Little Rock, AR 72204
Ph: (501)244-2363
Fax: (501)244-9903
E-mail: arna@arna.org
URL: www.arna.org

1656 ■ Arkansas Nursing Foundation - Dorothea Fund Scholarships *(Other/Scholarship)*

Purpose: To provide financial assistance to nurses throughout the state of Arkansas. **Focus:** Nursing. **Qualif.:** Applicants must be registered nurses who can give a statement of commitment to community health nursing, seeking a degree into result in an advanced practice nurse, and demonstrate a need. **Criteria:** Selection will be based on the committee's criteria.

Funds Avail.: No specific amount. **Duration:** Annual. **To Apply:** Applicants must complete the application packet and must include the following: completed application form; cover letter stating desire for the scholarship and intended use of funds (including a statement regarding other financial assistance); statement regarding institutional financial assistance toward the planned degree (tuition waivers or reductions); current resume (one page including education, work experience, achievements and honors, if applicable); two letters of recommendation (with one being from current supervisor or faculty) including information concerning leadership and academic ability of the applicant; official undergraduate and graduate transcript(s) from all nursing programs attended (in sealed envelope with Registrar's signature or stamp on flap); letter of acceptance into degree program accredited by NLNAC or CCNE; and extracurricular activities (achievements, organization memberships, volunteer work). **Deadline:** June 1.

1657 ■ Arkansas Nursing Foundation - Mary Gray Scholarships *(Other/Scholarship)*

Purpose: To provide financial assistance to nurses throughout the state of Arkansas. **Focus:** Nursing. **Qualif.:** Applicants must be registered nurses seeking an advanced degree in nursing, interested and/or involvement in advanced practice nursing (Advance Nurse Practitioner, Clinical Nurse Specialist, Certified Nurse Midwife, and Certified Nurse Anesthetist). **Criteria:** Selection will be based on the committee's criteria.

Funds Avail.: No specific amount. **Duration:** Annual. **To Apply:** Applicants must complete the application packet and must include the following: completed application form; cover letter stating desire for the scholarship and intended use of funds (including a statement regarding other financial assistance); statement regarding institutional financial assistance toward the planned degree (tuition waivers or reductions); current resume (one page including education, work experience, achievements, and honors, if applicable); two letters of recommendation (with one being from current supervisor or faculty) including information concerning leadership and academic ability of the applicant; official undergraduate and graduate transcript(s) from all nursing programs attended (in sealed envelope with Registrar's signature or stamp on flap); letter of acceptance into degree

Awards are arranged alphabetically below their administering organizations

program accredited by NLNAC or CCNE; and extracurricular activities (achievements, organization memberships, volunteer work). **Deadline:** June 1.

1658 ■ Arkansas Public Health Association (APHA)
PO Box 250327
Little Rock, AR 72225
E-mail: ar_apha@yahoo.com
URL: www.arkpublichealth.org

1659 ■ Arkansas Public Health Association Scholarships (Undergraduate/Scholarship)

Purpose: To provide financial support to Arkansas students. **Focus:** Public health. **Qualif.:** Applicants must: be Arkansas residents; be enrolled, or have planned to enroll in the field of public health; be currently classified as sophomores in college, university or approved Vo-Tech; have at least 2.5 GPA; and, demonstrate financial need. **Criteria:** Applicants will be judged based on the following criteria: (a) GPA; (b) Goals in public health; (c) Honors, organizations, volunteering with health-related organizations; (d) Letter from major professor; (e) Personal reference letter; (f) Present or past public health experience; (f) Full-time student; (g) Part-time student; (h) Financial need. **Funds Avail.:** $1,000. **Duration:** Annual. **To Apply:** Application forms are available online. Applicants must submit official college, university, or Vo-Tech transcripts; must have a letter of recommendation from major professor; must have a letter of personal reference; must have a statement/explanation of financial need; must have an explanation in 150 words or less concerning their goals and plans with the scholarship, their past and present public health experiences. **Deadline:** March 16. **Contact:** Arkansas Public Health Association at the above address.

1660 ■ Arkansas Single Parent Scholarship Fund (ASPSF)
614 E Emma Ave., Ste. 119
Springdale, AR 72764
Ph: (479)927-1402
Fax: (479)927-0755
URL: www.aspsf.org
Facebook: www.facebook.com/aspsf

1661 ■ Arkansas Single Parent Scholarships (Undergraduate, Graduate/Scholarship)

Purpose: To provide supplemental financial assistance to those single parents living in Arkansas who are pursuing a course of instruction that will improve their income-earning potential. **Focus:** General studies/Field of study not specified. **Qualif.:** Eligible applicants are the following: single parents living in Arkansas who are considered economically disadvantaged and who have custodial care of one or more children under the age of eighteen; and, those who have not previously earned a diploma or degree from a four-year institution of higher learning. **Criteria:** Selection shall be based on the aforementioned applicants' qualifications and compliance with the application details. **Funds Avail.:** Amount varies. **Duration:** Annual. **To Apply:** Applicants are encouraged to contact the Single Parent Scholarship Fund in their county (check website for counties with Single Parent Scholarship Fund). **Remarks:** Established in 1990.

1662 ■ Arkansas State University (ASU)
1600 S College St.
Mountain Home, AR 72653
Ph: (870)508-6100
URL: www.asumh.edu

1663 ■ Arkansas State University Mountain Home Scholarships (Undergraduate/Scholarship)

Purpose: To provide financial support to the students enrolled in ASUMH. **Focus:** General studies/Field of study not specified. **Qualif.:** Applicants must be enrolled at Arkansas State University Mountain Home; must be residents of Arkansas; must have a GPA average of 2.5-3.0; must have a minimum of 12 completed credit hours at ASUMH. **Criteria:** Selection of candidates will be based on the submitted application materials and academic criteria. **Funds Avail.:** $500, with $2,500 being awarded each semester. **To Apply:** Applicants must submit complete application form available online. **Deadline:** April 1.

1664 ■ Fondation J. Armand Bombardier
1155 Rue Metcalfe, Ste. 2100
Montreal, QC, Canada H3B 2V6
E-mail: fondation@fjab.qc.ca
URL: www.fondationbombardier.ca

1665 ■ Yvonne L. Bombardier Visual Arts Scholarships (Master's, Doctorate/Scholarship)

Purpose: To support the Quebec's next generation of artists. **Focus:** Drawing; Painting; Photography; Sculpture. **Qualif.:** Applicants must be Canadian citizens or have the status of permanent residents; must be students enrolled in a Master's or PhD art program in a Quebec university, who practice one or more of the following disciplines: drawing; engraving/stamping; painting; photography; sculpture. **Criteria:** Selection will be based on the committee's criteria. **Funds Avail.:** $15,000 to be paid over two years. **Duration:** Annual. **To Apply:** Applicants must submit a completed application form; a presentation letter describing the students' artistic and creative approach as well as their future projects and the developments of their approach (maximum 1,000 words); two letters of recommendation signed by a professor, a teacher, or a lecturer; a portfolio consisting of a DVD (maximum 5 minutes) or a CD (maximum 15 images) presenting original works produces by students over the last two year; a curriculum vitae (maximum 3 pages); an academic file containing all statement of grades for the current program of studies. If students are in the first year of their program, statement of grades for the last year in the previous program of studies must be submitted. **Deadline:** November 13.

1666 ■ Armed Forces Communications and Electronics Association San Diego Chapter
PO Box 80666
San Diego, CA 92138-0666
URL: sandiego.afceachapters.org

1667 ■ AFCEA San Diego Buck Bragunier Leadership Scholarship (Undergraduate/Scholarship)

Purpose: To provide scholarship for the students of San Diego military community. **Focus:** Computer and information sciences; Engineering; Mathematics and mathematical

Awards are arranged alphabetically below their administering organizations

sciences; Natural sciences; Science. **Qualif.:** Applicants must be: U.S. citizens and San Diego, California residents; and, high school seniors who are going to enroll and attend at any accredited four year college or university majoring in science, mathematics engineering, computer science or natural sciences. **Criteria:** Primary consideration will be based records of leadership and volunteering activities within the applicants' high school, church, community which are the focuses of the program.

Funds Avail.: $2,000. **Duration:** Annual. **To Apply:** Applicants may visit the website to download an application and other information. **Contact:** Mohan Krishnan at 619-299-2288.

1668 ■ Armenian Bar Association
c/o Lisa Boyadjian, Administrative Assistant
PO Box 29111
Los Angeles, CA 90029
Ph: (626)584-0043
URL: www.armenianbar.com

1669 ■ Armenian Bar Association Graduate Scholarships in Law *(Graduate/Scholarship)*

Purpose: To provide support students of Armenian descent attending, or accepted for admission to, an approved law school in the United States, Armenia or elsewhere. **Focus:** Law. **Qualif.:** Applicants must be enrolled in or admitted to, if in the United States, an American Bar Association-accredited or state-accredited law school, or if in Armenia or another country, a law school approved by the Armenia Bar Association; have a strong academic potential as demonstrated by academic performance. **Criteria:** Selection will be based on the committee's criteria.

Funds Avail.: No specific amount. **Duration:** Annual. **To Apply:** Applicants must submit a completed application package. Application package must include the following: completed application form; personal essay; two letters of recommendation (from professors, school administrators, Armenian community leaders or others in official capacities who have knowledge of the applicant's academic performance and potential and/or commitment to the Armenian community); official grade transcripts from undergraduate college and law school; and proof of entrance or acceptance into, or continuation in, an approved law school. **Deadline:** March 31.

1670 ■ Armenian Educational Foundation (AEF)
600 W Broadway, Ste. 130
Glendale, CA 91204
Ph: (818)242-4154
Fax: (818)242-4913
E-mail: aef@aefweb.org
URL: www.aefweb.org
Facebook: www.facebook.com/ArmenianEducationalFoundation

1671 ■ Richard R. Tufenkian Memorial Scholarships *(Undergraduate/Scholarship)*

Purpose: To provide financial support to qualified students of Armenian parentage. **Focus:** General studies/Field of study not specified. **Qualif.:** Applicants should have Armenian origin; have a 3.0 GPA; and be undergraduate students. **Criteria:** Awards are given based on academic merit; financial need.

Funds Avail.: $2,500. **Duration:** Annual. **Number Awarded:** 5. **To Apply:** Applicants must submit an application form; proof of acceptance to the university or college; first two pages of the most recent income tax returns; sealed official transcript; a letter of reference from university or college and from Armenian community service; an essay; and proof of parent's Armenian origin. **Deadline:** July 31. **Remarks:** Do not use mail which requires a signature upon delivery. **Contact:** For further information, applicants may e-mail: aef@aefweb.org.

1672 ■ Armenian General Benevolent Union (AGBU)
55 E 59th St.
New York, NY 10022-1112
Ph: (212)319-6383
E-mail: agbuny@agbu.org
URL: agbu.org
Facebook: www.facebook.com/agbu.org
Twitter: twitter.com/agbu

1673 ■ AGBU Heritage Scholar Grant *(Undergraduate/Scholarship, Grant)*

Purpose: To support the higher education of students graduated from AGBU high schools. **Focus:** General studies/Field of study not specified. **Qualif.:** Applicants must be college-bound high school seniors graduating from each of the three AGBU high schools in the United States with a GPA of 3.5 (out of 4.0) and above at any of the following: AGBU Manoogian-Demirdjian School in Canoga Park, CA; AGBU Alex and Marie Manoogian School in Southfield, MI; AGBU Vatche & Tamar Manoukian High School in Pasadena, CA. They must be admitted to a selective university and must be nominated for the grant by the principal and faculty of their respective high school. **Criteria:** Selection will be based on the aforesaid qualifications.

Funds Avail.: $2,000 each. **Duration:** Annual. **Number Awarded:** 2. **To Apply:** Application may contact AGBU for more information about application. **Deadline:** April 15. **Remarks:** Aside from the scholarship, there are other various awards that are being bestowed by AGBU.

1674 ■ Armenian Professional Society (APS)
117 S Louise St.
Glendale, CA 91205
Ph: (818)685-9946
E-mail: apsla@apsla.org
URL: www.apsla.org

1675 ■ Armenian Professional Society Graduate Student Scholarships *(Graduate/Scholarship)*

Purpose: To provide scholarships to Graduate students of Armenian decent who are or will be attending a university in the United States. **Focus:** General studies/Field of study not specified. **Qualif.:** Applicants must be students who have been accepted or enrolled in a graduate school in the United States. **Criteria:** Selection will be based on financial need, scholastic achievements, faculty recommendations and involvement in the Armenian Community.

Funds Avail.: No specific amount. **Duration:** Annual. **To Apply:** Applicants must submit print out of the scholarship application form (in portrait format, neatly typed) along with the official transcripts for the past four years; brief one-page essay about themselves, their involvement in the

Awards are arranged alphabetically below their administering organizations

Armenian community and why they should be scholarship recipients; copies of applicant's and parent's most recent IRS Tax Returns or equivalent financial information; and the obtained two college or university recommendations. **Deadline:** July 15.

1676 ■ Armenian Relief Society - Eastern United States

80 Bigelow Ave., Ste. 200
Watertown, MA 02472
Ph: (617)926-3801
Fax: (617)924-7238
E-mail: arseastus@gmail.com
URL: www.arseastusa.org

1677 ■ ARS Undergraduate Scholarships *(Undergraduate/Scholarship)*

Purpose: To encourage educational pursuits among undergraduate students of Armenian descent. **Focus:** General studies/Field of study not specified. **Qualif.:** Applicants must be of Armenian descent who are undergraduate students completed at least one semester at an accredited four-year college or university in the United States or must be enrolled in a two-year college and are transferring to a four-year college or university as full-time students in the Fall. **Criteria:** Grants are made on the basis of financial need, merit and involvement in the Armenian community.

Funds Avail.: No specific amount. **Duration:** Annual. **To Apply:** Application must include financial aid forms, recent official transcript, two letters of recommendation and tuition costs. **Deadline:** April 1. **Contact:** Scholarship Committee, Armenian Relief Society of Eastern USA, Inc., 80 Bigelow Avenue, Suite 200, Watertown, MA 02472.

1678 ■ Lazarian Graduate Scholarships *(Graduate/Scholarship)*

Purpose: To encourage educational pursuits among graduate students of Armenian descent. **Focus:** Business administration; Economics; History; International affairs and relations; Journalism; Law; Medicine; Political science; Public service. **Qualif.:** Applicants must be of Armenian descent pursuing their studies at the graduate level (Master's Degree or Doctorate) in the fields of law, history, political science, international relations, journalism, government, economics, business administration, medicine and public service. **Criteria:** Grants are made on the basis of financial need, merit and involvement in the Armenian community.

Funds Avail.: No specific amount. **Duration:** Annual. **To Apply:** Application package must include official transcript of college grades with raised seal, tuition costs, most recent Income Tax Return, three letters of recommendation and proof of acceptance into a graduate program. Application forms and instructions are available on the website. **Deadline:** April 1. **Contact:** Lazarian Scholarship Committee, Armenian Relief Society of Eastern USA, Inc., 80 Bigelow Avenue, Suite 200, Watertown, MA 02472.

1679 ■ Armenian Relief Society of Eastern U.S.A. (ARSER)

80 Bigelow Ave., Ste. 200
Watertown, MA 02472
Ph: (617)926-3801
Fax: (617)924-7238
E-mail: arseastus@gmail.com
URL: www.arseastusa.org
Facebook: www.facebook.com/ARSEasternUSA

1680 ■ ARS of Eastern USA Lazarian Graduate Scholarship *(Master's, Doctorate/Scholarship)*

Purpose: To support students who are in need of financial assistance in pursuing a graduate degree. **Focus:** Business; Economics; Government; History; International affairs and relations; Law; Medicine; Political science; Public service. **Qualif.:** Applicants must be of Armenian descent; must have graduated from an accredited four year college or university in the U.S.; must be in need of financial assistance; must be pursuing their studies at the gradate level in the field of law, history, political science, international relations, journalism, government, economics, business administration, medicine public service or a similar field. **Criteria:** Scholarships are awarded on the basis of financial need, academic merit, and involvement in the Armenian community.

Funds Avail.: No specific amount. **To Apply:** The following information must be sent with a completed application: official transcript of undergraduate, as well as graduate, college grades, including raised seal of the college or university and grades from the first semester of the current year; tuition costs for the current academic year; most recent Income Tax Return (form 1040). If an Income Tax Return has not been filed, a copy of FAFSA, SAR or the parents' Income Tax Return must be submitted; three letters of recommendation. One letter should be from a member of the Armenian Community, one from a member of academic community and third letter must be from a person of the applicants' choice; proof of enrollment in a graduate program or proof of acceptance into a graduate program. **Deadline:** April 1.

1681 ■ Armenian Students' Association of America Inc. (ASA)

333 Atlantic Ave.
Warwick, RI 02888
Ph: (401)461-6114
E-mail: asa@asainc.org
URL: www.asainc.org/index.php

1682 ■ Armenian American Citizen's League Scholarships *(Undergraduate/Scholarship)*

Purpose: To provide financial assistance to those students who are in need. **Focus:** General studies/Field of study not specified. **Qualif.:** Applicants must be permanent residents of the United States who have been living in California for at least two years and are enrolled full-time in an accredited college or university; must have a minimum GPA of 3.0 (B average). **Criteria:** Awards will be based on financial need, academic achievement and involvement in school and community services.

Funds Avail.: $1,000-$2,000. **Duration:** Annual. **To Apply:** Applicants may visit the website for the application process and other required materials. **Deadline:** March 1.

1683 ■ Armenian American Medical Association Scholarships *(Undergraduate/Scholarship)*

Purpose: To provide financial assistance to those students who are in need. **Focus:** Medicine. **Qualif.:** Applicants must be students enrolled in a U.S. medical school. Award is primarily intended for students residing and studying in a

Awards are arranged alphabetically below their administering organizations

private New England medical school. **Criteria:** Awards granted on the basis of need, merit and involvement in Armenian cultural affairs.

Funds Avail.: $1,000-$2,000. **Number Awarded:** 2-3. **To Apply:** Applicants must check the available website for the required materials. **Deadline:** October 20. **Contact:** For more information, please contact Dr. Edward Karian, Chairperson; 324 Common St. Watertown, MA 02472-4940.

1684 ■ Armenian American Pharmacists' Association Scholarships (Graduate/Scholarship)

Purpose: To provide financial support to those students who are pursuing pharmacy. **Focus:** Pharmacy. **Qualif.:** Applicants must be students of Armenian descent, pursuing a baccalaureate of pharmacy, doctor of pharmacy, or graduate degree program at a College of Pharmacy in the commonwealth of Massachusetts, Connecticut or Rhode Island. **Criteria:** Awards will be based on academic excellence and financial need.

Funds Avail.: No specific amount. **To Apply:** Applicants may contact the Association for the application process and other required materials. **Deadline:** September 15. **Contact:** Susan A. Krikorian, Chairman of Scholarship Committee, Department of Pharmacy Practice, 179 Longwood Ave., Boston, MA 02115.

1685 ■ Armenian General Athletic Union Scholarships (Undergraduate/Scholarship)

Purpose: To provide financial assistance to those students who are in need. **Focus:** General studies/Field of study not specified. **Qualif.:** Applicants must be high school students entering college; must be permanent U.S residents. **Criteria:** Awards will be based on academic merit and financial need.

Funds Avail.: $1,000. **To Apply:** Applicants must check the available website for the required materials. **Deadline:** May 15. **Contact:** Mrs. Ann Ajemian at 211 Grand Boulevard, Emerson, NJ 07630-1170.

1686 ■ Armenian Relief Society Scholarships (Graduate, Undergraduate/Scholarship)

Purpose: To provide financial assistance to those students who are in need. **Focus:** General studies/Field of study not specified. **Qualif.:** Applicants must be undergraduate or graduate students in a four-year college or university. **Criteria:** Awards will be based on academic merit, financial need and involvement in Armenian community.

Funds Avail.: Varies. **To Apply:** Applicants must submit three letters of recommendation, transcript and tax returns. **Deadline:** April 1. **Contact:** For more information, please contact: Mr. Sonanz Papazian; Phone: 617-926-02472.

1687 ■ Michael M. Assarian Scholarships (Undergraduate/Scholarship)

Purpose: To provide financial assistance to those students who are in need. **Focus:** General studies/Field of study not specified. **Qualif.:** Applicants must be full-time students of Armenian descent enrolled at Wayne State University. **Criteria:** Selection of scholars will be based on scholastic achievement, extracurricular activities and financial need.

Funds Avail.: Varies. **To Apply:** Applicants must submit an application, current academic transcript, FAFSA, and two letters of recommendation to the Office of Scholarships and Financial Aid at Wayne State University. **Deadline:** April 29. **Contact:** Private Scholarship Coordinator Office of Scholarships and Financial Aid Detroit, MI 48202; Tel: 313-577-4969.

1688 ■ John M. Azarian Memorial Armenian Youth Scholarship Fund (Undergraduate/Scholarship)

Purpose: To provide financial assistance to those students who are in need. **Focus:** General studies/Field of study not specified. **Qualif.:** Applicants must be full time enrolled in an accredited college or university; must be permanent residents of the United States. **Criteria:** Awards will be based on financial need, academic merit and involvement in the Armenian community.

Funds Avail.: $500-$3,000. **To Apply:** Applicants must submit a completed application form and two letters of reference. **Deadline:** May 1. **Contact:** Mr. John M. Azarian, Jr. c/o Azarian Management and Development Company at 6 Prospect Street, Suite 1B, Midland Park, NJ 07432; Tel: 201-444-711; Fax: 214-444-6655.

1689 ■ Hagop Bogigian Scholarship Fund (Undergraduate/Scholarship)

Purpose: To provide financial assistance to those students who are in need. **Focus:** Arts. **Qualif.:** Applicants must be students of Armenian descent who are enrolled in a four-year Bachelor of Arts degree program at Mt. Holyoke College; must maintain over a 3.0 GPA, and demonstrate financial need. **Criteria:** Priority will be given to those students with financial need.

Funds Avail.: No specific amount. **To Apply:** Applicants should apply directly to the financial aid office for financial aid and should indicate on the form that they are of Armenian descent. **Deadline:** March 1.

1690 ■ Armen H. Bululian Scholarships (Undergraduate/Scholarship)

Purpose: To provide financial assistance to those students who are in need. **Focus:** General studies/Field of study not specified. **Qualif.:** Applicants must be graduating high school seniors or enrolled full-time undergraduate students in an accredited college or university; must be residents of Monmouth or Ocean Counties in New Jersey. **Criteria:** Awards will be based on academic excellence and involvement in community services.

Funds Avail.: $1,000. **To Apply:** Interested applicants may contact the Association for the application process and other required materials. **Deadline:** June 30. **Contact:** For more information, Please contact: Mr. Harout Karakashian at 1184 Ocean Avenue, Elberon, NJ 07740.

1691 ■ Constantinople Armenian Relief Society Scholarships (CARS) (Undergraduate/Scholarship)

Purpose: To provide financial assistance to those students who are in need. **Focus:** General studies/Field of study not specified. **Qualif.:** Applicants must be undergraduate students of Armenian descent; must have a minimum of 3.0 GPA; must be attending college in or residing in the NY/NJ area. **Criteria:** Selection will be based on the committee's criteria.

Funds Avail.: $400-$600. **Duration:** Annual. **Number Awarded:** 10-20. **To Apply:** Applicants must check the available website for the required materials. **Deadline:** June 30. **Contact:** Talin Sesetyan, PO Box 769, Time Square Station, New York, NY 10108; Email: talins11@hotmail.com.

1692 ■ Karekin DerAvedision Memorial Endowment Fund (Undergraduate/Scholarship)

Purpose: To provide financial assistance to those who are in need. **Focus:** Armenian studies. **Qualif.:** Applicants must

Awards are arranged alphabetically below their administering organizations

be graduate students in Armenian Studies who have been accepted for admission to UCLA. **Criteria:** Preference will be given to those students who are in need.

Funds Avail.: Up to $8,000. **To Apply:** Applicants may contact the Association for the online application process and other required materials. **Deadline:** December 15.

1693 ■ Emmanuel Bible College Scholarships *(Undergraduate/Scholarship)*

Purpose: To provide financial support to those students who are in need. **Focus:** Education, Religious. **Qualif.:** Applicant must be willing to pledge to work as a minister, evangelist, missionary, or youth director after graduation; must study in one of the institutions of Emmanuel Bible College. **Criteria:** Awards will be based on merit and good character.

Funds Avail.: No specific amount. **To Apply:** Applicants must check the contact information for inquiries. **Deadline:** June 30. **Contact:** Dr. Yeghia Babikian, Director; 1605 East Elizabeth St., Pasadena, CA 91104; Phone: 818-791-2575; Fax 818-398-2424.

1694 ■ Garikian Scholarship Fund *(Undergraduate/Scholarship)*

Purpose: To provide financial assistance to those students who are in need. **Focus:** Armenian studies; Education; Journalism; Music; Near Eastern studies; Political science; Psychology; Sociology. **Qualif.:** Applicants must have completed their first academic year in college or university in California. **Criteria:** Preference will be given to those who meet the criteria.

Funds Avail.: $750-$1,000. **To Apply:** Applicants must apply to the Executive Board for application forms and return them, completed, before the deadline. **Deadline:** August 31. **Contact:** Berj S. Baghdoyan, c/o Western Prelacy, 4401 Russell Avenue, Los Angeles, CA 90027; Phone: 213-663-0438.

1695 ■ Hai Guin Scholarships Association *(Undergraduate/Scholarship)*

Purpose: To provide financial assistance to those students who are in need. **Focus:** General studies/Field of study not specified. **Qualif.:** Applicants must be students of Armenian descent, must reside in and attend school in Massachusetts. **Criteria:** Preference will be granted to college students who have completed the first semester of freshman year; selection will be based on scholarship achievement and financial need.

Funds Avail.: $1,000. **To Apply:** Applicants must check the available website for the required materials. **Deadline:** October 25. **Contact:** Hasmig Maserjian, Scholarship Chairperson, PO Box 509, Belmont, MA 024278.

1696 ■ Calouste Gulbenkian Foundation Scholarships *(Undergraduate/Scholarship)*

Purpose: To provide financial assistance to those students who are in need. **Focus:** General studies/Field of study not specified. **Qualif.:** Applicants must be sophomores or above who are enrolled full-time in an accredited college or university. **Criteria:** Awards will be based on academic merit and financial need; preference will be given to those applicants whose immediate family has not previously received a scholarship.

Funds Avail.: No specific amount. **To Apply:** Applicants must check the available website for the required materials. **Deadline:** April 15.

1697 ■ Kaspar Hovannisian Memorial Scholarships *(Graduate/Scholarship)*

Purpose: To provide financial assistance to those who are in need. **Focus:** General studies/Field of study not specified. **Qualif.:** Applicants must be graduate students in the field of Armenian Studies. **Criteria:** Preference will be given to those studying Armenian History.

Funds Avail.: Up to $8,000. **To Apply:** Applicants may contact the Association for the application process and other required materials. **Deadline:** December 15.

1698 ■ Hirair and Anna Hovnanian Foundation Presidential Scholarships *(Undergraduate/Scholarship)*

Purpose: To provide financial assistance to those students who are in need. **Focus:** General studies/Field of study not specified. **Qualif.:** Applicants must be students of Armenian ethnic origin who demonstrate financial need and outstanding academic achievements; must maintain a minimum 2.75 GPA. **Criteria:** Consideration will be given to all students of Armenian descent who apply and meet Villanova University's general admissions requirements.

Funds Avail.: No specific amount. **Duration:** Up to 4 academic years. **To Apply:** Applicants may contact the Association for the application process and other required materials. **Deadline:** March 15 for incoming freshman; April 15 all other students. **Contact:** Villanova University, Office of Student Financial Assistance, 800 Lancaster Ave., Villanova, PA 19085.

1699 ■ Hirair and Anna Hovnanian Foundation Scholarships *(Undergraduate/Scholarship)*

Purpose: To provide financial assistance to those students who are in need. **Focus:** General studies/Field of study not specified. **Qualif.:** Applicants must be full-time students enrolled at the Women's College at Georgian Court University, preferably of Armenian descent, who exhibit financial need. **Criteria:** Priority will be given to those who demonstrate financial need and with good academic standing.

Funds Avail.: No specific amount. **To Apply:** Applicants must check the contact information for inquiries.

1700 ■ Rev. and Mrs. A.K. Jizmejian Educational Fund *(Undergraduate/Scholarship)*

Purpose: To provide financial assistance to those students who are in need. **Focus:** Theology. **Qualif.:** Applicants must be full-time theological seminary students and fourth-year undergraduate students who intend to continue their education in a theological seminary. **Criteria:** Selection will be based on financial need, academic accomplishments, future leadership potential and good character references.

Funds Avail.: $500-$1,500. **To Apply:** Interested applicants may contact the Armenian Evangelical Church for the application form and must submit proof of enrollment at seminary or university. **Deadline:** June 30. **Contact:** Armenian Evangelical Church; Mr. Mihran Jizmejian, Chairman 816-60 Pavane Linkway Don Mills, Ontario, M3C 1A2 Canada.

1701 ■ Knights of Vartan, Fresno Lodge No. 9 Scholarships *(Undergraduate/Scholarship)*

Purpose: To provide financial assistance to those students who are in need. **Focus:** Armenian studies. **Qualif.:** Applicants must be new or continuing full-time students (12

Awards are arranged alphabetically below their administering organizations

units per semester) at Fresno State and maintain a 3.0 GPA or higher. **Criteria:** Scholarship will be given to those students who meet the criteria.

Funds Avail.: $750, one for an entering freshman and one for a continuing student at C.S.U.F. **Duration:** Annual. **Number Awarded:** 2. **To Apply:** Applicants must check the available website for the required materials. **Deadline:** November 1.

1702 ■ Mangasar M. Mangasarian Scholarship Fund *(Graduate/Scholarship)*

Purpose: To provide financial assistance to those students who are in need. **Focus:** General studies/Field of study not specified. **Qualif.:** Applicants must be full-time graduate students of Armenian parentage attending the University of California, Berkley. Scholarship is also offered to international students of Armenian descent. **Criteria:** Selection will be based on the committee's criteria.

Funds Avail.: $500-$3,000. **To Apply:** Interested applicants may contact the Association for the application process and other required materials. **Contact:** Mr. Tony Bernez, Scholarship Director, 210 Sproul Hall, Berkeley, CA 94720; Phone: 510-642-6363; Fax: 510-642-0672.

1703 ■ National Association for Armenian Studies and Research Scholarships *(Graduate, Postgraduate/Scholarship)*

Purpose: To provide financial assistance to those students who are in need. **Focus:** General studies/Field of study not specified. **Qualif.:** Applicants must be graduates or postgraduates doing research about Armenian Studies. **Criteria:** Selection will be based on the committee's criteria.

Funds Avail.: No specific amount. **To Apply:** Applicants may contact the Association for the application process and other required materials. **Deadline:** Early spring for fall grants; early fall for spring grants; and early winter for summer grants. **Contact:** National Association for Armenian Studies and Research, Inc., 395 Concord Ave., Belmont, MA 02478; Phone: 617-489-1610; Fax: 617-484-1759.

1704 ■ St. James Armenian Church Memorial Scholarships *(Undergraduate/Scholarship)*

Purpose: To provide financial assistance to those students who are in need. **Focus:** General studies/Field of study not specified. **Qualif.:** Applicants must be affiliated with St. James Armenian Church by being graduates of the Sunday school, Sunday school teachers, church choir members for at least one year, or in some other way acceptable to the scholarship committee. **Criteria:** Scholarships will be awarded based on the academic achievement, financial need, service to school, community and church and seriousness of purpose.

Funds Avail.: $250-$2,000. **To Apply:** Interested applicants may contact the Association for the application process and other required materials. **Deadline:** April 1. **Contact:** Ms. Anita Assarian; 465 Mount Auburn St., Watertown, MA 02172; Phone: 617-923-8860; Fax: 617-926-5503.

1705 ■ Hazaros Tabakoglu Scholarship Fund *(Undergraduate/Scholarship)*

Purpose: To provide financial assistance to those who are in need. **Focus:** General studies/Field of study not specified. **Qualif.:** Applicants must be full-time undergraduates of Armenian descent who are or will be enrolled at colleges in the United States; must be residents of New York, New Jersey or Connecticut. **Criteria:** Selection will be based on the demonstrated financial need, academic ability and commitment to the Armenian community and culture.

Funds Avail.: $1,000-$5,000. **To Apply:** Interested applicants may contact the Association for the application process and other required materials. **Deadline:** May 1. **Contact:** The New York Community Trust, 2 Park Avenue, New York, NY 1016; Phone: 212-686-0010.

1706 ■ Aram Torossian Memorial Scholarships *(Undergraduate/Scholarship)*

Purpose: To provide financial assistance to those students who are in need. **Focus:** General studies/Field of study not specified. **Qualif.:** Applicant must be a full-time student of Armenian parentage attending the University of California, Berkley. **Criteria:** Selection will be based on the committee's criteria.

Funds Avail.: $300-$3,000. **To Apply:** Interested applicant may contact the Association for the application process and other required materials. **Contact:** Mr. Tony Bernez, Scholarship Director, 210 Sproul Hall, Berkeley, CA 94720; Phone: 510-642-6363; Fax: 510-642-0672.

1707 ■ Union of Marash Armenian Scholarships *(Undergraduate, Graduate/Scholarship)*

Purpose: To provide financial assistance to those students who are in need. **Focus:** General studies/Field of study not specified. **Qualif.:** Applicant must be a matriculated, full-time undergraduate or graduate student accepted at an accredited institution of higher education; must demonstrate academic excellence; be of good moral character; be in financial need; and show involvement in community; and must be a descendant of a Marashtsi (a part of Armenia/Asia Minor). **Criteria:** Selection will be based on the committee's criteria.

Funds Avail.: $500-$1,000. **To Apply:** Interested applicant may contact the Association for the application process and other required materials. **Deadline:** July 31. **Contact:** Mrs. Siroon P. Shahinian, PhD, Secretary, The Student Fund, One Sussex Road, Great Neck, NY 11020-1828.

1708 ■ Harry and Angel Zerigian Scholarships *(Undergraduate/Scholarship)*

Purpose: To provide financial assistance to those students who are in need. **Focus:** Accounting. **Qualif.:** Applicant must be a full-time student with financial need and of Armenian ancestry; must be day-division sophomores majoring in Accounting at Bentley College who have satisfactorily completed all course work through the fall of sophomore year. **Criteria:** Preference will be given to those students who attended Haverhill, Lawrence, Waltham or Watertown High Schools.

Funds Avail.: No specific amount. **To Apply:** Applicants must check the available website for the required materials.

1709 ■ Army Aviation Association of America (AAAA)
593 Main St.
Monroe, CT 06468-2830
Ph: (203)268-2450
Fax: (203)268-5870
E-mail: aaaa@quad-a.org
URL: www.quad-a.org
Facebook: www.facebook.com/pages/ArmyAviationAssociationofAmerica/133801716678354

Awards are arranged alphabetically below their administering organizations

Twitter: www.twitter.com/army_aviation

1710 ■ AAAA Scholarship Program (Undergraduate, Graduate/Scholarship)

Purpose: To provide grants and loans to members who seek further education as well as the member's family who sought college-entry financial aid. **Focus:** General studies/Field of study not specified. **Qualif.:** Applicant must be a member of AAAA, the spouse of an AAAA member or deceased member, the unmarried son or daughter of an AAAA member or deceased member or the unmarried grandchild of an AAAA member or deceased member. Applicants must be attending an accredited college or university or selected for Fall entry as an undergraduate or graduate. **Criteria:** Scholarship recipients will be selected based on the selection committee's review of the application materials.

Duration: Annual. **To Apply:** Applicants must submit the completed application including the applicant's references made by two individuals; school recommendation; teacher's recommendation; academic reporting form; current transcript of grades; and a photograph. **Deadline:** May 1. **Remarks:** Established in 1963.

1711 ■ Army Nurse Corps Association (ANCA)
8000 IH-10
San Antonio, TX 78218-1235
Ph: (210)650-3534
Fax: (210)650-3494
E-mail: membership@e-anca.org
URL: e-anca.org

1712 ■ ANCA Scholarships (Undergraduate/Scholarship)

Purpose: To provide financial assistance to nursing students. **Focus:** Nursing. **Qualif.:** Applicants must be students in a nursing program approved by an agency acceptable to the United States Secretary of Education; have Internal Revenue Service tax-exempt status; have scholarship fund under the school control; been a supportive of Army Nurse Corps recruitment. **Criteria:** Applicants who are students planning to enter the Army Nurse Corps, Army Reserve or National Guard; previously served in the United States Army, Army Reserve or National Guard; Army Nurse Corps officers enrolled in undergraduate or graduate nursing programs not funded by United States Army, Army Reserve or National Guard; members of Army Medical Department pursuing baccalaureate degree in nursing not funded by United States Army, Army Reserve or National Guard will be given preference.

Funds Avail.: No specific amount. **Duration:** Annual. **To Apply:** Applicants must submit application template consist of school and location; agency accreditation; internal revenue status; scholarship program; support of army nurse corps recruitment activities; award criteria; application for specific student; and agreement to Education Committee.

1713 ■ Army Scholarship Foundation
11700 Preston Rd., Ste. 660-301
Dallas, TX 75230
E-mail: contactus@armyscholarshipfoundation.org
URL: www.armyscholarshipfoundation.org

1714 ■ First Lieutenant Scott McClean Love Memorial Scholarship - Children of Soldiers (Undergraduate, Vocational/Occupational/Scholarship)

Purpose: To financially support deserving children of current or former United States Army personnel in their pursuit of higher education. **Focus:** General studies/Field of study not specified. **Qualif.:** Applicants must be sons or daughters of regular duty, active duty Reserve or active duty National Guard U.S. Army members in good standing; or must be sons or daughters of former U.S. Army who received an honorable discharge or medical discharge or who were killed while serving in the U.S. Army; must be high school seniors, high school graduates or registered as undergraduate students at an accredited college or vocational/technical institution; must have a 2.0 GPA on a 4.0 system; must be U.S. citizens not reaching 30th birthday by application deadline. **Criteria:** Award will be given based on the submitted application materials.

Funds Avail.: $500 - $2,000. **Duration:** Annual. **To Apply:** Applicant must submit a completed scholarship application form along with a Free Application for Federal Student Aid (FAFSA); a signed copy of the appropriate income tax return for the previous year; a certificate of good service or the parent's/spouse's DD 214; a high school transcript and transcripts from all post high school educational institutions (if applicable); an essay; and a photograph. **Deadline:** May 1. **Contact:** Army Scholarship Foundation at the above address.

1715 ■ First Lieutenant Scott McClean Love Memorial Scholarship - Spouses of Soldiers (Undergraduate, Vocational/Occupational/Scholarship)

Purpose: To financially assist deserving spouses of current or former United States Army personnel in their pursuit of higher education. **Focus:** General studies/Field of study not specified. **Qualif.:** Applicants must be spouses of a serving enlisted regular active duty, active duty Reserve or active duty National Guard U.S. Army member in good standing; or must be spouses of former U.S. Army who received an honorable discharge or medical discharge or who were killed while serving in the U.S. Army. **Criteria:** Award will be given based on the submitted application materials.

Funds Avail.: $500 - $2,000. **Duration:** Annual. **To Apply:** Applicant must submit a completed scholarship application form along with a Free Application for Federal Student Aid (FAFSA); a signed copy of the appropriate income tax return for the previous year; a certificate of good service or the parent's/spouse's DD 214; a high school transcript and transcripts from all post high school educational institutions (if applicable); an essay; and a photograph. **Deadline:** May 1. **Contact:** Army Scholarship Foundation at the above address.

1716 ■ Captain Jennifer Shafer Odom Memorial Scholarships - Children of Soldiers (Undergraduate, Vocational/Occupational/Scholarship)

Purpose: To financially support deserving children of current or former United States Army personnel in their pursuit of higher education. **Focus:** General studies/Field of study not specified. **Qualif.:** Applicants must be sons or daughters of regular duty, active duty Reserve or active duty National Guard U.S. Army members in good standing; or must be sons or daughters of former U.S. Army who received an honorable discharge or medical discharge or who were killed while serving in the U.S. Army; must be high school seniors, high school graduates or registered as undergraduate students at an accredited college or vocational/technical institution; must have a 2.0 GPA on a 4.0 system; must be U.S. citizens not reaching 30th birthday by application deadline. **Criteria:** Selection will be based on the submitted application materials.

Awards are arranged alphabetically below their administering organizations

Funds Avail.: $500 - $2,000. **Duration:** Annual. **To Apply:** Applicant must submit a completed scholarship application form along with a Free Application for Federal Student Aid (FAFSA); a signed copy of the appropriate income tax return for the previous year; a certificate of good service or the parent's/spouse's DD 214; a high school transcript and transcripts from all post high school educational institutions (if applicable); an essay; and a photograph. **Deadline:** May 1. **Contact:** Army Scholarship Foundation at the above address.

1717 ■ Captain Jennifer Shafer Odom Memorial Scholarships - Spouses of Soldiers *(Undergraduate/Scholarship)*

Purpose: To financially assist deserving spouses of current or former United States Army personnel in their pursuit of higher education. **Focus:** General studies/Field of study not specified. **Qualif.:** Applicants must be spouses of a serving enlisted regular active duty, active duty Reserve or active duty National Guard U.S. Army member in good standing; or must be spouses of former U.S. Army who received an honorable discharge or medical discharge or who were killed while serving in the U.S. Army. **Criteria:** Selection will be based on the submitted application materials.

Funds Avail.: $500 - $2,000. **Duration:** Annual. **To Apply:** Applicants must submit a completed scholarship application form along with a Free Application for Federal Student Aid (FAFSA); a signed copy of the appropriate income tax return for the previous year; a certificate of good service or the parent's/spouse's DD 214; a high school transcript and transcripts from all post high school educational institutions (if applicable); an essay; and a photograph. **Deadline:** May 1. **Contact:** Army Scholarship Foundation at the above address.

1718 ■ Aaron Arnoldsen Memorial Golf Tournament
1325 Airmotive Way, Ste. 220
Reno, NV 89502
Ph: (775)560-7006
E-mail: info@aamemorial.com
URL: aamemorial.com

1719 ■ Aaron Edward Arnoldsen Memorial Scholarships *(Undergraduate/Scholarship)*

Purpose: To provide financial support to aid students' educational endeavors. **Focus:** General studies/Field of study not specified. **Qualif.:** Applicants must be junior or senior students; must be graduates of Nevada High School; must have minimum 3.2 cumulative high school GPA and a minimum 22 ACT concordant score. **Criteria:** Applicants will be evaluated by Scholarship Selection Committee.

Funds Avail.: $1,500. **Duration:** Annual. **To Apply:** Applicants must submit completed application form and the other requirements needed. **Deadline:** February 1.

1720 ■ ARRL Foundation (ARRLF)
225 Main St.
Newington, CT 06111-1494
Ph: (860)594-0200
Fax: (860)594-0259
E-mail: hq@arrl.org
URL: www.arrl.org/the-arrl-foundation

1721 ■ American Radio Relay League Louisiana Memorial Scholarships *(Undergraduate/Scholarship)*

Purpose: To provide financial assistance to students who have the license for higher education. **Focus:** Radio and television. **Qualif.:** Applicants must hold an FCC amateur radio license, and be Louisiana residents or attending a four-year college/university in Louisiana; must have a 3.0 GPA. **Criteria:** Award is given based on the submitted materials.

Funds Avail.: $750. **Duration:** Annual. **Number Awarded:** 1. **To Apply:** Applicants must submit a completed scholarship application form along with a recent high school (or equivalent) or college transcript. **Deadline:** January 31.

1722 ■ Earl I. Anderson Scholarships *(Undergraduate/Scholarship)*

Purpose: To provide financial assistance to students who have the license for post-secondary education. **Focus:** Radio and television. **Qualif.:** Applicant must hold an FCC amateur radio license; be a resident of, or attending classes in Illinois, Indiana, Michigan, or Florida; and must be an ARRL member. **Criteria:** Award is given based on the submitted materials. The ARRL Foundation Scholarship Committee will review all applicants for eligibility and award decisions. Preference will be given to applicants studying in Electronic Engineering or related technical field.

Funds Avail.: No specific amount. **Duration:** Annual. **To Apply:** Applicant must submit a completed scholarship application form online along with a pdf format of recent high school (or equivalent) or college transcript.

1723 ■ ARRL Foundation General Fund Scholarships *(Undergraduate/Scholarship)*

Purpose: To provide financial assistance to students who have the license for post-secondary education. **Focus:** Radio and television. **Qualif.:** Applicant must hold an FCC amateur radio license. **Criteria:** Award is given based on the submitted materials. The ARRL Foundation Scholarship Committee will review all applicants for eligibility and award decisions.

Funds Avail.: $2,000. **Duration:** Annual. **Number Awarded:** Varies. **To Apply:** Applicant must submit a completed scholarship application form online along with a pdf format of recent high school (or equivalent) or college transcript. **Deadline:** January 31.

1724 ■ ARRL Foundation PHD Scholarships *(Undergraduate/Scholarship)*

Purpose: To provide financial assistance to students who have the license for higher education. **Focus:** Computer and information sciences; Electronics; Journalism; Radio and television. **Qualif.:** Applicant must hold an FCC amateur radio license; be a resident of ARRL Midwest Division (IA, KS, MO, NE); with a course of study in journalism, computer science or electronic engineering; and be the child of a deceased radio amateur. **Criteria:** Award is given based on the submitted materials.

Funds Avail.: $1,000. **Duration:** Annual. **Number Awarded:** 1. **To Apply:** Applicant must submit a completed scholarship application form along with a recent high school (or equivalent) or college transcript. **Deadline:** January 31.

1725 ■ ARRLF Mississippi Scholarships *(Undergraduate/Scholarship)*

Purpose: To provide financial assistance to students who have the license for higher education. **Focus:** Communica-

Awards are arranged alphabetically below their administering organizations

tions; Electronics; Radio and television. **Qualif.:** Applicant must hold an FCC amateur radio license; be a Mississippi resident; be studying in baccalaureate or higher courses of study in electronics, communications or related fields; and be under 30 years of age. **Criteria:** Award is given based on the submitted materials.

Funds Avail.: $500. **Duration:** Annual. **Number Awarded:** 1. **To Apply:** Applicant must submit a completed scholarship application form along with a recent high school (or equivalent) or college transcript. **Deadline:** January 31.

1726 ■ Richard W. Bendicksen Memorial Scholarships (Undergraduate/Scholarship)

Purpose: To provide financial assistance to students who have the license for higher education. **Focus:** Radio and television. **Qualif.:** Applicant must hold an FCC amateur radio license and attending a four-year college/university. **Criteria:** Award is given based on the submitted materials.

Funds Avail.: $2,000. **Duration:** Annual. **Number Awarded:** 1. **To Apply:** Applicant must submit a completed scholarship application form along with a recent high school (or equivalent) or college transcript. **Deadline:** January 31.

1727 ■ William Bennett W7PHO Memorial Scholarships (Undergraduate/Scholarship)

Purpose: To support the education of students holding a valid FCC-granted Amateur Radio license for post-secondary education. **Focus:** Radio and television. **Qualif.:** Applicant must hold an FCC amateur radio license; be a Northwest, Pacific or Southwest Division resident; be enrolled in a four-year college/university; and have a GPA of 3.0 or better for an ongoing course of study. **Criteria:** Award is given based on submitted materials.

Funds Avail.: $500. **Duration:** Annual. **Number Awarded:** 1. **To Apply:** Applicant must submit a completed scholarship application form along with a recent high school (or equivalent) or college transcript. **Deadline:** January 31. **Contact:** ARRL Foundation Scholarship Committee at foundation@arrl.org.

1728 ■ Henry Broughton, K2AE Memorial Scholarships (Undergraduate/Scholarship)

Purpose: To provide financial support to students who are holding a license for post-secondary education. **Focus:** Engineering; Radio and television; Science. **Qualif.:** Applicant must hold an FCC amateur radio license; reside within 70 miles of Schenectady NY; studying in baccalaureate or higher courses of study in engineering, sciences or a similar field in an accredited four-year college/university. **Criteria:** Award is given based on the submitted materials.

Funds Avail.: $1,000. **Duration:** Annual. **Number Awarded:** 1. **To Apply:** Applicant must submit a completed scholarship application form along with a recent high school (or equivalent) or college transcript. **Deadline:** January 31.

1729 ■ Mary Lou Brown Scholarships (Undergraduate/Scholarship)

Purpose: To support the education of students holding a valid FCC-granted Amateur Radio license for post-secondary education. **Focus:** Radio and television. **Qualif.:** Applicant must hold an FCC amateur radio license; be a resident of ARRL Northwest Division (AK, ID, MT, OR, WA); studying baccalaureate or higher courses; and have a GPA of 3.0 or higher. **Criteria:** Awards are given based on the submitted materials. Preference will be given to those applicants who have demonstrated an interest in promoting Amateur Radio Service.

Funds Avail.: $2,500. **Duration:** Annual. **Number Awarded:** Varies. **To Apply:** Applicant must submit a completed scholarship application form along with a recent high school (or equivalent) or college transcript. **Deadline:** January 31.

1730 ■ L.B. Cebik, W4RNL, and Jean Cebik, N4TZP, Memorial Scholarships (Undergraduate/Scholarship)

Purpose: To provide financial support to students who are holding a license for post-secondary education. **Focus:** Radio and television. **Qualif.:** Applicant must hold an FCC amateur radio license; and be attending a four-year college/university. **Criteria:** Award is given based on the submitted materials.

Funds Avail.: $1,000. **Duration:** Annual. **Number Awarded:** 1. **To Apply:** Applicant must submit a completed scholarship application form along with a recent high school (or equivalent) or college transcript. **Deadline:** January 31.

1731 ■ Central Arizona DX Association Scholarships (Undergraduate/Scholarship)

Purpose: To provide financial support to students who are holding a license for post-secondary education. **Focus:** Radio and television. **Qualif.:** Applicant must hold an FCC amateur radio license; be a resident of Arizona; and have a GPA of 3.2 or above. **Criteria:** Graduating high school students will be considered before current college students.

Funds Avail.: $1,000. **Duration:** Annual. **Number Awarded:** 1. **To Apply:** Applicant must submit a completed scholarship application form along with a recent high school (or equivalent) or college transcript. **Deadline:** January 31.

1732 ■ Challenge Met Scholarships (Undergraduate/Scholarship)

Purpose: To provide financial support to students who are holding a license for post-secondary education. **Focus:** Radio and television. **Qualif.:** Applicant must hold an FCC amateur radio license; and be attending an accredited two or four-year college technical school or university. **Criteria:** Preference is given to application with documented learning disability (by physician or school) and indications that the applicant is putting forth substantial effort regardless of resulting academic grades.

Funds Avail.: $500. **Duration:** Annual. **Number Awarded:** Varies. **To Apply:** Applicant must submit a completed scholarship application form along with a recent high school (or equivalent) or college transcript. **Deadline:** January 31.

1733 ■ Chicago FM Club Scholarships (Undergraduate/Scholarship)

Purpose: To provide financial assistance to students who are pursuing post-secondary education. **Focus:** Radio and television. **Qualif.:** Applicant must hold an FCC amateur radio license; residency in FCC Ninth Call district (IN, IL, WI); be attending a post-secondary course of study at an accredited two or four-year college or trade school; and must be a U.S. citizen or within three months of citizenship. License requirement is Technician Class or higher; **Criteria:** Awards are given based on the submitted materials, eligibility and award decisions by the ARRL Foundation Scholarship Committee.

Funds Avail.: $500. **Duration:** Annual. **Number Awarded:** Varies. **To Apply:** Applicant must submit a completed scholarship application form online along with a pdf format of recent high school (or equivalent) or college transcript. **Deadline:** January 31.

Awards are arranged alphabetically below their administering organizations

1734 ■ Tom and Judith Comstock Scholarships
(Undergraduate/Scholarship)

Purpose: To support students with their education who have the license for post-secondary education. **Focus:** Radio and television. **Qualif.:** Applicant must hold an FCC amateur radio license; be a resident of Texas or Oklahoma; and be a high school senior accepted at a two or four-year college. **Criteria:** Award is given based on the submitted materials. The ARRL Foundation Scholarship Committee will review all applicants for eligibility and award decisions

Funds Avail.: $2,000. **Duration:** Annual. **Number Awarded:** 1. **To Apply:** Applicant must submit a completed scholarship application form online along with a pdf format of recent high school (or equivalent) or college transcript. **Deadline:** January 31.

1735 ■ Irving W. Cook WA0CGS Scholarships
(Undergraduate/Scholarship)

Purpose: To provide financial support to students who have the license for post-secondary education. **Focus:** Communications; Electronics; Radio and television. **Qualif.:** Applicant must hold an FCC amateur radio license; residency in Kansas; and be studying baccalaureate or higher courses in electronics, communications or a related field in any institution. **Criteria:** Award is given based on the submitted materials. The ARRL Foundation Scholarship Committee will review all applicants for eligibility and award decisions.

Funds Avail.: $1,000. **Duration:** Annual. **Number Awarded:** 1. **To Apply:** Applicant must submit a completed scholarship application form online along with a pdf format of recent high school (or equivalent) or college transcript. **Deadline:** January 31.

1736 ■ Charles Clarke Cordle Memorial Scholarships *(Undergraduate/Scholarship)*

Purpose: To provide financial assistance to students who have the license for post-secondary education. **Focus:** Communications; Electronics; Radio and television. **Qualif.:** Applicant must hold an FCC amateur radio license; be a resident of Georgia or Alabama; have a GPA of 2.5 or higher; and be attending an institution in Georgia or Alabama. **Criteria:** Award is given based on the submitted materials. The ARRL Foundation Scholarship Committee will review all applicants for eligibility and award decisions. Preference is given to applicants studying electronics, communications or related field.

Funds Avail.: $1,000. **Duration:** Annual. **Number Awarded:** 1. **To Apply:** Applicant must submit a completed scholarship application form online along with a pdf format of recent high school (or equivalent) or college transcript. **Deadline:** January 31.

1737 ■ Dayton Amateur Radio Association Scholarships *(Undergraduate/Scholarship)*

Purpose: To provide financial assistance to students who have the license for post-secondary education. **Focus:** Radio and television. **Qualif.:** Applicant must hold an FCC amateur radio license and be attending an accredited four-year college/university. **Criteria:** Award is given based on the submitted materials. The ARRL Foundation Scholarship Committee will review all applicants for eligibility and award decisions.

Funds Avail.: $1,000. **Duration:** Annual. **Number Awarded:** 4. **To Apply:** Applicant must submit a completed scholarship application form online along with a pdf format of recent high school (or equivalent) or college transcript. **Deadline:** January 31.

1738 ■ Charles N. Fisher Memorial Scholarships
(Undergraduate/Scholarship)

Purpose: To provide financial assistance to students who have the license for post-secondary education. **Focus:** Communications; Electronics; Radio and television. **Qualif.:** Applicant must hold an FCC amateur radio license; must be a resident of ARRL Southwestern Division (AZ, Los Angeles, Orange, San Diego, and Santa Barbara); studying in electronics, communications or related fields of a regionally accredited institution. **Criteria:** Award is given based on the submitted materials. The ARRL Foundation Scholarship Committee will review all applicants for eligibility and award decisions.

Funds Avail.: $1,000. **Duration:** Annual. **Number Awarded:** 1. **To Apply:** Applicant must submit a completed scholarship application form online along with a pdf format of recent high school (or equivalent) or college transcript. **Deadline:** February 31.

1739 ■ William R. Goldfarb Memorial Scholarships
(Undergraduate/Scholarship)

Purpose: To provide financial assistance to students who have the license for post-secondary education. **Focus:** Business; Computer and information sciences; Engineering; Medicine; Nursing; Radio and television; Science. **Qualif.:** Applicant must hold an FCC amateur radio license; must be studying baccalaureate courses in business-related, computers, medical, nursing, engineering or sciences; be a high school senior; and must demonstrate financial need. **Criteria:** Award is given based on the submitted materials. The ARRL Foundation Scholarship Committee will review all applicants for eligibility and award decisions.

Funds Avail.: $10,000. **Duration:** Annual. **Number Awarded:** 1. **To Apply:** Applicant must submit a completed scholarship application form along with a recent high school (or equivalent) or college transcript and the Free Application for Federal Student Aid (FAFSA) or Student Aid Report (SAR). **Deadline:** January 31.

1740 ■ Paul and Helen L. Grauer Scholarships
(Undergraduate/Scholarship)

Purpose: To provide financial assistance to students who have the license for post-secondary education. **Focus:** Communications; Electronics; Radio and television. **Qualif.:** Applicant must hold an FCC amateur radio license; be a resident of ARRL Midwest Division (IA, KS, MO, NE); be studying in baccalaureate or higher courses in electronics, communications or related field; and be attending school in the Midwest Division. **Criteria:** Award is given based on the submitted materials. The ARRL Foundation Scholarship Committee will review all applicants for eligibility and award decisions.

Funds Avail.: $1,000. **Duration:** Annual. **Number Awarded:** 1. **To Apply:** Applicant must submit a completed scholarship application form online along with a pdf format of recent high school (or equivalent) or college transcript. **Deadline:** January 31.

1741 ■ K2TEO Martin J. Green, Sr. Memorial Scholarships *(Undergraduate/Scholarship)*

Purpose: To provide financial assistance to students who have the license for post-secondary education. **Focus:** Radio and television. **Qualif.:** Applicant must hold an FCC amateur radio license. **Criteria:** Preference is given to a student from a "ham family".

Awards are arranged alphabetically below their administering organizations

Funds Avail.: $1,000. **Duration:** Annual. **Number Awarded:** 1. **To Apply:** Applicant must submit a completed scholarship application form along with a recent high school (or equivalent) or college transcript. **Deadline:** January 31.

1742 ■ Perry F. Hadlock Memorial Scholarships
(Undergraduate/Scholarship)

Purpose: To provide financial assistance to students who have the license for post-secondary education. **Focus:** Engineering, Electrical; Radio and television; Technology. **Qualif.:** Applicant must hold an FCC amateur radio license; must be studying in baccalaureate or higher courses in a technology-related field; preference to electrical and electronics engineering. **Criteria:** Preference is given to applicant studying at Clarkson University, Potsdam NY, or any Atlantic or Hudson Division.

Funds Avail.: $1,000. **To Apply:** Applicant must submit a completed scholarship application form along with a recent high school (or equivalent) or college transcript.

1743 ■ Albert H. Hix, W8AH Memorial Scholarships
(Undergraduate/Scholarship)

Purpose: To provide financial assistance to students who have the license for higher education. **Focus:** Radio and television. **Qualif.:** Applicant must hold an FCC amateur radio license; be a resident and attending school in the WV Section; and have a GPA of 3.0 or higher. **Criteria:** Award is given based on the submitted materials.

Funds Avail.: $500. **Duration:** Annual. **Number Awarded:** 1. **To Apply:** Applicant must submit a completed scholarship application form along with a recent high school (or equivalent) or college transcript. **Deadline:** January 31.

1744 ■ Seth Horen, K1LOM Memorial Scholarships
(Undergraduate/Scholarship)

Purpose: To provide financial assistance to students who have the license for higher education. **Focus:** Radio and television. **Qualif.:** Applicant must hold an FCC amateur radio license and be attending a four-year college/university. **Criteria:** Award is given based on the submitted materials.

Funds Avail.: $500. **To Apply:** Applicant must submit a completed scholarship application form along with a recent high school (or equivalent) or college transcript.

1745 ■ Dr. James L. Lawson Memorial Scholarships
(Undergraduate/Scholarship)

Purpose: To provide financial assistance to students who have the license for higher education. **Focus:** Communications; Electronics; Radio and television. **Qualif.:** Applicant must hold an FCC amateur radio license; be a resident of one of the New England states (ME, NH, VT, CT, RI) or New York State; and be studying in baccalaureate or higher courses in electronics, communications or related fields. **Criteria:** Award is given based on the submitted materials.

Funds Avail.: $500. **Duration:** Annual. **Number Awarded:** 1. **To Apply:** Applicant must submit a completed scholarship application form along with a recent high school (or equivalent) or college transcript. **Deadline:** January 31.

1746 ■ Fred R. McDaniel Memorial Scholarships
(Undergraduate/Scholarship)

Purpose: To provide financial assistance to students who have the license for higher education. **Focus:** Communications; Electronics; Radio and television. **Qualif.:** Applicant must hold an FCC amateur radio license; be a resident of the FCC 5th call district (TX, OK, AR, LA, MS, NM); be studying in baccalaureate or higher courses of study in electronics, communications or related fields. **Criteria:** Preference is given to students with GPA of 3.0 or higher.

Funds Avail.: $500. **Duration:** Annual. **Number Awarded:** 1. **To Apply:** Applicant must submit a completed scholarship application form along with a recent high school (or equivalent) or college transcript. **Deadline:** January 31.

1747 ■ Edmond A. Metzger Scholarships
(Undergraduate/Scholarship)

Purpose: To provide financial assistance to students who have the license for higher education. **Focus:** Engineering, Electrical; Radio and television. **Qualif.:** Applicants must hold an FCC amateur radio license; be residents of ARRL Central Division (IL, IN, WI); be studying in baccalaureate or higher courses of study in electrical engineering; be ARRL members; and attending school in the Central Division. **Criteria:** Award is given based on the submitted materials.

Funds Avail.: $500. **Duration:** Annual. **Number Awarded:** 1. **To Apply:** Applicants must submit a completed scholarship application form along with a recent high school (or equivalent) or college transcript. **Deadline:** January 31.

1748 ■ New England FEMARA Scholarships
(Undergraduate/Scholarship)

Purpose: To provide financial assistance to students who have the license for post-secondary education. **Focus:** Radio and television. **Qualif.:** Applicant must hold an FCC radio license (technical class or higher) ; and be a resident of one of the New England states (ME, NH, VT, CT, RI). **Criteria:** Award is given based on the submitted materials. The ARRL Foundation Scholarship Committee will review all applicants for eligibility and award decisions.

Funds Avail.: $1,000. **Duration:** Annual. **Number Awarded:** Varies. **To Apply:** Applicant must submit a completed scholarship application form online along with a pdf format of recent high school (or equivalent) or college transcript. **Deadline:** January 31.

1749 ■ Northern California DX Foundation Scholarships *(Undergraduate/Scholarship)*

Purpose: To provide financial assistance to students who have the license for higher education. **Focus:** Radio and television. **Qualif.:** Applicant must hold an FCC amateur radio license; be attending a junior college, four-year college/university or trade school in the U.S.; and must demonstrate activity and interest in DXing. **Criteria:** Awards are given based on the submitted materials.

Funds Avail.: No specific amount. **To Apply:** Applicant must submit a completed scholarship application form along with a recent high school (or equivalent) or college transcript.

1750 ■ Ray, NORP and Katie, WOKTE Pautz Scholarships *(Undergraduate/Scholarship)*

Purpose: To provide financial assistance to students who have the license for higher education. **Focus:** Computer and information sciences; Electronics; Radio and television. **Qualif.:** Applicant must hold an FCC amateur radio license; be a resident of the ARRL Midwest Division (IA, KS, MO, NE); be enrolled in electronics, computer science or related field at an accredited 4-year college/university; and be an ARRL member. **Criteria:** Award is given based on the submitted materials.

Funds Avail.: $500-$1,000. **Duration:** Annual. **Number**

Awards are arranged alphabetically below their administering organizations

Awarded: 1. **To Apply:** Applicant must submit a completed scholarship application form along with a recent high school (or equivalent) or college transcript. **Deadline:** January 31.

1751 ■ Peoria Area Amateur Radio Club Scholarships *(Undergraduate/Scholarship)*

Purpose: To provide financial assistance to students who have the license for higher education. **Focus:** Radio and television. **Qualif.:** Applicant must hold an FCC amateur radio license; be a resident of Central Illinois in one of these counties: Peoria, Tazewell, Woodford, Knox, McLean, Fulton, Logan, Marshall or Stark; and attending an accredited two or four-year college/university. **Criteria:** Award is given based on the submitted materials.

Funds Avail.: $500. **Duration:** Annual. **Number Awarded:** 1. **To Apply:** Applicant must submit a completed scholarship application form along with a recent high school (or equivalent) or college transcript. **Deadline:** January 31.

1752 ■ Thomas W. Porter, W8KYZ Scholarships Honoring Michael Daugherty, W8LSE *(Undergraduate/Scholarship)*

Purpose: To provide financial support to students who are in need. **Focus:** Radio and television. **Qualif.:** Applicant must hold an FCC amateur radio license and attending an accredited two or four-year college/university or technical school. **Criteria:** Preference is given to the resident of Ohio or West Virginia.

Funds Avail.: $1,000. **Duration:** Annual. **Number Awarded:** 1. **To Apply:** Applicant must submit a completed scholarship application form along with a recent high school (or equivalent) or college transcript. **Deadline:** January 31.

1753 ■ Donald Riebhoff Memorial Scholarships *(Undergraduate/Scholarship)*

Purpose: To provide financial support to students who are in need. **Focus:** Radio and television. **Qualif.:** Applicant must hold an FCC amateur radio license; be studying in baccalaureate or higher courses of study in international studies at an accredited post-secondary school; and be an ARRL member. **Criteria:** Award is given based on the submitted materials.

Funds Avail.: $1,000. **Duration:** Annual. **Number Awarded:** 1. **To Apply:** Applicants must submit a completed scholarship application form along with a recent high school (or equivalent) or college transcript. **Deadline:** January 31.

1754 ■ IRARC Memorial Joseph P. Rubino WA4MMD Scholarships *(Undergraduate/Scholarship)*

Purpose: To provide financial assistance to students who have the license for higher education. **Focus:** Electronics; Radio and television. **Qualif.:** Applicant must hold an FCC amateur radio license; have a minimum 2.5 GPA on a 4.0 scale; and be enrolled in an undergraduate degree or electronic technician certification program at an accredited institution. **Criteria:** Preference is given to the residents of Florida (Brevard County).

Funds Avail.: $750. **Duration:** Annual. **Number Awarded:** Varies. **To Apply:** Applicant must submit a completed scholarship application form along with a recent high school (or equivalent) or college transcript. **Deadline:** January 31.

1755 ■ The Bill, W2ONV, and Ann Salerno Memorial Scholarship *(Undergraduate/Scholarship)*

Purpose: To provide financial support to students who are in need. **Focus:** Radio and television. **Qualif.:** Applicant must hold an FCC amateur radio license; have a high school GPA of 3.7 or higher; have an annual family income not exceeding $100,000; and be enrolled at an accredited four-year college/university. **Criteria:** Award is given based on the submitted materials.

Funds Avail.: $1,000. **Duration:** Annual. **Number Awarded:** 2. **To Apply:** Applicant must submit a completed scholarship application form along with a recent high school (or equivalent) or college transcript. **Deadline:** January 31.

1756 ■ Eugene Gene Sallee, W4YFR Memorial Scholarships *(Undergraduate/Scholarship)*

Purpose: To provide financial support to students who are in need. **Focus:** Radio and television. **Qualif.:** Applicant must hold an FCC amateur radio license; be a resident of the state of Georgia; and have a GPA of 3.0 or higher. **Criteria:** Award is given based on the submitted materials.

Funds Avail.: No specific amount. **Number Awarded:** 1. **To Apply:** Applicant must submit a completed scholarship application form along with a recent high school (or equivalent) or college transcript.

1757 ■ Scholarships of the Morris Radio Club of New Jersey *(Undergraduate/Scholarship)*

Purpose: To provide financial assistance to students who have the license for higher education. **Focus:** Radio and television. **Qualif.:** Applicant must hold an FCC amateur radio license and be attending a four-year college/university. **Criteria:** Award is given based on the submitted materials.

Funds Avail.: $1,000. **Duration:** Annual. **Number Awarded:** 1. **To Apply:** Applicant must submit a completed scholarship application form along with a recent high school (or equivalent) or college transcript. **Deadline:** January 31.

1758 ■ Six Meter Club of Chicago Scholarships *(Undergraduate/Scholarship)*

Purpose: To provide financial support to students who are in need. **Focus:** Radio and television. **Qualif.:** Applicant must hold an FCC amateur radio license; a resident of Illinois; and be enrolled in a post-secondary course of study leading to undergraduate degree. If no qualified Illinois candidate, award is open to ARRL Central Division (IN, WI). **Criteria:** Award is given based on the submitted materials.

Funds Avail.: $500. **Duration:** Annual. **Number Awarded:** 1. **To Apply:** Applicant must submit a completed scholarship application form along with a recent high school (or equivalent) or college transcript. **Deadline:** January 31.

1759 ■ Zachary Taylor Stevens Memorial Scholarships *(Undergraduate/Scholarship)*

Purpose: To provide financial support to students who have the license for post-secondary education. **Focus:** Radio and television. **Qualif.:** Applicant must hold an FCC amateur radio license and be enrolled in an accredited two or four-year college/university or technical school. **Criteria:** Preference is given to the residents of Amateur radio call areas in MI, OH and WV.

Funds Avail.: $750. **Duration:** Annual. **Number Awarded:** 1. **To Apply:** Applicant must submit a completed scholarship application form along with a recent high school (or equivalent) or college transcript. **Deadline:** January 31.

1760 ■ Carole J. Streeter, KB9JBR Scholarships *(Undergraduate/Scholarship)*

Purpose: To provide financial support to students who have the license for post-secondary education. **Focus:** Radio

Awards are arranged alphabetically below their administering organizations

and television. **Qualif.:** Applicant must hold an FCC amateur radio license and be enrolled in an accredited college/university studying healing arts. **Criteria:** Preference is given to applicants with basic Morse Code proficiency; healing arts study may include courses at teaching hospitals or local colleges.
Funds Avail.: $1,000. **Duration:** Annual. **Number Awarded:** 1. **To Apply:** Applicant must submit a completed scholarship application form along with a recent high school (or equivalent) or college transcript. **Deadline:** January 31.

1761 ■ Norman E. Strohmeier, W2VRS Memorial Scholarships *(Undergraduate/Scholarship)*

Purpose: To provide financial support to students who have the license for post-secondary education. **Focus:** Radio and television. **Qualif.:** Applicant must hold an FCC amateur radio license; be a resident of Western New York; and have a cumulative GPA of 3.2 or better. **Criteria:** Preference is given to graduating high school seniors.
Funds Avail.: $500. **Duration:** Annual. **Number Awarded:** 1. **To Apply:** Applicant must submit a completed scholarship application form along with a recent high school (or equivalent) or college transcript. **Deadline:** January 31.

1762 ■ Gary Wagner, K3OMI Scholarships *(Undergraduate/Scholarship)*

Purpose: To provide financial support to students who have the license for post-secondary education. **Focus:** Engineering; Radio and television. **Qualif.:** Applicant must hold an FCC amateur radio license; be a resident of NC, VA, WV, MD or TN; enrolled in an accredited four-year college/university (NC, VA, WV, MD, or TN) working towards a Bachelor's of Science in any field of engineering; and have financial need. **Criteria:** Award is given based on the submitted materials.
Funds Avail.: $1,000. **Duration:** Annual. **Number Awarded:** 1. **To Apply:** Applicant must submit a completed scholarship application form along with a recent high school (or equivalent) or college transcript. **Deadline:** January 31.

1763 ■ The L. Phil and Alice J. Wicker Scholarship *(Undergraduate/Scholarship)*

Purpose: To provide financial support to students who have the license for post-secondary education. **Focus:** Communications; Electronics; Radio and television. **Qualif.:** Applicant must hold an FCC amateur radio license; be a resident of, and attending in ARRL Roanoke Division (NC, SC, VA, WV); enrolled in a baccalaureate or higher course in electronics, communications and related fields. **Criteria:** Award is given based on the submitted materials.
Funds Avail.: $500. **Duration:** Annual. **Number Awarded:** 1. **To Apply:** Applicant must submit a completed scholarship application form along with a recent high school (or equivalent) or college transcript. **Deadline:** January 31.

1764 ■ Yankee Clipper Contest Club, Inc. Youth Scholarships *(Undergraduate/Scholarship)*

Purpose: To provide financial support to students who have the license for post-secondary education. **Focus:** Radio and television. **Qualif.:** Applicant must hold an FCC amateur radio license; residency or college/university attendance within 175 miles of YCCC Center in Erving MA, including MA, RI, CT, Long Island NY, some of VT, NH, ME, PA, and NJ; and be enrolled in a two or four-year degree program at an accredited college/university. **Criteria:** Award is given based on the submitted materials.
Funds Avail.: $1,200. **Duration:** Annual. **Number Awarded:** 1. **To Apply:** Applicant must submit a completed scholarship application form along with a recent high school (or equivalent) or college transcript. **Deadline:** January 31.

1765 ■ Yasme Foundation Scholarships *(Undergraduate/Scholarship)*

Purpose: To provide financial support to students who have the license for post-secondary education. **Focus:** Engineering; Radio and television; Science. **Qualif.:** Applicant must have been licensed for at least two years and currently hold a General Class or higher Amateur Radio license. **Criteria:** Preference is given to high school applicants ranked in top 5%-10%, or to college students in the top 10%. Participation in local Amateur Radio club and community service is important to selection.
Funds Avail.: $3,000. **Duration:** Annual. **To Apply:** Applicant must submit a completed scholarship application form along with a recent high school (or equivalent) or college transcript. **Deadline:** January 31.

1766 ■ Art Dealers Association of Canada (ADAC)
401 Richmond St. W, Unit 393
Toronto, ON, Canada M5V 3A8
Ph: (416)934-1583
Fax: (866)280-9432
Free: 866-435-2322
E-mail: info@ad-ac.ca
URL: www.ad-ac.ca

1767 ■ ADAC Foundation Scholarships *(Undergraduate/Scholarship)*

Purpose: To support emerging artists from an institution chosen each year by ADAC. **Focus:** Art. **Qualif.:** Applicants must be Canadian citizens enrolled in a school of Arts degree program in the final year of their undergraduate studies. They must be devoted, committed and show talent and artistic ability. **Criteria:** Recipients will be chosen based on demonstrated academic significance and ongoing commitment to their practice.
Funds Avail.: No specific amount. **Duration:** Annual. **To Apply:** Applicants must submit a statement and curriculum vitae; must submit five examples of their work. Samples should be sent in JPG format and CD should be formatted with compatibility for both MAC and PC platforms. **Remarks:** Established in 1980.

1768 ■ Arthritis Foundation (AF)
1330 Peachtree St. NE, 6th Fl.
Atlanta, GA 30309
Ph: (404)872-7100
URL: www.arthritis.org
Facebook: www.facebook.com/Arthritis.org
LinkedIn: www.linkedin.com/company/arthritis-foundation
Twitter: twitter.com/ArthritisFdn

1769 ■ Arthritis Foundation Doctoral Dissertation Awards for Arthritis Health Professionals *(Doctorate/Fellowship)*

Purpose: To advance the research training of arthritis health professionals in their investigative or clinical teaching careers related to the rheumatic diseases. **Focus:**

Awards are arranged alphabetically below their administering organizations

Arthritis. **Qualif.:** Applicants must be health professionals whose research projects are related to arthritis management and/or comprehensive patient care in rheumatology practice, research or education. **Criteria:** Selection will be based on the committee's criteria.

Funds Avail.: $30,000. **To Apply:** Applicants may contact the Foundation for the application process.

1770 ■ Arthritis Foundation Innovative Research Grants *(Doctorate/Grant)*

Purpose: To broaden the base of inquiry in fundamental biomedical science, clinical science, and bio-behavioral research with relevance to osteoarthritis, rheumatoid arthritis, and juvenile arthritis. **Focus:** Arthritis. **Qualif.:** Applicants must have a doctoral degree at the assistant professor level or higher at any nonprofit US institution; must be independent, self-directed researchers for whom the institution provides space and other resources. Evidence of independence is required; must hold an NIH R01, K08, K23, NSF Grant, Howard Hughes, VA Merit or equivalent award at the time of application; must be US citizens or permanent residents at the time of the application. **Criteria:** Selection will be based on the committee's criteria.

Funds Avail.: $100,000. **Duration:** Two years. **To Apply:** Interested applicants must go to https://proposalcentral.altum.com to create an account. Instructions and application forms should be downloaded from the proposal CENTRAL website. Once the MS Word templates have been converted to PDF files, return/attach them through proposalCENTRAL along with the rest of the application, so that it can be transmitted electronically to the Arthritis Foundation. **Deadline:** August 30.

1771 ■ Arthritis Foundation Investigator Awards *(Doctorate/Award)*

Purpose: To support outstanding established investigator with innovative, creative ideas that have the potential to move arthritis research toward better treatments and a cure. **Focus:** Arthritis. **Qualif.:** Applicants must hold an MD, PhD, DO, DVM, or equivalent degree and a university faculty position at the associate professor level or above. Evidence of independence is required; must hold or have held in the past 12 months an NIH R01 or equivalent award at the time of application; must be US citizens or have permanent residence at the time of application. **Criteria:** Selection will be based on the committee's criteria.

Funds Avail.: $100,000. **Duration:** 5 years. **To Apply:** Applicants must go to https://proposalcentral.altum.com to create an account and for the application process. **Deadline:** August 30.

1772 ■ Arthritis Foundation Postdoctoral Fellowships *(Doctorate/Fellowship)*

Purpose: To encourage qualified scientists to embark on careers in research related to the understanding of arthritis and the rheumatic diseases. **Focus:** Arthritis. **Qualif.:** Applicants must be MDs, DVMs, PhDs or equivalent. Seventy-five percent of the applicant's time must be devoted to arthritis-related research. **Criteria:** Selection will be based on the committee's criteria.

Funds Avail.: $50,000 per year. **Duration:** Annual; 2 years. **To Apply:** Applicants may contact the Foundation for the application process. This award may be combined with other funding sources as long as all awards are concentrated on one research project.

1773 ■ Arthritis Foundation - Arizona
5009 E Washington St., Ste. 125
Phoenix, AZ 85034
Ph: (602)212-9900
Fax: (602)264-0563
URL: www.arthritis.org/arizona

1774 ■ Winterhoff Scholarships *(Undergraduate, Graduate/Scholarship)*

Purpose: To provide financial assistance to students with rheumatic diseases. **Focus:** Rheumatology. **Qualif.:** Applicants must be full-time undergraduate or graduate students diagnosed as rheumatic disease patient and must be willing to involve in the Arthritis Foundation. **Criteria:** Selection will be based on the committee's criteria.

Funds Avail.: No specific amount. **Duration:** Renewable. **To Apply:** Applicants may contact the Foundation for the application process and other information. **Deadline:** May 30.

1775 ■ Arts Council of Princeton (ACP)
Paul Robeson Center for the Arts
102 Witherspoon St.
Princeton, NJ 08542
Ph: (609)924-8777
Fax: (609)921-0008
E-mail: info@artscouncilofprinceton.org
URL: www.artscouncilofprinceton.org
Facebook: www.facebook.com/ArtsCouncilofPrinceton
Twitter: www.twitter.com/ArtsPrinceton

1776 ■ George Dale Scholarship Fund *(Undergraduate/Scholarship)*

Purpose: To make art experiences meaningful, instructive, fun and accessible for people of all ages, backgrounds and skill levels. **Focus:** General studies/Field of study not specified. **Qualif.:** Applicants must be children living in the John-Witherspoon neighborhood. **Criteria:** Selection will be based on the committee's criteria.

Funds Avail.: No specific amount. **Duration:** Annual. **To Apply:** Interested applicants must fill out the scholarship application available online and must return it to the Paul Robeson Center or may contact the Scholarship Awards Committee for the application process and other information.

1777 ■ ASAE: The Center for Association Leadership
1575 I St. NW
Washington, DC 20005-1103
Ph: (202)371-0940
Fax: (202)371-8315
Free: 888-950-ASAE
E-mail: asaeservice@asaecenter.org
URL: www.asaecenter.org

1778 ■ Diversity Executive Leadership Program Scholarships *(Other/Scholarship)*

Purpose: To provide support, education, access and service opportunities to individuals from identity groups who are under-represented in the association community. **Focus:** Leadership, Institutional and community; Manage-

Awards are arranged alphabetically below their administering organizations

ment. **Qualif.:** Applicants must be member of a racial or ethnic minority group, GLBT, or person with a disability; currently employed as a mid-to-senior level association employee with minimum of three years experience in association management or as an association CEO for a minimum of one year; has a professional, volunteer, civic or community leadership experience. **Criteria:** Preference is given to individuals who are members of ASAE & the Center and/or individuals who work with ASAE & the Center members; Recipients are selected on the basis of commitment to attend the DELP orientation, professional education programs and service on an ASAE and The Center or allied society committee or council.

Funds Avail.: No specific amount. **To Apply:** Application forms for this scholarship are available at the ASAE website. Applicants may also attach their resume; a personal statement that addresses why DELP participation is sought, leadership philosophy and how the applicant has to serve as an agent of change in the association community (one typewritten page in length); and program agreement form signed by the applicant's employer. **Deadline:** March 16.

1779 ■ Ascend
120 Wall St., 9th Fl.
New York, NY 10005
Ph: (212)248-4888
E-mail: info@ascendleadership.org
URL: www.ascendleadership.org
Facebook: www.facebook.com/ascendleadership
Twitter: twitter.com/ascendleader

1780 ■ Ernst and Young Scholarships
(Undergraduate/Scholarship)

Purpose: To support and honor students who have made excellent scholastic performance and contribution to the community. **Focus:** Accounting; Finance. **Qualif.:** Applicants must be current undergraduate or graduate students; must have a 3.3 GPA or higher; must be major in Accounting, Finance or IT; must be active Ascend members; must commit to attend the National Convention if selected as winner. **Criteria:** Selection will be based on the demonstrated leadership skills.

Funds Avail.: $5,000. **Number Awarded:** 5. **To Apply:** Applicants must complete and submit the application form together with the following materials: unofficial transcript, resume and 500-word minimum personal essay. **Deadline:** May 1.

1781 ■ Ashburn Institute (AI)
198 Okatie Village Dr., Ste. 103
PMB No. 301
Bluffton, SC 29909
Ph: (703)728-6482
Fax: (843)705-7643
URL: www.ashburninstitute.org

1782 ■ Mayme and Herb Frank Scholarship Program *(Graduate, Undergraduate/Scholarship)*

Purpose: To support the study of international integration and federalism at the graduate level. **Focus:** International affairs and relations. **Qualif.:** Applicants must be graduate students of strong academic standing; must have a thesis or dissertation relating to international integration and/or federalism and coursework that places major weight on international integration and/or federalism; or must have an independent study project relating to international integration and federalism to be conducted as part of a graduate program. **Criteria:** Selection of candidates will be based on the quality of the project and academic standing. Consideration is made by the Frank Education Fund Committee of the Ashburn Institute.

Funds Avail.: $500-$2,000 depending on relevance of the goals of the fund. **To Apply:** Applicants must complete the FEF Application form and must have the description of any course planned to be completed by the applicant during the period of the proposed grant; must submit the copy of the graduate transcripts if currently enrolled in a graduate program or a copy of the applicant's undergraduate transcripts if enrolled in a graduate program but have not yet started it. Application form and other supporting materials must be submitted to: Association to Unite the Democracies c/o The Ashburn Institute, The Frank Educational Fund, PO Box 77164, Washington, DC, 20013-7164, Phone: 202-220-1388, Fax: 202-220-1389. **Deadline:** April 1 for Fall term awards and October 1 for Spring term awards.

1783 ■ Asian Pacific American Advocates
1322 18th St. NW
Washington, DC 20036-1803
Ph: (202)223-5500
Fax: (202)296-0540
E-mail: oca@ocanational.org
URL: www.ocanational.org

1784 ■ Organization of Chinese Americans Scholarships *(Undergraduate/Scholarship)*

Purpose: To provide financial assistance to high school seniors in pursuing their educational career. **Focus:** General studies/Field of study not specified. **Qualif.:** Applicants must be current APA high school seniors entering their first year of college in the upcoming 2011 Fall Semester/Quarter; must demonstrate financial need; must be permanent residents or U.S. citizens; and have a cumulative Grade Point Average (GPA) of 3.0 or above (on a 4.0 scale). **Criteria:** Candidates will be selected based on achievements and financial needs.

Funds Avail.: No amount mentioned. **To Apply:** Applicants must submit resume; one-page essay; high school transcript(s); letter of acceptance from college or university; printed Student Aid Report (SAR); and financial Aid Award notification (FAN) from college or university. **Deadline:** January 10.

1785 ■ Asian Pacific American Bar Association of Silicon Valley (APABA-SV)
PO Box 60988
Palo Alto, CA 94306
E-mail: apabasv@gmail.com
URL: www.apabasv.org

1786 ■ APABA-SV Scholarships *(Advanced Professional/Scholarship)*

Purpose: To support law students in the Bay Area. **Focus:** Law. **Qualif.:** Applicants must be law students in the Bay Area who have overcome personal hardship or challenges, shown excellence and achievement in law school or demonstrated leadership and service to the Asian Pacific

Awards are arranged alphabetically below their administering organizations

American community. **Criteria:** Preference will be given to law students who will be interning at a non-profit organization that serves the Asian Pacific American community.

Funds Avail.: Amount varies. **To Apply:** Applicants must submit a resume (with GPA) and an essay (maximum of 2 pages, double-spaced). **Contact:** Email: apabasv@gmail.com.

1787 ■ Asian Pacific American Librarians Association (APALA)
PO Box 677593
Orlando, FL 32867-7593
URL: www.apalaweb.org

1788 ■ APALA Scholarship Award (Doctorate, Master's/Scholarship)

Purpose: To provide financial assistance to a student of Asian or Pacific background. **Focus:** Information science and technology; Library and archival sciences. **Qualif.:** Applicant must be of Asian/Pacific Islander heritage; must be a U.S. citizen or permanent resident of the United States or Canada; must be admitted full-time or part-time into a master's degree or doctoral program in library or information science at a library school accredited by ALA. **Criteria:** Recipients are selected based on the Scholarship Committee's review of the application materials.

Funds Avail.: $1,000. **Duration:** Annual. **Number Awarded:** 1. **To Apply:** Applicant must submit a completed application form available at the website together with a resume; copy of acceptance letter to an ALA accredited library school or library graduate school transcript; two letters of recommendation. **Deadline:** April 4. **Contact:** APALA Research & Travel Award Committee chair, Melanee Vicedo; Email: vicedo@usc.edu and co-chair Valeria Molteni; Email: valeria.molteni@sjsu.edu.

1789 ■ Asian/Pacific Bar Association of Sacramento (ABAS)
PO Box 2215
Sacramento, CA 95812-2215
E-mail: abassacramento@gmail.com
URL: www.abassacramento.com
Facebook: www.facebook.com/abassacramento
Twitter: www.twitter.com/abassacramento

1790 ■ Asian/Pacific Bar Association of Sacramento Law Foundation Scholarship (Graduate, Postgraduate/Scholarship)

Purpose: To support law students and recent law school graduates who possess extraordinary skills, desire and potential to serve and lead the greater Sacramento Asian-Pacific Islander community. **Focus:** Law. **Qualif.:** Applicants must: be either currently enrolled and in good standing at a Sacramento area (including U.C. Davis) law school or currently residing in the Sacramento area; and, have graduated from law school. **Criteria:** Recipients will be selected based on potential for community service; leadership in the Asian Pacific Islander community; academic achievement; and financial need.

Funds Avail.: Amount varies. **Duration:** Annual. **To Apply:** Applicants must submit evidence of scholarship eligibility (a copy of current law school registration or law school diploma will suffice); a personal statement; a current resume; current law school transcripts; financial information; and two references. Application form and other supporting documents should be sent to Nirav K. Desai. **Deadline:** February 19. **Contact:** Any questions about the scholarship program or its administration, please e-mail Latika Sharma at scholarships@abaslawfoundation.org.

1791 ■ Asian and Pacific Islander American Scholarship Fund (APIASF)
2025 M St. NW, Ste. 610
Washington, DC 20036
Ph: (202)986-6892
Fax: (202)530-0643
Free: 877-808-7032
E-mail: info@apiasf.org
URL: www.apiasf.org
Facebook: www.facebook.com/APIASF
Twitter: twitter.com/intent/user?screen_name=apiasf

1792 ■ APIASF Scholarships (Undergraduate/Scholarship)

Purpose: To support and encourage all Asian and Pacific Islander American students to pursue higher education by developing future leaders who will contribute back to their communities. **Focus:** General studies/Field of study not specified. **Qualif.:** Applicants must be: of Asian and/or Pacific Islander ethnicity as defined by the U.S. census; U.S. citizens, U.S. Nationals, legal permanent residents or citizens of the Federated States of Micronesia, Republic of the Marshall Islands or the Republic of Palau; and, first-time, incoming college students enrolled full-time in a two or four-year program at a U.S. accredited college or university in the U.S., Guam, American Samoa, or the Commonwealth of the Northern Mariana Islands for the coming school year. (In the Freely Associated States, this includes the Community Colleges of the Federated States of Micronesia, the Republic of Marshall Islands and the Republic of Palau.) Applicant must have cumulative, unweighted grade point average (GPA) of 2.7 or higher on a 4.0 scale. **Criteria:** Recipient will be selected based on academic record and future plans; community service and leadership; and financial need.

Funds Avail.: $2,500 to $20,000. **Duration:** Annual. **Number Awarded:** Varies. **To Apply:** Applicant must complete the application form online, available at the website of APIASF. Other instructions for the application **Deadline:** January 8.

1793 ■ ASIS International
1625 Prince St.
Alexandria, VA 22314-2882
Ph: (703)519-6200
Fax: (703)519-6299
E-mail: asis@asisonline.org
URL: www.asisonline.org/Pages/default.aspx

1794 ■ ASIS Foundation Chapter Matching Scholarships (Undergraduate/Scholarship)

Purpose: To provide educational assistance to chapter members, student members or student nonmembers pursuing a security career. **Focus:** General studies/Field of study not specified. **Qualif.:** Applicants must be part- or full-time students who have completed one year of study at an accredited college, university or community college towards a career in security profession; must be undergraduate students (their chapter will set the grade point average required, for them to be qualified for the scholarship) or graduate students who earned at least a 3.0 GPA on a 4.0 scale. **Criteria:** Applicants are evaluated based on their achievements and abilities.

Funds Avail.: $500-$1,000. **Duration:** Annual. **To Apply:** Applicants must submit a signed application form, an official transcript, and letter of recommendation from a faculty member to their sponsoring chapter. **Deadline:** November 18.

1795 ■ ASME International
2 Park Ave.
New York, NY 10016-5990
Ph: (973)882-1170
Fax: (973)882-1717
Free: 800-843-2763
E-mail: customercare@asme.org
URL: www.asme.org

1796 ■ Auxiliary Undergraduate Scholarships (Undergraduate/Scholarship)

Purpose: To provide scholarships and new developments in Mechanical Engineering; to honor students who demonstrate outstanding personal and academic characteristics. **Focus:** Engineering, Mechanical. **Qualif.:** Applicants must be full-time high school, undergraduate, or graduate students pursuing Mechanical Engineering courses or any related field of study in engineering; must be U.S citizens; and be enrolled at an accredited ABET Mechanical Engineering program in United States. **Criteria:** Recipients will be selected based on submitted application, needs, character, and ASME participation.

Funds Avail.: No specific amount. **Duration:** Annual. **To Apply:** Applicants must submit letter of recommendation by the Head of The Mechanical Engineering Faculty Advisor; letter from a non-academic reference, instructors or preferably in an Engineering School; an official transcript of records; and should have completed application form. Guidelines and application form is available from the ASME scholarship office or can be downloaded from the ASME website.

1797 ■ Lucy and Charles W.E. Clarke Scholarships (Undergraduate/Scholarship)

Purpose: To assist students in pursuing educational program in mechanical engineering or mechanical engineering technology. **Focus:** Engineering, Mechanical. **Qualif.:** Scholarship is open to schools accredited by the Accreditation Board for Engineering and Technology or substantially equivalent mechanical engineering technology departments who directly choose incoming freshmen beginning engineering studies in the fall to receive the scholarship. **Criteria:** Recipients are chosen by the departments on the basis of need, academic achievement, community involvement, work experience and recommendations.

Funds Avail.: $5,000. **Duration:** Annual. **To Apply:** Applications for deserving schools are made by the ASME Student Section as endorsed by the mechanical engineering technology department; Necessary forms are available in the website also indicating other instructions. **Deadline:** March 15. **Contact:** RuthAnn Bigley at bigleyr@asme.org.

1798 ■ Elisabeth M. and Winchell M. Parsons Scholarships (Graduate/Scholarship)

Purpose: To assist students in pursuing educational program in mechanical engineering or mechanical engineering technology. **Focus:** Engineering, Mechanical. **Qualif.:** Applicants must be full-time students seeking doctoral degree in mechanical engineering; must be U.S. citizens; and enrolled in U.S. school at an ABET accredited Mechanical Engineering Department. **Criteria:** Awards are given based on academic merit. Priority is given to students with financial need.

Funds Avail.: $2,000. **Duration:** Annual. **Number Awarded:** Up to 2. **To Apply:** Applicants must submit a letter of recommendation from the Head of the Mechanical Engineering Department or the Faculty Advisor; letter from a non-academic reference; list of scholastic recognition, honors or prizes won, membership in honorary or professional societies; list of extra-curricular college or civic activities in which they have participated and offices held; must submit an official transcript of records; grade and membership number in the American Society of Mechanical Engineers; should have completed application form; Guidelines and application form are available from the ASME scholarship office or can be downloaded from the ASME website. **Deadline:** March 1.

1799 ■ Rice-Cullimore Scholarships (Graduate/Scholarship)

Purpose: To assist students in pursuing educational program in mechanical engineering or mechanical engineering technology. **Focus:** Engineering, Mechanical. **Qualif.:** Candidate must be a foreign student intending to do graduate work for a Master's or Doctoral Degree in mechanical engineering in the United States. **Criteria:** Awards are given based on academic record, personal promise, character and financial need; Applicants must demonstrate their commitment to a career in mechanical engineering.

Funds Avail.: $2,000. **Duration:** Annual. **Number Awarded:** 1. **To Apply:** Applicant must submit a letter of recommendation from the Head of the Mechanical Engineering Department or the Faculty Advisor; Letter from a non-academic reference; and profile indicating scholastic recognition, honors or prizes won, membership in honorary or professional societies; extra-curricular college or civic activities in which they have participated, and offices held; official transcript; and completed application form. Guidelines and application form can be obtained from the ASME Scholarship Office or can be downloaded from the ASME website.

1800 ■ Marjorie Roy Rothermel Scholarships (Master's/Scholarship)

Purpose: To support students in pursuing their educational goal. **Focus:** Engineering, Mechanical. **Qualif.:** Applicants must be U.S. citizens and must be currently enrolled in a Master's degree program in a school at an ABET accredited Mechanical Engineering Department in United States. **Criteria:** Awards are given based on academic merit. Selection of applicants is based on academic performance character, need and ASME participation reviewed and scored by the Scholarship Committee.

Funds Avail.: $2,000. **Duration:** Annual. **Number Awarded:** Up to 2. **To Apply:** Applicants must submit letter of recommendation from the Head of The Mechanical Engineering Department or the Faculty Advisor; must file a letter from a non-academic reference; list of scholastic recognition, honors or prizes won; membership in honorary or professional societies; list of extra-curricular college or civic activities in which they have participated, and offices held; an official transcript of records; should have completed application form; Guidelines and application form are avail-

Awards are arranged alphabetically below their administering organizations

able from the ASME scholarship office or can be downloaded from the ASME website. **Deadline:** March 1.

1801 ■ ASPRS, The Imaging and Geospatial Information Society

5410 Grosvenor Ln., Ste. 210
Bethesda, MD 20814-2160
Ph: (301)493-0290
Fax: (301)493-0208
E-mail: asprs@asprs.org
URL: www.asprs.org

1802 ■ Robert E. Altenhofen Memorial Scholarships
(Graduate, Undergraduate/Scholarship)

Purpose: To encourage and commend college students who display exceptional interest and ability in the theoretical aspects of photogrammetry. **Focus:** Photogrammetry. **Qualif.:** Applicants must be undergraduate or graduate student members of ASPRS. **Criteria:** Recipients are selected based on the highest overall ranking.

Funds Avail.: $2,000 and a certificate. **To Apply:** Applicants must submit an application form; a statement (2 pages) regarding plans for continuing studies in theoretical photogrammetry; evidence of capabilities of the applicant in these fields; and academic transcripts.

1803 ■ Robert N. Colwell Memorial Fellowships
(Doctorate, Graduate/Fellowship)

Purpose: To encourage and commend college/university graduate students at the PhD level who display exceptional interest, desire, ability and aptitude in the field of remote sensing or other related geospatial information technologies, and who have a special interest in developing practical uses of these technologies. **Focus:** Remote sensing. **Qualif.:** Applicant must be a graduate student (Masters or PhD level); enrolled or planning to enroll in a college/university in the United States or Canada; or recently graduated post-doctoral researcher pursuing a study in remote sensing or related geospatial information technologies. **Criteria:** Recipients are selected based on the application materials submitted.

Funds Avail.: $6,500. **Duration:** Annual. **To Apply:** Applicants must submit completed application form; a listing of courses taken; transcript of all college/university level courses completed; a listing of internships, special projects or work experience; three letters of recommendation; and a statement (maximum of two pages) detailing the applicant's educational or research goals.

1804 ■ ERDAS Internship *(Graduate/Internship, Award)*

Purpose: To provide individuals an opportunity to carry out a small research project of their own choice, or to work on an existing ERDAS project as part of a team. **Focus:** Photogrammetry; Remote sensing. **Qualif.:** Applicant must be a graduate student of photogrammetry and remote sensing; and a student member of ASPRS. **Criteria:** Applicants are selected based on submitted applications.

Funds Avail.: $2,500. **Duration:** Eight weeks. **To Apply:** Applicants must submit an application form; two letters of recommendation; official transcripts from each college and university attended; a proposal (maximum of 1,000 words) stating the significance of the research, the proposed methodology, the expected results and a schedule. Research topics should be in the general area of digital photogrammetry and remote sensing. **Remarks:** Funded by ERDAS Inc. **Contact:** ASPRS Scholarship Administrator at scholarships@asprs.org.

1805 ■ William A. Fischer Memorial Scholarships *(Graduate/Scholarship)*

Purpose: To facilitate studies and career goals directed towards new and innovative uses of remote sensing data/techniques. **Focus:** Remote sensing. **Qualif.:** Applicants must be current or prospective graduate student members of ASPRS. **Criteria:** Applicants are selected based on the highest overall ranking.

Funds Avail.: $2,000 and a certificate. **Duration:** One year. **To Apply:** Applicant must submit an application form; a statement (2 pages) detailing educational and career plans for continuing studies in remote sensing applications; transcript of grades. **Deadline:** October 18. **Contact:** ASPRS Scholarship Administrator at scholarships@asprs.org.

1806 ■ Ta Liang Memorial Awards *(Graduate/Grant, Award)*

Purpose: To support research-related travel in remote sensing. **Focus:** Remote sensing. **Qualif.:** Applicant must be a graduate student member of ASPRS. **Criteria:** Applicants are selected based on scholastic record, research travel plan, letters of recommendation and community service activities.

Funds Avail.: $2,000 and a hand-engrossed certificate. **Duration:** Annual. **To Apply:** Applicants must submit an application form; a letter of recommendation; a statement (2 pages) detailing the plan for research-related travel; a transcript of all college-level courses completed and grades received; class rank; a description of extracurricular activities (particularly relating to community service).

1807 ■ Francis H. Moffitt Memorial Scholarships *(Graduate, Undergraduate/Scholarship)*

Purpose: To encourage upper-division undergraduate and graduate-level college students to pursue a course of study in surveying and photogrammetry leading to a career in the geospatial mapping profession. **Focus:** Photogrammetry; Remote sensing. **Qualif.:** Program is open to students currently enrolled or planning to enroll in a college/university in the United States or Canada pursuing a program of study in surveying or photogrammetry. **Criteria:** Applicants are selected based on the submitted applications.

Funds Avail.: $5,500. **Duration:** Annual. **To Apply:** Applicants must submit an application form; a listing of courses taken and/or those to be taken in surveying and photogrammetry and other related geospatial information technologies; a transcript of all college/university level courses completed; a listing of internships, special projects or work experience; two letters of recommendation or reference form; a statement (maximum of two pages) detailing the applicant's educational and research goals.

1808 ■ The Kenneth J. Osborn Memorial Scholarships *(Undergraduate/Scholarship)*

Purpose: To encourage and commend college students who display exceptional interest, desire, ability and aptitude to enter the profession of surveying, mapping, photogrammetry, or geospatial information and technology. **Focus:** Photogrammetry. **Qualif.:** Applicant must be an undergraduate student enrolled or planning to enroll in a college/university in the United States. **Criteria:** Scholarship will be given to an applicant who has the highest overall ranking.

Awards are arranged alphabetically below their administering organizations

Funds Avail.: $2,000. **Duration:** Annual. **To Apply:** Applicants must submit an application form; a listing of courses taken in surveying; mapping; photogrammetry and geospatial information and technology and the academic grades received; a transcript of all college or university level courses completed; two letters of recommendation from faculty members or professionals; evidence materials of the applicant's capabilities in this field; a statement of work experience; and a personal statement (maximum of 2 pages).

1809 ■ Paul R. Wolf Memorial Scholarships
(Graduate/Scholarship)

Purpose: To encourage and commend college students who displays exceptional interest, desire, ability, and aptitude to enter the profession of teaching Surveying, Mapping or Photography. **Focus:** Education; Photogrammetry. **Qualif.:** Applicant must be a graduate student member of ASPRS; enrolled or planning to enroll in a college/university in the United States; pursuing a program of study in preparation for entering the teaching profession in the general area of Surveying, Mapping or Photogrammetry. **Criteria:** The committee evaluates each application and will select the applicant who best meets the criteria.

Funds Avail.: $3,500 and a certificate. **To Apply:** Applicants must submit an application form; a listing of courses taken in Surveying, Mapping and Photogrammetry and the academic grades received; a transcript of all college or university level courses; two letters of recommendation from faculty members having knowledge of the applicant's capabilities as an educator in this field; evidence materials of the applicant's capabilities in this field; and a statement of teaching experience.

1810 ■ Z/I Imaging Scholarships *(Graduate/Scholarship)*

Purpose: To support graduate-level studies addressing new and innovative uses of signal processing, image processing techniques and the application of photogrammetry to real-world techniques. **Focus:** Photogrammetry. **Qualif.:** Applicant must be a member of ASPRS; planning to enroll for graduate studies in a college/university in the United States or elsewhere. **Criteria:** Scholarship will be given to an applicant who has the highest overall ranking.

Funds Avail.: $2,000. **Duration:** Annual. **To Apply:** Applicants must submit an application form; a statement (2 pages) detailing educational and career plans for continuing studies in photogrammetric applications; two reference forms/letters from faculty members who have knowledge of the applicant's capabilities; and evidence materials of the applicant's capabilities in this field.

1811 ■ Associated General Contractors of America (AGC)
2300 Wilson Blvd., Ste. 300
Arlington, VA 22201
Ph: (703)548-3118
Fax: (703)548-3119
Free: 800-242-1767
E-mail: info@agc.org
URL: www.agc.org
Facebook: www.facebook.com/AGCofA
LinkedIn: www.linkedin.com/company/associated-general
 -contractors-of-america
Twitter: twitter.com/AGCofA

Awards are arranged alphabetically below their administering organizations

1812 ■ AGC Foundation Outstanding Educator Awards *(Other/Award)*

Purpose: To recognize an educator who makes a significant mark in the field of construction education, and support the education of the students of the winning educator. **Focus:** Construction. **Qualif.:** Nominee must be a full-time teaching faculty member of a university construction program or a construction-related engineering program or with an institution-approved construction option, with at least four years full-time teaching experience. **Criteria:** Winner shall be chosen based on the teaching responsibilities and activities with AGC and/or other construction industry organizations.

Funds Avail.: $10,000 ($5,000 for the educator); $2,500 scholarships for the two students chosen by the winning educator. **Duration:** Annual. **To Apply:** Nominee must submit two copies of nomination form and attachments; the joint letter of nomination; the nomination checklist; a maximum of three letters of reference; and a "Notification of Receipt" Postcard. **Deadline:** November 15. **Remarks:** Established in 1985. **Contact:** Melinda Patrician, AGC Education and Research Foundation, at the above address; Email: patricianm@agc.org.

1813 ■ Associated General Contractors of New York State
10 Airline Dr., Ste. 203
Albany, NY 12205
Ph: (518)456-1134
Fax: (518)456-1198
E-mail: agcadmin@agcnys.org
URL: www.agcnys.org

1814 ■ AGC New York State Chapter Scholarship Program *(Undergraduate/Scholarship)*

Purpose: To provide financial assistance to students pursuing a degree in Civil engineering, Construction Technology and Construction Management at colleges or universities. **Focus:** Engineering, Civil. **Qualif.:** Applicant must be entering the 2nd, 3rd or 4th year of a two or four-year college; must seriously intent upon a career in the highway construction industry. Applicant must have 2.50 GPA. **Criteria:** Applicant will be evaluated by the Selection Committee of the New York State Chapter, Inc., Associated General Contractors.

Funds Avail.: $2,500-$5,000. **Duration:** Annual; One year. **Number Awarded:** 20. **To Apply:** Applicant must submit a signed, completed five-page application; three evaluation forms: one completed by a college faculty advisor, and two completed by adults not related to the applicant and preferably in the industry; and, official transcript of all college grades. **Deadline:** May 15. **Remarks:** Established in 1988. **Contact:** Email:bmanning@agcnys.org.

1815 ■ Associated Locksmiths of America (ALOA)
3500 Easy St.
Dallas, TX 75247
Ph: (214)819-9733
Free: 800-532-2562
URL: www.aloa.org
LinkedIn: www.linkedin.com/company/associated
 -locksmiths-of-america

1816 ■ ALOA Scholarship Foundation
(Undergraduate/Scholarship)

Purpose: To support the education of students entering the locksmithing field or already in the locksmithing field. **Focus:** Education, Vocational-technical. **Qualif.:** Applicants must be individuals desirous of entering the locksmithing field or individuals already in the field of locksmithing who wish to improve their professional skills through education. **Criteria:** Applicants will be evaluated based on their financial needs, character, aptitude for the skills necessary in locksmithing, desire for a career in locksmithing, availability to attend the event for which award is given, demonstrated commitment to the locksmith industry, letters of recommendation from locksmith industry reference, and previous scholarship awards.

Funds Avail.: No specific amount. **To Apply:** Applicants must complete the application form provided in the website of the Foundation and submit it along with the letters of recommendation from locksmith industry references.

1817 ■ Associated Press Television and Radio Association (APTRA)
1850 N Central Ave., Ste. 640
Phoenix, AZ 85004
URL: www.aptra.com

1818 ■ APTRA-Clete Roberts/Kathryn Dettman Memorial Journalism Scholarship *(Undergraduate/Scholarship)*

Purpose: To help students pursue a broadcast journalism course. **Focus:** Broadcasting. **Qualif.:** Applicants must be college students enrolled at a college or university in one of the 13 APTRA states; must be pursuing a career in Broadcast Journalism. (Incoming freshmen and high school seniors are not eligible). **Criteria:** Judges will evaluate applicants based on academic achievement, financial need and broadcast career goals.

Funds Avail.: $1,500. **Duration:** Annual. **Number Awarded:** 1. **To Apply:** Applicants must complete the application form and must attach tapes or writing samples of broadcast-related work. **Deadline:** February 27.

1819 ■ Associates of the American Foreign Service Worldwide (AAFSW)
4001 N 9th St., Ste. 214
Arlington, VA 22203
Ph: (703)820-5420
Fax: (703)820-5421
E-mail: office@aafsw.org
URL: www.aafsw.org
Facebook: www.facebook.com/aafsw
Twitter: twitter.com/aafsw

1820 ■ AAFSW College Merit Scholarship *(College, Undergraduate/Scholarship)*

Purpose: To recognize an outstanding student currently enrolled in college. **Focus:** Communications; Human relations. **Qualif.:** Applicants must be currently college students whose families are part of the foreign affairs community and an immediate family member must be a current member of AAFSW at time of the application. **Criteria:** Selection will be based on the committees' criteria.

Funds Avail.: $2,000. **To Apply:** Applicants must submit the following requirements: complete application form; original essay compose of 500 words or fewer; transcript of college courses that the applicants have taken so far; list of applicants' current courses and; two letters of recommendation from individuals with knowledge of the applicants' abilities in two of these areas - volunteering, paid employment, sports, art, music, etc. **Deadline:** April.

1821 ■ The Judy Felt Memorial Volunteerism Scholarship *(College, Undergraduate/Scholarship)*

Purpose: To recognize student with an exceptional record of community service. **Focus:** Communications; Human relations. **Qualif.:** Applicants must be high school seniors, gap year students or college students. **Criteria:** Selection will be based on the committees' criteria.

Funds Avail.: $1,000. **To Apply:** Applicants may contact the Association for application process and other information. **Deadline:** April.

1822 ■ Association for the Advancement of Baltic Studies (AABS)
University of Washington, Box 353420
Seattle, WA 98195-3420
Ph: (301)977-8491
Fax: (301)977-8492
E-mail: aabs@uw.edu
URL: www.aabs-balticstudies.org
Facebook: www.facebook.com/aabs.baltic.studies

1823 ■ Association for the Advancement of Baltic Studies Dissertation Grants for Graduate Students *(Doctorate/Grant)*

Purpose: To support doctoral dissertation research and write-up in any field of Baltic Studies. **Focus:** General studies/Field of study not specified. **Qualif.:** Applicants must be currently enrolled in a PhD program and have completed all requirements for a PhD except the dissertation. **Criteria:** Recipients are selected based on the scholarly potential of the applicant, quality and scholarly importance of the proposed work especially to the development of Baltic studies.

Funds Avail.: Up to $2,000. **Duration:** Annual. **To Apply:** Applicants must send three copies of a 500-word proposal, a one-page budget specifying expenses, a CV, evidence of current enrollment in a PhD program and a no more than 25-page writing sample. **Deadline:** December 19. **Contact:** Dr. Ivars Ijabs, Vice-President of Professional Development, at ivars.ijabs@lu.lv.

1824 ■ Association for the Advancement of Scandinavian Studies in Canada
University of Victoria
3800 Finnerty Rd.
Victoria, BC, Canada
URL: aassc.com

1825 ■ The AASSC Gurli Aagaard Woods Undergraduate Publication Awards *(Undergraduate/Award)*

Purpose: To develop skills and knowledge of undergraduate students about Scandinavian cultures and studies. **Focus:** General studies/Field of study not specified. **Qualif.:** Candidates must be an undergraduate students who have

Awards are arranged alphabetically below their administering organizations

interest in Scandinavian-Canadian Studies. **Criteria:** Selection will be based on the committee's criteria.

Funds Avail.: No specific amount. **To Apply:** Candidates must submit a 2,000 to 4,000 words essay (excluding footnotes and bibliography) in MLA style and must attach a title sheet with the following information: the student's name and contact information; the instructor's name; institutional affiliation; contact information; and the title and dates of the course in which the work was produced. **Deadline:** May 1.

1826 ■ The AASSC Marna Feldt Graduate Publication Awards (Graduate/Award)

Purpose: To develop skills and knowledge of the students about Scandinavian cultures and studies. **Focus:** General studies/Field of study not specified. **Qualif.:** Candidates must be graduate students who have interest in Scandinavian-Canadian Studies. **Criteria:** Selection will be based on the committee's criteria.

Funds Avail.: No specific amount. **To Apply:** Candidates must submit a 2,000 to 4,000 words essay (excluding footnotes and bibliography) in MLA style and must attach a title sheet with the following information: the student's name and contact information; the instructor's name; institutional affiliation; contact information; and the title and dates of the course in which the work was produced. **Deadline:** May 1.

1827 ■ AASSC Norwegian Travel Grants (Professional development/Grant)

Purpose: To help strengthen and encourage the presence of Norwegian language and culture in Canadian higher education. **Focus:** General studies/Field of study not specified. **Qualif.:** Applicants must be members of AASSC/AAESC; must be planning a visit to Norway with one or more of the following goals: attend a course, conference or seminar; do research or gather scientific information; establish or renew professional or academic contacts; seek out and gather teaching materials. **Criteria:** Selection will be based on the committee's criteria.

Funds Avail.: No specific amount. **To Apply:** Applicants may visit the website for the application process and other required materials. **Deadline:** May 1.

1828 ■ Association of American Geographers (AAG)
1710 16th St. NW
Washington, DC 20009
Ph: (202)234-1450
Fax: (202)234-2744
E-mail: gaia@aag.org
URL: www.aag.org
Facebook: www.facebook.com/geographers
LinkedIn: www.linkedin.com/groups/53689/profile
Twitter: twitter.com/theAAG

1829 ■ AAG Dissertation Research Grants (Doctorate/Grant)

Purpose: To provide support for doctoral dissertation research in the field of geography. **Focus:** Geography. **Qualif.:** Applicants must be AAG members for at least one year at the time of application submission. **Criteria:** Selection of recipients will be based on the submitted proposals. Proposals should demonstrate high standards of scholarship.

Funds Avail.: Around $1,000. **To Apply:** Application is via online. Digital submissions are required. All information must be entered in the online application form. **Deadline:** December 31. **Remarks:** In addition to the information applicants will provide on the online application form, their dissertation supervisors must certify their eligibility by sending an email prior to the deadline. **Contact:** Email at grantsawards@aag.org.

1830 ■ Darrel Hess Community College Geography Scholarships (Undergraduate/Scholarship)

Purpose: To provide financial assistance to qualified individuals who want to pursue their education. **Focus:** Geography. **Qualif.:** Applicants must be students currently enrolled at a US community college, junior college, city college, or similar two-year educational institution; must have completed at least two transfer courses in geography and plan to transfer to a four-year institution as a geography major during the coming academic year. **Criteria:** Selection of applicants will be based on the overall quality of the application, scholastic excellence and academic promise. Consideration will be given to those in need of financial support.

Funds Avail.: $1,000. **Duration:** Annual. **Number Awarded:** 2. **To Apply:** Applicants must complete the scholarship application available online at www.aag.org/grantsawards/hessform.rtf; must submit a two-page personal statement describing the applicant's academic and personal background, as well as the applicant's academic goals and interest in pursuing geography as a major at a baccalaureate institution; must have two letters of recommendation from college instructors; must have a copy of the applicant's current unofficial transcript. Application form and other supporting materials must be sent to Association of American Geographers, Hess Scholarship, 1710 16th St. NW, Washington, DC 20009-3198. **Deadline:** December 31.

1831 ■ Association on American Indian Affairs (AAIA)
966 Hungerford Dr., Ste. 12-B
Rockville, MD 20850
Ph: (240)314-7155
Fax: (240)314-7159
E-mail: general.aaia@indian-affairs.org
URL: indian-affairs.org
Facebook: www.facebook.com/Association-on-American-Indian-Affairs-216368710502
Twitter: twitter.com/IndianAffairs

1832 ■ Elizabeth and Sherman Asche Memorial Scholarships (Graduate, Undergraduate/Scholarship)

Purpose: To provide financial assistance to native people aiming for higher education. **Focus:** Public health; Science. **Qualif.:** Applicants must be full-time students from the Continental US or Alaska; must be graduate or undergraduate students pursuing a degree in public health or science. **Criteria:** Applicants will be selected based on the submitted materials.

Funds Avail.: $1,500. **Duration:** One academic year. **To Apply:** Applicants must submit the completed application form; Financial Need Analysis with FAO signature; certificate of at least 1/4 Indian blood; proof of tribal enrollment; a one-to-three-page essay stating educational goals and life experiences; two letters of recommendation; current Financial Aid Award Letter; copies of official transcript(s);

Awards are arranged alphabetically below their administering organizations

class schedule; and undergraduate class standing.

1833 ■ Florence Young Memorial Scholarships (Master's/Scholarship)

Purpose: To provide financial assistance to students for their educational expenses. **Focus:** Law. **Qualif.:** Applicants must be students pursuing a master's degree in art, public health or law and members of a tribe from the Continental U.S. or Alaska. Canadian students are not eligible. **Criteria:** Selection will be based on the committee's criteria.

Funds Avail.: $1,500. **Duration:** Annual. **To Apply:** Applicants may contact the Association for the application process and other information.

1834 ■ Sequoyah Graduate Scholarships (Master's/Scholarship)

Purpose: To provide financial assistance to students for their educational expenses. **Focus:** General studies/Field of study not specified. **Qualif.:** Applicants must be students in any curriculum who are seeking a master's degree and must be members of a tribe from the Continental U.S. or Alaska. Canadian students are not eligible. **Criteria:** Selection will be based on the committee's criteria.

Funds Avail.: $1,500. **Duration:** Annual. **To Apply:** Applicants may contact the Association for the application process and other information.

1835 ■ Allogan Slagle Memorial Scholarships (Undergraduate, Graduate/Scholarship)

Purpose: To provide financial assistance to non-federally recognize tribe members who are aiming higher education. **Focus:** Native American studies. **Qualif.:** Applicants must be students in any curriculum who are enrolled in tribes that are not recognized by the federal government. **Criteria:** Selection shall be based on the aforementioned qualifications and compliance with the application details.

Funds Avail.: No specific amount. **Duration:** Annual. **Number Awarded:** Varies. **To Apply:** Applicants must submit one application package only for the scholarship. Other details about application can be verified at the program website. **Deadline:** June 1. **Remarks:** Established in 2004.

1836 ■ Adolph Van Pelt Special Fund for Indians Scholarships (Undergraduate/Scholarship)

Purpose: To provide financial assistance to federally recognize tribe members who are aiming higher education. **Focus:** Native American studies. **Qualif.:** Applicants must be students who are enrolled in federally recognized tribes and who are seeking a degree in any curriculum. **Criteria:** Selection shall be based on the aforementioned qualifications and compliance with the application details.

Funds Avail.: No specific amount. **Duration:** Annual. **To Apply:** Applicants must submit one application package only for the scholarship. Other details about application can be verified at the program website. **Deadline:** June 1. **Remarks:** Established in 1987.

1837 ■ Association of American Indian Physicians (AAIP)

1225 Sovereign Row, Ste. 103
Oklahoma City, OK 73108-1854
Ph: (405)946-7072
Fax: (405)946-7651
URL: aaip.org

Awards are arranged alphabetically below their administering organizations

Facebook: www.facebook.com/The-Association-of-American-Indian-Physicians-156976135945
Twitter: www.twitter.com/AAIP1971

1838 ■ Association of American Indian Physicians Scholarships (Graduate, Undergraduate/Scholarship)

Purpose: To provide a framework for undergraduate and graduate students in the application process to a health professional school. **Focus:** Health education. **Qualif.:** Applicants must be undergraduate and graduate medical students; must be American Indian and Alaska Native Students. **Criteria:** Preference will be given to those students who meet the criteria.

Funds Avail.: Amount varies. **To Apply:** Applicants must submit the completed application form; AAIP Student Primary Data Sheet Scholarship Application; Recent College and/or University Transcripts; one letter of recommendation from a professor or academic advisor; copy of Certificate of Degree of Indian Blood or Tribal Identification Card; recent photograph for identification and publication purposes; one page personal statement answering: Why they are seeking a professional career in the health professions? What influenced them and the experience(s) they have had to support this decision? Their career goals and where they plan to work. The physician and medical students will use this in their mock interview.

1839 ■ Association of American Medical Colleges (AAMC)

655 K St. NW, Ste. 100
Washington, DC 20001-2399
Ph: (202)828-0400
E-mail: amcas@aamc.org
URL: www.aamc.org
Facebook: www.facebook.com/aamctoday
Twitter: twitter.com/aamctoday

1840 ■ Herbert W. Nickens Medical Student Scholarships (Advanced Professional/Scholarship)

Purpose: To support outstanding students who have shown leadership in efforts to eliminate inequities in medical education and health care and have demonstrated leadership efforts in addressing educational, societal, and health care needs of racial and ethnic minorities in the United States. **Focus:** Education, Medical. **Qualif.:** Applicants must be U.S. citizens or permanent residents who are entering third year of study in an accredited U.S. medical school. **Criteria:** Recipients will be selected based on academic standing.

Funds Avail.: $5,000. **Duration:** Annual. **Number Awarded:** 5. **To Apply:** Applicants must submit one original and nine photocopies of nomination letter from the medical school's dean or the dean's designate discussing the leadership, academic achievement, awards and honors; letters of recommendation from the medical school and faculty member; personal statement (does not exceed 250 words) discussing motivation for pursuing medical career; curriculum vitae; and official medical school academic transcript. **Deadline:** May 6. **Contact:** Angela Moses at NickensAwards@aamc.org.

1841 ■ Association of Applied Paleontological Sciences (AAPS)

96 E 700 S
Logan, UT 84321-5555

Ph: (435)752-7145
URL: www.aaps.net/index.html

1842 ■ A. Allen Graffham Research Grants
(Advanced Professional, Professional development/ Grant)

Purpose: To support researchers that will publish on specimens collected by, or in collaboration with, AAPS members. **Focus:** Geology; Paleontology. **Qualif.:** Applicants must be scientists, researchers or students in paleontology. **Criteria:** Selection will be based on the committee's criteria.

Funds Avail.: $1,000 per month for college and university graduate, and graduate studies students; $800 per month for college and university students. **Duration:** Annual. **Number Awarded:** Varies. **To Apply:** Interested applicants may apply by sending a letter of application explaining the focus of their research, which AAPS member they collected with or acquired the fossils from, and what they plan on using the money for. Applicants must also submit a copy of their resume, publication, and a copy of their paper. **Deadline:** March 7; July 18; October 30.

1843 ■ Dan Rigel Memorial Educational Grants
(Professional development, Advanced Professional/ Grant)

Purpose: To promote the education of their students in geology and paleontology. **Focus:** Geology; Paleontology. **Qualif.:** Applicants must be high school teachers or high school educators. **Criteria:** Awardees will be selected based upon need and the proposed use of funds.

Funds Avail.: $1,000. **Duration:** Annual. **To Apply:** Applicants must contact the Association to obtain an application form. Also, applicants need to write a letter stating how they propose to use the grant.

1844 ■ Charles Sternberg Scholarship *(Graduate/ Scholarship)*

Purpose: To support graduate level students in paleontology who are conducting various studies about macro vertebrate fossils. **Focus:** Paleontology. **Qualif.:** Applicants must be graduate level students in paleontology attending universities worldwide; must be active in field research and collecting. **Criteria:** Applicants are selected based on the criteria set by the Association and if they meet the approval of the board of directors and the membership.

Funds Avail.: $1,500. **Duration:** Annual. **To Apply:** Applicants must submit the following requirements: application letter explaining the focus of the study; recommendation letter from one or more professors; curriculum vitae or college transcript. **Deadline:** December 1. **Contact:** Neal Larson, Scholarship and Grant Chairperson; Email: ammoniteguy@gmail.com.

1845 ■ René M. Vandervelde Research Grants
(Undergraduate, Professional development/Grant)

Purpose: To encourage scientific research and publications on the fauna and flora of these deposits. **Focus:** Geology; Paleontology. **Qualif.:** Applicants must be students and researchers working in the marine paleontology, geology or stratigraphy of the Late Cretaceous Pierre and Bearpaw Shales of North America. **Criteria:** Selection will be based on the committee's criteria.

Funds Avail.: $1,000. **Duration:** Annual. **To Apply:** Interested applicants may contact the AAPS Scholarship Chairman and send a letter of request, a brief synopsis of planned research goals, resume, and a letter of support from either a professor and/or associates. **Contact:** Neal Larson, Scholarship and Grant Chairperson, ammoniteguy@gmail.com.

1846 ■ James R. Welch Scholarship *(Graduate/ Scholarship)*

Purpose: To support graduate level students in paleontology who are conducting various studies about macro invertebrate fossils. **Focus:** Paleontology. **Qualif.:** Applicants must be graduate level students in paleontology attending universities worldwide; must be active in field research and collecting. **Criteria:** Applicants are selected based on the criteria set by the Association and if they meet the approval of the board of directors and the membership.

Funds Avail.: $1,500. **Duration:** Annual. **To Apply:** Applicants must submit the following requirements: application letter explaining the focus of the study; recommendation letter from one or more professors; curriculum vitae or college transcript. **Deadline:** December 1. **Contact:** Neal Larson, Scholarship and Grant Chairperson; Email: ammoniteguy@gmail.com.

1847 ■ Association for Applied and Therapeutic Humor (AATH)
220 E State St., Fl. G
Rockford, IL 61104
Ph: (815)708-6587
E-mail: info@aath.org
URL: www.aath.org
Facebook: www.facebook.com/healthyhumor
Twitter: twitter.com/search?q=aath.org

1848 ■ The Dave Family "Humor Studies" Scholarships *(Undergraduate, Graduate/Scholarship)*

Purpose: To help cultivate the next generation of AATH members. **Focus:** Recreational therapy. **Qualif.:** Applicants must be college students pursuing humor/laughter studies with an interest in entering the field of applied or therapeutic humor. **Criteria:** Priority will be given to applicants entering colleges and universities in the United States.

Funds Avail.: No specific amount. **Duration:** Annual. **To Apply:** Applicants may contact Deb Price, AATH Scholarship co-chair. **Deadline:** December 31. **Contact:** Deb Price at debprice615@gmail.com.

1849 ■ Ed Dunkelblau Scholarships *(All/Scholarship, Award)*

Purpose: To honor the work, dedication, commitment and contribution to AATH and the field of therapeutic humor. **Focus:** Recreational therapy. **Qualif.:** Applicants must be practitioners of color or researchers interested in the cultural applications of therapeutic humor. **Criteria:** Selection will be based on the applicant's awareness of AATH mission.

Funds Avail.: No specific amount. **To Apply:** Applicants are required to submit an application demonstrating interest, statement of work and awareness to the AATH mission. **Contact:** E-mail submission should be made to: staff@aath.org.

1850 ■ The Margie Klein "Paper Plate" Scholarships *(Undergraduate/Scholarship)*

Purpose: To honor the work, dedication, commitment and contribution to AATH and in the field of therapeutic humor.

Focus: Recreational therapy. **Qualif.:** Applicants must show interest in therapeutic humor. **Criteria:** Selection will be based on the AATH's criteria: clarity; innovation/originality/creativity; and impact.

Funds Avail.: No specific amount. **Duration:** Annual. **To Apply:** Applicants must submit an essay describing how humor helped them in work-related situations. Examples can come from the corporate world, the nonprofit arena, or the self-employed. If possible, please provide at least three examples. Essays should range from approximately 250 to 500 words. They must also indicate their AATH membership status. **Deadline:** December 31. **Contact:** AATH Scholarship co-chair, Deb Price, at debprice615@gmail.com.

1851 ■ Lenny Ravich "Shalom" Scholarships (Advanced Professional/Scholarship)

Purpose: To help cultivate the next generation of AATH members. **Focus:** Recreational therapy. **Qualif.:** Applicants must be individuals whose works in humor and laughter clearly and tangibly demonstrate commitment to world peace. **Criteria:** Selection will be based on the impact of the applicant's essay.

Funds Avail.: $100. **Duration:** Annual. **To Apply:** Applicants must submit three essays (up to 250 words each) answering these questions: How do you presently apply (or plan to apply) your knowledge and experience in humor and laughter to advance world peace?; How has your mission and purpose in life brought you to this moment?; Why do you feel that you are deserving of this scholarship? **Remarks:** The scholarship is created by Lenny Ravich, Director of the Gestalt Institute of Tel Aviv.

1852 ■ Patty Wooten Scholarships (Professional development/Scholarship, Award, Recognition)

Purpose: To support nurses who are currently involved in creating humor interventions that are being used in a therapeutic manner for patients, family and/or staff. **Focus:** Recreational therapy. **Qualif.:** Applicants must be nurses (R.N., L.P.N., L.V.N. or C.N.A). **Criteria:** Selection will be based on the AATH's criteria.

Funds Avail.: No amount specified. **Duration:** Annual. **To Apply:** Applicants are required to write an essay describing how they perceive humor to be therapeutic and how they work, program, or intervention efforts have benefited patients, family, or staff. They must also indicate their AATH membership status. **Contact:** Deb Price, AATH Scholarship co-chair, at debprice615@gmail.com.

1853 ■ Association of Art Museum Curators (AAMC)
174 E 80th St.
New York, NY 10075
Ph: (646)405-8057
Fax: (212)537-5571
E-mail: aamc@artcurators.org
URL: www.artcurators.org
Twitter: twitter.com/Art_Curators

1854 ■ AAMC Foundation Engagement Program for International Curators Grants (Advanced Professional, Professional development/Grant)

Purpose: To provide opportunities for professional development and exchange, as well as to expand and strengthen the international curatorial community and give primacy to the curatorial voice in the international dialogue between museum professionals. **Focus:** Museum science. **Qualif.:** Application is open to non-U.S. based curators and U.S. liaisons working on or having worked within exhibitions and projects that explore historic American Art (c. 1500-1980), including painting; sculpture; works on paper, including prints, drawing and photography; decorative arts; and excluding architecture; design; and performance. U.S. liaisons must be AAMC members in good standing. Non-U.S. based curators must be proficient in oral and written English. **Criteria:** Selection will be based on the AAMC Foundation's criteria.

Funds Avail.: Amount varies. **Duration:** Annual; up to 2 years. **Number Awarded:** Varies. **To Apply:** Applicants must contact the AAMC Foundation for more information regarding the separate application process for the U.S. liaisons and non-U.S. based curators. **Deadline:** October 15.

1855 ■ Kress/AAR Fellowships (Professional development/Fellowship)

Purpose: To provide essential funding for curators to develop projects that require research in Italy. **Focus:** Museum science. **Qualif.:** Applicants must be AAMC members in good standing. **Criteria:** Selection will be based on the research proposal of the applicants. Priority will be given to those without fund to support travel research.

Funds Avail.: No specific amount. **Duration:** Annual. **To Apply:** Applicants must provide a letter of support from institution director, project director and/or host of project. They are required to list preferred period of residency, indicating a first and second choice. Research can be exhibition related or for written scholarly work, but should not be in conjunction with completing a dissertation. **Deadline:** January 9.

1856 ■ Association for Asian Studies (AAS)
825 Victors Way, Ste. 310
Ann Arbor, MI 48108
Ph: (734)665-2490
Fax: (734)665-3801
URL: www.asian-studies.org
Facebook: www.facebook.com/Association-for-Asian-Studies-Inc-AAS-104663456241055
LinkedIn: www.linkedin.com/company/association-for-asian-studies
Twitter: twitter.com/AASAsianStudies

1857 ■ AAS CIAC Small Grants (Graduate/Grant)

Purpose: To support funding requests for indirect costs of research. **Focus:** General studies/Field of study not specified. **Qualif.:** Applicants must be AAS members, junior and independent scholars, adjunct faculties, and dissertation-level graduate students. **Criteria:** Preference will be given to applicants who show sincere interest in research, particularly in Chinese or Inner Asia studies.

Funds Avail.: Up to $2,000. **Duration:** Annual. **To Apply:** Applicants need not fill out an application form; however, they must submit: a 250-word abstract of the project; a detailed budget of anticipated expenses, including other sources of funding; a two-page (maximum) curriculum vitae In the case of graduate students, a letter of support from their dissertation advisor, without which the application will not be considered. **Deadline:** February 1.

Awards are arranged alphabetically below their administering organizations

1858 ■ AAS Korean Studies Scholarship Program (Graduate/Scholarship)

Purpose: To provide scholarship for graduate students majoring in Korean studies in North America for their coursework and/or research. **Focus:** General studies/Field of study not specified. **Qualif.:** Applicants must be M.A. or Ph.D. students majoring in Korean studies in any university in North America. Applicants must exhibit sufficient ability to use Korean-language sources in their research and study. **Criteria:** Selection will be based on the submitted applications.

Funds Avail.: No specific amount. **Duration:** Annual. **To Apply:** Applicants must complete a Foundation Application Form, a three-page proposal outlining research interests and academic progress of the student, with a separate one-page bibliography; grade transcripts of coursework; and three letters of recommendation, one of which must be from someone able to attest to the applicant's language ability.

1859 ■ Association for Behavior Analysis International (ABAI)
550 W Centre Ave.
Portage, MI 49024
Ph: (269)492-9310
Fax: (269)492-9316
E-mail: mail@abainternational.org
URL: www.abainternational.org/welcome.aspx
Facebook: www.facebook.com/ABAInternational.org?v=wall

1860 ■ Marian Breland Bailey Award (Graduate, Undergraduate/Award)

Purpose: To promote research and scholarly activity by students in the applied analysis of animal behavior. **Focus:** Animal science and behavior. **Qualif.:** All current students and individuals who received degrees in the past year are eligible. Undergraduate submissions will receive special consideration as long as the project was conducted during bachelor's degree training. **Criteria:** Selection will be based on the committee's criteria and the application materials submitted.

Funds Avail.: No specific amount. **Duration:** Annual. **To Apply:** Applicants must submit any project (e.g., conceptual, review, empirical) that addresses issues relevant to the applied analysis of animal behavior. The paper should be prepared as if for submission to a journal, and must meet APA publication guidelines. Work project should not exceed 30 pages and should be in Word format. **Contact:** SIG president, Dr. Terri Bright, at terribright@comcast.net.

1861 ■ Student Research Awards from the Behavioral Gerontology SIG (Undergraduate, Graduate/Award, Monetary)

Purpose: To support research and scholarly activity by students in behavioral gerontology. **Focus:** Behavioral sciences; Gerontology. **Qualif.:** Applicant must be any graduate or undergraduate student who is first author on a behavioral gerontology related talk or poster. **Criteria:** Selection will be based on the committee's criteria and the application materials submitted.

Funds Avail.: $50. **Duration:** Annual. **Number Awarded:** 1. **To Apply:** There is no formal submission process. Any presentation (e.g., conceptual, review, empirical) that addresses issues relevant to behavioral gerontology is eligible.

1862 ■ Association of Black Women Lawyers of New Jersey
PO Box 22524
Trenton, NJ 08607
Ph: (609)614-7638
E-mail: abwl-nj@yahoogroups.com
URL: abwl-nj.org

1863 ■ Bernadine Johnson-Marshall and Martha Bell Williams Scholarships (Undergraduate/Scholarship)

Purpose: To encourage greater participation of African-American women in the field of law. **Focus:** Law. **Qualif.:** Applicants must be either enrolled at an accredited law school in New Jersey or New Jersey permanent residents enrolled at an accredited law school outside of New Jersey. **Criteria:** Scholarships will be awarded on the basis of demonstrated community service/civic involvement, personal financial need, academic achievement and a brief writing sample or essay.

Number Awarded: 1. **To Apply:** Interested applicants must visit the website to obtain an application. Completed applications can be sent via electronic mail or via US Postal Service mail. **Deadline:** March 15.

1864 ■ Association of Black Women Physicians (ABWP)
4712 Admiralty Way, Ste. 175
Marina del Rey, CA 90292
Ph: (310)321-8688
E-mail: abwpcorrespondence@gmail.com
URL: www.blackwomenphysicians.org
Facebook: www.facebook.com/Blackfemaledoctors
Twitter: twitter.com/ABWP2

1865 ■ Rebecca Lee Crumpler, M.D. Scholarships (Advanced Professional/Scholarship)

Purpose: To support medical students who demonstrate exceptional academic progress, community involvement, and financial need. **Focus:** Medicine. **Qualif.:** Applicants must be permanent residents of Southern California at any medical school, or students at a Southern California medical school, who are in good academic standing. **Criteria:** Applicants will be evaluated based on the committee's criteria.

Funds Avail.: No specific amount. **Duration:** Annual. **To Apply:** Interested applicants may contact the ABWP for more information.

1866 ■ Association of Business Information & Media Companies (ABM)
675 3rd Ave., 7th Fl.
New York, NY 10017-5704
Ph: (212)661-6360
Fax: (212)370-0736
E-mail: info@abmmail.com
URL: www.abmassociation.com

1867 ■ McAllister Fellowships (Professional development/Fellowship)

Purpose: To promote the study of business media. **Focus:** Business Communications. **Qualif.:** Recipients must be

Awards are arranged alphabetically below their administering organizations

editors or executives. **Criteria:** Selection will be based on the committee's criteria.

Funds Avail.: No specific amount. **Duration:** Annual. **To Apply:** Interested applicants may contact the ABM for the application process and other related information. **Contact:** Association of Business Information & Media Companies, at the above address.

1868 ■ Association of California Nurse Leaders Kern County Chapter
PO Box 13188
Bakersfield, CA 93389
URL: www.kcacnl.com

1869 ■ ACNL Research Scholarships (Graduate/Scholarship)

Purpose: To financially support graduate nursing students conducting nursing research study as part of their educational program of study. **Focus:** Nursing. **Qualif.:** Applicants must be enrolled in an accredited academic graduate nursing program and engaged in a research; and has had formal education/preparation in the conduct of nursing research (course work in conducting research). The research must show promise of having relevance to nursing practice, education, or research. **Criteria:** Selection is based on the student's qualifications, application materials, and on the research.

Funds Avail.: No specific amount. **To Apply:** Applicants must submit a completed application form along with an ACNL member application form if not a current ACNL member (optional); transcript of program courses to date including GPA; two current recommendation letters; a statement of purpose (no longer than 750 words); and resume and/or curriculum vitae. In addition, applicants must include the research abstract of the project (and status) or proposed project of no more than one page which includes purpose, aims, hypotheses (if applicable), methods, measures, and analysis plan.

1870 ■ Association of California Water Agencies (ACWA)
910 K St., Ste. 100
Sacramento, CA 95814-3577
Ph: (916)441-4545
Fax: (916)325-4849
Free: 888-666-2292
E-mail: acwabox@acwa.com
URL: www.acwa.com

1871 ■ Association of California Water Agencies Scholarships (Undergraduate/Scholarship)

Purpose: To promote study focusing on water resources. **Focus:** Water resources. **Qualif.:** Applicants must be residents of California attending one of the selected California schools full-time as juniors or seniors during the current academic year. **Criteria:** The award will be based not only on scholastic achievement but also on the individuals' commitment and motivation to their chosen vocation. Financial need will be considered.

Funds Avail.: $3,500. **Duration:** Annual. **Number Awarded:** 2. **To Apply:** Applicant must submit a completed scholarship application form along with an essay. **Deadline:** February 1. **Contact:** ACWA Scholarship Program at the above address.

1872 ■ Stephen K. Hall ACWA Water Law and Policy Scholarships (Graduate/Scholarship)

Purpose: To encourage talented and innovative students to join the effort to ensure California's water quality and to implement sound water management policies. **Focus:** Water resources. **Qualif.:** Applicants must be attending a public or private school located in the United States of America; have completed undergraduate work and at the time of the award; must be either part-time or full-time students in graduate studies; and must be carrying at least 8 units per term. **Criteria:** The award will be based not only on scholastic achievement, but also on the individual's commitment and motivation to their chosen vocation. Financial need will be considered.

Funds Avail.: $7,000. **Duration:** Annual. **To Apply:** Applicant must submit a completed scholarship application form along with the essay. **Deadline:** February 1. **Remarks:** Established in 2007.

1873 ■ Clair A. Hill Scholarships (Undergraduate/Scholarship)

Purpose: To support students pursuing degrees in water resources-related fields. **Focus:** Water resources. **Qualif.:** Applicants must be residents of California attending one of the selected California schools full-time as sophomores, juniors or seniors during the current academic year. **Criteria:** The award will be based not only on scholastic achievement but also on the individual's commitment and motivation to his/her chosen vocation. Financial need will be considered.

Funds Avail.: $5,000. **Duration:** Annual. **To Apply:** Applicant must complete scholarship application available online. Submit completed applications to Solano Irrigation District. **Deadline:** February 1.

1874 ■ Association for Canadian Studies in the United States (ACSUS)
1740 Massachusetts Ave. NW, Nitze 516
Washington, DC 20036
Ph: (202)670-1424
Fax: (202)663-5717
E-mail: info@acsus.org
URL: www.acsus.org
Twitter: twitter.com/ACSUS

1875 ■ ACSUS Distinguished Dissertation Awards (Doctorate/Award)

Purpose: To honor outstanding doctoral research on Canada at American institutions. **Focus:** General studies/Field of study not specified. **Qualif.:** Applicants must be nominated by a faculty serving on dissertation committees at universities in the United States; must be members of ACSUS; must have completed their PhD degree between August 2011 and August 2015. **Criteria:** Successful nominees should represent an original work that makes a contribution to the nominee's discipline; must contain at least 50% content on Canada; and the topic must be comparative in nature. The dissertation will be judged on substantive and methodological quality, originality of thought and clarity.

Funds Avail.: $500. **To Apply:** Nomination must be accompanied by a letter of support from the student's dissertation advisor and one from an additional reference who is not a member of ACSUS. Each nomination must be accompanied by a copy of the dissertation (not to exceed 500 words), typed and double-spaced; a one page resume of the nominee; and appendices containing charts, tables and bibliographies. **Deadline:** August 1.

1876 ■ Thomas O. Enders Graduate Fellowships
(Graduate/Fellowship)

Purpose: To encourage advanced scholarship on Canada-U.S. relations by funding fellowship for US scholars conducting research in Canada. **Focus:** General studies/Field of study not specified. **Qualif.:** Students in any discipline or professional school who are in the process of preparing a graduate thesis or doctoral dissertation related in substantial part to the study of Canada, Canada-U.S. relations or comparative policies in North America; must be U.S. citizens or permanent residents; must be enrolled in full-time masters or doctoral programs at any institution in the United States; and must have obtained, in writing, the support of a faculty member or research scientist at a Canadian university, or the head of an organization or business who agrees to act as the student's academic sponsor during the tenure of their award. **Criteria:** Recipients will be selected based on submitted materials.

Funds Avail.: $3,500. **To Apply:** Applicants must submit a curriculum vitae; one-page proposal outlining the thesis/dissertation project that states why research at the selected university is essential to the project and how such a visit will enhance the quality of the student's research; schedule of the activities; one letter of support from the student's thesis/dissertation chair and another one from the departmental chair or dean of the school; and a letter of invitation from the faculty member or organization head where student will be conducting research. **Deadline:** March 31. **Contact:** Professor Stephanie Golob, at the above address or Email: Stephanie.Golob@baruch.cuny.edu.

1877 ■ Association Canadienne des Chefs de Police
300 Terry Fox Dr., Unit 100
Kanata, ON, Canada K2K 0E3
Ph: (613)595-1101
Fax: (613)383-0372
URL: cacp.ca

1878 ■ Jack Ackroyd Scholarships *(Other/Scholarship)*

Purpose: To support members of police forces across Canada to further their education with a view of promoting professionalism and excellence throughout the policing community. **Focus:** Law enforcement. **Qualif.:** Applicants must be uniform and civilian members of police forces who have completed a degree or certificate program in police studies, criminology, law, or other programs related to law enforcement in an accredited Canadian university or community college. **Criteria:** Applicants who have demonstrated academic excellence in police related studies will be given preference.

Funds Avail.: 100 Canadian Dollars each. **Duration:** Annual. **Number Awarded:** 5. **To Apply:** Applicants must submit documents pertaining to their personal information, police service of employment, date of graduation, official transcripts of courses and grades, and any other information which may be considered relevant including any letter of support from the police service of which they are members. **Contact:** Further information or inquiries may be made to Trevor McCagherty, Executive Support, CACP Research Foundation, at 905-242-2146.

1879 ■ Association Canadienne Des Géographes (ACG)
McGill University
805 Sherbrooke St. W, Rm. 425
Montreal, QC, Canada H3A 2K6
Ph: (514)398-4946
Fax: (514)398-7437
URL: www.cag-acg.ca/en/index.html

1880 ■ Robin P. Armstrong Memorial Prize for Excellence in Native Studies Awards *(Graduate/Award)*

Purpose: To promote excellence in applied research related to First Nation/Aboriginal/Indigenous peoples in Canada. **Focus:** Geography. **Qualif.:** Applicants must be graduate students pursuing a geography program of study; must have completed a Master's or PhD thesis in native studies on aboriginal topic. **Criteria:** Candidates will be ranked based on the following categories: 1) significance of the problem; 2) conceptualization, design and execution of the study; 3) quality of the results; 4) potential for improving theory; and 5) clarity, insight and originality of the work. Research which involves quantitative data analysis using Statistics Canada and INAC data on aboriginal topics will be given extra points.

Funds Avail.: $500. **Duration:** Annual. **To Apply:** Applicants must submit a cover letter; curriculum vitae; and 1,000-1,500 words abstract outlining the problem or question studied, review of related literature, design and methodology, statistical results and conclusions, and statement of significance. **Deadline:** January 15. **Contact:** Evelyn Peters, University of Saskatchewan; Email: evelyn.peters@usask.ca.

1881 ■ CAG Health and Health Care Study Group Awards *(Graduate/Award)*

Purpose: To facilitate the exchange of ideas and information among researchers interested in health geography issues. **Focus:** General studies/Field of study not specified. **Qualif.:** Applicants must be members of the Canadian Association of Geographers; must be graduate students or supervisors who are members of the HHCSG at the time of the CAG meeting. **Criteria:** Award will be given to an applicant who conducted the best research.

Funds Avail.: No specific amount. **To Apply:** Applicants must submit an application form. **Contact:** Jennifer Dean, at jennifer.dean@uwaterloo.ca.

1882 ■ Canadian Association of Geographers Historical Geography Study Group Awards *(Master's, Graduate, Undergraduate/Award)*

Purpose: To promote collegiality and scholarly exchange among historical geographers, and to advance the interdisciplinary interests of historical geography within the academic community and beyond. **Focus:** Geography. **Qualif.:** Applicants must be full-time or part-time undergraduates or Master's students attending a credited Canadian college or university. **Criteria:** Candidates will be judged based on originality, research quality, and style of the submitted essay.

Funds Avail.: $100. **Duration:** Annual. **To Apply:** Applicants must submit an essay. It must be a research paper discussing Canadian historical geography and have been written anytime after January 2009. Essay must be submitted in French or English not exceeding 6,000 words includ-

Awards are arranged alphabetically below their administering organizations

ing references, footnotes or endnotes. In addition, applicants must also submit the following information: 1) name and contact details; 2) an abstract no longer than 250 words; 3) name of the institution attended at the time of writing the essay; 4) course by which the essay was written; and 5) name of the course instructor. **Contact:** Arn Keeling; Email: akeeling@mun.ca.

1883 ■ Association Canadienne d'Études Cinématographiques (ACEC)

4401 University Dr.
Lethbridge, AB, Canada T1K 3M4
Ph: (403)394-3922
URL: www.filmstudies.ca
Facebook: www.facebook.com/FSAC.ACEC
Twitter: www.twitter.com/#!/_filmstudies

1884 ■ Gerald Pratley Award *(Doctorate, Graduate/Award)*

Purpose: To inspire Quebec or Canadian cinema development by providing financial support for graduate students doing cinema research. **Focus:** Cinema. **Qualif.:** Applicants must be students entering or completing a graduate program in Film Studies (or any related discipline) at any recognized post-secondary institution in or outside Canada. Applicants need not be Canadian citizens. **Criteria:** Selection is based on the student's previous academic performance and his or her intentions for a specific paper or body of research on Canadian/Quebec cinema.

Funds Avail.: 1,000 Canadian Dollars. **Duration:** Annual. **To Apply:** Applicants must prepare a brief research proposal (500 words) including bibliography; two letters of recommendation; one sample of previous work (3000 to 5000 words); and official university transcripts. **Deadline:** July 31. **Remarks:** Established in 1991.

1885 ■ Association Canadienne du Diabete

1400-522 University Ave.
Toronto, ON, Canada M5G 2R5
Ph: (416)363-3373
E-mail: info@diabetes.ca
URL: www.diabetes.ca
Facebook: www.facebook.com/CanadianDiabetesAssociation
LinkedIn: www.linkedin.com/company/canadian-diabetes-association
Twitter: twitter.com/DiabetesAssoc

1886 ■ Eli Lilly Graduate Scholarship *(Graduate, Postgraduate/Scholarship)*

Purpose: To encourage members to pursue their graduate or post-secondary graduate studies in a diabetes field. **Focus:** Diabetes. **Qualif.:** Applicants must be active DES members for a minimum of two years; must be Canadian citizens or landed immigrants; must not have received another DES or Canadian Diabetes Association scholarships or bursary for the same academic year. **Criteria:** Preference will be given to those who are studying at a Canadian university. Recipient will be selected based on the deliberations of the DES Awards Selection Committee.

Funds Avail.: $5,000. **Duration:** Annual; 5 years only. **To Apply:** Applicants must type or submit in electronic format the application form available from the website; must submit two references and one current copy of the applicant's resume or curriculum vitae. **Deadline:** May 1.

1887 ■ Association Canadienne des Infirmières et Infirmiers en Sciences Neurologiques (ACIISN)

c/o Janet White, Membership Chairperson
212-324 Larry Uteck Blvd.
Halifax, NS, Canada B3M 0E7
E-mail: info@cann.ca
URL: www.cann.ca
Facebook: www.facebook.com/Canadian-Association-of-Neuroscience-Nurses-834278943328317
Twitter: www.twitter.com/CANNInfo

1888 ■ Lynn Ann Baldwin Scholarships *(Master's/Scholarship)*

Purpose: To provide financial support to qualified nurses to pursue master's level education with neuroscience nursing as a focus. **Focus:** Neuroscience. **Qualif.:** Applicants must be registered nurses who have worked in neurosciences and are members of Canadian Association of Neuroscience Nursing in good standing for at least two years; must be in the master's program of study. **Criteria:** Selection will be based on the committee's criteria.

Funds Avail.: No specific amount. **To Apply:** Applicants must submit a completed application form; proof of acceptance into the master's program for which the scholarship is being sought, or proof of registration to write the certification exam; evidence of amount of registration fees; proof of current registration with provincial nursing association; one letter of reference from a person who has had the opportunity to assess your work. **Remarks:** Established in 2007.

1889 ■ Neuroscience Certification Bursary Awards *(Other/Award)*

Purpose: To provide financial support to qualified nurses to pursue additional training in neuroscience nursing. **Focus:** Neuroscience. **Qualif.:** Applicants must be registered nurses who have worked in neurosciences and are members of the Canadian Association of Neuroscience Nurses in good standing. The program or course of study for the Jessie Young Bursary must have a clear Neuroscience focus or component. **Criteria:** Selection will be based on the committee's criteria.

Funds Avail.: No specific amount. **To Apply:** Applicants must submit a completed application form; proof of acceptance into the educational program or course of study which the bursary is being sought, or proof of registration to write the certification exam; evidence of amount of registration fees; proof of current registration with provincial nursing association; and one letter of reference from a person who has had the opportunity to assess the applicant's work.

1890 ■ Jessie Young Bursary Awards *(Other/Award)*

Purpose: To provide financial support to qualified nurses to pursue additional training in neuroscience nursing. **Focus:** Neuroscience. **Qualif.:** Applicants must be registered nurses who have worked in neurosciences and are members of the Canadian Association of Neuroscience Nurses in good standing. The program or course of study for the Jessie Young Bursary must have a clear Neuroscience focus or component. **Criteria:** Selection will be based on the committee's criteria.

Awards are arranged alphabetically below their administering organizations

Funds Avail.: No specific amount. **To Apply:** Applicants must submit a completed application form; proof of acceptance into the educational program or course of study which the bursary is being sought, or proof of registration to write the certification exam; evidence of amount of registration fees; proof of current registration with provincial nursing association; one letter of reference from a person who has had the opportunity to assess your work. **Deadline:** April 1. **Remarks:** Established in 1983.

1891 ■ Association Canadienne des Libertes Civiles
90 Eglinton Ave. E, Ste. 900
Toronto, ON, Canada M4P 1A6
Ph: (416)363-0321
Fax: (416)861-1291
E-mail: mail@ccla.org
URL: ccla.org
Facebook: www.facebook.com/cancivlib/info/?tab=overview
Twitter: www.twitter.com/cancivlib

1892 ■ CCLA Summer Legal Internships *(Graduate/Internship)*
Purpose: To help students engage in legal work relating to CCLA's ongoing advocacy efforts in civil liberties and human rights. **Focus:** Law. **Qualif.:** Internship opportunities are open to law students and law graduates. Applicants should be reliable, well-organized and self-motivated, with a demonstrated interest in civil liberties, human rights, and public policy. Strong writing skills are essential. Personal or professional experience working with non-governmental organizations is highly desirable. Bilingualism and the ability to read and write professionally in French is a strong plus. CCLA is an equal opportunity organization, and is committed to diversity and inclusiveness in its practices. **Criteria:** Applicants will be evaluated based on eligibility and submitted materials.

Funds Avail.: No specific amount. **Duration:** Annual. **To Apply:** Applicants must submit a resume, cover letter, and law school transcripts.

1893 ■ Bernard Chernos Essay Competition *(Undergraduate/Prize)*
Purpose: To provide opportunities among high school students. **Focus:** General studies/Field of study not specified. **Qualif.:** Applicants must be high school students. **Criteria:** Applicants will be selected based on submitted essay.

Funds Avail.: $500 cash; $250 forschool department. **Duration:** Annual. **Number Awarded:** 1. **To Apply:** Applicants must submit an essay addressing one of the questions given by the scholarship committee. **Deadline:** May 1.

1894 ■ Association Canadienne des Parajuristes
c/o Mrs. Cara Subirana
2606 Adhemar-Raynault Ave.
Montreal, QC, Canada J5W 0E1
E-mail: info@caplegal.ca
URL: www.caplegal.ca
Facebook: www.facebook.com/Caplegal
LinkedIn: www.linkedin.com/groups?gid=4420573
Twitter: twitter.com/CAPLegal

Awards are arranged alphabetically below their administering organizations

1895 ■ Lise M. Duchesneau Scholarship *(Undergraduate/Scholarship)*
Purpose: To encourage students who stood out during their paralegal studies. **Focus:** Paralegal studies. **Qualif.:** Applicants must be graduating students from participating institutions. **Criteria:** Selection shall be based on the criteria of the teachers of the Paralegal Program at participating institutions.

Funds Avail.: 500 Canadian Dollars. **Duration:** Annual. **To Apply:** Interested applicants may contact the Association for the application process and other information.

1896 ■ Association Canadienne des Professeurs de Langues Secondes (ACPLS)
2490 Don Reid Dr.
Ottawa, ON, Canada K1H 1E1
Ph: (613)727-0994
Free: 877-727-0994
E-mail: admin@caslt.org
URL: www.caslt.org
Twitter: twitter.com/CASLT_ACPLS

1897 ■ Robert Roy Awards *(Advanced Professional/Award, Recognition)*
Purpose: To recognize outstanding contributions by educators and researchers to the second language education field. **Focus:** Education, Bilingual and cross-cultural; Linguistics. **Qualif.:** Nominees must have been active members of the CASLT for at least two years; must have distinguished themselves in teaching, research, or writing to the improvement of second language teaching and learning in Canada. **Criteria:** Recipient will be selected based on submitted nomination.

Funds Avail.: No specific amount. **Duration:** Annual. **To Apply:** Applicants must submit the background information of the colleague they want to nominate to the contact provided. **Remarks:** Established in 1983. **Contact:** Robert Roy Award Nomination Committee, CASLT National Office, at the above address.

1898 ■ H.H. Stern Grant Awards *(Advanced Professional, Professional development/Award, Grant)*
Purpose: To support innovative classroom practices in second language learning. **Focus:** Education, Bilingual and cross-cultural. **Qualif.:** Applicants must be CASLT members. **Criteria:** Candidates will be chosen based on the submitted proposal which must: be innovative through the application of new techniques, strategies and/or approaches to learning; identify the impact of the project in the classroom, school or community; demonstrate the related improvement of student language learning; have the potential for duplication in other classrooms, schools, and communities; and include a brief plan for evaluating the innovation.

Funds Avail.: $200 - $500. **Duration:** Annual. **To Apply:** Applications should include: completed application form clearly identifying the teaching level and target second language, short applicant biography and a current electronic photograph; completed project description answering the five focus questions provided above; and, endorsement by a colleague or supervisor related to the impact of the project. **Deadline:** March 31. **Contact:** Send your applications to CASLT's National Office via email to admin@caslt.org.

1899 ■ Association Canadienne de Radio-Oncologie (ACRO)
20 Crown Steel Dr., Unit 6
Markham, ON, Canada L3R 9X9
Ph: (905)415-3917
Fax: (905)415-0071
Free: 855-415-3917
E-mail: caro-acro@secretariatcentral.com
URL: www.caro-acro.ca
Facebook: fr-ca.facebook.com/caroacrocommunication

1900 ■ CARO-ELEKTA Research Fellowship Program *(Professional development/Fellowship)*

Purpose: To foster the development of highly qualified clinicians, researchers and future Radiation Oncology leaders. **Focus:** Oncology. **Qualif.:** Applicants must be Canadian citizens or landed immigrants; must hold or intend to sit the Royal College of Physicians and Surgeons of Canada specialist certification examination in Radiation Oncology prior to the beginning of the fellowship; and must be resident members of CARO. **Criteria:** Applicants will be evaluated based on scientific merit; relevance to current or future Radiation Oncology practice in Canada; broad alignment with Elekta's research objectives to treat cancer and brain disorders.

Funds Avail.: No specific amount. **Duration:** One year. **To Apply:** Applicants must include a description of the proposed research project and its relevance to Radiation Oncology, identification of the host institution and supervisor, written confirmation from the supervisor that this fellowship will be supported by the host institution, current curriculum vitae and three letters of reference.

1901 ■ Association Canadienne de la Recherche Théâtrale
c/o Dr. Peter Kuling, Membership Coordinator
75 University Ave. W
Waterloo, ON, Canada N2L 3C5
Ph: (416)303-0441
URL: catracrt.ca
Facebook: www.facebook.com/CATRACRT
Twitter: twitter.com/catr_acrt

1902 ■ Robert G. Lawrence Prize *(Doctorate, Other, Graduate/Prize, Award)*

Purpose: To recognize research of scholars who have presented an outstanding paper during the CATR annual conference. **Focus:** Theater arts. **Qualif.:** Award is open to graduate students and scholars who recently completed their PhD (less than five years) and who make a presentation at the annual conference. **Criteria:** Recipients will be selected by the committee based on the depth and details of the submitted paper and quality of the presentation.

Funds Avail.: $200. **Duration:** Annual. **To Apply:** Applicants must forward a copy of their presentation to the president through e-mail attachment. **Remarks:** Established in 1995. **Contact:** Moira Day, Chair of the Lawrence Committee, at moira.day@usask.ca.

1903 ■ Heather McCallum Scholarships *(Doctorate, Other/Scholarship)*

Purpose: To allow researchers to enrich their projects in ways otherwise unaffordable, through travel, access to archives or events, or the purchase of materials. **Focus:** Interdisciplinary studies. **Qualif.:** Applicants must be graduate students and emerging scholars (within five years upon completion of a PhD) in the fields of theatre, drama and performance studies, with a preference given to topics with a Canadian focus. **Criteria:** Recipients will be chosen based on the following criteria: 1) excellence of the project and its contribution to the discipline; 2) a project which can be completed in a reasonable time; 3) academic records and potential of the applicants; 4) if the request indicates a purchase of anything at an archival value that can be deposited subsequently in the public domain. Preference will be given to those applicants who have not fully established their careers and are not eligible for funds for the particular project applied for from federal, provincial and municipal arts councils or institutions.

Funds Avail.: No specific amount. **Duration:** Annual. **To Apply:** Applicants must provide a maximum of two pages describing the project for which assistance is required; a detailed breakdown of costs; information concerning applications to other granting agencies; up-to-date curriculum vitae; and the name of a person who has been asked to send a letter of reference directly to the Secretary of the Committee. **Deadline:** March 31. **Contact:** Prof. Rosalind Kerr, at rkerr@ualberta.ca.

1904 ■ Association Canadienne des Ressources Hydriques (ACRH)
176 Gloucester St., Ste. 320
Ottawa, ON, Canada ON K2P 0A6
Ph: (613)237-9363
Fax: (613)594-5190
E-mail: services@aic.ca
URL: www.cwra.org/en/

1905 ■ Canadian Water Resources Association Scholarships *(Undergraduate/Scholarship)*

Purpose: To raise awareness of the value of water; to promote responsible and effective water resource management in Canada. **Focus:** Water resources. **Qualif.:** Applicants must be either Canadian citizens or Permanent Residents attending a Canadian University or college. **Criteria:** Recipients are selected based on academic excellence and project relevance to water management.

Funds Avail.: 1,500 Canadian dollars. **Number Awarded:** 3. **To Apply:** Applicants must provide a statement from the chairman/director of the department which verifies that the application is the one being submitted from that program for the graduate scholarship; completed application form; outlines of the applicant's research project and its relevance to sustainable water resources (500 words); official course transcript; two letters of reference; **Deadline:** January 30.

1906 ■ Ken Thomson Scholarships *(Undergraduate/Scholarship)*

Purpose: To raise awareness of the value of water; to promote responsible and effective water resource management in Canada. **Focus:** Water resources. **Qualif.:** Applicant must be the second-highest ranked graduate student whose program of study focuses upon applied, natural or social science aspects of water resources; must be Canadian citizen or landed immigrant attending a Canadian University or college; must be enrolled in full-time graduate studies in any discipline. **Criteria:** Recipients are selected based on academic excellence and project relevance to water management and development.

Funds Avail.: 2,000 Canadian Dollars. **Number Awarded:**

Awards are arranged alphabetically below their administering organizations

1. **To Apply:** Applicants must provide a statement from the chairman/director of the department which verifies that the application is reflective of the project; a 500-word statement which outlines the applicant's research project and its relevance to sustainable water resources; official transcript of records; two references to be sent directly to the Scholarship Committee by the referees or appropriate official of the university or college; a statement from the program chairman or director endorsing the application from that program, including confirmation of the applicant's full-time registration; and completed application form. **Deadline:** January 30. **Contact:** Canadian Water Resources Association at services@aic.ca.

1907 ■ Association Canadienne de Science Politique

260 Dalhousie St., Ste. 204
Ottawa, ON, Canada K1N 7E4
Ph: (613)562-1202
Fax: (613)241-0019
E-mail: cpsa-acsp@cpsa-acsp.ca
URL: www.cpsa-acsp.ca

1908 ■ Donald Smiley Prize (Advanced Professional/Prize, Award, Recognition)

Purpose: To encourage the ideals of scholarship represented by the great Canadian scientists. **Focus:** Political science. **Qualif.:** Books must be single-authored or multi-authored; authors or co-authors must be citizens or permanent residents of Canada and CPSA members in the year the book was published. **Criteria:** Awards will be given to the best book published in French or English in the field related to the study of government and politics in Canada.

Funds Avail.: No specific amount. **Duration:** Annual. **To Apply:** Authors must submit a book published in France or Canada. **Deadline:** December 10. **Contact:** CSPA-ACSP, at the above address.

1909 ■ Jill Vickers Prize (Other/Award)

Purpose: To support the authors of papers in the fields of Political Science and related studies. **Focus:** Political science. **Qualif.:** Applicants must be the authors of papers related to the topic of gender and politics presented in English or French. **Criteria:** Recipients will be selected based on the quality of their submissions.

Funds Avail.: No specific amount. **Duration:** Annual. **To Apply:** Applicants must submit their electronic copy of the paper to be e-mailed directly to each member of the Prize jury. **Deadline:** June 15.

1910 ■ Association Canadienne de Securite Incendie

2800 - 14th Ave., Ste. 210
Markham, ON, Canada L3R 0E4
Ph: (416)492-9417
Fax: (416)491-1670
E-mail: cfsa@taylorenterprises.com
URL: canadianfiresafety.com

1911 ■ CFSA Randal Brown & Associates Awards (Undergraduate/Award)

Purpose: To inspire pursuits on fire safety awareness by providing financial support for students attending an approved Fire Safety Technology Course in a post-secondary school in Canada. **Focus:** Fires and fire prevention. **Qualif.:** Applicants must be 2nd year students in a three-year full time Fire Protection Technology course at a Canadian college or university; must have exceptional overall skills in Codes/Standard Technology; have an academic proficiency of 3.3/4.00; and must be students entering the second and subsequent years of an approved course. **Criteria:** Applicants will be evaluated based on academic achievement and letter of application as required by the association.

Funds Avail.: 1,000 Canadian Dollars. **Duration:** Annual. **Number Awarded:** 2. **To Apply:** Applicants must submit their academic grades accompanied by completed application form. **Deadline:** March 18.

1912 ■ CFSA Aon Fire Protection Engineering Award (Undergraduate/Scholarship)

Purpose: To support and provide financial assistance to qualified persons who desire to make their careers in the field of fire safety. **Focus:** Fires and fire prevention. **Qualif.:** Applicants must be students enrolled in a Technician or Technology Program at a Canadian college or university with a primary focus on Sprinkler Technology - Code and Design and an academic proficiency or 3.3 GPA. **Criteria:** Selection will be based on the committees' criteria.

Funds Avail.: $1,000. **Duration:** Annual. **Number Awarded:** 1 to 2. **To Apply:** Applicants must submit a written response of up to 300 words in paragraph form, providing a brief description of: the applicants' interest in fire safety and knowledge of CFSA and the donor organization; the course of the applicants' they are enrolled in and how they would like to utilize their education; any experience of the applicants in the fire safety either work related, attendance of conferences, CFSA functions etc. and a statement of the applicants' extracurricular involvement and; letter of reference from faculty about individual. **Deadline:** March 18.

1913 ■ CFSA City of Markham, Buildings Standards Department Award (Undergraduate/Scholarship)

Purpose: To support and provide financial assistance to qualified persons who desire to make their careers in the field of fire safety. **Focus:** Fires and fire prevention. **Qualif.:** Applicants must be students enrolled in Fire Protection Engineering or related Fire and Life Safety Diploma Program at a Canadian college or university with academic good standing or 3.3 GPA. **Criteria:** Selection will be based on the committees' criteria.

Funds Avail.: $500. **Duration:** Annual. **Number Awarded:** 1. **To Apply:** Applicants must submit a written response of up to 300 words in paragraph form, providing a brief description of: the applicants' interest in fire safety and knowledge of CFSA and the donor organization; the course of the applicants' they are enrolled in and how they would like to utilize their education; any experience of the applicants in the fire safety either work related, attendance of conferences, CFSA functions etc. and a statement of the applicants' extracurricular involvement and; letter of reference from faculty about individual. **Deadline:** March 18.

1914 ■ CFSA Fire Safety Awards (Postgraduate/Award, Monetary)

Purpose: To expand fire safety awareness by providing financial assistance for individuals attending an approved Fire Safety Technology Course in a post-secondary school in Canada. **Focus:** Fires and fire prevention. **Qualif.:** Applicants must be enrolled in a Fire Protection Technology

Awards are arranged alphabetically below their administering organizations

course at a Canadian college or university; must have excelled with outstanding leadership, motivation and technical skills and an overall academic proficiency; must be students entering the second and subsequent years of an approved course. **Criteria:** Applicants will be evaluated based on academic achievement and letter of application as required by the association.
Funds Avail.: 1,000 Canadian Dollars. **Duration:** Annual. **To Apply:** Applicants must submit their academic grades together with completed application form.

1915 ■ CFSA Leber Rubes Inc. Awards
(Postgraduate/Award, Monetary)

Purpose: To inspire pursuits on fire safety awareness by providing financial support for students attending an approved Fire Safety Technology Course in a post-secondary school in Canada. **Focus:** Fires and fire prevention. **Qualif.:** Applicants must be 2nd year students in a three-year full-time Fire Protection Technology course at a Canadian college or university; must have exceptional overall skills in Fire Alarm System Technology; have an academic proficiency of 3.3/4.00; and must be students entering the second and subsequent years of an approved course. **Criteria:** Applicants will be evaluated based on academic achievement and letter of application as required by the association.
Funds Avail.: 850 Canadian Dollars. **Duration:** Annual. **To Apply:** Applicants must submit their academic grades together with completed application form. **Deadline:** March 14.

1916 ■ CFSA LRI Engineering Award
(Undergraduate/Scholarship)

Purpose: To support and provide financial assistance to qualified persons who desire to make their careers in the field of fire safety. **Focus:** Fires and fire prevention. **Qualif.:** Applicants must be students enrolled in a Fire Protection Technology Course at a Canadian college or university with exceptional overall skills in Fire Alarm System Technology in good academic standing or with 3.3 GPA. **Criteria:** Selection will be based on the committees' criteria.
Funds Avail.: $1,000. **Duration:** Annual. **Number Awarded:** 2. **To Apply:** Applicants must submit a written response of up to 300 words in paragraph form, providing a brief description of: the applicants' interest in fire safety and knowledge of CFSA and the donor organization; the course of the applicants' they are enrolled in and how they would like to utilize their education; any experience of the applicants in the fire safety either work related, attendance of conferences, CFSA functions etc. and a statement of the applicants' extracurricular involvement and; letter of reference from faculty about individual. **Deadline:** March 18.

1917 ■ CFSA Nadine International Inc. Awards
(Undergraduate/Award)

Purpose: To expand pursuits on fire safety awareness by providing financial assistance for students enrolled in an approved Fire Safety Technology Course in a post-secondary school in Canada. **Focus:** Fires and fire prevention. **Qualif.:** Applicants must be 2nd year students in a three-year full-time Fire Protection Technology course at a Canadian college or university; must have exceptional overall skills in Fire Suppression Technology; must have an academic proficiency of 3.3/4.00; must be students entering the second and subsequent years of an approved course. **Criteria:** Applicants will be evaluated based on academic achievement and letter of application as required by the association.
Funds Avail.: 1,000 Canadian Dollars. **Duration:** Annual. **Number Awarded:** 2. **To Apply:** Applicants must submit completed application form accompanied by copy of academic grades.

1918 ■ CFSA Siemens Canada Award
(Undergraduate/Scholarship)

Purpose: To support and provide financial assistance to qualified persons who desire to make their careers in the field of fire safety. **Focus:** Fires and fire prevention. **Qualif.:** Applicants must be students enrolled in a Technician or Technology Program at a Canadian college or university with a primary focus on Fire Alarm - Code and Design and an academic proficiency or 3.3 GPA. **Criteria:** Selection will be based on the committees' criteria.
Funds Avail.: $1,000. **Duration:** Annual. **Number Awarded:** 1 to 2. **To Apply:** Applicants must submit a written response of up to 300 words in paragraph form, providing a brief description of: the applicants' interest in fire safety and knowledge of CFSA and the donor organization; the course of the applicants' they are enrolled in and how they would like to utilize their education; any experience of the applicants in the fire safety either work related, attendance of conferences, CFSA functions etc. and a statement of the applicants' extracurricular involvement and; letter of reference from faculty about individual. **Deadline:** March 18.

1919 ■ CFSA Underwriters' Laboratories of Canada Awards *(Undergraduate/Award)*

Purpose: To inspire pursuits on fire safety awareness by providing financial assistance for students attending an approved Fire Safety Technology Course in a post-secondary school in Canada. **Focus:** Fires and fire prevention. **Qualif.:** Applicants must be top 1st and 2nd year students in a three-year full-time Fire Protection Technology course at a Canadian college or university; must have exceptional academic skills in Codes and Standards; must have an overall proficiency of 3.3/4.00. **Criteria:** Applicants will be evaluated based on academic achievement and letter of application as required by the association.
Funds Avail.: 500 Canadian Dollars. **Duration:** Annual. **To Apply:** Applicants must submit their academic grades and completed application form. **Deadline:** March 18.

1920 ■ Association Canadienne du Stationnement (ACS)
350-2255 St. Laurent Blvd.
Ottawa, ON, Canada K1G 4K3
Ph: (613)727-0700
Fax: (613)727-3183
E-mail: info@canadianparking.ca
URL: canadianparking.ca
Facebook: www.facebook.com/Canadian-Parking-Association-173429676044219
Twitter: twitter.com/canadianparking

1921 ■ Canadian Parking Association Scholarships
(Undergraduate/Scholarship)

Purpose: To provide financial assistance to students in their pursuit of academic excellence and to encourage post-secondary study that enhances the parking industry in Canada. **Focus:** General studies/Field of study not specified. **Qualif.:** Applicants for the employee scholarships must be registered CPA members whose job function is 50%

related to parking, their spouses and dependents, and members' employees whose job function is 50% related to parking, their spouses and dependents. For the academic scholarships, eligible are those with a minimum cumulative average of 70% (or equivalent) in the last three semesters of available marks. Non-academic courses such as career or personal development-related courses will not be considered. **Criteria:** Applicants will be evaluated based on academic performance; extracurricular activities or volunteer/community involvement, excluding those which are included in the high school curriculum; and quality of reference letters (one from a teacher and one from a person familiar with extracurricular activities or community involvement, excluding family members). **Funds Avail.:** 2,000 Canadian Dollars each. **Duration:** Annual. **Number Awarded:** 10. **To Apply:** Applicants must submit the completed application form; official transcript of the last three semesters; description of extracurricular activities or volunteer/community involvement; two signed letters of reference; and the parental consent form. **Deadline:** May 2. **Remarks:** Established in 2004.

1922 ■ Association of Certified Fraud Examiners (ACFE)
The Gregor Bldg.
716 West Ave.
Austin, TX 78701-2727
Ph: (512)478-9000
Fax: (512)478-9297
Free: 800-245-3321
URL: www.acfe.com
Facebook: www.facebook.com/AssociationofCertifiedFraudExaminers
Twitter: www.twitter.com/theacfe

1923 ■ Ritchie-Jennings Memorial Scholarships (Undergraduate, Graduate/Scholarship)
Purpose: To support the education of students who have an interest in pursuing a career in fraud examination. **Focus:** Accounting; Business administration; Criminal justice; Finance. **Qualif.:** Applicants must currently be enrolled full-time and similarly enrolled during the given academic year at an accredited, four-year college or university. They must have a declared major or minor in accounting, business administration, finance or criminal justice and demonstrate a desire to pursue a career in fraud examination or similar anti-fraud profession. **Criteria:** Scholarships are awarded on the basis of: completed application form; fraud-related interests, activities, goals, and desired career paths; overall academic achievement demonstrated by transcripts; and letters of recommendations.
Funds Avail.: $1,000-$10,000. **Duration:** Annual. **Number Awarded:** Varies. **To Apply:** Applicants must submit a completed Ritchie-Jennings Memorial Scholarship Application together with official transcript(s) showing all completed college or university courses; and three letters of recommendation (which must be submitted on behalf of the applicants). **Deadline:** February 5. **Contact:** scholarships@acfe.com.

1924 ■ Association of College Unions International (ACUI)
1 City Centre Ste. 200
120 W 7th St.
Bloomington, IN 47404-3925
Ph: (812)245-2284
Fax: (812)245-6710
E-mail: acui@acui.org
URL: www.acui.org
Twitter: twitter.com/@ACUITweets

1925 ■ ACUI Research and Education Grant (Undergraduate, Graduate, Professional development/Grant)
Purpose: To fund research-based projects that increase the knowledge base of the student activities, college unions, ACUI, and the profession in general. **Focus:** General studies/Field of study not specified. **Qualif.:** Applicants must be faculty, staff, and student members conducting research within the college union and student activities field. **Criteria:** Selection will be based on the credentials and research of the qualified applicants.
Funds Avail.: Up to $1,500. **Duration:** Annual. **To Apply:** Applicants must submit: a cover page identifying the research proposal title, the primary researcher's name, mailing address, institution, telephone number, and email address. A description of the research proposal, limited to 10 pages, including: purpose of the research; relevant literature; description of the methodology; detailed budget showing how the awarded funds will be utilized; justification as to how the project supports the published ACUI research agenda, and makes a significant contribution to the profession; anticipated project timeline; curriculum vitae including any relevant research previously conducted; all co-researchers should be listed and include a curriculum vitae; undergraduate and graduate student proposals must include a letter of support by the faculty member sponsoring the research; terms of agreement printed and signed. Applications must be submitted in either Word or PDF format.

1926 ■ Gretchen Laatsch Scholarships (Graduate/Scholarship)
Purpose: To encourage graduate students to submit professional quality articles in the field of college unions and students activities. **Focus:** General studies/Field of study not specified. **Qualif.:** Applicants must be recognized by an institution as students in pursuit of graduate degrees in any academic area. **Criteria:** Consideration will be given to students either currently in the field of college union and student activities or those intending to enter the profession.
Funds Avail.: $500. **Duration:** Annual. **To Apply:** Applicants must submit an article containing a minimum of 500 words; must have a letter of recommendation from a college union or student activities professional. **Deadline:** November. **Contact:** ACUI at jrudisil@acui.org.

1927 ■ Association for Compensatory Educators of Texas (ACET)
c/o Ken Schrader, Executive Director
PO Box 3516
Humble, TX 77347
Ph: (832)644-5020
Fax: (832)644-8520
URL: acetx.org

1928 ■ Association for Compensatory Educators of Texas Paraprofessionals Scholarships (Other/Scholarship)
Purpose: To support paraprofessionals who wish to return to school to pursue a degree and teacher certification.

Awards are arranged alphabetically below their administering organizations

Focus: General studies/Field of study not specified. **Qualif.:** Applicants must be paraprofessionals who wish to return to school to pursue a degree and teacher certification. They must be currently working with a school district in a compensatory program. **Criteria:** Preference will be given to those applicants who meet the criteria.

Funds Avail.: No specific amount. **Duration:** Annual. **Number Awarded:** 4. **To Apply:** Applicants must submit proof of a high school diploma or GED and must check the available website to download the scholarship application, information letter, scoring rubric and scoring grid.

1929 ■ Association for Compensatory Educators of Texas Scholarships (Undergraduate/Scholarship)

Purpose: To provide remedial assistance and support for students who have failed TAKS or are at-risk of dropping out of school. **Focus:** General studies/Field of study not specified. **Qualif.:** Applicants must be graduating high school students. **Criteria:** Selection will be made by the committee.

Funds Avail.: $1,000. **Duration:** Annual. **To Apply:** Applicants must submit a completed application form.

1930 ■ Association of Desk and Derrick Clubs (ADDC)
5321 S Sheridan Rd., Ste. 24
Tulsa, OK 74145
Ph: (918)622-1749
Fax: (918)622-1675
E-mail: ado@addc.org
URL: www.addc.org
Facebook: www.facebook.com/associationofdeskandderrickclubs?fref=ts

1931 ■ Association of Desk and Derrick Clubs Education Trust Scholarships (Undergraduate/Scholarship)

Purpose: To provide financial assistance for college students planning a career in the petroleum energy or allied industries. **Focus:** Energy-related areas; Engineering, Mechanical; Engineering, Nuclear; Engineering, Petroleum; Geology; Geophysics. **Qualif.:** Applicant must have completed at least two years or be currently enrolled in the second year of undergraduate study at an accredited college or university; be a U.S. or Canadian citizen; maintain a GPA of 3.2 or above on a 4.0 scale; be pursuing a career in the field of petroleum, energy or allied industry. **Criteria:** Preference will be given to applicants with financial need.

Funds Avail.: $1,500. **To Apply:** Applicants must submit a completed application form available at the website. **Contact:** Jill Coble, jillecoble@yahoo.com.

1932 ■ Association universitaire canadienne d'études nordique
2464 Sheffield Rd.
Ottawa, ON, Canada K1B 4E5
Ph: (613)290-8555
URL: acuns.ca

1933 ■ Canadian Polar Commission Scholarships (Doctorate, Graduate/Scholarship)

Purpose: To support Canadian students enrolled in a doctoral program at a Canadian university. **Focus:** General studies/Field of study not specified. **Qualif.:** Applicants must be Canadian citizens or permanent residents of Canada presently enrolled in a doctoral program at a Canadian university. **Criteria:** Selection is based on academic record, potential benefit of the research, originality, innovative approach and the applicant's interest in, and commitment to, polar studies.

Funds Avail.: $10,000. **Duration:** Annual. **To Apply:** Applicants must submit a completed application form together with two letters of reference; all transcript of grades; and a copy of the research license.

1934 ■ CNST Scholarships (Doctorate, Graduate/Scholarship)

Purpose: To support Canadian students enrolled in a doctoral program at a Canadian university. **Focus:** General studies/Field of study not specified. **Qualif.:** Applicants must be citizens or permanent residents of Canada presently enrolled in a doctoral program at a Canadian university. **Criteria:** Selection is based on academic record, the quality of the application, potential benefit of the research, originality, letters of reference and the applicants' interest in, and commitment to, the north and northern scholarship.

Funds Avail.: $10,000. **Duration:** Annual. **To Apply:** Applicants must submit a completed application form together with two letters of reference; all transcript of grades; and copy of the research license. **Deadline:** January 29.

1935 ■ Northern Resident Scholarships (Doctorate, Graduate/Scholarship)

Purpose: To support Canadian students who are long-term residents of Nunavut, Northwest Territories, Yukon or the Provincial North. **Focus:** General studies/Field of study not specified. **Qualif.:** Applicants must be Canadian citizens or permanent residents of Canada identified as long-term residents of Nunavut, Northwest Territories, Yukon or the Provincial North and currently enrolled in a masters or doctoral level program at a Canadian university. **Criteria:** Selection is based on academic record, the quality of the application, potential benefit of the research, letters of reference and the applicant's leadership skills and interest in, and commitment to, northern scholarship.

Funds Avail.: $10,000. **Duration:** Annual. **Number Awarded:** Varies. **To Apply:** Applicants must submit a completed application form together with two letters of reference; all official transcript of grades; and a copy of the research license.

1936 ■ Association of Donor Recruitment Professionals (ADRP)
PO Box 150790
Austin, TX 78715
Ph: (512)658-9414
Fax: (866)219-7008
URL: www.adrp.org

1937 ■ Association of Donor Recruitment Professionals Hughes Scholarships (Other/Scholarship)

Purpose: To help individuals enhance their professional development. **Focus:** General studies/Field of study not specified. **Qualif.:** Applicant must be a current member of ADRP; have been involved in donor recruitment/community relations for less than two years. ADRP board members are not eligible to apply. **Criteria:** Recipients will be selected based on submitted application.

Awards are arranged alphabetically below their administering organizations

Funds Avail.: No specific Amount. **Duration:** Annual. **To Apply:** Applicant must submit a typewritten 500 words essay describing a creative recruitment idea that he/she has developed or wants to implement; and a typewritten letter of endorsement from his/her immediate supervisor. **Remarks:** Established in 1999.

1938 ■ Association of Donor Recruitment Professionals Presidential Scholarships *(Other/Scholarship)*

Purpose: To provide financial assistance to members who wish to acquire education and networking opportunities. **Focus:** General studies/Field of study not specified. **Qualif.:** Applicant must be a member of ADRP; have been a donor recruiter for two or more years. ADRP board members are not eligible to apply. **Criteria:** Judging will be based on submitted application.

Funds Avail.: No specific amount. **Duration:** Annual. **To Apply:** Applicant must submit a 500 word essay stating why this scholarship would enhance his/her professional development; a letter of endorsement from his/her immediate supervisor; and a letter of endorsement from a blood drive coordinator. Materials must be submitted in a typewritten format. **Remarks:** Established in 1995.

1939 ■ Nancy J. Chapman Scholarships *(Other/Scholarship)*

Purpose: To help individuals enhance their professional development. **Focus:** General studies/Field of study not specified. **Qualif.:** Applicant must be a current member of ADRP; must be in a management position in donor recruitment. ADRP board members are not eligible to apply. **Criteria:** Recipients will be selected based on submitted application.

Funds Avail.: No specific amount. **Duration:** Annual. **To Apply:** Applicant must submit a typewritten 500-word essay stating why this scholarship would enhance his/her professional development and typewritten letter of endorsement from applicant's immediate supervisor. **Deadline:** December 6. **Remarks:** Established in 1991. **Contact:** Shirley Nimsky, Executive Director, Association of Donor Recruitment Professionals (ADRP), at the above address.

1940 ■ Charles Drew Scholarships *(Other/Scholarship)*

Purpose: To help individuals enhance their professional development. **Focus:** General studies/Field of study not specified. **Qualif.:** Applicants must be current members of ADRP. Board members are not eligible to apply. **Criteria:** Recipients will be selected based on submitted applications.

Funds Avail.: No specific amount. **Duration:** Annual. **To Apply:** Applicants must submit a 500-word essay describing a successful technique they have developed which resulted in an increase in minority donations; and a typewritten letter of endorsement from their immediate supervisor. **Remarks:** Established in 2002.

1941 ■ Association for Educational Communications and Technology (AECT)

320 W 8th St., Ste. 101
Bloomington, IN 47404-3745
Ph: (812)335-7675
Free: 877-677-2328
E-mail: aect@aect.org
URL: www.aect.org/newsite

Facebook: www.facebook.com/AECT1
Twitter: twitter.com/aect

1942 ■ AECT Foundation Mentor Endowment Scholarships *(Doctorate, Graduate/Scholarship)*

Purpose: To award scholarship to individuals that may be used for their graduate study. **Focus:** Education. **Qualif.:** Applicants must be graduate students in educational communications and technology pursuing a graduate study during an academic year or a summer session in any accredited college/university in the United States or Canada; must be members of AECT; and must be accepted in or enrolled in a doctoral level program. **Criteria:** Selection is based on: scholarship; leadership potential; experience in the field of educational communications and technology (such as employment, field experience, course work, assistantships, presentations, and publications); and letters of recommendation.

Funds Avail.: $3,000. **Duration:** One academic year or one summer session. **To Apply:** Applicants must submit a completed application form along with three letters of recommendation. **Contact:** ECT Foundation, c/o AECT, 1800 N. Stonelake Dr., Suite 2, Bloomington, IN 47404.

1943 ■ AECT Legacy Scholarship *(Master's, Graduate, Professional development/Scholarship)*

Purpose: To improve the teaching/learning process in the library and classroom and to supplement the recipient's training by extending the use of educational communications and technology. **Focus:** Education, Bilingual and cross-cultural; Education, Elementary; Education, Special; Library and archival sciences. **Qualif.:** Applicants must be practicing K-12 school teachers or school library/media specialists pursuing a Master's degree or professional certificate in the field. **Criteria:** Selection is based on: scholarship; experience in the field of educational media, information literacy, research skills and involvement in innovative programs; service and leadership in the profession; applicant's statement; and letters of recommendation.

Funds Avail.: No specific amount. **Duration:** one academic year or one summer session. **To Apply:** Applicants must complete and submit the application form and three letters of recommendation. Application and references may be emailed by the deadline, but letters of recommendation must be received from the writer no later than a week after the deadline. **Deadline:** August 15. **Contact:** Stephanie Moore, ECT Foundation President; Phone: 434-243-8906.

1944 ■ McJulien Minority Graduate Scholarships *(Graduate/Scholarship)*

Purpose: To support a minority graduate student pursuing educational communications and technology. **Focus:** Education. **Qualif.:** Applicant must be a full-time graduate student enrolled in a degree granting program in educational technology at the Master's, (MS), Specialist (EdS) or Doctoral (PhD/EdD) level; must provide evidence of an average of "B" or better; and must be a member of AECT. **Criteria:** Selection is based on the submitted applications.

Funds Avail.: No specific amount. **To Apply:** Applicant must submit a completed nomination form. **Deadline:** August 15.

1945 ■ Association of Energy Engineers (AEE)

3168 Mercer University Dr.
Atlanta, GA 30341
Ph: (770)447-5083

Awards are arranged alphabetically below their administering organizations

URL: www.aeecenter.org
Facebook: www.facebook.com/Association-of-Energy-Engineers-220059965150

1946 ■ Association of Energy Engineers Foundation Scholarship Program (Graduate, Undergraduate/Scholarship)

Purpose: To encourage qualified practitioners in energy engineering and energy management by awarding scholarships to further education in the field. **Focus:** Energy-related areas. **Qualif.:** Applicants must be undergraduates and graduate degree candidates who are enrolled in engineering or management programs at accredited colleges or universities; and must be nominated by AEE Chapters. **Criteria:** Applicants are evaluated based on the criteria designed by the Scholarship Selection Committee.

Funds Avail.: No specific amount. **Duration:** Annual. **To Apply:** Applicants must submit all the required application information. **Deadline:** May 1. **Contact:** Ms. Priscila Rivere, Scholarship Director; Phone: 770-447-5083; Email: priscila@aeecenter.org.

1947 ■ Association of Environmental & Engineering Geologists
1100-H Brandywine Blvd.
Zanesville, OH 43701
Fax: (740)452-2552
Free: 844-331-7867
E-mail: contact@aegweb.org
URL: www.aegweb.org
Facebook: www.facebook.com/AEGweb
Twitter: twitter.com/AEGweb

1948 ■ Marliave Scholarship Fund (Undergraduate/Scholarship, Grant)

Purpose: To support academic activity and reward outstanding scholarship in Engineering Geology and Geological Engineering. **Focus:** Engineering, Geological. **Qualif.:** Applicants must be senior or graduate students presently enrolled full-time in a college or university degree program that is directly applicable to engineering geology or geological engineering, and student members of AEG. **Criteria:** Selection shall be based on the aforesaid applicants' qualifications and compliance with the application details.

Funds Avail.: $3,000. **Duration:** Annual. **To Apply:** Applicants must submit a completed application form. **Deadline:** February 1. **Remarks:** Established in 1968. **Contact:** Association of Environmental and Engineering Geologists, at the above address.

1949 ■ Martin L. Stout Scholarships (Undergraduate, Graduate/Scholarship)

Purpose: To support environmental and engineering geologic studies by students at the undergraduate and graduate levels. **Focus:** Engineering, Geological. **Qualif.:** Applicants must be student members of AEG at time of award. **Criteria:** Selection shall be based on the best response to one of the required essay questions and on appraisals from two professors.

Funds Avail.: $1,000 Undergraduate; $1,500 Masters; $2,000 Doctoral. **Duration:** Annual. **To Apply:** Applicants must submit an original typed and signed application form along with four (4) legible photocopies. **Deadline:** February 1. **Contact:** Association of Environmental and Engineering Geologists, at the above address.

1950 ■ Association of Environmental Engineering and Science Professors Foundation (AEESP)
1211 Connecticut Ave NW, Suite 600
Washington, DC 20036
Ph: (202)640-6591
URL: www.aeespfoundation.org

1951 ■ CH2M Hill/AEESP Outstanding Doctoral Dissertation Award (Graduate, Doctorate/Award)

Purpose: To recognize outstanding doctoral dissertation that contributes to the advancement of environmental science and engineering. **Focus:** Engineering; Environmental science. **Qualif.:** Candidates must be doctoral students. **Criteria:** Submitted dissertations will be evaluated on the basis of: the scientific and technical merit of the research; originality of the research; contribution to the advancement of environmental engineering and science; clarity of presentation.

Funds Avail.: $1,500 for the student; $500 for the faculty advisor; $750 for travel support. **Duration:** Annual. **Number Awarded:** 2. **To Apply:** Faculty advisors are encouraged to nominate dissertations completed under their supervision but must limit themselves to a single entry. Nominations letter must contain the following information: the email and mailing address and telephone numbers for the students and advisors; an indication as to when the dissertations was completed; a one paragraph description of the importance of the student's work and its relevance to environmental engineering and science; concise statement defining the students' intellectual contribution to the work. The statement regarding intellectual contribution is necessary for all entries, but it is especially important if multiple authors contributed to the work under consideration. **Deadline:** March 15.

1952 ■ W. Wesley Eckenfelder Gradute Research Award (Graduate, Master's, Doctorate/Award)

Purpose: To recognize an environmental engineering or environmental science graduate student whose research contributes to the knowledge pool of wastewater management. **Focus:** Engineering; Environmental science. **Qualif.:** Applicant must either be a Master's or Ph.D. student. **Criteria:** Award selection will be based on academic program performance (45%), professional or community service (15%), project significance (25%), purpose and goals,(10%), and any other evidence provided (5%).

Funds Avail.: $1,500; $500 travel allotment. **Duration:** Annual. **To Apply:** Electronic nomination packages should include: letter from the faculty advisor of the applicant indicating completed substantive requirements for the graduate degree sought, and earned a minimum GPA of 3.3/4 in the current program; two academic letters of recommendation; 25-page copy of a publication (or manuscript submitted for publication) derived from the subject research for which the applicant is the first author; professional resume of the student applicant, listing all professional affiliations, publications, honors, service, and relevant experience; and applicant-prepared statement of professional purpose in pursuing the graduate degree and goals for the first five years of professional practice limited to 500 words. **Deadline:** March 15.

1953 ■ Paul V. Roberts/AEESP Outstanding Doctoral Dissertation Award *(Graduate, Doctorate/Prize, Monetary)*

Purpose: To recognize a rigorous and innovative doctoral thesis that advances the science and practice of water quality engineering for either engineered or natural systems. **Focus:** Engineering. **Qualif.:** Candidates must be doctoral students. **Criteria:** Submitted dissertations will be evaluated on the basis of: the scientific and technical merit of the research; originality of the research; contribution to the advancement of environmental engineering and science; clarity of presentation.

Funds Avail.: $1,500 for the student; $500 for the faculty advisor; $1,500 travel allotment. **Duration:** Annual. **To Apply:** Faculty advisors are encouraged to nominate dissertations completed under their supervision but must limit themselves to a single entry. Nominations letter must contain the following information: the email and mailing address and telephone numbers for the students and advisors; an indication as to when the dissertations was completed; a one paragraph description of the importance of the student's work and its relevance to environmental engineering and science; concise statement defining the students' intellectual contribution to the work. The statement regarding intellectual contribution is necessary for all entries, but it is especially important if multiple authors contributed to the work under consideration. **Deadline:** March 15.

1954 ■ William Brewster Snow Award *(Graduate/Award, Monetary)*

Purpose: To recognize an environmental engineering graduate student who has made significant accomplishments in an employment or academic engineering project. **Focus:** Engineering; Environmental science. **Qualif.:** Nominees for this award must be enrolled part- or full-time in an environmental engineering graduate program pursuing or have completed a master's degree in environmental engineering or a closely related program. **Criteria:** Eligible applicants will be judged based on academic program and performance (45%), professional or community service (15%), engineering project accomplishment (25%), purpose and goals (10%), and any other evidence provided (5%).

Funds Avail.: $250. **Duration:** Annual. **Number Awarded:** 1. **To Apply:** Electronic nomination packages should include: nomination form; transcript verifying that the student has achieved a minimum GPA of 3.3 (on a 4.0 scale) in Master's degree program coursework; documented successful completion of the Fundamentals of Engineering Exam; two academic letters of recommendation; evidence of active participation in a student or regular chapter of an engineering related professional society; statement of purpose in pursuing a Master's degree and goals for first 5 years of professional practice; any other evidence of merit, papers, honors, recognition; other documents the organization ask. **Deadline:** March 15.

1955 ■ Virginia Tech Student Travel Award *(Undergraduate, Graduate/Award)*

Purpose: To support the recipients' travel to attend the biennial AEESP Education and Research Conference. **Focus:** Engineering; Environmental science. **Qualif.:** Applicants must be undergraduate or graduate students of Virginia Tech. **Criteria:** Selection will be based on merit.

Funds Avail.: Up to $750. **Duration:** Biennial; in odd-numbered years. **To Apply:** Interested applicants may contact the Foundation or Virginia Tech for the application process and other information. **Remarks:** Established in 2007.

1956 ■ Association des Facultes de Pharmacie du Canada (AFPC)
PO Box 21053
Edmonton, AB, Canada T6R 2V4
URL: www.afpc.info

1957 ■ Merck Frosst Canada Ltd. Postgraduate Pharmacy Fellowships *(Graduate/Fellowship)*

Purpose: To encourage students to pursue their postgraduate studies in Pharmacy at a Canadian University. **Focus:** Pharmacy. **Qualif.:** Applicants must be in the final year in a pharmacy or pharmaceutical sciences degree program or pharmacy practitioners who are entering postgraduate studies in a faculty, College or School of Pharmacy in Canada or first year graduate students who have a pharmacy or pharmaceutical sciences degree and are enrolled in an M.Sc. or PhD degree in Faculty, College or School of Pharmacy in Canada; must be Canadian citizens or permanent residents of Canada. **Criteria:** Selection of applicants will be based on academic performance, publication activity, and fields of research in need of support.

Funds Avail.: Maximum of $30,000. **Duration:** Annual. **Number Awarded:** 2. **To Apply:** Applicants must submit the complete application form together with their official transcript of academic records. **Deadline:** December 15. **Contact:** Dr. Frank Abbott, Executive Director:hlopatka@telus.net.

1958 ■ Association of Family Practice Physician Assistants (AFPPA)
77 Wollcott Ave.
Dartmouth, MA 02747
Ph: (774)206-6774
Fax: (508)998-6001
E-mail: info@afppa.org
URL: www.afppa.org
Facebook: www.facebook.com/afppa
Twitter: twitter.com/afppa

1959 ■ AFPPA Student Scholarships *(Undergraduate/Scholarship)*

Purpose: To financially assist first and second year physician students. **Focus:** Medicine. **Qualif.:** Applicants must be PA students attending an accredited PA program for more than 12 months or students with 12 months or less of PA education. **Criteria:** Applicants who are AFPPA student members in good academic standing and demonstrate interest in family practice medicine will be given priority.

Funds Avail.: $1,500 per student. **Duration:** Annual. **Number Awarded:** 2. **To Apply:** Applicants must submit an essay (maximum of 750 words or less) describing the commitment to family practice medicine and how the current and past community involvement demonstrates this commitment. **Deadline:** September 1. **Contact:** Rene McCarty, PA-C, AFPPA Scholarship Committee Chair.; Email: info@afppa.org.

1960 ■ Association for Federal Information Resources Management (AFFIRM)
400 N Washington St., Ste. 300
Alexandria, VA 22314

Awards are arranged alphabetically below their administering organizations

Ph: (703)778-4646
Fax: (703)683-5480
E-mail: info@affirm.org
URL: www.affirm.org

1961 ■ AFFIRM University Scholarships
(Undergraduate/Scholarship)

Purpose: To support students who are scholars and are majoring in an IT related curriculum. **Focus:** Information science and technology; Technology. **Qualif.:** Applicants must be full-time students (12 credits or more); must be junior or above; must have a minimum of 3.0 cumulative GPA; and must be majoring in some aspect of information technology or related field. **Criteria:** U.S. Citizens are given preference.

Funds Avail.: No specific amount. **Duration:** Annual. **To Apply:** Scholarship applications will be provided by the universities. Applicants must prepare a letter of reference from a professor.

1962 ■ Association of Flight Attendants - CWA (AFA-CWA)
501 3rd St. NW
Washington, DC 20001
Ph: (202)434-1300
Free: 800-424-2401
E-mail: info@afacwa.org
URL: www.afanet.org

1963 ■ Association of Flight Attendants Scholarship Fund *(Undergraduate/Scholarship)*

Purpose: To further the education of promising young men and women who are dependents of AFA members in good standing who otherwise would not have the opportunity for higher education. **Focus:** Aviation. **Qualif.:** Applicants must be dependents of AFA members in good standing seeking to further education at an accredited college or university. **Criteria:** Selection will be based on the following criteria: students' rank on their high school class; SAT or ACT scores; demonstrated financial need.

Funds Avail.: Up to $5,000. **Duration:** Annual. **To Apply:** Applicants must submit a completed application form (available on the website), 300-word essay, three references; transcripts, grades and SAT scores. **Deadline:** April 10. **Contact:** Application must be sent to: Association of Flight Attendants Scholarship Fund, P. O. Box 56, Hartwood, VA. 22471-0056.

1964 ■ Association of Food and Drug Officials (AFDO)
2550 Kingston Rd., Ste. 311
York, PA 17402
Ph: (717)757-2888
Fax: (717)650-3650
E-mail: afdo@afdo.org
URL: www.afdo.org
Facebook: www.facebook.com/Association-of-Food-and-Drug-Officials-368401966580523
LinkedIn: www.linkedin.com/company/3091669?trk=NUS_CMPY_TWIT
Twitter: twitter.com/afdonews

1965 ■ George M. Burditt Scholarships
(Undergraduate/Scholarship)

Purpose: To provide financial assistance for students to further their education. **Focus:** General studies/Field of study not specified. **Qualif.:** Applicants should have demonstrated a desire to serve in a career of research, regulatory work, quality control, or teaching in an area related to some aspect of foods, drugs or consumer product safety; should have demonstrated leadership capabilities; and must have at least a 3.0 grade average during the first two years of undergraduate study on a scale of 4.0. **Criteria:** Selection will be based on the aforesaid qualifications.

Funds Avail.: $1,500. **Duration:** Annual. **To Apply:** Applicants must submit a completed application form; official and complete college transcript, and two letters of recommendation from faculty members. **Deadline:** February 1. **Remarks:** Established in 1981. **Contact:** Application form and supporting documents must be sent to Dr. Joanne Brown, Chair of the AFDO Awards Committee, AFDO, at the above address.

1966 ■ Betsy B. Woodward Scholarships
(Undergraduate/Scholarship)

Purpose: To provide financial assistance for students to further their education. **Focus:** General studies/Field of study not specified. **Qualif.:** Applicants should have demonstrated a desire to serve in a career of research, regulatory work, quality control, or teaching in an area related to some aspect of foods, drugs or consumer product safety; should have demonstrated leadership capabilities; and must have at least a 3.0 grade average during the first two years of undergraduate study on a scale of 4.0. **Criteria:** Selection will be based on the aforesaid qualifications.

Funds Avail.: $1,500. **Duration:** Annual. **To Apply:** Applicants must submit a completed application form, official and complete college transcript; and two letters of recommendation from faculty members. **Deadline:** February 1. **Remarks:** Established in 1981. **Contact:** Application form and supporting documents must be sent to Dr. Joanne Brown, Chair of the AFDO Awards Committee, AFDO, at the above address.

1967 ■ Association of Former Intelligence Officers (AFIO)
7700 Leesburg Pke., Ste. 324
Falls Church, VA 22043
Ph: (703)790-0320
Fax: (703)991-1278
E-mail: afio@afio.com
URL: www.afio.com

1968 ■ David L. Boren Undergraduate Scholarships
(Graduate, Undergraduate/Scholarship)

Purpose: To provide funding for graduate and undergraduate study in a number of targeted countries and fields. **Focus:** General studies/Field of study not specified. **Qualif.:** Applicants must be students currently enrolled in an undergraduate study or graduates planning to attend graduate school; and must have the desire to study foreign languages in addition to any major-related study. **Criteria:** Preference is given for those students who are interested in studying critical languages or fields related to security interest.

Funds Avail.: $10,000 per semester or $20,000 per academic year. **Duration:** Annual. **To Apply:** Applicants must complete an official application form which can be obtained from the Loyola College faculty representative. Applicants must also submit application forms online together with the three letters of recommendation, and four

Awards are arranged alphabetically below their administering organizations

semesters' worth of transcripts. **Deadline:** February 10. **Remarks:** For further information, applicants may write to Institute of International Education at the above address. Established in 1991.

1969 ■ CIA Undergraduate Scholarships
(Undergraduate/Scholarship)

Purpose: To assist minority, disabled and non-disabled deserving students to increase knowledge and academic skills. **Focus:** General studies/Field of study not specified. **Qualif.:** Applicants must be high school seniors planning to enroll or college sophomores attending a four or five-year college program; must be U.S. citizens; 1,000 SAT (Math or Verbal) or 21 ACT scores or higher (high school students); must have 3.0/4.0 scale high school or college GPA or higher. **Criteria:** Selection is based on applicants' demonstrated financial need.

Funds Avail.: $18,000. **Duration:** Annual. **To Apply:** Applicants must apply online and must successfully complete medical and psychological exam, polygraph interview and extensive background investigation; must attach the following documents: a) SAT or ACT scores (for high school seniors); b) most current FAFSA or SAR; c) school transcripts; and d) two letters of recommendation. **Deadline:** November 1.

1970 ■ Association of Government Accountants (AGA)
2208 Mt. Vernon Ave.
Alexandria, VA 22301-1314
Ph: (703)684-6931
Fax: (703)548-9367
Free: 800-AGA-7211
E-mail: agamembers@agacgfm.org
URL: www.agacgfm.org
Twitter: twitter.com/agacgfm

1971 ■ Association of Government Accountants Undergraduate/Graduate Scholarships for Community Service Accomplishments *(Graduate, Undergraduate/Scholarship)*

Purpose: To provide financial assistance to qualified professionals who exemplify and promote excellence in federal, state or local government financial management. **Focus:** Accounting; Economics; Public administration. **Qualif.:** Applicants must be pursuing a degree in a financial management academic discipline; must be actively involved in community service projects. **Criteria:** Applicants will be selected based on community service involvement and accomplishments. Candidates must have a minimum GPA of 3.0 on a 4.0 scale.

Funds Avail.: $1,500. **Number Awarded:** 2. **To Apply:** Applicants must complete the application form available online; must provide a recommendation letter and transcript of record; must submit an essay (cannot be more than two double-spaced pages). **Deadline:** April 15. **Contact:** AGA via U.S. Mail, or by email to awards@agacgfm.org.

1972 ■ Association of Government Accountants Undergraduate/Graduate Scholarships for Full-time study *(Graduate, Undergraduate/Scholarship)*

Purpose: To provide financial assistance to qualified professionals who exemplify and promote excellence in federal state or local government financial management. **Focus:** Accounting; Economics; Public administration. **Qualif.:** Applicants must be AGA members or family members; must be undertaking full-time undergraduate/graduate study in a financial management academic discipline; must have a minimum GPA of 3.0 on a 4.0 scale. **Criteria:** Applicants will be selected based on community service involvement and accomplishments.

Funds Avail.: Up to $3,000. **Number Awarded:** 2. **To Apply:** Applicants must complete the application form available online; must provide a recommendation letter and transcript of record; must submit an essay (cannot be more than two double-spaced pages). **Deadline:** April 15. **Contact:** AGA via U.S. Mail, or by email to awards@agacgfm.org.

1973 ■ Association of Government Accountants Undergraduate/Graduate Scholarships for Part-time study *(Graduate, Undergraduate/Scholarship)*

Purpose: To provide financial assistance to qualified professionals who exemplify and promote excellence in federal, state or local government financial management. **Focus:** Accounting; Economics; Public administration. **Qualif.:** Applicants must be AGA members or family members; must be applied toward full-time undergraduate/graduate study in a financial management academic discipline; must have a minimum GPA of 3.0 on a 4.0 scale. **Criteria:** Applicants will be selected based on community service involvement and accomplishments.

Funds Avail.: $1,500. **Number Awarded:** 2. **To Apply:** Applicants must complete the application form available online; must provide a recommendation letter and transcript of record; must submit an essay (cannot be more than two double-spaced pages). **Deadline:** April 15. **Contact:** AGA via U.S. Mail, or by email to awards@agacgfm.org.

1974 ■ Association of Independent Colleges and Universities of Pennsylvania (AICUP)
101 N Front St.
Harrisburg, PA 17101-1405
Ph: (717)232-8649
Fax: (717)233-8574
URL: www.aicup.org

1975 ■ Air Products and Chemicals, Inc. Scholarships *(Undergraduate/Scholarship)*

Purpose: To promote the engineering and information technology profession to individuals from groups historically underrepresented in engineering. **Focus:** Computer and information sciences; Engineering, Chemical; Engineering, Mechanical. **Qualif.:** Applicants must: be full-time undergraduate students majoring only in Chemical engineering, Mechanical engineering, Information technology (computer science, management information systems, IST); be enrolled as a junior in fall; have a minimum GPA of 3.0; be women and/or members of the following minority groups: American Indian or Alaska Native, Asian, Black or African American, Hispanic or Latino, Native Hawaiian or other Pacific Islander. Student must be accepted at, or currently attending, one of 84 member colleges and universities of the Association of Independent Colleges and Universities of Pennsylvania. **Criteria:** Selection will be based on the committee's criteria.

Funds Avail.: $7,500. **Duration:** Annual. **Number Awarded:** 1. **To Apply:** Application forms are available at the Financial Aid office; applicant must submit complete application materials to Mary Maronic, Foundation Associate,

Awards are arranged alphabetically below their administering organizations

Association of Independent Colleges and Universities of Pennsylvania. A complete application consists of a completed, signed application form, a copy of the student's transcript, a resume and an essay; the candidate may submit a letter of recommendation.

1976 ■ Michael Baker Corp. Scholarship for Diversity in Engineering *(Undergraduate/Scholarship)*

Purpose: To promote the engineering and information technology profession to individuals from groups historically underrepresented in engineering. **Focus:** Engineering, Architectural; Engineering, Civil. **Qualif.:** Applicants must be: full-time undergraduate students majoring in Civil, Environmental or Architectural Engineering only; enrolled as juniors in the fall; maintaining a minimum GPA of 3.0; women and/or members of the following minority groups: American Indians or Alaska Natives, Asians, Black or African Americans, Hispanics or Latinos, Native Hawaiians or Other Pacific Islanders. Student must be accepted at, or currently attending, one of 84 member colleges and universities of the Association of Independent Colleges and Universities of Pennsylvania. **Criteria:** Selection will be based on the committee's criteria.

Funds Avail.: $2,500. **Number Awarded:** 2. **To Apply:** Application forms are available at the Financial Aid office. Applicant must submit complete application to Mary Maronic, Foundation Associate, Association of Independent Colleges and Universities of Pennsylvania. A complete application consists of a completed, signed application form, a copy of the student's transcript, a resume and an essay; the candidate may submit a letter of recommendation.

1977 ■ Commonwealth "Good Citizen" Scholarships *(Undergraduate/Scholarship)*

Purpose: To provide scholarship to the students who have shown an extraordinary commitment to community service and who have demonstrated creativity in shaping their volunteer activities. **Focus:** General studies/Field of study not specified. **Qualif.:** Applicant must be a full-time undergraduate student with an extraordinary commitment to community service and who has demonstrated creativity in shaping his/her volunteer activities; and must attend a school that is a member of the Association of Independent Colleges and Universities of Pennsylvania. **Criteria:** Selection will be based on the Committee's criteria.

Funds Avail.: $1,500. **To Apply:** Applicant must write a brief essay describing their college experience and focusing upon the answers to the following: what volunteer/extracurricular activities do they participate in, either on or off campus; how do their community service activities relate to their major and what leadership roles have they taken; what are their career/academic goals upon graduation; how will they remain involved in their community upon graduation. Applicants should include any additional information that they feel will be helpful in choosing them as a recipients of the Commonwealth "Good Citizen" Scholarship; must limit essay to two double-spaced pages (essay must have 1-inch margins) with a font that is easily readable and set no smaller than 11. Completed applications should be returned to applicants' Financial Aid Office.

1978 ■ McLean Scholarships *(Undergraduate/Scholarship)*

Purpose: To help full-time undergraduate students who are enrolled in a Nursing or Physician's Assistant program. **Focus:** Nursing. **Qualif.:** Applicant must be a full-time undergraduate student enrolled in a Nursing or Physician Assistant program at one of the Association of Independent Colleges and Universities of Pennsylvania's member institutions; and have at least a 3.0 GPA. Ideal candidates are campus leaders and community volunteers. **Criteria:** Selection will be based on the committee's criteria.

Funds Avail.: No specific amount. **To Apply:** Application forms are available at the Financial Aid office. Along with the completed applications, students may submit a copy of their transcript, a letter of recommendation and any other materials that they feel will be helpful to the committee in making their decision. Students must also submit a brief essay describing their college experience, including the following information: why they chose their major; what steps they are taking to ensure that they succeed in their major; what they plan to do upon graduating and their academic/career goals. Applicants should also describe the primary volunteer/extracurricular activities in which they participate; how these activities relate to their major and what leadership roles they have taken. Completed applications should be returned to the applicants' Financial Aid office, which will then select one application to submit to AICUP.

1979 ■ Association for Institutional Research (AIR)
1435 E Piedmont Dr., Ste. 211
Tallahassee, FL 32308
Ph: (850)385-4155
Fax: (850)385-5180
E-mail: air@airweb.org
URL: www.airweb.org
Facebook: www.facebook.com/Association.for.Institutional.Research

1980 ■ AIR Dissertation Grants *(Doctorate/Grant)*

Purpose: To support dissertation research and writing under the guidance of a faculty dissertation advisor. **Focus:** General studies/Field of study not specified. **Qualif.:** Applicants must be doctoral students enrolled at U.S. post-secondary educational institutions. Such may be U.S. citizens, permanent residents, or non-U.S. citizens. **Criteria:** Selection shall be based on the applications review conducted by the panel of national experts.

Funds Avail.: $20,000. **Duration:** Annual. **To Apply:** Individuals are encouraged to begin the application process as soon as possible by providing initial contact information by going to https://apps.airweb.org/researchgrants. Complete the online application by following the Grant Guidelines. The application contains seven components. It is recommended that applicants write each section using word processing software and when finalized, cut and paste the text into the online application. Changes in formatting may occur when pasting into the application system. Submit the online proposal by following the directions at the end of the online application. When a proposal is successfully submitted, a confirmation email will be sent to the applicants. It is the applicants' responsibility to submit the final proposal and store the confirmation email as receipt of successful submission. **Deadline:** March 24. **Contact:** Email: grants@airweb.org; Phone: 850-385-4155 loc. 200.

1981 ■ AIR Research Grants *(Professional development/Grant)*

Purpose: To support research on a wide range of issues of critical importance to US higher education. **Focus:** General studies/Field of study not specified. **Qualif.:** Applicants must be faculties or practitioners affiliated with a US postsecondary institution or relevant non-profit higher education organization. **Criteria:** Selection will be based on the panel of national experts' criteria.

Funds Avail.: Up to $40,000. **Duration:** Annual. **To Apply:** Proposals must meet the following criteria: use data from one or more of the national datasets of NSF or NCES; address the NEPEC Focus topic, "The Impact of Data on the College Search and Selection Process." Individuals are encouraged to begin the application process as soon as possible by providing initial contact information as the first step by going to https://apps.airweb.org/researchgrants. Complete the online application by following the Research Grant Guidelines. The application contains seven components. It is recommended that applicants write each section using word processing software and when finalized, cut and paste the text into the online application. Changes in formatting may occur when pasting into the application system. Submit the online proposal by following the directions at the end of the online application. When a proposal is successfully submitted, a confirmation email will be sent to the applicants. It is the applicants' responsibility to submit the final proposal and store the confirmation email as receipt of successful submission.

1982 ■ Edward Delaney Scholarships *(Professional development/Scholarship)*

Purpose: To facilitate the professional growth and development of early career institutional research professionals by providing travel assistance to AIR's annual Forum. **Focus:** General studies/Field of study not specified. **Qualif.:** Applicants must meet the following criteria: hold current year AIR membership; be currently employed in the institutional research (IR) field; have worked for 3-5 years in a campus-based IR/assessment office for full- or part-time; and, have never attended the AIR Forum. **Criteria:** Selection will be based on the committee's criteria.

Funds Avail.: $1,000. **Duration:** Annual. **To Apply:** Applicants must submit an essay, maximum 750 words, addressing the impact this award is expected to have on their professional development. The essay should be written for blind review, which means that the essay should not include information that would personally identify them or their institutional affiliation. The essay should address each of the following prompts: Briefly describe the applicants' current work in IR and provide a summary review of their current skills; What three outcomes they hope to accomplish from their participation at the Forum?; What are the applicants' long-term career goals and how will their involvement with AIR and the Forum benefit them in this journey? A letter of support from the applicant's supervisor approving their participation in the professional development activity must also be submitted. **Deadline:** December 2. **Contact:** Email: scholarships@airweb.org; Phone: 850-385-4155 loc. 109.

1983 ■ Julia M. Duckwall Scholarships *(Professional development/Scholarship)*

Purpose: To facilitate the professional growth and development of early career institutional research professionals. **Focus:** General studies/Field of study not specified. **Qualif.:** Applicants must meet the following criteria: hold current year AIR membership; be currently employed in the institutional research (IR) field; have worked for 3-5 years in a campus-based IR/assessment office for full- or part-time; have never attended the AIR Forum; and, have never received a Data and Decisions Academy Scholarship. **Criteria:** Selection will be based on the committee's criteria.

Funds Avail.: No specific amount. **Duration:** Annual. **Number Awarded:** 3. **To Apply:** Applicants must submit an essay, maximum 750 words, addressing the impact this award is expected to have on their professional development. The essay should be written for blind review, which means that the essay should not include information that would personally identify them or their institutional affiliation. The essay should address each of the following prompts: briefly describe the applicants' current work in IR and provide a summary review of their current skills and accomplishments in the field; what outcomes do they anticipate from their participation in their selected professional development experience (state if the applicants desire to attend the Forum/Pre-Forum or to participate in the Data and Decisions Academy)?; Duckwall Award recipients are expected to honor Julia Duckwall's commitment to giving back to the IR field. How will the applicants assure that others will benefit from their experiences? A letter of support from the applicant's supervisor approving their participation in the professional development activity must also be submitted. **Deadline:** December 2. **Contact:** Email: scholarships@airweb.org; Phone: 850-385-4155 loc. 109.

1984 ■ Association of International Education Administrators (AIEA)
2204 Erwin Rd., Rm. 030
Durham, NC 27708-0404
Ph: (919)668-1928
Fax: (919)684-8749
E-mail: aiea@duke.edu
URL: www.aieaworld.org
Facebook: www.facebook.com/AIEA-Association-of
 -International-Education-Administrators
 -173003256103319
Twitter: twitter.com/AIEAWorld

1985 ■ AIEA Presidential Fellows Program *(Undergraduate/Fellowship)*

Purpose: To give mentorship to new Senior International Officers (SIO). **Focus:** Education. **Qualif.:** Candidates must be current AIEA members. **Criteria:** Selections will be based on the following criteria: need and perceived benefit; promise/potential of applicants; quality of statement and application materials.

Funds Avail.: $1,500. **Duration:** Annual. **Number Awarded:** 1. **To Apply:** Applicants may contact the Association for the application process and other information. **Deadline:** May 1.

1986 ■ Association of International Petroleum Negotiators (AIPN)
11767 Katy Freeway, Ste. 412
Houston, TX 77079
Ph: (281)558-7715
Fax: (281)558-7073
E-mail: membership@aipn.org
URL: www.aipn.org

1987 ■ AIPN Student Scholarships *(All/Scholarship)*

Purpose: To supports students in financial need who possess the potential to make a significant contribution tot he field of international oil and gas negotiations. **Focus:** Energy-related areas. **Qualif.:** Qualified applicants may be working towards an energy, commercial or law degree, but

Awards are arranged alphabetically below their administering organizations

must be attending a university that supports the AIPN by having professor on AIPN's Education Advisory Board. **Criteria:** Selection will be based on the following criteria: potential to make a significant contribution to the field of international oil and gas negotiations; academic ability; leadership and negotiation ability; year in school; financial need.
Funds Avail.: A total of $5,000. **Duration:** Annual. **To Apply:** Interested applicants may contact the Association for the application process and other information. **Remarks:** Established in 2009. **Contact:** education@aipn.org.

1988 ■ Association for Iron and Steel Technology (AIST)

186 Thorn Hill Rd.
Warrendale, PA 15086-7528
Ph: (724)814-3000
Fax: (724)814-3001
E-mail: memberservices@aist.org
URL: www.aist.org/home.aspx
Facebook: www.facebook.com/AIST-Association-for-Iron-Steel-Technology-354069413052
Twitter: twitter.com/AISTech

1989 ■ AIST Baltimore Member Chapter Scholarships *(Undergraduate/Scholarship)*

Purpose: To enhance education and careers in engineering or metallurgy. **Focus:** Engineering; Metallurgy. **Qualif.:** Applicants must be dependents or spouse of a commendable member of the AIST Baltimore Chapter Scholarship; must be attending an eligible, full-time course in the field of engineering at an institution; must demonstrate interest towards a career in the field of iron and steel industry. **Criteria:** Recipients are selected by the Scholarship Award Committee.
Funds Avail.: $1,500. **Duration:** Annual. **Number Awarded:** 1. **To Apply:** Applicants must submit an application form available at the website and must include the following materials: a resume; a copy of SAT/ACT scores; copy of transcripts; two essays (not exceeding 500 words) about the applicants' accomplishments, and the applicants' interest/involvement in the steel and iron industry. **Deadline:** April 30.

1990 ■ AIST Midwest Member Chapter - Engineering Scholarships *(Undergraduate/Scholarship)*

Purpose: To provide educational assistance for engineering students. **Focus:** Engineering. **Qualif.:** Applicants must be graduating high school students or full-time freshmen, sophomores or junior students in good academic standing from an accredited institution. **Criteria:** Recipients will be selected according to merit.
Funds Avail.: $1,500. **Duration:** Annual. **Number Awarded:** 2. **To Apply:** Applicants must submit an application form available at the website; a resume; a recommendation/evaluation from a counselor, teacher or professor; copy of SAT/ACT scores; a copy of transcripts; and an essay (maximum of 2 pages) describing the applicants' objectives for college and career. **Deadline:** March 15. **Contact:** Rich Trzcinski, EQ Engineers LLC; Address: 3400 179th Street, Hammond, IN 46323; Phone: 219-844-3500; Email: richt@eqengineers.com.

1991 ■ AIST Midwest Member Chapter - Non-Engineering Scholarships *(Undergraduate/Scholarship)*

Purpose: To support students in pursuing career within the iron and steel industry. **Focus:** General studies/Field of study not specified. **Qualif.:** Applicant must be a graduating high school student or a full-time freshman, sophomore or junior student in good academic standing from an accredited institution. **Criteria:** Beneficiary will be selected according to merit.
Funds Avail.: $1,500. **Duration:** Annual. **Number Awarded:** 2. **To Apply:** Applicants must submit an application form available at the website; a resume; a recommendation/evaluation from a Counselor, Teacher or Professor; copy of SAT/ACT scores; a copy of transcripts; and an essay (maximum of 2 pages) describing the applicants' objectives for college and career. **Deadline:** March 15. **Contact:** Rich Trzcinski, EQ Engineers LLC; Address: 3400 179th Street, Hammond, IN 46323; Phone: 219-844-3500; Email: richt@eqengineers.com.

1992 ■ AIST Midwest Member Chapter - Western States Scholarships *(Undergraduate/Scholarship)*

Purpose: To provide educational assistance for engineering students. **Focus:** Engineering. **Qualif.:** Applicant must be graduating high school students or a full-time freshmen, sophomores or junior students in good academic standing from an accredited institution. **Criteria:** Recipients will be selected according to merit.
Funds Avail.: $3,000. **Duration:** Annual. **Number Awarded:** 1. **To Apply:** Applicants must submit an application form available at the website together with the following materials: a resume; a recommendation/evaluation from a counselor, teacher or professor; copy of SAT/ACT scores; copy of transcripts; and an essay (maximum of 2 pages) describing the applicants' objectives for college and career. **Deadline:** March 15. **Contact:** Rich Trzcinski, EQ Engineers LLC; Address: 3400 179th Street, Hammond, IN 46323; Phone: 219-844-3500; Email: richt@eqengineers.com.

1993 ■ AIST Northwest Member Chapter Scholarships *(Undergraduate/Scholarship)*

Purpose: To provide educational assistance for students who wish to pursue their education. **Focus:** Engineering. **Qualif.:** Applicant must be a relative of a member of the AIST Northwest Member Chapter; must be a Pacific Northwest student; must demonstrate great interest in the iron and steel profession. Chemistry, metallurgy, mathematics, engineering and physics students are also qualified for the scholarships. **Criteria:** Priority will be given to engineering students. Academic achievements in chemistry, mathematics and physics are a major basis for the selection. Extra-curricular activities and student statements are also considered.
Funds Avail.: $3,000. **Duration:** Annual. **Number Awarded:** 1. **To Apply:** Applicants must submit an application form available at the website; a resume; a recommendation/evaluation from a counselor, teacher or professor; copy of SAT/ACT scores; copy of transcripts; and an essay (maximum of 2 pages) with one of the topics: Purpose in going to college; beneficial experience during the last two summers; most significant experiences and effect on future plans; accomplishments providing the greatest satisfaction; reason why the applicant should be chosen as the recipient of the award. **Deadline:** April 30. **Contact:** Patrick Jablonski, P.E., Environmental Engineer, Nucor Steel Seattle, Inc.; Address: 2424 SW Andover St. Seattle, WA 98106.

1994 ■ AIST Ohio Valley Chapter Scholarships *(Undergraduate/Scholarship)*

Purpose: To support students who are pursuing an education in engineering, metallurgy, physical science, computer

ASSOCIATION FOR IRON AND STEEL TECHNOLOGY

technology or an engineering technology field. **Focus:** Biology; Chemistry; Computer and information sciences; Engineering, Electrical; Engineering, Mechanical; Engineering, Metallurgical; Microbiology; Physical sciences. **Qualif.:** Applicant must be a dependent or member of Ohio Valley Chapter of the AIST; planning to attend or currently enrolled full-time curriculum at an accredited university or college. **Criteria:** Recipient is selected based on academic performance and achievements in mathematics and science, extracurricular activities and essays.

Funds Avail.: $1,000. **Duration:** Annual. **Number Awarded:** 1-2. **To Apply:** Applicant must submit an application form available at the website together with the following materials: a resume; a recommendation/evaluation from a counselor and teacher or professor; copy of SAT/ACT scores; copy of transcripts; an essay (maximum of 2 pages) with either one of the topics: purpose in going to college; beneficial experience during the last two summers; most significant experiences and effect on future plans; accomplishments providing the greatest satisfaction; reasons why he/she should be chosen as the recipient of the award. **Deadline:** March 31. **Contact:** Tom Euson; 3S Incorporated, Attn: AIST Scholarship; Address: 8686 Southwest Pkwy, Harrison, Ohio 45030; Phone: 812-656-8045.

1995 ■ AIST San Francisco Member Chapter Scholarships *(Undergraduate/Scholarship)*

Purpose: To support students who are pursuing education in iron- and steel-related industries. **Focus:** General studies/Field of study not specified. **Qualif.:** Applicant must be related to a San Francisco Chapter member; must be planning to attend or currently enrolled at an accredited university or college (full-time course only). **Criteria:** Recipients are selected by the Scholarship Award Committee.

Funds Avail.: $1,500 each. **Duration:** Annual. **Number Awarded:** Up to 2. **To Apply:** Applicants must submit an application form available at the website; resume; a recommendation/evaluation from a counselor, teacher or professor; copy of SAT/ACT scores; copy of transcripts; an essay (not more than 250 words) that answers the question, "Why are you motivated to attend college and how do you hope to utilize your degree after you graduate?". All requirements must be sent to: Frank Martucci Department Manager - Project Development USS-POSCO Industries 900 Loveridge Rd. Pittsburg, CA 94565. **Deadline:** April 30. **Contact:** Adam Krey, Purchasing Manager for Tin and Sheet, USS-POSCO Industries; Address: 900 Loveridge Rd. MS 64, P.O. Box 471, Pittsburg, CA 94565; Email: akrey@ussposco.com.

1996 ■ AIST Benjamin F. Fairless Scholarships *(Undergraduate/Scholarship)*

Purpose: To provide educational assistance for students who wish to pursue their education. **Focus:** Engineering; Metallurgy. **Qualif.:** Applicant must be enrolled full-time in an engineering, metallurgy or materials science program at an accredited North American university; have a minimum GPA of 3.0 on a 4.0 scale; demonstrate interest toward a career in the field of iron and steel industry. **Criteria:** Recipient is selected based on the application and other documents.

Funds Avail.: Up to $6,000. **To Apply:** Applicant must submit an application form available at the website; a resume; an essay (maximum of 2 pages) about the applicant's professional goals, interest in a career in the steel industry, and how the applicant's skills could be applied to enhance the industry; three letters of recommendation (addressing the character, academic status, leadership potential and career commitment) from a college academic advisor, professor and previous employer; and transcripts. **Deadline:** March 2. **Remarks:** Established in 1954.

1997 ■ AIST Midwest Member Chapter - Jack Gill Scholarships *(Undergraduate/Scholarship)*

Purpose: To provide educational assistance for engineering students. **Focus:** Engineering. **Qualif.:** Applicants must be graduating high school students or full-time freshmen, sophomores or junior students in good academic standing from an accredited institution. **Criteria:** Recipient will be selected according to merit.

Funds Avail.: $3,000. **Duration:** Annual. **Number Awarded:** 1. **To Apply:** Applicants must submit an application form available at the website; a resume; a recommendation/evaluation from a counselor, teacher or professor; copy of SAT/ACT scores; copy of transcripts; and an essay (maximum of 2 pages) describing the applicant's' objectives for college and career. **Deadline:** March 15. **Contact:** Rich Trzcinski, EQ Engineers LLC; Address: 3400 179th Street, Hammond, IN 46323; Phone: 219-844-3500; Email: richt@eqengineers.com.

1998 ■ Globe-Trotters Member Chapter Scholarships *(Undergraduate, Postgraduate/Scholarship)*

Purpose: To support students in pursuing career within the iron and steel industry. **Focus:** Metallurgy. **Qualif.:** Applicant must be a dependent of a member (Globe-Trotters member must also be a current member of AIST); be currently enrolled in an accredited college or university. Postgraduate students are also qualified for the scholarships. **Criteria:** Recipients are selected based on the submitted essay, academic and extracurricular activities.

Funds Avail.: $2,500 each. **Duration:** Annual. **Number Awarded:** Up to 4. **To Apply:** Applicants must submit an application form available at the website; resume; copy of SAT/ACT scores; a copy of transcripts; an essay (maximum of 300 words) about the reason the applicant has selected the particular field of study, and an explanation on how the scholarship will be applied, such as tuition, books, etc. **Deadline:** April 30. **Contact:** Gavin Noel; Address: 2100 Griffin Wheel Dr., Bessemer, AL 35020; Phone: 205-417-6820.

1999 ■ Alfred B. Glossbrenner Scholarships *(Undergraduate/Scholarship)*

Purpose: To provide educational assistance for students who wish to pursue their education and career in engineering and metallurgy. **Focus:** Engineering; Metallurgy. **Qualif.:** Applicant must be a dependent of an at least two-year member of the Association for Iron and Steel Technology, which must be a U.S. citizen or a U.S landed immigrant. Applicant should also be a full-time student from an accredited North American University; pursuing education in the field of engineering or metallurgy. Chemistry, geology, mathematics or physics students are also qualified for the scholarships. **Criteria:** Recipient is selected based on academic achievements in science (i.e. chemistry, mathematics and physics); extra-curricular activities and student statements will also be considered.

Funds Avail.: $2,000. **Duration:** Annual; up to four years. **To Apply:** Applicants must submit an application form available at the website; a resume; a recommendation/evaluation from a counselor, teacher or professor; copy of SAT/ACT scores; copy of transcripts; and an essay (maximum of 2 pages) with one of the topics: Purpose in

Awards are arranged alphabetically below their administering organizations

going to college; beneficial experience during the last two summers; most significant experiences and effect on future plans; accomplishments providing the greatest satisfaction; reason why the applicant should be chosen as the recipient of the award. **Deadline:** April 30. **Remarks:** Established in 1988. **Contact:** Yvonne VanCamp, AIST Northeastern Ohio Chapter Secretary-Treasurer, Globex Corporation; Address: 3620 Stutz Dr. Canfield, Ohio 44406.

2000 ■ AIST Willy Korf Memorial Fund (Undergraduate/Scholarship)

Purpose: To support students in pursuing a career within iron- and steel-related industries. **Focus:** Engineering; Metallurgy. **Qualif.:** Applicants must be enrolled full-time in an engineering, metallurgy or materials science program at an accredited North American university; have a minimum cumulative GPA of 3.0 on a 4.0 scale; demonstrate interest in a career in the iron and steel industry. **Criteria:** Recipients are selected based on the application materials submitted.

Funds Avail.: $3,000. **Duration:** Annual. **Number Awarded:** 4. **To Apply:** Applicants must submit an application form available at the website; a resume; three letters of recommendation which address the applicant's character, academic status, leadership potential and career commitment from a college academic advisor, professor and previous employer; transcripts; and an essay (maximum of 2 pages) about the applicant's professional goals, interest in a career in the iron and steel industry, and how the applicant's skills could be applied to enhance the industry.

2001 ■ AIST Ronald E. Lincoln Memorial Scholarships (Undergraduate/Scholarship)

Purpose: To support students who are pursuing education in iron- and steel-related industries. **Focus:** Engineering; Metallurgy. **Qualif.:** Applicant must be enrolled full-time in an engineering, metallurgy or materials science program at an accredited North American university; have a minimum cumulative GPA of 3.0 on a 4.0 scale; demonstrate interest toward a career in the field of iron and steel industry. **Criteria:** Recipients are selected based on the application materials submitted.

Funds Avail.: $3,000. **Duration:** Annual. **Number Awarded:** 3. **To Apply:** Applicant must submit an application form available at the website together with the following materials: a resume; three letters of recommendation (addressing character, academic status, leadership potential and career commitment) from a college academic advisor, professor and previous employer; transcripts; an essay (maximum of 2 pages) about the applicant's professional goals, interest in a career in the iron and steel industry, and how the applicant's skills could be applied to enhance the industry.

2002 ■ AIST Midwest Member Chapter - Betty McKern Scholarships (Undergraduate/Scholarship)

Purpose: To support students in pursuing career within the iron and steel industry. **Focus:** Engineering. **Qualif.:** Applicants must be graduating female high school students or full-time freshmen, sophomores or junior students in good academic standing from an accredited institution. **Criteria:** Recipient will be selected based on merits.

Funds Avail.: $3,000. **Duration:** Annual. **Number Awarded:** 1. **To Apply:** Applicants must complete and submit the application form available at the website together with the following materials: a resume; a recommendation/evaluation from a counselor, teacher or professor; copy of SAT/ACT scores; transcripts; and an essay (maximum of 2 pages) describing the applicants' objectives for college and career. **Deadline:** March 15. **Contact:** Rich Trzcinski, EQ Engineers LLC; Address: 3400 179th Street, Hammond, IN 46323; Phone: 219-844-3500; Email: richt@eqengineers.com.

2003 ■ AIST Midwest Member Chapter - Don Nelson Scholarships (Undergraduate/Scholarship)

Purpose: To provide educational assistance to engineering students. **Focus:** Engineering. **Qualif.:** Applicants must be graduating high school students or full-time freshmen, sophomores or junior students in good academic standing from an accredited institution. **Criteria:** Grantee will be selected according to merit.

Funds Avail.: $3,000. **Duration:** Annual. **Number Awarded:** 1. **To Apply:** Applicants must submit an application form available at the website; a resume; a recommendation/evaluation from a counselor, teacher or professor; copy of SAT/ACT scores; copy of transcripts; and an essay (maximum of 2 pages) describing the applicants' objectives for college and career. **Deadline:** March 15. **Contact:** Rich Trzcinski, EQ Engineers LLC; Address: 3400 179th Street, Hammond, IN 46323; Phone: 219-844-3500; Email: richt@eqengineers.com.

2004 ■ AIST Midwest Member Chapter - Mel Nickel Scholarships (Undergraduate/Scholarship)

Purpose: To provide educational assistance for engineering students. **Focus:** Engineering. **Qualif.:** Applicants must be graduating high school students or a full-time freshmen, sophomores or junior students in good academic standing from an accredited institution. **Criteria:** Recipients will be selected according to merit.

Funds Avail.: $3,000. **Duration:** Annual. **Number Awarded:** 1. **To Apply:** Applicants must submit an application form available at the website; a resume; a recommendation/evaluation from a counselor, teacher or professor; copy of SAT/ACT scores; copy of transcripts; and an essay (maximum of 2 pages) describing the applicants' objectives for college and career. **Deadline:** March 15. **Contact:** Rich Trzcinski, EQ Engineers LLC; Address: 3400 179th Street, Hammond, IN 46323; Phone: 219-844-3500; Email: richt@eqengineers.com.

2005 ■ AIST Judith A. Quinn Detroit Member Chapter Scholarship (Undergraduate/Scholarship)

Purpose: To provide financial support for students who are pursuing a career in engineering. **Focus:** Engineering; Metallurgy. **Qualif.:** Applicant must be a dependent of an AIST Detroit Chapter member in good standing for two or more consecutive years; have a minimum cumulative GPA of 3.0 on a 4.0 scale; must be enrolled full-time as an undergraduate student majoring in engineering, metallurgy or materials science program at an accredited North American university; demonstrate interest towards a career in the field of iron and steel industry. **Criteria:** Recipients are selected by the Scholarship Award Committee.

Funds Avail.: $2,500-$5,000. **Duration:** Annual. **Number Awarded:** Varies. **To Apply:** Applicant must submit an application form available at the website; a resume; three letters of recommendation (addressing character, academic status, leadership potential and career commitment) from a high school counselor or college academic advisor, teacher/professor or a previous employer; copy of SAT/ACT scores; copy of current transcripts; an essay (maximum of 2 pages) about the applicant's professional goals, interest in a career

Awards are arranged alphabetically below their administering organizations

in the iron and steel industry, and how the applicant's skills could be applied to enhance the industry. **Deadline:** April 30. **Contact:** Roger Kalinowsky; Email: rkalinowsky@sidockgroup.com.

2006 ■ AIST David H. Samson Canadian Scholarships *(Undergraduate/Scholarship)*

Purpose: To provide financial support for students who are pursuing a career in engineering. **Focus:** Engineering. **Qualif.:** Applicant must be a dependent of a Canadian citizen or an immigrant who is a commendable member of the Association for Iron and Steel Technology; must be attending full-time engineering course at an accredited Canadian university or college. Chemistry, geology, mathematics or physics students are also welcome for the scholarships. **Criteria:** Priority will be given to engineering students.

Funds Avail.: $3,000. **Duration:** Annual. **Number Awarded:** 1. **To Apply:** Applicant must submit an application form available at the website; a resume; a recommendation/evaluation (from a counselor, teacher or professor); a copy of SAT/ACT scores; a copy of current transcripts; an essay (1-2 pages) with either one of the topics: purpose in going to college; beneficial experience during the last two summers, most significant experiences and effect on future plans; accomplishments providing the greatest satisfaction; reasons why he/she should be chosen as the recipient of the award.

2007 ■ AIST William E. Schwabe Memorial Scholarships *(Undergraduate/Scholarship)*

Purpose: To support students who are pursuing education in iron- and steel-related industries. **Focus:** Engineering; Metallurgy. **Qualif.:** Applicant must be enrolled full-time in an engineering, metallurgy or materials science program at an accredited North American university; have a minimum cumulative GPA of 3.0 on a 4.0 scale; demonstrate interest in a career in the iron and steel industry. **Criteria:** Recipient will be selected based on the application materials submitted.

Funds Avail.: $3,000. **Duration:** Annual. **Number Awarded:** 1. **To Apply:** Applicants must submit an application form available at the website; a resume; three letters of recommendation (addressing character, academic status, leadership potential and career commitment) from a college academic advisor, professor and previous employer; transcripts; an essay (maximum of 2 pages) about the applicant's professional goals, interest in a career in the iron and steel industry, and how the applicant's skills could be applied to enhance the industry. **Remarks:** Established in 2005.

2008 ■ AIST Southeast Member Chapter Gene Suave Scholarships *(Undergraduate/Scholarship)*

Purpose: To provide financial support for students who are pursuing a career in engineering. **Focus:** Engineering. **Qualif.:** Applicant must be a Southeast Chapter student; planning to take up courses in engineering, sciences or other majors related to iron and steel production. **Criteria:** Recipient will be selected based on the SAT or ACT scores for college applicants and on the applicant's GPA from an accredited college or institution (non-first year student). Extracurricular activities and student's written essays are also considered.

Funds Avail.: $3,500. **Duration:** Annual. **Number Awarded:** 1. **To Apply:** Applicants must submit an application form available at the website; a resume; a recommendation/evaluation from a counselor, teacher or professor; copy of SAT/ACT scores; copy of transcripts; and an essay (maximum of 250 words) discussing the applicant's involvement in high school and the reason why the applicant deserves the scholarship. **Deadline:** April 30. **Contact:** Bob Buchanan, Rexnord, Address: 5210 Edwards Rd. Taylors, SC 29687; Phone: 864-679-7235.

2009 ■ Association of Jewish Libraries (AJL)
PO Box 1118
Teaneck, NJ 07666
Ph: (201)371-3255
E-mail: info@jewishlibraries.org
URL: www.jewishlibraries.org

2010 ■ AJL Conference Stipends *(Graduate/Grant)*

Purpose: To assist members with the expense of attending AJL's annual conference. **Focus:** General studies/Field of study not specified. **Qualif.:** Applicants must be current members of AJL at the time of application. **Criteria:** Applicants are selected based on the committee's review of the application materials.

Funds Avail.: No specific amount. **Duration:** Annual. **To Apply:** Applicants must complete the application form available online and send it via e-mail, fax, or regular mail. **Deadline:** March 21. **Contact:** Stipends Committee members Lenore Bell (bell1614@msn.com) and Rachel Glasser (rkglasser@gmail.com).

2011 ■ AJL Scholarship Fund *(Graduate/Scholarship)*

Purpose: To encourage students to train for, and enter, the field of Judaica librarianship. **Focus:** Library and archival sciences. **Qualif.:** Applicants must be attending or planning to attend an ALA-accredited graduate library school or equivalent; should have an interest in, and demonstrate a potential for, pursuing a career in Judaica librarianship. **Criteria:** Selection is based on the application.

Funds Avail.: $1,000. **To Apply:** Applicants must complete and submit the application form available online; a documentation of acceptance or enrollment; documentation of Jewish studies completed at an academic or less formal level or of experience working in Judaic libraries; and Personal statement as a Word or rtf format. **Deadline:** April 11. **Contact:** Shulamith Berger, Phone: 212-960-5451; Fax: 212-960-0066; email: sberger@yu.edu.

2012 ■ Association of Latino Professionals in Finance and Accounting (ALPFA)
801 S Grand Ave., Ste. 650
Los Angeles, CA 90017
Ph: (213)243-0004
Fax: (213)243-0006
URL: www.alpfa.org
Facebook: www.facebook.com/ALPFA
LinkedIn: www.linkedin.com/company/alpfa

2013 ■ ALPFA Scholarship Programs *(Graduate, Undergraduate/Scholarship)*

Purpose: To financially support Hispanic students pursuing studies in accounting, finance, IT or related field. **Focus:** Accounting; Business; Finance. **Qualif.:** Applicants must be full-time Hispanic students or of Hispanic descent; U.S. citizens or permanent residents of the United States or Puerto Rico; attending an accredited university; have a cumulative grade point average of 3.0 and above on a 4.0

Awards are arranged alphabetically below their administering organizations

scale; must demonstrate financial need; and pursuing an undergraduate or master's degree in business, finance and accounting. **Criteria:** Recipients are selected based on the selection committee's review of all applications.

Funds Avail.: $2,000-$10,000. **Duration:** Annual. **To Apply:** Applicants must register first in order to apply online (please visit the website). Applicants must submit an official transcript; proof of family income and citizen status; an essay; letter of recommendation; resume; and The Financial Aid Verification (for semi-finalist only). **Deadline:** April 30.

2014 ■ Association of Leadership Educators, Inc. (ALE)

c/o Jennifer Moss Breen, President
2500 California Plz.
Omaha, NE 68178
Ph: (402)280-3952
URL: www.leadershipeducators.org
Facebook: www.facebook.com/LeadershipEducators
Twitter: twitter.com/ALE_Leadership

2015 ■ Founding Mothers' Student Scholarships - Graduate *(Graduate/Scholarship)*

Purpose: To provide funds for outstanding students who show promise in the field and present at the conference. **Focus:** Leadership, Institutional and community. **Qualif.:** Applicants must be graduate students in good academic standing and may not have already received the award. Recipients for this award are required to present or co-present at the ALE Conference. **Criteria:** Selection will be based on the committees' criteria.

Funds Avail.: No specific amount. **Number Awarded:** Up to 4. **To Apply:** Applicants must submit the following requirements in PDF format and upload to the application website: personal info - name, address, phone number, e-mail, college/university, major, year in school and expected graduation date; current GPA; career goal(s) in 50 words or less; titles and categories of proposals submitted to the ALE conference and; name of person who will provide a letter of reference - name, position, address and e-mail. Applicants must also submit a response to the following questions (maximum of 50 words per question): What are your particular interests/concerns/goals in studying leadership?; How would you benefit from attending the ALE conference?; How would you share what you learned at the ALE with others?; What experiences drew you to leadership education? and; What role do you see leadership education playing in our world's future? **Deadline:** May 15. **Contact:** Kerry Priest, Director or Awards and Recognition, Assistant Professor, Kansas State Staley School of Leadership Studies, kerryp@k-state.edu, 785-532-3673.

2016 ■ Association for Library Service to Children (ALSC)

50 E Huron St.
Chicago, IL 60611-2795
Fax: (312)280-5271
Free: 800-545-2433
E-mail: alsc@ala.org
URL: www.ala.org/alsc

2017 ■ Bound to Stay Bound Books Scholarships *(Graduate/Scholarship)*

Purpose: To provide financial assistance for individuals pursuing a master's or advanced degree in children's librarianship. **Focus:** Library and archival sciences. **Qualif.:** Applicants must be U.S. or Canadian citizens pursuing a master or advanced degree in children's librarianship. **Criteria:** Applicants will be selected on the basis of academic excellence, leadership qualities and the desire to work with children in any type of library.

Funds Avail.: $7,500 each. **Duration:** Annual. **Number Awarded:** 4. **To Apply:** Applicants must submit a completed application form; a personal statement describing career interests and goals; a commitment to library service to children; and three references (must be completed online). **Deadline:** March 1.

2018 ■ Frederic G. Melcher Scholarships *(Graduate/Scholarship)*

Purpose: To provide financial assistance for individuals pursuing a master's or advanced degree in children's librarianship. **Focus:** Library and archival sciences. **Qualif.:** Applicants must be U.S. or Canadian citizens pursuing a master or advanced degree in children's librarianship. **Criteria:** Applicants will be selected on the basis of academic excellence, leadership qualities and the desire to work with children in any type of library.

Funds Avail.: $6,000. **Duration:** One year. **Number Awarded:** 2. **To Apply:** Applicants must submit a completed application form; a personal statement describing career interests and goals; a commitment to library service to children; and three references (must be completed online). **Deadline:** March 1. **Remarks:** The scholarship was established as a tribute to Frederic G. Melcher, a great leader in promoting better books for children. **Contact:** Questions regarding applications may be sent by e-mail to Caroline Jewell at cjewell@ala.org.

2019 ■ Association canadienne du droit des technologies de l'information

PO Box 918
Thornhill, ON, Canada L4J 8G7
Ph: (905)889-0640
URL: www.it-can.ca
Twitter: twitter.com/ITdotCan

2020 ■ Canadian IT Law Association Student Writing Contest *(Undergraduate/Prize)*

Purpose: To support law students who are encouraged to have an interest in information technology law. **Focus:** Law. **Qualif.:** Applicants must be students in any Canadian University. **Criteria:** Submissions will be reviewed based on quality, originality and creativity of argument, quality of writing, sophistication and depth of the research.

Funds Avail.: No specific amount. **Duration:** Annual. **To Apply:** Entries should be between approximately 25 to 50 typed pages, should contain endnotes and not footnotes, should be written in Word format, 12-point font and double-spaced. Submissions may be in English or French. Subject line for the entries should be "IT Can Student Writing Competition."

2021 ■ Association Minéralogique du Canada

490, rue de la Couronne
Quebec, QC, Canada G1K 9A9
Ph: (418)653-0333
Fax: (418)653-0777
E-mail: office@mineralogicalassociation.ca

Awards are arranged alphabetically below their administering organizations

URL: www.mineralogicalassociation.ca

2022 ■ Mineralogical Association of Canada Scholarships (Doctorate, Graduate/Scholarship)

Purpose: To support graduate students engaged in research in any field currently supported by MAC. **Focus:** Mineralogy. **Qualif.:** Applicants must be students entering their second year of an M.Sc. program or the second or third year of a Ph.D. program at any Canadian university or students who are Canadian citizens attending a university located outside of Canada. **Criteria:** Applications will be assessed by a committee consisting of three members of MAC council chaired by the Chairman of MACF.

Funds Avail.: 5,000 Canadian Dollars. **Duration:** Annual. **Number Awarded:** 2. **To Apply:** Applications must be accompanied by an official academic transcript (undergraduate and graduate). Applicants must provide an outline of their thesis project using two pages of single text. Five copies of the application form and thesis project should be provided. **Deadline:** May 2.

2023 ■ Association of Moving Image Archivists (AMIA)
1313 N Vine St.
Hollywood, CA 90028
Ph: (323)463-1500
Fax: (323)463-1506
E-mail: amia@amianet.org
URL: www.amianet.org
Facebook: www.facebook.com/Association-of-Moving-Image-Archivists-86854559717
Twitter: twitter.com/AMIAnet

2024 ■ Rick Chace Foundation Scholarships (Graduate/Scholarship)

Purpose: To provide financial assistance to deserving students who want to pursue a career in the field of moving image archiving. **Focus:** Library and archival sciences; Museum science. **Qualif.:** Applicants must be enrolled full-time in a graduate-level or other advanced program in moving image studies or production, library or information services, archival administration, museum studies or a related discipline; must have a GPA of at least 3.0. **Criteria:** Candidates will be judged based on their commitment in pursuing a career in the field of moving image archiving, academic records and strength of a student's program of study.

Funds Avail.: No specific amount. **To Apply:** Applicants must complete the application form available online; must have the official transcript from the applicants' most recent academic program; must provide an essay of not more than 1,000 words describing their major field of study, interest in moving image archiving, relevant experience and/or education and career goals; must submit two letters of recommendation.

2025 ■ Kodak Fellowships in Film Preservation (Graduate/Fellowship)

Purpose: To provide financial assistance to deserving students who want to pursue a career in the field of moving image archiving. **Focus:** Library and archival sciences; Museum science. **Qualif.:** Applicant must be enrolled full-time in a graduate-level or other advanced program in moving image studies or production, library or information services, archival administration, museum studies or a related discipline; must be accepted into such a program for the next academic year; must have a GPA of at least 3.0; must have strong organizational and interpersonal skills and demonstrate an interest in pursuing a career in the moving image archival field; must be at least 21 years of age and must possess a valid driver's license; must be a US citizen or have a US work visa. **Criteria:** Recipient will be selected based on the following criteria: (1) Commitment to pursuing a career in moving image archiving; (2) Academic record; (3) Program of study as it applies to moving image archiving.

Funds Avail.: No specific amount. **To Apply:** Applicant must complete the application form, available online; must submit an official transcript from the applicant's current or most recently completed academic program; must have an essay of not more than 1,000 words describing the applicant's interest and involvement in moving image archiving; must have two letters of recommendation.

2026 ■ Mary Pickford Scholarships (Graduate/Scholarship)

Purpose: To provide financial assistance to deserving students who want to pursue a career in the field of moving image archiving. **Focus:** Library and archival sciences; Museum science. **Qualif.:** Applicant must be enrolled full-time in a graduate-level or other advanced program in moving image studies or production, library or information services, archival administration, museum studies or a related discipline; must have a GPA of at least 3.0. **Criteria:** Recipient will be selected based on the scholarship application criteria.

Funds Avail.: No specific amount. **To Apply:** Applicant must complete the application form available online; must have the official transcript from the applicant's most recent academic program; must provide an essay of no more than 1,000 words describing applicant's major field of study, interest in moving image archiving, relevant experience and/or education and career goals; must submit two letters of recommendation.

2027 ■ Sony Pictures Scholarships (Graduate/Scholarship)

Purpose: To provide financial assistance to deserving students who want to pursue a career in the field of moving image archiving. **Focus:** Library and archival sciences; Museum science. **Qualif.:** Applicant must be enrolled full-time in a graduate-level or other advanced program in moving image studies or production, library or information services, archival administration, museum studies or a related discipline; must have a GPA of at least 3.0. **Criteria:** Recipient will be selected based on the scholarship application criteria.

Funds Avail.: No specific amount. **To Apply:** Applicant must complete the application form available online; must have the official transcript from the applicant's most recent academic program; must provide an essay of no more than 1,000 words describing applicant's major field of study, interest in moving image archiving, relevant experience and/or education and career goals; must submit two letters of recommendation.

2028 ■ Universal Studios Preservation Scholarships (Graduate/Scholarship)

Purpose: To provide financial assistance to deserving students who want to pursue their career in the field of moving image archiving. **Focus:** Library and archival sciences; Museum science. **Qualif.:** Applicants must be

Awards are arranged alphabetically below their administering organizations

enrolled full-time in a graduate-level or other advanced program in moving image studies or production, library or information services, archival administration, museum studies or a related discipline; must have a GPA of at least 3.0. **Criteria:** Candidates will be judged based on their commitment in pursuing a career in the field of moving image archiving, academic records, and strength of a student's program of study.

Funds Avail.: No specific amount. **To Apply:** Applicant must complete the application form available online; must have the official transcript from the applicants' most recent academic program; must provide an essay of not more than 1,000 words describing their major field of study, interest in moving image archiving, relevant experience and/or education and career goals; must submit two letters of recommendation.

2029 ■ Association for Nonprofit and Social Economy Research

c/o Institute for Nonprofit Studies
Mount Royal University
4825 Mount Royal Gate SW
Calgary, AB, Canada T3E 6K6
E-mail: anser.ares@gmail.com
URL: www.anser-ares.ca

2030 ■ ANSER Graduate Student Awards for Research on Nonprofits and the Social Economy (Graduate/Award)

Purpose: To encourage and foster graduate research excellence and innovation in the field of nonprofits and the social economy in Canada. **Focus:** Economics; Nonprofit sector. **Qualif.:** Applicants must be landed immigrants or Canadian graduate students who are focusing on non-profit and social economy research. **Criteria:** Selection will be based on: research scholarship; quality of research; relevance to nonprofits and the social economy; contribution to policy, governance, or sustainability of nonprofits and the social economy; and innovation in methodology, theory or area of focus.

Funds Avail.: 1,500 Canadian Dollars. **To Apply:** Applicants must submit the following by the deadline date: a two page outline of the research question/methodology/research partners/expected contribution/relationship to nonprofits and the social economy/research timetable; curriculum vitae (4 pages maximum) to include stage of study/expected completion date/bursaries or funding/publications/research experience; and a letter of support from supervisor or other to comment on quality of research scholarship and relevance to nonprofit and social economy. **Deadline:** December 19. **Contact:** ANSER-ARES Awards Committee Chair at luct@unb.ca.

2031 ■ Association of Occupational Health Professionals in Healthcare (AOHP)

125 Warrendale Bayne Rd., Ste. 375
Warrendale, PA 15086
Fax: (724)935-1560
Free: 800-362-4347
E-mail: info@aohp.org
URL: www.aohp.org/aohp
Facebook: www.facebook.com/AOHP-Association-of
 -Occupational-Health-Professional-in-Healthcare
 -128269079138

2032 ■ Sandra Bobbitt Continuing Education Scholarship (Undergraduate/Scholarship)

Purpose: To provide annual continuing education scholarships to subsidize the educational efforts of members. **Focus:** General studies/Field of study not specified. **Qualif.:** Applicants must be AOHP active members in good standing. **Criteria:** Applicants will be evaluated by the Scholarship Selection Committee.

Funds Avail.: $600. **Duration:** Annual. **Number Awarded:** Varies. **To Apply:** Applicants may verify the application process through the program website. **Deadline:** July 1. **Contact:** AOHP Headquarters at info@aohp.org.

2033 ■ Julie Schmid Research Scholarship (Advanced Professional/Scholarship)

Purpose: To encourage, promote and strengthen the knowledge base and expertise of the occupational health professional in healthcare. **Focus:** Occupational safety and health. **Qualif.:** Applicants must have proposals for an original research project on current and/or anticipated issues in healthcare-related occupational health. **Criteria:** Applicants will be selected based on merit in accordance with the evaluation tool.

Funds Avail.: $2,000. **Duration:** Annual. **To Apply:** Applicants must submit a formal title for the project; state the one category from the following list that best describes the area the research project will address: employment examinations, medical surveillance, immunizations, infectious diseases, employee health records, work injuries, administration, marketing occupational health services or other healthcare-related topics; briefly describe the impact/significance of the research project to the occupational health professional in a healthcare setting; list the objectives and goals of the research project; describe the activities that will be implemented to achieve the goals of the project, e.g., questionnaire. As appropriate, describe the target population, e.g., clinical (nursing, etc.) nonclinical employees. **Deadline:** July 1. **Contact:** AOHP Research Committee Chair at info@aohp.org.

2034 ■ Association of PeriOperative Registered Nurses (AORN)

2170 S Parker Rd., Ste. 400
Denver, CO 80231
Ph: (303)755-6300
Fax: (800)847-0045
Free: 800-755-2676
E-mail: custsvc@aorn.org
URL: www.aorn.org
Facebook: www.facebook.com/AORN
LinkedIn: www.linkedin.com/company/aorn
Twitter: twitter.com/aorn

2035 ■ AORN Academic Scholarships (Undergraduate, Master's, Doctorate/Scholarship)

Purpose: To support students who are pursuing a career in perioperative nursing; and to support registered nurses who are continuing their education in perioperative nursing by pursuing a bachelor's, master's or doctoral degree. **Focus:** Nursing. **Qualif.:** Applicants must be students who are pursuing a career in perioperative nursing and registered nurses who are continuing their education in perioperative nursing by pursuing a bachelor's, master's, or doctoral degree. **Criteria:** Selection will be based on the committee's criteria.

Awards are arranged alphabetically below their administering organizations

Funds Avail.: No specific amount. **Duration:** Annual. **To Apply:** Applicants must go to the website to create an account and for the online application process. Applicants must also submit an official transcript stating a 3.0 GPA or higher. **Deadline:** June 15.

2036 ■ AORN Administrator Skills Course *(Professional development/Recognition, Grant)*

Purpose: To develop the necessary skills needed to successfully manage every aspect of an ambulatory surgery facility; from daily operations to regulatory requirements. **Focus:** Nursing. **Qualif.:** Applicants must be registered nurses, physicians, administrators, and facility owners. **Criteria:** Selection will be based on financial need and professional goals for attending the Administrator Skills Course.

Funds Avail.: No specific amount. **Duration:** Annual. **To Apply:** Applicants must register for the AORN Administrator Skills Course to qualify for funds. Application can be obtained at the website and must be submitted via mail, electronic mail or fax. Applicants must also submit a typed, double-spaced and maximum of 1 page personal statement that includes the financial need and description of professional goals for attending the Administrator Skills Course. **Contact:** Ambulatory Surgery Division, c/o Association of PeriOperative Registered Nurses, at the above address.

2037 ■ AORN Foundation Scholarship Program *(Undergraduate, Doctorate, Master's/Scholarship)*

Purpose: To provide financial assistance to students enrolled in nursing schools and to perioperative nurses pursuing bachelors, masters, or doctoral degrees. **Focus:** Nursing. **Qualif.:** Applicants must be Nursing students (must be in an accredited program leading to initial licensure as RNs), baccalaureate, master, and doctoral candidates with a cumulative GPA of 3.0 or higher; International students are welcome to apply. **Criteria:** Recipient will be based on academics, essay and accurate completion of the scholarship application.

Funds Avail.: No specific amount. **To Apply:** Applicants must complete and submit all the required application materials. **Deadline:** June 15. **Contact:** AORN Foundation at foundation@aorn.org.

2038 ■ Association of Postgraduate Physician Assistant Programs (APPAP)
300 N Washington St., Ste. 710
Alexandria, VA 22314
Ph: (703)778-5570
Fax: (703)548-5539
E-mail: appap@appap.org
URL: www.appap.org

2039 ■ Linda Brandt Research Awards *(Postgraduate/Award)*

Purpose: To support research regarding physician assistant postgraduate training programs, PA residents/fellows and/or graduates. **Focus:** Medicine. **Qualif.:** Applicants must be Physician Assistant Post-Graduate Residents; must be Physician Assistant students who have a research focus on PA Post-Graduate training, impact or outcomes; must be professionals who have a research interest in PA Post-Graduate education, impact or outcomes. **Criteria:** Selection will be based on the committee's criteria.

Funds Avail.: $2,000. **Number Awarded:** One. **To Apply:** Applicants must submit a typed, double-spaced proposal that includes the following sections: title page; title; applicants' name, postal and email address, phone and fax numbers; abstract, not more than 500 words; research description, not more than four pages, which includes the background and rationale, methods, identification and qualifications of key personnel, and expected timeline for completion of the project; CV of applicants; CV of mentors; mentor statement of support; statement of institutional support. This may be a letter from an appropriate individual or representative who can affirm that the applicant has access to facilities and personnel to aid in the successful completion of the project. It may be included in the mentor statement if appropriate; students and residents should identify a mentor or mentor team. Up to 3 persons may be included. Mentor identification is optional for graduates and other professionals. However, mentor identification is encouraged for those with limited experience in research; importance to PA post-graduate education; feasibility and likelihood of completion (timeline, mentor, facility, etc.); considerations: writing organization, detail and style. **Deadline:** March 30.

2040 ■ Association for Preservation Technology International (APT)
3085 Stevenson Dr., Ste. 200
Springfield, IL 62703
Ph: (217)529-9039
Fax: (888)723-4242
E-mail: info@apti.org
URL: www.apti.org
Facebook: www.facebook.com/aptpreservation
LinkedIn: www.linkedin.com/groups/2146278/profile
Twitter: www.twitter.com/APT_Intl_Conf

2041 ■ Association for Preservation Technology International Student Scholarships *(Graduate, Undergraduate/Scholarship)*

Purpose: To promote research or projects on preservation technology. **Focus:** Historic preservation. **Qualif.:** Applicants must be enrolled in a trade, undergraduate or graduate program which is affiliated with a trade school, college or university. **Criteria:** Recipients are selected based on the quality of a submitted abstract and a personal statement.

Funds Avail.: No specific amount. **Duration:** Annual. **Number Awarded:** Varies. **To Apply:** Applicants are required to submit their personal as well as their professor's contact information; a 250-word abstract describing the scope of the project/research and summarizing its relationship to an aspect of preservation technology and/or heritage conservation that relates to the conference theme and/or paper tracks; and 250-word personal statement stating why the conference would be of value to them. Applicants are also required to create an electronic presentation and give an oral presentation during the conference. **Remarks:** Established in 1986.

2042 ■ Association of Professional Schools of International Affairs (APSIA)
1615 L St., NW 8th Flt.
Washington, DC 20036
Ph: (202)559-5831
URL: www.apsia.org
Facebook: www.facebook.com/APSIA-Association-of

Awards are arranged alphabetically below their administering organizations

-Professional-Schools-of-International-Affairs-195953972563/
LinkedIn: www.linkedin.com/company/1183164
Twitter: twitter.com/apsiainfo

2043 ■ Harold W. Rosenthal Fellowships in International Relations *(Professional development/Fellowship, Internship)*

Purpose: To expose young scholars of international relations to the inner workings of the U.S. Federal Government and Capitol Hill. **Focus:** International affairs and relations. **Qualif.:** Applicants must be full-time students at an APSIA full member school both at the time of nomination and during the fellowship; must return to school for at least the fall semester following their internship; and must be U.S. citizens or qualify for a J-1 visa through their internship placement, school or other method. **Criteria:** Selection will be conducted by the Fellowship Committee. The committee, in consultation with APSIA, will review all nomination documents to select semifinalists based on their commitment to public service, education and interest in international relations, experience and dedication to those values and professional standards set by Harold Rosenthal and the outstanding legacy of Rosenthal Fellowship alumni.

Funds Avail.: No specific amount. **To Apply:** Application is via nomination. The following nomination documents, including items supplied by the student nominees, must be sent electronically by the member school to the APSIA Executive Office by the deadline: Nomination Cover Letter signed by the Dean; Curriculum Vitae/Resume; signed letter of recommendation on letterhead stationery from a professor or former work supervisor; academic transcript from current university (unofficial accepted); academic transcript(s) from universities previously attended; and writing sample (2 pages maximum) on a topic in international affairs. Students must also submit their graduate transcripts (unofficial accepted) to the APSIA Executive Office as soon as they become available. **Deadline:** December 1.

2044 ■ Association for Psychological Science (APS)
1800 Massachusetts Ave. NW, Ste. 402
Washington, DC 20036
Ph: (202)293-9300
Fax: (202)293-9350
URL: www.psychologicalscience.org
Facebook: www.facebook.com/PsychologicalScience
Twitter: twitter.com/PsychScience

2045 ■ APS Student Research Award *(Undergraduate, Graduate/Award)*

Purpose: To promote and acknowledge outstanding research conducted by student members. **Focus:** Psychology. **Qualif.:** Applicants must be either graduate or undergraduate APS student members. **Criteria:** Award will be given on a competitive basis.

Funds Avail.: $250. **Duration:** Annual. **Number Awarded:** 5. **To Apply:** Students affiliated must submit the following information: project title and an abstract; project summary. The project should detail the purpose, methodology and results of the research and include introduction/background, methods, results and discussion/theoretical implications. **Deadline:** January 31.

2046 ■ Association for Psychological Science Student Grants (APS) *(Graduate, Undergraduate/Grant)*

Purpose: To provide assistance for the advanced research of APS students. **Focus:** Psychology. **Qualif.:** Applicant must be an APS undergraduate or graduate student. **Criteria:** Committees will evaluate each research proposal based on its clarity, ability to explain some psychological phenomenon and ability to advance research in a specified area.

Funds Avail.: $300-$500. **Duration:** Annual. **Number Awarded:** Varies. **To Apply:** Applicant must submit a cover letter; project summary; and review board approval. All materials must be submitted electronically, with a subject, APSSC Student Grant Submission. The cover letter and Project Summary should be in separate Microsoft Word or Open Format document. **Deadline:** November 17.

2047 ■ Association for Public Health Laboratories (APHL)
8515 Georgia Ave., Ste. 700
Silver Spring, MD 20910
Ph: (240)485-2745
Fax: (240)485-2700
E-mail: info@aphl.org
URL: www.aphl.org

2048 ■ APHL Emerging Infectious Diseases Fellowships *(Doctorate/Fellowship)*

Purpose: To train and prepare scientists for careers in public health laboratories and support public health initiatives related to infectious disease research. **Focus:** Public health. **Qualif.:** Applicants must be in doctoral level (PhD, MD or DVM) scientists who conduct high-priority research in infectious diseases. **Criteria:** Selection will be based on the committee's criteria.

Funds Avail.: No specific amount. **To Apply:** Applicants must submit a completed application, available at the website, before the deadline. It is the responsibility of the applicants to ensure that all materials are received at APHL. **Deadline:** February 8.

2049 ■ Association of Public Treasurers of the United States and Canada (APT US & C)
7044 S 13th St.
Oak Creek, WI 53154
Ph: (414)908-4947
Fax: (414)768-8001
E-mail: info@aptusc.org
URL: www.aptusc.org

2050 ■ APT US&C Scholarships *(Advanced Professional/Scholarship)*

Purpose: To give assistance to any active member who needs financial assistance to attend an APT US & C conference or to attend an affiliated APT US & C institute. **Focus:** General studies/Field of study not specified. **Qualif.:** Applicants must be active members in good standing. **Criteria:** Selection is based on financial need.

Funds Avail.: Up to $500 to attend a national APT US & C conference; $250 to attend an affiliated APT US & C institute. **Duration:** Annual. **To Apply:** Applicants must submit a completed APT US & C Scholarship application

Awards are arranged alphabetically below their administering organizations

form together with a letter from the applicants' city, town, county. **Deadline:** May 1. **Contact:** Application must be send through Fax: 414-908-8001.

2051 ■ Association of Rehabilitation Nurses (ARN)
8735 W Higgins Rd., Ste. 300
Chicago, IL 60631-2738
Free: 800-229-7530
E-mail: info@rehabnurse.org
URL: www.rehabnurse.org/about/content/About-ARN-index.html

2052 ■ Mary Ann Mikulic Scholarships *(Other/Scholarship)*

Purpose: To provide financial assistance covering full tuition of the Professional Rehabilitation Nursing course. **Focus:** Nursing. **Qualif.:** Applicants must be registered nurses with current license practicing in the specialty of rehabilitation nursing and able to meet all the financial responsibilities incurred by participating in the course. **Criteria:** Applicants will be evaluated by the Scholarship committee based on the application provided.

Funds Avail.: one full tuition. **To Apply:** Applicants must submit a completed application form along with current curriculum vitae or resume; a letter of support from an employer; and a statement on how the applicants will use the knowledge gained from completing the course and future plans as a rehabilitation nurse.

2053 ■ Association of Rehabilitation Nurses - Alabama Chapter
c/o Stephanie Burnett, Pres.
Spain Rehabilitation Center, Rm. 121
1717 6th Ave. S
Birmingham, AL 35233
Ph: (205)934-5786
E-mail: sburnett@uabmc.edu
URL: www.alabamaarn.org

2054 ■ Alabama ARN Scholarship *(Professional development/Scholarship)*

Purpose: To support and promote the advance professional rehabilitation nursing practice, through networking, education, and service among rehabilitation nurses in the state. **Focus:** Nursing; Rehabilitation, Physical/Psychological. **Qualif.:** Applicants must be current and active Alabama chapter members; must be employed or retired in health care services related to/in rehabilitation nursing. **Criteria:** Selection will be based on the committee's criteria.

Funds Avail.: No specific amount. **Duration:** Periodic. **To Apply:** Interested applicants must visit the website to obtain an application form. **Deadline:** September 24. **Contact:** Stephanie Burnett, Chapter President; email: sburnett@uabmc.edu; Phone: 205-934-5786.

2055 ■ Association for Research on Nonprofit Organizations and Voluntary Action (ARNOVA)
550 W North St., Ste. 301
Indianapolis, IN 46202
Ph: (317)684-2120
Fax: (317)684-2128
URL: www.arnova.org
Facebook: www.facebook.com/arnovafans
Twitter: www.twitter.com/ARNOVA

2056 ■ ARNOVA Emerging Scholar Awards *(Graduate/Award)*

Purpose: To help and support students and scholars spread their research into practice, and enhance their knowledge. **Focus:** Nonprofit sector. **Qualif.:** Applicants must have a paper accepted for the current year ARNOVA Conference. Winners of the past Emerging Scholars Award are not eligible to apply for the Emerging Scholars Award. **Criteria:** Selection of applicants will be based on the following criteria: (1) relevance of research to the field of nonprofit and voluntary action studies; (2) stage of research development; (3) demonstrated interest in nonprofit organization and voluntary action; (4) quality of conference proposal; and (5) letter of recommendation.

Funds Avail.: No specific amount. **Duration:** Annual. **To Apply:** Applicants must submit the following requirements: (1) cover letter; (2) copy of ARNOVA conference proposal; (3) letter of acceptance from the Conference Committee Chairs; (4) letter of recommendation from a faculty member or a letter of recommendation from someone who knows the research or work; (5) resume, containing a mailing address, email address, and telephone number; (6) official transcript of record. **Deadline:** August 31.

2057 ■ Association of School Business Officials of Maryland and the District of Columbia (ASBO-MD&DC)
c/o John Lang, Executive Director
10 Lord Mayors Ct.
Cockeysville, MD 21030
URL: www.asbo.org

2058 ■ Dwight P. Jacobus Scholarships *(Undergraduate/Scholarship)*

Purpose: To assist those individuals who require financial assistance to secure a college education. **Focus:** Business; Education. **Qualif.:** Applicants must have been: residents of Maryland or District of Columbia for at least one year preceding the date of the award; and, accepted for admission as full-time students. They must demonstrate financial need, and have a minimum 3.0 overall GPA. **Criteria:** Scholarships are made by the Association of School Business Officials of Maryland and the District of Columbia based upon: scholastic achievement; financial need; Scholastic Assessment Test (SAT) scores or American College Test (ACT) scores; and quality of extracurricular achievements.

Funds Avail.: $1,000 each. **Duration:** Annual. **Number Awarded:** 10. **To Apply:** Applicants must file an application and supporting documents with the Chair of the Scholarship Committee for ASBO of Maryland and the District of Columbia. Applications are available from guidance or financial aid offices, or may be requested in writing from the Chair of the Scholarship Committee. **Deadline:** March 1. **Contact:** Margaret Ellen Kalmanowicz at margaretellen.kalmanowicz@qacps.org.

2059 ■ Association of Schools and Programs of Public Health (ASPPH)
1900 M St. NW, Ste. 710
Washington, DC 20036

Awards are arranged alphabetically below their administering organizations

Ph: (202)296-1099
Fax: (202)296-1252
E-mail: info@asph.org
URL: www.aspph.org
Facebook: www.facebook.com/ASPPH
LinkedIn: www.linkedin.com/company/association-of
 -schools-and-programs-of-public-health
Twitter: twitter.com/ASPPHtweets

2060 ■ ASPPH/CDC Public Health Fellowship Program (Doctorate, Graduate/Fellowship)

Purpose: To address emerging needs of public health, and to provide leadership and professional opportunities at the Centers for Disease Control and Prevention (CDC) for students and graduate students of ASPH member graduate schools of public health. **Focus:** Public health. **Qualif.:** Applicant must have received an MPH or Doctorate degree prior to the beginning of the fellowship; or an early career professional with MPH or Doctorate degrees (within 5 years of graduation); have received his/her degree(s) from an ASPH-member, CEPH-accredited, graduate school of public health; and be a U.S. citizen or hold a visa permitting permanent residence in the U.S. **Criteria:** All Applications to the program undergo a two-phase review process.

Funds Avail.: No specific amount. **Duration:** 12 months. **To Apply:** Applicants must complete the application online. In addition, applicants must submit a hard copy documents of two generic recommendation letters; graduate transcripts (of all ASPH member school(s) of public health attended); and the signature page (available after submitting the online application). **Remarks:** Established in 1995.

2061 ■ ASPPH/EPA Environmental Health Fellowship Program (Doctorate, Postdoctorate/Fellowship)

Purpose: To provide professional training and opportunities for early career public health professionals by enabling them to work in EPA on current and emerging environmental public health needs. **Focus:** Public health. **Qualif.:** Applicant must have received an MPH or Doctorate degree prior to the beginning of the fellowship (no later than August of the application year); or an early career professional with MPH or Doctorate degree (within 5 years of graduation); must have received his/her degree(s) from an ASPH-member, CEPH-accredited, graduate school of public health; and must be a U.S. citizen or hold a visa permitting permanent residence in the U.S. **Criteria:** All Applications to the program undergo a two-phase review process.

Funds Avail.: No specific amount. **Duration:** one year. **To Apply:** Applicants must complete the application online. In addition, applicants must submit a hard copy documents of two generic recommendation letters; graduate transcripts (of all ASPH member school(s) of public health attended); and the signature page (available after submitting the online application).

2062 ■ ASPPH/NHTSA Public Health Fellowship Program (Postdoctorate/Fellowship)

Purpose: To provide training opportunities to graduates of accredited schools of public health. **Focus:** Public health. **Qualif.:** Applicant must have received an MPH or Doctorate degree prior to the beginning of the fellowship; or be a career professional with MPH or Doctorate degree (within 5 years of graduation); must have received his/her degree(s) from an ASPH-member, CEPH-accredited, graduate school of public health; and be a U.S. citizen or hold a visa permitting permanent residence in the U.S. **Criteria:** Selection is based on the quality of the essay, strength of credentials, previous professional experience; and letters of recommendation.

Funds Avail.: No specific amount. **Duration:** one year. **To Apply:** Applicants must complete the application online. In addition, applicants must submit a hard copy documents of two generic recommendation letters; graduate transcripts (of all ASPH member school(s) of public health attended); and the signature page (available after submitting the online application).

2063 ■ ASPPH Public Health Policy Fellowship Program (Doctorate, Postdoctorate/Fellowship)

Purpose: To provide opportunities for a motivated and experienced individual to play a role in helping to shape United States health policy. **Focus:** Public health. **Qualif.:** Applicant must have received an MPH or Doctorate degree prior to the beginning of the fellowship; or an early career professional with MPH or Doctorate degree (within 5 years of graduation); have received the degree(s) from an ASPH-member, CEPH-accredited, graduate school of public health; and a U.S. citizen or hold a visa permitting permanent residence in the U.S. **Criteria:** All Applications to the program undergo a two-phase review process.

Funds Avail.: No specific amount. **Duration:** 12 months. **To Apply:** Applicants must complete the application online. In addition, applicants must submit a hard copy documents of two generic recommendation letters; graduate transcripts (of all ASPH member school(s) of public health attended); and the signature page (available after submitting the online application).

2064 ■ ASPPH Public Health Preparedness Fellowship Program (Postdoctorate/Fellowship)

Purpose: To provide opportunities for a motivated and experienced individual to play a role in helping to shape United States health policy. **Focus:** Public health. **Qualif.:** Applicant must have received an MPH or Doctorate degree prior to the beginning of the fellowship; or an early career professional with MPH or Doctorate degrees (within 5 years of graduation); have received his/her degree(s) from an ASPH-member, CEPH-accredited, graduate school of public health; and a U.S. citizen or hold a visa permitting permanent residence in the U.S. **Criteria:** All Applications to the program undergo a two-phase review process.

Funds Avail.: No specific amount. **Duration:** 4 months. **To Apply:** Applicants must complete the application online. In addition, applicants must submit a hard copy documents of two generic recommendation letters; graduate transcripts (of all ASPH member school(s) of public health attended); and the signature page (available after submitting the online application).

2065 ■ ASPPH/CDC Allan Rosenfield Global Health Fellowship Program (Postdoctorate, Postgraduate/Fellowship)

Purpose: To enhance the training of graduates of schools of public health with an interest in global health. **Focus:** Public health. **Qualif.:** Applicant must have received his/her Master's or Doctorate degree prior to the beginning of the fellowship or within the last five years (graduate degrees must come from an ASPH member graduate school of public health accredited by the Council on Education for Public Health); and must be a U.S. citizen or hold a visa permitting permanent residence in the U.S. **Criteria:** Selection is based on quality of essay, strength of credentials, previous professional experience; and letters of recommendation.

Awards are arranged alphabetically below their administering organizations

Funds Avail.: No specific amount. **To Apply:** Applicants must complete the application online. In addition, applicants must submit a hard copy documents of two generic recommendation letters; graduate transcripts (of all ASPH member school(s) of public health attended); and the signature page (available after submitting the online application).

2066 ■ Association of Science-Technology Centers (ASTC)
818 Connecticut Ave. NW, 7th Fl.
Washington, DC 20006
Ph: (202)783-7200
Fax: (202)783-7207
E-mail: info@astc.org
URL: www.astc.org
Facebook: www.facebook.com/ScienceCenters
Twitter: twitter.com/ScienceCenters

2067 ■ Lee Kimche McGrath Worldwide Fellowships (Other/Fellowship)

Purpose: To support individuals from a science center or museum who wishes to participate in the ASTC Annual Conference. **Focus:** Museum science. **Qualif.:** Applicant must be an individual from a science center or museum (open or in development) outside the United States. **Criteria:** Applications are reviewed by the ASTC International Advisory Board. Preference will be given to an applicant whose/who: (1) institution cannot afford to send a representative to an ASTC conference; (2) participation will benefit other science centers in addition to their own; (3) have limited opportunities to meet professionally with science center colleagues; and, (4) is willing to participate in conference session, writing experiences or institution for an ASTC publication.

Funds Avail.: No specific amount. **Duration:** Annual. **Number Awarded:** Varies. **To Apply:** Application forms are available at the website. **Remarks:** Established in 2004. **Contact:** Walter Staveloz at wstaveloz@astc.org.

2068 ■ Association of Seventh-Day Adventist Librarians (ASDAL)
c/o Sarah Kimakwa, Treasurer
James White Library, Rm. 271
4910 Administration Dr.
Berrien Springs, MI 49104
URL: www.asdal.org

2069 ■ D. Glenn Hilts Scholarships (Graduate, Undergraduate/Scholarship)

Purpose: To recognize excellence in scholarship and to encourage individuals with leadership potential to seek employment in a Seventh-day Adventist library. **Focus:** General studies/Field of study not specified; Library and archival sciences. **Qualif.:** Applicant must be a Seventh-Day Adventist in good standing; be accepted in an American Library Association accredited library school; and must be a full-time student. **Criteria:** Priority is given to applicants with a complete application package.

Funds Avail.: $1,500. **To Apply:** Applicant must submit completed application form available at the website; submit a copy of the acceptance letter from the ALA-accredited library; GRE scores; an essay of 600 words; high school and college transcripts; and three letters of reference (there must be one from the applicant's Seventh-day Adventist pastor). **Deadline:** July 15. **Contact:** Marge Seifert, at meseifrt@southern.edu.

2070 ■ Association for the Sociology of Religion (ASR)
University of South Florida
Dept. of Sociology
4202 E Fowler Ave.
Tampa, FL 33620
Ph: (813)974-2758
Fax: (813)974-6455
URL: www.sociologyofreligion.com

2071 ■ Joseph H. Fichter Research Grants (Other/Grant)

Purpose: To financially assist scholars involved in promising research in the area of women and religion. **Focus:** Religion; Women's studies. **Qualif.:** Applicants must be ASR members at least during the year prior the submission of their application. **Criteria:** Recipients will be selected based on submitted materials.

Funds Avail.: $24,000. **Duration:** Annual. **To Apply:** Applicants must submit a proposal, one-page detailed budget, curriculum vitae and a statement of qualifications that specifically addresses the research project. Proposals should review briefly the previous research and theory that forms the background for the study, describe methods and research timetable and summarize succinctly what this research project aims to discover. Proposals and accompanying documents must be written in English. **Deadline:** May. **Contact:** Materials should be submitted electronically to Helen A. Berger at haberger@brandeis.edu.

2072 ■ Robert J. McNamara Student Paper Awards (Graduate/Award)

Purpose: To recognize outstanding student papers in the sociology of religion. **Focus:** Religion. **Qualif.:** Applicants must be currently enrolled graduate students who have not defended the PhD when the paper is submitted; membership in the Association for the Sociology of Religion is required either at the time of application or previously. **Criteria:** Applicants will be judged based on submitted paper.

Funds Avail.: $500. **Duration:** Annual. **To Apply:** Applicants must submit an abstract from the ASR Program Chair following the guidelines of all standard paper submissions. It should be in the form of articles with a maximum length of 40 double-spaced, single-sided pages inclusive of all materials: text, title, notes, table, figures, etc. The title page should include an abstract of no more than 200 words. Texts should not exceed 12,000 words, approximately 36 double-spaced pages of 12 point font. Applicants should attach their paper as a file, formatted in Microsoft Word. **Deadline:** June 1. **Contact:** Attached file should be forwarded to Kathleen Jenkins at kejenk@wm.edu.

2073 ■ Association of State Dam Safety Officials (ASDSO)
239 S Limestone
Lexington, KY 40508-2501
Ph: (859)550-2788
E-mail: info@damsafety.org
URL: www.damsafety.org

Awards are arranged alphabetically below their administering organizations

2074 ■ Association of State Dam Safety Officials Undergraduate Scholarships *(Undergraduate/Scholarship)*

Purpose: To promote the study of civil engineering and related fields as a career. **Focus:** Engineering, Civil. **Qualif.:** Applicant must be a U.S. citizen; enrolled in a civil engineering program and in their senior year; pursuing a career in hydraulics, hydrology or geotechnical disciplines or related to design, construction and operation of dams; have 2.5 GPA for the first three years in college and recommended by advisor. **Criteria:** Awards are given based on academic merit; financial need; work experience and essay.

Funds Avail.: Varies. **Duration:** Annual. **Number Awarded:** 2. **To Apply:** Applicant must send an application form; transcript; three letters of recommendation; and (500-word) essay describing the proposed study and its importance. **Deadline:** March 31.

2075 ■ Association of Surgical Technologists (AST)
6 W Dry Creek Cir., Ste. 200
Littleton, CO 80120-8031
Ph: (303)694-9130
Fax: (303)694-9169
Free: 800-637-7433
E-mail: memserv@ast.org
URL: www.ast.org
Facebook: www.facebook.com/AssociationofSurgicalTechnologists
LinkedIn: www.linkedin.com/company/association-of-surgical-technologists?trk=company_name
Twitter: twitter.com/AST_SurgTech

2076 ■ Foundation for Surgical Technology Scholarships *(Graduate/Scholarship)*

Purpose: To encourage and reward educational excellence as well as to respond to the financial need demonstrated by the surgical technology student and offer assistance to those who seek a career in surgical technology. **Focus:** Surgery. **Qualif.:** Applicants must be currently enrolled in an accredited surgical technology program and eligible to sit for the NBSTSA national surgical technologist certifying examination; must demonstrate superior academic ability; and must have a need for financial assistance. **Criteria:** Recipient selection is based on academic excellence and financial need.

Funds Avail.: No specific amount. **To Apply:** Applicants must complete the four parts of the application form: Student Responsibility; Official Transcript; Instructor Section; and Preceptor Section.

2077 ■ Association of Texas Professional Educators Foundation
305 E Huntland Dr., Ste. 300
Austin, TX 78752
Fax: (512)467-2203
Free: 800-777-2873
E-mail: info@atpe.org
URL: www.atpe.org

2078 ■ Barbara Jordan Memorial Scholarships *(Undergraduate, Graduate/Scholarship)*

Purpose: To support outstanding students currently enrolled in educator preparation programs. **Focus:** Education. **Qualif.:** Applicants must be juniors, seniors or graduate students enrolled in an accredited college/university educator preparation program. **Criteria:** Selection shall be based on the aforementioned applicants' qualifications and compliance with the application details.

Funds Avail.: No specific amount. **Duration:** Annual. **Number Awarded:** Varies. **To Apply:** Applicants must submit a completed application form along with college transcripts with official university imprint (do not fax); a detailed description of participation in any academic, honorary, civic or extracurricular activities in college; an essay (maximum of 2 typed, double-spaced 8 1/2x11 pages) including the applicant's personal educational philosophy, why the applicant wants to become an educator, who influenced the applicant the most in making career decision and why the applicant is applying for the award; and at least two (no more than three) letters of recommendation. **Deadline:** June 2. **Contact:** ATPE Foundation, at the above address.

2079 ■ Fred Wiesner Educational Excellence Scholarships *(Undergraduate, Graduate/Scholarship)*

Purpose: To support outstanding students currently enrolled in educator preparation programs. **Focus:** Education. **Qualif.:** Applicant must be college students enrolled in an accredited college/university educator preparation program. **Criteria:** Selection shall be based on the aforementioned applicants' qualifications and compliance with the application details.

Funds Avail.: No specific amount. **Duration:** Annual. **Number Awarded:** Varies. **To Apply:** Applicants must submit a completed application form along with college transcripts with official university imprint (do not fax); a detailed description of participation in any academic, honorary, civic or extracurricular activities in college; an essay (maximum of 2 typed, double-spaced 8 1/2x11 pages) including the applicant's personal educational philosophy, why the applicant wants to become an educator, who influenced the applicant the most in making career decision and why the applicant is applying for the award; and at least two (no more than three) letters of recommendation. **Deadline:** June 2. **Contact:** ATPE Foundation, at the above address.

2080 ■ Association of Textile, Apparel and Materials Professionals (AATCC)
1 Davis Dr.
Research Triangle Park, NC 27709-2215
Ph: (919)549-8141
Fax: (919)549-8933
URL: www.aatcc.org
Facebook: www.facebook.com/AATCC.org
LinkedIn: www.linkedin.com/groups/57984/profile
Twitter: twitter.com/AATCC

2081 ■ Charles H. Stone Scholarships *(Undergraduate/Scholarship)*

Purpose: To provide scholarships to junior and seniors, majoring in polymer or textile chemistry fields. **Focus:** Textile science. **Qualif.:** Applicants must be U.S. citizens; juniors or senior students in an undergraduate program; must have minimum GPA of 2.85 on a 4.0 scale; must be a student at Clemson Polymer and Fiber Chemistry or North Carolina State University Polymer and Color Chemistry; must be Piedmont Section Textile employees. **Criteria:** Recipients are selected based on extracurricular activities; employment experience and financial need.

Funds Avail.: $6,000 each. **Duration:** Annual. **Number**

Awards are arranged alphabetically below their administering organizations

Awarded: 4. **To Apply:** Applicants must submit all the required application information. **Deadline:** mid-February. **Contact:** Professor Gary Lickfield at lgary@clemson.edu; North Carolina State University, Mr. Kent Hester at kent_hester@ncsu.edu.

2082 ■ Association of the United States Navy (AUSN)
1619 King St.
Alexandria, VA 22314
Ph: (703)548-5800
Fax: (703)683-3647
Free: 877-628-9411
URL: www.ausn.org

2083 ■ Association of the United States Navy Scholarships (Undergraduate/Scholarship)

Purpose: To provide educational assistance for the sons and daughters of members of the Association of the United States Navy. **Focus:** General studies/Field of study not specified. **Qualif.:** Applicants must be: children of AUSN members in good standing; U.S. citizens; under 24 years of age; and, enrolled in or accepted for full-time enrollment at an accredited college, university or a fully-accredited technical school. **Criteria:** Selection will be based on financial need, scholastic and leadership ability, potential, character and personal qualities.

Funds Avail.: $1,000 to $2,000. **Duration:** Annual. **To Apply:** Applicants may download an application form available at the AUSN web site. **Deadline:** May 6.

2084 ■ Association of University Programs in Health Administration (AUPHA)
2000 N 14th St., Ste. 780
Arlington, VA 22201
Ph: (703)894-0940
Fax: (703)894-0941
E-mail: aupha@aupha.org
URL: www.aupha.org/home
Facebook: www.facebook.com/aupha
LinkedIn: www.linkedin.com/company/association-of
  -university-programs-in-health-administration
Twitter: www.twitter.com/aupha

2085 ■ Corris Boyd Scholarships (Master's/Scholarship)

Purpose: To support the education of students of color entering a Master's Degree program. **Focus:** Health care services. **Qualif.:** Applicants must have applied and been accepted to a Master's Degree AUPHA full-member program (but not yet enrolled); must be students of color; must have a minimum 3.0 GPA (out of 4.0) in undergraduate coursework; and must be U.S. citizens. **Criteria:** Selection is based on the applicant's leadership qualities; academic achievements; community involvement; commitment to healthcare; and financial need (may be considered when all other factors are equal).

Funds Avail.: $40,000. **Number Awarded:** 2. **To Apply:** Applicants must complete the application form online. In addition, applicants must submit GRE or GMAT score and score report (uploaded in PDF format or sent by mail or fax); current resume (uploaded in Word or PDF format); a personal statement (maximum of 1,000 words, uploaded in Word or PDF format); three signed letters of recommendation, one must be from a faculty member, one from an employer/supervisor (uploaded in PDF format or sent by mail or fax); and official transcripts (from all higher education institutions attended). **Deadline:** April 18. **Remarks:** Established in 2006.

2086 ■ Foster G. McGaw Scholarships (Undergraduate, Graduate/Scholarship)

Purpose: To provide financial support to students enrolled in health administration programs. **Focus:** Health services administration. **Qualif.:** Applicants must be undergraduate and graduate students in healthcare administration. **Criteria:** Selection will be based on the committee's criteria.

Funds Avail.: No specific amount. **To Apply:** Applicants may contact the Association for the application process and other required materials. **Contact:** Lacey Meckley at lmeckley@aupha.org.

2087 ■ David A. Winston Health Policy Scholarship (Graduate/Scholarship)

Purpose: To increase the number and quality of individuals trained in healthcare policy at the state and federal level. **Focus:** Health care services. **Qualif.:** Applicants must be U.S. citizens and first year graduate students studying health policy at an AUPHA member program. **Criteria:** Selection is based on the applicant's expressed and demonstrated commitment to health policy, leadership, academic achievement, community involvement and long term career interest.

Funds Avail.: $10,000. **Number Awarded:** 10. **To Apply:** Applicants must complete the application form online. In addition, applicants must submit a letter of nomination for the scholarship from a faculty member; a letter of nomination from a preceptor or employer; a personal statement; a CV detailing both professional and extracurricular activities; undergraduate and first semester graduate transcripts; and GRE or GMAT scores (waived if not required by academic program for admission). **Contact:** Lydia Middleton, Winston Fellowship Executive Director; Email: lmiddleton@winstonfellowship.org; Phone: 703-894-0940 x131.

2088 ■ Association for Women in Architecture + Design (AWA+D)
1315 Storm Pky.
Torrance, CA 90501
Ph: (310)534-8466
Fax: (310)257-1942
E-mail: parliamentarian@awaplusd.org
URL: awaplusd.org
Facebook: www.facebook.com/AWAplusD
LinkedIn: www.linkedin.com/groups/3863498/profile
Twitter: twitter.com/AWAplusD

2089 ■ Association for Women in Architecture Scholarships (Undergraduate/Scholarship)

Purpose: To advance and support the positions of women in architecture and allied fields. **Focus:** Architecture. **Qualif.:** Applicants must be residents of California or attending a California school; must be enrolled in one of the qualifying majors for the current school term; must have completed a minimum of 18 units in their major by the application due date. **Criteria:** Recipients are selected based on merit as evidenced by grades, personal statement, letter of recommendation and quality of student work.

Awards are arranged alphabetically below their administering organizations

Funds Avail.: $1,000. **Number Awarded:** 5. **To Apply:** Applicants must complete the application form; must submit an official transcript of records from each college and university attended, two sealed letters of recommendation with signature over the seal from an instructor who has taught in their major; must submit a typewritten personal statement stating the reasons for studying the chosen field and career objectives; must submit a portfolio in "11x17" format showing one-to-three projects from their school work and self-addressed stamped envelope, standard business size. **Deadline:** April 15. **Contact:** Questions can be addressed to Mary Werk at the above address; E-mail: scholarship@awa-la.org.

2090 ■ Association for Women in Computing - Houston Chapter
PO Box 421316
Houston, TX 77242-1316
E-mail: nationalrep@awchouston.org
URL: awchouston.org

2091 ■ Kathi Bowles Scholarships for Women in Technology *(Undergraduate, Graduate/Scholarship)*

Purpose: To support and assist women who are pursuing technology degrees and have contributed leadership and service to their school, university, or community. **Focus:** Computer and information sciences; Information science and technology; Technology. **Qualif.:** Applicants must reside within the Houston area; must be U.S. citizens or documented permanent residents of the U.S.; must have never been subject to any disciplinary action by any institution or entity, including, but not limited to, any educational or law enforcement agency; must have a high school GPA of 2.8 on a 4.0 scale, and planning to attend a four-year accredited college/university in Texas. **Criteria:** Selection shall be based on the aforementioned applicant's qualifications and compliance with the application details.

Funds Avail.: $1,000. **Duration:** Annual. **Number Awarded:** Varies. **To Apply:** Applicants must submit, in order, a fully completed and signed application/educational data form; resume; recommendation form and letter; transcript (high school students must include SAT/ACT scores); and a one-page written essay. Recommendation form must be sent separately by the recommender with transcript or transcript can be sent under separate cover. **Deadline:** April 30. **Remarks:** Established in 2000. **Contact:** awchouston.scholarship@yahoo.com.

2092 ■ Association for Women Geoscientists (AWG)
12000 N Washington St., Ste. 285
Thornton, CO 80241-3134
Ph: (303)412-6219
Fax: (303)253-9220
E-mail: office@awg.org
URL: www.awg.org
Facebook: www.facebook.com/AWGeoscientists

2093 ■ AWG Minority Scholarships *(Undergraduate/Scholarship)*

Purpose: To encourage young minority women to pursue an education and later a career in the geosciences. **Focus:** Geosciences. **Qualif.:** Applicants must be women who are African-American, Hispanic, or Native American and are full-time students pursuing undergraduate degree in geosciences at an accredited college or university. **Criteria:** Selection shall be based on the premises that the applicants may contribute to the larger world community through their academic and personal strengths.

Funds Avail.: Up to $6,000. **Duration:** Annual. **Number Awarded:** Varies. **To Apply:** Applicants must download the provided application form. The application calls for a statement of academic and career goals, two letters of recommendation, high school and college transcripts, and SAT or ACT scores. **Deadline:** June 30. **Contact:** Questions can be directed to Christina Tapia at office@awg.org.

2094 ■ Chrysalis Scholarships *(Graduate/Scholarship)*

Purpose: To support a geoscience graduate student with their thesis/ dissertation. **Focus:** Geosciences. **Qualif.:** Applicant must be a female geoscience graduate student who has had an interruption in her academic progress due to life circumstances. **Criteria:** Selection is based on the application materials.

Funds Avail.: $2,000. **Duration:** One year. **Number Awarded:** 2. **To Apply:** Applicants must submit a letter of application describing background, career goals and objectives, how the scholarship will be used, and the nature and length of the interruption of education. Applicants must also submit two reference letter electronically to chrysalis@awg.org, with a subject line: Chrysalis Scholarship. **Deadline:** March 31.

2095 ■ AWG Maria Luisa Crawford Field Camp Scholarships *(Undergraduate/Scholarship)*

Purpose: To encourage promising young women to pursue geoscience careers through attendance at field camp. **Focus:** Geosciences. **Qualif.:** Applicants must be full-time students who are pursuing an undergraduate degree in the geosciences at an accredited college or university, and have a GPA of 3.0 or higher. **Criteria:** Selection will be based on the committee's criteria.

Funds Avail.: $750 each. **Duration:** Annual. **Number Awarded:** 2. **To Apply:** Applicants must download and complete the provided application form. Also, applicants must provide the following: a 250-word essay explaining how the field-camp experience fits into their long-term academic and career goals; a transcript of all of their college work (an unofficial transcript is acceptable); names and contact information for two instructors who are acquainted with in the work and are willing to write letters of recommendation for the applicants (noting the ethnic origin, if applicable). The organization will contact them directly and ask them to submit their recommendations. **Deadline:** February 14. **Contact:** AWG Office at crawford@awg.org.

2096 ■ Janet Cullen Tanaka Scholarships *(Undergraduate/Scholarship)*

Purpose: To encourage the participation of women in the study of geosciences. **Focus:** Geosciences. **Qualif.:** Applicants should be undergraduate women (sophomore, junior, or senior women enrolled in a university or two-year college in Oregon or Washington State) committed to completing a Bachelor's Degree and pursuing a career or graduate work in the geosciences, including geology, environmental/engineering geology, geochemistry, geophysics, hydrogeology or hydrology. They must have a minimum of 3.2 GPA (or equivalent academic achievement). **Criteria:** Applicants will be judged based on their potential

Awards are arranged alphabetically below their administering organizations

for professional success, academic achievement and financial need. **Funds Avail.:** $1,500. **Duration:** Annual. **To Apply:** Applicants must submit their name, address, phone number, and email (if available); one paragraph each describing your (1) financial needs, (2) current resources, and (3) academic achievements; one-page essay summarizing your commitment to a career in the geosciences; copies of all college transcripts (photocopies accepted); three letters of reference; provide names, affiliations, phone numbers. **Deadline:** December 15. **Contact:** AWG Pacific Northwest Chapter, Attn: Scholarship Committee, P.O. Box 28391, Seattle, WA 98118; Email: scholarship@awg-ps.org.

2097 ■ Association for Women in Mathematics (AWM)
11240 Waples Mill Rd., Ste. 200
Fairfax, VA 22030
Ph: (703)934-0163
Fax: (703)359-7562
E-mail: awm@awm-math.org
URL: www.awm-math.org

2098 ■ AWM Mathematics Travel Grants (Doctorate/Grant)
Purpose: To enable women to attend research conferences in their fields and to provide valuable opportunities for them to advance their research activities and their visibility in the research community. **Focus:** Mathematics and mathematical sciences. **Qualif.:** Applicants must be women holding a doctorate degree and with a work address in the USA. **Criteria:** Awards will be determined on a competitive basis by a selection panel consisting of distinguished mathematicians appointed by the AWM.
Funds Avail.: $2,300 for domestic travel and $3,500 for foreign travel. **Duration:** Annual. **Number Awarded:** 3. **To Apply:** Application requirements and a complete step-by-step process are available online; application must be submitted online. **Deadline:** February 1; May 1; October 1. **Contact:** Jennifer Lewis; Phone: 703-934-0163 ext. 213.

2099 ■ Mathematics Mentoring Travel Grants for Women (Doctorate/Scholarship)
Purpose: To help young women to develop a long-term working and mentoring relationship with senior mathematicians. **Focus:** Mathematics and mathematical sciences. **Qualif.:** Applicants must be women holding a doctorate degree or equivalent with a work address in the United States; must be in a field supported by the Division of the Mathematical Sciences of the National Science Foundation. **Criteria:** Awards will be determined on a competitive basis by a selection panel consisting of distinguished mathematicians appointed by the AWM.
Funds Avail.: $5,000. **Duration:** Annual. **Number Awarded:** 7. **To Apply:** Applicants must have a curriculum vitae; must provide a research proposal which specifies why the proposed travel would be particularly beneficial; must submit a supporting letter from the proposed mentor with the curriculum vitae of the proposed mentor; must have a proposed budget and information about other sources of funding available. **Deadline:** February 1. **Contact:** Jennifer Lewis at 703-934-0163 ext. 213.

2100 ■ Association for Women in Sports Media (AWSM)
7742 Spalding Dr., No. 377
Norcross, GA 30092
E-mail: info@awsmonline.org
URL: www.awsmonline.org

2101 ■ Association for Women in Sports Media Internship/Scholarship Program (Undergraduate/Scholarship, Internship)
Purpose: To assist female college students interested in sports media careers through paid internships with employers. **Focus:** Media arts; Sports writing. **Qualif.:** Applicants must be full-time female students interested in sports media careers. **Criteria:** Applications will be evaluated by the AWSM board members and appropriate media professionals.
Funds Avail.: $1,000. **Duration:** Annual. **Number Awarded:** Varies. **To Apply:** Interested applicants may contact the AWSM for more information. **Remarks:** Established in 1990. **Contact:** Please e-mail any questions regarding to AWSM internship and scholarship program: awsminternship@gmail.com.

2102 ■ Association of Zoo Veterinary Technicians (AZVT)
c/o Marcie Oliva, CVT, Executive Director
White Oak Conservation Center
581705 White Oak Rd.
Yulee, FL 32097-2169
URL: www.azvt.org

2103 ■ Laurie Page-Peck Scholarship Fund (Undergraduate/Scholarship)
Purpose: To provide educational assistance for veterinary or medical technology students. **Focus:** Veterinary science and medicine. **Qualif.:** Applicant must be a veterinary or medical technology student interested in zoo veterinary technology. **Criteria:** Grantees will be selected based on the content, format and grammar of the submitted paper.
Funds Avail.: Up to $1,200. **To Apply:** Applicant must submit a paper about zoo veterinary technology. **Contact:** Grant Fuhrman, RVT at Houston Zoo, Inc., 1513 N. MacGregor, Houston, TX 77030, gfuhrman@houstonzoo.org.

2104 ■ Astronaut Scholarship Foundation (ASF)
6225 Vectorspace Blvd.
Titusville, FL 32780
Ph: (321)449-4876
Fax: (321)264-9176
E-mail: info@astronautscholarship.org
URL: www.astronautscholarship.org
Facebook: www.facebook.com/AstronautScholarship

2105 ■ Astronaut Scholarship Foundation Scholarships (Undergraduate/Scholarship)
Purpose: To support the promising students who want to pursue their masters in the fields of science and engineering. **Focus:** Engineering; Mathematics and mathematical sciences; Science. **Qualif.:** Applicants must be nominated by faculty members; must be U.S citizens; must be engineering or natural or applied science majors or mathematics students intending to pursue research or advance their field upon completion of their final degree; must be junior, senior or master's students; must have shown initiative, creativity and excellence in their chosen

Awards are arranged alphabetically below their administering organizations

field. **Criteria:** Recipients will be selected by the ASF Scholarship Committee.

Funds Avail.: $10,000. **Duration:** Annual. **To Apply:** Interested applicants may contact the Foundation for the application process and other required materials. **Contact:** Astronaut Scholarship Foundation, 6225 Vectorspace Blvd., Titusville, FL 32780.

2106 ■ Athenaeum of Philadelphia (PAT)
219 S 6th St.
Philadelphia, PA 19106-3794
Ph: (215)925-2688
Fax: (215)925-3755
URL: www.philaathenaeum.org
Facebook: www.facebook.com/philaathenaeum
LinkedIn: www.linkedin.com/company/athenaeum-of-philadelphia
Twitter: twitter.com/PhilaAthenaeum

2107 ■ Charles E. Peterson Senior Fellowships
(Other/Fellowship)

Purpose: To support professionals in the study, recording, and preservation of early American architecture and building technology (pre-1860) and the teaching of conservation skills in American schools of architecture. **Focus:** General studies/Field of study not specified. **Qualif.:** Applicants must be persons who hold a terminal degree and possess a distinguished record of accomplishment. **Criteria:** Applications are reviewed by a Committee of Architects, Architectural Historians and Educators appointed by the Athenaeum Board of Directors. Preference will be given to those applicants who have research on Delaware Valley topics.

Funds Avail.: Maximum of $15,000. **Duration:** Annual. **To Apply:** Applications should be submitted in the form of a single-page letter setting forth a brief statement of the project, with attached budget, schedule for completion, professional resume, and two letters of reference. **Deadline:** March 1. **Contact:** Peterson Fellowship Committee, The Athenaeum of Philadelphia, 219 S. 6th St., Philadelphia, PA 19106-3794.

2108 ■ Athletic Equipment Managers Association (AEMA)
460 Hunt Hill Rd.
Freeville, NY 13068-9643
Ph: (607)539-6300
Fax: (607)539-6340
E-mail: aema@frontiernet.net
URL: www.equipmentmanagers.org

2109 ■ Russell Athletics Scholarship
(Undergraduate/Scholarship)

Purpose: To assist students in furthering their professional abilities to athletic equipment management. **Focus:** General studies/Field of study not specified. **Qualif.:** Applicants must: be full-time college students with one year collegiate athletic equipment management experience; and, display an interest in the field of athletic equipment management. **Criteria:** Selection shall be based on academic achievement, community involvement, displayed interest in athletic Equipment management, completion of an essay and letters of recommendation.

Funds Avail.: $500 each. **Duration:** Annual. **Number Awarded:** 3. **To Apply:** Applicants must provide three (3) Character References with letters of recommendation. One of these references must come from the Supervising Equipment Manager. They must also submit an original essay of no more than 200 words on the topic of "What Athletic Equipment Management Means to Me". Submit the said documents along with the completed application form provided by AEMA. **Deadline:** March 15. **Contact:** AEMA Office, c/o Sam Trusner, 207 E. Bodman, Bement, IL 61813.

2110 ■ Atkinson Charitable Foundation
1 Yonge St., Ste. 702
Toronto, ON, Canada M5E 1E5
Ph: (416)368-5152
Fax: (416)865-3619
E-mail: info@atkinsonfoundation.ca
URL: atkinsonfoundation.ca

2111 ■ Atkinson Fellowships in Public Policy
(Professional development/Fellowship)

Purpose: To financially assist professionals with undertaking a research project on a topical public policy issue. **Focus:** Broadcasting; Journalism; Public affairs. **Qualif.:** Applicants must be Canadian citizens or landed immigrants who are full-time journalists in print or broadcast media. **Criteria:** The Selection Committee is open to research ideas on a wide range of topics. Preference will be given to issues that are at the forefront of public policy debate and have significant implications for Canadian society.

Funds Avail.: 75,000 Canadian Dollars stipend; 25,000 Canadian Dollars for research expenses. **Duration:** Annual; Program supports the fellows from September 1 to August 31 the following year. **To Apply:** Applicants must provide: curriculum vitae; story that contains the importance to Canadian society; and related articles in a three-page letter of intent. In the letter, they should demonstrate considerable familiarity with their chosen topic. They should also articulate the specific policy questions they want to pursue. Letters may be submitted in either English or French. **Deadline:** February 14. **Remarks:** Established in 1988.

2112 ■ Atlanta Association of Legal Administrators (AALA)
c/o Jennifer Brinkley, Executive Director
7433 Spout Springs Rd., Ste. 101, No. 54
Flowery Branch, GA 30542
Ph: (770)846-3402
URL: www.myaala.com
LinkedIn: www.linkedin.com/company/atlanta-association-of-legal-administrators

2113 ■ Gene Henson Scholarships *(Undergraduate/Scholarship)*

Purpose: To provide ongoing training and continuing education for the members of AALA, and support education in the community. **Focus:** General studies/Field of study not specified. **Qualif.:** Applicants must be U.S. citizens interested in attending a four-year college, university or specialized course of instruction within the state of Georgia, including private institutions. **Criteria:** Recipients will be selected based on financial need.

Funds Avail.: No specific amount. **Duration:** Annual. **To**

Awards are arranged alphabetically below their administering organizations

Apply: Applicants must submit a completed application form; must submit a transcript of records; must provide a list of extracurricular activities and enumerated community work; must write an essay (750 words or less) describing the candidate's opinions on current events happening locally, nationally or internationally; must submit a letter of acceptance. Incoming freshmen must include a signed statement from a non-affiliated organization. **Deadline:** March 23. **Remarks:** Established in 2004.

2114 ■ Atlantic County Bar Association
1201 Bacharach Blvd.
Atlantic City, NJ 08401
Ph: (609)345-3444
URL: www.atcobar.org
Facebook: www.facebook.com/Atcobara

2115 ■ Vincent S. Haneman-Joseph B. Perskie Memorial Foundation Scholarships *(Graduate, Undergraduate/Scholarship)*

Purpose: To support law students with their educational pursuit. **Focus:** Law. **Qualif.:** Applicants must be admitted to an American Bar Association accredited law school; must be residents of Atlantic County for one year prior to application; and be law students in any year including the first year. **Criteria:** Selection is based on academic ability, financial need, leadership potential and character.

Funds Avail.: No specific amount. **Duration:** Annual. **To Apply:** Applicants must submit a completed application form. **Deadline:** January 1 and May 1. **Contact:** Haneman-Perskie Scholarship Foundation, c/o Atlantic County Bar Association, 1201 Bacharach Blvd., Atlantic City, NJ 08401.

2116 ■ Atlantic Provinces Library Association (APLA)
Kenneth C. Rowe Management Bldg.
6100 University Ave., Ste. 4010
Halifax, NS, Canada B3H 4R2
Ph: (902)867-4883
E-mail: contact@apla.ca
URL: www.apla.ca

2117 ■ Atlantic Provinces Library Association Memorial Awards *(Undergraduate/Scholarship)*

Purpose: To provide financial assistance to individuals to undertake or complete the academic requirement leading to a degree in Library and Information Science. **Focus:** General studies/Field of study not specified; Library and archival sciences. **Qualif.:** Applicants must have a degree and must be currently doing research. **Criteria:** Priority will be given to those students with financial need.

Funds Avail.: No specific amount. **To Apply:** Applicants must send a letter outlining proposed research and estimated costs along with a copy of your curriculum vitae. **Deadline:** March 31.

2118 ■ Carin Alma E. Somers Scholarship Trust *(Undergraduate/Scholarship)*

Purpose: To provide financial assistance to individuals to undertake or complete the academic requirement leading to a degree in Library and Information Science. **Focus:** Library and archival sciences. **Qualif.:** Applicants must be Canadian citizens; must be residents of Atlantic Provinces; and must have demonstrated financial need. **Criteria:** Selection of recipients will be recommended by a committee of the four Provincial Vice Presidents and the President-Elect to the Executive Committee.

Funds Avail.: 2,000 Canadian Dollars. **To Apply:** Applicants must submit a completed application form. **Deadline:** March 31.

2119 ■ Atlantic Salmon Federation (ASF)
15 Rankine Mill Rd.
Chamcook, NB, Canada E5B 3A9
Ph: (506)529-4581
Fax: (506)529-1070
Free: 800-565-5666
E-mail: savesalmon@asf.ca
URL: www.asf.ca
Facebook: www.facebook.com/AtlanticSalmonFederation
Twitter: twitter.com/SalmonNews

2120 ■ Atlantic Salmon Federation Olin Fellowships *(Graduate/Fellowship)*

Purpose: To improve knowledge or skills in advanced fields while looking for solutions to current problems in Atlantic salmon biology, management and conservation. **Focus:** Biology, Marine. **Qualif.:** Applicants need not be enrolled in any degree program; must be legal residents of the United States or Canada; and must be enrolled in any accredited university, research laboratory or active management program. **Criteria:** Recipients are selected based on the committee's review of all applications.

Funds Avail.: $1,000-$3,000. **Duration:** Annual. **To Apply:** Application forms may be obtained from the Atlantic Salmon Federation Office in Canada or in USA; must attach a statement of qualifications; transcript of grades, if applicable; description of the program or project; and supporting documentation, if required. **Deadline:** March 15.

2121 ■ Audio Engineering Society (AES)
551 5th Ave., Ste. 1225
New York, NY 10165-2520
Ph: (212)661-8528
URL: www.aes.org

2122 ■ AES Educational Foundation Grants *(Graduate/Grant, Award)*

Purpose: To encourage entry of talented students into the profession of audio engineering and related fields. **Focus:** Engineering. **Qualif.:** All applicants are required to meet the following criteria: successful completion of an undergraduate degree program (typically four years) at a recognized college or university; demonstrated commitment to audio engineering (or a related field) as a career choice; acceptance or a pending application for graduate studies leading to a masters or higher degree, or an internationally recognized equivalent; and, be members in good standing of the Audio Engineering Society (any membership grade qualifies). **Criteria:** Selection will be based on the aforesaid qualifications and compliance with the application process.

Funds Avail.: No specific amount. **Duration:** Annual. **To Apply:** Applicants must submit two current letters of recommendation (one must be from major professor or academic advisors); a cover page; essays on past achievements and future plans; and list of references. Application forms may be requested from AES Headquarters via email. **Deadline:** May 15. **Remarks:** Established in 1984.

2123 ■ Auto Care Association
7101 Wisconsin Ave., Ste. 1300
Bethesda, MD 20814-3415
Ph: (301)654-6664
Fax: (301)654-3299
E-mail: info@autocare.org
URL: www.autocare.org

2124 ■ Tom Babcox Memorial Scholarships (Professional development/Scholarship)

Purpose: To support continuing education tailored specifically for the business needs of the automotive service industry. **Focus:** Automotive technology. **Qualif.:** Applicants must work in mechanical repair industry; must demonstrate an interest in self-improvement through management education; must own or work for a business as an ASA Collision division member in good standing. If applicants are not business owners, they must be recommended by a business owner. **Criteria:** Recipients are selected based on academic performance and demonstrated interest in automotive industry.

Funds Avail.: No specific amount. **To Apply:** Applicants must submit a completed application form.

2125 ■ Florida Automotive Industry Scholarships (Undergraduate/Scholarship)

Purpose: To provide and promote practical business management services. **Focus:** Automotive technology. **Qualif.:** Applicants must be high school seniors or high school graduates, or persons possessing a GED. Individual applicants must be nominated by a member of the association. **Criteria:** Recipients are selected based on academic achievement, merit and need.

Funds Avail.: No specific amount. **To Apply:** Applicants must submit a complete application form.

2126 ■ APSAIL's Ralph Silverman Memorial Scholarships (Undergraduate/Scholarship)

Purpose: To further promote quality and high standards through education within the automotive aftermarket industry. **Focus:** Automotive technology. **Qualif.:** Applicants must be students who intend to pursue a career in the automotive aftermarket industry. Applicants must be residents of Illinois and members of APSA Illinois. **Criteria:** Recipients are selected based on academic performance and demonstrated interest in the automotive industry.

Funds Avail.: No specific amount. **To Apply:** Applicants must submit a complete application form.

2127 ■ Sloan Northwood University Heavy-Duty Scholarships (Undergraduate/Scholarship)

Purpose: To provide and promote practical business management service. **Focus:** Automotive technology. **Qualif.:** Applicants must be enrolled in the university's Automotive Aftermarket Management curriculum, Heavy Duty Management program or the Heavy Duty Vehicle Technology program; must be U.S. citizens and maintain a 2.5 cumulative grade point average. **Criteria:** Recipients are selected based on financial need and demonstrated career interest.

Funds Avail.: No specific amount. **To Apply:** Applicants must submit a complete application form.

2128 ■ Auto-Pets
2900 Auburn St.
Auburn Hills, MI 48326
Fax: (248)253-1797
Free: 877-250-7729
URL: www.litter-robot.com

2129 ■ Auto-Pets "Out-of-the-Box Thinking" Scholarships (All/Award, Scholarship)

Purpose: To get young people thinking about innovation. **Focus:** Business; Engineering; Marketing and distribution. **Qualif.:** Applicants must be U.S. students. **Criteria:** Winners will be determined based on their essay of idea and pitch.

Funds Avail.: $50 to $1,500. **Number Awarded:** 3. **To Apply:** Applicants must apply by visiting the website. Contest rules will be sent to them by e-mail. **Deadline:** December 20. **Contact:** Send e-mail at christine@litter-robot.com for more questions.

2130 ■ Automotive Industries Association of Canada (AIAC)
180 Elgin St., Ste. 1400
Ottawa, ON, Canada K2P 2K3
Ph: (613)728-5821
Fax: (613)728-6021
Free: 800-808-2920
E-mail: info@aiacanada.com
URL: www.aiacanada.com
Facebook: www.facebook.com/AIAofCanada
LinkedIn: www.linkedin.com/company/aia-canada
Twitter: twitter.com/AIAOFCANADA

2131 ■ AIA and the Global Automotive Aftermarket Symposium Scholarships (Undergraduate/Scholarship)

Purpose: To support deserving secondary students, college and university students who want to pursue a career in the automotive aftermarket. **Focus:** Automotive technology. **Qualif.:** Applicants must be graduating high school seniors or have graduated from high school within the past two years; must be enrolled in a college-level program, university or an accredited automotive technical program through either a CAMPE college or a CARS-approved institute; must be attending a full-time program in Canada or the United States. **Criteria:** Applicants will be selected based on their academic merit.

Funds Avail.: 1,000 Canadian Dollars. **Duration:** Annual. **To Apply:** Application forms are available at the website. Applicants must prepare a copy of the current school transcript with official school seal; must submit an essay (at least 250 words in length, no longer than one page, double-spaced); letter of recommendation (from a non-family member, preferably an employer, teacher or someone other than a family friend). **Deadline:** June 15. **Remarks:** Established in 1996.

2132 ■ Hans McCorriston Motive Power Machinist Grant Programs (Undergraduate/Scholarship)

Purpose: To support students pursuing careers as motive power machinists. **Focus:** Automotive technology. **Qualif.:**

Applicants must be enrolled in the AIA Motive Power Machinist Training Program or a college-level machinist training program within Canada. **Criteria:** Applications and other supporting documents are reviewed by the Scholarship Committee.

Funds Avail.: 1,000 Canadian Dollars. **Duration:** Annual. **To Apply:** Applicant must fill up the application form available at the website. **Contact:** Didina Kyenge; Phone: (800) 808-2920 ext 231.

2133 ■ Arthur Paulin Automotive Aftermarket Scholarship Awards (Postgraduate, Undergraduate/Scholarship)

Purpose: To provide monetary assistance to deserving students in the automotive field. **Focus:** Automotive technology. **Qualif.:** Applicants must be enrolled in an automotive aftermarket industry-related program or curriculum at a Canadian college or university. **Criteria:** Recipients are selected based on Scholarship Committee's review of applications and other supporting documents.

Funds Avail.: 700 Canadian Dollars. **Duration:** Annual. **To Apply:** Application form is available at the website or upon request from the AIA National Office in Ottawa. Applicants must submit a letter stating his/her long-term automotive goals; and a letter from his/her automotive instructor; recent academic achievements, as well as achievements in the automotive sector. **Deadline:** November 30.

2134 ■ Marion Roberts Memorial Scholarships (Undergraduate/Scholarship)

Purpose: To provide financial assistance and encouragement enabling students to further their education at the post-secondary school level. **Focus:** General studies/Field of study not specified. **Qualif.:** Applicant must be a dependent child or spouse of a full-time employee in an active AIA member company; confirmation of the parent's/spouse employment must be provided by the member company. Applicant must be enrolled in a full-time post-secondary program leading to a degree, certificate or diploma at an accredited university, college, technical school or C.E.G.E.P. **Criteria:** Recipients are selected based on Scholarship Committee's review of applications.

Funds Avail.: 500 Canadian Dollars. **Duration:** Annual. **To Apply:** Applicants must fill up the application form available at the website; must prepare a letter that demonstrates leadership ability in school, social or other activities; must have a transcript indicating academic achievement, with an official seal or photocopy of the seal of the school; recent passport-sized photo. **Deadline:** July 15.

2135 ■ Automotive Recyclers Association (ARA)
9113 Church St.
Manassas, VA 20110
Ph: (571)208-0428
Fax: (571)208-0430
Free: 888-385-1005
URL: www.a-r-a.org
Twitter: twitter.com/AutoRecyclers

2136 ■ ARA Scholarship Awards (Undergraduate/Scholarship)

Purpose: To assist outstanding students to pursue their educational goal. **Focus:** Business; Education, Vocational-technical. **Qualif.:** Applicants must be children of an employee of a direct ARA member company; must be a high school senior or pursuing a full-time post high school program in an institution providing trade, business, or technical programs; have at least 3.0 GPA or equivalent. **Criteria:** Applicants will be selected based on their academic achievement.

Funds Avail.: No specific amount. **Duration:** Annual. **To Apply:** Applicants must submit a completed application form and profile sheet. Transcript of academic records must be sent by the applicant's school/college directly to the ARA Scholarship Advisor. Applicants must obtain a certification and letter of verification from the parents' employer who is a direct member of ARA (should include current employment and the hiring date). Send all requirements to the ARA Scholarship Foundation Advisor. **Deadline:** March 15. **Contact:** ARA Scholarship Advisor, 109 Defiant Way, Grass Valley, CA 95945, arascholar@sbcglobal.net.

2137 ■ Automotive Women's Alliance Foundation (AWAF)
PO Box 4305
Troy, MI 48099
Fax: (248)239-0291
Free: 877-393-2923
E-mail: admin@awafoundation.org
URL: www.awafoundation.org
LinkedIn: www.linkedin.com/groups/1919546/profile
Twitter: twitter.com/AutomotiveWomen

2138 ■ Automotive Women's Alliance Foundation Scholarships (Undergraduate/Scholarship)

Purpose: To support the advancement of automotive professionals and motivate current and future students studying an automotive related field. **Focus:** Automotive technology. **Qualif.:** Candidates must be North American citizens; must be high school seniors or accepted in a college or university; must have and maintain a minimum of 3.0 GPA. **Criteria:** Scholarships are given based on academic merit.

Funds Avail.: No specific amount. **To Apply:** Candidates must submit a completed application form; transcript from current educational institution; resume; and one-page cover letter stating the career goals. Freshmen applicants must provide a high school transcript and proof of acceptance from a college, university or class they wish to attend. **Deadline:** July 5.

2139 ■ AVAC: Global Advocacy for HIV Prevention
423 W 127th St., 4th Fl.
New York, NY 10027
Ph: (212)796-6423
Fax: (646)365-3452
URL: www.avac.org
Facebook: www.facebook.com/HIVpxresearch
Twitter: twitter.com/HIVpxresearch?ref_src=twsrc%5Egoogle%7Ctwcamp%5Eserp%7Ctwgr%5Eauthor

2140 ■ HIV Prevention Research Advocacy Fellowships (Professional development/Fellowship)

Purpose: To provide support to emerging and mid-career advocates to design and implement advocacy projects focused on biomedical HIV prevention research and implementation activities in their countries and communi-

Awards are arranged alphabetically below their administering organizations

ties. **Focus:** AIDS. **Qualif.:** Applicants must be emerging or mid-career community leaders and advocates involved or interested in advocacy around HIV prevention research and implementation; must be individuals with some experience or education in the areas of HIV and AIDS, public health, medicine, international development, women's rights, communications or advocacy with key populations, such as sex workers, LGBT people and drug users; must be based in low and middle-income countries where biomedical HIV prevention clinical research is planned or ongoing and/or where there is current work on implementation of voluntary medical male circumcision, pre-exposure prophylaxis, treatment as prevention and combination prevention packages that link biomedical strategies. Advocates can also develop proposals that seek to catalyze plans and policies in country where little activity on these issues has happened to date; must be able to collaborate with English-speaking mentors; must demonstrate strategic analysis of how Fellowship-related activities will relate to this work. **Criteria:** Selection will be based on the committee's criteria.

Funds Avail.: No specific amount. **To Apply:** Advocacy Fellowship application form can be downloaded at the website. Applicants must submit the individual and host organization information forms, the essay/short answer questions, the host organization letter of support and applicants' CV/resume.

2141 ■ AvaCare Medical
1665 Corporate Rd. West
Lakewood, NJ 08701
Fax: (732)813-7798
Free: 877-813-7799
URL: avacaremedical.com

2142 ■ AvaCare Medical Scholarships
(Undergraduate/Scholarship)

Purpose: To support students by providing them a scholarship toward college tuition. **Focus:** Dentistry; Medicine; Nursing; Nutrition. **Qualif.:** Applicants must be citizens of the United States or in a possession of an Alien Registration Card; must be high school seniors or enrolled in an accredited U.S. college or university; must achieved a minimum cumulative GPA of 3.0; must be pursuing a degree in the medical field such as therapy, nursing, medicine, nutrition, laboratory science, dentistry, etc. **Criteria:** Submissions will be judged on content, creativity and quality of work; must be own unique work and cannot be published anywhere else online.

Funds Avail.: $1,000. **Number Awarded:** 1. **To Apply:** Applicants must send a project about an act of kindness that inspired them along with their transcript, name, email address, phone number, and the field they are pursuing via mail or email. Applicants may choose to complete any one of the following projects: Blog post - up to 800 words (relevant pictures may be included); Video - up to 1.5 minutes, in one of the following formats: .mov, .mp4, .m4v, .flv, .3gp, .avi, .wmv; Image - up to 8.5" x 11", along with a short description. **Deadline:** December 15. **Contact:** scholarships@avacaremedical.com.

2143 ■ Aviation Distributors and Manufacturers Association (ADMA)
100 N 20th St., Ste. 400
Philadelphia, PA 19103-1462
Ph: (215)320-3872
Fax: (215)564-2175
E-mail: adma@fernley.com
URL: members.adma.org/adma

2144 ■ ADMA International Scholarship
(Undergraduate/Scholarship)

Purpose: To provide assistance for students pursuing careers in the aviation field. **Focus:** Aviation. **Qualif.:** Applicants must be third or fourth year students enrolled in a four-year program at an accredited Aviation institution and possess a minimum of 3.0 grade point average; or a second-year students in an A&P program at a two-year accredited institution. **Criteria:** Recipients are selected based on academic performance, financial need, recommendations, extracurricular activities and leadership contributions.

Funds Avail.: No specific amount. **Duration:** Annual. **To Apply:** Applicants must submit a filled out application form obtained at www.adma.org. Applicants must submit two letters of reference and a 500-word essay describing their desire to pursue a career in the aviation field. **Deadline:** May 26.

2145 ■ AVS Science and Technology Society (AVS)
125 Maiden Ln., 15th Fl.
New York, NY 10038
Ph: (212)248-0200
Fax: (212)248-0245
E-mail: yvonne@avs.org
URL: www.avs.org
Facebook: www.facebook.com/pages/AVS/143182759040976
Twitter: www.twitter.com/#!/AVS_Members

2146 ■ AVS Applied Surface Science Division Awards *(Graduate/Award)*

Purpose: To recognize and encourage excellence in continuing graduate studies in the sciences and technologies of interest to American Vacuum Society. **Focus:** Science technologies. **Qualif.:** Applicants must be graduate students that will need to present a poster or talk during any Applied Surface Science Division sessions, plus an additional capsule (3-slide, 5-minute) presentation to the judges. **Criteria:** Selection will be based on the scientific merit and originality of students' work.

Funds Avail.: $1,000. **Duration:** Annual. **To Apply:** Students wishing to participate in the competition should contact the ASSD Student Award Chair when submitting an abstract. **Deadline:** May 4. **Contact:** Angela Klink at angela@avs.org.

2147 ■ AVS Biomaterial Interfaces Division - Early Career Researchers Awards *(Graduate/Monetary)*

Purpose: To recognize and encourage excellence in continuing graduate studies in the sciences and technologies of interest to American Vacuum Society. **Focus:** Science technologies. **Qualif.:** Applicants must be students that will need to present a poster at one of the BI poster session on their thesis research. **Criteria:** Students will be judged on the scientific merit and originality of their research.

Funds Avail.: $250. **Duration:** Annual. **To Apply:** Students must submit a copy of their abstract along with a statement

Awards are arranged alphabetically below their administering organizations

of intent to compete for the student prize. **Deadline:** May 4.

2148 ■ **AVS Electronic Materials and Photonic Division Postdoctoral Award** *(Postdoctorate/Award)*

Purpose: To recognize postdoctoral fellows who will be presenting EMPD papers at the International Symposium. **Focus:** Science technologies. **Qualif.:** Interested applicants must be postdoctoral fellows who have an accepted abstract. **Criteria:** Selection will be based on the submitted materials.

Funds Avail.: $500. **To Apply:** Applicants must submit the following: a copy of the accepted abstract with Program Number; a recommendation letter from their advisor; their curriculum vitae; and a cover letter of request.

2149 ■ **AVS Manufacturing Science and Technology Group Awards** *(Graduate/Award)*

Purpose: To encourage participation of students in the MSTG program and to acknowledge the valuable contributions they make in advancing state-of-the-art in manufacturing science and technology. **Focus:** Science technologies. **Qualif.:** Applicants must be full-time university graduate students with primary appointments at universities. **Criteria:** Preference will be given to those who give oral presentations of their papers.

Funds Avail.: No specific amount. **Duration:** Annual. **Number Awarded:** Up to 2. **To Apply:** Applicants must submit the following: a 1-page letter of application describing the students research; letter of endorsement by the student's research advisor; copy of submitted abstract; completed application. **Deadline:** May 2.

2150 ■ **AVS MEMS and NEMS Technical Group Best Paper Awards** *(Undergraduate, Graduate/Monetary)*

Purpose: To promote outstanding scientific research and technological innovation. **Focus:** Science technologies. **Qualif.:** Candidates must be undergraduate or graduate students. **Criteria:** Candidates will be judged on the quality, originality of their research and their skill in presentation (oral/poster).

Funds Avail.: $500. **Duration:** Annual. **To Apply:** Interested candidates should submit a cover letter describing their intent to compete along with a copy of their AVS abstract, current resume and application to Angela Klink. **Deadline:** May 2.

2151 ■ **AVS Nanometer-Scale Science and Technology Division Graduate Award** *(Graduate/Monetary)*

Purpose: To give recognition to outstanding research by graduate students giving oral presentations in NSTD sessions at AVS international symposia. **Focus:** Science technologies. **Qualif.:** Applicants must be graduate students. **Criteria:** Selection is based on the quality of the talk, the responses to questions, and the level of the research.

Funds Avail.: $500. **Duration:** Annual. **To Apply:** Applicants must submit a completed application, a copy of the abstract, an extended abstract written by the student of no more than three pages, and a recommendation letter from the students' research advisor, who must be a member of AVS. **Deadline:** May 2.

2152 ■ **AVS Spectroscopic Ellipsometry Focus Topic Graduate Student Awards** *(Graduate/Award)*

Purpose: To recognize graduate students and young postdoc researchers in a Focus Topic on SE session at the Annual Symposium. **Focus:** Science technologies. **Qualif.:** Interested applicants must be competitive graduate students and young post-doctoral researchers. **Criteria:** Selection will be based on the submitted application materials.

Funds Avail.: $500. **Duration:** Annual. **Number Awarded:** 3. **To Apply:** Interested applicants must submit the following: curriculum vitae; a copy of their submitted AVS abstract; and a letter of recommendation from their research advisor.

2153 ■ **AVS Thin Film Division James Harper Awards** *(Graduate/Monetary)*

Purpose: To recognize the best oral presentation by a graduate student in a Thin Film Division session at the Annual Symposium. **Focus:** Science technologies. **Qualif.:** Applicants must be currently registered graduate students. **Criteria:** Selection will be based on the committee's criteria.

Funds Avail.: $800; two $500 for the runner-ups. **Duration:** Annual. **To Apply:** Interested applicants must submit the following: curriculum vitae; a copy of their submitted AVS abstract; and a letter of recommendation from their research advisor. **Deadline:** May 2.

2154 ■ **John Coburn and Harold Winters Student Award in Plasma Science and Technology** *(Graduate/Award)*

Purpose: To promote outstanding scientific research and technological innovation. **Focus:** Science technologies. **Qualif.:** Interested candidates must be students. **Criteria:** Winner will be selected from the finalists on the basis of the oral presentation, the quality of research, the clarity of the presentation and the potential for the research to advance the field of plasma science.

Funds Avail.: No specific amount. **Duration:** Annual. **To Apply:** Students must submit a curriculum vitae of the nominee; a one-page letter of endorsement from the student's research advisor/mentor; a copy of the nominee's submitted abstract for the AVS International Symposium. **Deadline:** March 31.

2155 ■ **Magnetic Interfaces and Nanostructures Division - The Leo M. Falicov Student Award** *(Graduate/Grant)*

Purpose: To recognize outstanding research performed by a graduate student in areas of interest to the MIND. **Focus:** Science technologies. **Qualif.:** Applicants must be graduate students. **Criteria:** Selection will be based on the oral presentation, considering quality of research and clarity of presentation.

Funds Avail.: No specific amount. **Duration:** Annual. **To Apply:** Interested applicants must visit the website for the online registration and nomination process. **Deadline:** May 2.

2156 ■ **Dorothy M. and Earl S. Hoffman Award** *(Graduate/Award)*

Purpose: To recognize and encourage excellence in continuing graduate studies in the sciences and technologies of interest to American Vacuum Society. **Focus:** Science technologies. **Qualif.:** Nominees must be registered graduate students in an accredited academic institution at the time when the applications are due.

Deadline: May 2. **Remarks:** Established in 2002.

2157 ■ **Morton M. Traum Surface Science Student Awards** *(Graduate, Doctorate/Prize)*

Purpose: To recognize and support the best student presenter at the AVS International Symposium. **Focus:** Sci-

Awards are arranged alphabetically below their administering organizations

ence technologies. **Qualif.:** Candidates must be either current graduate students or have received the Ph.D. degree in the year of the Symposium. **Criteria:** Selection will be based on the scientific content and presentation skill.

Funds Avail.: $1,000. **Duration:** Annual. **To Apply:** Candidates must submit the following: a copy of the abstract that includes the abstract submission number; an extended abstract that does not exceed two pages (including tables, figures and references; and expected graduation date. **Deadline:** May 2. **Remarks:** Established in 1981.

2158 ■ Russell and Sigurd Varian Award *(Graduate/Recognition)*

Purpose: To recognize and encourage excellence in continuing graduate studies in the sciences and technologies of interest to AVS. **Focus:** Science technologies. **Qualif.:** Applicants must be registered graduate students in an accredited academic institution at the time when the applications are due. Applicants are normally expected not to graduate before the award selection. **Criteria:** Selection will be based on the excellence in research and academic record.

Funds Avail.: No specific amount. **Duration:** Annual. **To Apply:** Applicants must submit a completed application form, the Report on Candidate Form, abstract to the AVS International Symposium for Division/Group awards and all supporting materials to Angela Klink. **Remarks:** Established in 1982.

2159 ■ Nellie Yeoh Whetten Award *(Graduate/Recognition)*

Purpose: To recognize and encourage excellence by women in graduate studies in the sciences and technologies of interest to AVS. **Focus:** Science technologies. **Qualif.:** Applicants must be registered female graduate students in an accredited academic institution at the time when the applications are due. Applicants are normally expected not to graduate before the award selection. **Criteria:** Selection will be based on the excellence in research and academic record.

Funds Avail.: No specific amount. **Duration:** Annual. **To Apply:** Applicants must submit a completed application form, the Report on Candidate Form, abstract to the AVS International Symposium for Division/Group awards and all supporting materials to Angela Klink. **Remarks:** Established in 1989.

2160 ■ AXA Equitable
1290 Avenue of the Americas
New York, NY 10104
Ph: (212)314-4600
Free: 888-292-4636
E-mail: service@axa-equitable.com
URL: www.axa-equitable.com

2161 ■ AXA Achievement Scholarships *(Undergraduate/Scholarship)*

Purpose: To provide scholarships to high school seniors and college students who demonstrated outstanding achievement. **Focus:** General studies/Field of study not specified. **Qualif.:** Applicants must be US citizens or legal residents; be current high school seniors who plan to enroll full-time in an accredited two-year or four-year college or university in the US; demonstrate ambition and self-drive as evidence by outstanding achievement in an activity in school, the community or the workplace; be recommended by an unrelated adult who can attest to the student's achievement. **Criteria:** Primary consideration will be given to the applicant's demonstrated achievement in a non-academic area as reported by the applicant and supported by the appraisal completed by an adult who is not related to the applicant.

Funds Avail.: $10,000 - $25,000 each. **Duration:** Annual. **Number Awarded:** 52. **To Apply:** Application form can be downloaded online. Applicants must submit the completed application form together with complete transcript of grades at the above address.

2162 ■ Ayn Rand Institute (ARI)
2121 Alton Pky., Ste. 250
Irvine, CA 92606
Ph: (949)222-6550
Fax: (949)222-6558
E-mail: mail@aynrand.org
URL: www.aynrand.org
Facebook: www.facebook.com/AynRandOrg
Twitter: twitter.com/aynrandorg

2163 ■ Atlas Shrugged Essay Contest *(Graduate, Undergraduate, High School/Prize)*

Purpose: To encourage students to use and practice their writing skills through essay contests. **Focus:** General studies/Field of study not specified. **Qualif.:** Applicant must be a 12th Grader, college undergraduate or a graduate student, and not a previous first place winner. **Criteria:** Essays will be judged on whether the student is able to argue for and justify his or her view--not on whether the Institute agrees with the view the student expresses. Judges will look for writing that is clear, articulate and logically organized. Winning essays must demonstrate an outstanding grasp of the philosophic meaning of Atlas Shrugged.

Funds Avail.: $20,000. **Duration:** Annual. **To Apply:** No application is required. Applicants must read Atlas Shrugged and write an 800-1,600-word essay on one of three assigned topics available on aynrand.org/contests. Applicants may submit the essay online or by mail. **Deadline:** April 28. **Contact:** For more information visit the website, aynrand.org/contests, or email essays@aynrand.org.

2164 ■ Ayn Rand Institute Anthem Essay Contest *(High School, Undergraduate/Prize)*

Purpose: To support high school and college students for the best essay on Ayn Rand's fiction. **Focus:** General studies/Field of study not specified. **Qualif.:** Students must be 8th, 9th and 10th Graders. **Criteria:** Essays will be judged on whether the student is able to argue for and justify his or her view—not on whether the Institute agrees with the view the student expresses. Judges will look for writing that is clear, articulate and logically organized. Winning essays must demonstrate an outstanding grasp of the philosophic meaning of Anthem.

Funds Avail.: $2,000 - 1st prize; $500 - 2nd prize; $200 - 3rd prize. **Duration:** Annual. **To Apply:** No application is required. Applicants must read Anthem and write a 600-1,200-word essay on one of three assigned topics available on aynrand.org/contests. Applicants may submit the essay online or by mail **Deadline:** March 29. **Contact:** Foe further information visit the website, aynrand.org/contests, or email essays@aynrand.org.

Awards are arranged alphabetically below their administering organizations

2165 ■ Ayn Rand Institute Fountainhead Essay Contest *(High School, Undergraduate/Prize)*

Purpose: To support and help high school students for the best essay on Ayn Rand's fiction. **Focus:** General studies/Field of study not specified. **Qualif.:** Students must be 11th and 12th graders. **Criteria:** Essays will be judged on whether the student is able to argue for and justify his or her view--not on whether the Institute agrees with the view the student expresses. Judges will look for writing that is clear, articulate and logically organized. Winning essays must demonstrate an outstanding grasp of the philosophic meaning of The Fountainhead.

Funds Avail.: $10,000 - 1st prize; $2,000 - 2nd prize; $1,000 - 3rd prize. **Duration:** Annual. **To Apply:** No application is required. Applicants must read The Fountainhead and write an 800-1,600-word essay on one of three assigned topics available on aynrand.org/contests. Applicants may submit the essay online or by mail. **Deadline:** April 26.

2166 ■ The Bailey Family Foundation
912 W Platt St.
Tampa, FL 33606-2108
Ph: (813)549-6140
Fax: (813)549-6141
E-mail: contact@bailey-family.org
URL: www.bailey-family.org
Facebook: www.facebook.com/BFFTampa
LinkedIn: www.linkedin.com/company/the-bailey-family-foundation?trk=tyah&trkInfo=clickedVertical%3Acompany%2CclickedEntityId%3A8696861%2Cidx%3A1-1-1%2CtarId%3A1448294549070%2Ctas%3Athe+bailey+family

2167 ■ The Bailey Family Foundation College Scholarship Program *(Undergraduate/Scholarship)*

Purpose: To financially assist students in continuing their education. **Focus:** General studies/Field of study not specified. **Qualif.:** Applicants must be legal U.S. residents, pursuing undergraduate degree or diploma; must have a minimum cumulative GPA of 2.5; and, must be enrolled or accepted to one of the participating schools listed on the scholarship application. **Criteria:** Applicants will be evaluated based on academic achievement and financial need.

Funds Avail.: $5,000. **Duration:** Annual. **To Apply:** Applicants must submit the completed scholarship application form and an essay of no more than 300 words describing any community service or other activities that have influenced the applicant's life or telling the reviewers about the applicant's goals. **Deadline:** March 15.

2168 ■ The Bailey Family Foundation High School Scholarships Program *(Undergraduate/Scholarship)*

Purpose: To provide financial assistance for high school seniors intending to continue their post-secondary education. **Focus:** General studies/Field of study not specified. **Qualif.:** Applicants must be U.S. residents; must possess a minimum cumulative GPA of 2.5; must demonstrate financial need; must be graduating seniors from a participating high school; and must be pursuing an undergraduate degree. **Criteria:** Applicants will be evaluated based on academic achievement and financial need.

Funds Avail.: $5,000. **To Apply:** Applicants must submit a completed scholarship application form including an essay of no more than 300 words describing any community service or other activities that have influenced them or telling the reviewers about the their goals. **Deadline:** March 15. **Contact:** The Bailey Family Foundation at the above address.

2169 ■ Baker, Donelson, Bearman, Caldwell and Berkowitz, P.C.
165 Madison Ave., Ste. 2000
Memphis, TN 38103
Ph: (901)526-2000
Fax: (901)577-2303
URL: www.bakerdonelson.com

2170 ■ Baker Donelson Diversity Scholarships *(Undergraduate/Scholarship)*

Purpose: To help law students defray the cost of law school tuition and related expenses. **Focus:** Law. **Qualif.:** Applicants must be diverse law students. **Criteria:** Selection will be based on the committee's criteria.

Funds Avail.: $10,000. **Duration:** Annual. **To Apply:** Interested applicants must visit the website for the online application tool.

2171 ■ Baker and Hostetler LLP
191 N Wacker Dr., Ste. 3100
Chicago, IL 60606-1901
Ph: (312)416-6200
Fax: (312)416-6201
E-mail: rokada@bakerlaw.com
URL: www.bakerlaw.com

2172 ■ Baker and Hostetler Diversity Fellowships *(Undergraduate/Fellowship)*

Purpose: To recruit candidates with diverse backgrounds and perspectives to foster an inclusive workplace. **Focus:** Law. **Qualif.:** Applicants must be enrolled full-time in an ABA-accredited law school and in good standing as a second-year law student at the time of application; A member of one of the under-represented racial/ethnic groups set forth by the Equal Employment Opportunity Commission or a member of the LGBT community; Not a recipient of a similar diversity award from another law firm for the same time period; Applicants must spend at least eight weeks with the firm. Splitting time between two offices may be permitted based upon approval of the two offices' Hiring Partners; A US citizens or otherwise authorized to work in the United States. **Criteria:** Selection will be based on the demonstrated superior academic performance during college and law school, significant personal achievements and strong community involvement. Law school students will need to possess strong oral and written communication skills, demonstrated leadership achievements and a sincere interest and commitment to join Baker Hostetler.

Funds Avail.: No specific amount. **To Apply:** Candidates must provide the following documents: completed application form; current resume; unofficial or official undergraduate and law school transcripts; personal statement; two professional or academic references

2173 ■ Paul D. White Scholarship *(Undergraduate/Scholarship)*

Purpose: To provide minority law students with valuable experience early in their careers. **Focus:** Law. **Qualif.:** Applicants must be law students of Black or African American,

Hispanic or Latino, Native Hawaiian or Pacific Islander, Asian, American Indian or Alaska Native descent. **Criteria:** Selection will be based on the committee's criteria.

Funds Avail.: $7,500. **Duration:** Annual. **To Apply:** Application form can be obtained at the website. Applicants must complete and submit completed application and personal statement. **Deadline:** December 1. **Remarks:** Established in 1997.

2174 ■ Baker and McKenzie L.L.P.
300 E Randolph St., Ste. 5000
Chicago, IL 60601
Ph: (312)861-8000
Fax: (312)861-2899
E-mail: info@bakernet.com
URL: www.bakernet.com

2175 ■ Baker and McKenzie Diversity Fellowships
(Postgraduate, Professional development/Fellowship)

Purpose: To encourage and support upcoming law students who are contributing essentially to the diversity of legal community. **Focus:** Law; Minorities. **Qualif.:** Applicants must be qualified rising second-year law students who show promise of contributing meaningfully to the diversity of the legal community; must meet the academic and hiring criteria of Baker and McKenzie's summer associate program; must receive an offer of summer employment for their second-year summer; and must be members of a population that historically has been underrepresented in the legal profession. **Criteria:** Selection will be based on the applicant's eligibility and compliance with the application process.

Funds Avail.: $10,000. **To Apply:** Applicants must complete the application and submit the following: current resume; a copy of undergraduate transcript; a copy of law school transcript; a personal statement, not to exceed 500 words, which describes their talents, qualities, and experiences and how they would contribute to Baker and McKenzie's diversity and inclusion efforts. Send the application and the supporting documents to the Diversity Fellowship mailbox. **Deadline:** August 31.

2176 ■ Baker and McKenzie Graduate Legal Studies Scholarships *(Graduate, Professional development/ Scholarship)*

Purpose: To support Firm associates in their full-time graduate legal study outside their home jurisdictions. **Focus:** Law. **Qualif.:** Applicants must be Baker and McKenzie associates who have been with the Firm for at least two years and are interested in studying for a graduate law degree (LI.M., M.C.L., or similar). **Criteria:** Scholarship winners are selected on the following bases: the associates' legal, intellectual and professional capabilities; the benefit and relevance to the associates of the proposed course of study; and additional criteria as outlined by the associate's local office.

Funds Avail.: No specific amount. **To Apply:** Applicants may contact the Firm for the application information. **Deadline:** Every January.

2177 ■ Baltimore City Community College (BCCC)
2901 Liberty Heights Ave.
Baltimore, MD 21215-7807
Ph: (410)462-8300
Free: 800-735-2258
URL: www.bccc.edu/site/default.aspx?PageID=1

2178 ■ BCCC Foundation General Scholarship Fund
(Undergraduate/Scholarship)

Purpose: To provide financial assistance to individuals who have the desire and commitment to pursue their educational goals. **Focus:** General studies/Field of study not specified. **Qualif.:** Applicants must: be BCCC students with 2.5 GPA or higher; demonstrate financial need; and, be Maryland residents. **Criteria:** Selection will be based on the aforesaid qualifications and compliance with the application details.

Funds Avail.: Amount varies. **Duration:** Annual. **To Apply:** Applicants must submit completed scholarship application along with a 300-500 word essay and a copy of transcript. **Deadline:** May 31.

2179 ■ BCCC Workforce Creation Scholarships
(Undergraduate/Scholarship)

Purpose: To provide financial assistance to those who have the desire and commitment to pursue their educational goals. **Focus:** General studies/Field of study not specified. **Qualif.:** Applicants must be U.S. citizens or eligible non-citizens who are Baltimore residents enrolled in an approved degree, certificate or critical workforce shortage program at BCCC (either full-time (12-15 credits), part-time (6-11 credits), or credit free approved status). **Criteria:** Selection will be based on academic achievement and financial need.

Funds Avail.: No specific amount. **Duration:** Annual. **To Apply:** Applicants must submit completed scholarship application along with a 300-500 word essay and a copy of transcript.

2180 ■ Banff Centre - Leadership Development
Box 1020
Banff, AB, Canada T1L 1H5
Ph: (403)762-6331
Fax: (403)762-6422
Free: 800-590-9799
E-mail: leadership@banffcentre.ca
URL: banffcentre.ca
Facebook: www.facebook.com/thebanffcentre
Twitter: www.twitter.com/thebanffcentre

2181 ■ Alliance Pipeline Scholarships *(Other/ Scholarship)*

Purpose: To support non-profit leaders of Canadian charities in improving their leadership skills. **Focus:** Leadership, Institutional and community. **Qualif.:** Applicants must be employees of a registered Canadian charity under the Income Tax Act (Canada). **Criteria:** Priority will be given to individuals with organizations operating in a location where Alliance Pipelines has a business interest or association.

Funds Avail.: No specific amount. **Duration:** Annual. **To Apply:** Applicants must submit a completed application form along with a brief outline (on letterhead) of the applicants' organization's history, mission and activities and the role, responsibilities and length of service with the organization; reasons why assistance is required; anticipated benefits from participating in the program; a description of how the applicants will share the learning from the program with the team, organization and throughout the

Awards are arranged alphabetically below their administering organizations

sector; the name of Supervisor or Board Chair; and the registered charity number with the Canada Revenue Agency (CRA).

2182 ■ Fraser Milner Casgrain Scholarships *(Other/Scholarship)*

Purpose: To support non-profit leaders of Canadian charities in improving their leadership skills. **Focus:** Leadership, Institutional and community. **Qualif.:** Applicant must be an employee, officer, director or designated agent of a registered Canadian charity under the Income Tax Act (Canada). **Criteria:** Selection is based on the submitted application materials.

Funds Avail.: $2,500. **To Apply:** Applicants must submit a completed application form together with a brief outline (on letterhead, one page) of the applicant's financial contribution to the program and the organization; the names of other agencies applied for funding and the amounts requested; reasons why assistance is required; the anticipated benefits from participating in the program; name of Supervisor of Board Chair; and the registered charity number with the Canada Revenue Agency (CRA). **Deadline:** June 30.

2183 ■ Investors Group Scholarships for Not-For-Profit Leaders *(Other/Scholarship)*

Purpose: To support non-profit leaders of Canadian charities in improving their leadership skills. **Focus:** Leadership, Institutional and community. **Qualif.:** Applicants must be employees of a registered Canadian charity under the Income Tax Act (Canada) and the organization must be located in Manitoba. **Criteria:** Priority will be given to individuals with organizations in the city of Winnipeg.

Funds Avail.: $4,583 each. **To Apply:** Applicants must submit a completed application form along with a brief outline (on letterhead) of the applicants' organization's history, mission, activities and the role, responsibilities and length of service with the organization; reasons why assistance is required; anticipated benefits from participating in the program; a description of how the applicants will sharing the learning from the program with the team, organization and throughout the sector; the name of Supervisor or Board Chair; and the registered charity number with the Canada Revenue Agency (CRA).

2184 ■ Lafarge Community Leaders Scholarships *(Other/Scholarship)*

Purpose: To support non-profit leaders of Canadian charities in improving their leadership skills. **Focus:** Leadership, Institutional and community. **Qualif.:** Applicant must be an employee of a Canadian non-profit organization. **Criteria:** Selection is based on the submitted application materials.

Funds Avail.: $4,000 each. **Duration:** Annual; 3 years. **Number Awarded:** 3. **To Apply:** Applicants must submit a completed application form along with a brief outline (on letterhead) of the applicant's organization's history, mission, activities and the role, responsibilities and length of service with the organization; reasons why assistance is required; anticipated benefits from participating in the program; a description of how the applicant will sharing the learnings from the program with the team, organization and throughout the sector; and the name of Supervisor or Board Chair.

2185 ■ Youth or the Environment Scholarships *(Other/Scholarship)*

Purpose: To support non-profit leaders of Canadian charities in improving their leadership skills. **Focus:** Leadership, Institutional and community. **Qualif.:** Applicant must be an employee, officer, director or designated agent of a Canadian registered charity under the Income Tax Act (Canada). The organization must have a substantial focus on either youth or the environment and be at a mid- or upper-level management position. The annual revenue of the organization must be under $3,000,000. **Criteria:** Selection is based on the submitted application materials.

Funds Avail.: No specific amount. **To Apply:** Applicants must submit a completed application form along with a brief outline (on letterhead) of the applicant's organization's history, mission, activities and role within the areas of focus; the applicant's role and responsibilities and length of service with the organization; the name of Supervisor or Board Chair; a resume; organization's most recent audited financial statements; and registered charity number with CRA.

2186 ■ Bank of Canada
234 Laurier Ave. W
Ottawa, ON, Canada K1A 0G9
Ph: (613)782-8111
Fax: (613)782-7713
Free: 800-303-1282
E-mail: info@bankofcanada.ca
URL: www.bankofcanada.ca

2187 ■ Bank of Canada Fellowship Award *(Doctorate, Other/Fellowship, Grant)*

Purpose: To provide financial support to students who have been recognized for their expertise and excellence in bank-related issues. **Focus:** Banking; Economics; Finance; Marketing and distribution. **Qualif.:** Applicants must be Canadian citizens, permanent residents or legally permitted to work in Canada; must have obtained a PhD degree; and be employed by a Canadian university during the tenure of the fellowship. **Criteria:** Candidates will be chosen based on 1) demonstrated excellence and innovation of their work; 2) applicability to Bank of Canada policy development and/or research; 3) potential to achieve recognition as leaders in the special fields as indicated by consistent high-quality work in publications or presentations; and 4) potential to make contributions in education and development of new researchers.

Funds Avail.: $50,000 for research grant; $40,000 for research expense allowance per year. **Duration:** Annual; up to five years. **To Apply:** Applicants must submit a cover page; letter of nomination from the university; curriculum vitae; current research program and plans (maximum of six, single-sided pages); current research paper and four abstracts; referee information. Materials should appear as a PDF document. Referees are also required to submit two letters of reference (signed and on official letterhead). **Deadline:** November 14. **Contact:** Bank of Canada Fellowship Award at: fellowship-bourses@bankofcanada.ca.

2188 ■ Bank of Canada Governor's Awards *(Doctorate, Other/Award, Grant)*

Purpose: To provide funds to exceptional assistant and associate professors working at Canadian universities who have made contributions in their fields. **Focus:** Business; Economics; Finance. **Qualif.:** Applicants must be Canadian citizens, permanent residents or legally permitted to work in Canada; must have obtained a PhD degree within ten years of application; and be employed by a Canadian university with a program in economics, business/finance as as-

Awards are arranged alphabetically below their administering organizations

sistants or associate professors during the tenure of the fellowship. **Criteria:** Candidates will be selected based on 1) demonstrated potential to make exemplary research contributions in the specified fields as indicated by publications of refereed and other articles; 2) applicability to Bank of Canada policy development and/or research; and 3) potential to make contributions in education and development of new researchers.
Funds Avail.: $25,000. **Duration:** Annual; up to two years. **To Apply:** Applicants must submit a cover page; letter of nomination from the university; curriculum vitae; current research program and plans (maximum six, single-sided pages); one current research paper and four abstracts (published and unpublished) and referee information. Materials should appear as a PDF document. Referees are also required to submit two letters of reference. **Deadline:** November 14. **Contact:** Governor's Award, Bank of Canada, Executive and Legal Services, at the above address; Email: fellowship-bourses@bankofcanada.ca.

2189 ■ Banner & Witcoff, Ltd.
10 S Wacker Dr., Ste. 3000
Chicago, IL 60606-7407
Ph: (312)463-5000
Fax: (312)463-5001
E-mail: info@bannerwitcoff.com
URL: www.bannerwitcoff.com

2190 ■ Donald W. Banner Diversity Scholarships for Law Students *(Graduate/Scholarship)*
Purpose: To foster the development of intellectual property lawyers from diverse backgrounds. **Focus:** Law. **Qualif.:** Applicants must be either 1L or 2L students who have entered into a JD program at an ABA-accredited law school in the United States. **Criteria:** Selection will be based on the committee's criteria. Priority will be given to those students who are members of a historically underrepresented minority group in IP law.
Funds Avail.: No specific amount. **Duration:** Annual. **To Apply:** Applicants must complete the Donald W. Banner Diversity Scholarship application form, available online; must submit a resume, academic transcripts (law, undergraduate/graduate school), a writing sample (5-10 pages), three references including contact information, and a one-page statement describing how diversity has impacted the candidate. **Contact:** Donald W. Banner Diversity Scholarship, c/o Christopher Hummel, at the above address.

2191 ■ Baptist Communicators Association (BCA)
c/o Margaret Colson, Executive Director
4519 Lashley Ct.
Marietta, GA 30068
Ph: (678)641-4457
E-mail: webmaster@baptistcommunicators.org
URL: www.baptistcommunicators.org
Facebook: www.facebook.com/BaptistComm
LinkedIn: www.linkedin.com/company/baptist
 -communicators-assn
Twitter: twitter.com/BaptistComm

2192 ■ Alan Compton and Bob Stanley Professional Scholarships *(Professional development/Scholarship)*
Purpose: To provide financial assistance to qualified or prospective members for attendance at a BCA-related workshop. **Focus:** General studies/Field of study not specified. **Qualif.:** Applicants must be minority-ethnic and international BCA members or prospective members. **Criteria:** Selection of scholarship recipients will be recommended to the Executive Committee by the Scholarship Committee.
Funds Avail.: Not to exceed $500.. **Duration:** Annual. **To Apply:** Application materials must include: a) name, address, and phone number of applicant; b) Current position/title, department and agency; c) Number of years worked in public relations/communications and number of years at the applicant's institution; d) Highest level of formal education attained and name of other professional development conferences or workshops attended in the past; e) copy of applicant's job description and resume; f) title and name of person to whom the applicant reports; g) statement of why financial assistance is needed and how much money is required. **Deadline:** March 1.

2193 ■ Al Shackleford and Dan Martin Professional Scholarships *(Professional development/Scholarship)*
Purpose: To provide financial assistance for attending BCA events. **Focus:** General studies/Field of study not specified. **Qualif.:** Applicants must be full-time BCA members. **Criteria:** Selection of scholarship recipients will be recommended to the Executive Committee by the Scholarship Committee.
Funds Avail.: $1,000. **Duration:** Annual. **To Apply:** Application materials must include: a) name, address, and phone number of applicant; b) Current position/title, department and agency; c) Number of years worked in public relations/communications and number of years at the applicant's institution; d) Highest level of formal education attained and name of other professional development conferences or workshops attended in the past; e) copy of applicant's job description and resume; f) title and name of person to whom the applicant reports; g) statement of why financial assistance is needed and how much money is required. **Deadline:** March 1.

2194 ■ Bar Association of San Francisco (BASF)
301 Battery St., 3rd Fl.
San Francisco, CA 94111
Ph: (415)982-1600
Fax: (415)477-2388
URL: www.sfbar.org

2195 ■ Bay Area Minority Law Student Scholarships *(Graduate, Undergraduate/Scholarship)*
Purpose: To provide financial assistance to qualified students from minority groups underrepresented in the law schools. **Focus:** Law. **Qualif.:** Applicants must be students from minority groups who are underrepresented in Bay Area law schools, and have received a "letter of admission" from one of the eight Northern California law schools. **Criteria:** Recipients will be selected based on the submitted application materials.
Funds Avail.: $10,000. **Duration:** Annual; Up to three years. **To Apply:** Applicants must submit the following: a completed application with official undergraduate or graduate transcript; 500-word personal statement; copies of current IRS tax forms; statement of economic need (optional); and, copies of "letters of admissions" from any ABA accredited law school in Northern California. **Deadline:** April 20. **Remarks:** Established in 1998. **Contact:** Elizabeth McGriff at emcgriff@sfbar.org.

Awards are arranged alphabetically below their administering organizations

2196 ■ Barrientos Scholarship Foundation (BSF)
PO Box 7173
Omaha, NE 68107
Ph: (402)215-5106
E-mail: info@barrientosscholarship.org
URL: www.barrientosscholarship.org

2197 ■ BSF General Scholarship Awards
(Undergraduate, Vocational/Occupational/Scholarship)

Purpose: To provide financial assistance to qualified students who want to pursue their studies. **Focus:** Interdisciplinary studies. **Qualif.:** Applicants must be students pursuing higher education and career goals that focus on disciplines other than arts; must be of Latino Heritage; must be high school graduating seniors, currently enrolled in college, or adults ready to pursue college; must plan to enroll in at least two classes and attend an accredited community college, university, or technical or vocational school in the State of Nebraska or surrounding greater Omaha Metropolitan area; must have a minimum of a 2.5 cumulative GPA. **Criteria:** Selection of applicants will be based on the criteria of the Scholarship Selection Committee.

Funds Avail.: Varies. **Number Awarded:** Multiple. **To Apply:** Applicants must have the application form available online; must have a personal essay with a minimum of two pages; must submit two letters of recommendation and official high school or college transcript. **Deadline:** May 1. **Contact:** Mail application to: Barrientos Scholarship Foundation, P.O. Box 7173, Omaha, NE 68107.

2198 ■ Barth Syndrome Foundation (BSF)
2005 Palmer Ave., No. 1033
Larchmont, NY 10538
Ph: (914)303-6323
Fax: (518)213-4061
Free: 855-662-2784
URL: www.barthsyndrome.org/home
Facebook: www.facebook.com/barthsyndromefoundation

2199 ■ BSF Science and Medicine Research Grants
(Professional development/Grant)

Purpose: To advance the state of knowledge about Barth Syndrome so that progress can be made in finding a specific treatment or cure for this unusual mitochondrial disease. **Focus:** Disabilities; Genetics. **Qualif.:** Applicants must be investigators at every professional level. **Criteria:** Applications will be scored on the basis of: importance and impact; feasibility; and prospect of long-term funding.

Funds Avail.: No specific amount. **Duration:** Annual. **To Apply:** Submitted application must be no more than 15 pages (including figures, tables and references) in length; single-sided, using a font size of 12 points and with one-inch margins; must contain the following elements: 1) completed information form; 2) an abstract summarizing the project; 3) a section presenting the specific aims of the project, stating both the objectives and the hypotheses to be tested in the project; 4) discussion of the background and significance of the work proposed, including a critical evaluation of previous research and existing knowledge, specifically identifying the gaps that the project is intended to fill, and explicitly stating the importance of the proposed research; 5) thorough summary of research design and methods, describing the experimental design and methods that will be used to accomplish the specific aims; 6) statement indicating whether human subjects or vertebrate animals will be involved in the research; 7) description of the resources and environment available for the project; 8) a list of project personnel (name, title, institution, and role of the project), including the percentage effort that each person is expected to devote to the project; and 9) detailed budget section for the proposed project, along with a separate narrative fully describing and justifying the expenses. **Deadline:** October 31.

2200 ■ Bat Conservation International (BCI)
PO Box 162603
Austin, TX 78716
Ph: (512)327-9721
Free: 800-538-BATS
URL: batcon.org

2201 ■ Bat Conservation International Student Research Scholarships *(Graduate, Undergraduate/Scholarship)*

Purpose: To support students in research initiatives that is essential in conserving bats and ecosystems. **Focus:** Wildlife conservation, management, and science. **Qualif.:** Applicants must be enrolled in any college or university who are conducting research that specifically addresses at least one of the specified areas of needs: (1) answering ecological or behavioral questions essential to conservation or management; (2) resolving an economic problem which will further conservation tolerance; (3) documenting key ecological or economic roles of bats; (4) educating people who are directly relevant to conservation success. **Criteria:** Award will be given to those applicants who have completed proposals that clearly address the conservation needs. Reviewers will rank all conservation-relevant proposals and fund those who have received the highest scores.

Funds Avail.: $1,000-$3,000. **Duration:** Annual. **Number Awarded:** 8-12. **To Apply:** Interested applicants may visit the website for the online application process. **Deadline:** April 30. **Remarks:** Established in 1982.

2202 ■ John Bayliss Broadcast Foundation
1771 N St. NW
Washington, DC 20036
Ph: (202)429-5355
Fax: (202)775-2981
URL: www.beaweb.org/bayliss.html
Facebook: www.facebook.com/The-John-Bayliss-Broadcast-Foundation-15731922609/info

2203 ■ John Bayliss Broadcast Foundation Internship Programs *(Undergraduate/Internship)*

Purpose: To assist students who are interested in a full-time career in Radio with innovative companies for an incomparable experience. **Focus:** Broadcasting. **Qualif.:** Applicants must be studying for a career in the radio industry and have taken basic journalism courses as well as specialized courses in the radio communication fields; must have previous radio-related experience; be enrolled in a degree program and entering their junior or senior year in college; must have a GPA of 3.0 or better; and must be at least 18 years of age. **Criteria:** Recipients are selected based on financial need and academic record.

Funds Avail.: No specific amount. **Duration:** Annual. **To Apply:** Applicants must submit a resume and complete the application form.

Awards are arranged alphabetically below their administering organizations

2204 ■ John Bayliss Broadcast Foundation Radio Scholarships *(Undergraduate/Scholarship)*

Purpose: To provide financial assistance to outstanding broadcast students. **Focus:** Broadcasting. **Qualif.:** Applicants must be entering their junior or senior year at an institution in the United States; must be preparing for a career in the radio industry, preferably commercial radio; must maintain a 3.0 GPA or better; and must demonstrate a high degree of integrity and a personal sense of responsibility. **Criteria:** Recipients are selected based on financial need, merit, history of radio-related activities, and based the demonstrated degree of integrity and a personal sense of responsibility.

Funds Avail.: $5,000. **Duration:** Annual. **To Apply:** Applicants must provide a typewritten resume; an official transcript; three letters of recommendation written by people other than relatives, a two-page typewritten essay describing their broadcasting goals as they relate to radio and the ways in which they hope to achieve their goals.

2205 ■ BDPA Education Technology Foundation (BETF)
4423 Lehigh Rd., No. 277
College Park, MD 20740
Ph: (513)284-4968
Fax: (202)318-2194
E-mail: info@betf.org
URL: www.betf.org

2206 ■ Eli Lilly and Company/Black Data Processing Associates Scholarships *(Undergraduate/Scholarship)*

Purpose: To provide outstanding minority students financial assistance in pursuing an information technology-related degree. **Focus:** Information science and technology. **Qualif.:** Applicants must be U.S. citizens or permanent residents and graduating high school seniors at the time of their application; must be pursuing an information technology-related degree at an accredited two or four-year college or university; must be student members of BDPA and participate in computer training activities. **Criteria:** Applicants are evaluated based on academic excellence; exceptional leadership potential; and impact through service to their communities.

Funds Avail.: $5,000. **Duration:** Annual. **To Apply:** Applicants must submit the completed application form; high school transcript; one 500-word essay explaining why information technology is important and the importance of personal commitment in giving back to your community; and two letters of recommendation. **Deadline:** July 7.

2207 ■ The Beatitudes Society
2345 Channing Way
Berkeley, CA 94704
URL: www.beatitudessociety.org
Facebook: www.facebook.com/BeatitudesSociety
Twitter: twitter.com/beats_society

2208 ■ Beatitudes Fellowships *(Professional development/Fellowship)*

Purpose: To assist young entrepreneurial faith leaders with the resources and relationships that empower them to create new models for church and the pursuit of social justice. **Focus:** Christian education. **Qualif.:** Eligible are emerging faith leaders who are: under the age of 40; within seven years of divinity school graduation; based in a community of faith; actively working to engage faith with social justice using a unique approach. **Criteria:** Selection will be based on a proven track record of leadership; a commitment to faith and to social justice; a willingness to take risks; a desire to collaborate with others; a specific project that matches up their deep gladness with the world's great need.

Funds Avail.: $5,000. **To Apply:** Fellows are nominated and then complete an application process that includes an online application and description of their project due, as well as a personal interview.

2209 ■ BECA Foundation
PO Box 936
Escondido, CA 92033
E-mail: webmaster@becafoundation.org
URL: www.becafoundation.org

2210 ■ BECA Foundation General Scholarships Fund *(Undergraduate/Scholarship)*

Purpose: To seek promising students and provide them with the necessary financial assistance, moral support and guidance to complete their education, thereby promoting higher educational and leadership standards within the Hispanic community. **Focus:** General studies/Field of study not specified. **Qualif.:** Applicant must be a San Diego County High School graduate who is entering college. **Criteria:** Recipients are selected based on financial need and merit; GPA; and community involvement.

Funds Avail.: $500 - $1,000. **To Apply:** Applicants must complete the application form online and must submit all required materials including an essay, two letters of recommendation in PDF or Word format and official transcripts. **Deadline:** April 1. **Contact:** scholarship@becafoundation.org.

2211 ■ Alice Newell Joslyn Medical Fund *(Undergraduate/Scholarship)*

Purpose: To seek promising students and provide them with the necessary financial assistance, moral support and guidance to complete their education, thereby promoting higher educational and leadership standards within the Hispanic community. **Focus:** Education, Medical. **Qualif.:** Applicants must be entering medical/health care professions (dental/medical assistant, nursing, physical therapist, or seeking their Bachelor of Science, Master's or Doctorate in the health field); must be residents of, or attending a high school or college in San Diego County at the time of application. **Criteria:** Recipients are selected based on financial need, scholastic determination, community and cultural awareness.

Funds Avail.: $500 - $2,000. **Duration:** Annual. **To Apply:** Applicants must complete the application form online and must submit all required materials including an essay, two letters of recommendation in PDF or Word format and official transcripts. **Deadline:** April 1. **Contact:** scholarship@becafoundation.org.

2212 ■ LAFS - Cal State University San Marcos General Scholarships *(Undergraduate/Scholarship)*

Purpose: To seek promising students and provide them with the necessary financial assistance, moral support and

Awards are arranged alphabetically below their administering organizations

guidance to complete their education, thereby promoting higher educational and leadership standards within the Hispanic community. **Focus:** General studies/Field of study not specified. **Qualif.:** Applicants must be Latino students enrolled at CSU San Marcos. Must be in good academic (2.0 GPA) administrative standing at CSUSM. Graduate students in an approved post-bachelors program. **Criteria:** Recipients are selected based on financial need, scholastic determination and community and cultural awareness.

Funds Avail.: No specific amount. **To Apply:** Applicants must complete the application form online and must submit all required materials including an essay, two letters of recommendation in PDF or Word format and official transcripts. **Deadline:** April 1. **Contact:** scholarship@becafoundation.org.

2213 ■ Beinecke Rare Book and Manuscript Library

121 Wall St.
New Haven, CT 06511
Ph: (203)432-2977
Fax: (203)432-4047
E-mail: beinecke.library@yale.edu
URL: beinecke.library.yale.edu

2214 ■ Beinecke Rare Book and Manuscript Library Visiting Postdoctoral Scholar Fellowships *(Postdoctorate/Fellowship)*

Purpose: To support visiting scholars, and provide access to the library for scholars who live outside the greater New Haven area. **Focus:** Library and archival sciences. **Qualif.:** Applicants must be visiting scholars pursuing post-doctoral or equivalent research in its collections. **Criteria:** Selection will be based on the committee's criteria.

Funds Avail.: No specific amount. **Duration:** Annual. **To Apply:** Applicants are asked to submit the following items to the Fellowship Selection Committee: online and printed copy of application form including the materials; curriculum vitae; a maximum of 1,200 words research proposal; detailed list of specific research materials to be consulted at Beinecke during the fellowship; two confidential letters of recommendation sent to the Beinecke Director, specifically addressing the merits of the proposed fellowship project; self-addressed, stamped postcard with the applicants' materials. **Deadline:** December 6.

2215 ■ Yale Graduate and Professional Students Research Fellowships *(Graduate, Professional development/Fellowship)*

Purpose: To support students who wish to use Beinecke collections as a primary resource for their dissertations or culminating projects. **Focus:** Library and archival sciences. **Qualif.:** Applicants must be graduate students who have completed their course work, passed their qualifying examinations and be prepared to pursue research based upon an approved prospectus; professional school students must be engaged in research for an approved culminating project required for their degree, with the expectation that their project will be undertaken in the final year of their program. **Criteria:** Selection will be based on a competitive basis.

Funds Avail.: Range from $3,000 to $13,650. **Duration:** Annual. **To Apply:** Applicants must submit the following materials to the Director of the Beinecke Library: an application form; curriculum vitae; a maximum of 1,200 words proposal explaining in detail the specific relationship between the Beinecke Collection and the applicant's research; a detailed list of specific research materials to be consulted at Beinecke during the fellowship; two confidential letters of recommendation sent to the Beinecke Director, one of which must come from the principal director of the applicant's dissertation or culminating project; for graduate students, approved or pending prospectus; for professional school students, a statement explaining how their project fulfills the culminating requirement in their school. **Deadline:** March 6; October 17.

2216 ■ Bel Canto Vocal Scholarship Foundation

55 Tremont St.
Cranston, RI 02920
URL: www.belcantoscholarship.com

2217 ■ Bel Canto Vocal Scholarship Foundation Vocal Competition *(Graduate/Award, Scholarship)*

Purpose: To support the education of young, talented opera singers. **Focus:** Opera. **Qualif.:** Contestants must be U.S. citizens with proof of citizenship, and must be 21 to 33 years old. **Criteria:** Selection is based on the application materials submitted.

Funds Avail.: No specific amount. **To Apply:** Candidates must audition for the Vocal Competition. **Contact:** Mr. Ronald DiPanni, Chairman/Auditions Committee; Email: rjdipanni@cox.net.

2218 ■ Max Bell Foundation

1201 5th St. SW Ste. 380
Calgary, AB, Canada T2R 0Y6
Ph: (403)215-7310
Fax: (403)215-7319
URL: www.maxbell.org

2219 ■ Max Bell Senior Fellow Grants *(Advanced Professional/Grant)*

Purpose: To add value to debates over critical public policy issues in health and wellness, education and environment. **Focus:** Environmental science; Health education; Public health. **Qualif.:** Candidates must be Canadian residents or eligible for retention in keeping with Canadian charitable law. **Criteria:** Selection of recipients will be based on the application.

Funds Avail.: Amount varies. **Duration:** Annual. **Number Awarded:** 1. **To Apply:** Candidates must follow the application process described on the "Apply For Support" page at the program website and indicate in the project title that they are applying for the Senior Fellow grant. The Foundation will review their Letter of Intent and contact them to follow up. Where warranted, they will be asked to develop a full proposal and will be interviewed in person by a Committee of the Board of Directors.

2220 ■ Ben Meadows Company Inc.

401 S Wright Rd.
Janesville, WI 53546
Fax: (800)628-2068
Free: 800-241-6401
E-mail: mail@benmeadows.com
URL: www.benmeadows.com

Awards are arranged alphabetically below their administering organizations

2221 ■ Ben Meadows Natural Resource Scholarships - Academic Achievement Scholarships (Undergraduate/Scholarship)

Purpose: To provide fund for students enrolled in a natural resource program. **Focus:** Environmental science; Fisheries sciences/management; Forestry; Natural resources; Wildlife conservation, management, and science. **Qualif.:** Applicant must be a junior or senior student enrolled in a natural resource program working toward a bachelor of arts or science degree, which includes, but not limited to, agro forestry, urban forestry, environmental studies, natural resource management, natural resource recreation, wildlife management, wood science and fisheries management. Student must have a GPA of 3.2 or higher on a 4.0 scale. **Criteria:** Award is given based on the application.

Funds Avail.: $2,500. **To Apply:** Applicant must complete the online scholarship application and must provide a letter of recommendation from educational superior (professor, teacher, advisor); must attach official copies of transcripts reflecting the GPA; must provide a list of clubs, activities and years involved; summary of accomplishments relating to the field of study; and 300 words essay on how these leadership roles help grow and expand interest of the chosen field. **Deadline:** June 30.

2222 ■ Ben Meadows Natural Resource Scholarships - Leadership Scholarships (Undergraduate/Scholarship)

Purpose: To provide fund for students enrolled in a natural resource program. **Focus:** Environmental science; Fisheries sciences/management; Forestry; Natural resources; Wildlife conservation, management, and science. **Qualif.:** Applicant must be a junior or senior student enrolled in a natural resource program working toward a bachelor of arts or science degree, which includes, but not limited to, agro forestry, urban forestry, environmental studies, natural resource management, natural resource recreation, wildlife management, wood science and fisheries management. Student must have a GPA of 2.5 or higher on a 4.0 scale. **Criteria:** Award is given based on the application.

Funds Avail.: $2,500. **To Apply:** Applicant must complete the online scholarship application and must provide a letter of recommendation from educational superior (professor, teacher, advisor), and attach official copies of transcripts reflecting the GPA; must provide a list of leadership roles, clubs and years involved; summary of involvement and projects within leadership roles relating to the field of study; and essay of 300 words on how these leadership roles have helped grow and expand interest of chosen field. **Deadline:** June 30.

2223 ■ Benign Essential Blepharospasm Research Foundation (BEBRF)
637 N 7th St., Ste. 102
Beaumont, TX 77702
Ph: (409)832-0788
Fax: (409)832-0890
E-mail: bebrf@blepharospasm.org
URL: www.blepharospasm.org

2224 ■ Benign Essential Blepharospasm Research Foundation Research Grants (Doctorate, Postdoctorate/Grant)

Purpose: To support research directly related to blepharospasm or Meige's Syndrome, both forms of cranial dystonia. **Focus:** Medicine. **Qualif.:** Principal investigators must hold M.D. or Ph.D. and intend to conduct researches that relate specifically to benign essential blepharospasm and Meige covering new treatments, pathophysiology and genetics, photophobia and dry eye; non-US citizens working at institutions abroad are eligible to apply. **Criteria:** Recipients are selected based on committee's review of the proposal.

Funds Avail.: $150,000. **Duration:** Annual. **To Apply:** Applicants must send curriculum vitae and eight copies of proposals with consent form and necessary signatures. Specific grant guidelines and forms are available on the website. **Deadline:** August 31.

2225 ■ Benton County Foundation (BCF)
660 NW Harrison Blvd.
Corvallis, OR 97330
Ph: (541)753-1603
URL: www.bcfgives.org

2226 ■ Margaret Dowell-Gravatt, M.D. Scholarships (Undergraduate/Scholarship)

Purpose: To encourage and support ethnic minority undergraduate women enrolled in the College of Science. **Focus:** Medical technology; Medicine; Microbiology; Nursing; Occupational therapy; Physical therapy; Zoology. **Qualif.:** Applicant must: be pursuing a degree in Zoology or Microbiology or one of the following pre-health programs: Medical Technology, Medicine, Nursing, Physical and/or Occupational therapy. Applicant must: be enrolled full-time at the sophomore, junior or senior level; have a GPA of 2.5 overall and 3.0 in science courses required in their major field or pre-health curriculum; qualify for financial assistance as defined by the Financial Aid Office of OSU. **Criteria:** Selection will be based on the committee's criteria.

Funds Avail.: No specific amount. **To Apply:** Applicant may contact the Foundation for application form and other requirements.

2227 ■ Joel R. Friend Scholarships (Undergraduate/Scholarship)

Purpose: To provide scholarship opportunity to the students from OSU. **Focus:** General studies/Field of study not specified. **Qualif.:** Applicants must be foreign students from Thailand, Taiwan (Republic of China) in attendance at OSU in any field of study; must qualify for financial assistance as defined by the Financial Aid Office of OSU. **Criteria:** Selection will be based on the committee's criteria.

Funds Avail.: No specific amount. **To Apply:** Applicant may contact the Foundation for application form and other requirements.

2228 ■ William Harrison Gill Education Fund (Undergraduate/Scholarship)

Purpose: To provide scholarship to the students of Oregon State University. **Focus:** General studies/Field of study not specified. **Qualif.:** Applicant must: be of Native American descent; be an American citizen with a permanent or guardian residence in one of the following states: Arizona, California, Colorado, Idaho, Montana, Nevada, New Mexico, Oregon, Utah, Washington or Wyoming; and must be students enrolled at Oregon State University. **Criteria:** Selection will be based on the committee's criteria.

Funds Avail.: No specific amount. **To Apply:** Applicant may contact the Foundation for application process and other requirements.

Awards are arranged alphabetically below their administering organizations

2229 ■ Lucy Hsu Ho Scholarships (Undergraduate/Scholarship)

Purpose: To award scholarship to the foreign students of ethnic Chinese descent. **Focus:** General studies/Field of study not specified. **Qualif.:** Applicants must be foreign students of ethnic Chinese descent; primary preference in awarding the scholarship shall be given to those candidates who have demonstrated leadership in student and/or community activities and organizations, as well as the desire to serve others in the candidate's future chosen field of work. Secondary preference shall be determined by level of financial need; must re-apply for this scholarship each year; must qualify for financial assistance as defined by the Financial Aid Office of OSU. **Criteria:** Selection will be based on the committee's criteria.

Funds Avail.: No specific amount. **To Apply:** Applicants may contact the Foundation for the application process and other required materials.

2230 ■ Kilbuck Family Native American Scholarships (Undergraduate/Scholarship)

Purpose: To provide scholarship opportunity to the students enrolled at Oregon State University. **Focus:** General studies/Field of study not specified. **Qualif.:** Applicant must have a cumulative GPA of 3.0 or above; have at least 1/16 enrolled or documented tribal affiliation; must be a graduate of Oregon or Alaska high schools. Scholarship is renewable for up to 12 terms if a 3.0 cumulative GPA is maintained. **Criteria:** Selection will be based on the committee's criteria.

Funds Avail.: No specific amount. **To Apply:** Applicant may contact the Foundation for application process and other requirements.

2231 ■ David W. Schacht Native American Student Scholarships (Undergraduate/Scholarship)

Purpose: To provide scholarship to the students of Oregon State University. **Focus:** General studies/Field of study not specified. **Qualif.:** Applicants must: be students of Native American descent, defined as self-identified individuals with tribal affiliation; have demonstrated ability and scholarship during high school or during previous college years; must qualify for financial assistance as defined by the Financial Aid Office of OSU. **Criteria:** Selection will be based on the committee's criteria.

Funds Avail.: No specific amount. **To Apply:** Applicant may contact the Foundation for application form and other requirements.

2232 ■ Helen J. and Harold Gilman Smith Scholarships (Graduate, Undergraduate/Scholarship)

Purpose: To provide scholarship to the students pursuing their first baccalaureate or graduate degree in any field of study. **Focus:** General studies/Field of study not specified. **Qualif.:** Applicant must: be a Native American student; have a minimum GPA of 2.75 for their undergraduate freshman year. Graduate students must maintain the minimum GPA level required by their college graduate degree program. Preference is given to students graduating from an American Indian high school. Applicant must qualify for financial assistance as defined by the Financial Aid Office of OSU. **Criteria:** Selection will be based on the committee's criteria.

Funds Avail.: No specific amount. **To Apply:** Applicant may contact the Foundation for application form and other requirements.

2233 ■ Hugh and Helen Wood Nepales Scholarships (Undergraduate/Scholarship)

Purpose: To provide scholarship to the students who are current citizens of Nepal. **Focus:** General studies/Field of study not specified. **Qualif.:** Applicants must be current students who are citizens of Nepal; primary preference in awarding the scholarship shall be given to those candidates who agree to become a public servant in Nepal for at least five years following graduation. Other requirements include: a 3.5 GPA; a minimum TOEFL score of 550 or other language competency score satisfactory to the university: and all preparatory work completed in Nepal. Secondary consideration will be given to African American students if no Nepalese students meet the requirements. **Criteria:** Selection will be based on the committee's criteria.

Funds Avail.: No specific amount. **To Apply:** Applicants may contact the Foundation for application form and other requirements.

2234 ■ Berks County Community Foundation (BCCF)
237 Court St.
Reading, PA 19601
Ph: (610)685-2223
Fax: (610)685-2240
E-mail: info@bccf.org
URL: www.bccf.org

2235 ■ Howard Fox Memorial Law Scholarships (Graduate/Scholarship)

Purpose: To provide scholarships to graduates of Berks County, PA, high schools who are entering their second year at an accredited law school, who demonstrate financial need, without discrimination to color, race, national origin or religion. **Focus:** Law. **Qualif.:** Applicants must be Berks County residents entering their second year at an accredited law school who demonstrate financial need, without discrimination to color, race, national origin or religion. **Criteria:** Recipients will be selected based on financial need.

Funds Avail.: $3,000. **Duration:** Annual. **To Apply:** Applicants must submit the following: completed application form with two letters of reference from people who are not related to them; a copy of law school transcript; and a written recommendation from a professor at the law school they are attending. **Deadline:** April 4. **Remarks:** The fund is in memory of Howard Fox who was a member of the Berks County Bar Association and an attorney in the Public Defenders Office at the time of his accidental death.

2236 ■ Best Price Nutrition
5 Earl Ct., Unit No. 160
Woodridge, IL 60517
Ph: (708)478-8143
Free: 800-499-4810
URL: www.bestpricenutrition.com

2237 ■ Best Price Nutrition and Health Scholarships (Undergraduate/Scholarship)

Purpose: To provide financial aid to students who are pursuing their educational goal. **Focus:** General studies/Field of study not specified. **Qualif.:** Applicants must be high school students; must be college students currently enrolled full-time, or alumni; must be residents of the United

Awards are arranged alphabetically below their administering organizations

States. **Criteria:** Selection will be based on the committee's criteria.

Funds Avail.: $1,000. **Number Awarded:** 1. **To Apply:** Interested applicants must go to http://www.bestpricenutrition.com/scholarship.html for the online application process. **Deadline:** December 31.

2238 ■ Beta Phi Mu
PO Box 42139
Philadelphia, PA 19101
Ph: (267)361-5018
E-mail: betaphimu@drexel.edu
URL: beta-phi-mu.org

2239 ■ Eugene Garfield Doctoral Dissertation Fellowship *(Doctorate/Fellowship)*

Purpose: To support doctoral students who are working on their dissertations in Library and Information Science, Information Studies, Informatics, or a related field. **Focus:** Information science and technology; Library and archival sciences. **Qualif.:** Candidates must be enrolled in a doctoral-level research program at an institution with ALA, CILIP, or other Beta Phi Mu Executive Board approved accreditation.

Funds Avail.: $3,000 each. **Duration:** Annual. **Number Awarded:** Up to 6. **To Apply:** Requirements include: curriculum vitae; meeting your program's requirements for advancement to candidacy; abstract of dissertation (300 word limit); letter from Dean or Director indicating dissertation topic has been approved; proof that applicant's candidacy has been advanced and that all requirements for degree except writing and defense of dissertation have been completed; three letters of recommendation; and personal statement from applicant not to exceed 500 words relating to post-dissertation plans. **Deadline:** March 15.

2240 ■ Harold Lancour Scholarship for Foreign Study *(Professional development/Scholarship)*

Purpose: Provided to Librarians for research or a special course of study to survey foreign libraries or programs outside North America. **Focus:** Library and archival sciences.

Funds Avail.: $1,750. **Duration:** Annual. **To Apply:** Requirements include: curriculum vitae; one or two page description of the planned foreign study with some indication of plans to use the information gained. Include any previous experience in foreign travel or study as well as any languages you can read or write. Scholarship will be awarded on a) Plan of study or research; and b) Usefulness of the study or research to the applicant and to the profession. **Deadline:** March 15.

2241 ■ Frank B. Sessa Scholarship *(Professional development/Scholarship)*

Purpose: Provided to a Beta Phi Mu member to increase his/her professional skills through additional study or attendance at a formal program or workshop. **Focus:** General studies/Field of study not specified. **Qualif.:** Must be a Beta Phi Mu member.

Funds Avail.: $1,500. **Duration:** Annual. **To Apply:** Requirements include: curriculum vitae; name of Beta Phi Mu chapter and year of induction; and one or two page description of applicant's plan for study and its relevance to the applicant's present job and plans for the future. **Deadline:** March 15.

2242 ■ Blanche E. Woolls Scholarships *(Graduate/Scholarship)*

Purpose: To provide support for a student beginning Library and Information Studies at an ALA-accredited school with the intention of pursuing a career in school library media service. **Focus:** Library and archival sciences. **Qualif.:** Applicants must be admitted to graduate programs in library and information studies accredited by the American Library Association and have not completed more than 12 hours by the Fall semester following to the application deadline. They must have the clear intention in pursuing a career in school library and media service. **Criteria:** Applicants will be judged on several factors but the autobiographical note is the prime importance.

Funds Avail.: $2,250. **Duration:** Annual. **Number Awarded:** 1. **To Apply:** Applicants must submit the completed application form together with typed one-page autobiography; current transcripts from all institutions of higher learning; and five letters of recommendation from academic instructors, employers or supervisors of paid volunteer work experience. All applications and documents must be scanned and sent via e-mail. **Deadline:** March 15. **Contact:** betaphimu@drexel.edu.

2243 ■ Beta Pi Sigma Sorority
256 Waterville St.
San Francisco, CA 94124
Ph: (415)467-0717
E-mail: bpssi@betapisigmasorority.org
URL: betapisigmasorority.org
LinkedIn: www.linkedin.com/company/beta-pi-sigma-sorority-inc

2244 ■ Beta Pi Sigma Sorority Scholarships (BPSSS) *(Undergraduate/Scholarship)*

Purpose: To provide educational assistance to graduating high school seniors. **Focus:** General studies/Field of study not specified. **Qualif.:** Applicants must be graduating high school seniors. **Criteria:** Application requirements are determined by the local chapter's scholarship committee.

Duration: Annual. **To Apply:** Applicants may contact the Association for application process and other information.

2245 ■ Beta Theta Pi
5134 Bonham Rd.
Oxford, OH 45056
Fax: (513)523-2381
Free: 800-800-2382
E-mail: beta@beta.org
URL: www.betathetapi.org
Facebook: www.facebook.com/betathetapi

2246 ■ Seth R. and Corrine H. Brooks Memorial Scholarships *(Undergraduate/Scholarship)*

Purpose: To financially assist students in their pursuit of academic achievement. **Focus:** General studies/Field of study not specified. **Qualif.:** Applicants must be students who will be attending college (including post-graduate students). They could also be sons or daughters of a Beta alumnus. **Criteria:** Recipients will be selected based on academic achievement and level of involvement on campus or community.

Funds Avail.: $1,300. **Duration:** Annual. **Number**

Awards are arranged alphabetically below their administering organizations

Awarded: 2. **To Apply:** Applicants must submit a complete application form; most current transcript of records; and a cover letter stating the reason for desiring a scholarship and academic plans. **Deadline:** April 15.

2247 ■ Bethesda Lutheran Communities
600 Hoffmann Dr.
Watertown, WI 53094
Ph: (920)261-3050
Fax: (920)261-8441
Free: 800-369-4636
URL: bethesdalutherancommunities.org

2248 ■ Lutheran Student Scholastic and Service Scholarships - College and University Students *(Undergraduate/Scholarship)*

Purpose: To financially support Lutheran students pursuing degrees in any area of service to people with developmental disabilities. **Focus:** Mental health. **Qualif.:** Applicants must be active communicant members of a Lutheran church; have achieved sophomore status or higher at a college or university; have a 3.0 overall GPA; and have an interest in a career in the field of developmental disabilities. **Criteria:** Selection of recipients will be in a competitive basis. Criteria include are the said qualifications and compliance with the application process.

Funds Avail.: $3,000. **Duration:** Annual. **Number Awarded:** 2. **To Apply:** Applicants must submit a completed application form together with an essay (250 to 300 words) on planned career in the field of developmental disabilities; four letters of recommendations; an official college transcript; an autobiography (one-page, double-spaced); a documentation of service to people who are developmentally disabled (minimum of 100 hours); and other materials helpful for the application. **Deadline:** May 1. **Contact:** Barb Schulz: Phone: 920-206-4427; 800-369-4636, ext. 4427; Email: barb.schultz@mailblc.org.

2249 ■ Bethune-Cookman University (B-CU)
640 Dr. Mary McLeod Bethune Blvd.
Daytona Beach, FL 32114-301
Ph: (386)481-2000
URL: www.cookman.edu
Facebook: www.facebook.com/bethunecookmanuniv
Twitter: twitter.com/bethunecookman

2250 ■ Bethune-Cookman University Excelsior Scholarship Level 1 *(Undergraduate/Scholarship)*

Purpose: To provide financial assistance for students intending to pursue their education. **Focus:** General studies/Field of study not specified. **Qualif.:** Applicants must be students who complete high school in May or June prior to enrolling into B-CU in the subsequent Fall semester. They must have a cumulative GPA of 3.5 (must earn and maintain 3.3 cumulative GPA to renew the award) and have test scores of SAT 1560 or ACT composite 23. **Criteria:** Selection will be based on merit.

Funds Avail.: No specific amount. **Duration:** Annual; Up to 3 years. **To Apply:** Applicants must provide enrollment fee (non-refundable) and a copy of Social Security Card.

2251 ■ Bethune-Cookman University Presidential Scholarships *(Undergraduate/Scholarship)*

Purpose: To provide financial assistance to students intending to pursue their education. **Focus:** General studies/Field of study not specified. **Qualif.:** Applicants must be students who complete high school in May or June prior to enrolling into B-CU in the subsequent Fall semester. They must have a cumulative GPA of 3.75 (must earn and maintain 3.4 cumulative GPA to renew the award) and have test scores of SAT 1820 or ACT composite 26. **Criteria:** Selection will be based on merit.

Funds Avail.: No spedific amount. **Duration:** Annual; Up to 4 years. **To Apply:** Applicants must provide enrollment fee (non-refundable) and a copy of Social Security Card.

2252 ■ Noorali Bharwani Professional Corp.
821A 5th St. SW
Medicine Hat, AB, Canada T1A 4H7
Ph: (403)527-0099
Fax: (403)529-0711
URL: nbharwani.com

2253 ■ Dr. Noorali and Sabiya Bharwani Endowment *(Undergraduate/Scholarship)*

Purpose: To provide financial assistance to qualified individuals who want to pursue their studies. **Focus:** Nursing. **Qualif.:** Applicants must be first year nursing students with a minimum GPA of B, equivalent of 3.0. **Criteria:** Preference will be given to students with financial need.

Funds Avail.: No specific amount. **Duration:** Annual. **To Apply:** For further information about the scholarship and application form, applicants are advice to contact Noorali Bharwani Professional Corporation.

2254 ■ Hussein Jina Bharwani Memorial Endowment *(Undergraduate/Scholarship)*

Purpose: To provide financial assistance to qualified individuals who want to pursue their studies. **Focus:** Nursing. **Qualif.:** Applicants must: be nursing students having completed the second year of the nursing program; have maintained a GPA of 3.0 or better; have demonstrated a keen interest in the nursing patient; demonstrate strong clinical skills including good organization and assessment skills; and, have the ability to establish a positive and constructive rapport with patients, their families and co-workers. **Criteria:** Recipients will be selected based on the committee's review of the application materials.

Funds Avail.: No specific amount. **Duration:** Annual. **To Apply:** For further information about the scholarship and application form, applicants are advice to contact Noorali Bharwani Professional Corporation.

2255 ■ Bibliographical Society of America (BSA)
PO Box 1537, Lenox Hill Sta.
New York, NY 10021
Ph: (212)452-2710
Fax: (212)452-2710
E-mail: bsa@bibsocamer.org
URL: www.bibsocamer.org

2256 ■ Katharine Pantzer Fellowships in the British Book Trades *(Other/Fellowship)*

Purpose: To support sustained research in topics relating to book production history in Britain and other related aspects. **Focus:** Library and archival sciences; Printing--History. **Qualif.:** Application is open to individuals conducting research on topics relating to book production and

Awards are arranged alphabetically below their administering organizations

distribution in Britain during the hand-press period as well as studies of authorship, reading and collecting based on the examination of British books published in that period. **Criteria:** Awards are given based on merit.

Funds Avail.: $3,000. **Duration:** Annual. **To Apply:** Applications should include the following: application form; project proposal of no more than 1,000 words; curriculum vitae; and, two signed letters of recommendation on official letterhead submitted independently by referees. Letters submitted electronically as a signed PDF via e-mail are preferable, although postal submissions will be accepted. **Deadline:** December 1. **Contact:** Fellowship Committee at: bsafellowships@bibsocamer.org.

2257 ■ Bibliographical Society of Canada (BSC)
360 Bloor St. W
Toronto, ON, Canada M5S 3C9
URL: www.bsc-sbc.ca

2258 ■ Bernard Amtmann Fellowships (Postgraduate, Other/Fellowship)

Purpose: To support the work of a scholar engaged in some area of bibliographical research, including textual studies and publishing history and with a particular emphasis on Canada. **Focus:** General studies/Field of study not specified. **Qualif.:** Applicants must be members of the Bibliographical Society of Canada. **Criteria:** Scholarship recipient will be selected based on scholastic ability. Preference is given to applicants who display great interest in research work.

Funds Avail.: No specific amount. **Duration:** Annual. **To Apply:** Application forms are available at the website.

2259 ■ Marie Tremaine Fellowships (Postgraduate, Other/Fellowship)

Purpose: To support the work of a scholar engaged in some area of bibliographical research, including textual studies and publishing history and with a particular emphasis on Canada. **Focus:** General studies/Field of study not specified. **Qualif.:** Applicants must be members of the Bibliographical Society of Canada. **Criteria:** Scholarship recipient will be selected based on scholastic ability. Preference is given to applicants who display great interest in research work.

Funds Avail.: $2,000. **Duration:** One year. **To Apply:** Application form will be available at the website. Application should includes the summary and description of the project, budget and must provide references. **Deadline:** February 28. **Remarks:** Established in 1987 in memory of and through the generosity of Marie Tremaine, the doyenne of Canadian bibliographers.

2260 ■ Big Sandy Community and Technical College (BSCTC)
1 Bert T. Combs Dr.
Prestonsburg, KY 41653
Ph: (606)886-3863
Free: 855-GOB-SCTC
URL: www.bigsandy.kctcs.edu

2261 ■ Kentucky Educational Excellence Scholarships (Undergraduate/Scholarship)

Purpose: To provide financial support for deserving Kentucky high school students and GED recipients who are intending to pursue their education. **Focus:** General studies/Field of study not specified. **Qualif.:** Applicants must: be high school students; be U.S. citizens, nationals or permanent residents; be residents of Kentucky; have earned at least a 2.5 GPA in any year of high school while meeting the KEES curriculum requirements; attend and graduate from a certified Kentucky high school or other approved high school; and, not be convicted felons. High school graduates applying for a KEES bonus award must have at least an ACT composite score of 15 or a score of 710 or higher on the SAT and must have earned at least a 2.5 GPA in any year of high school while meeting the KEES curriculum requirements. Home school graduates applying for a KEES bonus award must have an ACT composite score of 15 or better on a national exam; GED graduate applicants must have an ACT composite score of 15 or better on a national exam; must have earned a GED in Kentucky within five years of turning 18 years old. **Criteria:** Selection will be based on merit.

Funds Avail.: No specific amount. **Duration:** Annual. **To Apply:** Applicants are advised to contact KEES for scholarship information and instructions.

2262 ■ KHEAA Teacher Scholarship (Undergraduate/Scholarship)

Purpose: To provide financial aid for highly qualified Kentucky students intending to pursue initial teacher certification at participating Kentucky institutions. **Focus:** Teaching. **Qualif.:** Applicants must: be residents of Kentucky who are enrolled full-time in a teacher certification program; demonstrate financial need; and, meet their institution's educational program GPA requirements. **Criteria:** Priority will be given to financially incapable applicants.

Funds Avail.: No specific amount. **Duration:** Annual. **To Apply:** Applicants must complete application package which include the Free Application for Federal Student Aid and a Teacher Scholarship application. Applicants are advised to contact the Federal Student Aid Information Center at the above address.

2263 ■ BioCommunications Association (BCA)
c/o Connie Johansen, President
1394 Redwood Cir.
Laplata, MD 20646
Ph: (571)557-1971
URL: www.bca.org

2264 ■ Endowment Fund for Education Grants (Undergraduate/Grant)

Purpose: To provide funds for projects which assist in the education of persons actively pursuing careers in biological imaging. **Focus:** Biological and clinical sciences. **Qualif.:** Applicants must be students, trainees, biocommunicator or institutional program that can demonstrate a need for project funding. Students currently enrolled in sophomore, junior or senior years must be in good academic standing for all courses directly related to their major. **Criteria:** Fund Committee will evaluate the complete applications. Selection of applicants will be based on merit and availability of funds.

Funds Avail.: Maximum of $500. **Duration:** Annual. **To Apply:** Applicants must submit the following documentation: (1) Current curriculum vitae; (2) A full and complete statement of what the applicant/ applicants intend(s) to accomplish within the field of biological photography; (3) Time frame for the project; (4) Details of how the project will

Awards are arranged alphabetically below their administering organizations

benefit biomedical communications and biocommunicators as a whole, and of how this will be measured; (5) An agreement to provide the EFFE Committee with a final report describing the results of the project and its impact on biocommunication; (6) Description of plan to share the resulting educational benefits with the BCA membership; (7) An agreement that the BioCommunications Association, Inc., shall have the right of first publication on any results from project funded wholly or partially from the Endowment Fund for Education. **Deadline:** February 1.

2265 ■ Endowment Fund for Education, Loans *(Undergraduate/Loan)*

Purpose: To provide funds for projects which assist in the education of persons actively pursuing careers in biological imaging. **Focus:** Biological and clinical sciences. **Qualif.:** Applicants must be high school students or students currently enrolled in their freshman year at a university or college; must present documentary evidence to demonstrate that they are in good academic standing for all courses directly related to their major (for sophomore, junior and senior years of high school). **Criteria:** Fund Committees will evaluate the complete applications. Selection of applicants will be based on merit and availability of funds.

Funds Avail.: $500 or less. **Duration:** Annual. **To Apply:** Applicants must submit the following documentation: (1) Current curriculum vitae; (2) A financial statement; (3) High school graduates applying for a loan to be used as tuition for the freshman year must present documentation to assure the EFFE Committee that they are in good academic standing for their full senior year. Application forms are available online. **Deadline:** April 30.

2266 ■ Endowment Fund for Education, Loans/ Grants for Educational Materials *(Undergraduate/ Grant)*

Purpose: To provide funds for projects which assist in the education of persons actively pursuing careers in biological imaging. **Focus:** Biological and clinical sciences. **Qualif.:** Applicants must be currently enrolled in sophomore, junior or senior years and must present documentary evidence to demonstrate that they are in good academic standing for all courses directly related to their major. **Criteria:** Fund Committees will evaluate all the submitted applications. Selection of applicants will be based on merit and availability of funds.

Funds Avail.: Maximum of $500. **Duration:** Annual. **To Apply:** Applicants must submit the following materials: (1) A complete description of the materials to be purchased; (2) Information about where the materials will be housed and who is to be responsible for their security; (3) Details on how the materials will be made available to the students; (4) The life expectancy of the materials; (5) The relevance of the material to biophotography; (6) The number of students who will use the materials; (7) The total cost and supplier of the materials. **Deadline:** April 30.

2267 ■ Endowment Fund for Education, Loans/ Grants for Equipment *(Undergraduate/Grant)*

Purpose: To provide funds for projects which assist in the education of persons actively pursuing careers in biological imaging. **Focus:** Biological and clinical sciences. **Qualif.:** Applicants must be currently enrolled in sophomore, junior and senior years and must present documentary evidence to demonstrate that they are in good academic standing for all courses directly related to their major. **Criteria:** Fund Committees will evaluate all submitted applications. Selection of applicants will be based on merit and availability of funds.

Funds Avail.: Maximum of $500. **Duration:** Annual. **To Apply:** Applicants must submit the following documentation: (1) A complete description of each piece of equipment; (2) The life expectancy of each piece of equipment; (3) The role each piece of equipment will play in the education of biocommunicators; (4) The number of students who can be expected to benefit from the equipment; (5) The total cost of the equipment; (6) The intended supplier of the equipment; (7) An agreement to provide the EFFE Committee with reports at six and twelve months after installation stating how the equipment has been used to benefit the education of biophotography students.

2268 ■ Biomagnetic Therapy Association (BTA)
PO Box 394
Lyons, CO 80540
Ph: (303)823-0307
E-mail: biomagnetic@icloud.com
URL: www.biomagnetic.org

2269 ■ William Philpott Scholarships *(Undergraduate/Scholarship)*

Purpose: To encourage educational pursuits among Biomagnetic Therapy Association members who are pursuing certification as a Biomagnetic Specialist at the Biomagnetic Institute. **Focus:** Art therapy. **Qualif.:** Applicants must be enrolled at a post-secondary institution and must be pursuing certification as a Biomagnetic Specialist at the Biomagnetic Institute. **Criteria:** Selection is based on ability to complete the program successfully as well as on the applicants' ability to share Biomagnetic Therapy with their communities.

Funds Avail.: No specific amount. **Duration:** Annual. **To Apply:** Applicants must submit a copy of their personal information through e-mail indicating their names, e-mails, addresses and phone numbers and their answers to the question: "Why should you be honored with the scholarship". **Contact:** BTA at the above address.

2270 ■ Biomedical Engineering Society (BMES)
8201 Corporate Dr., Ste. 1125
Landover, MD 20785-2224
Ph: (301)459-1999
Fax: (301)459-2444
Free: 877-871-2637
URL: www.bmes.org
Facebook: www.facebook.com/BMESociety
LinkedIn: us.linkedin.com/company/biomedical-engineering-society
Twitter: twitter.com/BMESociety

2271 ■ BMES Graduate and Undergraduate Student Awards *(Graduate, Undergraduate/Award)*

Purpose: To promote the future of the biomedical engineering profession. **Focus:** Biomedical sciences; Engineering, Biomedical. **Qualif.:** Applicants must be graduates or undergraduate students and must be BMES members in good standing. **Criteria:** Selection will be based on the following: for the graduates: scientific merit, originality, and quality of written presentation; for undergraduates: originality, significance, thoroughness of design analysis, and performance evaluation.

Awards are arranged alphabetically below their administering organizations

Funds Avail.: $500 for graduate; $400 for undergraduate. **Duration:** Annual. **Number Awarded:** 5 graduate; 8 undergraduate. **To Apply:** Applicants must submit an abstract at the time of the official abstract-submission deadline for the Annual Meeting and pay the abstract-submission fee. For the Undergraduate submission: submit two-to-three pages, single spaced, (10-12 font type size) and one inch margins in all sides. A letter of support from the scientific advisor or department chair certifying the originality of the student effort must be uploaded at the time of submission. For the Graduate submission: submit three-to-four pages single spaced, (10-12 font type size) and one inch margins in all sides. A letter of support from the scientific advisor or department chair certifying the originality of the student effort must be uploaded at the time of submission. **Deadline:** May 31. **Contact:** Biomedical Engineering Society, at the above address.

2272 ■ Birmingham Public School (BPS)
31301 Evergreen Rd.
Beverly Hills, MI 48025-3800
Ph: (248)203-3000
Fax: (248)203-3144
URL: www.birmingham.k12.mi.us
Facebook: www.facebook.com/BirminghamPublicSchools
Twitter: twitter.com/BirminghamPS

2273 ■ Birmingham Student Scholarships (Undergraduate/Scholarship)

Purpose: To provide college financial assistance for students who reside within the boundaries of the Birmingham School District upon high school graduation. **Focus:** General studies/Field of study not specified. **Qualif.:** Applicants must be high school and/or college students living in the Birmingham Public School District at the time of the time of the high school graduation. **Criteria:** Selection will be based on the committee's criteria.

Funds Avail.: Amount varies. **Duration:** Annual. **Number Awarded:** Varies. **To Apply:** Applicants must submit completed application to the student's high school counselor prior to the filing date set by the Scholar Board each year. The application must be signed by both the student and one parent certifying the truth of the application. The application requires student's and parents' current income tax information, as well as information regarding family housing, unless there is independent written verification of an established pattern of non-support by a parent; scholarship grants will be reduced by 50 percent if information is not received from both parents. The application and instructions can be printed from the webpage. **Deadline:** February 28. **Contact:** Superintendent's Office, Birmingham Public Schools, at the above address.

2274 ■ Mary E. Bivins Foundation
2311 W 16th Ave.
Amarillo, TX 79102-2303
Ph: (806)379-9400
Fax: (806)379-9404
E-mail: info@bivinsfoundations.org
URL: www.bivinsfoundations.org

2275 ■ Mary E. Bivins Foundation Religious Scholarship Program (Graduate, Undergraduate/Scholarship)

Purpose: To educate ministers to preach the Christian religion. **Focus:** Education, Religious. **Qualif.:** Applicants must be dedicated to seeking an undergraduate or graduate education leading to a Bachelors or Masters Degree in a field that prepares the students to preach the Christian religion; must have the intent to serve as pulpit pastors; must be committed to studies and maintain a cumulative undergraduate GPA of 2.75 or above or a cumulative graduate GPA of 3.0 or above; must be permanent residents of one of the 26 counties of the Texas Panhandle; must enroll and pass a minimum of 12 hours each semester at the undergraduate level or 9 hours each semester at the graduate level; must enroll in an accredited college or university. **Criteria:** Preference will be given to those students who meet the criteria.

Funds Avail.: $2,500 for juniors or seniors; $3,500 for graduate students. **To Apply:** Applicants must check the available website for the required materials. **Deadline:** January 29. **Contact:** Linda Inks, Scholarship Program Officer, at 806-379-9400 or email: links@bivinsfoundation.org.

2276 ■ Black Business and Professional Association (BBPA)
675 King St. W, Ste. 210
Toronto, ON, Canada M5V 1M9
Ph: (416)504-4097
Fax: (416)504-7343
E-mail: information@bbpa.org
URL: www.bbpa.org
Facebook: www.facebook.com/thebbpa
Twitter: twitter.com/thebbpa

2277 ■ Hon. Lincoln Alexander Scholarships (Undergraduate, Graduate/Scholarship)

Purpose: To provide support for Black Canadian students who want to pursue education. **Focus:** General studies/Field of study not specified. **Qualif.:** Applicants must be: Canadian citizens or permanent residents who are members of the Canadian Black community (i.e. Black persons of discernible African ancestry and self identity); 17 to 30 years of age; and, enrolled in a full-time bachelor's degree, diploma or certificate program at a Canadian college or university for the academic year. **Criteria:** Selection will be based on academic achievement, financial need, and recognized contribution to the Black community.

Funds Avail.: 1,500 to 2,000 Canadian Dollars. **Duration:** Annual. **Number Awarded:** 1. **To Apply:** Applicants must complete the application form and submit along with a letter describing the reasons why he/she would be worthy recipient of a BBPA National Scholarship; a completed financial information schedule stating the budget for the coming year including information on the expected sources of funding, family income and related information; a letter of reference from the two individuals named in their application (must be a teacher from their high school, college or university, and an individual who is familiar with their community service); and two passport size photos - head shot. Application form and requirements must be sent to The Board of Trustees, BBPA National Scholarship Fund. **Deadline:** May 31. **Remarks:** The scholarship is in honor of the widely respected first Black Lieutenant Governor of Ontario, who continues to emphasize the need for fairness and equity for all citizens.

2278 ■ Robert K. Brown Scholarships (Undergraduate, Master's/Scholarship)

Purpose: To support a student pursuing a career in the field of Social Services at the bachelor's or master's degree level. **Focus:** Social work. **Qualif.:** Applicants must be: enrolled in a course of study in the field of social services; Canadian citizens or permanent residents; maximum of 30 years of age; and, enrolled in a full-time bachelor's or master's degree level at a Canadian college or university for the academic year. **Criteria:** Selection will be based on academic achievement, financial need, and recognized contribution to the Black community. Special consideration for Black males.

Funds Avail.: 1,500 Canadian Dollars. **Duration:** Annual. **Number Awarded:** 1. **To Apply:** Applicants must complete the application form and submit along with a letter describing the reasons why they would be worthy recipients of a BBPA National Scholarship; a completed financial information schedule stating their budget for the coming year including information on their expected sources of funding, family income and related information; a letter of reference from the two individuals named in their application (must be a teacher from their high school, college or university, and an individual who is familiar with their community service); and two passport size photos - head shot. Application form and requirements must be sent to The Board of Trustees, BBPA National Scholarship Fund. **Deadline:** May 31. **Remarks:** The scholarship is sponsored by Tropicana Community Services (Robert K. Brown was a founding father) which is a not-for-profit organization providing culturally appropriate social services to youth in east Toronto.

2279 ■ Herb Carnegie Scholarships (Undergraduate/ Scholarship)

Purpose: To provide support to under-privileged Black Canadian students. **Focus:** General studies/Field of study not specified. **Qualif.:** Applicants must be Canadian citizens or permanent residents; maximum of 30 years of age; and, enrolled in a full time bachelor's degree at a Canadian college or university for the academic year. **Criteria:** Selection will be based on academic achievement, financial need, and recognized contribution to the Black community.

Funds Avail.: 1,500 to 2,000 Canadian Dollars. **Duration:** Annual. **Number Awarded:** 1. **To Apply:** Applicants must complete the application form and submit along with a letter describing the reasons why they would be worthy recipients of a BBPA National Scholarship; a completed financial information schedule stating their budget for the coming year including information on their expected sources of funding, family income and related information; a letter of reference from the two individuals named in their application (must be a teacher from their high school, college or university, and an individual who is familiar with their community service); and two passport size photos head shot. Application form and requirements must be sent to The Board of Trustees, BBPA National Scholarship Fund. **Deadline:** May 31. **Remarks:** The scholarship is in honor of the late Mr. Herb Carnegie, an outstanding athlete who fought against systemic obstacles to be acknowledged as a first rate hockey player. He was awarded the Order of Canada, to recognize his contributions helping many youth overcome obstacles to their success.

2280 ■ Fraser Milner Casgrain LLP Scholarships (Graduate, Juris Doctorate/Scholarship)

Purpose: To provide support to Black Canadian students who want to pursue education. **Focus:** Law. **Qualif.:** Applicants must be Canadian citizens or permanent residents of up to 30 years of age, and enrolled in a LLB or JD degree course at a Canadian college or university for the academic year. **Criteria:** Selection will be based on academic achievement, financial need, and recognized contribution to the Black community.

Funds Avail.: 5,000 Canadian Dollars. **Duration:** Annual. **Number Awarded:** 1. **To Apply:** Applicants must complete the application form and submit along with a letter describing the reasons why they would be worthy recipients of a BBPA National Scholarship; a completed financial information schedule stating their budget for the coming year including information on their expected sources of funding, family income and related information; a letter of reference from the two individuals named in their application (must be a teacher from their high school, college or university, and an individual who is familiar with their community service); and two passport size photos - head shot. Application form and requirements must be sent to The Board of Trustees, BBPA National Scholarship Fund. **Deadline:** May 31. **Remarks:** The scholarship is sponsored by the FMC LLP (law firm).

2281 ■ CIBC Scholarships (Undergraduate, Graduate/ Scholarship)

Purpose: To provide support for Black Canadian students who demonstrated social responsibility through work in the community. **Focus:** Social work. **Qualif.:** Applicants must be: students attending college or university who have shown academic achievement, leadership potential and a commitment to helping in the community; Canadian citizens or permanent residents; 17 to 30 years of age; and, enrolled in a full-time bachelor's degree, diploma or certificate program at a Canadian college or university for the academic year. **Criteria:** Selection will be based on academic achievement, financial need, and recognized contribution to the Black community.

Funds Avail.: 5,000 Canadian Dollars. **Duration:** Annual. **Number Awarded:** 1. **To Apply:** Applicants must complete the application form and submit along with a letter describing the reasons why they would be worthy recipients of a BBPA National Scholarship; a completed financial information schedule stating their budget for the coming year including information on their expected sources of funding, family income and related information; a letter of reference from the two individuals named in their application (must be a teacher from their high school, college or university, and an individual who is familiar with their community service); and two passport size photos - head shot. Application form and requirements must be sent to The Board of Trustees, BBPA National Scholarship Fund. **Deadline:** May 31. **Contact:** The scholarship is sponsored by CIBC.

2282 ■ Harry Gairey Scholarships (Undergraduate/ Scholarship)

Purpose: To provide support to under-privileged Black Canadian students. **Focus:** General studies/Field of study not specified. **Qualif.:** Applicants must be Canadian citizens or permanent residents; maximum of 30 years of age; and, enrolled in a full time bachelor's degree at a Canadian college or university for the academic year. **Criteria:** Selection will be based on the applicants' academic achievement, financial need, and recognized contribution to the Black community.

Funds Avail.: 2,000 Canadian Dollars. **Duration:** Annual. **Number Awarded:** 1. **To Apply:** Applicants must complete the application form and submit along with a letter describing the reasons why they would be worthy recipients of a BBPA National Scholarship; a completed financial information schedule stating their budget for the coming year including information on their expected sources of funding,

Awards are arranged alphabetically below their administering organizations

family income and related information; a letter of reference from the two individuals named in their application (must be a teacher from their high school, college or university, and an individual who is familiar with their community service); and two passport size photos - head shot. Application form and requirements must be sent to The Board of Trustees, BBPA National Scholarship Fund. **Deadline:** May 31. **Remarks:** The scholarship is sponsored by the BBPA, in honor of Mr. Gairey's important role as a community activist and his many valuable contributions to the Black community over the years.

2283 ■ Lucille May Gopie Scholarships *(Undergraduate, Graduate/Scholarship)*

Purpose: To support a young person who has been encouraged by a single parent to pursue higher education as a means of self-fulfillment. **Focus:** General studies/Field of study not specified. **Qualif.:** Applicants must be: persons who have been encouraged by a single parent to pursue higher education; Canadian citizens or permanent residents; of 30 years old; and, enrolled in a full-time degree bachelor's degree at a Canadian college or university for the academic year. **Criteria:** Selection will be based on academic achievement, financial need, and recognized contribution to the Black community.

Funds Avail.: 2,000 Canadian Dollars. **Duration:** Annual. **Number Awarded:** 1. **To Apply:** Applicants must complete the application form and submit along with a letter describing the reasons why they would be worthy recipients of a BBPA National Scholarship; a completed financial information schedule stating their budget for the coming year including information on their expected sources of funding, family income and related information; a letter of reference from the two individuals named in their application (must be a teacher from their high school, college or university, and an individual who is familiar with their community service); and two passport size photos - head shot. Application form and requirements must be sent to The Board of Trustees, BBPA National Scholarship Fund. **Deadline:** May 31. **Remarks:** The scholarship is sponsored by Kamala Jean Gopie. Such is named for her mother, who came from humble beginnings and encouraged her children to dream and to achieve through education.

2284 ■ Guntley-Lorimer Science and Arts Scholarships *(Undergraduate/Scholarship)*

Purpose: To provide support to Black Canadian students enrolled in Science and Arts programs at the university and college levels. **Focus:** Arts; Science. **Qualif.:** Applicants must be Canadian citizens or permanent residents enrolled in Science and Arts programs at a Canadian college or university levels. **Criteria:** Selection will be based on academic achievement, financial need, and recognized contribution to the Black community.

Funds Avail.: 2,000 Canadian Dollars (for student in Arts); 3,000 Canadian Dollars (for student in Science). **Duration:** Annual. **Number Awarded:** 4. **To Apply:** Applicants must complete the application form and submit along with a letter describing the reasons why they would be worthy recipients of a BBPA National Scholarship; a completed financial information schedule stating their budget for the coming year including information on their expected sources of funding, family income and related information; a letter of reference from the two individuals named in their application (must be a teacher from their high school, college or university, and an individual who is familiar with their community service); and two passport size photos - head shot. Application form and requirements must be sent to The Board of Trustees, BBPA National Scholarship Fund. **Deadline:** May 31. **Remarks:** The scholarship is sponsored by Dr. Edith Guntley-Lorimer and Professor Michael Lorimer.

2285 ■ Al Hamilton Scholarships *(Undergraduate/Scholarship)*

Purpose: To provide support to under-privileged Black Canadian students. **Focus:** General studies/Field of study not specified. **Qualif.:** Applicants must be Canadian citizens or permanent residents; maximum of 30 years old; and, enrolled in a full time bachelor's degree at a Canadian college or university for the academic year. **Criteria:** Selection will be based on the applicants' academic achievement, financial need, and recognized contribution to the Black community.

Funds Avail.: 1,500 to 2,000 Canadian Dollars. **Duration:** Annual. **Number Awarded:** 1. **To Apply:** Applicants must complete the application form and submit along with a letter describing the reasons why they would be worthy recipients of a BBPA National Scholarship; a completed financial information schedule stating their budget for the coming year including information on their expected sources of funding, family income and related information; a letter of reference from the two individuals named in their application (must be a teacher from their high school, college or university, and an individual who is familiar with their community service); and two passport size photos - head shot. Application form and requirements must be sent to The Board of Trustees, BBPA National Scholarship Fund. **Deadline:** May 31. **Remarks:** The scholarship honors the late Al Hamilton, journalist, founder of an ethno-cultural newspaper for the Black community, and a respected community activist.

2286 ■ Hon. Michaelle Jean Scholarships *(Undergraduate/Scholarship)*

Purpose: To provide support to under-privileged Black Canadian students. **Focus:** General studies/Field of study not specified. **Qualif.:** Applicants must be Canadian citizens or permanent residents; 17 to 30 years of age; and, enrolled in a full-time degree (graduate or undergraduate), diploma or certificate program at a Canadian college or university for the academic year. **Criteria:** Selection will be based on the applicants' academic achievement, financial need, and recognized contribution to the Black community.

Funds Avail.: 1,500 to 2,000 Canadian Dollars. **Duration:** Annual. **Number Awarded:** 1. **To Apply:** Applicants must complete the application form and submit along with a letter describing the reasons why they would be worthy recipients of a BBPA National Scholarship; a completed financial information schedule stating their budget for the coming year including information on their expected sources of funding, family income and related information; a letter of reference from the two individuals named in their application (must be a teacher from their high school, college or university, and an individual who is familiar with their community service); and two passport size photos - head shot. Application form and requirements must be sent to The Board of Trustees. **Deadline:** May 31. **Contact:** The scholarship honors the first Afro-Canadian Governor General. After the expiration of her appointment in September 2010, she continues to contribute significantly to humanitarian issues. She was named UNESCO Special Envoy for Haiti, immediately after her term.

Awards are arranged alphabetically below their administering organizations

BLACK BUSINESS AND PROFESSIONAL ASSOCIATION

2287 ■ Harry Jerome Legacy Scholarships
(Undergraduate, Graduate/Scholarship)

Purpose: To provide support for Black Canadian students who have demonstrated superior achievement in academics, athletics and their involvement in helping those who need, assistance or support in the Black community. **Focus:** Athletics. **Qualif.:** Applicants must be Canadian citizens or permanent residents who are 18 years or older; have demonstrated superior achievement in academics, athletics and their involvement in helping those who need, assistance or support in the Black community; and, be enrolled in a full-time bachelor's degree, diploma or certificate program at a Canadian college or university for the academic year. **Criteria:** Selection will be based on academic achievement, financial need, and recognized contribution to the Black community. **Funds Avail.:** 5,000 Canadian Dollars. **Duration:** Annual. **Number Awarded:** 1. **To Apply:** Applicants must complete the application form and submit along with a letter describing the reasons why he/she would be worthy recipient of a BBPA National Scholarship; a completed financial information schedule stating the budget for the coming year including information on the expected sources of funding, family income and related information; a letter of reference from the two individuals named in the application (must be a teacher from their high school, college or university, and an individual who is familiar with their community service); and two passport size photos - head shot. Application form and requirements must be sent to The Board of Trustees, BBPA National Scholarship Fund. **Deadline:** May 31. **Remarks:** The scholarship is sponsored by the BBPA to honor Harry Jerome, an outstanding Black Canadian who was an Olympian, Officer of the Order of Canada and world renowned for his sports achievements.

2288 ■ Beverley Mascoll Scholarships
(Undergraduate/Scholarship)

Purpose: To provide support to under-privileged Black Canadian students. **Focus:** General studies/Field of study not specified. **Qualif.:** Applicants must be Canadian citizens or permanent residents; 17 to 30 years of age; and, enrolled in a full-time degree (graduate or undergraduate), diploma or certificate program at a Canadian college or university for the academic year. **Criteria:** Selection will be based on academic achievement, financial need, and recognized contribution to the Black community. **Funds Avail.:** 1,500 to 2,000 Canadian Dollars. **Duration:** Annual. **Number Awarded:** 1. **To Apply:** Applicants must complete the application form and submit along with a letter describing the reasons why they would be worthy recipients of a BBPA National Scholarship; a completed financial information schedule stating their budget for the coming year including information on their expected sources of funding, family income and related information; a letter of reference from the two individuals named in their application (must be a teacher from their high school, college or university, and an individual who is familiar with their community service); and two passport size photos - head shot. Application form and requirements must be sent to The Board of Trustees. **Deadline:** May 31. **Remarks:** The scholarship honors the memory of Mrs. Mascoll, a well known and respected entrepreneur who often helped out less fortunate members of our community.

2289 ■ Minerva Scholarships *(Undergraduate/Scholarship)*

Purpose: To provide support for under-privileged young Black Canadian students. **Focus:** General studies/Field of study not specified. **Qualif.:** Applicants must be: Canadian citizens or a permanent residents; maximum of 30 years old; and, enrolled in a full-time bachelor's degree at a Canadian college or university for the academic year. **Criteria:** Selection will be based on academic achievement, financial need, and recognized contribution to the Black community. **Funds Avail.:** 2,000 Canadian Dollars each. **Duration:** Annual. **Number Awarded:** 4. **To Apply:** Applicants must complete the application form and submit along with a letter describing the reasons why they would be worthy recipients of a BBPA National Scholarship; a completed financial information schedule stating their budget for the coming year including information on their expected sources of funding, family income and related information; a letter of reference from the two individuals named in their application (must be a teacher from their high school, college or university, and an individual who is familiar with their community service); and two passport size photos - head shot. Application form and requirements must be sent to The Board of Trustees, BBPA National Scholarship Fund. **Deadline:** May 31. **Remarks:** The scholarship is sponsored by Dr. Miriam Rossi and Mr. Renato Rossi.

2290 ■ Royal Bank Scholarships *(Undergraduate, Master's/Scholarship)*

Purpose: To provide support to under-privileged Black Canadian students. **Focus:** Business administration; Economics; Finance. **Qualif.:** Applicants must be: students enrolled in a course of study leading to a bachelor's or master's degree in Business Administration or a related program, and Canadian citizens or permanent residents of up to 30 years old. **Criteria:** Selection will be based on academic achievement, financial need, and recognized contribution to the Black community. **Funds Avail.:** 4,000 Canadian Dollars each. **Duration:** Annual. **Number Awarded:** 2. **To Apply:** Applicants must complete the application form and submit along with a letter describing the reasons why they would be worthy recipients of a BBPA National Scholarship; a completed financial information schedule stating their budget for the coming year including information on their expected sources of funding, family income and related information; a letter of reference from the two individuals named in their application (must be a teacher from their high school, college or university, and an individual who is familiar with their community service); and two passport size photos - head shot. Application form and requirements must be sent to The Board of Trustees, BBPA National Scholarship Fund. **Deadline:** May 31. **Remarks:** The scholarship is sponsored by the Royal Bank of Canada.

2291 ■ Scotiabank Scholarships *(Undergraduate/Scholarship)*

Purpose: To provide support to under-privileged Black Canadian students. **Focus:** Business. **Qualif.:** Applicants must be: students who have demonstrated high academic achievement as well as leadership skills and a commitment to helping in the community; enrolled in a course of study leading to a business degree; Canadian citizens or permanent residents; and, enrolled in a full-time bachelor's degree at a Canadian college or university for the academic year. **Criteria:** Selection will be based on academic achievement, financial need, and recognized contribution to the Black community. **Funds Avail.:** 5,000 Canadian Dollars each. **Duration:** Annual. **Number Awarded:** 2. **To Apply:** Applicants must

Awards are arranged alphabetically below their administering organizations

complete the application form and submit along with a letter describing the reasons why they would be worthy recipients of a BBPA National Scholarship; a completed financial information schedule stating their budget for the coming year including information on their expected sources of funding, family income and related information; a letter of reference from the two individuals named in their application (must be a teacher from their high school, college or university, and an individual who is familiar with their community service); and two passport size photos - head shot. Application form and requirements must be sent to The Board of Trustees, BBPA National Scholarship Fund. **Deadline:** May 31. **Remarks:** The scholarship is sponsored by the Bank of Nova Scotia.

2292 ■ Portia White Scholarships *(Undergraduate/Scholarship)*

Purpose: To provide support to under-privileged Black Canadian students. **Focus:** Music. **Qualif.:** Applicants must be Canadian citizens or permanent residents; 17 to 30 years of age; and, enrolled in a full-time degree (graduate or undergraduate), diploma or certificate program at a Canadian college or university for the academic year. **Criteria:** Selection will be based on the applicants' academic achievement, financial need, and recognized contribution to the Black community.

Funds Avail.: 1,500 to 2,000 Canadian Dollars. **Duration:** Annual. **Number Awarded:** 1. **To Apply:** Applicants must complete the application form and submit along with a letter describing the reasons why they would be worthy recipients of a BBPA National Scholarship; a completed financial information schedule stating their budget for the coming year including information on their expected sources of funding, family income and related information; a letter of reference from the two individuals named in their application (must be a teacher from their high school, college or university, and an individual who is familiar with their community service); and two passport size photos - head shot. Application form and requirements must be sent to The Board of Trustees. **Deadline:** May 31. **Remarks:** The scholarship is in honor of the late Ms. Portia White, a renowned opera singer in past decades, who overcame personal obstacles to establish an out-standing musical career.

2293 ■ Black Canadian Scholarship Fund
PO Box 8002
Ottawa, ON, Canada K1G 5H6
Ph: (613)567-7627
URL: www.bcsf.ca

2294 ■ BCSF Scholarships *(Undergraduate/Scholarship)*

Purpose: To encourage academic excellence among black students in their chosen fields of study. **Focus:** General studies/Field of study not specified. **Qualif.:** Applicants must be Black Canadian students graduating from a high school in the city of Ottawa. They must be admissible to a recognized Canadian university; demonstrate a need of financial assistance; be Canadian citizens; demonstrate leadership in community involvement; and, have an interim or final average of at least 75% in 6 grade 12 courses. **Criteria:** Selection will be based on the criteria set by the bestowing organization.

Funds Avail.: $6,000. **Duration:** Annual. **To Apply:** Applicants must submit a two-page essay explaining why the scholarship is important to them and how they will satisfy the eligibility criteria. They must also: provide a photocopy of the applicant's latest official transcript of 6 Grade 12 courses with above 75% average; have a letter of recommendation from a teacher/guidance counselor in current academic year; have proof of community service; have proof of Canadian citizenship; and, have a detailed statement indicating the amount of money expected from various sources. **Deadline:** May 31. **Remarks:** Established in 1996.

2295 ■ Black Caucus of the American Library Association (BCALA)
PO Box 5837
Chicago, IL 60680
E-mail: webmaster@bcala.org
URL: www.bcala.org

2296 ■ E.J. Josey Scholarships *(Graduate/Scholarship, Award)*

Purpose: To support African American students in library and information science. **Focus:** Library and archival sciences. **Qualif.:** Applicant must be an African American Citizen of the U.S. or Canada, and enrolled or accepted by ALA-accredited graduate program leading to a degree in library and information science at the time of application. **Criteria:** Selection is based on the essay's argument development and critical analysis, clear language, conciseness and creativity.

Funds Avail.: $2,000. **Duration:** One year. **Number Awarded:** 2. **To Apply:** Applicants must write an essay on a given theme. Essays (typed, double-spaced, and in Microsoft word or Corel) must include a cover letter providing the applicant's name, address, phone numbers, graduate program, and name of school and anticipated date of graduation. Only essays submitted via email to bbeal@mcc.cc.ms.us will be considered. **Deadline:** December 15. **Contact:** Billy C. Beal at bbeal@mcc.cc.ms.us.

2297 ■ Black Nurses Association of Greater Washington
PO Box 55285
Washington, DC 20040
Ph: (202)291-8866
URL: www.bnaofgwdca.org

2298 ■ Dr. Johnella Banks Memorial Scholarships *(Undergraduate/Scholarship)*

Purpose: To provide financial assistance to students who are in need. **Focus:** Nursing. **Qualif.:** Applicants must be African American with permanent residency in the District of Columbia or one of the adjacent counties of the State of Maryland (Anne Arundel, Calvert, Charles, Howard and Montgomery, Prince Georges); must be sophomore, junior or first-semester senior nursing students in a registered nursing or practical nursing program; must be currently enrolled in a National League for Nursing accredited program and be in good academic standing with a cumulative grade point average of at least 2.8; and must be U.S. citizens. **Criteria:** Recipients are selected based on financial need.

Funds Avail.: No specific amount. **Duration:** Annual. **To Apply:** Applicants must submit a current official transcript from their nursing program, two letters of recommendation from which one must come from current faculty member and one must come from the Nursing Faculty Advisor or Designee; must submit a written essay that describes the applicant's objectives and need-based reasons for scholarship application; documented evidence to add support for the applicant's desirability that includes participation in student and nursing activities, community service in the Greater Washington area, awards, letters and certificates; must provide a proof of United States citizenship and evidence of financial need. **Deadline:** January 31.

2299 ■ Margaret Pemberton Scholarships
(Undergraduate/Scholarship)

Purpose: To provide financial assistance to students who are in need. **Focus:** Nursing. **Qualif.:** Applicants must be African American with permanent residency in the District of Columbia or one of the adjacent counties of the State of Maryland (Anne Arundel, Calvert, Charles, Howard and Montgomery, Prince Georges); must be graduating senior, currently enrolled in a high school in the District of Columbia or one of the adjacent counties of the State of Maryland; must be in good academic standing with a cumulative grade point average of at least 2.8 (on a scale of 4.0). **Criteria:** Recipients are selected based on financial need.

Funds Avail.: No specific amount. **Duration:** Annual. **To Apply:** Applicants must submit at least one-page long written essay describing personal and educational goals, contributions to the community and reasons why they should be selected; must submit a documented evidence for support, including participation in activities and organizations, awards, certificates, and/or letters of commendation; must submit an official high school transcript, copy of letter of acceptance to a Baccalaureate Nursing Program in a college or university in the United States of America; must submit two letters of recommendation, from which one must come from a high school counselor or designee and the other one must come from non-related adult who has knowledge of the applicant's potential for success. **Deadline:** April 15.

2300 ■ Black Rock Arts Foundation (BRAF)
660 Alabama St.
San Francisco, CA 94110
Ph: (415)626-1248
URL: www.blackrockarts.org

2301 ■ BRAF Grants *(Graduate/Grant)*

Purpose: To support artists and organizations in promoting interactive arts in the community. **Focus:** Art. **Qualif.:** The grant is open to all individual artists, artist collectives or organizations regardless of their geographic location. The grant is applied towards creation of interactive artworks or towards the development of community programs that support interactive artworks. **Criteria:** Projects that are highly interactive, community-driven, and collaborative works of art that are accessible to the public and civic scope are given priority.

Funds Avail.: $500-$10,000. **Duration:** Annual. **To Apply:** Interested applicants must first submit their letter of inquiry in the online application service with a $5.00 fee; if selected by the committee, they will be invited to submit a full proposal **Deadline:** December 1.

2302 ■ Black Theatre Network (BTN)
2609 Douglas Rd. SE, Ste. 102
Washington, DC 20020
Ph: (202)274-5667
Fax: (202)806-6708
URL: www.blacktheatrenetwork.org

2303 ■ S. Randolph Edmonds Young Scholars Competition *(Graduate, Undergraduate/Scholarship)*

Purpose: To encourage research and scholarship in black theatre. **Focus:** Theater arts. **Qualif.:** Applicants must be college/university undergraduates or graduates working on a paper concerned with an aspect of the Black Theatre in either the United States or throughout the world. **Criteria:** Selection will be based on the criteria of the panel of judges.

Funds Avail.: 1st Place-$250; 2nd Place-$100. **To Apply:** Applicants must submit their own work. Papers must be typed, double-spaced and in MLA format with a works cited page. If applicable, also include endnotes that demonstrate awareness of formal methods of documentation. Papers should be approximately 10 pages in length, not including endnotes. **Deadline:** May 31. **Contact:** Artisia V. Green, Young Scholars Competition Coordinator, 757-221-2616, avgreen@wm.edu.

2304 ■ Blair Chiropractic Society
550 E Carson Plaza Dr., Ste. 122
Carson, CA 90746
E-mail: subluxationskill@hotmail.com
URL: www.blairchiropractic.com

2305 ■ Beatrice K. Blair Scholarships
(Undergraduate/Scholarship)

Purpose: To enhance the educational opportunities of chiropractic students with an interest in specific upper cervical Blair technique by providing financial assistance to eligible students attending chiropractic schools. **Focus:** Medicine, Chiropractic. **Qualif.:** The applicant must be a student in good standing at an accredited chiropractic college and a member of a student Blair club if available at their school. **Criteria:** The recipient will be selected based on his or her GPA of at least 2.5 out of 4.0 (C+), and he or she must have completed at least one Primary Blair Seminar.

Funds Avail.: No specific amount. **Duration:** Annual. **To Apply:** Applicants must submit a copy of their transcript; two letters of reference; list of Blair seminars they have attended; and an essay (1-2 pages) stating the reasons why they want to practice the Blair technique.

2306 ■ Blakemore Foundation
1201 3rd Ave., Ste. 4900
Seattle, WA 98101-3099
Ph: (206)359-8778
Fax: (206)359-9778
E-mail: blakemorefoundation@gmail.com
URL: www.blakemorefoundation.org

2307 ■ Blakemore Freeman Fellowships
(Undergraduate, Advanced Professional/Fellowship)

Purpose: To award fellowship to students for one academic year of advanced level language study in East or Southeast Asia in approved language programs. **Focus:** Foreign languages. **Qualif.:** Applicants must be pursuing a professional, business, technical or academic career that involves the regular use of a modern East or Southeast Asian

Awards are arranged alphabetically below their administering organizations

language; must have a college undergraduate degree; must be at or near an advanced level in the language as defined in the grant guidelines. Minimum requirement is 3 years of study of the language at college level or equivalent fluency; must be able to devote oneself exclusively to full-time intensive language study during the term of the grant; must be US citizens or permanent residents of the United States. **Criteria:** Selection will be based on the following criteria: a focused, well-defined career objective involving Asia in which regular use of the language is an important aspect; the potential to make a significant contribution to a field of study or area of professional or business activity in an Asian country; prior experience in the Asian country or involvement or participation in activities related to the country; good academic, professional or business background, appropriate to the career program.

Funds Avail.: No specific amount. **Duration:** Annual. **To Apply:** Application form can be downloaded at the website. Applicants must complete and submit the following materials: completed and signed application form; itemized list of all college-level language classes taken by applicants for the Asian language listed on grant application, including course names, dates and locations of study; curriculum vitae or resume; three to four pages in length, double-spaced essay discussing: 1) Applicants' academic, professional or business background; 2) Prior study and use of the language and involvement with the Asian country; 3) Career objective and how the language will be used to achieve them; two recent letters of recommendation from individuals familiar with applicants' academic, professional or business experience; official college and university transcripts from all institutions at which applicants have studied for one or more years. Electronic transcripts or official paper documents are both acceptable. If applicants have not completed three academic years of study of the language at the college level, submit the Foreign Language Reference Form, completed by a language instructor or other similar qualified individual able to evaluate the applicants' language competency. Applicants for programs involving tutorials should submit the following information with their application: description of the proposed tutorial program; information regarding the proposed tutors' professional qualifications; estimated costs for tutoring expenses; applicants' proposed affiliation during the grant period with a recognized educational institution in the Asian country. **Deadline:** December 30.

2308 ■ Blakemore Refresher Grants (Professional development/Grant)

Purpose: To provide mid-career professionals an opportunity to refresh their language skills by attending a full-time language program for a summer or semester. **Focus:** Foreign languages. **Qualif.:** Applicants must be professors who are teaching in an Asian-related field at a university or college in the United States; must be professionals working in an Asian field; must be former Blakemore Freeman Fellows; must be pursuing a professional, business, technical or academic career that involves the regular use of a modern East or Southeast Asian language; must have a college undergraduate degree; must be at an advanced level in the language; must be able to devote oneself exclusively to language study during the term of the grant; must be US citizens or permanent residents of the United States. Eligible languages are: Chinese, Indonesian, Japanese, Vietnamese, Korean, Khmer, Thai, and Burmese. **Criteria:** Selection will be based on the following criteria: a focused, well-defined career objective involving Asia in which regular use of the language is an important aspect; the potential to make a significant contribution to a field of study or area of professional or business activity in an Asian country; prior experience in the Asian country or involvement or participation in activities related to the country; good academic, professional or business background, appropriate to the career program.

Funds Avail.: No specific amount. **Duration:** Annual. **To Apply:** Application form can be downloaded at the website. Applicants must complete and submit the following materials: completed and signed application form; curriculum vitae or resume; three to four pages in length, double-spaced essay discussing: 1) Applicants' academic, professional or business background; 2) Prior study and use of the language and involvement with the Asian country; 3) Career objectives and how the language will be used to achieve them; one recent letter of recommendation from individuals familiar with applicants' academic, professional or business experience; official college and university transcripts from last institution attended. Electronic transcripts or official paper documents are both acceptable. Applicants for programs involving tutorials should submit the following information with their application: description of the proposed tutorial program; information regarding the proposed tutors' professional qualifications; estimated costs for tutoring expenses; applicants' proposed affiliation during the grant period with a recognized educational institution in the Asian country. **Deadline:** December 30.

2309 ■ Bleeding Disorders Alliance Illinois (BDAI)
210 S Desplaines St.
Chicago, IL 60661
Ph: (312)427-1495
Fax: (312)427-1602
E-mail: info@bdai.org
URL: www.bdai.org

2310 ■ Biogen Idec Hemophilia Scholarship Program (Undergraduate, Graduate, Doctorate/Scholarship)

Purpose: To enable students with hemophilia to pursue their passions through a wide range of academic scholarships. **Focus:** Hemophilia. **Qualif.:** Applicants must be U.S. citizens/legal residents with Hemophilia A or Hemophilia B pursuing a certification or undergraduate, graduate, or doctoral degree. **Criteria:** Applicants will be judged on academic record and involvement in their community.

Funds Avail.: $2,500-$7,000. **To Apply:** Applicants must prepare school transcripts, test scores and some basic information about the applicants. For further information kindly visit the website for detailed application process. **Deadline:** April 15.

2311 ■ Blinded Veterans Association (BVA)
477 H St. NW
Washington, DC 20001-2694
Ph: (202)371-8880
Fax: (202)371-8258
Free: 800-669-7079
E-mail: bva@bva.org
URL: www.bva.org

2312 ■ Kathern F. Gruber Scholarship Program (Undergraduate/Scholarship)

Purpose: To financially assist the spouses and dependent children of blinded veterans. **Focus:** General studies/Field of study not specified. **Qualif.:** Applicants must be spouses and dependent children of blinded veterans. **Criteria:** Recipients will be selected based on merit.

Funds Avail.: No specific amount. **Duration:** Annual. **To Apply:** Applicants must submit a completed application form along with three letters of reference. **Contact:** Scholarship Coordinator; Phone 202-371-8880, Ext. 313; or Email: cdumond@bva.org.

2313 ■ Blood Assurance Foundation
705 E 4th St.
Chattanooga, TN 37403-1916
Ph: (423)756-0966
Free: 800-962-0628
URL: www.bloodassurance.org

2314 ■ Crystal Green Memorial Scholarship *(Undergraduate/Scholarship)*

Purpose: To encourage educational pursuits by providing financial assistance. **Focus:** General studies/Field of study not specified. **Qualif.:** Applicants must be high school senior students planning to enter an accredited two or four-year college or university, and have at least "B" average and score of at least 20 on the ACT or 1100 on the SAT cumulative. **Criteria:** Recipients will be selected based on the written application, high school transcript, school and community service, letters of recommendation and a marketing plan for a blood drive.

Funds Avail.: $1,500 each. **Duration:** Annual. **Number Awarded:** 12. **To Apply:** Applicants must submit a detailed marketing plan for a new drive promotion; applicants must secure two letters of recommendation and obtain an official high school transcript which includes the first semester senior grades and ACT/SAT test scores. **Deadline:** April 15. **Remarks:** The scholarship fund is dedicated to Crystal Green who was a valiant and loving young woman that set forth the example of kindness and care to all that she met. Established in 1999.

2315 ■ Blues Heaven Foundation (BHF)
2120 S Michigan Ave.
Chicago, IL 60616
Ph: (312)808-1286
URL: www.bluesheaven.com

2316 ■ Muddy Waters Scholarships *(Undergraduate/Scholarship)*

Purpose: To provide financial assistance for students in Chicago. **Focus:** African-American studies; Education, Music; Folklore; Journalism; Music; Performing arts; Radio and television. **Qualif.:** Applicant must have a full-time enrollment status in a Chicago area college or university; must be in at least their first year of undergraduate studies or graduate program. **Criteria:** Awards are given based on academic achievement, concentration of studies and financial need.

Funds Avail.: $ 2,000. **To Apply:** Application form is available in website and must be sent to: Blues Heaven Foundation Inc., 2120 S Michigan Ave., Chicago, IL 60616. **Deadline:** April 30.

2317 ■ BMI Foundation
7 World Trade Ctr.
250 Greenwich St.
New York, NY 10007-0030
Ph: (212)220-3103
URL: bmifoundation.org

2318 ■ Pete Carpenter Fellowship *(Professional development/Fellowship)*

Purpose: To give aspiring TV and film composers the opportunity to work with the composer Mike Post at his studio in Los Angeles. **Focus:** Music composition. **Qualif.:** Applicant must be an aspiring composer under the age of 35. **Criteria:** Selection is based on the submitted music samples.

Funds Avail.: $3,000. **Duration:** Annual; 4-5 weeks. **To Apply:** Applicants must submit a completed, signed and notarized application form along with the original 1-3 minute music sample (should be on CD). **Deadline:** February 15. **Remarks:** Established in 1989. **Contact:** BMI Foundation, Inc., at the above address, or Email: carpenterfellowship@bmifoundation.org.

2319 ■ John Lennon Scholarships *(Undergraduate/Scholarship)*

Purpose: To support songwriters and composers who are current students. **Focus:** Music composition. **Qualif.:** Applicants must be current students or alumnus/alumna of a U.S. college or university and be between the ages of 17 and 24. **Criteria:** Selection is based on the submitted original song in any genre.

Funds Avail.: $20,000. **Duration:** Annual. **Number Awarded:** 3. **To Apply:** Applicants must submit a completed application form together with the CD of a song with original words and music (CD should be clearly labeled with the title of the song), and three typed copies of the lyrics (applicant's name must not appear on the CD or on the typed copies of the lyrics). Applicants applying through MENC must contact the Music Department of his/her college to locate the MENC Chapter Advisor at his/her college/university. **Remarks:** Established in 1997.

2320 ■ Peermusic Latin Scholarship *(Undergraduate/Scholarship)*

Purpose: To support songwriters and composers who are current students. **Focus:** Music composition. **Qualif.:** Applicant must be students enrolled at a college/university located in the U.S. or Puerto Rico; must be 16-25 years old prior to the application; and never had any musical work commercially recorded or distributed. **Criteria:** Selection is based on the submitted original song or instrumental work in a Latin genre.

Funds Avail.: $5,000. **Duration:** Annual. **To Apply:** Applicants must submit a completed application form along with the CD of a song or instrumental work with original words and music (CD should be clearly labeled with the title of the song), and three typed copies of the lyrics (applicant's name must not appear on the CD or on the typed copies of the lyric). **Deadline:** February 28.

2321 ■ Woody Guthrie Fellowship *(Professional development/Fellowship)*

Purpose: To support students pursuing research topics or themes related to Woody Guthrie which explore his creative work and contribution to American music and culture. **Focus:** History, American; Humanities; Musicology; Social sciences. **Qualif.:** Applicants must be pursuing research topics or themes related to Woody Guthrie. **Criteria:** Selection is based on the relevance and value of the project to the Foundation's mission and purposes; quality of the project;

Awards are arranged alphabetically below their administering organizations

evidence of the applicant's potential, motivation and ability to carry out the project successfully; and evidence of the applicant's prior record of achievement in the field covered by the project. **Funds Avail.:** Up to $5,000. **Duration:** Annual. **To Apply:** Applicants must submit a completed application form together with a curriculum vitae (maximum of 3 pages); a concise description of the proposed research project (maximum of 2 double-spaced pages); and a list of sources with amounts and dates of any other funding (past, present or future) awarded for the present project. **Deadline:** February 2. **Remarks:** Established in 2005.

2322 ■ B.O.G. Pest Control
645 Central Ave. E, Number 200
Edgewater, MD 21037
Ph: (410)867-1002
E-mail: office@bladesofgreen.com
URL: www.bogpestcontrol.com

2323 ■ B.O.G. Pest Control Scholarship Funds (Undergraduate, Graduate/Scholarship)

Purpose: To support students who demonstrate academic excellence, as well as a passion for the pursuit of further study in environmental education at an accredited college or university. **Focus:** Biology; Chemistry; Engineering, Chemical; Environmental science. **Qualif.:** Applicants must be seeking undergraduate or graduate level education in chemistry, chemical engineering, biology, environmental studies or related fields. **Criteria:** Selection will be based on the submitted application materials.

Funds Avail.: $1,000. **Duration:** Annual. **Number Awarded:** 1. **To Apply:** Applicants must prepare a 350 - 500 words essay describing the career path they plan to seek after graduation, passion for their intended field, and what inspired them to pursue their intended career path. Submit completed application form together with essay, letter of intent, and a high school transcript to Angela Osborne. **Deadline:** March 15. **Contact:** rpratt@bladesofgreen.com.

2324 ■ Bogliasco Foundation - Liguria Study Center for the Arts and Humanities
10 Rockefeller Plaza, 16th Fl.
New York, NY 10020-1903
Ph: (212)713-7628
Fax: (212)489-0787
E-mail: info@bfny.org
URL: www.bfge.org

2325 ■ Aaron Copland Bogliasco Fellowships in Music (Professional development/Fellowship)

Purpose: To provide funds to assist fellows who otherwise might not be able to afford the cost of travel to and from Genoa. **Focus:** Arts; Music. **Qualif.:** Applicants must be American composers. **Criteria:** Preference will be given to person whose applications suggest that they would be comfortable working in an intimate, international, multilingual community of scholars and artists.

Funds Avail.: No specific amount. **To Apply:** The Foundation only accepts applications submitted through the online application system. The following documents, which may be submitted in English, Italian, French, Spanish, or German will be required: completed application form; three letters of reference; a short-form curriculum vitae, three pages in length; a one-page description of the project that the applicants would pursue during their stay at the Liguria Study Center; a sample of the applicants' work that has been published, performed, exhibited or otherwise publicly presented during the last five years. **Deadline:** Varies.

2326 ■ Leo Biaggi de Blasys Bogliasco Fellowships (Professional development/Fellowship)

Purpose: To provide funds to assist fellows who otherwise might not be able to afford the cost of travel to and from Genoa. **Focus:** Arts; Humanities. **Qualif.:** Applicants must be living in those parts of the world where the cost of travel to Genoa may be prohibitive. **Criteria:** Preference will be given to person whose applications suggest that they would be comfortable working in an intimate, international, multilingual community of scholars and artists.

Funds Avail.: No specific amount. **To Apply:** The Foundation only accepts applications submitted through the online application system. The following documents, which may be submitted in English, Italian, French, Spanish, or German will be required: completed application form; three letters of reference; a short-form curriculum vitae, three pages in length; a one-page description of the project that the applicants would pursue during their stay at the Liguria Study Center; a sample of the applicants' work that has been published, performed, exhibited or otherwise publicly presented during the last five years. **Deadline:** Varies.

2327 ■ Bogliasco Fellowships (Professional development/Fellowship)

Purpose: To award qualified persons working in the various disciplines of the Arts and Humanities without regard to nationality, age, race or gender. **Focus:** Arts; Humanities. **Qualif.:** Applicants must be working in all disciplines of the Arts and Humanities without regard to nationality, age, race, religion or gender. **Criteria:** Preference will be given to person whose applications suggest that they would be comfortable working in an intimate, international, multilingual community of scholars and artists.

Funds Avail.: No specific amount. **Number Awarded:** 50. **To Apply:** The Foundation only accepts applications submitted through the online application system. The following documents, which may be submitted in English, Italian, French, Spanish, or German will be required: completed application form; three letters of reference; a short-form curriculum vitae, three pages in length; a one-page description of the project that the applicants would pursue during their stay at the Liguria Study Center; a sample of the applicants' work that has been published, performed, exhibited or otherwise publicly presented during the last five years. **Deadline:** January 15 and April 15.

2328 ■ John Burroughs Bogliasco Fellowships (Professional development/Fellowship)

Purpose: To provide funds to assist fellows who otherwise might not be able to afford the cost of travel to and from Genoa. **Focus:** Arts; Literature. **Qualif.:** Fellowship is open to all applicants regardless of nationality; must be working in the field of creative writing. **Criteria:** Preference will be given to person whose applications suggest that they would be comfortable working in an intimate, international, multilingual community of scholars and artists.

Funds Avail.: No specific amount. **To Apply:** The Foundation only accepts applications submitted through the online application system. The following documents, which may be submitted in English, Italian, French, Spanish, or Ger-

Awards are arranged alphabetically below their administering organizations

man will be required: completed application form; three letters of reference; a short-form curriculum vitae, three pages in length; a one-page description of the project that the applicants would pursue during their stay at the Liguria Study Center; a sample of the applicants' work that has been published, performed, exhibited or otherwise publicly presented during the last five years. **Deadline:** Varies.

2329 ■ Jerome Robbins Bogliasco Fellowships in Dance *(Professional development/Fellowship)*

Purpose: To provide funds to assist fellows who otherwise might not be able to afford the cost of travel to and from Genoa. **Focus:** Arts; Choreography. **Qualif.:** Applicants must be American choreographers. **Criteria:** Preference will be given to person whose applications suggest that they would be comfortable working in an intimate, international, multilingual community of scholars and artists.

Funds Avail.: No specific amount. **To Apply:** The Foundation only accepts applications submitted through the online application system. The following documents, which may be submitted in English, Italian, French, Spanish, or German will be required: completed application form; three letters of reference; a short-form curriculum vitae, three pages in length; a one-page description of the project that the applicants would pursue during their stay at the Liguria Study Center; a sample of the applicants' work that has been published, performed, exhibited or otherwise publicly presented during the last five years. **Deadline:** Varies.

2330 ■ New Museum Bogliasco Fellowship in Visual Art *(Professional development/Fellowship)*

Purpose: To provide funds to assist fellows who otherwise might not be able to afford the cost of travel to and from Genoa. **Focus:** Visual arts. **Qualif.:** Applicants must be working in the field of Visual Arts; fellowship is open to all applicants regardless of nationality. **Criteria:** Preference will be given to person whose applications suggest that they would be comfortable working in an intimate, international, multilingual community of scholars and artists.

Funds Avail.: No specific amount. **To Apply:** The Foundation only accepts applications submitted through the online application system. The following documents, which may be submitted in English, Italian, French, Spanish, or German will be required: completed application form; three letters of reference; a short-form curriculum vitae, three pages in length; a one-page description of the project that the applicants would pursue during their stay at the Liguria Study Center; a sample of the applicants' work that has been published, performed, exhibited or otherwise publicly presented during the last five years. **Deadline:** Varies.

2331 ■ Roger Sessions Memorial Bogliasco Fellowships in Music *(Professional development/Fellowship)*

Purpose: To provide funds to assist fellows who otherwise might not be able to afford the cost of travel to and from Genoa. **Focus:** Arts; Music. **Qualif.:** Applicants must be American composers. **Criteria:** Preference will be given to person whose applications suggest that they would be comfortable working in an intimate, international, multilingual community of scholars and artists.

Funds Avail.: No specific amount. **To Apply:** The Foundation only accepts applications submitted through the online application system. The following documents, which may be submitted in English, Italian, French, Spanish, or German will be required: completed application form; three letters of reference; a short-form curriculum vitae, three pages in length; a one-page description of the project that the applicants would pursue during their stay at the Liguria Study Center; a sample of the applicants' work that has been published, performed, exhibited or otherwise publicly presented during the last five years. **Deadline:** Varies.

2332 ■ Bohemian Lawyers Association of Chicago

c/o Joseph M. Dvorak IV, Manager
19 Riverside Rd., Ste. 5
Riverside, IL 60546-2606
Ph: (708)447-5331
E-mail: info@bohemianlawyers.org
URL: www.bohemianlawyers.org

2333 ■ Bohemian Lawyers Association of Chicago Scholarships *(Graduate/Scholarship)*

Purpose: To financially assist the qualified individuals who wish to pursue their law careers in Chicago. **Focus:** Law. **Qualif.:** Applicants must be of Bohemian descent, attending law school in the Chicago area. **Criteria:** Recipient will be selected based on the application materials given.

Funds Avail.: $2,500 - $5,000. **Duration:** Annual. **To Apply:** Applicants must complete the application form available in the website; must attach an essay indicating the reasons why they feel they should be awarded the scholarship and any special factors which they believe the committee should consider; must have a current copy of their law school transcript and resume. **Deadline:** April 9.

2334 ■ Boomer Benefits

5650 N Riverside Dr., Ste. 200
Fort Worth, TX 76137
Ph: (817)249-8600
Free: 855-732-9055
URL: boomerbenefits.com
Facebook: www.facebook.com/BoomerBenefits
Twitter: www.twitter.com/boomerbenefits

2335 ■ Boomer Benefits Scholarships *(Undergraduate/Scholarship)*

Purpose: To recognize and empower students who have returned to school later in life to better themselves, advance their current career path or pursue a new career. **Focus:** General studies/Field of study not specified. **Qualif.:** Applicants must be U.S. citizen age 50 or older who are currently enrolled in a two-year, four-year or graduate program at an accredited public or private school including community colleges, technical schools and four-year universities; must have a minimum 3.0 GPA. **Criteria:** Selection will be based on the applicants' GPA, amount and nature of his/her community service, and the strength of letters of recommendation submitted. Priority will be given to applicants who demonstrate a passion for service to others - particularly an older American, and a seriousness of purpose and sound character.

Funds Avail.: $1,000. **Duration:** Annual. **Number Awarded:** 1. **To Apply:** Applicants must download the provided scholarship application form from the website and submit per instructions given in the same packet. Additional documents include: recommendation letter from a professor in the last 2 years, or facilitator of a verifiable community service organization; transcript; and a letter describing current goals and how this education will help to achieve those goals, and community service history. **Deadline:** August 15. **Contact:** scholarship@boomerbenefits.com.

Awards are arranged alphabetically below their administering organizations

2336 ■ Boomer Esiason Foundation (BEF)
483 10th Ave., Ste. 300
New York, NY 10018
Ph: (646)292-7930
Fax: (646)292-7945
URL: esiason.org

2337 ■ BEF Scholarships of the Arts *(Graduate, Undergraduate/Scholarship)*

Purpose: To provide educational assistance for students engaged in arts. **Focus:** Art. **Qualif.:** Applicants must be artists with cystic fibrosis (CF). **Criteria:** Grantees will be selected according to credits.

Funds Avail.: $500-$1,000. **Duration:** Annual. **To Apply:** Applicants must submit an application form (available at the website); a recent photo; letter from the doctor confirming diagnosis of cystic fibrosis and list of daily medication routine; 2-part essay; an official/unofficial high school/college transcript; tuition breakdown; W2 form for verification for both parents and picture of the art entry. **Deadline:** May 20. **Contact:** Chris McEwan; Email: cmcewan@esiason.org.

2338 ■ Boomer Esiason Foundation General Academic Scholarships *(Undergraduate, Graduate/Scholarship)*

Purpose: To provide educational assistance for students with cystic fibrosis. **Focus:** General studies/Field of study not specified. **Qualif.:** Applicants must be proven to have been diagnosed with cystic fibrosis. **Criteria:** Grantees will be selected based on scholastic ability, character, leadership potential, service to the community and financial need.

Funds Avail.: $500-$2,500. **Duration:** Quarterly; one year only. **To Apply:** Applicants must submit a completed application form available at the website; recent photo; letter from physician confirming CF diagnosis and therapy routine; letter from social worker confirming need for financial assistance; recent W2 form; one-page essay stating goals; letter of acceptance from an academic institution; detailed breakdown of tuition costs; and transcript of records. **Deadline:** December 11; April 1; July 1; September 30; December 30. **Contact:** Chris McEwan; Email: cmcewan@esiason.org.

2339 ■ Exercise For Life Athletic Scholarships Program *(Undergraduate/Scholarship)*

Purpose: To provide educational assistance for student athletes with cystic fibrosis. **Focus:** General studies/Field of study not specified. **Qualif.:** Applicants must be high school senior athletes pursuing undergraduate degrees. **Criteria:** Grantees will be selected according to financial need, academic accomplishment and athletic ability.

Funds Avail.: $10,000. **Duration:** Annual. **Number Awarded:** 4. **To Apply:** Applicants must submit an application form (available at the website); EFL training log (print from website); an essay (one-page, single-spaced) on the importance of exercise and compliance; recent photo; letter from physician (on letterhead) confirming CF diagnosis and therapy routine; recent W2 form verification for both parents; high school transcript; letter of acceptance from a college institution; and signed waiver. Requirements must be mailed to: Boomer Esiason Foundation, Chris McEwan, 483 10th Ave., Ste. 300, New York, NY 10018. **Deadline:** June 10. **Contact:** Chris McEwan; Email: cmcewan@esiason.org.

2340 ■ Rimington Trophy Scholarships *(Undergraduate, Graduate/Scholarship)*

Purpose: To recognize and support individuals who are living, breathing and succeeding with cystic fibrosis. **Focus:** Cystic fibrosis. **Qualif.:** Applicants must be proven to have been diagnosed with cystic fibrosis. **Criteria:** Selection will be based on the applicants' demonstrated scholastic ability, character, leadership potential, service to the community and need for financial assistance.

Funds Avail.: $1,000-$2,000. **To Apply:** Applicants must submit all the following documents in order to be considered: application; essay discussing the applicants' post-graduation goals and importance of compliance to CF therapies and daily practices to stay healthy; recent photo; letter from physician (on letterhead) confirming CF diagnosis and therapy routine; transcript (high school, college and/or graduate school); letter of acceptance from academic institution; detailed breakdown of tuition costs from academic institution; and W2 form for both parents OR tax return if self-employed. **Deadline:** June 26. **Remarks:** Established in association with Rimington Trophy, the college football award named in honor of BEF President and former University of Nebraska center Dave Rimington.

2341 ■ Rosemary Quigley Memorial Scholarships *(Undergraduate, Graduate/Scholarship)*

Purpose: To enable and inspire young adults with cystic fibrosis to engage in academic studies that will lead them to lives and careers of personal and professional fulfillment. **Focus:** Cystic fibrosis. **Qualif.:** Applicants must be students with cystic fibrosis who are pursuing undergraduate or graduate degrees with a clear sense of life goals and whose commitment to living life to the fullest despite having CF is exemplary. **Criteria:** Scholarship committee will select finalists who will be interviewed on the phone. The award recipient will be chosen based on a majority vote based on ALL parts of the application.

Funds Avail.: $500-$2,000. **To Apply:** Applicants must submit all of the following requirements in order to be considered: application; essay discussing the applicants' post-graduation goals and importance of compliance to CF therapies and daily practices to stay healthy; recent photo; letter from physician (on letterhead) confirming CF diagnosis and therapy routine; transcript (high school, college and/or graduate school); letter of acceptance from academic institution; detailed breakdown of tuition costs from academic institution; and W2 form for both parents. **Deadline:** June 12.

2342 ■ Sacks For CF Scholarships *(Professional development/Scholarship)*

Purpose: To provide educational assistance for students with cystic fibrosis. **Focus:** General studies/Field of study not specified. **Qualif.:** Applicants must be proven to have been diagnosed with cystic fibrosis. **Criteria:** Grantees will be selected based on scholastic merits and type of lifestyle.

Funds Avail.: No specific amount. **Duration:** Annual. **Number Awarded:** Varies. **To Apply:** Applicants must submit an application form (downloaded from the website); recent photo; letter from a doctor confirming diagnosis of cystic fibrosis and list of daily medication routine; essay; an official/unofficial high school/college transcript; tuition breakdown; and W2 form for verification for both parents.

Awards are arranged alphabetically below their administering organizations

2343 ■ Bonnie Strangio Education Scholarships
(Graduate, Undergraduate/Scholarship)

Purpose: To provide educational assistance for students with cystic fibrosis. **Focus:** General studies/Field of study not specified. **Qualif.:** Applicants must be undergraduate or graduate students who have cystic fibrosis. **Criteria:** Grantees will be selected by a majority vote.

Funds Avail.: $500-$1,000. **Duration:** Annual. **To Apply:** Applicants must submit an application form (available at the website); an essay on post-graduation goals; a recent photo; a letter from a physician confirming CF diagnosis; most recent W2 form verification for both parents; transcript (high school, college, or graduate); and letter of acceptance from an academic institution. **Deadline:** June 17. **Remarks:** Established in 2005. **Contact:** Chris McEwan; Email: cmcewan@esiason.org.

2344 ■ Bourse de Montreal Inc.
800 Victoria Sq.
Montreal, QC, Canada H4Z 1A9
Ph: (514)871-2424
Fax: (514)871-3514
E-mail: info@tmx.com
URL: www.m-x.ca

2345 ■ The Canadian Derivatives Exchange Scholars Program *(Graduate, Postgraduate/Scholarship)*

Purpose: To support the education of the students interested in Canadian derivative markets. **Focus:** Finance. **Qualif.:** Applicants must be in full-time graduate or postgraduate programs in a Canadian university and must conduct a research projects (essay, paper, thesis or article) in whole or in part during the refereed academic year of the Canadian Derivatives Exchange Scholars Program regarding on exchange-traded derivatives, financial risk management or any topic related to the Montreal Exchange's business and the Canadian Capitals Market. **Criteria:** Selection will be based on how the applicants demonstrate the following criteria: innovative aspect of the research project; interest in research and show enthusiasm toward chosen topic; leadership and initiative in academic and professional activities; outstanding academic performance.

Funds Avail.: $15,000 and $20,000. **Number Awarded:** 4. **To Apply:** Applicants must submit the following required documents: application form duly completed; plan of the research project (maximum of two pages); one page letter of motivation; curriculum vitae; official transcript of all previous university studies; two referrals or evaluation form submitted individually. One of the referrals must be from the Research Director and the second can be academic or professional. **Deadline:** May 6.

2346 ■ Boys and Girls Club of Ottawa
2825 Dumaurier Ave.
Ottawa, ON, Canada K2B 7W3
Ph: (613)232-0925
Fax: (613)230-0891
URL: www.bgcottawa.org
Facebook: www.facebook.com/BoysandGirlsClubofOttawa
Twitter: twitter.com/bgcottawa

2347 ■ Ottawa Police 150th Anniversary Scholarships *(Undergraduate/Scholarship)*

Purpose: To promote, encourage and sponsor promising individuals who would otherwise experience extreme hardships in pursuing a post-secondary education. **Focus:** Criminal justice. **Qualif.:** Applicants must be students pursuing a career in policing or a related criminal justice field. **Criteria:** Recipients are selected based on financial need, academic achievement and community involvement.

Funds Avail.: $5,000. **To Apply:** Applicants must submit: a completed application form; completed expenses and income form; up-to-date resume; two letters of recommendation; copy of most recent school transcript; proof of citizenship status; copy of letter of acceptance to an accredited post-secondary school; professional quality color photo; and a 300-1,000 word essay discussing their community involvement, financial need, accomplishment and academics.

2348 ■ Brian Smith Memorial Scholarships *(Undergraduate/Scholarship)*

Purpose: To promote, encourage and sponsor promising individuals who would otherwise experience extreme hardships in pursuing a post-secondary education. **Focus:** General studies/Field of study not specified. **Qualif.:** Applicants must be graduating students from a high school in the Ottawa area planning to attend any university or college in the city of Ottawa. **Criteria:** Recipients will be selected based on financial need and demonstrated participation as a community volunteer.

Funds Avail.: $5,000. **Duration:** Annual. **Number Awarded:** 2. **To Apply:** Applicants must submit: a completed application form; completed expenses and income form; up-to-date resume; two letters of recommendation; copy of most recent school transcript; proof of citizenship status; copy of letter of acceptance to an accredited post-secondary school; professional quality color photo; and a 300-1,000-word essay discussing their community involvement, financial need, accomplishment and academics. **Deadline:** April 30. **Contact:** Ashley Tripp at 613-232-0925, x263 or atripp@bgcottawa.org.

2349 ■ Brain Canada Foundation
1200 McGill College Ave., Ste. 1600
Montreal, QC, Canada H3B 4G7
Ph: (514)989-2989
URL: www.braincanada.ca

2350 ■ Azrieli Neurodevelopmental Research Program *(Advanced Professional/Grant)*

Purpose: To support translational research in the area of neurodevelopmental disorders. **Focus:** Mental health; Neuroscience. **Qualif.:** Applicants must be teams of one or more Canadian investigators who are eligible to apply for research grants from the federal granting agencies (CIHR, NSERC, and SSHRC), with at least one international investigator (employed by and located at a non-Canadian research institution; Canadian citizens working outside Canada are eligible). **Criteria:** Selection will be based on the letter of intent and full application stages. Specific criteria include: innovation and originality; collaboration; feasibility; and impact.

Funds Avail.: No specific amount. **To Apply:** Applicants must submit a letter of intent (LOI) since the application for funding is competitive. LOI application components are: project summary; project team details; budget; attachments (figures and references); optional information such as names and contact information for up to three individuals who are not in conflict and would be competent to review the LOI and the subsequent full application, if invited; and signatures and certification. Submitted letters of intent will be subjected for review. Only those invited by Brain Canada following the LOI review will be able to submit full applications. All LOIs must be submitted using Brain Canada's electronic grant management system. **Deadline:** February 9 (letter of intent); May 19 (receipt of application). **Remarks:** The research program is made possible through the joint venture of Brain Canada Foundation and The Azrieli Foundation. **Contact:** programs@braincanada.ca.

2351 ■ Brain Canada-ALS Canada Career Transition Awards *(Postdoctorate, Advanced Professional, Professional development/Grant)*

Purpose: To identify and engage a rising star pursuing innovative research in laboratories and academic institutions in Canada. **Focus:** Amyotrophic lateral sclerosis; Neurology. **Qualif.:** Applicants must be either senior postdoctoral trainees or recently hired junior faculty members wanting to secure or maintain a faculty job in Canada. **Criteria:** Selection will be based on the committee's criteria.

Funds Avail.: No specific amount. **To Apply:** Applicants must submit a letter of intent describing the project to the Partners. Applicants whose letters of intent are considered highly promising and aligned with the program objectives will be invited to submit a full project proposal. **Deadline:** April 15. **Remarks:** The Career Transition Award is part of the joint funding program of the Brain Canada Foundation and the ALS Canada.

2352 ■ Brain Canada-ALS Canada Discovery Grants *(Advanced Professional, Professional development/Grant)*

Purpose: To encourage new basic research focused on identifying causes of, or treatments for ALS and related neurological disorders. **Focus:** Amyotrophic lateral sclerosis; Mental health; Neurology; Neuroscience. **Qualif.:** Applicants must be established ALS researchers and individuals from outside the field applying specific knowledge or expertise to ALS and related neurological disorders or teams of multiple investigators combining expertise in novel ways. **Criteria:** Selection will be based on the research proposals of the applicants and other criteria of the committee.

Funds Avail.: No specific amount. **To Apply:** Applicants may contact the Foundation for the application process and other required materials. **Deadline:** June 1. **Remarks:** The grant is part of the joint funding program of the Brain Canada Foundation and the ALS Canada.

2353 ■ Brain Canada-ALS Canada Hudson Translational Team Grants *(Advanced Professional, Professional development/Grant)*

Purpose: To support series of research that are relevant to ALS and related neurological disorders. **Focus:** Amyotrophic lateral sclerosis; Mental health; Neurology; Neuroscience. **Qualif.:** Applicants must be teams of independent investigators from multiple independent Canadian institutions proposing such a translational research approach with a sound and feasible rationale, supported by preliminary data. **Criteria:** Selection will be based on the research proposals of the applicants and other criteria of the committee.

Funds Avail.: No specific amount. **To Apply:** Applicants may contact the Foundation for the application process and other required materials. **Deadline:** March 23 (letter of intent submission); July 13 (full proposal submission). **Remarks:** The Hudson Translational Team Grant is part of the joint funding program of the Brain Canada Foundation and the ALS Canada.

2354 ■ Brain Canada/CQDM "Focus on Brain" Partnership Program *(Advanced Professional/Grant)*

Purpose: To identify, fund and support the development of breakthrough technologies that enhance biopharmaceutical research and development productivity and accelerate the development of new, safe and effective drugs for disorders of the brain and nervous system. **Focus:** Mental health; Neuroscience. **Qualif.:** Applicants must be investigators who are about to conduct research in Canada. **Criteria:** Selection will be based on the submitted letter of intent and full proposals.

Funds Avail.: Up to 1,500,000 Canadian Dollars. **Duration:** Three years. **Number Awarded:** Approximately 7 teams. **To Apply:** Applicants must submit a letter of intent describing the project to the Partners. Applicants whose letters of intent are considered highly promising and aligned with the program objectives will be invited to submit a full project proposal. **Deadline:** August 20 (letter of intent); November 7 (receipt of application). **Remarks:** The "Focus on Brain" is a joint program of Brain Canada Foundation and Quebec Consortium for Drug Discovery (CQDM).

2355 ■ Brain Canada/NeuroDevNet Developmental Neurosciences Research Training Awards *(Postdoctorate, Advanced Professional, Professional development/Grant)*

Purpose: To enhance the training of talented young scientists conducting research focused on the key aspects of developmental neurosciences under the direction of leading Canadian researchers. **Focus:** Mental health; Neuroscience. **Qualif.:** Applicants can be from any nation; however, training must be undertaken at a participating institution located within Canada. **Criteria:** Selection will be based on the committee's criteria.

Funds Avail.: 30,000 Canadian Dollars per year; 50,000 Canadian Dollars per year for postdoctoral fellowships; 5,000 Canadian Dollars per year for career development. **Duration:** Two years. **To Apply:** Applicants may verify the website for further instructions regarding the application process. **Deadline:** July 15. **Remarks:** The award is made possible by the joint cooperation of Brain Canada Foundation and NeuroDevNet. **Contact:** programs@braincanada.ca.

2356 ■ Brain Canada/RBC Research Partnership in Mental Health Services for Children and Youth Funds *(Advanced Professional/Grant)*

Purpose: To support multi-investigator research projects focused on improved delivery of mental health services through the identification and validation of innovative interventions and practices that are cost-effective, and delivered at the right place and time to support both affected individuals and their families. **Focus:** Mental health. **Qualif.:** Applicants must be two or more investigators in any scientific discipline who are eligible to apply for research grants from the Canadian federal granting agencies (CIHR, NSERC, and SSHRC). **Criteria:** Selection will be based on the research proposals and compliance with the application details. To be recommended for funding, proposals will demonstrate: innovation and originality; multidisciplinarity and teamwork; and potential for impact.

Funds Avail.: Total of 910,000 Canadian Dollars. **Dura-

tion: Three years. **Number Awarded:** 1 team. **To Apply:** Applicants must submit a letter of intent (LOI) since the application for funding is competitive. LOI application components are: project summary; project team details; budget; attachments (figures and references); optional information such as names and contact information for up to three individuals who are not in conflict and would be competent to review the LOI and the subsequent full application, if invited; and signatures and certification. Submitted letters of intent will be subjected for review. Only those invited by Brain Canada following the LOI review will be able to submit full applications. All LOIs must be submitted using Brain Canada's electronic grant management system. **Deadline:** April 3 (letter of intent); June 26 (receipt of application). **Remarks:** The research partnership is made possible by the Brain Canada Foundation and the Royal Bank of Canada. **Contact:** programs@braincanada.ca.

2357 ■ Platform Support Grants *(Advanced Professional/Grant)*

Purpose: To support major research platforms, local, regional or national, that provide enhanced technical and research capability to multiple investigators working in the brain sciences. **Focus:** Mental health; Neuroscience. **Qualif.:** Applicants must be User Groups of investigators working in the brain sciences. User Groups are composed of investigators based in Canada whose research depends on use of the platform for which support is requested, or who are involved in the development of the platform. Members of the User Group must be eligible to receive funding from the federal granting agencies. The User Group may be based in one or several research institutions. **Criteria:** Selection will be based on the following attributes of the applications: excellence and impact of the research that is conducted using the platform; distinctiveness of the platform; management of the platforms; the added value of Brain Canada and Partner(s) support; sustainable commitment to platform support; and data sharing and standardization.

Funds Avail.: Maximum of 1,000,000 Canadian Dollars (annual grant amounts, including matching funds). **Duration:** Three years. **To Apply:** Applicants must submit a letter of intent (LOI) since the application for funding is competitive. LOI application components are: platform summary; user group details; budget; impact; attachments (figures and references); optional information such as names and contact information for up to three individuals who are not in conflict and would be competent to review the LOI and the subsequent full application, if invited; and signatures and certification. Submitted letters of intent will be subjected for review. Only those invited by Brain Canada following the LOI review will be able to submit full applications. All LOIs must be submitted using Brain Canada's electronic grant management system. **Deadline:** January 30 (letter of intent); April 24 (receipt of application). **Contact:** programs@braincanada.ca.

2358 ■ Brandeis University - Hadassah-Brandeis Institute (HBI)
515 S St., MS 079
Waltham, MA 02454-9110
Ph: (781)736-2064
Fax: (781)736-2078
E-mail: reinharz@brandeis.edu
URL: www.brandeis.edu/hbi

2359 ■ HBI-BGI Scholar-in-Residence Program *(Undergraduate/Scholarship)*

Purpose: To provide scholars an opportunity to be in residence at Brandeis University with financial assistance. **Focus:** Jewish studies. **Qualif.:** Applicants must be scholars regardless of gender and religion, currently residing in, or who have emigrated from, the Former Soviet Union and willing to work on significant projects in the field of Jewish women's and gender studies. **Criteria:** Selection will be based on the committees' criteria.

Funds Avail.: No specific amount. **Duration:** Annual. **To Apply:** Applicants must submit each of the following items through online application: letter of introduction with the applicants preferred dates of residence; project abstract; project proposal; literature review (if appropriate); Curriculum Vitae; three professional letters of reference; writing sample maximum of 10 pages; three suggested topics for a public and/or academic lecture and; statement explaining where the applicants learned the scholarship opportunity. Hard copies must be sent to the program manager. **Contact:** Debby Olins, Program Manager at the above address.

2360 ■ Brandner Law Firm
1100 Poydras St., Ste. 1502
New Orleans, LA 70163
Ph: (504)552-5000
Free: 866-207-5437
URL: www.brandnerlawfirm.com
Facebook: www.facebook.com/Brandner-Law-Firm-LLC-151120065174
Twitter: www.twitter.com/MikeBrandner

2361 ■ Scholarships for a Higher Education in Law *(Graduate/Scholarship)*

Purpose: To support college-bound students wishing to pursue a legal degree. **Focus:** Law. **Qualif.:** Applicants must be currently enrolled in a Louisiana college or university and must have a minimum GPA of 3.0. **Criteria:** Recipients are determined solely by selection committee as appointed by Brandner Law Firm.

Funds Avail.: $1,500. **Duration:** Annual; non-renewable. **Number Awarded:** 1. **To Apply:** Applicants must submit the following application materials: official copy of high school transcript; essay of 500 to 1,400 words in PDF format, with the file name as: lastname_firstname_blf.pdf; filled-out application form. **Deadline:** November 30.

2362 ■ Hilda E. Bretzlaff Foundation (HEBF)
1550 N Milford Rd., Ste. 101
Milford, MI 48381
Ph: (248)684-3408
Fax: (248)684-2648
URL: www.hebf.org

2363 ■ Hilda E. Bretzlaff Foundation Scholarships *(Undergraduate/Scholarship, Grant)*

Purpose: To assist individuals in attending educational institutions in the United States of America and/or England. **Focus:** General studies/Field of study not specified. **Qualif.:** Applicants must: maintain a minimum 2.0 grade point average; demonstrate financial need; be moral, conservative, and ambitious; and, be credits to America. **Criteria:** Selection will be based on the aforesaid qualifications.

Awards are arranged alphabetically below their administering organizations

Funds Avail.: No specific amount. **To Apply:** Applicants must obtain an application by contacting a school, institution or organization having a proposal with the Foundation. Applicants must provide a complete, signed and dated application enclosed with the following items: previous year's tax return for self and parent/guardians; official transcript, (transcripts printed off the internet will not be accepted unless stamped by the school); two letters of recommendation from two different sources; and two essays, "What America Means to Me" and "Goals/Aspirations Essay."

2364 ■ British American Foundation of Texas (BAFTX)

PO Box 421234
Houston, TX 77242-1234
Ph: (713)587-9900
Fax: (713)784-7712
E-mail: info@baftx.org
URL: baftx.org

2365 ■ BAFTX Early Starters Awards
(Undergraduate/Scholarship)

Purpose: To provide assistance to students who are seeking financial resources for their education. **Focus:** General studies/Field of study not specified. **Qualif.:** Applicants must be permanent residents of Texas; enrolled in full-time education; must be attending in Middle School; must have maintain an average A grade and hold an excellent school attendance record. **Criteria:** Applicants are evaluated based on financial need.

Funds Avail.: $250-$1,000. **To Apply:** Applicants must submit the completed application form; essay between 300 and 500 words regarding a British person (past or present) whom they admire; current transcript signed by a member of their teaching staff; letter of recommendation which must come from a teacher in whose class they were enrolled within the past year, or from a guidance counselor at their school (letter must be on school letterhead paper); and a recent photograph.

2366 ■ BAFTX Graduate Awards *(Undergraduate/Scholarship)*

Purpose: To provide financial assistance to aspiring individuals from Great Britain or Texas, USA that are intent on furthering their education in their chosen field. **Focus:** General studies/Field of study not specified. **Qualif.:** Applicants must be permanent residents of Texas; must be enrolled in full time education; between 21 and above ; must hold an undergraduate degree with a GPA of 3.5 or above for U.S. applicants and 2.1 (65+) for U.K. applicants. **Criteria:** Applicants are evaluated based on academic achievement and financial need.

Funds Avail.: No specific amount. **To Apply:** Applicants must submit completed application form; essay, not less than 1,000 words, on one of the topics from the application form found at the website of BAFTX; current transcript of academic performance signed by a member of the teaching staff; letter of recommendation from a graduate or undergraduate professor in whose class they were enrolled or from a guidance counselor at their university (letter must be on university letterhead paper); financial statement declaring their eligibility for the program; budget outline stating the sum being requested for tuition fees and other costs associated with graduate tuition; and a recent photograph. **Deadline:** March 31.

2367 ■ BAFTX Junior Achievers Awards
(Undergraduate/Scholarship)

Purpose: To provide summer study program and cultural exchange for academically adept students. **Focus:** General studies/Field of study not specified. **Qualif.:** Applicants must be permanent residents of Texas; enrolled in full-time education; must be a high school junior; and must maintain a competitive GPA and excellent school attendance record. **Criteria:** Applicants are evaluated based on financial need.

Funds Avail.: No specific amount. **To Apply:** Applicants must submit completed application form; an essay between 500 and 750 words regarding a British person (past or present) whom they admire; current transcript of academic performance signed by a member of the teaching staff; letter of recommendation which must come from a teacher in whose class they were enrolled within the past year or from a guidance counselor at their school (letter must be on school letterhead); and a recent photograph. **Deadline:** January 31.

2368 ■ BAFTX Undergraduate Awards
(Undergraduate/Scholarship)

Purpose: To alleviate the financial burden of funding the college fees. **Focus:** General studies/Field of study not specified. **Qualif.:** Applicants must be permanent residents of Texas; must be enrolled in full time education; must be between 18 and above; and must maintain a GPA of 3.5. **Criteria:** Applicants are evaluated based on merit and financial need.

Funds Avail.: No specific amount. **To Apply:** Applicants must submit an essay, not less than 1,000 words, on one of the topics given in the application form found at the website of BAFTX; a letter of recommendation which must come from a teacher in whose class they were enrolled within the past year or from a guidance counselor at their university (letter must be on university letterhead paper); current transcript of their academic performance signed by a member of the teaching staff; financial statement declaring their eligibility for the program; budget outline stating the sum being requested for tuition fees and other costs associated with their education for one semester; and a recent photograph. **Deadline:** March 31.

2369 ■ Broadcast Education Association (BEA)

1771 N St. NW
Washington, DC 20036-2800
Ph: (202)602-0584
Fax: (202)609-9940
E-mail: help@beaweb.org
URL: www.beaweb.org/wp
Facebook: www.facebook.com/groups/34744282858
Twitter: twitter.com/BEAWebTweets

2370 ■ Walter S. Patterson Scholarships *(Graduate/Scholarship)*

Purpose: To provide a broad range of services to academic and professional members to keep them abreast with the latest electronic media developments in radio, television, news technologies, management, sales, news reporting, production, research, communication, law, policy and international systems. **Focus:** Broadcasting. **Qualif.:** Applicants must be professors, industry professionals and students involved in teaching and research related to radio, television and electronic media; must be juniors, seniors and graduate students at BEA Member institutions. **Criteria:**

Recipients are selected based on academic performance and potential as professionals.

Funds Avail.: $1,750 each. **Duration:** Annual. **Number Awarded:** 2. **To Apply:** Applicants must submit official application form from the campus faculty; must submit transcript of records, broadcast and other experiences; written statement of goals and supportive statement from three references. **Deadline:** October 13.

2371 ■ Helen J. Sioussat/Fay Wells Scholarships (Graduate/Scholarship)

Purpose: To provide a broad range of services to its academic and professional members to keep them abreast with the latest electronic media developments in radio, television, news technologies, management, sales, news reporting, production, research, communication, law, policy and international systems. **Focus:** Broadcasting. **Qualif.:** Applicants must be professors, industry professionals and students involved in teaching and research related to radio, television and electronic media; must be juniors, seniors and graduate students at BEA Member institutions. **Criteria:** Recipients are selected based on academic performance and potential as professionals.

Funds Avail.: No specific amount. **To Apply:** Applicants must submit an official application form from the campus faculty; must submit transcript of records, broadcast and other experiences; written statement of goals and supportive statement from three references. **Deadline:** October 12.

2372 ■ Alexander M. Tanger Scholarships (Graduate/Scholarship)

Purpose: To provide a broad range of services to academic and professional members to keep them abreast with the latest electronic media developments in radio, television, news technologies, management, sales, news reporting, production, research, communication, law, policy and international systems. **Focus:** Broadcasting. **Qualif.:** Applicants must be professors, industry professionals and students involved in teaching and research related to radio, television and electronic media; must be juniors, seniors and graduate students at BEA Member institutions. **Criteria:** Recipients are selected based on academic performance and potential as professionals.

Funds Avail.: No specific amount. **To Apply:** Applicants must submit official application form from the campus faculty; must submit transcript of records, broadcast and other experiences; written statement of goals and supportive statement from three references. **Deadline:** October 13.

2373 ■ Two Year/Community Broadcast Education Association Scholarship Awards (Graduate/Scholarship)

Purpose: To provide a broad range of services to academic and professional members to keep them abreast with the latest electronic media developments in radio, television, news technologies, management, sales, news reporting, production, research, communication, law, policy and international systems. **Focus:** Broadcasting. **Qualif.:** Applicants must be professors, industry professionals and students involved in teaching and research related to radio, television and electronic media; must be juniors, seniors and graduate students at BEA Member institutions. **Criteria:** Recipients are selected based on academic performance and potential as professionals.

Funds Avail.: No specific amount. **To Apply:** Applicants must submit official application form from the campus faculty; must submit transcript of records, broadcast and other experiences; written statement of goals and supportive statement from three references.

2374 ■ Abe Voron Scholarships (Graduate/Scholarship)

Purpose: To provide a broad range of services to academic and professional members to keep them abreast with the latest electronic media developments in radio, television, news technologies, management, sales, news reporting, production, research, communication, law, policy and international systems. **Focus:** Broadcasting. **Qualif.:** Applicants must be professors, industry professionals and students involved in teaching and research related to radio, television and electronic media; must be juniors, seniors and graduate students at BEA Member institutions; must be studying toward a career in radio. **Criteria:** Recipients are selected based on academic performance and potential as professionals.

Funds Avail.: $5,000. **To Apply:** Applicants must submit official application form from the campus faculty; must submit transcript of records, broadcast and other experiences; written statement of goals and supportive statement from three references. **Deadline:** October 13.

2375 ■ Vincent T. Wasilewski Scholarships (Graduate/Scholarship)

Purpose: To provide a broad range of services to academic and professional members to keep them abreast with the latest electronic media developments in radio, television, news technologies, management, sales, news reporting, production, research, communication, law, policy and international systems. **Focus:** Broadcasting. **Qualif.:** Applicants must be professors, industry professionals and students involved in teaching and research related to radio, television and electronic media; must be juniors, seniors and graduate students at BEA Member institutions. **Criteria:** Recipients are selected based on academic performance and potential as professionals.

Funds Avail.: $4,000. **Number Awarded:** 1. **To Apply:** Applicants must submit official application forms from the campus faculty; must submit transcript of records, broadcast and other experiences; written statement of goals and supportive statement from two references. **Deadline:** October 4. **Contact:** Dr. Orlik directly at orlik1pb@cmich.edu.

2376 ■ Bronx County Bar Association
New York State Supreme Ct. Bldg.
851 Grand Concourse, No. 124
Bronx, NY 10451
Ph: (718)293-2227
E-mail: info@bronxbar.com
URL: www.bronxbar.com

2377 ■ Hon. Peggy Bernheim Memorial Scholarships (Undergraduate/Scholarship)

Purpose: To provide financial assistance for the education of law school students who are domiciled in Bronx County. **Focus:** Law. **Qualif.:** Applicants must be: first, second or third year law students who are graduating in May or June; and, enrolled at an A.B.A. accredited school. They may also be first year students who have completed one semester of study. **Criteria:** Applicants will be evaluated based on academics, financial need, writing sample, personal interview and law school transcript.

Awards are arranged alphabetically below their administering organizations

Funds Avail.: $5,000. **Duration:** Annual. **Number Awarded:** 1. **To Apply:** Applicants must submit a general application. **Deadline:** February 5.

2378 ■ Craig Lensch Memorial Scholarships
(Undergraduate/Scholarship)

Purpose: To provide financial assistance for the education of law school students who are domiciled in Bronx County. **Focus:** Law. **Qualif.:** Applicants must be: first, second, or third year law students who are graduating in May or June; and, enrolled at an A.B.A. accredited school. They may also be first year students who have completed one semester of study. **Criteria:** Applicants will be evaluated based on academics, financial need, writing sample, personal interview, and law school transcript.

Funds Avail.: $5,000. **Duration:** Annual. **Number Awarded:** 1. **To Apply:** Applicants must submit a general application. **Deadline:** February 5.

2379 ■ The Brookdale Foundation
300 Frank W Burr Blvd., Ste. 13
Teaneck, NJ 07666
Ph: (201)836-4602
Fax: (201)836-4342
URL: www.brookdalefoundation.org

2380 ■ Brookdale Leadership in Aging Fellowships
(Other/Fellowship)

Purpose: To foster the development of a new generation of leaders in the field of aging by supporting investigators in the developmental stages of their careers. **Focus:** Gerontology. **Qualif.:** Applicants must demonstrate leadership potential; must provide evidence of an ongoing commitment to a career in aging; must have a mentor (or mentors) willing and able to provide professional guidance and to be helpful in the development of the their career and research project; must be willing to commit at least 75% of their time for career development for each of the two years of the Fellowship; must propose a project related to the field of aging; must have already earned a PhD or MD; and be between the first and tenth years of graduate degree. **Criteria:** Application will be scored as follows: Candidate: 10 points; Project: 5 points; Mentor/Institution: 5 points.

Funds Avail.: No specific amount. **Duration:** Annual. **To Apply:** Applicants must submit a completed online application. Materials needed for the application are: statement of Leadership Role in Aging; research project abstract; project description outlining the project's basic theoretical orientation, the goals and objectives of the project and its methodology; statement of project's current and future significance to the field; statement of 10 year career plan and action steps with special emphasis on relevance to the field of aging; participation in active grants and/or research projects; candidate's CV; up to three letters of support (one of which should be from the Department Chair or Dean); statement from the mentor(s); mentor's participation in active grants; mentor's CV(s); proposed project budget from the sponsoring institution; sponsoring institution's resource support; verification of Tax Exempt Status; and signed statement of support from sponsoring institution. **Remarks:** Established in 1985.

2381 ■ Brookings Doha Center (BDC)
1775 Massachusetts Ave. NW
Washington, DC 20036
Ph: (202)797-6000
E-mail: communications@brookings.edu
URL: www.brookings.edu

2382 ■ BDC Visiting Fellowships *(Advanced Professional, Professional development/Fellowship)*

Purpose: To assist PhD students in presenting their research at a seminar. **Focus:** General studies/Field of study not specified. **Qualif.:** Applicants must have a PhD in a field relevant to the area of research. Applicants without a PhD should have at least 10 years of professional experience in a relevant field. Applicants must have a demonstrated ability to conduct professional, in-depth research and a proven record of publishing and fluency in English. **Criteria:** Recipients will be selected based on submitted materials.

Funds Avail.: No specific amount. **Duration:** Annual. **Number Awarded:** 2. **To Apply:** Applicants must submit the following documents: a CV including professional and educational experience, citizenship, three references and full contact information; a writing sample in English, on a relevant topic. Writing samples should, if possible, be in a format similar to the analysis papers published by Brookings and must not be co-authored; a research proposal of at least 2,000 to 2,500 words and must include key questions being addressed, relevance to US and Middle East policymaking communities, method of research, and project objectives; a cover letter. **Deadline:** March 1; September 1.

2383 ■ John Carter Brown Library
94 George St.
Providence, RI 02906
Ph: (401)863-2725
Fax: (401)863-3477
E-mail: jcb-library@brown.edu
URL: www.brown.edu/academics/libraries/john-carter-brown
Facebook: www.facebook.com/jcblibrary
Twitter: twitter.com/jcblibrary

2384 ■ John Carter Brown Library Long-Term Fellowships *(Graduate, Doctorate/Fellowship)*

Purpose: To give scholars from the U.S. and abroad an opportunity to pursue their work in proximity to a distinguished collection of primary sources. **Focus:** General studies/Field of study not specified. **Qualif.:** Applicants must be American citizens or have been residents in the United States for three years. **Criteria:** Recipients will be selected based on academic standing and financial need.

Funds Avail.: $4,200 per month. **Duration:** Annual; From 5 to 10 months. **To Apply:** Applicants must complete the application form; must submit the Online Fellowship Application Cover sheet; must send three letters of recommendation. **Deadline:** December 15. **Remarks:** The fellowships are funded by the National Endowment for the Humanities (NEH).

2385 ■ John Carter Brown Library Short-Term Fellowships *(Doctorate, Postdoctorate/Fellowship)*

Purpose: To support and assist scholars in any area of research related to the Library's holdings. **Focus:** General studies/Field of study not specified. **Qualif.:** Applicants must be citizens of the United States and foreign nationals who are engaged in pre- or post-doctoral, or independent, research. Graduate students must have passed their

Awards are arranged alphabetically below their administering organizations

preliminary or general examinations at the time of application. **Criteria:** Recipients will be selected based on the academic standing and financial need.

Funds Avail.: $2,100 per month. **Duration:** Annual; From 2 to 4 months. **To Apply:** Applicants must complete the application form; must submit the Online Fellowship Application Cover sheet; must send two letters of recommendation.

2386 ■ Ron Brown Scholar Program
1160 Pepsi Pl., Ste. 206
Charlottesville, VA 22901
Ph: (434)964-1588
Fax: (434)964-1589
E-mail: info@ronbrown.org
URL: www.ronbrown.org
Twitter: twitter.com/ronbrownscholar

2387 ■ Ron Brown Scholars Program
(Undergraduate/Scholarship)

Purpose: To advance higher education and improve the lives of public service-minded and intellectually gifted African Americans and to accelerate their progress into impactful leadership roles and opportunities. **Focus:** General studies/Field of study not specified. **Qualif.:** Applicants must be senior high school students; must excel academically; exhibit exceptional leadership potential; participate in community service activities and demonstrate financial need; must be U.S. citizens or hold a permanent resident visa card. **Criteria:** Scholarship winners are selected based on their submitted applications, interviews and participation on weekend activities.

Funds Avail.: $40,000 ($10,000 per year for four years). **Duration:** Annual. **Number Awarded:** Varies. **To Apply:** Applicants must mail the application materials in one packet. Transcripts and letters of recommendation should not be sent under separate cover; incomplete, e-mailed or faxed applications will not be considered. **Deadline:** November 1; January 9. **Contact:** Ron Brown Scholar Program; Phone: 434-964-1588; Fax: 434-964-1589; Email: info@ronbrown.org.

2388 ■ Brown University - Pembroke Center for Teaching and Research on Women
172 Meeting St., Box 1958
Providence, RI 02912
Ph: (401)863-2643
Fax: (401)863-1298
E-mail: pembroke_center@brown.edu
URL: www.brown.edu/research/pembroke-center

2389 ■ Pembroke Center Faculty Fellowships
(Professional development/Fellowship)

Purpose: To support the participation of Brown faculty members in the Pembroke Seminar, an interdisciplinary research seminar that meets weekly throughout the academic year. **Focus:** General studies/Field of study not specified. **Qualif.:** Applicants must be campus-based full-time faculty members. **Criteria:** Selection will be based on the committee's criteria.

Funds Avail.: No specific amount. **To Apply:** Applicants must submit an application package which includes a current curriculum vitae and a 1,000 words project proposal that describes their research. Faculty participants should have an active interest in the seminar's topic, but the research project may be in any related field and need not directly address the topic. **Deadline:** January 14.

2390 ■ Pembroke Center Faculty Seed Grants
(Professional development/Grant)

Purpose: To support the formation of focused interdisciplinary groups working across fields and academic divisions to creatively explore social issues of representation. **Focus:** Arts; Health sciences; Humanities; Science technologies; Social sciences. **Qualif.:** Applicants must be from the humanities, social sciences, creative arts, health sciences, and science and technology studies. **Criteria:** Selection will be based on the committee's criteria. Preference will be given to projects that involve faculty across academic division.

Funds Avail.: $10,000. **To Apply:** Applicants must complete the following requirements: one faculty project director, plus a minimum of one additional faculty member from a different field; one-page bios of research group participants, including their disciplines, research interest as they relate to the seed grant application and their other interdisciplinary projects; title of research project and a two-to three-page description that details the central research questions, common themes and project goals; plan to involve other faculty researchers, visiting scholars, postdoctoral fellows, and students; dissemination plan for research findings. **Deadline:** April 1.

2391 ■ Pembroke Center Graduate Fellowships
(Graduate/Fellowship)

Purpose: To provide students an enhanced context that gives the opportunity for presentation of work and benefits or critique from an exciting group of Pembroke Center Faculty. **Focus:** General studies/Field of study not specified. **Qualif.:** Candidates must be graduate students enrolled and currently studying at Brown University. **Criteria:** Selection will be based on the committee's criteria.

Funds Avail.: $1,000 each. **Duration:** Annual. **Number Awarded:** Up to 3. **To Apply:** There is no application form. Interested students must submit a cover sheet indicating their name, current year, department and dissertation director; a three-page description of their research project, including a brief representative bibliography; a brief letter of support from a faculty member who knows their work. Materials should be sent or delivered to Donna Goodnow. **Deadline:** March 18.

2392 ■ Pembroke Center for Teaching and Research on Women Postdoctoral Fellowships
(Postdoctorate/Fellowship)

Purpose: To support the educational development of scholars from any field whose research relates to the theme of "Fatigue". **Focus:** General studies/Field of study not specified. **Qualif.:** Applicants must have a Ph.D. and may not hold a tenured position. **Criteria:** Candidates are selected on the basis of their scholarly potential and the relevance of their work to the research theme.

Funds Avail.: $50,000 stipend plus a supplement for health insurance and $1,500 for research expenses. **Duration:** Annual. **To Apply:** Applicants must complete and submit the following: completed application form; project statement of five typed pages with representative's bibliography; curriculum vitae; course proposal with a sample reading list; and, three confidential recommendation letters. **Deadline:** December 3. **Contact:** Email at: donna_goodnow@brown.edu or Phone: 401-863-2643.

Awards are arranged alphabetically below their administering organizations

2393 ■ Peggy Browning Fund
100 S Broad St., Ste. 1208
Philadelphia, PA 19110
Ph: (267)273-7990
Fax: (267)273-7688
URL: www.peggybrowningfund.org
Facebook: www.facebook.com/peggybrowningfund
LinkedIn: www.linkedin.com/groups/2746007/profile
Twitter: twitter.com/PeggyBFund

2394 ■ Peggy Browning Fund - Chicago School-Year Fellowships *(Graduate, Undergraduate/Fellowship)*

Purpose: To provide assistance for the education of law students about the human rights and needs of workers. **Focus:** Law. **Qualif.:** Applicants must be students in good standing at a participating law school in proximity to the fellowship location and must have completed at least one year of law school. **Criteria:** Selection is based on submitted application materials.

Funds Avail.: $5,000. **Duration:** Annual. **To Apply:** Applicants must submit a cover letter, a completed application form and resume.

2395 ■ Bryant Surety Bonds, Inc.
73 Old Dublin Pike Ste.10 No.306
Doylestown, PA 18901
Free: 866-450-3412
URL: www.bryantsuretybonds.com

2396 ■ Bryant Essay Scholarships *(Undergraduate, Graduate/Scholarship)*

Purpose: To help individuals start a new business that they have dreamed of by bonding their start up. **Focus:** General studies/Field of study not specified. **Qualif.:** Applicants must be currently enrolled in graduate or undergraduate degree program in an accredited U.S. college, university, or trade school. **Criteria:** Selection will be based on the committee's criteria.

Funds Avail.: $1,000. **Number Awarded:** 1. **To Apply:** Applicants must submit an essay of 500-2,000 words and an email regarding scholarships along with the following information: first and last name, school name, and expected date of graduation. **Deadline:** June 15. **Contact:** scholarships@bryantsuretybonds.com.

2397 ■ Bryant Visual Content Scholarships *(Undergraduate, Graduate/Scholarship)*

Purpose: To help individuals start a new business that they have dreamed of by bonding their start up. **Focus:** General studies/Field of study not specified. **Qualif.:** Applicants must be currently enrolled in a graduate or undergraduate degree program in an accredited U.S. college, university, or trade school. **Criteria:** Selection will be based on the committee's criteria.

Funds Avail.: $1,000. **Number Awarded:** 1. **To Apply:** Applicants must provide the following: images and infographics with high resolution in png, jpeg, jpg, or gif format; 1-3 minutes long video; slides deck with 5-20 slides; email regarding scholarships along with the following information: first and last name, school name and expected date of graduation. **Deadline:** June 15. **Contact:** scholarships@bryantsuretybonds.com.

2398 ■ Buckfire & Buckfire, P.C.
25800 Northwestern Hwy., No. 890
Southfield, MI 48075
Ph: (248)569-4646
Free: 888-797-8787
URL: www.buckfirelaw.com

2399 ■ Buckfire & Buckfire, P.C. Law School Diversity Scholarships *(Graduate/Scholarship)*

Purpose: To help law students who are in need of financial assistance achieve their academic and professional dreams. **Focus:** Law. **Qualif.:** Applicants must be U.S. citizens currently attending or have completed at least one semester of classes at an accredited law school within the United States; must have a minimum 3.0 GPA; must be members of ethnic or racial minority or any individuals who demonstrates a defined commitment to issues of diversity within their academic career. **Criteria:** Selection will be based on the committees' criteria.

Funds Avail.: $2,000. **Number Awarded:** 1. **To Apply:** Applicants must submit the following items: a completed scholarship application form; a one page typed essay describing how the applicants utilized their time promoting ethnic diversity within their community - alternatively, applicants may write about how they will use their law degree to promote ethnic diversity in the future; and a certified official copy of law school transcript. **Deadline:** April 1. **Remarks:** Established in 2013.

2400 ■ Buckfire & Buckfire, P.C. Medical Diversity Scholarships *(Advanced Professional/Scholarship)*

Purpose: To help students in need of financial assistance achieve their academic and professional dreams. **Focus:** Medical assisting. **Qualif.:** Applicants must be U.S. citizens currently attending or have completed at least one semester of classes at an accredited medical school within the United States; must have a minimum 3.0 GPA; must be members of ethnic or racial minority or any individuals who demonstrates a defined commitment to issues of diversity within their academic career. **Criteria:** Selection will be based on the committees' criteria.

Funds Avail.: $2,000. **Duration:** Annual. **Number Awarded:** 1. **To Apply:** Applicants must submit the following items: a completed scholarship application form; a one page typed essay describing how the applicants utilized their time promoting ethnic diversity within their community - alternatively, applicants may write about how they will use their medical degree to promote ethnic diversity in the future; and a certified official copy of medical school transcript. **Deadline:** April 1. **Remarks:** Established in 2014.

2401 ■ Susan Thompson Buffett Foundation
222 Kiewit Plz.
Omaha, NE 68131
Ph: (402)943-1383
E-mail: scholarships@stbfoundation.org
URL: www.buffettscholarships.org

2402 ■ Susan Thompson Buffett Foundation Scholarships *(Undergraduate/Scholarship)*

Purpose: To provide financial assistance to qualified individuals. **Focus:** General studies/Field of study not specified. **Qualif.:** Applicants must be residents of the State of Nebraska; must be graduating high school seniors or undergraduate students who have not already earned a bachelor's degree; must be attending or applying to a Nebraska state public school; must be in need of financial assistance; must have maintained at least a 2.5 GPA throughout high school; must have applied for federal financial aid and have already received back the Student Aid Report that contains their Expected Family Contribution. **Criteria:** Recipients will be selected based on financial need.

Funds Avail.: No specific amount. **Duration:** Annual. **To Apply:** Applicants must complete the application form available online; must submit a high school or college transcript; two letters of reference from teachers, employers or clergy members; must have a copy of the Information Summary of their financial aid; must provide one-page handwritten background and personal information. **Deadline:** February 1. **Contact:** Susan Thompson Buffett Foundation at 402-943-1383.

2403 ■ Building Owners and Managers Association of Greater New York (BOMANY)
11 Penn Plz., 22nd Fl., Ste. 2201
New York, NY 10001-2091
Ph: (212)239-3662
E-mail: president@bomany.com
URL: www.bomany.org

2404 ■ BOMA/NY Scholarships (Undergraduate/Scholarship)

Purpose: To financially assist students to further their professional education. **Focus:** General studies/Field of study not specified. **Qualif.:** Applicants must be currently enrolled RPA, FMA, SMA or SMT students, taking home study, classroom study or accelerated courses; must be employed by a BOMA/NY member firm and working within the 5 Boroughs of New York. **Criteria:** Applicants are evaluated on the basis of merit and demonstrated financial need.

Funds Avail.: No specific amount. **To Apply:** Applicants must submit completed application form along with a one page essay and letter of recommendation from current employer. **Deadline:** July 31. **Remarks:** Established in 1988. **Contact:** Mary Sorgente, Director of Education; Phone: 212-239-3662; E-mail: mary@bomany.com.

2405 ■ Bulletin of the Atomic Scientists
1155 E 60th St.
Chicago, IL 60637
Ph: (707)481-9372
E-mail: admin@thebulletin.org
URL: thebulletin.org
Facebook: www.facebook.com/BulletinOfTheAtomicScientists
LinkedIn: www.linkedin.com/company/bulletin-of-the-atomic-scientists
Twitter: twitter.com/BulletinAtomic

2406 ■ Rieser Fellowships (Undergraduate/Fellowship)

Purpose: To provide financial support for undergraduate students pursuing a project relating to interaction of science, global security, and public policy. **Focus:** National security; Peace studies. **Qualif.:** Applicant must be an undergraduate student at a U.S. college/university. **Criteria:** Awards are given based on academic interests, extracurricular activities and career aspiration.

Funds Avail.: $4,000. **Duration:** One year. **Number Awarded:** 2. **To Apply:** Applicant must send an application form (available at the website); resume; proposal (800-1000 words); official letters confirming internships, acceptance to conference; an essay (one-page, single-spaced) explaining how the fellowship would be benefit the applicant; project budget; and two letters of recommendation. **Deadline:** March 31.

2407 ■ Bunker Family Association (BFA)
c/o Gil Bunker, President
9 Sommerset Rd.
Turnersville, NJ 08012-2122
Ph: (856)589-6140
E-mail: membership@bunkerfamilyassn.org
URL: www.bunkerfamilyassn.org

2408 ■ Annabelle Moore Scholarship (Undergraduate/Scholarship)

Purpose: To support the continuing education of the relative of an Association member. **Focus:** General studies/Field of study not specified. **Qualif.:** Applicant must be a child or grandchild of a Bunker Family Association member in good standing, and must be a high school graduating senior or college freshman. **Criteria:** Selection will be based on the following: scholarship attainment, goals and worthiness, financial need, and activities and awards.

Funds Avail.: $500. **Duration:** Annual. **Number Awarded:** 1. **To Apply:** Every applicant is expected to comply with the following application process: complete the current application form; provide a genealogy chart showing Bunker lineage; and, forward a complete high school transcript (with official HS seal) containing marks for the most recent term or semester. **Deadline:** May 1.

2409 ■ Burger King McLamore Foundation
5505 Blue Lagoon Dr.
Miami, FL 33126
Ph: (305)378-3186
Fax: (305)378-7017
E-mail: bk_mclamorefoundation@whopper.com
URL: bkmclamorefoundation.org

2410 ■ Burger King Employee Scholars Program (Undergraduate/Scholarship)

Purpose: To provide scholarship awards to assist students who excel academically while also working part-time and being actively involved in their community. **Focus:** General studies/Field of study not specified. **Qualif.:** Applicants must be high school seniors who: are salaried or hourly team members of a Burger King restaurant; active on BK payroll for at least 12 months of the current year's application deadline; maintain at least a 2.0 GPA throughout high school or college; enrolled at an accredited college/vocational school in the fall of the scholarship year; participate in extracurricular activities or community service; receive written recommendation from his or her BK employer. **Criteria:** Selection will be based on financial need, community involvement, employment at a participating restaurant location, academic achievements and records.

Awards are arranged alphabetically below their administering organizations

Funds Avail.: No specific amount. **To Apply:** Applicants must log on to www.applyists.net to get an application and must follow the onscreen instructions. **Contact:** For additional information, applicants must contact the International Scholarship and Tuition Services, Inc.; Phone: 615-320-3149; Fax: 615-320-3151. Application form and supporting documents can be faxed at 615-627-9685 or 615-627-9673 or can be emailed at bkscholars@applyists.com.

2411 ■ Burger King Scholars Program
(Undergraduate/Scholarship)

Purpose: To provide scholarship awards to assist students who excel academically while also working part-time and being actively involved in their community. **Focus:** General studies/Field of study not specified. **Qualif.:** Applicants must be high school seniors who: maintain a cumulative GPA of 2.5 or higher on a 4.0 scale or the equivalent; work part-time an average of 15 hours per week; demonstrate participation in community service activities; demonstrate financial need; plan to enroll in an accredited two-year or four-year college, university or vocational/technical school; graduating high school seniors or graduating from home school education; must be U.S. or Canada residents. Companies and franchise restaurants, corporate and field employees are eligible to apply. **Criteria:** Selection will be based on the submitted application.

Funds Avail.: $1,000. **To Apply:** Applicants may apply online. **Deadline:** January 10.

2412 ■ Burroughs Wellcome Fund
21 T.W. Alexander Dr.
Research Triangle Park, NC 27709
Ph: (919)991-5100
Fax: (919)991-5160
E-mail: info@bwfund.org
URL: www.bwfund.org

2413 ■ Burroughs Wellcome Fund Collaborative Research Travel Grants (CRTG) *(Doctorate, Postdoctorate, Professional development/Grant)*

Purpose: To support researchers from degree-granting institutions with travel either domestically or internationally to acquire new research techniques, to promote collaborations and to attend courses. **Focus:** Biology; Chemistry; Computer and information sciences; Engineering; Mathematics and mathematical sciences; Physics; Statistics. **Qualif.:** Applicants must be postdoctoral fellows or faculty at degree-granting institutions in the U.S. or Canada; must hold a Ph.D. in mathematics, physics, chemistry, computer science, statistics, or engineering at the time of application; and interested in investigating research opportunities in the biological sciences; biologists holding a doctorate degree at the time of application who are interested in working with physical scientists, mathematicians, engineers, chemists, statisticians, or computer scientists to incorporate their ideas and approaches to answering biological questions are eligible as well; must be citizens or permanent residents of the U.S. or Canada at the time of application. **Criteria:** Selection of awards is made by a scientific advisory committee with final approval by the Burroughs Wellcome Fund Board of Directors. Selection is made on the basis of the proposal's scientific quality of the proposed activities and the career development potential and impact of the collaboration/visit. BWF does not provide critiques of unfunded proposals.

Funds Avail.: $15,000. **Duration:** Annual. **Number Awarded:** Varies. **To Apply:** Applicants must read all information provided in the program website to ensure successful application. Prepare, in advance, the documents required in the proposal elements. Combine and order the supporting materials into one (1) PDF file (prescribed formats are provided in the program website). Upload the combined file of supporting documents as one attachment on the "Attachments" page of the submission website. Other procedures must be confer to the program and submission websites. **Deadline:** February 2. **Contact:** Debra Holmes, Senior Program Associate, at the above address; Email: dholmes@bwfund.org.

2414 ■ Career Awards for Medical Scientists (CAMS) *(Postdoctorate, Advanced Professional, Professional development/Grant)*

Purpose: To support research and other scientific and educational activities of career medical scientists. **Focus:** Biomedical sciences; Medical research. **Qualif.:** Ideal candidates must be two years away from becoming independent investigators, have at least two years or more of postdoctoral research experience, and have significant publication records; must be nominated by their dean or department chair at the degree-granting institution where they will conduct the postdoctoral/fellowship training under the award; must hold an MD, DDS, DVM, PharmD or equivalent clinical degree; must be citizens or permanent residents of the U.S. or Canada at the time of application. **Criteria:** The CAMS Advisory Committee will review applications, interview finalists, and make recommendations for approval to BWF's Board of Directors.

Funds Avail.: $700,000. **Duration:** Annual. **Number Awarded:** Varies. **To Apply:** Candidates must be nominated by their dean or department chair at the degree-granting institution where they will conduct the postdoctoral/fellowship training under the award. They must read all information provided in the program website to ensure successful application. Prepare, in advance, the documents required in the proposal elements. Combine and order the supporting materials into one (1) PDF file (prescribed formats are provided in the program website). Upload the combined file of supporting documents as one attachment on the "Attachments" page of the submission website. Other procedures must be confer to the program and submission websites. **Deadline:** October 1. **Contact:** Debra Holmes, Senior Program Associate; Email: dholmes@bwfund.org.

2415 ■ Career Awards for Science and Mathematics Teachers *(Other/Award)*

Purpose: To recognize teachers who have demonstrated solid knowledge of science and/or mathematics content and have outstanding performance records in educating children. **Focus:** Mathematics and mathematical sciences; Science. **Qualif.:** Candidates in a middle school and high school must hold licensure to teach science and/or mathematics in North Carolina and have completed at least five years of teaching experience at the time of application with at least 70 percent of their time devoted to teaching science and/or mathematics courses. Candidates in elementary schools, who also can be science and/or mathematics specialists, must have completed at least five years of teaching at the time of application; with at least 30 percent of the candidate's time spent teaching science and/or mathematics. At least 20 percent of their time should be spent working with other teachers if they are specialists. Candidates must have superior knowledge of science and/or mathematics, excellent teaching skills, demonstrated leadership and a commitment to continue teaching in the North Carolina Public School system; must be currently licensed North Carolina public school science and/or mathematics teachers who teach in grades K-12 in North Carolina public schools; and must be citizens of the United States. **Criteria:** Selection will be based primarily on the following: candidate's qualifications and potential to conduct high-quality science and/or mathematics teaching; candidate's significant contributions to enhancing students' knowledge of science and/or mathematics; candidate's knowledge of subject content and effectiveness of communications skills; candidate's abilities in the classroom that should demonstrate learner-centered, knowledge-centered, assessment-centered and community-centered learning styles; candidate's support from the principal and superintendent. **Funds Avail.:** $175,000. **Duration:** Annual; five years. **To Apply:** All applications will require signatures and letters of support from the principal of the candidate's school and the superintendent of the school district. More than one candidate from a school or school district is eligible to apply. In support of the application, the principal and superintendent must demonstrate that the necessary environment for successful science and/or mathematics teaching exists at the school and that there are opportunities for the teacher to be mentored and to mentor other teachers. The principal and superintendent must clearly outline in letters of support how the teaching professional will be supported and developed as a teacher leader in the districts. **Deadline:** September 15. **Contact:** Melanie Scott, Senior Program Associate, at the above address; or Email: mscott@bwfund.org.

2416 ■ Career Awards at the Scientific Interface (CASI) (Doctorate, Postdoctorate, Advanced Professional, Professional development/Grant)

Purpose: To advance post-doctoral training and to foster the early career development of researchers whose works are dedicated to pursuing a career in academic research. **Focus:** Biochemistry; Biology; Biophysics; Chemistry; Computer and information sciences; Engineering; Mathematics and mathematical sciences; Medicine; Physics; Statistics. **Qualif.:** Candidates must hold a Ph.D. degree in one of the fields of mathematics, physics, chemistry, computer science, statistics, or engineering. Ph.D. is in biochemistry/biophysics/biology/cell biology/chemistry or who have an engineering degree, M.D. are also eligible, provided, they meet other eligibility criteria or any other qualifications set by the BWF for this program. **Criteria:** The Interfaces in Science Advisory Committee will review all preproposals, select candidates to invite for submission of full applications, interview finalists, and make recommendations for awards to the BWF Board of Directors. Selection will be based on: depth and rigor of training in a scientific discipline other than biology; importance of biological questions identified in the proposal, and innovation in the approaches chosen to answer them; nterdisciplinary nature of research plan, the degree to which non-biological methods are integrated, and the degree to which the proposed work will open new fields of inquiry; potential of candidate to establish a successful independent research career, evidenced by productivity during the postdoctoral period prior to application; and, quality of proposed collaborations. **Funds Avail.:** $500,000. **Duration:** Annual; five years. **Number Awarded:** Varies. **To Apply:** Applicants must read all information provided in the program website to ensure successful application. Prepare, in advance, the documents required in the proposal elements. Combine and order the supporting materials into one (1) PDF file (prescribed formats are provided in the program website). Upload the combined file of supporting documents as one attachment on the "Attachments" page of the submission website. Other procedures must be confer to the program and submission websites. **Deadline:** January 8. **Contact:** Rusty Kelley, Program Officer at rustykelley@bwfund.org.

2417 ■ Investigators in the Pathogenesis of Infectious Disease Awards (Doctorate, Postdoctorate, Professional development/Grant)

Purpose: To support accomplished investigators at the assistant professor level to study pathogenesis, with a focus on the interplay between human and microbial biology, shedding light on how human and microbial systems are affected by their encounters; and to provide opportunities for accomplished investigators still early in their careers to study what happens at the points where human and microbial systems connect. **Focus:** Biology; Infectious diseases; Pathology; Veterinary science and medicine. **Qualif.:** Candidates will generally have an M.D., D.V.M., or Ph.D. degree; must have an established record of independent research and hold a tenure-track position as an assistant professor or equivalent at the time the application is submitted; must be nominated by accredited, degree-granting institutions in the United States or Canada; must be citizens or permanent residents of the United States or Canada at the time of application. Rules for institutional nomination is provided at the program website. **Criteria:** BWF utilizes an external advisory committee composed of distinguished scientists from relevant pathogen and human biology fields to review applications and make funding recommendations for approval by BWF's Board of Directors. Proposal selection is based on a number of factors, including: candidate's qualifications and potential to conduct innovative research; quality and originality of the proposed research and its potential to advance understanding of fundamental issues of how infectious agents and human hosts interact; and, demonstration of an established record of independent research. **Funds Avail.:** $500,000. **Duration:** Annual. **To Apply:** Applicants must read all information provided in the program website to ensure successful application. Prepare, in advance, the documents required in the proposal elements. Combine and order the supporting materials into one (1) PDF file (prescribed formats are provided in the program website). Upload the combined file of supporting documents as one attachment on the "Attachments" page of the submission website. Other procedures must be confer to the program and submission websites. **Deadline:** November 5.

2418 ■ Bush Foundation
101 5th St. E, Ste. 2400
Saint Paul, MN 55101
Ph: (651)227-0891
Fax: (651)297-6485
E-mail: info@bushfoundation.org
URL: www.bushfoundation.org

2419 ■ Bush Artist Fellowships (Professional development/Fellowship)

Purpose: To support and develop more leaders who are better equipped and better networked to effectively lead change. **Focus:** Arts. **Qualif.:** Applicants must be residents of Minnesota, North Dakota or South Dakota; must be citizens or permanent residents of U.S.; must have lived in the listed region at least 24 months immediately prior to the application deadline; and at least 25-years-old on the application deadline. **Criteria:** Selection is based on applicant's strong vision; creative energy; commitment to excellence; and potential to fulfill the purpose of the Bush Artist Program.

Funds Avail.: Up to $100,000. **Duration:** Annual. **To Apply:** Applications will be accepted via online submission process. **Deadline:** September 29.

2420 ■ Bush Fellowship Program *(Other/Fellowship)*

Purpose: To motivate individuals who are eager to prepare themselves for greater leadership opportunities and to create positive change in their communities. **Focus:** Leadership, Institutional and community. **Qualif.:** Applicant must be a U.S. citizen or permanent resident; be 24 years or older at the application deadline date; have lived or worked for at least one continuous year immediately prior to the application deadline in Minnesota, North Dakota or South Dakota; and not a former Bush Leadership Fellows. **Criteria:** Selection committees review applicants' records with attention to leadership, learning and impact.

Funds Avail.: Up to $100,000. **Duration:** Annual. **To Apply:** Applications will be accepted via online submission process. **Deadline:** September 29.

2421 ■ Business and Professional Women's Foundation (BPWF)
1718 M St. NW, No. 148
Washington, DC 20036
Ph: (202)293-1100
Fax: (202)861-0298
E-mail: foundation@bpwfoundation.org
URL: www.bpwfoundation.org

2422 ■ BPW Foundation Career Advancement Scholarships *(Undergraduate/Scholarship)*

Purpose: To provide financial assistance to disadvantaged women seeking to further their education. **Focus:** General studies/Field of study not specified. **Qualif.:** Applicant must be a female at least 25 years of age; must be a U.S citizen or U.S national; must demonstrate critical financial need; must have an expected family contribution (EFC) of $2,500 or less; must be officially accepted into an accredited U.S college or university, including those in American Samoa, Puerto Rico, and the Virgin Islands; must demonstrate clear career plans; must not be earning a doctoral-level or terminal degree. **Criteria:** Applications will be reviewed by the scholarship committee.

Funds Avail.: No specific amount. **Duration:** Annual. **To Apply:** Scholarship application and other supporting documents must be sent to BPW foundation.

2423 ■ Business Professionals of America (BPA)
5454 Cleveland Ave.
Columbus, OH 43231-4021
Ph: (614)895-7277
Fax: (614)895-1165
Free: 800-334-2007
URL: www.bpa.org

2424 ■ National Technical Honor Society Scholarships *(Professional development/Scholarship)*

Purpose: To assist outstanding seniors of Business Professionals of America in the Secondary Division. **Focus:** Business. **Qualif.:** Applicants must be members of Business Professionals of America who are graduating high school seniors with minimum grade point average of 3.0. **Criteria:** Applicants are evaluated based on academic success and involvement within the organization.

Funds Avail.: $1,000. **Number Awarded:** 3. **To Apply:** Applicants must submit completed application form along with the school grade transcript or letter from his/her school principal verifying GPA; a one-page, typed resume of activities involving both Business Professionals of America and other school and community activities; three signed recommendation letters on official letterhead from local advisor and two individuals of their choice; a one-page, double-spaced, typed essay on topic, "What ideals have you taken from BPA and implemented into both your professional and personal lives?" and "How do you interpret the phrase"Uncover Your Magic" and give an example of how you have been embodied the phrase in your life?". **Deadline:** March 15. **Contact:** Heather Bunning, Director of Strategic Advancement at hbunning@bpa.org.

2425 ■ Business Solution Association (BSA)
3601 Joppa Rd.
Baltimore, MD 21234-3314
Ph: (410)931-8100
Fax: (410)931-8111
URL: www.businesssolutionsassociation.com

2426 ■ BSA Educational Scholarships *(Undergraduate/Scholarship)*

Purpose: To provide educational assistance to individuals affiliated with the office products industry. **Focus:** General studies/Field of study not specified. **Qualif.:** Applicants must be employees or relatives of an employee of a BSA member firm or a group affiliated with the office product industry. **Criteria:** Selection is based on academic success, interest, abilities, and financial need.

Funds Avail.: No specific amount. **Duration:** Annual. **To Apply:** Application form is available at the website. Applicants must prepare a transcript of grades and credits; a letter of recommendation from a person employed by a firm in the office products industry (must hold an executive or managerial position) and another from a teacher, professor or other educational professional. **Deadline:** March 21.

2427 ■ Cactus and Succulent Society of America (CSSA)
PO Box 1000
Claremont, CA 91711-1000
URL: www.cssainc.org

2428 ■ CSSA Research Grants *(Undergraduate, Graduate, Advanced Professional/Grant)*

Purpose: To support research on succulent plants. **Focus:** Botany. **Qualif.:** Program is open to all applicants, without respect to gender, age, nationality, or affiliation. **Criteria:** Selection will be based on the grant applications of the applicants. Grant applications will be reviewed on the basis of merit of the proposal and the competence of the investigator(s) to conduct the proposed research.

Funds Avail.: $1,200 to $3,000. **Duration:** Semiannual. **Number Awarded:** Varies. **To Apply:** Applicants must submit their respective research proposals on or before the deadline. All proposals must be written in English and

Awards are arranged alphabetically below their administering organizations

submitted in a format that can be copied directly onto 8.5 x 11 inch paper. If possible, the proposal should be submitted as a Microsoft Word document attached to an email addressed provided at the Contact. Components of the proposal are enumerated at the website. **Deadline:** February 1; July 1.

2429 ■ The Calgary Foundation
700, 999 8 St., SW
Calgary, AB, Canada T2R 1J5
Ph: (403)802-7700
Fax: (403)802-7701
E-mail: info@calgaryfoundation.org
URL: www.thecalgaryfoundation.org/

2430 ■ Kathryn Huget Leadership Awards *(Master's, Doctorate/Award)*

Purpose: To improve the role of leadership in business and specifically the advancement of women in leadership roles. **Focus:** Leadership, Institutional and community. **Qualif.:** Applicants must be studying at Master's or PhD level, preferably female students currently in leadership roles, whose focus is to improve the business workplace for women studying in the areas of: organizational behavior, business administration, business and commerce, sociology or psychology. **Criteria:** Selection will be based on the committee's criteria.

Funds Avail.: Minimum of $1,000. **To Apply:** Applicants must provide a one page brief summary of their involvement in business and views of leadership and two letters from business references. For further information applicants may contact the Society for the application process and other required materials. **Deadline:** June 30.

2431 ■ Calhoun Community College
PO Box 2216
Decatur, AL 35609
Ph: (256)306-2500
Free: 800-626-3628
E-mail: webmaster@calhoun.edu
URL: www.calhoun.edu
Facebook: www.facebook.com/Calhoun-Community
 -College-40190388729/?ref=nf
Twitter: twitter.com/CalhounCollege

2432 ■ Calhoun Valedictorian, Salutatorian/Top 5% Scholarships *(Undergraduate/Scholarship)*

Purpose: To provide educational assistance to Calhoun students. **Focus:** General studies/Field of study not specified. **Qualif.:** Applicants must be U.S. citizens who have a graduating cumulative GPA of 3.0 or higher and have a minimum composite score of 20 on the ACT. They must have been enrolled and accepted to Calhoun as full-time students. **Criteria:** Selection will be based on the committee's criteria.

Funds Avail.: No specific amount. **Duration:** Annual. **To Apply:** Applicants must complete a FAFSA (Free Application for Federal Student Aid) by March 1 in order to be considered. They must also complete the online scholarship application and submit along with other required materials and information. **Deadline:** March 1.

2433 ■ California Association for Health, Physical Education, Recreation, and Dance (CAHPERD)
1501 El Camino Ave., Ste. 3
Sacramento, CA 95815-2748
Ph: (916)922-3596
Fax: (916)922-0133
Free: 800-499-3596
E-mail: membership@cahperd.org
URL: www.cahperd.org
Facebook: www.facebook.com/CAHPERD
Twitter: twitter.com/cahperd

2434 ■ James Echols Scholarship Award *(Undergraduate/Scholarship)*

Purpose: To support the highest ranked minority applicants in their continuing education. **Focus:** Dance; Education, Physical; Health sciences. **Qualif.:** Applicants must: be students majoring in Health, Physical Education, Recreation or Dance; have completed (or be enrolled in) a minimum of 60 semester/90 quarter units of college work; be residents of California and attend a 2 or 4 year college/university within the State; have a minimum 3.0 overall GPA; be CAHPERD members for a minimum of 30 days prior to application. **Criteria:** Criteria for selection includes the following: scholastic proficiency; leadership ability; and, personal qualities.

Funds Avail.: $1,000. **Duration:** Annual. **To Apply:** Applicants must submit a completed application form, three letters of recommendation, and scholastic verification by the university registrar's office or transcripts of all college work. **Deadline:** December 31.

2435 ■ John F. Kennedy Scholarship Award *(Undergraduate/Scholarship)*

Purpose: To support the highest ranked undergraduate applicants in their continuing education. **Focus:** Dance; Education, Physical; Health sciences. **Qualif.:** Applicants must: be students majoring in Health, Physical Education, Recreation or Dance; have completed (or be enrolled in) a minimum of 60 semester/90 quarter units of college work; be residents of California and attend a 2 or 4 year college/university within the State; have a minimum 3.0 overall GPA; be CAHPERD members for a minimum of 30 days prior to application. **Criteria:** Criteria for selection includes the following: scholastic proficiency; leadership ability; and, personal qualities.

Funds Avail.: $1,000. **Duration:** Annual. **To Apply:** Applicants must submit a completed application form, three letters of recommendation, and scholastic verification by the university registrar's office or transcripts of all college work. **Deadline:** December 31.

2436 ■ Winifred Van Hagen/Rosalind Cassidy Scholarship Award *(Undergraduate/Scholarship)*

Purpose: To support the highest ranked applicants in their continuing education. **Focus:** Dance; Education, Physical; Health sciences. **Qualif.:** Applicants must: be students majoring in Health, Physical Education, Recreation or Dance; have completed (or be enrolled in) a minimum of 60 semester/90 quarter units of college work; be residents of California and attend a 2 or 4 year college/university within the State; have a minimum 3.0 overall GPA; be CAHPERD members for a minimum of 30 days prior to application. **Criteria:** Criteria for selection includes the following: scholastic proficiency; leadership ability; and, personal qualities.

Funds Avail.: $1,000. **Duration:** Annual. **To Apply:** Applicants must submit a completed application form, three letters of recommendation, and scholastic verification by the university registrar's office or transcripts of all college

Awards are arranged alphabetically below their administering organizations

work. **Deadline:** December 31.

2437 ■ California Association of Pest Control Advisers (CAPCA)
2300 River Plaza Dr., Ste. 120
Sacramento, CA 95833
Ph: (916)928-1625
Fax: (916)928-0705
URL: capca.com
Facebook: www.facebook.com/CAPestControlAdvisers

2438 ■ Stanley W. Strew Educational Fund Scholarships *(Undergraduate/Scholarship)*
Purpose: To support and promote agricultural pest control advisers or professional production consultants who serve California agricultural and horticultural producers. **Focus:** Agricultural sciences. **Qualif.:** Applicants must be incoming junior, senior or graduate students planning to pursue a career in pest management; must have a 2.5 GPA or better. **Criteria:** Recipients are selected based on academics; financial need; extra curricular activities; pest management experience; professional/career goals; class standing.

Funds Avail.: $3,000. **Duration:** Annual. **To Apply:** Applicants must submit a completed application form; must include a current official transcript of records; must submit at least two letters of recommendation. **Deadline:** May 8.

2439 ■ California Association of Private Postsecondary Schools (CAPPS)
555 Capitol Mall, Ste. 705
Sacramento, CA 95814
Ph: (916)447-5500
Fax: (916)440-8970
Free: 888-922-2777
E-mail: info@cappsonline.org
URL: www.cappsonline.org

2440 ■ Sue Fleming Memorial Scholarships *(Undergraduate/Scholarship)*
Purpose: To ensure that the needs of the entire sector, from small registered schools to large institutions are met from an educational, policy and business perspective. **Focus:** Cosmetology; Health sciences; Nursing. **Qualif.:** Applicants must be enrolled in an allied health program at a CAPP's member School; must be recommended by the School Director or President. **Criteria:** Recipients are selected based on academic performance.

Funds Avail.: No specific amount. **Duration:** Annual. **To Apply:** Applicants must submit one to two-page essay along with the completed application form, transcript and three letters of recommendation.

2441 ■ California Bar Foundation
180 Howard St.
San Francisco, CA 94105-1939
Ph: (415)856-0780
Fax: (415)856-0788
E-mail: info@calbarfoundation.org
URL: www.calbarfoundation.org

2442 ■ California Bar Foundation 1L Diversity Scholarships *(Graduate/Scholarship)*
Purpose: To defray the cost of the students' 1L year. **Focus:** Law. **Qualif.:** Applicants must be diverse law students throughout the state. Any diverse student who will matriculate in a California law school is eligible. **Criteria:** Selection will be based on the committees' criteria.

Funds Avail.: $7,500. **Duration:** Annual; each fall. **To Apply:** Applicants may contact the Foundation for the application process and other information. **Deadline:** May 31.

2443 ■ California Bar Foundation 3L Diversity Scholarships *(Undergraduate/Scholarship)*
Purpose: To help offset high cost of law school education. **Focus:** Law. **Qualif.:** Candidates must be enrolled in a California law school or must have completed at least one year of study at a California law school (the candidates' law school must certify good ethical standing of the candidates while attending law school and must also attest to the candidate's financial need). They must maintain at least a 2.5 or equivalent on a 4.0 scale (or provide an explanation of extenuating circumstances if GPA is lower than 2.5). **Criteria:** Selection will be based on the committee's criteria.

Funds Avail.: No specific amount. **Duration:** Annual. **To Apply:** Applicants must accomplish complete application package which includes: application; certification and authorization form (which includes certification of non-relationship, authorization to use information, name and likeness and consent and authorization to obtain information); resume; personal statement describing the candidate's commitment to and plans for a legal career in public service (not to exceed 400 words); three letters of recommendation; law school transcript; certification of financial need; certification of ethical standing and statement of nomination; and optional statement of financial circumstances. Candidate's name must appear in the upper right-hand corner of each page of every document submitted.

2444 ■ Rosenthal Bar Exam Scholarship Fund *(Advanced Professional/Scholarship)*
Purpose: To provide financial support to outstanding graduating California law students who are embarking on careers in public service law. **Focus:** Law. **Qualif.:** Candidates must be graduating or have graduated from a California law school; be taking the California Bar Exam for the first time; and, maintain at least a 2.5 GPA or equivalent on a 4.0 scale (or provide an explanation of extenuating circumstances if GPA is lower than 2.5). **Criteria:** Selection will be based on the committee's criteria.

Funds Avail.: $3,000 and/or cash awards of up to $1,000. **Duration:** Annual. **To Apply:** Candidates must be nominated by their law school. **Remarks:** Established in 1997.

2445 ■ California Grocers Association (CGA)
1215 K St., Ste. 700
Sacramento, CA 95814-3946
Ph: (916)448-3545
Fax: (916)448-2793
URL: www.cagrocers.com
Facebook: www.facebook.com/CAGrocers

2446 ■ Lou Amen Legacy Scholarships *(Undergraduate/Scholarship)*
Purpose: To provide proactive leadership, education, advocacy and information. **Focus:** General studies/Field of study not specified. **Qualif.:** Applicants must be high school seniors, college freshmen, sophomores and juniors who are dependents of employees or are themselves employees of a CGA member company; must be planning to enroll as

Awards are arranged alphabetically below their administering organizations

full-time college students at an accredited, non-profit college or university in the United States. **Criteria:** Recipients are selected based on academic merit, evidence of outstanding character and leadership potential.

Funds Avail.: No specific amount. **To Apply:** Applicants must submit a completed application form. **Deadline:** April 1.

2447 ■ Don C. Beaver Memorial Scholarships
(Undergraduate/Scholarship)

Purpose: To provide financial aid to student who pursuing a career in grocery industry. **Focus:** General studies/Field of study not specified. **Qualif.:** Applicants must be high school seniors, college freshmen, sophomores and juniors who are dependents of employees or are themselves employees of a CGA member company; must be planning to enroll as full-time college students at an accredited, non-profit college or university in the United States. **Criteria:** Recipients are selected based on academic merit, evidence of outstanding character and leadership potential.

Funds Avail.: $2,000. **To Apply:** Applicants must submit a completed application form. **Deadline:** April 1.

2448 ■ Jack H. Brown Scholarships *(Undergraduate/Scholarship)*

Purpose: To provide proactive leadership, education, advocacy and information. **Focus:** General studies/Field of study not specified. **Qualif.:** Applicants must be high school seniors, college freshmen, sophomores and juniors who are dependents of employees or are themselves employees of a CGA member company; must be planning to enroll as full-time college students at an accredited, non-profit college or university in the United States. **Criteria:** Recipients are selected based on academic merit, evidence of outstanding character and leadership potential.

Funds Avail.: No specific amount. **To Apply:** Applicants must submit a completed application form. **Deadline:** April 1.

2449 ■ Classic Wines of California Scholarships
(Undergraduate/Scholarship)

Purpose: To provide proactive leadership, education, advocacy and information. **Focus:** General studies/Field of study not specified. **Qualif.:** Applicants must be high school seniors, college freshmen, sophomores and juniors who are dependents of employees or are themselves employees of a CGA member company; must be planning to enroll as full-time college students at an accredited, non-profit college or university in the United States. **Criteria:** Recipients are selected based on academic merit, evidence of outstanding character and leadership potential.

Funds Avail.: $1,500. **Number Awarded:** 2. **To Apply:** Applicants must submit a completed application form. **Deadline:** April 1. **Contact:** CGA Educational Foundation; Email: foundation@cagrocers.com.

2450 ■ Hall of Achievement Scholarships
(Undergraduate/Scholarship)

Purpose: To provide proactive leadership, education, advocacy and information. **Focus:** General studies/Field of study not specified. **Qualif.:** Applicants must be high school seniors, college freshmen, sophomores and juniors who are dependents of employees or are themselves employees of a CGA member company; must be planning to enroll as full-time college students at an accredited, non-profit college or university in the United States. **Criteria:** Recipients are selected based on academic merit, evidence of outstanding character and leadership potential.

Funds Avail.: $2,000. **To Apply:** Applicants must submit a completed application form. **Deadline:** April 1.

2451 ■ Roger K. Hughes Legacy Scholarships
(Undergraduate/Scholarship)

Purpose: To provide proactive leadership, education, advocacy and information. **Focus:** General studies/Field of study not specified. **Qualif.:** Applicants must be high school seniors, college freshmen, sophomores and juniors who are dependents of employees or are themselves employees of a CGA member company; must be planning to enroll as full-time college students at an accredited, non-profit college or university in the United States. **Criteria:** Recipients are selected based on academic merit, evidence of outstanding character and leadership potential.

Funds Avail.: $1,000. **To Apply:** Applicants must submit a completed application form. **Deadline:** April 1.

2452 ■ Paul A. Hughes Memorial Scholarships
(Undergraduate/Scholarship)

Purpose: To provide proactive leadership, education, advocacy and information. **Focus:** General studies/Field of study not specified. **Qualif.:** Applicants must be high school seniors, college freshmen, sophomores and juniors who are dependents of employees or are themselves employees of a CGA member company; must be planning to enroll as full-time college students at an accredited, non-profit college or university in the United States. **Criteria:** Recipients are selected based on academic merit, evidence of outstanding character and leadership potential.

Funds Avail.: $1,000. **To Apply:** Applicants must submit a completed application form. **Deadline:** April 1.

2453 ■ Illuminator Educational Foundation Scholarships *(Undergraduate/Scholarship)*

Purpose: To provide proactive leadership, education, advocacy and information. **Focus:** General studies/Field of study not specified. **Qualif.:** Applicants must be high school seniors, college freshmen, sophomores and juniors who are dependents of employees or are themselves employees of a CGA member company; must be planning to enroll as full-time college students at an accredited, non-profit college or university in the United States. **Criteria:** Recipients are selected based on academic merit, evidence of outstanding character and leadership potential.

Funds Avail.: $1,000. **Number Awarded:** 10. **To Apply:** Applicants must submit a completed application form. **Deadline:** April 1.

2454 ■ Don Kaplan Legacy Scholarships
(Undergraduate/Scholarship)

Purpose: To provide proactive leadership, education, advocacy and information. **Focus:** General studies/Field of study not specified. **Qualif.:** Applicants must be high school seniors, college freshmen, sophomores and juniors who are dependents of employees or are themselves employees of a CGA member company; must be planning to enroll as full-time college students at an accredited, non-profit college or university in the United States. **Criteria:** Recipients are selected based on academic merit, evidence of outstanding character and leadership potential.

Funds Avail.: $1,000. **To Apply:** Applicants must submit a completed application form. **Deadline:** April 1.

Awards are arranged alphabetically below their administering organizations

2455 ■ Peter and Jody Larkin Legacy Scholarships
(Undergraduate/Scholarship)

Purpose: To provide proactive leadership, education, advocacy and information. **Focus:** General studies/Field of study not specified. **Qualif.:** Applicants must be high school seniors, college freshmen, sophomores and juniors who are dependents of employees or are themselves employees of a CGA member company; must be planning to enroll as full-time college students at an accredited, non-profit college or university in the United States. **Criteria:** Recipients are selected based on academic merit, evidence of outstanding character and leadership potential.

Funds Avail.: No specific amount. **To Apply:** Applicants must submit a completed application form. **Deadline:** April 1.

2456 ■ Bill MacAloney Legacy Scholarships
(Undergraduate/Scholarship)

Purpose: To provide proactive leadership, education, advocacy and information. **Focus:** General studies/Field of study not specified. **Qualif.:** Applicants must be high school seniors, college freshmen, sophomores and juniors who are dependents of employees or are themselves employees of a CGA member company; must be planning to enroll as full-time college students at an accredited, non-profit college or university in the United States. **Criteria:** Recipients are selected based on academic merit, evidence of outstanding character and leadership potential.

Funds Avail.: $1,000. **To Apply:** Applicants must submit a completed application form. **Deadline:** April 1.

2457 ■ Al Plamann Legacy Scholarships
(Undergraduate/Scholarship)

Purpose: To provide proactive leadership, education, advocacy and information. **Focus:** General studies/Field of study not specified. **Qualif.:** Applicants must be high school seniors, college freshmen, sophomores and juniors who are dependents of employees or are themselves employees of a CGA member company; must be planning to enroll as full-time college students at an accredited, non-profit college or university in the United States. **Criteria:** Recipients are selected based on academic merit, evidence of outstanding character and leadership potential.

Funds Avail.: No specific amount. **To Apply:** Applicants must submit a completed application form. **Deadline:** April 1.

2458 ■ Save Mart Legacy Scholarships
(Undergraduate/Scholarship)

Purpose: To provide proactive leadership, education, advocacy and information. **Focus:** General studies/Field of study not specified. **Qualif.:** Applicants must be high school seniors, college freshmen, sophomores and juniors who are dependents of employees or are themselves employees of a CGA member company; must be planning to enroll as full-time college students at an accredited, non-profit college or university in the United States. **Criteria:** Recipients are selected based on academic merit, evidence of outstanding character and leadership potential.

Funds Avail.: No specific amount. **To Apply:** Applicants must submit a completed application form. **Deadline:** April 1.

2459 ■ Trelut Family Legacy Scholarships
(Undergraduate/Scholarship)

Purpose: To provide proactive leadership, education, advocacy and information. **Focus:** General studies/Field of study not specified. **Qualif.:** Applicants must be high school seniors, college freshmen, sophomores and juniors who are dependents of employees or are themselves employees of a CGA member company; must be planning to enroll as full-time college students at an accredited, non-profit college or university in the United States. **Criteria:** Selection will be based on the commmittee's criteria.

Funds Avail.: No specific amount. **To Apply:** Applicants must submit a completed application form. **Deadline:** April 1.

2460 ■ Bob Wilson Legacy Scholarships
(Undergraduate/Scholarship)

Purpose: To provide proactive leadership, education, advocacy and information. **Focus:** General studies/Field of study not specified. **Qualif.:** Applicants must be high school seniors, college freshmen, sophomores and juniors who are dependents of employees or are themselves employees of a CGA member company; must be planning to enroll as full-time college students at an accredited, non-profit college or university in the United States. **Criteria:** Recipients are selected based on academic merit, evidence of outstanding character and leadership potential.

Funds Avail.: No specific amount. **To Apply:** Applicants must submit a completed application form. **Deadline:** April 1.

2461 ■ California Groundwater Association (CGA)
PO Box 14369
Santa Rosa, CA 95402-6369
Ph: (707)578-4408
Fax: (707)546-4906
E-mail: wellguy@groundh2o.org
URL: www.groundh2o.org

2462 ■ California Groundwater Association Scholarships *(Undergraduate/Scholarship)*

Purpose: To provide financial assistance to those students who are in need. **Focus:** General studies/Field of study not specified. **Qualif.:** Applicants must be California residents; must be pursuing a major course of study in groundwater; must have a family affiliation with a member of the California Groundwater Association; must show proof of current admission or entry acceptance at an educational institution within 6 months of scholarship award. **Criteria:** Preference will be given to those who meet the criteria.

Funds Avail.: $2,000. **Number Awarded:** 2. **To Apply:** Applicants must obtain a CGA sponsor; submit transcript and letter of recommendation; and provide a 500 word essay about their interest in the groundwater field or their chosen field of study. Applicants must check the available website for the additional requirements. **Deadline:** March 15. **Remarks:** Established in 1989.

2463 ■ California-Hawaii Elks Association (CHEA)
5450 E Lamona Ave.
Fresno, CA 93727
Ph: (559)255-4531
Fax: (559)456-2659
E-mail: chea@chea-elks.org
URL: www.chea-elks.org
Facebook: www.facebook.com/CaliforniaHawaiiElks

Awards are arranged alphabetically below their administering organizations

Twitter: twitter.com/CalHawaiiElks

2464 ■ CHEA Undergraduate Scholarship Program for Students with Disabilities *(Undergraduate/Scholarship)*

Purpose: To provide financial assistance to students with disabilities wishing to further their education. **Focus:** General studies/Field of study not specified. **Qualif.:** Applicants must be U.S. citizens and be residents of California or Hawaii; must have a physical impairment, neurological impairment, visual, hearing and/or speech-language disorder; must be current or graduating high school students; must have passed the General Educational Development (GED) Examination or the California High School Proficiency Examination (CHSPE). **Criteria:** Recipients will be selected based on academic achievement and financial need. **Funds Avail.:** $1,000 to $2,000 each. **Duration:** Annual. **Number Awarded:** 20-30. **To Apply:** Applicants must submit a completed application form, financial statement, official transcript of records, two letters of recommendation and essay. **Deadline:** March 15. **Remarks:** Established in 1981.

2465 ■ CHEA Vocational Grants *(Undergraduate/Grant)*

Purpose: To assist students who are planning to pursue eligible vocational/technical courses. **Focus:** General studies/Field of study not specified. **Qualif.:** Applicants must be high school students; must be residents of California or Hawaii who are American citizens; and must have plans to pursue vocational/technical courses. **Criteria:** Applicants will be judged based on motivation, need, skills, grades, completeness and neatness of the given directions. **Funds Avail.:** $500 to $2,000. **Duration:** Annual. **To Apply:** Applicants must complete the application form; must fill-out the date of application issued; must submit a BPO Elks Lodge endorsement, transcript of grades or work records; must provide a budget for school year projected, financial information and exhibit.

2466 ■ California Landscape Contractors Association (CLCA)

1491 River Park Dr., Ste. 100
Sacramento, CA 95815
Ph: (916)830-2780
Fax: (916)830-2788
E-mail: web_admin@clca.org
URL: www.clca.org

2467 ■ CLCA Landscape Educational Advancement Foundation Educational Grant Program *(Undergraduate/Grant)*

Purpose: To provide financial assistance to landscape programs for special needs. **Focus:** Landscape architecture and design. **Qualif.:** Applicants must be students attending an accredited California community college or state university, majoring in ornamental horticulture and taking a minimum of six units. **Criteria:** Recipients are selected based on academic performance and financial need. **Funds Avail.:** No specific amount. **Duration:** Annual. **To Apply:** Applicants must fill-up completely the provided application form available online.

2468 ■ California Police Youth Charities (CPYC)

7401 Galilee Rd., Ste. 350
Roseville, CA 95678-6931
Ph: (916)787-4201
Fax: (916)787-4246
URL: www.calpyc.com
Facebook: www.facebook.com/California-Police-Youth-Charities-305889306203688

2469 ■ Youth Leadership Scholarships *(Undergraduate/Scholarship)*

Purpose: To support twelfth grade students who have engaged in meaningful leadership and citizenship volunteer activities during the past year. **Focus:** General studies/Field of study not specified. **Qualif.:** Applicants must be high school seniors who wish to pursue their studies in college; must be residents of California, sons, daughters or wards of an active or retired California Peace Officer. **Criteria:** Recipients are selected based on the content, grammar, format creativity and structure of essay, demonstrated importance of good citizenship in their essay, demonstrated leadership, volunteerism, student's work in school and community and number of hours the students volunteered. **Funds Avail.:** $500-$1,000. **Number Awarded:** 5. **To Apply:** Applicants must submit a completed application form and essay. **Deadline:** August 1. **Contact:** Chris Eaton, 3800 Watt Ave., Ste. 125, Sacramento, CA, 95821, Phone: 916-482-4245, Fax: 916-482-4246, Email: cbuzzeaton@msn.com.

2470 ■ California Psychological Association (CPA)

1231 I St., Ste. 204
Sacramento, CA 95814-2933
Ph: (916)286-7979
Fax: (916)286-7971
E-mail: cpa@cpapsych.org
URL: www.cpapsych.org

2471 ■ CPA Foundation Minority Scholarships *(Graduate/Scholarship)*

Purpose: To strengthen the field of psychology by increasing the number of psychologists from California's ethnically diverse communities. **Focus:** Psychology. **Qualif.:** Applicants must: be members of one or more established ethnic minority groups; be graduated from a regionally accredited undergraduate institution; have been accepted into a doctoral program in psychology at a regionally accredited or approved institution in the State of California; and, enrolled as full-time graduate students. **Criteria:** Applicants will be judged on their potential for pursuing doctoral level work in psychology. **Funds Avail.:** $2,500 each. **Duration:** Annual. **Number Awarded:** 4. **To Apply:** Applicants must submit a completed application form which includes an essay along with three letters of recommendation (Applicant Evaluation Form); official copy of most recent transcript (mailed directly from the academic institution to the Foundation); a letter of acceptance directly from the respective graduate program; and financial information. **Contact:** CPA Foundation, through California Psychological Association, at the above address.

2472 ■ California School Library Association (CSLA)

6444 E Spring St., No. 237
Long Beach, CA 90815-1553

Awards are arranged alphabetically below their administering organizations

Fax: (888)655-8480
Free: 888-655-8480
E-mail: info@csla.net
URL: www.csla.net

2473 ■ Jewell Gardiner Scholarships *(Undergraduate/Scholarship)*

Purpose: To support members with their teacher librarian credential program. **Focus:** Library and archival sciences. **Qualif.:** Applicants must be: enrolled in a Library Media Teacher Credential program; current members of CSLA Northern Region; and, willing to serve as active CSLA volunteers as members of at least one committee. **Criteria:** Preference will be given to first-time recipients and applicants with teaching experience. **Funds Avail.:** $1,000. **Duration:** Semiannual. **To Apply:** Application forms are available online. Applicants must submit a letter of recommendation including the following: (a) length of time known and in what capacity; (b) evaluation of applicant's ability as teacher and as fellow worker; (c) evaluation of leadership abilities; (d) description of strengths; and (e) assessment of success as a library media teacher. **Deadline:** August 1 (Fall Term); November 1 (Spring Term).

2474 ■ School Library Paraprofessional Scholarships - Southern Region *(Advanced Professional/Scholarship)*

Purpose: To assist school library paraprofessionals in completing a school library technician/paraprofessional certificate program or obtaining a teaching credential with the ultimate goal of pursuing a Library Media Teacher Credential. **Focus:** Library and archival sciences. **Qualif.:** Applicants must be working in a classified position in the library media field, either in a school, district or County Office of Education; must be enrolled in a two-year paraprofessional program with the goal of becoming a qualified library technician or in a teacher credential program with the ultimate goal of pursuing a Library Media Teacher Services Credential; must be residents of the area served by the CSLA Southern Section; must be members of the California School Library Association. **Criteria:** Selection of applicants will be based on the criteria of the selection committee. **Funds Avail.:** $500. **Duration:** Annual. **To Apply:** Application forms are available online. Applicants must provide three letters of recommendation: (a) must be from a professor of the school in which the applicant is enrolled; (b) must be from a CSLA Southern Section member; (c) must be from a former or current supervisor. **Deadline:** September 19.

2475 ■ Teacher Librarian Scholarships *(Master's/Scholarship)*

Purpose: To assist those persons seeking preparation leading toward a degree or credential that will qualify the individual to work as a professional in the school library field in a school setting. **Focus:** Library and archival sciences. **Qualif.:** Applicants must be enrolled in a professional school library media teacher-credentialing program or a master's degree program; must be residents of the area served by the CSLA Southern Section; must be members of the California School Library Association. **Criteria:** Selection of applicants will be based on the criteria of the selection committee. **Funds Avail.:** $1,000 each. **Duration:** Annual. **Number Awarded:** 2. **To Apply:** Applicants must provide three letters of recommendation: (a) must be from a CSLA member; (b) must be from a professor in the library media; (c) must be from a former or current supervisor or a fellow teacher. **Deadline:** September 19.

2476 ■ California Scottish Rite Foundation

2100 N Broadway, Ste. 350
Santa Ana, CA 92706
Ph: (714)547-7325
Fax: (714)541-7602
E-mail: info@casrf.org
URL: www.casr-foundation.org

2477 ■ California Scottish Rite Foundation Scholarships *(Undergraduate/Scholarship)*

Purpose: To provide financial assistance to young men and women who want to pursue their education at university and graduate level. **Focus:** General studies/Field of study not specified. **Qualif.:** Applicants must be undergraduate students who are residents of California state with ages ranging from 17 to 25 years old; must have a grade point average of 3.0 or better. **Criteria:** Applicants are evaluated based on demonstrated high ideals and ability; high grades in school; financial need and part-time employment. **Funds Avail.:** $2,000 per year. **Duration:** One year. **To Apply:** Applicants must submit completed application form along with certified transcript of grades for previous semester; typed letter with handwritten signature by student of their employment, planned courses in the coming quarter/semester and current mailing address. **Deadline:** February 20.

2478 ■ California Sea Grant

University of California
9500 Gilman Dr., Dept. 0232
La Jolla, CA 92093-0232
Ph: (858)534-4440
Fax: (858)534-2231
E-mail: jeckman@ucsd.edu
URL: www-csgc.ucsd.edu

2479 ■ California Sea Grant State Fellowship *(Graduate/Fellowship)*

Purpose: To provide a unique educational opportunity for graduate students who are interested both in marine resources and in the policy decisions affecting those resources. **Focus:** Water resources. **Qualif.:** Applicants must be graduate students enrolled in the field of marine resources. **Criteria:** Recipients will be evaluated based on submitted application and supporting documents. Host selection will depend on the following categories: a) quality of the fellowship opportunity; b) level of educational benefit for the fellow; c) the host office's previous experience working with interns, fellows or other mentoring/educational programs; and d) level of financial commitment. **Funds Avail.:** $42,000. **Duration:** Annual. **To Apply:** Applicants must submit a completed application form. Applicants must visit the website for further information. **Deadline:** September 17.

2480 ■ California Society of Radiologic Technologists (CSRT)

575 Market St., Ste. 2125
San Francisco, CA 94105

Awards are arranged alphabetically below their administering organizations

Ph: (415)278-0441
Fax: (415)764-4933
E-mail: email@csrt.org
URL: www.csrt.org
Facebook: www.facebook.com/groups/298778630785
Twitter: twitter.com/CSRTorg

2481 ■ Anna Ames Clinical Excellence Student Grants *(Undergraduate/Grant)*

Purpose: To provide financial assistance to radiologic science students enrolled in JRCERT-approved California schools. **Focus:** Radiology. **Qualif.:** Applicants must be CSRT members or apply for membership at the time of application; must be enrolled full-time in California Department of Health Services approved and Joint Review Committee for Education in Radiologic Technology (JRCERT) accredited education program of Radiologic Sciences; must be enrolled in the program for at least 6 months at the time of receipt of the award; and, must possess exceptional skills in the clinical environment. **Criteria:** Applicants are evaluated based on academic merit.

Funds Avail.: $500. **Duration:** Annual. **To Apply:** Applicants must submit the completed application form and all other required materials for the Grant in a sealed envelope to Cecilia Ortiz. **Deadline:** July 1. **Contact:** California Society of Radiologic Technologists, 575 Market St., Ste. 2125, San Francisco, CA 94105; Phone: 415-278-0441; Email: email@csrt.org.

2482 ■ Ruth McMillan Student Grants *(Undergraduate/Grant)*

Purpose: To provide financial assistance to radiologic science students enrolled in approved California schools. **Focus:** Radiology. **Qualif.:** Applicants must be CSRT members enrolled full-time in a California Department of Health Services approved and CSRT-recognized education program of Radiologic Sciences (at least 6 months enrolled in the program at the time of receipt of the award); must possess a minimum grade point average of 2.5 in all college courses. **Criteria:** Applicants are evaluated based on academic merit.

Funds Avail.: $500. **Duration:** Annual. **To Apply:** Applicants must submit a completed application form obtained from the CSRT office and other required materials for the Grant. **Deadline:** July 1. **Contact:** California Society of Radiologic Technologists, 575 Market St., Ste. 2125, San Francisco, CA 94105, Phone: 415-278-0441, Email: email@csrt.org.

2483 ■ Superior District Legislative Mentoring Student Grants *(Undergraduate/Grant)*

Purpose: To provide an opportunity to radiologic science students enrolled in approved California schools, through financial assistance, in order for them to participate in the legislative process. **Focus:** Radiology. **Qualif.:** Applicants must be CSRT members enrolled full-time in a California Department of Health Services-approved and CSRT-recognized education program of Radiologic Sciences for at least 6 months at the time of receipt of the award; and, must possess exceptional interest in leadership and the legislative process. **Criteria:** Applicants are evaluated based on personal merit and attributes.

Funds Avail.: No specific amount. **To Apply:** Applicants must submit the completed application form obtained from the CSRT office and the all other required application information materials.

2484 ■ Superior District Legislative Mentoring Student Grants RT to DC *(Undergraduate/Grant)*

Purpose: To provide an opportunity to radiologic science students enrolled in approved California schools, through financial assistance, in order for them to participate in the legislative process. **Focus:** Radiology. **Qualif.:** Applicants must be CSRT members enrolled full-time in a California Department of Health Services approved and CSRT-recognized education program of Radiologic Sciences for at least 6 months at the time of receipt of the award; must possess exceptional interest in leadership and the legislative process. **Criteria:** Recipients are selected based on academic merit and financial need.

Funds Avail.: No specific amount. **To Apply:** Applicants must submit the completed application form obtained from the CSRT office and the other required materials for the award.

2485 ■ California State University San Marcos Alumni Association (CSUSM)

California State University-San Marcos
333 S Twin Oaks Valley Rd.
San Marcos, CA 92096-0001
Ph: (760)750-4406
E-mail: alumni@csusm.edu
URL: alumniweb.csusm.edu

2486 ■ Cal State San Macros Alumna Scholarships *(Undergraduate/Scholarship)*

Purpose: To support fellow and future alumni in furthering their education. **Focus:** General studies/Field of study not specified. **Qualif.:** Applicant must be admitted to a degree or certificate program and enrolled in at least six units. **Criteria:** Selection is based on academic merit, commitment to the community, leadership potential, and diverse interest.

Funds Avail.: No specific amount. **Duration:** Annual. **Number Awarded:** 4. **To Apply:** Applicant must submit an application to the Financial Aid and Scholarship Office.

2487 ■ California Waterfowl Association (CWA)

1346 Blue Oaks Blvd.
Roseville, CA 95678
Ph: (916)648-1406
Fax: (916)648-1665
URL: www.calwaterfowl.org

2488 ■ Dennis Raveling Scholarships *(Undergraduate/Scholarship)*

Purpose: To support student(s) with a desire to pursue a career in waterfowl or wetlands ecology. **Focus:** Botany; Ecology; Wildlife conservation, management, and science; Zoology. **Qualif.:** Applicants must be students with a desire to pursue a career in waterfowl or wetlands ecology. **Criteria:** Recipients are selected based on candidates resolve, high academic achievement and project merit.

Funds Avail.: $2,000 (Fist place); $1,000 (Second place). **Duration:** Annual. **Number Awarded:** 2. **To Apply:** Applicants must submit a "one-page" proposal summary description on an original research or management project; must submit a detailed proposal if required or "one-page" statement explaining the course of study for which they need to support. Applicants must also submit their resume,

Awards are arranged alphabetically below their administering organizations

letter of support from faculty member and names and phone numbers of two references. **Deadline:** October 31. **Contact:** California Waterfowl Association, Nicole Chavez, 1346 Blue Oaks Blvd., Roseville, CA 95678; Sabreena Britt, Education Coordinator; Phone: 916 648-1406 ext. 102; Email: sbritt@calaterfowl.org.

2489 ■ Calista Corp.
301 Calista Ct., Ste. A
Anchorage, AK 99518
Ph: (907)279-5516
Fax: (907)272-5060
Free: 800-277-5516
E-mail: calista@calistacorp.com
URL: www.calistacorp.com

2490 ■ Calista Education and Culture Scholarships *(Graduate, Undergraduate, Vocational/Occupational/Scholarship)*

Purpose: To provide financial assistance to Alaska Natives to enable them to participate in continuing educational activities, formal programs of study and programs to improve their status. **Focus:** General studies/Field of study not specified. **Qualif.:** Applicant must be accepted to an accredited school who is enrolled on a full-time basis; must be a high school graduate or have earned a GED and be in good academic standing with at least 2.0 GPA; must be an Alaska Native shareholder or a lineal descendant of an Alaska Native shareholder with ties to the Calista region. **Criteria:** Recipient will be selected based on scholarship application requirements.

Funds Avail.: $500 - $1,500. **Duration:** Annual. **To Apply:** Applicants must complete the application form available online; must have the official transcript of records; must have a copy of birth certificate or Certificate of Indian Blood; must have a letter of acceptance from their college, university or vocational school; must provide an essay (up to 500 words) describing their educational and career goals, their reasons for attending school and what they hope to accomplish in the future using the knowledge gained from their educational experience. New applicant must include the Cost Information Sheet from the school they plan to attend, personal statement and complete reference form. Returning applicant is not required to submit a copy of birth certificate and reference form. **Deadline:** June 30.

2491 ■ Calvin Alumni Association
3201 Burton St. SE
Grand Rapids, MI 49546-4301
Ph: (616)526-6000
Fax: (616)526-8551
Free: 800-688-0122
E-mail: info@calvin.edu
URL: www.calvin.edu/offices-services/alumni-association
Facebook: www.facebook.com/calvinalumni
Twitter: twitter.com/CalvinAlumni

2492 ■ Calvin Alumni Association British Columbia Scholarships *(Undergraduate/Scholarship)*

Purpose: To support students who display evidence of faith commitment in the areas of leadership, volunteerism and service to the community. **Focus:** General studies/Field of study not specified. **Qualif.:** Applicants must be enrolled as freshmen students. **Criteria:** Recipients are selected based on Christian character and personal involvement in life of their community, desire for a Christian higher education, evidence of leadership, volunteerism and service to the Community.

Funds Avail.: $1,000. **Number Awarded:** 1. **To Apply:** Applicants must submit a completed application form. **Deadline:** February 2. **Contact:** Elaine Smit; Phone: 604-271-0283; Email: elaine_smit@hotmail.com.

2493 ■ Calvin Alumni Association California- Bay Area Scholarships *(Undergraduate/Scholarship)*

Purpose: To help students by providing scholarships for entering freshmen. **Focus:** General studies/Field of study not specified. **Qualif.:** Applicants must be current high school seniors; must live in California Bay Area; must have a minimum GPA of 3.0. **Criteria:** Recipients are selected based on academic performance and financial need.

Funds Avail.: No specific amount. **To Apply:** Applicants must submit a completed application form. **Contact:** Mary Schrotenboer, mary@schrotenboer.com.

2494 ■ Calvin Alumni Association Florida-Gulf Coast Scholarships *(Undergraduate/Scholarship)*

Purpose: To help students by providing scholarships for entering freshmen. **Focus:** General studies/Field of study not specified. **Qualif.:** Applicants must be first year students from the Gulf Coast Florida; must live within the Gulf Coast Chapter area. **Criteria:** Recipients are selected based on academic performance and community involvement.

Funds Avail.: No specific amount. **To Apply:** Applicants must submit a completed application form. **Deadline:** February 2. **Contact:** Max Vreugdenhil; Phone: 941-794-3016; E-mail: vreugdenhil@verizon.net.

2495 ■ Calvin Alumni Association-Illinois Scholarships *(Undergraduate/Scholarship)*

Purpose: To support students who display evidence of faith commitment in the areas of leadership, volunteerism and service to the community. **Focus:** General studies/Field of study not specified. **Qualif.:** Applicants must be first year students from the Chicagoland Areas. **Criteria:** Recipients are selected based on scholastic achievement, commitment in the areas of leadership, volunteerism and service to the community.

Funds Avail.: $1,000. **To Apply:** Applicants must submit a completed application form; two completed recommendation forms; must submit a completed recommendation from their school Principal or Counselor; must submit an official high school transcript. **Deadline:** February 2. **Contact:** Susan Anderson; Phone: 630-462-0406; E-mail: essengee@juno.com.

2496 ■ Calvin Alumni Association-Michigan Lakeshore Scholarships *(Undergraduate/Scholarship)*

Purpose: To support students who display evidence of faith commitment in the areas of leadership, volunteerism and service to the community. **Focus:** General studies/Field of study not specified. **Qualif.:** Applicants must be first year students entering Calvin College; must attend a high school on Ottawa, Muskegon or Allegan Counties. **Criteria:** Recipients are selected based on the faith commitment in the areas of leadership, volunteerism and service to the community.

Funds Avail.: $1,000. **To Apply:** Applicants must submit a completed application form, short essay, transcript of records and two reference letters. **Deadline:** February 2.

Awards are arranged alphabetically below their administering organizations

Contact: Calvin College Alumni Office; Phone: 616-526-6142; E-mail: alumni@calvin.edu.

2497 ■ Calvin Alumni Association-Michigan, Lansing Scholarships *(Undergraduate/Scholarship)*

Purpose: To support students who display evidence of faith commitment in the areas of leadership, volunteerism and service to the community. **Focus:** General studies/Field of study not specified. **Qualif.:** Applicants must be first year students entering Calvin College; must have at least 2.5 GPA or better; must live in Mid-Michigan Chapter area. **Criteria:** Recipients are selected based on record of volunteer activities in church, community or school, GPA and written references.

Funds Avail.: $1,000. **Number Awarded:** Varies. **To Apply:** Applicants must submit a completed application form and two written references. **Deadline:** February 2. **Contact:** Derek Bajema at derekbajema@gmail.com.

2498 ■ Calvin Alumni Association-New Jersey Scholarships *(Undergraduate/Scholarship)*

Purpose: To support students who display evidence of faith commitment in the areas of leadership, volunteerism and service to the community. **Focus:** General studies/Field of study not specified. **Qualif.:** Applicants must be students planning to attend Calvin for the first time; must be from local area (New Jersey or New York City metro area). **Criteria:** Recipients are selected based on academic performance and not yet receiving other academic scholarships from Calvin or other sources. Consideration will be given to applicants who have demonstrated a Christian service, personal characters and professional promise.

Funds Avail.: $1,000. **Number Awarded:** Varies. **To Apply:** Applicants must submit a completed application, recommendation form and a high school transcript. **Deadline:** February 2. **Contact:** Jackie Streelman at jjkjk@me.com.

2499 ■ Calvin Alumni Association-South Florida Scholarships *(Undergraduate/Scholarship)*

Purpose: To help students by providing scholarships for entering freshmen. **Focus:** General studies/Field of study not specified. **Qualif.:** Applicants must be first year students entering Calvin college; students from Palm Beach and surrounding counties are eligible. **Criteria:** Recipients are selected based on GPA, Christian commitment, character, participation in extracurricular school activities, participation in church and community activities.

Funds Avail.: $1,000 to $1,500. **Number Awarded:** Varies. **To Apply:** Applicants must submit a completed application form. **Deadline:** February 2. **Contact:** Phil Wierenga at wierengap@bellsouth.net.

2500 ■ Calvin Alumni Association-Southeast Michigan Scholarships *(Undergraduate/Scholarship)*

Purpose: To help students by providing scholarships for entering freshmen. **Focus:** General studies/Field of study not specified. **Qualif.:** Applicants must be first year students entering Calvin College; must be resident of the Southeast Michigan Chapter area (generally defined as zip codes 48000-48399). **Criteria:** Recipients are selected based on academic performance.

Funds Avail.: $1,000. **Number Awarded:** 2. **To Apply:** Applicants must submit a completed application form and two written references. **Deadline:** February 2. **Contact:** Andrea House at 734-238-0554.

2501 ■ Calvin Alumni Association-Southeastern Wisconsin Scholarships *(Undergraduate/Scholarship)*

Purpose: To support students who display evidence of faith commitment in the areas of leadership, volunteerism and service to the community. **Focus:** General studies/Field of study not specified. **Qualif.:** Applicants must be undergraduate college students who have completed at least two years of undergraduate education; must be residents of Dodge, Jefferson, Kenosha, Milwaukee, Ozaukee, Racine, Walworth, Washington, or Waukesha County, Wisconsin who attended a church in one of those counties; must intend to attend Calvin College during the next academic year. **Criteria:** Recipients are selected based on cumulative GPA, financial need, Christian commitment and histories of extra-academic church and/or community activities.

Funds Avail.: No specific amount. **To Apply:** Applicants must submit a complete application form, a complete "Statement of Ways and Means" and a certified copy of transcript from each of the colleges attended. **Deadline:** February 2. **Contact:** Victor Plantinga at vplantinga@gmail.com.

2502 ■ Calvin Alumni Association Southern California Chapter Scholarships *(Undergraduate/Scholarship)*

Purpose: To help students by providing scholarships for entering freshmen. **Focus:** General studies/Field of study not specified. **Qualif.:** Applicants must be current high school senior students; must live within the Southern California Chapter area; must have a GPA of 3.0. **Criteria:** Recipients are selected based on the consistent pattern of volunteer service, character and scholastic ability.

Funds Avail.: No specific amount. **To Apply:** Applicants must submit a completed application form. **Contact:** Becky Kim; Phone: 616-647-7644; E-mail: rk28@calvin.edu.

2503 ■ Calvin Alumni Association-Southwest Michigan, Kalamazoo Scholarships *(Undergraduate/Scholarship)*

Purpose: To support students who display evidence of faith commitment in the areas of leadership, volunteerism and service to the community. **Focus:** General studies/Field of study not specified. **Qualif.:** Applicants must be high school senior students who live in Southwest Michigan Chapter area. **Criteria:** Recipients are selected based on answers to application questions and involvement in extra-curricular activities. Preference will be given to students who have not yet received a Calvin National Merit or Presidential Scholarship.

Funds Avail.: No specific amount. **To Apply:** Applicants must submit a completed application form including activities and awards. **Deadline:** February 2. **Contact:** Mary Jane Baylor; Phone: 269-370-5043; E-mail: rebaylor1@aol.com.

2504 ■ Calvin Alumni Association-Washington, D.C. Scholarships *(Undergraduate/Scholarship)*

Purpose: To support students who display evidence of faith commitment in the areas of leadership, volunteerism and service to the community. **Focus:** General studies/Field of study not specified. **Qualif.:** Applicants must be incoming first year or transfer Calvin students in the greater D.C./Baltimore area (approximately those living in the following zip code areas: 19900-21899, 22000-22599, 25400-25499 and 26700-26899) who will be entering Calvin. **Cri-**

Awards are arranged alphabetically below their administering organizations

teria: Recipients are selected based on Christian commitment, scholastic achievement, personal character and professional promise.

Funds Avail.: No specific amount. **To Apply:** Applicants must complete the application form, three copies of recommendation form, high school transcript and a one-page copy of resume. **Deadline:** February 2. **Contact:** Brandon Hunt at b.l.hunt@gmail.com.

2505 ■ Calvin Alumni Association-Washington, Lynden Scholarships (Undergraduate/Scholarship)

Purpose: To support students who display evidence of faith commitment in the areas of leadership, volunteerism and service to the community. **Focus:** General studies/Field of study not specified. **Qualif.:** Applicants must be students living within the Lynden Chapter area; must be high school seniors entering Calvin College with a minimum GPA of 2.50. **Criteria:** Recipients are selected based on demonstrated faith commitment in areas of leadership, volunteerism and service to the church, school and community.

Funds Avail.: No specific amount. **To Apply:** Applicants must complete the application form. **Deadline:** February 2. **Contact:** Kelly DeJong; Phone: 360-318-0794; E-mail: jkdejong@frontier.com.

2506 ■ Camden County Bar Association (CCBA)

1040 N Kings Highway, Ste. 201
Cherry Hill, NJ 08034
Ph: (856)482-0620
Fax: (856)482-0637
E-mail: info@camdencountybar.org
URL: www.camdencountybar.org
Facebook: www.facebook.com/Camden-County-Bar-Association-177789538905408

2507 ■ Benjamin Asbell Memorial Scholarships (Undergraduate/Scholarship)

Purpose: To help law students defray the cost of law school tuition. **Focus:** Law; Law enforcement. **Qualif.:** For the first award, applicants must be day or evening students at the Rutgers-Camden School of Law, who are residents of South Jersey and must not be first-year students. Applicants must also demonstrate genuine financial need, scholastic ability and a history or desire to work in the areas of law enforcement and/or the administration of justice. For the second award, applicants must be students at any of the following law schools: Rutgers-Camden, Rutgers-Newark, Penn, Seton Hall, Temple, Villanova or Widener. **Criteria:** Selection will be based on the committee's criteria.

Funds Avail.: $1,000 each. **Number Awarded:** 2. **To Apply:** Interested applicants must visit the website to download an application form. **Deadline:** February 28.

2508 ■ Eivind H. Barth, Jr. Memorial Scholarships (Undergraduate/Scholarship)

Purpose: To help law students defray the cost of law school tuition. **Focus:** Law. **Qualif.:** Applicants must be law students attending either the Rutgers-Camden School of Law or the Temple Law School. **Criteria:** Selection will be based on the committee's criteria.

Funds Avail.: $1,000. **To Apply:** Interested applicants must visit the website to download an application. **Deadline:** February 28.

2509 ■ Hon. Joseph W. Cowgill Memorial Scholarships (Undergraduate/Scholarship)

Purpose: To support law students defray the cost of law school tuition. **Focus:** Law. **Qualif.:** Applicants must be Rutgers-Camden School of Law students who are in the upper half of their class. Applicants must demonstrate genuine financial need as well as be a resident of Camden County. **Criteria:** Selection will be based on the committee's criteria.

Funds Avail.: $1,000. **To Apply:** Interested applicants must visit the website to download an application form. **Deadline:** February 28.

2510 ■ Hon. Ralph W.E. Donges Memorial Scholarships (Undergraduate/Scholarship)

Purpose: To assist law students defray the cost of law school tuition. **Focus:** Law. **Qualif.:** Applicants must be part-time, evening law students attending the following law schools: Rutgers-Camden, Rutgers-Newark, Penn, Seton Hall, Temple, Villanova or Widener. Applicants must show a bona fide intention to practice law in Camden County. Applicants should also demonstrate genuine financial need as well as scholastic achievement. **Criteria:** Selection will be based on the committee's criteria.

Funds Avail.: $1,000. **To Apply:** Interested applicants must visit the website to download an application form. **Deadline:** February 28.

2511 ■ DuBois Brothers Scholarships (Undergraduate/Scholarship)

Purpose: To assist law students defray the cost of law school tuition. **Focus:** Law. **Qualif.:** Applicants must be students of any Delaware Valley law school. Applicants must show a bona fide intention to practice law in South Jersey as well as exhibit professionalism and high character in their personal and academic lives. Applicants must also demonstrate genuine financial need. **Criteria:** Selection will be based on the committee's criteria.

Funds Avail.: $1,000. **To Apply:** Interested applicants must visit the website to download an application form. **Deadline:** February 28.

2512 ■ George F. Kugler, Jr. Scholarships (Undergraduate/Scholarship)

Purpose: To assist law students defray the cost of law school tuition. **Focus:** Law. **Qualif.:** Applicants must be second or third-year students attending any New Jersey law school. Applicants must demonstrate genuine financial need as well as a history of and/or desire to work in public service law. **Criteria:** Selection will be based on the committee's criteria.

Funds Avail.: $1,000. **To Apply:** Interested applicants must visit the website to download an application form. **Deadline:** February 28.

2513 ■ Harold and Harriet Plum Memorial Scholarships (Undergraduate/Scholarship)

Purpose: To support law students defray the cost of law school tuition. **Focus:** Law. **Qualif.:** Applicants must be students of any accredited law school; must demonstrate scholastic achievement as well as genuine financial need. **Criteria:** Selection will be based on the committee's criteria.

Funds Avail.: $1,000. **To Apply:** Interested applicants must visit the website to download an application form. **Deadline:** February 28.

2514 ■ Louis C. Portella Memorial Scholarships (Graduate/Scholarship)

Purpose: To support law students defray the cost of law school tuition. **Focus:** Law. **Qualif.:** Applicants must be

Awards are arranged alphabetically below their administering organizations

second or third year full-time students at either Rutgers-Camden or Temple law schools who reside in and intend to practice law in Camden County; must be in good academic standing; must be active in both extracurricular and community activities. **Criteria:** Selection will be based on the committee's criteria.

Funds Avail.: $1,000. **To Apply:** Interested applicants must visit the website to download an application form. **Deadline:** February 28.

2515 ■ Hon. Rudolph J. Rossetti Memorial Scholarships *(Undergraduate/Scholarship)*

Purpose: To support law students defray the cost of law school tuition. **Focus:** Law. **Qualif.:** Applicants must be students attending any Delaware Valley law school. Applicants must demonstrate scholastic achievement and a genuine financial need. **Criteria:** Selection will be based on the committee's criteria.

Funds Avail.: $1,000. **To Apply:** Interested applicants must visit the website to download an application form. **Deadline:** February 28.

2516 ■ Ann S. Salsberg Scholarship Awards *(Undergraduate/Award, Scholarship)*

Purpose: To award scholarship to young men/women who qualify for the honor. **Focus:** Paralegal studies. **Qualif.:** Applicants must be high school graduating seniors or high school graduates who are Camden City residents. **Criteria:** Selection will be based on the committee's criteria.

Funds Avail.: $2,000. **Duration:** Annual. **To Apply:** Interested applicants must submit the following: a one-page, typed and single spaced brief essay in which the applicants identifies plans they have for the future with regards to their possible pursuit of a legal career; recent transcript with a minimum 3.0 GPA (on a scale of 4.0=A); a provisional letter of acceptance to an accredited 4-year college or university, or any high school graduate currently enrolled in an accredited 4-year college or university; a disclosure of financial information revealing all sources of funding being received or being offered to the applicants including other scholarships, financial awards or other financial assistance. **Deadline:** May 1.

2517 ■ Jay A. Strassberg Memorial Scholarships *(Undergraduate/Scholarship)*

Purpose: To support law students pursuing degrees in Journalism, Public Relations, Advertising, Communications, or Theater Arts. **Focus:** Advertising; Journalism; Law; Public relations. **Qualif.:** Applicants must be any Temple, Drexel or Rutgers University law students or undergraduate students majoring in the Journalism, Public Relations and Advertising Department of the School of Communications and Theater Arts who demonstrates both financial need and academic achievement. **Criteria:** Preference will be given to candidates from Camden County or the South Jersey area.

Funds Avail.: $1,000. **Duration:** Annual. **To Apply:** Interested applicants must submit the following: a brief letter from the applicants detailing their personal and educational background, work history, course of study and plans after graduation; current transcript of undergraduate courses including GPA; letter of recommendation submitted by a member of the Journalism, Public Relations and Advertising Department at Temple University; a disclosure of financial information revealing all sources of funding being received or being offered to the applicants. **Deadline:** March 31.

2518 ■ Daniel B. Toll Memorial Scholarships *(Undergraduate/Scholarship)*

Purpose: To support law students defray the cost of law school tuition. **Focus:** Law. **Qualif.:** Applicants must be law students who are not in their final year of study; must be residents of South Jersey, preferably Camden County; must have demonstrated a commitment to the area in charitable, humanitarian and community service activities. **Criteria:** Selection will be based on the committee's criteria.

Funds Avail.: $1,000. **To Apply:** Interested students must visit the website to download an application form. **Deadline:** February 28.

2519 ■ William Tomar Memorial Scholarships *(Undergraduate/Scholarship)*

Purpose: To support law students defray the cost of law school tuition. **Focus:** Law. **Qualif.:** Applicants must be incoming, full or part-time law students at Rutgers School of Law - Camden. Applicants should demonstrate genuine financial need and scholastic achievement from previous educational experiences. **Criteria:** Selection will be based on the committee's criteria.

Funds Avail.: $1,000. **To Apply:** Interested students must visit the website to download an application form. An official acceptance letter from Rutgers must be submitted together with the application form. **Deadline:** February 28.

2520 ■ Bruce A. Wallace Memorial Scholarships *(Undergraduate/Scholarship)*

Purpose: To support law students defray the cost of law school tuition. **Focus:** Law. **Qualif.:** Applicants must be third-year students at Rutgers-Camden School of Law; must be from the South Jersey area; must be in the upper half of their class; must demonstrate genuine financial need. **Criteria:** Selection will be based on the committee's criteria.

Funds Avail.: $1,000. **To Apply:** Interested applicants must visit the website to download an application form. **Deadline:** January 31.

2521 ■ Camden County College
200 N Broadway
Camden, NJ 08102-1185
Ph: (856)338-1817
URL: www.camdencc.edu

2522 ■ Camden County College Foundation Scholarships *(Undergraduate/Scholarship)*

Purpose: To provide support to the outstanding individuals who want to pursue higher education and career goals at CCC. **Focus:** General studies/Field of study not specified. **Qualif.:** Applicants must: be full-time or part-time students returning to CCC; have a minimum of 3.0 GPA; and, have completed twelve (12) college credits. **Criteria:** Recipients will be chosen by the College's Scholarship Selection Committee and/ or by recommendation from department faculty.

Funds Avail.: No specific amount. **Duration:** Annual; one academic year. **To Apply:** Applicants must submit one recommendation from a faculty member or administrator at Camden County College. Application forms are available online. **Deadline:** March 15. **Contact:** Call 856-227-7200, ext. 4946.

2523 ■ Cameco Corp.
2121-11th St. W
Saskatoon, SK, Canada S7M 1J3

Awards are arranged alphabetically below their administering organizations

Ph: (306)956-6200
E-mail: info@cameco.com
URL: www.cameco.com
Facebook: www.facebook.com/Cameco.Careers
LinkedIn: www.linkedin.com/company/cameco-corporation
Twitter: www.twitter.com/camecocommunity

2524 ■ Cameco Corporation Scholarships in the Geological Sciences - Continuing Students (Undergraduate/Scholarship)

Purpose: To support students who want to pursue their career in geological sciences. **Focus:** Geology. **Qualif.:** Applicants must be full-time students who are Canadian citizens entering their second year of university study and pursuing Bachelor of Science degrees; must have declared majors in the geological sciences; must be registered in 200 level courses related to their majors; must have a sessional weighted average of at least 70% for all credit units attempted in the last regular session. **Criteria:** Recipient will be selected based on scholarship application form and requirements.

Funds Avail.: No specific amount. **Number Awarded:** 2. **To Apply:** Application form can be obtained from the Continuing Students, Student Central, University of Saskatchewan. **Deadline:** June 1. **Contact:** Continuing Students, Student Central, University of Saskatchewan, 105 Administration Place, Saskatoon, SK S7N 5A2; Phone: 306-966-1212; Email:askus@usask.ca.

2525 ■ Cameco Corporation Scholarships in the Geological Sciences - Entering Students (Undergraduate/Scholarship)

Purpose: To support students who want to pursue their career in geological sciences. **Focus:** Geology. **Qualif.:** Applicants must be full-time students who are Canadian citizens pursuing Bachelor of Science degrees and are entering their first year of university study and are registered in specified courses as outlined in guidelines. **Criteria:** Recipient will be selected based on scholarship application form and requirements.

Funds Avail.: No specific amount. **Number Awarded:** 2. **To Apply:** Application form can be obtained from the Recruitment and Admissions, University of Saskatchewan. **Deadline:** March 1. **Contact:** Phone: 306-966-5788; Email: admissions@usask.ca.

2526 ■ Bernard Michel Scholarships (Undergraduate/Scholarship)

Purpose: To provide financial support to a Saskatchewan aboriginal student who wants to pursue their studies. **Focus:** Engineering; Liberal arts. **Qualif.:** Applicants must be Saskatchewan aboriginal students entering their first or second year of study within the Colleges of Engineering, Commerce or Arts and Science at the University of Saskatchewan. **Criteria:** Recipient will be selected based on scholarship application form and requirements.

Funds Avail.: $5,000. **Duration:** Up to 2 years. **Number Awarded:** 2. **To Apply:** Applicant must complete the application form available online and must be sent to University of Saskatchewan. **Deadline:** June 1. **Contact:** 306-966-1212; awards@usask.ca.

2527 ■ Camp Network
1033 Demonbreun St., Ste. 300
Nashville, TN 37203
URL: www.campnetwork.com

2528 ■ Camp Network Counselor Appreciation Scholarships (Undergraduate/Scholarship)

Purpose: To reward and support the education of select few counselors. **Focus:** General studies/Field of study not specified. **Qualif.:** Applicants must be U.S. citizens who are currently high school seniors attending a school in the United States; must be anticipating completion of high school diploma at time of application; and must currently have a minimum of 3.0 GPA. **Criteria:** Selection will be based on the applicants' exhibited humility, passion, unity, servanthood, and thankfulness.

Funds Avail.: $1,000. **To Apply:** Applicants must create a short, exciting video (3-5 minutes max) that explains their experiences as camp counselors, how they exhibit the five qualities above, and how they intend to use the college degree. Upload the video to DropBox.com, YouTube, Vimeo, or another reputable file sharing service (make sure the visibility is set to public). To submit your application send an email to the contact provided. **Deadline:** November 1. **Contact:** Send e-mail to Andrew Downing at scholarships@campnetwork.com.

2529 ■ Campus Compact
45 Temple Pl.
Boston, MA 02111
Ph: (617)357-1881
Fax: (617)357-1889
E-mail: campus@compact.org
URL: www.compact.org
Facebook: www.facebook.com/CampusCompact
LinkedIn: www.linkedin.com/company/campus-compact
Twitter: twitter.com/campus_compact

2530 ■ Newman Civic Fellows Awards (Undergraduate/Award)

Purpose: To honor inspiring college student leaders who have demonstrated an investment in finding solutions for challenges facing communities throughout the country. **Focus:** General studies/Field of study not specified. **Qualif.:** Applicants must be undergraduate students at Campus Compact member colleges and universities. **Criteria:** Awards are given based on financial need and leadership.

Funds Avail.: No specific amount. **Duration:** Annual. **To Apply:** Applicants may contact the Campus Compact for the application process and other information.

2531 ■ Campus Discovery
c/o WiseChoice Brands, L.L.C.
PO Box 25457
Alexandria, VA 22313
URL: www.campusdiscovery.com

2532 ■ Campus Discovery Scholarships (Undergraduate/Scholarship)

Purpose: To support students in their educational pursuits. **Focus:** General studies/Field of study not specified. **Qualif.:** Applicants must be U.S. citizens or legal residents; enrolled full-time at a four-year college/university or a college graduate with a bachelor's degree and have completed at least one full year at one of the listed schools (list available at website). **Criteria:** Selection shall be based on writing ability (25%), wisdom (25%), originality (25%), and overall excellence (25%).

Awards are arranged alphabetically below their administering organizations

Funds Avail.: $5,000. **Duration:** Annual. **To Apply:** Applicants must submit a complete survey, including an answer to the required open-ended question online.

2533 ■ CampusDiscovery.com
3020 Hartley Rd., Ste. 220
Jacksonville, FL 32257
Ph: (904)483-2930
Fax: (904)483-2931
E-mail: info@campusdiscovery.com
URL: www.campusdiscovery.com

2534 ■ "Advice to Your High School Self" Scholarships *(Undergraduate/Scholarship)*

Purpose: To provide financial support to student who plans to pursue their education. **Focus:** General studies/Field of study not specified. **Qualif.:** Applicants must be college undergraduates and/or recent graduate students from either level B.A. or A.A.; must be US citizens. **Criteria:** Selection will be based on the committee's criteria.

Funds Avail.: $5,000. **To Apply:** Applicants must visit the website for the online application process and to create an online profile. Students must submit a complete survey about their college campus. Applicants must also provide a short, original, previously unpublished written response to the scholarship topic: "Assume you could go back in time and talk to yourself as a high school senior. Knowing what you know now about college life and making the transition, what advice would you give yourself?" The response must be in English and maximum of 200 words. **Deadline:** January 31.

2535 ■ Canadian Aeronautics and Space Institute (CASI)
350 Terry Fox Dr., Ste. 104
Kanata, ON, Canada K2K 2W5
Ph: (613)591-8787
Fax: (613)591-7291
E-mail: casi@casi.ca
URL: www.casi.ca

2536 ■ Charles Luttman Scholarship *(Undergraduate/Scholarship)*

Purpose: To support students who demonstrated qualities of leadership and involvement in any area of student affairs and excellence in communication and organizational skills. **Focus:** General studies/Field of study not specified. **Qualif.:** Nominees must be Canadian citizens and student members in good standing of CASI. **Criteria:** Selection will be based on the committee's criteria.

Funds Avail.: No specific amount. **Duration:** Annual. **To Apply:** Applicants may visit the website to obtain an application form. Applicants should provide a short outline of their activities and accomplishments in each of three areas: technical achievement; leadership and involvement in student affairs; communication and organizational skills. A statement about the goals the students have set for themselves should be included. Also required are three supporting narratives from faculty or community leaders which should emphasize the students' achievements. **Deadline:** April 30.

2537 ■ Canadian Anesthesiologists' Society (CAS)
1 Eglinton Ave. E, Ste. 208
Toronto, ON, Canada M4P 3A1
Ph: (416)480-0602
Fax: (416)480-0320
E-mail: anesthesia@cas.ca
URL: www.cas.ca/English/Home.aspx
Twitter: twitter.com/CASUpdate

2538 ■ Baxter Corporation Canadian Research Awards in Anesthesia *(Other/Award, Monetary)*

Purpose: To support anesthesia-related research in Canada. **Focus:** Anesthesiology. **Qualif.:** Applicants must be associate/active members of CAS who propose to carry out an original project and are eligible for the New Investigator Awards. **Criteria:** Award winner is chosen based on the scientific merit, importance, and feasibility of the project.

Funds Avail.: No specific amount. **Duration:** Annual. **To Apply:** Application forms are available online. Applicants must submit documentation of institutional approval of human and/or animal experimentation.

2539 ■ Canadian Anesthesiologists' Society Research Awards *(Other/Award)*

Purpose: To support anesthesia-related research in Canada. **Focus:** Anesthesiology. **Qualif.:** Applicants must be associate/active members of CAS who propose to carry out an original project and are eligible for the New Investigator Awards. **Criteria:** Award winner is chosen based on the scientific merit, importance, and feasibility of the project.

Funds Avail.: $60,000. **To Apply:** Application forms are available online. Applicants must submit documentation of institutional approval of human and/or animal experimentation. **Deadline:** January 8. **Contact:** For further information, applicants may send an e-mail at research@cas.ca.

2540 ■ CAS/GE Healthcare Canada Inc. Research Awards *(Other/Award)*

Purpose: To provide support for infrastructure costs related to a specific research project or program. **Focus:** Medical research. **Qualif.:** Nominees must be associate or active members of the society who are eligible for an award in the field of perioperative imaging related to anesthesia and/or critical care. **Criteria:** Award winner is chosen based on scientific merit, importance, and feasibility of the project.

Funds Avail.: No specific amount. **To Apply:** Application forms are available online. Applicants must submit documentation of institutional approval of human and or animal experimentation. **Contact:** For further information, applicants may send an e-mail at research@cas.ca.

2541 ■ CAS/Vitaid-LMA Residents' Research Grant Competition *(Other/Award)*

Purpose: To support anesthesia-related research performed by a resident in Canada. **Focus:** Anesthesiology. **Qualif.:** Nominees must be resident physicians who are in good standing at a Canadian university department of anesthesia. Nominees must be members of the CAS and must propose to carry out an original project within Canada. **Criteria:** Award winner is chosen based on scientific merit, importance, and feasibility of the project.

Funds Avail.: No specific amount. **To Apply:** Application forms are available online. Applicants must submit a curriculum vitae; letter from the supervisor that specifies the extent to which the applicant will contribute towards the research project; letter from the residency program director.

Awards are arranged alphabetically below their administering organizations

2542 ■ David S. Sheridan Canadian Research Awards (Other/Award)

Purpose: To support anesthesia-related research in Canada. **Focus:** Anesthesiology. **Qualif.:** Applicants must be associate/active members of CAS who propose to carry out an original project and are eligible for the New Investigator Awards. **Criteria:** Award winner is chosen based on the scientific merit, importance, and feasibility of the project.
Funds Avail.: 10,000 Canadian Dollars. **Duration:** Annual. **To Apply:** Applicants must fill up the application forms available online. Applicants must submit documentation of institutional approval of human and/or animal experimentation.

2543 ■ Canadian Association of Black Lawyers (CABL)
20 Toronto St., Ste. 300
Toronto, ON, Canada M5C 2B8
URL: www.cabl.ca
Facebook: www.facebook.com/Canadian-Association-of-Black-Lawyers-150574661678680

2544 ■ Lucie and Thornton Blackburn Scholarships (Graduate, Juris Doctorate/Scholarship)

Purpose: To financially assist minority students pursuing education at a Canadian law school. **Focus:** Law. **Qualif.:** Applicants must be minority students entering their second year of study in an LLB or JD program at a Canadian law school. **Criteria:** Applicants will be selected based on financial need. Determination of the scholarship recipient will be made by the Scholarship Awards Committee.
Funds Avail.: $5,000. **Duration:** Annual. **To Apply:** Applicants must submit a completed application form and other prescribed requirements to the contact provided. **Deadline:** January 16. **Contact:** Lucie and Thornton Blackburn Scholarship Awards Committee, c/o Canadian Association of Black Lawyers, at the above address; or Email: info@cabl.ca.

2545 ■ Canadian Association for Business Economics (CABE)
PO Box 898, Sta. B
Ottawa, ON, Canada K1P 5P9
Fax: (855)222-3321
Free: 855-222-3321
E-mail: info@cabe.ca
URL: www.cabe.ca
Facebook: www.facebook.com/CABEconomics
Twitter: twitter.com/cabe_economics

2546 ■ Doug Purvis Prize (Other/Prize)

Purpose: To recognize authors who made contributions to Canadian economic policy. **Focus:** Economics. **Qualif.:** Competition is available to authors working in all print media industries; must have written book(s)in relevance to Canadian economic policy; must have had a series of articles in newspapers or magazines, journals, or government studies including monographs done for Royal Commissions, other official documents and think-tank reports. Materials must be primarily, but not exclusively in the public domain. **Criteria:** Candidates will be chosen based on submitted piece.
Funds Avail.: $10,000. **Duration:** Annual. **To Apply:** Electronic submissions must be in PDF format. In case submissions need to be mailed, applicants must submit five copies of the nominated piece including the full details of the nominees, name and address of the nominator and affiliation. **Contact:** Canadian Association for Business Economics, at the above address.

2547 ■ Canadian Association of Cardiac Rehabilitation (CACR)
1390 Taylor Ave.
Winnipeg, MB, Canada R3M 3Y8
Ph: (204)928-7870
Fax: (204)928-7873
E-mail: admin@cacr.ca
URL: www.cacr.ca
Facebook: www.facebook.com/1CACPR/?ref=hl
LinkedIn: www.linkedin.com/in/cacpr
Twitter: twitter.com/CACPR_1

2548 ■ Canadian Association of Cardiac Rehabilitation Graduate Scholarship Awards (Graduate/Scholarship)

Purpose: To recognize the research of graduate students in the area of cardiac rehabilitation and to reflect CACR's support of their educational endeavors in this area. **Focus:** Medicine, Cardiology. **Qualif.:** Students must be a member of the CACR. **Criteria:** Selection will be based on strength of research methodology; feasibility of successfully completing the study; importance and relevance to the field of cardiac rehabilitation; strength of the letter of support; and applicant's potential for continuing to make a valuable contribution to the field of cardiac rehabilitation.
Funds Avail.: $3,000. **Duration:** Annual. **Number Awarded:** 4. **To Apply:** Applicants must submit the auto-fill abstract form in English in Word format together with one letter of reference from a current supervisor; and letter of application: a letter outlining the student's current research in the area of cardiac rehabilitation and future directions in this field. The letter should be maximum of two pages in length and must specifically address the rating criteria related to methodology, feasibility, importance and relevance. **Deadline:** May 1. **Contact:** Marilyn Thomas, 204-488-5857; email: mthomas@cacr.ca.

2549 ■ Canadian Association of Drilling Engineers (CADE)
PO Box 957
Calgary, AB, Canada T2P 2K4
Ph: (587)223-7016
E-mail: info@cadecanada.com
URL: www.cadecanada.com
Twitter: www.twitter.com/cade_can

2550 ■ CADE Bursary (Undergraduate/Scholarship)

Purpose: To financially support the qualified individuals who want to pursue their education in a Petroleum Industry. **Focus:** Engineering, Petroleum. **Qualif.:** Applicant must be a dependent of a CADE member or must be a CADE member. **Criteria:** Selection process will be based on enrollment in an engineering program as highest priority; financial need; industry experience; overall quality of submission.
Funds Avail.: No specific amount. **Duration:** Annual. **To**

Awards are arranged alphabetically below their administering organizations

Apply: Application form and instructions are available at the website. **Contact:** Mike Buker at 403-930-9015.

2551 ■ CADE Scholarships *(Undergraduate/Scholarship)*

Purpose: To financially support the qualified individuals who want to pursue their education in a Petroleum Industry. **Focus:** Engineering, Petroleum. **Qualif.:** Applicants must be an engineering student at the University of Alberta and the University of Calgary as well as Engineering Technology at the Southern Alberta Institute of Technology and the Northern Alberta Institute of Technology. **Criteria:** Selection process will be based on the criteria of the CADE executive committee.

Funds Avail.: No specific amount. **Duration:** Annual. **To Apply:** Application form and instructions are available at the website.

2552 ■ Canadian Association on Gerontology
263 McCaul St., Ste. 328
Toronto, ON, Canada M5T 1W7
Fax: (855)224-2240
Free: 855-224-2240
E-mail: contact@cagacg.ca
URL: cagacg.ca
Facebook: www.facebook.com/pages/Canadian-Association-on-Gerontology-Association-canadienne-de-gerontologie/187077537979477
LinkedIn: www.linkedin.com/company/canadian-association-on-gerontology

2553 ■ CAG Margery Boyce Bursary Awards *(Undergraduate/Award, Scholarship)*

Purpose: To support post-baccalaureate students who have made a significant contribution to their community through volunteer activities and who are registered in a program of study focused on aging or the aged. **Focus:** Gerontology. **Qualif.:** Applicant must be a CAG member; must be registered, or formally accepted at a recognized Canadian university at the time the application is submitted; must be a Canadian citizen or have permanent resident status. **Criteria:** Recipient will be recommended by the Awards Committee based on his/her contribution to the community through volunteer activities and based on his/her academic performance. Preference will be given to persons returning to university after an absence from formal study.

Funds Avail.: $500. **Duration:** Annual. **To Apply:** Applicants must submit an application form with transcripts; proof of registration or acceptance in a university program; letter of support from the faculty supervisor or program Chair which addresses the criteria for the bursary and the letter of support from any community organization that can address the amount and quality of the applicant's volunteer activities as related to the criteria; Applicant must submit a photo and a short biographical profile for the CAG Newsletter. **Deadline:** April 30.

2554 ■ CAG Donald Menzies Bursary Awards *(Postgraduate/Scholarship, Award)*

Purpose: To support post-baccalaureate students registered in a program of study focused on aging or the aged. **Focus:** Gerontology. **Qualif.:** Applicant must be a CAG member; must be registered, or formally accepted as a full-time student in a post-baccalaureate program at a recognized Canadian university at the time the application is submitted; must be a Canadian citizen or have permanent resident status. **Criteria:** Recipient will be selected by the Awards Committee based on academic merit among students demonstrating financial need.

Funds Avail.: $1,500. **Duration:** Annual. **To Apply:** Applicant must submit the application form with the university transcript; proof of registration, or acceptance in university program; a letter of support from the faculty supervisor; and an approved thesis/research project proposal (if applicable). Applicant must submit a photo and a short biographical profile for the CAG Newsletter. **Deadline:** April 30.

2555 ■ Schlegel-UW RIA Scholarships *(Doctorate/Scholarship)*

Purpose: To support students completing their first year of a doctoral program with a program of study related to gerontology. **Focus:** Gerontology. **Qualif.:** Applicants must be Canadian citizen or have permanent resident status; must be CAG members; must be completing their first year of a doctoral program, with a program of study relevant to the field of gerontology; must have a minimum of 80% academic average in the program of study preceding the doctoral program; and must have at least two years of practice and/or volunteer service with older adults. **Criteria:** Selection will be based on the committee's criteria.

Funds Avail.: $1,000. **To Apply:** Applicants must submit one original version of each of the following documents together with the online application form: all university transcripts; proof of registration in the first year of a doctoral program; a letter of support from the applicant's previous or current faculty supervisor or program Chair which addresses his/her program of study and its relevance to the field of gerontology; a maximum of two letter(s) of support from any community organizations (on letterhead) who can address the amount, quality and duration of the applicant's volunteer activities as related to the criteria. **Deadline:** May 22.

2556 ■ Canadian Association for HIV Research (CAHR)
One Rideau St., Ste. 744
Ottawa, ON, Canada K1N 8S7
Ph: (613)670-5842
Fax: (613)670-5701
E-mail: info@cahr-acrv.ca
URL: www.cahr-acrv.ca

2557 ■ CAHR Master's Level Scholarships *(Master's/Scholarship)*

Purpose: To support students who are planning a career in HIV/AIDS research. **Focus:** Medical research. **Qualif.:** Applicants must be enrolled in a Master's degree program and planning to conduct HIV/AIDS research; must be Canadian citizens or permanent residents of Canada. **Criteria:** Applicants will be evaluated based on achievements, characteristics and abilities of the applicants; quality and potential impact of the proposed research project; strength of the proposed training environment.

Funds Avail.: 17,500 Canadian Dollars. **Duration:** Annual. **To Apply:** Interested applicants may visit the website for the online application and other information. **Deadline:** February 5.

Awards are arranged alphabetically below their administering organizations

2558 ■ Canadian Association of Insolvency and Restructuring Professionals (CAIRP)

277 Wellington St. W
Toronto, ON, Canada M5V 3H2
Ph: (416)204-3242
Fax: (416)204-3410
E-mail: info@cairp.ca
URL: www.cairp.ca
Facebook: www.facebook.com/CAIRP.ca
LinkedIn: www.linkedin.com/company/3239103
Twitter: twitter.com/CAIRP_ACPIR

2559 ■ Lloyd Houlden Memorial Research Fellowships (Advanced Professional, Professional development/Fellowship)

Purpose: To support an original analysis of innovative ways to improve the insolvency system. **Focus:** Banking; Economics; Law. **Qualif.:** Applicants must be the authors of the paper that addresses those involved in insolvency practice, insolvency law, or in the development and analysis of insolvency policy. **Criteria:** Recipients will be selected based on submitted paper.

Funds Avail.: $20,000. **Duration:** Annual. **To Apply:** Applicants must submit a proposed research (i.e. research paper of 7000-10000 words in length), curriculum vitae, publications over the last two years and research in progress. **Contact:** CAIRP, at the above address.

2560 ■ Canadian Association of Law Libraries (CALL)

720 Spadina Ave., Ste. 202
Toronto, ON, Canada M5S 2T9
Ph: (647)346-8723
E-mail: office@callacbd.ca
URL: www.callacbd.ca
Facebook: www.facebook.com/callacbd
Twitter: twitter.com/callacbd

2561 ■ CALL/ACBD Education Reserve Fund Grants (Professional development/Grant)

Purpose: To provide funding support for members of CALL/ACBD intending to further their education in pursuits that do not fit the guidelines of the association's already established scholarships. **Focus:** Law. **Qualif.:** Applicants must be members of the Canadian Association of Law Libraries/Association canadienne des bibliotheques de droit who have been in good standing for a minimum of 12 months. Applicants' pursuits must be relevant to their career in law libraries or law librarianship. **Criteria:** Selection will be based on merit.

Funds Avail.: No specific amount. **Duration:** Annual. **To Apply:** Application form is available online. Applicants must submit completed application form along with a resume and a letter of support from your employer. **Contact:** Wendy Reynolds, Chair, CALL/ACBD Scholarships and Awards Committee, at wreynolds@ola.org.

2562 ■ CALL/ACBD Research Grants (Graduate/Grant)

Purpose: To provide members with financial assistance to carry out research in areas of interest to members and to the association. **Focus:** Law. **Qualif.:** Applicants must be members of CALL/ACBD who are intending to do research projects that promote an understanding of legal information sources or law librarianship. **Criteria:** Selection will be based on the recommendation of the committee to promote proposed research.

Funds Avail.: $1,400 to $4,400. **Duration:** Annual. **To Apply:** Applicants may apply individually or in partnership with another member of CALL/ACBD. They must submit completed application available in the website outlining the proposed project, the amount of money requested and a brief budget setting out how funds will be spent. They should be prepared to demonstrate that they have completed a preliminary investigation as to the feasibility of their proposed project. **Deadline:** March 15. **Remarks:** Established in 1996. **Contact:** Susan Barker, Co-Chair, CALL/ACBD Committee to Promote Research; e-mail: susan.barker@utoronto.ca. Or to Elizabeth Brutonm, Co-Chair, CALL/ACBD Committee to Promote Research; e-mail: ebruton@uwo.ca.

2563 ■ James D. Lang Memorial Scholarships (Graduate/Scholarship)

Purpose: To support attendance at a continuing education program, be it a workshop, certificate program or other similar activity deemed appropriate by the CALL/ACBD Scholarships and Awards Committee. **Focus:** Law. **Qualif.:** Applicants must be members of CALL/ACBD who have been in good standing for a minimum of 12 months. **Criteria:** Scholarship will be given based on merit.

Funds Avail.: No specific amount. **Duration:** Annual. **To Apply:** Application form is available online. Applicants must submit the completed application form along with resume and a letter of support from their employer. **Deadline:** March 15; June 15 and September 15. **Contact:** Wendy Reynolds, Chair, CALL/ACBD Scholarships and Awards Committee, at wreynolds@ola.org.

2564 ■ Diana M. Priestly Memorial Scholarships (Undergraduate/Scholarship)

Purpose: To encourage and support professional development in the area of law librarianship. **Focus:** Law. **Qualif.:** Applicants must: be Canadian citizens or landed immigrants; have previous law library experience and will be enrolled in an accredited Canadian Library School during the next academic term or year; have a degree from or are currently enrolled in an accredited Canadian Library School and will be enrolled in an approved Canadian Law School during the next academic term or year, or who have a degree from or are currently enrolled in an approved Canadian law School and will be enrolled in an accredited Canadian Library school during the next academic term/year, or who will be concurrently enrolled in an approved Canadian Law School and an accredited Canadian Library School during the next academic term/year. **Criteria:** Recipients will be chosen based on applicant's work experience, letter of application and letters of reference. Preference will be given to members of the Canadian Association of Law Libraries/Association canadienne des bibliotheques de droit.

Funds Avail.: $2,500. **Duration:** Annual. **Number Awarded:** 1. **To Apply:** Applicants must submit the completed application form available on the website along with resume; written statement from applicant; transcripts; and references. **Deadline:** February 1. **Contact:** Wendy Reynolds, Chair, CALL/ACBD Scholarships and Awards Committee, at wreynolds@ola.org.

Awards are arranged alphabetically below their administering organizations

2565 ■ Canadian Association of Law Teachers (CALT)
c/o Annie Rochette, President
Universite du Quebec a Montreal
Case postale 8888, succ. Centre-Ville
Montreal, QC, Canada H3C 3P8
URL: www.acpd-calt.org

2566 ■ Canadian Association of Law Teachers Award for Academic Excellence (Other/Award)
Purpose: To honor the exceptional contributions of a Canadian law teacher to research and law teaching. **Focus:** Law. **Qualif.:** Applicants must be Canadian law teachers in mid-career; and must be nominated by one or more colleagues. **Criteria:** Candidates will be evaluated based on the following criteria: (1) quality of teaching; (2) creation of new courses; and (3) research in relation to law reform or other legal matters.

Funds Avail.: No specific amount. **Duration:** Annual. **To Apply:** Applicants must submit a complete curriculum vitae; three letters of reference; and representative student's evaluation. Five copies of nomination documents must be submitted. **Deadline:** February 22.

2567 ■ Canadian Association for Neuroscience
2661 Queenswood Dr.
Victoria, BC, Canada V8N 1X6
URL: can-acn.org

2568 ■ Herbert H. Jasper Fellowships in Neurosciences (Postdoctorate/Fellowship)
Purpose: To support those who are undertaking postdoctoral research project with the investigator of their choice within the Neuroscience Research Group (Groupe de Recherche sur le Systeme Nerveux Central or GRSNC) of the University of Montreal. **Focus:** Neuroscience. **Qualif.:** Applicants must have obtained their Ph.D. no more than 4 years before the start of the fellowship. Those who plan to obtain their Ph.D. during the coming year are also eligible, as long as the planned dates of Ph.D. completion and beginning of the postdoctoral fellowship is before October of the current year. **Criteria:** Selection will be based on the committee's criteria.

Funds Avail.: 45,000 Canadian Dollars. **Duration:** Two years. **To Apply:** Applicants may visit the website for further information on the application. **Deadline:** January 29.

2569 ■ Canadian Association of Oilwell Drilling Contractors (CAODC)
Elveden House
2050, 717 - 7th Ave. SW
Calgary, AB, Canada T2P 0Z3
Ph: (403)264-4311
Fax: (403)263-3796
E-mail: communications@caodc.ca
URL: www.caodc.ca
Facebook: www.facebook.com/thecaodc
LinkedIn: www.linkedin.com/company/5607531?trk
=tyah&trkInfo=clickedVertical%3Acompany%2Cclicke
dEntityId%3A5607531%2Cidx%3A1-1-1%2CtarId%
3A1443548160756%2Ctas%3ACAODC
Twitter: twitter.com/thecaodc

2570 ■ CAODC Occupational Health and Safety Scholarships (Professional development/Scholarship)
Purpose: To help employees of CAODC achieve a higher education. **Focus:** General studies/Field of study not specified. **Qualif.:** Applicants must be CAODC drilling or service rig member employees with minimum of 12 months on-the-job experience and who are currently employed in one of the following: 1) as motorhands, derrickhands or drillers on a drilling rig; 2) as derrickhands or operators on a service rig; and 3) in a safety related position within the drilling or service rig member company. **Criteria:** Recipients will be selected based on submitted materials.

Funds Avail.: 6,920 Canadian Dollars. **Duration:** Annual. **To Apply:** Applicants must complete the application form; must provide a letter of referral and statement of goals. **Contact:** Kelli Tonge, ktonge@caodc.ca.

2571 ■ CAODC Scholarship Program (Undergraduate/Scholarship)
Purpose: To provide educational assistance to employees, children, or legal dependents of an employee of a CAODC drilling or service rig member company to continue their education. **Focus:** General studies/Field of study not specified. **Qualif.:** Applicants must be legal dependents of an employee or a bonafide employee of the CAODC proper, drilling or service rig member company; must be entering or continuing post-secondary education from an accredited college, university or trade program as full-time students. **Criteria:** Applicants will be evaluated based on submitted materials.

Funds Avail.: $1,000. **Duration:** Annual. **To Apply:** Applicants must complete the application form; must submit a transcript of records, statement of goals and a two-page essay. **Deadline:** July 8. **Contact:** Kelli Tonge, Manager, Safety and Training Services; Email: ktonge@caodc.ca.

2572 ■ Canadian Association for the Practical Study of Law in Education (CAPSLE)
c/o Lori Pollock, Secretary
37 Moultrey Cres.
Georgetown, ON, Canada L7G 4N4
Ph: (905)702-1710
Fax: (905)873-0662
E-mail: info@capsle.ca
URL: capsle.ca

2573 ■ Canadian Association for the Practical Study of Law in Education Fellowships (Graduate/Fellowship)
Purpose: To provide students an open forum who are studying legal issues affecting education. **Focus:** Law. **Qualif.:** Applicants must be Canadian citizens or landed immigrants enrolled in a Faculty of Law, Graduate School of Education or related discipline at a Canadian university. **Criteria:** Recipients will be selected based on submitted proposal.

Funds Avail.: No specific amount. **Duration:** Annual. **To Apply:** Applicants must submit a one-page proposal for a paper, project, or research that pertains to current practical issues in education law, exhibits academic rigor, is concerned with new or ongoing research or study and not with work that has been done; must be completed by April each year following the award and includes plans for a final paper which will be presented at a CAPSLE Annual Conference; must attach a two-page curriculum vitae and three letters of reference attesting to the applicant's ability. **Contact:** Canadian Association for the Practical Study of Law in Education, at the above address.

Awards are arranged alphabetically below their administering organizations

2574 ■ Canadian Association for Studies in Co-operation (CASC)
c/o Centre for the Study of Co-operatives
University of Saskatchewan
101 Diefenbaker Pl.
Saskatoon, SK, Canada S7N 5B8
E-mail: casc.acec@usask.ca
URL: www.coopresearch.coop

2575 ■ Amy and Tim Dauphinee Scholarships
(Graduate/Scholarship)

Purpose: To support research on co-operative studies. **Focus:** Banking; Finance. **Qualif.:** Applicants must either undertake studies at Canadian universities or university-equivalent colleges (regardless of citizenship) or are Canadian citizens or landed immigrants studying at such institutions outside Canada. **Criteria:** Selection will be based on the applicants' respective academic records, as well as on the importance of the proposed research activities to the development of the co-op movement in Canada or abroad.

Funds Avail.: 3,000 Canadian Dollars. **To Apply:** Applicants must fill-up completely the CASC Scholarships Application Form and attached the additional requirements enumerated in the Form. **Deadline:** March 31. **Contact:** Ashley Denny; Attn: CASC Scholarships, Co-operatives and Mutuals Canada, 4th flr., 275 Bank St., Ottawa, Ontario, Canada K2P 2L6; E-mail: adenny@canada.coop.

2576 ■ Alexander Fraser Laidlaw Fellowships
(Graduate/Fellowship, Scholarship)

Purpose: To support research on co-operative studies. **Focus:** Banking; Finance. **Qualif.:** Applicants must either undertake studies at Canadian universities or university-equivalent colleges (regardless of citizenship) or are Canadian citizens or landed immigrants studying at such institutions outside Canada. **Criteria:** Selection will be based on the applicants' respective academic records, as well as on the importance of the proposed research activities to the development of the co-op movement in Canada or abroad.

Funds Avail.: 1,000 Canadian Dollars. **To Apply:** Applicants must fill-up completely the CASC Scholarships Application Form. Please provide and attached the additional requirements enumerated in the Form. **Deadline:** March 31. **Contact:** Ashley Denny; Attn: CASC Scholarships, Co-operatives and Mutuals Canada, 4th flr., 275 Bank St., Ottawa, Ontario, Canada K2P 2L6; E-mail: adenny@canada.coop.

2577 ■ Lemaire Co-operative Studies Awards
(Undergraduate, Graduate/Scholarship)

Purpose: To encourage students to undertake studies and research which will help them contribute to the development of co-operative in Canada or elsewhere. **Focus:** Banking; Finance. **Qualif.:** Applicants must either undertake studies at Canadian universities or university-equivalent colleges (regardless of citizenship) or are Canadian citizens or landed immigrants studying at such institutions outside Canada. Full-time or part-time students, taking full- or partial-credit courses at any university or university equivalent college are eligible to apply. Eligible candidates must take a minimum of one course about co-operatives. **Criteria:** Selection will be based on the aforementioned qualifications.

Funds Avail.: 1,000 to 3,000 Canadian Dollars. **To Apply:** Applicants must fill-up completely the CASC Scholarships Application Form and attached the additional requirements enumerated in the Form. **Deadline:** March 31. **Contact:** Ashley Denny; Attn: CASC Scholarships, Co-operatives and Mutuals Canada, 4th flr., 275 Bank St., Ottawa, Ontario, Canada K2P 2L6; E-mail: adenny@canada.coop.

2578 ■ Canadian Authors Association-Ottawa Branch
163 Bell St. N
Ottawa, ON, Canada K1R 7E1
URL: www.canauthors-ottawa.org

2579 ■ CAA National Capital Region Writing Contests *(All/Award, Prize, Monetary)*

Purpose: To provide funds for written article(s) of an individual. **Focus:** Literature; Writing. **Qualif.:** Contest is open to members of CAA-NCR and/or residents of the National Capital Region. Applicant's essay must be original and unpublished work. **Criteria:** Winners will be selected based on submitted essays.

Funds Avail.: $300-1st Prize; $200-2nd Prize; $100-3rd Prize. **Duration:** Annual. **Number Awarded:** Up to 3. **To Apply:** Applicants must submit an essay or poem to be considered as entry for the contest. Formats are provided and can be found at the program website. **Deadline:** February 6. **Contact:** Sherrill Wark, CAA-NCR Contest Coordinator at the above address.

2580 ■ The Canadian Bar Association (CBA)
500-865 Carling Ave.
Ottawa, ON, Canada K1S 5S8
Ph: (613)237-2925
Fax: (613)237-0185
Free: 800-267-8860
E-mail: info@cba.org
URL: www.cba.org
Facebook: www.facebook.com/CanadianBarAssociation
Twitter: twitter.com/CBA_News

2581 ■ Viscount Bennett Fellowships *(Graduate/Fellowship)*

Purpose: To encourage a high standard of legal education, training and ethics. **Focus:** Law. **Qualif.:** Applicants must be Canadian citizens who have graduated from an approved law school in Canada, and be members of Canadian Bar Association in good standing. **Criteria:** The CBA Awards Committee is responsible for selecting the successful candidates. Recipients will be selected based on the result of the conducted interview.

Funds Avail.: $50,000. **Duration:** Annual; Up to 2 years. **Number Awarded:** 1. **To Apply:** Applicants must fill out completely the provided application form and such must be submitted together with the following: photocopy of birth certificate, one certified copy of law transcripts, academic distinctions, curriculum vitae, one-page synopsis of the extra-curricular interests as well as activities during the post-secondary studies, one-page statement outlining the course of study to be pursued, and three letters of reference. **Deadline:** November 15. **Remarks:** The Viscount Bennett Fellowship is made possible by a donation from the Right Honorable Viscount Bennett, a CBA Past President from 1929-30 who established a trust fund to provide income to be used to encourage a high standard of legal education, training and ethics.

Awards are arranged alphabetically below their administering organizations

2582 ■ Canadian Blood Services

1800 Alta Vista Dr.
Ottawa, ON, Canada K1G 4J5
Ph: (613)739-2300
Fax: (613)731-1411
Free: 888-236-6283
E-mail: feedback@blood.ca
URL: www.blood.ca/en
Facebook: www.facebook.com/itsinyoutogive

2583 ■ Canadian Blood Services Graduate Fellowship *(Graduate/Fellowship)*

Purpose: To attract and support young investigators to initiate or continue training in the field of blood transfusion science. **Focus:** Blood banking. **Qualif.:** Applicants must be engaged in full-time training in research in a Canadian graduate school leading to a PhD or combined health professional Ph.D. program; must demonstrate acceptance into a PhD program to receive continued support; in a training program which includes actual involvement in research and not only courses in research methods; and must not hold another award at the same time. **Criteria:** Selection is based on the applicant's academic qualifications, research experience and ability; relevance of the proposed project; and merit of the proposed project and research environment.

Funds Avail.: $4,000-$25,000. **Duration:** Annual. **To Apply:** Applicants must submit a completed application form including all attachments with four complete, collated copies and official, original transcript(s).

2584 ■ Canadian Blood Services Postdoctoral Fellowship *(Postdoctorate/Fellowship)*

Purpose: To foster careers related to transfusion science in Canada. **Focus:** Blood banking. **Qualif.:** Applicants must hold a relevant prerequisite degree (PhD, MD, DDS, or DVM) from a recognized academic institution; must be within five years of completing the degree; must not be holding another award. **Criteria:** Selection is based on the applicants' academic qualifications, research experience and ability; relevance of the proposed project; and merit of the proposed project and research environment.

Funds Avail.: $10,000. **Duration:** 1-3 years. **To Apply:** Applicants must submit a completed application form including all attachments with four complete, collated copies and official, original transcript(s).

2585 ■ Canadian Breast Cancer Foundation - BC/Yukon

300 - 1090 West Pender St.
Vancouver, BC, Canada V6E 2N7
Ph: (604)683-2873
Free: 800-561-6111
E-mail: cbcfbc@cbcf.org
URL: www.cbcf.org/bc/Pages/default.aspx

2586 ■ Annual Research Doctoral and Postgraduate Fellowship Grant Program *(Doctorate, Postdoctorate, Postgraduate, Advanced Professional/Fellowship, Grant)*

Purpose: To support the most qualified breast cancer research projects in BC. **Focus:** Medical research; Medicine; Oncology. **Qualif.:** Applicants for the program are the following: PhD students, health care professionals, MD graduates, or recent PhD graduates. **Criteria:** Selection will be based on the committee's criteria.

Funds Avail.: No specific amount. **Duration:** Annual. **To Apply:** Applicants must follow the following guidelines in application: confirm the program criteria and eligibility to apply by reviewing the Grants Fellowship Program Guidebook and Criteria; follow the registration instructions within the Fellowship Webgrants User Manual to register to use the WebGrants system; ensure that one must be familiarize with the user guide before completing application online; access WebGrants to complete application. **Contact:** bcgrants@cbcf.org.

2587 ■ CBCF - BC/Yukon Region Breast Cancer Research Grants Competition *(Advanced Professional/Grant)*

Purpose: To initiate new projects in breast cancer in British Columbia. **Focus:** Oncology. **Qualif.:** Applicants must be investigators from all research disciplines in British Columbia and Yukon Territory. **Criteria:** Recipients are selected based on the premise that projects must demonstrate direct impact on the issue of breast cancer, including strategies for knowledge translation so that the work being done in the laboratory transfers as quickly as possible to the clinic and to the people affected by breast cancer.

Funds Avail.: Up to 250,000 Canadian Dollars. **Duration:** Two years. **To Apply:** Applicants may verify the website for further information on the application process. **Contact:** Grants Allocation Manager at bcgrants@cbcf.org.

2588 ■ CBCF - BC/Yukon Region Breast Cancer Survivor Dragon Boat Grants *(Professional development/Grant)*

Purpose: To support breast cancer survivor dragon boat teams across the province. **Focus:** Oncology. **Qualif.:** Applicants must be members of breast cancer survivor dragon boat teams across British Columbia and Yukon Region. **Criteria:** Selection will be based on the committee's criteria.

Funds Avail.: No specific amount. **Number Awarded:** Over 20. **To Apply:** Applicants must visit the website for the online application process. **Deadline:** March 20. **Contact:** Grants Allocation Manager at bcgrants@cbcf.org.

2589 ■ CBCF - BC/Yukon Region Community Health Grants *(Professional development/Grant)*

Purpose: To provide locally tailored breast cancer programs throughout British Columbia and the Yukon, which allow sustainable and accountable community based initiatives in the areas of prevention, early detection, treatment and cure for breast cancer. **Focus:** Oncology. **Qualif.:** Applicants must be community organizations throughout British Columbia and the Yukon Territory that delve on breast cancer issues across the provinces. **Criteria:** Selection will be based on the committee's criteria.

Funds Avail.: No specific amount. **To Apply:** Applicants must visit the website for the online application process and other required materials. **Contact:** Grants Allocation Manager at bcgrants@cbcf.org.

2590 ■ CBCF - BC/Yukon Region Small Initiative Funds *(Professional development/Grant)*

Purpose: To provide funding for small scale community initiatives in breast cancer and breast health education and awareness. **Focus:** Oncology. **Qualif.:** Applicants must be

Awards are arranged alphabetically below their administering organizations

small scale community organizations throughout British Columbia and Yukon Territory. **Criteria:** Selection will be based on the committee's criteria. **Funds Avail.:** Up to 5,000 Canadian Dollars. **To Apply:** Applicants must visit the website for the online application process and other required materials. **Contact:** Grants Allocation Manager at bcgrants@cbcf.org.

2591 ■ Canadian Breast Cancer Foundation - Ontario

20 Victoria St. 6th Flr.
Toronto, ON, Canada M5C 2N8
Ph: (416)815-1313
Free: 866-373-6313
URL: www.cbcf.org/ontario

2592 ■ CBCF - Ontario Nurse and Allied Health Professional Fellowships *(Advanced Professional, Professional development/Fellowship)*

Purpose: To support nurses and allied health professionals with a strong emphasis on women's health to focus on pursuing formal or informal advanced study or training focused on gaining expertise in clinical disciplines involving the prevention, screening, diagnosis and/or treatment of breast cancer; survivorship; quality of life; conducting basic, translational, participatory or community-based research relevant to breast cancer, or a combination thereof. **Focus:** Nursing, Oncological; Oncology. **Qualif.:** Applicants must be Canadian residents or permanent residents and nurses or allied health professionals who are registered and licensed by their respective professional college. **Criteria:** Selection will be based on the following (in order of importance): relevance to breast cancer; applicants' supervision/training environment/training and career development plan; detailed project proposal; applicant academic performance; applicant publications/abstracts; knowledge translation plan; and anticipated impact. Preference will be given to candidates who demonstrate interest in and commitment to breast health/breast cancer issues, and intent to continue their careers in Ontario. **Funds Avail.:** 35,000 Canadian Dollars per 12 months of full-time training (three years) or part-time pro-rated to the percentage of research and/or clinical training time proposed (five years). **To Apply:** Interested applicants may apply via the WebGrants system and must provide all required application materials. **Deadline:** September 17 (intent to apply); October 15 (for both application and submission of letters of reference).

2593 ■ CBCF - Ontario Physician Fellowships *(Doctorate, Professional development/Fellowship)*

Purpose: To encourage medical doctors to focus on gaining expertise in research and/or clinical disciplines involving the prevention, screening, diagnosis and/or treatment of breast cancer; survivorship; quality of life; conducting basic, translational, participatory or community-based research relevant to breast cancer, or a combination thereof. **Focus:** Oncology. **Qualif.:** Applicants must be medical doctors who are registered in or have completed a Royal College of Physicians and Surgeons of Canada certified program or a College of Family Physicians certified program. **Criteria:** Selection will be based on the following (in order of importance): relevance to breast cancer; applicants' supervision/training environment/training and career development plan; applicants' mentor and mentorship plan; detailed project proposal; applicant academic performance; applicant publications/abstracts; knowledge translation plan; and anticipated impact. Preference will be given to candidates who demonstrate interest in and commitment to breast health/breast cancer issues, and intent to continue their careers in Ontario. **Funds Avail.:** 70,000 Canadian Dollars per 12 months of full-time training (three years) or part-time pro-rated to the percentage of research and/or clinical training time proposed (five years). **To Apply:** Interested applicants may apply via the WebGrants system and must provide all required application materials. **Deadline:** September 17 (intent to apply); October 15 (for both application and submission of letters of reference).

2594 ■ CBCF - Ontario Research Fellowships *(Doctorate, Postdoctorate, Professional development/Fellowship)*

Purpose: To develop the expertise and capacity of doctoral and postdoctoral researchers in the fields of breast cancer and breast health research. **Focus:** Oncology. **Qualif.:** Applicants must be Canadian citizens or permanent residents; must be university baccalaureate graduates; and must be enrolled for studies in a graduate program in Ontario, Canada at the doctoral level or accepted for postdoctoral studies in Ontario, Canada. **Criteria:** Selection will be based on the following (in order of importance): relevance to breast cancer; applicants' publications/abstracts; applicants' academic performance; applicants' supervision/training environment/training plan; detailed project proposal; knowledge translation plan; and anticipated impact. Preference will be given to candidates who demonstrate interest in and commitment to breast health/breast cancer issues, and intent to continue their careers in Ontario. **Funds Avail.:** 35,000 Canadian Dollars per 12 months of full-time training (doctoral); 45,000 Canadian Dollars per 12 months of full-time training (postdoctoral). **To Apply:** Applicants may apply via WebGrants system and must provide all required application materials. **Deadline:** September 17 (intent to apply); October 15 (for both application and submission of letters of reference).

2595 ■ CBCF - Ontario Research Project Grants *(Advanced Professional, Professional development/Grant)*

Purpose: To support individuals in their research on breast cancer. **Focus:** Oncology. **Qualif.:** Applicants must be individuals who are conducting research with direct impact and relevance to the breast cancer. **Criteria:** Selection will be on a competitive basis. **Funds Avail.:** Up to 450,000 Canadian Dollars. **Duration:** Five years. **To Apply:** Applicants must submit their respective research proposals. They may propose studies ranging from laboratory, pre-clinical and clinical investigations to psychosocial, survivorship, and health services research. All proposals must include a knowledge translation strategy. **Deadline:** September 17 (intent to apply); October 15 (application).

2596 ■ Canadian Breast Cancer Foundation - Prairies/NWT Region

First Edmonton Place
700 - 10665 Jasper Ave.
Edmonton, AB, Canada T5J 3S9
Ph: (780)452-1166
Free: 866-302-2223
URL: www.cbcf.org/prairies

Awards are arranged alphabetically below their administering organizations

2597 ■ CBCF - Prairies/NWT Grants in Basic Biomedical Research *(Advanced Professional, Professional development/Grant)*

Purpose: To support high-quality research in all areas including biology of breast cancer, prevention, screening, early detection, diagnosis, prognosis, treatment, cancer control, psychosocial, health care delivery and outcomes. **Focus:** Oncology. **Qualif.:** Applicants must be researchers in Manitoba, Saskatchewan, Alberta, Northwest Territories and Nunavut. **Criteria:** Selection will be on a competitive basis.

Funds Avail.: Up to 125,000 Canadian Dollars per year. **Duration:** Three years. **To Apply:** Applicants must provide their respective research proposals addressing biology of breast cancer, etiology, prevention, early detection, diagnosis, prognosis, treatment (discovery and development), development and characterization of model systems. **Deadline:** March 9.

2598 ■ CBCF - Prairies/NWT Grants in Clinical Research *(Advanced Professional, Professional development/Grant)*

Purpose: To support high-quality research in all areas including biology of breast cancer, prevention, screening, early detection, diagnosis, prognosis, treatment, cancer control, psychosocial, health care delivery and outcomes. **Focus:** Oncology. **Qualif.:** Applicants must be researchers in Manitoba, Saskatchewan, Alberta, Northwest Territories and Nunavut. **Criteria:** Selection will be on a competitive basis.

Funds Avail.: Up to 125,000 Canadian Dollars per year. **To Apply:** Applicants must provide their respective clinical projects and epidemiological studies addressing etiology, prevention, early detection, diagnosis, prognosis, treatment (clinical applications), evaluation of delivery methods and interventions. **Deadline:** March 9.

2599 ■ CBCF - Prairies/NWT Grants in Health Services and Policy Research *(Advanced Professional, Professional development/Grant)*

Purpose: To support high-quality research in all areas including biology of breast cancer, prevention, screening, early detection, diagnosis, prognosis, treatment, cancer control, psychosocial, health care delivery and outcomes. **Focus:** Oncology. **Qualif.:** Applicants must be researchers in Manitoba, Saskatchewan, Alberta, Northwest Territories and Nunavut. **Criteria:** Selection will be on a competitive basis.

Funds Avail.: Up to 125,000 Canadian Dollars per year. **To Apply:** Applicants must provide their respective research proposals on financial and health-care delivery issues such as quality of care, access to care (including timeliness and equity) and factors associated with variations in quality and access. **Deadline:** March 9.

2600 ■ CBCF - Prairies/NWT Postdoctoral Fellowships *(Postdoctorate, Professional development/Fellowship)*

Purpose: To provide assistance in launching a career in social, clinical or basic science breast cancer research. **Focus:** Oncology. **Qualif.:** Applicants must be recent Ph.D. graduates across Alberta, Saskatchewan, Manitoba, Northwest Territories and Nunavut. Research project must be relevant to the study of breast cancer. **Criteria:** Selection will be based on the submitted research proposals.

Funds Avail.: Maximum of 50,000 Canadian Dollars. **To Apply:** Applicants must submit one original signed hard copy of their completed application and one electronic copy, either through e-mail or USB to the CBCF-Prairies/NWT Region's Edmonton Office. **Deadline:** November 17.

2601 ■ CBCF - Prairies/NWT Research Grants in Psychosocial, Cultural and Environmental Determinants of Health *(Advanced Professional, Professional development/Grant)*

Purpose: To support high-quality research in all areas including biology of breast cancer, prevention, screening, early detection, diagnosis, prognosis, treatment, cancer control, psychosocial, health care delivery and outcomes. **Focus:** Oncology. **Qualif.:** Applicants must be researchers in Manitoba, Saskatchewan, Alberta, Northwest Territories and Nunavut. **Criteria:** Selection will be on a competitive basis.

Funds Avail.: Up to 125,000 Canadian Dollars per year. **To Apply:** Applicants must provide their respective research proposals addressing psychosocial issues, supportive care, survivorship and outcomes, quality of life issues and interventions, behavioural research, cancer control, education, communication. **Deadline:** March 9.

2602 ■ Canadian Bureau for International Education (CBIE)
220 Laurier Ave. W, Ste. 1550
Ottawa, ON, Canada K1P 5Z9
Ph: (613)237-4820
Fax: (613)237-1073
E-mail: info@cbie.ca
URL: www.cbie.ca

2603 ■ EDC International Business Scholarships *(Undergraduate/Scholarship)*

Purpose: To support Canadian students interested in pursuing studies in international business. **Focus:** Business. **Qualif.:** Applicants must be Canadian citizens or permanent residents enrolled in a full-time accredited bachelor's degree at a Canadian university or college; must be studying business (international business, commerce, finance, economics, accounting, etc.) or business combined with environmental or sustainability courses and returning to full-time studies for the upcoming academic year; and must be in excellent academic standing. **Criteria:** Scholarships are awarded by a selection committee who evaluates applications based on the following: demonstrated interest in pursuing a career in international business; academic achievement (as reflected in the transcripts and/or honors); experience in Canada and abroad (work, internships, volunteering, study exchanges) during the current program, or concrete plans for obtaining international experience during the academic year; leadership potential (as reflected in extracurricular activities); strength of letters of reference; and language skills.

Funds Avail.: 4,000 Canadian Dollars each. **Number Awarded:** Up to 30 (25 undergraduate/college students; 5 students in programs which combine business with environmental or sustainability studies). **To Apply:** Applicants may visit the program website for further information regarding the application process and other requirements needed to submit. **Deadline:** February 2 (online application); February 9 (submission of required references). **Remarks:** The EDC International Business Scholarship is administered on behalf of Export Development Canada by the Canadian

Awards are arranged alphabetically below their administering organizations

Bureau for International Education.

2604 ■ Canadian Cancer Society Research Institute (CCSRI)
55 Saint Clair Ave. W, Ste. 300
Toronto, ON, Canada M4V 2Y7
Ph: (416)961-7223
Fax: (416)961-4189
E-mail: research@cancer.ca
URL: www.cancer.ca/research
Twitter: twitter.com/CCSresearch

2605 ■ Canadian Cancer Society Travel Awards (Doctorate, Master's, Postdoctorate/Award)
Purpose: To defray the travel costs associated with making a scientific presentation as a first author or presenter at a conference, symposium or other appropriate professional meeting. **Focus:** Health sciences. **Qualif.:** Applicants must be one of the following: registered students in Ph.D. or M.D. program; post-doctoral fellows (within 5 years of attaining his/her Ph.D.); or medical residents/clinical fellows (within 5 years of attaining his/her M.D.). **Criteria:** Selection will be based on a competitive basis.
Funds Avail.: Maximum of $2,000. **Duration:** Annual. **Number Awarded:** 30. **To Apply:** Applicants must submit the following requirements: details of the conference; Curriculum Vitae; project summary including the relevance to cancer; budget along with information regarding the applicant's supervisor; and letter of support. **Deadline:** January 15; May 15; September 15.

2606 ■ Canadian Cartographic Association (CCA)
c/o Paul Heersink, Treasurer
39 Wales Ave.
Markham, ON, Canada L3P 2C4
Ph: (613)440-4425
Fax: (416)446-1639
E-mail: treasurer@cca-acc.org
URL: www.cca-acc.org
Facebook: www.facebook.com/Canadian-Cartographic-Association|Association-Canadienne-de-Cartographie-177748108946882/
Twitter: www.twitter.com/CdnCarto

2607 ■ Norman Nicholson Scholarships (Undergraduate/Scholarship)
Purpose: To recognize and encourage exceptional student achievement and ability in any aspect of cartography. **Focus:** Cartography/Surveying. **Qualif.:** Applicant must be a full-time student in a recognized college or university program; must be a Canadian citizen or landed immigrant. **Criteria:** Applicants are selected based on committee's review of the application materials.
Funds Avail.: $500. **Duration:** Annual. **To Apply:** Applicants must submit an official transcript of all college or university courses complete with grades received; letters of recommendation from two faculty members who are familiar with the student's works and capabilities; one-page statement from the student regarding plans for continuing education in cartography. **Deadline:** March 15. **Contact:** Claire Gosson; Email: secretary@cca-acc.org.

2608 ■ Canadian Centre for Occupational Health and Safety (CCOHS)
135 Hunter St. E
Hamilton, ON, Canada L8N 1M5
Ph: (905)572-2981
Fax: (905)572-2206
Free: 800-668-4284
E-mail: clientservices@ccohs.ca
URL: www.ccohs.ca
Facebook: www.facebook.com/CCOHS
Twitter: twitter.com/ccohs

2609 ■ Dick Martin Scholarships (Postgraduate/Scholarship)
Purpose: To support financially those students who wants to continue their career in occupational health and safety. **Focus:** Occupational safety and health. **Qualif.:** Applicants must be students, who are enrolled, either full-time or part-time, in an occupational health and safety related course or program. **Criteria:** Recipients will be selected based on Essay and Cover letter they submitted.
Funds Avail.: 500 Canadian dollars-3,000 Canadian dollars. **To Apply:** Applicants must submit complete online application form; one page cover letter and 1,000 to 1,200 word essay either of the two: Prevention Essay or Technical Essay. **Deadline:** October 1. **Remarks:** Established in 2002.

2610 ■ Canadian Co-operative Association (CCA)
275 Bank St., Ste. 400
Ottawa, ON, Canada K2P 2L6
Ph: (613)238-6711
Fax: (613)567-0658
E-mail: international@coopscanada.coop
URL: www.coopscanada.coop
Facebook: www.facebook.com/CoopsInCanada
Twitter: twitter.com/cca_intl

2611 ■ Canadian Association for Studies in Co-operation Scholarships Lemaire Co-operative Studies Awards (CASC) (Graduate, Undergraduate/Scholarship)
Purpose: To encourage students to undertake studies which will help them contribute to the development of co-operatives in Canada or elsewhere. **Focus:** Business. **Qualif.:** Applicants must be undergraduate or graduate students taking full or partial credit courses at any university or university-equivalent college, and must take a minimum of one course about co-operatives. **Criteria:** Selection is based on the submitted application materials.
Funds Avail.: No specific amount. **To Apply:** Applicants must submit a completed application form along with background information; previous degree(s) or official transcripts; academic awards/distinctions/scholarships; two letters of reference (one must be academic); statement of interest in co-operatives; experience with co-operatives (either as volunteer or employee); and a description of the project (3-5 pages for graduate students, 1 page for undergraduates). **Contact:** Canadian Co-operative Association, at the above address.

2612 ■ Canadian Association for Studies in Co-operation Scholarships - Amy and Tim Dauphinee Scholarships (CASC) (Graduate/Scholarship)
Purpose: To support studies about co-operative businesses and organizations. **Focus:** Business. **Qualif.:** Applicants must be graduate students either undertaking studies at a Canadian university or a university-equivalent

college (regardless of citizenship) or be Canadian citizens or landed immigrants studying at such institutions outside Canada. **Criteria:** Selection is based on the applicant's academic record as well as on the importance of the proposed research activities to the development of the co-op movement in Canada or abroad.

Funds Avail.: No specific amount. **To Apply:** Applicants must submit a completed application form along with background information; previous degree(s) or official transcripts; academic awards/distinctions/scholarships; two letters of reference (one must be academic); statement of interest in co-operatives; experience with co-operatives (either as volunteer or employee); and 3-5 pages description of project. **Contact:** Canadian Co-operative Association, at the above address.

2613 ■ Canadian Association for Studies in Co-operation Scholarships - Alexander Fraser Laidlaw Fellowships *(Graduate/Fellowship)*

Purpose: To support studies about co-operative businesses and organizations. **Focus:** Business. **Qualif.:** Applicants must be graduate students either undertaking studies at a Canadian university or a university-equivalent college (regardless of citizenship) or be Canadian citizens or landed immigrant studying at such institutions outside Canada. **Criteria:** Selection is based on the applicant's academic record as well as on the importance of the proposed research activities to the development of the co-op movement in Canada or abroad.

Funds Avail.: No specific amount. **To Apply:** Applicants must submit a completed application form along with background information; previous degree(s) or official transcripts; academic awards/distinctions/scholarships; two letters of reference (one must be academic); statement of interest in co-operatives; experience with co-operatives (either as volunteer or employee); and 3-5 pages description of project. **Contact:** Canadian Co-operative Association, at the above address.

2614 ■ Canadian Communication Association (CCA)
c/o Kirsten Kozonlanka, Treasurer
4207 River Bldg.
School of Journalism and Communication
Carleton University
1125 Colonel By Dr.
Ottawa, ON, Canada K1S 5B6
Ph: (613)520-7404
URL: www.acc-cca.ca
Facebook: www.facebook.com/groups/275796459129543

2615 ■ Beaverbrook Media at McGill Student Paper Prize *(Graduate/Prize)*

Purpose: To recognize the promising scholars in Canadian Communication Studies. **Focus:** Communications. **Qualif.:** Applicants must be students currently enrolled in a graduate program in Communications at a Canadian university; must be fully paid members of the CCA at the time they submit their paper for consideration. **Criteria:** Selection will be based on the following criteria: 1) engagement with communication studies; 2) scholarly insight and originality of research; 3) contribution to communication studies; 4) future research potential; and 5) maturity and sophistication of the argument.

Funds Avail.: 1,000 Canadian Dollars. **Duration:** Annual.

Number Awarded: 1. **To Apply:** Applicants must submit a single-authored essay. Paper must be between 6000-8000 words in Word, RTF, or PDF format. **Deadline:** April 1.

2616 ■ Gertrude J. Robinson Book Prize *(Professional development/Prize)*

Purpose: To recognize Canadian scholars and promote scholarly excellence in Communication fields. **Focus:** Communications. **Qualif.:** Nominees for the Prize must have published a monograph in the previous calendar year, and be members of the Canadian Communication Association. **Criteria:** Selection will be based on the following categories: 1) engagement with the field of communication studies; 2) scholarly insight and originality of the research; 3) contribution to the field of communication studies; 4) potential to promote or inspire further research by other Canadian scholars; and 5) maturity and sophistication of the argument.

Funds Avail.: No specific amount. **Duration:** Annual. **To Apply:** Applicants must submit a single or multi-authored monograph with publication date the same year as the prize. **Deadline:** March 1. **Remarks:** Established in 2001.

2617 ■ Canadian Consumer Specialty Products Association (CCSPA)
130 Albert St., Ste. 800
Ottawa, ON, Canada K1P 5G4
Ph: (613)232-6616
Fax: (613)233-6350
E-mail: assoc@ccspa.org
URL: www.ccspa.org
Twitter: www.twitter.com/CCSPA_ACPCS

2618 ■ Chevalier Award Scholarship *(Undergraduate/Scholarship)*

Purpose: To provide support to those students who demonstrated outstanding extracurricular contributions and accomplishments. **Focus:** General studies/Field of study not specified. **Qualif.:** Applicants must be sons or daughters of employees of a member company of the Canadian Consumer Specialty Products Association. **Criteria:** Selection will be based on good citizenship, humanitarian service, interest in communal affairs and leadership skills.

Funds Avail.: 2,500 Canadian Dollars. **Duration:** Annual. **To Apply:** Applicants may download an application form online. **Deadline:** July 8.

2619 ■ Canadian Energy Law Foundation
15th Flr., Dentons
850 - 2 St., SW
Calgary, AB, Canada T2P 0R8
URL: www.energylawfoundation.ca

2620 ■ Canadian Energy Law Foundation Graduate Scholarships in Law *(Advanced Professional/Scholarship)*

Purpose: To contribute to the advancement of energy law by means of supporting law students in their education. **Focus:** Law. **Qualif.:** Applicants must be Canadian and foreign students enrolled in a Canadian University LLM or PHD program who are confirmed as the Designated Candidate by the Law School. Only one designated candidate per law school is eligible. **Criteria:** CELF's Scholarship Subcommittee will make its recommendation

Awards are arranged alphabetically below their administering organizations

for award(s) on the basis of: thesis topic(s) that are of interest to Canadian energy lawyers; or recipient(s) intending to make a significant contribution to the Canadian energy legal practice. **Funds Avail.:** 20,000 Canadian Dollars. **To Apply:** Candidates must submit a statement describing their thesis topic and why it would be of interest to Canadian energy lawyers and/or a description of the activities undertaken by the applicants that are intended to make a significant contribution to the Canadian energy legal practice. This application must be accompanied by a letter from the Law School confirming that the applicants are the designated candidates for the Law School for the Scholarship Program.

2621 ■ Canadian Engineering Memorial Foundation

3-247 Barr St.
Renfrew, ON, Canada K7V 1J6
Free: 866-883-2363
E-mail: info@cemf.ca
URL: www.cemf.ca
Facebook: www.facebook.com/pages/CEMF/1434676350148112
Twitter: twitter.com/CEMF

2622 ■ CEMF Undergraduate Engineering Scholarships *(Undergraduate/Scholarship)*

Purpose: To provide financial assistance to qualified individuals who want to pursue their studies. **Focus:** Engineering. **Qualif.:** Applicants must be Canadian women in engineering in either their 1st, 2nd or 3rd year of study in an accredited program in Canada. **Criteria:** Selection of applicants will be based on the scholarship application requirements.

Funds Avail.: $5,000. **Duration:** Annual. **Number Awarded:** 5. **To Apply:** Applicants must submit a signed Applicant Declaration along with the a completed application form; an informational letter; community activities; reference letter; letter of support; proof of citizenship; a colored photograph; and voice sound clip.

2623 ■ Rona Hatt Master's Scholarships in Chemical Engineering *(Master's/Scholarship)*

Purpose: To encourage women to pursue their career path in engineering while inspiring others to follow in their footprints. **Focus:** Engineering. **Qualif.:** Applicants must be female Canadian citizens or landed immigrants with a permanent residence card; must be enrolled full-time in a graduate engineering program at the Masters level of study. **Criteria:** Applicants will be judge based on the following criteria: effectiveness of their Power Point presentation and short demonstration of an Engineering Principle Movie Clip; informational letter written by the applicants about their professional, volunteer, extracurricular and role model activities; scope of community involvement and extracurricular activities that demonstrate their leadership and outreach interests; professional achievements through research and work experience; achievements and leadership potential as perceived through the two reference letters and Dean's Letter of Support on provided forms; and overall quality of the submitted application, both electronic and hardcopy. Judges will base a large part of their assessment on the presentation; it must be unique, interesting and convincing.

Funds Avail.: $10,000. **Duration:** Annual. **To Apply:** Applicants must submit and complete the following documents: letter of support from the Dean or from the applicant's delegate; declaration and application form ensuring for the complete hard copy and electronic submission; list or chart of extracurricular activities; resume/curriculum vitae; reference letter; proof of citizenship; power point presentation geared to a high school level audience including a bibliography of all the presentation's resources, presentation must be within 20-30 minutes; informational letter that is no longer than four pages, in proper business format and should address to the CEMF and CEMF judging panel. Informational letter should include the following: a description of why the applicants think that their extracurricular activities make them a strong role model for other young women in engineering and what they have learned from their experiences; an essay of why they should be a leader and an ambassador for the profession; a brief outline of their academic curriculum (what you are studying, your research, undergraduate degrees, etc.) and how their professional experience makes them a leader without repeating their Curriculum Vitae; a list of awards received, including other scholarships, honours and recognitions; and some personal info like hobbies, membership in groups, organizations, athletic and cultural achievements and a kind of person the applicants think they are.

2624 ■ CEMF Claudette MacKay-Lassonde Graduate Scholarships *(Doctorate, Postdoctorate/Scholarship)*

Purpose: To encourage Canadian women to pursue careers in the field of engineering. **Focus:** Engineering. **Qualif.:** Applicants must be Canadian women who are pursuing studies in engineering at the PhD level. They must also have an undergraduate engineering degree from an accredited Canadian program, and must either be professional engineers or provincially registered as engineers-in-training/junior engineers. **Criteria:** Selection shall be based on: effectiveness of the presentation; community involvement and extra-curricular activities; professional achievements; achievements and leadership potential; overall quality of the electronic and hard copy package.

Funds Avail.: 15,000 Canadian Dollars. **Duration:** Annual. **To Apply:** Applicants must submit the following: an application form; letter of recommendation coming from the Dean's office; applicant declaration; maximum of four pages information letter; curriculum vitae; a colored photo; reference letter; proof of citizenship; media coverage; Power-Point presentation; and, approximately (20-30 minutes) movie on a CD presenting themselves. The entire application must be type in a (12-point) Times New Roman font, double-spaced, original, signed and in hard copy accompanied by an electronic copy on a Windows XP Platform CD. Reference letters and letter from the Dean can mail directly to CEMF. **Deadline:** January 15. **Remarks:** The scholarship is named in honor of the late Claudette MacKay-Lassonde, P.Eng. who spearheaded the initiative to form CEMF in recognition of her efforts and dedication as a founder. **Contact:** Applications must be submitted to: awards@cemf.ca.

2625 ■ Vale Master's in Engineering Scholarships *(Master's/Scholarship)*

Purpose: To support a woman enrolled full-time in an engineering master's program at a Canadian university. **Focus:** Engineering. **Qualif.:** Applicants must be women in Canada who are pursuing their studies in engineering at the Masters level. **Criteria:** Selection of applicants will be based on the scholarship application requirements.

Funds Avail.: 10,000 Canadian Dollars. **Duration:** Annual.

Number Awarded: 1. **To Apply:** Applicants must submit a signed Applicant Declaration along with a completed application form; an informational letter; curriculum vitae; a colored photograph; reference letters; proof of citizenship; presentation; demonstration video clip; voice sound clip; and a letter of recommendation.

2626 ■ Canadian Federation for Sexual Health (CFSH)
251 rue Bank St., 2nd Fl.
Ottawa, ON, Canada K2P 1X3
Ph: (613)241-4474
Fax: (613)241-7550
E-mail: admin@cfsh.ca
URL: www.cfsh.ca

2627 ■ John and Lois Lamont Graduate Scholarship (Graduate/Scholarship)
Purpose: To provide educational assistance for medical students enrolled in full-time graduate studies in a Canadian university. **Focus:** Education, Medical. **Qualif.:** Applicants must be Canadian citizens or landed immigrants who are graduates of any recognized university; possess an honour degree or its equivalent and intend to pursue a higher degree in the field of sexual and reproductive health. **Criteria:** Applicants will be selected based on the evaluation of the candidate's essay. Scholarship winners will be selected by a review committee constituted by the Canadian Federation for Sexual Health.

Funds Avail.: $3,000. **Duration:** Annual. **To Apply:** Applicants must submit a typewritten essay of 500-700 words, outlining their education, background in sex and reproductive health and/or women's issues, aspiration, and plans to access abortion provider training as an elective; must include the curriculum vitae, recent academic transcript and a full list of publications; and must submit a letter of recommendation.

2628 ■ Canadian Federation of University Women (CFUW)
331 Cooper St., Ste. 502
Ottawa, ON, Canada K2P 0G5
Ph: (613)234-8252
Fax: (613)234-8221
Free: 888-220-9606
URL: www.cfuw.org

2629 ■ Canadian Home Economics Association Fellowships (Master's, Doctorate/Fellowship)
Purpose: To support individuals in studying one or more aspects in the field of Human Ecology/Home Economics/Family and Consumer Sciences, at the masters or doctoral level. **Focus:** Home Economics. **Qualif.:** Candidates must be studying in one or more aspects in the field of Human Ecology/Home Economics/Family and Consumer Sciences at the masters or doctoral level. Applicants must be accepted or enrolled in a post-graduate program in Canada at the time of application. **Criteria:** Selection will be based on the committee's criteria.

Funds Avail.: 6,000 Canadian Dollars. **Duration:** Annual. **To Apply:** Application form can be obtained at the website. Applicants must complete and submit the following requirements: completed application form; completed filing fee payment form or a copy of the electronic receipt of the approved transaction for the online credit card payment of filing fee; completed personal information consent; statement of intent; curriculum vitae; completed referee assessment; confirmation of enrollment in a graduate program from the host institution; letter of acceptance into the program of proposed study from the host institution, if not enrolled at the time of application; ethics application/approval or approximate date of projected application, if applicable.

2630 ■ École Polytechnique Commemorative Awards (Master's, Doctorate, Graduate/Award, Fellowship)
Purpose: To promote the status of women. **Focus:** General studies/Field of study not specified. **Qualif.:** Applicants must be students at the masters or doctoral level of study. **Criteria:** Selection will be based on the committee's criteria.

Funds Avail.: $7,000 for doctoral; $5,000 for masters. **Duration:** Annual. **Number Awarded:** 2. **To Apply:** Application form can be obtained at the website. Applicants must complete and submit the following requirements: completed application form; completed filing fee payment form or a copy of the electronic receipt of the approved transaction for the online credit card payment of filing fee; completed personal information consent; statement of intent; curriculum vitae; completed referee assessment; confirmation of enrollment in a graduate program from the host institution; letter of acceptance into the program of proposed study from the host institution, if not enrolled at the time of application; ethics application/approval or approximate date of projected application, if applicable.

2631 ■ Elizabeth Massey Award (Postgraduate/Award)
Purpose: To support post-graduate students who are studying visual arts, such as painting or sculpture; or in music. **Focus:** Visual arts. **Qualif.:** Applicants must be post-graduate students in the visual arts. **Criteria:** Selection will be based on the committee's criteria.

Funds Avail.: 5,000 Canadian Dollars. **Duration:** Annual. **To Apply:** Application form can be obtained at the website. Applicants must complete and submit the following requirements: completed application form; completed filing fee payment form or a copy of the electronic receipt of the approved transaction for the online credit card payment of filing fee; completed personal information consent; statement of intent; curriculum vitae; completed referee assessment; confirmation of enrollment in a graduate program from the host institution; letter of acceptance into the program of proposed study from the host institution, if not enrolled at the time of application; ethics application/approval or approximate date of projected application, if applicable. **Remarks:** Established in 2006.

2632 ■ Dr. Alice E. Wilson Awards (Graduate, Doctorate/Award, Fellowship)
Purpose: To promote the status of women. **Focus:** General studies/Field of study not specified. **Qualif.:** Applicants must be masters or doctoral students. **Criteria:** Selection will be based on the committee's criteria.

Funds Avail.: 20,000 Canadian Dollars. **Duration:** Annual. **Number Awarded:** 4. **To Apply:** Application form can be obtained at the website. Applicants must complete and submit the following requirements: completed application form; completed filing fee payment form or a copy of the electronic receipt of the approved transaction for the online credit card payment of filing fee; completed personal information consent; statement of intent; curriculum vitae;

Awards are arranged alphabetically below their administering organizations

completed referee assessment; confirmation of enrollment in a graduate program from the host institution; letter of acceptance into the program of proposed study from the host institution, if not enrolled at the time of application; ethics application/approval or approximate date of projected application, if applicable.

2633 ■ Canadian Federation of University Women, Edmonton Branch
c/o Lynn Masters, Membership Chair
4205 Terwillegar Vista NW
Edmonton, AB, Canada T6R 2Z9
E-mail: cfuwedmonton@cfuwedmonton.org
URL: www.cfuwedmonton.org

2634 ■ Margaret Brine Graduate Scholarships (Graduate/Scholarship)

Purpose: To support women in their education. **Focus:** General studies/Field of study not specified. **Qualif.:** Applicants must be full-time female graduate students with a current minimum GPA of 3.8; must be registered in a research based degree program. Master's students must have completed at least one term of their Master's program at the University of Alberta and have received grades for courses taken at the graduate level. Doctoral students must have completed at least one year of their Doctoral program at the University of Alberta. **Criteria:** Selection will be based on the applicants' demonstrated academic excellence and embodying the values of CFUW.

Funds Avail.: 5,000 Canadian Dollars. **Duration:** Annual. **Number Awarded:** 4 (2 Master's, 2 Doctoral). **To Apply:** Applicants may download the Scholarship Application Form at the CFUW-Edmonton website. **Deadline:** February 26.

2635 ■ Canadian Fertility and Andrology Society (CFAS)
11649 Gouin Blvd. W, Ste. 104
Montreal, QC, Canada H8Y 1Y4
Ph: (514)524-9009
Fax: (514)524-2163
E-mail: info@cfas.ca
URL: www.cfas.ca

2636 ■ Dr. Biljan Memorial Awards (Advanced Professional/Award, Grant)

Purpose: To recognize a reproductive endocrinologist or fertility specialist who made a contribution to clinical research. **Focus:** Biological and clinical sciences; Endocrinology. **Qualif.:** Applicants must be CFAS members; must be clinicians working in the field of reproductive endocrinology and infertility. **Criteria:** Preference will be given to abstracts that address novel approaches to ovulation induction/IVF or that address innovations in patient-focused strategies that improve administrative or clinical care.

Funds Avail.: 5,000 Canadian Dollars. **Duration:** Biennial. **To Apply:** Every applicant must submit abstracts of their own. Abstracts must adhere to the CFAS and/or BFS requirements for submission as appropriate. **Contact:** CFAS, at the above address.

2637 ■ Canadian Frailty Network
Kidd House
100 Stuart St.
Kingston, ON, Canada K7L 3N6
Ph: (613)549-6666
URL: www.cfn-nce.ca

2638 ■ CFN Interdisciplinary Fellowships Program (Graduate, Postdoctorate, Advanced Professional/Fellowship)

Purpose: To provide a unique learning experience to trainees and adapt an experiential learning approach to allow fellows to: develop expertise on frailty and late life issues; understand interdisciplinary perspectives and collaborative practice; and, develop skills to be successful in professional settings. **Focus:** Gerontology. **Qualif.:** Applicants will be enrolled in and be in good standing, or have completed, a professional, master's or doctoral degree program at a recognized university, and will have relevant employment or life experience and the academic/other skills necessary to complete the fellowship requirements. The program is open to Canadian citizens and those with Canadian permanent residency only. **Criteria:** Preference will be given to applicants that have demonstrated current or prior personal or professional interest in late life issues related to frailty. Examples of demonstrated interest may include pursuing late-life courses or specializations, or relevant work, community service or leadership experience.

Funds Avail.: 25,000 Canadian Dollars (Master's level); 35,000 Canadian Dollars (doctorate level); 50,000 Canadian Dollars (postdoctorate/health professionals). **Number Awarded:** Varies. **To Apply:** A pre-application intent to apply is required with the fellowship competition, to be eligible to submit a full application package. Applications will not be considered unless a pre-application intent to apply has been submitted on-line. Please read the Application Instructions before registering at the Intent to Apply. A complete Application Package is comprised of: application form; applicants' respective CV; transcripts for all post-secondary and clinical/medical school studies; applicants' and supervisors' Capacity Disclosure Form; application signatures form; supervisor endorsement; two professional references form; partner letters of support. **Deadline:** October 16 (letter of intent); October 23 (full application).

2639 ■ Canadian Friends of the Hebrew University of Jerusalem (CFHU)
3080 Yonge St., Ste. 3020
Toronto, ON, Canada M4N 3N1
Ph: (416)485-8000
Fax: (416)485-8565
Free: 888-432-7398
E-mail: info@cfhu.org
URL: www.cfhu.org

2640 ■ Canadian Zionist Federation - Dr. Leon Aryeh Kronitz Scholarships (Undergraduate, Graduate/Scholarship)

Purpose: To support outstanding students looking to study abroad. **Focus:** Teaching. **Qualif.:** Applicants must be Canadian citizens; must be recent high school graduates, university students or graduate students pursuing teacher training or general studies in Israel; must be accepted for at least one year at an accredited postsecondary program; must demonstrate financial need. **Criteria:** Selection will be based on the Committees' criteria.

Funds Avail.: No specific amount. **To Apply:** Applicants must submit the three letters of recommendation required, one of which must be by a high school principal or university studies director and may contact the Association for other application information needed. **Deadline:** May 31. **Contact:** Florence Simon, Canadian Zionist Federation; 5151 Cote St. Catherine, Ste. 206, Montreal H3W 1M6; Phone: 514-739-7300 ext. 3100; czf.national@federationcja.org.

2641 ■ Hushy Lipton Memorial Scholarship Funds
(Undergraduate, Graduate, Postgraduate/Scholarship)

Purpose: To support outstanding students looking to study abroad. **Focus:** General studies/Field of study not specified. **Qualif.:** Applicants must be Canadian in need of financial aid; must be undergraduate, graduate or postgraduate students who are residing in Canada and planning to study for a full academic year; must have Ontario Secondary Diploma (OSSD) or its equivalent; and must be eligible for full-time attendance at associated recognized institutions of higher learning in Israel. **Criteria:** Selection will be based on the Committees' criteria.

Funds Avail.: No specific amount. **To Apply:** Applicants may visit the UJA website for updated application form and other relevant information. **Deadline:** May. **Contact:** Miriam Daniels; 416-635-2883 ext. 5116; mdaniels@ujafed.org; jewishtoronto.com/scholarships.

2642 ■ Morris M. Pulver Scholarship Funds
(Undergraduate, Graduate, Postgraduate/Scholarship)

Purpose: To support outstanding students looking to study abroad. **Focus:** General studies/Field of study not specified. **Qualif.:** Applicants must be Canadian in need of financial aid; must be undergraduate, graduate or postgraduate students who are residing in Canada and planning to study for a full academic year; must have Ontario Secondary Diploma (OSSD) or its equivalent; and must be eligible for full-time attendance at associated recognized institutions of higher learning in Israel. **Criteria:** Selection will be based on the Committees' criteria.

Funds Avail.: No specific amount. **To Apply:** Applicants may visit the UJA website for updated application form and other relevant information. **Deadline:** May. **Contact:** Miriam Daniels; 416-635-2883 ext. 5116; mdaniels@ujafed.org; jewishtoronto.com/scholarships.

2643 ■ Rothberg International School Graduate Merit Scholarships *(Graduate, Master's/Scholarship)*

Purpose: To support outstanding students looking to study abroad. **Focus:** General studies/Field of study not specified. **Qualif.:** Candidates must have completed their undergraduate degree and have a minimum GPA of 3.8 or equivalent. Any candidate for an M.A. program may apply and those selected will be eligible for a two-year fellowship, conditional on maintenance of academic performance. Candidates for any other graduate program are not eligible to apply for the Graduate Merit Scholarship. **Criteria:** Selection will be based on the Committees' criteria.

Funds Avail.: No specific amount. **To Apply:** Applicants may visit the website for online application and other information. **Contact:** overseas.huji.ac.il/scholarships; gradmiss@savion.huji.ac.il.

2644 ■ Canadian Gerontological Nursing Association (CGNA)
1202-71 Charles St. E
Toronto, ON, Canada M4Y 2T3
Ph: (416)927-8654
E-mail: CGNA.office@gmail.com
URL: www.cgna.net

2645 ■ Ann C. Beckingham Scholarships *(Graduate, Other/Scholarship)*

Purpose: To support outstanding registered nurses undertaking further education in a graduate degree program. **Focus:** Gerontology; Nursing. **Qualif.:** Applicants must: be Canadian citizens or landed immigrants at the time of taking up the award; be members of CGNA for more than two years immediately prior to the application submission; be registered to practice nursing in a Canadian province; have gained acceptance to a suitable program in a recognized educational institution at the time of taking up the award; exhibit an interest in, and potential for, a career in gerontological nursing. Applicants must be registered nurses undertaking further education in: a post-basic undergraduate nursing degree program; a graduate or post graduate degree program relevant to career development, preferably in the field of gerontological nursing - this includes nurse practitioner programs that focus on the care of older adults. **Criteria:** Selection will be based on the committee's criteria.

Funds Avail.: No specific amount. **Duration:** Annual. **To Apply:** Applicants must enclose a copy of their certificate to practice nursing in a Canadian province/territory; copy of current national/provincial/territorial gerontological nursing association membership card (or copy of completed CGNA/provincial/territorial association application form); evidence from an academic institution of part-time or full-time student status; academic transcript of most recently completed nursing degree program (please indicate as well those courses with gerontological content); curriculum vitae; and letter of support/recommendation from a current CGNA member. Applicants must complete the application by answering the following questions (in no more than one page for each): Describe your past contributions to gerontological nursing in Canada; Describe why you are interested in furthering your education in gerontological nursing and indicate how this additional education will assist your career plans. **Deadline:** April 4.

2646 ■ CGNA Memorial Scholarship *(Graduate, Other/Scholarship)*

Purpose: To help students further their education in a graduate degree program. **Focus:** Gerontology; Nursing. **Qualif.:** Applicants must be Canadian citizens or landed immigrants at the time of taking up the award; be member of CGNA for more than two years immediately prior to the application submission; be registered to practice nursing in a Canadian province; have gained acceptance to a suitable program in a recognized educational institution at the time of taking up the award; and must exhibit an interest in, and potential for, a career in gerontological nursing. **Criteria:** Selection will be based on the committee's criteria.

Funds Avail.: No specific amount. **Duration:** Annual. **To Apply:** Applicants must enclose a copy of their certificate to practice nursing in a Canadian province/territory; copy of current national/provincial/territorial gerontological nursing association membership card (or copy of completed CGNA/provincial/territorial association application form); evidence from an academic institution of part-time or full-time student status; academic transcript of most recently completed nursing degree program which should indicate as well those courses with gerontological content; curriculum vitae; and letter of support/recommendation from a current CGNA member. Applicants must complete the application by

Awards are arranged alphabetically below their administering organizations

answering the following questions (in no more than one page for each): Describe your past contributions to gerontological nursing in Canada; Describe why you are interested in furthering your education in gerontological nursing and indicate how this additional education will assist your career plans. **Deadline:** April 4.

2647 ■ Canadian Group Psychotherapy Association
c/o Sandy Ramsay
7633 Toombs Dr.
Prince George, BC, Canada V2K 4Z5
URL: cgpa.ca

2648 ■ CGPF Endowments Conference Scholarships (Undergraduate/Scholarship)

Purpose: To financially assist trainees who wish to acquire professional development and to defray the cost of attending the CGPA Annual conference. **Focus:** General studies/Field of study not specified. **Qualif.:** Applicants must be trainees in group psychotherapy in a GCPA-accredited training program or academic degree program. **Criteria:** Recipients will be evaluated based on training background, work experience, perspective on development of group therapy practice and being associated with the individual's life experience.

Funds Avail.: No specific amount. **Duration:** Annual. **Number Awarded:** 4. **To Apply:** Applicants must submit a letter of intent, curriculum vitae and letter of support from a mentor. **Deadline:** March 15.

2649 ■ Martin Fischer Awards (Undergraduate/Award)

Purpose: To recognize and support outstanding Canadian trainees or students who are receiving training in group therapy from an established program. **Focus:** General studies/Field of study not specified. **Qualif.:** Applicants must be students nominated by a training faculty member. **Criteria:** Applicants will be evaluated based on submitted paper, clinical and research achievements.

Funds Avail.: 500-1,500 Canadian Dollars. **To Apply:** Applicants must submit three copies of paper accompanying the letter of support and documentation of clinical and research achievements.

2650 ■ Canadian Hard of Hearing Association (CHHA)
2415 Holly Ln., Ste. 205
Ottawa, ON, Canada K1V 7P2
Ph: (613)526-1584
Fax: (613)526-4718
Free: 800-263-8068
E-mail: chhanational@chha.ca
URL: www.chha.ca

2651 ■ Canadian Hard of Hearing Association Scholarship Programs (Undergraduate/Scholarship)

Purpose: To offer financial assistance to hard of hearing and deafened students. **Focus:** General studies/Field of study not specified. **Qualif.:** Applicants must be students registered in a full-time program at a recognized Canadian college or university, with a goal of obtaining a diploma or degree; must be either hard-of-hearing, deafened or orally deaf. **Criteria:** Selection of applicants will be judged by a number of criteria including academic achievement, determination to cope with hearing loss and community involvement.

Funds Avail.: No specific amount. **Duration:** Annual. **To Apply:** Interested applicants must visit the website for the online application process. **Deadline:** March 4. **Remarks:** Established in 2002. **Contact:** scholarship@chha.ca.

2652 ■ Canadian Hemophilia Society (CHS)
301-666 Sherbrooke St. W
Montreal, QC, Canada H3A 1E7
Ph: (514)848-0503
Fax: (514)848-9661
Free: 800-668-2686
E-mail: chs@hemophilia.ca
URL: www.hemophilia.ca

2653 ■ CHS - Bursary Program Scholarships (Undergraduate/Scholarship)

Purpose: To bring young volunteers into the CHS while recognizing the importance of education. **Focus:** General studies/Field of study not specified. **Qualif.:** Applicants must possess academic standards sufficient to allow admission into the post-secondary educational institution and program to which the bursary would be applied. **Criteria:** Priority is given to those who have financial needs.

Funds Avail.: 5,000 Canadian Dollars. **Duration:** Annual. **Number Awarded:** 4. **To Apply:** Applicant must provide three letters of reference with the application stating the abilities and suitability of the candidate; must provide a letter from his/her physician or any medical authority confirming his/her medical status; must submit an original essay (500 words) to emphasize the logical thinking and adequate writing skills of the applicant; and must submit the original transcript of grades for the last year in secondary school. Application forms are available from the website. **Deadline:** April 30.

2654 ■ CHS - Mature Student Bursary Program Scholarships (Undergraduate/Scholarship)

Purpose: To support students returning to or beginning a course of studies at any post-secondary institution. **Focus:** General studies/Field of study not specified. **Qualif.:** Applicant must be at least 30 years of age. **Criteria:** Recipients are selected based on application materials and financial need as reviewed by a committee of academics and lay persons.

Funds Avail.: 5,000 Canadian Dollars. **Duration:** Annual. **To Apply:** Applicants must submit a detailed budget showing their source of income and their projected expenses for a year of study at the institution of their choice; must submit an essay of intent describing past employment and assessment of new career; must provide three letters of reference with their application, none of which may be from a relative (such letters should attest to the abilities and suitability of the candidate for the program being applied for as well as act as a character reference for the candidate); must provide a separate letter from their physician or some medical authority confirming their medical status regarding eligibility to this program. **Deadline:** April 30.

2655 ■ CHS Scholarships (Undergraduate/Scholarship)

Purpose: To bring young volunteers into the CHS while recognizing the importance of education. **Focus:** General studies/Field of study not specified. **Qualif.:** Applicants

Awards are arranged alphabetically below their administering organizations

must possess academic proficiency of 3.0 GPA on a 4.0 scale; must have an experience in community service at a volunteer level; and must possess leadership qualities. **Criteria:** Priority will be given to those who might not be able to succeed in a vocational course requiring strenuous physical labor.

Funds Avail.: 5,000 Canadian Dollars. **Duration:** Annual. **Number Awarded:** 4. **To Apply:** Applicant must provide three letters of reference with the application stating the abilities and suitability of the candidate; must provide a letter from his/her physician or any medical authority confirming his/her medical status; must submit an original 500-word essay to emphasize the logical thinking and adequate writing skills of the applicant; and must submit the original transcript of grades of the last year in secondary school. Application forms are available on the website. **Deadline:** April 30.

2656 ■ Canadian Hospitality Foundation (CHF)
300 Adelaide St. E, No. 339
Toronto, ON, Canada M5A 1N1
Ph: (416)363-3401
Fax: (416)363-3403
E-mail: chf@theohi.ca
URL: www.thechf.ca

2657 ■ Applied Hospitality Degree Scholarships *(Undergraduate/Scholarship)*

Purpose: To provide scholarship to the students enrolled in the first or second year of a community college. **Focus:** Hotel, institutional, and restaurant management; Travel and tourism. **Qualif.:** Applicants must be college students currently enrolled in the first or second year of a community college. Applicants must be Canadian citizens or permanent residents. **Criteria:** Selection will be based on work experience, scholastic record, leadership and ability to get along with others, professional promise, essay and discretionary points.

Funds Avail.: $2,500. **Duration:** Annual. **To Apply:** Applicants must complete the application form on-line. In addition, students must submit hard copies of the following documents (please note that missing or incomplete documents may be grounds for elimination): Most current official transcripts of your complete academic history at the college you are enrolled in at this time; one or more letters of recommendation from an instructor and/or administrator form your college; One letters of recommendation from past or present employers; Resume; An essay on one of the topics listed on application form (300 words). Employer and school letters must include telephone numbers and, where possible, e-mail addresses.

2658 ■ Canadian Hospitality Foundation College Entrance Scholarships *(Undergraduate/Scholarship)*

Purpose: To provide scholarship to the High School students in their final year of school. **Focus:** Culinary arts; Hotel, institutional, and restaurant management; Travel and tourism. **Qualif.:** Applicants must be high school students in their final year of school and who are enrolling in a minimum two-year college program in one of the following areas of training or study: Accommodation; Chef; Cook; Culinary; Events; Food and Beverages; Golf Club; Hospitality; Hotel; Resort; Restaurant; Tourism; Applicants must be Canadian citizens or permanent residents. **Criteria:** Selection will be based on work experience, scholastic record, leadership and ability to get along with others, professional promise and discretionary points.

Funds Avail.: No specific amount. **Duration:** Annual. **To Apply:** Applicants must complete the application form on-line. In addition, students must submit hard copies of the following documents (please note that missing or incomplete documents may be grounds for elimination): Final-year official transcripts from your previous academic year and report card from your current academic year (first semester/first term); Letter/s of recommendation from your school principal, teacher or guidance counselor; Letter/s of recommendation from past or present employers. School and employer letters must include telephone numbers and, where possible, e-mail addresses.

2659 ■ Canadian Hospitality Foundation University Entrance Scholarships *(Undergraduate/Scholarship)*

Purpose: To provide scholarships to High School students in their final year of school. **Focus:** Hotel, institutional, and restaurant management; Travel and tourism. **Qualif.:** Applicants must be high school students in their final year of school who are enrolling in a university degree program in one of the following areas of training or study: Hospitality; Hotel; Tourism. Applicants must be Canadian citizens or permanent residents. **Criteria:** Selection will be based on the following criteria: Work experience; Scholastic record; Leadership and ability to get along with others; Professional promise; Discretionary points.

Funds Avail.: No specific amount. **Duration:** Annual. **To Apply:** Applicants must complete the application form on-line; in addition, students must submit hard copies of the following documents (please note that missing or incomplete documents may be grounds for elimination): Final-year official transcripts from your previous academic year and report card from your current academic year (first semester/first term); Letter/s of recommendation from your school principal, teacher or guidance counselor; Letter/s of recommendation from past or present employers. School and employer letters must include telephone numbers and, where possible, e-mail addresses.

2660 ■ Culinary (1-Year Program) Scholarships *(Undergraduate/Scholarship)*

Purpose: To provide scholarship to the students enrolled in a one-year culinary program. **Focus:** Culinary arts. **Qualif.:** Applicants must: be college students currently enrolled in a one-year (minimum of eight months) culinary certificate program; not have received any other Canadian Hospitality Foundation scholarships; be Canadian citizens or permanent residents. **Criteria:** Selection will be based on work experience, scholastic record, leadership and ability to get along with others, professional promise and discretionary points. Applications selected by the judges are ranked and the scholarships are awarded based on dollar value.

Funds Avail.: No specific amount. **Duration:** Annual. **To Apply:** Applicants must complete the application form on-line. In addition, students must submit hard copies of the following documents (please note that missing or incomplete documents may be grounds for elimination): Final-year official transcripts from your previous academic year and report card from your current academic year (first semester/first term); Letter/s of recommendation from your school principal, teacher or guidance counselor; Letter/s of recommendation from past or present employers. School and employer letters must include telephone numbers and e-mail addresses.

Awards are arranged alphabetically below their administering organizations

2661 ■ Canadian Hydrographic Association (CHA)

4900 Yonge St., Ste. 1205
Toronto, ON, Canada M2N 6A6
Ph: (416)512-5815
Fax: (416)512-5830
URL: hydrography.ca/home.html

2662 ■ Canadian Hydrographic Association Student Awards (Undergraduate/Award, Monetary, Medal)

Purpose: To advance the knowledge of hydrography, cartography and associated disciplines. **Focus:** Engineering, Ocean; Hydrology; Oceanography. **Qualif.:** Applicants must be full time students in an accredited post-secondary program in the field of Geomatics in a university or technological college anywhere in Canada. **Criteria:** Selection will be based on the following criteria: demonstrated bona fide financial need, coupled with an above average academic performance.
Funds Avail.: No specific amount. **Duration:** Annual. **To Apply:** Applicants will be required to write a short paragraph explaining their financial need in a clear, concise manner on the application form or, if necessary, attached piece of paper. The importance of this aspect of the application is emphasized. Applicants must submit one letter of reference from an official of the university or college where the applicant spent the previous year. Letter of reference must include the address and phone number of this official. Also included is the completion of the provided application form. **Deadline:** June 30. **Contact:** Kirsten Greenfield, Canadian Hydrographic Association; E-mail: kirsten.greenfield@pwgsc.gc.ca.

2663 ■ Canadian Identification Society (CIS)

c/o Dwayne Raymond, President
555 Columbia St.
New Westminster, BC, Canada V3L 1B2
Ph: (604)529-2526
Fax: (604)529-2401
URL: cis-sci.ca

2664 ■ Canadian Identification Society Essay/Scholarship Awards (Advanced Professional, Professional development/Prize)

Purpose: To help CIS members conduct their research. **Focus:** Criminology; Law enforcement; Science. **Qualif.:** Applicants must be CIS members or immediate family members employed in law enforcement. **Criteria:** Essays will be evaluated based on originality of the technique, merit as a method of collecting/processing forensic evidence and the quality of writing.
Funds Avail.: 100 - 300 Canadian Dollars. **Duration:** Annual. **Number Awarded:** 3. **To Apply:** Applicants must submit an essay (minimum of 3000 words in either French or English) on forensic identification evidence that describes a successful method of locating, processing or presenting such evidence. **Contact:** Canadian Identification Society, at the above address.

2665 ■ William Donald Dixon Research Grants (Graduate, Undergraduate, Advanced Professional/Grant)

Purpose: To provide opportunities to individuals engaged in forensic research. **Focus:** Chemistry; Law enforcement; Science. **Qualif.:** Applicants must be members of CIS who have submitted a relevant research paper in the field of forensic science; must have a bachelor's degree in any discipline but should not be employed in law enforcement; graduates of three-year programs are required to be employed in law enforcement. **Criteria:** Recipients will be selected based on submitted research proposals. Priority may be given to graduates in science or chemistry.
Funds Avail.: 500 Canadian Dollars each. **Duration:** Annual. **Number Awarded:** 2. **To Apply:** Applicants must submit a research proposal, or outline on a topic related to forensic identification. The summary and/or research must be submitted for publishing in the Identification Canada Journal. Letters of recommendation should be obtained from a senior official of their police department, law enforcement official(s), or academic head and employer. **Contact:** Canadian Identification Society, at the above address.

2666 ■ Edward Foster Awards (Advanced Professional/Award)

Purpose: To encourage members to conduct research that will benefit the forensic identification profession. **Focus:** Criminology; Science. **Qualif.:** Applicants must be nominated by the two CIS members. **Criteria:** Awards will be given to applicants who best meet the qualifications.
Funds Avail.: No specific amount. **Duration:** Annual. **To Apply:** Applicants must submit an outline of their contributions to the field of forensic identification. **Contact:** Canadian Identification Society, at the above address.

2667 ■ Canadian Institute for the Administration of Justice (CIAJ)

3101 Chemin de la Tour Bureau A
3421 Succursalle Ctr. Ville
Montreal, QC, Canada H3C 3J7
Ph: (514)343-6157
Fax: (514)343-6296
LinkedIn: www.linkedin.com/company/ciaj-icaj

2668 ■ Charles D. Gonthier Research Fellowships (Graduate, Advanced Professional/Fellowship)

Purpose: To support and recognize an academic selected by the jury who will best research the topic of CIAJ's annual conference. **Focus:** Social sciences. **Qualif.:** Applicants must be faculty members and graduate students at Canadian universities. **Criteria:** Selection will be based on the CIAJ's criteria.
Funds Avail.: 7,500 Canadian Dollars. **Duration:** Annual. **To Apply:** Applicants should complete the application form provided at the website and submit it no later than the given deadline. They should also submit their respective research reports. **Deadline:** March 16.

2669 ■ Canadian Institute for Advanced Research (CIFAR)

180 Dundas St. W, Ste. 1400
Toronto, ON, Canada M5G 1Z8
Ph: (416)971-4251
Fax: (416)971-6169
Free: 888-738-1113
E-mail: info@cifar.ca
URL: www.cifar.ca

2670 ■ CIFAR Global Scholars Program (Advanced Professional, Professional development/Scholarship)

Purpose: To identify some of the world's most promising early-career researchers to become members of a CIFAR research program. **Focus:** General studies/Field of study not specified. **Qualif.:** Applicants must be individuals within the first three years of having completed their PhD; and must have demonstrated outstanding scholarship and research potential. **Criteria:** Selection will be based on the committee's criteria.

Funds Avail.: No specific amount. **To Apply:** Candidate must provide the following materials: a two-page backgrounder on the candidate (may visit the website for the template); a detailed letter from the nominator, outlining the candidates' academic achievements and their record of public engagement; a detailed project proposal from the candidates, outlining their proposal for a Trudeau project. The proposal is not required to include a budget, but if the candidate feels that a budget would help illustrate the proposal, a summary budget may be included. the proposal, including the budget if desired, should be between 5 and 10 pages; candidates' current resume; up to three publications, articles or book chapters written by the candidates; an optional, one or two testimonies or articles about the candidate containing substantially different elements than those contained in the letter of recommendation. **Contact:** Paula Driedger, Programs and Information Officer at pdriedger@cifar.ca.

2671 ■ Canadian Institute of Planners (CIP)
141 Laurier Ave. W, Ste. 1112
Ottawa, ON, Canada K1P 5J3
Ph: (613)237-7526
Fax: (613)237-7045
Free: 800-207-2138
E-mail: general@cip-icu.ca
URL: www.cip-icu.ca

2672 ■ CIP Fellow's Travel Scholarships
(Undergraduate/Scholarship)

Purpose: To provide opportunity for the student to travel, observe, and study, innovative, leading-edge planning projects first hand, thus contributing to their education, anticipation and excitement for the profession they are about to enter. **Focus:** General studies/Field of study not specified. **Qualif.:** Applicant must be a student member who is in the final year of an undergraduate planning program recognized by the Canadian Institute of Planners. **Criteria:** Recipients will be selected based on demonstrated leadership and commitment to their chosen profession and professional association; academic achievement; and a proposal to travel and explore a leading-edge, innovative or new planning initiative or project that will contribute to the depth and breadth of the student's educational experience as reviewed by a jury consisting of three members of the College of Fellows and the Vice President of the Student Scholarship Trust Fund.

Funds Avail.: 4,000 Canadian Dollars. **Duration:** Annual. **Number Awarded:** 1. **To Apply:** Applicants must provide their contact information, university and program enrollment information, official transcript, a recommendation letter from the department head and from someone who is familiar with the applicant's commitment to community service, a list of accomplishments and a travel proposal (not more than 4-5 pages in length). Applicants are required to submit six originals and one copy on CD of the submission materials. **Deadline:** February 17.

2673 ■ Canadian Institute of Ukrainian Studies (CIUS)
4-30 Pembina Hall
University of Alberta
Edmonton, AB, Canada T6G 2H8
Ph: (780)492-2972
E-mail: cius@ualberta.ca
URL: www.ualberta.ca/~cius
Facebook: www.facebook.com/canadian.institute.of.ukrainian.studies?ref=hl

2674 ■ Leo J. Krysa Family Undergraduate Scholarships *(Undergraduate/Scholarship)*

Purpose: To help students pursue their final year of study in the faculty of Arts or Education. **Focus:** Ukrainian studies. **Qualif.:** Candidates must be Canadian citizens or permanent residents of Canada at the time of application; must be students in the faculty of Arts and Education about to enter their final year of study in pursuit of an undergraduate degree; have a program which emphasizes Ukrainian and/or Ukrainian-Canadian studies based on the following areas: Education, History, Humanities and Social Sciences; must have a record of above average grades in their Ukrainian-content courses. **Criteria:** Applications will be judged on a point system that emphasizes academic achievement, performance in Ukrainian-content course, writing sample (paper or essay), and community involvement.

Funds Avail.: Up to $3,500. **Duration:** Annual. **To Apply:** Application form can be obtained at University of Alberta, Canadian Institute of Ukrainian Studies. Applicants must complete and submit the application form together with their official transcript of records. **Deadline:** March 1.

2675 ■ Ukrainian Canadian Professional and Business Club Scholarships in Education
(Undergraduate/Scholarship)

Purpose: To support students who wish to pursue their final year of study in the faculty of Education. **Focus:** Ukrainian studies. **Qualif.:** Applicant must be a full-time undergraduate student completing the third or fourth year in the faculty of Education at the University of Alberta; must have taken one course in language acquisition or teaching and one senior course in Ukrainian language or literature; must have both academic standing and demonstrated involvement in the Ukrainian community; and have an overall GPA of no less than 7.0. **Criteria:** Application will be judged on a points system that emphasizes academic achievement, performance in Ukrainian-content course, writing sample (paper or essay), and community involvement.

Funds Avail.: $800. **Duration:** Annual. **Number Awarded:** 1. **To Apply:** Application form can be obtained at University of Alberta, Canadian Institute of Ukrainian Studies. Applicants must complete and submit the application form together with their official transcript of records.

2676 ■ Canadian Iranian Foundation (CIF)
PO Box 91231
West Vancouver, BC, Canada V7V 3N6
Ph: (604)696-1121
Fax: (604)922-8584
E-mail: info@cif-bc.com
URL: canadianiranianfoundationinvancouver.com
Facebook: www.facebook.com/CanadianIranianFoundation

Awards are arranged alphabetically below their administering organizations

2677 ■ Canadian Iranian Foundation Scholarships (Undergraduate/Scholarship)

Purpose: To assist immigrant students who wish to pursue their academic goals. **Focus:** General studies/Field of study not specified. **Qualif.:** Applicants must have legal immigrant's status (Canadian Citizen or permanent resident of Canada) and reside in Canada; have shown a great effort in trying to integrate into Canadian Society by volunteering at least 100 hours of community service; have active interest in Iranian and Canadian culture and heritage; must be accepted into a Canadian post-secondary institute in a full degree program by the end of academic year. **Criteria:** Selection will be based on the committee's criteria.

Funds Avail.: $1,500. **Duration:** Annual. **To Apply:** Applicants must provide two academic references; letter of reference supporting volunteer services; and sealed official transcript of Grade 12 grades. **Deadline:** April 5.

2678 ■ Canadian Library Association (CLA)
1150 Morrison Dr., Ste. 400
Ottawa, ON, Canada K2H 8S9
Ph: (613)232-9625
Fax: (613)563-9895
E-mail: info@cla.ca
URL: www.cla.ca
Facebook: www.facebook.com/CanadianLibraryAssociation
LinkedIn: www.linkedin.com/groups/4137241/profile
Twitter: twitter.com/cla_web

2679 ■ CLA/ACB Dafoe Scholarships (Graduate/Scholarship)

Purpose: To encourage individuals to pursue their masters degree in library and information studies. **Focus:** Library and archival sciences. **Qualif.:** Candidates must be Canadian citizens or landed immigrants; must have professional library/information science degrees at an ALA-accredited institution. **Criteria:** Applicants are selected based on academic achievement, leadership potential and expressed interest in the profession.

Funds Avail.: $5,000. **Duration:** One year. **To Apply:** Application and scholarship reference forms are available at the website. Applicants must submit completed form along transcript of records and proof of admission to library and information studies program. **Deadline:** May 1. **Contact:** CLA/ACB Member Services Department at the above address or email at membership@cla.ca.

2680 ■ World Book Graduate Scholarships in Library and Information Science (Graduate/Scholarship)

Purpose: To support individuals who wish to pursue a PhD degree in library and information studies. **Focus:** Library and archival sciences. **Qualif.:** Applicant must be an individual who holds a MLS/MLIS degree and is pursuing a PhD degree in library and information studies in either Canada or the United States; must be a Canadian citizen or landed immigrant. **Criteria:** Recipients are selected based on the application and other supporting documents.

Funds Avail.: No specific amount. **Duration:** Annual. **To Apply:** Application form is available at the website. **Deadline:** May 1.

2681 ■ Canadian Meteorological and Oceanographic Society (CMOS)
5E197 - 200 Kent St.
Ottawa, ON, Canada K1P 6H7
Ph: (613)990-0300
Fax: (613)990-1617
URL: www.cmos.ca

2682 ■ CMOS-SCMO President's Prize (Professional development/Prize)

Purpose: To recognize members for a recent paper or book of special merit in the fields of meteorology or oceanography. **Focus:** Meteorology; Oceanography. **Qualif.:** Candidates must be members of the Society with a recent paper or book of special merit in the fields of meteorology or oceanography. The paper must have been accepted for publication in Atmosphere-Ocean or another refereed journal. **Criteria:** Selection will be based on the committee's criteria.

Funds Avail.: No specific amount. **Duration:** Annual. **To Apply:** Nominating letters should include the current title, full address and phone number of the nominee. An up-to-date CV and a summary of the candidate's work must be included. The nomination should be accompanied by, at least one and at most four, additional letters of support indicating the extent of influence of the candidate's work. Electronic format is preferred; however, hard-copy material will be accepted. **Deadline:** February 15. **Remarks:** Established in 1967. **Contact:** Email at awards-coord@cmos.ca.

2683 ■ Roger Daley Postdoctoral Publication Awards (Postdoctorate/Monetary)

Purpose: To recognize excellence of a publication in the fields of meteorology or oceanography that has appeared, or is in press, at the time of nomination. **Focus:** Meteorology; Oceanography. **Qualif.:** Candidates must be working in Canada in a non-permanent position as a postdoctoral fellows or research associates and must have received their doctoral degree within five years. **Criteria:** Award is based on the excellence of a publication in the fields of meteorology or oceanography that has appeared or is in press at the time of nomination.

Funds Avail.: 2,000 Canadian Dollars. **Duration:** Annual. **To Apply:** Nominating letters should include the current title, full address and phone number of the nominee. An up-to-date CV and a summary of the candidate's work must be included. The nomination should be accompanied by, at least one and at most four, additional letters of support indicating the extent of influence of the candidate's work. Electronic format is preferred; however, hard-copy material will be accepted. **Deadline:** February 15. **Remarks:** Established in 2005. **Contact:** Email at awards-coord@cmos.ca.

2684 ■ Tertia M.C. Hughes Memorial Graduate Student Prize (Graduate/Award, Prize)

Purpose: To promote meteorology and oceanography in Canada. **Focus:** Meteorology; Oceanography. **Qualif.:** Candidates must be graduate students registered at a Canadian university or by Canadian graduate students registered at a foreign university. **Criteria:** Selection will be based on the committee's criteria.

Funds Avail.: $500. **To Apply:** Nominating letters should include the current title, full address and phone number of the nominee. An up-to-date CV and a summary of the candidate's work must be included. The nomination should be accompanied by, at least one and at most four, additional letters of support indicating the extent of influence of the candidate's work. Electronic format is preferred; however, hard-copy material will be accepted.

Awards are arranged alphabetically below their administering organizations

2685 ■ François J. Saucier Prize in Applied Oceanography *(Professional development/Award, Prize)*

Purpose: To recognize an individual for an outstanding contribution to the application of oceanography in Canada. **Focus:** Meteorology; Oceanography. **Qualif.:** Candidates must be members of the Society with outstanding contribution to the application of meteorology in Canada. **Criteria:** Selection will be based on the committee's criteria.

Funds Avail.: No specific amount. **Duration:** Annual. **To Apply:** Nominating letters should include the current title, full address and phone number of the nominee. An up-to-date CV and a summary of the candidate's work must be included. The nomination should be accompanied by, at least one and at most four, additional letters of support indicating the extent of influence of the candidate's work. Electronic format is preferred; however, hard-copy material will be accepted. **Deadline:** February 15. **Remarks:** Established in 1982. **Contact:** awards-coord@cmos.ca.

2686 ■ Dr. Andrew Thomson Prize in Applied Meteorology *(Professional development/Award, Prize)*

Purpose: To recognize a member or members of the Society for an outstanding contribution to the application of meteorology in Canada. **Focus:** Meteorology; Oceanography. **Qualif.:** Candidates must be members of the Society with outstanding contribution to the application of meteorology in Canada. **Criteria:** Selection will be based on the committee's criteria.

Funds Avail.: No specific amount. **Duration:** Annual. **To Apply:** Nominating letters should include the current title, full address and phone number of the nominee. An up-to-date CV and a summary of the candidate's work must be included. The nomination should be accompanied by, at least one and at most four, additional letters of support indicating the extent of influence of the candidate's work. Electronic format is preferred; however, hard-copy material will be accepted. **Deadline:** February 15.

2687 ■ Canadian National Institute for the Blind (CNIB)
1929 Bayview Ave.
Toronto, ON, Canada M4G 3E8
Ph: (416)486-2500
Fax: (416)480-7700
Free: 800-563-2642
E-mail: info@cnib.ca
URL: www.cnib.ca

2688 ■ CNIB Master's Scholarships *(Master's/Scholarship)*

Purpose: To encourage and support people who are blind or partially sighted to undertake studies at the post-graduate level. **Focus:** General studies/Field of study not specified. **Qualif.:** Applicants must be blind or partially sighted (less than 20/70 corrected); must be university school graduates entering a post-graduate education program; and must be Canadian citizens (or landed immigrants, permanent residents, protected refugees for at least one year prior to the date of application). **Criteria:** Selection will be based on the applicants' academic standing and must have demonstrated superior intellectual ability and judgment. Preference will be given to those who will undertake theoretical and practical research at a Canadian university.

Funds Avail.: 12,500 Canadian Dollars. **Duration:** Annual. **To Apply:** Applicants must download the Application Form (either English or French application) and submit to Shampa Bose, Executive Assistant and Research Coordinator of CNIB. **Deadline:** May 31.

2689 ■ Nalini Perera Little Lotus Bud Master's Scholarships *(Master's/Scholarship)*

Purpose: To encourage and support people who are blind or partially sighted to undertake studies at the post-graduate level. **Focus:** General studies/Field of study not specified. **Qualif.:** Applicants must be blind or partially sighted (less than 20/70 corrected); must be university school graduates entering a post-graduate education program; and must be Canadian citizens (or landed immigrants, permanent residents, protected refugees for at least one year prior to the date of application). **Criteria:** Selection will be based on the applicants' academic standing and must have demonstrated superior intellectual ability and judgment. Preference will be given to those who will undertake theoretical and practical research at a Canadian university.

Funds Avail.: 5,000 Canadian Dollars. **Duration:** Annual. **To Apply:** Applicants must download the Application Form (either English or French application) and submit to Shampa Bose, Executive Assistant and Research Coordinator of CNIB. **Deadline:** May 31.

2690 ■ Scholarship Award of the Bell Aliant Pioneer Volunteers *(Undergraduate/Scholarship)*

Purpose: To provide financial assistance to a person with vision lost while attending a post-secondary educational program. **Focus:** General studies/Field of study not specified. **Qualif.:** Candidates must be aged 25 years or under, have visual acuity of 20/70 or less with correction and be Canadian Citizen residing in Nova Scotia or Prince Edward Island. They must also be graduating from Grade 12 during the application year (or be a high school graduate) and registered in a post-secondary educational program. **Criteria:** Candidates will be selected based on the Selection Committee's review of the application materials. Priority is given to candidates with financial need.

Funds Avail.: No specific amount. **Duration:** Annual. **To Apply:** Candidates must submit a completed application form (available on the website); must submit two letters of reference: (1) educational letter of recommendation, and (2) personal or community letter of recommendation including contact information (address, telephone, fax and e-mail); letter of acceptance from post-secondary education institution; must provide a documentation about the candidate's visual acuity. **Remarks:** Established in 2006. **Contact:** Selection Committee, Scholarship Award of the Bell Aliant Pioneer Volunteers, c/o Wendy Constable; Email: wendy.constable@cnib.ca.

2691 ■ Canadian National Railway Co.
935 de la Gauchetiere St. W
Montreal, QC, Canada H3B 2M9
Ph: (514)399-4821
Fax: (866)991-6184
Free: 888-888-5909
E-mail: contact@cn.ca
URL: www.cn.ca

2692 ■ CN Scholarships for Women *(Undergraduate/Scholarship)*

Purpose: To encourage women to pursue non-traditional careers in areas such as trade, technology and operations;

to promote employment equity in Canada. **Focus:** Technology. **Qualif.:** Applicants must be Canadian students who demonstrate desire in the field of trade, technology and operation, and have been accepted in one of those programs at an accredited educational institutions. **Criteria:** Applicants will be evaluated on the basis of their demonstrated interests in a non-traditional career. Scholarships are awarded regardless of whatever other financial assistance applicants may have obtained and may be used to ease financial constraints while studying.
Funds Avail.: 3,000 Canadian Dollars. **Duration:** Annual. **Number Awarded:** Varies. **To Apply:** Applicants must submit letter of recommendation written by one of their educators, employers, or someone who can assess their personality; and must include a (one-page) essay describing their interest with the chosen program. Aspiring applicants may also go to the website of the Canadian National Railways for other details regarding the application process. **Deadline:** May 13.

2693 ■ Canadian Nurses Foundation (CNF)
50 Driveway
Ottawa, ON, Canada K2P 1E2
Ph: (613)680-0879
Fax: (613)237-3520
Free: 844-204-0124
E-mail: info@cnf-fiic.ca
URL: www.cnf-fiic.ca
Facebook: www.facebook.com/cnf.fiic
Twitter: twitter.com/thecnf

2694 ■ Aplastic Anemia and Myelodysplasia Association of Canada Scholarships (Graduate/Scholarship)

Purpose: To support students who want to pursue their education. **Focus:** Hematology; Oncology. **Qualif.:** Applicants must be nurses who will be focusing their research in the field of hematology or oncology; must be willing to increase awareness of Aplastic, Anemia and Myelodysplasia issues by presenting to colleagues or sitting on the Board of the Association; must be Canadian citizens or permanent resident status; must be studying in Canada; must be RNs enrolled in a Masters program in a health related field; must be non-nurses who hold a degree in a health-related field or a nursing-related program, which will qualify them as RNs at the Master's level; must be full-time or part-time students, but part-time students must be taking minimum of 2 courses each semester. **Criteria:** Preference will be given to CANO members.
Funds Avail.: $5,000. **Duration:** Annual. **To Apply:** Applicants must complete and print the application form available online. **Deadline:** March 31.

2695 ■ AstraZeneca Scholarships (Doctorate/Scholarship)

Purpose: To support students who want to pursue their education. **Focus:** Nursing. **Qualif.:** Applicant must be a student doing research that will impact front line nursing care delivery to under serviced or marginalized populations in rural setting; must be a Canadian citizen or permanent resident status; must be studying in Canada; must be a full-time or part-time RN student, but part-time students must be taking a minimum of 2 courses each semester or doing thesis work; must not receive other awards or scholarships during the Scholar Year of the application. **Criteria:** Selection of applicants will be based on the Scholarship application criteria.
Funds Avail.: 9,000 Canadian Dollars. **Duration:** Annual. **To Apply:** Applicants must complete and print the application form available online. **Deadline:** March 31.

2696 ■ Dr. Ann C. Beckingham Scholarships (Doctorate/Scholarship)

Purpose: To support students who want to pursue their education. **Focus:** Nursing. **Qualif.:** Applicant must be a Canadian citizen or with a permanent resident status; must be studying in Canada; must be a full-time or part-time RN student, but part-time students must be taking a minimum of 2 courses each semester or doing thesis work; must not receive other awards or scholarships during the Scholar Year of the application. **Criteria:** Selection of applicants will be based on the Scholarship application criteria.
Funds Avail.: $5,000. **Duration:** Annual. **To Apply:** Applicants must complete and print the application form available online. **Deadline:** March 31.

2697 ■ Canadian Nurses Foundation Northern Award (Undergraduate/Scholarship)

Purpose: To support students who want to pursue their education. **Focus:** Nursing. **Qualif.:** Applicant must be a student intending to work in Canada's North; must be a Canadian citizen or permanent resident status; must be studying in Canada; must be entering at least year 2 as a full-time student of a baccalaureate-nursing program. **Criteria:** Preference will be given to aboriginal origin or nurses who have worked in the north for at least 2 years.
Funds Avail.: $3,000. **Duration:** Annual. **To Apply:** Applicants must complete and print the application form available online. **Deadline:** March 31.

2698 ■ Canadian Nurses Foundation Scholarships (Undergraduate, Master's, Doctorate/Scholarship)

Purpose: To support students in all areas of nursing practice. **Focus:** Nursing. **Qualif.:** Applicants must be Canadian citizens or permanent resident status; must be studying in Canada; must be entering at least year 2 as full-time students of a baccalaureate-nursing program. **Criteria:** Selection of applicants will be based on the Scholarship application criteria.
Funds Avail.: Varies. **Duration:** Annual. **To Apply:** Applicants must complete and print the application form available online. For further information, applicants are advice to contact, Jacqueline Solis, Foundation Coordinator at 613-237-2159. **Deadline:** March 31.

2699 ■ Extendicare Scholarships in Gerontology (Master's/Scholarship)

Purpose: To support students who want to pursue their education. **Focus:** Gerontology. **Qualif.:** Applicants must be nurses who intend to practice, teach or do research in gerontology/long term care; must be Canadian citizens or permanent resident status; must be studying in Canada; must be RNs enrolled in a Masters program in a health related field; must be non-nurses who hold a degree in a health-related field and are in a nursing-related program, which will qualify them as RNs at the Master's level; must be full-time or part-time students, but part-time students must be taking a minimum of 2 courses each semester. **Criteria:** Selection of applicants will be based on the scholarship application criteria.
Funds Avail.: $5,000. **Duration:** Annual. **To Apply:** Ap-

Awards are arranged alphabetically below their administering organizations

plicants must complete and print the application form available online. **Deadline:** March 31.

2700 ■ Dr. Helen Preston Glass Fellowships
(Doctorate/Fellowship)

Purpose: To support students who want to pursue their education. **Focus:** Nursing. **Qualif.:** Applicants must be Nurses from Manitoba who are studying in community health nursing, primary health care, health nursing and studies which focus on "at risk population"; must be registered nurses who are undertaking graduate studies in nursing; must be willing to practice in Canada for a period of not less than 6-12 months after the Scholarship has been received; must be Canadian citizens or permanent resident status; must be studying in Canada; must be full-time or part-time RN students, but part-time students must be taking minimum of 2 courses each semester or doing thesis work. **Criteria:** Selection of applicants will be based on the Scholarship application criteria.

Funds Avail.: $5,000. **Duration:** Annual. **To Apply:** Applicants must complete and print the application form available online. **Deadline:** March 31.

2701 ■ Judy Hill Memorial Scholarships
(Undergraduate/Scholarship)

Purpose: To support students who want to pursue their education. **Focus:** Nursing. **Qualif.:** Applicant must be a student who has worked in the north and must sign a statement that he/she will practice nursing in the north for a period of 12 months; must be a Canadian citizen or with a permanent resident status; must be studying in Canada; must be entering at least year 2 as a full-time student of a baccalaureate-nursing program. **Criteria:** Selection of applicants will be based on the Scholarship application criteria.

Funds Avail.: $3,000. **Duration:** Annual. **To Apply:** Applicants must complete and print the application form available online. **Deadline:** March 31.

2702 ■ Johnson & Johnson Scholarships
(Undergraduate/Scholarship)

Purpose: To support students who want to pursue their education. **Focus:** Nursing. **Qualif.:** Applicant must be a student who plans to practice nursing in an operating room or a critical care area; must be a Canadian citizen or permanent resident status; must be studying in Canada; must be entering at least year 2 as a full-time student of a baccalaureate-nursing program. **Criteria:** Selection of applicants will be based on the Scholarship application criteria.

Funds Avail.: $3,000. **Duration:** Annual. **To Apply:** Applicants must complete and print the application form available online. **Deadline:** March 31.

2703 ■ Dr. Dorothy J. Kergin Fellowships *(Doctorate, Master's/Fellowship)*

Purpose: To support students who want to pursue their education. **Focus:** Nursing. **Qualif.:** Applicant must be a Canadian citizen or permanent resident status; must be studying in Canada; must be a full-time or part-time RN student, but part-time students must be taking minimum of 2 courses each semester or doing thesis work; must be a student at the doctoral level. **Criteria:** Selection of applicants will be based on the Scholarship application criteria.

Funds Avail.: $5,000. **Duration:** Annual. **To Apply:** Applicants must complete and print the application form available online.

2704 ■ Tecla Lin & Nelia Laroza Memorial Scholarships *(Undergraduate/Scholarship)*

Purpose: To support students who want to pursue their education. **Focus:** Nursing. **Qualif.:** Applicant must be a foreign educated nurse working towards baccalaureate degree; must be a Canadian citizen or permanent resident status; must be studying in Canada; must be entering at least year 2 as a full-time student of a baccalaureate-nursing program. **Criteria:** Selection of applicants will be based on the Scholarship application criteria.

Funds Avail.: $3,000. **Duration:** Annual. **To Apply:** Applicants must complete and print the application form available online. **Deadline:** March 31.

2705 ■ Eleanor Jean Martin Award *(Master's/Scholarship)*

Purpose: To support students who want to pursue their education. **Focus:** Nursing. **Qualif.:** Applicants must be students interested in studying either Neurosurgical or Cancer nursing fields; must be Canadian citizens or permanent resident status; must be studying in Canada; must be RNs enrolled in a Masters program in a health related field; must be non-nurses who hold a degree in a health-related field and are in a nursing-related program, which will qualify them as RNs at the Master's level; must be full-time or part-time students, but part-time students must be taking a minimum of 2 courses each semester. **Criteria:** Selection of applicants will be based on the Scholarship application criteria.

Funds Avail.: $5,000. **Duration:** Annual. **To Apply:** Applicants must complete and print the application form available online. **Deadline:** March 31.

2706 ■ Military Nurses Association Scholarships
(Master's/Scholarship)

Purpose: To support students who want to pursue their education. **Focus:** Nursing. **Qualif.:** Applicants must be students at master level; must be Canadian citizens or permanent residents status; must be studying in Canada; must be RNs enrolled in a Masters program in a health related field; must be non-nurses who hold a degree in a health-related field and are in a nursing-related program, which will qualify them as RNs at the Master's level; must be full-time or part-time students, but part-time students must be taking minimum of 2 courses each semester. **Criteria:** Preference will be given to military nurses, or former military.

Funds Avail.: $5,000. **Duration:** Annual. **To Apply:** Applicants must complete and print the application form available online. **Deadline:** March 31.

2707 ■ Margaret Munro Award *(Undergraduate/Scholarship)*

Purpose: To support students who want to pursue their education. **Focus:** Nursing. **Qualif.:** Applicant must be a student from Prince Edward Island; must be a Canadian citizen or with a permanent resident status; must be studying in Canada; must be entering at least year 2 as a full-time student of a baccalaureate-nursing program. **Criteria:** Selection of applicants will be based on the Scholarship application criteria.

Funds Avail.: $3,000. **Duration:** Annual. **To Apply:** Applicants must complete and print the application form avail-

Awards are arranged alphabetically below their administering organizations

able online. **Deadline:** March 31.

2708 ■ Dr. Helen K. Mussallem Fellowships *(Master's/Scholarship)*

Purpose: To support students who want to pursue their education. **Focus:** Nursing. **Qualif.:** Applicants must be students at master level; must be Canadian citizens or permanent residents status; must be studying in Canada; must be RNs enrolled in a Masters program in a health related field; must be non-nurses who hold a degree in a health-related field and are in a nursing-related program, which will qualify them as RNs at the Master's level; must be full-time or part-time students, but part-time students must be taking a minimum of two courses each semester. **Criteria:** Recipients will be evaluated based on academic aptitude, personal strengths and leadership potential. Final decision will be made based on merit, strategic directions of CNF, financial and resources considerations.
Funds Avail.: $5,000. **Duration:** Annual. **To Apply:** Applicants must complete and print the application form available online. **Deadline:** March 31.

2709 ■ New Brunswick Nurses Association Scholarships *(Master's/Scholarship)*

Purpose: To support students who want to pursue their education. **Focus:** Nursing. **Qualif.:** Applicants must be students from New Brunswick; must be Canadian citizens or permanent resident status; must be studying in Canada; must be RNs enrolled in a Masters program in a health related field; must be non-nurses who hold a degree in a health-related field and are in a nursing-related program, which will qualify them as RNs at the Master's level; must be full-time or part-time students, but part-time students must be taking minimum of 2 courses each semester. **Criteria:** Selection of applicants will be based on the Scholarship application criteria.
Funds Avail.: $5,000. **Duration:** Annual. **To Apply:** Applicants must complete and print the application form available online. **Deadline:** March 31.

2710 ■ Sharon Nield Memorial Scholarships *(Undergraduate/Scholarship)*

Purpose: To support students who want to pursue their education. **Focus:** Nursing. **Qualif.:** Applicants must be registered nurses returning to school; must be Canadian citizens or have permanent resident status; must be studying in Canada; must be entering at least year 2 as full-time students of a baccalaureate-nursing program. **Criteria:** Selection of applicants will be based on the Scholarship application criteria.
Funds Avail.: $3,000. **Duration:** Annual. **To Apply:** Applicants must complete and print the application form available online. **Deadline:** March 31.

2711 ■ Senator Norman Paterson Fellowships *(Doctorate/Scholarship)*

Purpose: To support students who want to pursue their education. **Focus:** Nursing. **Qualif.:** Applicant must be a Canadian citizen or permanent resident status; must be studying in Canada; must be a full-time or part-time RN student, but part-time students must be taking a minimum of 2 courses each semester or doing thesis work; must be a student at the doctoral level. **Criteria:** Selection of applicants will be based on the Scholarship application criteria.
Funds Avail.: 3,000 Canadian Dollars. **Duration:** Annual. **To Apply:** Applicants must complete and print the application form available online. **Deadline:** March 31.

2712 ■ Sanofi Pasteur Scholarships *(Master's/Scholarship)*

Purpose: To support students who want to pursue their education. **Focus:** Nursing. **Qualif.:** Applicants must be Canadian citizens or permanent residents status; must be studying in Canada; must be RNs enrolled in a Masters program in a health related field; must be non-nurses who hold a degree in a health-related field or a nursing-related program, which will qualify them as RNs at the Master's level; must be full-time or part-time students, but part-time students must be taking minimum of 2 courses each semester. **Criteria:** Selection of applicants will be based on the Scholarship application criteria.
Funds Avail.: $5,000. **Duration:** Annual. **To Apply:** Applicants must complete and print the application form available online. **Deadline:** March 31.

2713 ■ Sigma Theta Tau International Scholarships *(Doctorate/Scholarship)*

Purpose: To support students who want to pursue their education. **Focus:** Nursing. **Qualif.:** Applicants must be nurses who are working on their PhD dissertation; must be Canadian citizens or permanent resident status; must be studying in Canada; must be full-time or part-time RN students, but part-time students must be taking a minimum of 2 courses each semester or doing thesis work. **Criteria:** Selection of applicants will be based on the Scholarship application criteria.
Funds Avail.: $1,800. **Duration:** Annual. **To Apply:** Applicants must complete and print the application form available online. **Deadline:** March 31.

2714 ■ TD Meloche-Monnex Scholarships *(Doctorate/Scholarship)*

Purpose: To support students who want to pursue their education. **Focus:** Nursing. **Qualif.:** Applicant must be a Canadian citizen or permanent resident status; must be studying in Canada; must be a full-time or part-time RN student but part-time students must be taking a minimum of two courses each semester or doing thesis work; must be a student at the doctoral level. **Criteria:** Recipients will be evaluated based on academic aptitude, personal strengths and leadership potential. Final decision will be made based on merit, strategic directions of CNF, financial and resources considerations.
Funds Avail.: $10,000. **Duration:** Annual. **To Apply:** Applicants must complete and print the application form available online. **Deadline:** March 31.

2715 ■ John Vanderlee Award *(Undergraduate/Scholarship)*

Purpose: To support students who want to pursue their education. **Focus:** Nursing. **Qualif.:** Applicant must be a male student entering at least year 2 as a full-time student of a baccalaureate-nursing program; must be a Canadian citizen or permanent resident status; must be studying in Canada. **Criteria:** Selection of applicants will be based on the Scholarship application criteria.
Funds Avail.: $3,000. **Duration:** Annual. **To Apply:** Applicants must complete and print the application form available online. **Deadline:** March 31.

2716 ■ Canadian Occupational Therapy Foundation (COTF)
2420 Bank St., Ste. 64
Ottawa, ON, Canada K1S 5R1

Awards are arranged alphabetically below their administering organizations

Ph: (613)523-2268
Fax: (613)523-2552
Free: 800-434-2268
URL: www.cotfcanada.org
Facebook: www.facebook.com/cotffce

2717 ■ Canadian Occupational Therapy Foundation Graduate Scholarships (Doctorate, Master's/Scholarship)

Purpose: To support an individual pursuing graduate studies and as such may be used at the recipient's discretion to offset the costs of fees, books, supplies, and so on. **Focus:** Occupational therapy. **Qualif.:** Applicants must be life or student members of CAOT enrolled full-time or part-time in a master's or doctoral program related to occupational therapy research. **Criteria:** Selection of applicants will be based on panel's criteria.

Funds Avail.: $3,000 doctoral and $1,500 master's. **Duration:** Annual. **To Apply:** Application details and process shall be determined by the scholarship program officers. **Deadline:** October 1.

2718 ■ Canadian Occupational Therapy Foundation Invacare Master's Scholarships (Master's/Scholarship)

Purpose: To support an individual pursuing graduate studies and as such may be used at the recipient's discretion to offset the costs of fees, books, supplies, and so on. **Focus:** Occupational therapy. **Qualif.:** Applicants must be individual, life or student members of CAOT enrolled full-time or part-time in a master's program related to occupational therapy. **Criteria:** Selection of applicants will be based on panel's criteria.

Funds Avail.: $2,000. **Duration:** Annual. **Number Awarded:** 1. **To Apply:** Application details and process shall be determined by the scholarship program officers. **Deadline:** October 1. **Remarks:** Established in 2006.

2719 ■ Thelma Cardwell Scholarships (Graduate/Scholarship)

Purpose: To support an individual pursuing graduate studies and as such may be used at the recipient's discretion to offset the costs of fees, books, supplies, and so on. **Focus:** Occupational therapy. **Qualif.:** Applicants must be individual, life or student members of CAOT enrolled full-time in a master's or doctoral level program who have demonstrated an outstanding contribution to occupational therapy; and must be in good standing. **Criteria:** Selection of applicants will be based on scholarship panel's criteria.

Funds Avail.: $2,000. **Duration:** Annual. **Number Awarded:** 1. **To Apply:** Application details and process shall be determined by the scholarship program officers. **Deadline:** October 1. **Remarks:** The scholarship is established to acknowledge Dr. Cardwell's outstanding contribution to occupational therapy, and is awarded to an individual enrolled in full-time studies who has demonstrated significant involvement and leadership in such field.

2720 ■ Goldwin Howland Scholarships (Graduate/Scholarship)

Purpose: To support an individual pursuing graduate studies and as such may be used at the recipient's discretion to offset the costs of fees, books, supplies, and so on. **Focus:** Occupational therapy. **Qualif.:** Applicants must be enrolled in graduate studies related to occupational therapy in Canada; must be CAOT individual, life or student members in good standing. Applicants enrolled in a university program outside Canada should indicate their intention to return to practice and/or to take up an academic appointment in Canada. **Criteria:** Selection of applicants will be based on scholarship reviewer criteria.

Funds Avail.: $2,000. **Duration:** Annual. **Number Awarded:** 1. **To Apply:** Application details and process shall be determined by the scholarship program officers. **Deadline:** October 1. **Remarks:** The scholarship was founded in appreciation of Dr. Howland's leadership and vision, and is awarded to an individual who has demonstrated these qualities within the profession of occupational therapy and is enrolled in full-time studies. Established in 1945.

2721 ■ Canadian Office Products Association (COPA)

101-1335 Morningside Ave.
Scarborough
Toronto, ON, Canada M1B 5M4
Ph: (905)624-9462
Fax: (905)624-0830
E-mail: info@copa.ca
URL: www.copa.ca
Facebook: www.facebook.com/CanadianOfficeProductsAssociation
LinkedIn: www.linkedin.com/company/2675440?trk=tyah&trkInfo=tas%3Acanadian%20office%2Cidx%3A1-1-1
Twitter: twitter.com/COPA_network

2722 ■ COPA Scholarship Fund (Undergraduate/Scholarship)

Purpose: To assist undergraduate students in their post-secondary education. **Focus:** General studies/Field of study not specified. **Qualif.:** Applicants must be students entering their first or second post-secondary studies. They must be former or current employees, or with parents, guardians, or grandparents who are currently employed by a COPA member company; must be citizens or permanent residents of Canada; must have received a high school diploma within the last five years; must have completed the final two years of high school in not more than two years (this should not be consecutive); must have achieved an overall average of at least 80% in the final two years of high school prior to graduation or a GPA of at least 75% in the first year of college or university; be enrolling the first or second year of study at a university or college recognized by the Association of Universities and Colleges of Canada. **Criteria:** Evaluation will be based on submitted materials.

Funds Avail.: Total of $9,000 ($1,500 each). **Duration:** Annual. **To Apply:** Applicants must complete the online application form; must submit two letters of reference from an academic or community official; a letter of employment verifying the connection to a COPA member company; a 500-word essay on the specified topic; must also submit a copy of the most recent unofficial transcript for the past two academic years. First year student applicants must submit a letter of acceptance and second year student applicants are required to provide a copy of the tuition invoice, if selected as finalists. **Deadline:** July 22.

2723 ■ Canadian Pain Society (CPS)

250 Consumers Rd., Ste. 301
Toronto, ON, Canada M2J 4V6
Ph: (416)642-6379

Fax: (416)495-8723
E-mail: office@canadianpainsociety.ca
URL: www.canadianpainsociety.ca
Facebook: www.facebook.com/CanadianPain
Twitter: twitter.com/CanadianPain

2724 ■ Canadian Pain Society Post-Doctoral Fellowship Awards *(Postdoctorate/Fellowship)*

Purpose: To financially assist PhD students to engage in pain research in and outside Canada. **Focus:** Education, Medical. **Qualif.:** Applicants must have completed their PhD in a pain-related field; must be Canadian citizens or landed immigrants with permanent Canadian residence. **Criteria:** Award will be given to applicants who best meet the requirements.

Funds Avail.: No specific amount. **To Apply:** Applicants must submit a cover letter; two-page summary of the proposed research; curriculum vitae; two letters of reference, one of which must come from a PhD supervisor; and a letter of support from the proposed supervisor.

2725 ■ CPS Clinical Pain Management Fellowship Awards *(Postgraduate/Fellowship)*

Purpose: To support graduates of Canadian post-graduate medical education programs who wish to further study in pain management at any institution in and outside Canada. **Focus:** Education, Medical. **Qualif.:** Applicants must have completed an MD; have completed a residency program accredited by the Royal College of Physicians and Surgeons of Canada or the College of Family Physicians of Canada; must be Canadian citizens or landed immigrants with permanent Canadian residence. **Criteria:** Award will be given to applicants who best meet the requirements.

Funds Avail.: No specific amount. **Duration:** Annual. **To Apply:** Applicants must submit a cover letter; curriculum vitae; two letters of reference, one of which must be from the Director of the residency program. If applicants have already completed specialty training, then a copy of the Royal College of Physicians and Surgeons of Canada or College of Family Physicians of Canada certificate should be submitted along with two letters of reference. A letter of support from the Director of the program the candidate proposes for their fellowship year is also required.

2726 ■ CPS Excellence in Interprofessional Pain Education Awards *(Other/Award)*

Purpose: To support CPS members who have made significant contributions in interprofessional pain education. **Focus:** Education, Medical. **Qualif.:** Applicants must be CPS members who have demonstrated excellence in interprofessional pain education in an accredited setting with various community healthcare professionals. **Criteria:** Submitted documents will be evaluated based on demonstration of innovation, scholarship, relevance to pain education, and contribution and impact of the work to the field.

Funds Avail.: No specific amount. **Duration:** Annual. **To Apply:** Each nomination should include a two-page letter submitted to the CPS that documents the nominee's area of educational focus. It should be accompanied by a supporting letter from another CPS member external to the nominee's institution but familiar with the nominee's achievements in IPE; and must submit a curriculum vitae.

2727 ■ CPS Interprofessional Nursing Project Awards *(Other/Award)*

Purpose: To support CPS members who have made significant contributions in interprofessional pain education. **Focus:** Education, Medical. **Qualif.:** Applicants must be registered nurses who have been members of the Canadian Pain Society (CPS) for at least one year and not been recipients of this award for three years. **Criteria:** This award will be given to applicants who best demonstrate excellence as principal investigators of an interprofessional project on changing pain management practices and improving patient outcomes. All submissions will be ranked according to innovation, feasibility, methodology, ethical considerations and relevance to current practice issues.

Funds Avail.: No specific amount. **Duration:** Annual. **To Apply:** Applicants must submit a brief proposal to the CPS that describes the project including the purpose, objectives, method, evaluation and budget. Proposal should be a maximum of two pages and the project must be completed within one year. Recipients must submit results in an abstract form to be considered for poster presentation at the subsequent scientific meeting; must present five minutes summary of the project at the CPS Special Interest Group-Nursing Issues Luncheon meeting and be present for the award presentation; and must submit receipts for all the travel costs.

2728 ■ CPS Knowledge Translation Research Awards *(Other/Grant)*

Purpose: To assist a pain-related knowledge translation research project. **Focus:** Education, Medical. **Qualif.:** Applicants must be registered nurses who have been members of the Canadian Pain Society (CPS) for at least one year and not been recipients of this grant for three years. **Criteria:** Submissions will be ranked according to feasibility, methodology, ethical considerations and relevance to current practice issues.

Funds Avail.: No specific amount. **Duration:** Annual. **To Apply:** Applicants must submit a two-page written proposal for the use of the money, purpose, objectives, method, evaluation and budget along with a reference letter from a CPS member; must submit a project which aims to improve patient outcomes using knowledge translation strategies and should be completed within one year; applicants must submit the results in an abstract form to be considered for the presentation at the subsequent CPS Scientific meeting.

2729 ■ CPS Nursing Excellence in Pain Management Awards *(Other/Award)*

Purpose: To assist and support nurses who consistently exemplify leadership in an area of nursing practice, education, or research in pain management. **Focus:** Education, Medical. **Qualif.:** Applicants must be registered nurses who have been members of the Canadian Pain Society (CPS) for at least the most recent three years and not been previous recipients of this award. Candidates must be nominated by three colleagues, at least one of whom is a CPS member. **Criteria:** Candidates will be ranked based on demonstrated leadership in an area of nursing practice, education, or research in pain management.

Funds Avail.: No specific amount. **Duration:** Annual. **To Apply:** Applicants must submit a completed nomination form made in writing; must include the nominee's curriculum vitae and narrative endorsement describing the qualifications of the candidate.

2730 ■ CPS Nursing Research and Education Awards *(Other/Grant)*

Purpose: To provide support a pain-related research project. **Focus:** Education, Medical. **Qualif.:** Applicants must be registered nurses who have been members of the

Canadian Pain Society (CPS) for at least one year and not been recipients of this award for three years. **Criteria:** Submissions will be ranked according to feasibility, methodology, ethical considerations and relevance to current practice issues.

Funds Avail.: No specific amount. **Duration:** Annual. **To Apply:** Applicants must submit a two-page written proposal for the use of money, purpose, objectives, method, evaluation and budget along with a reference letter from a CPS member; must submit the results in an abstract form to be considered for poster presentation at the subsequent CPS Scientific meeting.

2731 ■ CPS Outstanding Pain Mentorship Awards (Other/Award)

Purpose: To support and assist a researcher and/or clinician who consistently exemplifies outstanding mentorship in the training of future pain researchers and/or clinicians. **Focus:** Education, Medical. **Qualif.:** Applicants must be CPS members for at least two years and not been recipients of this award; and must be nominated by at least one colleague. **Criteria:** Award will be given to applicants who best meet the requirements.

Funds Avail.: $1,000. **Duration:** Annual. **To Apply:** Nominations must be made in writing; must include the nominee's curriculum vitae, narrative endorsement (maximum of 750 words) describing the mentorship qualities of the candidate. Endorsements must be signed by the nominee(s) before submission. **Deadline:** October 29. **Contact:** Canadian Pain Society office, at the above address or email: awards@canadianpainsociety.ca.

2732 ■ CPS Trainee Research Awards (Doctorate/Grant, Award)

Purpose: To support trainees who are working in any field of pain research projects. **Focus:** Education, Medical. **Qualif.:** Applicants must be trainees who are in the first three years of a PhD program; must be members of the Canadian Pain Society (CPS); must not hold other sources of external operating funds used to support research. **Criteria:** Judges will evaluate applications according to the trainee's qualifications/research background, academic excellence and merit of the proposed project.

Funds Avail.: $1,000. **Duration:** Annual. **Number Awarded:** 2. **To Apply:** Applicants must submit curriculum vitae; official (sealed) transcripts from all previous post-secondary institutions; one-page research summary outlining the research and indication of its related category; one-page budget with detailed justification of how funds will be used; and two letters of recommendation that address the trainee's academic and research abilities. Each letter must be sealed and signed across the seal by the writer. **Deadline:** October 29. **Remarks:** Established in 2007. **Contact:** Canadian Pain Society office at the above address; Email: awards@canadianpainsociety.ca.

2733 ■ Canadian Picture Pioneers (CPP)

225 The East Mall, Ste. 1762
Toronto, ON, Canada M9B 0A9
Ph: (416)368-1139
E-mail: cdnpicturepioneers@rogers.com
URL: www.canadianpicturepioneers.ca
Twitter: twitter.com/PicturePioneers

2734 ■ Canadian Picture Pioneers Scholarships (Undergraduate/Scholarship)

Purpose: To assist students who are in need of financial assistance, and who are enrolled in full time studies. **Focus:** Filmmaking; Media arts. **Qualif.:** Applicants must be legal residents of Canada; be 30 years of age and under; currently enrolled in full time studies at a post-secondary institution; and currently work or have worked in the film industry within the past 6 months, or children/grandchildren of individuals who currently work or who have worked in the film industry in the past 6 months (or has retired from a career in the film industry). **Criteria:** Scholarship will be selected by a panel of judges. Award is based on financial need of students.

Funds Avail.: No specific amount. **Duration:** Annual. **To Apply:** Applicants are asked to write a 500 word essay telling the judging Trustees about themselves and explain how the scholarship money would benefit them, and how their life and education will benefit society. **Deadline:** September 30. **Remarks:** Established in 2003. **Contact:** Canadian Picure Pioneers, at the above address.

2735 ■ Canadian Poultry Research Council

350 Sparks St., Ste. 1007
Ottawa, ON, Canada K1R 7S8
Ph: (613)566-5916
Fax: (613)241-5999
E-mail: info@cp-rc.ca
URL: www.cp-rc.ca

2736 ■ Canadian Poultry Research Council Postgraduate Scholarships (Postgraduate/Scholarship)

Purpose: To encourage and support graduate students to carry out research in an aspect of poultry science. **Focus:** Poultry science. **Qualif.:** Applicants must be entering the first year of a master's or doctoral program at a Canadian university; must be studying some aspect of poultry science and must also hold a Natural Sciences and Engineering Research Council scholarship at the Masters or Doctoral level. **Criteria:** Selection will be based on the committee's criteria.

Funds Avail.: $7,500. **Duration:** Annual. **To Apply:** Applicants must complete and submit the following: a completed CPRC Postgraduate Scholarship application form (available at the website); updated academic transcripts; a two-page resume describing the applicants' goals and academic and extracurricular activities that support their interests in poultry research; a statement of endorsement from applicants' research supervisor describing why they are particularly suitable for this award; outline of proposed research; contributions and statements.

2737 ■ Canadian Sanitation Supply Association (CSSA)

910 Dundas St. W
Whitby, ON, Canada L1P 1P7
Ph: (905)665-8001
Fax: (905)430-6418
Free: 866-684-8273
E-mail: info@cssa.com
URL: cssa.com

2738 ■ Canadian Sanitation Supply Association Scholarships (Undergraduate/Scholarship)

Purpose: To provide scholarship assistance to qualified Canadian students who will be attending college or university in Canada. **Focus:** General studies/Field of study

Awards are arranged alphabetically below their administering organizations

not specified. **Qualif.:** Applicant must be a student who will be graduating high school; must be an individual who is already enrolled in a college or university in Canada; must be a young Canadian who has achieved a high level of academic and leadership standards. **Criteria:** Applicant will be judged based on the following criteria: (1) Applicant's ability to read and fully comprehend the terms and conditions of the application procedure; (2) Applicant's ability to ensure that all components of the application-the Applicant Information Form, the 2"x3" photo, the essay, the transcripts, the evaluation form and the typed resume-are received by the CSSA Scholarship Foundation office; (3) Applicant's academic achievements as well as school/college activities, volunteerism and social achievements; (4) Quality of the essay - originality, clarity, grammar and presentation.

Funds Avail.: 2,000 Canadian Dollars. **Duration:** Annual. **Number Awarded:** 7. **To Apply:** Applicant must complete the application form available online; must have a photograph, and official high school or college transcript; must provide an essay on: "Does your school use EcoLogo certified products? If yes, do they believe it is effective against old style cleaning products? What products (brands) do they use? If not, what are the reasons that prevent them from using it?"; must have a typed resume with name, planned occupation or profession, high school information, college or university information, employment history, activity and leadership record, and applicant evaluation form completed by a counselor or teacher.

2739 ■ Sam Tughan Scholarships (Undergraduate/Scholarship)

Purpose: To provide scholarship assistance to qualified Canadian students who will be attending college or university in Canada. **Focus:** Medicine. **Qualif.:** Applicant must be a student who will be graduating high school; must be an individual who is already enrolled in a college or university in Canada; must be a young Canadian who has achieved a high level of academic and leadership standards. **Criteria:** Applicant will be judged based on the following criteria: (1) Applicant's ability to read and fully comprehend the terms and conditions of the application procedure; (2) Applicant's ability to ensure that all components of the application - the Applicant Information Form, the 2x3 photo, the essay, the transcripts, the evaluation form and the typed resume - are received by the CSSA Scholarship Foundation office; (3) Applicant's academic achievements as well as school/college activities, volunteerism and social achievements; (4) Quality of the essay - originality, clarity, grammar and presentation.

Funds Avail.: 2,000 Canadian dollars. **Number Awarded:** 7. **To Apply:** Applicant must complete the application form available online; must have a photograph, and official high school or college transcript; must provide an essay on: "Does your school use EcoLogo certified products? If yes, do they believe it is effective against old style cleaning products? What products (brands) do they use? If not, what are the reasons that prevent them from using it?"; must have a typed resume with name, planned occupation or profession, high school information, college or university information, employment history, activity and leadership record, and applicant evaluation form completed by a counselor or teacher.

2740 ■ Geoffrey H. Wood Scholarships (Undergraduate/Scholarship)

Purpose: To provide scholarship assistance to qualified Canadian students who will be attending college or university in Canada. **Focus:** Education. **Qualif.:** Applicant must be a student who will be graduating high school; must be an individual who is already enrolled in a college or university in Canada; must be a young Canadian who has achieved a high level of academic and leadership standards. **Criteria:** Applicant will be judged based on the following criteria: (1) Applicant's ability to read and fully comprehend the terms and conditions of the application procedure; (2) Applicant's ability to ensure that all components of the application (the Applicant Information Form, the 2"x3" photo, the essay, the transcripts, the evaluation form and the typed resume) are received by the CSSA Scholarship Foundation office; (3) Applicant's academic achievements as well as school/college activities, volunteerism and social achievements; (4) Quality of the essay (originality, clarity, grammar and presentation)

Funds Avail.: 2,000 Canadian dollars. **Number Awarded:** 7. **To Apply:** Applicant must complete the application form available online; must have a photograph and official high school or college transcript; must provide an essay on: "Does your school use EcoLogo certified products? If yes, do they believe it is effective against old style cleaning products? What products (brands) do they use? If not, what are the reasons that prevent them from using it?"; must have a typed resume with name, planned occupation or profession, high school information, college or university information, employment history, activity and leadership record, and applicant evaluation form completed by a counselor or teacher.

2741 ■ Canadian Simmental Association (CSA)
4101 19th St. NE, No. 13
Calgary, AB, Canada T2E 7C4
Ph: (403)250-7979
Fax: (403)250-5121
Free: 866-860-6051
E-mail: cansim@simmental.com
URL: www.simmental.com
Facebook: www.facebook.com/Canadian-Simmental-Association-186347918055419
Twitter: twitter.com/CdnSimmental

2742 ■ Dr. Allan A. Dixon Memorial Scholarships (Postgraduate/Scholarship)

Purpose: To support members of the Canadian Simmental Association and their children. **Focus:** General studies/Field of study not specified. **Qualif.:** Applicants must be members of the Canadian Simmental Association or children of members, for one year or more by the date of registration; must have past/present involvement with Simmental cattle; must be Canadian citizens; and must be studying at the following qualified educational institutions: a) Canadian universities and colleges recognized by the Association of Canadian Universities and Colleges; b) Canadian Community Colleges or institutions controlled by or under the supervision of provincial departments of education; c) Foreign Universities recommended by the Faculty to pursue the applicant's education and recognized by the Association of Canadian Universities and Colleges. **Criteria:** Preference will be given to applicants who are active members of the Canadian Simmental Association.

Funds Avail.: $1,000. **Duration:** One year. **To Apply:** Application forms will be available from the Garth Sweet Simmental Foundation Office. **Deadline:** October 1. **Remarks:** The scholarship is in the memory of Dr. Allan A. Dixon.

Awards are arranged alphabetically below their administering organizations

2743 ■ Canadian Society of Biblical Studies (CSBS)
c/o Alex Damm, Treasurer
Dept. of Religion & Culture
Wilfrid Laurier University
75 University Ave. W
Waterloo, ON, Canada N2L 3C5
E-mail: treasurer@csbs-sceb.ca
URL: www.csbs-sceb.ca

2744 ■ CSBS Student Prize Competition *(Graduate/Prize)*

Purpose: To help students demonstrate their research related to Biblical studies. **Focus:** Religion. **Qualif.:** Student essays must be related to the field of Biblical studies; must demonstrate graduate level research ability and show familiarity with the appropriate original and modern languages of scholarly research. Entries must be based on work already completed at the graduate level. **Criteria:** Winners will be selected based on submitted essays. Special attention will be paid to clarity and originality of the paper.

Funds Avail.: $250 each. **Duration:** Annual. **Number Awarded:** 2. **To Apply:** Entries must not be longer than 20 typed pages, should be double-spaced and in 12 point font; should be accompanied by a note from a professor or administrator verifying the candidate's status; must be written in English or French. Applicants are required to submit three copies of their essay. **Deadline:** January 15. **Contact:** Keith Bodner, Crandall University; Email: Keith.Bodner@crandallu.ca.

2745 ■ Canadian Society of Club Managers (CSCM)
2943B Bloor St. W
Etobicoke, ON, Canada M8X 1B3
Ph: (416)979-0640
Fax: (416)979-1144
Free: 877-376-CSCM
E-mail: national@cscm.org
URL: www.cscm.org

2746 ■ Val Mason Scholarships *(Postgraduate/Scholarship)*

Purpose: To provide financial assistance to individuals pursuing a career in club management. **Focus:** Management. **Qualif.:** Applicants must be nominated by a member of the society presently enrolled in a school, college or university and must intend to pursue a career in the Private Club Industry; must be employed or have been recently employed at a member club of the society; and must have shown a keen interest in pursuing a career in club management. **Criteria:** Applications and proposals will be reviewed and judged by the society's Scholarship Subcommittee.

Funds Avail.: $1,000. **To Apply:** Applicants must submit a letter of recommendation from the nominating member; transcript of records; a 500-word essay explaining their interests in the Private Club Industry; and must indicate how their education is presently funded. **Deadline:** July 18.

2747 ■ Canadian Society of Exploration Geophysicists (CSEG)
Roslyn Bldg., Ste.570
400 5th Ave. SW
Calgary, AB, Canada T2P 0L6
Ph: (403)262-0015
Fax: (403)262-7383
E-mail: office@cseg.ca
URL: www.cseg.ca
LinkedIn: www.linkedin.com/groups/4997418/profile
Twitter: twitter.com/csegonline

2748 ■ CSEG Scholarship Trust Fund *(Graduate, Undergraduate/Scholarship)*

Purpose: To provide financial support for promising graduate students pursuing careers in the field of exploration geophysics. **Focus:** Geophysics. **Qualif.:** Applicants must be undergraduates with above average standing or graduate students enrolled in an academic program directed toward an exploration geophysics career at any Canadian university. **Criteria:** Applicants are selected based on academic performance, financial need, interest in geophysics and extra-curricular activities.

Funds Avail.: No specific amount. **Duration:** Annual. **To Apply:** Applicants must provide a transcript of post-secondary education accompanied by a list of courses currently in progress and recommendation letters from two faculty members or a past or current employer mailed directly to the Committee by the author. **Deadline:** November 1. **Remarks:** Established in 1970.

2749 ■ Canadian Society for Medical Laboratory Science (CSMLS)
33 Wellington St. N
Hamilton, ON, Canada L8R 1M7
Ph: (905)528-8642
Fax: (905)528-4968
Free: 800-263-8277
E-mail: info@csmls.org
URL: www.csmls.org
Twitter: twitter.com/csmls

2750 ■ CSMLS Student Scholarship Awards *(Postgraduate/Scholarship)*

Purpose: To help aid two students in their final year of a Canadian training program. **Focus:** Medical laboratory technology. **Qualif.:** Applicants must be current members of CSMLS and enrolled in the final year of a full-time Canadian training program in general medical laboratory technology, diagnostic cytology, and clinical genetics; must be Canadian citizens or permanent residents. **Criteria:** Applicants will be evaluated based on academic achievement, leadership and volunteer service and financial need. Scholarship applications will be reviewed by the CSMLS Grants and Scholarships Committee.

Funds Avail.: No specific amount. **To Apply:** Applicants must submit the application forms together with the official transcript of records; two letters of recommendation, one should be from a faculty member or college official and one should be from a community leader or other person.

2751 ■ Canadian Society for Otolaryngology - Head and Neck Surgery (CSOHNS)
68 Gilkison Rd.
Elora, ON, Canada N0B 1S0
E-mail: cso.hns@sympatico.ca
URL: www.entcanada.org

Awards are arranged alphabetically below their administering organizations

2752 ■ CSOHNS Fellowships (Graduate/Fellowship)

Purpose: To help students pursue advanced training in Canada. **Focus:** General studies/Field of study not specified. **Qualif.:** Applicants must be MD or equivalent in good standing and must be permanent residents or in an accredited otolaryngology training program in Canada. Otolaryngologists who wish to undergo advanced training may also apply. Host institutions must be affiliated with a Canadian medical school or an accredited medical school abroad. Eligible supervisors must demonstrate competence in the field of further study, must be prepared to supervise fellows for a period not less than a year, and must not be supervising a CSOHNS funded fellow in the concurrent year as the applicant. **Criteria:** Applications will be ranked based on demonstrated academic and clinical productivity of the applicants and supervisors, interest in subspecialty area, clinical and academic exposure at host institution, need for advanced training, letters of reference and evaluations of supervisor from the Society and Fund sponsored fellows.
Funds Avail.: No specific amount. **To Apply:** Application forms must be completed by the applicants and supervisors. Candidates must submit the supporting documents which include curriculum vitae, four letters of recommendation and supporting documentation from a Canadian institution outlining any clinical position that the institution might offer. All documents must be emailed as PDF attachments to Dr. Trina Uwiera, Chair, and Fellowship Committee.

2753 ■ Canadian Society of Petroleum Geologists (CSPG)
110, 333 - 5th Ave. SW
Calgary, AB, Canada T2P 3B6
Ph: (403)264-5610
Fax: (403)264-5898
URL: www.cspg.org
Facebook: www.facebook.com/CSPGeologists
Twitter: twitter.com/CSPGeologists

2754 ■ Glen Ruby Memorial Scholarships (Undergraduate/Scholarship)

Purpose: To promote excellence in petroleum geology and geophysics by assisting in the development of future geoscientists. **Focus:** Geosciences. **Qualif.:** Applicants must be students in their second, third or fourth year of studies in areas related to petroleum geology and geophysics. **Criteria:** Selection will be based on merit.
Funds Avail.: $2,000 (2nd year students); $3,000 (3rd year students); $5,000 (4th year students). **Duration:** Annual. **Number Awarded:** Varies. **To Apply:** Applicants must submit the completed application form together with copy of transcripts. Application forms are available online.

2755 ■ Canadian Society for the Study of Higher Education (CSSHE)
260 Dalhousie St., Ste. 204
Ottawa, ON, Canada K1N 7E4
Ph: (613)241-0018
Fax: (613)241-0019
E-mail: csshe-scees@csse.ca
URL: csshe-scees.ca

2756 ■ CSSHE Masters Thesis/Project Awards (Master's/Award)

Purpose: To support outstanding Master's thesis or project in Canadian universities in the area of higher education. **Focus:** Education; Educational administration. **Qualif.:** Applicants must have completed the requirements for a Master's degree at a Canadian university; must be nominated by a faculty member. **Criteria:** Applicants will be chosen based on submitted project or thesis.
Funds Avail.: No specific amount. **Duration:** Annual. **To Apply:** Faculty members must submit two nominations. Each submission must include five copies of an expanded abstract (1000-1500 words). It should contain the problem statement, significance of the study, methodology, major findings and recommendations. A separate file with the full text of the thesis or project should also be submitted. **Deadline:** January 31. **Contact:** M. Alexandre Beaupré-Lavallée, Masters Award Chair; Email: alexandre.beaupre-lavallee@umontreal.ca; and Mr. Tim Howard CSSHE Secretariat; Email: csshe-scees@csse.ca.

2757 ■ CSSHE Research Awards (Professional development/Award)

Purpose: To honor scholars in mid-career for publishing outstanding research on any aspect of Canadian post-secondary education. **Focus:** Education; Educational administration. **Qualif.:** Applicants must be scholars with demonstrated contributions in research focusing on Canadian post-secondary education. **Criteria:** Award will be made on the basis of published research with particular emphasis given to work published in the last five years.
Funds Avail.: No specific amount. **Duration:** Annual. **To Apply:** Applicants must submit a letter of nomination describing the candidate and stating the reason(s) why he/she has been chosen for a research award; must also submit a curriculum vitae or example(s) of the published scholarship. **Deadline:** January 31.

2758 ■ Canadian Student Leadership Association (CSLA)
c/o Nicole Haire, President
Three Oaks Senior High School
10 Kenmoore Ave.
Summerside, PE, Canada C1N 4V9
Ph: (902)888-8460
Fax: (902)888-8261
E-mail: info@studentleadership.ca
URL: studentleadership.ca
Facebook: www.facebook.com/CanadianStudentLeadershipAssociation
Twitter: twitter.com/CSLA_Leaders

2759 ■ CSLA Leaders of Distinction Award (Professional development/Recognition)

Purpose: To recognize and support professionals for their outstanding leadership at the advisor level. **Focus:** General studies/Field of study not specified. **Qualif.:** Applicants must be active or past members of CSLA or a provincial association; must demonstrate excellence in leadership; must be committed to professional growth; must teach, coach and help others; must foster imagination in bringing about positive change; must show extraordinary commitment to student leadership; must demonstrate service to students, institution and profession; have evidence of impact on and involvement with students. **Criteria:** Recipients will be selected based on demonstrated leadership.
Funds Avail.: No specific amount. **To Apply:** Applicants must submit a completed application form online. **Deadline:** June 30.

Awards are arranged alphabetically below their administering organizations

2760 ■ CSLA Leadership Scholarships
(Undergraduate/Scholarship)

Purpose: To support eligible students who have made significant contribution to student leadership initiatives in their home community. **Focus:** General studies/Field of study not specified. **Qualif.:** Applicants must be enrolled in their senior year in a Canadian high school; must be currently members of CSLA; must have minimum average of 70% in their graduating year; must have plan to attend an accredited Canadian post-secondary institution; must have superior contribution through membership; and must have made a significant contribution to student leadership initiatives in their community. **Criteria:** Applicants will be selected based on merit.

Funds Avail.: $1,000. **Duration:** Annual. **Number Awarded:** 5. **To Apply:** Applicants must submit a completed application form, resume, list of leadership activities completed during high school years, transcript of records and letter of reference from the chairperson or leadership advisor. Applicants must also submit an essay on how they would engage student leaders to make a positive and democratic difference in their school and community. **Deadline:** April 25.

2761 ■ Canadian Technical Asphalt Association (CTAA)
895 Fort St., Ste. 300
Victoria, BC, Canada V8W 1H7
Ph: (250)361-9187
Fax: (250)361-9187
E-mail: admin@ctaa.ca
URL: www.ctaa.ca

2762 ■ Canadian Technical Asphalt Association Scholarships *(Undergraduate/Scholarship)*

Purpose: To support students preparing for careers related to asphalt paving technology. **Focus:** Engineering, Chemical; Engineering, Civil. **Qualif.:** Applicants must have been admitted or currently enrolled in a technical college or a university leading to either a diploma or degree. **Criteria:** Recipients will be chosen based on their submitted application form and supporting documents.

Funds Avail.: $2,000. **Duration:** Annual. **To Apply:** Applicants must submit a completed application form; resume; current academic transcripts; maximum of 500 words statement explaining why they deserve to receive the scholarship; and three letters of reference (one from advisor and two from individuals knowledgeable in technical or academic qualifications of the applicant). **Deadline:** July 1.

2763 ■ Canadian Transportation Research Forum (CTRF)
PO Box 23033
Woodstock, ON, Canada N4T 1R9
Ph: (519)421-9701
Fax: (519)421-9319
URL: www.ctrf.ca
LinkedIn: www.linkedin.com/grps/CTRF-GRTC-8205076
Twitter: twitter.com/ForCTRF

2764 ■ CTRF Scholarships for Graduate Study in Transportation *(Graduate/Scholarship)*

Purpose: To encourage graduate students to specialize in the transportation field. **Focus:** Business administration; Economics; Geography; Law; Religion. **Qualif.:** Applicants must be Canadian citizens or immigrants. **Criteria:** Selection shall be based on academic ability, relevant work experience, stated career objectives and supporting letters of reference. Preference will be given to applicants who are enrolled in policy and business oriented studies at any Canadian institutions.

Funds Avail.: $4,000-$6,000. **Duration:** Annual. **Number Awarded:** Varies. **To Apply:** Applicants must submit a covering letter (including name, address, telephone/fax numbers and e-mail address); official transcript(s) (scanned as a .pdf file); description of work experience or resume (optional); a 300-word summary outlining graduate research project or field of study; and two letters of reference. Submit all documentation (including transcripts) on a CD via mail. Reference letters must be submitted to cawoudsma@ctrf.ca. **Deadline:** January 31.

2765 ■ Canadian Water and Wastewater Association (CWWA)
1010 Polytek St., Unit 11
Ottawa, ON, Canada K1J 9H9
Ph: (613)747-0524
Fax: (613)747-0523
E-mail: admin@cwwa.ca
URL: www.cwwa.ca

2766 ■ Steve Bonk Scholarships *(Postgraduate/Scholarship)*

Purpose: To provide educational assistance to those embarking on careers associated with municipal water supply or wastewater. **Focus:** General studies/Field of study not specified. **Qualif.:** Applicants must be Canadian citizens or permanent residents of Canada; must be residents of current CWWA municipal members, or attend college or university in a municipal or CWWA Academic members; must have completed successfully one year of post-secondary education; must be registered as full-time students in further studies; must intend to pursue a career related to the municipal water or wastewater industry. **Criteria:** Candidates will be selected based on the academic achievement, statement/essay, and work experience/extracurricular activities.

Funds Avail.: $500. **To Apply:** Applicants must have a copy of the post-secondary course transcripts completed to date; must have a description/list of planned further studies; must provide a statement or essay (500 words) of the applicant's interest, knowledge and future goals in the water/wastewater industry together with applicable work experience or extracurricular activities. **Deadline:** June 1. **Remarks:** Established in 1995. **Contact:** Application and other supporting documents must be sent to CWWA - Steve Bonk Scholarship, at the above address.

2767 ■ Canadians for Access to Professional Education
166 St. Andrew St.
Ottawa, ON, Canada K1N 5G6
Ph: (613)866-8629
URL: capescholarship.ca/

2768 ■ CAPE Scholarships *(Undergraduate, Postdoctorate/Scholarship)*

Purpose: To allow students to pursue a professional education without recourse to private debt by providing them

Awards are arranged alphabetically below their administering organizations

financial assistance. **Focus:** Education. **Qualif.:** Applicants must have been admitted to an eligible program of study; must be eligible for or have applied for provincial/territorial and federal government financial assistance programs, including loan and grant programs. **Criteria:** Applicants will be assessed on the following criteria: whether the applicant is a member of a group under-represented in a particular professional program or field; financial need not covered by government financial assistance or other sources; commitment to community service, as shown by the cover letter, resume, and references; and evidence of applicants' ability to succeed in their program of study. **Funds Avail.:** Up to $5,000. **Duration:** Four years; renewable. **To Apply:** Applicants must submit the following: proof of admission to an eligible professional program (If admission has not been received by the time of application, applicants must indicate which program(s) they have applied to and when they expect to receive a decision); resume outlining applicant's educational, employment, and volunteer experience and should also highlight academic and professional accomplishments; copy of the applicant's application and Notice of Assessment for student financial assistance (i.e. student loans or grants) from their provincial or territorial student financial assistance program - these documents should provide a breakdown of the costs of the applicants program, their expected personal and parental contributions, and the loan and/or grant amounts for which they are eligible (If you have not yet received a Notice of Assessment, a printout of the application information, online pre-assessment or online estimation is acceptable. Applicants will be required to provide the official Notice of Assessment once it is received); disclosure of any additional financial resources (either personal or received from other sources) that may be used to fund applicants professional studies, such as other scholarships, RESPs, family contributions, etc; copy of the official transcript of their most recent post-secondary program; two letters of reference; and a letter of intent no longer than 1000 words. Letter of intent must contain the following: motivation to pursue the applicants' chosen field of study; family background and the challenges that the applicants have overcome in pursuing their studies thus far; how applicants have financed their education thus far, and how they plan to finance their professional; applicants dedication to community service, including their community service experience so far; applicants plans upon graduation from their chosen field of study, including both career and community service plans; and a description of the professionally-relevant volunteer work and/or projects that the applicants intend to do during their studies as a part of the CAPE Scholarship. **Deadline:** June 14.

2769 ■ Cancer for College (CFC)
981 Park Center Dr.
Vista, CA 92081
Ph: (760)599-5096
E-mail: info@cancerforcollege.org
URL: www.cancerforcollege.org
Facebook: www.facebook.com/cancerforcollege

2770 ■ Cancer for College Scholarships *(Graduate, Undergraduate/Scholarship)*

Purpose: To support current and former cancer patients in their educational pursuits. **Focus:** General studies/Field of study not specified. **Qualif.:** Applicants must be U.S. residents enrolled in an accredited university, community college or trade school; and must be cancer patients, cancer survivors and/or amputees. **Criteria:** Selection is based on the submitted application materials. **Funds Avail.:** $1,000-$5,000. **Duration:** Annual. **To Apply:** Applicants must submit a completed application form together with a summary of cancer treatments including date of diagnosis, place of treatment, doctor's contact information and health status; a personal statement (minimum of one page double-spaced, type written page); a description of how the applicants' college education is being financed with a copy of all financial aid being received; a copy of an acceptance letter or a letter of good standing from the registrar's office; two letters of recommendation (doctor, nurse, teacher, counselor, mentor, etc.), one letter must be from the treating physician/nurse. Applicants applying from a junior college only need to complete the application form and supply a single letter from the treating doctor. **Deadline:** January 31.

2771 ■ Cancer Research Institute (CRI)
1 Exchange Plz.
55 Broadway, Ste. 1802
New York, NY 10006
Ph: (212)688-7515
Fax: (212)832-9376
Free: 800-992-2623
URL: www.cancerresearch.org

2772 ■ CRI Clinic and Laboratory Integration Program Grants (CLIP) *(Professional development/Grant)*

Purpose: To support scientists who are working to explore clinically relevant questions aimed at improving the effectiveness of cancer immunotherapies. **Focus:** Immunology. **Qualif.:** Candidates must hold a faculty appointment as a tenure-track assistant professor at the time of award activation. **Criteria:** Selection will be based on the committee's criteria. **Funds Avail.:** $100,000. **Duration:** Two years. **To Apply:** The process for applying for a CLIP Grant consists of two parts: letter of intent and invited application. Letters of intent must be submitted electronically. Applicants must visit the website to access the online application. Applicants will be asked to create a user account unique to them, which will catalogue all applications they submit to CRI. After the applicants filled-out all required fields on the online application, they will be asked on the final page of the application to upload, in this order, the following supporting documentation in one PDF document: abstract of research in nontechnical English explaining the importance of the proposed research and its clinical relevance, not to exceed 250 words; an initial research concept, not to exceed 3 pages; brief description of current research; curriculum vitae and bibliography. **Deadline:** November 1 for the letter of intent; February 1 for the full application.

2773 ■ CRI Irvington Postdoctoral Fellowship Program *(Postdoctorate/Fellowship)*

Purpose: To support and train young scientists who wish to receive training in cancer immunology or general immunology. **Focus:** Immunology. **Qualif.:** Applicant must have a doctoral degree prior to the award activation. **Criteria:** A panel of 23 scientists drawn from our Scientific Advisory Council rigorously evaluates each candidate, the intended sponsor and training environment, and the nature and feasibility of the proposed project. **Funds Avail.:** $50,000 for the first year, $53,000 for the second year and $57,000 for the third year, and an allowance of $1,500 per year. **Duration:** Annual; Three years. **To Apply:** Applicants must submit completed application and materials in electronic format. Documents to be uploaded are: brief description of the applicants' background and research accomplishments; list of other funding sources with due dates; curriculum vitae and bibliography; abstract of research in non-technical English; concise research proposal (maximum of 10 pages); letter from the sponsor introducing the applicant and describing the sponsor's qualifications to direct the proposed research; sponsor's curriculum vitae; and two letters of recommendation. **Deadline:** April 1 and October 1. **Remarks:** Established in 1971.

2774 ■ CRI Irvington Postdoctoral Fellowships
(Postdoctorate, Doctorate/Fellowship)

Purpose: To support qualified young scientists at leading universities and research centers around the world who wish to receive training in cancer immunology. **Focus:** Immunology. **Qualif.:** Applicants must working in areas directly related to cancer immunology. An eligible project must fall into the broad field of immunology and must show relevance to solving the cancer problem; must have a doctoral degree by the date of award activation and must conduct their proposed research under a sponsor who holds a formal appointment at the host institution. **Criteria:** Selection will be based on the committee's criteria.

Funds Avail.: $50,000 for the first year, $53,000 for the second year and $57,000 for the third year. In addition, an allowance of $1,500 is allotted to the host institution. **To Apply:** Applicants must visit the website to obtain a PDF application form. Applications must be submitted electronically. Applicants must also complete the electronic application form at http://www.cancerresearch.org/postdoc/apply. Applicants will be prompted to create a user account unique to them which will catalogue all applications they submit to CRI. Applicants must upload, in this order, the following supporting documentation in one PDF document: 1. the entire PDF application form, beginning with the cover sheet. Please make sure all signatures have been obtained for section three; 2. Brief description of the applicants' background and research accomplishments; 3. List of other funding sources to which application has been or will be submitted, with due dates; 4. Applicants' curriculum vitae and bibliography; 5. Brief summary of the project, including a description of how the proposed research is relevant to understanding the role of the immune system in cancer and/or the treatment of cancer through immunological means. Relevance to cancer immunology must also be reflected throughout the research proposal; 6. Abstract of research in nontechnical English explaining the importance of the proposed research and its potential clinical relevance. The abstract will be used for fundraising purposes and submitted to CRI's lay Board of Trustees; 7. Concise research proposal not to exceed 6 pages inclusive of tables and figures, exclusive of references; 8. Letter from the sponsor introducing the applicants and describing the sponsors' qualifications to direct the proposed research. The letter must contain assurance that the applicants' project will be conducted under the direct supervision of the sponsor. The sponsor should also emphasize the relevance of the proposed project to cancer immunology; 9. Sponsors' curriculum vitae, bibliography and a list of sponsors' current research support; 10. Two letters of recommendation. One letter must be from the applicants' thesis advisor. Applicants who received an MD or otherwise who do not have a thesis advisor should have some other qualified individual submit the letter. The second letter should be from an individual well-acquainted with the applicants' work. **Deadline:** April 1 and October 1.

2775 ■ Student Training and Research in Tumor Immunology Grants *(Graduate/Grant)*

Purpose: To attract students to promising careers as cancer immunologists. **Focus:** Immunology. **Qualif.:** Applicants must be graduate students conducting thesis research in the area of tumor immunology. **Criteria:** Selection will be based on the committee's criteria.

Funds Avail.: $60,000. **To Apply:** Applicants may contact the Institute for the application process and other information.

2776 ■ Cancer Research Society (CRS)
625 President-Kennedy Ave., Ste. 402
Montreal, QC, Canada H3A 3S5
Ph: (514)861-9227
Fax: (514)861-9220
Free: 888-766-2262
E-mail: info@src-crs.ca
URL: www.crs-src.ca
Facebook: www.facebook.com/cancerresearchsociety
LinkedIn: www.linkedin.com/company/cancer-research-society-soci-t-de-recherche-sur-le-cancer
Twitter: twitter.com/SRC_CRS

2777 ■ Scholarships for the Next Generation of Scientists *(Postdoctorate/Scholarship)*

Purpose: To support the transition of postdoctoral researchers, who become members of team of researchers in universities, and those who want to continue their work as independent researchers in a Canadian university. **Focus:** Medical research. **Qualif.:** Applicants must be Canadian citizens or permanent residents for the entire scholarship; must be registered as a postdoctoral fellow in a university or accredited institution; must commit to start a work as a researcher in a university or accredited Canadian institution; must make the commitment to devote at least 75% of his/her time to research; must demonstrate his/her capacity or potential to be a competitive researcher at the provincial, national and international levels. **Criteria:** Panel reviewers use the following criteria: file of the candidate must demonstrate his/her capacity or potential to be a competitive researcher at the provincial, national and international level; originality of the research plan; ability of the investigator to conduct the research in his/her respective milieu; significance of the project to cancer research; strengths and weaknesses of the proposal; budget relevance.

Funds Avail.: $160,000. **Duration:** Triennial. **To Apply:** Applicants must send his/her filled out application and documents using file transfer service of the website or thru mail or courier with two electronic copies saved on two CDs or two USB keys. The format title of the file should be "Last name_First name_2015 NGS" and the application documents must include proof of residency and three letters of references together with name and contact information. **Deadline:** April 30.

2778 ■ Cancer Survivors' Fund
PO Box 792
Missouri City, TX 77459-0792
Ph: (281)437-7142
Fax: (281)596-7244

E-mail: csf@cancersurvivorsfund.org
URL: www.cancersurvivorsfund.org

2779 ■ Cancer Survivors' Fund Scholarships (Undergraduate/Scholarship)

Purpose: To augment the expenses associated with the college education of young cancer survivors. **Focus:** General studies/Field of study not specified. **Qualif.:** Applicants must be cancer survivors or currently diagnosed with cancer; must be enrolled in or accepted for enrollment in an undergraduate school. **Criteria:** Recipients are selected by a Committee based on applicant's personal hardship, financial and emotional needs and academic qualifications.

Funds Avail.: No specific amount. **Duration:** Annual. **To Apply:** Applicants must complete the online scholarship application; must submit two letters of recommendation from two different academic teachers addressing why they should receive the scholarship; a letter from an attending physician verifying their medical history and current medical situation; must agree to do volunteer work to use their cancer experience to help other young cancer patients and survivors coping with a life threatening or life-altering event; must submit an essay discussing the following question: How has my experience with cancer impacted my life values and career goals? Essays must be minimum of 500 words and a maximum of 1200 words. **Contact:** Cancer Survivors' Fund, P.O. Box 792, Missouri City, Texas 77459; Phone: 281-437-7142; Fax: 281-437-9568; E-mail: csf@cancersurvivorsfund.org.

2780 ■ C&F Abogados
271 W Short St., Ste. 101
Security Trust Building
Lexington, KY 40507
Ph: (859)971-0060
E-mail: dancarmanlawyer@gmail.com
URL: lexingtonabogado.com

2781 ■ CF Abogados Legal Scholarships (Graduate/Scholarship)

Purpose: To encourage and award creative authorship. **Focus:** Law. **Qualif.:** Applicants must be first-year law school students; must be commencing law school (1L) in August of the current year; must have a published article in print or digital media. **Criteria:** Selection will be based on creativity, originality, and ability to clearly convey a complex message of the submitted article.

Funds Avail.: $2,000. **Duration:** Non-renewable. **Number Awarded:** 1. **To Apply:** Applicants must submit the following: completed scholarship application form; copy of law school acceptance letter; and copy of previously published article or link to its online location. **Deadline:** May 1.

2782 ■ Cape Coral Community Foundation (CCCF)
1405 SE 47th St., Unit 2
Cape Coral, FL 33904
Ph: (239)542-5594
Fax: (239)542-8307
E-mail: cccf@capecoralcf.org
URL: www.capecoralcf.org
Facebook: www.facebook.com/Cape-Coral-Community-Foundation-235740559776341

2783 ■ The Helen and Edward Brancati Teacher Development Scholarships (Other/Scholarship)

Purpose: To assist teachers employed by an accredited school in the United States who wish to continue their education. **Focus:** General studies/Field of study not specified. **Qualif.:** Applicants must be teachers employed by an accredited school in the United States who are seeking post-graduate education or need funds to continue their education classes, workshops, conferences or certification courses; must be U.S. citizens. **Criteria:** Recipients are selected based on demonstrated ability to create an atmosphere of learning for students across the broad spectrum of a mainstream classroom, complete application, letter of recommendation, essay and other materials.

Funds Avail.: $750. **Duration:** Annual. **To Apply:** Applicants must show proof of employment; must provide a copy of teaching certificate, written evaluations from their school principal; must outline a plan for how these funds will be used to increase their professional development or enhance their classroom; must provide a 500-word original essay discussing their reasons for becoming a teacher and how this scholarship will be beneficial; must submit a proof of enrollment or most recent transcript. **Deadline:** October 31. **Contact:** jacque@capecoralcg.org.

2784 ■ The Rotary Club of Cape Coral Goldcoast Scholarship Fund (Undergraduate/Scholarship)

Purpose: To assist eligible high school seniors to further their education by attending college. **Focus:** General studies/Field of study not specified. **Qualif.:** Applicants must be graduating seniors of any high school in Lee County; must have a 3.2 GPA or better; must be accepted to at least one accredited junior college, college or university; must be residents of Cape Coral; must be U.S. citizens and active in school and community. **Criteria:** Recipients are selected based on academic standing, academic history, school and community involvement, career and academic goals and three letters of recommendation.

Funds Avail.: $4,000. **Duration:** Up to 4 years. **To Apply:** Applicants must submit a completed application form. **Deadline:** April 1.

2785 ■ Cape Fear Community College Foundation
411 N Front St.
Wilmington, NC 28401-3910
Ph: (910)362-7207
E-mail: foundation@cfcc.edu
URL: cfcc.edu/foundation

2786 ■ Cape Fear Community College Merit Scholarships (Undergraduate/Scholarship)

Purpose: To assist the local high school students of North Carolina throughout the course of their studies. **Focus:** General studies/Field of study not specified. **Qualif.:** Applicants must be U.S. citizens; must be high school senior students who have applied for or been approved to enroll in Cape Fear Community College in a curriculum program and possess academic potential as shown by high school grades, rank in class; must maintain 3.0 GPA and have completed 12 credit hours during their fall semester. **Criteria:** Applicants are judged based on academic achievement and financial need. Consideration will be given to non-school activities, work record, community service and

Awards are arranged alphabetically below their administering organizations

association with the applicant's vocational field of interest. **Funds Avail.:** $1,800. **Duration:** Annual. **Number Awarded:** Varies. **To Apply:** Applicants must submit all required application information including the letter of recommendation from high school principal, guidance counselor or high school teacher. **Deadline:** March 31. **Contact:** Dana McKoy, CFCC Foundation; Phone: 910-362-7207; E-mail: dmckoy@cfcc.edu.

2787 ■ Capital City AIDS Fund (CCAF)
1912 F St., Ste. 105
Sacramento, CA 95811
Ph: (916)448-1110
E-mail: capcityaidsfund@yahoo.com
URL: www.capcityaidsfund.org

2788 ■ Helen Veress-Mitchell Scholarship Fund
(Undergraduate/Scholarship)

Purpose: To help and support people living with HIV/AIDS attend college and pursue a two-year, four-year, or graduate degree. **Focus:** General studies/Field of study not specified. **Qualif.:** Applicants must be enrolled in a college or technical school with a minimum nine hours of class work; must remain in good standing with a minimum GPA of 2.0 or higher. **Criteria:** Selection will be based on evaluation of submitted documents and specific criteria.

Funds Avail.: No specific amount. **To Apply:** Applicants should submit a completed application form; transcripts from the last two academic years including GPA; proof of enrollment for current academic year; two recommendation letters from a medical provider and/or educator. **Remarks:** Established in 2002.

2789 ■ Cardiac Health Foundation of Canada
901 Lawrence Ave., W Ste. 306
Toronto, ON, Canada M6A 1C3
Ph: (416)730-8299
Fax: (416)730-0421
E-mail: info@cardiachealth.ca
URL: cardiachealth.ca/

2790 ■ Cardiac Health Foundation of Canada Scholarships *(Graduate/Scholarship)*

Purpose: To support educational endeavors of graduate students in the area of cardiac rehabilitation. **Focus:** Health care services. **Qualif.:** Applicants must be graduate student members of Canadian Association of Cardiovascular Prevention and Rehabilitation (CACPR) and must submit a scientific abstract and it must be accepted for presentation at the CACPR Annual Symposium. **Criteria:** Selection will be based on the committee's criteria.

Funds Avail.: $3,000. **Duration:** Annual. **Number Awarded:** 4. **To Apply:** Applicants must submit letter outlining the student's current research in the area of cardiac rehabilitation and future directions in this field. The letter should be a maximum of two pages in length and must specifically address the rating criteria related to methodology, feasibility, importance and relevance; plus one letter of reference from a current supervisor and photo to accompany your abstract within the CICRP. **Deadline:** May 4.

2791 ■ Dr. Terry Kavanagh Fellowships *(Graduate/Fellowship)*

Purpose: To support educational endeavors of graduate students. **Focus:** Health care services. **Qualif.:** Applicants must be graduate students of University of Toronto. **Criteria:** Selection will be based on the committee's criteria.

Funds Avail.: $6,000-$7,000. **Number Awarded:** 2. **To Apply:** Applicants may contact the Society for the application process and other required materials.

2792 ■ Career Transition For Dancers (CTFD)
5757 Wilshire Blvd., Ste. 400
Los Angeles, CA 90036
Ph: (212)221-7300
E-mail: careercentereast@actorsfund.org
URL: www.actorsfund.org/services-and-programs/sideline-work-new-careers/career-transition-dancers

2793 ■ Caroline H. Newhouse Scholarship Fund
(Professional development/Scholarship, Grant)

Purpose: To support current and former professional dancers who can demonstrate earning their livelihood from performing as a dancer. **Focus:** Dance. **Qualif.:** Applicants must be dancers who have performing dance careers of 7 or more years. Performing years need not be consecutive or current; must have 100 weeks or more of paid dance employment in the United States within a career-span of 7 or more years; must have total gross earnings of minimum of $56,000 arrived at by combining the annual gross income of the 7 highest earning years of performing dance careers. **Criteria:** Selection shall be based on the applicants' respective work history as professional dancers.

Funds Avail.: $2,000 each. **Duration:** Bimonthly. **Number Awarded:** Varies. **To Apply:** Applicants must complete an application form and provide documentation of a performing work history. Other information about the program can be verified at the website. **Deadline:** January 7; March 11; May 13; July 15; September 9; November 11. **Remarks:** Established in 2002. **Contact:** Ann Barry, Grants Administrator; Phone: 212-764-0172 ext. 224.

2794 ■ CareerFitter.com
PO Box 134
Pisgah Forest, NC 28768-0134
Ph: (918)477-2280
E-mail: 2008@careerfitter.com
URL: www.careerfitter.com

2795 ■ CareerFitter Scholarships *(Undergraduate, Graduate/Scholarship)*

Purpose: To support students in their educational pursuits. **Focus:** General studies/Field of study not specified. **Qualif.:** Applicants must be students who are planning to enroll or participate in a college, university or graduate school program during an upcoming spring/summer/fall term. It is recommended that students who apply have a better than 2.4 Grade Point Average. **Criteria:** Selection shall be based on the aforementioned applicants' qualifications and compliance with the application details.

Funds Avail.: $500 each. **Duration:** Annual. **Number Awarded:** Varies. **To Apply:** Applicants may visit the scholarship section of the bestowing organization's website for further information regarding the application details. **Deadline:** September 15.

2796 ■ Caribbean Hotel and Tourism Association (CHTA)
2655 Le Jeune Rd., Ste. 910
Coral Gables, FL 33134

Awards are arranged alphabetically below their administering organizations

Ph: (305)443-3040
Fax: (305)675-7977
E-mail: events@caribbeanhotelandtourism.com
URL: www.caribbeanhotelassociation.com
Twitter: twitter.com/chTAfeeds

2797 ■ Caribbean Hotel and Tourism Association Academic Scholarships (Graduate, Undergraduate/Scholarship)

Purpose: To support the education of Caribbean tourism industry personnel and students pursuing tourism & hospitality careers. **Focus:** Hotel, institutional, and restaurant management. **Qualif.:** Applicants must be full-time or must be secondary school graduates pursuing a diploma or degree in hotel and restaurant management or culinary arts in a two-year or four-year program at an affiliated CHA institution; or either be full-time students who are currently pursuing a diploma or degree in hotel and restaurant management, culinary arts in a two-year, four-year, or a graduate program at an affiliated CHA institution and who have completed first semester of the program; must be born in Caribbean and registered as Caribbean National. **Criteria:** Recipients are selected based on potential for success in the hotel industry and financial need.

Funds Avail.: $500-$5,000. **Duration:** Annual. **To Apply:** Applicants must complete the application form; must submit a copy of certificates or awards; must include a current photo; must submit references or recommendations. **Deadline:** April 15. **Contact:** CHTA Office; Phone: 571-436-4386; E-mail: foundation@caribbeanhotelandtourism.com.

2798 ■ Carnegie Institution for Science
1530 P St. NW
Washington, DC 20005
Ph: (202)387-6400
Fax: (202)387-8092
URL: carnegiescience.edu
Facebook: www.facebook.com/carnegiescience
Twitter: twitter.com/carnegiescience

2799 ■ Carnegie Observatories Graduate Research Fellowships (Graduate, Doctorate/Fellowship)

Purpose: To support graduate students interested in carrying out all or part of their thesis research under the supervision of a Carnegie Staff member. **Focus:** General studies/Field of study not specified. **Qualif.:** Applicants must have completed all requisite coursework and examinations at their home institution, and be ready to conduct full-time research toward their PhD dissertation, at the start of the appointment. Since a PhD degree will be awarded by the home institution, applicants must obtain written approval from the department chair or head granting permission for the applicant to participate in the program. **Criteria:** Selection will be based on the committee's criteria.

Funds Avail.: No specific amount. **Duration:** Annual. **To Apply:** Applicants must submit a brief cover letter summarizing the application and its contents; department head/chair approval letter; a list of potential advisors and projects; title of research project to be conducted with the Carnegie advisor; letters of recommendation sent by the three individuals familiar with the academic qualifications and scientific potential of the applicant. If English is not the native language, letters should assess their English proficiency. letters should be submitted by email; an official transcript of the Applicants' courses and grades to be mailed by the university Registrar; curriculum vitae and publication record; a four page maximum statement of previous and current research; a four page maximum summary of the research project. All application materials, except for the transcript of grades should be submitted online. Documents should be uploaded in PDF format. **Deadline:** April 19. **Contact:** Carnegie Observatories, at the above address; Email: gradfellowships@obs.carnegiescience.edu.

2800 ■ Carpenters' Company of the City and County of Philadelphia
320 Chestnut St., Carpenters Hall
Philadelphia, PA 19106
Ph: (215)925-0167
E-mail: carphall@carpentershall.com
URL: www.carpentershall.org/company

2801 ■ Carpenters' Company Scholarships (Undergraduate/Scholarship)

Purpose: To aid young adults pursuing a career in Architecture, Structural Engineering, or Construction Management/Engineering. **Focus:** Architecture; Construction; Engineering, Architectural. **Qualif.:** Applicants must be full-time students in their third or fourth year of an accredited degree program in Architecture, Structural Engineering, or Construction Engineering/Management maintaining overall cumulative GPA of 3.3; and be certified as having financial need by the Financial Aid Advisor at the school they are attending. **Criteria:** Selection shall be based on the aforementioned applicants' qualifications and compliance with the application details.

Funds Avail.: $5,000. **Duration:** Annual; up to 4 years. **To Apply:** Applicants must submit a completed scholarship application form. **Deadline:** May 2.

2802 ■ Cascade Blues Association (CBA)
PO Box 6566
Portland, OR 97228-6566
Ph: (503)223-1850
E-mail: cascadebluesstaff@gmail.com
URL: cascadebluesassociation.org

2803 ■ Christopher Mesi Memorial Music Scholarships (Undergraduate/Scholarship)

Purpose: To encourage anyone to pursue an undergraduate degree at a local college. **Focus:** Music. **Qualif.:** Applicants must be high school seniors or college music students; must have GPA of 2.75 or better. **Criteria:** Recipients are selected based on demonstrated achievement through their involvement in school or community activities.

Funds Avail.: $500. **To Apply:** Applicants must submit their transcript of records; two letters of recommendation from which one must come from a music teacher and one must come from a counselor, employer or teacher; and a proof of college enrollment. **Deadline:** July 1. **Remarks:** CBA Scholarship Committee P.O. Box 14493, P.O. Box 14493 Portland, OR 97293-0493, Portland, OR 97293-0493. Established in 1997.

2804 ■ Cascara Vacation Rentals
57100 Beaver Dr., Bldg. 6, Ste. 160
Sunriver, OR 97707

Fax: (541)593-6652
Free: 800-531-1130
URL: www.cascaravacations.com

2805 ■ Cascara Vacation Rentals Hospitality Matters Scholarships *(Undergraduate, Graduate/Scholarship)*

Purpose: To offer scholarships to students to use at the college of choice. **Focus:** General studies/Field of study not specified. **Qualif.:** Applicants must be students currently enrolled in a graduate or undergraduate degree program at an accredited U.S. college, university or trade school. **Criteria:** Submitted essay will be evaluated based on the following criteria: a thoroughness of thought; creative approach; correct spelling and grammar; a representation of hospitality service true to the values of personal contact; supporting evidence behind claims.

Funds Avail.: $500. **Duration:** Annual. **Number Awarded:** 1. **To Apply:** Applicants must prepare a 750-word essay describing what personal service is and ways it can be implemented in a modern accommodation businesses. Submission will be at the company's scholarship entry page (http://www.cascaravacations.com/hospitality-matters-scholarship-entry-page). **Deadline:** June 19. **Contact:** evan@cascaravacations.com.

2806 ■ Fundación Educativa Carlos M. Castañeda (FECMC)

1925 Brickell Ave. D-1108
Miami, FL 33129
Ph: (305)859-9617
E-mail: fundacion_educativa_cmc@yahoo.com
URL: fecmc.tripod.com/carlosmcastaedaeducationalfoundation

2807 ■ Carlos M. Castaneda Journalism Scholarships *(Graduate/Scholarship)*

Purpose: To support the education and development of Spanish speaking journalists. **Focus:** Journalism. **Qualif.:** Applicants must be Spanish speaking journalists or journalism students who have completed a four-year undergraduate program with a minimum 3.0 GPA (of 4.0) average or the equivalent to a B average (undergraduate major in journalism is not necessary); be pursuing a career in the field of journalism in Spanish and must have mastered the Spanish language at the professional level and must be able to translate thoughts into words proficiently. **Criteria:** Selection shall be based on the aforementioned applicants' qualifications and compliance with the application details.

Funds Avail.: $7,000 each. **Duration:** Annual. **Number Awarded:** Varies. **To Apply:** Applicants must submit a completed application form together with all transcript(s) of academic work (in sealed envelopes with official school seal or a signature across the flap); proof of acceptance into a graduate journalism program; applicant's (or applicant's parents') most recent 1040 tax form or equivalent tax documents (if from a foreign country); Curriculum Vitae listing educational background, work history, awards, internships, language proficiency and any work done for school/community newspaper; three reference letters in separate sealed envelopes (professors, advisors, employers, etc.); a portfolio with three of the best stories published by professional or school publications in Spanish (photocopied and adapted to fit an 8 1/2" by 11" page); and a 2000-word essay. **Deadline:** April 15. **Remarks:** Established in 2005.

2808 ■ Casualty Actuarial Society (CAS)

4350 N Fairfax Dr., Ste. 250
Arlington, VA 22203
Ph: (703)276-3100
Fax: (703)276-3108
E-mail: office@casact.org
URL: www.casact.org

2809 ■ CAS Trust Scholarship *(Undergraduate/Scholarship)*

Purpose: To support students' interest in the property/casualty actuarial profession. **Focus:** Actuarial science. **Qualif.:** Applicants must be U.S. or Canadian citizens or permanent residents; must be continuing or currently attending a U.S. or Canadian college or university as full-time students in the current academic year; must have SAT for at least one actuarial exam by March of the current year. Applicants should demonstrate high scholastic achievement and strong interest in the casualty actuarial profession, mathematical aptitude, and communication skills. **Criteria:** Preference will be given to applicants who have not yet won the CAS Trust Scholarship.

Funds Avail.: $10,000 for the first place and $5,000 each for the second and third place. **Duration:** Annual. **To Apply:** Applicants must submit the following requirements: 4-page CAS Trust Scholarship application and attached essay; two recommendation letters, preferably completed by internship supervisors, instructors and/or advisors at the applicants' educational institution who know them well; and a current official transcript. **Deadline:** March 2.

2810 ■ Harold W. Schloss Memorial Scholarship Fund *(Undergraduate/Scholarship)*

Purpose: To support and give benefit to deserving and academically outstanding students in the actuarial program of the Department of Statistics and Actuarial Science at the University of Iowa. **Focus:** Actuarial science. **Qualif.:** Applicants must be members of CAS society. **Criteria:** Selection will be based on the committee's criteria.

Funds Avail.: $500. **Duration:** Annual. **To Apply:** Interested applicants may contact the CAS society for the application details. **Remarks:** Established in 1984.

2811 ■ Catholic Biblical Association of America (CBA)

Catholic University of America
433 Caldwell Hall
Washington, DC 20064
Ph: (202)319-5519
Fax: (202)319-4799
E-mail: cba-office@cua.edu
URL: catholicbiblical.org
Facebook: www.facebook.com/CatholicBiblicalAssociation

2812 ■ Catholic Biblical Association of America Scholarships *(Undergraduate/Scholarship)*

Purpose: To provide support to students who want to pursue their biblical studies. **Focus:** Bible studies. **Qualif.:** Applicant must be a full-time student in doctoral programs on biblical studies at four institutions: (a) Catholic University of America; (b) Graduate Theological Union at Berkeley; (c) University of Notre Dame; (d) Fordham University. **Criteria:** Selection will be based on the following criteria: (1) Doctoral programs in both Old Testament and New Testament, which

Awards are arranged alphabetically below their administering organizations

include a theological component; (2) Quality programs, as judge on faculty and on course requirements, including biblical language requirements resembling those of the Pontifical Biblical Institute for the S.S.L., including both Hebrew and Greek. **Funds Avail.:** Full tuition fee and a stipend of $15,500. **Duration:** Annual. **To Apply:** For further information, applicants are advised to contact the Association at Catholic University of America. **Contact:** CBA Executive Secretary, Joseph Atkinson at atkinson@cua.edu.

2813 ■ Catholic Library Association (CLA)
205 W Monroe St., Ste. 314
Chicago, IL 60606-5061
Ph: (312)739-1776
Fax: (312)739-1778
Free: 855-739-1776
E-mail: sbaron@regent.edu
URL: www.cathla.org

2814 ■ Rev. Andrew L. Bouwhuis Memorial Scholarship Program (Graduate/Scholarship)
Purpose: To foster advanced studies in the field of Library Science. **Focus:** Library and archival sciences; Science. **Qualif.:** Applicant must be attending a graduate library school and in need of financial assistance. **Criteria:** Recipient is selected based on collegiate records, evidence of need for financial help and acceptance in a graduate school program.
Funds Avail.: $1,500. **Duration:** Annual. **To Apply:** Applicant must prepare a copy of an acceptance letter at a graduate library school; resume; personal statement on the applicant's interest in librarianship; statement of financial need; reference letter (from a librarian, employer or college instructor); and official transcript. Application materials must be forwarded to the Scholarship Committee. **Deadline:** February 1. **Remarks:** In memory of Reverend Andrew L. Bouwhuis.

2815 ■ Catholic Relief Services (CRS)
228 W Lexington St.
Baltimore, MD 21201-3443
Free: 888-277-7575
E-mail: info@crs.org
URL: www.crs.org
Facebook: www.facebook.com/CatholicReliefServices
Twitter: twitter.com/catholicrelief

2816 ■ Catholic Relief Services Summer Internships (Undergraduate, Graduate, Professional development/Internship)
Purpose: To provide interns the professional experience, knowledge and skills that could help them enter the world of international non-government organizations. **Focus:** General studies/Field of study not specified. **Qualif.:** Applicants must be currently enrolled undergraduate or graduate college students or have graduated within the last year. **Criteria:** CRS will look for interns who possess strong organizational skills and the ability to collaborate in a team environment. Proactive individuals with strong interpersonal skills and oral/written communications and the commitment and ability to produce high quality, accurate work in an efficient and timely manner are the most successful. Proficiency in MS Outlook, Word, Excel, and PowerPoint is highly desirable.

Funds Avail.: No specific amount. **To Apply:** Applicants who want to apply may visit the website for the internship postings. Interested applicants are encouraged to apply for the internship(s) that most closely in their field of study and skills set. Afterwards, they will receive an email for a video interview within 3 to 5 days of their application submission. Application and video interviews are reviewed and eligible candidates are contacted for a phone or Skype interview with the hiring manager for their internship. **Deadline:** May 1.

2817 ■ Catholic United Financial
3499 Lexington Ave. N
Saint Paul, MN 55126
Ph: (651)490-0170
E-mail: info@catholicunited.org
URL: www.catholicunitedfinancial.org
Facebook: www.linkedin.com/company/catholic-aid-association
Twitter: twitter.com/catholicuf

2818 ■ Catholic Aid Association's Post-High School Tuition Scholarships (Undergraduate/Scholarship)
Purpose: To provide financial assistance to students to pursue their education. **Focus:** General studies/Field of study not specified. **Qualif.:** Applicants must be members of Catholic Aid for at least two years (prior to application deadline and at the time the award is given); must be entering their first or second year of post-high school education. **Criteria:** Recipients will be selected based on submitted application.
Funds Avail.: $500 for students attending a Catholic college or university; $300 for those attending a non-Catholic educational institution. **Duration:** Annual. **Number Awarded:** 2. **To Apply:** Applicants must submit a filled out application form; an insurance certificate or annuity; and GPA for the last year of school attended either high school, college, or trade school. **Deadline:** February 15.

2819 ■ Cave Conservancy Foundation
c/o Ms. Bonnie Whitlock
13131 Overhill Lake Lane
Glen Allen, VA 23059
Ph: (804)798-3432
Fax: (804)798-4894
URL: www.caveconservancyfoundation.org

2820 ■ CCF Academic Fellowships in Karst Studies - Graduate (Master's, Doctorate/Fellowship)
Purpose: To promote the study of caves and conservation. **Focus:** Cave studies; Environmental conservation. **Qualif.:** Applicants must be students who are currently enrolled in either a master's or doctorate degree level at any accredited U.S. university or college, and interested in the study of caves and karst. **Criteria:** Selection will be based on the committee's criteria.
Funds Avail.: $5,000 for Master's degree; $15,000 for Doctorate degree. **To Apply:** Applicants for the fellowship must include a letter of intent, a curriculum vita, a thesis proposal, graduate transcripts, and two letters of recommendation, one being from the thesis advisor. Application must be submitted via email, with request receipt notation. **Deadline:** May 1. **Contact:** Dr. Annette S. Engel, at aengel1@utk.edu; cavecv@aol.com.

Awards are arranged alphabetically below their administering organizations

2821 ■ CCF Academic Fellowships in Karst Studies - Undegraduate *(Undergraduate/Fellowship)*

Purpose: To assist graduate students, particularly in the master's level, in their further education on cave studies. **Focus:** Cave studies; Conservation of natural resources. **Qualif.:** Applicants must be students who are currently enrolled in an undergraduate degree level at any accredited U.S. university or college, and interested in the study of caves and karst. **Criteria:** Selection will be based on the committee's criteria.

Funds Avail.: $5,000. **To Apply:** Applicants for the fellowship must include a letter of intent, a research proposal not exceeding 5,000 words, a letter of support from the undergraduate advisor, and undergraduate transcripts. Application must be submitted via email, with "request receipt" notation. **Deadline:** May 1. **Contact:** Dr. Horton H. Hobbs III at hhobbs@wittenberg.edu; cavecv@aol.com.

2822 ■ Cave Conservancy of the Virginias (CCV)
13131 Overhill Lake Ln.
Glen Allen, VA 23059
Ph: (804)798-4893
URL: www.caveconservancyofvirginia.org

2823 ■ Cave Conservancy Foundation Graduate and Undergraduate Fellowships *(Doctorate, Graduate, Undergraduate/Fellowship)*

Purpose: To promote study and research on caves and karst in any field. **Focus:** Archeology; Biology; Cave studies; Engineering, Geological; Geography; Geology; Social sciences. **Qualif.:** Applicants must be full-time graduate or undergraduate students at any U.S. college/university studying caves and karst in any field, including but not limited to archeology, biology, engineering, geography, geology and social sciences. **Criteria:** Selection shall be based on the aforementioned applicants' qualifications and compliance with the application details.

Funds Avail.: $5,000 (undergraduate and graduate students) and $15,000 (PhD Students). **Duration:** Annual. **Number Awarded:** Varies. **To Apply:** Undergraduate applicants must submit a letter of intent, a proposal of the research (maximum of 500 words), a letter of support and undergraduate transcripts. Graduate applicants (MS and PhD) must submit a letter of intent, a curriculum vitae, a thesis proposal, graduate transcript and two letters of recommendation (one from the thesis advisor). Application materials must be submitted to Cave Conservancy Foundation. **Deadline:** May 2. **Contact:** Dr. Annette S. Engel, via email at aengel1@utk.edu.

2824 ■ CCNMA: Latino Journalists of California
ASU Walter Cronkite School of Journalism and Mass Communication
725 Arizona Ave., Ste. 206
Santa Monica, CA 90401-1734
Ph: (424)229-9482
Fax: (424)238-0271
E-mail: ccnmainfo@ccnma.org
URL: ccnma.org

2825 ■ Joel Garcia Memorial Scholarship *(Undergraduate/Scholarship)*

Purpose: To provide support qualified Latino students who are planning to pursue a career in journalism. **Focus:** Journalism. **Qualif.:** Applicant must be a Latino college student or graduating high school senior attending a college or university in California (California resident may attend a college or university outside of California). **Criteria:** Selection is based on commitment to the field of journalism, scholastic achievement, community awareness and financial need.

Funds Avail.: $500-$1,000. **Duration:** Annual. **To Apply:** Applicants must submit a completed application form together with an autobiographical essay (300-500 words); two reference letters, including at least one from a family member (no family members); current official transcripts; and work samples (which include newspaper articles, TV or radio audition tapes, or photographs produced by student applicant).

2826 ■ Frank del Olmo Memorial Scholarships *(Undergraduate/Scholarship)*

Purpose: To support qualified Latino students who are planning to pursue a career in journalism. **Focus:** Journalism. **Qualif.:** Applicants must be Latino college students or graduating high school seniors attending a college or university in California (California residents may attend a college or university outside of California). **Criteria:** Selection will be based on commitment to the field of journalism, scholastic achievement, community awareness and financial need.

Funds Avail.: No specific amount. **Duration:** Annual. **To Apply:** Applicants must submit a completed application form together with an autobiographical essay (300-500 words); two reference letters, including at least one from a faculty member (no family members); current official transcripts; and work samples (which include newspaper articles, TV or radio audition tapes, or photographs produced by student applicants).

2827 ■ CDA Foundation
1201 K St., 15 Fl.
Sacramento, CA 95814
Free: 800-232-7645
URL: www.cdafoundation.org
Facebook: www.facebook.com/cdacares

2828 ■ CDA Foundation Allied Dental Student Scholarships *(Undergraduate/Scholarship)*

Purpose: To provide support to dental hygiene, assistant or lab tech students toward completing their education. **Focus:** Dental hygiene; Dental laboratory technology; Dentistry. **Qualif.:** Applicants must be interested in becoming or already enrolled in a California dental hygienist, dental assistant, or a dental laboratory technician program; must demonstrate responsibility/leadership, community organization involvement or any outstanding achievements; and possess a positive desire to have a career in the dental field. **Criteria:** Selection is based on the submitted application and materials.

Funds Avail.: No specific amount. **To Apply:** Applicants must contact the local dental society to retrieve an application form, criteria and application submission deadline date.

2829 ■ CDA Foundation Dental Student Scholarships *(All/Scholarship)*

Purpose: To support dental students working towards completing their education. **Focus:** Dental hygiene; Dental laboratory technology; Dentistry. **Qualif.:** Applicants must

Awards are arranged alphabetically below their administering organizations

be enrolled full-time in a California dental school; must demonstrate financial need, responsibility/leadership, volunteer community/organization involvement; and must be in good academic and ethical standing with the dental school. **Criteria:** Selection is based on: Financial need (34%); Community leadership (66%); and Proven good academic and ethical standing.

Funds Avail.: Up to $5,000. **Number Awarded:** Varies. **To Apply:** Applicants must complete the online application along with all requested and applicable attachments (scan into file format).

2830 ■ Latinos for Dental Careers Scholarships (Undergraduate/Scholarship)

Purpose: To increase the number of Latinos in the dental profession. **Focus:** Dental hygiene; Dental laboratory technology; Dentistry. **Qualif.:** Applicants must be dental students, dental hygiene students (accepted to or in a DH program based in a California dental school) or international student dentists accepted to or enrolled at a California dental school; must be of Latino descent, and currently enrolled or accepted in a California dental school program; and must be enrolled full time. **Criteria:** Selection is based on the submitted application and materials.

Funds Avail.: $1,000. **To Apply:** Applicants must complete the online application along with all requested and applicable attachments (scan into file format).

2831 ■ Bettie Underwood Dental Assisting Scholarships (Undergraduate/Scholarship)

Purpose: To support students in pursuing their educational goals. **Focus:** Dental hygiene; Dental laboratory technology; Dentistry. **Qualif.:** Applicants must be interested in becoming dental assistants and are currently enrolled in a state-approved program; must demonstrate financial need, responsibility/leadership, volunteer community/organization involvement and any outstanding academic achievements; and must possess a strong desire for a career in the dental field. **Criteria:** Selection is based on financial need, community service/leadership and achievement.

Funds Avail.: Up to $1,000. **To Apply:** Applicants must complete the online application along with all requested and applicable attachments (scan into file format). Applicants are required to provide a proof/certification of hours in any volunteer community services or involvement.

2832 ■ CDC Foundation
55 Park Pl., Ste. 400
Atlanta, GA 30303
Ph: (404)653-0790
Fax: (404)653-0330
Free: 888-880-4232
E-mail: info@cdcfoundation.org
URL: www.cdcfoundation.org

2833 ■ Pappaioanou Veterinary Public Health and Applied Epidemiology Fellowships (Undergraduate/Fellowship)

Purpose: To provide an opportunity for third and fourth-year medical and veterinary students to gain public health experience in an international setting. **Focus:** Medicine; Veterinary science and medicine. **Qualif.:** Applicants must be third or fourth year students in the veterinary medicine. **Criteria:** Applicants will be selected on a highly competitive basis.

Funds Avail.: No specific amount. **Duration:** up to one full year. **To Apply:** Applicants are required to submit one to two page research proposal (not to exceed two single-spaced pages with an 11-font size) that contains the following information: name of the applicants and their respective contact information; date of submission; brief description of career objectives, focus/pursuits/plans; title/name of proposed fellowship opportunity; public health purpose/objective of the proposed opportunity; learning objective of proposed opportunity (how will the experience assist achieving career pursuits); CDC program that would be hosting the experience; name of CDC mentor that would supervise/oversee learning experience; proposed start date and time period to be spent at CDC for learning opportunity; and, amount of funding being sought and what funding would be used to support. **Contact:** dhonaman@cdcfoundation.org.

2834 ■ CEDAM International
2 Fox Rd.
Croton on Hudson, NY 10520
Ph: (914)271-5365
URL: cedaminternational.org

2835 ■ Lloyd Bridges Scholarships (Graduate, Other/Scholarship)

Purpose: To inspire individuals to go and help protect one of the world's most fragile ecosystems; to have educators experience the wonders of the underwater world and share it to their students. **Focus:** Aquaculture. **Qualif.:** Applicant must be a certified scuba diver, a teacher (elementary or secondary level), or actively engaged in an education program at an institution or environmental organization, such as an aquarium, science center or relevant non-profit organization. **Criteria:** Scholarship will be awarded based on the applicant's merit and financial need.

Funds Avail.: No specific amount. **Duration:** Annual. **To Apply:** Applicant must complete the application form available on the website; must submit a 500-word essay and two recommendation letters. **Deadline:** April 15.

2836 ■ Celler Legal, P.A.
7450 Griffin Rd., Ste. 230
Davie, FL 33314
Ph: (954)903-7475
URL: www.floridaovertimelawyer.com

2837 ■ Celler Legal P.A. Employment Skills Scholarship Program (Undergraduate/Scholarship)

Purpose: To support exceptional young students looking to advance their work and career skills with the intent of using their education in service of their community. **Focus:** General studies/Field of study not specified. **Qualif.:** Applicants must be entering or attending first year in a Florida college or university; must have maintained a high school GPA of 3.0 of higher; must be U.S. citizens or have permanent residency. **Criteria:** Applicants will be reviewed by members of Celler Legal P.A. and evaluated based on factors including financial need, the personal story share, and the accomplishment of the students.

Funds Avail.: $1,000. **Duration:** Annual. **Number Awarded:** 1. **To Apply:** In order for submissions to be considered, applicants must include a copy of high school transcripts, SAT or ACT scores. Entrants are strongly encouraged to share any extracurricular activities and athletic accomplishments they were involved in during high school. Applicants are encouraged to share how they intend to use their education for the benefit of the community and others and share any reasons they feel they should be selected for the award. **Deadline:** November 12. **Contact:** richard@floridaovertimelawyer.com.

2838 ■ Cengage Learning Inc.
20 Channel Center St.
Boston, MA 02210
Ph: (617)289-7700
Fax: (617)289-7844
E-mail: investors@cengage.com
URL: www.cengage.com

2839 ■ Cengage Learning Scholarships Program
(Undergraduate/Scholarship)

Purpose: To support the continuing education of U.S. employees' children. **Focus:** General studies/Field of study not specified. **Qualif.:** Applicants must be U.S. employees' children who are starting or continuing in a two- or four-year college or a post-secondary vocational school. **Criteria:** Applicants are selected based on merit.

Funds Avail.: $1,500 each. **Duration:** Annual. **Number Awarded:** 18. **To Apply:** Applicants must download the provided application form at the website. **Contact:** Scholarship Management Services at 507-931-1682.

2840 ■ Center for Advanced Study in the Behavioral Sciences (CASBS)
75 Alta Rd.
Stanford, CA 94305
Ph: (650)736-0100
Fax: (650)736-0221
E-mail: casbs-library@stanford.edu
URL: casbs.stanford.edu

2841 ■ CASBS Fellowships *(Doctorate, Other/Fellowship)*

Purpose: To extend knowledge of the principles governing human behavior to help solve the critical problems of contemporary society. **Focus:** Behavioral sciences. **Qualif.:** Applicants must have a PhD, professional degree (e.g., J.D., M.D.) or equivalent foreign degree; have achieved an equivalent level of professional reputation. Faculty at all academic levels or independent scholars may apply, provided they exhibit a high level of achievement (adjusted for rank) including a strong record of research publications. Ethnic minorities, women, international scholars and scholars from less research-oriented colleges and universities are also encouraged to apply. **Criteria:** Selection process is based on an online application system. All scholars requesting consideration must apply via this website. Several reviewers, including experts in the applicants' field(s), evaluate each application meeting our basic criteria. The Center's Fellow Selection Committee, consisting of members from the CASBS Board of Directors and past CASBS Fellows, consider the best-rated applications for CASBS Fellowship awards.

Funds Avail.: $65,000. **Duration:** Annual. **To Apply:** Applicants may visit the website for the online application. **Remarks:** Established in 1954. **Contact:** Center for Advanced Study in the Behavioral Sciences, Stanford University, at the above address.

2842 ■ Center for Book Arts (CBA)
28 W 27th St., 3rd Fl.
New York, NY 10001
Ph: (212)481-0295
E-mail: info@centerforbookarts.org
URL: centerforbookarts.org
Facebook: www.facebook.com/CenterForBookArts
Twitter: www.twitter.com/center4bookarts

2843 ■ Artist-in-Residence Workspace Grant *(Professional development/Grant)*

Purpose: To promote experimentation in making book art. **Focus:** Art. **Qualif.:** Applicants must be artists, live/work in New York State and must reside in the greater NYC metropolitan area at the time of application and during the residency. **Criteria:** Selection will be based on the committees' criteria.

Funds Avail.: $750-$1,000. **Duration:** Annual. **Number Awarded:** Up to 5. **To Apply:** Applicants may contact the Association for application process and other information. **Deadline:** October 15.

2844 ■ Center for Craft, Creativity and Design (CCCD)
67 Broadway St.
Asheville, NC 28801
Ph: (828)785-1357
Fax: (828)785-1372
E-mail: info@craftcreativitydesign.org
URL: www.craftcreativitydesign.org
Facebook: www.facebook.com/centerforcraft

2845 ■ Craft Research Fund Grants *(Other/Grant)*

Purpose: To support innovative research on artistic and critical issues in craft theory and history. **Focus:** Crafts. **Qualif.:** Applicants must be researchers, scholars or museum curators. **Criteria:** Peer panel of readers will evaluate applications based on the following criteria: 1) if completed properly, the proposal will advance scholarship and knowledge in U.S. Craft; 2) the plan for dissemination identifies the audience and have supporting documents; 3) project must be feasible based on timeline, expertise and budget reflected in the application; 4) addresses the goals of Craft Research Fund.

Funds Avail.: Up to $15,000. **Duration:** Annual. **To Apply:** Applicants must submit five copies of the proposal in the following order by page: 1) cover sheet; 2) one-page summary of the proposal; 3) three other scholars/colleagues who have written the three most significant works of the chosen topic; 4) timeline and schedule for completing the project; 5) budget page; 6-7) curriculum vitae; 8-12) no more than five pages project description; 13-14) letter of support from a field scholar and from an institution, publication, organization, participant or anyone who is affiliated with the project; 15) image(s) that would compliment or may add to the clarity of the proposal (optional). **Deadline:** October 9.

2846 ■ Center for Global Initiatives
FedEx Global Education Ctr.
CB 5145

Awards are arranged alphabetically below their administering organizations

301 Pittsboro St., Ste. 3002
Chapel Hill, NC 27599-5145
Ph: (919)962-3094
Fax: (919)962-5375
E-mail: cgi@unc.edu
URL: cgi.unc.edu

2847 ■ UNC-CGI C.V. Starr Scholarships
(Undergraduate, Graduate/Scholarship)

Purpose: To support University of North Carolina students who demonstrate financial need to undertake an independent internationally-oriented experience. **Focus:** General studies/Field of study not specified. **Qualif.:** Applicants must be undergraduate and graduate students. Undergraduate applicants should be "Pell-eligible" based on demonstrated financial need; must have at least 2.8 GPA. Graduate applicants must not be U.S. citizens or permanent residents (green card holders). They must have plan of returning to UNC for at least one semester upon completing their internationally-oriented experience. **Criteria:** Applications will be evaluated based on feasibility and planning, need, impact and budget.

Funds Avail.: Amount varies. **Number Awarded:** Varies. **To Apply:** Applicants must complete an online application form and must include the following: a) basic biography; b) project title and summary; c) short answer questions; d) letter of affiliation; e) list of three references; f) detailed budget; g) list of additional funding sources; h) unofficial transcript; and i) international student need analysis worksheet. **Remarks:** Established in 2004. **Contact:** Mr. Tripp Tuttle, Programs Officer, Center for Global Initiatives; Email at tripp.tuttle@unc.edu.

2848 ■ Center for International Environmental Law (CIEL)
1350 Connecticut Ave. NW, Ste. 1100
Washington, DC 20036
Ph: (202)785-8700
Fax: (202)785-8701
E-mail: info@ciel.org
URL: www.ciel.org
LinkedIn: www.linkedin.com/company/the-center-for
  -international-environmental-law-ciel-
Twitter: twitter.com/ciel_tweets

2849 ■ Louis B. Sohn Fellowships in Human Rights and Environment *(Graduate/Fellowship)*

Purpose: To offer fellowship positions to recent law school graduates and members of the bar who wish to develop or increase their knowledge of the practice of public interest, international environmental law. **Focus:** Law. **Qualif.:** Applicants must be recent law school graduates or members of the bar. **Criteria:** Selection is based on the submitted application materials.

Funds Avail.: No specific amount. **Duration:** Annual. **To Apply:** Applicants must submit a letter, resume, writing sample, and an additional essay that describes applicants' interest and background in human rights and the environment and how these legal instruments can or should be used to protect human rights and the environment (maximum of 500 words). The applicants must indicate in the cover letter that they would like to be considered for the fellowship.

2850 ■ Center for Jewish History (CJH)
15 W 16th St.
New York, NY 10011
Ph: (212)294-8301
E-mail: inquiries@cjh.org
URL: www.cjh.org
Facebook: www.facebook.com/centerforjewishhistory

2851 ■ CJH Graduate Research Fellowships *(Doctorate/Fellowship)*

Purpose: To support original research at the Center for Jewish History in the field of Jewish Studies. **Focus:** Jewish studies. **Qualif.:** Open to all qualified doctoral candidates in accredited institutions. Applicants must have the appropriate visa for acceptance of the stipend and for the required duration of the award. **Criteria:** Preference will be given to those candidates who draw on the library and archival resources of more than one partner.

Funds Avail.: A stipend of up to $17,500 plus up to $5,000 to offset moving expenses. **Duration:** Up to one year. **To Apply:** Applicants must complete the following requirements: cover letter stating area of interest, knowledge of relevant languages, and how the project relates to the mission of the Center for Jewish History; curriculum vitae, including contact information, education, publications, scholarly and/or museum activities, teaching experience and any other relevant work experience; specific research proposal of no more than five pages, including specific reference to the collections at the Center and clearly stated goals for research during the period of the fellowship; official graduate school transcript; three letters of recommendation, including from the students' academic advisors, which address the significance of the candidate's work for the field as well as the candidate's ability to fulfill the proposed work. Send all application materials together electronically as one PDF continuous document. Letters of recommendation may arrive under separate cover. **Deadline:** February 2. **Contact:** Christopher Barthel, PhD, Senior Manager for Academic and Public Programs, Center for Jewish History; Email: fellowships@cjh.org.

2852 ■ CJH Visiting Scholars Program *(Doctorate/Fellowship)*

Purpose: To support visiting scholars as they worked to complete their dissertations using the partner collections. **Focus:** Jewish studies. **Qualif.:** Applicants must be scholars who have their PhD or equivalent terminal degree; must be scholars working on projects that make use of the Center partner collections. **Criteria:** Selection will be based on the committee's criteria.

Funds Avail.: No specific amount. **Duration:** Up to three months. **To Apply:** Applicants must complete the following requirements: a complete curriculum vitae; a description of the proposed research, maximum of three pages in length, including an explanation of which of the Center partners' collections will be used; the names and contact information of two references. Send all application materials together electronically as one continuous PDF document. **Contact:** Christopher Barthel, PhD, Senior Manager for Academic and Public Programs, Center for Jewish History; Email: fellowships@cjh.org.

2853 ■ NEH Fellowships for Senior Scholars *(Doctorate/Fellowship)*

Purpose: To support college and university faculty as they worked to complete their dissertations using the partner collections. **Focus:** European studies; German studies; Humanities; Jewish studies; Russian studies. **Qualif.:** Open to all college and university faculty who received a PhD more than six years prior to the start of the fellowship; must be US citizens as well as foreigners who have lived in the US for at least three years prior to the application deadline; must have the appropriate visa for acceptance of the stipend for the duration of the award. **Criteria:** Selection will be based on the committee's criteria.

Funds Avail.: A stipend of up to $50,400. **Duration:** Annual. **To Apply:** Applicants must complete the following requirements: cover letter stating area of interest, knowledge of relevant languages, and how the project relates to the mission of the Center for Jewish History; curriculum vitae, including contact information, education, publications, scholarly and/or museum activities, teaching experience and any other relevant work experience; specific research proposal of no more than five pages, including specific reference to the collections at the Center and clearly stated goals for research during the period of the fellowship; three letters of recommendation, which address the significance of the candidates' work for their field as well as the candidates' ability to fulfill the proposed work. Send all application materials together electronically as one continuous PDF document. Letters of recommendation may arrive under separate cover. **Deadline:** December 1.

2854 ■ Prins Foundation Fellowship for Senior Scholars *(Doctorate/Fellowship)*

Purpose: To provide support international senior scholars as they worked to complete their dissertations using the partner collections. **Focus:** European studies; German studies; Humanities; Jewish studies; Russian studies. **Qualif.:** Applicants must be foreign senior scholars in any field who have completed a PhD more than six years prior to the start of the fellowship and whose research will benefit substantially from consultation of materials housed at the Center. **Criteria:** Selection will be based on the committee's criteria. Preference will be given to candidates from Eastern Europe and the former Soviet Union.

Funds Avail.: A stipend of $75,000 as well as a relocation stipend of up to $15,000. **Duration:** One year. **To Apply:** Applicants must complete the following requirements: curriculum vitae, including information, education, publications, scholarly and/or museum activities, teaching experience and any other relevant work experience; detailed research proposal consisting of four to five pages, including specific reference to the collections at the Center and clearly stated goals for research during the period of the fellowship; three letters of recommendation that address the significance of the candidate's work for their field as well as the candidate's ability to fulfill the proposed research project; two recent publications consisting of either an article published in a scholarly journal, a chapter in an edited collection, or the introduction and a subsequent chapter from a recently published book; 1- to 2-page essay articulating why they wish to emigrate and what they hope to accomplish after concluding the fellowship. Send all application materials together electronically as one PDF continuous document. Applicants are responsible for ensuring that letters of recommendation are submitted electronically by recommenders by the deadline. **Deadline:** January 5. **Contact:** Christopher Barthel, PhD, Senior Manager for Academic and Public Programs Center for Jewish History; Email: fellowships@cjh.org.

2855 ■ Prins Foundation Post-Doctoral and Early Career Fellowship for Emigrating Scholars *(Professional development, Postdoctorate/Fellowship)*

Purpose: To support international scholars as they worked to complete their dissertations using the partner collections. **Focus:** European studies; German studies; Humanities; Jewish studies; Russian studies. **Qualif.:** Applicants must be scholars from outside the United States who seek permanent teaching and research positions who are at the beginning of their career; must have the appropriate visa for acceptance of the stipend for the duration of the award. **Criteria:** Selection will be based on the committee's criteria. Preference will be given to candidates from Eastern Europe and the former Soviet Union.

Funds Avail.: $35,000. **Duration:** Annual. **To Apply:** Applicants must complete the following materials: cover letter stating area of interest, knowledge of relevant languages, and how the project relates to the mission of the Center for Jewish History; curriculum vitae, including contact information, education, publications, scholarly and/or museum activities, teaching experience and any other relevant work experience; specific research proposal of no more than five pages, including specific reference to the collections at the Center and clearly stated goals for research during the period of the fellowship; three letters of recommendation, which address the significance of the candidates' work for their field as well as the candidates' ability to fulfill the proposed work. Send all application materials together electronically as one PDF continuous document. Letters of recommendation may arrive under separate cover. **Deadline:** January 11. **Contact:** Christopher Barthel, PhD, Senior Manager for Academic and Public Programs; Email: fellowships@cjh.org.

2856 ■ Joseph S. Steinberg Emerging Jewish Filmmaker Fellowships *(Undergraduate, Graduate/Fellowship)*

Purpose: To help further existing projects, or to start new projects, whose subject matter is in line with the collections housed at the Center. **Focus:** Jewish studies. **Qualif.:** Applicants must be undergraduate and graduate emerging filmmakers working on their own original projects on topics related to modern Jewish history. **Criteria:** Students will be selected for one academic year of research through a rigorous and competitive process.

Funds Avail.: Up to $5,000. **Duration:** Annual. **To Apply:** Applicants must look at the website to obtain an application form. They must also submit at least one but not more than two letter of reference from instructors or professional contacts. Send all application materials together electronically on one PDF document.

2857 ■ The Center for Justice & Accountability
1 Hallidie Plz., Ste. 406
San Francisco, CA 94102
Ph: (415)544-0444
Fax: (415)544-0456
E-mail: center4justice@cja.org
URL: www.cja.org
Facebook: www.facebook.com/
CenterForJusticeAndAccountability
Twitter: twitter.com/cja_news

2858 ■ CJA Legal Internships *(Professional development/Internship)*

Purpose: To encourage and train law students in preparation for their chosen profession. **Focus:** Law. **Qualif.:** Applicants must be second and third year law students who want to undergo training at CJA's office in San Francisco. Exceptional first year law students may be considered for the summer term. **Criteria:** Selection will be based on need. The Center are particularly interested in students with some familiarity with human rights and evidence. **Funds Avail.:** No specific amount. **To Apply:** Applicants must send an email which contains the following: cover letter, resume, and transcript. They must state their names and the term for which they are applying in the subject line. Cover letter of the applicants should consist of the following: the term which they are applying; any relevant coursework (especially evidence, advanced civil procedure, federal courts, trial advocacy, international criminal law, international humanitarian law, human rights law, public international or comparative law, and immigration law), and your professor(s) for any human rights law, humanitarian law, or related international law courses; any language abilities, especially Spanish, French, Somali, Khmai, Arabic, Farsi, Haitian, Creole, Swahili or any Southeast Asian languages; and any deadlines the applicants need to secure funding for their internship. **Deadline:** July 3 (fall term). **Contact:** Email applications to intern@cja.org.

2859 ■ Center for Justice and International Law
1630 Connecticut Ave., NW Ste. 401
Washington, DC 20009-1053
Ph: (202)319-3000
Fax: (202)319-3019
URL: cejil.org

2860 ■ CEJIL Communications Internships
(Undergraduate, Graduate/Internship)

Purpose: To encourage students and graduates who wish to have more practical experience in the field of human rights to complement their academic and professional training. **Focus:** Communications; Human rights. **Qualif.:** Applicants must be students or graduates with concentrations in communications or journalism that are interested in promoting and protecting human rights, with a particular emphasis in Latin America. Students or graduates with a career orientation towards human rights work are also considered. **Criteria:** Selection will be based on the applications of the aspiring interns.

Funds Avail.: No specific amount. **To Apply:** Interested applicants should fill out the online application form for the office in which they hope to carry out the internship. After filling out all of the necessary information on the application, they will also have the option of attaching a copy of their resume. **Deadline:** October 15; February 15; June 15. **Contact:** For more information, please contact the person in charge of the program in different offices: pasantiasur@cejil.org (Buenos Aires, Argentina); pasantiasbrasil@cejil.org (Rio de Janeiro, Brazil); pasantiasmeso@cejil.org (San Jose, Costa Rica); pasantiasdc@cejil.org (Washington D.C., U.S.A.).

2861 ■ CEJIL Legal Internships *(Graduate, Professional development/Internship)*

Purpose: To encourage students and graduates who wish to have more practical experience in the field of human rights to complement their academic and professional training. **Focus:** Human rights; Law. **Qualif.:** Applicants must be law students or law graduates interested in a career in international human rights law, with a particular interest in Latin America. Students or graduates with careers oriented towards human rights work will also be considered. Furthermore, applicants must have solid command of the Spanish language; have excellent writing skills; have willingness and ability to handle a wide variety of tasks; and have experience in working in non-government organizations. Knowledge of Portuguese and/or English language is valuable, depending also upon the office where the internship is held. **Criteria:** Selection will be based on the applications of the aspiring interns.

Funds Avail.: No specific amount. **To Apply:** Applications for the internship (in Washington D.C.) will be accepted on a rolling basis. Interested applicants should fill out the online application form for the office in which they hope to carry out the internship. After filling out all of the necessary information on the application, they will also have the option of attaching a copy of their resume. **Deadline:** October 15; February 15; June 15. **Contact:** For more information, please contact the person in charge of the program in different offices: pasantiasur@cejil.org (Buenos Aires, Argentina); pasantiasbrasil@cejil.org (Rio de Janeiro, Brazil); pasantiasmeso@cejil.org (San Jose, Costa Rica); pasantiasdc@cejil.org (Washington D.C., U.S.A.).

2862 ■ Center for LGBTQ Studies (CLAGS)
365 5th Ave., Rm. 7115
New York, NY 10016
Ph: (212)817-1955
Fax: (212)817-1567
E-mail: info@clags.org
URL: www.clags.org
Facebook: www.facebook.com/clags.org
Twitter: twitter.com/CLAGSNY

2863 ■ Center for Lesbian and Gay Studies Fellowships *(Graduate/Fellowship)*

Purpose: To provide fund to support research, travel or writing. **Focus:** Homosexuality. **Qualif.:** Applicants must be graduate students, academic or independent scholars who work on dissertation. **Criteria:** Applicants will be selected by the fellowships committee of the Center for Lesbian and Gay Studies based on the review of the application materials.

Funds Avail.: $2,000. **To Apply:** Applicants must submit a cover letter with contact information; a 5-10-page proposal; a curriculum vitae; and two letters of recommendation. **Deadline:** June 1. **Contact:** Letters of recommendation should be sent by e-mail directly from recommenders to clagsfellowships@gmail.com.

2864 ■ Martin Duberman Fellowships *(Other/Fellowship)*

Purpose: To award a senior scholar from any country doing scholarly research on the lesbian, gay, bisexual, transgender, and queer experience. **Focus:** Homosexuality. **Qualif.:** Applicant must be a tenured university professor; advanced independent scholar; must be able to show a prior contribution to the field of LGBTQ. **Criteria:** Applicants will be selected based on the fellowships committee's review of the application materials.

Funds Avail.: $7,500. **Duration:** Annual. **To Apply:** Applicants must submit a completed application form; a cover letter with contact information; a proposal of 5-10 pages; curriculum vitae; an evidence of contribution to the field of LGTBQ studies; and two letters of recommendation. **Deadline:** June 1. **Contact:** clagsfellowships@gmail.com.

2865 ■ Joan Heller-Diane Bernard Fellowships *(Graduate, Undergraduate/Fellowship)*

Purpose: To supports research into the impact of lesbians and/or gay men on U.S. society and culture. **Focus:** Homosexuality. **Qualif.:** Applicants must be junior scholars, graduate students, untenured professors, independent researchers, or senior scholars. Applicants conducting a research on lesbians are encouraged to apply. **Criteria:** Applicants will be selected based on the fellowships committee's review of the application materials.

Funds Avail.: $6,250. **Number Awarded:** 2. **To Apply:** Applicants must submit a cover letter with contact information; a proposal of 5-10 pages; evidence of contribution to the field of LGTBQ studies; curriculum vitae; and two letters of recommendation. **Deadline:** November 15. **Contact:** For further information, applicants may contact the Fellowship Coordinator by phone: 212-817-1958 or by e-mail: clagsfellowships@gmail.com.

2866 ■ Center for Plant Conservation (CPC)
15600 San Pasqual Valley Rd.
Escondido, CA 92027-7000
Ph: (760)796-5686
E-mail: cpc@sandiegozoo.org
URL: www.centerforplantconservation.org
Facebook: www.facebook.com/CenterForPlantConservation

2867 ■ Catherine H. Beattie Fellowships *(Graduate/Fellowship)*

Purpose: To enable individuals to conduct research on a rare or endangered U.S. plant. **Focus:** Biology; Horticulture. **Qualif.:** Applicants must be graduate students in biology or horticulture. **Criteria:** Preference will be given to students focusing on endangered flora of the Carolinas or the southeastern United States.

Funds Avail.: $1,000 - $4,500 and will serve as compensation for work done by a graduate student. **Duration:** Annual. **To Apply:** Applications should be submitted to the Center for Plant Conservation and must include the following: (a) a 2-3 page proposal which includes a description of the research project and how it relates to the student's academic and professional development; (b) an itemized budget for the funds requested; (c) a current resume; (d) a letter of endorsement by an academic advisor from the institution where the student is pursuing graduate studies; (e) the names of three additional persons qualified to describe the student's character and ability; (f) official transcripts for both undergraduate and graduate academic records. **Deadline:** November 30. **Contact:** Beattie Fellowship, Center for Plant Conservation, at the above address.

2868 ■ Central Florida Jazz Society (CFJS)
3208 W Lake Mary Blvd., Ste. 1720
Lake Mary, FL 32746-3476
Ph: (407)539-2357
E-mail: Jazz@CentralFloridaJazzSociety.com
URL: centralfloridajazzsociety.com
Facebook: www.facebook.com/centralfloridajazzsociety/timeline?ref=page_internal

2869 ■ Central Florida Jazz Society Scholarships *(Undergraduate/Award, Scholarship)*

Purpose: To support amateur jazz musicians in furthering their education. **Focus:** Music, Jazz. **Qualif.:** Applicants must be amateur jazz musicians who are high school seniors or students in the first 3 years of college; be interested in furthering their studies in jazz music; and be residents of, or attend/plan to attend a college in, Central Florida: Orange, Seminole, Osceola, Brevard or Volusia counties. There is no age restriction. **Criteria:** Applicants will be judged based on: technique, expression, style (interpretation), performance presence (showmanship) and overall performance.

Funds Avail.: $7,000. **Number Awarded:** 4. **To Apply:** An initial screening of all applicants will require an audition cassette tape, CD or DVD containing 1 or 2 improvised choruses of two selections of different tempos (labeled with the student's name on the recording). In addition to the musical recording, a letter of recommendation, from an individual familiar with the applicant's musicianship, character and commitment to jazz study, must be submitted. **Deadline:** March 8.

2870 ■ Central Ohio Diabetes Association (CODA)
1100 Dennison Ave.
Columbus, OH 43201
Ph: (614)884-4400
Fax: (614)884-4484
E-mail: coda@diabetesohio.org
URL: www.diabetesohio.org
Facebook: www.facebook.com/diabetesohio
Twitter: twitter.com/diabetesohio

2871 ■ The Youth Scholarship Program *(Undergraduate/Scholarship)*

Purpose: To provide scholarships to those students with diabetes. **Focus:** Diabetes. **Qualif.:** Applicants must be full-time undergraduate students with diabetes in the Central Ohio area; must demonstrate exemplary adjustment to living with diabetes; show financial need; and demonstrate involvement in extracurricular activities which help others and foster personal growth. **Criteria:** Preference will be given to those students who will meet the criteria.

Funds Avail.: No specific amount. **To Apply:** Applicants must submit a completed application form.

2872 ■ Central Texas Bluegrass Association (CTBA)
PO Box 9816
Austin, TX 78766-9816
Ph: (512)415-3177
E-mail: ctba@centraltexasbluegrass.org
URL: www.centraltexasbluegrass.org

2873 ■ Willa Beach-Porter Music Scholarships *(Undergraduate/Scholarship)*

Purpose: To further the enjoyment of bluegrass music through teaching, sharing and playing; to promote bluegrass music in Central Texas. **Focus:** Music. **Qualif.:** Applicants must be 12 years of age or over and must be Texas residents. **Criteria:** Recipients are selected based on financial need.

Funds Avail.: No specific amount. **Duration:** Annual. **To Apply:** Applicants must complete an application form and two recommendation letters (mailed separately). **Deadline:** June 1.

2874 ■ CentraState Healthcare Foundation
916 Route 33, Ste. 6
Freehold, NJ 07728

Awards are arranged alphabetically below their administering organizations

Ph: (732)294-7030
URL: www.centrastatefoundation.org

2875 ■ CentraState Associated Auxiliaries Scholarships *(Undergraduate/Scholarship)*

Purpose: To provide scholarship assistance to deserving students who want to pursue the health care field. **Focus:** Health care services. **Qualif.:** Applicants must be students or adult who live and volunteer in the CentraState service area. They must be pursuing a career in the health care field. **Criteria:** Selection will be based on the aforesaid qualifications and compliance with the application process. **Funds Avail.:** $500 each. **Duration:** Annual. **Number Awarded:** 3. **To Apply:** Applicants must submit a current transcript, letters of recommendation from two teachers and/or counselors and the completed essay requirement. The application form may be obtained from the CentraState Healthcare Foundation office. **Deadline:** April 30. **Contact:** Mrs. Valerie MacPhee, PO Box 32, Perrineville, NJ 08535.

2876 ■ CentraState Band Aid Open Committee Scholarships *(Undergraduate/Scholarship)*

Purpose: To support students who are planning to pursue a career in the health professions. **Focus:** Health sciences. **Qualif.:** Applicants must be high school seniors enrolled in the Medical Sciences Program at Freehold Regional High School. **Criteria:** Selection will be based on the aforesaid qualifications and compliance with the application process. **Funds Avail.:** $2,000. **Duration:** Annual. **To Apply:** Applicants must submit a current transcript, letters of recommendation from two teachers and/or counselors and the completed essay requirement. The application form may be obtained from the CentraState Healthcare Foundation office. **Deadline:** March 21. **Contact:** Ms. Marybeth Ruddy at the Freehold Regional High School or Lyn Cannon, at the above address.

2877 ■ CentraState Healthcare Foundation Health Professions Scholarships *(Undergraduate/Scholarship)*

Purpose: To provide scholarship assistance to deserving students who want to pursue the healthcare field. **Focus:** Health care services. **Qualif.:** Applicants must be high school seniors who live and/or attend school within the CentraState Healthcare System service area and have chosen to pursue a career in the health professions. **Criteria:** Selection will be based on the aforesaid qualifications and compliance with the application process. **Funds Avail.:** $1,000 each. **Duration:** Annual. **Number Awarded:** 3. **To Apply:** Applicants must submit a current transcript, letters of recommendation from two teachers and/or counselors and the completed essay requirement. The application form may be obtained from the CentraState Healthcare Foundation office. **Deadline:** May 1. **Contact:** Lynn Cannon, at the above address.

2878 ■ DCH Freehold Toyota Scholarships *(Undergraduate/Scholarship)*

Purpose: To support students who are planning to pursue a career in the health professions. **Focus:** Health sciences. **Qualif.:** Applicants must be high school seniors enrolled in the Medical Sciences Program at Freehold Regional High School. **Criteria:** Selection will be based on the aforesaid qualifications and compliance with the application process. **Funds Avail.:** $1,000. **Duration:** Annual. **To Apply:** Applicants must submit a current transcript, letters of recommendation from two teachers and/or counselors and the completed essay requirement. The application form may be obtained from the CentraState Healthcare Foundation office. **Deadline:** March 21. **Contact:** Ms. Marybeth Ruddy at the Freehold Regional High School or Lyn Cannon, at the above address.

2879 ■ Centre for International Sustainable Development Law (CISDL)

Chancellor Day Hall
3644 Peel St.
Montreal, QC, Canada H3A 1W9
Ph: (818)685-9931
Fax: (514)398-4659
E-mail: secretariat@cisdl.org
URL: www.cisdl.org
Facebook: www.facebook.com/Centre-for-International-Sustainable-Development-Law-211145808904765

2880 ■ CISDL Global Research Fellowship - Associate Fellows *(Graduate/Fellowship)*

Purpose: To promote sustainable societies and the protection of ecosystems by advancing understanding, development and implementation of international sustainable development law. **Focus:** Law. **Qualif.:** Applicant may be a law or legal graduate student from a developing country or from one of the leading international law programmes of university law faculties around the world. **Criteria:** Selection is based on CISDL research priorities, the candidate's academic and professional qualifications and indication from a Lead Counsel that they will work with the candidate on a particular project. Preference is given to research fellows presently based in Montreal or in the country of a CISDL Lead Counsel. **Funds Avail.:** No specific amount. **Duration:** Annual; one year. **To Apply:** Applicants must submit a completed application form along with a cover letter and current CV. **Deadline:** October 1. **Contact:** Marie-Claire Cordonier Segger at mcsegger@cisdl.org or Ashfaq Khalfan at akhalfan@cisdl.org.

2881 ■ CISDL Global Research Fellowship - Legal Research Fellows *(Graduate/Fellowship)*

Purpose: To promote sustainable societies and the protection of ecosystems by advancing understanding, development and implementation of international sustainable development law. **Focus:** Law. **Qualif.:** Applicant must hold a law degree or graduate degree in law; must have more than 5 years of legal experience in his/her field; must hold an excellent academic and professional credentials; and can demonstrate a specific interest in international law related to sustainable development, particularly in the areas of current research and undertaking within the CISDL. **Criteria:** Selection is based on academic and professional qualifications. Preference is given to applications from research fellows presently based in Montreal or in the country of a CISDL Lead Counsel. **Funds Avail.:** No specific amount. **Duration:** Annual; two years. **To Apply:** Applicants must submit a completed application form together with a curriculum vitae and a cover letter. **Deadline:** October 1. **Contact:** Marie-Claire Cordonier Segger at mcsegger@cisdl.org or Ashfaq Khalfan at akhalfan@cisdl.org.

2882 ■ CISDL Global Research Fellowships - Senior Research Fellows *(Other/Fellowship)*

Purpose: To promote sustainable societies and the protection of ecosystems by advancing understanding, develop-

Awards are arranged alphabetically below their administering organizations

ment and implementation of international sustainable development law. **Focus:** Law. **Qualif.:** Applicant may be a professor of international law or hold an equivalent professional experience in the field of international expertise; must have an internationally recognized level of expertise and must be backed by superb academic and professional credentials; must have years of experience in international law related to sustainable development. **Criteria:** Preference is given to CISDL fellows from developing countries, and those who are based in universities or international law institutions affiliated with CISDL.

Funds Avail.: No specific amount. **Duration:** Annual; four years. **To Apply:** Applicants must submit a completed application form together with a current resume. **Deadline:** October 1.

2883 ■ Centre pour l'Innovation dans la Gouvernance Internationale
67 Erb St. W
Waterloo, ON, Canada N2L 6C2
Ph: (519)885-2444
Fax: (519)885-5450
URL: www.cigionline.org

2884 ■ International Law Research Program Fellowships *(Advanced Professional, Professional development/Fellowship)*

Purpose: To encourage leading scholars, senior practitioners and legal experts in the government or private sector to take part in research on international law. **Focus:** Law. **Qualif.:** Applicants must be widely recognized or established individuals who are legal scholars, lawyers and others with extensive expertise and interest in one or more of the core ILRP streams: intellectual property law; international economic, financial and investment law, regulation and governance; and environmental law and treaties. Applicants must also be able to demonstrate capability to exercise independence in research, as evidenced by, for example, senior authorship/sole authorship of publications, and invited presentations at conferences. Canadian citizens and permanent residents will be given priority. Non-Canadian applicants are responsible for obtaining their own work permits. **Criteria:** Selection will be based on the applicants' high quality academic qualifications, professional experience, established networks, a proven track record of publications in prominent journals, and participation in public discourse and debate. Applications are subjected to a two stage ranking and review process by a Selection Committee consisting of CIGI senior management and external members. Priority will be given to proposals that align with the three core streams of the ILRP and programmatic streams of CIGI. CIGI is especially interested in supporting research that align with the priorities of its programs and can result in work that reaches a broad audience.

Funds Avail.: No specific amount. **Duration:** Up to 5 years. **To Apply:** Consideration of applications will occur regularly throughout the year. Please submit applications by e-mail. Applicants should provide the following: a current curriculum vitae; a copy of the Project Proposal including anticipated deliverables and timelines (not to exceed five single-spaced typed pages, using 12-point type); an indication as to whether external funding has been sought to support their project, and, if so, the current stage it is in the adjudication process (being developed, under consideration, or awarded); a brief statement explaining the relevance of the project to the programmatic goals of the ILRP and why an affiliation with CIGI would be of mutual benefit is strongly encouraged; and, names and addresses of at least three references. It is essential to make projects clear to individuals outside their own field and to explain its broader implications. The following elements should be addressed in the proposal: detailed description of the topic and its importance; the originality of the proposed study (explain what makes the project distinctive); the basic ideas and hypotheses; the methodology to be used (including the activities you will undertake to gather the data you need for your project and the techniques that you will use to analyze the data in order to prove your thesis); a timeline of activities/benchmarks; the present status of your research, including how much has already been done in relevant collections and archives, and what you would hope to accomplish at CIGI; how the research will contribute to international legal frameworks; and, the relevance of the project to the programmatic goals of CIGI. **Contact:** E-mail at lawcareers@cigionline.org.

2885 ■ Centre de Recherches pour le Développement International (CRDI)
150 Kent St.
Ottawa, ON, Canada K1P 0B2
Ph: (613)236-6163
Fax: (613)238-7230
E-mail: info@idrc.ca
URL: www.idrc.ca
Facebook: www.facebook.com/IDRC.CRDI
Twitter: twitter.com/Idrc_crdi

2886 ■ The Bentley Cropping Systems Fellowship *(Graduate/Fellowship)*

Purpose: To provide funding for field research aimed at increasing the yield of food crops, improving farmers' livelihoods, and improving soil fertility. **Focus:** Agricultural sciences; Food science and technology. **Qualif.:** Applicant must be a citizen or permanent resident of Canada, or a citizen of a developing country; be enrolled full-time at a recognized university at the master's, doctoral, or post-doctoral level in Canada or in a developing country for the duration of the award period. **Criteria:** Selection shall be based on the qualifications of the applicant, as well as to the submitted proposal of the person.

Funds Avail.: No specific amount. **Duration:** Biennial. **To Apply:** Applicant must be able to submit a research proposal focusing on very simple cropping-systems research that can benefit smallholder farmers in developing countries, especially rural women farmers. For more information, visit the program page or website.

2887 ■ ChairScholars Foundation
16101 Carencia Lane
Odessa, FL 33556-3278
Ph: (813)926-0544
E-mail: programs@chairscholars.org
URL: chairscholars.org

2888 ■ ChairScholars Florida Scholarship Program *(Undergraduate/Scholarship)*

Purpose: To provide tuition for college or vocational school with Florida Prepaid Tuition Scholarships. **Focus:** Disabilities. **Qualif.:** Applicants must: have serious physical disability; be eligible for their school's "Free or Reduced

Awards are arranged alphabetically below their administering organizations

Lunch Program"; have at least a B average; be enrolled in any Florida public school. **Criteria:** Selection will be based on the committee's criteria.

Funds Avail.: No specific amount. **Duration:** Annual. **To Apply:** Interested applicants may contact the Foundation for the application process and other information.

2889 ■ ChairScholars National Scholarship Program
(Undergraduate/Scholarship)

Purpose: To support low-income students with severe physical disabilities - giving them the opportunity to pursue their dreams because "no physical impairment should deter a motivated mind". **Focus:** General studies/Field of study not specified. **Qualif.:** Applicants must: have serious physical challenge and may or may not use a wheelchair for mobility (no minor disability will be considered); have verifiable unmet financial need; have at least a B average; be a high school senior or college undergraduate; and, show some form of significant community service or social contribution in the past. **Criteria:** Selection will be based on the committee's criteria.

Funds Avail.: $30,000. **Duration:** Annual. **To Apply:** Applicants must submit: good quality recent photograph, full body shot as opposed to head shot; 300 to 500 word essay that outlines how became physically challenged, how the situation has affected the family, and goals and aspirations for the future; three letters of recommendation; Parent's or Guardian's Federal income tax return from last year (if parents are divorced, please send both tax returns); High School transcripts, including SAT and ACT scores and any honors or achievements earned; Physician's documentation of your disability; and if obtained any other scholarships already, inform the bestowing organization of that fact.

2890 ■ Chemical Heritage Foundation (CHF)
315 Chestnut St.
Philadelphia, PA 19106
Ph: (215)925-2222
URL: www.chemheritage.org

2891 ■ Chemical Heritage Foundation Travel Grants (CHF) *(All/Grant)*

Purpose: To promote research about history of chemical and molecular sciences, technologies and industries. **Focus:** Chemistry. **Qualif.:** Applicants must be researchers residing more than 75 miles from Philadelphia. **Criteria:** Recipients are selected based on committee's review of the research.

Funds Avail.: $750 per week. **Duration:** 1 to 2 weeks. **Number Awarded:** 1. **To Apply:** Applicants must send a one-page statement of research project; curriculum vitae less than three pages; budget estimate; and a letter of reference.

2892 ■ Cherokee Nation
17675 S Muskogee Ave.
Tahlequah, OK 74464
Ph: (918)453-5000
Free: 800-256-0671
E-mail: communications@cherokee.org
URL: www.cherokee.org
Facebook: www.facebook.com/TheCherokeeNation

2893 ■ Cherokee Nation Graduate Scholarships
(Graduate/Scholarship)

Purpose: To support Cherokee Nation Tribal Citizens pursuing degrees at a college or university. **Focus:** General studies/Field of study not specified. **Qualif.:** Applicant must be a Cherokee Nation Tribal citizen seeking graduate degrees; permanent resident in the Cherokee Nation area, which is defined as counties within the Cherokee boundaries; or permanent resident in the contiguous counties to the Cherokee Nation boundaries, (including contiguous counties in Arkansas, Kansas, Missouri, and Oklahoma). **Criteria:** Selection is based on the following preferences: First: Continuing students; Second: Classification order of new applicants (Senior, Junior, Sophomore, Freshman); Third: Academic performance.

Funds Avail.: $1,000. **Duration:** 1 semester. **To Apply:** Applicants must submit a completed application form together with a copy of Social Security card; copy of Tribal Citizenship card (blue); official undergraduate transcript with Bachelor's Degree conferment; and a letter of acceptance to graduate program.

2894 ■ Cherokee Nation Pell Scholarships
(Undergraduate/Scholarship)

Purpose: To support Cherokee Nation Tribal Citizens pursuing degrees at a college or university. **Focus:** General studies/Field of study not specified. **Qualif.:** Applicant must be a Cherokee Nation tribal citizen who qualified for Federal Pell Grant funding regardless of permanent residence. **Criteria:** Selection is based on the following preferences: First: Continuing students; Second: Classification order of new applicants (Senior, Junior, Sophomore, Freshman); Third: Academic performance.

Funds Avail.: No specific amount. **To Apply:** Applicants must submit a completed application form together with Student Aid Report (all pages); copy of Social Security card; copy of Tribal Citizenship card (blue); official high school transcript (7 semester) or GED scores (Freshmen only); copy of ACT/SAT or College Placement Test Scores (Freshmen only); and official Undergraduate Transcript with most recent semester grades (if applicable).

2895 ■ Cherokee Nation Scholarships
(Undergraduate/Scholarship)

Purpose: To support Cherokee Nation Tribal Citizens pursuing degrees at a college or university. **Focus:** General studies/Field of study not specified. **Qualif.:** Applicant must be a Cherokee Nation tribal citizen who does not qualify for Federal Pell Grant funding; a permanent resident in the Cherokee Nation area, which is defined as counties within the Cherokee Nation boundaries; or permanent resident in the contiguous counties to the Cherokee Nation boundaries (including contiguous counties in Arkansas, Kansas, Missouri, and Oklahoma). **Criteria:** Selection is based on the following preferences: First: Continuing students; Second: Classification order of new applicants (Senior, Junior, Sophomore, Freshman); Third: Academic performance.

Funds Avail.: No specific amount. **To Apply:** Applicants must submit a completed application form together with Student Aid Report (all pages); copy of Social Security card; copy of Tribal Citizenship card (blue); official high school transcript (7 semester) or GED scores (Freshmen only); copy of ACT/SAT or College Placement Test Scores (Freshmen only); and official Undergraduate Transcript with most recent semester grades (if applicable).

2896 ■ Chicago Bar Foundation (CBF)
321 S Plymouth Ct., Ste. 3B
Chicago, IL 60604-3917
Ph: (312)554-1204
Fax: (312)554-1203

Awards are arranged alphabetically below their administering organizations

URL: www.chicagobarfoundation.org

2897 ■ Abraham Lincoln Marovitz Public Interest Law Scholarships (Undergraduate/Scholarship)

Purpose: To support needy law students pursuing a public interest legal career. **Focus:** Law. **Qualif.:** Applicants must be first-year students attending one of the nine Illinois law schools (Chicago-Kent College of Law, University of Chicago Law School, DePaul University College of Law, University of Illinois College of Law, John Marshall Law School, Loyola University School of Law, Northern Illinois University Law School, Northwestern University School of Law and Southern Illinois University School of Law). **Criteria:** Recipients will be selected on the basis of the following: (1) solid commitment to public interest issues, as demonstrated by past and present activities; (2) desire to practice public interest law; (3) commitment to pursue a career in public interest law, as demonstrated by an application essay and personal interview; (4) ability to achieve success as a lawyer; (5) demonstrated financial need; and (6) demonstrated commitment to live and work in Chicago area after law school graduation.

Funds Avail.: $10,000 in the first year, $15,000 in the second year and another $15,000 on the third year. **Duration:** Annual. **To Apply:** Applicants must submit a cover letter with attached application form; resume; official transcript from undergraduate institution and graduate institution; two letters of reference about commitment to public interest work; brief essay (no more than three pages, explaining commitment to pursue a career in public interest law). **Deadline:** May 9. **Remarks:** Established in 2004. **Contact:** Ryanne Easley at reasley@chicagobar.org; phone: 312-554-1247.

2898 ■ Chicago Railroad Mechanical Association (CRMA)
c/o Kenneth V. Denby, Jr., Secretary-Treasurer
2303 Flemming Rd.
Valparaiso, IN 46383
URL: www.thecrma.org

2899 ■ CRMA Scholarships (Graduate, Undergraduate/Scholarship)

Purpose: To provide financial assistance to eligible college or university students. **Focus:** General studies/Field of study not specified. **Qualif.:** Applicants must be either sons, daughters, adopted children, grandchildren or stepchildren of CRMA members who have maintained current membership in the association; must be enrolled at the time of application as full-time undergraduate or graduate students at an accredited junior college offering associate degree, a college or university offering bachelor or graduate degrees; must demonstrate successful completion of the previous year of study by maintaining at least a 2.75 accumulated GPA on a scale of 1 to 4 with an "A" equal to 4; must have accumulated enough credits from accredited school(s) in time for the fall semester to have obtained at least a sophomore level standing at the college or university of enrollment. **Criteria:** Selection will be based on the evaluation of narrative; transcript; recommendations; activities; honors and overall abilities.

Funds Avail.: Up to $2,000. **Duration:** Annual. **Number Awarded:** 2. **To Apply:** Applicants must submit a completed application form including the narrative requested in Section E of the application; official transcript from learning institute's Bursar office including work completed; two recommendation letters. The application, narrative statement, transcript and recommendation letters must be submitted in one envelope. **Deadline:** July 15.

2900 ■ Chicana/Latina Foundation (CLF)
1419 Burlingame Ave., Ste. W2
Burlingame, CA 94010
Ph: (650)373-1083
Fax: (650)373-1090
E-mail: clfinfo@chicanalatina.org
URL: www.chicanalatina.org

2901 ■ Chicana Latina Scholarship Fund (Graduate, Undergraduate/Scholarship)

Purpose: To assist Latina students in completing their undergraduate and graduate college education. **Focus:** General studies/Field of study not specified. **Qualif.:** Applicants must be Chicana/Latina women of the Northern California counties; must be enrolled in accredited colleges, universities and community colleges in one of the listed Northern California counties; must have been residents for at least two years in one of the listed Northern California counties; must be enrolled as full-time college students, have completed a minimum of 15 college semester units after high school graduation, and have at least a 2.5 GPA; must have demonstrated leadership and civic/community involvement. **Criteria:** Preference will be given to those who meet the criteria.

Funds Avail.: $1,500. **Duration:** Annual. **Number Awarded:** 31. **To Apply:** Applicants must submit a completed application form, two letters of recommendation; completed confidential demographic information, college transcript, resume and two essays (300-600 words) "describing your most valued community commitments, academic achievements, and/or leadership activities as a Chicana/Latina? What and/or who motivated you to action? and Imagine yourself ten years from now. What role will you play and how will you impact the social justice issues facing Latinas?" **Deadline:** March 31.

2902 ■ Childhood Cancer Canada Foundation
21 St. Clair Ave. E, Ste. 801
Toronto, ON, Canada M4T 1L9
Ph: (416)489-6440
Fax: (416)489-9812
Free: 800-363-1062
E-mail: info@childhoodcancer.ca
URL: www.childhoodcancer.ca
Facebook: www.facebook.com/ChildhoodCancerCanada
Twitter: twitter.com/chldhdcancercan

2903 ■ Childhood Cancer Survivor Scholarships (Undergraduate/Scholarship)

Purpose: To support young Canadians and assist them financially with their first year of post-secondary school education. **Focus:** Oncology. **Qualif.:** Applicants must be young Canadians who are childhood cancer survivors; must be Canadian citizens or landed immigrants between the ages of 17-25 years. **Criteria:** Recipients are selected based on financial need.

Funds Avail.: $1,500. **To Apply:** Applicants must write a 300-500 word letter describing their future academic goals and highlighting their reasons for applying for this scholar-

Awards are arranged alphabetically below their administering organizations

ship; must provide a copy of the letter of acceptance to a university, college or any post-secondary educational program and a copy of their most recent transcript, if not first year students; must provide a statement from a doctor/pediatrician and oncologist stating that they had some form of childhood cancer; must complete the application form.

2904 ■ TEVA Canada Scholarship (Undergraduate/Scholarship)

Purpose: To provide scholarships to young Canadians who are in treatment or who have survived childhood care. **Focus:** Oncology. **Qualif.:** Applicants must be entering (or already enrolled in) a Canadian university in programs such as pharmacy, medicine, or health sciences post-graduate programs of study. Applicants may be in any year of their studies provided that they are enrolled in school for the fall term that the scholarships are awarded in; must been treated (or are currently being treated) for childhood cancer (diagnosis must have occurred before 19th birthday); must be a Canadian resident. **Criteria:** Selection will be based on financial need. Preference will be given to individual sharing at Teen Connector via blog post/video about themselves describing experiences with cancer, hobbies and interests, plans or goals for their future (optional) but highly recommended in order to be considered competitive applicants.

Funds Avail.: 5,000 Canadian dollars. **Duration:** Annual. **Number Awarded:** Maximum of 10. **To Apply:** Applicants must submit a completed application form, statement from an oncologist or physician confirming treatment (or currently receiving treatment) for childhood cancer; a personal essay describing "how the journey with cancer inspired you to follow a career in the field of pharmacy/medicine/health sciences."; copy of undergraduate degree; letter of acceptance from the university; current photo; membership at online site "Teen Connector". **Contact:** Zoey Friedman at zoey@childhoodcancer.ca.

2905 ■ Children's Hospital of Philadelphia
34th St. & Civic Center Blvd.
Philadelphia, PA 19104
Free: 800-879-2467
URL: www.chop.edu
Facebook: www.facebook.com/ChildrensHospitalofPhiladelphia
Twitter: twitter.com/ChildrensPhila

2906 ■ Eagles Fly for Leukemia Scholarships (Undergraduate/Scholarship)

Purpose: To abolish childhood cancers and enhance the lives of children and families in their communities. **Focus:** Health care services. **Qualif.:** Applicants must be high school seniors currently battling cancer or survivors of childhood cancer. **Criteria:** Recipients are selected based on the financial need.

Funds Avail.: No specific amount. **To Apply:** Applicants must submit a complete application form. **Contact:** Trish Fulvio, Phone: 484-433-7767; Email: pafulvio@aol.com.

2907 ■ Michael A. Hunter Memorial Scholarships (Undergraduate/Scholarship)

Purpose: To help improve the quality of life for those affected with leukemia/lymphoma. **Focus:** Health care services. **Qualif.:** Applicants must be graduating high school seniors, community college and four-year university students who are leukemia patients and/or children of non-surviving leukemia patients; must be enrolled full-time; and must have a minimum GPA of 3.0 or "B" average. **Criteria:** Recipients are selected based on financial need.

Funds Avail.: $2,000 - $3,000. **Duration:** Annual. **To Apply:** Applicants must submit a complete application form and a 600-words essay about how leukemia or lymphoma has affected your life.

2908 ■ Children's Literature Association (ChLA)
1301 W 22nd St., Ste. 202
Oak Brook, IL 60523
Ph: (630)571-4520
Fax: (708)876-5598
E-mail: info@childlitassn.org
URL: www.childlitassn.org
Facebook: www.facebook.com/ChildLitAssn

2909 ■ Hannah Beiter Graduate Student Research Grants (Doctorate, Graduate/Grant)

Purpose: To encourage young individuals to pursue their research that may be related to the dissertation or Master's thesis. **Focus:** Literature, Children's. **Qualif.:** Applicants must be a member of the Children's Literature Association. **Criteria:** Applicants will be selected based on their proposal and reference letter.

Funds Avail.: $500-$1,500 individual awards. **Duration:** Annual. **To Apply:** Applicants must provide a cover letter including the name, telephone number, mailing address and email address, academic institution and status; must submit curriculum vitae and two reference letter. **Deadline:** February 1.

2910 ■ The Children's Tumor Foundation (CTF)
120 Wall St., 16th Fl.
New York, NY 10005-3904
Ph: (212)344-6633
Fax: (212)747-0004
Free: 800-323-7938
E-mail: info@ctf.org
URL: www.ctf.org
Facebook: www.facebook.com/childrenstumor
LinkedIn: www.linkedin.com/company/children's-tumor-foundation
Twitter: twitter.com/childrenstumor

2911 ■ CTF Young Investigator Awards (CTF-YIA) (Graduate, Postdoctorate, Doctorate/Award)

Purpose: To accelerate progress toward finding effective NF therapies. **Focus:** Neuroscience. **Qualif.:** Applicants must be postdoctoral fellows (MD, PhD or equivalent) but no more than seven years past the completion of their first doctoral degree; must be graduate students pursuing their MD, PhD or equivalent; must be affiliated with the laboratory of a senior researcher who is the applicants' research sponsor. The sponsor must offer a training environment that is conducive for the growth and education of an early NF career researcher. As part of the application, the mentor is asked to describe the intended training plan.

Funds Avail.: Varies. **Duration:** Annual. **Contact:** grants@ctf.org.

2912 ■ A Child's Hope International
2430 E Kemper Rd.
Cincinnati, OH 45241

Awards are arranged alphabetically below their administering organizations

Ph: (513)771-2244
E-mail: info@achildshopeintl.org
URL: www.achildshopeintl.org

2913 ■ Linsley Scholarship Fund (Undergraduate/Scholarship)

Purpose: To support young adults pursuing post-secondary education for their tuition and certain approved living expenses. **Focus:** General studies/Field of study not specified. **Qualif.:** Applicants must be young adults pursuing post-secondary education; must have been in public or private foster care for the 12 consecutive months prior to their 18th birthday; must have been adopted or placed into legal guardianship from foster care; must have been orphaned for at least one year at the time of their 18th birthday; must have been accepted into or exact to be accepted into an accredited Pell-eligible college, post-secondary school or vocational program; must be under the age of 25; have been in foster care or orphaned while living in the United States. U.S. citizenship is required. **Criteria:** Selection will be based on the combination of merits and needs of the applicants.

Funds Avail.: $1,500 to $5,000. **Duration:** Annual. **To Apply:** Interested applicants may contact the Linsley Scholarship Fund for the application process and other information. **Remarks:** The scholarship was established in recognition of Paul and Deanna Linsley's selfless lives.

2914 ■ Jane Coffin Childs Memorial Fund for Medical Research

333 Cedar St.
New Haven, CT 06520-8000
Ph: (203)785-4612
E-mail: jccfund@yale.edu
URL: www.jccfund.org

2915 ■ Jane Coffin Childs Memorial Fund - Medical Research Fellowships (Postdoctorate/Fellowship)

Purpose: To award fellowships to suitably qualified individuals for full-time postdoctoral studies in the medical and related sciences bearing on cancer. **Focus:** Oncology. **Qualif.:** Applicants in general should not have more than one year of postdoctoral experience; must hold either the MD degree or the PhD degree in the field in which they propose to study or furnish evidence of equivalent training and experience; must be citizens of any country but for foreign nationals awards will be made only for study in the United States. American citizens may hold a fellowship either in the United States or in a foreign country. **Criteria:** Selection will be based on the committee's criteria.

Funds Avail.: Basic stipend at present, the first year, the second year, and the third year is $50,000, with an additionl 1,000 for each dependent child. **To Apply:** Applicant must submit evidence as to pre and postdoctoral training must supply (a) the names and addresses of three individuals personally acquainted both with the applicant and with the applicant's professional work, one of whom should be the principal pre-doctoral advisor, (b) a suitably documented outline of the research problem proposed, and (c) the written consent of the chief of laboratory and a responsible fiscal officer of the host institution indicating their willingness to accept and provide necessary facilities for the Fellow. **Deadline:** February 1. **Contact:** Jane Coffin Childs Memorial Fund for Medical Research, at the above address.

2916 ■ Chinese American Medical Society (CAMS)

265 Canal St., Ste. 515
New York, NY 10013
Ph: (212)334-4760
Fax: (646)304-6373
URL: chineseamericanmedicalsociety.cloverpad.org

2917 ■ Chinese American Medical Society Summer Research Fellowships Program (Undergraduate/Fellowship)

Purpose: To promote and support clinical and basic science research among Chinese American medical and dental students. **Focus:** Dental laboratory technology; Medical technology. **Qualif.:** Applicants must be current students in an accredited medical or dental school in the United States; working on a project in the basic science or clinical research. **Criteria:** Special consideration will be given to projects involving Chinese American health issues.

Funds Avail.: $400 per week. **Duration:** 8 to 10 weeks. **To Apply:** Applicants must submit completed CAMS Summer Research Fellowship Application; project description; personal statement; curriculum vitae; a two letters from a supervising investigator supporting the research project and from the Dean verifying good standing. **Deadline:** April 30.

2918 ■ Esther Lim Memorial Scholarships (Undergraduate/Scholarship)

Purpose: To provide educational assistance to medical, dental students, and scientists. **Focus:** Dental laboratory technology; Medical technology. **Qualif.:** Applicant must be a medical or dental student or scientist matriculated in a medical or dental school. **Criteria:** Selection is based on merit.

Funds Avail.: No specific amount. **Duration:** Annual. **To Apply:** Application form is available at the website. Applicant must submit completed application form along with a letter from the Dean of Students verifying good standing; two letters of recommendation; a personal statement; and a current vitae. **Deadline:** April 30.

2919 ■ Ruth Liu Memorial Scholarships (Undergraduate/Scholarship)

Purpose: To provide scholarships to outstanding medical students in need of financial assistance. **Focus:** Dental laboratory technology; Medical technology. **Qualif.:** Applicant must be a medical or dental student or scientist matriculated in a medical or dental school. **Criteria:** Selection is based on merit.

Funds Avail.: $1,000 each. **Duration:** Annual. **Number Awarded:** 3-5. **To Apply:** Application form is available at the website. Applicants must submit completed application form along with a letter from the Dean of Students verifying good standing; two letters of recommendation; a personal statement; and a current vitae. **Deadline:** April 30.

2920 ■ Chinese Professionals Association of Canada (CPAC)

4150 Finch Ave. E
Toronto, ON, Canada M1S 3T9
Ph: (416)298-7885
Fax: (416)298-0068
E-mail: office@cpac-canada.ca
URL: www.cpac-canada.ca

Awards are arranged alphabetically below their administering organizations

2921 ■ CC Times Scholarships (Undergraduate/Scholarship)

Purpose: To help needy students further their education. **Focus:** General studies/Field of study not specified. **Qualif.:** Applicants must be secondary or post-secondary students or either be CPAC members and/or children with financial difficulties; must be enrolled in a degree program and have completed at least two semesters in a recognized university. **Criteria:** Recipients will be selected based on demonstrated leadership and academic achievements.

Funds Avail.: No specific amount. **To Apply:** Applicants must contact Howard Shen, President of the Education Foundation of CPAC, for further information.

2922 ■ Chinese Professionals Association of Canada BMO Diversity Scholarships (Undergraduate/Scholarship)

Purpose: To help needy students further their education. **Focus:** General studies/Field of study not specified. **Qualif.:** Applicants must be secondary or post-secondary students or either be CPAC members and/or children with financial difficulties; must be enrolled in a degree program and have completed at least two semesters in a recognized university. **Criteria:** Recipients will be selected based on demonstrated leadership and academic achievements.

Funds Avail.: No specific amount. **To Apply:** Applicants must contact Howard Shen, President of the Education Foundation of CPAC, for further information.

2923 ■ Chinese Professionals Association of Canada Education Foundation Awards (High School/Award)

Purpose: To encourage high school students to pursue higher education. **Focus:** General studies/Field of study not specified. **Qualif.:** Applicants must have completed grade 10, 11 or 12. **Criteria:** Recipients will be selected based on academic excellence and community involvement.

Funds Avail.: $1,000. **Number Awarded:** 6. **To Apply:** Applicants must contact Howard Shen, President of the Education Foundation of CPAC, for further information.

2924 ■ Chinese Professionals Association of Canada Journalism Scholarships (Undergraduate/Scholarship)

Purpose: To help needy students further their education. **Focus:** General studies/Field of study not specified. **Qualif.:** Applicants must be secondary or post-secondary students or either be CPAC members and/or children with financial difficulties; must be enrolled in a degree program and have completed at least two semesters in a recognized university. **Criteria:** Recipients will be selected based on demonstrated leadership and academic achievements.

Funds Avail.: No specific amount. **To Apply:** Applicants must contact Howard Shen, President of the Education Foundation of CPAC, for further information.

2925 ■ Chinese Professionals Association of Canada Professional Achievement Awards (Other/Award)

Purpose: To recognize and celebrate the achievements of professional immigrants. **Focus:** General studies/Field of study not specified. **Qualif.:** Applicants must have achieved an outstanding stature in their profession in Canada; must have used CPAC's services (including bridging program) for them to land new jobs; and must have achieved a successful accomplishment on a different profession other than the training they had before. **Criteria:** Award will be given to those who best meet the qualifications.

Funds Avail.: No specific amount. **To Apply:** Applicants must contact Howard Shen, President of the Education Foundation of CPAC, for further information. **Deadline:** December 6. **Remarks:** Established in 2009.

2926 ■ Pang Xiaoyan Scholarships (Undergraduate/Scholarship)

Purpose: To help needy students further their education. **Focus:** General studies/Field of study not specified. **Qualif.:** Applicants must be secondary or post-secondary students or either be CPAC members and/or children with financial difficulties; must be enrolled in a degree program and have completed at least two semesters in a recognized university. **Criteria:** Recipients will be selected based on demonstrated leadership and academic achievements.

Funds Avail.: No specific amount. **To Apply:** Applicants must contact Howard Shen, President of the Education Foundation of CPAC, for further information.

2927 ■ Chopin Foundation of the United States
1440 79th Street Cswy., Ste. 117
Miami, FL 33141
Ph: (305)868-0624
Fax: (305)865-5150
E-mail: info@chopin.org
URL: www.chopin.org
Facebook: www.facebook.com/chopinus
Twitter: twitter.com/ChopinMiami

2928 ■ Chopin Foundation of the United States Scholarships (Undergraduate/Scholarship)

Purpose: To support and encourage young, talented American pianists. **Focus:** Music, Piano. **Qualif.:** Applicants must be American pianists (citizens or legal residents); not younger than 14 and not older than 17 years; studying in the field of music, majoring in piano, and enrolled at the secondary or undergraduate school level as a full-time student. **Criteria:** Applicants are selected based on merit.

Funds Avail.: $500-$1,000. **Duration:** Annual. **Number Awarded:** Up to 10. **To Apply:** Applicants must submit a statement of career goals; minimum of two references from piano teachers or performers; a video tape of Chopin's works, registration fee of $25 and proof of enrollment. **Deadline:** May 15.

2929 ■ Choristers Guild (CG)
12404 Park Central Dr., Ste. 100
Dallas, TX 75251-1802
Ph: (469)398-3606
Fax: (469)398-3611
Free: 800-246-7478
E-mail: membership@mailcg.org
URL: www.choristersguild.org
Facebook: www.facebook.com/ChoristersGuild/?ref=tsg
Twitter: twitter.com/ChoristersGuild

2930 ■ Ruth K. Jacobs Memorial Scholarships (Graduate, Undergraduate/Scholarship)

Purpose: To provide financial aid to full-time students preparing for church music ministry. **Focus:** Music. **Qualif.:**

Applicants must be juniors, seniors or graduate students majoring in music who holds choral music with children and youth as a primary interest. **Criteria:** Recipient will be selected on the basis of academic merit, interest in church music, ministry of church music as a vocation and financial need.

Funds Avail.: Up to $1,500. **Duration:** Annual. **To Apply:** Applicants must submit an application form; transcript of records; and four references who are acquainted with the applicants' qualifications. **Deadline:** February 1. **Contact:** Choristers Guild Memorial Scholarship Committee, 12404 Park Central Drive, Suite 100, Dallas, TX 75251; Email: ehehn@mailcg.org.

2931 ■ Christian Missionary Scholarship Foundation (CMSF)
1899 Orchard Lake Rd., Ste. 203
Sylvan Lake, MI 48320
Ph: (616)526-7731
Fax: (616)526-6777
E-mail: cmsf01@gmail.com
URL: www.christianmissionaryscholarship.org
Facebook: www.facebook.com/christianmissionaryscholarshipfoundation

2932 ■ CMSF Scholarships (Undergraduate, Graduate/Scholarship)

Purpose: To provide financial support for the education of the children of missionaries. **Focus:** General studies/Field of study not specified. **Qualif.:** Applicants must be the children of missionaries who are currently on or recently returned from the mission field in a country other than their own passport country. **Criteria:** Selection shall be based on the aforementioned applicants' qualifications and compliance with the application details.

Funds Avail.: No specific amount. **Duration:** Annual. **Number Awarded:** Varies. **To Apply:** Applicants must fill up completely the Scholarship application form. **Contact:** Christian Missionary Scholarship Foundation, at the above address.

2933 ■ Christian Pharmacists Fellowship International (CPFI)
PO Box 1154
Bristol, TN 37621-1154
Ph: (423)844-1043
E-mail: office@cpfi.org
URL: www.cpfi.org

2934 ■ Christian Pharmacists Fellowship International (Advanced Professional/Fellowship)

Purpose: To assist Christian students in pursuing a career on pharmacy. **Focus:** Pharmacy. **Qualif.:** Applicant must be a national CPFI member; enrolled in an accredited pharmacy college/university or training program. **Criteria:** Awards are given based on the merit of the application and the Christian relevance of the project. Preference will be given to applicants whose plans or projects are experiential in nature or become the component of the curriculum.

Funds Avail.: No specific amount. **Duration:** Annual. **To Apply:** Applicant must send completed application form; description of the plan or project; an email support from the Dean and from an instructor/mentor; and a resume.

2935 ■ Christian Scholarship Foundation (CSF)
c/o Dr. Gregory E. Sterling, President
Yale Divinity School
409 Prospect St.
New Haven, CT 06511
URL: www.christianscholars.org

2936 ■ CSF Graduate Fellowships (Graduate/Fellowship)

Purpose: To provide financial assistance to ministers enrolled in doctoral programs in religion and related fields. **Focus:** Bible studies; Religion; Theology. **Qualif.:** Eligible applicants are members of the Churches of Christ who are teaching or who plan to teach religion and related subjects in universities, colleges, schools of theology, and Bible chairs. Previous recipients are eligible to apply. They must also have completed at least one full year of study as candidates for the Ph.D. or equivalent post-graduate degree prior to the year of application. **Criteria:** Selection shall be based on the aforesaid qualifications and compliance with the application details.

Funds Avail.: $2,000-$10,000. **Duration:** Annual. **Number Awarded:** 3-5. **To Apply:** Prospective applicants should: make application on the official form supplied by The Christian Scholarship Foundation; supply transcripts of all previous academic work, graduate and undergraduate; secure letters of recommendation regarding personal, religious, and intellectual development; supply a research paper, or other example of the applicants' most scholarly written work (not more than 50 pp. in length); submit a summary statement of plans for the academic year for which application is made, including signature of approval by the applicant's' faculty advisor or major professor; and, present an estimated budget showing income and expenditures. **Deadline:** January 15. **Remarks:** Established in 1982. **Contact:** Christian Scholarship Foundation, c/o Gregory Sterling; Email: gregory.sterling@yale.edu.

2937 ■ Church Hill Classics Ltd.
594 Pepper St.
Monroe, CT 06468
Ph: (203)268-1535
Fax: (203)268-2468
Free: 800-477-9005
E-mail: info@diplomaframe.com
URL: www.diplomaframe.com

2938 ■ Frame My Future Scholarships Contest (Undergraduate, Graduate/Scholarship)

Purpose: To provide students the funds they need for their educational expenses. **Focus:** General studies/Field of study not specified. **Qualif.:** Applicants must be legal U.S. residents and attending U.S. college or university full-time for the current academic year. **Criteria:** Judges will select finalist based on creativity of the full entry, including the image and accompanying description.

Funds Avail.: $1,000. **Duration:** Annual. **Number Awarded:** 5. **To Apply:** Applicants must submit their creative, original entry piece using the entry form online. The full entry must be the applicants' work and relate to the theme - "This is how I Frame My Future", and contain correct grammar and spelling. **Deadline:** March 8.

2939 ■ Winston Churchill Foundation of the United States (WCFUS)
600 Madison Ave., Ste. 1601
New York, NY 10022-1737

Awards are arranged alphabetically below their administering organizations

Ph: (212)752-3200
Fax: (212)246-8330
E-mail: info@winstonchurchillfoundation.org
URL: www.winstonchurchillfoundation.org

2940 ■ The Churchill Scholarships (Postgraduate/Scholarship)

Purpose: To provide finance to American students seeking doctorate degree opportunities in United Kingdom. **Focus:** Engineering; Mathematics and mathematical sciences. **Qualif.:** Applicants must be citizens of the United States enrolled in one of the institutions participating in the scholarship program competition or students who have recently graduated from one of those institutions. They must be between the ages of 19 and 26. **Criteria:** Recipients will be selected based on the following: academic achievement in all disciplines; the capacity to contribute to the advancement of knowledge in the sciences, engineering or mathematics by pursuing original, creative work at advanced levels as demonstrated by awards and prizes as reference. **Funds Avail.:** No specific amount. **Duration:** Annual. **To Apply:** Applicants must complete the application form; four letters of reference; proposed program of the study; personal statement. **Deadline:** November 10.

2941 ■ CIHR Training Program in Health Law and Policy

57 Louis Pasteur
Ottawa, ON, Canada K1N 6K5
Ph: (613)562-5800
Fax: (613)562-5124
E-mail: info@healthlawtraining.ca
URL: hlep.ca
Facebook: www.facebook.com/healthlawtraining

2942 ■ CIHR Health Law, Ethics and Policy Fellowships (Graduate/Fellowship)

Purpose: To increase research capacity in the area of health law and policy. **Focus:** Law. **Qualif.:** Applicants must be admitted into the Faculty of Law graduate program at one of the three participating institutions (Dalhousie University, University of Alberta, and University of Toronto). **Criteria:** Selection is based on the submitted application and materials. **Funds Avail.:** Up to 17,850 Canadian Dollars. **Duration:** Annual; up to 3 years. **Number Awarded:** Varies. **To Apply:** Applicants must submit a completed application form together with the transcripts from all universities attended (certified copies); two academic letters of reference; and a one-page statement of interest in health law and policy. **Deadline:** March 15.

2943 ■ Cincinnati Scholarship Foundation (CSF)

602 Main St., Ste. 1000
Cincinnati, OH 45202
Ph: (513)345-6701
Fax: (513)345-6705
E-mail: info@cincinnatischolarshipfoundation.org
URL: www.cincinnatischolarshipfoundation.org
Facebook: www.facebook.com/CincinnatiScholarshipFoundation
Twitter: twitter.com/CincinnatiSF

2944 ■ Michael Bany Memorial Scholarships (Undergraduate/Scholarship)

Purpose: To help students of Greater Cincinnati area achieve a college education. **Focus:** General studies/Field of study not specified. **Qualif.:** Applicant must be a resident of Greater Cincinnati; student with a proven musical ability and financial need pursing a degree in a field of music; with a minimum 2.5 GPA freshman year and 2.75 thereafter. **Criteria:** Awards are given based on need. **Funds Avail.:** No specific amount. **Duration:** Annual. **To Apply:** Applicant must submit a completed scholarship application form along with a copy of recent transcript; expected Family Contribution (EFC) from Student Aid Report (SAR), which comes as a result of filing the FAFSA; and a copy of Financial Aid Award Letter from the chosen college to be attended. **Deadline:** April 30.

2945 ■ Walter and Marilyn Bartlett Scholarships (Undergraduate/Scholarship)

Purpose: To support students from Greater Cincinnati area to pursue a college education. **Focus:** General studies/Field of study not specified. **Qualif.:** Applicant must be a resident of Greater Cincinnati and attending college as a full-time student. **Criteria:** Awards are given based on need. **Funds Avail.:** No specific amount. **Duration:** Annual. **To Apply:** Applicant must submit a completed scholarship application form along with a copy of recent transcript; expected Family Contribution (EFC) from Student Aid Report (SAR), which comes as a result of filing the FAFSA; and a copy of Financial Aid Award Letter from the chosen college to be attended. **Deadline:** April 30.

2946 ■ Milton and Edith Brown Memorial Scholarships (Undergraduate/Scholarship)

Purpose: To help students of Greater Cincinnati area achieve a college education. **Focus:** General studies/Field of study not specified. **Qualif.:** Applicant must be a resident of Greater Cincinnati and attending college as a full-time student. **Criteria:** Awards are given based on need. **Funds Avail.:** No specific amount. **Duration:** Annual. **To Apply:** Applicant must submit a completed scholarship application form along with a copy of recent transcript; expected Family Contribution (EFC) from Student Aid Report (SAR), which comes as a result of filing the FAFSA; and a copy of Financial Aid Award Letter from the chosen college to be attended. **Deadline:** April 30.

2947 ■ Eugene Carroll Scholarships (Undergraduate/Scholarship)

Purpose: To support students from Greater Cincinnati area to pursue a college education. **Focus:** General studies/Field of study not specified. **Qualif.:** Applicant must be a resident of Greater Cincinnati and attending college as a full-time student. **Criteria:** Awards are given based on need. **Funds Avail.:** No specific amount. **Duration:** Annual. **To Apply:** Applicant must submit a completed scholarship application form along with a copy of recent transcript; expected Family Contribution (EFC) from Student Aid Report (SAR), which comes as a result of filing the FAFSA; and a copy of Financial Aid Award Letter from the chosen college to be attended. **Deadline:** April 30.

2948 ■ CFT/ACPSOP Scholarships (Undergraduate/Scholarship)

Purpose: To help students from Greater Cincinnati area to achieve their dream of a college education. **Focus:** General studies/Field of study not specified. **Qualif.:** Applicant must be a resident of Greater Cincinnati and attending college

Awards are arranged alphabetically below their administering organizations

as a full-time student. **Criteria:** Awards are given based on need.

Funds Avail.: No specific amount. **To Apply:** Applicant must submit a completed scholarship application form along with a copy of recent transcript; expected Family Contribution (EFC) from Student Aid Report (SAR), which comes as a result of filing the FAFSA; and a copy of Financial Aid Award Letter from the chosen college to be attended. **Deadline:** April 17. **Remarks:** Faxed applications will not be considered. **Contact:** Cincinnati Scholarship Foundation; Phone: 513-345-6701; Fax: 513-345-6705; E-mail: info@cincinnatischolarshipfoundation.org.

2949 ■ Cincinnati High School Scholarships
(Undergraduate/Scholarship)

Purpose: To encourage students to achieve their highest academic potential. **Focus:** General studies/Field of study not specified. **Qualif.:** Applicant must attend a Cincinnati Public School in grades 7-12; meet the Federal Poverty Income Guidelines; maintains a minimum 2.50 GPA with no "Fs", "Xs" or "Is" in any subject; and be referred by a designated counselor or school representative. **Criteria:** Selection will be based on the submitted application.

Funds Avail.: No specific amount. **Duration:** Annual. **Number Awarded:** Varies. **To Apply:** Applications are only available from the representative at the student's school. The CSF representatives provide applications to students they recommend for the program. **Deadline:** Varies. **Contact:** Cincinnati Scholarship Foundation; Phone: 513-345-6701; Fax: 513-345-6705; E-mail: info@cincinnatischolarshipfoundation.org.

2950 ■ T.L. Conlan Scholarships *(Undergraduate/Scholarship)*

Purpose: To help students from Greater Cincinnati area to achieve the dream of a college education. **Focus:** General studies/Field of study not specified. **Qualif.:** Applicant must be a resident of Greater Cincinnati and attending college as a full-time student. **Criteria:** Awards are given based on need.

Funds Avail.: No specific amount. **Duration:** Annual. **To Apply:** Applicant must submit a completed scholarship application form along with a copy of recent transcript; expected Family Contribution (EFC) from Student Aid Report (SAR), which comes as a result of filing the FAFSA; and a copy of Financial Aid Award Letter from the chosen college to be attended. **Deadline:** April 30.

2951 ■ CSF Ach Family Scholarships
(Undergraduate/Scholarship)

Purpose: To support students from Greater Cincinnati area to pursue a college education. **Focus:** General studies/Field of study not specified. **Qualif.:** Applicant must be a resident of Greater Cincinnati and attending college as a full-time student. **Criteria:** Awards are given based on need.

Funds Avail.: No specific amount. **To Apply:** Applicant must submit a completed scholarship application form along with a copy of recent transcript; expected Family Contribution (EFC) from Student Aid Report (SAR), which comes as a result of filing the FAFSA; and a copy of Financial Aid Award Letter from the chosen college to be attended. **Deadline:** April 30.

2952 ■ CSF Barr Foundation Scholarships
(Undergraduate/Scholarship)

Purpose: To help students from Greater Cincinnati area to achieve the dream of a college education. **Focus:** General studies/Field of study not specified. **Qualif.:** Applicant must be a resident of Greater Cincinnati and attending college as a full-time student. **Criteria:** Awards are given based on need.

Funds Avail.: No specific amount. **Duration:** Annual. **To Apply:** Applicant must submit a completed scholarship application form along with a copy of recent transcript; expected Family Contribution (EFC) from Student Aid Report (SAR), which comes as a result of filing the FAFSA; and a copy of Financial Aid Award Letter from the chosen college to be attended. **Deadline:** April 30.

2953 ■ CSF Barrett Family Scholarships
(Undergraduate/Scholarship)

Purpose: To help students from Greater Cincinnati area to achieve the dream of a college education. **Focus:** General studies/Field of study not specified. **Qualif.:** Applicant must be a resident of Greater Cincinnati and attending college as a full-time student. **Criteria:** Awards are given based on need.

Funds Avail.: No specific amount. **Duration:** Annual. **To Apply:** Applicant must submit a completed scholarship application form along with a copy of recent transcript; expected Family Contribution (EFC) from Student Aid Report (SAR), which comes as a result of filing the FAFSA; and a copy of Financial Aid Award Letter from the chosen college to be attended. **Deadline:** April 30.

2954 ■ CSF Borden Inc. Scholarships
(Undergraduate/Scholarship)

Purpose: To help students from Greater Cincinnati area to achieve the dream of a college education. **Focus:** General studies/Field of study not specified. **Qualif.:** Applicant must be a resident of Greater Cincinnati and attending college as a full-time student. **Criteria:** Awards are given based on need.

Funds Avail.: No specific amount. **Duration:** Annual. **To Apply:** Applicant must submit a completed scholarship application form along with a copy of recent transcript; expected Family Contribution (EFC) from Student Aid Report (SAR), which comes as a result of filing the FAFSA; and a copy of Financial Aid Award Letter from the chosen college to be attended. **Deadline:** April 30.

2955 ■ CSF Castellini Foundation Scholarships
(Undergraduate/Scholarship)

Purpose: To help students from Greater Cincinnati area to achieve the dream of a college education. **Focus:** General studies/Field of study not specified. **Qualif.:** Applicant must be a resident of Greater Cincinnati and attending college as a full-time student. **Criteria:** Awards are given based on need.

Funds Avail.: No specific amount. **Duration:** Annual. **To Apply:** Applicant must submit a completed scholarship application form along with a copy of recent transcript; expected Family Contribution (EFC) from Student Aid Report (SAR), which comes as a result of filing the FAFSA; and a copy of Financial Aid Award Letter from the chosen college to be attended. **Deadline:** April 30.

2956 ■ CSF Cincinnati Bell Scholarships
(Undergraduate/Scholarship)

Purpose: To support students from Greater Cincinnati area to pursue a college education. **Focus:** General studies/Field of study not specified. **Qualif.:** Applicant must be a resident of Greater Cincinnati and attending college as a

Awards are arranged alphabetically below their administering organizations

full-time student. **Criteria:** Awards are given based on need.

Funds Avail.: No specific amount. **To Apply:** Applicant must submit a completed scholarship application form along with a copy of recent transcript; expected Family Contribution (EFC) from Student Aid Report (SAR), which comes as a result of filing the FAFSA; and a copy of Financial Aid Award Letter from the chosen college to be attended. **Deadline:** April 30.

2957 ■ CSF Cincinnati Financial Corporation Scholarships *(Undergraduate/Scholarship)*

Purpose: To support students from Greater Cincinnati area to pursue a college education. **Focus:** General studies/Field of study not specified. **Qualif.:** Applicant must be a resident of Greater Cincinnati and attending college as a full-time student. **Criteria:** Awards are given based on need.

Funds Avail.: No specific amount. **To Apply:** Applicant must submit a completed scholarship application form along with a copy of recent transcript; expected Family Contribution (EFC) from Student Aid Report (SAR), which comes as a result of filing the FAFSA; and a copy of Financial Aid Award Letter from the chosen college to be attended. **Deadline:** April 30.

2958 ■ CSF Crosset Family Scholarships *(Undergraduate/Scholarship)*

Purpose: To support students from Greater Cincinnati area to pursue a college education. **Focus:** General studies/Field of study not specified. **Qualif.:** Applicant must be a resident of Greater Cincinnati and attending college as a full-time student. **Criteria:** Awards are given based on need.

Funds Avail.: No specific amount. **To Apply:** Applicant must submit a completed scholarship application form along with a copy of recent transcript; expected Family Contribution (EFC) from Student Aid Report (SAR), which comes as a result of filing the FAFSA; and a copy of Financial Aid Award Letter from the chosen college to be attended. **Deadline:** April 30.

2959 ■ CSF Dater Foundation Scholarships *(Undergraduate/Scholarship)*

Purpose: To support students from Greater Cincinnati area to pursue a college education. **Focus:** General studies/Field of study not specified. **Qualif.:** Applicants must be students coming from Hamilton, Clermont, Butler and Warren counties attending college in Ohio, Indiana or Kentucky with priority given to students attending Dater Junior or Senior High School. Must have proven financial need. **Criteria:** Awards are given based on need.

Funds Avail.: No specific amount. **To Apply:** Applicant must submit a completed scholarship application form along with a copy of recent transcript; expected Family Contribution (EFC) from Student Aid Report (SAR), which comes as a result of filing the FAFSA; and a copy of Financial Aid Award Letter from the chosen college to be attended. **Deadline:** April 30.

2960 ■ CSF Duke Energy Scholarships *(Undergraduate/Scholarship)*

Purpose: To support students from Greater Cincinnati area to pursue a college education. **Focus:** General studies/Field of study not specified. **Qualif.:** Applicant must be a resident of Greater Cincinnati and attending college as a full-time student. **Criteria:** Awards are given based on need.

Funds Avail.: No specific amount. **To Apply:** Applicant must submit a completed scholarship application form along with a copy of recent transcript; expected Family Contribution (EFC) from Student Aid Report (SAR), which comes as a result of filing the FAFSA; and a copy of Financial Aid Award Letter from the chosen college to be attended. **Deadline:** April 30.

2961 ■ CSF Farmer Family Foundation Scholarships *(Undergraduate/Scholarship)*

Purpose: To help students from Greater Cincinnati area to achieve the dream of a college education. **Focus:** General studies/Field of study not specified. **Qualif.:** Applicant must be a resident of Greater Cincinnati and attending college as a full-time student. **Criteria:** Awards are given based on need.

Funds Avail.: No specific amount. **Duration:** Annual. **To Apply:** Applicant must submit a completed scholarship application form along with a copy of recent transcript; expected Family Contribution (EFC) from Student Aid Report (SAR), which comes as a result of filing the FAFSA; and a copy of Financial Aid Award Letter from the chosen college to be attended. **Deadline:** April 30.

2962 ■ CSF Fifth Third Bank Combined Scholarships *(Undergraduate/Scholarship)*

Purpose: To help students from Greater Cincinnati area to achieve the dream of a college education. **Focus:** General studies/Field of study not specified. **Qualif.:** Applicant must be a resident of Greater Cincinnati and attending college as a full-time student. **Criteria:** Awards are given based on need.

Funds Avail.: No specific amount. **Duration:** Annual. **To Apply:** Applicant must submit a completed scholarship application form along with a copy of recent transcript; expected Family Contribution (EFC) from Student Aid Report (SAR), which comes as a result of filing the FAFSA; and a copy of Financial Aid Award Letter from the chosen college to be attended. **Deadline:** April 30.

2963 ■ CSF Fletemeyer Family Scholarships *(Undergraduate/Scholarship)*

Purpose: To help students from Greater Cincinnati area to achieve the dream of a college education. **Focus:** General studies/Field of study not specified. **Qualif.:** Applicant must be a resident of Greater Cincinnati and attending college as a full-time student. **Criteria:** Awards are given based on need.

Funds Avail.: No specific amount. **Duration:** Annual. **To Apply:** Applicant must submit a completed scholarship application form along with a copy of recent transcript; expected Family Contribution (EFC) from Student Aid Report (SAR), which comes as a result of filing the FAFSA; and a copy of Financial Aid Award Letter from the chosen college to be attended. **Deadline:** April 30.

2964 ■ CSF Gardner Foundation Scholarships *(Undergraduate/Scholarship)*

Purpose: To help students from Greater Cincinnati area to achieve the dream of a college education. **Focus:** General studies/Field of study not specified. **Qualif.:** Applicant must be a resident of Greater Cincinnati and attending college as a full-time student. **Criteria:** Awards are given based on need.

Awards are arranged alphabetically below their administering organizations

Funds Avail.: No specific amount. **Duration:** Annual. **To Apply:** Applicant must submit a completed scholarship application form along with a copy of recent transcript; expected Family Contribution (EFC) from Student Aid Report (SAR), which comes as a result of filing the FAFSA; and a copy of Financial Aid Award Letter from the chosen college to be attended. **Deadline:** April 30.

2965 ■ CSF Goldman, Sachs and Company Scholarships (Undergraduate/Scholarship)

Purpose: To help students from Greater Cincinnati area to achieve the dream of a college education. **Focus:** General studies/Field of study not specified. **Qualif.:** Applicant must be a resident of Greater Cincinnati and attending college as a full-time student. **Criteria:** Awards are given based on need.

Funds Avail.: No specific amount. **Duration:** Annual. **To Apply:** Applicant must submit a completed scholarship application form along with a copy of recent transcript; expected Family Contribution (EFC) from Student Aid Report (SAR), which comes as a result of filing the FAFSA; and a copy of Financial Aid Award Letter from the chosen college to be attended. **Deadline:** April 30.

2966 ■ CSF H.C. Schott Foundation Scholarships (Undergraduate/Scholarship)

Purpose: To help students from Greater Cincinnati area to achieve the dream of a college education. **Focus:** General studies/Field of study not specified. **Qualif.:** Applicant must be a resident of Greater Cincinnati and attending college as a full-time student. **Criteria:** Awards are given based on need.

Funds Avail.: No specific amount. **Duration:** Annual. **To Apply:** Applicant must submit a completed scholarship application form along with a copy of recent transcript; expected Family Contribution (EFC) from Student Aid Report (SAR), which comes as a result of filing the FAFSA; and a copy of Financial Aid Award Letter from the chosen college to be attended. **Deadline:** April 30.

2967 ■ CSF Heidelberg Distributing Co. Scholarships (Undergraduate/Scholarship)

Purpose: To help students from Greater Cincinnati area to achieve the dream of a college education. **Focus:** General studies/Field of study not specified. **Qualif.:** Applicant must be a resident of Greater Cincinnati and attending college as a full-time student. **Criteria:** Awards are given based on need.

Funds Avail.: No specific amount. **Duration:** Annual. **To Apply:** Applicant must submit a completed scholarship application form along with a copy of recent transcript; expected Family Contribution (EFC) from Student Aid Report (SAR), which comes as a result of filing the FAFSA; and a copy of Financial Aid Award Letter from the chosen college to be attended. **Deadline:** April 30.

2968 ■ CSF Heinz Pet Products Scholarships (Undergraduate/Scholarship)

Purpose: To help students from Greater Cincinnati area to achieve the dream of a college education. **Focus:** General studies/Field of study not specified. **Qualif.:** Applicant must be a resident of Greater Cincinnati and attending college as a full-time student. **Criteria:** Awards are given based on need.

Funds Avail.: No specific amount. **Duration:** Annual. **To Apply:** Applicant must submit a completed scholarship application form along with a copy of recent transcript; expected Family Contribution (EFC) from Student Aid Report (SAR), which comes as a result of filing the FAFSA; and a copy of Financial Aid Award Letter from the chosen college to be attended. **Deadline:** April 30.

2969 ■ CSF Juilfs Foundation Scholarships (Undergraduate/Scholarship)

Purpose: To help students from Greater Cincinnati area to achieve the dream of a college education. **Focus:** General studies/Field of study not specified. **Qualif.:** Applicant must be a resident of Greater Cincinnati and attending college as a full-time student. **Criteria:** Awards are given based on need.

Funds Avail.: No specific amount. **Duration:** Annual. **To Apply:** Applicant must submit a completed scholarship application form along with a copy of recent transcript; expected Family Contribution (EFC) from Student Aid Report (SAR), which comes as a result of filing the FAFSA; and a copy of Financial Aid Award Letter from the chosen college to be attended. **Deadline:** April 30.

2970 ■ CSF Kroger Cincinnati/Dayton Scholarships (Undergraduate/Scholarship)

Purpose: To help students from Greater Cincinnati area to achieve the dream of a college education. **Focus:** General studies/Field of study not specified. **Qualif.:** Applicant must be a resident of Greater Cincinnati and attending college as a full-time student. **Criteria:** Awards are given based on need.

Funds Avail.: No specific amount. **Duration:** Annual. **To Apply:** Applicant must submit a completed scholarship application form along with a copy of recent transcript; expected Family Contribution (EFC) from Student Aid Report (SAR), which comes as a result of filing the FAFSA; and a copy of Financial Aid Award Letter from the chosen college to be attended. **Deadline:** April 30.

2971 ■ CSF McCall Educational Scholarships (Undergraduate/Scholarship)

Purpose: To help students of Greater Cincinnati area achieve a college education. **Focus:** General studies/Field of study not specified. **Qualif.:** Applicant must be a resident of Greater Cincinnati; must be African-American students attending a college in Hamilton County or Miami University. **Criteria:** Awards are given based on need.

Funds Avail.: No specific amount. **Duration:** Annual. **To Apply:** Applicant must submit a completed scholarship application form along with a copy of recent transcript; expected Family Contribution (EFC) from Student Aid Report (SAR), which comes as a result of filing the FAFSA; and a copy of Financial Aid Award Letter from the chosen college to be attended. **Deadline:** April 30.

2972 ■ CSF Midland Company Scholarships (Undergraduate/Scholarship)

Purpose: To help students from Greater Cincinnati area to achieve the dream of a college education. **Focus:** General studies/Field of study not specified. **Qualif.:** Applicant must be a resident of Greater Cincinnati and attending college as a full-time student. **Criteria:** Awards are given based on need.

Funds Avail.: No specific amount. **Duration:** Annual. **To Apply:** Applicant must submit a completed scholarship application form along with a copy of recent transcript; expected Family Contribution (EFC) from Student Aid

Awards are arranged alphabetically below their administering organizations

Report (SAR), which comes as a result of filing the FAFSA; and a copy of Financial Aid Award Letter from the chosen college to be attended. **Deadline:** April 30.

2973 ■ CSF Nethercott Family Scholarships *(Undergraduate/Scholarship)*

Purpose: To help students from Greater Cincinnati area to achieve the dream of a college education. **Focus:** General studies/Field of study not specified. **Qualif.:** Applicant must be a resident of Greater Cincinnati and attending college as a full-time student. **Criteria:** Awards are given based on need.

Funds Avail.: No specific amount. **Duration:** Annual. **To Apply:** Applicant must submit a completed scholarship application form along with a copy of recent transcript; expected Family Contribution (EFC) from Student Aid Report (SAR), which comes as a result of filing the FAFSA; and a copy of Financial Aid Award Letter from the chosen college to be attended. **Deadline:** April 30.

2974 ■ CSF Ohio National Foundation Scholarships *(Undergraduate/Scholarship)*

Purpose: To support students from Greater Cincinnati area to pursue a college education. **Focus:** General studies/Field of study not specified. **Qualif.:** Applicant must be a resident of Greater Cincinnati and attending college as a full-time student. **Criteria:** Awards are given based on need.

Funds Avail.: No specific amount. **Duration:** Annual. **To Apply:** Applicant must submit a completed scholarship application form along with a copy of recent transcript; expected Family Contribution (EFC) from Student Aid Report (SAR), which comes as a result of filing the FAFSA; and a copy of Financial Aid Award Letter from the chosen college to be attended. **Deadline:** April 30.

2975 ■ CSF Pepper Family Scholarships *(Undergraduate/Scholarship)*

Purpose: To help students from Greater Cincinnati area to achieve the dream of a college education. **Focus:** General studies/Field of study not specified. **Qualif.:** Applicant must be a resident of Greater Cincinnati and attending college as a full-time student. **Criteria:** Awards are given based on need.

Funds Avail.: No specific amount. **Duration:** Annual. **To Apply:** Applicant must submit a completed scholarship application form along with a copy of recent transcript; expected Family Contribution (EFC) from Student Aid Report (SAR), which comes as a result of filing the FAFSA; and a copy of Financial Aid Award Letter from the chosen college to be attended. **Deadline:** April 30.

2976 ■ CSF Pichler Family Scholarships *(Undergraduate/Scholarship)*

Purpose: To help students from Greater Cincinnati area to achieve the dream of a college education. **Focus:** General studies/Field of study not specified. **Qualif.:** Applicant must be a resident of Greater Cincinnati and attending college as a full-time student. **Criteria:** Awards are given based on need.

Funds Avail.: No specific amount. **Duration:** Annual. **To Apply:** Applicant must submit a completed scholarship application form along with a copy of recent transcript; expected Family Contribution (EFC) from Student Aid Report (SAR), which comes as a result of filing the FAFSA; and a copy of Financial Aid Award Letter from the chosen college to be attended. **Deadline:** April 30.

2977 ■ CSF PNC Bank Scholarships *(Undergraduate/Scholarship)*

Purpose: To help students from Greater Cincinnati area to achieve the dream of a college education. **Focus:** General studies/Field of study not specified. **Qualif.:** Applicant must be a resident of Greater Cincinnati and attending college as a full-time student. **Criteria:** Awards are given based on need.

Funds Avail.: No specific amount. **Duration:** Annual. **To Apply:** Applicant must submit a completed scholarship application form along with a copy of recent transcript; expected Family Contribution (EFC) from Student Aid Report (SAR), which comes as a result of filing the FAFSA; and a copy of Financial Aid Award Letter from the chosen college to be attended. **Deadline:** April 30.

2978 ■ CSF Procter and Gamble Scholarships *(Undergraduate/Scholarship)*

Purpose: To help students from Greater Cincinnati area to achieve the dream of a college education. **Focus:** General studies/Field of study not specified. **Qualif.:** Applicant must be a resident of Greater Cincinnati and attending college as a full-time student. **Criteria:** Awards are given based on need.

Funds Avail.: No specific amount. **Duration:** Annual. **To Apply:** Applicant must submit a completed scholarship application form along with a copy of recent transcript; expected Family Contribution (EFC) from Student Aid Report (SAR), which comes as a result of filing the FAFSA; and a copy of Financial Aid Award Letter from the chosen college to be attended. **Deadline:** April 30.

2979 ■ CSF Scripps Headliners Scholarships *(Undergraduate/Scholarship)*

Purpose: To support students from Greater Cincinnati area to pursue a college education. **Focus:** General studies/Field of study not specified. **Qualif.:** Applicant must be a resident of Greater Cincinnati and attending college as a full-time student. **Criteria:** Awards are given based on need.

Funds Avail.: No specific amount. **Duration:** Annual. **To Apply:** Applicant must submit a completed scholarship application form along with a copy of recent transcript; expected Family Contribution (EFC) from Student Aid Report (SAR), which comes as a result of filing the FAFSA; and a copy of Financial Aid Award Letter from the chosen college to be attended. **Deadline:** April 30.

2980 ■ CSF Semple Foundation Scholarships *(Undergraduate/Scholarship)*

Purpose: To help students from Greater Cincinnati area to achieve the dream of a college education. **Focus:** General studies/Field of study not specified. **Qualif.:** Applicant must be a resident of Greater Cincinnati and attending college as a full-time student. **Criteria:** Awards are given based on need.

Funds Avail.: No specific amount. **Duration:** Annual. **To Apply:** Applicant must submit a completed scholarship application form along with a copy of recent transcript; expected Family Contribution (EFC) from Student Aid Report (SAR), which comes as a result of filing the FAFSA; and a copy of Financial Aid Award Letter from the chosen college to be attended. **Deadline:** April 30.

Awards are arranged alphabetically below their administering organizations

CINCINNATI SCHOLARSHIP FOUNDATION

2981 ■ CSF Union Central 135th Anniversary Scholarships (Undergraduate/Scholarship)

Purpose: To support students from Greater Cincinnati area to pursue a college education. **Focus:** General studies/Field of study not specified. **Qualif.:** Applicant must be a resident of Greater Cincinnati and attending college as a full-time student. **Criteria:** Awards are given based on need.

Funds Avail.: No specific amount. **Duration:** Annual. **To Apply:** Applicant must submit a completed scholarship application form along with a copy of recent transcript; expected Family Contribution (EFC) from Student Aid Report (SAR), which comes as a result of filing the FAFSA; and a copy of Financial Aid Award Letter from the chosen college to be attended. **Deadline:** April 30.

2982 ■ CSF U.S. Bank N.A. Scholarships (Undergraduate/Scholarship)

Purpose: To help students from Greater Cincinnati area to achieve the dream of a college education. **Focus:** General studies/Field of study not specified. **Qualif.:** Applicant must be a resident of Greater Cincinnati and attending college as a full-time student. **Criteria:** Awards are given based on need.

Funds Avail.: No specific amount. **Duration:** Annual. **To Apply:** Applicant must submit a completed scholarship application form along with a copy of recent transcript; expected Family Contribution (EFC) from Student Aid Report (SAR), which comes as a result of filing the FAFSA; and a copy of Financial Aid Award Letter from the chosen college to be attended. **Deadline:** April 30.

2983 ■ CSF Western-Southern Foundation Scholarships (Undergraduate/Scholarship)

Purpose: To help students from Greater Cincinnati area to achieve the dream of a college education. **Focus:** General studies/Field of study not specified. **Qualif.:** Applicant must be a resident of Greater Cincinnati and attending college as a full-time student. **Criteria:** Awards are given based on need.

Funds Avail.: No specific amount. **Duration:** Annual. **To Apply:** Applicant must submit a completed scholarship application form along with a copy of recent transcript; expected Family Contribution (EFC) from Student Aid Report (SAR), which comes as a result of filing the FAFSA; and a copy of Financial Aid Award Letter from the chosen college to be attended. **Deadline:** April 30.

2984 ■ CSF Woodward Trustees Scholarships (Undergraduate/Scholarship)

Purpose: To help students from Greater Cincinnati area to achieve the dream of a college education. **Focus:** General studies/Field of study not specified. **Qualif.:** Applicant must be a resident of Greater Cincinnati and attending college as a full-time student. **Criteria:** Awards are given based on need.

Funds Avail.: No specific amount. **Duration:** Annual. **To Apply:** Applicant must submit a completed scholarship application form along with a copy of recent transcript; expected Family Contribution (EFC) from Student Aid Report (SAR), which comes as a result of filing the FAFSA; and a copy of Financial Aid Award Letter from the chosen college to be attended. **Deadline:** April 30.

2985 ■ CSF Wynne Family Memorial Scholarships (Undergraduate/Scholarship)

Purpose: To help students from Greater Cincinnati area to achieve the dream of a college education. **Focus:** General studies/Field of study not specified. **Qualif.:** Applicant must be a resident of Greater Cincinnati and attending college as a full-time student. **Criteria:** Awards are given based on need.

Funds Avail.: No specific amount. **Duration:** Annual. **To Apply:** Applicant must submit a completed scholarship application form along with a copy of recent transcript; expected Family Contribution (EFC) from Student Aid Report (SAR), which comes as a result of filing the FAFSA; and a copy of Financial Aid Award Letter from the chosen college to be attended. **Deadline:** April 30. **Contact:** Cincinnati Scholarship Foundation; Phone: 513-345-6701; Fax: 513-345-6705; E-mail: info@cincinnatischolarshipfoundation.org.

2986 ■ Curtis/Breeden Scholarships (Doctorate/Scholarship)

Purpose: To help students of Greater Cincinnati area who are pursuing Doctorate Degree. **Focus:** General studies/Field of study not specified. **Qualif.:** Applicant must be a resident of Greater Cincinnati and attending college as a full-time student. **Criteria:** Awards are given based on need.

Funds Avail.: No specific amount. **Duration:** Annual. **To Apply:** Applicant must submit a completed scholarship application form along with a copy of recent transcript; expected Family Contribution (EFC) from Student Aid Report (SAR), which comes as a result of filing the FAFSA; and a copy of Financial Aid Award Letter from the chosen college to be attended. **Deadline:** April 30.

2987 ■ Estelle Davis Memorial Scholarships (Undergraduate/Scholarship)

Purpose: To help students from Greater Cincinnati area to achieve the dream of a college education. **Focus:** General studies/Field of study not specified. **Qualif.:** Applicant must be a resident of Greater Cincinnati and attending college as a full-time student. **Criteria:** Awards are given based on need.

Funds Avail.: No specific amount. **To Apply:** Applicant must submit a completed scholarship application form along with a copy of recent transcript; expected Family Contribution (EFC) from Student Aid Report (SAR), which comes as a result of filing the FAFSA; and a copy of Financial Aid Award Letter from the chosen college to be attended.

2988 ■ Thomas J. Emery Memorial Scholarships (Undergraduate/Scholarship)

Purpose: To help students from Greater Cincinnati area to achieve the dream of a college education. **Focus:** General studies/Field of study not specified. **Qualif.:** Applicant must be a resident of Greater Cincinnati and attending college as a full-time student. **Criteria:** Awards are given based on need.

Funds Avail.: No specific amount. **Duration:** Annual. **To Apply:** Applicant must submit a completed scholarship application form along with a copy of recent transcript; expected Family Contribution (EFC) from Student Aid Report (SAR), which comes as a result of filing the FAFSA; and a copy of Financial Aid Award Letter from the chosen college to be attended. **Deadline:** April 30.

2989 ■ Lyle and Rlene Everingham Family Scholarships (Undergraduate/Scholarship)

Purpose: To help students of Greater Cincinnati area achieve a college education. **Focus:** General studies/Field

Awards are arranged alphabetically below their administering organizations

of study not specified. **Qualif.:** Applicant must be a resident of Greater Cincinnati and attending college as a full-time student. **Criteria:** Awards are given based on need.

Funds Avail.: No specific amount. **Duration:** Annual. **To Apply:** Applicant must submit a completed scholarship application form along with a copy of recent transcript; expected Family Contribution (EFC) from Student Aid Report (SAR), which comes as a result of filing the FAFSA; and a copy of Financial Aid Award Letter from the chosen college to be attended. **Deadline:** April 30.

2990 ■ Lyle Everingham Scholarships
(Undergraduate/Scholarship)

Purpose: To help students of Greater Cincinnati area achieve a college education. **Focus:** General studies/Field of study not specified. **Qualif.:** Applicant must be a resident of Greater Cincinnati and attending college as a full-time student. **Criteria:** Awards are given based on need.

Funds Avail.: No specific amount. **Duration:** Annual. **To Apply:** Applicant must submit a completed scholarship application form along with a copy of recent transcript; expected Family Contribution (EFC) from Student Aid Report (SAR), which comes as a result of filing the FAFSA; and a copy of Financial Aid Award Letter from the chosen college to be attended. **Deadline:** April 30.

2991 ■ William A. Friedlander Scholarships
(Undergraduate/Scholarship)

Purpose: To help students from Greater Cincinnati area to achieve the dream of a college education. **Focus:** General studies/Field of study not specified. **Qualif.:** Applicant must be a resident of Greater Cincinnati and attending college as a full-time student. **Criteria:** Awards are given based on need.

Funds Avail.: No specific amount. **Duration:** Annual. **To Apply:** Applicant must submit a completed scholarship application form along with a copy of recent transcript; expected Family Contribution (EFC) from Student Aid Report (SAR), which comes as a result of filing the FAFSA; and a copy of Financial Aid Award Letter from the chosen college to be attended. **Deadline:** April 30.

2992 ■ Priscilla Gamble Scholarships
(Undergraduate/Scholarship)

Purpose: To help students from Greater Cincinnati area to achieve the dream of a college education. **Focus:** General studies/Field of study not specified. **Qualif.:** Applicant must be a resident of Greater Cincinnati and attending college as a full-time student. **Criteria:** Awards are given based on need.

Funds Avail.: No specific amount. **Duration:** Annual. **To Apply:** Applicant must submit a completed scholarship application form along with a copy of recent transcript; expected Family Contribution (EFC) from Student Aid Report (SAR), which comes as a result of filing the FAFSA; and a copy of Financial Aid Award Letter from the chosen college to be attended. **Deadline:** April 30.

2993 ■ G.E. Aviation Scholarships *(Undergraduate/Scholarship)*

Purpose: To help students from Greater Cincinnati area to achieve the dream of a college education. **Focus:** General studies/Field of study not specified. **Qualif.:** Applicant must be a resident of Greater Cincinnati, and attending college as a full-time student. **Criteria:** Award will be given based on need.

Funds Avail.: No specific amount. **Duration:** Annual. **To Apply:** Applicant must submit a completed scholarship application form along with a copy of recent transcript; expected Family Contribution (EFC) from Student Aid Report (SAR), which comes as a result of filing the FAFSA; and a copy of Financial Aid Award Letter from the chosen college to be attended. **Deadline:** April 30.

2994 ■ Milacron Geier Scholarships *(Undergraduate/Scholarship)*

Purpose: To support students from Greater Cincinnati area to pursue a college education. **Focus:** General studies/Field of study not specified. **Qualif.:** Applicant must be a resident of Greater Cincinnati and attending college as a full-time student. **Criteria:** Awards are given based on need.

Funds Avail.: No specific amount. **To Apply:** Applicant must submit a completed scholarship application form along with a copy of recent transcript; expected Family Contribution (EFC) from Student Aid Report (SAR), which comes as a result of filing the FAFSA; and a copy of Financial Aid Award Letter from the chosen college to be attended. **Deadline:** April 30.

2995 ■ Greater Cincinnati Scholarships Association
(Undergraduate/Scholarship)

Purpose: To support students from Greater Cincinnati area to pursue a college education. **Focus:** General studies/Field of study not specified. **Qualif.:** Applicant must be a resident of Greater Cincinnati and attending college as a full-time student. **Criteria:** Awards are given based on need.

Funds Avail.: No specific amount. **Duration:** Annual. **To Apply:** Applicant must submit a completed scholarship application form along with a copy of recent transcript; expected Family Contribution (EFC) from Student Aid Report (SAR), which comes as a result of filing the FAFSA; and a copy of Financial Aid Award Letter from the chosen college to be attended. **Deadline:** April 30.

2996 ■ Richard Heekin Scholarships *(Undergraduate/Scholarship)*

Purpose: To help students from Greater Cincinnati area to achieve the dream of a college education. **Focus:** General studies/Field of study not specified. **Qualif.:** Applicant must be a resident of Greater Cincinnati and attending college as a full-time student. **Criteria:** Awards are given based on need.

Funds Avail.: No specific amount. **Duration:** Annual. **To Apply:** Applicant must submit a completed scholarship application form along with a copy of recent transcript; expected Family Contribution (EFC) from Student Aid Report (SAR), which comes as a result of filing the FAFSA; and a copy of Financial Aid Award Letter from the chosen college to be attended. **Deadline:** April 30.

2997 ■ Helen Steiner Rice Scholarships
(Undergraduate/Scholarship)

Purpose: To help students from Greater Cincinnati area to achieve the dream of a college education. **Focus:** General studies/Field of study not specified. **Qualif.:** Applicant must be a resident of Greater Cincinnati and attending college as a full-time student. **Criteria:** Awards are given based on need.

Funds Avail.: No specific amount. **Duration:** Annual. **To Apply:** Applicant must submit a completed scholarship ap-

Awards are arranged alphabetically below their administering organizations

plication form along with a copy of recent transcript; expected Family Contribution (EFC) from Student Aid Report (SAR), which comes as a result of filing the FAFSA; and a copy of Financial Aid Award Letter from the chosen college to be attended. **Deadline:** April 30.

2998 ■ Dwight Hibbard Scholarships
(Undergraduate/Scholarship)

Purpose: To support students from Greater Cincinnati area to pursue a college education. **Focus:** General studies/Field of study not specified. **Qualif.:** Applicant must be a resident of Greater Cincinnati and attending college as a full-time student. **Criteria:** Awards are given based on need.

Funds Avail.: No specific amount. **Duration:** Annual. **To Apply:** Applicant must submit a completed scholarship application form along with a copy of recent transcript; expected Family Contribution (EFC) from Student Aid Report (SAR), which comes as a result of filing the FAFSA; and a copy of Financial Aid Award Letter from the chosen college to be attended. **Deadline:** April 30.

2999 ■ Florette B. Hoffheimer Scholarships
(Undergraduate/Scholarship)

Purpose: To help students from Greater Cincinnati area to achieve the dream of a college education. **Focus:** General studies/Field of study not specified. **Qualif.:** Applicant must be a resident of Greater Cincinnati and attending college as a full-time student. **Criteria:** Awards are given based on need.

Funds Avail.: No specific amount. **Duration:** Annual. **To Apply:** Applicant must submit a completed scholarship application form along with a copy of recent transcript; expected Family Contribution (EFC) from Student Aid Report (SAR), which comes as a result of filing the FAFSA; and a copy of Financial Aid Award Letter from the chosen college to be attended. **Deadline:** April 30.

3000 ■ Roger and Joyce Howe Scholarships
(Undergraduate/Scholarship)

Purpose: To help students from Greater Cincinnati area to achieve the dream of a college education. **Focus:** General studies/Field of study not specified. **Qualif.:** Applicant must be a resident of Greater Cincinnati and attending college as a full-time student. **Criteria:** Awards are given based on need.

Funds Avail.: No specific amount. **Duration:** Annual. **To Apply:** Applicant must submit a completed scholarship application form along with a copy of recent transcript; expected Family Contribution (EFC) from Student Aid Report (SAR), which comes as a result of filing the FAFSA; and a copy of Financial Aid Award Letter from the chosen college to be attended. **Deadline:** April 30.

3001 ■ Johnny Bench Scholarships *(Undergraduate/Scholarship)*

Purpose: To help students from Greater Cincinnati area to achieve the dream of a college education. **Focus:** General studies/Field of study not specified. **Qualif.:** Applicants must be students residing within the I-275 boundary and attending the University of Cincinnati, Miami University, College of Mt. St. Joseph, Northern Kentucky University, Thomas More College and Cincinnati State. Also for students residing in Binger OK attending college in Oklahoma; must have participated in athletics. **Criteria:** Awards are given based on need.

Funds Avail.: No specific amount. **Duration:** Annual. **To Apply:** Applicant must submit a completed scholarship application form along with a copy of recent transcript; expected Family Contribution (EFC) from Student Aid Report (SAR), which comes as a result of filing the FAFSA; and a copy of Financial Aid Award Letter from the chosen college to be attended. **Deadline:** April 30.

3002 ■ Ella Wilson Johnson Scholarships
(Undergraduate/Scholarship)

Purpose: To help students from Greater Cincinnati area to achieve the dream of a college education. **Focus:** General studies/Field of study not specified. **Qualif.:** Applicant must be a resident of Greater Cincinnati and attending college as a full-time student. **Criteria:** Awards are given based on need.

Funds Avail.: No specific amount. **Duration:** Annual. **To Apply:** Applicant must submit a completed scholarship application form along with a copy of recent transcript; expected Family Contribution (EFC) from Student Aid Report (SAR), which comes as a result of filing the FAFSA; and a copy of Financial Aid Award Letter from the chosen college to be attended. **Deadline:** April 30.

3003 ■ David J. Joseph Company Scholarships
(Undergraduate/Scholarship)

Purpose: To support students from Greater Cincinnati area to pursue a college education. **Focus:** General studies/Field of study not specified. **Qualif.:** Applicant must be a resident of Greater Cincinnati and attending college as a full-time student; must be dependent children of employees of the David J. Joseph Company. **Criteria:** Awards are given based on need.

Funds Avail.: No specific amount. **To Apply:** Applicant must submit a completed scholarship application form along with a copy of recent transcript; expected Family Contribution (EFC) from Student Aid Report (SAR), which comes as a result of filing the FAFSA; and a copy of Financial Aid Award Letter from the chosen college to be attended. **Deadline:** April 30.

3004 ■ Raymond and Augusta Klink Scholarships
(Undergraduate/Scholarship)

Purpose: To help students from Greater Cincinnati area to achieve the dream of a college education. **Focus:** General studies/Field of study not specified. **Qualif.:** Applicant must be a resident of Greater Cincinnati and attending college as a full-time student. **Criteria:** Awards are given based on need.

Funds Avail.: No specific amount. **Duration:** Annual. **To Apply:** Applicant must submit a completed scholarship application form along with a copy of recent transcript; expected Family Contribution (EFC) from Student Aid Report (SAR), which comes as a result of filing the FAFSA; and a copy of Financial Aid Award Letter from the chosen college to be attended. **Deadline:** April 30.

3005 ■ Bob and Linda Kohlhepp Scholarships
(Undergraduate/Scholarship)

Purpose: To help students from Greater Cincinnati area to achieve the dream of a college education. **Focus:** General studies/Field of study not specified. **Qualif.:** Applicant must be a resident of Greater Cincinnati and attending college as a full-time student. **Criteria:** Awards are given based on need.

Funds Avail.: No specific amount. **Duration:** Annual. **To**

Awards are arranged alphabetically below their administering organizations

Apply: Applicant must submit a completed scholarship application form along with a copy of recent transcript; expected Family Contribution (EFC) from Student Aid Report (SAR), which comes as a result of filing the FAFSA; and a copy of Financial Aid Award Letter from the chosen college to be attended. **Deadline:** April 30.

3006 ■ Carl H. Lindner Family Scholarships
(Undergraduate/Scholarship)

Purpose: To help students from Greater Cincinnati area to achieve the dream of a college education. **Focus:** General studies/Field of study not specified. **Qualif.:** Applicant must be a resident of Greater Cincinnati and attending college as a full-time student. **Criteria:** Awards are given based on need.

Funds Avail.: No specific amount. **Duration:** Annual. **To Apply:** Applicant must submit a completed scholarship application form along with a copy of recent transcript; expected Family Contribution (EFC) from Student Aid Report (SAR), which comes as a result of filing the FAFSA; and a copy of Financial Aid Award Letter from the chosen college to be attended. **Deadline:** April 30.

3007 ■ Corwin Nixon Scholarships *(Undergraduate/Scholarship)*

Purpose: To support students from Greater Cincinnati area to pursue a college education. **Focus:** General studies/Field of study not specified. **Qualif.:** Applicant must be a student residing in the 84th Ohio Congressional District pursuing a degree in the medical field and with a proven financial need. **Criteria:** Awards are given based on need.

Funds Avail.: No specific amount. **To Apply:** Applicant must submit a completed scholarship application form along with a copy of recent transcript; expected Family Contribution (EFC) from Student Aid Report (SAR), which comes as a result of filing the FAFSA; and a copy of Financial Aid Award Letter from the chosen college to be attended. **Deadline:** April 30.

3008 ■ CSF Charles and Claire Phillips Scholarships *(Undergraduate/Scholarship)*

Purpose: To help students from Greater Cincinnati area to achieve their dream of a college education. **Focus:** General studies/Field of study not specified. **Qualif.:** Applicant must be a resident of Greater Cincinnati and attending college as a full-time student. **Criteria:** Awards are given based on need.

Funds Avail.: No specific amount. **To Apply:** Applicant must submit a completed scholarship application form along with a copy of recent transcript; expected Family Contribution (EFC) from Student Aid Report (SAR), which comes as a result of filing the FAFSA; and a copy of Financial Aid Award Letter from the chosen college to be attended. **Deadline:** April 30. **Remarks:** Faxed applications will not be considered. **Contact:** Cincinnati Scholarship Foundation; Phone: 513-345-6701; Fax: 513-345-6705; E-mail: info@cincinnatischolarshipfoundation.org.

3009 ■ Marvin Rammelsberg Scholarships
(Undergraduate/Scholarship)

Purpose: To help students of Greater Cincinnati area achieve a college education. **Focus:** General studies/Field of study not specified. **Qualif.:** Applicant must be a graduate of Cincinnati Public Schools attending Morehead State University. **Criteria:** Awards are given based on need.

Funds Avail.: No specific amount. **Duration:** Annual. **To Apply:** Applicant must submit a completed scholarship application form along with a copy of recent transcript; expected Family Contribution (EFC) from Student Aid Report (SAR), which comes as a result of filing the FAFSA; and a copy of Financial Aid Award Letter from the chosen college to be attended. **Deadline:** April 30.

3010 ■ Robert H. Reakirt Scholarships
(Undergraduate/Scholarship)

Purpose: To help students from Greater Cincinnati area to achieve the dream of a college education. **Focus:** General studies/Field of study not specified. **Qualif.:** Applicant must be a resident of Greater Cincinnati and attending college as a full-time student. **Criteria:** Awards are given based on need.

Funds Avail.: No specific amount. **Duration:** Annual. **To Apply:** Applicant must submit a completed scholarship application form along with a copy of recent transcript; expected Family Contribution (EFC) from Student Aid Report (SAR), which comes as a result of filing the FAFSA; and a copy of Financial Aid Award Letter from the chosen college to be attended. **Deadline:** April 30.

3011 ■ William J. Rielly/MCURC Scholarships
(Undergraduate/Scholarship)

Purpose: To help students from Greater Cincinnati area to achieve the dream of a college education. **Focus:** General studies/Field of study not specified. **Qualif.:** Applicant must be a resident of Greater Cincinnati and attending college as a full-time student. **Criteria:** Awards are given based on need.

Funds Avail.: No specific amount. **Duration:** Annual. **To Apply:** Applicant must submit a completed scholarship application form along with a copy of recent transcript; expected Family Contribution (EFC) from Student Aid Report (SAR), which comes as a result of filing the FAFSA; and a copy of Financial Aid Award Letter from the chosen college to be attended. **Deadline:** April 30.

3012 ■ Mary Roberts Scholarships *(Undergraduate/Scholarship)*

Purpose: To help students of Greater Cincinnati area achieve a college education. **Focus:** General studies/Field of study not specified. **Qualif.:** Applicant must be a resident of Greater Cincinnati; must be a student majoring in Nursing. **Criteria:** Awards are given based on need.

Funds Avail.: No specific amount. **Duration:** Annual. **To Apply:** Applicant must submit a completed scholarship application form along with a copy of recent transcript; expected Family Contribution (EFC) from Student Aid Report (SAR), which comes as a result of filing the FAFSA; and a copy of Financial Aid Award Letter from the chosen college to be attended. **Deadline:** April 30.

3013 ■ S.C. Johnson, A Family Company Scholarships *(Undergraduate/Scholarship)*

Purpose: To help students from Greater Cincinnati area to achieve the dream of a college education. **Focus:** General studies/Field of study not specified. **Qualif.:** Applicant must be a resident of Greater Cincinnati and attending college as a full-time student. **Criteria:** Awards are given based on need.

Funds Avail.: No specific amount. **Duration:** Annual. **To Apply:** Applicant must submit a completed scholarship application form along with a copy of recent transcript; expected Family Contribution (EFC) from Student Aid

Awards are arranged alphabetically below their administering organizations

Report (SAR), which comes as a result of filing the FAFSA; and a copy of Financial Aid Award Letter from the chosen college to be attended. **Deadline:** April 30.

3014 ■ CSF Charlotte R. Schmidlapp Scholarships *(Undergraduate/Scholarship)*

Purpose: To support students from Greater Cincinnati area to pursue a college education. **Focus:** General studies/Field of study not specified. **Qualif.:** Applicant must be a resident of Greater Cincinnati and attending college as a full-time student. **Criteria:** Awards are given based on need.

Funds Avail.: No specific amount. **To Apply:** Applicant must submit a completed scholarship application form along with a copy of recent transcript; expected Family Contribution (EFC) from Student Aid Report (SAR), which comes as a result of filing the FAFSA; and a copy of Financial Aid Award Letter from the chosen college to be attended. **Deadline:** April 30.

3015 ■ Nelson Schwab Jr. Scholarships *(Undergraduate/Scholarship)*

Purpose: To help students from Greater Cincinnati area to achieve the dream of a college education. **Focus:** General studies/Field of study not specified. **Qualif.:** Applicant must be a resident of Greater Cincinnati and attending college as a full-time student. **Criteria:** Awards are given based on need.

Funds Avail.: No specific amount. **Duration:** Annual. **To Apply:** Applicant must submit a completed scholarship application form along with a copy of recent transcript; expected Family Contribution (EFC) from Student Aid Report (SAR), which comes as a result of filing the FAFSA; and a copy of Financial Aid Award Letter from the chosen college to be attended. **Deadline:** April 30.

3016 ■ Judge Benjamin Schwartz Scholarships *(Undergraduate/Scholarship)*

Purpose: To help students from Greater Cincinnati area to achieve the dream of a college education. **Focus:** General studies/Field of study not specified. **Qualif.:** Applicant must be a resident of Greater Cincinnati and attending college as a full-time student. **Criteria:** Awards are given based on need.

Funds Avail.: No specific amount. **Duration:** Annual. **To Apply:** Applicant must submit a completed scholarship application form along with a copy of recent transcript; expected Family Contribution (EFC) from Student Aid Report (SAR), which comes as a result of filing the FAFSA; and a copy of Financial Aid Award Letter from the chosen college to be attended. **Deadline:** April 30.

3017 ■ CSF E.W. Scripps Foundation Scholarship Fund *(Undergraduate/Scholarship)*

Purpose: To help students from Greater Cincinnati area to achieve the dream of a college education. **Focus:** General studies/Field of study not specified. **Qualif.:** Applicants must be high school graduates who reside in Greater Cincinnati and are beginning college in the fall of their graduation. **Criteria:** Selection shall be based on the applicants' proven financial need, and other criteria set by the selection committee.

Funds Avail.: No specific amount. **Duration:** Annual. **To Apply:** Applicant must submit a completed scholarship application form along with a copy of recent transcript; expected Family Contribution (EFC) from Student Aid Report (SAR), which comes as a result of filing the FAFSA; and a copy of Financial Aid Award Letter from the chosen college to be attended. **Deadline:** April 30.

3018 ■ S. David Shor Scholarships *(Undergraduate/Scholarship)*

Purpose: To help students from Greater Cincinnati area to achieve the dream of a college education. **Focus:** General studies/Field of study not specified. **Qualif.:** Applicant must be a resident of Greater Cincinnati and attending college as a full-time student. **Criteria:** Awards are given based on need.

Funds Avail.: No specific amount. **Duration:** Annual. **To Apply:** Applicant must submit a completed scholarship application form along with a copy of recent transcript; expected Family Contribution (EFC) from Student Aid Report (SAR), which comes as a result of filing the FAFSA; and a copy of Financial Aid Award Letter from the chosen college to be attended. **Deadline:** April 30.

3019 ■ Lowe Simpson Scholarships *(Undergraduate/Scholarship)*

Purpose: To help students of Greater Cincinnati area achieve a college education. **Focus:** General studies/Field of study not specified. **Qualif.:** Applicant must be a resident of Greater Cincinnati and attending college as a full-time student. **Criteria:** Awards are given based on need.

Funds Avail.: No specific amount. **Duration:** Annual. **To Apply:** Applicant must submit a completed scholarship application form along with a copy of recent transcript; expected Family Contribution (EFC) from Student Aid Report (SAR), which comes as a result of filing the FAFSA; and a copy of Financial Aid Award Letter from the chosen college to be attended. **Deadline:** April 30.

3020 ■ Frank Foster Skillman Scholarships *(Undergraduate/Scholarship)*

Purpose: To help students from Greater Cincinnati area to achieve the dream of a college education. **Focus:** General studies/Field of study not specified. **Qualif.:** Applicant must be a resident of Greater Cincinnati and attending college as a full-time student. **Criteria:** Awards are given based on need.

Funds Avail.: No specific amount. **Duration:** Annual. **To Apply:** Applicant must submit a completed scholarship application form along with a copy of recent transcript; expected Family Contribution (EFC) from Student Aid Report (SAR), which comes as a result of filing the FAFSA; and a copy of Financial Aid Award Letter from the chosen college to be attended. **Deadline:** April 30.

3021 ■ Joseph S. Stern, Jr. Scholarships *(Undergraduate/Scholarship)*

Purpose: To help students from Greater Cincinnati area to achieve the dream of a college education. **Focus:** General studies/Field of study not specified. **Qualif.:** Applicant must be a resident of Greater Cincinnati and attending college as a full-time student. **Criteria:** Awards are given based on need.

Funds Avail.: No specific amount. **Duration:** Annual. **To Apply:** Applicant must submit a completed scholarship application form along with a copy of recent transcript; expected Family Contribution (EFC) from Student Aid Report (SAR), which comes as a result of filing the FAFSA; and a copy of Financial Aid Award Letter from the chosen college to be attended. **Deadline:** April 30. **Contact:** Cincin-

Awards are arranged alphabetically below their administering organizations

nati Scholarship Foundation; Phone: 513-345-6701; Fax: 513-345-6705; E-mail: info@cincinnatischolarshipfoundation.org.

3022 ■ Martha W. Tanner Memorial Scholarships
(Undergraduate/Scholarship)

Purpose: To help students of Greater Cincinnati area achieve a college education. **Focus:** General studies/Field of study not specified. **Qualif.:** Applicant must be a student of Appalachian descent; resident of Greater Cincinnati and attending college as a full-time student. **Criteria:** Awards are given based on need.

Funds Avail.: No specific amount. **Duration:** Annual. **To Apply:** Applicant must submit a completed scholarship application form along with a copy of recent transcript; expected Family Contribution (EFC) from Student Aid Report (SAR), which comes as a result of filing the FAFSA; and a copy of Financial Aid Award Letter from the chosen college to be attended. **Deadline:** April 30.

3023 ■ CSF Christopher Todd Grant Memorial Scholarships *(Undergraduate/Scholarship)*

Purpose: To support students from Greater Cincinnati area to pursue a college education. **Focus:** General studies/Field of study not specified. **Qualif.:** Applicant must be a graduating senior of a Northern Kentucky high school in defined as Kenton, Boone, and Campbell counties and has played soccer in grade or high school and has proven financial need. **Criteria:** Awards are given based on need.

Funds Avail.: No specific amount. **To Apply:** Applicant must submit a completed scholarship application form along with a copy of recent transcript; expected Family Contribution (EFC) from Student Aid Report (SAR), which comes as a result of filing the FAFSA; and a copy of Financial Aid Award Letter from the chosen college to be attended. **Deadline:** April 30.

3024 ■ Dee Wacksman Scholarships
(Undergraduate/Scholarship)

Purpose: To support students from Greater Cincinnati area to pursue a college education. **Focus:** General studies/Field of study not specified. **Qualif.:** Applicant must be a resident of Greater Cincinnati and attending college as a full-time student majoring in the performing arts. **Criteria:** Awards are given based on need.

Funds Avail.: No specific amount. **To Apply:** Applicant must submit a completed scholarship application form along with a copy of recent transcript; expected Family Contribution (EFC) from Student Aid Report (SAR), which comes as a result of filing the FAFSA; and a copy of Financial Aid Award Letter from the chosen college to be attended. **Deadline:** April 30.

3025 ■ HCRTA/Glen O. and Wyllabeth Wise Scholarships *(Undergraduate/Scholarship)*

Purpose: To help students from Greater Cincinnati area to achieve the dream of a college education. **Focus:** General studies/Field of study not specified. **Qualif.:** Applicant must be a resident of Greater Cincinnati and attending college as a full-time student. **Criteria:** Awards are given based on need.

Funds Avail.: No specific amount. **Duration:** Annual. **To Apply:** Applicant must submit a completed scholarship application form along with a copy of recent transcript; expected Family Contribution (EFC) from Student Aid Report (SAR), which comes as a result of filing the FAFSA; and a copy of Financial Aid Award Letter from the chosen college to be attended. **Deadline:** April 30.

3026 ■ L and T Woolfolk Memorial Scholarships
(Undergraduate/Scholarship)

Purpose: To help students of Greater Cincinnati area achieve a college education. **Focus:** General studies/Field of study not specified. **Qualif.:** Applicant must be a resident of Greater Cincinnati and attending college as a full-time student. **Criteria:** Awards are given based on need.

Funds Avail.: No specific amount. **Duration:** Annual. **To Apply:** Applicant must submit a completed scholarship application form along with a copy of recent transcript; expected Family Contribution (EFC) from Student Aid Report (SAR), which comes as a result of filing the FAFSA; and a copy of Financial Aid Award Letter from the chosen college to be attended. **Deadline:** April 30.

3027 ■ Louis B. Zapoleon Memorial Scholarships
(Undergraduate/Scholarship)

Purpose: To help students of Greater Cincinnati area achieve a college education. **Focus:** General studies/Field of study not specified. **Qualif.:** Applicant must be a resident of Greater Cincinnati and attending college as a full-time student. **Criteria:** Awards are given based on need.

Funds Avail.: No specific amount. **Duration:** Annual. **To Apply:** Applicant must submit a completed scholarship application form along with a copy of recent transcript; expected Family Contribution (EFC) from Student Aid Report (SAR), which comes as a result of filing the FAFSA; and a copy of Financial Aid Award Letter from the chosen college to be attended. **Deadline:** April 30.

3028 ■ Cinestory Foundation
PO Box 661962
Los Angeles, CA 90066
Ph: (323)900-0502
URL: www.cinestory.org

3029 ■ Cinestory Fellowship *(Professional development/Fellowship)*

Purpose: To help writers to advance their craft and career. **Focus:** Screenwriting. **Qualif.:** Applicants must be writers who are members of the Foundation. **Criteria:** Selection will be based on the committee's criteria.

Funds Avail.: No specific amount. **Duration:** Annual. **To Apply:** Interested applicants may reach the Cinestory Foundation for the application process and other details.

3030 ■ Cintas Foundation
c/o Nancy Reisman, Esq., Sec.
Morris & McVeigh
767 3rd Ave., 4th Fl.
New York, NY 10017
URL: www.cintasfoundation.org

3031 ■ Cintas Foundation Fellowships in Architecture *(Professional development/Fellowship)*

Purpose: To encourage the development of artists in architecture. **Focus:** Architecture. **Qualif.:** Applicants must be artists living outside of Cuba; must be Cuban citizens or with direct lineage (having a Cuban parent or grandparent). **Criteria:** Applicants will be evaluated based on submitted materials.

Awards are arranged alphabetically below their administering organizations

Funds Avail.: No specific amount. **Duration:** Annual. **To Apply:** Applicants must submit a completed, original application (completed either in English or Spanish); must prepare two narrative statements, two letters of recommendation and work samples. Acceptable formats are DVDs and CDs accompanied by a corresponding image list. Materials must be accompanied by the work sample form. Limit submission to ten samples. **Deadline:** August 1.

3032 ■ Cintas Foundation Fellowships in Visual Arts *(Professional development/Fellowship)*

Purpose: To encourage the development of artists in visual arts. **Focus:** Visual arts. **Qualif.:** Applicants must be creative artists living outside of Cuba; of Cuban citizens or with direct lineage (having a Cuban parent or grandparent). **Criteria:** Applicants will be evaluated based on submitted materials.

Funds Avail.: No specific amount. **Duration:** Annual. **To Apply:** Applicants must submit an original application (completed either in English or Spanish); must prepare two narrative statements, two letters of recommendation and work samples. Applicants may submit maximum of 10 digital images. Acceptable formats are DVDs and CDs accompanied by a corresponding image list. **Contact:** Eliza Gonzalez, Assistant Registrar and CINTAS Administrator, MDC Museum of Art and Design Freedom Tower at Miami Dade College, 600 Biscayne Blvd. Miami, Florida 33132; Telephone: 305-237-7741; Email: egonza10@mdc.edu.

3033 ■ Brandon Fradd Fellowship *(Professional development/Fellowship)*

Purpose: To encourage the development of artists in music composition. **Focus:** Music. **Qualif.:** Applicants must be creative artists living outside of Cuba; of Cuban citizenship or with direct lineage (having a Cuban parent or grandparent). **Criteria:** Applicants will be evaluated based on submitted materials.

Funds Avail.: No specific amount. **Duration:** Annual. **To Apply:** Applicants must submit an original application (completed either in English or Spanish); must submit two narrative statements, two letters of recommendation and work samples (three to five recordings). Samples should be in DVDs or CDs in MP3 format. **Deadline:** July 1. **Contact:** Eliza Gonzalez, Assistant Registrar and CINTAS Administrator, MDC Museum of Art and Design Freedom Tower at Miami Dade College, 600 Biscayne Blvd. Miami, Florida 33132; Telephone: 305-237-7741; Email: egonza10@mdc.edu.

3034 ■ Circuits & Systems Inc.
59 2nd St.
East Rockaway, NY 11518
Ph: (516)593-4301
URL: www.arlynscales.com

3035 ■ Arlyn Scales Awards for Science and Technology *(Undergraduate/Scholarship)*

Purpose: To promote the education and the future of science and technology in New York state. **Focus:** Computer and information sciences; Engineering; Mathematics and mathematical sciences; Science. **Qualif.:** Applicants must be graduating high school students in New York state who will attend a four-year engineering or related program within the state; must have a minimum GPA of 3.5 on a 4.0 scale; must be majoring in Mathematics or Mathematical Sciences, Science, Engineering, or Computer and Information Sciences; and have a household income of $50,000 or less. **Criteria:** Applicants are selected based on merit and compliance with the application process.

Funds Avail.: $1,000 each. **Number Awarded:** 2. **To Apply:** Applicants must submit the following: completed Common Scholarship Application together with a 500+ word essay describing why they should receive this award; two recommendation letters on official letterhead written within the last six months; official transcript in an official sealed envelope; and copy of their most recent tax form. **Deadline:** July 3 (application); July 24 (all other documentations). **Contact:** leilany@optimum7.com.

3036 ■ Civic Music Association of Milwaukee
2625 S Greeley St., Ste. 3A
Milwaukee, WI 53207
Ph: (414)483-3223
E-mail: info@civicmusicmilwaukee.org
URL: www.civicmusicmilwaukee.org

3037 ■ CMA Private Lesson Program: Instrumental Scholarships for Elementary and Middle School Students *(Undergraduate/Scholarship)*

Purpose: To encourage one or more students who have demonstrated exceptional musical potential but are not presently taking private lessons. **Focus:** Music. **Qualif.:** Applicants must be 4th to 9th grade band and orchestra students who have not yet had the opportunity for private study. **Criteria:** Recipients are selected based on the quality of the audition, musical ability, potential, attitude and reliability, parent's statement describing their commitment and support for the lessons and home practice and student's essay about his/her musical experiences and participation in school music activities.

Funds Avail.: No specific amount. **To Apply:** Applicants must undergo an audition and must prepare an essay about his or her experiences in school music activities. **Deadline:** March 2.

3038 ■ Civil Air Patrol (CAP)
105 S Hansell St., Bldg. 714
Maxwell AFB, AL 36112-6332
Free: 877-227-9142
URL: www.gocivilairpatrol.com
Facebook: www.facebook.com/capnhq/
Twitter: twitter.com/civilairpatrol

3039 ■ Civil Air Patrol Flight Scholarships *(Undergraduate/Scholarship)*

Purpose: To provide academic and flight scholarships to deserving cadets and seniors. **Focus:** Aeronautics; Aviation. **Qualif.:** Applicants must be current CAP members; have earned the Billy Mitchell Award (Cadets only or received a Senior Rating in any specialty track (Seniors only); possess and maintain an academic and discipline standard acceptable to the school; must be enrolled in a full-time course of study during the academic year for which the scholarship is awarded; have not received the scholarship in the past that the applicant is applying for. **Criteria:** Selection will be based on the submitted application.

Funds Avail.: No specific amount. **To Apply:** Applicants may apply online. Selected applicants for scholarships must provide official school transcripts and other supporting documents to validate the information that is provided in

Awards are arranged alphabetically below their administering organizations

the application. **Deadline:** January 15. **Contact:** Questions can be addressed to strupp@capnhq.gov.

3040 ■ Civitan International (CI)
PO Box 130744
Birmingham, AL 35213-0744
Ph: (205)591-8910
E-mail: civitan@civitan.org
URL: civitan.org
Facebook: www.facebook.com/Civitan.International

3041 ■ Civitan Shropshire Scholarships
(Undergraduate, Vocational/Occupational/Scholarship)

Purpose: To provide financial assistance to students enrolled in undergraduate or graduate studies. **Focus:** General studies/Field of study not specified. **Qualif.:** Applicants must be Civitans (or Civitans' children or grandchildren) and must have been Civitan for at least two years and/or must be or have been Junior Civitans for no less than two years; must be students pursuing careers which help further the ideals and purposes of Civitan International as embodied in its Creed; must be enrolled in a degree or certificate program at an accredited community college, vocational school, four-year college or graduate school. **Criteria:** Recipients are selected based on academic record; professional objectives; civitan involvement; community-service activities; and financial need.

Funds Avail.: $1,000. **Duration:** Annual. **To Apply:** Applicants must submit all required application materials. Junior Civitan candidates must submit a letter of endorsement coming from an advisor or school principal. Applicants must call the Foundation if unable to access their website. **Deadline:** January 31. **Contact:** Lauren Turrigilo at lauren@civitan.org.

3042 ■ Clan Ross America
PO Box 6341
River Forest, IL 60305
E-mail: info@clanross.org
URL: clanross.org

3043 ■ Clan Ross Foundation Scholarships
(Undergraduate/Scholarship)

Purpose: To enhance the knowledge of the youth about Scottish culture. **Focus:** Scottish studies. **Qualif.:** Applicants must be current members of Clan Ross Association of the United States, Inc. for at least a year. Applicants who are also related with the current members of the Association are also welcome to apply. Families or members of the Clan Ross Scholarship Committee are disqualified for the scholarships. **Criteria:** Recipients will be selected based on their keen interests and dedications in studying Scottish culture, accomplishments in the chosen area of study, and academic capability.

Funds Avail.: $1,000 each. **Duration:** One year. **Number Awarded:** 2. **To Apply:** Applicants must write or call the Clan Ross Association for complete information and application form. **Contact:** Virgil Bumann, 1867 Via Acorde, Camarillo, CA 93010.

3044 ■ Claremont McKenna College - Henry Kravis Leadership Institute
850 Columbia Ave.
Claremont, CA 91711-6420
Ph: (909)621-8743
Fax: (909)607-5252
E-mail: kravis.institute@cmc.edu
URL: kravisleadershipinstitute.org

3045 ■ CMC-KLI Leadership Research Fellowship
(Undergraduate/Fellowship)

Purpose: To encourage and support students research on projects related to all areas of leadership. **Focus:** Leadership, Institutional and community. **Qualif.:** Applicants must be a Claremont McKenna College students and have a minimum GPA of 8.5 and be in good standing with the college. **Criteria:** Selections will be based on the following criteria: proposed research must be interesting and relevant to the study of leadership; significant learning will be as a result of the proposed research; proposed research are well-planned and can reasonably be completed in an academic year; methodology are appropriate and well considered.

Funds Avail.: $1,000. **Duration:** Annual. **To Apply:** Applicants must submit the following requirements: online application form; resume; CMC transcript; research proposal; faculty sponsor confirmation. **Deadline:** October 6. **Contact:** Dr. Sherylle J. Tan; 909-607-8136; stan@cmc.edu.

3046 ■ CMC-KLI Social Sector Internship Program
(Undergraduate/Internship)

Purpose: To allow student involvement in the management of the organization. **Focus:** Leadership, Institutional and community. **Qualif.:** Applicants must be Claremont McKenna College students. **Criteria:** Selection will be based on the committees' criteria.

Funds Avail.: $5,000. **Duration:** Annual. **To Apply:** Applicants may contact the CMC Career Services Center for the application process and other information. **Deadline:** March 23.

3047 ■ CMC-KLI Social Sector Research Fellowship
(Undergraduate/Fellowship)

Purpose: To encourage and support students research on projects related to social entrepreneurship and the social sector. **Focus:** Leadership, Institutional and community. **Qualif.:** Applicants must be a Claremont McKenna College students and have a minimum GPA of 8.5 and be in good standing with the college. **Criteria:** Selections will be based on the following criteria: proposed research must be interesting and relevant to the study of leadership; significant learning will be as a result of the proposed research; proposed research are well-planned and can reasonably be completed in an academic year; methodology are appropriate and well considered.

Funds Avail.: $1,000. **Duration:** Annual. **To Apply:** Applicants must submit the following requirements: online application form; resume; CMC transcript; research proposal; faculty sponsor confirmation. **Deadline:** October 6. **Contact:** Dr. Sherylle J. Tan; 909-607-8136; stan@cmc.edu.

3048 ■ Willis W. and Ethel M. Clark Foundation
PO Box 89
Pebble Beach, CA 93953-0089
Ph: (831)625-1175
E-mail: clarkfoundation@redshift.com
URL: www.theclarkfoundation.org

3049 ■ Willis W. and Ethel M. Clark Foundation Fellowships *(Graduate/Fellowship)*

Purpose: To provide financial assistance to deserving students who are attending graduate school or who have

Awards are arranged alphabetically below their administering organizations

been accepted to a graduate school. **Focus:** Public service. **Qualif.:** Applicants must have been born, raised and/or have lived in one of the coastal communities of the Monterey Peninsula (Marina, Sand City, Seaside, Del Rey Oaks, Monterey, Pacific Grove, Pebble Beach, Carmel, Carmel Valley Village, and Big Sur); must be enrolled in an advanced program of study in a field of significant public interest benefit; must have above average academic achievement; have potential to make a significant contribution to society in general and, in particular, the coastal communities of the Monterey Peninsula; must have proven commitment to volunteerism and public service; must have demonstrated passion for community betterment and must be able to document a continuing philosophy toward community service for the area; and have responsible career goals for advancement in the chosen field. **Criteria:** Selection is based on submitted application materials and oral interview.
Funds Avail.: Up to $10,000. **Duration:** Annual; one academic year. **To Apply:** Applicants must submit a completed, typed original plus one copy of the application form together with a resume/curriculum vitae (original plus one copy); a narrative autobiography (original plus one copy, maximum of two pages, double-spaced); statement of community service (original plus one copy, maximum of two pages, double-spaced); career goals (original plus one copy, maximum of one page, double-spaced); official transcripts (original plus one copy); proof of enrollment; and two letters of recommendation. **Deadline:** January 31. **Remarks:** Established in 2002.

3050 ■ Cleveland Leadership Center
One Cleveland Ctr.
1375 E 9th St., Ste. 2430
Cleveland, OH 44114
Ph: (216)592-2400
Fax: (216)621-7733
URL: www.cleveleads.org

3051 ■ Cleveland Executive Fellowships (CEF) *(Other/Fellowship)*
Purpose: To accelerate the professional development of civic leaders for Greater Cleveland. **Focus:** Public affairs. **Qualif.:** Applicants must have significant professional achievements and substantial organizational responsibilities; must have an average of 5-10 years of experience; have a minimum of five years of experience and/or a master's degree. **Criteria:** Selection is based on submitted applications.
Funds Avail.: $40,000. **Duration:** Annual. **Number Awarded:** Varies. **To Apply:** Applicants must submit a completed application electronically. Application requires: two copies of completed application form, including written essays; two copies of a professional-quality resume (maximum of 2 pages); three letters of recommendation; and official academic transcripts for all higher education institutions attended. **Contact:** hbelsito@cleveleads.org.

3052 ■ Clinic for the Rehabilitation of Wildlife (CROW)
3883 Sanibel Captiva Rd.
Sanibel, FL 33957
Ph: (239)472-3644
Fax: (239)472-8544
E-mail: info@crowclinic.org
URL: crowclinic.org

3053 ■ CROW Fellowships *(All/Fellowship)*
Purpose: To provide individuals with a thorough understanding of the rehabilitation process for injured and orphaned wildlife on the Gulf Coast of Southwest Florida. **Focus:** Wildlife conservation, management, and science. **Qualif.:** Applicants must be interested in wildlife rehabilitation and medicine, and must have the pre-exposure rabies vaccine prior to beginning employment. **Criteria:** Selection shall be based on the applicants' promptness, positive attitude, willingness to work long hours, and good communication skills.
Funds Avail.: $250 bi-weekly stipend. **Duration:** Semiannual. **To Apply:** Applicants must contact the clinic for the application information.

3054 ■ Clinical Nurse Specialist Foundation
801 E Park Dr., Ste. 100
Harrisburg, PA 17111
Ph: (717)703-0033
Fax: (717)234-6798
E-mail: deb@pronursingresources.com
URL: www.cns-foundation.org

3055 ■ Jan Bingle Scholarships *(Master's, Doctorate/Scholarship)*
Purpose: To increase the number of CNSs who are educated and prepared and thus, address the shortage of CNSs in the United States. **Focus:** Nursing. **Qualif.:** Applicants must be students who are pursuing a master's degree in an accredited CNS program or Clinical Nurse Specialists pursuing a research or practice doctorate. **Criteria:** Scholarship is competitive and is based on academic performance, clinical excellence, and demonstrated leadership.
Funds Avail.: $1,000. **To Apply:** Applicants must complete and submit their application and must attach the following documents: documentation of admission as a student in a CNS master's or DNP program, or a CNS DNP or PhD program; documentation of current active student status by registrar, faculty member or dean; a current official transcript provided by a Registrar or by an academic advisor that confirms their current minimum cumulative GPA of 3.0 or higher; evidence of outstanding achievement in CNS course work in their specialty by recommendation of two program faculty; evidence of past or present (five years preceding entry into the academic program) leadership activity related to nursing; evidence of experiences resulting in improvement or positive change with other cultures, minority groups and/or vulnerable populations; evidence of professional citizenship as exemplified in local, state, national initiative to improve nursing or health care. **Deadline:** January 31.

3056 ■ Katie Brush Memorial Scholarships *(Master's, Doctorate/Scholarship)*
Purpose: To increase the number of CNSs who are educated and prepared and thus, address the shortage of CNSs in the United States. **Focus:** Nursing. **Qualif.:** Applicants must be students who are pursuing a master's degree in an accredited CNS program or Clinical Nurse Specialists pursuing a research or practice doctorate. **Criteria:** Scholarship is competitive and is based on academic performance, clinical excellence, and demonstrated leadership.

Awards are arranged alphabetically below their administering organizations

Funds Avail.: $1,000. **To Apply:** Applicants must complete and submit their application and must attach the following documents: documentation of admission as a student in a CNS master's or DNP program, or a CNS DNP or PhD program; documentation of current active student status by registrar, faculty member or dean; a current official transcript provided by a Registrar or by an academic advisor that confirms their current minimum cumulative GPA of 3.0 or higher; evidence of study in the field of acute or critical care nursing specialty by recommendation of two program faculty; evidence of clinical competence in the area of critical care; evidence of leadership abilities/activity in the area of critical care. **Deadline:** January 31.

3057 ■ Christine Filipovich Scholarships *(Master's, Doctorate/Scholarship)*

Purpose: To increase the number of CNSs who are educated and prepared and thus, address the shortage of CNSs in the United States. **Focus:** Nursing. **Qualif.:** Applicants must be students who are pursuing a master's degree in an accredited CNS program or Clinical Nurse Specialists pursuing a research or practice doctorate. **Criteria:** Scholarship is competitive and is based on academic performance, clinical excellence, and demonstrated leadership.

Funds Avail.: $500 each. **Number Awarded:** 2. **To Apply:** Applicants must complete and submit their application and must attach the following documents: documentation of admission as a student in a CNS master's or DNP program, or a CNS DNP or PhD program; documentation of current active student status by registrar, faculty member or dean; a current official transcript provided by a Registrar or by an academic advisor that confirms their current minimum cumulative GPA of 3.0 or higher; current curriculum vitae and description of their background/expertise related to the project; letter from the current employer. Applicants applying for funds to support research related to CNS outcomes must attach the following: overview of the project, abstract and timeline; letters of support; proposed budget; plans for dissemination of findings; IRB review documentation or anticipated date of IRB review. Applicants applying to support health policy activities must attach a description of intended use of funds and a description of expected outcome or how they will use the project. **Deadline:** January 31.

3058 ■ Lippincott Williams and Wilkins Scholarships *(Master's, Doctorate/Scholarship)*

Purpose: To increase the number of CNSs who are educated and prepared and thus, address the shortage of CNSs in the United States. **Focus:** Nursing. **Qualif.:** Applicants must be students who are pursuing a master's degree in an accredited CNS program or Clinical Nurse Specialists pursuing a research or practice doctorate. **Criteria:** Scholarship is competitive and is based on academic performance, clinical excellence, and demonstrated leadership.

Funds Avail.: No specific amount. **To Apply:** Applicants must complete and submit their application and must attach the following documents: documentation of admission as a student in a CNS master's or DNP program, or a CNS DNP or PhD program; documentation of current active student status by registrar, faculty member or dean; a current official transcript provided by a Registrar or by an academic advisor that confirms their current minimum cumulative GPA of 3.0 or higher; evidence of outstanding achievement in CNS course work in their specialty by recommendation of two program faculty; evidence of past or present (five years preceding entry into the academic program) leadership activity related to nursing; evidence of experiences resulting in improvement or positive change with other cultures, minority groups and/or vulnerable populations; evidence of professional citizenship as exemplified in local, state, national initiative to improve nursing or health care.

3059 ■ Club Managers Association of America (CMAA)
1733 King St.
Alexandria, VA 22314
Ph: (703)739-9500
Fax: (703)739-0124
URL: www.cmaa.org

3060 ■ The Club Foundation Faculty Research Grants *(Professional development/Grant)*

Purpose: To support research that is significant to the club management industry. **Focus:** Management. **Qualif.:** Applicants must be university faculty members. **Criteria:** Candidates are evaluated by The Club Foundation Allocation Committee (CFAC) using the following criteria: a) problem conceptualization; b) research technique; c) contribution to the field; d) clarity and thoroughness; e) project budget.

Funds Avail.: Up to $2,500. **Number Awarded:** 2-4. **To Apply:** Applicants must download application form from the CMAA website. The application, narrative and other required attachments must be typed using 12-point font and one-inch margins. **Deadline:** November 1.

3061 ■ CMAA Student Conference Travel Grants *(Undergraduate/Grant)*

Purpose: To help student chapters offset the costs associated with attending the CMAA World Conference on Club Management. **Focus:** Management. **Qualif.:** Applicants must be student chapters of CMAA. **Criteria:** Recipients will be selected based on the quality of application material submitted.

Funds Avail.: No specific amount. **Duration:** Annual. **To Apply:** Applicant student chapters must hold a fundraising event; submit a president's annual report; submit the current chapter budget; submit an application for the grant; and submit a grantee form stipulating that funds will be used for its intended purpose.

3062 ■ Willmoore H. Kendall Scholarships *(Professional development/Scholarship)*

Purpose: To provide tuition support to assist club managers interested in pursuing the Certified Club Manager (CCM) designation. **Focus:** Management. **Qualif.:** Candidate must be a CMAA member; an assistant manager; currently pursuing the CMMA designation; have at least one remaining BMI course to complete; must be nominated by their chapter. **Criteria:** Applicants who are recommended by The Club Foundation Allocation Committee and approved by The Club Foundation Board of Governors will be given preference.

Funds Avail.: No specific amount. **Duration:** Annual. **To Apply:** Applicant must submit an official application form and must provide the following materials: a letter provided by the applicant's chapter supporting his/her application and must be signed by a chapter officer; a letter of recommendation from a member and the general manager of the applicant's club; a resume; a 500-1000 words addressing the following components: a) a detailed description of the applicant's career objectives and goals; b) detail the reason(s) he/she wished to pursue the CCM designation; c) what his/her specific interests within the private club management field; d) a characteristic of Mr. Kendall's with which the applicant identifies and the reason why.

3063 ■ Joe Perdue Scholarships (Undergraduate/Scholarship)

Purpose: To support and enhance the life cycle of a club managers professional development, beginning at the university level and building throughout their career. **Focus:** Management. **Qualif.:** Candidates must be pursuing managerial careers in the private club industry; must have completed their freshman year of college and be enrolled for the full academic year in an accredited four-year institution; and must have achieved and maintained a grade point average of at least 2.5 on a 4.0 scale, or 4.5 on a 6.0 scale. **Criteria:** Applicants who are CMAA student chapter members are given additional points.

Funds Avail.: No specific amount. **Duration:** Annual. **To Apply:** Candidates must submit an official application available online; a sealed copy of official college transcripts; a recommendation form and recommendation letter from a faculty advisor/professor and a private club industry professional; a resume; and a 500-1000 words addressing the following components: 1) the applicant's career objectives and goals; 2) the characteristics he/she possesses that will enable him/her to succeed as a club manager; 3) his/her perception of CMAA and the private club industry; 4) specific interests within the private club management field; 5) why the applicant feel that he/she should be a Club Foundation Scholarship recipient.

3064 ■ Clubs of America
484 Wegner Rd.
Lakemoor, IL 60051
Ph: (815)363-4000
URL: www.greatclubs.com

3065 ■ The Clubs of America Scholarships Award for Career Success (Undergraduate/Scholarship)

Purpose: To help students consider their aspirations as well as ease the burden of the costs of higher education. **Focus:** General studies/Field of study not specified. **Qualif.:** Applicants must be current college students enrolled in any accredited U.S. college or university with a cumulative GPA of at least 3.0 **Criteria:** Selection will be based on the scholarship committee's criteria.

Funds Avail.: $1,000. **Duration:** Annual. **Number Awarded:** 1. **To Apply:** Applicants must submit an essay of no fewer than 600 words about their career aspirations and how their current course load will help them achieve success in their careers; where do the applicants see themselves 10 years from now? Thinking outside the box is encouraged. Essay must be submitted as a .doc or .pdf attachment via email. Youtube submissions are optional, although not required. Video should be no longer than 5 minutes. **Deadline:** August 31. **Contact:** scholarship@greatclubs.com.

3066 ■ COACH: Canada's Health Informatics Association
250 Consumers Rd., Ste. 301
Toronto, ON, Canada M2J 4V6
Ph: (416)494-9324
Fax: (416)495-8723
Free: 888-253-8554
E-mail: info@coachorg.com
URL: www.coachorg.com

3067 ■ Steven Huesing Scholarships (Graduate, Undergraduate/Scholarship)

Purpose: To encourage health education by providing financial assistance for post-secondary education. **Focus:** Health education. **Qualif.:** Applicants must be enrolled in a health informatics or related program at an accredited post-secondary institution; and must demonstrate active involvement and achievement in health informatics. **Criteria:** Recipients will be selected based on academic standing and potential contribution to advance Health Informatics.

Funds Avail.: $1,000. **Duration:** One year. **To Apply:** Applicants must submit a transcript of records and an assessment from academic advisor; must have proof of enrollment in a recognized Canadian post-secondary institution and current attendance in a health informatics and related program; must prepare a (500-word) description of their involvement and achievements in health informatics. **Remarks:** Established in 1999 in recognition of Founding President Steven Huesing's contribution to COACH.

3068 ■ Coaching Association of Canada (CAC)
1155 Lola St., Ste. 201
Ottawa, ON, Canada K1K 4C1
Ph: (613)235-5000
Fax: (613)235-9500
URL: www.coach.ca
Facebook: www.facebook.com/coach.ca
Twitter: twitter.com/CAC_ACE

3069 ■ Women in Coaching National Coaching Institute Scholarships (Undergraduate/Scholarship)

Purpose: To financially assist women attending one of the seven National Coaching Institutes in Canada. **Focus:** General studies/Field of study not specified. **Qualif.:** Applicants must be Canadian citizens or landed immigrants currently coaching Canadian athletes; must be certified NCCP level 3; and must be accepted in a full-time or part-time diploma program at one of the seven National Coaching Institutes across Canada. **Criteria:** Recipients will be selected based on submitted application form and supporting documents.

Funds Avail.: Varies. **Duration:** Annual. **To Apply:** Applicants must contact Ms. Sheilagh Croxon for application form and needed materials. **Deadline:** August 19.

3070 ■ Coalition of Higher Education Assistance Organizations (COHEAO)
1101 Vermont Ave. NW, Ste. 400
Washington, DC 20005-3521
Ph: (202)289-3910
Fax: (202)371-0197
URL: www.coheao.com
Twitter: twitter.com/COHEAO

3071 ■ COHEAO Scholarships (Undergraduate/Scholarship)

Purpose: To provide financial assistance to those students who are in need. **Focus:** General studies/Field of study not

Awards are arranged alphabetically below their administering organizations

specified. **Qualif.:** Applicants must be U.S citizens; must attend a COHEAO member school; must have a minimum GPA of 3.75 on a 4.0 scale. Only undergraduate students who are entering their sophomore, junior or senior year are eligible to apply; freshmen and graduate students are not eligible. **Criteria:** Preference will be given to those students who meet the criteria.

Funds Avail.: $1,000. **Duration:** Annual. **Number Awarded:** Up to 4. **To Apply:** Applicants must submit the following: completed application form; essay/testimonial response(s); academic recommendation letter; sealed official copy of transcript. **Deadline:** April 1. **Contact:** Wes Huffman at whuffman@wpllc.net.

3072 ■ Coalition for Networked Information (CNI)
21 Dupont Cir., Ste. 800
Washington, DC 20036
Ph: (202)296-5098
Fax: (202)872-0884
URL: www.cni.org
Facebook: www.facebook.com/cni.org
Twitter: twitter.com/cni_org

3073 ■ Paul Evan Peters Fellowship (Master's, Doctorate/Fellowship)

Purpose: To support and assist students pursuing graduate studies in the information sciences, librarianship, or closely related field, that advance the frontiers of digital information and technology. **Focus:** Information science and technology; Library and archival sciences. **Qualif.:** Applicant must be entering or enrolled in a master's or doctoral program in information science or librarianship at an accredited U.S. university, or a program that has received American Library Association (ALA) accreditation (including reciprocal), or one that is a member of the iSchools iCaucus. Students in other, closely related disciplines may also be considered, provided that the course of study relates directly to information management/studies; must be a U.S. citizen or permanent resident of the United States. **Criteria:** Applicants will be judged on how well they meet the academic and personal standards for the award, not on financial need.

Funds Avail.: $5,000 for doctoral; $2,500 for master's. **Duration:** Biennial. **Number Awarded:** 2. **To Apply:** The application process will be posted to the CNI-ANNOUNCE listserv and CNI News feed. Completed applications must include the following: a completed form, which includes space for a 300-500-word essay explaining the applicants' qualification, intellectual interests, and academic and career objectives. The essay must include a discussion of how applicants will advance scholarship in digital information and technology and apply their knowledge to problems of scholarship, intellectual productivity, or public life; a curriculum vitae or resume that includes the applicants' complete contact information (address, phone number and email); two letters of recommendation from faculty members, work supervisors or others who can comment on the applicants' academic and personal qualifications for the fellowship. These letters must be sent by email directly from the recommenders' email accounts; a copy of students' letter of acceptance into a university graduate program in information science or librarianship, or closely related field; proof of US citizenship or permanent residency; official transcript may also be requested, if applicants have already completed courses toward the graduate degree.

3074 ■ Coast Guard Foundation
394 Taugwonk Rd.
Stonington, CT 06378
Ph: (860)535-0786
Fax: (860)535-0944
E-mail: info@cgfdn.org
URL: www.coastguardfoundation.org
Facebook: www.facebook.com/coastguardfoundation

3075 ■ Commander Ronald J. Cantin Scholarships (Undergraduate/Scholarship)

Purpose: To support Coast Guard enlisted personnel and their dependents. **Focus:** General studies/Field of study not specified. **Qualif.:** Applicants must be dependent children of enlisted men and women of the US Coast Guard on active duty, retired or deceased and dependent children of enlisted personnel in the Coast Guard Reserve currently on extended active duty 180 days or more. **Criteria:** Selection will be based on scholastic promise, motivation, moral character, leadership qualities and good citizenship.

Funds Avail.: $2,500. **Duration:** Annual. **To Apply:** Applicants must submit an application package which includes: completed foundation scholarship application form; student's college entrance scores; letter of recommendation from a school official where the student is currently attending high school, or college transcript signed by school official; letter to the president of the selection committee; letter of acceptance from the college or vocational school the student plans to attend; and completed Foundation financial statement. Application packages should include originals plus five copies of all original materials, with the exception of official transcripts which are to remain sealed. **Deadline:** March 15. **Contact:** Commandant (G-1112), 2100 2nd St., SW, STOP 7902 Washington, DC 20593-7902.

3076 ■ Commander Daniel J. Christovich Scholarship Fund (Undergraduate/Scholarship)

Purpose: To provide support to Coast Guard personnel and to their family in aiming higher education. **Focus:** General studies/Field of study not specified. **Qualif.:** Applicants must be dependent children of enlisted men and women of the US Coast Guard on active duty, retired or deceased and dependent children of enlisted personnel in the Coast Guard Reserve currently on extended active duty 180 days or more. **Criteria:** Selection will be based on scholastic promise, motivation, moral character, leadership qualities and good citizenship.

Funds Avail.: $2,500. **Duration:** Annual. **To Apply:** Applicants must submit an application package which includes: completed foundation scholarship application form; student's college entrance scores; letter of recommendation from a school official where the student is currently attending high school, or college transcript signed by school official; letter to the president of the selection committee; letter of acceptance from the college or vocational school the student plans to attend; and completed Foundation financial statement. Application packages should include originals plus five copies of all original materials, with the exception of official transcripts which are to remain sealed. **Deadline:** March 15. **Contact:** Commandant (G-1112), 2100 2nd St., SW, STOP 7902 Washington, DC 20593-7902.

3077 ■ Clay Maitland CGF Scholarship (Undergraduate/Scholarship)

Purpose: To provide support to Coast Guard personnel and to their family in aiming higher education. **Focus:**

General studies/Field of study not specified. **Qualif.:** Applicants must be dependent children of enlisted men and women of the US Coast Guard on active duty, retired or deceased and dependent children of enlisted personnel in the Coast Guard Reserve currently on extended active duty 180 days or more. **Criteria:** Selection will be based on scholastic promise, motivation, moral character, leadership qualities and good citizenship.

Funds Avail.: $5,000. **Duration:** Annual; Renewable for up to four consecutive years. **To Apply:** Applicants must submit an application package which includes: completed foundation scholarship application form; student's college entrance scores; letter of recommendation from a school official where the student is currently attending high school, or college transcript signed by school official; letter to the president of the selection committee; letter of acceptance from the college or vocational school the student plans to attend; and completed Foundation financial statement. Application packages should include originals plus five copies of all original materials, with the exception of official transcripts which are to remain sealed. **Deadline:** March 15. **Contact:** Commandant (G-1112), 2100 2nd St., SW, STOP 7902 Washington, DC 20593-7902.

3078 ■ Coast Guard Foundation Enlisted Education Grants (Advanced Professional/Grant)

Purpose: To provide support to Coast Guard personnel and to their family in aiming higher education. **Focus:** General studies/Field of study not specified. **Qualif.:** Applicants must be active enlisted personnel in pay grades E-3 to E-9 with two or more years of Coast Guard service. **Criteria:** Selection will be based on scholastic promise, motivation, moral character, leadership qualities and good citizenship.

Funds Avail.: No specific amount. **Duration:** Annual. **To Apply:** Applicants should complete the application form 1560/10a, available through the Coast Guard Institute. **Remarks:** Established in 1999. **Contact:** Commandant (G-1112), 2100 2nd St., SW, STOP 7902 Washington, DC 20593-7902.

3079 ■ The Fallen Heroes Scholarships (Undergraduate/Scholarship)

Purpose: To provide support to Coast Guard personnel and to their family in aiming higher education. **Focus:** General studies/Field of study not specified. **Qualif.:** Applicants must be CG dependent children of enlisted AND commissioned officers **Criteria:** Selection will be based on scholastic promise, motivation, moral character, leadership qualities and good citizenship.

Funds Avail.: No specific amount. **Duration:** Annual. **To Apply:** Applicants must submit a completed foundation application form; college entrance scores; letter of recommendation from high school official or college transcript signed by college official; applicant letter to the president of the selection committee; letter of acceptance from the college the student plans to attend; and Foundation financial statement. **Deadline:** March 15. **Contact:** Commandant (G-1112), 2100 2nd St., SW, STOP 7902 Washington, DC 20593-7902.

3080 ■ Captain Ernest Fox Perpetual Scholarships (Undergraduate/Scholarship)

Purpose: To provide support to Coast Guard personnel and to their family in aiming higher education. **Focus:** General studies/Field of study not specified. **Qualif.:** Applicants must be employees of Aircraft Repair and Supply Center (active duty, federal civil service and their dependents). **Criteria:** Selection will be based on scholastic promise, motivation, moral character, leadership qualities and good citizenship.

Funds Avail.: $1,000. **Duration:** Annual; One year. **To Apply:** Applicants must submit an original and five copies of the application package to Aircraft Repair and Supply Center. **Contact:** Commandant (G-1112), 2100 2nd St., SW, STOP 7902 Washington, DC 20593-7902.

3081 ■ Arnold Sobel Scholarships (Undergraduate/Scholarship)

Purpose: To provide support to Coast Guard personnel and to their family in aiming higher education. **Focus:** General studies/Field of study not specified. **Qualif.:** Applicants must be dependent children of enlisted men and women of the US Coast Guard on active duty, retired or deceased and dependent children of enlisted personnel in the Coast Guard Reserve currently on extended active duty 180 days or more. **Criteria:** Selection will be based on scholastic promise, motivation, moral character, leadership qualities and good citizenship.

Funds Avail.: $5,000. **Duration:** Annual. **To Apply:** Applicants must submit an application package which includes: completed foundation scholarship application form; student's college entrance scores; letter of recommendation from a school official where the student is currently attending high school, or college transcript signed by school official; letter to the president of the selection committee; letter of acceptance from the college or vocational school the student plans to attend; and completed Foundation financial statement. Application packages should include originals plus five copies of all original materials, with the exception of official transcripts which are to remain sealed. **Deadline:** March 15. **Contact:** Commandant (G-1112), 2100 2nd St., SW, STOP 7902 Washington, DC 20593-7902.

3082 ■ The Vander Putten Family Scholarships (Advanced Professional/Scholarship)

Purpose: To assist active duty and reserve Coast Guard personnel with their educational expenses. **Focus:** General studies/Field of study not specified. **Qualif.:** Applicants must be active enlisted personnel in pay grades E-3 to E-9 with two or more years of Coast Guard service. **Criteria:** Selection will be based on scholastic promise, motivation, moral character, leadership qualities and good citizenship.

Funds Avail.: Up to $500. **To Apply:** Applicants should complete the application form 1560/10a, available through the Coast Guard Institute.

3083 ■ Coastal Bend Community Foundation (CBCF)

615 N Upper Broadway Ste. 1950
Corpus Christi, TX 78401
Ph: (361)882-9745
Fax: (361)882-2865
URL: www.cbcfoundation.org

3084 ■ Alejandro "Alex" Abecia Reaching High Scholarships (Undergraduate/Scholarship)

Purpose: To provide resources for educational opportunities including vocational schools, two and four-year universities. **Focus:** General studies/Field of study not specified. **Qualif.:** Applicants must be senior members of the Mary Caroll High School Band or graduating senior

Awards are arranged alphabetically below their administering organizations

members of the Mary Caroll High School soccer team; must be members of the A/B Honor Roll; must have taken honor classes in high school and maintained a course load of at least 12 hours per semester. **Criteria:** Applicants are evaluated based on merit.

Funds Avail.: $100. **Number Awarded:** 4. **To Apply:** Interested applicants may contact the Foundation for the application process and other information. **Contact:** Karen Wesson, Director of Scholarships; Phone 361-882-9745; Email: kwesson@cbcfoundation.org.

3085 ■ Allen - Marty Allen Scholarships
(Undergraduate/Scholarship)

Purpose: To provide financial assistance to students who are majoring in Music. **Focus:** Music. **Qualif.:** Applicants must be a graduating senior or current college student with a permanent residence in the CBCF seven-county area; must be a music major; must be enrolled full time at an accredited college or university; must maintain a GPA of 2.5 on a 4.0 scale. **Criteria:** Applicants who are jazz musicians will be given preference.

Funds Avail.: $225. **To Apply:** Interested applicants may contact the Foundation for the application process and other information. **Contact:** Karen Wesson, Director of Scholarships; Phone 361-882-9745; Email: kwesson@cbcfoundation.org.

3086 ■ Zachary Barriger Memorial Scholarships
(Undergraduate/Scholarship)

Purpose: To provide financial assistance to high school seniors who are planning to pursue a career in computer/electrical engineering. **Focus:** Engineering, Computer; Engineering, Electrical. **Qualif.:** Applicants must be seniors at Tuloso-Midway High School; must be attending an accredited two- or four-year college in Texas; must maintain a GPA of 2.75 on a 4.0 scale. **Criteria:** Applicants are evaluated based on merit. Preference will be given to jazz musicians.

Funds Avail.: $1,500. **To Apply:** Applicants must complete and submit the application and other required materials. **Contact:** Karen Wesson, Director of Scholarships; Phone 361-882-9745; Email: kwesson@cbcfoundation.org.

3087 ■ O.J. Beck, Jr. Memorial Scholarships
(Undergraduate/Scholarship)

Purpose: To provide educational assistance to students who are seeking a bachelor's degree in building construction. **Focus:** Construction. **Qualif.:** Applicants must be graduating high school seniors or current college students planning to or currently pursuing a bachelor of science degree in building construction; must be permanent residence in the area served by the South Texas Chapter of Associated General Contractors (22 counties); must attend any accredited four year college or university. **Criteria:** Recipients will be selected based on financial need.

Funds Avail.: $2,000. **To Apply:** Interested applicants may contact the Foundation for the application process and other information. **Contact:** South Texas Associated General Contractors; Phone: 361-289-0996.

3088 ■ Reverend E.F. Bennett Scholarships
(Undergraduate/Scholarship)

Purpose: To provide financial support to graduating seniors from a Coastal Bend high school. **Focus:** General studies/Field of study not specified. **Qualif.:** Applicants must be: graduating seniors from a CBCF seven-county area high school; in the top 10% of their graduating class; attending Del Mar College, Texas A&M University-Corpus Christi or Texas A&M University-Kingsville. **Criteria:** Applicants will be evaluated based on financial need.

Funds Avail.: $850. **To Apply:** Interested applicants may contact the Foundation for the application process and other information. **Contact:** Karen Wesson, Director of Scholarships; Phone 361-882-9745; Email: kwesson@cbcfoundation.org.

3089 ■ Marion Luna Brem/Pat McNeil Health and Education Scholarships *(Undergraduate/Scholarship)*

Purpose: To provide financial assistance to teenage parents in Coastal Bend to pursue a college education while raising and supporting their children. **Focus:** General studies/Field of study not specified. **Qualif.:** Applicants must: attended high school in Coastal Bend; have a high school diploma or GED certification and a minimum GPA of 2.5; must attend Coastal Bend College, Del Mar College, Texas A&M University-Corpus Christi or Texas A&M University-Kingsville; must maintain a 2.0 GPA on a 4.0 scale and a minimum of 9 credit hours per semester. **Criteria:** Applicants are evaluated based on academic achievement and financial need.

Funds Avail.: $1,000. **Duration:** Annual. **Number Awarded:** 2. **To Apply:** Applicants must submit all the required application information. **Deadline:** March 1. **Contact:** Karen Wesson, Director of Scholarships; Phone: 361-882-9745; E-mail: kwesson@cbcfoundation.org.

3090 ■ D.C. and Virginia Brown Scholarships
(Undergraduate/Scholarship)

Purpose: To provide financial assistance to students in need. **Focus:** General studies/Field of study not specified. **Qualif.:** Applicants must be graduates or current students of Mathis High School who have earned their GED certificate and who have good potential and character; must maintain a course load of 12 semester hours and a 2.5 GPA on a 4.0 scale. **Criteria:** Applicants will be evaluated based on academic merit and personal attributes.

Funds Avail.: $4,000 for four-year college student; $2,200 for two-year and trade school student; $1,000 for handicapped student. **Number Awarded:** 4. **To Apply:** Interested applicants may contact the Foundation for the application process and other information. **Contact:** Karen Wesson, Director of Scholarships; Phone 361-882-9745; Email: kwesson@cbcfoundation.org.

3091 ■ Cecil E. Burney Scholarships
(Undergraduate/Scholarship)

Purpose: To provide financial assistance to high school seniors or graduates of a Coastal Bend high school in furthering their college education. **Focus:** Education; History; Liberal arts; Music; Political science. **Qualif.:** Applicants must be a graduating senior or current college student who graduated from a high school in the CBCF seven-county area; must maintain a GPA of 3.0 on a 4.0 scale; attend an accredited college or university in the United States of America and be enrolled full-time. **Criteria:** Applicants are evaluated based on academic performance.

Funds Avail.: $2,000. **Number Awarded:** 1. **To Apply:** Interested applicants may contact the Foundation for the application process and other information. **Deadline:** March 1. **Contact:** Karen Wesson, Director of Scholarships; Phone: 361-882-9745; E-mail: kwesson@cbcfoundation.org.

Awards are arranged alphabetically below their administering organizations

COASTAL BEND COMMUNITY FOUNDATION

3092 ■ C.C.H.R.M.A. Scholarships *(Undergraduate/Scholarship)*

Purpose: To assist students majoring in business with an interest in human resources. **Focus:** Business; Personnel administration/human resources. **Qualif.:** Applicants must be residents and college students enrolled full-time in the Coastal Bend seven-county service area universities, including University of the Incarnate Word online courses; must maintain a 3.0 GPA on a 4.0 scale. **Criteria:** Applicants will be evaluated based on academic achievement and financial need.

Funds Avail.: $700. **Number Awarded:** 1. **To Apply:** Applicants must submit a complete application form, including a one page essay on "Why I am interested in Human Management?" and college transcript.

3093 ■ Justin Forrest Cox "Beat the Odds" Memorial Scholarships *(Undergraduate/Scholarship)*

Purpose: To provide educational support to students who are in need. **Focus:** General studies/Field of study not specified. **Qualif.:** Applicants must be students who graduated from a Victoria ISD high School; must have a "C" average or better; must be pursuing a four-year baccalaureate degree; must complete at least 12 credit hours per semester; must overcome a significant difficulty in graduating from high school and have maintained a 2.5 GPA. **Criteria:** Applicants will be evaluated based on academic achievement and financial need.

Funds Avail.: $2,500. **Number Awarded:** 1. **To Apply:** Interested applicants may contact the Foundation for the application process and other information. **Deadline:** April 1. **Contact:** Karen Wesson, Director of Scholarships; Phone 361-882-9745; Email: kwesson@cbcfoundation.org.

3094 ■ Derek Lee Dean Soccer Scholarships *(Undergraduate/Scholarship)*

Purpose: To assist outstanding high school students of W.B. Ray High School who have a passion for soccer. **Focus:** General studies/Field of study not specified. **Qualif.:** Applicants must be members of the soccer team who exhibit love for soccer, teamwork and sportsmanship. **Criteria:** Applicants are evaluated based on academic achievement and personal involvement in the sport.

Funds Avail.: $1,000. **Number Awarded:** 2. **To Apply:** Interested applicants may contact the Foundation for the application process and other information. **Deadline:** April 1. **Contact:** Karen Wesson, Director of Scholarships; Phone 361-882-9745; Email: kwesson@cbcfoundation.org.

3095 ■ Jay and Rheba Downes Memorial Scholarships *(Undergraduate/Scholarship)*

Purpose: To provide financial assistance to students who are pursuing college. **Focus:** General studies/Field of study not specified. **Qualif.:** Applicants must be graduating Alice High School seniors who lettered in UIL-sanctioned golf for at least two years; have an overall high school GPA of "B" or better; participated in extracurricular activities other than athletics; have high ideals, and spirit of good conduct and sportsmanship benefiting the "Fighting Alice Coyote"; must attend a four-year college or university, register for at least 12 hours of classes and maintain a minimum college GPA of 2.5 on 4.0 scale. **Criteria:** Applicants are evaluated based on academic achievement and financial need.

Funds Avail.: $1,500. **Number Awarded:** 1. **To Apply:** Applicants must be nominated by the athletic director and head golf coach at Alice High School. Interested applicants may contact the Foundation for the application process and other information. **Contact:** Karen Wesson, Director of Scholarships; Phone 361-882-9745; Email: kwesson@cbcfoundation.org.

3096 ■ John R. Eidson Jr., Scholarships *(Undergraduate/Scholarship)*

Purpose: To provide financial assistance to Coastal Bend students who intend to study engineering in college. **Focus:** Engineering. **Qualif.:** Applicants must be students (sophomore year or more) attending Texas A & M University - College Station; graduate of high school in one of seven counties served by CBCF; majoring in Engineering; must have participated in professional and social societies; and maintained full-time status and a GPA of 3.0 higher. **Criteria:** Recipients are selected based on financial need. Preference given to students of Asian or Eastern Indian heritage.

Funds Avail.: $1,000. **Number Awarded:** 1. **To Apply:** Applicants must obtain application form from the financial aid office at Texas A&M University in College Station. **Contact:** Karen Wesson, Director of Scholarships; Phone: 361-882-9745; E-mail: kwesson@cbcfoundation.org.

3097 ■ Barney Flynn Memorial Scholarships *(Undergraduate/Scholarship)*

Purpose: To provide financial assistance to graduating seniors of Corpus Christi, Flour Bluff or Tuloso-Midway ISD high schools in furthering their education. **Focus:** General studies/Field of study not specified. **Qualif.:** Applicants must be graduating seniors from any high school in CCISD, Tuloso-Midway or Flour Bluff; must be currently active, with a high performance level and achievement level in band; and must be enrolled full-time at any accredited college or university. **Criteria:** Applicants will be evaluated based on merit.

Funds Avail.: $1,000. **Number Awarded:** 1. **To Apply:** Interested applicants may contact the Foundation for the application process and other information. **Deadline:** March 1. **Contact:** Karen Wesson, Director of Scholarships; Phone: 361-882-9745; E-mail: kwesson@cbcfoundation.org.

3098 ■ Melissa Ann Guerra Scholarships *(Undergraduate/Scholarship)*

Purpose: To provide educational assistance to senior students of Mary Caroll High School. **Focus:** General studies/Field of study not specified. **Qualif.:** Applicants must be Mary Caroll High School seniors; must attend a publicly state-funded college or university in Texas; and maintain a minimum of a 3.0 GPA and 12 credit hours per semester. Applicants must demonstrate financial need. **Criteria:** Applicants are evaluated based on academic performance. Preference will be given to students who are Tigerette Drill team members and/or members of the National Honor Society, those who plan to study pre-law, education or nursing, and those attending Del Mar College or TAMUCC.

Funds Avail.: $1,000. **Number Awarded:** 1. **To Apply:** Interested applicants may contact the Foundation for the application process and other information. Applications are also available in the Mary Caroll High School counselor's office. **Deadline:** March 1. **Contact:** Karen Wesson, Director of Scholarships; Phone: 361-882-9745; E-mail: kwesson@cbcfoundation.org.

Awards are arranged alphabetically below their administering organizations

3099 ■ Manuel Hernandez, Jr. Foundation Scholarships *(Undergraduate/Scholarship)*

Purpose: To provide students the financial assistance they need. **Focus:** General studies/Field of study not specified. **Qualif.:** Applicants must be graduating seniors of Roy Miller High School; must have been accepted at an accredited college or university; minimum GPA of 80% on a 100% scale. **Criteria:** Applicants will be evaluated based on financial need.

Funds Avail.: $1,000. **To Apply:** Interested applicants may contact the Foundation for the application process and other information. Applications may be downloaded from the Foundation website or obtained from the Roy Miller High School Counselor's office together with an essay titled "Keeping these United States Free and Peace with the World". **Contact:** Karen Wesson, Director of Scholarships; Phone 361-882-9745; Email: kwesson@cbcfoundation.org.

3100 ■ A. Joseph Huerta "Puedo" Scholarships *(Undergraduate/Scholarship)*

Purpose: To provide financial assistance to students who pursue education in college. **Focus:** General studies/Field of study not specified. **Qualif.:** Applicants must be a graduating seniors from Carroll, Collegiate, King, Moody, Miller or WB Ray high schools in Corpus Christi, Texas; must be enrolled as full-time college students (at least 12 semester credits) at a four-year accredited college or university; and must maintain a course load of at least 12 college credits per semester and a GPA of 3.0 or higher. **Criteria:** Applicants are evaluated based on academic achievement and financial need.

Funds Avail.: $5,000-$5,000. **Duration:** Annual. **Number Awarded:** 12. **To Apply:** Interested applicants may contact the Foundation for the application process and other information. **Contact:** Karen Wesson, Director of Scholarships; Phone 361-882-9745; Email: kwesson@cbcfoundation.org.

3101 ■ Casey Laine Armed Forces Scholarships *(Undergraduate/Scholarship)*

Purpose: To assist students who are seeking financial resources to further their college education. **Focus:** General studies/Field of study not specified. **Qualif.:** Applicants must graduate in top 50% of the class from any high school in the CBCF seven-county service area; maintain a GPA of 2.5 and enrolled in at least 12 hours per semester; must be graduating seniors or current graduates from a Coastal Bend high school, or dependent of a member or honorably discharged veterans of the armed services, or R.O.T.C. members (high school seniors must agree to join an R.O.T.C. program upon entering college). **Criteria:** Applicants are evaluated based on academic performance. Preference will be given to an applicant residing in a single parent home, where parent is not remarried, and female if all other criteria are met (ROTC/veteran and single parent).

Funds Avail.: $800 (paid $200/year over 4 years). **To Apply:** Interested applicants may contact the Foundation for the application process and other information. **Contact:** Karen Wesson, Director of Scholarships; Phone 361-882-9745; Email: kwesson@cbcfoundation.org.

3102 ■ Sue Kay Lay Memorial Scholarships *(Undergraduate/Scholarship)*

Purpose: To assist high school seniors seeking financial resources to further their education. **Focus:** General studies/Field of study not specified. **Qualif.:** Applicants must be graduating seniors from any high school in the CBCF seven-county service area; must be enrolled in college full-time (12 hours or more); must have high school GPA of 3.0 on a 4.0 scale; and maintain a permanent residence in the Coastal Bend. **Criteria:** Applicants are evaluated based on financial need.

Funds Avail.: $6,000. **To Apply:** Interested applicants may contact the Foundation for the application process and other information. **Contact:** Karen Wesson, Director of Scholarships; Phone 361-882-9745; Email: kwesson@cbcfoundation.org.

3103 ■ Brian and Colleen Miller Math and Science Scholarships *(Undergraduate/Scholarship)*

Purpose: To provide financial assistance to students who needs college education. **Focus:** General studies/Field of study not specified. **Qualif.:** Applicants must be graduating high school seniors in the CBCF seven-county service area; must attend any accredited four-year college or university; must be resident of the CBCF service area. **Criteria:** Applicants will be evaluated based on financial need. Preference will be given to applicants taking AP Math and Science courses, and involved in extracurricular math and science competitions, groups and events.

Funds Avail.: $500. **To Apply:** Applicants must submit completed application form along with the documentation of participation and/or awards in the areas of mathematics and/or science. **Contact:** Karen Wesson, Director of Scholarships; Phone 361-882-9745; Email: kwesson@cbcfoundation.org.

3104 ■ J.J. Rains Memorial Scholarships *(Undergraduate/Scholarship)*

Purpose: To provide financial assistance to senior students for their college education. **Focus:** General studies/Field of study not specified. **Qualif.:** Applicants must be graduating CCISD high school seniors with preference for students who have participated in speech or debate; have a cumulative high school GPA of 2.5; must maintain a cumulative college GPA of 2.5 on a 4.0 scale and enroll in a minimum of 12 semester hours. **Criteria:** Applicants are evaluated based on academic achievement and financial need.

Funds Avail.: $1,000. **To Apply:** Applicants must submit all the required application information. **Contact:** Karen Wesson, Director of Scholarships; Phone 361-882-9745; Email: kwesson@cbcfoundation.org.

3105 ■ W.B. Ray HS Class of '56 Averill Johnson Scholarships *(Undergraduate/Scholarship)*

Purpose: To provide financial assistance to graduating seniors of W.B. Ray High School. **Focus:** General studies/Field of study not specified. **Qualif.:** Applicants must be W.B. Ray high school seniors; enrolled as full-time (12 semester hours) students in an accredited college or university in the United States in the fall semester following graduation with a minimum GPA of 90% on a 100% scale. **Criteria:** Recipients are selected based on academic achievement and financial need.

Funds Avail.: $1,000. **To Apply:** Interested applicants may contact the Foundation for the application process and other information. **Contact:** Karen Wesson, Director of Scholarships; Phone 361-882-9745; Email: kwesson@cbcfoundation.org.

3106 ■ Rotary Club of Corpus Christi Scholarships *(Undergraduate/Scholarship)*

Purpose: To support the advancement of higher education in the immediate Corpus Christi area. **Focus:** General studies/Field of study not specified. **Qualif.:** Applicants must be graduating high school seniors from any high school within the city limits of Corpus Christi, Texas; must be enrolled full time at Del Mar College or Texas A&M - Corpus Christi; and must maintain a minimum GPA of 2.0 on a 4.0 scale for renewal of scholarship. **Criteria:** Applicants are evaluated based on financial need.

Funds Avail.: $3,000. **To Apply:** Interested applicants may contact the Foundation for the application process and other information. **Contact:** Karen Wesson, Director of Scholarships; Phone 361-882-9745; Email: kwesson@cbcfoundation.org.

3107 ■ Kevin Saunders Wheelchair Success Scholarships (Undergraduate/Scholarship)

Purpose: To provide an opportunity for people permanently confined to a wheelchair to attend college or technical school. **Focus:** General studies/Field of study not specified. **Qualif.:** Applicants must be graduating seniors or current college students who are permanent residents of the CBCF seven-county service area; permanently confined to a wheelchair or have a family member who is confined to a wheelchair, and be involved in sports competition and activities necessary for success in competition. **Criteria:** Applicants will be evaluated based on scholastic performance and financial need.

Funds Avail.: $500. **To Apply:** Interested applicants may contact the Foundation for the application process and other information. **Contact:** Karen Wesson, Director of Scholarships; Phone 361-882-9745; Email: kwesson@cbcfoundation.org.

3108 ■ Seaman Family Scholarships (Undergraduate/Scholarship)

Purpose: To provide financial assistance for Coastal Bend students who are home-schooled and need financial aid. **Focus:** General studies/Field of study not specified. **Qualif.:** Applicants must be a graduating home-schooled seniors or returning recipients from the CBCF seven-county service area or Calhoun County, Texas; must be a member in the Home Schoolers Association; be enrolled full-time at an accredited college or university. **Criteria:** Applicants are judged on the basis of academic performance and financial need. Preference will be given to first time applicants.

Funds Avail.: $1,000. **To Apply:** Interested applicants may contact the Foundation for the application process and other information. **Contact:** Karen Wesson, Director of Scholarships; Phone 361-882-9745; Email: kwesson@cbcfoundation.org.

3109 ■ Judge Terry Shamsie Scholarships (Undergraduate/Scholarship)

Purpose: To provide financial support to students with their post-secondary school education. **Focus:** General studies/Field of study not specified. **Qualif.:** Applicants must be graduating high school seniors from: Banquete High School, Robstown High School, or Nueces or Kleberg counties, attending Texas A&M Corpus Christi or Texas A&M Kingsville; must have a GPA of 3.0 on a 4.0 scale. Applicants may also be graduating high school seniors from any high school in the seven-county service area, majoring in economics or agriculture at any accredited college or university with a minimum GPA of 3.5 on a 4.0 scale. Applicants must be permanent residents in the CBCF seven-county service area. **Criteria:** Applicants will be evaluated based on academic achievement and financial need.

Funds Avail.: $1,000. **Number Awarded:** 4. **To Apply:** Interested applicants may contact the Foundation for the application process and other information. **Contact:** Karen Wesson, Director of Scholarships; Phone 361-882-9745; Email: kwesson@cbcfoundation.org.

3110 ■ Jim Springer Memorial Scholarships (Undergraduate/Scholarship)

Purpose: To provide financial assistance to further the education of deserving students in Coastal Bend. **Focus:** Advertising; Marketing and distribution; Public relations. **Qualif.:** Applicants must be Coastal Bend residents; full-time college sophomore, junior or senior students with grade point average of 2.5; majoring in public relations, marketing, advertising or communications. **Criteria:** Applicants are evaluated based on academic performance and financial need.

Funds Avail.: $500. **To Apply:** Applicants must submit all the required application information. **Contact:** Karen Wesson, Director of Scholarships; Phone 361-882-9745; Email: kwesson@cbcfoundation.org.

3111 ■ Talbert Family Memorial Scholarships (Undergraduate/Scholarship)

Purpose: To provide financial support to deserving students who are studying accounting. **Focus:** Accounting. **Qualif.:** Applicants must be full-time college juniors majoring in accounting or financial management at a Texas college with 3.0 grade point average; must be graduates from a Coastal Bend high school and permanently residents of Coastal Bend. **Criteria:** Applicants must submit all the required application information.

Funds Avail.: $4,000. **To Apply:** Interested applicants may contact the Foundation for the application process and other information. **Contact:** Karen Wesson, Director of Scholarships; Phone 361-882-9745; Email: kwesson@cbcfoundation.org.

3112 ■ Faye and Rendell Webb Scholarships (Undergraduate/Scholarship)

Purpose: To provide financial assistance to students who are in need. **Focus:** Education. **Qualif.:** Applicants must be students graduated from Miller or Moody high schools, with preference for students who attended Los Encinos, Lamar or Lozano elementary schools for at least one year; must be education majors who are attending college in the state of Texas; must be students who have an average of 85 percent or better or maintain 3.0 GPA on 4.0 scale and complete at least 12 credits per semester. **Criteria:** Applicants will be evaluated based on academic achievement and financial need.

Funds Avail.: $1,000. **To Apply:** Interested applicants may contact the Foundation for the application process and other information. **Contact:** Karen Wesson, Director of Scholarships; Phone 361-882-9745; Email: kwesson@cbcfoundation.org.

3113 ■ Dr. Dana Williams Scholarships (Undergraduate/Scholarship)

Purpose: To provide educational assistance to students planning to become teachers or public school administrators. **Focus:** Education. **Qualif.:** Applicants must be graduating high school seniors from any high school in the CCISD, with preference for permanent residents of Nueces County and education majors pursuing a teaching certificate. Applicants must maintain a GPA of 3.0 in a 4.0 scale. **Criteria:** Applicants will be judged based on financial need.

Awards are arranged alphabetically below their administering organizations

Funds Avail.: $4,000. **To Apply:** Interested applicants may contact the Foundation for the application process and other information. **Contact:** Karen Wesson, Director of Scholarships; Phone 361-882-9745; Email: kwesson@cbcfoundation.org.

3114 ■ Coca-Cola Scholars Foundation
PO Box 442
Atlanta, GA 30301
Ph: (404)733-5420
Free: 800-306-2653
E-mail: scholars@coca-cola.com
URL: www.coca-colascholars.org

3115 ■ Coca-Cola Scholars Program Scholarships *(Undergraduate/Scholarship)*

Purpose: To provide scholarships to high school seniors for them to pursue higher education. **Focus:** General studies/Field of study not specified. **Qualif.:** Applicants must be: current high school (or home-schooled) seniors attending school in the United States (or select DoD schools); U.S. Citizens; U.S. Nationals; U.S. Permanent Residents; Refugees; Asylees; Cuban-Haitian Entrants; or Humanitarian Parolees; anticipating completion of high school diploma at the time of application; planning to pursue a degree at an accredited U.S. post-secondary institution; and, carrying a minimum 3.00 GPA at the end of their junior year of high school. **Criteria:** Selection will be based on the committee's criteria.

Funds Avail.: $20,000. **Duration:** Annual. **Number Awarded:** Varies. **To Apply:** Applicants may apply online and must complete all parts of the application process. **Deadline:** October 31.

3116 ■ The Coleopterists Society (CS)
c/o Insect Biodiversity Lab
South Dakota State University
Box 2207A, SAG 361
Brookings, SD 57007
Ph: (605)688-4438
Fax: (605)688-4602
E-mail: coleopsoctreas@gmail.com
URL: www.coleopsoc.org
Facebook: www.facebook.com/coleopterists.society
Twitter: twitter.com/coleopsoc

3117 ■ Coleopterists Society - Youth Incentive Award *(Undergraduate/Award)*

Purpose: To provide encouragement and assistance to young beetle enthusiasts (grades 7-12). **Focus:** Education. **Qualif.:** Applicants must be grades 7-12. **Criteria:** Selection will be based on the committees' criteria.

Funds Avail.: up to $300. **Duration:** Annual. **Number Awarded:** 2. **To Apply:** Applicants may contact the Coleopterists Society for the application process and other information. **Deadline:** September 1.

3118 ■ College Art Association (CAA)
50 Broadway, 21st Fl.
New York, NY 10004
Ph: (212)691-1051
Fax: (212)627-2381
E-mail: nyoffice@collegeart.org
URL: www.collegeart.org
Facebook: www.facebook.com/collegeartassociation

3119 ■ College Art Association Wyeth Publication Grants *(Other/Grant)*

Purpose: To support book-length, scholarly manuscripts in the history of American art. **Focus:** History, American; Publishing; Visual arts. **Qualif.:** Applicants must be publishers of book-length scholarly manuscripts in the history of American art, visual studies, and related subjects that have been accepted by the publishers on their merits but cannot be published in the most desirable form without a subsidy. **Criteria:** Selection will be based on the qualifications and compliance with the application process.

Funds Avail.: No specific amount. **Duration:** Annual. **To Apply:** Applicants must submit a curriculum vitae, narrative description, authors' response to peer reviews, publishers' cover letter, partial manuscript and two or more peer reviews of the manuscript that have been submitted to the publishers. **Deadline:** September 15. **Remarks:** Established in 2005. **Contact:** Sarah Zabrodski, CAA editorial manager; Email: szabrodski@collegeart.org.

3120 ■ College of Healthcare Information Management Executives (CHIME)
710 Avis Dr., Ste. 200
Ann Arbor, MI 48108
Ph: (734)665-0000
Fax: (734)665-4922
E-mail: staff@chimecentral.org
URL: chimecentral.org
Facebook: www.facebook.com/CIOCHIME
Twitter: twitter.com/CIOCHIME

3121 ■ John Glaser Scholarships *(Undergraduate/Scholarship)*

Purpose: To acknowledge IT staff members who show potential for advancement to a CIO and who are dedicated to professional development. **Focus:** Health care services. **Qualif.:** Candidates must be employed and nominated by a current CHIME member. **Criteria:** Recipients are selected based on Committee's review of the CIO potential and dedication to professional development.

Funds Avail.: $3,000. **Duration:** One year. **Number Awarded:** 2. **To Apply:** Applicants must provide resume; and (500 to 1,000-word) essay describing: visions and goals; handling their responsibilities; financial challenges that prohibit them to participate in leadership development activities; and benefits they can get to the program they choose to attend. Applicant's direct supervisor is required to complete the questions on the application. **Deadline:** August 16. **Contact:** Application form and materials should be mailed to CHIME Scholarship Committee at the above address.

3122 ■ College Reading and Learning Association (CRLA)
7044 S 13th St.
Oak Creek, WI 53154
Ph: (414)908-4961
E-mail: customercare@crla.net
URL: www.crla.net
Facebook: www.facebook.com/

Awards are arranged alphabetically below their administering organizations

CollegeReadingAndLearningAssoc
LinkedIn: www.linkedin.com/groups/8108376/profile
Twitter: www.twitter.com/CRLApd

3123 ■ Cengage Travel Award for Teachers of Reading at a Community College *(Professional development/Monetary)*

Purpose: To support a member who seeks professional development. **Focus:** Education; Reading. **Qualif.:** Applicant must be a CRLA member teaching reading at a community college who seeks professional development through participation in the annual CRLA conference.
Funds Avail.: $500. **Duration:** Annual. **Deadline:** August 1.

3124 ■ College Success Foundation (CSF)
1605 NW Sammamish Rd., Ste. 200
Issaquah, WA 98027-5388
Ph: (425)416-2000
Fax: (425)416-2001
Free: 877-655-4097
URL: www.collegesuccessfoundation.org

3125 ■ College Success Foundation Chateau Ste. Michelle Scholarship Fund *(Undergraduate/Scholarship)*

Purpose: To provide financial support for underserved students who would like to obtain four-year college degree. **Focus:** General studies/Field of study not specified. **Qualif.:** Applicants must have plan to attend, or currently attending an eligible four-year college or university in Washington State; must be residents of Washington; must have plan to file or have already filed a FAFSA, if eligible; must have 2.75 cumulative GPA; and be enrolled full-time (12 credits per quarter or equivalent for semester) as college students. **Criteria:** Recipients will be selected based on submitted materials.
Funds Avail.: No specific amount. **Duration:** Four years. **Number Awarded:** Varies. **To Apply:** Applicants must complete the application form and contact CSF for further information. **Remarks:** Established in 2001.

3126 ■ College Success Foundation Leadership 1000 Scholarships *(Undergraduate/Scholarship)*

Purpose: To provide college scholarships to deserving students who need assistance attending an eligible four-year college or university in Washington State. **Focus:** General studies/Field of study not specified. **Qualif.:** Applicants must have plan to attend, or currently attending an eligible four-year college or university in Washington State; must be enrolled in a full-time basis; must be Washington State residents; must have plan to file or have already filed a FAFSA, if eligible; must have 2.75 cumulative GPA. **Criteria:** Recipients will be selected based on submitted materials.
Funds Avail.: $2,500 to $5,000. **Duration:** Annual. **To Apply:** Applicants must complete the application form and must contact CSF office for other required materials. **Deadline:** February 24.

3127 ■ College Success Foundation Realize the Dream Scholarships *(Undergraduate/Scholarship)*

Purpose: To support high school undergraduates who do not qualify for federal and state financial aid programs, but who do qualify for resident student status for state tuition and fees. **Focus:** General studies/Field of study not specified. **Qualif.:** Applicants must be undocumented residents of the United States and therefore do not qualify to apply for federal or state financial aid programs; must receive their high school diploma from a Washington State High School; must have 2.0 or higher high school GPA; must have plan to enroll in a college in full-time and complete an associate's and/or bachelor's degree at an eligible Washington educational institution; must be eligible to file the HB 1079 affidavit with public colleges and universities in order to permit them to quality for tuition rates that Washington State residents pay; and must have family size and income level that meets the program requirements. **Criteria:** Recipients will be evaluated based on GPA, cost of attendance, financial aid and scholarships awarded at the college or university to be attended.
Funds Avail.: $5,000 each. **Duration:** One year. **Number Awarded:** Around 100. **To Apply:** Applicants must submit a completed application form. **Deadline:** June 18.

3128 ■ College Success Foundation Washington State Governors' Scholarship for Foster Youth *(Undergraduate/Scholarship)*

Purpose: To help young men and women who are currently in an open dependency court order in Washington State, or an open dependency tribal court order, continue their education and earn a college degree. **Focus:** General studies/Field of study not specified. **Qualif.:** Applicants must be Washington State High School seniors and on track to graduate from high school; must have cumulative GPA of 2.0 or higher; must have plan to enroll in a college on a full-time basis; must have resided in Washington State for at least three academic years prior to high school graduation; must be currently in an open dependency court order that resulted from intervention by Washington State on their behalf and have been placed in any of the following living situations: a) foster care; b) dependency guardianship; and c) guardianship. **Criteria:** Applicants will be selected based on eligibility and submitted materials.
Funds Avail.: $2,000 (two-year community colleges); $3,000 (four-year public colleges and universities); $4,000 (independent college and universities). **Duration:** Five years. **Number Awarded:** Varies. **To Apply:** Applicants must contact CSF office for further information.

3129 ■ Colombian Education Fund
5-11 47th Ave.
Long Island City, NY 11101
Ph: (347)458-6665
URL: colombianeducationfund.org

3130 ■ Colombian Education Fund Scholarships *(Undergraduate/Scholarship)*

Purpose: To support the education of Colombian-American students. **Focus:** General studies/Field of study not specified. **Qualif.:** Applicants must be graduating high school seniors accepted at a college or university and/or college students in their sophomore year; must be Colombian, of Colombian descent or have a strong interest in helping the Colombian community. **Criteria:** Selection will be based on the following considerations: application; financial need; and personal statements.
Funds Avail.: $2,000 each. **Number Awarded:** 5. **To Apply:** Applicants must complete the following materials: application form; official transcript; a statement of financial

Awards are arranged alphabetically below their administering organizations

need describing their financial situation and their family, eligibility for financial aid, employment, health and other issues; a personal statement that explains what makes them the perfect candidates including their involvement with the immigrant community and plan to give back to the Columbian community when they accomplish their professional goals, their commitment to community advancement, any obstacles they have faced in their educational career and what this scholarship would mean to them; one letter of recommendation to be emailed as an attachment with applicants name in the subject line. **Deadline:** March 31. **Contact:** Kimberly Rodriguez, Director of Educational Programs, at kimberly.colef@gmail.com.

3131 ■ Colorado Association of Stormwater and Floodplain Managers (CASFM)
c/o Shea Thomas, Chairperson
Urban Drainage & Flood Control District
2480 W 26th Ave., Ste. 156B
Denver, CO 80211
Ph: (303)455-6277
URL: www.casfm.org

3132 ■ CASFM-Ben Urbonas Scholarships
(Graduate/Scholarship)

Purpose: To promote interest among students and the engineering community in CASFM and to promote the goals of the organization. **Focus:** Atmospheric science; Hydrology; Meteorology. **Qualif.:** Applicants must be U.S. citizens enrolled in a graduate program closely related to CASFM's goals at a College or University in the State of Colorado and be registered to take at least three credit-hours of coursework per semester. Eligible programs of study include, but are not limited to hydrology, hydraulics, watershed management, floodplain management, stormwater management, stormwater quality, emergency response, meteorology and climatology. **Criteria:** Selection will be based on the evaluation of applications and specific criteria.

Funds Avail.: $2,500. **Duration:** Annual. **To Apply:** Applicants must submit a completed application form; a short essay (up to 500 words) describing personal and career goals. **Deadline:** October 16. **Remarks:** Established in 2002.

3133 ■ Colorado Broadcasters Association (CBA)
333 W Hampden Ave., Ste. 400
Englewood, CO 80110
Ph: (720)536-5427
Fax: (720)536-5259
E-mail: CBA@ColoradoBroadcasters.org
URL: www.coloradobroadcasters.org

3134 ■ Broadcast Education and Development Program *(Other/Scholarship)*

Purpose: To foster continual development of Colorado's radio and television workforce. **Focus:** Broadcasting. **Qualif.:** Applicants must be full-time employees of a Colorado broadcast station; must have been employed by that station for a minimum of one year; and the station must be a member in good standing of the CBA. Applicants must be residents of Colorado, as defined by the Colorado Commission of Higher Education. **Criteria:** Award will be on a first-come, first-served basis until funds are depleted.

Funds Avail.: $10,000. **Duration:** Annual. **To Apply:** Applicants must visit the CBA website to download the application form. Applications must be submitted using the official CBA Continuing Education Scholarship form and must be accompanied by the indicated attachments. **Deadline:** June 30. **Contact:** Colorado Broadcasters Association, at the above address or Email: CBA@ColoradoBroadcasters.org.

3135 ■ Colorado Christian University Alumni Association
8787 W Alameda Ave.
Lakewood, CO 80226
Ph: (303)963-3330
Free: 800-44F-AITH
E-mail: alumni@ccu.edu
URL: www.ccu.edu/alumni

3136 ■ CCU Alumni Endowed Scholarships
(Undergraduate/Scholarship)

Purpose: To assist students with the cost of post-secondary education. **Focus:** General studies/Field of study not specified. **Qualif.:** Applicant must be pursuing a baccalaureate degree; completed at least 85 credits, with a minimum of 24 credits earned at CCU; have a GPA of 3.3 or above; demonstrated the need of financial assistance; shows local church or community involvement; and have an alumni sponsor. **Criteria:** Selection is based on merit.

Funds Avail.: No specific amount. **Duration:** Annual. **To Apply:** Applicants may contact the Alumni Relations for more details on the scholarship.

3137 ■ Colorado Hotel and Lodging Association (CH&LA)
4700 S Syracuse St., Ste. 410
Denver, CO 80237-3023
Ph: (303)297-8335
Fax: (303)297-8104
E-mail: info@chla.com
URL: www.coloradolodging.com
Facebook: www.facebook.com/coloradohotelandlodging
Twitter: twitter.com/coloradolodging

3138 ■ Karl Mehlmann Scholarships *(Undergraduate/Scholarship)*

Purpose: To support students pursuing degrees in the hospitality and tourism industry. **Focus:** Culinary arts. **Qualif.:** Applicants must be enrolled in an accredited four-year university or college and be majoring in hotel and/or restaurant management; must also be enrolled in the final year at the Culinary Institute of America; must be freshmen, sophomores, juniors or seniors who are going to graduate school; must carry a minimum workload of 12 hours per quarter or semester; must have maintain a minimum overall GPA of 3.0 on a 4.0 scale; must be U.S. citizens. **Criteria:** Recipients are selected based on the grammar and spelling of the essay.

Funds Avail.: $8,000. **To Apply:** Applicants must submit one official transcript from current school or most recent if not currently attending school; must submit a brief autobiography; a one-page, typewritten essay answering why you've selected the hospitality industry for your career and what definition of hospitality is; must submit a type, signed and on letterhead recommendation letter from College or

University; signature from Director/Dean. **Deadline:** April 10.

3139 ■ Colorado Nurses Foundation (CNF)
2851 S Parker Rd., Ste. 250
Aurora, CO 80014
Fax: (303)200-7099
Free: 800-205-6655
E-mail: info@coloradonursesfoundation.com
URL: www.coloradonursesfoundation.com

3140 ■ Roy Anderson Memorial Scholarships *(Graduate, Undergraduate/Scholarship)*

Purpose: To provide scholarships for qualified nursing students from both rural and urban settings. **Focus:** Nursing. **Qualif.:** Applicants must be Colorado residents committed to practicing nursing in Colorado; must be students in an approved Colorado Nursing Program; must have a minimum of 3.25 GPA (for undergraduate applicants) or 3.5 GPA (for graduate applicants); and must have one of the following student statuses: (1) Junior or senior level BSN undergraduate students; (2) RN enrolled in a baccalaureate or higher degree nursing program in a school of nursing; (3) Students in second year of nursing studies in an associate degree in nursing program; (4) RN with master's degree in nursing, currently practicing in Colorado and enrolled in a doctoral program; (5) Students in second or third year of a Doctorate Nursing Practice (DNP) program. **Criteria:** Scholarship application will be rated based on the following: (1) Professional philosophy and goals; (2) Dedication to the improvement of patient care in Colorado; (3) Demonstrated commitment to nursing, critical thinking skills and potential for leadership; (4) Involvement in community and professional organizations; (5) GPA-minimum of 3.25 undergraduate, 3.5 graduate; (6) Financial need; (7) Recommendation of one faculty member; and (8) Employer/Supervisor recommendation.

Funds Avail.: No specific amount. **Duration:** Annual. **Number Awarded:** Varies. **To Apply:** Applicants must submit a cover sheet, financial need statement, resume, recommendation form from Faculty and Employer in a separated sealed envelope, copy of transcript including the last semester grades. Student essay must be no more than three pages, double-spaced in a 12pt. font with 1" each margin. **Contact:** Vicki Carroll; Phone: 970-416-6811; Fax: 970-416-6820; Email: CNFScholarships@aol.com.

3141 ■ Colorado Nurses Foundation Nightingale Scholarships *(Graduate, Undergraduate/Scholarship)*

Purpose: To provide scholarships for qualified nursing students from both rural and urban settings. **Focus:** Nursing. **Qualif.:** Applicants must be Colorado residents committed to practicing nursing in Colorado; must be students in an approved Colorado Nursing Program; must have a minimum of 3.25 GPA (for undergraduate applicants) or 3.5 GPA (for graduate applicants); and must have one of the following student statuses: (1) Junior or senior level BSN undergraduate students; (2) RN enrolled in a baccalaureate or higher degree nursing program in a school of nursing; (3) Students in second year of nursing studies in an associate degree in nursing program; (4) RN with master's degree in nursing, currently practicing in Colorado and enrolled in a doctoral program; (5) Students in second or third year of a Doctorate Nursing Practice (DNP) program. **Criteria:** Scholarship application will be rated based on the following: (1) Professional philosophy and goals; (2) Dedication to the improvement of patient care in Colorado; (3) Demonstrated commitment to nursing, critical thinking skills and potential for leadership; (4) Involvement in community and professional organizations; (5) GPA-minimum of 3.25 undergraduate, 3.5 graduate; (6) Financial need; (7) Recommendation of one faculty member; and (8) Employer/Supervisor recommendation.

Funds Avail.: No specific amount. **Duration:** Annual. **To Apply:** Applicants must submit a cover sheet, financial need statement, resume, recommendation form from Faculty and Employer in a separated sealed envelope, copy of transcript including the last semester grades. Student essay must be no more than three pages, double-spaced in a 12pt. font with 1" each margin. **Contact:** Vicki Carroll; Phone: 970-416-6811; Fax: 970-416-6820; Email: CNFScholarships@aol.com.

3142 ■ Lola Fehr: Nightingale Scholarships *(Graduate, Undergraduate/Scholarship)*

Purpose: To provide scholarships for qualified nursing students from both rural and urban settings. **Focus:** Nursing. **Qualif.:** Applicants must be Colorado residents committed to practicing nursing in Colorado; must be students in an approved Colorado Nursing Program; must have a minimum of 3.25 GPA (for undergraduate applicants) or 3.5 GPA (for graduate applicants); and must have one of the following student statuses: (1) Junior or senior level BSN undergraduate students; (2) RN enrolled in a baccalaureate or higher degree nursing program in a school of nursing; (3) Students in second year of nursing studies in an associate degree in nursing program; (4) RN with master's degree in nursing, currently practicing in Colorado and enrolled in a doctoral program; (5) Students in second or third year of a Doctorate Nursing Practice (DNP) program. **Criteria:** Scholarship application will be rated based on the following: (1) Professional philosophy and goals; (2) Dedication to the improvement of patient care in Colorado; (3) Demonstrated commitment to nursing, critical thinking skills and potential for leadership; (4) Involvement in community and professional organizations; (5) GPA-minimum of 3.25 undergraduate, 3.5 graduate; (6) Financial need; (7) Recommendation of one faculty member; and (8) Employer/Supervisor recommendation.

Funds Avail.: No specific amount. **To Apply:** Applicants must submit a cover sheet, financial need statement, resume, recommendation form from Faculty and Employer in a separated sealed envelope, copy of transcript including the last semester grades. Student essay must be no more than three pages, double-spaced in a 12pt. font with 1" each margin. **Contact:** Vicki Carroll; Phone: 970-416-6811; Fax: 970-416-6820; Email: CNFScholarships@aol.com.

3143 ■ H.M. Muffly Memorial Scholarships *(Graduate, Undergraduate/Scholarship)*

Purpose: To provide scholarships for qualified nursing students from both rural and urban settings. **Focus:** Nursing. **Qualif.:** Applicants must be Colorado residents committed to practicing nursing in Colorado; must be students in an approved Colorado Nursing Program; must have a minimum of 3.25 GPA (for undergraduate applicants) or 3.5 GPA (for graduate applicants); and must have one of the following student statuses: (1) Junior or senior level BSN undergraduate students; (2) RN enrolled in a baccalaureate or higher degree nursing program in a school of nursing; (3) Students in second year of nursing studies in an associate degree in nursing program; (4) RN with master's degree in nursing, currently practicing in Colorado and enrolled in a doctoral program; (5) Students in second or

Awards are arranged alphabetically below their administering organizations

third year of a Doctorate Nursing Practice (DNP) program. **Criteria:** Scholarship application will be rated based on the following: (1) Professional philosophy and goals; (2) Dedication to the improvement of patient care in Colorado; (3) Demonstrated commitment to nursing, critical thinking skills and potential for leadership; (4) Involvement in community and professional organizations; (5) GPA-minimum of 3.25 undergraduate, 3.5 graduate; (6) Financial need; (7) Recommendation of one faculty member; and (8) Employer/Supervisor recommendation.

Funds Avail.: No specific amount. **Number Awarded:** Varies. **To Apply:** Applicants must submit a cover sheet, financial need statement, resume, recommendation form from Faculty and Employer in a separated sealed envelope, copy of transcript including the last semester grades. Student essay must be no more than three pages, double-spaced in a 12pt. font with 1" each margin. **Contact:** Vicki Carroll; Phone: 970-416-6811; Fax: 970-416-6820; Email: CNFScholarships@aol.com.

3144 ■ Colorado Nurses Association: Virginia Paulson Memorial Scholarships *(Graduate, Undergraduate/Scholarship)*

Purpose: To provide scholarships for qualified nursing students from both rural and urban settings. **Focus:** Nursing. **Qualif.:** Applicants must be Colorado residents committed to practicing nursing in Colorado; must be students in an approved Colorado Nursing Program; must have a minimum of 3.25 GPA (for undergraduate applicants) or 3.5 GPA (for graduate applicants); and must have one of the following student statuses: (1) Junior or senior level BSN undergraduate students; (2) RN enrolled in a baccalaureate or higher degree nursing program in a school of nursing; (3) Students in second year of nursing studies in an associate degree in nursing program; (4) RN with master's degree in nursing, currently practicing in Colorado and enrolled in a doctoral program; (5) Students in second or third year of a Doctorate Nursing Practice (DNP) program. **Criteria:** Scholarship application will be rated based on the following: (1) Professional philosophy and goals; (2) Dedication to the improvement of patient care in Colorado; (3) Demonstrated commitment to nursing, critical thinking skills and potential for leadership; (4) Involvement in community and professional organizations; (5) GPA-minimum of 3.25 undergraduate, 3.5 graduate; (6) Financial need; (7) Recommendation of one faculty member, and (8) Employer/Supervisor recommendation.

Funds Avail.: No specific amount. **To Apply:** Applicant must submit a cover sheet, financial need statement, resume, recommendation form from Faculty and Employer in a separated sealed envelope, copy of transcript including the last semester grades. Student essay must be no more than three pages, double-spaced in a 12pt. font with 1" each margin. **Contact:** Vicki Carroll; Phone: 970-416-6811; Fax: 970-416-6820; Email: CNFScholarships@aol.com.

3145 ■ Patty Walter Memorial Scholarships *(Graduate, Undergraduate/Scholarship)*

Purpose: To provide scholarships for qualified nursing students from both rural and urban settings. **Focus:** Nursing. **Qualif.:** Applicants must be Colorado residents committed to practicing nursing in Colorado; must be students in an approved Colorado Nursing Program; must have a minimum of 3.25 GPA (for undergraduate applicants) or 3.5 GPA (for graduate applicants); and must have one of the following student statuses: (1) Junior or senior level BSN undergraduate students; (2) RN enrolled in a baccalaureate or higher degree nursing program in a school of nursing; (3) Students in second year of nursing studies in an associate degree in nursing program; (4) RN with master's degree in nursing, currently practicing in Colorado and enrolled in a doctoral program; (5) Students in second or third year of a Doctorate Nursing Practice (DNP) program. **Criteria:** Scholarship application will be rated based on the following: (1) Professional philosophy and goals; (2) Dedication to the improvement of patient care in Colorado; (3) Demonstrated commitment to nursing, critical thinking skills and potential for leadership; (4) Involvement in community and professional organizations; (5) GPA-minimum of 3.25 undergraduate, 3.5 graduate; (6) Financial need; (7) Recommendation of one faculty member, and (8) Employer/Supervisor recommendation.

Funds Avail.: No specific amount. **To Apply:** Applicants are advised to contact the foundation at Colorado Nurses Foundation for further information. **Contact:** Vicki Carroll; Phone: 970-416-6811; Fax: 970-416-6820; Email: CNFScholarships@aol.com.

3146 ■ Colorado Society of Certified Public Accountants (COCPA)
7887 E Belleview Ave., Ste. 200
Englewood, CO 80111
Ph: (303)773-2877
Fax: (303)773-6344
Free: 800-523-9082
E-mail: info@cocpa.org
URL: www.cocpa.org
LinkedIn: www.linkedin.com/company/colorado-society-of-certified-public-accountants

3147 ■ CSCPA College Scholarships *(Graduate, Undergraduate/Scholarship)*

Purpose: To support undergraduate and graduate accounting students. **Focus:** Accounting. **Qualif.:** Applicant must be an accounting major who has completed at least eight semester hours of accounting courses including one upper division accounting course; attend a Colorado college/university with an accredited accounting program; enrolled in courses equal to six semester/quarter hours or more for the semester/quarter for which the student is applying; have a college/university cumulative GPA of 3.0 or better on a 4.0 scale; and a U.S. citizen, or non-U.S. citizen legally living and studying in Colorado with a valid visa. **Criteria:** Selection is based on the application materials submitted.

Funds Avail.: $2,500. **Duration:** one year. **Number Awarded:** Varies. **To Apply:** Applicants must submit a completed application form together with an official or unofficial transcript from the current school that includes cumulative overall GPA. **Deadline:** June 1.

3148 ■ CSCPA High School Scholarships *(Undergraduate/Scholarship)*

Purpose: To support high school seniors who plan to major in accounting at Colorado community colleges and Colorado colleges/universities. **Focus:** Accounting. **Qualif.:** Applicant must be a Colorado high school senior who will major in accounting at a Colorado community college or Colorado college or university with an accredited accounting program; enrolled in courses equal to six semester/quarter hours or more for the semester/quarter for which the student is applying; have a 3.0 or better cumulative GPA on a 4.0 scale; and a U.S. citizen, or non-U.S. citizen legally living and studying in Colorado with a valid visa. **Criteria:** Selection is based on the application materials submitted. **Funds Avail.:** $1,000. **To Apply:** Applicants must submit a completed application form together with an official high school transcript that includes the applicant's cumulative GPA, class ranking and SAT/ACT test scores.

3149 ■ CSCPA Sophomore Scholarships
(Undergraduate/Scholarship)

Purpose: To financially support outstanding sophomore accounting students. **Focus:** Accounting. **Qualif.:** Applicant must be a sophomore who has maintained a 3.0 or better GPA on a 4.0 scale during the prior year and plans to major in accounting; enrolled in a Principles of Accounting class with a 3.0 GPA, and enroll in courses equal to six semester/quarter hours or more for the term for which the student is applying; and be a U.S. citizen, or non-U.S. citizen legally living and studying in Colorado with a valid visa. **Criteria:** Selection is based on the application materials submitted. **Funds Avail.:** $1,000. **To Apply:** Applicants must submit a completed application form along with an official or unofficial transcript that includes the previous year's cumulative overall GPA.

3150 ■ Columbus Citizens Foundation
8 E 69th St.
New York, NY 10021-4906
Ph: (212)249-9923
Fax: (212)737-4413
E-mail: ccf@columbuscitizens.org
URL: www.columbuscitizensfd.org

3151 ■ Columbus Citizens Foundation College Scholarships *(Undergraduate/Scholarship)*

Purpose: To provide financial assistance to underwrite the cost of Italian descent students' college tuition. **Focus:** General studies/Field of study not specified. **Qualif.:** Applicants must be students who are of Italian descent with GPA of 3.0 or higher; and who are from households where the total gross income does not exceed $25,000 per capita; only seniors in high school who will enter college as freshmen are eligible to apply. **Criteria:** Applicants are evaluated based on existence of Italian-American ancestry; financial need; academic excellence; and service to school and community. **Funds Avail.:** No specific amount. **To Apply:** Applicants must complete the application form; must submit a copy of their parent's or guardian's State and Federal Income Tax Returns; two letters of recommendation; an essay; academic performance verification; and must pay the $25 application fee. **Deadline:** February 15. **Remarks:** Established in 1984.

3152 ■ Columbus Citizens Foundation High School Scholarships *(Undergraduate/Scholarship)*

Purpose: To provide educational assistance for students of Italian descent. **Focus:** General studies/Field of study not specified. **Qualif.:** Applicants must be students of Italian descent; with GPA of 3.0 or higher; and must come from households where the total gross income does not exceed $20,000 per capita; only 8th graders who will enter high school as freshman are eligible; must maintain 3.25 GPA and demonstrate that they have performed community service activities. **Criteria:** Applicants are evaluated based on existence of Italian-American ancestry; academic achievement and school/community service; and financial need. **Funds Avail.:** No specific amount. **To Apply:** Applicants must complete the application form; must submit a copy of their parent's or guardian's State and Federal Income Tax Returns; three letters of recommendation; an essay; academic performance verification; and must pay the $25 application fee. **Deadline:** February 15. **Remarks:** Established in 1994.

3153 ■ Colvin Law Offices
205 S High St.
Winchester, TN 37398
Ph: (931)962-1044
Fax: (931)962-1094
Free: 844-683-6220
URL: www.colvin-law.com

3154 ■ John R. Colvin Legal Scholarships
(Graduate/Scholarship)

Purpose: To help students finance their first semester of law school and give them a strong foothold for continuing their law degree. **Focus:** Law. **Qualif.:** Applicants must be U.S. citizens or authorized to work/go to school in the United States; must have a published article in print or digital; must be commencing law school (1L) in August of the current year. **Criteria:** Selection will be based on creativity, originality, and ability to clearly convey a complex message of the submitted article. **Funds Avail.:** $1,000. **Duration:** Non-renewable. **Number Awarded:** 1. **To Apply:** Applicants must submit the following: a completed scholarship application form; a copy of law school acceptance letter; copy of previously published article or link to its online location. **Deadline:** May 1. **Contact:** jrclaw309@gmail.com.

3155 ■ Committee of 200 (C200)
980 N Michigan Ave., Ste. 1575
Chicago, IL 60611
Ph: (312)255-0296
Fax: (312)255-0789
E-mail: info@c200.org
URL: www.c200.org
Facebook: www.facebook.com/committeeof200
LinkedIn: www.linkedin.com/company/the-committee-of-200
Twitter: twitter.com/committeeof200

3156 ■ C200 Scholar Awards *(Graduate/Scholarship)*

Purpose: To support outstanding MBA women students for their extraordinary leadership potential, entrepreneurial spirit, and a commitment to giving back and supporting other women. **Focus:** Business. **Qualif.:** Applicants must be women MBA students enrolled in business school hosting a C200 Outreach Seminar. **Criteria:** Selections are based on work experience, GPA, recommendations and essays. **Funds Avail.:** Up to $10,000. **Duration:** Annual. **Number Awarded:** Varies. **To Apply:** Applicant must submit a recommendation and essay. **Contact:** Meghan McRae at mmcrae@c200.org.

3157 ■ The Commonwealth Fund
1 E 75th St.
New York, NY 10021

Awards are arranged alphabetically below their administering organizations

Ph: (212)606-3800
Fax: (212)606-3500
E-mail: info@cmwf.org
URL: www.commonwealthfund.org
Facebook: www.facebook.com/commonwealthfund
Twitter: twitter.com/commonwealthfnd

3158 ■ AHCJ Reporting Fellowships on Health Care Performance (Other/Fellowship)

Purpose: To pursue a significant reporting project examining health care systems. **Focus:** Health care services. **Qualif.:** Applicants must be health care journalists. **Criteria:** Selection will be based on the committee's criteria.

Funds Avail.: $2,500; $4,000 project allowance. **Duration:** Annual. **To Apply:** Applicants must visit the AHCJ website at www.healthjournalism.org to obtain an application form and other required attachments. **Deadline:** November 2. **Contact:** Ev Ruch-Graham, ev@healthjournalism.org.

3159 ■ Australian-American Health Policy Fellowships (Doctorate, Graduate/Fellowship)

Purpose: To offer a unique opportunity for outstanding, mid-career U.S. health policy researchers and practitioners to spend up to 10 months in Australia. **Focus:** Health care services. **Qualif.:** Applicants must be citizens of the United States; must be mid-career health services researchers or practitioners; have demonstrated expertise in health policy issues and track record of informing health policy through research, policy analysis, health services or clinical leadership; have completed a master's degree, doctorate or equivalent in health services research, health administration, health policy or a related discipline, such as economics or political science; and if academically based, be at a mid-career level. **Criteria:** Candidates will be selected based on their qualifications and leadership potential; their commitment to improving health care through research and practice; quality of their research proposal; relevance of their proposed research to the Fund's areas of interest and to policy development in their home country and strength of their supporting letters.

Funds Avail.: Up to 87,000 Australian Dollars. **To Apply:** Applicants must complete a formal application including an applicant summary sheet, statement of professional objectives, preliminary research proposal for a policy-oriented research project that fits within the program's priority areas, curriculum vitae, institutional letter of reference from the director of the applicant's institution or organization; two other professional references from senior health policymakers, managers or researchers who can comment on the applicant's past work and potential contributions of their proposed project and samples of up to three published articles or reports. **Deadline:** October 2. **Contact:** Robin Osborn, Vice President and Director, International Health Policy and Practice Innovations, The Commonwealth Fund; Email: ro@cmwf.org.

3160 ■ Harkness Fellowships in Health Care Policy and Practice (Doctorate, Graduate/Fellowship)

Purpose: To provide opportunities for mid-career health services researchers and practitioners from Australia, Canada, Germany, The Netherlands, New Zealand, Norway, Sweden, Switzerland and the United Kingdom. **Focus:** Economics; Health care services; Political science. **Qualif.:** Applicants must be citizens of Australia, Canada, Germany, New Zealand, The Netherlands, Norway, Sweden, Switzerland and the United Kingdom; must show significant promise as policy-oriented health services researchers or practitioners; have demonstrated expertise in health policy issues and a track record of informing health policy through research, policy analysis, health services or clinical leadership; have a master's degree or doctorate in health care services, health policy research or a related discipline, such as economics or political science. Consideration will be given to candidates with a bachelor's degree only, depending on work experience; and if academically based, be at a mid-career level. **Criteria:** Recipients will be selected based on their qualifications and leadership potential; their commitment to improving health care through research and practice; quality of their research proposal; relevance of their proposed research to the fund's areas of interest and to policy development in their home country and strength of their supporting letters.

Funds Avail.: No specific amount. **To Apply:** Candidates must complete a formal application, including: statement of professional objectives, curriculum vitae, five page preliminary proposal for a policy-oriented research project that fits within the fund's national program areas; letter of reference from the applicant's department chair or from the director of their institution; three professional references from senior health policy researchers, policymakers or senior level managers who can comment on the applicants' past work and the potential contribution of their proposed project. **Deadline:** September 8; November 16.

3161 ■ Mongan Commonwealth Fund Fellowship in Minority Health Policy (Other/Fellowship)

Purpose: To promote a high performing health care system that achieves better access, improved quality, and greater efficiency. **Focus:** General studies/Field of study not specified. **Qualif.:** Applicants must be physicians who have completed residency, either BE/BC in the United States; must have additional experience beyond residency, such as chief residency is preferred; have experience or interest in addressing and improving the health needs of minorities, disadvantaged and vulnerable populations; have strong evidence of leadership experience or potential, especially as related to community efforts, quality improvements and/or health policy; have an intention to pursue a career in policy, public health practice or academia; and must be U.S. citizens. **Criteria:** Applications will be reviewed for academic and training qualifications; commitment to a multicultural perspective in program planning, program implementation and policy analysis; experience in projects devoted to increasing quality care and access and improving the capacity of the health care system to address health needs of minority, disadvantaged and vulnerable populations; and evidence of leadership potential.

Funds Avail.: No specific amount. **To Apply:** Applicants must complete the application form, both the Commonwealth Fund/Harvard University Fellowship in Minority Health Policy and the Master of Public Health Program of the Harvard School of Public Health, including application for financial aid at HSPH. For those applicants who already have an MPH degree, applications to both the Commonwealth Fund/Harvard University Fellowship (CFHUF) in Minority Health Policy and the Master of Public Administration Program of the Harvard Kennedy School will be required, including application for financial aid at HKS. Once applicants have filled out and submitted all of the required information in the Request for Application Form, they should download the appropriate CFHUF application documents online. **Contact:** The Commonwealth Fund, at the above address.

Awards are arranged alphabetically below their administering organizations

3162 ■ Communal Studies Association (CSA)
PO Box 122
Amana, IA 52203
Ph: (319)622-6446
E-mail: info@communalstudies.org
URL: www.communalstudies.info

3163 ■ Communal Studies Association Research Fellowships (Graduate/Fellowship)

Purpose: To support research on historic or contemporary intentional communities. **Focus:** General studies/Field of study not specified. **Qualif.:** Applicants must be CSA members in good standing at the time of application and at presentation of the research. **Criteria:** Fellowships will be given to those who meet the qualifications.

Funds Avail.: $1,200. **Duration:** Annual. **To Apply:** Applicants should provide: a curriculum vita or resume and letters from two relevant references; a two-page description of the overall project, how he/she plans to accomplish such research, its goals, a timeline and how it will be presented at the CSA conference (paper, panel, A/V presentation, performance, exhibition, etc.); a bibliography of intended resources to be consulted during the grant project and a statement that these resources are open to the applicants; and a detailed budget (specify if funds other than this grant are to be used and their sources). **Deadline:** March 1. **Contact:** CSA at info@communalstudies.org.

3164 ■ Communications Workers of America Canada (CWA)
301-2200 Prince of Wales Dr.
Ottawa, ON, Canada K2E 6Z9
Ph: (613)820-9777
Fax: (613)820-8188
Free: 877-486-4292
E-mail: info@cwa-scacanada.ca
URL: www.cwa-scacanada.ca

3165 ■ Morton Bahr Scholarships (Undergraduate/Scholarship)

Purpose: To assist union members and other workers by furthering their educational goals and enhancing educational access through distance learning. **Focus:** General studies/Field of study not specified. **Qualif.:** Applicants must be Union workers, family members and/or domestic partners interested in registering for degree studies with Empire State College. **Criteria:** Preference will be given to members of the Communications Workers of America. Criteria include an ability to succeed in college studies, a program match with educational and career goals, leadership qualities, financial need and diversity.

Funds Avail.: No specific amount. **To Apply:** Interested applicants may download an application form online and must submit all required materials. **Deadline:** May 15.

3166 ■ Communities Adolescent Nutrition and Fitness Program (CANFIT)
2140 Shattuck Ave., Ste. 1110
Berkeley, CA 94704
Ph: (510)644-1533
Fax: (510)644-1535
E-mail: info@canfit.org
URL: www.canfit.org
Facebook: www.facebook.com/canfit
Twitter: twitter.com/canfit

3167 ■ CANFIT Nutrition, Physical Education and Culinary Arts Scholarships (Graduate, Undergraduate/Scholarship)

Purpose: To encourage students to consider careers that will improve adolescent nutrition and fitness. **Focus:** Culinary arts; Education, Physical; Nutrition; Public health. **Qualif.:** Applicants must California students of African-American, American Indian, Alaska Native, Asian-American, Pacific Islander or Latino/Hispanic descent; graduate applicants must be enrolled in an approved master level or doctoral graduate program in Nutrition, Public Health, Physical Education, or American Dietetic Association; must have approved pre-professional practice program at an accredited university in California; must have 12-15 units of graduate course work; must have 3.0 GPA or higher; applicants must be enrolled in an approved bachelor level program in Nutrition or Physical Education at an accredited university in California; must have 50 semester units of college credits completed; must have a 2.5 GPA or higher. **Criteria:** Selection will be based on the evaluation of submitted documents and specific criteria.

Funds Avail.: No specific amount. **Duration:** Annual. **To Apply:** Applicants must submit a completed application form; completed Statement of Financial Status; two recommendation letters from two individuals; letter describing academic goals and involvement in community nutrition; a 500-1,000-word essay; photograph of own self (billfold size or larger); one copy of an official transcript of graduate course work to 12-15 units (for graduate applicants) or official transcripts of all college work to accrue 50 units (for undergraduate applicants). **Deadline:** March 31.

3168 ■ Community Forestry and Environmental Research Partnerships (CEFRP)
University of California-Berkeley
101 Gianinni Hall, No. 3100
Berkeley, CA 94720
Ph: (510)642-3431
E-mail: cffellow@nature.berkeley.edu
URL: nature.berkeley.edu/community_forestry

3169 ■ Community-based Natural Resource Management Assistantships (Undergraduate, Advanced Professional/Internship)

Purpose: To provide financial assistance to those students who are in need. **Focus:** Environmental science. **Qualif.:** Applicants must be faculty or students at any U.S. college or university, in any department. **Criteria:** Priority will be given to those who meet the criteria.

Funds Avail.: $5,200. **To Apply:** Applicants must check the available website for more information.

3170 ■ Community Foundation of the Eastern Shore (CFES)
1324 Belmont Ave., Ste. 401
Salisbury, MD 21804
Ph: (410)742-9911
Fax: (410)742-6638
E-mail: cfes@cfes.org
URL: cfes.org
Facebook: www.facebook.com/CFEasternShore

Awards are arranged alphabetically below their administering organizations

Twitter: twitter.com/cfesnonprofit

3171 ■ William R. Bowen Scholarships
(Undergraduate/Scholarship)

Purpose: To assist high school graduating students in their pursuit of continuing education. **Focus:** General studies/Field of study not specified. **Qualif.:** Applicants must be graduating seniors of Snow Hill High School. **Criteria:** Recipients are selected based on academic performance and financial need.

Funds Avail.: $1,000. **To Apply:** Applicants must submit a completed application form. Application forms are available from Snow Hill High School Guidance Office. **Contact:** Community Foundation of the Eastern Shore, at the above address.

3172 ■ William T. Burbage Family Memorial Scholarships *(Undergraduate/Scholarship)*

Purpose: To aid up-and-coming tertiary level students in their continuing education. **Focus:** General studies/Field of study not specified. **Qualif.:** Applicants must be graduating seniors of Stephen Decatur High School who have selected their college and have been accepted for admission as full-time students and have 3.0 GPA. **Criteria:** Recipients are selected based on leadership potential.

Funds Avail.: $1,000. **Duration:** Annual. **To Apply:** Applicants must submit a completed application form; an official high school transcript of grades; letter of acceptance from college or university; two letters of recommendation from non-family members; a detailed listing by high school year of activities and an essay explaining how growing up on the Eastern Shore has contributed the individual leadership style. **Deadline:** April 15. **Contact:** Community Foundation of the Eastern Shore, at the above address.

3173 ■ Irene Culver Collins and Louis Franklin Collins Scholarships *(Undergraduate/Scholarship)*

Purpose: To assist past or current graduating high school senior from Parkside High School in their pursuance of higher education. **Focus:** General studies/Field of study not specified. **Qualif.:** Applicants must be past graduates or current 12th grade students of Parkside High School, Wicomico County, Maryland who: have been accepted for admission as full-time college students; and, have successfully completed a minimum of three advanced placement social studies during the enrollment at Parkside High School. **Criteria:** Recipients are selected based on academic performance and financial need.

Funds Avail.: $5,000. **Duration:** Annual. **To Apply:** Applicants must submit a completed application form; official high school transcript of grades; letter of acceptance from college or university; and an essay describing the personal character and two letters of recommendation from non-family members. **Deadline:** April 1. **Contact:** Community Foundation of the Eastern Shore, at the above address.

3174 ■ Eastern Shore Building Industry Association Scholarships *(Undergraduate/Scholarship)*

Purpose: To encourage and support those students who are pursuing a career in architecture, engineering, or a construction related study. **Focus:** Architecture; Construction; Engineering. **Qualif.:** Applicants must be current 12th grade students of high schools in Eastern Shore of Maryland counties of Kent, Queen Anne's, Caroline, Talbot, Dorchester, Somerset and Worcester who have been accepted for admission as full-time students. They must have a minimum of 2.5 GPA on a 4.0 scale and participated in some extracurricular activities. **Criteria:** Recipients are selected based on academic performance, financial need and extracurricular activities.

Funds Avail.: $500. **Duration:** Annual. **To Apply:** Applicants must submit a completed application form; an official high school transcript of grades; letter of acceptance from college or university; an essay describing the reasons of choosing the career path and two letters of recommendation from non-family members. **Deadline:** April 1. **Contact:** Home Builders Association of Maryland, Eastern Shore Chapter Scholarship, 11825 W. Market Place, Fulton, Maryland 20759.

3175 ■ Federalsburg Rotary Club Scholarships
(Undergraduate/Scholarship)

Purpose: To aid graduates of Colonel Richardson High School for their pursuit of higher education in their respective colleges or universities. **Focus:** General studies/Field of study not specified. **Qualif.:** Applicants must be graduating seniors of Colonel Richardson High School who have selected their college and have been accepted for admission as full-time students; must have 2.5 GPA. **Criteria:** Recipients are selected based on financial need.

Funds Avail.: Minimum of $500. **Duration:** Annual. **To Apply:** Applicants must submit a completed application form; an official high school transcript of grades and letter of acceptance from college or university. **Deadline:** April 1. **Contact:** Community Foundation of the Eastern Shore, at the above address.

3176 ■ Herb and Anne Fincher Memorial Scholarships *(Undergraduate/Scholarship)*

Purpose: To support Maryland students who are about to pursue Mathematics or Engineering courses. **Focus:** Engineering; Mathematics and mathematical sciences. **Qualif.:** Applicants must be graduates of the four public high schools in Wicomico County, Maryland (James M. Bennett High, Wicomico High, Parkside High, and Mardela High) who have been accepted into a course of study for either math or engineering. **Criteria:** Recipients shall be selected based on demonstrated maturity and commitment to succeed in college level courses of study.

Funds Avail.: $1,500 per annum. **Duration:** Annual; up to 4 years. **To Apply:** Applicants must submit a completed application form, an official high school transcript of grades, letter of acceptance from college or university and two letters of recommendation from non-family members. **Deadline:** April 1. **Contact:** Community Foundation of the Eastern Shore, at the above address.

3177 ■ Green Hill Yacht and Country Club Scholarships *(Undergraduate/Scholarship)*

Purpose: To empower donors to make a profound difference in the quality of life in Maryland's Lower Eastern Shore; to provide community leadership through grants, non-profit support programs, charitable partnerships and local initiatives in Somerset, Wicomico and Worcester counties. **Focus:** General studies/Field of study not specified. **Qualif.:** Applicants must be past graduates or current 12th grade students of Wicomico, Somerset or Worcester County School who have been accepted for admission as full-time students in an accredited four-year college or university or accredited two-year educational/vocational institution. **Criteria:** Recipients are selected based on academic achievement and financial need.

Funds Avail.: $1,000. **Duration:** Annual. **To Apply:** Applicants must submit a completed application form, an official high school transcript of grades and two letters of recommendation from non-family member. Completed application must be submitted to the contact provided. **Deadline:** April 15. **Contact:** Scholarship Advisory Committee Chair, Green Hill Yacht and Country Club, 5471 Whitehaven Rd., Quantico, Maryland 21856-2134.

3178 ■ Gruwell Scholarships *(Undergraduate/Scholarship)*

Purpose: To help students in their pursuance of higher education. **Focus:** General studies/Field of study not specified. **Qualif.:** Applicants must be residents of Lake Forest School District, Kent County, Delaware who have selected their college and have been accepted for admission as full-time students. **Criteria:** Recipients are selected based on financial need, community involvement, academic achievement and extracurricular activities.

Funds Avail.: $1,000. **Duration:** Annual. **To Apply:** Applicants must submit a completed application form, an official high school transcript of grades and letter of acceptance from college or university; a copy of parent/guardian and student's most recent income tax return and two letters of recommendation from non-family members. **Deadline:** April 1. **Contact:** Community Foundation of the Eastern Shore, at the above address.

3179 ■ Hancock Family Snow Hill High School Scholarships *(Undergraduate/Scholarship)*

Purpose: To support graduating high school seniors from Snow Hill High School in their continuing education. **Focus:** General studies/Field of study not specified. **Qualif.:** Applicants must: be graduating seniors at Snow Hill High School who have been accepted by an Accredited academic college program; have 2.5 GPA in appropriate course work indicating the students are able to be successful at the college level; have three or more year residents of Snow Hill area; be active in school activity, church, community and youth clubs; and, have a good moral character. **Criteria:** Recipients are selected based on academic performance, financial need and participation in extracurricular activities.

Funds Avail.: $2,000. **Duration:** Annual. **To Apply:** Applicants must submit a completed application form; an official high school transcript of grades; letter of acceptance from college or university; a copy of parent/guardian and student's most recent income tax return and two letters of recommendation from non-family members. **Deadline:** April 21. **Contact:** Community Foundation of the Eastern Shore, at the above address.

3180 ■ Dick and Pat Hazel Minority Scholarships *(Undergraduate/Scholarship)*

Purpose: To support the education of minority students who are about to commit to teaching for two years within the public education systems of Somerset, Wicomico, or Worcester Counties. **Focus:** Education. **Qualif.:** Applicants must be members of a minority group and must commit teaching for two years within the public education systems of Somerset, Wicomico or Worcester counties. They must also be residents of Wicomico, Somerset or Worcester County, Maryland who have selected their college and have been accepted for admission as full-time students whose pursuit must be education/teaching. **Criteria:** Recipients are selected based on financial need, community involvement, academic achievement and extracurricular activities.

Funds Avail.: $1,000 to $2,000. **Duration:** Annual. **To Apply:** Applicants must submit a completed application form; "one-page" describing the reasons of wanting to teach; an official high school transcript of grades; letter of acceptance from college or university and summary of financial assistance from college/university financial aid and office; must also submit a copy of parent/guardian and student's most recent income tax return and two letters of recommendation from non-family members. **Deadline:** May 1. **Contact:** Community Foundation of the Eastern Shore, at the above address.

3181 ■ Martin S. Kane Memorial Community Service Award Scholarships *(Undergraduate/Scholarship)*

Purpose: To aid the continuing education of high school seniors from Wicomico High School. **Focus:** General studies/Field of study not specified. **Qualif.:** Applicants must be graduating high school seniors from Wicomico High School. **Criteria:** Recipients are selected based on financial need.

Funds Avail.: $600. **To Apply:** Application can be obtain from Wicomico High School Guidance Office. **Contact:** Community Foundation of the Eastern Shore, at the above address.

3182 ■ TFC Edward A. Plank, Jr. Memorial Scholarships *(Undergraduate/Scholarship)*

Purpose: To support those graduating in the public school systems of Maryland in Somerset County. **Focus:** General studies/Field of study not specified. **Qualif.:** Applicants must be graduating seniors from any Somerset County School, and have 3.0 overall GPA. **Criteria:** Recipients are selected based on academic achievement and financial need.

Funds Avail.: $2,000. **Duration:** Annual. **To Apply:** Applicants must submit a completed application form, a 500-word essay on how crimes and/or drug abuse have been affected today's society and personal letters of recommendation from two responsible adults other than relatives. **Deadline:** March 31. **Contact:** Community Foundation of the Eastern Shore, at the above address.

3183 ■ Progress Lane Scholarships *(Undergraduate/Scholarship)*

Purpose: To support the continuing education of high school graduating seniors from Washington High School. **Focus:** General studies/Field of study not specified. **Qualif.:** Applicants must be current graduating 12th grade students of Washington High School, Princess Anne, Maryland who are financially advantaged and have been accepted for admission as students with a minimum of six credit hours in a course of study that will serve the educational requirements for their chosen career. **Criteria:** Recipients are selected based on academic performance and financial need.

Funds Avail.: $500. **Duration:** Annual. **To Apply:** Applicants must submit a completed application form; an official high school transcript of grades; a letter of acceptance from college; university or training institute and "250-word" essay describing the reasons of wanting to attend college. **Deadline:** April 1. **Contact:** Community Foundation of the Eastern Shore, at the above address.

3184 ■ Duane V. Puerde Memorial Scholarships *(Undergraduate/Scholarship)*

Purpose: To aid graduating students from Parkside High School in their pursuit of higher education. **Focus:** General studies/Field of study not specified. **Qualif.:** Applicants

Awards are arranged alphabetically below their administering organizations

must be past graduates or current 12th grade students of Parkside High school who are residents of rural Eastern Wicomico County, Maryland including but not exclusive to the communities of Parsonburg, Pittsville, Powellville, Williards or Melson who have been accepted for admission as full-time college students or vocational school. **Criteria:** Recipients are selected based on academic performance and participation in extracurricular activities.

Funds Avail.: $500. **Duration:** Annual. **To Apply:** Applicants must submit a completed application form, an official high school transcript of grades and two letters of recommendation from non-family members. **Deadline:** April 1. **Contact:** Elaine W. Purdue, Chair, Duane V. Perdue Memorial Scholarship, P.O. Box 5, Willards, Maryland 26874.

3185 ■ Elizabeth Pusey Scholarships
(Undergraduate/Scholarship)

Purpose: To support those outstanding students who are about to enter tertiary education level. **Focus:** General studies/Field of study not specified. **Qualif.:** Applicants must be graduating seniors at any Wicomico County high school who have selected their college and have been accepted from admission as full-time students and are in the top 10% of their class. **Criteria:** Recipients shall be selected based on financial need.

Funds Avail.: $1,500 each. **Duration:** Annual; up to 4 years. **Number Awarded:** 3. **To Apply:** Applicants must submit a completed application form, an official transcript of grades ad letter of acceptance from college or university. **Deadline:** April 1. **Contact:** Community Foundation of the Eastern Shore, at the above address.

3186 ■ Lana K. Rinehart Scholarships
(Undergraduate/Scholarship)

Purpose: To support the students from Parkside High School who are pursuing higher education. **Focus:** General studies/Field of study not specified. **Qualif.:** Applicants must be graduating senior students at Parkside High School. **Criteria:** Recipients are selected based on academic performance and financial need.

Funds Avail.: $1,000. **To Apply:** Applicants must submit a completed application form. Applications are available from Parkside High School Guidance Office. **Contact:** Community Foundation of the Eastern Shore, at the above address.

3187 ■ Drew Smith Memorial Scholarships
(Undergraduate/Scholarship)

Purpose: To assist a turfgrass management student who has a similar passion for the golf industry and one who demonstrates the drive, determination and financial need that Drew would have had himself. **Focus:** Turfgrass management. **Qualif.:** Applicants must be adults or graduating public or private high school seniors who are pursuing a degree in golf turf management from an accredited college or university and must be domiciled residents of the Eastern Shore Counties of Maryland and Virginia or the State of Delaware. They must also be enrolled in college for a minimum of six credit hours per scholastic year. **Criteria:** Recipients are selected based on academic record, financial need, extracurricular activities or community service.

Funds Avail.: Minimum of $1,000. **Duration:** Annual. **To Apply:** Applicants must submit a completed application form, Career Goal Information, and two letters of recommendation to the contact provided. **Deadline:** July 14. **Contact:** Drew Smith Memorial Scholarship, P.O. Box 1607, Ocean Pines, Maryland 21811.

3188 ■ Esther M. Smith Scholarships
(Undergraduate/Scholarship)

Purpose: To support selected students with disabilities from Maryland in their continuing education. **Focus:** General studies/Field of study not specified. **Qualif.:** Applicants must: be graduating seniors with a disability as accepted defined by the Americans with Disabilities Act (ADA) who attended in Wicomico County; be nominated by their school principal, guidance counselor or teacher; have a minimum GPA of 2.0; and, have been accepted for admission as full-time students at an accredited four-year college or university or a two-year education or career training institution. **Criteria:** Recipients are selected based on academic performance and financial need.

Funds Avail.: $2,000 for one academic year, ($1,000 per semester). **Duration:** Annual. **To Apply:** Applicants must submit completed application form; an official high school transcript of grades and letter of recommendation from non-family members. **Deadline:** April 15. **Contact:** Ms. Kathy Redden, Esther M. Smith Fund, 1813 Holly Swamp Rd., Pocomoke, Maryland 21851.

3189 ■ Wi-Hi Class of '55 Scholarship
(Undergraduate/Scholarship)

Purpose: To assist the graduates of Wicomico High School in their pursuance of higher education. **Focus:** General studies/Field of study not specified. **Qualif.:** Applicants must: be graduating senior students of Wicomico High School who have spent at least their junior and senior years in that school's program; have selected their college and have been accepted for admission as full-time students; and, have 3.0 cumulative GPA. **Criteria:** Recipients are selected based on community involvement, academic achievement and extracurricular activities.

Funds Avail.: $1,000. **Duration:** Annual. **To Apply:** Applicants must submit a completed application form; an official high school transcript of grades; letter of acceptance from college or university; three letters of recommendation from non-family members and "250-word" essay on "How they can make a difference". **Deadline:** April 15. **Contact:** Community Foundation of the Eastern Shore, at the above address.

3190 ■ M. William and Frances J. Tilghman Scholarships
(Undergraduate/Scholarship)

Purpose: To support high school graduates from Maryland for them to continue study at the tertiary level. **Focus:** General studies/Field of study not specified. **Qualif.:** Applicants must be graduating high school senior students from Wicomico or Somerset County public high school. **Criteria:** Selection shall be based on academic achievement, extracurricular activities and financial need.

Funds Avail.: Minimum of $1,000. **Duration:** Annual. **To Apply:** Applicants must submit a completed application form; an official high school transcript of grades; letter of acceptance from a college or university and two letters of recommendation from non-family members. **Deadline:** April 1. **Contact:** Community Foundation of the Eastern Shore, at the above address.

3191 ■ Community Foundation of the Fox River Valley
111 W Downer Pl., Ste. 312
Aurora, IL 60506-6106

Awards are arranged alphabetically below their administering organizations

Ph: (630)896-7800
Fax: (630)896-7811
E-mail: info@communityfoundationfrv.org
URL: www.communityfoundationfrv.org
Facebook: www.facebook.com/cffrv
LinkedIn: www.linkedin.com/company/community-foundation-of-the-fox-river-valley
Twitter: www.twitter.com/CFFRVfoundation

3192 ■ Community Foundation of the Fox River Valley Scholarships *(Undergraduate/Scholarship)*

Purpose: To enhance and support the quality of life in the Fox River Valley of Illinois. **Focus:** General studies/Field of study not specified. **Qualif.:** Applicants must be students who will attend an accredited institution of higher learning on a full-time basis and whose permanent residence is within the Foundation's service area. **Criteria:** Recipients are selected based on academic ability and financial need.

Funds Avail.: No specific amount. **Duration:** Annual. **Number Awarded:** 1. **To Apply:** Applicants must submit a completed application form. **Deadline:** February 1.

3193 ■ Community Foundation for Greater Atlanta
191 Peachtree St. NE, Ste. 1000, 10th Fl.
Atlanta, GA 30303
Ph: (404)688-5525
Fax: (404)688-3060
E-mail: info@cfgreateratlanta.org
URL: www.cfgreateratlanta.org
Facebook: www.facebook.com/cfgreateratlanta

3194 ■ Steve Dearduff Scholarships *(Graduate, Undergraduate/Scholarship)*

Purpose: To provide financial assistance to undergraduate and graduate students pursuing degrees in medicine and social work. **Focus:** Medicine; Social work. **Qualif.:** Applicants must be legal residents of Georgia; must be enrolled or accepted in an accredited higher learning institution pursuing undergraduate or graduate degrees in medicine or social work; must have demonstrated history of commitment to community service; must have potential for success in chosen field; and have a minimum GPA of 2.0; must demonstrate financial need. **Criteria:** Recipients will be selected based on submitted documents and financial need.

Funds Avail.: No specific amount. **Duration:** Annual. **To Apply:** Applicants must visit the Foundation's website to obtain the link for online application.

3195 ■ George and Pearl Strickland Scholarships *(Graduate, Undergraduate/Scholarship)*

Purpose: To provide financial assistance to undergraduate and graduate students pursuing a degree at Atlanta University Center colleges. **Focus:** General studies/Field of study not specified. **Qualif.:** Applicants must be legal residents of Georgia; must be enrolled or accepted at Clark Atlanta University, Morehouse College, Morehouse School of Medicine or Spelman College; and have a minimum GPA of 2.0. **Criteria:** Recipients will be selected based on demonstrated commitment to community service, potential for success in chosen field and financial need.

Funds Avail.: No specific amount. **Duration:** Annual. **Number Awarded:** Varies. **To Apply:** Applicants must visit the Foundation's website to obtain the link for online application. **Contact:** Community Foundation for Greater Atlanta, at the above address.

3196 ■ Community Foundation for Greater New Haven
70 Audubon St.
New Haven, CT 06510-9755
Ph: (203)777-2386
Fax: (203)787-6584
E-mail: contactus@cfgnh.org
URL: www.cfgnh.org
Facebook: www.facebook.com/cfgnh
Twitter: twitter.com/cfgnh

3197 ■ Bambi Bailey Scholarships *(Undergraduate/Scholarship)*

Purpose: To create positive and sustainable change in Greater New Haven by increasing the amount of and enhancing the impact of community philanthropy and to provide college scholarships based on financial need. **Focus:** General studies/Field of study not specified. **Qualif.:** Applicants must be students from New Haven who may not consider college as an option; must demonstrate an interest and ability in writing; must attend or plan to attend Wellesley College. **Criteria:** Recipients are selected based on financial need. Preference will be given to students demonstrating an interest and ability in writing and/or who plan to or do attend Wellesley College.

Funds Avail.: $1,000. **Duration:** Annual. **To Apply:** Applicants must complete the application form and attach a personal essay; academic verification; letter of recommendation; and Parent/Guardian IRS Form. **Remarks:** Established in 2001. **Contact:** Denise Canning at 203-777-7076 or dcanning@cfgnh.org.

3198 ■ George J. Bysiewicz Scholarship Fund *(Undergraduate/Scholarship)*

Purpose: To create changes in Greater New Haven by enhancing the impact of community philanthropy. **Focus:** General studies/Field of study not specified. **Qualif.:** Applicants must be students from New Haven, Catholic School planning to attend Sacred Heart Academy and Notre Dame High School. **Criteria:** Recipients are selected based on financial need.

Funds Avail.: No specific amount. **To Apply:** Applicants must complete the application form and attach a personal essay; academic verification; two letter of recommendation; letter of acceptance from either Sacred Heart Academy or Notre Dame; and Parent/Guardian IRS Form. **Contact:** Denise Canning at 203-777-7076 or dcanning@cfgnh.org.

3199 ■ Murtha Cullina LLP Scholarships Fund *(Undergraduate/Scholarship)*

Purpose: To create changes in Greater New Haven by enhancing the impact of community philanthropy. **Focus:** General studies/Field of study not specified. **Qualif.:** Applicants must be students from the greater New Haven area planning to attend a Metropolitan Business Academy. **Criteria:** Recipients are selected based on financial need.

Funds Avail.: No specific amount. **To Apply:** Applicants must complete the application form and attach a personal essay; academic verification; letter of recommendation; and

Awards are arranged alphabetically below their administering organizations

Parent/Guardian IRS Form. **Contact:** Denise Canning at 203-777-7076 or dcanning@cfgnh.org.

3200 ■ John S. Martinez and Family Scholarship Fund *(Undergraduate/Scholarship)*

Purpose: To create changes in Greater New Haven by enhancing the impact of community philanthropy. **Focus:** General studies/Field of study not specified. **Qualif.:** Applicants must be students in an institution or university. **Criteria:** Recipients are selected based on financial need.

Funds Avail.: No specific amount. **To Apply:** Applicants must complete the application form and must attach a personal essay; academic verification; letter of recommendation; and Parent/Guardian IRS Form. **Contact:** Denise Canning at 203-777-7076 or dcanning@cfgnh.org.

3201 ■ Curtis M. Saulsbury Scholarship Fund *(Undergraduate/Scholarship)*

Purpose: To provide young people the opportunity to obtain an education in music. **Focus:** Music. **Qualif.:** Applicants must be graduating from secondary school (James Hillhouse High School) in the region serviced by the community foundation. **Criteria:** Recipients are selected based on financial need.

Funds Avail.: No specific amount. **To Apply:** Applicants must complete the application form and attach a personal essay; academic verification; letter of recommendation; and Parent/Guardian IRS Form. **Contact:** Denise Canning at 203-777-7076 or dcanning@cfgnh.org.

3202 ■ Ruth and Sherman Zudekoff Scholarships *(Undergraduate/Scholarship)*

Purpose: To create positive and sustainable change in Greater New Haven by increasing the amount of and enhancing the impact of community philanthropy. **Focus:** General studies/Field of study not specified. **Qualif.:** Applicants must be students from Hyde Leadership School. **Criteria:** Recipients are selected based on financial need.

Funds Avail.: No specific amount. **To Apply:** Applicants must complete the application form and attach a personal essay; academic verification; letter of recommendation; and Parent/Guardian IRS Form. **Contact:** Denise Canning at 203-777-7076 or dcanning@cfgnh.org.

3203 ■ Community Foundation of Greene County (CFGC)

PO Box 768
Waynesburg, PA 15370
Ph: (724)627-2010
Fax: (724)627-2011
E-mail: cfgcpa@gmail.com
URL: www.cfgcpa.org

3204 ■ The William H. Davis, Jr. Scholarship Fund *(Undergraduate/Scholarship)*

Purpose: To support students attending the Westmoreland County Community College. **Focus:** General studies/Field of study not specified. **Qualif.:** Applicants must be residents of Green County; must be graduating students or previous graduates of any Greene County high school; have made application and be accepted at Westmoreland County Community College as full-time students or registered for a minimum of 12 credit hours. **Criteria:** Recipients are selected based on financial need.

Funds Avail.: No specific amount. **To Apply:** Applicants must submit the following requirements: complete application form; a copy of their FAFSA Student Report, including the Estimated Family Contribution; official transcript; copy of WCCC acceptance letter; and any financial aid or scholarship letters. **Deadline:** June 1.

3205 ■ The Thelma S. Hoge Memorial Scholarship Fund *(Undergraduate/Scholarship)*

Purpose: To support students of West Greene School District who are pursuing a college education. **Focus:** General studies/Field of study not specified. **Qualif.:** Applicants must be graduating seniors from West Greene; must be accepted at a post-secondary or four-year college degree program; must have a minimum GPA of 3.0. **Criteria:** Recipients are selected based on essay, results of an interview and completed application.

Funds Avail.: $2,500. **Number Awarded:** 2. **To Apply:** Applicants must provide a brief essay about themselves; copy of high school transcript and two character references.

3206 ■ The Renardo A. Matteucci Scholarship Fund *(Undergraduate/Scholarship)*

Purpose: To provide an annual need-based scholarship to the Jefferson-Morgan High School students. **Focus:** General studies/Field of study not specified. **Qualif.:** Applicants must be graduating students from Jefferson-Morgan High School; must be planning to pursue a Bachelor Degree, an Associate Degree or a Diploma from a trade school; must have a minimum GPA of 2.75. **Criteria:** Recipients are selected based on financial need.

Funds Avail.: $1,000. **Number Awarded:** 2. **To Apply:** Applicants must submit five copies of their FAFSA, Special Condition Form, verification of their GPA from guidance counselor, an official attendance record and post-secondary acceptance letter. **Deadline:** April 1.

3207 ■ The Walter Samek III Memorial Scholarship Fund *(Undergraduate/Scholarship)*

Purpose: To assist graduating senior class members of Carmichaels High School to continue post-secondary education. **Focus:** General studies/Field of study not specified. **Qualif.:** Applicants must be Carmichaels senior boys or girls who are enrolled in an approved post-secondary college/university; must have a 3.5 GPA. **Criteria:** Recipients are selected based on financial need and community service.

Funds Avail.: No specific amount. **To Apply:** Applicants must submit a completed application form. **Deadline:** April 15.

3208 ■ Community Foundation of Middle Tennessee (CFMT)

3833 Cleghorn Ave., Ste. 400
Nashville, TN 37215-2519
Ph: (615)321-4939
Fax: (615)327-2746
Free: 888-540-5200
E-mail: mail@cfmt.org
URL: www.cfmt.org

3209 ■ Lt. Holly Adams Memorial Scholarships *(Undergraduate/Scholarship)*

Purpose: To provide financial assistance to students pursuing a specific field of study and who are most in need.

Focus: General studies/Field of study not specified. **Qualif.:** Applicants must be students from the Page High School area in Williamson County who not only achieve, but also possess the integrity, courage and caring spirit to help others achieve. **Criteria:** The Board of The Community Foundation will choose a volunteer selection committee which will review each application and select the recipients based on the criteria established by donors.

Funds Avail.: No specific amount. **To Apply:** Applicants must complete the application form; must submit two applicant appraisals; transcript of grades; student's essay describing educational plans and how these will help in career goals; and one recent photograph. **Deadline:** March 15. **Remarks:** Established in 2006. **Contact:** Pat Cole, Scholarship Coordinator; Phone: 615-321-4939; Email: pcole@cfmt.org.

3210 ■ Kathy D. and Stephen J. Anderson Scholarships *(Undergraduate/Scholarship)*

Purpose: To provide financial assistance to students pursuing a specific field of study and who are most in need. **Focus:** General studies/Field of study not specified. **Qualif.:** Applicants must be graduate students from the Public High School area in Williamson County who have attended for a minimum of three years; must be in good standing as citizens in the school and community; have 3.2 or better GPA and minimum ACT score of 22 or SAT of 1100; and must be involved in at least one extracurricular activity (which could include working part-time). **Criteria:** Recipients are selected based on financial need.

Funds Avail.: Maximum amount of $10,000 per student. **Duration:** Up to 4 years. **To Apply:** Applicants must complete the application form; must submit two applicant appraisals; transcript of grades; student's essay describing educational plans and how these will help in career goals; and one recent photograph. **Deadline:** March 15. **Remarks:** Established in 2005. **Contact:** Pat Cole, Scholarship Coordinator; Phone: 615-321-4939; Email: pcole@cfmt.org.

3211 ■ Cynthia and Alan Baran Fine Arts and Music Scholarships *(Undergraduate/Scholarship)*

Purpose: To provide financial assistance to students pursuing a specific field of study and who are most in need. **Focus:** Art; Music. **Qualif.:** Applicants must be rising sophomores, juniors, seniors in college and graduate students at an accredited college, university, or institute full-time or part-time (six or more credits); and must maintain at least 3.0 GPA or better. **Criteria:** Recipients are selected based on financial need, extracurricular and civic participation. Preference will be given to those applicants pursuing a course of study in Music degree (courses in acoustic mandolin or acoustic guitar) and Fine arts or Studio art (courses in painting, drawing, sculpture, ceramics, photography or printmaking).

Funds Avail.: No specific amount. **To Apply:** Applicants must complete the application form; must submit two applicant appraisals; transcript of grades; student's essay describing educational plans and how these will help in career goals; and one recent photograph. **Deadline:** March 15. **Remarks:** Established in 2004. **Contact:** Pat Cole, Scholarship Coordinator; Phone: 615-321-4939; Email: pcole@cfmt.org.

3212 ■ Belmont University Commercial Music Showcase Scholarships *(Undergraduate/Scholarship)*

Purpose: To provide financial assistance to students pursuing a specific field of study and who are most in need. **Focus:** Music. **Qualif.:** Applicants must be high school seniors, college freshmen, sophomores, or juniors accepted to or attending Belmont University in Nashville, Tennessee as commercial music majors. **Criteria:** Recipients are selected based on financial need.

Funds Avail.: No specific amount. **To Apply:** Applicants must complete the application form; must submit two applicant appraisals; transcript of grades; student essay describing their educational plans and how these will help in career goals; and one recent photograph. **Deadline:** March 15. **Remarks:** Established in 1998. **Contact:** Pat Cole, Scholarship Coordinator; Phone: 615-321-4939; Email: pcole@cfmt.org.

3213 ■ George Oliver Benton Memorial Scholarships *(Undergraduate/Scholarship)*

Purpose: To provide financial assistance to students pursuing a specific field of study and who are most in need. **Focus:** Government. **Qualif.:** Applicants must be Legislative Interns; students who attend an accredited four-year college/university in the state of Tennessee; and must be residents of Tennessee. **Criteria:** Recipients will be selected based on extracurricular activities especially those indicative of an interest in government.

Funds Avail.: No specific amount. **To Apply:** Applicants must complete the application form; must submit two applicant appraisals; transcript of grades; student essay describing educational plans and how these will help in career goals; and one recent photograph. **Deadline:** March 15. **Remarks:** Established in 2001. **Contact:** Pat Cole, Scholarship Coordinator; Phone: 615-321-4939; Email: pcole@cfmt.org.

3214 ■ Dody Boyd Scholarships *(Undergraduate/Scholarship)*

Purpose: To provide financial assistance to students pursuing a specific field of study and who are most in need. **Focus:** General studies/Field of study not specified. **Qualif.:** Applicants must be seniors graduating from Cheatham County Central High School and wishing to attend a two-year community college/technical school or four-year university; must have GPA of at least 2.5 or better and an ACT score of 20 or better. **Criteria:** Recipients are selected based on financial need.

Funds Avail.: No specific amount. **To Apply:** Applicants must complete the application form; must submit two applicant appraisals; transcript of grades; student's essay describing educational plans and how these will help in career goals; and one recent photograph. **Deadline:** March 15. **Remarks:** Established in 2006. **Contact:** Pat Cole, Scholarship Coordinator; Phone: 615-321-4939; Email: pcole@cfmt.org.

3215 ■ JoAhn Brown-Nash Memorial Scholarships *(Undergraduate/Scholarship)*

Purpose: To provide financial assistance to students pursuing a specific field of study and who are most in need. **Focus:** General studies/Field of study not specified. **Qualif.:** Applicants must be female students at Fisk University, entering their junior year, who exemplify outstanding leadership skills, with a GPA of 3.2 or above. **Criteria:** Recipients are selected based on the financial need.

Funds Avail.: No specific amount. **To Apply:** Applicants must submit a completed application form along with a High School and/or College Transcripts (sealed in a separate envelope), and two appraisal letters (sealed in a

Awards are arranged alphabetically below their administering organizations

separate envelope). **Deadline:** March 15. **Remarks:** Established in 2002. **Contact:** Pat Cole, Scholarship Coordinator; Phone: 615-321-4939; Email: pcole@cfmt.org.

3216 ■ William and Clara Bryan Scholarships *(Undergraduate/Scholarship)*

Purpose: To provide financial assistance to students pursuing a specific field of study and who are most in need. **Focus:** General studies/Field of study not specified. **Qualif.:** Applicants must be high school seniors, or college freshmen, sophomores or juniors who are from Giles County, Tennessee and have lived there for the majority of their pre-college schooling. **Criteria:** Recipients are selected based on merit and financial need.

Funds Avail.: No specific amount. **To Apply:** Applicants must complete the application form; must submit two applicant appraisals; transcript of grades; student's essay describing educational plans and how these will help in career goals; and one recent photograph. **Deadline:** March 15. **Remarks:** Established in 1994. **Contact:** Pat Cole, Scholarship Coordinator; Phone: 615-321-4939; Email: pcole@cfmt.org.

3217 ■ Leigh Carter Scholarships *(Undergraduate/Scholarship)*

Purpose: To provide financial support to students who wish to attend chiropractic college upon completion of their undergraduate degree programs. **Focus:** Health care services. **Qualif.:** Applicants must be full-time students attending one of the nation's accredited chiropractic colleges or universities. **Criteria:** Recipients are selected based on financial need, interest in health care delivery, extracurricular and civic participation. Preference will be given to students from Tennessee.

Funds Avail.: No specific amount. **To Apply:** Applicants must complete the application form; must submit two applicant appraisals; transcript of grades; student's essay describing educational plans and how these will help in career goals; and one recent photograph. **Remarks:** Established in 2001.

3218 ■ Cheatham County Community Foundation Scholarships *(Undergraduate/Scholarship)*

Purpose: To provide financial assistance to students pursuing a specific field of study. **Focus:** General studies/Field of study not specified. **Qualif.:** Applicants must be Cheatham County, Tennessee residents for a minimum period of one year; must have a high school diploma or GED with a GPA of 2.0 or better; must attend an accredited college, university, or technical school and maintain a grade point average of 2.0 or better. **Criteria:** Recipients are selected based on financial need, extracurricular and civic participation.

Funds Avail.: No specific amount. **To Apply:** Applicants must complete the application form. Applicants must submit two applicant appraisals; transcript of grades; student's essay describing educational plans and how these will help in career goals. Applicants must submit one recent photograph. **Remarks:** Established in 2002. **Contact:** Pat Cole, Scholarship Coordinator at 615-321-4939 or by email at pcole@cfmt.org.

3219 ■ Choose Your Future Scholarships *(Undergraduate/Scholarship)*

Purpose: To provide financial assistance to students pursuing a specific field of study and who are most in need. **Focus:** General studies/Field of study not specified. **Qualif.:** Applicants must be graduates of the Metropolitan Nashville Public School of Davidson County with a minimum GPA of 2.5 and a score of 21 on the ACT; and must be attending a college or university in the United States. **Criteria:** Recipients are selected based on financial need, extracurricular and civic participation. Preference will be given to students who are the first in their families to attend college.

Funds Avail.: No specific amount. **To Apply:** Applicants must complete the application form; must submit two applicant appraisals; transcript of grades; student's essay describing educational plans and how these will help in career goals; one recent photograph. **Deadline:** March 15. **Remarks:** Established in 2007. **Contact:** Pat Cole, Scholarship Coordinator; Phone: 615-321-4939; Email: pcole@cfmt.org.

3220 ■ Howard A. Clark Horticulture Scholarships *(Undergraduate/Scholarship)*

Purpose: To provide financial assistance to students pursuing a specific field of study and who are most in need. **Focus:** Horticulture. **Qualif.:** Applicants must be graduating seniors from Avery County High School, North Carolina attending a two or four-year college to study horticulture or agriculture; and must have at least a 2.5 GPA in high school. **Criteria:** Recipients are selected based on financial need, extracurricular and civic participation.

Funds Avail.: No specific amount. **To Apply:** Applicants must complete the application form; must submit two applicant appraisals; transcript of grades; student's essay describing educational plans and how these will help in career goals; and one recent photograph. **Deadline:** March 15. **Remarks:** Established in 2008. **Contact:** Pat Cole, Scholarship Coordinator; Phone: 615-321-4939; Email: pcole@cfmt.org.

3221 ■ The Community Foundation Student Education Loan Funds for Gay and Lesbians *(Undergraduate/Loan)*

Purpose: To provide financial assistance to students pursuing a specific field of study and who are most in need. **Focus:** General studies/Field of study not specified. **Qualif.:** Applicants must be young men or women whose parents have discontinued financial support for their education because they are gay or lesbian. **Criteria:** Recipients are selected based on financial need, extracurricular and civic participation.

Funds Avail.: No specific amount. **To Apply:** Applicants must complete the application form; must submit two applicant appraisals; transcript of grades; student's essay describing the educational plans and how these will help in career goals; and one recent photograph. **Deadline:** March 15. **Contact:** Pat Cole, Scholarship Coordinator; Phone: 615-321-4939; Email: pcole@cfmt.org.

3222 ■ Colonel Richard M. Dawson Highway Patrol Scholarship Fund *(Undergraduate/Scholarship)*

Purpose: To provide financial assistance to students pursuing a specific field of study and who are most in need. **Focus:** Criminal justice. **Qualif.:** Applicants must be children of employees of the Tennessee Highway Patrol who serve in uniform, undercover, or plainclothes; must be rising sophomores, juniors, or seniors in college who demonstrate a commitment to a career in criminal justice through their course of study. **Criteria:** Recipients are selected based on financial need, extracurricular and civic participation.

Awards are arranged alphabetically below their administering organizations

COMMUNITY FOUNDATION OF MIDDLE TENNESSEE

Funds Avail.: No specific amount. **To Apply:** Applicants must complete the application form; must submit two applicant appraisals; transcript of grades; student's essay describing educational plans and how these will help in career goals; and one recent photograph. **Deadline:** March 15. **Remarks:** Established in 2004. **Contact:** Pat Cole, Scholarship Coordinator; Phone: 615-321-4939; Email: pcole@cfmt.org.

3223 ■ DBI Scholarships Fund (Undergraduate/Scholarship)

Purpose: To provide financial assistance to students pursuing a specific field of study and who are most in need. **Focus:** General studies/Field of study not specified. **Qualif.:** Applicants must be graduating high school seniors, undergraduates and graduates enrolling or enrolled at an accredited college/university, junior college or technical/vocational school on a full-time basis maintaining "B" average or better; must be the children of current employees of Ingram Entertainment Inc. or DBI Distributing Inc. with at least two years of service. **Criteria:** Recipients are selected based on financial need, extracurricular and civic participation.

Funds Avail.: No specific amount. **To Apply:** Applicants must complete the application form; must submit two applicant appraisals; transcript of grades; student's essay describing educational plans and how these will help in career goals; and one recent photograph. **Deadline:** March 15. **Remarks:** Established in 2003. **Contact:** Pat Cole, Scholarship Coordinator; Phone: 615-321-4939; Email: pcole@cfmt.org.

3224 ■ B.J. Dean Scholarships (Undergraduate/Scholarship)

Purpose: To provide financial assistance to students pursuing a specific field of study and who are most in need. **Focus:** General studies/Field of study not specified. **Qualif.:** Applicants must be females preparing for full-time Christian ministry, but scholarship is not limited to those seeking ordination or serving in any particular denomination. Applicants must be residents of Tennessee or Texas or be enrolled in Yale Divinity School. **Criteria:** Recipients are selected based on financial need, extracurricular and civic participation.

Funds Avail.: No specific amount. **To Apply:** Applicants must complete the application form. Applicants must submit two applicant appraisals; transcript of grades; student essay describing educational plans and how these will help in career goals. Applicants must submit one recent photograph. **Deadline:** March 15. **Remarks:** Established in 1995. **Contact:** Pat Cole, Scholarship Coordinator; Phone: 615-321-4939; Email: pcole@cfmt.org.

3225 ■ Dr. Mac Scholarships (Undergraduate/Scholarship)

Purpose: To provide financial assistance to students pursuing a specific field of study and who are most in need. **Focus:** Dentistry. **Qualif.:** Applicants must be enrolled at the University of Tennessee at Memphis School of Dentistry and entering their third year of school with a minimum of 2.7 GPA. **Criteria:** Recipients are selected based on financial need, extracurricular and civic participation.

Funds Avail.: No specific amount. **To Apply:** Applicants must complete the application form; must submit two applicant appraisals; transcript of grades; student's essay describing educational plans and how these will help in career goals; and one recent photograph. **Deadline:** March 15. **Remarks:** Established in 2004. **Contact:** Pat Cole, Scholarship Coordinator; Phone: 615-321-4939; Email: pcole@cfmt.org.

3226 ■ Jimmy Edwards Scholarships (Undergraduate/Scholarship)

Purpose: To provide financial assistance to students pursuing a specific field of study and who are most in need. **Focus:** General studies/Field of study not specified. **Qualif.:** Applicants must be past students or graduates of Donelson High School, Donelson, Tennessee and any descendents of alumni of Donelson High School. **Criteria:** Recipients are selected based on financial need, extracurricular and civic participation.

Funds Avail.: No specific amount. **To Apply:** Applicants must complete the application form; must submit two applicant appraisals; transcript of grades; student's essay describing educational plans and how these will help in career goals; and one recent photograph. **Deadline:** March 15. **Remarks:** Established in 2001. **Contact:** Pat Cole, Scholarship Coordinator; Phone: 615-321-4939; Email: pcole@cfmt.org.

3227 ■ Pauline LaFon Gore Scholarships (Undergraduate/Scholarship)

Purpose: To provide financial assistance to students pursuing a specific field of study and who are most in need. **Focus:** General studies/Field of study not specified. **Qualif.:** Applicants must be high school seniors and current college underclassmen who are from Smith County, Tennessee and have lived there for the majority of their pre-college schooling. **Criteria:** Recipients are selected based on financial need, extracurricular and civic participation.

Funds Avail.: No specific amount. **To Apply:** Applicants must complete the application form; must submit two applicant appraisals; transcript of grades; student's essay describing educational plans and how these will help in career goals; and one recent photograph. **Deadline:** March 15. **Remarks:** Established in 1998. **Contact:** Pat Cole, Scholarship Coordinator; Phone: 615-321-4939; Email: pcole@cfmt.org.

3228 ■ Frank and Charlene Harris Scholarships (Undergraduate/Scholarship)

Purpose: To provide financial assistance to students pursuing a specific field of study and who are most in need. **Focus:** General studies/Field of study not specified. **Qualif.:** Applicants must be seniors of Cumberland Gap High School in Clairborne County, TN; and must have GPA of 3.0 or higher at the time of the application. **Criteria:** Recipients are selected based on financial need, extracurricular and civic participation.

Funds Avail.: No specific amount. **To Apply:** Applicants must complete the application form; must submit two applicant appraisals; transcript of grades; student's essay describing educational plans and how these will help in career goals; and one recent photograph. **Deadline:** March 15. **Remarks:** Established in 2005. **Contact:** Pat Cole, Scholarship Coordinator; Phone: 615-321-4939; Email: pcole@cfmt.org.

3229 ■ Regina Higdon Scholarships (Undergraduate/Scholarship)

Purpose: To provide financial assistance to students pursuing a specific field of study and who are most in need. **Focus:** Art. **Qualif.:** Applicants must be graduating eighth

Awards are arranged alphabetically below their administering organizations

graders of Christ the King School and/or former graduates of Christ the King School attending Father Ryan High School or St. Cecilia Academy; must have at least a 2.5 GPA or equivalent; and must exhibit a love for the arts. **Criteria:** Recipients are selected based on financial need, extracurricular and civic participation.

Funds Avail.: No specific amount. **To Apply:** Applicants must complete the application form; must submit two applicant appraisals; transcript of grades; student's essay describing educational plans and how these will help in career goals; and one recent photograph. **Deadline:** March 15. **Remarks:** Established in 2003. **Contact:** Pat Cole, Scholarship Coordinator; Phone: 615-321-4939; Email: pcole@cfmt.org.

3230 ■ Jennifer Ingrum Scholarships (Undergraduate/Scholarship)

Purpose: To provide financial assistance to students pursuing a specific field of study and who are most in need. **Focus:** General studies/Field of study not specified. **Qualif.:** Applicants must be students of Gallatin High School and Station Camp High School area who qualify academically for college but need financial assistance. **Criteria:** Recipients are selected based on financial need, extracurricular and civic participation.

Funds Avail.: $2,000. **Duration:** Annual. **Number Awarded:** 2. **To Apply:** Applicants must complete the application form; must submit two applicant appraisals; transcript of grades; student's essay describing educational plans and how these will help in career goals; and one recent photograph. **Deadline:** March 15. **Remarks:** Established in 2005. **Contact:** Pat Cole, Scholarship Coordinator; Phone: 615-321-4939; Email: pcole@cfmt.org.

3231 ■ Maude Keisling/Cumberland County Extension Homemakers Scholarships (Undergraduate/Scholarship)

Purpose: To provide financial assistance to students pursuing a specific field of study and who are most in need. **Focus:** Ecology; Education; Social work. **Qualif.:** Applicants must be residents of Cumberland County, Tennessee for a period of four years or more; must be graduating high school seniors, GED graduates, or current college undergraduates with GPA of 2.5 or better; must pursue a field of study such as, but not limited to, human ecology, family and consumer science, education, and social services; and must be enrolled as full or part-time students with six or more semester hours at an accredited college, university, or community college. **Criteria:** Recipients are selected based on financial need, extracurricular and civic participation. Extra consideration will be given to adults out of school for five years or more seeking higher education.

Funds Avail.: No specific amount. **To Apply:** Applicants must complete the application form; must submit two applicant appraisals; transcript of grades; student's essay describing educational plans and how these will help in career goals; and one recent photograph. **Deadline:** March 15. **Remarks:** Established in 2000. **Contact:** Pat Cole, Scholarship Coordinator; Phone: 615-321-4939; Email: pcole@cfmt.org.

3232 ■ Knox-Hume Scholarships (Undergraduate/Scholarship)

Purpose: To provide financial assistance to students pursuing a specific field of study and who are most in need. **Focus:** General studies/Field of study not specified. **Qualif.:** Applicants must be graduates of Hume-Fogg High School who exhibit academic merit and financial need. **Criteria:** Recipients are selected based on financial need, extracurricular and civic participation.

Funds Avail.: No specific amount. **To Apply:** Applicants must complete the application form; must submit two applicant appraisals; transcript of grades; student's essay describing educational plans and how these will help in career goals; and one recent photograph. **Deadline:** March 15. **Remarks:** Established in 2007. **Contact:** Pat Cole, Scholarship Coordinator; Phone: 615-321-4939; Email: pcole@cfmt.org.

3233 ■ Senator Carl O. Koella, Jr. Memorial Scholarships (Undergraduate/Scholarship)

Purpose: To provide financial assistance to students pursuing a specific field of study and who are most in need. **Focus:** Law. **Qualif.:** Applicants must be legislative interns, either public or private, currently enrolled or planning to enroll in a four-year college the year of the application; and must be residents of Blount and Sevier Counties of Tennessee. **Criteria:** Recipients are selected based on financial need, extracurricular and civic participation. Extra consideration will be given to extracurricular activities in the areas of government and politics.

Funds Avail.: No specific amount. **To Apply:** Applicants must complete the application form; must submit two applicant appraisals; transcript of grades; student's essay describing educational plans and how these will help in career goals and one recent photograph. **Deadline:** March 15. **Remarks:** Established in 1999. **Contact:** Pat Cole, Scholarship Coordinator; Phone: 615-321-4939; Email: pcole@cfmt.org.

3234 ■ Michael B. Kruse Scholarships (Graduate, Undergraduate/Scholarship)

Purpose: To provide financial assistance to students pursuing a specific field of study and who are most in need. **Focus:** Accounting. **Qualif.:** Applicants must be rising juniors, seniors and graduate students majoring in accounting with goals in becoming a Certified Public Accountant; must be residents of Tennessee and attend an accredited college/university in the State of Tennessee; and must maintain a minimum GPA of 3.2 or better. **Criteria:** Recipients are selected based on financial need, extracurricular and civic participation. Special consideration will be given to married applicants.

Funds Avail.: No specific amount. **To Apply:** Applicants must complete the application form; must submit two applicant appraisals; transcript of grades; student's essay describing educational plans and how these will help in career goals; and one recent photograph. **Deadline:** March 15. **Remarks:** Established in 2003. **Contact:** Pat Cole, Scholarship Coordinator; Phone: 615-321-4939; Email: pcole@cfmt.org.

3235 ■ Heloise Werthan Kuhn Scholarships (Undergraduate/Scholarship)

Purpose: To provide financial assistance to students pursuing a specific field of study and who are most in need. **Focus:** General studies/Field of study not specified. **Qualif.:** Applicants must be pregnant or parenting teens living in the State of Tennessee; must be enrolled or planning to enroll in post-secondary education at an accredited college, university, junior college, technical school, or job training program as a way to increase their job skills and become more employable. **Criteria:** Recipients are selected based on financial need, extracurricular and civic participation.

Awards are arranged alphabetically below their administering organizations

Funds Avail.: No specific amount. **To Apply:** Applicants must complete the application form; must submit two applicant appraisals; transcript of grades; student's essay describing the educational plans and how these will help in career goals; and one recent photograph. **Deadline:** March 15. **Remarks:** Established in 2001. **Contact:** Pat Cole, Scholarship Coordinator; Phone: 615-321-4939; Email: pcole@cfmt.org.

3236 ■ Diane G. Lowe and John Gomez, IV Scholarships *(Undergraduate/Scholarship)*

Purpose: To provide financial assistance to students who would be otherwise unable to take qualifying entrance exams to institutions of higher learning and to provide gifted students financial assistance to attend academic programs that offer intellectually-accelerated content. **Focus:** General studies/Field of study not specified. **Qualif.:** Applicants must be students with financial need in Grades 6-12 who reside in Rutherford, Cannon, Dekalb, or Wilson Counties. Students taking qualifying entrance exams to institutions of higher learning, such as the SAT and ACT exams, and will attend academic programs that offer special challenges or accelerated content. **Criteria:** Recipients are selected based on financial need, extracurricular and civic participation.

Funds Avail.: No specific amount. **To Apply:** Applicants must complete the application form; must submit two applicant appraisals; transcript of grades; student's essay describing educational plans and how these will help in career goals; one recent photograph. **Deadline:** March 15. **Remarks:** Established in 2006. **Contact:** Pat Cole, Scholarship Coordinator; Phone: 615-321-4939; Email: pcole@cfmt.org.

3237 ■ Edna L. Martin Scholarships *(Undergraduate/Scholarship)*

Purpose: To provide financial assistance to students pursuing a specific field of study and who are most in need. **Focus:** Education. **Qualif.:** Applicants must be graduating high school seniors, or individuals who previously graduated from the Davidson County-Metropolitan Nashville Public School System; must have desire to pursue a career in teaching in elementary, middle or high school. **Criteria:** Recipients are selected based on financial need, extracurricular and civic participation.

Funds Avail.: No specific amount. **To Apply:** Applicants must complete the application form; must submit two applicant appraisals; transcript of grades; student essay describing educational plans and how these will help in career goals; and one recent photograph. **Deadline:** March 15. **Remarks:** Established in 2004. **Contact:** Pat Cole, Scholarship Coordinator; Phone: 615-321-4939; Email: pcole@cfmt.org.

3238 ■ Juliann and Joe Maxwell Scholarships *(Undergraduate/Scholarship)*

Purpose: To provide financial assistance to students pursuing a specific field of study and who are most in need. **Focus:** General studies/Field of study not specified. **Qualif.:** Applicants must be high school seniors, college freshmen, sophomores and juniors who are dependent children, including adopted and stepchildren of full or part-time employees of the Tractor Supply Company. Employees must have minimum of one year of service with Tractor Supply Company by January 1 of the year in which the application is received. **Criteria:** Recipients are selected based on financial need, extracurricular and civic participation.

Funds Avail.: No specific amount. **To Apply:** Applicants must complete the application form; must submit two applicant appraisals; transcript of grades; student essay describing their educational plans and how these will help in career goals; and one recent photograph. **Deadline:** March 15. **Remarks:** Established in 2006. **Contact:** Pat Cole, Scholarship Coordinator; Phone: 615-321-4939; Email: pcole@cfmt.org.

3239 ■ Juliann King Maxwell Scholarships for Riverview High School *(Undergraduate, Vocational/Occupational/Scholarship)*

Purpose: To provide financial assistance to students pursuing a specific field of study and who are most in need. **Focus:** General studies/Field of study not specified. **Qualif.:** Applicants must be graduating seniors from Riverview High School in Searcy, Arkansas, or prior recipients of the scholarship, who wants to pursue vocational training as well as those pursuing a college degree. **Criteria:** Recipients are selected based on financial need, extracurricular and civic participation. Preference to those whose teachers recognize effort, a desire to learn and determination.

Funds Avail.: No specific amount. **To Apply:** Applicants must complete the application form. Applicants must submit two applicant appraisals; transcript of grades; student essay describing educational plans and how these will help in career goals. Applicants must submit one recent photograph. **Deadline:** March 15. **Remarks:** Established in 2006. **Contact:** Pat Cole, Scholarship Coordinator; Phone: 615-321-4939; Email: pcole@cfmt.org.

3240 ■ John E. Mayfield ABLE Scholarships *(Undergraduate/Scholarship)*

Purpose: To provide financial assistance to students pursuing a specific field of study and who are most in need. **Focus:** General studies/Field of study not specified. **Qualif.:** Applicants must be graduating seniors and be participants of the ABLE program; must attend an accredited college, university, junior college, technical school or job training program. Individuals who have previously received scholarship assistance are welcome to re-apply. **Criteria:** Recipients are selected based on financial need, extracurricular and civic participation.

Funds Avail.: No specific amount. **To Apply:** Applicants must complete the application form; must submit two applicant appraisals; transcript of grades; student essay describing educational plans and how these will help in career goals; and one recent photograph. **Deadline:** March 15. **Remarks:** Established in 2002. **Contact:** Pat Cole, Scholarship Coordinator; Phone: 615-321-4939; Email: pcole@cfmt.org.

3241 ■ John E. Mayfield Scholarship Fund for Cheatham County Central High School *(Undergraduate/Scholarship)*

Purpose: To provide financial assistance to students pursuing a specific field of study and who are most in need. **Focus:** General studies/Field of study not specified. **Qualif.:** Applicants must be alumni and/or graduating seniors of Cheatham County Central High School in Cheatham County, Tennessee; must be residents of Cheatham County and have grade point average of 2.0 or better. **Criteria:** Recipients are selected based on financial need, extracurricular and civic participation.

Funds Avail.: No specific amount. **To Apply:** Applicants must complete the application form; must submit two ap-

Awards are arranged alphabetically below their administering organizations

plicant appraisals; transcript of grades; student essay describing educational plans and how these will help in career goals; one recent photograph. **Deadline:** March 15. **Remarks:** Established in 2000. **Contact:** Pat Cole, Scholarship Coordinator; Phone: 615-321-4939; Email: pcole@cfmt.org.

3242 ■ John E. Mayfield Scholarship Fund for Harpeth High School *(Undergraduate/Scholarship)*

Purpose: To provide financial assistance to students pursuing a specific field of study and who are most in need. **Focus:** General studies/Field of study not specified. **Qualif.:** Applicants must be alumni and/or graduating seniors of Harpeth High School in Cheatham County, Tennessee; must be residents of Cheatham County and have GPA of 2.0 or better. **Criteria:** Recipients are selected based on financial need, extracurricular and civic participation.

Funds Avail.: No specific amount. **To Apply:** Applicants must complete the application form; must submit two applicant appraisals; transcript of grades; student essay describing educational plans and how these will help in career goals; one recent photograph. **Deadline:** March 15. **Remarks:** Established in 2000. **Contact:** Pat Cole, Scholarship Coordinator; Phone: 615-321-4939; Email: pcole@cfmt.org.

3243 ■ John E. Mayfield Scholarship Fund for Pleasant View Christian High School *(Undergraduate/Scholarship)*

Purpose: To provide financial assistance to students pursuing a specific field of study and who are most in need. **Focus:** General studies/Field of study not specified. **Qualif.:** Applicants must be alumni and/or graduating seniors of Pleasant View Christian School in Cheatham County, Tennessee; must be residents of Cheatham County and have GPA of 2.0 or better. **Criteria:** Recipients are selected based on financial need, extracurricular and civic participation.

Funds Avail.: No specific amount. **To Apply:** Applicants must complete the application form; must submit two applicant appraisals; transcript of grades; student essay describing educational plans and how these will help in career goals; and one recent photograph. **Deadline:** March 15. **Remarks:** Established in 2001. **Contact:** Pat Cole, Scholarship Coordinator; Phone: 615-321-4939; Email: pcole@cfmt.org.

3244 ■ John E. Mayfield Scholarship Fund for Sycamore High School *(Undergraduate/Scholarship)*

Purpose: To provide financial assistance to students pursuing a specific field of study and who are most in need. **Focus:** General studies/Field of study not specified. **Qualif.:** Applicants must be alumni and/or graduating seniors of Sycamore High School in Cheatham County, Tennessee; must be residents of Cheatham County and have GPA of 2.0 or better. **Criteria:** Recipients are selected based on financial need, extracurricular and civic participation.

Funds Avail.: No specific amount. **To Apply:** Applicants must complete the application form; must submit two applicant appraisals; transcript of grades; student essay describing educational plans and how these will help in career goals; and one recent photograph. **Deadline:** March 15. **Remarks:** Established in 2000. **Contact:** Pat Cole, Scholarship Coordinator; Phone: 615-321-4939; Email: pcole@cfmt.org.

3245 ■ Archie Hartwell Nash Memorial Scholarships *(Graduate, Undergraduate/Scholarship)*

Purpose: To provide financial assistance to students pursuing a specific field of study and who are most in need. **Focus:** General studies/Field of study not specified. **Qualif.:** Applicants must be Middle Tennessee State University sophomores or above including graduate students who are working at a minimum of 20 hours and have a GPA of 2.0 or better. **Criteria:** Recipients are selected based on financial need, extracurricular and civic participation.

Funds Avail.: No specific amount. **To Apply:** Applicants must complete the application form; must submit two applicant appraisals; transcript of grades; student essay describing educational plans and how these will help in career goals. Applicants must submit; and one recent photograph. **Deadline:** March 15. **Remarks:** Established in 1997. **Contact:** Pat Cole, Scholarship Coordinator; Phone: 615-321-4939; Email: pcole@cfmt.org.

3246 ■ Jerry Newson Scholarships *(Undergraduate/Scholarship)*

Purpose: To provide financial assistance to students pursuing a specific field of study and who are most in need. **Focus:** General studies/Field of study not specified. **Qualif.:** Applicants must currently reside in Davidson County, Tennessee; must have high school diploma or GED; must attend a four-year accredited institution of higher education which may be out-of-state; must be pursuing degree in the social sciences or areas where they will be helping and giving back to their community. High school graduates and adults are encouraged to apply. **Criteria:** Recipients are selected based on financial need, extracurricular and civic participation.

Funds Avail.: No specific amount. **To Apply:** Applicants must complete the application form; must submit two applicant appraisals; transcript of grades; student essay describing educational plans and how these will help in career goals; and one recent photograph. **Deadline:** March 15. **Remarks:** Established in 1997. **Contact:** Pat Cole, Scholarship Coordinator; Phone: 615-321-4939; Email: pcole@cfmt.org.

3247 ■ Eloise Pitts O'More Scholarships *(Undergraduate/Scholarship)*

Purpose: To provide financial assistance to students pursuing a specific field of study and who are most in need. **Focus:** Interior design. **Qualif.:** Applicants must be interior design students who are currently pursuing a degree in interior design at O'More College of Design; must be classified as juniors or higher and have GPA of 3.0 or higher at the time of application; be actively participating members of either the American Society of Interior Design and/or International Design Association's student chapters. **Criteria:** Recipients are selected based on financial need, extracurricular and civic participation.

Funds Avail.: No specific amount. **To Apply:** Applicants must complete the application form; must submit two applicant appraisals; transcript of grades; student essay describing educational plans and how these will help in career goals; and one recent photograph. **Deadline:** March 15. **Remarks:** Established in 2001. **Contact:** Pat Cole, Scholarship Coordinator; Phone: 615-321-4939; Email: pcole@cfmt.org.

3248 ■ Buster Pool Memorial Scholarships *(Undergraduate/Scholarship)*

Purpose: To provide financial assistance to students pursuing a specific field of study and who are most in need.

Awards are arranged alphabetically below their administering organizations

Focus: General studies/Field of study not specified. **Qualif.:** Applicants must be graduating seniors of Meridian High School in Meridian, Mississippi and/or previous recipients of this scholarship; must have GPA of 2.5 or higher at the time of application. **Criteria:** Recipients are selected based on financial need, extracurricular and civic participation. Preference will be given to those applicants who are members of Meridian High School Golf Team and/or golfers in difference to Buster pool's passion for the game of golf.

Funds Avail.: No specific amount. **To Apply:** Applicants must complete the application form; must submit two applicant appraisals; transcript of grades; student essay describing educational plans and how these will help in career goals; and one recent photograph. **Deadline:** March 15. **Remarks:** Established in 2002. **Contact:** Pat Cole, Scholarship Coordinator; Phone: 615-321-4939; Email: pcole@cfmt.org.

3249 ■ Barbara Hagan Richards Scholarships *(Undergraduate/Scholarship)*

Purpose: To provide financial assistance to students pursuing a specific field of study and who are most in need. **Focus:** General studies/Field of study not specified. **Qualif.:** Applicants must be graduating seniors, undergraduates, and/or graduate students currently enrolled in a college/university and/or alumni of any high school located and serving Giles County, Tennessee; must have GPA of 3.0. **Criteria:** Recipients are selected based on financial need, extracurricular and civic participation.

Funds Avail.: No specific amount. **To Apply:** Applicants must complete the application form; must submit two applicant appraisals; transcript of grades; student essay describing educational plans and how these will help in career goals; and one recent photograph. **Deadline:** March 15. **Remarks:** Established in 2001. **Contact:** Pat Cole, Scholarship Coordinator; Phone: 615-321-4939; Email: pcole@cfmt.org.

3250 ■ James Edward "Bill" Richards Scholarships *(Undergraduate/Scholarship)*

Purpose: To provide financial assistance to students pursuing a specific field of study and who are most in need. **Focus:** General studies/Field of study not specified. **Qualif.:** Applicants must be high school seniors, undergraduates or graduate students who have graduated from East High School in Nashville, Tennessee; and must have GPA of at least 3.0. **Criteria:** Recipients are selected based on financial need, extracurricular and civic participation.

Funds Avail.: No specific amount. **To Apply:** Applicants must complete the application form; must submit two applicant appraisals; transcript of grades; student's essay describing educational plans and how these will help in career goals; and one recent photograph. **Deadline:** March 15. **Remarks:** Established in 2001. **Contact:** Pat Cole, Scholarship Coordinator; Phone: 615-321-4939; Email: pcole@cfmt.org.

3251 ■ Meyer D. and Dorothy C. Silverman Scholarship *(Undergraduate/Scholarship)*

Purpose: To provide financial assistance to students pursuing a specific field of study and who are most in need. **Focus:** General studies/Field of study not specified. **Qualif.:** Applicants must be students in Grade 7 to 12 in Oak Ridge Public Schools who are committed in developing their talents as string instrument players but who, otherwise, would be financially unable to take private string instruction; and must be recommended by an instructor. **Criteria:** Recipients will be selected based on financial need and demonstrated commitment to music.

Funds Avail.: No specific amount. **To Apply:** Applicants must complete the application form; must submit two applicant appraisals; transcript of grades; student essay describing educational plans and how these will help in career goals; and one recent photograph. **Deadline:** March 15. **Remarks:** Established in 2007. **Contact:** Pat Cole, Scholarship Coordinator; Phone: 615-321-4939; Email: pcole@cfmt.org.

3252 ■ Drue Smith/Society of Professional Journalists Scholarships *(Undergraduate/Scholarship)*

Purpose: To provide financial assistance to students pursuing a specific field of study and who are most in need. **Focus:** Journalism. **Qualif.:** Applicants must be college juniors, seniors or graduate students who have graduated from high school in Middle Tennessee and have chosen journalism or broadcast news for a career, or mid-career working journalists who seek training to develop professionally or further their careers. **Criteria:** Recipients are selected based on financial need, extracurricular and civic participation.

Funds Avail.: No specific amount. **To Apply:** Applicants must complete the application form; must submit two applicant appraisals; transcript of grades; student's essay describing educational plans and how these will help in career goals and one recent photograph. **Deadline:** March 15. **Remarks:** Established in 2004. **Contact:** Pat Cole, Scholarship Coordinator; Phone: 615-321-4939; Email: pcole@cfmt.org.

3253 ■ Richie Stevenson Scholarships *(Undergraduate, Vocational/Occupational/Scholarship)*

Purpose: To provide financial assistance to students pursuing a specific field of study and who are most in need. **Focus:** General studies/Field of study not specified. **Qualif.:** Applicants must be graduates of Benton Hall School who wish to attend a technical school, vocational school, community college, junior or four-year college or university. **Criteria:** Recipients are selected based on financial need, extracurricular and civic participation.

Funds Avail.: No specific amount. **To Apply:** Applicants must complete the application form; must submit two applicant appraisals; transcript of grades; student essay describing educational plans and how these will help in career goals; and one recent photograph. **Deadline:** March 15. **Remarks:** Established in 2000. **Contact:** Pat Cole, Scholarship Coordinator; Phone: 615-321-4939; Email: pcole@cfmt.org.

3254 ■ Tennessee Trucking Foundation Scholarships *(Undergraduate/Scholarship)*

Purpose: To provide financial assistance to students pursuing a specific field of study and who are most in need. **Focus:** General studies/Field of study not specified. **Qualif.:** Applicants must be Tennessee residents who are dependent children, spouses or employees who are members in good standing of the Tennessee Trucking Association; must be entering their junior or senior years at accredited colleges or universities located in the State of Tennessee. **Criteria:** Recipients are selected based on financial need, extracurricular and civic participation.

Funds Avail.: No specific amount. **To Apply:** Applicants must complete the application form; must submit two applicant appraisals; transcript of grades; student's essay

Awards are arranged alphabetically below their administering organizations

describing the educational plans and how these will help in career goals; and one recent photograph. **Deadline:** March 15. **Remarks:** Established in 2003. **Contact:** Pat Cole, Scholarship Coordinator; Phone: 615-321-4939; Email: pcole@cfmt.org.

3255 ■ Emmett H. Turner Scholarships
(Undergraduate/Scholarship)

Purpose: To provide financial assistance to students pursuing a specific field of study and who are most in need. **Focus:** Criminal justice. **Qualif.:** Applicants must be students enrolling or currently enrolled at Tennessee University in the Criminal Justice program. **Criteria:** Recipients are selected based on financial need, extracurricular and civic participation.

Funds Avail.: No specific amount. **To Apply:** Applicants must complete the application form. Applicants must submit two applicant appraisals; transcript of grades; student essay describing educational plans and how these will help in career goals. Applicants must submit one recent photograph. **Deadline:** March 15. **Remarks:** Established in 2003. **Contact:** Pat Cole, Scholarship Coordinator; Phone: 615-321-4939; Email: pcole@cfmt.org.

3256 ■ Teddy Wilburn Scholarships *(Undergraduate/Scholarship)*

Purpose: To provide financial assistance to students pursuing a specific field of study and who are most in need. **Focus:** General studies/Field of study not specified. **Qualif.:** Applicants must be students enrolling or currently enrolled at Tennessee State University or Vanderbilt University; must have at least "B" overall GPA during the last two years of high school; must have attended high school within the 40 counties of Middle Tennessee for the majority of high school. **Criteria:** Recipients are selected based on financial need, extracurricular and civic participation.

Funds Avail.: No specific amount. **To Apply:** Applicants must complete the application form; must submit two applicant appraisals; transcript of grades; student's essay describing educational plans and how these will help in career goals; and one recent photograph. **Deadline:** March 15. **Remarks:** Established in 2005. **Contact:** Pat Cole, Scholarship Coordinator; Phone: 615-321-4939; Email: pcole@cfmt.org.

3257 ■ The Woman's Club of Nashville Scholarship Endowment Fund *(Undergraduate/Scholarship)*

Purpose: To provide financial assistance to students pursuing a specific field of study and who are most in need. **Focus:** General studies/Field of study not specified. **Qualif.:** Applicants must be women residing in Davidson County, Tennessee. Applicants must be graduating high school seniors or high school graduates with a GPA of 3.0 or higher. **Criteria:** Recipients are selected based on financial need, extracurricular and civic participation.

Funds Avail.: No specific amount. **To Apply:** Applicants must complete the application form. Applicants must submit two applicant appraisals; transcript of grades; student essay describing educational plans and how these will help in career goals. Applicants must submit one recent photograph. **Deadline:** March 15. **Contact:** Pat Cole, Scholarship Coordinator; Phone: 615-321-4939; Email: pcole@cfmt.org.

3258 ■ John W. Work III Memorial Foundation Scholarships *(Undergraduate/Scholarship)*

Purpose: To provide financial assistance to students pursuing a specific field of study and who are most in need. **Focus:** Music. **Qualif.:** Applicants must be undergraduate juniors, seniors or graduate students pursuing a degree in music at an accredited university, college or institute; must have "B" average and demonstrate potential for excellence in music. **Criteria:** Recipients are selected based on financial need, extracurricular and civic participation. Special preference will be given to African Americans.

Funds Avail.: No specific amount. **To Apply:** Applicants must complete the application form; must submit two applicant appraisals; transcript of grades; student's essay describing educational plans and how these will help in career goals; and one recent photograph. **Deadline:** March 15. **Remarks:** Established in 2002. **Contact:** Pat Cole, Scholarship Coordinator; Phone: 615-321-4939; Email: pcole@cfmt.org.

3259 ■ Community Foundation of Northeast Alabama (CFNEA)
Quintard Towers
1130 Quintard Ave., Ste. 100
Anniston, AL 36201
Ph: (256)231-5160
URL: www.yourcommunityfirst.org
Facebook: www.facebook.com/Community-Foundation-of-Northeast-Alabama-212407278799983

3260 ■ Calhoun County Auburn University Scholarships *(Undergraduate/Scholarship)*

Purpose: To provide financial resources enabling local students to pursue higher education at Auburn University. **Focus:** General studies/Field of study not specified. **Qualif.:** Applicants must be graduates of any accredited public or private high school within Calhoun County; must have maintained 2.5 GPA on a 4.0 scale; must be ranked within the top 25% of high school graduating class. **Criteria:** Recipients are selected based on financial need.

Funds Avail.: $1,000. **To Apply:** Applicants must submit a completed application form and an essay describing their personal aspirations, educational and career goals. **Deadline:** March 13.

3261 ■ Melanie and Todd Edmonson Memorial Scholarships *(Undergraduate/Scholarship)*

Purpose: To encourage young people to follow their dreams and to help lessen some of life's challenges. **Focus:** General studies/Field of study not specified. **Qualif.:** Applicants must be graduates of Oxford High School or its successor; must have 3.0 or "B" average; must be actively involved in their community, school and religious activities; must be full or part-time enrolled students at an accredited institution of higher learning in the United States; may be pursuing any field of academic study or technical training. **Criteria:** Recipients are selected based on financial need and academic performance.

Funds Avail.: $1,000. **Number Awarded:** 2. **To Apply:** Applicants must submit a completed application form, transcript of records, an essay describing their personal aspirations, educational or career goals and how this scholarship will help in achieving their career goals. **Deadline:** March 13.

3262 ■ Farley Moody Galbraith Scholarship Fund
(Undergraduate/Scholarship)

Purpose: To encourage high school seniors to attain a four-year college degree. **Focus:** General studies/Field of

Awards are arranged alphabetically below their administering organizations

study not specified. **Qualif.:** Applicants must be graduating seniors from any public or private high school including home school; must have 3.0 average on a 4.0 scale; must be enrolled as part- or full-time students. **Criteria:** Recipients are selected based on financial need, academic ability and good character.

Funds Avail.: $2,000. **To Apply:** Applicants must submit a completed application form and an essay describing their personal aspirations, educational or career goals and how this scholarship will help in achieving their career goals. Guideline and applications are available from the Community Foundation or online at www.yourcommunityfirst.org. **Deadline:** March 13.

3263 ■ Whitney Laine Gallahar Memorial Scholarship Fund *(Undergraduate/Scholarship)*

Purpose: To provide supplement funding for full- or part-time enrolled students at an accredited state college or university within Alabama. **Focus:** General studies/Field of study not specified. **Qualif.:** Applicants must be graduating seniors of Ohatchee High school or its successor institution; must have 2.5 GPA; must be enrolled as part- or full-time. **Criteria:** Recipients are selected based on financial need, academic ability and good character.

Funds Avail.: $1,000. **To Apply:** Applicants must submit a completed application form and an essay describing their personal aspirations, educational or career goals and how this scholarship will help in achieving their career goals. **Deadline:** March 13.

3264 ■ Guin-Stanford Scholarships *(Advanced Professional/Scholarship)*

Purpose: To enhance the quality of life in Calhoun County, Alabama. **Focus:** General studies/Field of study not specified. **Qualif.:** Applicants must have earned a bachelor's degree from an accredited college or university; must hold a current Teaching Certificate from the State of Alabama. **Criteria:** Recipients are selected based on financial need and character.

Funds Avail.: $1,000. **To Apply:** Applicants must submit a completed application form, letter of enrollment and two letters of recommendation. **Deadline:** March 13.

3265 ■ Cleve Holloway Memorial Scholarship Fund *(Undergraduate/Scholarship)*

Purpose: To provide full or supplemental funding for full-time enrolled students at an accredited state college or university within Alabama. **Focus:** General studies/Field of study not specified. **Qualif.:** Applicants must be graduating seniors of Anniston High School or its successor institution; must maintain high personal standards and moral character; must have a minimum of 2.5 or "C" average on a 4.0 scale; must be enrolled full-time. **Criteria:** Recipients are selected based on financial need, academic ability and good character.

Funds Avail.: $1,000. **To Apply:** Applicants must submit a completed application form, transcript of records and an essay describing their personal aspirations, educational or career goals and how this scholarship will help in achieving their career goals. **Deadline:** March 13.

3266 ■ E.C. Lloyd and J.C.U. Johnson Scholarship Fund *(Undergraduate/Scholarship)*

Purpose: To provide supplement funding for full or part-time enrolled students at any accredited two-or-four-year college or university within the United States. **Focus:** General studies/Field of study not specified. **Qualif.:** Applicants must be graduating seniors from any public or private high school including home schools; must have 2.5 or "C" average on a 4.0 scale; must be enrolled as part- or full-time students. **Criteria:** Preference will be given to applicants who are the first in their family to attend college.

Funds Avail.: $2,500. **To Apply:** Applicants must submit a completed application form and an essay describing their personal aspirations, educational or career goals and how this scholarship will help in achieving the career goal. **Deadline:** March 13.

3267 ■ Gertie S. Lowe Nursing Scholarship Awards *(Undergraduate/Scholarship)*

Purpose: To promote and celebrate the nursing profession. **Focus:** Nursing. **Qualif.:** Applicants must be full- or part-time students in the LPN or RN program at Gadsten State Community College; must be graduates of any accredited public or private high school within Calhoun County currently attending Gadsden State Community College. **Criteria:** Recipients are selected based on character, academic ability, school/community service and financial need.

Funds Avail.: No specific amount. **To Apply:** Applicants must submit a completed application form and an essay describing their personal aspirations and contributions to nursing profession.

3268 ■ Reverend John S. Nettles Scholarships *(Undergraduate/Scholarship)*

Purpose: To foster hope, self-confidence and ambition in the graduates of Anniston High School. **Focus:** General studies/Field of study not specified. **Qualif.:** Applicants must be graduating seniors from Anniston high School; must have 2.5 GPA or above on a 4.0 scale. **Criteria:** Recipients are selected based on character, academic ability, school, church and community service and financial need.

Funds Avail.: $1,000. **To Apply:** Applicants must submit a completed application form and an essay describing the personal aspirations, educational and career goals. **Deadline:** February 1.

3269 ■ Gerald Powell Scholarships *(Undergraduate/Scholarship)*

Purpose: To support tuition assistance for students attending Sacred Heart of Jesus Catholic School in Anniston, Alabama. **Focus:** General studies/Field of study not specified. **Qualif.:** Applicants must be enrolled on a full-time basis at Sacred Heart of Jesus Catholic School either in elementary or high school levels; must maintain a GPA of 2.5 or "C" on a 4.0 scale. **Criteria:** Recipients are selected based on background, financial need and clarity and completeness of application.

Funds Avail.: No specific amount. **To Apply:** Applicants must submit a completed application form.

3270 ■ Joseph and Amelia Saks Scholarship Fund *(Undergraduate/Scholarship)*

Purpose: To foster educational opportunities for graduates of Saks High School; to provide full or supplemental funding for full-time enrolled students over a four-year period at an accredited college or university within the United States. **Focus:** General studies/Field of study not specified. **Qualif.:** Applicants must be graduating senior students of Saks High School or its successor institution; must have

Awards are arranged alphabetically below their administering organizations

maintained high personal standards and moral character; must have a minimum of 2.5 or "C" average on a 4.0 scale; must be full-time students completing academics aligned with their specific major or degree. **Criteria:** Recipients are selected based on financial need and academic performance. **Funds Avail.:** No specific amount. **Duration:** Annual. **Number Awarded:** 2. **To Apply:** Applicants must submit: a completed application form; an essay describing their personal aspirations, educational or career goals and how this scholarship will help in achieving their career goals; a signed letter of acceptance; certified proof of enrollment from an institution and confirmation that the recipient is enrolled; and an official college or university transcript at the end of academic term. **Deadline:** March 13.

3271 ■ Leslie and Mary Ella Scales Memorial Scholarships (Undergraduate/Scholarship)

Purpose: To recognize the value of higher education and provide support for graduates of Anniston High School. **Focus:** General studies/Field of study not specified. **Qualif.:** Applicants must be full-time or part-time students attending any accredited institution of higher learning in United States; may pursue any field of academic study or technical training. **Criteria:** Recipients are selected based on financial need. **Funds Avail.:** $1,000. **To Apply:** Applicants must submit a completed application form. **Deadline:** March 13.

3272 ■ Nathan Sparks Memorial Scholarships (Undergraduate/Scholarship)

Purpose: To provide supplemental funding for full or part-time enrolled students at an accredited college, university or technical institution within United States. **Focus:** General studies/Field of study not specified. **Qualif.:** Applicants must be graduating seniors of Saks High School or its successor institution. **Criteria:** Recipients are selected based on financial need. **Funds Avail.:** $1,000. **To Apply:** Applicants must submit a completed application form, an essay describing their personal character and two letters of recommendation. **Deadline:** March 1.

3273 ■ Mary Katherine "Kathy" Williamson Scholarship Fund (Undergraduate/Scholarship)

Purpose: To provide financial aid to deserving individuals pursuing an associate or bachelor degree in medical field. **Focus:** General studies/Field of study not specified. **Qualif.:** Applicants must be individuals who have a diploma from any accredited public or private high school or who have earned the General Education Development (GED) certificate; must be residents of Calhoun County; must have a 2.5 overall GPA or better on a 4.0 scale. **Criteria:** Recipients are selected based on financial need, passion to serve the needs of others and community service. **Funds Avail.:** $2,500. **To Apply:** Applicants must submit a completed application form, transcript of records, and an essay describing their personal aspirations, educational or career goals and how this scholarship will help in achieving their career goals. Applications are available to the guidance counselors at schools in Calhoun County or directly from the Community Foundation office or website (www.yourcommunityfirst.org). **Deadline:** March 13.

3274 ■ Community Foundation of Northern Illinois
946 N 2nd St.
Rockford, IL 61107
Ph: (815)962-2110
Fax: (815)962-2116
E-mail: info@cfnil.org
URL: www.cfnil.org
Twitter: twitter.com/The_CFNIL?ref_src=twsrc%5Etfw

3275 ■ Charles Lee Anderson Memorial Scholarships (Undergraduate/Scholarship)

Purpose: To support students achieve their educational goals. **Focus:** Education. **Qualif.:** Applicants must be Rock Valley or Sycamore High School graduating seniors who will enter a college or university to pursue a degree in education. **Criteria:** Recipients are selected based on demonstrated optimism, determination and love of neighbor. **Funds Avail.:** No specific amount. **To Apply:** Applicants must submit a completed application form, verification form, an official college transcript in a sealed envelope and two completed recommendation forms. **Deadline:** February 1.

3276 ■ Richard L. Bernardi Memorial Scholarships (Undergraduate/Scholarship)

Purpose: To provide financial support to those students who are pursuing their educational goal. **Focus:** General studies/Field of study not specified. **Qualif.:** Applicants must be attending or planning to attend Rock Valley College; must be committed to completing a bachelor's degree; must have an at least 2.0 GPA. **Criteria:** Recipients are selected based on demonstrated enthusiasm and leadership. **Funds Avail.:** No specific amount. **To Apply:** Applicants must submit a completed application form, verification form, an official college transcript in a sealed envelope and two completed recommendation forms. **Deadline:** February 1. **Contact:** Laura Schweitzer at 815-926-2110 x17 or lschweitzer@cfnil.org.

3277 ■ Lindsay Buster Memorial Scholarships (Undergraduate/Scholarship)

Purpose: To provide financial support to those students who are pursuing their educational goal. **Focus:** General studies/Field of study not specified. **Qualif.:** Applicants must be graduating senior athletes from Jefferson High school who have participated in high school sports for a minimum of three years including their senior year; must have 2.5 or higher cumulative GPA; must have plans to attend a two-or-four year college or university. **Criteria:** Recipients are selected based on financial need. **Funds Avail.:** No specific amount. **To Apply:** Applicants must submit a completed application form, verification form, an official transcript in a sealed envelope and two letters of recommendation. **Deadline:** February 1. **Contact:** Laura Schweitzer at 815-926-2110 x17 or lschweitzer@cfnil.org.

3278 ■ CFNIL Community Foundation Scholarships (Undergraduate/Scholarship)

Purpose: To serve the four county area (Boone, Ogle, Stephenson and Winnebago) through philanthropy; to provide leadership in meeting charitable needs and to be a responsible steward to the Foundation's donors and of the Foundation's endowment. **Focus:** General studies/Field of study not specified. **Qualif.:** Applicants must be graduating senior students and residents of Winnebago county; must have an at least 2.75 or higher GPA and have plans to attend a college, university or trade school. **Criteria:** Recipients are selected based on financial need.

Awards are arranged alphabetically below their administering organizations

Funds Avail.: No specific amount. To Apply: Applicants must submit a completed application form, verification form, an official transcript in a sealed envelope, two letters of recommendation and a copy of their FAFSA. Deadline: March 1. Contact: Laura Schweitzer at 962-2110 ext. 17 or e-mail at lschweitzer@cfnil.org.

3279 ■ CFNIL Senior Memorial Scholarships
(Undergraduate/Scholarship)

Purpose: To serve the four county area (Boone, Ogle, Stephenson and Winnebago) through philanthropy; to provide leadership in meeting charitable needs and to be a responsible steward to the Foundation's donors and of the Foundation's endowment. Focus: General studies/Field of study not specified. Qualif.: Applicants must be graduating senior students from a Rockford School District No. 205 high school; must plan to attend a college, university or higher institution of learning; must be students completing high school who are pursuing the challenge and benefits of higher education, current college students, and non-traditional students seeking to return to school. Criteria: Recipients are selected based on academic potential and financial need.

Funds Avail.: No specific amount. To Apply: Applicants must be nominated by their high school principal. Deadline: March 1. Contact: Laura Schweitzer at 962-2110 ext. 17; E-mail - lschweitzer@cfnil.org.

3280 ■ Harry H. and Floy B. Chapin Scholarships
(Undergraduate/Scholarship)

Purpose: To serve the four county area (Boone, Ogle, Stephenson and Winnebago) through philanthropy; to provide leadership in meeting charitable needs and to be a responsible steward to the Foundation's donors and of the Foundation's endowment. Focus: General studies/Field of study not specified. Qualif.: Applicants must be graduating senior students from Durand, Dakota or Pecatonica High school; must rank in top 15% of graduating class; must plan to attend a recognized college or university. Criteria: Recipients are selected based on financial need and involvement in school, community and/or church activities.

Funds Avail.: No specific amount. To Apply: Applicants must submit a completed application form, verification form, an official transcript in a sealed envelope and two letters of recommendation. Deadline: March 1. Contact: Laura Schweitzer at 962-2110 ext. 17 or e-mail at lschweitzer@cfnil.org.

3281 ■ Margaret T. Craig Community Service Scholarships *(Undergraduate/Scholarship)*

Purpose: To reward, promote and encourage youth to be involved in their community. Focus: General studies/Field of study not specified. Qualif.: Applicants must be high school graduates under the age of 23 or graduating seniors with a permanent address in Winnebago County; must have a plan to pursue a two or four-year degree at an accredited college, university or trade school; must have a minimum of 2.75 GPA. Criteria: Recipients are selected based on financial need, community involvement and strong commitment to improving the quality of life for people in their school, community and country.

Funds Avail.: No specific amount. To Apply: Applicants must submit a completed application form, verification form, an official transcript in a sealed envelope and two letters of recommendation. Deadline: March 1.

3282 ■ William R. Durham/Theater Scholarships
(Undergraduate/Scholarship)

Purpose: To serve the four county area (Boone, Ogle, Stephenson and Winnebago) through philanthropy; to provide leadership in meeting charitable needs and to be a responsible steward to the Foundation's donors and of the Foundation's endowment. Focus: Theater arts. Qualif.: Applicants must be high school graduates or graduating seniors with a permanent address within Winnebago or Boone county with a GPA of at least 3.0 on a 4.0 scale; must plan to attend an accredited four-year college or university to obtain an M.A. or B.A.; must intend to teach theater or work professionally as a performer or technician in theater. Criteria: Recipients are selected based on financial need.

Funds Avail.: No specific amount. To Apply: Applicants must submit a completed application form, verification form, an official transcript in a sealed envelope and two letters of recommendation. Deadline: March 1. Contact: Laura Schwetzer at 962-2110 ext. 17 or e-mail at lschweitzer@cfnil.org.

3283 ■ Helen R. Finley-Loescher and Stephen Loescher Scholarships *(Undergraduate/Scholarship)*

Purpose: To financially support those students who are in pursuit of a college degree. Focus: Arts. Qualif.: Applicants must be Freeport High School students demonstrating academic achievement, self-motivation and an interest in the arts; must have exhibited artistic talent through participation in the high school arts curriculum; must have plans to pursue education in fine arts. Criteria: Recipients are selected based on financial need and demonstrated active involvement in social studies organizations, clubs and classes such as student government, political campaigns, social service and community service.

Funds Avail.: No specific amount. To Apply: Applicants must contact a Freeport High school Art Department Instructor for an application form. Deadline: March 1.

3284 ■ John Flynn Memorial Scholarships
(Undergraduate/Scholarship)

Purpose: To provide educational resources to Pecatonica High School Senior students who are pursuing higher education. Focus: General studies/Field of study not specified. Qualif.: Applicants must be graduating Pecatonica High School senior students who are pursuing higher education; must have at least a 2.0 GPA on a 4.0 scale and have been involved in community service. Criteria: Recipients are selected based on financial need.

Funds Avail.: No specific amount. To Apply: Applicants must submit a completed application form, verification form, an official transcript in a sealed envelope and two letters of recommendation. Deadline: March 1.

3285 ■ Susan Kay Munson Gilmore Memorial Scholarships *(Undergraduate, Vocational/Occupational/Scholarship)*

Purpose: To provide financial support to those students who are pursuing their educational goal. Focus: General studies/Field of study not specified. Qualif.: Applicants must be graduating senior students or former graduates of a Guilford or Mendota Township high school; must have 2.0/4.0 GPA; and must be pursuing a vocational career. Criteria: Recipients are selected based on financial need.

Funds Avail.: No specific amount. To Apply: Applicants must submit a completed application form, verification form,

Awards are arranged alphabetically below their administering organizations

an official transcript in a sealed envelope, two letters of recommendation and a copy of their FAFSA. **Deadline:** March 1. **Contact:** Laura Schweitzer at 815-926-2110 x17 or lschweitzer@cfnil.org.

3286 ■ Nettie and Jesse Gorov Scholarships (Undergraduate/Scholarship)

Purpose: To provide educational resources to students planning to attend a college or university to pursue a degree. **Focus:** General studies/Field of study not specified. **Qualif.:** Applicants must plan to attend an accredited two or four-year school. **Criteria:** Recipients are selected based on financial need, character and academic achievement.

Funds Avail.: No specific amount. **To Apply:** Applicants must submit a completed application form, verification form, an official transcript in a sealed envelope, two letters of recommendation and a copy of their FAFSA. **Deadline:** March 1. **Contact:** Laura Schweitzer at 815-926-2110 x17 or lschweitzer@cfnil.org.

3287 ■ Amber Huber Memorial Scholarships (Undergraduate/Scholarship)

Purpose: To provide financial support to those students who are pursuing their educational goal. **Focus:** General studies/Field of study not specified. **Qualif.:** Applicants must be graduating senior female from Byron High School who have participated in the Byron High School girls track program and/or Byron High School Cheerleading program for at least three seasons including their senior year; must have a minimum GPA of 2.0/4.0. **Criteria:** Recipients are selected based on financial need.

Funds Avail.: No specific amount. **To Apply:** Applicants must submit a completed application form, verification form, an official transcript in a sealed envelope and two letters of recommendation. **Deadline:** February 1. **Contact:** Laura Schweitzer at 815-926-2110 x17 or lschweitzer@cfnil.org.

3288 ■ International Management Council Scholarships (IMC) (Undergraduate/Scholarship)

Purpose: The provide quality leadership and management development for supervisors and managers to enhance professional growth, community roles and individual personal development. **Focus:** Business. **Qualif.:** Applicants must be graduating seniors residing in Winnebago County who are pursuing a degree in business; must have a GPA of at least 3.0 on a 4.0 scale and have been active in community service. **Criteria:** Recipients are selected based on financial need.

Funds Avail.: No specific amount. **To Apply:** Applicants must submit a completed application form, verification form, an official transcript in a sealed envelope and two letters of recommendation. **Deadline:** February 1. **Contact:** Laura Schweitzer at 815-926-2110 x17 or lschweitzer@cfnil.org.

3289 ■ Ashley E. Ketcher Memorial Scholarships (Undergraduate/Scholarship)

Purpose: To provide educational support to students who are planning to attend an accredited college or university. **Focus:** General studies/Field of study not specified. **Qualif.:** Applicants must be graduating Auburn High School seniors in the CAPA program who have an interest in and prior experience in the performing arts; must have a cumulative GPA of at least 2.5/4.0. **Criteria:** Recipients are selected based on financial need.

Funds Avail.: No specific amount. **To Apply:** Applicants must submit a completed application form, verification form, an official transcript in a sealed envelope, two letters of recommendation and a copy of FAFSA. **Deadline:** March 1. **Contact:** Laura Schweitzer at 815-926-2110 x17 or lschweitzer@cfnil.org.

3290 ■ La Voz Latina Scholarships (Undergraduate/Scholarship)

Purpose: To serve the four county area (Boone, Ogle, Stephenson and Winnebago) through philanthropy; to provide leadership in meeting charitable needs and to be a responsible steward to the Foundation's donors and of the Foundation's endowment. **Focus:** Education, Secondary. **Qualif.:** Applicants must be high school graduates of Hispanic origin who reside in Winnebago County; must be enrolled in a post-secondary education program; must be students completing high school who are pursuing the challenge and benefits of higher education, current college students, and non-traditional students seeking to return to school. **Criteria:** Recipients are selected based on financial need.

Funds Avail.: No specific amount. **To Apply:** Applicants must submit a completed application form. **Deadline:** January 15.

3291 ■ Leopold Education Project Scholarships (Undergraduate/Scholarship)

Purpose: To provide students the financial assistance they need in pursuing their chosen degree of education. **Focus:** General studies/Field of study not specified. **Qualif.:** Applicants must be graduating high school seniors or high school graduates who are enrolled or planning to enroll in a full-time course of study at an accredited four-year college or university in a natural resources filed; must have a GPA of at least 3.0 on a 4.0 scale and have their permanent address in Boone, Cook, Dekalb, DuPage, Kane, Lake, Mchenry, Will or Winnebago counties; must be students completing high school who are pursuing the challenge and benefits of higher education, current college students, and non-traditional students seeking to return to school. **Criteria:** Recipients are selected based on financial need.

Funds Avail.: No specific amount. **To Apply:** Applicants must contact Jackie Falkenstein for more information.

3292 ■ Keith Maffioli Scholarships (Undergraduate/Scholarship)

Purpose: To provide financial support to those students who are pursuing their educational goal. **Focus:** General studies/Field of study not specified. **Qualif.:** Applicants must be graduating senior students from a Boone, Stephenson, Ogle or Winnebago County School who have a cumulative GPA of 3.0 or higher. **Criteria:** Recipients are selected based on financial need.

Funds Avail.: No specific amount. **To Apply:** Applicants must submit a completed application form, verification form, an official transcript in a sealed envelope, two letters of recommendation and a copy of their FAFSA. **Deadline:** March 1. **Contact:** Laura Schweitzer at 815-926-2110 x17 or lschweitzer@cfnil.org.

3293 ■ May-Cassioppi Scholarships (Undergraduate/Scholarship)

Purpose: To provide financial support to those students who are pursuing their educational goal. **Focus:** General studies/Field of study not specified. **Qualif.:** Applicants must be former Guilford High school swimmers and/or div-

COMMUNITY FOUNDATION OF NORTHERN ILLINOIS

ers; must exhibit character traits of strength, discipline, leadership, teamwork and loyalty. **Criteria:** Recipients are selected based on financial need.

Funds Avail.: No specific amount. **To Apply:** Applicants must submit a completed application form, verification form, an official transcript in a sealed envelope, two letters of recommendation and a copy of their FAFSA. **Deadline:** March 1. **Contact:** Laura Schweitzer at 815-926-2110 x17 or lschweitzer@cfnil.org.

3294 ■ Paul and Ruth Neidhold Business Scholarships *(Undergraduate/Scholarship)*

Purpose: To provide financial support to those students who are pursuing their educational goal. **Focus:** Business. **Qualif.:** Applicants must be Harvard High School seniors with a minimum GPA of 2.0; must have plans to pursue an education or training in a business field. **Criteria:** Recipients are selected based on financial need.

Funds Avail.: No specific amount. **To Apply:** Applicants must submit a completed application form, verification form, an official transcript in a sealed envelope, two letters of recommendation and a copy of their FAFSA. **Deadline:** February 1. **Contact:** Laura Schweitzer at 815-926-2110 x17 or lschweitzer@cfnil.org.

3295 ■ Northwest Community Center Scholarships *(Undergraduate/Scholarship)*

Purpose: To provide financial support to those students who are pursuing their educational goal. **Focus:** General studies/Field of study not specified. **Qualif.:** Applicants must be graduating senior students or graduates from a Rockford high school who have a GPA of at least 2.0; must have plans to attend a college, university or trade school; must be residents of northwest Rockford or have a history of involvement at the Northwest Community Center as either a volunteer or participant. **Criteria:** Recipients are selected based on financial need.

Funds Avail.: No specific amount. **To Apply:** Applicants must submit a completed application form, verification form, an official transcript in a sealed envelope, two letters of recommendation and a copy of their FAFSA. **Deadline:** March 1. **Contact:** Laura Schweitzer at 815-926-2110 x17 or lschweitzer@cfnil.org.

3296 ■ William Pigott Memorial Scholarships *(Undergraduate/Scholarship)*

Purpose: To provide financial support to those students who are pursuing post-secondary studies. **Focus:** Engineering. **Qualif.:** Applicants must be graduating senior students from McHenry, Boone or Winnebago county majoring in engineering. **Criteria:** Recipients are selected based on financial need.

Funds Avail.: No specific amount. **To Apply:** Applicants must submit a completed application form, verification form, an official transcript in a sealed envelope and two letters of recommendation. **Deadline:** February 1. **Contact:** Laura Schweitzer at 815-926-2110 x17 or lschweitzer@cfnil.org.

3297 ■ Mark A. Reid Memorial Scholarship Grants *(Undergraduate/Scholarship)*

Purpose: To provide students the financial assistance they need in pursuing their chosen degree of education. **Focus:** Music. **Qualif.:** Applicants must be graduating seniors at Oregon High School who actively participate in music or drama; must be students completing high school who are pursuing the challenge and benefits of higher education, current college students, and non-traditional students seeking to return to school. **Criteria:** Recipients are selected based on demonstrated leadership.

Funds Avail.: No specific amount. **To Apply:** Applicants must contact Mitch Lauer for more information.

3298 ■ Rockford Area Habitat for Humanity College Scholarships *(Undergraduate/Scholarship)*

Purpose: To provide educational resources for Rockford residents of Habitat for Humanity homes who wish to begin or continue their college education. **Focus:** General studies/Field of study not specified. **Qualif.:** Applicants must have plans to attend an accredited junior college or university; must be current homeowner residents or dependents of homeowner residents of a home built by Rockford Area Habitat for Humanity; must be residing in that home at time of scholarship application. **Criteria:** Recipients are selected based on financial need.

Funds Avail.: No specific amount. **To Apply:** Applicants must submit a completed application form, verification form, an official transcript in a sealed envelope, two letters of recommendation and a copy of FAFSA. **Deadline:** February 1. **Contact:** Laura Schweitzer at 815-926-2110 x17 or lschweitzer@cfnil.org.

3299 ■ Deborah Jean Rydberg Memorial Scholarships *(Undergraduate/Scholarship)*

Purpose: To provide financial support to those students who are pursuing their educational goal. **Focus:** General studies/Field of study not specified. **Qualif.:** Applicants must be graduating female senior athletes at Guilford High school who have a minimum GPA of 2.3/4.0 or better average and have plans to attend college. **Criteria:** Recipients are selected based on financial need.

Funds Avail.: No specific amount. **To Apply:** Applicants must submit a completed application form, verification form, an official transcript in a sealed envelope and two letters of recommendation. **Deadline:** February 1. **Contact:** Laura Schweitzer at 815-926-2110 x17 or lschweitzer@cfnil.org.

3300 ■ Richard J. Schnell Memorial Scholarships *(Postdoctorate/Scholarship)*

Purpose: To provide financial support to those students who are pursuing their educational goal. **Focus:** General studies/Field of study not specified. **Qualif.:** Applicants must have been accepted into or enrolled in an American Dental Association accredited dental or dental hygiene program or a graduate post-doctoral program in United States. **Criteria:** Recipients are selected based on financial need.

Funds Avail.: No specific amount. **To Apply:** Applicants must submit a completed application form, verification form, an official transcript in a sealed envelope, two letters of recommendation and a copy of their FAFSA. **Deadline:** July 1. **Contact:** Laura Schweitzer at 815-926-2110 x17 or lschweitzer@cfnil.org.

3301 ■ Bonnie Sorenson Scudder Scholarships *(Undergraduate/Scholarship)*

Purpose: To serve the four county area (Boone, Ogle, Stephenson and Winnebago) through philanthropy; to provide leadership in meeting charitable needs and to be a responsible steward to the Foundation's donors and of the Foundation's endowment. **Focus:** Education, Physical. **Qualif.:** Applicants must be female senior students at Harvard High School who have exhibited an interest in

Awards are arranged alphabetically below their administering organizations

women's physical education and who wish to pursue a degree in women's physical education; must be students completing high school who are pursuing the challenge and benefits of higher education, current college students, and non-traditional students seeking to return to school. **Criteria:** Recipients are selected based on financial need.

Funds Avail.: No specific amount. **To Apply:** Applicants must submit a completed application form and must contact Melissa Laffey for more information. **Contact:** Mellisa Laffey, Harvard High School, 1103 N Jefferson, Harvard, IL 60033.

3302 ■ Ernest and Charlene Stachowiak Memorial Scholarships *(Undergraduate/Scholarship)*

Purpose: To provide financial support to those students who are pursuing their educational goal. **Focus:** General studies/Field of study not specified. **Qualif.:** Applicants must be graduating seniors or college students with a permanent address within Boone, Ogle, Stephenson or Winnebago county; must have a GPA of at least 2.5 on 4.0 scale. **Criteria:** Recipients are selected based on financial need.

Funds Avail.: No specific amount. **To Apply:** Applicants must submit a completed application form, verification form, an official transcript in a sealed envelope, two letters of recommendation and a copy of their FAFSA. **Deadline:** March 1. **Contact:** Laura Schweitzer at 815-926-2110 x17 or lschweitzer@cfnil.org.

3303 ■ Gary S. Wilmer/RAMI Music Scholarships *(Undergraduate/Scholarship)*

Purpose: To provide financial support to those students who are pursuing an education in music. **Focus:** Music. **Qualif.:** Applicants must be graduating senior students from Boone or Winnebago County who have a GPA of at least 2.5; must have plans to pursue a degree in music performance, education or composition and be actively involved in school or community musical groups; must be nominated by a music teacher. **Criteria:** Recipients are selected based on financial need.

Funds Avail.: No specific amount. **To Apply:** Applicants must submit a completed application form, verification form, an official transcript in a sealed envelope, two letters of recommendation and a five minute or less performance tape or C.D. **Deadline:** February 1. **Contact:** Laura Schweitzer at 815-926-2110 x17 or lschweitzer@cfnil.org.

3304 ■ Women of Today's Manufacturing Scholarships *(Undergraduate/Scholarship)*

Purpose: To provide financial support to those students who are pursuing their educational goal. **Focus:** Manufacturing. **Qualif.:** Applicants must be male or female residents of Ogle, Winnebago, Boone, Stephenson or Rock County who are attending or plan to attend a college, university or trade/technical school; must demonstrate how their course work will impact manufacturing technology in the region. **Criteria:** Recipients are selected based on financial need.

Funds Avail.: No specific amount. **To Apply:** Applicants must submit a completed application form, verification form, an official transcript in a sealed envelope and two letters of recommendation. **Deadline:** February 1. **Contact:** Laura Schweitzer at 815-926-2110 x17 or lschweitzer@cfnil.org.

3305 ■ Carolyn Wones Recruitment Scholarship Grants *(Undergraduate/Scholarship)*

Purpose: To provide financial support to those students who are pursuing post-secondary degree in teaching. **Focus:** General studies/Field of study not specified. **Qualif.:** Applicants must be females who graduated from a public high school within Boone or Winnebago county; must have plans to pursue a degree in secondary teaching; must exhibit academic potential and have participated in a number of high school activities. **Criteria:** Recipients are selected based on financial need.

Funds Avail.: No specific amount. **To Apply:** Applicants must submit a completed application form, verification form, an official transcript in a sealed envelope and two letters of recommendation. **Deadline:** February 1. **Contact:** Laura Schweitzer at 815-926-2110 x17 or lschweitzer@cfnil.org.

3306 ■ Margaret Wyeth Scholarships *(Undergraduate/Scholarship)*

Purpose: To provide financial support to those students who are pursuing their educational goal. **Focus:** General studies/Field of study not specified. **Qualif.:** Applicants must be graduating public high school senior students and residing in Boone, Ogle or Winnebago County; must plan to attend a college or university. **Criteria:** Recipients are selected based on financial need and demonstrated active involvement in social studies organizations, clubs and classes such as student government, political campaigns, social service and community service.

Funds Avail.: No specific amount. **To Apply:** Applicants must submit a completed application form, verification form, an official transcript in a sealed envelope, two letters of recommendation and a copy of their FAFSA. **Deadline:** March 1. **Contact:** Laura Schweitzer at 815-926-2110 x17 or lschweitzer@cfnil.org.

3307 ■ Zeta Chapter Memorial Scholarship Awards *(Undergraduate/Scholarship)*

Purpose: To provide financial support to those students who are pursuing their educational goal. **Focus:** General studies/Field of study not specified. **Qualif.:** Applicants must be females who are graduating from a public high school within Boone or Winnebago county; must have plans to teach at any level; must exhibit academic potential and have participated in a number of high school activities. **Criteria:** Recipients are selected based on financial need and demonstrated active involvement in social studies organizations, clubs and classes such as student government, political campaigns, social service and community service.

Funds Avail.: No specific amount. **To Apply:** Applicants must submit a completed application form, verification form, an official transcript in a sealed envelope and two letters of recommendation. **Deadline:** February 1. **Contact:** Laura Schweitzer at 815-926-2110 x17 or lschweitzer@cfnil.org.

3308 ■ Community Foundation of Prince Edward Island (CFPEI)
Queen Square Ctr., Ste. 105
119-121 Queen St.
Charlottetown, PE, Canada C1A 4B3
Ph: (902)892-3440
Fax: (902)892-0880
Free: 800-566-7307
E-mail: cfpei@pei.aibn.com
URL: www.cfpei.ca

3309 ■ Architects Association of PEI Scholarships *(Undergraduate/Scholarship)*

Purpose: To provide financial assistance to qualified individuals who want to pursue their education. **Focus:**

Awards are arranged alphabetically below their administering organizations

Architecture. **Qualif.:** Applicant must be a Prince Edward Island student who graduated from a PEI High School and has been accepted into a recognized architectural program. **Criteria:** Recipient will be selected based on the scholarship application requirements.

Funds Avail.: $1,500. **To Apply:** Applicant must complete the application form available online; must submit an official transcript of marks, copy of letter of acceptance from the university, an essay, two reference letters and portfolio of work. **Deadline:** June 1.

3310 ■ Joan Auld Scholarships *(Undergraduate/Scholarship)*

Purpose: To provide financial assistance to qualified individuals who want to pursue their education. **Focus:** Art; Crafts; Design. **Qualif.:** Applicant must be a Canadian citizen; must have been a resident of P.E.I for at least the 6 months prior to application; must be undertaking full-time studies in a craft-related field at a recognized institution of applied art, craft and design; must demonstrate high school graduation or equivalence. **Criteria:** Recipient will be selected based on the scholarship application criteria.

Funds Avail.: No specific amount. **To Apply:** Applicants must complete the application form available online; must provide an outline of the proposed course of study and the name of the institution where they will attend the class; must submit an essay about their background, interest, aims and ambitions; must submit a letter of reference and portfolio demonstrating previous work, samples of craft-related work, sketches, video or pictures; must include written verification of acceptance. **Deadline:** October 17.

3311 ■ Lorne and Ruby Bonnell Scholarships *(Undergraduate/Scholarship)*

Purpose: To provide scholarship assistance to qualified individuals who want to pursue their studies. **Focus:** General studies/Field of study not specified. **Qualif.:** Applicant must be a graduate of a Prince Edward Island high school; must be a graduate of the University of Prince Edward Island with high academic standing; must be accepted into graduate studies in the sciences at a Canadian university. **Criteria:** Recipient will be selected by the selection committee following the guidelines of conditions of eligibility.

Funds Avail.: $1,000. **To Apply:** Applicant must complete the application form available online; must submit an official letter of acceptance from a Canadian graduate school. Application form and other supporting documents must be sent to Lorne and Ruby Bonnell Scholarship Fund c/o The Community Foundation of Prince Edward Island, 119-121 Queen St. Ste. 105, Charlottetown, PE C1A 4B3. **Deadline:** June 1.

3312 ■ Orin Carver Scholarships *(Undergraduate/Scholarship)*

Purpose: To provide financial assistance to qualified individuals who want to pursue their education. **Focus:** General studies/Field of study not specified. **Qualif.:** Applicants must be high school graduates in the top 25% of their class; must exhibit excellence and leadership in either athletics, arts and/or community service; must be accepted into a post-secondary program at UPEI or Holland College. **Criteria:** Recipient will be selected based on the scholarship application requirements.

Funds Avail.: No specific amount. **To Apply:** Applicants must complete the application form available online; must have a formal statement of academic standing and official academic transcript for most recent academic year, as verified by educational institute attended; must have two letters of reference (one from the educational institution and one from a community member); must provide a 500-word essay or portfolio of their excellent works. **Deadline:** June 1. **Contact:** Orin Carver Scholarship Selection Committee, at the above address.

3313 ■ Lowell Phillips Scholarships *(Undergraduate/Scholarship)*

Purpose: To provide financial assistance to qualified individuals who want to pursue their education. **Focus:** General studies/Field of study not specified. **Qualif.:** Applicant must be a high school graduate from the Western School District with a physical disability; must be a resident of Prince County; must have financial need; must have been accepted at a recognized post-secondary institution. **Criteria:** Recipient will be selected based on the scholarship application criteria.

Funds Avail.: No specific amount. **To Apply:** Applicant must complete the application form available online; must submit a copy of their final grades; must have a brief description of their physical disability and what they hope to gain from their studies; must have a letter of acceptance for the next year's study. **Deadline:** June 1.

3314 ■ Summerside-Natick International Friendship Hockey Scholarships *(Undergraduate/Scholarship)*

Purpose: To provide financial assistance to qualified individuals who want to pursue their education. **Focus:** General studies/Field of study not specified. **Qualif.:** Applicant must be a high school graduate of Prince Edward Island; must be accepted at a post-secondary institution; must be entering the first year of study; must have played in the Summerside Area Minor Hockey Association. **Criteria:** Recipient will be selected based on the scholarship application criteria.

Funds Avail.: $500. **To Apply:** Applicant must complete the application form available online; must include a letter detailing how he/she meets the selection criteria; must have an official letter of acceptance from a recognized post-secondary institution; must submit two letters of reference; and most recent transcript. Application form and other supporting documents must be sent to The Summerside-Natick International Friendship Fund. **Deadline:** June 1.

3315 ■ Community Foundation of Sarasota County
2635 Fruitville Rd.
Sarasota, FL 34237
Ph: (941)955-3000
Fax: (941)952-1951
E-mail: info@cfsarasota.org
URL: www.cfsarasota.org
Facebook: www.facebook.com/
 CommunityFoundationSarasotaCounty
LinkedIn: www.linkedin.com/company/community
 -foundation-of-sarasota-county
Twitter: twitter.com/CFSarasota

3316 ■ Emily and Roland Abraham Educational Funds *(Undergraduate/Scholarship)*

Purpose: To help students pursue a college degree or vocational training. **Focus:** General studies/Field of study not specified. **Qualif.:** Applicants must be public high school

Awards are arranged alphabetically below their administering organizations

senior students from Sarasota, Manatee or Charlotte counties; must have a 3.2 GPA or higher. **Criteria:** Selection will be based on financial need.

Funds Avail.: No specific amount. **To Apply:** Applicants must complete the application form and must submit all required documents including transcript, parent's or guardian's most recent 1040 federal tax form and two letters of reference from people who know the applicants well. **Contact:** Rebekah Fleming, Program Assistant at rebekah@cfsarasota.org.

3317 ■ American Business Women's Association Sarasota Sunrise Chapter Scholarships
(Undergraduate, Vocational/Occupational/Scholarship)

Purpose: To provide financial assistance to needy individuals to attend an accredited college or university. **Focus:** Business. **Qualif.:** Applicants must be female students with 3.0 unweighted high school GPA and must be of good character and have a career goal related to their college or university studies; must be residents of Manatee or Sarasota Counties. **Criteria:** Recipients are selected based on financial need.

Funds Avail.: No specific amount. **To Apply:** Applicants must complete the application form and must submit all required documents including transcript, parent's or guardian's most recent 1040 federal tax form and two letters of reference from people who know the applicants well. **Remarks:** Established in 2003.

3318 ■ byourself Scholarship Fund *(Undergraduate, Vocational/Occupational/Scholarship)*

Purpose: To provide financial assistance to students who are pursuing their educational goal. **Focus:** Nursing. **Qualif.:** Applicants must be adult learners, men or women in Sarasota County pursuing RN, LPN, or CNA; must be accepted into the nursing programs at Manatee Community College or Sarasota County Technical Institute; and must maintain a 2.8 GPA. **Criteria:** Recipients are selected based on financial need.

Funds Avail.: No specific amount. **To Apply:** Applicants must complete the application form and must submit all required documents including the following: transcript; parent's or guardian's most recent 1040 federal tax form; two letters of reference from people who know the applicants well; official acceptance letter from college or vocational school; and a copy of SAT and ACT scores. **Remarks:** Established in 2002.

3319 ■ Clifford W. and Doris E. Davis Educational Scholarship Fund *(Undergraduate, Vocational/Occupational/Scholarship)*

Purpose: To help students obtain a college degree or vocational training to pursue a career in nursing or the medical field. **Focus:** Education, Medical. **Qualif.:** Applicants must be adult learners, men and women, who are residents of Sarasota County. **Criteria:** Recipients are selected based on financial need and on their educational objectives that will lead to a career in the health care field.

Funds Avail.: No specific amount. **To Apply:** Applicants must complete the application form and must submit all required documents including the following: transcript; parent's or guardian's most recent 1040 federal tax form; two letters of reference from people who know the applicants well; official acceptance letter from college or vocational school; and a copy of SAT and ACT scores.

3320 ■ Father Connie Dougherty Scholarships
(Undergraduate, Vocational/Occupational/Scholarship)

Purpose: To support students to attend a college, university, or institution of higher learning including education in advanced vocational training. **Focus:** General studies/Field of study not specified. **Qualif.:** Applicants must be graduates of Sarasota County public and private school. **Criteria:** Recipients are selected based on academic performance and financial need.

Funds Avail.: No specific amount. **To Apply:** Applicants must submit a completed application form and all required materials including the following: an official transcript; SAT or ACT scores; copy of Student Aid Report; and three letters of recommendation (one must come from a teacher and one from a community member who is not a teacher or relative). **Deadline:** April 1.

3321 ■ James Franklin and Dorothy J. Warnell Scholarship Fund *(Undergraduate, Vocational/Occupational/Scholarship)*

Purpose: To provide financial assistance to students who are pursuing their educational goal. **Focus:** General studies/Field of study not specified. **Qualif.:** Applicants must be residents of Sarasota County for post high school education. **Criteria:** Recipients are selected based on financial need and on their educational objectives.

Funds Avail.: No specific amount. **To Apply:** Applicants must complete the application form and must submit all required documents including the following: transcript; parent's or guardian's most recent 1040 federal tax form; two letters of reference from people who know the applicants well; official acceptance letter from college or vocational school; and a copy of SAT and ACT scores.

3322 ■ George W. and Ethel B. Hoefler Fund *(Undergraduate/Scholarship)*

Purpose: To provide educational assistance to students who wish to study again. **Focus:** General studies/Field of study not specified. **Qualif.:** Applicants must be adult learners who are Sarasota County residents. **Criteria:** Recipients will be selected on the basis of financial need and demonstrated aptitude and seriousness of purpose.

Funds Avail.: No specific amount. **To Apply:** Applicants must complete the application form and must submit all required documents including transcript, parent's or guardian's most recent 1040 federal tax form and two letters of reference from people who know the applicants well.

3323 ■ Helen F. "Jerri" Rand Memorial Scholarships *(Undergraduate, Vocational/Occupational/Scholarship)*

Purpose: To provide financial assistance to students who are pursuing their educational goal. **Focus:** Cosmetology. **Qualif.:** Applicants must be adult learners who are accepted to any accredited beauty school in Sarasota County pursuing a professional certificate in hairdressing. **Criteria:** Recipients are selected based on financial need and on their educational objectives that will lead to a career.

Funds Avail.: No specific amount. **To Apply:** Applicants must complete the application form and must submit all required documents including the following: transcript; parent's or guardian's most recent 1040 federal tax form; two letters of reference from people who know the applicants well; official acceptance letter from college or vocational school; and a copy of SAT and ACT scores. **Remarks:** Established in 2006.

Awards are arranged alphabetically below their administering organizations

3324 ■ Community Foundation for Southeast Michigan (CFSEM)

333 W Fort St., Ste. 2010
Detroit, MI 48226-3134
Ph: (313)961-6675
Fax: (313)961-2886
E-mail: cfsem@cfsem.org
URL: cfsem.org

3325 ■ Dick Depaolis Memorial Scholarships
(Undergraduate/Scholarship)

Purpose: To provide educational scholarship support to scholar-athletes who are graduates of North Farmington High School. **Focus:** General studies/Field of study not specified. **Qualif.:** Applicants must: be members of the graduating class at North Farmington High School; demonstrate exemplary desire, ability and have a GPA of 3.0 or higher; be male athletes demonstrating leadership, academic discipline and good sportsmanship on and off the field; and, be playing varsity sports (football preferred). Those applicants will take a major in Liberal Studies, especially History and English, in college. **Criteria:** Recipients will be evaluated based on their academic records, recommendations, statement of goals and financial need.

Funds Avail.: No specific amount. **Duration:** Annual. **To Apply:** Application form contains the following: (a) scholarship guidelines and deadlines; (b) statement of academic and career goals; (c) recommendation form; and (d) transcript release form. They must use a computer, typewriter or print neatly in blue or black ink in completing the application form. **Deadline:** March 26. **Remarks:** Established in 2004. **Contact:** scholarships@cfsem.org.

3326 ■ Detroit Economic Club Scholarship
(Undergraduate/Scholarship)

Purpose: To assist students from Detroit and Macomb, Oakland, and Wayne counties in pursuing a program of undergraduate education. **Focus:** General studies/Field of study not specified. **Qualif.:** Applicants must be graduates of any high school located in the City of Detroit, or Wayne, Oakland, or Macomb counties and entering their first year of college in the fall. **Criteria:** Recipients will be selected based on their: scholastic performance while in high school; demonstrated character and leadership; personal statement; and, financial need.

Funds Avail.: $2,000 each. **Duration:** Annual. **Number Awarded:** 2. **To Apply:** Applicants must first be nominated by their counselor and then invited to apply, for scholarship consideration. They must fill-out the Scholarship Application form. High school principal, advisor, counselor, or a teacher should be asked to complete the High School Certification Form and Applicant Recommendation Form. These forms should be filled-out by two different individuals. **Deadline:** April 15. **Contact:** scholarships@cfsem.org.

3327 ■ Robert Holmes Scholarship *(Undergraduate/Scholarship)*

Purpose: To assist the legal dependents of Michigan Teamsters in pursuing a program of undergraduate education. **Focus:** General studies/Field of study not specified. **Qualif.:** Applicants must be: dependents of eligible Michigan Teamsters and high school seniors who will attend a Michigan College or University as full-time students; and, active (or have been) placed on a seniority list. **Criteria:** Recipients will be selected based on their: strong scholastic performance while in high school; class rank; and demonstrated qualities of leadership in school, extracurricular activities and community involvement.

Funds Avail.: $1,000 each. **Duration:** Annual. **Number Awarded:** 6. **To Apply:** Applicants must submit the completed application form; must ask a high school principal or advisor/counselor to complete the enclosed high School Certification Form and to a high school teacher or other adult to complete the enclosed the Applicant Recommendation Form. **Deadline:** April 15. **Contact:** scholarships@cfsem.org.

3328 ■ Detroit Tigers Willie Horton Scholarship
(Undergraduate/Scholarship)

Purpose: To provide educational scholarship support to the graduates of Detroit Collegiate Preparatory High School at Northwestern. **Focus:** General studies/Field of study not specified. **Qualif.:** Applicants must: be graduating seniors at Northwestern High School in Detroit; show leadership and character through extracurricular activities, volunteer involvement and work experience in school and in the community; have applied or have been accepted as full-time students in an accredited educational institution in the United States; and, demonstrate desire, ability and good grades. **Criteria:** Applicants will be evaluated based on their scholastic, personal attributes and experience in school or community.

Funds Avail.: No specific amount. **Duration:** Annual. **To Apply:** Applicants must use a computer, typewriter or print neatly in blue or black ink all appropriate forms. They must submit a complete application form including the following: (1) scholarship guidelines and deadlines; (2) student application; (3) statement of academic and career goals; (4) recommendation forms; and (5) transcript release form. **Deadline:** April 15. **Remarks:** The Detroit Tigers established the Detroit Tigers Willie Horton Scholarship to honor the on field and civic contributions of hometown hero, Willie Horton. Established in 2000. **Contact:** scholarships@cfsem.org.

3329 ■ Chris Kurzweil Scholarship *(Undergraduate/Scholarship)*

Purpose: To assist the legal dependents of employees of Intertape Polymer Group in pursuing a program of undergraduate education. **Focus:** General studies/Field of study not specified. **Qualif.:** Applicants must be dependents of members of the Intertape Polymer Group, formerly American Tape; and must be high school seniors. **Criteria:** Recipients will be selected based on their: strong scholastic performance; leadership qualities in school, extracurricular activities and community involvement; and, class rank.

Funds Avail.: $1,000 each. **Duration:** Annual. **Number Awarded:** 2. **To Apply:** Applicants must use a computer, typewriter or print neatly in blue or black ink all appropriate forms. They must complete the application form and ask a high school principal or advisor/counselor to complete the High School Certification Form and a high school teacher or another adult to complete the Applicant Recommendation Form. **Deadline:** April 15. **Remarks:** The scholarship was established by Mr. Chris M. Kurzweil, former Chief Executive Officer of American Tape. **Contact:** scholarships@cfsem.org.

3330 ■ Imelda "Mel" and Ralph LeMar Scholarship
(Undergraduate/Scholarship)

Purpose: To provide educational scholarship support to scholar-athletes who graduate of Fowlerville High School. **Focus:** Chemistry; Engineering, Electrical; Engineering,

Awards are arranged alphabetically below their administering organizations

Mechanical; Physics. **Qualif.:** Applicants must: be members of a graduating class in a public high school in Fowlerville, Michigan; demonstrate exemplary desire, ability and good grades; show leadership and character through extracurricular activities, volunteer involvement and work experience in school and in the community; have applied or been accepted as full-time students in an accredited educational institution in the United States; and, be planning to study chemistry, physics or electrical or mechanical engineering in college. **Criteria:** Applicants will be evaluated based on their academic records, recommendations and the students' statement of goals.

Funds Avail.: No specific amount. **Duration:** Annual. **To Apply:** Forms may be computerized or typewritten or printed neatly in blue or black ink as appropriate. They must submit a complete application form including the following: (1) scholarship guidelines and deadlines; (2) student application; (3) statement of academic and career goals; (4) recommendation form; (5) transcript release form. **Deadline:** March 22. **Remarks:** The scholarship was established by Imelda and Ralph LeMar to support student who graduate from Fowlerville public schools. Established in 2000. **Contact:** scholarships@cfsem.org.

3331 ■ Virgil K. Lobring Scholarship *(Undergraduate/Scholarship)*

Purpose: To provide educational scholarship support to graduates of Western International High School. **Focus:** General studies/Field of study not specified. **Qualif.:** Applicants must: be members of the graduating class at Southwestern High School in Detroit, Michigan; demonstrate exemplary desire, ability and good grades; demonstrate leadership and character through extracurricular activities, volunteers involvement and work experience in school and in the community; have applied or been accepted as full-time students in an accredited educational institution in the United States; be students who have demonstrated the greatest improvement from the time during freshman year in high school as determined by the Lobring Scholarship committee; and, demonstrate financial need. **Criteria:** Applicants will be evaluated based on their academic records, recommendations and statement of goals.

Funds Avail.: No specific amount. **Duration:** Annual. **To Apply:** Applicants must submit the application containing scholarship guidelines and deadlines, student application, essay question, recommendation forms from counselor, teacher and community service forms; and transcripts release form. **Deadline:** April 15. **Contact:** scholarships@cfsem.org.

3332 ■ Jean and Tom Rosenthal Scholarship Program *(Undergraduate/Scholarship)*

Purpose: To provide educational scholarship support to graduates of Pontiac High School. **Focus:** General studies/Field of study not specified. **Qualif.:** Applicants must: be members of the graduating class at Pontiac Northern High School or Pontiac Central High School demonstrating exemplary desire, ability and good grades of at least 2.5 or higher; show leadership and character through extracurricular activities, volunteer involvement and work experience in school and in the community; and, have applied or been accepted as full-time students in an accredited educational institution in the United States. **Criteria:** Applicants will be evaluated based on their academic records, recommendations and essay on personal commitment of service to others.

Funds Avail.: No specific amount. **Duration:** Annual. **To Apply:** Applicants must submit the application containing scholarship guidelines and deadlines, student application, essay question, recommendation forms from counselor, teacher and community service forms, and transcripts release form. **Deadline:** April 15. **Contact:** scholarships@cfsem.org.

3333 ■ Jeptha Wade Schureman Scholarship Program *(Undergraduate/Scholarship)*

Purpose: To provide financial assistance to students of Southeast Michigan region for their education. **Focus:** Dentistry; Law; Medicine; Nursing. **Qualif.:** Applicants must be: residents of Wayne, Oakland, Macomb, Lenawee, Monroe, Livingston, Washtenaw, or St. Clair counties at the time of high school graduation; fatherless either through death or through termination of parental rights before age 18; and, pursuing, or planning to pursue a degree in the fields of law, nursing, medicine or dentistry. They must: demonstrate a strong scholastic performance while in high school or college with an equivalent of 3.0 GPA on a 4.0 scale; demonstrate leadership and character through extracurricular activities, school and community service, volunteer involvement and paid work experience; and, be admitted to one of the 15 non-profit public universities in Michigan. **Criteria:** Applicants will be evaluated based on academic records; recommendations and statement of goals; and demonstrated financial need. Preference will be given to candidates between the ages of 17-27 at the time of application and pursuing a full-time education.

Funds Avail.: $7,500 each. **Duration:** Annual. **Number Awarded:** Up to 10. **To Apply:** Applicants must submit the completed application form; and must provide a written personal statement which describes the following: (1) educational plans and career goals; (2) motivating factors and important experiences which may help them shape their personal philosophy and future goals. **Deadline:** April 15. **Contact:** scholarships@cfsem.org.

3334 ■ Community Foundation of Western Massachusetts
1500 Main St., Ste. 2300
Springfield, MA 01115-5769
Ph: (413)732-2858
Fax: (413)733-8565
E-mail: wmass@communityfoundation.org
URL: www.communityfoundation.org
Facebook: www.facebook.com/CommunityFoundationWMass
LinkedIn: www.linkedin.com/company/community-foundation-of-western-massachusetts?trk=hb_tab_compy_id_113605
Twitter: twitter.com/CFWM413

3335 ■ Community Foundation of Western Massachusetts Community Scholarship Program *(Undergraduate/Scholarship)*

Purpose: To help bring higher education within reach of residents in Massachusetts who might not otherwise be able to afford it. **Focus:** General studies/Field of study not specified. **Qualif.:** Applicants must be residents from Franklin, Hampden, Hampshire or combination or city/town; must be freshmen, sophomores, juniors, graduating seniors or graduates of specific high school. **Criteria:** Applicants are evaluated based on scholastic ability, financial need, extracurricular activities, volunteer and community services or athletic activities.

Funds Avail.: Amount varies. **Duration:** Annual. **To Apply:** Applicants must submit all the required application information. **Deadline:** March 31. **Contact:** scholar@communityfoundation.org.

3336 ■ Community Legal Services of Philadelphia (CLS)
1424 Chestnut St.
Philadelphia, PA 19102-2505
Ph: (215)981-3700
URL: clsphila.org
Facebook: www.facebook.com/clsphila
LinkedIn: www.linkedin.com/company/community-legal-services
Twitter: twitter.com/CLSphila

3337 ■ Community Legal Services of Philadelphia Fellowships *(Postgraduate/Fellowship)*

Purpose: To deliver high quality legal services to a diverse client population. **Focus:** Law; Paralegal studies. **Qualif.:** Candidates must be graduates or judicial law clerks interested in a public interest law career. Candidates with diverse cultural backgrounds and/or oral proficiency in languages other than English, people of color, gay men and lesbians, and members of under-served or disadvantage communities are also encouraged to apply. **Criteria:** Selection will be based on the committee's criteria.

Funds Avail.: No specific amount. **Duration:** Annual. **Number Awarded:** Varies. **To Apply:** Applicants must submit the following requirements: resume; cover letter addressing their interest and experience in public interest and poverty law and describing any ideas for a fellowship proposal; two brief legal writing samples; law school transcript; list of three references. Materials should be sent via email to fellowship@clsphila.org to the attention of: Carol Horne Penn, Esq., Deputy Dir., Community Legal Services, Inc., 1424 Chestnut St., Philadelphia, PA 19102. **Deadline:** July 1.

3338 ■ Composite Panel Association (CPA)
19465 Deerfield Ave., Ste. 306
Leesburg, VA 20176
Ph: (703)724-1128
Fax: (703)724-1588
E-mail: admin@decorativesurfaces.org
URL: www.compositepanel.org

3339 ■ Robert E. Dougherty Scholarships *(Undergraduate, Postgraduate/Scholarship)*

Purpose: To provide financial assistance to students pursuing a career in the composite panel and affiliated industries. **Focus:** Chemistry; Engineering; Forestry. **Qualif.:** Applicant must be a North American citizen; and be nominated by a member of the Robert E. Dougherty Education Foundation. **Criteria:** Member companies are permitted to nominate one or more individuals for scholarship consideration.

Funds Avail.: $5,000. **Duration:** Annual. **Number Awarded:** 5. **To Apply:** Scholarship Application forms can be downloaded at the website and must be filled out and returned to the Foundation.

3340 ■ Conference on Asian Pacific American Leadership (CAPAL)
PO Box 65073
Washington, DC 20035
Free: 877-892-5427
E-mail: info@capal.org
URL: www.capal.org
Facebook: www.facebook.com/capaldc
LinkedIn: www.linkedin.com/company/conference-on-asian-pacific-american-leadership-capal-

3341 ■ CAPAL Public Service Scholarships *(Graduate, Undergraduate/Scholarship)*

Purpose: To provide financial assistance to students with leadership potential to pursue public service internships in Washington, DC. **Focus:** Public service. **Qualif.:** Applicants must be undergraduate and graduate students working in a full-time summer internship in the public sector within the Washington, DC metropolitan area. **Criteria:** Selection will be based on demonstrated commitment to public service, including service to the APA community, demonstrated leadership and potential for continued growth in leadership skills, relevance and consistency with overall public sector goals, academic achievement and financial need.

Funds Avail.: $3,500. **To Apply:** Applicants must submit a completed online application form; resume and academic transcripts; one to three letters of recommendation; a statement of purpose that answers two out of three questions found on the online application. **Deadline:** March 7. **Contact:** Conference on Asian Pacific American Leadership, at the above address.

3342 ■ Conference of State Bank Supervisors (CSBS)
1129 20th St. NW, 9th Fl.
Washington, DC 20036
Ph: (202)296-2840
Fax: (202)296-1928
URL: www.csbs.org/Pages/default.aspx

3343 ■ Conference of State Bank Supervisors Graduate School Scholarships *(Graduate/Award)*

Purpose: To encourage and assist qualified bank and trust examiners to prepare themselves for expanded duties and responsibilities in their banking departments. **Focus:** Banking. **Qualif.:** Applicants must be outstanding and deserving examiners who demonstrate excellence in their work by supporting their attendance at the graduate banking or graduate trust school of their choice. They must: have three (3) years of experience in bank or trust supervision as examiners-in-charge or 3 years of experience as bank or trust examiners plus 2 years of experience in a bank or trust company; have a degree from an accredited college and must have successfully completed the CSBS Senior School; have demonstrated fully to the State Bank that they have the potential to assume senior-level responsibilities; and, continue to be employed by a state banking department. **Criteria:** Recipients will be selected based on experience, education, promotion potential and other requirements set by the schools and the banking departments.

Funds Avail.: Up to $3,000 plus $1,250 from the Graduate School of Banking at Colorado. **Duration:** Annual. **Number Awarded:** 3. **To Apply:** State Bank Supervisors must nominate candidates using nomination forms provided by the Foundation. **Deadline:** December 18. **Remarks:** Established in 1972.

Awards are arranged alphabetically below their administering organizations

3344 ■ Congressional Black Caucus Foundation (CBCF)

1720 Massachusetts Ave. NW
Washington, DC 20036
Ph: (202)263-2800
Fax: (202)775-0773
E-mail: info@cbcfinc.org
URL: www.cbcfinc.org
Facebook: www.facebook.com/CBCFInc
LinkedIn: www.linkedin.com/company/congressional-black-caucus-foundation

3345 ■ CBC Spouses Education Scholarship Fund
(Graduate, Undergraduate/Scholarship)

Purpose: To provide support to students in pursuing their educational goals. **Focus:** General studies/Field of study not specified. **Qualif.:** Applicants must intend to pursue full-time undergraduate, graduate degrees at an accredited college/university; must have minimum 2.5 GPA; must exhibit leadership ability and participate in community service activities; and must be residing or attending school in a congressional district represented by a CBC member. **Criteria:** Selection is based on submitted application and materials.

Funds Avail.: No specific amount. **To Apply:** Applicants must submit a completed CBC Spouses scholarship application; a sealed official high school or college transcript; a personal statement essay from the student (500-1,000 words) that addresses all four (4) of the topics listed on the application in one essay; two letters of recommendation (one should come from a community or public service leader-church leader, community leader, etc.); if a first year student, an acceptance letter from the college/university where the student will enroll; and a recent photograph suitable for publication. **Deadline:** May 20. **Contact:** Phone: 202-263-2800; Email: scholarships@cbcfinc.org.

3346 ■ CBC Spouses Heineken USA Performing Arts Scholarships *(Undergraduate/Scholarship)*

Purpose: To support students pursuing a career in the field of performing arts. **Focus:** Performing arts. **Qualif.:** Applicants must be U.S. citizen or permanent U.S. resident; must be currently/planning to be enrolled in the upcoming academic year as a full-time undergraduate student; must have minimum 2.5 GPA on a 4.0 scale; must be pursuing a major and career in a performing art; must exhibit leadership ability and participate in community service activities. **Criteria:** Selection is based on submitted application and materials.

Funds Avail.: Up to $3,000. **To Apply:** Applicants must submit personal statement (500-1,000 words) addressing four topics in one cohesive essay; two recommendation letters; electronic copy of detailed Federal Student Aid Report (SAR); resume (3 pages maximum) detailing the academics, extracurricular activities, honors, employment, community service, and special skills, recent photograph suitable for publication; 2 minute visual recording sample. **Deadline:** April 29. **Contact:** Phone:202-263-2800; Email: scholarships@cbcfinc.org.

3347 ■ CBC Spouses Visual Arts Scholarships *(Undergraduate/Scholarship)*

Purpose: To support students pursuing a career in the visual arts to achieve their goals. **Focus:** Visual arts. **Qualif.:** Applicants must be U.S. citizen or permanent U.S. resident; must be currently/planning to be enrolled in the upcoming academic year as a full-time undergraduate student; must have minimum 2.5 GPA on a 4.0 scale; must be pursuing major and career in visual art; and must exhibit leadership and community service. **Criteria:** Selection is based on submitted application and materials.

Funds Avail.: $3,000. **To Apply:** Applicants must submit personal statement (500-1,000 words) addressing four topics in one cohesive essay; 2 (two) electronically submitted letters of recommendation; Electronic PDF copy of detailed Federal Student Aid Report (SAR); resume (3 pages maximum) detailing academics, extracurricular activities, honors, employment, community service, and special skills; and five original pieces of artwork from the art genre for which are applying, with each file name showing the piece's title, dimensions, and media. **Deadline:** April 29. **Contact:** Phone: 202-263-2800; Email: scholarships@cbcfinc.org.

3348 ■ CBCF Congressional Fellows Program
(Other/Fellowship)

Purpose: To increase the number of African Americans working as professional staff in the U.S. Congress. **Focus:** General studies/Field of study not specified. **Qualif.:** Applicant must be a U.S. citizen or permitted to work in the U.S.; a graduate or have professional degree completed prior to the start date fellowship program; familiar with the federal legislative process, Congress and the Congressional Black Caucus (CBC) and its members; and have demonstrated interest in public policy and commitment to creating and implementing policy to improve the living conditions for underserved and underrepresented individuals. **Criteria:** Selection is based on a combination of the following criteria: a record of academic and professional achievement; evidence of leadership skills and the potential for further growth; demonstrated interest in public policy; and quality of paper application and interview performance.

Funds Avail.: No specific amount. **Duration:** Annual. **To Apply:** Applicant must submit a completed application form along with a resume; three letters of recommendation; three Transcript (at least one must be an official transcript); and three essays (each essay no more than two pages in length). Submit three copies of the complete application under one cover. Bind application with paperclips (do not use staples). **Deadline:** April 8.

3349 ■ Louis Stokes Health Scholars Program
(Undergraduate/Scholarship)

Purpose: To provide support to students in pursuing their educational goals. **Focus:** Health care services; Health education; Health sciences; Health services administration; Occupational safety and health; Public health. **Qualif.:** Applicants must: be U.S. citizens or legal U.S. residents who have a minimum 3.0 GPA on a 4.0 scale; be currently enrolled or planning to enroll in a full-time undergraduate course of study at an accredited two- or four-year college, university, vocational or technical school (degree must be in a subject that will lead to a career in a health field); planning seek work in an underserved community; and have demonstrated financial need. **Criteria:** Preference will be given to students who demonstrate an interest to work in underserved communities.

Funds Avail.: Up to $8,000. **To Apply:** Applicants must submit personal statement essay (500-1,000 words) that addresses all four of the topics listed in the application in one cohesive essay; two electronically submitted letters of recommendation; electronic copy of detailed Federal Student Aid Report (SAR); one-page resume listing extracurricular activities, honors, employment, community service, and special skills; and recent photograph suitable for publication. **Deadline:** May 3.

3350 ■ Louis Stokes Urban Health Policy Fellows Program *(Other/Fellowship)*

Purpose: To bring together individuals with diverse interests in policy areas in order to complement and enrich the experiences of all program participants. **Focus:** Behavioral sciences; Biological and clinical sciences; Health sciences; Social sciences. **Qualif.:** Applicants must be U.S. citizens or permitted to work in the United States; must be graduate or have professional degree in a health-related field (behavioral science, social sciences, biological sciences and health professions) from an accredited institution completed prior to the fellowship start date; must familiar with the federal legislative process, Congress and the Congressional Black Caucus (CBC); and must have demonstrated interest in public policy, and commitment to creating and implementing policy to improve the living conditions for underserved and underrepresented individuals. **Criteria:** Selection is based on a combination of the following criteria: a record of academic and professional achievement; evidence of leadership skills and the potential for further growth; study of how health policies affect African Americans and minorities; demonstrated interest in public health policy; and quality of paper application and interview performance.

Funds Avail.: No specific amount. **Duration:** Annual. **To Apply:** Applicants must submit a completed application form along with a resume; three letters of recommendation; three transcripts (at least one must be an official transcript); and three essays (each essay no more than two pages in length). Submit three copies of the complete application under one cover. Bind application with paperclips (do not use staples). **Deadline:** April 8.

3351 ■ Congressional Hispanic Caucus Institute
300 M St., SE 5th Flr., Ste. 510
Washington, DC 20003
Ph: (202)543-1771
Fax: (202)546-2143
URL: www.chci.org

3352 ■ CHCI Graduate Fellowships *(Graduate/Fellowship)*

Purpose: To enhance individuals' leadership abilities, strengthen professional skills and ultimately produce more competent and competitive Latino professionals in public policy areas. **Focus:** Education; Engineering; Health care services; Housing; Law; Mathematics and mathematical sciences; Public administration; Public service; Science; Technology. **Qualif.:** Applicants must be U.S. citizens, lawful permanent residents, asylees, or individuals who are lawfully authorized to work full-time without restriction for any U.S. employer and who, at the time of application, possess lawful evidence of employment authorization. Applicants must have earned a Bachelor's degree within two years of the program start date; have high academic achievement (preference of 3.0 GPA or higher); have evidence of leadership skills and potential for leadership growth; have demonstrated commitment to public service-oriented activities; and have superior analytical skills and outstanding oral and written communication skills. **Criteria:** Selection will be on competitive basis.

Funds Avail.: $2,900. **To Apply:** Applicants may contact the CHCI regarding the application process and other necessary information. **Contact:** CHCI Internship and Fellowship Programs at rdecerega@chci.org.

3353 ■ CHCI Public Policy Fellowships *(Professional development/Fellowship)*

Purpose: To enhance individuals' leadership abilities, strengthen professional skills and ultimately produce more competent and competitive Latino professionals in public policy areas. **Focus:** Public administration; Public service. **Qualif.:** Applicants must be U.S. citizens, lawful permanent residents, asylees, or individuals who are lawfully authorized to work full-time without restriction for any U.S. employer and who, at the time of application, possess lawful evidence of employment authorization. Applicants must have earned a Bachelor's degree within two years of the program start date; have high academic achievement (preference of 3.0 GPA or higher); have evidence of leadership skills and potential for leadership growth; have demonstrated commitment to public service-oriented activities; and have superior analytical skills and outstanding oral and written communication skills. **Criteria:** Selection will be on competitive basis.

Funds Avail.: $2,400. **To Apply:** Applicants may contact the CHCI regarding the application process and other necessary information. **Deadline:** February 20. **Contact:** CHCI Internship and Fellowship Programs at rdecerega@chci.org.

3354 ■ CHCI Scholarships *(Undergraduate, Graduate/Scholarship)*

Purpose: To provide critical financial assistance that will increase graduation rates among Latino students in postsecondary education. **Focus:** General studies/Field of study not specified. **Qualif.:** Applicants must be U.S. citizens, lawful permanent residents, asylees, or individuals who are lawfully authorized to work full-time without restriction for any U.S. employer and who, at the time of application, possess lawful evidence of employment authorization; must be full-time enrolled students in a U.S. Department of Education accredited community college, university, or graduate/professional program within the United States and Puerto Rico during the scholarship; must have demonstrated financial need; must have consistent, active participation in public and/or community service activities; and must have strong writing skills. **Criteria:** Selection will be on competitive basis.

Funds Avail.: $1,000 (for an associate degree); $2,500 (for an undergraduate degree); $5,000 (for a graduate/professional level study). **To Apply:** Applicants may contact the CHCI regarding the application process and other necessary information. **Contact:** For all questions regarding CHCI Scholarship applications please send an email at scholarships@chci.org.

3355 ■ Connecticut Association of Assessing Officers (CAAO)
PO Box 427
Windsor, CT 06095-0427
URL: www.caao.com

3356 ■ CAAO Scholarship *(Professional development/Scholarship)*

Purpose: To support member of CAAO in career development. **Focus:** General studies/Field of study not specified. **Qualif.:** Applicants must be members of Connecticut Association of Assessing Officers; must be employed in a

Awards are arranged alphabetically below their administering organizations

Connecticut Assessor's Office at the time of request. **Criteria:** Selection will be based on the Professional Designation and Awards Committee's criteria.

Funds Avail.: No specific amount. **Duration:** Annual. **To Apply:** Application form can be downloaded at the website. Applicants must provide a letter signed by the Finance Director or Chief Executive Officer of their employing municipality, stating that said Municipality will not pay for, nor reimburse the applicants for the full cost of the course for which the Scholarship is requested.

3357 ■ Connecticut Association of Land Surveyors (CALS)
78 Beaver Rd.
Wethersfield, CT 06109
Ph: (860)563-1990
Fax: (860)529-9700
URL: ctsurveyors.org

3358 ■ Connecticut Association of Land Surveyors Memorial Scholarships *(Undergraduate/Scholarship)*

Purpose: To provide students the financial assistance they need in surveying. **Focus:** Cartography/Surveying. **Qualif.:** Applicants must be residents of Connecticut; must be enrolled in a program leading to a degree in surveying or related fields; must be accepted to attend the program and could be a freshman; must show an interest or work history in being a part of the surveying profession. **Criteria:** Recipients are selected based on academic performance and interest in surveying profession.

Funds Avail.: No specific amount. **To Apply:** Applicants must submit a statement outlining qualifications, transcript, resume and other pertinent information. **Deadline:** June 1.

3359 ■ Connecticut Association of Latinos in Higher Education (CALAHE)
Willard Hall, Rm. 110
Central Connecticut State University
1615 Stanley St.
New Britain, CT 06050
URL: calahe.org
Facebook: www.facebook.com/CALAHE

3360 ■ Thomas M. Blake Memorial Scholarships *(Undergraduate/Scholarship)*

Purpose: To promote different areas of postsecondary education participated by Latinos. **Focus:** Education. **Qualif.:** Applicant must be accepted for admission to an accredited institution of higher education; have a "B" average (3.0 GPA) for all completed enrollment periods at the time of application; a U.S. citizen or permanent resident; have been a Connecticut resident during the preceding 12 months; a Latino student from Connecticut; and must demonstrate financial need. **Criteria:** Selection is based on the application materials.

Funds Avail.: $1,000. **To Apply:** Applicants must submit a completed scholarship application together with an official copy of educational transcripts; copy of Student Aid Report (SAR) sent by the U.S. Department of Education; and an essay on "How do you feel education is going to impact your ability to continue assisting others to pursue an education?" (Maximum of 2 pages typewritten, double spaced statement). **Deadline:** April 15. **Contact:** Dr. Wilson Luna, Gateway Community College, at the above address.

3361 ■ Rosa Quezada Memorial Education Scholarships *(Undergraduate/Scholarship)*

Purpose: To promote different areas of postsecondary education participated by Latinos. **Focus:** Education. **Qualif.:** Applicant must be accepted for admission to an accredited institution of higher education; have a "B" average (3.0 GPA) for all completed enrollment periods at the time of application; a U.S. citizen or permanent resident; have been a Connecticut resident during the preceding 12 months; a Latino student from Connecticut; and must demonstrate financial need. **Criteria:** Selection is based on the application materials.

Funds Avail.: $1,000. **To Apply:** Applicants must submit a completed scholarship application together with an official copy of educational transcripts; copy of Student Aid Report (SAR) sent by the U.S. Department of Education; and an essay on "How do you feel education is going to impact your ability to continue assisting others to pursue an education?" (Maximum of 2 pages typewritten, double spaced statement). **Deadline:** April 15. **Contact:** Dr. Wilson Luna, Gateway Community College, at the above address.

3362 ■ John Soto Scholarships *(Undergraduate/Scholarship)*

Purpose: To promote different areas of postsecondary education participated by Latinos. **Focus:** Education. **Qualif.:** Applicant must be accepted for admission to an accredited institution of higher education; have a "B" average (3.0 GPA) for all completed enrollment periods at the time of application; a U.S. citizen or permanent resident; have been a Connecticut resident during the preceding 12 months; a Latino student from Connecticut; and must demonstrate financial need. **Criteria:** Selection is based on the application materials.

Funds Avail.: $1,000. **To Apply:** Applicants must submit a completed scholarship application together with an official copy of educational transcripts; copy of Student Aid Report (SAR) sent by the U.S. Department of Education; and an essay on "How do you feel education is going to impact your ability to continue assisting others to pursue an education?" (Maximum of 2 pages typewritten, double spaced statement). **Deadline:** April 15. **Contact:** Dr. Wilson Luna, Gateway Community College, at the above address.

3363 ■ Marta Vallin Memorial Scholarships *(Undergraduate/Scholarship)*

Purpose: To promote the participation of Latinos in different areas of postsecondary education in Connecticut. **Focus:** Education. **Qualif.:** Applicant must be attending Gateway Community College; have a "B" average (3.0 GPA) for all completed enrollment periods at the time of application; a U.S. citizen or permanent resident; have been a Connecticut resident during the preceding 12 months; a Latino student from Connecticut; and must demonstrate financial need. **Criteria:** Selection is based on the application materials.

Funds Avail.: $1,000. **To Apply:** Applicants must submit a completed scholarship application together with an official copy of educational transcripts; copy of Student Aid Report (SAR) sent by the U.S. Department of Education; and an essay on "How do you feel education is going to impact your ability to continue assisting others to pursue an education?" (Maximum of 2 pages typewritten, double spaced statement). **Deadline:** April 15.

Awards are arranged alphabetically below their administering organizations

3364 ■ Connecticut Construction Industries Association (CCIA)
912 Silas Deane Hwy.
Wethersfield, CT 06109-3433
Ph: (860)529-6855
Fax: (860)563-0616
E-mail: ccia-info@ctconstruction.org
URL: www.ctconstruction.org
Twitter: twitter.com/CCIA_info

3365 ■ Associated General Contractors of Connecticut Scholarships (Undergraduate/Scholarship)

Purpose: To support students enrolled in a construction management or construction related engineering programs. **Focus:** Construction; Engineering, Civil. **Qualif.:** Applicants must be graduating high school seniors entering college as freshmen or entering a two-year technical school with a construction course of study with the intent of entering a four-year college upon completion of the technical school; must desire a career in construction; must pursue a B.S. degree in construction technology or construction civil engineering; must be U.S. citizens or documented residents of the United States. **Criteria:** Recipients are selected based on academic performance and interest in the field of construction.

Funds Avail.: $5,000 ($2,500 per year for two years). **To Apply:** Applicants must complete the "four-page" signed application; must submit one faculty evaluation form completed by high school faculty member with scholastic achievement and school history, two personal evaluation forms and official transcript of records. **Deadline:** March 31. **Contact:** John W. Butts at 860-529-6855.

3366 ■ Connecticut Space Grant College Consortium
University of Hartford
200 Bloomfield Ave.
West Hartford, CT 06117
Ph: (860)768-4846
Fax: (860)768-5073
E-mail: ctspgrant@hartford.edu
URL: ctspacegrant.org

3367 ■ Connecticut Space Grant College Consortium Undergraduate Research Fellowships (Undergraduate/Fellowship)

Purpose: To support outstanding students' education and research who exemplify interest in STEM field. **Focus:** Space and planetary sciences. **Qualif.:** Applicants must be undergraduate full-time students with a minimum GPA of 3.0 or higher. All applicants must provide a proof of U.S. Citizenship through the Grant Verification Form. **Criteria:** Selection will be based on the committees' criteria.

Funds Avail.: $5,000. **Number Awarded:** 4. **To Apply:** Applicants must submit complete requirements via email. The email must include two attachments, the Contact/Demographic Info form and a single PDF containing the appropriate cover sheet, abstract, proposal narrative, letters of support, resume/CV, transcript and the Grant Verification Form. **Deadline:** March 15. **Contact:** csgcinfo@hartford.edu.

3368 ■ Conquer Cancer Foundation
2318 Mill Road, Suite 800
Alexandria, VA 22314
E-mail: info@conquercancerfoundation.org
URL: www.conquercancerfoundation.org

3369 ■ ASCO/CCF Young Investigator Awards (Professional development, Advanced Professional/Grant)

Purpose: To fund physicians during the transition from a fellowship program to a faculty appointment. **Focus:** Oncology. **Qualif.:** Applicants must: be physicians working with MD, DO, or international equivalent working in any country; be on their last two years in a clinical department at an academic medical institution at the time of grant submission; have a valid and active medical license at the time of application; be members of ASCO; and, have a mentor from the sponsoring institution who must provide a letter of support. **Criteria:** Preference will be given to those with proposals that are hypothesis-driven with a clinical research focus on generating the rationale for future clinical studies; strength of the mentor in supporting the applicants' proposal and in facilitating the applicants' career development; potential to pursue an academic clinical oncology career; availability of institutional resources to support the proposed project.

Funds Avail.: $50,000. **Duration:** Annual. **To Apply:** Applicants must accomplish their online application process at Grants Website and should be submitted in accordance to the requirements and instructions of the Request for Proposals (RFP). All application materials must be in English and must include the following components: contact information; project information (includes Abstract, IRB and Animal Use Assurances); specific aims; personal statements; applicants' biosketch; research strategy; cited references; project timeline; budget and justification; mentor's biosketch; mentor's letter of support; institutional letter of support from Department Chair or Dean; institutional approval face sheet signed by the Institutional Approver. **Deadline:** September 22.

3370 ■ Bradley Stuart Beller Special Merit Award (Doctorate, Postdoctorate/Award)

Purpose: To support fellows who have the highest ranking abstract overall in the Merit Award category as determined by the Scientific Program Committee. **Focus:** Medical research; Oncology. **Qualif.:** Applicants must hold a doctoral degree or be doctoral candidates at the time of abstract submission; must be enrolled in an oncology fellowship training program or equivalent; must work in an oncology laboratory or clinical research setting; must agree to present the abstract at the annual meeting; should provide letter of support from their training program director; and a two-page curriculum vitae. **Criteria:** Selection will be based on the committee's criteria.

Funds Avail.: $1,000 - $1,500. **Duration:** Annual. **To Apply:** Interested applicants may contact the Foundation for the application process and other details. **Contact:** Conquer Cancer Foundation, at the above address.

3371 ■ CCF Career Development Award (Professional development/Grant)

Purpose: To provide funding to clinical investigators who have received their initial faculty appointment to establish an independent clinical cancer research program. **Focus:** Oncology. **Qualif.:** Applicants must be physicians working in any country and in the first to third year of a full-time, primary faculty appointment in a clinical department at an academic medical institution; must have a valid and active medical license at the time of application; must have

Awards are arranged alphabetically below their administering organizations

completed productive postdoctoral research; must be ASCO members; should not have any current career development award and have not been a Principal Investigator on any large project grants; and must have a mentor from the sponsoring institution who must provide a letter of support. **Criteria:** The Conquer Cancer Foundation Grants Selection Committee will select the recipient based on the following criteria: potential for the applicants to pursue an academic clinical oncology career; strength of the hypothesis-driven proposal with a clinical research focus; strength of the mentor in supporting the applicants' proposal and in facilitating the applicants' career development; and availability of institutional resources to support the proposed project.

Funds Avail.: $200,000. **Duration:** Annual; Paid in three annual increments. **To Apply:** Applicants must accomplish their online application process and must be submitted in accordance to the requirements and instructions of the Request for Proposals (RFP); all application materials must be in English. **Deadline:** September 22.

3372 ■ CCF Improving Cancer Care Grants (Professional development, Doctorate/Grant)

Purpose: To encourage multi-disciplinary research that will have a major impact in breast cancer care. **Focus:** Oncology. **Qualif.:** The research teams must be focused on implementing and/or evaluating new solutions to existing problems in quality of, access to, and delivery of care with general applicability to breast cancer; must be led by a single Principal Investigator, who must be an active ASCO member (or have submitted a membership application) with an MD, DO, PhD or equivalent degree; must have a multidisciplinary team of investigators that may include clinicians, nurses, pharmacists, statisticians, epidemiologists, information technologists and other research experts. **Criteria:** Selection will be based on the committee's criteria.

Funds Avail.: $1.35 million for 3 years. **Number Awarded:** 1. **To Apply:** Interested applicants must visit the Easygrants website at https://grants.ascocancerfoundation.org to create an account and to access the online application system. Applicants must provide a letter of intent to be submitted online **Remarks:** Established in 2010. **Contact:** ASCO Cancer Foundation at grants@asco.org.

3373 ■ CCF Merit Award (Professional development, Doctorate/Award)

Purpose: To support fellows and residents whose research is addressed in high-quality abstracts and recognized for its scientific merit. **Focus:** Oncology. **Qualif.:** Authors of an abstract must hold a doctoral degree or doctoral degree candidates at the time of abstract submission; must be enrolled in an oncology fellowship training program to equivalent; must work in an oncology laboratory or clinical research setting. **Criteria:** Selection will be based on the committee's criteria.

Funds Avail.: $1,000 to $1,500. **Duration:** Annual. **To Apply:** Consideration for the award is available on the abstract submitter for the appropriate meeting. Applicants must present the abstract at the annual meeting and must provide a letter of support from their training program director and two-page curriculum vitae.

3374 ■ Comparative Effectiveness Research Professorship (CERP) (Professional development, Doctorate/Grant)

Purpose: To assist consumers, clinicians, purchasers, and policy makers to make informed decisions that will improve health care at both the individual and population levels. **Focus:** Oncology. **Qualif.:** Applicants must have an MD, PhD or equivalent degree; must have the rank of full professors; must have full-time faculty appointment at an academic medical center; must have a full-time faculty appointment at an academic medical center; must have made significant contributions that have changed the direction of breast cancer research; must be serving as a research mentor to one or more researcher(s) in training; must lead a research team in conducting research on comparative effectiveness in breast cancer; must be active members of ASCO; must commit to spend 75% of time during the award period dedicated to research including leading a team of researchers and mentoring physician-scientists. **Criteria:** Selection will be based on the following criteria: qualifications, experience and productivity of the applicants; commitment to mentoring the next generation of researchers in comparative effectiveness research; scientific impact, merit and originality of the applicants' ongoing research, and the ongoing research that the applicants are mentoring; documented effective research team leadership; facilities and resources available to the applicants to continue their research career and attain their career goals.

Funds Avail.: A total of $500,000. **Duration:** Annual; Paid in 5 annual increments. **To Apply:** Domestic and international applications must be submitted in accordance with the requirements and instructions of request for proposal (RFP). Applicants must provide a letter of intent. All application materials must be in English and must be submitted online.

3375 ■ Drug Development Research Professorship (Professional development/Internship)

Purpose: To provide flexible funding to outstanding researchers who have made, and are continuing to make significant contributions that may change the direction of cancer research. **Focus:** Medical research. **Qualif.:** Applicants must be physicians working in any country with a full-time faculty appointment in a clinical department at an academic medical center; must currently hold the rank of full professor at an academic medical center. If applicants does not hold the rank of full professor, but meets all other eligibility criteria, they must provide written explanation of why their current rank at their institution should be considered equivalent; must made significant contributions to the development of new therapies for cancer; must be serving as a research mentor to researcher(s) in training, and must be planning to continue to provide leadership in the area of drug development throughout the award period; must lead a research team in the conduct of drug development research that includes clinical trials; must be full members of the American Society of Clinical Oncology in good standing or submit a membership application with grant application; must expect to spend 75% of time during the award period dedicated to research and drug development activities, leading a team of researchers and mentoring junior faculty and trainees on research and drug development. **Criteria:** The selection committee will select recipients based on the following: qualifications, experience, and productivity of the applicants; commitment to mentoring the next generation of researchers in scientific and regulatory aspect of drug development; scientific impact, merit, and originality of the applicants' ongoing research; documented effective research team leadership; and facilities and resources available to the applicants to pursue their research career.

Funds Avail.: $100,000 per year. **Duration:** Annual; Up to 5 years. **To Apply:** All applications must be submitted in accordance to the requirements and instructions of the Request for Applications. To initiate an application, applicants must go to https://grants.conquercancerfoundation.org. An application must include the following mandatory components: contact information; project information; applicants' biosketch; list of collaborators; a maximum 10-page research plan; cited references; budget and justification; letter from researcher-in-training; institutional letter of support from Department Chair or Dean; institutional approved face sheet signed by Institutional Approver Officer. Applicants may also include the following optional components: clinical trial protocol; prior publication; supporting documentation. **Contact:** Conquer Cancer Foundation, at the above address.

3376 ■ International Development and Education Award in Palliative Care *(Professional development/Award)*

Purpose: To provide medical education in palliative care, assist with career development and helps establish strong relationships with leading ASCO members in the field of palliative care who serves as scientific Mentors to each recipient. **Focus:** Oncology. **Qualif.:** Applicants must have a current passport that does not expire before December of the current year; must be current residents of a country classified by the World Bank as Low-Income, Lower-Middle-Income, or Upper-Middle-Income, and have limited resources to attend the ASCO Annual Meeting; must be full members, members in training or international corresponding members of ASCO or willing to submit an application for ASCO membership; must have a demonstrated interest in integrating palliative and supportive care into their institution; must be less than ten years past their oncology program training; must be fluent in English. **Criteria:** Selection will be based on the submitted applications.

Funds Avail.: No specific amount. **Duration:** Annual. **To Apply:** All applications must be submitted in accordance to the requirements and instructions of the Request for Applications. To initiate an application, applicants must go to https://grants.conquercancerfoundation.org. An application must include the following mandatory components: contact information; personal statement; applicant information; biographical sketch; senior oncologist or palliative care specialist letter of recommendation; institutional approval. **Deadline:** January 6.

3377 ■ International Development and Education Awards *(Professional development, Doctorate/Grant)*

Purpose: To support early-career oncologists in developing countries and facilitates the sharing of knowledge between these oncologists and ASCO members. **Focus:** Oncology. **Qualif.:** Applicants must have a current passport; must be current residents of a country classified by the World Bank as Low-Income, Lower-Middle-Income or Upper-Middle-Income and have limited resources to attend the ASC Annual Meeting; must be members of ASCO (full, member-in-training, or international corresponding); must be less than ten years past their oncology program; must be fluent in English. **Criteria:** Selection will be based on the committee's criteria.

Funds Avail.: Amount not specified. **Duration:** Annual. **To Apply:** Interested applicants must go to https://grants.conquercancerfoundation.org for the online application process.

3378 ■ International Innovation Grants *(Professional development/Grant)*

Purpose: To provide research funding in support of novel and innovative project that can have a significant impact on cancer control in low- and middle-income countries. **Focus:** Oncology. **Qualif.:** Principal investigators must be ASCO members and must be affiliated with the Grantee Organization; must be residents of the low-income or middle-income country. Grantee organizations must be nonprofit or governmental agency in a low-income or middle-income country. Grantee organizations and principal investigators will be expected to share and disseminate the knowledge gained during their research project. **Criteria:** Selection will be based on the committee's criteria.

Funds Avail.: Up to $20,000. **Duration:** Annual. **To Apply:** All application materials must be in English and must be submitted through the Easygrants website; letter of intent must also be provided. **Remarks:** Established in 2013.

3379 ■ Brigid Leventhal Special Merit Award *(Postdoctorate, Professional development/Award)*

Purpose: To support fellows who submitted the top abstract in Pediatric Oncology. **Focus:** Oncology. **Qualif.:** Authors of an abstract must hold a doctoral degree or doctoral degree candidates at the time of abstract submission; must be enrolled in an oncology fellowship training program to equivalent; must work in an oncology laboratory or clinical research setting. **Criteria:** Selection criteria will be based on the committee's criteria.

Funds Avail.: $1,000-$1,500. **Duration:** Annual. **To Apply:** Consideration for the award is available on the abstract submitter for the appropriate meeting. Applicants must present the abstract at the annual meeting and must provide a letter of support from their training program director and two-page curriculum vitae.

3380 ■ Long-term International Fellowships *(Professional development/Fellowship)*

Purpose: To provide early-career oncologists in low- to middle-income countries the support and resources needed to advance their training. **Focus:** Oncology. **Qualif.:** Applicants must be full members or international corresponding members of ASCO; must be a physicians who have completed a subspecialty training program or the equivalent; must have less than 10 years of experience; must commit to returning to their home country within one year following the completion of the fellowship; must have a pre-existing relationship with a mentor of ASCO and are employed in U.S. or Canada. **Criteria:** Selection will be based on the committee's criteria.

Funds Avail.: A total of $115,000. **Duration:** Annual. **To Apply:** Applicants must accomplish their online application process at https://grants.conquercancerfoundation.org and must be submitted in accordance to the requirements and instructions of the Request for Proposals (RFP). All application materials must be in English and must include the following components: Contact Information; Project Information; Personal Statement Questions; Biographical Sketch; Letter of Recommendation from Home Institution; Publications; Budget; Mentor Information. The following must be completed by the mentor: Fellowship description from US or Canadian Mentor; Mentor NIH Biographical Sketch; Mentor Letter of Support; Institutional Approval Facesheet, signed by Host Institution.

3381 ■ Medical Student Rotation for Underrepresented Populations *(Graduate/Grant)*

Purpose: To facilitate the recruitment and retention of individuals from populations underrepresented in medicine to cancer careers and increase access to quality care for underserved communities. **Focus:** Oncology. **Qualif.:** Ap-

Awards are arranged alphabetically below their administering organizations

plicants must be enrolled in an MD or DO, U.S. medical school program and be of an underrepresented population; must be U.S. citizens, nationals or permanent residents; must demonstrate interest in pursuing oncology as a career; and must have good academic record. **Criteria:** Selection will be based on the committee's criteria.

Funds Avail.: $5,000 stipend for the rotation; $1,500 for future travel to the ASCO Annual Meeting; additional $2,000 to students' mentor. **Duration:** Annual. **To Apply:** Interested applicants may visit the website to obtain an application form. **Deadline:** December 7.

3382 ■ James B. Nachman ASCO Junior Faculty Award in Pediatric Oncology *(Doctorate, Professional development/Grant)*

Purpose: To support faculty members who submits the highest ranking abstract in pediatric oncology for the ASCO Annual Meeting. **Focus:** Oncology. **Qualif.:** Applicants must be holding a medical or doctoral degree; must be within seven years of their first faculty appointment at the time of abstract submission; must conduct laboratory, population-based, or clinical research focused on childhood cancer; agrees to present the abstract at the ASCO Annual Meeting. **Criteria:** Selection will be based on the committee' s criteria.

Funds Avail.: $3,000. **Duration:** Annual. **To Apply:** Consideration for the award is available on the abstract submitter for the appropriate meeting. Applicants must present the abstract at the annual meeting and must provide a letter of support from their training program director and two-page curriculum vitae.

3383 ■ Oncology Trainee Travel Awards *(Professional development/Grant)*

Purpose: To support the continuing education and professional development of trainee oncologists by providing them with an individual travel grant to defray travel expenses for attending the ASCO Annual Meeting. **Focus:** Oncology. **Qualif.:** Applicants must be ASCO members. **Criteria:** Selection will be based on the committee's criteria.

Funds Avail.: $1,100 Travel fare plus complimentary registration for the Annual Meeting. **Duration:** Annual. **To Apply:** Interested applicants may contact the Foundation for the application process and other information.

3384 ■ The Pain Special Merit Award *(Postdoctorate, Professional development/Award)*

Purpose: To support fellow who submitted the top abstract in Pain and Symptom Management Research. **Focus:** Oncology. **Qualif.:** Authors of an abstract must hold a doctoral degree or doctoral degree candidates at the time of abstract submission; must be enrolled in an oncology fellowship training program to equivalent; must work in an oncology laboratory or clinical research setting. **Criteria:** Selected will be based on the committee's criteria.

Funds Avail.: No specific amount. **Duration:** Annual. **To Apply:** Consideration for the award is available on the abstract submitter for the appropriate meeting. Applicants must present the abstract at the annual meeting and must provide a letter of support from their training program director and two-page curriculum vitae.

3385 ■ Patient Advocate Scholarship Program *(Professional development/Scholarship)*

Purpose: To support the awardees to be able to attend the Annual Meeting of The American Society of Clinical Oncology (ASCO) and ASCO Symposia. **Focus:** Medical research; Oncology. **Qualif.:** Advocates must be either operating from an individual or organizational level, locally or nationally. **Criteria:** Selection will be based on the committee's criteria.

Funds Avail.: No amount specified. **Duration:** Annual. **To Apply:** Interested applicants may contact the Conquer Cancer Foundation for the application process and other information details.

3386 ■ Resident Travel Award for Underrepresented Populations *(Professional development/Award)*

Purpose: To support residents from underrepresented populations to attend the ASCO Annual Meeting. **Focus:** Oncology. **Qualif.:** Applicants must be enrolled in an ACGME-accredited residency program and be of an underrepresented population; candidates must be U.S. nationals or permanent residents; must show interest in pursuing oncology as a career; and must have good academic record. **Criteria:** Selection will be based on the following criteria; demonstration of an interest in pursuing oncology as a career; demonstration of leadership, volunteerism and/or commitment to underserved populations or health disparities; letters of support; and personal statement.

Funds Avail.: $1,500. **Duration:** Annual. **To Apply:** Interested applicants must visit the website for the online application process. All applications must be submitted in accordance with the requirements and instructions of the RFA. Applicants must also provide the following requirements: contact information; applicants information; references; current resume; personal statement; proof of US citizenship and residency; travel and academic verification form; letters of recommendation.

3387 ■ Translational Research Professorship *(Professional development/Internship)*

Purpose: To provide flexible funding to outstanding translational researchers who have made, and are continuing to make significant contributions that have changed the direction of cancer research. **Focus:** Medical research. **Qualif.:** Applicants must be physicians working in any country with a full-time faculty appointment in a clinical department at an academic medical center; must currently hold the rank of full professor at an academic medical center. If applicants does not hold the rank of full professor, but meets all other eligibility criteria, they must provide written explanation of why their current rank at their institution should be considered equivalent; must made significant contributions to the development of new therapies for cancer; must be serving as a research mentor to researcher(s) in training, and must be planning to continue to provide leadership in the area of drug development throughout the award period; must lead a research team in the conduct of drug development research that includes clinical trials; must be full members of the American Society of Clinical Oncology in good standing or submit a membership application with grant application; must expect to spend 75% of time during the award period dedicated to research and drug development activities, leading a team of researchers and mentoring junior faculty and trainees on research and drug development. **Criteria:** The selection committee will select recipients based on the following: qualifications, experience, and productivity of the applicants; commitment to mentoring the next generation of researchers in scientific and regulatory aspect of drug development; scientific impact, merit, and originality of the applicants' ongoing research; documented effective research team leadership; and facilities and resources

Awards are arranged alphabetically below their administering organizations

available to the applicants to pursue their research career. **Funds Avail.:** No specific amount. **Duration:** Annual. **To Apply:** All applications must be submitted in accordance to the requirements and instructions of the Request for Applications. To initiate an application, applicants must go to https://grants.conquercancerfoundation.org. An application must include the following mandatory components: contact information; project information; applicants' biosketch; list of collaborators; a maximum 10-page research plan; cited references; budget and justification; letter from researcher-in-training; institutional letter of support from Department Chair or Dean; institutional approved face sheet signed by Institutional Approver Officer. Applicants may also include the following optional components: clinical trial protocol; prior publication; supporting documentation.

3388 ■ Conseil Canadien pour le Commerce Autochtone
2 Berkeley St., Ste. 310
Toronto, ON, Canada M5A 4J5
Ph: (416)961-8663
Fax: (416)961-3995
E-mail: info@ccab.com
URL: www.ccab.com

3389 ■ Foundation for the Advancement of Aboriginal Youth Bursary Program (Undergraduate/Scholarship)

Purpose: To provide scholarship assistance to qualified individuals who want to pursue their post-secondary education. **Focus:** General studies/Field of study not specified. **Qualif.:** Applicant must be a Canadian resident, of First Nation, Metis or Inuit heritage and attending either a high school or a post-secondary institute full-time within Canada. **Criteria:** Recipient will be selected based on financial need, academic and career commitment, contribution to family and community and leadership and role model qualities.

Funds Avail.: No specific amount. **Duration:** Annual. **To Apply:** Applicant must complete the application form available online; must provide a proof of First Nations, Inuit or Metis ancestry; must have two signed, original letters of support; must provide a copy of the most recent official school transcripts and report card; must include a letter of acceptance; must provide a recent color photo. **Deadline:** October 8. **Contact:** 1-866-566-3229.

3390 ■ Foundation for the Advancement of Aboriginal Youth Scholarships (Undergraduate/Scholarship)

Purpose: To provide scholarship assistance to qualified individuals who want to pursue their post-secondary education. **Focus:** General studies/Field of study not specified. **Qualif.:** Applicant must be a Canadian resident, of First Nation, Metis or Inuit heritage and attending either high school or a post-secondary institute full-time within Canada. **Criteria:** Recipient will be selected based on financial need, academic and career commitment, contribution to family and community, and leadership and role model qualities.

Funds Avail.: No specific amount. **To Apply:** Applicant must complete the application form available online; must provide proof of First Nation, Inuit or Metis ancestry; must have two signed, original letters of support; must provide a copy of the most recent official school transcripts and report card; must include a letter of acceptance; must provide a recent color photo. Application form and other supporting documents must be sent to Foundation for the Advancement of Aboriginal Youth, c/o Canadian Council for Aboriginal Business, 250 The Esplanade, Ste. 204, Toronto, ON M5A 1J2. **Deadline:** October 8. **Contact:** 1-866-566-3229.

3391 ■ Conseil Canadien des Techniciens et Technologues (CCTT)
400 - 14 Concourse Gate
Ottawa, ON, Canada K2E 7S6
Ph: (613)238-8123
Fax: (613)238-8822
E-mail: ccttadm@cctt.ca
URL: www.cctt.ca
Twitter: twitter.com/CCTTCanada

3392 ■ Canadian Council of Technicians and Technologists Scholarships for Technology Students (Undergraduate/Scholarship)

Purpose: To assist the son or daughter of a certified member with expenses incurred to undertake a course of studies leading to a technician or technology diploma in a recognized program of studies in Engineering or Applied Science Technology. **Focus:** Engineering; Science technologies. **Qualif.:** Applicant must be a son or daughter of an individual member of a Constituent member (CM) of CCTT. **Criteria:** Selection shall be based on the aforementioned qualifications and compliance with the application details.

Funds Avail.: 1,000 Canadian Dollars. **Duration:** Annual. **Number Awarded:** 2. **To Apply:** Applicant must secure a letter from a Constituent member of the council, attesting to the fact that his or her parents are members in good standing; must confirm by official transcripts that he/she is a graduate from grade 12 secondary school program with second-class, or with better standing and has been proven that she/he is enrolled as full-time student in an Engineering or Applied Science Technology Program in Canada. **Deadline:** December 15. **Contact:** For additional information, please contact the CCTT office: Phone: 613-238-8123 ext. 225.

3393 ■ Conseil Consultatif Canadiene de la Radio
811-116 Albert St.
Ottawa, ON, Canada K1P 5G3
Ph: (613)230-3261
Free: 888-902-5768
E-mail: rabc.gm@on.aibn.com
URL: www.rabc-cccr.ca

3394 ■ Future Leader in Radiocommunications Scholarships (Undergraduate/Scholarship)

Purpose: To encourage careers in telecommunications especially among engineering students. **Focus:** Telecommunications systems. **Qualif.:** Applicants must be enrolled in an accredited Canadian university and must have completed at least the second year in an engineering programme. **Criteria:** Selection of applicants will be based on their academic excellence and community involvement.

Funds Avail.: $3,500. **Duration:** Annual. **To Apply:** Scholarship applications may be obtained by contacting RABC or log on to www.electrofed.com. Completed applications must be submitted to RABC. **Deadline:** July 31. **Remarks:**

Awards are arranged alphabetically below their administering organizations

Administered by the Electro-Federation Canada.

3395 ■ Conseil de recherches en sciences humaines
350 Albert St.
Ottawa, ON, Canada K1P 6G4
Ph: (613)995-4273
E-mail: webmaster@sshrc-crsh.gc.ca
URL: www.sshrc-crsh.gc.ca

3396 ■ SSHRC Doctoral Fellowship Program
(Doctorate/Fellowship, Scholarship)

Purpose: To develop research skills and assist in the training of highly-qualified academic personnel by supporting students who demonstrate a high standard of scholarly achievement in undergraduate and graduate studies in the social sciences and humanities. **Focus:** Humanities; Social sciences. **Qualif.:** Applicants must: be citizens or permanent residents of Canada; be applying for support to pursue their first PhD; be pursuing doctoral studies (or a combined MA/PhD) in the social sciences and humanities; not have already received a scholarship or fellowship from SSHRC, NSERC or CIHR to undertake or complete a doctoral degree or combined MA/PhD; not be applying in the current academic year to NSERC or CIHR; and not be pursuing a degree program that combines undergraduate and graduate degrees. CGS Doctoral Scholarships are tenable only at recognized universities in Canada; SSHRC Doctoral Fellowships are tenable at any recognized university in Canada or abroad, provided that the award holder has completed at least one previous degree at a Canadian university. On the proposed start date of the award, applicants must: be registered as a full-time student undertaking or continuing a doctoral program in the social sciences or humanities; and not have exceeded the allowable number of months already spent in doctoral study, as set out in the section above. **Criteria:** Selection will be based on academic merit.

Funds Avail.: 20,000 Canadian Dollars. **To Apply:** Applicants must ensure that they meet the requirements; complete and submit only one application form with the required attachments. Applicants will find the application instructions inside their application when they begin to create it online. Applicants must determine their current registration status and submit their complete application to the appropriate institution. Candidates eligible for both the CGS Doctoral Scholarship and the SSHRC Doctoral Fellowship will be considered for both awards. All candidates will be assigned a rank order on the basis of the selection committee's recommendations. **Deadline:** November 6.

3397 ■ Conseil International d'Études Canadiennes (CIEC)
Holland Cross RO
1620 Scott St., Unit 8
Ottawa, ON, Canada K1Y 4V1
Ph: (819)205-0359
URL: www.iccs-ciec.ca
Facebook: www.facebook.com/ICCS.CIEC.page
Twitter: twitter.com/ICCS_CIEC

3398 ■ Canadian Studies Postdoctoral Fellowships
(Postdoctorate/Fellowship)

Purpose: To enable young Canadian and foreign academics to visit a Canadian or foreign university with a Canadian Studies program for a teaching or research fellowship. **Focus:** Canadian studies. **Qualif.:** Applicants must be in post-doctoral level that have completed a doctoral thesis on a topic primarily related to Canada and are not employed as a full-time; must obtain a formal commitment from such universities concerning the services and teaching and/or research opportunities which would be available to them. **Criteria:** Selection will be based on the committee's criteria.

Funds Avail.: $2,500. **Duration:** Minimum of one month and maximum of three months. **To Apply:** Applicants must submit the following materials: up-to-date curriculum vitae; copy of the doctoral thesis; full description of the project proposed by the applicant during his/her fellowship; an official letter from the host university indicating its support of the young researcher (availability of research tools, library, archives, computer, office, accommodation, teaching load and other responsibilities); two letters of reference from university professors knowledgeable with the candidates' studies; and letter from the senior researcher's host outlining the research project and the work to be assigned to the young researcher during the fellowship. For applicant applying for a research fellowship, they must include a budget detailing travel expenses, material, photocopies, etc. and for applicant applying for a teaching fellowship, they must also include a course outline maximum of two pages. Application files must be submitted to the ICCS with a recommendation from the national Canadian Studies Association. **Deadline:** November 24.

3399 ■ International Council for Canadian Studies Graduate Student Scholarships (Graduate/Scholarship)

Purpose: To support the works of young scholars, by enabling successful candidates for their research related to their thesis or dissertation in the field of Canadian Studies. **Focus:** Canadian studies. **Qualif.:** Applicants must be students in the social sciences or humanities who are in the process of preparing a graduate thesis or doctoral dissertation in Canada; must be at the thesis or dissertation stage; and must obtained in writing the support of a faculty member at a Canadian University who has agreed to act as the students' academic sponsor during the tenure of their award. **Criteria:** Applicants will be evaluated based on clarity of the proposal and its methodology; the proposal's potential contribution; must demonstrate the need for the research to be carried out in Canada and by the strength of the letter of support. Nominations will be evaluated and ranked by the adjudication committee appointed by the International Council for Canadian Studies.

Funds Avail.: Up to 4,000 Canadian Dollars. **Duration:** Annual. **Number Awarded:** 6. **To Apply:** Applicants must submit a two-page proposal outlining the thesis/dissertation project; an official university transcript; copy of a letter from the faculty member in a Canadian University indicating their willingness to act as the student's academic sponsor; and a letter of support from the student's thesis/dissertation supervisor. **Deadline:** November 24.

3400 ■ Conseil de Recherches en Sciences Naturelles et en Génie du Canada
350 Albert St., 16th Fl.
Ottawa, ON, Canada K1A 1H5
Ph: (613)995-4273
Fax: (613)992-5337
Free: 855-275-2861
E-mail: exec@nserc-crsng.gc.ca

CONSEIL DE RECHERCHES EN SCIENCES NATURELLES ET EN GÉNIE

URL: www.nserc-crsng.gc.ca
Facebook: www.facebook.com/EurekaCanadaEnglish
LinkedIn: www.linkedin.com/company/natural-sciences-and-engineering-research-council-of-canada
Twitter: twitter.com/nserc_crsng

3401 ■ Alexander Graham Bell Canada Graduate Scholarship Program *(Doctorate, Master's/Scholarship)*

Purpose: To provide financial support for outstanding eligible students pursuing master's or doctoral studies in a Canadian university. **Focus:** Natural sciences; Pre-Columbian studies. **Qualif.:** Applicants must be Canadian citizens or permanent residents of Canada; must hold, or expect to hold (at the time award is taken) a degree in science or engineering from a university whose standing is acceptable to NSERC (if you have a degree in a field other than science or engineering, NSERC may accept your application at its discretion); must intend to pursue, in the following year, full-time graduate studies and research at the master's or doctoral level in an eligible program in one of the areas of the natural sciences and engineering supported by NSERC; and must have obtained a first-class average (a grade of "A-") in each of the last two completed years of study. **Criteria:** Selection of recipients is based on merit.

Funds Avail.: 35,000 Canadian Dollars. **Duration:** Maximum of four years. **To Apply:** Applicants must complete the online Form 201 (available on-line) and submit with other supporting materials. **Deadline:** October 15. **Contact:** For further information, applicants may send an email to schol@nserc-crsng.gc.ca.

3402 ■ Banting Postdoctoral Fellowships *(Postdoctorate/Fellowship)*

Purpose: To provide financial assistance to postdoctoral applicants and to develop their careers. **Focus:** General studies/Field of study not specified. **Qualif.:** Applicants must fulfill or have fulfilled all degree requirements for a PhD, PhD equivalent or health professional degree with proposed host institution. Canadian citizens, permanent residents of Canada and foreign citizens are all eligible to apply with the following conditions: applicants who are not Canadian citizens or permanent residents of Canada may only hold their Banting Postdoctoral Fellowship at a Canadian institution; applicants who are Canadian citizens or permanent residents of Canada and who obtained their PhD, PhD-equivalent or health professional degree from a foreign university may only hold their Banting Postdoctoral Fellowship at a Canadian institution; and applicants who are Canadian citizens or permanent residents of Canada and who obtained their PhD, PhD-equivalent or health professional degree from a Canadian university may hold their Banting Postdoctoral Fellowship at either a Canadian institution or an institution outside of Canada. In choosing the right host institutions, applicants must consider one of the following: Canadian and foreign universities; affiliated research hospitals; colleges; and not-for-profit organizations with a strong research mandate. **Criteria:** Applicants will be selected based on qualifications and submitted materials.

Funds Avail.: $70,000. **Duration:** Biennial; non-renewable. **To Apply:** Applicants must submit the completed application in either French or English language including all host institution documents and referee assessments. **Deadline:** Septemar 23.

3403 ■ Industrial R&D Fellowships *(Postdoctorate/Fellowship)*

Purpose: To provide financial support and to enable recent doctoral graduates to engage in research and development in the private sector. **Focus:** Engineering. **Qualif.:** Applicants must be Canadian citizens or permanent resident of Canada or foreign nationals with Ph.D. and graduated from a Canadian postsecondary institution; must hold a doctoral degree in a discipline of science or engineering that NSERC supports; must have completed a doctoral degree within the last five years; must not have been employed for more than six months in an R&D position in the Canadian private sector after receipt of his or her doctoral degree; and must not have received an offer of employment from the nominating company except an offer of this fellowship, conditional upon NSERC approval, or short-term employment of up to six months while awaiting a decision on the fellowship. **Criteria:** Two members of the NSERC IRDF College of Reviewers, composed of federal government employees from departments and agencies with an interest in research and development, and academic researchers who have experience with industrial research collaborations will review each nomination. The members evaluate applicants based on the following criteria: research ability or potential; and communication, interpersonal and leadership abilities. The reviewers evaluate the research proposal based on the following criteria: the research and development environment/opportunity for an industrial R&D experience; the scientific and technical merit of the proposed R&D activities; the significance and feasibility of the proposed R&D activities; incrementality; and the company's overall commitment, including its financial commitment, to the fellow and the project.

Funds Avail.: No specific amount. **Duration:** Annual. **To Apply:** Applicants must first contact a company that is willing to support their nomination. The candidates and the company must negotiate the details of the research project(s) and position. The company will submit the nomination to NSERC. The nomination must include and submit the original of each of the following: Form 200 (Application for an Industrial Postgraduate Scholarship, Industrial R&D Fellowship or Visiting Fellowship in Canadian Government Laboratories), to be completed by the candidate; attach Contributions and statements; Proof of completion of Ph.D. (if completed at time of nomination); Proof of Canadian citizenship, permanent residency or post-graduation work permit; report on the applicant of Form 200, two reports to be completed by persons very familiar with the candidate's previous work; nomination for an Industrial R&D Fellowship (Form 183C); company's official letter/contract offering employment to, and co-signed by, the candidate; letter from the collaborating company(s) outlining the nature of its/their participation and contributions (if applicable); terms and Conditions of Applying Form to be completed by the nominee; and terms and Conditions of Applying Form to be completed by the authorized organization representative.

3404 ■ Natural Sciences and Engineering Research Council Postgraduate Scholarships *(Doctorate/Scholarship)*

Purpose: To provide financial support for outstanding eligible students pursuing master's or doctoral studies in a Canadian university. **Focus:** Natural sciences; Pre-Columbian studies. **Qualif.:** Applicants must be Canadian citizens or permanent residents of Canada; must hold, or expect to hold (at the time award is taken) a degree in science or engineering from a university whose standing is

Awards are arranged alphabetically below their administering organizations

acceptable to NSERC (if you have a degree in a field other than science or engineering, NSERC may accept your application at its discretion); must intend to pursue, in the following year, full-time or part-time graduate studies and research at the master's or doctoral level in an eligible program in one of the areas of the natural sciences and engineering supported by NSERC; and must have obtained a first-class average (a grade of "A-") in each of the last two completed years of study. Foreign candidates are also eligible to apply. **Criteria:** Selection of recipients is based on merit.

Funds Avail.: 21,000 Canadian Dollars. **Duration:** Up to three years. **To Apply:** Applicants must complete the Form 200 (available on-line) and submit with other supporting materials. **Contact:** For further information, applicants may send an email to schol@nserc-crsng.gc.ca.

3405 ■ Vanier Canada Graduate Scholarships (Graduate/Scholarship)

Purpose: To support students who demonstrate a high standard of scholarly achievement in graduate studies in the social sciences and humanities, natural sciences and engineering, and health and to those who demonstrate leadership skills. **Focus:** Health sciences; Humanities; Natural sciences; Social sciences. **Qualif.:** Program is open to both Canadian and international students who must be nominated for a Vanier Canada Graduate Scholarship. **Criteria:** Selection will be based on the committee's criteria.

Funds Avail.: 50,000 Canadian Dollars per year. **Duration:** Three years. **To Apply:** Applicants must visit the Vanier CGS website for further instructions and application procedures. **Contact:** For additional information, applicants may email at vanier@cihr-irsc.gc.ca.

3406 ■ Constangy, Brooks, Smith & Prophete L.L.P.
230 Peachtree St. NW, Ste. 2400
Atlanta, GA 30303-1557
Fax: (404)525-6955
E-mail: humanresources@constangy.com
URL: www.constangy.com

3407 ■ Constangy, Brooks and Smith Diversity Scholars Awards (Undergraduate/Award)

Purpose: To honor and recognize the achievements of law students who have demonstrated academic achievement, a commitment to diversity in their community, school or work environment, and personal achievements in overcoming challenges to reach goals. **Focus:** Law. **Qualif.:** Applicants must be second-year students enrolled in an accredited law school that is located in one of the following three regions: Southern; Mid-West/West Coast; Eastern. **Criteria:** Scholarship will be awarded based on accomplishments in academics, a commitment to diversity in the community, school or work environment, and personal achievement in overcoming challenges to reach goals.

Funds Avail.: $2,500. **Number Awarded:** 1. **To Apply:** Interested applicants must visit the website for the application process. **Deadline:** November 12.

3408 ■ Contra Costa County Bar Association (CCCBA)
2300 Clayton Rd., Ste. 520
Concord, CA 94520
Ph: (925)686-6900
Fax: (925)686-9867
URL: www.cccba.org

3409 ■ Richard E. Arnason Court Scholarships (Undergraduate/Scholarship)

Purpose: To help adults or juveniles gain the education they need to get ahead. **Focus:** Criminal justice. **Qualif.:** Applicants must be adults or juveniles currently residing in Contra Costa County who have been through the criminal justice system resulting in a conviction; must be out of custody as of March 31st of the current year and not in a residential treatment program or on electronic home detention. **Criteria:** Award is based on education expenses.

Funds Avail.: Up to $2,500. **To Apply:** Applicants must submit a completed application form. If selected for consideration, applicants must provide references and documentation to support their request, including school transcripts. **Deadline:** April 30.

3410 ■ Jack Kent Cooke Foundation (JKCF)
44325 Woodridge Pky.
Lansdowne, VA 20176
Ph: (703)723-8000
Fax: (703)723-8030
Free: 855-509-5253
URL: www.jkcf.org
Facebook: www.facebook.com/JackKentCookeFoundation
LinkedIn: www.linkedin.com/company/the-jack-kent-cooke-foundation

3411 ■ Jack Kent Cooke Foundation College Scholarships (Undergraduate/Scholarship)

Purpose: To support deserving students with their educational expenses. **Focus:** Education. **Qualif.:** Applicants must be high school senior students; must have a cumulative unweighted GPA of 3.5 or above and score in the top 15%; must have an SAT combined score of 1200 or above (CR and M) and/or ACT composite score of 26 or above; and must have demonstrated unmet financial need and intend to enroll full-time in an accredited college. **Criteria:** Selection will be based on exceptional academic ability and achievement, financial need, persistence, a desire to help others, and leadership.

Funds Avail.: Up to $40,000. **Duration:** Annual. **Number Awarded:** Up to 40. **To Apply:** Applicants must visit the Foundation's website for the online application system. The College Scholarship Program application requires information from several different people. Each person must have a unique email address in order to receive the required forms via email from the online application system. **Deadline:** November.

3412 ■ Jack Kent Cooke Foundation Graduate Scholarships (Graduate/Scholarship)

Purpose: To support students pursuing graduate or professional study. **Focus:** General studies/Field of study not specified. **Qualif.:** Applicants must be college seniors or recent graduates (within the last five years) from an accredited college/university in the U.S.; must have a cumulative GPA of 3.50 or better on a 4.0 scale (or equivalent); must have a plan to begin their first graduate degree program; and be nominated by their undergraduate institution. **Criteria:** Selection is based on academic achievement and critical thinking ability, financial need, will to succeed and a breadth of interest and activities.

Awards are arranged alphabetically below their administering organizations

Funds Avail.: No specific amount. **Duration:** Annual. **Number Awarded:** Varies. **To Apply:** Applicants must be nominated by their undergraduate institutions (students cannot apply directly). Applicants must contact the Foundation's Faculty Representative at his/her institution.

3413 ■ Jack Kent Cooke Foundation Undergraduate Transfer Scholarships *(Undergraduate/Scholarship)*

Purpose: To support community college students to transfer and complete their bachelor's degrees at the top four-year colleges/universities. **Focus:** General studies/Field of study not specified. **Qualif.:** Applicants must be current students at an accredited U.S. community college or two-year institution with sophomore status, or recent graduates; plan to enroll full-time in a baccalaureate program at an accredited college/university; have a cumulative undergraduate GPA of 3.50 or better on a scale of 4.0 (or the equivalent); nominated by their two-year institution; have unmet financial need; and have not previously been nominated for the Jack Kent Cooke Foundation Undergraduate Transfer Scholarship. **Criteria:** Selection is based on academic excellence and critical thinking ability, financial need, will to succeed and breadth of interest and activities.

Funds Avail.: Up to $40,000. **Duration:** Annual. **Number Awarded:** 85. **To Apply:** Applicants must contact the Faculty Representative at their two-year college.

3414 ■ Jack Kent Cooke Foundation Young Scholars *(Undergraduate/Scholarship)*

Purpose: To support students in their educational pursuits. **Focus:** General studies/Field of study not specified. **Qualif.:** Applicants must be in the 7th grade entering 8th grade; have mostly 'A' grades and no 'Cs' or below in the past two years; have a family with unmet financial need; and planning to attend high school in the U.S. **Criteria:** Selection is based on academic ability and high achievement and intelligence, unmet financial need, will to succeed, leadership and public service, critical-thinking ability and appreciation for, or participation in, the arts and humanities, music, art, literature or similar fields.

Funds Avail.: No specific amount. **Duration:** Annual. **Number Awarded:** Varies. **To Apply:** Applicants must submit a completed application (application checklist: student application, parent/guardian form, custodial parent(s)/guardian(s) financial form and tax forms; noncustodial parent(s)/guardian(s) financial form and tax forms (if applicable); school report; teacher recommendation; personal recommendation; survey form).

3415 ■ Cooley L.L.P.
3175 Hanover St.
Palo Alto, CA 94304-1130
Ph: (650)843-5000
Fax: (650)849-7400
URL: www.cooley.com
Facebook: www.facebook.com/CooleyLLP
LinkedIn: www.linkedin.com/company/cooleyllp
Twitter: www.twitter.com/CooleyLLP

3416 ■ Cooley Diversity Fellowship *(Graduate, Undergraduate/Fellowship)*

Purpose: To financially assist law students. **Focus:** Law. **Qualif.:** Applicants must: be law students enrolled full-time in an ABA accredited law school and in the 1L year at the time of application; be committed to join the Firm's Summer Associate Program following the 2L year; and must not be recipients of a similar diversity award from other law firm for the same time period. **Criteria:** Selection is based on the student's commitment to promoting goals of diversity; academic performance; personal achievements; leadership abilities; community service; and commitment to joining the Cooley Godward Kronish Summer Associate Program.

Funds Avail.: Up to $30,000. **To Apply:** Applicants must submit a completed application form along with a brief personal statement; a current resume; law school transcript; and undergraduate transcript. In addition, applicants may also submit up to two letters of recommendation; up to three references; and a legal writing sample. **Deadline:** January 4. **Contact:** Amie Santos, Cooley's Diversity and Inclusion Manager; Email: diversityfellowship@cooley.com.

3417 ■ Coordinating Council for Women in History (CCWH)
URL: theccwh.org
Facebook: www.facebook.com/Coordinating-Council-for-Women-in-History-674185169261548

3418 ■ CCWH/Berkshire Conference of Women Historians Graduate Student Fellowships *(Doctorate/Fellowship)*

Purpose: To support the completion of a dissertation in a history department either in the crucial stage of research or in the final year of writing. **Focus:** History. **Qualif.:** Applicants must be graduate student historians in a history department in a US institution; must have passed to ABD status by the time of application; may specialize in any field of history; may hold this award and others simultaneously; need not attend the award ceremony to receive the award; must be current CCWH members. **Criteria:** Selection will be based on the committee's criteria.

Funds Avail.: $1,000. **Number Awarded:** 1. **To Apply:** Candidates should submit all of the following items as attachments in one email with applicants name and CCWH/Berks in the subject line: a scan of the completed signature from verifying ABD status and current CCWH membership; a current curriculum vitae; a summary of the dissertation project, an explanation of how the dissertation project will advance the understanding of the issue(s) under study, a survey of the major primary sources, a discussion of the historiography, a summary of research already accomplished, and an indication of plans for completion of the dissertation in no more than 1,200 words, double-spaced; a letter of recommendation from a member of the dissertation committee in a separate email with name of applicants and CCWH/Berks Award in the subject line. **Deadline:** May 15. **Contact:** ccwhberksaward@theccwh.org.

3419 ■ CCWH Nupur Chaudhuri First Article Prizes *(Professional development/Prize)*

Purpose: To support the best first article published in the field of history. **Focus:** History. **Qualif.:** Applicants must be current CCWH members; need not attend the award ceremony to receive the award; have published an article with full scholarly apparatus in a refereed journal. **Criteria:** Selection will be based on the committee's criteria.

Funds Avail.: $1,000. **To Apply:** Applicants must submit the following information in an email and attachments: Name; Mailing address; Home phone; Email; Institutional affiliation if any; Bibliographical Information; Article Title; Journal, volume and date of publication and page numbers;

Awards are arranged alphabetically below their administering organizations

current CV; Article. **Deadline:** May 15.

3420 ■ Copper and Brass Servicenter Association (CBSA)
6734 W 121st St.
Overland Park, KS 66209
Ph: (913)396-0697
Fax: (913)345-1006
E-mail: cbsahq@copper-brass.org
URL: www.copper-brass.org

3421 ■ Copper and Brass Servicenter Association Inc. Scholarship Program *(Undergraduate/Scholarship)*

Purpose: To provide financial educational assistance to a child of CBSA employees or any associate member companies. **Focus:** General studies/Field of study not specified. **Qualif.:** Applicants must be dependents of an individual employed in CBSA's service center or any associate member company; must be college students entering sophomore, junior or senior year in the fall; must be taking at least six credit hours in the upcoming year; and must have a GPA of at least 3.0 on a 4.0 scale. **Criteria:** Scholarships will be granted only to children of CBSA's service center or associate member companies. Applicants will be selected based on academic performance and financial need.

Funds Avail.: No specific amount. **Duration:** Annual. **To Apply:** Candidates must fill out the online application form. Must submit two letters of recommendation (one from an educator and one from a past or present employer); 500-word essay explaining the reason of pursuing the chosen field; and transcript of records. Freshmen candidates must submit a high school transcript. **Deadline:** March 1. **Contact:** Jean McClure; Phone: 913-396-0697.

3422 ■ Coro
Ph: (202)585-6548
E-mail: info@coro.org
URL: www.coro.org

3423 ■ Coro Fellows Program in Public Affairs *(Postgraduate/Fellowship)*

Purpose: To train and prepare committed individuals for effective and ethical leadership in the public affairs arena. **Focus:** Public affairs. **Qualif.:** Applicants must be graduate students committed to effective and ethical leadership in the public affairs arena. **Criteria:** Selection shall be based on the aforementioned applicants' qualifications and compliance with the application details.

Funds Avail.: No specific amount. **Duration:** Annual. **Number Awarded:** Varies. **To Apply:** Applicants must first complete the online pre-application form. Applicants may then submit electronically the three written essays; resume (maximum of 2 pages); three letters of recommendation; official academic transcripts for all higher education institutions attended; and a $75 non-refundable application fee.

3424 ■ Corporate Counsel Women of Color (CCWC)
Radio City Sta.
New York, NY 10101-2095
Ph: (646)483-8041
E-mail: info@ccwomenofcolor.org
URL: ccwomenofcolor.org/ccwomen-2016.html

3425 ■ My Life As A Lawyer Scholarships *(Graduate, Undergraduate/Scholarship)*

Purpose: To support law students with their educational pursuit. **Focus:** Law. **Qualif.:** Applicants must be first or second year students enrolled in an accredited law school in any state of the United States of America. **Criteria:** Selection is based on the submitted application materials.

Funds Avail.: No specific amount. **To Apply:** Applicants must submit (through first-class mail only) a completed application form together with a list of any publications, academic awards, honors, scholarships, memberships, and/or extracurricular activities; an essay of no more 350 words; and a copy of law school transcript. **Deadline:** June 30.

3426 ■ Correctional Education Association (CEA)
PO Box 3430
Laurel, MD 20709
Ph: (443)459-3080
Fax: (443)459-3088
E-mail: office@ceanational.org
URL: www.ceanational.org/index2.htm

3427 ■ Correctional Education Association Scholarships *(Graduate, Undergraduate/Scholarship)*

Purpose: To encourage students to continue a course of study in correctional education. **Focus:** Criminal justice. **Qualif.:** Applicant must be a graduate or undergraduate student in correctional education; must be a voting member of the Correctional Education Association and have been a member for a minimum of two years prior to application. **Criteria:** Application materials (quality of the application will be taken into consideration) will be evaluated by the Scholarship Committee. Priority will be given to first time applicants.

Funds Avail.: No specified amount. **To Apply:** Application forms are available in the website (application format must be completed in full in order to be considered by the Committee). Application materials must be sent to Correctional Educational Association, Scholarship Committee.

3428 ■ Council for the Advancement of Science Writing (CASW)
PO Box 910
Hedgesville, WV 25427
Ph: (304)754-6786
URL: www.casw.org
Facebook: www.facebook.com/SciWriting
Twitter: twitter.com/ScienceWriting

3429 ■ Taylor/Blakeslee University Fellowships *(Other, Undergraduate/Fellowship)*

Purpose: To provide financial support to students who want to pursue a career in science writing. **Focus:** Journalism. **Qualif.:** Applicants must be professional journalists and students enrolled in a U.S graduate-level science writing program; must be U.S citizens or long-time residents. **Criteria:** Scholarship application will be evaluated by CASW Selection Committee based on criteria. Journalists with at least two years of mass media experience will receive preferential treatment in the selection process.

Funds Avail.: $5,000. **Duration:** Annual. **To Apply:** Applicants must complete the application form; must submit resume; samples of writing; description of science-writing program and list of courses to be pursued; and statement (not to exceed 500 words). **Deadline:** July 1. **Contact:** Rennie Taylor at P.O Box 910 Hedgesville, WV 25427.

3430 ■ Council of American Overseas Research Centers (CAORC)

PO Box 37012
Washington, DC 20013-7012
Ph: (202)633-1599
Fax: (202)633-3141
E-mail: info@caorc.org
URL: www.caorc.org

3431 ■ Multi-Country Research Fellowships *(Doctorate/Fellowship)*

Purpose: To support advanced regional or trans-regional research in the humanities, social sciences or allied natural sciences for US doctoral candidates and scholars who have already earned their PhD. **Focus:** Humanities; Natural sciences; Social sciences. **Qualif.:** Applicants must be US citizens or permanent resident; must have a PhD or be doctoral candidates who have completed all PhD requirements with the exception of the dissertation; must be engaged in the study of and research in the humanities, social sciences and allied natural sciences; must wish to conduct research of regional or trans-regional significance in two or more countries outside the US, one of which must host a participating American overseas research center (ORC). **Criteria:** Selection will be based on the following criteria: merits of the proposal for significance, relevance and potential contribution to regional and/or trans-regional scholarly research; qualifications; research design and methodology; significance to the applicants' field; significance to needs and interests of host country and CAORC; feasibility in terms of resources and amount of time allocated to the project; need for residence in host country to accomplish the project; proficiency in language required to complete research project, if applicable.

Funds Avail.: Up to $10,500 each. **Duration:** Annual. **Number Awarded:** 9. **To Apply:** A complete application must consists the following: application form; project description; project bibliography/literature review; two separate letters of recommendation; a maximum three pages curriculum vitae; graduate transcripts. The project description must be 1,500 words or less, describing the nature of the applicants' proposed project and their competence to carry out the required research. State their research question and the methods and procedures they will use to conduct their research. Give the reasons why their project requires their presence in the countries they indicated and indicate the facilities that they plan to use while conducting their research. Applicants must also indicate the relationship they will have with the host-country ORC(s) and the extent to which they have investigated other funding sources. Submit the application form, project description, project bibliography/literature review and curriculum vitae, in MS Word format, via email. Letters of recommendation must be sent directly from the applicants' referee. Transcript must be mailed directly to CAORC.

3432 ■ Council for Children with Behavior Disorders

Council for Exceptional Children
2900 Crystal Dr., Ste. 1000
Arlington, VA 22202-3557
URL: www.ccbd.net
Facebook: www.facebook.com/CCBDmembers/posts/1020559394672988
LinkedIn: www.linkedin.com/company/2756373
Twitter: twitter.com/CCBDmembers

3433 ■ Eleanor Guetzloe Undergraduate Scholarship *(Undergraduate/Scholarship)*

Purpose: To support an outstanding undergraduate students who are pursuing teaching certification in the area of behavioral needs. **Focus:** Behavioral sciences. **Qualif.:** Applicants must be current members of the Council for Exceptional Children (CEC), and registered to attend either graduate or undergraduate studies directly related to working with students with behavioral needs at an accredited institution of higher education. **Criteria:** Selection will be based on the committee's criteria.

Funds Avail.: No specific amount. **Duration:** Annual. **To Apply:** Applicants may visit the website for the online application and must submit their transcript of all higher education coursework and latter of support.

3434 ■ Council of Energy Resource Tribes (CERT)

8200 S Quebec St., No. 509
Centennial, CO 80112
Ph: (303)345-5632
URL: 74.63.154.129

3435 ■ CERT College Scholarships *(Graduate, Undergraduate/Scholarship)*

Purpose: To meet the unforeseen need of today's Indian college students. **Focus:** Business; Computer and information sciences; Engineering; Mathematics and mathematical sciences; Science. **Qualif.:** Applicants must have been selected and/or successfully participated in one of the CERT education programs: TRIBES Program (1981-2005), CERT Intern Program (1986-2009), CERT Scholars Program (2006-2008); must be a full-time undergraduate (12 hrs/semester) or graduate (9 hrs/semester) student enrolled at an accredited two or four year tribal, private, or public university/college; majoring in business, engineering, science, math, computer technology, or related fields; and maintain an acceptable GPA (2.5 cumulative GPA or higher) according to CERT Scholarship guidelines. **Criteria:** Selection is based on the application.

Funds Avail.: No specific amount. **To Apply:** Applicants must submit a completed application form together with university/college enrollment verification for forthcoming semester/quarter (if not shown on transcript); and most recent official transcripts from university/college registrar's office after completion of each semester or quarter. **Deadline:** September 15 (Fall); February 15 (Spring). **Contact:** Clint LeBeau by email at clebeau@certredearth.com or 3545 S Tamarac Drive, Suite 320, Denver, CO 80237.

3436 ■ Council for European Studies (CES)

Columbia University
420 W 118 St., MC 3307
New York, NY 10027

Awards are arranged alphabetically below their administering organizations

Ph: (212)854-4172
Fax: (212)854-8808
E-mail: info@ces-europe.org
URL: councilforeuropeanstudies.org
Facebook: www.facebook.com/CESEurope
LinkedIn: www.linkedin.com/company/council-for-european-studies
Twitter: twitter.com/ces_europe

3437 ■ CES Conference Travel Grants *(Graduate, Professional development/Grant)*

Purpose: To provide support trans-Atlantic travel for junior faculty and graduate students already scheduled to present at the Council's International Conference of Europeanists. **Focus:** European studies. **Qualif.:** Presenters must be accepted to present a paper at the International Conference of Europeanists; must be currently working at and affiliated with an academic, research or policy institution in North America; must be graduate students or hold the rank of Assistant Professor (or its equivalent) and below; must be committed to presenting at the CES conference regardless of eventual grant status. **Criteria:** Selection will be based on the committee's criteria.

Funds Avail.: $500. **To Apply:** Interested applicants must visit the website for the online application process. **Deadline:** February 1.

3438 ■ CES First Article Prize *(Professional development/Prize)*

Purpose: To honor the writers of the best first articles in European studies published within a two-year period. **Focus:** European studies; Humanities; Social sciences. **Qualif.:** Nominated article must be the first article published by the nominee in the field of European Studies in a peer-reviewed journal; must be published between January 1, 2010 and December 31, 2011; must be the work of one author only or be an article on which the nominee is the first author; must be authored by a member of the Council for European Studies or a faculty/student of an institution that is a member. **Criteria:** Strong preference will be given to submissions in English, French, German and Spanish.

Funds Avail.: $500. **Number Awarded:** 2. **To Apply:** Nominations must be submitted by the publisher, editor, author or admiring colleagues, and must be accompanied by a nomination form and digital copy of the nominated article.

3439 ■ CES Pre-Dissertation Research Fellowships *(Graduate/Fellowship)*

Purpose: To facilitate the transition from coursework to fieldwork, and to enable students to make rapid progress in refining their initial ideas into a feasible, interesting and fundable doctoral project. **Focus:** European studies. **Qualif.:** Applicants must be enrolled in a doctoral program at a university that is a member of the council for European Studies Academic Consortium; must possess any language skills required to carry out the proposed research; must have completed the majority of doctoral coursework; must have not yet begun substantial dissertation research in Europe. **Criteria:** Selection will be based on the committee's criteria.

Funds Avail.: $4,000. **To Apply:** Applicants must submit the CES Pre-Dissertation Fellowship Application Form and return three completed Faculty Recommendation Forms. Also, applicants must submit a Language Competency Form for every language in which they will require functional knowledge to complete their proposed research. **Deadline:** January 16.

3440 ■ Mellon-CES Dissertation Completion Fellowships *(Graduate/Fellowship)*

Purpose: To facilitate the timely completion of the doctoral degree by late-stage graduate students on topics that focus on European Studies. **Focus:** European studies. **Qualif.:** Applicants must be ABD; must be enrolled at a higher education institution in the US that is a member of the CES Academic Consortium; must have no more than one full year of dissertation work remaining at the start of the fellowship year as certified by their dissertation advisor. Applicants must also have exhausted the dissertation completion funding normally provided by their academic department or university, and must be working on a topic within or substantially overlapping European Studies. **Criteria:** Selection will be based on the committee's criteria.

Funds Avail.: A stipend of $25,000. **To Apply:** Interested applicants must visit the website for the online application process. **Deadline:** January 26.

3441 ■ Council on Foreign Relations (CFR)

The Harold Pratt House
58 E 68th St.
New York, NY 10065
Ph: (212)434-9400
Fax: (212)434-9800
E-mail: corporate@cfr.org
URL: www.cfr.org
Facebook: www.facebook.com/councilonforeignrelations
LinkedIn: www.linkedin.com/company/council-on-foreign-relations
Twitter: twitter.com/CFR_org

3442 ■ CFR Military Fellowships *(Professional development/Fellowship)*

Purpose: To enable selected military officers to broaden their understanding of international relations **Focus:** International affairs and relations. **Qualif.:** Applicants must be military officers nominated by the Chiefs of Staff of the Army and the Air Force, the Chief of Naval Operations, and the Commandants of the Coast Guard and the Marine Corps. **Criteria:** Selection will be based on the CFR's criteria.

Funds Avail.: No specific amount. **Number Awarded:** 4 to 5. **To Apply:** Interested applicants from the U.S. Army, U.S. Air Force, U.S. Coast Guard, U.S. Marine Corps, and U.S. Navy should contact their human resources officer to learn more about the fellowship application process. **Contact:** Email at fellowships@cfr.org.

3443 ■ CFR National Intelligence Fellowships *(Professional development/Fellowship)*

Purpose: To provide the opportunity to senior intelligence officers to participate in and contribute to the Council on Foreign Relations activities and events. **Focus:** Intelligence service; International affairs and relations. **Qualif.:** Applicants must be senior intelligence officers. **Criteria:** Selection will be based on the CFR's criteria.

Funds Avail.: No specific amount. **To Apply:** Applicants from the intelligence community are nominated by the Office of the Director of National Intelligence and interviewed by CFR. Interested candidates should contact their human resources officer to learn more about the application process. **Contact:** Email at fellowships@cfr.org.

Awards are arranged alphabetically below their administering organizations

3444 ■ CFR Stanton Nuclear Security Fellowships
(Doctorate, Postdoctorate, Advanced Professional/ Fellowship)

Purpose: To encourage younger scholars studying nuclear security issues and stimulate the development of the next generation of thought leaders in nuclear security. **Focus:** International affairs and relations; National security. **Qualif.:** Applicants must be U.S. citizens and permanent residents who are eligible to work in the United States; and must be junior (non-tenured) faculty, postdoctoral fellows, or predoctoral candidates from any discipline, including law, who are working on a nuclear security related issue. **Criteria:** Selection will be based on the CFR's criteria.

Funds Avail.: $110,000 (junior, non-tenured); $80,000 (postdoctoral); $50,000 (predoctoral). **Number Awarded:** Up to 3. **To Apply:** Interested applicants who meet the program's eligibility requirements can apply online. **Deadline:** December 15. **Contact:** Email at fellowships@cfr.org.

3445 ■ CFR Volunteer Internships *(Undergraduate, Graduate/Internship)*

Purpose: To offer outstanding volunteer opportunities for college students and graduate students focusing on international relations and who are pursuing a career in foreign policy or a related field. **Focus:** International affairs and relations. **Qualif.:** Applicants must be U.S. citizens and permanent residents who are pursuing a career in foreign policy or a related field. **Criteria:** Selection will be on highly competitive basis.

Funds Avail.: No specific amount. **To Apply:** Interested applicants may visit the website or contact CFR for more information. **Contact:** Council on Foreign Relations Human Resources Department, at the above address.

3446 ■ Edward R. Murrow Press Fellowships
(Professional development/Fellowship)

Purpose: To assist individuals in the field of journalism. **Focus:** Journalism. **Qualif.:** Applicants must be those who have distinguished credentials in the field of journalism and who have covered international news as a working journalist for print, broadcast, or online media widely available in the United States. Applicants are limited to those individuals who are authorized to work in the United States and who will continue to be authorized for the duration of the fellowship. **Criteria:** Selection will be highly competitive and will be based on a combination of the following criteria: depth and breadth of professional experience as a foreign correspondent or editor, firm grounding in foreign policy and international relations, and a clear, creative, and original application statement.

Funds Avail.: $65,000. **To Apply:** Interested candidates who meet the program's eligibility requirements can apply online. **Deadline:** March 1. **Contact:** Email at fellowships@cfr.org.

3447 ■ International Affairs Fellowships in Japan (IAF-J) *(Professional development/Fellowship)*

Purpose: To provide the opportunity to mid-career U.S. citizens to expand their professional horizons by spending a period of research or other professional activity in Japan. **Focus:** International affairs and relations. **Qualif.:** Applicants must be group of mid-career U.S. citizens between the ages of twenty-seven and forty-five. **Criteria:** Selection will be based on the applicants' academic and professional accomplishments and promise, the merits and feasibility of their specific research or action proposals, character and personal qualities conducive to promising cross-cultural communication and cooperation, and the contribution that the proposed research or professional activity will make to the applicants' career development.

Funds Avail.: No specific amount. **To Apply:** Interested candidates who meet the program's eligibility requirements can apply online. **Deadline:** October 31. **Remarks:** The fellowship is sponsored by Hitachi, Ltd. **Contact:** Email at fellowships@cfr.org.

3448 ■ International Affairs Fellowships in Nuclear Security (IAF-NS) *(Professional development/ Fellowship)*

Purpose: To offer university-based scholars valuable hands-on experience in the nuclear security policymaking field. **Focus:** International affairs and relations. **Qualif.:** Applicants must be faculty members with tenure or on tenure-track lines at accredited universities and who propose to conduct policy-relevant research on nuclear security issues; must be U.S. citizens or permanent residents who are eligible to work in the United States; and must be between the ages of twenty-nine and fifty. CFR does not sponsor for visas. Former Stanton nuclear security fellows who meet the eligibility requirements can apply. **Criteria:** Selection will be based on a combination of the following criteria: scholarly qualifications, achievements and promise, depth and breadth of professional experience, firm grounding in foreign policy and international relations, and the contribution the fellowship will make to the applicants' career development.

Funds Avail.: $125,000. **Number Awarded:** 2. **To Apply:** Interested candidates who meet the program's eligibility requirements can apply online. **Deadline:** January 16. **Remarks:** The fellowship is sponsored by the Stanton Foundation. **Contact:** Email at fellowships@cfr.org.

3449 ■ Council on Library and Information Resources (CLIR)
1707 NW L St., Ste. 650
Washington, DC 20036
Ph: (202)939-4750
Fax: (202)939-4765
E-mail: chenry@clir.org
URL: www.clir.org
Twitter: twitter.com/clirnews

3450 ■ Mellon Fellowships for Dissertation Research in the Humanities *(Doctorate, Graduate/ Fellowship, Scholarship)*

Purpose: To help junior scholars in the humanities and related social science fields gain skill and creativity in developing knowledge from original sources. **Focus:** Humanities; Social sciences. **Qualif.:** Applicants must be enrolled in a doctoral program in a graduate school in the United States; have completed all doctoral requirements except the dissertation; planning to do dissertation research primarily in original source material in the holdings of archives, libraries, historical societies, museums, related repositories or a combination. Candidates for the Ed.D, J.D., or D.D. degrees are not eligible. **Criteria:** Selection of applicants will be based on quality of the research proposal with reference to the following category: (1) originality and creativity; (2) importance of the proposed dissertation to the applicant's field; (3) appropriateness of the primary source collection(s) and institutions in which the applicant

Awards are arranged alphabetically below their administering organizations

proposes to do research; (4) competence of the research; and (5) prospects for completing specified research within the time projected and funds awarded.

Funds Avail.: $2,000 per month plus $1,000 upon participating in symposium on research. **Duration:** Annual; 9-12 months. **Number Awarded:** 15. **To Apply:** Applicants must complete and submit the online application form; official transcripts; a letter from the appropriate dean, department head or dissertation advisor certifying that the candidate has completed or will complete all doctoral work except the dissertation; and three letters of reference. All documents must be submitted in triplicate by mail. **Contact:** mellon@clir.org.

3451 ■ Mellon Fellowships for Dissertation Research in Original Sources (Doctorate/Fellowship)

Purpose: To help junior scholars in the humanities and related social science fields gain skills and creativity in developing knowledge from original sources. **Focus:** Humanities; Social sciences. **Qualif.:** Applicants must: be currently enrolled in a doctoral program in a graduate school in the United States; have plan to do dissertation research primarily in original source material in the holdings of archives, libraries, historical societies, museums, related repositories, or a combination; and write the dissertation and receive the Ph.D. degree in a field of the humanities or in a related element of the social sciences. **Criteria:** The committee will assess quality with reference to the following criteria: originality and creativity of the research proposal; importance of the proposed dissertation to the applicants' field; appropriateness of the primary-source collections and institutions in which the applicants proposes to do research; competence of the applicants for proposed research as indicated by references, transcripts, language skills, research experience and other academic achievements; prospects for completing specified research within the time projected and funds awarded.

Funds Avail.: $25,000. **Duration:** Annual. **To Apply:** Interested applicants may visit the website for the online application system. Applicants must provide transcripts covering all graduate study and three letters of reference. All reference letters must be submitted by reference providers through the online application system. **Deadline:** December 2.

3452 ■ Rovelstad Scholarship in International Librarianship (Undergraduate, Graduate/Award, Scholarship)

Purpose: To provide financial support to students of library and information science who wish to attend the World Library and Information Congress of the International Federation of Library Associations and Institutions (IFLA). **Focus:** Humanities; Library and archival sciences. **Qualif.:** Applicants must be enrolled in an accredited school of library and information science at the time of the current IFLA annual meeting. They must be citizens or permanent residents of the United States, and should have an interest in cooperative endeavors with international libraries, international standards or other international library and information issues. **Criteria:** Selection will be based on the committee's criteria.

Funds Avail.: No specific amount. **Duration:** Annual. **To Apply:** Applicants must complete and submit the application form available online together with official transcripts of undergraduate and graduate school records and two letters of reference submitted by reference providers through the online application system. **Deadline:** January 27.

3453 ■ Council on Social Work Education (CSWE)
1701 Duke St., Ste. 200
Alexandria, VA 22314
Ph: (703)683-8080
Fax: (703)683-8099
E-mail: info@cswe.org
URL: www.cswe.org
Facebook: www.facebook.com/pages/CSWE-Annual-Program-Meeting/519861458043267
LinkedIn: www.linkedin.com/company/council-on-social-work-education?trk=tyah
Twitter: www.twitter.com/CSocialWorkEd

3454 ■ Council on Social Work Education Minority Fellowship Program for Doctoral Students (Postdoctorate/Fellowship)

Purpose: To help racial/ethnic minority individuals pursuing a doctoral degree in social work. **Focus:** Mental health; Social work. **Qualif.:** Applicants must be currently enrolled in a doctoral program in a school of social work. **Criteria:** Recipients will be selected based on the academic standing and letters of recommendation.

Funds Avail.: No specific amount. **Duration:** Annual. **To Apply:** Applicants must submit an application instruction sheet. All permanent residents must provide the following: photocopy of Permanent Resident Card signed by the notary public; official transcript of records; GRE and MAT scores; letter of admission; resume; financial list of information including the resources applied for, personal financial costs and anticipated income.

3455 ■ Council on Social Work Education Scholars Program (Doctorate/Scholarship)

Purpose: To provide opportunities for senior and junior scholars to work on research projects or programmatic initiatives of their choosing that is in line with the priorities of CSWE. **Focus:** Social work. **Qualif.:** Applicants must be senior scholars, faculty members and junior scholars such as doctoral students or individuals recently completing their doctoral dissertation. **Criteria:** Selection will be based on proposed research.

Funds Avail.: No specific amount. **Duration:** Annual. **To Apply:** Applicants must submit completed application together with project proposal; budget; task list; and curriculum vitae. **Contact:** Jessica Holmes, director of the Office of Social Work Education and Research, jholmes@cswe.org.

3456 ■ Carl A. Scott Book Scholarships (Undergraduate/Scholarship)

Purpose: To promote equity and social justice in social work. **Focus:** Social work. **Qualif.:** Applicants must be in the last year of study for a social work degree in a baccalaureate or master's degree program accredited by the Council on Social Work Education; must be African American, American Indian, Asian American, Mexican American or Puerto Rican; must have a cumulative GPA of at least 3.0 on a 4.0 scale; and must be enrolled in 12 credit hours. **Criteria:** Recipients are selected based on the demonstrated commitment in promoting equity and social justice.

Funds Avail.: $500. **Duration:** Annual. **Number Awarded:** 2. **To Apply:** Applicants must submit a two-three page, double-spaced, typewritten statement that include professional interests, and experiences; two letters of recommendation preferably from a professor, a field instructor, or a community-based leader; an official letter from the school's registrar verifying that the applicant is enrolled and in good standing with the university or college; and an official academic transcript from university/college.

3457 ■ Counseil Canadien de droit International
275 Bay St.
Ottawa, ON, Canada K1R 5Z5
Ph: (613)235-0442
Fax: (613)236-2727
E-mail: manager@ccil-ccdi.ca
URL: www.ccil-ccdi.ca

3458 ■ Leslie C. Green Veterans Scholarships *(Juris Doctorate, Advanced Professional/Scholarship)*

Purpose: To provide tuition support to Canadian Armed Forces veterans entering or pursuing legal studies in a Canadian law school. **Focus:** Law. **Qualif.:** Applicants must be Canadian Armed Forces veterans who are entering or pursuing legal studies at the JD or LL.B. level in a Canadian law school. **Criteria:** Applicants with operational experience will be favored in the selection process. Preference will be given to candidates whose past activities and future career plans suggest an intent and ability to make an active contribution to the development of international humanitarian law. Consideration will also be given to the caliber of the candidates' academic and professional record. Where applicable, financial need will also be considered.

Funds Avail.: 2,000 Canadian Dollars. **To Apply:** Candidates must apply by sending the following materials to the Scholarship Committee: a cover letter detailing the candidates' service history in the Canadian Forces, their plans for legal studies and demonstrating their interest in international humanitarian law; an explanation in the event that the applicants wish to raise financial need as a consideration; proof of first year admission to or enrolment in a JD or LL.B. program at a Canadian law school; academic records in the form of transcripts (of post-secondary education) wherein scanned copies will also be accepted; and a certification that all of the information supplied in support of the application is truthful. **Deadline:** October 30. **Contact:** Application materials must be e-mailed to manager@ccil-ccdi.ca.

3459 ■ John Peters Humphrey Student Fellowships *(Graduate/Fellowship)*

Purpose: To inspire educational achievement by providing support for outstanding students pursuing graduate studies at leading graduate institutions in Canada or worldwide. **Focus:** Law; Political science. **Qualif.:** Applicants must be students of Canadian law and political science (or their equivalent) faculties. **Criteria:** Selection committee appointed by the President of the CCIL will review the applications and base its determination on the applicant's academic accomplishments, proposed program of study, letter of reference, and other information contained in the application.

Funds Avail.: Up to 40,000 Canadian Dollars. **Duration:** Annual. **Number Awarded:** Up to 3. **To Apply:** Applicants must submit the official transcript from each post-secondary academic institution, three letters of reference which speak both of the candidate's academic strengths and weaknesses and his/her likelihood of success in a programme of graduate studies. **Deadline:** December 1.

3460 ■ Courage to Grow
PO Box 2507
Chelan, WA 98816
Ph: (509)731-3056
E-mail: Support@CourageToGrowScholarship.com
URL: couragetogrowscholarship.com

3461 ■ Courage to Grow Scholarships *(Undergraduate/Scholarship)*

Purpose: To help and support students achieve their higher education goals. **Focus:** General studies/Field of study not specified. **Qualif.:** Applicants must be U.S. citizens who are juniors or high school seniors or college students with a minimum GPA of 2.5. **Criteria:** Recipients will be selected based on submitted application materials.

Funds Avail.: No specific amount. **Duration:** Monthly. **To Apply:** Applicants must provide proof of enrollment obtained from the college administration department, proof of GPA and maximum of 250 words description on why the applicant deserves to get the award.

3462 ■ The Cover Guy
5054 Fairview St.
Burlington, ON, Canada L7L0B4
Ph: (905)320-8706
Free: 866-652-6837
E-mail: info@thecoverguy.com
URL: www.thecoverguy.com

3463 ■ The Cover Guy Annual Scholarships *(Undergraduate, Graduate/Scholarship)*

Purpose: To provide financial support to students to help them with their studies and expenses. **Focus:** General studies/Field of study not specified. **Qualif.:** Applicants must be students enrolled in an undergraduate or graduate program at a university, college or trade school in the United States or Canada. **Criteria:** Selection will be based on the submitted application, studies and community involvement.

Funds Avail.: $500. **Duration:** Annual. **Number Awarded:** 2. **To Apply:** Interested applicants must visit the website for the online application process and other information. **Deadline:** March 31.

3464 ■ George W. Crawford Black Bar Association
PO Box 2715
Hartford, CT 06145-2715
Ph: (860)578-4764
E-mail: info@georgecrawfordblackbar.org
URL: www.georgecrawfordblackbar.org
Twitter: twitter.com/GWCBlackBarCT

3465 ■ Priscilla Green Scholarships *(Undergraduate/Scholarship)*

Purpose: To support minority students who are practicing law in the State of Connecticut. **Focus:** Law. **Qualif.:** Applicants must be minority law students at accredited law schools who demonstrate a commitment to both practicing law in the State of Connecticut and furthering Crawford's

Awards are arranged alphabetically below their administering organizations

mission. **Criteria:** Selection will be based on academic and extracurricular achievement and submitted application. **Funds Avail.:** $1,000. **Duration:** Annual. **To Apply:** Applicants must submit a completed application form together with the following: updated resume which includes their year of matriculation, expected year of graduation, GPA, all secondary and professional schools attended and degrees received, honors and awards received and extracurricular activities; a maximum of 1,000 words essay, describing the applicants' view in the significance of the expanded definition of diversity and the costs and benefits of broadening the definition of what is considered a diverse workplace; personal statement, double-spaced, explaining how the applicants' past or current societal contribution have been in furtherance of Crawford's mission. **Deadline:** March 16. **Contact:** Thamar Esperance at TEsperance@ghla.org; or Stephanie Johnson at StephanieA.Johnson@TheHartford.com.

3466 ■ Creative Glass Center of America (CGCA)
1501 Glasstown Rd.
Millville, NJ 08332-1566
Ph: (856)825-6800
Fax: (856)825-2410
Free: 800-998-4552
E-mail: cgca@wheatonarts.org
URL: www.wheatonarts.org/artists-2/creative-glass-center-of-america

3467 ■ Creative Glass Center of America Fellowships (Advanced Professional/Fellowship)

Purpose: To accommodate artist's needs with custom fellowship of various lengths and flexible schedules. **Focus:** General studies/Field of study not specified. **Qualif.:** Applicants must be artists with young families, artists whose professional commitments do not afford them the option of a three-month residency and for teams of artists wishing to collaborate on a particular project. **Criteria:** Applicants will be evaluated by the Fellowship Selection Committee based on their designed criteria.

Funds Avail.: No specific amount. **Duration:** Annual; Three months or six weeks. **To Apply:** Applicants must submit completed application form; two letters of recommendation; a CD containing ten images of the applicant's work, image information sheet, one paragraph biography, statement of intent and current resume/CV.

3468 ■ Credit Union Central of Saskatchewan
2055 Albert St.
Regina, SK, Canada S4P 3G8
Ph: (306)566-1200
Free: 866-403-7499
URL: www.saskcentral.com

3469 ■ Norm Bromberger Research Bursaries (Undergraduate, Graduate/Scholarship)

Purpose: To support research relating to co-operatives and/or credit unions. **Focus:** Banking. **Qualif.:** Applicants must be involved in co-operatives and/or credit unions as volunteers or employees. Those who have unable to secure sponsorship for their study from the co-operative or credit union with which they are associated are also urged to apply. **Criteria:** Selection will be based on the aforementioned qualifications, as well as the applicants' compliance with the application process. Preference will be given, but not limited, to Saskatchewan candidates.

Funds Avail.: 2,000 Canadian Dollars. **To Apply:** Applicants must complete the provided Norm Bromberger Research Bursary Application Form; must also submit a supporting statement explaining how the proposed study will contribute to credit unions and/or co-operatives and an understanding that a copy of the completed work will be submitted to Canadian credit union and co-op resource centers. Applications should be sent to the contact provided. **Deadline:** June 30. **Remarks:** The bursary has been established in recognition of the outstanding contributions made by Norm Bromberger to the development of credit unions and co-operatives in Saskatchewan and across Canada. **Contact:** Centre for the Study of Cooperatives, University of Saskatchewan, 101 Diefenbaker Place, Saskatoon, Saskatchewan, Canada S7N 5B8; Phone: (306) 966-8509; Fax: (306) 966-8517; E-Mail: coop.studies@usask.ca.

3470 ■ Crisis Intervention and Suicide Prevention Centre of British Columbia
763 E Broadway
Vancouver, BC, Canada V5T 1X8
Ph: (604)872-1811
Fax: (604)879-6216
Free: 800-784-2433
E-mail: info@crisiscentre.bc.ca
URL: crisiscentre.bc.ca

3471 ■ Steve Cowan Memorial Scholarships (Undergraduate/Scholarship)

Purpose: To support individuals who have made a positive contribution to their school and/or local or global community. **Focus:** General studies/Field of study not specified. **Qualif.:** Applicants must be currently enrolled in grade 12 at a Lower Mainland/Sea-to-Sky Corridor high school; must possess the academic skills to successfully enter and complete a post-secondary education. **Criteria:** Selection will be based on applicant's dedication to the humanitarian ideals and community service ideals of the Crisis Centre, their volunteer experience, community leadership and their participation in community service.

Funds Avail.: $500-$1,000. **To Apply:** Applicants must submit an application form, two reference letters and an official transcript of the past two years of schooling. **Deadline:** April 4.

3472 ■ Crohn's and Colitis Canada
600-60 St. Clair Ave. E
Toronto, ON, Canada M4T 1N5
Ph: (416)920-5035
Fax: (416)929-0364
Free: 800-387-1479
E-mail: support@crohnsandcolitis.ca
URL: www.crohnsandcolitis.ca/site/c.dtJRL9NUJmL4H/b.9012407/k.BE24/Home.htm
Facebook: www.facebook.com/crohnsandcolitis.ca
Twitter: twitter.com/getgutsyCanada

3473 ■ Crohn's and Colitis Canada Grants in Aid of Research (Advanced Professional, Professional development/Grant)

Purpose: To advance prevention, treatments, health policy, and ultimately find cures on inflammatory bowel disease

Awards are arranged alphabetically below their administering organizations

(IBD). **Focus:** Gastroenterology. **Qualif.:** Applicants must be investigators who hold an academic appointment at a Canadian University in a Faculty of Medicine, Nursing, Pharmacy, Veterinary Medicine or other Graduate Faculty. **Criteria:** Selection will be based on the committee's criteria.

Funds Avail.: 125,000 Canadian Dollars per year. **Duration:** Three years. **To Apply:** Applicants may visit the website for further application instructions and to gain access to the necessary forms for the program. **Deadline:** November 3 (letter of intent); January 20 (application and other forms). **Contact:** Electronic applications should be emailed to researchassistant@crohnsandcolitis.ca. Printed copies should be mailed to the Research Grants and Awards Coordinator.

3474 ■ Crohn's and Colitis Canada Innovations in IBD Research Grants *(Advanced Professional, Professional development/Grant)*

Purpose: To stimulate and support research which may not be encompassed within the boundaries of traditional medical research. **Focus:** Gastroenterology; Medical research. **Qualif.:** Applicants must be principal investigators. Principal investigators can be postdoctoral fellows or those with faculty or equivalent appointments at the institution. **Criteria:** Selection will be based on the committee's criteria.

Funds Avail.: Maximum of 50,000 Canadian Dollars. **To Apply:** Applicants must visit the website to obtain an application form and to submit a letter of intent. **Deadline:** January 20. **Contact:** Electronic applications should be emailed to researchassistant@crohnsandcolitis.ca. Printed copies should be mailed to the Research Grants and Awards Coordinator.

3475 ■ Crohn's and Colitis Foundation of America (CCFA)
733 3rd Ave., Ste. 510
New York, NY 10017
Ph: (212)685-3440
Fax: (212)779-4098
Free: 800-932-2423
E-mail: info@ccfa.org
URL: www.ccfa.org
Facebook: www.facebook.com/ccfafb
Twitter: twitter.com/CCFA

3476 ■ CCFA Career Development Awards *(Doctorate/Grant)*

Purpose: To support a research that will help prepare for a career of independent basic or clinical investigation in the area of inflammatory bowel disease. **Focus:** Medicine. **Qualif.:** Applicants must be employed in an institution; engaged in health care or health-related research within the United States; have MD, PhD or equivalent; must not be in excess of ten years beyond the attainment of the doctoral degree; and have at least two years of documented post-doctoral research relevant to IBD. Proposals must be relevant to inflammatory bowel disease (Crohn's Disease or ulcerative colitis). **Criteria:** Applicants will be selected on the basis of intellectual background; mentor's record; number of important techniques to be learned; importance of the research area; relevance to IBD; and applicant's career objectives.

Funds Avail.: Total of $90,000. **Duration:** Annual. **To Apply:** Applicants must download, complete and submit the application form, CDA Letter of Intent and CDA forms available at the website. Only compiled application on a CD or disk will be considered. **Deadline:** January 14 and July 1.

3477 ■ CCFA Research Fellowship Awards *(Doctorate, Graduate/Fellowship)*

Purpose: To support a research that will help prepare for a career of independent basic or clinical investigation in the area of Crohn's disease and ulcerative colitis. **Focus:** Medicine. **Qualif.:** Applicants must be employed in an institution; engaged in health care or health related research within the United States; have MD, PhD or equivalent. Applicants with MD degrees must have at least two years of post doctoral experience. Candidates with PhD degrees must have at least one year of post-doctoral research experience related to IBD. Proposals must be relevant to inflammatory bowel disease (Crohn's Disease or ulcerative colitis). **Criteria:** Applicants will be selected on the basis of intellectual background; research experience; mentor's track record; number of important techniques to be learned; importance of the research area; relevance to IBD; and career objectives.

Funds Avail.: Up to $58,250. **Duration:** Annual; one to three years. **To Apply:** Applicants must download, complete and submit the application form, RFA Letter of Intent and RFA forms available at the website. **Deadline:** January 14 and July 1.

3478 ■ CCFA Student Research Fellowship Awards *(Graduate, Undergraduate/Grant)*

Purpose: To fund a research on topics relevant to inflammatory bowel disease. **Focus:** Medicine. **Qualif.:** Applicants must be undergraduate, medical, or graduate students at an accredited institution in United States. **Criteria:** Applicants will be judged based on novelty, feasibility and significance of the proposal; attributes of the candidate; mentor's record; evidence of the institutional commitment and laboratory environment.

Funds Avail.: Up to $2,500. **Duration:** Annual. **Number Awarded:** Up to 16. **To Apply:** Applicants must download, complete and submit the application form and SRFA forms available at the website. **Deadline:** March 15.

3479 ■ Crohn's and Colitis Foundation of America Senior Research Awards *(Doctorate, Graduate/Grant)*

Purpose: To provide funds for research to generate sufficient preliminary data from other sources such as National Institute of Health (NIH). **Focus:** Medicine. **Qualif.:** Applicants must have MD, PhD or equivalent degree; must be employed in an institution or engaged in health care or health related research; must have attained independence from their mentors. Proposals must be relevant to inflammatory bowel disease (Crohn's Disease or ulcerative colitis). **Criteria:** Awards will be given on the basis of scientific merit; relevance to IBD; excellence of investigator and research environment.

Funds Avail.: $115,830. **Duration:** One to three years. **To Apply:** Applicants must download, complete and submit the application form, SRA Letter of Intent and SRA forms available at the website; must submit a research plan with evidence; curriculum vitae; appendix and application index (optional). Formats for all attachments must be .doc, .xls or .pdf only. **Deadline:** January 14. **Contact:** E-mail: grants@ccfa.org.

3480 ■ CrossLites
c/o Samuel Certo, Faculty Advisor
1000 Holt Ave.
Winter Park, FL 32789

Awards are arranged alphabetically below their administering organizations

E-mail: Crosslites@gmail.com
URL: www.crosslites.com

3481 ■ CrossLites Scholarships *(Undergraduate, Graduate/Scholarship)*

Purpose: To provide financial aid to students who wish to pursue their education. **Focus:** General studies/Field of study not specified. **Qualif.:** Applicants must be high school, college or graduate school students. **Criteria:** Selection shall be based on the submitted essay's originality, reflection, punctuation/grammar, and content.

Funds Avail.: No specific amount. **Duration:** Annual. **Number Awarded:** Varies. **To Apply:** Applicants must submit their name; email address; name of the institution that the applicant is attending or planning to attend; a 400-600 word reflective essay (based on Dr. Parker's quotes or messages). Official transcripts must be sent via snail mail.

3482 ■ CSA Fraternal Life
2050 Finley Rd., Ste. 70
Lombard, IL 60148
Ph: (630)472-0500
Fax: (630)472-1100
Free: 800-543-3272
URL: csalife.com

3483 ■ CSA Fraternal Life Scholarships *(Undergraduate/Scholarship)*

Purpose: To help students on their financial needs for studying in college. **Focus:** General studies/Field of study not specified. **Qualif.:** Applicants must be student-members with satisfactory class standing no less than a "B" or Better or 3.0 in average (minimum of two years); have at least $5,000 face value in permanent life insurance or $1,000 in a CSA annuity at the time of application. **Criteria:** Selection will be made based on class rank, grade point average, college placement test scores, extracurricular activities including CSA activities, and essay made.

Funds Avail.: No specific amount. **Number Awarded:** Varies. **To Apply:** Applicants must submit a completed application form to the Fraternal Department; a complete official transcript to be sent to CSA; submit a photo for publication in the Journal to be attached to the first page of the application over the cap and diploma and a 400-600 words essay about the applicants' interests. **Deadline:** March 25.

3484 ■ Cuban American Bar Association (CABA)
c/o Annie Hernandez, President
Holland & Knight
701 Brickell Ave., Ste. 3300
Miami, FL 33131
Ph: (305)646-0046
E-mail: info@cabaonline.com
URL: cabaonline.com
Facebook: www.facebook.com/Cuban-American-Bar-Association-211022262253929

3485 ■ Cuban American Bar Association Scholarships *(All/Scholarship)*

Purpose: To provide financial assistance for students enrolled in accredited law schools. **Focus:** Law. **Qualif.:** Applicant must be a Cuban-American law student who has distinguished himself/herself academically and/or in service-oriented activities; any law student who has distinguished himself/herself in research, writing, community services, and/or other activities of importance to the Cuban-American community; must not be currently enrolled at the University of Miami, Florida International University, University of Florida, St. Thomas University, Nova Southern University and Florida State University. **Criteria:** Selection will be based on the committee's criteria.

Funds Avail.: $2,500. **Duration:** Annual. **To Apply:** Applicants must submit a completed formal application together with a competitive essay (no more than 1,000 words) focusing on and describing in detail the activities and achievements that the applicant qualify for the award; an updated resume; and a copy of applicant's transcript. **Deadline:** October 1. **Contact:** Victoria Mendez, victoriamendez@aol.com; Sandra Ferrera, sferrera@melandrussin.com.

3486 ■ The Culinary Trust (TCT)
PO Box 5485
Portland, OR 97228-5485
E-mail: info@theculinarytrust.org
URL: www.theculinarytrust.org
Facebook: www.facebook.com/culinarytrust
Twitter: twitter.com/culinarytrust

3487 ■ The French Culinary Institute Classic Pastry Arts Scholarships *(Other, Undergraduate/Scholarship)*

Purpose: To assist individuals who wish to advance their knowledge in culinary arts. **Focus:** Culinary arts. **Qualif.:** Applicant must be a new student or career professional toward the nine months Classic Pastry Arts Diploma Program; have a GPA of 3.0 or higher (for applicants who have been students during the five years prior to the application). **Criteria:** Recipients are selected based on merit, work experience, culinary goals and skills, and references.

Funds Avail.: No specific amount. **Duration:** Annual. **To Apply:** Applicants must submit a completed Culinary Trust Scholarship application form, a current resume, a two-page essay illustrating culinary goals, or a three-page project proposal and one-page budget and timeline describing independent study project; two letter of professional reference from employers, educational institutions or volunteer organizations on personal or business letterhead; non-refundable $25 fee.

3488 ■ Cultural Vistas
440 Park Ave. S, 2nd Fl.
New York, NY 10016-8012
Ph: (212)497-3500
E-mail: info@culturalvistas.org
URL: www.culturalvistas.org

3489 ■ IAESTE United States Internships *(Undergraduate/Internship)*

Purpose: To allow students and recent graduates experience the cultural exchange and mutual understanding between the United States and other countries. **Focus:** Cross-cultural studies. **Qualif.:** Applicants must be students majoring in technical fields at host companies in the United States. **Criteria:** Selection shall be based on the aforementioned qualifications and compliance with the application details.

Awards are arranged alphabetically below their administering organizations

THE CURE STARTS NOW FOUNDATION

Funds Avail.: No specific amount. Duration: Annual. Number Awarded: Varies. To Apply: Applicants may verify the application process through the program website. Remarks: Established in 1950.

3490 ■ Jessica King Scholarships (Other/Scholarship)

Purpose: To enable talented, driven, and adventurous young Americans to have a life-changing international experience and succeed in the international hospitality field. Focus: Management; Public relations. Qualif.: Applicants must: be at least 18 years old but not older than 35 having an offer of training/work contract from an employer in the hospitality industry for a position outside the US; be participants in an AIPT program; have an educational degree (Associate or Bachelor degree or ACF certification) from a hospitality/culinary school or program; have had at least 2 years of employment in the hospitality industry; and, be US citizens. Criteria: Selection shall be based on the merit, and not on the financial need. Funds Avail.: No specific amount. Duration: Annual. To Apply: Applicants must complete and submit a filled-out application form and must include two letters of reference, two copies of resume and a copy of school transcripts. They must also submit an essay of at least 500 words but not exceeding 1000 words, describing the applicant's motivation for participating in a practical work experience abroad; describing the skills that they expect to learn from their international work experience. Applicants must also include how they will apply the experience to their future endeavors upon return to the US. Remarks: Established in 2002.

3491 ■ The Cure Starts Now Foundation
10280 Chester Road
Cincinnati, OH 45215
Ph: (513)772-4888
URL: www.thecurestartsnow.org

3492 ■ The Cure Starts Now Foundation Grants (Graduate, Doctorate/Grant)

Purpose: To support research that investigates the cure for pediatric brain cancers with a focus on Diffuse Intrinsic Brainstem Glioma. Focus: Medicine; Oncology. Qualif.: Applicants must be MD, DO, PhD, DrPH or equivalent degree holder; must be members of a non-profit organization or a valid medical/scientific organization; must be up to date with any previous funding through The Cure Starts Now, which includes progress submissions. Criteria: Applicants shall be assessed based on the following criteria: scientific merit, disease impact, innovation, feasibility, and expertise of investigators. Funds Avail.: $100,000-$200,000. Duration: Annual. To Apply: Applicants must submit a completed application form and their proposal. Applications should be single spaced and 12 point font. Margins should be not less than 0.5 inches on all sides. Page size is 8.5 x 11 inches. Two hard copies of the application with original signatures and proposal along with a CD-ROM or flash drive with the application in PDF format and proposal should be submitted to the foundation. Application materials should be sent to Dr. Gavin Baumgardner. Deadline: June 1. Contact: Dr. Gavin Baumgardner, Chairman, at the above address.

3493 ■ Cystic Fibrosis Foundation
6931 Arlington Rd., Ste. B
Bethesda, MD 20814
Ph: (301)657-8444
Fax: (301)652-9571
Free: 877-657-8444
E-mail: metro-dc@cff.org
URL: www.cff.org/Chapters/metrodc
Facebook: www.facebook.com/cysticfibrosisfoundation
Twitter: twitter.com/CF_Foundation

3494 ■ Cystic Fibrosis Scholarship Foundation (Undergraduate/Scholarship)

Purpose: To provide financial support for individuals who are pursuing college program or vocational program. Focus: General studies/Field of study not specified. Qualif.: Applicants may either be individuals entering college or vocational school or those who have already completed two semesters of college or vocational school. Criteria: Scholarships are awarded based on a combination of financial need, academic achievement and leadership. Funds Avail.: $1,000 each. Duration: Annual. To Apply: Application forms and instructions are available at the website.

3495 ■ DACOR
1801 F St. NW
Washington, DC 20006
Ph: (202)682-0500
Fax: (202)842-3295
URL: www.dacorbacon.org

3496 ■ DACOR Graduate Fellowships for Study of International Affairs (Graduate, Master's/Fellowship)

Purpose: To support students pursuing Master's degree in international affairs. Focus: International affairs and relations. Qualif.: Recipients must be U.S. citizens pursuing Master's degree in international affairs; must be planning to study at any accredited graduate school in the United States. Criteria: Selection will be based on the Education Committee's criteria. Funds Avail.: $10,000 each. Duration: Annual. To Apply: Interested applicants may contact the Organization for the application process and other details.

3497 ■ Gantenbein Medical Fund Fellowship (Graduate/Fellowship)

Purpose: To provide financial assistance, in education aspect, to American students pursuing medical degree/studies. Focus: Medicine. Qualif.: Applicants must be first-year American students enrolled in accredited U.S. medical schools with a program in Global Health that is integrated into the regular medical school program. Criteria: Selection will be based on the committee's criteria. Funds Avail.: $30,000. Duration: Annual. To Apply: Interested applicants may contact the Organization for the application process and other details. Remarks: The Gantenbein Medical Fund was established through the bequest of Mary F. Gantenbein in memory of her husband, FSO James W. Gantenbein.

3498 ■ Daedalian Foundation (DF)
PO Box 249
Universal City, TX 78148-0249
Ph: (210)945-2111
Fax: (210)945-2112

Awards are arranged alphabetically below their administering organizations

E-mail: membership@daedalians.org
URL: www.daedalians.org

3499 ■ Daedalian Foundation Matching Scholarships Program (Undergraduate/Scholarship)

Purpose: To support high school students who wants to be a military pilot. **Focus:** Aerospace sciences. **Qualif.:** Applicants must be college/university students pursuing a career as military aviators. **Criteria:** Selection is based on the application.

Funds Avail.: No specific amount. **Duration:** Annual. **To Apply:** Applicants must submit a completed application form together with a 3" x 5" photograph to the Chairman.

3500 ■ Descendant Scholarships (Undergraduate/Scholarship)

Purpose: To encourage the youth to become military pilots. **Focus:** Aerospace sciences. **Qualif.:** Applicant must be a direct descendant (natural or adopted) of a Founder, Named, or Hereditary member in good standing (living or deceased) of the Order of Daedalians; a citizen of the United States of America; accepted by or attending an accredited college/university and enrolled in an academic program which leads to a baccalaureate or higher degree; physically and mentally qualified with demonstrated aptitude for commissioned US military service; in good scholastic standing; and not a recipient of another Daedalian scholarship in the same year. **Criteria:** Selection is based on the application.

Funds Avail.: $2,000. **Number Awarded:** 3. **To Apply:** Applicants must submit a completed application form together with a 3" x 5" photograph and a letter stating the rank, name and number of the sponsoring Daeldalian. **Deadline:** August 1.

3501 ■ John and Alice Egan Multi-Year Mentioning Scholarships (Undergraduate/Scholarship)

Purpose: To support high school students who wants to be a military pilot. **Focus:** Aerospace sciences. **Qualif.:** Applicants must be college/university students pursuing a career as military aviators. **Criteria:** Selection is based on the application.

Funds Avail.: $500-$2,000. **Duration:** Annual. **To Apply:** Applicants must submit a completed application form together with a 3" x 5" photograph; complete transcripts (sent directly by the educational institution); a copy of FAA medical certificate and annotated copy of the Flight Physical Standards Questionnaire.

3502 ■ Navy, Army or Air Force ROTC Scholarship Program (Undergraduate/Scholarship)

Purpose: To support high school students who wants to be a military pilot. **Focus:** Aerospace sciences. **Qualif.:** Applicants must be college/university students pursuing a career in military and must be nominated by local commander. **Criteria:** Selection is made by various ROTC headquarters.

Funds Avail.: No specific amount. **Duration:** Annual. **Number Awarded:** Varies. **To Apply:** Applicants may contact the foundation for application information.

3503 ■ Daily Lineups
Highland Beach, FL 33487
Ph: (561)274-6504
URL: www.dailylineups.com

3504 ■ Daily Lineups Scholarship Awards (Undergraduate, Master's/Award, Scholarship)

Purpose: To support and motivate students to value and make the most of their education. **Focus:** General studies/Field of study not specified. **Qualif.:** Applicants must be legal residents of the United States who are at least 16 years of age and enrolled in an accredited post-secondary academic institution in the United States. Students enrolled in a two year, four year, or graduate programs are also eligible to apply. If under the age of 18, they must have the consent of their parents or legal guardians to participate. **Criteria:** Applicants must answer four personal, open-ended, and thought-provoking questions. The students whose responses are the most persuasive, compelling, and well-written, as judged by our executive management team, will be considered finalists.

Funds Avail.: $1,000 each. **Number Awarded:** 2. **To Apply:** Applicants may enter the contest by submitting a contest application via sponsor's website. All information fields in the contest application must be completed in full, in the English language, and the application must be received by the deadline to be eligible. They may submit only one application, and no revisions to the application may be made after such has been submitted. **Deadline:** September 1. **Contact:** Send email at Michelle@DailyLineups.com.

3505 ■ Dairy Farmers of America Inc. (DFA)
10220 N Ambassador Dr.
Kansas City, MO 64153
Ph: (816)801-6455
Free: 888-337-2407
E-mail: gsevilla@dfamilk.com
URL: www.dfamilk.com
LinkedIn: www.linkedin.com/company/dairy-farmers-of-america
Twitter: www.twitter.com/dfamilk

3506 ■ Dairy Farmers of America Scholarships (Undergraduate/Scholarship)

Purpose: To support outstanding students pursuing careers in the dairy industry. **Focus:** Dairy science. **Qualif.:** Applicants must be pursuing a career in the dairy industry and enrolled in or applying for an accredited degree program. **Criteria:** Selection is based on applicant's commitment and passion to have a career in the dairy industry, and responses to essay questions; extracurricular activities, awards, recognition and work experience; academic achievement; and financial need.

Funds Avail.: No specific amount. **To Apply:** Applicants must submit a completed application form along with a recent transcript and two letters of recommendation. **Deadline:** January 15.

3507 ■ Dalai Lama Trust
1228 17th St. NW
Washington, DC 20036
Ph: (212)213-5010
E-mail: info@dalailamatrust.org
URL: www.dalailamatrust.org

3508 ■ Dalai Lama Trust Graduate Scholarships (Graduate/Scholarship)

Purpose: To further human capital development of the Tibetan people by supporting the pursuit of excellence among Tibetan students in the graduate field of their choice. **Focus:** General studies/Field of study not specified. **Qualif.:** Applicants must be enrolled in or already accepted to a graduate degree program in a university in Europe, Australia or Americas and must demonstrate proof of Tibetan heritage. **Criteria:** Selection will be based on submitted documents and selected applicants will be contacted for a phone interview.

Funds Avail.: Up to $10,000. **Duration:** Annual. **Number Awarded:** 10 to 15. **To Apply:** Applicants must submit a completed application form; photograph of themselves in digital format attached to the application form; official undergraduate transcript of records; curriculum vitae; copy of acceptance letter or enrollment form for intended graduate institution; two written letters of recommendation; two essay responses; copy of valid Green Book; financial statement: copy of most recent income tax return, or SAR/FAFSA forms if applicable. **Deadline:** May 8. **Contact:** The Dalai Lama Trust, at the above address, or Email: scholarship@dalailamatrust.org.

3509 ■ Dalcroze Society of America (DSA)
c/o Anne Farber
161 W. 86th St., No. 7A
New York, NY 10024-3411
Ph: (212)724-5009
E-mail: president@dalcrozeusa.org
URL: www.dalcrozeusa.org

3510 ■ Dalcroze Society of America Memorial Scholarships *(Graduate/Scholarship)*

Purpose: To provide financial aid to students attending institutions offering Dalcroze certification or graduate credits devoted to the Dalcroze approach. **Focus:** Education, Music. **Qualif.:** Applicants must be attending an institution offering Dalcroze graduate credits and must not have been previously awarded a DSA scholarship. **Criteria:** Committees will award scholarships based on merit, financial need, intention to work towards Dalcroze certification within United States, residency and previous experience.

Funds Avail.: No specific amount. **Duration:** 3 weeks to one semester. **To Apply:** Applicants must submit a resume, proof of acceptance at a Dalcroze Training Center, three letters of recommendation, statement of financial need such as recent tax return or other documents, and a personal statement describing teaching and Dalcroze experiences or reasons for pursuing the training. **Deadline:** April 30. **Contact:** Jessica Schaeffer, Secretary at secretary@dalcrozeusa.org.

3511 ■ Dallas Area Paralegal Association
c/o Mariela Cawthon, Exec. Dir.
2100 Ross Ave., Ste. 2700
Dallas, TX 75201
Ph: (214)284-0091
E-mail: executivedirector@dallasparalegals.org
URL: dallasparalegals.org

3512 ■ DAPA Student Member Scholarships *(Undergraduate/Scholarship)*

Purpose: To promote the professional development of the paralegal profession and individual paralegal. **Focus:** Paralegal studies. **Qualif.:** Applicants must: be enrolled and actively participating in a minimum of six hours of study in a Baccalaureate, Post-baccalaureate or Associate Degree paralegal education program at a college and/or paralegal school which has attained American Bar Association approval or in institutionally accredited and in substantial compliance with the ABA Guidelines within Dallas/Fort Worth and the contiguous counties; demonstrate financial need; have not been convicted of a felony; have and maintain a minimum 3.0 GPA on a 4.0 scale average at the institution they are currently attending. **Criteria:** Scholarships will be awarded without regard to race, color, creed, sex or age.

Funds Avail.: No specific amount. **Duration:** Annual. **Number Awarded:** Varies. **To Apply:** Applicants must complete and submit the following: fully completed on-line application, which is appointed by Communities Foundation of Texas, Inc.; an essay, to be submitted on-line, which shall be 750 words or less on a topic to be chosen by the Selection Committee; two letters of recommendation. One should be from an instructor or counselor who can attest to the applicants' working ethic and general character; copy of current transcript. Students who maintain a minimum of 3.0 GPA may apply and/or reapply for additional scholarship funds on an annual basis. The institutions will be asked to submit an unlimited number of applications on behalf of applicants meeting all scholarship recipient requirements to the selection committee. Each institution and the programs presented shall be licensed and accredited. **Deadline:** July 1.

3513 ■ Damon Runyon Cancer Research Foundation
1 Exchange Plz.
55 Broadway, Ste. 302
New York, NY 10006-3720
Ph: (212)455-0500
E-mail: info@damonrunyon.org
URL: www.damonrunyon.org

3514 ■ Damon Runyon Cancer Research Foundation Fellowships *(Doctorate, Graduate, Postdoctorate/Fellowship)*

Purpose: To support the training of the brightest postdoctoral scientists as they embark upon their research careers. **Focus:** Medical research. **Qualif.:** Applicants must have completed one or more degrees or its equivalent: MD, PhD, MD/PhD, DDS, DVM (applicants must include a copy of their diploma to confirm date of conferral); application must be under the guidance of a Sponsor - a scientist (tenured, tenure-track or equivalent position); applicants who have already accepted a postdoctoral research fellowship award are not eligible. **Criteria:** Selection is based on the quality of the research proposal; qualifications, experience and productivity of both the candidate and the Sponsor; and the quality of the research training environment in which the proposed research is to be conducted.

Funds Avail.: $50,000-$60,000. **Duration:** Annual. **Number Awarded:** Varies. **To Apply:** Applicants must submit an application cover sheet with all required original signatures; the Sponsor's biographical sketch in NIH format and a list of current funding; sponsor's letter including: a)description of training plan for the candidate, b) track record of mentorship with list of graduate and postdoctoral fellows trained, c) percentage of proposal written by the candidate (numerical percentage); applicant's curriculum vitae, including a bibliography of all published works; a letter from the applicant describing his/her previous research and teaching

Awards are arranged alphabetically below their administering organizations

experience (the letter must state that the applicant is committed to a career in cancer research); and the research proposal, which shall not exceed five pages of single-spaced 12-point type with at least 0.5 inch margins. **Deadline:** March 15 and August 15.

3515 ■ Damon Runyon Physician-Scientist Training Awards *(Postdoctorate, Professional development/Award)*

Purpose: To provide funds to developing physician-scientists to pursue research intensively. **Focus:** General studies/Field of study not specified. **Qualif.:** Applicants must be physician-scientist; must be completed his/her residency and clinical training; must be U.S. Specialty Board eligible at the time of the application; and must be able to devote at least 80% of his/her time and effort to Damon Runyon-supported research. **Criteria:** Selection is based on the following: quality of a format research proposal written by the applicants; commitment of the institution to the development and training of future physician-scientists, including providing the necessary protected time for research; importance of the proposed research to the understanding of cancer and/or prevention, diagnosis or treatment of cancer; and capacity of the mentor to provide a robust training experience that will accelerate the development of the applicants' scientific skills and prepare him/her to independently conduct high quality, innovative cancer-related research. **Funds Avail.:** $460,000. **Duration:** Annual. **Number Awarded:** 3. **To Apply:** Applicants must propose a research together with the help of his/her mentor and submit a letter of commitment from Institution/Department. A letter endorsed by both the Dean or Center Director, and the Head/Chair of the Department, should confirm the applicant's and mentor's academic appointments, state the institution's commitment to support the applicant's research efforts, the nature of the support that will be provided, and guarantee a minimum of 80% protected time for the applicant's research to fulfill the terms of the award. **Deadline:** December 1.

3516 ■ Damon Runyon-Rachleff Innovation Awards *(Postdoctorate/Fellowship)*

Purpose: To provide funding for extraordinary early career researchers who have an innovative new idea but lack sufficient preliminary data to obtain traditional funding. **Focus:** Medical research. **Qualif.:** Applicants, including non-U.S. citizens, must be conducting independent research at a U.S. research institution. must have a background in multiple disciplines; must belong to either tenure-track Assistant Professors within the first four years of obtaining the position, Clinical Instructors and Senior Clinical Fellows (with an MD) pursuing a period of independent research before taking a faculty position, or Postdoctoral Fellows and highly motivated recent PhD and MD graduates pursuing a period of independent research before taking a faculty position; must commit 80% of their time to conducting research; and must demonstrate access to the resources and infrastructures necessary to conduct the research. **Criteria:** Recipients are chosen based on the applicants' capacity to conduct bold, exceptionally creative research; the novelty and potential for breakthrough innovation of the proposed research; the likelihood of impact to cancer understanding if research is successful; and the applicants' lack of resources to pursue the proposed research. **Funds Avail.:** $150,000 per year. **Duration:** Annual. **To Apply:** Applicants must submit the pre-proposal materials including the following: (1) a completed cover sheet; (2) one-page description of the proposed research; (3) one paragraph description of the resources and core facilities; (4) NIH biosketch; (5) three reference letters from a Tenure-track Assistant professor and clinical instructors and/or Senior Clinical Fellows. Semi finalist applicants will be asked to submit a full proposal including the following: (a) an expanded description of the research proposal (maximum of three pages); (b) full curriculum vitae; (c) a proposed budget for the term of the award; (d) a written statement guaranteeing adequate safety precautions and approved by the appropriate Institutional Review Board; and two letters of reference.

3517 ■ Damon Runyon-Sohn Pediatric Cancer Fellowship Awards *(Master's, Doctorate/Fellowship)*

Purpose: To provide funds to basic scientists and clinicians who conduct research with the potential to significantly impact the prevention, diagnosis or treatment of one or more pediatric cancers. **Focus:** Medical research. **Qualif.:** Applicants must have completed one or more of the following degrees or its equivalent: MD, PHD, MD/PHD, DDS, and DVM. **Criteria:** Applicants are evaluated based on the following criteria: potential impact of the research on pediatric cancer; the quality of the research proposal (importance of the problem, originality of approach, and appropriateness of techniques and clarity of presentation); the qualifications, experience and productivity of both the candidate and the sponsor; the quality of the research training environment in which the proposed research is to be conducted and its potential for broadening and strengthening the applicants' ability to conduct innovative and substantive research. **Funds Avail.:** $50,000-$60,000. **To Apply:** Applicants must propose a research that conducted at a university, hospital or research institution.

3518 ■ Damon Runyon Clinical Investigator Awards *(Doctorate, Graduate, Postdoctorate/Fellowship, Award)*

Purpose: To increase the number of physicians capable of moving seamlessly between the laboratory and the patient's bedside in search of breakthrough treatments. **Focus:** Medical research. **Qualif.:** Applicants must be U.S. citizens or permanent legal residents; must be nominated by their institution; must have received an MD or MD/PhD degree(s) from an accredited institution and are board-eligible; must be committed to spending 80% of their time conducting research; must apply in conjunction with a mentor who is established in the field of clinical translational cancer research. **Criteria:** Recipients are chosen based on excellence of the applicant and the mentor; innovation, creativity, quality and originality of research proposal; commitment of the mentor and institution to the development and training of the applicant as an independent clinical research investigator; evidence of the applicant's commitment to clinical translational and/or cancer prevention research and their ability to apply these advances; importance of the proposed research; and adherence of the proposal to the definition of clinical research. **Funds Avail.:** No specific amount. **Duration:** Annual. **To Apply:** Applicants submit a curriculum vitae; cover sheet; At-a-Glance form; nomination letter from institution/department; applicant's letter and accomplishments; mentor's biographical sketch and letter of support; mentor's proposal training; applicant's research proposal; human subjects, radiation safety and environmental health issues statement; summary of research form; and two letters of recommendation. All application materials should be sent in a CD/DVD. **Deadline:** February 2.

Awards are arranged alphabetically below their administering organizations

3519 ■ Dan Carman Attorney at Law, PLLC
271 W Short St., Ste. 110
Lexington, KY 40507
Ph: (859)685-1055
E-mail: dancarmanlawyer@gmail.com
URL: www.lexingtondefense.com

3520 ■ Dan Carman Attorney at Law Criminal Defense Scholarships *(Advanced Professional/ Scholarship)*

Purpose: To reward an aspiring law student finance his or her first year of law school. **Focus:** Law. **Qualif.:** Applicants must be law school students enrolled at any accredited college or university. **Criteria:** Selection will be based on the applicants' persuasive and creative authorship in a previously published (print or digital) article. The topic of the article may be determined by the applicants. The article must also have the following characteristics: creativity; originality; and ability to clearly convey a complex message. **Funds Avail.:** $2,000. **Number Awarded:** 1. **To Apply:** Applicants must submit the following requirements: a copy of Law School Acceptance Letter (commencing fall of the current year); published article in print or digital; and completed online application. **Deadline:** May 1.

3521 ■ Danish America Heritage Society (DAHS)
1717 Grant St.
Blair, NE 68008
Ph: (402)426-9610
URL: www.danishamericanheritagesociety.org

3522 ■ Edith and Arnold N. Bodtker Grants *(Undergraduate, Graduate/Grant, Internship)*

Purpose: To provide stipends for students interested in studying and performing research in the area of Danish immigration to North America. **Focus:** Cross-cultural studies. **Qualif.:** Applicants must be currently enrolled at or graduated from a university level institution. They must have a designed research or internship project that makes a stay in the USA or Canada (for Danish or North American students) or in Denmark (for North American students) necessary for their research. **Criteria:** Selection shall be based on the aforementioned qualifications and compliance with the application details. **Funds Avail.:** Up to $5,000. **Duration:** Annual. **Number Awarded:** Varies. **To Apply:** Applicants must submit proposals for grant projects, as well as a proposed budget, and least two letter of reference. **Deadline:** April 15 or September 15. **Remarks:** Established in 1998. **Contact:** Timothy Jensen, President, Danish American Heritage Society, 1717 Grant Street. Blair, Nebraska 68008, USA.

3523 ■ Dante Society of America (DSA)
PO Box 600616
Newtonville, MA 02460
Ph: (617)831-9288
E-mail: dantesociety@gmail.com
URL: www.dantesociety.org

3524 ■ DSA Dante Prizes *(Undergraduate/Prize, Monetary)*

Purpose: To support best student essay in competition on a subject related to the life or works of Dante. **Focus:** Renaissance studies. **Qualif.:** Applicants must be undergraduates in any American or Canadian college or university, or by anyone not enrolled as graduate students who have received the degree of A.B., or its equivalent, within the past year. **Criteria:** Selection will be based on the committee's criteria. **Funds Avail.:** $500. **Duration:** Annual. **To Apply:** All submissions must be made by e-mail attachment of a file in either Word or WordPerfect and sent to the Dante Society. Files should have the extension .doc or .rtf if saved in Word, .wpd if saved in WordPerfect. Undergraduate essays should be no longer than 7,500 words in length including bibliographies and any other material. The writer's name should not appear on the essay title page or on any other page of the essay since the essays are submitted anonymously to the readers. Quotations from Dante's works should be cited in the original language and the format of an essay should conform to either the Chicago or MLA Style Sheet guidelines. **Deadline:** June 30.

3525 ■ Charles Hall Grandgent Awards *(Graduate/Award, Monetary)*

Purpose: To support best student essay in competition on a subject related to the life or works of Dante. **Focus:** Renaissance studies. **Qualif.:** Applicants must be American or Canadian students enrolled in any graduate program. **Criteria:** Selection will be based on the committee's criteria. **Funds Avail.:** $750. **Duration:** Annual. **To Apply:** All submissions must be made by e-mail attachment of a file in either Word or WordPerfect and sent to the Dante Society. Files should have the extension .doc or .rtf if saved in Word, .wpd if saved in WordPerfect. Graduate essays should be no longer than 10,000 words in length, including bibliographies and any other material. Each writer should provide a cover page giving the writer's name, local, permanent and email addresses, the title of the essay, the essay category and the writer's institutional affiliation. The writer's name should not appear on the essay title page or on any other page of the essay since the essays are submitted anonymously to the readers. Quotations from Dante's works should be cited in the original language and the format of an essay should conform to either the Chicago or MLA Style Sheet guidelines. **Deadline:** June 30.

3526 ■ David Library of the American Revolution
1201 River Rd.
Washington Crossing, PA 18977
Ph: (215)493-6776
Fax: (215)493-5492
E-mail: librarian@dlar.org
URL: www.dlar.org

3527 ■ David Library Fellowships *(Doctorate, Postdoctorate/Fellowship)*

Purpose: To support the education of doctoral and postdoctoral students and encourage the scholarly use of the Library's Resources. **Focus:** General studies/Field of study not specified. **Qualif.:** Open to both doctoral and postdoctoral applicants. Doctoral candidates must have passed their general examinations before beginning their fellowships. **Criteria:** Selection will be based on the committee's criteria. **Funds Avail.:** Range from $1,000 to $1,600. **Duration:** One month. **To Apply:** Applicants should submit seven sets of the following: cover sheet with applicants name,

Awards are arranged alphabetically below their administering organizations

mailing address, email address, phone number, academic affiliation and title of project; a brief project statement (3 to 5 pages) describing the project and stating what David Library resources will be used; a detailed C.V.; writing sample (10 to 20 pages of recent work, preferably from the proposed fellowship project). Each application must be supported by two letters of reference sent directly by the referee, not sent by the applicant). All application materials must be submitted in a single package. **Deadline:** March 6. **Remarks:** Established in 1985. **Contact:** Brian Graziano, Operations Manager, at 215-493-6776 ext. 100, or email fellows@dlar.org.

3528 ■ David Mann Law Office
130 N Crest Blvd.
Macon, GA 31210
Ph: (478)742-3381
Fax: (478)746-3354
Free: 855-507
E-mail: davidmanninjurylaw@gmail.com
URL: www.manninjurylaw.com

3529 ■ Mann Law Firm Scholarships *(Advanced Professional/Scholarship)*

Purpose: To reward clear and concise communication which conveys a message to the target audience. **Focus:** Law. **Qualif.:** Applicants must be U.S. citizens or authorized to work/go to school in the United States. **Criteria:** Selection will be based on creativity, originally and ability to clearly convey a complex message of the submitted article.

Duration: Non-renewable. **Number Awarded:** 1. **To Apply:** Applicants must visit the website for the online application process; must submit a copy of law school acceptance letter and published article in print or digital. **Deadline:** May 1.

3530 ■ Davis Levin Livingston
851 Fort St., Ste. 400
Honolulu, HI 96813
Ph: (866)806-4349
URL: www.davislevin.com

3531 ■ Davis Levin Livingston Public Interest Law Scholarships *(Postgraduate/Scholarship)*

Purpose: To support law students intending to pursue public interest law. **Focus:** Law. **Qualif.:** Applicants must be U.S. citizens or otherwise authorized to work in the United States; must be accepted and will be attending law school in the fall of the same year following the application; and must have academic achievement as reflected by an undergraduate cumulative minimum 3.0 GPA. **Criteria:** Selection will be based on the applicants' eligibility and compliance with the application process.

Funds Avail.: $3,000. **To Apply:** Applicants must complete the application form and submit the following: one to three page typed essay; a stated intention of pursuing a legal career in public interest law; an official and complete copy of undergraduate college transcripts; an acceptance letter from an accredited law school within the United States; and proof of legal residency in the U.S. (i.e., birth certificate, passport, permanent resident card, etc.). **Deadline:** July 15. **Contact:** Application materials should be mailed (or e-mailed in PDF format) to Lynne Agbalog at lynne@davislevin.com.

3532 ■ Davis Memorial Foundation
275 Tennant Ave., No. 106
Morgan Hill, CA 95037
Ph: (650)938-5441
Fax: (650)938-5407
E-mail: dmf@wsrca.com
URL: www.davisfoundation.org

3533 ■ Davis Memorial Foundation Scholarships *(Graduate, Undergraduate/Scholarship)*

Purpose: To develop qualified professionals through education and to award those who have the desire to continue to improve their quality of life. **Focus:** General studies/Field of study not specified. **Qualif.:** Applicants must be: high school students, undergraduate or graduate students or technical trade school students who are provisionally accepted as students into undergraduate or graduate degree programs for the coming academic year by accredited colleges or universities; and, WSRCA members in good standing, their employees or their respective immediate family (spouse or child). The child may be natural, legally adopted or a step child. **Criteria:** Applicants will be evaluated based on both academic and personal performance.

Funds Avail.: $5,000 each. **Duration:** Annual. **Number Awarded:** 6. **To Apply:** Applicants must submit six copies of each: official application form; official transcript of all high school and college records; letter from college, university or technical trade school where the undergraduate or graduate work will be undertaken, indicating provisional acceptance of the proposed course of study; and current picture. **Deadline:** April 15. **Contact:** Board of Trustees, Davis Memorial Foundation Scholarship Fund, at the above address.

3534 ■ Davis Wright Tremaine L.L.P. (DWT)
188 W Northern Lights Blvd., Ste. 1100
Anchorage, AK 99503-3985
Ph: (907)257-5300
E-mail: info@dwt.com
URL: www.dwt.com/offices/Anchorage

3535 ■ Davis Wright Tremaine 1L Diversity Scholarships *(Undergraduate/Scholarship)*

Purpose: To provide financial assistance to qualified students intending to pursue their law degree. **Focus:** Law. **Qualif.:** Applicants must: be first-year law students; have a record of academic achievement in both undergraduate school and the first year of law school; demonstrate promise for a successful career in law; be committed to civic involvement that promotes diversity; be willing to continue that commitment upon entering the legal profession; and, commit to become Summer Associates in any of DWT's Offices (Seattle, New York, or Portland) between the student's first and second years of law school. **Criteria:** Applicants will be selected based on their academic performance and commitment to a successful career in law.

Funds Avail.: $7,500. **Duration:** Annual. **Number Awarded:** Varies. **To Apply:** Applicants must submit a current resume; a complete undergraduate transcript; a grade from the first semester of law school; a short, personal essay indicating the applicant's eligibility for and interest in the scholarship, and a legal writing sample; and two or three references (one of whom should be a person qualified to comment on the applicant's law school work). **Deadline:** January 13. **Contact:** Seattle Scholarship, Brook Dormaier; email: BrookDormaier@dwt.com; Portland Scholarship, Hiroko Peraza; email: HirokoPeraza@dwt.com.

3536 ■ Death Valley '49ers, Inc.
24601 Glen Ivy Rd., No. 39
Corona, CA 92883
URL: www.deathvalley49ers.org

3537 ■ Death Valley '49ers Scholarships
(Undergraduate/Scholarship)

Purpose: To assist high school graduates living in the Death Valley Unified School District. **Focus:** Historic preservation. **Qualif.:** Applicants must be residents of the Death Valley Unified School District and/or Death Valley National Park for a minimum of two years and/or parent(s) are employed within the boundaries of Death Valley National Park and/or attended Death Valley Elementary School for a minimum of two years; must have completed all the required subjects for high school graduation in their junior and senior academic years at Beatty, Pahrump, or Shoshone High Schools; must maintain 24 to 30 required units per academic year. Freshmen must have 2.5 GPA, Sophomores must have 2.75, Juniors and Seniors must have 3.0 GPA. **Criteria:** Scholarships are awarded based on a four-year program and will be renewed each year based on the academic progress of the student. The scholarship committee will review academic progress at the end of each semester.

Funds Avail.: $4,000. **Duration:** Annual. **To Apply:** Applicants must submit a Death Valley '49ers Scholarship Application to the Scholarship Committee by the application deadline in the senior year of high school. **Remarks:** Established in 1976. **Contact:** Virginia E. Stockman, Chairman, Death Valley '49ers Scholarship Committee at Rvstockman@aol.com.

3538 ■ Debt.com
5701 W Sunrise Blvd., Ste. 100
Plantation, FL 33313
Free: 800-810-0989
URL: www.debt.com

3539 ■ Debt.com Scholarships *(All/Scholarship)*

Purpose: To offer scholarships to students pursuing higher education. **Focus:** General studies/Field of study not specified. **Qualif.:** Applicants must be students in the United States. **Criteria:** Selection will be based on the committee's criteria.

Funds Avail.: $500. **Number Awarded:** 1. **To Apply:** Applicants may contact the Debt.com or may visit the website for the application process and other required materials. **Deadline:** August 1. **Contact:** editor@debt.com.

3540 ■ The Decorative Arts Trust
20 S Olive St., Ste. 304
Media, PA 19063
Ph: (610)627-4970
E-mail: thetrust@decorativeartstrust.org
URL: www.decorativeartstrust.org
Facebook: www.facebook.com/The-Decorative-Arts-Trust-128778940541114

Twitter: twitter.com/DecArtsTrust

3541 ■ Dewey Lee Curtis Scholarships *(Advanced Professional/Scholarship)*

Purpose: To support individuals actively working in the field of American decorative arts with their education. **Focus:** Art. **Qualif.:** Applicants must be individuals who are actively working in the field of American decorative arts. **Criteria:** Candidates will be selected based on the application.

Funds Avail.: No specific amount. **Number Awarded:** 1. **To Apply:** Applicants may contact the organization or their Institute's office for the application information.

3542 ■ DefensiveDriving.com
11 Greenway Plaza, Ste. 3150
Houston, TX 77046
Ph: (713)488-4000
URL: www.defensivedriving.com
Facebook: www.facebook.com/defensivedrivingonline

3543 ■ DefensiveDriving.com Scholarships
(Undergraduate/Scholarship)

Purpose: To supply college students with funds to pay for their school. **Focus:** General studies/Field of study not specified. **Qualif.:** Applicants must be high school seniors or college students who are legal residents of the United States and enrolled in semester beginning no later than fall of the current year. Home-schooled students may apply as long as their course of study is equivalent to a high school senior.Relatives of DefensiveDriving.com staff may not enter. **Criteria:** Selection will be based on creativity and originality of the submitted video application.

Funds Avail.: $1,000. **Number Awarded:** 1. **To Apply:** Applicants are required to like DefensiveDriving.com Facebook page to be considered. They are also required to submit a video (see the "Make A Video" tab on the scholarship website for further details). **Deadline:** May 31. **Contact:** scholarshipdefensivedriving@gmail.com.

3544 ■ Delaware Community Foundation (DCF)
100 W 10th St., Ste. 115
Wilmington, DE 19801-1632
Ph: (302)571-8004
Fax: (302)571-1553
E-mail: info@delcf.org
URL: delcf.org

3545 ■ Chrysler Technical Scholarship Fund
(Undergraduate/Scholarship)

Purpose: To support students pursuing their respective careers in design, engineering, manufacturing or repair of automotive products. **Focus:** General studies/Field of study not specified. **Qualif.:** Applicants must be residents of Delaware and not older than 23 years of age at the time of application; have an at least 2.75 GPA and plan to obtain a degree or certificate from a community college, trade school or university in a technical field related to the design, engineering, manufacturing or repair of automotive products, including but not limited to, automotive repair, skilled trades and engineering. **Criteria:** Recipients will be selected based on demonstrated academic ability, leadership traits and financial need.

Funds Avail.: $1,000 each per academic year. **Duration:**

Awards are arranged alphabetically below their administering organizations

Annual. **Number Awarded:** 20. **To Apply:** Applicants must download and fill out the application form at the Delaware Community Foundation website. **Deadline:** April 1. **Contact:** Joyce Darling at jdarling@delcf.org or call 302-571-8004.

3546 ■ Delta Delta Delta
2331 Brookhollow Plaza Dr.
Arlington, TX 76006
Ph: (817)633-8001
Fax: (817)652-0212
E-mail: info@trideltaeo.org
URL: www.tridelta.org

3547 ■ Nancy Ashley Adams/Ashley Adams Koetje Scholarships *(Undergraduate/Scholarship)*

Purpose: To provide financial assistance to qualified undergraduate students. **Focus:** General studies/Field of study not specified. **Qualif.:** Applicants must be Alpha Eta chapter members in Florida State University and be initiated sophomore or junior members. **Criteria:** Applicants will be evaluated based on their academic achievement, chapter and campus activities, and financial need. Preference will be given to officers or members from out-of-state.

Funds Avail.: No specific amount. **Duration:** Annual; one academic year. **To Apply:** Application forms are available on the website. Applicants must provide a personal statement about their educational and vocational goals; must have a recommendation letter from a faculty member; must have an official transcript from each undergraduate institution. **Deadline:** March 1. **Contact:** Applicants must contact Tawnya Braeutigam at the Foundation office; Email: tbraeutigam@trideltaeo.org.

3548 ■ Margaret M. Alkek Scholarships *(Undergraduate/Scholarship)*

Purpose: To provide financial assistance to qualified undergraduate students. **Focus:** Education; Music; Theater arts. **Qualif.:** Applicants must be Theta Xi chapter members at the University of Southern California; have academic achievement at the collegiate level of 3.0 or better; and be initiated sophomore or junior members. **Criteria:** Preference will be given to those majoring in education, music or theater.

Funds Avail.: No specific amount. **Duration:** Annual. **To Apply:** Application forms are available on the website. Applicants must provide a personal statement about their educational and vocational goals; must have a recommendation letter from a faculty member; must have an official transcript from each undergraduate institution. **Deadline:** March 1. **Contact:** For further information, applicants must e-mail Tawnya Braeutigam at tbraeutigam@rideltaeo.org.

3549 ■ Durning Sisters Scholarships *(Graduate/Scholarship)*

Purpose: To provide financial assistance to graduate students. **Focus:** General studies/Field of study not specified. **Qualif.:** Applicants must be Tri Delta members who have completed 12 hours of graduate study and are unmarried. **Criteria:** Applicants will be evaluated based on academic merit, chapter and campus or community activities.

Funds Avail.: No specific amount. **Duration:** Annual; one academic year. **To Apply:** Applicants must complete the application form available on the website; must have a personal statement about educational and vocational goals; must have two letters of academic recommendation and one Tri Delta recommendation letter; must provide a transcript and financial information. **Deadline:** March 1.

3550 ■ Harriet Erich Graduate Fellowships *(Graduate/Fellowship, Scholarship)*

Purpose: To provide financial assistance to graduate students. **Focus:** General studies/Field of study not specified. **Qualif.:** Applicants must be Tri Delta members enrolled in an accredited graduate program at the University of Alabama. **Criteria:** Applicants will be judged based on academic merit as well as chapter and campus or community activities.

Funds Avail.: No specific amount. **Duration:** Annual; one academic year. **To Apply:** Applicants must complete the application form available on the website; must have a personal statement about educational and vocational goals; must have two letters of academic recommendation and one Tri Delta recommendation letter; must provide a transcript and financial information. **Deadline:** March 1. **Contact:** Applicants must contact Tawnya Braeutigam at the Foundation office; Email: tbraeutigam@trideltaeo.org.

3551 ■ Louise Bales Gallagher Scholarships *(Undergraduate/Scholarship)*

Purpose: To provide financial assistance to qualified undergraduate students. **Focus:** General studies/Field of study not specified. **Qualif.:** Applicants must be Delta Epsilon chapter members at Millikin University; must be initiated sophomore or junior members. **Criteria:** Scholarship application will be based on the following criteria: financial need (50%); academic achievement (25%); and, chapter and campus involvement (25%).

Funds Avail.: No specific amount. **Duration:** Annual. **To Apply:** Application forms are available on the website. Applicants must provide a personal statement about educational and vocational goals; must have a recommendation letter from a faculty member; must have an official transcript from each undergraduate institution. **Deadline:** March 1. **Contact:** For further information, applicants must e-mail Tawnya Braeutigam at tbraeutigam@rideltaeo.org.

3552 ■ Peg Hart Harrison Memorial Scholarships *(Undergraduate/Scholarship)*

Purpose: To provide financial assistance to qualified undergraduate students. **Focus:** General studies/Field of study not specified. **Qualif.:** Applicants must be: Beta Lambda chapter members at the University of Central Florida; members who have overcome insurmountable odds; and, initiated sophomore or junior members. **Criteria:** Applicants will be judge based on academic standing, chapter and campus activities, and financial need.

Funds Avail.: No specific amount. **Duration:** Annual; one academic year. **To Apply:** Application forms are available in the website. Applicants must provide a personal statement about their educational and vocational goals; must have a recommendation letter from a faculty member; must have an official transcript from each undergraduate institution. **Deadline:** March 1. **Contact:** Applicants must contact Tawnya Braeutigam at the Foundation office; Phone: 817-633-8001; Email: tbraeutigam@trideltaeo.org.

3553 ■ Hazel D. Isbell Fellowships *(Graduate/Fellowship, Scholarship)*

Purpose: To provide financial assistance to graduate students. **Focus:** General studies/Field of study not specified. **Qualif.:** Applicants must be Tri Delta members pursuing a graduate study. **Criteria:** Preference will be given to Theta Delta alumnae attending the University of Oregon, Theta Mu chapter members.

Funds Avail.: No specific amount. **Duration:** Annual; one academic year. **To Apply:** Applicants must complete the application form available on the website; must have a personal statement about educational and vocational goals; must have two letters of academic recommendation and one Tri Delta recommendation letter; must provide a transcript and financial information. **Deadline:** March 1. **Contact:** Applicants must contact Tawnya Braeutigam at the Foundation office; Email: tbraeutigam@trideltaeo.org.

3554 ■ Sarah Shinn Marshall Scholarships
(Undergraduate/Scholarship)

Purpose: To provide financial assistance to qualified undergraduate students. **Focus:** General studies/Field of study not specified. **Qualif.:** Applicants must be initiated sophomore or junior members in good standing of Delta Delta. **Criteria:** Applicants will be judge based on academic standing, chapter and campus activities, and financial need.

Funds Avail.: No specific amount. **Duration:** Annual. **To Apply:** Application forms are available on the website. Applicants must provide a personal statement about educational and vocational goals; must have a recommendation letter from a faculty member; must have an official transcript from each undergraduate institution. **Deadline:** March 1.

3555 ■ Martin Sisters Scholarships *(Undergraduate/ Scholarship)*

Purpose: To provide financial assistance to qualified undergraduate students. **Focus:** General studies/Field of study not specified. **Qualif.:** Applicants must be initiated sophomore or junior members in good standing of Delta Delta. **Criteria:** Applicants are judged based on academic standing, chapter and campus activities, and financial need.

Funds Avail.: No specific amount. **Duration:** Annual; one academic year. **To Apply:** Application forms are available in the website. Applicants must provide a personal statement about educational and vocational goals; must have a recommendation letter from a faculty member; must have an official transcript from each undergraduate institutions. **Deadline:** March 1. **Contact:** Applicants must contact Tawnya Braeutigam at the Foundation office; Email: tbraeutigam@trideltaeo.org.

3556 ■ McKinney Sisters Undergraduate Scholarships *(Undergraduate/Scholarship)*

Purpose: To provide financial assistance to qualified undergraduate students. **Focus:** General studies/Field of study not specified. **Qualif.:** Applicants must be graduates from high school in San Antonio, TX or have permanent residence in San Antonio. They must also be initiated sophomore or junior members. **Criteria:** Applicants will be judged based on academic achievement, campus and community involvement, and financial need.

Funds Avail.: No specific amount. **Duration:** Annual; one academic year. **To Apply:** Application forms are available on the website. Applicants must provide a personal statement about educational and vocational goals; must have a recommendation letter from a faculty member; must have an official transcript from each undergraduate institution. **Deadline:** March 1. **Contact:** Applicants must contact Tawnya Braeutigam at the Foundation office; Email: tbraeutigam@trideltaeo.org.

3557 ■ Cissy McDaniel Parker Scholarships
(Undergraduate/Scholarship)

Purpose: To provide financial assistance to qualified undergraduate students. **Focus:** General studies/Field of study not specified. **Qualif.:** Applicants must be Theta Zeta chapter members at the University of Texas; have an academic achievement of 3.0 or better GPA; and be initiated sophomore or junior members. **Criteria:** Applicants will be judged based on academic achievement, campus and community involvement, and financial need.

Funds Avail.: No specific amount. **Duration:** Annual; one academic year. **To Apply:** Application forms are available on the website. Applicants must provide a personal statement about educational and vocational goals; must have a recommendation letter from a faculty member; must have an official transcript from each undergraduate institution. **Deadline:** March 1. **Contact:** Applicants must contact Tawnya Braeutigam at the Foundation office; Email: tbraeutigam@trideltaeo.org.

3558 ■ Cheryl White Pryor Memorial Scholarships
(Undergraduate/Scholarship)

Purpose: To provide financial assistance to qualified undergraduate students. **Focus:** General studies/Field of study not specified. **Qualif.:** Applicants must be members of Delta Sigma chapter member at Tennessee; and be initiated sophomore or junior members. **Criteria:** Scholarship selection committee shall determine the number of recipients and amounts of each scholarship. Applicants will be evaluated based on the following criteria: past and present service to the Delta Sigma chapter at the University of Tennessee (60%); academic achievement (30%); and, financial need (10%).

Funds Avail.: No specific amount. **Duration:** Annual. **To Apply:** Application forms are available on the website. Applicants must provide a personal statement about educational and vocational goals; must have a recommendation letter from a faculty member; must have an official transcript from each undergraduate institution. **Deadline:** March 1. **Contact:** For further information, applicants must e-mail Tawnya Braeutigam at tbraeutigam@rideltaeo.org.

3559 ■ Tri Delta Alpha Eta Scholarships
(Undergraduate/Scholarship)

Purpose: To provide financial assistance to qualified undergraduate students. **Focus:** General studies/Field of study not specified. **Qualif.:** Applicants must be members of Alpha Eta chapter member at Florida State University; and be initiated sophomore or junior members. **Criteria:** Applicants will be judged based on academic standing, chapter and campus activities, and financial need.

Funds Avail.: No Specific amount. **Duration:** Annual; one academic year. **To Apply:** Application forms are available on the website. Applicants must provide a personal statement about their educational and vocational goals; must have a recommendation letter from a faculty member; must have an official transcript from each undergraduate institution. **Deadline:** March 1. **Contact:** Applicants must contact Tawnya Braeutigam at the Foundation office; Email: tbraeutigam@trideltaeo.org.

3560 ■ Tri Delta Alpha Rho Leadership Scholarships *(Undergraduate/Scholarship)*

Purpose: To provide financial assistance to qualified undergraduate students. **Focus:** General studies/Field of study not specified. **Qualif.:** Applicants must be Alpha Rho

Awards are arranged alphabetically below their administering organizations

chapter members at the University of Georgia and be initiated sophomore or junior members. **Criteria:** Applicants will be judge based on academic standing, chapter and campus activities, and financial need.

Funds Avail.: No specific amount. **Duration:** Annual; one academic year. **To Apply:** Application forms are available on the website. Applicants must provide a personal statement about their educational and vocational goals; must have a recommendation letter from a faculty member; must have an official transcript from each undergraduate institution. **Deadline:** March 1. **Contact:** Applicants must contact Tawnya Braeutigam at the Foundation office: Email: tbraeutigam@trideltaeo.org.

3561 ■ Tri Delta Atlanta Alumnae Achievement Scholarships (Undergraduate/Scholarship)

Purpose: To provide financial assistance to qualified undergraduate students. **Focus:** General studies/Field of study not specified. **Qualif.:** Applicant must be: currently enrolled in an undergraduate Tri Delta member in good standing at any public or private college or university; a collegiate member who graduated from a Georgia high school in one of the following four counties: Fulton, Dekalb, Cobb or Gwinnett; and, a junior during the application year. **Criteria:** Selection of applicant will be based on the following criteria: must have a minimum GPA of 3.3 on a 4.0 scale; collegiate chapter service (must have served or be serving at an elected or appointed position(s)); and, leadership or community service on campus.

Funds Avail.: No specific amount. **Duration:** Annual. **To Apply:** Application forms are available on the website. Applicant must provide a personal statement about educational and vocational goals; must have a recommendation letter from a faculty member; must have an official transcript from each undergraduate institution. **Deadline:** March 1.

3562 ■ Tri Delta Beta Gamma Memorial Scholarships (Undergraduate/Scholarship)

Purpose: To provide financial assistance to qualified undergraduate students. **Focus:** General studies/Field of study not specified. **Qualif.:** Applicants must: be Beta Gamma chapter members at Jacksonville University; be full-time undergraduates at Jacksonville University; have a minimum GPA of 2.5; and be members who have overcome personal hardship or life struggle. **Criteria:** Applicants will be judged based on academic standing, chapter and campus activities, and financial need.

Funds Avail.: No specific amount. **Duration:** Annual; one academic year. **To Apply:** Application forms are available on the website. Applicants must provide a personal statement about their educational and vocational goals; must have a recommendation letter from a faculty member; must have an official transcript from each undergraduate institution. **Deadline:** March 1. **Contact:** Applicants must contact Tawnya Braeutigam at the Foundation office: Phone: 817-633-8001; Email: tbraeutigam@trideltaeo.org.

3563 ■ Tri Delta Houston Alumnae Chapter Graduate Fellowships (Graduate/Fellowship, Scholarship)

Purpose: To provide financial assistance to graduate students. **Focus:** General studies/Field of study not specified. **Qualif.:** Applicants must be Tri Delta members enrolled in an accredited graduate program full-time whose permanent residence is in Houston, Texas. **Criteria:** Applicants will be selected based on academic merit as well as chapter and campus or community activities.

Funds Avail.: No specific amount. **Duration:** Annual; one academic year. **To Apply:** Applicants must complete the application form available on the website; must have a personal statement about educational and vocational goals; must have two letters of academic recommendation and one Tri Delta recommendation letter; must provide a transcript and financial information. **Deadline:** March 1.

3564 ■ Tri Delta Northern Virginia Alumnae Chapter Scholarships (Undergraduate/Scholarship)

Purpose: To provide financial assistance to qualified undergraduate students. **Focus:** General studies/Field of study not specified. **Qualif.:** Applicants must have academic achievement of 3.0 or better GPA; must have a financial need; and be initiated sophomore or junior members. **Criteria:** Priority will be given to members from a Virginia Tri Delta chapter, then members of any Tri Delta chapter with a permanent residence in Northern Virginia.

Funds Avail.: No specific amount. **Duration:** Annual. **To Apply:** Application forms are available on the website. Applicants must provide a personal statement about educational and vocational goals; must have a recommendation letter from a faculty member; must have an official transcript from each undergraduate institution. **Deadline:** March 1. **Contact:** Applicants must contact Tawnya Braeutigam at the Foundation office; Email: tbraeutigam@trideltaeo.org.

3565 ■ Delta Epsilon Sigma (DES)
c/o Dr. Claudia Marie Kovach, Secretary-Treasurer
1 Neumann Dr.
Aston, PA 19014-1298
E-mail: contact@deltaepsilonsigma.org
URL: www.deltaepsilonsigma.org

3566 ■ Delta Epsilon Sigma Graduate Fellowships (Graduate/Fellowship)

Purpose: To provide financial support for the education of member students. **Focus:** General studies/Field of study not specified. **Qualif.:** Applicants must be members who are in the senior years of study. **Criteria:** Applicants will be judged by the Scholarship Committee based on scholastic achievement, leadership and service activities.

Funds Avail.: No specified amount. **Duration:** Annual. **To Apply:** Applicants must submit typed application accompanied by three letters of recommendation including one from the Chapter Advisor and official transcripts of all college work through the current fall semester. **Deadline:** March 1. **Contact:** Scanned document should be emailed to: Contact@DeltaEpsilonSigma.org.

3567 ■ Delta Epsilon Sigma Undergraduate Scholarships (Undergraduate/Scholarship)

Purpose: To provide financial support for the education of member students. **Focus:** General studies/Field of study not specified. **Qualif.:** Applicants must be members who are in their junior years of study. **Criteria:** Applicants will be judged by the Scholarship Committee based on scholastic achievement, leadership and service activities.

Funds Avail.: No specified amount. **Duration:** Annual. **To Apply:** Applicants must submit typed application accompanied by three letters of recommendation including one from the Chapter Advisor and official transcripts of all college work through the current fall semester. **Deadline:** March 1. **Contact:** Scanned document should be emailed to: Contact@DeltaEpsilonSigma.org.

3568 ■ Delta Gamma
3250 Riverside Dr.
Columbus, OH 43221

Awards are arranged alphabetically below their administering organizations

Ph: (614)481-8169
Free: 800-644-5414
E-mail: DG-EO@deltagamma.org
URL: www.deltagamma.org

3569 ■ Delta Gamma Undergraduate Merit-Based Scholarships *(Undergraduate/Scholarship)*

Purpose: To encourage the Delta Gammas to pursue a career in science. **Focus:** Science. **Qualif.:** Candidates must have a 3.0 or higher GPA; must have completed either three semesters or four quarters of college work. **Criteria:** Selection will be based on scholastic excellence, participation and leadership roles in chapter, campus and community activities and required recommendations. **Funds Avail.:** No specific amount. **Duration:** Annual. **To Apply:** Applicants must submit a complete Delta Gamma Foundation scholarship application. **Deadline:** March 1. **Contact:** Contact Director of Scholarships and Fellowships at scholarshipfellowship@deltagamma.org.

3570 ■ The Delta Kappa Gamma Society International

P.O. Box 1589
Austin, TX 78767
Ph: (512)478-5748
Fax: (512)478-3961
Free: 888-762-4685
URL: www.dkg.org
Facebook: www.facebook.com/dkgorg

3571 ■ Delta Kappa Gamma Society International World Fellowships *(Professional development/Fellowship)*

Purpose: To enable international female students to pursue advanced study in the United States and/or Canada. **Focus:** General studies/Field of study not specified. **Qualif.:** Applicants must be female graduate students from various countries other than the United States or Canada. **Criteria:** Selection will be based on the following: (1) for the applications to study in the United States, the Institute of International Education (IIE) staff will review successful international candidates and will forward applications for those who meet the criteria for Delta Kappa Gamma fellowships; (2) for the applications to study in Canada: application forms are submitted to the international World Fellowship Committee for evaluation and ranking. **Funds Avail.:** Amount varies. **Number Awarded:** Varies. **To Apply:** Applicants who wish to study in the United States may ask the Cultural Affairs Office of the United States Embassy in their home country to obtain further information on the application process. Meanwhile, those who wish to study in Canada must submit the application forms and other documents required to the international World Fellowship committee for evaluation and ranking. **Remarks:** The World Fellowship Program began as a project to aid women in war-torn countries.

3572 ■ Delta Nu Alpha Transportation Fraternity (DNA)

1720 Manistique Ave.
South Milwaukee, WI 53172
Ph: (414)764-3063
Fax: (630)499-8505
E-mail: admin@deltanualpha.org
URL: www.deltanualpha.org

3573 ■ Delta Nu Alpha Foundation Scholarships *(Undergraduate/Scholarship)*

Purpose: To emphasize financial assistance and mentoring for students, excellent continuing education opportunities for the work force, and vigilance in communicating changes in regulations. **Focus:** Logistics; Transportation. **Qualif.:** Program is open to all students studying in the field of Transportation, Logistics and Supply Chain Management. Students pursuing associate and bachelor degrees are encouraged to apply. **Criteria:** Recipients are selected based on academic success, potential, motivation, career plans, recommendation, evaluation of Faculty members and internship experience related to transportation and logistics. **Funds Avail.:** No amount specified. **To Apply:** Applicants must submit a completed application form along with transcripts of all college/university level work completed and two letters of recommendation (one should be from the transportation, logistics or supply chain management instructor). **Deadline:** June 30. **Contact:** Tom Bock, Scholarship Chair, at bocko@mindspring.com or deltanualphafoundation@cableone.net.

3574 ■ Delta Phi Epsilon Sorority (DPHIE)

251 S Camac St.
Philadelphia, PA 19107
Ph: (215)732-5901
Fax: (215)732-5906
E-mail: info@dphie.org
URL: www.dphie.org
Facebook: www.facebook.com/DeltaPhiEpsilonSorority

3575 ■ Delta Phi Epsilon Educational Foundation Scholarships *(Undergraduate, Graduate/Scholarship)*

Purpose: To develop social conscience and a willingness to think in terms of the common good in order to assure for its members continuous development and achievement in the collegiate and fraternity world. **Focus:** General studies/Field of study not specified. **Qualif.:** Applicants must be undergraduate and graduate students who are initiated members of Delta Phi Epsilon in good standing, who will be enrolled as full-time students. **Criteria:** Scholarships will be based on three criteria: service and involvement, academics, and need. **Funds Avail.:** $500-$3,000. **Duration:** Annual; one academic year. **To Apply:** Application forms are available on the website. Applicants must submit an official transcript of grades, letter of introduction and need for scholarship, typed autobiographical sketch (1,000 words max), two recent photos suitable for publication, letter of recommendation from (must provide at least 2): Chapter President; Chapter Advisor; College Professor or Administrator; High School Teacher/Principal; Alumna; Employer. Applicant must provide a name and address of financial aid director for the school. **Deadline:** January 15. **Contact:** Nicole DeFeo, at ndefeo@dphie.org.

3576 ■ Delta Tau Lambda Sorority, Inc. (DTL)

PO Box 7714
Ann Arbor, MI 48107-7714
E-mail: dtl-info@deltataulambda.org
URL: www.deltataulambda.org
Facebook: www.facebook.com/deltataulambda

Awards are arranged alphabetically below their administering organizations

Twitter: twitter.com/DeltaTauLambda

3577 ■ Lydia Cruz and Sandra Maria Ramos Scholarships *(Undergraduate/Scholarship)*

Purpose: To assist young Latinas in reaching their goals through education. **Focus:** General studies/Field of study not specified. **Qualif.:** Applicants must be current Latina high school seniors who are entering their first year of college at a two or four year higher learning institution. **Criteria:** Selection of applicants will be based on academic excellence and community service.

Funds Avail.: No specific amount. **To Apply:** Applicants must complete the application form, available on the website, including the essays; must provide the official high school transcript and a copy of University/College Acceptance Letter. Scholarship application materials must be sent to Delta Tau Lambda Sorority, Inc.

3578 ■ Delta Zeta Sorority
202 E Church St.
Oxford, OH 45056
Ph: (513)523-7597
E-mail: dzs@dzshq.com
URL: www.deltazeta.org
Facebook: www.facebook.com/DeltaZetaSororityNational
LinkedIn: www.linkedin.com/
 grps?gid=107634&trk=myg_ugrp_ovr
Twitter: www.twitter.com/DeltaZetaNatl

3579 ■ Sandra Sebrell Bailey Scholarships *(Undergraduate/Scholarship)*

Purpose: To provide financial assistance to all qualified undergraduate students. **Focus:** General studies/Field of study not specified. **Qualif.:** Applicants must be junior or senior women who have been initiated members at least one year and who are in good standing. **Criteria:** Applicants will be evaluated based on academic achievements, financial need, campus leadership and activities, and services to Delta Zeta. Preference will be given to those members entering the field of education.

Funds Avail.: No specific amount. **Duration:** Annual. **To Apply:** Scholarship applications are available on the website and must be completed properly. Applicants must have the FAFSA reply form. **Deadline:** February 15. **Contact:** dzfoundation@dzshq.com.

3580 ■ Charline Chilson Scholarships *(Undergraduate/Scholarship)*

Purpose: To provide financial assistance for qualified graduate students. **Focus:** Science. **Qualif.:** Applicants must be Delta Zeta members in good standing; must be in their junior or senior year or as graduate students; must have a high grade point in their major; must show financial need; must have a history of active leadership and participation in Delta Zeta activities; and must have a commitment to a degree in science. **Criteria:** Applicants will be selected based on academic achievements and financial need.

Funds Avail.: No specific amount. **Duration:** Annual. **To Apply:** Scholarship applications are available on the website and must be completed properly. Applicants must have the FAFSA reply form. **Deadline:** February 15. **Contact:** dzfoundation@dzshq.com.

3581 ■ Arlene Davis Scholarships *(Undergraduate/Scholarship)*

Purpose: To provide financial assistance to all qualified undergraduate students. **Focus:** Aviation. **Qualif.:** Applicants must be initiated, active, continuing members entering their sophomore or junior year, who are enrolled in courses showing an interest in aviation; must have a 3.0 grade average. **Criteria:** Candidate will be selected based on academic standing and financial need.

Funds Avail.: No specific amount. **Duration:** Annual. **To Apply:** Scholarship applications are available on the website and must be completed properly. Applicant must have the FAFSA reply form. **Deadline:** February 15. **Contact:** Application must be submitted at dzfoundation@dzshq.com.

3582 ■ Delta Zeta Undergraduate Scholarships *(Undergraduate/Scholarship)*

Purpose: To provide financial assistance to all qualified undergraduate students. **Focus:** General studies/Field of study not specified. **Qualif.:** Applicants must be initiated, active, continuing members of Delta Zeta entering junior or senior year; be outstanding in campus and chapter activities, and have maintained at least a B average (3.0). **Criteria:** Scholarship applications will be reviewed and evaluated by the committee. Recommendation for scholarship recipients will be made by the scholarship committees to the Foundation Board of Trustees for final selection.

Funds Avail.: $500-$2,500. **Duration:** Annual; one academic year. **To Apply:** Scholarship applications are available on the website and must be completed properly. Applicants must have the FAFSA reply form. **Deadline:** February 15. **Contact:** dzfoundation@dzshq.com.

3583 ■ Elizabeth M. Gruber Scholarships *(Graduate/Scholarship)*

Purpose: To provide financial assistance to all qualified undergraduate student. **Focus:** Liberal arts. **Qualif.:** Applicants must be Delta Zeta graduate students working toward a degree in a liberal arts area. **Criteria:** Preference will be given to Alpha Beta Chapter members or to Delta Zeta attending a university in the Midwest.

Funds Avail.: No specific amount. **Duration:** Annual. **To Apply:** Applicants must provide a transcript of record; must submit a statement indicating their special service to Delta Zeta, activities and/or community involvement, academic honors and/or honor societies, and personal statement about their need and desire to get the award; must have a list of employment records and at least two recommendation letter from a Delta Zeta (Alumnae Chapter President, College Chapter Director, and/or Regional Collegiate Coordinator), and one from Academic Graduate Advisor and/or Employer. **Deadline:** February 15. **Contact:** Application must be submitted at dzfoundation@dzshq.com.

3584 ■ Edith Head Scholarships *(Undergraduate/Scholarship)*

Purpose: To provide financial assistance to all qualified undergraduate students. **Focus:** Fashion design. **Qualif.:** Applicants must be initiated, active, continuing members of Delta Zeta pursuing a course study leading to a career in design, production, and merchandising of textile and apparel products, and/or costume design; must be junior or senior students, graduate level, or a professional school which offers fashion merchandising, textiles, and clothing or costume design; must have at least a 3.0 average. **Criteria:** Candidates will be selected based on the academic standing and financial need.

Funds Avail.: No specific amount. **Duration:** Annual. **To Apply:** Scholarship applications are available on the website and must be completed properly. Applicants must have the FAFSA reply form. **Deadline:** February 15. **Contact:** Application must be submitted at dzfoundation@dzshq.com.

3585 ■ Lavonne Heghinian Scholarships
(Undergraduate/Scholarship)

Purpose: To provide financial assistance to all qualified undergraduate students. **Focus:** General studies/Field of study not specified. **Qualif.:** Applicants must be initiated, active, continuing members of Delta Zeta in need of financial assistance; must have a 3.0 average. **Criteria:** Application will be evaluated based on the sorority service, campus involvement and employment. Preference will be given to Southern California applicants in accordance with Mrs. Heghinian's will.

Funds Avail.: No specific amount. **Duration:** Annual. **To Apply:** Scholarship applications are available on the website and must be completed properly. Applicantd must have the FAFSA reply form. **Deadline:** February 15. **Contact:** Application must be submitted at dzfoundation@dzshq.com.

3586 ■ Houston/Nancy Holliman Scholarships
(Undergraduate/Scholarship)

Purpose: To provide financial assistance to all qualified undergraduate students. **Focus:** Health sciences; Hearing and deafness; Speech and language pathology/Audiology. **Qualif.:** Applicant must be a junior or senior active, continuing member majoring in hearing and speech, audiology or an allied field; must have an academic achievements (maintaining a 3.0 average), campus honors and activities, and service to Delta Zeta. **Criteria:** Candidates will be selected based on academic standing, honors, and financial need.

Funds Avail.: No specific amount. **Duration:** Annual. **To Apply:** Scholarship applications are available on the website and must be completed properly. Applicant must have the FAFSA reply form. **Deadline:** February 15. **Contact:** Application must be submitted at dzfoundation@dzshq.com.

3587 ■ Sarah Jane Houston Scholarships
(Undergraduate/Scholarship)

Purpose: To provide financial assistance to all qualified undergraduate students. **Focus:** Education, English as a second language. **Qualif.:** Applicants must be undergraduate Delta Zeta members in good standing with 3.0 or higher grade point average and who are major field in English or in related fields such as speech, debate, drama, theater, or education. **Criteria:** Applicants from Delta Zeta chapters in Illinois will be given preference if all other qualifications are equal. Applicants will be evaluated based on academic achievements and campus activities.

Funds Avail.: No specific amount. **Duration:** Annual. **To Apply:** Scholarship applications are available in the website and must be completed properly. Applicants must have the FAFSA reply form. **Deadline:** February 15. **Contact:** dzfoundation@dzshq.com.

3588 ■ Huenefeld/Denton Scholarships
(Undergraduate/Scholarship)

Purpose: To provide financial assistance to all qualified undergraduate students. **Focus:** Child development; Education; Library and archival sciences. **Qualif.:** Applicants must be junior or senior initiated, active continuing members in need of financial help, seeking an undergraduate degree in child development/primary education or library science. **Criteria:** Applicants will be evaluated based on their academic achievements, campus activities, and service to Delta Zeta.

Funds Avail.: No specific amount. **Duration:** Annual. **To Apply:** Scholarship applications are available on the website and must be completed properly. Applicants must have the FAFSA reply form. **Deadline:** February 15. **Contact:** Application must be submitted at dzfoundation@dzshq.com.

3589 ■ Betsy B. and Garold A. Leach Scholarships for Museum Studies *(Undergraduate/Scholarship)*

Purpose: To provide financial assistance to all qualified undergraduate students. **Focus:** Museum science. **Qualif.:** Applicant must be an initiated, continuing member of Delta Zeta pursuing a course of study that could lead to a career in museum work; must be entering his/her junior or senior year or graduate level; must have a financial need and have at least 3.0 average. **Criteria:** Selection of candidates will be based on academic achievements, and campus activities.

Funds Avail.: No specific amount. **Duration:** Annual. **To Apply:** Scholarship applications are available on the website and must be completed properly. Applicant must have the FAFSA reply form. **Deadline:** February 15. **Contact:** Application must be submitted at dzfoundation@dzshq.com.

3590 ■ Elsa Ludeke Graduate Scholarships
(Graduate/Scholarship)

Purpose: To provide financial assistance to all qualified graduate students. **Focus:** General studies/Field of study not specified. **Qualif.:** Applicants must be initiated members in need of financial assistance; must have at least a B average (3.0); must be outstanding in undergraduate campus activities and in special service and leadership to Delta Zeta chapter. **Criteria:** Selection of applicant will be based on financial need and academic achievements.

Funds Avail.: No specific amount. **Duration:** Annual. **To Apply:** Applicants must provide a transcript of record; must submit a statement indicating special service to Delta Zeta, activities and/or community involvement, academic honors and/or honor societies, and personal statement about their need and desire to get the award; must have a list of employment records and at least two recommendation letters from a Delta Zeta (Alumnae Chapter President, College Chapter Director, and/or Regional Collegiate Coordinator), and one from Academic Graduate Advisor and/or Employer. **Deadline:** February 15. **Contact:** Application must be submitted at dzfoundation@dzshq.com.

3591 ■ John L. and Eleanore I. Mckinley Scholarships *(Undergraduate/Scholarship)*

Purpose: To provide financial assistance to all qualified undergraduate students. **Focus:** General studies/Field of study not specified. **Qualif.:** Applicants must be junior or senior Delta Zeta members in good standing; must have earned a B or better average at the conclusion of their sophomore year; must have achieved a high level of service to the Delta Zeta Sorority and their college community. **Criteria:** Financial need is considered.

Funds Avail.: No specific amount. **Duration:** Annual. **To Apply:** Scholarship applications are available on the website and must be completed properly. Applicants must

Awards are arranged alphabetically below their administering organizations

have the FAFSA reply form. **Deadline:** February 15. **Contact:** dzfoundation@dzshq.com.

3592 ■ Helen Woodruff Nolop Scholarships in Audiology and Allied Fields *(Graduate/Scholarship)*

Purpose: To assist qualified female students in pursuing an education. **Focus:** Health sciences; Speech and language pathology/Audiology. **Qualif.:** Applicant must be a graduate student in audiology or in allied field and with 3.0 cumulative grade average. **Criteria:** Selection of applicant will be based on academic achievement and financial need.

Funds Avail.: No specific amount. **Duration:** Annual. **To Apply:** Applicant must provide a transcript of record; must submit a statement indicating special service to Delta Zeta, activities and/or community involvement, academic honors and/or honor societies, and personal statement about need and desire to get the award; must have a list of employment records and at least two recommendation letters from a Delta Zeta (Alumnae Chapter President, College Chapter Director, and/or Regional Collegiate Coordinator), and one from Academic Graduate Advisor and/or Employer. **Deadline:** February 15. **Contact:** dzfoundation@dzshq.com.

3593 ■ Gail Patrick Charitable Trust Scholarships *(Undergraduate/Scholarship)*

Purpose: To provide financial assistance to all qualified undergraduate student. **Focus:** General studies/Field of study not specified. **Qualif.:** Applicants must be initiated, active, continuing Delta Zeta members in need of financial assistance; must be entering their junior or senior year. **Criteria:** Applicants will be evaluated based on academic achievements and campus activities.

Funds Avail.: $2,500. **Duration:** Annual. **To Apply:** Scholarship applications are available on the website and must be completed properly. Applicants must have the FAFSA reply form. **Deadline:** February 15. **Contact:** dzfoundation@dzshq.com.

3594 ■ Dorothy Worden Ronken Scholarships *(Graduate/Scholarship)*

Purpose: To provide financial assistance to all qualified graduate students. **Focus:** Business; Education. **Qualif.:** Applicants must be Delta Zeta graduate students working on a degree in education or business; must be initiated continuing members in good standing in a collegiate chapter with 3.0 cumulative grade average. **Criteria:** Preference will be given to applicants from the Alpha Alpha chapter of Northwestern University.

Funds Avail.: No specific amount. **Duration:** Annual. **To Apply:** Applicants must provide a transcript of record; must submit a statement indicating their special service to Delta Zeta, activities and/or community involvement, academic honors and/or honor societies, and personal statement about need and desire to get the award; must have a list of employment records and at least two recommendation letters from a Delta Zeta (Alumnae Chapter President, College Chapter Director, and/or Regional Collegiate Coordinator), and one from Academic Graduate Advisor and/or employer. **Deadline:** February 15. **Contact:** dzfoundation@dzshq.com.

3595 ■ Elizabeth Coulter Stephenson Scholarships *(Undergraduate/Scholarship, Grant)*

Purpose: To provide financial assistance to all qualified undergraduate students. **Focus:** General studies/Field of study not specified. **Qualif.:** Applicants must be outstanding in campus and chapter activities; must have held, or must currently hold, an executive board position; must have at least 3.0 average; must have been adversely affected, or parents have been adversely affected by a disaster. **Criteria:** Preference will be given to initiated, active, continuing members of Delta Zeta in their junior or senior year who need a financial assistant.

Funds Avail.: $1,000. **Duration:** Annual. **To Apply:** Application forms are available in the website. Applicants must provide the official transcript; must have statement about special service to Delta Zeta, campus activities and/or community involvement, and academic honors; must have the list of employment record; must submit a recommendation letter from the college chapter director (CCD) and if chapter has no CCD, a letter from RCC will suffice. **Deadline:** February 15. **Contact:** Application materials must be sent at dzfoundation@dzshq.com.

3596 ■ Thornberg/Havens Scholarships *(Undergraduate/Scholarship)*

Purpose: To provide financial assistance to all qualified undergraduate students. **Focus:** General studies/Field of study not specified. **Qualif.:** Applicants must be undergraduate and/or graduate Delta Zeta students in good standing; must be initiated members in need of financial assistance who have shown outstanding campus and chapter activities; must have at least 3.0 undergraduate average. **Criteria:** Candidates will be selected based on their academic standing and financial need.

Funds Avail.: No specific amount. **Duration:** Annual. **To Apply:** Scholarship applications are available on the website and must be completed properly. Applicants must have the FAFSA reply form. **Deadline:** February 15. **Contact:** Application must be submitted at dzfoundation@dzshq.com.

3597 ■ DeMolay International
10200 NW Ambassador Dr.
Kansas City, MO 64153
Ph: (816)891-8333
Fax: (816)891-9062
Free: 800-336-6529
E-mail: demolay@demolay.org
URL: demolay.org
Facebook: www.facebook.com/DeMolay.International
Twitter: twitter.com/demolay

3598 ■ Frank S. Land Scholarships *(Undergraduate/Scholarship)*

Purpose: To provide financial assistance for eligible members of DeMolay. **Focus:** General studies/Field of study not specified. **Qualif.:** Applicants must be active members of DeMolay who have not yet reached their majority or 21st birthday. **Criteria:** Applicants are evaluated based on personal attributes.

Funds Avail.: No specific amount. **Duration:** Annual. **To Apply:** Applicants may download the scholarship application form from the Foundation's website. **Deadline:** April 1.

3599 ■ Denver Scholarship Foundation (DSF)
303 E 17th Ave., Ste. 200
Denver, CO 80203
Ph: (303)951-4140

Awards are arranged alphabetically below their administering organizations

Fax: (720)746-5139
E-mail: info@denverscholarship.org
URL: www.denverscholarship.org
Facebook: www.facebook.com/DSFScholars
Twitter: twitter.com/DenvScholarFdtn

3600 ■ Denver Scholarship Foundation Scholarships (Undergraduate/Scholarship)

Purpose: To inspire and empower Denver Public School (DPS) students to achieve their post-secondary goals. **Focus:** General studies/Field of study not specified. **Qualif.:** Applicant must be a DPS graduate, enrolled and included in the State Census (October 1st Count) at a participating DPS school for at least one year immediately preceding graduation; and eligible to receive federal student financial aid; must be a U.S. citizen, permanent resident or other eligible non-citizen. **Criteria:** Awards will be given based on merit and need.

Funds Avail.: No specific amount. **To Apply:** Applicant must complete and submit the DSF Scholarship Application online. **Deadline:** July 15. **Remarks:** All mailings, fax coversheets or e-mail messages must include the student's full name, student ID number, phone number and e-mail address.

3601 ■ Deutscher Akademischer Austausch Dienst (DAAD)

871 United Nations Plz.
New York, NY 10017
Ph: (212)758-3223
Fax: (212)755-5780
E-mail: daadny@daad.org
URL: www.daad.org
Facebook: www.facebook.com/DAADNorthAmerica
Twitter: twitter.com/daadnewyork

3602 ■ Leo Baeck Institute - DAAD Fellowships (Doctorate/Fellowship)

Purpose: To provide financial assistance for students doing dissertation research work and to academics writing a scholarly essay or book. **Focus:** German studies. **Qualif.:** Applicants must be US citizens and Ph.D. candidates or recent Ph.D.'s (degree awarded within the last two years). **Criteria:** Selection shall be based on the aforementioned qualifications and compliance with the application details.

Funds Avail.: $2,000. **Duration:** Annual. **Number Awarded:** 2. **To Apply:** Applicants must submit the following: completed application form; curriculum vitae; a full description of the research project; for doctoral students, send official transcripts for graduate and undergraduate work, evidence of enrollment in a PhD program, one letter of recommendation by their doctoral advisor and one by another scholar familiar with their work; for PhDs, evidence of their degree (transcripts not required); and two letters of recommendation from two colleagues familiar with their research. **Contact:** Leo Baeck Institute, Address: 15 W 16th St. New York, New York 10011; Phone: 212-744-6400; Fax: 212-988-1305; Email: lbaeck@lbi.cjh.org.

3603 ■ DAAD Learn German in Germany Grants (Doctorate/Grant)

Purpose: To encourage faculty members who are not in German Studies, German Language and Literature, and German Translation and Interpretation to attend intensive language courses at Goethe-Instituts in Germany. **Focus:** German studies. **Qualif.:** Applicants must be citizens or permanent residents of the United States or Canada and they are scholars who hold a Ph.D. (or equivalent) and have been working in research or teaching full-time at a university or research institution in the United States or Canada for at least two years after receipt of the doctorate; must be in mid-career and are under 46 years of age; must have a basic knowledge of German; must not have previously studied in a German-speaking country for more than two months and/or received a grant to attend a German language course from DAAD or any other organization within the last three years. **Criteria:** Preference will be given to applicants in the social sciences, the natural sciences, engineering and professional schools.

Funds Avail.: 1,800 Euros. **Duration:** Annual. **Number Awarded:** 2. **To Apply:** Applicants must submit a completed DAAD application form; curriculum vitae not to exceed five pages; a detailed statement explaining why the applicant wants to attend a Goethe Institute language course in Germany; accomplish the language evaluation (self-test form enclosed with application); must have the list of publications and a list of courses taught during the previous academic year. **Deadline:** January 31. **Contact:** E-mail: thomanek@daad.org.

3604 ■ DAAD Study Scholarship Awards (Graduate/Scholarship)

Purpose: To provide the opportunity to study in Germany, or complete a Master's degree course and obtain a degree from a German higher education institution. **Focus:** Dentistry; Medicine; Pharmacy; Veterinary science and medicine. **Qualif.:** Applicants must be graduating seniors (fourth or final year of undergraduate studies) or those with undergraduate degree in all academic fields; must be enrolled full-time at any North American University; citizens of US or Canada but foreigners should have studied at any accredited US or Canadian university for two years; requested to have a study project to make a stay in Germany essential. **Criteria:** Preference will be given to applicants who have been invited by a faculty member at a German university to study at a particular university department.

Funds Avail.: No specific amount. **Duration:** Annual. **To Apply:** Applicant must submit the application form with the supplemental form (for music, fine arts, dance only), CV/Resume, study proposal, two letters of recommendation, evidence of contact with German Institution, DAAD Language evaluation form and transcript of records. **Deadline:** November 4 for applicants outside the field of music, visual arts and performring arts. **Contact:** kim@daad.org.

3605 ■ DAAD Undergraduate Scholarship Program (Undergraduate/Scholarship)

Purpose: To support undergraduate US and Canadian students interested in studying, doing research or completing an internship in Germany. **Focus:** General studies/Field of study not specified. **Qualif.:** Applicants must be currently second or third year students and will be in their third and fourth year during their stay in Germany; must be U.S., Canadian citizens or permanent residents; has interest in contemporary German and European affairs; and full-time students in an undergraduate degree-granting program at an accredited North American college or university. Students with outstanding academic records and personal integrity as evinced by both their grades and letters of recommendation are eligible to apply. **Criteria:** Preference will be given to students whose projects or programs are

Awards are arranged alphabetically below their administering organizations

based at an organized by a German university.

Funds Avail.: 650 Euros. **Duration:** One semester. **To Apply:** Applicants must submit the original printout of the application with their signature and three copies of the following supplemental documents: resume; an approximately three pages of project proposal; two recommendation letters from major professors; acceptance into Study Abroad Program, Exchange Program, letter by mentor or invitation from a German university; transcripts; and language evaluation certificate. **Deadline:** January 31.

3606 ■ Faculty Research Visit Grants (Doctorate/Grant, Award)

Purpose: To pursue research at universities, libraries, archives, institutes or laboratories in Germany. **Focus:** General studies/Field of study not specified. **Qualif.:** Applicants must be scholars at United States, Canadian universities or research institutions holding a PhD. (or equivalent); have been working in research or teaching as full time for at least two years after receipt of the doctorate; be U.S. or Canadian citizens (German nationals must have been working in a U.S. or Canadian institution for six consecutive years); should possess adequate knowledge of the German language; applicants may not hold a DAAD grant and a grant from another German or German-American organization concurrently for the same project. Previous grantees can only be qualified after three years. **Criteria:** Scholarship decisions are made by an independent academic selection committee based on an outstanding academic record and potential; validity and feasibility of the proposed project; and the necessity to carry it out in Germany.

Funds Avail.: 2,000 Euros; 2,150 Euros; 2,300 Euros. **Duration:** Biennial; one to three months program. **To Apply:** Applicants must submit completed DAAD application form entitled "Research Visit for Faculty"; a not to exceed five pages curriculum vitae; complete list of publications; an up to five pages detailed description of the research project which includes a literature review and information on significance, methodology, availability or quality of data and the need for carrying out research in Germany; and letter(s) of invitation from the German institution(s). **Deadline:** October 15; May 15.

3607 ■ German Studies Research Grants (Undergraduate/Grant, Award)

Purpose: To encourage research and promote the study of cultural, political, historical, economic, and social aspects of modern and contemporary German affairs from an inter and multidisciplinary perspective. **Focus:** German studies. **Qualif.:** Applicants must be undergraduate students with at least junior standing pursuing German Studies nominated by their department and/or program chair; must be U.S. citizens who are enrolled full time at the university that nominates them; have completed at least two years of college degree in German; and with a minimum of three courses in German Studies. **Criteria:** Selection of applicants will be based on the application and other supporting documents.

Funds Avail.: $1,500-$3,000. **To Apply:** Applicants must submit a completed DAAD application form; curriculum vitae; detailed description of the research project or the pre-dissertation proposal; budget statement; list of German language and German Studies courses taken; two letters of recommendation wherein, one must come from professor supervising the German Studies curriculum or the research project; DAAD language evaluation form signed by a German Department faculty member; and an official transcript of records. **Contact:** thomanek@daad.org.

3608 ■ Hochschulsommerkurse (Undergraduate/Grant, Award)

Purpose: To attend a broad range of summer courses at German universities which focus mainly on literary, cultural, political and economic aspects of modern and contemporary Germany. **Focus:** German studies. **Qualif.:** Applicants must be full-time students at any colleges or universities in U.S. and Canada; must have focus in any field of study; must at least reached their junior standing or third year (10 full-course credits for Canadians) at the time of application. **Criteria:** Applicants will be assessed on the basis of their academic and professional future.

Funds Avail.: 850 Euros. **To Apply:** Applicants must submit a completed DAAD application form; autobiographical essay in German; a detailed, English statement of approximately 500 words explaining why the applicant wants to attend a university summer course; recommendation letter written by a professor in the applicant's major field of study but the recommendation should be different from professor who evaluates the language proficiency; complete, official transcripts of all post-secondary studies; DAAD language evaluation form (Sprachzeugnis) signed by any member of German Department at the applicant's institution or by an official of a Goethe Institute. **Deadline:** December 15. **Contact:** gaedeke@daad.org.

3609 ■ Intensive Language Course Grants (Doctorate/Grant)

Purpose: To enhance language proficiency in Germany. **Focus:** German studies. **Qualif.:** Applicants must be full-time students currently enrolled in a graduate program in all fields of study except English, German, or any other modern language or literature; must have completed three semesters of college German or have achieved an equivalent level of language proficiency; foreign nationals other than U.S. and Canada must be full-time graduate students in a U.S. or Canadian university for at least one academic year; must have completed three semesters of college German or equivalent level of language proficiency; not a previous grantee for the past three years; must be no older than 32. **Criteria:** Applicants will be assessed based on academic record and statements of project and professional future.

Funds Avail.: 2,300 Euros plus 300-450 Euros travel subsidy. **Duration:** Eight weeks. **To Apply:** Applicants must submit a complete DAAD application form; a detailed statement (in English) of approximately 500 words explaining why the applicant wants to attend the intensive language course; resume; a recommendation letter from a professor in the applicant's major field of study; complete transcript of records; DAAD language evaluation form (Sprachzeugnis); list of German language courses taken. Application must be sent to: DAAD New York office. **Deadline:** December 15.

3610 ■ Study Scholarships for Artists or Musicians (Graduate/Scholarship)

Purpose: To provide the opportunity to study in Germany, or complete a postgraduate degree course and obtain a degree from a German higher education institution. **Focus:** Architecture; Art; Dance; Music. **Qualif.:** Applicants in the fields of Fine Arts, Architecture, Music and Dance, other academic fields are welcome to apply for the regular Study Scholarship; graduating seniors must be full-time at an accredited university for two years; U.S. or Canadian citizens.

Awards are arranged alphabetically below their administering organizations

Criteria: Preference will be given to applicants who have been invited by a faculty member at a German university to study at a particular university department.
Funds Avail.: 750 Euros. **Duration:** Annual. **To Apply:** Applicant must complete the online application form available in the website and must have the following: Supplemental materials, CV/Resume, Study proposal, two letters of recommendation, evidence of contact with German Institution and transcript of records.

3611 ■ Development Fund for Black Students in Science and Technology (DFBSST)
2705 Bladensburg Rd. NE
Washington, DC 20018
Ph: (202)635-3604
URL: www.dfbsstscholarship.org

3612 ■ Development Fund for Black Students in Science and Technology Scholarships
(Undergraduate/Scholarship)

Purpose: To provide scholarships to African American undergraduate students. **Focus:** Science; Technology. **Qualif.:** Applicants must meet the following criteria: African-American heritage; undergraduate students majoring (or intending to major) in a technical field of study (i.e., engineering, math, science, etc.); enrollment at one of the predominantly Black colleges or universities; U.S. citizenship or permanent residency. **Criteria:** Awards will be based on academic achievement, personal essay describing career goals, current and past relevant extracurricular activities, recommendations from teachers and guidance counselors and financial need.
Funds Avail.: $2,000. **Duration:** Annual; up to 4 years. **To Apply:** Applicants must submit a completed application form. **Deadline:** June 15. **Contact:** Development Fund for Black Students in Science and Technology at the above address.

3613 ■ Diabetes Hope Foundation
6150 Dixie Rd., Unit 1
Mississauga, ON, Canada L5T 2E2
Ph: (905)670-0557
Fax: (905)565-7296
E-mail: info@diabeteshopefoundation.com
URL: www.diabeteshopefoundation.com
Facebook: www.facebook.com/diabeteshopefoundation

3614 ■ Diabetes Hope Foundation Scholarships
(Undergraduate/Scholarship)

Purpose: To provide educational assistance to students with diabetes in continuing their studies. **Focus:** General studies/Field of study not specified. **Qualif.:** Applicant must be a resident of Ontario, Canada; must be in the transition year of Diabetes Care by a Pediatric Health Care team; must have received care for type 1 or 2 Diabetes by a Pediatric Health Care team for a minimum of 1 year; must demonstrate competence in self management. **Criteria:** Preference will be given for those who are in need.
Funds Avail.: No specific amount. **Duration:** Annual; One year. **Number Awarded:** 25 to 40. **To Apply:** Applicant must provide an endorsement letter from a member of their Pediatric Health Care team confirming their attendance and documenting successful self-management. **Deadline:** March 9; March 30.

3615 ■ Diabetes Scholars Foundation (DSF)
2118 Plum Grove Rd., No. 356
Rolling Meadows, IL 60008
Ph: (312)215-9861
Fax: (847)991-8739
E-mail: m.podjasek@diabetesscholars.org
URL: www.diabetesscholars.org

3616 ■ Diabetes Scholars Foundation College Scholarships *(Undergraduate/Scholarship)*

Purpose: To financially support incoming freshmen seeking a higher education at an accredited four year university, college, technical or trade school. **Focus:** Arts; Athletics; Business; Diabetes; Health care services; Mental health; Nursing; Political science. **Qualif.:** Applicants must be high school seniors and incoming freshmen with Type 1 diabetes seeking a higher education at an accredited four year university, college, technical or trade school. Must also be U.S. citizens or permanent residents. **Criteria:** Selection will be based on the committee's criteria.
Funds Avail.: Amount varies. **Duration:** Annual. **To Apply:** Application package, including letters of recommendations, must be fully submitted online. **Deadline:** April 15.

3617 ■ Dickey Rural Networks (DRN)
9628 Hwy. 281
Ellendale, ND 58436
Ph: (701)344-5000
Free: 877-559-4692
E-mail: marketing@drtel.com
URL: www.drtel.net
Facebook: www.facebook.com/dickeyruralnetworks
Twitter: www.twitter.com/dickeyrural

3618 ■ Dickey Rural Networks College Scholarship Program *(Undergraduate, Vocational/Occupational/ Scholarship)*

Purpose: To provide financial assistance to those students who wants to further their college education. **Focus:** Telecommunications systems. **Qualif.:** Applicants must be graduating high school seniors; must receive local telecommunications service from a current NTCA member (except for students sponsored by an associate member company); must be accepted by an accredited two or four-year college, university or vocational-technical school; must have at least a C grade point average (GPA); must have academic credentials within an average to above-average range; must express an interest to return to a rural community following graduation; and must be sponsored by a contributor to, or supporter of, the Foundation for Rural Service. **Criteria:** Applicants are evaluated based on academic credentials and financial need.
Funds Avail.: $3,000. **Number Awarded:** 30. **To Apply:** Applicants must complete and print the DRN/FRS Scholarship Application online, which is also available from the school counselor, with the complete instructions and checklist of items to be considered. **Deadline:** February 13.

3619 ■ Bill Dickey Scholarship Association
1301 E Washington St., Ste. 200
Phoenix, AZ 85034
Ph: (602)258-7851
Fax: (602)258-3412

Awards are arranged alphabetically below their administering organizations

URL: www.nmjgsa.org

3620 ■ Bill Dickey Scholarship Association Scholarships (Undergraduate/Scholarship)

Purpose: To provide financial support to deserving undergraduate students. **Focus:** General studies/Field of study not specified. **Qualif.:** Applicants must be high school seniors who are already in BDSA database as well as undergraduate students that previously received a scholarship as freshmen. **Criteria:** Selection will be based on academic achievement, entrance exam scores, financial need, references, evidence of community service and golfing ability.

Funds Avail.: Up to $14,000. **Duration:** Annual; up to 4 years. **To Apply:** Applicants must check the available website to enter their database profile and to gain further information regarding the award. **Deadline:** May 11. **Contact:** Bill Dickey Scholarship Association, at the above address.

3621 ■ Dietetics in Health Care Communities (DHCC)

c/o Academy of Nutrition and Dietetics
PO Box 4489
Carol Stream, IL 60197-4489
Ph: (319)235-0991
Fax: (319)235-7224
Free: 800-877-1600
E-mail: dhccdpg@mchsi.com
URL: www.dhccdpg.org
Facebook: www.facebook.com/dieteticsinhealthcarecommunities15

3622 ■ Gaynold Jensen Education Stipends (Postdoctorate, Other/Scholarship)

Purpose: To provide learning programs to improve the contributions of consultant dietitians to health care. **Focus:** Health care services. **Qualif.:** Applicants must be American Dietetic Association members; must be at least a two-year member in Consultant Dietitians in Health Care Facilities; a registered dietitian; currently practicing as a consultant dietitian; planning to expand knowledge in the consultant role. **Criteria:** Recipients are selected based on the committee's review of how and why the program will improve the applicant's contributions as a consultant dietitian in health care.

Funds Avail.: No specific amount. **Duration:** Annual. **To Apply:** Applicants must send the application forms (available at the website).

3623 ■ Directed Energy Professional Society (DEPS)

7770 Jefferson St. NE, Ste. 440
Albuquerque, NM 87109
Ph: (505)998-4910
Fax: (505)998-4917
E-mail: office@deps.org
URL: www.deps.org

3624 ■ DEPS Graduate Scholarship Program (Graduate/Scholarship)

Purpose: To provide support of research and development of DE technology. **Focus:** Chemistry; Engineering, Aerospace/Aeronautical/Astronautical; Engineering, Chemical; Engineering, Electrical; Engineering, Optical; Materials research/science; Physics. **Qualif.:** Applicants must be U.S. citizens or individuals who have demonstrated interest in American citizenship; must be full-time graduate students at a U.S. school; must be pursuing or currently studying DE technology areas of HEL or HPM with scopes similar to those researches published in the Journal of Directed Energy. **Criteria:** Applicants are selected based on the reviews conducted by the DEPS Board of Scientific and Engineering Advisors' (BSEA).

Funds Avail.: Amount varies. **Duration:** Annual. **Number Awarded:** Varies. **To Apply:** Applicants must submit completed application form available at the website; official transcripts of undergraduate and graduate studies sent directly from the school; letter of interest in DE technology and statement of proposed research; and a reference letter from a potential or current research advisor including an assessment of the applicant's potential and description of facilities to be employed for the research; and letter of intent to become U.S. citizen. **Deadline:** April 15. **Contact:** Mark Neice, DEPS Executive Director, at mark@deps.org.

3625 ■ Dirksen Congressional Center

2815 Broadway
Pekin, IL 61554-4219
Ph: (309)347-7113
Fax: (309)347-6412
E-mail: info@dirksencenter.org
URL: www.dirksencenter.org

3626 ■ Congressional Research Awards (Graduate/Award)

Purpose: To fund research on congressional leadership and related studies about the U.S. Congress. **Focus:** Government. **Qualif.:** Applicants must have a serious interest in studying the Congress; must be political scientists, historians, biographers, scholars of public administration or American studies, and journalists; must be graduate students who have successfully defended their dissertation prospectus to apply and awards a significant portion of the funds for dissertation research; must be U.S. citizens who reside in the United States. **Criteria:** Recipients are selected based on the project design; plan of work; dissemination; applicant's qualifications; relationship of the project to the Centers Program goals and to current work in the field; and appropriateness of the project request for the requirements.

Funds Avail.: $35,000. **Duration:** Annual. **To Apply:** Applicants must submit the original and four copies of application summary sheet listing the name and contact information not exceeding 100-words; a description of the project goals, methods, and intended results, demonstrating clearly its importance to the award program priorities; A vitae including a list of publications; Original and five copies of a letter of reference from the person directing their dissertation work; a proposal letter from the responsible official stipulating that no indirect or overhead costs will be charged against the grant. **Deadline:** March 1. **Contact:** Frank H. Mackaman at the above address, fmackaman@dirksencenter.org.

3627 ■ Ray and Kathy LaHood Scholarships for the Study of American Government (Undergraduate/Scholarship)

Purpose: To provide financial support for Bradley University juniors who are majoring in a discipline related to The Dirksen Center's purpose and interest or in subjects related to the study of Federal Government. **Focus:** Government. **Qualif.:** Applicants must: be juniors in good standing entering their senior year of study in a field related to the study of the U.S. government; be attending Bradley University; have a grade point average (on a four-point scale) of at least 3.5 overall and 3.5 in their major; and, agree to meet with Ray or Kathy LaHood during the second semester of their senior year. **Criteria:** Recipients will be selected based on scholastic records.

Funds Avail.: No specific amount. **Duration:** Annual. **To Apply:** Applicants must fill out the required scholarship form. They must agree to write a 250-word evaluation of the impact of their scholarship before the end of their senior year. **Contact:** Brad McMillan, Executive Director Institute for Principled Leadership, bmcmillan@bradley.edu.

3628 ■ The Disability Care Center
2875 S Orange Ave., Ste. 500
Orlando, FL 32806
Fax: (877)570-0649
Free: 888-504-0035
URL: www.disabilitycarecenter.org

3629 ■ Disability Care Center Disabled Student Scholarships (Undergraduate/Scholarship)

Purpose: To assist students who are suffering from a debilitating condition(s) while continuing their education at a college institution. **Focus:** General studies/Field of study not specified. **Qualif.:** Applicants must be enrolled in a U.S. college institution with at least 12 credit hours of classes for the upcoming fall semester; must be legal residents of the United States; must have a GPA of 2.5 from their most recent transcript (high school or college); and must have a medically diagnosed impairment. **Criteria:** Selection will be based on the aforementioned qualifications and the submitted essays.

Funds Avail.: $500. **Number Awarded:** 1. **To Apply:** Applicants will be required to write a short essay between 500 and 1,500 words about the essay topic given here. Topic is about describing an obstacle or hardship that arose due to their conditions and how they were able to overcome such. They should explain the impact it has had on their lives and how such will influence their future. Additional requirement is their most recent transcript. **Deadline:** August 1. **Contact:** Send e-mail at scholarship@disabilitycarecenter.org.

3630 ■ Disability Care Center Special Education Scholarships (Undergraduate/Scholarship)

Purpose: To support students who are pursuing a degree in special education. **Focus:** Education; Education, Special. **Qualif.:** Applicants must be enrolled in a U.S. college institution with at least 12 credit hours of classes for the upcoming fall semester; must be legal residents of the United States; must have a GPA of 2.5 from their most recent transcript (high school or college); and must be currently majoring in special education. **Criteria:** Selection will be based on the aforementioned qualifications and the submitted essays.

Funds Avail.: $500. **Number Awarded:** 1. **To Apply:** Applicants will be required to write a short essay between 500 and 1,500 words about the essay topic given here. They must explain why they are pursuing a degree in special education and how they plan to make a difference in the lives of the disabled. Additional requirement is a letter of recommendation from a creditable source. **Deadline:** August 1. **Contact:** Send e-mail at scholarship@disabilitycarecenter.org.

3631 ■ Disabled American Veterans (DAV)
PO Box 14301
Cincinnati, OH 45250-0301
Free: 877-426-2838
URL: www.dav.org
Facebook: www.facebook.com/DAV
Twitter: twitter.com/davhq

3632 ■ Jesse Brown Memorial Youth Scholarship Program (Advanced Professional/Scholarship)

Purpose: To provide financial assistance to young volunteers who play active roles in the Department of Veterans Affairs Voluntary Service programs to continue their education. **Focus:** General studies/Field of study not specified. **Qualif.:** Applicants must be any volunteers who are at the age of 21 or younger and have volunteered for a minimum of 100 hours at a VA medical center during the previous year; immediate family members of the DAV national organization are also eligible. **Criteria:** Applicants will be evaluated based on criteria designed by the Scholarship Selection Committee.

Funds Avail.: Varies. **Duration:** Annual. **Number Awarded:** 8. **To Apply:** Nominations must be submitted by the Voluntary Service Program Manager at the VA medical center, DAV Department Commander. Students must submit a self-nomination form which is available online, including an essay and any supporting documentation. **Deadline:** February.

3633 ■ Discover Financial Services (DFS)
2500 Lake Cook Rd.
Riverwoods, IL 60015
Fax: (224)405-0900
Free: 800-347-2683
E-mail: legal@discoverfinancial.com
URL: www.discover.com
Facebook: www.facebook.com/discover
Twitter: www.twitter.com/discover

3634 ■ Discover Bar Exam Loans (Graduate/Loan)

Purpose: To help cover the bar exam prep classes and living expenses. **Focus:** Law. **Qualif.:** Applicants must have graduated within the past 6 months or be enrolled at least half-time and making satisfactory academic progress in their final year of study in a graduate law degree program; must be US citizens; permanent residents or international students. International students require a Social Security number and a cosigner; must be 16 years or older at the time of application; must pass a credit check. **Criteria:** Selection will be based on the committee's criteria.

Funds Avail.: Up to $16,000 for bar exam preparation; minimum of $1,000 for each loan. **Duration:** Annual. **To Apply:** Interested students must visit the website for the online application process.

3635 ■ Discover Graduate Loans (Graduate, Master's, Doctorate/Loan)

Purpose: To address the needs of students enrolled in a master's or doctoral degree programs. **Focus:** General studies/Field of study not specified. **Qualif.:** Applicants must be students enrolled at least half-time in a graduate program at an eligible school; must be seeking a degree; must be making satisfactory academic progress as defined by their school; must be US citizens, permanent residents or international students. International students require a Social Security number and a cosigner; must be 16 years or older at the time of application; must pass a credit check. **Criteria:** Selection will be based on the committee's criteria. **Funds Avail.:** Varies. **Duration:** Annual. **To Apply:** Interested applicants must visit the website for the online application process.

3636 ■ Discover Health Professions Loans
(Graduate/Loan)

Purpose: To address the needs of students enrolled in a health professions graduate program. **Focus:** Dentistry; Medical assisting; Medicine, Osteopathic; Nursing; Occupational therapy; Optometry; Pharmacy; Physical therapy; Podiatry; Veterinary science and medicine. **Qualif.:** Applicants must be students enrolled at least half-time in a health professions graduate program at an eligible school; must be seeking a degree; must be making satisfactory academic progress as defined by their school; must be US citizens, permanent residents or international students. International students require a Social Security number and a cosigner; must be 16 years or older at the time of application; must pass a credit check. **Criteria:** Selection will be based on the committee's criteria. **Funds Avail.:** Minimum of $1,000 per year. **Duration:** Annual. **To Apply:** Interested applicants may visit the website for the online application.

3637 ■ Discover Law Loans *(Graduate/Loan)*

Purpose: To address the needs of students enrolled in a graduate program at an eligible law school. **Focus:** Law. **Qualif.:** Applicants must be students enrolled at least half-time in a graduate program at an eligible law school; must be seeking a degree; must be making satisfactory academic progress as defined by their school; must be US citizens, permanent residents or international students. International students require a Social Security number and a cosigner; must be 16 years or older at the time of application; must pass a credit check. **Criteria:** Selection will be based on the committee's criteria. **Funds Avail.:** Minimum of $1,000. **Duration:** Annual. **To Apply:** Interested students must visit the website for the online application.

3638 ■ Discover MBA Loans *(Graduate/Loan)*

Purpose: To address the needs of students enrolled in a graduate program at an eligible business school. **Focus:** Business. **Qualif.:** Applicants must be students enrolled at least half-time in a graduate program at an eligible business school; must be seeking a degree; must be making satisfactory academic progress as defined by their school; must be US citizens, permanent residents or international students. International students require a Social Security number and a cosigner; must be 16 years or older at the time of application; must pass a credit check. **Criteria:** Selection will be based on the committee's criteria. **Funds Avail.:** Minimum of $1,000. **Duration:** Annual. **To Apply:** Interested students must visit the website for the online application.

3639 ■ Discover Residency Loans *(Graduate/Loan)*

Purpose: To cover the cost of residency, internship, relocation and board exam review. **Focus:** Dentistry; Medical assisting; Medicine, Osteopathic; Nursing; Occupational therapy; Optometry; Pharmacy; Physical sciences; Podiatry; Veterinary science and medicine. **Qualif.:** Applicants must have graduated within the past 12 months or be enrolled at least half-time and making satisfactory academic progress in their final year of study in a graduate health professions program; must be US citizens, permanent residents or international students. International students require a Social Security number and a cosigner; must be 16 years or older at the time of application; must pass a credit check. **Criteria:** Selection will be based on the committee's criteria. **Funds Avail.:** Varies. **Duration:** Annual. **To Apply:** Interested students must visit the website for the online application process.

3640 ■ The Distinguished Flying Cross Society (DFCS)
PO Box 502408
San Diego, CA 92150
Free: 866-332-6332
E-mail: dfcs@dfcsociety.org
URL: www.dfcsociety.org

3641 ■ Distinguished Flying Cross Society Scholarships *(Undergraduate/Scholarship)*

Purpose: To support dependents of DFC Society members in the pursuit of continuing higher education. **Focus:** Aviation. **Qualif.:** Applicants must be descendants (or legally adopted children) of a DFC Society member; must be attending the Spring Semester at an accredited institution of higher education in the pursuit of an undergraduate degree. **Criteria:** Recipients will be selected based on academic achievement. **Funds Avail.:** $1,000. **Number Awarded:** 4. **To Apply:** Applicants must provide (500-word) essay on why they deserve a DFCS Scholarship; SAT/SCAT scores; official high school transcript; and a letter from DFCS member attesting that he/she is a descendant of a DFCS member. **Deadline:** November 15.

3642 ■ Distinguished Young Women
751 Government St.
Mobile, AL 36602
Ph: (251)438-3621
Fax: (251)431-0063
URL: distinguishedyw.org
Facebook: www.facebook.com/DistinguishedYW

3643 ■ Distinguished Young Women Scholarships
(Undergraduate/Scholarship)

Purpose: To give every young woman the opportunity to further their education and prepare for a successful future. Awarded in two categories: Cash Scholarships; College-Granted Scholarships. **Focus:** General studies/Field of study not specified. **Qualif.:** Applicants must be enrolled in their chosen field of study at an approved school or institution. **Criteria:** Selection will be based on the submitted application. **Funds Avail.:** No specific amount. **To Apply:** Applicants must submit a completed application and must complete a Scholarship Funds Request and Transcript Release Statement from and return it to the Foundation.

3644 ■ Dixon Hughes Goodman L.L.P.
440 Monticello Ave., Ste. 1400
Norfolk, VA 23510-2103

Ph: (757)624-5100
Fax: (757)624-5233
Free: 866-455-3261
E-mail: tasinfo@dhgllp.com
URL: www.dhgllp.com

3645 ■ Dixon Hughes Goodman LLP Annual Scholarship (Undergraduate/Scholarship)

Purpose: To help promising students pursue public accounting as a profession. **Focus:** Accounting. **Qualif.:** Applicant must be a U.S. citizen; a junior or senior accounting major; currently enrolled in an accredited Virginia college or university with the intent to take the CPA Exam; and have a minimum overall and accounting GPA of 3.0 or higher. **Criteria:** Award is given based on the merit of the application.

Funds Avail.: $10,000. **Duration:** Annual. **Number Awarded:** 1. **To Apply:** Applicants must submit a completed scholarship application together with the essay; letter of recommendation from a faculty member; a current resume; and recent official transcript reflecting GPA; application must be typed or printed.

3646 ■ Dog Fence DIY
13101 Preston
Dallas, TX 75240
Free: 888-936-4349
URL: www.dogfencediy.com

3647 ■ Veterinary and Pre-Veterinary Academic Scholarships (Undergraduate/Scholarship)

Purpose: To provide assistance to pre-veterinary and veterinary students with their education. **Focus:** Biology; Veterinary science and medicine. **Qualif.:** Applicants must be undergraduate students enrolled in a Doctor of Veterinary Medicine program, undergraduate biology or pre-veterinary studies program or the equivalent; must have completed at least the first two years of undergraduate education; must be enrolled full-time and in good standing at an accredited university; must hold a minimum of 3.5 GPA or equivalent. **Criteria:** Selection will be based on the committee's criteria.

Funds Avail.: $2,000. **To Apply:** Interested applicants must submit a 2,000-word essay on the topic: "How to Be A Better Pet-Owner: Advice from a Veterinary Student". **Deadline:** June 1.

3648 ■ Dollar-A-Day Scholarship Fund
PO Box 811882
Boca Raton, FL 33481-1882
Free: 888-728-2521
E-mail: info@muslimscholarship.org
URL: www.muslimscholarship.org

3649 ■ Dollar-A-Day Academic Scholarships (Graduate, Undergraduate/Scholarship)

Purpose: To provide educational assistance to Muslim university students in their chosen field of study. **Focus:** General studies/Field of study not specified. **Qualif.:** Applicants must be permanent residents or citizens of the United States; college or graduate students; must be Muslims; must demonstrate financial need; and have filed the FAFSA for the applicable year. **Criteria:** Selection will be based on evaluation of submitted documents and specific criteria. Preference will be given to students enrolled in an advanced degree program, but undergraduate students are still encouraged to apply.

Funds Avail.: $1,000. **Duration:** Annual. **To Apply:** Applicants must submit a completed application form; university enrollment form; most recent transcripts; two recommendation letters; student aid report; and updated resume. **Deadline:** August 26. **Contact:** Dollar-A-Day Scholarship Fund, at the above address.

3650 ■ Dolphin Scholarship Foundation
4966 Euclid Rd., Ste. 109
Virginia Beach, VA 23462
Ph: (757)671-3200
Fax: (757)671-3330
E-mail: info@dolphinscholarship.org
URL: www.dolphinscholarship.org

3651 ■ Dolphin Scholarships (Undergraduate/Scholarship)

Purpose: To support the education of children/stepchildren of members or former members of the Submarine Force or who have served in the Submarine Force. **Focus:** General studies/Field of study not specified. **Qualif.:** Applicant must be a high school senior or college student; child or stepchild of a member or former member of the U.S. Navy Submarine Force; unmarried; under age 24; must attend a four-year accredited college or university and intend to work toward a BS or BA degree. **Criteria:** Scholarships are awarded based on academic proficiency, financial need and commitment to and excellence in school and community activities.

Funds Avail.: Varies. **Duration:** Annual. **Number Awarded:** Varies. **To Apply:** Applicants must submit a completed scholarship application form. **Remarks:** Established in 1960.

3652 ■ Dominican Bar Association (DBA)
PO Box 203
New York, NY 10013
E-mail: dominicanbarassoc@gmail.com
URL: www.dominicanbarassociation.org

3653 ■ DBA Student Scholarships (Undergraduate/Scholarship)

Purpose: To help undergraduate students pursue their education in a law school. **Focus:** Law. **Qualif.:** Applicants must be first, second or third year undergraduate students in the field of law; must be enrolled full-time or part-time. **Criteria:** Applicants will be evaluated based on demonstrated involvement in and commitment to serve the Latino community through the legal profession, academic, personal achievement and financial need.

Funds Avail.: $3,000. **Duration:** Annual. **To Apply:** Applicants must submit a completed and signed DBA scholarship application form, current resume, cover letter, an official undergraduate transcript or a photocopy and letter from the law school's financial aid office indicating the amount of aid awarded.

3654 ■ Douglas-Coldwell Foundation (DCF)
300-279 Laurier Ave. W
Ottawa, ON, Canada K1P 5J9

Awards are arranged alphabetically below their administering organizations

Ph: (613)232-1918
Fax: (613)230-9950
E-mail: info@dcf.ca
URL: www.dcf.ca

3655 ■ Beverlee Bell Scholarships in Human Rights and Democracy *(Graduate/Scholarship)*

Purpose: To provide support to qualified students who want to pursue their education. **Focus:** Human rights. **Qualif.:** Applicants must be graduate students making a significant contribution to human rights and democracy in developing countries. **Criteria:** Applicants are selected based on the committee's review of the application materials.

Funds Avail.: 1,000 Canadian Dollars. **Duration:** Annual. **To Apply:** Applicants are advised to contact the Carleton University for further information about the scholarship application form and requirements. **Remarks:** Established in 2002. **Contact:** Carleton University, Academic Department, 1125 Colonel By Dr., Ottawa, ON; Phone: 613-520-2525; Fax: 613-520-4049.

3656 ■ Douglas-Coldwell Foundation Scholarships in Social Affairs *(Graduate/Scholarship)*

Purpose: To support deserving student who wants to pursue their study. **Focus:** Education, English as a second language; History; Political science; Social work; Sociology. **Qualif.:** Applicants must be fully-qualified graduate students preparing a thesis on a topic involving some aspect of Canadian social theory or history. **Criteria:** Applicants are selected based on the Scholarship Committee's review of the application materials.

Funds Avail.: 3,000 Canadian Dollars. **To Apply:** Scholarship application form and requirements are available at University of Regina, Graduate Studies and Research. **Deadline:** October 31. **Contact:** Carleton University, Academic Department, 1125 Colonel By Dr., Ottawa, ON; Phone: 613-520-2525; Fax: 613-520-4049.

3657 ■ Kalmen Kaplansky Scholarships in Economic and Social Rights *(Graduate/Scholarship)*

Purpose: To provide support to qualified students who want to pursue their education. **Focus:** Civil rights; Economics. **Qualif.:** Applicants must be graduate students researching economic and social rights in a School or Department in the Faculty of Public Affairs and Management at Carleton University. **Criteria:** Recipients will be selected based on their research work.

Funds Avail.: 1,000 Canadian Dollars. **To Apply:** Applicants are advised to contact the Carleton University, Academic Unit, 1125 Colonel By Dr., Ottawa, ON for further information about the scholarship application form and other requirements. **Deadline:** February 1. **Contact:** Carleton University, Academic Department, 1125 Colonel By Dr., Ottawa, ON; Phone: 613-520-2525; Fax: 613-520-4049.

3658 ■ Downeast Energy and Building Supply
18 Spring St.
Brunswick, ME 04011
Free: 800-339-9921
URL: www.downeastenergy.com

3659 ■ Downeast Energy Scholarships *(Undergraduate/Scholarship)*

Purpose: To provide support to students in pursuing their educational goal. **Focus:** General studies/Field of study not specified. **Qualif.:** Applicants must be students who are high school seniors or graduates planning to enroll, or students already enrolled in a full-time course of study leading to a bachelor's degree at an accredited post-secondary college or university, an associate's degree at a junior or community post secondary school, or a certificate at an approved vocational technical institute. **Criteria:** Award will be based on a combination of selection factors including, but not limited to, scholastic merit and participation in extracurricular activities.

Funds Avail.: Varies. **Duration:** Annual; One academic year. **Number Awarded:** Varies. **To Apply:** Applicants must submit completed word process application; transcripts of high school; two or more non-family character references; and a word processed cover letter describing your intended course of study and anything else that might help us in our decision.

3660 ■ Drake University Law School
2621 Carpenter Ave.
Des Moines, IA 50311
Ph: (515)271-2824
Free: 800-443-7253
E-mail: lawadmit@drake.edu
URL: www.law.drake.edu

3661 ■ William Stone Ayres Scholarship *(Undergraduate/Scholarship)*

Purpose: To support the education of law students at the Drake University Law School. **Focus:** Law. **Qualif.:** Applicants must be students of Drake University Law School. **Criteria:** Recipients will be selected based on merit and academic achievement.

Funds Avail.: No specific amount. **Duration:** Annual. **To Apply:** Applicants must file FAFSA and application form. **Remarks:** The scholarship was established by a bequest from Gladys L. Ayres in memory of her husband, an 1894 Law School graduate. **Contact:** E-mail at law-admit@drake.edu.

3662 ■ Beverly Estate Scholarship *(Undergraduate/Scholarship)*

Purpose: To support the education of law students at the Drake University Law School. **Focus:** Law. **Qualif.:** Applicants must be students of Drake University Law School. **Criteria:** Recipients will be selected based on merit and academic achievement.

Funds Avail.: No specific amount. **Duration:** Annual. **To Apply:** Applicants must file FAFSA and application form. **Remarks:** The scholarships are made possible by bequests from Francis Cecile Beverly, LW'15, and Adda Brown Beverly, ED'14. **Contact:** E-mail at law-admit@drake.edu.

3663 ■ George and Mary Brammer Scholarship *(Undergraduate/Scholarship)*

Purpose: To support the education of law students at the Drake University Law School. **Focus:** Law. **Qualif.:** Applicants must be students of Drake University Law School. **Criteria:** Recipients will be selected based on merit and academic achievement.

Funds Avail.: No specific amount. **Duration:** Annual. **To Apply:** Applicants must file FAFSA and application form. **Remarks:** The scholarship was established by Mary and John Harper as a memorial to Mary's parents, 1908 and

Awards are arranged alphabetically below their administering organizations

DRAKE UNIVERSITY LAW SCHOOL

1907 graduates of the Law School. **Contact:** E-mail at law-admit@drake.edu.

3664 ■ Raymond DiPaglia Endowment Scholarship (Undergraduate/Scholarship)

Purpose: To support the education of law students at the Drake University Law School. **Focus:** Law. **Qualif.:** Applicants must be returning law students who are in good standing at the Drake University Law School. **Criteria:** Recipients will be selected based on merit and academic achievement.

Funds Avail.: No specific amount. **Duration:** Annual. **To Apply:** Applicants must file FAFSA and application form. **Remarks:** The endowed scholarship was established by Mr. Raymond DiPaglia, LW'91. **Contact:** E-mail at law-admit@drake.edu.

3665 ■ Grace O. Doane Scholarship (Undergraduate/Scholarship)

Purpose: To support the education of law students at the Drake University Law School. **Focus:** Law. **Qualif.:** Applicants must be second year Iowa residents who rank in the top one-half of their class. **Criteria:** Recipients will be selected based on merit and academic achievement.

Funds Avail.: No specific amount. **Duration:** Annual. **To Apply:** Applicants must file FAFSA and an application form. **Contact:** E-mail at law-admit@drake.edu.

3666 ■ Joseph M. Dorgan Scholarship (Undergraduate/Scholarship)

Purpose: To support the education of law students at the Drake University Law School. **Focus:** Law. **Qualif.:** Applicants must be African-American law students. **Criteria:** Recipients will be selected based on merit and academic achievement, as well as financial need.

Funds Avail.: No specific amount. **Duration:** Annual. **To Apply:** Applicants must file FAFSA and application form. **Contact:** E-mail at law-admit@drake.edu.

3667 ■ Drake University Law School Law Opportunity Scholarships - Disadvantage (Undergraduate/Scholarship)

Purpose: To support the education of disadvantaged law students at Drake University Law School. **Focus:** Law. **Qualif.:** Applicants must have been admitted to the Law School and able to demonstrate financial need as determined by the Free Application for Federal Student Aid. **Criteria:** Recipients will be selected based on the following factors: (1) applicants' showing of diversity, disadvantage or both; (2) academic record; (3) personal achievements and leadership; and (4) financial need. Preference will be given to students whose enrollment will significantly contribute to the diversity of the Drake Law School student body, or to those who have overcome economic, educational or other significant disadvantages.

Funds Avail.: No specific amount. **Duration:** Annual. **To Apply:** Applicants must have the FAFSA form completed between January 1 and March 1, and must submit the completed scholarship application form. **Contact:** Office of Admission and Financial Aid at 515-271-2782.

3668 ■ Drake University Law School Law Opportunity Scholarships - Diversity (Undergraduate/Scholarship)

Purpose: To promote the diversity of students in Drake University. **Focus:** Law. **Qualif.:** Applicants must have been admitted to the law school and able to demonstrate financial need as determined by the Free Application for Federal Student Aid. **Criteria:** Recipients will be selected based on the following factors: (1) applicants' showing of diversity, disadvantage or both; (2) academic record; (3) personal achievements and leadership; and (4) financial need. Preference will be given to students whose enrollment will significantly contribute to the diversity of the Drake University law school student body, or to those who have overcome economic, educational or other significant disadvantages.

Funds Avail.: No specific amount. **Duration:** Annual. **To Apply:** Applicants must have the FAFSA form completed between January 1 and March 1, and must submit the completed scholarship application form. **Contact:** Office of Admission and Financial Aid at 515-271-2782.

3669 ■ Drake University Law School Public Service Scholarships (Undergraduate/Scholarship)

Purpose: To support the education of law students at the Drake University Law School. **Focus:** Law. **Qualif.:** Applicants must be entering students who exhibit an extraordinary history of public service work and plan to continue that commitment during and after law school. **Criteria:** Recipients will be selected based merit, academic achievement, and financial need.

Funds Avail.: No specific amount. **Duration:** Annual. **To Apply:** Applicants must submit completed application form along with essay, a short description of past work experiences/activities, letters of recommendation, relevant academic curriculum and statement of reasons for award. **Deadline:** April 1. **Contact:** Office of Admission and Financial Aid at 515-271-2782.

3670 ■ Robert E. Early Memorial Scholarship (Undergraduate/Scholarship)

Purpose: To support the education of law students at the Drake University Law School. **Focus:** Law. **Qualif.:** Applicants must be second or third year full time students who are in need of financial assistance. **Criteria:** Recipients will be selected based on merit, academic achievement, and financial need.

Funds Avail.: No specific amount. **Duration:** Annual. **To Apply:** Applicants must file FAFSA and application form. **Remarks:** The scholarship was established by Margaret M. Early in memory of her husband, LW'41. **Contact:** E-mail at law-admit@drake.edu.

3671 ■ Herman E. Elgar Memorial Scholarship (Undergraduate/Scholarship)

Purpose: To support the education of law students at the Drake University Law School. **Focus:** Law. **Qualif.:** Applicants must be third year law students at Drake University. **Criteria:** Recipients will be selected based on merit, academic achievement, and financial need.

Funds Avail.: No specific amount. **Duration:** Annual. **To Apply:** Applicants must file FAFSA and application form. **Remarks:** The scholarship was established in memory of Mr. Elgar, LW'11, by his wife Clara Elgar and children, John Elgar, LW'50, Alanson Elgar, LW'51 and Elizabeth Elgar Anderson, ED'41. **Contact:** E-mail at law-admit@drake.edu.

3672 ■ D.J. Fairgrave Education Trust (Undergraduate/Scholarship)

Purpose: To support the education of law students at the Drake University Law School. **Focus:** Law. **Qualif.:** Ap-

Awards are arranged alphabetically below their administering organizations

plicants must be students of Drake University Law School. **Criteria:** Recipients will be selected based on: financial need; character; academic record; personal achievements; future goals and anticipated contributions to the profession.
Funds Avail.: No specific amount. **Duration:** Annual. **To Apply:** Applicant must file FAFSA and application form. **Remarks:** The scholarship trust was established by Denio John Fairgrave. **Contact:** E-mail at law-admit@drake.edu.

3673 ■ Leland Stanford Forrest Scholarship
(Undergraduate/Scholarship)

Purpose: To support the education of law students at the Drake University Law School. **Focus:** Law. **Qualif.:** Applicants must be students who are graduates of Iowa high schools or colleges, and whose high school and college experiences took place outside the state. **Criteria:** Recipients will be selected from among entering students who are graduates of Iowa high schools or colleges.
Funds Avail.: No specific amount. **Duration:** Annual. **To Apply:** Applicants must fill up the General Information Form of Scholarship. **Remarks:** The scholarship was established through the bequest of Leland Stanford Forrest, former dean of the law school. **Contact:** E-mail at law-admit@drake.edu.

3674 ■ Lex and Scott Hawkins Endowed Scholarship *(Undergraduate/Scholarship)*

Purpose: To support the education of law students. **Focus:** Law. **Qualif.:** Applicants must be the president of the Law School's Moot Court Board. **Criteria:** Recipients will be selected based on merit.
Funds Avail.: No specific amount. **Duration:** Annual. **To Apply:** Applicants may contact Office of Admission and Financial Aid for more information. **Contact:** E-mail at law-admit@drake.edu.

3675 ■ Edward and Cora Hayes Scholarship
(Undergraduate/Scholarship)

Purpose: To assist law students who are not graduates of Iowa high schools or colleges. **Focus:** Law. **Qualif.:** Applicants must be accepted as first year students at Drake University Law School and not graduates of Iowa high schools or colleges. They must be students whose high school and college experiences took place outside the state. **Criteria:** Recipients will be selected based on merit.
Funds Avail.: No specific amount. **Duration:** Annual. **To Apply:** Applicants must fill up the General Information Form of Scholarship. **Remarks:** The scholarship was established by the former associate dean (Edward) and his wife (Cora). **Contact:** E-mail at law-admit@drake.edu.

3676 ■ Annamae Heaps Law Scholarship
(Undergraduate/Scholarship)

Purpose: To support the education of law students at the Drake University Law School. **Focus:** Law. **Qualif.:** Applicants must be second year students who demonstrate financial need. **Criteria:** Recipients will be selected based on merit and academic achievement.
Funds Avail.: No specific amount. **Duration:** Annual. **To Apply:** Applicants must file FAFSA and application form. **Contact:** E-mail at law-admit@drake.edu.

3677 ■ John M. Helmick Law Scholarship
(Undergraduate/Scholarship)

Purpose: To support students who plan to enter the legal or educational professions in Iowa. **Focus:** Law. **Qualif.:** Applicants must be students of Iowa backgrounds planning to enter the legal or educational professions in Iowa. **Criteria:** Recipients will be selected based on merit and academic achievement.
Funds Avail.: No specific amount. **Duration:** Annual. **To Apply:** Applicants must file FAFSA and application form. **Remarks:** The scholarship was established by Robert H. Helmick, LW'60, in memory of his grandfather, John Miller Helmick. **Contact:** E-mail at law-admit@drake.edu.

3678 ■ Iowa Association of Electric Cooperatives - Electric Cooperative Pioneer Trust Fund Scholarship *(Undergraduate/Scholarship)*

Purpose: To support the education of law students at the Drake University Law School. **Focus:** Law. **Qualif.:** Applicants must be second or third year law students interested in agricultural law. **Criteria:** Selection will be based on merit and academic achievement. Preference will be given to students planning to practice in Iowa.
Funds Avail.: No specific amount. **Duration:** Annual. **To Apply:** Applicants may contact Office of Admission and Financial Aid for more information. **Contact:** E-mail at law-admit@drake.edu.

3679 ■ James P. Irish Scholarship *(Undergraduate/Scholarship)*

Purpose: To support the education of law students at the Drake University Law School. **Focus:** Law. **Qualif.:** Applicants must be students graduated from Southeast Polk High School or members of the Law Review Board of Editor. **Criteria:** Recipients will be selected based on merit and academic achievement.
Funds Avail.: No specific amount. **Duration:** Annual. **To Apply:** Applicants may contact Office of Admission and Financial Aid for more information. **Remarks:** The scholarship was established by Edwin Skinner and Donald Beattie in honor of their associate and law partner, James P. Irish, LW'31. **Contact:** E-mail at law-admit@drake.edu.

3680 ■ Martin Luther King Law Scholarship
(Undergraduate/Scholarship)

Purpose: To support the education of law students at the Drake University Law School. **Focus:** Law. **Qualif.:** Applicants must be female African-American law students who embody the spirit and values of Martin Luther King and who have demonstrated financial need. **Criteria:** Recipients will be selected based on merit and academic achievement.
Funds Avail.: No specific amount. **Duration:** Annual. **To Apply:** Applicant must file FAFSA and application form. **Remarks:** The scholarship was established by Naomi Mercer, LW'68. **Contact:** E-mail at law-admit@drake.edu.

3681 ■ Forest A. King Scholarship *(Undergraduate/Scholarship)*

Purpose: To support the education of law students at the Drake University Law School. **Focus:** Law. **Qualif.:** Applicants must be students of Drake University Law School. **Criteria:** Recipients will be selected based on merit and academic achievement.
Funds Avail.: No specific amount. **Duration:** Annual. **To Apply:** Applicants must file FAFSA and application form. **Remarks:** The scholarship was established in memory of Mr. King, LW'25, by his wife, Nonnie. **Contact:** E-mail at law-admit@drake.edu.

Awards are arranged alphabetically below their administering organizations

DRAKE UNIVERSITY LAW SCHOOL

3682 ■ Verne Lawyer Scholarship *(Undergraduate/Scholarship)*

Purpose: To support the education of law students at the Drake University Law School. **Focus:** Law. **Qualif.:** Applicants must be students of Drake University Law School. **Criteria:** Recipients will be selected based on merit and academic achievement.

Funds Avail.: No specific amount. **Duration:** Annual. **To Apply:** Applicants must file FAFSA and application form. **Remarks:** The scholarship was established by an anonymous donor to honor D. Verne Lawyer, a 1949 graduate of the Law School. Established in 1992. **Contact:** E-mail at law-admit@drake.edu.

3683 ■ Frederick D. Lewis Jr. Scholarships *(Undergraduate/Scholarship)*

Purpose: To support the education of law students at the Drake University Law School. **Focus:** Law. **Qualif.:** Applicants must be students of Drake University Law School. **Criteria:** Recipients will be selected based on merit and academic achievement.

Funds Avail.: No specific amount. **Duration:** Annual. **To Apply:** Applicants must file FAFSA and application form. **Remarks:** The scholarship fund was established by Patrick D. Kelly, LW'53, in memory of Frederick D. Lewis Jr., a professor at Drake Law School from 1949 to 1959. **Contact:** E-mail at law-admit@drake.edu.

3684 ■ Gordon and Delores Madson Scholarship *(Undergraduate/Scholarship)*

Purpose: To support the education of law students at the Drake University Law School. **Focus:** Law. **Qualif.:** Applicants must be students of Drake University Law School. **Criteria:** Recipients will be selected based on merit and academic achievement.

Funds Avail.: No specific amount. **Duration:** Annual. **To Apply:** Applicants must file FAFSA and application form. **Remarks:** The scholarship was established by Gordon Madson, LW'57, and his wife, Delores. **Contact:** E-mail at law-admit@drake.edu.

3685 ■ Jake S. More Scholarship *(Undergraduate/Scholarship)*

Purpose: To support the education of law students at the Drake University Law School. **Focus:** Law. **Qualif.:** Applicants must be students of Drake University Law School. **Criteria:** Recipients will be selected based on merit and academic achievement.

Funds Avail.: No specific amount. **Duration:** Annual. **To Apply:** Applicants must file FAFSA and scholarship application form. **Remarks:** The scholarship was established by Jake S. More, LW'28. **Contact:** E-mail at law-admit@drake.edu.

3686 ■ Dwight D. Opperman Scholarships *(Undergraduate/Scholarship)*

Purpose: To support the education of law students at the Drake University Law School. **Focus:** Law. **Qualif.:** Applicants must: be accepted as first year students at Drake Law School; show evidence of superior academic record and potential; have a high score in law entrance exam; and, demonstrate significant community and extracurricular experiences. **Criteria:** Selection will be based on merit and academic achievement.

Funds Avail.: $10,000 each. **Duration:** Annual. **Number Awarded:** 5. **To Apply:** Applicants must complete the application packet (application for admission and the general scholarship information sheet). **Contact:** E-mail at law-admit@drake.edu.

3687 ■ Janet Reynoldson Memorial Scholarship *(Undergraduate/Scholarship)*

Purpose: To support the education of law students at the Drake University Law School. **Focus:** Law. **Qualif.:** Applicants must be students of Drake University Law School. **Criteria:** Recipients will be selected based on students' contributions to community and family, academic achievement, need and significant change in career.

Funds Avail.: No specific amount. **Duration:** Annual. **To Apply:** Applicants must file FAFSA and application form. **Remarks:** The scholarship was established by the family of Janet Reynoldson, LW'65. **Contact:** E-mail at law-admit@drake.edu.

3688 ■ Walter and Rita Selvy Scholarship *(Undergraduate/Scholarship)*

Purpose: To support the education of law students at the Drake University Law School. **Focus:** Law. **Qualif.:** Applicants must be students of Drake University Law School. **Criteria:** Recipients will be selected based on merit and academic achievement.

Funds Avail.: No specific amount. **Duration:** Annual. **To Apply:** Applicants must file FAFSA and application form. **Remarks:** The scholarship was established by Walter, LW'28, and his late wife, Rita Selvy. Awarded under the direction of the president of Drake University. **Contact:** E-mail at law-admit@drake.edu.

3689 ■ Charles "Buck" and Dora Taylor Scholarship *(Undergraduate/Scholarship)*

Purpose: To support the education of law students at the Drake University Law School. **Focus:** Law. **Qualif.:** Applicants must be students with financial need and have demonstrated a history of academic success while participating in sports at the undergraduate school level. **Criteria:** Recipients will be selected based on merit, academic achievement, and financial need.

Funds Avail.: No specific amount. **Duration:** Annual. **To Apply:** Applicants must submit the General Information Form for Scholarships along with the application for admission. **Remarks:** The scholarship was established in honor of Charles Taylor, LW'33. **Contact:** E-mail at law-admit@drake.edu.

3690 ■ Haemer Wheatcraft Scholarship *(Undergraduate/Scholarship)*

Purpose: To support the education of law students at the Drake University Law School. **Focus:** Law. **Qualif.:** Applicants must be students of Drake University Law School. **Criteria:** Recipients are selected based on merit and academic achievement.

Funds Avail.: No specific amount. **Duration:** Annual. **To Apply:** Applicants must file the FAFSA and the scholarship application. **Remarks:** The scholarship was established by friends and associates in honor of Haemer Wheatcraft, LW'33. **Contact:** E-mail at law-admit@drake.edu.

3691 ■ Zarley, McKee, Thomte, Voorhees, Sease Law Scholarship *(Undergraduate/Scholarship)*

Purpose: To support the education of law students at the Drake University Law School. **Focus:** Law. **Qualif.:** Ap-

Awards are arranged alphabetically below their administering organizations

plicants must be students interested in intellectual property law. **Criteria:** Recipients will be selected based on merit and academic achievement.

Funds Avail.: No specific amount. **Duration:** Annual. **To Apply:** Applicants must file FAFSA and application form. **Remarks:** The scholarship was established by Donald H. Zarley, LW'54; Bruce W. McKee; Dennis L. Thomte; Michael G. Voorhees, LW'68; Edmund J. Sease, LW'67; and John Beehner. **Contact:** E-mail at law-admit@drake.edu.

3692 ■ Drama Therapy Fund
1626 Leavenworth St.
Manhattan, KS 66502
E-mail: info@dramatherapyfund.org
URL: www.dramatherapyfund.org

3693 ■ Wilder Dimension Scholarships for Advanced Study in Theatre Arts *(Graduate/Scholarship)*

Purpose: To provide drama therapist the assistance they need. **Focus:** Theater arts. **Qualif.:** Applicants must be registered drama therapists working on continuing education and graduate students preparing for careers as drama therapists either through an approved NADT university program or through NADT alternative learning program. **Criteria:** Selection will be based on evaluation of submitted documents and specific criteria. Applications will be reviewed by a team of three registered drama therapists.

Funds Avail.: Up to $400. **To Apply:** Applicants must submit a contact information page along with a letter of intent which includes contact information, name of proposed course, where the course will be offered, and dates of the course, rational for wanting to study theater history or literature and contribution to practice as drama therapist. Send via online or send via mail (applicants must send four hard copies for mail applications). **Contact:** Sally Bailey, Treasurer, at the above address; or Email: dtfund@dramatherapyfund.org.

3694 ■ Camille and Henry Dreyfus Foundation, Inc.
555 Madison Ave., 20th Fl.
New York, NY 10022-3301
Ph: (212)753-1760
Fax: (212)593-2256
E-mail: admin@dreyfus.org
URL: www.dreyfus.org
Facebook: www.dreyfus.org

3695 ■ Camille and Henry Dreyfus Foundation - Senior Scientist Mentor Program *(Professional development/Grant)*

Purpose: To support emeritus faculty who maintain active research programs with undergraduates in the chemical sciences. **Focus:** Science. **Qualif.:** Open to all academic institutions in the States, Districts, and Territories of the United States of America that grant a bachelor's degree or higher in the chemical sciences, including biochemistry, materials chemistry, and chemical engineering; faculty with emeritus status on or before October of the current year, and who maintain active research programs in the chemical sciences, may apply. **Criteria:** Selection will be based on the assessment of the research proposed and the plans for undergraduate participation in the research.

Funds Avail.: $20,000. **Duration:** Annual; two years. **To Apply:** Applicants may visit the website to obtain an application form. The original application should be formatted on 8 1/2 x 11-inch paper, using 12-point font size, and assembled as: the online application form; a no more than four pages describing the specific projects or project types in which the undergraduates will participate, ongoing research with undergraduates, and how they will interact with and mentor the undergraduates; a maximum of five pages CV that includes a list of up to 15 relevant publications in which contributions by undergraduate co-authors are clearly identified; a letter from an institutional representative highlighting the applicants' achievements with undergraduates and confirming that the institutional facilities required for the proposed research are available. Letter of support must be sent directly to the Foundation from a colleague, preferably from outside the institution, which is familiar with the applicants' research, teaching and experience in mentoring and advising undergraduates. Generate all the materials as a single PDF document and should be sent through email. **Deadline:** May 18.

3696 ■ Dublin San Ramon Services District
7051 Dublin Blvd.
Dublin, CA 94568-3018
Ph: (925)828-0515
Fax: (925)829-1180
URL: www.dsrsd.com

3697 ■ DSRSD James B. Kohnen Scholarships *(Undergraduate, High School/Scholarship)*

Purpose: To promote a career in water resources. **Focus:** Water resources. **Qualif.:** Applicants must be high school seniors living in the DSRSD service area and graduating students from one of the following schools: Dublin High School, Valley High School, Dougherty Valley High School, California High School, Valley Christian High School, or Quarry Lane School; intending to study a field or discipline related to water resources at an accredited, publicly funded college or university in California; planning to attend college full-time for the current academic year; must have a 3.0 GPA or better. **Criteria:** Selection will be based on a combination of scholastic achievement, an essay, and applicants' commitment to a field related to water resources.

Funds Avail.: $2,000. **Number Awarded:** 1. **To Apply:** Applicants must submit a completed application form, two letters of recommendation on official school or business letterhead, official sealed high school transcript through December of their senior year, and a 500-word essay describing why the applicants intend to study a field related to water resources. **Deadline:** April 30. **Contact:** Sue Stephenson, stephenson@dsrsd.com, 925-875-2295.

3698 ■ Doris Duke Charitable Foundation (DDCF)
650 5th Ave., 19th Fl.
New York, NY 10019
Ph: (212)974-7000
Fax: (212)974-7590
E-mail: webmaster@ddcf.org
URL: www.ddcf.org
Facebook: twitter.com/DorisDukeFdn

3699 ■ Clinical Research Fellowship for Medical Students *(Graduate/Fellowship)*

Purpose: To encourage medical students who are pursuing careers in clinical research. **Focus:** Biological and clinical sciences. **Qualif.:** Applicants must be students matriculated at any US medical school who are in good academic standing and have completed two or more years of medical school prior to the start of the fellowship. **Criteria:** Selection will be based on the committee's criteria.

Funds Avail.: No specific amount. **To Apply:** Applicants must visit the website for the online application form. Complete all sections of the online application form, which requests the following information: contact information; education history; areas of clinical research you are interested in during the fellowship year; schools to which you are applying (this information will be released to all schools you apply to); names and emails of medical school dean and faculty submitting letters of support; descriptions of prior research experience, if applicable. Completed application should include the following: online application form; letter from the dean; letter of support; personal statement, curriculum vitae; medical school transcript; additional school requirements. **Contact:** Leslie Engel, at the above address.

3700 ■ Duke University and University of North Carolina Rotary Peace Center
Sanford School of Public Policy
Duke Center for International Development
Rubenstein Hall, Room 286
PO Box 90237
Durham, NC 27708-0237
Ph: (919)613-9222
URL: rotarypeacecenternc.org

3701 ■ Rotary Peace Fellowship Program (Graduate, Master's/Fellowship)

Purpose: To empower, educate, and increase the capacity of peace builders through rigorous academic training, practice, and global networking opportunities. **Focus:** Peace studies. **Qualif.:** Applicants must: have strong commitment to international understanding and peace demonstrated through professional and academic achievements and personal and community service activities; have demonstrated leadership skills; have obtain four-year bachelor's degree, with strong academic achievement (the equivalent of a cumulative undergraduate grade point average of at least 3.0); have relevant work experience minimum of three years' combined paid or unpaid full-time or preferably more; have proficiency in a second language; take the TOEFL or IELTS exams; take the GRE exam (for all applicants from University of North Carolina). **Criteria:** Applicants are selected in a globally competitive process based on personal, academic, and professional achievements.

Funds Avail.: No specific amount. **Duration:** Annual. **To Apply:** Applicants must submit completely the necessary requirements which include curriculum vitae (CV), personal statement, complete transcripts, two to three copies of recommendations and test scores. Applicants must contact their local Rotary club to begin the process of endorsement and pass the interview, either in person or via phone, by the Rotary district. Those who want to study at Duke or UNC should rank the Duke-UNC Rotary Center as number one. **Deadline:** July 1.

3702 ■ Duluth Superior Area Community Foundation
222 E Superior St., Ste. 302
Duluth, MN 55802
Ph: (218)726-0232
URL: www.dsacommunityfoundation.com

3703 ■ Darrell and Palchie Asselin Scholarships (Undergraduate/Scholarship)

Purpose: To provide financial assistance to the non-traditional, older students in financial resources for their education. **Focus:** General studies/Field of study not specified. **Qualif.:** Applicants must be students over the age of 22 who are the primary care givers to one or more children under the age of 18; must have a grade point average of 2.5 (based on a 4.0 system) or higher for a completed of at least 50% of the course of instruction at the time of the award. **Criteria:** Applicants are evaluated based on academic achievement, financial need, written recommendations, seriousness of purpose.

Funds Avail.: $2,000 each. **Duration:** Annual. **Number Awarded:** Varies. **To Apply:** Applicants must complete the application form; academic transcript; letters of recommendation; and financial need documentation. **Remarks:** Established in 1993. **Contact:** Duluth-Superior Area Community Foundation, at the above address.

3704 ■ William E. Barto Scholarships (Undergraduate/Scholarship)

Purpose: To provide financial assistance for art students. **Focus:** Arts; Visual arts. **Qualif.:** Applicants must be: graduating seniors of public and private high schools in Duluth and Superior; planning to major in arts or visual arts at the University of Minnesota Duluth or the University of Wisconsin-Superior; and, included in the upper 25% of their class. **Criteria:** Applicants are evaluated based on financial need, academic record, written recommendations, and seriousness of purpose.

Funds Avail.: $2,000. **Duration:** Annual. **To Apply:** Applicants must submit a completed application form; academic transcript; letters of recommendation; and financial need documentation. **Remarks:** Established in 1995. **Contact:** Duluth-Superior Area Community Foundation, at the above address.

3705 ■ Bernard B. and Mary L. Brusin Scholarships (Undergraduate/Scholarship)

Purpose: To provide assistance to Jewish and Roman Catholic students who are in need financial of aid for their college education. **Focus:** General studies/Field of study not specified. **Qualif.:** Applicants must be either Jewish or Roman Catholic graduating seniors from St. Louis County public or private high schools who are in the top 25% of their high school. **Criteria:** Applicants are evaluated based on financial need, academic record, written recommendations (one of which must be from a clergy) and seriousness of purpose.

Funds Avail.: About $5,000. **Duration:** Annual. **To Apply:** Applicants should complete and submit an application form; academic transcript (including standardized test scores); recommendations from one educator and one to the clergy; and financial need documentation. **Remarks:** Established in 1987. **Contact:** Duluth-Superior Area Community Foundation, at the above address.

3706 ■ DSACF Modern Woodmen of America Scholarships (Undergraduate/Scholarship)

Purpose: To provide financial assistance to the non-traditional students who are in financial need. **Focus:** General studies/Field of study not specified. **Qualif.:** Applicants

Awards are arranged alphabetically below their administering organizations

must be single parents who are the primary care-givers to one or more children, and have completed at least 50 percent of their course of instruction at the time of the award. **Criteria:** Applicants are evaluated based on academic record, written recommendations, and involvement in community and church activities.
Funds Avail.: $1,000. **Duration:** Annual. **Number Awarded:** 1. **To Apply:** Applicants must submit a completed application form together with academic transcript (including standardized test scores), two recommendations, and financial need documentation. **Remarks:** Established in 1988. **Contact:** Duluth-Superior Area Community Foundation, at the above address.

3707 ■ Duluth Building and Construction Trades Council Scholarships (Undergraduate/Scholarship)

Purpose: To provide financial assistance to children of members of unions affiliated with the Duluth Building Trades Council. **Focus:** Health care services. **Qualif.:** Applicants must be graduating high school seniors, whose parent/guardian is a member of one of the 17 unions affiliated with the Duluth Building Trades Council; and, have grade point average of 2.75, based on 4.0 scale, or higher. They also must be students from the Foundation's geographic service areas. **Criteria:** Applicants are evaluated based on academic record (including GPA, class rank, and test scores when relevant), written recommendations, and seriousness of purpose. Preference will be given to students entering the health care field.
Funds Avail.: $2,500. **Duration:** Annual. **To Apply:** Applicants must submit all the required application information. **Contact:** Duluth-Superior Area Community Foundation, at the above address.

3708 ■ Duluth Central High School Alumni Scholarships (Undergraduate/Scholarship)

Purpose: To assist students who ever attended Central High School to help them achieve their educational goals. **Focus:** General studies/Field of study not specified. **Qualif.:** Applicants must be graduating seniors from Duluth Central High School who will attend the College of St. Scholastica, University of Minnesota-Duluth, University of Wisconsin-Superior, Lake Superior College, or Wisconsin Indianhead Technical College. **Criteria:** Applicants are evaluated based on academic record, financial need, written recommendations, and seriousness of purpose.
Funds Avail.: $1,000. **Duration:** Annual. **To Apply:** Applicants must submit a completed application form; academic transcript (including standardized test scores); two letters of recommendation; and financial need documentation. **Remarks:** Established in 1944. **Contact:** Duluth-Superior Area Community Foundation, at the above address.

3709 ■ Peter M. Gargano Scholarship Fund (Undergraduate/Scholarship)

Purpose: To provide financial assistance for post-secondary education to the children of employees of Ulland Brothers. **Focus:** General studies/Field of study not specified. **Qualif.:** Applicants must be: children of Ulland Brothers employees who have been employed with the company for a minimum of two years (for salaried employees) or for a minimum of two seasons (for seasonal employees); students who are unmarried child under age 25 who are not self-supporting and who are full-time high school seniors or post-secondary students; and, graduating high school seniors from the Geographic Service Areas. They must also have a grade point average of 3.0 (based on 4.0 system) or higher. **Criteria:** Applicants are evaluated based on academic record (including GPA, class rank, and test scores when relevant), financial need, written recommendations, and seriousness of purpose.
Funds Avail.: $2,000. **Duration:** Annual. **Number Awarded:** 1. **To Apply:** Applicants must submit a completed application form and recently completed Student Aid Report (SAR) from the Free Application for Federal Student Aid (FAFSA). A completed application must also include an academic transcript (including standardized test scores), one recommendation and financial need documentation. **Remarks:** Established in 1992. **Contact:** Duluth-Superior Area Community Foundation, at the above address.

3710 ■ Patricia S. Gustafson '56 Memorial Scholarships (Undergraduate/Scholarship)

Purpose: To provide financial assistance to graduating female seniors from Denfeld High School or the Marshall School who exemplifies the characteristics and life exhibited by Patricia Gustafson. **Focus:** General studies/Field of study not specified. **Qualif.:** Applicants must: be young women who will graduate from Denfeld High School or Marshall High School; plan to attend either the University of Minnesota Duluth, Lake Superior College or the College of St. Scholastica; have a high school grade point average of 3.4 or higher; be active participants or leaders in school activities; and, have some measure of financial need. **Criteria:** Recipients are selected based on ability to live a full life following the example of Patricia Gustafson; contributions to their schools; high academic achievement; potential and intention to make contributions in the field of education; high level of moral character; and, level of financial need.
Funds Avail.: $800 each. **Duration:** Annual. **Number Awarded:** Varies. **To Apply:** Applicants must submit a completed application form and a personal statement answering the question "Considering what you know of Patricia Gustafson, why do you think you would be a worthy recipient of a scholarship honoring her memory?" **Remarks:** Established in 2007. **Contact:** Duluth-Superior Area Community Foundation, at the above address.

3711 ■ Jeanne H. Hemmingway Scholarships (Undergraduate/Scholarship)

Purpose: To assist students with financial need from the three counties of Minnesota's Arrowhead region to attend the area's largest school, the University of Minnesota Duluth. **Focus:** General studies/Field of study not specified. **Qualif.:** Applicants must be graduate seniors of public or private high schools in St. Louis, Lake and Cook counties who are planning to attend UMD and included in the top 15% of their high school. **Criteria:** Applicants are evaluated based on financial need, academic record, written recommendations, and seriousness of purpose.
Funds Avail.: Around $2,250 to $2,500 each person. **Duration:** Annual. **Number Awarded:** Varies. **To Apply:** Applicants must submit a completed application form and a recently completed Student Aid Report (SAR) from the Free Application for Federal Student Aid (FAFSA). **Remarks:** Established in 1990. **Contact:** Duluth-Superior Area Community Foundation, at the above address.

3712 ■ Gus and Henrietta Hill Scholarships (Undergraduate/Scholarship)

Purpose: To provide financial assistance to graduates of Duluth East High School pursuing post-secondary educa-

Awards are arranged alphabetically below their administering organizations

tion. **Focus:** General studies/Field of study not specified. **Qualif.:** Applicants must be graduating seniors from Duluth East High School who are active in the sport of pole vaulting and/or music activities; must be on top third of their high school class. **Criteria:** Applicants will be evaluated based on participation in pole vaulting and/or music activities, financial need, academic record, written recommendations, and seriousness of purpose. **Funds Avail.:** About $5,000 per year. **Duration:** Annual. **Number Awarded:** Varies. **To Apply:** Applicants must submit a completed application form; academic transcript (including standardized test scores); two letters of recommendation; and financial documentation. **Remarks:** Established in 2000. **Contact:** Duluth-Superior Area Community Foundation, at the above address.

3713 ■ Max and Julia Houghton Duluth Central Scholarships *(Undergraduate/Scholarship)*

Purpose: To provide financial assistance to graduating Central seniors for post-secondary education. **Focus:** General studies/Field of study not specified. **Qualif.:** Applicants must be graduating seniors from Duluth Central High School who are in the top 25% of their high school class. **Criteria:** Applicants are evaluated based on financial need, academic performance, and involvement in community and/or school activities. **Funds Avail.:** Amount varies. **Number Awarded:** Varies. **To Apply:** Applicants must submit all the required application information. **Remarks:** Established in 2003. **Contact:** Duluth-Superior Area Community Foundation, at the above address.

3714 ■ Greg Irons Award Fund *(Undergraduate/Scholarship)*

Purpose: To recognize and reward the efforts of students in Duluth Public Schools and teachers who help students succeed. **Focus:** General studies/Field of study not specified. **Qualif.:** Applicants must: be 12th grade students who have been able to attain their personal goals through self motivation, perseverance and through guidance of a mentor who characterizes Greg Irons; have positive influences through their enthusiastic participation in school activities; and, be students with academic, physical, or emotional needs. **Criteria:** Recipients will be selected based on academic record and other factors described on the application. Preference will be given to students who have desire to enter the teaching profession or other helping professions. **Funds Avail.:** About $1,000 each per year. **Duration:** Annual. **Number Awarded:** Varies. **To Apply:** Applicants must submit a completed application form including transcript of records. **Remarks:** Established in 1990. **Contact:** Duluth-Superior Area Community Foundation, at the above address.

3715 ■ The Jackson Club Scholarships *(Undergraduate/Scholarship)*

Purpose: To provide financial awards for post secondary education, including college and vocational training to graduating seniors from Hermantown High School. **Focus:** General studies/Field of study not specified. **Qualif.:** Applicants must be residents of Hermantown and graduates of Hermantown High School planning to attend any accredited post-secondary institution on a full-time basis, and have a 2.3 grade point average. **Criteria:** Applicants are evaluated based on academic record, written recommendation, and involvement in community activities. **Funds Avail.:** Amount varies. **Duration:** Annual. **To Apply:** Applicants must submit a completed application form; transcript of records (including standardized test scores); one letter of recommendation; and an essay stating the meaning of growing up in Hermantown. **Remarks:** Established in 2005. **Contact:** Duluth-Superior Area Community Foundation, at the above address.

3716 ■ Cory Jam Memorial Award Fund *(Undergraduate/Scholarship)*

Purpose: To provide financial assistance to Duluth East High School graduates. **Focus:** General studies/Field of study not specified. **Qualif.:** Applicants must be graduating seniors from Duluth East High School who attended Congdon Park Elementary School, Homecroft Elementary School or Lowell Elementary School; must have participated in at least two extracurricular activities sponsored by Duluth East High School and at least one community based activity during their high school enrollment years; must intend to pursue education or training at any accredited university, college or technical school; must possess a 3.5 grade point average or higher based on 4.0 system. **Criteria:** Applicants are evaluated based on academic records, written recommendations, and involvement in community and church activities. **Funds Avail.:** $1,000. **Duration:** Annual. **Number Awarded:** 1. **To Apply:** Applicants must submit a completed application form; academic transcript (including standardized test scores); and two letters of recommendation. **Remarks:** Established in 1988. **Contact:** Duluth-Superior Area Community Foundation, at the above address.

3717 ■ Minnesota Power Community Involvement Scholarships *(Undergraduate/Scholarship)*

Purpose: To provide financial assistance for graduating high school seniors within Minnesota Power's service area who are active volunteers in their communities. **Focus:** General studies/Field of study not specified. **Qualif.:** Applicants must be full-time high school seniors residing within Minnesota Power's service territory who have a 3.0 GPA or above. **Criteria:** Applicants are evaluated based on community involvement and financial need. **Funds Avail.:** $2,500 each per year. **Duration:** Annual. **Number Awarded:** 20. **To Apply:** Applicants must submit an application form; supporting documentation from community leaders; a copy of the applicant's parents' 1040 form; and a high school transcript. **Remarks:** Established in 1998. **Contact:** Duluth-Superior Area Community Foundation, at the above address.

3718 ■ Hubert A. Nelson Scholarships *(Undergraduate/Scholarship)*

Purpose: To provide financial assistance for students studying business and accounting. **Focus:** Accounting; Business. **Qualif.:** Applicants must be: graduating seniors of public or private high schools in Duluth and Superior; planning to major in business/accounting at the University of Minnesota-Duluth or the University of Wisconsin-Superior; and, in the top 25% of their high school. **Criteria:** Applicants are evaluated based on academic record, financial need, written recommendations, involvement in community; and extra-curricular activities. **Funds Avail.:** $1,000 each. **Duration:** Annual. **Number Awarded:** Varies. **To Apply:** Applicants must submit a completed application form; academic transcript (including standardized test scores); one letter of recommendation;

Awards are arranged alphabetically below their administering organizations

and financial need documentation. **Remarks:** Established in 1995. **Contact:** Duluth-Superior Area Community Foundation, at the above address.

3719 ■ Amelia and Emanuel Nessell Scholarships
(Undergraduate/Scholarship)

Purpose: To provide educational opportunities for students who are in financial need, especially those Jewish applicants. **Focus:** General studies/Field of study not specified. **Qualif.:** Applicants must be: graduating seniors of Duluth public or private high schools; Jewish students who are planning to pursue a post-secondary education, including community colleges, four-year colleges and universities; and, in the top 25% of their high school class. **Criteria:** Applicants are evaluated based on academic record, financial need, written recommendations (one of which must come from a clergy), involvement in community and extra-curricular activities. Priority consideration will be given to Jewish applicants.

Funds Avail.: $1,000 each. **Duration:** Annual. **Number Awarded:** Varies. **To Apply:** Applicants must submit a completed DSACF Common Scholarship Application form; academic transcript (including standardized test scores); two letters of recommendation (one from educator and the other one must come from the clergy); and financial documentation. **Remarks:** Established in 1997. **Contact:** Duluth-Superior Area Community Foundation, at the above address.

3720 ■ Anderson Niskanen Scholarships
(Undergraduate/Scholarship)

Purpose: To provide financial assistance to Duluth public high schools graduating students who are in financial need for post-secondary education at the University of Minnesota Duluth or the University of Minnesota-Twin Cities. **Focus:** General studies/Field of study not specified. **Qualif.:** Applicants must be graduating seniors from Duluth public high schools who will attend either the University of Minnesota-Duluth or the University of Minnesota-Twin Cities; and must be in the top 25% of their class. **Criteria:** Applicants are evaluated based on financial need, academic achievement, written recommendations and seriousness of purpose.

Funds Avail.: $2,000 each. **Duration:** Annual. **Number Awarded:** Varies. **To Apply:** Applicants must submit a completed application form; academic transcript (including standardized test scores); two letters of recommendation; and financial documentation. **Remarks:** Established in 1998. **Contact:** Duluth-Superior Area Community Foundation, at the above address.

3721 ■ Dr. Mark Rathke Family Scholarships
(Undergraduate/Scholarship)

Purpose: To help future generations of Marshall School students to pursue their educational goals. **Focus:** General studies/Field of study not specified. **Qualif.:** Applicants must: be graduating seniors of the Marshall School who will be attending a college or university as full-time students; have a grade point average of 2.75 (on a 4.0 scale) or higher; and, have demonstrated school and/or community involvement, leadership qualities and hardworking behavior. **Criteria:** Applicants are evaluated based on academic record; hard-working behavior; good citizenship; leadership qualities; serious commitment to college education; written recommendations; and involvement in community and extra-curricular activities. Preference will be given to those students who are not in the top ten percent of their graduating class.

Funds Avail.: $1,000 each. **Duration:** Annual. **Number Awarded:** Varies. **To Apply:** Applicants must submit a completed application form; academic transcript (including standardized test scores); and two letter of recommendation. **Remarks:** Established in 1999. **Contact:** Duluth-Superior Area Community Foundation, at the above address.

3722 ■ Lawrence E. and Mabel Jackson Rudberg Scholarships
(Undergraduate/Scholarship)

Purpose: To provide financial assistance to students pursuing a college degree. **Focus:** General studies/Field of study not specified. **Qualif.:** Applicants must be graduating seniors from Duluth public and Two Harbors Senior High intending to pursue a post-secondary education at an accredited four-year public or private college or university. **Criteria:** Applicants are evaluated based on academic record, financial need, written recommendations, involvement in community and extra-curricular activities. Two Harbors graduates will be given preference.

Funds Avail.: $5,000 each. **Duration:** Annual. **Number Awarded:** 2. **To Apply:** Applicants must submit a completed DSACF Common Scholarship Application form; academic transcript (including standardized test scores); two letters of recommendation; and financial need documentation. **Remarks:** Established in 1999. **Contact:** Duluth-Superior Area Community Foundation, at the above address.

3723 ■ Phil Shykes Memorial Scholarships
(Undergraduate/Scholarship)

Purpose: To provide financial assistance to graduating seniors from Hermantown High School for post-secondary education at vocational school, college or university. **Focus:** General studies/Field of study not specified. **Qualif.:** Applicants must be graduating seniors from Hermantown High School who are intending to pursue post-secondary education at a vocational college, community college, or other college or university on a full-time basis, and have achieved a 2.5 or higher cumulative GPA (on a 4.0 scale) in high school. **Criteria:** Recipients will be selected based on the following criteria: (1) financial need; (2) family profile; (3) involvement in community service; (4) major field of interest; (5) determination to pursue a higher education or vocation; and (6) employment (optional).

Funds Avail.: $1,000. **Duration:** Annual. **To Apply:** Applicants must submit a completed DSACF Common Scholarship Application form; academic transcript (including standardized test scores); one letter of recommendation; and financial need documentation. **Remarks:** Established in 1999. **Contact:** Duluth-Superior Area Community Foundation, at the above address.

3724 ■ Dale and Betty George Sola Scholarships
(Undergraduate/Scholarship)

Purpose: To provide financial assistance for graduating seniors who reside in the central area of Duluth, who attend the Marshall School or several alternative schools in Duluth. **Focus:** General studies/Field of study not specified. **Qualif.:** Applicants must be students of Duluth Central High School, the Marshall School, Lakeview Christian Academy and alternative schools (including Unity School and the Harbor City International School) in the central areas of Duluth; or, graduates residing within the Central Hillside or Park Point areas who have a grade point average of 2.75 (on a 4.0 scale) or higher. **Criteria:** Recipients will be selected based on the following criteria: (1)

demonstrated leadership; (2) hard-working behavior; (3) financial need; (4) good work ethic; (5) involvement in community and school activities; and (6) academic performance. Preference will be given to students who are not in the top ten percent of the graduating class.

Funds Avail.: $1,000. **To Apply:** Applicants must complete the DSACF Common Scholarship Application available from the Guidance Offices; academic transcript (including standardized test scores); two letters of recommendation; and financial need documentation. **Remarks:** Established in 2003. **Contact:** Duluth-Superior Area Community Foundation, at the above address.

3725 ■ John A. and Jean Quinn Sullivan Scholarship Funds *(Undergraduate/Scholarship)*

Purpose: To provide financial assistance for students majoring in education who are in financial need. **Focus:** Education. **Qualif.:** Applicants must be graduates of Senior High in Superior, Wisconsin who will attend their junior and senior years at the University of Wisconsin-Superior majoring in education. **Criteria:** Recipients will be selected based on financial need, academic record, written recommendations, and seriousness of purpose.

Funds Avail.: Around $1,000 per year. **Duration:** Annual. **Number Awarded:** 1. **To Apply:** Applicants must contact the University of Wisconsin Education Department for application form. **Remarks:** Established in 1996. **Contact:** Duluth-Superior Area Community Foundation, at the above address.

3726 ■ Robert B. and Sophia Whiteside Scholarships *(Undergraduate/Scholarship)*

Purpose: To provide financial assistance to students of Duluth high schools who are going to attend college. **Focus:** General studies/Field of study not specified. **Qualif.:** Applicants must be high school seniors graduating from schools, including home schools, in Duluth and seek admission to any fully-accredited, degree granting college or university; and must be in top 10% of their class. **Criteria:** Applicants are evaluated based on academic achievement.

Funds Avail.: $6,000. **Duration:** Annual. **Number Awarded:** Varies. **To Apply:** Applicants must submit a completed application form; academic transcript (including standardized test scores); and two letters of recommendation. **Remarks:** Established in 1976. **Contact:** Duluth-Superior Area Community Foundation, at the above address.

3727 ■ Dumbarton Oaks Research Library and Collection
1703 32nd St. NW
Washington, DC 20007
Ph: (202)339-6401
Fax: (202)625-0279
E-mail: museum@doaks.org
URL: www.doaks.org
Facebook: www.facebook.com/DumbartonOaksResearchLibraryandCollection

3728 ■ Dumbarton Oaks Fellowships *(Doctorate, Graduate/Fellowship)*

Purpose: To promote research in Byzantine studies, Pre-Columbian studies and Garden and Landscape Studies. Awarded in various categories. **Focus:** Byzantine studies; Pre-Columbian studies. **Qualif.:** Applicant must be a graduate students who expects to have a PhD prior to taking up residence at Dumbarton Oaks. **Criteria:** Selection is based on the submitted application materials.

Funds Avail.: No specific amount. **Duration:** One academic year. **To Apply:** Applicants are required to complete the application online. In addition, applicants must submit three letters of recommendation. **Deadline:** November 1.

3729 ■ Dumbarton Oaks Junior Fellowships *(Graduate/Fellowship)*

Purpose: To promote research in Byzantine studies, Pre-Columbian studies and Garden and Landscape Studies. **Focus:** Byzantine studies; Pre-Columbian studies. **Qualif.:** Applicants must be degree candidates who, at the time of application, have fulfilled all preliminary requirements for a PhD (or appropriate final degree) and will be working on a dissertation or final project at Dumbarton Oaks. **Criteria:** Selection is based on the submitted application materials.

Funds Avail.: No specific amount. **Duration:** one academic year. **To Apply:** Applicants are required to complete the application online. In addition, applicants must submit three letters of recommendation and a transcript of graduate record (sent by university registrar). **Deadline:** November 1.

3730 ■ Dumbarton Oaks Research Library and Collection Bliss Symposium Awards *(Undergraduate, Graduate/Award)*

Purpose: To provide travel expenses for Harvard students wishing to attend the annual symposia in Byzantine, Pre-Columbian, or Garden and Landscape studies at Dumbarton Oaks. **Focus:** Byzantine studies. **Qualif.:** Applicants must be currently-enrolled graduate students or undergraduate juniors or seniors at Harvard University. Preference will be given to students in concentrations relevant to the programs of study at Dumbarton Oaks. **Criteria:** Selection will be based on the committee's criteria.

Funds Avail.: No specific amount. **To Apply:** Applicants should prepare an application consisting of a brief cover letter stating why the conference is of interest, curriculum vitae, and one letter of recommendation, which should be from the applicant's advisor or department chair. Applications must be received at least four weeks prior to the symposium, and should be marked "Bliss Awards" and directed to the appropriate study program. Recipients of the Bliss Symposium Awards are responsible for making their own arrangements for travel and accommodation. No housing will be available at Dumbarton Oaks during the symposia. Funds will be disbursed only after the successful applicant has submitted a travel expense form and original receipts.

3731 ■ Dumbarton Oaks Research Library and Collection Graduate Research Workshops *(Undergraduate, Graduate/Fellowship)*

Purpose: To support group of students on their research workshops that intersect with the Institute's particular fields of study and resources. **Focus:** Byzantine studies. **Qualif.:** Applicants must be group of students about 4-8 members, graduate or undergraduate, and have already formed or planning to form a research workshop at Harvard University. **Criteria:** Selection will be based on the committee's criteria.

Funds Avail.: No specific amount. **Duration:** No less than two days and no longer than a week. **To Apply:** Applicants must submit a 250-word proposal outlining the nature and purpose of the workshop, the names and resumes of

Awards are arranged alphabetically below their administering organizations

student participants and the principal student coordinator. The proposal should include at least three possible bands of time when the visits to Dumbarton Oaks could take place. **Contact:** Proposals should be sent to Professor Jan Ziolkowski, Director; Dumbarton Oaks Research Library and Collection; 1703 32nd St., NW, Washington DC 20007-2934.

3732 ■ Dumbarton Oaks Research Library and Collection One-Month Research Stipends *(Doctorate/Monetary)*

Purpose: To engage students in advance research in one of Dumbarton Oaks subject specialties. **Focus:** Byzantine studies. **Qualif.:** Applicants must be scholars holding PhD or other relevant terminal degree and working on research projects in Byzantine studies, Pre-Columbian studies, or Garden and Landscapes studies. **Criteria:** Preference will be given to applicants who live 75 or more miles from Washington, D.C.

Funds Avail.: $3,000. **To Apply:** Applicants must submit an online application prior to the deadline of the applicants proposed research visit and must notify the department to which they are applying via email. A completed online application must include a project proposal of no more than 1,000 words and two letters of reference. Proposed project must contain the following: an overview of the project, its significance in the applicant's discipline and ways in which research will complement; and the challenge in studying their field. Applicants must also describe in the statement the importance of Dumbarton Oaks library holdings or museum collections to their project. Successful U.S. citizen's applicants must provide a copy of an original Social Security card and a U.S. Social Security number or an International Taxpayer Identification Number (ITIN) for the non-U.S. citizens for stipend disbursement. Dumbarton Oaks provides J-1 visas for the month, as part of our U.S. Department of State-designated Exchange Visitor Program. In order to qualify, scholars must provide proof of health insurance that fulfills the criteria of the J-1 visa.

3733 ■ Dumbarton Oaks Research Library and Collection Post-Baccalaureate Media Fellowships *(Graduate/Fellowship)*

Purpose: To develop and apply their research skills while gaining experience in related professional fields and contributing to the institutional mission of Dumbarton Oaks. **Focus:** Byzantine studies. **Qualif.:** Applicants must be Harvard college graduates. **Criteria:** Selection will be based on the committee's criteria.

Funds Avail.: No specific amount. **Duration:** Annual. **To Apply:** Applicants must send a cover letter and resume. **Contact:** fellowshipprograms@doaks.org.

3734 ■ Dumbarton Oaks Research Library and Collection Project Grants *(Doctorate/Grant)*

Purpose: To assist scholars in conducting research about Byzantine, Pre-Columbian, or Garden and Landscape Studies. **Focus:** Byzantine studies. **Qualif.:** Applicants must be holding a doctorate or appropriate final degree and not currently affiliated with Dumbarton Oaks. **Criteria:** Selection of applicants will be based on the ability and preparation of the principal project personnel (including knowledge of the requisite languages) and interest in and value of the project to the specific field of the study.

Funds Avail.: $3,000-$10,000. **To Apply:** Applicants must submit a project proposal regarding on either one of the following: Pre-Columbian project, Garden and Landscape project or Byzantine project. Applicants must contact the appropriate director of the studies before applying, to determine if the planning project is within the purview of Dumbarton Oaks. Completed applications must include three letter of reference posted directly by the recommenders to the online application. Upon completion of their projects, grant recipients will be asked to submit brief reports of their work suitable for dissemination on the Dumbarton Oaks website. For projects involving photography, Dumbarton Oaks requests that successful applicants provide a set of digital images to document their work. Reports, no longer than 2,000 words, should be submitted as both Microsoft Word and PDF documents, with one to three illustrations sent separately in .tif or .jpg format. All photographs and illustrations for documentation and for project grant reports must be submitted in digital format, and as separate high resolution files--not embedded in another type of document. All images must be of sufficient quality for print publication--at least 7" wide at 300 dpi, or about 2100 pixels wide. Maps, graphs, and line drawings should be supplied as vector graphics, such as Adobe Illustrator .ai or .eps. Byzantine project grant recipients may also be asked to submit longer reports covering more than one season for publication in Dumbarton Oaks Papers; while it does not guarantee publication. All applications must be in English and submitted electronically.

3735 ■ Dumbarton Oaks Research Library and Collection Short-Term Predoctoral Residencies Grants *(Doctorate/Grant)*

Purpose: To support scholars in doing their research in the field of Byzantine, Pre-Columbian, or Garden and Landscape studies. **Focus:** Byzantine studies. **Qualif.:** Applicants must be advanced graduate students who are preparing for their PhD general exams, writing their doctoral dissertations, or expecting relevant final degrees in the field of Byzantine, Pre-Columbian, or Garden and Landscape studies. Preference will be given to those who need access to the fieldwork and photo collections or to the Rare Book Room, or who wish to examine museum objects. **Criteria:** Selection will be based on the committee's criteria.

Funds Avail.: No specific amount. **Duration:** Two to four weeks. **To Apply:** Applicants must send the following to the appropriate Director of Studies and subject librarian, at least 60 days before the preferred residency dates: letter of request specifically the desired period of stay and the purpose of the visit; and brief curriculum vitae with address and telephone number, U.S. Social Security number, education, awards and honors, present and past positions (if applicable), publication, papers read, field research, etc. and a statement about language competences. In addition, applicants must have their academic adviser send a letter of recommendation directly to the appropriate Director of Studies at Dumbarton Oaks.

3736 ■ Dumbarton Oaks Research Library and Collection Summer Fellowships *(Graduate/Fellowship)*

Purpose: To support students who are interested in learning and conducting research in Byzantine, Garden and Landscape, and Pre-Columbian studies. **Focus:** Byzantine studies. **Qualif.:** Applicants must be Byzantine, Pre-Columbian, or Garden and Landscape Scholars on any level of advancement beyond the first year of graduate (post-baccalaureate) study. **Criteria:** Selection will be based on the committee's criteria.

Funds Avail.: No specific amount. **To Apply:** Applicants must present a proposal considering all aspects of these

Awards are arranged alphabetically below their administering organizations

interdisciplinary and international fields: agricultural; architectural; art historical; botanical; cultural; ecological; economic; geographical; horticultural; social; and technological.

3737 ■ Dumbarton Oaks Research Library and Collection Summer Internships for Harvard Students
(Undergraduate, Graduate/Internship)

Purpose: To support educational expenses of the students in studying Byzantine, Pre-Columbian, or Garden and Landscape Studies. **Focus:** Byzantine studies. **Qualif.:** Applicants must be undergraduate or graduate students of Harvard. **Criteria:** Selection will be based on the committee's criteria.

Funds Avail.: No specific amount. **Duration:** Eight to ten weeks. **To Apply:** Applicants must submit through online the following requirements: resume; a statement of interest describing any relevant experience and how internship fits into personal and professional development of the applicant; and a separate sheet with the names of two referees familiar with the applicant's scholar work, along with their titles and contact information (preferably as one PDF document). **Deadline:** March 2. **Contact:** internships@doaks.org.

3738 ■ Dumbarton Oaks Research Library and Collection Post-Doctoral Teaching Fellowships
(Postdoctorate/Fellowship)

Purpose: To promote research in Byzantine studies, Pre-Columbian studies, and Garden and Landscape Studies. **Focus:** Byzantine studies; Pre-Columbian studies. **Qualif.:** Applicant must have completed all requirements for the doctoral degree; a citizen of the U.S. or Canada or a graduate of a North American university; and must have an excellent command of spoken and written English. **Criteria:** Selection is based on demonstrated scholarly accomplishment and overall academic excellence and promise; potential future impact on the field of Byzantine studies through teaching and writing; significance and quality of the research project(s) to be carried out at Dumbarton Oaks; knowledge of the relevant ancient and modern languages; and ability to contribute to the academic community at Dumbarton Oaks and local area universities.

Funds Avail.: No specific amount. **Duration:** three years. **To Apply:** Applicants must submit six copies of an application consisting of a cover letter that includes a statement of teaching experience and proposed courses; a curriculum vitae; a writing sample of not more than forty pages; a 1000-word description of the research project(s) to be carried out during the term of the fellowship; and three letters of recommendation.

3739 ■ Mellon Fellowships in Urban Landscape Studies
(Graduate, Master's, Doctorate/Fellowship)

Purpose: To support devoted students to pursue research about garden and landscape studies. **Focus:** Landscape architecture and design. **Qualif.:** Applicants must be scholars and designers pursuing on the history and current conditions of urban landscapes. Preference will be given to applicants with final degree such as PhD or MLA. **Criteria:** Applicants will be evaluated based on the suitability and clarity of the research objectives, the relevance to the fellowship project, the feasibility of the budget and schedule, and the potential contribution to the field of urban landscape studies.

Funds Avail.: No specific amount. **To Apply:** Applicants must submit three letters of recommendation. A supplemental application is required, which should be uploaded, as a separate attachment, in section 8 of the online application. The request, which may be in narrative form, should explain the location, timing, and purpose of the proposed field research, the anticipated outcomes, the relation to the larger fellowship project, and the preparation and suitability of the applicants for the proposed research. Proposals should also include a preliminary budget and schedule of work. For non-U.S. citizens, Dumbarton Oaks provides J-1 visas for the term of the Fellowship appointment, as part of our U.S. Department of State-designated Exchange Visitor Program. Please be advised that scholars who have been in the United States with J status within the past 12 months may not qualify for a Dumbarton Oaks J-1 visa unless they were in the United States for a total time of less than six months. These individuals and all other non-U.S. citizens are strongly urged to check their prospective visa status for the requested period of the Fellowship prior to submitting an application. **Contact:** mellon@doaks.org.

3740 ■ William R. Tyler Fellowships *(Graduate/Fellowship)*

Purpose: To provide funds to graduate students with genuine intellectual interests on Pre-Columbian/early Colonial or Mediterranean/Byzantine worlds or in Garden and Landscape history. **Focus:** Byzantine studies. **Qualif.:** Applicants must be Harvard graduate students in art history, archaeology, history and literature of the Pre-Columbian/early Colonial or Mediterranean/Byzantine worlds or in Garden and Landscape history, who have completed all departmental requirements for the PhD before the application deadline. **Criteria:** Selection will be based on the committee's criteria.

Funds Avail.: No specific amount. **To Apply:** Applicants must provide three letters of recommendation, two of which should be from professors in their department at Harvard Universities and one of which should be from their dissertation supervisor. For further application information kindly visits the society's website.

3741 ■ Gabriel Dumont Institute of Native Studies and Applied Research (GDI)
917 - 22nd St. W
Saskatoon, SK, Canada S7M 0R9
Ph: (306)242-6070
Fax: (306)242-0002
Free: 877-488-6888
E-mail: info@gdins.org
URL: www.gdins.org

3742 ■ Gabriel Dumont College Graduate Student Bursary *(Postgraduate, Master's, Doctorate/Scholarship)*

Purpose: To provide financial assistance and encourage Saskatchewan Metis to pursue full time graduate studies and conduct research in fields related to Metis people. **Focus:** Culture. **Qualif.:** Applicants must be Metis students who are pursuing full-time academics at the postgraduate level, Masters or Doctorate at a recognized university in Canada or abroad. **Criteria:** Applicants will be selected by criteria of the selection committee.

Funds Avail.: No specific amount. **Duration:** Annual. **Number Awarded:** Varies. **To Apply:** Applicants must submit the most recent two years of the official transcript of post-

Awards are arranged alphabetically below their administering organizations

secondary education and photocopy of membership card or a letter from Metis Nation (Saskatchewan Local President or Area Director) as a proof of being a Metis. **Deadline:** April 6 and October 6.

3743 ■ Dutchess County Bar Association (DCBA)
PO Box 4865
Poughkeepsie, NY 12602
Ph: (845)473-2488
Fax: (845)485-1484
URL: www.dutchesscountybar.org

3744 ■ Joseph H. Gellert/Dutchess County Bar Association Scholarships (Undergraduate/Scholarship)
Purpose: To provide financial assistance for the residents of Dutchess County intending to attend an accredited law school. **Focus:** Law. **Qualif.:** Applicants must be Dutchess County residents who completed at least one year of law school. **Criteria:** Applicants will be evaluated based on financial need.

Funds Avail.: No specific amount. **Duration:** Annual. **Number Awarded:** 2. **To Apply:** Applicants must submit application; copy of law school transcript; essay of approximately 500 words describing interest in the law and career aspirations; letter of recommendation; and resume.

3745 ■ Dystonia Medical Research Foundation (DMRF)
1 E Wacker Dr., Ste. 2810
Chicago, IL 60601-1905
Ph: (312)755-0198
Fax: (312)803-0138
Free: 800-377-3978
E-mail: dystonia@dystonia-foundation.org
URL: www.dystonia-foundation.org
Facebook: www.facebook.com/Dystonia-Medical-Research-Foundation-46820882711
Twitter: twitter.com/dmrf

3746 ■ Dystonia Medical Research Foundation Clinical Fellowships (Postdoctorate/Fellowship)
Purpose: To assist post-doctoral fellows in establishing careers in research relevant to dystonia. **Focus:** Muscular dystrophy. **Qualif.:** Applicants must be in their post-doctoral degree. **Criteria:** Applicant will be selected based on their proposal.

Funds Avail.: $75,000 per year. **Duration:** One year. **To Apply:** Applicants must submit a proposal. In addition, applicants should include the following attachments: Application Cover Sheet (use form provided); Budget (use form provided); biographical sketch of principal investigator and all key personnel (Use standard NIH form); Research Funding Terms and Conditions, signed by applicant and applicant's institutional official; letters of support (one letter from a mentor); and relevant articles, video clips, or other items, if applicable. **Deadline:** February 22.

3747 ■ Early American Industries Association (EAIA)
PO Box 524
Hebron, MD 21830-0524
Ph: (508)993-9578
E-mail: eaia@comcast.net
URL: www.earlyamericanindustries.org
Facebook: www.facebook.com/EarlyAmericanIndustries

3748 ■ EAIA Research Grants (Other/Grant)
Purpose: To preserve and present historic trades, crafts and tools that will reflect their impact in our lives. **Focus:** Crafts; Industry and trade. **Qualif.:** Applicants must be individuals with a research related to trades, crafts and tools. **Criteria:** Recipients will be evaluated based on submitted research.

Funds Avail.: Up to $3,000. **Duration:** Annual. **To Apply:** Applicants must submit a research; project must be related to the purpose of the EAIA; the total length including the form may not exceed ten pages; successful applicants will be required to file a report on the project attached on a form; one copy of the final form of the completed project must be deposited to the Research Grants Committee, whether or not the final form is published; applicants are asked to give the names and addresses of their local newspapers, so the Research Grants Committee can announce new grant recipients. **Deadline:** March 15. **Contact:** For information and applications contact: John H. Verrill, Executive Director, at the above address.

3749 ■ Earthquake Engineering Research Institute (EERI)
499 14th St., Ste. 320
Oakland, CA 94612-1934
Ph: (510)451-0905
Fax: (510)451-5411
E-mail: eeri@eeri.org
URL: www.eeri.org
Facebook: www.facebook.com/EERI.org

3750 ■ EERI/FEMA Graduate Fellowship in Earthquake Hazard Reduction (Graduate/Fellowship)
Purpose: To support study and research that may contribute to the science and practice of earthquake hazard mitigation. **Focus:** Earth sciences. **Qualif.:** Applicants must be enrolled in a graduate degree program at an accredited U.S. college/university and must hold U.S. citizenship or permanent resident status. **Criteria:** Selection is based on the submitted application and materials.

Funds Avail.: $12,000 with $8,000 for tuition, fees and research expenses. **Duration:** Annual; 9 months. **To Apply:** Applicants must submit a completed application form along with the letter of nomination by faculty sponsor; academic transcript; a statement (maximum of 300 words) of educational and career goals; and a resume (maximum of two pages). In addition, two letters of recommendation must be sent by the author directly to EERI. **Deadline:** May 29.

3751 ■ East Tennessee Foundation (ETF)
520 W Summit Hill Dr., Ste. 1101
Knoxville, TN 37902-2219
Ph: (865)524-1223
Fax: (865)637-6039
Free: 877-524-1223
URL: www.easttennesseefoundation.org
Facebook: www.facebook.com/etfdn

3752 ■ B&W Y-12 Scholarship Fund (Undergraduate/Scholarship)
Purpose: To benefit graduating high school seniors wishing to pursue careers in science, math or pre-engineering

Awards are arranged alphabetically below their administering organizations

related fields. **Focus:** Engineering; Mathematics and mathematical sciences; Science. **Qualif.:** Applicants must be enrolled as full-time students at either Roane State Community College or Pellissippi State Technical College; must be U.S citizens; must have a minimum GPA of at least 3.0; be a graduating senior from a high school located in Anderson, Blount, Campbell, Claiborne, Cocke, Knox, Loudon, Morgan, Roane or Sevier counties. **Criteria:** A selection committee will be pre-selected and approved by ETF's board of Directors. The committee's primary function shall be the one to select the scholarship recipient, not only by considering the applicants' qualifications under criteria established above but also in consideration of the following factors: Scholastic and academic achievements; general aptitude for advanced educational work and seriousness of purpose; qualities of citizenship in school and in community such as volunteer work and employment history; participation in extracurricular activities at school or in the community; demonstrated financial need.

Funds Avail.: $1,400. **Number Awarded:** 1. **To Apply:** Applicants must check the application process online. **Deadline:** March 13. **Remarks:** Established in 2004.

3753 ■ Ruby A. Brown Memorial Scholarships (Undergraduate/Scholarship)

Purpose: To benefit health nurses seeking to continue their nursing education. **Focus:** Nursing. **Qualif.:** Applicants must be currently employed as a public health nurse; must be residents in one of 15 counties (Anderson, Blount, Campbell, Claiborne, Cocke, Grainger, Hamblen, Jefferson, Loudon, Monroe, Morgan, Roane, Scott, Sevier or Union); may pursue their education at any accredited, not-for-profit nursing program on a full-time or part-time basis. **Criteria:** Selection of recipient and alternate will be based upon current level of education, additional training being pursued, length of employment, current county of employment, financial need and GPA.

Funds Avail.: $3,000. **To Apply:** Applicants must check the application process online and must submit two reference letters. Applicants must send five copies of the application and attachments plus the originals. **Deadline:** March 13. **Remarks:** Established in 2003.

3754 ■ Gordon W. and Agnes P. Cobb Scholarships (Undergraduate/Scholarship)

Purpose: To benefit graduates of high schools in Blount, Loudon, and Knox counties in Tennessee who wish to pursue or who are pursuing college education in a health care or medical-related field. **Focus:** Health sciences. **Qualif.:** Applicants must show proof of maintaining full-time enrollment and a 3.0 or better academic standing in a health care or medical related curriculum each year through the submission of academic transcripts to the foundation at the end of each semester. **Criteria:** Selection will be based on the following criteria: Academic promise and achievement; enrolled in a health care or medical-related curriculum; desire to pursue advanced education in a health care or medical-related field; evidence of a strong work or volunteer history; must demonstrate financial need. Applicants from single-parent families will be given special consideration.

Funds Avail.: $10,000 per year. **Duration:** Up to 4 years. **To Apply:** Applicants must check the application process online. **Deadline:** March 13. **Remarks:** Established in 1996.

3755 ■ Steven L. Coffey Memorial Scholarships (Undergraduate/Scholarship)

Purpose: To assist students who possess the potential for excellence but may require some additional support in achieving their educational goals. **Focus:** General studies/Field of study not specified. **Qualif.:** Applicants must either be Anderson County residents and graduates of Anderson County High School, Clinton Senior High School or Oak Ridge High School. **Criteria:** Grants are awarded based on academic excellence; must have financial need; must also present an evidence of a 2.5 GPA or better; and the desire to pursue a post secondary education.

Funds Avail.: $1,500-$2,000. **To Apply:** Applicants must check the application online for the required materials. **Deadline:** April 20. **Remarks:** Established in 1988.

3756 ■ R.G. and Ruth Crossno Memorial Scholarships (Undergraduate/Scholarship)

Purpose: To benefit graduating seniors of Anderson County High School who wish to pursue an advanced degree. **Focus:** General studies/Field of study not specified. **Qualif.:** Applicants must be enrolled as full-time students in an accredited public or private not-for-profit university or community college. **Criteria:** Selection of scholars will be based on applicants' demonstrated financial need, career motivation, academic promise and evidence of strong work experience.

Funds Avail.: $1,400. **Duration:** Renewable up to four years. **To Apply:** Applicants must check the application process online as well as the required materials. **Deadline:** March 13. **Remarks:** Mr. R.G. Crossno, past mayor of Norris, Tennessee and 21-year member of the Anderson County School Board dedicated his life to promoting better education throughout the state of Tennessee. Established in 1990.

3757 ■ Michael D. Curtin Renaissance Student Memorial Scholarships (Undergraduate/Scholarship)

Purpose: To recognize and benefit students who demonstrate leadership or achievement in a balanced array of activities, including the arts, athletics, citizenship, community/religious service and academics. **Focus:** General studies/Field of study not specified. **Qualif.:** Applicants must be enrolled as full time students in an accredited public or private not-for-profit university. **Criteria:** Selection of scholars will be selected by the scholarship committee consisting of five faculty members from Anderson County High School; they will review all applications, conduct interviews and make funding recommendations to East Tennessee Foundation Board of Directors.

Funds Avail.: $1,000. **Duration:** Up to 4 years. **To Apply:** Applicants must check the application process online. **Deadline:** March 13. **Remarks:** Established in 2000.

3758 ■ East-West Center (EWC)
1601 E West Rd.
Honolulu, HI 96848-1601
Ph: (808)944-7111
Fax: (808)944-7376
URL: www.eastwestcenter.org

3759 ■ Asian Development Bank - Japan Scholarships (Graduate/Scholarship)

Purpose: To support students to participate in educational programs at the East-West Center while pursuing graduate study in the ADB approved fields at the University of Hawaii at Manoa. **Focus:** General studies/Field of study not specified. **Qualif.:** Applicants must be citizens of a developing member country of the Asian Development Bank; must have a 4-year bachelor's degree or the equivalent of a 4-year bachelor's degree at the time of application; must have a Master's degree that is equivalent to a US Master's degree to apply for Doctoral studies; must have at least two years of full-time professional work experience at the time of application; must take one of the English proficiency tests. The minimum acceptable scores are 550 for TOEFL or 6.5 for IELTS. **Criteria:** Selection will be based on the committee's criteria.

Funds Avail.: No specific amount. **To Apply:** Applicants must complete the following materials: ADB Scholarship Application Form; University of Hawai'i Graduate Admissions Application; curriculum vitae; completed essays 1-3; writing sample; application fee; two official transcripts from each institution attended; one official degree certificate for every degree earned; three letters of reference; official TOEFL or IELTS test score report received directly by East-West Center from the Testing Center; official GRE; official GMAT test scores. Application form, letter of reference form and letter of reference-community service can be downloaded at the website. **Deadline:** November 1. **Contact:** East-West Center, Award Services/ADB-JSP Scholarship, John A. Burns Hall, Room 2066, 1601 East-West Road, Honolulu, HI 96848-1601; Phone: 808-944-7738; Fax: 808-944-7730; E-mail: adbjsp@eastwestcenter.org.

3760 ■ East-West Center Graduate Degree Fellowships *(Master's, Doctorate, Graduate/Fellowship)*

Purpose: To support students to participate in educational and research programs at the East-West Center while pursuing graduate study at the University of Hawai'i. **Focus:** General studies/Field of study not specified. **Qualif.:** Applicants must be citizens or permanent residents of the United States and citizens of countries in the Pacific and Asia, including Russia. **Criteria:** Selection will be based on the committee's criteria.

Funds Avail.: No specific amount. **Duration:** One year. **To Apply:** Interested applicants may contact the Center for the application process and other information. **Deadline:** November 1. **Contact:** East-West Center, Award Services Office; Phone: 808-944-7735; Fax: 808-944-7730; Email: scholarships@eastwestcenter.org.

3761 ■ Indonesian Directorate General of Higher Education Scholarships *(Graduate/Scholarship)*

Purpose: To support students to participate in educational and research program at the East-West Center while pursuing graduate study at the University of Hawaii. **Focus:** General studies/Field of study not specified. **Qualif.:** Applicants must be citizens of Indonesia pursuing graduate study at the University of Hawaii. **Criteria:** Selection will be based on the committee's criteria.

Funds Avail.: No specific amount. **To Apply:** Interested applicants may contact the Center for the application process and other information. **Deadline:** November 1. **Contact:** East-West Center at scholarships@eastwestcenter.org.

3762 ■ Obuchi Student Scholarships *(Graduate/Scholarship)*

Purpose: To support students to participate in educational, cultural, residential and leadership programs at the East-West Center while pursuing a Master's degree at the University of Hawaii or for study in the Asia Pacific Leadership Program. **Focus:** General studies/Field of study not specified. **Qualif.:** Applicants must be residents of Okinawa, Japan, who have the intention of returning to Okinawa on completion of study, to contribute to the development needs of Okinawa; must be enrolled or planning to enroll in an MA program at the University of Hawaii at Manoa. **Criteria:** Selection will be based on the committee's criteria.

Funds Avail.: No specific amount. **To Apply:** Interested applicants may contact the Center for the application process and other information. **Deadline:** November 1. **Contact:** East-West Center, Award Services Office; Phone: 808-944-7735; Fax: 808-944-7730; Email: scholarships@eastwestcenter.org.

3763 ■ Southeast Asian Ministers of Education Organization-Vietnam Scholarship Program *(Graduate/Scholarship)*

Purpose: To support students to participate in educational and research program at the East-West Center while pursuing graduate study at the University of Hawaii. **Focus:** General studies/Field of study not specified. **Qualif.:** Applicants must be citizens of Vietnam. **Criteria:** Selection will be based on the committee's criteria.

Funds Avail.: No specific amount. **To Apply:** Interested applicants may contact the Center for the application process and other information. **Contact:** East-West Center, Award Services Office; Phone: 808-944-7735; Fax: 808-944-7730; Email: scholarships@eastwestcenter.org.

3764 ■ Easter Seals Ontario
1 Concorde Gate, Ste. 700
Toronto, ON, Canada M3C 3N6
Ph: (416)421-8377
Fax: (416)696-1035
Free: 800-668-6252
E-mail: info@easterseals.org
URL: www.easterseals.org
Facebook: www.facebook.com/EasterSealsON
LinkedIn: www.linkedin.com/company/107859
Twitter: twitter.com/eastersealson

3765 ■ The Leaders of Tomorrow Scholarships *(Undergraduate, Vocational/Occupational/Scholarship)*

Purpose: To assist young adults with physical disabilities with the cost of post-secondary education or vocational training. **Focus:** Education, Vocational-technical. **Qualif.:** Applicants must be seeking for post-secondary education; demonstrated consistent level of scholastic achievement throughout their secondary school curriculum; participated as a spokesperson for The Easter Seal Society; must served as models and inspirations to fellow students; and have applied for alternate financial assistance and still require assistance. **Criteria:** Applicants are evaluated based on financial need.

Funds Avail.: No specific amount. **To Apply:** Applicants must submit the completed application form along with typed, one-page letter outlining the qualifications for the award, including scholastic achievement, motivation, initiative and extra-curricular activities; copy of secondary and, if applicable, post-secondary transcripts; any interim marks that are available before the deadline; and, proof of application to applicable alternate sources of financial assistance. **Remarks:** Established in 2007. **Contact:** Tina

Shier at scholarships@easterseals.org.

3766 ■ Beatrice Drinnan Spence Scholarships
(Undergraduate, Vocational/Occupational/Scholarship)

Purpose: To assist young adults with physical disabilities with the cost of post-secondary education or vocational training. **Focus:** Education, Vocational-technical. **Qualif.:** Applicants must be resident students of Ontario with disabilities who are currently applying to or enrolled in a post-secondary educational facility like university or community college. **Criteria:** Applicants are evaluated based on personal attributes and financial need.

Funds Avail.: $5,000. **Duration:** Annual. **Number Awarded:** 1. **To Apply:** Applicants must submit the completed application form along with a one-page letter outlining qualifications for the award including scholastic achievement, motivation, initiative and extra-curricular activities; copy of secondary and, if applicable, post-secondary transcripts; any interim marks that are available before the deadline; and, proof of application to applicable alternate sources of financial assistance. **Deadline:** May 8. **Remarks:** Established in 2004. **Contact:** Tina Shier at scholarships@easterseals.org.

3767 ■ Eastern Communication Association (ECA)
Duquesne University
Department of Communication & Rhetorical Studies
340 College Hall
600 Forbes Ave.
Pittsburgh, PA 15219
E-mail: info@ecasite.org
URL: associationdatabase.com

3768 ■ ECA Applied Urban Communication Research Grants *(Professional development/Grant)*

Purpose: To foster and promote significant inter-disciplinary communication research contributions that extend the boundaries of "applied research". **Focus:** Communications. **Qualif.:** Applicants must be members of the Eastern Communication Association. **Criteria:** Applicants will be evaluated based on potential impact of their work as well as the quality and rigor of their contributions.

Funds Avail.: $2,500. **Duration:** Annual. **To Apply:** Applicants must include the following: 1) a cover letter explaining why the applicant deserves the award; 2) 500-word essay describing their career goals, outlining the anticipated outcomes, intended mode of dissemination of the research; 3) anticipated budget and timetable for completion of the project; 4) copy of the curriculum vitae; and at least one supporting letter from someone well-acquainted with the nominee. **Deadline:** March 4. **Contact:** ECA Past President Thomas R. Flynn at thomas.flynn@sru.edu.

3769 ■ ECA Centennial Scholarships *(Master's, Doctorate/Scholarship)*

Purpose: To assist deserving PhD and M.A. students in their education. **Focus:** Communications. **Qualif.:** Applicants must be PhD or M.A. students in Communication who are current ECA members. **Criteria:** Recipients will be selected based on submitted materials and academic achievement.

Funds Avail.: No specific amount. **Duration:** Annual. **To Apply:** Application is via nomination. Nominations must include a letter of nomination from the thesis/dissertation advisor attesting the nominees' student status. Must submit a four page, 1500-word project summary. **Deadline:** March 15. **Contact:** Thomas R. Flynn, ECA Past President, at thomas.flynn@sru.edu.

3770 ■ Eastman Community Music School (ECMS)
Eastman School of Music
University of Rochester
26 Gibbs St.
Rochester, NY 14604-2505
Ph: (585)274-1400
Fax: (585)274-1005
E-mail: community@esm.rochester.edu
URL: www.esm.rochester.edu/community

3771 ■ ECMS Scholarships *(Undergraduate/Scholarship)*

Purpose: To assist ECMS students in their continuing education. **Focus:** Music. **Qualif.:** Applicants must be ECMS students enrolled in a diploma program. **Criteria:** Selection shall be based on merit and financial need.

Funds Avail.: No specific amount. **Duration:** Annual. **To Apply:** Applicants must submit a completed application form along with Financial Assistance Application Form; teacher recommendation; and copy of the first page of the applicant's federal tax form. **Remarks:** The scholarships are awarded in various names.

3772 ■ Echoing Green
494 8th Ave., 2nd Fl.
New York, NY 10165
Ph: (212)689-1165
Fax: (212)689-9010
E-mail: info@echoinggreen.org
URL: www.echoinggreen.org

3773 ■ Echoing Green Black Male Achievement Fellowships *(Professional development/Fellowship)*

Purpose: To encourage individuals who are dedicated to improving the life outcomes of black men and boys in the United States. **Focus:** Social work. **Qualif.:** Applicants must be social entrepreneurs who are starting up new and innovative organizations in the field of black male achievement. **Criteria:** Selection will be based on the committee's criteria.

Funds Avail.: $80,000 for individuals; $90,000 for two-person partnerships. **To Apply:** Applicants may apply as individuals or as partners. They may contact Echoing Green for the application process.

3774 ■ Echoing Green Climate Fellowships *(Professional development/Fellowship)*

Purpose: To encourage individuals who are committed to working on innovations in mitigation and adaptation to climate change. **Focus:** Social work. **Qualif.:** Applicants must be next-generation social entrepreneurs committed to working on innovations in mitigation and adaptation to climate change. **Criteria:** Selection will be based on the committee's criteria.

Funds Avail.: $80,000 for individuals; $90,000 for two-person partnerships. **To Apply:** Applicants may apply as individuals or as partners. They may contact Echoing Green for the application process.

Awards are arranged alphabetically below their administering organizations

3775 ■ Echoing Green Global Fellowships *(Professional development/Fellowship)*

Purpose: To support emerging leaders working to bring about positive social change. **Focus:** Leadership, Institutional and community. **Qualif.:** Applicants must be emerging social entrepreneurs from any part of the world working to disrupt the status quo. **Criteria:** Selection will be based on the committee's criteria.

Funds Avail.: $80,000 for individuals; $90,000 for two-person partnerships. **To Apply:** Applicants may apply as individuals or as partners. They may contact Echoing Green for the application process.

3776 ■ Ecological Society of America (ESA)
1990 M St. NW, Ste. 700
Washington, DC 20036
Ph: (202)833-8773
Fax: (202)833-8775
E-mail: esahq@esa.org
URL: www.esa.org
Facebook: www.facebook.com/esa.org
Twitter: twitter.com/esa_org

3777 ■ Jasper Ridge Restoration Fellowships Jasper Ridge Biological Preserve *(Graduate, Postdoctorate/Fellowship)*

Purpose: To provide financial support to deserving students. **Focus:** General studies/Field of study not specified. **Qualif.:** Applicants must be post-doctoral students up to senior faculty. **Criteria:** Applications will be assessed based on an individual's past accomplishments and on potential to take full advantage of the ecosystems and past research at Jasper Ridge, as well as the intellectual community at Stanford.

Funds Avail.: $80,000. **To Apply:** Applicants must submit a CV, a 3-page description of their proposed program, and contact information for 3 references. **Deadline:** May 1. **Contact:** For additional information or to submit an application, please contact: Dr. Philippe Cohen at philippe.cohen@stanford.edu. Administrative Director, Jasper Ridge Biological Preserve, 4001 Sand Hill Road, Woodside, CA 94062. Applications should be submitted as email attachments.

3778 ■ Economic History Association (EHA)
McClelland Hall, 401GG
Dept. of Economics
University of Arizona
Tucson, AZ 85721
Ph: (520)621-4421
Fax: (520)621-8450
E-mail: fishback@email.arizona.edu
URL: eh.net/eha

3779 ■ Arthur H. Cole Grants in Aid *(Doctorate/Grant, Award)*

Purpose: To support research in economic history, regardless of time period or geographic area. **Focus:** History, Economic. **Qualif.:** Applicant must be a member of the association and must hold a Ph.D. degree. **Criteria:** Applicants with recent PhD degrees are given preference.

Funds Avail.: Up to $5,000. **Duration:** Annual. **To Apply:** Applicants must email required information: name, home address, institutional affiliation and contact information; submit a (five-page, single-spaced) proposal, inclusive of any footnotes, tables, and bibliography. Proposal should discuss how this grant will facilitate completion of the research; a curriculum vitae; and a project budget. **Deadline:** March 1. **Contact:** Professor Kirsten Wandschneider, Committee on Research in Economic History; Email: Kirsten@oxy.edu.

3780 ■ EHA Exploratory Travel and Data Grants *(Doctorate/Grant)*

Purpose: To provide students the financial assistance they need in research. **Focus:** History, Economic. **Qualif.:** Applicants must be doctoral students and current association members. **Criteria:** Recipients will be selected based on Committee's review of the application materials submitted.

Funds Avail.: Up to $2,500. **Duration:** Annual. **To Apply:** Applicants must e-mail required information: name, home address, institutional affiliation, contact information and the name of the chair of the dissertation committee; submit a copy of current curriculum vitae; a (one-page) itemized budget; a (three-page, double-spaced) proposal (inclusive of any footnotes, tables, and bibliography) that describes the topic, how the fellowship will help to complete the thesis, describes the work to date, time-table of completion and a brief bibliography. **Deadline:** January 15. **Contact:** Professor Kirsten Wandschneider, chair, Committee on Research in Economic History; Email: Kirsten@oxy.edu.

3781 ■ EHA Graduate Dissertation Fellowships *(Doctorate/Fellowship)*

Purpose: To support students whose thesis topics have been approved and who have made some progress towards writing their dissertation. **Focus:** History, Economic. **Qualif.:** Applicants must be current association members. **Criteria:** Recipients will be selected based on the committee's review of the application materials submitted.

Funds Avail.: $10,000. **Duration:** Annual. **To Apply:** Applicants must e-mail the following materials: name, home address, institutional affiliation, contact information and two reference letters (one from the chair of the thesis committee); submit a copy of current curriculum vitae; (five-page, single-spaced) proposal (inclusive of any footnotes, tables, and bibliography) that describes the topic, how the fellowship will help to complete the thesis, describes the work to date, time-table of completion and a brief bibliography; and a draft of a completed thesis chapter. **Deadline:** January 15.

3782 ■ EDiS Company
110 S. Poplar St., Ste.400
110 S Poplar St.
Wilmington, DE 19801
Free: 800-995-3347
URL: www.ediscompany.com
Facebook: www.facebook.com/ediscompany
LinkedIn: www.linkedin.com/company/edis-company
Twitter: www.twitter.com/EDiSCompany

3783 ■ Generation III Scholarships *(Undergraduate/Scholarship)*

Purpose: To support students who are planning to pursue an associate or bachelor's degree. **Focus:** Architecture; Business; Engineering. **Qualif.:** Applicants must be residents within the community in which EDiS is currently

Awards are arranged alphabetically below their administering organizations

working; must not be any employee of an EDiS Company or a relative of an employee of an EDiS Company; must be pursuing either an Associate's degree or Bachelor's degree; field of study is limited to business or construction-related degrees; and must have a cumulative GPA of 2.5 or greater for renewal. **Criteria:** Awards are given based on academic achievement, financial aid and field of study.

Funds Avail.: $1,000. **Duration:** Annual; up to four years. **Number Awarded:** 1. **To Apply:** Applicants must submit a completed scholarship application together with official transcript (from current institution) and a copy of best SAT score. **Deadline:** April 1. **Remarks:** Established in 1998.

3784 ■ EditMyPaper.ca
5863 Leslie St.
Toronto, ON, Canada M2h1J8
Ph: (647)428-1143
URL: editmypaper.ca

3785 ■ The Edit My Paper Proofreading Scholarships (Undergraduate/Scholarship)

Purpose: To reward great writers and allow them to showcase their rhetoric skills. **Focus:** Writing. **Qualif.:** Applicants must be enrolled in high school, college or university (North America/Europe). **Criteria:** Selection will be based on the following criteria: depth of thought; creativity; spelling and grammar.

Funds Avail.: $500-$1,000. **Number Awarded:** 3. **To Apply:** Applicants must write a 500 to 1000 word essay on the prompt located on the scholarship info page and submit it along with some basic information. Applicants may contact the Foundation for application process and other information. **Deadline:** December 30.

3786 ■ Editors' Association of Canada (EAC)
505-27 Carlton St.
Toronto, ON, Canada M5B 1L2
Ph: (416)975-1379
Fax: (416)975-1637
Free: 866-226-3348
E-mail: info@editors.ca
URL: www.editors.ca

3787 ■ Claudette Upton Scholarships (Undergraduate/Scholarship)

Purpose: To support continuing professional development in editing. **Focus:** Editors and editing. **Qualif.:** Applicants must be student members of EAC. **Criteria:** Scholarship will be given to a student who demonstrates an aptitude for editing, commitment to pursuing a career as an editor, and other qualifications reminiscent of honorary life member Claudette Upton.

Funds Avail.: $1,000. **Duration:** Annual. **To Apply:** Applicants must submit the following documents: 1) a reference letter from an instructor; 2) maximum two-page resume; and 3) 300-word statement in response to the question "At the end of a long career as an editor, what would be the one thing you hope to be the most proud of?" **Deadline:** January 31. **Remarks:** Established in 2009. **Contact:** Application form and supporting documents may be sent via e-mail at claudetteuptonscholarship@editors.ca.

3788 ■ Edmonton Community Foundation
9910 103 St. NW
Edmonton, AB, Canada T5K 2K7
Ph: (780)426-0015
Free: 866-626-0015
E-mail: info@ecfoundation.org
URL: www.ecfoundation.org

3789 ■ Lowry Awards for Women of Excellence (Undergraduate, Graduate, Advanced Professional/Award, Scholarship)

Purpose: To provide assistance to women of all ages in pursuit of their goals in the fields of water, power, finance, energy, accounting, healthcare, safety and/or community relations. **Focus:** General studies/Field of study not specified. **Qualif.:** Applicants must be female residents in the City of Edmonton who are able to demonstrate permanent residence or citizenship of Canada; must be pursuing a program of study in the fields of water, power, finance, energy, accounting, healthcare, safety and/or community relations leading to a recognized certificate, diploma, undergraduate or graduate degree, or professional designation at a school operating in Edmonton; and must clearly demonstrate how the proposed course of study will help the applicants reach their career aspirations. **Criteria:** Consideration and priority will be given to those with commitment to an ongoing career in their field of study in Edmonton, community involvement or leadership, participation in sports and recreation, educational goals related to establishing their excellence as a leader in their chosen field, and financial need.

Funds Avail.: Amount varies. **Duration:** Annual. **Number Awarded:** Varies. **To Apply:** Applicants must submit the completed application form and must provide two reference letters which recommend the student and the course of study. Reference letters must be from a third party individual (e.g. employer, volunteer contact, teacher); should clearly address how the applicants meet the criteria and priorities described above; should be signed, dated and current, and with contact information for the writer; should have summary which outlines the applicants' employment and educational history; and should have statement of marks for most recent studies. Official transcripts are not required, a photocopy or print out from a school website is acceptable. Before an award is confirmed, recipients must provide proof of enrolment in the program of choice. **Deadline:** May 31.

3790 ■ Al Maurer Awards (Undergraduate, Graduate, Advanced Professional/Award, Scholarship)

Purpose: To assist public service employees with furthering their education in areas that will promote public service excellence. **Focus:** Public service. **Qualif.:** Applicants must be permanent public sector employees; must demonstrate permanent public service employment within Edmonton city limits; must be residence in the greater Edmonton area and permanent residence or citizenship of Canada; and must pursuit a program of study leading to a recognized certificate, diploma, undergraduate or graduate degree, or professional designation at a school operating in Edmonton. **Criteria:** Priority will be given to applicants who demonstrate commitment to an ongoing career in the public service, educational goals related to refining the employees' ability to promote public service excellence, and financial need to cover educational costs beyond those provided by the employer.

Funds Avail.: Amount varies. **Duration:** Annual. **Number Awarded:** Varies. **To Apply:** Applicants must submit the completed application form; must provide a reference letter from their managers or supervisors which recommends the

Awards are arranged alphabetically below their administering organizations

students and the course of study (reference letters should clearly address how the applicant meets the criteria and priorities); must provide a personal reference from someone (not a relative) who can address how the applicants meet the criteria; must provide a resume which outlines the applicants' employment and educational (including training provided by the employer) history. Before an award is confirmed, recipients must provide proof of enrollment in the program of choice. **Deadline:** August 31.

3791 ■ Edmonton Epilepsy Association (EEA)
11215 Groat Rd. NW
Edmonton, AB, Canada T5M 3K2
Ph: (780)488-9600
Fax: (780)447-5486
Free: 866-374-5377
E-mail: info@edmontonepilepsy.org
URL: www.edmontonepilepsy.org

3792 ■ Edmonton Epilepsy Continuing Education Scholarships *(Undergraduate/Scholarship)*

Purpose: To open doors for incoming or continuing Canadian college students who are under epilepsy care. **Focus:** General studies/Field of study not specified. **Qualif.:** Applicants must be Canadian citizens entering or continuing in college or University studies who have landed immigrant status and currently be under a Canadian physician's care for epilepsy. **Criteria:** Recipients will be selected based on Committee's review of all applications and supporting documents.

Funds Avail.: $1,000. **Duration:** Annual. **Number Awarded:** 2. **To Apply:** Applicants must submit three letter of recommendation of which one must come from someone from academia; a copy of immigration papers (if landed immigrant); an unofficial copy of the current academic transcript; and a copy of university, college, or graduate school application(s)/acceptance letter, or confirmation of enrollment. **Deadline:** March 1.

3793 ■ Edon Farmers Cooperative Association Inc.
205 S Michigan St.
Edon, OH 43518
Ph: (419)272-2121
Fax: (419)272-2304
Free: 800-878-4093
E-mail: rdunbar@edonfarmerscoop.com
URL: www.edonfarmerscoop.com

3794 ■ Edon Farmers Cooperative Scholarships *(Undergraduate/Scholarship)*

Purpose: To provide financial assistance for high school seniors to further their education as full-time students in any post high school institution. **Focus:** Agricultural sciences. **Qualif.:** Applicants must be dependents of a stockholder going into any field of study or any students going into an agricultural field; and must be high school seniors in any post high school institutions. **Criteria:** Recipients are selected based on demonstrated scholarship potential, spirit of hard work, leadership ability, interest in extracurricular activities and commitment to reach personal goals. Financial need will be one of the considerations but not necessarily the primary factor.

Funds Avail.: $1,000. **To Apply:** Applicants must submit all the required application information.

3795 ■ Educational Audiology Association (EAA)
700 McKnight Park Dr., Ste. 708
Pittsburgh, PA 15237
Fax: (888)729-3489
Free: 800-460-7322
E-mail: admin@edaud.org
URL: edaud.org
Facebook: www.facebook.com/educationalaudiology
LinkedIn: www.linkedin.com/groups/4300870/profile
Twitter: twitter.com/EduAud

3796 ■ Fred Berg Awards *(Undergraduate/Award)*

Purpose: To promote educational audiology. **Focus:** Speech and language pathology/Audiology. **Qualif.:** Applicants may be members or nonmembers of EAA. **Criteria:** Awards will be given based on the committee's criteria. The Nominations and Awards Committee reviews the nominations and makes recommendations to the EAA Executive Committee for approval.

Funds Avail.: No specific amount. **Duration:** Annual. **Number Awarded:** Varies. **To Apply:** Nominator must submit a letter stating the applicant's specific qualifications for the award; two additional letters of support; and the applicant's vitae. **Remarks:** Established in 1991.

3797 ■ Educational Audiology Association Doctoral Scholarships *(Doctorate/Scholarship)*

Purpose: To provide financial assistance to a member of EAA, practicing as an educational audiologist who are pursuing doctoral degree. **Focus:** Speech and language pathology/Audiology. **Qualif.:** Applicant must be a member of EAA; practicing as an educational audiologist; be matriculated in an official doctoral program. **Criteria:** Recipient is awarded based on committee's review of their application.

Funds Avail.: $500. **Duration:** Annually. **To Apply:** Applicants must submit all supporting documentation. **Deadline:** Rolling submissions will be accepted all year.

3798 ■ Noel D. Matkin Awards *(Undergraduate/Award)*

Purpose: To promote educational audiology. **Focus:** Speech and language pathology/Audiology. **Qualif.:** Applicant must be a member of EAA. **Criteria:** Award will be given to practitioners and students who are EAA members.

Funds Avail.: No specific amount. **Duration:** Annual. **To Apply:** Members are encouraged to submit proposals for these awards. The proposals should be typed, double-spaced, and should include the requested information on the pdf rule. The proposals should include section headings and number pages. Applicants must submit a letter of support from their academic advisor, research mentor or program director. **Deadline:** February 1. **Contact:** EAA Headquarters, 3030 W 81st Ave., Westminster, Colorado 80031.

3799 ■ The Educational Foundation for Women in Accounting (EFWA)
136 S Keowee St.
Dayton, OH 45402
Ph: (937)424-3391
Fax: (937)222-5794

E-mail: info@efwa.org
URL: www.efwa.org

3800 ■ EFWA Moss Adams Foundation Scholarships *(Undergraduate/Scholarship)*

Purpose: To provide financial assistance to female reentry students who wish to pursue a degree in accounting. **Focus:** Accounting. **Qualif.:** Applicants must be women returning to school with undergraduate status; incoming, current, or reentry junior or seniors; must be minority women; or pursuing their fifth year requirement through either general studies or within a graduate program. **Criteria:** Scholarship recipients will be selected based on commitment of the career goals, aptitude for accounting and business and financial need. Preference will be given to those individuals who have demonstrated financial need.

Funds Avail.: $1,000. **Duration:** Annual. **To Apply:** Applicants must submit a completed application with all attachments (scholastic record; employment record; volunteer activities; professional activities; honors; career goals; personal goals; financial need; tax returns; references; and complete school contact information) to Educational Foundation for Women in Accounting.

3801 ■ Michele L. McDonald Scholarships *(Undergraduate/Scholarship)*

Purpose: To provide financial assistance to female reentry students who wish to pursue a degree in accounting. **Focus:** Accounting. **Qualif.:** Applicants must be women returning to college from the work force or after raising children. **Criteria:** Scholarship recipients will be selected based on commitment of the career goals, aptitude for accounting and business, established plans for achieving goals, both personal and professional, financial need and demonstration of how this scholarship will impact their lives. Preference will be given to those female applicants returning to college from the work force or after raising children.

Funds Avail.: $1,000. **Duration:** Annual. **To Apply:** Applicants must submit a completed application with all attachments (scholastic record; employment record; volunteer activities; professional activities; honors; career goals; personal goals; financial need; tax returns; references; and complete school contact information) to Educational Foundation for Women in Accounting.

3802 ■ Rhonda J.B. O'Leary Memorial Scholarship *(Undergraduate, Graduate/Scholarship)*

Purpose: To support students who are pursuing a degree in accounting. **Focus:** Accounting. **Qualif.:** Applicants must be part-time or full-time students, pursuing either an associate's of applied science, bachelor's or master's degree in accounting or an equivalent designated post-baccalaureate certificate of accounting; must have completed a minimum of 30 semester hours or 45 quarter hours within four weeks of the application deadline; must have maintained a minimum grade point average of 2.05 overall and 3.0 in accounting; must be attending an accredited community college, college, university or professional school of accounting. **Criteria:** Scholarship recipients will be selected based on commitment of the career goals, communication skills, financial need and circumstances, personal circumstances and grade point average.

Funds Avail.: Up to $2,000. **Duration:** One year. **To Apply:** Applicants must submit a complete Seattle Chapter application form (typed, if possible); original current official college transcript (in sealed envelope) for each application; financial aid transcripts from the college; two original, signed, letters of recommendation; evidence of acceptance to program if either transferring to another college or beginning a post-baccalaureate education at a new university.

3803 ■ Educational Research Center of America (ERCA)
2 Dubon Ct.
Farmingdale, NY 11735
Ph: (561)586-1003
E-mail: info@studentresearch.org
URL: www.studentresearch.org

3804 ■ ERCA Community Contribution Scholarships *(Undergraduate/Scholarship)*

Purpose: To help high school students further their education and professional development. **Focus:** General studies/Field of study not specified. **Qualif.:** Applicants must be high school students and legal residents of the United States. They must also have recognized a need/problem in their community and have determined a way to address such need or solve the problem with their respective developed action plan. **Criteria:** Applications are sorted by graduation year. Judges will select 25 finalists from the 50 semi-finalists based on project quality, grades, honors and activities.

Funds Avail.: $25,000 ($5,000 top scholar; $2,500 each for 2 runner-ups; $1,000 each for 15 students). **Duration:** Annual. **Number Awarded:** 18. **To Apply:** Applicants must submit a completed official ERCA Community Contribution Scholarship Competition Application.

3805 ■ Educational Testing Service (ETS)
225 Phillips Blvd.
Ewing, NJ 08628
Ph: (609)921-9000
Fax: (609)734-5410
URL: www.ets.org

3806 ■ ETS Postdoctoral Fellowships *(Postdoctorate/Fellowship)*

Purpose: To provide research opportunities to individuals who have recently earned their doctoral degrees. **Focus:** Linguistics; Psychology; Speech and language pathology/Audiology; Statistics; Teaching. **Qualif.:** Applicants must be doctorate in a relevant discipline within the past three years and have evidence of prior research. **Criteria:** Selection shall be based on the applicants' scholarship and the technical strength of the proposed research topic.

Funds Avail.: No specific amount. **Duration:** Annual. **To Apply:** Applicants must send a one-page abstract about the research and a letter of intent. If the submitted abstract is approved, applicants must submit a detailed proposal (approximately 5 double-spaced pages) describing the research that will be carried out at ETS and how it relates to current ETS research; a current curriculum vita; official graduate academic transcripts; and names and e-mail addresses of three individuals familiar with the applicant's work and willing to complete a recommendation form. Submit all application materials via e-mail (provided at the contact) as PDF attachments, except for the transcripts which must be sent via regular mail. **Deadline:** January 1 (Preliminary application materials) March 1 (Final application materials). **Contact:** Email: internfellowships@ets.org; Phone: 609-734-5543.

Awards are arranged alphabetically below their administering organizations

3807 ■ Harold Gulliksen Psychometric Research Fellowships *(Doctorate, Graduate/Fellowship)*

Purpose: To increase the number of well-trained scientists in educational assessment, psychometrics and statistics. **Focus:** Linguistics; Psychology; Speech and language pathology/Audiology; Statistics; Teaching. **Qualif.:** Applicants must: be enrolled in a doctoral program; have completed all the coursework toward the PhD; be at the dissertation stage of the program (dissertation topics in the areas of psychometrics, statistics, educational/psychological measurement, or quantitative methods will be given priority). **Criteria:** Selection shall be based on the strength of the applicants' academic credentials and the suitability and technical strength of the proposed research project.

Funds Avail.: No specific amount. **Duration:** Annual. **To Apply:** Applicants must submit a letter of interest (approximately five double-spaced pages) describing the research that would be undertaken during the award year and how the research fits with ETS research efforts; a nomination letter (either as an e-mail or as an e-mail with a PDF attachment) from an academic advisor; and a current curriculum vitae. For final application, applicants must submit a detailed project description (approximately 15 double-spaced pages) of the research the applicant will carry out at the host university, including the purpose, goals and methods of the research; official graduate academic transcripts; and evidence of scholarship (presentations, manuscripts, etc.). Submit all application materials via e-mail (provided at the contact) as PDF attachments. **Deadline:** January 1 (preliminary application), March 1 (final application). **Contact:** Email: internfellowships@ets.org; Phone: 609-734-5543.

3808 ■ Sylvia Taylor Johnson Fellowships in Educational Measurement *(Doctorate/Fellowship)*

Purpose: To encourage original and significant research for early-career scholars. **Focus:** Linguistics; Psychology; Speech and language pathology/Audiology; Statistics; Teaching. **Qualif.:** Applicants must have received doctorate degrees within the past ten years and be U.S. citizens or permanent residents. **Criteria:** Selection shall be based on applicants' record of accomplishments, proposed topic of research, commitment to education and independent body of scholarship that signals the promise of continuing outstanding contributions to educational measurement.

Funds Avail.: No specific amount. **Duration:** Annual. **To Apply:** Applicants must submit a letter of interest; a detailed proposal (approximately five double-spaced pages in length) of the type of research the applicant will conduct at ETS; current curriculum vita; the names and e-mail addresses of three individuals familiar with the applicant's work and willing to complete a recommendation form; samples of published research; and official graduate academic transcripts. Submit all application materials via e-mail (provided at the contact) as PDF attachments. **Deadline:** January 1 (Preliminary application materials); March 1 (Final application materials). **Contact:** Email: internfellowships@ets.org; Phone: 609-734-5543.

3809 ■ The Edwards Law Firm
8282 S Memorial, Ste., 100
Tulsa, OK 74133
Free: 800-304-9246
E-mail: medwards@edwardslawok.com
URL: www.edwardslawok.com

3810 ■ The Edwards Annual College Scholarships *(Undergraduate/Scholarship)*

Purpose: To provide scholarships to deserving students towards their tuition costs. **Focus:** General studies/Field of study not specified. **Qualif.:** Applicants must be currently enrolled in an Oklahoma college or university, and must have a minimum GPA of 2.5. **Criteria:** Selection will be based on the committee's criteria.

Funds Avail.: $1,500. **Duration:** Annual. **Number Awarded:** 1. **To Apply:** Interested applicants must visit the website to complete the application process and must provide the following: official copy of high school transcript and a minimum 500 word essay using the specified prompt. Prepare an essay in a .PDF format, with the file name: lastname_firstname_blf.pdf. **Deadline:** November 15.

3811 ■ The Eichholz Law Firm
530 Stephenson Ave. No.200
Savannah, GA 31405
Ph: (912)232-2791
Fax: (912)629-2560
Free: 866-947-7449
URL: www.thejusticelawyer.com

3812 ■ Scholarships for an Education Towards Law *(Graduate/Scholarship)*

Purpose: To further students' education in Law. **Focus:** Law. **Qualif.:** Applicants must be currently enrolled in public or private high school located in any of the following counties: Chatham County, Effingham Count, or Bulloch County; and must have a minimum GPA of 2.9 weighted. **Criteria:** Recipients are determined solely by selection committee as appointed by The Eichholz Law Firm.

Funds Avail.: $1,000. **Duration:** Annual; non-renewable. **Number Awarded:** 1. **To Apply:** Applicants must submit the following application materials: official copy of high school transcript (official sealed copy required prior to award); original essay of at least 1,400 words, but no more than 1500 words on the provided topic; and filled-out application forms. **Deadline:** October 15.

3813 ■ Eisbrouch Marsh, LLC
50 Main St., Ste. 6
Hackensack, NJ 07601
Ph: (201)977-6040
URL: emlawoffices.com

3814 ■ Eisbrouch & Marsh Scholarship Awards *(Undergraduate, Graduate/Scholarship)*

Purpose: To assist single mothers who are equally committed to completing their degree and raising their families. **Focus:** General studies/Field of study not specified. **Qualif.:** Applicants must be accepted/enrolled in a junior college with plans to attend a 4-year college or university program, or accepted/enrolled in a 4-year college or university program, or accepted/enrolled in a graduate program, or enrolled in high school with plans to attend a 4-year college or university program; must be single mothers; and must have maintained a minimum 3.0 GPA at their current educational institution according to their most recent transcript. **Criteria:** Selection will be based on the committee's criteria.

Funds Avail.: $1,000. **To Apply:** Applicants are required to

Awards are arranged alphabetically below their administering organizations

write about their dual roles as both mothers and students. Essays should be a minimum of 1,000 words and should address the following: "describe some of the challenges motherhood has imposed on your academic goals", "how your role as a mother prepared you for the challenges you face as a student?" and "what will earning your degree mean to you?". The following additional requirements are necessary for all applicants: application attachments must be in word or PDF formats only (kindly complete and sign the attached PDF application form and submit with other required materials); applications must be sent via email (only emailed applications will be considered); applicants must include their most current contact information including full name, mailing address, email address and phone number; proof of attendance or acceptance at one of the learning institutions; copy of the applicants' official transcript for their most recently completed semester of school that reflects the minimum 3.0 GPA requirement. **Deadline:** December 31.

3815 ■ El Dorado County Mineral and Gem Society
PO Box 950
Placerville, CA 95667-0950
Ph: (530)676-2472
E-mail: info@eldoradomineralandgem.org
URL: www.eldoradomineralandgem.org

3816 ■ El Dorado County Mineral and Gem Society Scholarships *(Undergraduate/Scholarship)*

Purpose: To provide support to students who are pursuing a degree and/or career in earth sciences, lapidary arts and other related fields at an accredited college or university. **Focus:** Earth sciences. **Qualif.:** Applicant must be a graduate of an El Dorado County high school, who may now be attending a college or graduate school outside of the County. **Criteria:** Selection is based on the application.

Funds Avail.: $500 - $1,000. **Duration:** Annual. **Number Awarded:** 1. **To Apply:** Applicant must submit a completed application form along with the following: a current transcript; a personal essay of 300-500 words; and two letters of reference, one of which is from a faculty member and the other from someone who is not a member of the applicant's family. **Deadline:** May 1.

3817 ■ El Pomar Foundation
10 Lake Cir.
Colorado Springs, CO 80906
Ph: (719)633-7733
Fax: (719)577-5702
Free: 800-554-7711
E-mail: grants@elpomar.org
URL: www.elpomar.org
Facebook: www.facebook.com/elpomarfoundation

3818 ■ El Pomar Fellowships *(Graduate/Fellowship)*

Purpose: To provide students the opportunity that combines on-the-job training with a solid background in leadership theory. **Focus:** General studies/Field of study not specified. **Qualif.:** Applicant must be a graduate of a four-year university/college; have a Colorado connection (a Colorado resident, have attended a Colorado college/university, or have immediate family who are residents or past residents); must demonstrate strong leadership capability and potential; must exhibit the highest standards of professionalism and behavior; possess strong verbal and writing skills; must demonstrate personal initiative and determination; and have the ability to travel throughout the state of Colorado on official Foundation business. **Criteria:** Selection is based on submitted application materials.

Funds Avail.: No specific amount. **To Apply:** Applicant must submit a 1-2 page letter on leadership experience, career objectives, and interest in the Fellowship program; a resume; college transcript(s); and two letters of recommendation. **Contact:** Ann Fenley, 719-577-7057; Email: recruiting@elpomar.org.

3819 ■ eLearning.net
12345 Lakecity Way, No. 150
Seattle, WA 98125
Free: 866-771-4449
URL: elearning.net

3820 ■ Instructional Design & Learning Technologies Scholarships *(Undergraduate, Graduate/Scholarship)*

Purpose: To help learning and development professionals pursue their own continuing education and apply the latest in instructional design theory and educational technologies to their work to build better training programs. **Focus:** General studies/Field of study not specified. **Qualif.:** Applicants must possess a minimum of 5 years of post-high school work experience; must have applied for and been accepted to an eligible program of study. **Criteria:** Essays will be reviewed for items including: essay completeness, detail, and thoughtfulness; alignment of the program of study to the applicants' stated goals; grammatical correctness.

Funds Avail.: $750-$1,500. **Duration:** Annual. **Number Awarded:** 4. **To Apply:** Interested applicants must submit a type written (PDF document) essay that include the following: describe a little about yourself including your professional work history and your experiences in learning form and/or developing online adult education. At a minimum including first and last name, name of your current employer or most recent employer if currently between jobs, describe your experience in developing online training programs either individually or as part o a team, and a link to your LinkedIn profile (if you have one) or other online professional biography; why are you pursuing an education in instructional design, eLearning development, learning technologies, or related field?; How do you intend to apply what you learn to the work you will do in the future?; What educational institution did you select and how did you go about selecting that institution as the one best suited to your learning needs?; What program of study did you select and how did you go about selecting that program as the one best suited to your learning needs; List any other information you feel will help the scholarship judges evaluate your application. Applicants must provide two scholarship recommendation letters from professional associates. Letters should include: first and last name of your referral source; name of current employer; relationship of referral source to applicants (e.g. direct supervisor, co-worker, former manager, etc.); a description of why the referral source believes the applicants would benefit from the chosen program of study. **Deadline:** August 12. **Contact:** learningscholarships@gmail.com.

3821 ■ Electro-Federation Canada (EFC)
180 Attwell Dr., Ste. 300
Toronto, ON, Canada M9W 6A9

Ph: (905)602-8877
Fax: (416)679-9234
Free: 866-602-8877
URL: www.electrofed.com
Twitter: twitter.com/EFC_Tweets

3822 ■ Affiliated Distributors Electrical Industry Scholarship Awards *(Undergraduate/Scholarship)*

Purpose: To help students across Canada reach their education and career objectives. **Focus:** Engineering, Electrical. **Qualif.:** Applicants must be students in any post-secondary institution across Canada who have successfully completed at least the first year of any degree, diploma or electrical apprenticeship program. **Criteria:** Priority will be given to students who have an electrical or electronics concentration. The successful students will have above-average marks in their current program and will have shown leadership in their school and community.
Funds Avail.: 3,500 Canadian Dollars. **To Apply:** Applicants may visit the website for them to create an account to apply for the scholarship, as well as for the other application materials required. **Deadline:** May 31. **Remarks:** The scholarship is co-sponsored by the Affiliated Distributors.

3823 ■ Burndy Canada Inc. Academic Achievement Awards *(Undergraduate/Scholarship)*

Purpose: To help students across Canada reach their education and career objectives. **Focus:** Engineering, Electrical. **Qualif.:** Applicants must be college or university students who have completed at least one year of study in any area related to the electrical industry; and must either be current employees of Burndy Canada Inc. or related to someone currently employed with the Company or employed or related to a current employee of any electrical distributor or manufacturer in the Canadian Electrical Industry. **Criteria:** Selection will be based on the committee's criteria.
Funds Avail.: 3,500 Canadian Dollars. **To Apply:** Applicants may visit the website to create an account to apply for the scholarship and for other application requirements. **Deadline:** May 31. **Remarks:** The scholarship is co-sponsored by Burndy Canada, Inc.

3824 ■ Convectair Sustainable Development Scholarship Awards *(Undergraduate/Scholarship)*

Purpose: To help students across Canada reach their education and career objectives. **Focus:** Electronics; Engineering, Electrical; Engineering, Mechanical; Environmental science. **Qualif.:** Applicants must be college or university students across Canada in sustainable development, engineering (electrical and mechanical), electronics and environmental studies; and must have completed at least one year of academic studies with an above-average mark. Also open to employees or relatives of full-time employees of any Electro-Federation Canada members. **Criteria:** Selection will be based on the applicants' eligibility and other criteria of the committee.
Funds Avail.: 3,500 Canadian Dollars. **To Apply:** Applicants may visit the website to create an account to apply for the scholarship and for the other application requirements. **Deadline:** May 31. **Remarks:** The scholarship is co-sponsored by the Convectair.

3825 ■ Bob Dyer/OEL Apprenticeship Scholarships *(Undergraduate/Scholarship)*

Purpose: To help students across Canada reach their education and career objectives. **Focus:** Electronics; Engineering, Electrical. **Qualif.:** Applicants must be apprentices who have, within the last 12 months, completed any of the levels of schooling at an approved Ontario College Electrical Apprenticeship program; must have at least a 75% average; and must be OEL member company employees or immediate relatives of an OEL member company employee. **Criteria:** Selection will be based on the applicants' eligibility and other criteria of the committee.
Funds Avail.: 500 Canadian Dollars each. **Number Awarded:** 5. **To Apply:** Applicants may visit the website for them to create an account to apply for the scholarship, as well as for the other application materials required. **Deadline:** May 31. **Remarks:** The scholarship is co-sponsored by the Ontario Electrical League.

3826 ■ Eaton Awards of Academic Achievement *(Undergraduate/Scholarship)*

Purpose: To help students across Canada reach their education and career objectives. **Focus:** Electronics; Engineering, Electrical. **Qualif.:** Applicants must be university or college students who have completed at least one year of academic studies with a minimum 80% average (2.5 GPA) whose parent/legal guardian is a full-time employee of an Electro-Federation Canada member in good standing. **Criteria:** Selection will be based on the applicants' eligibility and other criteria of the committee.
Funds Avail.: 3,500 Canadian Dollars each. **Number Awarded:** 2. **To Apply:** Applicants may visit the website for them to create an account to apply for the scholarship, as well as for the other application materials required. **Deadline:** May 31. **Remarks:** The scholarship is co-sponsored by Eaton.

3827 ■ EFC Atlantic Region Scholarships *(Undergraduate/Scholarship)*

Purpose: To help students across Canada reach their education and career objectives. **Focus:** Electronics; Engineering, Electrical. **Qualif.:** Applicants must be students enrolled full-time in a two-year electrical/electronics program at either Nova Scotia Community College, New Brunswick Community College or PEI Holland College and successfully completed their first year of study with a minimum 75% average. **Criteria:** Selection will be based on the applicants' eligibility and other criteria of the committee.
Funds Avail.: 1,000 Canadian Dollars each. **Number Awarded:** 5. **To Apply:** Applicants may visit the website for them to create an account to apply for the scholarship, as well as for the other application materials required. **Deadline:** May 31. **Remarks:** The scholarship is co-sponsored by the EFC Atlantic Region.

3828 ■ EFC University and College Scholarships *(Undergraduate/Scholarship)*

Purpose: To help students across Canada reach their education and career objectives. **Focus:** Electronics; Engineering, Electrical. **Qualif.:** Applicants must be students who have completed at least their first year of study in electrical engineering, electrical technology, or business administration, and maintained a minimum cumulative average of 75%. **Criteria:** Selection will be based on the applicants' eligibility and other criteria of the committee.
Funds Avail.: 1,000 Canadian Dollars each. **Number Awarded:** 14. **To Apply:** Applicants may visit the website for them to create an account to apply for the scholarship,

as well as for the other application materials required. **Deadline:** May 31.

3829 ■ Franklin Empire Scholarship Awards
(Undergraduate/Scholarship)

Purpose: To help students across Canada reach their education and career objectives. **Focus:** Engineering, Electrical. **Qualif.:** Applicants must be university, college, or trade school students, in Quebec or Ontario; must have completed two years of study in the field of electrical apprenticeship, electrical technician, engineering/technology (electrical, mechanical, industrial), or a discipline related to the electrical industry; and must have maintained an average of 80%. **Criteria:** Selection will be based on the applicants' eligibility and other criteria of the committee.

Funds Avail.: 3,500 Canadian Dollars. **To Apply:** Applicants may visit the website to create an account to apply for the scholarship and for the other application requirements. **Deadline:** May 31. **Remarks:** The scholarship is co-sponsored by the Franklin Empire.

3830 ■ G.E. Lighting Canada Community Leadership Awards *(Undergraduate/Award)*

Purpose: To help students across Canada reach their education and career objectives. **Focus:** Business; Engineering, Electrical. **Qualif.:** Applicants must be undergraduate university students in either an Engineering or Business program who have completed at least their first year of study with a minimum cumulative average of 80% and have also established a commitment to community service through volunteerism. **Criteria:** Selection will be based on the applicants' eligibility and other criteria of the committee.

Funds Avail.: 3,500 Canadian Dollars. **To Apply:** Applicants may visit the website for them to create an account to apply for the scholarship, as well as for the other application materials required. **Deadline:** May 31. **Remarks:** The scholarship is co-sponsored by the G.E. Lighting Canada.

3831 ■ Gerrie Electric Memorial Scholarship Awards *(Undergraduate/Scholarship)*

Purpose: To help students across Canada reach their education and career objectives. **Focus:** Engineering, Electrical. **Qualif.:** Applicants must be Canadian citizens; must be students entering second year at Ontario college or university in the field of electrical apprenticeship, electrical engineering technology, or electrical technician; must have demonstrated community service through volunteerism; and must have achieved a cumulative average of 75%. **Criteria:** Preference will be given to relatives of Gerrie Electric, its customers and its vendor partners.

Funds Avail.: 3,500 Canadian Dollars. **To Apply:** Applicants may visit the website to create an account to apply for the scholarship and for the other application requirements. **Deadline:** May 31. **Remarks:** The scholarship is co-sponsored by the Gerrie Electric.

3832 ■ Graybar Canada Award of Excellence Scholarships *(Undergraduate/Scholarship)*

Purpose: To help students across Canada reach their education and career objectives. **Focus:** Arts; Business; Electronics; Engineering, Electrical; Information science and technology. **Qualif.:** Applicants must be students who have completed their first year of post-secondary education in either a business program, general arts, IT or a discipline related to the electrical industry; and must have maintained a minimum cumulative average of at least 80%. **Criteria:** Selection will be based on the applicants' eligibility and other criteria of the committee.

Funds Avail.: 3,500 Canadian Dollars. **To Apply:** Applicants may visit the website for them to create an account to apply for the scholarship, as well as for the other application materials required. **Deadline:** May 31. **Remarks:** The scholarship is co-sponsored by the Graybar Canada.

3833 ■ Hammond Power Solutions Inc. Outstanding Electrical Scholar Awards *(Undergraduate/Award)*

Purpose: To help students across Canada reach their education and career objectives. **Focus:** Electronics; Engineering, Electrical. **Qualif.:** Applicants must be Ontario or Quebec university/college students currently enrolled in an approved post-secondary electrical program; must have completed at least their second year of study in Electrical Engineering, Electrical Technology, Electrical Technician, Electrical Technologist, Industrial Electrician, or working towards completing an electrical apprenticeship; and must have a minimum cumulative average of 75%. **Criteria:** Selection will be based on the applicants' eligibility. Preference will be given to students who commit to their industry through active membership with OACETT and/or PEO, or to those who demonstrate active leadership in their school or community.

Funds Avail.: 3,500 Canadian Dollars. **To Apply:** Applicants may visit the website to create an account to apply for the scholarship and for the other application requirements. **Deadline:** May 31. **Remarks:** The scholarship is co-sponsored by the Hammond Power Solutions Inc.

3834 ■ E.B. Horsman & Son Scholarships *(Undergraduate/Scholarship)*

Purpose: To help students across Canada reach their education and career objectives. **Focus:** Engineering, Electrical. **Qualif.:** Applicants must be students attending any post-secondary institution in a region where EBH is located; must have completed at least their first year of study in electrical apprenticeship, electrical technician, engineering/technology electrical, or a discipline related to the electrical industry. **Criteria:** Preference will be given to relatives of EBH, its customers and its supplier partners.

Funds Avail.: 3,500 Canadian Dollars. **To Apply:** Applicants may visit the website to create an account to apply for the scholarship and for the other application requirements. **Deadline:** May 31. **Remarks:** The scholarship is co-sponsored by the E.B. Horsman & Son.

3835 ■ Hubbell Canada LP "Electrical Industry Leadership" Scholarship Awards *(Undergraduate/Scholarship)*

Purpose: To support students who have demonstrated interests in a career path that will drive innovation and leadership in the electrical industry in Canada. **Focus:** Electronics; Engineering, Electrical. **Qualif.:** Applicants must be students enrolled in a Canadian university who have completed at least their first year of study in Business, Engineering or Science with a minimum cumulative average of 80%. **Criteria:** Selection will be based on the applicants' eligibility and other criteria of the committee.

Funds Avail.: 3,500 Canadian Dollars. **To Apply:** Applicants may visit the website for them to create an account to apply for the scholarship, as well as for the other application materials required. **Deadline:** May 31. **Remarks:** The scholarship is co-sponsored by the Hubbell, Inc.

Awards are arranged alphabetically below their administering organizations

3836 ■ Ideal Supply Scholarship Awards
(Undergraduate/Scholarship)

Purpose: To help students across Canada reach their education and career objectives. **Focus:** Electronics; Engineering, Electrical. **Qualif.:** Applicants must be entering into an electrical or electronic related program or apprenticeship in an Ontario college or university. **Criteria:** Additional consideration will be given to students who have achieved an accumulated average of 75% or greater, are Canadian citizens, and have displayed ongoing community engagement.

Funds Avail.: 3,500 Canadian Dollars. **To Apply:** Applicants may visit the website to create an account to apply for the scholarship and for the other application requirements. **Deadline:** May 31. **Remarks:** The scholarship is co-sponsored by the Ideal Supply.

3837 ■ Kerrwil's J.W. Kerr Continuing Education Scholarship Awards *(Undergraduate/Scholarship)*

Purpose: To help students across Canada reach their education and career objectives. **Focus:** Business; Electronics; Engineering, Electrical; Marketing and distribution. **Qualif.:** Applicants must be university or college graduates in a Canadian school; must have completed at least their second year in an engineering or business program with a minimum cumulative average of 75% and with a desire to drive forward in a marketing or product management in the electrical industry; and must also be either current employees or relatives of someone currently employed within the Canadian Electrical industry, including electrical wholesale, electrical equipment manufacturing representatives or electrical manufacturing. **Criteria:** Selection will be based on the applicants' eligibility and other criteria of the committee.

Funds Avail.: 3,500 Canadian Dollars. **To Apply:** Applicants may visit the website for them to create an account to apply for the scholarship, as well as for the other application materials required. **Deadline:** May 31. **Remarks:** The scholarship is co-sponsored by the Kerrwil.

3838 ■ Osram Sylvania Scholastic Achievement Awards *(Undergraduate/Scholarship)*

Purpose: To help students across Canada reach their education and career objectives. **Focus:** Business administration; Engineering, Electrical; Engineering, Mechanical. **Qualif.:** Applicants must be university students who have completed at least the second year of study with a minimum cumulative average of 85%. Eligible fields of study include electrical and mechanical engineering and business administration. **Criteria:** Selection will be based on the applicants' eligibility and other criteria of the committee.

Funds Avail.: 3,500 Canadian Dollars. **To Apply:** Applicants may visit the website for them to create an account to apply for the scholarship, as well as for the other application materials required. **Deadline:** May 31. **Remarks:** The scholarship is co-sponsored by the Osram Sylvania.

3839 ■ Philips Lighting Continuing Education Awards *(Undergraduate/Scholarship)*

Purpose: To help students across Canada reach their education and career objectives. **Focus:** Business administration; Engineering, Electrical; Engineering, Mechanical. **Qualif.:** Applicants must be university students who have completed at least the second year of study with a minimum cumulative average of 85%. Eligible fields of study include electrical and mechanical engineering and business administration. **Criteria:** Selection will be based on the applicants' eligibility and other criteria of the committee.

Funds Avail.: 3,500 Canadian Dollars. **To Apply:** Applicants may visit the website for them to create an account to apply for the scholarship, as well as for the other application materials required. **Deadline:** May 31. **Remarks:** The scholarship is co-sponsored by the Philips Lighting Canada.

3840 ■ RAB Design Lighting Award of Excellence
(Undergraduate/Scholarship)

Purpose: To help students across Canada reach their education and career objectives. **Focus:** Electronics; Engineering, Electrical; Engineering, Mechanical. **Qualif.:** Applicants must be Canadian university or college students who have completed at least their first year of study in an Electrical, Electronics or Mechanical Engineering program; must demonstrate a minimum overall average of at least 75%. **Criteria:** Selection will be based on the applicants' eligibility and other criteria of the committee.

Funds Avail.: 3,500 Canadian Dollars. **To Apply:** Applicants may visit the website for them to create an account to apply for the scholarship, as well as for the other application materials required. **Deadline:** May 31. **Remarks:** The scholarship is co-sponsored by the RAB Design Lighting Inc.

3841 ■ Schneider Electric Student Merit Awards
(Undergraduate/Scholarship)

Purpose: To help students across Canada reach their education and career objectives. **Focus:** Business administration; Engineering, Electrical. **Qualif.:** Applicants must be university, college or apprenticeship students who have completed at least their first year of study in Engineering, Business Administration or an Electrical Apprenticeship program; and maintained a minimum cumulative average of 85%. **Criteria:** Selection will be based on the applicants' eligibility and other criteria of the committee.

Funds Avail.: 5,000 Canadian Dollars. **To Apply:** Applicants may visit the website for them to create an account to apply for the scholarship, as well as for the other application materials required. **Deadline:** May 31. **Remarks:** The scholarship is co-sponsored by the Schneider Electric.

3842 ■ Siemens Canada Academic Awards
(Undergraduate/Scholarship)

Purpose: To help students across Canada reach their education and career objectives. **Focus:** Engineering, Electrical; Engineering, Mechanical. **Qualif.:** Applicants must be university or college students who have completed at least their second year of study in an electrical, mechanical engineering/technology program with a minimum 80% average. **Criteria:** Selection will be based on the applicants' eligibility and other criteria of the committee.

Funds Avail.: 3,500 Canadian Dollars each. **Number Awarded:** 4. **To Apply:** Applicants may visit the website for them to create an account to apply for the scholarship, as well as for the other application materials required. **Deadline:** May 31. **Remarks:** The scholarship is co-sponsored by the Siemens Canada.

3843 ■ Sonepar Canada Scholarship Awards
(Undergraduate/Scholarship)

Purpose: To help students across Canada reach their education and career objectives. **Focus:** Electronics; Engineering, Electrical. **Qualif.:** Applicants must be

Awards are arranged alphabetically below their administering organizations

university or college students in a Canadian school who have completed at least their second year in an Engineering or Business program with a minimum cumulative average of 80%. **Criteria:** Selection will be based on the applicants' eligibility and other criteria of the committee.

Funds Avail.: 3,500 Canadian Dollars. **To Apply:** Applicants may visit the website for them to create an account to apply for the scholarship, as well as for the other application materials required. **Deadline:** May 31. **Remarks:** The scholarship is co-sponsored by the Sonepar Canada.

3844 ■ Standard Recognition of Excellence Awards (Undergraduate/Scholarship)

Purpose: To assist Canadian university or college students who demonstrate academic excellence. **Focus:** Electronics; Engineering, Electrical. **Qualif.:** Applicants must be Canadian university or college students who have completed two years of study in business administration/commerce and must have maintained a minimum cumulative average of 80%. **Criteria:** Selection will be based on the applicants' eligibility and other criteria of the committee.

Funds Avail.: 3,500 Canadian Dollars. **To Apply:** Applicants may visit the website for them to create an account to apply for the scholarship, as well as for the other application materials required. **Deadline:** May 31. **Remarks:** The scholarship is co-sponsored by the Standard Products, Inc.

3845 ■ Stelpro Scholarships 360: Energizing Potential (Undergraduate/Scholarship)

Purpose: To support native Quebec students in their continuing education. **Focus:** Electronics; Engineering, Electrical. **Qualif.:** Applicants must be native Quebec residents, studying within the province, whose academic and/or professional path have led them to pursue a career in the electrical industry; must be enrolled in either a vocational training program, college or university degree program. **Criteria:** Selection will be based on the applicants' eligibility and other criteria of the committee.

Funds Avail.: 3,500 Canadian Dollars. **To Apply:** Applicants may visit the website for them to create an account to apply for the scholarship, as well as for the other application materials required. **Deadline:** May 31. **Remarks:** The scholarship is co-sponsored by the Stelpro.

3846 ■ RABC William Taylor Scholarships (Undergraduate/Scholarship)

Purpose: To help students across Canada reach their education and career objectives. **Focus:** Telecommunications systems. **Qualif.:** Applicants must be engineering students who have completed at least their second year in an accredited Canadian University and plan on pursuing a career in telecommunications. **Criteria:** Selection will be based on the applicants' eligibility and other criteria of the committee.

Funds Avail.: 3,500 Canadian Dollars. **To Apply:** Applicants may visit the website for them to create an account to apply for the scholarship, as well as for the other application materials required. **Deadline:** May 31. **Remarks:** The scholarship is co-sponsored by the Radio Advisory Board of Canada.

3847 ■ Thomas & Betts Scholarship Awards (Undergraduate/Scholarship)

Purpose: To help students across Canada reach their education and career objectives. **Focus:** Engineering, Electrical; Engineering, Industrial; Engineering, Mechanical. **Qualif.:** Applicants must be students who have completed at least the second year of a post-secondary program in engineering (industrial, mechanical or electrical) or in operation management; must have maintained a minimum cumulative average of 75%; and must have demonstrated community involvement. **Criteria:** Selection will be based on the applicants' eligibility and other criteria of the committee.

Funds Avail.: 3,500 Canadian Dollars. **To Apply:** Applicants may visit the website for them to create an account to apply for the scholarship, as well as for the other application materials required. **Deadline:** May 31. **Remarks:** The scholarship is co-sponsored by the Thomas & Betts, a member of the ABB Group of Companies.

3848 ■ WESCO Student Achievement Awards (Undergraduate/Scholarship)

Purpose: To help students across Canada reach their education and career objectives. **Focus:** Business administration; Electronics; Engineering, Electrical. **Qualif.:** Applicants must be university or college students who have completed at least their first year of study in electrical engineering, electrical technology, or business administration, and maintained a minimum cumulative average of 80%. **Criteria:** Selection will be based on the applicants' eligibility and other criteria of the committee.

Funds Avail.: 3,500 Canadian Dollars. **To Apply:** Applicants may visit the website for them to create an account to apply for the scholarship, as well as for the other application materials required. **Deadline:** May 31. **Remarks:** The scholarship is co-sponsored by the WESCO Distribution Canada.

3849 ■ Electrochemical Society (ECS)
Bldg. D
65 S Main St.
Pennington, NJ 08534-2827
Ph: (609)737-1902
Fax: (609)737-2743
E-mail: ecs@electrochem.org
URL: www.electrochem.org
Facebook: www.facebook.com/TheElectrochemicalSociety
LinkedIn: www.linkedin.com/grps/ECS-74067/about?trk=anet_ug_grppro
Twitter: twitter.com/ECSorg

3850 ■ Oronzio de Nora Industrial Electrochemistry Fellowships (Postdoctorate/Fellowship)

Purpose: To support students who are conducting research about industrial electrochemistry. **Focus:** Electrochemistry. **Qualif.:** Applicant must be a postdoctoral scientist or engineer continuing research in industrial electrochemistry. **Criteria:** Selection is based on the proposed research topics in the areas of electrochemistry.

Funds Avail.: $25,000. **Duration:** Annual. **To Apply:** Applicants must submit an essay (1,000 words or less) addressing personal interests/career goals related to the fellowship position, and talents brought to the fellowship, along with a curriculum vitae; three letters of recommendation (should include letter of support from the group receiving the fellow); and transcripts. **Deadline:** January 1. **Contact:** ECS; E-mail: awards@electrochem.org.

Awards are arranged alphabetically below their administering organizations

3851 ■ Electronic Document Systems Foundation (EDSF)
1845 Precinct Line Rd., Ste. 212
Hurst, TX 76054
Ph: (817)849-1145
Fax: (817)849-1185
E-mail: info@edsf.org
URL: www.edsf.org

3852 ■ Document Management and Graphic Communications Industry Scholarships (Undergraduate/Scholarship)

Purpose: To recognize and support the next generation of professionals for the document management and communication companies worldwide. **Focus:** Communications technologies; Computer and information sciences; Engineering. **Qualif.:** Applicants must be full-time students who are committed to pursuing careers in document management and communications marketplace which include computer science and engineering, graphic and media communications and those students interested in Business in the document management and communications industry; must have a minimum GPA of 3.0 or a 'B' average; must be technical, trade school, community college, undergraduate and advanced-degree students in the U.S. and/or diploma or tertiary students outside of the U.S. may be considered for scholarships; must be students who are attending full-time, an accredited college or university. **Criteria:** Applicants are evaluated based on any one or a combination of the following: Scholastic achievement, application essay, participation in school activities, community service, honors and organizational affiliations and education objectives.

Funds Avail.: $1,000-$5,000. **Number Awarded:** Minimum of 40. **To Apply:** Applicants must submit all the required application information. **Deadline:** May 1.

3853 ■ Elks National Foundation (ENF)
2750 N Lakeview Ave.
Chicago, IL 60614-1889
Ph: (773)755-4700
Fax: (773)755-4790
URL: www.elks.org/enf

3854 ■ ENF Most Valuable Student Scholarships (Undergraduate/Scholarship)

Purpose: To provide educational support to outstanding students for their college or university expenses. **Focus:** General studies/Field of study not specified. **Qualif.:** Applicants must be high school seniors who are citizens of the United States at the date of their applications. **Criteria:** Recipients are selected based on leadership, financial need and scholastic standing.

Funds Avail.: $4,000 to $50,000. **Duration:** Annual. **Number Awarded:** 500. **To Apply:** Application form can be obtained at the Foundation's website. Completed application must be submitted to the Elks Lodge nearest to the applicant's home. **Deadline:** Varies.

3855 ■ Clay Elliott Scholarship Foundation
975-A Elgin St. W, Ste. 263
Cobourg, ON, Canada K9A 5J3
Ph: (905)372-7549
E-mail: info@attitudesforeducation.com
URL: www.attitudesforeducation.com

3856 ■ Clay Elliott Scholarship Foundation Scholarships (Undergraduate/Scholarship)

Purpose: To provide a student with monetary assistance to attend Canadian post-secondary institution of their choice. **Focus:** General studies/Field of study not specified. **Qualif.:** Applicant must be a graduating student in the current school year; must be a Canadian citizen; must have notification of acceptance into a full-time post-secondary program; must be a current resident of Northumberland County; must be attending a high school within Northumberland County. **Criteria:** Selection is based on the application materials.

Funds Avail.: $1,500 for the first academic year; $1,000 for each additional year. **Duration:** Annual. **To Apply:** Applicant must submit a personal information and two reference letter (one must be an academic reference); must provide a written future academic plan. **Deadline:** May 2.

3857 ■ Emergency Nurses Association (ENA)
915 Lee St.
Des Plaines, IL 60016-6569
Ph: (847)460-4123
Free: 800-900-9659
E-mail: education@ena.org
URL: www.ena.org
Facebook: www.facebook.com/ENAorg
Twitter: twitter.com/ENAorg

3858 ■ ENA Foundation State Challenge Undergraduate Scholarship (Undergraduate/Scholarship)

Purpose: To provide support to individuals and emergency nurses who are seeking a higher level of education. **Focus:** Nursing. **Qualif.:** Applicants must be attending a NLN, CCNE, or AACN accredited school; must be ENA members for at least one year; and must have a minimum GPA of 3.0. **Criteria:** Applicants will be evaluated by the ENA Foundation review panel.

Funds Avail.: $3,000. **Duration:** Annual. **Number Awarded:** Varies. **To Apply:** Applicants must provide a letter verifying the school's current accreditation together with the application form. If not a member, applicant must provide a letter of reference from an ENA member.

3859 ■ ENA Foundation
915 Lee St.
Des Plaines, IL 60016-6569
Free: 800-900-9659
URL: www.ena.org

3860 ■ Board of Certification for Emergency Nursing (BCEN) Undergraduate Scholarships (Undergraduate/Scholarship)

Purpose: To provide support to individuals and emergency nurses who are seeking a higher level of education. **Focus:** Nursing. **Qualif.:** Applicants must be nurses with a current BCEN credential (CEN, CPEN, CFRN or CTRN) who are pursuing a baccalaureate degree in nursing; must be ENA members for at least one year; and with a minimum GPA of 3.0 **Criteria:** Applicants will be evaluated by the ENA Foundation review panel.

Awards are arranged alphabetically below their administering organizations

Funds Avail.: $2,000 each. **Duration:** Annual. **Number Awarded:** 13. **To Apply:** Applicants must provide a letter verifying the school's current accreditation with the application (visit the website for the application). If not a member, applicant must provide a letter of reference from an ENA member. Applications submitted electronically must include scanned copies of the required documents: signed copy of the application; official transcripts; and reference letters. Applications must be mailed or e-mailed only. **Deadline:** April 29.

3861 ■ ENA Foundation Annual Conference Scholarships *(Advanced Professional, Professional development/Scholarship)*

Purpose: To support members to attend the Annual Conference. **Focus:** Nursing. **Qualif.:** Applicants must be members of ENA. **Criteria:** Selection will be based on the committee's criteria.

Funds Avail.: $500 each. **Number Awarded:** 20. **To Apply:** Applicants must fill-up completely the application form provided by ENA Foundation, then submit such, together with other documents asked by the organization. **Deadline:** July 1. **Contact:** ENA Foundation; E-mail: Foundation@ena.org.

3862 ■ ENA Foundation Seed Research Grants *(Master's, Advanced Professional/Grant)*

Purpose: To provide funding for research that will advance the specialized practice of emergency nursing. **Focus:** Nursing. **Qualif.:** Applicants must be registered nurse with master's degree; must be ready to or have already research project; not have served the ENA board of directors, ENA Foundation board of trustees, or ENA Foundation grant review team in the immediate past three years; and must be current ENA members. **Criteria:** Selection will be based on the committee's criteria.

Funds Avail.: $500 each. **Duration:** Annual. **To Apply:** Applicants must fill-up completely the entire application form available at the website and submit the complete application together with the signed research agreement electronically or via mail. **Deadline:** November 1. **Contact:** Development Department; E-mail at ENA.Foundation@ena.org.

3863 ■ Endocrine Society
2055 L St. NW, Ste. 600
Washington, DC 20036
Ph: (202)971-3636
Fax: (202)736-9705
Free: 888-363-6274
E-mail: societyservices@endocrine.org
URL: www.endocrine.org
Facebook: www.facebook.com/EndocrineSociety
Twitter: twitter.com/TheEndoSociety

3864 ■ Endocrine Society Summer Research Fellowships *(Graduate, Undergraduate/Fellowship)*

Purpose: To encourage promising undergraduate students, medical students and first year graduate school students to pursue careers in endocrinology. **Focus:** Endocrinology. **Qualif.:** Applicants must be currently enrolled full-time in school and may not be employed as research assistants. Students' academic levels must fall into one of the three categories at the time they apply: undergraduate students who are currently in their third year of schooling or beyond; first year graduate students; medical students who are beyond their first year of schooling. Mentors must be active members of the Endocrine Society and projects must be under the direction of the mentor. Only one application per mentor must be submitted. **Criteria:** Selection will be based on the committee's criteria.

Funds Avail.: No specific amount. **Duration:** 10-12 weeks. **Number Awarded:** Varies. **To Apply:** Applicants must contact the society for the application process. **Contact:** Applicants may e-mail their questions to awards@endosociety.org.

3865 ■ Lilly Endocrine Scholars Fellowship Awards *(Doctorate, Other/Fellowship)*

Purpose: To support fellows who perform clinical research related to pituitary disorders, bone disorders or diabetes mellitus. **Focus:** Endocrinology. **Qualif.:** Applicants must be DO, MD or MD/PhD fellows either enrolled in their first through third year of training in a U.S. adult or pediatric clinical endocrinology program, or have completed an adult or pediatric endocrinology training program who are now proposing to do a research fellowship in a U.S. training program. **Criteria:** Selection will be based on the committee's criteria.

Funds Avail.: No specific amount. **Duration:** Annual. **To Apply:** Applicants may contact the society for the application process. **Contact:** Applicants may e-mail their questions to awards@endocrine.org.

3866 ■ Endourological Society
4100 Duff Pl., Lower Level
Seaford, NY 11783
Ph: (516)520-1224
Fax: (516)520-1225
URL: www.endourology.org

3867 ■ Endourological Society Fellowships *(Professional development/Fellowship)*

Purpose: To facilitate the development of academic and clinical excellence in endourology and minimally Invasive Surgery. **Focus:** Urology. **Qualif.:** Applicants must be chief residents, junior academic faculty and members of the Endourological Society with an academic appointment; must have plan to continue their academic career after completing their fellowship training. **Criteria:** Recipients will be selected based on qualifications and submitted materials.

Funds Avail.: No specific amount. **Duration:** Annual; One year. **To Apply:** Applicants must submit a curriculum vitae, letters of recommendation from three urologists who have practiced with the individual and are familiar with their surgical abilities, letter from the Chairman of department or division of Urology; must provide a one to two-page narrative outlining the following: 1) reasons for seeking the fellowship position; 2) reasons for selecting one or two places they plan to visit; and 3) how fellowship will impact their career future plans once completed; must submit a one-page description of the research project and letter of support from the head of endourological program.

3868 ■ Energy and Mineral Law Foundation (EMLF)
340 S Broadway, Ste. 101
Lexington, KY 40508
Ph: (859)231-0271
Fax: (859)226-0485

Awards are arranged alphabetically below their administering organizations

URL: www.emlf.org

3869 ■ EMLF Law Student Scholarships
(Undergraduate/Scholarship)

Purpose: To provide law school students an educational assistance. **Focus:** Energy-related areas; Environmental law; Environmental science; Mineralogy; Natural resources. **Qualif.:** Applicants must be law school students for the current academic year and must demonstrate an interest in the study of natural resources, energy or mineral law. **Criteria:** Recipient will be selected based on the following criteria: a) potential to make a significant contribution in the field of energy, mineral and natural resources law; b) academic ability; c) leadership ability; and d) financial need.

Funds Avail.: $1,000-$5,000. **Duration:** Annual. **To Apply:** Applicants must submit a complete application form; transcript of records; and two letters of recommendation from school dean, faculty member, or member of the legal profession. **Deadline:** April 15. **Contact:** Application form and other supporting documents may be sent electronically at carolyn@emlf.org.

3870 ■ Enlisted Association of National Guard of the United States (EANGUS)
3133 Mount Vernon Ave.
Alexandria, VA 22305-2640
Fax: (703)519-3849
Free: 800-234-3264
E-mail: eangus@eangus.org
URL: eangus.org
Facebook: www.facebook.com/Enlisted-Association-of-the-National-Guard-of-the-United-States-119938698056650
Twitter: twitter.com/eangus72

3871 ■ CSM Virgil R. Williams Scholarships
(Undergraduate/Scholarship)

Purpose: To support the education of EANGUS members, their spouses and their unmarried children. **Focus:** General studies/Field of study not specified. **Qualif.:** Applicant must be EANGUS Auxiliary members; must be unmarried, dependent sons and daughters of EANGUS Auxiliary members; must be spouses of EANGUS Auxiliary members. **Criteria:** Awards will be made based on the applicant's character, leadership and financial need.

Funds Avail.: $3,000. **To Apply:** Applicant must submit a transcript of high school credits and/or a transcript of college credits for applicants already in an institution of higher learning; must have a letter from the applicant with personal, specific facts as to his/ her desire to continue his/ her education and why financial assistance is required; must have three letters of academic recommendation verifying the application and giving moral, personal and leadership traits. Application form and other documents must be submitted electronically via the internet to the Chairman of the Scholarship Committee except the school transcript. **Deadline:** June 1. **Contact:** MSG(R) Ronal E. Emerson, Scholarship Chm., 586 Deerfield Dr., Ringgold, VA 24586-5660; 434-822-7303; rsemerson2@verizon.net.

3872 ■ Ennis Arts Association (EAA)
PO Box 201
Ennis, MT 59729
E-mail: info@ennisartsassociation.org
URL: www.ennisartsassociation.org

3873 ■ EAA Tuition Scholarships *(Undergraduate/Scholarship)*

Purpose: To help students pursue their education in an arts related curriculum. **Focus:** Arts. **Qualif.:** Applicants must be: college or vocational technical school students who are currently or have the plan to enroll in an arts curriculum; and, living or have lived within the boundaries of the Ennis/Harrison School Districts. **Criteria:** Recipients will be evaluated based on submitted materials.

Funds Avail.: Amount varies. **Duration:** Annual. **Number Awarded:** 2. **To Apply:** Applicants must contact the Guidance Counselor at their prospective school. **Deadline:** April 15.

3874 ■ EAA Workshop Scholarships *(Undergraduate/Scholarship)*

Purpose: To support the total cost of an art related single activity, workshop, adult education class or camp. **Focus:** Arts. **Qualif.:** Applicants must be individuals living in Madison County (Ennis, Harrison, Sheridan or Twin Bridges) school district boundaries. **Criteria:** Selection will be based on the committee's criteria.

Funds Avail.: $100 to $200. **Duration:** Annual. **To Apply:** Applicants must contact the Guidance Counselor at their prospective school.

3875 ■ Ensurify
222 3rd St.
Cambridge, MA 02142
Ph: (781)369-5695
URL: ensurify.com

3876 ■ Ensurify Safe Driving Scholarships *(Undergraduate/Scholarship)*

Purpose: To support the next generation of innovators with a college scholarship contest. **Focus:** General studies/ Field of study not specified. **Qualif.:** Applicants must be enrolled at any accredited four-year university, two-year college, graduate school, community college, or trade school; must be willing to prove their active student status. **Criteria:** Selection will be based on the written essay of the applicants.

Funds Avail.: $1,000. **Duration:** Non-renewable. **Number Awarded:** 1. **To Apply:** Applicants should write a well-developed thought-provoking essay on one of the topics regarding safe driving. Topics are as follows: "What made me stop?" (in 750 to 1,250 words about the moment that the applicants (either as drivers or passengers) realized the risks of using a smartphone while driving); "When it all stopped being fun?" (in 750 to 1,250 words about the moment that the applicants (either as drivers or passengers) realized the risks of being intoxicated while driving); "Are self-driving cars safer?" (in 750 to 1,250 words about their opinion as regards to driver incapacitation, the societal changes that would come in place, and the risks would autonomous vehicles eliminate or impose). Additional requirement is a transcript or official letter of enrollment from the university. **Deadline:** April 15. **Contact:** Send the essay to scholarship@ensurify.com.

3877 ■ Entertainment Software Association (ESA)
575 7th St. NW, Ste. 300
Washington, DC 20004

Awards are arranged alphabetically below their administering organizations

E-mail: esa@theesa.com
URL: www.theesa.com
Facebook: www.facebook.com/
TheEntertainmentSoftwareAssociation
Twitter: twitter.com/RichatESA

3878 ■ ESA Foundation Scholarship Program
(Undergraduate/Scholarship)

Purpose: To assist women and minority students who plan to continue their education in fields supporting Video Game Development. **Focus:** Computer and information sciences; Graphic art and design. **Qualif.:** Applicants must be: women or minority students who are pursuing degrees leading to careers in computer and video game arts (high school seniors must already be accepted into a program); enrolling or enrolled in a full-time undergraduate course of study at an accredited four-year college or university in the United States; maintaining a GPA of 2.75 or above on a 4.0 scale (or its equivalent); and, U.S. citizens. **Criteria:** Recipients will be selected based on academic standing.

Funds Avail.: $3,000 each. **Duration:** Annual. **Number Awarded:** 30 (15 graduating high school seniors and 15 current college students). **To Apply:** Applicants must complete an online application form. They must provide a proof that they are currently enrolled in a college, university, or institution. **Deadline:** April 1. **Remarks:** The scholarships are administered by the ESA Foundation. Established in 2007.

3879 ■ Entomological Foundation
3 Park Pl., Ste. 307
Annapolis, MD 21401-3722
Ph: (301)731-4535
E-mail: cstelzig@entsoc.org
URL: www.entfdn.org
Facebook: www.facebook.com/EntFdn
Twitter: www.twitter.com/@EntFdn

3880 ■ Lillian and Alex Feir Graduate Student Travel Awards *(Master's, Doctorate/Award)*

Purpose: To encourage graduate students working with insects or other arthropods in the broad areas of physiology, biochemistry and molecular biology to affiliate with ESA's Integrative Physiological and Molecular Insect Systems Section and to attend the ESA Annual Meeting or an International Congress of Entomology. **Focus:** Entomology. **Qualif.:** Applicants must be students who are using arthropods to study any aspect of basic or applied physiology, biochemistry or molecular biology in the broadest sense for their Master's or doctoral research; must be ESA student members. Students from all science departments are encouraged to apply. **Criteria:** Candidates will be judged using the following criteria: enthusiasm and interest in attending the meeting; academic credentials; reasonable budget to attend meeting; topic or areas of thesis research; recommendations from colleagues, peer groups, etc.

Funds Avail.: No specific amount. **To Apply:** All nomination packages must be submitted electronically. The entire nomination package must not exceed 20 pages total. This includes letters of nomination or recommendation and publication lists. Letters of nomination and recommendation must be included in the electronic package. Only the following file formats will be accepted: PDF, RTF, TIF or JPG graphic files. Files created on either PC or MAC platforms will be accepted; font size for text may not be smaller than 10 point; the package must contain no more than six separate files and the size of each file must not exceed 3 MB. Complete packages may be submitted either by the nomination submission website or by email as attached files to the awards administrator. Nominators must provide the information called for in the CV template, either in the template's format or in their own format. Nominators must provide the following other materials: letter of nomination that provides a brief explanation of how the individual excelled in performing their duties, including innovations in training, programs and methods; up to three letters of endorsement from professional colleagues and clientele; topic or areas of thesis research; official or unofficial transcripts of all prior undergraduate and graduate education; reasons for attending the meeting; budget to attending the meeting. **Deadline:** July 1. **Contact:** ipmworks@ipminstitute.org.

3881 ■ Shripat Kamble Urban Entomology Graduate Student Awards for Innovative Research *(Doctorate/Recognition, Grant)*

Purpose: To support and recognize a doctoral student who is currently conducting research which demonstrates innovative and realistic approaches to urban entomology. **Focus:** Entomology. **Qualif.:** Candidates must be students for a doctoral degree at an accredited university in the U.S.; must be ESA members with a genuine interest in urban entomology excluding turf and ornamental pests. **Criteria:** Candidates will be judged using the following criteria: candidates' honors, awards, achievements and recognition; recommendations of professors, advisors, etc.; leadership/grants; publications; BCE-Intern; research proposal's feasibility, scientific contribution to the knowledge of the biology or control of pests in the urban environment, creativity and innovation, contribution and scientific impact.

Funds Avail.: $500. **Duration:** Annual. **To Apply:** All nomination packages must be submitted electronically. The entire nomination package must not exceed 20 pages total. This includes letters of nomination or recommendation and publication lists. Letters of nomination and recommendation must be included in the electronic package. Only the following file formats will be accepted: PDF, RTF, TIF or JPG graphic files. Files created on either PC or MAC platforms will be accepted; font size for text may not be smaller than 10 point; contain no more than six separate files and the size of each file must not exceed 3 MB. Complete packages may be submitted either by Nomination Submission Website or by email as attached files to the awards administrator. **Deadline:** July 1.

3882 ■ Jeffery P. LaFage Graduate Student Research Award *(Master's, Doctorate/Grant)*

Purpose: To recognize graduate students who proposes innovative research that advances or contributes significantly to the knowledge of the biology or control of pests in the urban environment, especially termites or other wood-destroying organisms. **Focus:** Biology; Entomology. **Qualif.:** Applicants must be candidates for a Master's or doctoral degree at an accredited university. Priority will be given to proposals demonstrating a creative and realistic approach to the fields of interest.

Funds Avail.: No specific amount. **Duration:** Annual. **To Apply:** All nomination packages must be submitted electronically. The entire nomination package must not exceed 20 pages total. This includes letters of nomination or recommendation and publication lists. Letters of nomination and recommendation must be included in the electronic package. Only the following file formats will be accepted:

Awards are arranged alphabetically below their administering organizations

PDF, RTF, TIF or JPG graphic files. Files created on either PC or MAC platforms will be accepted; font size for text may not be smaller than 10 point; contain no more than six separate files and the size of each file must not exceed 3 MB. Complete packages may be submitted either by Nomination Submission Website or by email as attached files to the awards administrator. **Deadline:** July 1.

3883 ■ Henry and Sylvia Richardson Research Grant *(Postdoctorate/Grant)*

Purpose: To provide research funds to postdoctoral members of the Entomological Society of America. **Focus:** Entomology. **Qualif.:** Candidates must be postdoctoral members of the Entomological Society of America who: have at least one year of promising work experience; are undertaking research in selected areas; demonstrated a high level of scholarship. **Criteria:** Selection will be based on the committee's criteria.

Funds Avail.: No specific amount. **Duration:** Annual. **To Apply:** Nominator must visit the website of The Entomological Foundation or Entomological Society of America to obtain a nomination CV format for organizing the summary of the nominee's biographical and professional information. Nomination must be completed, including letters of recommendation and other supporting materials and must be submitted electronically. Applicable information of the following is required: Name; Affiliation; Current Professional Title; Appointment Split; Contact Information; Educational Background; Relevant Employment; Memberships and Affiliations; Awards and Honors. **Deadline:** July 1.

3884 ■ Kenneth and Barbara Starks Plant Resistance to Insects Graduate Student Research Awards *(Graduate/Grant)*

Purpose: To support graduate students with their studies in entomology or plant breeding/genetics for innovative research that contributes significantly to knowledge of plant resistance to insect. **Focus:** Entomology. **Qualif.:** Candidates must be graduate students in entomology or plant breeding/genetics for innovative research that contributes significantly to knowledge of plant resistance to insects. **Criteria:** Candidates will be judged using the following criteria: candidates' honors, awards, achievements and recognition; recommendations of professors, advisors, etc.; grantmanship; publications; research proposal's feasibility, contribution, creativity and innovation, national impact.

Funds Avail.: Amount varies based on the earnings from the investment. **Duration:** Annual. **To Apply:** All nomination packages must be submitted electronically. The entire nomination package must not exceed 20 pages total. This includes letters of nomination or recommendation and publication lists. Letters of nomination and recommendation must be included in the electronic package. Only the following file formats will be accepted: PDF, RTF, TIF or JPG graphic files. Files created on either PC or MAC platforms will be accepted; font size for text may not be smaller than 10 point; packages must contain no more than six separate files and the size of each file must not exceed 3 MB. Complete packages may be submitted either by the nomination submission website or by email as attached files to the awards administrator. **Deadline:** July 1.

3885 ■ Entomological Society of Canada (ESC)
500-386 Broadway
Winnipeg, MB, Canada R3C 3R6
Ph: (204)282-9823
Free: 888-821-8387
E-mail: info@esc-sec.ca
URL: www.esc-sec.ca

3886 ■ Ed Becker Conference Travel Awards *(Undergraduate, Graduate/Award)*

Purpose: To provide financial assistance to students to attend a Joint Annual Meetings and present a paper or poster. **Focus:** Entomology. **Qualif.:** Applicants must be students in graduate or undergraduate program at a Canadian university and an active member in the ESC. **Criteria:** Applications will be reviewed by a committee of the Society.

Funds Avail.: $500. **Duration:** Annual. **To Apply:** Applicants must submit the application in a single PDF file with the following documents: cover page including award being applied for, name and email address of the applicant and email addresses of those providing letters of support; Curriculum Vitae containing name and address, phone number, email address, date, education (degrees and dates), work and volunteer experience, awards and scholarships, list of scientific contributions like refereed and non-refereed publications, talks and posters at meetings, other communications and other interests or achievements; scanned set of transcripts, either of originals, or copies certified as such by a graduate secretary/administrator or graduate supervisor, showing undergraduate and post graduate (if applicable) grades; an abstract of the paper or poster with the maximum words of 250; letter from the applicant's supervisor of research stating that the applicant is engaged in a graduate or undergraduate program; recommendation letter from a faculty member who is familiar to the applicant's research. **Deadline:** February 16.

3887 ■ Biological Survey of Canada Scholarships *(Postgraduate/Scholarship)*

Purpose: To assist a student studying insect or terrestrial arthropod biodiversity in Canada. **Focus:** Entomology. **Qualif.:** Applicants must be post-graduate students studying at a Canadian university and carrying out a project on insect (or terrestrial arthropod) faunistics in a Canadian habitat. **Criteria:** Applications will be reviewed by a committee of the Society.

Funds Avail.: $1,000. **Duration:** Biennial; in even numbered years. **Number Awarded:** 1. **To Apply:** Applicants must submit the application in a single PDF file with the following documents: cover page including award being applied for, name and email address of the applicant and email addresses of those providing letters of support; Curriculum Vitae containing name and address, phone number, email address, date, education (degrees and dates), work and volunteer experience, awards and scholarships, list of scientific contributions like refereed and non-refereed publications, talks and posters at meetings, other communications and other interests or achievements; scanned set of transcripts, either of originals, or copies certified as such by a graduate secretary/administrator or graduate supervisor, showing undergraduate and post graduate (if applicable) grades; a one page statement answering to the question "why you are studying entomology?" and a summary of the applicant's thesis research and; reference letters from applicant's supervisor and one other person which clearly indicate the applicant's academic abilities, communication skills, progress as a graduate student and the novelty and scholastic contribution of the applicant's research to the field of entomology. Letter of the applicant should indicate the contribution of his/her work. **Deadline:** February 16.

Awards are arranged alphabetically below their administering organizations

ENTOMOLOGICAL SOCIETY OF CANADA

3888 ■ John H. Borden Scholarships *(Postgraduate/Scholarship)*

Purpose: To assist students in postgraduate programs who are studying Integrated Pest Management (IPM) with an entomological emphasis. **Focus:** Entomology. **Qualif.:** Applicants must be full time postgraduate students studying Integrated Pest Management (IPM) at a degree granting institution in Canada. **Criteria:** Applications will be reviewed by a committee of the Society.

Funds Avail.: $1,000. **Number Awarded:** 1. **To Apply:** Applicants must submit the application in a single PDF file with the following documents: cover page including award being applied for, name and email address of the applicant and email addresses of those providing letters of support; Curriculum Vitae containing name and address, phone number, email address, date, education (degrees and dates), work and volunteer experience, awards and scholarships, list of scientific contributions like refereed and non-refereed publications, talks and posters at meetings, other communications and other interests or achievements; scanned set of transcripts, either of originals, or copies certified as such by a graduate secretary/administrator or graduate supervisor, showing undergraduate and post graduate (if applicable) grades; a one page statement answering to the question "why you are studying entomology?"; a summary of the applicant's thesis research; and reference letters from applicant's supervisor and one other person which clearly indicate the applicant's academic abilities, communication skills, progress as a graduate student and the novelty and scholastic contribution of the applicant's research to the field of entomology. Letter of the applicant should indicate the contribution of his/her work. **Deadline:** February 16.

3889 ■ Lloyd M. Dosdall Memorial Scholarships *(Postgraduate/Scholarship)*

Purpose: To assist students conducting research in the area of arthropod community ecology. **Focus:** Entomology. **Qualif.:** Applicants must be full-time postgraduate students in the field of arthropod community ecology and studying at a degree granting institution in Canada. Preference will be given to those applicants with a focus on aquatic or agroecosystems. **Criteria:** Applications will be reviewed by a committee of the Society.

Funds Avail.: $1,000. **Duration:** Annual. **Number Awarded:** 2. **To Apply:** Applicants must submit the application in a single PDF file with the following documents: cover page including award being applied for, name and email address of the applicant and email addresses of those providing letters of support; curriculum vitae containing name, address, phone number, email address, date, education, work and volunteer experience, awards and scholarships, list of scientific contributions like refereed and non-refereed publications, talks and posters at meetings, other communications and other interests or achievements; scanned set of transcripts, either of originals, or copies certified as such by a graduate secretary/administrator or graduate supervisor, showing undergraduate and post graduate (if applicable) grades; one page statement answering to the question "why you are studying entomology?" and summary of the applicant's thesis research; reference letters from applicant's supervisor and one other person which clearly indicate the applicant's academic abilities, communication skills, progress as a graduate student and the novelty and scholastic contribution of the applicant's research to the field of entomology. **Deadline:** July 31.

3890 ■ Entomological Society of Canada Postgraduate Awards *(Postgraduate/Award)*

Purpose: To assists students in studies and researches leading to a postgraduate degree in entomology. **Focus:** Entomology. **Qualif.:** Applicants must be postgraduate students enrolled at a Canadian university and his/her studies and research must be carried out at a Canadian university. **Criteria:** Applications will be reviewed by a committee of the Society.

Funds Avail.: $2,000. **Duration:** Annual. **Number Awarded:** 2. **To Apply:** Applicants must submit the application in a single PDF file with the following documents: cover page including award being applied for, name and email address of the applicant and email addresses of those providing letters of support; Curriculum Vitae containing name and address, phone number, email address, date, education (degrees and dates), work and volunteer experience, awards and scholarships, list of scientific contributions like refereed and non-refereed publications, talks and posters at meetings, other communications and other interests or achievements; scanned set of transcripts, either of originals, or copies certified as such by a graduate secretary/administrator or graduate supervisor, showing undergraduate and post graduate (if applicable) grades; a one page statement answering to the question "why you are studying entomology?"; a summary of the applicant's thesis research; and reference letters from applicant's supervisor and one other person which clearly indicate the applicant's academic abilities, communication skills, progress as a graduate student and the novelty and scholastic contribution of the applicant's research to the field of entomology. **Deadline:** February 16.

3891 ■ Graduate Research-Travel Scholarships *(Graduate/Scholarship)*

Purpose: To foster graduate education in entomology and to help students increase the scope of the graduate training. **Focus:** Entomology. **Qualif.:** Applicants must be enrolled as full-time graduate students at a Canadian university and pursuing scientific studies on insects or other related terrestrial arthropods. **Criteria:** Selection criteria will be based on a competitive basis.

Funds Avail.: Maximum of $2,000. **Duration:** Annual. **Number Awarded:** 2. **To Apply:** Applicants must submit the application in a single PDF file with the following documents: cover page including award being applied for, name and email address of the applicant and email addresses of those providing letters of support; curriculum vitae containing name and address, phone number, email address, date, education (degrees and dates), work and volunteer experience, awards and scholarships, list of scientific contributions like refereed and non-refereed publications, talks and posters at meetings, other communications and other interests or achievements; scanned set of transcripts, either of originals, or copies certified as such by a graduate secretary/administrator or graduate supervisor, showing undergraduate and post graduate (if applicable) grades; and approximately four pages of proposal. Proposal will be in the format of a grant proposal and the applicant will provide the following information: the subject of the thesis; a pertinent review of the literature in the field; a concise presentation of the status of the ongoing thesis research; a description of the research or course work to be undertaken, clearly indicating the relevance to the overall goal of the thesis, an explanation of why such work cannot be carried out at the student's own university and the justification of the site where the research/course work will be carried out; a budget for the proposed project; and anticipated dates of

Awards are arranged alphabetically below their administering organizations

travel and date on which scholarship money is needed. **Deadline:** February 16.

3892 ■ Keith Kevan Award *(Postgraduate/Award)*

Purpose: To assist students in postgraduate programs who are studying systematic in entomology. **Focus:** Entomology. **Qualif.:** Applicants must be post-graduate students studying at Canadian university or Canadian citizens studying abroad and members of Entomological Society of Canada. **Criteria:** Applications will be reviewed by a committee of the Society.

Funds Avail.: $1,000. **Duration:** Biennial; in odd numbered years. **To Apply:** Applicants must submit the application in a single PDF file with the following documents: cover page including award being applied for, and name and email addresses including the email addresses of those providing letters of support; Curriculum Vitae containing name and address, phone number, email address, date, education (degrees and dates), work and volunteer experience, awards and scholarships, list of scientific contributions like refereed and non-refereed publications, talks and posters at meetings, other communications and other interests or achievements; scanned set of transcripts, either of originals, or copies certified as such by a graduate secretary/administrator or graduate supervisor, showing undergraduate and post graduate (if applicable) grades; one page statement answering to the question "why you are studying entomology?"; summary of the thesis research; and reference letters from the supervisor and one other person which clearly indicate the applicants' academic abilities, communication skills, progress as a graduate student and the novelty and scholastic contribution of the applicants' research to the field of entomology. Letters of the applicants should indicate the contribution of his/her work to biosystematics. **Deadline:** February 16.

3893 ■ Entomological Society of Saskatchewan

c/o Iain Phillips, Treasurer
No. 101-108 Research Dr.
Saskatoon, SK, Canada S7N 3R3
Ph: (306)933-7474
Fax: (306)933-6820
E-mail: iain.phillips@wsask.ca
URL: www.entsocsask.ca

3894 ■ Brooks Scholarships *(Graduate/Scholarship)*

Purpose: To support students in studies related to Entomology and to provide them the opportunity to gain research experience in the field of entomology. **Focus:** Entomology. **Qualif.:** Applicants must be registered for at least one academic year as full-time students in the field of entomology in the College of Graduate Studies and Research at the Universities of Saskatchewan or Regina; must have an academic average equivalent to a "B" standing or above; and must have demonstrated the ability to make an outstanding contribution to entomology in Saskatchewan. **Criteria:** Selection will be based on the committee's criteria.

Funds Avail.: $500. **Duration:** Annual. **To Apply:** Applicants must send their academic records, a list of publications, and a statement of interests, activities and accomplishments related to entomology. **Deadline:** October 1.

3895 ■ Entomological Society of Saskatchewan Student Presentation Awards *(Undergraduate/Award)*

Purpose: To support students giving a scientific presentation at the Entomological Society of Saskatchewan ESS Annual Meeting. **Focus:** Entomology. **Qualif.:** Applicants must be students studying entomology at any level including those from universities outside Saskatchewan. **Criteria:** Selection criteria will be based at competitive basis.

Funds Avail.: $100. **Duration:** Annual. **Number Awarded:** Varies. **To Apply:** Interested applicants may contact the Society for the application process and other required materials.

3896 ■ Entomological Society of Saskatchewan Travel Awards *(Professional development/Award)*

Purpose: To support members of ESS by helping them attend an entomological conference or conduct entomological research or activities. **Focus:** Entomology. **Qualif.:** Recipients must be members of the Entomological Society of Saskatchewan in good standing. **Criteria:** Selection will be based on the committee's criteria.

Funds Avail.: $1,000. **Duration:** Fiscal year. **To Apply:** Recipients must submit a statement indicating why it is important for the ESS to lend its support and budget. The budget should include a breakdown of the expected costs, the anticipated sources of funding for the conference, project or event and where the ESS support will be applied. Recipients must submit the applications electronically.

3897 ■ Environmental Law Institute (ELI)

2000 L St. NW, Ste. 620
Washington, DC 20036
Ph: (202)939-3824
URL: www.eli.org
Facebook: www.facebook.com/EnvironmentalLawInstitute/
Twitter: twitter.com/ELIORG

3898 ■ Public Interest Environmental Law Fellowships *(Graduate/Fellowship)*

Purpose: To provide a recent law school graduate a year of legal experience and training. **Focus:** Law. **Qualif.:** Applicant must be a law school graduate or a candidate, who has graduated recently, and have a top academic record and possess superior legal research and writing skills. **Criteria:** Selection is based on the application materials.

Funds Avail.: $30,000, with benefits. **Duration:** Annual. **To Apply:** Applicants must submit a complete application package which must include: cover letter; current resume; completed "ELI Application for Employment"; law school transcript; three references; and writing sample of approximately 10 (but no more than 15) pages.

3899 ■ Environmental Research and Education Foundation (EREF)

3301 Benson Dr., Ste. 101
Raleigh, NC 27609
Ph: (919)861-6876
Fax: (919)861-6878
E-mail: foundation@erefdn.org
URL: www.erefdn.org
Facebook: www.facebook.com/erefauction
LinkedIn: www.linkedin.com/grps/Environmental-Research-Education-Foundation-4240923/about
Twitter: twitter.com/erefnews

3900 ■ Environmental Research and Education Foundation Scholarships *(Master's, Doctorate, Postdoctorate/Scholarship)*

Purpose: To promote the waste management research and education. **Focus:** Waste management. **Qualif.:** Applicants must be full-time master's students, doctoral or post-doctoral researchers; must have demonstrated interest in waste management research. **Criteria:** Recipients are selected based on academic performance; professional experience; relevance of one's work to the advancement of solid waste management; potential for success.

Funds Avail.: $14,400 for doctoral and post-doctoral; $6,000 for master's degree. **Duration:** Annual. **To Apply:** Applicant must complete an application form; must submit an official college transcript; admission test scores; three recommendations; an essay of not more than 500 words that includes an autobiographical statement and discussion of research topic. Essay should be typewritten, double-spaced, unbound and unstapled. **Deadline:** May1. **Contact:** Environmental Research and Education Foundation, at the above address.

3901 ■ Epilepsy Foundation
8301 Professional Pl. E, Ste. 200
Landover, MD 20785-2353
Fax: (301)459-1569
Free: 866-332-1000
E-mail: contactus@efa.org
URL: www.epilepsyfoundation.org

3902 ■ Epilepsy Foundation Behavioral Sciences Post-Doctoral Fellowships *(Postdoctorate/Fellowship)*

Purpose: To provide financial assistance for post-doctoral training of behavioral scientists committed to epilepsy research. **Focus:** Behavioral sciences; Epilepsy; Social sciences. **Qualif.:** Applicants must receive their doctoral degrees in the field of social sciences by the time the fellowship commences; have an acceptable research plan; and have an access to institutional resources in conducting the project. **Criteria:** Applications are evaluated based on the quality of the proposed project; applicant's and preceptor's qualifications; and adequacy of the facility.

Funds Avail.: No specific amount. **To Apply:** Applicants must complete an application form with letters of recommendation included.

3903 ■ Epilepsy Foundation Behavioral Sciences Student Fellowships *(Graduate, Undergraduate/Fellowship)*

Purpose: To encourage individuals to pursue careers in epilepsy in either the research or practice setting. **Focus:** Behavioral sciences; Epilepsy. **Qualif.:** Applicants must be undergraduates or graduate students who are studying a field related to epilepsy research or clinical care; have (three months) free period to conduct the research; have qualified mentor; and have an access to institutional resources including clinics and laboratories to conduct the project. **Criteria:** Applications are evaluated based on the quality of the proposed project; interest in the field; applicant's and mentor's qualifications; adequacy of facilities and quality of the training environment.

To Apply: Applicants must complete an application form with letters of recommendation included.

3904 ■ Epilepsy Foundation Health Sciences Student Fellowships *(Doctorate, Graduate/Fellowship)*

Purpose: To stimulate individuals to pursue careers in epilepsy in either research or practice settings. **Focus:** Epilepsy; Health sciences. **Qualif.:** Applicants must be pre-doctoral training students in Health Sciences; be enrolled or accepted for enrollment in medical school, in doctoral program or other graduate program; have an epilepsy-related study or research plan; have three months free period; have a qualified mentor; have an access to institutional resources including clinics or laboratories in conducting the project. **Criteria:** Applications are evaluated based on the quality of the proposed project; relevance of the proposed work to epilepsy; interest in the field of epilepsy; applicants' qualifications; adequacy of facility and quality of the training environment.

Funds Avail.: No specific amount. **To Apply:** Applicants must complete an application form with letters of recommendation included.

3905 ■ Epilepsy Foundation Post-doctoral Research and Training Fellowships *(Postdoctorate/Fellowship)*

Purpose: To support the post-doctoral training of academic physicians and scientists committed to epilepsy research. **Focus:** Epilepsy; Neuroscience. **Qualif.:** Applicants must be physicians or PhD neuroscientists. **Criteria:** Applications are evaluated based on the quality of the proposed project. Applications are considered from individuals interested in acquiring experience either in basic laboratory research or in the conduct of human clinical studies.

Funds Avail.: No specific amount. **To Apply:** Applicants may visit the website or contact Epilepsy Foundation for more details.

3906 ■ Epilepsy Foundation Pre-doctoral Research Training Fellowships *(Graduate/Fellowship)*

Purpose: To supports pre-doctoral students with dissertation research related to epilepsy. **Focus:** Biochemistry; Epilepsy; Genetics; Neuroscience; Nursing, Cardiovascular and cerebrovascular; Pharmacology; Pharmacy; Physiology; Psychology. **Qualif.:** Applicants must be graduate students enrolled in a full-time doctoral (PhD) program with academic focus on Neuroscience, Physiology, Pharmacology, Psychology, Biochemistry, Genetics, Nursing, or Pharmacy. **Criteria:** Applications are evaluated based on the quality of the proposed project.

Funds Avail.: No specific amount. **To Apply:** Applicants may visit the website or contact Epilepsy Foundation for more details.

3907 ■ Epilepsy Foundation Research Grants *(Doctorate/Grant)*

Purpose: To support clinical investigators or basic scientists by providing funds for biological or behavioral research that will advance the understanding, treatment, and prevention of epilepsy. **Focus:** Behavioral sciences; Epilepsy. **Qualif.:** Applicants must be conducting a biological or behavioral research that may advance the treatment, understanding and prevention of epilepsy. **Criteria:** Applications are evaluated based on the quality of the proposed project.

Funds Avail.: No specific amount. **Duration:** Annual. **To Apply:** Applicants may visit the website or contact Epilepsy Foundation for more details.

3908 ■ Epilepsy Foundation Research and Training Fellowships for Clinicians *(Doctorate, Other/Grant)*

Purpose: To provide support for study and research by clinically trained professionals. **Focus:** Epilepsy; Medicine, Internal; Neurology; Psychiatry. **Qualif.:** Applicants must be clinically trained professionals (PharmD, Doctor of Nursing); must have an MD or DO who have completed residency training in neurology, neurosurgery, pediatrics, internal medicine, or psychiatry by the time the fellowship commences. **Criteria:** Applications are evaluated based on the quality of the proposed project.

Funds Avail.: No specific amount. **Duration:** Annual. **To Apply:** Applicants may visit the website or contact Epilepsy Foundation for more details.

3909 ■ Targeted Research Initiative for Health Outcomes (Doctorate/Grant)

Purpose: To support research that generates initial data leading to more extensive projects that will generate knowledge and will ultimately improve the healthcare of persons with epilepsy. **Focus:** Behavioral sciences; Epilepsy. **Qualif.:** Applicants must hold a relevant advanced degree; have completed all research training; and must be based at corporations as well as academic/university settings. **Criteria:** Applications are evaluated based on proposal's scientific validity; relevance to the program's goals and feasibility; applicant's qualifications and adequacy of the research. Grants will be awarded to applicants who have provided a clear justification based on need and timetable of the work proposed.

Funds Avail.: No specific amount. **To Apply:** Applicants may visit the website or contact Epilepsy Foundation for more details.

3910 ■ Epilepsy Newfoundland and Labrador (ENL)
351 Kenmount Rd.
Saint John's, NL, Canada A1B 3P9
Ph: (709)722-0502
Free: 866-EPI-LEPSY
E-mail: info@epilepsynl.com
URL: www.epilepsynl.com

3911 ■ Jim Hierlihy Memorial Scholarship (Undergraduate/Scholarship)

Purpose: To widen horizons of ENL student members by providing financial support as they pursue college or university studies. **Focus:** General studies/Field of study not specified. **Qualif.:** Applicants must be diagnosed with epilepsy and be members in good standing of Epilepsy Newfoundland and Labrador at the time of scholarship application. Scholarship is not open to current ENL board and staff members. Former board or staff members and/or their family members may apply for scholarships if they have been out of the service of Epilepsy Newfoundland and Labrador for two years. **Criteria:** Recipient is chosen based on grades, extracurricular activities and financial need.

Funds Avail.: $1,000. **Duration:** Annual. **Number Awarded:** 1. **To Apply:** Applicants must submit the completed application form available from the website along with a copy of the most recent academic transcript. **Deadline:** November 1.

3912 ■ Mature Student Scholarship (Undergraduate/Scholarship)

Purpose: To widen horizons of ENL student members by providing financial support as they pursue college or university studies. **Focus:** General studies/Field of study not specified. **Qualif.:** Applicants must be 21 years or older; must be diagnosed with epilepsy; and be members in good standing of Epilepsy Newfoundland and Labrador at the time of the scholarship application. Scholarship is not open to current ENL board and staff members. Former board or staff members and/or their family members can apply for scholarships if they have been out of the service of Epilepsy Newfoundland and Labrador for two years. **Criteria:** Selection is based on the review of application records.

Funds Avail.: $1,000. **Duration:** Annual. **Number Awarded:** 1. **To Apply:** Applicants must complete application form available at the website and submit it along with a copy of the most recent academic transcript to: Epilepsy Newfoundland and Labrador, 261 Kenmount Rd., St. John's, NF A1B 3P9. **Deadline:** January 15. **Contact:** 261 Kenmount Road, St. John's, NL A1B 3P9; Telephone: 709-722-0502; Toll Free: 1-866-epilepsy; Fax: 709-722-0999; Email: info@epilepsynl.com.

3913 ■ Epsilon Sigma Alpha (ESA)
363 W Drake Rd.
Fort Collins, CO 80526
Ph: (970)223-2824
Fax: (970)223-4456
E-mail: esainfo@epsilonsigmaalpha.org
URL: www.epsilonsigmaalpha.org/Homepage

3914 ■ ESA Foundation Life Grants (Undergraduate/Grant)

Purpose: To assist persons who seek further study/training, workshops, seminars, intern training, etc. for the development of their skills and job advancement. **Focus:** Leadership, Institutional and community. **Qualif.:** Applicants must be individuals seeking help/support for self and career development. **Criteria:** Selection will be based on the committees' criteria.

Funds Avail.: $1,500. **To Apply:** Applicants must fill-up the Life Grant Application form and may contact the Association for other information needed. **Contact:** Cathy Holsted, Grants Chairman.

3915 ■ Equal Justice Initiative (EJI)
122 Commerce St.
Montgomery, AL 36104
Ph: (334)269-1803
Fax: (334)269-1806
E-mail: contact_us@eji.org
URL: www.eji.org
Facebook: www.facebook.com/equaljusticeinitiative

3916 ■ EJI Justice Fellowship (Graduate, Postgraduate, Professional development/Fellowship)

Purpose: To provide opportunity to those talented and ambitious recent college graduates, post graduates and young professionals to work for two years as a full-time, paid staff member at EJI. **Focus:** Nonprofit sector; Social work. **Qualif.:** Applicants must be a recent college graduates, post graduates and young professionals. **Criteria:** Selection will be based on the committee's criteria.

Funds Avail.: No specific amount. **To Apply:** Applicants must send a letter of interest and resume. **Deadline:** December 31. **Contact:** Jennae Swiergula at jswiergula@eji.org.

3917 ■ Equal Justice Works
1730 M St. NW, Ste. 1010
Washington, DC 20036-4511
Ph: (202)466-3686

Awards are arranged alphabetically below their administering organizations

URL: www.equaljusticeworks.org

3918 ■ Equal Justice Works Fellowship Program
(Graduate, Undergraduate/Fellowship)

Purpose: To support qualified and passionate lawyers in developing new and innovative legal projects that can impact lives and serve communities in desperate need of legal assistance. **Focus:** Law. **Qualif.:** Applicants must be third year law students, graduates or experienced attorneys from an EJW law school who are committed to public interest. **Criteria:** Applications will be judged based on quality of the proposed project.

Funds Avail.: No specific amount. **To Apply:** Applicants must provide a completed application, including a project proposal, a fellowship candidate to carry out the project, and a nonprofit public interest organization identified to host the project; Applicants must also submit a certification form and two hard copies of letters of recommendation; and must attend a scheduled interview if evaluated successfully. **Deadline:** September 16.

3919 ■ Equity Foundation
221 NW 2nd Ave.
Portland, OR 97209
Ph: (503)231-5759
E-mail: info@equityfoundation.org
URL: www.equityfoundation.org
Facebook: www.facebook.com/EquityFoundation
Twitter: twitter.com/EquityFdn

3920 ■ Gregori Jakovina Endowment Scholarships
(Undergraduate/Scholarship)

Purpose: To encourage and facilitate post-secondary education in the arts for people who are gay, lesbian, bisexual or transgender (GLBT). **Focus:** Art. **Qualif.:** Applicants must be Oregon or Clark County Washington residents who demonstrate financial need. **Criteria:** Preference will be given to those who meet the criteria.

Funds Avail.: No specific amount. **To Apply:** Applicants must check the application process online. **Deadline:** July 31.

3921 ■ Portland Area Business Association Scholarships *(Undergraduate/Scholarship)*

Purpose: To provide financial assistance to post secondary GLBT students. **Focus:** General studies/Field of study not specified. **Qualif.:** Applicants must be members of the gay, lesbian, bisexual or transgendered communities. **Criteria:** Preference will be given to those who meet the criteria.

Funds Avail.: No specific amount. **To Apply:** Applicants must check the available website for the required materials.

3922 ■ Pride of the Rose Scholarship Fund
(Undergraduate/Scholarship)

Purpose: To provide financial assistance to those students who are in need. **Focus:** General studies/Field of study not specified. **Qualif.:** Applicants must be post-secondary education to members of the gay, lesbian, bisexual and transgender communities and their children residing in the Quad-county area of Portland, OR and Clark County, WA. **Criteria:** Preference will be given to those who meet the criteria.

Funds Avail.: No specific amount. **To Apply:** Applicants must check the application process online. **Deadline:** July 31.

3923 ■ Bill and Ann Sheperd Legal Scholarship Fund *(Undergraduate/Scholarship)*

Purpose: To provide financial support to those who are in need. **Focus:** Law. **Qualif.:** Applicants must be third-year and fourth-year law students dedicated to keeping Oregon a hate-free state; be committed to equal rights and justice for gays, lesbians, bisexuals and transgendered persons; be citizens of the United States; must demonstrate the potential to complete their law program successfully; and demonstrate the intent to practice law and promote the rights of the gay, lesbian, bisexual and transgendered community. **Criteria:** Preference will be given to those who meet the criteria.

Funds Avail.: No specific amount. **To Apply:** Applicants must check the available website for the required materials.

3924 ■ Erickson Merkel Foundation
1475 Eldridge Ave. E
Maplewood, MN 55109
Ph: (952)212-3195
URL: www.ericksonmerkel.org

3925 ■ Erickson Merkel Foundation Scholarships
(Undergraduate/Scholarship)

Purpose: To select and reward scholarship candidates who exemplify the values of hard work, creativity and services. **Focus:** General studies/Field of study not specified. **Qualif.:** Applicants must be students currently enrolled or will be enrolled at an accredited college, university or trade school by fall. **Criteria:** Selection will be based on the compliance with the application process.

Funds Avail.: Three $1,000; One $3,000. **Number Awarded:** 4. **To Apply:** Applicants must download the application form at the website. They should also submit an essay discussing efforts being made to limit student loan debt and contribution being made to the community. **Deadline:** April 15. **Contact:** E-mail at scholarships@ericksonmerkel.org.

3926 ■ Etruscan Foundation (EF)
PO Box 26
Fremont, MI 49412-0026
Ph: (231)519-0675
Fax: (231)924-0777
E-mail: office@etruscanfoundation.org
URL: www.etruscanfoundation.org
Facebook: www.facebook.com/Etruscanfoundation

3927 ■ Fieldwork Fellowships *(Undergraduate/Award, Fellowship)*

Purpose: To help defray the costs of participation in field schools, archaeological conservation programs and research projects at Etruscan and other pre-Roman sites across Italy. **Focus:** Archeology; Culture. **Qualif.:** Applicants must be U.S., Canadian or European citizens who are students enrolled at an accredited college or university in North America or England. All applicants must be members of The Etruscan Foundation. **Criteria:** Applicants will be evaluated by The Etruscan Foundation Fellowship Review Committee. The recommendations of the Committee will be forwarded to the Board of Directors for final approval.

Funds Avail.: $2,000. **To Apply:** Applicants may contact

Awards are arranged alphabetically below their administering organizations

the Foundation for the application process and other information. **Deadline:** March 18. **Contact:** Richard String, Executive Director, at the above address.

3928 ■ Eurasia Foundation
1350 Connecticut Ave. NW, Ste. 1000
Washington, DC 20036
Ph: (202)234-7370
Fax: (202)234-7377
E-mail: eurasia@eurasia.org
URL: www.eurasia.org

3929 ■ Bill Maynes Fellowships *(Professional development/Fellowship)*

Purpose: To build personal and professional bridges between emerging leaders in the Eurasia region and their counterparts in the United States. **Focus:** General studies/Field of study not specified. **Qualif.:** Applicants must be: citizens of Armenia, Azerbaijan, Belarus, Georgia, Kazakhstan, Kyrgyzstan, Moldova, Russia, Tajikistan, Turkmenistan, Ukraine or Uzbekistan; individuals working at local, national and international levels with a record of achievement or exceptional future promise in the fields of micro and small business, independent media, open and responsive governance, community development, youth or gender advocacy or other areas that support civil society; have a commitment to fully take advantage of a rigorous program of meetings, speaking engagements, presentations and practical involvement at various institutions during the course of the fellowship; be an experienced partners of the Eurasia Foundation Network; be candidates with a good command of the English language. **Criteria:** Selection will be based on the committee's criteria.

Funds Avail.: No specific amount. **To Apply:** Interested applicants must contact Zhenya Khilji for the application process and further inquiries.

3930 ■ Everglades Foundation
18001 Old Cutler Rd., Ste. 625
Miami, FL 33157
Ph: (305)251-0001
E-mail: info@evergladesfoundation.org
URL: www.evergladesfoundation.org
Facebook: www.facebook.com/evergladesfoundation
LinkedIn: www.linkedin.com/company/everglades
 -foundation?trk=cws-cpw-coname-0-0
Twitter: twitter.com/evergfoundation?ref_src=twsrc%5Etfw

3931 ■ Everglades Foundation Fellowship *(Graduate, Doctorate, Master's/Fellowship)*

Purpose: To support graduate research students in pursuing the development of innovative scientific methods in advancing the understanding of Everglades physical, chemical, or biological processes, or research in economic impacts of environmental changes. **Focus:** Biological and clinical sciences; Earth sciences; Economics; Engineering; Geography; Resource management. **Qualif.:** Applicants must be full-time graduate research students pursuing degrees in earth sciences, biological sciences, engineering, geography, planning and resource management, and economics. **Criteria:** All applications will be reviewed by experts to determine the potential contribution of the work to Everglades restoration; recommendations from leading professors and investigators currently active in Everglades are important; and factors including the applicants' prior research and/or publication and academic record, personal essay, and interdisciplinary nature of the research.

Funds Avail.: $10,000 - $20,000. **Duration:** Annual. **Number Awarded:** 2. **To Apply:** Application entries should contain the following: a cover letter; a proposal describing the research that the award would support (no more than 5,000 words); proposed budget; a personal essay of no more than 2 pages on the candidates' career goals and how scholarship will support those goals; a curriculum vitae including transcripts; at least one and up to three academic or professional letter(s) of reference; and other relevant or supporting work products or documentation. Electronic submission is preferred, and the package and letters of reference should be emailed. **Deadline:** July 31. **Contact:** Everglades Foundation, at the above address or Email to fellowship@evergladesfoundation.org.

3932 ■ Everglades Foundation Internship *(Postgraduate, Postdoctorate/Internship)*

Purpose: To support graduate research students in pursuing the development of innovative scientific methods in advancing the understanding of Everglades physical, chemical, or biological processes, or research in economic impacts of environmental changes. **Focus:** Biological and clinical sciences; Earth sciences; Economics; Engineering; Geography; Resource management. **Qualif.:** Applicants must have an interest in a range of topics related to Everglades restoration. **Criteria:** Selection criteria will be based on the submitted application.

Funds Avail.: No specific amount. **Duration:** Annual. **To Apply:** Interested applicants may contact the Foundation for the application process and other information.

3933 ■ Everglades Foundation Scholarships *(Graduate, Master's, Doctorate/Scholarship)*

Purpose: To support graduate research students in pursuing the development of innovative scientific methods in advancing the understanding of Everglades physical, chemical, or biological processes, or research in economic impacts of environmental changes. **Focus:** Biological and clinical sciences; Earth sciences; Economics; Engineering; Geography; Resource management. **Qualif.:** Applicants must be full-time graduate research students pursuing degrees in earth sciences, biological sciences, engineering, geography, planning and resource management and economics. **Criteria:** All applications will be reviewed by experts to determine the potential contribution of the work to Everglades restoration; recommendations from leading professors and investigators currently active in Everglades are important; and factors including the applicant's prior research and/or publication and academic record, personal essay, and interdisciplinary nature of the research.

Funds Avail.: $10,000 - $20,000. **Duration:** Annual. **To Apply:** Application entries should contain the following: a cover letter; a proposal describing the research that the award would support (no more than 5,000 words); proposed budget; a personal essay of no more than 2 pages on the candidates' career goals and how scholarship will support those goals; a curriculum vitae including transcripts; at least one and up to three academic or professional letter(s) of reference; and other relevant or supporting work products or documentation. Electronic submission is preferred, and the package and letters of reference should be emailed. **Deadline:** July 31.

Awards are arranged alphabetically below their administering organizations

3934 ■ Executive Women International (EWI)
3860 South 2300 East, Ste. 211
Salt Lake City, UT 84109
Ph: (801)355-2800
Fax: (801)355-2852
E-mail: ewi@ewiconnect.com
URL: www.ewiconnect.com
Twitter: twitter.com/ewicorporate

3935 ■ Adult Students in Scholastic Transition Scholarships (ASIST) *(Professional development/Scholarship)*

Purpose: To financially support students for their continuous education. **Focus:** General studies/Field of study not specified. **Qualif.:** Applicants must be single parents or non-traditional students including individuals past high school age who are entering a college, university or trade school and/or the workforce for the first time; or either be non-traditional students already enrolled who are in need of re-training due to changes in the workplace; must be 18 years of age or older; and must be residing within the boundaries of the EWI chapter to which application is submitted. **Criteria:** Recipients are selected based on: financial need; socially, physically and economically challenged adults; responsibility for small children. **Funds Avail.:** $2,000-$10,000. **Duration:** Annual. **Number Awarded:** 13. **To Apply:** Applicants must complete the application form; must include a copy of the most recent federal or state tax return and W-2 form; must enclosed personal recommendation form; and must obtain an official transcript of grades from the educational provider or ACT scores. Applicants must contact the nearest EWI Chapter for more information.

3936 ■ Executive Women International Scholarship Program (EWISP) *(Undergraduate/Scholarship)*

Purpose: To financially help qualified applicants achieve their academic goals. **Focus:** General studies/Field of study not specified. **Qualif.:** Applicants must be full-time junior students currently enrolled in a school located within the geographical boundaries of a participating EWI Chapter; and must have plan to pursue a degree at an accredited post-secondary institution. **Criteria:** Applicants will be selected based on character, personal merit and background. **Funds Avail.:** $1,000-$5,000. **Duration:** Annual. **To Apply:** Applicants must submit a completed application form available on the website; two letters of recommendation (use the Personal Recommendation Form) and official transcript of grades. Applications should be submitted to the EWI Chapter near the applicant's residency.

3937 ■ Executive Women's Golf Association (EWGA)
8895 N Military Trl., Ste. 102e
Palm Beach Gardens, FL 33410
Ph: (561)691-0096
E-mail: info@myewga.com
URL: www.ewga.com
Facebook: www.facebook.com/EWGA1
LinkedIn: www.linkedin.com/groups/1435337/profile
Twitter: twitter.com/ewga

3938 ■ Women on Par Scholarships *(Undergraduate/Scholarship)*

Purpose: To provide financial assistance to nontraditional female students who are interested in beginning or completing their undergraduate education to allow them to get "on par" with their peers and advance themselves both professionally and personally. **Focus:** General studies/Field of study not specified. **Qualif.:** Candidates must be female of at least 30 years old as of January 1st of the current year; must be U.S. or Canadian citizens, or legal residents who are currently enrolled or accepted to an accredited school, college or university; must be pursuing a technical/vocational, associate, or bachelor's degree (candidates must be first time applicants to school, or must be returning to school after an absence to complete a degree); and must exhibit a need for financial assistance. **Criteria:** Candidates will be selected based on the aforesaid qualifications and compliance with the application process. **Funds Avail.:** One $1,000; One $500. **Duration:** Annual. **Number Awarded:** 2. **To Apply:** Application process has two phases. For the Phase One, candidates must submit the following materials to be considered: completed application form (all information must be provided as required in Sections 1-11 of the form for their applications to be considered); proof of current enrollment in, or acceptance to, an accredited school; and a self-addressed, stamped envelope if they do not have email address. If selected to advance to Phase Two of the application process as scholarship finalists, the following materials are required in order for the application to be considered: official transcripts from schools previously attended; three sealed letters of reference; and official financial documentation of their previous year's income (Form 1040 as filed with the IRS or foreign equivalent). **Deadline:** April 15 (Phase One). **Remarks:** The scholarship is funded by the EWGA Foundation. **Contact:** EWGA Foundation at foundation@myewga.com.

3939 ■ ExeptionalNurse.com
13019 Coastal Cir.
Palm Beach Gardens, FL 33410
E-mail: exceptionalnurse@aol.com
URL: www.exceptionalnurse.com

3940 ■ ExeptionalNurse.com Scholarships *(Undergraduate, Graduate/Scholarship)*

Purpose: To support students with disabilities who wish to continue their education in a nursing education program. **Focus:** Nursing. **Qualif.:** Applicants must be students with a documented disability who have applied to, or already been admitted to, a college or university program on a full-time basis. **Criteria:** Selection shall be based on the aforementioned applicants' qualifications and compliance with the application details. **Funds Avail.:** No specific amount. **Duration:** Annual. **Number Awarded:** Varies. **To Apply:** Applicants must submit a completed and signed application form along with three letters of recommendation attesting to the applicant's academic abilities and personal character (may not be relatives); a 1-2 page essay; official transcripts of high school/and or college courses completed; and Medical Verification of Disability Form. **Deadline:** June 1. **Remarks:** The scholarships are awarded in various categories. Established in 2003.

3941 ■ The Expert Institute
75 Maiden Ln., Ste. 704
New York, NY 10038
Free: 888-858-9511
URL: www.theexpertinstitute.com

3942 ■ The Expert Institute Legal Blog Post Writing Contest (Graduate/Award)

Purpose: To help law students ease some of their financial burden. **Focus:** Law. **Qualif.:** Applicants must be current law school students. **Criteria:** The Expert Institute editorial staff, as well as a panel of practicing trial lawyers will judge the contest.

Funds Avail.: $250-$500. **Duration:** Semiannual. **Number Awarded:** 2. **To Apply:** Applicants must submit a 1,500-2,500 words essay written in a blog post format with the following factors: clarity, style, and poise of writing; originality of topic; thoroughness of research and quality of analysis; and comprehensibility by lay and professional audiences. **Deadline:** December 31.

3943 ■ Experts Exchange
2701 McMillan Ave.,Ste. 160
San Luis Obispo, CA 93401
Ph: (805)787-0603
Fax: (805)540-6064
URL: www.experts-exchange.com

3944 ■ Experts Exchange Scholarships Contest (Undergraduate, Graduate/Scholarship)

Purpose: To support the creative genius in those who have made a difference in the lives of others in some innovative or technological fashion. **Focus:** General studies/Field of study not specified. **Qualif.:** Applicants must be U.S. citizens, permanent residents, or hold a valid student visa; must be currently enrolled in or accepted to a college, university, or trade school as undergraduate or graduate students within the United States as of the application deadline. **Criteria:** Selection will be based on the aforesaid qualifications and compliance with the application process.

Funds Avail.: $500 to $1,500. **Duration:** Semiannual. **Number Awarded:** 3. **To Apply:** Student applicants must submit their original pieces of work via articles or videos on a technology topic of their choosing to the Experts Exchange website. The idea or creation must be the applicants' original work. **Deadline:** June 30; December 31. **Contact:** Send e-mail at scholarship@experts-exchange.com.

3945 ■ The Explorers Club
46 E 70th St.
New York, NY 10021
Ph: (212)628-8383
Fax: (212)288-4449
E-mail: president@explorers.org
URL: www.explorers.org
Facebook: www.facebook.com/pages/The-Explorers-Club/691604090855340
Twitter: twitter.com/explorersclub

3946 ■ Scott Pearlman Field Awards for Science and Exploration (Other/Award)

Purpose: To provide grants to artists, writers, filmmakers, still and video photographers, and journalists recommended by a member of The Explorers Club who is also leading the expedition. **Focus:** Filmmaking; Journalism; Photography. **Qualif.:** Applicants must be professional artists, writers, photographers, filmmakers and journalists. **Criteria:** Selection will be based on the committee's criteria.

Funds Avail.: No specific amount. **To Apply:** Applicants may visit the website to download the application form. Four copies of the completed application, samples of the candidate's work, and letters from two peers familiar with the candidate's work and a written recommendation from the expedition leader must be received together for consideration. **Deadline:** May 30. **Contact:** Will Roseman at wroseman@explorers.org.

3947 ■ Express Medical Supply
218 Seebold Spur
Fenton, MO 63026
Ph: (800)633-2139
E-mail: rstorz@exmed.net
URL: www.exmed.net

3948 ■ Express Medical Supply Scholarships (Undergraduate/Scholarship)

Purpose: To encourage students to tap into their creative side. **Focus:** General studies/Field of study not specified. **Qualif.:** Applicants must be students enrolled in fall of the current year at any two- or four-year college or university in the United States. **Criteria:** Selection will be based on the applicants' photo, which will be deemed as displayed to be most creative in their Twitter account.

Funds Avail.: $500. **Number Awarded:** 1. **To Apply:** Applicants must tweet their respective photo entries (@Express_Medical) that best represent the word "express" to them. The link is at the scholarship page. **Deadline:** June 30. **Contact:** E-mail at scholarships@exmed.net.

3949 ■ Facebook Inc.
156 University Ave.
Palo Alto, CA 94301-1688
Ph: (650)543-4800
URL: www.facebook.com

3950 ■ Facebook Fellowships Program (Doctorate/Fellowship)

Purpose: To encourage and support promising doctoral students who are engaged in innovative and relevant research in areas related to computer science and engineering. **Focus:** Computer and information sciences; Engineering. **Qualif.:** Applicants must be full-time PhD students who are currently involved in on-going research, and enrolled in an accredited university in any country during the academic year(s) that the Fellowship is awarded. Students' work must be related to one or more of the following disciplines: Artificial Intelligence; Computer Vision; Connectivity; Data Mining; Databases; Distributed Systems, Networking & Operating Systems; Economics and Computation; Human-Computer Interaction; Machine Learning; Natural Language Processing &Speech Technologies; Programming Languages & Compilers; Security & Privacy; Social Computing; Software Engineering. **Criteria:** Selection will be based on the submitted applications.

Funds Avail.: A stipend of $37,000 each year, and up to $5,000 in conference travel support. **Duration:** Up to two years. **To Apply:** Applicants must submit a 1-2 page research summary which clearly identifies the area of focus, importance to the field, and applicability to Facebook of the anticipated research during the award; a current CV with email, phone and mailing address, including applicable coursework; 2 letters of recommendation (one must be from an academic advisor). **Deadline:** November 1.

3951 ■ Fadel Educational Foundation, Inc. (FEF)
3137 Village W Dr.
Augusta, GA 30907-3148
Ph: (484)694-1783
URL: fadelfoundation.wordpress.com
Facebook: www.facebook.com/FadelFoundation
Twitter: twitter.com/fadelfoundation

3952 ■ FEF Scholarships (Undergraduate/Scholarship)

Purpose: To encourage American Muslims to pursue post-secondary education. **Focus:** General studies/Field of study not specified. **Qualif.:** Applicants must be non-incarcerated Muslim U.S. citizens and permanent residents who are about to pursue post-secondary education. **Criteria:** Selection shall be based on merit and financial need. **Funds Avail.:** No specific amount. **Duration:** Annual. **To Apply:** Applicants may visit the website to verify the application process and other pieces of information. **Contact:** Fadel Educational Foundation, Inc., at the above address.

3953 ■ Faegre Baker Daniels L.L.P.
90 S Seventh St.
Minneapolis, MN 55402-3903
Ph: (612)766-7000
Fax: (612)766-1600
Free: 800-328-4393
E-mail: info@faegre.com
URL: www.faegre.com
Facebook: www.facebook.com/FaegreBD
LinkedIn: www.linkedin.com/company/faegre-baker-daniels-llp
Twitter: www.twitter.com/FaegreBD

3954 ■ Faegre Baker Daniels Diversity & Inclusion Fellowships (Graduate/Fellowship)

Purpose: To promote diversity in the legal profession. **Focus:** Law. **Qualif.:** Applicants must be enrolled in a J.D. program at any accredited law school in the United States; must be interested in a summer associate position in one of FaegreBD's U.S. offices. **Criteria:** Selection will be based on the submitted application materials. **Funds Avail.:** $10,000. **Duration:** Annual. **To Apply:** Applicants must complete the online application and must provide the following materials: a resume and a cover letter indicating office preference; a law school transcript; a two-page personal statement explaining how or why they will contribute meaningfully to diversity and inclusion at Faegre Baker Daniels and/or in the legal profession.

3955 ■ Families of Freedom Scholarship Fund
Scholarship America
1 Scholarship Way
Saint Peter, MN 56082
Free: 877-862-0136
E-mail: info@familiesoffreedom.org
URL: www.familiesoffreedom.org

3956 ■ Families of Freedom Scholarship Fund - America Scholarships (Undergraduate, Vocational/Occupational/Scholarship)

Purpose: To provide education assistance for post-secondary study to dependents - children and spouses - of those killed of permanently disabled as a result of terrorist attacks on September 11, 2001 and during the rescue activities to those attacks. **Focus:** General studies/Field of study not specified. **Qualif.:** Applicants must be dependents of those killed or permanently disabled as a result of the terrorist attacks on September 11, 2001 and during the rescue activities relating to those attacks. Specifically, families of Freedom benefits children and spouses of the victims, including airplane crew and passengers, World Trade Center and Pentagon workers and visitors, and relief workers, including firefighters and emergency medical personnel and law enforcement personnel. Participants must enroll in a course of study at an accredited two- or four-year college, university or vocational-technical school based in the United States. **Criteria:** Recipients are selected based on merit. **Funds Avail.:** No specific amount. **To Apply:** Applicants must submit all the required application information.

3957 ■ Families USA
1201 New York Ave. NW, Ste. 1100
Washington, DC 20005
Ph: (202)628-3030
Fax: (202)347-2417
E-mail: info@familiesusa.org
URL: www.familiesusa.org
Facebook: facebook.com/familiesusa
Twitter: twitter.com/familiesusa

3958 ■ Villers Fellowships for Health Care Justice (Graduate/Fellowship)

Purpose: To develop a network of young leaders who share a passion for social and health care justice. **Focus:** Health care services. **Qualif.:** Applicants must be authorized to work in the United States and have a college degree or plan to receive a degree. **Criteria:** Selection shall be based on applicants' demonstrable passion for justice in the health care system. **Funds Avail.:** $38,000. **Duration:** Annual. **To Apply:** Applicants must submit a completed application form along with a personal essay and a resume. In addition, Families USA must receive an official copy of most recent college or graduate school transcript sent directly from the school registrar's office, three letters of recommendation from academic and/or professional references who can attest the applicant's community involvement sent directly from the references themselves. **Deadline:** January 23. **Contact:** Send application materials to: villersfellowship@familiesusa.org.

3959 ■ Wellstone Fellowships for Social Justice (Graduate/Fellowship)

Purpose: To foster the advancement of social justice through participation in health care advocacy work that focuses on the unique challenges facing many communities of color. **Focus:** Social work. **Qualif.:** Applicants must be authorized to work in the United States and have a college degree or plan to receive a degree. **Criteria:** Selection will be based on the applicants' demonstrable passion for social justice. **Funds Avail.:** $38,000. **Duration:** Annual. **To Apply:** Applicants must submit a completed application form along with a personal essay and a resume. In addition, Families USA must receive an official copy of most recent college or graduate school transcript sent directly from the school

Awards are arranged alphabetically below their administering organizations

registrar's office, three letters of recommendation from academic and/or professional references who can attest the applicant's community involvement. **Deadline:** February 6. **Contact:** Send application materials to: wellstonefellowship@familiesusa.org.

3960 ■ Family, Career and Community Leaders of America (FCCLA)
1910 Association Dr.
Reston, VA 20191-1584
Ph: (703)476-4900
Fax: (703)439-2662
E-mail: inbox@fcclainc.org
URL: www.fcclainc.org
Facebook: www.facebook.com/nationalfccla
Twitter: twitter.com/nationalfccla

3961 ■ Beth Middleton Memorial Scholarships
(Undergraduate/Scholarship)

Purpose: To support leadership potential and develop skills for life planning, goal setting, problem solving, decision making and interpersonal communications. **Focus:** General studies/Field of study not specified. **Qualif.:** Applicants must be member for minimum of 2 years; must me current or former FCCLA state or national officer; must be currently senior (grade 12) in high school; must have minimum 3.5 cumulative GPA (based on a non-weighted 4.0 scale); must maintain 3.0 GPA in their post-secondary; must be affiliated with National FCCLA. **Criteria:** Recipients will be selected based on academic records and contributions made as an officer as well as outstanding leadership, academic excellence, community service, and demonstration of well-roundedness through various activities.

Funds Avail.: $400 for tuition, room and/or board. **Number Awarded:** 1. **To Apply:** Applicants must fill out the on-line application form using a 10pt. Times New Roman font; must attach the most recent official high school transcript of record including the first semester of the senior year including standardized college entrance exam scores(ACT and/or SAT); must provide a copy of the chapter affiliation verifying national dues paid by March 1, 2013; applicant must include recommendations from his/her local adviser, state adviser, and one other person knowledgeable of student's non-FCCLA activities. **Deadline:** March 1.

3962 ■ National Technical Honor Society Scholarships *(Undergraduate/Scholarship)*

Purpose: To support qualified FCCLA members that have applied to a degree granting institution leading to an associate's or bachelor's degree in any field of study. **Focus:** General studies/Field of study not specified. **Qualif.:** Applicant must be a member of the National Technical Honor Society; must be a senior and must have taken the ACT or SAT examination; must have applied to a degree granting institution leading to an associate's or bachelor's degree in any field of study. **Criteria:** Recipient will be selected based on outstanding leadership, academic excellence and significant volunteer experience; also, judges will base the evaluation to the style and expression as well as content.

Funds Avail.: $1,000. **Number Awarded:** 2. **To Apply:** Applicant must fill out the online application form using the 10pt. Times New Roman font; most recent official high school transcript including the first semester grades of the senior year and standardized college entrance exam scores(ACT and/or SAT); a copy of the chapter affiliation verifying national dues paid by March 1, 2013; applicant must include a letter of recommendation from his/her local adviser, state adviser, and one other person knowledgeable of student's non-FCCLA activities; all signatures must be included. **Deadline:** April 1.

3963 ■ Fanconi Anemia Research Fund (FARF)
1801 Willamette St., Ste. 200
Eugene, OR 97401
Ph: (541)687-4658
Free: 888-326-2664
E-mail: info@fanconi.org
URL: www.fanconi.org

3964 ■ Fanconi Anemia Research Grants *(Postdoctorate/Grant)*

Purpose: To help researchers advance the science relating to Fanconi anemia. **Focus:** Health sciences. **Qualif.:** Applicants must be principal investigators, postdoctoral fellows or grant coordinators. **Criteria:** Selection will be based on the committee's criteria.

Funds Avail.: No specific amount. **To Apply:** Applicants must contact the Fanconi Anemia Research Fund office to request an application packet. The packet contains application forms and guidelines, conditions of award and criteria for peer review. **Remarks:** Established in 1989. **Contact:** Fanconi Anemia Research Fund, at the above address.

3965 ■ The Fantasy Sports Daily
2540 South Ocean Blvd.
Highland Beach, FL 33487
Ph: (561)274-6504
Fax: (561)274-6507
URL: www.fantasysportsdaily.com

3966 ■ The Fantasy Sports Daily Scholarship Program - General Scholarship for Advanced Education *(Undergraduate, Graduate, Master's/Scholarship)*

Purpose: To support and motivate students to value and make the most of their education, and to give scholarship awards to deserving students to achieve higher quality education, and actively promote education to encourage students to improve their knowledge and strive for excellence. **Focus:** General studies/Field of study not specified. **Qualif.:** Applicants must be legal residents of the United States and must be students who are at least 16 years of age enrolled in an accredited post-secondary academic institution in the United States in a two year, four year or a graduate program. **Criteria:** Students are selected based on their responses, as judged by the executive management team.

Funds Avail.: $1,000. **Duration:** Annual; each fall and spring semester. **To Apply:** Applicants must submit one complete contest application via sponsor's website in English language before the deadline and must answer four personal, open-ended, and thought-provoking questions to be considered as finalist. **Deadline:** October 15.

3967 ■ Farella Braun Martel L.L.P.
Russ Bldg., 235 Montgomery St., 17th Fl.
235 Montgomery St., 17th Fl.
San Francisco, CA 94104

Ph: (415)954-4400
Fax: (415)954-4480
E-mail: cloof@fbm.com
URL: www.fbm.com

3968 ■ Farella Braun + Martel LLP 1L Diversity Scholarship Program (Undergraduate/Scholarship)

Purpose: To assist diverse Bay Area law students who are pursuing their legal careers. **Focus:** Law. **Qualif.:** Applicants must be current first-year students with full- or part-time class loads attending one of the following law schools: University of California, Berkeley, School of Law; University of California Davis School of Law; University of California, Hastings College of the Law; Santa Clara University School of Law; Stanford Law School; or University of San Francisco School of Law. The program is open to law students of underrepresented groups whose background or personal experience would otherwise contribute to the diversity of the legal profession. **Criteria:** Recipients will be selected based on a combination of merit and financial need. Preference will be given to applicants who demonstrate a commitment to working and living in the Bay Area.

Funds Avail.: $30,000 ($10,000 each). **Duration:** Annual. **Number Awarded:** 3. **To Apply:** Applicants must submit the completed application form together with the other requirements asked by the bestowing organization. **Deadline:** March 7. **Contact:** Priscilla Zaccalini, Diversity & Professional Development Programs Coordinator, at pzaccalini@fbm.com, or call 415-954-3547.

3969 ■ Farm Equipment Manufacturers Association (FEMA)

1000 Executive Pky., Ste. 100
Saint Louis, MO 63141-6369
Ph: (314)878-2304
Fax: (314)732-1480
E-mail: info@farmequip.org
URL: www.farmequip.org

3970 ■ Harold B. Halter Memorial Scholarship (Undergraduate/Scholarship)

Purpose: To provide scholarship to outstanding students to apply at any two-year or four-year college of their choice. **Focus:** General studies/Field of study not specified. **Qualif.:** Applicants must be students who have been enrolled in the Pope County Community High School for at least two previous years; must have a GPA of 2.5 based upon a 4 point system; must have been accepted for enrollment as full-time students in a junior or four-year accredited college or university. **Criteria:** Selection will be based on the following criteria: excellence in scholarship; contribution to the favorable image of Pope County Community High School, including improvement in academic work; demonstrated leadership ability; outstanding character and personal development; desire to grow academically and socially; and has shown a level of financial self-support.

Funds Avail.: $1,000. **Duration:** Annual. **To Apply:** Interested applicants may contact the Association for the application processes and other information.

3971 ■ FCBA Foundation

1020 19th St. NW, Ste. 325
Washington, DC 20036-6101
Ph: (202)293-4000
Fax: (202)293-4317
E-mail: fcba@fcba.org
URL: www.fcba.org/foundation

3972 ■ FCBA Foundation College Scholarship Program (Undergraduate/Scholarship)

Purpose: To provide financial assistance for local high school students intending to pursue college studies. **Focus:** General studies/Field of study not specified. **Qualif.:** Applicants must be high school students attending in any of the 9 local public high schools located in the District of Columbia. **Criteria:** The Foundation will review applications from high school students of diverse backgrounds with an interest in communications-related fields, including media, journalism, technology, engineering or law.

Funds Avail.: $10,000 to $28,000. **Duration:** Annual; Up to 4 years. **Number Awarded:** Varies. **To Apply:** Application is via online. Applicants may visit the website for further information on the application process. **Deadline:** March 4.

3973 ■ FCBA Foundation Internship Stipends for Law Students (Professional development/Internship)

Purpose: To support law students in their job trainings with a connection to their field of study. **Focus:** Law. **Qualif.:** Applicants must be U.S. law students attending an accredited college or university. **Criteria:** Selection will be based on the committee's criteria.

Funds Avail.: Amount varies. **Number Awarded:** Varies. **To Apply:** Interested applicants may contact the Foundation for the application process and other required materials.

3974 ■ FCBA Foundation Law School Scholarships (Postgraduate/Scholarship)

Purpose: To support the education of law students across the country. **Focus:** Law. **Qualif.:** Applicants must be U.S. law students attending an accredited college or university. **Criteria:** Selection will be based on need and merit.

Funds Avail.: $2,000 to $10,000. **Number Awarded:** Varies. **To Apply:** Interested applicants may contact the Foundation for the application process and other required materials.

3975 ■ Federal Alliance For Safe Homes (FLASH)

1427 E Piedmont Dr., Ste. 2
Tallahassee, FL 32308
Fax: (850)201-1067
Free: 877-221-7233
E-mail: flash@flash.org
URL: www.flash.org
Facebook: www.facebook.com/federalalliance/?ref=ts
Twitter: twitter.com/FederalAlliance

3976 ■ FLASH Social Science Scholarships (Graduate/Scholarship)

Purpose: To support graduate students seeking academic degrees that underpin disaster safety and mitigation, including construction, engineering, financial services, risk communication, social sciences and other related fields. **Focus:** Engineering; Risk management; Social sciences. **Qualif.:** Applicants must be master or doctorate degree students performing research on behavior change, societal effects, or other social aspects as they relate to natural disaster mitigation. **Criteria:** Selection will be based on the committee's criteria.

Funds Avail.: $1,500. **Duration:** Annual. **To Apply:** Applicants must submit the following: a fully-completed application form; unofficial transcripts of undergraduate and graduate records; a statement of appraisal and agreement to direct the applicants' graduate research program from the proposed faculty advisor. Applicants must respond to all questions on the application form in typewritten and no additional sheet should be attached.

3977 ■ Huber Engineered Woods Product Evaluation Scholarships *(Graduate/Scholarship)*

Purpose: To support graduate students seeking academic degrees that underpin disaster safety and mitigation, including construction, engineering, financial services, risk communication, social sciences and other related fields. **Focus:** Architecture; Construction; Engineering; Materials research/science. **Qualif.:** Applicants must be master or doctorate degree students performing research on new structural product testing/evaluation and new structural product testing/evaluation procedures. **Criteria:** Selection will be based on the committee's criteria.

Funds Avail.: $1,500. **Duration:** Annual. **To Apply:** Applicants must submit the following: a fully-completed application form; unofficial transcripts of undergraduate and graduate records; a statement of appraisal and agreement to direct the applicants' graduate research program from the proposed faculty advisor. Applicants must respond to all questions on the application form in typewritten and no additional sheet should be attached.

3978 ■ International Code Council Scholarships *(Graduate/Scholarship)*

Purpose: To support graduate students seeking academic degrees that underpin disaster safety and mitigation, including construction, engineering, financial services, risk communication, social sciences and other related fields. **Focus:** Construction; Engineering. **Qualif.:** Applicants must be master or doctorate degree students performing research in any of the following areas: the effectiveness of building codes against natural disasters; education/outreach research focused on building codes; research into the incentives and impediments for building code adoption/enforcement. **Criteria:** Applicants will be selected based on the merits of the application.

Funds Avail.: $1,500. **Duration:** Annual. **To Apply:** Applicants must submit the following: a fully-completed application form; unofficial transcripts of undergraduate and graduate records; a statement of appraisal and agreement to direct the applicants' graduate research program from the proposed faculty advisor. Applicants must respond to all questions on the application form in typewritten and no additional sheet should be attached.

3979 ■ John Jeffries Meteorology Scholarships *(Graduate/Scholarship)*

Purpose: To support graduate students seeking academic degrees that underpin disaster safety and mitigation, including construction, engineering, financial services, risk communication, social sciences and other related fields. **Focus:** Meteorology. **Qualif.:** Applicants must be master or doctorate degree students performing research on meteorology or meteorological risk modeling as it relates to natural disasters. **Criteria:** Selection will be based on the committee's criteria.

Funds Avail.: $1,500. **Duration:** Annual. **To Apply:** Applicants must submit the following: a fully-completed application form; unofficial transcripts of undergraduate and graduate records; a statement of appraisal and agreement to direct the applicants' graduate research program from the proposed faculty advisor. Applicants must respond to all questions on the application form in typewritten and no additional sheet should be attached.

3980 ■ Portland Cement Association Scholarships *(Graduate/Scholarship)*

Purpose: To support graduate students seeking academic degrees that underpin disaster safety and mitigation, including construction, engineering, financial services, risk communication, social sciences and other related fields. **Focus:** Construction. **Qualif.:** Applicants must be master or doctorate degree students or fourth or fifth year architectural students performing research on the following topics: innovative use of concrete systems to improve the resilience of new production homes; quantification of the impacts significant loss of housing stock has on post disaster community recovery and continuity; life cycle cost analysis examining short and long term financial and social impacts of more resilient concrete home construction; innovative use of concrete to improve the resilience of homes that are rebuilt after being damaged or destroyed in a natural disaster. **Criteria:** Selection will be based on the committee's criteria.

Funds Avail.: $1,500. **Duration:** Annual. **To Apply:** Applicants must submit the following: a fully-completed application form; unofficial transcripts of undergraduate and graduate records; a statement of appraisal and agreement to direct the applicants' graduate research program from the proposed faculty advisor. Applicants must respond to all questions on the application form in typewritten and no additional sheet should be attached.

3981 ■ Resilience Action Fund Scholarships *(Graduate/Scholarship)*

Purpose: To support graduate students seeking academic degrees that underpin disaster safety and mitigation, including construction, engineering, financial services, risk communication, social sciences and other related fields. **Focus:** Architecture; Business; Construction; Economics; Urban affairs/design/planning. **Qualif.:** Applicants must be master and doctorate degree students performing research on policy cost-benefit analysis, risk assessment and construction economics, or correlation between housing prices/affordability and construction costs related to mitigation. **Criteria:** Selection will be based on the committee's criteria.

Funds Avail.: $1,500. **Duration:** Annual. **To Apply:** Applicants must submit the following: a fully-completed application form; unofficial transcripts of undergraduate and graduate records; a statement of appraisal and agreement to direct the applicants' graduate research program from the proposed faculty advisor. Applicants must respond to all questions on the application form in typewritten and no additional sheet should be attached.

3982 ■ Federal Circuit Bar Association (FCBA)
1620 I St. NW, Ste. 801
Washington, DC 20006-4033
Ph: (202)466-3923
Fax: (202)833-1061
URL: www.fedcirbar.org

Awards are arranged alphabetically below their administering organizations

3983 ■ William S. Bullinger Scholarships *(Doctorate/Scholarship)*

Purpose: To support individuals who have an interest in the subject matter of the Federal Circuit's legal community. **Focus:** Law. **Qualif.:** Applicants must be pursuing a juris doctor degree; must be enrolling for the upcoming academic year in any law school accredited by the American Bar Association; must demonstrate financial need and interest in one of the many topics that lie within the procedure, substance or scope of the jurisdiction of the United States Court of Appeal for the Federal Circuit. **Criteria:** Selection is based primarily on economic need, although other criteria including academic promise and an interest in the subject matter of the Federal Circuit's legal community are considered.

Funds Avail.: $5,000. **Duration:** Annual. **Number Awarded:** 1. **To Apply:** An application must include the following: curriculum vitae; undergraduate and, if applicable, graduate law school transcripts; an original, typed essay written by the applicant alone. The essay is limited to no more than 450 words on one page and should address the applicants' financial need, any interests in particular areas of the law, and any qualifications for a particular scholarship considered relevant by the applicants. Submissions must be transmitted as a single document in PDF format only by email to the co-chairs of the FCBA Scholarship Committee, Joseph Reisman and Emily Tait. Applicants must identify their submission by FCBA Scholarship Submission in the subject line.

3984 ■ Douglas B. Henderson Leadership Scholarships *(Doctorate/Scholarship)*

Purpose: To support law students showing financial need and demonstrating both academic excellence and outstanding leadership. **Focus:** Law. **Qualif.:** Applicants must be pursuing a juris doctor degree; must be enrolling for the upcoming academic year in any law school accredited by the American Bar Association; must demonstrate financial need and interest in one of the many topics that lie within the procedure, substance or scope of the jurisdiction of the United States Court of Appeal for the Federal Circuit. **Criteria:** Selection will be based on the committee's criteria.

Funds Avail.: No specific amount. **To Apply:** An application must include the following: curriculum vitae; undergraduate and, if applicable, graduate law school transcripts; an original, typed essay written by the applicant alone. The essay is limited to no more than 450 words on one page and should address the applicants' financial need, any interests in particular areas of the law, and any qualifications for a particular scholarship considered relevant by the applicants. Submissions must be transmitted as a single document in PDF format only by email to the cochairs of the FCBA Scholarship Committee, Joseph Reisman and Emily Tait. Applicants must identify their submission by FCBA Scholarship Submission in the subject line.

3985 ■ Howard T. Markey Memorial Scholarship *(Undergraduate/Scholarship)*

Purpose: To provide financial support for qualified individuals intending to pursue their studies. **Focus:** Law. **Qualif.:** Applicants must be law students showing financial need, demonstrated academic promise, and service, either in undergraduate or in law school. **Criteria:** Awards will be given based on a written submission of no more than one page setting out the applicant's financial need, any interests in particular areas of the law, and any qualifications for the awards considered relevant by the applicant. Application materials will be considered, and prior academic performance will not be the primary criteria for selection.

Funds Avail.: $10,000. **Duration:** Annual; one year. **Number Awarded:** 1. **To Apply:** Applicants must submit a college and law school transcript and a one-page curriculum vitae. **Deadline:** April 15.

3986 ■ Need-Based Scholarships *(Doctorate/Scholarship)*

Purpose: To provide scholarship to law students in need of financial help. **Focus:** Law. **Qualif.:** Applicants must be pursuing a juris doctor degree; must be enrolling for the upcoming academic year in any law school accredited by the American Bar Association; must demonstrate financial need and interest in one of the many topics that lie within the procedure, substance or scope of the jurisdiction of the United States Court of Appeal for the Federal Circuit. **Criteria:** Selection will be based on the committee's criteria.

Funds Avail.: $5,000. **Duration:** Annual. **To Apply:** An application must include the following: curriculum vitae; undergraduate and, if applicable, graduate law school transcripts; an original, typed essay written by the applicant alone. The essay is limited to no more than 450 words on one page and should address the applicants' financial need, any interests in particular areas of the law, and any qualifications for a particular scholarship considered relevant by the applicants. Submissions must be transmitted as a single document in PDF format only by email to the cochairs of the FCBA Scholarship Committee, Joseph Reisman and Emily Tait. Applicants must identify their submission by FCBA Scholarship Submission in the subject line.

3987 ■ Helen W. Nies Memorial Scholarship *(Postgraduate/Scholarship)*

Purpose: To provide financial support for qualified individuals intending to pursue their studies. **Focus:** Law. **Qualif.:** Applicants must be women law students showing financial need, demonstrated academic promise and service, either in undergraduate or in law school. **Criteria:** Selection will be based on aforesaid qualifications and compliance with the application process.

Funds Avail.: $10,000. **Duration:** Annual. **To Apply:** Applicants must submit a college and law school transcript and a one-page curriculum vitae. In addition to that is a written submission of no more than one page setting out the applicants' financial need, any interests in particular areas of the law, and any qualifications for the awards considered relevant by the applicants. **Deadline:** April 15.

3988 ■ Federal Employee Education and Assistance Fund (FEEA)

3333 S Wadsworth Blvd., Ste. 300
Lakewood, CO 80227
Ph: (303)933-7580
Fax: (303)933-7587
Free: 800-323-4140
E-mail: fedshelpingfeds@feea.org
URL: www.feea.org

3989 ■ FEEA-NTEU Scholarships *(Graduate, Postgraduate, Undergraduate/Scholarship)*

Purpose: To provide financial assistance to civilian employees of the US Federal Government. **Focus:** General studies/Field of study not specified. **Qualif.:** Applicants

Awards are arranged alphabetically below their administering organizations

must be current civilian federal employees and their dependent family members (spouse/child); adult children and other relatives are eligible if claimed on the sponsoring employee's tax return; active duty military members and their dependents are eligible only through a sponsoring civilian employee spouse; military retirees and dependents are eligible if the retiree (or retiree's spouse) is a current civilian federal employee; must have at least three (3) years of civilian federal service; must have at least a 3.0 cumulative grade point average (CGPA) unweighted on a 4.0 scale; must be current high school seniors or college students working toward an accredited degree and enrolled in a two or four year undergraduate, graduate or postgraduate program; dependents must be full-time students; and federal employees may be part-time students. **Criteria:** Applicants will be judged by Scholarship Committee. **Funds Avail.:** $5,000. **Duration:** Annual. **Number Awarded:** Up to 7. **To Apply:** Applicants must submit FEEA Scholarship Application Form; essay; written recommendation/character reference; transcript; a list and brief description of awards, extracurricular and community service activities; copy of ACT, SAT or other examination scores; copy of most recent standard form 50 "notice of personnel action", and two self-addressed, stamped, No. 10 business-size envelopes with first class postage properly affixed. **Remarks:** Established in 2006. **Contact:** Niki Gleason, Program Director, Scholarships: Phone: 303-933-7580; Fax: 303-933-7587; Email: ngleason@feea.org.

3990 ■ Federal Law Enforcement Officers Association (FLEOA)
7945 MacArthur Blvd., Ste. 201
Cabin John, MD 20818
Ph: (202)870-5503
Free: 866-553-5362
E-mail: fleoa@fleoa.org
URL: www.fleoa.org

3991 ■ FLEOA Foundation Scholarship Program
(Undergraduate/Scholarship)

Purpose: To provide educational assistance for the children of current, retired or deceased Federal Law Enforcement Officers. **Focus:** General studies/Field of study not specified. **Qualif.:** Applicants must be high school graduates; dependents of a current, retired or deceased Federal Law Enforcement Officer. **Criteria:** Scholarship will be awarded to the applicant with the highest cumulative ranking as independently reviewed by FLEAO Foundation Scholarship Committee; scholastic ability; and social character. Special consideration will be given to those applicants who are the children of federal law enforcement officers killed or disabled in the line of duty. **Funds Avail.:** No specific amount. **Duration:** Annual. **To Apply:** Applicants must submit completed application form available from the website; transcript of records (with class ranking, SAT scores); and an acceptance letter from a college or university.

3992 ■ Federal Managers Association (FMA)
1641 Prince St.
Alexandria, VA 22314-2818
Ph: (703)683-8700
Fax: (703)683-8707
E-mail: info@fedmanagers.org
URL: www.fedmanagers.org

3993 ■ FMA-FEEA Scholarship Program
(Undergraduate/Scholarship)

Purpose: To provide financial assistance for the educational pursuits of current civilian employees and retirees who are FMA members and their dependent family members. **Focus:** General studies/Field of study not specified. **Qualif.:** Applicants must be at least college freshmen who have a 3.0 cumulative grade point average on 4.0 scale, and current high school seniors or college students working toward an accredited degree and enrolled in two- or four-year post-secondary, graduate or postgraduate program; full-time students (if dependents), or part-time students (if federal employees). **Criteria:** Candidates will be evaluated based on academic performance.
Funds Avail.: $1,000. **Duration:** Annual. **Number Awarded:** Varies. **To Apply:** Applicants must submit: complete application package containing the FMA-FEEA Scholarship Application Form; essay; written recommendation/character reference; transcript of scholastic record; brief description of awards, extracurricular and community service activities; copy of ACT, SAT or other examination scores; copy of most recent standard Form 50 "Notice of Personnel Action"; and two self-addressed, stamped, No. 10 business-size envelopes with first class postage properly affixed. **Remarks:** Established in 1994.

3994 ■ The Federalist Society
1776 I St. NW, Ste. 300
Washington, DC 20006
Ph: (202)822-8138
Fax: (202)296-8061
E-mail: info@fed-soc.org
URL: www.fed-soc.org
Facebook: www.facebook.com/Federalist.Society
LinkedIn: www.linkedin.com/company/the-federalist-society

3995 ■ Olin/Searle Fellows in Law *(Other/Fellowship)*

Purpose: To provide young legal thinkers the opportunity to spend one or two years working full time on writing and developing their scholarship with the goal of entering the legal academy. **Focus:** Law. **Qualif.:** Applicants must be J.D. and have extremely strong academic qualifications; committed to the rule of law and intellectual diversity and legal academia; and have the promise of a distinguished career as a legal scholar and teacher. **Criteria:** A distinguished group of academics will select the Fellows based on qualifications and the submitted application materials.
Funds Avail.: $60,000 plus benefits. **Duration:** Annual. **To Apply:** Applicants must submit a resume and law school transcript; academic writing sample(s) (50 page limit); a brief discussion of the applicants' areas of intellectual interest (approximately 2 pages); a statement of commitment to teaching law; and at least two, and generally no more than three, letters of support. **Deadline:** March 15.

3996 ■ Federated Women's Institutes of Ontario
7382 Wellington Rd. 30, RR5
Guelph, ON, Canada N1H 6J2
Ph: (519)836-3078
Fax: (519)836-9456
URL: fwio.on.ca

3997 ■ Ontario Women's Institute Scholarships
(Undergraduate/Scholarship)

Purpose: To assist students studying at the University of Guelph, College of Social and Applied Human Sciences.

Awards are arranged alphabetically below their administering organizations

Focus: Hotel, institutional, and restaurant management; Management. **Qualif.:** Applicants must be female students from Ontario with a minimum of 70% cumulative average at the end of the second semester of the BASc Program or the Marketing Management, Housing and Real Estate Management, or Hotel and Food Administration majors who have been involved in extracurricular activities; must be currently studying at the University of Guelph. **Criteria:** Recipients will be selected based on submitted materials. **Funds Avail.:** 1,000 Canadian Dollars. **Duration:** Annual. **Number Awarded:** 3. **To Apply:** Applicants must visit the website for further information. **Deadline:** May 15. **Remarks:** Established in 1947.

3998 ■ Federation of American Consumers and Travelers (FACT)
318 Hillsboro Ave.
Edwardsville, IL 62025
Fax: (618)656-5369
Free: 800-872-3228
E-mail: cservice@usafact.org
URL: www.usafact.org

3999 ■ FACT "Second Chance" Scholarship Program (Undergraduate/Scholarship)
Purpose: To support the education of FACT members and their families. **Focus:** General studies/Field of study not specified. **Qualif.:** Applicants must be FACT members and their immediate families. They must be graduating from an accredited public, private or parochial high school and maintain a "C" grade point average to remain in the funds (if considered). Applicants may be students currently enrolled in two- or four-year education in accredited colleges or universities. **Criteria:** Applicants will be evaluated by the Scholarship Committee based on academic records and quality of the essay submitted. **Funds Avail.:** $2,500 to $10,000. **Duration:** Annual. **Number Awarded:** 2. **To Apply:** Applicants must submit completed application form; Release Authorization and Membership Verification Form; Certification Form; Official Copy of High School Transcript signed by the applicant's high school principal or academic advisor; and a two-page, double-spaced essay. **Deadline:** January 15.

4000 ■ Federation of Asian Canadian Lawyers
20 Toronto St., Ste. 300
Toronto, ON, Canada M5C 2B8
E-mail: facl.admin@facl.ca
URL: facl.ca

4001 ■ Omatsu FACL Scholarships (Juris Doctorate, Advanced Professional/Scholarship)
Purpose: To support FACL student members in their legal education. **Focus:** Law. **Qualif.:** Applicants must be FACL members who are students pursuing a JD/LLB/BCL at a law school in Canada; must have demonstrated some past, current, and/or future involvement in promoting social justice; must have appropriate status in Canada (either citizens or permanent residents); and must be self-identify as of Asian descents (East Asian, Southeast Asian, or South Asian). **Criteria:** Selection will be based on leadership and community involvement, law student vision, academics, financial need, and personal statement. **Funds Avail.:** 1,000 Canadian Dollars each. **Number Awarded:** 2. **To Apply:** Applicants must complete the provided Application Form and submit via email, along with their curriculum vitae, university and law school transcripts. **Deadline:** May 31. **Contact:** Submit scholarship applications via e-mail at external.public@facl.ca.

4002 ■ Fédération Canadienne des Épiciers Indépendants
105 Gordon Baker Rd., Ste. 401
North York, ON, Canada M2H 3P8
Ph: (416)492-2311
Fax: (416)492-2347
Free: 800-661-2344
E-mail: info@cfig.ca
URL: www.cfig.ca
Facebook: www.facebook.com/CFIGFCEI
LinkedIn: ca.linkedin.com/company/canadian-federation-of-independent-grocers
Twitter: twitter.com/cfigfcei

4003 ■ Canadian Federation of Independent Grocers National Scholarships (Undergraduate/Scholarship)
Purpose: To provide financial assistance to Canadian students for their further educational enrichment. **Focus:** General studies/Field of study not specified. **Qualif.:** Applicants must be Canadian residents studying in Canada; enrolled or expecting to be enrolled in a post-secondary program of at least two years. High school applicants must be in their last year of secondary studies; college or university applicants must be enrolled in at least one more full year of study as of spring. **Criteria:** Applicants are evaluated based on the essay they have written, respectively. **Funds Avail.:** 6,000 Canadian dollars. **Duration:** Annual. **Number Awarded:** 1. **To Apply:** Applicants must submit (1,000-word) essay on topic given by the Scholarship Committee; list of academic achievements, awards and extracurricular activities; official grade transcript of the last completed year; and the completed application form with all pertinent information properly filled in. **Deadline:** June 19.

4004 ■ Federation of Diocesan Liturgical Commissions (FDLC)
415 Michigan Ave. NE
Washington, DC 20017-4503
Ph: (202)635-6990
Fax: (202)529-2452
E-mail: nationaloffice@fdlc.org
URL: www.fdlc.org

4005 ■ The Tabat Scholarship Fund (Graduate/Scholarship)
Purpose: To support graduate students in liturgical studies by providing assistance with the payment of tuition, the purchase of books, or the continuation of research. **Focus:** Religion; Theology. **Qualif.:** Applicants must be pursuing a graduate degree in a program of liturgical studies to prepare for service in the Church of the United States in an academic, diocesan, or parish setting. **Criteria:** Candidates will be evaluated by the Scholarship Committee. **Funds Avail.:** $1,000. **Duration:** Annual. **To Apply:** Applicants must submit curriculum vitae; a short description of

Awards are arranged alphabetically below their administering organizations

how the grant will be used; and two letters of recommendation, in a sealed envelope, from professors or from someone knowledgeable about the person's work. **Deadline:** June 1. **Remarks:** Established in 2001.

4006 ■ FEI Co.
5350 NE Dawson Creek Dr.
Hillsboro, OR 97124-5793
Ph: (503)726-7500
Fax: (503)726-2767
Free: 866-693-3426
URL: www.investor.fei.com

4007 ■ Casey Bennett Scholarships (Undergraduate/Scholarship)

Purpose: To assist high school seniors who plan careers in the fields of Physical Sciences or Materials Sciences. **Focus:** Physical sciences. **Qualif.:** Applicants must be high school seniors who are planning to pursue a career in Physical Sciences or Materials Sciences, and have 3.5 GPA or above. **Criteria:** Awards are given based on financial need.

Funds Avail.: $2,000. **Duration:** Annual. **Number Awarded:** 1. **To Apply:** Applicants must complete the online scholarship application; submit a brief essay (approximately 1/2-1 page) explaining why they should receive the award and an explanation of education/career "roadmap"; a letter of recommendation from a science-related faculty member; and high school transcript (copy or scan). **Deadline:** May 1. **Remarks:** Established in 2004.

4008 ■ The Feldman Law Firm, PLLC
1 E Washington St., Ste. 500
Phoenix, AZ 85004
Ph: (602)540-7887
URL: www.afphoenixcriminalattorney.com

4009 ■ Feldman Law Firm Disabled Veterans Scholarships (All/Scholarship)

Purpose: To provide scholarships for disabled veterans. **Focus:** General studies/Field of study not specified. **Qualif.:** Applicants must be disable veterans of the United States Armed Forces with a disability rating of at least 30 percent. **Criteria:** Winners will be chosen in part by the online interest that is generated by their application. The specifics of their application, as well as its style, emotional appeal, etc., may generate online interest and therefore may increase their chances of success in the process. However, the final decision will be made at the discretion of Adam Feldman.

Funds Avail.: $1,000. **Duration:** Annual. **Number Awarded:** 2. **To Apply:** Applicants must complete the online application form on the scholarship website, including agreeing to the terms and conditions of the scholarship program. Applicants must also upload the following materials: a short statement of no more than 100 words explaining their educational goals; an essay (between 650 and 1,000 words) that discusses how their life have been affected by their military service and/or disability. **Deadline:** November 10.

4010 ■ Feldman & Royle, Attorneys at Law
2828 N Central Ave., Ste. 1203
Phoenix, AZ 85004
Ph: (602)899-8000
URL: www.foldmanroyle.com

4011 ■ Feldman & Royle, Attorneys at Law Autism Scholarships (All/Scholarship)

Purpose: To provide scholarships for those diagnosed with Autism. **Focus:** General studies/Field of study not specified. **Qualif.:** Applicants must be individuals diagnosed with ASD (DSM-5). **Criteria:** The decision on the winners of the scholarship shall be in the sole discretion of Feldman & Royle, Attorneys at Law. It will be based, at least in part, upon the amount of online interest in their application.

Funds Avail.: $1,000. **Duration:** Annual. **Number Awarded:** 2. **To Apply:** Applicants must complete the online application form and submit the following materials: a brief statement of up to 100 words telling the reader what educational plans that the applicants have if they are awarded the scholarship; an essay of not less 650 words and not more than 1,000 words on the subject of how having ASD have affected the applicants' education. **Deadline:** November 7. **Contact:** Email: Michael@feldmanroyle.com.

4012 ■ Fibrose Kystique Canada
2323 Yonge St., Ste. 800
Toronto, ON, Canada M4P 2C9
Ph: (416)485-9149
Fax: (416)485-0960
Free: 800-378-2233
E-mail: info@cysticfibrosis.ca
URL: www.cysticfibrosis.ca
Facebook: www.facebook.com/CysticFibrosisCanada
Twitter: twitter.com/CFCanada

4013 ■ CCFF Clinical Fellowships (Doctorate, Graduate/Fellowship)

Purpose: To train physicians to become CF specialists so that they can provide ongoing clinical care to individuals with CF in Canada. **Focus:** Cystic fibrosis. **Qualif.:** Applicant must be a Canadian citizen or permanent resident; have an MD degree; have recently completed the clinical training, exam and have obtained medical licensure in Canada. **Criteria:** Selection is based on the applicant's merit and potential.

Funds Avail.: No specific amount. **Duration:** one year. **To Apply:** Applicants must submit three letters of recommendation (one from the recent supervisor); description of the proposed clinical training program; and official transcripts. Eleven copies of the application are must be submitted, one of which must contain original signatures. **Deadline:** October 1.

4014 ■ CCFF Fellowships (Doctorate, Graduate/Fellowship)

Purpose: To support basic or clinical research training in the areas of biomedical or behavioral sciences pertinent to cystic fibrosis. **Focus:** Cystic fibrosis. **Qualif.:** Applicants must hold an MD or PhD degree or must be graduates who have already completed basic residency training and are eligible for Canadian licensure. **Criteria:** Selection is based on the applicant's merit and potential.

Funds Avail.: Varies. **Duration:** 2 years. **To Apply:** Applicants must submit three letters of recommendation (one from a current supervisor); a description of the proposed research and training program; and official transcripts.

Awards are arranged alphabetically below their administering organizations

Twelve copies of the application are required (1 with original signatures and 11 double-sided photocopies, with each copy stapled in the upper left hand corner). **Deadline:** October 1. **Contact:** amackesy@cysticfibrosis.ca.

4015 ■ CCFF Scholarships *(Doctorate, Graduate/Scholarship)*

Purpose: To attract investigators to cystic fibrosis research. **Focus:** Cystic fibrosis. **Qualif.:** Applicant must hold an MD or PhD degree; must be sponsored by the chairman of the appropriate department and by the dean of the faculty; and has recently completed the training and wish to devote the majority of the time to cystic fibrosis research. **Criteria:** Selection is based on the caliber of the applicant's research and the potential of the applicant to make an outstanding contribution to cystic fibrosis research.

Funds Avail.: $60,000. **Duration:** three years. **To Apply:** Applicants must submit a completed application form together with the required materials. **Deadline:** October 1.

4016 ■ Field Museum of Natural History
1400 S Lake Shore Dr.
Chicago, IL 60605-2496
Ph: (312)922-9410
E-mail: action@fieldmuseum.org
URL: www.fieldmuseum.org
Facebook: www.facebook.com/fieldmuseum
Twitter: twitter.com/fieldmuseum

4017 ■ Field Museum Graduate Student Fellowships *(Graduate/Fellowship)*

Purpose: To support graduate students engaged in dissertation research associated with the Field Museum. **Focus:** General studies/Field of study not specified. **Qualif.:** Applicants must be graduate students residing in the Chicago area. **Criteria:** Selection will be based on evaluation of submitted research including relevance of the Field museum's collections to the project, collaboration(s) with Field Museum curators (if any), procedures and methods used in the project.

Funds Avail.: $30,000. **Duration:** Annual. **Number Awarded:** 2. **To Apply:** Applicants must submit proposed research summary (one or two pages, double-spaced); full curriculum vitae with names and contact information of two references in addition to sponsor; copy of thesis proposal uploaded as supplemental material with the application; two reference letters sent 10 days after the application deadline. **Deadline:** January 30.

4018 ■ Fields Institute
222 College St.
Toronto, ON, Canada M5T 3J1
Ph: (416)348-9710
Fax: (416)348-9714
E-mail: inquiries@fields.utoronto.ca
URL: www.fields.utoronto.ca

4019 ■ Fields Institute - Fields Research Immersion Fellowships *(Postdoctorate/Fellowship)*

Purpose: To support individuals with high potential to re-enter an active research career after an interruption due to family responsibilities. **Focus:** Mathematics and mathematical sciences. **Qualif.:** Applicants must have been in a postdoctoral or faculty position at the time their active career was interrupted; may be in complete or partial hiatus from research activities at the time of application; and should not be engaged in full-time paid research activities. **Criteria:** Selection is based on the submitted application materials.

Funds Avail.: No specific amount. **To Apply:** Applicants must submit a cover sheet indicating applicant's interest; a CV; and a research proposal which includes the name(s) of faculty who may be appropriate as supervisors/research advisors. **Deadline:** March 31.

4020 ■ Postdoctoral Fellowships at the Fields Institute *(Postdoctorate/Fellowship)*

Purpose: To support postdoctoral fellows in the field of mathematical sciences. **Focus:** Mathematics and mathematical sciences. **Qualif.:** Applicants must be expecting to receive a PhD in a related area of the mathematical sciences. **Criteria:** Applicants must submit their applications before the deadline to be considered.

Funds Avail.: 20,000 Canadian Dollars. **Duration:** 6 months. **To Apply:** Applicants must submit online a cover letter; curriculum vitae; a research statement; publication list; and three reference letters (submitted by the reference writers).

4021 ■ Filipino Bar Association of Northern California (FBANC)
268 Bush St., No. 2928
San Francisco, CA 94104-3503
E-mail: fbancinfo@gmail.com
URL: fbanc.org
Facebook: www.facebook.com/groups/23799184288
LinkedIn: www.linkedin.com/groups/3230676/profile
Twitter: www.twitter.com/fbancorg

4022 ■ Filipino Bar Association of Northern California Scholarships (FBANC) *(Advanced Professional/Scholarship)*

Purpose: To support law students in their educational pursuit. **Focus:** Law. **Qualif.:** Applicant must be a current law student in good academic standing and admitted to a law school. **Criteria:** Selection is based on the applicant's ability to address the essay questions as well as demonstrated interest in serving the Filipino community.

Funds Avail.: No specific amount. **Duration:** Annual. **To Apply:** Applicants must submit a current law school transcript or admittance letter from a law school; a resume; and not longer than two page essay (double-spaced). **Remarks:** Established in 1998.

4023 ■ FinancialCAD Corp.
13450 102nd Ave., Ste. 1750 Central City,
Surrey, BC, Canada V3T 5X3
E-mail: support@fincad.com
URL: www.fincad.com
LinkedIn: www.linkedin.com/company/fincad

4024 ■ FINCAD Women in Finance Scholarships *(Graduate/Scholarship)*

Purpose: To encourage and support outstanding women in the field of finance. **Focus:** Finance. **Qualif.:** Applicants must be students in any age who are studying Finance in an accredited graduate-level program. **Criteria:** Selection

Awards are arranged alphabetically below their administering organizations

will be based on the committees' criteria.

Funds Avail.: $10,000. **Duration:** Annual. **To Apply:** Applicants may contact the Company for the application process and other information.

4025 ■ Fine Arts Association (FAA)
38660 Mentor Ave.
Willoughby, OH 44094
Ph: (440)951-7500
Fax: (440)975-4592
URL: www.fineartsassociation.org

4026 ■ Fine Arts Association Minority Scholarships (Undergraduate/Scholarship)

Purpose: To ensure that the opportunity for art education is available to all who deserve it and to create customized educational arts experiences in music, dance, drama, visual arts and music therapy. **Focus:** Art. **Qualif.:** Students applying must be residents of Lake County who are members of a minority population as defined by the Ohio Arts Council. **Criteria:** Recipients are selected based on financial need.

Funds Avail.: No specific amount. **To Apply:** Applicants must complete the application form with parents/guardians if they are dependents. Forms are available at the FAA Customer Service Center and are also available for download at the website. First time applicants must include a copy of the first page of their most recent IRS 1040 form. **Contact:** Customer Service Center at 440-951-7500.

4027 ■ Fine Arts Association United Way Scholarships (Undergraduate/Scholarship)

Purpose: To ensure that the opportunity for art education is available to all who deserve it and to create customized educational arts experiences in music, dance, drama, visual arts and music therapy. **Focus:** Art. **Qualif.:** Applicants must be students residing in Lake County and must have total family income not exceeding $22,400 annually, unless there are extenuating financial circumstances. **Criteria:** Recipients are selected based on financial need.

Funds Avail.: No specific amount. **To Apply:** Applicants must complete the application form with parents/guardians if they are dependents. Forms are available at the FAA Customer Service Center and are also available for download at the website. First time applicants must include a copy of the first page of their most recent IRS 1040 form. **Contact:** Customer Service Center at 440-951-7500.

4028 ■ Gwen Yarnell Theatre Scholarships (Undergraduate/Scholarship)

Purpose: To ensure that the opportunity for art education is available to all who deserve it and to create customized educational arts experiences in music, dance, drama, visual arts and music therapy. **Focus:** Art; Theater arts. **Qualif.:** Applicants must have enrolled in classes or lessons at The Fine Arts Association within the past year. Preference will be given to currently enrolled students. Applicants must have achievements in art, dance, music or theater. **Criteria:** Scholarships are awarded based on the individual's achievements relative to his/her age, without regard for race, sex, religion, age, disability or national origin.

Funds Avail.: No specific amount. **To Apply:** Applicants must complete and submit the achievement scholarship application to the Customer Service Center together with the instructor recommendation form for achievement scholarship. **Contact:** Customer Service Center at 440-951-7500.

4029 ■ Finnegan, Henderson, Farabow, Garrett and Dunner L.L.P.
901 New York Ave. NW
Washington, DC 20001-4413
Ph: (202)408-4000
Fax: (202)408-4400
E-mail: info@finnegan.com
URL: www.finnegan.com

4030 ■ Finnegan Diversity Scholarships (Juris Doctorate/Scholarship)

Purpose: To develop diversity in the workplace and in the field of intellectual property law. **Focus:** Law. **Qualif.:** Applicants must: be enrolled in an ABA-accredited law school in the JD class; meet Finnegan's hiring criteria (a degree in life sciences/chemistry, engineering, or computer science, or substantial prior trademark experience); and, contribute to enhancing diversity. Successful applicants have included members of racial, ethnic, disabled, and sexual orientation groups that have been historically underrepresented in the legal profession. **Criteria:** Selection of recipients is vested to Finnegan Diversity Scholarship Selection Committee. Criteria for selecting the applicants shall be determined by the committee.

Funds Avail.: $15,000. **Duration:** Annual. **To Apply:** Students must submit: an application; resume; official or unofficial transcripts wherein law school grades should be forwarded once received; and 1-2 page personal statement which include a description of how the applicant will contribute to Finnegan's practice and diversity mission. **Deadline:** January 25. **Remarks:** Established in 2003. **Contact:** Finnegan Diversity Scholarship, c/o Laurie Taylor, Recruitment Manager Personal Statement, Finnegan, Henderson, Farabow, Garrett & Dunner, L.L.P, diversityscholarship@finnegan.com.

4031 ■ Firefly Foundation
87 Avenue Rd.
Toronto, ON, Canada M5R 3R9
E-mail: contact@fireflyfoundation.org
URL: www.fireflyfoundation.org

4032 ■ Firefly Foundation/ASRP Spark Award (Postdoctorate, Advanced Professional/Grant)

Purpose: To support unique, creative research ideas that will impact brain health and prevent, defer or effectively treat neurodegenerative disease. **Focus:** Alzheimer's disease. **Qualif.:** Applicants must be within the 18 months of completing their Ph.D. and pursue their postdoctoral fellowship in Canada. **Criteria:** Selection will be based on the research proposals of the applicants.

Funds Avail.: 100,000 Canadian Dollars per year (50,000 per annum). **Duration:** Up to 2 years. **To Apply:** Applicants are required to submit proposals for studies using the Alzheimer Society of Canada (ASC) online application system for work that explicitly address the Firefly Foundation's mission to find treatment for prevention or cures to eradicate neurodegenerative disease. **Remarks:** The Spark Award is a partnership program between the Firefly Foundation and the Alzheimer Society of Canada, through its Alzheimer Society Research Program. **Contact:** Research Department, Alzheimer Society of Canada, at research@alzheimer.ca.

4033 ■ Firland Foundation
1700 NE 150th St.
Shoreline, WA 98155
Ph: (206)363-4349
Fax: (206)365-4751
URL: www.firland.org

4034 ■ Firland Foundation Graduate Pulmonary Nursing Fellowships *(Professional development/Fellowship)*

Purpose: To recruit and retain high caliber graduate nursing students who are committed to nursing practice, education, or research in tuberculosis (TB) or other pulmonary diseases. **Focus:** Tuberculosis. **Qualif.:** Applicants must be graduate nursing students in the MS, MN, DNP or PhD programs at the University of Washington School of Nursing (UW SoN). **Criteria:** Selection will be on a competitive basis. Funding preference will be given to students who are focused on nursing care of individuals with TB and plan to practice in the Pacific Northwest after graduation. **Funds Avail.:** $30,000 per year. **Duration:** Two years. **Number Awarded:** 1. **To Apply:** Applicants may contact the Foundation for the application process and other required materials. **Contact:** Questions can be sent to Terri Simpson, Chair of the Firlands Grant Committee, at tsimpson@uw.edu.

4035 ■ Cedric Northrop Fellowships *(Professional development/Fellowship)*

Purpose: To provide opportunity to develop independent faculty-level tuberculosis research funding. **Focus:** Tuberculosis. **Qualif.:** Applicants must be investigators interested in tuberculosis research. **Criteria:** Selection will be based on the committee's criteria. **Funds Avail.:** No specific amount. **Duration:** Three years. **To Apply:** Applicants must submit a letter of intent via online application. If approved, within a few days a unique link to the application proper will be received. **Deadline:** March 31. **Contact:** Questions can be sent to Terri Simpson, Chair of the Firlands Grant Committee, at tsimpson@uw.edu.

4036 ■ First Community Foundation of Pennsylvania, Williamsport-Lycoming
330 Pine St., Ste. 400
Williamsport, PA 17701
Ph: (570)321-1500
Fax: (570)321-6434
Free: 866-901-2372
E-mail: fcfp@fcfpartnership.org
URL: www.wlfoundation.org

4037 ■ Ruth D. Adams Fund *(Undergraduate/Scholarship)*

Purpose: To provide financial assistance for Montoursville Area High School seniors who are seeking higher education beyond graduation from high school (full-time) and who represent the top 10% GPA of graduating seniors. **Focus:** General studies/Field of study not specified. **Qualif.:** Applicants shall be approved for full-time admission to any accredited two or four-year college or university of their choice and be enrolled in a course of study of their choice which leads to a degree. **Criteria:** Selection will be based on the committee's criteria and financial need. Preference will be given to those who should not otherwise be able to pursue a higher education by any other means. **Funds Avail.:** No specific amount. **Number Awarded:** 5. **To Apply:** Applicants may contact and request an application from the Montoursville Area High School; Tax return; attach an essay (250 words, double-spaced) about the topic "What motivated me to seek a degree at a higher institution of education." **Contact:** Betty Gilmour, Director of Grantmaking, the First Community Foundation Partnership of PA; Phone: 570-321-1500; Email: BettyG@fcfpartnership.org.

4038 ■ Anne L. Alexander and Blaise Robert Alexander Memorial Scholarships *(Undergraduate/Scholarship)*

Purpose: To provide scholarship for graduating seniors from Mount Carmel Area High School and Montoursville Area High School. **Focus:** General studies/Field of study not specified. **Qualif.:** Applicants must attend an accredited four-year college or university and enrolled in a business or technical program; exhibits good citizenship and community involvement; **Criteria:** Selection will be based on the committee's criteria and financial need. **Funds Avail.:** No specific amount. **Number Awarded:** 2. **To Apply:** Applicants may contact and request an application from the Montoursville Area High School and the Mount Carmel School District; attach an essay (not exceeding two pages) outlining "Why he or she is applying for the scholarship and summarizing his/her ultimate career objectives." **Contact:** Betty Gilmour, Director of Grantmaking, the First Community Foundation Partnership of PA; Phone: 570-321-1500; Email: BettyG@fcfpartnership.org.

4039 ■ B-Brave McMahon/Stratton Scholarship Fund *(Undergraduate/Scholarship)*

Purpose: To provide financial assistance for graduates who have been in the foster care system or have legal adopted status and who have shown remarkable achievement despite the obstacles in their life. **Focus:** General studies/Field of study not specified. **Qualif.:** Applicant must be a graduating senior from a Lycoming County High School or Clinton County High School that has believed in herself/himself; must have been accepted into a full-time continuing education program, preferably in Pennsylvania; must have exhibited good citizenship and have no known drug or alcohol record or juvenile offenses; have an unmet financial need; and must show evidence that they have a current minimum GPA of 2.8. **Criteria:** Selection will be based on the committee's criteria. **Funds Avail.:** No specific amount. **Duration:** Annual. **To Apply:** Candidates must complete the application and submit it along with any requested additional information to the Williamsport-Lycoming Community Foundation. **Deadline:** April 15. **Contact:** Betty Gilmour, Director of Grantmaking, the First Community Foundation Partnership of PA; Phone: 570-321-1500; Email: BettyG@fcfpartnership.org.

4040 ■ Gina L. Barnhart Memorial Scholarship Fund *(Undergraduate/Scholarship)*

Purpose: To provide financial assistance for Milton Area High school seniors planning to pursue a major in elementary education. **Focus:** Education, Elementary. **Qualif.:** Applicants must be seniors in good standing and members of the cheerleading squad; must have been accepted by a

Awards are arranged alphabetically below their administering organizations

qualified institution of higher education and plan to major in elementary education. Applicants who are planning to major in secondary education may be considered if there are no candidates that are planning to major in elementary education. Preference will be given to applicants with educational and/or career objectives focused on working with children or community service. **Criteria:** Selection will be based on the committee's criteria.

Funds Avail.: No specific amount. **To Apply:** Applicants must submit of a 200-word short essay on the following topic: "How has my participating in cheerleading and sports helped to prepare me for a career in elementary education or other work on behalf of children?" **Contact:** Betty Gilmour, Director of Grantmaking, the First Community Foundation Partnership of PA; Phone: 570-321-1500; Email: BettyG@fcfpartnership.org.

4041 ■ Joseph R. Calder, Jr., MD Scholarship Fund
(Undergraduate/Scholarship)

Purpose: To support the education of current and/or aspiring Lycoming County medical professionals who plan to dedicate their lives to helping others. **Focus:** Health sciences; Medicine; Nursing; Pharmacy. **Qualif.:** Applicants must be graduating seniors residing in Lycoming County; accepted into a full-time or part-time medical or any other related specialty at an accredited institution of higher education. **Criteria:** Selection will be based on merit.

Funds Avail.: No specific amount. **Duration:** Annual. **To Apply:** Applicants must submit a completed application form together with a proof of acceptance into an accredited two or four year college or university in a medical related program; Applicants must submit an essay not to exceed one page outlining why they are pursuing a career in the medical field and summarizing their ultimate career objectives; and at least one letter of reference or testimonial; resume including job experience, volunteer experience and community or school involvement. Applicants may download an application form the Foundation's web site. **Deadline:** April 15. **Contact:** Betty Gilmour, Director of Grantmaking, the First Community Foundation Partnership of PA; Phone: 570-321-1500; Email: BettyG@fcfpartnership.org.

4042 ■ Warren E. "Whitey" Cole American Society of Highway Engineers Scholarships *(Undergraduate/Scholarship)*

Purpose: To provide scholarship awards for students enrolled in a Civil Engineering curriculum. **Focus:** Engineering, Civil. **Qualif.:** Applicants must be enrolled in a civil engineering, civil engineering technology or civil technology curriculum; have completed at least the sophomore year of a four-year curriculum or the freshman year of a two-year curriculum; be either enrolled at Pennsylvania State University, Bucknell University or Pennsylvania College of Technology or have residence in the counties of Bradford, Columbia, Lycoming, Montour, Northumberland, Snyder, Sullivan, Tioga or Union and attend another college. **Criteria:** Selection will be based on the committee's criteria.

Funds Avail.: No specific amount. **Duration:** Annual. **To Apply:** Applicants must complete the application and submit it along with any requested additional information to the Williamsport-Lycoming Community Foundation. **Contact:** JR Wolyniec, American Society Highway Engineers; Phone: 570-326-4428; Email: jr@wolyniec.com.

4043 ■ Marion Jones Donaldson Scholarship Fund
(Undergraduate/Scholarship)

Purpose: To provide financial assistance for Canton Area High School seniors who are pursuing a course of study in elementary or secondary education. **Focus:** Education, Elementary; Education, Secondary. **Qualif.:** Applicants must be attending an accredited institution of higher education, pursuing a major in the area of Elementary or Secondary Education; must have a four-year overall minimum grade average of 85%. **Criteria:** Selection will be based on involvement in community service, extra-curricular activities, and financial need.

Funds Avail.: No specific amount. **Duration:** Annual. **To Apply:** Applicants must complete and submit an application, a 500-word or fewer essay describing why they want to enter the field of education, and three letters of reference. **Contact:** Canton High School Guidance Office at Phone: 570-673-5134.

4044 ■ Lindsay M. Entz Memorial Scholarships
(Undergraduate/Scholarship)

Purpose: To provide financial assistance for the Jersey Shore High School seniors intending to pursue a course of study in elementary education, preferably with an emphasis on education of special-needs children. **Focus:** Education, Elementary. **Qualif.:** Applicants must plan to pursue a course of study in elementary education, preferably with an emphasis on education of special-needs children; must have exhibited good citizenship and community involvement; must be leaders with a sense of humor; must be grounded; must show tolerance to others; must be honest; must have integrity; and must make a difference in the school community. **Criteria:** Selection will be based on the committee's criteria.

Funds Avail.: No specific amount. **Duration:** Annual. **Number Awarded:** 2. **To Apply:** Applicants must complete and submit the application; must attach a cover letter (not to exceed two pages) outlining why they are applying for the scholarship and summarizing their ultimate career objectives; must provide proof that they have been accepted to an accredited two-/four-year college/university; and must provide at least one letter of reference. **Contact:** Betty Gilmour, Director of Grantmaking, the First Community Foundation Partnership of PA; Phone: 570-321-1500; Email: BettyG@fcfpartnership.org.

4045 ■ Nolan W. Feeser Scholarship Fund
(Undergraduate/Scholarship)

Purpose: To provide financial assistance for South Williamsport Area High School seniors who are pursuing a higher education degree at an accredited college or university. **Focus:** General studies/Field of study not specified. **Qualif.:** Applicants must have displayed academic achievements; must have unmet financial need; and must be planning to enroll at or pursuing a degree at Lycoming College, Gettysburg College or Pennsylvania College of Technology. **Criteria:** Selection will be based on the committee's criteria.

Funds Avail.: No specific amount. **Duration:** Annual. **Number Awarded:** 2. **To Apply:** Applicants may contact and request an application from the South Williamsport Area High School. **Contact:** Betty Gilmour, Director of Grantmaking, the First Community Foundation Partnership of PA; Phone: 570-321-1500; Email: BettyG@fcfpartnership.org.

4046 ■ Benjamin Franklin Trust Fund *(Undergraduate, Vocational/Occupational/Scholarship)*

Purpose: To provide academic support for students who are attending Pennsylvania College and have graduated from Bradford County, Clinton County, Lycoming County, Potter County, Sullivan County or Tioga County. **Focus:**

Awards are arranged alphabetically below their administering organizations

General studies/Field of study not specified. **Qualif.:** Applicants must be enrolled at the Pennsylvania College of Technology; must be enrolled in an approved Tech prep high school program and subsequently enroll in a Certificate, Associate or Bachelor's Degree program at the Pennsylvania College of Technology. In schools without approved Tech Prep programs, students must enroll in a high school vocational-technical program and subsequently enroll in a Certificate, Associate, or Bachelor's Degree program at the Pennsylvania College of Technology. Applicants must have a GPA of "B" or higher and must be enrolled full-time. Preference will be given to continuing students in subsequent years if a cumulative GPA of 2.80 is maintained in the program. **Criteria:** Selection will be based on the committee's criteria.

Funds Avail.: No specific amount. **Duration:** Annual. **To Apply:** Applicants must submit a writing sample as defined by the Pennsylvania College of Technology Prep office. **Contact:** Betty Gilmour, Director of Grantmaking, the First Community Foundation Partnership of PA; Phone: 570-321-1500; Email: BettyG@fcfpartnership.org.

4047 ■ Daniel G. and Helen I. Fultz Scholarship Fund (Undergraduate/Scholarship)

Purpose: To encourage educational pursuits by providing scholarship for Indian Valley High School seniors. **Focus:** General studies/Field of study not specified. **Qualif.:** Applicants must be graduating seniors from the Mifflin County High School (formerly Indian Valley Senior High School) who have been accepted into a full-time undergraduate Program at Lycoming College, Williamsport, PA; have exhibit good citizenship and community involvement, leadership, humility, tolerance of others, honesty, integrity, and makes a difference in the school community. **Criteria:** Selection will be based on the committee's criteria. Preference on class rank, grade point average will only be used if needed to distinguish between multiple potential candidates.

Funds Avail.: No specific amount. **Duration:** Annual. **Number Awarded:** 1. **To Apply:** Applicants may contact and request an application from the Mifflin County High School. **Contact:** Betty Gilmour, Director of Grantmaking, the First Community Foundation Partnership of PA; Phone: 570-321-1500; Email: BettyG@fcfpartnership.org.

4048 ■ Morton and Beatrice Harrison Scholarship Fund (Undergraduate/Scholarship)

Purpose: To provide financial assistance for Lycoming County young adults who demonstrate the potential to succeed in pursuing higher education goals. **Focus:** General studies/Field of study not specified. **Qualif.:** Applicants must be young adults who, as a result of legal offenses as juveniles or young adults, have come to the attention of Lycoming County's Probation Department; must demonstrate a strong willingness to make positive changes in their lives and pursue educational and/or job training goals that will enable them to fulfill their human potential; and plan to attend a qualified institution of higher education, including but not limited to a 2- or 4-year college or university, a technical college, trade school, or other approved education or training program. **Criteria:** Selection will be based on the committee's criteria.

Funds Avail.: No specific amount. **Duration:** Annual. **Number Awarded:** 1. **To Apply:** Applicants must complete the application and submit it along with any requested additional information to the Williamsport-Lycoming Community Foundation. **Contact:** Betty Gilmour, Director of Grantmaking, the First Community Foundation Partnership of PA; Phone: 570-321-1500; Email: BettyG@fcfpartnership.org.

4049 ■ ISCALC International Scholarship Fund (Undergraduate/Scholarship)

Purpose: To provide financial assistance for Lycoming County high school seniors who have demonstrated an interest in furthering their education in international studies. **Focus:** Foreign languages; International affairs and relations. **Qualif.:** Applicant must be a graduating high school senior within Lycoming county high school who will be attending an accredited institution of higher education and who plans to pursue major coursework in the area of international studies, including but not limited to international affairs, foreign languages, overseas exchange programs, multicultural studies, and related areas. **Criteria:** Selection will be based on the committee's criteria.

Funds Avail.: No specific amount. **To Apply:** Applicant may request an application form from any Lycoming County High School Guidance Office or by contacting the Williamsport-Lycoming Community Foundation. Applicants must submit a completed application from together with their high school transcript, a typed essay (not exceeding two pages) describing "Why they qualify for this scholarship, highlighting past international experiences and future goals; List of school and/r community involvement ;and at least one letter of reference. **Deadline:** April 15. **Contact:** Betty Gilmour, Director of Grantmaking, the First Community Foundation Partnership of PA; Phone: 570-321-1500; Email: BettyG@fcfpartnership.org.

4050 ■ Carl and Lucille Jarrett Scholarship Fund (Undergraduate/Scholarship)

Purpose: To provide scholarship for Montgomery Area High School seniors and/or graduated alumni who have been accepted and will attend an accredited 2 or 4-year college or university, full-time or part-time. **Focus:** General studies/Field of study not specified. **Qualif.:** Applicants should be accepted, part-time or full-time, at an accredited 2- or 4-year institution of higher education; must exhibit good citizenship; must be honest; must have integrity; must have shown through job or volunteer history their ability to succeed; must be self-motivated; and must have strong ethics. **Criteria:** Selection will be based on the committee's criteria.

Funds Avail.: No specific amount. **Number Awarded:** 5. **To Apply:** Applicants must complete the application. Applicants may request an application by contacting the Guidance Counselors of Montgomery Area High School or download it through the Foundation's web site. **Contact:** Betty Gilmour, Director of Grantmaking, the First Community Foundation Partnership of PA; Phone: 570-321-1500; Email: BettyG@fcfpartnership.org.

4051 ■ Joseph and Catherine Missigman Memorial Nursing Scholarships (Undergraduate/Scholarship)

Purpose: To provide financial assistance for Bloomsburg University students who are pursuing a career in nursing. **Focus:** Nursing. **Qualif.:** Applicants must be Bloomsburg University students who have identified nursing as their major; must be completing their second or third year's curricula in the University's nursing education program; have a GPA of 2.5 or greater for all nursing coursework; and have a demonstrated financial need as determined by Bloomsburg University's methods and practices for assessing its student's financial capacities. **Criteria:** Selection will be based on the committee's criteria.

Awards are arranged alphabetically below their administering organizations

Funds Avail.: No specific amount. **To Apply:** Applicants must have completed and filed an application for the scholarship and must include a one-page cover letter describing his/her rational for applying for the scholarship as well as his/her interest in the nursing field. **Contact:** Dr. Margie Eckroth-Bucher; Phone: 570-389-4607; Email: meckroth@bloomu.edu.

4052 ■ Missigman Scholarship Fund
(Undergraduate/Scholarship)

Purpose: To provide financial assistance for Sullivan County High School seniors who have been accepted into a full-time undergraduate program at an accredited institution of higher education, preferably in Pennsylvania. **Focus:** General studies/Field of study not specified. **Qualif.:** Candidate must be a graduating senior at Sullivan County High School and must demonstrate a strong potential to succeed in pursuing their higher education objectives. **Criteria:** Selection will be based on the committee's criteria.

Funds Avail.: No specific amount. **To Apply:** Applicants may request an application from the Sullivan County High School or from the First Community Foundation of Pennsylvania. **Contact:** Jill Sysock, Guidance Office, Sullivan County High School, Beech and South St., Laporte, PA 18626, 570-947-7001, sysojill@sulcosd.k12.pa.us.

4053 ■ Robert E. and Judy More Scholarship Fund
(Undergraduate/Scholarship)

Purpose: To provide financial assistance for Montgomery Area High School students intending to pursue higher education in finance, engineering, business or science. **Focus:** Business; Engineering; Finance; Science. **Qualif.:** Applicants must be accepted, full-time, at an accredited institution of higher education, preferably in Pennsylvania; must exhibit leadership qualities, academic excellence and a cooperative spirit. **Criteria:** Selection will be based on the committee's criteria.

Funds Avail.: No specific amount. **Duration:** Annual. **To Apply:** Applicants must complete and submit the application. Scholarship application can be requested from Montgomery Area High School or may be downloaded from the Foundation's web site. **Contact:** Betty Gilmour, Director of Grantmaking, the First Community Foundation Partnership of PA; Phone: 570-321-1500; Email: BettyG@fcfpartnership.org.

4054 ■ Muncy Rotary Club Scholarship Fund
(Undergraduate/Scholarship)

Purpose: To provide financial assistance for Muncy High School seniors who have been accepted into a full-time continuing education program. **Focus:** General studies/Field of study not specified. **Qualif.:** Applicants must have exhibited community involvement. Other than a strong potential for success, such factors as class rank and GPA will not be criteria in making a selection unless, in the judgment of the Muncy Rotary Club Scholarship Committee, such factors are needed to distinguish between multiple potential candidates. **Criteria:** Financial need will be a considering factor.

Funds Avail.: No specific amount. **Duration:** Annual. **To Apply:** Applicants may request an application from Erik Berthold of Muncy High School. **Contact:** Betty Gilmour, Director of Grantmaking, the First Community Foundation Partnership of PA; Phone: 570-321-1500; Email: BettyG@fcfpartnership.org.

4055 ■ Muncy Scholars Award Fund
(Undergraduate/Scholarship)

Purpose: To provide financial assistance for graduating seniors in the Muncy Area School District who have completed grades 9, 10, and 11 at the Muncy High School and who have been accepted and will attend a 4-year college, full-time. **Focus:** General studies/Field of study not specified. **Qualif.:** Applicants must attend Muncy High School from freshman year through senior year; attend full-time, a four-year college or university. Applicants must also exhibit continued growth in his/her citizenship; possess qualities of leadership, honesty and integrity, and determination to succeed. **Criteria:** Selection will be based on the committee's criteria.

Funds Avail.: No specific amount. **To Apply:** Applicants will be selected from the top 10 academic performers and must have attained at least one varsity letter (either in sports or band). **Contact:** Betty Gilmour, Director of Grantmaking, the First Community Foundation Partnership of PA; Phone: 570-321-1500; Email: BettyG@fcfpartnership.org.

4056 ■ Albert and Alice Nacinovich Music Scholarships
(Undergraduate/Scholarship)

Purpose: To provide financial assistance for Lycoming County high school seniors graduating from public or private schools with a demonstrated interest in music, planning to attend a qualified institution of higher education in a music-related field of study. **Focus:** Music. **Qualif.:** Applicants must be graduating high school seniors from any Lycoming County high school, public or private (secular or Christian), or as part of a qualified home-schooling arrangement within Lycoming County; must have been accepted to a qualified institution of higher education with the intention of pursuing further education or a career in music in a degree-granting program in music education or a music-related field of study; and must have a demonstrated interest in music, which may include participation in band, chorus, music theory and composition, and performance service at school, church, or community. Applicants must have maintained a GPA of 80 or higher. **Criteria:** Selection will be based on the committee's criteria.

Funds Avail.: No specific amount. **To Apply:** Applicants will be required to complete an application, provide copies of transcripts, at least one letter of reference; list of school and/or community involvement; and attach a 500-word of essay or less outlining his or her interest in music and how a scholarship award will help to advance his or her goals within a musical field or discipline. A recording of the applicant's work must also be submitted with completed application and essay. **Deadline:** April 15. **Contact:** Betty Gilmour, Director of Grantmaking, the First Community Foundation Partnership of PA; Phone: 570-321-1500; Email: BettyG@fcfpartnership.org.

4057 ■ Kimberly Marie Rogers Memorial Scholarship Fund
(Undergraduate, Vocational/Occupational/Scholarship)

Purpose: To provide scholarship for Montoursville Area High School seniors who are planning to attend a vocational/technical college or a two or four-year accredited college. **Focus:** General studies/Field of study not specified. **Qualif.:** Applicants must be Montoursville Area High School seniors who are planning to attend a vocational/technical college or a two or four-year accredited college. Their major should fall under the vocational/technical field. **Criteria:** Selection will be based on financial need but with equal emphasis on academics. The recipient must have a GPA of 3.0 or higher.

Awards are arranged alphabetically below their administering organizations

Funds Avail.: No specific amount. To Apply: Applicants may contact and request an application from the Montoursville Area High School; attach an essay (250 words, double-spaced) on the topic: "Why I feel a technical or vocational education is important to me?" Contact: Betty Gilmour, Director of Grantmaking, the First Community Foundation Partnership of PA; Phone: 570-321-1500; Email: BettyG@fcfpartnership.org.

4058 ■ Dr. Wayne F. Rose Scholarship Fund
(Undergraduate/Scholarship)

Purpose: To provide financial assistance for Loyalsock High School seniors intending to attend a qualified institution of higher education in pursuit of a career in education who have a demonstrated interest in working with children and who exhibit an appreciation of the arts. Focus: General studies/Field of study not specified. Qualif.: Applicants must be attending a qualified institution of higher education; pursuing a career in education; and demonstrates interest in working with children; must demonstrate family financial need; must demonstrate active involvement working or volunteering with children outside of their own school and typical class responsibilities; must demonstrate participation in the arts while in school and/or through extracurricular activities; and must be in good academic standing with potential for success. Criteria: Selection will be based on the committee's criteria.

Funds Avail.: No specific amount. To Apply: Applicants may request an application to the Loyalsock Township High School. Applicants must have a recommendation of at least one teacher. Contact: Betty Gilmour, Director of Grantmaking, the First Community Foundation Partnership of PA; Phone: 570-321-1500; Email: BettyG@fcfpartnership.org.

4059 ■ John A. Savoy Scholarship Fund
(Undergraduate/Scholarship)

Purpose: To provide financial assistance for South Williamsport Area High School seniors who have been accepted into a full-time undergraduate program at an accredited institution of higher education, preferably in Pennsylvania. Focus: General studies/Field of study not specified. Qualif.: Applicants must attend, full-time, an undergraduate program at an accredited institution of higher education, preferably in Pennsylvania; must have exhibited good citizenship and community involvement; have unmet financial need; and must not have been the recipient of other major scholarship awards. Criteria: Selection will be based on committee's criteria.

Funds Avail.: $2,000. Duration: Annual. To Apply: Scholarship is renewable as long as the recipient remains in good standing at an accredited college or university but shall not exceed a maximum of 4 years. Applicant must submit an application to the Guidance Counselor's Office; must include a cover letter (not to exceed two pages) outlining why he or she is applying for the scholarship and summarizing his/her ultimate career objectives; must provide at least one letter of reference; and must provide proof that he or she has been accepted to a qualified two or four-year college/university. Contact: Betty Gilmour, Director of Grantmaking, the First Community Foundation Partnership of PA; Phone: 570-321-1500; Email: BettyG@fcfpartnership.org.

4060 ■ Ralph and Josephine Smith Scholarship Fund
(Undergraduate/Scholarship)

Purpose: To defray all or a portion of the costs of attending college or other undergraduate institutions of higher learning beyond the secondary level for Warrior Run High School seniors. Focus: General studies/Field of study not specified. Qualif.: Applicants must maintain a GPA of 2.5. Applicant's financial needs shall always be a primary consideration. Extra-curricular activities will not be considered in the selection process. Criteria: Selection will be based on the committee's criteria.

Funds Avail.: No specific amount. Duration: Annual. To Apply: Applicants may request an application from the Guidance Office of Warrior Run High School. Contact: Betty Gilmour, Director of Grantmaking, the First Community Foundation Partnership of PA; Phone: 570-321-1500; Email: BettyG@fcfpartnership.org.

4061 ■ Margaret E. Waldron Scholarship Fund
(Undergraduate/Scholarship)

Purpose: To provide financial assistance for Muncy High School seniors who are pursuing higher education. Focus: General studies/Field of study not specified. Qualif.: Applicants must have completed grades 10, 11, 12 at Muncy High School and have graduated from academic courses at Muncy High School; must rank in upper 1/5 of the class during junior and senior years; must present letter of acceptance from a postsecondary institution of higher learning. Criteria: Selection will be based on the committee's criteria.

Funds Avail.: $14,000 paid over four years ($3,000 for the freshman and sophomore years; $4,000 for the junior and senior years). Duration: Annual. Number Awarded: 2. To Apply: Applicants may contact Guidance Office of Muncy High School to request an application or download the application from the Foundation's web site. Applicant must submit a copy of his/her parents' current U.S. Individual Income Tax Return and a copy of his or her school transcript through the third marking period of his or her senior year. Contact: Betty Gilmour, Director of Grantmaking, the First Community Foundation Partnership of PA; Phone: 570-321-1500; Email: BettyG@fcfpartnership.org.

4062 ■ Monica M. Weaver Memorial Fund
(Undergraduate/Scholarship)

Purpose: To provide scholarship for Montoursville Area High School seniors of high scholastic standing who are enrolled at a college or other educational institution. Focus: Physical therapy. Qualif.: Applicants must be female students with high scholastic standing; attending an accredited four-year college or university or other educational institution, majoring in physical therapy; Majors in occupational therapy, nursing or other related health care profession can also apply, but preference to majors in physical therapy. Applicants must have resided in Montoursville Area School District for a minimum of three (3) years prior to graduation. Criteria: Selection will be based on the committee's criteria. Preference will be given to a student who has not received other scholarships and demonstrates financial need.

Funds Avail.: No specific amount. To Apply: Applicants may contact and request an application from the Montoursville Area High School; attach with a copy of tax return for consideration. Contact: Betty Gilmour, Director of Grantmaking, the First Community Foundation Partnership of PA; Phone: 570-321-1500; Email: BettyG@fcfpartnership.org.

4063 ■ Eleanor M. Wolfson Memorial Scholarship Fund
(Undergraduate/Scholarship)

Purpose: To provide scholarship for Montoursville Area High School seniors who will be attending Yale College.

Awards are arranged alphabetically below their administering organizations

Focus: Creative writing. **Qualif.:** Applicants must be graduating seniors at Montoursville Area High School. If there are no graduating students planning to attend Yale College, a graduating student attending an accredited four-year college or university with an outstanding academic record and a demonstrated talent in creative writing will be considered. **Criteria:** Selection will be based on academic merit and potential.

Funds Avail.: No specific amount. **To Apply:** Applicants may contact and request an application from the Montoursville Area High School. **Contact:** Betty Gilmour, Director of Grantmaking, the First Community Foundation Partnership of PA; Phone: 570-321-1500; Email: BettyG@fcfpartnership.org.

4064 ■ Wendy Y. Wolfson Memorial Scholarship Fund (Undergraduate/Scholarship)

Purpose: To provide scholarship for Montoursville Area High School seniors who will be attending Yale College. **Focus:** Criticism (Art, Drama, Literary); Music. **Qualif.:** Applicants must be graduating seniors of Montoursville Area High School. If there are no graduating students planning to attend Yale College, graduating students with an outstanding academic record and a demonstrated talent in music or drama will be considered. **Criteria:** Selection will be based on academic merit and potential.

Funds Avail.: No specific amount. **To Apply:** Applicants may contact and request an application from the Montoursville Area High School. **Contact:** Betty Gilmour, Director of Grantmaking, the First Community Foundation Partnership of PA; Phone: 570-321-1500; Email: BettyG@fcfpartnership.org.

4065 ■ Fish & Richardson P.C.
One Marina Park Dr.
Boston, MA 02210
Ph: (617)542-5070
Fax: (617)542-8906
E-mail: info@fr.com
URL: www.fr.com
LinkedIn: www.linkedin.com/company/fish-&-richardson-p.c
Twitter: www.twitter.com/fishrichardson

4066 ■ Fish & Richardson 1L Diversity Fellowships (Undergraduate/Scholarship)

Purpose: To promote diversity in the legal profession. **Focus:** Law. **Qualif.:** Applicants must be first year law students. **Criteria:** Selection is based on the submitted application and materials.

Funds Avail.: $5,000. **Duration:** Annual. **Number Awarded:** Varies. **To Apply:** Applicants must submit a completed application which includes an essay question, a resume, undergraduate transcript, legal writing sample, and a letter of recommendation from a law school or college professor. **Remarks:** Established in 2005.

4067 ■ Allison E. Fisher Memorial Fund
PO Box 43402
Baltimore, MD 21236
Ph: (410)679-0595
E-mail: info@allisonfisherfund.org
URL: www.allisonfisherfund.org

4068 ■ Allison E. Fisher Scholarships (Undergraduate, Graduate/Scholarship)

Purpose: To provide financial assistance to students who are attending an accredited four-year university. **Focus:** Journalism; Photography; Radio and television. **Qualif.:** Applicants must be any foreign or U.S. students who are majoring in journalism-print, photography or radio and television or planning a career in one of those fields; must be currently attending accredited four-year university; must have cumulative grade point average of 3.0 and be enrolled in undergraduate or graduate school during the award year. **Criteria:** Applicants are evaluated based on academic and financial need.

Funds Avail.: $2,500. **Duration:** Annual. **To Apply:** Applicants must submit all the required application information. **Deadline:** February 13.

4069 ■ Flamenco de la Isla Society
2568 Vancouver St.
Victoria, BC, Canada V8T 4A7
E-mail: info@flamencodelaisla.org
URL: www.flamencodelaisla.org

4070 ■ Flamenco Student Scholarships (Undergraduate, Professional development/Scholarship)

Purpose: To support students defray the cost of obtaining an education. **Focus:** Dance. **Qualif.:** Applicants must be members of the Flamenco de la Isla Society; must have a minimum of two years flamenco dance training; must be taking a minimum of two classes per week; must be willing to, or have in the past, volunteered for the society's events. **Criteria:** Preference will be given to those students who meet the criteria.

Funds Avail.: Up to $500. **Duration:** Annual. **To Apply:** Applicants must submit a completed application form and must provide a statement (no more than half a page) stating the importance of the scholarship. **Deadline:** May 1. **Contact:** Flamenco de la Isla Society, at the above address.

4071 ■ Flexible Packaging Association (FPA)
185 Admiral Cochrane Dr., Ste. 105
Annapolis, MD 21401
Ph: (410)694-0800
Fax: (410)694-0900
E-mail: fpa@flexpack.org
URL: www.flexpack.org

4072 ■ FPA Summer Internships Program (Undergraduate/Internship)

Purpose: To support students financially regarding their internship. **Focus:** Education, Industrial; Industrial design. **Qualif.:** Applicants must be enrolled in an AA, BA, BS or MS degree program; have a 2.7 GPA; have 24 credit hours, nine credits of which are in packaging, printing or other areas in the converting industry. **Criteria:** Recipient is selected based on submitted application and supporting materials.

Funds Avail.: $3,000. **Duration:** Annual. **To Apply:** Applicants are advised to visit the website for the online application system. Prepare a recommendation letter (academic or professional); and an essay (maximum of 500

Awards are arranged alphabetically below their administering organizations

words). **Deadline:** February 13. **Remarks:** Established in 2005.

4073 ■ Flexographic Technical Association (FTA)
3920 Veterans Memorial Hwy., Ste. 9
Bohemia, NY 11716-1074
Ph: (631)737-6020
Fax: (631)737-6813
URL: www.flexography.org

4074 ■ FIRST Operator Certification Awards *(Professional development/Internship)*

Purpose: To assist individuals who desire to improve their skills in the pursuit of certification training. **Focus:** Printing trades and industries. **Qualif.:** Applicants must pursue FIRST Operator Certification (Levels I, II & III) in one of the three areas of concentration: Press, Prepress, or Implementation Specialist; must have at least two years of full-time direct work experience in any area related to flexographic printing/converting. **Criteria:** Selection will be based on submitted applications.

Funds Avail.: No specific amount. **Duration:** Annual. **To Apply:** Applicants must submit an electronic format of a completed application form together with supporting documents such as work history, letters of recommendation and must attach a school transcript. **Contact:** Flexographic Technical Association, at the above address; or Email: memberinfo@flexography.org.

4075 ■ Florida A&M University - Environmental Sciences Institute (ESI)
Frederick Humphries Science Research Ctr., 305-D
1515 Martin Luther King Blvd.
Tallahassee, FL 32307
Ph: (850)599-3550
Fax: (850)599-8183
E-mail: famuesi@famu.edu
URL: www.famu.edu/index.cfm?environmentalscience&About

4076 ■ FAMU Presidential Scholarship - Florida Community College Scholarships *(Undergraduate/Scholarship)*

Purpose: To assist high achieving Florida community/junior college graduates. **Focus:** Environmental science. **Qualif.:** Applicants must be AA/AS degree transfer students who have the minimum 2.50 GPA and not enrolled as FAMU students. All applicants must enroll in a minimum of 15 credit hours each semester and must complete the Free Application for Federal Student Aid (FAFSA) each year. **Criteria:** Selection will be based on the committees' criteria.

Funds Avail.: $1,500 to $10,000. **Duration:** Annual. **To Apply:** Applicants may contact the Center for application process and other information.

4077 ■ FAMU Presidential Scholarship - George W. Gore Assistantship Scholarship *(Undergraduate/Scholarship)*

Purpose: To assist incoming freshmen students in meeting the cost of college education. **Focus:** Education. **Qualif.:** Applicants must be incoming freshmen who have at least 1650 on the SAT or 23 on the ACT and a minimum unweighted 3.0 high school GPA. **Criteria:** Selection will be based on the committees' criteria.

Funds Avail.: $8,000-$24,000. **Duration:** Up to four years. **To Apply:** Applicants may contact the University for the application process and other information.

4078 ■ Florida Association of Directors of Nursing Administration (FADONA)
400 Executive Center Dr., No. 208
West Palm Beach, FL 33401
Ph: (561)683-0037
Fax: (561)689-6324
E-mail: fadona@fadona.org
URL: www.fadona.org

4079 ■ Imogene Ward Nursing Scholarships *(Undergraduate/Scholarship)*

Purpose: To provide financial assistance to individuals who wants to pursue their education in the LTC setting. **Focus:** Nursing. **Qualif.:** Applicants must be pursuing education to become registered nurses; must be enrolled in an accredited Florida Nursing program; must be willing to pledge a minimum of two years, working full-time in long-term care in the state of Florida. **Criteria:** Recipients are selected based on demonstrated determination to overcome personal and/or professional obstacles to pursue nursing education, track record of excellence and the potential for future leadership in long-term care.

Funds Avail.: No specific amount. **To Apply:** Applicants must submit a completed application form including name and full contact information; must submit a 300-word or less narrative essay which outlines what it takes to be an exceptional nurse and also expresses reasons they should be considered for the Imogene Ward Nursing Scholarship Award.

4080 ■ Florida Association for Media in Education (FAME)
PO Box 4778
Haines City, FL 33845-4778
Ph: (863)585-6802
E-mail: floridamediaed@gmail.com
URL: www.floridamediaed.org

4081 ■ Sandy Ulm Scholarships *(Undergraduate/Scholarship)*

Purpose: To help students in Florida be involved in and have open access to a quality school library media program, administered by a highly competent, certified library media specialist. **Focus:** Media arts. **Qualif.:** Applicants must be individuals: who are registered in a university certificate or Master's course of study in Library Science or Educational Media or related field as approved by the Scholarship Committee; who are currently enrolled in at least one course for credit in their designated program; who maintain a minimum of 3.0 average on a 4-point scale for previous academic work; who live and/or work in a county in the State of Florida; who are or plan to be a school library media specialist; who are members in good standing of FAME; who sign the notarized statement that is part of the application form stating the they will obtain Florida media specialist certification and serve in an educational media related position within the State of Florida for a minimum of one year following completion of their education. **Criteria:** Recipients are selected based on academic performance.

Awards are arranged alphabetically below their administering organizations

Funds Avail.: No specific amount. **Duration:** Annual. **To Apply:** Applicants must submit a completed application form and a copy of the transcript of all college credits for the graduate program in which they are currently enrolled, two letters of recommendation (one must come from a professor) and a notarized statement (found in application). **Deadline:** September 15.

4082 ■ Florida Department of Business and Professional Regulation (DBPR)
1940 N Monroe St.
Tallahassee, FL 32399-1027
Ph: (850)487-1395
Fax: (352)333-2508
Free: 866-532-1440
E-mail: call.center@dbpr.state.fl.us
URL: www.myfloridalicense.com

4083 ■ Clay Ford Florida Board of Accountancy Minority Scholarships (Undergraduate/Scholarship)
Purpose: To encourage students to remain in school for the fifth year required to sit for the CPA exam. **Focus:** Accounting. **Qualif.:** Applicants must be individuals with ethnicity, gender or racial minority status pursuant to section 288.703(3) F.S.; and be Florida residents who are in the fifth year of an accounting program at an accredited Florida institution. **Criteria:** Selection shall be based on financial need, on the aforementioned applicants' qualifications, and compliance with the application details.

Funds Avail.: $3,000 to $6,000 per semester. **Duration:** Annual. **To Apply:** Applicants must submit a completed application form along with a copy current transcripts; a copy of most recent FAFSA; and a financial release form completed by the financial aid office. **Deadline:** June 1. **Contact:** Florida Board of Accountancy Clay Ford Scholarship Application, 240 NW 76th Drive, Suite A, Gainesville, Florida 32607.

4084 ■ Florida Education Fund (FEF)
201 E Kennedy Blvd., Ste. 1525
Tampa, FL 33602
Ph: (813)272-2772
Fax: (813)272-2784
E-mail: office@fefonline.org
URL: www.fefonline.org

4085 ■ Florida Education Fund McKnight Doctoral Fellowships (Graduate/Fellowship)
Purpose: To address the under-representation of African American and Hispanic faculty at colleges and universities in the state of Florida by increasing the pool of citizens qualified with PhD degrees to teach at the college and university levels. **Focus:** Arts; Business; Engineering; Health sciences; Nursing; Performing arts; Science; Visual arts. **Qualif.:** Applicants must be African American or Hispanic, US citizens, and hold a minimum of a bachelor's degree from a regionally accredited college or university. Currently enrolled doctoral students are not eligible to apply. The Fellowships must be used at one of the participating Florida universities and will be awarded only to those eligible individuals who have been accepted for graduate study at one of the participating universities. **Criteria:** Selection will be based on the committee's criteria.

Funds Avail.: $17,000 in tuition, fees and stipend. **Duration:** Annual. **Number Awarded:** Up to 50. **To Apply:** Interested applicants may visit the website for the application process. Paper application forms are also available upon request. **Deadline:** January 15. **Remarks:** Established in 1984.

4086 ■ Florida Engineering Society (FES)
125 S Gadsden St.
Tallahassee, FL 32301
Ph: (850)224-7121
Fax: (850)222-4349
E-mail: fes@fleng.org
URL: www.fleng.org
Facebook: www.facebook.com/FloridaEngineeringSociety
LinkedIn: www.linkedin.com/in/florida-engineering-society-696b3311
Twitter: twitter.com/FICE_ACECFL

4087 ■ Cesar A. Calas/FES Miami Chapter Scholarships (Undergraduate/Scholarship)
Purpose: To encourage and assist students in pursuing engineering careers; to educate the public about engineering; and to promote and enhance engineering education in Florida in order to position the state as a technological leader in global economy. **Focus:** Engineering. **Qualif.:** Applicants must be attending an accredited college of higher learning and enrolled in an engineering program approved by the Florida Engineering Society Scholarship Committee; must have at least 3.0 GPA; must maintain 12 credit hours per semester; and must be permanent residents of Miami-Dade or Monroe County. **Criteria:** Recipients are selected based on academic performance and financial need.

Funds Avail.: $1,000. **To Apply:** Applicants must submit completed application form; an official transcript; and letter of recommendation from any appropriate source. **Contact:** Kelly Jones; email: kelly@fleng.org.

4088 ■ Fecon Scholarships (Undergraduate/Scholarship)
Purpose: To encourage and assist students in pursuing engineering careers; to educate the public about engineering; and to promote and enhance engineering education in Florida in order to position the state as a technological leader in global economy. **Focus:** Engineering. **Qualif.:** Applicant must be currently enrolled or accepted into a Florida university engineering program; must be in or entering his/her junior or senior year; must have at least 3.0 average on a 4.0 scale; must be recommended by an engineering faculty member; and must be interested in pursuing a career in the field of construction. **Criteria:** Recipients are selected based on academic performance and financial need.

Funds Avail.: $1,000. **To Apply:** Applicants must submit a complete application form and an official transcript. **Deadline:** April 15. **Contact:** Attn: Kelly Harris-Jones, Florida Engineering Society, kelly@fleng.org.

4089 ■ FICE Scholarships (Undergraduate/Scholarship)
Purpose: To encourage and assist students in pursuing engineering careers; to educate the public about engineering; and to promote and enhance engineering education in Florida in order to position the state as a technological leader in global economy. **Focus:** Engineering. **Qualif.:** Applicants must be U.S. citizens pursuing a bachelor's degree

in an Accreditation Board Engineering and Technology (ABET) program and must be entering their junior, senior or fifth year of college. **Criteria:** Recipients are selected based on academic performance and financial need.

Funds Avail.: $5,000. **To Apply:** Applicants must submit completed application form and an official transcript. **Deadline:** February 12.

4090 ■ Florida Engineering Society University Scholarships (Undergraduate/Scholarship)

Purpose: To encourage and assist students in pursuing engineering careers; to educate the public about engineering; and to promote and enhance engineering education in Florida in order to position the state as a technological leader in global economy. **Focus:** Engineering. **Qualif.:** Applicant must be entering his or her junior or senior year in the Florida University Engineering Program; must have at least 3.0 grade point average on a 4.0 scale; must be recommended by an engineering faculty member; and must be a U.S. citizen or resident of Florida. **Criteria:** Recipients are selected based on academic performance and financial need.

Funds Avail.: No specific amount. **To Apply:** Applicants must submit a completed application form; an official transcript; and letter of recommendation from an engineering faculty member. **Deadline:** February 12.

4091 ■ David F. Ludovici Scholarships (Undergraduate/Scholarship)

Purpose: To encourage and assist students in pursuing engineering careers; to educate the public about engineering; and to promote and enhance engineering education in Florida in order to position the state as a technological leader in global economy. **Focus:** Engineering. **Qualif.:** Applicants must be enrolled in an ABET-accredited Florida engineering school and must be interested in civil, structural or consulting engineering. **Criteria:** Recipients are selected based on academic performance and financial need.

Funds Avail.: $1,000. **To Apply:** Applicants must submit completed application form; an official transcript; and letter of recommendation from any appropriate source. **Contact:** Kelly Jones; email: kelly@fleng.org.

4092 ■ Raymond W. Miller, PE and Alice E. Miller Scholarships (Undergraduate/Scholarship)

Purpose: To encourage and assist students in pursuing engineering careers; to educate the public about engineering; and to promote and enhance engineering education in Florida in order to position the state as a technological leader in global economy. **Focus:** Engineering. **Qualif.:** Applicants must be enrolled in an ABET-accredited Florida engineering school and must plan to attend the University of Florida. **Criteria:** Recipients are selected based on academic performance and financial need.

Funds Avail.: $1,000. **To Apply:** Applicants must submit completed application form; an official transcript; and letter of recommendation from any appropriate source. **Contact:** Kelly Jones; email: kelly@fleng.org.

4093 ■ Raymond W. Miller, PE Scholarships (Undergraduate/Scholarship)

Purpose: To encourage and assist students in pursuing engineering careers; to educate the public about engineering; and to promote and enhance engineering education in Florida in order to position the state as a technological leader in global economy. **Focus:** Engineering. **Qualif.:** Applicants must be enrolled in an ABET-accredited Florida engineering school and must plan to attend the University of Florida. **Criteria:** Recipients are selected based on academic performance and financial need.

Funds Avail.: $2,500. **To Apply:** Applicants must submit a complete application form; an official transcript; and letter of recommendation from any appropriate source. **Contact:** Kelly Jones; email: kelly@fleng.org.

4094 ■ Eric Primavera Memorial Scholarships (Undergraduate/Scholarship)

Purpose: To encourage and assist students in pursuing engineering careers; to educate the public about engineering; and to promote and enhance engineering education in Florida in order to position the state as a technological leader in global economy. **Focus:** Engineering. **Qualif.:** Applicants must be enrolled in an ABET-accredited Florida engineering school and plan to attend the Florida Institute of Technology. **Criteria:** Recipients are selected based on academic performance and financial need. Preference will be given to students desiring to attend Florida Institute of Technology.

Funds Avail.: $1,000. **To Apply:** Applicants must submit completed application form; an official transcript; and letter of recommendation from any appropriate source. **Contact:** Kelly Jones; email: kelly@fleng.org.

4095 ■ Florida Fertilizer & Agrichemical Association (FFAA)
411 E Orange St., Ste. 119
Lakeland, FL 33801
Ph: (863)686-4827
Fax: (863)682-8626
URL: www.ffaa.org
Facebook: www.facebook.com/Florida-Fertilizer-Agrichemical-Association-115164458792

4096 ■ Florida Fertilizer and Agrichemical Association Scholarships (Undergraduate/Scholarship)

Purpose: To promote the study of agriculture in higher education and to encourage students pursuing agriculture studies. **Focus:** Agricultural sciences. **Qualif.:** Applicants must be agriculture junior, senior or graduate students at the University of Florida A&M or Florida Southern; must plan to enroll for the semester immediately following the fall semester; must have a minimum GPA of 3.0 on a 4.0 scale. **Criteria:** Recipients are selected based on academic performance and financial need.

Funds Avail.: No specific amount. **Duration:** Annual. **To Apply:** Applicants must submit a completed application form. **Deadline:** October 15.

4097 ■ Florida Institute of Certified Public Accountants (FICPA)
325 W College Ave.
Tallahassee, FL 32301
Ph: (850)224-2727
Fax: (850)222-8190
Free: 800-342-3197
E-mail: msc@ficpa.org
URL: www.ficpa.org

4098 ■ FICPA Educational Foundation 1040K Race Scholarships (Undergraduate/Scholarship)

Purpose: To offset the educational costs for accounting students at Florida's colleges and universities. **Focus:** Accounting. **Qualif.:** Applicant must be an African American; a permanent resident of Miami-Dade, Broward, Palm Beach, or Monroe Counties; and must be a full-time, 4th or 5th year accounting major at: Barry University, Florida Atlantic University, Florida International University, Florida Memorial College, Nova Southeastern University, St. Thomas University, and University of Miami. **Criteria:** Awards will be given based on the application materials submitted.

Funds Avail.: $3,000 each. **Duration:** Annual. **Number Awarded:** Varies. **To Apply:** Applicant must submit a completed application along with a complete official transcript to the Accounting Scholarship Chairman at their school.

4099 ■ Florida Nursery, Growers and Landscape Association (FNGLA)
1533 Park Center Dr.
Orlando, FL 32835-5705
Ph: (407)295-7994
Fax: (407)295-1619
Free: 800-375-3642
E-mail: info@fngla.org
URL: www.fngla.org
Facebook: www.facebook.com/FNGLA
Twitter: twitter.com/fngla

4100 ■ James H. Davis Scholarships
(Undergraduate/Scholarship)

Purpose: To encourage students to pursue careers in Florida's horticulture industry and related pursuits by providing financial assistance for undergraduate, post-graduate, or other advanced education programs in Florida. **Focus:** Horticulture. **Qualif.:** Applicants must be incoming college freshmen, sophomores, juniors, seniors and/or graduate students planning to attend a community college, college or university in the state of Florida; must be full-time students in horticulture program or related field with the intent to graduate in the field; must have a 2.0 or above GPA. **Criteria:** Recipients are selected based on financial need and students' ability to maintain a 2.0 grade point average.

Funds Avail.: No specific amount. **Duration:** Annual. **To Apply:** Applicants must complete the application form; must submit a high school or college transcript; an essay and two letters of recommendation. **Deadline:** January 15.

4101 ■ Florida Nurses Association (FNA)
1235 E Concord St.
Orlando, FL 32803
Ph: (407)896-3261
Fax: (407)896-9042
E-mail: info@floridanurse.org
URL: www.floridanurse.org

4102 ■ Florida Nurses Foundation Scholarships
(Undergraduate, Master's, Doctorate/Scholarship)

Purpose: To serve and support all registered nurses through professional development, advocacy and the promotion of excellence at every level of professional nursing practice. **Focus:** Nursing. **Qualif.:** Applicants must be enrolled in a nationally accredited nursing program; must be students including those in associate, baccalaureate, and master's degree nursing programs or doctoral programs; and must have a minimum GPA of 2.5 for undergraduate and 3.0 GPA for graduate students. **Criteria:** Recipients are selected based on academic performance and potential contribution to the Nursing Professionals Society.

Funds Avail.: No specific amount. **To Apply:** Applicants must submit all necessary documents with the application form online. **Deadline:** June 1.

4103 ■ Florida Outdoor Writers Association (FOWA)
24 NW 33rd Ct., Ste. A
Gainesville, FL 32607-2556
Ph: (352)284-1763
E-mail: info@fowa.org
URL: www.fowa.org

4104 ■ Florida Outdoor Writers Association Scholarships
(Undergraduate/Scholarship)

Purpose: To motivate and encourage young people to enter outdoor communications career fields. **Focus:** Communications; Journalism. **Qualif.:** Applicants must be students at Florida Colleges and Universities, or must be students whose applications are endorsed by a FOWA member or a faculty advisor. **Criteria:** Recipients are selected based on the essay, endorsement of the faculty advisor or FOWA member, scholastic merit and extracurricular activities as indicated in the applicant's resume or supporting materials submitted.

Funds Avail.: $500-$1,000. **Duration:** Annual. **To Apply:** Applicants must submit a completed application form; must submit an essay, 500-1,000-words, that expresses their appreciation for the outdoor experience; an up-to-date resume; a letter of endorsement from a FOWA member or faculty advisor. **Deadline:** May 16.

4105 ■ Florida Police Chiefs Association (FPCA)
2636 Mitcham Dr.
Tallahassee, FL 32308
Ph: (850)219-3631
URL: www.fpca.com
Facebook: www.facebook.com/TheFPCA

4106 ■ Police Explorer Scholarships Program
(Undergraduate/Scholarship)

Purpose: To support number of programs including youth career development. **Focus:** Government. **Qualif.:** Applicants must have been involved in a police explorer post, and have been a member of the post for a minimum of one year by the time of award presentation; must maintain a minimum of a 2.0 overall grade point average and should be completing their senior year in high school, already enrolled in college or planning to attend college. **Criteria:** Recipients are selected based on the information they submit to the foundation.

Funds Avail.: $1,000. **Duration:** Annual. **To Apply:** Applicants must submit a completed application form and supporting documents should be forwarded in a 9" x 12" envelope. **Deadline:** April 15.

4107 ■ Florida Public Health Association (FPHA)
1605 Pebble Beach Blvd.
Green Cove Springs, FL 32043-8077
Ph: (904)657-2009

Awards are arranged alphabetically below their administering organizations

Fax: (904)657-2235
E-mail: floridapha@bellsouth.net
URL: fpha.org
Facebook: www.facebook.com/FLPublicHealth

4108 ■ Florida Public Health Association Public Health Graduate Scholarships (Graduate/Scholarship)

Purpose: To support the studies of students who are studying public health. **Focus:** Public health. **Qualif.:** Applicant must be a FPHA member; must be in a Master's Degree or Doctoral Degree program in the field of public health; must intend to remain in Florida and contribute to Florida's Public Health System following graduation. **Criteria:** Selection is based on the application.

Funds Avail.: No specific amount. **Duration:** Annual. **To Apply:** Applicants must submit the complete application form together with a narrative (1-2 pages) that explains professional goals and reasons for seeking Master's or Doctoral degree, curriculum vitae, two original letters of recommendation from two non-family references, and copy of current transcript showing GPA.

4109 ■ Florida Public Health Association Public Health Undergraduate Scholarships (Undergraduate/Scholarship)

Purpose: To support the studies of students who are studying public health. **Focus:** Public health. **Qualif.:** Applicants must be working on degrees in health-related or public health programs. **Criteria:** Selection is based on the application.

Funds Avail.: $300. **Duration:** Annual. **To Apply:** Applicants must submit the completed application form together with a narrative (1-2 pages) that explains professional goals and reasons for interest in health or public health, curriculum vitae, two original letters of recommendation from two non-family references, and a copy of current transcript showing GPA.

4110 ■ Florida Retired Educators Association (FREA)
10051 5th St. N Ste. 108
Saint Petersburg, FL 33702
Ph: (727)577-6400
Fax: (727)577-6445
E-mail: info@frea.org
URL: www.frea.org

4111 ■ FREA Scholarship (Undergraduate/Scholarship)

Purpose: To provide an opportunity to high school seniors who wish to teach in the State of Florida. **Focus:** Education. **Qualif.:** Applicants must be graduating high school seniors. **Criteria:** Selection will be based on the committee's criteria.

Funds Avail.: Amount varies. **Duration:** Annual. **To Apply:** Interested applicants may visit the website to obtain an application form. Applicants must complete and submit the application form on or before the deadline. **Remarks:** Established in 1980.

4112 ■ Fondation Asie Pacifique du Canada
900-675 W Hastings St.
Vancouver, BC, Canada V6B 1N2

Ph: (604)684-5986
Fax: (604)681-1370
E-mail: info@asiapacific.ca
URL: www.asiapacific.ca
Facebook: www.facebook.com/asiapacificfoundationofcanada
Twitter: twitter.com/AsiaPacificFdn

4113 ■ Asia Pacific Foundation of Canada Junior Research Fellowships (Undergraduate, Master's/Fellowship)

Purpose: To support undergraduates and master's level program graduates with their work and research in Vancouver. **Focus:** General studies/Field of study not specified. **Qualif.:** Applicants must be Canadian citizens or permanent residents (international students with an off-campus work permit will be considered in some cases); must be available to work at the Foundation's Vancouver or Toronto offices; and must be enrolled in an undergraduate or master's-level program. **Criteria:** Selection will be based on the committee's criteria.

Funds Avail.: $1,000-$4,000. **To Apply:** Applicants must submit the following documents: resume detailing the applicants' academic background, skills and professional experiences; a short writing sample (published or unpublished); copy of the applicants' university transcript (scanned or electronic copies will suffice); a 1-2 page cover letter detailing the applicants' career interests and goals, how they hope to benefit from the fellowship and why are they interested in working in the thematic area specified in the call for applications; name, title and contact information (email and phone number) for two references. Applications are accepted in English and French. **Contact:** Erin Williams at erinwilliams@asiapacific.ca.

4114 ■ Asia Pacific Foundation of Canada Media Fellowships (Professional development/Fellowship)

Purpose: To help Canadian journalists provide more insightful reportage and analysis on Asia and the Canada-Asia relationship while connecting journalists working on this dynamic part of the world. **Focus:** Journalism. **Qualif.:** Applicants must be journalists who are citizens or permanent residents of Canada; must be employed by a Canadian magazine, newspaper, news service, business publication, radio, television station, new media or multimedia outlet as reporters, feature writers, columnists or as freelancers; must have at least three years of experience in their field and have an established history of publication in Canadian news media. **Criteria:** Selection of applicants will be based on the jury formed by APF Canada. The key criteria are significance of the topic, project feasibility, potential impact and personal qualifications.

Funds Avail.: $7,000-$10,000. **Number Awarded:** 3. **To Apply:** Applicants must submit the following requirements: curriculum vitae; two examples of written or broadcast work, if possible, provide links to the examples of previous work or include copies as a PDF format or as digital media files; budget proposal of up to $7,000 including materials and other basic expenses but excluding trans-Pacific travel; letter from their prospective editor/producer, stating a willingness, in principle, to run stories resulting from this trip, subject to normal editorial judgment; and 750 words research proposal. **Deadline:** March 13. **Contact:** Erin Williams at erin.williams@asiapacific.ca.

Awards are arranged alphabetically below their administering organizations

4115 ■ Asia Pacific Foundation of Canada Post-Graduate Research Fellowships *(Master's, Doctorate/Fellowship)*

Purpose: To support Masters or PhD graduates in their work and conducting research. **Focus:** General studies/Field of study not specified. **Qualif.:** Applicants must be Canadian citizens and permanent residents who have graduated from a Master's or doctoral program within 18 months of the application as defined by the date of the graduation ceremony. **Criteria:** Selection will be based on the committee's criteria.

Funds Avail.: $38,000-$40,000. **Duration:** Annual; non-renewable. **Number Awarded:** 3. **To Apply:** Applicants must submit the following documents: resume detailing the applicants' academic background; writing sample (published or unpublished); 500-750 words description of the project that would be undertaken at the Foundation; and two letters of recommendation from individuals who know the applicant. If sending hard copies, referees should mail them directly to the Foundation at the address. If sending by email, the letter should be in the form of a signed PDF document, sent from the referee's institutional email address. **Deadline:** February 16.

4116 ■ Fondation pour le journalisme canadien
595 Bay St., Ste. 401
Toronto, ON, Canada M5G 2C2
Ph: (416)955-0394
Fax: (416)532-6879
E-mail: info@cjf-fjc.ca
URL: cjf-fjc.ca
Facebook: www.facebook.com/cjffjc

4117 ■ CJF Canadian Journalism Fellowships *(Graduate, Other, Undergraduate/Fellowship)*

Purpose: To help fellows achieve their future potential as effective and responsible journalists. **Focus:** Journalism. **Qualif.:** Applicants must have at least five years experience and be full-time news or editorial employees with Canadian newspapers, news services, radio, television or magazines. Freelance journalists who have been working consistently in the media over a five-year period will also be considered. Fellows are free to enroll in any graduate or undergraduate courses and use the full facilities of the University of Toronto. **Criteria:** Fellows are selected by a committee appointed by the President of the University of Toronto and the Master of Massey College.

Funds Avail.: 3,000 Canadian Dollars. **To Apply:** Applicants must include a proposal for a plan of study; statement of the applicant's experience; samples of work; and supporting letters from an employer or references. **Deadline:** March 6.

4118 ■ Greg Clerk Awards *(Advanced Professional, Professional development/Award)*

Purpose: To recognize and offer a professional development opportunity to working journalists. **Focus:** Journalism; Media arts; Radio and television. **Qualif.:** Applicants must be Canadian journalists who have been employed for one to five years and are employed by, under contract to, or freelancing on the news and editorial side of regularly published newspapers and periodicals, TV and radio news broadcasters, and online publications. **Criteria:** Applicants will be judged based on submitted materials. The jury will be looking for innovative proposals from journalists interested in expanding their knowledge and understanding of issues rather than their reporting skills.

Funds Avail.: $5,000. **Duration:** Annual. **To Apply:** Applicants must submit a detailed proposal of no more than two pages outlining the use of professional development opportunity; two samples of works; resume; and one letter of recommendation from a relevant employer. TV or radio clips should be no longer than 30 minutes. It should be on disc or available online for download. Original clippings should be accompanied by a printout text (mail), or in PDF format (e-mail). **Deadline:** February 27. **Contact:** For information, contact Email: programs@cjf-fjc.ca.

4119 ■ Tom Hanson Photojournalism Awards *(All/Internship)*

Purpose: To give photographers trying to break into photojournalism the chance to perform on the national stage. **Focus:** Photography, Journalistic. **Qualif.:** Applicants must be Canadian photojournalists who have been in the business less than five years. Applicants can be students, freelance photographers or photographers currently employed at regional or non-daily publications. **Criteria:** Successful applicant will be selected based on submitted materials. Selection is vested to the selection committee made up of Canadian Journalism Foundation board members, photographers and photo editors from The Canadian Press and daily newspapers and members of Tom's family.

Funds Avail.: $875 weekly salary. **Duration:** Annual; Program runs for six weeks between April and September. **Number Awarded:** 1. **To Apply:** Applicants must submit the following: a detailed proposal of no more than 1,000 words on how you would use this internship to expand your experience as a photojournalist; a portfolio of at least 12 and no more than 25 photos. Each photo should be captioned and may include a brief background explanation on how the photo was captured; a multimedia presentation that includes video; resume; and a letter of recommendation from a current employer or teacher, although such is not mandatory. **Deadline:** January 8. **Remarks:** The program was established in memory of Tom Hanson, an award-winning photographer for The Canadian Press who travelled around the world and across the country, shooting some of the most iconic news and sports images of the last 15 years. The Hanson Award is administered by The Canadian Journalism Foundation and offers a six-week paid internship at The Canadian Press head office in Toronto for a photojournalist in the early stages of his or her career. **Contact:** graeme.roy@thecanadianpress.com or Wendy Kan at wkan@cjf-fjc.ca for questions and concerns.

4120 ■ Fondation des Prix Michener
c/o The Ottawa Citizen
Box 5020
1101 Baxter Rd.
Ottawa, ON, Canada K2C 3M4
E-mail: information@michenerawards.ca
URL: www.michenerawards.ca

4121 ■ Michener-Deacon Fellowship for Journalism Education *(Professional development/Fellowship)*

Purpose: To strengthen the education of both of the successful applicant and the regular student in the journalism program. **Focus:** Journalism. **Qualif.:** Applicants must be Canadian citizens or residents of Canada who are active in

Awards are arranged alphabetically below their administering organizations

Canadian journalism, must have a minimum of five years' experience in news or editorial departments of newspapers, news agencies, radio and television, magazines, websites or online publications. Freelancers who have five years' experience in journalism are also encouraged to apply. **Criteria:** Judges will award the fellowship on the merits of the applicant's proposal for a course of study over one semester.

Funds Avail.: $30,000. **To Apply:** Applicants must submit the following requirements: written outline for a course of study in PDF format; resume that includes detailed work history; written authorization for leave from an employer and; letter from the host department providing approval from the application and describing how it will support the candidate. The letter should confirm that the school will organize one public lecture for the journalist-in-residence and facilitate arrangements for other lectures and/or mentoring during the semester.

4122 ■ Fondation Savoy
230 Foch St.
Saint-Jean-sur-Richelieu, QC, Canada J3B 2B2
Ph: (450)358-9779
Fax: (450)346-1045
E-mail: epilepsy@savoy-foundation.ca
URL: www.savoy-foundation.ca

4123 ■ Savoy Foundation Postdoctoral and Clinical Research Fellowships (Postdoctorate/Fellowship)

Purpose: To support study and research in the field of epilepsy. **Focus:** Epilepsy. **Qualif.:** Applicants must be scientists or medical specialist (PhD or MD) who wish to carry out a full-time research project in the field of epilepsy. **Criteria:** Selection is based on the submitted application.

Funds Avail.: 30,000 Canadian Dollars; plus additional 1,500 Canadian Dollars for the fellow with the highest mark. **Duration:** 1 year. **To Apply:** Applicants must submit a completed application form. Two letters of reference must be sent directly by the writers to the foundation. **Deadline:** January 15.

4124 ■ Fonds de la Société canadienne d' évaluation pour l'éducation
c/o The Willow Group
1485 Laperriere Ave.
Ottawa, ON, Canada K1Z 7S8
Ph: (613)725-2526
Fax: (613)729-6206
E-mail: secretariat@evaluation-education.org
URL: cesef.memberlodge.org

4125 ■ Canadian Evaluation Society Educational Fund Scholarships (Graduate/Scholarship)

Purpose: To provide scholarship for graduate students wishing to further their knowledge within the field of program evaluation. **Focus:** General studies/Field of study not specified. **Qualif.:** Program is open to students of program evaluation who are pursuing studies for the purpose of improving the theory and practice of program evaluation. They must be in master's or doctoral level. **Criteria:** Selection will be based on merit and contribution to the field.

Funds Avail.: Amount varies. **Duration:** Annual. **Number Awarded:** Varies. **To Apply:** Applicants may contact the society for information about the submission process and deadlines. **Deadline:** December 15.

4126 ■ Food and Drug Law Institute (FDLI)
1155 15th St. NW, Ste. 910
Washington, DC 20005-2706
Ph: (202)371-1420
Fax: (202)371-0649
Free: 800-956-6293
E-mail: service@fdli.org
URL: www.fdli.org

4127 ■ H. Thomas Austern Memorial Writing Competition (Doctorate/Award, Prize)

Purpose: To encourage students interested in the areas of law that affect food, drugs, animal drugs, biologics, cosmetics, diagnostics, dietary supplements, medical devices and tobacco. **Focus:** Law. **Qualif.:** Applicants must be currently enrolled in a J.D. program at any of the nations' "ABA accredited" law schools. **Criteria:** Committees of practicing attorneys and law professors with relevant food and drug expertise will judge the papers according to the following category: 1) thoroughness and depth of legal analysis; 2) originality and difficulty of topic; 3) evaluation of judicial precedents, status and regulations; 4) discussion of conclusions and future impact; 5) quality of legal research; 6) writing style; 7) conciseness; 8) form and quality of citations; and 9) conformity with rules and competition.

Funds Avail.: $4,000 (1st Place); $1,000 (2nd Place). **Duration:** Annual. **Number Awarded:** 2. **To Apply:** Submissions shall be typewritten, double-spaced on 81/2 x 11 inch paper. Electronic submissions in word documents are acceptable. Students joining the short paper competition shall not exceed 40 pages in length including appendices and footnotes, which may be single-spaced. Candidates submitting in a long paper category shall reach the 100 pages including footnotes. Text and footnote shall be typewritten, 12 pt. Times New Roman format. Papers shall have one-inch margin in all sides. Applicants must also include a cover sheet with entrant's full name and contact information, law school, year of study and date of submission. **Deadline:** June 6. **Contact:** comments@fdli.org.

4128 ■ Food Processing Suppliers Association (FPSA)
1451 Dolley Madison Blvd., Ste. 101
McLean, VA 22101
Ph: (703)663-1200
Fax: (703)761-4334
E-mail: info@fpsa.org
URL: www.fpsa.org
Facebook: www.facebook.com/FPSAorg/?ref=ts
Twitter: twitter.com/fpsaorg

4129 ■ Career Development Scholarships (Postdoctorate, Postgraduate/Scholarship)

Purpose: To attract and retain qualified personnel for the food processing industry. **Focus:** Food science and technology; Food service careers. **Qualif.:** Applicants can be FPSA member employees who work full-time or their immediate family members (spouse and children). Applicants must be high school seniors, college students, or graduate students. **Criteria:** Selection is based on aca-

Awards are arranged alphabetically below their administering organizations

demic achievement; character & integrity; essay content; community involvement and leadership.

Funds Avail.: $5,000. **Duration:** One year. **Number Awarded:** 10. **To Apply:** Candidates must complete the online application. In addition, candidates must mail or fax a 500-word essay, the cover page, and all required documents. **Deadline:** April 1. **Remarks:** Established in 1983. **Contact:** Robyn Roche at rroche@fpsa.org.

4130 ■ Foot Locker Foundation, Inc.
112 W 34th St.
New York, NY 10120
Ph: (212)254-2390
Fax: (212)243-2391
E-mail: footlocker@tmiagency.org
URL: www.footlockerscholarathletes.com

4131 ■ Foot Locker Scholar Athletes (Undergraduate/Scholarship)

Purpose: To help phenomenal student-athletes pursue their dreams of attending and excelling at four-year college/university. **Focus:** General studies/Field of study not specified. **Qualif.:** Applicants must be U.S. citizens or legal permanent residents who are college-bound students in the fall of the current year; must have at least a 3.0 GPA throughout their high school career; and must be able to participate in a sports-related activity in their high school or community. **Criteria:** Applicants will be evaluated based on the following: embody good sportsmanship and strong moral character; are passionate and committed to empowering the community in which they live; are confident and enthusiastic leaders; display academic excellence; or have come from diverse backgrounds.

Funds Avail.: $20,000 each, plus $5,000 to one of the winners. **Number Awarded:** 20. **To Apply:** Application is via online. **Deadline:** December 17.

4132 ■ For the Love of Chocolate Scholarship Foundation
226 W Jackson Blvd., Ste. 106
Chicago, IL 60606
Ph: (312)726-2419
E-mail: info@fortheloveofchocolatefoundation.org
URL: www.fortheloveofchocolatefoundation.org
Facebook: www.facebook.com/ftloc
Twitter: twitter.com/FLoveChocolate

4133 ■ For the Love of Chocolate Foundation Scholarships (Undergraduate, Graduate, Professional development/Scholarship)

Purpose: To encourage and assist aspiring students, career changers and culinary career professionals to advance their knowledge of the pastry arts. **Focus:** Culinary arts. **Qualif.:** Applicants must demonstrate a desire to develop pastry art skills; accepted into L'Art de la Patisserie program; must work a minimum of 40 hours in a foodservice establishment prior to the beginning of the semester (work must be documented by a direct supervisor); must demonstrate financial need; must be accepted by The French Pastry School for the upcoming semester; and must be U.S. citizens. **Criteria:** Selection will be based on the submitted application materials and demonstrated financial need.

Funds Avail.: No specific amount. **Duration:** 3/year. **To Apply:** Applicants must submit a completed scholarship application form along with a personal essay, two letters of recommendation and a copy of previous year's tax return. **Deadline:** May 1, June 1 and October 1.

4134 ■ Forensic Sciences Foundation (FSF)
410 N 21st St.
Colorado Springs, CO 80904
Ph: (719)636-1100
Fax: (719)636-1993
URL: fsf.aafs.org

4135 ■ FSF Student Travel Grant (Undergraduate, Graduate/Grant)

Purpose: To assist students by helping them attend the American Academy of Forensic Sciences (AAFS) Annual Meeting. **Focus:** Criminology. **Qualif.:** Applicants must be AAFS members/affiliates or AAFS applicants applying for membership; Must be 4th year undergraduate or graduate students at an accredited four-year college, university, or professional school whose accreditation is acceptable to the FSF Board of Trustees.

Funds Avail.: Up to $1,500 per student. **Duration:** Annual. **Number Awarded:** 8. **To Apply:** Applicants submit an abstract either as presenters or co-authors for the annual meeting they will be attending; Must have a letter of recommendation from their advisor or professor; Must submit a 400-600 word essay explaining how attendance at an AAFS meeting will impact their career decision; Must submit a curriculum vitae to include specific regarding their involvement in forensic science and their current GPA. **Deadline:** October 15.

4136 ■ Forest History Society (FHS)
701 William Vickers Ave.
Durham, NC 27701
Ph: (919)682-9319
Fax: (919)682-2349
E-mail: stevena@duke.edu
URL: www.foresthistory.org

4137 ■ Alfred D. Bell, Jr. Travel Grants (Graduate/Grant)

Purpose: To provide financial assistance for researchers conducting in-depth studies using resources in the society's archive and library. **Focus:** General studies/Field of study not specified. **Qualif.:** Candidates must be researchers conducting in-depth studies and who use FHS research resources to support their work. **Criteria:** Preference is given to applicants whose research topics are well-covered in the FHS library and archives. Preference is also given to young scholars per the wishes of the Bell family.

Funds Avail.: $950. **Duration:** Annual. **To Apply:** Applicants must submit a completed hard copy of the application form at the FHS office. **Remarks:** Established in 1990. **Contact:** Cheryl Oakes at coakes@duke.edu.

4138 ■ Frederick K. Weyerhaeuser Forest History Fellowships (Graduate/Fellowship)

Purpose: To support the research of a Duke University graduate student whose research examines in some way forest and conservation history. **Focus:** Environmental conservation; Forestry; History. **Qualif.:** Applicants must be

Duke University graduate students pursuing research in the fields of forest, conservation or environmental history. **Criteria:** Fellowship recipient is selected on the basis of merit. Proposals are judged in terms of overall significance and quality of presentation.

Funds Avail.: $11,000. **Duration:** Annual. **Number Awarded:** 1. **To Apply:** Applicants must submit a narrative description of research (up to eight pages), including significance of topic, research approach, author's background, research and writing schedule and budget. Attachments are not necessary but may include previous publications, written chapters and basic bibliography; curriculum vitae and 2-3 letters of recommendation from persons knowledgeable of the applicant's research. Letters of recommendation should address the author's qualifications and may describe the significance of the topic to forest and conservation history; five hard copies of the proposal and an electronic copy of the proposal without supporting documents. Applicants must provide a cover letter that states the title of the proposed research, a one-paragraph summary of the significance of the project and a description of the historical nature of the project. **Deadline:** January 31. **Remarks:** Established to honor the memory of Frederick K. Weyerhaeuser. Established in 1986. **Contact:** Andrea Anderson at: andrea.anderson@foresthistory.org.

4139 ■ Formsbirds.com
South Ashland Ave.
Chicago, IL 60608
E-mail: support@formbirds.com
URL: www.formsbirds.com

4140 ■ The FormsBirds Scholarships
(Undergraduate/Scholarship)

Purpose: To help outstanding students to complete their college education. **Focus:** General studies/Field of study not specified. **Qualif.:** Applicants must be full-time students enrolled in a university, college or technical institute; must have an overall 3.0 GPA. **Criteria:** Selection will be based on the committee's criteria.

Funds Avail.: $500. **Duration:** Annual; renewable. **Number Awarded:** 1. **To Apply:** Applicants must compose a 500-1,000 word essay in Word or PDF format telling about: "Would you often use forms in daily life? What convenience forms have brought to you?" In addition, applicants are also required to include their full name, email address, mailing address, country, city, phone number, college name, college website, major in college, year of graduation as well as at least two recommendation letters from their teacher, department head or headmaster. **Deadline:** August 31. **Contact:** Essay should be submitted to: scholarship@formbirds.com.

4141 ■ Fort Atkinson Community Foundation
244 N Main St.
Fort Atkinson, WI 53538
Ph: (920)563-3210
E-mail: facf@fortfoundation.org
URL: fortfoundation.org
Facebook: www.facebook.com/fortfoundation

4142 ■ Walter and Louise Buell Graduate Scholarships *(Graduate/Scholarship)*

Purpose: To provide financial assistance to students residing within the Fort Atkinson area. **Focus:** General studies/Field of study not specified. **Qualif.:** Applicants must be residents of the Fort Atkinson area or graduates of Fort Atkinson High School; must be accepted into a graduate school at an accredited college or university in a program leading to an advanced degree within the United States; must be full or part-time graduate students with ongoing registration; must make steady progress towards a degree; and must demonstrate financial need. **Criteria:** Applicants will be evaluated based on academic achievement, interest and potential for community involvement, citizenship and need for financial assistance.

Funds Avail.: No specific amount. **Number Awarded:** Varies. **To Apply:** Applicants must submit a completed application form; an essay consisting of career goals and how obtaining their education will be an advantage for the community; appended college transcripts including undergraduate study and any graduate work completed; two recommendation letters. **Contact:** Fort Atkinson Community Foundation, at the above address.

4143 ■ Jason Dahnert Memorial Scholarships
(Undergraduate/Scholarship)

Purpose: To assist students pursuing a career in engineering. **Focus:** Engineering. **Qualif.:** Applicants must be residents of Fort Atkinson area; must be in current high school senior years, college undergraduate or graduate students concentrating in any disciplines involving engineering; must be pursuing degrees at a recognized U.S. college or university. **Criteria:** Selection will be based on academic records, financial need, participation in extra-curricular activities and community involvement.

Funds Avail.: No specific amount. **To Apply:** Applicants must submit a completed application form; an essay consisting of interest in technology and career goals; high school or college transcripts including undergraduate study and any graduate work completed to date; test scores; two recommendation letters. **Contact:** Fort Atkinson Community Foundation, at the above address.

4144 ■ Jerome Hake Engineering Scholarships
(Undergraduate/Scholarship)

Purpose: To provide financial assistance to students who are currently pursuing a degree in engineering at a college or university. **Focus:** Engineering. **Qualif.:** Applicants must be current high school seniors graduating in the top one-third of their class, college undergraduate or graduate students pursuing engineering degrees (candidates studying electrical engineering should be given special consideration assuming that all other selection criteria are met); must be residents of the Fort Atkinson area; must attend a four-year degree granting college or university. **Criteria:** Selection will be based on financial need, academic records especially in math and science courses, good character and strong work ethic.

Funds Avail.: No specific amount. **To Apply:** Applicants must submit a completed application form; an essay describing interest in technology; high school or college transcripts including undergraduate study and any graduate work completed to date; test scores; two recommendation letters. **Contact:** Fort Atkinson Community Foundation, at the above address.

4145 ■ Gene Halker Memorial Scholarships *(Graduate, Undergraduate/Scholarship)*

Purpose: To provide financial assistance to students pursuing a degree in economics, business, literature or any related field. **Focus:** Business; Economics; Literature. **Qualif.: Applicants must be residents of the Fort Atkinson area or graduates of Fort Atkinson High School pursuing degrees in economics, business, literature or any related fields; undergraduate applicants must be full-time students at a four-year degree granting college or university with junior standing in the next academic year; graduate applicants may be either full-time or part-time students at an accredited U.S college or university which grants postgraduate degrees; must have a minimum GPA of 3.0 in post-secondary study. **Criteria:** Selection is based on academic records, indication of potential success from letters of reference and financial need.

Funds Avail.: No specific amount. **To Apply:** Applicants must submit a completed application form; an essay consisting of career goals and explanation for choosing area of study; high school and college transcripts including undergraduate study and any graduate work completed to date; test scores; two letters of recommendation. **Contact:** Fort Atkinson Community Foundation, at the above address.

4146 ■ Eileen Harrison Education Scholarships
(Graduate, Undergraduate/Scholarship)

Purpose: To provide financial assistance to students pursuing an undergraduate or graduate degree in education. **Focus:** Education. **Qualif.:** Applicants must be residents of Fort Atkinson area, graduates of Fort Atkinson High School or employees of Fort Atkinson School District; must be currently pursuing an undergraduate or graduate degree in Education (graduate students may be full or part-time students); must attend a four-year degree granting college or university; must obtain a GPA of 3.0 on a 4.0 scale; must be in good standing in undergraduate/graduate program. **Criteria:** Selection will be based on evaluation of submitted documents and specific criteria.

Funds Avail.: No specific amount. **To Apply:** Applicants must submit a completed application form; an essay describing commitment to education; high school or college transcripts including undergraduate study and any graduate work completed to date; test scores; two recommendation letters. **Contact:** Fort Atkinson Community Foundation, at the above address.

4147 ■ Robert C. and Judith L. Knapp Scholarships
(Graduate, Undergraduate/Scholarship)

Purpose: To financially support students who have the potential for achieving their professional goals. **Focus:** Education, Music; Engineering; Mathematics and mathematical sciences; Physics. **Qualif.:** Applicants must be residents of the Fort Atkinson area pursuing undergraduate or graduate degrees in mathematics, mathematics education, physics, physics education, engineering, engineering education, music performance or music education at a college or university; must have completed at least one year full-time college study and earned at least 3.0 GPA in post secondary study; must attend a four-year degree granting college or university. **Criteria:** Evaluations will be based on academic records plus indication of potential success from letters of reference.

Funds Avail.: No specific amount. **To Apply:** Applicants must submit a completed application form; an essay consisting of career goals and choosing of area of study; high school and college transcripts including undergraduate study and any graduate work completed to date; two letters of recommendation. **Contact:** Fort Atkinson Community Foundation, at the above address.

4148 ■ Jane Shaw Knox Graduate Scholarships
(Graduate/Scholarship)

Purpose: To provide tuition aid to women pursuing postgraduate degrees. **Focus:** General studies/Field of study not specified. **Qualif.:** Applicants must be residents of Fort Atkinson area (graduates of Fort Atkinson High School, employed in Fort Atkinson, have a Fort Atkinson mailing address or phone number). **Criteria:** Selection will be based on evaluation of submitted documents and specific criteria.

Funds Avail.: No specific amount. **To Apply:** Applicants must submit a completed application form; official copy of university transcript(s); personal resume; three recommendation letters; financial data. **Contact:** Fort Atkinson Community Foundation, at the above address.

4149 ■ Ralph and Clara Rutledge Memorial Scholarships *(Graduate/Scholarship)*

Purpose: To provide financial support to students residing within Fort Atkinson area. **Focus:** General studies/Field of study not specified. **Qualif.:** Applicants must be residents of Fort Atkinson area or graduates of Fort Atkinson High School; must be accepted into a graduate school at an accredited college or university in a program leading to an advanced degree within the United States; must be full or part-time graduate students with an ongoing registration; must be making steady progress towards a degree. **Criteria:** Applicants will be evaluated based on academic achievement, interest and potential for community involvement and citizenship.

Funds Avail.: No specific amount. **To Apply:** Applicants must submit a completed application form; an essay consisting of career goals and how obtaining their education will be an advantage for the community; appended college transcripts including undergraduate study and any graduate work completed; two recommendation letters. **Contact:** Fort Atkinson Community Foundation, at the above address.

4150 ■ Forté Foundation
9600 Escarpment, Ste. 745
Austin, TX 78749
Ph: (512)535-5157
URL: www.fortefoundation.org

4151 ■ Forté Fellowships *(Master's/Fellowship)*

Purpose: To increase the number of women applying to and enrolling in MBA programs by offering fellowships. **Focus:** Business. **Qualif.:** Candidates should exhibit exemplary leadership in one or more ways: academic leadership, team leadership, community leadership, and creative leadership; should demonstrate a commitment to women and girls via personal mentorship or community involvement. Such commitment is in alignment with the mission of Forte Foundation; must be women pursuing a full-time, part-time or executive MBA education at any of the sponsor business schools. **Criteria:** Selection will be based on the committee's criteria.

Funds Avail.: No specific amount. **To Apply:** Interested individuals must first submit an MBA application to a participating school. Schools are encourage to nominate fellows who represent diverse educational and work backgrounds, career goals, ethnicities and citizenship.

4152 ■ Forum for Theological Exploration (FTE)
160 Clairemont Ave., Ste. 300
Decatur, GA 30030

Awards are arranged alphabetically below their administering organizations

Ph: (678)369-6755
Fax: (678)369-6757
URL: fteleaders.org
Facebook: www.facebook.com/fteleaders

4153 ■ FTE Dissertation Fellowships (Graduate, Doctorate/Fellowship)

Purpose: To encourage new scholars from a variety of fields to undertake research relevant to the improvement of education. **Focus:** Bible studies; Religion; Theology. **Qualif.:** Applicants must be U.S. citizens; must be in the final writing stage of dissertation; must be African-American doctoral students in religion, theology and biblical studies. **Criteria:** Selection will be based on evaluation of submitted documents and specific criteria.

Funds Avail.: $10,000. **Number Awarded:** 4. **To Apply:** Applicants must submit a completed application form, dissertation proposal and writing plan approved by the dissertation committee. Applicants may also contact the Organization for other application requirements. **Deadline:** February 1.

4154 ■ FTE Doctoral Fellowships (Doctorate, Graduate/Fellowship)

Purpose: To provide assistance for African-American students pursuing graduate degrees in religious, theological or biblical studies. **Focus:** Bible studies; Religion; Theology. **Qualif.:** Applicants must be African-American students preparing to enter first year of an accredited Ph.D. or Th.D. program in religion, theology or biblical studies; must be committed to becoming a leader within theological education; must have strong consideration to teaching at a theological school; must be U.S. citizens; must hold bachelor's degree from an accredited college or university. **Criteria:** Selection is based on evaluation of submitted documents and specific criteria.

Funds Avail.: Up to $20,000. **To Apply:** Applicants must submit a completed application form; curriculum vitae; two to three page essay; transcripts of all undergraduate and graduate schools attended; photocopy of GRE school report; two reference letters; completed budget statement form; documentation from school showing amount of financial award to be received; provide six copies of each requirements except for letters of reference and transcripts. **Deadline:** February 1.

4155 ■ FTE North American Doctoral Fellowships (Doctorate, Graduate/Fellowship)

Purpose: To provide financial assistance to talented students from racial and ethnic groups that are traditionally underrepresented in graduate education. **Focus:** Bible studies; Religion; Theology. **Qualif.:** Applicants must be members of a racial or ethnic group that is traditionally underrepresented in graduate education; enrolled full-time in a Ph.D. or Th.D. program in religion or theology and demonstrate high academic performance; U.S. or Canadian citizens or permanent residents of either countries; demonstrates commitment to teaching and scholarship and capacity for leadership in theological education. **Criteria:** Selection is based on the evaluation of the submitted documents and specific criteria. Preference will be given to students nearing the end of their studies.

Funds Avail.: Up to $10,000. **Duration:** Annual. **To Apply:** Applicants must submit a completed application form; curriculum vitae; two-page essay; graduate transcripts; academic form; two reference letters; completed budget statement form; documentation from school showing amount of financial award to be received; provide six copies of each of the requirements except for letters of reference and transcripts.

4156 ■ Foster Care to Success (FC2S)
21351 Gentry Dr., Ste. 130
Sterling, VA 20166
Ph: (571)203-0270
Fax: (571)203-0273
E-mail: info@fc2success.org
URL: www.fc2success.org
Facebook: www.facebook.com/FosterCare2Success
Twitter: twitter.com/fc2success

4157 ■ Casey Family Services Alumni Scholarships (Graduate, Undergraduate, Vocational/Occupational/Scholarship)

Purpose: To provide funds for students to cover their tuition and/or other expenses directly related to educational pursuits. **Focus:** Health care services. **Qualif.:** Applicants must be alumnus of Casey Family Services Foster Care in Connecticut, Maine, Maryland, Massachusetts, New Hampshire, Rhode Island and Vermont; must be between the ages of 16 and 49 at the time of application; must be currently enrolled or planning to attend a college or university in pursuit of a certificate, associate, bachelor, master's or a professional degree including law or medicine; or currently enrolled or planning to attend a technical or vocational school in pursuit of a certificate or certification. **Criteria:** Recipients are selected based on financial needs and scholastic standing.

Funds Avail.: $10,000. **To Apply:** Interested applicants are suggested to visit the website to create an account and for the online application process. **Contact:** 571-203-0270; scholarships@fc2success.org.

4158 ■ Dr. Nancy Foster Scholarship Program
NOAA Office of National Marine Sanctuaries
N/ORM 6 SSMC 4 11th Fl.
1305 E West Hwy., Rm. 11146
Silver Spring, MD 20910
E-mail: fosterscholars@noaa.gov
URL: fosterscholars.noaa.gov

4159 ■ Dr. Nancy Foster Scholarships (Graduate/Scholarship)

Purpose: To provide support for independent graduate-level studies in oceanography, marine biology, or maritime archaeology (including all science, engineering, social science and resource management of ocean and coastal areas), particularly by women and members of minority groups. **Focus:** Biology, Marine; Maritime studies; Oceanography. **Qualif.:** Applicants must: be U.S. citizens enrolled or accepted at an accredited U.S. graduate institution, and pursuing or intending to pursue a master's or doctoral level degree in oceanography, maritime archaeology or marine biology; have and maintain a minimum cumulative and term grade point average of 3.3 or higher; and, maintain full-time student status for the duration of the scholarship award. **Criteria:** Selection is based on: academic record and statement of intent (20%); quality of project and applicability to program priorities (30%); recommendations and/or endorsement letters (15%); relevant experience related to diversity of education, extra-curricular activities, honors and awards, interpersonal, written and oral communication skills (20%) and financial need (15%).

Funds Avail.: Up to $42,000 each. **Duration:** Annual. **Number Awarded:** Varies. **To Apply:** Applicants may visit the scholarship section of the bestowing organization's website for further information regarding the application details.

4160 ■ Foundation of the American Institute for Conservation of Historic & Artistic Works
1156 15th St. NW, Ste. 320
Washington, DC 20005-1714
Ph: (202)452-9545
Fax: (202)452-9328
E-mail: info@conservation-us.org
URL: www.conservation-us.org

4161 ■ Individual Professional Development Scholarship *(Professional development/Scholarship)*

Purpose: To help defray professional development costs for individual members of AIC who are Professional Associates or Fellows. **Focus:** Art conservation. **Qualif.:** Applicants must be AIC members seeking professional development. **Criteria:** Preference may be given to applicants who have not received FAIC funding within the past three years; and to applicants who will publish/lecture on the proposed project (thereby disseminating knowledge/skills gained).

Funds Avail.: Up to $1,000. **Duration:** Annual. **To Apply:** Applicants must complete and submit five copies of application and supporting materials to FAIC. Applicants may also submit application electronically only if all of materials (with the exception of letters of support) can be submitted electronically. Send the application form and all supporting materials in PDF, RTF or Microsoft Word format via email attachments. Name the files to include last name ("Lastname.doc" or "Lastname.pdf"). **Deadline:** February 15 or September 15.

4162 ■ Foundation for Anesthesia Education and Research (FAER)
200 First Street SW, WF6-674
Rochester, MN 55905
Ph: (507)284-0291
E-mail: faer@faer.org
URL: www.faer.org

4163 ■ FAER Mentored Research Training Grants *(Professional development/Grant)*

Purpose: To help anesthesiologists develop the skills, preliminary data for subsequent grant applications and research publications needed to become independent investigators. **Focus:** Anesthesiology. **Qualif.:** Applicants must be U.S. citizens, permanent residents, or holders of H-1 visa with minimum of three years remaining; must be graduate physician with an unexpired, permanent, unconditional and unrestricted license to practice medicine or osteopathy in at least one state or jurisdiction of the United States; must be certified by the American Board of Anesthesiology or in the examination system; must be active members of the American Society of Anesthesiologists; and must have no more than ten years from completion of initial core anesthesiology residency training, whether or not from an ACGME-accredited program. **Criteria:** Selection will be based on the committee's criteria.

Funds Avail.: $175,000 ($75,000 for the 1st year; $100,000 for the 2nd year). **Duration:** Two years. **To Apply:** Applicants must be able to provide research projects in basic science, clinical or translational, or health service research. Applicants and mentors must submit their biographical sketches (applicants must use the latest FAER version of the current NIH biosketch template while mentors must use the standard NIH biosketch template). Other documents required are abstracts; resubmission statement (if the applicants have previously submitted any research proposal to FAER); research plan; budget; letters of commitment and recommendation; and human use or animal review (with IRB or IACUC approval). Applicants must also remember that the mentorship and career development sections are major elements of FAER research grant applications and are weighted heavily in the scoring. **Deadline:** August 15 (summer/fall); February 15 (winter/spring). **Contact:** For questions, contact Jody Clikeman, Grants Program Specialist, at JodyClikeman@faer.org.

4164 ■ FAER Research in Education Grants *(Advanced Professional/Grant)*

Purpose: To advance the careers and knowledge of anesthesiologists interested in improving the concepts, methods and techniques of education in anesthesiology. **Focus:** Anesthesiology. **Qualif.:** Applicants must: be U.S. citizens, permanent residents, or holders of H-1 or O-1 visa with minimum of three years remaining; be graduate physicians with an unexpired, permanent, unconditional and unrestricted license to practice medicine or osteopathy in at least one state or jurisdiction of the United States; be certified by the American Board of Anesthesiology or in the examination system; be active members of the American Society of Anesthesiologists; and, have no more than ten years from completion of initial core anesthesiology residency training, whether or not from an ACGME-accredited program. **Criteria:** Selection will be based on the committee's criteria.

Funds Avail.: $100,000 ($50,000 per annum). **Duration:** up to two years. **To Apply:** Applicants and mentors must submit their biographical sketches (applicants must use the latest FAER version of the current NIH biosketch template while mentors must use the standard NIH biosketch template). Other documents required are abstracts; resubmission statement (if the applicants have previously submitted any research proposal to FAER); research plan; budget; letters of commitment and recommendation; and human use or animal review (with IRB or IACUC approval). Applicants must also remember that the mentorship and career development sections are major elements of FAER research grant applications and are weighted heavily in the scoring. **Deadline:** August 15 (summer/fall); February 15 (winter/spring). **Contact:** For questions, contact Jody Clikeman, Grants Program Specialist, at jodyclikeman@faer.org.

4165 ■ FAER Research Fellowship Grants *(Postdoctorate, Postgraduate, Graduate/Grant)*

Purpose: To provide anesthesiology residents and fellows the opportunity to obtain significant training in research techniques and scientific methods. **Focus:** Anesthesiology. **Qualif.:** Applicants must be U.S. citizens, permanent U.S. residents, or holder of H-1 visa with minimum of three years remaining; must be graduate physicians who are enrolled in an ACGME-accredited residency program in anesthesiology or who are accepted into a clinical fellowship program sponsored by an ACGME-accredited residency program in anesthesiology; and must be active or resident members of the American Society of Anesthesiologists. **Criteria:** Selection will be based on the committee's criteria.

Funds Avail.: $75,000. **Duration:** Annual. **To Apply:** Interested applicants may reach FAER for the application process and other related information. **Deadline:** August 15 fall; February 15 spring. **Contact:** Jody Clikeman, grants program specialist, at JodyClikeman@faer.org.

4166 ■ Foundation for Appalachian Ohio
35 Public Sq.
Nelsonville, OH 45764
Ph: (740)753-1111
Fax: (740)753-3333
E-mail: info@ffao.org
URL: www.appalachianohio.org
Facebook: www.facebook.com/foundationforappalachianohio

4167 ■ Ora E. Anderson Scholarships (Undergraduate, High School/Scholarship)

Purpose: To provide financial support to the most outstanding eligible scholars who are committed to environmental protection and conservation. **Focus:** Natural sciences. **Qualif.:** Applicants must be graduating high school seniors who possess a GED; must be residents of and attending school within any of the 32 counties of Appalachian Ohio; must have a plan to pursue post-secondary studies associated with the natural sciences, including but not limited to, forest and wildlife management, environmental restoration, natural and historical interpretation, ecotourism and related disciplines associated with broadly protecting plants, animals and the environment; must have a proof of acceptance at an accredited vocational school, college or university. **Criteria:** Applicants will be selected based on academic performance and demonstrated commitment to environmental protection and conservation.

Funds Avail.: No specific amount. **Duration:** Annual. **To Apply:** Applicants must complete the application form available online; must attach a transcript of records and personal statement. **Deadline:** March 31. **Contact:** Foundation for Appalachian Ohio, at the above address.

4168 ■ Zelma Gray Medical School Scholarships (Graduate, Doctorate/Fellowship)

Purpose: To provide scholarship assistance to promising medical provider from Guernsey County High School in order to improve the medical access and healthcare in Ohio. **Focus:** Education, Medical. **Qualif.:** Applicants must be residents and high school graduates of Guernsey County who are pursuing a Doctor of Medicine or Doctor of Osteopathic Medicine degree; must be enrolled full-time in an accredited medical school and must remain in good standing as defined by the policy in effect at the individual's school enrollment. **Criteria:** Applicants will be selected based on MCAT scores and college transcripts on a non-discriminatory basis without regard to race, creed, national origin, religion, or sex and the amount is at the discretion of the Fund Trustee.

Funds Avail.: No specific amount. **Duration:** Annual. **To Apply:** Applicants must complete the application form; must submit a certified copy of academic transcripts from all colleges or undergraduate institutions attended, indicating grades per class or course, and cumulative undergraduate grade point average; must provide proof of scores on the Medical College Admission Test (MCAT) or other test designed to measure their ability and aptitude for medical school; must have a copy of Free Application for Federal Student Aid (FAFSA) or the most recent federal income tax return. **Deadline:** March 31. **Contact:** Foundation for Appalachian Ohio, at the above address; or Email: to tmann@ffao.org.

4169 ■ Susan K. Ipacs Nursing Legacy Scholarships (Undergraduate, High School/Scholarship)

Purpose: To provide financial assistance to nursing students. **Focus:** Nursing. **Qualif.:** Applicants must be second year Hocking College students pursuing a degree in a nursing program; must have at least 3.0 GPA on a 4.00 scale. **Criteria:** Selection of applicants will be based on financial need and character as evidenced by personal conduct, values, attitude and behavior applicable to the nursing field, and submitted statement and nomination forms. Application requirements will be evaluated by the Scholarship Committee and the final approval is made by the Foundation's Board of Trustees.

Funds Avail.: No specific amount. **Duration:** Annual. **To Apply:** Applicants must submit a complete application which includes the following: original application form available on the website, including all required signatures; current Hocking College transcript of records signed by the school official; two applicant nominations in a sealed envelope; student aid report listing their EFC from the FAFSA. **Deadline:** March 31. **Contact:** Foundation for Appalachian Ohio, at the above address, or Email: to tmann@ffao.org.

4170 ■ Wayne F. White and Bob Evans Legacy Scholarships (Undergraduate, High School/Scholarship)

Purpose: To financially assist senior high school students in Appalachian Ohio. **Focus:** General studies/Field of study not specified. **Qualif.:** Applicants must be graduating high school seniors who possess a GED; must be residents of and attending school within any of the 32 counties of Appalachian Ohio; must demonstrate outstanding character, academic excellence and involvement with extra-curricular activities; must have an Expected Family Contribution (EFC) of $8,000 or less. **Criteria:** Preference will be given to those with financial need, who demonstrate the desire to succeed and overcome obstacles.

Funds Avail.: $14,500. **Duration:** Annual. **Number Awarded:** 29. **To Apply:** Applicants must complete the application form available online; must attach a transcript of records and personal statement. **Deadline:** March 31. **Contact:** Foundation for Appalachian Ohio, at the above address, or Email: tmann@ffao.org.

4171 ■ Foundation for the Carolinas (FFTC)
220 N Tryon St.
Charlotte, NC 28202
Ph: (704)973-4500
Free: 800-973-7244
URL: www.fftc.org

4172 ■ Henry S. and Carolyn Adams Scholarship Fund (Undergraduate/Scholarship)

Purpose: To provide educational assistance for deserving students with financial need who are residents of Union County, NC. **Focus:** General studies/Field of study not specified. **Qualif.:** Applicants must have a minimum

Awards are arranged alphabetically below their administering organizations

cumulative grade point average of 3.0 (on a 4.0 scale); must be legal residents of Union County, NC; must be nominated by the principal of their high school; and must demonstrate a substantial need for financial assistance. **Criteria:** Recipients are selected based on academic achievement; school and community involvement and personal achievements.

Funds Avail.: No specific amount. **To Apply:** Applicants must submit completed application form; official copy of high school transcript(s), including SAT/ACT scores; one to two-paged typed statement expressing qualifications for the scholarship, educational goals and financial need for scholarship assistance; two completed recommendation forms including at least one from a current teacher; and a copy of SAR from FAFSA. **Deadline:** march 16. **Contact:** Qiana Austin at qaustin@fftc.org.

4173 ■ Herb Adrian Memorial Scholarship Fund
(Undergraduate/Scholarship)

Purpose: To provide financial assistance for students at the University of North Carolina at Charlotte who have expressed an interest in the multi-family housing field. **Focus:** Construction; Finance; Management. **Qualif.:** Applicants must be rising Virginia Tech junior or senior; must have interest in the multi-housing industry, including but not limited to finance, construction and management; and must demonstrate financial need. **Criteria:** Recipients are selected based on financial need.

Funds Avail.: No specific amount. **To Apply:** Applicants must contact the Virginia Tech Residential Property Management School, 540-231-4784. **Contact:** Qiana Austin at qaustin@fftc.org.

4174 ■ African American Network - Carolinas Scholarship Fund *(Undergraduate/Scholarship)*

Purpose: To provide scholarships for college-bound students from North and South Carolina who are pursuing a major in engineering, math, science, computer science, accounting, finance or business administration. **Focus:** Accounting; Business administration; Computer and information sciences; Engineering; Finance; Mathematics and mathematical sciences; Science. **Qualif.:** Applicants must be graduating seniors at a North or South Carolina high school; must attend a four-year college or university located in North or South Carolina; must plan to major in engineering, computer science, the sciences, accounting, finance or business administration. **Criteria:** Applicants are judged based on grade point average; residence; leadership skills and financial need.

Funds Avail.: No specific amount. **Duration:** Annual. **Number Awarded:** 2. **To Apply:** Applicants must submit all the required application information. **Contact:** Advocates for African Americans, Attn: Advocates for African Americans Scholarship Committee, P. O. Box 30234, Charlotte, NC 28230-0234; Email: AANCarolinasScholarship@duke-energy.com.

4175 ■ William Tasse Alexander Scholarship Fund
(Undergraduate/Scholarship)

Purpose: To provide financial assistance to students who are studying primarily in the field of education. **Focus:** Education. **Qualif.:** Applicants must be legal residents of Mecklenburg County, NC who are matriculating full-time juniors or seniors in college; must have a minimum cumulative grade point average of 3.0 on a 4.0 scale; and must be majoring in the field of education or taking courses leading to a career in teaching. **Criteria:** Applicants are evaluated based on academic performance; school and community involvement and personal achievements; and demonstrated potential for a career as an educator.

Funds Avail.: No specific amount. **To Apply:** Applicants must submit completed application form; official transcript(s) of academic coursework and grades for at least the last two years; copy of applicants' NTE/Praxis Series scores, if available; three recommendation forms (two from instructors or other campus administrators and one from an employer or other non-related individual); one to two pages typewritten statement expressing reasons for applying for scholarship, qualifications, and educational/career goals; and a copy of the estimated expense budget for tuition, room and board, books, etc. at the school they attended. **Remarks:** Established in 1982. **Contact:** Qiana Austin at qaustin@fftc.org.

4176 ■ Andersen Nontraditional Scholarships for Women's Education and Retraining (ANSWER)
(Undergraduate/Scholarship)

Purpose: To provide financial support and encouragement for adult women. **Focus:** General studies/Field of study not specified. **Qualif.:** Applicants must be nontraditional female students age 25 or older at the time of the application deadline; legal residents of Mecklenburg County, NC or contiguous county in North Carolina or South Carolina; enrolled or planning to enroll as full-time, degree-seeking students at an accredited institution in North Carolina or South Carolina; and must be primary caregivers to at least one school-age child (enrolled in K-12). This includes natural born or legally adopted children for whom legal guardianship has been granted. **Criteria:** Applicants who are single parents are given preference, with the following basis criteria: financial need as determined by the costs of college attendance compared with an applicants' household income and other financial factors; demonstrated potential for academic success.

Funds Avail.: No specific amount. **To Apply:** Applicants must submit a completed application form; copy of the Student Aid Report from FAFSA; official transcripts of grades for the applicant's most recently completed coursework; three recommendation forms from non-related adults such as instructors or other campus administrators, employers, mentors, etc.; updated, typed resume; one to two-page typed personal statement expressing why the applicant is applying for the scholarship and the applicant's educational and career goals; and copy of the applicant's federal tax return for the preceding year showing dependents and adjusted gross income. **Deadline:** March 29. **Contact:** Qiana Austin at qaustin@fftc.org.

4177 ■ Bank of America Junior Achievement Scholarship Fund *(Undergraduate/Scholarship)*

Purpose: To provide financial support for undergraduate students who have expressed an interest in business through their service to Junior Achievement in Atlanta, GA. **Focus:** Business; Technology. **Qualif.:** Applicants must be graduating high school seniors with a minimum cumulative GPA of 3.0 on a 4.0 scale and who have actively participated in Junior Achievement of Georgia; and must be planning to major in business or computer technology. **Criteria:** Applicants are evaluated based on academic merit and financial need.

Funds Avail.: No specific amount. **To Apply:** Applicants must submit all the required application information. **Contact:** Qiana Austin at qaustin@fftc.org.

Awards are arranged alphabetically below their administering organizations

FOUNDATION FOR THE CAROLINAS

4178 ■ Pete and Ellen Bensley Memorial Scholarship Fund *(Undergraduate/Scholarship)*

Purpose: To assist graduating seniors at East Mecklenburg High School who demonstrates interest in foreign languages and/or journalism. **Focus:** Foreign languages; Journalism. **Qualif.:** Applicants must be legal residents of Mecklenburg County and graduating seniors at East Mecklenburg High School who are planning to major in foreign languages and/or journalism. **Criteria:** Applicants are selected based on the criteria designed by the Scholarship Selection Committee.

Funds Avail.: No specific amount. **To Apply:** Applicants must submit all the required materials and complete application information. **Contact:** Qiana Austin at qaustin@fftc.org.

4179 ■ Donald H. Bernstein/John B. Talbert, Jr. Scholarships *(Undergraduate/Scholarship)*

Purpose: To provide educational support to students who are children of employees of Hanes Companies, Inc., USA. **Focus:** General studies/Field of study not specified. **Qualif.:** Applicants must be graduating high school seniors who have a minimum cumulative grade point average of 3.0 (on a 4.0 scale). Parents or legal guardians of applicants must be employees who have completed at least two years (24 months) of full-time service with Hanes Companies, Inc. USA prior to the application deadline. Applicants shall be defined to include natural-born or legally-adopted dependent children, stepchildren, and wards of employees. **Criteria:** Applicants are evaluated based on academic/personal achievement; financial need; school and community involvement.

Funds Avail.: No specific amount. **To Apply:** Applicants must submit a completed application form; copy of high school transcript(s), including SAT/ACT scores; three recommendation forms (two from teachers or other school personnel and one from an employer or other non-related adult); one to two-paged typed statement expressing the reason for applying for the scholarship, qualifications, and educational/career goals; and letter from an official of Hanes Companies, Inc. USA where parent or legally-appointed guardians are employed. **Deadline:** March 17. **Contact:** Qiana Austin at qaustin@fftc.org.

4180 ■ T. Frank Booth Memorial Scholarship Fund *(Undergraduate/Scholarship)*

Purpose: To provide financial assistance to accounting students at East Carolina University. **Focus:** Accounting. **Qualif.:** Applicants must be legal residents of North Carolina who are juniors or seniors with a 3.0 minimum cumulative grade point average (on 4.0 scale) who have declared major in accounting. **Criteria:** Applicants are evaluated based on merit and financial need.

Funds Avail.: No specific amount. **To Apply:** Applicants must submit all the required application information. **Contact:** Qiana Austin at qaustin@fftc.org.

4181 ■ Cadmus Communications Corporation Graphics Scholarship Endowment Fund *(Undergraduate/Scholarship)*

Purpose: To assist students who are enrolled in the associate degree in Graphic Arts Management Program at Central Piedmont Community College. **Focus:** Graphic art and design. **Qualif.:** Applicants must have completed at least two semesters of the CPCC Graphic Arts and Imaging Technology Program with 3.0 minimum cumulative grade point average on 4.0 scale. **Criteria:** Applicants are evaluated based on criteria designed by the Scholarship Selection Committee.

Funds Avail.: No specific amount. **Duration:** Annual. **To Apply:** Applicants must submit all the required application information and materials. **Contact:** CPCC Graphic Arts and Imaging Technology Program, Phone: 704-330-4437.

4182 ■ Kasie Ford Capling Memorial Scholarship Endowment Fund *(Undergraduate/Scholarship)*

Purpose: To provide financial assistance for high school seniors graduating from Charlotte-Mecklenburg high schools (public or private) who have experienced the death of one or both parents. **Focus:** General studies/Field of study not specified. **Qualif.:** Applicants must be graduating high school seniors from a Charlotte-Mecklenburg high school (public or private) who has attended atleast two full academic years; must be legal residents of Mecklenburg County, NC; must have experienced the death of one or both parents; and must be in good standing at the time of application. Applicants must plan to attend an accredited four-year college or university. **Criteria:** Recipients will be selected based on academic achievements; record of leadership as evidenced by the school, athletic and community involvement; and financial need. Preference will be given to students planning to attend a college in North Carolina.

Funds Avail.: No specific amount. **Duration:** Annual. **To Apply:** Applicants must complete the application form; must submit a copy of Student Aid Report (SAR); official transcript of high school and/or college coursework and grades for at least the last two years, including SAT/ACT scores if taken; and two recommendation forms: one from a teacher or other school personnel and one from a non-related adult such as employer, mentor, coach, etc. **Contact:** Qiana Austin at qaustin@fftc.org.

4183 ■ Julian E. Carnes Scholarship Fund *(Undergraduate/Scholarship)*

Purpose: To provide financial assistance to students of Clemson University and the University of North Carolina at Charlotte who are preparing for a career in a technological field appropriate to meet the requirements of the U.S. Patent Office as a patent agent or attorney. **Focus:** Biology; Chemistry; Computer and information sciences; Engineering; Physics. **Qualif.:** Applicants must be legal residents of North or South Carolina; must be rising juniors or seniors at Clemson University or UNC Charlotte whose academic major is appropriate to meet the requirements of the U.S. Patent Office for admission as a patent agent or attorney (including but not limited to engineering, chemistry, physics, biology and computer science); and must have at least a 3.0 cumulative grade point average (on a 4.0 scale). **Criteria:** Applicants are evaluated based on merit.

Funds Avail.: No specific amount. **To Apply:** Applicants must submit all the required application information. **Contact:** Qiana Austin at qaustin@fftc.org.

4184 ■ Carolinas-Virginias Retail Hardware Scholarships *(Undergraduate/Scholarship)*

Purpose: To support the children of employees of member firms of the Carolinas-Virginias Region of the National Retail Hardware Association. **Focus:** General studies/Field of study not specified. **Qualif.:** Applicants must have a minimum cumulative grade point average of 2.5 on a 4.0 scale; whose parents or legally-appointed guardians are employees who have completed at least two years of full-

Awards are arranged alphabetically below their administering organizations

time service with a member firm of the Carolinas-Virginias Region of the National Retail Hardware Association; children of employees shall be defined to include natural-born or legally-adopted dependent children, stepchildren, and wards of employees. **Criteria:** Applicants are evaluated based on academic achievement including grade point average and performance on tests designed to measure preparation and ability for postsecondary study; school and community involvement and personal achievements; work experience particularly in retail hardware.

Funds Avail.: No specific amount. **To Apply:** Applicants must submit a completed application form; copy of the Student Aid Report (SAR) from FAFSA; official transcript(s) of high school and/or college coursework and grades for at least the last two years, including SAT/ACT scores if taken; three recommendation forms, two from teachers or other school personnel and one from an employer or other non-related adult; one to two-page typed statement expressing the reason on why applicant is applying for the scholarship, qualifications and educational and career goals; a letter from an official of the member firm of the Carolinas-Virginias Region of the National Retail Hardware Association where parent or legally-appointed guardian is employed. **Deadline:** March 24. **Contact:** Qiana Austin at qaustin@fftc.org.

4185 ■ Charlotte Housing Authority Scholarship Fund (CHASF) *(Undergraduate, Vocational/Occupational/Scholarship)*

Purpose: To provide educational assistance for young residents of housing owned or managed by the Charlotte Housing Authority. **Focus:** General studies/Field of study not specified. **Qualif.:** Applicants must be residents of public housing owned or managed by the Charlotte Housing Authority. Applicants attending a college, vocational or technical school for the first time must not be over 21 years of age as of September 1 of the school year for which the scholarship award is to be made; those who have previously attended a college, vocational or technical school must not be over 24 years of age as of September 1 of the school year for which the scholarship award is to be made. **Criteria:** Applicants are evaluated based on financial need; academic performance; personal achievements; school and community involvement; and commitment to and demonstrated potential for success in college, technical or vocational school.

Funds Avail.: No specific amount. **To Apply:** Applicants must submit a completed application form; official transcript(s) of coursework and grades for at least the first two years, including SAT/ACT scores if taken; three recommendation forms (one from an adult in the housing community where the applicant lives, one from a teacher, counselor or other school administrator, and one from an employer, minister, community leader or other non-related adult); one to two pages typed personal statement expressing the applicant's educational and career goals and financial need for scholarship assistance; and a copy of the applicant's FAFSA or student aid report. **Deadline:** April 25. **Contact:** Qiana Austin at qaustin@fftc.org.

4186 ■ Charlotte-Mecklenburg Schools Scholarship Incentive Program *(Undergraduate/Scholarship)*

Purpose: To provide motivation and encouragement for Charlotte-Mecklenburg public high school students with financial need to stay in school, graduate and pursue postsecondary education. **Focus:** General studies/Field of study not specified. **Qualif.:** Applicants must be graduating seniors at a Charlotte-Mecklenburg public high school; must be participants in the Communities in Schools ThinkCOLLEGE Program or the Charlotte-Mecklenburg Schools AVID Program; must be legal residents of Mecklenburg County, NC; and must have 2.5 minimum cumulative grade point average on a 4.0 scale. **Criteria:** Applicants will be evaluated based on financial need; academic/personal achievement; and school/community involvement.

Funds Avail.: No specific amount. **To Apply:** Applicants must submit completed application form; official copy of high school transcript(s), including SAT/ACT scores; two recommendation forms from a teacher, counselor or other school administrator, and the other one from an employer, community leader or non-related adult; one to two pages typed personal statement; and copy of SAR from FAFSA. **Deadline:** April 21. **Contact:** Qiana Austin at qaustin@fftc.org.

4187 ■ Children's Scholarship Fund of Charlotte *(Undergraduate/Scholarship)*

Purpose: To provide scholarship assistance to students who are in grades K-8. **Focus:** General studies/Field of study not specified. **Qualif.:** Applicants must be legal residents children of Mecklenburg County, NC in grades K-8 attending or planning to attend a tuition-based school in the Charlotte-Mecklenburg region. **Criteria:** Recipients will be selected based on financial need.

Funds Avail.: No specific amount. **Duration:** Annual. **To Apply:** Applicants must submit all the required application information. **Deadline:** December 31. **Contact:** Lisa Clarke at lclarke@fftc.org.

4188 ■ Lula Faye Clegg Memorial Scholarship Fund *(Undergraduate/Scholarship)*

Purpose: To provide financial assistance to students who are majoring in education. **Focus:** Education. **Qualif.:** Applicants must be graduates of a high school in the Charlotte-Mecklenburg public school system; must rank in the top 10% of graduating high school class; and must have strong interest and commitment to a career in teaching. **Criteria:** Applicants are evaluated based on the criteria designed by the Scholarship Selection Committee.

Funds Avail.: No specific amount. **To Apply:** Applicants must submit all the required application information. **Contact:** Qiana Austin at qaustin@fftc.org.

4189 ■ Cole Foundation Undergraduate Scholarship Program *(Undergraduate/Scholarship)*

Purpose: To increase the number of high school graduates from Richmond County, NC pursuing a post-secondary education. **Focus:** General studies/Field of study not specified. **Qualif.:** Applicants must be legal residents of Richmond County, NC; must be high school seniors scheduled to graduate in the spring of the current school year. Students applying for four-year scholarships must have a minimum cumulative grade point average of 3.0 (on 4.0 scale). **Criteria:** Preference will be given to applicants whose parents do not have a college degree and will be evaluated based on financial need; academic achievement; school and community involvement; and personal achievements.

Funds Avail.: No specific amount. **To Apply:** Applicants must submit a completed application form; copy of SAR from FAFSA; official copy of the applicants' high school transcript(s), including SAT/ACT scores if taken; typewritten statement expressing educational and career goals, reasons for applying for the scholarship and why they deserve the scholarship; and copy of both parents' federal

Awards are arranged alphabetically below their administering organizations

tax return(s) for the preceding year showing dependents and adjusted gross income. **Deadline:** March 16. **Contact:** Qiana Austin at qaustin@fftc.org.

4190 ■ Sally Cole Visual Arts Scholarship Fund *(Undergraduate/Scholarship)*

Purpose: To provide financial assistance to Richmond County, NC students with demonstrated talent and career interests in the visual arts. **Focus:** Visual arts. **Qualif.:** Applicants must be planning to attend an accredited two-year or four-year post-secondary institution with a degree program in visual arts; must be high school seniors in good academic standing scheduled to graduate in the spring of the current school year; must have an expressed and demonstrated interest in the visual and/or studio arts which primarily includes, but are not limited to, painting, drawing, sculpture, illustration and ceramics; must be legal residents of Richmond County, NC. **Criteria:** Applicants are evaluated based on academic achievement; school and community involvement and personal achievements; and demonstrated aptitude and career potential in the visual arts.

Funds Avail.: No specific amount. **To Apply:** Applicants must submit a completed application form; official copy of high school transcript(s), including SAT/ACT scores if taken; three recommendation forms, two of which must come from individuals able to evaluate the applicants' aptitude and career potential in the visual arts; one to two pages typewritten statement expressing a) applicants' reasons for applying for the scholarship, b) applicants' interest in the arts, c) applicants' educational and career goals in the field of visual arts; and samples (3-5 labeled color slides) of applicants' original artwork. **Deadline:** March 16. **Contact:** Qiana Austin at qaustin@fftc.org.

4191 ■ Judy Crocker Memorial Scholarship Fund *(Undergraduate/Scholarship)*

Purpose: To provide financial assistance to students with an interest in Education, Human Services and related majors. **Focus:** Education. **Qualif.:** Applicants must be legal residents of York County, SC; must be rising juniors or seniors at Winthrop University, located in Rock Hill, SC, majoring in education, human services or a related field; must have 2.9 minimum cumulative grade point average (on a 4.0 scale) and who demonstrate financial need. **Criteria:** Recipients are selected based on financial need.

Funds Avail.: No specific amount. **To Apply:** Applicants must submit all the required application information. **Contact:** Qiana Austin at qaustin@fftc.org.

4192 ■ Crowder Scholarships *(Undergraduate/Scholarship)*

Purpose: To provide financial assistance for children of employees of general contracting companies headquartered in Mecklenburg County, NC. **Focus:** General studies/Field of study not specified. **Qualif.:** Applicants must be defined as natural born or legally adopted dependent children, stepchildren, and wards of employees. Parents or legally-appointed guardians of applicants must have worked for their respective general contracting company for at least three years prior to the application deadline. A minimum cumulative grade point average of 2.0 (on a 4.0 scale) is required. **Criteria:** Applicants will be evaluated based on academic achievement; financial need; school and community involvement; and personal achievements. Preference will be given to children of employees of Crowder Construction Company.

Funds Avail.: No specific amount. **To Apply:** Applicants must submit a completed application form; copy of SAR from FAFSA; official transcript(s) of high school and/or college coursework and grades for at least the last two years, including SAT/ACT scores if taken; three recommendation forms; a one to two-paged typed statement expressing why the applicant is applying for the scholarship, applicant's qualifications and the applicant's educational and career goals; a letter from an official of the general contracting company where the applicant's parent is employed, certifying that the parent is an employee and stating the employee's position and length of service; and a copy of both parents' federal tax return for the preceding year showing dependents and adjusted gross income. **Deadline:** March 21. **Contact:** Qiana Austin at qaustin@fftc.org.

4193 ■ The E.R. and Lilian B. Dimmette Scholarship Fund *(Undergraduate/Scholarship)*

Purpose: To provide financial assistance to students who deserves it. **Focus:** General studies/Field of study not specified. **Qualif.:** Applicants must be nominated by the Superintendent of Schools in their county; must have a minimum cumulative grade point average of 2.5 (on a 4.0 scale); and must be legal residents of Gaston, Iredell, Mecklenburg, Rowan or Wilkes County, North Carolina. **Criteria:** Applicants are evaluated based on demonstrated substantial need for financial assistance.

Funds Avail.: No specific amount. **To Apply:** Applicants must submit completed application form; copy of the SAR from FAFSA; official copy of high school transcript(s), including SAT/ACT scores; three recommendation forms (two from teachers or other school personnel and one from an employer or other non-related adult); one to two-paged typed statement expressing qualifications for the scholarship, educational goals and financial need for scholarship assistance; copy of both parents' federal tax return for the preceding year showing dependents and adjusted gross income; and copy of estimated expense budget for tuition, fees, room, board, books, etc. for the school planning to attend. **Deadline:** April 7. **Contact:** Qiana Austin at qaustin@fftc.org.

4194 ■ Laura M. Fleming Scholarships *(Undergraduate, Vocational/Occupational/Scholarship)*

Purpose: To provide financial assistance to children of Founders Federal Credit Union members to attend an accredited college, vocational or technical school of their choice. **Focus:** Education, Vocational-technical. **Qualif.:** Applicants must be children of Founders Federal Credit Union members defined as natural born or legally adopted children and stepchildren and wards of employees; must be high school seniors graduating in the spring of the current school year; must have a minimum 3.5 cumulative grade point average (on a 4.0 scale). Applicant's parents or legally appointed guardians must be Founders Credit Union members in good standing for a minimum of two years (24 months) prior to the application deadline. **Criteria:** Applicants are evaluated based on financial need; record of good citizenship evidenced by school and community involvement; and academic achievement.

Funds Avail.: No specific amount. **To Apply:** Applicants must submit completed application form; official copy of most recent high school transcript; three recommendation forms (two from current teachers or other school personnel and one from an employer or other non-relative); two typed essays of 400 words or less on topics provided in the application form; documentation of school and community involvement; and a copy of Student Aid Report (SAR) from

Awards are arranged alphabetically below their administering organizations

FAFSA. **Deadline:** March 17. **Contact:** Qiana Austin at qaustin@fftc.org.

4195 ■ Foundation for the Carolinas Rotary Scholarship Fund *(Undergraduate/Scholarship)*

Purpose: To provide financial assistance to students who are pursuing college. **Focus:** General studies/Field of study not specified. **Qualif.:** Applicants must be at least college juniors or seniors at a four-year institution enrolling as full-time students; must have a minimum 3.0 cumulative grade point average (on a 4.0 scale); and must demonstrate financial need. **Criteria:** Recipients are selected based on academic merit, financial need and community service.

Funds Avail.: No specific amount. **To Apply:** Applicants must submit completed application form; copy of Student Aid Report (SAR) from Free Application for Federal Student Aid; official transcript(s) of academic coursework and grades for at least the last two years; three recommendation forms (two from instructors or other campus administrators and one from an employer or other non-related individual in Charlotte-Mecklenburg area); one to two-paged typed statement expressing reasons for applying for the scholarship; and a copy of the estimated expense budget for tuition, room and board, books, etc. **Contact:** Qiana Austin at qaustin@fftc.org.

4196 ■ Richard Goolsby Scholarship Fund *(Graduate, Undergraduate/Scholarship)*

Purpose: To provide financial assistance to graduate undergraduate students who have shown a career interest or demonstrate practical experiences in the plastics industry. **Focus:** General studies/Field of study not specified. **Qualif.:** Applicants must be full-time rising college sophomore, junior or senior students at a four-year college or two-year technical school, who are in good academic standing and majoring in or taking courses that would be suited to a career in the plastics industry (includes but not limited to chemistry, physics, chemical engineering, mechanical engineering, industrial engineering and business administration); or must be graduate students seeking to obtain a post-secondary graduate degree. **Criteria:** Applicants are evaluated on the basis of academic performance; demonstrated interest in plastics industry; financial need; school and community involvement; and personal achievements. Preference will be given to applicants living in the Geographical area served by the Carolinas Section of the Society of Plastics Engineers (central and western North Carolina and all South Carolina).

Funds Avail.: No specific amount. **To Apply:** Applicants must submit a completed application form; copy of the Student Aid Report (SAR) from Free Application for Federal Student Aid; official transcript(s) of academic coursework and grades for at least the last two years; three recommendation forms (two from teachers or other school administrators and one from an employer or other non-related individual); and a personal statement expressing reasons for applying for the scholarship, qualifications, educational and career goals in plastics industry. **Deadline:** March 25. **Contact:** Qiana Austin at qaustin@fftc.org.

4197 ■ Howard B. Higgins South Carolina Dental Scholarships *(Undergraduate/Scholarship)*

Purpose: To provide financial assistance to students who are attending College at the Medical University of South Carolina. **Focus:** Dentistry. **Qualif.:** Applicants must be students at the College of Dental Medicine at the Medical University of South Carolina; must have at least 3.0 cumulative grade point average (on a 4.0 scale); and must be legal residents of South Carolina. **Criteria:** Applicants are evaluated based on the criteria designed by the Scholarship Selection Committee.

Funds Avail.: No specific amount. **To Apply:** Applicants must submit all the required application information. **Contact:** Qiana Austin at qaustin@fftc.org.

4198 ■ Wilbert L. and Zora F. Holmes Scholarship Endowment Fund *(Undergraduate/Scholarship)*

Purpose: To provide financial assistance for graduating seniors from South Carolina's York School District One intending to attend an accredited college or technical school of their choice. **Focus:** Education, Vocational-technical. **Qualif.:** Applicants must be graduating seniors at York Comprehensive High School (currently the only high school in the York School District One) and must have been students at York Comprehensive High School for a minimum of two years as of the application deadline; must be legal residents of York County, South Carolina; and must have a minimum of 3.0 cumulative grade point average (on 4.0 scale) at the end of the first semester of senior year. **Criteria:** Recipients are selected based on academic achievement and financial need.

Funds Avail.: No specific amount. **To Apply:** Applicants must submit all the required application information. **Contact:** Qiana Austin at qaustin@fftc.org.

4199 ■ James V. Johnson Scholarship Fund *(Undergraduate/Scholarship)*

Purpose: To provide financial assistance to students at Pfeiffer University in Misenheimer, NC and Mitchell Community College in Statesville, NC. **Focus:** General studies/Field of study not specified. **Qualif.:** Applicants must be legal residents of Iredell or Alexander County in North Carolina; must be incoming freshmen at Pfeiffer University in Misenheimer, NC or first-year students at Mitchell Community College in Statesville, NC. **Criteria:** Applicants are evaluated based on criteria designed by the Scholarship Selection Committee.

Funds Avail.: No specific amount. **To Apply:** Applicants must submit all the required application information. **Contact:** Qiana Austin at qaustin@fftc.org.

4200 ■ Annabel Lambeth Jones Scholarships *(Undergraduate/Scholarship)*

Purpose: To provide financial assistance to students at Queens University and Brevard College. **Focus:** General studies/Field of study not specified. **Qualif.:** Applicants must be incoming freshmen at Queens University of Charlotte in Charlotte, NC or Brevard College in Brevard, NC; must have high academic merit; and must have demonstrated leadership potential. **Criteria:** Applicants are evaluated based on personal attributes.

Funds Avail.: No specific amount. **To Apply:** Applicants must submit all the required application information. **Contact:** Qiana Austin at qaustin@fftc.org.

4201 ■ Mary and Millard Kiker Scholarships *(Undergraduate/Scholarship)*

Purpose: To support deserving students with financial need who are residents of Anson or Union Countries in North Carolina. **Focus:** General studies/Field of study not specified. **Qualif.:** Applicants must be legal residents of Anson or Union County, NC who are nominated by the Superintendent of Schools in their county with a minimum cumulative grade point average of 2.5 (on a 4.0 scale) and must demonstrate substantial need for financial assistance. **Criteria:** Selection will be based on financial need.

Funds Avail.: No specific amount. **To Apply:** Applicants must submit a completed application form; copy of the Student Aid Report from FAFSA; official copy of high school transcript(s), including SAT/ACT scores; three recommendation forms (two from teachers or other school personnel and one from an employer or other non-related adult); one to two-paged typed statement expressing qualifications for the scholarship, educational goals and financial need for scholarship assistance; and a copy of both parents' federal tax return for the preceding year showing dependents and adjusted gross income. **Deadline:** March 16. **Contact:** Qiana Austin at qaustin@fftc.org.

4202 ■ Law Enforcement Memorial Scholarship Fund *(Undergraduate/Scholarship)*

Purpose: To provide financial support to students who are studying law enforcement. **Focus:** Law enforcement. **Qualif.:** Applicants must be students at Central Piedmont Community College or the University of North Carolina at Charlotte who have a 2.5 minimum cumulative grade point average (on a 4.0 scale); and majoring in a law enforcement field. **Criteria:** Applicants are judged based on academic merit.

Funds Avail.: No specific amount. **To Apply:** Applicants must submit all the required application information. **Contact:** Qiana Austin at qaustin@fftc.org.

4203 ■ George T. Lewis, Jr. Academic Scholarship Fund *(Undergraduate/Scholarship)*

Purpose: To provide motivation and encouragement to George T. Lewis, Jr. Academic Center graduates intending to pursue post-secondary education or training. **Focus:** General studies/Field of study not specified. **Qualif.:** Applicants must meet or exceed the benchmark goals for attendance set for the George T. Lewis, Jr. Academic Center during their senior year; must have earned a minimum 2.0 cumulative grade point average (on a 4.0 scale) at the end of the first semester of senior year; and must be graduating seniors at the George T. Lewis, Jr. Academic Center and must have at least one full academic year of enrollment and participation in the ThinkCOLLEGE Program (upon graduation). **Criteria:** Applicants are evaluated based on academic achievement; school involvement and personal achievements and financial need.

Funds Avail.: No specific amount. **To Apply:** Applicants must submit completed application form; copy of the SAR from FAFSA; official copy of high school transcript(s), including SAT/ACT scores; two recommendation forms (one from a teacher, counselor or other school administrator and one from employer, community leader or other non-related adult); a one to two-paged typed personal statement on one of the following topics: (1) Discuss who or what has been the biggest influence on your decisions to attend college and why or (2) Present and explain the 'personal mission' or 'personal vision' you have adopted for yourself and discuss why you think these goals are important; and a copy of the applicant's completed FAFSA. **Contact:** Qiana Austin at qaustin@fftc.org.

4204 ■ Albert and Eloise Midyette Memorial Scholarship Fund *(Undergraduate/Scholarship)*

Purpose: To provide educational support to students who are pursuing degrees in the fields of religious and ministry studies, nursing and other medical academic fields. **Focus:** Education, Medical; Nursing. **Qualif.:** Applicants must be full-time U.S. citizen students attending Limestone College in Gaffney, South Carolina; must be majoring in the fields of religious and ministry studies, nursing or other medical academic fields; and must have a cumulative grade point average of at least 2.5 (on a 4.0 scale). **Criteria:** Applicants are evaluated on the basis of academic achievement and financial need.

Funds Avail.: No specific amount. **To Apply:** Applicants must submit all the required application information and materials. **Contact:** Qiana Austin at qaustin@fftc.org.

4205 ■ Carolina Panthers Players Sam Mills Memorial Scholarship Fund *(Undergraduate/Scholarship)*

Purpose: To assist athletes from Mecklenburg County, NC and Spartanburg County, SC who wish to pursue a four-year undergraduate degree. **Focus:** General studies/Field of study not specified. **Qualif.:** Applicants must be graduating senior athletes at high schools (public or private) located in Mecklenburg County, NC or Spartanburg County, SC; have earned a varsity letter in high school; with 3.0 minimum cumulative unweighted grade point average on a 4.0 scale; demonstrated outstanding leadership and citizenship; and must attend an accredited four-year college or university as full-time students. **Criteria:** Applicants are evaluated based on academic achievement; school and community involvement; evidence of leadership and citizenship.

Funds Avail.: No specific amount. **Duration:** Annual. **To Apply:** Applicants must submit a completed application form; copy of the Student Aid Report (SAR) from Free Application for FAFSA; official copy of high school transcript, including SAT/ACT scores; three recommendation forms, one from a faculty member/school official and one from a member of the coaching staff of the sport in which the athletes participate; and must attend a personal interview with the Selection Committee, if requested. **Contact:** Qiana Austin, Vice President and Scholarships Program Officer; Phone: 704-973-4535; Email: qaustin@fftc.org.

4206 ■ Carolina Panthers Players Sam Mills Memorial Scholarships *(Graduate/Scholarship)*

Purpose: To assist athletes from North and South Carolina who wish to pursue their next level of education. **Focus:** General studies/Field of study not specified. **Qualif.:** Applicants must have earned an intercollegiate varsity letter in college; must be graduating senior athletes at an accredited North or South Carolina college or university; have minimum cumulative grade point average of 3.0 on a 4.0 scale; must receive a nomination for scholarship consideration from their current Athletic Director. Female athletes may letter in any sport and male athletes must letter in football. **Criteria:** Applicants are evaluated based on academic performance; record of leadership and citizenship; school and community involvement and personal achievements.

Funds Avail.: No specific amount. **Duration:** Annual. **To Apply:** Applicants must submit a completed application form; official transcript; copy of score report from the Graduate Record Exam (GRE), Law School Admissions Test (LSAT), Medical College Admissions Test (MCAT) or other appropriate graduate admission test scores, if available; three recommendation forms which include one from a faculty member in major course of study, one from a member of the Athletic Department and one from another school official or other non-related individual familiar with the applicants' extracurricular and leadership involvement;

Awards are arranged alphabetically below their administering organizations

and a typed double-spaced personal statement not to exceed 1,000 words expressing the reason for applying for the scholarship, involvement in athletics, and educational/career goals. **Deadline:** March 25. **Contact:** Qiana Austin, Vice President and Scholarships Program Officer; Phone: 704-973-4535; Email: qaustin@fftc.org.

4207 ■ North Carolina League for Nursing Academic Scholarships *(Graduate/Scholarship)*

Purpose: To provide financial assistance for graduate students pursuing either a master's degree in nursing or a doctoral degree in nursing or a related discipline. **Focus:** Nursing. **Qualif.:** Applicants must be legal residents of North Carolina; must have completed a minimum of six semester hours of course work in their graduate program of study by the application deadline; and must be granted unconditional admission to a master's degree program in nursing or doctoral degree program in nursing or a related discipline and be classified as a graduate degree student by the college or university. **Criteria:** Applicants are evaluated based on academic performance and financial need.

Funds Avail.: No specific amount. **To Apply:** Applicants must submit a completed application form; copy of the Student Aid Report from Free Application for Federal Student Aid; official transcripts; two recommendation forms (one from a faculty member familiar with the applicant's progress in the program and one from any other non-related individual); a one to two-paged typed statement expressing qualifications for the scholarship; and commitment to full-time employment in North Carolina either in nursing practice or in teaching in a nursing education program. **Deadline:** March 16. **Contact:** Qiana Austin at qaustin@fftc.org.

4208 ■ North Mecklenburg Teachers' Memorial Scholarships *(Undergraduate/Scholarship)*

Purpose: To provide financial support to students who intend to pursue a degree in education. **Focus:** Education. **Qualif.:** Applicants must be graduating seniors at North Mecklenburg High School; must be planning to attend a four-year college or university; and must be majoring in education. **Criteria:** Applicants are evaluated based on academic achievement; extracurricular and community involvement; statement of personal aspirations and educational goals; and financial need.

Funds Avail.: No specific amount. **To Apply:** Applicants must submit a completed application form; copy of the Student Aid Report (SAR) from Free Application for Federal Student Aid; official transcript of academic coursework and grades; and a typewritten statement expressing the applicants' educational and career goals and reasons for applying for the scholarship. **Remarks:** Established in 2007. **Contact:** Qiana Austin at qaustin@fftc.org.

4209 ■ Ted H. Ousley Scholarship Fund *(Undergraduate/Scholarship)*

Purpose: To provide undergraduate scholarships for graduating seniors at North Mecklenburg High School in Huntersville, NC. **Focus:** General studies/Field of study not specified. **Qualif.:** Applicants must be graduating seniors at North Mecklenburg High School; must have a minimum cumulative grade point average of 2.5 (on a 4.0 scale); and must be planning to attend a post-secondary institution in North Carolina. **Criteria:** Applicants are evaluated based on criteria designed by the Scholarship Selection Committee.

Funds Avail.: No specific amount. **To Apply:** Applicants must submit all the required application information. **Contact:** Qiana Austin at qaustin@fftc.org.

4210 ■ Henry DeWitt Plyler Scholarship Fund *(Undergraduate/Scholarship)*

Purpose: To provide financial support to students who are attending Winthrop University. **Focus:** General studies/Field of study not specified. **Qualif.:** Applicants must be graduating seniors or graduates of Lancaster County public high schools; must have 3.0 minimum cumulative grade point average (on a 4.0 scale); and must be legal residents of Lancaster County, SC. **Criteria:** Applicants are evaluated based on financial need as determined by the costs of college attendance compared with applicants' household income and other financial factors; academic performance and achievement; and school and community involvement. Preference will be given to students with a career interest in the field of teaching.

Funds Avail.: No specific amount. **To Apply:** Applicants must submit completed application form; copy of the SAR from FAFSA; official transcript(s) of high school and/or college coursework and grades for at least the last two years, including SAT/ACT scores if taken; three recommendation forms (two from teachers or other school personnel and one from employer or other non-related adult); one to two-paged typed statement expressing reason for applying for the scholarship, qualifications and the educational and career goals. **Deadline:** April 13. **Contact:** Qiana Austin at qaustin@fftc.org.

4211 ■ Ben Robinette Scholarship Endowment Fund *(Undergraduate/Scholarship)*

Purpose: To assist graduates of high schools in Charlotte-Mecklenburg (public or private schools) to attend the University of North Carolina at Chapel Hill. **Focus:** General studies/Field of study not specified. **Qualif.:** Applicants must be graduating seniors at public or private high school in Charlotte-Mecklenburg with minimum of 3.0 grade point average on 4.0 scale. **Criteria:** Preference will be given to competitive runners who have been members of their high school track or cross country teams.

Funds Avail.: No specific amount. **To Apply:** Applicants must submit all the required application information. **Contact:** Qiana Austin at qaustin@fftc.org.

4212 ■ Rotary Public Safety Scholarships *(Undergraduate/Scholarship)*

Purpose: To provide financial assistance to the children of Mecklenburg County first responders. **Focus:** Public service. **Qualif.:** Applicants must be high school seniors intending to enter a two-year or four-year degree program with a minimum of 2.5 cumulative grade point average (on a 4.0 scale), whose mother or father are full time employees of the Charlotte Fire Department, Charlotte-Mecklenburg Police Department, Mecklenburg County Sheriff's Office or MEDIC with minimum of one year of service. **Criteria:** Recipients are selected based on academic performance; financial need; and record of good citizenship as evidenced by school and community involvement beyond required activities.

Funds Avail.: No specific amount. **To Apply:** Applicants must submit a completed application form; copy of SAR from FAFSA; official transcripts of academic coursework and grades for at least the last two years; four recommendation forms (two from instructors or other school administrators and two from employers or other non-related individuals in the Charlotte-Mecklenburg area); one to two-paged typed statement expressing reasons for applying for the scholarship, qualifications, and educational and career goals; and a copy of estimated expense budget for tuition, room and board, books, etc. at the school the applicant wants to attend. **Deadline:** March 29. **Contact:** Qiana Austin at qaustin@fftc.org.

4213 ■ Tacy Anna Smith Memorial Scholarships *(Undergraduate/Scholarship)*

Purpose: To provide financial support to seniors who are studying at Providence High School in Charlotte, NC. **Focus:** General studies/Field of study not specified. **Qualif.:** Applicants must be graduating seniors at Providence High School with a 2.5 minimum cumulative grade point average (on a 4.0 scale), planning to attend a four-year college or university. **Criteria:** Applicants are evaluated based on criteria designed by the Scholarship Committee.

Funds Avail.: No specific amount. **To Apply:** Applicants must submit all the required application information. **Contact:** Qiana Austin at qaustin@fftc.org.

4214 ■ The Spirit Square Center for Arts and Education Scholarship Fund *(Undergraduate/Scholarship)*

Purpose: To provide financial assistance for undergraduate students who can demonstrate aptitude and career potential in arts. **Focus:** General studies/Field of study not specified. **Qualif.:** Applicants must be college juniors or senior students in good academic standing who have demonstrated talent and with a declared major that indicates potential for a significant career contribution to arts. **Criteria:** Recipients are selected based on academic performance; school and community involvement and personal achievements; and commitment to and demonstrated potential for a career in arts. Preference will be given to students who are legal residents of Mecklenburg or contiguous counties in North or South Carolina and those who attend colleges and universities in North Carolina.

Funds Avail.: No specific amount. **To Apply:** Applicants must submit a completed application form; official transcript(s) of academic coursework and grades for at least the last two years; three recommendation forms, two of which must come from individuals who are able to evaluate the applicants' aptitude and career potential in arts; one to two pages typed statement expressing 1) reasons for applying for the scholarship, 2) interest in arts, 3) educational and career goals in arts; and 4) a copy of the estimated expense budget for tuition, room and board, books, etc. **Deadline:** March 16. **Contact:** Qiana Austin at qaustin@fftc.org.

4215 ■ Mary Stewart and William T. Covington, Jr. Scholarship Fund *(Undergraduate/Scholarship)*

Purpose: To provide financial support to students who graduated from a public high school. **Focus:** General studies/Field of study not specified. **Qualif.:** Applicants must be legal residents of Hoke County, NC; must have 2.75 minimum cumulative grade point average (on a 4.0 scale); and must attend a four-year college or university. **Criteria:** Applicants are evaluated based on the criteria designed by the Scholarship Selection Committee.

Funds Avail.: No specific amount. **To Apply:** Applicants must submit all the required application information and materials. **Contact:** Qiana Austin at qaustin@fftc.org.

4216 ■ Jack Tate/ThinkCOLLEGE Scholarship Fund *(Undergraduate/Scholarship)*

Purpose: To provide educational assistance to participants who attend Central Piedmont Community College. **Focus:** General studies/Field of study not specified. **Qualif.:** Applicants must achieve 90% of the benchmark goal for attendance set for their high school during their senior year (Charlotte-Mecklenburg School System sets individual school goals each year for attendance, academics and behavior, copies are available in the school offices); must have earned a minimum 2.5 cumulative grade point average (on a 4.0 scale) at the end of the first semester of senior year; must be graduating seniors at Communities In Schools site; and must have at least one full academic year of enrollment and participation in the ThinkCOLLEGE Program (upon graduation). **Criteria:** Recipients will be selected based on financial need; academic achievement; school and community involvement; and personal achievements.

Funds Avail.: No specific amount. **To Apply:** Applicants must submit a completed application form; official copy of high school transcript(s), including SAT/ACT scores; two recommendation forms (one from a teacher, counselor or other school administrator and one from an employer, community leader or other non-related adult); one to two-paged typed personal statement; and a copy of Student Aid Report from Free Application for Federal Student Aid (FAFSA). **Deadline:** April 12. **Contact:** Qiana Austin at qaustin@fftc.org.

4217 ■ Turner Family Scholarships *(Undergraduate, Vocational/Occupational/Scholarship)*

Purpose: To provide financial assistance for graduating high school seniors in Mecklenburg County intending to attend an accredited college or vocational school in Mecklenburg County. **Focus:** Education, Vocational-technical. **Qualif.:** Applicants must be graduating high school seniors who have a minimum cumulative grade point average of 2.5 (on a 4.0 scale); residing in Mecklenburg County, NC. Applicants must attend an accredited college or vocational school in Mecklenburg County, North Carolina. **Criteria:** Applicants are evaluated based on academic achievement including grade point average and performance on tests designed to measure preparation and ability for postsecondary study; involvement in extracurricular activities and leadership roles held; and record of community service and other personal achievements. Preference will be given to applicants who are children of National Welders Suppliers employees.

Funds Avail.: No specific amount. **To Apply:** Applicants must submit completed application form; copy of the Student Aid Report (SAR) from Free Application for Federal Student Aid (FAFSA); three recommendation forms (two from teachers or other school personnel and one from an employer or other non-related adult); one to two pages typed statement expressing reasons for applying for the scholarship, qualifications and educational/career goals; and a letter from an official of National Welders Supply Company, Inc. where the applicants' parents or legally appointed guardians are employed. **Contact:** Qiana Austin at qaustin@fftc.org.

4218 ■ The Sybil Jennings Vorheis Memorial Undergraduate Scholarships *(Undergraduate/Scholarship)*

Purpose: To assist North Iredell High School graduates in obtaining a degree in physical therapy, medicine or nursing from a post-secondary accredited institution. **Focus:** Medicine; Nursing; Physical therapy. **Qualif.:** Applicants must be graduating or have graduated from North Iredell High School with a minimum cumulative grade point average of 3.0 (on 4.0 scale). **Criteria:** Recipients are selected on the

Awards are arranged alphabetically below their administering organizations

basis of academic achievement; school and community involvement; and personal achievements.

Funds Avail.: No specific amount. **To Apply:** Applicants must submit completed application form; verification of acceptance into the accredited graduate program; official copy of college transcript; two recommendation forms and letters of recommendation; and a typewritten application statement of eligibility expressing applicant's educational and career goals, reasons for applying for the scholarship, and why the applicant feels they are a good candidate for the scholarship. **Deadline:** March 16. **Contact:** Qiana Austin at qaustin@fftc.org.

4219 ■ Laramie Walden Memorial Fund
(Undergraduate/Scholarship)

Purpose: To provide financial assistance to children of Charlotte, NC firefighters. **Focus:** General studies/Field of study not specified. **Qualif.:** Applicants must be seniors scheduled to graduate in the spring of the academic year; must have 3.5 minimum cumulative weighted grade point average (on a 4.0 scale) whose parent(s) are full-time employees of the Charlotte Fire Department with at least one year of service; and must participate in state-sanctioned school sport. **Criteria:** Applicants are evaluated based on academic merit and extracurricular involvement.

Funds Avail.: No specific amount. **Duration:** Annual. **To Apply:** Applicants must submit completed application form; official transcript(s) of academic coursework and grades for at least the last two years; three recommendation forms (two from instructor or other school administrator and one from a non-related adult in the Charlotte-Mecklenburg area such as an employer, coach, scout leader, etc.); and a one-paged typed statement expressing the reason for applying for the scholarship, qualifications, educational and career goals. **Deadline:** March 16. **Contact:** Qiana Austin at qaustin@fftc.org.

4220 ■ Fred C. Wikoff, Jr. Scholarships *(Undergraduate, Vocational/Occupational/Scholarship)*

Purpose: To provide educational support to students who are children of employees of Wikoff Color Corporation. **Focus:** General studies/Field of study not specified. **Qualif.:** Applicants must be children of employees (defined to include natural-born or legally-adopted dependent children and stepchildren and wards of employees). Parents or legally-appointed guardians of applicants must be full-time employees who have worked for Wikoff Color Corporation for at least two years prior to the application deadline. Applicants enrolled in high school at the time of application must have a minimum cumulative grade point average 2.5 (on a 4.0 scale). Applicants enrolled in college at the time of application must have a minimum cumulative grade point average of 2.0 (on a 4.0 scale). Applicant's age must not be over 25 as of the application deadline but a student over the age of 25 will be considered on a case to case basis if the student is permanently disabled or has some other special circumstance that requires him or her to be financially dependent upon their parents. **Criteria:** Applicants are evaluated based on academic achievement; school and community involvement and personal achievements; and financial need.

Funds Avail.: No specific amount. **To Apply:** Applicants must submit a completed application form; copy of SAR from FAFSA; official transcript(s) of high school and/or college coursework and grades for at least the last two years, including SAT/ACT scores if taken; three recommendation forms (two from teachers or other school personnel and one from an employer or other non-related adult); one to two-page typed statement expressing the reason for applying for the scholarship, qualifications and educational and career goals; and a letter from an official of Wikoff Color Corporation where parents or legally appointed guardians are employed. **Deadline:** March 16. **Contact:** Qiana Austin at qaustin@fftc.org.

4221 ■ Harriet Glen Wilmore Scholarship
(Undergraduate, Vocational/Occupational/Scholarship)

Purpose: To provide financial assistance to residents who are intending to attend college or vocational school. **Focus:** Education, Vocational-technical. **Qualif.:** Applicants must be residents of the Wilmore Neighborhood which is defined by Summit Avenue on the north, Interstate 77 on the west, South Tryon Street on the east and Wilmore Drive on the south; must have lived in Wilmore Neighborhood for at least one year (12 months) prior to the application deadline; and must have a minimum cumulative grade point average of 2.0 (on a 4.0 scale) for the last completed years of education. **Criteria:** Applicants are judged based on academic achievement; financial need; and leadership potential evidenced by school and/or community involvement. Preference will be given to applicants who are current high school seniors.

Funds Avail.: No specific amount. **To Apply:** Applicants must submit a completed application form; official transcript(s) of high school and/or college coursework and grades for at least the last two years attended, including SAT/ACT score reports if taken; one recommendation form from a teacher, other school personnel or employer; one to two page personal statement expressing the applicants' educational and career goals and financial need for scholarship assistance; and a copy of the Student Aid Report (SAR) from Free Application for Federal Student Aid (FAFSA). **Deadline:** May 2. **Contact:** Qiana Austin at qaustin@fftc.org.

4222 ■ Mary and Elliot Wood Foundation Graduate Scholarship Fund *(Graduate/Scholarship)*

Purpose: To further the knowledge of the scholars for their careers that will contribute to the Goals of the Foundation. **Focus:** Ecology; Economics; Education; Environmental science; Government; Humanities; Nutrition; Peace studies. **Qualif.:** Applicants must have been chosen as recipients or finalists for MEWF undergraduate scholarships; must commit a course of graduate study and an eventual career that will contribute to the goals of the foundation; must maintain a full-time enrollment (nine semester hours) for which the scholarship is paid. Applicants must specify in the application, the graduate school and the degree to be earned. **Criteria:** Applicants are evaluated on the basis of academic achievement, extracurricular activities and statement of personal goals and references.

Funds Avail.: No specific amount. **To Apply:** Applicants must submit a completed application form, curriculum vitae, personal statement, letters of recommendation and official transcripts in a sealed envelope. **Deadline:** April 18.

4223 ■ Mary and Elliot Wood Foundation Undergraduate Scholarship Fund *(Undergraduate/Scholarship)*

Purpose: To provide financial support for the most gifted future leaders who have the capability, desire, energy, enthusiasm and determination to improve our civilization and to enhance the quality of all life cultural, civic, and ecological. **Focus:** General studies/Field of study not specified. **Qualif.:** Applicants must be students graduating from high schools in the districts in Guilford County, Davidson County, Randolph County, Moore County; must have a GPA of atleast 4.0 and 1800 on SAT total scores. **Criteria:** Applicants are evaluated based on personal character; leadership potential; and scholastic achievement.

Funds Avail.: No specific amount. **Duration:** Annual. **To Apply:** Applicants must submit completed application form and all other required materials for the scholarship. **Contact:** Qiana Austin at qaustin@fftc.org.

4224 ■ Foundation for Community Association Research
6402 Arlington Blvd., Ste. 500
Falls Church, VA 22042
Ph: (703)970-9220
Fax: (703)970-9558
Free: 888-224-4321
E-mail: foundation@caionline.org
URL: www.cairf.org

4225 ■ Byron Hanke Fellowships (Doctorate, Graduate, Undergraduate/Fellowship)

Purpose: To promote positive charge for all stakeholders who live in homeowner associations by discovering future trends and opportunities; to support and conduct research; to facilitate and promote cooperation among industry partners and provide resources that help educate the public. **Focus:** General studies/Field of study not specified. **Qualif.:** Applicants must be enrolled in an accredited master's, doctoral or law program in United States of America or Canada. Students in all discipline are welcome to apply provided their research projects or studies are related to community associations. **Criteria:** Recipients are selected based on academic achievements; faculty recommendations; research and writing ability; and the nature of the proposed topic and its benefit to the study and understanding of community associations.

Funds Avail.: $3,000-$5000. **To Apply:** Applicants must submit a completed application form and research proposal. **Deadline:** May 1.

4226 ■ Foundation for Contemporary Arts (FCA)
820 Greenwich St.
New York, NY 10014
Ph: (212)807-7077
Fax: (212)807-7177
E-mail: info@contemporary-arts.org
URL: www.foundationforcontemporaryarts.org

4227 ■ FCA Grants to Artists (Advanced Professional/Grant)

Purpose: To provide recipients with the financial means to engage in whatever artistic endeavors they wish to pursue, to research and develop ideas, embark on projects, and complete projects already under way. **Focus:** Dance; Music; Performing arts; Poetry; Visual arts. **Qualif.:** Candidates must be artists working in any of the following areas: dance, music/sound, theater/performance art, poetry and the visual arts. **Criteria:** Selection will be based on merit and imaginativeness of their work and the effect such recognitions and support might have at this point in their careers.

Funds Avail.: No specific amount. **Duration:** Annual. **To Apply:** The FCA invites distinguished artists and arts professionals to serve as nominators and propose one exceptional individual, collective or performing group whom they feel deserves and will benefit from an award.

4228 ■ Foundation for Educational Exchange between Canada and the United States of America
350 Albert St., Ste. 2015
Ottawa, ON, Canada K1R 1A4
Ph: (613)688-5540
Fax: (613)237-2029
URL: www.fulbright.ca

4229 ■ Killam Fellowships (Undergraduate/Fellowship)

Purpose: To provide an opportunity for exceptional undergraduate students from universities in the United States to spend either one semester or a full academic year as an exchange student in Canada. **Focus:** General studies/Field of study not specified. **Qualif.:** Applicants must be citizens of Canada or the United States who are also full-time undergraduate students in good standing at a degree-granting institution in Canada or the United States. They must also: meet the eligibility requirements of their home university; be fluent in English; have a superior academic record; complete all the steps of the application process prior to the published deadlines, and, in the case of the direct exchange applicant; and, be nominated by their respective universities to receive a Killam Fellowship. **Criteria:** Selection is open and competitive, based on a combination of academic standing, personal statement, and letters of reference. Applications will be reviewed by an independent adjudication committee comprised of faculty members from Canadian and American universities.

Funds Avail.: $10,000. **Duration:** Annual. **To Apply:** Applications and instructions can be obtained online. **Deadline:** January 31.

4230 ■ Foundation for Enhancing Communities
200 N 3rd St.
Harrisburg, PA 17108-0678
Ph: (717)236-5040
Fax: (717)231-4463
E-mail: info@tfec.org
URL: www.tfec.org

4231 ■ G. Thomas Balsbaugh Memorial Scholarship Fund (Undergraduate/Scholarship)

Purpose: To provide financial assistance for a Dauphin County high school senior planning to attend a four-year college or university. **Focus:** General studies/Field of study not specified. **Qualif.:** Applicants must be high school seniors from Dauphin County planning to attend a four-year college or university; must be legal residents of Dauphin County; have high academic standing and achievement; must exemplify good character; must exhibit a variety of interests and activities in both academic and personal life; and must demonstrate financial need. **Criteria:** Recipients will be selected based in demonstrated good character; interest and activities in both academic and personal life; and financial need.

Funds Avail.: Up to $1,000. **Number Awarded:** 1. **To Apply:** Application for the scholarship should include: student

Awards are arranged alphabetically below their administering organizations

resume; official academic transcript issued by school; completed personal information; completed financial statement; and personal statement (300 words maximum, typewritten, 12 pt. font, double spaced) describing current interests and activities as well as future goals and ambitions; FAFSA Student Aid Report Form; and two personal reference letters. One letter should come from a high school teacher. **Deadline:** April 1. **Contact:** Faith Elmes, Scholarship Associate; Phone: 717-236-5040; Email: felmes@tfec.org.

4232 ■ Robbie Barron Memorial Scholarships *(Undergraduate/Scholarship)*

Purpose: To provide financial support for a graduating senior of Cedar Cliff High School who attended Hillside Elementary School. **Focus:** General studies/Field of study not specified. **Qualif.:** Applicant must be a graduating senior at Cedar Cliff High School and have attended Hillside Elementary. **Criteria:** Scholarship will be given based on the following: academic achievement; extracurricular activities; services to the community; an essay which identifies the applicant's opinion on values and youth leadership; and financial need.

Funds Avail.: Amount varies. **Number Awarded:** 1. **To Apply:** Applicant may download the application at the TFEC web site. Applicant must submit the following required attachments: completed student application; high school transcript; completed student essay (question attached); and one personal reference letter. Applicants may return their completed application to the High School Guidance Office. **Deadline:** April 1. **Remarks:** Established in 1996. **Contact:** Faith Elmes, Scholarship Associate; Phone: 717-236-5040; Email: felmes@tfec.org.

4233 ■ Friends of Megan Bolton Memorial Fund *(Undergraduate/Scholarship)*

Purpose: To assist students with their college expenses. **Focus:** General studies/Field of study not specified. **Qualif.:** Applicants must be graduating high school seniors of Camp Hill High School; must have high academic standing and achievement; and must exemplify good character. **Criteria:** Selection will be based on: financial need; high academic standing and achievement; leadership; and character.

Funds Avail.: $1,000. **Number Awarded:** Varies. **To Apply:** Application form can be obtained online. Applicants must submit an official school transcript of their complete high school records including GPA, through the first half of final year, on which the raised school seal is imprinted. Students should indicate evidence of meaningful leadership and positive character traits, volunteer work or involvement in community or church activities/charities that contribute to the betterment of that community or organization. Submit a resume if available, though not required, and a reference letter written by one of the contacts from the resume. Students are also asked to submit an essay (300 words or less) describing their idea of friendship and the significance of having close friends in their lives. **Deadline:** April 1. **Contact:** Faith Elmes, Scholarship Associate; Phone: 717-236-5040; Email: felmes@tfec.org.

4234 ■ Chambersburg/Fannett-Metal School District Scholarship Fund *(Undergraduate/Scholarship)*

Purpose: To provide educational assistance to students of Chambersburg High School and Fannett-Metal High School. **Focus:** Computer and information sciences; Engineering, Computer. **Qualif.:** Applicants must be graduating students from Chambersburg Area High School and Fanett-Metal High School; have a desire to pursue a career in computer engineering or computer science; and must have an academic achievement of a cumulative GPA of 2.0 or higher on a 4.0 scale. **Criteria:** Selection will be based on financial need; submitted essay; academic achievement; extracurricular activities; volunteer services to the community; and demonstrated financial need.

Funds Avail.: Amount varies. **Number Awarded:** 2. **To Apply:** Applicants must submit a completed scholarship application form; a high school transcript with GPA; completed personal essay identifying their interest in computer science and/or computer engineering including professional goals; FAFSA Student Aid Report; and two letters of recommendation from a teacher and the other one must be from an employer or a supervisor of a community service volunteer agency. Letters from family members will not be accepted. **Deadline:** April 1. **Contact:** Faith Elmes, Scholarship Associate; Phone: 717-236-5040; Email: felmes@tfec.org.

4235 ■ CODY Foundation Fund *(Undergraduate/Scholarship)*

Purpose: To promote Christian initiatives through education and athletics. **Focus:** General studies/Field of study not specified. **Qualif.:** Applicants must be graduating high school senior students from Greenwood High School, Susquenita High School, West Perry High School or Newport High School. **Criteria:** Selection will be based on the following: GPA (academic achievements); community involvement; recommendation letters (one from a teacher, the other from an employer, supervisor, or community advisor); completed essay; high moral character (must attend and/or be involved in church activities); and financial need.

Funds Avail.: $500. **Number Awarded:** 2. **To Apply:** Applicants must complete the required attachments: completed application; official high school transcript; FAFSA student aid report; completed student essay; and two personal reference letters. To the persons writing the reference letters should list the applicant's leadership attributes and examples where they demonstrate their faith or belief system. **Deadline:** April 1. **Contact:** Faith Elmes, Scholarship Associate; Phone: 717-236-5040; Email: felmes@tfec.org.

4236 ■ Jan DiMartino Delany Memorial Scholarships *(Undergraduate/Scholarship)*

Purpose: To assist students with their college tuition expenses. **Focus:** General studies/Field of study not specified. **Qualif.:** Applicant must be a graduating senior of Cumberland Valley High School who will attend a two or four-year institution of higher learning. **Criteria:** Selection criteria will be based on financial need; scholastic ability; leadership abilities within the school or community; community service; essay; and personal challenges that have been overcome. Preference will be given to those applicants who are graduating seniors of Cumberland Valley High School.

Funds Avail.: $2,000. **Number Awarded:** 1. **To Apply:** Applicant must complete and submit the application to the Cumberland Valley High School Guidance Office. Include an official transcript of complete high school records with GPA, through the first half of final year on which the raised school seal is imprinted. On a separate sheet of paper, applicant must list his/ her most significant extracurricular or non-academic activities, noting work experience and community service with the dates of these activities; completed personal essay explaining how you have overcome per-

Awards are arranged alphabetically below their administering organizations

sonal challenges. **Deadline:** April 1. **Contact:** Faith Elmes, Scholarship Associate; Phone: 717-236-5040; Email: felmes@tfec.org.

4237 ■ Lou Drane Music Scholarships
(Undergraduate/Scholarship)

Purpose: To provide educational assistance to deserving music students in the areas of classical music composition, teaching, and/or performance. **Focus:** Music, Classical. **Qualif.:** Applicant must have a serious interest in classical music and display unusual ability and/or creativity; must apply for financial aid from the school he/she plans to attend; must attend an accredited post-secondary institution of higher learning or have been accepted and plan to attend same; be a citizen of the United States and must maintain a permanent residence on one of the following counties in central Pennsylvania: Adams, Cumberland; Dauphin, Franklin, Fulton, Juniata, Lancaster, Lebanon, Montour, Northumberland, Perry, Snyder or York. **Criteria:** Recipients will be selected based on technical quality of their recording. **Funds Avail.:** Up to $5,000. **Number Awarded:** Varies. **To Apply:** Applicant must attach FAFSA Student Aid Report and a letter detailing applicant's financial need; and must submit, along with the application, an example of their ability, in one of the following fields: Composition or composition-teaching - a CD not to exceed 20 minutes in length - and a written music score - of two separate works of you own composition. Identify yourself, your instrument and title at the beginning of the tape. Label the recording with this information also. Audition recordings of original compositions must be of live performances. MIDI and other electronic performances are not accepted. For applications in Performance or performance-teaching submit a CD, not to exceed 20 minutes in length, of two separate works reflecting a variety of style. Identify yourself, your instrument and title at the beginning of the recording. Label the tape with this information also. All instruments with the exception of piano and classical guitar must be accompanied, but avoid lengthy introductions by accompaniment. **Deadline:** March 30. **Contact:** Faith Elmes, Scholarship Associate; Phone: 717-236-5040; Email: felmes@tfec.org.

4238 ■ Sue and Ken Dyer Foundation Travel Scholarships *(Undergraduate/Scholarship)*

Purpose: To assist students with travel expenses for educational or service trips. **Focus:** Travel and tourism. **Qualif.:** Applicants must be junior or senior students enrolled at one of the following schools: Cedar Cliff, Camp Hill, Mechanicsburg, Trinity or the Harrisburg Academy. **Criteria:** Selection criteria include purpose of the travel (must be for educational purposes or service) ; financial need; character of the applicants and information provided by the written references. **Funds Avail.:** $2,000. **Number Awarded:** Varies. **To Apply:** Applicants must complete and return the application and required attachments to the Foundation. Required attachments include: scholastic record and extracurricular activities; an essay on the topic: "The purpose of my proposed trip and what I expect to gain from this experience". Essay should be titled, type-written, double-spaced and maximum of 300 words; two reference letters from individuals who can speak to the quality of your character, your academic prowess and/or your likelihood of utilizing the proposed travel experience as a tool for personal growth; also include financial information. **Deadline:** April 1. **Contact:** Faith Elmes, Scholarship Associate; Phone: 717-236-5040; Email: felmes@tfec.org.

4239 ■ Family and Children's Services of Lebanon County Fund *(Undergraduate/Scholarship)*

Purpose: To provide financial assistance to Lebanon County residents who are pursuing higher education degrees. **Focus:** Medicine; Mental health; Nursing; Social work. **Qualif.:** Applicants must be enrolled full-time in schools of advanced education in the fields of medicine, nursing, social work, mental health and other specialized therapies in the treatment of physical and mental disabilities; must demonstrate financial need, academic aptitude and achievement, and commitment to a career in human services; and must be residents of Lebanon County. **Criteria:** Applicants will be judged based on financial need, academic aptitude and achievement, and commitment to a career in human services. **Funds Avail.:** Amount varies. **Number Awarded:** Varies. **To Apply:** Applicants may obtain the application online. Applicants must provide the most recent, either a certified high school transcript or a certified college transcript; (300-word) essay. It should be typewritten, 12 pt. font and double-spaced; and one personal reference letter who can attest their commitment in human services career. **Deadline:** March 30. **Contact:** Faith Elmes, Scholarship Associate; Phone: 717-236-5040; Email: felmes@tfec.org.

4240 ■ Adrienne Zoe Fedok Art and Music Scholarships *(Undergraduate/Scholarship)*

Purpose: To provide financial support to students of either Central Dauphin High School or Central Dauphin East High School. **Focus:** Art; Music. **Qualif.:** Applicant must be from either Central Dauphin High School or Central Dauphin East High School entering his or her freshman year in post-secondary education in the field of Art and Music. **Criteria:** Selection will be based on the following criteria: interest in art and/or music education; financial need; SAT scores; GPA; demonstrated leadership and community service; and personal essay on the applicant's educational and career goals. **Funds Avail.:** $1,000. **Number Awarded:** 1. **To Apply:** Application and the required attachments must be completed and postmarked on or before the deadline. Required attachments include: completed application; high school transcript including GPA; SAT scores; FAFSA Student Aid Report Form (Financial Aid Form); two letters of recommendation (one from a faculty member in the art or music department); a list of extra-curricular activities demonstrating leadership and community service; and personal essay on the applicant's educational and career goals. **Deadline:** April 1. **Contact:** Faith Elmes, Scholarship Associate; Phone: 717-236-5040; Email: felmes@tfec.org.

4241 ■ Norma Gotwalt Scholarship Fund *(Undergraduate/Scholarship)*

Purpose: To provide financial assistance to students for their college tuition expenses. **Focus:** Education, Elementary. **Qualif.:** Applicants must be female junior or senior students studying Elementary Education at the Penn State Capital College and who have maintained a minimum of 3.25 cumulative GPA while at Capital College. **Criteria:** Recipients will be selected based on financial need; community service; submitted essay; and career goals. **Funds Avail.:** $3,000. **Number Awarded:** 1. **To Apply:** Applicants must complete the application form; must submit an official transcript of post-secondary academic records; FAFSA Student Aid Report Form; (300-word) personal es-

Awards are arranged alphabetically below their administering organizations

say; and a written recommendation from a professor who can assess the potential ability as an elementary school teacher. **Deadline:** March 15. **Contact:** Faith Elmes, Scholarship Associate; Phone: 717-236-5040; Email: felmes@tfec.org.

4242 ■ Roberta L. Houpt Scholarship Fund
(Undergraduate/Scholarship)

Purpose: To provide financial support to students who are studying nursing at college or university. **Focus:** Nursing. **Qualif.:** Applicants must be nursing undergraduate students and residents of Dauphin, Cumberland or Perry Counties. **Criteria:** Selection will be based on the following criteria: desire to pursue a career in nursing; academic achievement; extracurricular activities; services to the community; an essay which identifies the applicant's interest in nursing; and financial need.

Funds Avail.: $2,000. **Duration:** Annual. **Number Awarded:** Varies. **To Apply:** Application and the required attachments must be completed and postmarked on or before the deadline. Required attachments include: completed student background sheet; high school transcript or college transcript; letter of acceptance in nursing program or college transcript showing enrollment in program; FAFSA student aid report form (financial aid form); completed essay (question attached); and two personal reference letters (one letter should be from a science teacher and the other letter should be from an individual who can speak to applicant's ability to successfully complete studies), such as a teacher, employer, or mentor. Application form can be obtained online. **Deadline:** April 1. **Remarks:** Established in 1998. **Contact:** Faith Elmes, Scholarship Associate; Phone: 717-236-5040; Email: felmes@tfec.org.

4243 ■ Carol Hoy Scholarship Fund *(Undergraduate/Scholarship)*

Purpose: To provide educational support to students who are pursuing a career in early childhood education. **Focus:** Education, Early childhood; Education, Elementary. **Qualif.:** Applicants must be graduating seniors from Mechanicsburg Area High School; must have desire to pursue a career in elementary education or early childhood education. **Criteria:** Selection will be based on the following criteria: academic achievements; leadership and community service; one or two paragraph essay; personal interview; and financial need.

Funds Avail.: No specific amount. **Duration:** Annual. **Number Awarded:** 1. **To Apply:** Application and the required attachments must be completed and postmarked on or before the deadline. The required attachments include: completed student background sheet; high school transcript; FAFSA student aid report form (financial aid form); completed student essay; resume including leadership and community service; and two personal reference letters. One letter should be from a teacher and the other letter should be from an individual who can speak to applicant's ability to successfully complete studies, such as a teacher, employer, or mentor. Application form can be obtained online. **Deadline:** April 1. **Remarks:** Established in 2006. **Contact:** Faith Elmes, Scholarship Associate; Phone: 717-236-5040; Email: felmes@tfec.org.

4244 ■ Erin L. Jenkins Memorial Scholarship Fund
(Undergraduate/Scholarship)

Purpose: To provide educational support to deserving students attending Cumberland Valley High School. **Focus:** General studies/Field of study not specified. **Qualif.:** Applicants must reside in the area defined by the Cumberland Valley School District or its successor; must have desire to a career in elementary education or early childhood education. **Criteria:** Recipients will be selected based on financial need; academic achievement; community service; and essay.

Funds Avail.: $1,500. **Number Awarded:** 1. **To Apply:** Applicants must complete and return the application and attachments to the Foundation. Students must also submit the following: official school transcript; two recommendations; FAFSA Student Aid Report Form; and (300-word) personal essay. **Deadline:** April 1. **Contact:** Faith Elmes, Scholarship Associate; Phone: 717-236-5040; Email: felmes@tfec.org.

4245 ■ Ken and Romaine Kauffman Scholarship Fund *(Undergraduate/Scholarship)*

Purpose: To provide assistance to students with their college tuitions expenses. **Focus:** Automotive technology. **Qualif.:** Applicants must be residents of Cumberland Perry Counties pursuing a degree in the mechanical or technical field; must be graduating seniors of Cumberland Valley High School or Cumberland-Perry Vo-Tech planning to attend a four-year college, university, technical school or community college. **Criteria:** Selection will be based on the committee's criteria. Preference will be given to students studying an automotive technology.

Funds Avail.: $500. **Duration:** Annual. **Number Awarded:** 1. **To Apply:** Applicants must complete the application form; must submit an official transcript including GPA; FAFSA Student Aid Report Form; and one personal reference letter from an individual such as teacher, employer or mentor. **Deadline:** April 1. **Contact:** Faith Elmes, Scholarship Associate; Phone: 717-236-5040; Email: felmes@tfec.org.

4246 ■ Leon I. Lock and Barbara R. Lock Scholarship Fund *(Undergraduate/Scholarship)*

Purpose: To provide assistance to students with their college tuitions expenses. **Focus:** Automotive technology. **Qualif.:** Applicants must be graduating seniors in any high school in the Harrisburg School District (including Bishop McDevitt High School) who will attend Harrisburg Area Community College, or Penn State, or students who have graduated from one of the two high schools in no more than five years before the year of application; must have minimum GPA of 2.5 on a 4.0 scale; must be enrolled in an automotive technology either at HACC or Penn State. **Criteria:** Recipients will be selected based on financial need; academic achievements; demonstrated work and study ethic from an employer or volunteer group supervisors; and impact of essay. Preference will be given to those students enrolled at Harrisburg Area Community College in an automotive technology field.

Funds Avail.: $500. **Number Awarded:** Varies. **To Apply:** Applicants must complete the application form; must submit an official transcript including GPA; FAFSA Student Aid Report; reference letter from an employer or a volunteer group about how students demonstrate a good work or study ethic; and maximum of 300 words essay explaining the choice of the course undertaken. Essay should be in 12-point font and double-spaced. **Deadline:** April 1. **Contact:** Faith Elmes, Scholarship Associate; Phone: 717-236-5040; Email: felmes@tfec.org.

4247 ■ Carie and George Lyter Scholarship Fund
(Undergraduate/Scholarship)

Purpose: To provide educational assistance for students attending Greenwood High School, Newport High School,

Awards are arranged alphabetically below their administering organizations

Susquenita High School and West Perry High School. **Focus:** Education, Elementary; Mathematics and mathematical sciences; Science. **Qualif.:** Applicants must be Graduate of Greenwood High School, Newport High School, Susquenita High School or West Perry High School and have a desire to pursue a career in elementary or middle school education with emphasis in science or mathematics; an academic achievement of a cumulative GPA of 2.5 to 3.0 on a 4.0 scale in their junior/senior year; demonstrated talent for leadership; a high moral character (must have attended and be involved in church activities); and must demonstrate financial need. **Criteria:** Selection will be based on the committee's criteria. **Funds Avail.:** Amount varies. **Number Awarded:** 1. **To Apply:** Applicants must submit the following required attachments: completed student background sheet; official high school transcript with raised school seal; FAFSA student aid report; completed student 300-word essay identifying their interest in Elementary or Middle School Education with an emphasis in science and mathematics (include professional goals); and two personal reference letters. One letter should be from a teacher and the other letter should be from an employer or a supervisor of a community service volunteer agency. Letters of reference may not be from a family member. **Deadline:** April 1. **Remarks:** Established in 2002. **Contact:** Faith Elmes, Scholarship Associate; Phone: 717-236-5040; Email: felmes@tfec.org.

4248 ■ Sam Mizrahi Memorial Scholarships
(Undergraduate/Scholarship)

Purpose: To assist students with their college tuition expenses. **Focus:** General studies/Field of study not specified. **Qualif.:** Applicants must be students from Northern York High School who plan to attend a two or four-year college, university or trade school; must demonstrate financial need; must have a minimum 2.5 GPA; and must have a high moral character. **Criteria:** Recipients will be selected based on financial need; leadership/community service; character; and personal essay. **Funds Avail.:** $1,000. **Number Awarded:** Varies. **To Apply:** Applicants must complete the attached form and any other requested supporting documents and return on or before the deadline to the guidance counselor at Northern York High School. Applicants must include an official transcript of complete high school records including GPA, through first half of final year, on which the raised school seal is imprinted. On a separate sheet of paper, list the most significant extracurricular or nonacademic activities, noting work experience and community service with the dates of these activities. Applicants must also write a one to two-page essay on the subject "My biggest life challenge and what I learned from the experience". **Deadline:** April 16. **Contact:** Faith Elmes, Scholarship Associate; Phone: 717-236-5040; Email: felmes@tfec.org.

4249 ■ Leo F. Moro Baseball Memorial Scholarships
(Undergraduate/Scholarship)

Purpose: To assist students with their college tuition expenses. **Focus:** General studies/Field of study not specified. **Qualif.:** Applicants must be graduating senior students of Malden High School or Malden Catholic High School in Malden, Massachusetts who will attend a two or four-year college or university; must have accomplishments in baseball at the high school level and have plan to continue a baseball career in college; and must have success in the sport of baseball. **Criteria:** Recipients will be selected based on financial need; leadership ability; academic achievement based on GPA and SAT scores; and sportsmanship. **Funds Avail.:** Amount varies. **Number Awarded:** Varies. **To Apply:** Applicants must complete and return the attached form and other requested supporting documents to the foundation. Applicants must include an official transcript of complete high school records including GPA, through the first half of final year, on which the raised school seal is imprinted. On a separate sheet of paper, list the most significant extracurricular or no-academic activities, noting work experience and community service with the dates of these activities. Please include a photocopy of your FAFSA with your completed scholarship application; and must attach a baseball information sheet. Application form can be obtained online. **Deadline:** May 31. **Contact:** Faith Elmes, Scholarship Associate; Phone: 717-236-5040; Email: felmes@tfec.org.

4250 ■ Dr. Harry V. Pfautz Memorial Scholarship Fund *(Undergraduate/Scholarship)*

Purpose: To assist Susquenita High School students with their college expenses in the field of Forestry and/or Agriculture with an emphasis in forestry. **Focus:** Forestry. **Qualif.:** Applicants must be graduating senior students of Susquenita High School who have a GPA of 2.5 on a 4.0 point scale. **Criteria:** Selection will be based on financial need, community involvement and work ethic, scholastic performance and student essay. **Funds Avail.:** Amount varies. **Number Awarded:** 1. **To Apply:** Applicants must complete the attached form and requested supporting documents and send to the foundation. The supporting documents include: official transcript of the complete high school records including GPA, through the first half of final year, on which the raised school seal is imprinted; FAFSA Student Aid Report Form; completed personal essay explaining the reasons of choosing the Forestry as a career path and description of educational plans in achieving goals; and two personal reference letters from a teacher. Letters from family members will not be accepted. References should be sealed in an envelope. **Deadline:** April 1. **Contact:** Faith Elmes, Scholarship Associate; Phone: 717-236-5040; Email: felmes@tfec.org.

4251 ■ Ruth Cook Pfautz Memorial Scholarship Fund *(Undergraduate/Scholarship)*

Purpose: To assist Susquenita High School students with their college expenses in the field of Elementary Education. **Focus:** Education, Elementary. **Qualif.:** Applicants must be graduating senior students of Susquenita High School who have a GPA of 2.5 on a 4.0 point scale; plans to study early elementary education. **Criteria:** Selection will be based on financial need, community service, leadership qualities and career plans. **Funds Avail.:** Amount varies. **Number Awarded:** 1. **To Apply:** Application form can be obtained online. Applicants must complete the attached form and requested supporting documents and send to the Foundation. The supporting documents include: official transcript of the complete high school record, including GPA, through the first half of final year, on which the raised school seal is imprinted; list of extracurricular or non-academic activities; reference letter; and a 300-word student essay explaining why they have chosen Elementary Education as a career path and describing their educational plans to achieve their career goal. **Deadline:** April 1. **Contact:** Faith Elmes, Scholarship Associate; Phone: 717-236-5040; Email: felmes@tfec.org.

4252 ■ Bertha and Byron L. Reppert Scholarship Fund *(Undergraduate/Scholarship)*

Purpose: To encourage and recognize two senior students from the Mechanicsburg Area School District who demonstrate good citizenship. **Focus:** Horticulture; Political science. **Qualif.:** Applicants must have an interest in political science or horticulture; must be in the top one-third of the graduating class; must be accepted to an accredited college or university; must demonstrate good citizenship within the school and local community; and must complete an essay explaining how they meet the criteria. **Criteria:** Selection will be based on the committee's criteria.

Funds Avail.: Amount varies. **Number Awarded:** 2 (1 male; 1 female). **To Apply:** Application form can be obtained online. Applicants must attach the following documents: official transcript of the complete high school/college records including GPA, through the first half of the present year, with the raised school seal imprinted; list of extracurricular or non-academic activities; FAFSA Student Aid Report; and an essay describing how they meet the eligibility criteria of this scholarship. **Deadline:** April 1. **Remarks:** Established in 2001. **Contact:** Faith Elmes, Scholarship Associate; Phone: 717-236-5040; Email: felmes@tfec.org.

4253 ■ Ollie Rosenberg Educational Trust *(Undergraduate/Scholarship)*

Purpose: To assist students with business, technical or trade school tuition expenses. **Focus:** General studies/Field of study not specified. **Qualif.:** Applicants must be students who are graduating seniors from Harrisburg High School, Sci-Tech High, Bishop McDevitt, or Dauphin County Technical school are eligible to apply; must attend a state supported school in Pennsylvania; must have a job; must have a Pennsylvania student loan; and must demonstrate financial need. **Criteria:** Selection will be based on the committee's criteria; extracurricular and/or non-academic activities; completed personal essay; and financial need.

Funds Avail.: Amount varies. **Number Awarded:** Varies. **To Apply:** Applicants must complete and submit the application and required documents to the Foundation. Required documents include official transcript of the complete high school records including GPA, through first half of final year, on which the raised school seal is imprinted, and a 300-word essay explaining how applicant has overcome the challenges in life and how he or she will apply these lessons to his or her vocation. Applicants must list their most significant extracurricular or non-academic activities, emphasizing work experience and community volunteer service. Scholarships require a copy of SAR to be included in application. Applications missing the SAR will not be considered. **Deadline:** April 1. **Contact:** Application form and supporting documents should be submitted to: The Foundation for Enhancing Communities, The Ollie Rosenberg Scholarship Fund, Attn: Allison Moesta, Program Associate for Educational Enhancement, 200 N. 3rd Street, 8th Floor, PO Box 678, Harrisburg, PA 17108-0678; Phone: 717-236-5040; Email: felmes@tfec.org.

4254 ■ J. Ward Sleichter and Frances F. Sleichter Memorial Scholarship Fund *(Undergraduate/Scholarship)*

Purpose: To provide aid for needy and deserving students who otherwise would not have the financial means to obtain a four-year college education. **Focus:** General studies/Field of study not specified. **Qualif.:** Applicants must be full-time students who maintain a "B" or 2.5 grade point average or equivalent; must reside in the area defined by the Shippensburg Area School District, or its successor; and must have plan to attend a four-year college or university. **Criteria:** Recipients will be selected based on financial need; and demonstrated motivation, character, ability and potential.

Funds Avail.: Up to $5,000. **Duration:** Up to 4 years. **Number Awarded:** 1. **To Apply:** Applicants must complete the following required attachments: application; official school transcript; two recommendations (one from the student's guidance counselor and one from a teacher who can discuss the student's personal characteristics such as motivation, character, ability and potential); and FAFSA Student Aid Report (make sure to include the cover letter of the report, which will indicate the student's Estimated Family contribution). **Deadline:** April 1. **Contact:** Faith Elmes, Scholarship Associate; Phone: 717-236-5040; Email: felmes@tfec.org.

4255 ■ Soroptimist International of Chambersburg Scholarship Fund *(Undergraduate/Scholarship)*

Purpose: To provide assistance for female seniors of Chambersburg Area Senior High School. **Focus:** General studies/Field of study not specified. **Qualif.:** Applicants must be female senior students of Chambersburg Area High School; and must be accepted at an accredited college or university at the time the awards are made. **Criteria:** Selection will be based on academic performance; citizenship; interest and aptitude; leadership qualities; responsibility; enthusiasm; motivation to learn and improve; attitude and cooperative spirit; dependability; financial need; and recommendations from a teacher and also a counselor.

Funds Avail.: Amount varies. **Number Awarded:** 1. **To Apply:** Applicants must complete the required attachments. Required attachments include: application; two letters of recommendation (one from your guidance counselor, containing your GPA, course of study and general character assessment and the other from one of your teacher containing a general character assessment of you as a person and a student); FAFSA Student Aid Report; a paragraph of approximately 150 words answering the question "Why I Have Chosen to Continue My Education". **Deadline:** April 1. **Contact:** Faith Elmes, Scholarship Associate; Phone: 717-236-5040; Email: felmes@tfec.org.

4256 ■ Joseph L. and Vivian E. Steele Music Scholarship Fund *(Undergraduate/Scholarship)*

Purpose: To assist needy students of classical music in the fields of composition, teaching and performance. **Focus:** Music. **Qualif.:** Applicants must have a serious interest in classical music and display unusual ability and/or creativity; must apply for financial aid from the school they plan to attend; must attend an accredited post-secondary institution of higher learning or have been accepted and plan to attend same; must be citizens of the United States and must maintain permanent residence in one of the following counties in central Pennsylvania: Adams, Cumberland, Dauphin, Franklin, Fulton, Juniata, Lancaster, Lebanon, Montour, Northumberland, Perry, Snyder or York. **Criteria:** Recipients will be selected based on financial need and technical quality of recording.

Funds Avail.: Up to $5,000 each. **Duration:** Annual. **Number Awarded:** Varies. **To Apply:** Each applicant is required to submit the attached application on or before the deadline. Submit along with the application, an example of ability in one of the following fields: Composition or composition-teaching - a CD not to exceed 20 minutes in length and a written music score for two separate works of own composition. Identify self, instrument and title at the beginning of the tape. Label the tape with this information also; Performance or performance-teaching - a CD, not to exceed 20 minutes in length, of two separate works reflecting a variety of style. Identify self, instrument and title at the beginning of the recording. **Deadline:** March 30. **Contact:** Faith El-

Awards are arranged alphabetically below their administering organizations

mes, Scholarship Associate; Phone: 717-236-5040; Email: felmes@tfec.org.

4257 ■ Anil and Neema Thakrar Family Fund No. 1 (Undergraduate/Scholarship)

Purpose: To encourage educational pursuits by providing financial assistance; to assist students for the study of a medical related discipline attending a school in Dauphin, Cumberland or Perry Counties. **Focus:** Engineering; Mathematics and mathematical sciences; Science. **Qualif.:** Program is open to students intending to study Math, Science and Engineering from the City of Harrisburg School District and Sci-Tech High School, or to high school students in Dauphin, Cumberland and Perry Counties intending to study in a medical-related discipline; must have a minimum GPA between 2.0 and 3.0. **Criteria:** Selection will be based on leadership/community service; character; and financial need.

Funds Avail.: Amount varies. **Duration:** Annual. **Number Awarded:** 1. **To Apply:** Applicants must complete and submit the application and other required attachments on or before the deadline. Applicants must provide the following attachments: official transcript of complete high school/college records including GPA; must attach a 300-word essay stating the biggest life challenge and the lesson acquired from the experience; and two personal reference letters from a high school teacher. Letters from family members will not be accepted. Reference should be sealed in an envelope. **Deadline:** April 1. **Contact:** Faith Elmes, Scholarship Associate; Phone: 717-236-5040; Email: felmes@tfec.org.

4258 ■ Jack and Edna May Yost Scholarships (Undergraduate/Scholarship)

Purpose: To assist students with their college tuition expenses. **Focus:** General studies/Field of study not specified. **Qualif.:** Applicants must be graduating seniors of a Dauphin or Cumberland County High School who will attend a two or four-year degree program at an accredited college; must have a minimum SAT score of 1,000; must be full-time students planning to attend a two or four-year accredited college; must be graduates of any Dauphin or Cumberland County high school; must have minimum GPA of 2.5 on a 4.0 scale; and must be able to demonstrate past or current community service and willingness to work to attain future goals. **Criteria:** Selection will be based on the committee's criteria. Preference will be given to students who demonstrate financial need; children of postal employees; and students who have plan on majoring nursing or have teaching profession.

Funds Avail.: Up to $5,000. **Number Awarded:** Varies. **To Apply:** Applicants must complete and submit the following attachments: official transcript of complete high school records with GPA; FAFSA Student Aid Report; two personal reference letters come from a teacher and the other one must come from someone who can attest the applicant's personal characteristics such as motivation, character, ability and potential; and personal essay. Essay should be titled, type-written, 12 point font, double-spaced and maximum of 300 words. **Deadline:** April 1. **Contact:** Faith Elmes, Scholarship Associate; Phone: 717-236-5040; Email: felmes@tfec.org.

4259 ■ Foundation of the Federal Bar Association (FFBA)
1220 N Fillmore St., Ste. 444
Arlington, VA 22201

URL: www.fedbar.org/Foundation.aspx

4260 ■ Foundation of the Federal Bar Association Public Service Scholarship Award (Undergraduate/Scholarship)

Purpose: To provide financial assistance to high school students for their continuing higher education. **Focus:** General studies/Field of study not specified. **Qualif.:** Applicants must be: graduating high school seniors planning to attend a four-year college or university; and, students currently enrolled full-time at a four-year college or university or graduate students enrolled full-time in a graduate or professional degree program. At least one of the applicants' parents or guardians must be current federal government attorneys or federal judges and members of the Federal Bar Association. **Criteria:** Applicants will be evaluated based on academic record, leadership recognition, school and community activities and service, and compelling essay response - exhibiting both substance and written communication skills.

Funds Avail.: $5,000. **Duration:** Annual. **To Apply:** Applicants must submit the following: completed application along with most recent transcripts (official copy); letter of acceptance from their college, university or graduate/professional school for new enrollees; and an essay. **Deadline:** April 30. **Contact:** Foundation of the Federal Bar Association at foundation@fedbar.org.

4261 ■ Foundation Fighting Blindness (FFB)
890 Yonge St., 12th Fl.
Toronto, ON, Canada M4W 3P4
Ph: (416)360-4200
Fax: (416)360-0060
Free: 800-461-3331
E-mail: info@ffb.ca
URL: ffb.ca

4262 ■ FFB-C Postdoctoral Fellowships (Postdoctorate/Fellowship)

Purpose: To increase the number of Canadian scientists being trained to investigate the causes, means of detection, prevention and cure of retinitis pigmentosa (RP), macular degeneration and related diseases of the retina. **Focus:** Optometry. **Qualif.:** Applicants must hold an MD, PhD, DDS, DVM, PharmD, or equivalent degree in a field appropriate to retinal degenerative disease research (molecular genetics, molecular biology, physiology, biochemistry, cell biology, or immunology). **Criteria:** Selection is based on the submitted application and materials.

Funds Avail.: No specific amount. **To Apply:** Applicants must complete the application online.

4263 ■ Foundation of the Hospitality Sales and Marketing Association International
1760 Old Meadow Rd., Ste. 500
McLean, VA 22102
Ph: (703)506-3280
Fax: (703)506-3266
E-mail: info@hsmai.org
URL: www.hsmai.org

4264 ■ FHSMAI Scholarship Program (Graduate/Scholarship)

Purpose: To provide financial assistance to students pursuing associate, baccalaureate and graduate degrees in

Awards are arranged alphabetically below their administering organizations

Hospitality Management or related fields. **Focus:** Hotel, institutional, and restaurant management. **Qualif.:** Applicant must be enrolled as a student in a hospitality management or related curriculum; pursuing a degree; must have hospitality work experience; must demonstrate an interest in a career in hospitality sales and marketing; must be in good academic standing. **Criteria:** Recipients are evaluated based on Grade Point Average, Industry-related work experience, Presentation of application, Involvement in HSMAI, Responses to essay questions, Recommendations, and Extracurricular involvement.

Funds Avail.: No specific amount. **Duration:** Annual. **To Apply:** Applicants must submit completed typed application form; transcript from current college or university; two recommendation forms; current resume; and three personal essays. Applicants must send their completed applications to Foundation Scholarship Committee. **Remarks:** Established in 1983. **Contact:** info@hsmai.org.

4265 ■ Foundation of the International Association of Defense Counsel (IADC)
303 W Madison, Ste. 925
Chicago, IL 60606
Ph: (312)368-1494
Fax: (312)368-1854
E-mail: info@iadclaw.org
URL: www.iadclaw.org

4266 ■ Gary Walker Memorial Scholarships (Other/Scholarship)

Purpose: To provide assistance to minority and women students, as well as those demonstrating financial need. **Focus:** Law. **Qualif.:** Applicants must be attorneys who have some level of actual trial experience; must have been in trial practice for between 2 and 10 years; and must demonstrate commitment to the advancement of the defense trial bar. **Criteria:** Preference is given to minority and women students as well as those demonstrating financial need.

Funds Avail.: No specific amount. **Duration:** Annual. **To Apply:** Applicants must submit a completed application form available in the website along with a statement of the applicant's actual trial experience (indicating number of trials, nature of the litigation, nature of role in defense team, etc.); copy of resume; list of any professional, civic or volunteer activities that may demonstrate a commitment to the legal profession and the defense bar; description of additional factors supporting scholarship application; and two letters of recommendation from attorneys who have supervised applicant's work. **Deadline:** May 18.

4267 ■ Foundation of the National Student Nurses Association (FNSNA)
45 Main St., Ste. 606
Brooklyn, NY 11201
Ph: (718)210-0705
Fax: (718)797-1186
URL: www.forevernursing.org
Facebook: www.facebook.com/FNSNA
Twitter: twitter.com/ForeverNursing

4268 ■ Breakthrough to Nursing Scholarships (Undergraduate/Scholarship)

Purpose: To provide financial support to qualified nursing students. **Focus:** Nursing. **Qualif.:** Applicant must be a student committed to providing quality health care services to underserved population; must possess the necessary leadership skills to influence the delivery of quality care; must be a U.S citizen or Alien with U.S permanent resident status/Alien Registration Number; must establish academic achievement; must have an involvement in student nursing organizations and community health activities; must be attending classes and taking no less than six credits per semester. **Criteria:** Selection of applicants will be based on academic achievement, financial need and involvement in student nursing organizations and community health activities. Selection committee of faculty and students from various nursing programs is appointed to select recipients.

Funds Avail.: No specific amount. **Duration:** Annual. **To Apply:** Applicants must submit and complete the application form available online; must submit an official transcript of records. Application form and other supporting documents must be sent to Foundation of the National Nurses' Association. **Deadline:** January 11.

4269 ■ Career Mobility Scholarships (Graduate, Undergraduate, Vocational/Occupational/Scholarship)

Purpose: To provide financial support to qualified nursing students. **Focus:** Nursing. **Qualif.:** Applicants must be nursing or pre-nursing students who are registered nurses (RNs) enrolled in RN and BSN and RN to MSN completion programs or a licensed practical/vocational nurses enrolled in programs leading to RN licensure; must be U.S. citizens or Alien with U.S. permanent residents status/Alien Registration Number; must have established academic achievement; must have an involvement in student nursing organizations and community health activities; must be attending classes and taking no less than six credits per semester. **Criteria:** Selection of Scholarships recipients will be based on academic achievement, financial need and involvement in student nursing organizations and community health activities.

Funds Avail.: No specific amount. **Duration:** Annual. **To Apply:** Applicants must submit and complete the application form available online; must submit an official transcript of records; application form and other supporting documents must be sent to Foundation of the National Nurses' Association. **Deadline:** January.

4270 ■ Specialty Nursing Scholarships (Undergraduate/Scholarship)

Purpose: To provide financial support to qualified nursing students. **Focus:** Nursing. **Qualif.:** Applicant must be a student interested in pursuing specialized areas of nursing practice; must be a U.S citizen or Alien with U.S permanent resident status/Alien Registration Number; must establish academic achievement; must have an involvement in student nursing organizations and community health activities; must be attending classes and taking no less than six credits per semester. **Criteria:** Selection of applicants will be based on academic achievement, financial need, and involvement in student nursing organizations and community health activities. Selection committee of faculty and students from various nursing programs is appointed to select recipients.

Funds Avail.: No specific amount. **Duration:** Annual. **To Apply:** Applicants must submit and complete the application form available online; must submit an official transcript of records. Application form and other supporting documents must be sent to Foundation of the National Nurses' Association. **Deadline:** January 11.

Awards are arranged alphabetically below their administering organizations

4271 ■ Foundation for Neonatal Research and Education (FNRE)
c/o Anthony J. Jannetti, Chief Financial Officer
200 E Holly Ave., Box 56
Sewell, NJ 08080
Ph: (856)256-2343
Fax: (856)589-7463
E-mail: contact@fnre.com
URL: ajj.com/fnre
Facebook: www.facebook.com/Foundation-for-Neonatal-Research-and-Education-326866947443380

4272 ■ Foundation for Neonatal Research and Education Scholarships (Doctorate, Graduate, Postgraduate, Undergraduate/Scholarship)

Purpose: To support students and professionals pursue a higher education. **Focus:** Nursing, Neonatal. **Qualif.:** Applicants must be neonatal nurses admitted to a college or school of higher education on one of the following: a) Bachelor of Science in Nursing (current RN); b) Master in Science in Nursing for Advance Practice in Neonatal Nursing; c) Doctoral degree in Nursing; and d) Master's or Post-Master degree in Nursing Administration or Business Management; must have 3.0 GPA or higher; must be actively engaged in a service, research, or educational role; active members of a professional association and must demonstrate an ongoing professional education in neonatal nursing; must have not received a FNRE scholarship or grant in the past five years. **Criteria:** Recipients will be selected based on qualifications and submitted materials.

Funds Avail.: No specific amount. **Duration:** Annual. **To Apply:** Applicants must submit a completed application form, current resume or curriculum vitae, an official transcript from each college or school of higher education, a letter of verification of enrollment and acceptance to a college or school. Evaluation forms shall be submitted in the following manner: a) CNS applicants - a separate form from a nurse manager or supervisor and two members of the health team; b) NNP applicants - a separate form from a nurse manager or supervisor, a practicing NNP and a neonatologist or other pediatric physician practicing in neonatal care; c) Nursing Administration or Business Management applicants - a separate form from a nurse manager or supervisor and two members of the health team; d) Doctoral applicants - a separate form from a supervisor and one member of program faculty and one member of the health team; e) BSN applicants - a separate form from a nursing supervisor and two members of the health team. Applicants are also required to submit a (250 words or less) statement addressing the plans of making a significant difference in neonatal nursing practice. **Deadline:** May 1. **Contact:** Foundation for Neonatal Research and Education (FNRE), FNRE Coordinator, c/o Anthony J. Jannetti, Inc., at the above address.

4273 ■ Foundation of the Pennsylvania Medical Society
777 E Park Dr.
Harrisburg, PA 17105-8820
Ph: (717)558-7750
Fax: (717)558-7818
E-mail: foundation@pamedsoc.org
URL: www.foundationpamedsoc.org

Awards are arranged alphabetically below their administering organizations

4274 ■ Allegheny County Medical Society Medical Student Scholarships (ACMS) (Undergraduate/Scholarship)

Purpose: To assist local students with the cost of attending a Pennsylvania medical school. **Focus:** Medicine. **Qualif.:** Applicants must be Pennsylvania residents from one of the following counties: Allegheny, Armstrong, Beaver, Butler, Washington, or Westmoreland; must be enrolled full-time in an accredited Pennsylvania medical school or entering his/her 3rd or 4th year of medical school. **Criteria:** Applicants are evaluated based on financial need.

Funds Avail.: $4,000. **Duration:** Annual. **To Apply:** Applicants must submit: completed scholarship application form; two reference letters from persons other than family members, documenting integrity, interpersonal skills and potential as a future physician (one must come from either a medical school professor or a physician); a letter, on school letterhead, from the applicants' medical school verifying that they are enrolled full time as a third or fourth-year medical student at that institution; and a typed, one-page essay addressing the following: Where do you see yourself in 10 years? How do you plan to give back to the community? **Deadline:** September 30. **Contact:** studentservices-foundation@pamedsoc.org.

4275 ■ Alliance Medical Education Scholarship Fund (AMES) (Undergraduate/Scholarship)

Purpose: To financially assist a deserving medical student enrolled in a Pennsylvania medical school. **Focus:** Medicine. **Qualif.:** Applicants must be residents of Pennsylvania who are enrolled in a Pennsylvania medical school as full-time second- or third-year medical students. **Criteria:** Applicants are evaluated based on financial need, merit, leadership and service.

Funds Avail.: $2,500. **Duration:** Annual. **Number Awarded:** Varies. **To Apply:** Applicants must submit: the completed application form; two reference letters from persons who know them well (other than their families); letter from their medical school verifying that they are enrolled full-time and currently second or third-year medical students; and a typed statement of one page describing their vision for the future of Pennsylvania Medicine. **Deadline:** February 28. **Contact:** studentservices-foundation@pamedsoc.org.

4276 ■ Scott A. Gunder, MD, DCMS Presidential Scholarships (Undergraduate/Scholarship)

Purpose: To financially assist deserving second-year medical students at Penn State College of Medicine. **Focus:** Medicine. **Qualif.:** Applicants must have been residents of Pennsylvania for at least 12 months before registering as medical students; must be second-year medical students; must be enrolled full-time at Penn State College of Medicine; and must be members of Pennsylvania Medical Society and their county medical society. **Criteria:** Applicants are evaluated based on financial need.

Funds Avail.: $1,500. **Duration:** Annual. **To Apply:** Applicants must submit: completed application form; two reference letters, from persons other than family members, documenting the applicants' integrity, interpersonal skills and potential as future physicians; letter, on school letterhead, from Penn State College of Medicine verifying that they are enrolled full-time and second-year medical students; one-page typed essay describing the person or event that most influenced them to become physicians and how they see themselves leading others into medicine; and completed Pennsylvania Medical Society membership applications if students are not current members. **Remarks:** Established in 2000. **Contact:** studentservices-foundation@pamedsoc.org.

4277 ■ Lycoming County Medical Society Scholarships (LCMS) *(Undergraduate/Scholarship)*

Purpose: To provide financial assistance for medical students who are residents of Lycoming County. **Focus:** Medicine. **Qualif.:** Applicants must be residents of Lycoming County in the state of Pennsylvania; must be enrolled full-time in an accredited allopathic or osteopathic medical school within the United States. **Criteria:** Applicants are evaluated based on financial need.

Funds Avail.: $3,000. **Duration:** Annual. **To Apply:** Applicants must submit: completed application form; two reference letters, from persons other than family members, documenting the applicants' integrity, interpersonal skills, and potential as future physicians; a letter, on school letterhead, from applicants' medical school verifying that they are enrolled full-time as medical students at their respective institutions; and, one-page, typed essay specifically describing why they chose to become physicians and what contributions they expect to make to the health profession. **Deadline:** September 30. **Contact:** studentservices-foundation@pamedsoc.org.

4278 ■ Montgomery County Medical Society Scholarships (MCMS) *(Undergraduate/Scholarship)*

Purpose: To provide financial assistance for medical students who are residents of Montgomery County. **Focus:** Medicine. **Qualif.:** Applicants must be residents of Montgomery County in the state of Pennsylvania; must have been Pennsylvania residents for at least 12 months prior to registering as medical students; must be enrolled full-time in an accredited United States medical school; must be enrolled or entering their first year of medical school. **Criteria:** Applicants are evaluated based on financial need.

Funds Avail.: $2,500. **Duration:** Annual. **Number Awarded:** 2. **To Apply:** Applicants must submit a completed application form; two reference letters, from persons other than family members, documenting the applicants' integrity, interpersonal skills and potential as physicians; a letter, on school letterhead, from their medical schools verifying that they are enrolled full time as first-year medical students at that institution; one-page, typed essay addressing the reasons for pursuing medical career, personal goals and plans for future within the profession. **Deadline:** September 30.

4279 ■ Myrtle Siegfried, MD and Michael Vigilante, MD Scholarships *(Undergraduate/Scholarship)*

Purpose: To provide financial assistance to qualified first-year medical students residing in Berks, Lehigh, or Northampton County. **Focus:** Medicine. **Qualif.:** Applicants must be residents of Berks, Lehigh or Northampton County; must be entering first year of medical school; must be enrolled full-time in an accredited United States medical school. **Criteria:** Applicants are evaluated based on financial need.

Funds Avail.: $1,000. **Duration:** Annual. **To Apply:** Applicants must submit a completed application form; two reference letters documenting the applicants' integrity, interpersonal skills and potential as future physicians (letters must come from persons who know the applicants well but are not family members); a letter, on school letterhead, from their medical school verifying that they are enrolled full-time at that institution and first-year medical students; one-page, typed essay specifically describing why they chose to become physicians and what contributions they expect to make to the health profession. **Deadline:** September 30.

4280 ■ Foundation for the Preservation of Honey Bees, Inc.
Bldg. 5, Ste. 300
3525 Piedmont Rd. NE
Atlanta, GA 30305
Fax: (404)240-0998
URL: preservationofhoneybees.org

4281 ■ Foundation for the Preservation of Honey Bees Graduate Scholarships *(Graduate/Scholarship)*

Purpose: To allow the recipients to attend the annual North American Beekeeping Conference, where they will have an opportunity to meet other researchers and beekeepers and to present their research to the industry. **Focus:** Life sciences. **Qualif.:** Applicant must be a graduate student in apiculture. **Criteria:** Selection is based on the application.

Funds Avail.: No specific amount. **Duration:** Annual. **To Apply:** Applicants must submit a cover letter from the advisor outlining the applicant's progress toward graduate degree, tentative graduation date, and any other information about the applicant and the research that would help the committee "get to know" the applicant; a curriculum vitae, or resume, not to exceed 2 pages; and the research proposal (not to exceed 3 pages). **Contact:** Foundation for the Preservation of Honey Bees, at the above address.

4282 ■ Foundation for Seacoast Health
100 Campus Dr., Ste. 1
Portsmouth, NH 03801
Ph: (603)422-8200
Fax: (603)422-8207
E-mail: ffsh@communitycampus.org
URL: www.ffsh.org

4283 ■ Foundation for Seacoast Health Scholarships *(Undergraduate, Graduate/Scholarship)*

Purpose: To support students pursuing a health-related field of study. **Focus:** Health care services; Health education. **Qualif.:** Applicants must have been and continue to be residents of New Hampshire (Portsmouth, North Hampton, Greenland, Rye, Newington, New Castle) or Maine (Kittery, Eliot, or York) for a minimum of two years prior to the Scholarship Program and pursuing a health-related field of study as undergraduate or graduate students in an accredited institution of learning. **Criteria:** Selection will be based on academic achievement (class rank, GPA and test scores), course difficulty, work shortage areas of need in Seacoast, job experience, community service, evidence of dedication to chosen field of study and financial need.

Funds Avail.: Amount varies. **Duration:** Annual. **Number Awarded:** 2 (1 undergraduate; 1 graduate). **To Apply:** Applicants must submit a completed Scholarship Application form along with three Student Assessment Forms (in sealed envelopes); official school transcripts; test scores; essay; and current resume. **Deadline:** March 1. **Remarks:** The scholarships are offered into two: the Edwina Foye Scholarship for graduates, and the Steven Scott Cutter Scholarship for undergraduates.

4284 ■ FPDA Motion and Control Network
105 Eastern Ave., Ste. 104
Annapolis, MD 21403-3300

FRAGILE X RESEARCH FOUNDATION OF CANADA — Sponsors and Their Scholarships

Ph: (410)940-6347
Fax: (410)263-1659
E-mail: info@fpda.org
URL: www.fpda.org

4285 ■ Tom D. Ralls Memorial Scholarship *(Professional development/Scholarship)*

Purpose: To support young executives for their full tuition to the University of Innovative Distribution. **Focus:** Industrial design. **Qualif.:** Applicant must be an employee in good standing of an FPDA Regular (Distributor) Member organization; must be a qualified member of the FPDA Young Executives (YES).

Funds Avail.: No specific amount. **Duration:** Annual. **To Apply:** Applicant must provide a letter of recommendation from a company principal; must provide an essay detailing his/her desire to attend the University of Innovative Distribution program. **Deadline:** November 14.

4286 ■ Fragile X Research Foundation of Canada (FXRFC)

167 Queen St. W
Brampton, ON, Canada L6Y 1M5
Ph: (905)453-9366
Fax: (905)453-0095
E-mail: info@fragilexcanada.ca
URL: www.fragilexcanada.ca/index.php?home&lng=en

4287 ■ FXRFC Medical Research Postdoctoral Fellowships *(Postdoctorate/Fellowship)*

Purpose: To promote research aimed at finding a specific treatment for Fragile X syndrome. **Focus:** Medical research. **Qualif.:** Applicants must be nominated by institutions and should have training and experience at least equal to the PhD or MD level. **Criteria:** Selection is based on submitted application materials.

Funds Avail.: Up to 40,000 Canadian Dollars. **Duration:** Annual. **To Apply:** Application package must include a brief letter of inquiry describing the proposed project; a 6-12 page description of the proposed project (background, objectives, approach, methodological detail, significance, originality, and key references); curriculum vitae for the principal investigator; curriculum vitae for the postdoctoral fellow to be supported under the grant; three references; financial accounting of how the funds will be spent; a full accounting of any other current and submitted sources of support for the project; and requested start date of the project. Send one complete copy of the application to fxrfc@on.aibn.com in PDF file, and two copies (may be sent on a CD) to Carlo Paribello MSM, MD, President, Fragile X Research Foundation of Canada. **Deadline:** October 1. **Contact:** Dr. Carlo Paribello at the above address.

4288 ■ Joe Francis Haircare Scholarship Foundation

PO Box 50625
Minneapolis, MN 55405
Ph: (651)769-1757
E-mail: contact@joefrancis.com
URL: www.joefrancis.com

4289 ■ Joe Francis Haircare Scholarships *(Undergraduate/Scholarship)*

Purpose: To provide support to deserving students who want to pursue their professional training in hairstyling. **Focus:** Cosmetology. **Qualif.:** Applicant must be actively enrolled in cosmetology school or planning to enroll in cosmetology/barber school. **Criteria:** Recipient will be selected by the independent committee composed of individuals drawn from the professional beauty industry. Selection is based on their potential, financial need, and commitment to a long-term career in cosmetology.

Funds Avail.: $1,000. **Duration:** Annual. **To Apply:** Applicant must complete the application form available online; must have a letter of recommendation from an employer, instructor, counselor, or someone qualified to offer testimony of his/her character. **Deadline:** June 1. **Contact:** Kim Larson, 651-769-1757, kimlarsonmn@gmail.com.

4290 ■ Franklin District Medical Society

85 Post Office Pk., Ste. 8518
Wilbraham, MA 01095
Ph: (413)596-9231
Fax: (413)596-9901
Free: 800-522-3112
E-mail: franklin@massmed.org
URL: www.massmed.org/franklin/#.VdUW4LKqqko

4291 ■ Percy W. Wadman, M.D. Scholarship *(Postgraduate/Scholarship)*

Purpose: To support medical students based on merit and financial need. **Focus:** Medicine. **Qualif.:** Applicants' one or both parents or guardians must live in Franklin County.

Funds Avail.: $1,000-$2,000. **Duration:** Annual. **To Apply:** A letter of matriculation must be submitted from applicants' medical school; a copy of the letter of recommendation from the applicants' undergraduate school to the medical school must be submitted; and a copy of parent's or guardian's 1040 Federal Tax Form for the last tax year. **Deadline:** December 31.

4292 ■ Fraser Stryker

500 Energy Plz., 409 S 17th St.
Omaha, NE 68102-2663
Ph: (402)341-6000
Fax: (402)341-8290
Free: 800-544-6041
URL: www.fraserstryker.com

4293 ■ Fraser Stryker Diversity Scholarships *(Undergraduate/Scholarship)*

Purpose: To provide financial aid for college-bound students from low-income families in the Omaha metro area who are interested in pursuing a career in law. **Focus:** Law. **Qualif.:** Applicants must be high school seniors of African-American, Asian, Latino or Native-American origins who attend public or private high schools in the greater Omaha area. They must have been accepted to an accredited college or university located in the United States. **Criteria:** Recipients are selected based on interest in pursuing a career in law, financial need, top 20% in class rank, and U.S. citizenship or residency in the Omaha area for the previous six consecutive years.

Funds Avail.: $2,500 per academic year. **Duration:** Annual. **To Apply:** Applicants must pick up Scholarship Application from high school counselor. **Deadline:** March 6. **Contact:** Stephen M. Bruckner, 500 Energy Plaza, 409 S 17th St., Omaha, NE 68102-2663; Phone: 402-341-6000;

Awards are arranged alphabetically below their administering organizations

Fax: 402-341-8290; Email: sbruckner@fraserstryker.com.

4294 ■ FRAXA Research Foundation
10 Prince Pl., Ste. 203
Newburyport, MA 01950
Ph: (978)462-1866
E-mail: info@fraxa.org
URL: www.fraxa.org
Facebook: www.facebook.com/fraxaresearch
Twitter: twitter.com/fraxaresearch

4295 ■ FRAXA Postdoctoral Fellowships *(Postdoctorate, Master's/Fellowship)*
Purpose: To encourage research aimed at finding a specific treatment for fragile X syndrome. **Focus:** General studies/Field of study not specified. **Qualif.:** Applicants must be full time and have MD, PhD, or MD/PhD. **Criteria:** Selection will be based on the committee's criteria.
Funds Avail.: $45,000 per year. **Duration:** Two years. **Number Awarded:** 6-8 total fellowships depending on available funds. **To Apply:** Candidates must be nominated by their institutions. Applicants must provide the following information with their application: description of the proposed project (6-12 pages recommended); curriculum vitae for the principal investigator; curriculum vitae for the postdoctoral fellow to be supported under the grant; names of three references who are willing to be contacted to provide recommendations for candidate postdoctoral fellow; financial accounting of how the funds will be spent, with dollar distribution into major component items; a full accounting of any other current and submitted sources of support for this project and other lab research; requested start date of the project. The earliest possible state date is three months after receipt of the application. Completed application must be submitted via email. Application must be in a PDF format of less than 10 MB. **Deadline:** February 1. **Contact:** Dr. Michael Tranfaglia, CSO of FRAXA, at mtranfaglia@fraxa.org.

4296 ■ Fredrikson and Byron P.A.
200 S Sixth St., Ste. 4000
Minneapolis, MN 55402-1425
Ph: (612)492-7000
Fax: (612)492-7077
E-mail: jkoneck@fredlaw.com
URL: www.fredlaw.com

4297 ■ Fredrikson and Byron Foundation Minority Scholarships *(Undergraduate/Scholarship)*
Purpose: To sponsor educational opportunities for minority law students. **Focus:** Law. **Qualif.:** Applicants must be currently enrolled, first-year minority law students. **Criteria:** Selection is based on the application materials submitted.
Funds Avail.: $15,000. **Duration:** Annual. **To Apply:** Applicants must submit a completed application form along with two written recommendations (Applicant Appraisal Form for Law School Professors or Applicant Appraisal Form for Employers of Other Reference); one writing sample from a first year legal writing course; current law school transcripts; undergraduate transcripts from all undergraduate institutions attended; and a resume. Applicants may apply online. **Deadline:** March 31. **Contact:** Curt Okerson; Email: cokerson@fredlaw.com; All required materials should be directed to: Greta Larson at glarson@fredlaw.com.

4298 ■ Freedom Alliance
22570 Markey Ct., Ste. 240
Dulles, VA 20166
Ph: (703)444-7940
Fax: (703)444-9893
Free: 800-475-6620
E-mail: info@freedomallinge.org
URL: freedomalliance.org

4299 ■ Freedom Alliance Scholarships *(Undergraduate/Scholarship)*
Purpose: To support the children of American heroes. **Focus:** General studies/Field of study not specified. **Qualif.:** Applicant must be a dependent child of an active service member killed or disabled military as the result of an operational mission/training accident; a senior high school, high school graduate or enrolled in an institution of higher learning; and must be 26 years old and below. **Criteria:** Applicants are selected based on the committee's review of the application materials.
Funds Avail.: No specific amount. **To Apply:** Applicants must complete online application and forward a copy of Government Issued Photo Identification (drivers License, ID Card); must submit a certificate of death or rating letter from the Veterans Administration disability; an essay; scholastic record; and a photo (photo of parents are optional). **Deadline:** June 30. **Remarks:** Freedom of Alliance will mail scholarship check to the school. **Contact:** Adam Morgan, Phone: 800-475-6620; Email: info@fascholarship.com.

4300 ■ Freedom From Religion Foundation (FFRF)
PO Box 750
Madison, WI 53701
Ph: (608)256-8900
Fax: (608)204-0422
E-mail: info@ffrf.org
URL: ffrf.org
Facebook: www.facebook.com/4ffrf
Twitter: twitter.com/FFRF

4301 ■ Brian Bolton Graduate/Mature Student Essay Awards *(Undergraduate, Graduate/Award)*
Purpose: To promote the constitutional principle of separation of state and church. **Focus:** General studies/Field of study not specified. **Qualif.:** Applicants must be currently enrolled graduate students of any age or any currently enrolled undergraduate ages 25 to 30. **Criteria:** Selection will be based on the committee's criteria.
Funds Avail.: $200-$3,000. **To Apply:** Applicants must submit an essay with 750-950 words; must be typed, stapled and double-spaced with standard margins. Include word count. Place name and essay title on each page. Choose own title and include one-paragraph biography on separate page at end of essay. Include name, age and birth date, hometown, university or college, year in school, intended major and interests, previous degrees and anticipated graduation date. Must be e-mail to gradessay@ffrf.org. **Deadline:** July 1.

4302 ■ Fried, Frank, Harris, Shriver and Jacobson L.L.P.
One New York Plz.
New York, NY 10004

Awards are arranged alphabetically below their administering organizations

Ph: (212)859-8000
Fax: (212)859-4000
URL: www.friedfrank.com

4303 ■ Fried, Frank, Harris, Shriver and Jacobson Fellowships (Graduate/Fellowship)

Purpose: To support recent law school graduates. **Focus:** Law. **Qualif.:** Applicants must be third-year law students or recent graduates currently in a judicial clerkship. **Criteria:** Selection is based on the application materials.

Funds Avail.: No specific amount. **Duration:** Annual. **To Apply:** Applicants must submit a resume, two letters of recommendation (one each from a law school faculty member and an employer), a legal writing sample, a 500-word essay, and a law school transcript. **Contact:** Please contact: Phone: 212-859-8345; Email: fellowship@friedfrank.com.

4304 ■ Friends of Canadian Broadcasting (FCB)

200/238 - 131 Bloor St. W
Toronto, ON, Canada M5S 1R8
Free: 866-833-1282
E-mail: friends@friends.ca
URL: www.friends.ca
Facebook: www.facebook.com/friendscb
Twitter: twitter.com/friendscb

4305 ■ Dalton Camp Awards (Undergraduate/Award, Monetary)

Purpose: To support individuals who write essays on the link between democracy and the media in Canada. **Focus:** Media arts. **Qualif.:** Applicants must be Canadian citizens or permanent residents of Canada. **Criteria:** Selection will be based on the committee's criteria.

Funds Avail.: 10,000 Canadian Dollars for the first award; 2,500 Canadian Dollars for the second award. **Duration:** Annual. **To Apply:** Applicants must submit an essay that is written in English and does not exceed 2,000 words. Each entry shall be accompanied by the author's full name and contact information including postal address, email address and a telephone number. Each entry shall also include: a biographical sketch not exceeding 50 words; the word count of the essay; written confirmation that the entry complies with the Rules of The Dalton Camp Award. Essays submitted by email attachment should include, on the first page of the essay, a title followed by the full name of the author. Subsequent pages should be numbered and contain no information identifying the author. Essays submitted using the online submission form shall contain no information identifying the author in the body of the essay. Applicants may submit their essays through email at submissions@daltoncampaward.ca or may visit the website for the online submission. **Remarks:** Established in 2002.

4306 ■ Friends of Project 10 Inc.

115 W California Blvd., Ste. 116
Pasadena, CA 91105
Ph: (626)577-4553
E-mail: project10@hotmail.com
URL: friendsofproject10.org

4307 ■ Friends of Project 10 Models of Excellence Scholarships (Undergraduate/Scholarship)

Purpose: To support students who have advanced the civil rights of the lesbian, gay, bisexual, and transgender communities. **Focus:** Sexuality. **Qualif.:** Applicants are limited to graduating senior high school students residing in these Southern California counties: Imperial, Kern, Los Angeles, Orange, Riverside, Santa Barbara, San Bernardino, San Diego, San Luis Obispo, Ventura. They must be from public, private and parochial schools who have advanced the civil rights of the lesbian, gay, bisexual, and transgender (LGBT) population. **Criteria:** Selection shall be based on the aforementioned applicants' qualifications and compliance with the application details.

Funds Avail.: $1,000-$3,000. **Duration:** Annual. **Number Awarded:** Varies. **To Apply:** Applicants must submit a completed scholarship application. Applicants must also enclose the following: a transcript of high school grades and grades in progress; a list of activities with particular emphasis on work done in the LGBT community; proposed course of study at college, university, or technical school; one or more letters of recommendation; autobiography describing the background, the aspirations after college, and the connection to the LGBT community (2 pages maximum); and examples of any work that such applicant think would be of interest to the scholarship committee (optional). **Deadline:** May 7. **Remarks:** Established in 1994. **Contact:** Friends of Project 10, Inc., at the above address.

4308 ■ Fund for American Studies (TFAS)

1706 New Hampshire Ave. NW
Washington, DC 20009
Ph: (202)986-0384
Fax: (202)986-0390
E-mail: info@tfas.org
URL: www.tfas.org
Facebook: www.facebook.com/TFASorg
LinkedIn: www.linkedin.com/groups/25022/profile
Twitter: twitter.com/TFASorg

4309 ■ TFAS Congressional Scholarship Awards (Undergraduate/Award, Scholarship)

Purpose: To provide financial support for students who wish to attend the Institute on Business and Government Affairs (IBGA) at Georgetown University. **Focus:** Business; Local government. **Qualif.:** Applicant must be an undergraduate student. **Criteria:** Selection will be based on leadership skills, academics, campus and community involvement.

Funds Avail.: No specific amount. **Duration:** Annual. **To Apply:** Applicants may visit the TFAS website for the scholarship information and application. **Remarks:** Established in 1990. **Contact:** TFAS; Phone: 202-986-0384; Fax: 202-986-0390; Email: info@TFAS.org.

4310 ■ Eben Tisdale Fellowships (Undergraduate/Fellowship)

Purpose: To support outstanding students who are interested technology and public policy. **Focus:** Technology. **Qualif.:** Applicants must be junior or senior students interested in public policy and the high-tech industry, or in a graduate program. **Criteria:** The Advisory Committee will evaluate submitted materials.

Funds Avail.: Full scholarship of $8,695; $1,000 Stipends. **Duration:** Annual. **To Apply:** Applicants must submit a completed application form; professional resume; official academic transcripts; evaluation forms from two academic references (in a sealed envelope, author's signature must

Awards are arranged alphabetically below their administering organizations

be across the seal); a 500-word statement on reasons of wanting to be a Tisdale fellow. **Deadline:** February 10. **Remarks:** Established after the death of Eben Tisdale, general manager of government affairs for the Hewlett-Packard Company. **Contact:** Joel Troutman, Program Associate, Institute on Business and Government Affairs, 1621 New Hampshire Ave., NW Washington, DC 20009; Phone: 202-986-0384; Fax: 202-318-0441; Email: Tisdale@TFAS.org.

4311 ■ Funeral Service Foundation (FSF)
13625 Bishops Dr.
Brookfield, WI 53005-6607
Free: 877-402-5900
E-mail: info@funeralservicefoundation.org
URL: www.funeralservicefoundation.org

4312 ■ Joseph E. Hagan Memorial Scholarships
(Undergraduate/Scholarship)

Purpose: To provide financial assistance for mortuary science school students. **Focus:** Mortuary science. **Qualif.:** Applicants must be full-time students who will be enrolled or have been accepted for enrollment in the Fall semester in programs accredited by the American Board of Funeral Service Education. **Criteria:** Applicants are evaluated by the judges from the FSF Board of Trustees based on essay submitted by them.

Funds Avail.: $2,500. **Duration:** Annual. **To Apply:** Applicants must submit all the required application information. **Deadline:** June 15. **Remarks:** Established in 2000.

4313 ■ Brenda Renee Horn Memorial Scholarship
(Undergraduate/Scholarship)

Purpose: To provide financial assistance for top-scoring mortuary science students via the Key Memories scholarship essay contest. **Focus:** Mortuary science. **Qualif.:** Applicants must be students who are enrolled or accepted for enrollment in a mortuary science school accredited by the American Board of Funeral Service Education. **Criteria:** Applicants are judged by members of the Keystone Advisory Board and a Funeral Service Foundation representative.

Funds Avail.: $3,000. **Duration:** Annual. **To Apply:** Applicants must visit the Foundation's website for the online application process. **Contact:** campus.relations@sci-us.com.

4314 ■ NFDA Professional Women's Conference Scholarships *(Undergraduate/Scholarship)*

Purpose: To provide financial assistance for tuition and travel stipend for selected individuals who attended the National Funeral Directors Association Professional Women's Conference. **Focus:** Funeral services; Mortuary science. **Qualif.:** Applicants must be verifiably employed in funeral service or a related occupation or mortuary science school students enrolled in school accredited by the American Board of Funeral Service Education. **Criteria:** Applicants are evaluated based on answers to essay.

Funds Avail.: $1,000. **To Apply:** Applicants must submit all the required application information. **Deadline:** June 15.

4315 ■ Fur Takers of America (FTA)
PO Box 3
Buckley, IL 60918
Ph: (217)394-2577
URL: www.furtakersofamerica.com

4316 ■ Charles Dobbins FTA Scholarships
(Undergraduate, Vocational/Occupational/Scholarship)

Purpose: To promote interest in the accumulation and dissemination of knowledge concerning the trapping of fur bearing animals among persons interested therein. **Focus:** Agricultural sciences; Biology; Wildlife conservation, management, and science. **Qualif.:** Applicants must be members of FTA or their immediate relatives; must be majoring in agriculture, biology, wildlife management or related courses in an accredited two-year or four-year college, university, or vocational/technical school. **Criteria:** Recipients are selected based on academic records and quality of the essay submitted.

Funds Avail.: $500. **Duration:** Annual. **To Apply:** Applicants must provide a proof of high school graduation or pending graduation; official documents indicating that they have been accepted in an institution as first year students, or registration of classes if applicants are already in school. Applicants must also submit an essay that discusses career goals and how the scholarship would help to achieve these goals. **Deadline:** May 1. **Contact:** Jerry Schilling; Address: 21 Schilling Lane, New Harmony, IN 47631; Phone: 812-783-1097.

4317 ■ Gallery Collection
65 Challenger Rd.
Ridgefield Park, NJ 07660
Ph: (201)641-0070
Fax: (201)641-7694
Free: 800-950-7064
E-mail: service@gallerycollection.com
URL: www.gallerycollection.com

4318 ■ The Gallery Collection's Create-A-Greeting Card Scholarships *(Undergraduate/Scholarship)*

Purpose: To encourage students to use their talents and pursue their education. **Focus:** Art; Graphic art and design; Photography. **Qualif.:** Applicants must be currently enrolled in high school, college or university; must have a talent in fine arts, graphic design or photography; and must be U.S. citizens. **Criteria:** Winning greeting card will be determined based on overall aesthetic appeal, quality of execution, creativity and originality, successful incorporation of design elements, appropriateness, attractiveness towards customers and suitability as a design in Prudent's Gallery Collection greeting card line.

Funds Avail.: $10,000 for the winner, and $1,000 for the selected school. **Duration:** Annual. **To Apply:** Applicants must submit an original photograph - a piece of artwork or graphics file for the front cover. **Contact:** Scholarship Administrator, The Gallery Collection, Prudent Publishing Company, Inc.; E-mail: scholarshipadmin@gallerycollection.com.

4319 ■ Gamewardens Association, Vietnam to Present
PO Box 83
Parsons, KS 67357
Free: 866-220-7477
URL: www.tf116.org

Awards are arranged alphabetically below their administering organizations

4320 ■ Gamewarden Scholarship program *(High School, Undergraduate, Vocational/Occupational/Scholarship)*

Purpose: To discuss military history, military news and other topics of concern or interest about Vietnam. **Focus:** Vietnamese studies. **Qualif.:** Applicant must be needing the assistance; must be the son, daughter or grandchild of a member of Game wardens; an applicant must be receiving an education from a four-year or two-year college, university, or vocational school. **Criteria:** Committee will consider the application based on the need of the applicant. **Funds Avail.:** $1,500. **Duration:** Annual. **To Apply:** Applicant must fill out the application form and send to Game warden of Vietnam Association Office. **Deadline:** July 30. **Contact:** Glen Fry, normlguy@gmail.com.

4321 ■ Gamma Sigma Alpha (GSA)
PO Box 3948
Parker, CO 80134
Free: 866-793-5406
E-mail: director@gammasigmaalpha.org
URL: gammasigmaalpha.org

4322 ■ Gamma Sigma Alpha Graduate Scholarships *(Graduate/Scholarship)*

Purpose: To assist qualified members pursuing graduate studies at an accredited institution. **Focus:** General studies/Field of study not specified. **Qualif.:** Applicants must be members of Gamma Sigma Alpha with a cumulative GPA of 3.5 or better (applicants must have been initiated prior to their application submission). **Criteria:** Selection will be based upon academic record, recommendations submitted, the applicant's statement, and scholarly, campus and community activities. **Funds Avail.:** $2,000 each. **Number Awarded:** 2. **To Apply:** Applicants must submit a completed application form together with a letter of recommendation; resume; one page essay; and official transcript(s) of all academic work. **Deadline:** May 2. **Contact:** Wes Schaub, Selection Committee Chair at director@gammasigmaalpha.org.

4323 ■ Garden Club of America (GCA)
14 E 60th St., 3rd Fl.
New York, NY 10022
Ph: (212)753-8287
Fax: (212)753-0134
E-mail: gca@gcamerica.org
URL: www.gcamerica.org

4324 ■ Garden Club of America Awards in Tropical Botany (GCA) *(Doctorate/Award)*

Purpose: To assist doctoral candidates enrolled in a U.S. PhD program to undertake field work in the tropics. **Focus:** Botany. **Qualif.:** Applicants must be PhD enrolled in United States university. **Criteria:** Applicants are selected based on Committee's review of the application materials. **Funds Avail.:** $5,500. **Number Awarded:** 2. **To Apply:** Applicants must submit a curriculum vitae; (two-page) statement of proposed research; personal letter describing plans for the future and commitment to tropical conservation; letter of recommendation from student's graduate advisor including an evaluation of the student's progress. **Remarks:** Established in 1983. **Contact:** Andrea Santy, Senior Program Officer, phone: 202-495-4447; e-mail: andrea.santy@wwfus.org.

4325 ■ Katherine M. Grosscup Scholarships *(Undergraduate, Graduate/Scholarship)*

Purpose: To provide financial assistance to students who wish to pursue study of horticulture and related field. **Focus:** Horticulture. **Qualif.:** Applicants must be current college sophomores, juniors, seniors or graduate students from Ohio, Pennsylvania, West Virginia, Michigan, Indiana and Kentucky, and have "B" GPA or better. **Criteria:** Applicants will be selected based on Committee's review of the application materials and personal interview. **Funds Avail.:** $3,500. **Duration:** Annual. **Number Awarded:** 1. **To Apply:** Applicants must submit a completed application form; one letter of recommendation; transcript of college records; and personal statement explaining the career goals and how the chosen area of study will help achieve the objectives. **Deadline:** January 16. **Remarks:** Established in 1981. **Contact:** The Garden Club of America, attn: Scholarship Applications, 14 East 60th Street, New York, NY 10022-1006; Phone: 212-753-8287; fax: 212-753-0134; grosscupscholarship@gmail.com; and scholarshipapplications@gcamerica.org.

4326 ■ Gay Asian Pacific Alliance Foundation (GAPA)
PO Box 22482
San Francisco, CA 94142
Ph: (415)857-4272
E-mail: info@gapafoundation.org
URL: gapafoundation.org
Facebook: www.facebook.com/gapafoundation
Twitter: twitter.com/GAPAFoundation

4327 ■ GAPA Scholarships *(Undergraduate/Scholarship)*

Purpose: To provide financial assistance to lesbian, gay, bisexual and transgender Asian and Pacific Islanders in educational pursuits. **Focus:** Homosexuality. **Qualif.:** Applicant must be an Asian/Pacific Islander; applying or attending school in one of the nine Bay Area counties; and have a minimum GPA of 2.75. **Criteria:** Priority is given to those self-identified as lesbian, gay, bisexual or transgender, or involved in the l/g/b/t community. **Funds Avail.:** $1000. **To Apply:** Applicants must submit a completed Horizons Foundation's scholarship application form together with a transcript, a letter of recommendation and a 500-word essay. **Deadline:** October 31. **Remarks:** In memory of George Choy. The scholarship is administered by the Horizons Foundation. **Contact:** Horizons Foundation, 870 Market St., Suite 728, San Francisco, CA 94102; Ty Lim, ty@gapa.org.

4328 ■ Gay and Lesbian Business Association of Santa Barbara (GLBA)
PO Box 90907
Santa Barbara, CA 93190
Ph: (805)684-4442
URL: glbasb.org

4329 ■ Carl Joseph Adelhardt Memorial Scholarships *(Undergraduate/Scholarship)*

Purpose: To provide financial assistance to those students who are in need. **Focus:** General studies/Field of study not

Awards are arranged alphabetically below their administering organizations

specified. **Qualif.:** Applicants must be students enrolled or planning to enroll at a post-secondary institution in Santa Barbara County. **Criteria:** Scholarships are awarded based upon the potential for lasting contribution to the Santa Barbara gay and lesbian community, career goals, and financial need.
Funds Avail.: No specific amount. **Duration:** Annual. **To Apply:** Applicants must submit the following: completed application including statements of community involvement and financial need; an autobiography/personal statement; a copy of current college and/or high school transcript of records; two letters of recommendation from a community member and the other one must come from a teacher or faculty member of their institution. **Deadline:** July 30. **Remarks:** Established in 2005.

4330 ■ Stephen Logan Memorial Scholarships (Undergraduate/Scholarship)

Purpose: To provide financial assistance to students who are in need. **Focus:** General studies/Field of study not specified. **Qualif.:** Applicants must be enrolled or planning to enroll at a post-secondary institution in Santa Barbara County. **Criteria:** Recipients will be selected based upon the potential contribution to the Santa Barbara gay and lesbian community; career goals; and financial need.
Funds Avail.: No specific amount. **Duration:** Annual. **To Apply:** Applicants must submit the following: completed application including statements of community involvement and financial need; an autobiography/personal statement; a copy of current college and/or high school transcript of records; two letters of recommendation from a community member and the other one must come from a teacher or a faculty member of their institution. **Deadline:** July 30. **Remarks:** Established in 2000.

4331 ■ The Raffin-Gathercole Scholarships (Undergraduate/Scholarship)

Purpose: To help LGBT youth succeed academically. **Focus:** General studies/Field of study not specified. **Qualif.:** Applicants must be enrolled or planning to enroll at a post-secondary institution in Santa Barbara County. **Criteria:** Scholarships are awarded based upon the potential for lasting contribution to the Santa Barbara gay and lesbian community, career goals, and financial need.
Funds Avail.: No specific amount. **Duration:** Annual. **To Apply:** Applicants must submit the following: completed application including statements of community involvement and financial need; an autobiography/personal statement; a copy of current college and/or high school transcript of records; two letters of recommendation from a community member and the other one must come from a teacher or faculty member of their institution. **Deadline:** July 30. **Remarks:** Established in 2003.

4332 ■ Gemological Institute of America (GIA)
The Robert Mouawad Campus
5345 Armada Dr.
Carlsbad, CA 92008
Ph: (760)603-4000
Fax: (760)603-4080
Free: 800-421-7250
E-mail: admissions@gia.edu
URL: www.gia.edu

4333 ■ ColorMasters Scholarships (Undergraduate/Scholarship)

Purpose: To provide financial support to applicants employed by a jewelry store that carries ColorMasters products. **Focus:** Gemology. **Qualif.:** Applicants must be U.S. citizens and permanent residents; must be at least 18 years old; must have a high school diploma or GED equivalency; must be applying for Distance Education School of Gemology Accredited Jewelry Professionals (AJP) diploma program. **Criteria:** Preference will be given to applicants employed by a jewelry store that carries ColorMasters products.
Funds Avail.: $1,000. **Duration:** Annual. **To Apply:** Applicants must complete the GIA Scholarship application (available on the website), with a letter of recommendation from a person in the jewelry industry. **Deadline:** April 30 and September 30.

4334 ■ GIA Scholarship- Distance Education eLearning (Graduate/Scholarship)

Purpose: To promote the study of gemology. **Focus:** Gemology. **Qualif.:** Applicants must be students enrolled in any Distance Education eLearning course. They must also be U.S. citizens or U.S. permanent residents. **Criteria:** Applications will be reviewed by the GIA scholarship committee.
Funds Avail.: $4,000. **Duration:** Annual. **To Apply:** Applicant must complete the GIA Scholarship application (available at the website), with a letter of recommendation from a person in the jewelry industry.

4335 ■ GIA Scholarships - On Campus (Graduate/Scholarship)

Purpose: To promote the study of gemology. **Focus:** Gemology. **Qualif.:** Applicants must be students enrolled in on-campus programs including the Graduate Diamonds program, the Graduate Colored Stones program, or the following Jewelry Manufacturing Arts programs: Jewelry Design and Comprehensive CAD/CAM for Jewelry. **Criteria:** Applications will be reviewed by the GIA scholarship committee.
Funds Avail.: $22,000. **To Apply:** Applicant must complete the GIA Scholarship application (available at the website), with a letter of recommendation from a person in the jewelry industry. **Deadline:** April 30.

4336 ■ William Goldberg Diamond Corp. Scholarships (Undergraduate/Scholarship)

Purpose: To support individuals who are pursuing a gemology program. **Focus:** Gemology. **Qualif.:** Applicant must be U.S. citizen and permanent resident; at least 18 years old; have a high school diploma or GED equivalency; currently employed or planning to enter in the jewelry industry; applying for any School of Gemology course or program; past recipient of GIA scholarship within last five years are not eligible. **Criteria:** Applications will be reviewed by the GIA scholarship committee.
Funds Avail.: $10,000. **Number Awarded:** 1. **To Apply:** Applicant must complete the GIA Scholarship application (available at the website), with a letter of recommendation from a person in the jewelry industry. Send application and supporting documents to: Gemological Institute of America, Office of Student Financial Assistance. **Deadline:** April 30 and October 31.

4337 ■ Morris Hanauer Scholarships (Undergraduate/Scholarship)

Purpose: To support individuals who are pursuing a gemology program. **Focus:** Gemology. **Qualif.:** Applicant must be U.S. citizen and permanent resident; at least 18 years

Awards are arranged alphabetically below their administering organizations

old; have a high school diploma or GED equivalency; currently employed or planning to enter in the jewelry industry; applying for Distance Education School of Gemology course or program; past recipient of GIA scholarship within last five years are not eligible. **Criteria:** Applications will be reviewed by the GIA scholarship committee.

Funds Avail.: $600. **Number Awarded:** 1. **To Apply:** Applicants must complete the GIA Scholarship application (available at the website), with a letter of recommendation from a person in the jewelry industry. **Deadline:** April 30 and September 30.

4338 ■ Peter Hess Scholarships *(Undergraduate/Scholarship)*

Purpose: To provide educational assistance to students. **Focus:** General studies/Field of study not specified. **Qualif.:** Applicants must be California residents. They must also be California Jewelers Association members or related to CJA members or willing to join the CJA if awarded the scholarship. **Criteria:** Applications will be reviewed by the GIA scholarship committee.

Funds Avail.: $1,000. **Duration:** Annual. **Number Awarded:** 1. **To Apply:** Applicants must complete the GIA Scholarship application (available at the website), with a letter of recommendation from a person in the jewelry industry. **Deadline:** October 15. **Contact:** Phone: 760-603-4131, 800-421-7250 ext. 4131; Email scholarship@gia.edu.

4339 ■ George W. Juno Memorial Scholarships *(Undergraduate/Scholarship)*

Purpose: To promote the study of gemology. **Focus:** Gemology. **Qualif.:** Applicants must be students enrolled in Distance Education eLearning gemology courses. **Criteria:** Applications will be reviewed by the GIA scholarship committee.

Funds Avail.: $1,000. **Number Awarded:** 1. **To Apply:** Applicant must complete the GIA Scholarship application (available at the website), with a letter of recommendation from a person in the jewelry industry. **Contact:** Phone: 760-603-4131, 800-421-7250 ext. 4131; Email scholarship@gia.edu.

4340 ■ Richard T. Liddicoat Scholarships *(Graduate/Scholarship)*

Purpose: To support individuals who are pursuing a gemology program. **Focus:** Gemology. **Qualif.:** Applicant must be U.S. citizen and permanent resident; at least 18 years old; have a high school diploma or GED equivalency; currently employed or planning to enter in the jewelry industry; applying for On Campus and Distance Education School of Gemology Graduate Gemologist (GG) program (includes 3 Lab classes of Diamond Grading, Colored Stone Grading, and Gem Identification); past recipient of GIA scholarship within last five years are not eligible. **Criteria:** Applications will be reviewed by the GIA scholarship committee.

Funds Avail.: $22,000. **To Apply:** Applicant must complete the GIA Scholarship application (available at the website), with a letter of recommendation from a person in the jewelry industry. Send application and supporting documents to Gemological Institute of America, Office of Student Financial Assistance. **Deadline:** April 30 and September 30.

4341 ■ Lone Star GIA Associate and Alumni Scholarships *(Undergraduate/Scholarship)*

Purpose: To provide educational assistance for students. **Focus:** General studies/Field of study not specified. **Qualif.:** Applicants must: be U.S. citizens and permanent residents; at least 18 years old; have a high school diploma or GED equivalency; be currently employed or planning to enter in the jewelry industry; and, be applying for any On Campus School or Distance Education course or program. **Criteria:** Applications will be reviewed by the GIA scholarship committee. Preference will be given to applicants residing in Texas, Oklahoma, Louisiana, New Mexico and Arkansas.

Funds Avail.: $500. **Number Awarded:** 1. **To Apply:** Applicants must complete the GIA Scholarship application (available at the website), with a letter of recommendation from a person in the jewelry industry.

4342 ■ Mikimoto Scholarships *(Graduate/Scholarship)*

Purpose: To support individuals who are pursuing a gemology program. **Focus:** Gemology. **Qualif.:** Applicants must be U.S. citizens and permanent residents; must be at least 18 years old; must have a high school diploma or GED equivalency; must be currently employed or planning to enter in the jewelry industry; must be applying for Distance Education School of Gemology Graduate Pearls diploma program. **Criteria:** Applications will be reviewed by the GIA scholarship committee.

Funds Avail.: $915. **Duration:** Annual. **To Apply:** Applicants must complete the GIA Scholarship application (available at the website), with a letter of recommendation from a person in the jewelry industry. **Deadline:** April 30 and September 30.

4343 ■ Eunice Miles Scholarships *(Undergraduate/Scholarship)*

Purpose: To provide educational assistance for students. **Focus:** General studies/Field of study not specified. **Qualif.:** Applicants must: be U.S. citizens and permanent residents; at least 18 years old; have a high school diploma or GED equivalency; be currently employed or planning to enter in the jewelry industry; and, be applying for any On Campus School or Distance Education course or program. **Criteria:** Applications will be reviewed by the GIA scholarship committee.

Funds Avail.: $500. **Duration:** Annual. **Number Awarded:** 5. **To Apply:** Applicants must complete the GIA Scholarship application (available at the website), with a letter of recommendation from a person in the jewelry industry.

4344 ■ North Texas GIA Alumni Association Scholarships *(Undergraduate/Scholarship)*

Purpose: To provide educational assistance for students. **Focus:** General studies/Field of study not specified. **Qualif.:** Applicants must: be U.S. citizens and permanent residents; at least 18 years old; have a high school diploma or GED equivalency; be currently employed or planning to enter in the jewelry industry; and, be applying for any On Campus School or Distance Education course or program. **Criteria:** Applications will be reviewed by the GIA scholarship committee. Preference will be given to applicants residing in Texas with zip codes ending in 75000-75799, 76000-76999, and 79000-79799.

Funds Avail.: $1,500. **Number Awarded:** 1. **To Apply:** Applicant must complete the GIA Scholarship application (available at the website), with a letter of recommendation from a person in the jewelry industry.

4345 ■ Daniel Swarovski and Company Scholarships *(Graduate/Scholarship)*

Purpose: To support individuals who are pursuing a gemology program. **Focus:** Gemology. **Qualif.:** Applicant must

Awards are arranged alphabetically below their administering organizations

be a U.S. citizen and permanent resident; at least 18 years old; have a high school diploma or GED equivalency; have 2-3 years work experience in jewelry industry; applying for On Campus School of Gemology Graduate Gemologist (GG) courses; past recipient of GIA scholarship within last five years are not eligible. **Criteria:** Applications will be reviewed by the GIA scholarship committee. **Funds Avail.:** $1,565. **Number Awarded:** 1. **To Apply:** Applicant must complete the GIA Scholarship application (available on the website), with two letters of recommendation, both of which must be from a person in the jewelry industry. Send application and supporting documents to: Gemological Institute of America, Office of Student Financial Assistance. **Deadline:** April 30 and October 31.

4346 ■ Kurt Wayne Scholarships *(Graduate/Scholarship)*

Purpose: To support individuals who are pursuing a gemology program. **Focus:** Art industries and trade; Gemology. **Qualif.:** Applicant must be U.S. citizen and permanent resident; at least 18 years old; have a high school diploma or GED equivalency; currently employed or planning to enter in the jewelry industry; applying for On Campus School of Jewelry Manufacturing Arts Graduate Jeweler (GJ) program courses; past recipient of GIA scholarship within last five years are not eligible. **Criteria:** Applications will be reviewed by the GIA scholarship committee. **Funds Avail.:** $1,000. **Number Awarded:** 1. **To Apply:** Applicant must complete the GIA Scholarship application (available at the website), with a letter of recommendation from a person in the jewelry industry. Send application and supporting documents to Gemological Institute of America, Office of Student Financial Assistance. **Deadline:** April 30 and October 31.

4347 ■ Robert B. Westover Scholarships *(Undergraduate/Scholarship)*

Purpose: To provide educational assistance to students. **Focus:** General studies/Field of study not specified. **Qualif.:** Applicants must be California residents. They must also be California Jewelers Association members or related to CJA members or willing to join the CJA if awarded the scholarship. **Criteria:** Applications will be reviewed by the GIA scholarship committee. **Funds Avail.:** $1,000. **Duration:** Annual. **Number Awarded:** 1. **To Apply:** Applicants must complete the GIA Scholarship application (available at the website), with a letter of recommendation from a person in the jewelry industry. **Deadline:** October 15. **Contact:** Phone: 760-603-4131, 800-421-7250 ext. 4131; Email scholarship@gia.edu.

4348 ■ General Aviation Manufacturers Association (GAMA)
1400 K St. NW, Ste. 801
Washington, DC 20005-2485
Ph: (202)393-1500
Fax: (202)842-4063
URL: www.gama.aero
Facebook: www.facebook.com/General.Aviation.Manufacturers.Association

4349 ■ Dr. Harold S. Wood Awards for Excellence *(Undergraduate/Award)*

Purpose: To support a college student attending a National Intercollegiate Flying Association member college or university program. **Focus:** Aviation. **Qualif.:** Candidate for the award must: be an enrolled college student; have completed a semester at a NIFA participating institution with GPA of 3.0 on a 4.0 scale or better; have rendered service to NIFA, aviation clubs or aviation-related activities or non-aviation extra-curricular service and contribution to school and community. **Criteria:** The applicant must be nominated and will be judged on the basis of GPA, community and school activities and aviation-related contributions. **Funds Avail.:** $1,000. **Duration:** One year. **Number Awarded:** 1. **To Apply:** Applicants must submit a completed application form together with their transcript and letters of recommendation. **Deadline:** April 18. **Contact:** Kate Fraser at 202-393-1500 or e-mail kfraser@gama.aero.

4350 ■ General Federation of Women's Clubs of Massachusetts
245 Dutton Rd.
Sudbury, MA 01776
Ph: (978)443-1617
E-mail: gfwcma@aol.com
URL: www.gfwcma.org

4351 ■ Boston City Federation "Return to School" Scholarships *(Undergraduate, Graduate/Scholarship)*

Purpose: To support a woman returning to college after an absence of at least four years. **Focus:** General studies/Field of study not specified. **Qualif.:** Applicants must be women maintaining legal residence in Massachusetts and returning to college after an absence of at least four years. **Criteria:** Selection will be based on the submitted application materials. **Funds Avail.:** $500. **Duration:** Annual. **To Apply:** Applicants must submit a completed application form along with a personal statement (maximum of 500 words) addressing professional goals and financial need; letter of reference from recent employer, or mentor in field of study; and official transcript of college grades. Applicants are required to submit the original and three additional copies of the application packet. **Deadline:** March 1.

4352 ■ Dorchester Woman's Club Music Scholarship - Voice *(Undergraduate/Scholarship)*

Purpose: To support undergraduate voice majors. **Focus:** Music, Vocal. **Qualif.:** Applicants must be Massachusetts residents and undergraduate students currently enrolled in a four-year accredited college, university or school of music, majoring in voice. **Criteria:** Selection shall be based on the aforementioned applicants' qualifications and compliance with the application details. **Funds Avail.:** $500. **Duration:** Annual. **To Apply:** Applicants must submit a completed application form along with a personal statement (maximum of 500 words) addressing professional goals, financial need, experience and repertoire; letter of recommendation from college department head, major professor or voice instructor (original on college letterhead); and official transcript of college grades. **Deadline:** March 1. **Contact:** Virginia T. Williams; Email: dlvtwilliams@aol.com.

4353 ■ GFWCMA Communication Disorder/Speech Therapy Scholarships *(Graduate/Scholarship)*

Purpose: To support students in their pursuit of communication disorder/speech therapy education. **Focus:**

Speech and language pathology/Audiology. **Qualif.:** Applicants must be maintaining legal residences in Massachusetts. **Criteria:** Selection shall be based on the aforementioned applicants' qualifications and compliance with the application details.

Funds Avail.: Up to $500. **Duration:** Annual. **To Apply:** Applicants must submit a completed application form along with a personal statement (maximum of 500 words) addressing professional goals and financial need; a letter of reference from the department chair (original on school letterhead); and official transcript of college grades. Applicants are required to submit the original and additional three copies of the application packet. **Deadline:** March 1.

4354 ■ Nickels for Notes Music Scholarship (Undergraduate/Scholarship)

Purpose: To support students majoring in Piano, Instrument, Music Education, Music Therapy or Voice. **Focus:** Education, Music; Music therapy; Music, Piano; Music, Vocal. **Qualif.:** Applicants must be senior students in a Massachusetts High School who will major in Piano, Instrument, Music Education, Music Therapy or Voice. **Criteria:** Selection shall be based on the aforementioned applicants' qualifications and compliance with the application details.

Funds Avail.: $500. **Duration:** Annual. **To Apply:** Applicants must submit a completed application form along with a personal statement (maximum of 500 words) addressing professional goals, experience and repertoire (if applicable) and financial need; a letter of recommendation from either High School Principal or Music Instructor (original, on school letterhead); and official transcript of high school grades. **Deadline:** March 1. **Contact:** Virginia T. Williams, GFWC of Massachusetts Music Chairman; Email: dlvtwilliams@aol.com.

4355 ■ Pennies for Art Scholarships (Undergraduate/Scholarship)

Purpose: To support talented students in their educational pursuits. **Focus:** Art. **Qualif.:** Applicant must be a senior in a Massachusetts High School, or home schooled and have achieved the standards for graduation set by the town of residence. **Criteria:** Selection shall be based on the aforementioned applicant's qualifications and compliance with the application details.

Funds Avail.: Up to $500. **Duration:** Annual. **To Apply:** Applicant must submit a completed application form together with a personal statement (maximum of 500 words) addressing professional goals and financial need; a letter of recommendation from high school art instructor (original on school letterhead); official transcript of grades; and a portfolio of three examples of original artwork, matted, not framed, not larger than 12" X 18" overall dimension (printed name and address on the back of each example and on the portfolio). **Deadline:** March 1.

4356 ■ Catherine E. Philbin Scholarships (Undergraduate, Graduate/Scholarship)

Purpose: To support graduate or undergraduate students residing in Massachusetts and majoring in Public Health. **Focus:** Public health. **Qualif.:** Applicants must be undergraduate or graduate students maintaining legal residence in Massachusetts and pursuing study in Public Health. **Criteria:** Selection will be based on the committee's criteria.

Funds Avail.: $500. **Duration:** Annual. **To Apply:** Applicants must submit a completed application form together with a personal statement (maximum of 500 words) addressing professional goals and financial need; a letter of reference from the department chair (original on school letterhead); and official transcript of college grades. Applicants are required to submit the original and three additional copies of the application packet. **Deadline:** March 1.

4357 ■ Women's Italian Club of Boston Scholarships (Undergraduate/Scholarship)

Purpose: To support students of Italian heritage in their educational pursuits. **Focus:** Music. **Qualif.:** Applicant must be a senior in a Massachusetts High School, or home schooled and have achieved the standards for graduation set by the town of residence. **Criteria:** Selection will be based on the submitted application materials.

Funds Avail.: $1,000. **Duration:** Annual. **To Apply:** Applicant must submit a completed application form together with a personal statement (maximum of 500 words) addressing goals, Italian heritage and work experience; official transcript of high school grades; and two letters of recommendation from counselor or teachers (original on school letterhead). Applicant is also required to submit one original and three additional copies of the application packet. **Deadline:** March 1. **Contact:** Mary Ann Pierce, Scholarship Chairman at mapgfwc@msn.com.

4358 ■ General Motors Foundation
300 Renaissance Ctr.
Detroit, MI 48265-3000
URL: www.gm.com

4359 ■ Buick Achievers Scholarship Program (Undergraduate/Scholarship)

Purpose: To support students who demonstrate excellence in the classroom and communities to attend college. **Focus:** Business; Design; Engineering; Mathematics and mathematical sciences; Science; Technology. **Qualif.:** Applicants must be high school seniors or college undergraduate students who plan to enroll full-time and major in a specified course of study that focuses on engineering, technology, design or business at an accredited four-year college or university in the United States or Puerto Rico; must be US citizens and have a permanent residence in the United States or Puerto Rico. **Criteria:** Scholarships will be awarded based on participation and leadership in community and school activities, interest in the automotive industry, academic achievement and financial need. Special consideration will be given to those who are first-generation college students, females, minorities, military veterans or dependents of military personnel.

Funds Avail.: $25,000. **Duration:** Annual. **To Apply:** Applicants must the website at http://wwwbuickachievers.com for the online application process or may contact the Scholarship America for other information.

4360 ■ Genesee Finger Lakes Chapter of Air and Waste Management Association (GFL AWMA)
PO Box 92006
Rochester, NY 14692
URL: www.gflawma.com

4361 ■ GFLC AWMA Scholarships (Undergraduate, Graduate/Scholarship)

Purpose: To support and recognize R.I.T. environmental management students. **Focus:** Environmental science.

Awards are arranged alphabetically below their administering organizations

Qualif.: Applicants must be undergraduate or graduate students in an environmental engineering, environmental science or environmental management program attending a recognized college/university located within the New York counties of Allegany, Chemung, Genesee, Livingston, Monroe, Orleans, Schuyler, Seneca, Steuben, Wyoming or Yates. **Criteria:** Award is given based on academic records, leadership in academics and in the community and future academic and career potential.

Funds Avail.: No specific amount. **Duration:** Annual. **To Apply:** Applicants must submit a completed scholarship application form along with two most recent academic transcripts. **Contact:** Genesee Finger Lakes Chapter Air and Waste Management Association, at the above address.

4362 ■ Geological Society of America (GSA)
3300 Penrose Pl.
Boulder, CO 80301
Ph: (303)357-1000
Fax: (303)357-1070
E-mail: gsaservice@geosociety.org
URL: www.geosociety.org/index.htm
Facebook: www.facebook.com/GSA.1888
Twitter: twitter.com/geosociety

4363 ■ Farouk El-Baz Student Research Grants
(Graduate, Undergraduate/Grant)

Purpose: To encourage and support desert studies by students in their senior year of undergraduate studies, or at the Master's or Ph.D. level. **Focus:** Geology. **Qualif.:** Applicants must be GSA members in their senior year of their undergraduate studies, or at the Master's or Ph.D. level. **Criteria:** Recipients will be selected based on the significance of the project proposal.

Funds Avail.: No specific amount. **Duration:** Annual. **To Apply:** Applicants must submit a one-page description of proposed research under title; letter of recommendation by university research advisor. **Deadline:** February 1. **Contact:** E-mail at awards@geosociety.org.

4364 ■ Geological Society of America Graduate Student Research Grants *(Doctorate, Graduate/Grant)*

Purpose: To provide partial support of master's and doctoral thesis research in geological science for graduate students enrolled in universities in the United States, Canada, Mexico, and Central America. **Focus:** Geology. **Qualif.:** Applicants must be GSA members currently enrolled in a U.S., Canadian, Mexican, or Central American university or college in an earth science degree program with geologic component. **Criteria:** Recipients will be selected based on the qualifications of the candidate and their academic standing.

Funds Avail.: $2,500. **Duration:** Annual. **To Apply:** Applicants must fill out the online application form. **Deadline:** February 1. **Contact:** Applicants may e-mail their questions at awards@geosociety.org or call 303-357-1028.

4365 ■ George Cedric Metcalf Charitable Foundation
38 Madison Ave.
Toronto, ON, Canada M5R 2S1
Fax: (416)926-0370
URL: metcalffoundation.com

Awards are arranged alphabetically below their administering organizations

4366 ■ Metcalf Innovation Fellowships *(Advanced Professional, Professional development/Fellowship)*

Purpose: To support individuals who have vision, passion for their issue, intellectual rigour and willingness to ask hard questions and propose novel solutions. **Focus:** Medical research. **Qualif.:** Applicants must be policymakers, managers, academicians, or entrepreneurs; must have a significant record of achievement and be recognized within their field; and must have worked in an area related to their proposed exploration for a minimum of ten years. **Criteria:** Selection will be based on the applicants' respective research proposals.

Funds Avail.: Maximum of 30,000 Canadian Dollars. **To Apply:** The Foundation does not accept unsolicited applications for the program. Applicants may verify the website for the release of request for proposals (RFP).

4367 ■ Georgetown Working League
PO Box 262
Georgetown, ME 04548
URL: georgetownworkingleague.org

4368 ■ Georgetown Working League Scholarships *(Undergraduate/Scholarship)*

Purpose: To provide financial assistance to students seeking higher education. **Focus:** General studies/Field of study not specified. **Qualif.:** Applicants must be students seeking higher education who reside in Georgetown, Maine; must have been accepted or wait-listed at an accredited school for further advances education. **Criteria:** Selection will be based on the committee's criteria.

Funds Avail.: No specific amount. **Duration:** Annual; One year. **To Apply:** Applicants must submit complete application form from high school guidance counselor; copy of most recent transcript; computer generated essay; and copy of school or college acceptance letter or waitlist letter. **Deadline:** April 30.

4369 ■ Riggs Cove Foundation Scholarships *(Undergraduate/Scholarship)*

Purpose: To provide financial assistance to students seeking higher education. **Focus:** General studies/Field of study not specified. **Qualif.:** Applicants must be students seeking higher education who reside in Georgetown, Maine; must have been accepted or wait-listed at an accredited school for further advances education. **Criteria:** Selection will be based on the committee's criteria.

Funds Avail.: No specific amount. **Duration:** Annual; One year. **To Apply:** Applicants must submit complete application form from high school guidance counselor; copy of most recent transcript; computer generated essay; and copy of school or college acceptance letter or waitlist letter. **Deadline:** April 30.

4370 ■ Benjamin Riggs Scholarships *(Undergraduate/Scholarship)*

Purpose: To provide financial assistance to students seeking higher education. **Focus:** General studies/Field of study not specified. **Qualif.:** Applicants must be students seeking higher education who reside in Georgetown, Maine; must have been accepted or wait-listed at an accredited school for further advances education. **Criteria:** Selection will be based on the committee's criteria.

Funds Avail.: No specific amount. **Duration:** Annual; One year. **To Apply:** Applicants must submit complete application form from high school guidance counselor; copy of most recent transcript; computer generated essay; and copy of school or college acceptance letter or waitlist letter. **Deadline:** April 30.

4371 ■ Robinhood Marine Center Scholarships
(Undergraduate/Scholarship)

Purpose: To provide financial assistance to students seeking higher education. **Focus:** General studies/Field of study not specified. **Qualif.:** Applicants must be students seeking higher education who reside in Georgetown, Maine; must have been accepted or wait-listed at an accredited school for further advances education. **Criteria:** Selection will be based on the committee's criteria.

Funds Avail.: No specific amount. **Duration:** Annual; One year. **To Apply:** Applicants must submit complete application form from high school guidance counselor; copy of most recent transcript; computer generated essay; and copy of school or college acceptance letter or waitlist letter. **Deadline:** April 30.

4372 ■ Josephine Hooker Shain Scholarships
(Undergraduate/Scholarship)

Purpose: To provide financial assistance to students seeking higher education. **Focus:** General studies/Field of study not specified. **Qualif.:** Applicants must be students seeking higher education who reside in Georgetown, Maine; must have been accepted or wait-listed at an accredited school for further advances education. **Criteria:** Selection will be based on the committee's criteria.

Funds Avail.: No specific amount. **Duration:** Annual; One year. **To Apply:** Applicants must submit complete application form from high school guidance counselor; copy of most recent transcript; computer generated essay; and copy of school or college acceptance letter or waitlist letter. **Deadline:** April 30.

4373 ■ Woodex Bearing Company Scholarships
(Undergraduate/Scholarship)

Purpose: To provide financial assistance to students seeking higher education. **Focus:** General studies/Field of study not specified. **Qualif.:** Applicants must be students seeking higher education who reside in Georgetown, Maine; must have been accepted or wait-listed at an accredited school for further advances education. **Criteria:** Selection will be based on the committee's criteria.

Funds Avail.: No specific amount. **Duration:** Annual; One year. **To Apply:** Applicants must submit complete application form from high school guidance counselor; copy of most recent transcript; computer generated essay; and copy of school or college acceptance letter or waitlist letter. **Deadline:** April 30.

4374 ■ Georgia Association of Broadcasters (GAB)
6 W Druid Hills Dr. NE, Ste. 330
Atlanta, GA 30329-2150
Ph: (770)395-7200
E-mail: admin@gab.org
URL: gab.org

4375 ■ E. Lanier Finch Scholarships *(Undergraduate/Scholarship)*

Purpose: To provide financial assistance to deserving students who will carry on the tradition of excellence in Georgia's broadcasting industry. **Focus:** Broadcasting. **Qualif.:** Applicant must be registered as a full time student at a fully accredited college or university; a rising junior or senior studying for a degree in some aspect of the broadcasting industry and a bona fide resident of the state of Georgia. **Criteria:** GAB participating member stations will select the winning candidates.

Funds Avail.: $1,500. **Duration:** Annual. **To Apply:** Application form can be downloaded online. Applicants must complete the form, and attach additional sheets as necessary. **Deadline:** April 30.

4376 ■ Georgia Association of Water Professionals (GAWP)
1655 Enterprise Way
Marietta, GA 30067
Ph: (770)618-8690
Fax: (770)618-8695
URL: www.gawp.org

4377 ■ GAWP Graduate Scholarships *(Graduate/Scholarship)*

Purpose: To provide financial assistance to Georgia Association of Water Professionals members and their children who want to pursue their education. **Focus:** General studies/Field of study not specified. **Qualif.:** Applicants must hold an active, individual membership in GAWP; must be graduates of an accredited college or university. **Criteria:** Applicants will be selected by the scholarship committee based on their academic achievements.

Funds Avail.: $2,000. **To Apply:** Applicants must complete the application available in the website. **Deadline:** February 28. **Remarks:** Established in 2003.

4378 ■ Philip R. Karr, III Scholarship Fund
(Graduate/Scholarship)

Purpose: To provide financial assistance to GAWP members and their children who want to pursue their education. **Focus:** General studies/Field of study not specified. **Qualif.:** Applicants must be residents of Georgia, or entering or attending a college or university graduate school located in Georgia; must be graduates of an accredited college or university. **Criteria:** Applicants will be selected by the scholarship committee based on their academic achievements.

Funds Avail.: $2,000. **Duration:** one year. **To Apply:** Applicants are required submit a short essay (not to exceed 1,500 words); must complete the application available in the website. **Deadline:** February 28. **Remarks:** Established in 1996.

4379 ■ Georgia Engineering Foundation
Harris Tower, Ste. 700
233 Peachtree St.
Atlanta, GA 30303
Ph: (404)521-2324
Fax: (404)521-0283
URL: www.gefinc.org

4380 ■ Georgia Engineering Foundation Scholarships *(Graduate/Scholarship)*

Purpose: To provide financial assistance to those students who are in need. **Focus:** Engineering. **Qualif.:** Applicants

Awards are arranged alphabetically below their administering organizations

must be Georgia students (college freshmen, upperclassmen and graduate students) who are preparing for a career in engineering or engineering technology; must be U.S citizens; must be enrolled in an engineering or engineering technology ABET-accredited program leading to a B.S or graduate degree. **Criteria:** Preference will be given to students who meet the criteria.

Funds Avail.: $1,000-$5,000. **Duration:** Annual. **Number Awarded:** Varies. **To Apply:** Applicants must complete an online application form; must submit official transcript(s) in a sealed envelope; letter of recommendations; photograph (no larger than 4"x 6"); and SAT scores. **Deadline:** August 31. **Contact:** John Boneberg, Scholarship Chair at John.Boneberg@obg.com.

4381 ■ Georgia Gerontology Society
P.O. Box 7905
Atlanta, GA 30357
Ph: (706)296-9795
URL: www.georgiagerontologysociety.org

4382 ■ Virginia M. Smyth Scholarships *(Graduate/Scholarship)*

Purpose: To offer financial support to a person committed to embarking upon, or seeking to advance, a career in aging. **Focus:** Gerontology. **Qualif.:** Applicants must be full-time graduate students in the field of aging. **Criteria:** Selection will be based on the committee's criteria.

Funds Avail.: $3,000. **Number Awarded:** 1. **To Apply:** Applicants must complete and submit the scholarship application packet to Abby Cox. **Deadline:** April 24. **Contact:** Abby Cox at administrator@georgiagerontologysociety.org.

4383 ■ Georgia Library Association (GLA)
PO Box 793
Rex, GA 30273
Ph: (678)466-4334
Free: 800-999-8558
URL: gla.georgialibraries.org

4384 ■ GLA Beard Scholarships *(Master's/Scholarship)*

Purpose: To provide financial assistance towards completing a Master's degree in library science. **Focus:** Library and archival sciences. **Qualif.:** Applicants must be completing their senior year at an accredited college or university and have been accepted as students in a Master's degree program at a library school accredited by the American Library Association; must be ready to begin the program of study not later than the fall term of the year in which the scholarship is awarded; must indicate an intention to complete degree requirements within three years; must maintain a passing grade average throughout the program; must agree to work for one year following graduation from a library school. **Criteria:** Selection will be based on the application and supporting documents. Residents of Georgia will be given preference, but not a requirement.

Funds Avail.: $1,000. **Duration:** Annual. **To Apply:** Applicants must complete the application form; must submit a proof of admission to an American Library Association-accredited Master's program, two letters of reference, official transcripts of all academic coursework and short essay stating the reasons why choosing to become a librarian and ultimate professional goals. **Deadline:** May 23. **Contact:** Email at glascholarships2015@gmail.com (for sending all documents, except transcripts). Transcripts may be mailed to Mack Freeman, GLA Scholarship Committee Vice-chair, c/o West Georgia Regional Library, 710 Rome Street, Carrollton, GA 30117.

4385 ■ GLA Hubbard Scholarships *(Master's/Scholarship)*

Purpose: To recruit excellent librarians for Georgia and provide financial assistance towards completing a Master's degree in library science. **Focus:** Library and archival sciences. **Qualif.:** Applicants must be completing their senior year at an accredited college or university and have been accepted as students in a Master's degree program at a library school accredited by the American Library Association; must be ready to begin the program of study not later than the fall term of the year in which the scholarship is awarded; must indicate an intention to complete degree requirements within three years; must maintain a passing grade average throughout the program; must agree to work for one year following graduation from a library school. **Criteria:** Selection will be based on the application and supporting documents. Residents of Georgia will be given preference, but not a requirement.

Funds Avail.: $3,000. **Duration:** Annual. **To Apply:** Applicants must complete the application form; must submit a proof of admission to an American Library Association-accredited Master's program, two letters of reference, official transcripts of all academic coursework and short essay stating the reasons why choosing to become a librarian and ultimate professional goals. **Deadline:** May 23. **Contact:** Email at glascholarships2015@gmail.com.

4386 ■ Georgia Press Educational Foundation (GPEF)
3066 Mercer University Dr., Ste. 200
Atlanta, GA 30341-4137
Ph: (770)454-6776
Fax: (770)454-6778
E-mail: mail@gapress.org
URL: gapress.org/georgia-press-educational-foundation

4387 ■ Durwood McAlister Scholarships *(Undergraduate/Scholarship)*

Purpose: To provide scholarship for outstanding students majoring in print journalism at a Georgia college or university. **Focus:** Journalism; Publishing. **Qualif.:** Applicants must be junior or senior students majoring in either the news-editorial or public relations sequence at the Henry W. Grady College of Journalism and Mass Communication at the University of Georgia. They must be legal residents of Georgia for two years or must be residents of the state for three years. **Criteria:** Selection will be based on the committee's criteria.

Funds Avail.: $2,000. **Duration:** Annual. **To Apply:** Scholarship application can be obtained from the GPEF website. The following documents must be enclosed in the application: most recent grade transcript; anticipated budget; school photograph; copy of SAT scores; parents'/applicant's tax return; and recommendations of high school counselor, principal, college professor, or Georgia Press Association member. **Deadline:** March 1. **Remarks:** Established in 1992.

4388 ■ Morris Newspaper Corp. Scholarships *(Undergraduate/Scholarship)*

Purpose: To provide scholarships for outstanding print journalism students attending a Georgia college or univer-

sity. **Focus:** Journalism; Publishing. **Qualif.:** Applicants must be junior or senior students majoring in either the news-editorial or public relations sequence at the Henry W. Grady College of Journalism and Mass Communication at the University of Georgia. They must be legal residents of Georgia for two years or must be residents of the state for three years. **Criteria:** Selection will be based on the committee's criteria.
Funds Avail.: $2,000. **Duration:** Annual. **To Apply:** Applications are submitted through newspapers in the Morris Newspaper Corporation chain. **Deadline:** March 1. **Remarks:** Established in 1987.

4389 ■ William C. Rogers Scholarships
(Undergraduate/Scholarship)

Purpose: To assist Georgia residents attending Georgia colleges and universities who are pursuing careers in journalism and mass communication. **Focus:** Communications; Journalism; Media arts; Public affairs; Public relations. **Qualif.:** Applicants must be junior or senior students majoring in either the news-editorial sequence at the Henry W. Grady College of Journalism and Mass Communication at the University of Georgia. They must be legal residents of Georgia for two years or must be residents of the state for three years. **Criteria:** Recipients will be selected from three nominations submitted by the University of Georgia. Factors considered include family income and established individual need.
Funds Avail.: $2,000. **Duration:** Annual. **To Apply:** Scholarship application can be obtained from the GPEF website. The following documents must be enclosed in the application: most recent grade transcript; anticipated budget; school photograph; copy of SAT scores; parents'/applicant's tax return; and recommendations of high school counselor, principal, college professor, or Georgia Press Association member. **Deadline:** March 1. **Remarks:** Established in 1981.

4390 ■ Kirk Sutlive Scholarships *(Undergraduate/Scholarship)*

Purpose: To assist Georgia residents attending Georgia colleges and universities who are pursuing careers in journalism and mass communication. **Focus:** Communications; Journalism; Media arts; Public affairs; Public relations. **Qualif.:** Applicants must be junior or senior students majoring in either the news-editorial or public relations sequence at the Henry W. Grady College of Journalism and Mass Communication at the University of Georgia. They must be legal residents of Georgia for two years or must be residents of the state for three years. **Criteria:** Recipients will be selected from three nominations submitted by the University of Georgia. Factors considered include family income and established individual need.
Funds Avail.: $1,000. **Duration:** Annual. **To Apply:** Scholarship application can be obtained from the GPEF website. The following documents must be enclosed in the application: most recent grade transcript; anticipated budget; school photograph; copy of SAT scores; parents'/your tax return; and recommendations of high school counselor, principal, college professor, or Georgia Press Association member. **Deadline:** March 1. **Remarks:** Established in 1986.

4391 ■ Gerber Foundation
4747 W 48th St., Ste. 153
Fremont, MI 49412-8119
Ph: (231)924-3175
Fax: (231)924-7906
E-mail: tgf@gerberfoundation.org
URL: www.gerberfoundation.org

4392 ■ Gerber Foundation Merit Scholarships
(Undergraduate/Scholarship)

Purpose: To support graduating seniors from Newaygo and Muskegon Counties with the expenses of higher education. **Focus:** General studies/Field of study not specified. **Qualif.:** Applicants must: be high school students graduating from one a high school in Newaygo and Muskegon Counties in Michigan planning to pursue a course of study leading to a four year baccalaureate degree, two year associate degree, or a vocational or technical training program leading to a certificate, at an accredited, non-profit college or university in the United States; and, have a GPA of 3.70 or below. **Criteria:** Recipients will be selected based on overall academic record and achievements, school recommendation, leadership qualities, high moral character, a constructive attitude and involvement in diverse curricular, extracurricular, and community activities with evidence of community service.
Funds Avail.: $2,300. **Duration:** Annual. **To Apply:** Applications are of two types: online, and paper applications. Aspiring applicants must visit either the program or the bestowing organization's website for the checklist or the necessary application requirements. **Deadline:** February 28. **Remarks:** Established in 1999.

4393 ■ Daniel Gerber, Sr. Medallion Scholarships
(Undergraduate/Scholarship)

Purpose: To support graduating seniors from Newaygo County with the expenses of higher education. **Focus:** General studies/Field of study not specified. **Qualif.:** Applicants must: be high school students graduating from one of the five school districts in Newaygo County, Michigan and planning to pursue a course of study leading to a four year baccalaureate degree, two year associate degree, or a vocational or technical training program leading to a certificate, at an accredited, non-profit college or university in the United States; and, have a GPA of 3.71 or higher. **Criteria:** Recipients will be selected based on overall academic record and achievements, school recommendation, leadership qualities, high moral character, a constructive attitude and involvement in diverse curricular, extracurricular, and community activities with evidence of community service.
Funds Avail.: $9,200. **Duration:** Annual. **To Apply:** Applications are of two types: online, and paper applications. Aspiring applicants must visit either the program or the bestowing organization's website for the checklist or the necessary application requirements. **Deadline:** February 28. **Remarks:** Established in 2002.

4394 ■ German Historical Institute (GHI)
1607 New Hampshire Ave. NW
Washington, DC 20009-2562
Ph: (202)387-3355
Fax: (202)387-6437
E-mail: info@ghi-dc.org
URL: www.ghi-dc.org

4395 ■ German Historical Institute Doctoral and Postdoctoral Fellowships *(Doctorate, Postgraduate/Fellowship)*

Purpose: To provide financial assistance to German and American students. **Focus:** German studies; History,

Awards are arranged alphabetically below their administering organizations

American. **Qualif.:** Applicants must be German and American doctoral students and post-doctoral scholars in the fields of German history, the history of German-American relations, historical role of Germany and the USA in international relations. **Criteria:** Scholarship recipients will be selected based on the jury's review of the application materials.

Funds Avail.: 1,700 Euros for doctoral students; 3,000 Euros for post-doctoral scholars. **Duration:** Annual. **To Apply:** Applicants must submit two copies of: cover letter; curriculum vitae; last diploma; project descriptions (in 3,000 words); research schedule; letter of reference. **Deadline:** April 1.

4396 ■ German Historical Institute Fellowships at the Horner Library *(Doctorate/Fellowship)*

Purpose: To provide travel subsidy and allowance to PhD and MA students for their research. **Focus:** General studies/Field of study not specified. **Qualif.:** Applicants must be PhD or MA students. **Criteria:** Scholarship recipient will be selected based on the Selection Committee's review of the application materials.

Funds Avail.: $1,000-$3,500. **Duration:** Up to four weeks. **Number Awarded:** 2-4. **To Apply:** Applicants must submit a (two-page) project description; curriculum vitae, copies of transcripts; and the name of the referee. Applications (in English or German) should be made electronically to the GHI. **Deadline:** March 5.

4397 ■ German Marshall Fund of the United States (GMF)
1744 R St. NW
Washington, DC 20009
Ph: (202)683-2650
Fax: (202)265-1662
E-mail: info@gmfus.org
URL: www.gmfus.org
Facebook: www.facebook.com/gmfus
Twitter: twitter.com/gmfus

4398 ■ APSA Congressional Fellowships *(Other/Fellowship)*

Purpose: To expand public knowledge and awareness of the U.S. Congress around the world. **Focus:** Political science. **Qualif.:** Applicants must be German citizens, possess superior written and spoken English language skills, and have a minimum of three years work experience. Candidates should demonstrate how their professional path would benefit from the APSA Congressional Fellowship. Potential candidates include political journalists, early-to-mid-career academics with outstanding records, and experts from the fields of foreign policy, economics, migration, environment, science and social issues. Representatives from business, trade organizations and labor unions are invited to apply provided they can demonstrate existing political and public policy ties. **Criteria:** Selection will be based on applicants' commitment to transatlantic relations, quality of their written and oral presentation, preparation for the program, professional excellence and current and future involvement in the public policy in Germany.

Funds Avail.: No specific amount. **To Apply:** Applicants must submit the following: application form (available at the website); a curriculum vitae with accompanying cover letter; two fellowship-specific letters of reference; and an essay addressing the significance of the Congressional Fellowship program for the applicants' future career and what value they would bring to a congressional office or committee. **Deadline:** January 15. **Contact:** Ursula Soyez, Senior Program Officer; Email: usoyez@gmfus.org.

4399 ■ Marshall Memorial Fellowships *(Other/Fellowship)*

Purpose: To provide a unique opportunity for emerging leaders from U.S. and Europe to explore policies, institutions and culture on the other side of the Atlantic. **Focus:** General studies/Field of study not specified. **Qualif.:** Applicants must be nominated by a recognized leader in their community or professional field. All Marshall Memorial Fellowship alumni are also eligible to nominate for the program. Nominators should be in a senior position and be able to evaluate the candidate's leadership potential. **Criteria:** Selection will be based on the committee's criteria.

Funds Avail.: No specific amount. **Duration:** Annual. **Number Awarded:** 75. **To Apply:** Applicants must complete the online application, which currently includes an application form, essays, a resume/CV and two letters of recommendation. Nominators should also submit a letter of recommendation. Upon submitting the applications to the selection partner, candidates will be further informed of the interview and selection process. **Remarks:** Established in 1982. **Contact:** German Marshall Fund of the United States, at the above address.

4400 ■ Transatlantic Fellows Program *(Other/Fellowship)*

Purpose: To develop a range of program and initiatives and build important networks of policymakers and analysts in the Euroatlantic community. **Focus:** General studies/Field of study not specified. **Qualif.:** Applicants must be policy-practitioners, journalists, business people and academics. **Criteria:** Selection will be based on the committee's criteria.

Funds Avail.: No specific amount. **Duration:** Annual. **To Apply:** Applicants may contact GMF office for more information on the application process.

4401 ■ Urban and Regional Policy (Comparative Domestic Policy) Fellowships *(Other/Fellowship)*

Purpose: To provide opportunities for practitioners and policy-makers working on economic and social issues at the urban and regional policy levels to meet with their counterparts across the Atlantic and discuss policies and measures that have been implemented. **Focus:** General studies/Field of study not specified. **Qualif.:** Applicants must be practitioners and policymakers working on local and state policy in the United States and Europe; be mid-career professionals engaged in targeted policy areas with an interest in gaining an understanding of how these issues are approached in a policy context other than their own and ability to translate lessons learned into policy action in their own community. Applicants must be civic leaders, policymakers or practitioners in state/local government, leaders from the private sector or representative of nonprofit and policy organizations. **Criteria:** Selection will be based on the committee's criteria.

Funds Avail.: No specific amount. **Duration:** Annual. **To Apply:** Interested candidates should see the program summary on the website for further details on the program and application process. **Deadline:** April 15. **Contact:** Bartek Starodaj, program coordinator; Email: bstarodaj@gmfus.org.

Awards are arranged alphabetically below their administering organizations

4402 ■ Peter R. Weitz Prize *(Other/Prize)*

Purpose: To acknowledge excellence and originality in reporting European or transatlantic affairs in the American media. **Focus:** General studies/Field of study not specified. **Qualif.:** Must be journalists covering European issues for American newspapers, magazines and online media, whether they are correspondents based in Europe or cover Europe from the United States. **Criteria:** Selection will be made by a jury of senior American and European journalists based on work published either in print or online by American news media during the previous calendar year. **Funds Avail.:** $10,000. **Duration:** Annual. **To Apply:** Candidates may contact the German Marshall Fund office for the application process. **Remarks:** Established in 1999. **Contact:** For more information on the Peter R. Weitz Prize and other opportunities for journalists, please contact Kristina Field at kfield@gmfus.org.

4403 ■ German Society of Pennsylvania (GSP)
611 Spring Garden St.
Philadelphia, PA 19123-3505
Ph: (215)627-2332
Fax: (215)627-5297
E-mail: info@germansociety.org
URL: www.germansociety.org
Facebook: www.facebook.com/GermanSocietyPA
Twitter: www.twitter.com/GermanSocietyPA

4404 ■ German Society Scholarships *(Undergraduate/Scholarship)*

Purpose: To provide financial assistance for students majoring in German language and literature. **Focus:** Foreign languages; German studies. **Qualif.:** Applicant must be a resident of the Greater Delaware Valley and a high school senior intending to major in German, or a German major (Double majors are also eligible). **Criteria:** Awards are based on the student's achievement and promise. Financial need may also be considered. **Funds Avail.:** $3,000. **Duration:** Annual. **To Apply:** Applicant must submit a completed application form; a German writing sample (up to one typewritten page); recent transcript; and two letters of reference. **Deadline:** March 7.

4405 ■ Getty Foundation
1200 Getty Ctr. Dr.
Los Angeles, CA 90049
Ph: (310)440-7300
E-mail: gettyfoundation@getty.edu
URL: www.getty.edu/foundation

4406 ■ Getty Conservation Guest Scholar Grants *(Professional development/Grant)*

Purpose: To provide an opportunity for professionals to pursue scholarly research in an interdisciplinary manner across traditional boundaries in areas of interest to the international conservation community. **Focus:** Conservation of natural resources. **Qualif.:** Applicants must be conservators, scientists or professionals who have attained distinction in conservation and allied fields. Applicants should have at least five years experience in the field of conservation and should have an established record of publications and other contributions to the field. **Criteria:** Grants are awarded on a competitive basis. Applications are reviewed by committee and evaluated by the Conservation Institute based on: an applicant's past achievements; their qualifications to undertake the project; how the project would benefit from the resources at the Getty, including its library and collections; and how the project would contribute to the advancement of practice in the conservation field. **Funds Avail.:** $3,500 per month. **Duration:** Annual; from 3 to 6 consecutive months. **To Apply:** Applicants are required to complete and submit the online Getty Conservation Guest Scholar Grant application form, which includes completing an online information sheet, uploading a project proposal, curriculum vitae, selected bibliography and a single optional writing sample. **Deadline:** November 3. **Contact:** Phone: 310-440-7374; Fax: 310-440-7703; Email: researchgrants@getty.edu.

4407 ■ Getty Foundation Library Research Grants *(Professional development/Grant)*

Purpose: To provide partial, short-term support for costs relating to travel and living expenses to scholars whose research requires use of specific collections housed in the Getty Research Institute. **Focus:** Library and archival sciences. **Qualif.:** Applicants must be scholars of all nationalities and at any level who demonstrate a compelling need to use materials housed in the Research Library, and whose place of residence is more than eighty miles from the Getty Center. **Criteria:** Selection will be based on the committee's criteria. **Funds Avail.:** Range from $500 to $2,500. **Duration:** Annual; Up to 3 months. **To Apply:** Applicants will be required to complete and submit the online Getty Library Research Grant application form which includes uploading a project proposal; curriculum vitae; selected bibliography of Getty Research Library Collections you wish to consult; and proposed estimated travel costs. Applicants must have two confidential letters of recommendation forwarded by their recommenders via e-mail to the Getty Foundation. Recommenders should attach a scanned original letter to the e-mail or may provide the recommendation in the body of the email. In all cases, letters of recommendation must come directly from the recommender's e-mail account and must clearly indicate the applicant's name and "Library Research Grant" in the subject line, and include the recommender's name and title. **Deadline:** October 15. **Contact:** Phone: 310-440-7374; Fax: 310-440-7703; Email: researchgrants@getty.edu.

4408 ■ Getty GRI-NEH Postdoctoral Fellowships *(Postdoctorate/Fellowship)*

Purpose: To support emerging scholars who are working on projects related to the Getty Research Institute's annual theme. **Focus:** General studies/Field of study not specified. **Qualif.:** Applicants must be United States citizens or foreign nationals who can document that they have lived in the U.S. for the three years immediately preceding the fellowship application deadline. **Criteria:** Fellowships are awarded on a competitive basis. Applications will be evaluated by the Getty Research Institute based on: the overall quality of the application; how the proposed project bears upon the annual research theme; the applicants' past achievements; and how the project would benefit from the resources at the Getty, including its library and collections. **Funds Avail.:** $4,200 per month to each applicant. **Duration:** Annual. **Number Awarded:** 2. **To Apply:** Applicants are required to complete and submit the online fellowship application form, which includes completing an online information form and uploading a project proposal, doctoral

Awards are arranged alphabetically below their administering organizations

dissertation plan or abstract, curriculum vitae, writing sample, selected bibliography and confirmation letter of academic status. Applicants are required to have two confidential recommendation letters forwarded by their recommenders via e-mail to the Getty Foundation. **Deadline:** October 1. **Contact:** Phone: 310-440-7374; Fax: 310-440-7703; Email: researchgrants@getty.edu.

4409 ■ Getty Postdoctoral Fellowships
(Postdoctorate/Fellowship)

Purpose: To support emerging scholars who are working on projects related to the Getty Research Institute's annual theme. **Focus:** General studies/Field of study not specified. **Qualif.:** Applications are welcome from scholars of all nationalities. **Criteria:** Fellowships are awarded on a competitive basis. Applications will be evaluated by the Getty Research Institute based on: the overall quality of the application; how the proposed project bears upon the annual research theme; the applicants' past achievements; and how the project would benefit from the resources at the Getty, including its library and collections.

Funds Avail.: $30,000. **Duration:** Annual; Nine months. **To Apply:** Applicants are required to complete and submit the online fellowship application form, which includes completing an online information form and uploading a project proposal, doctoral dissertation plan or abstract, curriculum vitae, writing sample, selected bibliography and confirmation letter of academic status. Applicants are required to have two confidential recommendation letters forwarded by their recommenders via e-mail to the Getty Foundation. **Deadline:** October 1. **Contact:** Phone: 310-440-7374; Fax: 310-440-7703; Email: researchgrants@getty.edu.

4410 ■ Getty Postdoctoral Fellowships in Conservation Science *(Postdoctorate/Fellowship)*

Purpose: To provide a unique two-year research and learning experience in the field of conservation science. **Focus:** Chemistry; Conservation of natural resources; Physical sciences. **Qualif.:** Applications are welcome from scientists of all nationalities who are interested in pursuing a career in conservation science and have received a PhD in chemistry/physical science. A background in the humanities is helpful, and strong science working practices are essential. **Criteria:** Selection will be based on the committee's criteria.

Funds Avail.: No specific amount. **Duration:** Annual. **To Apply:** Applicants must complete and submit an online application which includes completing an online information form, and uploading a Statement of Interest in Conservation Science, Doctoral Dissertation Abstract, Curriculum Vitae or Resume, Writing Sample and Degree Confirmation Letter. Applicants are also required to submit two confidential letters of recommendation in support of their application. **Contact:** Phone: 310-440-7374; Fax: 310-440-7703; Email: researchgrants@getty.edu.

4411 ■ Getty Predoctoral Fellowships *(Doctorate/Fellowship)*

Purpose: To support emerging scholars who are working on projects related to the Getty Research Institute's annual theme. **Focus:** General studies/Field of study not specified. **Qualif.:** Applications are welcome from scholars of all nationalities. Applicants must have advanced to candidacy by the time of the fellowship start date and should expect to complete their dissertations during the fellowship period. **Criteria:** Fellowships are awarded on a competitive basis. Applications will be evaluated by the Getty Research Institute based on: the overall quality of the application; how the proposed project bears upon the annual research theme; the applicants' past achievements; and how the project would benefit from the resources at the Getty, including its library and collections.

Funds Avail.: $25,000. **Duration:** Annual; Nine months. **To Apply:** Applicants are required to complete and submit the online fellowship application form, which includes completing an online information form and uploading a project proposal, doctoral dissertation plan or abstract, curriculum vitae, writing sample, selected bibliography and confirmation letter of academic status. Applicants are required to have two confidential recommendation letters forwarded by their recommenders via e-mail to the Getty Foundation. **Deadline:** October 1. **Contact:** Phone: 310-440-7374; Fax: 310-440-7703; Email: researchgrants@getty.edu.

4412 ■ Getty Scholar Grants *(Professional development/Grant)*

Purpose: To support and encourage established scholars, or writers who have attained distinction in their fields. **Focus:** Art; Humanities; Social sciences. **Qualif.:** Applicants must be scholars, artists or writers who have attained distinction in their fields. Applications are also accepted from researchers of all nationalities who are working in the arts, humanities or social sciences. **Criteria:** Grants are awarded on a competitive basis. Applications will be evaluated by the Getty Research Institute based on: the overall quality of the application; how the proposed project bears upon the annual research theme; the applicants' past achievements; and how the project would benefit from the resources at the Getty, including its library and collections.

Funds Avail.: $65,000. **Duration:** Annual. **To Apply:** Applicants are required to complete and submit the online Getty Residential Scholar application form which includes completing an online information sheet and uploading a project proposal, curriculum vitae and optional writing sample. **Deadline:** October 1. **Contact:** Phone: 310-440-7374; Fax: 310-440-7703; Email: researchgrants@getty.edu.

4413 ■ Gettysburg College - Eisenhower Institute
818 Connecticut Ave. NW, Ste. 800
Washington, DC 20006
Ph: (202)628-4444
Fax: (202)628-4445
E-mail: ei@eisenhowerinstitute.org
URL: www.eisenhowerinstitute.org
Twitter: twitter.com/eigbc

4414 ■ Conrad N. Hilton Scholarships
(Undergraduate/Scholarship)

Purpose: To help American students study abroad with strong international orientation to their studies. **Focus:** Business administration; Economics; Government; History; International affairs and relations. **Qualif.:** Applicant must be a Gettysburg College senior or junior undergraduate student planning to study abroad; have at least a 3.0 cumulative GPA (can be waived for applicants with strong needs or qualifications); and must be social science or interdisciplinary majors. **Criteria:** Selection is based on merit.

Funds Avail.: $2,500. **Number Awarded:** 4. **To Apply:**

Awards are arranged alphabetically below their administering organizations

Applicant must submit an academic transcript; a resume; a statement of career aspirations (maximum of 1,000 words); a letter of recommendation from the candidate's faculty advisor or department chair; and a copy of a (10-15 page) paper (within the last four months) from a course in the applicant's major field of study. Submit it at Gettysburg College. **Deadline:** February 15.

4415 ■ Clifford Roberts Graduate Fellowships
(Doctorate/Fellowship)

Purpose: To support study and education dealing with the role of government in a free society, the relationship between international and domestic issues and improved understanding of world affairs. **Focus:** Public affairs. **Qualif.:** Applicant must be at an advanced stage of their doctoral candidacies, preferably preparing a dissertation. **Criteria:** Selection is based on merit. The Institute will consider the applications of less advanced graduate students or persons who recently earned their PhD and pursuing the Institute's field of interest.

Funds Avail.: $10,000. **To Apply:** Applicants must submit a curriculum vitae; a statement describing the nature and scope of the dissertation; a 10- to 15-page writing sample on a topic related to the dissertation; a 1,000-word statement of career aspirations; two letters of recommendation; and other required materials by the university. Submit materials at the participating universities. **Deadline:** March 14. **Remarks:** The program is available only at the participating universities. **Contact:** Rick Farwell at 202-628-4444, or rfarwell@gettysburg.edu.

4416 ■ Ann Cook Whitman Scholarships for Perry High School *(Undergraduate/Scholarship)*

Purpose: To assist graduating seniors from Perry High School, Perry, Ohio, based on need and merit, in obtaining an undergraduate degree in furtherance of their education and leadership skills. **Focus:** General studies/Field of study not specified. **Qualif.:** Applicant must be a high school senior student at Perry High School planning to receive an undergraduate education; and have an average of B and above (can be waived for applicants with strong needs or qualifications). **Criteria:** Selection is based on need and merit.

Funds Avail.: $4,000 each year for four years. **Duration:** Annual. **Number Awarded:** 2. **To Apply:** Applicant must submit an academic transcript; a resume; a statement of career aspirations (maximum of 1,000 words); a letter of recommendation from the candidate's faculty advisor or guidance counselor; another letter of recommendation from a member of the Perry, Ohio community other than a family member; and documentation from Perry High School on its needs-based assessment procedures for its nominees. Submit materials at the Perry High School. **Deadline:** April 4. **Contact:** Application materials should be forwarded to David Wemer at dwemer@gettysburg.edu.

4417 ■ Ann Cook Whitman Washington, DC Scholarships *(Undergraduate/Scholarship)*

Purpose: To assist graduating African-American seniors from the District of Columbia public education system in obtaining an undergraduate degree in furtherance of their education and leadership skills. **Focus:** General studies/Field of study not specified. **Qualif.:** Applicant must be an African-American senior student from any of four eligible high schools (Spingarn, H.D. Woodson, Ballou, and Eastern) pursuing an undergraduate education; and have a 2.8 GPA or above (can be waived for applicants with strong needs or qualifications). **Criteria:** Selection is based on need and merit.

Funds Avail.: $4,000 each year for four years. **Duration:** Annual. **Number Awarded:** 2. **To Apply:** Applicants must submit a completed application form; academic transcript; a statement of career aspirations (maximum of 500 words); identification of colleges/universities applied to; a letter of recommendation from a faculty member or the guidance counselor; and another letter of recommendation from a member of the Washington, DC community, other than a family member. Submit materials at the applicant's respective high school. **Deadline:** April 4. **Contact:** Application materials should be forwarded to David Wemer at dwemer@gettysburg.edu.

4418 ■ Ghana-Canada Association of British Columbia (GCABC)
141-6200 McKay Ave., Ste. 499
Burnaby, BC, Canada V5H 4M9
E-mail: info@ghanaiansinbc.org
URL: www.ghanaiansinbc.org

4419 ■ GCABC Youth Scholarship Awards
(Undergraduate/Scholarship)

Purpose: To help Ghanaian-Canadian students pursue their education. **Focus:** General studies/Field of study not specified. **Qualif.:** Applicants must be Ghanaian-Canadian post-secondary students in B.C. and Ghanaian secondary school students in Ghana; must be 17 to 30 years old; must be of Ghanaian descent; must have plan or currently enrolled in an undergraduate degree in any field of study; and must have minimum of six months voluntary community service prior to the application. **Criteria:** Recipients will be evaluated based on submitted materials.

Funds Avail.: No specific amount. **Duration:** Annual. **To Apply:** Applicants must complete the application form; must submit three letters of recommendation, a 150-word essay explaining the financial need and reason for competing, and essay explaining the role to make GCABC a better community organization.

4420 ■ Gibbons P.C.
One Gateway Ctr.
Newark, NJ 07102-5310
Ph: (973)596-4500
Fax: (973)596-0545
URL: www.gibbonslaw.com

4421 ■ John J. Gibbons Fellowships in Public Interest and Constitutional Law *(Professional development/Fellowship)*

Purpose: To provide law students who wants to have a practical experience and training in the public sector. **Focus:** Law. **Qualif.:** Applicant must be a person of high academic achievement and professional accomplishment, served as a judicial clerk or have been actively working in the field of public interest law. **Criteria:** Selection is based on the application materials submitted.

Funds Avail.: No specific amount. **To Apply:** Applicants must submit a completed application form together with a law school transcript; two letters of recommendation; resume; and a writing sample. **Deadline:** February 23. **Contact:** Gibbons Fellowship Program, Gibbons P.C., at the above address.

Awards are arranged alphabetically below their administering organizations

4422 ■ Keith Gilmore Foundation
5160 Skyline Way NE
Calgary, AB, Canada T2E 6V1
Ph: (403)275-2662
Free: 888-836-7242
URL: keithgilmorefoundation.com

4423 ■ Keith Gilmore Foundation - Diploma Scholarships (Other/Scholarship)
Purpose: To offer scholarship to those individuals who have their career leading to the field of agriculture. **Focus:** Agriculture, Economic aspects; Communications; Journalism. **Qualif.:** Applicants must be individuals enrolled in a recognized diploma program in agriculture, journalism and/or communications, leading to a career in the field of agriculture. **Criteria:** Selection of recipients is based on academic merit, contribution to school and/or community and indication of academic promise.
Funds Avail.: 1,500 Canadian dollars. **Number Awarded:** Varies. **To Apply:** Application forms are available online at www.keithgilmorefoundation.com.

4424 ■ Keith Gilmore Foundation - Postgraduate Scholarships (Postgraduate/Scholarship)
Purpose: To provide support for the education of the aspiring students. **Focus:** Agriculture, Economic aspects; Communications; Journalism; Veterinary science and medicine. **Qualif.:** Applicant must be an individual enrolled in a postgraduate degree program in agriculture, veterinary medicine, journalism and/or communications at a recognized university, leading to a career in the field of agriculture. **Criteria:** Selection of recipients is based on academic merit, contribution to school and/or community and indication of academic promise.
Funds Avail.: 2,500 Canadian dollars. **Number Awarded:** 2. **To Apply:** Application forms are available online at www.keithgilmorefoundation.com.

4425 ■ Keith Gilmore Foundation - Undergraduate Scholarships (Undergraduate/Scholarship)
Purpose: To provide educational support to students who are in need. **Focus:** Agriculture, Economic aspects; Communications; Journalism; Veterinary science and medicine. **Qualif.:** Applicant must be an individual enrolled in an undergraduate degree program in agriculture, veterinary medicine, journalism and/or communications at a recognized university, leading to a career in the field of agriculture. **Criteria:** Selection of recipients is based on academic merit, contribution to school and/or community and indication of academic promise.
Funds Avail.: 2,000 Canadian dollars. **Duration:** Annual. **Number Awarded:** Varies. **To Apply:** Application forms are available online at www.keithgilmorefoundation.com.

4426 ■ Girls Incorporated of the Greater Capital Region
962 Albany St.
Schenectady, NY 12307-1513
Ph: (518)374-9800
E-mail: info@gcr.girls-inc.org
URL: www.girlsinccapitalregion.org
Facebook: www.facebook.com/girlsinccapitalregion
Twitter: www.twitter.com/GirlsIncGCR

4427 ■ Dorothea E. Allen Scholarship (Undergraduate/Scholarship)
Purpose: To assist current or former members of Girls Incorporated in enhancing their potentials and talents. **Focus:** General studies/Field of study not specified. **Qualif.:** Applicants must be current or former members of Girls Incorporated. **Criteria:** Preference for applicants who have promise and potential in enhancing their talents.
Funds Avail.: $3,022. **Duration:** Annual. **To Apply:** Interested applicants may call Girls Incorporated for more information about this scholarship.

4428 ■ Anna C. Hume Scholarship (Undergraduate/Scholarship)
Purpose: To supplement the normal sources of financial aid. **Focus:** General studies/Field of study not specified. **Qualif.:** Applicants must be females who are members of Girls Incorporated and require normal financial aid. **Criteria:** Selection will be based on the committee's criteria.
Funds Avail.: $25,000. **Duration:** Annual. **To Apply:** Interested applicants may contact the Girls Incorporated for the application process and personal interview.

4429 ■ GLAAD
5455 Wilshire Blvd., Ste. 1500
Los Angeles, CA 90036
Ph: (212)629-3322
E-mail: info@glaad.org
URL: www.glaad.org
Facebook: www.facebook.com/GLAAD
Twitter: twitter.com/glaad

4430 ■ Design and Multimedia Internships - New York (Undergraduate, Graduate/Internship)
Purpose: To promote understanding, increase acceptance, and advance equality. **Focus:** Media arts. **Qualif.:** Applicants must have the following qualifications: strong proficiency in the Adobe Suite; knowledge of design for web and print media; experience and/or enthusiasm in using visual media for social change; excellent verbal, written and visual communications skills; serious attention to detail; tech and Internet savvy; video editing experience is a plus; experience with HTML, CSS, and/or Drupal are a plus; be genuinely concerned and conversant about LGBTQ issues and have a passion and desire to make a difference. The ideal candidate would be someone who is passionate about LGBTQ, love info graphics, makes .gifs for fun and has a strong interest in the intersection of good design and social good. All GLAAD interns are required to be students attending an institution with courses leading to a degree, certificate or diploma, such as college or graduate school. Interns must have graduated from high school. **Criteria:** Selection will be based on the committee's criteria.
Funds Avail.: No specific amount. **To Apply:** The following must be included in application: a brief cover letter outlining their interest and experience specific to the position; a current resume. The title of the position must appear in the first line of the email; an online portfolio of recent work demonstrating proficiency in graphic design across web and print media; one original and effective piece of visual content (optional) for distribution on GLAAD's social media channels that is related to an area of GLAAD's work or mission. **Deadline:** Varies. **Contact:** Human Resources at jobs@glaad.org.

4431 ■ Entertainment Media Internships - Los Angeles (Undergraduate, Graduate/Internship)
Purpose: To promote understanding, increase acceptance, and advance equality. **Focus:** Media arts. **Qualif.:** Ap-

Awards are arranged alphabetically below their administering organizations

plicants must have the following qualifications: knowledge of entertainment industry and/or lesbian, gay, bisexual and transgender issues; strong written and oral communication skills and strong organizational skills; an ability to manage multiple tasks to meet deadlines and desire to be a self-starter; attention to detail and the ability to think creatively; computer proficiency in word processing, spreadsheets, database work, email and Internet research; ability to work collaboratively and effectively with people of diverse races, ages, ethnicities, orientations and gender identities. All GLAAD interns are required to be students attending an institution with courses leading to a degree, certificate or diploma, such as college or graduate school. Interns must have graduated from high school. **Criteria:** Selection will be based on the committee's criteria.

Funds Avail.: No specifc amount. **Duration:** Annual. **To Apply:** Applicants must submit a brief cover letter outlining their interest and experience specific to the position and their current resume. The title of the position must appear in the first line of the email. **Contact:** jobs@glaad.org.

4432 ■ Faith Initiatives Internships - New York
(Undergraduate, Graduate/Internship)

Purpose: To promote understanding, increase acceptance, and advance equality. **Focus:** Journalism; Media arts. **Qualif.:** Applicants must have the following qualifications: an extremely positive attitude; demonstrated interest in advocacy work around LGBT and progressive issues; skills in communication or journalism; research and writing skills; interest in religion and LGBT issues; computer proficiency in word processing, database work, email and Internet research; ability to manage multiple tasks to meet deadlines and to be a self-starter; creative thinker who is able to work with people of diverse races, ages, ethnicities and sexual identities; willingness to learn, grow and be inspired to greatness. All GLAAD interns are required to be students attending an institution with courses leading to a degree, certificate or diploma, such as college or graduate school. Interns must have graduated from high school. **Criteria:** Selection will be based on the committee's criteria.

Funds Avail.: No specific amount. **To Apply:** The following must be included in application: a brief cover letter outlining their interest and experience specific to the position; a current resume. The title of the position must appear in the first line of the email. **Deadline:** Varies. **Contact:** jobs@glaad.org.

4433 ■ Foundation Relations Internships - Los Angeles *(Undergraduate, Graduate/Internship)*

Purpose: To promote understanding, increase acceptance, and advance equality. **Focus:** Media arts. **Qualif.:** Applicants must have the following qualifications: a self-starter and creative thinker with interest in foundation relations and grant writing; excellent written and verbal communication skills; ability to work in a fast paced environment, with limited supervision; computer proficient in word processing, email and Internet research; genuinely concerned and conversant about LGBT issues and have a passion and desire to make a difference; able to work collaboratively and effectively with people of diverse races, ages, ethnicities and sexual identities; interest fundraising, media and LGBT issues; good organizational and time management skills. All GLAAD interns are required to be students attending an institution with courses leading to a degree, certificate or diploma, such as college or graduate school. Interns must have graduated from high school. **Criteria:** Selection will be based on the committee's criteria.

Funds Avail.: No specific amount. **Duration:** Annual. **To Apply:** Applicants must submit a brief cover letter outlining their interest and experience specific to the position and their current resume. The title of the position must appear in the first line of the email. **Contact:** jobs@glaad.org.

4434 ■ GLAAD Communications/PR Internships - New York *(Undergraduate, Graduate/Internship)*

Purpose: To promote understanding, increase acceptance, and advance equality. **Focus:** Communications; Public administration. **Qualif.:** The ideal candidate will have had previous internship experience or coursework related to public relations. The successful applicants will be: self-starter and creative thinkers with interest and experience in public relations; knowledgeable about LGBT media outlets and familiar with LGBT newspapers and blogs; successful and experienced in drafting media pitches, press releases, new articles and other communications materials; computer proficient in word processing, database work, email and Internet research; genuinely concerned and conversant about LGBT issues and have a passion and desire to make a difference; able to work collaboratively and effectively with people of diverse races, ages ethnicities and sexual identities. All GLAAD interns are required to be students attending an institution with courses leading to a degree, certificate or diploma, such as college or graduate school. Interns must have graduated from high school. **Criteria:** Selection will be based on the committee's criteria.

Funds Avail.: No specific amount. **Duration:** Annual. **To Apply:** Applicants must submit a brief cover letter outlining their interest and experience specific to the position and their current resume. The title of the position must appear in the first line of the email. **Contact:** jobs@glaad.org.

4435 ■ GLAAD News Internships - New York *(Undergraduate, Graduate/Internship)*

Purpose: To provide equal employment opportunity to all employees and applicants for employment without regard to their race, color, religious creed, sex, gender identity, gender expression, age, national origin, ancestry, citizenship status, physical or mental disability, medical condition, pregnancy, marital or veteran status, sexual orientation, height and weight, or other personal characteristics as may be protected by applicable law. **Focus:** Media arts. **Qualif.:** Applicants must have the following qualifications: an extremely positive attitude; demonstrated interest in advocacy work around LGBT and progressive issues, progressive communications or journalism; exceptional research and writing skills; computer proficiency in word processing, database work, email and Internet research; strong oral communication skills; knowledge of, and commitment to, gay, lesbian, bisexual and transgender issues; the ability to work effectively with people of diverse races, ages, ethnicities and sexual identities; willingness to learn, grow and be inspired to greatness. All GLAAD interns are required to be students attending an institution with courses leading to a degree, certificate or diploma, such as college or graduate school. Interns must have graduated from high school. **Criteria:** Selection will be based on the committee's criteria.

Funds Avail.: No specific amount. **To Apply:** Applicants must submit a brief cover letter outlining their interest and experience specific to the position and their current resume. The title of the position must appear in the first line of the email. **Contact:** interns@glaad.org.

Awards are arranged alphabetically below their administering organizations

4436 ■ GLAAD Spanish-Language and Latino Media Internships - Los Angeles *(Undergraduate, Graduate/Internship)*

Purpose: To provide equal employment opportunity to all employees and applicants for employment without regard to their race, color, religious creed, sex, gender identity, gender expression, age, national origin, ancestry, citizenship status, physical or mental disability, medical condition, pregnancy, marital or veteran status, sexual orientation, height and weight, or other personal characteristics as may be protected by applicable law. **Focus:** Communications; Journalism; Public relations. **Qualif.:** Candidates must be fluent in both English and Spanish. Fluent oral, verbal, reading and writing Spanish-language skills are a must; have a strong written and oral communication skills; have a professional demeanor and appearance; have a strong organizational skills, ability to manage multiple tasks to meet deadline, and desire to be a self-starter; have an ability to work under pressure; have an interest in Spanish language media and the desire to learn more about media outreach and media work in general. Skills necessary to create a more diverse and inclusive environment are a plus. All GLAAD interns are required to be students attending an institution with courses leading to a degree, certificate or diploma, such as college or graduate school. Interns must have graduated from high school. **Criteria:** Selection will be based on the committee's criteria.

Funds Avail.: No specific amount. **Duration:** Annual. **To Apply:** Applicants must submit a brief cover letter outlining their interest and experience specific to the position and their current resume. The title of the position must appear in the first line of the email. **Contact:** interns@glaad.org.

4437 ■ GLAAD Youth Issues Internships - New York *(Undergraduate, Graduate/Internship)*

Purpose: To support those from LGBT community in acquiring knowledge related to youth issues. **Focus:** Communications; Journalism. **Qualif.:** Applicants should have a demonstrated interest in progressive communications, local and grassroots activism or advocacy work around issues of LGBT equality; have good written and oral communication skills; have an Internet research skills. Some experience and a working knowledge and understanding of the media and its history of covering trans issues are a plus. All GLAAD interns are required to be students attending an institution with courses leading to a degree, certificate or diploma, such as college or graduate school. Interns must have graduated from high school. **Criteria:** Selection will be based on the committee's criteria.

Funds Avail.: No specific amount. **Duration:** Annual. **To Apply:** Applicants must submit a brief cover letter outlining their interest and experience specific to the position and their current resume. The title of the position must appear in the first line of the email.

4438 ■ Special Events Internships - Los Angeles *(Undergraduate, Graduate/Internship)*

Purpose: To provide students the opportunity to gain experience in event management and fundraising in a professional work environment during a 12-week internship. **Focus:** Media arts. **Qualif.:** Applicants must have the following qualifications: interest in fundraising, events, media and LGBT issues; good organizational and time management skills; willingness and ability to work well with others; knowledge of Microsoft Office; polished written and verbal communication skills; knowledge of and commitment to the LGBT community; ability to work in a fast paced environment; must be able and willing to pick up 40 lbs. All GLAAD interns are required to be students attending an institution with courses leading to a degree, certificate or diploma, such as college or graduate school. Interns must have graduated from high school. **Criteria:** Selection will be based on the committee's criteria.

Funds Avail.: No specific amount. **To Apply:** Applicants must submit a brief cover letter outlining their interest and experience specific to the position and their current resume. The title of the position must appear in the first line of the email.

4439 ■ Special Events Internships - New York *(Undergraduate, Graduate/Internship)*

Purpose: To provide students the opportunity to gain experience in event management and fundraising in a professional work environment. **Focus:** Media arts. **Qualif.:** Applicants must have the following qualifications: interest in fundraising, events, media and LGBT issues; good organizational and time management skills; willingness and ability to work well with others; knowledge of Microsoft Office; polished written and verbal communication skills; knowledge of and commitment to the LGBT community; ability to work in a fast paced environment; must be able and willing to pick up 40 lbs. All GLAAD interns are required to be students attending an institution with courses leading to a degree, certificate or diploma, such as college or graduate school. Interns must have graduated from high school. **Criteria:** Selection will be based on the committee's criteria.

Funds Avail.: No specific amount. **To Apply:** Applicants must submit a brief cover letter outlining their interest and experience specific to the position and their current resume. The title of the position must appear in the first line of the email.

4440 ■ Sports Internships - Los Angeles *(Undergraduate, Graduate/Internship)*

Purpose: To provide students the opportunity to engage with journalists and industry professionals in print, broadcast, radio and online outlets. **Focus:** Communications; Journalism. **Qualif.:** Applicants should have a demonstrated interest in both LGBT issues and professional and/or amateur sports, as well as interest in local and grassroots activism or advocacy work around issues of LGBT equality; have good written and oral communication skills; have Internet research skills. Some experience and a working knowledge and understanding of the sports media and its history of covering LGBT issues are a plus. All GLAAD interns are required to be students attending an institution with courses leading to a degree, certificate or diploma, such as college or graduate school. Interns must have graduated from high school. **Criteria:** Selection will be based on the committee's criteria.

Funds Avail.: No specific amount. **To Apply:** Applicants must submit a brief cover letter outlining their interest and experience specific to the position and their current resume. The title of the position must appear in the first line of the email.

4441 ■ Trans Issues Internships - New York *(Undergraduate, Graduate/Internship)*

Purpose: To provide students the opportunity to engage with journalists in print, broadcast, radio and online outlets to ensure fair, accurate and inclusive media coverage of the LGBT community. **Focus:** Communications; Journalism. **Qualif.:** Applicants should have a demonstrated interest in progressive communications, local and grassroots

Awards are arranged alphabetically below their administering organizations

activism or advocacy work around issues of trans equality; have good written and oral communication skills; have an Internet research skills. Some experience and a working knowledge and understanding of the media and its history of covering trans issues are a plus. All GLAAD interns are required to be students attending an institution with courses leading to a degree, certificate or diploma, such as college or graduate school. Interns must have graduated from high school. **Criteria:** Selection will be based on the committee's criteria.

Funds Avail.: No specific amount. **To Apply:** Applicants must submit a brief cover letter outlining their interest and experience specific to the position and their current resume. The title of the position must appear in the first line of the email.

4442 ■ J. Robert Gladden Orthopaedic Society (JRGOS)
9400 W Higgins Rd., Ste. 500
Rosemont, IL 60018-4238
Ph: (847)698-1633
Fax: (847)823-4921
E-mail: jrgos@aaos.org
URL: www.gladdensociety.org

4443 ■ J. Robert Gladden Orthopaedic Society International Traveling Fellowship (Undergraduate/Fellowship)

Purpose: To support outstanding young individuals to increase their surgical skills, learn new techniques, or expand their practice interests. **Focus:** Muscular dystrophy. **Qualif.:** Applicants must be members of JRGOS in good standing with 2-3 years in practice. **Criteria:** Preference will be given to those applicants that elect to work with a Senior JRGOS member.

Funds Avail.: Up to $2,500. **To Apply:** Applicants must submit completed application form, which includes: proposed visitation site address; duration of travel; proposal including anticipated experience and enrichment potential; sponsor letter from responsible individual at visitation site and; applicants' CV. **Deadline:** December 1.

4444 ■ Glass Art Association of Canada (GAAC)
c/o Wendy McPeak
13, 52449 Range Rd. 222
Ardrossan, AB, Canada T8E 2G6
E-mail: gaacanada@gmail.com
URL: www.glassartcanada.ca

4445 ■ GAAC Project Grants (Undergraduate, Professional development/Grant)

Purpose: To support the development of a project that benefits the artist's studio practice and promotes excellence in Canadian Glass. **Focus:** Art. **Qualif.:** Applicants must be students currently enrolled in a glass program in Canada or abroad, or practicing professionals who are not currently attending college or university. **Criteria:** Selection will be based on the submitted project proposal.

Funds Avail.: $1,000 - student; $1,500 - professional. **Duration:** Annual. **To Apply:** Applicants must submitted their project proposal to Gabby Wilson via email along with their contact information, indicating whether they are students or professionals. Applicants' curriculum vitae, digital images with corresponding information, and biography should be uploaded at the GAAC Artist Directory at http://glassartcanada/public/user/login. Project proposals should be 1-2 page detailed description of applicants' project and its benefits to their studio practice including a budget outlining expenses as a Word document file, labeled lastname_firstname_proposal.doc. **Deadline:** May 9. **Contact:** Project proposal should be submitted to Gabby Wilson at gaac.submissions@gmail.com.

4446 ■ Gleaner Life Insurance Society (GLIS)
5200 W US Highway 223
Adrian, MI 49221-9461
Fax: (517)265-7745
Free: 800-992-1894
E-mail: gleaner@gleanerlife.org
URL: www.gleanerlife.org

4447 ■ Gleaner Life Insurance Society Scholarships (Undergraduate/Scholarship)

Purpose: To strengthen the brotherhood; to help Gleaner family members pursuing their post-secondary education. **Focus:** General studies/Field of study not specified. **Qualif.:** Applicants must be family members who are high school graduates or high school senior students; and have at least 10 or more semester credit hours enrolled. **Criteria:** Recipients will be selected based on completion and quality of application, leadership, quality of activities, letters of recommendation and personal statement.

Funds Avail.: $3,000. **Duration:** Annual. **Number Awarded:** 1. **To Apply:** Applicants must fill out the application form and present any information and/or reasons for applying; must attach an official transcript of high school records (applicants already graduated from high school are also required to submit high school transcripts or attach an official transcript of college records if applicable); result of an aptitude test at junior or senior level; evaluation of students (leadership, perseverance, prediction of post-high school success); three letters of personal recommendation that can provide a brief statement on the applicant's behalf. **Deadline:** November 1. **Contact:** Fraternal Department; Phone: 800-992-1894; Email: scholarships@gleanerlife.org.

4448 ■ Glendale Latino Association (GLA)
PO Box 806
Verdugo City, CA 91046
URL: www.glendalelatinoassociation.com

4449 ■ Glendale Latino Association Scholarships (Undergraduate/Scholarship)

Purpose: To provide encouragement and financial support to Latino students pursuing higher education in colleges and universities. **Focus:** Aeronautics; Engineering; Mathematics and mathematical sciences; Photography; Physics; Science. **Qualif.:** Applicants must be Latino high school or college students who demonstrate potential for successful college careers and who demonstrate financial need. **Criteria:** Recipients will be selected based on demonstrated academic achievement, volunteerism and a future return to their community.

Funds Avail.: No specific amount. **Duration:** Annual. **To Apply:** Applicants must complete the application form; must submit a personal essay, a 50-word personal biography, academic transcripts, recommendation letter and employer/supervisor recommendation letter. Qualified applicants will

Awards are arranged alphabetically below their administering organizations

be considered for a personal interview. **Deadline:** March 2.

4450 ■ Glenn Miller Birthplace Society (GMBS)
122 W Clark St.
Clarinda, IA 51632
Ph: (712)542-2461
Fax: (712)542-2868
E-mail: gmbs@glennmiller.org
URL: glennmiller.org
Facebook: www.facebook.com/Glenn-Miller-Birthplace-Society-Museum-270496579641251

4451 ■ Glenn Miller Scholarships *(Undergraduate/Scholarship)*

Purpose: To assist promising young talents in any field of applied music who may be musical leaders of tomorrow. **Focus:** Music. **Qualif.:** Applicants must be graduating high school seniors or first year college students intending to make music a central part of their future life and high school seniors, unless they have been previous first place winners. **Criteria:** Recipients will be selected based on questions of eligibility, conformance to the rules and their intent.

Funds Avail.: $1,000; $2,000; $3,000. **Duration:** Annual. **To Apply:** Applicants must submit a clear high-quality audio CD or tape; completed application; and statement of musical intentions. **Deadline:** March 1. **Contact:** Glenn Miller Birthplace Society; Phone: 712-542-2461; Fax: 712-542-2868; Email: gmbs@glennmiller.org.

4452 ■ Glens Falls Foundation
237 Glen St.
Glens Falls, NY 12801
Ph: (518)761-7350
E-mail: administrator@glensfallsfoundation.org
URL: www.glensfallsfoundation.org
Facebook: www.facebook.com/glensfallsfoundation

4453 ■ Gilberto and Lennetta Pesquera Medical School Scholarships *(Graduate, Doctorate/Scholarship, Grant)*

Purpose: To assist qualified students who have graduated from local area schools and have successfully completed the first year of medical school. **Focus:** Education, Medical; Medicine. **Qualif.:** Applicants must be second, third or fourth year medical students. **Criteria:** Selection will be based on submitted documents and specific criteria.

Funds Avail.: $4,000. **Duration:** Annual. **Number Awarded:** 4. **To Apply:** Applicants should submit a completed application form; official medical school transcripts; brief personal statement describing applicant's academic and occupational goals, interests and activities; names, phone numbers and e-mail addresses of two personal references. **Deadline:** 4th Friday of June. **Contact:** Chairperson, Pesquera Medical Scholarship Committee by email at: administrator@glensfallsfoundation.org; or by mail to: Glens Falls Foundation, at the above address.

4454 ■ Harry B. Pulver Scholarships *(Undergraduate/Scholarship)*

Purpose: To provide financial assistance to area students attending Dartmouth College or Harvard University. **Focus:** General studies/Field of study not specified. **Qualif.:** Applicants must be in their incoming freshmen college year; must be residents of Warren, Washington, or Saratoga Counties in New York State; must have good moral character; good academic standing and financial need. **Criteria:** Selection will be based on submitted documents and specific criteria.

Funds Avail.: $8,000. **Duration:** Annual; maximum of four years. **To Apply:** Applicants must submit a completed application form; financial aid letter from Darmouth College or Harvard University; copy of high school transcript including grades through the first semester of the senior year; complete list of extracurricular activities and volunteer work; at least two letters of recommendation; documentation that the applicant will be attending Dartmouth or Harvard; an essay on how the scholarship will assist the applicant in achieving undergraduate goals. **Deadline:** May 15. **Contact:** Glens Falls Foundation, at the above address.

4455 ■ Global Business Travel Association (GBTA)
123 N Pitt St.
Alexandria, VA 22314
Ph: (703)684-0836
Fax: (703)342-4324
E-mail: info@gbta.org
URL: www.gbta.org

4456 ■ Mike Kabo Global Scholarships *(Other/Scholarship)*

Purpose: To provide individuals with the opportunity to attend the two day Global Leadership Program (GLP) session and NBTA's International Convention and Exposition. **Focus:** Travel and tourism. **Qualif.:** Applicant must be: a corporate travel professional from the buyer community; a resident outside of the United States of America; a member of NBTA or one of its Paragon Partner Members. **Criteria:** Recipients will be selected by the NBTA Foundation and the National Business Travel Association based on standard recipient review and selection procedures including: value of experience to corporate enterprise and travel management; educational background; responsibilities within company; potential growth; and industry involvement.

Funds Avail.: No specific amount. **Number Awarded:** 1. **To Apply:** Applicants must complete the form available at the website and must include an essay (500-1000 words) stating the reasons of being interested in receiving this scholarship and how would help the professional growth or bring value to the company. **Deadline:** June 15. **Contact:** Magda Halim; Phone: 703.236.1164; E-mail: mhalim@gbtafoundation.org.

4457 ■ Global Scholarship Alliance (GSA)
1700 Madison Road
Cincinnati, OH 45206
E-mail: info@globalscholarship.net
URL: globalscholarship.net

4458 ■ GSA Scholarships for International Nurses *(Undergraduate, Master's/Scholarship)*

Purpose: To support both local and international nursing students in further enhancement of their skills in the field of nursing. **Focus:** Nursing. **Qualif.:** Applicants must: successfully completed at least three year registered nursing degree program; be active and unencumbered registered nurse license in country of residence; have knowledge on

Awards are arranged alphabetically below their administering organizations

both theory and clinical rotations during nursing training in surgical, obstetrics, pediatrics, psychiatry, and medical nursing; and have minimum of one year of recent postgraduation and licensure acute care hospital based nursing experience in specialties such as critical/intensive care, coronary care, emergency, medical, surgical, operating room/theater or telemetry. **Criteria:** Selection will be based on the committee's criteria.

Funds Avail.: No specific amount. **To Apply:** Applicants must complete and return a Scholarship Agreement in which they agree to: meet GSA standards for selection; be admitted to a GSA approved University Partner; secure US nursing license and US visa; complete their education obligations; enroll, attend classes, maintain an adequate GPA, remain in good standing with the university, and graduate within a prescribed timeframe; maintain compliance with visa work restrictions and complete practical training and on-campus employment obligations; remain in visa status throughout the program period; repay the scholarship amount plus interest if they fail to fulfill their program obligations pursuant to the terms of their Scholarship Agreement; repay the Scholarship Amounts plus interest if they fail to complete their graduate program within the prescribed timeframe; begin fulfilling home service obligation according to visa requirements within thirty days of completing their graduate program and any subsequent practical training.Applicants can make appeal or request GSA offices in their country for seeking information about the program and for the processing of applications.

4459 ■ Global Sustainable Electricity Partnership
505, de Maisonneuve Blvd. West Lobby
Montreal, QC, Canada H3A 3C2
URL: www.globalelectricity.org

4460 ■ e8 Sustainable Energy Development Post-Doctoral Scholarship Programme (ESED)
(Postdoctorate/Scholarship)

Purpose: To support outstanding students pursuing advanced studies in sustainable energy development, and to promote the efficient generation and use of electricity. **Focus:** Energy-related areas. **Qualif.:** Applicants must be citizens of the developing countries and territories identified for OECD official development aid in the DAC List of ODA Recipients and planning to undertake studies at the Masters level in areas directly related to sustainable energy development. **Criteria:** An Academic Panel consisting of accomplished representatives of notable academic institutions from Europe, North America and Japan will review the applications. All selections are final and all applicants will be notified.

Funds Avail.: $23,000. **Duration:** Biennial. **Number Awarded:** 10. **To Apply:** Applicants must provide the following: proof of citizenship; letter of acceptance from approved academic institution to undertake studies in sustainable energy development; copies of transcripts; curriculum vitae; complete application form; two letters of reference - one academic and one personal; applicants' statement; and research plan. The academic letter of reference should be dated and speak to the following points: the reference provider's status and relationship to the applicants; academic ranking and/or professional accomplishments; interest in sustainable energy development; maturity and judgment; ability to communicate, both orally and in writing, and to interact productively with individuals and groups; professional potential, including possible impacts the scholarship may have; and interest and experience in applying their expertise to the issues of sustainable energy development. The personal letter of reference must be dated and come from a person who can discuss other personal qualities or interests that make the applicants especially qualified to receive the scholarship. For master's applicants, they must submit a statement about their qualifications for the scholarship and their career goals. It should not exceed 1,000 words in length and should cover the following points: reason of wanting the scholarship; qualifications; the studies they intend to pursue and how they relate to sustainable energy development; how their Masters studies will affect their community and their career and, ultimately, the field of sustainable energy development; and the commitment to return to their country. Post-Doctoral applicants must submit statement about their qualifications for the scholarship and their career goals but should not exceed 500 words in length and should cover the following points: reason of wanting the scholarship; applicants' qualifications; research interest and how it relates to sustainable energy development; reasons on how Post-Doctoral research will affect the field of knowledge on sustainable energy development, their community and their career; and the commitment to return to their country. Also post-doctoral applicants are required to submit research plan that is clear and concise, describing on how it is related to sustainable energy development that they intend to pursue using a maximum 2,000 words (excluding the Abstract). Applicants may use additional pages for figures and references. In doing research plan, the statement should demonstrate the understanding of the research principles necessary to pursue the research objectives. Present the plan with clear hypotheses or questions to be addressed in the research and include: abstract; principle objectives; background information (broader research or other activities of which the research would be a part); data sources; methodology or approach; expected results; and significance or application of results to sustainable energy development. If the applicants have not yet formulated a plan of research, the statement should include: abstract; description of two or three research questions related to sustainable energy development and any link to their previous research; analysis of how the applicants think these questions may best be answered and description of their methodology and data sources.

4461 ■ Goddard Systems
1016 W 9th Ave., Ste. 210
King of Prussia, PA 19406
URL: www.goddardschoolfranchise.com
Facebook: www.facebook.com/goddardschool
Twitter: www.twitter.com/goddardsystems

4462 ■ Anthony A. Martino Memorial Scholarships
(Undergraduate/Scholarship)

Purpose: To provide scholarships for students who demonstrate the work ethic and perseverance that exemplified Martino's commitment to his career, family and community. **Focus:** General studies/Field of study not specified. **Qualif.:** Applicants must be graduates of a Goddard School pre-kindergarten or kindergarten program; must be high school seniors who are U.S. citizens, permanent residents or non-U.S. citizens living legally in the United States. **Criteria:** Selection will be based on the committee's criteria.

Funds Avail.: $10,000. **Duration:** Non-renewable. **To Apply:** Applicants must provide one 30- to 120-second video addressing the question, "How did your Goddard School experience influence your career path or education?" Video essays should be saved to a USB drive or DVD and mailed with the completed application. The written essay and video submitted with each application must be the original work of the applicants and may not contain the work, including the intellectual property, of others, such as non-original music. Applicants must submit a transcript from all high schools attended and must indicate a cumulative GPA. **Deadline:** March 11.

4463 ■ **Godparents for Tanzania**
PO Box 20221
Roanoke, VA 24018
E-mail: tellmemore@godparents4tz.org
URL: www.godparents4tz.org

4464 ■ Godparents for Tanzania Scholarship
(Undergraduate/Scholarship)

Purpose: To provide financial assistance for projects that are intended to help educate young people in Tanzania. **Focus:** General studies/Field of study not specified. **Qualif.:** Applicants must: be Tanzanian citizens from the Kilimanjaro or Karatu areas of Tanzania; demonstrate a satisfactory academic record at current level of education; be attending school in Tanzania; be studying on the secondary or first degree university level; and, agree to work in Tanzania for five years following graduation. **Criteria:** Recipients will be selected based on multiple criteria including academic ability, family circumstances and financial need.

Funds Avail.: $1,000 each. **Duration:** Annual. **Number Awarded:** 50. **To Apply:** Applicants must submit completed application along with a letter of reference from a non-related adult, preferably an educator or clergy person.

4465 ■ **Goethe Society of North America (GSNA)**
c/o Professor Birgit Tautz, Executive Secretary
Bowdoin College
Dept. of German
7700 College Sta.
Brunswick, ME 04011-8477
URL: www.goethesociety.org

4466 ■ Gloria Flaherty Scholarships *(Graduate/Scholarship)*

Purpose: To provide financial aid to worthy graduate students who wish to further their education in areas related to the interests promoted by the society. **Focus:** General studies/Field of study not specified. **Qualif.:** Applicants must be graduate students working on Goethe and/or the Age of Goethe; must able to complete the research project before receiving a doctoral degree are eligible. **Criteria:** Candidates will be selected based on their research proposal.

Funds Avail.: $500. **Duration:** Annual. **To Apply:** Interested students should send their dissertation prospectus as email attachments and a separate attachment of recommendation letter from their dissertation advisers. **Deadline:** March 31. **Contact:** Prof. Clark Muenzer, clark.muenzer@gmail.com.

4467 ■ **Golden Belt Community Foundation**
1307 Williams St.
Great Bend, KS 67530
Ph: (620)792-3000
Fax: (620)792-7900
E-mail: gbcf@goldenbeltcf.org
URL: goldenbeltcf.org
Facebook: www.facebook.com/GoldenBeltCommunityFoundation

4468 ■ John J. Mingenback Memorial Scholarships *(Graduate, Undergraduate/Scholarship)*

Purpose: To provide financial assistance to medical students with personal and professional commitment to the community. **Focus:** Education, Medical. **Qualif.:** Applicants must be from Barton County, Kansas; must be full time undergraduate or graduate students at a university or college with preference given to Kansas schools; must be majoring in a health/medical related field; must have a minimum 3.0 GPA. **Criteria:** Selection will be based on the evaluation of submitted documents and specific criteria.

Funds Avail.: No specific amount. **Duration:** Annual. **To Apply:** Applicants should submit a completed application form; recommendation letter; official transcripts; personal essay.

4469 ■ **Golden Eagle Coins L.L.C.**
3386 Fort Meade Rd.
Laurel, MD 20724
Ph: (301)206-9222
Fax: (301)206-9278
Free: 800-735-1311
E-mail: info@goldeneaglecoin.com
URL: www.goldeneaglecoin.com

4470 ■ Golden Eagle Coins Scholarships *(Undergraduate/Scholarship)*

Purpose: To support students in their pursuit of higher education. **Focus:** General studies/Field of study not specified. **Qualif.:** Applicants must be American citizens, permanent residents, or hold a valid student visa; must be currently enrolled as high school or college/university students within the United States; must have a cumulative GPA of at least 3.0 or equivalent; and must have designed an innovative project that makes a difference in the lives of others (This could be a website, series of blogs, an app, fundraising event, etc.). **Criteria:** Selection will be based on the aforementioned qualifications and the submitted entries of the applicants.

Funds Avail.: $500. **Duration:** Monthly. **Number Awarded:** 1 per month. **To Apply:** Applicants must submit an essay describing the goal of the particular project (with supporting documentation).

4471 ■ **Golden Key International Honour Society (GKIHS)**
1040 Crown Pointe Pky., Ste. 900
Atlanta, GA 30338
Ph: (678)689-2200
Fax: (678)689-2297
Free: 800-377-2401
E-mail: memberservices@goldenkey.org
URL: www.goldenkey.org

4472 ■ Golden Key Study Abroad Scholarships *(Undergraduate/Scholarship)*

Purpose: To assist members who participate in a study abroad program. **Focus:** General studies/Field of study not

Awards are arranged alphabetically below their administering organizations

specified. **Qualif.:** Applicants must be undergraduate members currently enrolled in a study abroad program; or will be enrolled the academic year immediately following the granting of the award. **Criteria:** Selection committee will review applicants based on academic achievement and relevance of study abroad program to major field of study.

Funds Avail.: $1,000. **To Apply:** Applicants must register scholarship application online. Print the cover page from online registration and uses it as a cover for the entire application and attaches a description of the planned academic program (maximum of 5 pages), a one-page statement signed by a professor, and a current comprehensive official academic transcript.

4473 ■ Goldia.com
P.O. Box 5557
New York, NY 10185
Ph: (212)840-6099
E-mail: service@goldia.com
URL: www.goldia.com

4474 ■ Goldia.com Jewelry Scholarships
(Undergraduate, Graduate/Scholarship)

Purpose: To offer a scholarship to students towards their academic costs for the current academic year. **Focus:** Gemology. **Qualif.:** Applicants must be residents of the United States, Brazil, India, South Korea, Australia, Japan, United Kingdom or Canada; must be currently enrolled full-time in college or an alumni. **Criteria:** Submitted materials will be judged based on punctuation, grammar, clarity and organization, and content.

Funds Avail.: $500. **Duration:** Annual. **Number Awarded:** 1. **To Apply:** Applicants must visit the website to fill out a survey related to jewelry; must also answer one of the last three essay questions in the survey with 750 words or less. **Deadline:** December 31.

4475 ■ Golf Canada
1333 Dorval Dr.
Oakville, ON, Canada L6M 3Z4
Ph: (905)849-9700
Fax: (905)845-7040
Free: 800-263-0009
E-mail: info@golfcanada.ca
URL: golfcanada.ca

4476 ■ Suzanne Beauregard Scholarships
(Undergraduate/Scholarship)

Purpose: To support young golfers who wish to pursue their studies. **Focus:** General studies/Field of study not specified. **Qualif.:** Applicants (Canadian citizen born or resident in the territory governed by Golf Quebec) must have completed at least one full year in a post-secondary degree program and show a minimum average of 70%; must be full-time students at a university, college or CEGEP; must demonstrate a record of athletic and academic excellence; must be members in good standing of Golf Quebec; must demonstrate regular participation in community and or extracurricular activities. **Criteria:** Candidates will be judged based on the information contained within their applications and support materials.

Funds Avail.: $2,000 each. **Duration:** Annual. **Number Awarded:** 2. **To Apply:** Application forms are available online and must be sent to Golf Canada Foundation.

4477 ■ Canadian Seniors' Golf Association Scholarships
(Undergraduate/Scholarship)

Purpose: To provide financial assistance to young Canadian men and women. **Focus:** Athletics; General studies/Field of study not specified. **Qualif.:** Applicants must be Canadian men and women who elect to obtain an education and participate in the golf program at a RCGA Foundation-recognized university in Canada; must have successfully completed at least one full year in a post-secondary degree program and show a minimum average of 70% in each year of the program; must have experience in competitive golf at a regional, provincial or national level; must have been accepted at and plan to attend an RCGA Foundation recognized college or university; and must have been named or be becoming named to the institution's golf team. **Criteria:** Candidates will be judged based on the information contained in their applications and support materials.

Funds Avail.: $3,000. **Duration:** Annual. **To Apply:** Application forms are available online and must be sent to Golf Canada Foundation. **Contact:** Golf Canada Foundation, at the above address.

4478 ■ Connor/Spafford Scholarships
(Undergraduate/Scholarship)

Purpose: To assist promising Nova Scotia Atlantic Canada men and women to obtain a degree and participate in the golf program at a university. **Focus:** General studies/Field of study not specified. **Qualif.:** Applicants must be Canadian citizens or residents in Atlantic Canada; must have successfully completed at least one full year in a postsecondary degree program and have maintained a minimum average of 70%; must have been accepted at a university or college and have been named or will be named to the institution's golf team; must have experience in competitive golf at a regional, provincial or natural level. **Criteria:** Preference will be given to applicants who were born in or are residents in Nova Scotia.

Funds Avail.: $5,000. **Duration:** Annual. **To Apply:** Application forms are available online. Applicants must submit official transcripts from last two years of high school/CEGEP showing 70% average each year; official transcripts from each year of post-secondary degree program showing 70% average each year; proof of acceptance and enrollment in RCGA Foundation recognized school; typed personal letter outlining academic and golf achievements, goals and career objectives; and outlined full details of golf background. Application forms are available online and must be sent to Golf Canada Foundation. **Contact:** Golf Canada Foundation, at the above address.

4479 ■ Mary Ellen Driscoll Scholarships
(Undergraduate/Scholarship)

Purpose: To provide financial assistance to Canadian women. **Focus:** General studies/Field of study not specified. **Qualif.:** Applicants must be female Canadian citizens or residents in New Brunswick; have successfully completed at least one full year in a post-secondary degree program at a recognized educational institution; have been accepted at a university or college and have been named or will be named to the institution's golf team; and, have experience in competitive golf at the regional, provincial or national level. **Criteria:** Applicants will be judged based on submitted applications and supporting materials. Preference will be given to those who have been accepted to a college or university in Canada with a recognized golf program.

Funds Avail.: $1,000. **Duration:** Annual. **Number**

Awarded: 1. **To Apply:** Application forms are available online and must be sent to Golf Canada Foundation.

4480 ■ Geordie Hilton Academic Scholarships
(Undergraduate/Scholarship)

Purpose: To assist a promising university student. **Focus:** Business administration; Sports studies. **Qualif.:** Applicants must be university students studying towards a degree in sport/business administration; must show a minimum average of 80% in the last two years of high school or CEGEP and have attained a graduation diploma (minimum Grade 12); must have completed at least one full year of education in a post-secondary degree program at a recognized institution; must intend to continue in an undergraduate or graduate program in sport/business administration; must have experience in competitive golf at a regional, provincial or national level; must have participated in community and/or extracurricular activities; must be Canadian citizens or landed immigrants. **Criteria:** Candidates will be judged based on the information contained in their applications and support materials.

Funds Avail.: No specific amount. **To Apply:** Application forms are available online and must be sent to Golf Canada Foundation. **Contact:** Golf Canada Foundation, at the above address.

4481 ■ Marlene Streit Golf Scholarships
(Undergraduate/Scholarship)

Purpose: To support the Canadian female golfers attending Canadian universities and colleges recognized by the RCGA Foundation. **Focus:** General studies/Field of study not specified. **Qualif.:** Applicants must be Canadian female golfers; must have a minimum of 70% in the last two years of high school/CEGEP and have graduated (minimum grade 12). Applicants must also complete at least one full year in a post-secondary degree program and show a minimum average of 70%; must have experience in competitive golf at a regional, provincial or national level; must have been accepted at an RCGA Foundation recognized college or university; and have been named or will be named to the institution's golf team; must be Canadian citizens or landed immigrants. **Criteria:** Applicants will be judged based on the information contained in their applications and support materials.

Funds Avail.: $3,000. **Number Awarded:** 2. **To Apply:** Application forms are available online and must be sent to Golf Canada Foundation. **Contact:** Golf Canada Foundation, at the above address.

4482 ■ Golf Course Superintendents Association of America (GCSAA)
1421 Research Park Dr.
Lawrence, KS 66049-3859
Ph: (785)841-2240
Fax: (785)832-3643
Free: 800-472-7878
E-mail: mbrhelp@gcsaa.org
URL: www.gcsaa.org

4483 ■ GCSAA Scholars Competition
(Undergraduate/Scholarship)

Purpose: To encourage students who wish to pursue a career in golf course management. **Focus:** Turfgrass management. **Qualif.:** Applicants must be undergraduate students who are currently enrolled in two or more years of an accredited program related to golf course management; must have completed the first year (24 credit hours or equivalent); and must be GCSAA members. Graduating seniors prior to the application deadline are ineligible. **Criteria:** Applicants will be evaluated based on academic achievement, potential to become a leading professional, employment history, extracurricular activities, recommendation of a superintendent with whom students have worked with and a current academic advisor.

Funds Avail.: $500 - $6,000. **Duration:** Annual. **To Apply:** Applicants must submit their transcript of records, Advisor's Report and Superintendent's Report. The essay component must not exceed two double-spaced pages. Additional application forms can be obtained from the Environmental Institute for Golf or may visit the GCSAA website. **Deadline:** June 1. **Contact:** Mischia Wright, associate director, EIFG; mwright@gcsaa.org.

4484 ■ GCSAA Student Essay Contest *(Graduate, Undergraduate/Prize)*

Purpose: To provide assistance to students pursuing degrees in turfgrass science. **Focus:** Agricultural sciences; Turfgrass management. **Qualif.:** Applicants must be undergraduate and graduate students pursuing degrees in turfgrass science, agronomy, or any related fields to golf course management; and must be GCSAA members. **Criteria:** Selected applicants should have an essay that is original, compelling, well-organized, readable, persuasive and creative. Technical accuracy, composition skills and the student's adherence to the contest rules will be considered.

Funds Avail.: $4,500. **Number Awarded:** 3. **To Apply:** Applicant's essay should be 7 to 12 pages in length, double-spaced and must be in type-written format; must include a cover page with the student's name, school and year attended, home and campus addresses, contact numbers and signature. Each page should be numbered including the student's last name. **Contact:** Mischia Wright, EIFG; Email: mwright@gcsaa.org.

4485 ■ Dr. James Watson Fellowship Program
(Doctorate, Graduate/Fellowship)

Purpose: To provide financial assistance for the future educators and researchers of the turfgrass industry. **Focus:** Turfgrass management. **Qualif.:** Applicants must be candidates for masters' or doctoral degrees; be in their second year of a recognized program in turfgrass science or any related fields; must have plans to pursue a career in research, instruction, or extension service in a university setting. **Criteria:** Selection of applicants will be based on academic excellence, peer recommendations, communication skills, commitment to a career as instructors and/or scientists, accomplishment in research and/or education and potential contributions to the industry.

Funds Avail.: $5,000. **Duration:** Annual. **Number Awarded:** 3. **To Apply:** Applicants must attach a resume, one-page summaries of any research projects, educational efforts, extension programs, or other relevant activities in which they have been involved; letters of professional recommendation from an adviser or other academic instructors; one letter of recommendation from a superintendent with whom they have had professional contact; and transcript of records. **Deadline:** October 1.

4486 ■ Gonzaga University School of Law
721 N Cincinnati St.
Spokane, WA 99202-2021
Ph: (509)313-5532

Awards are arranged alphabetically below their administering organizations

GOODMAN ACKER, P.C. — Sponsors and Their Scholarships

E-mail: admissions@lawschool.gonzaga.edu
URL: www.law.gonzaga.edu
Facebook: www.facebook.com/GonzagaLawSchool
LinkedIn: www.linkedin.com/edu/school?id=19644&trk=edu-cp-title
Twitter: twitter.com/GonzagaLaw

4487 ■ Thomas More Scholarships *(Undergraduate/Scholarship)*

Purpose: To help individuals in the pursuit of their educational goals. **Focus:** Law. **Qualif.:** Applicants must be U.S. or Canadian citizens who are entering a law school as first year students, and have a 3.5 GPA or higher and have taken the LSAT. **Criteria:** Recipients will be selected based on academic achievement, life, and work experience.

Funds Avail.: No specific amount. **Duration:** Annual. **To Apply:** Applicants must submit their completed application and two letters of recommendation. **Deadline:** February 1. **Remarks:** Established in 1980. **Contact:** Thomas More Scholarship Program staff at tmscholarship@lawschool.gonzaga.edu.

4488 ■ Goodman Acker, P.C.
17000 W 10 Mile Rd., 2nd Flr.
Southfield, MI 48075
Ph: (248)483-5000
Fax: (248)483-3131
Free: 866-483-6714
URL: www.goodmanacker.com

4489 ■ Goodman Acker Scholarships *(Graduate/Scholarship)*

Purpose: To assist students who are completing and pursuing their degree in law school. **Focus:** Law. **Qualif.:** Applicants must be students who are currently attending or have been accepted to an accredited law school in the United States; must be enrolled at an accredited 4-year university and have been accepted to a law school; must have academic achievement as reflected by a minimum 3.0 GPA; must be U.S. citizens. **Criteria:** Essays will be judged by a panel from Goodman Acker and associated parties. Submissions will be judged on academic achievement and essay submission.

Funds Avail.: $1,000. **To Apply:** Applicants must submit the following requirements: complete online application form and essay; certified official copy of law school transcript or undergraduate transcript; and if entering law school, copy of acceptance letter. Essay must be no more than three pages long (double spaced, Time New Roman, size 12 font) answering one of the following essay topics: "As a victim, what are the top 10 things you should ask your personal injury lawyer?" and "how would the world be different if there were no personal injury lawyers?". **Deadline:** December 1.

4490 ■ Goodwin Procter L.L.P.
53 State St.
Boston, MA 02109
Ph: (617)570-1000
Fax: (617)523-1231
URL: www.goodwinprocter.com
Facebook: www.facebook.com/home.php#!/pages/Goodwin-Procter-LLP/118266874895544
LinkedIn: www.linkedin.com/company/goodwin-procter-llp
Twitter: www.twitter.com/goodwinlaw

4491 ■ Public Interest Fellowships for Law Students of Color *(Undergraduate/Fellowship)*

Purpose: To help support students who plan to work in public interest law positions. **Focus:** Law. **Qualif.:** Applicants must be full-time, currently enrolled, first-year students of color pursuing a JD at an accredited law school. **Criteria:** Selection will be based on the committee's criteria.

Funds Avail.: $7,500. **Duration:** Annual. **To Apply:** Interested applicants may contact the Firm for the application process and other information. **Contact:** fellowships@goodwinprocter.com.

4492 ■ Google Inc.
1600 Amphitheatre Pky.
Mountain View, CA 94043
Ph: (650)253-0000
Fax: (650)253-0001
E-mail: info@google.com
URL: www.google.com

4493 ■ Dr. Anita Borg Memorial Scholarships - USA *(Graduate, Undergraduate/Scholarship)*

Purpose: To support and encourage women to excel in computing and technology and become active role models and leaders in the field. **Focus:** Computer and information sciences; Engineering, Computer. **Qualif.:** Applicants must be female students entering their senior year of undergraduate study or be enrolled in a graduate program in the current academic year at a university in the US; must be enrolled in computer science or computer engineering or a closely related technical field as a full-time student for the current year; must maintain a cumulative GPA of at least 3.5 on a 4.0 scale or 4.5 on a 5.0 scale. **Criteria:** Scholarships will be awarded based on the strength of each candidate's academic background and demonstrated leadership.

Funds Avail.: $10,000. **Duration:** Annual. **To Apply:** Applicants may apply online. Applicants must submit their electronic resume, essay responses, transcripts and name and email of referrers (PDF format preferred for all requested documents). **Deadline:** January 15. **Remarks:** Established in 2004. **Contact:** anitaborgscholars@google.com.

4494 ■ China Google PhD Fellowships *(Doctorate/Fellowship)*

Purpose: To recognize outstanding graduate students doing exceptional work in computer science, related disciplines, or promising research areas. **Focus:** Computer and information sciences. **Qualif.:** Candidates must be outstanding PhD students. **Criteria:** Selection will be based on the committee's criteria.

Funds Avail.: No specific amount. **To Apply:** Applications are not accepted directly from students. The invited university will be asked to submit application materials.

4495 ■ Google-American Indian Science and Engineering Society Scholarships *(Graduate, Undergraduate/Scholarship)*

Purpose: To encourage students to excel in their studies and become active role models and leaders. **Focus:** Com-

Awards are arranged alphabetically below their administering organizations

puter and information sciences; Engineering, Computer. **Qualif.:** Applicants must be currently pursuing undergraduate and graduate degrees in computer science or computer engineering. **Criteria:** Selection will be based on the committee's criteria.

Funds Avail.: Varies. **To Apply:** Applicants may contact the society for the application process.

4496 ■ Google European Doctoral Fellowships
(Doctorate/Fellowship)

Purpose: To provide educational support to students doing exceptional research in Computer Science or closely related areas. **Focus:** Computer and information sciences. **Qualif.:** Candidates must be PhD students at any stage of research in the areas of expertise represented by the fellowships; must attend a full-time PhD position at one of the selected universities. Students must remain enrolled in the PhD program or forfeit the fellowship award; must be nominated by their department/university. **Criteria:** Selection will be based on the committee's criteria.

Funds Avail.: No specific amount. **Number Awarded:** Varies. **To Apply:** The university's computer science department or invited department should submit the following: name of fellowship for which the students are being considered; students' CV; official transcripts of previous and current academic records; research/dissertation proposal of maximum 6 pages including references; 2-3 letters of recommendation from those familiar with the nominees' work, at least one coming from the thesis advisor; short CV from the proposed supervisor. **Deadline:** February 1.

4497 ■ Google Hispanic College Fund Scholarships
(Graduate, Undergraduate/Scholarship)

Purpose: To encourage students to excel in their studies and become active role models and leaders. **Focus:** Computer and information sciences; Engineering, Computer. **Qualif.:** Applicants must be of Hispanic background; must be US citizens or permanent residents of the US or Puerto Rico; must be studying at an accredited university in the US or Puerto Rico for the upcoming academic year; must be enrolled for the upcoming academic year; must have a minimum GPA of a 3.5 on a 4.0 scale; must be junior or senior undergraduate or graduate students pursuing a degree in computer science or computer engineering for the upcoming academic year. **Criteria:** Selection will be based on demonstrated academic excellence and financial need.

Funds Avail.: $500 - $5,000. **Duration:** Annual. **To Apply:** Applicants may apply to the Google scholarship program by completing the STEM Majors Application. Applicants must submit their official transcript, proof of family income and proof of citizenship status. Applicant's essay, letter of recommendation, resume and financial aid verification must be submitted online.

4498 ■ Google US/Canada PhD Fellowships *(Graduate, Doctorate/Fellowship)*

Purpose: To recognize outstanding graduate students doing exceptional work in computer science, related disciplines, or promising research areas. **Focus:** Computer and information sciences. **Qualif.:** Candidates must be full-time graduate students pursuing a PhD in the research areas represented by the fellowships; must attend one of the eligible schools and universities. Students must remain enrolled in the PhD program or forfeit the fellowship award; must be nominated by their department; must have completed their graduate coursework in the PhD program and be embarking on or continuing their graduate research. **Criteria:** Selection will be based on the committee's criteria.

Funds Avail.: $34,000. **Duration:** Annual. **To Apply:** The university will be asked to submit the following: name of fellowship for which students are being considered; students' CV; transcript of current and previous academic records; a 4-5 page research/dissertation proposal; 2-3 letters of recommendation from those familiar with the nominees' work, at least one coming from the thesis advisor. **Deadline:** November 3.

4499 ■ The Gordon Foundation
11 Church St., Ste. 400
Toronto, ON, Canada M5E 1W1
Ph: (416)601-4776
Fax: (416)601-1689
URL: gordonfoundation.ca

4500 ■ Jane Glassco Northern Fellowships *(Professional development/Fellowship)*

Purpose: To support those individuals from the Northern region in their research and understanding of important issues faced by their region by helping them to develop policy ideas which can help to address such issues. **Focus:** Canadian studies. **Qualif.:** Applicants must be Canadian citizens or permanent residents, or residents or former residents of Yukon, Northwest Territories, Nunavut, Nunavik, or Nunatsiavut; must be interested in professional development, education and lifelong learning, public policy, indigenous knowledge, and northern issues; and must be fluent in English. **Criteria:** Applicants are evaluated and selected on the following criteria: history of community engagement as demonstrated through volunteering, engagement with aboriginal governments, bands, or nonprofit organizations; interest in public policy and activism as an effective means to positive change; knowledge of issues facing the North; demonstration of leadership potential; ability to fulfill the program requirements and stay engaged in the program for years to come; and overall quality of the application.

Funds Avail.: 5,000 Canadian Dollars. **Number Awarded:** 10. **To Apply:** Applicants may contact the Foundation for the application process and other information.

4501 ■ Government Finance Officers Association of United States and Canada (GFOA)
203 N LaSalle St., Ste. 2700
Chicago, IL 60601-1210
Ph: (312)977-9700
Fax: (312)977-4806
URL: www.gfoa.org

4502 ■ GFOA Minorities in Government Finance Scholarship *(Graduate, Undergraduate/Scholarship)*

Purpose: To recognize outstanding performance by minority students, and support them, in their preparation for careers in state and local government finance. **Focus:** Business administration; Economics; Finance; Political science; Public administration. **Qualif.:** Applicants must: be current full- or part-time upper-division undergraduate or graduate students in public administration, accounting, finance, political science, economics or business administration (with a specific focus on government or nonprofit management);

Awards are arranged alphabetically below their administering organizations

belong to one of the following groups (as defined by the U.S. Census Bureau): Black or African American, American Indian or Alaska Native, Asian, Native Hawaiian or other Pacific islander, Hispanic or Latino; be citizens or permanent residents of the United States or Canada; be recommended by academic advisor, the dean of the graduate program (graduate students) or department chair (undergraduate students); and, be students who have not received scholarships administered by the Government Finance Officers Association of the United States and Canada. **Criteria:** Recipients will be selected on the basis of their: plan to pursue a career in state and local government finance; past academic record and work experience; strength of past coursework and present plan of study; and undergraduate and graduate grade point averages.

Funds Avail.: $8,000. **Duration:** Annual. **To Apply:** Applicants must submit the following: application form; statement of proposed state and local government finance career plan and if applicable, plan of graduate study; undergraduate and graduate grade transcripts; resume; and academic advisor's, department chair's or dean's letter of recommendation; and other letters of recommendation (optional). **Deadline:** February 19.

4503 ■ Daniel B. Goldberg Scholarship *(Graduate/Scholarship)*

Purpose: To support outstanding performance in graduate programs by students preparing for a career in state and local government finance. **Focus:** Finance. **Qualif.:** Applicants must: be current full-time students in a graduate program that prepares students for careers in state and local government finance and are expecting to be enrolled in the spring semester of the current year in a baccalaureate degree or its equivalent; be citizens or permanent residents of the United States or Canada; and, have not been winners of scholarship program administered by the GFOA of the US and Canada. **Criteria:** Candidates will be assessed on the basis of their: plans to pursue a career in state or local government finance; strength of past coursework and present plan of study; letters of recommendation from academic advisor, the dean of the graduate program and others; and undergraduate and graduate grade point averages.

Funds Avail.: $13,000. **Duration:** Annual. **To Apply:** Applicants must submit completed application form; statement of proposed career plan in state and local government finance; undergraduate and graduate transcript of grades; resume; academic advisor's or dean's letter of recommendation; and other graduate program faculty letters of recommendation. **Deadline:** February 19. **Remarks:** Established in 1985.

4504 ■ Frank L. Greathouse Government Accounting Scholarship *(Graduate, Undergraduate/Scholarship)*

Purpose: To recognize outstanding performance in accounting studies by students preparing for a career in state and local government finance. **Focus:** Finance. **Qualif.:** Applicants must: be current full-time undergraduate or graduate students in an accounting program preparing for a career in state and local government finance (both advanced undergraduate and graduate students); be citizens or permanent residents of the United States or Canada; be recommended by the academic advisor or the accounting program chair; and, have not been past winners of a scholarship program administered by the Government Finance Officers Association of the US and Canada. **Criteria:** Applicants will be selected based on: the statement of proposed career plan in state and local government finance or proposed plan of graduate studies in government accounting or public administration; strength of past coursework and present plan of study; letters of recommendation by academic advisor, chair of the accounting program and others; and undergraduate/ graduate grade point averages.

Funds Avail.: $8,000. **Duration:** Annual. **To Apply:** Applicants must submit the following: completed application form; statement of proposed career plan in state and local government finance; plan of graduate study (if applicable); undergraduate and graduate grade transcripts; resume; academic advisor's or department chair's letter of recommendation; and other letters of recommendation (optional). **Deadline:** February 19. **Remarks:** Established in 1985.

4505 ■ Graham and Dunn P.C.
2801 Alaskan Way, Ste. 300
Seattle, WA 98121
Ph: (206)624-8300
Fax: (206)340-9599
E-mail: info@grahamdunn.com
URL: www.grahamdunn.com

4506 ■ Graham and Dunn 1L Diversity Fellowships *(Graduate/Fellowship)*

Purpose: To promote diversity in the legal profession. **Focus:** Law. **Qualif.:** Applicant must be a first year law school student in good standing pursuing a Juris Doctor at an ABA-accredited law; must possess a record of academic, employment, community and/or other achievement indicating potential for success in law school and in the legal profession; must contribute to the diversity of the law school student body and the legal community; must demonstrate commitment to fostering diversity in the legal community; must be able to commit to participation in a 12-week summer clerkship program with the firm; and must be ultimately committed to a long-term practicing of law in Seattle. **Criteria:** Selection is based on the submitted application materials.

Funds Avail.: $7,500. **Duration:** one academic year. **To Apply:** Applicants must submit a resume, complete transcript of undergraduate grades, first semester law school grades, a short personal statement (maximum of 500 words), a legal writing sample (maximum of 5 pages), and a list of two academic or professional references. **Deadline:** January 15. **Contact:** Marisa Velling Lindell at the above address.

4507 ■ Grand Canyon Historical Society (GCHS)
PO Box 31405
Flagstaff, AZ 86003-1405
E-mail: President@grandcanyonhistory.org
URL: www.grandcanyonhistory.org/index.html

4508 ■ Grand Canyon Historical Society Scholarships *(Graduate/Scholarship)*

Purpose: To develop and promote appreciation, understanding and education of the earlier history of the inhabitants. **Focus:** Environmental conservation; Historic preservation; History. **Qualif.:** Applicants must be any Arizona university graduate student doing work in history and historic or environmental preservation fields. **Criteria:** Selection will be based on evaluation of submitted documents and specific criteria.

Awards are arranged alphabetically below their administering organizations

Funds Avail.: $1,000. **To Apply:** Applicants must submit a research project concerning historical individuals and environmental issues in the Grand Canyon region; one-page application letter with a short biography that includes name, address, phone, number, undergraduate or graduate degrees, current degree program, department and advisor; and must submit a short paragraph describing how this award would be applied on the proposed project. **Deadline:** March 1. **Contact:** Al Richmond; Email: AlRichmond@npgcable.com.

4509 ■ Grand Haven Area Community Foundation

1 S Harbor Dr.
Grand Haven, MI 49417
Ph: (616)842-6378
Fax: (616)842-9518
URL: www.ghacf.org

4510 ■ Charles A. Bassett Endowed Memorial Scholarship Fund *(Undergraduate/Scholarship)*

Purpose: To improve and enhance the quality of life in the Tri-Cities area by serving as a leader, catalyst and resource for philanthropy; to strive for community improvement through strategic grantmaking in such fields as arts, education, health, environment, youth, social services and other human needs. **Focus:** General studies/Field of study not specified. **Qualif.:** Applicants must be graduating seniors from Spring Lake High School who have played on the tennis team. **Criteria:** Recipients will be selected based on positive thought, strong personal conviction and outstanding character. Financial need is not a priority.

Funds Avail.: No specific amount. **To Apply:** Applicants must submit: completed application form; current high school or college transcript; Student Aid Report (SAR) from the Free Application for Federal Student Aid (FAFSA) with EFC number, unless applying for scholarships that do not consider financial need; and letter of recommendation. **Deadline:** March 2. **Contact:** Kim McLaughlin; Phone: 616-842-6378; Email: kmclaughlin@ghacf.org.

4511 ■ Geri Coccodrilli Culinary Scholarship Fund *(Undergraduate/Scholarship)*

Purpose: To provide scholarship assistance to a Tri-Cities area students. **Focus:** Culinary arts. **Qualif.:** Applicants must be graduating high school seniors from the Tri-Cities area and Fruitport High School who wish to pursue studies in the Culinary Arts. **Criteria:** Recipients are selected based on leadership ability; community involvement; financial need; creativity; and academic achievement.

Funds Avail.: No specific amount. **To Apply:** Applicants must submit: completed application form; current high school or college transcript; Student Aid Report (SAR) from the Free Application for Federal Student Aid (FAFSA) with EFC number, unless applying for scholarships that do not consider financial need; and letter of recommendation. **Deadline:** March 2. **Contact:** Kim McLaughlin; Phone: 616-842-6378; Email: kmclaughlin@ghacf.org.

4512 ■ Dake Community Manufacturing Scholarships *(Undergraduate/Scholarship)*

Purpose: To provide encouragement and support to a student who wants to further his/her manufacturing education. **Focus:** Manufacturing. **Qualif.:** Applicants must be current high school graduating seniors from Northwest Ottawa County, Muskegon County or Oceana County; must be high school graduating seniors, current college students or adult students; must be interested to further his/her career in manufacturing education including: industrial, vocational, and technical training. **Criteria:** Recipients are selected based on financial need; academic achievement; leadership ability; creativity; community and volunteer service; and special circumstances.

Funds Avail.: No specific amount. **To Apply:** Applicants must submit: completed application form; current high school or college transcript; Student Aid Report (SAR) from the Free Application for Federal Student Aid (FAFSA), unless applying for scholarships that do not consider financial need; and letter of recommendation. **Deadline:** March 2. **Contact:** Kim McLaughlin; Phone: 616-842-6378; Email: kmclaughlin@ghacf.org.

4513 ■ Erickson Education Scholarships *(Undergraduate/Scholarship)*

Purpose: To improve and enhance the quality of life in the Tri-Cities area by serving as a leader, catalyst and resource for philanthropy; to strive for community improvement through strategic grantmaking in such fields as arts, education, health, environment, youth, social services and other human needs. **Focus:** Education. **Qualif.:** Applicants must be graduating seniors of Grand Haven or Spring Lake High Schools who have excelled not only academically but who have also demonstrated leadership qualities and an outstanding record of community involvement; financial need is a consideration. **Criteria:** Recipients will be selected based on the following: financial need; academic achievement; leadership ability; creativity; community and volunteer service; and special circumstances.

Funds Avail.: No specific amount. **To Apply:** Applicants must submit: completed application form; current high school or college transcript; Student Aid Report (SAR) from the Free Application for Federal Student Aid (FAFSA) with EFC number, unless applying for scholarships that do not consider financial need; and letter of recommendation. **Deadline:** March 2. **Contact:** Kim McLaughlin; Phone: 616-842-6378; Email: kmclaughlin@ghacf.org.

4514 ■ Kevin Ernst Memorial Scholarship Fund *(Undergraduate/Scholarship)*

Purpose: To support students from the Tri-Cities area pursuing studies in the field of mathematics or accounting. **Focus:** Mathematics and mathematical sciences. **Qualif.:** Applicants must be students in the Foundation's service area who wish to continue their education in the field of mathematics. **Criteria:** Recipients are selected based on financial need; academic achievement; leadership ability; creativity; community and volunteer service; and special circumstances.

Funds Avail.: No specific amount. **To Apply:** Applicants must submit: completed application form; current high school or college transcript; Student Aid Report (SAR) from the Free Application for Federal Student Aid (FAFSA) with EFC number, unless applying for scholarships that do not consider financial need; and letter of recommendation. **Deadline:** March 2. **Contact:** Kim McLaughlin; Phone: 616-842-6378; Email: kmclaughlin@ghacf.org.

4515 ■ Bertha M. Fase Memorial Scholarship Fund *(Undergraduate/Scholarship)*

Purpose: To provide scholarship assistance to a Grand Haven High School student. **Focus:** Education. **Qualif.:** Applicants must be Grand Haven High School graduating

GRAND HAVEN AREA COMMUNITY FOUNDATION

seniors with a 3.5 GPA or better; must plan to pursue studies in the field of Education. Applicants must demonstrate interest in youth through volunteer mentoring (for consideration). In addition, a student who is a member of St. Paul's United Church of Christ will be given special consideration. **Criteria:** Recipients will be selected based on academic achievement; leadership ability; creativity; community and volunteer service; financial need; and special circumstances.
Funds Avail.: No specific amount. **To Apply:** Applicants must submit: completed application form; current high school or college transcript; Student Aid Report (SAR) from the Free Application for Federal Student Aid (FAFSA) with EFC number, unless applying for scholarships that do not consider financial need; and letter of recommendation. **Deadline:** March 2. **Contact:** Kim McLaughlin; Phone: 616-842-6378; Email: kmclaughlin@ghacf.org.

4516 ■ Scott A. Flahive Memorial Scholarship Fund
(Undergraduate/Scholarship)

Purpose: To provide scholarship assistance to a Tri-Cities area students. **Focus:** Law. **Qualif.:** Applicants must be students pursuing career in the field of law enforcement and/or criminal justice. **Criteria:** Recipients are selected based on demonstrated academic excellence; financial need; leadership ability; community and volunteer service; creativity; and special circumstances.
Funds Avail.: No specific amount. **To Apply:** Applicants must submit: completed application form; current high school or college transcript; Student Aid Report (SAR) from the Free Application for Federal Student Aid (FAFSA) with EFC number, unless applying for scholarships that do not consider financial need; and letter of recommendation. **Deadline:** March 2. **Contact:** Kim McLaughlin; Phone: 616-842-6378; Email: kmclaughlin@ghacf.org.

4517 ■ Floto-Peel Family Scholarship Fund
(Undergraduate, Vocational/Occupational/Scholarship)

Purpose: To improve and enhance the quality of life in the Tri-Cities area by serving as a leader, catalyst and resource for philanthropy; to strive for community improvement through strategic grantmaking in such fields as arts, education, health, environment, youth, social services and other human needs. **Focus:** Business; Nursing. **Qualif.:** Applicants must be Tri-Cities area residents planning to attend a two-to-four year college, university or vocational school; must plan to study in the field of nursing or business; must have 2.5 GPA. **Criteria:** Recipients are selected based on financial need; academic achievement; leadership ability; community and volunteer service; creativity; and special circumstances.
Funds Avail.: No specific amount. **To Apply:** Applicants must submit: completed application form; current high school or college transcript; Student Aid Report (SAR) from the Free Application for Federal Student Aid (FAFSA) with EFC number, unless applying for scholarships that do not consider financial need; and letter of recommendation. **Deadline:** March 2. **Contact:** Kim McLaughlin; Phone: 616-842-6378; Email: kmclaughlin@ghacf.org.

4518 ■ John L. and Victory E. Frantz Scholarship
(Undergraduate/Scholarship)

Purpose: To improve and enhance the quality of life in the Tri-Cities area by serving as a leader, catalyst and resource for philanthropy; to strive for community improvement through strategic grantmaking in such fields as arts, education, health, environment, youth, social services and other human needs; to assist high school graduating seniors of northwest Ottawa County to pursue a college education. **Focus:** General studies/Field of study not specified. **Qualif.:** Applicants must be high school graduating seniors of northwest Ottawa County. **Criteria:** Recipients are selected based on demonstrated academic excellence and financial need.
Funds Avail.: No specific amount. **To Apply:** Applicants must submit: completed application form; current high school or college transcript; Student Aid Report (SAR) from the Free Application for Federal Student Aid (FAFSA), unless applying for scholarships that do not consider financial need; and letter of recommendation. **Deadline:** March 2. **Contact:** Kim McLaughlin; Phone: 616-842-6378; Email: kmclaughlin@ghacf.org.

4519 ■ Gauthier Family Scholarship Fund
(Undergraduate/Scholarship)

Purpose: To support students from the Tri-Cities area pursuing studies in Mechanical or Electrical Engineering. **Focus:** Engineering. **Qualif.:** Applicants must be high school students from the Tri-Cities area who wish to pursue studies in mechanical or electrical engineering at Michigan Technical Institute. **Criteria:** Recipients are selected based on demonstrated academic excellence and financial need.
Funds Avail.: No specific amount. **To Apply:** Applicants must submit: completed application form; current high school or college transcript; Student Aid Report (SAR) from the Free Application for Federal Student Aid (FAFSA) with EFC number, unless applying for scholarships that do not consider financial need; and letter of recommendation. **Deadline:** March 2. **Contact:** Kim McLaughlin; Phone: 616-842-6378; Email: kmclaughlin@ghacf.org.

4520 ■ Tom Gifford Scholarships *(Undergraduate/Scholarship)*

Purpose: To improve and enhance the quality of life in the Tri-Cities area by serving as a leader, catalyst and resource for philanthropy; to strive for community improvement through strategic grantmaking in such fields as arts, education, health, environment, youth, social services and other human needs. **Focus:** General studies/Field of study not specified. **Qualif.:** Applicants must be planning to attend Amherst College within 30 months of high school graduation will be given consideration. Applicants who will be attending one of the top ten colleges or university (based in the current year US News and World Report) will be considered if no Amherst applicant is available. Application is also available to graduates of Spring Lake high School who have been a student for three (3) semesters immediately prior to graduation and who have attended SLHS for atleast three (3) years. **Criteria:** Recipients are selected based on demonstrated academic excellence and financial need.
Funds Avail.: No specific amount. **To Apply:** Applicants must submit: completed application form; current high school or college transcript; Student Aid Report (SAR) from the Free Application for Federal Student Aid (FAFSA) with EFC number, unless applying for scholarships that do not consider financial need; and letter of recommendation. **Deadline:** March 2. **Contact:** Kim McLaughlin; Phone: 616-842-6378; Email: kmclaughlin@ghacf.org.

4521 ■ Grand Haven Offshore Challenge Scholarship Fund *(Undergraduate/Scholarship)*

Purpose: To improve and enhance the quality of life in the Tri-Cities area by serving as a leader, catalyst and resource

Awards are arranged alphabetically below their administering organizations

for philanthropy; to strive for community improvement through strategic grantmaking in such fields as arts, education, health, environment, youth, social services and other human needs. **Focus:** Natural resources. **Qualif.:** Applicants must be graduating high school seniors from the Tri-Cities area who plan to pursue a career in natural resources such as fisheries, wildlife and environmental water quality at any public or private college or university. **Criteria:** Recipients are selected based on demonstrated academic excellence and financial need.

Funds Avail.: No specific amount. **To Apply:** Applicants must submit: completed application form; current high school or college transcript; Student Aid Report (SAR) from the Free Application for Federal Student Aid (FAFSA) with EFC number, unless applying for scholarships that do not consider financial need; and letter of recommendation. **Deadline:** March 2. **Contact:** Kim McLaughlin; Phone: 616-842-6378; Email: kmclaughlin@ghacf.org.

4522 ■ Barbara and Nicole Heacox Foreign Travel and Study Scholarship Fund *(Undergraduate/Scholarship)*

Purpose: To improve and enhance the quality of life in the Tri-Cities area by serving as a leader, catalyst and resource for philanthropy; to strive for community improvement through strategic grantmaking in such fields as arts, education, health, environment, youth, social services and other human needs. **Focus:** General studies/Field of study not specified. **Qualif.:** Applicants must be a northwest Ottawa County Tri-Cities Area high school student, or college student wanting to pursue educational or travel opportunities in foreign countries; financial need is a primary consideration. **Criteria:** Recipients are selected based on financial need; academic achievement; leadership ability; community and volunteer service; creativity; and special circumstances.

Funds Avail.: No specific amount. **To Apply:** Applicants must submit: completed application form; current high school or college transcript; Student Aid Report (SAR) from the Free Application for Federal Student Aid (FAFSA) with EFC number, unless applying for scholarships that do not consider financial need; and letter of recommendation. Applicants must also provide a course description. **Deadline:** March 2. **Contact:** Kim McLaughlin; Phone: 616-842-6378; Email: kmclaughlin@ghacf.org.

4523 ■ Marjorie M. Hendricks Environmental Education Scholarship Fund *(Undergraduate/Scholarship)*

Purpose: To assist an upperclassman or graduate student majoring in environmental science field. **Focus:** Environmental science. **Qualif.:** Applicants must be Tri-Cities area residents or graduates of a Tri-Cities High School, attending a university and majoring in an environmental science course of study. **Criteria:** Recipients are selected based on financial need. First priority will be given to students attending GVSU or Aquinas College.

Funds Avail.: No specific amount. **To Apply:** Applicants must submit: completed application form; current high school or college transcript; Student Aid Report (SAR) from the Free Application for Federal Student Aid (FAFSA) with EFC number, unless applying for scholarships that do not consider financial need; and letter of recommendation. **Deadline:** March 2. **Contact:** Kim McLaughlin; Phone: 616-842-6378; Email: kmclaughlin@ghacf.org.

4524 ■ Michael Herman Scholarships *(Undergraduate, Vocational/Occupational/Scholarship)*

Purpose: To improve and enhance the quality of life in the Tri-Cities area by serving as a leader, catalyst and resource for philanthropy; to strive for community improvement through strategic grantmaking in such fields as arts, education, health, environment, youth, social services and other human needs. **Focus:** General studies/Field of study not specified. **Qualif.:** Applicants must be a current high school graduate of any Tri-Cities area; intending to pursue a degree or certification at any two- or four-year accredited college, university or vocational/technical school. Applicants who played on a soccer team and wishes to continue playing in college on an intramural, club or college team will be given consideration. Applicants with financial need will also be considered. Applicants from middle-income families are encouraged to apply. **Criteria:** Recipients will be selected based on financial need; community and volunteer service; creativity; leadership ability; and special circumstances.

Funds Avail.: No specific amount. **To Apply:** Applicants must submit the following: a completed application form; current high school or college transcript; Student Aid Report (SAR) from the Free Application for Federal Student Aid (FAFSA), unless applying for scholarships that do not consider financial need; and letter of recommendation. **Deadline:** March 2. **Contact:** Kim McLaughlin; Phone: 616-842-6378; Email: kmclaughlin@ghacf.org.

4525 ■ Hierholzer-Fojtik Scholarship Fund *(Undergraduate/Scholarship)*

Purpose: To provide scholarship assistance to a Tri-Cities area students. **Focus:** Law. **Qualif.:** Applicants must be Grand Haven High School graduates planning to pursue law as a career. **Criteria:** Recipients are selected based on financial need; academic achievement; leadership ability; creativity; community and volunteer service; and special circumstances.

Funds Avail.: No specific amount. **To Apply:** Applicants must submit: completed application form; current high school or college transcript; Student Aid Report (SAR) from the Free Application for Federal Student Aid (FAFSA) with EFC number, unless applying for scholarships that do not consider financial need; and letter of recommendation. **Deadline:** March 2. **Contact:** Kim McLaughlin; Phone: 616-842-6378; Email: kmclaughlin@ghacf.org.

4526 ■ Hoffman Family Scholarship Fund *(Undergraduate/Scholarship)*

Purpose: To improve and enhance the quality of life in the Tri-Cities area by serving as a leader, catalyst and resource for philanthropy; to strive for community improvement through strategic grantmaking in such fields as arts, education, health, environment, youth, social services and other human needs. **Focus:** General studies/Field of study not specified. **Qualif.:** Applicants must be graduating high school seniors at Grand Haven, Spring Lake or Fruitport high schools; must have a 3.0 GPA; special consideration will be given to an individual who is a member of the first generation in their family to attend college. **Criteria:** Recipients are selected based on demonstrated academic excellence and financial need.

Funds Avail.: No specific amount. **To Apply:** Applicants must submit: completed application form; current high school or college transcript; Student Aid Report (SAR) from the Free Application for Federal Student Aid (FAFSA), unless applying for scholarships that do not consider financial need; and letter of recommendation. **Deadline:** March 2. **Contact:** Kim McLaughlin; Phone: 616-842-6378; Email: kmclaughlin@ghacf.org.

Awards are arranged alphabetically below their administering organizations

GRAND HAVEN AREA COMMUNITY FOUNDATION

4527 ■ James W. Junior and Jane T. Brown Scholarships *(Undergraduate, Vocational/Occupational/Scholarship)*

Purpose: To assist men and women in the Tri-Cities in returning to school to further their education after a period of working. **Focus:** General studies/Field of study not specified. **Qualif.:** Applicants must be residents of Tri-Cities seeking to return to school to pursue their education after a period of working. Applicants must be over the age of 21 and has financial needs. **Criteria:** Recipients are selected based on financial need; academic achievement; leadership ability; community and volunteer service; creativity; and special circumstances.

Funds Avail.: No specific amount. **To Apply:** Applicants must submit: completed application form; current high school or college transcript; Student Aid Report (SAR) from the Free Application for Federal Student Aid (FAFSA) with EFC number, unless applying for scholarships that do not consider financial need; and letter of recommendation. **Deadline:** March 2. **Contact:** Kim McLaughlin; Phone: 616-842-6378; Email: kmclaughlin@ghacf.org.

4528 ■ Seth Koehler Central High School Scholarship Fund *(Undergraduate, Vocational/Occupational/Scholarship)*

Purpose: To provide educational financial assistance to a graduating senior from Central High School. **Focus:** General studies/Field of study not specified. **Qualif.:** Applicants must be graduating seniors from Central High School; must have plan to attend any two-to-four year college, university, vocational or technical school. **Criteria:** Recipients are selected based on financial need; academic achievement; leadership ability; community and volunteer service; creativity; and special circumstances.

Funds Avail.: No specific amount. **To Apply:** Applicants must submit: completed application form; current high school or college transcript; Student Aid Report (SAR) from the Free Application for Federal Student Aid (FAFSA) with EFC number, unless applying for scholarships that do not consider financial need; and letter of recommendation. **Deadline:** March 2. **Contact:** Kim McLaughlin; Phone: 616-842-6378; Email: kmclaughlin@ghacf.org.

4529 ■ Paul J. Laninga Memorial Scholarship Fund *(Undergraduate/Scholarship)*

Purpose: To improve and enhance the quality of life in the Tri-Cities area by serving as a leader, catalyst and resource for philanthropy; to strive for community improvement through strategic grantmaking in such fields as arts, education, health, environment, youth, social services and other human needs. **Focus:** Accounting; Business. **Qualif.:** Applicants must be graduating high school seniors of Northwest Ottawa County who plan to attend a public university; must be pursuing education and long-term careers in the areas of business and/or accounting. **Criteria:** Recipients will be selected based on academic achievement; financial need; leadership ability; community and volunteer service; creativity; and special circumstances.

Funds Avail.: No specific amount. **To Apply:** Applicants must submit: completed application form; current high school or college transcript; Student Aid Report (SAR) with EFC number from the Free Application for Federal Student Aid (FAFSA), unless applying for scholarships that do not consider financial need; and letter of recommendation. **Deadline:** March 2. **Contact:** Kim McLaughlin; Phone: 616-842-6378; Email: kmclaughlin@ghacf.org.

4530 ■ Rick and Beverly Lattin Education Scholarship Fund *(Undergraduate/Scholarship)*

Purpose: To provide financial assistance to graduates of Spring Lake or Grand Haven High school who demonstrate financial need. **Focus:** Business. **Qualif.:** Applicants must be current graduates of Spring Lake or Grand Haven High School who demonstrate financial need; must be pursuing skills in the area of business or technical training and plans to attend either Grand Valley State University or Western Michigan University. **Criteria:** Recipients are selected based on financial need; academic achievement; leadership ability; community and volunteer service; and special circumstances. Strong consideration will be given to students who are pursuing skills in the area of business or technical training.

Funds Avail.: No specific amount. **To Apply:** Applicants must submit completed application form; current high school or college transcript; Student Aid Report (SAR) from the Free Application for Federal Student Aid (FAFSA), unless applying for scholarships that do not consider financial need; and letter of recommendation. **Deadline:** March 2. **Contact:** Kim McLaughlin; Phone: 616-842-6378; Email: kmclaughlin@ghacf.org.

4531 ■ Jack W. Leatherman Family Scholarship Fund *(Undergraduate, Vocational/Occupational/Scholarship)*

Purpose: To improve and enhance the quality of life in the Tri-Cities area by serving as a leader, catalyst and resource for philanthropy; to strive for community improvement through strategic grantmaking in such fields as arts, education, health, environment, youth, social services and other human needs. **Focus:** General studies/Field of study not specified. **Qualif.:** Applicants must be current Grand Haven High School seniors and who are pursuing vocational or technology training and/or certification or plan to attend any 2 or 4 year accredited public college/university. **Criteria:** Recipients are selected based on financial need. Preference shall be given to students who faced or overcome adversity in life. Strong motivation and desire to achieve will be considered in lieu of past academic performance.

Funds Avail.: No specific amount. **To Apply:** Applicants must submit: completed application form; current high school or college transcript; Student Aid Report (SAR) from the Free Application for Federal Student Aid (FAFSA), unless applying for scholarships that do not consider financial need; and letter of recommendation. **Deadline:** March 2. **Contact:** Kim McLaughlin; Phone: 616-842-6378; Email: kmclaughlin@ghacf.org.

4532 ■ Pat and John MacTavish Scholarship Fund *(Undergraduate/Scholarship)*

Purpose: To improve and enhance the quality of life in the Tri-Cities area by serving as a leader, catalyst and resource for philanthropy; to strive for community improvement through strategic grantmaking in such fields as arts, education, health, environment, youth, social services and other human needs. **Focus:** Science. **Qualif.:** Applicants must be high school or college students seeking to pursue any of the following areas of study: math, chemistry, geology, technical writing, physics or computer science. **Criteria:** Recipients are selected based on demonstrated academic excellence and financial need. Preference to female students.

Funds Avail.: No specific amount. **To Apply:** Applicants must submit: completed application form; current high school or college transcript; Student Aid Report (SAR) from

Awards are arranged alphabetically below their administering organizations

the Free Application for Federal Student Aid (FAFSA) with EFC number, unless applying for scholarships that do not consider financial need; and letter of recommendation. **Deadline:** March 2. **Contact:** Kim McLaughlin; Phone: 616-842-6378; Email: kmclaughlin@ghacf.org.

4533 ■ Kyle R. Moreland Memorial Scholarships (Undergraduate/Scholarship)

Purpose: To provide assistance to a Grand Haven High School graduating senior student. **Focus:** General studies/Field of study not specified. **Qualif.:** Applicants must be Grand Haven High School graduating seniors planning to attend a two or four-year college degree program; must be active in their Christian faith community; must have participated on high school golf or tennis team; must have a 3.0 GPA or above. Scholarship is also open to current graduates of Spring Lake High School and/or Western Christian Michigan High School. **Criteria:** Recipients are selected based on academic performance.

Funds Avail.: No specific amount. **To Apply:** Applicants must submit: completed application form; current high school or college transcript; Student Aid Report (SAR) from the Free Application for Federal Student Aid (FAFSA) with EFC number, unless applying for scholarships that do not consider financial need; and letter of recommendation. **Deadline:** March 2. **Contact:** Kim McLaughlin; Phone: 616-842-6378; Email: kmclaughlin@ghacf.org.

4534 ■ North Ottawa Hospital Auxiliary Scholarship Fund (Undergraduate/Scholarship)

Purpose: To provide scholarship assistance to a Tri-Cities area students. **Focus:** Nursing. **Qualif.:** Applicants must be from the Tri-Cities area; currently enrolled as college students who have taken their core requirements and been accepted into their health-care related program of study. **Criteria:** Recipients are selected based on financial need, academic achievement, extracurricular activities, work history, educational goals and personal aspirations.

Funds Avail.: No specific amount. **To Apply:** Applicants must submit: completed application form; current high school or college transcript; Student Aid Report (SAR) from the Free Application for Federal Student Aid (FAFSA) with EFC number, unless applying for scholarships that do not consider financial need; and letter of recommendation. **Deadline:** March 2. **Contact:** Kim McLaughlin; Phone: 616-842-6378; Email: kmclaughlin@ghacf.org.

4535 ■ Marvin R. and Pearl E. Patterson Family Scholarships Fund (Undergraduate/Scholarship)

Purpose: To improve and enhance the quality of life in the Tri-Cities area by serving as a leader, catalyst and resource for philanthropy; to strive for community improvement through strategic grantmaking in such fields as arts, education, health, environment, youth, social services and other human needs. **Focus:** Art. **Qualif.:** Applicants must be students who will be graduating or graduated from a Tri-Cities area public high school; must have at least 3.0 GPA and plan to attend any two-year or four-year college or university to study graphic arts or fine arts. **Criteria:** Recipients will be selected based on academic achievement; leadership ability; community and volunteer service; creativity; and special circumstances.

Funds Avail.: No specific amount. **To Apply:** Applicants must submit: completed application form; current high school or college transcript; Student Aid Report (SAR) from the Free Application for Federal Student Aid (FAFSA) with EFC number, unless applying for scholarships that do not consider financial need; and letter of recommendation. **Deadline:** March 2. **Contact:** Kim McLaughlin; Phone: 616-842-6378; Email: kmclaughlin@ghacf.org.

4536 ■ P.E.O. Chapter DS Scholarships (Undergraduate, Vocational/Occupational/Scholarship)

Purpose: To improve and enhance the quality of life in the Tri-Cities area by serving as a leader, catalyst and resource for philanthropy; to strive for community improvement through strategic grantmaking in such fields as arts, education, health, environment, youth, social services and other human needs. **Focus:** General studies/Field of study not specified. **Qualif.:** Applicants must be graduating female students or non-traditional students who graduated from any Tri-Cities area public or private high school; must plan to pursue a degree or certification at any two or four-year accredited college, university, vocational or technical school. Applicants planning to attend Cottey College, the college owned and supported by P.E.O. International will be given priority. **Criteria:** Recipients are selected based on academic performance.

Funds Avail.: No specific amount. **To Apply:** Applicants must submit: completed application form; current high school or college transcript; Student Aid Report (SAR) from the Free Application for Federal Student Aid (FAFSA) with EFC number, unless applying for scholarships that do not consider financial need; and letter of recommendation. **Deadline:** March 2. **Contact:** Kim McLaughlin; Phone: 616-842-6378; Email: kmclaughlin@ghacf.org.

4537 ■ Terry Linda Potter Scholarship Fund (Undergraduate/Scholarship)

Purpose: To improve and enhance the quality of life in the Tri-Cities area by serving as a leader, catalyst and resource for philanthropy; to strive for community improvement through strategic grantmaking in such fields as arts, education, health, environment, youth, social services and other human needs. **Focus:** Health education. **Qualif.:** Applicants must reside in the Northwest Ottawa County area; must demonstrate scholastic ability and academic performance, interest in pursuing further education, preferably in a health-related field, financial need, and acceptance at an accredited two- or four-year college. **Criteria:** Recipients are selected based on financial need; academic achievement; leadership ability; creativity; community and volunteer service; and special circumstances.

Funds Avail.: No specific amount. **To Apply:** Applicants must submit: completed application form; current high school or college transcript; Student Aid Report (SAR) from the Free Application for Federal Student Aid (FAFSA) with EFC number, unless applying for scholarships that do not consider financial need; and letter of recommendation. **Deadline:** March 2. **Contact:** Kim McLaughlin; Phone: 616-842-6378; Email: kmclaughlin@ghacf.org.

4538 ■ Jacob L. Reinecke Memorial Scholarship Fund (Undergraduate/Scholarship)

Purpose: To provide scholarship assistance to a Grand Haven High School student. **Focus:** General studies/Field of study not specified. **Qualif.:** Applicants must be Grand Haven High School graduating seniors planning to attend a two-to-four year college, university or trade school; consideration will be given to male students who participated in high school athletics, specifically basketball or baseball; must have a 3.0 GPA or above. **Criteria:** Recipients are selected based on hard-working attitude and strong motivation to succeed.

Funds Avail.: No specific amount. **To Apply:** Applicants must submit: completed application form; current high school or college transcript; Student Aid Report (SAR) with EFC number from the Free Application for Federal Student Aid (FAFSA), unless applying for scholarships that do not consider financial need; and letter of recommendation. **Deadline:** March 2. **Contact:** Kim McLaughlin; Phone: 616-842-6378; Email: kmclaughlin@ghacf.org.

4539 ■ Daniel L. Reiss Memorial Scholarship Fund *(Undergraduate/Scholarship)*

Purpose: To improve and enhance the quality of life in the Tri-Cities area by serving as a leader, catalyst and resource for philanthropy; to strive for community improvement through strategic grantmaking in such fields as arts, education, health, environment, youth, social services and other human needs. **Focus:** General studies/Field of study not specified. **Qualif.:** Applicants must be graduating Grand Haven High School students who have at least a 3.8 GPA; must plan to pursue studies at Grand Valley State University or Western Michigan University in an Aeronautical Engineering or Political Science program study. **Criteria:** Recipients are selected based on demonstrated academic excellence and financial need. **Funds Avail.:** No specific amount. **To Apply:** Applicants must submit: completed application form; current high school or college transcript; Student Aid Report (SAR) from the Free Application for Federal Student Aid (FAFSA) with EFC number, unless applying for scholarships that do not consider financial need; and letter of recommendation. **Deadline:** March 2. **Contact:** Kim McLaughlin; Phone: 616-842-6378; Email: kmclaughlin@ghacf.org.

4540 ■ Harold and Eleanor Ringelberg Scholarships *(Undergraduate/Scholarship)*

Purpose: To improve and enhance the quality of life in the Tri-Cities area by serving as a leader, catalyst and resource for philanthropy; to strive for community improvement through strategic grantmaking in such fields as arts, education, health, environment, youth, social services and other human needs. **Focus:** General studies/Field of study not specified. **Qualif.:** Applicants must be Grand Haven High School graduating seniors with a minimum 3.8 GPA; must plan to pursue a college degree at Michigan State University; must have attended Grand Haven Christian School prior to high school. **Criteria:** Recipients are selected based on academic achievement. **Funds Avail.:** No specific amount. **To Apply:** Applicants must submit: completed application form; current high school or college transcript; Student Aid Report (SAR) from the Free Application for Federal Student Aid (FAFSA) with EFC number, unless applying for scholarships that do not consider financial need; and letter of recommendation. **Deadline:** March 2. **Contact:** Kim McLaughlin; Phone: 616-842-6378; Email: kmclaughlin@ghacf.org.

4541 ■ Charles and Eleanor Rycenga Education Scholarship Fund *(Undergraduate/Scholarship)*

Purpose: To improve and enhance the quality of life in the Tri-Cities area by serving as a leader, catalyst and resource for philanthropy; to strive for community improvement through strategic grantmaking in such fields as arts, education, health, environment, youth, social services and other human needs. **Focus:** General studies/Field of study not specified. **Qualif.:** Applicants must be graduating seniors of Grand Haven, Spring Lake or Western Michigan Christian High School; must have the desire to continue their education at an accredited four-year college, junior college, trade school or apprenticeship, preferably in Michigan. **Criteria:** Recipients are selected based on financial need. **Funds Avail.:** No specific amount. **To Apply:** Applicants must submit: completed application form; current high school or college transcript; Student Aid Report (SAR) from the Free Application for Federal Student Aid (FAFSA), unless applying for scholarships that do not consider financial need; and letter of recommendation. **Deadline:** March 2. **Contact:** Kim McLaughlin; Phone: 616-842-6378; Email: kmclaughlin@ghacf.org.

4542 ■ Millicent M. Schaffner Endowed Memorial Scholarships *(Undergraduate/Scholarship)*

Purpose: To improve and enhance the quality of life in the Tri-Cities area by serving as a leader, catalyst and resource for philanthropy; to strive for community improvement through strategic grantmaking in such fields as the arts, education, health, environment, youth, social services and other human needs. **Focus:** General studies/Field of study not specified. **Qualif.:** Applicants must be female students who have a strong motivation to continue their education at an accredited four-year college. **Criteria:** Recipients are selected based on financial need. **Funds Avail.:** No specific amount. **To Apply:** Applicants must submit: completed application form; current high school or college transcript; Student Aid Report (SAR) from the Free Application for Federal Student Aid (FAFSA), unless applying for scholarships that do not consider financial need; and letter of recommendation. **Deadline:** March 2. **Contact:** Kim McLaughlin; Phone: 616-842-6378; Email: kmclaughlin@ghacf.org.

4543 ■ David and Jinny Schultz Family Scholarship *(Undergraduate/Scholarship)*

Purpose: To improve and enhance the quality of life in the Tri-Cities area by serving as a leader, catalyst and resource for philanthropy; to strive for community improvement through strategic grantmaking in such fields as arts, education, health, environment, youth, social services and other human needs. **Focus:** General studies/Field of study not specified. **Qualif.:** Applicants must be graduating seniors who wish to continue their education at a four-year college, junior college, trade school or apprenticeship. Strong academic records are not required. **Criteria:** Recipients are selected based on financial need. **Funds Avail.:** No specific amount. **To Apply:** Applicants must submit: completed application form; current high school or college transcript; Student Aid Report (SAR) from the Free Application for Federal Student Aid (FAFSA), unless applying for scholarships that do not consider financial need; and letter of recommendation. **Deadline:** March 2. **Contact:** Kim McLaughlin; Phone: 616-842-6378; Email: kmclaughlin@ghacf.org.

4544 ■ David and Sharon Seaver Family Scholarship Fund *(Undergraduate/Scholarship)*

Purpose: To improve and enhance the quality of life in the Tri-Cities area by serving as a leader, catalyst and resource for philanthropy; to strive for community improvement through strategic grantmaking in such fields as arts, education, health, environment, youth, social services and other human needs. **Focus:** Business. **Qualif.:** Applicants must be graduating seniors of Grand Haven High School who plan to pursue a career in Business. **Criteria:** Recipients are selected based on financial need; creativity; community and volunteer service; leadership ability; and special circumstances.

Awards are arranged alphabetically below their administering organizations

Funds Avail.: No specific amount. **To Apply:** Applicants must submit: completed application form; current high school or college transcript; Student Aid Report (SAR) from the Free Application for Federal Student Aid (FAFSA), unless applying for scholarships that do not consider financial need; and letter of recommendation. **Deadline:** March 2. **Contact:** Kim McLaughlin; Phone: 616-842-6378; Email: kmclaughlin@ghacf.org.

4545 ■ Ken and Sandy Sharkey Family Scholarship Fund *(Undergraduate/Scholarship)*

Purpose: To improve and enhance the quality of life in the Tri-Cities area by serving as a leader, catalyst and resource for philanthropy; to strive for community improvement through strategic grantmaking in such fields as arts, education, health, environment, youth, social services and other human needs. **Focus:** General studies/Field of study not specified. **Qualif.:** Applicants must be graduating seniors from Grand Haven High School who demonstrate civic responsibility and plan to be involved in improving their community in the future; must have a 3.0 minimum GPA. **Criteria:** Recipients are selected based on academic performance; leadership ability; community and volunteer service; financial need; and special circumstances. **Funds Avail.:** No specific amount. **To Apply:** Applicants must submit: completed application form; current high school or college transcript; Student Aid Report (SAR) from the Free Application for Federal Student Aid (FAFSA), unless applying for scholarships that do not consider financial need; and letter of recommendation. **Deadline:** March 2. **Contact:** Kim McLaughlin; Phone: 616-842-6378; Email: kmclaughlin@ghacf.org.

4546 ■ Marion A. and Ruth Sherwood Family Fund Education Scholarships *(Undergraduate/Scholarship)*

Purpose: To provide scholarship assistance to a Tri-Cities area High School student. **Focus:** Education. **Qualif.:** Applicants must be planning to pursue a career in the field of Education. **Criteria:** Recipients are selected based on academic excellence and financial need. **Funds Avail.:** No specific amount. **To Apply:** Applicants must submit: completed application form; current high school or college transcript; Student Aid Report (SAR) from the Free Application for Federal Student Aid (FAFSA) with EFC number, unless applying for scholarships that do not consider financial need; and letter of recommendation. **Deadline:** March 2. **Contact:** Kim McLaughlin; Phone: 616-842-6378; Email: kmclaughlin@ghacf.org.

4547 ■ Marion A. and Ruth K. Sherwood Family Fund Engineering Scholarships *(Undergraduate/Scholarship)*

Purpose: To provide scholarship assistance to a Tri-Cities area High School student. **Focus:** Engineering. **Qualif.:** Applicants must be students planning to pursue a career in the field of engineering. **Criteria:** Recipients are selected based on academic excellence; financial need; leadership ability; creativity; community and volunteer service; and special circumstances. **Funds Avail.:** No specific amount. **To Apply:** Applicants must submit: completed application form; current high school or college transcript; Student Aid Report (SAR) from the Free Application for Federal Student Aid (FAFSA) with EFC number, unless applying for scholarships that do not consider financial need; and letter of recommendation. **Deadline:** March 2. **Contact:** Kim McLaughlin; Phone: 616-842-6378; Email: kmclaughlin@ghacf.org.

4548 ■ Miller G. Sherwood Family Scholarship Fund *(Undergraduate/Scholarship)*

Purpose: To improve and enhance the quality of life in the Tri-Cities area by serving as a leader, catalyst and resource for philanthropy; to strive for community improvement through strategic grantmaking in such fields as arts, education, health, environment, youth, social services and other human needs. **Focus:** Environmental science. **Qualif.:** Applicants must be graduating seniors of Grand Haven or Spring Lake High School who plan to pursue an education in the areas of environment or social services. Academic grade point excellence is not required. **Criteria:** Recipients are selected based on financial need; academic achievement; leadership ability; community and volunteer service; creativity; and special circumstances. **Funds Avail.:** No specific amount. **To Apply:** Applicants must submit: completed application form; current high school or college transcript; Student Aid Report (SAR) from the Free Application for Federal Student Aid (FAFSA) with EFC number, unless applying for scholarships that do not consider financial need; and letter of recommendation. **Deadline:** March 2. **Contact:** Kim McLaughlin; Phone: 616-842-6378; Email: kmclaughlin@ghacf.org.

4549 ■ Edward P. Suchecki Family Scholarship Fund *(Undergraduate/Scholarship)*

Purpose: To improve and enhance the quality of life in the Tri-Cities area by serving as a leader, catalyst and resource for philanthropy; to strive for community improvement through strategic grantmaking in such fields as arts, education, health, environment, youth, social services and other human needs. **Focus:** Business. **Qualif.:** Applicants must be graduating high school senior athletes from Grand Haven High School, preferably planning to pursue a career in business. **Criteria:** Recipients are selected based on financial need. **Funds Avail.:** No specific amount. **To Apply:** Applicants must submit: completed application form; current high school or college transcript; Student Aid Report (SAR) from the Free Application for Federal Student Aid (FAFSA), unless applying for scholarships that do not consider financial need; and letter of recommendation. **Deadline:** March 2. **Contact:** Kim McLaughlin; Phone: 616-842-6378; Email: kmclaughlin@ghacf.org.

4550 ■ Henry D. and Ruth G. Swartz Family Scholarship Fund *(Undergraduate/Scholarship)*

Purpose: To improve and enhance the quality of life in the Tri-Cities area by serving as a leader, catalyst and resource for philanthropy; to strive for community improvement through strategic grantmaking in such fields as arts, education, health, environment, youth, social services and other human needs. **Focus:** Computer and information sciences. **Qualif.:** Applicants must be graduating high school seniors from Grand Haven High School, Spring Lake High School, Holland Christian High School or Western Michigan Christian High School in North Ottawa County; must be pursuing a career in engineering, computer science, pre-law or medicine. **Criteria:** Recipients are selected based on leadership ability, community involvement and academic achievement; creativity; financial need; and special circumstances. Preference will be given to those students pursuing a career in engineering, computer science, pre-law and medicine. **Funds Avail.:** No specific amount. **To Apply:** Applicants must submit: completed application form; current high school or college transcript; Student Aid Report (SAR) from

Awards are arranged alphabetically below their administering organizations

the Free Application for Federal Student Aid (FAFSA); and letter of recommendation. **Deadline:** March 2. **Contact:** Kim McLaughlin; Phone: 616-842-6378; Email: kmclaughlin@ghacf.org.

4551 ■ H. Wayne Van Agtmael Cosmetology Scholarship Fund *(Undergraduate/Scholarship)*

Purpose: To improve and enhance the quality of life in the Tri-Cities area by serving as a leader, catalyst and resource for philanthropy; to strive for community improvement through strategic grantmaking in such fields as arts, education, health, environment, youth, social services and other human needs. **Focus:** Cosmetology. **Qualif.:** Applicants must be residing in Tri-Cities area; high school graduate; and planning to attend a certified cosmetology program at a Cosmetology School such as Aveda Institute, CHIC University of Cosmetology, French Academy of Cosmetology, or Booker Institute of Cosmetology. **Criteria:** Recipients are selected based on academic excellence and financial need.

Funds Avail.: No specific amount. **To Apply:** Applicants must submit: completed application form; current high school or college transcript; Student Aid Report (SAR) from the Free Application for Federal Student Aid (FAFSA), unless applying for scholarships that do not consider financial need; and letter of recommendation. **Deadline:** March 2. **Contact:** Kim McLaughlin; Phone: 616-842-6378; Email: kmclaughlin@ghacf.org.

4552 ■ West Michigan Nursery and Landscape Association Scholarship Fund *(Undergraduate/Scholarship)*

Purpose: To assist graduating high school seniors and currently enrolled college students to pursue a horticulture or green industry career. **Focus:** Horticulture. **Qualif.:** Applicants must be graduating high school seniors or currently enrolled college students planning to pursue a horticulture or green industry career at a two-or-four-year college or university; must be residents of Ottawa, Oceana, Newaygo, Muskegon or Allegan Counties. **Criteria:** Recipients are selected based on demonstrated academic excellence and financial need.

Funds Avail.: No specific amount. **To Apply:** Applicants must submit: completed application form; current high school or college transcript; Student Aid Report (SAR) from the Free Application for Federal Student Aid (FAFSA), unless applying for scholarships that do not consider financial need; and letter of recommendation. **Deadline:** March 2. **Contact:** Kim McLaughlin; Phone: 616-842-6378; Email: kmclaughlin@ghacf.org.

4553 ■ Louise Wachter Wickham Scholarships *(Undergraduate/Scholarship)*

Purpose: To assist local graduating high school seniors interested in obtaining a college degree in elementary education. **Focus:** Education. **Qualif.:** Applicants must be graduating high school seniors interested in obtaining a college degree in elementary education; must have a good (but not necessarily perfect) academic record. **Criteria:** Recipients are selected based on academic performance; financial need; leadership ability; creativity; community and volunteer service; and special circumstances.

Funds Avail.: No specific amount. **To Apply:** Applicants must submit: completed application form; current high school or college transcript; Student Aid Report (SAR) from the Free Application for Federal Student Aid (FAFSA) with EFC number, unless applying for scholarships that do not consider financial need; and letter of recommendation. **Deadline:** March 2. **Contact:** Kim McLaughlin; Phone: 616-842-6378; Email: kmclaughlin@ghacf.org.

4554 ■ Women's Club of Grand Haven Scholarships *(Undergraduate/Scholarship)*

Purpose: To improve and enhance the quality of life in the Tri-Cities area by serving as a leader, catalyst and resource for philanthropy; to strive for community improvement through strategic grantmaking in such fields as the arts, education, health, environment, youth, social services and other human needs. **Focus:** General studies/Field of study not specified. **Qualif.:** Applicants may be non-traditional students; Tri-Cities adult resident seeking to gain additional education of career training at a college, university, technical or vocational school. Applicants must be a student whose secondary education has been delayed or interrupted. **Criteria:** Recipients are selected based on financial need, academic achievement, community service and college plans. Preference will be given to a female, age 21 or older, with demonstrated financial need.

Funds Avail.: No specific amount. **To Apply:** Applicants must submit: completed application form; current high school or college transcript; Student Aid Report (SAR) from the Free Application for Federal Student Aid (FAFSA) with EFC number, unless applying for scholarships that do not consider financial need; and letter of recommendation. **Deadline:** March 2. **Contact:** Kim McLaughlin; Phone: 616-842-6378; Email: kmclaughlin@ghacf.org.

4555 ■ Zenko Family Scholarship Fund *(Undergraduate/Scholarship)*

Purpose: To provide assistance to students to further their education. **Focus:** General studies/Field of study not specified. **Qualif.:** Applicants must be Tri-Cities graduates of Spring Lake, Grand Haven or Fruitport High School; and have made their own financial contribution through employment to further their education at an accredited four-year college, junior college, trade school or apprenticeship. **Criteria:** Recipients are selected based on financial need.

Funds Avail.: No specific amount. **To Apply:** Applicants must submit: completed application form; current high school or college transcript; Student Aid Report (SAR) from the Free Application for Federal Student Aid (FAFSA), unless applying for scholarships that do not consider financial need; and letter of recommendation. **Deadline:** March 2. **Contact:** Kim McLaughlin; Phone: 616-842-6378; Email: kmclaughlin@ghacf.org.

4556 ■ Leo Zupin Memorial Scholarship Fund *(Undergraduate, Vocational/Occupational/Scholarship)*

Purpose: To support students from Michigan accredited public college/university. **Focus:** Mathematics and mathematical sciences. **Qualif.:** Applicants must plan to attend any Michigan two-to-four year accredited public college, university, vocational or technology training and/or certification institution; must be students wishing to pursue a degree in mathematics. **Criteria:** Recipients are selected based on financial need, motivation, desire to achieve and academic performance. Preference will be given to applicants who have faced and overcome adversity in their lives.

Funds Avail.: No specific amount. **To Apply:** Applicants must submit: completed application form; current high school or college transcript; Student Aid Report (SAR) from the Free Application for Federal Student Aid (FAFSA) with EFC number, unless applying for scholarships that do not consider financial need; and letter of recommendation.

Awards are arranged alphabetically below their administering organizations

Deadline: March 2. **Contact:** Kim McLaughlin; Phone: 616-842-6378; Email: kmclaughlin@ghacf.org.

4557 ■ Grand Island Community Foundation
1811 W 2nd St., Ste. 365
Grand Island, NE 68803
Ph: (308)381-7767
Fax: (308)384-4069
E-mail: info@gicf.org
URL: www.gicf.org
Facebook: www.facebook.com/GICommunityFoundation

4558 ■ Ahrens Charitable Trust Scholarship
(Undergraduate/Scholarship)

Purpose: To provide financial support to students in pursuit of furthering their education and pursuing their dreams. **Focus:** Medicine. **Qualif.:** Applicants must be enrolled full-time; must have 3.5 or higher GPA and demonstrated financial need. **Criteria:** Selection is based on the online application.

Funds Avail.: No specific amount. **Duration:** Annual. **To Apply:** Applicants must fill up and submit complete online application.

4559 ■ Edgar Barge Memorial Scholarships
(Undergraduate/Scholarship)

Purpose: To provide financial support to students in pursuit of furthering their education and pursuing their dreams. **Focus:** General studies/Field of study not specified. **Qualif.:** Applicants must be enrolled full-time; must have 3.5 or higher GPA and demonstrated financial need. **Criteria:** Selection is based on the online application.

Funds Avail.: No specific amount. **Duration:** Annual. **To Apply:** Applicants must fill up and submit complete online application.

4560 ■ Karen Connick Memorial Scholarships
(Undergraduate/Scholarship)

Purpose: To provide financial support to students in pursuit of furthering their education and pursuing their dreams. **Focus:** General studies/Field of study not specified. **Qualif.:** Applicants must be enrolled full-time; must have 3.5 or higher GPA and demonstrated financial need. **Criteria:** Selection is based on the online application.

Funds Avail.: No specific amount. **Duration:** Annual. **To Apply:** Applicants must fill up and submit complete online application.

4561 ■ Doniphan Community Foundation Scholarships
(Undergraduate/Scholarship)

Purpose: To provide financial support to students in pursuit of furthering their education and pursuing their dreams. **Focus:** General studies/Field of study not specified. **Qualif.:** Applicants must be enrolled full-time; must have 3.5 or higher GPA and demonstrated financial need. **Criteria:** Selection is based on the online application.

Funds Avail.: No specific amount. **Duration:** Annual. **To Apply:** Applicants must submit a completed application form along with a typewritten personal statement, high school and college/university transcripts, high school class rank, and ACT scores.

4562 ■ Howard G. and Gladys A. Eakes Memorial Scholarships
(Undergraduate/Scholarship)

Purpose: To provide financial support to students in pursuit of furthering their education and pursuing their dreams. **Focus:** General studies/Field of study not specified. **Qualif.:** Applicants must be enrolled full-time high school senior; must be child or stepchild of Eakes Office Solutions employee; must have 3.0 or higher GPA and demonstrated financial need. **Criteria:** Selection is based on the online application.

Funds Avail.: No specific amount. **Duration:** Annual. **To Apply:** Applicants must fill up and submit complete online application.

4563 ■ Hall County Medical Society Scholarships
(Undergraduate/Scholarship)

Purpose: To provide financial support to students in pursuit of furthering their education and pursuing their dreams. **Focus:** Medicine. **Qualif.:** Applicants must be enrolled full-time; must have 3.5 or higher GPA and demonstrated financial need. **Criteria:** Selection is based on the online application.

Funds Avail.: No specific amount. **To Apply:** Applicants must fill up and submit complete online application.

4564 ■ Pleasantview Public Schools Fund
(Undergraduate/Scholarship)

Purpose: To provide financial support to students in pursuit of furthering their education and pursuing their dreams. **Focus:** General studies/Field of study not specified. **Qualif.:** Applicants must be enrolled full-time; must have 3.5 or higher GPA and demonstrated financial need. **Criteria:** Selection is based on the online application.

Funds Avail.: No specific amount. **Duration:** Annual. **To Apply:** Applicants must fill up and submit complete online application.

4565 ■ Jim and Dee Price Scholarships
(Undergraduate/Scholarship)

Purpose: To provide financial support to students in pursuit of furthering their education and pursuing their dreams. **Focus:** General studies/Field of study not specified. **Qualif.:** Applicants must be enrolled full-time; must be children of Kriz-Davis Co. employees; must have 3.5 or higher GPA and demonstrated financial need. **Criteria:** Selection is based on the online application.

Funds Avail.: No specific amount. **Duration:** Annual. **To Apply:** Applicants must fill up and submit complete online application.

4566 ■ Carl C. and Abbie Rebman Trust Scholarships
(Undergraduate/Scholarship)

Purpose: To provide financial support to students in pursuit of furthering their education and pursuing their dreams. **Focus:** Automotive technology; Nursing. **Qualif.:** Applicants must be enrolled full-time; must have 3.5 or higher GPA and demonstrated financial need. **Criteria:** Selection is based on the online application.

Funds Avail.: No specific amount. **Duration:** Annual. **To Apply:** Applicants must fill up and submit complete online application.

4567 ■ Teammates Mentoring Scholarship Program
(Undergraduate/Scholarship)

Purpose: To provide financial support to students in pursuit of furthering their education and pursuing their dreams. **Focus:** General studies/Field of study not specified. **Qualif.:** Applicants must be enrolled full-time; must have 3.5 or higher GPA and demonstrated financial need. **Criteria:**

Awards are arranged alphabetically below their administering organizations

Selection is based on the online application.

Funds Avail.: No specific amount. **Duration:** Annual. **To Apply:** Applicants must fill up and submit complete online application.

4568 ■ Woodyard Family Scholarships
(Undergraduate/Scholarship)

Purpose: To provide financial support to students in pursuit of furthering their education and pursuing their dreams. **Focus:** General studies/Field of study not specified. **Qualif.:** Applicants must be enrolled full-time; must have at least 3.0 GPA and a class rank in the top 25%; and demonstrated financial need. **Criteria:** Selection is based on the online application.

Funds Avail.: No specific amount. **Duration:** Annual. **To Apply:** Applicants must fill up and submit complete online application.

4569 ■ James and Joy Zana Memorial Scholarships
(Undergraduate/Scholarship)

Purpose: To provide financial support to students in pursuit of furthering their education and pursuing their dreams. **Focus:** Art. **Qualif.:** Applicants must be enrolled full-time; must have 3.5 or higher GPA and demonstrated financial need. **Criteria:** Selection is based on the online application.

Funds Avail.: No specific amount. **Duration:** Annual. **To Apply:** Applicants must fill up and submit complete online application.

4570 ■ Grand Lodge of Saskatchewan
1930 Lorne St.
Regina, SK, Canada S4P 2M1
Ph: (306)522-5686
Fax: (306)522-5687
Free: 877-661-2231
E-mail: glsask@atssaskmasons.ca
URL: www.saskmasons.ca

4571 ■ Murray Montague Memorial Scholarships
(Undergraduate/Scholarship)

Purpose: To provide financial support to students in the higher learning institutions. **Focus:** General studies/Field of study not specified. **Qualif.:** Applicants must be Saskatchewan High School graduates who proceed to an institution of higher learning anywhere in Canada; must be registered for a full academic load for a full academic year as required by the institution chosen. **Criteria:** Selection will be based on academic achievement, leadership skills, community and school activities and special awards.

Funds Avail.: 1,000 Canadian Dollars. **Duration:** Annual. **To Apply:** Applicants must submit the following requirements: completed application form; official final transcript of Grade 12 marks issued by the Saskatchewan Ministry of Education; character reference from a community leader; letter of reference from high school principal or guidance counselor; letter from the applicant outlining extracurricular activities and educational goals; proof of registration in the chosen institute of higher learning. **Deadline:** August 10.

4572 ■ Grand Rapids Community Foundation (GRCF)
185 Oakes St. SW
Grand Rapids, MI 49503
Ph: (616)454-1751
Fax: (616)454-6455
E-mail: grfound@grfoundation.org
URL: www.grfoundation.org

4573 ■ Altrusa International of Grand Rapids Scholarships *(Undergraduate/Scholarship)*

Purpose: To provide financial support to those students who are in need. **Focus:** General studies/Field of study not specified. **Qualif.:** Applicants must be students from Kent, Allegan, Iona, Ottawa, Montcalm or Muskegon counties (6 months residency minimum). Applicants must be entering or returning to college after sitting out of school for two years. Applicants must demonstrate financial need. **Criteria:** Priority will be given to those students with financial need.

Funds Avail.: No specific amount. **Duration:** Annual. **To Apply:** Complete general online application; List of Awards, Volunteer Activities, Employment/School Extra-Curricular Activities; Academic Transcript from most recent semester (High School Students: must include first semester senior year); An essay about yourself that includes: reasons for choice of college, chosen course of study, career goals, plans for financing education, and information on past activities benefitting community; must provide two (2) letters of recommendation. **Deadline:** April 1. **Contact:** Ruth Bishop, Education Program Officer; Phone: 616-454-1751 Ext. 103; Email: rbishop@grfoundation.org.

4574 ■ Arts Council of Greater Grand Rapids Minority Scholarships *(Undergraduate/Scholarship)*

Purpose: To support students of color in their pursuit of higher education and future career choices. **Focus:** Performing arts; Visual arts. **Qualif.:** Applicants must be students of color (African American, Hispanic, Native American, Pacific Islander) attending a non-profit public or private college/university; must be majoring in Fine Arts including all visual and performing art forms; must be Kent County residents; must have a minimum 2.5 GPA; and must have a financial need. **Criteria:** Selection will be based on the Foundation's criteria.

Funds Avail.: No specific amount. **To Apply:** Applicants must contact the Foundation for further information. **Deadline:** April 1.

4575 ■ Dr. Noyes L. Avery, Jr. and Ann E. Avery Scholarships *(Undergraduate, Graduate/Scholarship)*

Purpose: To provide financial assistance to those students who are in need. **Focus:** Medicine. **Qualif.:** Applicants must be full-time students from Kent County (3 years minimum) who are attending the University of Michigan for a medical doctor degree. Applicants must have a minimum of 3.0 GPA. Applicants must have financial need. **Criteria:** Preference will be given to those students who meet the criteria.

Funds Avail.: No specific amount. **Duration:** Annual. **To Apply:** Applicants must complete the following: general online application; list of awards, volunteer activities, employment/school extra-curricular activities; academic transcript from most recent semester (High School Students: must include first semester senior year); an essay about yourself that includes: reasons for choice of college, chosen course of study, career goals, plans for financing education, and information on past activities benefitting community. **Deadline:** April 1. **Contact:** Ruth Bishop, Education Program Officer; Phone: 616-454-1751 Ext. 103;

Awards are arranged alphabetically below their administering organizations

Email: rbishop@grfoundation.org.

4576 ■ Black Men Building Resources Scholarships
(Undergraduate/Scholarship)

Purpose: To support African American students from Kent County in their pursuit of higher education and future career choices. **Focus:** General studies/Field of study not specified. **Qualif.:** Applicants must be African American male or female students; must be residing in Kent County and graduated or received a GED from a Grand Rapids area high school; must also have demonstrated financial need. **Criteria:** Selection will be based on the Foundation's criteria.

Funds Avail.: No specific amount. **To Apply:** Applicants must contact the Foundation for further information. **Deadline:** April 1.

4577 ■ Geraldine Geistert Boss Scholarships
(Undergraduate/Scholarship)

Purpose: To provide financial support to those students who are in need. **Focus:** General studies/Field of study not specified. **Qualif.:** Applicants must be full-time students with financial need residing in Kent County (5 years minimum) and pursuing an undergraduate degree at an accredited college in Michigan. Applicants must have a minimum of 3.0 GPA. **Criteria:** Preference will be given to those students who meet the criteria.

Funds Avail.: No specific amount. **Duration:** Annual. **To Apply:** Complete general online application; List of Awards, Volunteer Activities, Employment/School Extra-Curricular Activities; Academic Transcript from most recent semester (High School Students: must include first semester senior year); An essay about yourself that includes: reasons for choice of college, chosen course of study, career goals, plans for financing education, and information on past activities benefitting community. **Deadline:** April 1. **Contact:** Ruth Bishop, Education Program Officer; Phone: 616-454-1751 x103; E-mail: rbishop@grfoundation.org.

4578 ■ Harry and Lucille Brown Scholarships
(Undergraduate/Scholarship)

Purpose: To provide financial support to those students who are in need. **Focus:** General studies/Field of study not specified. **Qualif.:** Applicants must be residents of Kent County (3 year minimum); must have financial need; must be pursuing an undergraduate degree at any accredited college in the U.S; must have a minimum of 3.3 GPA. **Criteria:** Preference will be given to those students who meet the criteria.

Funds Avail.: No specific amount. **Duration:** Annual. **To Apply:** Complete general online application; List of Awards, Volunteer Activities, Employment/School Extra-Curricular Activities; Academic Transcript from most recent semester (High School Students: must include first semester senior year); An essay about yourself that includes: reasons for choice of college, chosen course of study, career goals, plans for financing education, and information on past activities benefitting community. **Deadline:** April 1. **Contact:** Ruth Bishop, Education Program Officer; Phone: 616-454-1751 Ext. 103; Email: rbishop@grfoundation.org.

4579 ■ Orrie and Dorothy Cassada Scholarships
(Undergraduate/Scholarship)

Purpose: To provide financial assistance to those students who are in need. **Focus:** General studies/Field of study not specified. **Qualif.:** Applicants must be residents of Kent County (3 years minimum) who will be attending Aquinas, Calvin, Cornerstone, Davenport, GRCC, GVSU or Kendall. Applicants must have financial need and a 3.0 minimum GPA. **Criteria:** Preference will be given to those students who meet the criteria.

Funds Avail.: No specific amount. **Duration:** Annual. **To Apply:** Applicants must complete the following: general online application; list of awards, volunteer activities, employment/school extra-curricular activities; academic transcript from most recent semester (High School Students: must include first semester senior year); An essay about yourself that includes: reasons for choice of college, chosen course of study, career goals, plans for financing education, and information on past activities benefitting community. **Deadline:** April 1. **Contact:** Ruth Bishop, Education Program Officer; Phone: 616-454-1751 Ext. 103; Email: rbishop@grfoundation.org.

4580 ■ Llewellyn L. Cayvan String Instrument Scholarships *(Undergraduate/Scholarship)*

Purpose: To assist those students with talent in musical instruments by supporting them financially. **Focus:** Music. **Qualif.:** Applicants must be undergraduate or graduate level students studying the violin, viola, violoncello, or the bass violin. No residency or financial need requirements. **Criteria:** Preference will be based on talent.

Funds Avail.: No specific amount. **Duration:** Annual. **To Apply:** Applicants must complete the following: general online application; list of awards, volunteer activities, employment/school extra-curricular activities; academic transcript from most recent semester (High School Students: must include first semester senior year); An essay about yourself that includes: reasons for choice of college, chosen course of study, career goals, plans for financing education, and information on past activities benefitting community. **Deadline:** April 1. **Contact:** Ruth Bishop, Education Program Officer; Phone: 616-454-1751 x103; E-mail: rbishop@grfoundation.org.

4581 ■ Aim High Jerry Clay Scholarships
(Undergraduate/Scholarship)

Purpose: To support students in their pursuit of higher education and future career choices. **Focus:** Welding. **Qualif.:** Applicants must be students from Kent, Barry, Ionia, Montcalm, Muskegon, Newaygo, or Ottawa County pursuing a full-time undergraduate degree or certification in the welding technology field of study at an accredited program located at or affiliated with Grand Rapids Community College or Ferris State University. They must also have demonstrated financial need. **Criteria:** Selection will be based on the Foundation's criteria.

Funds Avail.: No specific amount. **To Apply:** Applicants must contact the Foundation for further information. **Deadline:** April 1.

4582 ■ Thomas D. Coffield Scholarships
(Undergraduate/Scholarship)

Purpose: To provide financial assistance to those students who are in need. **Focus:** General studies/Field of study not specified. **Qualif.:** Applicants must be senior students at Central High School who will be entering a two or four-year accredited college or university; must have a 2.5 minimum GPA; must have demonstrated financial need. **Criteria:** Preference will be given to those who meet the criteria.

Funds Avail.: No specific amount. **Duration:** Annual. **To Apply:** Complete general online application; List of Awards,

Awards are arranged alphabetically below their administering organizations

Volunteer Activities, Employment/School Extra-Curricular Activities; Academic Transcript from most recent semester (High School Students: must include first semester senior year); An essay about yourself that includes: reasons for choice of college, chosen course of study, career goals, plans for financing education, and information on past activities benefitting community. **Deadline:** April 1. **Contact:** Ruth Bishop, Education Program Officer; Phone: 616-454-1751 x103; E-mail: rbishop@grfoundation.org.

4583 ■ Paul Collins Scholarships *(Undergraduate/Scholarship)*

Purpose: To provide financial assistance to deserving students. **Focus:** Art; Art industries and trade. **Qualif.:** Applicants must be undergraduate level students studying Fine or Applied Arts at Aquinas, Calvin, GVSU, GRCC or Kendall; must be residents of Kent County; must have a minimum of 2.5 GPA, financial need and demonstrate artistic talent. **Criteria:** Selection will be based on criteria.

Funds Avail.: No specific amount. **Duration:** Annual. **To Apply:** Applicants must complete the following: general online application; list of awards, volunteer activities, employment/school extra-curricular activities; academic transcript from most recent semester (High School Students: must include first semester senior year); An essay about yourself that includes: reasons for choice of college, chosen course of study, career goals, plans for financing education, and information on past activities benefitting community. **Deadline:** April 1. **Contact:** Ruth Bishop, Education Program Officer; Phone: 616-454-1751 Ext. 103; Email: rbishop@grfoundation.org.

4584 ■ Rosemary Cook Education Scholarships *(Undergraduate/Scholarship)*

Purpose: To support students from Kent County who are majoring in education. **Focus:** Education. **Qualif.:** Applicants must be students who are Kent County residents; must be graduates of a Grad Rapids Public High School; must be pursuing an undergraduate degree in Education full-time at any accredited Michigan public or private college/university; must have a financial need; and must have a minimum GPA of 2.75. **Criteria:** Selection will be based on the Foundation's criteria.

Funds Avail.: No specific amount. **To Apply:** Applicants must contact the Foundation for further information. **Deadline:** April 1.

4585 ■ Gerald M. Crane Music Award Scholarships *(Undergraduate/Scholarship)*

Purpose: To provide funding to students for their music lessons, seminars, workshops, summer enrichment programs, music concerts, instruments, books, vocal music lessons or any other kinds of musical materials. **Focus:** Music. **Qualif.:** Applicants must be high school music students in Kent or Ottawa County who are requesting money for music lessons, seminars, workshops, summer enrichment programs, music concerts, instruments, books, vocal music lessons or any other kinds of musical materials. **Criteria:** Selection will be based on the Foundation's criteria.

Funds Avail.: No specific amount. **To Apply:** Interested applicants may download the application form at the website. **Deadline:** April 1. **Remarks:** The award money may not be used for undergraduate college tuition.

4586 ■ Darooge Family Scholarships *(Undergraduate/Scholarship)*

Purpose: To support students in their pursuit of higher education and future career choices. **Focus:** Construction. **Qualif.:** Applicants must be high school seniors residing in Kent County and entering college to pursue an undergraduate degree in a construction-related field of study at an accredited two or four year college/university/trade school in Michigan. They must also have financial need. **Criteria:** Selection will be based on the Foundation's criteria.

Funds Avail.: No specific amount. **To Apply:** Applicants must contact the Foundation for further information. **Deadline:** April 1.

4587 ■ Achille and Irene Despres, William and Andre Scholarships *(Undergraduate/Scholarship)*

Purpose: To provide financial assistance to those students who are in need. **Focus:** General studies/Field of study not specified. **Qualif.:** Applicants must be of Mexican heritage; must be Kent or Ottawa residents; must be enrolled in an accredited college or university; must have demonstrated financial need; must have a cumulative GPA of at least 2.75. **Criteria:** Priority will be given to those students with financial need.

Funds Avail.: No specific amount. **Duration:** Annual. **To Apply:** Applicants may visit the website for the application process and other required materials. **Deadline:** April 1. **Contact:** Ruth Bishop, Education Program Officer; Phone: 616-454-1751 Ext. 103; Email: rbishop@grfoundation.org.

4588 ■ Donald J. DeYoung Scholarships *(Undergraduate/Scholarship)*

Purpose: To support current or former wards of the court in their pursuit of higher education and future career choices. **Focus:** General studies/Field of study not specified. **Qualif.:** Applicants must be current or former wards of the court in Kent County, Michigan; must be pursuing an undergraduate college or vocational education; must have a minimum cumulative GPA of 2.5; and must have a financial need. **Criteria:** Selection will be based on the Foundation's criteria.

Funds Avail.: No specific amount. **To Apply:** Applicants must submit an application form (available at the website) and a recommendation letter from a caseworker. **Deadline:** April 1.

4589 ■ Economic Club Business Study Abroad Scholarships *(Undergraduate/Scholarship)*

Purpose: To support students in their pursuit of higher education and future career choices. **Focus:** General studies/Field of study not specified. **Qualif.:** Applicants must be residents of Kent, Allegan, Ottawa or Muskegon County for at least three years, or resident students at a public college or university in the West Michigan area for at least two years; must be full-time undergraduate students (second year or above) pursuing a degree in business and will be studying abroad through a public college or university; must have a minimum GPA of 3.0; and must also exhibit financial need. **Criteria:** Selection will be based on the Foundation's criteria.

Funds Avail.: No specific amount. **To Apply:** Applicants must download the application form at the website. **Deadline:** April 1.

4590 ■ Economic Club of Grand Rapids Scholarships *(Undergraduate/Scholarship)*

Purpose: To support students in their pursuit of higher education and future career choices. **Focus:** Business. **Qualif.:** Applicants must be undergraduate students pursuing a degree in business; must be residents of Kent or Ot-

Awards are arranged alphabetically below their administering organizations

tawa County for a minimum of three years with demonstrated financial need; and must have a minimum GPA of 3.0. **Criteria:** Selection will be based on the Foundation's criteria.

Funds Avail.: No specific amount. **To Apply:** Applicants must contact the Foundation for further information. **Deadline:** April 1.

4591 ■ Virginia Valk Fehsenfeld Scholarships *(Undergraduate/Scholarship)*

Purpose: To provide financial support to those students who are in need. **Focus:** General studies/Field of study not specified. **Qualif.:** Applicants must be full-time undergraduate students pursuing a degree in Dietetics, Nutrition, Education or General Human Services. Applicants must be residents of Kent County, must have financial need and minimum of 3.4 GPA is required. **Criteria:** Preference will be given to those who meet the criteria.

Funds Avail.: No specific amount. **Duration:** Annual. **To Apply:** Applicants must complete the following: general online application; list of awards, volunteer activities, employment/school extra-curricular activities; academic transcript from most recent semester (High School Students: must include first semester senior year); An essay about yourself that includes: reasons for choice of college, chosen course of study, career goals, plans for financing education, and information on past activities benefitting community. **Deadline:** April 1. **Contact:** Ruth Bishop, Education Program Officer; Phone: 616-454-1751 x103; E-mail: rbishop@grfoundation.org.

4592 ■ Melbourne and Alice E. Frontjes Scholarships *(Undergraduate/Scholarship)*

Purpose: To provide financial assistance to those students who are in need. **Focus:** General studies/Field of study not specified. **Qualif.:** Applicants must be Kent County residents (3 years minimum) who are pursuing an undergraduate degree at Central Michigan University, Western Michigan University, GRCC, University of Michigan or Michigan State University. Applicants must have demonstrated financial need and have a minimum of 2.75 GPA. **Criteria:** Preference will be given to those students who meet the criteria.

Funds Avail.: No specific amount. **Duration:** Annual. **To Apply:** Applicants must complete the following: general online application; list of awards, volunteer activities, employment/school extra-curricular activities; academic transcript from most recent semester (High School Students: must include first semester senior year); An essay about yourself that includes: reasons for choice of college, chosen course of study, career goals, plans for financing education, and information on past activities benefitting community. **Deadline:** April 1. **Contact:** Ruth Bishop, Education Program Officer; Phone: 616-454-1751 Ext. 103; Email: rbishop@grfoundation.org.

4593 ■ Carolyn Gallmeyer Scholarships *(Undergraduate/Scholarship)*

Purpose: To provide financial support to those students who are in need. **Focus:** General studies/Field of study not specified. **Qualif.:** Applicants must be Kent County residents who are pursuing an undergraduate degree at any U.S college; must have financial need and a minimum 2.75 GPA. **Criteria:** Recipients will be selected based on financial need.

Funds Avail.: No specific amount. **Duration:** Annual. **To Apply:** Applicants must complete the following: general online application; list of awards, volunteer activities, employment/school extra-curricular activities; academic transcript from most recent semester (High School Students: must include first semester senior year); An essay about yourself that includes: reasons for choice of college, chosen course of study, career goals, plans for financing education, and information on past activities benefitting community. **Deadline:** April 1. **Contact:** Ruth Bishop, Education Program Officer; Phone: 616-454-1751 Ext. 103; Email: rbishop@grfoundation.org.

4594 ■ Mathilda and Carolyn Gallmeyer Scholarships *(Undergraduate/Scholarship)*

Purpose: To provide financial assistance to those students who are in need. **Focus:** Art. **Qualif.:** Applicants must be Kent County residents (5 years minimum); must be pursuing Painting or Fine arts; must demonstrate artistic talent, financial need and a minimum of 2.75 GPA. **Criteria:** Preference will be given to those students who meet the criteria.

Funds Avail.: No specific amount. **Duration:** Annual. **To Apply:** Complete general online application; List of Awards, Volunteer Activities, Employment/School Extra-Curricular Activities; Academic Transcript from most recent semester (High School Students: must include first semester senior year); An essay about yourself that includes: reasons for choice of college, chosen course of study, career goals, plans for financing education, and information on past activities benefitting community. **Deadline:** April 1. **Contact:** Ruth Bishop, Education Program Officer; Phone: 616-454-1751 Ext. 103; Email: rbishop@grfoundation.org.

4595 ■ Grand Rapids Scholarship Association *(Undergraduate/Scholarship)*

Purpose: To provide financial assistance to those students who are in need. **Focus:** General studies/Field of study not specified. **Qualif.:** Applicants must be Kent County residents (3 years minimum) who will be attending Aquinas, Calvin, Cornerstone, Davenport, GRCC, GVSU or Kendall. Applicants must have financial need and must have a 3.0 minimum GPA. **Criteria:** Preference will be given to those students who meet the criteria.

Funds Avail.: No specific amount. **Duration:** Annual. **To Apply:** Complete general online application; List of Awards, Volunteer Activities, Employment/School Extra-Curricular Activities; Academic Transcript from most recent semester (High School Students: must include first semester senior year); An essay about yourself that includes: reasons for choice of college, chosen course of study, career goals, plans for financing education, and information on past activities benefitting community. **Deadline:** April 1. **Contact:** Ruth Bishop, Education Program Officer; Phone: 616-454-1751 Ext. 103; Email: rbishop@grfoundation.org.

4596 ■ Grand Rapids University Prep Founder's Scholarships *(Undergraduate/Scholarship)*

Purpose: To support students in their pursuit of higher education and future career choices. **Focus:** General studies/Field of study not specified. **Qualif.:** Applicants must be senior students at Grand Rapids University Prep Academy; must be pursuing an undergraduate degree or certification at an accredited two- or four-year college/university or trade school program located within the United States; must have a financial need; and must have a minimum cumulative GPA of 2.5. **Criteria:** Selection will be based on the Foundation's criteria.

Funds Avail.: No specific amount. **To Apply:** Applicants must contact the Foundation for further information. **Deadline:** April 1.

4597 ■ Hackett Family Scholarships *(Undergraduate/ Scholarship)*

Purpose: To support students in their pursuit of higher education and future career choices. **Focus:** General studies/Field of study not specified. **Qualif.:** Applicants must be senior students or have graduated from any GR public high school in Grand Rapids, Michigan, and attending an accredited college/university or skilled trade school of their choice. **Criteria:** Preference will be given to women of color.

Funds Avail.: No specific amount. **To Apply:** Interested applicants may contact the Foundation for further information. **Deadline:** April 1.

4598 ■ Guy D. and Mary Edith Halladay Graduate Scholarships *(Undergraduate/Scholarship)*

Purpose: To provide financial support to those students who are in need. **Focus:** General studies/Field of study not specified. **Qualif.:** Applicants must be residents of Kent County (2 years minimum); and must be graduate level students at a Michigan college. Applicants must have demonstrated financial need and must have a minimum of 3.0 GPA. **Criteria:** Preference will be given to those who meet the criteria.

Funds Avail.: No specific amount. **Duration:** Annual. **To Apply:** Complete general online application; List of Awards, Volunteer Activities, Employment/School Extra-Curricular Activities; Academic Transcript from most recent semester (High School Students: must include first semester senior year); An essay about yourself that includes: reasons for choice of college, chosen course of study, career goals, plans for financing education, and information on past activities benefitting community. **Deadline:** April 1. **Contact:** Ruth Bishop, Education Program Officer; Phone: 616-454-1751 Ext. 103; Email: rbishop@grfoundation.org.

4599 ■ Guy D. and Mary Edith Halladay Music Scholarships *(Graduate, Undergraduate/Scholarship)*

Purpose: To provide financial assistance to deserving students. **Focus:** Music. **Qualif.:** Applicants must be residents of Kent County (2 years minimum) who are majoring in Music at any college or university in the U.S. Applicants must have financial need. Applicants must have a cumulative GPA of 3.0. **Criteria:** Priority will be given to those students with high financial need.

Funds Avail.: No specific amount. **Duration:** Annual. **To Apply:** Applicants must complete the following: general online application; list of awards, volunteer activities, employment/school extra-curricular activities; academic transcript from most recent semester (High School Students: must include first semester senior year); An essay about yourself that includes: reasons for choice of college, chosen course of study, career goals, plans for financing education, and information on past activities benefitting community. **Deadline:** April 1. **Contact:** Ruth Bishop, Education Program Officer; Phone: 616-454-1751 Ext. 103; Email: rbishop@grfoundation.org.

4600 ■ Donald and Florence Hunting Scholarships *(Undergraduate/Scholarship)*

Purpose: To provide financial assistance to those students who are in need. **Focus:** General studies/Field of study not specified. **Qualif.:** Applicants must be senior students at Rockford High School who will be entering college in the fall; must have demonstrated financial need. **Criteria:** Priority will be given to those students with financial need.

Funds Avail.: No specific amount. **Duration:** Annual. **To Apply:** Applicants must complete the following: general online application; list of awards, volunteer activities, employment/school extra-curricular activities; academic transcript from most recent semester (High School Students: must include first semester senior year); An essay about yourself that includes: reasons for choice of college, chosen course of study, career goals, plans for financing education, and information on past activities benefitting community. **Deadline:** April 1. **Contact:** Ruth Bishop, Education Program Officer; Phone: 616-454-1751 Ext. 103; Email: rbishop@grfoundation.org.

4601 ■ Jack Family Scholarships *(Undergraduate/ Scholarship)*

Purpose: To provide financial assistance to those students who are in need. **Focus:** General studies/Field of study not specified. **Qualif.:** Applicants must be undergraduate students residing in Kent County (3 years minimum) who demonstrate financial need. Applicants must have a minimum of 3.3 GPA. **Criteria:** Preference will be given to those students who meet the criteria.

Funds Avail.: No specific amount. **Duration:** Annual. **To Apply:** Complete general online application; List of Awards, Volunteer Activities, Employment/School Extra-Curricular Activities; Academic Transcript from most recent semester (High School Students: must include first semester senior year); An essay about yourself that includes: reasons for choice of college, chosen course of study, career goals, plans for financing education, and information on past activities benefitting community. **Deadline:** April 1. **Contact:** Ruth Bishop, Education Program Officer; Phone: 616-454-1751 Ext. 103; Email: rbishop@grfoundation.org.

4602 ■ Camilla C. Johnson Scholarships *(Undergraduate/Scholarship)*

Purpose: To provide financial support to those deserving students. **Focus:** General studies/Field of study not specified. **Qualif.:** Applicants must be senior students at Union High School entering college full-time in the fall; must have financial need; must have a cumulative of 2.6 GPA. **Criteria:** Preference will be given to those students who meet the criteria.

Funds Avail.: No specific amount. **Duration:** Annual. **To Apply:** Complete general online application; List of Awards, Volunteer Activities, Employment/School Extra-Curricular Activities; Academic Transcript from most recent semester (High School Students: must include first semester senior year); An essay about yourself that includes: reasons for choice of college, chosen course of study, career goals, plans for financing education, and information on past activities benefitting community. **Deadline:** April 1. **Contact:** Ruth Bishop, Education Program Officer; Phone: 616-454-1751 Ext. 103; Email: rbishop@grfoundation.org.

4603 ■ Vivian M. Kommer Scholarships *(Undergraduate/Scholarship)*

Purpose: To support students in their pursuit of higher education and future career choices. **Focus:** Business. **Qualif.:** Applicants must be senior students at West Catholic High School entering undergraduate studies in business or pre-law; must demonstrate financial need; and have a minimum GPA of 3.0. **Criteria:** Selection will be based on the Foundation's criteria.

Awards are arranged alphabetically below their administering organizations

Sponsors and Their Scholarships

GRAND RAPIDS COMMUNITY FOUNDATION

Funds Avail.: No specific amount. **To Apply:** Applicants must contact the Foundation for further information. **Deadline:** April 1.

4604 ■ Roger and Jacquelyn Vander Laan Family Scholarships *(Undergraduate/Scholarship)*

Purpose: To support students in their pursuit of higher education and future career choices. **Focus:** General studies/Field of study not specified. **Qualif.:** Applicants must be seniors at South Christian High School; must be entering a full time program in the fall at any accredited college, university, vocational or technical school; must be majoring in healthcare, education, or business; must have a financial need; and must have a minimum 3.0 GPA. **Criteria:** Selection will be based on the Foundation's criteria.

Funds Avail.: No specific amount. **To Apply:** Applicants must contact the Foundation for further information. **Deadline:** April 1.

4605 ■ Ladies Literary Club Scholarships *(Undergraduate/Scholarship)*

Purpose: To support students in their pursuit of higher education and future career choices. **Focus:** Arts. **Qualif.:** Applicants must be students who are also residents of Kent, Ottawa, Muskegon, Allegan, Montcalm, or Barry County; must be majoring in literary arts at any accredited Michigan college or university; must have a financial need; and must have a minimum GPA of 3.0. **Criteria:** Selection will be based on the Foundation's criteria.

Funds Avail.: No specific amount. **To Apply:** Applicants must contact the Foundation for further information. **Deadline:** April 1.

4606 ■ Lavina Laible Scholarships *(Undergraduate/Scholarship)*

Purpose: To provide financial assistance to those students who are in need. **Focus:** General studies/Field of study not specified. **Qualif.:** Applicants must be female students in their third year or above of undergraduate studies at the University of Michigan. Applicants must be Kent County residents. Applicants must have financial need. Applicants must have a minimum of 3.0 GPA. **Criteria:** Preference will be given to those students who meet the criteria.

Funds Avail.: No specific amount. **Duration:** Annual. **To Apply:** Applicants must complete the following: general online application; list of awards, volunteer activities, employment/school extra-curricular activities; academic transcript from most recent semester (High School Students: must include first semester senior year); An essay about yourself that includes: reasons for choice of college, chosen course of study, career goals, plans for financing education, and information on past activities benefitting community. **Deadline:** April 1. **Contact:** Ruth Bishop, Education Program Officer; Phone: 616-454-1751 x103; E-mail: rbishop@grfoundation.org.

4607 ■ Stephen Lankester Scholarships *(Undergraduate/Scholarship)*

Purpose: To provide financial assistance to those students who are in need. **Focus:** General studies/Field of study not specified. **Qualif.:** Applicants must be Kent County residents (3 years minimum); must be attending an undergraduate program at a Michigan college; must have financial need; must have a minimum of 3.0 GPA. **Criteria:** Preference will be given to those who meet the criteria.

Funds Avail.: No specific amount. **Duration:** Annual. **To Apply:** Applicants must complete the following: general online application; list of awards, volunteer activities, employment/school extra-curricular activities; academic transcript from most recent semester (High School Students: must include first semester senior year); An essay about yourself that includes: reasons for choice of college, chosen course of study, career goals, plans for financing education, and information on past activities benefitting community. **Deadline:** April 1. **Contact:** Ruth Bishop, Education Program Officer; Phone: 616-454-1751 Ext. 103; Email: rbishop@grfoundation.org.

4608 ■ Sherman L. and Mabel C. Lepard Scholarships *(Undergraduate/Scholarship)*

Purpose: To provide financial assistance to deserving students. **Focus:** General studies/Field of study not specified. **Qualif.:** Applicants must be pursuing an undergraduate degree at any accredited college or university in the U.S; must be Kent County residents (3 years minimum); must have demonstrated financial need; must have a minimum of 3.3 GPA. **Criteria:** Preference will be given to those students who meet the criteria.

Funds Avail.: No specific amount. **Duration:** Annual. **To Apply:** Applicants must complete the following: general online application; list of awards, volunteer activities, employment/school extra-curricular activities; academic transcript from most recent semester (High School Students: must include first semester senior year); An essay about yourself that includes: reasons for choice of college, chosen course of study, career goals, plans for financing education, and information on past activities benefitting community. **Deadline:** April 1. **Contact:** Ruth Bishop, Education Program Officer; Phone: 616-454-1751 Ext. 103; Email: rbishop@grfoundation.org.

4609 ■ John T. and Frances J. Maghielse Scholarships *(Undergraduate/Scholarship)*

Purpose: To provide financial assistance to students who are in need. **Focus:** General studies/Field of study not specified. **Qualif.:** Applicants must be graduates of Grand Rapids Public High School; must be Kent County residents; must be currently pursuing a full-time undergraduate degree in the field of Education at any Michigan public or private college/ university. Applicants must have financial need and must have a minimum of 3.0 GPA. **Criteria:** Preference will be given to those students who meet the criteria.

Funds Avail.: No specific amount. **Duration:** Annual. **To Apply:** Applicants must complete the following: general online application; list of awards, volunteer activities, employment/school extra-curricular activities; academic transcript from most recent semester (High School Students: must include first semester senior year); An essay about yourself that includes: reasons for choice of college, chosen course of study, career goals, plans for financing education, and information on past activities benefitting community. **Deadline:** April 1. **Contact:** Ruth Bishop, Education Program Officer; Phone: 616-454-1751 x103; E-mail: rbishop@grfoundation.org.

4610 ■ Fred & Lena Meijer Scholarships *(Undergraduate/Scholarship)*

Purpose: To support Meijer team members or their dependents in their pursuit of higher education and future career choices. **Focus:** General studies/Field of study not specified. **Qualif.:** Applicants must be students who are

Awards are arranged alphabetically below their administering organizations

Meijer Team Members or children (natural, legally adopted, or stepchildren) of Meijer Team Members who have been employed for at least one year by the time of the application deadline. Children of Team Members must be full-time students to apply, while Meijer team member applicants may be part-time students. **Criteria:** Selection will be based on the Foundation's criteria.

Funds Avail.: No specific amount. **To Apply:** Application is via online. **Deadline:** April 1.

4611 ■ Joshua Esch Mitchell Aviation Scholarships
(Undergraduate/Scholarship)

Purpose: To provide financial support to those students who study flight science. **Focus:** Aviation. **Qualif.:** Applicants must be U.S citizens; must be enrolled full or part-time at a college or university in the United States providing an accredited flight science curriculum; must be 2nd year students or above with a minimum of 2.75 GPA; must be pursuing studies in the field of professional piloting with an emphasis in General Aviation, Aviation Management, or Aviation Safety. **Criteria:** Selection will be based on the committee's criteria.

Funds Avail.: No specific amount. **Duration:** Annual. **To Apply:** Applicants must complete the following: general online application; list of awards, volunteer activities, employment/school extra-curricular activities; academic transcript from most recent semester (High School Students: must include first semester senior year); An essay about yourself that includes: reasons for choice of college, chosen course of study, career goals, plans for financing education, and information on past activities benefitting community. **Deadline:** April 1. **Contact:** Ruth Bishop, Education Program Officer; Phone: 616-454-1751 x103; E-mail: rbishop@grfoundation.org.

4612 ■ Robert L. and Hilda Treasure Mitchell Scholarships *(Undergraduate/Scholarship)*

Purpose: To provide financial assistance to deserving students. **Focus:** General studies/Field of study not specified. **Qualif.:** Applicants must be pursuing an undergraduate degree at any accredited college or university in the United States; must be Kent County residents (3 years minimum); must demonstrate financial need; must have a minimum of 3.3 GPA. **Criteria:** Preference will be given to those students who meet the criteria.

Funds Avail.: No specific amount. **Duration:** Annual. **To Apply:** Applicants must complete the following: general online application; list of awards, volunteer activities, employment/school extra-curricular activities; academic transcript from most recent semester (High School Students: must include first semester senior year); An essay about yourself that includes: reasons for choice of college, chosen course of study, career goals, plans for financing education, and information on past activities benefitting community. **Deadline:** April 1. **Contact:** Ruth Bishop, Education Program Officer; Phone: 616-454-1751 Ext. 103; Email: rbishop@grfoundation.org.

4613 ■ Harry J. Morris, Jr. Emergency Services Scholarships *(Undergraduate/Scholarship)*

Purpose: To support students in their pursuit of higher education and future career choices in the field of emergency services. **Focus:** Emergency and disaster services; Fires and fire prevention; Paramedics. **Qualif.:** Applicants must be residents of Kent, Allegan, Barry, Ionia, Ottawa, Montcalm, Muskegon or Newaygo County; must be pursuing an undergraduate degree or certificate at an accredited education program in Michigan in the field of emergency medical technician, paramedic, or firefighting training; must have a minimum GPA of 2.5 or verified GED certificate; and have demonstrate a financial need. **Criteria:** Selection will be based on the Foundation's criteria.

Funds Avail.: No specific amount. **To Apply:** Applicants must contact the Foundation for further information. **Deadline:** April 1.

4614 ■ NAIFA West Michigan Scholarships
(Undergraduate/Scholarship)

Purpose: To support students in their pursuit of higher education and future career choices. **Focus:** Business; Finance. **Qualif.:** Applicants must be residents of Kent or contiguous counties; must be students pursuing a full-time undergraduate (third year or above) or graduate degree as business/financial majors at a Michigan public or private college/university; must have a financial need; and must a minimum 3.0 GPA. **Criteria:** Selection will be based on the Foundation's criteria.

Funds Avail.: No specific amount. **To Apply:** Applicants must contact the Foundation for further information. **Deadline:** April 1.

4615 ■ Peggy Kommer Novosad Scholarships
(Graduate, Postgraduate/Scholarship)

Purpose: To provide financial support to those students who are in need. **Focus:** Business; Law. **Qualif.:** Applicants must be residents of Kent County who are currently completing or possessing an undergraduate degree from GVSU or MSU and will be pursuing a full-time graduate or post-graduate degree in business or law at any accredited university in Michigan. Applicants must have financial need and a minimum of 3.5 GPA. **Criteria:** Preference will be given to those who meet the criteria.

Funds Avail.: No specific amount. **Duration:** Annual. **To Apply:** Applicants must complete the following: general online application; list of awards, volunteer activities, employment/school extra-curricular activities; academic transcript from most recent semester (High School Students: must include first semester senior year); An essay about yourself that includes: reasons for choice of college, chosen course of study, career goals, plans for financing education, and information on past activities benefitting community. **Deadline:** April 1. **Contact:** Ruth Bishop, Education Program Officer; Phone: 616-454-1751 x103; E-mail: rbishop@grfoundation.org.

4616 ■ Patricia and Armen Oumedian Scholarships
(Undergraduate/Scholarship)

Purpose: To provide financial support to those students who are in need. **Focus:** Engineering. **Qualif.:** Applicants must be second year or above full-time student at Kettering or transferring from GRCC to Kettering; must be a resident of West Michigan or currently be employed by a West Michigan Kettering Co-op employer; must demonstrate financial need and have a minimum 3.0 GPA. **Criteria:** Preference will be given to those students who meet the criteria.

Funds Avail.: No specific amount. **Duration:** Annual. **To Apply:** Applicants must complete the following: general online application; list of awards, volunteer activities, employment/school extra-curricular activities; academic transcript from most recent semester (High School Students: must include first semester senior year); An essay about yourself that includes: reasons for choice of college,

Awards are arranged alphabetically below their administering organizations

chosen course of study, career goals, plans for financing education, and information on past activities benefitting community. **Deadline:** April 1. **Contact:** Ruth Bishop, Education Program Officer; Phone: 616-454-1751 Ext. 103; Email: rbishop@grfoundation.org.

4617 ■ Reach for Your Goal Scholarships
(Undergraduate/Scholarship)

Purpose: To support students in their pursuit of higher education and future career choices. **Focus:** General studies/Field of study not specified. **Qualif.:** Applicants must be residents of Kent County; must be high school seniors who have been accepted into an accredited Michigan trade school, college or university; must have a financial need; and must have a minimum 3.0 GPA. **Criteria:** Selection will be based on the Foundation's criteria.

Funds Avail.: No specific amount. **To Apply:** Applicants must contact the Foundation for further information. **Deadline:** April 1.

4618 ■ Josephine Ringold Scholarships
(Undergraduate/Scholarship)

Purpose: To provide financial support to those students who are in need. **Focus:** General studies/Field of study not specified. **Qualif.:** Applicants must be Kent County residents (3 years minimum) who will be attending Aquinas, Calvin, Cornerstone, Davenport, GRCC, GVSU or Kendall. Applicants must have financial need and a 3.0 minimum GPA is required. **Criteria:** Preference will be given to those students who meet the criteria.

Funds Avail.: No specific amount. **Duration:** Annual. **To Apply:** Applicants must complete the following: general online application; list of awards, volunteer activities, employment/school extra-curricular activities; academic transcript from most recent semester (High School Students: must include first semester senior year); An essay about yourself that includes: reasons for choice of college, chosen course of study, career goals, plans for financing education, and information on past activities benefitting community. **Deadline:** April 1. **Contact:** Ruth Bishop, Education Program Officer; Phone: 616-454-1751 Ext. 103; Email: rbishop@grfoundation.org.

4619 ■ Dave & Laurie Russell Family Scholarships for Habitat for Humanity of Kent County Families
(Undergraduate/Scholarship)

Purpose: To support students in their pursuit of higher education and future career choices. **Focus:** General studies/Field of study not specified. **Qualif.:** Applicants must be students who are Habitat for Humanity of Kent County home owners or immediate family members (spouses/partners, children, stepchildren) residing in the home, and pursuing an undergraduate degree or certification at an accredited vocational trade program, two- or four-year college or accredited graduate level program located in the United States. They must also have demonstrated financial need. **Criteria:** Selection will be based on the Foundation's criteria.

Funds Avail.: No specific amount. **To Apply:** Applicants must contact the Foundation for further information. **Deadline:** April 1.

4620 ■ Margery J. Seeger Scholarships
(Undergraduate/Scholarship)

Purpose: To provide financial assistance to those students who are in need. **Focus:** General studies/Field of study not specified. **Qualif.:** Applicants must be Kent County residents (3 years minimum) who are pursuing an undergraduate degree at any accredited college in the U.S.; must have financial need; must have a minimum of 3.3 GPA. **Criteria:** Preference will be given to those students who meet the criteria.

Funds Avail.: No specific amount. **Duration:** Annual. **To Apply:** Applicants must complete the following: general online application; list of awards, volunteer activities, employment/school extra-curricular activities; academic transcript from most recent semester (High School Students: must include first semester senior year); An essay about yourself that includes: reasons for choice of college, chosen course of study, career goals, plans for financing education, and information on past activities benefitting community. **Deadline:** April 1. **Contact:** Ruth Bishop, Education Program Officer; Phone: 616-454-1751 Ext. 103; Email: rbishop@grfoundation.org.

4621 ■ Ronald T. Smith Family Scholarships
(Undergraduate, Graduate/Scholarship)

Purpose: To support individuals in their pursuit of higher education and future career choices. **Focus:** General studies/Field of study not specified. **Qualif.:** Applicants must be students who are employees of or spouses/domestic partners or children (natural, legally adopted, or stepchildren) of employees of Bodycote Grand Rapids or Holland Plants; must be pursuing an undergraduate or graduate degree at any accredited college/university or trade school in the United States; must have a financial need; and must have a minimum GPA of 3.0. **Criteria:** Selection will be based on the Foundation's criteria.

Funds Avail.: No specific amount. **To Apply:** Applicants must contact the Foundation for further information. **Deadline:** April 1.

4622 ■ Gladys Snauble Scholarships
(Undergraduate/Scholarship)

Purpose: To provide financial support to those students who are in need. **Focus:** General studies/Field of study not specified. **Qualif.:** Applicants must be senior students at Cedar Springs High School who will be entering college in the fall. Applicants must have financial need. **Criteria:** Priority will be given to those students with financial need.

Funds Avail.: No specific amount. **Duration:** Annual. **To Apply:** Complete general online application; List of Awards, Volunteer Activities, Employment/School Extra-Curricular Activities; Academic Transcript from most recent semester (High School Students: must include first semester senior year); An essay about yourself that includes: reasons for choice of college, chosen course of study, career goals, plans for financing education, and information on past activities benefitting community. **Deadline:** April 1. **Contact:** Ruth Bishop, Education Program Officer; Phone: 616-454-1751 x103; E-mail: rbishop@grfoundation.org.

4623 ■ Christine Soper Scholarships
(Undergraduate/Scholarship)

Purpose: To provide financial support to those students who are in need. **Focus:** General studies/Field of study not specified. **Qualif.:** Applicants must be Kent County residents (3 years minimum) who will be attending Aquinas, Calvin, Cornerstone, Davenport, GRCC, GVSU or Kendall; must have financial need; must have a cumulative of 3.0 GPA. **Criteria:** Priority will be given to those students who meet the criteria.

Funds Avail.: No specific amount. **Duration:** Annual. **To**

Awards are arranged alphabetically below their administering organizations

Apply: Applicants must complete the following: general online application; list of awards, volunteer activities, employment/school extra-curricular activities; academic transcript from most recent semester (High School Students: must include first semester senior year); An essay about yourself that includes: reasons for choice of college, chosen course of study, career goals, plans for financing education, and information on past activities benefitting community. **Deadline:** April 1. **Contact:** Ruth Bishop, Education Program Officer; Phone: 616-454-1751 Ext. 103; Email: rbishop@grfoundation.org.

4624 ■ Dr. William E. and Norma Sprague Scholarships (Undergraduate, Graduate/Scholarship)

Purpose: To provide financial assistance to those students who are in need. **Focus:** Medicine. **Qualif.:** Applicants must be full-time students and permanent residents in the Michigan counties of Kent, Allegan, Barry, Ionia, Montcalm, Muskegon, Newaygo or Athens County, Ohio, who are pursuing a full-time undergraduate or graduate degree in medicine at Ohio University. Applicants must have financial need. Applicants must have a minimum of 3.0 GPA. **Criteria:** Preference will be given to those students who meet the criteria.

Funds Avail.: No specific amount. **Duration:** Annual. **To Apply:** Complete general online application; List of Awards, Volunteer Activities, Employment/School Extra-Curricular Activities; Academic Transcript from most recent semester (High School Students: must include first semester senior year); An essay about yourself that includes: reasons for choice of college, chosen course of study, career goals, plans for financing education, and information on past activities benefitting community. **Deadline:** April 1. **Contact:** Ruth Bishop, Education Program Officer; Phone: 616-454-1751 Ext. 103; Email: rbishop@grfoundation.org.

4625 ■ Dorothy B. and Charles E. Thomas Scholarships (Undergraduate/Scholarship)

Purpose: To provide financial assistance to those students who are in need. **Focus:** General studies/Field of study not specified. **Qualif.:** Applicants must be Kent County residents (3 years minimum) who will be attending Aquinas, Calvin, Cornerstone, Davenport, GRCC, GVSU or Kendall; must have a minimum of 3.0 GPA; must have financial need. **Criteria:** Priority will be given to those students with financial need.

Funds Avail.: No specific amount. **Duration:** Annual. **To Apply:** Applicants must complete the following: general online application; list of awards, volunteer activities, employment/school extra-curricular activities; academic transcript from most recent semester (High School Students: must include first semester senior year); An essay about yourself that includes: reasons for choice of college, chosen course of study, career goals, plans for financing education, and information on past activities benefitting community. **Deadline:** April 1. **Contact:** Ruth Bishop, Education Program Officer; Phone: 616-454-1751 Ext. 103; Email: rbishop@grfoundation.org.

4626 ■ Dorothy J. Thurston Graduate Scholarships (Undergraduate/Scholarship)

Purpose: To provide financial assistance to those students who are in need. **Focus:** General studies/Field of study not specified. **Qualif.:** Applicants must be Kent County residents who are pursuing full or part-time study at any accredited school in Michigan. Applicants must have financial need. Applicants must have a minimum of 3.0 GPA. **Criteria:** Preference will be given to those students who meet the criteria.

Funds Avail.: No specific amount. **Duration:** Annual. **To Apply:** Applicants must complete the general online application; List of Awards, Volunteer Activities, Employment/School Extra-Curricular Activities; Academic Transcript from most recent semester (High School Students: must include first semester senior year); An essay about yourself that includes: reasons for choice of college, chosen course of study, career goals, plans for financing education, and information on past activities benefitting community. **Deadline:** April 1. **Contact:** Ruth Bishop, Education Program Officer; Phone: 616-454-1751 x103; E-mail: rbishop@grfoundation.org.

4627 ■ Mildred E. Troske Music Scholarships (Undergraduate/Scholarship)

Purpose: To provide financial support to those students who are in need. **Focus:** General studies/Field of study not specified. **Qualif.:** Applicants must be residents of Kent County (2 years minimum) who are studying music at a camp or are undergraduate music majors; must have demonstrated financial need; must have a minimum of 3.0 GPA. **Criteria:** Preference will be given to those students who meet the criteria.

Funds Avail.: No specific amount. **Duration:** Annual. **To Apply:** Applicants must complete the following: general online application; list of awards, volunteer activities, employment/school extra-curricular activities; academic transcript from most recent semester (High School Students: must include first semester senior year); An essay about yourself that includes: reasons for choice of college, chosen course of study, career goals, plans for financing education, and information on past activities benefitting community. **Deadline:** April 1. **Contact:** Ruth Bishop, Education Program Officer; Phone: 616-454-1751 Ext. 103; Email: rbishop@grfoundation.org.

4628 ■ U-M Alumnae Club (University of Michigan) Scholarships (Undergraduate/Scholarship)

Purpose: To support female students in their pursuit of higher education and future career choices. **Focus:** General studies/Field of study not specified. **Qualif.:** Applicants must be female students entering the second year or above at the University of Michigan; must have a permanent residency (three years minimum) in Kent or adjoining counties of Allegan, Barry, Ionia, Montcalm, Muskegon, Newaygo, or Ottawa; must have a financial need; and must have a minimum GPA of 3.0. **Criteria:** Selection will be based on the Foundation's criteria.

Funds Avail.: No specific amount. **To Apply:** Applicants must contact the Foundation for further information. **Deadline:** April 1.

4629 ■ Keith C. Vanderhyde Scholarships (Undergraduate/Scholarship)

Purpose: To provide financial assistance to those students who are in need. **Focus:** General studies/Field of study not specified. **Qualif.:** Applicants must be senior students or graduates of Ottawa Hills High School who are pursuing a full-time undergraduate degree. Applicants must demonstrate financial need. Applicants must have a minimum of 3.0 GPA. **Criteria:** Priority will be given to those students with financial need.

Funds Avail.: No specific amount. **Duration:** Annual. **To Apply:** Applicants must complete the following: general online application; list of awards, volunteer activities, employment/school extra-curricular activities; academic transcript from most recent semester (High School Students: must include first semester senior year); An essay about yourself that includes: reasons for choice of college, chosen course of study, career goals, plans for financing education, and information on past activities benefitting community. **Deadline:** April 1. **Contact:** Ruth Bishop, Education Program Officer; Phone: 616-454-1751 x103; E-mail: rbishop@grfoundation.org.

4630 ■ Jacob R. and Mary M. VanLoo and Lenore K. VanLoo Scholarships *(Undergraduate/Scholarship)*

Purpose: To provide financial assistance to those students who are in need. **Focus:** General studies/Field of study not specified. **Qualif.:** Applicants must be Kent County residents (3 years minimum) who will be attending Grand Rapids Community College or Grand Valley State University. Applicants must have financial need. Applicants must have a minimum of 3.0 GPA. **Criteria:** Preference will be given to those students who meet the criteria.

Funds Avail.: No specific amount. **Duration:** Annual. **To Apply:** Complete general online application; List of Awards, Volunteer Activities, Employment/School Extra-Curricular Activities; Academic Transcript from most recent semester (High School Students: must include first semester senior year); An essay about yourself that includes: reasons for choice of college, chosen course of study, career goals, plans for financing education, and information on past activities benefitting community. **Deadline:** April 1. **Contact:** Ruth Bishop, Education Program Officer; Phone: 616-454-1751 Ext. 103; Email: rbishop@grfoundation.org.

4631 ■ Chad Vollmer Scholarships *(Undergraduate/Scholarship)*

Purpose: To support students who will attend Grand Rapids Community College for their pursuit of higher education and to encourage them in their future career choices. **Focus:** General studies/Field of study not specified. **Qualif.:** Applicants must be senior high school students at Central High School and will attend Grand Rapids Community College; must have a financial need; must have a 2.3 minimum GPA to renew; and must have an acceptable work history. **Criteria:** Selection will be based on the Foundation's criteria.

Funds Avail.: No specific amount. **To Apply:** Applicants must contact the Foundation for further information. **Deadline:** April 1.

4632 ■ Donald M. Wells Scholarships *(Undergraduate/Scholarship)*

Purpose: To provide financial assistance to those students who are in need. **Focus:** General studies/Field of study not specified. **Qualif.:** Applicants must be senior students or graduates of Central High School who are pursuing undergraduate studies at GRCC, University of Chicago or University of Michigan. Applicants must have financial need and must have a minimum of 2.5 GPA. **Criteria:** Preference will be given to those students who meet the criteria.

Funds Avail.: No specific amount. **Duration:** Annual. **To Apply:** Applicants must complete the following: general online application; list of awards, volunteer activities, employment/school extra-curricular activities; academic transcript from most recent semester (High School Students: must include first semester senior year); An essay about yourself that includes: reasons for choice of college, chosen course of study, career goals, plans for financing education, and information on past activities benefitting community. **Deadline:** April 1. **Contact:** Ruth Bishop, Education Program Officer; Phone: 616-454-1751 x103; E-mail: rbishop@grfoundation.org.

4633 ■ Elmo Wierenga Alumni Scholarships *(Undergraduate/Scholarship)*

Purpose: To provide financial support to those students who are in need. **Focus:** General studies/Field of study not specified. **Qualif.:** Applicants must be senior students at Ottawa Hills High School pursuing full-time undergraduate studies at any 2 or 4-year accredited school in the U.S. Applicants must have financial need and a minimum of 2.5 GPA. **Criteria:** Priority will be given to those students with financial need.

Funds Avail.: No specific amount. **Duration:** Annual. **To Apply:** Complete general online application; List of Awards, Volunteer Activities, Employment/School Extra-Curricular Activities; Academic Transcript from most recent semester (High School Students: must include first semester senior year); An essay about yourself that includes: reasons for choice of college, chosen course of study, career goals, plans for financing education, and information on past activities benefitting community. **Deadline:** April 1. **Contact:** Ruth Bishop, Education Program Officer; Phone: 616-454-1751 x103; E-mail: rbishop@grfoundation.org.

4634 ■ Walter C. Winchester Scholarships *(Undergraduate/Scholarship)*

Purpose: To support students in their pursuit of higher education and future career choices. **Focus:** General studies/Field of study not specified. **Qualif.:** Applicants must be senior students graduating from a Grad Rapids Public High School; have demonstrate financial need; and have a minimum 3.3 GPA. **Criteria:** Selection will be based on the Foundation's criteria.

Funds Avail.: No specific amount. **To Apply:** Applicants must contact the Foundation for further information. **Deadline:** April 1.

4635 ■ Michael J. Wolf Scholarships *(Undergraduate/Scholarship)*

Purpose: To support students in their pursuit of higher education and future career choices. **Focus:** General studies/Field of study not specified. **Qualif.:** Applicants must be senior graduating students from a Grand Rapids Public High School; must be residing in the City of Grand Rapids; must be pursuing an undergraduate degree at the University of Michigan; must demonstrate a financial need; and must have a minimum GPA of 3.0. **Criteria:** Selection will be based on the Foundation's criteria.

Funds Avail.: No specific amount. **To Apply:** Applicants must contact the Foundation for further information. **Deadline:** April 1.

4636 ■ Violet Wondergem Health Science Scholarships *(Undergraduate/Scholarship)*

Purpose: To support students majoring in a health service related field. **Focus:** Health care services. **Qualif.:** Applicants must be residents of Kent or Ottawa County; must be majoring in a health service related field at any accredited Michigan college or university; must have a financial need; and must have a minimum 3.0 cumulative GPA. **Criteria:** Selection will be based on the Foundation's criteria.

Funds Avail.: No specific amount. **To Apply:** Applicants

Awards are arranged alphabetically below their administering organizations

must contact the Foundation for further information. **Deadline:** April 1.

4637 ■ Audrey L. Wright Scholarships
(Undergraduate/Scholarship)

Purpose: To provide financial support to deserving students. **Focus:** Education--Curricula; Foreign languages. **Qualif.:** Applicants must be residents of Kent County (3 years minimum); must be pursuing an undergraduate degree in Foreign Language or Education; must have financial need; must have a minimum of 3.0 GPA. **Criteria:** Preference will be given to those students who meet the criteria.

Funds Avail.: No specific amount. **Duration:** Annual. **To Apply:** Complete general online application; List of Awards, Volunteer Activities, Employment/School Extra-Curricular Activities; Academic Transcript from most recent semester (High School Students: must include first semester senior year); An essay about yourself that includes: reasons for choice of college, chosen course of study, career goals, plans for financing education, and information on past activities benefitting community. **Deadline:** April 1. **Contact:** Ruth Bishop, Education Program Officer; Phone: 616-454-1751 Ext. 103; Email: rbishop@grfoundation.org.

4638 ■ Grandmothers for Peace International (GPI)
PO Box 1292
Elk Grove, CA 95759-1292
Ph: (916)730-6476
URL: www.grandmothersforpeace.org
Facebook: www.facebook.com/GrandmothersForPeace

4639 ■ Barbara Wiedner and Dorothy Vandercook Memorial Peace Scholarships *(Undergraduate/Scholarship)*

Purpose: To provide financial assistance to students across the United States, Africa, Kyrgyzstan, Canada, Norway and Ukraine. **Focus:** General studies/Field of study not specified. **Qualif.:** Applicants must be high school seniors or in their first year of college. **Criteria:** Recipients will be evaluated by the Scholarship Selection Committees based on some criteria.

Funds Avail.: No specific amount. **Duration:** Annual. **To Apply:** Applicants must submit the completed application form; brief autobiography of activities relating to peace and social justice, nuclear disarmament issues, or conflict resolution; two letters of recommendation; and must describe how they will contribute to a peaceful and just society in the future. **Deadline:** March 1. **Contact:** Leal Portis, President, 301 Redbud Way, Nevada City, CA 95959, Phone/Fax: 530-265-3887, E-mail: portis.leal@gmail.com.

4640 ■ Granger Business Association (GBA)
PO Box 427
Granger, IN 46530
Ph: (574)274-8554
Fax: (574)271-7150
E-mail: info@grangertoday.com
URL: www.grangertoday.com

4641 ■ Granger Business Association College Scholarships *(Undergraduate/Scholarship)*

Purpose: To help defray college expenses of students from Granger area. **Focus:** General studies/Field of study not specified. **Qualif.:** Applicants must reside in the 46530 zip code and demonstrate financial need. **Criteria:** Criteria for selection include (but not limited to) academics; extra curricular activities; volunteer work and personal narratives.

Funds Avail.: $1,000 each. **Duration:** Annual. **Number Awarded:** Typically 10. **To Apply:** Applicants must check the application process online. **Deadline:** March 1. **Contact:** Kathy Smith; Phone: 574-243-7746; Email: kathy.smith@lakecitybank.com.

4642 ■ Grass Foundation
PO Box 241458
Los Angeles, CA 90024
Ph: (424)832-4188
Fax: (310)986-2252
E-mail: info@grassfoundation.org
URL: www.grassfoundation.org

4643 ■ Grass Fellowships at the Marine Biological Laboratory *(Doctorate, Postdoctorate/Fellowship)*

Purpose: To support investigator-designed, independent research projects by scientists early in their career. **Focus:** Biophysics; Neurology; Neurophysiology; Neuroscience. **Qualif.:** Applicants must be early investigators (late stage predoctoral trainees and beyond) including those with prior experience at MBL or with the Grass Foundation. **Criteria:** Priority is given to applicants with a demonstrated commitment to a research career and no prior research experience at the MBL.

Funds Avail.: No specific amount. **Duration:** Annual. **Number Awarded:** Varies. **To Apply:** Applicants must complete the application package and must be submitted electronically as a single pdf or MS Word file. **Deadline:** December 5. **Contact:** Ann Woolford, the Grass Fellowship Program Coordinator at MBL; Email: gfp@grassfoundation.org; Phone: 508.289.7521.

4644 ■ Gravure Education Foundation (GEF)
PO Box 25617
Rochester, NY 14625-0617
Ph: (201)523-6042
Fax: (201)523-6048
E-mail: gaa@gaa.org
URL: www.gaa.org/gravure-education-foundation

4645 ■ ALCOA Foundation Corporate Scholarships *(Undergraduate, Graduate/Scholarship)*

Purpose: To help undergraduate and graduate students pursue their education through the support of ALCOA employee volunteers. **Focus:** General studies/Field of study not specified. **Qualif.:** Applicants must be undergraduate or graduate students enrolled in a full-time basis in one of the GEF designated learning resource centers; must have GPA of 3.0 or greater on a 4.0 scale. **Criteria:** Applicants will be chosen based on demonstrated leadership and academic accomplishments.

Funds Avail.: $1,500. **Duration:** Annual. **Number Awarded:** 1. **To Apply:** Applicants must submit a completed application form; must contact the Executive Director for further information. **Deadline:** May 1. **Remarks:** In collaboration with ALCOA Foundation. **Contact:** Rod Sosa, GEF Trustee, at rsosa@fresco.com.

4646 ■ Cerutti Group Scholarships *(Undergraduate/Scholarship)*

Purpose: To provide financial assistance to undergraduate and graduate students. **Focus:** General studies/Field of

Awards are arranged alphabetically below their administering organizations

study not specified. **Qualif.:** Applicants must be sophomore, junior, senior, or graduate students at the time the scholarships are awarded; declared major in Printing, Graphic Arts, or Graphic Communications must be demonstrated; must demonstrate leadership development efforts through clubs or associations, sports, community participation, or volunteer activity; must exhibit scholarly performance and demonstrate academic success; with a GPA of 3.0 or greater (on a 4.0 scale) is required. **Criteria:** Recipients will be chosen based on submitted materials.

Funds Avail.: Not less than $1,500 each awardee. **Duration:** Annual. **Number Awarded:** 1. **To Apply:** Applicants must submit an essay of 300-500 words describing "My interest in gravure technology and the print communications industry"; must submit a "student copy" of their college/university transcripts; and mail or e-mail completed application and must have completed the attached GEF scholarship application form. **Deadline:** May 1. **Remarks:** The scholarship is made possible with Cerutti Group. **Contact:** Rod Sosa, GEF Trustee at rsosa@fresco.com.

4647 ■ GEF Scholarship Program (Undergraduate, Graduate/Scholarship)

Purpose: To financially assist students interested in graphic communications or any related fields of study. **Focus:** Graphic art and design. **Qualif.:** Applicants must be undergraduate or graduate students enrolled full-time at any of the GEF-funded colleges or universities; must be majoring printing, graphic arts or any fields of study related in graphic communications; must have 3.0 GPA or greater on a 4.0 scale. **Criteria:** Applicants will be selected based on merit.

Funds Avail.: Amount not specified. **To Apply:** Applicants must submit a completed application form. Faxed applications will not be accepted. **Deadline:** May 1. **Contact:** Bernadette Carlson, bcarlson@gaa.org.

4648 ■ Gravure Publishing Council Scholarships (Undergraduate, Graduate/Scholarship)

Purpose: To encourage students who are in financial need and encourage them to enter the gravure industry. **Focus:** Printmaking. **Qualif.:** Applicants must be sophomore, junior, senior, or graduate students at the time the scholarships are awarded; declared major in Printing, Graphic Arts, or Graphic Communications must be demonstrated; must demonstrate leadership development efforts through clubs or associations, sports, community participation, or volunteer activity; must exhibit scholarly performance and demonstrate academic success; with a GPA of 3.0 or greater (on a 4.0 scale) is required. **Criteria:** Recipients will be selected based on submitted materials.

Funds Avail.: Not less than $1,500 each awardee. **Duration:** Annual. **Number Awarded:** 1. **To Apply:** Applicants must submit an essay of 300-500 words describing "My interest in gravure technology and the print communications industry"; must submit a "student copy" of their college/university transcripts; and mail or e-mail completed application and must have completed the attached GEF scholarship application form. **Deadline:** May 1. **Remarks:** The scholarship is made possible with Gravure Publishing Council. **Contact:** Rod Sosa, GEF Trustee at rsosa@fresco.com.

4649 ■ Harry V. Quadracci Memorial Scholarships (Undergraduate, Graduate/Scholarship)

Purpose: To provide financial assistance to students and encourage them to be involved in Gravure industry. **Focus:** Graphic art and design; Printmaking. **Qualif.:** Applicants must be undergraduate and graduate students; must be enrolled full-time at any of the printing management/graphic arts programs at one of the GEF designed learning resource centers; must maintain a GPA of 3.0 or greater. **Criteria:** Applicants will be chosen based on demonstrated academic success, extracurricular/community involvement and financial need.

Funds Avail.: $1,000. **Duration:** Annual. **Number Awarded:** 1. **To Apply:** Applicants must complete and submit the following: GEF scholarship application form; a 300-500 words essay entitled "Why I Have Chosen Printing as a Career Choice"; a student copy of college/university transcripts. Email completed application to Rod Sosa, GEF Trustee. **Deadline:** May 1. **Contact:** Rod Sosa, GEF Trustee at rsosa@fresco.com.

4650 ■ Grays Harbor Community Foundation
705 J St.
Hoquiam, WA 98550
Ph: (360)532-1600
Fax: (360)532-8111
E-mail: info@gh-cf.org
URL: gh-cf.org
Facebook: www.facebook.com/GraysHarborCommunityFoundation

4651 ■ Grays Harbor Community Foundation Scholarships (Undergraduate, Graduate/Scholarship)

Purpose: To support outstanding undergraduate and vocational students from Grays Harbor County. **Focus:** General studies/Field of study not specified. **Qualif.:** Applicants must: be residents of Grays Harbor; have graduated from a Grays Harbor or Pacific County high school; be in need of financial assistance; undergraduate students enrolled as full-time (12 credits minimum) at an accredited college/university and have earned a cumulative GPA of 3.0 (or equivalent B average); or graduate students accepted into a graduate program at an accredited university and have earned a cumulative GPA of 3.0 (or equivalent B average) both in college and in the first year of graduate school. **Criteria:** Selection shall be based on applicants' academic performance, financial need, character, ability, industry and service.

Funds Avail.: No specific amount. **Duration:** Annual. **To Apply:** Applicants must submit a completed, printed and signed application form along with a personal essay (1-page, typed); three written letters of recommendation; history of employment; certified transcripts from all schools attended; and a documentation of acceptance by a graduate program at an accredited university (graduate students). **Deadline:** March 15. **Contact:** Grays Harbor Community Foundation, at the above address.

4652 ■ Great Lakes Athletic Trainers Association (GLATA)
PO Box 436
Crystal Lake, IL 60039
Ph: (815)455-8512
E-mail: info@glata.org
URL: www.glata.org
Twitter: twitter.com/d4updates

4653 ■ GLATA Living Memorial Doctorate Scholarships (Doctorate, Graduate/Fellowship)

Purpose: To honor the memory and accomplishments of the deceased members of the GLATA by providing scholarships to students who want to pursue their graduate studies. **Focus:** General studies/Field of study not specified. **Qualif.:** Applicant must be a member in good standing of the National Athletic Trainers Association; must be a current GLATA Certified member; must have a grade point average of 3.0, its equivalent, or above. **Criteria:** Selection of applicants will be based on the criteria of the Scholarship Committee.

Funds Avail.: $2,000. **To Apply:** Applicants must complete the application form available on the website; must submit an official statement from the registrar of the college or university indicating the applicants current GPA, and that the applicant is enrolled in a PhD, EdD or equivalent terminal degree program and has qualified for dissertation level credits; must have an official transcript through the most recently completed school term; must provide three candidate recommendation forms sent to the District Vice-President (one form must be completed by the applicant's Major Advisor, an Athletic Administrator or another Professor, and a sponsoring Athletic Trainer). **Contact:** Great Lakes Athletic Trainers Association, at the above address.

4654 ■ GLATA Living Memorial Graduate Scholarships *(Graduate/Fellowship, Scholarship)*

Purpose: To honor the memory and accomplishments of the deceased members of the GLATA by providing scholarships to students who want to pursue their graduate studies. **Focus:** General studies/Field of study not specified. **Qualif.:** Applicant must be a member in good standing of the National Athletic Trainers Association; must be a full time student within GLATA or must be a current GLATA member; must have the intention to pursue certification by the NATA; must have a GPA of B or above. For Graduate applicants: must be a degree-seeking candidate for the upcoming fall academic term; must have worked at least two academic years as an athletic training student on the college level under the supervision of an NATA certified athletic trainer. For Undergraduate applicants: must have a senior standing for the next fall academic term; must have worked at least one academic year as an athletic training student on the college level under the supervision of an NATA certified athletic trainer; must currently be a full time student enrolled in a curriculum leading to a Bachelor's degree at the time of application. **Criteria:** Selection of applicants will be based on the criteria of the Scholarship Committee.

Funds Avail.: No specific amont. **To Apply:** Applicants must complete the application form available on the website; must submit an official statement from the registrar of the college or university indicating the applicant's current GPA, and also indicating that the applicant is a full-time student; must submit an official transcript through the most recently completed school term; must have three candidate recommendation forms sent to the district vice-president (one form must be completed by a professor who is an Athletic Trainer in the applicant's major field, and one form must be completed by a Non-ATC Academic professor in the applicant's major field). **Contact:** David Craig, GLATA Vice-President; Email: dhcraig3@yahoo.com.

4655 ■ Great Lakes Commission (GLC)
2805 S Industrial Hwy., Ste. 100
Ann Arbor, MI 48104-6791
Ph: (734)665-9135
Fax: (734)665-9150
URL: glc.org

Awards are arranged alphabetically below their administering organizations

4656 ■ Great Lakes Commission Sea Grant Fellowships *(Graduate/Scholarship)*

Purpose: To provide fund to work and advance the environmental quality and sustainable economic development goals. **Focus:** Natural resources; Public health. **Qualif.:** Applicants must be graduate or professional students in the field of public policy, public health, natural resources, aquatic sciences or other related field at an accredited institution of higher education in the United States. **Criteria:** Evaluations will be based on academic ability; communication skills; diversity and appropriateness of background; and interests to fellowship experience.

Funds Avail.: $42,000. **Duration:** One year. **To Apply:** Applicants must complete the required documents; personal and academic resume (maximum of two pages); education and career goal statement (1,000 words or less); two letters of recommendation with at least one from the student's major professor; a letter of endorsement from the sponsoring Sea Grant Director; a copy of undergraduates and graduates transcript of records. Must be sent to the Great Lakes Commission. **Deadline:** February 28. **Contact:** E-mail Christine Manninen at manninen@glc.org.

4657 ■ Greater Seattle Business Association (GSBA)
400 E Pine St., Ste. 322
Seattle, WA 98122-2300
Ph: (206)363-9188
Fax: (206)568-3123
E-mail: office@thegsba.org
URL: www.thegsba.org
Facebook: www.facebook.com/theGSBA.org

4658 ■ Greater Seattle Business Association Scholarships (GSBA Scholarships) *(Undergraduate/Scholarship)*

Purpose: To support undergraduate students by providing financial resources to pursue their educational goals. **Focus:** General studies/Field of study not specified. **Qualif.:** Applicant must be a current resident of Washington pursuing an undergraduate degree at any college in the US. **Criteria:** Applicants will be evaluated based on leadership potential; academic strength/special skills and talents; and diversity.

Funds Avail.: $11,000. **Duration:** Annual. **To Apply:** Applicants must complete and return scholarship application, letters of reference and transcripts by application deadline. **Deadline:** January 15. **Remarks:** GSBA Scholarships are being awarded to undergraduate LGBTQ and Aliied students who exhibit leadership potential, demonstrate strong academic abilities, and who are actively involved in school and community organizations. The program was started by two teachers who realized there was a huge need to support students who, because of their sexual orientation, were often discriminated against in school, disowned by their families and shunned by their friends. These were students who had the ability and drive to be successful in college, but who did not have the money or support to go to college. Established in 1990.

4659 ■ Greater Valley Chamber of Commerce
10 Progress Dr., 2nd Fl.
Shelton, CT 06484
Ph: (203)925-4981

Fax: (203)925-4984
E-mail: info@greatervalleychamber.com
URL: www.greatervalleychamber.com

4660 ■ Gerald J. and Helen Bogen Fund
(Undergraduate/Scholarship)

Purpose: To support those most in need of financial aid to assist their pursuing studies beyond the secondary school level to an accredited junior or senior college. **Focus:** General studies/Field of study not specified. **Qualif.:** Applicants must be graduating students from any of the following schools: Ansonia, Derby, Oxford, Seymour, Shelton High Schools, or Emmett O'Brien Vocational Technical School. **Criteria:** Preference will be given to applicants whose applications imply their academic ability, need of financial aid, and those who have showed good citizenship and concern in the community during their high school years.

Funds Avail.: No specific amount. **Duration:** Annual. **Number Awarded:** 2 (1 male and 1 female). **To Apply:** In order to apply for this scholarship, applicants must complete the following: an attached application form, available online, with complete signatures; high school transcript; financial aid acknowledgement form which indicates the family's contribution (provide single side pages only without staples). **Deadline:** March 27. **Remarks:** Established in 1984.

4661 ■ Julia B. DeCapua Fund *(Undergraduate/ Scholarship)*

Purpose: To support those most in need of financial aid to assist them in pursuing their studies beyond the secondary school level to an accredited junior or senior college. **Focus:** General studies/Field of study not specified. **Qualif.:** Applicants must be students pursuing teaching as a vocation and who are from Ansonia, Beacon Falls, Derby, Oxford, Seymour, or Shelton. **Criteria:** Preference will be given to applicants who are pursuing teaching as a vocation; needs financial aid; and have good academic ability.

Funds Avail.: No specific amount. **Duration:** Annual. **To Apply:** In order to apply for this scholarship, an applicant must complete the following: an attached application form online with complete signatures; high school transcript; and a financial aid acknowledgement form which indicates the family's contribution (provide single side pages only without staples). **Deadline:** March 27. **Remarks:** Established in 1996.

4662 ■ Herman and Bess Glazer Scholarship Fund
(Undergraduate/Scholarship)

Purpose: To support those most in need of financial aid to assist their pursuing studies beyond the secondary school level to an accredited junior or senior college. **Focus:** General studies/Field of study not specified. **Qualif.:** Applicants must be graduating students from any of the following schools: Ansonia, Derby, Oxford, Seymour, Shelton High Schools, or Emmett O'Brien Vocational Technical School. **Criteria:** Preference will be given to applicants whose applications imply their need of financial aid in pursuing studies beyond secondary level to an accredited junior or senior college.

Funds Avail.: No specific amount. **Duration:** Annual. **Number Awarded:** 2. **To Apply:** In order to apply for this scholarship, applicants must complete the following: an attached application form, available online, with complete signatures; high school transcript; financial aid acknowledgement form which indicates the family's contribution (provide single side pages only without staples). **Deadline:** March 27. **Remarks:** Established in 1979.

4663 ■ Greater Washington Society of Certified Public Accountants (GWSCPA)
1140 Connecticut Ave. NW, Ste. 606
Washington, DC 20036
Ph: (202)601-0560
E-mail: info@gwscpa.org
URL: www.gwscpa.org

4664 ■ GWSCPA Scholarships *(Undergraduate/ Scholarship)*

Purpose: To support students aspiring to become a Certified Public Accountant. **Focus:** Accounting. **Qualif.:** Applicants must be students attending a GWSCPA eligible school/university on a full time basis and must meet all the other criteria. **Criteria:** Selection is based on the application materials submitted.

Funds Avail.: $3,000-$4,000 each. **Duration:** Annual. **Number Awarded:** Up to 4. **To Apply:** Applicants must contact their respective schools/universities for the application details. **Deadline:** March 3. **Remarks:** Established in 1963.

4665 ■ Greek Orthodox Archdiocese of America
8 E 79th St., No. 10
New York, NY 10075
Ph: (212)570-3500
Fax: (212)570-3569
E-mail: administration@goarch.org
URL: www.goarch.org
Facebook: www.facebook.com/goarch

4666 ■ Greek Orthodox Archdiocese of America Paleologos Graduate Scholarships *(Graduate/ Scholarship)*

Purpose: To provide financial assistance towards the education of young people from the Orthodox Christian community. **Focus:** General studies/Field of study not specified. **Qualif.:** Applicants must be Orthodox Christians from a church who belong to SCOBA (Standing Conference of Canonical Orthodox Bishops in the Americas); must be active in church activities; must be college graduates and in the next academic year, must be either commencing their graduate studies or continuing their graduate program studies on a full-time basis at an accredited university in a non-theological field of study leading to a graduate degree; must be U.S. citizens or permanent residents of the United States. **Criteria:** Selection will be based on evaluation of submitted documents and specific criteria.

Funds Avail.: $5,000. **Duration:** Annual. **To Apply:** Applicants must submit a completed application form; academic records including undergraduate and graduate transcripts (past and present); statement of financial need; a copy or transcript of baptismal or chrismation certificate; resume or curriculum vitae; scholarship proposal; personal statement (optional); five recommendation letters. **Deadline:** April 27. **Contact:** Greek Orthodox Archdiocese of America, at the above address or Email: at scholarships@goarch.org.

4667 ■ Green Knight Economic Development Corporation (GKEDC)
PO Box 4
Pen Argyl, PA 18072-0004

E-mail: questions@gkedc.com
URL: www.gkedc.com

4668 ■ Green Knight Economic Development Corporation Scholarships (Undergraduate/Scholarship)

Purpose: To support students who wish to continue higher education. **Focus:** General studies/Field of study not specified. **Qualif.:** Applicants must be graduating high school seniors who live in the Pen Argyl School District and who will be continuing their education in a college program. **Criteria:** Selection will be based on the aforesaid qualifications and compliance with the application process.

Funds Avail.: $4,000. **Duration:** Annual. **To Apply:** Applicants must submit a completed scholarship application form together with a one-page essay. Guidance counselor must sign and the date the last page of the application verifying the SAT scores, class rank and GPA. **Deadline:** May 22.

4669 ■ Greenlining Institute
1918 University Ave., 2nd Fl.
Berkeley, CA 94704
Ph: (510)926-4000
Fax: (510)926-4010
E-mail: questions@greenlining.org
URL: greenlining.org

4670 ■ Greenlining Institute Fellowships (Graduate/Fellowship)

Purpose: To encourage and train young leaders that have completed their undergraduate degree and are seeking hands-on public policy experience. **Focus:** Leadership, Institutional and community. **Qualif.:** Applicants must be students of color or from must be from other disadvantaged groups, and must have completed at least an undergraduate degree. **Criteria:** Selection shall be based on the aforementioned applicants' qualifications and compliance with the application details.

Funds Avail.: $37,500-$40,000. **Duration:** Annual. **To Apply:** Applicants must submit a completed application form along with a personal statement; resume; two letters or recommendation; and copies of all higher education transcripts.

4671 ■ Greenwich Scholarship Association (GSA)
PO Box 4627
Greenwich, CT 06831
E-mail: GSAapplications@gmail.com
URL: greenwichscholarship.org

4672 ■ Greenwich Scholarship Association Scholarships (GSA) (Undergraduate/Scholarship)

Purpose: To assist students to attend a public, private or parochial school to pursue their studies. **Focus:** General studies/Field of study not specified. **Qualif.:** Applicants must be graduating seniors residing in Greenwich, CT; must be currently attending a public, private, or parochial school located in Greenwich; must have demonstrated financial need. **Criteria:** Recipients will be selected based on financial need.

Funds Avail.: Varies. **To Apply:** Applicants must submit a completed application form; attach an activity sheet; financial statement; completed and filed FAFSA. **Deadline:** March 12.

4673 ■ Griffin Foundation
303 W Prospect Rd.
Fort Collins, CO 80526
Ph: (970)482-3030
Fax: (970)484-6648
URL: www.thegriffinfoundation.org

4674 ■ Griffin Foundation Scholarships (Undergraduate/Scholarship)

Purpose: To support qualified applicants who have an associate degree from a junior or community college. **Focus:** General studies/Field of study not specified. **Qualif.:** Applicants must have an associate degree or at least 60 hours from a junior or community college and seeking to complete a baccalaureate degree; have a cumulative GPA of at least a 3.5 on a 4.0 scale in all college level work; and, be admitted as full-time, on-campus students in a baccalaureate degree program at the participating university they have selected. **Criteria:** Scholarships will be awarded on a competitive basis by ranking applicants in the following areas for their activities since graduation from high school: scholarship; leadership and service; personal traits; and financial need.

Funds Avail.: $5,000. **Duration:** Annual. **To Apply:** Application form can be downloaded from the Griffin Foundation website. Applicants must type or print their application legibly; applicants must attach three letters of recommendation, at least one of which is from a college faculty member, counselor or administrator who can comment on applicant qualifications (be sure recommendations are signed). Applicants must attach an official copy of grade transcript(s) from each college attended. Scholarship can only be used at Colorado State University (Fort Collins Campus), the University of Northern Colorado, or the University of Wyoming (Larimie Campus). **Deadline:** March 1.

4675 ■ Guajardo & Marks LLP
13355 Noel Rd., Ste. 1370
Dallas, TX 75240
Ph: (972)774-9800
Fax: (972)774-9801
URL: www.guajardomarks.com

4676 ■ Guajardo & Marks Law School Scholarships (Graduate/Scholarship)

Purpose: To encourage and award creative authorship. **Focus:** Law. **Qualif.:** Applicants must be U.S. citizens or authorized to work in the United States; must be commencing law school (1L) in August of the current year; must have a published article in print or digital media. **Criteria:** Selection will be based on the creativity, originality and ability to clearly convey a complex message of the submitted sample writings.

Funds Avail.: $1,000. **Duration:** Non-renewable. **To Apply:** Applicants must visit the website for the online application process; must prepare a completed scholarship application form, copy of law school acceptance letter, and copy of previously published article or link to its online location. **Deadline:** May 1.

4677 ■ Guelph Caribbean Canadian Association
7 Clair Rd. W
Guelph, ON, Canada N1L 0A0

Awards are arranged alphabetically below their administering organizations

E-mail: info@guelphcaribbean.ca
URL: guelphcaribbean.ca

4678 ■ Guelph Caribbean Canadian Association Graduate Scholarships (Undergraduate/Scholarship)

Purpose: To support students who have been admitted to a post secondary institution in Canada. **Focus:** Culture. **Qualif.:** Applicants must be residents of the City of Guelph or Wellington County and students of Caribbean/West Indian heritage enrolled in graduate studies at the University of Guelph with proof of acceptance and/or ongoing registration. Applicants must have demonstrated leadership skills and involvement in extra-curricular end/or volunteer activities at university campus and/or the community. **Criteria:** Selection will be based on the committees' criteria.

Funds Avail.: $500. **Duration:** Annual. **To Apply:** Applicants must submit a completed application form together with one of the following: letter of acceptance from an eligible post secondary Institution or proof of ongoing registration at an eligible post secondary Institution. Applicants must also submit a short essay or resume describing the reasons of why the applicants would be worthy recipients of the award including their contributions to school and community life, work history and any additional volunteer work.

4679 ■ Guelph Caribbean Canadian Association Undergraduate Scholarships (Undergraduate/Scholarship)

Purpose: To assist deserving students who have been admitted to post-secondary institution in Canada. **Focus:** General studies/Field of study not specified. **Qualif.:** Applicants must be students of Caribbean/West Indian heritage who are Canadian citizens; must be residents of the City of Guelph or Wellington County; must be students either entering first year of post-secondary education with a copy of letter of acceptance at a recognized post-secondary institution or second year with proof of ongoing registration. **Criteria:** Recipients will be selected based on academic achievement and demonstrated leadership skills and involvement in extra-curricular activities.

Funds Avail.: $500 each. **Duration:** Annual; One year. **To Apply:** Applicants must complete the application form; must submit one letter of acceptance from an eligible post-secondary institution or proof of ongoing registration, resume, or short essay describing the reasons why they deserve the award. **Deadline:** October 1.

4680 ■ Harry Frank Guggenheim Foundation (HFG)
25 W 53rd St.
New York, NY 10019-5401
Ph: (646)428-0971
Fax: (646)428-0981
E-mail: info@hfg.org
URL: www.hfg.org
Twitter: twitter.com/HFGuggenheim

4681 ■ Harry Frank Guggenheim Dissertation Fellowships (Doctorate/Fellowship)

Purpose: To support the doctoral candidates to enable them to complete the thesis in a timely manner and are only appropriate for students approaching the final year of their Ph.D. work. **Focus:** Humanities; Social sciences. **Qualif.:** Applicants must be citizens of any country and studying as doctoral candidates in colleges and universities in any country. They must be entering the dissertation stage of the graduate school. **Criteria:** Recipients will be selected based on the comparison of the candidates' theses.

Funds Avail.: $20,000 each. **Duration:** Annual. **Number Awarded:** 10 or more. **To Apply:** Applicants must submit the following: three copies of typewritten title page; abstract; advisors letter; applicant's background; a research plan; protection of subjects. **Deadline:** February 1.

4682 ■ Harry Frank Guggenheim Foundation Research Grants (Professional development/Grant)

Purpose: To support research that can increase understanding and amelioration of urgent problems of violence and aggression in the modern world. **Focus:** Humanities; Social sciences. **Qualif.:** Applicants must be citizens of any country who have a project proposal in the field of natural sciences and humanities. While almost all recipients of the research grant possess a PhD, M.D. or equivalent degree, there are no formal degree requirements for the grant. **Criteria:** Recipients are selected based on the project proposal.

Funds Avail.: $15,000 to $40,000. **Duration:** Annual. **To Apply:** Applicants must submit three copies of typewritten title page; abstract; personnel; budget; budget justification; research plan; protection of subjects; tax exempt status; referees' comments. **Deadline:** August 1.

4683 ■ John Simon Guggenheim Memorial Foundation
90 Park Ave.
New York, NY 10016
Ph: (212)687-4470
Fax: (212)697-3248
URL: www.gf.org

4684 ■ John Simon Guggenheim Memorial Fellowships - U.S. and Canadian Competition (Advanced Professional/Fellowship)

Purpose: To support individuals in their respective research and artistic creations. **Focus:** Arts; Humanities; Natural sciences; Social sciences. **Qualif.:** Applicants must be individuals who have already demonstrated exceptional capacity for productive scholarship or exceptional creative ability in the arts, and must be U.S. or Canadian citizens. **Criteria:** Selection shall be based on the aforementioned applicants' qualifications and compliance with the application details.

Funds Avail.: No specific amount. **Duration:** Annual. **Number Awarded:** Varies. **To Apply:** Applicants must submit a completed application form together with the three separate supplementary statements. The three supplementary statements are: a brief narrative account of the applicant's career, describing previous accomplishments; a list of: Publications (scholar, scientist, or writer), Exhibitions (artist), Performances (choreographer), Compositions (composer), or Films/Videotapes (film or video maker); and a statement of plans for the period for which the Fellowship is requested. Application form must be submitted in PDF format. **Remarks:** Established in 1926. **Contact:** John Simon Guggenheim Memorial Foundation, at the above address.

4685 ■ Gulf and Caribbean Fisheries Institute (GCFI)
Florida Fish and Wildlife Conservation Commission
Marine Research Institute

2796 Overseas Hwy., Ste. 119
Marathon, FL 33050
Ph: (305)289-2330
Fax: (305)289-2334
URL: www.gcfi.org
Facebook: www.facebook.com/Gulf-and-Caribbean-Fisheries-Institute-GCFI-205610209456578

4686 ■ Ronald L. Schmied Scholarships (Other, Undergraduate/Scholarship)

Purpose: To encourage students with interest in marine recreational fisheries. **Focus:** Biology, Marine; Fisheries sciences/management. **Qualif.:** Applicant must be enrolled at a college/university degree program in the wider Caribbean or in one of Gulf of Mexico states (Mexico and the United States); or a student engaged in a research project in the Gulf of Mexico and wider Caribbean region. **Criteria:** Applicants will be selected based on the following: involvement with recreational fisheries issues, level of achievement, innovation, and financial need.

Funds Avail.: $1,500 (covers airfare, lodging, and research-related expenses). **Duration:** Annual. **Number Awarded:** 1. **To Apply:** Applicants must submit electronically an application letter (includes name, address, contact numbers, educational institution department, degree level, description of current marine research, career goals, and reasons for the needing financial assistance); an endorsement letter from a faculty; and a vita. **Deadline:** July 31. **Contact:** Dr. Stephen Holland, Chair, at sholland@ufl.edu.

4687 ■ Hagley Museum and Library
298 Buck Rd. E
Wilmington, DE 19807-0630
Ph: (302)658-2400
Fax: (302)658-0568
URL: www.hagley.org
Facebook: www.facebook.com/HagleyMuseumandLibrary
Twitter: twitter.com/hagleyde

4688 ■ Henry Belin du Pont Dissertation Fellowships (Doctorate, Graduate/Fellowship)

Purpose: To support graduate students conducting research for their dissertation. **Focus:** General studies/Field of study not specified. **Qualif.:** Applicants must be graduate students who have completed all course work for the doctoral degree and conducting research for their dissertation. **Criteria:** Selection is based on demonstrated superior intellectual quality and presentation of a persuasive methodology for the project. Applicants must show that there are significant research materials at Hagley pertinent to the dissertation.

Funds Avail.: $6,500. **Duration:** Up to 4 months. **To Apply:** Applicants must submit a completed application form together with the dissertation prospectus; statement concerning the relevance of Hagley's research collections to the project; two letters of recommendation; and writing samples. **Deadline:** November 15. **Contact:** Carol Lockman; Email: clockman@Hagley.org.

4689 ■ Henry Belin du Pont Research Grants (Graduate/Fellowship)

Purpose: To support research and study in the library, archival and artifact collections of the Hagley Museum and Library. **Focus:** Library and archival sciences. **Qualif.:** Applicants must be pursuing an advanced research and study in the library, archival and artifact collections of the Hagley Museum and Library, and must be from out of state. **Criteria:** Preference will be given to those whose travel costs to Hagley will be higher.

Funds Avail.: $200-$400. **Duration:** Up to 8 weeks. **To Apply:** Applicants must submit a completed application form along a cover letter noting the requested period of residency; a copy of curriculum vitae (maximum of four pages); and a 4-5 page description of the proposed research project. **Deadline:** March 31; June 30; October 31. **Contact:** Carol Lockman; Email: clockman@Hagley.org.

4690 ■ Hamilton Industrial Environmental Association (HIEA)
PO Box 56113
Stoney Creek, ON, Canada L8H 5C9
Ph: (905)662-2131
E-mail: info@hiea.org
URL: www.hiea.org

4691 ■ Hamilton Industrial Environmental Association Bursaries-Mohawk College (Undergraduate/Scholarship)

Purpose: To provide financial assistance to those students who are in need. **Focus:** Engineering; Environmental technology; Technology. **Qualif.:** Applicants must be 2nd year students in their final semester; must have been raised in Hamilton or graduated from Hamilton High School. **Criteria:** Applications will be considered based on their year's work in an internship for a Hamilton employer and a written essay on area of study and career goals.

Funds Avail.: No specific amount. **Number Awarded:** 1. **To Apply:** Applicants must check the available website for more information.

4692 ■ George and Mary Josephine Hamman Foundation
3336 Richmond, Ste. 310
Houston, TX 77098
Ph: (713)522-9891
Fax: (713)522-9693
E-mail: hammanfdn@aol.com
URL: hammanfoundation.org

4693 ■ George and Mary Josephine Hamman Foundation Scholarships (Undergraduate/Scholarship)

Purpose: To provide undergraduate scholarships for Houston area high school seniors. **Focus:** General studies/Field of study not specified. **Qualif.:** Applicants must be Houston area high school seniors who attend schools or are homeschooled in the following eight counties: Brazoria, Chambers, Fort Bend, Galveston, Harris, Liberty, Montgomery or Waller; must be US citizens. **Criteria:** Applicants are evaluated based on scholastic ability and financial need.

Funds Avail.: $18,000. **Duration:** Annual. **Number Awarded:** 70. **To Apply:** Applicants must write for the one-page scholarship application and the three-page financial qualification statement or it may be downloaded from the website. Completed scholarship applications must be submitted with these documents (in the following order): (1) Financial Qualification Statement, (2) complete, legible,

Awards are arranged alphabetically below their administering organizations

signed copy of parents'/guardians' and student's most recent federal income tax return (including all schedules) plus, if applicable, corporate or partnership returns, (3) proof of ACT and/or SAT results, and (4) high school transcript (unofficial is accepted). **Deadline:** February 19.

4694 ■ Hampton Roads Community Foundation

101 W Main St., Ste. 4500
Norfolk, VA 23510
Ph: (757)622-7951
Fax: (757)622-1751
URL: www.hamptonroadscf.org
Facebook: www.facebook.com/hamptonroadscf

4695 ■ Richard D. and Sheppard R. Cooke Memorial Scholarships *(Graduate/Scholarship)*

Purpose: To provide financial assistance to qualified individuals who want to pursue their educational goals. **Focus:** Religion. **Qualif.:** Applicants must be students at Union Theological Seminary in Richmond who are candidates for the ministry; must be enrolled in a degree program. **Criteria:** Selection of recipients will be based on financial need and the scholarship criteria. Preference will be given to students from the Norfolk churches within the Presbytery of Eastern Virginia.

Funds Avail.: No specific amount. **To Apply:** Applicants must complete the application form available from the website; provide a copy of transcripts, recommendation letter and statement of family income. **Deadline:** April 1.

4696 ■ Palmer Farley Memorial Scholarships *(Graduate/Scholarship)*

Purpose: To provide financial assistance to qualified individuals who want to pursue their educational goals. **Focus:** Communications. **Qualif.:** Applicants must be students pursuing the creative brand management track at the Virginia Commonwealth University Brandcenter. **Criteria:** Selection of recipients will be based on financial need and the scholarship criteria.

Funds Avail.: No specific amount. **Duration:** Renewable up to 2 years. **To Apply:** Applicants must complete the application form available from the website; provide a copy of their transcripts, recommendation letter and statement of family income. **Deadline:** May 1.

4697 ■ Victor and Ruth N. Goodman Memorial Scholarships *(Graduate/Scholarship)*

Purpose: To provide financial assistance to qualified individuals who want to pursue their educational goals. **Focus:** Education, Medical. **Qualif.:** Applicants must be students studying medicine or other health professions. **Criteria:** Selection of recipients will be based on financial need and the scholarship criteria.

Funds Avail.: No specific amount. **To Apply:** Applicants must complete the application form available from the website; provide a copy of their transcripts, recommendation letter and statement of family income.

4698 ■ Hampton Roads Association of Social Workers Scholarships *(Graduate/Scholarship)*

Purpose: To provide financial assistance to qualified individuals who want to pursue their educational goals. **Focus:** Social work. **Qualif.:** Applicants must be graduate students in social work; must be from Virginia. **Criteria:** Selection of recipients will be based on financial need and the scholarship criteria.

Funds Avail.: No specific amount. **To Apply:** Applicants must complete the application form available from the website; provide a copy of their transcripts, recommendation letter and statement of family income.

4699 ■ Hampton Roads Sanitation District Environmental Scholarships *(Graduate/Scholarship)*

Purpose: To provide financial assistance to qualified individuals who want to pursue their educational goals. **Focus:** Environmental technology. **Qualif.:** Applicants must be full-time graduate students from the Hampton Roads Sanitation District service area studying environmental health, environmental chemistry, biology or civil or environmental engineering at a public Virginia university. **Criteria:** Selection of recipients will be based on financial need and the scholarship criteria.

Funds Avail.: No specific amount. **To Apply:** Applicants must complete the application form available from the website; provide a copy of transcripts, recommendation letter and statement of family income. **Deadline:** March 1.

4700 ■ Louis I. Jaffe Memorial Scholarships-NSU Alumni *(Graduate/Scholarship)*

Purpose: To provide financial assistance to qualified individuals who want to pursue their educational goals. **Focus:** General studies/Field of study not specified. **Qualif.:** Applicants must be graduates of Norfolk State University who are enrolled in a graduate program at any institution; must be from anywhere in Virginia. **Criteria:** Selection of recipients will be based on financial need and the scholarship criteria. Priority will be given to applicants from Hampton Roads.

Funds Avail.: No specific amount. **To Apply:** Applicants must complete the application form available from the website; must provide a copy of transcripts, recommendation letter and statement of family income.

4701 ■ Louis I. Jaffe Memorial Scholarships-ODU *(Graduate/Scholarship)*

Purpose: To provide financial assistance to qualified individuals who want to pursue their educational goals. **Focus:** Art history; Humanities. **Qualif.:** Applicants must be students at Old Dominion University studying humanities or must be students at any other University studying art history. **Criteria:** Selection of recipients will be based on financial need and the scholarship criteria.

Funds Avail.: No specific amount. **To Apply:** Applicants must complete the application form available from the website; provide a copy of their transcripts, recommendation letter and statement of family income.

4702 ■ William F. Miles Scholarships *(Undergraduate/Scholarship)*

Purpose: To provide financial assistance to qualified individuals who want to pursue their educational goals. **Focus:** Religion. **Qualif.:** Applicants must be students preparing for leadership in the field of religious service. **Criteria:** Selection of recipients will be based on financial need and the scholarship criteria. Recipients are recommended by Westminster Chapter No. 99, Order of the Eastern Star.

Funds Avail.: No specific amount. **To Apply:** Applicants must complete the application form available from the website; provide a copy of their transcripts, recommendation letter and statement of family income. **Deadline:** April 1.

4703 ■ Ellis W. Rowe Scholarships (Undergraduate/Scholarship)

Purpose: To provide financial assistance to qualified individuals who want to pursue their educational goals. **Focus:** Agriculture, Economic aspects; Biology, Marine; Humanities; Nursing. **Qualif.:** Applicants must be students from Gloucester County; must be studying marine science, nursing, ministry, medicine, humanities, agriculture, biology or any other basic science. **Criteria:** Selection of recipients will be based on financial need and the scholarship criteria. Preference will be given to students from the York District attending Virginia Wesleyan College or another Methodist college.

Funds Avail.: No specific amount. **To Apply:** Applicants must complete the application form available from the website; provide a copy of their transcripts, recommendation letter and statement of family income.

4704 ■ Hy Smith Endowment Fund (Undergraduate/Scholarship)

Purpose: To provide financial assistance to qualified individuals who want to pursue their educational goals. **Focus:** Religion. **Qualif.:** Applicants must be students at Virginia Theological Seminary in Alexandria who are candidates for the ministry; must be residents of the geographic region served by the Diocese of Southern Virginia. **Criteria:** Selection on applicants will be based on financial need and the scholarship criteria. Recipients are recommended by the Eastern Star Training Awards Committee for Religious Leadership of Westminster Chapter No. 99.

Funds Avail.: No specific amount. **To Apply:** Applicants must complete the application form available from the website; provide a copy of the transcripts, recommendation letter and statement of family income. **Deadline:** April 1.

4705 ■ Florence L. Smith Medical Scholarships (Graduate/Scholarship)

Purpose: To provide financial assistance to qualified individuals who want to pursue their educational goals. **Focus:** Education, Medical. **Qualif.:** Applicants must be Virginia residents attending Eastern Virginia Medical School, University of Virginia School of Medicine or Virginia Commonwealth University School of Medicine. **Criteria:** Selection of recipients will be based on financial need and the scholarship criteria.

Funds Avail.: No specific amount. **To Apply:** Applicants must complete the application form available from the website; provide a copy of transcripts from their postsecondary education; and attach a statement of financial need.

4706 ■ Enid W. and Bernard B. Spigel Architectural Scholarships (Graduate, Undergraduate/Scholarship)

Purpose: To provide financial assistance to qualified individuals who want to pursue their educational goals. **Focus:** Landscape architecture and design. **Qualif.:** Applicants must be Virginia residents who are junior, senior or graduate students in architecture, architectural history or architectural preservation. **Criteria:** Selection of recipients will be based on financial need and the scholarship criteria. Preference will be given to students from the York District attending Virginia Wesleyan College or another Methodist college.

Funds Avail.: No specific amount. **To Apply:** Applicants must complete the application form available from the website; provide a copy of their transcripts, recommendation letter and statement of family income.

4707 ■ Handweavers Guild of America (HGA)
1255 Buford Hwy., Ste. 211
Suwanee, GA 30024-8421
Ph: (678)730-0010
Fax: (678)730-0836
E-mail: hga@weavespindye.org
URL: www.weavespindye.org

4708 ■ Convergence Assistantship Grants (Undergraduate/Grant)

Purpose: To provide opportunity to students to assist internationally known instructors and to participate in the Convergence experience. **Focus:** Art. **Qualif.:** Applicant must be currently enrolled in an accredited academic program and available to attend a Training Class Saturday at the Convention Center. **Criteria:** Selection will be based on the submitted application materials.

Funds Avail.: Varies. **To Apply:** Awardee must submit a Letter of Nomination from the Professor; must provide the Convergence complete registration form and personal statement. **Deadline:** April 1.

4709 ■ Mearl K. Gable II Memorial Grants (Other/Grant)

Purpose: To provide educational opportunities to members for study in non-accredited programs for any skill level. **Focus:** Art. **Qualif.:** Recipients must be HGA members. **Criteria:** Selection will be based on the submitted application.

Funds Avail.: $100. **Duration:** One year. **To Apply:** Application form must be printed and must have the following: Name of school or provider of instruction, title and short description of course (attach brochure). Applicants must provide a resume of the background, current activities, and future goals in the fiber field. **Deadline:** March 1. **Remarks:** Established in 2000.

4710 ■ Handweavers Guild of America and Dendel Scholarships (Graduate, Undergraduate/Scholarship)

Purpose: To further the education in the field of fiber arts, including training for research, textile history and conservation. **Focus:** Art. **Qualif.:** Applicants must be enrolled at accredited undergraduate or graduate programs in the United States and Canada. **Criteria:** Recipients will be selected based on artistic and technical merit rather than financial needs.

Funds Avail.: $4,000. **Duration:** One year. **To Apply:** Application forms are available on the website. Applicants must have the following: Transcript (a copy of the transcript must accompany the application); maximum of 16 slides or digital images; and an image description sheet. Applicants must provide a self-addressed, stamped envelope suitable for the return of slides or CD. **Deadline:** March 15. **Contact:** Application and other required materials must be sent to HGA Scholarship Chair at the above address.

4711 ■ Silvio and Eugenia Petrini Grants (Other/Grant)

Purpose: To provide educational opportunities to members for study in non-accredited programs for any skill level.

Awards are arranged alphabetically below their administering organizations

Focus: Art. **Qualif.:** Recipients must be HGA members. **Criteria:** Selection of applicants will be based on application materials.

Funds Avail.: $300. **Duration:** One year. **To Apply:** Application forms are available on the website. **Deadline:** March 1. **Remarks:** Established in 1994.

4712 ■ The Haraldson Foundation
25025 I-45 N, Ste. 410
The Woodlands, TX 77380
Ph: (281)362-9909
URL: www.haraldsonfoundation.org

4713 ■ Haraldson Foundation Scholarships
(Undergraduate, Graduate/Scholarship)

Purpose: To assist University of Texas-bound high school seniors who have high SAT or ACT scores. **Focus:** General studies/Field of study not specified. **Qualif.:** Applicants must be high school seniors planning to attend the University of Texas, or currently enrolled in a University of Texas undergraduate or graduate program; have volunteered in community service activities; demonstrated academic excellence, leadership and character; and have financial need. Students must maintain a 3.0 GPA each semester and must complete at least 12 hours of course work each semester. **Criteria:** Selection shall be based on the aforementioned applicants' qualifications and compliance with the application details.

Funds Avail.: No specific amount. **Duration:** Annual. **Number Awarded:** Varies. **To Apply:** Applicants must submit a completed application form along with three letters of recommendation (at least one from a Math or English teacher); Official high school transcript; one page essay on chosen career and goals; 500-word essay on "How I Will Personally Contribute to Meeting Society's Future Challenges"; and a completed Financial Information. **Remarks:** Established in 1992. **Contact:** The Haroldson Foundation, at the above address.

4714 ■ Harbor Breeze Corp.
100 Aquarium Way, Dock No. 2
Long Beach, CA 90802
Ph: (562)432-4900
E-mail: harborbreezecruises@gmail.com
URL: 2seewhales.com

4715 ■ Captain James H. Peterson Memorial Scholarships *(Undergraduate/Scholarship)*

Purpose: To assist deserving students in their future endeavors. **Focus:** General studies/Field of study not specified. **Qualif.:** Applicants must be American citizens, permanent residents, or hold a valid student visa; must have plans to be enrolled as college/university students within the United States; must have a cumulative GPA of at least 3.0. **Criteria:** Selection will be based on the submitted essay.

Funds Avail.: $2,500. **Duration:** Annual. **To Apply:** Applicants must submit an original essay that answers the following questions: How do you foresee social media and advertising evolving in the future? What will the next generations of customers expect? How can Harbor Breeze Cruises, as a whale watch operations, engage these customers going into the future? How can Harbor Breeze Cruises stand out from the competition going forward in the future?; must also submit a letter of recommendation and their photo online. **Deadline:** April 30.

4716 ■ Hardanger Fiddle Association of America (HFAA)
PO Box 23046
Minneapolis, MN 55423-0046
Ph: (612)568-7448
E-mail: info@hfaa.org
URL: www.hfaa.org

4717 ■ Bernt Balchen, Jr. and Olav Jorgen Hegge Hardingfele Scholarships *(Other/Scholarship)*

Purpose: To provide support students who are intending to attend the HFAA Annual Workshops. **Focus:** Music. **Qualif.:** Applicants must have an experience in playing a string instrument in either classical or folk tradition. **Criteria:** Scholarship will be given to the applicants who best meet the requirements.

Funds Avail.: No specific amount. **Duration:** Annual. **To Apply:** Applicants must submit a completed application form (available at the website www.hfaa.org); a personal statement; a letter of reference from a person not related to the applicant, preferably an instructor or a fellow musician; three copies of a 3-5 minute cassette tape or CD recording of the applicant's string instrument playing ability in classical or folk tradition. **Deadline:** April 15.

4718 ■ Hardy Wolf & Downing Injury Lawyers
477 Congress St., 5th Flr.
Portland, ME 04101
Ph: (207)878-0000
URL: hardywolf.com

4719 ■ Hardy, Wolf & Downing Scholarships
(Undergraduate, Graduate/Scholarship)

Purpose: To provide financial assistance to students who want to pursue their dreams in legal profession. **Focus:** Law enforcement. **Qualif.:** Applicants must be one of the following: high school students who plan to attend an accredited U.S. college; college students attending an accredited U.S. College; or law students currently accepted or enrolled in an ABA-accredited law school. Applicants must either be active, retired or immediate family relatives of such members of any branch of U.S. military or any branch of law enforcement. **Criteria:** Selection will be based on the strength of the applicants' essays.

Funds Avail.: $100-$2,500. **Number Awarded:** 13. **To Apply:** Applicants must write an essay on the following topics: for members and family members of U.S. military - "what is/are the greatest challenge(s) facing veterans when they return home from serving their country?"; for members of law enforcement and family members of law enforcement workers - "what is/are the greatest challenge(s) facing law enforcement personnel today?". Essays must be 1500-2000 words in length; applications must be submitted via email; all materials must be submitted in Word of PDF format; applicants must provide their full name and all current contact information including mailing address, email address and phone number and must complete and sign the attached PDF application form and submit with other required materials (proof of attendance or acceptance at school, proof of minimum 3.0 GPA from the school of the applicants currently attend or most recently attended, and

Awards are arranged alphabetically below their administering organizations

proof of personal affiliation or family affiliation with any branch of the U.S. military or law enforcement agency). **Deadline:** June 30.

4720 ■ Bryce Harlow Foundation
1700 New York Ave. NW, Ste. 400
Washington, DC 20006
Ph: (202)654-7812
E-mail: info@bryceharlow.org
URL: www.bryceharlow.org

4721 ■ Bryce Harlow Fellowship Program *(Graduate/Fellowship)*

Purpose: To provide financial assistance to students who are pursuing a career in professional advocacy through public affairs, government relations or lobbying. **Focus:** Government; Public affairs. **Qualif.:** Applicants must be students who have been accepted for admission to a graduate program in certain universities (check website for list of universities); planning to enroll in part-time graduate studies for credit at the participating university for at least two semesters of the next academic year; demonstrate an interest and strong ability for a career in public affairs, government relations or lobbying; and U.S. citizens. **Criteria:** The Bryce Harlow Foundation Fellowship Committee will review and select finalists from all of the application. Applicants are evaluated based on demonstrated strong interest in public affairs, government relations or lobbying; professional achievement and leadership potential; academic achievement and potential; and financial need.

Funds Avail.: $8,000. **To Apply:** Applicants must download and complete the application and written statements (250 words each) discussing details about career interests, leadership abilities, financial need and advocacy with integrity. Submit it along with two letters of recommendation from persons familiar with the applicants; brief resume; and official transcripts from all undergraduate universities. **Deadline:** April 29. **Remarks:** Established in 1985.

4722 ■ Harness Horse Youth Foundation (HHYF)
16575 Carey Rd.
Westfield, IN 46074-8925
Ph: (317)867-5877
Fax: (317)867-1886
URL: www.hhyf.org
Facebook: www.facebook.com/Harness-Horse-Youth-Foundation-160769000644309

4723 ■ Charles Bradley Memorial Scholarships *(Undergraduate/Scholarship)*

Purpose: To provide financial assistance to the children or relatives of racing officials who were members of the North American Judges and Stewards and licensed pari-mutuel officials. **Focus:** General studies/Field of study not specified. **Qualif.:** Applicants must be at least in high school and children or relatives of racing officials who were members of the North American Judges and Stewards Association and/or licensed USTA pari-mutuel officials in the following categories: presiding judges, associate judges, paddock judges and starters. **Criteria:** Candidates will be assessed based on scholastic achievement, grade point average, financial need, completeness of application and quality of essay.

Funds Avail.: No amount mentioned. **To Apply:** Applicants must complete and submit application form; must attach (1,000 words) typewritten statement including background, career goals and experiences; a copy of the latest transcript; two letters of recommendation. **Deadline:** April 30. **Contact:** ellen@hhyf.org.

4724 ■ Gallo Blue Chip Scholarships *(Undergraduate/Scholarship)*

Purpose: To support the continuing education of the children of harness racing families in New York, New Jersey and Pennsylvania. **Focus:** General studies/Field of study not specified. **Qualif.:** Applicants must be child of harness horse trainer or caretaker licensed in New York, New Jersey; must have been raised and/or reside in the three-state region; must be at least high school seniors; must be (plan to be) enrolled as full-time students (minimum 12 credit hours). **Criteria:** Applicants will be evaluated based on demonstrated scholastic achievement, including but not limited to their GPA, financial need and quality of essay.

Funds Avail.: $15,000. **Duration:** Annual. **To Apply:** Applicants must submit a completed application form and must attach the following required materials: (1) a copy of transcripts; (2) parent's current racing commission license; (3) resume; and (4) 1,000-word essay explaining the accomplishments, plans or career goals and relationship to New York and New Jersey region. **Deadline:** April 30.

4725 ■ Curt Greene Memorial Scholarships *(Undergraduate/Scholarship)*

Purpose: To provide financial support for senior high school students who may or may not be pursuing harness racing but demonstrates passion for the sport. **Focus:** General studies/Field of study not specified. **Qualif.:** Applicant must be at least a high school senior. **Criteria:** Candidates will be assessed based on scholastic achievement, grade point average, financial need, completeness of application and quality of essay.

Funds Avail.: $2500. **To Apply:** Applicants must complete and submit application form. **Deadline:** April 30. **Contact:** ellen@hhyf.org.

4726 ■ Harness Tracks of America (HTA)
12025 E Dry Gulch Pl.
Tucson, AZ 85749-9727
Ph: (520)529-2525
Fax: (520)529-3235
E-mail: info@harnesstracks.com
URL: www.harnesstracks.com

4727 ■ Harness Tracks of America Scholarship Fund *(Undergraduate/Scholarship)*

Purpose: To provide financial assistance to students for post-secondary education. **Focus:** General studies/Field of study not specified. **Qualif.:** Applicants must be sons or daughters of licensed drivers, trainers, caretakers, management or young people actively engaged in the harness racing industry. **Criteria:** Recipients will be selected based on his or her academic merit, financial need and active harness racing involvement.

Funds Avail.: $5,000. **Duration:** Annual. **Number Awarded:** 3. **To Apply:** Applicants must submit completed application form together with essays; official academic transcripts; federal tax forms; student aid report; fee rates schedule; and any other supporting documents. Letters of recommendation are not required but may be included.

Awards are arranged alphabetically below their administering organizations

Deadline: June 17. **Contact:** Delight Craddock:(520) 529-2525; delight@harnesstracks.com.

4728 ■ Harris Corp.
1025 W NASA Blvd.
Melbourne, FL 32919-0001
Ph: (321)727-9100
Fax: (321)674-4740
Free: 800-442-7747
URL: www.harris.com

4729 ■ National Merit Harris Corporation Scholarship Program *(Undergraduate/Scholarship)*

Purpose: To financially assist high school students. **Focus:** General studies/Field of study not specified. **Qualif.:** Applicants must be high school students who are children of Harris Corporation current employees; must be U.S. citizens or have applied for permanent residence. Applicants who do not take the PSAT/NMSQT because of illness, emergency or other circumstance but meet all the requirements will be accepted. **Criteria:** Applicants will be judged based on PSAT/NMSQT scores; academic records; activities and contributions to school and community; recommendation letter; and essay about characteristics, plans, and goals.

Funds Avail.: $2,000 per year. **Duration:** Annual; 4 years. **Number Awarded:** 2. **To Apply:** Applicants must obtain a copy of PSAT/NMSQT Official Student Guide and take the qualifying exam. **Deadline:** March 1.

4730 ■ Harris Personal Injury Lawyers, Inc.
301 Mission Ave., Ste. 203
Oceanside, CA 92054
Ph: (760)231-9970
Fax: (760)231-9919
URL: harrispersonalinjury.com

4731 ■ Injury Scholarships *(Undergraduate/Scholarship)*

Purpose: To provide financial assistance to students who have suffered a serious injury. **Focus:** General studies/Field of study not specified. **Qualif.:** Applicants must be college students who have suffered a serious injury and have committed to demonstrating a determination to rebuild his/her life by attending college. **Criteria:** Selection will be based on the committee's criteria.

Funds Avail.: $1,000. **To Apply:** Applicants must submit a letter about his/her injury experience. **Deadline:** May 31.

4732 ■ Harry Hampton Memorial Wildlife, Inc.
P.O. Box 2641
Columbia, SC 29202
Ph: (803)600-1570
URL: www.hamptonwildlifefund.org

4733 ■ Harry Hampton Fund Scholarship *(Undergraduate/Scholarship)*

Purpose: To support excellent students in pursuing and promoting higher education in the natural resources area in South Carolina. **Focus:** Biology; Environmental science; Fisheries sciences/management; Forestry; Wildlife conservation, management, and science; Zoology. **Qualif.:** Applicants must be full-time residents of South Carolina; must be seniors in public or private high school in South Carolina; must attend an institution of higher learning in South Carolina; must have a major in natural resources discipline such as wildlife biology, fisheries biology, forestry, marine science or environmental science; must maintain a GPR of 2.5 or above. **Criteria:** Selection criteria will be determined by the board of directors of the Harry Hampton Wildlife Fund.

Funds Avail.: $2,500. **Duration:** Annual. **Number Awarded:** 1. **To Apply:** Applications are available on the website and must be submitted on or before the due date along with applicants' essay and autobiography, transcript of high school grades, college board scores, rank in high school class and a recent photograph. **Deadline:** January 31. **Remarks:** Established in 1992. **Contact:** Hampton Fund Scholarships, at the above address or via email at jim.goller@hamptonwildlifefund.org.

4734 ■ Hartford Foundation for Public Giving
10 Columbus Blvd., 8th Fl.
Hartford, CT 06106-1976
Ph: (860)548-1888
Fax: (860)249-3561
E-mail: hfpg@hfpg.org
URL: www.hfpg.org
Facebook: www.facebook.com/HartfordFoundation
Twitter: twitter.com/HartfordFdn

4735 ■ Frederick G. Adams Scholarships *(Undergraduate/Scholarship)*

Purpose: To provide scholarship for graduating high school seniors of Greater Hartford area. **Focus:** General studies/Field of study not specified. **Qualif.:** Applicants must be graduating seniors who live in or are attending school in Greater Hartford; must be entering a four-year college or university (full-time enrollment); must have a financial need; must be on a top third of the class or a good academic record; and must be active volunteer in school, community, or other extracurricular activities. **Criteria:** Selection will be based on the committee's criteria.

Funds Avail.: $3,000. **To Apply:** Applicants must download and fill out the online application and attach the following requirements: letter of recommendation from your guidance counselor or a teacher; official high school transcript, including SAT or ACT scores; copy of the essay you submitted with your college application (if you did not have to submit one, write a brief essay, no more than 2 pages, regarding your future goals); copy of pages 1 and 2 of your parents' or guardians' most recent completed federal tax form 1040; and mail everything to Hartford Foundation College Scholarship Program. **Deadline:** February 1.

4736 ■ Alliance Francaise of Hartford Harpin/Rohinsky Scholarships *(Undergraduate/Scholarship)*

Purpose: To provide educational assistance for graduating high school seniors who live in or are attending school in Greater Hartford. **Focus:** French studies. **Qualif.:** Applicants must be entering a four-year college or university (full-time enrollment); must pursue French studies in college; must have a financial need; must rank top third of their class; and must be active volunteers in school, community, or other extracurricular activities. **Criteria:** Selection will be based on the committee's criteria.

Funds Avail.: $3,000. **Number Awarded:** 1. **To Apply:**

Awards are arranged alphabetically below their administering organizations

Applicants must download and fill out the online application and attach the following requirements: letter of recommendation from your guidance counselor or a from your teacher; official high school transcript, including SAT or ACT scores; copy of the essay you submitted with your college application (if you did not have to submit one, write a brief essay (no more than 2 pages) regarding your future goals); copy of pages 1 and 2 of your parents' most recent completed federal tax form 1040; and mail everything to Hartford Foundation College Scholarship Program. **Deadline:** February 1.

4737 ■ Officer Brian A. Aselton Memorial Scholarships *(Undergraduate/Scholarship)*

Purpose: To provide educational assistance for students entering or enrolled as undergraduate students at Manchester Community College. **Focus:** Criminal justice. **Qualif.:** Applicants must be Connecticut residents, majoring in Criminal Justice and planning a career in law enforcement. **Criteria:** Selection will be based on the committee's criteria.

Funds Avail.: $500-$1,000. **To Apply:** Applicants may obtain the application materials from the Manchester Community College. **Deadline:** March 1.

4738 ■ John Bell and Lawrence Thornton Scholarship Fund *(Undergraduate/Scholarship)*

Purpose: To provide educational assistance for students presently enrolled at Hampton University. **Focus:** General studies/Field of study not specified. **Qualif.:** Applicant must be a Greater Hartford resident; must demonstrate academic excellence, financial need, extracurricular activities and community service; must have a GPA of 3.0 and above; and must be rising sophomore and rising junior status. **Criteria:** Selection will be based on the committee's criteria.

Funds Avail.: No specific amount. **To Apply:** Applicants may obtain application materials from Connecticut River Valley Chapter National Hampton University Alumni Association, Inc. Scholarship Committee. **Deadline:** March 25. **Contact:** Sarah Carlson at scarlson@hfpg.org; Scholarship Committee, PO Box 2734 Hartford, CT 06146-2734.

4739 ■ Lebbeus F. Bissell Scholarships *(Undergraduate/Scholarship)*

Purpose: To provide educational assistance to graduating high school seniors of Rockville, Vernon or Ellington High Schools. **Focus:** General studies/Field of study not specified. **Qualif.:** Applicants must demonstrate academic excellence, financial need, extracurricular activities and community service. **Criteria:** Selection will be based on the committee's criteria.

Funds Avail.: $4,000. **Number Awarded:** 3. **To Apply:** Applicants may obtain application materials from Guidance Departments of Rockville, Tolland or Ellington High Schools or from Lebbeus F. Bissel Scholarship Advisory Committee. **Deadline:** March 25. **Contact:** Sarah Carlson at scarlson@hfpg.org.

4740 ■ Maria Gonzales Borrero Scholarships *(Undergraduate/Scholarship)*

Purpose: To provide funds for the education of Hispanic descent graduating students from City high schools who are preparing for a career in a health related field. **Focus:** Health care services. **Qualif.:** Applicants must be entering a four-year college or university (full-time enrollment) pursuing a health-related field; must demonstrate financial need; must be top third with good academic record; and must be active volunteers in school, community, or other extracurricular activities. **Criteria:** Selection will be based on the committee's criteria.

Funds Avail.: $3,000. **To Apply:** Application form can be downloaded online. Applicants must complete the scholarship application. Applicants must also attach the following requirements: letter of recommendation from your guidance counselor or a teacher; official high school transcript (including SAT or ACT scores); copy of the essay you submitted with your college application (If you did not have to submit one, write a brief (no more than two pages) essay regarding your future goals); and copy of pages 1 and 2 of your parents' or guardians' most recent completed federal tax form 1040. Mail everything to Hartford Foundation College Scholarship Program. **Deadline:** February 1.

4741 ■ W. Philip Braender and Nancy Coleman Braender Scholarships *(Undergraduate/Scholarship)*

Purpose: To provide financial assistance to those students who are in need. **Focus:** General studies/Field of study not specified. **Qualif.:** Applicants must be entering a four-year college or university (full-time enrollment); must demonstrate financial need; must be in the top third with good academic record; and must be active volunteer in school, community, or other extracurricular activities. **Criteria:** Selection will be based on the committee's criteria.

Funds Avail.: $3,000. **To Apply:** Application form can be downloaded on-line. Applicants must complete the scholarship application. Applicants must also attach the following requirements: letter of recommendation from your guidance counselor or a teacher; official high school transcript. Including SAT or ACT scores; copy of the essay you submitted with your college application. If you did not have to submit one, write a brief (no more than two pages) essay regarding your future goals; copy of pages 1 and 2 of your parents' or guardians' most recent completed federal tax form 1040. Mail everything to Hartford Foundation College Scholarship Program. **Deadline:** February 1.

4742 ■ Rhea Sourifman Caplin Memorial Scholarships *(Undergraduate/Scholarship)*

Purpose: To provide scholarship to the Jewish high school senior or college students. **Focus:** Health care services; Nursing. **Qualif.:** Applicants must: be Greater Hartford residents; be pursuing nursing or health care profession; have a minimum B average in sciences; have a good citizenship and active involvement in the community. **Criteria:** Selection will be based on the committee's criteria.

Funds Avail.: $1,000-$2,000. **Number Awarded:** 1-2. **To Apply:** Applicants may obtain application materials from Jewish Community Foundation of Greater Hartford's website at http://www.jchartford.org/scholarships. **Deadline:** April 15. **Contact:** Jewish Community Foundation of Greater Hartford, 333 Bloomfield Ave. Ste. D West Hartford, CT 06117; Phone: 860-523-7460; Fax: 860-231-0576; Email: grants@jchartford.org.

4743 ■ The College Club of Hartford Scholarships *(Undergraduate/Scholarship)*

Purpose: To provide scholarship for graduating high school students. **Focus:** General studies/Field of study not specified. **Qualif.:** Applicants must be graduating public high school seniors residing in Avon, Bloomfield, Canton, East Hartford, Farmington, Glastonbury, Hartford, Manchester, Newington, Rocky Hill, Simsbury, West Hartford, Wethersfield or Windsor; must be attending in an accredited two or four-year school; must demonstrate financial need and

Awards are arranged alphabetically below their administering organizations

community service; must be on a class rank upper 10% (Applicant's grades through 2nd quarter of senior year are required); and must be students who attend Trinity College or St. Joseph College in Connecticut. **Criteria:** Selection will be based on the committee's criteria.

Funds Avail.: $1,500. **To Apply:** Interested applicants may visit the website at http://www.collegeclubofhartford.org/scholarships to obtain an application. **Deadline:** March 25. **Contact:** Patricia Kane, Chairperson, The College Club of Hartford, 222 North Hollow Road, East hartland, CT 06027.

4744 ■ Connecticut Association of Latinos in Higher Education Scholarships *(Undergraduate/Scholarship)*

Purpose: To award scholarship to the students entering or enrolled as undergraduates in an accredited college or university. **Focus:** General studies/Field of study not specified. **Qualif.:** Applicants must be residents of Connecticut; must be of Latino background; must have financial need and community service; and must have an academic excellence ("B" average). **Criteria:** Selection will be based on the committee's criteria.

Funds Avail.: $1,000. **Number Awarded:** 15. **To Apply:** Students may log on to www.calahe.org to obtain an application. **Deadline:** April 15. **Contact:** Application form and supporting documents must be submitted to: CALAHE Scholarship Chair c/o Office of Dean of Students, Dr. Wilson Luna, Gateway Community College, 60 Sergent Dr., New Haven, CT 06511; Phone: 203-285-2210; Fax: 203-285-2211; E-mail: wilsonluna@aol.com.

4745 ■ Connecticut Mortgage Bankers Social Affairs Committee Scholarships *(Undergraduate/Scholarship)*

Purpose: To provide scholarship assistance to Connecticut high school graduates who are pursuing undergraduate studies in business, finance and/ or real estate. **Focus:** Business; Real estate. **Qualif.:** Applicants must be entering a four-year college or university (full-time enrollment) pursuing a career in business, mortgage or real estate; must have a financial need; must be on a class rank - top third with good academic record; and must be active volunteers in school, community, or other extracurricular activities. **Criteria:** Selection will be based on the committee's criteria.

Funds Avail.: $3,000. **To Apply:** Application form can be downloaded on-line. Applicants must complete the scholarship application. Applicants must also attach the following requirements: letter of recommendation from your guidance counselor or a teacher; official high school transcript. Including SAT or ACT scores; copy of the essay you submitted with your college application. If you did not have to submit one, write a brief (no more than two pages) essay regarding your future goals; copy of pages 1 and 2 of your parents' most recent completed federal tax form 1040. Mail everything to Hartford Foundation College Scholarship Program. **Deadline:** February 1.

4746 ■ Brian Cummins Memorial Scholarships *(Undergraduate/Scholarship)*

Purpose: To provide scholarship for college junior or senior or graduate students enrolled in a full-time program to teach blind and visually impaired students in Connecticut. **Focus:** General studies/Field of study not specified. **Qualif.:** Applicants must demonstrate financial need, community service, and academic excellence. **Criteria:** Selection will be based on the committee's criteria.

Funds Avail.: $5,000. **Number Awarded:** 1. **To Apply:** Application can be obtain at the National Federation of the Blind CT's website. **Deadline:** October 15. **Contact:** National Federation of the Blind of Connecticut, Phone: 860-298-1971; Fax: 860-291-2795; info@nfbct.org.

4747 ■ C. Rodney Demarest Memorial Scholarships *(Undergraduate/Scholarship)*

Purpose: To provide scholarship for students who are legally blind. **Focus:** General studies/Field of study not specified. **Qualif.:** Applicants must be graduating high school seniors or college students residing or attending school full-time in Connecticut; must be legally blind; must demonstrate financial need, community service and academic excellence. **Criteria:** Selection will be based on the committee's criteria.

Funds Avail.: $3,000. **Number Awarded:** 1. **To Apply:** Applicants may obtain application materials from National Federation of the Blind of CT. **Deadline:** September 15. **Contact:** National Federation of the Blind of CT, 477 Connecticut Blvd., Ste. 217 E, Hartford, CT 06108; Phone: 860-289-1971; E-mail: info@nfbct.org or may log on to www.nfbct.org.

4748 ■ Albert and Jane Dewey Scholarships *(Undergraduate/Scholarship)*

Purpose: To provide financial assistance to those students who are attending Trinity College. **Focus:** General studies/Field of study not specified. **Qualif.:** Applicants must be residents of Manchester who demonstrate financial need. Preference will be given to minority students. **Criteria:** Selection will be based on the committee's criteria.

Funds Avail.: $1,000-$4,000. **To Apply:** Application form can be downloaded on-line. Applicants must complete the scholarship application. Applicants must also attach the following requirements: letter of recommendation from your guidance counselor or a teacher; official high school transcript. Including SAT or ACT scores; copy of the essay you submitted with your college application. If you did not have to submit one, write a brief (no more than two pages) essay regarding your future goals; copy of pages 1 and 2 of your parents' or guardians' most recent completed federal tax form 1040. Mail everything to Hartford Foundation College Scholarship Program. **Deadline:** May 1. **Contact:** Molly Devanney, Scholarship Chair, at 860-783-5823 or molly@highlandparkmarket.com.

4749 ■ Harry A. Donn Scholarships *(Undergraduate/Scholarship)*

Purpose: To support students from the Greater Hartford region who are pursuing four-year college degrees. **Focus:** General studies/Field of study not specified. **Qualif.:** Applicants must: be entering a four-year college or university (full-time enrollment); demonstrate financial need; be on a class rank - top third with good academic record; be active volunteer in school, community, or other extracurricular activities. **Criteria:** Selection will be based on the committee's criteria.

Funds Avail.: $3,000. **Number Awarded:** 1. **To Apply:** Application form can be downloaded online. Applicants must complete the scholarship application. Applicants must also attach the following requirements: letter of recommendation from your guidance counselor or a teacher; official high school transcript. Including SAT or ACT scores; copy of the essay you submitted with your college application. If you did not have to submit one, write a brief (no more than two pages) essay regarding your future goals;

Awards are arranged alphabetically below their administering organizations

copy of pages 1 and 2 of your parents' most recent completed federal tax form 1040. Mail everything to Hartford Foundation College Scholarship Program. **Deadline:** February 1.

4750 ■ Charles Dubose Scholarships
(Undergraduate/Scholarship)

Purpose: To provide scholarship to the students attending five-year accredited colleges or universities offering Architecture. **Focus:** Architecture. **Qualif.:** Applicants must: completed a two years of Bachelor in Architecture Program; be a Connecticut connection; demonstrated financial need and academic excellence. **Criteria:** Selection will be based on the committee's criteria.

Funds Avail.: $1,200-$5,000. **Number Awarded:** 1-2. **To Apply:** Applicants may obtain application materials from the Connecticut Architecture Foundation's website at www.aiact.org. **Deadline:** April 20. **Contact:** Diana Harp Jones, Connecticut Architecture Foundation, 370 James St. Ste. 402, New Haven, CT 06513. Phone: 203-865-2195; Fax: 203-562-5378.

4751 ■ Farmington UNICO Scholarships
(Undergraduate/Scholarship)

Purpose: To provide financial assistance to Farmington students or adjacent communities who are members of UNICO. **Focus:** General studies/Field of study not specified. **Qualif.:** Applicants must: be a Farmington or West Hartford resident; be a graduating high school senior; demonstrated financial need and academic excellence. **Criteria:** Selection will be based on the committee's criteria.

Funds Avail.: $2,000. **To Apply:** Application form can be downloaded on-line. Applicants must complete the scholarship application. Applicants must also attach the following requirements: letter of recommendation from your guidance counselor or a teacher; official high school transcript. Including SAT or ACT scores; copy of the essay you submitted with your college application. If you did not have to submit one, write a brief (no more than two pages) essay regarding your future goals; copy of pages 1 and 2 of your parents' or guardians' most recent completed federal tax form 1040. Mail everything to Hartford Foundation College Scholarship Program. **Deadline:** March 16. **Contact:** James F. Kane, Scholarship Chairman; Phone: 860-224-6999; Fax: 860-826-1897; Email: jkane@jkanelaw.com.

4752 ■ Symee Ruth Feinberg Memorial Scholarships
(Undergraduate/Scholarship)

Purpose: To provide scholarship to needy Hartford residents under age 22 who are seeking careers in human services and have experience helping others. **Focus:** General studies/Field of study not specified. **Qualif.:** Applicants must: be entering a four-year college or university; pursuing a career in human services; be in a class rank- top third with good academic record; be an active volunteer in school, community, or other extracurricular activities. **Criteria:** Selection will be based on the committee's criteria.

Funds Avail.: $3,000. **To Apply:** Application form can be downloaded online. Applicants must complete the scholarship application. Applicants must also attach the following requirements: letter of recommendation from your guidance counselor or a teacher; official high school transcript. Including SAT or ACT scores; copy of the essay you submitted with your college application. If you did not have to submit one, write a brief (no more than two pages) essay regarding your future goals; copy of pages 1 and 2 of your parents' or guardians' most recent completed federal tax form 1040. Mail everything to Hartford Foundation College Scholarship Program. **Deadline:** February 1.

4753 ■ James L. and Genevieve H. Goodwin Scholarships
(Undergraduate/Scholarship)

Purpose: To provide financial assistance to those students who are in need. **Focus:** Forestry. **Qualif.:** Applicants must be enrolled in an undergraduate or graduate curriculum in silviculture or forest resource management; and must be a Connecticut resident. **Criteria:** Selection will be based on the committee's criteria.

Funds Avail.: $1,000-$5,000. **Number Awarded:** 1-10. **To Apply:** Applicants may complete the General Scholarship Application and include a personal statement indicating why you are interested in Forest Management and submit to Connecticut forest and Park Association, Inc. **Deadline:** March 20. **Contact:** Eric Hammerling, Executive Director; Phone: 860-346-2372; Fax: 860-347-7463; Email: info@ctwoodlands.org.

4754 ■ William G. and Mayme J. Green Scholarships
(Undergraduate/Scholarship)

Purpose: To award scholarship to a graduating high school senior from Newington or Hartford Public High School. **Focus:** Nursing. **Qualif.:** Applicants must: be entering a four-year college or university (full-time enrollment) pursuing a degree in Nursing; must demonstrate financial need; be on the class rank - top third with a good academic record; be an active volunteer in school, community, or other extracurricular activities. **Criteria:** Selection will be based on the committee's criteria.

Funds Avail.: $2,500. **Number Awarded:** 1. **To Apply:** Application form can be downloaded online. Applicants must complete the scholarship application. Applicants must also attach the following requirements: letter of recommendation from your guidance counselor or a teacher; official high school transcript. Including SAT or ACT scores; copy of the essay you submitted with your college application. If you did not have to submit one, write a brief (no more than two pages) essay regarding your future goals; copy of pages 1 and 2 of your parents' most recent completed federal tax form 1040. Mail everything to Hartford Foundation College Scholarship Program. **Deadline:** February 13. **Contact:** Hartford Foundation College Scholarship Program, Scholarship Management Services, Scholarship America, One Scholarship Way, PO Box 297, St. Peter, MN 56082. 800-537-4180.

4755 ■ Ida L. Hartenberg Charitable Scholarships
(Undergraduate/Scholarship)

Purpose: To provide scholarship to the graduating high school senior who lives in or attends school in Greater Hartford. **Focus:** Teaching. **Qualif.:** Applicants must: be entering a four-year college or university (full-time enrollment); be pursuing a career in teaching; demonstrate financial need; be on a class rank - top third with good academic record; be an active volunteer in school, community, or other extracurricular activities. **Criteria:** Selection will be based on the committee's criteria.

Funds Avail.: $3,000. **Number Awarded:** 1. **To Apply:** Application form can be downloaded online. Applicants must complete the scholarship application. Applicants must also attach the following requirements: letter of recommendation from your guidance counselor or a teacher; official high school transcript. Including SAT or ACT scores; copy of the essay you submitted with your college application. If you did not have to submit one, write a brief (no

Awards are arranged alphabetically below their administering organizations

more than two pages) essay regarding your future goals; copy of pages 1 and 2 of your parents' or guardians' most recent completed federal tax form 1040. Mail everything to Hartford Foundation College Scholarship Program. **Deadline:** February 1.

4756 ■ Hartford Grammar School Scholarships
(Undergraduate/Scholarship)

Purpose: To award scholarship to a graduating high school senior from a public high school in the City of Hartford. **Focus:** General studies/Field of study not specified. **Qualif.:** Applicants must be entering a four-year college or university (full-time enrollment); demonstrate financial need; be on class rank with good academic record; be an active volunteer in school, community, or other extracurricular activities. **Criteria:** Selection will be based on the committee's criteria.

Funds Avail.: $3,000. **Number Awarded:** 1. **To Apply:** Application form can be downloaded on-line. Applicants must complete the scholarship application. Applicants must also attach the following requirements: letter of recommendation from your guidance counselor or a teacher; official high school transcript. Including SAT or ACT scores; copy of the essay you submitted with your college application. If you did not have to submit one, write a brief (no more than two pages) essay regarding your future goals; copy of pages 1 and 2 of your parents' or guardians' most recent completed federal tax form 1040. Mail everything to Hartford Foundation College Scholarship Program. **Deadline:** February 1.

4757 ■ Walter Doc Hurley Scholarship
(Undergraduate/Scholarship)

Purpose: To provide financial support to those students in need. **Focus:** General studies/Field of study not specified. **Qualif.:** Student must be entering college in the fall semester after graduation. Eligible school can be found on www.docscholar.org. Students demonstrate financial need, academic excellence and community service. **Criteria:** Selection will be based on the committee's criteria.

Funds Avail.: $3,000. **Number Awarded:** 1. **To Apply:** Applicants may obtain application materials from eligible high school guidance office. Applications will not be mailed to students. Valid applications must include: Student Air Report (SAR) from FAFSA showing Estimated Family Contribution (EFC); three letter of recommendation (teacher, guidance counselor, and non-educational person); typed essay (no more than 1 1/2 pages); High School Transcript; SAT or ACT scores. All materials must be submitted to Doc Hurley Scholarship Foundation, Inc. **Deadline:** February 1.

4758 ■ Interracial Scholarship Fund of Greater Hartford *(Undergraduate/Scholarship)*

Purpose: To provide scholarship awards to students from the Greater Hartford region who are pursuing a four-year college degree. **Focus:** General studies/Field of study not specified. **Qualif.:** Applicants must: be graduating high school senior who lives in or attends school in Greater Hartford; be on a class rank - top third with good academic record; be active volunteer in school, community, or other extracurricular activities; be involved in community service. **Criteria:** Selection will be based on the committee's criteria.

Funds Avail.: $3,000. **Number Awarded:** 1. **To Apply:** Application form can be downloaded online. Applicants must complete the scholarship application. Applicants must also attach the following requirements: letter of recommendation from your guidance counselor or a teacher; official high school transcript. Including SAT or ACT scores; copy of the essay you submitted with your college application. If you did not have to submit one, write a brief (no more than two pages) essay regarding your future goals; copy of pages 1 and 2 of your parents' most recent completed federal tax form 1040. Mail everything to Hartford Foundation College Scholarship Program. **Deadline:** February 1.

4759 ■ Walter Kapala Scholarships *(Undergraduate/Scholarship)*

Purpose: To support students who are in need of help with their college finances. **Focus:** General studies/Field of study not specified. **Qualif.:** Applicants must be entering a four-year college or university in the fall after high school graduation; demonstrate financial need and have an academic excellence. **Criteria:** Selection will be based on the committee's criteria.

Funds Avail.: $1,500. **Number Awarded:** 1. **To Apply:** Applicants must complete and submit the General Scholarship Application available at the website. **Deadline:** March 25. **Contact:** Sarah Carlson at scarlson@hfpg.org. Submit completed application to Merrill Lynch Trust Company, Walter Kapala Scholarship, Hopewell Charitable Trust Center, 1300 Merill Lynch Drive, Pennington, NJ 08534.

4760 ■ American Marketing Association-Connecticut Chapter, Anna C. Klune Memorial Scholarships *(Graduate/Scholarship)*

Purpose: To assist in the personal and professional career development of marketing professionals in addition to advancing the science and ethical practice of the marketing discipline. **Focus:** Marketing and distribution. **Qualif.:** Applicants must: be a Connecticut resident, may or may not be studying in Connecticut; be a second-year MBA students; be a Marketing or related major; demonstrated leadership record; have entrepreneurial/innovative spirit. **Criteria:** Selection will be based on the committee's criteria.

Funds Avail.: $1,000-$1,500. **Number Awarded:** 1. **To Apply:** Applicants may obtain application materials from the AMA-CT website at www.amact.org. **Deadline:** March 30.

4761 ■ Herman P. Kopplemann Scholarships *(Undergraduate/Scholarship)*

Purpose: To award scholarship to a graduating high school senior who lives in or attends school in Greater Hartford. **Focus:** General studies/Field of study not specified. **Qualif.:** Applicants must: be entering a four-year college or university; demonstrate financial need; be on a top third with good academic record; be an active volunteer in school, community, or other extracurricular activities; has been a newspaper carrier in Hartford County. **Criteria:** Selection will be based on the committee's criteria.

Funds Avail.: $3,000. **Number Awarded:** 1-4. **To Apply:** Application form can be downloaded on-line. Applicants must complete the scholarship application. Applicants must also attach the following requirements: letter of recommendation from your guidance counselor or a teacher; official high school transcript. Including SAT or ACT scores; copy of the essay you submitted with your college application. If you did not have to submit one, write a brief (no more than two pages) essay regarding your future goals; copy of pages 1 and 2 of your parents' or guardians' most recent completed federal tax form 1040. **Deadline:** February 1. **Contact:** Submit completed application to Scholar-

Awards are arranged alphabetically below their administering organizations

ship America, Hartford Foundation College Scholarship Program, Scholarship Management Services, 1505 Riverview Rd, PO Box 297, St. Peter, MN 56082. 800537-4180.

4762 ■ Mary Main Memorial Scholarships
(Undergraduate/Scholarship)

Purpose: To provide scholarship to the graduating senior or college student residing or attending school full-time in Connecticut. **Focus:** General studies/Field of study not specified. **Qualif.:** Applicants must be legally blind and demonstrate financial need, community service, and academic excellence. **Criteria:** Selection will be based on the committee's criteria.

Funds Avail.: $3,000. **Number Awarded:** 1. **To Apply:** Applicants may obtain application materials from the National Federation of the Blind of Connecticut's website at www.nfbct.org. **Deadline:** September 15. **Contact:** National Federation of the Blind of Connecticut 477 Connecticut Blvd. Ste. 217, East Hartford, CT 06108; Phone: 860-289-1971; Fax: 860-291-2795; Email: info@nfbct.org.

4763 ■ Manchester Scholarship Foundation - Adult Learners Scholarships *(Undergraduate/Scholarship)*

Purpose: To support adults who were returning to or beginning a college education after a lapse since high school graduation. **Focus:** General studies/Field of study not specified. **Qualif.:** Applicants must be adults of age 21 or older who resided in Manchester for at least six months and who have been accepted to a college or other postsecondary school; must demonstrate financial need. **Criteria:** Selection will be based on the committee's criteria.

Funds Avail.: $600 for one course; $1,000 for two courses. **To Apply:** Students may obtain application materials from their Guidance Office or from Manchester Scholarship Foundation, Inc.. **Deadline:** April 14. **Contact:** Ms. Carol Powell, Adult Learner Scholarship Chairperson; Phone: 860-649-2153; Email: johngp@cox.net.

4764 ■ Dr. Frank and Florence Marino Scholarships
(Undergraduate/Scholarship)

Purpose: To provide educational support to those students who are attending medical school in Connecticut. **Focus:** Medicine. **Qualif.:** Applicants must: have attended Connecticut school for at least 8 years (K-12) and graduated from Connecticut public or parochial high school; demonstrate financial need; have academic excellence; must be 2nd, 3rd, or 4th year medical students. **Criteria:** Selection will be based on the committee's criteria.

Funds Avail.: $1,000. **To Apply:** Applicants may obtain an application from the financial aid office of their medical school or may contact Sarah Carlson. **Deadline:** May 8. **Contact:** Sarah Carlson at scarlson@hfpg.org.

4765 ■ ARTC Glenn Moon Scholarships
(Undergraduate/Scholarship)

Purpose: To provide scholarship for graduating seniors from any public or private high school in Connecticut. **Focus:** Education. **Qualif.:** Applicants must be graduating seniors from any public or private high school in Connecticut who are about to enter a four-year college or university, major in teaching career education. **Criteria:** Selection shall be based on the aforesaid qualifications, financial need, academic excellence, and compliance with the application process.

Funds Avail.: $3,000 (Two $1,500 one-time awards); $2,000 renewable. **Duration:** Annual. **Number Awarded:** 3. **To Apply:** Application is via online. **Deadline:** March 31. **Contact:** Judy Morganroth, Chairperson, Association of Retired Teachers of Connecticut - Glenn Moon Scholarship Fund, Inc. 26 Route 87, Columbia, CT 06237; Phone: 860-228-1245; Email: freuenwald@yahoo.com.

4766 ■ Sylvia Parkinson Scholarships
(Undergraduate/Scholarship)

Purpose: To support medical students at University of Connecticut School of Medicine who intended to practice in the Hartford area. **Focus:** Medicine. **Qualif.:** Applicants must: be Capitol Region residents; demonstrate financial need; have an academic excellence; intend to practice in the Greater Hartford area. **Criteria:** Selection will be based on the committee's criteria.

Funds Avail.: $1,500-$3,000. **Number Awarded:** Varies. **To Apply:** Applicants may obtain application materials from University of Connecticut School of Medicine. **Deadline:** March 2. **Contact:** devereux@uchc.edu.

4767 ■ Dorothy E. Hofmann Pembroke Scholarships
(Undergraduate/Scholarship)

Purpose: To support students in Greater Hartford region. **Focus:** General studies/Field of study not specified. **Qualif.:** Applicants must be female residents of Harford, currently enrolled in a public, private, charter or magnet high school in the 29 town Greater Hartford region; must be planning to attend in one of the following colleges/universities: Trinity College, University of Hartford, University of Connecticut, University of Saint Joseph, Central CT State University, Brown University. **Criteria:** Selection will be based on the committee's criteria.

Funds Avail.: No specific amount. **Number Awarded:** 2. **To Apply:** Interested applicants may contact the Foundation for the application process and other information. **Deadline:** March 25. **Contact:** Sarah Carlson at scarlson@hfpg.org.

4768 ■ Nicholas J. Piergrossi Scholarships
(Undergraduate/Scholarship)

Purpose: To provide support to first-year students who are attending at University of Connecticut School of Dental Medicine. **Focus:** Dentistry. **Qualif.:** Applicants must be residents of Connecticut who demonstrates financial need and academic excellence. **Criteria:** Selection will be based on the committee's criteria.

Funds Avail.: $1,000. **Number Awarded:** 1. **To Apply:** Applicants may obtain application materials from University of Connecticut School of Dental Medicine. **Deadline:** March 2.

4769 ■ Day Pitney LLP Scholarships
(Undergraduate/Scholarship)

Purpose: To provide scholarship to the graduating high school senior in the City of Hartford. **Focus:** General studies/Field of study not specified. **Qualif.:** Applicants must: be entering a four-year college or university (full-time enrollment); demonstrate financial need; be on the class rank - top third with good academic record; be active volunteer in school, community, or other extracurricular activities. **Criteria:** Selection will be based on the committee's criteria.

Funds Avail.: $3,000. **Number Awarded:** 1. **To Apply:** Application form can be downloaded on-line. Applicants must complete the scholarship application. Applicants must also attach the following requirements: letter of recom-

Awards are arranged alphabetically below their administering organizations

mendation from your guidance counselor or a teacher; official high school transcript. Including SAT or ACT scores; copy of the essay you submitted with your college application. If you did not have to submit one, write a brief (no more than two pages) essay regarding your future goals; copy of pages 1 and 2 of your parents' or guardians' most recent completed federal tax form 1040. Mail everything to Hartford Foundation College Scholarship Program. **Deadline:** February 1. **Remarks:** Established in 1990.

4770 ■ Dr. Sidney Rafal Memorial Scholarships
(Undergraduate/Scholarship)

Purpose: To provide assistance to students who are attending the University of Connecticut School of Dental Medicine. **Focus:** Dental hygiene; Dentistry. **Qualif.:** Applicants must demonstrate financial need and academic excellence. **Criteria:** Selection will be based on the committee's criteria.

Funds Avail.: $500-$1,000. **Number Awarded:** 1. **To Apply:** Applicants may obtain application materials from University of Connecticut School of Dental Medicine. **Deadline:** March 2.

4771 ■ Mary C. Rawlins Scholarships
(Undergraduate/Scholarship)

Purpose: To award financial support to the graduating high school senior. **Focus:** General studies/Field of study not specified. **Qualif.:** Applicants must: be a resident of Connecticut; graduating high school senior; be entering a two- or four-year college or university; have a GPA of 2.5 or higher at end of Fall semester. **Criteria:** Selection will be based on the committee's criteria.

Funds Avail.: $500-$1,000. **Number Awarded:** 1-2. **To Apply:** Applicants may obtain application materials from Division of Criminal Justice, The CTAAAP Scholarship Committee. **Deadline:** March 13. **Contact:** Division of Criminal Justice, The CTAAAP Scholarship Committee, 300 Corporate Place Rocky Hill, CT 06067; Marcia Bonitto at mbpanama4@aol.com.

4772 ■ Peter T. Steinwedell Scholarships
(Undergraduate/Scholarship)

Purpose: To provide scholarship to graduate students in the field of education. **Focus:** Education. **Qualif.:** Applicant must be an Education major with strong preference given to applicants pursuing teaching career; must demonstrate financial need and academic excellence. **Criteria:** Selection will be based on the committee's criteria.

Funds Avail.: $1,000-$1,500. **Number Awarded:** 1-2. **To Apply:** Application form can be downloaded on-line. Applicants must complete the scholarship application. Applicants must also attach the following requirements: letter of recommendation from your guidance counselor or a teacher; official high school transcript. Including SAT or ACT scores; copy of the essay you submitted with your college application. If you did not have to submit one, write a brief (no more than two pages) essay regarding your future goals; copy of pages 1 and 2 of your parents' most recent completed federal tax form 1040. Mail everything to Hartford Foundation College Scholarship Program. **Deadline:** March 25. **Contact:** Sarah Carlson at scarlson@hfpg.org.

4773 ■ Town and County Club Scholarships
(Undergraduate/Scholarship)

Purpose: To support adult women who are pursuing their educational goal. **Focus:** General studies/Field of study not specified. **Qualif.:** Applicant must be a female adult learner; must be a resident of Greater Hartford region; must be enrolled full or part-time in an accredited community undergraduate college or university in the Greater Hartford region; must have a completion of 15 semester hours or the equivalent of academic work with a 2.5 GPA; and must demonstrate financial need. **Criteria:** Selection will be based on the committee's criteria.

Funds Avail.: $3,000. **To Apply:** Students may contact the Town and County Club or access the website www.town-county.com for application form.

4774 ■ Elmer Cooke Young - Taylor Young Scholarships
(Undergraduate/Scholarship)

Purpose: To provide financial assistance for high school graduates who are pursuing their academic dreams. **Focus:** General studies/Field of study not specified. **Qualif.:** Students must be graduating seniors from Glastonbury or Windsor High School; must demonstrate financial need; must be on a class rank - top third with good academic record; and must be active volunteers in school, community, or other extracurricular activities. **Criteria:** Selection will be based on the committee's criteria.

Funds Avail.: $3,000. **Number Awarded:** 2-4. **To Apply:** Application forms can be downloaded on-line. Applicants must complete the scholarship application. Applicants must also attach the following requirements: letter of recommendation from your guidance counselor or a teacher; official high school transcript (including SAT or ACT scores); copy of the essay you submitted with your college application (If you did not have to submit one, write a brief essay of no more than two pages regarding your future goals); copy of pages 1 and 2 of your parents' or guardians' most recent completed federal tax form 1040. Mail everything to Hartford Foundation College Scholarship Program. **Deadline:** February 1.

4775 ■ Hartford Public Library
500 Main St.
Hartford, CT 06103-3075
Ph: (860)695-6300
Fax: (860)722-6900
E-mail: reference@hplct.org
URL: www.hplct.org

4776 ■ Caroline M. Hewins Scholarships *(Graduate/Scholarship)*

Purpose: To support students planning to specialize in library work with children. **Focus:** Library and archival sciences. **Qualif.:** Applicants must have received, or about to receive, a four year undergraduate degree and have applied for admission to a library school accredited by the American Library Association. **Criteria:** Preference will be given to applicants who plan to pursue a career in public library service.

Funds Avail.: $4,000. **Duration:** Annual. **To Apply:** Applicants must submit a completed application form along with transcript of credits through the first semester of the senior year and an evidence of application to an accredited school of library service. **Deadline:** May 1. **Remarks:** Established in 1926. **Contact:** Caroline M. Hewins Scholarship, c/o Mary Billings, Chief Public Services Officer, Hartford Public Library, at the above address.

4777 ■ Hartford Whalers Booster Club (HWBC)
PO Box 273
Hartford, CT 06141

Awards are arranged alphabetically below their administering organizations

Ph: (860)956-3839
E-mail: hwbcub@sbcglobal.net
URL: whalerwatch.com

4778 ■ Hartford Whalers Booster Club Scholarships (Undergraduate/Scholarship)

Purpose: To provide scholarship to those students who are outstanding in academic and as hockey players. **Focus:** General studies/Field of study not specified. **Qualif.:** Applicants must: intend to play collegiate hockey; have an outstanding hockey abilities; be a Connecticut resident; have an academic excellence. **Criteria:** Selection will be based on the committee's criteria.

Funds Avail.: No specific amount. **Duration:** Annual. **To Apply:** Applicants must complete the General Scholarship Application and include a letter of recommendation from your hockey coach outlining your hockey performance and submit to Hartford Whalers Booster Club. **Deadline:** March 1.

4779 ■ Harvard-Smithsonian Center for Astrophysics (CFA)
60 Garden St.
Cambridge, MA 02138
Ph: (617)495-7100
URL: www.cfa.harvard.edu
Twitter: www.twitter.com/saoastro

4780 ■ CfA Postdoctoral Fellowships (Postdoctorate/Fellowship)

Purpose: To advance knowledge of the Universe through research in astronomy and astrophysics and in related areas of fundamental physics and geophysics. **Focus:** Geophysics; Physics. **Qualif.:** Applicants must be outstanding researchers displaying significant promise in theory, observation, instrumentation, and/or laboratory experiments; must be first-author refereed journal paper and who already received their PhD at the time of application. **Criteria:** Selection will be based on the committee's criteria.

Funds Avail.: Approximately $66,500 with a research budget of $16,000. **Duration:** Annual. **To Apply:** Interested applicants must visit the website for the online application process. Applicants must also upload the following forms in PDF or Text format: curriculum vitae; publication list; summary of previous and current research (up to four pages); research proposal (up to four pages); and three reference letters. **Deadline:** January 1 and September 1.

4781 ■ Clay Postdoctoral Fellowships (Postdoctorate/Fellowship)

Purpose: To support an outstanding researcher(s) displaying significant promise in theory, observation, instrumentation, and/or laboratory experiments. **Focus:** Geophysics; Physics. **Qualif.:** Applicants must be outstanding researchers displaying significant promise in theory, observation, instrumentation, and/or laboratory experiments. **Criteria:** Selection will be based on the committee's criteria.

Funds Avail.: A stipend of approximately $67,500 plus a research budget of $16,000. **Duration:** Annual; up to five years. **To Apply:** Interested applicants must visit the website for the online application process. The following forms must be uploaded in PDF or Text format: curriculum vitae; publication list; summary of previous and current research (maximum of 4 pages); research proposal (maximum of 4 pages). Applicants must also prepare three letters of reference. **Deadline:** October 30.

4782 ■ SAO (Smithsonian Astrophysical Observatory) Predoctoral Fellowships (Graduate/Fellowship)

Purpose: To advance the knowledge of the Universe through research in astronomy and astrophysics and in related areas of fundamental physics and geophysics. **Focus:** Geophysics; Physics. **Qualif.:** Applicants must be current graduate students pursuing thesis research in astrophysics or related fields. **Criteria:** Selection will be based on the committee's criteria.

Funds Avail.: No specific amount. **Duration:** Six months. **To Apply:** Interested applicants must visit the website for the application form and other informations about current research and facilities. Applicants should directly contact any Smithsonian scientist in their area of interest to discuss possible research topics. Applicants must upload the following files in 12-point font: curriculum vitae, summary of previous and current research (limited to three pages including references and figures); research proposal (limited to three pages including references and figures).

4783 ■ Harvard University Faculty of Arts & Sciences - Institute for Quantitative Social Science - Henry A. Murray Research Archive
CGIS Knafel Bldg.
1737 Cambridge St.
Cambridge, MA 02138
E-mail: support@dataverse.org
URL: murray.harvard.edu

4784 ■ Jeanne Humphrey Block Dissertation Award (Postdoctorate/Award)

Purpose: To encourage and recognize an outstanding individual for the excellent dissertation regarding social sciences. **Focus:** Social sciences. **Qualif.:** Applicants must be Harvard Ph.D. students (3rd year or above) in the social sciences. **Criteria:** Award decision will be based on: significance to science research; innovation and; investigator evaluation.

Funds Avail.: $2,500. **Duration:** Annual; each Spring. **To Apply:** Applicants must submit through email the following requirements: dissertation paper maximum of two pages; letter of recommendation from dissertation adviser; completed application form; CV/Resume and; project budget. Dissertation must utilize data archived in the Harvard Dataverse. **Deadline:** March 13. **Contact:** funding@iq.harvard.edu.

4785 ■ Harvard University Law School
1563 Massachusetts Ave.
Cambridge, MA 02138
Ph: (617)495-3109
E-mail: jdadmiss@law.harvard.edu
URL: www.law.harvard.edu

4786 ■ Henigson Human Rights Fellowships (Graduate, Master's, Juris Doctorate/Fellowship)

Purpose: To encourage the HLS students to build human rights work and to expand their interest in working in the field. **Focus:** Human rights; Law. **Qualif.:** Applicants must be: current and former J.D. students (3Ls expecting to receive the J.D. degree, as well as J.D graduates who are

Awards are arranged alphabetically below their administering organizations

currently clerks for judges); engaged in full-time public interest work; active in human rights or public interest work while students at HLS; LL.M. students who expect to receive the LL.M. degree and who come from and will return to a country other than the United States; and/or, HLS students and recent graduates with a demonstrated commitment to international human rights and have an interest working in the field. **Criteria:** Selection of recipients will be based on the application materials.

Funds Avail.: Up to $27,000 plus $1,500 toward international health insurance. **Duration:** Annual. **To Apply:** Applicants must submit their curriculum vitae, including information about classes, work and extracurricular activities in public interest and human rights inside and outside of Harvard Law School; a personal statement (500 words maximum) about the applicant's relevant experience, interest, and future aspirations with respect to public interest and human rights work; a project description; a letter and supporting materials from sponsoring organization detailing their purpose, function, and particular interest in the work of the applicant; two or three letters of recommendation including at least one from an HLS professor; and an HLS transcript. **Deadline:** March 21. **Contact:** Human Rights Program at hrp@law.harvard.edu.

4787 ■ Satter Human Rights Fellowships *(Graduate, Master's, Juris Doctorate/Fellowship)*

Purpose: To enable students to make a significant contribution to addressing human rights violations involving mass atrocities and similar situations during the year of the fellowship and to help students develop careers in human rights. **Focus:** Human rights; Law. **Qualif.:** Applicants must be: Harvard Law School J.D. students (3Ls expecting to receive the J.D. degree, as well as recent J.D. graduates); and/or, Harvard Law School LL.M. students who expect to receive the LL.M. degree. **Criteria:** Selection of recipients will be based on the submitted application materials.

Funds Avail.: Up to $45,000. **Duration:** Annual. **To Apply:** Applicants must submit their curriculum vitae, including information about classes, work and extracurricular activities in public interest and human rights inside and outside of Harvard Law School; a personal statement (500 words maximum) about the applicants' relevant experience, interest, and future aspirations with respect to public interest and human rights work; a project description; a letter and supporting materials from sponsoring organization detailing their purpose, function, and particular interest in the work of the applicant; two or three letters of recommendation including at least one from an HLS professor; and an HLS transcript. **Deadline:** March 21. **Contact:** Human Rights Program at hrp@law.harvard.edu; phone: 617-495-9362.

4788 ■ Harvard University - Law School - Program on Negotiation (PON)
501 Pound Hall
1563 Massachusetts Ave.
Cambridge, MA 02138
Ph: (617)495-1684
Fax: (617)495-7818
E-mail: pon@law.harvard.edu
URL: www.pon.harvard.edu

4789 ■ PON Graduate Student Grants *(Graduate/Grant)*

Purpose: To support cutting-edge research at the graduate level. **Focus:** Consulting; Law. **Qualif.:** Applicants must be graduate students conducting or planning to conduct a research. Students from any Boston-area school may apply. **Criteria:** Grant applications will be evaluated on the basis of: academic merit; originality and; potential for producing material for an academic paper or thesis.

Funds Avail.: $1,000. **To Apply:** Applicants must submit the following requirements: one to two page description of the proposed project; budget including all other sources of support for the project; curriculum vitae maximum of two pages and; letter of reference from a faculty member familiar with the students' work. Recipients are required to submit a one-page project overview upon completion of their project, to be posted on the PON website, outlining their research question (s) or project and briefly describing their initial findings. **Deadline:** November 30 and May 3.

4790 ■ PON Next Generation Grants *(Doctorate, Postdoctorate/Grant)*

Purpose: To support research in negotiation and conflict resolution by non-tenured faculty and doctoral students. **Focus:** Consulting; Law. **Qualif.:** Applicants must be non-tenured faculty or doctoral students from any school or department within PON's inter-university consortium (Harvard, MIT, and Tufts Fletcher School). Post-doctoral students with a formal affiliation to Harvard or one of the consortium schools of PON are also eligible to apply. **Criteria:** Grant application will be evaluated on the basis of: academic merit; originality and; potential for yielding publishable material in leading academic journals.

Funds Avail.: $5,000-$10,000. **To Apply:** Applicants must submit a three to five page proposal electronically together with the following: description of the proposed research, justifying the request for funds; qualification of applicants to carry out the research, referencing appropriate courses or training that provide the basis for competency in the proposed method; budget including all other sources of support for the project; curriculum vitae and; for students: name and contact information for a faculty member familiar with the students' work. **Deadline:** November 30 and May 31.

4791 ■ PON Summer Fellowships *(Graduate/Fellowship)*

Purpose: To forge new links between our academic community and worldwide organizations involved in the practice of negotiation and dispute resolution, and to encourage students to reach for opportunities that would otherwise not be available to them due to financial constraints. **Focus:** Consulting; Law. **Qualif.:** Applicants must be returning graduate students at schools in the Boston-area. Eligible internships and research projects must be unpaid, undertaken in partnership with a public, non-profit or academic organization, and a minimum of eight weeks in duration. Fellowship applicants must have already secured or applied for the position/project for which they are seeking PON Summer Fellowship support. Grants will be dispersed once documentation confirming the internship or project is provided by the host organization or, in the case or research projects, by a supervising faculty member. **Criteria:** Selection will be based on the Committees' criteria.

Funds Avail.: $3,500. **To Apply:** Applicants must complete and submit the following requirements: cover page; letter from host organization (internship) or academic supervisor (research); resume or curriculum vitae; project proposal; budget detailing estimated expenses; letter of recommendation and; Signed Acknowledgement of Risk and General Release Form (to be provided by PON if/when a

Awards are arranged alphabetically below their administering organizations

fellowship is awarded). **Deadline:** March 21.

4792 ■ Hasbrook & Hasbrook
400 N Walker Ave., No. 130
Oklahoma City, OK 73102
Ph: (405)235-1551
E-mail: hasbrooklawfirm@gmail.com
URL: www.oklahomalawyer.com

4793 ■ Make Us Proud Scholarships *(Undergraduate/Scholarship)*

Purpose: To support students to achieve their educational goals. **Focus:** General studies/Field of study not specified. **Qualif.:** Applicants must be U.S. citizens living and attending school in the United States; must be graduating high school seniors or college freshmen or sophomores who have completed no more than 60 credit hours. **Criteria:** Selection will be based on the relevance to one of the practice areas, composition and creativity of the submitted essay.

Funds Avail.: $1,000. **Duration:** Annual. **Number Awarded:** 1. **To Apply:** Applicants must write a 140-word essay and 140-character tweet-worthy summary of the essay on a topic related to one of Hasbrook & Hasbrook's nine practice areas. The essay may inform or advocate or both. Applicants must submit a cover page that contains the following information: name; address; date of birth; phone number; email; current school; school planning to attend next semester. A cover page, essay and tweet must be submitted as a single PDF document and a photo of yourself via email attachments. **Deadline:** July 31. **Contact:** scholarship@hasbrooklaw.com.

4794 ■ Hawaii Community Foundation
827 Fort Street Mall
Honolulu, HI 96813
Ph: (808)537-6333
Fax: (808)521-6286
Free: 888-731-3863
E-mail: info@hcf-hawaii.org
URL: www.hawaiicommunityfoundation.org

4795 ■ Victoria S. and Bradley L. Geist Scholarships *(Undergraduate/Scholarship)*

Purpose: To provide opportunities to students currently or formerly in the foster care system. **Focus:** General studies/Field of study not specified. **Qualif.:** Applicants must be currently or formerly placed in the foster care system in the state of Hawai'i. They must currently be or have been in the State of Hawaii foster care system for at least one day since the age of 14. **Criteria:** Recipients will be selected based on demonstrated financial need.

Funds Avail.: No specific amount. **Duration:** Annual. **To Apply:** Applicants must submit a confirmation letter from a DHS or Foster Family Program case worker to verify foster status. The letter should indicate whether they aged out of the foster care system. **Deadline:** January 1; May 16; September 15.

4796 ■ HCF Community Scholarships Fund *(Undergraduate, Graduate/Scholarship)*

Purpose: To assist students aiming to further their education. **Focus:** General studies/Field of study not specified. **Qualif.:** Applicants must be residents of Hawaii; must be full-time undergraduate or graduate students who have plan to attend an accredited two- or four-year college or university; must have a minimum GPA of 2.7 and must exhibit good moral character. **Criteria:** Applicants will be selected based on demonstrated financial need and academic achievement.

Funds Avail.: No specific amount. **Duration:** Annual. **To Apply:** Application is via online. Those who are first time applicants must create an online account and log in by providing a username and password while those returning applicants shall use their existing accounts. Second is that they must complete the basic application, then upload the supporting materials. Afterwards, complete the optional selections. Finally, review and submit the online application.

4797 ■ Hawaii Lodging and Tourism Association (HLTA)
2270 Kalakaua Ave., Ste. 1506
Honolulu, HI 96815-2519
Ph: (808)923-0407
Fax: (808)924-3843
E-mail: info@hawaiilodging.org
URL: hawaiilodging.org

4798 ■ R.W. "Bob" Holden Memorial Scholarships *(Undergraduate/Scholarship)*

Purpose: To support students who have the potential to work toward the standard of excellence. **Focus:** Hotel, institutional, and restaurant management. **Qualif.:** Applicants must be students who are Hawaii residents enrolled full-time at an accredited university/college in the United States; majoring in hotel/lodging management and have a minimum 3.0 GPA. **Criteria:** Selection will be based on the aforesaid qualifications and compliance with the application process.

Funds Avail.: $1,000 each. **Duration:** Annual. **Number Awarded:** 3. **To Apply:** Applicants must submit the following application checklist (enclosures required with application): proof of residency (either Hawaii state identification card or Hawaii state driver's license); most recent official transcript from current college; autobiography; career goals essay; recommendation from university professor, counselor, or dean; and photograph (optional). **Deadline:** July 1.

4799 ■ Clem Judd Jr. Memorial Scholarships *(Undergraduate/Scholarship)*

Purpose: To support students who have the potential to work toward the standard of excellence. **Focus:** Hotel, institutional, and restaurant management. **Qualif.:** Applicants must be students who are Hawaii residents of Hawaiian ancestry enrolled full-time at an accredited university/college in the United States; majoring in hotel/lodging management and have a minimum 3.0 GPA. **Criteria:** Selection will be based on the aforesaid qualifications and compliance with the application process.

Funds Avail.: $1,000 to $2,500. **Duration:** Annual. **Number Awarded:** Up to 2. **To Apply:** Applicants must submit the following application checklist (enclosures required with application): proof of residency (either Hawaii state identification card or Hawaii state driver's license); most recent official transcript from current college; autobiography; career goals essay; recommendation from university professor, counselor, or dean; and photograph (optional). **Deadline:** July 1.

Awards are arranged alphabetically below their administering organizations

4800 ■ Hawaii Pacific Gerontological Society (HPGS)
PO Box 3714
Honolulu, HI 96812
E-mail: hpgs.hawaii@gmail.com
URL: hpgs.org

4801 ■ HPGS/ALOH Graduate Scholarships
(Graduate/Scholarship)

Purpose: To support graduate, law and medical students registered in a program of study focused on gerontology or geriatrics. **Focus:** Gerontology; Medicine, Geriatric. **Qualif.:** Applicants must be graduate, law or medical students at the University of Hawaii, Hawaii Pacific University and Chaminade University who want to pursue careers related to Gerontology and Geriatrics. **Criteria:** Preference will be given to students who meet the scholarship criteria and provide evidence of financial need. Applicants must have demonstrated interest in aging through one or more of the following: (a) currently taking, or having taken, one or more aging-related credit courses or certificate programs; (b) paid professional or para-professional work experience with older adults or in an aging-related setting; (c) attendance at one or more non-credit aging-related courses or seminars; (d) volunteer work or internship in an aging-related community site; (e) work on an aging-related project that the applicants as students initiated; (f) assisting or having assisted by a professor on a research project;(g) playing a leadership role in a class or services learning project that helps older persons.

Funds Avail.: $1,000. **Duration:** Annual. **Number Awarded:** 1. **To Apply:** Application forms are available online. Applicants must submit evidence of financial need and proof of residency in the State of Hawaii; must provide a copy of recommendation letter from their academic adviser, former professor, instructor, or supervisor at their internship or volunteer site; must submit an essay that addresses their qualifications for receiving the scholarship, including experience in and dedication to the field of gerontology, their future career plans, and financial need; must have a copy of latest community college or university transcript and a valid ID. **Deadline:** May 31. **Contact:** Hawaii Pacific Gerontological Society, Attn: HPGS Scholarship Committee, at the above address, or Email: hpgs.hawaii@gmail.com.

4802 ■ HPGS Undergraduate Scholarships
(Undergraduate/Scholarship)

Purpose: To support professionals pursuing their career related to gerontology or geriatrics. **Focus:** Gerontology; Medicine, Geriatric. **Qualif.:** Applicants must be Hawaiian residents, undergraduates and community college students in the University of Hawaii System, Hawaii Pacific University and Chaminade University pursuing careers in gerontology and geriatrics; must demonstrate a 3.0 GPA or higher for the past academic year at the community or undergraduate level. **Criteria:** Preference will be given to students who have taken, or are currently taking, at least one aging related community college or university course, or to students who demonstrate an interest in the field of gerontology in an aging-related community site, for example: doing volunteer work or performing an internship at an aging related community site; working on an aging related project that you as a student initiated; assisting or having assisted a professor on an aging related project; having played a leadership role in working on a class or service learning project that helped older persons.

Funds Avail.: $1,000. **Duration:** Annual. **Number Awarded:** Varies. **To Apply:** Application forms are available online. Applicants must provide a proof of residency in the State of Hawaii; must submit a letter of recommendation from their academic adviser, former professors, instructors, or supervisors at their internship or volunteer site; must submit an essay that addresses their qualifications for receiving the scholarship, including experience in and dedication to the field of gerontology, their future career plans and expression of financial need; must have a copy of latest community college or university transcript. **Deadline:** May 31. **Contact:** Hawaii Pacific Gerontological Society, at the above address.

4803 ■ Health in Aging Foundation
40 Fulton St., 18th Fl.
New York, NY 10038
Free: 800-563-4916
E-mail: info@healthinaging.org
URL: www.healthinaging.org

4804 ■ T. Franklin Williams Research Scholars Award Program *(Other/Grant)*

Purpose: To support the academic career development of a promising geriatrics physician-scientist. **Focus:** Medicine, Geriatric. **Qualif.:** Applicants must: have an MD or DO degree; be within four years of the first faculty appointment at the time the grant becomes effective; must devote 75% of their time to conduct research with 40% specifically devoted to this project; be internal medicine geriatrician who have completed all of the requirements to be eligible to sit for a Certificate of Added Qualifications by the time the award commences; have at least two sponsors committed to providing guidance and collaboration throughout the course of the proposed project (at least one sponsor should represent geriatrics and at least one sponsor should represent a subspecialty of internal medicine); and must be citizens or lawfully admitted permanent residents of the United States. **Criteria:** Selection is based on the qualifications of the applicant; impact of the proposed project on the applicant's career; the applicant's commitment to an academic research career devoted to improving the care of older adults; scientific merit of the research proposal and its relevance to improving subspecialty care of older adults; evidence of the sub-specialty and geriatrics sponsors' commitment to the applicant as well as the sponsors' experience in research and training in the applicant's area of research interest; and commitment of the applicant's institution to supporting the career development of the junior faculty member.

Funds Avail.: Amount varies. **Duration:** Two years. **To Apply:** Applicants may request for an application online.

4805 ■ Health Effects Institute (HEI)
75 Federal St., Ste. 1400
Boston, MA 02110-1817
Ph: (617)488-2300
Fax: (617)488-2335
E-mail: pubs@healtheffects.org
URL: www.healtheffects.org

4806 ■ Walter A. Rosenblith New Investigator Award *(Postdoctorate/Award)*

Purpose: To provide funding for outstanding investigators who are beginning independent research on the health effects of air pollution. **Focus:** Air pollution. **Qualif.:** Applicants must be scientists of any nationality holding a PhD, ScD, MD, DVM, or DrPH degree or equivalent; should have two to six years of research experience after obtaining the highest degree; must be assistant professors or equivalent position at an academic or research institution. **Criteria:** All applications will be evaluated in the two-stage process described as external and internal review. The external review includes the relevance of expertise in the area of proposed research, its environment, and the mentoring plan; the internal review evaluates letters of support, institutional support, and the applicants' career development and mentoring plan.

Funds Avail.: $450,000. **Duration:** Annual; 3 years. **To Apply:** Interested applicants must accomplish and send the online application form found in the website; must provide a one to two pages letter of intent summarizing the proposed project prior to submitting an application, and specifying the research goals of the project and indicate the general approach to be used; must provide a curriculum vitae maximum of two pages. **Deadline:** June 3. **Contact:** Dr. Geoffrey Sunshine, at the above address.

4807 ■ Health Physics Society (HPS)
1313 Dolley Madison Blvd., Ste. 402
McLean, VA 22101
Ph: (703)790-1745
Fax: (703)790-2672
E-mail: hps@burkinc.com
URL: www.hps.org

4808 ■ Richard J. Burk, Jr. Fellowships *(Graduate/Fellowship)*

Purpose: To support students enrolled in bona fide U.S. graduate programs in health physics or a closely related field. **Focus:** Health sciences; Radiology. **Qualif.:** Applicants must be full-time entering or continuing student enrolled in U.S. graduate programs in health physics or related field. Previous HPS Fellowship holders are ineligible. **Criteria:** Selection is based on the application.

Funds Avail.: $5,000 cash; and $800 travel grant. **Duration:** Annual. **To Apply:** Applicants must complete the online application. **Deadline:** March 28. **Contact:** Jill Drupa, Health Physics Society; 1313 Dolley Madison Blvd., Suite 402, McLean, VA 22101; Phone: 703-790-1745; Fax: 703-790-2672; Email: jdrupa@burkinc.com.

4809 ■ Robert Gardner Memorial Fellowships *(Graduate/Fellowship)*

Purpose: To support students enrolled in bona fide U.S. graduate programs in health physics or a closely related field. **Focus:** Health sciences; Radiology. **Qualif.:** Applicants must be full-time entering or continuing students enrolled in U.S. graduate programs in health physics or related field. Previous HPS Fellowship holders are ineligible. **Criteria:** Selection is based on the application.

Funds Avail.: $5,000 cash; $800 travel grant. **Duration:** Annual. **To Apply:** Applicants must complete the online application. **Deadline:** March 28. **Contact:** Jill Drupa, Health Physics Society; 1313 Dolley Madison Blvd., Suite 402, McLean, VA 22101; Phone: 703-790-1745; Fax: 703-790-2672; Email: jdrupa@burkinc.com.

4810 ■ Robert S. Landauer, Sr. Memorial Fellowships *(Graduate/Fellowship)*

Purpose: To provide financial support to students enrolled in bona fide U.S. graduate programs in health physics or a closely related field. **Focus:** Health sciences; Radiology. **Qualif.:** Applicants must be full-time entering or continuing students enrolled in U.S. graduate programs in health physics or related field. Previous HPS Fellowship holders are ineligible. **Criteria:** Selection is based on the application.

Funds Avail.: $5,000 cash; $800 travel grant. **Duration:** Annual. **To Apply:** Applicants must complete the online application. **Deadline:** March 28.

4811 ■ Burton J. Moyer Memorial Fellowships *(Graduate/Fellowship)*

Purpose: To support students enrolled in bona fide U.S. graduate programs in health physics or a closely related field. **Focus:** Health sciences; Radiology. **Qualif.:** Applicants must be full-time entering or continuing students enrolled in U.S. graduate programs in health physics or related field. Previous HPS Fellowship holders are ineligible. **Criteria:** Selection is based on the application.

Funds Avail.: $10,000 cash; $800 travel grant to be used to attend the HPS annual meeting. **Duration:** Annual. **Number Awarded:** 1. **To Apply:** Applicants must complete the online application. **Deadline:** March 28. **Contact:** Jill Drupa, Health Physics Society; 1313 Dolley Madison Blvd., Suite 402, McLean, VA 22101; Phone: 703-790-1745;Fax: 703-790-2672; Email: jdrupa@burkinc.com.

4812 ■ J. Newell Stannard Fellowships *(Graduate/Fellowship)*

Purpose: To support students enrolled in bona fide U.S. graduate programs in health physics or a closely related field. **Focus:** Health sciences; Radiology. **Qualif.:** Applicants must be full-time entering or continuing students enrolled in U.S. graduate programs in health physics or related field. Previous HPS Fellowship holders are ineligible. **Criteria:** Selection is based on the application.

Funds Avail.: $5,000 cash; and $800 travel grant. **Duration:** Annual. **To Apply:** Applicants must complete the online application. **Deadline:** March 28. **Contact:** Jill Drupa, Health Physics Society; 1313 Dolley Madison Blvd., Suite 402, McLean, VA 22101; Phone: 703-790-1745; Fax: 703-790-2672; Email: jdrupa@burkinc.com.

4813 ■ Health Resources in Action
95 Berkeley St.
Boston, MA 02116
Ph: (617)451-0049
Fax: (617)451-0062
URL: www.hria.org
LinkedIn: www.linkedin.com/company/health-resources-in-action

4814 ■ Davis Foundation Postdoctoral Fellowships *(Doctorate, Master's/Fellowship)*

Purpose: To support postdoctoral fellows working in non-profit academic, medical and research institutions in the United States. **Focus:** Health sciences. **Qualif.:** Applicants must be MD, PhD or equivalent awarded from an accredited domestic or foreign institution; have completed no more than three years of full-time postdoctoral research experience by the time funding begins; conduct the proposed research project at a hospital, university or other non-profit research institution where applicants hold their postdoctoral fellowship appointment. **Criteria:** Selection will be based on the following criteria: applicant's demonstrated competency and potential for a career in research; qualifications

Awards are arranged alphabetically below their administering organizations

of the mentor and the degree of commitment to supervise and train the applicant during the proposed research period; letters of recommendation; research hypothesis is novel and/or builds on current knowledge; proposal reviews the relevant literature; objectives are well conceived, realistic and important; research methodology, data collection and date analysis are feasible and appropriate to the proposal's aims; project that will contribute to the professional training and growth of the applicant; and advancing knowledge that may someday lead to improving the quality of human life. **Funds Avail.:** $141,000-$177,000. **Duration:** Three years. **To Apply:** Applicants must submit a research project which focuses the relevant aspects of the biological causes of anorexia nervosa and bulimia nervosa as defined by clinical criteria; must upload a signed letter of support from their research project mentor; and supply two confidential letters of recommendation, one of which must be from thesis advisor for applicants holding a PhD. If the thesis advisor is unavailable to write a letter of recommendation, a brief explanation of his/her unavailability must be included in the uploaded document. Complete application process required an online submission as well as a mailed copy of the application materials that are submitted online. **Contact:** Jeanne Brown, Program Officer; Phone: 617-279-2240, ext. 709; Email: jbrown@hria.org.

4815 ■ Charles H. Hood Foundation Child Health Research Awards Program *(Doctorate/Grant)*

Purpose: To support newly independent faculty, provide the opportunity to demonstrate creativity, and assist in the transition to other sources of research funding. **Focus:** Medical research. **Qualif.:** Applicants must be researchers who are within five years of their first faculty appointment by the funding start date; must be working in nonprofit academic, medical or research institutions within the six New England states; must hold a doctoral degree with a demonstrated level of independence confirmed by the department or division chair. **Criteria:** Selection shall be based on the applicants' showing of potential for a future career as an independent investigator in research relevant to child health. **Funds Avail.:** $150,000 ($75,000 per year inclusive of 10% indirect costs) each. **Duration:** Annual; up to two years. **Number Awarded:** Up to 5. **To Apply:** Applicants must visit the website to obtain an application form. **Deadline:** March 30. **Contact:** Gay Lockwood at glockwood@hria.org.

4816 ■ Jeffress Trust Awards Program in Interdisciplinary Research *(Professional development/Award)*

Purpose: To promote scientific discovery through interdisciplinary collaboration and integration of innovative computational and quantitative strategies. **Focus:** Astronomy and astronomical sciences; Biological and clinical sciences; Chemistry; Computer and information sciences; Engineering; Environmental science; Materials research/science; Mathematics and mathematical sciences; Physics. **Qualif.:** Principal investigators must be full-time faculty members at a nonprofit academic or research institution in Virginia. For undergraduate students' participation, a proportion of the award is required to be allotted towards funding undergraduate students' research through stipend support. The research areas that are currently eligible include: astronomy; biosciences; chemistry; computer sciences; engineering, environmental sciences; material science; mathematics and physics. **Criteria:** The Scientific Review Committee uses the following criteria to evaluate applications: project's scientific merit, impact and innovation exploiting computational and quantitative strategies within the relevant field of science or engineering; qualifications of applicants and co-investigators to carry out the proposed research; research objectives, methodology, data collection and data analysis that are feasible and appropriate to meet the proposal's goals; detailed plan for undergraduate students research opportunities in the work. **Funds Avail.:** $100,000. **To Apply:** Application form can be obtained at the website. In order to balance funding opportunities for nonprofit academic or research institutions across Virginia, a maximum of four applications may be nominated per institution, inclusive of all schools and colleges therein. Complete applications must include the following: application face sheet; table of contents; research project summary and performance sites; nontechnical project summary; biosketches; letter of recommendation and commitment from department chair; letters of collaboration; budget form A; budget justification form B; current, pending and post award funding; research proposal. Research proposal must be ten pages maximum, inclusive of a bibliography of references. Proposal sections include specific aims, background and significance, preliminary studies/preliminary data, research design and methods, potential limitations and/or pitfalls, project timeline, future direction and impact of the research and literature cited. Include all figures, graphs, tables, images and bibliography of references related to the project in the ten pages. **Deadline:** January 15 - Online submission; January 17 - Printed materials submission. **Contact:** Jeanne Brown, Program Officer at jbrown@hria.org or 617-279-2240 x709.

4817 ■ Charles A. King Trust Postdoctoral Research Fellowships *(Postdoctorate/Fellowship)*

Purpose: To support postdoctoral scientists in non-profit academic, medical or research institutions in Massachusetts. **Focus:** Biological and clinical sciences; Health sciences. **Qualif.:** Applicants must be working in an academic or medical research institution in the state of Massachusetts and have required minimum/maximum years of experience; must hold a fellowship position under the supervision of a faculty member; mentors must confirm that degrees obtained outside the United States are equivalent to the MD, DMD, PhD or other doctoral degree; only one applicant per mentor may apply per application cycle. **Criteria:** Selection will be based on the following criteria: applicant's demonstrated competency and potential for a career in research; qualifications of the mentor and the degree of commitment to supervise and train the applicant during the proposed research period; letters of recommendation; novelty of research hypothesis is novel and ability to build on current knowledge; proposal reviews the relevant literature; objectives are well conceived, realistic and important; research methodology, data collection and date analysis are feasible and appropriate to the proposal's aims; project that will contribute to the professional training and growth of the applicant; and advancing knowledge that may someday lead to improving the quality of human life. **Funds Avail.:** $43,700 to $53,175, inclusive of a $2,000 expense allowance. **Duration:** Annual; 2 years. **To Apply:** Applicants must visit the website to obtain an application form. The complete application process requires an online submission as well as mailed package containing the Face Sheet with original signatures, four printed copies of the document uploaded online and three confidential letters of recommendation. **Deadline:** January 29. **Remarks:** Established in 1936. **Contact:** Erin Johnstone, Program Officer; E-mail: EJohnstone@hria.org.

Awards are arranged alphabetically below their administering organizations

4818 ■ Klarman Family Foundation Grants Program in Eating Disorders Research *(Professional development/Grant)*

Purpose: To provide strategic investment in translational research that will accelerate progress in developing effective treatments for anorexia nervosa, bulimia nervosa and binger eating disorder. **Focus:** Medical research. **Qualif.:** Applicants must be investigators who hold a faculty appointment at nonprofit academic, medical or research institutions in the United States, Canada and Israel. **Criteria:** Selection will be based on the submitted application and research project.

Funds Avail.: $400,000 ($200,000 per year, up to two years); $150,000 (one-year pilot studies). **Duration:** Two years. **To Apply:** Application form can be obtained at the website. The complete application process requires an online submission as well as four printed copies of the uploaded PDF. The following sections must be completed for the online submission: institution's tax ID number; eligibility quiz; application data; research project information; research classification; research area; certification; attachment (document upload). The following attached documents and forms must be combined and converted into one PDF file in the order for upload: application face sheet; table of contents; research project summary and performance sites; nontechnical summary; biosketch(es) of applicants and co-investigator(s); department or division chair's letter; letter of collaboration; budget forms; research proposal. **Contact:** Gay Lockwood, Senior Program Officer at glockwood@hria.org or 617-279-2240, x702.

4819 ■ Robert E. Leet and Clara Guthrie Patterson Trust Awards Program in Clinical Research *(Professional development/Grant)*

Purpose: To accelerate clinical research by offering K23 and K08 Award Recipients the resources to explore research activities not supported by NIH K Awards. **Focus:** Medical research. **Qualif.:** Applicants must be mentored investigators conducting clinical research across a range of research disciplines, broadly defined to include patient-oriented research and translational laboratory research. **Criteria:** Selection will be based on the committee's criteria.

Funds Avail.: $100,000. **Duration:** One year. **Number Awarded:** Up to 4. **To Apply:** Interested applicants may contact the Foundation for the application process and other information. **Contact:** Gay Lockwood, Senior Program Officer at GLockwood@hria.org; Phone: 617-279-2240, x702.

4820 ■ Lymphatic Research Foundation Additional Support for NIH-funded F32 Postdoctoral Fellows Awards *(Postdoctorate/Award)*

Purpose: To help foster career interest in the field of lymphatic research by offering additional funds for F32 postdoctoral research projects. **Focus:** Medical research. **Qualif.:** Applicants must be postdoctoral fellows who are currently working in a field relevant to the lymphatic system. **Criteria:** Scientific Review Committee uses the following criteria to evaluate applications: novelty of research and relevance to the mission of LRF; applicants' demonstrated competency and potential for a career in research; qualifications of the mentor and the degree of commitment to supervise and train the fellow during the research period.

Funds Avail.: No specific amount. **To Apply:** Interested applicants must visit the website to obtain an application form.

4821 ■ Lymphatic Research Foundation Postdoctoral Fellowship Awards Program *(Postdoctorate/Fellowship)*

Purpose: To expand and strengthen the pool of outstanding junior investigators in the field of lymphatic research. **Focus:** Medical research. **Qualif.:** Applicants must be postdoctoral scientists in academic, medical or research institutions throughout the world. **Criteria:** Selection will be based on the committee's criteria.

Funds Avail.: $87,396-$98,304. **Duration:** Two years. **To Apply:** Interested applicants must visit the website to obtain an application form. **Deadline:** January 15.

4822 ■ Deborah Munroe Noonan Memorial Research Awards *(Professional development/Grant)*

Purpose: To support innovative clinical and service system research and demonstration projects from both nonprofit organizations and academic institutions that serve children with physical or developmental disabilities and associated health-related complications. **Focus:** Disabilities; Medical research. **Qualif.:** Applicants must hold a position within a nonprofit institution or organization. Project must address the target age range of birth through 23 years old. **Criteria:** Selection will be based on the following criteria: relevance to the Fund's focus; potential impact on the care and quality of life for children and adolescents with disabilities; significance, innovation and feasibility of the project; quality and appropriateness of project design procedures, methods and analytic plans; qualification of the applicants and team to conduct the research project; quality of the letters of support/collaboration.

Funds Avail.: $80,000. **Duration:** Annual. **To Apply:** All application information must be completed online and the proposal uploaded as a PDF by the deadline. In addition, three hard copies of the uploaded PDF must be mailed. The complete application includes an application face sheet, project summary, proposal (eight pages excluding bibliography), CV, proposed budget and letter(s) of support and letter(s) of collaboration. Research projects must be conducted within the Fund's geographic area of interest. **Deadline:** March 13 (online submission); March 17 (mailed materials). **Contact:** Jeanne Brown, Program Officer; E-mail: jbrown@hria.org or Phone: 617-279-2240 loc. 709.

4823 ■ Smith Family Awards Program for Excellence in Biomedical Research *(Advanced Professional, Professional development/Grant)*

Purpose: To launch the careers of newly independent biomedical researchers with the ultimate goal of achieving medical breakthroughs. **Focus:** Medical research. **Qualif.:** Applicants must be full-time faculty members at a nonprofit academic, medical, or research institution in Massachusetts, at Brown or Yale University. They must have completed their postdoctoral training. **Criteria:** Selection will be based on the following criteria: project's scientific merit and the applicants' familiarity with the pertinent literature and the work of other investigators in their field of interest; applicants' potential to carry out independent research and clear ability to develop a sound research plan; objectives that are technically feasible and personnel who are qualified to carry out the proposed research; institutional commitment to the applicants.

Funds Avail.: $300,000 ($100,000 per year inclusive of 5% indirect costs). **Duration:** Annual; Up to 3 years. **To Apply:** All applicants must be internally selected by their institutions. Any school or college within an academic

Awards are arranged alphabetically below their administering organizations

institution in Massachusetts may each submit up to two applications. Each hospital or free standing biomedical research facility in Massachusetts may also submit two applications. Two applications will also be accepted from Brown University and two applications from Yale University. These applications may be submitted from any academic department or school within Brown or Yale or one of their affiliated entities after going through these institutions' internal review process. The department or division Chair must explain how the award will enhance the applicants' research career. The chair must also complete the applicant independence/institutional commitment form. **Deadline:** September 3 (online submission); September 8 (printed materials). **Remarks:** Established in 1992. **Contact:** Gay Lockwood at glockwood@hria.org.

4824 ■ Thome Foundation Awards Program in Age-Related Macular Degeneration Research *(Professional development/Grant)*

Purpose: To support translational research that will lead to improved therapies for individuals suffering from age-related macular degeneration. **Focus:** Visual impairment. **Qualif.:** Applicants must hold a faculty appointment at a nonprofit academic, medical or research institution in the United States. Scientists who have conducted research exploring the biological causes of related disorders and/or similar translational research programs are encouraged to apply. Preference will be given to originality of ideas, regardless of faculty seniority. **Criteria:** The Scientific Review Committee uses the following criteria to evaluate applications: Qualifications of the applicants and prior experience in conducting innovative research; hypothesis that is clearly stated, based on sound precedents and supported by relevant literature; objectives that are well thought out, realistic and technically feasible; research methodology, data collection and data analysis that are feasible and appropriate to the proposal's aims; quality and originality of the research project; potential of the research project to lead to effective treatment of AMD. **Funds Avail.:** $500,000 ($250,000 per year). **Duration:** Two years. **Number Awarded:** Up to 6. **To Apply:** Applicants must visit the website to obtain an application. Initial proposal application must be submitted to the online application system. Applicants who are invited to submit Full Proposals will be notified by email. The full proposal application includes the Application face Sheet, Department or Division Head Letter, Budget Forms, Budget Justification, Applicants' Biosketch and a 10-page Research Proposal. **Contact:** Erin Johnstone, Program Officer at EJohnstone@hria.org; Phone: 617-279-2240, x710.

4825 ■ Thome Foundation Awards Program in Alzheimer's Disease Drug Discovery Research *(Professional development/Grant)*

Purpose: To support pilot studies towards innovative drug discovery research that will lead to improved therapies for individuals suffering from Alzheimer's disease. **Focus:** Alzheimer's disease. **Qualif.:** Applicants must hold a faculty appointment at a nonprofit academic, medical, nongovernmental or research institution in the United States. The sponsoring institution accepts responsibility for the scientific, administrative and financial management of overall projects including any subcontracts used for the project. **Criteria:** The Scientific Review Committee uses the following criteria to evaluate applications: qualifications of the applicants and prior experience in conducting innovative research; hypotheses that is clearly stated, based on sound precedents and supported by relevant literature; objectives that are well thought out, realistic and technically feasible; research methodology, data collection and data analysis that are feasible and appropriate to the proposal's aims; quality and originality of the research project; potential research project contributing to effective treatment of Alzheimer's disease. **Funds Avail.:** $200,000 ($100,000 per year). **Duration:** Two years. **To Apply:** Application form can be obtained at the website. The initial proposal must be submitted to the online application system. Applicants who are invited to submit full research proposals will be notified by email. The full proposal includes the application face sheet, department or division head letter, budget forms, budget justification, applicant's biosketch and a 10-page research proposal. **Deadline:** June 15 - Initial Proposal; September 15 - Full Proposal. **Contact:** Linda Lam, Program Officer at llam@hria.org or 617-279-2240, ext.710.

4826 ■ Healthcare Financial Management Association - Connecticut Chapter

c/o Shannon St. Hilaire, MBA-HCM, FHFMA, President
Middlesex Hospital
28 Crescent St.
Middletown, CT 06457-3650
Ph: (860)358-6890
URL: www.cthfma.org

4827 ■ HFMA Connecticut Chapter Scholarships *(Undergraduate, Graduate/Scholarship)*

Purpose: To encourage and support individuals who are furthering their formal education in healthcare as graduate or undergraduate students based upon the quality of the written response to a question about a current issue in health care. **Focus:** Health care services. **Qualif.:** Applicants must be undergraduate or graduate students in the health care area. **Criteria:** Selection shall be based on the quality of the written response to the question about a current issue in health care. **Funds Avail.:** $4,000 (first place); $1,000 (second place). **Duration:** Annual. **Number Awarded:** Varies. **To Apply:** Applicants must submit a completed scholarship application form along with the required documents. **Deadline:** September 4. **Contact:** Mary G. Messina, HFMA Scholarship Committee, c/o Yale-New Haven Health System One Church Street, Fourth Floor, New Haven, CT 06510; Phone: 203-688-8543; Fax: 203-688-6005; Email: mary.messina@ynhh.org.

4828 ■ Healthcare Information and Management Systems Society (HIMSS)

33 W Monroe St., Ste. 1700
Chicago, IL 60603-5616
Ph: (312)664-4467
Fax: (312)664-6143
E-mail: himss@himss.org
URL: www.himss.org
Facebook: www.facebook.com/HIMSSpage
LinkedIn: www.linkedin.com/groups/93115/profile
Twitter: twitter.com/himss

4829 ■ Dvora Brodie Scholarships *(Graduate, Postgraduate, Undergraduate/Scholarship)*

Purpose: To provide financial support to a HIMSS student member who exhibits excellence and future leadership

potential in the healthcare information and management system industry. **Focus:** Health care services. **Qualif.:** Applicant must be a member in good standing of HIMSS attending a school in New England, or originally be from the New England area; and the primary occupation of the applicant at the time the scholarship is awarded must be that of a student in an accredited undergraduate, Masters, or PhD program related to the healthcare information management systems field. **Criteria:** Recipient will be selected according to merit, financial need, and other factors.
Funds Avail.: No specific amount. **Duration:** Annual. **To Apply:** Applicant must submit a completed application form. **Contact:** scholarships@himss.org.

4830 ■ Richard P. Covert, Ph.D./FHIMSS Scholarships for Management Systems (Graduate, Postgraduate, Undergraduate/Scholarship)
Purpose: To provide financial assistance to students pursuing a degree in Management Engineering. **Focus:** Engineering. **Qualif.:** Applicant must be a member in good standing of HIMSS and the primary occupation of the applicant at the time the scholarship is awarded must be that of student in an accredited undergraduate, Masters or PhD program related to the healthcare information management systems field. **Criteria:** Recipient will be selected according to merit, financial need, and other factors.
Funds Avail.: $5,000. **Duration:** Annual. **To Apply:** Applicant must submit a completed application form. **Deadline:** August 28. **Contact:** scholarships@himss.org.

4831 ■ Healthcare Information Management Systems Scholarships (Graduate, Postgraduate, Undergraduate/Scholarship)
Purpose: To provide financial assistance to students in healthcare and IT-related fields. **Focus:** Health care services. **Qualif.:** Applicant must be a member in good standing of HIMSS and a student in an accredited undergraduate, Master's or PhD program related to the healthcare information or management systems field. **Criteria:** Recipient will be selected according to merit, financial need, and other factors.
Funds Avail.: $5,000. **Duration:** Annual. **Number Awarded:** 3. **To Apply:** Applicant must submit a completed application form. **Contact:** scholarships@himss.org.

4832 ■ Northern California Chapter of HIMSS Scholarships (Graduate, Postgraduate, Undergraduate/Scholarship)
Purpose: To provide financial assistance for a student in healthcare informatics who exhibits academic excellence and future leadership potential in the healthcare information and management systems industry. **Focus:** Health care services. **Qualif.:** Applicant must be a member in good standing of HIMSS or member of National HIMSS and the Northern California Chapter attending a school in the Northern California area and the primary occupation of the applicant at the time the scholarship is awarded must be that of student in an accredited undergraduate, Master's or PhD program related to the healthcare information management systems field. **Criteria:** Recipient will be selected according to merit, financial need and other factors.
Funds Avail.: $5,000. **Duration:** Annual. **To Apply:** Applicant must submit a completed application form. **Deadline:** August 28. **Contact:** scholarships@himss.org.

4833 ■ Hearing Foundation of Canada (TFHC)
1 Yonge St., Ste. 1801
Toronto, ON, Canada M5E 1W7
Ph: (416)364-4060
Fax: (416)369-0515
Free: 866-432-7968
E-mail: info@hearingfoundation.ca
URL: www.hearingfoundation.ca
LinkedIn: www.linkedin.com/company/the-hearing-foundation-of-canada

4834 ■ THFC Medical Research Grants (Professional development/Grant)
Purpose: To support medical research into different areas of hearing loss. **Focus:** Hearing and deafness; Medical research. **Qualif.:** Applicants must be young investigators. Research must be in the categories of basic or clinical research, and focus on biological and clinical projects rather than the psycho-social aspects of hearing loss. **Criteria:** Selection will be based on the scientific merit of the research proposals of the applicants.
Funds Avail.: Up to 25,000 Canadian Dollars. **To Apply:** Applicants must submit a proposal that should be relevant to the cause, prevention, intervention, morbidity, economic or personal impact, and cure of hearing loss. Applications from individuals with or without institutional affiliations will be considered. Applications should be in narrative form and no longer than five single-spaced typewritten pages in length. Two additional pages of supportive attachments from figures or other related data are acceptable, but they must be relevant. All applications must include the following: cover sheet to be completed by the Principal Investigator. Include PI name bottom of every page; co-investigator(s) cover page for each co-investigator; proposed research form, signed by PI; curriculum vitae form for all research personnel; proposed research description, signed by PI. The format for all submission text must be 12 point font, one inch margins and single spaced. **Deadline:** October 25 (by mail); October 31 (by email). **Contact:** Questions can be directed to Jamie Wood, Manager of Programs, at jwood@hearingfoundation.ca.

4835 ■ Heisler Law Office
1011 N Calvert St.
Baltimore, MD 21202
Ph: (410)625-4878
Fax: (410)659-7111
Free: 855-946-0464
E-mail: sheislerlaw@gmail.com
URL: www.theinjurylawyermd.com

4836 ■ Steven H. Heisler Law Scholarships (Graduate/Scholarship)
Purpose: To support an individual who has shown dedication to and involvement in their local community. **Focus:** Law. **Qualif.:** Applicants must be U.S. citizens or authorized to work/go to school in the United States. **Criteria:** Selection will be based on length of community service history, depth of dedication to the community, and ability to clearly convey a complex message.
Funds Avail.: $2,500. **Number Awarded:** 1. **To Apply:** Applicants must visit the website for the online application process. Applicants must provide a copy of Law School acceptance letter and an essay on benefit of community service. **Deadline:** May 1.

4837 ■ Helicopter Foundation International (HFI)
1920 Ballenger Ave.
Alexandria, VA 22314-2898

Awards are arranged alphabetically below their administering organizations

Ph: (703)683-4646
URL: www.helicopterfoundation.org
Facebook: www.facebook.com/helicopterfoundation

4838 ■ Helicopter Foundation International Commercial Helicopter Rating Scholarships *(Other/Scholarship)*

Purpose: To assist private helicopter pilot candidates who wish to obtain their commercial helicopter ratings. **Focus:** Aviation. **Qualif.:** Applicants must already have obtained their Private license and be enrolled in a Commercial Helicopter Rating program at an FAA-approved Part 141 school or international equivalent. **Criteria:** Recipients will be selected based on skills and abilities to be commercial helicopter pilots and interest in pursuing a career as pilot in the helicopter industry.
Funds Avail.: No specific amount. **Duration:** Annual. **Number Awarded:** Up to 4. **To Apply:** Applicants may check the website for further information.

4839 ■ Helicopter Foundation International Maintenance Technician Certificate Scholarships *(Other/Scholarship)*

Purpose: To assist candidates who wish to obtain Maintenance Technician certificate. **Focus:** Aviation. **Qualif.:** Applicants must already be enrolled in a Maintenance Technician Certificate program at an FAA-approved Part 147 school or international equivalent. **Criteria:** Recipients are selected based on financial need.
Duration: Annual. **Number Awarded:** Up to 6. **To Apply:** Applicants may check the website for further information.

4840 ■ Michelle North Scholarships for Safety *(Other/Scholarship)*

Purpose: To assist private helicopter pilot candidates who wish to obtain their commercial helicopter ratings. **Focus:** Aviation. **Qualif.:** Applicants must be pilots who have already attained a commercial rating and demonstrate an outstanding aptitude for safe flying and aviation best practices. **Criteria:** Recipients are selected based on the aforesaid qualifications.
Funds Avail.: No specific amount. **Duration:** Annual. **Number Awarded:** 1. **To Apply:** Applicants may check the website for further information.

4841 ■ Bill Sanderson Aviation Maintenance Technician Scholarships *(Postgraduate/Scholarship)*

Purpose: To assist private helicopter pilot candidates who wish to obtain their commercial helicopter ratings. **Focus:** Aviation. **Qualif.:** Applicants must be about to graduate from an FAA approved Part 147 AMT school or be recent recipients within the last three years of an Airframe and Powerplant Certificate. **Criteria:** Recipients are selected based on demonstrated interest in the field of aviation.
Funds Avail.: Maximum of $1,600. **Duration:** Annual. **Number Awarded:** Up to 8. **To Apply:** Applicants may check the website for further information.

4842 ■ Hellenic Times Scholarship Fund
823 11th Ave., 5th Fl.
New York, NY 10019-3557
Fax: (212)977-3662
E-mail: htsfund@aol.com
URL: www.htsf.org

4843 ■ Hellenic Times Scholarships *(Undergraduate, Graduate/Scholarship)*

Purpose: To provide financial support to Greek descent students. **Focus:** General studies/Field of study not specified. **Qualif.:** Applicants must be undergraduate or graduate students; must be enrolled in an accredited college or university in the United States; must be of Greek descent aged between 17 and 25. **Criteria:** Selection will be based on necessity and merit.
Funds Avail.: No specific amount. **Duration:** Annual. **To Apply:** Applicants must submit a completed application form, applicants' photo, official school transcripts and a copy of tax returns. Winners are required to submit a copy of their Bursar tuition bill. **Deadline:** April 30.

4844 ■ Hellenic University Club of Philadelphia (HUC)
PO Box 42199
Philadelphia, PA 19101-2199
Ph: (215)483-7440
E-mail: hucphiladelphia@gmail.com
URL: hucphiladelphia.org
Facebook: www.facebook.com/pages/Hellenic-University-Club-of-Philadelphia/107120016016523
Twitter: twitter.com/HUCPhila

4845 ■ Christopher Demetris Memorial Scholarships *(Undergraduate/Scholarship)*

Purpose: To support students who are of Eastern Orthodox faith, and in need. **Focus:** Greek studies. **Qualif.:** Applicants must be of Greek descent, U.S. citizens or lawful permanent residents of Berks, Bucks, Chester, Delaware, Lancaster, Lehigh, Montgomery or Philadelphia Counties in Pennsylvania, Atlantic, Burlington, Camden, Cape May, Cumberland, Gloucester or Salem Counties in New Jersey. Students who are declared majors in Greek Studies may also apply, regardless of their heritage. They must be also enrolled full-time in a degree program at an accredited four-year college or university. High school seniors accepted for enrollment in such a degree program may also apply. **Criteria:** Selection will be based on merit and financial need.
Funds Avail.: $2,000. **Duration:** Annual. **To Apply:** Application forms can be obtained from the HUCPhila website. Applicants must complete the application form and mail to Scholarship Chairman. Applicants must also provide one letter of recommendation and scholastic transcripts. **Deadline:** April 4.

4846 ■ Dr. Michael Dorizas Memorial Scholarships *(Undergraduate/Scholarship)*

Purpose: To provide scholarship for students with outstanding academic qualifications and financial need. **Focus:** Greek studies. **Qualif.:** Applicants must be of Greek descent, U.S. citizens or lawful permanent residents of Berks, Bucks, Chester, Delaware, Lancaster, Lehigh, Montgomery or Philadelphia Counties in Pennsylvania, Atlantic, Burlington, Camden, Cape May, Cumberland, Gloucester or Salem Counties in New Jersey. Students who are declared majors in Greek Studies may also apply, regardless of their heritage. They must be also enrolled full-time in a degree program at an accredited four-year college or university. High school seniors accepted for enrollment in such a degree program may also apply. **Criteria:** Selection will be based on academic merit and financial need.

Awards are arranged alphabetically below their administering organizations

Funds Avail.: $3,000. **Duration:** Annual. **To Apply:** Application form can be obtained from the HUCPhila website. Applicants must complete the application form and mail to Scholarship Chairman. Applicants must also provide one letter of recommendation and scholastic transcripts. **Deadline:** April 4. **Remarks:** The scholarship was established in honor of the late Dr. Michael Dorizas, a widely respected Philadelphia educator, lecturer and athlete.

4847 ■ Hellenic University Club of Philadelphia Founders Scholarships *(Undergraduate/Scholarship)*

Purpose: To provide scholarships for students with outstanding academic qualifications and financial need. **Focus:** Greek studies. **Qualif.:** Applicants must be of Greek descents, U.S. citizens or lawful permanent residents of Berks, Bucks, Chester, Delaware, Lancaster, Lehigh, Montgomery or Philadelphia Counties in Pennsylvania, Atlantic, Burlington, Camden, Cape May, Cumberland, Gloucester or Salem Counties in New Jersey. Students who are declared majors in Greek Studies may also apply, regardless of their heritage. They must be also enrolled full-time in a degree program at an accredited four-year college or university. High school seniors accepted for enrollment in such a degree program may also apply. **Criteria:** Scholarship will be given based on merit.

Funds Avail.: $3,000. **Duration:** Annual. **To Apply:** Application form can be obtained from the HUCPhila website. Applicants must complete the application form and mail to Scholarship Chairman. Applicants must also provide one letter of recommendation and scholastic transcripts. **Deadline:** April 4. **Remarks:** The scholarship was established to honor the deceased founders of the Hellenic University Club of Philadelphia.

4848 ■ Nicholas S. Hetos, DDS, Memorial Graduate Scholarships *(Graduate, Doctorate/Scholarship)*

Purpose: To provide scholarships for students with outstanding academic qualifications and financial need. **Focus:** Dentistry. **Qualif.:** Applicants must be of Greek descent, U.S. citizens or lawful permanent residents of Berks, Bucks, Chester, Delaware, Lancaster, Lehigh, Montgomery or Philadelphia Counties in Pennsylvania, Atlantic, Burlington, Camden, Cape May, Cumberland, Gloucester or Salem Counties in New Jersey. Students who are declared majors in Greek Studies may also apply, regardless of their heritage. They must be also enrolled full-time in a degree program at an accredited four-year college or university, and senior undergraduate or graduate students with financial need pursuing studies leading to a Doctoral of Dental Medicine (D.M.D.) or Doctoral of Dental Surgery (D.D.S.) Degree. **Criteria:** Selection will be based on merit and financial need.

Funds Avail.: $2,000. **Duration:** Annual. **To Apply:** Application forms can be obtained from the HUCPhila website. Applicants must send their name and address to Scholarship Chairman. Applicants must also provide one letter of recommendation and scholastic transcripts. **Deadline:** April 4. **Remarks:** The scholarship was established to honor Dr. Nicholas S. Hetos, Philadelphia dentist, past president and founding member of the Hellenic University Club of Philadelphia. This scholarship is funded by Dr. Maria G. Hetos. Established in 2001.

4849 ■ Dr. Nicholas Padis Memorial Graduate Scholarships *(Graduate/Scholarship)*

Purpose: To provide educational support to students who are in need. **Focus:** General studies/Field of study not specified. **Qualif.:** Applicants must be of Greek descents, U.S. citizens or lawful permanent residents of Berks, Bucks, Chester, Delaware, Lancaster, Lehigh, Montgomery or Philadelphia Counties in Pennsylvania, Atlantic, Burlington, Camden, Cape May, Cumberland, Gloucester or Salem Counties in New Jersey. **Criteria:** The Scholarship Committee will select students who have the highest academic achievement to be the recipients of the award.

Funds Avail.: $5,000. **Duration:** Annual. **To Apply:** Application form can be obtained from the HUCPhila website. Applicants must send their name and address to Scholarship Chairman. Applicants must also submit a transcript, resume, two letters of recommendation, essay and page 1 of FAFSA Student Aid Report. **Deadline:** April 4. **Remarks:** The scholarship was established to honor Philadelphia physician, first president and founding member of the Hellenic University Club of Philadelphia, Dr. Nicholas Padis. Established in 1986.

4850 ■ Dr. Peter A. Theodos Memorial Graduate Scholarships *(Undergraduate, Graduate/Scholarship)*

Purpose: To provide scholarship for students with outstanding academic qualifications and financial need. **Focus:** Medicine. **Qualif.:** Applicants must be of Greek descent, U.S. citizens or lawful permanent residents of Berks, Bucks, Chester, Delaware, Lancaster, Lehigh, Montgomery or Philadelphia Counties in Pennsylvania, Atlantic, Burlington, Camden, Cape May, Cumberland, Gloucester or Salem Counties in New Jersey. Students who are declared majors in Greek Studies may also apply, regardless of their heritage. They must be also enrolled full-time in a degree program at an accredited four-year college or university; senior undergraduate or graduate students with financial need pursuing studies leading to a Doctor of Medicine (M.D.) Degree. **Criteria:** Selection will be based on academic merit and financial need.

Funds Avail.: $1,500. **Duration:** Annual. **To Apply:** Application form can be obtained from the HUCPhila website. Applicants must send their name and address to the Scholarship Chairman and provide one letter of recommendation and scholastic transcripts. **Deadline:** April 4. **Remarks:** The scholarship was established to honor Philadelphia physician, past president and founding member of the Hellenic University Club of Philadelphia, Dr. Peter A. Theodos. The scholarship is funded by Mrs. Peter A. Theodos. Established in 2001.

4851 ■ Dimitri J. Ververelli Memorial Scholarship for Architecture and/or Engineering *(Undergraduate/Scholarship)*

Purpose: To provide educational support to students who are in need. **Focus:** Architecture; Engineering. **Qualif.:** Applicants must be of Greek descent, U.S. citizens or lawful permanent residents of Berks, Bucks, Chester, Delaware, Lancaster, Lehigh, Montgomery or Philadelphia Counties in Pennsylvania, Atlantic, Burlington, Camden, Cape May, Cumberland, Gloucester or Salem Counties in New Jersey. Students who are declared majors in Greek Studies may also apply, regardless of their heritage; they must be also enrolled full-time in a degree program at an accredited four-year college or university. High school seniors accepted for enrollment in such a degree program may also apply. **Criteria:** Selection will be based on merit and financial need.

Funds Avail.: $2,000. **Duration:** Annual. **To Apply:** Application form can be obtained from the HUCPhila website. Applicants must complete the application form and mail to

Awards are arranged alphabetically below their administering organizations

Scholarship Chairman. Applicants must also provide one letter of recommendation and scholastic transcripts. **Deadline:** April 4. **Remarks:** The scholarship was established by Mrs. Anastasia Ververelli to honor her husband, Dimitri J. Ververelli, a past president of the Hellenic University Club of Philadelphia.

4852 ■ Helsell Fetterman L.L.P.
1001 4th Ave., Ste. 4200
Seattle, WA 98154-1154
Ph: (206)292-1144
Fax: (206)340-0902
E-mail: info@helsell.com
URL: www.helsell.com
Facebook: www.facebook.com/pages/Helsell-Fetterman/320135294701862
LinkedIn: www.linkedin.com/company/helsell-fetterman-llp

4853 ■ Richard S. White Fellowships
(Undergraduate/Fellowship)

Purpose: To assist law students in their educational pursuit. **Focus:** Law. **Qualif.:** Applicants must be second year law students in good standing pursuing a law degree at an ABA-accredited law school; possess an academic record, leadership abilities and a commitment to personal and professional initiatives that indicate promise for a successful legal career; demonstrate an interest and commitment to both the practice areas represented at Helsell Fetterman and to building a practice in the Seattle area. **Criteria:** Scholarship will be based on the committee's criteria.

Funds Avail.: $7,500. **Duration:** 12 weeks. **To Apply:** Applicants must prepare a 1- to 2-page personal statement on a topic of their choice that allows the firm to fully evaluate their candidacy and ability to enrich the diversity of the legal community. Completed application form must be submitted together with the following: current resume; copy of final undergraduate transcript and current law school transcript, unofficial is acceptable; legal writing sample up to 10 pages; three professional and/or academic references with contact information.

4854 ■ Hemingway Foundation and Society
c/o Gail Sinclair
Rollins College
1000 Holt Ave. 2770
Winter Park, FL 32789
URL: www.hemingwaysociety.org
Facebook: www.facebook.com/HemingwaySociety
Twitter: www.twitter.com/theEHSociety

4855 ■ Ernest Hemingway Research Grants *(Other/Grant)*

Purpose: To provide funds for scholars and students who are doing research in the Ernest Hemingway Collection. **Focus:** General studies/Field of study not specified. **Qualif.:** Applicant must be a scholar and student interested or doing research in Ernest Hemingway Collection. **Criteria:** Grant applications are evaluated on the basis of expected utilization of the Hemingway Collection. Preference is given to dissertation research by Ph.D. candidates working in newly opened or relatively unused portions of the collection, but all proposals are welcome and will receive careful consideration.

Funds Avail.: $200 - $1,000. **To Apply:** Application forms are available at the website and must be accompanied by a brief proposal (three to four pages) in the form of a letter or more describing the planned research, its significance; must submit two letters of recommendation from academic or other appropriate references; must have a sample of applicant's writing, a project budget, and a vitae. **Deadline:** November 2. **Contact:** Application forms and other supporting materials must be sent to: Grant and Fellowship Coordinator, John F. Kennedy Presidential Library and Museum, Columbia Point, Boston, MA 02125; Phone: 617-514-1630; Fax: 617-514-1325; Email: stephen.plotkin@nara.gov.

4856 ■ Jim and Nancy Hinkle Travel Grants
(Graduate/Grant)

Purpose: To assist graduate students to attend the biennial international conferences. **Focus:** General studies/Field of study not specified. **Qualif.:** Recipients must be members in good standing of the Hemingway Society; must currently be enrolled in a graduate degree program, and must be planning to present a paper at the conference. **Criteria:** Applications are selected by the Hickle Travel Grant Committee and evaluated by the following criteria: clarity, originality, and value in furthering Hemingway scholarship, criticism, or instruction. Application from previous Hinkle winners are welcome, applications from students who have not won before will be given priority.

Funds Avail.: No specific amount. **To Apply:** Application must include the following information: (1) Full name of applicant, (2) address, phone, email, (3) Social Security Number, (4) Paper title & abstract, (5) Degree program and school, (6) Letter of recommendation. Applications should be sent to Hinkle Selection Committee Chair: Suzanne del Gizzo, 380 Wellington Terrace, Jenkintown, PA 19046. **Deadline:** October 1.

4857 ■ Lewis-Reynolds-Smith Founders Fellowship
(Graduate/Fellowship)

Purpose: To support the development of a Hemingway-related project. **Focus:** General studies/Field of study not specified. **Qualif.:** Applicant must be a graduate student, independent scholar, or post-doctoral up through the rank of assistant professor. **Criteria:** Applications are ranked by the committee based on the following criteria: clarity, originality, and feasibility, criticism, or instruction; and the likelihood of its publication.

Funds Avail.: $1,000 each. **Duration:** Annual. **To Apply:** Applicant must submit as a Microsoft word attachment or send by mail the following information and agreements: (1) Full name and Social Security Number, (2) Addresses, phone numbers and email address (including summer and between session), (3) Degree program and school, (4) Verification of graduate enrollment status or awarded degree (if appropriate); must have the description of Hemingway Project (200-word limit). **Deadline:** February 1. **Contact:** Application form and supporting documents must be sent to: Prof. Debra A. Moddelmog, Fellowship Committee Chair, Dept. of English, Ohio State University, 421 Denney Hall, 164 W, 17th Ave., Colombus, OH 43210.

4858 ■ Hemophilia Federation of America (HFA)
820 1st St. NE, Ste. 720
Washington, DC 20002
Ph: (202)675-6984
Fax: (202)675-6983
Free: 800-230-9797
E-mail: info@hemophiliafed.org

Awards are arranged alphabetically below their administering organizations

URL: www.hemophiliafed.org
Facebook: www.facebook.com/hemophiliafed
Twitter: twitter.com/hemophiliafed

4859 ■ Millie Gonzalez Memorial Scholarships (Undergraduate/Scholarship)

Purpose: To encourage educational pursuits among women with bleeding disorders through providing financial assistance. **Focus:** General studies/Field of study not specified. **Qualif.:** Eligible applicants for the scholarship are women with hemophilia or von Willebrand disease and their immediate family members. **Criteria:** Recipients are chosen based on combined merit and need.

Funds Avail.: $1,000. **Duration:** Annual. **To Apply:** Applicants are encouraged to submit their applications electronically. All the necessary instructions and application forms can be downloaded from the website. **Deadline:** August 1. **Contact:** Linda Leigh Sulser, Scholarship Liaison: Phone: 877-376-4968; Email: Scholarships@FactorSupport.com.

4860 ■ Hemophilia Federation of America Educational Scholarships (Undergraduate/Scholarship)

Purpose: To assists and advocates for the bleeding disorders community. **Focus:** Hemophilia. **Qualif.:** Applicants must have hemophilia or von Willebrand (VWD) and must be seeking a post-secondary education from a college, university, or trade school; must be members of the bleeding disorders community. Applicants must be able to demonstrate a commitment in improving quality of life by pursuing his/her goals with determination. **Criteria:** Selection will be based on the scholarship Committee of HFA.

Funds Avail.: $1,500. **Number Awarded:** 10. **To Apply:** Applicants must submit a completed application; essay; proof of academic standing; statement of financial need and parents previous year's tax return (if applicant is a dependent, otherwise the applicant's tax return); proof of enrollment; two letters of reference (one professional reference the other from the HTC or physician) **Deadline:** April 30.

4861 ■ Mike Hylton and Ron Niederman Memorial Scholarships (Undergraduate/Scholarship)

Purpose: To encourage educational pursuits among men with bleeding disorders through providing financial assistance. **Focus:** General studies/Field of study not specified. **Qualif.:** Eligible applicants for the scholarship are individuals with hemophilia or von Willebrand disease and their immediate family members. **Criteria:** Recipients are chosen based on combined merit and need.

Funds Avail.: $1,000. **Duration:** Annual. **Number Awarded:** 10. **To Apply:** Application requirements and instructions are available from the website. **Deadline:** August 1. **Contact:** Linda Leigh Sulser, Scholarship Liaison: Phone: 877-376-4968; Email: scholarships@factorsupport.com.

4862 ■ Herb Society of America (HSA)

9019 Kirtland Chardon Rd.
Kirtland, OH 44094
Ph: (440)256-0514
Fax: (440)256-0541
E-mail: herbs@herbsociety.org
URL: www.herbsociety.org
Facebook: www.facebook.com/The-Herb-Society-of-America-10720845126

4863 ■ Nashville Unit Scholarships (Undergraduate/Scholarship)

Purpose: To provide financial assistance to those students who are in need. **Focus:** Horticulture. **Qualif.:** Applicants must be permanent residents of Tennessee; must be current college freshman, sophomore or junior students who are American citizens. **Criteria:** Recipients are selected based on financial need and academic performance.

Funds Avail.: $1,500. **To Apply:** Applicants must submit a completed application form and two letters of reference. **Deadline:** April 1.

4864 ■ Pennsylvania Heartland Unit Scholarships (Undergraduate/Scholarship)

Purpose: To provide support to students who are active within the field of horticulture. **Focus:** Horticulture. **Qualif.:** Applicants must be third or fourth year students of an associate degree program within the study of horticulture; must be residents of Berks, Montgomery, York, Lancaster or Schuylkill county. **Criteria:** Recipients are selected based on financial need and academic performance.

Funds Avail.: $1,000 - $1,500. **Duration:** Annual. **Number Awarded:** 2. **To Apply:** Applicants must submit: a completed application form; two letters of reference from which one must come from an advisor or professor and one from a reference of the student's choice; must submit an official school transcript; and an essay stating their reasons for choosing the field of horticulture and future plans. **Deadline:** April 1. **Contact:** Jeannette Lanshe, jetlan1@aol.com.

4865 ■ South Texas Unit Scholarships (Undergraduate/Scholarship)

Purpose: To provide support to students who are in need. **Focus:** Horticulture. **Qualif.:** Applicants must be students who are studying agronomy, horticulture, botany or a closely-related discipline at an accredited four-year college or university; must be either permanent residents of Texas or attending an accredited college or university in Texas; must have completed two full years of college and be entering their junior or senior year of studies. **Criteria:** Recipients are selected based on academic performance and financial need.

Funds Avail.: $1,000. **Duration:** Annual. **To Apply:** Applicants must submit a completed application form and recommendation from professor or guidance counselor. **Contact:** Application form and other supporting documents should be sent to PO Box 6515 Houston, TX 77265-6515.

4866 ■ Western Reserve Herb Society Scholarships (Undergraduate/Scholarship)

Purpose: To support students with their studies in horticulture or any related fields. **Focus:** Horticulture. **Qualif.:** Applicants must be: undergraduate students; Ohio residents; studying horticulture or a related field such as landscape architecture or horticultural therapy; planning a career involving teaching/research or work in the public sector; entering their second to fifth year of an undergraduate program at an accredited college or university. **Criteria:** Recipients are selected based on academic performance and financial need.

Funds Avail.: $6,750. **Number Awarded:** 1. **To Apply:** Applicants must submit a completed application form. **Deadline:** April 1.

Awards are arranged alphabetically below their administering organizations

4867 ■ Francis Sylvia Zverina Scholarships
(Undergraduate/Scholarship)

Purpose: To provide financial assistance to students who are in need. **Focus:** Horticulture. **Qualif.:** Applicants must be students in good scholastic standing who are studying horticulture or related fields such as landscape architecture or horticultural therapy; must have horticultural career goals involving teaching/research or work in the public sector; must be U.S. citizens; must have completed their second or third year of undergraduate school at an accredited college or university anywhere in United States. **Criteria:** Recipients are selected based on academic records and financial need.

Funds Avail.: $9,380. **Duration:** Annual. **Number Awarded:** 2. **To Apply:** Applicants must submit a completed application form.

4868 ■ Hereditary Disease Foundation (HDF)
3960 Broadway, 6th Fl.
New York, NY 10032
Ph: (212)928-2121
Fax: (212)928-2172
E-mail: cures@hdfoundation.org
URL: www.hdfoundation.org

4869 ■ Hereditary Disease Foundation Basic Research Grants *(Advanced Professional/Grant)*

Purpose: To support projects that contribute in identifying and understanding the fundamental defects in Huntington's disease and related disorders. **Focus:** Huntington's disease. **Qualif.:** Applicants are those who are conducting research on Huntington's disease. **Criteria:** Applications will be reviewed by the Scientific Advisory Board. Consideration is given to treatments and cures for Huntington's disease. Selected applicants will receive a written notification of the funding decision.

Funds Avail.: $50,000 per year. **Duration:** Annual. **To Apply:** Applicants may visit the website to verify the application process and other pieces of information.

4870 ■ Herpetologists' League (HL)
c/o Meredith Mahoney, Treasurer
ISM Research and Collections Ctr.
1011 E Ash St.
Springfield, IL 62703
Ph: (217)785-4843
URL: www.herpetologistsleague.org
Facebook: www.facebook.com/HerpetologistsLeague

4871 ■ The Herpetologists' League Graduate Research Award *(Graduate/Award)*

Purpose: To support graduate students devoted to studying herpetology. **Focus:** Herpetology. **Qualif.:** Applicants must be member of The Herpetologists' League in good standing; must be either a registered graduate student or have completed their graduate degree within 14 months of their presentation. **Criteria:** Selection will be based on the committee's criteria.

Funds Avail.: $200-$500. **Duration:** Annual. **Number Awarded:** Up to 5. **To Apply:** Applicants must submit an abstract, of which they must be the senior author and have done the majority of the work, by the deadline for submission of abstracts to the Joint Meetings, indicating their desire to complete for the HL Graduate Research Award. Applicants must give the oral presentation at the meeting.

4872 ■ Jones-Lovich Grants in Southwestern Herpetology *(Master's, Doctorate/Grant)*

Purpose: To support herpetological field research in the American Southwest. **Focus:** Herpetology. **Qualif.:** Applicants must be members in good standing of The Herpetologists' League; must be MS or PhD graduate students; must be registered and in good standing in a degree-granting program. The project must be original work that is authored and conducted by the applicants. The research must involve amphibians or reptiles that occur in the southwestern United States and northwestern Mexico. **Criteria:** Selection will be based on the committee's criteria.

Funds Avail.: $1,000. **To Apply:** Applicants must submit a 1,200 words proposal, excluding citations, budget, cover page or CV, double-spaced, with one inch margins and 12-pt. font. Applicants must also include the following: a cover page provided at the HL website; a detailed budget, as well as sources and amounts of current and pending support; a two-page CV that includes applicants' telephone number, email and mailing address. Arrange in advance for one letter of support to be sent separately by the supporter to Carol Spencer. **Deadline:** January 7. **Contact:** Carol Spencer at atrox@berkeley.edu.

4873 ■ E. E. Williams Research Grants *(Master's, Doctorate/Grant)*

Purpose: To support the research of graduate students. **Focus:** Biology; Herpetology. **Qualif.:** Applicants must be members in good standing of The Herpetologists' League; must be MS or PhD candidates, registered and in good standing in a degree-granting program; project must be original work, authored and conducted by the applicants. **Criteria:** Selection will be based on the committee's criteria.

Funds Avail.: $1,000. **To Apply:** Application forms can be obtained at the website. Proposals must be maximum 1,200 words, double spaced, with 12 pt. font and one inch margins. Name the file with applicants' name and category. Applicants must include the cover page, available at the website, a detailed budget, as well as sources, and amounts of current and pending support. Applicants must clearly designate the proposal category on the cover page. Arrange in advance for one letter of support to be sent separately by the supporter. Include a two-page CV that includes telephone, email and mailing addresses. Send complete application as a single PDF electronically to Ann Paterson. **Deadline:** December 15. **Contact:** Ann Paterson at apaterson@wbcoll.edu.

4874 ■ The Hertz Foundation
2300 First St., Ste 250
Livermore, CA 94550
Ph: (925)373-1642
URL: www.hertzfoundation.org

4875 ■ Hertz Foundation Graduate Fellowship Award *(Graduate/Fellowship)*

Purpose: To support the students of the applied physical, biological and engineering science who are willing to morally commit to make their skills available in time of national emergency. **Focus:** Engineering; Science. **Qualif.:** Applicants must be students of the applied physical, biological and engineering sciences who are citizens or permanent residents of the United States of America, and who are will-

Awards are arranged alphabetically below their administering organizations

ing to morally commit to make their skills available to the United States in time of national emergency; must be college seniors wishing to pursue the PhD degree in any of the fields of particular interest to the Foundation, as well as graduate students already in the process of doing so. **Criteria:** Award is based on merit.

Funds Avail.: $32,000; $38,000; $6,000. **Duration:** Annual. **To Apply:** Interested applicants must visit the website to create a log in and password to view and access the application. Applicants must submit the necessary application requirements and other documents asked by the Foundation. **Deadline:** October 31.

4876 ■ Hertz Foundation Thesis Prize *(Graduate/Prize)*

Purpose: To support graduate students in the applied physical, biological, and engineering sciences for the purpose of solving difficult, real-world problems. **Focus:** Engineering; Science. **Qualif.:** Applicants must be graduate student in the applied physical, biological and engineering sciences. **Criteria:** Selection will be based on the overall excellence and pertinence to high-impact applications of the physical sciences.

Funds Avail.: $5,000. **Duration:** Annual. **To Apply:** Applicants are required to furnish the Foundation with copies of doctoral dissertation upon receiving the Ph.D. Applicants may contact the Foundation for the application process and other details.

4877 ■ Higher Education Consortium for Urban Affairs (HECUA)
2233 University Ave. W, Ste. 210
Saint Paul, MN 55114
Ph: (651)287-3300
Fax: (651)659-9421
E-mail: hecua@hecua.org
URL: www.hecua.org
Facebook: www.facebook.com/pages/Higher-Education
 -Consortium-for-Urban-Affairs-HECUA/
 28262965017?ref=aymt_homepage_panel
LinkedIn: www.linkedin.com/
 groups?home=&gid=6793581&trk=anet_ug_hm
Twitter: twitter.com/HECUA_offcampus

4878 ■ HECUA Scholarship for Community Engagement *(Undergraduate/Scholarship)*

Purpose: To support students who have worked for social change and whose future goals will be strengthened by a HECUA semester program. **Focus:** Urban affairs/design/planning. **Qualif.:** Applicants must be enrolled in HECUA program (semester-long or short-term programs abroad or in the U.S. are all eligible). For students to be considered enrolled, their application must have been accepted by the HECUA Student Services Department and the must have subsequently submitted a completed and signed Participation Agreement Letter and non-refundable program deposit. **Criteria:** Selection will be based on the committees' criteria.

Funds Avail.: $750. **To Apply:** Applicants must submit the following requirements: Scholarship for Community Engagement Application Form; reflective essay answering to questions of "How have past experiences led you to consider yourself a person who values community engagement?" and "How do you expect the HECUA program will enable you to further your goals and projects for social change?". A complete program application to one of HECUA's semester-long or short-term programs must be on file at HECUA. **Deadline:** December 1; April 15.

4879 ■ HECUA Scholarship for Social Justice *(Undergraduate/Scholarship)*

Purpose: To fund the first generation college students with low-income to support their studies. **Focus:** Education. **Qualif.:** Applicants must be first generation college students, or students from a low-income family, or students of color who are currently enrolled in one of HECUA's member colleges/universities in a semester-long domestic or international HECUA program (HECUA's short-term programs are not eligible). For students to be considered enrolled, their application must have been accepted by the HECUA Student Services Department and the student must have subsequently submitted a completed and signed Participation Agreement Letter and a non-refundable program deposit. **Criteria:** Selection will be based on the committees' criteria.

Funds Avail.: $1,500. **To Apply:** Applicants must submit scholarship application form, copy of students' FAFSA form and reflective essay composed of: drawing of the applicants' life experience and personal and academic goals; explanation of the applicants on how they believe they can contribute to and receive from a program with the mission to equip students with the knowledge, experiences, tools and passion to address nowadays pressing social justice issues and; reflect on how the HECUA program will benefit the applicants, people, issues and communities they care about. **Deadline:** April 15; December 1.

4880 ■ Hill Country Master Gardeners
AgriLife Ext., Kerr County Office
3655 Highway 27
Kerrville, TX 78028
Ph: (830)257-6568
Fax: (830)257-6573
E-mail: kerr@ag.tamu.edu
URL: www.hillcountrymastergardeners.org

4881 ■ Hill Country Master Gardeners Horticulture Scholarships *(Undergraduate/Scholarship)*

Purpose: To provide financial support to two undergraduate or graduate students at Texas A&M, Texas Tech, Tarleton State or Stephen F. Austin State University. **Focus:** Horticulture. **Qualif.:** Applicants must be pursuing a horticultural sciences degree; must be full-time students (12 hours for undergraduate and nine hours for graduate students) in one of the four universities mentioned; must be in junior level with a GPA of 3.0; must be Texas residents; preference will be given to students residing at Kerr, Kendal, Gillespie and Bandera Counties. **Criteria:** Selection will be based on the evaluation of submitted documents and specific criteria.

Funds Avail.: $2,000. **Duration:** Annual. **Number Awarded:** 2. **To Apply:** Applicants must submit a completed application form; two letters of recommendation from an instructor and other qualified persons; college transcripts, including the most recent semester, sealed in an envelope. **Deadline:** May 31. **Contact:** Hill Country Master Gardeners, at the above address.

4882 ■ Hispanic Association of Colleges and Universities (HACU)
8415 Datapoint Dr., Ste. 400
San Antonio, TX 78229

Awards are arranged alphabetically below their administering organizations

Ph: (210)692-3805
Fax: (210)692-0823
E-mail: hacu@hacu.net
URL: www.hacu.net/hacu/default.asp
Facebook: www.facebook.com/HACUnews
LinkedIn: www.linkedin.com/company/hispanic-association-of-colleges-and-universities

4883 ■ HACU/Denny's Hungry for Education Scholarships *(Undergraduate, Graduate/Scholarship)*

Purpose: To assist students in defraying some of the educational expenditures. **Focus:** Child care. **Qualif.:** Applicants must be full or part-time undergraduate or graduate students attending a two-year or four-year HACU-member institutions within the following states: Arizona, California, Colorado, D.C., Florida, Georgia, Illinois, North Carolina, New Mexico, Nevada, New York, South Carolina, Texas and Washington; and must possess a minimum cumulative GPA of 2.5. **Criteria:** Selection will be based on the committee's criteria.

Funds Avail.: $1,000. **To Apply:** Applicants must submit a 500-word essay on how Denny's can help in the fight against childhood hunger in the United States together with enrollment verification form and transcript. **Deadline:** April 2.

4884 ■ HACU/Empacadora Fruticola Santa Ines S.A. de C.V. Scholarships *(Undergraduate, Graduate/Scholarship)*

Purpose: To assist students in defraying some of the educational expenditures. **Focus:** Environmental science. **Qualif.:** Applicants must be full time and part time undergraduate and graduate students attending a two-year or four-year institution; and must have a minimum cumulative GPA of 3.0 with a declared major in agriculture or ecological/environmental sciences. **Criteria:** Preference will be given to students who live in (originate from) Southern Arizona or Southern California.

Funds Avail.: $1,000. **To Apply:** Applicants must submit an enrollment verification form and transcript. **Deadline:** May 29.

4885 ■ HACU/Gilberto Salazar Escoboza Scholarships *(Undergraduate, Graduate/Scholarship)*

Purpose: To assist students in defraying some of the educational expenditures. **Focus:** Environmental science. **Qualif.:** Applicants must be full time and part time undergraduate and graduate students attending a two-year or four-year institution; and must have a minimum cumulative GPA of 3.0 with a declared major in agriculture or ecological/environmental sciences. **Criteria:** Preference will be given to students who live in (originate from) Southern Arizona or Southern California.

Funds Avail.: $1,000. **To Apply:** Applicants must submit an enrollment verification form and transcript. **Deadline:** May 29.

4886 ■ HACU/JCPenny Leadership Excellence Scholarships *(Undergraduate, Graduate/Scholarship)*

Purpose: To assist students in defraying some of the educational expenditures. **Focus:** Business. **Qualif.:** Applicants must be full-time undergraduate or graduate students attending four-year HACU member institution within the United States or Puerto Rico; must possess a minimum cumulative GPA of 3.0. **Criteria:** Selection will be based on the committee's criteria.

Funds Avail.: $2,500. **To Apply:** Applicants must submit an enrollment verification form and transcript. **Deadline:** May 22.

4887 ■ HACU/KIA Motors America, Inc. Scholarships *(Undergraduate, Graduate/Scholarship)*

Purpose: To assist students in defraying some of the educational expenditures. **Focus:** General studies/Field of study not specified. **Qualif.:** Applicants must be full-time undergraduate and graduate students attending a four-year HACU-member institution within the United States or Puerto Rico; must possess a minimum cumulative GPA of 3.0. **Criteria:** Selection will be based on the committee's criteria.

Funds Avail.: $4,000. **To Apply:** Applicants must submit the two supporting documents: enrollment verification form and transcript. **Deadline:** May 29.

4888 ■ HACU/NASCAR Scholarships *(Graduate, Undergraduate/Scholarship)*

Purpose: To assist students in defraying some of the college expenditures of students in HACU-member institutions. **Focus:** Broadcasting; Business; Engineering; Management; Public relations; Technology. **Qualif.:** Applicants must be full-time undergraduate and graduate students majoring in business, engineering, public relations, mass media, technology, sports marketing and marketing/management and attending a HACU-member four-year institution in Florida, North Carolina or Georgia. **Criteria:** Selection will be based on the committee's criteria.

Funds Avail.: $2,200 each. **Duration:** Annual. **Number Awarded:** 6. **To Apply:** Applicants must fill out the application form and must provide any documents showing that they are currently enrolled or accepted by a college, university, or institution. **Deadline:** May 29. **Remarks:** The scholarship is awarded by HACU, in partnership with NASCAR. **Contact:** HACU scholarship program at scholarship@hacu.net.

4889 ■ HACU/Videxport S.A. de C.V. Scholarships *(Undergraduate, Graduate/Scholarship)*

Purpose: To assist students in defraying some of the educational expenditures. **Focus:** Environmental science. **Qualif.:** Applicants must be full-time or part-time undergraduate or graduate students majoring in agriculture or ecological/environmental sciences and have a minimum cumulative GPA of 3.0. **Criteria:** Preference will be given to students who live in (originate from) Southern Arizona or Southern California, but may attend any HACU-member college or university.

Funds Avail.: $1,000. **To Apply:** Applicants must submit the two supporting documents: enrollment verification form and transcript. **Deadline:** May 29.

4890 ■ Hispanic Association of Colleges and Universities Scholarships *(Undergraduate/Scholarship)*

Purpose: To assist students in defraying some of the college expenditures of students enrolled in HACU-member institutions. **Focus:** General studies/Field of study not specified. **Qualif.:** Applicants must: be enrolled college students who have completed their first semester of freshman year at the time of applying; attend a HACU-member college or university in the U.S. or Puerto Rico at the time applications are completed and scholarship awards are made (for the most up-to-date listing of HACU member

Awards are arranged alphabetically below their administering organizations

institutions, please refer to the HACU website); and, demonstrate financial need if required by scholarship sponsor (typically determined by FAFSA). **Criteria:** Selection will be based on the aforesaid qualifications and compliance with the application process.

Funds Avail.: No specific amount. **Duration:** Annual. **Number Awarded:** Varies. **To Apply:** Application is via online. Also, applicants must fill out the application form and provide documents showing that they are currently enrolled or accepted by a college, university, or institution. **Contact:** HACU scholarship program at scholarship@hacu.net.

4891 ■ Hispanic Dental Association (HDA)
3910 South IH 35., Ste. 245
Austin, TX 78704-7441
Ph: (512)904-0252
E-mail: hispanicdental@hdassoc.org
URL: www.hdassoc.org

4892 ■ Colgate-Palmolive/HDA Foundation Scholarships (Master's, Postgraduate/Scholarship)

Purpose: To support students who seek to advance their scientific and applied clinical knowledge in the area of dentistry to further their commitment to aiding and supporting the Hispanic community. **Focus:** Dental hygiene; Dentistry. **Qualif.:** Applicant must be a member of the Hispanic Dental Association who has been accepted into or is currently enrolled in an accredited Masters or above program in a Dentistry Related Field; must have an undergraduate or graduate degree in an oral health related field (dental hygienist, dentistry etc.) from the U.S. or abroad; and must have permanent resident status in the U.S. **Criteria:** Selection is based on students' commitment and dedication to improving the oral health of the Hispanic community; community service (volunteer efforts in school, medical facilities, church, etc.); leadership skills; and scholastic achievement.

Funds Avail.: Up to $4,000. **To Apply:** Applicants must submit a complete application. **Deadline:** May 1. **Contact:** Hispanic Dental Association Foundation, at the above address or Email: cpena@hdassoc.org.

4893 ■ Procter & Gamble Professional Oral Health/ HDA Foundation Scholarships (Undergraduate/Scholarship)

Purpose: To support promising students as they enter into their academic training. **Focus:** Dental hygiene; Dental laboratory technology; Dentistry. **Qualif.:** Applicant must be a student member of the Hispanic Dental Association who has been accepted into an accredited dental, dental hygiene, dental assisting or dental technician program; and must have permanent resident status in the U.S.; must have a minimum GPA of 3.0 on a 4.0 scale; must show interest in improving the oral health of the Hispanic community; must show evidence of commitment and dedication to serve the Hispanic community. **Criteria:** Selection is based on students' commitment and dedication to improving the oral health of the Hispanic community; community service (volunteer efforts in school, medical facilities, church, etc.); leadership skills; and scholastic achievement.

Funds Avail.: $2,000 for Dental Students and $1,000 for Dental Auxiliaries. **To Apply:** Applicants must submit a complete application and must be typed in English. **Deadline:** May 1. **Contact:** Hispanic Dental Association Foundation, at above address or Email: cgaleano@hdassoc.org.

4894 ■ Dr. Juan D. Villarreal/HDA Foundation Scholarships (Undergraduate/Scholarship)

Purpose: To support promising students as they enter into their academic training. **Focus:** Dental hygiene; Dentistry. **Qualif.:** Applicant must be a student member of the Hispanic Dental Association who has been accepted into or is currently enrolled in an accredited dental school or dental hygiene program in the state of Texas (student may be at any stage of the undergraduate program, first through fourth year); and must have permanent resident status in the U.S. **Criteria:** Selection is based on students' commitment and dedication to improving the oral health of the Hispanic community; community service (volunteer efforts in school, medical facilities, church, etc.); leadership skills; and scholastic achievement.

Funds Avail.: $1,000 and $500. **To Apply:** Applicants must submit a complete application. **Contact:** Hispanic Dental Association Foundation, at the above address or Email: cgaleano@hdassoc.org.

4895 ■ Hispanic Faculty Staff Association (HFSA)
PO Box 8184
Austin, TX 78713
URL: www.utexas.edu/staff/hfsa

4896 ■ Jamail/Long Challenge Grant Scholarships (Undergraduate/Scholarship)

Purpose: To support deserving Hispanic students at The University of Texas at Austin. **Focus:** General studies/Field of study not specified. **Qualif.:** Applicants must be Hispanic students enrolled as full-time undergraduate, graduate or transfer students at the University of Texas, Austin; must maintain satisfactory progress toward completion of their degree requirements as determined by the regular procedures of the Texas Exes. **Criteria:** Recipients are selected based on academic performance.

Funds Avail.: $1,000. **Duration:** Annual. **To Apply:** Applicants must complete the online Continuing & Transfer Scholarship Application provided by the Office of Student Financial Services. Applicants must select "Texas Exes Scholarships" on the "Scholarship Choices" page of the application and then enter the correct scholarship code, ESA-HISPANIC, in the space provided. **Deadline:** March 1.

4897 ■ Hispanic Lawyers Association of Illinois (HLAI)
321 S Plymouth Ct., Ste. 600
Chicago, IL 60604
Ph: (312)554-2045
URL: www.hlai.org

4898 ■ Kaplan Scholarships (Graduate/Scholarship)

Purpose: To help increase excellence among individuals who are pursuing careers in the legal field. **Focus:** Law. **Qualif.:** Applicants must be law students who demonstrate a genuine interest in pursuing a legal career. **Criteria:** Scholarship will be given based on merit.

Funds Avail.: No specific amount. **To Apply:** Applicants must submit completed application (available at the website) and submit along with two short essays about your commitment to public interest law and to serving the legal and social needs of the Hispanic community. They must also provide a copy of law school transcript.

4899 ■ Hispanic Metropolitan Chamber (HMC)
333 SW 5th Ave., Ste. 100
Portland, OR 97204

Awards are arranged alphabetically below their administering organizations

Ph: (503)222-0280
Fax: (503)243-5597
E-mail: info@hmccoregon.com
URL: www.hmccoregon.com
Facebook: www.facebook.com/hispanic.chamber.1
LinkedIn: www.linkedin.com/company/hispanic-metropolitan-chamber
Twitter: twitter.com/OregonHispanic

4900 ■ Hispanic Metropolitan Chamber Scholarships (Graduate, Undergraduate/Scholarship)

Purpose: To provide support and encourage Hispanics to pursue higher education. **Focus:** General studies/Field of study not specified. **Qualif.:** Applicant must be of Hispanic ancestry; residing in Oregon or Clark County Washington; have at least a 2.75 GPA as evidenced by a certified high school or college transcript; and enrolled in an accredited Community College, 4 year University or an accredited Graduate Degree Program. **Criteria:** Selection is based on academic achievements, extracurricular activities in the community and a written essay.

Funds Avail.: No specific amount. **Duration:** Annual. **To Apply:** Applicants must submit a completed application form together with the required materials. **Deadline:** January 31.

4901 ■ Hispanic Scholarship Fund (HSF)
1411 W 190th St., Ste. 700
Gardena, CA 90248
Ph: (310)975-3700
Fax: (310)349-3328
URL: www.hsf.net

4902 ■ Becas Univision Scholarship Program (Undergraduate, Graduate/Scholarship)

Purpose: To assist students of Hispanic heritage obtain a college degree. **Focus:** General studies/Field of study not specified. **Qualif.:** Applicants must be of Hispanic heritage; must have a minimum of 3.0 GPA for high school students or 2.5 GPA for college of graduate students on a 4.0 scale; must plan to enroll full-time in an accredited, not-for-profit, 4-year university or graduate school. **Criteria:** Selection will be based on the committee's criteria.

Duration: Annual. **To Apply:** Applicants must complete and submit the FAFSA or state based financial aid application. **Deadline:** March 30.

4903 ■ The Gates Millennium Scholars (Undergraduate/Scholarship)

Purpose: To provide greater access and opportunity to higher education for outstanding students from underrepresented backgrounds. **Focus:** Education; Engineering; Library and archival sciences; Mathematics and mathematical sciences; Public health; Science. **Qualif.:** Applicant must be a graduating high school senior student; be an African American, American Indian/Alaska Native, Asian Pacific Islander American and Hispanic American heritage; a U.S. citizen or legal permanent resident; have a minimum 3.3 GPA on a 4.0 scale; must demonstrate leadership skills; must demonstrate financial need. **Criteria:** Recipients will be selected based on the merits of the application.

Funds Avail.: No specific amount. **To Apply:** Applicant must complete all three required forms available at the award site www.gmsp.org. American Indian/Alaska Native must submit proof of tribal enrollment or a certificate of descent if selected as finalist. **Deadline:** January 14.

4904 ■ Hispanic Scholarship Fund General College Scholarship Program (HSF) (Undergraduate/Scholarship)

Purpose: To assist students of Hispanic heritage in obtaining a college degree. **Focus:** General studies/Field of study not specified. **Qualif.:** Applicant must be of Hispanic heritage; U.S. citizen or legal permanent resident with a valid permanent resident card or passport stamped I-551; have a minimum 3.0 GPA on a 4.0 scale or the equivalent; must apply for federal financing aid using the Free Application for Federal Student Aid (FAFSA) at www.fafsa.ed.gov; must be pursuing his/her first undergraduate of graduate degree; must have plans to enroll full-time in a degree seeking program at a two-year or four-year U.S. accredited institution in the U.S., Puerto Rico, U.S. Virgin Islands or Guam. **Criteria:** Recipients will be selected based on the merits of the application.

Funds Avail.: $1,000 to $5,000. **To Apply:** Applications must be submitted using the HSF online application system; Student Aid Report (SAR); and school or HSF enrollment verification form. Submit all required documents in one envelope. **Deadline:** April 2.

4905 ■ HSF/Marathon Oil College Scholarship Program (Undergraduate/Scholarship)

Purpose: To provide students the opportunity to participate in a possible paid 8-10 week summer internship at various Marathon Oil Corporation locations. **Focus:** Accounting; Engineering, Chemical; Engineering, Civil; Engineering, Electrical; Engineering, Mechanical; Engineering, Petroleum; Geology; Geophysics; Land management; Logistics; Marketing and distribution; Transportation. **Qualif.:** Applicants must be of Hispanic American, African American, Asian Pacific Islander American or American Indian/Alaskan Native heritage; U.S. citizens or legal permanent residents with a valid Social Security Number and a permanent resident card or passport stamped I-551; have a minimum 3.0 GPA on a 4.0 scale; a sophomore majoring in chemical engineering, civil engineering, electrical engineering, mechanical engineering, petroleum engineering, geology, geophysics, accounting, marketing, global procurement or supply chain management, environmental health & safety, energy management or petroleum land management, transportation & logistics or geotechnical engineering; or a senior pursuing a Masters degree in geology or geophysics; must participate in a possible paid summer internship opportunity in Marathon Oil Corporation; must apply for federal financing aid using the Free Application for Federal Student Aid (FAFSA) at www.fafsa.ed.gov. **Criteria:** Preference will be given to the applicants who best meet the requirements.

Funds Avail.: $10,000. **Duration:** Annual. **To Apply:** Applications must be submitted using the HSF online application system. **Deadline:** October 1.

4906 ■ HSF/Wells Fargo Scholarship Program (Undergraduate/Scholarship)

Purpose: To assist college students who are interested in financial and banking based careers. **Focus:** Banking; Finance. **Qualif.:** Applicants must be of Hispanic heritage; U.S. citizens or permanent residents with a valid card or passport stamped I-551; sophomores enrolled full-time at a four-year accredited college/university in the U.S. (must be enrolled as juniors in the following academic year); pursuing a degree in Business, Economics, Finance, Accounting or IT, including CIS, MIS and Computer Engineering; have a minimum 3.0 GPA on a 4.0 scale or the equivalent; must apply for Federal Financing Aid. **Criteria:** Priority will be given to students from the following universities: Arizona State University, California State University - Fresno, California State University - Fullerton, California State University - San Francisco, Columbia University, Iowa State University, San Jose State University, Santa Clara University, Stanford University, Texas A&M University, University of Arizona, University of California - Berkeley, University of California - Davis, University of California - Los Angeles, University of California - San Diego, University of Minnesota, University of Southern California, University of Texas at Austin, University of Washington. Priority will also be given to residents of: Alaska, Arizona, California, Colorado, Iowa, Idaho, Illinois, Indiana, Michigan, Minnesota, Montana, Nebraska, Nevada, New Mexico, North Dakota, Ohio, Oregon, South Dakota, Texas, Utah, Washington, Wisconsin, Wyoming.

Funds Avail.: No specific amount. **To Apply:** Applicants must use the HSF online application system; Student Aid Report (SAR); and school or HSF enrollment verification form. Submit all required documents in one envelope.

4907 ■ Historians of Islamic Art Association (HIAA)
c/o Glaire D. Anderson, Treasurer
UNC-Chapel Hill
115 S Columbia St., CB 3405
Chapel Hill, NC 27514
Fax: (919)962-0722
URL: www.historiansofislamicart.org

4908 ■ HIAA Graduate Student Travel Grants (Graduate/Grant)

Purpose: To defray the travel costs of students who are presenting papers at the Annual Meeting. **Focus:** Area and ethnic studies. **Qualif.:** Applicants must be graduate students who have been invited or accepted to present papers at an annual meeting of a professional society. **Criteria:** Preference will be given to applicants whose papers will be presented at HIAA-sponsored panels.

Funds Avail.: $500. **Duration:** Annual. **Number Awarded:** Varies. **To Apply:** Applicants must submit a cover letter summarizing the application; a separate sheet listing the applicant's name, institutional affiliation and status (e.g. Ph.D. candidate; 3rd year), email address, name of the primary institutional advisor, conference title, dates and venue, paper title, and itemized travel budget; a letter of support from the advisor; abstract of the paper to be presented; and the notification of acceptance from the conference/session organizer(s). **Contact:** Dr. Nancy Micklewright, Head of Scholarly Programs and Publications, FreerlSackler, Smithsonian's Museums of Asian Art; Email: searssj@si.edu.

4909 ■ Margaret B. Ševenko Prize in Islamic Art and Culture (Doctorate/Prize)

Purpose: To support young scholars who have unpublished articles on any aspect of Islamic visual culture. **Focus:** Art history; Culture. **Qualif.:** Applicants must be junior scholars (pre-dissertation to three years after the PhD degree) on any aspect of Islamic visual culture. **Criteria:** Selection will be based on submitted articles.

Funds Avail.: $500. **Duration:** Annual. **To Apply:** Applicants must submit their attachments (must be in DOC., .DOCX, or .PDF format) with the authors' contact information. A letter of recommendation should be sent separately by an advisor or referee through e-mail. **Deadline:** November 15. **Contact:** Professor Bernard O'Kane, The American University in Cairo; Email: bokane@aucegypt.edu.

4910 ■ Ho-Chunk Nation
Tribal Office Bldg.
W9814 Airport Rd.
Black River Falls, WI 54615
Ph: (715)284-9343
Fax: (715)284-2632
Free: 800-294-9343
URL: www.ho-chunknation.com

4911 ■ Josephine P. White Eagle Scholarships (Undergraduate, Graduate/Scholarship)

Purpose: To provide funding to Ho-Chunk student members to complete their Master's and/or Doctoral degree at a non-profit Title IV institution. **Focus:** Business; Education; Health sciences; Law. **Qualif.:** Applicants must be enrolled members of the Ho-Chunk Nation; must be accepted into a non-profit Title IV institution offering graduate level degrees within the borders or jurisdiction of the United States. They must be interested in the fields of Education, Business, Health Sciences and Law; must be enrolled in a full-time basis; must have GPA of 3.0 on a 4.0 scale. Those who are accepted in an approved Title IV law school must be accredited by the American Bar Association. **Criteria:** Applicants will be evaluated based on submitted materials.

Funds Avail.: Amount varies. **Duration:** Annual. **To Apply:** Applicants must complete the application form; must submit a letter of acceptance, an official transcript from all prior post-secondary institutions attended, a 500-1000-word personal essay, three letters of recommendation from non-related persons, graduate outline and the Higher Education Division's academic plan, official class schedule, Ho-Chunk Nation background check and written verification of application for funding from minimum of two other sources. **Deadline:** March 1 (summer term); May 1 (fall term); October 1 (spring term).

4912 ■ Hogg Foundation for Mental Health
Lake Austin Centre, 4th Fl.
3001 Lake Austin Blvd.
Austin, TX 78703
Ph: (512)471-5041
Fax: (512)471-9608
Free: 888-404-4336
E-mail: Hogg-Grants@austin.utexas.edu
URL: www.hogg.utexas.edu/funding.html

4913 ■ HFMH Bilingual Scholarships for Mental Health Workforce Diversity (Graduate/Scholarship)

Purpose: To raise awareness of, and begin to meet the need for, more cultural and linguistic diversity in the state's mental health workforce. **Focus:** Social work. **Qualif.:** Applicants must be accepted as new students by a Texas graduate social work program that is accredited or in candidacy for accreditation by the National Council on Social Work Education; must be fluent in English and a second language chosen by the school, typically Spanish; must commit to work in Texas after graduation providing

Awards are arranged alphabetically below their administering organizations

mental health services for a period equal to the timeframe of the scholarship; must meet any additional selection criteria required by the program of their choice. **Criteria:** Selection will be based on the committee's criteria.

Funds Avail.: Amount varies. **To Apply:** Students must apply for the scholarship through their school and should contact their graduate program's office for more information. **Remarks:** Established in 2008.

4914 ■ Hollis NorEasters Snowmobile Club
PO Box 517
Hollis, NH 03049
URL: www.noreasters.org

4915 ■ Nor' Easters Scholarships - Four-year Program *(Undergraduate/Scholarship)*

Purpose: To support the education of a student member. **Focus:** General studies/Field of study not specified. **Qualif.:** Applicant must be a high school senior of exemplary character; a club member; must demonstrate an active interest primarily in the sport of snowmobiling, or secondarily in trail management and maintenance; and must exemplify a commitment to community service. **Criteria:** Selection will be based on the submitted application.

Funds Avail.: $1,000. **Duration:** Annual. **To Apply:** Applicant must submit a completed application form along with the required documents. **Deadline:** May 2.

4916 ■ Nor' Easters Scholarships - Two-year Program *(Undergraduate/Scholarship)*

Purpose: To support the education of a student member. **Focus:** General studies/Field of study not specified. **Qualif.:** Applicant must be a high school senior of exemplary character; a club member; must demonstrate an active interest primarily in the sport of snowmobiling, or secondarily in trail management and maintenance; and must exemplify a commitment to community service. **Criteria:** Selection is based on the application.

Funds Avail.: $1,000. **Duration:** Annual. **Number Awarded:** 1. **To Apply:** Applicant must submit a completed application form along with the required documents. **Deadline:** May 2.

4917 ■ Joseph A. Holmes Safety Association (JAHSA)
PO Box 9375
Arlington, VA 22219
Ph: (304)256-3223
Fax: (304)256-3319
E-mail: mail@holmessafety.org
URL: www.holmessafety.org
Facebook: www.facebook.com/holmessafety
LinkedIn: www.linkedin.com/company/joseph-a-holmes
-safety-association?trk=biz-companies-cym
Twitter: twitter.com/JosephAHolmes

4918 ■ Joseph A. Holmes Safety Association Scholarships *(Undergraduate, Graduate/Scholarship)*

Purpose: To assist persons who are pursuing careers in the mining industry, safety and health-related fields. **Focus:** Mining. **Qualif.:** Applicants must be: U.S. citizens or permanent residents (green-card holders) pursuing a career in the mining industry, safety and health-related field; or, high school graduates enrolled in a college/university degree program, or undergraduate students currently enrolled in a college/university degree program, or graduates of a college/university pursuing a graduate degree. **Criteria:** Selection shall be based on demonstrated outstanding academic achievement, financial need, GPA, leadership and future career interest in a mine related field.

Funds Avail.: Amount varies. **Duration:** Annual. **To Apply:** Applicants must submit a completed application form together with transcript of grades for the last three years of completed education; completed financial disclosure information; short essay (200-300 words); and list of extracurricular activities and/or a list of other academic achievements. **Deadline:** May 1. **Contact:** Sylvia Ortiz: silvieort@yahoo.com.

4919 ■ Holocaust and Human Rights Center of Maine (HHRC)
University of Maine at Augusta
46 University Dr.
Augusta, ME 04330-1644
Ph: (207)621-3530
Fax: (207)621-3534
E-mail: infohhrc@maine.edu
URL: www.hhrc.uma.edu
Facebook: www.facebook.com/HHRCMaine
Twitter: www.twitter.com/search?q=Holocaust%20and%
 20Human%20Rights%20Center%20of%20Maine&src
 =typd

4920 ■ Lawrence Alan Spiegel Remembrance Scholarships *(Undergraduate/Scholarship)*

Purpose: To support students who submitted a winning essay. **Focus:** General studies/Field of study not specified. **Qualif.:** Applicants must be high school seniors or homeschoolers who are residents of Maine and who have been accepted at any accredited and Title IV eligible college, university or technical school. **Criteria:** Applicants are evaluated by a panel of judges based on submitted essay.

Funds Avail.: $1,000. **Duration:** Annual. **To Apply:** Applicants must write an essay on "Why is it important that the remembrance, history and lessons of the Holocaust be passed to a new generation?" The essay must not exceed four pages, must be double-spaced and be accompanied by a self-addressed, stamped envelope and a completed application. **Deadline:** April 8. **Contact:** Holocaust and Human Rights Center of Maine; Phone: 207-621-3530; Email: infohhrc@maine.edu.

4921 ■ Home Builders Association of Kentucky (HBAK)
1040 Burlington Ln.
Frankfort, KY 40601
Fax: (502)875-5480
Free: 800-489-4225
URL: www.hbak.com
Facebook: www.facebook.com/HBAofKy
Twitter: twitter.com/hbaofky

4922 ■ Betty Bell Scholarship Fund *(Undergraduate/Scholarship)*

Purpose: To assist students in obtaining higher education in a building industry related field. **Focus:** General studies/Field of study not specified. **Qualif.:** Applicant must: be a student presently enrolled in an institution of higher education; be a member, spouse, child, or employee of a member of the association; live in the jurisdiction of the Home Builders Association of Kentucky; and, exhibit good character. **Criteria:** Selection will be based on the committee's criteria.

Funds Avail.: $500. **Duration:** Annual. **To Apply:** Applicant must provide two letters of recommendation. One must be from the teacher within the last two years and one must be someone other than a relative. The recommendations must include an address or phone number so that they can be contacted if necessary. **Deadline:** April 15.

4923 ■ Tommy Bright Scholarship Fund
(Undergraduate/Scholarship)

Purpose: To assist students in achieving a more comprehensive understanding of how the United States government operates. **Focus:** General studies/Field of study not specified. **Qualif.:** Applicants must: be students presently enrolled in high school or college; live in the jurisdiction of the Home Builders Association of Kentucky; be the children or grandchildren of a member or members' employee of the HBAK; and, exhibit good character. **Criteria:** Selection will be based on the submitted applications, personal references, recommendations and scholastic records.

Funds Avail.: $1,000. **Duration:** Annual. **To Apply:** Applicants must complete the application for the award; must secure a written recommendation from two people other than family members, who can offer personal references for the applicant. Applications must be mailed or delivered to the Home Builders Association of Kentucky. **Deadline:** April 15.

4924 ■ HomeCity Real Estate
7000 Bee Caves Rd., Ste. 350
Austin, TX 78746
Ph: (972)521-3800
E-mail: page@homecity.com
URL: www.homecity.com

4925 ■ HomeCity Real Estate Scholarships
(Undergraduate/Scholarship)

Purpose: To help students interested in pursuing a career in the real estate industry afford the rising cost of education. **Focus:** Real estate. **Qualif.:** Applicants must be college students or incoming freshmen enrolled in an undergraduate degree program in a spring, summer, or fall of the current semester; must be enrolled at an accredited American college, university or trade school. **Criteria:** Selection will be based on the submitted application and essay.

Funds Avail.: $1,000. **Number Awarded:** 1. **To Apply:** Applicants must prepare a 800-1,000 words essay on a topic: "What specific, actionable advice would you give to home buyers in the current real estate market?". Applicants must visit the website to enter their personal information and to submit a copy of their essay. **Deadline:** July 15.

4926 ■ Homeless Children's Education Fund
2020 Smallman St., 2nd Flr.
Pittsburgh, PA 15222
Ph: (412)562-0154
Fax: (412)562-1109
E-mail: info@homelessfund.org
URL: www.homelessfund.org

4927 ■ Hope Through Learning Awards
(Undergraduate/Scholarship)

Purpose: To assist currently or formerly homeless youth in attending post-secondary education or training. **Focus:** General studies/Field of study not specified. **Qualif.:** Applicants must be currently residing in Allegheny County; must be 24 years of age or younger; must be high school graduates or GED recipients, or due to complete secondary education at the end of the school year; must be accepted into a postsecondary education or career program (e.g. college, university, community college, business school, technical school, vocational school, career training, internship, apprenticeship) for the first time, and are scheduled to begin classes/training before the end of the current year. and must be experiencing or have experienced homelessness during school attendance years. **Criteria:** Selection will be based on the following: commitment to education despite homelessness; compelling challenges due to homelessness; financial need for college; academic achievement and accomplishments; writing style and ability; statement of goals and career interests; and community involvement.

Funds Avail.: $2,500. **To Apply:** Applicants must retrieve the application form at the program website. Such must be completely filled and should be submitted along with the following: resume; high school transcript (in sealed envelope with counselors signature or school stamp over seal); copy of post-secondary program acceptance letter; two recommendation letters (letters should be on letterhead and include the authors title, address, phone number, email address, and signature. Each letter should be in a sealed envelope and signed over the seal. Examples include teachers, mentors, clergy, community leaders, case managers, or homeless housing staff, excluding any family members); and two to three pages of essay responding to each item (describing their experience with homelessness and how such condition affected their education; how they overcome the challenges of housing instability to succeed in school; and what do they think should be done, or would they do, to increase awareness or address the issue of student homelessness). **Deadline:** May 31. **Contact:** Carrie Pavlik at cpavlik@homelessfund.org.

4928 ■ Honor Society of Phi Kappa Phi - North Dakota State University Chapter 10
Office of Registration and Records
1301 Administration Ave.
Fargo, ND 58102
Ph: (701)231-7987
Fax: (701)231-8959
Free: 800-608-6378
URL: www.ndsu.nodak.edu/ndsu/pkp

4929 ■ Matilda B. Thompson Scholarship
(Undergraduate/Scholarship)

Purpose: To provide scholarship to members of Phi Kappa Phi. **Focus:** General studies/Field of study not specified. **Qualif.:** Applicants must be members of Phi Kappa Phi and enrolled at NDSU fall semester. **Criteria:** Selection will be based on the committee's criteria.

Funds Avail.: $100-$300. **Duration:** Annual. **Number Awarded:** Varies. **To Apply:** Interested applicants may visit the website to obtain an application. **Deadline:** November 30.

Awards are arranged alphabetically below their administering organizations

4930 ■ Hoover Presidential Foundation
302 Parkside Dr.
West Branch, IA 52358
Ph: (319)643-5327
Fax: (319)643-2391
E-mail: info@hooverpf.org
URL: www.hooverpresidentialfoundation.org
Facebook: www.facebook.com/HooverPresFoundation
Twitter: twitter.com/HooverPresFndn

4931 ■ Herbert Hoover Uncommon Student Awards (Undergraduate/Scholarship)

Purpose: To encourage academic excellence and innovativeness among young students of Iowa by providing educational assistance. **Focus:** General studies/Field of study not specified. **Qualif.:** Applicants must be students in their junior level in an Iowa high school or a home schooled program in the spring of the current year, with a high school graduation date of spring of the following year. **Criteria:** Selection shall be based on the project proposal and letters of recommendation of selected students from Iowa High School. (Grades, test score, essays and financial need are not evaluated).

Funds Avail.: Amount Varies. **Duration:** Annual. **Number Awarded:** Up to 15. **To Apply:** Applicants must submit a completed application form, project proposal and two letters of recommendation. Forms are available at the website and must be sent to Hoover Library Association. **Deadline:** March 15. **Contact:** Delene McConnaha; Phone: 319-643-5327; E-mail: info@hooverPF.org.

4932 ■ Hope for the Warriors
5101C Backlick Rd.
Annandale, VA 22003
Free: 877-246-7349
E-mail: info@hopeforthewarriors.org
URL: www.hopeforthewarriors.org
Facebook: www.facebook.com/HopeForTheWarriors
LinkedIn: www.linkedin.com/groups/3761606/profile
Twitter: twitter.com/Hope4Warriors

4933 ■ Hope for the Warriors Spouse/Caregiver Scholarships (Undergraduate, Graduate/Scholarship)

Purpose: To identify, recognize and reward exceptional spouses to aid in their continued education at a reputable, accredited college or trade school as they assume critical roles in the financial well being of their families. **Focus:** General studies/Field of study not specified. **Qualif.:** Applicant must possess a valid military ID card and be the legal spouse of a U.S. military member who was wounded/injured or killed in the line of duty between 2001 and the present; currently reside in the United States; intend to make application to or be currently enrolled in an accredited college or trade school, in pursuit of a bachelors/masters degree or vocational program pursuing certification; and must show proof of satisfactory academic progress (score of at least 650 on the GED, a high school diploma with a 2.6 overall GPA based on a 4.0 scale or similar rating of current studies if within the last five years). **Criteria:** Selection shall be based on eligibility, commitment to succeed as indicated by academic achievement, personal goals, letters of recommendation, resume and an original essay response.

Funds Avail.: No specific amount. **Duration:** Annual. **To Apply:** Applicant must submit a completed application form along with the proof of service, proof of injury/death, original essay, two-page questionnaire and two letters of recommendation. **Deadline:** May 31. **Contact:** E-mail: scholarships@hopeforthewarriors.org.

4934 ■ Horatio Alger Association of Distinguished Americans (HAADA)
99 Canal Center Plz., Ste. 320
Alexandria, VA 22314-1588
Ph: (703)684-9444
Free: 844-422-4200
URL: www.horatioalger.com

4935 ■ Ak-Sar-Ben Scholarships (Undergraduate/Scholarship)

Purpose: To provide financial assistance to students in the state of Iowa. **Focus:** General studies/Field of study not specified. **Qualif.:** Applicants must be enrolled full time as high school seniors, progressing normally toward graduation and planning to enter college not later than the fall following graduation; must have a strong commitment to pursue a bachelor's degree at an accredited institution (students may start their studies at a two-year institution and then transfer to a four-year institution); must have critical financial need ($50,000 or less adjusted gross income per family is preferred; if higher, an explanation must be provided); must be involved in co-curricular and community activities; must have a minimum grade point average of 2.0; must be residents of Nebraska and western Iowa; and be citizens or permanent residents of the United States. **Criteria:** Recipients will be selected based on financial need.

Funds Avail.: $6,000. **Number Awarded:** 50. **To Apply:** Applicants must submit an official high school transcript; a copy of parents/guardians federal income tax return; have one letter of support and must be logged in to the application process at the HAA website. Faxes/e-mails will not be accepted. Students must download the certification page from the HAA web site, complete it and obtain the proper signatures prior to mailing.

4936 ■ Horatio Alger Delaware Scholarships (Undergraduate/Scholarship)

Purpose: To provide financial assistance to students in the state of Delaware. **Focus:** General studies/Field of study not specified. **Qualif.:** Applicants must be U.S. citizens who are residents of Delaware, enrolled full time as high school seniors in the United States, and progressing normally toward graduation in spring/summer of the current year with the plan to enter a college in the United States no later than the fall following graduation. They must also: be involved in co-curricular and community service activities; display integrity and perseverance in overcoming adversity; demonstrate critical financial need ($55,000 or lower adjusted gross family income is required); and, exhibit a strong commitment to pursue and complete a bachelor's degree at an accredited non-profit public or private institution in the United States (students may start their studies at a two-year institution and then transfer to a four-year institution). **Criteria:** Selection will be based on the aforesaid qualifications and compliance with the application process.

Funds Avail.: $7,000. **Duration:** Annual. **Number Awarded:** 14. **To Apply:** Applicants must have one letter of support and must be logged in to the application process at the HAA website. Faxes/e-mails will not be accepted.

Awards are arranged alphabetically below their administering organizations

HORATIO ALGER ASSOCIATION OF DISTINGUISHED AMERICANS

Students must download the certification page from the HAA web site, complete it and obtain the proper signatures prior to mailing. **Deadline:** February 15. **Remarks:** The scholarships are made in honor of John W. Rollins, Sr.

4937 ■ Horatio Alger District of Columbia, Maryland and Virginia Scholarships (Undergraduate/Scholarship)

Purpose: To support deserving students from the Washington D.C., Metro area in the following counties: District of Columbia, Maryland, Virginia. **Focus:** General studies/Field of study not specified. **Qualif.:** Applicants must be U.S. citizens (residents of District of Columbia, Maryland, and/or Virginia) enrolled full time as high school seniors in the United States, and progressing normally toward graduation in spring/summer of the current year with the plan to enter a college in the United States no later than the fall following graduation. They must also: be involved in co-curricular and community service activities; display integrity and perseverance in overcoming adversity; demonstrate critical financial need ($55,000 or lower adjusted gross family income is required); and, exhibit a strong commitment to pursue and complete a bachelor's degree at an accredited non-profit public or private institution in the United States (students may start their studies at a two-year institution and then transfer to a four-year institution). **Criteria:** Selection will be based on the aforesaid qualifications and compliance with the application process.

Funds Avail.: $7,000. **Duration:** Annual. **Number Awarded:** 20. **To Apply:** Applicants must have one letter of support and must be logged in to the application process at the HAA website. Faxes/e-mails will not be accepted. Students must download the certification page from the HAA web site, complete it and obtain the proper signatures prior to mailing. **Deadline:** February 15. **Remarks:** The scholarships are made possible through its funder, Anthony Welters.

4938 ■ Horatio Alger Florida Scholarships (Undergraduate/Scholarship)

Purpose: To provide financial assistance to students in the counties of Broward, Martin and St. Lucie in the state of Florida. **Focus:** General studies/Field of study not specified. **Qualif.:** Applicants must be U.S. citizens who are Florida residents, enrolled full time as high school seniors in the United States, and progressing normally toward graduation in spring/summer of the current year with the plan to enter a college in the United States no later than the fall following graduation. They must also: be involved in co-curricular and community service activities; display integrity and perseverance in overcoming adversity; demonstrate critical financial need ($55,000 or lower adjusted gross family income is required); and, exhibit a strong commitment to pursue and complete a bachelor's degree at an accredited non-profit public or private institution in the United States (students may start their studies at a two-year institution and then transfer to a four-year institution). **Criteria:** Selection will be based on the aforesaid qualifications and compliance with the application process.

Funds Avail.: $7,000. **Duration:** Annual. **Number Awarded:** 43. **To Apply:** Applicants must have one letter of support and must be logged in to the application process at the HAA website. Faxes/e-mails will not be accepted. Students must download the certification page from the HAA web site, complete it and obtain the proper signatures prior to mailing. **Deadline:** February 15. **Remarks:** The scholarships are made in honor of John A. Moran.

4939 ■ Horatio Alger Georgia Scholarships (Undergraduate/Scholarship)

Purpose: To provide financial assistance to students in the state of Georgia. **Focus:** General studies/Field of study not specified. **Qualif.:** Applicants must be U.S. citizens who are Georgia residents, enrolled full time as high school seniors in the United States, and progressing normally toward graduation in spring/summer of the current year with the plan to enter a college in the United States no later than the fall following graduation. They must also: be involved in co-curricular and community service activities; display integrity and perseverance in overcoming adversity; demonstrate critical financial need ($55,000 or lower adjusted gross family income is required); and, exhibit a strong commitment to pursue and complete a bachelor's degree at an accredited non-profit public or private institution in the United States (students may start their studies at a two-year institution and then transfer to a four-year institution). **Criteria:** Selection will be based on the aforesaid qualifications and compliance with the application process.

Funds Avail.: $7,000. **Duration:** Annual. **Number Awarded:** 50. **To Apply:** Applicants must have one letter of support and must be logged in to the application process at the HAA website. Faxes/e-mails will not be accepted. Students must download the certification page from the HAA web site, complete it and obtain the proper signatures prior to mailing. **Deadline:** February 15. **Remarks:** The scholarships are funded by O. Wayne Rollins Foundation.

4940 ■ Horatio Alger Illinois Scholarships (Undergraduate/Scholarship)

Purpose: To provide financial assistance to students in the state of Illinois. **Focus:** General studies/Field of study not specified. **Qualif.:** Applicants must be U.S. citizens who are residing in Illinois, and enrolled full time as high school seniors in the United States, and progressing normally toward graduation in spring/summer of the current year with the plan to enter a college in the United States no later than the fall following graduation. They must also: be involved in co-curricular and community service activities; display integrity and perseverance in overcoming adversity; demonstrate critical financial need ($55,000 or lower adjusted gross family income is required); and, exhibit a strong commitment to pursue and complete a bachelor's degree at an accredited non-profit public or private institution in the United States (students may start their studies at a two-year institution and then transfer to a four-year institution). **Criteria:** Selection will be based on the aforesaid qualifications and compliance with the application process.

Funds Avail.: $7,000. **Duration:** Annual. **Number Awarded:** 20. **To Apply:** Applicants must submit an official high school transcript; a copy of parents/guardians federal income tax return; and have one letter of support and must be logged in to the application process at the HAA website. Faxes/e-mails will not be accepted. Students must download the certification page from the HAA web site, complete it and obtain the proper signatures prior to mailing. **Deadline:** February 15. **Remarks:** The scholarships are funded by Brinson Foundation & Doris K. Christopher.

4941 ■ Horatio Alger Indiana Scholarships (Undergraduate/Scholarship)

Purpose: To provide financial assistance to students in the state of Indiana. **Focus:** General studies/Field of study not specified. **Qualif.:** Applicants must be U.S. citizens who are residing in Indiana, and enrolled full time as high school seniors in the United States, and progressing normally

Awards are arranged alphabetically below their administering organizations

toward graduation in spring/summer of the current year with the plan to enter a college in the United States no later than the fall following graduation. They must also: be involved in co-curricular and community service activities; display integrity and perseverance in overcoming adversity; demonstrate critical financial need ($55,000 or lower adjusted gross family income is required); and, exhibit a strong commitment to pursue and complete a bachelor's degree at an accredited non-profit public or private institution in the United States (students may start their studies at a two-year institution and then transfer to a four-year institution). **Criteria:** Selection will be based on the aforesaid qualifications and compliance with the application process. **Funds Avail.:** $7,000. **Duration:** Annual. **Number Awarded:** 10. **To Apply:** Applicants must submit an official high school transcript; one copy of parents/guardians federal income tax return; and have one letter of support and must be logged in to the application process at the HAA website. Faxes/e-mails will not be accepted. Students must download the certification page from the HAA web site, complete it and obtain the proper signatures prior to mailing. **Deadline:** February 15. **Remarks:** The scholarships are funded by Suzanne and Walter Scott Foundation.

4942 ■ Horatio Alger Kentucky Scholarships
(Undergraduate/Scholarship)

Purpose: To provide financial assistance to students in the state of Kentucky. **Focus:** General studies/Field of study not specified. **Qualif.:** Applicants must be U.S. citizens who are Kentucky residents, and enrolled full time as high school seniors in the United States, and progressing normally toward graduation in spring/summer of the current year with the plan to enter a college in the United States no later than the fall following graduation. They must also: be involved in co-curricular and community service activities; display integrity and perseverance in overcoming adversity; demonstrate critical financial need ($55,000 or lower adjusted gross family income is required); and, exhibit a strong commitment to pursue and complete a bachelor's degree at an accredited non-profit public or private institution in the United States (students may start their studies at a two-year institution and then transfer to a four-year institution). **Criteria:** Recipients will be selected based on financial need.
Funds Avail.: $7,000. **Duration:** Annual. **Number Awarded:** 8. **To Apply:** Applicants must submit an official high school transcript; a copy of parents/guardians federal income tax return; have one letter of support and must be logged in to the application process at the HAA website. Faxes/e-mails will not be accepted. Students must download the certification page from the HAA web site, complete it and obtain the proper signatures prior to mailing. **Deadline:** February 15. **Remarks:** The scholarships are funded by Horatio Alger Endowment Fund.

4943 ■ Horatio Alger Lola and Duane Hagadone Idaho Scholarships (Undergraduate/Scholarship)

Purpose: To provide scholarships to students in the State of Idaho. **Focus:** General studies/Field of study not specified. **Qualif.:** Applicants must be U.S. citizens enrolled full time as high school seniors in the United States, and progressing normally toward graduation in spring/summer of the current year with the plan to enter a college in the United States no later than the fall following graduation. They must also: be involved in co-curricular and community service activities; display integrity and perseverance in overcoming adversity; demonstrate critical financial need ($55,000 or lower adjusted gross family income is required); and, exhibit a strong commitment to pursue and complete a bachelor's degree at an accredited non-profit public or private institution in the United States (students may start their studies at a two-year institution and then transfer to a four-year institution). Furthermore, applicants must: reside in the Idaho counties of Benewah, Boundary, Bonner, Kootenai, Latah, or Shoshone; and, attend North Idaho College, Lewis-Clark State College (Coeur d'Alene or Lewiston campus) or the University of Idaho. **Criteria:** Selection will be based on the aforesaid qualifications and compliance with the application process.
Funds Avail.: $7,000. **Duration:** Annual. **Number Awarded:** 25. **To Apply:** Applicants must submit an official high school transcript; a copy of parents/guardians federal income tax return; and have one letter of support and must be logged in to the application process at the HAA website. Faxes/e-mails will not be accepted. Students must download the certification page from the HAA web site, complete it and obtain the proper signatures prior to mailing. **Deadline:** April 15.

4944 ■ Horatio Alger Louisiana Scholarships
(Undergraduate/Scholarship)

Purpose: To provide financial assistance to students in the state of Louisiana. **Focus:** General studies/Field of study not specified. **Qualif.:** Applicants must be U.S. citizens enrolled full time as high school seniors in the United States, and progressing normally toward graduation in spring/summer of the current year with the plan to enter a college in the United States no later than the fall following graduation. They must also: be involved in co-curricular and community service activities; display integrity and perseverance in overcoming adversity; demonstrate critical financial need ($55,000 or lower adjusted gross family income is required); and, exhibit a strong commitment to pursue and complete a bachelor's degree at an accredited non-profit public or private institution in the United States (students may start their studies at a two-year institution and then transfer to a four-year institution). Furthermore, applicants must pursue a bachelor's degree at a college in Louisiana **Criteria:** Selection will be based on the aforesaid qualifications and compliance with the application process.
Funds Avail.: $10,500. **Duration:** Annual. **Number Awarded:** 25. **To Apply:** Applicants must submit an official high school transcript; a copy of parents/guardians federal income tax return; have one letter of support and must be logged in to the application process at the HAA website. Faxes/e-mails will not be accepted. Students must download the certification page from the HAA web site, complete it and obtain the proper signatures prior to mailing. **Deadline:** February 15. **Remarks:** The scholarships are made possible through its funder, William J. Doré.

4945 ■ Horatio Alger Minnesota Scholarships
(Undergraduate/Scholarship)

Purpose: To provide financial assistance to students in the state of Minnesota. **Focus:** General studies/Field of study not specified. **Qualif.:** Applicants must be U.S. citizens who are Minnesota residents, enrolled full time as high school seniors in the United States, and progressing normally toward graduation in spring/summer of the current year with the plan to enter a college in the United States no later than the fall following graduation. They must also: be involved in co-curricular and community service activities; display integrity and perseverance in overcoming adversity; demonstrate critical financial need ($55,000 or lower adjusted gross family income is required); and, exhibit a strong commitment to pursue and complete a bachelor's

Awards are arranged alphabetically below their administering organizations

degree at an accredited non-profit public or private institution in the United States (students may start their studies at a two-year institution and then transfer to a four-year institution). **Criteria:** Selection will be based on the aforesaid qualifications and compliance with the application process. **Funds Avail.:** $7,000. **Duration:** Annual. **Number Awarded:** 10. **To Apply:** Applicants must submit an official high school transcript; a copy of parents/guardians federal tax return; have one letter of support and must be logged in to the application process at the HAA website. Faxes/e-mails will not be accepted. Students must download the certification page from the HAA web site, complete it and obtain the proper signatures prior to mailing. **Deadline:** February 15. **Remarks:** The scholarships are funded by Al and Cathy Annexstad and Horatio Alger Scholarship Fund.

4946 ■ Horatio Alger Missouri Scholarships
(Undergraduate/Scholarship)

Purpose: To provide financial assistance to students in the state of Missouri. **Focus:** General studies/Field of study not specified. **Qualif.:** Applicants must be U.S. citizens who are Missouri residents and enrolled full time as high school seniors in the United States, and progressing normally toward graduation in spring/summer of the current year with the plan to enter a college in the United States no later than the fall following graduation. They must also: be involved in co-curricular and community service activities; display integrity and perseverance in overcoming adversity; demonstrate critical financial need ($55,000 or lower adjusted gross family income is required); and, exhibit a strong commitment to pursue and complete a bachelor's degree at an accredited non-profit public or private institution in the United States (students may start their studies at a two-year institution and then transfer to a four-year institution). **Criteria:** Selection will be based on the aforesaid qualifications and compliance with the application process. **Funds Avail.:** $7,000. **Duration:** Annual. **Number Awarded:** 10. **To Apply:** Applicants must submit an official high school transcript; a copy of parents/guardians federal income tax return; have one letter of support and must be logged in to the application process at the HAA website. Faxes/e-mails will not be accepted. Students must download the certification page from the HAA web site, complete it and obtain the proper signatures prior to mailing. **Deadline:** February 15. **Remarks:** The scholarships are made possible through its funder, Paul Anthony Novelly.

4947 ■ Horatio Alger Montana Scholarships
(Undergraduate/Scholarship)

Purpose: To provide financial assistance to students in the state of Montana. **Focus:** General studies/Field of study not specified. **Qualif.:** Applicants must be U.S. citizens enrolled full time as high school seniors in the United States, and progressing normally toward graduation in spring/summer of the current year with the plan to enter a college in the United States no later than the fall following graduation. They must also: be involved in co-curricular and community service activities; display integrity and perseverance in overcoming adversity; demonstrate critical financial need ($55,000 or lower adjusted gross family income is required); and, exhibit a strong commitment to pursue and complete a bachelor's degree at an accredited non-profit public or private institution in the United States (students may start their studies at a two-year institution and then transfer to a four-year institution). Furthermore, they must pursue a bachelor's degree at the University of Montana, The University of Montana-Western, The University of Montana-Missoula College of Technology, Helena College of Technology of The University of Montana, or Montana Tech of The University of The University of Montana. **Criteria:** Selection will be based on the aforesaid qualifications and compliance with the application process. **Funds Avail.:** $7,000. **Duration:** Annual. **Number Awarded:** 50. **To Apply:** Applicants must submit an official high school transcript; a copy of parents/guardians federal tax return; have one letter of support and must be logged in to the application process at the HAA website. Faxes/e-mails will not be accepted. Students must download the certification page from the HAA web site, complete it and obtain the proper signatures prior to mailing. **Remarks:** The scholarships are made possible through the funding from Phyllis and Dennis Washington.

4948 ■ Horatio Alger National Scholarships
(Undergraduate/Scholarship)

Purpose: To assist high school students who have faced and overcome great obstacles in their young lives. **Focus:** General studies/Field of study not specified. **Qualif.:** Applicants must be U.S. citizens enrolled full time as high school seniors in the United States, and progressing normally toward graduation in spring/summer of the current year with the plan to enter a college in the United States no later than the fall following graduation. They must also: be involved in co-curricular and community service activities; display integrity and perseverance in overcoming adversity; demonstrate critical financial need ($55,000 or lower adjusted gross family income is required); and, exhibit a strong commitment to pursue and complete a bachelor's degree at an accredited non-profit public or private institution in the United States (students may start their studies at a two-year institution and then transfer to a four-year institution). **Criteria:** Selection will be based on the aforesaid qualifications and compliance with the application details. **Funds Avail.:** No specific amount. **Duration:** Annual. **Number Awarded:** Varies. **To Apply:** Applicants must submit an official high school transcript; a copy of parents/guardian federal income tax return; and have one letter of support and must be logged in to the application process at the HAA website. Faxes/e-mails will not be accepted. Students must download the certification page from the HAA web site, complete it and obtain the proper signatures prior to mailing. **Deadline:** April 15.

4949 ■ Horatio Alger North Dakota Scholarships
(Undergraduate/Scholarship)

Purpose: To provide financial assistance to students in the state of North Dakota. **Focus:** General studies/Field of study not specified. **Qualif.:** Applicants must be U.S. citizens who are North Dakota residents, enrolled full time as high school seniors in the United States, and progressing normally toward graduation in spring/summer of the current year with the plan to enter a college in the United States no later than the fall following graduation. They must also: be involved in co-curricular and community service activities; display integrity and perseverance in overcoming adversity; demonstrate critical financial need ($55,000 or lower adjusted gross family income is required); and, exhibit a strong commitment to pursue and complete a bachelor's degree at an accredited non-profit public or private institution in the United States (students may start their studies at a two-year institution and then transfer to a four-year institution). **Criteria:** Recipients will be selected based on financial need. **Funds Avail.:** $7,000. **Duration:** Annual. **Number Awarded:** 28. **To Apply:** Applicants must submit an official

Awards are arranged alphabetically below their administering organizations

high school transcript; a copy of parent's/guardian's federal tax return; have one letter of support and must be logged in to the application process at the HAA website. Faxes/e-mails will not be accepted. Students must download the certification page from the HAA web site, complete it and obtain the proper signatures prior to mailing. **Deadline:** February 15. **Remarks:** The scholarships are funded by BNSF Railway Foundation.

4950 ■ Horatio Alger Pennsylvania Scholarships
(Undergraduate/Scholarship)

Purpose: To provide financial assistance to students in the State of Pennsylvania. **Focus:** General studies/Field of study not specified. **Qualif.:** Applicants must be U.S. citizens who are Pennsylvania residents, enrolled full time as high school seniors in the United States, and progressing normally toward graduation in spring/summer of the current year with the plan to enter a college in the United States no later than the fall following graduation. They must also: be involved in co-curricular and community service activities; display integrity and perseverance in overcoming adversity; demonstrate critical financial need ($55,000 or lower adjusted gross family income is required); and, exhibit a strong commitment to pursue and complete a bachelor's degree at an accredited non-profit public or private institution in the United States (students may start their studies at a two-year institution and then transfer to a four-year institution). **Criteria:** Selection will be based on the aforesaid qualifications and compliance with the application process.

Funds Avail.: $7,000. **Duration:** Annual. **Number Awarded:** 50. **To Apply:** Applicants must submit an official high school transcript; have one letter of support and must be logged in to the application process at the HAA website. Faxes/e-mails will not be accepted. Students must download the certification page from the HAA web site, complete it and obtain the proper signatures prior to mailing. **Deadline:** February 15. **Remarks:** The scholarships are funded by Neubauer Family Foundation and Alan B. Miller.

4951 ■ Horatio Alger South Dakota Scholarships
(Undergraduate/Scholarship)

Purpose: To provide financial assistance to students in the state of South Dakota. **Focus:** General studies/Field of study not specified. **Qualif.:** Applicants must be U.S. citizens who are South Dakota residents, enrolled full time as high school seniors in the United States, and progressing normally toward graduation in spring/summer of the current year with the plan to enter a college in the United States no later than the fall following graduation. They must also: be involved in co-curricular and community service activities; display integrity and perseverance in overcoming adversity; demonstrate critical financial need ($55,000 or lower adjusted gross family income is required); and, exhibit a strong commitment to pursue and complete a bachelor's degree at an accredited non-profit public or private institution in the United States (students may start their studies at a two-year institution and then transfer to a four-year institution). **Criteria:** Selection will be based on the aforesaid qualifications and compliance with the application process.

Funds Avail.: $7,000. **Duration:** Annual. **Number Awarded:** 32. **To Apply:** Applicants must submit an official high school transcript; a copy of parents/guardians federal tax return; have one letter of support and must be logged in to the application process at the HAA website. Faxes/e-mails will not be accepted. Students must download the certification page from the HAA web site, complete it and obtain the proper signatures prior to mailing. **Deadline:** February 15. **Remarks:** The scholarships are funded by MidAmerican Energy Foundation and Dean Buntrock.

4952 ■ Horatio Alger Texas - Fort Worth Scholarships
(Undergraduate/Scholarship)

Purpose: To provide financial assistance to students from Fort Worth, Texas. **Focus:** General studies/Field of study not specified. **Qualif.:** Applicants must be U.S. citizens who are residents of Forth Worth, Texas, enrolled full time as high school seniors in the United States, and progressing normally toward graduation in spring/summer of the current year with the plan to enter a college in the United States no later than the fall following graduation. They must also: be involved in co-curricular and community service activities; display integrity and perseverance in overcoming adversity; demonstrate critical financial need ($55,000 or lower adjusted gross family income is required); and, exhibit a strong commitment to pursue and complete a bachelor's degree at an accredited non-profit public or private institution in the United States (students may start their studies at a two-year institution and then transfer to a four-year institution). **Criteria:** Selection will be based on the aforesaid qualifications and compliance with the application process.

Funds Avail.: $7,000. **Duration:** Annual. **Number Awarded:** 12. **To Apply:** Applicants must have one letter of support and must be logged in to the application process at the HAA website. Faxes/e-mails will not be accepted. Students must download the certification page from the HAA web site, complete it and obtain the proper signatures prior to mailing. **Deadline:** February 15. **Remarks:** The scholarships are funded by BNSF Railway Foundation.

4953 ■ Horatio Alger Texas Scholarships
(Undergraduate/Scholarship)

Purpose: To provide financial assistance to students in the state of Texas. **Focus:** General studies/Field of study not specified. **Qualif.:** Applicants must be U.S. citizens who are Texas residents, enrolled full time as high school seniors in the United States, and progressing normally toward graduation in spring/summer of the current year with the plan to enter a college in the United States no later than the fall following graduation. They must also: be involved in co-curricular and community service activities; display integrity and perseverance in overcoming adversity; demonstrate critical financial need ($55,000 or lower adjusted gross family income is required); and, exhibit a strong commitment to pursue and complete a bachelor's degree at an accredited non-profit public or private institution in the United States (students may start their studies at a two-year institution and then transfer to a four-year institution). **Criteria:** Selection will be based on the aforesaid qualifications and compliance with the application process.

Funds Avail.: $7,000. **Duration:** Annual. **Number Awarded:** 7. **To Apply:** Applicants must have one letter of support and must be logged in to the application process at the HAA website. Faxes/e-mails will not be accepted. Students must download the certification page from the HAA web site, complete it and obtain the proper signatures prior to mailing. **Deadline:** February 15. **Remarks:** The scholarships are funded by Ebby Halliday Scholarship.

4954 ■ Horatio Alger Utah Scholarships
(Undergraduate/Scholarship)

Purpose: To provide financial assistance to students in the state of Utah. **Focus:** General studies/Field of study not specified. **Qualif.:** Applicants must be U.S. citizens who are Utah residents, enrolled full time as high school seniors in the United States, and progressing normally toward graduation in spring/summer of the current year with the plan to enter a college in the United States no later than the fall following graduation. They must also: be involved in co-curricular and community service activities; display integrity and perseverance in overcoming adversity; demonstrate critical financial need ($55,000 or lower adjusted gross family income is required); and, exhibit a strong commitment to pursue and complete a bachelor's degree at an accredited non-profit public or private institution in the United States (students may start their studies at a two-year institution and then transfer to a four-year institution). **Criteria:** Selection will be based on the aforesaid qualifications and compliance with the application process. **Funds Avail.:** $7,000. **Duration:** Annual. **Number Awarded:** 7. **To Apply:** Applicants must have one letter of support and must be logged in to the application process at the HAA website. Faxes/e-mails will not be accepted. Students must download the certification page from the HAA web site, complete it and obtain the proper signatures prior to mailing. **Deadline:** February 15. **Remarks:** The scholarships are made possible by its funder, John A. Moran.

4955 ■ Horatio Alger Washington Scholarships
(Undergraduate/Scholarship)

Purpose: To provide financial assistance to students in the state of Washington. **Focus:** General studies/Field of study not specified. **Qualif.:** Applicants must be U.S. citizens who are Washington residents, enrolled full time as high school seniors in the United States, and progressing normally toward graduation in spring/summer of the current year with the plan to enter a college in the United States no later than the fall following graduation. They must also: be involved in co-curricular and community service activities; display integrity and perseverance in overcoming adversity; demonstrate critical financial need ($55,000 or lower adjusted gross family income is required); and, exhibit a strong commitment to pursue and complete a bachelor's degree at an accredited non-profit public or private institution in the United States (students may start their studies at a two-year institution and then transfer to a four-year institution). **Criteria:** Selection will be based on the aforesaid qualifications and compliance with the application process. **Funds Avail.:** $7,000. **Duration:** Annual. **Number Awarded:** 10. **To Apply:** Applicants must have one letter of support and must be logged in to the application process at the HAA website. Faxes/emails will not be accepted. Students must download the certification page from the HAA web site, complete it and obtain the proper signatures prior to mailing. **Deadline:** February 15. **Remarks:** The scholarships are made possible by its funder, Joseph Clark.

4956 ■ Horatio Alger Wyoming Scholarships
(Undergraduate/Scholarship)

Purpose: To provide financial assistance to students in the state of Wyoming. **Focus:** General studies/Field of study not specified. **Qualif.:** Applicants must be U.S. citizens who are Wyoming residents, enrolled full time as high school seniors in the United States, and progressing normally toward graduation in spring/summer of the current year with the plan to enter a college in the United States no later than the fall following graduation. They must also: be involved in co-curricular and community service activities; display integrity and perseverance in overcoming adversity; demonstrate critical financial need ($55,000 or lower adjusted gross family income is required); and, exhibit a strong commitment to pursue and complete a bachelor's degree at an accredited non-profit public or private institution in the United States (students may start their studies at a two-year institution and then transfer to a four-year institution). **Criteria:** Selection will be based on the aforesaid qualifications and compliance with the application process. **Funds Avail.:** $7,000. **Duration:** Annual. **Number Awarded:** 5. **To Apply:** Applicants must have one letter of support and must be logged in to the application process at the HAA website. Faxes/e-mails will not be accepted. Students must download the certification page from the HAA web site, complete it and obtain the proper signatures prior to mailing. **Deadline:** February 15. **Remarks:** The scholarships are funded by the Suzanne and Walter Scott Foundation.

4957 ■ Horatio Alger Ak-Sar-Ben Scholarships
(Undergraduate/Scholarship)

Purpose: To provide financial assistance to students in the state of Nebraska and western Iowa. **Focus:** General studies/Field of study not specified. **Qualif.:** Applicants must be enrolled full time as high school seniors, progressing normally toward graduation and planning to enter college not later than the fall following graduation; must have a strong commitment to pursue a bachelor's degree at an accredited institution (students may start their studies at a two-year institution and then transfer to a four-year institution); must have critical financial need ($50,000 or less adjusted gross income per family is preferred; if higher, an explanation must be provided); must be involved in co-curricular and community activities; must have a minimum grade point average of 2.0; must be residents of Nebraska or western Iowa; be citizens or permanent residents of the United States. **Criteria:** Recipients will be selected based on financial need. **Funds Avail.:** $5,000. **Number Awarded:** 50. **To Apply:** Applicants must submit an official transcript; a copy of parents/guardians federal tax return; have one letter of support and must be logged in to the application process at the HAA website. Faxes/e-mails will not be accepted. Students must download the certification page from the HAA web site, complete it and obtain the proper signatures prior to mailing.

4958 ■ Horatio Alger Idaho University Scholarships
(Undergraduate/Scholarship)

Purpose: To provide educational support to students who are in need. **Focus:** General studies/Field of study not specified. **Qualif.:** Applicants must attend Idaho State University and be enrolled in the College of Business; must have critical financial need based on the Student Aid Report; must be residents of the State of Idaho; must have a minimum cumulative grade point average of 2.0 or better. **Criteria:** Recipients will be selected based on the committee's review of all applications. **Funds Avail.:** $55,000. **Duration:** Annual. **To Apply:** Applicants must submit an official high school and college transcript of records; a copy of parents/guardians federal income tax return; must provide a copy of Student Aid Report (SAR); and have one letter of support and must be logged in to the application process at the HAA website. Faxes/e-mails will not be accepted. Students must download the certification page from the HAA web site, complete it and obtain the proper signatures prior to mailing.

4959 ■ HotelsCheap.org
420 Jericho Tpk., No. 328
Jericho, NY 11753
Ph: (516)478-8322

Awards are arranged alphabetically below their administering organizations

Fax: (516)622-9630
Free: 800-311-4307
URL: www.hotelscheap.org/

4960 ■ General Scholarships for Higher Learning
(Undergraduate, Graduate, Master's/Scholarship)

Purpose: To support and motivate students to value and make the most of their education, and to give scholarship awards to deserving students to achieve higher quality education, and actively promoting education to encourage students to improve their knowledge and strive for excellence. **Focus:** General studies/Field of study not specified. **Qualif.:** Applicants must be legal residents of the United States and students who are at least 16 years of age enrolled in an accredited post-secondary academic institution in the United States in a two year, four year or a graduate program. **Criteria:** Students are selected based on their responses, as judged by the executive management team.

Funds Avail.: $1,500. **Duration:** Annual; each fall and spring semester. **To Apply:** Applicants must submit one complete contest application via sponsor's website in English language before the deadline and must answer four personal, open-ended, and thought-provoking questions to be considered as finalist. Students under the age of 18, must have the consent of their parents or legal guardians to participate. **Deadline:** April 15.

4961 ■ Houghton Mifflin Harcourt Co.
222 Berkeley St.
Boston, MA 02116
Ph: (617)351-5000
E-mail: tradecustomerservice@hmhpub.com
URL: www.hmhco.com

4962 ■ Gerda and Kurt Klein Scholarships
(Undergraduate/Scholarship)

Purpose: To recognize and support high school students who foster ethnic and religious tolerance and actively minimize bigotry within their community. **Focus:** General studies/Field of study not specified. **Qualif.:** Applicant must be a high school student who works to affect change in the community by fostering ethnic and religious tolerance and acting against bigotry and hatred. **Criteria:** Award is given based on the submitted application materials.

Funds Avail.: No specific amount. **Duration:** Annual. **To Apply:** Applicant may visit the website to verify the application process and other pieces of information. **Remarks:** Established in 2007.

4963 ■ House of Puerto Rico San Diego
PO Box 81982
San Diego, CA 92138
Ph: (619)234-3445
E-mail: hprsd@houseofpuertorico.com
URL: www.houseofpuertorico.com
Facebook: www.facebook.com/HouseofPuertoRico

4964 ■ Casilda Pagan Educational/Vocational Scholarships (Graduate, Undergraduate, Postgraduate/Scholarship)

Purpose: To assist individuals attain their educational and professional goals. **Focus:** General studies/Field of study not specified. **Qualif.:** Applicants must be high school seniors, graduates, or college/post-graduate students; must be current active members of House of Puerto Rico San Diego or San Diego County residents of Puerto Rican descent who have contributed at least 10 hours of community service through HPRSD. **Criteria:** Evaluations will be based on need, goal, motivation, application and contribution.

Funds Avail.: No specific amount. **Duration:** Annual. **To Apply:** Applicants must submit a personal essay (minimum of 250 words) including educational goals, financial needs, contribution to community service through the house of Puerto Rico, prior history of community service; proof of current enrollment in an educational or vocational institution; transcripts reflecting most recent academic achievement; three recommendation letters from teachers, counselors, employers or community leaders; completed application form; any additional materials that could enhance application. **Deadline:** July 31. **Remarks:** Established in 1972. **Contact:** Joe Carballo at jcarballo@san.rr.com.

4965 ■ Houston Geological Society (HGS)
14811 St. Marys Ln., Ste. 250
Houston, TX 77079
Ph: (713)463-9476
Fax: (281)679-5504
URL: www.hgs.org
Facebook: www.facebook.com/hgs.org

4966 ■ W.L. Calvert Memorial Scholarships
(Graduate/Scholarship)

Purpose: To assist graduate students to pursue a career in some area of economic geology. **Focus:** Earth sciences. **Qualif.:** Applicants must be graduate students who are admitted to a graduate degree program leading to an M.S. or PhD at any accredited U.S. college or university; must be U.S. citizens who are interested in earth sciences or any related field of study. **Criteria:** Applicants will be chosen based on academic record, demonstrated potential to complete graduate degree requirements as attested by professional earth scientists in academia, government and industry. Financial need will be a secondary consideration.

Funds Avail.: $3,500 tp $4,500. **Duration:** Annual. **To Apply:** Applicants must complete the application form and must provide an evidence of their acceptance for a graduate study. **Deadline:** June 15. **Remarks:** Established in 1974. **Contact:** Dr. Alison Henning, Rice University, Department of Earth Science, 6100 Main St., Houston, TX 77005.

4967 ■ HGS Foundation Undergraduate Scholarships (Undergraduate/Scholarship)

Purpose: To provide scholarships to deserving undergraduate students majoring in geosciences. **Focus:** Geosciences. **Qualif.:** Applicants must be juniors and seniors in the current academic year; must be enrolled full-time carrying a normal academic load in geosciences; and must be U.S. citizens. **Criteria:** Recipients will be selected based on academic achievement.

Funds Avail.: $1,500. **Duration:** Annual. **To Apply:** Nominated candidates must contact the head of geosciences department for further information.

4968 ■ Houston Intellectual Property Law Association (HIPLA)
c/o Theodore Ro, President
National Aeronautics & Space Administration

HOUTAN SCHOLARSHIP FOUNDATION

2101 NASA Pky., MC AL
Houston, TX 77058
URL: www.hipla.org

4969 ■ HIPLA Judicial Fellowships (Undergraduate/Fellowship)

Purpose: To promote development and understanding of the Intellectual Property Law to law students. **Focus:** Law. **Qualif.:** Applicants must be full-time students at the University of Law Center, the Thurgood Marshall School of Law or the South Texas College of Law who are not receiving law school credit for their internship and intends to practice intellectual property law. The applicants must be U.S. citizens have completed at least 30 hours of course work at the time their internship begins and have a GPA average that ranks in the top half of the applicant's law school class. **Criteria:** Selection is based on student's qualifications and on submitted application materials.

Funds Avail.: Up to $3,000. **Duration:** at least six weeks. **To Apply:** Applicants must submit a resume, a letter describing interest in intellectual property law, a letter from the court or USPTO stating that student has been accepted for an internship and a description of any circumstances to be considered.

4970 ■ HIPLA Scholarships for University of Houston Law Center Students (Graduate, Undergraduate/Scholarship)

Purpose: To support students interested in intellectual property. **Focus:** Law. **Qualif.:** Applicants must be University of Houston Law Center student who have demonstrated interest in intellectual property law, have completed at least 30 hours of law study and have not previously received a HIPLA scholarship or fellowship. **Criteria:** Consideration will be given to students who have interned for a Houston Federal Judge, the U.S. Court of Appeals for the Federal Circuit, or the USPTO.

Funds Avail.: $1,500. **Duration:** Annual. **Number Awarded:** Up to 3. **To Apply:** Application materials, including transcript and a copy of financial aid award, should be returned to the Office of Student Services or sent via electronic mail to Associate Dean Sondra Tennessee. **Deadline:** October 30.

4971 ■ Houtan Scholarship Foundation

300 Central Ave.
Egg Harbor Township, NJ 08234
E-mail: info@houtan.org
URL: www.houtan.org

4972 ■ Houtan Scholarships (Graduate/Scholarship)

Purpose: To support students who have high academic performance and proven interest in promoting Iran's great culture. **Focus:** Area and ethnic studies. **Qualif.:** Applicants should have a working knowledge of Farsi and should demonstrate an active interest in Iranian culture, heritage and literature; must be attending or anticipating to attend an accredited graduate school; must have superior academic performance or a significant increase of academic performance over the course of the academic career; and may have financial need. **Criteria:** Recipient is selected based on submitted documents, financial need, and the interview.

Funds Avail.: $3,500. **Duration:** Annual. **Number Awarded:** 1. **To Apply:** Applicants must submit a completed application form along with two letters of recommendation, college transcript, and goals and aspirations essay. **Deadline:** June 1 and October 1.

4973 ■ Howard Hughes Medical Institute (HHMI)

4000 Jones Bridge Rd.
Chevy Chase, MD 20815-6720
Ph: (301)215-8500
E-mail: commpub@hhmi.org
URL: www.hhmi.org
Facebook: www.facebook.com/HowardHughesMed
Twitter: twitter.com/hhminews

4974 ■ Gilliam Fellowships for Advanced Study (Doctorate/Fellowship)

Purpose: To offer an extraordinary opportunity to pursue graduate studies in the life sciences. **Focus:** Biomedical research. **Qualif.:** Applicants must be past participants in the HHMI Exceptional Research Opportunities Program must be graduating seniors or must be enrolled or planning to enroll in a PhD program in the biomedical or related sciences. In addition, applicants must not have completed more than one year in a PhD program by the application date. **Criteria:** Fellowships are awarded on the basis of the candidate's promise as a scientific investigator and potential for leadership in the scientific community, as reflected by academic records, relevant educational and personal experiences, previous accomplishment and goals, research experience, proposed research plan, references and scores attained on the Graduate Record Examination general test or the Medical College Admission Test.

Funds Avail.: $46,000. **Duration:** Annual; up to 3 years. **To Apply:** Applicants are expected to complete an application, which will be made available electronically to all eligible Exceptional Research Opportunities Program (EXROP) students. The application will be submitted via HHMI's web-based competition system at www.hhmi.org/competitions. A complete application consists of the following items: applicant information including name, current and permanent addresses, email address and other pertinent information; educational history including names of all colleges and universities attended, dates of attendance and degrees obtained; all undergraduate transcripts (to be sent to HHMI directly by institutions attended); list of relevant honors, awards and professional activities; educational and personal experiences relevant to applicant's career goals and objectives; research experiences, including dates, project summary and the applicant's role in the project; list of publications, presentations and posters, if applicable; proposed research plan with literature cited; leadership statement demonstrating leadership potential and/or how receipt of the Gilliam Fellowship will help advance scientific careers of underrepresented students; three letters of reference sent directly to HHMI. Letters should be from those who can speak best to potential as a scientist, and one from HHMI program director; recent score on the Graduate Record Examination General Test or Medical College Admission Test. **Deadline:** February 4.

4975 ■ HHMI International Student Research Fellowships (Doctorate/Fellowship)

Purpose: To support outstanding international pre-doctoral students studying in the United States who are ineligible for fellowships or training grants through U.S. federal agencies. **Focus:** Biomedical research. **Qualif.:** Applicants must be in their 3rd or 4th year of a PhD program in the biomedical or related sciences at a designated nominating institution; have demonstrated exceptional talent for research; have entered laboratory in which they will conduct their dissertation research; must not be U.S. citizens, non-citizens or permanent residents of the United States. **Criteria:** Fellows will be chosen based on their promise as scientific investigators.

Funds Avail.: $43,000. **Duration:** Up to 3 years. **To Apply:** Application will be submitted online using HHMI's web-based competition system at www.hhmi.org/competitions. A complete application will consist of the following: applicant information, including name, contact information and email address; graduate degree information, including name of department/program, date of entry into the graduate program and name and email address of the dissertation advisor(s); description of intended dissertation research with a limited bibliography of key references; brief discussion of the significance and innovation of the intended research project; research experiences, including dates, project summary and the applicant's role in the project; list of publications, presentations and posters, if applicable; list of relevant honors, awards and professional activities; letters of reference. One letter must be from the applicant's dissertation advisor. Other letters should be from those who can speak best to the applicant's potential as a researcher. These letters must be uploaded in the competition system by the reference writer; educational history, including names of all colleges and universities attended, dates of attendance and degrees obtained; graduate transcripts (to be uploaded by the applicant); scores on the GRE or MCAT and TOEFL. **Deadline:** February 11.

4976 ■ HHMI Medical Research Fellowships
(Undergraduate/Fellowship)

Purpose: To support students to pursue biomedical research training. **Focus:** Biomedical research. **Qualif.:** Applicants must be enrolled in a medical, dental or veterinary school located in the United States. The fellowship research may be conducted at any academic or nonprofit institution in the United States, except the National Institutes of Health. **Criteria:** Fellowships are awarded on the basis of the applicant's ability and promise for a research career as a physician-scientist or medically trained researcher and the quality of the training that will be provided.

Funds Avail.: No specific amount. **Number Awarded:** Varies. **To Apply:** Applicants may visit the Institute's website for the web-based submission process and other application requirements.

4977 ■ Howard Hughes Medical Institute (HHMI) - Janelia Farm Research Campus
19700 Helix Drive
Ashburn, VA 20147
Ph: (571)209-4000
URL: www.janelia.org

4978 ■ Janelia Farm Graduate Program *(Graduate/Award)*

Purpose: To provide assistance to students with passion for engaging in high-quality research in neuroscience or imaging technology. **Focus:** Neuroscience; Technology. **Qualif.:** Applicants must be graduate students planning to attend in a collaborative PhD program at the University of Cambridge, the University of Chicago or the Johns Hopkins University. **Criteria:** Selection will be based on the committee's criteria.

Funds Avail.: No specific amount. **Duration:** Annual. **To Apply:** Interested applicants must apply to their chosen institutes as well as to the graduate program. Application is not complete without the required supporting documentation: curriculum vitae, research proposal with 500 words or less, statement of research, undergraduate transcripts, names and contact information for three references, GRE scores, TOEFL or IELTS for non-English-speaking countries, and names of three Janelia scientists that the applicants want to work with. All accomplished applications must be submitted on the online service.

4979 ■ Hudson River Foundation (HRF)
17 Battery Pl., Ste. 915
New York, NY 10004
Ph: (212)483-7667
Fax: (212)924-8325
E-mail: info@hudsonriver.org
URL: www.hudsonriver.org

4980 ■ Mark B. Bain Graduate Fellowship *(Doctorate, Master's, Graduate/Fellowship)*

Purpose: To support advanced graduate students conducting research on the Hudson River system. **Focus:** General studies/Field of study not specified. **Qualif.:** Applicants must be enrolled in an accredited doctoral or master's program, must have thesis advisor and advisory committee (if appropriate to the institution), and must have thesis research plan approved by the student's institution or department. **Criteria:** Selection is based on the submitted application and materials.

Funds Avail.: $15,000 for doctoral students; $11,000 for Master's level students. **Duration:** Annual. **Number Awarded:** up to 6. **To Apply:** Applicants must submit a proposal cover page; a description of the thesis project (maximum of 10 pages); a timetable for the completion of the research; an estimated cost of supplies, travel, etc.; applicant's curriculum vitae; a letter from the University stating that the applicant will receive a tuition waiver or reimbursement for the period of the fellowship; and two letters of recommendation (one from an advisor, mailed directly to the Foundation). **Deadline:** March 16.

4981 ■ Tibor T. Polgar Fellowships *(Graduate, Undergraduate/Fellowship)*

Purpose: To provide summertime grant and research funds for college students to conduct research on the Hudson River. **Focus:** General studies/Field of study not specified. **Qualif.:** Applicants must be undergraduate or graduate students who will conduct research on the Hudson River. **Criteria:** Selection is based on submitted application materials.

Funds Avail.: $1,000-$3,800. **Duration:** Annual. **Number Awarded:** 8. **To Apply:** Applications should include a letter of interest in the program, a short description (4-6 pages) of the research project, a timetable of the research, an estimated cost of supplies and travel expenses, a letter of support from student's advisor and curriculum vitae. **Deadline:** February 22. **Contact:** Helena Andreyko at 212-483-7667.

4982 ■ Hughes Memorial Foundation
223 Riverview Dr., Ste. I
Danville, VA 24540
Ph: (434)799-2412

Awards are arranged alphabetically below their administering organizations

Fax: (434)799-3089
URL: www.hughesmemorialfoundation.org
Facebook: www.facebook.com/HughesMemorialFoundatio

4983 ■ Hughes Memorial Foundation Scholarships (Graduate/Scholarship)

Purpose: To provide financial assistance to needy students and be able to further their career. **Focus:** General studies/Field of study not specified. **Qualif.:** Applicants must be needy and/or at-risk children living in the Virginia counties of Pittsylvania, Halifax, Mecklenburg, Charlotte, Campbell, Bedford, Franklin, Henry and Patrick; the North Carolina counties of Stokes, Rockingham, Caswell and Person; and the cities of Virginia and North Carolina that are located geographically within those counties; must have a minimum of 2.5 GPA. **Criteria:** Recipients will be selected based on the degree of need, demonstrated ability to succeed in educational endeavor, impact towards beneficiary, accuracy, completeness and reasonableness of application.

Funds Avail.: No specific amount. **To Apply:** Applicants must submit a completed application form for Federal Student Aid; Student aid report; parents' federal Income Tax Return; description of all motor vehicles owned by the family with year, make and model; description of all real estate owned by the family with the tax-appraised value; description of any other significant debts by the family; official transcripts from high schools and colleges attended; official SAT, ACT or graduate/professional exam scores. **Deadline:** April 1. **Contact:** Hughes Memorial Foundation, at the above address.

4984 ■ Huguenot Society of South Carolina
138 Logan St.
Charleston, SC 29401-1941
Ph: (843)723-3235
Fax: (843)853-8476
URL: www.huguenotsociety.org

4985 ■ Mary Mouzon Darby Undergraduate Scholarships (Undergraduate/Scholarship)

Purpose: To financially support undergraduate students. **Focus:** General studies/Field of study not specified. **Qualif.:** Applicants must be of Huguenot descent and either members of the Huguenot Society of South Carolina or the child or grandchild of a current member of the Society. **Criteria:** Preference will be given to those qualified applicants entering first year of college and/or those with demonstrated financial need.

Funds Avail.: $1,000. **Duration:** Annual. **To Apply:** Applicants must submit: the cover sheet with contact information; the lineage sheet listing the applicant's lineage to the Huguenot ancestor; a brief (three pages, double-spaced) paper that includes a biographical sketch of the applicant's Huguenot ancestor and what this Huguenot heritage means to the applicants. **Deadline:** December 31. **Contact:** Huguenot Society of South Carolina, at the above address.

4986 ■ Huguenot Society of South Carolina Graduate Scholarships (Graduate/Scholarship)

Purpose: To support students working toward a graduate degree in history. **Focus:** History. **Qualif.:** Applicants must be students working toward a graduate degree in history. **Criteria:** Selection will be based on submitted essay.

Funds Avail.: $1,000. **To Apply:** Applicants must submit two hard copies of the essay, as well as a cover letter giving full name, address, telephone number, details of the undergraduate degree and also the graduate degree currently in progress, and the thesis and significance of the paper. The text should not exceed 25 typed and double-spaced pages, excluding footnotes, illustrations and bibliography (one-inch margins for the top, bottom, left, and right). All submissions must include footnotes and any other necessary documentation. Titles of the works cited in the essay and notes should be typed in italics and indexed if possible, using the standards set forth in the Chicago Manual of Style, 15th Edition. The essay must be a work of scholarship on a Huguenot topic; may examine any aspect of the religious, political, economic, social, or intellectual history of the French or Walloon Protestants from the sixteenth century to the present; may deal with any appropriate geographical area. Submissions must be original, not previously published and not under consideration by another publication. The author of the winning essay will be asked to submit a copy of his/her paper on a MS Word-Compatible CD. **Deadline:** December 31. **Contact:** Graduate Scholarship, Huguenot Society of South Carolina, at the above address.

4987 ■ Human Race Theatre Company
126 N Main St., Ste. 300
Dayton, OH 45402-1710
Ph: (937)461-3823
Fax: (937)461-7223
E-mail: contact@humanracetheatre.org
URL: www.humanracetheatre.org

4988 ■ Stephen Schwartz Musical Theatre Scholarships (Undergraduate/Scholarship)

Purpose: To support student singers/actors in the greater Dayton area. **Focus:** Theater arts. **Qualif.:** Applicants must have a permanent address in Montgomery County or one of seven contiguous counties (Preble, Darke, Miami, Clark, Greene, Warren or Butler) or be currently enrolled at a college in one of the eight counties previously listed. **Criteria:** Awards are given based on the auditions and applications.

Funds Avail.: $1,000 for high school senior; $1,500 for college student. **Duration:** Annual. **Number Awarded:** 2. **To Apply:** Applicants must submit a completed application; two letters of recommendation: one from a faculty including a private lessons instructor; and one from a Director or Music Director from a show where applicants appeared in the past two years; current photograph; resume; and must prepare two contrasting songs that best show the vocal and acting ability. **Deadline:** February 16. **Remarks:** Established in 2007. **Contact:** John Faas, Development Director, at 937-461-3823 ext. 3111 or via email: john@humanracetheatre.org.

4989 ■ Human Resources Research Organization (HumRRO)
66 Canal Center Plz., Ste. 700
Alexandria, VA 22314-1578
Ph: (703)549-3611
Fax: (703)549-9025
URL: www.humrro.org
Facebook: www.facebook.com/Human-Resources-Research-Organization-HumRRO-161583990533313
Twitter: twitter.com/HumRROorg

Awards are arranged alphabetically below their administering organizations

4990 ■ Meredith P. Crawford Fellowships in I/O Psychology (Doctorate/Fellowship)

Purpose: To provide financial support while the student completes his/her dissertation in the field of Industrial-Organizational (I-O) Psychology, or in a field congruent with the objectives of the Society for Industrial Psychology, Inc. (SIOP). **Focus:** Psychology. **Qualif.:** Applicants must be doctoral candidates whose dissertation topic has been proposed and approved by his/ her graduate faculty in Industrial-Organizational (I-O) Psychology, Inc. **Criteria:** Applicants will be evaluated on the basis of merit, research promise, academic achievement and professional productivity.

Funds Avail.: $12,000. **Number Awarded:** 1. **To Apply:** Applicants must provide a completed application form, a personal statement, three completed recommendation forms and an official transcript from each institution attended for graduate academic work. **Deadline:** July 1. **Contact:** For questions, just call Jessica Terner at 703-706-5687.

4991 ■ Human Rights Campaign (HRC)
1640 Rhode Island Ave. NW
Washington, DC 20036-3278
Ph: (202)628-4160
Fax: (202)347-5323
Free: 800-777-4723
E-mail: membership@hrc.org
URL: www.hrc.org
Facebook: www.facebook.com/humanrightscampaign
Twitter: twitter.com/HRC

4992 ■ McCleary Law Fellows Program (Graduate, Undergraduate/Fellowship)

Purpose: To provide training opportunities for law students. **Focus:** Law. **Qualif.:** Applicants must possess a strong academic record at an accredited American law school, excellent interpersonal, legal research and writing skills and an interest in civil rights, policy and/or nonprofit lawyering. 1Ls, 2Ls, 3Ls and LL.M. candidates are eligible. **Criteria:** Selection is based on the submitted application materials.

Funds Avail.: No specific amount. **Duration:** 11-13 weeks. **Number Awarded:** Up to 4. **To Apply:** Applicants must submit, via e-mail, a cover letter; resume; brief legal writing sample (five pages or less); names of two references and; a law school transcript.

4993 ■ Human Rights in China (HRIC)
450 7th Ave., Ste. 1301
New York, NY 10123
Ph: (212)239-4495
Fax: (212)239-2561
E-mail: hrichina@hrichina.org
URL: www.hrichina.org/en

4994 ■ Robert L. Bernstein Fellowships in International Human Rights (Graduate/Fellowship)

Purpose: To enable an NYU Law School graduate to devote a year to full-time human rights work at HRIC. **Focus:** Human rights; Law. **Qualif.:** Applicants must be graduate students of NYU Law School; must have demonstrated commitment to and knowledge of international human rights; must have excellent writing and communication skills; must have strong research skills; must have relevant coursework. Mandarin proficiency is a plus. **Criteria:** Selection will be based on the committee's criteria.

Funds Avail.: $50,000 plus benefits. **To Apply:** Application must include the following: cover letter, resume, two letters of recommendation, at least one individually written and edited writing sample; an official transcript, an essay of no more than 250 words, describing one key human rights challenge facing China. **Deadline:** November 7. **Contact:** HRIC at fellowships@hrichina.org.

4995 ■ Human Rights Resource Center (HRRC)
University of Minnesota Law School
229 19th Ave. S, Ste. N-120
Minneapolis, MN 55455
Ph: (612)626-0041
Fax: (612)625-2011
Free: 888-HRE-DUC8
E-mail: humanrts@umn.edu
URL: www.hrusa.org

4996 ■ Upper Midwest Human Rights Fellowship Program (Graduate/Scholarship, Fellowship)

Purpose: To promote social justice by providing practical experience related to international human rights. **Focus:** Human rights. **Qualif.:** Applicants must be law students and graduate students at the University of Minnesota. **Criteria:** Primary criterion for selection is a demonstrated interest in, and commitment to, the promotion of international human rights. Subcommittee of the Human Rights Center's Advisory Board will select the grant recipients. Awards will be determined by considering an individual's qualifications and interests together with the needs of the supervising organization.

Funds Avail.: $1,000 - $5,000 for transportation, lodging, and food expenses incurred during the fellowship period. **Duration:** Annual. **To Apply:** Applicants must submit a complete application form available online; must provide the confirmation letter from host; transcript (from last ten years only); a cover letter/resume; one letter of reference; and a 2-3-page essay detailing the following: (1) Significance of the experience for your academic or professional training, (2) Relationship of the fellowship to your future goals, (3) How the host organization will benefit from a fellowship, (4) Description of the key aspects of a current human rights issue in the country/location of your proposed fellowship and how the sponsoring organization addresses it; (5) Description of how you will use your new human rights experiences in your community upon your return home. **Deadline:** February 6. **Contact:** Willa Gelvick, Fellowship Coordinator at 612-626-2226 or hrfellow@umn.edu.

4997 ■ Human Rights Watch (HRW)
350 5th Ave., 34th Fl.
New York, NY 10118-3299
Ph: (212)290-4700
Fax: (212)736-1300
E-mail: hrwpress@hrw.org
URL: www.hrw.org
Facebook: www.facebook.com/HumanRightsWatch
Twitter: twitter.com/hrw

4998 ■ Alan R. and Barbara D. Finberg Fellowships (Graduate/Fellowship)

Purpose: To support and mentor graduates of law schools or graduates of journalism, international relations, area

Awards are arranged alphabetically below their administering organizations

studies, or other relevant disciplines. **Focus:** Area and ethnic studies; International affairs and relations; Journalism; Law. **Qualif.:** Applicants must be graduate students (at the master's level) in the fields of law, journalism, international relations, or other relevant studies; must have exceptional analytic skills, an ability to write and speak clearly; must be committed working in the human rights field in the future; must be proficient in one language in addition to English; and must be familiar with countries or regions where serious human rights violations occur. **Criteria:** Selection is based on applicant's qualifications and submitted application materials.

Funds Avail.: $55,000. **Duration:** One year. **To Apply:** Applicants must submit a complete application packet which includes a cover letter; resume (curriculum vitae); two letters of recommendation; at least one unedited, unpublished writing sample; and an official law or graduate school transcript. Applications should be sent by e-mail, under a single cover and as PDF files with the name of the fellowship being applied in the subject line. **Deadline:** October 8.

4999 ■ NYU School of Law Fellowships at HRW
(Graduate/Fellowship)

Purpose: To support and mentor graduates of New York University School of Law. **Focus:** Law. **Qualif.:** Applicants must be J.D. graduate of New York University School of Law who have exceptional analytic skills; have an ability to write and speak clearly; must be committed working in the human rights field in the future; must be proficient in one language in addition to English; must be familiar with countries or regions where serious human rights violations occur. **Criteria:** Selection is based on applicant's qualification and submitted application materials.

Funds Avail.: $55,000. **Duration:** One year. **To Apply:** Applicants must submit a complete application packet which must include a cover letter; resume (curriculum vitae); two letters of recommendation; at least one unedited, unpublished writing sample; and an official law or graduate school transcript. Applications should be sent by e-mail, under a single cover and as PDF files with the name of the fellowship being applied in the subject line. **Deadline:** October 8.

5000 ■ Leonard H. Sandler Fellowships *(Graduate/Fellowship)*

Purpose: To support and mentor graduates of Columbia Law School. **Focus:** Law. **Qualif.:** Applicants must be a J.D. graduate of Columbia Law School; must have exceptional analytic skills and an ability to write and speak clearly; must be committed working in the human rights field in the future; must be proficient in one language in addition to English; and must be familiar with countries or regions where serious human rights violations occur. **Criteria:** Selection is based on applicant's qualification and submitted application materials.

Funds Avail.: $55,000. **Duration:** one year. **To Apply:** Applicants must submit a complete application packet which must include a cover letter; resume (curriculum vitae); two letters of recommendation; at least one unedited, unpublished writing sample; and an official law or graduate school transcript. Applications should be sent by e-mail, under a single cover and as PDF files with the name of the fellowship being applied in the subject line. **Deadline:** October 8.

5001 ■ The Humane Society of the United States (HSUS)
2100 L St. NW
Washington, DC 20037
Ph: (202)452-1100
Free: 866-720-2676
E-mail: donorcare@humanesociety.org
URL: www.humanesociety.org

5002 ■ Shaw-Worth Memorial Scholarship *(Undergraduate/Scholarship)*

Purpose: To help students achieve their dreams of working in the service of animals, the environment and humankind. **Focus:** Animal rights. **Qualif.:** Applicants must be high school seniors who have made contributions to animal protection; must be from New England public, private and vocational schools. **Criteria:** Recipients will be selected based on submitted application materials. Scholastic standing and financial need are not the basis for the award.

Funds Avail.: No specific amount. **To Apply:** Applicants must submit letter of narrative statement of achievements and attitude towards animal protection. Applicants must submit a documentation of activities such as recommendations from at least three persons and description of future plans for humane work. Supporting letters from teachers, mentors, supervisors, peers and other observers are not required but may help. Applications should include the student's home address and phone numbers. **Deadline:** March 25.

5003 ■ Humboldt State University - Schatz Energy Research Center (SERC)
1 Harpst St.
Arcata, CA 95521
Ph: (707)826-4345
Fax: (707)826-4347
E-mail: serc@humboldt.edu
URL: www.schatzlab.org

5004 ■ Schatz Energy Fellowships for Graduate Studies *(Graduate/Fellowship)*

Purpose: To provide training and experience to graduate students who intend to focus on renewable energy or energy efficiency related work. **Focus:** Energy-related areas. **Qualif.:** Applicant must be admitted to the Environmental Resources Engineering (ERE) and Energy, Technology, and Policy (ETaP) graduate program at Humboldt State University and intend to focus on renewable energy or energy efficiency related work. **Criteria:** Selection is based on the application.

Funds Avail.: $10,000. **To Apply:** Applicants must submit a carefully written 500-word essay that describes the reasons for applying for the Schatz Energy Fellowship and the line of research or project work that the student propose to pursue while studying at Humboldt State and briefly discuss how prior studies and work experience help to prepare the student to engage in the proposed work; and a completed application for admission to the ETaP or ERE graduate program. **Deadline:** February 15.

5005 ■ Hungarian American Coalition (HAC)
2400 N St. NW, Ste. 603
Washington, DC 20037
Ph: (202)296-9505

Awards are arranged alphabetically below their administering organizations

Fax: (202)775-5175
E-mail: hac@hacusa.org
URL: www.hacusa.org
Facebook: www.facebook.com/HungarianAmericanCoalition

5006 ■ Dr. Elemér and Éva Kiss Scholarship Fund
(Undergraduate/Scholarship)

Purpose: To support Hungarian students who will be admitted at any U.S. college or university. **Focus:** General studies/Field of study not specified. **Qualif.:** Applicants must be citizens of Hungary or members of an ethnic Hungarian community in Slovakia, Romania, Voivodina, Serbia, or Ukraine; must have gained admission as full-time students to a U.S. college or university. **Criteria:** Preference will be given to deserving students who are eligible to apply and will able to comply with the instructions for the application in the said program.

Funds Avail.: $1,000. **Duration:** Annual. **To Apply:** Applicants must provide proof of scholarship and other sources of financial support; record of excellent academic standing; and two letters of recommendation regarding the applicant's personal and academic achievements. **Remarks:** Established in 1997. **Contact:** Dr. Elemér and Éva Kiss Scholarship Fund, scholarship@hacusa.org.

5007 ■ Hungarian-American Enterprise Scholarship Fund (HAESF)
300 Fore St.
Portland, ME 04101
Ph: (207)553-4194
Fax: (207)553-5194
URL: www.haesf.org

5008 ■ HAESF Graduate Scholarships *(Graduate/Scholarship)*

Purpose: To provide opportunities for Hungarian Society leaders to receive an international education that leads to professional occupations. **Focus:** General studies/Field of study not specified. **Qualif.:** Applicants must be recent graduate students who have obtained their five-year program in any Hungarian university. Applicants who have obtained their three years of education under the old curriculum and continued their remaining two years under the new higher education system are eligible to apply; must maintain a minimum of 3.0 GPA; must hold a Hungarian passport; and must be accepted to an American university/college, or certificate-granting institution. **Criteria:** Applicants will be judged based on, but not limited to: 1) potential future contributions to Hungarian Society; 2) professional objectives to the values and mission of HAESF; 3) articulated professional goals; 4) personality; 5) strength of recommendations; 6) ability to serve as ambassadors of Hungary; 7) communication skills; 8) diversity of majors and professional interests; 9) financial need.

Funds Avail.: No specific amount. **To Apply:** Applicants must fill out the HAESF Graduate Scholarship Application form; must submit an acceptance letter from the receiving academic institution, detailed budget proposal, personal statement, current curriculum vitae, a copy of transcript of records, a letter signed in English which includes the average of all subjects taken and any related to the major field of study, a copy of diploma, copies of relevant certificates of completion and three letters of reference discussing the following: 1) relationship with the applicants; 2) program's relevance for applicant's future and career goals; 3) assessment of applicant's character, abilities, strength and weaknesses; 4) English language communication skill; 5) detailed contact information of the referee. Supporting documents should be in translated in English. **Contact:** HAESF's Program Officer, at the above address or Email: info@haesf.org.

5009 ■ HAESF Professional Internship Program *(Doctorate/Internship)*

Purpose: To provide opportunities for Hungarian society leaders to have an international training experience. **Focus:** Agriculture, Economic aspects; Art; Business; Communications; Media arts; Medicine; Public administration; Public health; Social sciences. **Qualif.:** Program is open to PhD students who have started their studies within six months of completing their university degree program; full-time students who have completed their four years out of a five-year university degree program under the old curriculum; students who have completed their three years plus two-year program in the same or related discipline under the new higher education system; graduated a five-year university program or three years plus two-year program no more than six months before the application deadline. Applicants must pursue studies at an accredited Hungarian university; must hold a Hungarian passport; and level of English must be sufficient to perform in a native English-speaking environment. **Criteria:** Applicants will be judged based on, but not limited to: 1) potential future contributions to Hungarian Society; 2) professional objectives to the values and mission of HAESF; 3) articulated professional goals; 4) personality; 5) strength of recommendations; 6) ability to serve as ambassadors of Hungary; 7) communication skills; 8) diversity of majors and professional interests; 9) clear understanding on what the program can offer.

Funds Avail.: $30,000. **Duration:** 12 months. **To Apply:** Applicants must fill out the HAESF Professional Internship Program Application form; must submit a personal statement, current curriculum vitae, a copy of transcript of records (translated in English), a letter signed in English which includes the average of all subjects taken and any related to the major field of study, a copy of diploma, copies of relevant certificates of completion and three letters of reference discussing the following: 1) Relationship with applicants; 2) Internship's relevance for applicant's future and career goals; 3) Assessment of applicant's character, abilities, strength and weaknesses; 4) English language communication skill. **Deadline:** April 1 and October 15. **Contact:** HAESF Hungary Office at the above address or Email: info@haesf.org.

5010 ■ HAESF Senior Leaders and Scholars Fellowships *(Other/Fellowship)*

Purpose: To help mid-level and senior-level Hungarian professionals who are pursuing their projects in the United States. **Focus:** Business; Public administration. **Qualif.:** Program is open to mid-level and senior-level Hungarian professionals in Business, Public Administration, non-profit organizations and academia. Candidates should hold a PhD degree or at least five years of professional or relevant experience; must hold a Hungarian passport; must not have been physically present in the United States as nonimmigrants on a J-1 visa within the 12-month period unless their presence in the United States was less than six months duration or short-term scholar exchange activity; level of English must be sufficient to perform in a native English-speaking work environment. **Criteria:** Applicants will be judged based on, but not limited to: 1) potential future contributions to Hungarian Society; 2)professional objectives to the values and mission of HAESF; 3) articulated professional goals; 4) professionalism; 5) strength of recommendations; 6) ability to serve as ambassadors of Hungary; 7) communication skills; 8) diversity of majors and professional interests; 9) project proposal. **Funds Avail.:** $60,000. **Duration:** Annual; 3-12 month. **To Apply:** Applicants must fill out the HAESF Senior Leaders and Scholars Fellowship Application form; must submit a detailed budget proposal, personal statement, current curriculum vitae, letter(s) of invitation from the host organization(s) in the United States, project proposal and two letters of reference discussing the following: 1) Relationship with applicants; 2) Relevance of the proposed project to applicant's future and career goals; 3) Assessment of applicant's character, abilities, strength and weaknesses; 4) English language communication skill; 5) Detailed contact information of the referee. Supporting documents should be in translated in English. **Deadline:** April 1 and October 15.

5011 ■ Beatrice Hunter Cancer Research Institute (BHCRI)

Ste. 2L-A2, Tupper Link, 5850 College St.
Halifax, NS, Canada B3H 4R2
Ph: (902)494-8970
Fax: (902)494-8472
URL: bhcri.ca

5012 ■ BHCRI Bridge Funds (Advanced Professional, Professional development/Grant)

Purpose: To support professionals in their cancer-related research. **Focus:** Oncology. **Qualif.:** Applicants must be BHCRI senior scientists, associate members or honorary members (qualifying as senior scientists or associate members) in good standing and whose project is clearly focused on cancer. **Criteria:** Selection will be based on the Institute's criteria.

Funds Avail.: 25,000 Canadian Dollars per annum. **Duration:** Up to 2 years. **To Apply:** Interested applicants are pleased to submit the following: a signed cover letter which includes confirmation of cancer-related research; completed application form (provided at the BHCRI website), signed and dated; completed funding overlap declaration, signed and dated; and full common curriculum vitae of applicants with appropriate Tri-Council formatting. Send complete application package via e-mail or mail the original application to the BHCRI.

5013 ■ BHCRI Cancer Research Training Program Awards (Graduate, Postdoctorate, Advanced Professional, Professional development/Grant)

Purpose: To provide training and funding to graduate students, medical residents, postdoctoral fellows and clinical research fellows involved in cancer research at recognized institutions in Atlantic Canada. **Focus:** Oncology. **Qualif.:** Applicants must be graduate students, medical residents, postdoctoral fellows and clinical research fellows involved in cancer research at recognized institutions in Atlantic Canada. Meanwhile, supervisors must be senior scientists, associate members or honorary members (qualifying a senior scientists or associate members) of the Institute. **Criteria:** Selection will be based on the Institute's criteria.

Funds Avail.: No specific amount. **Duration:** Semiannual.

Number Awarded: Varies. **To Apply:** Interested applicants may contact the Institute for the application information.

5014 ■ BHCRI Matching Funds (Advanced Professional, Professional development/Grant)

Purpose: To support professionals in their cancer-related research. **Focus:** Oncology. **Qualif.:** Applicants must be BHCRI senior scientists, associate members or honorary members (qualifying as senior scientists or associate members) in good standing and whose project is clearly focused on cancer. **Criteria:** Selection will be based on the Institute's criteria.

Funds Avail.: 25,000 Canadian Dollars per annum. **Duration:** Up to 3 years. **To Apply:** Interested applicants are pleased to submit the following: a signed cover letter which includes confirmation of cancer-related research; completed application form (provided at the BHCRI website), signed and dated; completed funding overlap declaration, signed and dated; a copy of the approved grant, including full budget, score and approval letter from granting agency; documentation showing application to other funding sources; reviewers' and scientific officers' comments from the granting agency regarding the approved grant; and full common curriculum vitae of applicants with appropriate Tri-Council formatting. Send complete application package via e-mail or mail the original application to the BHCRI.

5015 ■ BHCRI Miscellaneous Funds (Advanced Professional, Professional development/Grant)

Purpose: To support professionals in their cancer-related research. **Focus:** Oncology. **Qualif.:** Applicants must be BHCRI senior scientists, associate members or honorary members (qualifying as senior scientists or associate members) in good standing and whose project is clearly focused on cancer. **Criteria:** Selection will be based on the Institute's criteria.

Funds Avail.: 10,000 Canadian Dollars. **To Apply:** Interested applicants are pleased to submit the following: a signed cover letter which includes confirmation of cancer-related research; completed application form (provided at the BHCRI website), signed and dated; completed funding overlap declaration, signed and dated; and full common curriculum vitae of applicants with appropriate Tri-Council formatting. Send complete application package via e-mail, or mail the original application to the BHCRI.

5016 ■ BHCRI Seed Funds (Advanced Professional, Professional development/Grant)

Purpose: To support professionals in their cancer-related research. **Focus:** Oncology. **Qualif.:** Applicants must be BHCRI senior scientists, associate members or honorary members (qualifying as senior scientists or associate members) in good standing and whose project is clearly focused on cancer. **Criteria:** Selection will be based on the Institute's criteria.

Funds Avail.: 10,000 Canadian Dollars. **To Apply:** Interested applicants are pleased to submit the following: a signed cover letter which includes confirmation of cancer-related research; completed application form (provided at the BHCRI website), signed and dated; completed funding overlap declaration, signed and dated; and full common curriculum vitae of applicants with appropriate Tri-Council formatting. Send complete application package via e-mail or mail the original application to the BHCRI.

5017 ■ BHCRI Studentship Awards (Undergraduate, Graduate, Advanced Professional/Grant)

Purpose: To support cancer research of students and medical professionals. **Focus:** Oncology. **Qualif.:** Ap-

Awards are arranged alphabetically below their administering organizations

plicants must be undergraduate students, medical residents or students registered in a graduate program in Atlantic Canada commencing the following September, undertaking cancer research or participating in a clinical training project. Meanwhile, supervisors must be senior scientists, associate members or honorary members (qualifying a senior scientists or associate members) of the Institute. **Criteria:** Selection will be based on the Institute's criteria.

Funds Avail.: 6,500 Canadian Dollars each. **Duration:** Annual. **Number Awarded:** 10. **To Apply:** Interested applicants may contact the Institute for the application information.

5018 ■ Huntington's Disease Society of America (HDSA)
505 8th Ave., Ste. 902
New York, NY 10018
Ph: (212)242-1968
Free: 800-345-4372
URL: www.hdsa.org
Facebook: www.facebook.com/HDSofA
LinkedIn: www.linkedin.com/company/huntington's-disease-society-of-america
Twitter: twitter.com/HDSA

5019 ■ HDSA Research Grants (Graduate/Grant)
Purpose: To provide seed funding for new or innovative research projects. **Focus:** Huntington's disease. **Qualif.:** Applicants must be principal investigators. **Criteria:** Recipients are selected based on the potential of their research.

Funds Avail.: No specific amount. **To Apply:** Applicants may visit the website or contact Huntington's Disease Society of America for more details.

5020 ■ Huntington's Disease Society of America Research Fellowships (Postdoctorate/Fellowship)
Purpose: To provide support to young scientist for their research. **Focus:** Huntington's disease. **Qualif.:** Applicants must be investigators who want to enter the field of HD research. **Criteria:** Recipients are selected according to the potential of their research.

Funds Avail.: No specific amount. **To Apply:** Applicants may visit the website or contact Huntington's Disease Society of America for more details.

5021 ■ Don King Student Fellowships (Undergraduate/Fellowship)
Purpose: To sponsor HD investigations that can be conducted over a 10-week period. **Focus:** Huntington's disease. **Qualif.:** Applicants must be matriculated undergraduate life sciences students, pre-medical students, and first-year medical students who are currently attending accredited institutions in the United States where HDSA sponsors ongoing HD research. **Criteria:** Recipient will be selected based on the academic credentials, scientific merit of the proposed project and the relevance of the proposal to HD.

Funds Avail.: $4,000. **Deadline:** March 6.

5022 ■ Hydro Research Foundation (HRF)
25 Massachusetts Ave. NW, Ste. 450
Washington, DC 20001
Ph: (303)674-5254
E-mail: info@hydrofoundation.org
URL: www.hydrofoundation.org

5023 ■ Hydro Research Foundation Fellowships (Advanced Professional/Fellowship)
Purpose: To stimulate new student research and academic interest in research and careers in conventional or pumped storage hydropower. **Focus:** Hydrology. **Qualif.:** Applicants must be Master's or Post-Master's graduate students enrolled full-time at a U.S. university. **Criteria:** Fellows will be selected based on research vision, innovation, academic performance, potential for leadership and overall strength of the research proposal.

Funds Avail.: Approximately $55,000-$141,000 over the one to three year period of study. **Duration:** Annual. **Number Awarded:** Varies. **To Apply:** Applicants must complete an application form; must submit a research proposal, release form, copy of transcript(s), copy of GRE scores, resume, two references, letter of support from university department, supporting documents (optional).

5024 ■ Hydrocephalus Association (HA)
4340 East-West Hwy., Ste. 905
Bethesda, MD 20814-4447
Ph: (301)202-3811
Fax: (301)202-3913
Free: 888-598-3789
E-mail: info@hydroassoc.org
URL: www.hydroassoc.org
Facebook: www.facebook.com/HydroAssoc
LinkedIn: www.linkedin.com/company/hydrocephalus-association?trk=nav_account_sub_nav_company_admin
Twitter: twitter.com/hydroassoc

5025 ■ Anthony Abbene Scholarships (Undergraduate/Scholarship)
Purpose: To provide financial assistance to capable and promising young adults who live with the ongoing challenges and complexities of hydrocephalus. **Focus:** General studies/Field of study not specified. **Qualif.:** Applicants must be between 17 and 30 years old and have hydrocephalus. **Criteria:** Priority will be given to those students who meet the criteria.

Funds Avail.: $1,000 each. **Duration:** Annual. **Number Awarded:** 2. **To Apply:** Applicants must email their contact information to the association to obtain an application form. **Deadline:** April 19. **Remarks:** Established in 2002.

5026 ■ Justin Scot Alston Memorial Scholarships (Undergraduate/Scholarship)
Purpose: To provide financial assistance to capable and promising young adults who live with the ongoing challenges and complexities of hydrocephalus. **Focus:** General studies/Field of study not specified. **Qualif.:** Applicants must be between 17 and 30 years old and have hydrocephalus. **Criteria:** Priority will be given to those students who meet the criteria.

Funds Avail.: $1,000. **Duration:** Annual. **Number Awarded:** 1. **To Apply:** Applicants must email their contact information to the association to obtain an application form. **Deadline:** April 19.

5027 ■ Gerard Swartz Fudge Memorial Scholarships (Undergraduate/Scholarship)
Purpose: To offer scholarships to young adults with hydrocephalus. **Focus:** General studies/Field of study not specified. **Qualif.:** Applicants must be between 17 and 30

years old and have hydrocephalus. **Criteria:** Priority will be given to those students who meet the criteria. **Funds Avail.:** $1,000. **Number Awarded:** 2. **To Apply:** Applicants may visit the website or contact the Assocation for more information on the application process. **Deadline:** April 10. **Remarks:** This fund was established in 1994 by the Fudge family. Their son, Gerard, had hydrocephalus and died in 1992 at the age of 22 in the midst of his college experience. **Contact:** Hydrocephalus Association at the above address.

5028 ■ Mario J. Tocco Hydrocephalus Foundation Scholarships *(Undergraduate/Scholarship)*
Purpose: To provide financial assistance to capable and promising young adults who live with the ongoing challenges and complexities of hydrocephalus. **Focus:** General studies/Field of study not specified. **Qualif.:** Applicants must be between 17 and 30 years old and have hydrocephalus. **Criteria:** Priority will be given to those students who meet the criteria. **Funds Avail.:** $1,000. **Duration:** Annual. **To Apply:** Applicants must email their contact information to the association to obtain an application form. **Deadline:** April 19. **Remarks:** Established in 2007.

5029 ■ Morris L. and Rebecca Ziskind Memorial Scholarships *(Undergraduate/Scholarship)*
Purpose: To offer scholarships to young adults with hydrocephalus. **Focus:** General studies/Field of study not specified. **Qualif.:** Applicants must be between 17 and 30 years old and have hydrocephalus. **Criteria:** Priority will be given to those students who meet the criteria. **Funds Avail.:** $1,000. **To Apply:** Applicants must email their contact information to the association to obtain an application form. **Deadline:** April 10. **Remarks:** This fund was established in 2001 by Rebecca Ziskind and her family in memory of her husband, Dr. Morris Ziskind, who had NPH. After Rebecca Ziskind's death in 2005, their three surviving children and their spouses-Carrie and Dee Norton, Jerome and Rosemary Ziskind, and Janet and Charles Tarino-graciously funded one more scholarship in loving memory of their parents, so that two scholarships are now awarded from this fund.

Awards are arranged alphabetically below their administering organizations

WITHDRAWN

FOR REFERENCE
not to be taken from this building

CPSIA information can be obtained
at www.ICGtesting.com
Printed in the USA
FFOW04n0448211016
28683FF